Thank you for picking up
The 1993 Information Please Sports Al...

NOW IN ITS FOURTH YEAR AS AMERICA'S FAVORITE SPORTS REFERENCE BOOK.

PRAISE FOR PREVIOUS EDITIONS:

"This is a remarkable book—complete, accurate and interesting. After my over 60 years announcing sports, I should know a great record book. This is certainly it."
—Red Barber

"It's fast, it's accurate and it's all there. I find myself going back-back-back-back-back to it all the time."
—Chris Berman, ESPN

"A valuable tool to anyone who needs to know anything about sports. I don't know how I got along without it."
—Jim Lehrer, "The MacNeil/Lehrer Newshour"

"I keep the *IPSA* next to my computer and I'm much more confident using it than I am using my computer."
—Dick Shaap, ABC News

"The baseball section alone has sustained me through many a cold winter's night. A must for any sports fan."
—Jon Miller
Baltimore Orioles

"Tops. Absolutely the best. There's nothing it doesn't have."
—Brent P. Holshouser, Sports Editor, *Petersburg (VA) Progress-Index*

"A commodious compendium."
—Gene Shalit, "The Today Show"

"Fabulous reference book. We would be lost without it!"
—Mike Huss, WGNU, St. Louis

"Remarkable. Will be an invaluable addition to sports libraries for writers and fans."
—Rod Rose, *The Lebanon (IN) Reporter*

The Champions of 1992
The quick reference to the year's best.

Auto Racing

NASCAR Circuit
Daytona 500 .... Davey Allison
Winston 500 .... Davey Allison
Coca-Cola 600 .... Dale Earnhardt
Southern 500 .... Darrell Waltrip
Winston Cup Champion............ Alan Kulwicki

IndyCar Circuit
Indianapolis 500 .... Al Unser Jr.
PPG Cup Champion .... Bobby Rahal

Formula One Circuit
World Driving Championship ...... Nigel Mansell

Baseball

World Series ... Toronto def. Atlanta, 4 games to 2
MVP..................... Pat Borders, Toronto, C
ALCS .... Toronto def. Oakland, 4 games to 2
MVP................ Roberto Alomar, Toronto, 2B
NLCS........ Atlanta def. Pittsburgh, 4 games to 3
MVP .... John Smoltz, Atlanta, P
All-Star Game .... AL, 13-6 (at San Diego)
MVP .... Ken Griffey, Seattle, OF
College World Series. Pepperdine 3, CS-Fullerton 2
MVP................. Phil Nevin, CS-Fullerton, 3B

College Basketball

Men's NCAA Final Four
Championship............ Duke 71, Michigan 51
Semifinals.................. Duke 81, Indiana 78
.... Michigan 76, Cincinnati 72
MVP..................... Bobby Hurley, Duke, G

Women's NCAA Final Four
Championship ...... Stanford 78, Western Ky. 62
Semifinals .... Stanford 66, Virginia 65
.... Western Ky. 84, SW Missouri St. 72
MVP .... Molly Goodenbour, Stanford G

Pro Basketball

NBA Finals... Chicago def. Portland, 4 games to 2
MVP................ Michael Jordan, Chicago, G
Eastern Final .. Chicago def. Cleve., 4 games to 2
Western Final ... Portland def. Utah, 4 games to 2
All-Star Game .... West, 153-113 (at Orlando)
MVP .... Magic Johnson, LA Lakers (ret.)

College Football (1991)

National Champions
Associated Press (media) .... Miami-FL (12-0)
USA Today/CNN (coaches) ... Washington (12-0)

Major Bowls
Orange .... Miami-FL 22, Nebraska 0
Rose .... Washington 34, Michigan 14
Fiesta .... Penn St. 42, Tennessee 17
Cotton .... Florida St. 10, Texas A&M 2
Sugar .... Notre Dame 39, Florida 28

Heisman Trophy. Desmond Howard, Michigan, WR

Pro Football (1991)

Super Bowl XXVI ..... Washington 37, Buffalo 24
MVP ...... Mark Rypien, Washington, QB
AFC Championship .... Buffalo 10, Denver 7
NFC Championship ... Washington 41, Detroit 10
Pro Bowl .... NFC, 21-15 (at Honolulu)
MVP .... Michael Irvin, Dallas, WR
CFL Grey Cup Final .... Toronto 36, Calgary 21
MVP .... Rocket Ismail, Toronto, WR-KR

Golf

Men's Major Championships
Masters .... Fred Couples
U.S. Open........................... Tom Kite
British Open ....:... Nick Faldo
PGA Championship .... Nick Price

Seniors Major Championships
The Tradition...................... Lee Trevino
PGA Seniors .... Lee Trevino
Senior Players Championship ...... Dave Stockton
U.S. Senior Open .... Larry Laoretti

Women's Major Championships
Nabisco Dinah Shore .... Dottie Mochrie
LPGA Championship .... Betsy King
U.S. Women's Open .... Patty Sheehan
du Maurier Classic .... Sherri Steinhauer

Hockey

Stanley Cup Final ... Pitts. def. Chi., 4 games to 0
MVP............... Mario Lemieux, Pittsburgh, C
Campbell Final. Chicago def. Edmonton, 4 games to 0
Wales Final .. Pittsburgh def. Boston, 4 games to 0
All-Star Game .. Campbell, 10-6 (at Philadelphia)
MVP..................... Brett Hull, St. Louis, RW
NCAA Div. I Final. Lake Superior St. 5, Wisconsin 3
MVP .... Paul Constantin, Lake Superior St., F

Horse Racing

Triple Crown Champions
Kentucky Derby............... Lil E. Tee (Pat Day)
Preakness Stakes ..... Pine Bluff (Chris McCarron)
Belmont Stakes ... A.P. Indy (Eddie Delahoussaye)

Harness Racing
Hambletonian ..... Alf Palema (Mickey McNichol)

Winter Olympics
(at Albertville, France)

Most Medals Won:
Top 3 Countries .... 26 Germany (10-10-6)
23 Unified Team (9-6-8)
20 Norway (9-6-5)

Men........... 4 Bjorn Dahlie, Norway (3-1-0)
4 Vegard Ulvang, Norway (3-1-0)
Women . 5 Lyubov Egorova, Unified Team (3-2-0)
5 Elena Valbe, Unified Team (1-0-4)

Summer Olympics
(at Barcelona, Spain)

Most Medals Won:
Top 3 Countries ... 112 Unified Team (45-38-29)
108 USA (37-34-37)
82 Germany (33-21-28)

Men..... 6 Vitaly Scherbo, Unified Team (6-0-0)
5 Grigory Misiutin, Unified Team (1-4-0)
Women........... 5 Shannon Miller, USA (0-2-3)
4 Four-way tie.

Tennis

Men's Grand Slam Championships
Australian Open ....Jim Courier
French Open........................ Jim Courier
Wimbledon...................... Andre Agassi
U.S. Open....................... Stefan Edberg

Women's Grand Slam Championships
Australian Open .... Monica Seles
French Open .... Monica Seles
Wimbledon..................... Steffi Graf
U.S. Open....................... Monica Seles

THE 1993
INFORMATION PLEASE®
SPORTS
ALMANAC

Mike Meserole

EDITOR

PRODUCTION COORDINATOR
Michael Michaud

Research and typing assistance by
**Vinny Vassallo, Dawn Longo,
Howard Courtney, Rob Guijarro**
and **Howie Schwab**

Typesetting by
Publication Services, Inc. of Boston, Mass.

HOUGHTON MIFFLIN COMPANY   BOSTON

The Information Please Sports Almanac

ISSN: 1045-4980

Copyright © 1992 by Houghton Mifflin Company. All rights reserved. No part of this work may be reproduced or transmitted in any form or by any means, electronic or mechanical, including photocopying, recording, or any information storage and retrieval system, except as may be expressly permitted by the 1976 Copyright Act or in writing from the publisher. Requests for permission should be addressed in writing to Houghton Mifflin Company, 2 Park Street, Boston, Massachusetts 02108.

Comments and Suggestions

Comments and suggestions from readers are invited. Because of the many letters received, however, it is not possible to respond personally to every correspondent. Nevertheless, all letters are welcome and each will be carefully considered. **The Information Please Sports Almanac** does not rule on bets or wagers. Address all correspondence to Houghton Mifflin Company, 2 Park Street, Boston, Massachusetts 02108.

Additional copies of **The 1993 Information Please Sports Almanac** may be ordered directly by mail from:
Customer Service Department
Houghton Mifflin Company
Burlington, MA 01803
Phone toll-free (800) 225-3362 for price and shipping information. In Massachusetts, phone (617) 272-1500.

Information Please is a registered trademark of Houghton Mifflin Company.

Printed in the United States of America

WP 10 9 8 7 6 5 4 3 2 1

CONTENTS

Preface 7
Bibliography 8
Updates 11
   Late News 13
   College Football by Ivan Maisel 15
   Pro Football by Vito Stellino 17
   Red Barber Feature by George Vecsey ....
The Sweet Sixteen 23
   Top Personalities of 1991-92 ....
The Year in Review 29
   Cartoon by Mort Drucker 30
   Year in Review by Scott Ostler 37
   Extra Points by Charles A. Monagan 45
   Month-by-Month Review Calendar 58
   Preview Calendar ....
Baseball 59
   Year in Review by Peter Gammons 71
   1992 Statistics 91
   Through the Years ....
College Football 127
   Year in Review by Ivan Maisel 135
   1991-92 Statistics 145
   Through the Years ....
Pro Football 189
   Year in Review by Gary Myers 197
   1991-92 Statistics 215
   Through the Years ....
College Basketball 245
   Year in Review by Gene Wojciechowski 253
   1991-92 Statistics 267
   Through the Years ....
Pro Basketball 297
   Year in Review by Bob Ryan 305
   1991-92 Statistics 317
   Through the Years ....
Hockey 331
   Year in Review by Eric Duhatschek 339
   1991-92 Statistics 355
   Through the Years ....
College Sports 375
   Year in Review by David Davidson 383
   Div.I Basketball Schools 387
   Div.I-A Football Schools 389
   Div.I-AA Football Schools 396
   Annual NCAA Div. I Team Champions 391
   1991-92 NCAA Champions ....
Halls of Fame & Awards 403
   Halls of Fame 408
   Connie Hawkins feature by Terry Pluto 430
   Retired Numbers 433
   Awards ....
SPECIAL: Trophies by Clark Booth 437
   Cartoon by Jeff MacNelly 437
Who's Who 451
   Sports Personalities ....

Arenas & Ballparks **471**
Business & Media
   Year in Review by Richard Sandomir **493**
   Media Statistics and Awards **501**
   Howard Cosell feature by Howard Rosenberg **507**
   Sports Directory **510**
Olympics
   Olympics Overview by Phil Hersh **531**
   Winter Games by Christine Brennan **535**
   Albertville Statistics **541**
   Winter Games Through the Years **546**
   Summer Games by Phil Hersh **555**
   Barcelona Statistics **565**
   Summer Games Through the Years **579**
International Sports
   Year in Review by Phil Hersh **601**
   1992 World Track & Field Championships **606**
   World and U.S. Records (Track & Field and Swimming) **607**
   Winter Sports **614**
   Summer Sports **616**
   Through the Years **617**
Soccer
   Year in Review by Paul Gardner **625**
   1991-92 Statistics **633**
   Through the Years **637**
Horse Racing
   Year in Review by Sharon Smith **647**
   1991-92 Statistics **655**
   Through the Years **660**
Bowling
   Year in Review by Dick Evans **677**
   1991-92 Statistics **683**
   Through the Years **686**
Tennis
   Year in Review by Jim Martz **691**
   1991-92 Statistics **699**
   Through the Years **705**
Golf
   Year in Review by Marino Parascenzo **719**
   1991-92 Statistics **727**
   Through the Years **733**
Auto Racing
   Year in Review by Mike Harris **749**
   1991-92 Statistics **757**
   Through the Years **762**
Boxing
   Year in Review by Bernard Fernandez **771**
   1991-92 Statistics **779**
   Through the Years **784**
Miscellaneous **795**
Deaths
   Obituaries for 1991-92 .... **809**
   Bill France feature by Herman Hickman **813**
   Jean Yawkey feature by George Sullivan **821**
Time-Out **823**
Coming Attractions **832**

As much as it pains me to admit it, I was fast asleep the moment Francisco Cabrera of the Braves delivered the biggest pennant-winning base hit since Bobby Thomson took Ralph Branca deep in 1951. It was practically midnight here in the East and I had long since crawled into bed and drifted off listening to Vin Scully's call of the game on radio.

Back in 1961, when Roger Maris and Mickey Mantle were each chasing Babe Ruth and 60 home runs, I often tuned in Scully's mentor, Red Barber, and listened in the dark from a transistor radio under my pillow. I didn't care much for the Yankees, but I loved hearing Barber describe a game. Red had some very flattering things to say about this book on National Public Radio last year and his passing during the World Series left me and his many other admirers saddened.

The 12 months covered by this fourth edition of The Sports Almanac, November 1991 through October 1992, were bracketed by the retirement (Nov. 7) and unretirement (Sept. 29) of the year's overwhelming sports personality: Magic Johnson. Magic was all over the sports map in 1991-92 and he's all over this book, too. The year also featured the exploits of the Dream Team; the last double dip of the Olympic Games in one year; back-to-back championships for Duke basketball, the Chicago Bulls and the Pittsburgh Penguins; three more Grand Slam titles for Monica Seles; football championships in Washington state and Washington, D.C.; and another terrific, if way-past-my-bedtime, World Series.

Chronicling those stories and many others in The 1993 Sports Almanac was an effort made easier by the steadying influence of production coordinator Michael Michaud and the support of publisher Steve Lewers. This book has grown from 562 to 832 pages in the last three years thanks, in no small way, to these two.

My thanks, as usual, also goes to Charley Monagan and the 26 writers whose essays put meat on the almanac's statistical skeleton; cartoonists Jeff MacNelly and Mort Drucker; illustrator Lynn Michaud; everyone at Publication Services in Boston; Margaret Anne Miles, Greg Mroczek, Chris Leonesio, Mab Gray and Marnie Patterson at Houghton Mifflin; Jim Murphy and his crew at Western Publishing; Nat Andriani at Wide World Photos and Stephanie Mullen at Allsport; Gary Johnson, Cynthia Gable and everybody at the NCAA; Bill Dean at the Baseball Hall of Fame; Pete Newcomb, Bob Kuenster, Tim Barrett, John Kelly, George Dostaler, Chuck Pagano, Paul Rufo, Jim Thompson, John Brister, Paul Kennedy, Peggy Hendershot and all the communications and public relations folks at the other end of the phone or fax machine who were nice enough to provide needed information.

Finally, this year's almanac is dedicated to the memories of Tom Cookman and Peter Evans. When we were growing up and the World Series was played in daylight, Tom and Peter were my two best friends. Tom was the most athletic kid I knew and Peter was easily the most creative. All these years later, I think of them often.

—Mike Meserole

Wolcott, Conn.
October, 1992

Research Material

Many sources were used in the gathering of information for this almanac. Day to day material was almost always found in copies of **USA Today**, **The Boston Globe**, and **The New York Times**.

Several weekly and bi-weekly periodicals were also used in the past year's pursuit of facts and figures, among them—**Baseball America**, **Boxing Illustrated**, **The European**, **FIFA** (Soccer) **News**, **The Hockey News**, **The NCAA News**, **On Track**, **Soccer America**, **Sports Illustrated**, **The Sporting News**, **Track & Field News**, and **USA Today Baseball Weekly**.

In addition, the following books provided background material for one or more chapters of the almanac.

Arenas & Ballparks

Ballparks of North America, by Michael Benson; McFarland & Company, Inc. (1989); Jefferson, N.C.

The Ballparks, by Bill Shannon and George Kalinsky; Hawthorn Books, Inc. (1975); New York.

Green Cathedrals (Revised Edition), by Philip Lowry; Addison-Wesley Publishing Co. (1992); Reading, Mass.

The NFL's Encyclopedic History of Professional Football, Macmillan Publishing Co. (1977); New York.

Take Me Out to the Ballpark, by Lowell Reidenbaugh; The Sporting News Publishing Co. (1983); St.Louis.

24 Seconds to Shoot (An Informal History of the NBA), by Leonard Koppett; Macmillan Publishing Co. (1968); New York.

Plus many major league baseball, NBA, NFL, NHL league and team guides, and major college football and basketball guides.

Auto Racing

1992 IndyCar Media Guide, edited by Dave Elshoff; Championship Auto Racing Teams; Bloomfield Hills, Mich.

1992 Indianapolis 500 Media Fact Book, compiled Bob Laycock and Kurt Hunt; Indianapolis Motor Speedway; Indianapolis.

Indy: 75 Years of Racing's Greatest Spectacle, by Rich Taylor; St. Martin's Press (1991); New York.

Marlboro Grand Prix Guide, 1950-91 (1992 Edition), compiled by Jacques Deschenaux; Charles Stewart & Company Ltd; Brentford, England.

1992 Winston Cup Media Guide, compiled and edited by Ty Norris; NASCAR Winston Cup Series; Winston-Salem, N.C.

Baseball

The All-Star Game (A Pictorial History, 1933 to Present), by Donald Honig; The Sporting News Publishing Co. (1987); St. Louis.

1992 American League Red Book, published by The Sporting News Publishing Co.; St. Louis.

Baseball America's 1992 Almanac, edited by Allan Simpson; Baseball America, Inc.; Durham, N.C.

Baseball America's 1992 Directory, edited by Allan Simpson; Baseball America, Inc.; Durham, N.C.

The Baseball Chronology, edited by James Charlton; Macmillian Publishing Co. (1991); New York.

The Baseball Encyclopedia (Eighth Edition), editorial director, Rick Wolff; Macmillan Publishing Co. (1989); New York.

The Complete 1992 Baseball Record Book, edited by Craig Carter; The Sporting News Publishing Co.; St. Louis.

The Official Major League Baseball 1992 Stat Book, by the editors of The Baseball Encyclopedia; Macmillan Publishing Co.; New York.

1992 National League Green Book, published by The Sporting News Publishing Co.; St. Louis.

1992 NCAA Baseball and Softball, compiled by John Painter, Sean Straziscar and James Wright; edited by Theodore Breidenthal; NCAA Books; Overland Park, Kan.

The Scrapbook History of Baseball by Jordan Deutsch, Richard Cohen, Roland Johnson and David Neft; Bobbs-Merrill Company, Inc. (1975); Indianapolis/New York.

1992 Sporting News Official Baseball Guide, edited by Craig Carter; The Sporting News Publishing Co.; St. Louis.

1992 Sporting News Official Baseball Register, edited by Mark Shimabukuro; The Sporting News Publishing Co.; St. Louis.

The Sports Encyclopedia Baseball (1992 Edition), edited by David Neft and Richard Cohen; St. Martin's Press; New York.

Total Baseball (Second Edition), edited by John Thorn and Pete Palmer; Warner Books (1991); New York.

College Basketball

All the Moves (A History of College Basketball), by Neil D. Issacs; J.B. Lippincott Company (1975); New York.

1991-92 Blue Ribbon College Basketball Yearbook, edited by Chris Wallace; Bantam Books; New York.

College Basketball, U.S.A. (Since 1892), by John D.McCallum; Stein and Day (1978); New York.

Collegiate Basketball: Facts and Figures on the Cage Sport, by Edwin C. Caudle; The Paragon Press (1960); Montgomery, Ala.

The Encyclopedia of the NCAA Basketball Tournament, written and compiled by Jim Savage; Dell Publishing (1990); New York.

The Final Four (Reliving America's Basketball Classic), compiled by Billy Reed; Host Communications, Inc. (1988); Lexington, Ky.

Final Four Records, 1939-91, compiled by Gary Johnson and James Van Valkenburg; edited by Michael V. Earle; NCAA Books; Overland Park, Kan.

The Modern Encyclopedia of Basketball (Second Revised Edition), edited by Zander Hollander; Dolphins Books (1979); Doubleday & Company, Inc.; Garden City, N.Y.

1992 NCAA Basketball, compiled by Gary Johnson, Richard Campbell, John Painter, Sean Straziscar, James Wright and James Van Valkenburg; edited by Michelle A. Pond; NCAA Books; Overland Park, Kan.

1992 NIT Tournament Guide, Madison Square Garden; New York.

Plus many NCAA Division I conference guides from the ACC to the WAC.

Pro Basketball

The Official NBA Basketball Encyclopedia, edited by Zander Hollander and Alex Sachere; Villard Books (1989); New York.

1991-92 Philadelphia 76ers Statistical Yearbook, edited by Harvey Pollack; Philadelphia 76ers; Philadelphia.

1991-92 Sporting News Official NBA Guide, edited by Craig Carter and Alex Sachare; The Sporting News Publishing Co.; St. Louis.

1991-92 Sporting News Official NBA Register, edited by Alex Sachare and Dave Sloan; The Sporting News Publishing Co.; St. Louis.

Bowling

Bowlers Journal Annual, January, 1992; Chicago.

1992 LPBT Guide, Ladies Pro Bowlers Tour; Rockford, Ill.

1992 PBA Press-Radio-TV Guide; Professional Bowlers Association; Akron, Ohio.

Boxing

1992 Computer Boxing Update (volumes 7-9), compiled by Ralph Citro; Ralph Citro Inc.; Blackwood, N.J.

The Ring 1985 Record Book & Boxing Encyclopedia, edited by Herbert G. Goldman; The Ring Publishing Corp.; New York.

College Sports

1990-91 National Collegiate Championships, edited by Theodore Breidenthal; NCAA Books; Overland Park, Kan.

1992 NCAA Basketball, compiled by Gary Johnson, Richard Campbell, John Painter, Sean Straziscar, James Wright and James Van Valkenburg; edited by Michelle A. Pond; NCAA Books; Overland Park, Kan.

1991 NCAA Football, compiled by Richard Campbell, John Painter, Sean Straziscar and James Van Valkenburg; edited by J. Gregory Summers; NCAA Books; Overland Park, Kan.

NCAA: The Voice of College Sports (A Diamond Anniversary History, 1906-81), by Jack Falla; NCAA Books; Overland Park, Kan.

NAIA Championship History and Records Book (1990-91), National Assn. of Intercollegiate Athletics; NAIA Books; Kansas City, Mo.

College Football

Football: A College History, by Tom Perrin; McFarland & Company, Inc. (1987); Jefferson, N.C.

Football: Facts & Figures, by Dr. L.H. Baker; Farrar & Rinehart, Inc. (1945); New York.

Great College Football Coaches of the Twenties and Thirties, by Tim Cohane; Arlington House (1973); New Rochelle, N.Y.

1991 NCAA Football, compiled by Richard Campbell, John Painter, Sean Straziscar and James Van Valkenburg; edited by J. Gregory Summers; NCAA Books; Overland Park, Kan.

Saturday Afternoon, by Richard Whittingham; Workman Publishing Co., Inc. (1985); New York.

Saturday's America, by Dan Jenkins; Sports Illustrated Books; Little, Brown & Company (1970); Boston.

Tournament of Roses, The First 100 Years, by Joe Hendrickson; Knapp Press (1989); Los Angeles.

Plus numerous college football team and conference guides, especially the 1991 guides compiled by Notre Dame, the Atlantic Coast Conference, Southeastern Conference and Southwest Conference.

Pro Football

1991 Canadian Football League Guide, compiled by the CFL Communications Dept.; Toronto.

The Football Encyclopedia (The Complete History of NFL Football from 1892 to the Present), compiled by David Neft and Richard Cohen; St. Martin's Press (1991); New York.

The Official NFL Encyclopedia, by Beau Riffenburgh; New American Library (1986); New York.

Official NFL 1991 Record and Fact Book, edited by Leslie Hammond and Chuck Garrity, Jr.; produced by NFL Properties, Inc.; New York.

The Scrapbook History of Pro Football, by Richard Cohen, Jordan Deutsch, Roland Johnson and David Neft; Bobbs-Merrill Company, Inc. (1976); Indianapolis/New York.

1991 Sporting News Football Guide, edited by Craig Carter; The Sporting News Publishing Co.; St. Louis.

1991 Sporting News Football Register, edited Mark Shimabukuro; The Sporting News Publishing Co.; St. Louis.

1991 Sporting News Super Bowl Book, edited by Tom Dienhart, Joe Hoppel and Dave Sloan; The Sporting News Publishing Co.; St. Louis.

Golf

The Encyclopedia of Golf (Revised Edition), compiled by Nevin H. Gibson; A.S. Barnes and Company (1964); New York.

Guinness Golf Records: Facts and Champions, by Donald Steel; Guinness Superlatives Ltd. (1987); Middlesex, England.

The History of the PGA Tour, by Al Barkow; Doubleday (1989); New York.

The Illustrated History of Women's Golf, by Rhonda Glenn, Taylor Publishing Co. (1991); Dallas.

The PGA World Golf Hall of Fame Book, by Gerald Astor, Prentice Hall Press (1991); New York.

1992 LPGA Player Guide, produced by LPGA Communications Dept.; Ladies Professional Golf Assn. Tour; Daytona Beach, Fla.

1992 Official PGA Tour Book, produced by PGA Tour Creative Services; Professional Golfers Assn. Tour; Ponte Vedra, Fla.

1992 Official Senior PGA Tour Book, produced by PGA Tour Creative Services; Professional Golfers Assn. Tour; Ponte Vedra, Fla.

Pro-Golf '92, PGA European Tour Media Guide, Virginia Water, Surrey, England.

The Random House International Encyclopedia of Golf, by Malcolm Campbell; Random House (1991); New York.

USGA Record Books (1895-1959, 1960-80 and 1981-90); U.S. Golf Association; Far Hills, N.J.

Hockey

Canada Cup '87: The Official History, No.1 Publications Ltd.; Toronto.

Checking Back (A History of the National Hockey League), by Neil D. Isaacs; W.W.Norton & Company, Inc. (1977); New York.

1990-91 Division I College Hockey Record Manual, edited by Andrew K. Finnie; Andrew K. Finnie and Hockey East Association; Boston.

The Hockey Encyclopedia, by Stan Fischler and Shirley Walton Fischler; research editor, Bob Duff; Macmillan Publishing Co. (1983); New York.

Hockey Hall of Fame (The Official History of the Game and Its Greatest Stars), by Dan Diamond and Joseph Romain; Doubleday (1988); New York.

The National Hockey League, by Edward F. Dolan Jr.; W H Smith Publishers Inc. (1986); New York.

The Official National Hockey League 75th Anniversary Commemorative Book, edited by Dan Diamond; McClelland & Stewart, Inc. (1991); Toronto.

1991-92 Official NHL Guide & Record Book, compiled by the NHL Communications Dept.; New York/Montreal.

The Stanley Cup, by Joseph Romain and James Duplacey; Gallery Books (1989); New York.

The Trail of the Stanley Cup (Volumns I-III), by Charles L. Coleman; Progressive Publications Inc. (1969); Sherbrooke, Quebec.

Horse Racing

1992 American Racing Manual, compiled by the Daily Racing Form; Hightstown, N.J.

1991 Breeders' Cup Statistics; Breeders' Cup Limited; Lexington, Ky.

1992 Directory and Record Book, Thoroughbred Racing Associations of North America Inc.; Elkton, Md.

1992 Kentucky Derby Media Guide, compiled by Churchill Downs Public Relations Dept.; Louisville, Ky.

1992 NYRA Media Guide, The New York Racing Association Inc.; Jamaica, N.Y.

1992 Preakness Press Guide, compiled and edited by Damon Thayer and Joe Kelly; Maryland Jockey Club; Baltimore, Md.

1992 Trotting and Pacing Guide, compiled and edited by John Pawlak; United States Trotting Association; Columbus, Ohio.

International Sports

Athletics: A History of Modern Track and Field (1860-1990, Men and Women), by Roberto Quercetani; Vallardi & Associati (1990); Milan, Italy.

Athletics 1992 (The International Track and Field Annual), Association of Frack & Field Statisticians; edited by Peter Matthews; Burlington Publishing Ltd.; Berkshire, England.

Track & Field News' Little Blue Book; Metric conversion tables; From the editors of Track & Field News (1989); Los Altos, Calif.

Miscellaneous

The America's Cup 1851-1987 (Sailing for Supremacy), by Gary Lester and Richard Sleeman; Lester-Townsend Publishing (1986); Sydney, Australia.

The Encyclopedia of Sports (Fifth Revised Edition), by Frank G. Menke; revisions by Suzanne Treat; A.S. Barnes and Co., Inc. (1975); Cranbury, N.J.

The Great American Sports Book, by George Gipe; Doubleday & Company, Inc. (1978); Garden City, N.Y.

The 1992 Information Please Almanac, edited by Otto Johnson; Houghton Mifflin Co.; Boston.

1992 Official PRCA Media Guide, edited by Steve Fleming; Professional Rodeo Cowboys Association; Colorado Springs.

The Sail Magazine Book of Sailing, by Peter Johnson; Alfred A. Knopf (1989); New York.

1992 Sports Illustrated Sports Almanac, by the editors of Sports Illustrated; Little, Brown and Co.; Boston.

The Sportspages Almanac 1992, edited by Matthew Engel and Ian Morrison; Simon and Schuster; London.

"Ten Years of the Ironman," Triathlete Magazine; October, 1988; Santa Monica, Calif.

The 1992 World Almanac and Book of Facts, edited by Mark Hoffman; Pharos Books; New York.

Olympics

All That Glitters Is Not Gold (An Irreverent Look at the Olympic Games); by William O. Johnson, Jr.; G.P. Putnam's Sons (1972); New York.

An Approved History of the Olympic Games, by Bill Henry and Patricia Henry Yeomans; Alfred Publishing Co., Inc. (1984); Sherman Oaks, Calif.

An Illustrated History of the Olympics (Third Edition); by Dick Schaap; Alfred A. Knopf (1975); New York.

The Complete Book of the Olympics (1992 Edition); by David Wallechinsky; Little, Brown and Co.; Boston.

The Games Must Go On (Avery Brundage and the Olympic Movement), by Allen Guttmann; Columbia University Press (1984); New York.

Hitler's Games (The 1936 Olympics), by Duff Hart-Davis; Harper & Row (1986); New York/London.

The Nazi Olympics, by Richard D. Mandell; Souvenir Press (1972); London.

The Official USOC Book of the 1984 Olympic Games, by Dick Schaap; Random House/ABC Sports; New York.

The Olympic Games Handbook, by David Chester; Charles Scribner's Sons (1975); New York.

The Olympic Record Book, compiled by Bill Mallon; Garland Publishing Inc. (1988); New York & London.

The Olympics: A History of the Games, by William Oscar Johnson; Oxmoor House (1992); Birmingham, Ala.

Pursuit of Excellence (The Olympic Story), by The Associated Press and Grolier; Grolier Enterprises Inc. (1979); Danbury, Conn.

The Story of the Olympic Games (776 B.C. to 1948 A.D.), by John Kieran and Arthur Daley; J.B. Lippincott Company (1948); Philadelphia/New York.

United States Olympic Books (Seven Editions): 1936,48,52,56,60,61-65,68; U.S. Olympic Association; New York.

The USA and the Olympic Movement, produced by the USOC Information Dept.; edited by Gayle Plant; U.S. Olympic Committee (1988); Colorado Springs.

Plus official IOC and USOC records from the 1992 Winter Olympics in Albertville and 1992 Summer Olympics in Barcelona.

Soccer

The American Encyclopedia of Soccer, edited by Zander Hollander; Everest House Publishers (1980); New York.

The European Football Yearbook (1991-92 Edition), edited by Mike Hammond; Sports Projects Ltd; West Midlands, England.

The Guinness Book of Soccer Facts & Feats, by Jack Rollin; Guinness Superlatives Ltd. (1978); Middlesex, England.

History of Soccer's World Cup, by Michael Archer; Chartwell Books, Inc. (1978); Secaucus, N.J.

The History of the World Cup, by Brian Glanville; Faber and Faber Limited (1984); London/Boston.

1991-92 MSL Official Guide, Major (Indoor) Soccer League; Overland Park, Kan.

The World Cup (The Players, Coaches, History and Excitement), by Filip Bondy; Mallard Press (1991); New York.

Tennis

The Illustrated Encyclopedia of World Tennis, by John Haylett and Richard Evans; Exeter Books (1989); New York.

Official Encyclopedia of Tennis, edited by the staff of the U.S. Lawn Tennis Assn.; Harper & Row (1972); New York.

1992 Official ATP Tour Player Guide, edited by Greg Sharko and Jay Beck; Association of Tennis Professionals; Ponte Vedra Beach, Fla.

1992 Official Kraft Tour Media Guide, compiled by WTA Public Relations staff; Women's Tennis Association; St. Petersburg, Fla.

1992 Official USTA Tennis Yearbook; by United States Tennis Association; H.O. Zimman, Inc.; Lynn, Mass.

Who's Who

The Encyclopedia of North American Sports History, by Ralph Hickok; Facts on File (1992); New York.

Facts & Dates of American Sports, by Gorton Carruth & Eugene Ehrlich; Harper & Row, Publishers, Inc. (1988); New York.

101 Greatest Athletes of the Century, by Will Grimsley and the Associated Press Sports Staff; Bonanza Books (1987); Crown Publishers, Inc.; New York.

The New York Times Book of Sports Legends, edited by Joseph Vecchione; Simon & Shuster (1991); New York.

Superstars, by Frank Litsky; Vineyard Books, Inc. (1975); Secaucus, N.J.

Other Reference Books

The New York Public Library Desk Reference, edited by Felice Levy and Lisa Wolff; Webster's New World (1989); Simon & Schuster; New York.

TV Facts, (Revised and Updated), by Cobbett Steinberg; Facts On File Publications (1985); New York.

The World Book Encyclopedia (1988 Edition); World Book, Inc.; Chicago.

The World Book Yearbook (Annual Supplements, 1954-92); World Book, Inc.; Chicago.

Wide World Photos

New heavyweight champion **Riddick Bowe** wraps himself in title belts after winning a unanimous 12-round decision over Evander Holyfield on Nov. 13 in Las Vegas.

UPDATES

News items that occurred after chapter deadlines.

BOXING

Bowe Wins Heavyweight Championship

LAS VEGAS, Nov. 13—Challenger **Riddick Bowe** scored a unanimous 12-round decision over a courageous but overmatched **Evander Holyfield** to become the new undisputed world heavyweight champion before 18,000 at the Thomas & Mack Center.

Both fighters entered the ring undefeated, although at 6-foot-5 and 235 pounds, the 25-year-old Bowe was two and half inches taller, 30 pounds heavier and five years younger than Holyfield. In what quickly turned into a rousing slugfest Bowe proved to be the stronger man, nearly knocking Holyfield out in both the 10th and 11th rounds. But Holyfield, defending his title for the fourth time, refused to yield even after being knocked down early in the 11th.

Afterward, Bowe (32-0, 27 KOs) was noncommittal about whether he would make his first defense against 43-year-old former champion **George Foreman** or 27-year-old Briton **Lennox Lewis**, who beat Bowe for the gold medal at the 1988 Olympics and stunned Razor Ruddock with a second-round knockout in London on Oct. 31. A battered Holyfield (29-1, 22 KOs) talked of retirement at the post-fight news conference.

PRO BASKETBALL

Magic Re-Retires, Citing "Controversies"

LOS ANGELES, Nov. 2—Just four days before the opening of the 1992-93 NBA season and his scheduled return as an active player with the L.A. Lakers, **Magic Johnson** quit again after several players, including Karl Malone of Utah and Gerald Wilkins of Cleveland, voiced their concern about the possibility of contracting the AIDS virus from Johnson.

Johnson stunned the sports world on Nov. 7, 1991, by disclosing that he had been infected by the virus that causes AIDS and would retire immediately. Then on Sept. 29, 1992, after successful performances in the NBA All-Star Game and with the U.S. Olympic basketball team, he announced he was coming back and hoped to play as many as 70 games. On Oct. 1, the Lakers signed him to the most lucrative contract in sports history—a one-year extension for the 1994-95 season worth $14.6 million.

Magic played in five exhibition games, but as the new season approached he realized that more than a few players were uneasy about his comeback. Although medical experts maintained that the chances of catching the virus from him during a game were extremely remote, Magic decided to call off his return.

In a statement released by the Lakers, he said, "It has become obvious that the various controversies surrounding my return are taking away from both basketball as a sport and the larger issue of living with HIV, for me and the many people affected."

AUTO RACING

Kulwicki and Rahal Capture Titles

Bobby Rahal and **Alan Kulwicki**, two drivers who also own their racing teams, won the PPG IndyCar World Series and NASCAR Winston Cup championships in the final races of the season.

Rahal became IndyCar's first driver-owner-champion on Oct. 18, when he clinched his third PPG Cup (and $1 million) with a third-place finish at the Toyota Monterey Grand Prix. Pole sitter Michael Andretti won the race, his last before joining the Formula One circuit in 1993, but fell four points short of overtaking Rahal in the final PPG Cup standings.

Four weeks later, Kulwicki became the first driver-owner to win the NASCAR title (and $1.3 million) since Richard Petty in 1979 with a second-place finish in the Hooters 500 at Atlanta Motor Speedway. He edged Hooters winner Bill Elliott by just 10 points in the final standings. Davey Allison, who entered the race with a 30-point lead on Kulwicki and a 40-point bulge on Elliott, fell from contention when he crashed into Ernie Irvan with 75 laps to go. The race also marked **Richard Petty's** final appearance as a NASCAR driver after 35 years and 200 victories. Petty, 55, crashed on the 95th lap and finished 35th, but his crew patched the familiar No. 43 Pontiac back together for a final career victory lap.

COLLEGE FOOTBALL

Hurricanes and Huskies

by Ivan Maisel
The Dallas Morning News

Even heavyweight title fights only last 12 rounds. Washington and Miami's battle for college football supremacy appeared at mid-season as if it would continue indefinitely.

After sharing the mythical national title last year, the Hurricanes and Huskies do-si-do'd in and out of the top spot in the two major polls for the first seven weeks.

Miami led the Associated Press poll for three weeks. Washington led for three weeks. Then they tied, the first first-place tie in the AP vote in 51 years. In the Oct. 25 poll, Miami returned to No. 1 by a one-point margin.

Mike Stewart/Allsport

Coach **Dennis Erickson** and Miami of Florida were undefeated and ranked No. 1 in games through Nov. 22.

Both teams suffered not only by comparison to each other but by comparison to their predecessors. If there's a sympathy vote, however, Miami won far and away.

First came the shocking deaths of former Miami players Jerome Brown and Shane Curry. In late August, two players were indicted for receiving federal student aid through fraudulent means.

Yet even that paled in comparison to the wreckage of Hurricane Andrew, which tore apart the Coral Gables campus and the homes of players and coaches, including head coach Dennis Erickson. He took the team to Dodgertown in Vero Beach for the last 10 days of preseason practice. The Hurricanes opened at Iowa with an emotional 24-7 victory dedicated to the victims at home.

However, injuries on the offensive line soon emasculated the offense. Miami defeated Arizona 8-7 when Wildcats kicker Steve McLaughlin's 51-yard game-ending kick went wide right. Voters shifted to Washington in significant numbers.

But the Hurricanes fought back in the next two weeks. As in its 17-16 victory in 1991, Miami defeated Florida State 19-16 because a last-minute Seminoles field goal drifted wide right. The following week, the Hurricanes gained only 218 yards of total offense yet won at Penn State 17-14.

Washington had no such close calls through October, building an 8-0 record by an average score of 29-9. But then the Huskies lost twice in three weeks—16-3 to Arizona on Nov. 7, and 42-23 to Washington State on Nov. 21—and fell from second to 11th in the AP poll. Going into Thanksgiving, Alabama (10-0) moved up to No. 2, followed by Florida State (9-1) and Texas A&M (11-0).

As the 12-team Southeastern Conference prepared for its first championship game on Dec. 5, between Western Division winner Alabama and Eastern challenger Florida, the league was still reeling from two coaching changes and a player revolt.

Arkansas dropped its opener, 10-3, to The Citadel of Division I-AA, and coach Jack Crowe lost his job the next day. Athletic director Frank Broyles, who had extended Crowe's contract in December 1991, promoted defensive coordinator Joe Kines, but the Razorbacks were only 2-6-1 going into their final game with LSU. Players at winless South Carolina took a vote on Oct. 12 and decided they didn't want to suit up for coach Sparky Woods anymore. After a reconciliation, the Gamecocks won five of their last six. One of their victims was Tennessee, which lost three straight games in October after a 5-0 start. The swoon cost coach Johnny Majors his job after 16 years, even though the rebuilding Vols were 7-3 going into their regular season finale with Vanderbilt.

HORSE RACING
A.P. Indy Takes Breeders' Cup Classic

HALLANDALE, Fla., Oct. 31—Belmont Stakes champion **A.P. Indy**, with **Eddie Delahoussaye** in the saddle, won the $3 million Breeders' Cup Classic at Gulfstream Park, beating **Pleasant Tap** by three lengths to all but clinch Horse of the Year honors.

Tragedy, however, struck in the afternoon's first of seven races, the Breeders' Cup Sprint, when British-bred **Mr Brooks** fell and broke his right foreleg and had to be humanely destroyed. Jockey **Lester Piggott**, the most accomplished rider in European racing, suffered a fractured collarbone and two broken ribs in the fall.

Arazi, the French horse who became a superstar in the 1991 Breeders' Cup at Churchill Downs with a spectacular finishing kick in the Juvenile and then came in a disappointing eighth in the '92 Kentucky Derby, flopped again in the Mile, running 11th in a field of 14.

Results from the seven Breeders' Cup races held Saturday, Oct. 31, 1992, at Gulfstream Park in Hallandale, Fla..

Race	Time	Top 3 Finishers	Jockeys	Trainers	Money Won
Sprint (6 furlongs)	1:08⅕	1 Thirty Slews	Eddie Delahoussaye	Bob Baffert	$520,000
		2 Meafara	Jorge Velasquez	Leslie Ahrens	200,000
		3 Rubiano	Julie Krone	Scotty Schulhofer	120,000
Juvenile Fillies (1¹/₁₆) miles	1:42⅘	1 Eliza	Pat Valenzuela	Alex Hassinger	$520,000
		2 Educated Risk	Jerry Bailey	Shug McGaughey	200,000
		3 Boots 'n Jackie	M.A. Lee	Emanuel Tortora	120,000
Distaff (1⅛ miles)	1:48	1 Paseana	Chris McCarron	Ron McAnally	$520,000
		2 Versailles Treaty	Mike Smith	Shug McGaughey	200,000
		3 Magical Maiden	Gary Stevens	Warren Stute	120,000
Mile	1:32⅘	1 Lure	Mike Smith	Shug MGaughey	$520,000
		2 Paradise Creek	Pat Day	Bill Mott	200,000
		3 Brief Truce	Michael Kinane	Dermot Weld	120,000
Juvenile (1¹/₁₆ miles)	1:43⅖	1 Gilded Time	Chris McCarron	Darrell Vienna	$520,000
		2 It'sali'Iknowfact	Laffit Pincay, Jr.	Cam Gambolati	200,000
		3 River Special	Kent Desormeaux	Bob Hess, Jr.	120,000
Turf (1½ miles)	2:24	1 Fraise	Pat Valenzuela	Bill Mott	$1,040,000
		2 Sky Classic	Pat Day	James Day	400,000
		3 Quest for Fame	Pat Eddery	Bobby Frankel	240,000
Classic (1¼ miles)	2:00⅕	1 A.P. Indy	Eddie Delahoussaye	Neil Drysdale	$1,560,000
		2 Pleasant Tap	Gary Stevens	Chris Speckert	600,000
		3 Jolypha	Pat Eddery	Andre Fabre	360,000

BASEBALL
Giants' Move Voted Down

SCOTTSDALE, Ariz., Nov. 10—National League owners, by a vote of 9-4, rejected the proposed move of the **San Francisco Giants** to Tampa/St. Petersburg, Fla. Only Chicago, Florida, Philadephia and St. Louis voted in favor of the shift. While the decision cleared the way for local S.F. investors to buy the club for $100 million, Tampa Bay officials, who bought the club for $115 million on Aug. 7, planned to contest the vote in court.

On Nov. 13, arbitrator **George Nicolau** reinstated relief pitcher **Steve Howe**, who had been banned for life by former commissioner **Fay Vincent** on June 8 for repeated problems with drugs.

Oakland reliever **Dennis Eckersley** led the parade of postseason prize-winners, picking up both the AL Most Valuable Player and Cy Young awards. Other trophies went to NL MVP **Barry Bonds** of Pittsburgh; NL Cy Young **Greg Maddux** of Chicago; rookies **Pat Listach** of Milwaukee (AL) and **Eric Karros** of Los Angeles (NL); and managers **Tony La Russa** of Oakland (AL) and **Jim Leyland** of Pittsburgh (NL).

PRO FOOTBALL

Players Gain Upper Hand

by Vito Stellino
The Baltimore Sun

Wide World Photos

Free agent **Keith Jackson** left Philadelphia and signed with Miami on Sept. 30.

In the first half of the NFL's 73rd season, the off-the-field court wrangling between owners and players often upstaged the action on the field.

The players, who failed to win free agency on the picket line during a 1987 strike, finally appeared to be nearing their goal after a five-year legal fight.

On Sept. 10 in Minneapolis, a federal court jury of eight women ruled the NFL's Plan B restrictive free agency system was illegal in a case named for Freeman Mc-Neil of the New York Jets.

The immediate result was that four players who were holding out were declared free agents by federal judge David Doty.

Tight end Keith Jackson of the Philadelphia Eagles was the biggest prize of the group and he quickly signed a four-year, $6 million deal with the Miami Dolphins while wide receiver Webster Slaughter of the Cleveland Browns signed with the Houston Oilers and defensive lineman Garin Veris of the New England Patriots signed with the San Francisco 49ers. D.J. Dozier, who's trying baseball for a career, was released by the Detroit Lions and no team showed interest in him.

Reggie White of the Philadelphia Eagles immediately filed a suit that the players hope will result in the courts either declaring the players whose contracts expire Feb. 1, 1993 are total free agents or at least make the players with four years of experience free agents.

The owners, meanwhile, are drawing up a much more restrictive plan that would limit free agency to players with six to eight years experience under certain conditions.

In two other cases that did not have direct bearing on the McNeil case but added to the perception that the players have the edge in court, the players won more than $60 million in damages in separate verdicts handed down Oct. 5.

One ramification of the legal fight was a delay of expansion. The league, which had announced it hoped to name two teams in 1992 to play in 1994, delayed the timetable for at least a year. It previously narrowed the field down to five finalists—St. Louis, Baltimore, Charlotte, Memphis and Jacksonville.

The league also decided to suspend the World League for one season. The spring league, which was a success in Europe, but struggled in the U.S., lost money for two years before the NFL pulled the plug. It's uncertain if the league will return.

On the field, the most significant development of the season was that San Francisco continued its winning ways without quarterback Joe Montana, who led the 49ers to four Super Bowls in the 1980s. With Montana sidelined through November, Steve Young directed the 'Niners to a 9-2 start that tied Dallas and Buffalo for the best record in the NFL by Thanksgiving.

The Miami Dolphins celebrated the 20th anniversary of their perfect 17-0 record in 1972 by winning their first six games before losing to Indianapolis. Meanwhile, New England lost its first nine in a row before beating the Colts.

In the record category, Art Monk of the Washington Redskins and James Lofton of the Buffalo Bills broke two of the career records held by Steve Largent, the retired wide receiver of the Seattle Seahawks. Monk broke his career reception mark of 819 catches and Lofton snapped his yardage mark of 13,089 yards.

GOLF

Couples, Faldo Top Money Winners

Fred Couples and **Nick Faldo** ended the 1992 season on Nov. 1 as the best players on the American and European PGA tours.

By placing fifth in the Tour Championship at Pinehurst, N.C., Couples clinched both the Arnold Palmer Award as the tour's leading money winner with $1,344,188 and his second straight Vardon Trophy for lowest scoring average at 69.38. Faldo, with a 23rd at the Volvo Masters in Spain, won the Order of Merit with a record £708,522 and also had the Euro Tour's low average of 69.10. In the Sony rankings, Faldo finished the year nearly six points ahead of runner-up Couples, 22.34 to 16.59.

TENNIS

Seles and Courier End Year at No. 1

NEW YORK, Nov. 22—**Monica Seles** finished her second straight year as the Number One player in women's tennis by routing **Martina Navratilova** in the best-of-five final of the Virginia Slims Championship, 7-5, 6-3, 6-1. The 18-year-old Seles, winner of six Grand Slam singles titles in the last two years, won $250,000 (plus a $500,000 bonus) to set a single-season earnings record of $2,622,352.

On the men's tour, **Jim Courier** lost to **Boris Becker**, 6-4, 6-3, 7-5, in the final of the ATP Tour World Championship at Frankfurt, Germany, but ended the season at No. 1. Courier is the first American Player of the Year since John McEnroe in 1984.

COLLEGE BASKETBALL

NCAA Puts Syracuse on Probation

SYRACUSE, N.Y., Oct. 1—The NCAA put the entire **Syracuse** athletic program on two years' probation for infractions made by men's and women's basketball and men's lacrosse, wrestling and football. Coach Jim Boeheim's basketball team was banned from the 1993 NCAA tournament, but allowed to appear on television.

That action took place after an investigation by the *Syracuse Post-Standard* revealed that substantial cash gifts, meals and clothes had been given to players by boosters, that a "street agent" had been used for recruiting, that an extra coach had been illegally employed, and that the school had failed to properly monitor the situation.

DEATHS

Walter Lanier (Red) Barber, 84, the Mississippi-born baseball broadcaster who called games for the Cincinnati Reds, Brooklyn Dodgers and New York Yankees from 1934-66, died Oct. 22 in Tallahassee, Fla., of pneumonia and other complications following emergency surgery on Oct. 10 to remove an intestinal blockage. He was the first broadcaster, along with Mel Allen, to be honored by the Baseball Hall of Fame.

Other sports figures who died in late October included **Dottie Green**, 71, a catcher who played four seasons for the original Rockford (Ill.) Peaches, the dominant team in the All-American Girls Professional Baseball League from 1943-54; and **Arthur Wint**, 72, the Jamaican middle distance runner who won his country's first Olympic gold medal in 1948 when he captured the 400 meters at the Summer Olympics in London.

MISCELLANEOUS

NEW YORK, Nov. 1—**Willie Mtolo**, a 28-year-old black South African, won the New York City Marathon in a time of 2 hours 9 minutes and 29 seconds. Australia's **Lisa Ondieki**, 32, was the women's winner, covering the 26.2-mile course in 2:24:40.

On Oct. 10, **Mark Allen** (8:09:08) and **Paula Newby-Fraser** (8:55:28) each set new course records in the 15th running of the Ironman Triathlon in Hawaii.

Elsewhere, U.S. Olympic Committee treasurer **LeRoy Walker** was elected the 23rd president of the USOC on Oct. 11, becoming the first black to hold the position in the group's 92-year history.

THE 1993 INFORMATION PLEASE SPORTS ALMANAC

U P D A T E D
S T A T I S T I C S

Through NOV. 23

THE SEASON IN REVIEW
1992
LATE WINNERS • STANDINGS

SEC A

PAGE 17

AUTO RACING

Late 1992 Results

NASCAR

Date	Event	Winner (Pos.)	Avg.mph	Earnings	Pole	Qual.mph
Sept.28	Goody's 500	Geoff Bodine (7)	75.424	$ 60,550	K.Petty	92.497
Oct. 6	Tyson Holly Farms 400	Geoff Bodine (3)	107.360	71,625	A.Kulwicki	117.133
Oct. 11	Mello Yello 500	Mark Martin (4)	153.602	101,500	A.Kulwicki	179.027
Oct. 25	AC Delco 500	Kyle Petty (1)	130.748	153,100*	K.Petty	149.675
Nov. 1	Pyroil 500	Davey Allison (12)	103.885	65,285	R.Wallace	128.141
Nov. 15	Hooters 500	Bill Elliott (11)	133.322	93,600	R.Mast	180.183

*Includes carryover Unocal 76 bonus for winning race from pole—Petty ($98,800).
Winning Cars: Ford Thunderbird 5 (Bodine 2, Allison, Elliott, Martin); Pontiac Grand Prix (K.Petty).

IndyCar

Date	Event	Winner (Pos.)	Time	Avg.mph	Pole	Qual.mph
Oct. 4	Bosch Spark Plug GP	Bobby Rahal (3)	1:03:07.8	128.848	Mi.Andretti	181.435
Oct. 18	Toyota Monterey GP	Michael Andretti (1)	1:51:34.4	99.996	Mi.Andretti	111.967

Winning car: Lola Chevrolet (Rahal); Lola Ford (Mi.Andretti).

Formula One

Date	Grand Prix	Winner (Pos.)	Time	Avg.mph	Pole	Qual.mph
Sept.27	Portugal	Nigel Mansell (1)	1:34:46.659	121.491	N.Mansell	133.222
Oct. 25	Japan	Riccardo Patrese (2)	1:33:09.553	124.379	N.Mansell	134.731
Nov. 8	Australia	Gerhard Berger (4)	1:46:54.786	106.780	N.Mansell	114.680

Winning Constructors: Williams-Renault 2 (Mansell, Patrese); McLaren-Honda (Berger).

BOWLING

1992 Fall Tour Results

PBA

Final	Event	Winner	Earnings	Final	Runner-up
Oct.11	Japan Cup '92 (Tokyo)	Parker Bohn III	$18,500	258-235	Tsuguo Tsukahara
Oct.21	Touring Players Champs	Pete Weber	27,000	219-192	Harry Sullins
Oct.28	Rochester Open	Marc McDowell	23,000	267-215	Randy Pederson
Nov. 4	Taylor Lanes Open	Amleto Monacelli	23,000	246-193	Chris Warren
Nov. 11	Brunswick World Open	Jeff Lizzi	39,000	247-192	Amleto Monacelli

Seniors

Final	Event	Winner	Earnings	Final	Runner-up
Sept.30	Don Carter Classic	Les Zikes	$ 5,000	235-185	John Handegard
Oct. 7	Naples Hammer Open	John Hricsina	8,000	245-207	Jerry Brunette
Oct.14	Pinellas Suncoast Open	Robert Gibbs	8,000	235-187	Gene Stus

LPBT

Final	Event	Winner	Earnings	Final	Runner-up
Oct. 7	Columbia 300 Delaware Open	Carol Gianotti	$13,500	178-168	Dede Davidson
Oct.14	Hammer Eastern Open	Leanne Barrette	9,000	254-219	Carol Gianotti
Oct.25	Three Rivers Open	Carol Norman	5,000	227-169	Carol Gianotti
Nov. 1	Hammer Midwest Open	Carol Gianotti	9,000	194-158	Wendy Macpherson
Nov. 8	Ebonite Fall Classic	Carol Gianotti	7,000	200-191	C.Coburn-Carroll
Nov. 21	**Sam's Town Invitational**	Tish Johnson	20,000	279-189	Robin Romeo

BOXING

Late 1992 Major Bouts
(Oct. 1–Nov. 13)

WBA, WBC and IBF champions are listed in **bold** type. Note the following Result column abbreviations: KO (knockout); TKO (technical knockout); Wu (won by unanimous decision); Ws (won by split decision); Wm (won by majority decision); TW (won by majority technical decision); No Dec. (no decision).

New champions: Undisputed heavyweight—**Riddick Bowe** (32-0, 27 KO); WBC super middleweight—**Nigel Benn** (34-2-0, 30 KO); WBA welterweight—**Crisanto Espana** (28-0-0, 24 KO); WBA lightweight—**Tony (the Tiger) Lopez** (41-3-1, 29 KO).

Heavyweights

Date	Winner	Loser	Result	Title	Site
Oct.31	Lennox Lewis	Razor Ruddock	KO 2	Non-title	London
Nov.13	Riddick Bowe	**Evander Holyfield**	Wu 12	**WBA/WBC/IBF**	Las Vegas
Nov.13	Michael Moorer	Billy Wright	TKO 2	Non-title	Las Vegas

Junior Heavyweights
(Cruiserweights)

Date	Winner	Loser	Result	Title	Site
Oct.16	**Anaclet Wamba**	Andrew Maynard	Wu 12	**WBC**	Paris

Super Middleweights

Date	Winner	Loser	Result	Title	Site
Oct. 3	Nigel Benn	**Mauro Galvano**	TKO 3	**WBC**	Marino, Italy

Middleweights

Date	Winner	Loser	Result	Title	Site
Oct.27	**Reggie Johnson**	Lamar Parks	Wu 12	**WBA**	Houston

Welterweights

Date	Winner	Loser	Result	Title	Site
Oct.31	Crisanto Espana	**Meldrick Taylor**	TKO 8	**WBA**	London

Lightweights

Date	Winner	Loser	Result	Title	Site
Oct.24	Tony (the Tiger) Lopez	**Joey Gamache**	TKO 11	**WBA**	Portland, Me.

Junior Lightweights
(Super Featherweight)

Date	Winner	Loser	Result	Title	Site
Nov.13	**Azumah Nelson**	Calvin Grove	Wu 12	**WBC**	Lake Tahoe, Nev.

Junior Bantamweights
(Super Flyweight)

Date	Winner	Loser	Result	Title	Site
Oct.31	**Sung-Kil Moon**	Greg Richardson	Ws 12	**WBC**	Inchon, S.Kor.

Flyweights

Date	Winner	Loser	Result	Title	Site
Oct.20	**Yuri Arbachakov**	Yunun Chin	Wu 12	**WBC**	Tokyo

COLLEGE FOOTBALL

AP Top 25 Poll
(as of Sunday, Nov. 22, 1992)

Sportswriters and broadcasters poll, including games through Nov. 21, 1992. First place votes in parentheses, followed by record, total points (based on 25 for 1st, 24 for 2nd, etc.) and preseason rank.

		Record	Pts	Preseason			Record	Pts	Preseason
1	Miami (61)	10-0-0	1549	1	14	Stanford	9-3-0	828	17
2	Alabama (1)	10-0-0	1483	9	15	Ohio St	8-2-1	653	19
3	Florida St	9-1-0	1407	5	16	Mississippi St	7-3-0	575	22
4	Texas A&M	11-0-0	1389	7	17	Boston College	8-2-1	516	36
5	Notre Dame	8-1-1	1289	3	18	Tennessee	7-3-0	432	21
6	Florida	8-2-0	1166	4	19	USC	6-3-1	357	26
7	Michigan	8-0-3	1084	6	20	North Carolina	8-3-0	351	42
8	Syracuse	9-2-0	1077	10	21	Washington St	8-3-0	314	51
9	Georgia	8-2-0	1030	14	22	Penn St	7-4-0	282	8
10	Colorado	9-1-1	976	12	23	Arizona	6-4-1	257	45
11	Washington	9-2-0	928	2	24	Mississippi	7-3-0	204	NR
12	Nebraska	7-2-0	914	11	25	BYU	8-4-0	114	24
13	N.C.State	9-2-1	856	27					

Others receiving votes: Hawaii (41); Bowling Green (31); Kansas (16); Illinois (9); Southern Miss (5); Virginia (4); Wake Forest (3); Arizona St., Baylor and Rice (2); Fresno St., Rutgers, Texas and UCLA (1).

BUSINESS AND MEDIA
Highest-Paid Athletes

Andre Agassi, Jim Courier and Monica Seles, all winners of Grand Slam tournaments on the men's and women's tennis tours this year and all under the age of 23, were among the Top 10 highest-paid athletes of 1992, according to the annual *Forbes* magazine Top 40 survey scheduled for publication on Nov. 23.

Basketball star Michael Jordan, who earned $32 million off the court, took over the No. 1 spot from heavyweight boxing champion Evander Holyfield.

Courier, the Australian and French Open champion, was ranked ninth on the list—the highest of all 17 newcomers to the Top 40. Other new names included boxers Larry Holmes and Julio Cesar Chavez, tennis player Michael Chang, golfers Fred Couples and Lee Trevino, football quarterback Dan Marino and nine baseball players.

Note that the survey was completed before basketball's Magic Johnson and hockey's Mario Lemieux signed new mega-contracts in October.

The *Forbes* Top 40

The 40 highest-paid athletes of 1992 (including salary, winnings, endorsements, etc) according to the Nov. 23, 1992, issue of *Forbes* magazine. Nationality, birthdate and each athlete's 1991 rank are also listed. Age refers to athlete's age as of Dec. 31, 1992.

		Sport	Salary/ Winnings	Other Income	Total	Nat	Birthdate (Age)	1991 Rank
1	Michael Jordan	Basketball	$ 3.9	$32.0	**$35.9**	USA	Feb. 17, 1963 (29)	3
2	Evander Holyfield	Boxing	27.0	1.0	**28.0**	USA	Oct. 19, 1962 (30)	1
3	Ayrton Senna	Auto Racing	17.5	5.0	**22.0**	BRA	Mar. 21, 1960 (32)	5
4	Nigel Mansell	Auto Racing	12.5	2.0	**14.5**	GBR	Aug. 8, 1953 (39)	9
5	Andre Agassi	Tennis	2.0	9.0	**11.0**	USA	Apr. 29, 1970 (22)	16t
6	Arnold Palmer	Golf	0.1	10.0	**10.1**	USA	Sept.10, 1929 (63)	8
7	Joe Montana	Football	3.5	6.0	**9.5**	USA	June 11, 1956 (36)	13
8	Jack Nicklaus	Golf	0.2	9.0	**9.2**	USA	Jan. 21, 1940 (52)	10
9	Jim Courier	Tennis	3.0	6.0	**9.0**	USA	Aug. 17, 1970 (22)	—
10	Monica Seles	Tennis	2.5	6.0	**8.5**	YUG	Dec. 2, 1973 (19)	12
11	Larry Holmes	Boxing	8.0	0.2	**8.2**	USA	Nov. 3, 1949 (42)	—
12	Gerhard Berger	Auto Racing	7.5	0.5	**8.0**	AUT	Aug. 27, 1959 (33)	19t
13	Michael Chang	Tennis	1.5	6.5	**8.0**	USA	Feb. 22, 1972 (20)	—
14	Wayne Gretzky	Hockey	3.0	4.5	**7.5**	CAN	Jan. 26, 1961 (31)	19t
15	Riccardo Patrese	Auto Racing	7.0	0.5	**7.5**	ITA	Apr. 17, 1954 (38)	—
16	Greg Norman	Golf	0.2	7.0	**7.2**	AUS	Feb. 10, 1955 (37)	14t
17	George Foreman	Boxing	6.0	1.0	**7.0**	USA	Jan. 10, 1949 (43)	4
18	Julio Ceasar Chavez	Boxing	6.0	1.0	**7.0**	MEX	July 12, 1962 (30)	—
19	Fred Couples	Golf	1.5	5.5	**7.0**	USA	Oct. 3, 1959 (33)	—
20	Steffi Graf	Tennis	1.8	5.0	**6.8**	GER	June 14, 1969 (23)	16t
21	David Robinson	Basketball	2.5	4.2	**6.7**	USA	Aug. 6, 1965 (27)	24t
22	Magic Johnson	Basketball	2.5	4.0	**6.5**	USA	Aug. 14, 1959 (33)	23
23	Gabriela Sabatini	Tennis	1.5	5.0	**6.5**	ARG	May 16, 1970 (22)	22
24	Bobby Bonilla	Baseball	6.1	0.2	**6.3**	USA	Feb. 23, 1963 (29)	—
25	Stefan Edberg	Tennis	2.3	4.0	**6.3**	SWE	Jan. 19, 1966 (26)	14t
26	Dan Marino	Football	5.0	1.0	**6.0**	USA	Sept.15, 1961 (31)	—
27	Nick Faldo	Golf	0.5	5.5	**6.0**	GBR	July 18, 1957 (35)	24t
28	Pete Sampras	Tennis	1.6	4.0	**5.6**	USA	Aug. 12, 1971 (21)	32
29	Danny Tartabull	Baseball	5.3	0.2	**5.5**	USA	Oct. 30, 1962 (30)	—
30	Roger Clemens	Baseball	4.6	0.8	**5.4**	USA	Aug. 4, 1962 (30)	—
31	Dwight Gooden	Baseball	4.9	0.5	**5.4**	USA	Nov. 16, 1964 (28)	—
32	Ruben Sierra	Baseball	5.0	0.1	**5.1**	PUR	Oct. 6, 1965 (27)	—
33	Ivan Lendl	Tennis	1.0	4.0	**5.0**	USA	Mar. 7, 1960 (32)	30
34	Patrick Ewing	Basketball	4.0	1.0	**5.0**	USA	Aug. 5, 1962 (29)	27t
35	Frank Viola	Baseball	4.7	0.3	**5.0**	USA	Apr. 19, 1960 (32)	—
36	Lee Trevino	Golf	1.0	4.0	**5.0**	USA	Dec. 1, 1939 (52)	—
37	Will Clark	Baseball	4.3	0.5	**4.8**	USA	Mar. 13, 1964 (28)	36t
38	Barry Bonds	Baseball	4.7	0.1	**4.8**	USA	July 24, 1964 (28)	—
39	Doug Drabek	Baseball	4.7	0.1	**4.8**	USA	July 25, 1962 (30)	—
40	Cecil Fielder	Baseball	4.5	0.1	**4.6**	USA	Sept.21, 1963 (29)	—

Falling off the list (17): Mike Tyson (2nd in 1991); Alain Prost (6th); Razor Ruddock (7th); Larry Bird (11th); Boris Becker (18th); Jean Alesi (21st); Jennifer Capriati (26th); Rocket Ismail (27th-tie); Hot Rod Williams (29th); Bo Jackson (31st); Hakeem Olajuwon, Darryl Strawberry and Greg LeMond (all tied for 33rd); Nelson Piquet (36th-tie); Kevin Mitchell (38th); Curtis Strange (39th); Joe Carter (40th).

PRO FOOTBALL

NFL Standings
(through Nov. 23, 1992)

American Football Conference

Eastern Division

	W	L	T	PF	PA	vs Div	vs AFC
Buffalo	9	2	0	301	183	5-1-0	6-2-0
Miami	8	3	0	269	193	3-3-0	6-3-0
Indianapolis	4	7	0	147	253	2-3-0	3-7-0
NY Jets	3	8	0	166	226	2-3-0	3-5-0
New England	2	9	0	162	260	2-4-0	2-6-0

Central Division

	W	L	T	PF	PA	vs Div	vs AFC
Pittsburgh	8	3	0	226	153	3-1-0	7-2-0
Houston	6	5	0	246	197	2-3-0	5-5-0
Cleveland	5	6	0	167	176	2-1-0	4-5-0
Cincinnati	4	7	0	197	249	1-3-0	3-4-0

Western Division

	W	L	T	PF	PA	vs Div	vs AFC
Denver	7	4	0	175	207	3-2-0	6-2-0
Kansas City	7	4	0	228	172	5-1-0	5-3-0
San Diego	6	5	0	187	179	2-3-0	5-5-0
LA Raiders	5	6	0	176	171	3-2-0	4-4-0
Seattle	1	10	0	73	218	0-5-0	1-7-0

National Football Conference

Eastern Division

	W	L	T	PF	PA	vs Div	vs NFC
Dallas	9	2	0	263	162	5-1-0	6-2-0
Philadelphia	7	4	0	255	168	4-2-0	5-3-0
Washington	6	5	0	178	187	1-3-0	4-4-0
NY Giants	5	6	0	248	249	2-2-0	4-4-0
Phoenix	3	8	0	184	241	1-5-0	3-8-0

Central Division

	W	L	T	PF	PA	vs Div	vs NFC
Minnesota	8	3	0	276	174	6-1-0	6-2-0
Green Bay	5	6	0	168	218	2-3-0	3-5-0
Chicago	4	7	0	227	261	3-4-0	4-6-0
Tampa Bay	4	7	0	198	256	3-4-0	4-5-0
Detroit	3	8	0	196	229	2-4-0	2-7-0

Western Division

	W	L	T	PF	PA	vs Div	vs NFC
San Francisco	9	2	0	319	182	6-0-0	7-1-0
New Orleans	8	3	0	211	141	2-2-0	7-3-0
Atlanta	4	7	0	200	302	1-3-0	3-5-0
LA Rams	4	7	0	200	233	0-4-0	2-5-0

GOLF

Late 1992 Tournament Results

PGA Tour

Last Rd	Tournament	Winner	Earnings	Runner-Up
Sep.27	B.C.Open	John Daly (266)	$144,000	4-way tie (272)
Oct. 4	Buick Southern Open	Gary Hallberg (206)†	126,000	J.Gallagher (207)
Oct.11	Las Vegas Invitational	John Cook (334)	234,000	D.Frost (336)
Oct.18	Disney World/Olds Classic	John Huston (262)	180,000	M.O'Meara (265)
Oct.25	H-E-B Texas Open	Nick Price (263)*	162,000	S.Elkington (263)
Nov. 1	PGA Tour Championship	Paul Azinger (276)	360,000	L.Janzen & C.Pavin (279)
Nov. 8	World Cup of Golf (Madrid)	USA—Fred Couples & Davis Love III (548)	120,000 120,000	SWE—Forsbrand & Johansson (549)
Nov. 8	Centel Championship	Don Pooley (268)	115,000	G.Morgan (269)
Nov. 15	Kapalua International	Davis Love III (275)	144,000	M.Hulbert (276)
Nov. 22	Shark Shootout	Tom Kite & Davis Love III (190)	125,000 125,000	3-way tie (192)

*Playoff: Texas—Price won on 2nd hole.
†Rain shortened
Second place ties (3 players or more): 4-WAY—**B.C.Open** (J.Edwards, K.Green, J.Hass, N.Henke). 3-WAY—**Shootout** (F.Couples & R.Floyd, H.Irwin & B.Lietzke, N.Price & B.R.Brown).
Remaining events (2): Skins Game (Nov.26-29); JCPenny Classic (Dec.5-8) and Sazale Classic (Dec.3-6).

European PGA Tour

Last Rd	Tournament	Winner	Earnings	Runner-Up
Sept.27	Piaget Belgian Open	Miguel Jimenez (274)	£100,000	B.Lane (277)
Oct. 4	Mercedes German Masters	Barry Lane (272)	100,000	3-way tie (274)
Oct. 11	World Match Play	Nick Faldo (8&7)	160,000	Jeff Sluman
Oct. 11	Honda Open (Hamberg)	Bernhard Langer (273)	75,000	D.Clarke (276)
Oct. 18	Alfred Dunhill Cup	England (2-0)	300,000	Scotland
Oct. 25	Iberia Madrid Open	David Feherty (272)	66,660	M.McNulty (276)
Nov. 1	Volvo Masters (Spain)	Sandy Lyle (287)*	110,000	C.Montgomerie (287)
Nov. 8	World Cup of Golf (Madrid)	USA—Fred Couples & Davis Love III (548)	120,000 120,000	SWE—Forsbrand & Johansson (549)

*Playoff: Volvo—Lyle won on 1st hole.
Second place ties (3 players or more): 3-WAY—**German Masters** (R.Davis, B.Langer, I.Woosnam).
Remaining event: Johnny Walker World Championship (Dec.16-19).

Seniors Tour

Last Rd	Tournament	Winner	Earnings	Runner-Up
Sep.27	Nationwide Championship	Isao Aoki (136)†	$120,000	R.Floyd (137)
Oct. 4	Vantage Championship	Jim Colbert (132)†	202,500	J.Dent (134)
Oct.11	Raley's Gold Rush	Bob Charles (201)	75,000	C.C.Rodriguez & G.Player (208)
Oct.18	TransAmerica Championship	Bob Charles (200)	75,000	D.Stockton (201)
Oct.25	Ralph's Classic	Ray Floyd (195)	90,000	I.Aoki (198)
Nov. 1	Kaanapali Classic	Tommy Aaron (198)	75,000	D.Stockton (199)
Nov. 8	Ko Olina Invitational	Chi Chi Rodriguez (206)	75,000	C.Coodt (212)
Nov. 15	Du Pont Cup (Kitaura, Japan)	USA (10)	—	Japan (6)

†Rain shortened
Remaining event: Senior Tour Champions (Dec.10-13).

LPGA Tour

Last Rd	Tournament	Winner	Earnings	Runner-Up
Sep.27	Los Coyotes Classic	Nancy Scranton (279)	$ 75,000	M.Mallon (280)
Oct. 4	Solheim Cup (Edinburgh)	Europe (11½)	—	USA (6½)
Nov. 1	Nichirei International	USA (21½)	—	Japan (10½)
Nov. 8	Japan Classic	Betsy King (205)*	97,500	H.Alfredsson (205)

*Playoff: Japan—King won on 4th hole.
Remaining events (2): JCPenny Classic (Dec.3-6) and JBP Cup Match Play Championship (Dec.10-13).

Team Competition
MEN
Dunhill Cup
at St. Andrews, Scotland (Oct.15-18)

Semifinals (England def. USA, 2-1): David Gilford (ENG) def. Fred Couples (USA), 69-70; Steve Richardson (ENG) def. Davis Love III (USA), 68-71; Tom Kite (USA) def. Jamie Spence (ENG), 71-72.

Semifinals (Scotland def. Australia, 2-1): Colin Montgomerie (SCO) def. Ian Baker-Finch (AUS), 68-72; Sandy Lyle (SCO) def. Rodger Davis (AUS), 69-73; Greg Norman (AUS) def. Gordon Brand Jr. (SCO), 68-73.

Final (England def. Scotland, 2-0): Richardson def. Brand, 71-73; Spence ties Montgomerie, 69-69; Gilford def. Lyle, 71-74.

WOMEN
Solheim Cup
Dalmahoy Hotel Golf & Country Club, Edinburgh, Scotland (Oct.2-4).

Day One (foursomes): Laura Davies & Alison Nicholas (EUR) def. Betsy King & Beth Daniel (USA) 1 up at 18th; Liselotte Neumann & Helen Alfredsson (EUR) def. Pat Bradley & Dottie Mochrie (USA) 2&1; Danielle Ammaccapane & Meg Mallon (USA) def. Florence Descampe & Trish Johnson (EUR) 1 up at 18th; Dale Reid & Pamela Wright (EUR) halved with Patty Sheehan & Juli Inkster (USA). Europe leads 2½ to 1½.

Day Two (four-ball): Davies & Nicholas def. Sheehan & Inkster one up at 18th; Descampe & Johnson halved with Brandie Burton & Deb Richard (USA); King & Mallon def. Reid & Wright 1 up at 18th; Alfredsson & Neumann halved with Bradley & Mochrie. Europe leads 4½ to 3½.

Day Three (singles): Davies def. Burton 4&2; Alfredsson def. Ammaccapane 4&3; Johnson def. Sheehan 2&1; Inkster def. Nicholas 3&2; Daniel def. Descampe 3&1; Wright def. Bradley 4&3; Catrin Nilsmark def. Mallon 3&2; Kitrina Douglas def. Richard 7&6; Neumann def. King 2&1; Reid def. Mochrie 3&2. Europe wins 11½ to 6½.

HORSE RACING

Thoroughbreds
Late 1992 Major Stakes Races
(See page 14 for Breeders' Cup results.)

Date	Race	Location	Miles	Winner	Jockey	Value to Winner
Sept.27	Super Derby XIII	La.Downs	1¼	Senor Thomas	Aaron Gryder	$450,000
Oct. 3	Turf Classic	Belmont	1½ (T)	Sky Classic	Pat Day	300,000
Oct. 4	Prix de L'Arc de Triomphe	Longchamp	1½ (T)	Subotica (FRA)	Thierry Jarnet	956,000
Oct. 10	Jockey Club Gold Cup	Belmont	1¼	Pleasant Tap	Gary Stevens	510,000
Oct. 10	Oak Tree Invitational	Santa Anita	1½ (T)	Navarone	Pat Valenzuela	240,000
Oct. 10	Champagne Stakes	Belmont	1	Sea Hero	Jerry Bailey	300,000
Oct. 16	Meadowlands Cup	Meadowlands	1⅛	Sea Cadet	Alex Solis	300,000
Oct. 17	Budweiser International	Laurel	1¼ (T)	Zoman	Alan Munro	450,000
Oct. 17	My Dear Stakes	Calder	1¹⁄₁₆	Boots 'n Jackie	Mike Lee	246,000
Oct. 17	In Reality Stakes	Calder	1¹⁄₁₆	Silver of Silver	Jacinto Vasquez	246,000
Oct. 18	Rothmans International	Woodbine	1½ (T)	Snurge (IRE)	Richard Quinn	636,000
Oct. 24	NYRA Mile Handicap	Aqueduct	1	Ibero (ARG)	Laffit Pincay Jr.	300,000

Harness Racing
Late 1992 Major Stakes Races

Date	Race	Raceway	Winner	Driver	Value to Winner
Sept.24	Little Brown Jug	Delaware, OH	Fake Left	Ron Waples	$160,744
Oct. 9	Kentucky Futurity	The Red Mile	Armbro Keepsake	John Campbell	72,005
Oct. 9	BC Aged Horse/Gelding Pace	Mohawk Raceway	Artsplace	John Campbell	184,050
Oct. 9	BC Aged Horse/Gelding Trot	Mohawk Raceway	No Sex Please	Ron Waples	184,050
Oct. 9	BC Aged Mare Pace	Mohawk Raceway	Shady Daisy	Ron Pierce	153,375
Oct. 9	BC Aged Mare Trot	Mohawk Raceway	Peace Corps	Torbjorn Jansson	192,639
Oct. 23	BC 2-Yr-Old Colt/Gelding Trot	Pompano	Giant Chill	John Patterson	150,000
Oct. 23	BC 3-Yr-Old Colt/Gelding Trot	Pompano	Baltic Striker	Mike Lachance	150,000
Oct. 23	BC 2-Yr-Old Filly Trot	Pompano	Winky's Goal	Catello Manzi	150,000
Oct. 23	BC 3-Yr-Old Filly Trot	Pompano	Imperfection	Mike Lachance	150,000
Oct. 23	BC 2-Yr-Old Filly Pace	Pompano	Immortality	John Campbell	150,000
Oct. 23	BC 2-Yr-Old Colt/Gelding Pace	Pompano	Village Jiffy	Ron Waples	150,000
Nov. 6	BC 3-Yr-Old Colt/Gelding Pace	Northfield, OH	Kingsbridge	Roger Mayotte	150,000
Nov. 6	BC 3-Yr-Old Filly Race	Northfield, OH	So Fresh	John Campbell	150,000

TENNIS

Late 1992 Tournament Results
Men's Tour

Finals	Tournament	Winner	Earnings	Loser	Score
Oct. 4	Swiss Indoors (Basel)	Boris Becker	$100,800	P.Korda	36 63 62 64
Oct. 4	Queensland Open (Brisbane)	Guillaume Raoux	33,800	K.Carlson	64 76
Oct. 4	Championship of Sicily	Sergi Bruguera	41,000	E.Sanchez	61 63
Oct.11	Australian Indoor (Sydney)	Goran Ivanisevic	135,000	S.Edberg	64 62 64
Oct.11	Toulouse Grand Prix	Guy Forget	39,600	P.Korda	63 62
Oct.11	Athens International	Jordi Arrese	18,700	S.Bruguera	75 30(ret)
Oct.18	Seiko Super Tennis (Toyko)	Ivan Lendl	135,000	H.Holm	76 64
Oct.18	Bolzano Indoor	Thomas Enquist	38,800	A.Boetsch	62 16 76
Oct.17	Riklis Classic (Tel Aviv)	Jeff Tarango	18,700	S.Simiam	46 63 64
Oct.25	Taipei Classic	Jim Grabb	38,800	J.Morgan	63 63
Oct.25	CA Tennis Trophy (Vienna)	Petr Korda	40,300	G.Pozzi	63 62 57 61
Oct.25	Lyon Grand Prix	Pete Sampras	79,200	C.Poiline	64 62
Nov. 1	Stockholm Open	Goran Ivanisevic	170,000	G.Forget	76 46 76 62
Nov. 8	Paris Open Indoor	Boris Becker	297,000	G.Forget	76 63 36 63
Nov. 8	Tour de Buzios	Jaime Oncins	33,800	L.Herrera	63 62
Nov.15	European Community Champs.(Antwerp)	Richard Krajicek	144,000	M.Woodforde	62 62
Nov.15	Kremlin Cup (Moscow)	Marc Rosset	45,000	C.U.Steeb	62 62
Nov.22	ATP World Championship (Frankfurt)	Boris Becker	625,000	J.Courier	64 63 75

Remaining ATP events (2): ATP Doubles World Championship (at Johannesburg, Nov.23-29); Davis Cup final (Switzerland vs. U.S. at Ft.Worth, Dec. 4-6).

Women's Tour

Finals	Tournament	Winner	Earnings	Loser	Score
Sept.27	Nichirei International (Tokyo)	Monica Seles	$ 70,000	G. Sabatini	62 60
Oct. 4	Volkswagen Cup (Leipzig)	Steffi Graf	45,000	J. Novotna	63 16 64
Oct. 4	Open Whirlpool (Bayonne)	M.Maleeva-Fragniere	27,000	N. Tauziat	67 62 63
Oct. 4	Taiwan Open (Taipei)	Shaun Stafford	18,000	A. Grossman	61 63
Oct. 11	European Indoor (Zurich)	Steffi Graf	70,000	M.Navratilova	26 75 75
Oct. 18	Porsche Grand Prix (Filderstadt)	Martina Navratilova	70,000	G. Sabatini	76 63
Oct. 25	Midland Bank Champs.(Brighton)	Steffi Graf	70,000	J.Novotna	46 64 76
Nov. 1	Puerto Rican Open (San Juan)	Mary Pierce	27,000	G.Fernandez	61 75
Nov. 8	Bank of the West Classic (Oakland)	Monica Seles	70,000	M.Navratilova	63 64
Nov.14	Indianapolis Classic	Helena Sukova	27,000	L.Harvey-Wild	64 63
Nov.15	Va.Slims/Philadelphia	Steffi Graf	70,000	A.S-Vicario	63 36 61
Nov.21	Va.Slims Doubles Champs.(New York)	Arantxa Sanchez Vicario & Helena Sukova	45,000 45,000	L.Neiland & J.Novotna	76 61
Nov.22	Va.Slims Championship (New York)	Monica Seles	250,000*	M.Navratilova	75 63 61

*Winner's share of $250,000, plus $500,000 bonus for year-long play.
Remaining events: none (season over).

Wide World Photos

NHL franchise players **Mario Lemieux** of Pittsburgh (left) and **Eric Lindros** of Philadelphia comprise one-eighth of the 1992 Sweet Sixteen.

THE SWEET SIXTEEN

Top Personalities of The Year

Coming up with a list of the year's top performers, personalities and landmarks is bound to generate a debate or two about who really belongs in such company, so here is *The Sports Almanac's* contribution to the discussion after polling its editors, writers and researchers.

The voting criteria were these: Who made news and who made a difference in 1992? Rather than settle on a Top 10 list (impossible) or a Top 20 (too many), we've opted for the middle ground—a group of 16 individuals, teams and places that reflect the events, both good and bad, of the past 12 months.

We've chosen to call this list "The Sweet 16," although one of its members—former heavyweight champion and convicted rapist Mike Tyson—can be called anything but sweet. While the Tyson trial was undeniably the major sports story of last winter and the story of the year in boxing, we feel a little like *Time* magazine must have felt in 1979, when it named the Ayatollah Khomeini Man of the Year.

The calendar months covered by the fourth edition of *The Sports Almanac*—November 1991 through October 1992—produced such an array of worthy contenders that 60 candidates, from Davey Allison to Dave Winfield, received votes. The 44 runners-up are given on page 28.

The Sports Almanac Sweet 16

(in alphabetical order)

Andre Agassi	Ray Floyd	Eric Lindros
Camden Yards	Magic Johnson	Monica Seles
Gail Devers	Michael Jordan	Mike Tyson
Dream Team	Jackie Joyner-Kersee	Fay Vincent
Duke Basketball	Mario Lemieux	Kristi Yamaguchi
	Carl Lewis	

A. Murray/Allsport

Andre Agassi

Sometimes image isn't everything. At 22, Agassi has been called everything from a choker to a tank artist, but he became the tennis season's most unlikely hero at Wimbledon in July when he captured his first Grand Slam title in a gutsy, five-set final against Goran Ivanisevic.

While his Davis Cup play also showed a strong competitive heartbeat, Agassi lost to Jim Courier again at Paris and Flushing. Still, Barbra Streisand never called Courier a Zen master.

Janice Rettallata/Allsport

Camden Yards

Officially, Oriole Park at Camden Yards, but just call it 1992's "Field of Dreams." Three and half million fans pushed past the turnstiles to experience this architectural return to traditional baseball values and very few were disappointed.

With its brick and steel construction, short home run porch down the right field line, sparse foul territory and grassy playing field, Camden Yards is a worthy descendant of Wrigley Field and Fenway Park. All that and state of the art luxury boxes, too.

Chris Cole/Allsport

Gail Devers

Eighteen months after her feet were nearly amputated as a result of radiation treatment for Graves' disease, Devers, 25, became the comeback story of the year by winning the Olympic gold medal in the women's 100 meters and just missing a bronze in the 100-meter hurdles.

Her determination to overcome the hyperthyroid condition that appeared to ruin her promising career in 1988 was one of the most inspiring profiles in courage of this or any other Olympiad.

Duke University

Duke Basketball

In his 12th season in Durham, coach Mike Krzyzewski guided the Blue Devils to a 34-2 record, their sixth Final Four appearance in seven years and a second straight NCAA championship. Ranked No. 1 from start to finish, Duke was the first repeat national champion in 19 years.

The roster: Christian Ast, Kenny Blakeney, Ron Burt, Marty Clark, Brian Davis, Bobby Hurley, Christian Laettner, Antonio Lang, Eric Meek, Grant Hill, Thomas Hill and Cherokee Parks.

Gary Newkirk/Allsport

The Dream Team

Simply the most awesome collection of talent ever assembled in any sport, at any time. Okay, so coach Chuck Daly's squad of NBA All-Stars won the Olympic gold medal without breaking a sweat. It didn't matter. What mattered was that the world couldn't get enough of them.

The roster: Charles Barkley, Larry Bird, Clyde Drexler, Patrick Ewing, Magic Johnson, Michael Jordan, Christian Laettner, Karl Malone, Chris Mullin, Scottie Pippen, David Robinson and John Stockton.

PGA Tour

Ray Floyd

In March, shortly after a fire destroyed his suburban Miami home, Floyd won the Doral-Ryder Open, becoming only the second golfer, after Sam Snead, to win a PGA Tour event in four different decades. Five weeks later, he finished second in the Masters at age 49.

On Sept. 20, he won his first Seniors event, becoming the only golfer to win on both tours in the same year. He then donated his winnings to the Hurricane Andrew relief effort in southern Florida.

Wide World Photos

Magic Johnson

His brilliant basketball career appeared over at age 32 when he stunned the nation on Nov. 7, 1991, with the news that he had the HIV virus that causes AIDS and was retiring immediately.

But that was only the beginning. In the next 11 months, he came back to win MVP honors in the NBA All-Star Game, was the sensation of the Olympics as the foremost Dream Teamer, then rejoined the Lakers in the fall and signed a $14.5 million one-year contract extension.

Wide World Photos

Jackie Joyner-Kersee

Perhaps, at age 30, the best women's track and field performer ever. She followed up her 1991 world championship in the seven-event heptathlon with a gold medal in Barcelona, giving her two golds and a silver since 1984. No other Olympic athlete, man or woman, has ever medaled in the heptathlon or decathlon three times.

She also won a bronze medal in the long jump, making her the only woman in Barcelona to win two individual track and field medals.

Wide World Photos

Michael Jordan

Enhanced his standing as the world's best basketball player by leading the NBA in scoring for the sixth year in a row, winning his second straight regular season and playoff MVP awards, and carrying the Bulls to their second consecutive NBA title. Even won another Olympic gold medal.

Jordan, 29, also topped the *Forbes* Top 40 list of highest-paid athletes, but a $57,000 gambling debt (first denied then admitted to in court) tarnished his otherwise sterling reputation.

Wide World Photos

Mario Lemieux

Left little doubt in 1992 that he had supplanted Wayne Gretzky as the NHL's main man. Despite missing 16 regular season games with a bad back and six playoff games with a broken left hand, he won his third scoring title, led the Penguins to their second straight Stanley Cup and became the first player to win back-to-back playoff MVP awards.

He celebrated his 27th birthday on Oct. 6 by signing a league record, seven year, $42 million contract to stay in Pittsburgh.

Wide World Photos

Carl Lewis

At 31, he was supposed to be over the hill. The Olympic trials confirmed that notion when he failed to qualify for either the 100 or 200 meters. He went to Barcelona as an underdog in the long jump and a long shot to run on the U.S. 4x100 relay team.

So what happened? He won the long jump and anchored a world record in the relay, pushing his career gold medal count to eight. Afterward, experts were calling him the biggest star in the history of the Olympics.

Chris Cole/Allsport

Monica Seles

The top-ranked women's tennis player in the world for two years running and winner of three Grand Slam titles in both 1991 and 1992. No player, man or woman, has ever won as many Grand Slam events (7) before turning 19.

Grunt-and-volleyed her way past Steffi Graf in an epic French Open final in June, but then fell silent in the Wimbledon final and lost to Graf in straight sets. Also the only woman to crack the *Forbes* Top 40 list of highest-paid athletes.

Philadelphia Flyers

Eric Lindros

The most hyped and controversial player in the history of the NHL. And he's only 19. Debuted as a rookie with the Flyers on Oct. 6, a year after refusing to sign with Quebec, the team that picked him first in the 1991 draft.

By sitting out a year, the 6-4, 239-pound center forced the Nordiques to trade his rights for five players, a No. 1 draft pick and $15 million. The Flyers then signed him for over $3 million a year, second only to Lemieux.

Gary Mook/Allsport

Mike Tyson

His trial and eventual conviction on Feb. 10, for the rape of an 18-year-old beauty contestant in the summer of 1991 was the most sensational and sordid sports story of the year. The 26-year-old ex-heavyweight champion was subsequently sentenced to six years in jail, but many believe he may be paroled after three.

If the conviction date sounds familiar, it should. On Feb. 10, 1990, Tyson lost his title in Tokyo when Buster Douglas knocked him out in the 10th round.

Wide World Photos

Fay Vincent

Stubborn, 54-year-old former baseball commissioner who was forced out of office in a September owners' coup.

Although he enjoyed good relations with fans, players and the media, Vincent served at the pleasure of the owners and they were not pleased with his handling of such issues as expansion money allocation and National League realignment. His ouster removed the best hope for avoiding a possible labor showdown with the players' union in 1993.

Mike Powell/Allsport

Kristi Yamaguchi

Returned the women's figure skating gold medal to the United States for the first time since 1976, by combining artistry with athletic ability and keeping her balance while those around her crashed and burned. The 20-year-old then followed her Olympic triumph by repeating as world champion.

Joined with double gold medalist Bonnie Blair, Cathy Turner and Donna Weinbrecht to capture all five of America's gold medals at the Albertville Winter Games.

Also Receiving Votes
(in alphabetical order)

Davey Allison (auto racing)
City of Barcelona
Charles Barkley (basketball)
Larry Bird (basketball)
Bonnie Blair (speedskating)
Barry Bonds (baseball)
Pat Borders (baseball)
George Brett & Robin Yount (baseball)
Sergei Bubka (track & field)
Chicago Bulls (basketball)
Francisco Cabrera (baseball)
Julio Cesar Chavez (boxing)
Fred Couples (golf)

Jim Courier (tennis)
Pat Day (horse racing)
Danish national soccer team
Dennis Eckersley (baseball)
Stefan Edberg (tennis)
Krisztina Egerszegi (swimming)
Marshall Faulk (college football)
Nick Faldo (golf)
Greg Garrison (prosecutor in Tyson trial)

Evander Holyfield (boxing)
Bill Koch and the crew of *America*[3] (yachting)
Petra Kronberger (skiing)
Christian Laettner (college basketball)
Nigel Mansell (auto racing)
Miami of Florida football
Shannon Miller (gymnastics)
Terry Norris (boxing)

Dan O'Brien (track & field)
Pittsburgh Penguins (hockey)
Russian hockey players
Deion Sanders (baseball & football)
Juan Antonio Samaranch (Olympics)
Citizens of Sarajevo
Vitaly Scherbo (gymnastics)
Gary Sheffield (baseball)
Thurman Thomas (football)
Alberto Tomba (skiing)
Gwen Torrence (track & field)
U.S. womens national soccer team
Washington Redskins (football)
Dave Winfield (baseball)

THE YEAR IN REVIEW

by Scott Ostler

Moonstruck

Sports seemed to be played under a year-long full moon in 1992; luckily several women emerged to save the day.

God retired. That's what kind of year 1992 was.

Not THE God, thank God. The God who retired was Doug Harvey, the National League umpire who picked up the catchy nickname "God" several years ago when he tried to wave off a rainstorm.

Still, who WAS calling the shots in '92? Something weird was in the air. Sports were played under a year-long full moon. Jupiter was aligned with Pluto and Pluto was aligned with Goofy and Snoopy and Schottzie.

The Bird stopped flying, The Great One sat one out, Little Leaguers were the biggest cheaters and the mightiest Olympic battles were fought between shoe companies and cola makers.

Pure, old-fashioned sports triumph was in short supply. The magic moments, those that shine in our memories, are usually the Kirk Gibson home runs and the Joe Montana passes. This year the headlines were dominated by scenes behind the scenes. The field of valor was overshadowed by the craziness.

There were exceptions, of course. Baseball gave us another classic Fall Classic. Canada, after sitting out the first 88 World Serieses, joined the party by sending the Toronto Blue Jays to battle

the valiant Atlanta forces, led by Ted Turner and Jane Fonda. The chopping and chanting of the Braves' fans, the flashing feet of Deion Sanders couldn't stop the Jays.

The rock-steady hitting of Series MVP Pat Borders, and an 11th inning double by Ancient Dave Winfield (41) in the sixth and deciding game sent Toronto and all of Canada into ecstacy.

But even the World Series was almost upstaged by sideline schtick. Prime Time Sanders got himself in hot water by tossing buckets of ice water on TV Tim McCarver during the Braves' clubhouse pennant celebration, an incident that became the Big Story prior to Series Game 1.

When a U.S. Marine color guard at Game 2 in Atlanta accidentally carried a Canadian flag upside down, a huge furor ensued, fueled by Canadian insecurity and, in the end, diffused by Canadian equanimity.

The Series' socko finish aside, baseball as a whole was beset by controversy, as were most sports. Ninety-two was like "The Phantom of the Opera"—the main action swirled and unfurled in the wings and secret corners of the theater, rather than on stage.

Why? Was it because the media, and perhaps the public, has become obsessed with the titillating and the tawdry, has grown bored with the glory of the games themselves? Or did we simply hap-

Scott Ostler, formerly of the *Los Angeles Times* and *The National*, is now a columnist for the *San Francisco Chronicle*.

Wide World Photos

Wide World Photos

While **Doug Harvey** (left) walked away with dignity from a 31-year NL umpiring career on Oct. 4, there was nothing dignified about the upside-down Canadian flag presented by the U.S. Marine color guard before Game 2 of the World Series.

pen across a year in which crimes, quotes and off-field mishaps bumped the *sports* part of sports to the agate columns?

Example: The U.S. Olympic basketball Dream Team was the centerpiece of the Summer Games in Barcelona. But do we remember the Dream Team's games—won by an average of 45 points—or do we recall more vividly the team's training outposts in La Jolla and Monte Carlo, the luxury hotel in Barcelona, Charles Barkley's outrageous quotes, Michael Jordan's golf or Magic Johnson's messiah-like spell over the fans?

Even with the Dream Team, it was money that mattered. A squabble between Pepsi and Coke threatened to knock Pepsi-man Magic out of the Olympics before they started. Then, at the medal ceremony, Magic, Michael and Sir Charles—all Nike corporate loyalists—covered a rival logo with American Flags. Oh, say can you see any Reebok on me?

As for the Olympics as a whole, what Olympic stat is more significant than this one: Two. The two cities that hosted the Winter and Summer Games of 1984—Sarajevo and Los Angeles—were engulfed in flames of civil strife eight years later. Sarajevo was caught in a bloody civil war while riots broke out in South Central L.A. after four white policemen were acquitted in the Rodney King beating case.

In tennis, will 1992 be remembered as the year Andre Agassi made his big breakthrough at Wimbledon, winning his first Grand Slam event? Or did he raise more eyebrows by striking up a deeeep friendship at the U.S. Open with Barbra Streisand, who sighed of her charming prince, "He's playing like a Zen master. He's very much in the moment"?

Like, where else would he be?

At Wimbledon, the London tabloids, bored with the tennis, made catty remarks about Monica Seles' rear end, and aimed "grunt-o-meters" at her to measure the decibel level of her unladylike (or so was the implication; the tabloids didn't meter the men) grunts.

31

Magic Can't Say Goodbye

Earvin (Magic) Johnson is strolling along one of the main boulevards in Barcelona during the 1992 Olympics. A crowd of several hundred people stroll with him.

He finishes a snack of potato chips and tosses away the bag—into a trash can, of course. Swish. Instantly, dozens of grown men dive for the wrapper.

Years from now that crumpled wrapper, mounted on a walnut plaque, will hang above the mantle in the home of some lucky Barcelonian.

Such is the hold Magic Johnson has taken over the hearts of fans everywhere, that his trash is sacred.

In the more dignified setting of the Opening Ceremonies, Magic was besieged by athletes of every nation, desperate for a snapshot, a handshake, a smile.

It was Magic Johnson's year. He had retired from the NBA on Nov. 7, 1991, in the aftershock of learning he had contracted the deadly HIV virus.

But Magic never really went away. He was in the public eye constantly—talking, being interviewed, visiting the sick, smiling, playing pickup basketball, sending out the message that life is to be lived, for a day or for a decade.

He joined the President's Commission on AIDS, then resigned in the fall to protest the government's inactivity. Magic never could stand to sit on the ball.

Never was he tougher than in '92, not even in that game at the end of his rookie season, when he played every position and scored 42 points and brought an NBA championship to Los Angeles.

Magic could not leave basketball. He played HORSE with his Laker pals before the fans arrived at the Forum, and he played ball in half the gyms in L.A.

Then, surprised at how well he was feeling, he accepted the vote of the fans and started in the '92 NBA All-Star game, ignoring considerable protests from the general population and even from some fellow players.

The game had the makings of a final, melancholy curtain call. But with the help of guys like Dennis Rodman, who had too

Wide World Photos

Magic Johnson with new uniform the day he signed with the Lakers in 1979.

much pride in himself and respect for Magic to concede a basket ("He'll have to earn anything he gets off me"), Magic re-entered the NBA.

He took over the game with a dazzling performance of no-look passes, no-pass looks and no-way hooks, with a *coup de grace* over-your-face three pointer at the buzzer.

Then, after leading the Dream Team to the gold in Barcelona, Magic officially un-retired from NBA ball on Sept. 30. Again there were public protests. It's not safe. It's not fair to his family.

But to Magic, his family is everyone who watches basketball, who lives for the moment when the 6-9 point guard is thundering downcourt, pounding the ball, dreaming up 100-mph chess moves.

"It's winnin' time," Magic said at the press conference to announce his return.

That's the exact same phrase he uttered just before that last game in 1980. He also said back then, "I thrive on pressure," and somehow the man never changes.

Larry Bird retired because, due to his back, he could not play. Magic un-retired because he could.

He and Bird are true brothers of the soul, and Magic's one regret was that he could not actually perform miracles. If he could, he would have brought Bird back with him.

—Scott Ostler

Bird Can And Does

by Bob Ryan

Aging superstar athletes retire for one of two reasons: a) they have seen their skills erode to the point where they risk embarrassment, and b) they are physically unable to perform.

Larry Bird goes out as a b).

The greatest forward who has ever played basketball officially announced his retirement from the Boston Celtics and the NBA on Aug. 18. It was, he said, an easy decision. He was a wonderfully conditioned athlete, but he had a bad back, and that was that.

"I would like to have played a little longer," he explained, "but I've had enough pain to last me a lifetime."

Larry Bird did not stumble around like some has-been this past season. He averaged 19 points a game and was the team's best passer and defensive rebounder, as indeed he was from the first moment he slipped on a Celtics' uniform 13 years ago. But due to the persistent back problem—an operation in June 1991 proved to be only partly successful—he had his great days, his good days and his just-get-by days.

Imagine the frustration Bird felt on the just-get-by days. "You know," he said one day during the Dream Team experience, "when I'm healthy, I can still play."

The Portland Trail Blazers would second the motion. On the afternoon of Mar. 15, Bird reminded a national television audience of his ongoing greatness as he led the Celtics to a double overtime victory over the Western Conference champions by submitting a line of 49 points, 14 rebounds, 12 assists and four steals. Five months later, he was forced into premature retirement.

Bird retires with three league MVP awards, three championship rings and everyone's acclamation as the greatest forward of all-time. He may even have been the greatest player, period. Skeptics wondered aloud if his well-documented running and jumping deficiencies would prevent him from matching his collegiate exploits when he came into the NBA, but Bird quickly demonstrated that he was even better than advertised as he earned Rookie of the Year and first-team All-Star honors. From then on, he only got better. What he couldn't get, in the end, was healthier.

Wide World Photos

Larry Bird with new uniform the day he signed with the Celtics in 1979.

Along with his friend Magic Johnson, he reminded people that the greatest thing in basketball was the pass. Boston Garden fans warmed up to him as they had to no other Celtic. The last unsold seat for a Celtic home game was in December of 1981, and Bird is the reason.

He wasn't always a physically fragile being. He missed a total of 13 games during his first seven seasons. Not playing games he was being paid to play was a monumental aggravation and embarrassment, and he would do anything humanly possible to get ready for action.

The irony of his physical situation is that following the 1986-87 season he got fitness religion and transformed his body into its leanest and strongest state ever. But neither his heels, from which bone spurs were removed in 1988, nor his back were interested in the news. The back had the final say.

Larry Bird played through the pain as long as he could. He was amazingly tough, so much so that Red Auerbach said, "Nobody in my 42 years in Boston ever played hurt the way he did."

Most people in Boston figure you can leave out the word "hurt."

Bob Ryan is a columnist for *The Boston Globe* and wrote the 1990 best-seller, Drive: the Story of My Life, with Larry Bird.

Daniel Mainzer

Indianapolis 500 Rookie of the Year **Lyn St. James** with the girls who swept the three divisions of the All-American Soapbox Derby on Aug. 8th (from left to right): **Bonnie Thornton** of Las Vegas, **Carolyn Fox** of Salem, Ore. and **Loren Hurst** of Akron.

Monica's rivals picked up the gruntball and ran with it. They protested Monica's squeal and had her silenced. With hushed tones once again wafting over center court, Seles fell quietly to Steffi Graf in the finals, 6-2, 6-1.

Elsewhere, Monica's grunt and volley game did not produce a national outcry to shut up and, free to exhale with gusto, she won three of the four Grand Slam titles for the second year in a row.

London tabloids weren't the only heartless hounds of news. *USA Today* "outed" Arthur Ashe, revealing a secret he wished to keep secret: That he has AIDS.

An angry Ashe, his life needlessly roiled, asked the nation's press: "Are you going to be cold, hard, crass purveyors of the facts just for the people's right to know, under the guise of freedom of the press, or are you going to show a little sensitivity about some things?"

USA Today went for Plan A.

Speaking of cold and crass, how about the heavyweight boxing division? Former champs Mike Tyson, John Tate, Buster Douglas, Trevor Berbick and Tony Tucker—they all fought the law and the law won.

Tyson was the role model. He went on trial for luring a Miss Black America contestant to his Indianapolis hotel room and failing to stop at the bell.

Tyson's attorney, William Fuller, said Desiree Washington was simply angry at Tyson because he refused to walk her to the lobby after their, uh, date.

"We admit he was rude," Fuller conceded.

Rude, plus. The jury called it rape, and no quote from the brutal boxing world was more chilling than the victim's testimony that Tyson told her during the attack, "Don't fight me, mommy."

Tyson was sentenced to six years in prison, where he'll have plenty of time to read Emily Post.

Baseball also plunged into a spiritual valley. The major league owners panicked as their century-old golden goose came closer to being goosed out. Hard financial times? In spring training games, the Dodgers asked fans sitting behind the outfield fence to return home-run balls.

The team owners wanted Fay Vincent to wield their collective sword in the power/money war against the players, but Fay had this funny idea about representing all of baseball.

The owners met and voted no confidence in Vincent, and, in the best interests of what was left of the game, he resigned, possibly paving the way for a 1993 spring training lockout, which would save the Dodgers the trouble of chasing down home-run balls.

Ah, but baseball is for kids, right? In August, the team from Zamboanga City in the Philippines trounced Long Beach, Calif., 15-4, in the championship game of the Little League World Series. Then a Philippine reporter uncovered evidence that 8 of the 14 Philippine players were ringers from far outside the Zamboanga area. Forfeit city.

Humbled, contrite? No, the Philippine adults were angry. A Zamboanga radio personality seemed to speak for many of them when he suggested that the whistle-blowing scribe be hanged in public.

After which, let's take the kids out for sno-cones.

You like fiery violence? Then you had to love the Indy 500, where an ambulance should have taken the checkered flag. "The Greatest Spectacle In Racing"? How about the greatest debacle?

The Indy box score: 17 crashes before the race; 10 crashes during the race, involving 13 cars; 1 death; and 16 drivers with broken bones. Rookie driver Jovy Marcelo crashed and died, the first Brickyard fatality in 10 years.

The flying Andrettis got off easier. Jeff broke both lower legs, ankles, and feet, while Mario broke bones in toes of both feet.

Limping right along, we move to college football, the championship of which is decided annually by means of politically motivated regional squabbling, culminating in a vote. The national champion was Miami. Or was it Washington? We need a poll to decide which poll is most valid.

At least college athletics build character. Bobby Knight, king of grimace humor, built it by mock-threatening his players with a bullwhip. Jackie Sherrill built it, before a game against the Texas Longhorns, by making his players watch the castration of a steer named Wild Willie.

Sherrill later apologized. Wild Willie did not accept.

In this coaching trio, Jerry Tarkanian came off as a veritable Mother Theresa. All he did was resign from UNLV, then rescind his resignation in anger, then rescind the rescinding, then hire on to coach the NBA San Antonio Spurs, then sign free-agent Lloyd Daniels, who would have played for Tark at UNLV had he (Daniels) not been busted in a crack house.

Yes, yes, of course, there was good news too in 1992, although much of it, too, was off-the-field stuff.

The NHL continued to flounder, weathering its first strike, continued player brawling and a back injury that sidelined the Great Gretzky. But the league did manage to sack inept president John Zeigler, get 19-year-old superkid (and Quebec City favorite) Eric Lindros traded to Philadelphia for six players and $15 million, and break the pro sports sex barrier when the expansion Tampa Bay Lightning put a 20-year-old female named Manon Rheaume in goal for one period of an exhibition game with St. Louis.

The team's aim, perhaps, was cheap publicity, but Rheaume played well, stopping seven of nine shots. "I think she played very well for her first NHL game," said Lightning general manager Phil Esposito. "I remember my first game: I was scared to death."

It was one small step for womankind in a year in which women dominated the sports news as never before, beginning with Desiree Washington.

Even though '92 was the 20th anniversary of Title IX, women were still battling for equality. As rodeo star Lynn Jancowski said of the women's rodeo circuit: "We don't even get the quality clowns."

The quality often comes from within. If you needed an Athlete of the Year, you could find none more courageous than Gail Devers, who ran the Olympic 100 meters two years after Graves Disease had reduced her to a bleeding, crawling, shattered shell of an athlete.

Wide World Photos

Tampa Bay Lightning goaltender **Manon Rheaume** held her own against St. Louis in an NHL exhibition game on Sept. 23, stopping seven of nine shots by the Blues.

When Devers was slow out of the blocks in the 100-meter semifinals, her coach Bob Kersee asked what was wrong.

Devers: "I can't feel my feet."

Kersee: "This is the Olympic Games. You've worked hard to get here. If you can't feel your feet, you work your arms and tell your feet to keep up."

She did, they did, and she won the 100 meters, and then narrowly missed another medal in the 100-meter hurdles.

Kersee's wife, Jackie Joyner-Kersee, won her second straight gold medal in the heptathlon, and vowed to go for a three-peat in '96.

Gwen Torrance finished fourth in the 100, announced that others in the race were "not clean," steroid-wise, then won the 400, thus proving she could run more than just her mouth.

In the Winter Olympics, Kristi Yamaguchi became the first U.S. woman since Dorothy Hamill in '76 to win the figure skating gold medal and Bonnie "The Blur" Blair speedskated her way to two golds. Throw in Cathy Turner's gold in short-track speedskating and Donna Weinbrecht's in freestyle skiing and you have every gold medal the U.S. brought home from Albertville.

Seles was the dominant player in world tennis; French figure skater Surya Bonaly earned our Hotdog-of-the-Year honors with rival-psyching backflips in Olympics warmups; and, two women even broke ground by taking over as athletic directors at two Division I-A football schools—Barbara Hedges at Washington and Merrily Dean Baker at Michigan State.

And we can finally put to rest the myth of the woman driver. Lyn St. James was Rookie of the Year at Indy with an 11th place finish, girls swept the top three spots at the All-American Soap Box Derby in Akron, and Esther Canseco nimbly survived a bumper-car battle with hubby Jose.

Behind the scenes, Cookie Johnson was a guiding light for a man named Magic, and mother to Earvin III; British Open champion Nick Faldo, the world's best golfer, never went anywhere near a golf course without caddie Fanny Sunesson; and eight women jurists struck down the NFL's Plan B free agency, a blow for player freedom.

Women took their lumps, too. Martina Navratilova was reduced to whining about Seles' grunting at Wimbledon, then lost in straight sets to Jimmy Connors in a hokey Las Vegas shootout. World champion sprinter Katrin Krabbe of Germany was scratched from the Olympics after a steroid scandal. And Reds' owner Marge Schott dealt a chop block to feminist enlightenment. When asked about a new commissioner Marge said, "If they want someone to please the owners, they should hire Madonna."

But Madonna was busy *playing* baseball, in "A League of Their Own."

For women, '92 was a year of their own.

Not to sell the men short. There were true heroes—Carl Lewis, Rare Jordan, Mario Lemieux, Mark Rypien, Vitaly Scherbo, and Dave Winfield, to name a few.

The biggest male hero, though, had to be Wild Willie. As country music star Billy Ray Cyress sang (albeit in a different context)—"All gave some, some gave all." □

Gary Newkirk/Allsport

GAME FACE OF THE YEAR

A focused **Iran Barkley** before taking on and beating champion
Thomas Hearns for the WBA light heavyweight title in March.

EXTRA POINTS

EXTRA POINTS
by Charles A. Monagan

H. Darr Beiser/USA Today

OLYMPIC MASCOTS FROM HELL

For those who thought incredibly goofy Olympics mascots were the sole province of European nations, meet Whatizit—America's latest contribution to international infantilism. Whatizit, which has been described as resembling a sperm with legs, will supposedly serve as the spunky official maitre 'd to the 1996 Olympics in Atlanta.

That leaves us three years to turn Whatizit into Whatwazit.

THE FINAL CUT

Mississippi State football coach Jackie Sherrill had his team witness the castration of a bull as an "educational" experience, he told the press. He said he wanted to show his players the difference between a bull and a steer, which is what the bull is called after its voice goes up an octave. The operation, incidentally, took place during the week leading up to Mississippi State's game with the Texas Longhorns.

Charles A. Monagan is the editor of *Connecticut* magazine.

THE RED ZONE

As the baseball season entered its final month, the Cincinnati Reds once again made more news off the field than on it.

—First of all, with about a month to go and a pennant race with the Braves still a possibility, owner Marge Schott called a clubhouse meeting during which, for inspiration, she showed the players a photo of deceased team-mascot-Schottzie's grave.

—A week later, when scouting director Julian Mock had to go to Billings, Mont., to see a farm team in action, Schott, citing budgetary problems, made him drive to Montana from Cincinnati.

—In mid-September, manager Lou Piniella and relief pitcher Rob Dibble got into an expletive-filled fistfight in the Reds' locker room in front of cameras and reporters.

—Several days later, Schott was forced to miss a game with the Padres because of a dogbite.

The Braves beat the Reds by 8 games.

HORSE OF THE YEAR

Treboh Joe, a nine-year-old pacing gelding, set a harness racing record when he ran to his 166th straight defeat. Said the steed's owner-trainer-driver Willie Mitchell after the race, "Joe was raring to go in the starting gate, but by the time we reached the first turn, I knew we had the record."

QUOTES OF THE YEAR, PART I

"If I'm going down, I'm going down standing up."
> —Indiana's Chuck Person before the Pacers were swept from the playoffs by Boston.

"Tommy went on the Slim Fast diet and lost 75 games."
> —Milton Berle, on manager Tommy Lasorda of the last place Dodgers.

"You've been indicted."
> —How former tight end John Mackey learned, from a hotel receptionist, that he'd be inducted into the Pro Football Hall of Fame.

"Great trade. Who did we get?"
> —Phillies' Len Dykstra, after hearing Von Hayes had been traded to the Angels.

"I came, I saw, they kicked my butt."
> —U.S. Olympic figure skater Christopher Bowman after finishing fourth in Albertville.

Indiana Pacers

Person

Wide World Photos

Flanagan

"You know you're having a bad day when the fifth inning rolls around and they drag the warning track."
> —Oriole pitcher Mike Flanagan.

"All you see are these big kookaloos. That's why the game looks like it's played by robots. They're all like trees."
> —Hockey Hall-of-Famer Bobby Hull on the state of the NHL.

"The movie or the airport?"
> —Dodger reliever Roger McDowell, when asked if he'd seen JFK.

SYGMA

HAPPENING COUPLE

Wimbledon champ Andre Agassi and Barbra Streisand became quite an item during the U.S. Open, especially when Streisand delivered this over-the-top assessment of her new pal: "He's very intelligent; very, very sensitive, very evolved—more than his linear years. And he's an extraordinary human being. He plays like a Zen master. It's very in the moment."

WHAT WOULD MOOCHIE SAY?

The dream team from the Philippines was stripped of its Little League World Series title after officials learned some players were too old and not all the players were from the same town. The Philippines' senior Little League official countered that the U.S. rescinded the championship because it could not take losing to Filipinos.

Meanwhile, in a Whiteville, N.C., youth-league game, one coach slashed the throat of another as they argued over a rules infraction in front of their players. Richard Blackwell was charged with assault with intent to kill for his attack on Marty Butler, who needed 50 stitches to stop the bleeding.

THE MASS PIKERS

How bad were things for baseball fans in Boston during the '92 season? A T-shirt being hawked near Fenway Park read: "The Red Sox Magic Number: 911."

IndyCar

DRIVER OF THE YEAR

Racecar driver Roberto Guerrero set a new qualifying record for the Indianapolis 500 with an average speed of some 232.48 m.p.h. In the race itself, however, Guerrero lost control of his car and crashed during the parade lap.

BOX SCORE OF THE YEAR

Troy State (Ala.) rang up a nosebleed-inducing NCAA basketball scoring record in its 258-141 win over DeVry Institute. The Trojans were 102-for-190 from the field, including an astonishing 51-for-109 from three-point range. After reaching the 200-point mark with 7 minutes, 57 seconds left, Troy State actually turned up the juice a notch, scoring at a 7-point-a-minute clip over the remainder of the game.

ADIOS, PASCUAL

The Yankees' Pascual Perez arrived at camp each day during spring training in a chauffeur-driven black stretch limousine with room for eight, a TV, VCR and CD player. Less than a month after shelling out some $57,000 for the new wheels, however, Perez was on his way back home, having tested positive for cocaine and thus forfeiting his $1.9 million salary.

PROM NIGHT

A Manchester, N.H., high school baseball team had to forfeit a state tournament quarterfinal game when six players decided they'd rather go to the prom. Only eight players from the Memorial High School team showed up for the game, the others apparently deciding they had a better chance of getting past first base at the big dance.

A STACK OF FLOPJOCKS

It was a year of hype and disappointment for many of the world's top athletes, most notably:

—Dan O'Brien, half of Reebok's wildly-touted "Dan and Dave" Olympics decathlon exacta, failed to make a height in the pole vault at the trials and was left off the U.S. squad.

—Sergei Bubka, holder of 30 world records in the pole vault, no-heighted in Barcelona.

—Midori Ito of Japan felt the need to apologize publicly to her countrymen after failing to win an Olympic figure skating gold medal.

—The French racehorse Arazi was a consensus lock for the Kentucky Derby (and, by extension, the Triple Crown)—but unfortunately it actually had to run the race. Arazi finished out of the money and was essentially never heard from again.

—Gymnast Kim Zmeskal bumbled and stumbled her way out of medal consideration at the Summer Olympics.

Gerard Vandystadt/Allsport

QUOTES OF THE YEAR, PART II

"I'm very excited to be named head coach of the Baltimore Colts."

—Ted Marchibroda, on being introduced as the new coach of the Indianapolis Colts.

"I thought we probably played this week like I thought maybe we could have played last week, and I didn't even think we could play that bad last week if we played like this."

—Marchibroda, still apparently confused, following the Colts' second preseason game.

"It's not how good you are when you play good. It's how good you are when you play bad. And we played pretty good, even though we played bad. Imagine if we'd played good."

—Georgia guard Litterial Green, after the Bulldogs beat Georgia Tech, 66-65.

Indianapolis Colts
Marchibroda

Univ. of Georgia
Green

"When the pitcher threw a fastball low and outside, it looked like a fastball high and inside."

—Indian catcher Junior Ortiz, after playing a game with his contact lenses switched.

"I usually don't like to complain, but I felt there was a lot of air in the ball."

—Sacramento guard Mitch Richmond, after going 2-for-33 from the field in consecutive games.

"Millionaire."

—Russian gymnast Vitaly Scherbo, winner of six Olympic gold medals, when asked what his ambitions were upon arriving in the U.S.

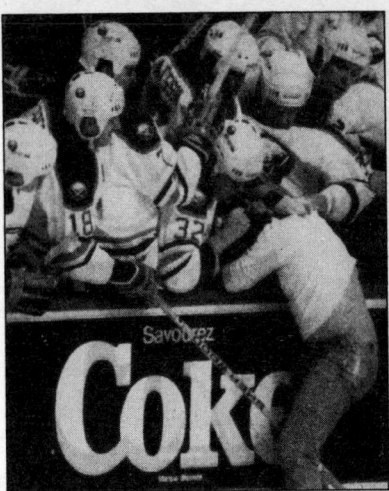
Wide World Photos

FAN APPRECIATION NIGHT

A drunken fan in Quebec attacked the visiting Buffalo Sabres' bench and was soundly thrashed for his efforts. It was one of the few instances in NHL history where players actually came back to the bench to join in a fight.

A FINE MADNESS

When Derrick Coleman of the New Jersey Nets was fined $1,000 by coach Bill Fitch for being late to practice, Coleman wrote out a check for $5,000 to cover the next four infractions as well.

Wide World Photos

BUBBLEHEAD

Indians reliever Steve Olin (left) managed to put 71 pieces of bubble gum into his mouth at one time, breaking the record of teammate Steve Wicklander (right).

NIGHTCRAWLERS 101

In an epic lake battle the likes of which had not been seen since Admiral Perry subdued the British on Lake Erie, Purdue topped Indiana in the first intercollegiate bass fishing tournament. Each college set 22 student-athletes loose for eight hours on Lake Monroe, near Bloomington, Ind., but these 352 man-hours yielded only five bass for the Boilermakers and three for the Hoosiers. Purdue was duly awarded the first Old Minnow Bucket in recognition of its come-from-below victory.

AN INJURY FOR OUR TIMES

Padres outfielder Tony Gwynn broke the tip of his finger when he slammed it in the door of his Porsche on his way to the bank.

Wide World Photos

Bruce Bennett/BBS

THE PENGUIN AND BATMAN

Mario Lemieux (left) led the Penguins to their second straight Stanley Cup title, while Pittsburgh native Michael Keaton (right) starred in his second Batman blockbuster. During the year, the Pens were sold for $60 million, while "Batman Returns" grossed $160 million.

DO THE JERK

It was another scintillating year for .244 hitter Jose Canseco. He was arrested during the off-season after using his Porsche to ram the BMW driven by his wife Esther, and then spitting on her car window. Later, after not reporting early to spring training, as the A's had requested, he said, "All they can do is spank me. What are they going to do, bench me?"

Finally, after alienating virtually all his teammates, he was traded to the Texas Rangers, where the change of scenery is apparently more conducive to his lifetsyle. "It's more relaxed here," he said. "It's an atmosphere I can relate to. In Oakland it was always win, win, win—and you get fed up with it."

THE GOSPEL ACCORDING TO ST. CHARLES

"I'm on the lovely island of St. Thomas."
—Charles Barkley, informing a reporter that he was on a vacation from talking to the press

"Poor people can't live here—so I guess I fit in."
—Barkley, on life in Monte Carlo

"I got the superstar treatment. Everybody else got bologna and water. I got bologna and milk."
—Barkley, after spending four hours in jail on a Milwaukee assault charge

"Why don't they take their butt-whipping like people and go home?"
—Barkley, after beating up on the Angolans

Wide World Photos

SORE SIGHTS FOR EYES

—Bo Jackson trying to run down the first base line during spring training with the White Sox.

—Bjorn Borg continuing his "comeback" even while declaring bankruptcy. At last look, he was ranked 1,043rd worldwide.

—Baseball's Jack Clark declaring bankrupcty and revealing he owns 18 cars, including three 1992 Mercedes, each of which he bought for over $100,000.

—The violent behavior in Chicago that followed the Bulls' successful defense of their NBA title. Revelers set fire to cars and looted stores as more than 100 people were injured and over 1,000 arrested.

—Bobby Fischer's sour and paranoid behavior as he emerged from two decades of hiding to take on Boris Spassky in a much-ballyhooed chess match in Yugoslavia.

MEDIA NOTES

—A May 17 delivery strike shut down Pittsburgh's two daily newspapers—two weeks before the Penguins won the Stanley Cup. Five months later, the Pirates lost the NL playoffs in the most exciting bottom of the ninth inning in baseball history and the locals still had to buy an out-of-town paper to read about it.

—A reporter for the *New York Post* described the Mets collectively as "spoiled 20-year-old millionaire boys with pornographic minds, sixth grade vocabularies and good throwing arms.

—*The Sporting News*, long considered to be "the bible of baseball," decided not to run box scores any longer.

—A London tabloid reporter covering Wimbledon asked Monica Seles, "Have they told you not to wear figure-hugging outfits because your bottom's too big?"

—In Portland, *The Oregonian* dropped the use of ethnic nicknames. "We will not be a passive participant in perpetuating racial or cultural stereotypes in our community," the paper said. So much for the Blazers drafting Cherokee Parks.

SLAM DINK

The Suns' Cedric Ceballos impressed onlookers (and the judges) at the NBA's Slam Dunk competition when he jammed home an acrobatic winner while blindfolded. He was awarded first place, but later revealed that he actually could see perfectly well through the blindfold.

SEPARATED AT BIRTH?

Wide World Photos

Pat Riley
Knicks coach

Orion Home Video

Anthony Hopkins
Oscar winner

Wide World Photos

Felipe Alou
Expos manager

Simon & Schuster

Ossie Davis
Veteran actor

Hanna-Barbera Prod.

Huckleberry Hound
Cartoon legend

World Cup USA 94

Striker
World Cup mascot

Wide World Photos

YOU'RE OUTTA HERE!

Thirty-nine major league head coaches and managers were either fired, demoted, kicked upstairs or got out on their own over the last 12 months. Here's the list:

NFL
Jerry Burns, Vikings (retired)
Dan Henning, Chargers (fired)
Lindy Infante, Packers (fired)
Chuck Knox, Seahawks (quit)
Chuck Noll, Steelers (retired)
John Robinson, Rams (quit)
Rick Venturi, Colts (demoted)
Richard Williamson, Bucs (fired)
Sam Wyche, Bengals (fired)

NBA
Larry Brown, Spurs (fired)
Don Chaney, Rockets (fired)
Chuck Daly, Pistons (quit)
Bill Fitch, Nets (quit)
Cotton Fitzsimmons, Suns (retired)
Frank Hamblen, Bucks (fired)
Del Harris, Bucks (quit)
Rex Hughes, Kings (fired)
K.C. Jones, Sonics (fired)
Jim Lynam, 76ers (promoted to GM)
Dick Motta, Kings (fired)
Mike Schuler, Clippers (fired)
Paul Westhead, Nuggets (fired)

BASEBALL
Lou Piniella, Reds (quit)
Bill Plummer, Mariners (fired)
Greg Riddoch, Padres (fired)
Tom Runnells, Expos (fired)
Bobby Valentine, Rangers (fired)

NHL
Rick Bowness, Bruins (fired)
Pat Burns, Canadiens (quit)
Dave Chambers, Nordiques (fired)
Rick Dudley, Buffalo (fired)
Paul Holmgren, Flyers (fired)
Mike Keenan, Blackhawks (GM only)
Tom McVie, Devils (fired)
Doug Risebrough, Flames (GM only)
Jim Roberts, Whalers (fired)
Brian Sutter, Blues (fired)
Tom Watt, Maple Leafs (fired)
Tom Webster, Kings (fired)

FASHION NOTES

—The big fashion hit of the Summer Olympics was tie-dyed shirt of the Lithuanian basketball team, which had been designed and donated to the team by the Grateful Dead. Some 25,000 of the shirts were sold—at $30 a pop—in the weeks immediately following the Games, with part of the proceeds going to the financially-strapped Lithuanians.

—The red, white and blue sweaters worn by the U.S. team for the Winter Olympics' opening ceremony were made in Hong Kong.

—Nadia Comaneci, the 5-time gold medalist, made her biggest splash in years by appearing in her underwear in a Jockey advertisement.

—Sharp-dressed boxing man Hector "Macho" Camacho (below) sure looked good before his fight with Julio Cesar Chavez. He didn't look too good afterward, though.

Holly Stein/Allsport

BUSH LEAGUE

George Bush's bad year got off to a bad start in Baltimore, when his Opening Day first pitch bounced in the dirt and rolled to the backstop.

Ron Vesely

George Brett (standing) and **Robin Yount** each reached 3,000 career hits in September; Yount on the 9th and Brett on the 30th.

1991-1992 CALENDAR

Sun	Mon	Tue	Wed	Thu	Fri	Sat
					1	2
3	4	5	6	7	8	9
10	11	12	13	14	15	16
17	18	19	20	21	22	23
24	25	26	27	28	29	30

Wide World Photos

Dale Earnhardt
Wins fifth Winston Cup.

2 Black Tie Affair wins the Classic and French-based two-year-old Arazi runs off with the Juvenile as Breeders' Cup races return to Churchill Downs.

3 Salvador Garcia of Mexico (2:09.28) and Liz Mc-Colgan of Scotland (2:27.23) are first across finish line in 22nd running of New York City Marathon.

4 Texas A&M basketball program placed on two years' probation and barred from 1992 NCAA tournament for recruiting violations under former coach Kermit Davis, Jr.

7 Magic Johnson stuns the nation by announcing that he has been infected by the HIV virus that causes AIDS and is retiring from basketball at age 32. The virus was discovered while the L.A. Lakers' star guard was undergoing tests for an insurance policy.

10 Cleveland quarterback Bernie Kosar breaks Bart Starr's 26-year-old NFL record of 294 passes without an interception, reaching 308 before being picked off by Ben Smith in the second quarter of a 32-30 loss to Philadelphia.

Martina Navratilova beats Monica Seles to win Virginia Slims of California tournament. The victory is Navratilova's 157th career title, tying her with all-time leader Chris Evert.

13 Roger Clemens of Boston wins third AL Cy Young Award. Only four other pitchers have won three times—Sandy Koufax, Jim Palmer, Tom Seaver and four-time winner Steve Carlton.

14 NFL suspends Pittsburgh guard Terry Long for four weeks without pay for violating league rules on steroid use.

15 Cleveland Indians trade left-handed pitcher Greg Swindell to Cincinnati for right-handers Jack Armstrong, Scott Scudder and Joe Turek.

UCLA surprises Indiana, 87-72, in Hall of Fame Tip-off Classic as 1991-92 college basketball season begins.

16 Second-ranked Miami topples No. 1 Florida St., 17-16, in Tallahassee as last-second, 34-yard Seminoles' field goal try misses wide right. Hurricane win is fifth in six years against FSU.

17 Dale Earnhardt captures fifth NASCAR Winston Cup title with fifth place finish in Hardee's 500 in Atlanta.

Pete Sampras downs Jim Courier in four sets to win second annual ATP Championship in Frankfurt.

18 Detroit Lions lineman Mike Utley remains paralyzed following neck surgery for fractured vertebra suffered in Nov. 17 game against L.A. Rams.

Auburn basketball program placed on two years' probation and barred from 1992 NCAA tournament for recruiting violations.

20 Terry Pendleton of Atlanta gets MVP nod in NL, edging Pittsburgh's Barry Bonds by 15 points as baseball's final postseason baseball award is announced. Other winners include AL MVP Cal Ripken; NL Cy Young choice Tom Glavine; Rookies Chuck Knoblauch (AL) and Jeff Bagwell (NL); and managers Tom Kelly (AL) and Bobby Cox (NL).

23 Heavyweight champ Evander Holyfield survives first knockdown of his career (in 3rd round) then TKOs Bert Cooper, a 32-1 shot, in 7th round to defend title in Atlanta.

24 Previously unbeaten Washington upset by Dallas, 24-21, at RFK as all six NFL division leaders lose in Week 13.

Monica Seles beats Martina Navratilova in four sets to win Virginia Slims Championship and finish year at No. 1.

Rocket Ismail is named MVP of CFL Grey Cup game as Toronto beats Calgary, 36-21, in Winnipeg.

Independent investigation concludes that former U.S. Olympic Committee president Bob Helmick committed at least six conflict of interest violations, but recommends no action. Helmick resigned his post Sept. 18.

26 Bob Johnson, coach of the Pittsburgh Penguins, dies of brain cancer at age 60.

27 Cincinnati sends outfielder Eric Davis and pitcher Kip Gross to LA Dodgers for pitchers Tim Belcher and John Wetteland.

30 United States beats Norway, 2-1, in Canton, China, to win inaugural FIFA Women's World Championship in soccer.

Sun	Mon	Tue	Wed	Thu	Fri	Sat
1	2	3	4	5	6	7
8	9	10	11	12	13	14
15	16	17	18	19	20	21
22	23	24	25	26	27	28
29	30	31				

Wide World Photos

Yannick Noah
Davis Cup captain rejoices.

1 France wins Davis Cup for first time since 1932 as Guy Forget clinches title in Lyon with four-set victory over Pete Sampras.

2 Bobby Bonilla becomes baseball's latest highest-paid player ever, as New York Mets sign free agent for five years and $29 million.

4 Former USOC chief Robert Helmick resigns from International Olympic Committee amid IOC inquiries into conflict of interest charges.

5 Lou Holtz ends rumors of a possible move to Minnesota of the NFL by signing a five-year contract extension at Notre Dame.

6 Jeff Smulyan puts Seattle Mariners up for sale at $100 million. According to the club's Kingdome lease, if no local buyer emerges in 120 days, Smulyan can move the franchise.

8 Virginia beats Santa Clara, 1-0, on penalty kicks to win NCAA soccer championship.

10 Long Beach St. drops out of Division I-A football for 1992 season, citing lack of money and fan support.

11 Kansas City deals pitcher Bret Saberhagen and infielder Bill Pecota to New York Mets for outfielder Kevin McReynolds and infielders Gregg Jefferies, Kevin Miller.

San Francisco sends outfielder Kevin Mitchell to Seattle for pitchers Bill Swift, Mike Jackson and Dave Burba.

Mark Messier signs a five-year, $13 million contract with the New York Rangers, making him the NHL's third highest-paid player behind Wayne Gretzky and Mario Lemieux.

12 John Mackovic resigns as head football coach and athletic director at Illinois to become head coach at Texas.

Former All-Pro defensive end Dexter Manley, now with Tampa Bay, announces retirement after failed drug test makes him a four-time violator of NFL's drug abuse policy.

14 Michigan wide receiver Desmond Howard wins Heisman Trophy by widest margin (1,574 votes) since O.J. Simpson in 1968.

15 David Wheaton's straight-set victory over Michael Chang in the Grand Slam Cup final at Munich nets him the biggest winner's check in tennis: $2 million.

17 Cleveland routs Miami, 148-80, setting an all-time NBA victory margin of 68 points. Previous mark was 63 by L.A. Lakers over Golden St. in 1972.

18 World Series hero and free agent pitcher Jack Morris signs with Toronto for three years and $10.85 million.

John Robinson tells Los Angeles Rams that he's retiring when season ends. The Rams are 3-12 and last in NFC West.

20 New York Yankees pitcher Steve Howe, who has been suspended from baseball five times for drug and alcohol abuse, pleads not guilty to drug possession charges in Montana.

Free agent pitcher Frank Viola signs with Boston for three years and $13.9 million.

High-scoring forward Pat LaFontaine, acquired by Buffalo on Oct. 25 in a seven-player deal with N.Y. Islanders, returns from five-week absence after breaking his jaw. Sabres tie Edmonton, 4-4, at the Aud.

22 NFL regular season ends as San Francisco (10-6) routs Chicago (11-5) by 52-14 score. Despite win, 49ers fail to reach playoffs for first time in eight years.

23 San Diego Chargers fire coach Dan Henning after finishing 4-12 and last in AFC West.

24 Dick Motta is fired by NBA Sacramento Kings the day after saying he'll retire at the end of the year.

Cincinnati Bengals say Sam Wyche has quit as head coach, but Wyche says he was fired. Either way, he's gone after a 3-13 last-place finish in AFC Central.

26 Chuck Noll retires as Pittsburgh coach after 23 years, 209 victories and four Super Bowl championships.

27 David Shula is named head coach in Cincinnati at age 32, becoming youngest head coach in NFL's modern era. Meanwhile, Chuck Knox will not return as Seattle coach and Tampa Bay fires Richard Williamson.

29 Tampa Bay owner Hugh Culverhouse says former N.Y. Giants coach Bill Parcells backed out of an agreement to coach the Buccaneers.

31 Bobby Ross resigns at Georgia Tech to become head coach of San Diego Chargers.

Sun	Mon	Tue	Wed	Thu	Fri	Sat
			1	2	3	4
5	6	7	8	9	10	11
12	13	14	15	16	17	18
19	20	21	22	23	24	25
26	27	28	29	30	31	

1 Miami and Washington both finish at 12-0 and share national college football championship. Hurricanes beat Nebraska, 22-0, in Orange Bowl and win AP poll, while Huskies down Michigan, 34-14, in Rose Bowl and get nod from coaches.

2 Calgary and Toronto complete 10-player trade; center Doug Gilmour goes to Maple Leafs and winger Gary Leeman to Flames.

6 Free agent outfielder Danny Tartabull signs five-year contract with NY Yankees worth $25.5 million.

Seattle Seahawks president-GM Tom Flores becomes team's head coach four years after resigning as head coach of LA Raiders.

7 Baseball Hall of Fame elects pitchers Tom Seaver and Rollie Fingers. Seaver polls highest percentage of vote ever (98.8%), surpassing Ty Cobb (98.2% in 1936).

8 Los Angeles Rams name Chuck Knox to second tour of duty as head coach. Knox, who quit his post in Seattle on Dec. 27, coached Rams to five NFC West titles from 1973-77.

NCAA toughens Proposition 48 requirements for incoming freshmen by raising required number of college preparatory courses and minimum grade point average.

10 Minnesota Vikings name Stanford's Dennis Green, making him second black head coach in pro football's modern era.

Former Cincinnati head coach Sam Wyche signs to coach Tampa Bay.

11 U.S. Figure Skating championships in Orlando won by Christopher Bowman and Kristi Yamaguchi.

12 Buffalo and Washington clinch Super Bowl berths at home; Bills edge Denver, 10-7, while Redskins rout Detroit, 41-10.

Troy State of Alabama beats DeVry Institute, 258-141, breaking eight NCAA records—including most points in a game, set in 1991-92 when it beat DeVry, 187-116.

Hall of Fame jockey Angel Cordero Jr., listed in stable condition after surgery to remove spleen following four-horse spill Jan. 12 at Aqueduct which also broke his left arm and three ribs.

15 Seattle fires head coach K.C. Jones after 18-18 start. Sonics name assistant Bob Kloppenburg as interim coach.

City of San Jose and NL's San Francisco Giants announce conditional move to San Jose, provided local voters approve $195 million financing of new stadium on June ballot.

16 Bill Walsh named as head coach at Stanford 13 years after leaving to become head coach of San Francisco 49ers. Contract is for five years at $350,000 per.

Wide World Photos

Rollie Fingers & Tom Seaver
Off to Cooperstown.

19 Cincinnati signs shortstop Barry Larkin to five-year contract worth $25.6 million, making him second highest-paid player in baseball (behind Mets' Bonilla).

21 Pittsburgh Steelers name 34-year-old Kansas City defensive coordinator Bill Cowher as new head coach, succeeding Chuck Noll.

San Antonio Spurs fire Larry Brown as head coach after 21-17 start, name V.P. of basketball operations Bob Bass as interim.

23 College football bowl alliance officially announces nine-year agreement involving four major bowls, four secondary bowls, six conferences and Notre Dame.

George Karl returns from Europe to become head coach of Seattle SuperSonics, loses first game to Portland, 113-109, at home.

24 Monica Seles wins second straight Australian Open title, beating Mary Joe Fernandez, 6-2, 6-3.

25 Jim Courier defeats top-seeded Stefan Edberg, 6-3, 3-6, 6-4, 6-2, to become first American men's player to win Australian Open in 10 years.

Football Hall of Fame announces election of Al Davis, John Mackey, Lem Barney, and John Riggins.

26 Washington beats Buffalo, 37-24, in Super Bowl XXVI; Redskins quarterback Mark Rypien named Most Valuable Player.

27 Jury selection begins in Indianapolis rape trial of former heavyweight champion Mike Tyson.

28 Buffalo Bills assistant Ted Marchibroda named as new head coach at Indianapolis. He previously coached Colts in Baltimore (1975-79).

31 Basketball Hall of Fame announces election of Connie Hawkins, Bob Lanier and seven others.

Sun	Mon	Tue	Wed	Thu	Fri	Sat
						1
2	3	4	5	6	7	8
9	10	11	12	13	14	15
16	17	18	19	20	21	22
23	24	25	26	27	28	29

Mike Powell/Allsport

Bonnie Blair
Two more gold medals.

2 LA Clippers fire Mike Schuler after 21-24 start, name Mack Calvin interim coach.

United States defeats Argentina, 5-0, in opening round of 1992 Davis Cup competition at Kohala Coast, Hawaii.

NFC rallies in fourth quarter to beat AFC, 21-15, in Pro Bowl. Dallas wide receiver Michael Irvin (eight catches) is MVP.

5 Michael Jordan serves one-game suspension for bumping official in Jan. 3 triple-overtime loss to Utah. Jordan also fined $5,000 and forfeits $40,000 in lost salary.

6 LA Clippers sign Larry Brown to five-year contract as head coach, two-and-a-half weeks after being fired as Spurs coach.

7 Ex-heavyweight champion Larry Holmes, 42, wins unanimous 12-round decision over Ray Mercer in Atlantic City.

St. Louis Blues trade center Adam Oates to Boston for center Craig Janney and defenseman Stephane Quintal.

Mark Everett breaks 22-year-old world indoor 600-yard record in 1:07.53 at Millrose Games in New York.

8 Winter Olympics open in Albertville, France. Cross-country skiing veteran Bill Koch carries American flag in opening ceremonies.

9 MVP Magic Johnson has 25 points and nine assists as Western Conference routs East, 153-113, in NBA All-Star Game at Orlando.

10 Mike Tyson guilty on all three counts as rape trial jury of eight men and four women returns verdict after 9½ hours of deliberation. Conviction comes two years to the day after losing his heavyweight title to Buster Douglas.

Bonnie Blair captures first American gold medal of Winter Games by winning 500 meters in speedskating.

Jim Courier moves up to No. 1 in ATP computer rankings; first American to reach top of men's tennis ladder since 1985.

11 Second-ranked Virginia beats No. 1 Maryland, 75-74, in women's college basketball showdown at College Park, Md.

13 Donna Weinbrecht wins Olympic skiing gold medal in women's moguls; U.S. Hockey team upsets Finland, 4-1.

Jose Canseco arrested in Miami and charged with aggravated battery after ramming estranged wife's car.

14 Bonnie Blair becomes first American woman to win three career gold medals after taking 1,000-meter speedskating title in Albertville (her second gold of the Games).

16 Davey Allison wins Daytona 500, following footsteps of father Bobby, who won NASCAR's biggest race three times.

Magic Johnson's No. 32 retired by LA Lakers at halftime of NBA game with Boston Celtics.

Martina Navratilova wins 158th singles title, the most ever by a pro tennis player, beating Jana Novotna in three sets to win Virginia Slims of Chicago.

18 Houston Rockets fire 1991 Coach of the Year Don Chaney after 26-26 start, name assistant Rudy Tomjanovich as interim.

19 Three-team, seven-player NHL deal sends defenseman Paul Coffey to LA Kings, right wing Mark Recchi to Philadelphia, and right wing Rick Tocchet to Pittsburgh.

21 Kristi Yamaguchi becomes first American woman to win figure skating gold medal since 1976; U.S. hockey team's gold medal hopes end in 5-2 loss to Unified Team in semifinals.

22 Alberto Tomba of Italy falls short of repeating 1988 Olympic sweep of slalom and giant slalom Alpine events, finishing second in the slalom to Christian Jagge of Norway.

23 Unified Team beats Eric Lindros and Canada, 3-1, to win eighth Olympic hockey gold medal since 1956.

UNLV basketball coach Jerry Tarkanian, who submitted his resignation in June, announces he has changed his mind and will stay in order to fight new allegations against program.

27 Prairie View A&M basketball team beaten, 112-79, by Mississippi Valley St., breaking single season record for losses with 28.

Sun	Mon	Tue	Wed	Thu	Fri	Sat
1	2	3	4	5	6	7
8	9	10	11	12	13	14
15	16	17	18	19	20	21
22	23	24	25	26	27	28
29	30	31				

Wide World Photos

Martin Buser
Wins fastest Iditarod.

1 **Larry Bird** returns after missing two months with sore back, gets 26 points, 13 rebounds and nine assists as Celtics beat Mavericks, 101-91, at Boston Garden.

2 **Ryne Sandberg** becomes baseball's newest highest-paid player as Chicago Cubs announce signing of second baseman to five-year contract worth $30.5 million.

Long jump world record-holder Mike Powell named winner of 63rd annual Sullivan Award as nation's top amateur athlete.

3 **Jerry Tarkanian's** 19-year run as basketball coach at UNLV comes to a likely conclusion as Rebels beat Utah St. Tark bows out with a 508-105 record at Vegas.

Calgary GM Doug Risebrough resigns as coach of Flames, names assistant Guy Charron as replacement.

5 **Baseball owners** vote to change rules of amateur draft, allowing teams to retain rights to high school graduates for four years.

6 **NY Yankees pitcher** Pascual Perez suspended one year by baseball commissioner Fay Vincent after testing positive for cocaine.

9 **Twelve former** Soviet republics agree to compete as Unified Team at upcoming Summer Olympics in Barcelona.

10 **Bo Jackson** signs new one-year contract for $109,000 minimum with Chicago White Sox, plans to undergo hip replacement surgery during summer.

U.S. Olympic goalie Ray LeBlanc wins NHL debut, backstopping Chicago Blackhawks in 5-1 victory over San Jose.

11 **Martin Buser** wins Alaska's 1,158-mile Iditarod sled dog race in record time of 10 days, 19 hours and 17 minutes.

12 **Former Boston** Celtics guard Charles Smith convicted of vehicular homicide in hit-and-run deaths of two college students on Mar. 22, 1991.

16 **California pitcher** Matt Keough, 36, who was attempting to return to the major leagues after five years, undergoes emergency surgery after being struck in head by line drive at training camp in Scottsdale, Ariz.

17 **Baseball Hall of Fame** veterans' committee names pitcher Hal Newhouser and umpire Bill McGowan.

Pittsburgh Pirates trade 20-game winner John Smiley to Minnesota for two minor league prospects.

NFL trims list of expansion hopefuls to seven—Baltimore, St. Louis, Oakland, Jacksonville, Memphis, Charlotte and Sacramento—but says that lack of collective bargaining agreement with players may delay timetable.

18 **Instant replay** falls four votes short of renewal as NFL owners, meeting in Phoenix, favor continuation by only 17-11 (a majority of 21 votes was needed to pass).

Monica Seles' 27-match winning streak snapped in straight-set loss to Jennifer Capriati in quarterfinals of Lipton Tennis in Key Biscayne, Fla.

20 **WBA light heavyweight** champion Thomas Hearns loses title to Iran Barkley in 12-round split decision at Las Vegas.

NHL players, seeking a new collective bargaining agreement with owners, set a strike deadline of noon on Mar. 30.

New England Patriots owner Victor Kiam accepts St. Louis businessman James Orthwein's offer to buy his 51% of team for approximately $50 million.

Jim Courier loses No. 1 ranking following semifinal round loss to Michael Chang in Lipton Tennis. Stefan Edberg takes over top spot.

23 **Sites announced** for 1994 World Cup; Rose Bowl, Silverdome and Giants Stadium among nine stadiums selected to host soccer tournament.

26 **Mike Tyson sentenced** to six years in prison and fined $30,000 for rape conviction.

29 **U.S. defeats** Czechoslovakia, 3-2, as Andre Agassi beats Petr Korda in straight sets in deciding match of Davis Cup quarterfinals at Fort Myers, Fla.

Olympic champion Kristi Yamaguchi retains world figure skating title in Oakland, beating out teammate Nancy Kerrigan.

Milwaukee trades infielder Gary Sheffield to San Diego for pitcher Ricky Bones.

30 **NHL players** move back strike deadline two days; new deadline now April 1 at 3 P.M.

Sun	Mon	Tue	Wed	Thu	Fri	Sat
			1	2	3	4
5	6	7	8	9	10	11
12	13	14	15	16	17	18
19	20	21	22	23	24	25
26	27	28	29	30		

1 Strike shuts down NHL season with five days remaining in regular season as players vote 560-4 to reject owners' latest offer.

Rollie Massimino leaves Villanova to become basketball coach at UNLV; signs five-year contract worth $2 million.

NFL owners vote to shorten 1992 season to 17 weeks and give $28 million ($1 million per team) rebate to television networks in 1993.

2 NFL's Plan B signing period ends with 166 players changing teams (up from 139 in 1991).

3 Seattle Mariners owner Jeff Smulyan signs agreement to sell AL club for $100 million to local group backed by Japanese investors. Principal investor is Nintendo president Hiroshi Yamauchi.

Michigan State board of trustees appoints NCAA assistant executive director Merrily Dean Baker to succeed football coach George Perles as athletic director.

LSU junior center Shaquille O'Neal announces he will leave LSU and apply for NBA Draft.

4 Michigan and Duke reach NCAA basketball final as Wolverines beat Cincinnati, 76-72, and Blue Devils down Indiana, 81-78 in semifinals.

Bo Jackson undergoes hip reconstruction surgery in suburban Chicago, plans to rejoin White Sox after lengthy rehabilitation.

Lake Superior St. wins second NCAA hockey title, beating Wisconsin, 5-3, in Albany, N.Y.

5 Stanford captures second NCAA women's basketball title in three years, defeating Western Kentucky, 78-62, in L.A.

6 Duke becomes first team in 19 years to repeat as NCAA basketball champion, routing Michigan, 71-51, in Minneapolis. Last repeat champ was UCLA, winners of seven in a row from 1967-73.

Baseball season opens with President Bush throwing out first ball at new Camden Yards ballpark in Baltimore.

8 Arthur Ashe reveals he has had the AIDS virus since 1988, cites tainted blood transfusion during 1983 open heart surgery as cause.

10 NHL strike ends after 10 days as players win some concessions on licensing and reduced compensation for free agents. Season to resume on Apr. 12.

12 Fred Couples claims first major title, winning Masters by two strokes over 49-year-old Ray Floyd.

13 Lou Carnesecca announces retirement after 24 seasons as St. John's basketball coach; steps down with 526-200 record and 18 NCAA tournament appearances.

15 San Antonio signs Jerry Tarkanian to three-year deal worth $400,000 a year plus incentives to coach Spurs beginning with 1992-93 season.

Wide World Photos

Hirochi Yamauchi
Investing in Mariners.

19 NHL playoffs begin, but Mario Lemieux misses Pittsburgh opener with sore shoulder.

NBA regular season ends with Michael Jordan winning his sixth straight scoring title and Miami clinching its first playoff berth.

20 Defending champion Ibrahim Hussein of Kenya wins third Boston Marathon in 2:08:14; women's winner is Russian Olga Markova (2:23:43).

23 NBA playoffs begin and three coaching changes are announced—Frank Hamblen is out in Milwaukee, Paul Westhead is out in Denver and Paul Westphal will replace retiring Cotton Fitzsimmons in Phoenix after the playoffs.

Tampa Bay names Terry Crisp as coach of NHL expansion Lightning.

25 Minnesota trades two-time All-Pro defensive tackle Keith Millard to Seattle for second round draft choice.

26 Indianapolis picks defensive standouts Steve Emtman and Quentin Coryatt 1-2 in NFL Draft, then deals Eric Dickerson to LA Raiders for fourth and eighth round choices.

29 Riots break out in South Central Los Angeles after four white policemen are acquitted in Rodney King beating case. Violence causes postponement of Utah-LA Clippers playoff game and Philadelphia-LA Dodgers baseball game.

NFL suspends Pittsburgh running back Tim Worley for one year for violating league substance abuse policy.

30 Dusk-to-dawn curfew in wake of Los Angeles riots causes postponement of Utah-LA Clippers and Portland-LA Lakers playoff games and all LA Dodgers games through the weekend.

Sun	Mon	Tue	Wed	Thu	Fri	Sat
					1	2
3	4	5	6	7	8	9
10	11	12	13	14	15	16
17	18	19	20	21	22	23
24	25	26	27	28	29	30
31						

Wide World Photos

Buck Rodgers
Recovering from injuries.

1 **Seventh game wins** enable Boston, Montreal, NY Rangers and Pittsburgh to advance in NHL playoffs.

*America*³ **beats** *Stars & Stripes* to win defender series and advance to America's Cup final against *Il Moro di Venezia* of Italy.

Weekend NBA playoff games between Utah-LA Clippers and Portland-LA Lakers are shifted to Anaheim and Las Vegas, respectively.

2 **Lil E. Tee** wins Kentucky Derby as heavily-favored French horse Arazi finishes eighth.

5 **Chuck Daly** resigns as head coach of Detroit Pistons after nine seasons and back-to-back NBA titles in 1989 and 1990.

6 **Pittsburgh's** Mario Lemieux out indefinitely with broken left hand after being slashed by NY Rangers' Adam Graves.

7 **Hall of Fame** jockey Angel Cordero Jr., 49, announces retirement due to injuries suffered in Jan. 12 racing accident; leaves as No.3 on all-time wins list (7,076) and No. 2 in money earned ($164,571,847).

9 **America's Cup** final begins off San Diego as *America*³ beats Italy's *Il Moro di Venezia* in first race of best-of-seven series.

Terry Norris defeats challenger Meldrick Taylor with fourth round TKO in defense of WBC junior middleweight title in Las Vegas.

Strike the Gold, winner of 1991 Kentucky Derby, ends 12-race losing streak by winning Pimlico Special in Baltimore.

11 **James Orthwein** completes purchase of New England Patriots from Victor Kiam, assures Pats' fans he has no intention of moving team.

IAAF upholds two-year suspension of American track star Butch Reynolds for alleged steroid use.

12 **Mike Dunleavy** quits as LA Lakers coach after two years to accept eight-year deal as GM-coach in Milwaukee.

Portland guard Clyde Drexler and Duke center Christian Laettner selected to fill final two slots on U.S. Olympic team.

15 **Jovy Marcelo** of Philippines becomes first racing fatality in 10 years at Indianapolis Motor Speedway when he is killed in crash during qualifying run for Indy 500.

16 **Pine Bluff** wins Preakness Stakes as Kentucky Derby winner Lil E. Tee finishes fifth.

*America*³ **successfully** defends America's Cup, beating Italy's *Il Moro di Venezia* four to one in closest racing in Cup history (average winning margin of five races was 49 seconds).

17 **Orlando Magic** win NBA Draft lottery, almost certain to make LSU junior center Shaquille O'Neal overall number one pick on June 24.

Betsy King wins LPGA Championship by 11 strokes in Bethesda, Md.

18 **Wimp Sanderson** resigns as Alabama basketball coach after longtime secretary accuses him of striking her in the face.

19 **Mario Lemieux** returns after missing two weeks with broken left hand, scores twice as Pittsburgh takes 2-0 lead over Boston in NHL Wales Conference final.

Angels' pitcher Bert Blyleven, 41, returns to mound after two years and two rotator cuff operations, pitches six innings against NY Yankees but gets no decision.

20 **Penn State**, left out of newly-formed football bowl alliance, lands bid to 1993 Blockbuster Bowl on New Year's Day.

21 **California Angels'** manager Buck Rodgers breaks right elbow and left knee in early morning bus crash en route to Baltimore from New York.

22 **Final "Tonight Show,"** starring Johnny Carson airs.

24 **Al Unser Jr.** edges Scott Goodyear to win closest-ever Indianapolis 500; victory makes Unsers first winning father-son combination.

25 **Lyn St. James**, 45, officially named as first woman and oldest driver to win Indy 500 Rookie of Year.

28 **Chuck Daly** named head coach of New Jersey Nets, signs three-year deal for $4 million.

29 **Montreal coach** Pat Burns quits Canadiens to accept four-year contract to coach in Toronto.

Sun	Mon	Tue	Wed	Thu	Fri	Sat
	1	2	3	4	5	6
7	8	9	10	11	12	13
14	15	16	17	18	19	20
21	22	23	24	25	26	27
28	29	30				

1 Pittsburgh completes four-game sweep of Chicago to win second straight Stanley Cup; Mario Lemieux named Conn Smythe Trophy winner as MVP.

2 San Jose voters reject new Giants' stadium proposal by 55% to 45%; ballot defeat is fourth in the Bay Area in less than six years.

U.S. Senate passes bill banning all government-sponsored sports betting.

6 Monica Seles wins third French Open title in a row, beating Steffi Graf, 6-2, 3-6, 10-8.

A.P. Indy wins Belmont Stakes in 2:26.0, tying 1989 winner Easy Goer for second fastest time ever.

Pepperdine wins NCAA baseball title, beating Cal State-Fullerton, 3-2, in Omaha.

7 Jim Courier repeats as French Open champion, defeating Petr Korda in straight sets, 7-5, 6-2, 6-1.

11 Baseball owners, meeting in New York, officially approve sale of Seattle Mariners to Japanese-led group by 25-1 vote.

12 John Ziegler quits as NHL president after 15 years in office.

13 Sergei Bubka resets world outdoor pole vault record with jump of 20 feet, one-half inch in Dijon, France.

14 Chicago rallies from 15 points down in fourth quarter to beat Portland, 97-93, winning second straight NBA championship in six games; Bulls' Michael Jordan first-ever back-to-back winner of playoff MVP award.

15 Boston reliever Jeff Reardon becomes baseball's all-time saves leader with 342 as Red Sox down NY Yankees, 1-0.

16 McNeil vs. NFL free agency trial officially begins in Minneapolis with opening testimony.

Mark Messier of NY Rangers wins second Hart Trophy in three years as NHL MVP.

17 Philadelphia 76ers deal unhappy forward Charles Barkley to Phoenix for Jeff Hornacek, Tim Perry and Andrew Lang.

19 Heavyweight champion Evander Holyfield wins unanimous 12-round decision over 42-year-old former champ Larry Holmes in Las Vegas.

Hockey Hall of Fame elects former players Marcel Dionne, Lanny McDonald and Bob Gainey and veteran Woody Dumart.

20 Federal court, in 11th hour ruling, allows Butch Reynolds to compete in 400 meters at Olympic trials in New Orleans (competition in event is pushed back to Sunday).

21 Tom Kite wins U.S. Open by two shots over Jeff Sluman at Pebble Beach; title is 42-year-old Kite's first major.

Wide World Photos

Shaquille O'Neal
First pick in NBA Draft.

22 Eric Lindros trade goes to arbitration as Philadelphia and NY Rangers each claim that Quebec traded 19-year-old superstar to them on June 20.

NHL legal counsel Gil Stein, 64, appointed to succeed John Ziegler as NHL president until new commissioner is named.

24 NY Yankee pitcher Steve Howe permanently suspended by commissioner Fay Vincent for violating baseball's drug policy.

Orlando Magic make LSU junior center Shaquille O'Neal top pick in NBA Draft.

25 Philadelphia Eagles' All-Pro defensive tackle Jerome Brown killed in single car accident in Brooksville, Fla.

26 Butch Reynolds finishes fifth in 400-meter finals at Olympic trials, does not make U.S. team.

27 World champion Dan O'Brien fails to qualify for Olympic decathlon when he no-heights in pole vault at U.S. trials.

28 U.S. Olympic Dream Team routs Cuba, 136-57, in opening round of Tournament of the Americas Olympic qualifying competition in Portland.

Michael Johnson wins 200 meters as Carl Lewis finishes fourth at Olympic trials.

29 Rose Bowl chosen to host championship game, consolation and one semifinal of 1994 World Cup; other semifinal to be played at Giants Stadium in New Jersey.

30 Arbitrator awards rights to Eric Lindros to Philadelphia; Flyers send goalie Ron Hextall, center Mike Ricci and three others, plus a 1993 first-round draft pick and $15 million to Quebec.

Sun	Mon	Tue	Wed	Thu	Fri	Sat
			1	2	3	4
5	6	7	8	9	10	11
12	13	14	15	16	17	18
19	20	21	22	23	24	25
26	27	28	29	30	31	

Chris Cole/Allsport

Vitaly Scherbo
One man gold rush.

1 Three-cornered NBA trade sends guard Dale Ellis to San Antonio, forward Alaa Abdelnaby to Milwaukee and the rights to forward Tracy Murray to Portland.

2 France selected over Morocco by 12-7 vote to host 1998 World Cup.

4 Steffi Graf wins fourth Wimbledon title in five years, beating Monica Seles, 6-2, 6-1, in most lopsided final in nine years.

5 Andre Agassi captures first Grand Slam title, defeating Goran Ivanisevic in five-set men's final at Wimbledon.

Dream Team trounces Venezuela, 127-80, in Tournament of Americas final. Americans win six games by average of 51.5 points.

6 Baseball commissioner Fay Vincent orders National League realignment, moving Atlanta and Cincinnati to the Eastern Division and Chicago and St. Louis to the West.

John McEnroe wins fifth Wimbledon doubles title, teaming with Michael Stich to beat Jim Grabb and Richey Reneberg in longest championship match in Wimbledon history (5-7, 7-6, 3-6, 7-6, 19-17).

7 Chicago Cubs file suit to stop commissioner's edict to realign National League.

9 Texas Rangers fire manager Bobby Valentine after 45-41 start, name coach Toby Harrah interim manager.

10 Major Soccer League folds after 14 years when league officials fail to recruit sixth franchise for 1992-93 indoor season.

11 Two-time U.S. Open champion Tracy Austin, 29, and three others inducted into International Tennis Hall of Fame at Newport, R.I.

14 American League wins fifth straight All-Star Game, 13-6, at Jack Murphy Stadium in San Diego. Seattle's Ken Griffey Jr. named MVP.

15 Eric Lindros signs six-year contract with Philadelphia Flyers for reported $15-to-$18 million.

19 Nick Faldo rallies to birdie two of last four holes to edge John Cook by a stroke in British Open at Muirfield; Open title is Faldo's third in six years.

Germany defeats Spain, 2-1, to win in women's Federation Cup tennis in Frankfurt.

Davey Allison hospitalized after breaking right arm, right wrist and collarbone when car flips 11 times late in running of Pocono 500. Accident occurs when Allison's rear is clipped by eventual winner Darrell Waltrip.

23 Illinois federal judge issues injunction blocking Chicago Cubs' forced move to NL West; baseball commissioner Fay Vincent immediately appeals ruling.

24 George Steinbrenner cleared by commissioner's office to resume control of NY Yankees on Mar. 1, 1993.

Houston Astros owner John McMullen agrees to sell club to Texas businessman Drayton McLane Jr. for $115 million.

25 Summer Olympics officially begin in Barcelona as a record 172 countries march in opening ceremonies; dramatic festivities are watched by an estimated 3.5 billion on worldwide TV.

26 Swimmer Nelson Diebel wins first U.S. gold medal of Games, taking 100-meter breaststroke in Olympic record time (1:01.50).

Spanish cyclist Miguel Indurain wins second straight Tour de France by 4:35 over Claudio Chiappucci of Italy.

27 Patty Sheehan defeats Juli Inkster by two strokes in 18-hole playoff to win U.S. Women's Open at Oakmont, Pa.

McNeil vs NFL free agency trial resumes following collapse of settlement talks over weekend.

28 U.S. women set world record in 4x100-meter freestyle relay (3:38.46); Matt Biondi fifth in 100-meter free.

29 Mike Barrowman sets world record in 200-meter breaststroke (2:10.16); Mark Lenzi wins springboard diving gold.

30 U.S. wins eight swimming medals; women set world record in 4x100-meter medley relay (4:02.54).

31 Vitaly Scherbo of Unified Team captures men's all-around gold medal on way to eventual haul of six golds in gymnasts.

Sun	Mon	Tue	Wed	Thu	Fri	Sat
						1
2	3	4	5	6	7	8
9	10	11	12	13	14	15
16	17	18	19	20	21	22
23	24	25	26	27	28	29
30	31					

Chris Cole/Allsport

Jennifer Capriati
Upsets Graf in Barcelona.

1 Olympic 100-meter gold medals won by Britain's Linford Christie and Gail Devers of U.S. American favorite Eric Griffin upset in boxing.

2 Jackie Joyner-Kersee captures second straight Olympic gold medal in heptathlon; U.S. gymnast Trent Dimas wins high bar.

3 Mike Conley wins Olympic triple jump, but world record leap is wind-aided.

Detroit Tigers fire team president Bo Schembechler and chairman Jim Campbell.

4 Phar-Mor Inc. president Mickey Monash and his father Nathan are implicated in a $350 million embezzlement scheme; withdraw from part-ownership in Colorado Rockies and LPGA golf sponsorships.

5 U.S. women's basketball squad upset by Unified Team, 79-73, in Olympic semifinals.

6 Kevin Young sets world record of 46.78 seconds in 400-meter hurdles as U.S. track and field team wins nine Olympic medals; U.S. hammer thrower Jud Logan expelled after testing positive for banned substance.

7 Jennifer Capriati surprises Steffi Graf, 3-6, 6-3, 6-4, to win Olympic gold in tennis; Jackie Joyner-Kersee is third in long jump and Sergei Bubka fails to win any medal in pole vault.

Tampa announces conditional agreement to buy San Francisco Giants for $110 million and move club to Florida for 1993 season.

Shaquille O'Neal signs seven-year deal with Orlando Magic for a reported $40 million.

8 Dream Team routs Croatia, 117-85 to win Olympic basketball gold medal; U.S. men set two world relay records in track and field; Oscar De La Hoya wins only U.S. boxing gold.

9 Summer Olympics end, Unified Team edges U.S. in total medals, 112-108, and by 45-37 in gold medals.

11 Redskins' quarterback Mark Rypien ends holdout, signs for $9 million over three years.

16 Nick Price wins PGA Championship by two strokes, while **Sherri Steinhauer** takes LPGA du Maurier Classic by two.

Nigel Mansell clinches his first Formula One driving championship with a second place finish in the Hungarian Grand Prix.

17 Dodgers' Kevin Gross pitches baseball season's only complete game no-hitter, blanking San Francisco 2-0 in L.A.

18 Larry Bird announces retirement from basketball after 13 seasons and three NBA titles with Boston; 35-year-old three-time MVP cites bad back.

19 Third generation of Boone family plays in majors as Bret Boone debuts with Seattle and singles in first time up.

22 Miami-FL and **Washington** ranked 1-2 in AP preseason college football poll.

23 Houston Astros complete marathon, 26-game road trip with 12-14 record following 3-1 win over Philadelphia.

24 Hurricane Andrew, packing 164-mile-per-hour winds, slams into southern Florida killing 33, destroying 63,000 homes and causing $30 billion in damage.

Oriole ironman Cal Ripken signs five-year contract with Baltimore worth $30.5 million.

25 NHL owners toughen rules against fighting and stick infractions; also make helmets optional and accept resignation of executive VP Brian O'Neill.

26 Texas A&M beats Stanford, 10-7, in season's football opener, spoiling Bill Walsh's return to college ranks.

27 Toronto acquires pitcher David Cone from NY Mets for infielder Jeff Kent and outfielder Ryan Thompson.

29 Philippines routs Long Beach, 15-4, to win Little League World Series in Williamsport, Pa.

30 Boston trades all-time saves leader Jeff Reardon to Atlanta for two players to be named later.

Sergei Bubka breaks world pole vault record for 31st time with leap of 20-feet, 1-inch in Padua, Italy.

31 Oakland trades outfielder Jose Canseco to Texas for outfielder Ruben Sierra and pitchers Bobby Witt and Jeff Russell.

Sun	Mon	Tue	Wed	Thu	Fri	Sat
		1	2	3	4	5
6	7	8	9	10	11	12
13	14	15	16	17	18	19
20	21	22	23	24	25	26
27	28	29	30			

1   **Notre Dame linebacker** Demetrius DuBose suspended two games by NCAA for accepting loan from Seattle-based ND booster.

49ers quarterback Joe Montana placed on injured reserve for minimum of four weeks.

2   **NHL and ESPN** announce $80 million, five-year cable TV deal (one year, plus four-year option).

Former world chess champions Bobby Fischer and Boris Spassky begin $5 million challenge match in Sveti Stefan, Yugoslavia. First player to win 10 games takes home $3.35 million.

3   **Baseball owners**, meeting in Chicago, vote 18-10 urging commissioner Fay Vincent to resign. Vincent, however, restates intention to stay in office.

Michael Andretti announces he will leave IndyCar and join Formula One circuit in 1993. His father Mario won Grand Prix driving title in 1978.

5   **Dan O'Brien** sets world record in decathlon with 8,891 points in Talence, France. Old record of 8,847 was set by Britain's Daley Thompson at 1984 Olympics in L.A.

6   **Arkansas football** coach Jack Crowe forced out one day after 10-3 loss to Div. I-AA Citadel at home; assistant Joe Kines named interim coach.

7   **Fay Vincent** resigns as baseball commissioner four days after owners' no-confidence vote.

9   **Milwaukee owner** Bud Selig named chairman of baseball's executive council, making him, in effect, acting baseball commissioner.

Brewers' Robin Yount singles to right in bottom of seventh to become only the 17th player in baseball history to reach 3,000 hits.

10   **All-woman jury** in Minneapolis decides in favor of players in Freeman McNeil vs. NFL free agency trial.

Deion Sanders signs amended contract with Atlanta Falcons for $2 million in 1992; is free to play postseason baseball with Atlanta Braves.

12   **Monica Seles** beats Arantxa Sanchez Vicario in straight sets to win second consecutive U.S. Open.

Notre Dame rallies for 10 points in fourth quarter to tie Michigan, 17-17, in South Bend.

Julio Cesar Chavez retains WBC super lightweight title with unanimous decision over Hector (Macho) Camacho in Las Vegas.

13   **Stefan Edberg** defeats Pete Sampras in four sets to successfully defend U.S. Open title.

Greg Norman wins first tournament in 27 months, beating Bruce Lietzke on second hole of sudden death to take Canadian Open.

Nigel Mansell announces before Italian Grand Prix that he will leave Formula One for IndyCar circuit in 1993.

Wide World Photos

Bud Selig
Acting baseball commissioner.

17   **NFL owners** push back expansion announcement date indefinitely, put World League on hold until 1994.

Philippines stripped of Little League World Series title for using ineligible players.

19   **Sergei Bubka** breaks world pole vault record for 32nd time with leap of 20-feet, 1½-inch in Tokyo.

20   **Second baseman** Mickey Morandini of Philadelphia becomes only ninth player to turn unassisted triple play; but Phils lose to Pirates, 3-2.

Ray Floyd, who turned 50 on Sept. 4, wins second Seniors tournament he enters to become first player to win on both PGA tours in same year.

22   **Wayne Gretzky** sidelined indefinitely with herniated thoracic disk (back).

Three-way NBA deal sends forward Charles Smith and guards Doc Rivers and Bo Kimble to New York; center Stanley Roberts and guard Mark Jackson to LA Clippers; and three draft picks to Orlando.

23   **Tampa Bay goalie** Manon Rheaume becomes first woman to play in NHL exhibition game, stopping seven of nine St. Louis shots in first period.

27   **John Daly** wins B.C. Open by six strokes for first PGA win of 1992.

28   **Philadelphia free agent** tight end Keith Jackson signs four-year contract with Miami for $6 million.

29   **Magic Johnson** announces his return to LA Lakers, says he will play 50-60 games of the 82-game schedule.

30   **Royals' George Brett** goes 4-for-4 against Angels in Anaheim to become only the 18th player in baseball history to reach 3,000 hits.

Sun	Mon	Tue	Wed	Thu	Fri	Sat
				1	2	3
4	5	6	7	8	9	10
11	12	13	14	15	16	17
18	19	20	21	22	23	24
25	26	27	28	29	30	31

Wide World Photos

Joe Carter
Blue Jays win Series.

1 Lakers sign Magic Johnson to one-year contract extension that will pay him $14.6 million in 1994-95.

NCAA places entire Syracuse athletic program on two-year probation for violations in five sports; basketball team barred from 1993 NCAA tournament for recruiting infractions.

NHL makes acting president Gil Stein full-time president.

3 No. 2 Miami beats No. 3 Florida St., 19-16, as last-second Seminoles' field goal attempt goes wide right for second year in a row.

Stanford upsets No. 6 Notre Dame, 33-16, at South Bend after trailing 16-6 at half.

4 Europe surprises United States, 11½ to 6½ to capture Solheim Cup women's golf in Edinburgh, Scotland.

5 Pittsburgh captain Mario Lemieux celebrates 27th birthday by signing seven-year contract worth $42 million, making him highest-paid NHL player ever.

NFL loses two more court cases, one relating to developmental squads, the other to players' strike of 1987.

6 NL playoffs begin as Braves' John Smoltz beats Pirates, 5-1, in Atlanta.

Lou Piniella says he will not be back as Cincinnati manager in 1993, plans to explore other options.

Eric Lindros scores once in NHL debut as Flyers rally to tie Penguins, 3-3, in Pittsburgh.

7 AL playoffs begin as Oakland beats Toronto, 4-3, on Harold Baines' solo homer in 9th inning.

Expansion Tampa Bay Lightning routs Chicago, 7-3, in NHL debut as forward Chris Kontos scores four goals.

8 Expansion Ottawa Senators open with 5-3 victory over Montreal in NHL debut.

11 College football polls split, Washington is No. 1 in AP vote, while Miami gets nod from coaches.

Nick Faldo beats Jeff Sluman, 8 and 7, to win World Match Play title in Virginia Water, England.

12 Art Monk catches seven passes to overtake Steve Largent as NFL's all-time receptions leader with 820 as Washington pounds Denver, 34-3, at RFK.

13 Seattle fires manager Bill Plummer after finishing last in AL West with 64-98 record.

14 Francisco Cabrera delivers two-out, two-run single in bottom of 9th as Atlanta rallies to beat Pittsburgh, 3-2, and win NL pennant.

Toronto routs Oakland, 9-2, at SkyDome to win first AL pennant.

15 New York City beats out Dallas-Fort Worth, Miami and St. Louis to host 1998 Goodwill Games.

17 World Series opens in Atlanta as Braves beat Blue Jays, 3-1, on Damon Berryhill's three-run homer in 6th inning.

18 Miami and Washington, both 6-0, tie for No. 1 in AP college football poll; Miami remains first in coaches' poll.

Bobby Rahal wins third IndyCar PPG Cup title with third place at Toyota Monterey Grand Prix.

20 NFL commissioner Paul Tagliabue announces league will delay expansion until 1995, cites unresolved labor issues.

22 Michael Jordan testifies in money laundering trial of James (Slim) Bouler that he paid defendant $57,000 to cover gambling losses.

Toronto judge rules that NHL must pay $22 million plus interest back to pension fund of players who were in league from 1948-82.

23 Florida Marlins name Oakland third base coach Rene Lachemann as first manager.

24 Toronto wins World Series in six games with 11-inning, 4-3 victory over Braves in Atlanta. Catcher Pat Borders named MVP.

26 Texas names Montreal farm director Kevin Kennedy as new manager.

27 Oakland manager Tony La Russa named AL Manager of the Year by baseball writers.

Colorado Rockies name St. Louis batting coach Don Baylor as first manager.

28 Pittsburgh manager Jim Leyland named NL Manager of the Year by baseball writers.

30 Cincinnati Reds promote first base coach and batting instructor Tony Perez to manager's job.

DECEMBER, 1992

4 Baseball Winter Meetings begin in Louisville.
4 National Finals Rodeo begins (Las Vegas).
4 NCAA Men's Soccer Final Four begins (Davidson, N.C.).
5 Army-Navy Game (Philadelphia).
5 SEC championship game (Birmingham, Ala.)
12 Heisman Trophy winner announced (New York).
28 NFL regular season ends (Detroit at S.F.).

JANUARY

1 Major bowl games (8): Blockbuster (Miami); Citrus (Orlando); Cotton (Dallas); Fiesta (Tempe); Hall of Fame (Tampa); Orange (Miami); Rose (Pasadena) and Sugar (New Orleans).
2 NFL playoffs (2): AFC/NFC wild card games.
3 NFL playoffs (2): AFC/NFC wild card games.
9 NFL playoffs (2): AFC/NFC semifinal games.
10 NFL playoffs (2): AFC/NFC semifinal games.
12 NCAA Convention begins (Dallas).
17 NFL playoffs (2): AFC/NFC championship games.
17 U.S. Figure Skating Championships begin (Phoenix).
18 Australian Open tennis begins (Melbourne).
30 24 Hours at Daytona begins (Daytona Beach).
31 Super Bowl XXVII (Pasadena)

FEBRUARY

4 National Girls & Women in Sports Day.
6 NHL Hockey All-Star Game (Montreal).
7 NFL Pro Bowl (Honolulu).
14 Daytona 500 (Daytona Beach).
21 NBA All-Star Game (Orlando).
21 U.S. Women's Open bowling begins (Garland, Texas)
26 U.S. Mobil Indoor Track Championships (New York)

MARCH

6 Iditarod Trail Sled Dog race begins (Anchorage to Nome).
9 World Figure Skating Championships begin (Prague).
12 World Indoor Track & Field Championships begin (Toronto).
12 NCAA Indoor Track & Field Championships begin (Indianapolis).
14 NCAA Division I Basketball tournament seeds announced.
14 NFL Annual Meeting begins (Palm Springs, Calif.).
17 NCAA Women's Division I Basketball tournament begins.
18 NCAA Men's Division I Basketball tournament begins.
18 NCAA Division I Wrestling tournament begins (Ames, Iowa).
18 NCAA Women's Swimming Championships begin (Minneapolis).
21 PBA National bowling begins (Toledo).
25 PGA Players Championship golf begins (Ponte Vedra, Fla.).
25 NCAA Men's Swimming Championships begin (Bloomington, Ind.).
25 LPGA Dinah Shore golf begins (Rancho Mirage, Calif.).
26 Davis Cup tennis first round begins (eight sites).
28 World Cross-country Championships (Amorebieta, Spain).

APRIL

1 NCAA Division I Hockey Final Four begins (Milwaukee).
3 NCAA Women's Basketball Final Four begins (Atlanta).
3 NCAA Men's Basketball Final Four begins (New Orleans).
4 U.S. Men's Open bowling begins (Canandaigua, N.Y.).
5 Baseball Opening Day.
8 Masters golf begins (Augusta).
13 World Gymnastics Championships begin (Birmingham, England).
15 NHL regular season ends.
18 NHL Stanley Cup playoffs begin.
19 Boston Marathon.
20 PBA Firestone Tournament of Champions bowling begins (Akron).
25 NBA regular season ends.
25 NFL Draft begins (New York).
29 NBA playoffs begin.

MAY

1 Kentucky Derby (Louisville).
4 ABC Masters bowling begins (Tulsa).
6 Tour duPont cycling race begins (eastern U.S.).
10 LPGA Championship golf begins (Bethesda, Md.).
15 Preakness Stakes (Baltimore).
24 French Open tennis begins (Paris).
29 NCAA Lacrosse Final Four begins (College Park, Md.).
30 Indianapolis 500.

JUNE

2 NCAA Men's and Women's Track & Field Championships begin (New Orleans).
4 NCAA College World Series begins (Omaha).
5 Belmont Stakes (Elmont,NY).
12 National Collegiate Rowing Championships begin (Cincinnati).
17 U.S. Open golf begins (Springfield, N.J.)
19 24 Hours of Le Mans auto race begins (Le Mans, France).
21 Wimbledon tennis begins.
26 NHL Draft (Quebec City)
30 NBA Draft (TBA).

JULY

3 Tour de France cycling race begins (through July 25).
8 U.S. Senior Open golf begins (Englewood, Colo.).
13 Baseball All-Star Game (Baltimore).
15 British Open golf begins (Royal St. George's).
16 Davis Cup tennis second round begins (four sites).
19 Women's Federation Cup tennis begins (Frankfurt).
22 U.S. Women's Open golf begins (Carmel, Ind.).

AUGUST

7 Hambletonian harness race (E.Rutherford, N.J.).
7 All-American Soap Box Derby (Akron).
9 U.S. Women's Amateur golf begins (San Diego).
12 PGA Championship golf begins (Toledo).
14 World Track & Field Championships begin (Stuttgart).
16 World Chess Championship begins (TBA).
23 Little League Baseball World Series begins (Williamsport, Pa).
24 U.S. Men's Amateur golf begins (Houston).
26 U.S. Gymnastics Championships begin (Salt Lake City).
26 LPGA du Maurier Classic begins (London, Ont.).
30 U.S. Open tennis begins (Flushing, N.Y.).

SEPTEMBER

5 NFL regular season opens.
24 Ryder Cup golf matches begin (The Belfry, England).
24 Davis Cup tennis semifinal round begins (two sites).

OCTOBER

3 Baseball regular season ends.
5 Baseball AL/NL Championship Series begin.
9 College football: Miami-FL at Florida St.
9 College football: Oklahoma vs Texas (Dallas).
16 World Series begins (in city of NL champion).
23 College football: USC at Notre Dame.

NOVEMBER

6 Breeders' Cup horse racing (Santa Anita).
14 New York City Marathon.
15 ATP Men's Tennis Championships begin (Frankfurt).
15 Virginia Slims Tennis Championships begin (New York).
20 College football: Harvard at Yale; Ohio St. at Michigan; Oklahoma at Nebraska; UCLA at USC.
27 Alabama vs Auburn (Birmingham).
28 CFL Grey Cup (Toronto).

DECEMBER

3 Davis Cup tennis final begins.
3 National Finals Rodeo begins (Las Vegas).
4 College football: SEC Championship Game (Birmingham); Army vs Navy (E.Rutherford, N.J.).
27 NFL regular season ends.

Wide World Photos

Toronto's **Dave Winfield** delivers a two-run double in the top of the 11th inning in the Blue Jays' 4-3 victory over Atlanta in the deciding game of the World Series.

BASEBALL

WORLD SERIES
by Peter Gammons

Oh Canada!

*Toronto captures baseball's first real World Series
as the national pastime is embraced by two countries.*

It all ended with a flash, a bunt pulled down the first base line by Otis Nixon. As pinch runner John Smoltz streaked from third toward home plate with the potential tying run, young Blue Jay relief pitcher Mike Timlin calmly cut off the bunt before it could trickle out to first baseman Joe Carter, spun and tossed to Carter.

And so the 1992 baseball season bolted to an end, culminated by the first real World Series, one that threw together flag-waving patriotism, Dousing Deion Sanders and four one-run losses for the Braves. "They can keep telling us that we've played in two of the great successive World Series," said Atlanta manager Bobby Cox, "but when your last six World Series defeats have been by one run, they get pretty tough to take."

Indeed, this was a World Series that could have been a four-game sweep by either team, one that turned on a dramatic pinch-hit homer in Game 2 and an historic Devon White catch in Game 3 and, in the end, was won by a Toronto bullpen that Cox had to concede "is one of the best ever." For all else, even the unlikely MVP, Pat Borders, this was a Series decided in the bullpen, where Toronto's relievers won three games, saved three and allowed one earned run in 18⅓ innings, while Atlanta's bullpen lost the second, third and, finally, the sixth games. "When two teams hit a combined .225, you know that pitching and defense wins

out," said Toronto's Roberto Alomar.

The Series had begun innocently enough with Tom Glavine besting Morris 3-1 in the opener in a battle of homers. Joe Carter hit a solo shot off Glavine in the fourth, but after three innings of laying off Morris's assortment of breaking balls, catcher Damon Berryhill finally got a hanging forkball and hit a three-run homer for the victory. And when the Braves knocked out David Cone and got to the ninth inning of the second game up 4-3, it appeared that they would continue their unbeatable ways in Fulton County Stadium. But Cox brought veteran Jeff Reardon in for the ninth, and after walking Derek Bell with one out, the 36-year old reliever who five months earlier had established the career save record laid a fastball right down the middle to pinch hitter Ed Sprague. Toronto's young catcher smashed it deep into the left field stands, Tom Henke closed the ninth and the Series went across the border tied 1-1.

Not only was this a baseball first, but it was an hysterical worst. During the singing of the Canadian anthem before Game 2, a U.S. Marine (Gomer Pyle?) accidently presented the Canadian flag upside down. The phone lines at CBS, the stadium and all Toronto media outlets were flooded by irate Canadians suggesting this was an intentional slap at their country by a nation afraid of losing its national game to another country. Of

Wide World Photos

Fans at SkyDome in Toronto wave American and Canadian flags
before Game 3 of baseball's first international World Series.

course, there isn't a Canadian player on
Toronto, but...

Not only was there the flag flap, there
was the Deion watch. After the Braves
dramatically won the playoffs, Sanders
dumped four buckets of ice water on CBS
broadcaster Tim McCarver in retaliation
for critical comments McCarver had
made concerning Sanders playing in an
NFL and baseball playoff game in the
same day. Yet, as it turned out, Sanders
was the best player the Braves had. He
went 8-for-15, stole three bases and
made a great throw in Game 6 to force
extra innings. "It's really too bad, but we
don't expect he'll ever be a full time baseball player," said Braves president Stan
Kasten. "His thing is to be Deion. But he
could be one of the best baseball players
on the planet."

When the flags were calmed and they
got to Game 3, it was Deion and not
veteran MVP candidate Terry Pendleton
who demonstrated the right instincts on
the play of the Series. With none out in the
fourth inning of a scoreless game, Sanders was on second, Pendleton on first
when David Justice smoked a line drive to
the center field fence. Mortally, it was an
impossible catch, hit directly over Devon

White's head, with no elevation. But the
game's best center fielder streaked back,
leaped and caught the ball, managed to
feather his fall against the wall, landed
and came up throwing a perfect strike to
the cutoff man, Alomar.

Sanders had made the right play, tag-
ging up at second. "There was no human
way that ball could have been caught,"
said Pendleton. "So I took off. I forgot
that when it comes to playing center field,
White isn't human."

Pendleton was ruled out for passing
Sanders, although Alomar had no way of
knowing as he wheeled in center and
fired a strike to first baseman John Olerud. But as the ball got to Olerud, Sanders bolted off second and was suddenly in
a rundown. Kelly Gruber dived and did
catch Sanders' heel for what should have
been a triple play and one of the most
unforgettable moments in Series history,
only umpire Bob Davidson couldn't see
the tag and ruled him safe. The next day,
Davidson admitted he had erred.

But, once again, the game came down
to the bullpens, and Reardon again was
touched—this time by a Candy Maldonado single with two out in the bottom of
the ninth for a 3-2 Toronto victory. In the

fourth game, while Cox stuck with his three man rotation, Blue Jays manager Cito Gaston went to veteran lefty Jimmy Key, who worked seven strong innings, turned it over to Duane Ward and Henke and eked out a 2-1 squeaker that made it 3-1 in games.

When the two teams got to SkyDome Thursday, the city of Toronto had already announced plans for a Friday parade. Wrong. Morris, perhaps exhausted from carrying the Toronto staff for five weeks in July and August, had little left on his fastball, and when Lonnie Smith cracked an opposite field grand slam homer in the fifth inning the Braves went back to Atlanta down 3-2 with a 7-2 romp for John Smoltz and reliever Mike Stanton.

Game 6 was delayed 20 minutes because Ross Perot had bought time from CBS, not a good omen for the state of baseball. But, like the other historic sixth games—1975, 1986—this one was unforgettable for those who stayed awake—for, like the others, it ended between 12:30 and 1 A.M. Sanders had tied it 1-1 for Steve Avery in the third when he singled, stole and scored on a sacrifice fly, but Avery, bothered by a blister, gave up a Maldonado homer in the fourth for a 2-1 Toronto lead. That stood, with Cone going six, then Todd Stottlemyre, then David Wells and Ward. When Henke, Toronto's traditional closer, entered in the ninth, the Jays had set a World Series record of 15⅓ straight scoreless innings.

But Henke did not hold it. In a wild and crazy ninth in which playoff hero Fransisco Cabrera nearly won it with a line drive that Maldonado almost misjudged, Nixon slapped a two-out single that put the game into extra innings. There, Gaston went to his fourth game starter and winner, Key, who shut down Atlanta in the tenth. In the 11th, against 1991 sixth game loser Charlie Leibrandt, the Jays had White at second, Alomar at first, two out and a 3-2 count to Dave Winfield. Leibrandt did not get his changeup where he wanted. Instead of being on the outside corner, it was down the middle, and instead of his ground ball going to Pendleton, correctly playing off the line, the ball went over the bag for a two-run double that made it 4-2, and forever buried the "Mr. May" slight Winfield had so long lived under.

Only, it still wasn't over. In the bottom of the 11th, Jeff Blauser singled. Berryhill hit a perfect double play ball to shortstop Alfredo Griffin, only the ball took a bad hop, ricocheted off his shoulder into the outfield and the Braves had runners at first and third, no one out. 1986, anyone?

After a bunt to advance pinch runner Smoltz to second and a ground ball that scored the third run and put Smoltz at third, Gaston brought on Timlin. The previous November, Timlin had undergone arm surgery, and it wasn't until September that his fastball—which his catchers claim is the best in the league—came back. Timlin had one save and a 4.12 ERA for the season. And had to face Nixon.

Timlin blew one fastball on the inside corner for a strike, and when he wheeled in the next one, Nixon had made up his mind to bunt. As the pitch bore in, he knew he couldn't push the ball to the left side, away from where Timlin was falling, and had to pull it towards Carter, normally not a good defensive first baseman. But the pitch ran in so far on Nixon's hands that he didn't get the barrell of the bat on the bunt, Timlin cut it off and the Blue Jays were world champions.

For Borders, a .450 average, three runners gunned down and endless forkballs blocked perfectly earned him the MVP. For Gaston, toughness and dignity answered his critics with a world championship. And, finally, for Canada, the best America's National Pastime has to offer.

THE PLAYOFFS

They are two baseball portraits that insure that each 1992 playoff series will be long hung on the walls of baseball's museum of memories.

One is Braves' first baseman Sid Bream sliding into home plate, his foot inches from the glove of diving Pirates catcher Mike LaValliere. The other is Roberto Alomar with his arms raised, gazing impishly towards right field at his home run that dramatically crushed Dennis Eckersley and the Oakland Athletics in the fourth game.

Each captures a Series that will not long be forgotten, either in Pittsburgh, where the Pirates became the most stunned losers in the 24-year history of the playoffs, or in Toronto, which had long been waiting to host the first international World

Wide World Photos

Atlanta's **Sid Bream** slides past the outstretched glove of Pittsburgh catcher **Mike LaValliere** to score the winning run of the NLCS with two out in the bottom of the 9th inning of Game 7.

Series. "It's not something from which we'll recover quickly or easily," said Pirates' manager Jim Leyland, while the Blue Jays' Dave Winfield said, "it's as if we won for an entire country." All over Toronto, people wore T-shirts that read, "My Canada Includes The World Series." At home in Pittsburgh, Andy Van Slyke, having lost two straight years to Atlanta in bitter seventh games and in 1990 in six to Cincinnati, said, "There will never be words to describe what this feels like."

The Pirates-Braves NLCS will essentially be remembered for that one inning in which Pittsburgh had it all, then had nothing. The Braves had run off to a 3-1 lead and a seeming rout, only to have Barry Bonds awaken and the Bucs rally, win the fifth game at home, the sixth 13-4 in Atlanta and send Doug Drabek out against John Smoltz for the game of his life.

The Pirates jumped out against Smoltz with a run in the top of the first on a walk, a Van Slyke single and Orlando Merced's fly ball. That held until the sixth, when Jay Bell doubled and Van Slyke singled him

in. Meanwhile, Drabek, who had not pitched well in his two previous starts, was rolling. Leyland had spun Braves manager Bobby Cox out of players, so that the Braves no longer had Deion Sanders or their best reliever (Mike Stanton), and with three outs to go, his team that had performed with such character for an entire season after losing Bobby Bonilla to free agency was set for a great comeback and piece of justice.

But at that point, Drabek seemingly hit the wall. Terry Pendleton, called by Braves president Stan Kasten "the best free agent signing in baseball history," doubled into the right field corner. Drabek then made a good pitch and got David Justice to hit a ground ball towards the middle. Pittsburgh second baseman Chico Lind, the best in the league, skittered to his right to field the ball, but it kicked off his glove and rolled a few feet away. "That was when we knew this could be our miracle," said Pendleton. "When Lind misses a ball, something has to happen." The exhausted Drabek walked Sid

Wide World Photos

Pinch hitter **Francisco Cabrera** of Atlanta strokes his pennant-winning, two-run single to left in the bottom of the 9th of Game 7.

Bream to load the bases and Leyland went to reliever Stan Belinda.

Leyland had avoided his bullpen with leads in the series, but at that point, had no choice. Belinda gave up a sacrifice fly, then walked Damon Berryhill to re-load the bases. For years, Pirates fans will lament that umpire Randy Marsh squeezed Belinda, calling balls on two pitches that looked like pennant-winning third strikes. Even so, Belinda got Brian Hunter to pop up, and with Cox out of players, all that stood between Pittsburgh and the pennant was Francisco Cabrera—a career minor leaguer added to the roster Aug. 31 because of an injury to regular catcher Greg Olson. Cox was so strapped for players that he had no one to run for the deadlegged Bream at second, and if the game had been tied, he had no one to play second base. Ah, for the Bucs, the pennant that was won and lost again finally seemed won.

But Cabrera pulled a single into left field, and in a frozen moment right out of the ending to "Bonnie and Clyde," Bream lumbered around third and to-

wards home as Bonds fired for the plate. The throw was slightly to the pitcher's side of home, LaValliere fielded it, dived...and reached Bream's foot a flash after it had caught the plate. After a second's stop to realize reality, Justice piled on top of Bream, Fulton County Stadium erupted and one of the great moments in playoff history was over.

Forgotten was Bonds' "It's over" that he hollered when he broke a three-year playoff nightmare by doubling in a run in the first inning of the fifth game that started the Pirate comeback. Forgotten was journeyman Bob Walk's brilliant three-hit shutout in that game. Forgotten was a year's worth of managing by Leyland that could only be compared to one recent performance, that by his friend Tony La Russa in Oakland.

Like Leyland, La Russa's magic finally ran out in the ALCS. Toronto was the heavy favorite, but the A's had overcome injuries, age and adversity all season in what they all knew, with 16 potential free agents, was their last hurrah. "We know that with Jack Morris, David Cone and Juan Guzman, they seem the favorites," said La Russa. "But we have to find a way to steal a game four times, and we can."

They stole the opener in Toronto when Harold Baines hit a ninth-inning homer off '91 hero Morris, and went home to Oakland tied 1-1 after Cone beat them 3-1. Then came a two-act play that unravelled La Russa's well-laid plan.

All season, the A's had won with their bullpen, especially Dennis Eckersley. When they traded Jose Canseco on Aug. 31, one of the key ingredients of the deal was reliever Jeff Russell, whom they acquired to get to The Eck. But the third game was turned over to the bullpen going into the seventh inning with the A's down 3-2, and, as Eckersley said, "the bleeding began."

The A's didn't quit, but five Oakland relievers couldn't stop Toronto. The Jays went up 5-2 in the seventh; the A's scored two to get back to 5-4. The Jays scored a run in the top of the eighth, Oakland one in the bottom, and, finally, still within a run, the Oakland bullpen allowed another run in the ninth to lose 7-5. Not only did they feel exhausted from the chase, but, worse, the invincible Eckersley, who had 51 saves in 54 opportunities, was hit.

So was Russell. And when Rick Honeycutt pitched, he, too, was ineffective.

Worse, the A's knew their bullpen was shot. Eckersley had felt a strain in his elbow right before the playoffs and was in pain. Russell reinjured his elbow in Game 3, and was done. Honeycutt's hip was killing him.

So, when the A's went into the eighth inning of the fourth game with a 6-1 lead, Bob Welch, injured most of the season, could go no longer. After a Roberto Alomar double and singles by Joe Carter and Dave Winfield, La Russa had to go to Eckersley in an unfamiliar position—the eighth, none out, the lefthanded-hitting John Olerud at the plate. It was the earliest Eck had been used all season, but there was no one else.

Olerud raked a single into right, 6-3. Candy Maldonado hit his next pitch to right-center, 6-4. Then Eckersley got three outs, and when he struck out Ed Sprague to end the inning, he nervously pumped his fist. "I was so afraid that I couldn't stop the bleeding, when I struck him out I let out a burst of emotion," said Eckersley. From the visiting dugout came screams of derision at the great Oakland pitcher, and from the on-deck circle, Devon White screamed obscenities. Eckersley looked back to glare at White. "We thought he was glaring at the whole team," said Alomar. "It seemed to get us even more pumped." As it turned out, the bleeding had not stopped.

White led off the ninth with a single. Alomar followed by reaching out and drilling a line drive that hit in the left field corner, two feet foul. "If Eckersley was healthy and throwing well, things would have been different," said Alomar. "But he wasn't normal." Eckersley figured that Alomar was looking away after the shot to the corner and came in with a fastball. Alomar snapped his bat and sent a line drive into the right field seats, 6-6. "Robby Alomar is the best player in our league," Eckersley said the next morning. "God, he's great. But I was crushed. I felt like a ten-year-old who just wanted to be sheltered by his mother."

The A's had one more chance in the bottom of the ninth when they got pinch runner Eric Fox to third with one out and Terry Steinbach, their best clutch hitter, at the plate. But Toronto's overpowering re-

Wide World Photos

ALCS Most Valuable Player **Roberto Alomar** raises his arms in triumph after belting a two-run, 9th inning homer off Dennis Eckersley in Game 4.

liever Duane Ward got Steinbach to ground to Alomar, Fox committed the baserunning blunder of going to the plate, and Alomar threw him out. In the 11th inning, the Jays scored the winner off the tattered A's bullpen. "Choke no more," said Carter. "All we've heard about all season is that we choke. Not this time."

"There's no question that this is the most important win in the history of this franchise," said Rance Mulliniks, the Toronto elder statesman. Indeed, although Dave Stewart got the A's back to Toronto with a complete game masterpiece in Game 5, he only postponed the inevitable. In the sixth game, Carter hit a two-run homer in the first, Maldonado a three-run homer in the third, Toronto had a quick 6-0 lead and won 9-2 to become the first team outside the United States to win a pennant. "The best team won," said La Russa in a statement that summed up his dignity, and the dignity this team had in winning four divisions in five years.

"It's hard to look back at what they've done," said Blue Jays manager Cito Gaston, the first black man to manage in the World Series. "We've been so close for so long and had lived with so many negative tags, we probably don't appreciate what they've done. But it was an exhausting series, emotional, exhausting and fiery. It was as intense as baseball gets as every game seemed to go back and forth across the line of dislike and respect."

Roberto Alomar, arms raised, and Sid Bream, foot raised, will not soon be forgotten in Oakland or Pittsburgh.

THE REGULAR SEASON

One September afternoon, a visitor to Dodger Stadium went to visit Tommy Lasorda's office and discovered that the escalators were shut off. It being a long haul downstairs, he went to the elevator. It was shut off. As the day progressed, he learned that the digital clock underneath the scoreboard had been shut off—disrupting batting practice—and that in the dining room, desserts and toothpicks had been eliminated. Yes, Scrooge, the Dodgers not only went from a two-game lead with a week to play in 1991 to last place, 32 games out, but their attendance dropped by more than 780,000.

Welcome to baseball in the year 1992, the year the market started crashing and all around the game, from Shea to County to Dodger Stadium, from the Bronx to San Francisco Bay, panic spread about the financial future of the game. While owners paid more than $100M to players on the disabled list, the unrest became so great that by (ironically) Labor Day, Commissioner Fay Vincent had been forced to resign. The Astros were sold. Tiger owner Tom Monaghan was in such a financial bind that he had to borrow money to make a payroll, then was forced to sell the club and take the dough from his pizza rival Mike Ilitch. Giants owner Bob Lurie sold his team to a group from Tampa Bay, which set off another set of problems, while the Mariners were prevented from moving to St. Petersburg when a Japanese concern that owns Nintendo was allowed to anchor a local group saving the franchise. The San Diego Padres were so strapped for cash that they almost didn't make a September payroll. The Yankees cut back on two minor league teams, the Instructional League and extended spring programs and reduced their scouting staff. And as more than two-thirds of the teams

dropped in attendance, the exciting, upstart Brewers and remarkable Pirates each drew barely 8,000 for September pennant race games.

"It became a year in which the only thing you ever heard was 'money, money, money,'" said Oakland's general manager Sandy Alderson. "I must have tried to make five thousand trades from June on," said Boston GM Lou Gorman, "and instead of *who* are we trying to trade, it was always *how much* of a contract are we looking to unload."

Vincent's resignation came on Sept. 7, and two days later he was replaced by the owners' Executive Committee, with Brewer owner Bud Selig the de facto, pro tem, interim and titular commissioner.

There had been dissatisfaction and unrest concerning Vincent for months. Some owners and general managers disliked his stubborn nature; for instance, he threatened to suspend one general manager because of criticism of Vincent's allocation of the expansion money. There had been concern about the handling of the George Steinbrenner ban and hard feeling still prevailed about his intervention in the 1990 lockout, which some owners felt undermined their strategy and gave the players the upper hand. In October 1991, when the owners' Player Relations Committee hired former New York mayoral candidate Richard Ravitch as its director, they paid him $100,000 more than Vincent, a direct slap in the face.

Then this May, Selig, Ravitch and White Sox owner Jerry Reinsdorf met with Vincent to try to get him to step out of the labor process entirely in the event of a 1993 lockout. Vincent refused, arguing that no commissioner had ever allowed such a weakening of the office.

The first week of June, the PRC—along with American League President Dr. Bobby Brown and the National League's Bill White—voted 7-2 to formally ask Vincent to remove himself from the labor process. Vincent again refused. The sentiment grew to oust Vincent. There was a controversy during hearings on his lifetime ban of Yankee pitcher Steve Howe, when Vincent reportedly bullied three Yankee executives. Then he ruled that since no one could agree on the expanded 1993 schedule, he was realigning the National League. The Cubs and

Wide World Photos

Former commissioner **Fay Vincent** (left) and **Fred Kuhlmann** of the St. Louis Cardinals, chairman of baseball's ownership committee, meeting with reporters in New York on June 10 after the owners agreed to the sale of the Seattle Mariners to a group headed by Nintendo president Hiroshi Yamauchi.

Cardinals were moved to the West, the Braves and Reds to the East. While most agreed, the Cubs' parent Tribune Co., owner of the superstation that broadcasts its games, filed an injunction halting the realignment and questioning the power of the commissioner. Finally, the opposition put together an 18-10 coalition, met in Chicago and drafted the resignation proposal. That was it for Vincent.

"The problems," he said, "are far greater than one man. When I took office, I said it was the best job in America. Now, I would probably not say that."

The resignation culminated one of the most remarkable two-week stretches in baseball history, one that summarized the economic turmoil—and popularity crisis—that the game is encountering.

On August 26, the Blue Jays made the first bombshell deal of the pennant race. They traded two kids—center fielder Ryan Thompson and second baseman Jeff Kent—to the Mets for David Cone. This deal for one of the game's most dominating pitchers sent Gotham City into shock, but it was a simple business mat-

ter. The Mets had made the decision that they would not, under any circumstances, give Cone a four- or five-year contract, knew they'd lose him, and the Jays had two middle-of-the-field kids that they felt could help them. In turn, Toronto had no intention of signing Cone. "It's not a matter of whether we sign Cone, because we probably won't," said Blue Jays GM Pat Gillick. "We put a lot of emphasis on developing our own players for two reasons—the first is to develop players for Toronto, the second is to develop assets to allow us to go get what we need if we're in the race every year. (In 1990, Gillick traded three pitchers for Bud Black; in 1991, he traded three players for Tom Candiotti, and each deal kept him in the race.) It used to be that teams worried about what they had to show for a deal. Today, what you have to show is whether or not you give your team and your fans a chance to win. Next year, you regroup again."

Then on August 31 came the biggest bombshell of all: Alderson traded Jose Canseco to Texas for Ruben Sierra, Bobby Witt and Jeff Russell. The A's were already seven games up on Minnesota, but Tony La Russa for weeks had said, "This is a thin equation; every day we come to the park, we're worried about starting a ten-game losing streak." At the time of the trade, Sierra was suffering from chicken pox, but they figured he would be a tradeoff for the oft-injured Canseco, and that Witt and Russell would bolster their sagging pitching staff. But what got Alderson criticized was that Sierra and Russell were free agents and could walk away.

"People kept focusing on whether or not we sign Sierra," said Alderson. "That's not the point. This is a business in freefall, and the old system where one judged trades lineally doesn't apply any more. The point is to have flexibility in one's payroll, and cash in hand. Baseball now has a form of salary cap, the problem is that we have 26 different ones. But we all have to operate under them. Cash is now king, and you'd better have flexibility with your cash flow and flexibility on your roster, because player values are plummeting and he who has the cash and flexibility can do a lot."

The personality of Canseco, who had alienated teammates by leaving one game early and being found asleep in the clubhouse during another, was part of the deal. He later engaged in a verbal war with La Russa and Oakland's management. Canseco said after the trade, "It's more relaxed here, it's an atmosphere I can relate to. In Oakland, it was always win, win, win, and you get fed up with it. I'm more comfortable here." When he arrived in the Oakland Coliseum a week later, a guard stopped him at the A's clubhouse door. The players had voted to ban him from his old locker room.

Back on June 15, 1976, the day that Charles Oscar Finley tried to sell Vida Blue, Joe Rudi and Rollie Fingers, baseball realized that the old Reserve System era was over and the free agent system was in effect. Well, those 12 days in which Cone, Canseco and Vincent moved on was the end of the player-controlled and guided Free Agent Era, and the beginning of a new, uncharted period. On the one hand, Cal Ripken (five years, $32.5M), Ryne Sandberg (four years, $28M) and Bobby Bonilla (five years, $29M) were signing huge contracts while Greg Maddox (five years, $28M) and Barry Bonds (five years, $25M) turned down megabucks, while on the other hand, some players sat waiting for the phone to ring. "For the first time," said Selig, "everyone realizes that we've got an industry with a lot of serious problems. This game I love is not moving forward. It's losing its audience and its financial balance."

A recent study prepared for ESPN showed that of the three major professional sports, the interest in baseball is far and away in the greatest decline. They found that baseball tends to lose people at 20 and doesn't pick them back up until 45, after the prime spending age. National TV ratings are abysmal, and three years ago, when Time-Warner did a survey on American athletes, only one baseball player was among the 25 most visible athletes in America, and he was Bo Jackson, who was seen as Bo, not as a baseball player.

Take, for instance, that Labor Day weekend. Instead of centering on the final turn of three interesting pennant races, one of which involved one of the most fascinating young teams (the Expos) in years, the move to unseat Vincent was all the baseball news. A friend recently was searching for a nationally-televised baseball game, only to discover that the pennant race had been dumped in favor of a practice football game. Therein lies a terrible problem that has to be addressed—by dramatic regional realignment, shortened schedules, three divisions and the increased pennant race participation of a possible wild card addition, to name a few possibilities—and addressed soon.

Nevertheless, there was a lot within the game that made 1992 fun despite the fact that only one of the four pennant races went down to the final weekend.

Two of the last players who are heroes the way they used to be, Robin Yount and George Brett, became the 18th and 19th players to reach 3,000 hits. Brett did it on Sept. 30 in Anaheim, after two nights of sitting out with a bad shoulder. He went 4-for-5, got No. 3,000 with brother Ken broadcasting for the Angels and, after all the perfunctory hugging, got picked off first. It was grand that two men who play baseball because they love it, not for what it does for them, should get to 3,000—

Wide World Photos   Wide World Photos

Milwaukee's **Robin Yount** (left) collected his 3,000th career hit Sept. 9, at home against Cleveland. Three weeks later, **George Brett** of Kansas City reached 3,000 with a 4-for-5 performance in Anaheim against the Angels.

and likely Cooperstown—within a month of one another.

There was the unveiling of Baltimore's Camden Yards, the ultimate baseball stadium. Carved out of the bricks of old Baltimore, Camden became a national sensation, attracting nearly 40 consecutive sellouts (curiously, the O's played worse there than on the road). A year after the phenomenal success of Chicago's new Comiskey Park, the '90s are seeing a new wave of baseball-only parks. Cleveland and Texas will open theirs in 1994, Denver will have one in 1996.

There was Gary Sheffield's run at the Triple Crown, which got Ducky Medwick more publicity than he'd ever had. Sheffield had been traded from the Brewers to San Diego in spring training because he was unhappy in Milwaukee (at one point, he claimed he intentionally threw balls away because he was so unhappy, but later denied it), and until he broke a finger in the final week, had a legitimate shot at the crown. As it was, he finished with the batting title at .330, trailed teammate Fred McGriff in homers, 35-33 and his 100 RBI was not far behind the 109 of

Phillies catcher Darren Daulton. By the end of the year, people were calling Doc Gooden "Gary Sheffield's uncle" after years of the reverse.

It was a year in which the teams with the three highest payrolls, the Dodgers, Mets and Red Sox, all finished last or next to it. It got so bad for the Dodgers that Lasorda was rumored to be headed to Tampa Bay, didn't get a vote of confidence from Peter O'Malley, and called a press box to complain about a story and even called a St. Louis talk show to refute criticism.

In New York, Mets manager Jeff Torborg—called "Jeff from Flushing" for his radio shows—called it "the worst year of my life," while Bonilla got caught calling the press box after an error, then denied it, thus getting back page tabloid headlines of "Cry Bobby" (*Post*) and "Liars and Losers" (*Daily News*). In Boston, Matt Young started the season by throwing an eight-inning no-hitter in Cleveland, and losing; Young hasn't won since May 20, 1991, and has won 11 of his last 65 starts dating back to April 15, 1986. In perfect symmetry, Frank Viola threw a one-hitter on Sept. 1 in Toronto—as the Red Sox officially clinched last place.

Other than the Dodgers, Mets and Red Sox, the Reds were probably the most disappointed contender, despite the fact that they lasted until the final week. Their season had begun with considerable anticipation after the acquisitions of pitchers Tim Belcher and Greg Swindell and lead-off man Bip Roberts, but injuries and bullpen inconsistency—not to mention the Braves—wiped them out. Atlanta started 20-27, but when their pitching got in gear in late May, they went on a 53-18 streak that included three bursts of three consecutive shutouts. Tommy Glavine won 12 in a row, was 18-3 at one point and was the first pitcher to win 20, as well as baseball's winningest pitcher over the last two years. Tomahawk Chops Revisited: the Braves had attracted as many fans by June 1 as they had in 71 of their 91 previous entire seasons. The Padres stayed in it for a while on the offensive force of The Four Tops—Tony Fernandez, Tony Gwynn, Sheffield and McGriff—but faded with a lack of pitching depth, and finally manager Greg Riddoch was fired.

The managerial firing that impacted the races came in Montreal, where young, intense Tom Runnells was replaced by 57-year old Felipe Alou. On June 20, Les Expos were in last place. But they came together. With baseball's best young outfield—stolen-base king Marquis Grissom, Larry Walker and Alou's son Moises—as well as the multidimensional DeLino DeShields at second, the Expos used the best young talent in the game. General manager Dan Duquette had made off-season deals for the league's No. 2 closer (John Wetteland) and a 17-game winner (Kenny Hill), and it wasn't until the final two weeks that the Pirates clinched their third straight title.

But Pittsburgh's climb should never be underestimated. "What's so impressive about the Pirates is that they're so unimpressive when you look at the lineup casually," said the Cardinals' Joe Torre. "They do all the little things managers would like to get their players to do, but can't. And they play the best defense on earth."

Montreal's climb was pure fun, as was the rise of the Brewers and Orioles in the East. The Brewers chased the Blue Jays to the final weekend with great pitching. Cal

Wide World Photos

Dennis Eckersley of Oakland led the majors in saves with 51 and became the first reliever to record 40 saves in four different seasons.

Eldred came up in late July and proceeded to go 11-2. Chris Bosio won ten straight starts. Jamie Navarro and Bill Wegman were among the league leaders in innings, while rookie manager Phil Garner unleashed a stealing mania; the Brewers stole 256 bases, and had 11 players with 10 or more steals, a feat that had not been accomplished since 1901.

The Orioles faded in September when, other than young ace Mike Mussina, the pitching faded, but they had a remarkable run thanks to their version of Bonds and Van Slyke: Brady Anderson and Mike Devereaux. Anderson was the first American League player ever to have 50 steals, 20 homers and 75 RBI, while Devereux played a brilliant center field and knocked in 107 runs.

And finally, it was a year in which the Houston Astros had to go on a 28-day, 26-game road trip because the Republican Convention was booked in the Astrodome. It was also the year that Dan Quayle told Milwaukee's Paul Molitor, "I hope you guys have a good year and play the Orioles in the World Series." □

THE 1993 INFORMATION PLEASE SPORTS ALMANAC

BASEBALL STATISTICS

THE SEASON IN REVIEW

1992

LEAGUE LEADERS • POSTSEASON

SEC A

PAGE 71

Final Major League Standings

Division champions (*) are noted. Number of seasons listed after each manager refers to current tenure with club.

American League

East Division

	W	L	Pct	GB	Home	Away
*Toronto	96	66	.593	—	53-28	43-38
Milwaukee	92	70	.568	4	53-28	39-42
Baltimore	89	73	.549	7	43-38	46-35
Cleveland	76	86	.469	20	41-40	35-46
New York	76	86	.469	20	41-40	35-46
Detroit	75	87	.463	21	38-42	37-45
Boston	73	89	.451	23	44-37	29-52

1992 Managers: Tor—Cito Gaston (4th season); **Mil**—Phil Garner (1st); **Bal**— Johnny Oates (2nd); **Cle**—Mike Hargrove (2nd); **NY**—Buck Showalter (1st); **Det**—Sparky Anderson (14th); **Bos**—Butch Hobson (1st).

1991 Standings: 1. Toronto (91-71); 2. Boston (84-78) and Detroit (84-78); 4. Milwaukee (83-79); 5. New York (71-91); 6. Baltimore (67-95); 7. Cleveland (57-105).

West Division

	W	L	Pct	GB	Home	Away
*Oakland	96	66	.593	—	51-30	45-36
Minnesota	90	72	.556	6	48-33	42-39
Chicago	86	76	.531	10	50-32	36-44
Texas	77	85	.475	19	36-45	41-40
Kansas City	72	90	.444	24	44-37	28-53
California	72	90	.444	24	41-40	31-50
Seattle	64	98	.395	32	38-43	26-55

1992 Managers: Oak—Tony La Russa (7th season); **Min**—Tom Kelly (7th); **Chi**—Gene Lamont (1st); **Tex**—replaced Bobby Valentine (8th, 45-41) with Toby Harrah (32-44) on July 9; **Cal**—while Buck Rodgers (2nd, 33-40) was sidelined 99 days with injuries suffered in a May 21 team bus accident, John Wathan (39-50) served as interim manager; **KC**—Hal McRae (2nd); **Sea**—Bill Plummer (1st).

1991 Standings: 1. Minnesota (95-67); 2. Chicago (87-75); 3. Texas (85-77); 4. Oakland (84-78); 5. Seattle (83-79); 6. Kansas City (82-80); 7. California (81-81).

National League

East Division

	W	L	Pct	GB	Home	Away
*Pittsburgh	96	66	.593	—	53-28	43-38
Montreal	87	75	.537	9	43-38	44-37
St. Louis	83	79	.512	13	45-36	38-43
Chicago	78	84	.481	18	43-38	35-46
New York	72	90	.444	24	41-40	31-50
Philadelphia	70	92	.432	26	41-40	29-52

1992 Managers: Pit—Jim Leyland (7th season); **Mon**—replaced Tom Runnells (2nd, 17-20) with Felipe Alou (70-55) on May 22; **StL**—Joe Torre (3rd); **Chi**—Jim Lefebvre (1st); **NY**—Jeff Torborg (1st); **Phi**—Jim Fregosi (2nd).

1991 Standings: 1. Pittsburgh (98-64); 2. St. Louis (84-78); 3. Philadelphia (78-84); 4. Chicago (77-83) and New York (77-83); 6. Montreal (71-90).

West Division

	W	L	Pct	GB	Home	Away
*Atlanta	98	64	.605	—	51-30	47-34
Cincinnati	90	72	.556	8	53-28	37-44
San Diego	82	80	.506	16	45-36	37-44
Houston	81	81	.500	17	47-34	34-47
San Francisco	72	90	.444	26	42-39	30-51
Los Angeles	63	99	.389	35	37-44	26-55

1992 Managers: Atl—Bobby Cox (3rd season); **Cin**—Lou Piniella (3rd); **SD**—replaced Greg Riddoch (3rd, 78-72) with Jim Riggleman (4-8) on Sept. 23; **Hou**—Art Howe (4th); **SF**—Roger Craig (8th); **LA**—Tom Lasorda (17th).

1991 Standings: 1. Atlanta (94-68); 2. Los Angeles (93-69); 3. San Diego (84-78); 4. San Francisco (75-87); 5. Cincinnati (74-88); 6. Houston (65-97).

The 1992 *Sporting News* Awards

Released Oct. 27, 1992; AL and NL awards voted on by players in each league; all players eligible to vote on new Major League Player of the Year award; only managers eligible to vote on Manager of the Year awards.

Player of the Year: Gary Sheffield, SD, 3B. **Pitchers of the Year: AL**—Dennis Eckersley, Oak.; **NL**—Greg Maddux, Chi. **Managers of the Year: AL**—Tony La Russa, Oak.; **NL**—Jim Leyland, Pit. **Rookies of the Year: AL**—Pat Listach, Mil., 2B, and Cal Eldred, Mil., P; **NL**—Eric Karros, LA, 1B, and Tim Wakefield, Pit., P. **Comebacks of the Year: AL**—Rick Sutcliffe, Bal., P; **NL**—Gary Sheffield, SD, 3B.

AL All-Star Team

C—Mickey Tettleton, Detroit; **1B**—Mark McGwire, Oakland; **2B**—Roberto Alomar, Toronto; **SS**—Travis Fryman, Detroit; **3B**—Edgar Martinez, Seattle; **OF**—Kirby Puckett, Minnesota, Joe Carter, Toronto and Mike Devereaux, Baltimore; **DH**—Dave Winfield, Toronto; **RHP**—Jack McDowell, Chicago; **LHP**—Dave Fleming, Seattle.

NL All-Star Team

C—Darren Daulton, Philadelphia; **1B**—Fred McGriff, San Diego; **2B**—Ryne Sandberg, Chicago; **SS**—Barry Larkin, Cincinnati; **3B**—Gary Sheffield, San Diego; **OF**—Barry Bonds, Pittsburgh, Andy Van Slyke, Pittsburgh and Larry Walker, Montreal; **RHP**—Greg Maddux, Chicago; **LHP**—Tom Glavine, Atlanta.

American League Regular Season Individual Leaders

Batting
Minimum of 502 plate appearances.

	Avg	AB	R	H	HR	RBI
Edgar Martinez, Sea	.343	528	100	181	18	73
Kirby Puckett, Min	.329	639	104	210	19	110
Frank Thomas, Chi	.323	573	108	185	24	115
Paul Molitor, Mil	.320	609	89	195	12	89
Shane Mack, Min	.315	600	101	189	16	75
Carlos Baerga, Cle	.312	657	92	205	20	105
Roberto Alomar, Tor	.310	571	105	177	8	76
Ken Griffey, Sea	.308	565	83	174	27	103
Brian Harper, Min	.307	502	58	154	9	73
Mike Bordick, Oak	.300	504	62	151	3	48
Darryl Hamilton, Mil	.298	470	67	140	5	62
Chuck Knoblauch, Min	.297	600	104	178	2	56
Tim Raines, Chi	.294	551	102	162	7	54
Omar Vizquel, Sea	.294	483	49	142	0	21
Pat Listach, Mil	.290	579	93	168	1	47
Dave Winfield, Tor	.290	583	92	169	26	108

Pitching
Minimum of 162 innings pitched.

	ERA	W-L	IP	H	SO
Roger Clemens, Bos	2.41	18-11	246.2	203	208
Kevin Appier, KC	2.46	15- 8	208.1	167	150
Mike Mussina, Bal	2.54	18- 5	241.0	212	130
Juan Guzman, Tor	2.64	16- 5	180.2	135	165
Jim Abbott, Cal	2.77	7-15	211.0	208	130
Melido Perez, NY	2.87	13-16	247.2	212	218
Charles Nagy, Cle	2.96	17-10	252.0	245	169
Jack McDowell, Chi	3.18	20-10	260.2	247	178
Bill Wegman, Mil	3.20	13-14	261.2	251	127
John Smiley, Min	3.21	16- 9	241.0	205	163
Kevin Brown, Tex	3.32	21-11	265.2	262	173
Jaime Navarro, Mil	3.33	17-11	246.0	224	100
Dave Fleming, Sea	3.39	17-10	228.1	225	112
Scott Erickson, Min	3.40	13-12	212.0	197	101
Frank Viola, Bos	3.44	13-12	238.0	214	121

Home Runs
Gonzalez, Tex	43
McGwire, Oak	42
Fielder, Det	35
Belle, Cle	34
Carter, Tor	34
Deer, Det	32
Tettleton, Det	32
Griffey, Sea	27
Canseco, Oak-Tex	26
Palmer, Tex	26
Winfield, Tor	26

Runs Batted In
Fielder, Det	124
Carter, Tor	119
Thomas, Chi	115
Bell, Chi	112
Belle, Cle	112
Puckett, Min	110
Gonzalez, Tex	109
Winfield, Tor	108
Devereaux, Bal	107
Baega, Cle	105
McGwire, Oak	104

Wins
Morris, Tor	21- 6
Brown, Tex	21-11
McDowell, Chi	20-10
Mussina, Bal	18- 5
Clemens, Bos	18-11
Fleming, Sea	17-10
Nagy, Cle	17-10
Navarro, Mil	17-11
Moore, Oak	17-12
Six tied with 16 each.	

Saves
	SV	BS
Eckersley, Oak	51	3
Aguilera, Min	41	7
Montgomery, KC	39	7
Olson, Bal	36	8
Henke, Tor	34	3
Farr, NY	30	6
Russell, Tex-Oak	30	9
Henry, Mil	29	4
Olin, Cle	29	7
Reardon, Bos	27	8

Stolen Bases
	SB	CS
Lofton, Cle	66	12
Listach, Mil	54	18
Anderson, Bal	53	16
Polonia, Cal	51	21
Alomar, Tor	49	9
R.Henderson, Oak	48	11
Raines, Chi	45	6
Curtis, Cal	43	18
Hamilton, Mil	41	14
Johnson, Chi	41	14

Hits
Puckett, Min	210
Baerga, Cle	205
Molitor, Mil	195
Mack, Min	189
Thomas, Chi	185
Mattingly, NY	184
E.Martinez, Sea	181
Devereaux, Bal	180
Knoblauch, Min	178
Alomar, Tor	177
Fryman, Det	175

Appearances
Rodgers, Tex	81
D.Ward, Tor	79
Olin, Cle	72
Lilliquist, Cle	71
Harris, Bos	70
Eckersley, Oak	69

Innings
Brown, Tex	265.2
Wegman, Mil	261.2
McDowell, Chi	260.2
Nagy, Cle	252.0
Perez, NY	247.2
Clemens, Bos	246.2

Triples
Johnson, Chi	12
Devereaux, Bal	11
Anderson, Bal	10
Raines, Chi	9
Alomar, Tor	8
Lofton, Cle	8

Doubles
E.Martinez, Sea	46
Thomas, Chi	46
Mattingly, NY	40
Yount, Mil	40
Griffey, Sea	39

Games Started
Moore, Oak	36
Sutcliffe, Bal	36
Brown, Tex	35
McDonald, Bal	35
Wegman, Mil	35
Viola, Bos	35

Games Finished
Eckersley, Oak	65
Montgomery, KC	62
Olin, Cle	62
Aguilera, Min	61
Henry, Mil	56
Olson, Bal	56

Runs
Phillips, Det	114
Thomas, Chi	108
Alomar, Tor	105
Knoblauch, Min	104
Puckett, Min	104

On Base Pct.
Thomas, Chi	.439
Tartabull, NY	.409
Alomar, Tor	.405
E.Martinez, Sea	.404
Mack, Min	.394

Complete Games
McDowell, Chi	13
Brown, Tex	11
Clemens, Bos	11
Nagy, Cle	10
Perez, NY	10
Langston, Cal	8
Mussina, Bal	8

Shutouts
Clemens, Bos	5
Fleming, Sea	4
Mussina, Bal	4
Darling, Oak	3
Erickson, Min	3
Nagy, Cle	3
Navarro, Mil	3

Total Bases
Puckett, Min	313
Carter, Tor	310
Gonzalez, Tex	309
Thomas, Chi	307
Devereaux, Bal	303

Slugging Pct.
McGwire, Oak	.585
E.Martinez, Sea	.544
Thomas, Chi	.536
Griffey, Sea	.535
Gonzalez, Tex	.529

Strikeouts
Johnson, Sea	241
Perez, NY	218
Clemens, Bos	208
Guzman, Tex	179
McDowell, Chi	178
Langston, Cal	174

Walks
Johnson, Sea	144
Witt, Tex-Oak	114
Moore, Oak	103
Finley, Cal	98
McCaskill, Chi	95
Perez, NY	93

Times Walked
Tettleton, Det	122
Thomas, Chi	122
Phillips, Det	114
Milligan, Bal	106

Times Struck Out
Palmer, Tex	154
Fielder, Det	151
Buhner, Sea	146
Fryman, Det	144

Losses
Hanson, Sea	8-17
Perez, NY	13-16
Armstrong, Cle	6-15
Abbott, Cal	7-15
Sutcliffe, Bal	16-15
Five tied with 14 each.	

HRs Given Up
Gullickson, Det	35
McDonald, Bal	32
Cook, Cle	29
Sanderson, NY	28
Wegman, Mil	28
Bones, Mil	27

American League Leaders

Wide World Photos

Edgar Martinez
Batting Avg. & Doubles

Wide World Photos

Juan Gonzalez
Home Runs

Wide World Photos

Cecil Fielder
Runs Batted In

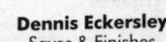
Wide World Photos

Kenny Lofton
Stolen Bases

Wide World Photos

Roger Clemens
ERA & Shutouts

Wide World Photos

Dennis Eckersley
Saves & Finishes

Wide World Photos

Jack Morris
Wins

Wide World Photos

Kevin Brown
Wins

Wide World Photos

Randy Johnson
Strikeouts & Walks

National League Regular Season Individual Leaders

Batting

Minimum of 502 plate appearances.

	Avg	AB	R	H	HR	RBI
Gary Sheffield, SD	.330	557	87	184	33	100
Andy Van Slyke, Pit	.324	614	103	199	14	89
John Kruk, Phi	.323	507	86	164	10	70
Bip Roberts, Cin	.323	532	92	172	4	45
Tony Gwynn, SD	.317	520	77	165	6	41
Terry Pendleton, Atl	.311	640	98	199	21	105
Barry Bonds, Pit	.311	473	109	147	34	103
Brett Butler, LA	.309	553	86	171	3	39
Mark Grace, Chi	.307	603	72	185	9	79
Barry Larkin, Cin	.304	533	76	162	12	78
Ryne Sandberg, Chi	.304	612	100	186	26	87
Larry Walker, Mon	.301	528	85	159	23	93
Will Clark, SF	.300	513	69	154	16	73
Willie McGee, SF	.297	474	56	141	1	36
Ozzie Smith, St.L	.295	518	73	153	0	31
Felix Jose, St.L	.295	509	62	150	14	75

Pitching

Minimum of 162 innings pitched.

	ERA	W-L	IP	H	SO
Bill Swift, SF	2.08	10- 4	164.2	144	77
Bob Tewksbury, St.L	2.16	16- 5	233.0	217	91
Greg Maddux, Chi	2.18	20-11	268.0	201	199
Curt Schilling, Phi	2.35	14-11	226.1	165	147
Dennis Martinez, Mon	2.47	16-11	226.1	172	147
Mike Morgan, Chi	2.55	16- 8	240.0	203	123
Jose Rijo, Cin	2.56	15-10	211.0	185	171
Ken Hill, Mon	2.68	16- 9	218.0	187	150
Greg Swindell, Cin	2.70	12- 8	213.2	210	138
Sid Fernandez, NY	2.73	14-11	214.2	162	193
Tom Glavine, Atl	2.76	20- 8	225.0	197	129
Doug Drabek, Pit	2.77	15-11	256.2	218	177
John Smoltz, Atl	2.85	15-12	246.2	206	215
Tom Candiotti, LA	3.00	11-15	203.2	177	152
Kevin Gross, LA	3.17	8-13	204.2	182	158

Home Runs

McGriff, SD	35
Bonds, Pit	34
Sheffield, SD	33
Daulton, Phi	27
Hollins, Phi	27
Sandberg, Chi	26
Walker, Mon	23
Dawson, Chi	22
Justice, Atl	21
Pendleton, Atl	21

Runs Batted In

Daulton, Phi	109
Pendleton, Atl	105
McGriff, SD	104
Bonds, Pit	103
Sheffield, SD	100
Bagwell, Hou	96
Hollins, Phi	93
Murray, NY	93
Walker, Mon	93
Dawson, Chi	90

Wins

Glavine, Atl	20- 8
Maddux, Chi	20-11
Tewksbury, St.L	16- 5
Morgan, Chi	16- 8
Hill, Mon	16- 9
Martinez, Mon	16-11
Leibrandt, Atl	15- 7
Rijo, Cin	15-10
Drabek, Pit	15-11
Smoltz, Atl	15-12
Belcher, Cin	15-14

Saves

	SV	BS
L.Smith, St.L	43	8
Myers, SD	38	8
Wetteland, Mon	37	9
D.Jones, Hou	36	6
M.Williams, Phi	29	7
Charlton, Cin	26	8
Dibble, Cin	25	5
Belinda, Pit	18	6
Beck, SF	17	6
Three tied with 15 each.		

Stolen Bases

	SB	CS
Grissom, Mon	78	13
DeShields, Mon	46	15
Finley, Hou	44	9
Roberts, Cin	44	16
O.Smith, St.L	43	9
Lankford, St.L	42	24
Butler, LA	41	21
Nixon, Atl	41	18
Bonds, Pit	39	8
Biggio, Hou	38	15

Hits

Pendleton, Atl	199
Van Slyke, Pit	199
Sandberg, Chi	186
Grace, Chi	185
Sheffield, SD	184
Grissom, Mon	180
Finley, Hou	177
Lankford, St.L	175
Roberts, Cin	172
Butler, LA	171
Fernandez, SD	171

Appearances

Boever, Hou	81
D.Jones, Hou	80
Hernandez, Hou	77
Perez, St.L	77
Innis, NY	76
Carpenter, St.L	73

Innings

Maddux, Chi	268.0
Drabek, Pit	256.2
Smoltz, Atl	246.2
Morgan, Chi	240.0
Avery, Atl	233.2
Tewksbury, St.L	233.0

Triples

Sanders, Atl	14
Finley, Hou	13
Van Slyke, Pit	12
Alicea, St.L	11
Butler, LA	11

Doubles

Van Slyke, Pit	45
Clark, SF	40
Duncan, Phi	40
Lankford, St.L	40
Two tied with 39 each.	

Games Started

Avery, Atl	35
Maddux, Chi	35
Smoltz, Atl	35
Six tied with 34 each.	

Games Finished

Jones, Hou	70
Wetteland, Mon	58
Myers, SD	57
M.Williams, Phi	56
L.Smith, St.L	55

Runs

Bonds, Pit	109
Hollins, Phi	104
Van Slyke, Pit	103
Sandberg, Chi	100
Grissom, Mon	99

On Base Pct.

Bonds, Pit	.456
Kruk, Phi	.423
Butler, LA	.413
McGriff, SD	.394
Roberts, Cin	.393

Complete Games

Mulholland, Phi	12
Drabek, Pit	10
Schilling, Phi	10
Maddux, Chi	9
Smoltz, Atl	9
Cone, NY	7
Glavine, Atl	7

Shutouts

Cone, NY	5
Glavine, Atl	5
Astacio, LA	4
Drabek, Pit	4
Hurst, SD	4
Maddux, Chi	4
Schilling, Phi	4

Total Bases

Sheffield, SD	323
Sandberg, Chi	312
Van Slyke, Pit	310
Pendleton, Atl	303
Bonds, Pit	295
McGriff, SD	295

Slugging Pct.

Bonds, Pit	.624
Sheffield, SD	.580
McGriff, SD	.556
Daulton, Phi	.524
Sandberg, Chi	.510
Walker, Mon	.506

Strikeouts

Smoltz, Atl	215
Cone, NY	214
Maddux, Chi	199
Fernandez, NY	193
Drabek, Pit	177
Rijo, Cin	171

Walks

Cone, NY	82
Ojeda, LA	81
Belcher, Cin	80
Smoltz, Atl	80
Morgan, Chi	79
Two tied with 77 each.	

Times Walked

Bonds, Pit	127
McGriff, SD	96
Butler, LA	95
Biggio, Hou	94
Kruk, Phi	92

Times Struck Out

Lankford, St.L	147
Hollins, Phi	110
Williams, SF	109
Deshields, Mon	108
Duncan, Phi	108
McGriff, SD	108

Losses

Hershiser, LA	10-15
Candiotti, LA	11-15
Abbott, Phi	1-14
Young, NY	2-14
Wilson, SF	8-14
Benes, SD	13-14
Belcher, Cin	15-14

HRs Given Up

Black, SF	23
Hurst, SD	22
Abbott, Phi	20
Olivares, St.L	20
Castillo, Chi	19
Harnisch, Hou	18
Wilson, SF	18

National League Leaders

Wide World Photos

Gary Sheffield
Batting & Total Bases

Wide World Photos

Fred McGriff
Home Runs

Wide World Photos

Darren Daulton
Runs Batted In

Wide World Photos

Marquis Grissom
Stolen Bases

Wide World Photos

Bill Swift
ERA

Wide World Photos

Lee Smith
Saves

Wide World Photos

Tom Glavine
Wins

Wide World Photos

Greg Maddux
Wins & Innings

Wide World Photos

John Smoltz
Strikeouts

1992 All Star Game

63rd Baseball All-Star Game. **Date:** July 14 at Jack Murphy Stadium in San Diego; **Managers:** Tom Kelly, Minnesota (AL) and Bobby Cox, Atlanta (NL); **MVP:** CF Ken Griffey Jr., Seattle (AL): 3-for-3, solo HR in third inning.

American League

	AB	R	H	BI	PO	A	E
Roberto Alomar, Tor, 2b	3	1	1	0	1	3	0
Carlos Baerga, Cle, 2b	1	1	1	1	0	0	0
Charles Nagy, Cle, p	1	1	1	0	0	0	0
Rick Aguilera, Min, p	1	0	0	0	0	0	0
Wade Boggs, Bos, 3b	3	1	1	0	1	0	0
Robin Ventura, Chi, 3b	2	1	2	1	1	1	0
Kirby Puckett, Min, lf	3	1	1	0	3	0	0
Ruben Sierra, Tex, rf	2	2	1	2	2	0	0
Joe Carter, Tor, rf	3	1	2	1	0	0	0
Travis Fryman, Det, ss	1	1	1	1	0	2	0
Mark McGwire, Oak, 1b	3	1	1	2	4	0	0
Paul Molitor, Mil, 1b	2	0	1	0	5	0	1
Cal Ripken Jr, Bal, ss	3	0	1	1	1	2	0
Roberto Kelly, NY, cf	2	0	1	2	0	0	0
Ken Griffey Jr, Sea, cf	3	2	3	2	1	0	0
Ivan Rodriguez, Tex, c	2	0	0	0	4	0	0
Sandy Alomar Jr, Cle, c	3	0	1	0	3	0	0
Chuck Knoblauch, Min, 2b	1	0	0	0	1	0	0
Kevin Brown, Tex, p	1	0	0	0	0	0	0
Edgar Martinez, Sea, ph	1	0	0	0	0	0	0
Brady Anderson, Bal, lf	3	0	0	0	0	0	0
TOTALS	44	13	19	13	27	8	1

National League

	AB	R	H	BI	PO	A	E
Ozzie Smith, St.L, ss	3	0	1	0	2	1	0
Tony Fernandez, SD, ss	2	1	1	0	1	1	0
Tony Gwynn, SD, rf	2	0	0	0	0	0	0
John Kruk, Phi, rf	2	1	2	0	0	2	1
Barry Bonds, Pit, lf	3	1	1	0	3	1	0
Bip Roberts, Cin, lf	2	1	2	2	0	0	0
Fred McGriff, SD, 1b	3	0	2	1	6	1	0
Tom Pagnozzi, St.L, ph	1	0	0	0	0	0	0
Norm Charlton, Cin, p	1	0	0	0	0	2	0
Terry Pendleton, Atl, 3b	2	0	1	0	0	2	0
Will Clark, SF, 1b	2	1	1	3	1	0	0
Andy VanSlyke, Pit, cf	2	0	0	0	0	0	0
Ron Gant, Atl, ph-cf	2	0	0	0	1	0	0
Ryne Sandberg, Chi, 2b	2	0	0	0	2	3	0
Craig Biggio, Hou, 2b	2	0	0	0	0	0	0
Benito Santiago, SD, c	1	0	0	0	3	0	0
Darren Daulton, Phi, c	3	1	0	0	4	0	0
Larry Walker, Mon, ph	1	0	1	0	0	0	0
Gary Sheffield, SD, 3b	2	0	0	0	1	0	0
Mike Sharperson, LA, 3b	1	0	0	0	0	0	0
TOTALS	39	6	12	6	27	12	1

	1	2	3	4	5	6	7	8	9	R	H	E
American League	4	1	1	0	0	4	0	3	0—13		19	1
National League	0	0	0	0	0	1	0	3	2— 6		12	1

E—Molitor, AL; Kruk, NL. **DP**—American (6); National (7). **2B**—Baerga, Ventura, Kelly and Griffey, AL; O.Smith and Bonds, NL. **HR**—Sierra (off Tewksbury) and Griffey (off Maddux), AL; Clark (off Aguilera), NL. **SB**—Alomar (2), AL.

AL Pitching	IP	H	R	ER	BB	SO
Kevin Brown, Tex (W)	1.0	0	0	0	0	1
Jack McDowell, Chi	1.0	0	0	0	0	0
Juan Guzman, Tor	1.0	2	0	0	1	2
Roger Clemens, Bos	1.0	2	0	0	0	0
Mike Mussina, Bal	1.0	0	0	0	0	0
Mark Langston, Cal	1.0	0	0	0	0	1
Charles Nagy, Cle	1.0	0	0	0	0	1
Jeff Montgomery, KC	0.2	2	2	2	0	0
Rick Aguilera, Min	0.2	1	1	1	0	0
Dennis Eckersley, Oak	0.2	3	2	0	0	2
TOTALS	9.0	12	6	4	1	7

NL Pitching	IP	H	R	ER	BB	SO
Tom Glavine, Atl (L)	1.2	9	5	5	0	2
Greg Maddux, Chi	1.1	1	1	1	0	0
David Cone, NY	1.0	0	0	0	0	1
Bob Tewksbury, St.L	1.2	4	4	4	1	0
John Smoltz, Atl	0.1	1	0	0	0	0
Dennis Martinez, Mon	1.0	0	0	0	0	1
Doug Jones, Hou	1.0	4	3	3	0	2
Norm Charlton, Cin	1.0	0	0	0	1	1
TOTALS	9.0	19	13	13	2	7

Umpires—Doug Harvey (NL) plate; Rich Garcia (AL) 1b; Harry Wendlestedt (NL) 2b; Greg Kosc (AL) 3b; Tom Hallian (NL) lf; Tim Tschida (AL) rf. **Time**—2:55. **Attendance**—59,372. **TV Rating**—14.9/27 share (CBS).

Home Attendance

Overall 1992 regular season attendance in Major League Baseball was 56,858,010 in 2076 games for an average per game crowd of 27,388; numbers in parentheses indicate ranking in 1991; HD indicates home dates.

American League
Based on tickets sold.

	Attendance	HD	Average
1 Toronto (1)	4,028,318	81	49,732
2 Baltimore (5)	3,567,819	80	44,598
3 Chicago (2)	2,681,156	81*	33,101
4 Oakland (3)	2,494,160	81	30,792
5 Minnesota (8)	2,482,428	81	30,647
6 Boston (4)	2,468,514	78	31,648
7 Texas (7)	2,198,231	80	27,478
8 California (6)	2,065,444	81	25,499
9 Kansas City (9)	1,867,689	79	23,642
10 Milwaukee (13)	1,857,351	79	23,511
11 New York (11)	1,748,737	80	21,859
12 Seattle (10)	1,651,367	81	20,387
13 Detroit (12)	1,423,963	78*	18,256
14 Cleveland (14)	1,224,094	78	15,694
TOTAL	31,759,331	1118	28,407

National League
Based on turnstile count.

	Attendance	HD	Average
1 Atlanta (6)	3,077,400	80	38,468
2 Los Angeles (1)	2,473,266	77	32,120
3 St.Louis (2)	2,418,483	80	30,231
4 Cincinnati (3)	2,315,946	80	28,949
5 Chicago (4)	2,126,720	80	26,584
6 Philadelphia (8)	1,927,448	78	24,711
7 Pittsburgh (7)	1,829,395	81	22,585
8 New York (5)	1,779,534	76	23,415
9 San Diego (9)	1,721,406	81	21,252
10 Montreal (12)	1,669,127	80	20,864
11 San Fran. (10)	1,560,998	79	19,759
12 Houston (11)	1,211,412	81	14,956
TOTAL	24,111,135	953	25,300

*One rained out Chicago at Detroit game was rescheduled and played in Chicago.

AL Team by Team Statistics

Baltimore Orioles

Batting (150 AB)	Avg	AB	R	H	HR	RBI	SB
Joe Orsulak	.289	391	45	113	4	39	5
Glenn Davis	.276	398	46	110	13	48	1
Mike Devereaux	.276	653	76	180	24	107	10
Chris Hoiles	.274	310	49	85	20	40	0
Brady Anderson	.271	623	100	169	21	80	53
Chito Martinez	.268	198	26	53	5	25	0
Leo Gomez	.265	468	62	124	17	64	2
Cal Ripken	.251	637	73	160	14	72	4
Mark McLemore	.246	228	40	56	0	27	11
Randy Milligan	.240	462	71	111	11	53	0
Jeff Tackett*	.240	179	21	43	5	24	0
Sam Horn	.235	162	13	38	5	19	0
David Segui	.233	189	21	44	1	17	1
Billy Ripken	.230	330	35	76	4	36	2

Acquired: P Craig Lefferts from SD (Aug.31) for minor league P Erik Schullstrom.

Pitching (40 IP)	ERA	W-L	Gm	IP	BB	SO
Gregg Olson	2.05	1-5	60	61.1	24	58
Todd Frohwirth	2.46	4-3	65	106.0	41	58
Mike Mussina	2.54	18-5	32	241.0	48	130
Alan Mills	2.61	10-4	35	103.1	54	60
Storm Davis	3.43	7-3	48	89.1	36	53
Arthur Rhodes*	3.63	7-5	15	94.1	38	77
Ben McDonald	4.24	13-13	35	227.0	74	158
Rick Sutcliffe	4.47	16-15	36	237.1	74	109
Bob Milacki	5.84	6-8	23	115.2	44	51

Saves: Olson (36); S.Davis and Frothwirth (2); Mills (2); Milacki and Mark Williamson (1). **Complete games:** Mussina (8); Sutcliffe (5); McDonald (4); Rhodes (2); Craig Lefferts (1). **Shutouts:** Mussina (4); McDonald and Sutcliffe (2); Rhodes (1).

Boston Red Sox

Batting (150 AB)	Avg	AB	R	H	HR	RBI	SB
Scott Cooper*	.276	337	34	93	5	33	1
John Valentin*	.276	185	21	51	5	25	1
Bob Zupcic*	.276	392	46	108	3	43	2
Tom Brunansky	.266	458	47	122	15	74	2
Wade Boggs	.259	514	62	133	7	50	1
Ellis Burks	.255	235	35	60	8	30	5
Jody Reed	.247	550	64	136	3	40	7
Phil Plantier	.246	349	46	86	7	30	2
Tony Pena	.241	410	39	99	1	38	3
Billy Hatcher	.238	315	37	75	1	23	4
Herm Winningham	.235	234	27	55	1	14	6
Mo Vaughn	.234	355	42	83	13	57	3
Mike Greenwell	.233	180	16	42	2	18	2
Tim Naehring	.231	186	12	43	3	14	0
Luis Rivera	.215	288	17	62	0	29	4
Jack Clark	.210	257	32	54	5	33	1

Acquired: OF Hatcher from Cin. (July 9) for P Tom Bolton.
Traded: P Reardon to Atl.(Aug.30) for P Nate Minchey and OF Sean Ross.

Pitching (40 IP)	ERA	W-L	Gm	IP	BB	SO
Paul Quantrill*	2.19	2-3	27	49.1	15	24
Roger Clemens	2.41	18-11	32	246.2	62	208
Greg Harris	2.51	4-9	70	107.2	60	73
Frank Viola	3.44	13-12	35	238.0	89	121
Danny Darwin	3.96	9-9	51	161.1	53	124
John Dopson	4.08	7-11	25	141.1	38	55
Jeff Reardon	4.25	2-2	46	42.1	7	32
Joe Hesketh	4.36	8-9	30	148.2	58	104
Matt Young	4.58	0-4	28	70.2	42	57
Mike Gardiner	4.75	4-10	28	130.2	58	79

Saves: Reardon (27); Harris (4); Darwin (3); Tony Fosses (2); Hesketh, Quantrill and Ken Ryan (1). **Complete games:** Clemens (11); Viola (6); Darwin (2); Harris, Hesketh and Young (1). **Shutouts:** Clemens (5); Viola (1).

California Angels

Batting (150 AB)	Avg	AB	R	H	HR	RBI	SB
Luis Polonia	.286	577	83	165	0	35	51
Rene Gonzales	.277	329	47	91	7	38	7
Luis Sojo	.272	368	37	100	7	43	7
Chad Curtis*	.259	441	59	114	10	46	43
Damion Easley*	.258	151	14	39	1	12	9
Gary DiSarcina*	.247	518	48	128	3	42	9
Junior Felix	.246	509	63	125	9	72	8
Gary Gaetti	.226	456	41	103	12	48	3
Von Hayes	.225	307	35	69	4	29	11
Lee Stevens	.221	312	25	69	7	37	1
Hubie Brooks	.216	306	28	66	8	36	3
Mike Fitzgerald	.212	189	19	40	6	17	2

Acquired: P Valera and player to be named from NY Mets (Apr.12) for SS Dick Schofield.

Pitching (40 IP)	ERA	W-L	Gm	IP	BB	SO
Jim Abbott	2.77	7-15	29	211.0	68	130
Joe Grahe	3.52	5-6	46	94.2	39	39
Steve Frey	3.57	4-2	51	45.1	22	24
Mark Langston	3.66	13-14	32	229.0	74	174
Julio Valera*	3.73	8-11	30	188.0	64	113
Chuck Finley	3.96	7-12	31	204.1	98	124
Bert Blyleven	4.74	8-12	25	133.0	29	70
Chuck Crim	5.17	7-6	57	87.0	29	30
Tim Fortugno*	5.18	1-1	14	41.2	19	31

Saves: Grahe (21); Bryan Harvey (13); Frey (4); Crim and Fortugno (1). **Complete games:** Langston (8); Abbott (7); Finley and Valera (4); Blyleven and Fortugno (1). **Shutouts:** Langston and Valera (2); Finley and Fortugno (1).

Chicago White Sox

Batting (150 AB)	Avg	AB	R	H	HR	RBI	SB
Frank Thomas	.323	573	108	185	24	115	6
Tim Raines	.294	551	102	162	7	54	45
Robin Ventura	.282	592	85	167	16	93	2
Shawn Abner	.279	208	21	58	1	16	1
Lance Johnson	.279	567	67	158	3	47	41
Craig Grebeck	.268	287	24	77	3	35	0
George Bell	.255	627	74	160	25	112	5
Ron Karkovice	.237	342	39	81	13	50	10
Steve Sax	.236	567	74	134	4	47	30
Carlton Fisk	.229	188	12	43	3	21	3
Dan Pasqua	.211	265	26	56	6	33	0

Pitching (40 IP)	ERA	W-L	Gm	IP	BB	SO
Roberto Hernandez*	1.65	7-3	43	71.0	20	68
Terry Leach	1.95	6-5	51	73.2	20	22
Scott Radinsky	2.73	3-7	68	59.1	34	48
Jack McDowell	3.18	20-10	34	260.2	75	178
Charlie Hough	3.93	7-12	27	176.1	66	76
Kirk McCaskill	4.18	12-13	34	209.0	95	109
Alex Fernandez	4.27	8-11	29	187.2	50	95
Greg Hibbard	4.40	10-7	31	176.0	57	69
Bobby Thigpen	4.75	1-3	55	55.0	33	45
Donn Pall	4.93	5-2	39	73.0	27	27
Wilson Alvarez	5.20	5-3	34	100.1	65	66

Saves: Thigpen (22); Radinsky (15); Hernandez (12); Alvarez, Hibbard and Pall (1). **Complete games:** McDowell (13); Fernandez and Hough (4). **Shutouts:** Fernandez (2); MacDowell (1).

Cleveland Indians

Batting (150 AB)	Avg	AB	R	H	HR	RBI	SB
Carlos Baerga........	.312	657	92	205	20	105	10
Kenny Lofton*.......	.285	576	96	164	5	42	66
Thomas Howard......	.277	358	36	99	2	32	15
Felix Fermin..........	.270	215	27	58	0	13	0
Paul Sorrento........	.269	458	52	123	18	60	0
Mark Lewis	.264	413	44	109	5	30	4
Carlos Martinez	.263	228	23	60	5	35	1
Brook Jacoby	.261	291	30	76	4	36	0
Albert Belle	.260	585	81	152	34	112	8
Mark Whiten	.254	508	73	129	9	43	16
Sandy Alomar........	.251	299	22	75	2	26	3
Junior Ortiz	.250	244	20	61	0	24	1
Glenallen Hill	.241	369	38	89	18	49	9

Acquired: OF Howard from SD (Apr.14) for SS Jason Hardtke and P Chris Maffatt; P Mesa from Bal. (July 14) for minor league OF Kyle Washington.

Pitching (40 IP)	ERA	W-L	Gm	IP	BB	SO
Derek Lilliquist........	1.75	5-3	71	61.2	18	48
Steve Olin	2.34	8-5	72	88.1	27	47
Ted Power	2.54	3-3	64	99.1	35	51
Charles Nagy	2.96	17-10	33	252.0	57	169
Kevin Wickander......	3.07	2-0	44	41.0	28	38
Eric Plunk	3.64	9-6	58	71.2	38	50
Dennis Cook.........	3.82	5-7	32	158.0	50	96
Rod Nichols.........	4.53	4-3	30	105.1	31	56
Jose Mesa	4.59	7-12	28	160.2	70	62
Jack Armstrong.......	4.64	6-15	35	166.2	67	114
Scott Scudder	5.28	6-10	23	109.0	55	66
Denis Boucher.......	6.37	2-2	8	41.0	20	17
Dave Otto	7.06	5-9	18	80.1	33	32

Saves: Olin (29); Lilliquist and Power (6); Plunk (4); Wickander (1). **Complete games:** Nagy (10); Armstrong, Cook and Mesa (1). **Shutouts:** Nagy (3); Mesa (1).

Detroit Tigers

Batting (150 AB)	Avg	AB	R	H	HR	RBI	SB
Scott Livingstone*...	.282	354	43	100	4	46	1
Lou Whitaker........	.278	453	77	126	19	71	6
Tony Phillips	.276	606	114	167	10	64	12
Skeeter Barnes	.273	165	27	45	3	25	3
Travis Fryman	.266	659	87	175	20	96	8
Dan Gladden	.254	417	57	106	7	42	4
Chad Kreuter	.253	190	22	48	2	16	0
Rob Deer	.247	393	66	97	32	64	4
Cecil Fielder	.244	594	80	145	35	124	0
Milt Cuyler..........	.241	291	39	70	3	28	8
Mickey Tettleton.....	.238	525	82	125	32	83	0
Mark Carreon	.232	336	34	78	10	41	3
Dave Bergman	.232	181	17	42	1	10	1

Pitching (40 IP)	ERA	W-L	Gm	IP	BB	SO
John Kiely*	2.13	4-2	39	55.0	28	18
Mike Munoz	3.00	1-2	65	48.0	25	23
John Doherty*.......	3.88	7-4	47	116.0	25	37
David Haas*.........	3.94	5-3	12	61.2	16	29
Mike Henneman	3.96	2-6	60	77.1	20	58
Mark Leiter	4.18	8-5	35	112.0	43	75
Bill Gullickson	4.34	14-13	34	221.2	50	64
Frank Tanana	4.39	13-11	32	186.2	90	91
Kurt Knudsen*......	4.58	2-3	48	70.2	41	51
Walt Terrell	5.20	7-10	36	136.2	48	61
Eric King	5.22	4-6	17	79.1	28	45
Kevin Ritz...........	5.60	2-5	23	80.1	44	57
Les Lancaster	6.33	3-4	41	86.2	51	35
Scott Aldred........	6.78	3-8	16	65.0	33	34

Saves: Hennemann (24); Knudsen (5); Doherty (3); Munoz (2); Groom and King (1). **Complete games:** Gullickson (4); Tanana (3); Haas, Leiter and Terrell (1). **Shutouts:** Gullickson and Haas (1).

Kansas City Royals

Batting (150 AB)	Avg	AB	R	H	HR	RBI	SB
George Brett........	.285	592	55	169	7	61	8
Gregg Jefferies.......	.285	604	66	172	10	75	19
Keith Miller	.284	416	57	118	4	38	16
Wally Joyner	.269	522	66	154	9	66	11
Jim Eisenreich.......	.269	353	31	95	2	28	11
Curtis Wilkerson	.250	296	27	74	2	29	18
Kevin McReynolds.....	.247	373	45	92	13	49	7
Gary Thurman	.245	200	25	49	0	20	9
Mike Macfarlane......	.234	402	51	94	17	48	1
Brent Mayne	.225	213	16	48	0	18	0
David Howard	.224	219	19	49	1	18	3
Brian McRae.........	.223	533	63	119	4	52	18

Acquired: Ps Haney and Bill Sampen from Mon.(Aug.29) for P Archie Cordin and 3B Sean Berry; P Juan Berenguer from Atl.(July 21) for P Mark Davis.

Pitching (40 IP)	ERA	W-L	Gm	IP	BB	SO
Jeff Montgomery......	2.18	1-6	65	82.2	27	69
Kevin Appier	2.46	15-8	30	208.1	68	150
Steve Shifflett*.......	2.60	1-4	34	52.0	17	25
Rusty Meacham*......	2.74	10-4	64	101.2	21	64
Rick Reed...........	3.68	3-7	19	100.1	20	49
Mark Gubicza	3.72	7-6	18	111.1	36	81
Chris Haney	3.86	2-3	7	42.0	16	27
Hipolito Pichardo*....	3.95	9-6	31	143.2	49	59
Luis Aquino	4.52	3-6	15	67.2	20	11
Tom Gordon.........	4.59	6-10	40	117.2	55	98
Mike Magnante	4.94	4-9	44	89.1	35	31
Mike Boddicker......	4.98	1-4	29	86.2	37	47
Juan Berenguer	5.64	1-4	19	44.2	20	26

Saves: Montgomery (39); Boddicker (3); Meacham (2). **Complete games:** Appier (3); Gubicza (2); Haney, Pichardo, Dennis Rasmussen and Reed (1). **Shutouts:** Gubicza, Haney, Pichardo, Rasmussen and Reed (1).

Milwaukee Brewers

Batting (150 AB)	Avg	AB	R	H	HR	RBI	SB
Paul Molitor........	.320	609	89	195	12	89	31
Darryl Hamilton	.298	470	67	140	5	62	41
Pat Listach*.........	.290	579	93	168	1	47	54
Dante Bichette.......	.287	387	37	111	5	41	18
Scott Fletcher.......	.275	386	53	106	3	51	17
Kevin Seitzer........	.270	540	74	146	5	71	13
Robin Yount	.264	557	71	147	8	77	15
B.J. Surhoff	.252	480	63	121	4	62	14
Jim Gantner.........	.246	256	22	63	1	18	6
Dave Nilsson*.......	.232	164	15	38	4	25	2
Franklin Stubbs	.229	288	37	66	9	42	11
Greg Vaughn	.228	501	77	114	23	78	15

Signed: free agent P Heaton to minor league contract (Aug.12) and brought up (Sept.11).

Pitching (40 IP)	ERA	W-L	Gm	IP	BB	SO
Cal Eldred*..........	1.79	11-2	14	100.1	23	62
James Austin*.......	1.85	5-2	47	58.1	32	30
Mike Fetters	1.87	5-1	50	62.2	24	43
Darren Holmes.......	2.55	4-4	41	42.1	11	31
Dan Plesac	2.96	5-4	44	79.0	35	54
Bill Wegman	3.20	13-14	35	261.2	55	127
Jaime Navarro	3.33	17-11	34	246.0	64	100
Chris Bosio	3.62	16-6	33	231.1	44	120
Doug Henry	4.02	1-4	68	65.0	24	52
Neal Heaton........	4.07	3-1	32	42.0	23	31
Ricky Bones	4.57	9-10	31	163.1	48	65
Bruce Ruffin........	6.67	1-6	25	58.0	41	45

Saves: Henry (29); Holmes (6); Fetters (2); Jesse Orosco and Plesac (1). **Complete games:** Wegman (7); Navarro (5); Bosio (4); Eldred (2); Ruffin (1). **Shutouts:** Navarro (3); Bosio (2); Eldred (1).

Minnesota Twins

Batting (150 AB)

	Avg	AB	R	H	HR	RBI	SB
Kirby Puckett	.329	639	104	210	19	110	17
Shane Mack	.315	600	101	189	16	75	26
Brian Harper	.307	502	58	154	9	73	0
Chuck Knoblauch	.297	600	104	178	2	56	34
Chili Davis	.288	444	63	128	12	66	4
Pedro Munoz	.270	418	44	113	12	71	4
Scott Leius	.249	409	50	102	2	35	6
Gene Larkin	.246	337	38	83	6	42	7
Greg Gagne	.246	439	53	108	7	39	6
Kent Hrbek	.244	394	52	96	15	58	5
Randy Bush	.214	182	14	39	2	22	1

Pitching (40 IP)

	ERA	W-L	Gm	IP	BB	SO
Gary Wayne	2.63	3-3	41	48.0	19	29
Carl Willis	2.72	7-3	59	79.1	11	45
Tom Edens	2.83	6-3	52	76.1	36	57
Rick Aguilera	2.84	2-6	64	66.2	17	52
Mark Guthrie	2.88	2-3	54	75.0	23	76
John Smiley	3.21	16-9	34	241.0	65	163
Mike Trombley*	3.30	3-2	10	46.1	17	38
Scott Erickson	3.40	13-12	32	212.0	83	101
Kevin Tapani	3.97	16-11	34	220.0	48	138
Bill Krueger	4.30	10-6	27	161.1	46	86
Pat Mahomes*	5.04	3-4	14	69.2	37	44
Willie Banks*	5.70	4-4	16	71.0	37	37

Saves: Aguilera (41); Guthrie (5); Edens (3); Willis (1). **Complete games:** Erickson and Smiley (5); Tapani (4); Krueger (2). **Shutouts:** Erickson (3); Krueger and Smiley (2); Tapani (1).

New York Yankees

Batting (150 AB)

	Avg	AB	R	H	HR	RBI	SB
Don Mattingly	.288	640	89	184	14	86	3
Bernie Williams	.280	261	39	73	5	26	7
Mel Hall	.280	583	67	163	15	81	4
Roberto Kelly	.272	580	81	158	10	66	28
Randy Velarde	.272	412	57	112	7	46	7
Andy Stankiewicz*	.268	400	52	107	2	25	9
Danny Tartabull	.266	421	72	112	25	85	2
Charlie Hayes	.257	509	52	131	18	66	3
Mike Gallego	.254	173	24	44	3	14	0
Mike Stanley	.249	173	24	43	8	27	0
Kevin Maas	.248	286	35	71	11	35	3
Pat Kelly	.226	318	38	72	7	27	8
Matt Nokes	.224	384	42	86	22	59	0

Signed: free agent P Young to minor league contract (June 16) and brought up July 4.

Pitching (40 IP)

	ERA	W-L	Gm	IP	BB	SO
Steve Farr	1.56	2-2	50	52.0	19	37
Melido Perez	2.87	13-16	33	247.2	93	218
Rich Monteleone	3.30	7-3	47	92.2	27	62
Sam Militello*	3.45	3-3	9	60.0	32	42
John Habyan	3.84	5-6	56	72.2	21	44
Curt Young	3.99	4-2	33	67.2	17	20
Bob Wickman*	4.11	6-1	8	50.1	20	21
Greg Cadaret	4.25	4-8	46	103.2	74	73
Scott Kamieniecki	4.36	6-14	28	188.0	74	88
Scott Sanderson	4.93	12-11	33	193.1	64	104
Jeff Johnson	6.66	2-3	13	52.2	23	14

Saves: Farr (30); Habyan (7); Steve Howe (6); Cadaret (1). **Complete games:** Perez (10); Kamieniecki (4); Sanderson (2); Cadaret (1). **Shutouts:** Cadaret, Perez and Sanderson (1).

Oakland Athletics

Batting (150 AB)

	Avg	AB	R	H	HR	RBI	SB
Mike Bordick	.300	504	62	151	3	48	12
Jerry Browne	.287	324	43	93	3	40	3
Rickey Henderson	.283	396	77	112	15	46	48
Terry Steinbach	.279	438	48	122	12	53	2
Ruben Sierra	.278	601	83	167	17	87	14
Willie Wilson	.270	396	38	107	0	37	28
Mark McGwire	.268	467	87	125	42	104	0
Carney Lansford	.262	496	65	130	7	75	7
Harold Baines	.253	478	58	121	16	76	1
Lance Blankenship	.241	349	59	84	3	34	21
Jamie Quirk	.220	177	13	39	2	11	0
Walt Weiss	.212	316	36	67	0	21	6

Acquired: OF Sierra and Ps Russell and Witt from Tex. (Aug.31) for OF Jose Canseco. **Signed:** free agent P Downs (June 30); free agent P Hillegas to minor league contract (Aug.31) and brought up (Sept.1).

Pitching (40 IP)

	ERA	W-L	Gm	IP	BB	SO
Jim Corsi	1.43	4-2	32	44.0	18	19
Jeff Russell	1.63	4-3	59	66.1	25	48
Dennis Eckersley	1.91	7-1	69	80.0	11	93
Vince Horsman*	2.49	2-1	58	43.1	21	18
Jeff Parrett	3.02	9-1	66	98.1	42	78
Bob Welch	3.27	11-7	20	123.2	43	47
Kelly Downs	3.29	5-5	18	82.0	46	38
Dave Stewart	3.66	12-10	31	199.1	79	130
Ron Darling	3.66	15-10	33	206.1	72	99
Mike Moore	4.12	17-12	36	223.0	103	117
Bobby Witt	4.29	10-14	31	193.0	114	125
Kevin Campbell*	5.12	2-3	32	65.0	45	38
Shawn Hillegas	5.23	1-8	26	86.0	37	49
Joe Slusarski	5.45	5-5	15	76.0	27	38
Gene Nelson	6.45	3-1	28	51.2	22	23

Saves: Eckersley (51); Russell (30); Honeycutt (3); Campbell and Horseman (1). **Complete games:** Darling (4); Moore and Stewart (2); Hillegas (1). **Shutouts:** Darling (3); Hillegas (1).

Seattle Mariners

Batting (150 AB)

	Avg	AB	R	H	HR	RBI	SB
Edgar Martinez	.343	528	100	181	18	73	14
Ken Griffey	.308	565	83	174	27	103	10
Omar Vizquel	.294	483	49	142	0	21	15
Kevin Mitchell	.286	360	48	103	9	67	0
Greg Briley	.275	200	18	55	5	12	9
Henry Cotto	.259	294	42	76	5	27	23
Tino Martinez	.257	460	53	118	16	66	2
Dave Cochrane	.250	152	10	38	2	12	1
Harold Reynolds	.247	458	55	113	3	33	15
Jay Buhner	.243	543	69	132	25	79	0
Dave Valle	.240	367	39	88	9	30	0
Lance Parrish	.233	275	26	64	12	32	1
Pete O'Brien	.222	396	40	88	14	52	2

Acquired: P Fisher from Cin. (June 29) for future considerations; P Leary from NY Yanks (Aug.23) for minor league OF Shane Twitty. **Claimed:** C Parrish on waivers from Cal. (June 28).

Pitching (40 IP)

	ERA	W-L	Gm	IP	BB	SO
Dave Fleming*	3.39	17-10	33	228.1	60	112
Jeff Nelson*	3.44	1-7	66	81.0	44	46
Randy Johnson	3.77	12-14	31	210.1	144	241
Mark Grant	3.89	2-4	23	81.0	22	42
Brian Fisher	4.53	4-3	22	91.1	47	26
Dennis Powell	4.58	4-2	49	57.0	29	35
Mike Schooler	4.70	2-7	53	51.2	24	33
Russ Swan	4.74	3-10	55	104.1	45	45
Erik Hanson	4.82	8-17	31	186.2	57	112
Tim Leary	5.36	8-10	26	141.0	87	46
Rich DeLucia	5.49	3-6	30	83.2	35	66
Calvin Jones	5.69	3-5	38	61.2	47	49

Saves: Schooler (13); Swan (9); Nelson (6); DeLucia, Fisher (1). **Complete games:** Fleming (7); Hanson and Johnson (6); Leary (3); Swan (1). **Shutouts:** Fleming (4); Johnson (2); Hanson (1).

Texas Rangers

Batting (150 AB)	Avg	AB	R	H	HR	RBI	SB
Brian Downing	.278	320	53	89	10	39	1
Rafael Palmeiro	.268	608	84	163	22	85	2
Kevin Reimer	.267	494	56	132	16	58	2
Jeff Huson	.261	318	49	83	4	24	18
Juan Gonzalez	.260	584	77	152	43	109	0
Ivan Rodriguez	.260	420	39	109	8	37	0
Jeff Frye*	.256	199	24	51	1	12	1
Dickie Thon	.247	275	30	68	4	37	12
Jose Canseco	.244	439	74	107	26	87	6
Dean Palmer	.229	541	74	124	26	72	10
Al Newman	.220	246	25	54	0	12	9
Monty Fariss*	.217	166	13	36	3	21	0
Geno Petralli	.198	192	11	38	1	18	0

Acquired: OF Canseco from Oak.(Aug.31) for OF Ruben Sierra and Ps Jeff Russell and Bobby Witt; P Nunez from Mil.(May 25) for P Mark Hampton.

Pitching (40 IP)	ERA	W-L	Gm	IP	BB	SO
Kenny Rogers	3.09	3-6	81	78.2	26	70
Kevin Brown	3.32	21-11	35	265.2	76	173
Jose Guzman	3.66	16-11	33	224.0	73	179
Nolan Ryan	3.72	5-9	27	157.1	69	157
Todd Burns	3.84	3-5	35	103.0	32	55
Roger Pavlik*	4.21	4-4	13	62.0	34	45
Edwin Nunez	4.85	1-3	49	59.1	22	49
Jeff Robinson	5.72	4-4	16	45.2	21	18
Terry Mathews	5.95	2-4	40	42.1	31	26
Brian Bohanon	6.31	1-1	18	45.2	25	29

Saves: Rogers (6); Matt Whiteside (4); Nunez (3); Burns (1). **Complete games:** Brown (11); Guzman (5); Ryan (2); Pavlik. **Shutouts:** Brown (1).

Toronto Blue Jays

Batting (150 AB)	Avg	AB	R	H	HR	RBI	SB
Roberto Alomar	.310	571	105	177	8	76	49
Dave Winfield	.290	583	92	169	26	108	2
John Olerud	.284	458	68	130	16	66	1
Candy Maldonado	.272	489	64	133	20	66	2
Joe Carter	.264	622	97	164	34	119	12
Manuel Lee	.263	396	49	104	3	39	6
Devon White	.248	641	98	159	17	60	37
Derek Bell*	.242	161	23	39	2	15	7
Pat Borders	.242	480	47	116	13	53	1
Jeff Kent	.240	192	36	46	8	35	2
Alfredo Griffin	.233	150	21	35	0	10	3
Kelly Gruber	.229	446	42	102	11	43	7

Acquired: P Eichhorn from Cal.(July 30) for C Greg Myers and OF Rob Ducey; P Cone from NY Mets (Aug.27) for 3B Jeff Kent and OF Ryan Thompson.

Pitching (40 IP)	ERA	W-L	Gm	IP	BB	SO
Duane Ward	1.95	7-4	79	101.1	39	103
Tom Henke	2.26	3-2	57	55.2	22	46
David Cone	2.55	4-3	8	53.0	29	47
Juan Guzman	2.64	16-5	28	180.2	72	165
Mark Eichhorn	3.08	4-4	65	87.2	25	61
Jimmy Key	3.53	13-13	33	216.2	59	117
Jack Morris	4.04	21-6	34	240.2	80	132
Mike Timlin	4.12	0-2	26	43.2	20	35
Bob MacDonald	4.37	1-0	27	47.1	16	26
Todd Stottlemyre	4.50	12-11	28	174.0	63	98
Dave Stieb	5.04	4-6	21	96.1	43	45
Pat Hentgen	5.36	5-2	28	50.1	32	39
David Wells	5.40	7-9	41	120.0	36	62

Saves: Henke (34); Ward (12); Eichhorn and Wells (2); Timlin (1). **Complete games:** Morris and Stottlemyre (6); Key (4); Guzman and Stieb (1). **Shutouts:** Key and Stottlemyre (2); Morris (1).

Team Leaders

AL

Batting	Avg	AB	R	H	HR	RBI	SB
Minnesota	.277	5582	747	1544	104	701	123
Milwaukee	.268	5504	740	1477	82	683	256
Cleveland	.266	5620	674	1495	127	637	144
Seattle	.263	5564	679	1466	149	638	100
Toronto	.263	5536	780	1458	163	737	129
New York	.261	5593	733	1462	163	703	78
Chicago	.261	5498	738	1434	110	686	160
Baltimore	.259	5485	705	1423	148	680	89
Oakland	.258	5387	745	1389	142	693	143
Kansas City	.256	5501	610	1411	75	568	131
Detroit	.256	5515	791	1411	182	746	66
Texas	.250	5587	682	1387	159	646	61
Boston	.246	5461	599	1343	84	567	44
California	.243	5364	579	1306	88	537	160

Pitching	ERA	W	Sv	CG	ShO	HR	BB	SO
Milwaukee	3.43	92	39	19	14	127	435	793
Boston	3.58	73	39	22	13	107	535	943
Minnesota	3.70	90	50	16	13	121	479	923
Oakland	3.73	96	58	8	9	129	601	843
Baltimore	3.79	89	48	20	16	124	518	846
Kansas City	3.81	72	44	9	12	106	512	834
Chicago	3.82	86	52	21	5	123	550	810
California	3.84	72	42	25	13	130	532	888
Toronto	3.91	96	49	18	14	124	541	954
Texas	4.09	72	42	19	3	113	598	1034
Cleveland	4.11	76	46	13	7	159	566	890
New York	4.21	76	44	20	9	129	612	851
Seattle	4.55	64	30	21	9	129	661	894
Detroit	4.60	75	36	10	4	155	564	693

NL

Batting	Avg	AB	R	H	HR	RBI	SB
St.Louis	.262	5594	631	1464	94	599	208
Cincinnati	.260	5460	660	1418	99	606	125
San Diego	.255	5476	617	1396	135	576	69
Pittsburgh	.255	5527	693	1409	106	656	110
Chicago	.254	5590	593	1420	104	566	77
Atlanta	.254	5480	682	1391	138	641	126
Philadelphia	.253	5500	686	1392	118	638	127
Montreal	.252	5477	648	1381	102	601	196
Los Angeles	.248	5368	548	1333	72	499	142
Houston	.246	5480	608	1350	96	582	139
San Francisco	.244	5456	574	1330	105	532	112
New York	.235	5340	599	1254	93	564	129

Pitching	ERA	W	Sv	CG	ShO	HR	BB	SO
Atlanta	3.14	98	41	26	24	89	489	948
Montreal	3.25	87	49	11	14	92	525	1014
Pittsburgh	3.35	96	43	20	20	101	455	844
St.Louis	3.38	83	47	10	9	118	400	842
Chicago	3.39	78	37	16	11	107	575	901
Los Angeles	3.41	63	29	18	13	82	553	981
Cincinnati	3.46	90	55	9	11	109	470	1060
San Diego	3.56	82	46	9	11	111	439	971
San Francisco	3.61	72	30	9	12	128	502	927
New York	3.66	72	34	17	13	98	482	1025
Houston	3.72	81	45	5	12	114	539	978
Philadelphia	4.11	70	34	27	7	113	549	851

NL Team by Team Statistics

Atlanta Braves

Batting (150 AB)	Avg	AB	R	H	HR	RBI	SB
Terry Pendleton.......	.311	640	98	199	21	105	5
Deion Sanders	.304	303	54	92	8	28	26
Otis Nixon	.294	456	79	134	2	22	41
Jeff Blauser	.262	343	61	90	14	46	5
Sid Bream	.261	372	30	97	10	61	6
Ron Gant............	.259	544	74	141	17	80	32
David Justice	.256	484	78	124	21	72	2
Lonnie Smith	.247	158	23	39	6	33	4
Brian Hunter	.239	238	34	57	14	41	1
Greg Olson...........	.238	302	27	72	3	27	2
Damon Berryhill	.228	307	21	70	10	43	0
Mark Lemke	.227	427	38	97	6	26	0
Rafael Belliard........	.211	285	20	60	0	14	0

Acquired: P Mark Davis from KC (July 21) for P Juan Berenguer; P Jeff Reardon from Bos.(Aug.30) for P Nate Minchey and OF Sean Ross.

Pitching (40 IP)	ERA	W-L	Gm	IP	BB	SO
Pete Smith	2.05	7-0	12	79.0	28	43
Mike Bielecki	2.57	2-4	19	80.2	27	62
Tom Glavine	2.76	20-8	33	225.0	70	129
John Smoltz..........	2.85	15-12	35	246.2	80	215
Steve Avery	3.20	11-11	35	233.2	71	129
Marvin Freeman	3.22	7-5	58	64.1	29	41
Charlie Leibrandt	3.36	15-7	32	193.0	42	104
Kent Mercker.........	3.42	3-2	53	68.1	35	49
Alejandro Pena.......	4.07	1-6	41	42.0	13	34
Mike Stanton	4.10	5-4	65	63.2	20	44

Saves: Pena (15); Stanton (8); Mercker (6); Mark Wohlers (4); Freeman and Reardon (3); Berenguer and Armando Reynoso (1). **Complete games:** Smoltz (9); Glavine (7); Smoltz (5); Leibrandt (5); Avery and P.Smith (2); Bielecki (1). **Shutouts:** Glavine (5); Smoltz (3); Avery and Leibrandt (2); Bielecki and P.Smith (1).

Chicago Cubs

Batting (150 AB)	Avg	AB	R	H	HR	RBI	SB
Mark Grace	.307	603	72	185	9	79	6
Ryne Sandberg	.304	612	100	186	26	87	17
Andre Dawson	.277	542	60	150	22	90	6
Dwight Smith	.276	217	28	60	3	24	9
Derrick May*.........	.274	351	33	96	8	45	5
Rick Wilkins	.270	244	20	66	8	22	0
Joe Girardi	.270	270	19	73	1	12	0
Steve Buechele	.261	524	52	137	9	64	1
Sammy Sosa	.260	262	41	68	8	25	15
Doug Dascenzo	.255	376	37	96	0	20	6
Ray Sanchez*	.251	255	24	64	1	19	2
Kal Daniels	.241	212	21	51	6	25	0
Jose Vizcaino........	.225	285	26	64	1	17	3
Luis Salazar	.208	255	20	53	5	25	1

Acquired: OF Daniels from LA (June 27) for player to be named; 3B Buechele from Pit.(July 10) for P Danny Jackson.

Pitching (40 IP)	ERA	W-L	Gm	IP	BB	SO
Greg Maddux........	2.18	20-11	35	268.0	70	199
Mike Morgan	2.55	16-8	34	240.0	79	123
Bob Scanlan	2.89	3-6	69	87.1	30	42
Jeff Robinson........	3.00	4-3	49	78.0	40	46
Frank Castillo	3.46	10-11	33	205.1	63	135
Chuck McElroy	3.55	4-7	72	83.2	51	83
Ken Patterson	3.89	2-3	32	41.2	27	23
Paul Assenmacher	4.10	4-4	70	68.0	26	67
Jim Bullinger*	4.66	2-8	39	85.0	54	36
Shawn Boskie	5.01	5-11	23	91.2	36	39

Saves: Scanlan (14); Assenmacher (8); Bullinger (7); McElroy (6); Robinson and Heathcliff Slocomb (1). **Complete games:** Maddux (9); Morgan (6); Bullinger (1). **Shutouts:** Maddux (4); Morgan (1).

Cincinnati Reds

Batting (150 AB)	Avg	AB	R	H	HR	RBI	SB
Bip Roberts	.323	532	92	172	4	45	44
Barry Larkin..........	.304	533	76	162	12	78	15
Hal Morris	.271	395	41	107	6	53	6
Reggie Sanders*......	.270	385	62	104	12	36	16
Joe Oliver	.270	485	42	131	10	57	2
Dave Martinez........	.254	393	47	100	3	31	12
Paul O'Neill	.246	496	59	122	14	66	6
Chris Sabo	.244	344	42	84	12	43	4
Glenn Braggs........	.237	266	40	63	8	38	3
Bill Doran	.235	387	48	91	8	47	7
Fred Benavides*......	.231	173	14	40	1	17	0

Acquired: P Bolton from Bos.(July 9) for OF Billy Hatcher.

Pitching (40 IP)	ERA	W-L	Gm	IP	BB	SO
Jose Rijo	2.56	15-10	33	211.0	44	171
Tim Pugh*	2.58	4-2	7	45.1	13	18
Greg Swindell	2.70	12-8	31	213.2	41	138
Steve Foster*	2.88	1-1	31	50.0	13	34
Scott Bankhead......	2.93	10-4	54	70.2	29	53
Norm Charlton.......	2.99	4-2	64	81.1	26	90
Rob Dibble	3.07	3-5	63	70.1	31	110
Dwayne Henry	3.33	3-3	60	83.2	44	72
Tim Belcher	3.91	15-14	35	227.2	80	149
Chris Hammond......	4.21	7-10	28	147.1	55	79
Scott Ruskin.........	5.03	4-3	57	53.2	20	43
Tom Browning	5.07	6-5	16	87.0	28	33
Tom Bolton	5.24	3-3	16	46.1	23	27

Saves: Charlton (26); Dibble (25); Foster (2); Bankhead and Milton Hill (1). **Complete games:** Swindell (5); Belcher and Rijo (2). **Shutouts:** Swindell (3); Belcher (1).

Houston Astros

Batting (150 AB)	Avg	AB	R	H	HR	RBI	SB
Ken Caminiti	.294	506	68	149	13	62	10
Steve Finley	.292	607	84	177	5	55	44
Craig Biggio	.277	613	96	170	6	39	38
Jeff Bagwell	.273	586	87	160	18	96	10
Pete Incaviglia	.266	349	31	93	11	44	2
Rafael Ramirez	.250	176	17	44	1	13	0
Luis Gonzalez	.243	387	40	94	10	55	7
Scott Servais*........	.239	205	12	49	0	15	0
Eric Anthony	.239	440	45	105	19	80	5
Ed Taubensee*	.222	297	23	66	5	28	2
Casey Candaele......	.213	320	19	68	1	18	7
Andujar Cedeno......	.173	220	15	38	2	13	2

Pitching (40 IP)	ERA	W-L	Gm	IP	BB	SO
Doug Jones	1.85	11-8	80	111.2	17	93
Xavier Hernandez.....	2.11	9-1	77	111.0	42	96
Joe Boever...........	2.51	3-6	81	111.1	45	67
Mark Portugal.......	2.66	6-3	18	101.1	41	62
Pete Harnisch	3.70	9-10	34	206.2	64	164
Brian Williams*	3.92	7-6	16	96.1	42	54
Darryl Kile	3.95	5-10	22	125.1	63	90
Willie Blair	4.00	5-7	29	78.2	25	48
Butch Henry*........	4.02	6-9	28	165.2	41	96
Rob Murphy	4.04	3-1	59	55.2	21	42
Jimmy Jones	4.07	10-6	25	139.1	39	69
Al Osuna............	4.23	6-3	66	61.2	38	37

Saves: D.Jones (36); Hernandez (7); Boever (2). **Complete games:** Henry and Kile (2); Portugal (1). **Shutouts:** Henry and Portugal (1).

Los Angeles Dodgers

Batting (150 AB)	Avg	AB	R	H	HR	RBI	SB
Brett Butler	.309	553	86	171	3	39	41
Mike Sharperson	.300	317	48	95	3	36	2
Lenny Harris	.271	347	28	94	0	30	19
Mitch Webster	.267	262	33	70	6	35	11
Jose Offerman	.260	534	67	139	1	30	23
Carlos Hernandez*	.260	173	11	45	3	17	0
Eric Karros*	.257	545	63	140	20	88	2
Todd Benzinger	.239	293	24	70	4	31	2
Darryl Strawberry	.237	156	20	37	5	25	3
Eric Davis	.228	267	21	61	5	32	19
Mike Scioscia	.221	348	19	77	3	24	3
Dave Hansen	.214	341	30	73	6	22	0

Pitching (40 IP)	ERA	W-L	Gm	IP	BB	SO
Jay Howell	1.54	1-3	41	46.2	18	36
Pedro Astacio*	1.98	5-5	11	82.0	20	43
Jim Gott	2.45	3-3	68	88.0	41	75
Tom Candiotti	3.00	11-15	32	203.2	63	152
Kevin Gross	3.17	8-13	34	204.2	77	158
Bob Ojeda	3.63	6-9	29	166.1	81	94
Orel Hershiser	3.67	10-15	33	210.2	69	130
Ramon Martinez	4.00	8-11	25	150.2	69	101
Roger McDowell	4.09	6-10	65	83.2	42	50
Steve Wilson	4.19	2-5	60	66.2	29	54
Tim Crews	5.19	0-3	49	78.0	20	43

Saves: McDowell (14); Gott (6); John Candelaria (5); Howell (4). **Complete games:** Candiotti (6); Astacio and Gross (4); Ojeda (2); Hershiser and Martinez (1). **Shutouts:** Astacio (4); Gross (3); Candiotti (2); Martinez and Ojeda (1).

New York Mets

Batting (150 AB)	Avg	AB	R	H	HR	RBI	SB
Chico Walker	.289	253	26	73	4	38	15
Dave Magadan	.283	321	33	91	3	28	1
Vince Coleman	.275	229	37	63	2	21	24
Kevin Bass	.269	402	40	108	9	39	14
Eddie Murray	.261	551	64	144	16	93	4
Willie Randolph	.252	286	29	72	2	15	1
Daryl Boston	.249	289	37	72	11	35	12
Bobby Bonilla	.249	438	62	109	19	70	4
Dave Gallagher	.240	175	20	42	1	21	4
Bill Pecota	.227	269	28	61	2	26	9
Howard Johnson	.223	350	48	78	7	43	22
Charlie O'Brien	.212	156	15	33	2	13	0
Todd Hundley*	.209	358	32	75	7	32	3
Dick Schofield	.205	420	52	86	4	36	11

Acquired: SS Schofield from Cal.(Apr.12) for P Julio Valera and player to be named; P Guetterman from NY Yanks (June 9) for P Tim Burke; OF Bass from SF (Aug.7) for player to be named; 3B Jeff Kent and OF Ryan Thompson from Tor.(Aug.27) for P David Cone. **Claimed:** OF Walker on waivers from Chi.Cubs (May 7).

Pitching (40 IP)	ERA	W-L	Gm	IP	BB	SO
Sid Fernandez	2.73	14-11	32	214.2	67	193
Jeff Innis	2.86	6-9	76	88.0	36	39
David Cone	2.88	13-7	27	196.2	82	214
Bret Saberhagen	3.50	3-5	17	97.2	27	81
Wally Whitehurst	3.62	3-9	44	97.0	33	70
Pete Schourek	3.64	6-8	22	136.0	44	60
Dwight Gooden	3.67	10-13	31	206.0	70	145
Anthony Young*	4.17	2-14	52	121.0	31	64
Paul Gibson	5.23	0-1	43	62.0	25	49
Eric Hillman*	5.33	2-2	11	52.1	10	16
Barry Jones	5.68	7-6	61	69.2	35	30
Lee Guetterman	5.82	3-4	43	43.1	14	15

Saves: John Franco and Young (15); Guetterman (2); Innis and Jones (1). **Complete games:** Cone (7); Fernandez (5); Gooden (3); Saberhagen and Young (1). **Shutouts:** Cone (5); Fernandez (2); Saberhagen (1).

Montreal Expos

Batting (150 AB)	Avg	AB	R	H	HR	RBI	SB
Larry Walker	.301	528	85	159	23	93	18
Delino Deshields	.292	530	82	155	7	56	46
Moises Alou*	.282	341	53	96	9	56	16
Marquis Grissom	.276	653	99	180	14	66	78
Spike Owen	.269	386	52	104	7	40	9
Greg Colbrunn*	.268	168	12	45	2	18	3
Ivan Calderon	.265	170	19	45	3	24	1
Darrin Fletcher	.243	222	13	54	2	26	0
Archi Cianfrocco*	.241	232	25	56	6	30	3
John Vanderwal*	.239	213	21	51	4	20	3
Bret Barberie	.232	285	26	66	1	24	9
Tim Wallach	.223	537	53	120	9	59	2
Gary Carter	.218	285	24	62	5	29	0

Acquired: P Heredia from SF (Aug.18) for INF Brett Jenkins.

Pitching (40 IP)	ERA	W-L	Gm	IP	BB	SO
Mel Rojas	1.43	7-1	68	100.2	34	70
Dennis Martinez	2.47	16-11	32	226.1	60	147
Ken Hill	2.68	16-9	33	218.0	75	150
Jeff Fassero	2.84	8-7	70	85.2	34	63
John Wetteland	2.92	4-4	67	83.1	36	99
Brian Barnes	2.97	6-6	21	100.0	46	65
Bill Sampen	3.13	1-4	44	63.1	29	23
Chris Nabholz	3.32	11-12	32	195.0	74	130
Gil Heredia*	4.23	2-3	20	44.2	20	22
Mark Gardner	4.36	12-10	33	179.2	60	132

Saves: Wetteland (37); Rojas (10); Kent Bottenfield and Fassero (1). **Complete games:** Martinez (6); Hill (3); Chris Haney and Nabholz (1). **Shutouts:** Hill (3); C.Haney and Nabholz (1).

Philadelphia Phillies

Batting (150 AB)	Avg	AB	R	H	HR	RBI	SB
John Kruk	.323	507	86	164	10	70	3
Ricky Jordan	.304	276	33	84	4	34	3
Lenny Dykstra	.301	345	53	104	6	39	30
Darren Daulton	.270	485	80	131	27	109	11
Dave Hollins	.270	586	104	158	27	93	9
Mariano Duncan	.267	574	71	153	8	50	23
Mickey Morandini	.265	422	47	112	3	30	8
Wes Chamberlain	.258	275	26	71	9	41	4
Stan Javier	.249	334	42	83	1	29	18
Ruben Amaro*	.219	374	43	82	7	34	11

Acquired: OF Javier from LA (July 2) for P Steve Searcy and player to be named; P Rivera from Atl.(May 28) for minor league P Donnie Elliott.

Pitching (40 IP)	ERA	W-L	Gm	IP	BB	SO
Curt Schilling	2.35	14-11	42	226.1	59	147
Ben Rivera*	3.07	7-4	28	117.1	45	77
Bob Ayrault*	3.12	2-2	30	43.1	17	27
Mike Hartley	3.44	7-6	46	55.0	23	53
Mitch Williams	3.78	5-8	66	81.0	64	74
Terry Mulholland	3.81	13-11	32	229.0	46	125
Brad Brink*	4.14	0-4	8	41.1	13	16
Jose DeLeon	4.37	2-8	32	117.1	48	79
Cliff Brantley*	4.60	2-6	28	76.1	58	32
Kyle Abbott*	5.13	1-14	31	133.1	45	88
Greg Mathews	5.16	2-3	14	52.1	24	27
Tommy Greene	5.32	3-3	13	64.1	34	39
Don Robinson	6.18	1-4	8	43.2	4	17

Saves: Mitch Williams (29); Schilling and Shepherd (2); Wally Ritchie (1). **Complete games:** Mulholland (12); Schilling (10); Rivera (4); Mike Williams (1). **Shutouts:** Schilling (4); Mulholland (2); Rivera (1).

Pittsburgh Pirates

Batting (150 AB)	Avg	AB	R	H	HR	RBI	SB
Don Slaught	.345	255	26	88	4	37	2
Andy Van Slyke	.324	614	103	199	14	89	12
Barry Bonds	.311	473	109	147	34	103	39
Alex Cole	.278	205	33	57	0	10	7
Jay Bell	.264	632	87	167	9	55	7
Cecil Espy	.258	194	21	50	1	20	6
Mike LaValliere	.256	293	22	75	2	29	0
Gary Redus	.256	176	26	45	3	12	11
Lloyd McClendon	.253	190	26	48	3	20	1
Orlando Merced	.247	405	50	100	6	60	5
Jose Lind	.235	468	38	110	0	39	3
Jeff King	.231	480	56	111	14	65	4
Gary Varsho	.222	162	22	36	4	22	5

Acquired: OF Cole from Cle.(July 3) for OF Tony Mitchell and P John Carter; P Jackson from Chi.Cubs (July 10) for 3B Steve Buechele.

Pitching (40 IP)	ERA	W-L	Gm	IP	BB	SO
Tim Wakefield*	2.15	8-1	13	92.0	35	51
Doug Drabek	2.77	15-11	34	256.2	54	177
Bob Patterson	2.92	6-3	60	64.2	23	43
Zane Smith	3.06	8-8	23	141.0	19	56
Stan Belinda	3.15	6-4	59	71.1	29	57
Bob Walk	3.20	10-6	36	135.0	43	60
Randy Tomlin	3.41	14-9	35	208.2	42	90
Danny Jackson	3.84	8-13	34	201.1	77	97
Roger Mason	4.09	5-7	65	88.0	33	56
Vicenté Palacios	4.25	3-2	20	53.0	27	33
Denny Neagle*	4.48	4-6	55	86.1	43	77
Danny Cox	4.60	5-3	25	62.2	27	48

Saves: Belinda (18); Patterson (9); Mason (8); Cox (3); Neagle and Walk (2); and Cooke (1). **Complete games:** Drabek (10); Smith and Wakefield (4); Tomlin and Walk (1). **Shutouts:** Drabek (4); Smith (3); Tomlin and Wakefield (1).

St. Louis Cardinals

Batting (150 AB)	Avg	AB	R	H	HR	RBI	SB
Geronimo Pena	.305	203	31	62	7	31	13
Bernard Gilkey	.302	384	56	116	7	43	18
Ozzie Smith	.295	518	73	153	0	31	43
Felix Jose	.295	509	62	150	14	75	28
Milt Thompson	.293	208	31	61	4	17	18
Ray Lankford	.293	598	87	175	20	86	42
Todd Zeile	.257	439	51	113	7	48	7
Tom Pagnozzi	.249	485	33	121	7	44	2
Luis Alicea	.245	265	26	65	2	32	2
Andres Galarraga	.243	325	38	79	10	39	5
Brian Jordan	.207	193	17	40	5	22	7

Pitching (40 IP)	ERA	W-L	Gm	IP	BB	SO
Mike Perez*	1.84	9-3	77	93.0	32	46
Tod Worrell	2.11	5-3	67	64.0	25	64
Bob Tewksbury	2.16	16-5	33	233.0	20	91
Chris Carpenter	2.97	5-4	73	88.0	27	46
Lee Smith	3.12	4-9	70	75.0	26	60
Bob McClure	3.17	2-2	71	54.0	25	24
Rheal Cormier	3.68	10-10	31	186.0	33	117
Donovan Osborne*	3.77	11-9	34	179.0	38	104
Omar Olivares	3.84	9-9	32	197.0	63	124
Mark Clark*	4.45	3-10	20	113.1	36	44

Saves: L.Smith (43); Worrell (3); Carpenter (1). **Complete games:** Tewksbury (5); Cormier (3); Clark and Olivares (1). **Shutouts:** Clark (1).

San Diego Padres

Batting (150 AB)	Avg	AB	R	H	HR	RBI	SB
Gary Sheffield	.330	557	87	184	33	100	5
Tony Gwynn	.317	520	77	165	6	41	3
Fred McGriff	.286	531	79	152	35	104	8
Tony Fernandez	.275	622	84	171	4	37	20
Dan Walters*	.251	179	14	45	4	22	1
Benito Santiago	.251	386	37	97	10	42	2
Darrin Jackson	.249	587	72	146	17	70	14
Jerald Clark	.242	496	45	120	12	58	3
Kurt Stillwell	.227	379	35	86	2	24	4
Tim Teufel	.224	246	23	55	6	25	2
Oscar Azocar	.190	168	15	32	0	8	1

Traded: P Lefferts to Bal.(Aug.31) for minor league P Erik Schullstrom.

Pitching (40 IP)	ERA	W-L	Gm	IP	BB	SO
Mike Maddux	2.37	2-2	50	79.2	24	60
Rich Rodriguez	2.37	6-3	61	91.0	29	64
Jose Melendez	2.92	6-7	56	89.1	20	82
Jim Deshaies	3.28	4-7	15	96.0	33	46
Andy Benes	3.35	13-14	34	231.1	61	169
Frank Seminara*	3.68	9-4	19	100.1	46	61
Craig Lefferts	3.69	13-9	27	163.1	35	81
Bruce Hurst	3.85	14-9	32	217.1	51	131
Greg Harris	4.12	4-8	20	118.0	35	66
Randy Myers	4.29	3-6	66	79.2	34	66

Saves: Myers (38); Maddux (5); Larry Andersen (2); Jeremy Hernandez (1). **Complete games:** Hurst (6); Benes (2); Harris (1). **Shutouts:** Hurst (4); Benes (2).

San Francisco Giants

Batting (150 AB)	Avg	AB	R	H	HR	RBI	SB
Will Clark	.300	513	69	154	16	73	12
Willie McGee	.297	474	56	141	1	36	13
Mike Felder	.286	322	44	92	4	23	14
Cory Snyder	.269	390	48	105	14	57	4
Robby Thompson	.260	443	54	115	14	49	5
Kirt Manwaring	.244	349	24	85	4	26	2
Chris James	.242	248	25	60	5	32	2
Jose Uribe	.241	162	24	39	2	13	2
Darren Lewis	.231	320	38	74	1	18	28
Matt Williams	.227	529	58	120	20	66	7
Royce Clayton*	.224	321	31	72	4	24	8

Pitching (40 IP)	ERA	W-L	Gm	IP	BB	SO
Rod Beck	1.76	3-3	65	92.0	15	87
Bill Swift	2.08	10-4	30	164.2	43	77
Jeff Brantley	2.95	7-7	56	91.2	45	86
Bryan Hickerson*	3.09	5-3	61	87.1	21	68
Kelly Downs	3.47	1-2	19	62.1	24	33
Pedro Pena*	3.48	1-1	25	44.0	20	32
Francisco Oliveras	3.63	0-3	16	44.2	10	17
Mike Jackson	3.73	6-6	67	82.0	33	80
John Burkett	3.84	13-9	32	189.2	45	107
Bud Black	3.97	10-12	28	177.0	59	82
Trevor Wilson	4.21	8-14	26	154.0	64	88
Dave Burba	4.97	2-7	23	70.2	31	47
Dave Righetti	5.06	2-7	54	78.1	36	47

Saves: Beck (17); Brantley (7); Righetti (3); Jackson (2); Swift (1). **Complete games:** Burkett and Swift (3); Black (2); Wilson (1). **Shutouts:** Swift (2); Black, Burkett and Wilson (1).

American League Championship Series
Composite Box Score

Toronto Blue Jays

Batting (1 AB)	Avg	AB	R	H	HR	RBI
Ed Sprague, ph	.500	2	0	1	0	0
Roberto Alomar, 2b	.423	26	4	11	2	4
John Olerud, 1b	.348	23	4	8	1	4
Devon White, cf	.348	23	2	8	0	2
Pat Borders, c	.318	22	3	7	1	3
Manuel Lee, ss	.278	18	2	5	0	3
Candy Maldonado, lf	.273	22	3	6	2	6
Dave Winfield, dh	.250	24	7	6	2	3
Joe Carter, rf-1b	.192	26	2	5	1	3
Kelly Gruber, 3b	.091	22	3	2	1	2
Alfredo Griffin, pr-ss	.000	2	0	0	0	0
Derek Bell, pr-rf	—	0	1	0	0	0
TOTALS	.281	210	31	59	10	30

Pitching	W-L	ERA	Gm	IP	H	BB	SO
Tom Henke	0-0	0.00	4	4.2	4	2	2
Jimmy Key	0-0	0.00	1	3.0	2	1	1
Mark Eichhorn	0-0	0.00	1	1.0	0	1	0
Juan Guzman	2-0	2.08	2	13.0	12	5	11
Todd Stottlemyre	0-0	2.46	1	3.2	3	0	1
David Cone	1-1	3.00	2	12.0	11	5	9
Jack Morris	0-1	6.57	2	12.1	11	9	6
Duane Ward	1-0	6.75	3	4.0	5	1	2
Mike Timlin	0-0	6.75	2	1.1	4	0	1
TOTALS	4-2	3.44	6	55.0	52	24	33

Saves: Henke (3). **CG:** Morris. **WP:** Morris. **PB:** Borders (3). **HBP:** Guzman (McGwire).

Oakland Athletics

Batting (1 AB)	Avg	AB	R	H	HR	RBI
Harold Baines, dh	.440	25	6	11	1	4
Jerry Browne, ph-cf-3b	.400	10	3	4	0	2
Ruben Sierra, rf	.333	24	4	8	1	7
Terry Steinbach, c	.292	24	1	7	1	5
Rickey Henderson, lf	.261	*23	5	6	0	1
Lance Blankenship, 2b-pr	.231	13	2	3	0	0
Willie Wilson, cf	.227	22	0	5	0	0
Carney Lansford, 3b	.167	18	0	3	0	1
Walt Weiss, ss	.167	6	1	1	0	0
Mark McGwire, 1b	.150	20	1	3	1	3
Mike Bordick, ss-2b	.053	19	1	1	0	0
Eric Fox, pr-dh-lf	.000	1	0	0	0	0
Jamie Quirk, ph	.000	1	0	0	0	0
Randy Ready, ph	.000	1	0	0	0	0
TOTALS	.251	207	24	52	4	23

Pitching	W-L	ERA	Gm	IP	H	BB	SO
Jim Corsi	0-0	0.00	3	2.0	2	3	0
Rick Honeycutt	0-0	0.00	2	2.0	0	0	1
Bob Welch	0-0	2.57	1	7.0	7	1	7
Dave Stewart	1-0	2.70	2	16.2	14	6	7
Ron Darling	0-1	3.00	1	6.0	4	2	3
Kelly Downs	0-1	3.86	2	2.1	3	1	0
Dennis Eckersley	0-0	6.00	3	3.0	8	0	2
Mike Moore	0-2	7.45	2	9.2	11	5	7
Jeff Russell	1-0	9.00	3	2.0	2	4	0
Jeff Parrett	0-0	11.57	3	2.1	6	0	1
Bobby Witt	0-0	18.00	1	1.0	2	1	1
TOTALS	2-4	4.50	6	54.0	59	23	29

Save: Eckersley. **CG:** Stewart. **WP:** Darling (2), Russell.

Score by Innings

	1	2	3	4	5	6	7	8	9	10	11	R	H	E
Toronto	2	2	4		2	5	1		4	7	3	0	1 —**31**	59	8
Oakland	2	3	6		2	3	2		2	2	2	0	0 —**24**	52	7

DP: Oakland 5, Toronto 7. **LOB:** Oakland 48, Toronto 45; **2B:** Oakland—Sierra 2, Baines 2, Wilson; Toronto—White 2, Olerud 2, Alomar, Lee, Winfield, Gruber. **3B:** Oakland—Sierra; Toronto—Lee. **HR:** Oakland—Wilson 7, Weiss 2, Henderson 2, Fox 2, Blankenship, Bordick, Sierra; Toronto—Alomar 5, Carter 2. **CS:** Oakland—Sierra 2; Toronto—White 4, Maldonado. **S:** Oakland—Browne, McGwire, Baines; Toronto—Gruber. **SF:** Oakland—Sierra 2; Toronto—Lee, Borders, White.

Umpires: Don Denkinger, Larry Young, Al Clark, Durwood Merrill, Joe Brinkman, Drew Coble.

ALCS
Toronto wins series, 4 games to 2.

Date	Winner	Home Field
Oct. 7	Athletics, 4-3	at Toronto
Oct. 8	Blue Jays, 3-1	at Toronto
Oct.10	Blue Jays, 7-5	at Oakland
Oct.11	Blue Jays, 7-6 (11 inn.)	at Oakland
Oct.12	Athletics, 6-2	at Oakland
Oct.14	Blue Jays, 9-2	at Toronto

Game 1
Wednesday, Oct. 7 at Toronto

	1	2	3	4	5	6	7	8	9	R	H	E
Oakland	0	3	0	0	0	0	0	0	1 —4	6	1
Toronto	0	0	0	0	1	1	0	1	0 —3	9	0

Win: Russell, Oak. (1-0). **Save:** Eckersley (1). **Loss:** Morris, Tor.(0-1).
2B: Toronto—Winfield. **HR:** Oakland—Baines (1), McGwire (1), Steinbach (1); Toronto—Winfield (1), Borders (1). **RBI:** Oakland—McGwire 2, Baines, Steinbach; Toronto—Winfield, Olerud, Borders. **SB:** Oakland—Wilson; Toronto—Alomar.
Attendance—51,039. **Time**—2:47.

Game 2
Thursday, Oct. 8 at Toronto

	1	2	3	4	5	6	7	8	9	R	H	E
Oakland	0	0	0	0	0	0	0	0	1 —1	6	0
Toronto	0	0	0	0	2	0	1	0	x —3	4	0

Win: Cone, Tor. (1-0). **Save:** Henke (1). **Loss:** Moore, Oak. (0-1).
2B: Oakland—Wilson; Toronto—Gruber. **3B:** Oakland—Sierra. **HR:** Oakland—Wilson 2; Toronto—Baines; Toronto—Gruber 2, Lee. **SB:** Oakland—Wilson 3 (4), Weiss 2 (2), Bordick (1); Toronto—Alomar (2), Carter (1).
Attendance—51,114. **Time**—2:58.

Game 3
Saturday, Oct. 10 at Oakland

	1	2	3	4	5	6	7	8	9	R	H	E
Toronto	0	1	0	1	1	0	2	1	1 —7	9	1
Oakland	0	0	0	2	0	0	2	1	0 —5	13	3

Win: Guzman, Tor. (1-0). **Save:** Henke (2). **Loss:** Darling, Oak. (0-1).
2B: Toronto—White; Oakland—Sierra. **3B:** Toronto—Lee. **HR:** Toronto—Alomar (1), Maldonaldo (1). **RBI:** Toronto—Maldonaldo 2, Lee 2, Alomar, Winfield; Oakland—Sierra 2, Steinbach 2, Baines. **SB:** Toronto—Carter (2); Oakland—Wilson 2 (6), Henderson (1).
Attendance—46,911. **Time**—3:41.

Game 4
Sunday, Oct. 11 at Oakland

	1	2	3	4	5	6	7	8	9	10	11	R	H	E
Toronto	0	1	0	0	0	0	3	2	0	1	—	7	17	4
Oakland	0	0	5	0	0	1	0	0	0	0	—	6	12	2

Win: D.Ward, Tor. (1-0). **Save:** Henke, Tor. (3). **Loss:** Downs, Oak. (0-1).
2B: Toronto—Alomar, Olerud; Oakland—Sierra, Baines. **HR:** Toronto—Alomar (2). **RBI:** Toronto—Alomar 2, Olerud 2, Carter, Maldonado, Borders; Oakland—Sierra 2, Henderson, Baines, Steinbach, Lansford. **SB:** Toronto—Alomar (3); Oakland—Henderson (2), Fox (1), Blankenship (1).
Attendance—47,732. **Time**—4:25.

Game 5
Monday, Oct. 12 at Oakland

	1	2	3	4	5	6	7	8	9	R	H	E
Toronto	0	0	0	1	0	0	1	0	0	—	2	7	3
Oakland	2	0	1	0	3	0	0	0	x	—	6	8	0

Win: Stewart, Oak. (1-0). **Loss:** Cone, Tor. (1-1).
2B: Toronto—White. **HR:** Toronto—Winfield (2); Oakland—Sierra (1). **RBI:** Toronto—White, Winfield; Oakland—Sierra 3, Browne 2.
Attendance—44,955. **Time**—2:51.

Game 6
Wednesday, Oct. 14 at Toronto

	1	2	3	4	5	6	7	8	9	R	H	E
Oakland	0	0	0	0	0	1	0	1	0	—	2	7	1
Toronto	2	0	4	0	1	0	0	2	x	—	9	13	0

Win: Guzman, Tor. (2-0). **Loss:** Moore, Oak. (0-2).
2B: Oakland—Baines; Toronto—Olerud. **HR:** Toronto—Carter (1), Maldonado (2). **RBI:** Oakland—McGwire, Steinbach; Toronto—Maldonado 3, Carter 2, White, Alomar, Olerud, Borders. **SB:** Oakland—Sierra (1), Wilson (7), Fox (2); Toronto—Alomar 2 (5).
Attendance—51,335. **Time**—3:15.

Most Valuable Player
Roberto Alomar, Toronto
2nd baseman

Avg	AB	R	H	2B	3B	HR	RBI	SB
.423	26	4	11	1	0	2	4	5

National League Championship Series
Composite Box Score

Atlanta Braves

Batting (1 AB)	Avg	AB	R	H	HR	RBI
Mike Stanton, p	1.000	1	1	1	0	1
Jeff Treadway, ph	.667	3	1	2	0	0
Francisco Cabrera, ph	.500	2	0	1	0	2
Mark Lemke, 2b	.333	21	2	7	0	2
Lonnie Smith, ph	.333	6	1	2	0	1
Otis Nixon, cf	.286	28	5	8	0	2
John Smoltz, p	.286	7	1	2	0	1
David Justice, rf	.280	25	5	7	2	6
Sid Bream, 1b	.273	22	5	6	1	2
Terry Pendleton, 3b	.233	30	2	7	0	3
Jeff Blauser, ss	.208	24	3	5	1	4
Brian Hunter, 1b-ph	.200	5	1	1	0	0
Ron Gant, lf	.182	22	5	4	2	6
Damon Berryhill, c	.167	24	1	4	0	1
Deion Sanders, ph-lf-cf	.000	5	0	0	0	0
Steve Avery, p	.000	2	0	0	0	1
Rafael Belliard, pr-ss-2b	.000	2	1	0	0	0
Tom Glavine, p	.000	2	0	0	0	0
Charlie Leibrandt, p	.000	1	0	0	0	0
Javier Lopez, c	.000	1	0	0	0	0
Pete Smith, p	.000	1	0	0	0	0
TOTALS	.244	234	34	57	6	32

Pitching	W-L	ERA	Gm	IP	H	BB	SO
Mike Stanton	0-0	0.00	5	4.1	2	2	5
Kent Mercker	0-0	0.00	2	3.0	1	1	1
Jeff Reardon	1-0	0.00	3	3.0	0	2	3
Mark Wohlers	0-0	0.00	3	3.0	2	1	2
Charlie Leibrandt	0-0	1.93	2	4.2	4	3	3
Pete Smith	0-0	2.45	2	3.2	2	3	3
John Smoltz	2-0	2.66	3	20.1	14	10	19
Steve Avery	1-1	9.00	3	8.0	13	2	3
Tom Glavine	0-2	12.27	2	7.1	13	3	2
Marvin Freeman	0-0	14.73	3	3.2	8	2	1
TOTALS	4-3	4.72	7	61.0	59	29	42

Save: Reardon (1). **WP:** Smoltz, Avery, Reardon. **HBP:** Glavine 2 (Bonds, Bell). **PB:** Berryhill.

Pittsburgh Pirates

Batting (1 AB)	Avg	AB	R	H	HR	RBI
Lloyd McClendon, rf	.727	11	4	8	1	4
Cecil Espy, ph-rf	.667	3	0	2	0	0
Gary Varsho, ph	.500	2	0	1	0	0
Gary Redus, 1b-ph	.438	16	4	7	0	3
Don Slaught, c-ph	.333	12	5	4	1	5
Andy Van Slyke, cf	.276	29	1	8	0	4
Barry Bonds, lf	.261	23	5	6	1	2
Jeff King, 3b	.241	29	4	7	0	0
Jose Lind, 2b	.222	27	5	6	1	5
Alex Cole, rf-ph	.200	10	2	2	0	1
Mike LaValliere, c	.200	10	1	2	0	0
Jay Bell, ss	.172	29	3	5	1	4
Orlando Merced, 1b-ph	.100	10	0	1	0	2
Doug Drabek, p	.000	6	0	0	0	0
Tim Wakefield, p	.000	6	1	0	0	0
Bob Walk, p	.000	5	0	0	0	0
John Wehner, ph	.000	2	0	0	0	0
Carlos Garcia, 2b	.000	1	0	0	0	0
TOTALS	.255	231	35	59	5	32

Pitching	W-L	ERA	Gm	IP	H	BB	SO
Roger Mason	0-0	0.00	2	3.1	0	2	1
Stan Belinda	0-0	0.00	2	1.2	2	0	2
Danny Cox	0-0	0.00	2	1.1	1	1	1
Tim Wakefield	2-0	3.00	2	18.0	14	5	7
Doug Drabek	0-3	3.71	3	17.0	18	7	10
Bob Walk	1-0	3.86	2	11.2	6	7	6
Bob Patterson	0-0	5.40	2	1.2	3	1	1
Randy Tomlin	0-0	6.75	2	2.2	5	1	0
Danny Jackson	0-1	21.60	1	1.2	4	2	0
Denny Neagle	0-0	27.00	2	1.2	4	3	0
TOTALS	3-4	4.45	7	60.2	57	29	28

CG: Wakefield (2); Walk. **WP:** Wakefield. **PB:** Slaught 2.

National League Championship Series (Cont.)
Composite Box Score
Score by Innings

	1	2	3	4	5	6	7	8	9	R	H	E
Atlanta	0	7	0	4	7	2	8	1	5—34	57	2
Pittsburgh	5	10	2	0	5	4	7	2	0—35	59	5

DP: Pittsburgh 6, Atlanta 3. **LOB:** Pittsburgh 50, Atlanta 51. **2B:** Pittsburgh—Redus 4, King 4, Van Slyke 3, McClendon 2, Lind 2, Bell 2, Slaught, Bonds, Merced; Atlanta—Bream 3, Nixon 2, Pendleton 2, Stanton, Lemke, Justice, Berryhill. **3B:** Pittsburgh—Redus, Van Slyke, Lind; Atlanta—Blauser, L.Smith. **SB:** Pittsburgh—Bonds; Atlanta—Nixon 3, Gant, Smoltz. **CS:** Pittsburgh—Merced, King. **S:** Pittsburgh—Wakefield 2, Drabek; Atlanta—Gant, Blauser. **SF:** Pittsburgh—Van Slyke, McClendon, Merced; Atlanta—Gant, Avery.

Umpires: John McSherry, Randy Marsh, Steve Rippley, Gary Darling, Gerry Davis, Ed Montague.

NLCS
Atlanta wins series, 4 games to 3.

Date	Winner	Home Field
Oct. 6	Braves, 5-1	at Atlanta
Oct. 7	Braves, 13-5	at Atlanta
Oct. 9	Pirates, 3-2	at Pittsburgh
Oct.10	Braves, 6-4	at Pittsburgh
Oct.11	Pirates, 7-1	at Pittsburgh
Oct.13	Pirates, 13-4	at Atlanta
Oct.14	Braves, 3-2	at Atlanta

Game 1
Tuesday, Oct. 6 at Atlanta

	1	2	3	4	5	6	7	8	9	R	H	E
Pittsburgh	0	0	0	0	0	0	0	1	0—1	5	1
Atlanta	0	1	0	2	1	0	1	0	x—5	8	0

Win: Smoltz, Atl. (1-0). **Loss:** Drabek, Pit. (0-1).
2B: Pittsburgh—King; Atlanta—Justice, Bream. **HR:** Pittsburgh—Lind (1); Atlanta—Blauser. **RBI:** Pittsburgh—Lind; Atlanta—Blauser, Pendleton, Bream, Lemke. **SB:** Atlanta—Nixon (1), Gant (1).
Attendance—51,971. **Time**—3:00.

Game 2
Wednesday, Oct. 7 at Atlanta

	1	2	3	4	5	6	7	8	9	R	H	E
Pittsburgh	0	0	0	0	0	0	4	1	0—	5	7	0
Atlanta	0	4	0	0	4	0	5	0	x—13	14	0

Win: Avery, Atl. (1-0). **Loss:** Jackson, Pit. (0-1).
2B: Pittsburgh—McClendon; Atlanta—Pendleton, Stanton. **3B:** Pittsburgh—Lind; Atlanta—Blauser. **HR:** Atlanta—Gant (1). **RBI:** Pittsburgh—Lind 2, McClendon, Slaught; Atlanta—Gant 4, Pendleton 2, Justice 2, Blauser, Berryhill, Lemke, Avery, Stanton. **SB:** Atlanta—Nixon (2).
Attendance—51,975. **Time**—3:20.

Game 3
Friday, Oct. 9 at Pittsburgh

	1	2	3	4	5	6	7	8	9	R	H	E
Atlanta	0	0	0	1	0	0	1	0	0—2	5	0
Pittsburgh	0	0	0	0	1	1	1	0	x—3	8	1

Win: Wakefield, Pit. (1-0). **Loss:** Glavine, Atl. (0-1).
2B: Atlanta—Nixon, Lemke; Pittsburgh—Redus, Bell, Van Slyke, King. **3B:** Pittsburgh—Redus. **HR:** Atlanta—Bream (1), Gant (2); Pittsburgh—Slaught (1). **RBI:** Atlanta—Bream, Gant; Pittsburgh—Van Slyke, King, Slaught.
Attendance—56,610. **Time**—2:37.

Game 4
Saturday, Oct. 10 at Pittsburgh

	1	2	3	4	5	6	7	8	9	R	H	E
Atlanta	0	2	0	0	2	2	0	0	0—6	11	1
Pittsburg	0	2	1	0	0	0	1	0	0—4	6	1

Win: Smoltz, Atl. (2-0). **Save:** Reardon, Atl. (1). **Loss:** Drabek, Pit. (0-2).
2B: Atlanta—Nixon; Pittsburgh—Van Slyke, Merced. **3B:** Pittsburgh—Van Slyke. **RBI:** Atlanta—Nixon 2, Blauser, Justice, Smoltz; Pittsburgh—Cole, Van Slyke, Merced. **SB:** Atlanta—Nixon (3), Smoltz (1).
Attendance—57,164. **Time**—3:10.

Game 5
Sunday, Oct. 11 at Pittsburgh

	1	2	3	4	5	6	7	8	9	R	H	E
Atlanta	0	0	0	0	0	0	0	1	0—1	3	0
Pittsburg	4	0	1	0	0	1	1	0	x—7	13	0

Win: Walk, Pit. (1-0). **Loss:** Avery, Atl. (1-1).
2B: Atlanta—Bream; Pittsburgh—Redus 2, Bonds, King, McClendon. **3B:** Atlanta—L.Smith. **RBI:** Atlanta—Blauser; Pittsburgh—McClendon 2, Redus, Bell, Bonds, King, Slaught. **SB:** Pittsburgh—Bonds (1).
Attendance—52,929. **Time**—2:52.

Game 6
Tuesday, Oct. 13 at Atlanta

	1	2	3	4	5	6	7	8	9	R	H	E
Pittsburgh	0	8	0	0	4	1	0	0	0—13	13	1
Atlanta	0	0	0	1	0	0	1	2	x—4	9	1

Win: Wakefield, Pit. (2-0). **Loss:** Glavine, Atl. (0-2).
2B: Pittsburgh—Redus, Slaught, Lind; **HR:** Pittsburgh—Bell (1), Bonds (1), McClendon (1); Atlanta—Justice 2 (2). **RBI:** Pittsburgh—Bell 3, Redus 2, Slaught 2, Lind 2, Van Slyke, Bonds, McClendon; Atlanta—Justice 3, L.Smith.
Attendance—51,975. **Time**—2:50.

Game 7
Wednesday, Oct. 14 at Atlanta

	1	2	3	4	5	6	7	8	9	R	H	E
Pittsburgh	1	0	0	0	0	1	0	0	0—2	7	1
Atlanta	0	0	0	0	0	0	0	3—3	7	0

Win: Reardon, Atl. (1-0). **Loss:** Drabek, Pit. (0-3).
2B: Pittsburgh—Bell, Van Slyke, King, Lind; Atlanta—Pendleton, Bream, Berryhill. **RBI:** Pittsburgh—Van Slyke, Merced; Atlanta—Cabrera 2, Gant.
Attendance—51,975. **Time**—3:22.

Most Valuable Player
John Smoltz, Atlanta
Pitcher

W-L	ERA	Gm	IP	H	BB	SO
2-0	2.66	3	20.1	14	10	19

World Series
Composite Box Score

Toronto Blue Jays

Batting (1 AB)	Avg	AB	R	H	HR	RBI
David Cone, p	.500	4	0	2	0	1
Ed Sprague, ph	.500	2	1	1	1	2
Pat Borders, c	.450	20	2	9	1	3
John Olerud, 1b	.308	13	2	4	0	0
Joe Carter, 1b-lf-rf	.273	22	2	6	2	3
Devon White, cf	.231	26	2	6	0	2
Dave Winfield, rf-dh	.227	22	0	5	0	3
Roberto Alomar, 2b	.208	24	3	5	0	0
Candy Maldonado, lf-ph	.158	19	1	3	1	2
Kelly Gruber, 3b	.105	19	2	2	1	1
Manny Lee, ss	.105	19	1	2	0	0
Jack Morris	.000	2	0	0	0	0
Pat Tabler, ph	.000	2	0	0	0	0
Derek Bell, ph	.000	1	1	0	0	0
Jimmy Key, p	.000	1	0	0	0	0
TOTALS	.230	196	17	45	6	17

Pitching	W-L	ERA	GM	IP	H	BB	SO
David Wells	0-0	0.00	4	4.1	1	2	3
Todd Stottlemyre	0-0	0.00	4	3.2	4	0	4
Duane Ward	2-0	0.00	4	3.1	1	1	6
Mark Eichhorn	0-0	0.00	1	1.0	0	0	1
Mike Timlin	0-0	0.00	2	1.1	0	0	0
Jimmy Key	2-0	1.00	2	9.0	6	0	6
Juan Guzman	0-0	1.13	2	8.0	8	1	7
Tom Henke	0-0	2.70	3	3.1	2	2	1
David Cone	0-0	3.48	2	10.1	9	8	8
Jack Morris	0-2	8.44	2	10.2	13	6	12
TOTALS	4-2	2.78	6	55.0	44	20	48

Saves: Henke (2), Timlin (1). **WP:** Morris, Cone, Ward. **HBP:** Henke (L.Smith).

Atlanta Braves

Batting (1 AB)	Avg	AB	R	H	HR	RBI
Deion Sanders, lf	.533	15	4	8	0	1
Otis Nixon, cf	.296	27	3	8	0	1
Jeff Blauser, ss	.250	24	2	6	0	0
Terry Pendleton, 3b	.240	25	2	6	0	2
Mark Lemke, 2b	.211	19	0	4	0	2
Sid Bream, 1b	.200	15	1	3	0	0
Brian Hunter, ph-1b-pr	.200	5	0	1	0	2
Lonnie Smith, ph-dh	.167	12	1	2	1	5
David Justice, rf	.158	19	4	3	1	3
Ron Gant, lf-ph-pr	.125	8	2	1	0	0
Damon Berryhill, c	.091	22	1	2	1	3
John Smoltz, p	.000	3	0	0	0	0
Tom Glavine, p	.000	1	0	0	0	0
Steve Avery, p	.000	1	0	0	0	0
Francisco Cabrera, ph	.000	1	0	0	0	0
Jeff Treadway, ph	.000	1	0	0	0	0
Pete Smith, p	.000	1	0	0	0	0
TOTALS	.220	200	20	44	3	19

Pitching	W-L	ERA	GM	IP	H	BB	SO
Mike Stanton	0-0	0.00	4	5.0	3	2	1
Mark Wohlers	0-0	0.00	2	0.2	0	1	0
Pete Smith	0-0	—	1	3.0	3	0	0
Tom Glavine	1-1	1.59	2	17.0	10	4	8
John Smoltz	1-0	2.70	2	13.1	13	7	12
Steve Avery	0-1	3.75	2	12.0	11	3	11
Charlie Leibrandt	0-1	9.00	1	2.0	3	0	0
Jeff Reardon	0-1	13.50	2	1.1	2	1	1
TOTALS	2-4	2.65	6	54.1	45	18	33

Saves: Stanton (1). **WP:** Smoltz (2). **HBP:** Leibrandt (White).

Score by Innings

	1	2	3	4	5	6	7	8	9	10	11	R	H	E
Toronto	1	1	1	4	2	0	1	2	3	0	2	17	45	4
Atlanta	1	1	1	2	7	4	0	2	1	0	1	20	44	2

DP: Toronto 5, Atlanta 7. **LOB:** Toronto 38, Atlanta 40. **2B:** Toronto—Borders 3, Carter 2, Winfield, White, Alomar; Atlanta—Pendleton 2, Sanders 2, Nixon, Gant. **SB:** Toronto—Alomar 3, White, Gruber, Carter; Atlanta—Nixon 5, Sanders 5, Gant 2, Blauser 2, Justice. **CS:** Atlanta—Hunter, Blauser, Nixon. **S:** Toronto—Winfield, Gruber; Atlanta—Berryhill, Belliard. **SF:** Toronto—Carter; Atlanta—Hunter, Pendleton.

Umpires: AL—Mike Reilly, Dan Morrison, John Shulock; NL—Jerry Crawford, Joe West, Bob Davidson.

WORLD SERIES
Toronto wins series, 4 games to 2.

Date	Winner	Home Field
Oct.17	Braves, 3-1	at Atlanta
Oct.18	Blue Jays, 5-4	at Atlanta
Oct.20	Blue Jays, 3-2	at Toronto
Oct.21	Blue Jays, 2-1	at Toronto
Oct.22	Braves, 7-2	at Toronto
Oct.24	Blue Jays, 4-3 (11 inn.)	at Atlanta

Game 1
Saturday, Oct. 17 at Atlanta

	1	2	3	4	5	6	7	8	9	R	H	E
Toronto	0	0	0	1	0	0	0	0	0	1	4	0
Atlanta	0	0	0	0	0	3	0	0	x	3	4	0

Win: Glavine, Atl. (1-0). **Loss:** Morris, Tor. (0-1).
HR: Toronto—Carter (1); Atlanta-Berryhill (1). **RBI:** Toronto—Carter; Atlanta—Berryhill 3. **SB:** Atlanta—Nixon (1), Gant (1).
Attendance: 51,763. **Time:** 2:37.

Game 2
Sunday, Oct. 18 at Atlanta

	1	2	3	4	5	6	7	8	9	R	H	E
Toronto	0	0	0	2	0	0	0	1	2	5	9	2
Atlanta	0	1	0	1	2	0	0	0	—	4	5	1

Win: Ward, Tor. (1-0). **Save:** Henke, Tor. (1). **Loss:** Reardon, Atl. (0-1).
2B: Toronto—Alomar, Borders. **HR:** Toronto—Sprague (1).
RBI: Toronto—Sprague 2, Cone, Winfield, White; Atlanta—Justice, Hunter, Lemke. **SB:** Atlanta—Sanders 2 (2), Justice (1), Blauser (1), Gant (2).
Attendance: 51,763. **Time:** 3:30.

Game 3
Tuesday, Oct. 20 at Toronto

	1	2	3	4	5	6	7	8	9	R	H	E
Atlanta	0	0	0	0	0	1	0	1	0	2	9	0
Toronto	0	0	0	1	0	0	1	0	1	3	6	1

Win: Ward, Tor. (2-0). **Loss:** Avery, Atl. (0-1).
2B: Atlanta—Sanders. **HR:** Toronto—Carter (2), Gruber (1).
RBI: Atlanta—Justice, L.Smith; Toronto—Carter, Maldonado, Gruber. **SB:** Atlanta—Nixon (2), Sanders (3); Toronto—Alomar (1), Gruber (1).
Attendance: 51,813. **Time:** 2:49.

World Series (Cont.)

Game 4
Wednesday, Oct. 21 at Toronto

	1	2	3	4	5	6	7	8	9	R	H	E
Atlanta	0	0	0	0	0	0	1	0		1	5	0
Toronto	0	0	1	0	0	0	1	0	x	2	6	0

Win: Key, Tor. (1-0). **Save:** Henke, Tor. (2). **Loss:** Glavine, Atl. (1-1).

2B: Atlanta—Gant; Toronto—White. **HR:** Toronto—Borders. **RBI:** Atlanta—Lemke; Toronto—White, Borders. **SB:** Atlanta—Nixon (3), Blauser (2); Toronto—Alomar (2).
Attendance: 52,090. **Time:** 2:21.

Game 5
Thursday, Oct 22 at Toronto

	1	2	3	4	5	6	7	8	9	R	H	E
Atlanta	1	0	0	1	5	0	0	0	0	7	13	0
Toronto	0	1	0	1	0	0	0	0	0	2	6	0

Win: Smoltz, Atl. (1-0). **Save:** Stanton, Atl. (1). **Loss:** Morris, Tor. (0-2).

2B: Atlanta—Pendleton 2, Nixon; Toronto—Borders. **HR:** Justice (1), L.Smith (1). **RBI:** Atlanta—L.Smith 4, Justice, Pendleton, Sanders; Toronto—Borders 2. **SB:** Atlanta—Nixon 2 (5).
Attendance: 52,268. **Time:** 3:05.

Game 6
Saturday, Oct. 24 at Atlanta

	1	2	3	4	5	6	7	8	9	10	11	R	H	E
Toronto	1	0	0	1	0	0	0	0	0	0	2	4	14	1
Atlanta	0	0	1	0	0	0	0	0	1	0	1	3	8	1

Win: Key, Tor. (2-0). **Save:** Timlin, Tor. (1). **Loss:** Leibrandt, Atl. (0-1).

2B: Toronto—Carter 2, Winfield, Borders; Atlanta—Sanders. **HR:** Toronto—Maldonado (1). **RBI:** Toronto—Winfield 2, Carter, Maldonado; Atlanta—Nixon, Pendleton, Hunter. **SB:** Toronto—White (1), Alomar (3); Atlanta-Sanders 2 (5).
Attendance: 51,763. **Time:** 4:07.

Most Valuable Player
Pat Borders, Toronto
Catcher

Avg	AB	R	H	2B	3B	HR	RBI
.450	20	2	9	3	0	1	3

Colleges

Final *Baseball America* Top 25

Final 1992 *Baseball America* Division I poll, released after the NCAA College World Series. records include all postseason games.

	W	L			W	L			W	L
1 Pepperdine	48	11	10	Oklahoma	43	24	19	Texas A&M	41	20
2 CS-Fullerton	46	17	11	Stanford	39	23	20	N.C.State	46	18
3 Miami-FL	55	10	12	Hawaii	49	14	21	UCLA	37	26
4 Texas	48	17	13	Arizona	34	23	22	Georgia Tech	45	19
5 Wichita St	56	11	14	California	35	28	23	Western Carolina	45	21
6 LSU	50	16	15	Notre Dame	48	15	24	VCU	35	12
7 Clemson	50	14	16	Florida	44	20	25	South Alabama	44	16
8 Oklahoma St	49	16	17	Long Beach St.	36	21				
9 Florida St.	49	21	18	South Carolina	42	22				

College World Series

Seventh-seeded Pepperdine defeated Cal State Fullerton, 3-2, to win the first NCAA Division I College World Series championship game between two teams from the same state on June 6 at Rosenblatt Stadium in Omaha. The Waves went through the CWS unbeaten, led by a pitching staff that gave up only four earned runs in 36 innings.

Results

Game 1— (1) Miami-FL 4 . . . . (8) California 3 (13 inn)
Game 2— (4) CS-Fullerton 7 . . . . (5) Florida St. 2
Game 3— (7) Pepperdine 6 . . . . (2) Wichita St. 0
Game 4— (3) Texas 15 . . . . (6) Oklahoma 3
Game 5— Florida St. 5 . . . . California 4 (Cal out)
Game 6— Miami-FL 4 . . . . CS-Fullerton 3
Game 7— Oklahoma 8 . . . . Wichita St. 4 (WSU out)
Game 8— Pepperdine 7 . . . . Texas 0
Game 9— CS-Fullerton 6 . . . . Florida St. 0 (FSU out)
Game 10— Texas 8 . . . . Oklahoma 5 (Okla. out)
Game 11— CS-Fullerton 7 . . . . Miami-FL 5
Game 12— Pepperdine 5 . . . . Texas 4 (Texas out)
Game 13— CS-Fullerton 8 . . . . . . Miami-FL 1 (Miami out)
Game 14— Pepperdine 3 . . . . CS-Fullerton 2

Most Outstanding Player
Phil Nevin, CS-Fullerton
3rd baseman

Avg	AB	R	H	2B	3B	HR	RBI
.526	19	7	10	2	0	2	11

Championship Game
Saturday, June 6 at Omaha, Neb.

	1	2	3	4	5	6	7	8	9	R	H	E
Pepperdine	2	0	0	0	1	0	0	0	0	3	8	0
Wichita St	0	0	0	1	0	0	0	0	1	2	4	0

Win—Patrick Ahearne, Pep (15-2); **Save**—Steve Montgomery (9); **Loss**—Dan Naulty (13-4).

2B: Pepperdine—David Main (16), Dan Melendez (15). **HR:** Pepperdine—Eric Ekdahl 1). **RBI:** Pepperdine—Main, Mark Wasikowski, Ekdahl; CS-Fullerton—Jason Moler. **SB:** CS-Fullerton—Nate Rodriguez (35).
Attendance—17,962. **Time**—2:56.

All-Tournament Team

C—Scott Vollmer. Pepperdine; **1B**—Dan Melendez, Pepperdine; **2B**—Steve Rodriguez, Pepperdine; **SS**—Nate Rodriguez, CS-Fullerton; **3B**—Phil Nevin, CS-Fullerton; **OF**—Byron Mathews, Oklahoma, Chris Powell, CS-Fullerton, and Johnathen Smith, Miami-FL; **DH**—Brooks Kieschnick, Texas; **P**—Patrick Ahearne, Pepperdine and James Popoff, CS-Fullerton.

Confident Waves Win First CWS

by Jim Callis

Coach Andy Lopez of Pepperdine likes to stress substance over image, and his Waves rode that credo to the 1992 College World Series championship.

Pepperdine won its first national title June 6 by beating Cal State-Fullerton, 3-2, before a final-game record crowd of 17,692 at Rosenblatt Stadium in Omaha. By winning the title, the team proved something to itself and to the NCAA baseball committee.

The Waves won with essentially the same personnel they had in 1991, when they lost seven of their last nine games and went 0-2 at the West I Regionals. The difference was self-confidence.

"I think the minute we stepped on the field in September, from that point on we knew we were going to do something special this year," All-America first baseman Dan Melendez said. "We didn't know it was going to end like this, though."

As the Waves won four straight Series games, they dodged discussion about why they were ranked third in the nation by *Baseball America* but seeded seventh among the eight teams in Omaha. After beating Fullerton, Lopez admitted his team was inspired by the perceived lack of respect.

"I think we were looked upon as, 'They had a great season, but . . .' or, 'They had a nice year, but . . .' " Lopez said. "We came in here as a seventh seed, and I'll say it now, our guys took it as a slap in the face."

No lower seed ever has won the College World Series. This year's championship game was also historic as the first to feature two teams from the same state.

Cal State Fullerton entered the game after eliminating top-seeded Miami, 8-1, in the 13th game of the Series. The defeat ended Hurricanes coach Ron Fraser's dream of retiring after 30 seasons with a third NCAA championship to go with his 1982 and '85 titles.

Pepperdine had opened the Series with a record 24 straight scoreless innings, so two first-inning runs loomed large against Fullerton. All-America righthander Patrick Ahearne, the Orel Hershiser wannabe who didn't allow

Wide World Photos

Cal State Fullerton lost the title game, but third baseman **Phil Nevin** was the Most Outstanding Player of the Series.

an earned run in 14 Series innings, surrendered just one unearned run while pitching into the seventh of the title game.

Shortstop Eric Ekdahl's first home run of the year, a fifth-inning solo shot, gave the Waves a 3-1 lead they carried into the bottom of the eighth. Then the Titans made one last run.

All-America closer Steve Montgomery hit Nate Rodriquez and Jeremy Carr before Carl Powell bunted the tying runs into scoring position. Montgomery intentionally walked Phil Nevin, the tournament's first Most Outstanding Player from a losing team since Minnesota's Dave Winfield in 1973, to load the bases. Jason Moler hit a sacrifice fly to cut the lead to 3-2, and Tony Banks then smashed a fastball between first and second that seemed destined to tie the game.

But destiny favored the Waves. All-America second baseman Steve Rodriguez dove to his left, caught the ball cleanly on a true hop and threw Banks out.

One inning later, Rodriguez squeezed a Bret Hemphill pop-up to end the game and show that substance and image can go hand-in-hand.

Jim Callis is the associate editor of Baseball America.

Colleges (Cont.)
1992 All-America Team
Selected by *Baseball America*.

Player of the Year
Phil Nevin, CS-Fullerton, 3B

First Team			
Pos		**Class**	**Hgt**	**Wgt**

Pos		Class	Hgt	Wgt
C—	Jason Varitek, Georgia Tech	So.	6-2	209
1B—	Doug Hecker, Tennessee	Jr.	6-4	210
2B—	Brian Eldridge, Oklahoma	Sr.	5-10	175
SS—	Craig Wilson, Kansas St.	Sr.	6-0	175
3B—	Phil Nevin, CS-Fullerton	Jr.	6-2	180
OF—	Jeffrey Hammonds, Stanford	Jr.	6-0	185
OF—	Chad McConnell, Creighton	Jr.	6-1	185
OF—	Calvin Murray, Texas	Jr.	5-11	185
DH—	Troy Penix, California	Jr.	6-4	230
P—	Patrick Ahearne, Pepperdine	Sr.	6-3	195
P—	Jeff Alkire, Miami-FL	Jr.	6-1	205
P—	Darren Dreifort, Wichita St.	So.	6-2	200
P—	Lloyd Peever, LSU	Jr.	6-0	180
P—	Mike Romano, Tulane	So.	6-1	170

Second Team			

Pos		Class	Hgt	Wgt
C—	Bobby Hughes, USC	So.	6-4	210
1B—	Dan Melendez, Pepperdine	Jr.	6-4	195
2B—	Todd Walker, LSU	Fr.	6-0	165
SS—	Chris Wimmer, Wichita St.	Jr.	5-11	165
3B—	Mike Gulan, Kent	Jr.	6-1	190
OF—	Todd Dreifort, Wichita St.	Sr.	6-1	200
OF—	John LaMar, Indiana St.	Sr.	6-3	190
OF—	Kevin Northrup, Clemson	Sr.	6-1	185
DH—	Derek Hacopian, Maryland	Sr.	6-0	200
P—	Roger Bailey, Florida St.	Jr.	6-1	170
P—	Matt Donahue, N.C.State	Sr.	6-1	205
P—	Benji Grigsby, San Diego St	Jr.	6-1	200
P—	Scott Karl, Hawaii	Jr.	6-3	192
P—	B.J. Wallace, Mississippi St	Jr.	6-1	200

NCAA Division I Leaders

Batting

Average

	Cl	Gm	AB	H	Avg
Mike Smith, Indiana	Sr.	55	202	99	.490
Derek Hacopian, Maryland	Sr.	56	194	95	.490
Dan Koptiva, Louisville	Sr.	61	256	125	.488
Jay Logwood, Towson St	Jr.	47	171	81	.474
Glenn Hamel, St. Bona	Jr.	37	123	56	.455

Home Runs

	Cl	Gm	HR	P/Gm
Mike Smith, Indiana	Sr.	55	27	0.49
John Tomasello, San Francisco	Sr.	54	24	0.44
Derek Hacopian, Maryland	Sr.	56	23	0.41
Rod Walker, E.Tenn St	Jr.	50	20	0.40
Bill Selby, Southern Miss	Sr.	59	23	0.39

Runs Batted In

	Cl	Gm	RBI	P/Gm
Mike Smith, Indiana	Sr.	55	95	1.73
Derek Hacopian, Maryland	Sr.	56	84	1.50
Les Jennette, Va.Tech	Sr.	50	73	1.46
Rob Newman, Louisville	Sr.	61	88	1.44
Phil Nevin, CS-Fullerton	Jr.	61	86	1.41

Pitching

Earned Run Average

	Cl	Gm	IP	ERA
Rick Navarro, San Diego St	Sr.	12	59.0	1.373
David Hawkins, Nichools St	Sr.	16	78.1	1.379
John O'Brien, N'eastern	Jr.	9	57.1	1.41
John Wesley, IL-Chicago	Jr.	16	70.0	1.54
Paxton Briley, Clemson	Jr.	13	80.0	1.69

Wins

	Cl	Gm	IP	W-L
Mike Romano, Tulane	So.	23	165.1	17-4
Patrick Ahearne, Pepperdine	Sr.	21	142.2	15-2
Roger Bailey, Florida St	Jr.	22	139.1	15-5
Four tied with 14 each.				

Strikeouts

	Cl	IP	So	P/G
Ron Villone, UMass	Jr.	59.1	89	13.5
Sean Hogan, Morehead St	Jr.	73.1	102	12.5
Steve Reich, Army	Jr.	53.2	73	12.2
Benji Grigsby, S.Diego St	Jr.	79.0	107	12.2
Gettys Glaze, Citadel	Sr.	79.1	104	11.8

MLB Amateur Draft
First round selections at the 28th Amateur Draft held on June 1, 1991.

First Round

No			Pos
1	Houston	Phil Nevin, CS-Fullerton	3B
2	Cleveland	Paul Shuey, North Carolina	RHP
3	Montreal	B.J. Wallace, Miss. St.	LHP
4	Baltimore	Jeffrey Hammonds, Stanford	OF
5	Cincinnati	Chad Mottola, Central Fla.	OF
6	NY Yankees	Derek Jeter, HS Kalamazoo, Mich.	SS
7	San Francisco	Calvin Murray, Texas	OF
8	California	Pete Janicki, UCLA	RHP
9	MY Mets	Preston Wilson, HS Bamberg, S.C.	SS
10	Kansas City	Michael Tucker, Longwood Coll.	SS
11	Chi.Cubs	Derek Wallace, Pepperdine	RHP
12	Milwaukee	Kenny Felder, Florida St.	OF
13	Philadelphia	Chad McConnell, Creighton	OF
14	Seattle	Ron Villone, UMass	LHP

No			Pos
15	St.Louis	Sean Lowe, Arizona St.	RHP
16	Detroit	Ricky Greene, LSU	RHP
17	Kansas City	Jim Pittsley, HS DuBois, Pa.	RHP
18	NY Mets	Chris Roberts, Florida St.	LHP-OF
19	Toronto	Shannon Stewart, HS Miami, Fla.	OF
20	Oakland	Benji Grigsby, San Diego St.	RHP
21	Atlanta	Jamie Arnold, HS Kissimmee, Fla.	RHP
22	Texas	Rick Helling, Stanford	RHP
23	Pittsburgh	Jason Kendall, HS Torrance, Calif.	C
24	Chisox	Eddie Pearson, Bishop St. (Ala.)	1B
25	Toronto	Todd Steverson, Arizona St.	OF
26	Minnesota	Dan Serafini, HS San Mateo, Calif.	LHP
27	Colorado	John Burke, Florida	RHP
28	Florida	Charles Johnson, Miami-FL	C

THE 1993 INFORMATION PLEASE SPORTS ALMANAC

BASEBALL STATISTICS

THROUGH THE YEARS
1900-1992
WORLD SERIES • ALL-TIMERS

SEC B

PAGE 91

The World Series

The World Series began in 1903 when Pittsburgh of the older National League (founded in 1876) invited Boston of the American League (founded in 1901) to play a best-of-9 game series to determine which of the two league champions was the best. Boston was the surprise winner, 5 games to 3. The 1904 NL champion New York Giants refused to play Boston the following year, so there was no series. Giants' owner John T. Brush hated AL president Ban Johnson and considered the junior circuit to be a minor league. By the following year, however, Brush and Johnson had smoothed out their differences and the Giants agreed to play Philadelphia in a best-of-7 game series. Since then the World Series has been best-of-7 format, except from 1919-21 when it returned to best-of-9.

In the chart below, the National League teams are listed in CAPITAL letters. Also, each World Series champion's wins and losses are noted in parentheses after the series score.

Year	Winner	Manager	Series	Loser	Manager
1903	Boston Red Sox	Jimmy Collins	5-3 (LWLLWWWW)	PITTSBURGH	Fred Clarke
1904	Not held				
1905	NY GIANTS	John McGraw	4-1 (WLWWW)	Philadelphia A's	Connie Mack
1906	Chicago White Sox	Fielder Jones	4-2 (WLWLWW)	CHICAGO CUBS	Frank Chance
1907	CHICAGO CUBS	Frank Chance	4-0-1 (TWWWW)	Detroit	Hugh Jennings
1908	CHICAGO CUBS	Frank Chance	4-1 (WWLWW)	Detroit	Hugh Jennings
1909	PITTSBURGH	Fred Clarke	4-3 (WLWLWLW)	Detroit	Hugh Jennings
1910	Philadelphia A's	Connie Mack	4-1 (WWWLW)	CHICAGO CUBS	Frank Chance
1911	Philadelphia A's	Connie Mack	4-2 (LWWWLW)	NY GIANTS	John McGraw
1912	Boston Red Sox	Jake Stahl	4-3-1 (WTLWWLLW)	NY GIANTS	John McGraw
1913	Philadelphia A's	Connie Mack	4-1 (WLWWW)	NY GIANTS	John McGraw
1914	BOSTON BRAVES	George Stallings	4-0	Philadelphia A's	Connie Mack
1915	Boston Red Sox	Bill Carrigan	4-1 (LWWWW)	PHILA. PHILLIES	Pat Moran
1916	Boston Red Sox	Bill Carrigan	4-1 (WWLWW)	BKLN. DODGERS	Wilbert Robinson
1917	Chicago White Sox	Pants Rowland	4-2 (WWLLWW)	NY GIANTS	John McGraw
1918	Boston Red Sox	Ed Barrow	4-2 (WLWWLW)	CHICAGO CUBS	Fred Mitchell
1919	CINCINNATI	Pat Moran	5-3 (WWLWWLLW)	Chicago White Sox	Kid Gleason
1920	Cleveland	Tris Speaker	5-2 (WLLWWWW)	BKLN. DODGERS	Wilbert Robinson
1921	NY GIANTS	John McGraw	5-3 (LLWWLWWW)	NY Yankees	Miller Huggins
1922	NY GIANTS	John McGraw	4-0-1 (WTWWW)	NY Yankees	Miller Huggins
1923	NY Yankees	Miller Huggins	4-2 (LWLWW)	NY GIANTS	John McGraw
1924	Washington	Bucky Harris	4-3 (LWLWLWW)	NY GIANTS	John McGraw
1925	PITTSBURGH	Bill McKechnie	4-3 (LWLLWWW)	Washington	Bucky Harris
1926	ST.L. CARDINALS	Rogers Hornsby	4-3 (LWWLLWW)	NY Yankees	Miller Huggins
1927	NY Yankees	Miller Huggins	4-0	PITTSBURGH	Donie Bush
1928	NY Yankees	Miller Huggins	4-0	ST.L. CARDINALS	Bill McKechnie
1929	Philadelphia A's	Connie Mack	4-1 (WWLWW)	CHICAGO CUBS	Joe McCarthy
1930	Philadelphia A's	Connie Mack	4-2 (WWLLWW)	ST.L. CARDINALS	Gabby Street
1931	ST.L. CARDINALS	Gabby Street	4-3 (LWWLWLW)	Philadelphia A's	Connie Mack
1932	NY Yankees	Joe McCarthy	4-0	CHICAGO CUBS	Charlie Grimm
1933	NY GIANTS	Bill Terry	4-1 (WWLWW)	Washington	Joe Cronin
1934	ST.L. CARDINALS	Frankie Frisch	4-3 (WLWLLWW)	Detroit	Mickey Cochrane
1935	Detroit	Mickey Cochrane	4-2 (LWWWLW)	CHICAGO CUBS	Charlie Grimm
1936	NY Yankees	Joe McCarthy	4-2 (LWWWLW)	NY GIANTS	Bill Terry
1937	NY Yankees	Joe McCarthy	4-1 (WWWLW)	NY GIANTS	Bill Terry
1938	NY Yankees	Joe McCarthy	4-0	CHICAGO CUBS	Gabby Hartnett
1939	NY Yankees	Joe McCarthy	4-0	CINCINNATI	Bill McKechnie
1940	CINCINNATI	Bill McKechnie	4-3 (LWLWLWW)	Detroit	Del Baker
1941	NY Yankees	Joe McCarthy	4-1 (WLWWW)	BKLN. DODGERS	Leo Durocher
1942	ST.L. CARDINALS	Billy Southworth	4-1 (LWWWW)	NY Yankees	Joe McCarthy
1943	NY Yankees	Joe McCarthy	4-1 (LWWWW)	ST.L. CARDINALS	Billy Southworth
1944	ST.L. CARDINALS	Billy Southworth	4-2 (LWLWWW)	St.Louis Browns	Luke Sewell
1945	Detroit	Steve O'Neill	4-3 (LWLWLWW)	CHICAGO CUBS	Charlie Grimm
1946	ST.L. CARDINALS	Eddie Dyer	4-3 (LWLWLWW)	Boston Red Sox	Joe Cronin
1947	NY Yankees	Bucky Harris	4-3 (WWLLWLW)	BKLN. DODGERS	Burt Shotton

World Series (Cont.)

Year	Winner	Manager	Series	Loser	Manager
1948	Cleveland	Lou Boudreau	4-2 (LWWWLW)	BOSTON BRAVES	Billy Southworth
1949	NY Yankees	Casey Stengel	4-1 (WLWWW)	BKLN. DODGERS	Burt Shotton
1950	NY Yankees	Casey Stengel	4-0	PHILA. PHILLIES	Eddie Sawyer
1951	NY Yankees	Casey Stengel	4-2 (LWLWW)	NY GIANTS	Leo Durocher
1952	NY Yankees	Casey Stengel	4-3 (LWLWLWW)	BKLN. DODGERS	Charlie Dressen
1953	NY Yankees	Casey Stengel	4-2 (WWLLWW)	BKLN. DODGERS	Charlie Dressen
1954	NY GIANTS	Leo Durocher	4-0	Cleveland	Al Lopez
1955	BKLN. DODGERS	Walter Alston	4-3 (LLWWWLW)	NY Yankees	Casey Stengel
1956	NY Yankees	Casey Stengel	4-3 (LLWWWLW)	BKLN. DODGERS	Walter Alston
1957	MILW. BRAVES	Fred Haney	4-3 (LWLWWLW)	NY Yankees	Casey Stengel
1958	NY Yankees	Casey Stengel	4-3 (LLWLWWW)	MILW. BRAVES	Fred Haney
1959	LA DODGERS	Walter Alston	4-2 (LWWWLW)	Chicago White Sox	Al Lopez
1960	PITTSBURGH	Danny Murtaugh	4-3 (WLLWWLW)	NY Yankees	Casey Stengel
1961	NY Yankees	Ralph Houk	4-1 (WLWWW)	CINCINNATI	Fred Hutchinson
1962	NY Yankees	Ralph Houk	4-3 (WLWLWLW)	SF GIANTS	Alvin Dark
1963	LA DODGERS	Walter Alston	4-0	NY Yankees	Ralph Houk
1964	ST.L. CARDINALS	Johnny Keane	4-3 (WLLWWLW)	NY Yankees	Yogi Berra
1965	LA DODGERS	Walter Alston	4-3 (LLWWLWW)	Minnesota	Sam Mele
1966	Baltimore	Hank Bauer	4-0	LA DODGERS	Walter Alston
1967	ST.L. CARDINALS	Red Schoendienst	4-3 (WLWLWLW)	Boston Red Sox	Dick Williams
1968	Detroit	Mayo Smith	4-3 (LWLLWWW)	ST.L. CARDINALS	Red Schoendienst
1969	NY METS	Gil Hodges	4-1 (LWWWW)	Baltimore	Earl Weaver
1970	Baltimore	Earl Weaver	4-1 (WWWLW)	CINCINNATI	Sparky Anderson
1971	PITTSBURGH	Danny Murtaugh	4-3 (LLWWWLW)	Baltimore	Earl Weaver
1972	Oakland A's	Dick Williams	4-3 (WWLWLLW)	CINCINNATI	Sparky Anderson
1973	Oakland A's	Dick Williams	4-3 (WLWLLWW)	NY METS	Yogi Berra
1974	Oakland A's	Alvin Dark	4-1 (LWWWW)	LA DODGERS	Walter Alston
1975	CINCINNATI	Sparky Anderson	4-3 (LWWLWLW)	Boston Red Sox	Darrell Johnson
1976	CINCINNATI	Sparky Anderson	4-0	NY Yankees	Billy Martin
1977	NY Yankees	Billy Martin	4-2 (WLWWLW)	LA DODGERS	Tommy Lasorda
1978	NY Yankees	Bob Lemon	4-2 (LLWWWW)	LA DODGERS	Tommy Lasorda
1979	PITTSBURGH	Chuck Tanner	4-3 (LWLLWWW)	Baltimore	Earl Weaver
1980	PHILA. PHILLIES	Dallas Green	4-2 (WWLLWW)	Kansas City	Jim Frey
1981	LA DODGERS	Tommy Lasorda	4-2 (LLWWWW)	NY Yankees	Bob Lemon
1982	ST.L. CARDINALS	Whitey Herzog	4-3 (LWWLLWW)	Milwaukee Brewers	Harvey Kuenn
1983	Baltimore	Joe Altobelli	4-1 (LWWWW)	PHILA. PHILLIES	Paul Owens
1984	Detroit	Sparky Anderson	4-1 (WLWWW)	SAN DIEGO	Dick Williams
1985	Kansas City	Dick Howser	4-3 (LLWWLWW)	ST.L. CARDINALS	Whitey Herzog
1986	NY METS	Davey Johnson	4-3 (LLWWWLW)	Boston Red Sox	John McNamara
1987	Minnesota	Tom Kelly	4-3 (WWLLLWW)	ST.L. CARDINALS	Whitey Herzog
1988	LA DODGERS	Tommy Lasorda	4-1 (WWLWW)	Oakland A's	Tony La Russa
1989	Oakland A's	Tony La Russa	4-0	SF GIANTS	Roger Craig
1990	CINCINNATI	Lou Piniella	4-0	Oakland A's	Tony La Russa
1991	Minnesota	Tom Kelly	4-3 (WWLLLWW)	ATLANTA BRAVES	Bobby Cox
1992	Toronto	Cito Gaston	4-2 (LWWWLW)	ATLANTA BRAVES	Bobby Cox

Most Valuable Players

Currently selected by media panel made up of representatives of CBS Sports, CBS Radio, AP, UPI, and World Series official scorers. Presented by *Sport* magazine from 1955-88 and by Major League Baseball since 1989. Winners who did not play for World Series champions are in **bold** type.
  Multiple winners: Bob Gibson, Reggie Jackson and Sandy Koufax (2).

Year		Year		Year	
1955	Johnny Podres, Bkyln, P	1970	Brooks Robinson, Bal., 3B	1982	Darrell Porter, St.L., C
1956	Don Larsen, NY, P	1971	Roberto Clemente, Pit., OF	1983	Rick Dempsey, Bal., C
1957	Lew Burdette, Mil., P	1972	Gene Tenace, Oak., C	1984	Alan Trammell, Det., SS
1958	Bob Turley, NY, P	1973	Reggie Jackson, Oak., OF	1985	Bret Saberhagen, KC, P
1959	Larry Sherry, LA, P	1974	Rollie Fingers, Oak., P	1986	Ray Knight, NY, 3B
		1975	Pete Rose, Cin., 3B	1987	Frank Viola, Min., P
1960	**Bobby Richardson**, NY, 2B	1976	Johnny Bench, Cin., C	1988	Orel Hershiser, LA, P
1961	Whitey Ford, NY, P	1977	Reggie Jackson, NY, OF	1989	Dave Stewart, Oak., P
1962	Ralph Terry, NY, P	1978	Bucky Dent, NY, SS		
1963	Sandy Koufax, LA, P	1979	Willie Stargell, Pit., 1B	1990	Jose Rijo, Cin., P
1964	Bob Gibson, St.L., P			1991	Jack Morris, Min., P
1965	Sandy Koufax, LA, P	1980	Mike Schmidt, Phi., 3B	1992	Pat Borders, Tor., C
1966	Frank Robinson, Bal., OF	1981	Pedro Guerrero, LA, OF;		
1967	Bob Gibson, St.L., P		Ron Cey, LA, 3B;		
1968	Mickey Lolich, Det., P		& Steve Yeager, LA, C		
1969	Donn Clendenon, NY, 1B				

All-Time World Series Leaders
CAREER
World Series leaders through 1991. Years listed indicate number of World Series appearances.
Hitting

Games

	Yrs	Gm
Yogi Berra, NY Yankees	14	75
Mickey Mantle, NY Yankees	12	65
Elston Howard, NY Yankees-Boston	10	54
Hank Bauer, NY Yankees	9	53
Gil McDougald, NY Yankees	8	53

At Bats

	Yrs	AB
Yogi Berra, NY Yankees	14	259
Mickey Mantle, NY Yankees	12	230
Joe DiMaggio, NY Yankees	10	199
Frankie Frisch, NY Giants-St.L Cards	8	197
Gil McDougald, NY Yankees	8	190

Batting Avg. (minimum 50 AB)

	AB	H	Avg
Pepper Martin, St.L Cards	55	23	.418
Lou Brock, St.Louis	87	34	.391
Thurman Munson, NY Yankees	67	25	.373
George Brett, Kansas City	51	19	.373
Hank Aaron, Milw. Braves	55	20	.364

Hits

	AB	H	Avg
Yogi Berra, NY Yankees	259	71	.274
Mickey Mantle, NY Yankees	230	59	.257
Frankie Frisch, NYG-St.L Cards	197	58	.294
Joe DiMaggio, NY Yankees	199	54	.271
Hank Bauer, NY Yankees	188	46	.245
Pee Wee Reese, Brooklyn	169	46	.272

Runs

	Gm	R
Mickey Mantle, NY Yankees	65	42
Yogi Berra, NY Yankees	75	41
Babe Ruth, NY Yankees	41	37
Lou Gehrig, NY Yankees	34	30
Joe DiMaggio, NY Yankees	51	27

Home Runs

	AB	HR
Mickey Mantle, NY Yankees	230	18
Babe Ruth, NY Yankees	129	15
Yogi Berra, NY Yankees	259	12
Duke Snider, Brooklyn-LA	133	11
Lou Gehrig, NY Yankees	119	10
Reggie Jackson, Oakland-NY Yankees	98	10

Runs Batted In

	Gm	RBI
Mickey Mantle, NY Yankees	65	40
Yogi Berra, NY Yankees	75	39
Lou Gehrig, NY Yankees	34	35
Babe Ruth, NY Yankees	41	33
Joe DiMaggio, NY Yankees	51	30

Stolen Bases

	Gm	SB
Lou Brock, St.Louis	21	14
Eddie Collins, Phi.A's-Chisox	34	14
Frank Chance, Chi.Cubs	20	10
Davey Lopes, Los Angeles	23	10
Phil Rizzuto, NY Yankees	52	10

Total Bases

	Gm	TB
Mickey Mantle, NY Yankees	65	123
Yogi Berra, NY Yankees	75	117
Babe Ruth, NY Yankees	41	96
Lou Gehrig, NY Yankees	34	87
Joe DiMaggio, NY Yankees	51	84

Slugging Avg. (50 AB)

	AB	Avg
Reggie Jackson, Oakland-NY Yankees	98	.755
Babe Ruth, NY Yankees	129	.744
Lou Gehrig, NY Yankees	119	.731
Al Simmons, Phi.A's-Cincinnati	73	.658
Lou Brock, St.Louis	87	.655

Pitching
Games

	Yrs	Gm
Whitey Ford, NY Yankees	11	22
Rollie Fingers, Oakland	3	16
Allie Reynolds, NY Yankees	6	15
Bob Turley, NY Yankees	5	15
Clay Carroll, Cincinnati	3	14

Wins

	Gm	W-L
Whitey Ford, NY Yankees	22	10-8
Bob Gibson, St.Louis	9	7-2
Allie Reynolds, NY Yankees	15	7-2
Red Ruffing, NY Yankees	10	7-2
Lefty Gomez, NY Yankees	7	6-0
Chief Bender, Philadelphia A's	10	6-4
Waite Hoyt, NY Yankees-Phi.A's	12	6-4

World Series Appearances

In the 88 years that the World Series has been contested, American League teams have won 51 championships while National League teams have won 37.

The New York Yankees have appeared in the Series on 33 occasions and won a record 22 titles. The Brooklyn-Los Angeles Dodgers are second in appearances with 18. The following teams are ranked by number of appearances through the 1991 World Series; (*) indicates AL teams.

	App	W	L	Pct.	Last Series	Last Title
NY Yankees*	33	22	11	.667	1981	1978
Bklyn/LA Dodgers	18	6	12	.333	1988	1988
NY/SF Giants	16	5	11	.313	1989	1954
St.L.Cardinals	15	9	6	.600	1987	1982
Phi/KC/Oak.A's*	14	9	5	.643	1990	1989
Chicago Cubs	10	2	8	.200	1945	1908
Boston Red Sox*	9	5	4	.556	1986	1918
Cincinnati Reds	9	5	4	.556	1990	1990
Detroit Tigers*	9	4	5	.444	1984	1984
Pittsburgh Pirates	7	5	2	.714	1979	1979
St.L/Bal.Orioles*	7	3	4	.429	1983	1983
Wash/Min.Twins*	6	3	3	.500	1991	1991
Bos/Mil/Atl.Braves	6	2	4	.333	1992	1957
Chi.White Sox*	4	2	2	.500	1959	1917
Phi.Phillies	4	1	3	.250	1983	1980
Cle.Indians*	3	2	1	.667	1954	1948
NY Mets	3	2	1	.667	1986	1986
KC Royals*	2	1	1	.500	1985	1985
Tor. Blue Jays	1	1	0	1.000	1992	1992
Sea/Mil.Brewers*	1	0	1	.000	1982	—
SD Padres	1	0	1	.000	1984	—

All-Time World Series Leaders (Cont.)

Losses

	Gm	W-L
Whitey Ford, NY Yankees	22	10-8
Christy Mathewson, NY Giants	11	5-5
Joe Bush, Phi.A's-Bosox-NY Yankees	9	2-5
Rube Marquard, NY Giants-Brooklyn	11	2-5
Eddie Plank, Philadelphia A's	7	2-5
Schoolboy Rowe, Detroit	8	2-5

Strikeouts

	Gm	IP	SO
Whitey Ford, NY Yankees	22	146	94
Bob Gibson, St.Louis	9	81	92
Allie Reynolds, NY Yankees	15	77	62
Sandy Koufax, Los Angeles	8	57	61
Red Ruffing, NY Yankees	10	86	61

ERA (minimum 25 IP)

	Gm	IP	ERA
Jack Billingham, Cincinnati	7	25	0.36
Harry Brecheen, St.Louis	7	33	0.83
Babe Ruth, Boston Red Sox	3	31	0.87
Sherry Smith, Brooklyn	3	30	0.89
Sandy Koufax, Los Angeles	8	57	0.95

Bases on Balls

	Gm	IP	BB
Whitey Ford, NY Yankees	22	146	34
Allie Reynolds, NY Yankees	15	77	32
Art Nehf, NY Giants-Chi.Cubs	12	79	32
Jim Palmer, Baltimore	9	65	31
Bob Turley, NY Yankees	15	54	29

Innings Pitched

	Gm	IP
Whitey Ford, NY Yankees	22	146
Christy Mathewson, NY Giants	11	102
Red Ruffing, NY Yankees	10	86
Chief Bender, Philadelphia A's	10	85
Waite Hoyt, NY Yankees-Phi.A's	12	84

Complete Games

	GS	CG	W-L
Christy Mathewson, NY Giants	11	10	5-5
Chief Bender, Philadelphia A's	10	9	6-4
Bob Gibson, St.Louis	9	8	7-2
Whitey Ford, NY Yankees	22	7	10-8
Red Ruffing, NY Yankees	10	7	7-2

Saves

	Gm	IP	Sv
Rollie Fingers, Oakland	16	33	6
Allie Reynolds, NY Yankees	15	77	4
Johnny Murphy, NY Yankees	8	16	4
Seven pitchers tied with 3 each.			

Shutouts

	GS	CG	ShO
Christy Mathewson, NY Giants	11	10	4
Three Finger Brown, Chi. Cubs	7	5	3
Whitey Ford, NY Yankees	22	7	3
Seven pitchers tied with 2 each.			

League Championship Series

Division play came to the major leagues in 1969 when both the American and National Leagues expanded to 12 teams. With an East and West Division in each league, League Championship Series (LCS) became necessary to determine the NL and AL pennant winners. In the charts below, the East Division champions are noted by the letter E and the West Division champions by W. Also, each playoff winner's wins and losses are noted in parentheses after the series score. The LCS changed from best-of-5 to best-of-7 in 1985.

National League

Year	Winner	Manager	Series	Loser	Manager
1969	E- New York	Gil Hodges	3-0	W- Atlanta	Lum Harris
1970	W- Cincinnati	Sparky Anderson	3-0	E- Pittsburgh	Danny Murtaugh
1971	E- Pittsburgh	Danny Murtaugh	3-1 (LWWW)	W- San Francisco	Charlie Fox
1972	W- Cincinnati	Sparky Anderson	3-2 (LWWLW)	E- Pittsburgh	Bill Virdon
1973	E- New York	Yogi Berra	3-2 (LWWLW)	W- Cincinnati	Sparky Anderson
1974	W- Los Angeles	Walter Alston	3-1 (WWLW)	E- Pittsburgh	Danny Murtaugh
1975	W- Cincinnati	Sparky Anderson	3-0	E- Pittsburgh	Danny Murtaugh
1976	W- Cincinnati	Sparky Anderson	3-0	E- Philadelphia	Danny Ozark
1977	W- Los Angeles	Tommy Lasorda	3-1 (WLWW)	E- Philadelphia	Danny Ozark
1978	W- Los Angeles	Tommy Lasorda	3-1 (WWLW)	E- Philadelphia	Danny Ozark
1979	E- Pittsburgh	Chuck Tanner	3-0	W- Cincinnati	John McNamara
1980	E- Philadelphia	Dallas Green	3-2 (WLLWW)	W- Houston	Bill Virdon
1981	W- Los Angeles	Tommy Lasorda	3-2 (WLLWW)	E- Montreal	Jim Fanning
1982	E- St. Louis	Whitey Herzog	3-0	W- Atlanta	Joe Torre
1983	E- Philadelphia	Paul Owens	3-1 (WLWW)	W- Los Angeles	Tommy Lasorda
1984	W- San Diego	Dick Williams	3-2 (LLWWW)	E- Chicago	Jim Frey
1985	E- St. Louis	Whitey Herzog	4-2 (LLWWWW)	W- Los Angeles	Tommy Lasorda
1986	E- New York	Davey Johnson	4-2 (LWWLWW)	W- Houston	Hal Lanier
1987	E- St. Louis	Whitey Herzog	4-3 (WLWWLLW)	W- San Francisco	Roger Craig
1988	W- Los Angeles	Tommy Lasorda	4-3 (LWLWWLW)	E- New York	Davey Johnson
1989	W- San Francisco	Roger Craig	4-1 (WLWWW)	E- Chicago	Don Zimmer
1990	W- Cincinnati	Lou Piniella	4-2 (LWWWLW)	E- Pittsburgh	Jim Leyland
1991	W- Atlanta	Bobby Cox	4-3 (LWWLLWW)	E- Pittsburgh	Jim Leyland
1992	W- Atlanta	Bobby Cox	4-3 (WWLWLLW)	E- Pittsburgh	Jim Leyland

NLCS Most Valuable Players

Year		Year		Year	
1977	Dusty Baker, LA, OF	1983	Gary Matthews, Phi., OF	1989	Will Clark, SF, 1B
1978	Steve Garvey, LA, 1B	1984	Steve Garvey, SD, 1B	1990	Rob Dibble, Cin., P
1979	Willie Stargell, Pit., 1B	1985	Ozzie Smith, St.L., SS		& Randy Myers, Cin., P
1980	Manny Trillo, Phi., 2B	1986	Mike Scott, Houston, P	1991	Steve Avery, Atl., P
1981	Burt Hooton, LA, P	1987	Jeff Leonard, San Fran., OF	1992	John Smoltz, Atl., P
1982	Darrell Porter, St.L., C	1988	Orel Hershiser, LA, P		

American League

Year	Winner	Manager	Series	Loser	Manager
1969	E- Baltimore	Earl Weaver	3-0	W- Minnesota	Billy Martin
1970	E- Baltimore	Earl Weaver	3-0	W- Minnesota	Bill Rigney
1971	E- Baltimore	Earl Weaver	3-0	W- Oakland	Dick Williams
1972	W- Oakland	Dick Williams	3-2 (WWLLW)	E- Detroit	Billy Martin
1973	W- Oakland	Dick Williams	3-2 (LWWLW)	E- Baltimore	Earl Weaver
1974	W- Oakland	Alvin Dark	3-1 (LWWW)	E- Baltimore	Earl Weaver
1975	E- Boston	Darrell Johnson	3-0	W- Oakland	Alvin Dark
1976	E- New York	Billy Martin	3-2 (WLWLW)	W- Kansas City	Whitey Herzog
1977	E- New York	Billy Martin	3-2 (LWLWW)	W- Kansas City	Whitey Herzog
1978	E- New York	Bob Lemon	3-1 (WLWW)	W- Kansas City	Whitey Herzog
1979	E- Baltimore	Earl Weaver	3-1 (WWLW)	W- California	Jim Fregosi
1980	W- Kansas City	Jim Frey	3-0	E- New York	Dick Howser
1981	E- New York	Bob Lemon	3-0	W- Oakland	Billy Martin
1982	E- Milwaukee	Harvey Kuenn	3-2 (LLWWW)	W- California	Gene Mauch
1983	E- Baltimore	Joe Altobelli	3-1 (LWWW)	W- Chicago	Tony La Russa
1984	E- Detroit	Sparky Anderson	3-0	W- Kansas City	Dick Howser
1985	W- Kansas City	Dick Howser	4-3 (LLWLWWW)	E- Toronto	Bobby Cox
1986	E- Boston	John McNamara	4-3 (LWLLWWW)	W- California	Gene Mauch
1987	W- Minnesota	Tom Kelly	4-1 (WWLWW)	E- Detroit	Sparky Anderson
1988	W- Oakland	Tony La Russa	4-0	E- Boston	Joe Morgan
1989	W- Oakland	Tony La Russa	4-1 (WWLWW)	E- Toronto	Cito Gaston
1990	W- Oakland	Tony La Russa	4-0	E- Boston	Joe Morgan
1991	W-Minnesota	Tom Kelly	4-1 (WLWWW)	E-Toronto	Cito Gaston
1992	E-Toronto	Cito Gaston	4-2 (LWWWLW)	W-Oakland	Tony La Russa

ALCS Most Valuable Players

Year		Year		Year	
1980	Frank White, KC, 2B	1985	George Brett, KC, 3B	1989	Rickey Henderson, Oak., OF
1981	Graig Nettles, NY, 3B	1986	Marty Barrett, Bos., 2B	1990	Dave Stewart, Oak., P
1982	Fred Lynn, Cal., OF	1987	Gary Gaetti, Min., 3B	1991	Kirby Puckett, Min., OF
1983	Mike Boddicker, Bal., P	1988	Dennis Eckersley, Oak., P	1992	Roberto Alomar, Tor., 2B
1984	Kirk Gibson, Det., OF				

Other Playoffs

Seven times from 1946-80, playoffs were necessary to decide league or division championships when two teams tied for first place at the end of the regular season. In the strike year of 1981, there were playoffs between the first and second half-season champions in both leagues.

National League

Year	NL	W	L	Manager	Year	NL West	W	L	Manager
1946	Brooklyn	96	58	Leo Durocher	1980	Houston	92	70	Bill Virdon
	St.Louis	96	58	Eddie Dyer		Los Angeles	92	70	Tommy Lasorda
	Playoff: (Best-of-3) St.Louis, 2-0					Playoff: (1 game) Houston, 7-1 (at LA)			
	NL	**W**	**L**	**Manager**		**NL East**	**W**	**L**	**Manager**
1951	Brooklyn	96	58	Charlie Dressen	1981	(1st Half) Phila.	34	21	Dallas Green
	New York	96	58	Leo Durocher		(2nd Half) Montreal	30	23	Jim Fanning
	Playoff: (Best-of-3) New York, 2-1 (WLW)					Playoff: (Best-of-5) Montreal, 3-2 (WWLLW)			
	NL	**W**	**L**	**Manager**		**NL West**	**W**	**L**	**Manager**
1959	Milwaukee	86	68	Fred Haney		(1st Half) Los Ang.	36	21	Tommy Lasorda
	Los Angeles	86	68	Walter Alston		(2nd Half) Houston	33	20	Bill Virdon
	Playoff: (Best-of-3) Los Angeles, 2-0					Playoff: (Best-of-5) Los Angeles, 3-2 (LLWWW)			
	NL	**W**	**L**	**Manager**					
1962	Los Angeles	101	61	Walter Alston					
	San Francisco	101	61	Alvin Dark					
	Playoff: (Best-of-3) San Francisco, 2-1 (WLW)								

Other Playoffs (Cont.)
American League

Year	AL	W	L	Manager
1948	Boston	96	58	Joe McCarthy
	Cleveland	96	58	Lou Boudreau
	Playoff: (1 game) Cleveland, 8-3 (at Boston)			

	AL East	W	L	Manager
1978	Boston	99	63	Don Zimmer
	New York	99	63	Bob Lemon
	Playoff: (1 game) New York, 5-4 (at Boston)			

Year	AL East	W	L	Manager
1981	(1st Half) N.Y.	34	22	Bob Lemon
	(2nd Half) Milw.	31	22	Buck Rodgers
	Playoff: (Best-of-5) New York, 3-2 (WWLLW)			

	AL West	W	L	Manager
	(1st Half) Oakland	37	23	Billy Martin
	(2nd Half) Kan.City....	30	23	Jim Frey
	Playoff: (Best-of-5), Oakland, 3-0			

Major League Franchise Origins

Here is what the current 28 teams in Major League Baseball have to show for the years they have put in as members of the National League (NL) and American League (AL).

National League

	1st Year	Pennants & World Series	Franchise Stops

Atlanta Braves...............	1876	6 NL (1914,48,57-58,91-92)
		2 WS (1914,57)
			Boston (1876-1952)
			  Milwaukee (1953-65)
			  Atlanta (1966—)

Chicago Cubs...............	1876	10 NL (1906-08,10,18,29,32,35,38,45) 2 WS (1907-08)	Chicago (1876—)
Cincinnati Reds..............	1876	9 NL (1919,39-40,61,70,72,75-76,90) 5 WS (1919,40,75-76,90)	Cincinnati (1876-80) Cincinnati (1890—)
Colorado Rockies	1993	None	Denver (1993—)
Florida Marlins	1993	None	Miami (1993—)
Houston Astros	1962	None	Houston (1962—)

Los Angeles Dodgers	1890	18 NL (1916,20,41,47,49,52-53,55-56,59,63,
		    65-66,74,77-78, 81,88)
		6 WS (1955,59,63,65,81,88)
			Brooklyn (1890-1957)
			  Los Angeles (1958—)

Montreal Expos..............	1969	None	Montreal (1969—)
New York Mets	1962	3 NL (1969,73,86) 2 WS (1969,86)	New York (1962—)
Philadelphia Phillies	1880	4 NL (1915,50,80,83) 1 WS (1980)	Philadelphia (1883—)
Pittsburgh Pirates............	1887	7 NL (1903,09,25,27,60,71,79) 5 WS (1909,25,60,71,79)	Pittsburgh (1887—)
St.Louis Cardinals............	1892	15 NL (1926,28,30-31,34,42-44,46,64, 67-68,82,85,87) 9 WS (1926,31,34,42,44,46,64,67,82)	St.Louis (1892—)
San Diego Padres............	1969	1 NL (1984)	San Diego (1969—)

San Francisco Giants	1883	16 NL (1905,11-13,17,21-24,33,36-37,51,
		    54,62,89)
		5 WS (1905,21-22,33,54)
			New York (1883–1957)
			  San Francisco (1958—)

American League

	1st Year	Pennants & World Series	Franchise Stops

Baltimore Orioles	1901	7 AL (1944,66,69-71,79,83)
		3 WS (1966,70,83)
			Milwaukee (1901)
			  St.Louis (1902-53)
			  Baltimore (1954—)

Boston Red Sox..............	1901	9 AL (1903,12,15-16,18,46,67,75,86) 5 WS (1903,12,15-16,18)	Boston (1901—)
California Angels	1961	None	Los Angeles (1961-65) Anaheim, CA (1966—)
Chicago White Sox...........	1901	4 AL (1906,17,19,59) 2 WS (1906,17)	Chicago (1901—)
Cleveland Indians............	1901	3 AL (1920,48,54) 2 WS (1920,48)	Cleveland (1901—)
Detroit Tigers................	1901	9 AL (1907-09,34-35,40,45,68,84) 4 WS (1935,45,68,84)	Detroit (1901—)
Kansas City Royals	1969	2 AL (1980,85) 1 WS (1985)	Kansas City (1969—)

	1st Year	Pennants & World Series	Franchise Stops
Milwaukee Brewers	1969	1 AL (1982)	Seattle (1969) / Milwaukee (1970—)
Minnesota Twins	1901	6 AL (1924-25,33,65,87,91) / 3 WS (1924,87,91)	Washington, DC (1901-60) / Bloomington, MN (1961-81) / Minneapolis (1982—)
New York Yankees	1901	33 AL (1921-23,26-28,32,36-39,41-43,47, / 49-53,55-58,60-64,76-78,81) / 22 WS (1923,27-28,32,36-39,41,43,47,49-53, / 56,58,61-62,77-78)	Baltimore (1901-02) / New York (1903—)
Oakland Athletics	1901	14 AL (1905,10-11,13-14,29-31,72-74,88-90) / 9 WS (1910-11,13,29-30,72-74,89)	Philadelphia (1901-54) / Kansas City (1955-67) / Oakland (1968—)
Seattle Mariners	1977	None	Seattle (1977—)
Texas Rangers	1961	None	Washington, DC (1961-71) / Arlington, TX (1972—)
Toronto Blue Jays	1977	1 AL (1992) / 1 WS (1992)	Toronto (1977—)

The Growth of Major League Baseball

The National League (founded in 1876) and the American League (founded in 1901) were both eight-team circuits at the turn of the century and remained that way until expansion finally came to Major League Baseball in the 1960s. The AL added two teams in 1961 and the NL did the same a year later. Both leagues went to 12 teams and split into two divisions in 1969. The AL then grew by two more teams in 1977, but the NL didn't follow suit until adding its 13th and 14th clubs in 1993.

Expansion Timetable (Since 1901)

1961—Los Angeles Angels (now California) and Washington Senators (now Texas Rangers) join AL; **1962**—Houston Colt .45s (now Astros) and New York Mets join NL; **1969**—Kansas City Royals and Seattle Pilots (now Milwaukee Brewers) join AL, while Montreal Expos and San Diego Padres join NL; **1977**—Seattle Mariners and Toronto Blue Jays join AL; **1993**—Colorado Rockies and Florida Marlins join NL.

City and Nickname Changes

American League

1902—Milwaukee Brewers move to St. Louis and become Browns; **1903**—Baltimore Orioles move to New York and become Highlanders; **1913**—NY Highlanders renamed Yankees; **1954**—St. Louis Browns move to Baltimore and become Orioles; **1955**—Philadelphia Athletics move to Kansas City; **1961**—Washington Senators move to Bloomington, Minn., and become Minnesota Twins; **1965**—LA Angels renamed California Angels; **1966**—California Angels move to Anaheim; **1968**—KC Athletics move to Oakland and become A's; **1970**—Seattle Pilots move to Milwaukee and become Brewers; **1972**—Washington Senators move to Arlington, Texas, and become Rangers; **1982**—Minnesota Twins move to Minneapolis; **1987**—Oakland A's renamed Athletics.

Other nicknames: Boston (Pilgrims, Puritans, Plymouth Rocks and Somersets through 1906); **Cleveland** (Bronchos, Blues, Naps and Molly McGuires through 1914); **Washington** (Senators through 1904, then Nationals from 1905-44, then Senators again from 1945-60).

National League

1953—Boston Braves move to Milwaukee; **1958**—Brooklyn Dodgers move to Los Angeles and New York Giants move to San Francisco; **1965**—Houston Colt .45s renamed Astros; **1966**—Milwaukee Braves move to Atlanta.

Other nicknames: Boston (Beaneaters and Doves through 1908, and Bees from 1936-40); **Brooklyn** (Superbas through 1926, then Robins from 1927-31; then Dodgers from 1932-57); **Cincinnati** (Red Legs from 1944-45, then Redlegs from 1954-60, then Reds since 1961); **Philadelphia** (Blue Jays from 1943-44).

Champions of Leagues That No Longer Exist

A Special Baseball Records Committee appointed by the commissioner found in 1968 that four extinct leagues qualified for major league status—the American Association (1882-91), the Union Association (1884), the Players' League (1890) and the Federal League (1914-15). The first years of the American League (1900) and Federal League (1913) were not recognized.

American Association

Year	Champion	Manager	Year	Champion	Manager	Year	Champion	Manager
1882	Cincinnati	Pop Snyder	1886	St.Louis	Charlie Comiskey	1889	Brooklyn	Bill McGunnigle
1883	Philadelphia	Lew Simmons	1887	St.Louis	Charlie Comiskey	1890	Louisville	Jack Chapman
1884	New York	Jim Mutrie	1888	St.Louis	Charlie Comiskey	1891	Boston	Arthur Irwin
1885	St.Louis	Charlie Comiskey						

Union Association			Players' League			Federal League		
Year	Champion	Manager	Year	Champion	Manager	Year	Champion	Manager
1884	St.Louis	Henry Lucas	1890	Boston	King Kelly	1914	Indianapolis	Bill Phillips
						1915	Chicago	Joe Tinker

Annual Batting Leaders (since 1900)
Batting Average
National League

Multiple winners: Honus Wagner (8); Rogers Hornsby and Stan Musial (7); Roberto Clemente, Tony Gwynn and Bill Madlock (4); Pete Rose and Paul Waner (3); Hank Aaron, Richie Ashburn, Jake Daubert, Tommy Davis, Ernie Lombardi, Willie McGee, Lefty O'Doul, Dave Parker and Edd Roush (2).

Year		Avg	Year		Avg	Year		Avg
1900	Honus Wagner, Pit.	.381	1932	Lefty O'Doul, Bklyn	.368	1963	Tommy Davis, LA.	.326
1901	Jesse Burkett, St.L.	.382	1933	Chuck Klein, Phi.	.368	1964	Roberto Clemente, Pit	.339
1902	Ginger Beaumont, Pit	.357	1934	Paul Waner, Pit.	.362	1965	Roberto Clemente, Pit	.329
1903	Honus Wagner, Pit.	.355	1935	Arkie Vaughan, Pit.	.385	1966	Matty Alou, Pit	.342
1904	Honus Wagner, Pit.	.349	1936	Paul Waner, Pit.	.373	1967	Roberto Clemente, Pit	.357
1905	Cy Seymour, Cin	.377	1937	Joe Medwick, St.L.	.374	1968	Pete Rose, Cin	.335
1906	Honus Wagner, Pit.	.339	1938	Ernie Lombardi, Cin	.342	1969	Pete Rose, Cin	.348
1907	Honus Wagner, Pit.	.350	1939	Johnny Mize, St.L	.349			
1908	Honus Wagner, Pit.	.354				1970	Rico Carty, Atl.	.366
1909	Honus Wagner, Pit.	.339	1940	Debs Garms, Pit.	.355	1971	Joe Torre, St.L	.363
			1941	Pete Reiser, Bklyn	.343	1972	Billy Williams, Chi	.333
1910	Sherry Magee, Phi	.331	1942	Ernie Lombardi, Bos	.330	1973	Pete Rose, Cin	.338
1911	Honus Wagner, Pit.	.334	1943	Stan Musial, St.L.	.357	1974	Ralph Garr, Atl.	.353
1912	Heinie Zimmerman, Chi	.372	1944	Dixie Walker, Bklyn	.357	1975	Bill Madlock, Chi	.354
1913	Jake Daubert, Bklyn.	.350	1945	Phil Cavarretta, Chi	.355	1976	Bill Madlock, Chi	.339
1914	Jake Daubert, Bklyn.	.329	1946	Stan Musial, St.L.	.365	1977	Dave Parker, Pit	.338
1915	Larry Doyle, NY	.320	1947	Harry Walker, St.L-Phi	.363	1978	Dave Parker, Pit	.334
1916	Hal Chase, Cin	.339	1948	Stan Musial, St.L.	.376	1979	Keith Hernandez, St.L	.344
1917	Edd Roush, Cin	.341	1949	Jackie Robinson, Bklyn	.342			
1918	Zack Wheat, Bklyn.	.335				1980	Bill Buckner, Chi.	.324
1919	Edd Roush, Cin	.321	1950	Stan Musial, St.L.	.346	1981	Bill Madlock, Pit	.341
			1951	Stan Musial, St.L.	.355	1982	Al Oliver, Mon	.331
1920	Rogers Hornsby, St.L	.370	1952	Stan Musial, St.L.	.336	1983	Bill Madlock, Pit	.323
1921	Rogers Hornsby, St.L.	.397	1953	Carl Furillo, Bklyn	.344	1984	Tony Gwynn, SD	.351
1922	Rogers Hornsby, St.L.	.401	1954	Willie Mays, NY	.345	1985	Willie McGee, Mon	.353
1923	Rogers Hornsby, St.L.	.384	1955	Richie Ashburn, Phi	.338	1986	Tim Raines, Mon	.334
1924	Rogers Hornsby, St.L.	.424	1956	Hank Aaron, Mil	.328	1987	Tony Gwynn, SD	.370
1925	Rogers Hornsby, St.L.	.403	1957	Stan Musial, St.L.	.351	1988	Tony Gwynn, SD	.313
1926	Bubbles Hargrave, Cin	.353	1958	Richie Ashburn, Phi	.350	1989	Tony Gwynn, SD	.336
1927	Paul Waner, Pit.	.380	1959	Hank Aaron, Mil	.355			
1928	Rogers Hornsby, Bos	.387				1990	Willie McGee, St.L.	.335
1929	Lefty O'Doul, Phi	.398	1960	Dick Groat, Pit	.325	1991	Terry Pendleton, Atl	.319
			1961	Roberto Clemente, Pit	.351	1992	Gary Sheffield, SD	.330
1930	Bill Terry, NY	.401	1962	Tommy Davis, LA.	.346			
1931	Chick Hafey, St.L	.349						

American League

Multiple winners: Ty Cobb (12); Rod Carew (7); Ted Williams (6); Wade Boggs (5); Harry Heilmann (4); George Brett, Nap Lajoie, Tony Oliva and Carl Yastrzemski (3); Luke Appling, Joe DiMaggio, Ferris Fain, Jimmie Foxx, Pete Runnels, Al Simmons, George Sisler and Mickey Vernon (2).

Year		Avg	Year		Avg	Year		Avg
1901	Nap Lajoie, Phi	.422	1923	Harry Heilmann, Det	.403	1945	Snuffy Stirnweiss, NY	.309
1902	Ed Delahanty, Wash	.376	1924	Babe Ruth, NY	.378	1946	Mickey Vernon, Wash	.353
1903	Nap Lajoie, Cle	.355	1925	Harry Heilmann, Det	.393	1947	Ted Williams, Bos.	.343
1904	Nap Lajoie, Cle	.381	1926	Heine Manush, Det	.378	1948	Ted Williams, Bos.	.369
1905	Elmer Flick, Cle	.306	1927	Harry Heilmann, Det	.398	1949	George Kell, Det	.343
1906	George Stone, St.L.	.358	1928	Goose Goslin, Wash	.379			
1907	Ty Cobb, Det	.350	1929	Lew Fonseca, Cle	.369	1950	Billy Goodman, Bos	.354
1908	Ty Cobb, Det	.324				1951	Ferris Fain, Phi	.344
1909	Ty Cobb, Det	.377	1930	Al Simmons, Phi	.381	1952	Ferris Fain, Phi	.327
			1931	Al Simmons, Phi.	.390	1953	Mickey Vernon, Wash	.337
1910	Ty Cobb, Det	.385	1932	Dale Alexander, Det-Bos	.367	1954	Bobby Avila, Clev.	.341
1911	Ty Cobb, Det	.420	1933	Jimmie Foxx, Phi.	.356	1955	Al Kaline, Det	.340
1912	Ty Cobb, Det	.410	1934	Lou Gehrig, NY	.363	1956	Mickey Mantle, NY.	.353
1913	Ty Cobb, Det	.390	1935	Buddy Myer, Wash.	.349	1957	Ted Williams, Bos.	.388
1914	Ty Cobb, Det	.368	1936	Luke Appling, Chi	.388	1958	Ted Williams, Bos.	.328
1915	Ty Cobb, Det	.369	1937	Charlie Gehringer, Det	.371	1959	Harvey Kuenn, Det.	.353
1916	Tris Speaker, Cle	.386	1938	Jimmie Foxx, Bos	.349			
1917	Ty Cobb, Det	.383	1939	Joe DiMaggio, NY	.381	1960	Pete Runnels, Bos.	.320
1918	Ty Cobb, Det	.382				1961	Norm Cash, Det	.361
1919	Ty Cobb, Det	.384	1940	Joe DiMaggio, NY	.352	1962	Pete Runnels, Bos.	.326
			1941	Ted Williams, Bos.	.406	1963	Carl Yastrzemski, Bos	.321
1920	George Sisler, St.L.	.407	1942	Ted Williams, Bos.	.356	1964	Tony Oliva, Min	.323
1921	Harry Heilmann, Det	.394	1943	Luke Appling, Chi	.328	1965	Tony Oliva, Min	.321
1922	George Sisler, St.L.	.420	1944	Lou Boudreau, Clev	.327	1966	Frank Robinson, Bal.	.316

Batting Average (Cont.)

Year		Avg	Year		Avg	Year		Avg
1967	Carl Yastrzemski, Bos	.326	1976	George Brett, KC	.333	1985	Wade Boggs, Bos.	.368
1968	Carl Yastrzemski, Bos	.301	1977	Rod Carew, Min	.388	1986	Wade Boggs, Bos.	.357
1969	Rod Carew, Min	.332	1978	Rod Carew, Min	.333	1987	Wade Boggs, Bos.	.363
1970	Alex Johnson, Cal	.329	1979	Fred Lynn, Bos	.333	1988	Wade Boggs, Bos.	.366
1971	Tony Oliva, Min	.337	1980	George Brett, KC	.390	1989	Kirby Puckett, Min	.339
1972	Rod Carew, Min	.318	1981	Carney Lansford, Bos	.336	1990	George Brett, KC	.329
1973	Rod Carew, Min	.350	1982	Willie Wilson, KC	.332	1991	Julio Franco, Tex	.341
1974	Rod Carew, Min	.364	1983	Wade Boggs, Bos.	.361	1992	Edgar Martinez, Sea	.343
1975	Rod Carew, Min	.359	1984	Don Mattingly, NY	.343			

Home Runs
National League

Multiple winners: Mike Schmidt (8); Ralph Kiner (7); Gavvy Cravath and Mel Ott (6); Hank Aaron, Chuck Klein, Willie Mays, Johnny Mize, Cy Williams and Hack Wilson (4); Willie McCovey (3); Ernie Banks, Johnny Bench, George Foster, Rogers Hornsby, Tim Jordan, Dave Kingman, Eddie Mathews, Dale Murphy, Bill Nicholson, Dave Robertson, Wildfire Schulte and Willie Stargell (2).

Year		Avg	Year		HR	Year		HR
1900	Herman Long, Bos	12	1932	Chuck Klein, Phi	38	1962	Willie Mays, SF	49
1901	Sam Crawford, Cin	16		& Mel Ott, NY	38	1963	Hank Aaron, Mil	44
1902	Tommy Leach, Pit	6	1933	Chuck Klein, Phi	28		& Willie McCovey, SF	44
1903	Jimmy Sheckard, Bklyn	9	1934	Rip Collins, St.L	35	1964	Willie Mays, SF	47
1904	Harry Lumley, Bklyn	9		& Mel Ott, NY	35	1965	Willie Mays, SF	52
1905	Fred Odwell, Cin	9	1935	Wally Berger, Bos	34	1966	Hank Aaron, Atl	44
1906	Tim Jordan, Bklyn	12	1936	Mel Ott, NY	33	1967	Hank Aaron, Atl	39
1907	Dave Brain, Bos	10	1937	Joe Medwick, St.L	31	1968	Willie McCovey, SF	36
1908	Tim Jordan, Bklyn	12		& Mel Ott, NY	31	1969	Willie McCovey, SF	45
1909	Red Murray, NY	7	1938	Mel Ott, NY	36	1970	Johnny Bench, Cin	45
1910	Fred Beck, Bos	10	1939	Johnny Mize, St.L	28	1971	Willie Stargell, Pit.	48
	& Wildfire Schulte, Chi	10	1940	Johnny Mize, St.L	43	1972	Johnny Bench, Cin	40
1911	Wildfire Schulte, Chi	21	1941	Dolf Camilli, Bklyn	34	1973	Willie Stargell, Pit.	44
1912	Heinie Zimmerman, Chi.	14	1942	Mel Ott, NY	30	1974	Mike Schmidt, Phi	36
1913	Gavvy Cravath, Phi	19	1943	Bill Nicholson, Chi.	29	1975	Mike Schmidt, Phi	38
1914	Gavvy Cravath, Phi	19	1944	Bill Nicholson, Chi.	33	1976	Mike Schmidt, Phi	38
1915	Gavvy Cravath, Phi	24	1945	Tommy Holmes, Bos	28	1977	George Foster, Cin	52
1916	Cy Williams, Chi	12	1946	Ralph Kiner, Pit	23	1978	George Foster, Cin	40
	& Dave Robertson, NY	12	1947	Ralph Kiner, Pit	51	1979	Dave Kingman, Chi	48
1917	Gavvy Cravath, Phi	12		& Johnny Mize, NY	51	1980	Mike Schmidt, Phi	48
	& Dave Robertson, NY	12	1948	Ralph Kiner, Pit	40	1981	Mike Schmidt, Phi	31
1918	Gavvy Cravath, Phi.	8		& Johnny Mize, NY	40	1982	Dave Kingman, NY	37
1919	Gavvy Cravath, Phi	12	1949	Ralph Kiner, Pit	54	1983	Mike Schmidt, Phi	40
1920	Cy Williams, Phi.	15	1950	Ralph Kiner, Pit	47	1984	Dale Murphy, Atl	36
1921	George Kelly, NY	23	1951	Ralph Kiner, Pit	42		& Mike Schmidt, Phi	36
1922	Rogers Hornsby, St.L.	42	1952	Ralph Kiner, Pit	37	1985	Dale Murphy, Atl	37
1923	Cy Williams, Phi.	41		& Hank Sauer, Chi	37	1986	Mike Schmidt, Phi	37
1924	Jack Fournier, Bklyn	27	1953	Eddie Mathews, Mil	47	1987	Andre Dawson, Chi.	49
1925	Rogers Hornsby, St.L.	39	1954	Ted Kluszewski, Cin.	49	1988	Darryl Strawberry, NY	39
1926	Hack Wilson, Chi	21	1955	Willie Mays, NY	51	1989	Kevin Mitchell, SF.	47
1927	Cy Williams, Phi.	30	1956	Duke Snider, Bklyn	43	1990	Ryne Sandberg, Chi	40
	& Hack Wilson, Chi.	30	1957	Hank Aaron, Mil	44	1991	Howard Johnson, Ny	38
1928	Jim Bottomley, St.L	31	1958	Ernie Banks, Chi	47	1992	Fred McGriff, SD	35
	& Hack Wilson, Chi.	31	1959	Eddie Mathews, Mil	46			
1929	Chuck Klein, Phi	43	1960	Ernie Banks, Chi	41			
1930	Hack Wilson, Chi	56	1961	Orlando Cepeda, SF	46			
1931	Chuck Klein, Phi	31						

American League

Multiple winners: Babe Ruth (12); Harmon Killebrew (6); Home Run Baker, Harry Davis, Jimmie Foxx, Hank Greenberg, Reggie Jackson, Mickey Mantle and Ted Williams (4); Lou Gehrig and Jim Rice (3); Dick Allen, Tony Armas, Jose Canseco, Joe DiMaggio, Larry Doby, Cecil Fielder, Frank Howard, Wally Pipp, Al Rosen and Gorman Thomas (2).

Year		HR	Year		HR	Year		HR
1901	Nap Lajoie, Phi	14	1906	Harry Davis, Phi.	12	1911	Home Run Baker, Phi	11
1902	Socks Seybold, Phi.	16	1907	Harry Davis, Phi.	8	1912	Home Run Baker, Phi	10
1903	Buck Freeman, Bos	13	1908	Sam Crawford, Det	7		& Tris Speaker, Bos.	10
1904	Harry Davis, Phi.	10	1909	Ty Cobb, Det	9	1913	Home Run Baker, Phi	12
1905	Harry Davis, Phi.	8	1910	Jake Stahl, Bos	10	1914	Home Run Baker, Phi	9

Annual Batting Leaders (Cont.)
Home Runs
American League

Year		HR	Year		HR	Year		HR
1915	Braggo Roth, Chi-Cle	7	1943	Rudy York, Det.	34	1972	Dick Allen, Chi.	37
1916	Wally Pipp, NY	12	1944	Nick Etten, NY	22	1973	Reggie Jackson, Oak	32
1917	Wally Pipp, NY	9	1945	Vern Stephens, St.L	24	1974	Dick Allen, Chi.	32
1918	Babe Ruth, Bos	11	1946	Hank Greenberg, Det.	44	1975	Reggie Jackson, Oak	36
	& Tilly Walker, Phi	11	1947	Ted Williams, Bos	32		& George Scott, Mil.	36
1919	Babe Ruth, Bos	29	1948	Joe DiMaggio, NY	39	1976	Graig Nettles, NY	32
			1949	Ted Williams, Bos	43	1977	Jim Rice, Bos	39
1920	Babe Ruth, NY	54				1978	Jim Rice, Bos	46
1921	Babe Ruth, NY	59	1950	Al Rosen, Cle.	37	1979	Gorman Thomas, Mil	45
1922	Ken Williams, St.L	39	1951	Gus Zernial, Chi-Phi	33			
1923	Babe Ruth, NY	41	1952	Larry Doby, Cle	32	1980	Reggie Jackson, NY	41
1924	Babe Ruth, NY	46	1953	Al Rosen, Cle	43		& Ben Ogilvie, Mil.	41
1925	Bob Meusel, NY.	33	1954	Larry Doby, Cle	32	1981	Tony Armas, Oak	22
1926	Babe Ruth, NY	47	1955	Mickey Mantle, NY	37		Dwight Evans, Bos.	22
1927	Babe Ruth, NY	60	1956	Mickey Mantle, NY	52		Bobby Grich, Cal.	22
1928	Babe Ruth, NY	54	1957	Roy Sievers, Wash.	42		& Eddie Murray, Bal	22
1929	Babe Ruth, NY	46	1958	Mickey Mantle, NY	42	1982	Reggie Jackson, Cal	39
			1959	Rocky Colavito, Cle.	42		& Gorman Thomas, Mil	39
1930	Babe Ruth, NY	49		& Harmon Killebrew, Wash.	42	1983	Jim Rice, Bos	39
1931	Lou Gehrig, NY	46				1984	Tony Armas, Bos	43
	& Babe Ruth, NY	46	1960	Mickey Mantle, NY	40	1985	Darrell Evans, Det	40
1932	Jimmie Foxx, Phi	58	1961	Roger Maris, NY	61	1986	Jesse Barfield, Tor	40
1933	Jimmie Foxx, Phi	48	1962	Harmon Killebrew, Min.	48	1987	Mark McGwire, Oak.	49
1934	Lou Gehrig, NY	49	1963	Harmon Killebrew, Min.	45	1988	Jose Canseco, Oak.	42
1935	Jimmie Foxx, Phi	36	1964	Harmon Killebrew, Min.	49	1989	Fred McGriff, Tor.	36
	& Hank Greenberg, Det.	36	1965	Tony Conigliaro, Bos	32			
1936	Lou Gehrig, NY	49	1966	Frank Robinson, Bal	49	1990	Cecil Fielder, Det.	51
1937	Joe DiMaggio, NY.	46	1967	Harmon Killebrew, Min.	44	1991	Jose Canseco, Oak.	44
1938	Hank Greenberg, Det.	58		& Carl Yastrzemski, Bos	44		& Cecil Fielder, Det.	44
1939	Jimmie Foxx, Bos.	35	1968	Frank Howard, Wash.	44	1992	Juan Gonzalez, Tex.	43
1940	Hank Greenberg, Det.	41	1969	Harmon Killebrew, Min.	49			
1941	Ted Williams, Bos	37	1970	Frank Howard, Wash.	44			
1942	Ted Williams, Bos	36	1971	Bill Melton, Chi	33			

Runs Batted In
National League

Multiple winners: Hank Aaron, Rogers Hornsby, Sherry Magee, Mike Schmidt and Honus Wagner (4); Johnny Bench, George Foster, Joe Medwick, Johnny Mize and Heinie Zimmerman (3); Ernie Banks, Jim Bottomley, Orlando Cepeda, Gavvy Cravath, George Kelly, Chuck Klein, Willie McCovey, Dale Murphy, Stan Musial, Bill Nicholson and Hack Wilson (2).

Year		RBI	Year		RBI	Year		RBI
1900	Elmer Flick, Phi	110	1922	Rogers Hornsby, St.L.	152	1946	Enos Slaughter, St.L	130
1901	Honus Wagner, Pit	126	1923	Irish Meusel, NY	125	1947	Johnny Mize, NY.	138
1902	Honus Wagner, Pit	91	1924	George Kelly, NY	136	1948	Stan Musial, St.L	131
1903	Sam Mertes, NY	104	1925	Rogers Hornsby, St.L.	143	1949	Ralph Kiner, Pit	127
1904	Bill Dahlen, NY	80	1926	Jim Bottomley, St.L.	120			
1905	Cy Seymour, Cin.	121	1927	Paul Waner, Pit	131	1950	Del Ennis, Phi.	126
1906	Jim Nealon, Pit	83	1928	Jim Bottomley, St.L.	136	1951	Monty Irvin, NY	121
	& Harry Steinfeldt, Chi	83	1929	Hack Wilson, Chi	159	1952	Hank Sauer, Chi	121
1907	Sherry Magee, Phi.	85				1953	Roy Campanella, Bkln	142
1908	Honus Wagner, Pit	109	1930	Hack Wilson, Chi	190	1954	Ted Kluszewski, Cin	141
1909	Honus Wagner, Pit	100	1931	Chuck Klein, Phi	121	1955	Duke Snider, Bkln	136
			1932	Don Hurst, Phi.	143	1956	Stan Musial, St.L	109
1910	Sherry Magee, Phi.	123	1933	Chuck Klein, Phi.	120	1957	Hank Aaron, Mil	132
1911	Wildfire Schulte, Chi	121	1934	Mel Ott, NY.	135	1958	Ernie Banks, Chi	129
1912	Heinie Zimmerman, Chi.	103	1935	Wally Berger, Bos	130	1959	Ernie Banks, Chi	143
1913	Gavvy Cravath, Phi.	128	1936	Joe Medwick, St.L	138			
1914	Sherry Magee, Phi.	103	1937	Joe Medwick, St.L	154	1960	Hank Aaron, Mil	126
1915	Gavvy Cravath, Phi.	115	1938	Joe Medwick, St.L	122	1961	Orlando Cepeda, SF	142
1916	Heinie Zimmerman, Chi-NY	83	1939	Frank McCormick, Cin	128	1962	Tommy Davis, LA	153
						1963	Hank Aaron, Mil	130
1917	Heinie Zimmerman, NY	102	1940	Johnny Mize, St.L	137	1964	Ken Boyer, St.L	119
1918	Sherry Magee, Cin	76	1941	Dolph Camilli, Bklyn	120	1965	Deron Johnson, Cin	130
1919	Hy Myers, Bklyn	73	1942	Johnny Mize, NY.	110	1966	Hank Aaron, Atl	127
			1943	Bill Nicholson, Chi	128	1967	Orlando Cepeda, St.L	111
1920	Rogers Hornsby, St.L.	94	1944	Bill Nicholson, Chi	122	1968	Willie McCovey, SF	105
	& George Kelly, NY.	94	1945	Dixie Walker, Bklyn	124	1969	Willie McCovey, SF	126
1921	Rogers Hornsby, St.L.	126						

Year		RBI	Year		RBI	Year		RBI
1970	Johnny Bench, Cin	148	1979	Dave Winfield, SD.	118	1985	Dave Parker, Cin.	125
1971	Joe Torre, St.L.	137	1980	Mike Schmidt, Phi	121	1986	Mike Schmidt, Phi	119
1972	Johnny Bench, Cin	125	1981	Mike Schmidt, Phi	91	1987	Andre Dawson, Chi	137
1973	Willie Stargell, Pit.	119	1982	Dale Murphy, Atl.	109	1988	Will Clark, SF.	109
1974	Johnny Bench, Cin	129		& Al Oliver, Mon.	109	1989	Kevin Mitchell, SF	125
1975	Greg Luzinski, Phi	120	1983	Dale Murphy, Atl.	121			
1976	George Foster, Cin	121	1984	Gary Carter, Mon	106	1990	Matt Williams, SF	122
1977	George Foster, Cin	149		& Mike Schmidt, Phi	106	1991	Howard Johnson, NY	117
1978	George Foster, Cin	120				1992	Darren Daulton, Phi	109

American League

Multiple winners: Babe Ruth (6); Lou Gehrig (5); Ty Cobb, Hank Greenberg and Ted Williams (4); Sam Crawford, Cecil Fielder, Jimmie Foxx, Jackie Jensen, Harmon Killebrew, Vern Stephens and Bobby Veach (3); Home Run Baker, Cecil Cooper, Harry Davis, Joe DiMaggio, Buck Freeman, Nap Lajoie, Roger Maris, Jim Rice, Al Rosen, and Bobby Veach (2).

Year		RBI	Year		RBI	Year		RBI
1901	Nap Lajoie, Phi	125	1933	Jimmie Foxx, Phi	163	1962	Harmon Killebrew, Min	126
1902	Buck Freeman, Bos	121	1934	Lou Gehrig, NY	165	1963	Dick Stuart, Bos	118
1903	Buck Freeman, Bos	104	1935	Hank Greenberg, Det.	170	1964	Brooks Robinson, Bal	118
1904	Nap Lajoie, Cle.	102	1936	Hal Trosky, Cle	162	1965	Rocky Colavito, Cle.	108
1905	Harry Davis, Phi.	83	1937	Hank Greenberg, Det.	183	1966	Frank Robinson, Bal	122
1906	Harry Davis, Phi.	96	1938	Jimmie Foxx, Bos.	175	1967	Carl Yastrzemski, Bos	121
1907	Ty Cobb, Det.	116	1939	Ted Williams, Bos	145	1968	Ken Harrelson, Bos.	109
1908	Ty Cobb, Det.	108				1969	Harmon Killebrew, Min	140
1909	Ty Cobb, Det.	107	1940	Hank Greenberg, Det.	150			
			1941	Joe DiMaggio, NY	125	1970	Frank Howard, Wash	126
1910	Sam Crawford, Det.	120	1942	Ted Williams, Bos	137	1971	Harmon Killebrew, Min	119
1911	Ty Cobb, Det.	144	1943	Rudy York, Det	118	1972	Dick Allen, Chi	113
1912	Home Run Baker, Phi	133	1944	Vern Stephens, St.L	109	1973	Reggie Jackson, Oak	117
1913	Home Run Baker, Phi	126	1945	Nick Etten, NY	111	1974	Jeff Burroughs, Tex	118
1914	Sam Crawford, Det.	104	1946	Hank Greenberg, Det.	127	1975	George Scott, Mil	109
1915	Sam Crawford, Det.	112	1947	Ted Williams, Bos	114	1976	Lee May, Bal	109
	& Bobby Veach, Det	112	1948	Joe DiMaggio, NY	155	1977	Larry Hisle, Min	119
1916	Del Pratt, St.L.	103	1949	Ted Williams, Bos	159	1978	Jim Rice, Bos	139
1917	Bobby Veach, Det	103		& Vern Stephens, Bos	159	1979	Don Baylor, Cal	139
1918	Bobby Veach, Det	78						
1919	Babe Ruth, Bos	114	1950	Walt Dropo, Bos	144	1980	Cecil Cooper, Mil	122
				& Vern Stephens, Bos	144	1981	Eddie Murray, Bal	78
1920	Babe Ruth, NY	137	1951	Gus Zernial, Chi-Phi	129	1982	Hal McRae, KC	133
1921	Babe Ruth, NY	171	1952	Al Rosen, Cle.	105	1983	Cecil Cooper, Mil	126
1922	Ken Williams, St.L	155	1953	Al Rosen, Cle.	145		& Jim Rice, Bos	126
1923	Babe Ruth, NY	131	1954	Larry Doby, Cle.	126	1984	Tony Armas, Bos	123
1924	Goose Goslin, Wash	129	1955	Ray Boone, Det	116	1985	Don Mattingly, NY	145
1925	Bob Meusel, NY	138		& Jackie Jensen, Bos.	116	1986	Joe Carter, Cle	121
1926	Babe Ruth, NY	145	1956	Mickey Mantle, NY	130	1987	George Bell, Tor	134
1927	Lou Gehrig, NY	175	1957	Roy Sievers, Wash.	114	1988	Jose Canseco, Oak	124
1928	Lou Gehrig, NY	142	1958	Jackie Jensen, Bos	122	1989	Ruben Sierra, Tex	119
	& Babe Ruth, NY	142	1959	Jackie Jensen, Bos	112			
1929	Al Simmons, Phi	157				1990	Cecil Fielder, Det.	132
1930	Lou Gehrig, NY	174	1960	Roger Maris, NY	112	1991	Cecil Fielder, Det.	133
1931	Lou Gehrig, NY	184	1961	Roger Maris, NY	142	1992	Cecil Fielder, Det.	124
1932	Jimmie Foxx, Phi	169						

30 Homers & 30 Stolen Bases in One Season

National League

	Year	Gm	HR	SB
Willie Mays, NY Giants	1956	152	36	40
Willie Mays, NY Giants	1957	152	35	38
Hank Aaron, Milwaukee	1963	161	44	31
Bobby Bonds, San Francisco	1969	158	32	45
Bobby Bonds, San Francisco	1973	160	39	43
Dale Murphy, Atlanta	1983	162	36	30
Eric Davis, Cincinnati	1987	129	37	50
Howard Johnson, NY Mets	1987	157	36	32
Darryl Strawberry, NY Mets	1987	154	39	36
Howard Johnson, NY Mets	1989	153	36	41
Ron Gant, Atlanta	1990	152	32	33
Barry Bonds, Pittsburgh	1990	151	33	52
Ron Gant, Atlanta	1991	154	32	34
Howard Johnson, NY Mets	1991	156	38	30
Barry Bonds, Pittsburgh	1992	140	34	39

American League

	Year	Gm	HR	SB
Kenny Williams, St. Louis	1922	153	39	37
Tommy Harper, Milwaukee	1970	154	31	38
Bobby Bonds, New York	1975	145	32	30
Bobby Bonds, California	1977	158	37	41
Bobby Bonds, Chicago-Texas	1978	156	31	43
Joe Carter, Cleveland	1987	149	32	31
Jose Canseco, Oakland	1988	158	42	40

Annual Batting Leaders (Cont.)
Stolen Bases
National League

Multiple winners: Max Carey (10); Lou Brock (8); Vince Coleman and Maury Wills (6); Honus Wagner (5); Bob Brescher, Kiki Cuyler, Willie Mays and Tim Raines (4); Bill Bruton, Frankie Frisch and Pepper Martin (3); George Burns, Frank Chance, Augie Galan, Marquis Grissom, Stan Hack, Sam Jethroe, Davey Lopes, Omar Moreno, Pete Reiser and Jackie Robinson (2).

Year		SB	Year		SB	Year		SB
1900	Patsy Donovan, St.L	45	1932	Chuck Klein, Phi	20	1964	Maury Wills, LA	53
	& George Van Haltren, NY	45	1933	Pepper Martin, St.L	26	1965	Maury Wills, LA	94
1901	Honus Wagner, Pit	49	1934	Pepper Martin, St.L	23	1966	Lou Brock, St.L	74
1902	Honus Wagner, Pit	42	1935	Augie Galan, Chi	22	1967	Lou Brock, St.L	52
1903	Frank Chance, Chi	67	1936	Pepper Martin, St.L	23	1968	Lou Brock, St.L	62
	& Jimmy Sheckard, Bklyn	67	1937	Augie Galan, Chi	23	1969	Lou Brock, St.L	53
1904	Honus Wagner, Pit	53	1938	Stan Hack, Chi	16	1970	Bobby Tolan, Cin	57
1905	Art Devlin, NY	59	1939	Stan Hack, Chi	17	1971	Lou Brock, St.L	64
	& Billy Maloney, Chi	59		& Lee Handley, Pit	17	1972	Lou Brock, St.L	63
1906	Frank Chance, Chi	57	1940	Lonny Frey, Cin	22	1973	Lou Brock, St.L	70
1907	Honus Wagner, Pit	61	1941	Danny Murtaugh, Phi	18	1974	Lou Brock, St.L	118
1908	Honus Wagner, Pit	53	1942	Pete Reiser, Bklyn	20	1975	Davey Lopes, LA	77
1909	Bob Bescher, Cin	54	1943	Arky Vaughan, Bklyn	20	1976	Davey Lopes, LA	63
1910	Bob Bescher, Cin	70	1944	Johnny Barrett, Pit	28	1977	Frank Tavares, Pit	70
1911	Bob Bescher, Cin	81	1945	Red Schoendienst, St.L	26	1978	Omar Moreno, Pit	71
1912	Bob Bescher, Cin	67	1946	Pete Reiser, Bklyn	34	1979	Omar Moreno, Pit	77
1913	Max Carey, Pit	61	1947	Jackie Robinson, Bklyn	29	1980	Ron LeFlore, Mon	97
1914	George Burns, NY	62	1948	Richie Ashburn, Phi	32	1981	Tim Raines, Mon	71
1915	Max Carey, Pit	36	1949	Jackie Robinson, Bklyn	37	1982	Tim Raines, Mon	78
1916	Max Carey, Pit	63	1950	Sam Jethroe, Bos	35	1983	Tim Raines, Mon	90
1917	Max Carey, Pit	46	1951	Sam Jethroe, Bos	35	1984	Tim Raines, Mon	75
1918	Max Carey, Pit	58	1952	Pee Wee Reese, Bklyn	30	1985	Vince Coleman, St.L	110
1919	George Burns, NY	40	1953	Bill Bruton, Mil	26	1986	Vince Coleman, St.L	107
1920	Max Carey, Pit	52	1954	Bill Bruton, Mil	34	1987	Vince Coleman, St.L	109
1921	Frankie Frisch, NY	49	1955	Bill Bruton, Mil	25	1988	Vince Coleman, St.L	81
1922	Max Carey, Pit	51	1956	Willie Mays, NY	40	1989	Vince Coleman, St.L	66
1923	Max Carey, Pit	51	1957	Willie Mays, NY	38	1990	Vince Coleman, St.L	77
1924	Max Carey, Pit	49	1958	Willie Mays, SF	31	1991	Marquis Grissom, Mon	76
1925	Max Carey, Pit	46	1959	Willie Mays, SF	27	1992	Marquis Grissom, Mon	78
1926	Kiki Cuyler, Pit	35	1960	Maury Wills, LA	50			
1927	Frankie Frisch, St.L	48	1961	Maury Wills, LA	35			
1928	Kiki Cuyler, Chi	37	1962	Maury Wills, LA	104			
1929	Kiki Cuyler, Chi	43	1963	Maury Wills, LA	40			
1930	Kiki Cuyler, Chi	37						
1931	Frankie Frisch, St.L	28						

American League

Multiple winners: Rickey Henderson (11); Luis Aparicio (9); Bert Campaneris, George Case and Ty Cobb (6); Ben Chapman, Eddie Collins and George Sisler (4); Bob Dillinger, Minnie Minoso and Bill Werber (3); Elmer Flick, Tommy Harper, Clyde Milan, Johnny Mostil, Bill North and Snuffy Stirnweiss (2).

Year		SB	Year		SB	Year		SB
1901	Frank Isbell, Chi	52	1915	Ty Cobb, Det	96	1930	Marty McManus, Det	23
1902	Topsy Hartsel, Phi	47	1916	Ty Cobb, Det	68	1931	Ben Chapman, NY	61
1903	Harry Bay, Cle	45	1917	Ty Cobb, Det	55	1932	Ben Chapman, NY	38
1904	Elmer Flick, Cle	42	1918	George Sisler, St.L	45	1933	Ben Chapman, NY	27
1905	Danny Hoffman, Phi	46	1919	Eddie Collins, Chi	33	1934	Bill Werber, Bos	40
1906	John Anderson, Wash	39	1920	Sam Rice, Wash	63	1935	Bill Werber, Bos	29
	& Elmer Flick, Cle	39	1921	George Sisler, St.L	35	1936	Lyn Lary, St.L	37
1907	Ty Cobb, Det	49	1922	George Sisler, St.L	51	1937	Ben Chapman, Wash-Bos	35
1908	Patsy Dougherty, Chi	47	1923	Eddie Collins, Chi	47		& Bill Werber, Phi	35
1909	Ty Cobb, Det	76	1924	Eddie Collins, Chi	42	1938	Frank Crosetti, NY	27
1910	Eddie Collins, Phi	81	1925	Johnny Mostil, Chi	43	1939	George Case, Wash	51
1911	Ty Cobb, Det	83	1926	Johnny Mostil, Chi	35	1940	George Case, Wash	35
1912	Clyde Milan, Wash	88	1927	George Sisler, St.L	27	1941	George Case, Wash	33
1913	Clyde Milan, Wash	75	1928	Buddy Myer, Bos	30	1942	George Case, Wash	44
1914	Fritz Maisel, NY	74	1929	Charlie Gehringer, Det	28	1943	George Case, Wash	61

Year		SB	Year		SB	Year		SB
1944	Snuffy Stirnweiss, NY	55	1962	Luis Aparicio, Chi	31	1980	Rickey Henderson, Oak	100
1945	Snuffy Stirnweiss, NY	33	1963	Luis Aparicio, Bal	40	1981	Rickey Henderson, Oak	56
1946	George Case, Cle	28	1964	Luis Aparicio, Bal	57	1982	Rickey Henderson, Oak	130
1947	Bob Dillinger, St.L	34	1965	Bert Campaneris, KC	51	1983	Rickey Henderson, Oak	108
1948	Bob Dillinger, St.L	28	1966	Bert Campaneris, KC	52	1984	Rickey Henderson, Oak	66
1949	Bob Dillinger, St.L	20	1967	Bert Campaneris, KC	55	1985	Rickey Henderson, NY	80
			1968	Bert Campaneris, Oak	62	1986	Rickey Henderson, NY	87
1950	Dom DiMaggio, Bos	15	1969	Tommy Harper, Sea	73	1987	Harold Reynolds, Sea	60
1951	Minnie Minoso, Cle-Chi	31				1988	Rickey Henderson, NY	93
1952	Minnie Minoso, Chi	22	1970	Bert Campaneris, Oak	42	1989	R.Henderson, NY-Oak	77
1953	Minnie Minoso, Chi	25	1971	Amos Otis, KC	52			
1954	Jackie Jensen, Bos	22	1972	Bert Campaneris, Oak	52	1990	Rickey Henderson, Oak	65
1955	Jim Rivera, Chi	25	1973	Tommy Harper, Bos	54	1991	Rickey Henderson, Oak	58
1956	Luis Aparicio, Chi	21	1974	Bill North, Oak	54	1992	Kenny Lofton, Cle	62
1957	Luis Aparicio, Chi	28	1975	Mickey Rivers, CA	70			
1958	Luis Aparicio, Chi	29	1976	Bill North, Oak	75			
1959	Luis Aparicio, Chi	56	1977	Freddie Patek, KC	53			
			1978	Ron LeFlore, Det	68			
1960	Luis Aparicio, Chi	51	1979	Willie Wilson, KC	83			
1961	Luis Aparicio, Chi	53						

Batting Triple Crown Winners

Players who led either league in Batting Average, Home Runs and Runs Batted In over a single season.

National League

	Year	Avg	HR	RBI
Paul Hines, Providence	1878	.358	4	50
Hugh Duffy, Boston	1894	.438	18	145
Heinie Zimmerman, Chicago	1912	.372	14	103
Rogers Hornsby, St.Louis	1922	.401	42	152
Rogers Hornsby, St.Louis	1925	.403	39	143
Chuck Klein, Philadelphia	1933	.368	28	120
Joe Medwick, St.Louis	1937	.374	31*	154

*Tied for league lead in HRs with Mel Ott, NY.

American League

	Year	Avg	HR	RBI
Nap Lajoie, Philadelphia	1901	.422	14	125
Ty Cobb, Detroit	1909	.377	9	115
Jimmie Foxx, Philadelphia	1933	.356	48	163
Lou Gehrig, New York	1934	.363	49	165
Ted Williams, Boston	1942	.356	36	137
Ted Williams, Boston	1947	.343	32	114
Mickey Mantle, New York	1956	.353	52	130
Frank Robinson, Baltimore	1966	.316	49	122
Carl Yastrzemski, Boston	1967	.326	44*	121

*Tied for league lead in HRs with Harmon Killebrew, Min.

Consecutive Game Streaks

Regular season games through 1992.

Games Played

Active streak in **bold** type.

Gm		Dates of Streak	
2130	Lou Gehrig, NY	6/1/25	to 4/30/39
1735	**Cal Ripken Jr**, Bal	5/30/82	to —
1307	Everett Scott, Bos-NY	6/20/16	to 5/5/25
1207	Steve Garvey, LA-SD	9/3/75	to 7/29/83
1117	Billy Williams, Cubs	9/22/63	to 9/2/70
1103	Joe Sewell, Cle	9/13/22	to 4/30/30
895	Stan Musial, St.L	4/15/52	to 8/23/57
829	Eddie Yost, Wash	4/30/49	to 5/11/55
822	Gus Suhr, Pit	9/11/31	to 6/4/37
798	Nellie Fox, Chisox	8/8/55	to 9/3/60
745	Pete Rose, Cin-Phi	9/2/78	to 8/23/83
740	Dale Murphy, Atl	9/26/81	to 7/8/86
730	Richie Ashburn, Phi	6/7/50	to 4/13/55
717	Ernie Banks, Cubs	8/28/56	to 6/22/61
678	Pete Rose, Cin	9/28/73	to 5/7/78

Others

Gm		Gm	
673	Earl Averill	565	Aaron Ward
652	Frank McCormick	540	Candy LaChance
648	Sandy Alomar	535	John Freeman
618	Eddie Brown	533	Fred Luderus
585	Roy McMillan	511	Clyde Milan
577	George Pinckley	511	Charlie Gehringer
574	Steve Brodie	508	Vada Pinson

Hitting

	Gm	Year
Joe DiMaggio, New York (AL)	56	1941
Willie Keeler, Baltimore (NL)	44	1897
Pete Rose, Cincinnati (NL)	44	1978
Bill Dahlen, Chicago (NL)	42	1894
George Sisler, St.Louis (AL)	41	1922
Ty Cobb, Detroit (AL)	40	1911
Paul Molitor, Milwaukee (AL)	39	1987
Tommy Holmes, Boston (NL)	37	1945
Billy Hamilton, Philadelphia (NL)	36	1894
Fred Clarke, Louisville (NL)	35	1895
Ty Cobb, Detroit (AL)	35	1917
George Sisler, St.Louis (AL)	34	1925
John Stone, Detroit (AL)	34	1930
George McQuinn, St.Louis (AL)	34	1938
Dom DiMaggio, Boston (AL)	34	1949
Benito Santiago, San Diego (NL)	34	1987
George Davis, New York (NL)	33	1893
Hal Chase, New York (AL)	33	1907
Rogers Hornsby, St. Louis (NL)	33	1922
Heinie Manush, Washington (AL)	33	1933
Ed Delahanty, Philadelphia (NL)	31	1899
Nap Lajoie, Cleveland (AL)	31	1906
Sam Rice, Washington (AL)	31	1924
Willie Davis, Los Angeles (NL)	31	1969
Rico Carty, Atlanta (NL)	31	1970
Ken Landreaux, Minnesota (AL)	31	1980

Annual Pitching Leaders (since 1900)
Winning Percentage
At least 15 wins, except in strike year of 1981 when minimum was 10.
National League
Multiple winners: Ed Reulbach and Tom Seaver (3); Larry Benton, Harry Brecheen, Jack Chesbro, Paul Derringer, Freddie Fitzsimmons, Don Gullet, Claude Hendrix, Carl Hubbell, Sandy Koufax, Bill Lee, Christy Mathewson, Don Newcombe and Preacher Roe (2).

Year		W-L	Pct	Year		W-L	Pct
1900	Jesse Tannehill, Pittsburgh	20-6	.769	1948	Harry Brecheen, St. Louis	20-7	.741
1901	Jack Chesbro, Pittsburgh	21-10	.677	1949	Preacher Roe, Brooklyn	15-6	.714
1902	Jack Chesbro, Pittsburgh	28-6	.824	1950	Sal Maglie, New York	18-4	.818
1903	Sam Leever, Pittsburgh	25-7	.781	1951	Preacher Roe, Brooklyn	22-3	.880
1904	Joe McGinnity, New York	35-8	.814	1952	Hoyt Wilhelm, New York	15-3	.833
1905	Christy Mathewson, New York	31-8	.795	1953	Carl Erskine, Brooklyn	20-6	.769
1906	Ed Reulbach, Chicago	19-4	.826	1954	Johnny Antonelli, New York	21-7	.750
1907	Ed Reulbach, Chicago	17-4	.810	1955	Don Newcombe, Brooklyn	20-5	.800
1908	Ed Reulbach, Chicago	24-7	.774	1956	Don Newcombe, Brooklyn	27-7	.794
1909	Howie Camnitz, Pittsburgh	25-6	.806	1957	Bob Buhl, Milwaukee	18-7	.720
	& Christy Mathewson, New York	25-6	.806	1958	Warren Spahn, Milwaukee	22-11	.667
1910	King Cole, Chicago	20-4	.833		& Lew Burdette, Milwaukee	20-10	.667
1911	Rube Marquard, New York	24-7	.774	1959	Roy Face, Pittsburgh	18-1	.947
1912	Claude Hendrix, Pittsburgh	24-9	.727	1960	Ernie Broglio, St. Louis	21-9	.700
1913	Bert Humphries, Chicago	16-4	.800	1961	Johnny Podres, Los Angeles	18-5	.783
1914	Bill James, Boston	26-7	.788	1962	Bob Purkey, Cincinnati	23-5	.821
1915	Grover Alexander, Phila.	31-10	.756	1963	Ron Perranoski, Los Angeles	16-3	.842
1916	Tom Hughes, Boston	16-3	.842	1964	Sandy Koufax, Los Angeles	19-5	.792
1917	Ferdie Schupp, New York	21-7	.750	1965	Sandy Koufax, Los Angeles	26-8	.765
1918	Claude Hendrix, Chicago	19-7	.731	1966	Juan Marichal, San Francisco	25-6	.806
1919	Dutch Ruether, Cincinnati	19-6	.760	1967	Dick Hughes, St. Louis	16-6	.727
1920	Burleigh Grimes, Brooklyn	23-11	.676	1968	Steve Blass, Pittsburgh	18-6	.750
1921	Bill Doak, St.Louis	15-6	.714	1969	Tom Seaver, New York	25-7	.781
1922	Pete Donohue, Cincinnati	18-9	.667	1970	Bob Gibson, St. Louis	23-7	.767
1923	Dolf Luque, Cincinnati	27-8	.771	1971	Don Gullett, Cincinnati	16-6	.727
1924	Emil Yde, Pittsburgh	16-3	.842	1972	Gary Nolan, Cincinnati	15-5	.750
1925	Bill Sherdel, St.Louis	15-6	.714	1973	Tommy John, Los Angeles	16-7	.696
1926	Ray Kremer, Pittsburgh	20-6	.769	1974	Andy Messersmith, Los Angeles	20-6	.769
1927	Larry Benton, Boston-NY	17-7	.708	1975	Don Gullett, Cincinnati	15-4	.789
1928	Larry Benton, New York	25-9	.735	1976	Steve Carlton, Philadelphia	20-7	.741
1929	Charlie Root, Chicago	19-6	.760	1977	John Candelaria, Pittsburgh	20-5	.800
1930	Freddie Fitzsimmons, NY	19-7	.731	1978	Gaylord Perry, San Diego	21-6	.778
1931	Paul Derringer, St.Louis	18-8	.692	1979	Tom Seaver, Cincinnati	16-6	.727
1932	Lon Warneke, Chicago	22-6	.786	1980	Jim Bibby, Pittsburgh	19-6	.760
1933	Ben Cantwell, Boston	20-10	.667	1981	Tom Seaver, Cincinnati	14-2	.875
1934	Dizzy Dean, St.Louis	30-7	.811	1982	Phil Niekro, Atlanta	17-4	.810
1935	Bill Lee, Chicago	20-6	.769	1983	John Denny, Philadelphia	19-6	.760
1936	Carl Hubbell, New York	26-6	.813	1984	Rick Sutcliffe, Chicago	16-1	.941
1937	Carl Hubbell, New York	22-8	.733	1985	Orel Hershiser, Los Angeles	19-3	.864
1938	Bill Lee, Chicago	22-9	.710	1986	Bob Ojeda, New York	18-5	.783
1939	Paul Derringer, Cincinnati	25-7	.781	1987	Dwight Gooden, New York	15-7	.682
1940	Freddie Fitzsimmons, Bklyn	16-2	.889	1988	David Cone, New York	20-3	.870
1941	Elmer Riddle, Cincinnati	19-4	.826	1989	Mike Bielecki, Chicago	18-7	.720
1942	Larry French, Brooklyn	15-4	.789	1990	Doug Drabek, Pittsburgh	22-6	.786
1943	Mort Cooper, St. Louis	21-8	.724	1991	John Smiley, Pittsburgh	20-8	.714
1944	Ted Wilks, St. Louis	17-4	.810		& Jose Rijo, Cincinnati	15-6	.714
1945	Harry Brecheen, St. Louis	14-4	.778	1992	Bob Tewksbury, St. Louis	16-5	.762
1946	Murray Dickson, St. Louis	15-6	.714				
1947	Larry Jansen, New York	21-5	.808				

Note: In 1984, Sutcliffe was also 4-5 with Cle.(AL) for a combined record of 20-6 (.769).

American League
Multiple winners: Lefty Grove (5); Chief Bender and Whitey Ford (3); Johnny Allen, Eddie Cicotte, Roger Clemens, Mike Cuellar, Lefty Gomez, Catfish Hunter, Walter Johnson, Jim Palmer, Pete Vuckovich and Smokey Joe Wood (2).

Year		W-L	Pct	Year		W-L	Pct
1901	Clark Griffith, Chicago	24-7	.774	1904	Jack Chesbro, New York	41-12	.774
1902	Bill Bernhard, Phila-Cleve	18-5	.783	1905	Andy Coakley, Philadelphia	20-7	.741
1903	Cy Young, Boston	28-9	.757	1906	Eddie Plank, Philadelphia	19-6	.760

Year		W-L	Pct	Year		W-L	Pct
1907	Wild Bill Donovan, Detroit	25-4	.862	1952	Bobby Shantz, Philadelphia	24-7	.774
1908	Ed Walsh, Chicago	40-15	.727	1953	Ed Lopat, New York	16-4	.800
1909	George Mullin, Detroit	29-8	.784	1954	Sandy Consuegra, Chicago	16-3	.842
				1955	Tommy Byrne, New York	16-5	.762
1910	Chief Bender, Philadelphia	23-5	.821	1956	Whitey Ford, New York	19-6	.760
1911	Chief Bender, Philadelphia	17-5	.773	1957	Dick Donovan, Chicago	16-6	.727
1912	Smokey Joe Wood, Boston	34-5	.872		& Tom Sturdivant, New York	16-6	.727
1913	Walter Johnson, Washington	36-7	.837	1958	Bob Turley, New York	21-7	.750
1914	Chief Bender, Philadelphia	17-3	.850	1959	Bob Shaw, Chicago	18-6	.750
1915	Smokey Joe Wood, Boston	15-5	.750				
1916	Eddie Cicotte, Chicago	15-7	.682	1960	Jim Perry, Cleveland	18-10	.643
1917	Reb Russell, Chicago	15-5	.750	1961	Whitey Ford, New York	25-4	.862
1918	Sad Sam Jones, Boston	16-5	.762	1962	Ray Herbert, Chicago	20-9	.690
1919	Eddie Cicotte, Chicago	29-7	.806	1963	Whitey Ford, New York	24-7	.774
				1964	Wally Bunker, Baltimore	19-5	.792
1920	Jim Bagby, Cleveland	31-12	.721	1965	Mudcat Grant, Minnesota	21-7	.750
1921	Carl Mays, New York	27-9	.750	1966	Sonny Siebert, Cleveland	16-8	.667
1922	Joe Bush, New York	26-7	.788	1967	Joe Horlen, Chicago	19-7	.731
1923	Herb Pennock, New York	19-6	.760	1968	Denny McLain, Detroit	31-6	.838
1924	Walter Johnson, Washington	23-7	.767	1969	Jim Palmer, Baltimore	16-4	.800
1925	Stan Coveleski, Washington	20-5	.800				
1926	George Uhle, Cleveland	27-11	.711	1970	Mike Cuellar, Baltimore	24-8	.750
1927	Waite Hoyt, New York	22-7	.759	1971	Dave McNally, Baltimore	21-5	.808
1928	General Crowder, St. Louis	21-5	.808	1972	Catfish Hunter, Oakland	21-7	.750
1929	Lefty Grove, Philadelphia	20-6	.769	1973	Catfish Hunter, Oakland	21-5	.808
				1974	Mike Cuellar, Baltimore	22-10	.688
1930	Lefty Grove, Philadelphia	28-5	.848	1975	Mike Torrez, Baltimore	20-9	.690
1931	Lefty Grove, Philadelphia	31-4	.886	1976	Bill Campbell, Minnesota	17-5	.773
1932	Johnny Allen, New York	17-4	.810	1977	Paul Splittorff, Kansas City	16-6	.727
1933	Lefty Grove, Philadelphia	24-8	.750	1978	Ron Guidry, New York	25-3	.893
1934	Lefty Gomez, New York	26-5	.839	1979	Mike Caldwell, Milwaukee	16-6	.727
1935	Eldon Auker, Detroit	18-7	.720				
1936	Monte Pearson, New York	19-7	.731	1980	Steve Stone, Baltimore	25-7	.781
1937	Johnny Allen, Cleveland	15-1	.938	1981	Pete Vuckovich, Milwaukee	14-4	.778
1938	Red Ruffing, New York	21-7	.750	1982	Pete Vuckovich, Milwaukee	18-6	.750
1939	Lefty Grove, Boston	15-4	.789		& Jim Palmer, Baltimore	15-3	.750
				1983	Rich Dotson, Chicago	22-7	.759
1940	Schoolboy Rowe, Detroit	16-3	.842	1984	Doyle Alexander, Toronto	17-6	.739
1941	Lefty Gomez, New York	15-5	.750	1985	Ron Guidry, New York	22-6	.786
1942	Ernie Bonham, New York	21-5	.808	1986	Roger Clemens, Boston	24-4	.857
1943	Spud Chandler, New York	20-4	.833	1987	Roger Clemens, Boston	20-9	.690
1944	Tex Hughson, Boston	18-5	.783	1988	Frank Viola, Minnesota	24-7	.774
1945	Hal Newhouser, Detroit	25-9	.735	1989	Bret Saberhagen, Kansas City	23-6	.793
1946	Boo Ferriss, Boston	25-6	.806				
1947	Allie Reynolds, New York	19-8	.704	1990	Bob Welch, Oakland	27-6	.818
1948	Jack Kramer, Boston	18-5	.783	1991	Scott Erickson, Minnesota	20-8	.714
1949	Ellis Kinder, Boston	23-6	.793	1992	Mike Mussina, Baltimore	18-5	.783
1950	Vic Raschi, New York	21-8	.724				
1951	Bob Feller, Cleveland	22-8	.733				

Earned Run Average

Earned Run Averages were based on at least 10 complete games pitched (1900-50), at least 154 innings pitched (1950-60), and at least 162 innings pitched since 1961 in the AL and 1962 in the NL. In the strike year of 1981, qualifiers had to pitch at least as many innings as the total number of games their team played that season.

National League

Multiple winners: Grover Alexander, Sandy Koufax and Christy Mathewson (5); Carl Hubbell, Tom Seaver, Warren Spahn and Dazzy Vance (3); Bill Doak, Ray Kremer, Dolf Luque, Howie Pollett, Nolan Ryan, Bill Walker and Bucky Walters (2).

Year		ERA	Year		ERA	Year		ERA
1900	Rube Waddell, Pit.	2.37	1910	George McQuillan, Phi	1.60	1920	Grover Alexander, Chi	1.91
1901	Jesse Tannehill, Pit	2.18	1911	Christy Mathewson, NY	1.99	1921	Bill Doak, St.L.	2.59
1902	Jack Taylor, Chi	1.33	1912	Jeff Tesreau, NY	1.96	1922	Rosy Ryan, NY	3.01
1903	Sam Leever, Pit.	2.06	1913	Christy Mathewson, NY	2.06	1923	Dolf Luque, Cin	1.93
1904	Joe McGinnity, NY	1.61	1914	Bill Doak, St.L.	1.72	1924	Dazzy Vance, Bklyn	2.16
1905	Christy Mathewson, NY	1.27	1915	Grover Alexander, Phi	1.22	1925	Dolf Luque, Cin	2.63
1906	Three Finger Brown, Chi.	1.04	1916	Grover Alexander, Phi	1.55	1926	Ray Kremer, Pit.	2.61
1907	Jack Pfiester, Chi	1.15	1917	Grover Alexander, Phi	1.86	1927	Ray Kremer, Pit.	2.47
1908	Christy Mathewson, NY	1.43	1918	Hippo Vaughn, Chi	1.74	1928	Dazzy Vance, Bklyn	2.09
1909	Christy Mathewson, NY	1.14	1919	Grover Alexander, Chi	1.72	1929	Bill Walker, NY	3.09

Annual Pitching Leaders (Cont.)
Earned Run Average
National League

Year		ERA	Year		ERA	Year		ERA
1930	Dazzy Vance, Bklyn	2.61	1952	Hoyt Wilhelm, NY	2.43	1973	Tom Seaver, NY	2.08
1931	Bill Walker, NY	2.26	1953	Warren Spahn, Mil	2.10	1974	Buzz Capra, Atl	2.28
1932	Lon Warneke, Chi	2.37	1954	Johnny Antonelli, NY	2.30	1975	Randy Jones, SD	2.24
1933	Carl Hubbell, NY	1.66	1955	Bob Friend, Pit	2.83	1976	John Denny, St.L	2.52
1934	Carl Hubbell, NY	2.30	1956	Lew Burdette, Mil	2.70	1977	John Candelaria, Pit	2.34
1935	Cy Blanton, Pit	2.58	1957	Johnny Podres, Bklyn	2.66	1978	Craig Swan, NY	2.43
1936	Carl Hubbell, NY	2.31	1958	Stu Miller, SF	2.47	1979	J.R. Richard, Hou	2.71
1937	Jim Turner, Bos	2.38	1959	Sam Jones, SF	2.83			
1938	Bill Lee, Chi	2.66				1980	Don Sutton, LA	2.21
1939	Bucky Walters, Cin	2.29	1960	Mike McCormick, SF	2.70	1981	Nolan Ryan, Hou	1.69
			1961	Warren Spahn, Mil	3.02	1982	Steve Rogers, Mon	2.40
1940	Bucky Walters, Cin	2.48	1962	Sandy Koufax, LA	2.54	1983	Atlee Hammaker, SF	2.25
1941	Elmer Riddle, Cin	2.24	1963	Sandy Koufax, LA	1.88	1984	Alejandro Pena, LA	2.48
1942	Mort Cooper, St.L	1.78	1964	Sandy Koufax, LA	1.74	1985	Dwight Gooden, NY	1.53
1943	Howie Pollet, St.L	1.75	1965	Sandy Koufax, LA	2.04	1986	Mike Scott, Hou	2.22
1944	Ed Heusser, Cin	2.38	1966	Sandy Koufax, LA	1.73	1987	Nolan Ryan, Hou	2.76
1945	Hank Borowy, Chi	2.13	1967	Phil Niekro, Atl	1.87	1988	Joe Magrane, St.L	2.18
1946	Howie Pollet, St.L	2.10	1968	Bob Gibson, St.L	1.12	1989	Scott Garrelts, SF	2.28
1947	Warren Spahn, Bos	2.33	1969	Juan Marichal, SF	2.10			
1948	Harry Brecheen, St.L	2.24				1990	Danny Darwin, Hou	2.21
1949	Dave Koslo, NY	2.50	1970	Tom Seaver, NY	2.81	1991	Dennis Martinez, Mon	2.39
			1971	Tom Seaver, NY	1.76	1992	Bill Swift, SF	2.08
1950	Jim Hearn, St.L-NY	2.49	1972	Steve Carlton, Phi.	1.98			
1951	Chet Nichols, Bos	2.88						

Note: In 1945, Borowy had a 3.13 ERA in 18 games with New York (AL) for a combined ERA of 2.65.

American League

Multiple winners: Lefty Grove (9); Walter Johnson (5); Roger Clemens (4); Spud Chandler, Stan Coveleski, Red Faber, Whitey Ford, Lefty Gomez, Ron Guidry, Addie Joss, Hal Newhouser, Jim Palmer, Gary Peters, Luis Tiant and Ed Walsh (2).

Year		ERA	Year		ERA	Year		ERA
1901	Cy Young, Bos	1.62	1932	Lefty Grove, Phi	2.84	1963	Gary Peters, Chi	2.33
1902	Ed Siever, Det	1.91	1933	Monte Pearson, Cle	2.33	1964	Dean Chance, LA	1.65
1903	Earl Moore, Cle	1.77	1934	Lefty Gomez, NY	2.33	1965	Sam McDowell, Cle	2.18
1904	Addie Joss, Cle	1.59	1935	Lefty Grove, Bos	2.70	1966	Gary Peters, Chi	1.98
1905	Rube Waddell, Phi	1.48	1936	Lefty Grove, Bos	2.81	1967	Joe Horlen, Chi	2.06
1906	Doc White, Chi	1.52	1937	Lefty Gomez, NY	2.33	1968	Luis Tiant, Cle	1.60
1907	Ed Walsh, Chi	1.60	1938	Lefty Grove, Bos	3.08	1969	Dick Bosman, Wash	2.19
1908	Addie Joss, Cle	1.16	1939	Lefty Grove, Bos	2.54			
1909	Harry Krause, Phi	1.39				1970	Diego Segui, Oak	2.56
			1940	Bob Feller, Cle	2.61	1971	Vida Blue, Oak	1.82
1910	Ed Walsh, Chi	1.27	1941	Thorton Lee, Chi	2.37	1972	Luis Tiant, Bos	1.91
1911	Vean Gregg, Cle	1.81	1942	Ted Lyons, Chi	2.10	1973	Jim Palmer, Bal	2.40
1912	Walter Johnson, Wash	1.39	1943	Spud Chandler, NY	1.64	1974	Catfish Hunter, Ock	2.49
1913	Walter Johnson, Wash	1.09	1944	Dizzy Trout, Det	2.12	1975	Jim Palmer, Bal	2.09
1914	Dutch Leonard, Bos	1.01	1945	Hal Newhouser, Det	1.81	1976	Mark Fidrych, Det	2.34
1915	Smokey Joe Wood, Bos	1.49	1946	Hal Newhouser, Det	1.94	1977	Frank Tanana, Cal	2.54
1916	Babe Ruth, Bos	1.75	1947	Spud Chandler, NY	2.46	1978	Ron Guidry, NY	1.74
1917	Eddie Cicotte, Chi	1.53	1948	Gene Bearden, Cle	2.43	1979	Ron Guidry, NY	2.78
1918	Walter Johnson, Wash	1.27	1949	Mel Parnell, Bos	2.77			
1919	Walter Johnson, Wash	1.49				1980	Rudy May, NY	2.47
			1950	Early Wynn, Cle	3.20	1981	Steve McCatty, Oak	2.32
1920	Bob Shawkey, NY	2.45	1951	Saul Rogovin, Det-Chi	2.78	1982	Rick Sutcliffe, Cle	2.96
1921	Red Faber, Chi	2.48	1952	Allie Reynolds, NY	2.06	1983	Rick Honeycutt, Tex	2.42
1922	Red Faber, Chi	2.80	1953	Ed Lopat, NY	2.42	1984	Mike Boddicker, Bal	2.79
1923	Stan Coveleski, Cle	2.76	1954	Mike Garcia, Cle	2.64	1985	Dave Stieb, Tor	2.48
1924	Walter Johnson, Wash	2.72	1955	Billy Pierce, Chi	1.97	1986	Roger Clemens, Bos	2.48
1925	Stan Coveleski, Wash	2.84	1956	Whitey Ford, NY	2.47	1987	Jimmy Key, Tor	2.76
1926	Lefty Grove, Phi	2.51	1957	Bobby Shantz, NY	2.45	1988	Allan Anderson, Min	2.45
1927	Wilcy Moore, NY	2.28	1958	Whitey Ford, NY	2.01	1989	Bret Saberhagen, KC	2.16
1928	Garland Braxton, Wash	2.51	1959	Hoyt Wilhelm, Bal	2.19			
1929	Lefty Grove, Phi	2.81				1990	Roger Clemens, Bos	1.93
			1960	Frank Baumann, Chi	2.67	1991	Roger Clemens, Bos	2.62
1930	Lefty Grove, Phi	2.54	1961	Dick Donovan, Wash	2.40	1992	Roger Clemens, Bos	2.41
1931	Lefty Grove, Phi	2.06	1962	Hank Aguirre, Det	2.21			

Note: In 1940, Ernie Bonham of NY had a 1.90 ERA and 10 complete games, but appeared in only a total of 12 games and 99 innings.

Strikeouts
National League

Multiple winners: Dazzy Vance (7); Grover Alexander (6); Steve Carlton, Christy Mathewson and Tom Seaver (5); Dizzy Dean, Sandy Koufax and Warren Spahn (4); Don Drysdale, Sam Jones and Johnny Vander Meer (3); David Cone, Dwight Gooden, Bill Hallahan, J.R. Richard, Robin Roberts, Nolan Ryan and Hippo Vaughn (2).

Year		SO	Year		SO	Year		SO
1900	Rube Waddell, Pit	130	1932	Dizzy Dean, St.L	191	1962	Don Drysdale, LA	232
1901	Noodles Hahn, Cinn	239	1933	Dizzy Dean, St.L	199	1963	Sandy Koufax, LA	306
1902	Vic Willis, Bos.	225	1934	Dizzy Dean, St.L	195	1964	Bob Veale, Pit	250
1903	Christy Mathewson, NY	267	1935	Dizzy Dean, St.L	182	1965	Sandy Koufax, LA	382
1904	Christy Mathewson, NY	212	1936	Van Lingle Mungo,Bklyn.	238	1966	Sandy Koufax, LA	317
1905	Christy Mathewson, NY	206	1937	Carl Hubbell, NY	159	1967	Jim Bunning, Phi	253
1906	Fred Beebe, Chi-St.L	171	1938	Clay Bryant, Chi	135	1968	Bob Gibson, St.L	268
1907	Christy Mathewson, NY	178	1939	Claude Passeau,Phi-Chi.	137	1969	Ferguson Jenkins, Chi	273
1908	Christy Mathewson, NY	259		& Bucky Walters, Cin	137			
1909	Orval Overall, Chi	205				1970	Tom Seaver, NY	283
			1940	Kirby Higbe, Phi	137	1971	Tom Seaver, NY	289
1910	Earl Moore, Phi	185	1941	John Vander Meer,Cin	202	1972	Steve Carlton, Phi	310
1911	Rube Marquard, NY	237	1942	John Vander Meer,Cin	186	1973	Tom Seaver, NY	251
1912	Grover Alexander, Phi	195	1943	John Vander Meer,Cin	174	1974	Steve Carlton, Phi	240
1913	Tom Seaton, Phi	168	1944	Bill Voiselle, NY	161	1975	Tom Seaver, NY	243
1914	Grover Alexander, Phi	214	1945	Preacher Roe, Pitt	148	1976	Tom Seaver, NY	235
1915	Grover Alexander, Phi	241	1946	Johnny Schmitz, Chi	135	1977	Phil Niekro, Atl	262
1916	Grover Alexander, Phi	167	1947	Ewell Blackwell, Cin	193	1978	J.R. Richard, Hou	303
1917	Grover Alexander, Phi	201	1948	Harry Brecheen, St.L	149	1979	J.R. Richard, Hou	313
1918	Hippo Vaughn, Chi.	148	1949	Warren Spahn, Bos.	151			
1919	Hippo Vaughn, Chi.	141				1980	Steve Carlton, Phi	286
			1950	Warren Spahn, Bos.	191	1981	F. Valenzuela,LA	180
1920	Grover Alexander, Chi	173	1951	Don Newcombe, Bklyn.	164	1982	Steve Carlton, Phi	286
1921	Burleigh Grimes, Bklyn	136		& Warren Spahn, Bos.	164	1983	Steve Carlton, Phi	275
1922	Dazzy Vance, Bklyn	134	1952	Warren Spahn, Bos.	183	1984	Dwight Gooden, NY	276
1923	Dazzy Vance, Bklyn	197	1953	Robin Roberts, Phi	198	1985	Dwight Gooden, NY	268
1924	Dazzy Vance, Bklyn	262	1954	Robin Roberts, Phi	185	1986	Mike Scott, Hou	306
1925	Dazzy Vance, Bklyn	221	1955	Sam Jones, Chi	198	1987	Nolan Ryan, Hou	270
1926	Dazzy Vance, Bklyn	140	1956	Sam Jones, Chi	176	1988	Nolan Ryan, Hou	228
1927	Dazzy Vance, Bklyn	184	1957	Jack Sanford, Phi	188	1989	Jose DeLeon, St.L	201
1928	Dazzy Vance, Bklyn	200	1958	Sam Jones, St.L	225			
1929	Pat Malone, Chi	166	1959	Don Drydale, LA	242	1990	David Cone, NY	233
						1991	David Cone, NY	241
1930	Bill Hallahan, St.L	177	1960	Don Drysdale, LA	246	1992	John Smoltz, Alt.	215
1931	Bill Hallahan, St.L	159	1961	Sandy Koufax, LA	269			

American League

Multiple winners: Walter Johnson (12); Nolan Ryan (9); Bob Feller and Lefty Grove (7); Rube Waddell (6); Sam McDowell (5); Lefty Gomez, Camilo Pascual and Mark Langston (3); Len Barker, Tommy Bridges, Jim Bunning, Roger Clemens, Hal Newhouser, Allie Reynolds, Herb Score, Ed Walsh and Early Wynn (2).

Year		SO	Year		SO	Year		SO
1901	Cy Young, Bos.	158	1920	Stan Coveleski, Cle	133	1939	Bob Feller, Cle.	246
1902	Rube Waddell, Phi.	210	1921	Walter Johnson, Wash	143	1940	Bob Feller, Cle.	261
1903	Rube Waddell, Phi.	302	1922	Urban Shocker, St.L	149	1941	Bob Feller, Cle.	260
1904	Rube Waddell, Phi.	349	1923	Walter Johnson, Wash	130	1942	Tex Hughson, Bos	113
1905	Rube Waddell, Phi.	287	1924	Walter Johnson, Wash	158		& Bobo Newsom,Wash	113
1906	Rube Waddell, Phi.	196	1925	Lefty Grove, Phi.	116	1943	Allie Reynolds, Cle	151
1907	Rube Waddell, Phi.	232	1926	Lefty Grove, Phi.	194	1944	Hal Newhouser, Det	187
1908	Ed Walsh, Chi	269	1927	Lefty Grove, Phi.	174	1945	Hal Newhouser, Det	212
1909	Frank Smith, Chi	177	1928	Lefty Grove, Phi.	183	1946	Bob Feller, Cle.	348
			1929	Lefty Grove, Phi.	170	1947	Bob Feller, Cle.	196
1910	Walter Johnson, Wash .	313				1948	Bob Feller, Cle.	164
1911	Ed Walsh, Chi	255	1930	Lefty Grove, Phi.	209	1949	Virgil Trucks, Det	153
1912	Walter Johnson, Wash	303	1931	Lefty Grove, Phi.	175			
1913	Walter Johnson, Wash	243	1932	Red Ruffing, NY	190	1950	Bob Lemon, Cle	170
1914	Walter Johnson, Wash	225	1933	Lefty Gomez, NY	163	1951	Vic Raschi, NY	164
1915	Walter Johnson, Wash	203	1934	Lefty Gomez, NY	158	1952	Allie Reynolds, NY	160
1916	Walter Johnson, Wash	228	1935	Tommy Bridges, Det	163	1953	Billy Pierce Chi.	186
1917	Walter Johnson, Wash	188	1936	Tommy Bridges, Det	175	1954	Bob Turley, Bal	185
1918	Walter Johnson, Wash	162	1937	Lefty Gomez, NY	194	1955	Herb Score, Cle.	245
1919	Walter Johnson, Wash	147	1938	Bob Feller, Cle.	240			

Annual Pitching Leaders (Cont.)
Strikeouts

Year		SO	Year		SO	Year		SO
1956	Herb Score, Cle.	263	1970	Sam McDowell, Cle	304	1982	Floyd Bannister, Sea	209
1957	Early Wynn, Cle.	184	1971	Mickey Lolich, Det.	308	1983	Jack Morris, Det	232
1958	Early Wynn, Chi	179	1972	Nolan Ryan, Cal	329	1984	Mark Langston, Sea	204
1959	Jim Bunning, Det.	201	1973	Nolan Ryan, Cal	383	1985	Bert Blyleven,Cle-Min	206
1960	Jim Bunning, Det.	201	1974	Nolan Ryan, Cal	367	1986	Mark Langston, Sea	245
1961	Camilo Pascual, Min.	221	1975	Frank Tanana, Cal	269	1987	Mark Langston, Sea	262
1962	Camilo Pascual, Min.	206	1976	Nolan Ryan, Cal	327	1988	Roger Clemens, Bos	291
1963	Camilo Pascual, Min.	202	1977	Nolan Ryan, Cal	341	1989	Nolan Ryan, Tex	301
1964	Al Downing, NY	217	1978	Nolan Ryan, Cal	260	1990	Nolan Ryan, Tex	232
1965	Sam McDowell, Cle.	325	1979	Nolan Ryan, Cal	223	1991	Roger Clemens, Bos	241
1966	Sam McDowell, Cle	225	1980	Len Barker, Cle	187	1992	Randy Johnson, Sea	241
1967	Jim Lonborg, Bos	246	1981	Len Barker, Cle	127			
1968	Sam McDowell, Cle	283						
1969	Sam McDowell, Cle	279						

Pitching Triple Crown Winners

Pitchers who led either league in Earned Run Average, Wins and Strikeouts over a single season.

National League

	Year	ERA	W-L	SO
Tommy Bond, Bos	1877	2.11	40-17	170
Hoss Radbourn, Prov	1884	1.38	60-12	441
Tim Keefe, NY	1888	1.74	35-12	333
John Clarkson, Bos.	1889	2.73	49-19	284
Amos Rusie, NY	1894	2.78	36-13	195
Christy Mathewson, NY	1905	1.27	31-8	206
Christy Mathewson, NY	1908	1.43	37-11	259
Grover Alexander, Phi	1915	1.22	31-10	241
Grover Alexander, Phi	1916	1.55	33-12	167
Grover Alexander, Phi	1917	1.86	30-13	201
Hippo Vaughn, Chi	1918	1.74	22-10	148
Grover Alexander, Chi	1920	1.91	27-14	173
Dazzy Vance, Bklyn.	1924	2.16	28-6	262
Bucky Walters, Cin	1939	2.29	27-11	137
Sandy Koufax, LA	1963	1.88	25-5	306
Sandy Koufax, LA	1965	2.04	26-8	382
Sandy Koufax, LA	1966	1.73	27-9	317

	Year	ERA	W-L	SO
Steve Carlton, Phi	1972	1.97	27-10	310
Dwight Gooden, NY	1985	1.53	24-4	268

Ties: in 1894, Rusie tied for league lead in wins with Jouett Meekin, NY (36-10); in 1939, Walters tied for league lead in strikeouts with Claude Passeau, Phi-Chi; in 1963, Koufax tied for the league lead in wins with Juan Marichal, SF.

American League

	Year	ERA	W-L	SO
Cy Young, Bos	1901	1.62	33-10	158
Rube Waddell, Phi	1905	1.48	26-11	287
Walter Johnson, Wash	1913	1.09	36-7	243
Walter Johnson, Wash	1918	1.27	23-13	162
Walter Johnson, Wash	1924	2.72	23-7	158
Lefty Grove, Phi.	1930	2.54	28-5	209
Lefty Grove, Phi.	1931	2.06	31-4	175
Lefty Gomez, NY	1934	2.33	26-5	158
Lefty Gomez, NY	1937	2.33	21-11	194
Hal Newhouser, Det.	1945	1.81	25-9	212

Perfect Games

Fifteen pitchers have thrown perfect games (27 up, 27 down) in major league history.

National League

	Game	Date	Score
Lee Richmond	Wor.vs Cle.	6/12/1880	1-0
Monte Ward	Prov.vs Bos.	6/17/1880	5-0
Harvey Haddix	Pit.at Mil.	5/26/1959	0-1*
Jim Bunning	Phi.at NY	6/21/1964	6-0
Sandy Koufax	LA vs Chi.	9/9/1965	1-0
Tom Browning	Cin.vs LA	9/16/1988	1-0
Dennis Martinez	Mon. at LA	7/28/1991	2-0

American League

	Game	Date	Score
Cy Young	Bos.vs Phi.	5/5/1904	3-0
Adrian Joss	Cle.vs Chi.	10/2/1908	1-0
Ernie Shore	Bos.vs Wash.	6/23/1917	4-0*
Charlie Robertson	Chi.at Det.	4/30/1922	2-0
Catfish Hunter	Oak.vs Min.	5/8/1968	4-0
Len Barker	Cle.vs Tor.	5/15/1981	3-0
Mike Witt	Cal.at Tex.	9/30/1984	1-0

*Haddix pitched 12 perfect innings before losing in the 13th. Braves' lead-off batter Felix Mantilla reached on a throwing error by Pirates 3B Don Hoak, Eddie Mathews sacrificed Mantilla to 2nd, Hank Aaron was walked intentionally, and Joe Adcock hit a 3-run HR. Adcock, however, passed Aaron on the bases and was only credited with a 1-run double.

*Babe Ruth started for Boston, walking Senators' lead-off batter Ray Morgan, then was thrown out of game by umpire Brick Owens for arguing the call. Shore came on in relief. Morgan was caught stealing and Shore retired the next 26 batters in a row. While technically not a perfect game—since he didn't start—Shore gets credit anyway.

World Series

Pitcher	Game	Date	Score
Don Larson	NY vs Bklyn	10/8/1956	2-0

All-Time Major League Leaders

Based on statistics compiled by *The Baseball Encyclopedia* (8th ed.); through 1992 regular season.

CAREER

Players active in 1992 in **bold** type.

Batting

Note that (*) indicates left-handed hitter and (†) indicates switch-hitter.

Batting Average

		Yrs	AB	H	Avg
1	Ty Cobb*	24	11,429	4191	.367
2	Rogers Hornsby	23	8,137	2930	.358
3	Joe Jackson*	13	4,981	1774	.356
4	Ed Delahanty*	16	7,502	2591	.345
5	Ted Williams*	19	7,706	2654	.344
6	Tris Speaker*	22	10,208	3515	.344
7	Billy Hamilton*	14	6,284	2163	.344
8	Willie Keeler*	19	8,585	2947	.343
9	Dan Brouthers*	19	6,711	2296	.342
10	Babe Ruth*	22	8,399	2873	.342
11	Harry Heilmann	17	7,787	2660	.342
12	Pete Browning	13	4,820	1646	.341
13	Bill Terry*	14	6,428	2193	.341
14	George Sisler*	15	8,267	2812	.340
15	Lou Gehrig*	17	8,001	2721	.340
16	Jesse Burkett*	16	8,413	2853	.339
17	Nap Lajoie	21	9,592	3244	.338
18	**Wade Boggs***	11	6,213	2098	.338
19	Riggs Stephenson	14	4,508	1515	.336
20	Al Simmons	20	8,761	2927	.334
21	Paul Waner*	20	9,459	3152	.333
22	Eddie Collins*	25	9,949	3311	.333
23	Stan Musial*	22	10,972	3630	.331
24	Sam Thompson*	14	6,005	1986	.331
25	Heinie Manush*	17	7,653	2524	.330

Hits

		Yrs	AB	H	Avg
1	Pete Rose†	24	14,053	4256	.303
2	Ty Cobb*	24	11,429	4191	.367
3	Hank Aaron*	23	12,364	3771	.305
4	Stan Musial*	22	10,972	3630	.331
5	Tris Speaker*	22	10,208	3515	.344
6	Carl Yastrzemski*	23	11,988	3419	.285
7	Honus Wagner	21	10,443	3418	.327
8	Eddie Collins*	25	9,949	3311	.333
9	Willie Mays	22	10,881	3283	.302
10	Nap Lajoie	21	9,592	3244	.338
11	Paul Waner*	20	9,459	3152	.333
12	Rod Carew*	19	9,315	3053	.328
13	Robin Yount	19	10,554	3025	.287
14	Lou Brock*	19	10,332	3023	.293
15	Al Kaline	22	10,116	3007	.297
16	George Brett	20	9,789	3005	.307
17	Cap Anson	22	9,108	3000	.329
	Roberto Clemente*	18	9,454	3000	.317
19	Sam Rice*	20	9,269	2987	.322
20	Sam Crawford*	19	9,580	2964	.309
21	Willie Keeler*	19	8,585	2947	.343
22	Frank Robinson	21	10,006	2943	.294
23	Jake Beckley*	20	9,527	2931	.308
24	Rogers Hornsby	23	8,173	2930	.358
25	Al Simmons	20	8,761	2927	.334

Players Active in 1992

		Yrs	AB	H	Avg
1	Wade Boggs*	11	6,213	2098	.338
2	Tony Gwynn*	11	5,701	1864	.327
3	Kirby Puckett	9	5,645	1812	.321
4	Don Mattingly*	11	5,643	1754	.311
5	George Brett*	20	9,789	3005	.307
6	Mike Greenwell*	8	2,980	912	.306
7	Paul Molitor	15	7,520	2281	.303
8	Will Clark*	7	3,778	1139	.301
9	Ken Griffey, Jr*	4	2,165	652	.301
10	Julio Franco	11	5,416	1630	.301

Players Active in 1992

		Yrs	AB	H	Avg
1	Robin Yount	19	10,554	3025	.287
2	George Brett	20	9,789	3005	.307
3	Dave Winfield	19	10,047	2866	.285
4	Eddie Murray	16	9,124	2646	.290
5	Andre Dawson	17	8,890	2504	.282
6	Carlton Fisk	23	8,703	2346	.270
7	Paul Molitor	15	7,520	2281	.303
8	Willie Randolph	18	8,018	2210	.276
9	Willie Wilson	17	7,489	2145	.286
10	Ozzie Smith	15	8,087	2108	.261

Games Played

1	Pete Rose	3562
2	Carl Yastrzemski	3308
3	Hank Aaron	3298
4	Ty Cobb	3034
5	Stan Musial	3026
6	Willie Mays	2992
7	Rusty Staub	2951
8	Brooks Robinson	2896
9	Al Kaline	2834
10	Eddie Collins	2826
11	Reggie Jackson	2820
12	Frank Robinson	2808
13	Tris Speaker	2789
	Honus Wagner	2789
15	Tony Perez	2777
16	Mel Ott	2734
17	Robin Yount	2729
18	Dave Winfield	2707
19	Graig Nettles	2700
20	Darrell Evans	2687

At Bats

1	Pete Rose	14,053
2	Hank Aaron	12,364
3	Carl Yastrzemski	11,988
4	Ty Cobb	11,429
5	Stan Musial	10,972
6	Willie Mays	10,881
7	Brooks Robinson	10,654
8	Robin Yount	10,554
9	Honus Wagner	10,441
10	Lou Brock	10,332
11	Luis Aparicio	10,230
12	Tris Speaker	10,208
13	Al Kaline	10,116
14	Rabbit Maranville	10,078
15	Dave Winfield	10,047
16	Frank Robinson	10,006
17	Eddie Collins	9,949
18	Reggie Jackson	9,864
19	George Brett	9,789
20	Tony Perez	9,778

Total Bases

1	Hank Aaron	6856
2	Stan Musial	6134
3	Willie Mays	6066
4	Ty Cobb	5863
5	Babe Ruth	5793
6	Pete Rose	5752
7	Carl Yastrzemski	5539
8	Frank Robinson	5373
9	Tris Speaker	5104
10	Lou Gehrig	5059
11	Mel Ott	5041
12	Jimmie Foxx	4956
13	Ted Williams	4884
14	Honus Wagner	4868
15	Dave Winfield	4867
16	Al Kaline	4852
17	Reggie Jackson	4834
18	George Brett	4801
19	Rogers Hornsby	4712
20	Ernie Banks	4706

All-Time Major League Leaders (Cont.)
Batting

Home Runs

		Yrs	AB	HR	Pct
1	Hank Aaron	23	12,364	755	6.1
2	Babe Ruth*	22	8,399	714	8.5
3	Willie Mays	22	10,881	660	6.1
4	Frank Robinson	21	10,006	586	5.9
5	Harmon Killebrew	22	8,147	573	7.0
6	Reggie Jackson*	21	9,864	563	5.7
7	Mike Schmidt	18	8,352	548	6.6
8	Mickey Mantle†	18	8,102	536	6.6
9	Jimmie Foxx	20	8,134	534	6.6
10	Ted Williams*	19	7,706	521	6.8
	Willie McCovey*	22	8,197	521	6.4
12	Eddie Mathews†	17	8,537	512	6.0
	Ernie Banks	19	9,421	512	5.4
14	Mel Ott*	22	9,456	511	5.4
15	Lou Gehrig*	17	8,001	493	6.2
16	Willie Stargell*	21	7,927	475	6.0
	Stan Musial*	22	10,972	475	4.3
18	Carl Yastrzemski*	23	11,988	452	3.8
19	Dave Kingman	16	6,677	442	6.6
20	**Dave Winfield**	19	10,047	432	4.3
21	Billy Williams*	18	9,350	426	4.6
22	Darrell Evans	21	8,973	414	4.6
	Eddie Murray†	16	9,124	414	4.5
24	Duke Snider*	18	7,161	407	5.7
25	**Andre Dawson**	17	8,890	399	4.5
	Al Kaline*	22	10,116	399	3.9

Runs Batted In

		Yrs	Gm	RBI	P/G
1	Hank Aaron	23	3298	2297	.70
2	Babe Ruth*	22	2503	2211	.88
3	Lou Gehrig*	17	2164	1990	.92
4	Ty Cobb*	24	3034	1961	.65
5	Stan Musial*	22	3026	1951	.64
6	Jimmie Foxx	20	2317	1921	.83
7	Willie Mays	22	2992	1903	.64
8	Mel Ott*	22	2732	1861	.68
9	Carl Yastrzemski*	23	3308	1844	.56
10	Ted Williams*	19	2292	1839	.80
11	Al Simmons	20	2215	1827	.82
12	Frank Robinson	21	2808	1812	.65
13	Honus Wagner	21	2786	1732	.62
14	Cap Anson	22	2276	1715	.75
15	**Dave Winfield**	19	2707	1710	.63
16	Reggie Jackson*	21	2820	1702	.60
17	Tony Perez	23	2777	1652	.59
18	Ernie Banks	19	2528	1636	.65
19	Goose Goslin*	18	2287	1609	.70
20	Nap Lajoie	21	2475	1599	.65
21	Mike Schmidt	18	2404	1595	.66
22	Rogers Hornsby	23	2259	1584	.70
	Harmon Killebrew	22	2435	1584	.65
24	Al Kaline	22	2834	1583	.56
25	Jake Beckley*	20	2386	1575	.66

Players Active in 1992

		Yrs	AB	HR	Pct
1	Dave Winfield	19	10,047	432	4.3
2	Eddie Murray	16	9,124	414	4.5
3	Andre Dawson	17	8,890	399	4.5
4	Dale Murphy	17	7,918	398	5.0
5	Carlton Fisk	23	8,703	375	4.3
6	Jack Clark	18	6,847	340	5.0
7	Gary Carter	19	7,971	324	4.1
8	Lance Parrish	16	6,743	316	4.7
9	George Brett	20	9,789	298	3.0
10	Darryl Strawberry	10	4,564	285	6.2
11	Brian Downing	20	7,853	275	3.5
12	Cal Ripken	12	6,942	273	3.9
13	Kent Hrbek	12	5,526	258	4.7
14	Tom Brunansky	12	5,860	255	4.4
15	George Bell	11	5,713	252	4.4

Players Active in 1992

		Yrs	Gm	RBI	P/G
1	Dave Winfield	19	2707	1710	.63
2	Eddie Murray	16	2444	1562	.64
3	George Brett	20	2562	1520	.59
4	Andre Dawson	17	2310	1425	.62
5	Robin Yount	19	2729	1355	.50
6	Carlton Fisk	23	2474	1326	.54
7	Dale Murphy	17	2154	1259	.58
8	Gary Carter	19	2296	1225	.53
9	Jack Clark	18	1994	1180	.59
10	Brian Downing	20	2344	1073	.46
11	Harold Baines	13	1844	1066	.58
12	Lance Parrish	16	1868	1030	.55
13	Cal Ripken	12	1800	1014	.56
14	Kent Hrbek	12	1543	950	.62
15	George Bell	11	1485	938	.63

Runs

1	Ty Cobb	2245
2	Babe Ruth	2174
	Hank Aaron	2174
4	Pete Rose	2165
5	Willie Mays	2062
6	Stan Musial	1949
7	Lou Gehrig	1888
8	Tris Speaker	1881
9	Mel Ott	1859
10	Frank Robinson	1829
11	Eddie Collins	1818
12	Carl Yastrzemski	1816
13	Ted Williams	1798
14	Charlie Gehringer	1774
15	Jimmie Foxx	1751
16	Honus Wagner	1735
17	Willie Keeler	1727
18	Cap Anson	1719
19	Jesse Burkett	1718
20	Billy Hamilton	1692

Extra Base Hits

1	Hank Aaron	1477
2	Stan Musial	1377
3	Babe Ruth	1356
4	Willie Mays	1323
5	Lou Gehrig	1190
6	Frank Robinson	1186
7	Carl Yastrzemski	1157
8	Ty Cobb	1139
9	Tris Speaker	1132
10	Ted Williams	1117
	Jimmie Foxx	1117
12	Reggie Jackson	1075
13	Mel Ott	1071
14	**George Brett**	1066
15	Pete Rose	1041
16	Mike Schmidt	1015
17	Rogers Hornsby	1011
18	Ernie Banks	1009
19	**Dave Winfield**	1008
20	Honus Wagner	996

Slugging Average

1	Babe Ruth	.690
2	Ted Williams	.634
3	Lou Gehrig	.632
4	Jimmie Foxx	.609
5	Hank Greenberg	.605
6	Joe DiMaggio	.579
7	Rogers Hornsby	.577
8	Johnny Mize	.562
9	Stan Musial	.559
10	Willie Mays	.557
11	Mickey Mantle	.557
12	Hank Aaron	.555
13	Ralph Kiner	.548
14	Hack Wilson	.545
15	Chuck Klein	.543
16	Duke Snider	.540
17	Frank Robinson	.537
18	Al Simmons	.535
19	Dick Allen	.534
20	Earl Averill	.533

Stolen Bases

1 **Rickey Henderson** 1042
2 Lou Brock 938
3 Billy Hamilton 915
4 Ty Cobb 892
5 Eddie Collins 743
6 Arlie Latham 739
7 Max Carey 738
8 **Tim Raines** 730
9 Honus Wagner 720
10 Joe Morgan 689
11 **Willie Wilson** 660
12 Bert Campaneris 649
13 Tom Brown 627
14 George Davis 615
15 **Vince Coleman** 610
16 Hugh Duffy 583
17 Dummy Hoy 597
18 Maury Wills 586
19 George Van Haltren 583
20 Davey Lopes 557

Walks

1 Babe Ruth 2056
2 Ted Williams 2019
3 Joe Morgan 1865
4 Carl Yastrzemski 1845
5 Mickey Mantle 1734
6 Mel Ott 1708
7 Eddie Yost 1614
8 Darrell Evans 1605
9 Stan Musial 1599
10 Pete Rose 1566
11 Harmon Killebrew 1559
12 Lou Gehrig 1508
13 Mike Schmidt 1507
14 Eddie Collins 1503
15 Willie Mays 1463
16 Jimmie Foxx 1452
17 Eddie Mathews 1444
18 Frank Robinson 1420
19 Hank Aaron 1402
20 Dwight Evans 1391

Strikeouts

1 Reggie Jackson 2597
2 Willie Stargell 1936
3 Mike Schmidt 1883
4 Tony Perez 1867
5 Dave Kingman 1816
6 Bobby Bonds 1757
7 **Dale Murphy** 1733
8 Lou Brock 1730
9 Mickey Mantle 1710
10 Harmon Killebrew 1699
11 Dwight Evans 1697
12 Lee May 1570
13 Dick Allen 1556
14 Willie McCovey 1550
15 Dave Parker 1537
16 Frank Robinson 1532
17 Willie Mays 1526
18 Rick Monday 1513
19 Greg Luzinski 1495
20 **Dave Winfield** 1493

Pitching

Note that (*) indicates left-handed pitcher. Active pitcher leaders are listed for wins, strikeouts and saves.

Wins

		Yrs	GS	W	L	Pct
1	Cy Young	22	815	511	313	.620
2	Walter Johnson	21	666	416	279	.599
3	Christy Mathewson	17	551	373	188	.665
	Grover Alexander	20	598	373	208	.642
5	Warren Spahn*	21	665	363	245	.597
6	Kid Nichols	15	561	361	208	.634
	Pud Galvin	14	682	361	308	.540
8	Tim Keefe	14	594	342	225	.603
9	Steve Carlton*	24	709	329	244	.574
10	Eddie Plank*	17	527	327	193	.629
11	John Clarkson	12	518	326	177	.648
12	Don Sutton	23	756	324	256	.559
13	Nolan Ryan	26	760	319	287	.526
14	Phil Niekro	24	716	318	274	.537
15	Gaylord Perry	22	690	314	265	.542
16	Old Hoss Radbourn	12	503	311	194	.616
	Tom Seaver	20	647	311	205	.603
18	Mickey Welch	13	549	308	209	.596
19	Lefty Grove*	17	456	300	141	.680
	Early Wynn	23	612	300	244	.551
21	Tommy John*	26	700	288	231	.555
22	Bert Blyleven	22	685	287	250	.534
23	Robin Roberts	19	609	286	245	.539
24	Tony Mullane	13	505	285	220	.564
25	Ferguson Jenkins	19	594	284	226	.557
26	Jim Kaat*	25	625	283	237	.544
27	Red Ruffing	22	536	273	225	.548
28	Burleigh Grimes	19	495	270	212	.560
29	Jim Palmer	19	521	268	152	.638
30	Bob Feller	18	484	266	162	.621

Strikeouts

		Yrs	IP	SO	P/9
1	Nolan Ryan	26	5320.2	5668	9.59
2	Steve Carlton*	24	5217.1	4136	7.13
3	Bert Blyleven	22	4970.1	3701	6.70
4	Tom Seaver	20	4782.2	3640	6.85
5	Don Sutton	23	5282.1	3574	6.09
6	Gaylord Perry	22	5350.1	3534	5.94
7	Walter Johnson	21	5923.2	3509	5.33
8	Phil Niekro	24	5404.1	3342	5.57
9	Ferguson Jenkins	19	4500.2	3192	6.38
10	Bob Gibson	17	3884.1	3117	7.22
11	Jim Bunning	17	3760.1	2855	6.83
12	Mickey Lolich*	16	3638.1	2832	7.01
13	Cy Young	22	7354.2	2800	3.42
14	Frank Tanana*	20	3984.0	2657	6.00
15	Warren Spahn*	21	5243.2	2583	4.43
16	Bob Feller	18	3827.0	2581	6.07
17	Jerry Koosman*	19	3839.1	2556	5.99
18	Tim Keefe	14	5061.1	2527	4.50
19	Christy Mathewson	17	4781.0	2502	4.71
20	Don Drysdale	14	3432.0	2486	6.52
21	Jim Kaat*	25	4530.1	2461	4.89
22	Sam McDowell*	15	2492.1	2453	8.86
23	Luis Tiant	19	3486.1	2416	6.24
24	Sandy Koufax*	12	2324.1	2396	9.28
25	Robin Roberts	19	4688.2	2357	4.52
26	Early Wynn	23	4564.0	2334	4.60
27	Rube Waddell*	13	2961.1	2316	7.04
28	Juan Marichal	16	3507.1	2303	5.91
29	Jack Morris	16	3530.2	2275	5.80
30	Lefty Grove*	17	3940.2	2266	5.17

Pitchers Active in 1992

		Yrs	GS	W	L	Pct
1	Nolan Ryan	26	760	319	287	.526
2	Bert Blyleven	22	685	287	250	.534
3	Jack Morris	16	477	237	168	.585
4	Frank Tanana	20	585	233	219	.515
5	Charlie Hough	23	385	202	191	.514
6	Bob Welch	15	426	199	129	.607
7	Dennis Martinez	17	442	193	156	.553
8	Dennis Eckersley	18	361	181	145	.555
9	John Candelaria	18	356	177	119	.598
10	Dave Stieb	14	405	174	132	.569

Pitchers Active in 1992

		Yrs	IP	SO	P/9
1	Nolan Ryan	26	5320.2	5668	9.59
2	Bert Blyleven	22	4970.1	3701	6.70
3	Frank Tanana	20	3984.0	2657	6.00
4	Jack Morris	16	3530.2	2275	5.80
5	Charlie Hough	23	3482.1	2171	5.61
6	Dennis Eckersley	18	2971.1	2118	6.42
7	Roger Clemens	9	2031.0	1873	8.30
8	Bob Welch	15	2856.0	1862	5.87
9	Mark Langston	9	2072.2	1805	7.84
10	Floyd Bannister	15	2387.2	1723	6.49

All-Time Major League Leaders (Cont.)
Pitching

Winning Pct.

		Yrs	W-L	Pct
1	Bob Caruthers	9	218-97	.692
2	Dave Foutz	11	147-66	.690
3	Whitey Ford*	16	236-106	.690
4	**Dwight Gooden**	9	142-66	.683
5	**Roger Clemens**	9	152-73	.680
6	Lefty Grove*	17	300-141	.680
7	Vic Raschi	10	132-66	.667
8	Christy Mathewson	17	373-188	.665
9	Larry Corcoran	8	177-90	.663
10	Sam Leever	13	194-101	.658
11	Sal Maglie	10	119-62	.657
12	Sandy Koufax*	12	165-87	.655
13	Johnny Allen	13	142-75	.654
14	Ron Guidry*	14	170-91	.651
15	Lefty Gomez*	14	189-102	.649

Losses

		Yrs	GS	W	L	Pct
1	Cy Young	22	815	511	313	.620
2	Pud Galvin	14	682	361	310	.538
3	**Nolan Ryan**	26	760	319	287	.526
4	Walter Johnson	21	666	416	279	.599
5	Phil Niekro	24	716	318	274	.537
6	Gaylord Perry	22	690	314	265	.542
7	Jack Powell	16	517	245	256	.489
	Don Sutton	23	756	324	256	.559
9	Eppa Rixey*	21	552	266	251	.515
10	**Bert Blyleven**	22	685	287	250	.534
11	Robin Roberts	19	609	286	245	.539
	Warren Spahn*	21	665	363	245	.597
13	Early Wynn	23	612	300	244	.551
	Steve Carlton*	24	709	329	244	.574
15	Jim Kaat*	25	625	283	237	.544

Appearances

1	Hoyt Wilhelm	1070
2	Kent Tekulve	1050
3	Lindy McDaniel	987
4	Rollie Fingers	944
5	Gene Garber	931
6	**Rich Gossage**	927
7	Cy Young	906
8	Sparky Lyle	899
9	Jim Kaat	898
10	Don McMahon	874
11	Phil Niekro	864
12	Roy Face	848
13	Tug McGraw	824
14	**Jeff Reardon**	811
15	**Charlie Hough**	803

Innings Pitched

1	Cy Young	7354.2
2	Pud Galvin	5941.1
3	Walter Johnson	5923.2
4	Phil Niekro	5404.1
5	Gaylord Perry	5350.1
6	**Nolan Ryan**	5320.2
7	Don Sutton	5282.1
8	Warren Spahn	5243.2
9	Steve Carlton	5217.1
10	Grover Alexander	5189.1
11	Tim Keefe	5061.1
12	Kid Nichols	5057.1
13	**Bert Blyleven**	4970.1
14	Mickey Welch	4802.0
15	Tom Seaver	4782.2

Earned Run Avg.

1	Ed Walsh	1.82
2	Addie Joss	1.88
3	Three Finger Brown	2.06
4	Monte Ward	2.10
5	Christy Mathewson	2.13
6	Rube Waddell	2.16
7	Walter Johnson	2.17
8	Orval Overall	2.24
9	Tommy Bond	2.25
10	Will White	2.28
11	Ed Reulbach	2.28
12	Jim Scott	2.32
13	Eddie Plank	2.34
14	Larry Corcoran	2.36
15	Eddie Cicotte	2.37

Shutouts

1	Walter Johnson	110
2	Grover Alexander	90
3	Christy Mathewson	80
4	Cy Young	76
5	Eddie Plank	69
6	Warren Spahn	63
7	**Nolan Ryan**	61
	Tom Seaver	61
9	**Bert Blyleven**	60
10	Don Sutton	58
11	Three Finger Brown	57
	Pud Galvin	57
	Ed Walsh	57
14	Bob Gibson	56
15	Steve Carlton	55

Walks Allowed

1	**Nolan Ryan**	2755
2	Steve Carlton	1833
3	Phil Niekro	1809
4	Early Wynn	1775
5	Bob Feller	1764
6	Bobo Newsom	1732
7	Amos Rusie	1704
8	Gus Weyhing	1566
9	**Charlie Hough**	1542
10	Red Ruffing	1541
11	Bump Hadley	1442
12	Warren Spahn	1434
13	Earl Whitehill	1431
14	Tony Mullane	1409
15	Sad Sam Jones	1396

HRs Allowed

1	Robin Roberts	505
2	Ferguson Jenkins	484
3	Phil Niekro	482
4	Don Sutton	472
5	Warren Spahn	434
6	**Bert Blyleven**	430
7	**Frank Tanana**	420
8	Steve Carlton	414
9	Gaylord Perry	399
10	Jim Kaat	395
11	Tom Seaver	380
12	Catfish Hunter	374
13	Jim Bunning	372
14	Mickey Lolich	347
15	Luis Tiant	346

Saves

1	**Jeff Reardon**	357
2	**Lee Smith**	355
3	Rollie Fingers	341
4	**Rich Gossage**	308
5	Bruce Sutter	300
6	**Dave Righetti**	251
7	Dan Quisenberry	244
8	**Dennis Eckersley**	239
9	Sparky Lyle	238
10	Hoyt Wilhelm	227
11	**John Franco**	226
12	**Tom Henke**	220
13	Gene Garber	218
14	**Dave Smith**	216
15	**Bobby Thigpen**	200
16	Roy Face	193
17	Mike Marshall	188
18	Steve Bedrosian	184
	Kent Tekulve	184
20	Tug McGraw	180
21	Ron Perranoski	179
22	Lindy McDaniel	172
23	**Doug Jones**	164
24	Stu Miller	154
25	**Jay Howell**	153
	Don McMahon	153
27	Greg Minton	150
28	**Roger McDowell**	149
29	Ted Abernathy	148
30	Willie Hernandez	147

SINGLE SEASON
Through 1992 regular season.
Batting

Home Runs

		Year	Gm	AB	HR
1	Roger Maris, NY-AL	1961	162	590	61
2	Babe Ruth, NY-AL	1927	151	540	60
3	Babe Ruth, NY-AL	1921	152	540	59
4	Hank Greenberg, Det.	1938	155	556	58
	Jimmie Foxx, Phi-AL	1932	154	585	58
6	Hack Wilson, Chi-NL	1930	155	585	56
7	Babe Ruth, NY-AL	1920	142	458	54
	Mickey Mantle, NY-AL	1961	153	514	54
	Babe Ruth, NY-AL	1928	154	536	54
	Ralph Kiner, Pit	1949	152	549	54
11	Mickey Mantle, NY-AL	1956	150	533	52
	Willie Mays, SF.	1965	157	558	52
	George Foster, Cin	1977	158	615	52
14	Ralph Kiner, Pit	1947	152	565	51
	Cecil Fielder, Det.	1990	159	573	51
	Willie Mays, NY-NL	1955	152	580	51
	Johnny Mize, NY-NL	1947	154	586	51
18	Jimmie Foxx, Bos-AL	1938	149	565	50

Hits

		Year	AB	H	Avg
1	George Sisler, StL-AL	1920	631	257	.407
2	Bill Terry, NY-NL	1930	633	254	.401
	Lefty O'Doul, Phi-NL	1929	638	254	.398
4	Al Simmons, Phi-AL	1925	658	253	.384
5	Rogers Hornsby, StL-NL	1922	623	250	.401
6	Chuck Klein, Phi-NL	1930	648	250	.386
7	Ty Cobb, Det	1911	591	248	.420
8	George Sisler, StL-AL	1922	586	246	.420
9	Babe Herman, Bklyn	1930	614	241	.393
	Heinie Manush, StL-AL	1928	638	241	.378
11	Wade Boggs, Bos	1985	653	240	.368
12	Rod Carew, Min	1977	616	239	.388
13	Don Mattingly, NY-AL	1986	677	238	.352
14	Harry Heilmann, Det.	1921	602	237	.394
	Paul Waner, Pit	1927	623	237	.380
	Joe Medwick, StL-NL	1937	633	237	.374
17	Jack Tobin, StL-AL	1921	671	236	.352
18	Rogers Hornsby, StL-NL	1921	592	235	.397

Batting Average

From 1900-49

		Year	AB	H	Avg
1	Rogers Hornsby, StL-NL	1924	536	227	.424
2	Nap Lajoie, Phi-AL	1901	543	229	.422
3	George Sisler, StL-AL	1922	586	246	.420
	Ty Cobb, Det	1911	591	248	.420
5	Ty Cobb, Det	1912	533	227	.410
6	Joe Jackson, Cle	1911	571	233	.408
7	George Sisler, StL-AL	1920	631	257	.407
8	Ted Williams, Bos-AL	1941	456	185	.406
9	Rogers Hornsby, StL-NL	1925	504	203	.403
10	Harry Heilmann, Det.	1923	524	211	.403

Since 1950

		Year	AB	H	Avg
1	George Brett, KC	1980	449	175	.390
2	Ted Williams, Bos	1957	420	163	.388
	Rod Carew, Min	1977	616	239	.388
4	Tony Gwynn, SD	1987	589	218	.370
5	Wade Boggs, Bos	1985	653	240	.368
6	Wade Boggs, Bos	1988	584	214	.366
	Rico Carty, Atl	1970	478	175	.366
8	Mickey Mantle, NY-AL	1957	474	173	.365
9	Rod Carew, Min	1974	599	218	.364
10	Joe Torre, St.L	1971	634	230	.363
	Wade Boggs, Bos	1987	551	200	.363

Total Bases

From 1900-49

		Year	TB
1	Babe Ruth, New York-AL	1921	457
2	Rogers Hornsby, St.Louis-NL	1922	450
3	Lou Gehrig, New York-AL	1927	447
4	Chuck Klein, Philadelphia-NL	1930	445
5	Jimmie Foxx, Philadelphia-AL	1932	438
6	Stan Musial, St.Louis-NL	1948	429
7	Hack Wilson, Chicago-NL	1930	423
8	Chuck Klein, Philadelphia-NL	1932	420
9	Lou Gehrig, New York-AL	1930	419
10	Joe DiMaggio, New York-AL	1937	418

Since 1950

		Year	TB
1	Jim Rice, Boston	1978	406
2	Hank Aaron, Milwaukee	1959	400
3	George Foster, Cincinnati	1977	388
	Don Mattingly, New York-AL	1986	388
5	Willie Mays, New York-NL	1955	382
	Willie Mays, San Francisco	1962	382
	Jim Rice, Boston	1977	382
8	Frank Robinson, Cincinnati	1962	380
9	Ernie Banks, Chicago-NL	1958	379
10	Duke Snider, Brooklyn	1954	378

Runs Batted In

From 1900-49

		Year	Avg	HR	RBI
1	Hack Wilson, Chi-NL	1930	.356	56	190
2	Lou Gehrig, NY-AL	1931	.341	46	184
3	Hank Greenberg, Det.	1937	.337	40	183
4	Lou Gehrig, NY-AL	1927	.373	47	175
	Jimmie Foxx, Bos-AL	1938	.349	50	175
6	Lou Gehrig, NY-AL	1930	.379	41	174
7	Babe Ruth, NY-AL	1921	.378	59	171
8	Chuck Klein, Phi-NL	1930	.386	40	170
	Hank Greenberg, Det.	1935	.328	36	170
10	Jimmie Foxx, Phi-AL	1932	.364	58	169

Since 1950

		Year	Avg	HR	RBI
1	Tommy Davis, LA-NL	1962	.346	27	153
2	George Foster, Cin	1977	.320	52	149
3	Johnny Bench, Cin	1970	.293	45	148
4	Al Rosen, Cle	1953	.336	43	145
	Don Mattingly, NY-AL	1985	.324	35	145
6	Walt Dropo, Bos-AL	1950	.322	34	144
	Vern Stephens, Bos-AL	1950	.295	30	144
8	Ernie Banks, Chi-NL	1959	.304	45	143
9	Roy Campanella, Bklyn	1953	.312	41	142
	Orlando Cepeda, SF	1961	.311	46	142
	Roger Maris, NY-AL	1961	.269	61	142

All-Time Major League Leaders (Cont.)
Batting

Runs

		Year	Runs
1	Babe Ruth, New York-AL	1921	177
2	Lou Gehrig, New York-AL	1936	167
3	Babe Ruth, New York-AL	1928	163
	Lou Gehrig, New York-AL	1931	163
5	Babe Ruth, New York-AL	1920	158
	Babe Ruth, New York-AL	1927	158
	Chuck Klein, Philadelphia-NL	1930	158
8	Rogers Hornsby, Chicago-NL	1929	156
9	Kiki Cuyler, Chicago-NL	1930	155
10	Lefty O'Doul, Philadelphia-NL	1929	152
	Woody English, Chicago-NL	1930	152
	Al Simmons, Philadelphia-AL	1930	152
	Chuck Klein, Philadelphia-NL	1932	152
14	Babe Ruth, New York-AL	1923	151
	Jimmie Foxx, Philadelphia-AL	1932	151
	Joe DiMaggio, New York-AL	1937	151
17	Babe Ruth, New York-AL	1930	150
	Ted Williams, Boston-AL	1940	150
19	Lou Gehrig, New York-AL	1927	149
	Babe Ruth, New York-AL	1931	149

Walks

		Year	BB
1	Babe Ruth, New York-AL	1923	170
2	Ted Williams, Boston-AL	1947	162
	Ted Williams, Boston-AL	1949	162
4	Ted Williams, Boston-AL	1946	156
5	Eddie Yost, Washington	1956	151
6	Eddie Joost, Philadelphia-AL	1949	149
7	Babe Ruth, New York-AL	1920	148
	Eddie Stanky, Brooklyn	1945	148
	Jimmy Wynn, Houston	1969	148
10	Jimmy Sheckard, Chicago-NL	1911	147

Extra Base Hits

		Year	EBH
1	Babe Ruth, New York-AL	1921	119
2	Lou Gehrig, New York-AL	1927	117
3	Chuck Klein, Philadelphia-NL	1930	107
5	Chuck Klein, Philadelphia-NL	1932	103
	Hank Greenberg, Detroit	1937	103
	Stan Musial, St.Louis-NL	1948	103
7	Rogers Hornsby, St.Louis-NL	1922	102
8	Lou Gehrig, New York-AL	1930	100
	Jimmie Foxx, Philadelphia-AL	1933	100

Three tied with 99.

Slugging Average
From 1900-49

		Year	Avg
1	Babe Ruth, New York-AL	1920	.847
2	Babe Ruth, New York-AL	1921	.846
3	Babe Ruth, New York-AL	1927	.772
4	Lou Gehrig, New York-AL	1927	.765
5	Babe Ruth, New York-AL	1923	.764
6	Rogers Hornsby, St.Louis-NL	1925	.756
7	Jimmie Foxx, Philadelphia-AL	1932	.749
8	Babe Ruth, New York-AL	1924	.739
9	Babe Ruth, New York-AL	1926	.737
10	Ted Williams, Boston-AL	1941	.735

Since 1950

		Year	Avg
1	Ted Williams, Boston-AL	1957	.731
2	Mickey Mantle, New York-AL	1956	.705
3	Mickey Mantle, New York-AL	1961	.687
4	Hank Aaron, Atlanta	1971	.669
5	Willie Mays, New York-NL	1954	.667

Stolen Bases

		Year	SB
1	Rickey Henderson, Oakland	1982	130
2	Lou Brock, St.Louis	1974	118
3	Vince Coleman, St.Louis	1985	110
4	Vince Coleman, St.Louis	1987	109
5	Rickey Henderson, Oakland	1983	108
6	Vince Coleman, St.Louis	1986	107
7	Maury Wills, Los Angeles-NL	1962	104
8	Rickey Henderson, Oakland	1980	100
9	Ron LeFlore, Montreal	1980	97
10	Ty Cobb, Detroit	1915	96
11	Omar Moreno, Pittsburgh	1980	96
12	Maury Wills, Los Angeles	1965	94
13	Rickey Henderson, New York-AL	1988	93
14	Tim Raines, Montreal	1983	90
15	Clyde Milan, Washington	1912	88
16	Rickey Henderson, New York-AL	1986	87
17	Ty Cobb, Detroit	1911	83
	Willie Wilson, Kansas City	1979	83
19	Bob Bescher, Cincinnati	1911	81
	Eddie Collins, Philadelphia-AL	1910	81
	Vince Coleman, St.Louis	1988	81

Strikeouts

		Year	SO
1	Bobby Bonds, San Francisco	1970	189
2	Bobby Bonds, San Francisco	1969	187
3	Rob Deer, Milwaukee	1987	186
4	Pete Incaviglia, Texas	1986	185
5	Cecil Fielder, Detroit	1990	182
6	Mike Schmidt, Philadelphia	1975	180
7	Rob Deer, Milwaukee	1986	179
8	Dave Nicholson, Chicago-AL	1963	175
	Gorman Thomas, Milwaukee	1979	175
	Jose Canseco, Oakland	1986	175
	Rob Deer, Detroit	1991	175

Pinch Hits
Career pinch hits in parentheses.

		Year	PH	
1	Jose Morales, Montreal	1976	25	(123)
2	Dave Philley, Baltimore	1961	24	(93)
	Vic Davalillo, St.Louis	1970	24	(95)
	Rusty Staub, New York-NL	1983	24	(100)
5	Wallace Johnson, Montreal	1988	22	(78)
	Peanuts Lowrey, St.Louis	1953	22	(62)
	Sam Leslie, New York-NL	1932	22	(59)
	Red Schoendienst, St.Louis	1962	22	(56)

Note: The all-time career pinch hit leader is Manny Mota (150), followed by Smoky Burgess (145) and Greg Gross (143).

Four Home Runs in One Game
National League

	Date	H/A	Inn
Bobby Lowe, Boston	5/30/1894	H	9
Ed Delahanty, Philadelphia	7/13/1896	A	9
Chuck Klein, Philadelphia	7/10/1936	A	10
Gil Hodges, Brooklyn	8/31/1950	H	9
Joe Adcock, Milwaukee	7/31/1954	A	9
Willie Mays, San Francisco	4/30/1961	A	9
Mike Schmidt, Philadelphia	4/17/1976	A	10
Bob Horner, Atlanta	7/6/1986	H	9

American League

	Date	H/A	Inn
Lou Gehrig, New York	6/3/1932	A	9
Pat Seerey, Chicago	7/18/1948	A	11
Rocky Colavito, Cleveland	6/10/1959	A	9

Pitching

Wins

From 1900-49

		Year	W	L	Pct
1	Jack Chesbro, NY-AL	1904	41	12	.774
2	Ed Walsh, Chi-AL	1908	40	15	.727
3	Christy Mathewson, NY-NL	1908	37	11	.771
4	Walter Johnson, Wash	1913	36	7	.837
5	Joe McGinnity, NY-NL	1904	35	8	.814
6	Smokey Joe Wood, Bos-AL	1912	34	5	.872
7	Cy Young, Bos-AL	1901	33	10	.767
	Grover Alexander, Phi-NL	1916	33	12	.733
	Christy Mathewson, NY-NL	1904	33	12	.733

Since 1950

		Year	W	L	Pct
1	Denny McLain, Det	1968	31	6	.838
2	Robin Roberts, Phi-NL	1952	28	7	.800
3	Bob Welch, Oak	1990	27	6	.818
4	Don Newcombe, Bklyn	1956	27	7	.794
	Sandy Koufax, LA	1966	27	9	.750
6	Steve Carlton, Phi	1972	27	10	.730
7	Sandy Koufax, LA	1965	26	8	.765
	Juan Marichal, SF	1968	26	9	.743

Note: 11 pitchers tied with 25 wins, including Marichal twice.

Earned Run Average

From 1900-1949

		Year	ShO	ERA
1	Dutch Leonard, Bos-AL	1914	7	1.01
2	Three Finger Brown,	1906	10	1.04
3	Walter Johnson, Wash	1913	11	1.09
4	Bob Gibson, St.L	1968	13	1.12
5	Christy Mathewson, NY-NL	1909	8	1.14
6	Jack Pfiester, Chi-NL	1907	3	1.15
7	Addie Joss, Cle	1908	9	1.16
8	Carl Lundgren, Chi-NL	1907	7	1.17
9	Grover Alexander, Phi-NL	1915	12	1.22
10	Cy Young, Bos-AL	1908	3	1.26

Since 1950

		Year	ShO	ERA
1	Bob Gibson, St.L	1968	13	1.12
2	Dwight Gooden, NY-NL	1985	8	1.53
3	Luis Tiant, Cle	1968	9	1.60
4	Dean Chance, LA-AL	1964	11	1.65
5	Nolan Ryan, Cal	1981	3	1.69
6	Sandy Koufax, LA	1966	5	1.73
7	Sandy Koufax, LA	1964	7	1.74
8	Ron Guidry, NY-AL	1978	9	1.74
9	Tom Seaver, NY-NL	1971	4	1.76
10	Sam McDowell, Cle	1968	3	1.81

Winning Pct.

		Year	W-L	Pct
1	Roy Face, Pit	1959	18-1	.947
2	Rick Sutcliffe, Chi-NL*	1984	16-1	.941
3	Johnny Allen, Cle	1937	15-1	.938
4	Ron Guidry, NY-AL	1978	25-3	.893
5	Freddie Fitzsimmons, Bklyn	1940	16-2	.889
6	Lefty Grove, Phi-AL	1931	31-4	.886
7	Bob Stanley, Bos	1978	15-2	.882
8	Preacher Roe, Bklyn	1951	22-3	.880
9	Tom Seaver, Cin	1981	14-2	.875
10	Smokey Joe Wood, Bos-AL	1912	34-5	.872

*Sutcliffe began 1984 with Cleveland and was 4-5 before being traded to the Cubs; his overall winning pct. was .769 (20-6).

Strikeouts

		Year	SO	P/G
1	Nolan Ryan, Cal	1973	383	10.57
2	Sandy Koufax, LA	1965	382	10.24
3	Nolan Ryan, Cal	1974	367	9.92
4	Rube Waddell, Phi-AL	1904	349	8.12
5	Bob Feller, Cle	1946	348	8.45
6	Nolan Ryan, Cal	1977	341	10.26
7	Nolan Ryan, Cal	1972	329	10.43
8	Nolan Ryan, Cal	1976	327	10.36
9	Sam McDowell, Cle	1965	325	10.71
10	Sandy Koufax, LA	1966	317	8.83

Appearances

		Year	App	Sv
1	Mike Marshall, LA	1974	106	21
2	Kent Tekulve, Pit	1979	94	31
3	Mike Marshall, LA	1973	92	31
4	Kent Tekulve, Pit	1978	91	31
5	Wayne Granger, Cin	1969	90	27
	Mike Marshall, Min	1979	90	32
	Kent Tekulve, Phi	1987	90	3

Saves

		Year	App	Sv
1	Bobby Thigpen, Chi-AL	1990	77	57
2	Dennis Eckersley, Oak	1992	69	51
3	Dennis Eckersley, Oak	1990	63	48
4	Lee Smith, St. L	1991	67	47
5	Dave Righetti, NY-AL	1986	74	46
	Bryan Harvey, Cal	1991	67	46

Innings Pitched (since 1920)

		Year	IP	W-L
1	Wilbur Wood, Chi-AL	1972	377	24-17
2	Mickey Lolich, Det	1971	376	25-14
3	Bob Feller, Cle	1946	371	26-15
4	Grover Alexander, Chi-NL	1920	363	27-14
5	Wilbur Wood, Chi-AL	1973	359	24-20

Shutouts

		Year	ShO	ERA
1	Grover Alexander, Phi-NL	1916	16	1.55
2	Jack Coombs, Phi-AL	1910	13	1.30
	Bob Gibson, St.L	1968	13	1.12
4	Christy Mathewson, NY-NL	1908	12	1.43
	Grover Alexander, Phi-NL	1915	12	1.22

Walks Allowed

		Year	BB	SO
1	Bob Feller, Cle	1938	208	240
2	Nolan Ryan, Cal	1977	204	341
3	Nolan Ryan, Cal	1974	202	367
4	Bob Feller, Cle	1941	194	260
5	Bobo Newsom, St.L-AL	1938	192	226

Home Runs Allowed

		Year	HRs
1	Bert Blyleven, Minnesota	1986	50
2	Robin Roberts, Philadelphia	1956	46
	Bert Blyleven, Minnesota	1987	46
4	Pedro Ramos, Washington	1957	43
5	Denny McLain, Detroit	1966	42

The All-Star Game

Baseball's first All-Star Game was held on July 6, 1933, before 47,595 at Comiskey Park in Chicago. From that year on, the All-Star Game has matched the best players in the American League against the best in the National. From 1959-62, two All-Star Games were played and in 1945, World War II travel restrictions made it necessary to call the All-Star Game off. The NL leads the series, 37-24-1. In the chart below, the American League is listed in **bold** type.

Year		Host (Ballpark)	AL Manager	NL Manager
1933	**American,** 4-2	Chicago (Comiskey Park)	Connie Mack	John McGraw
1934	**American,** 9-7	New York (Polo Grounds)	Joe Cronin	Bill Terry
1935	**American,** 4-1	Cleveland (Cleveland Stadium)	Mickey Cochrane	Frankie Frisch
1936	National, 4-3	Boston (Braves Field)	Joe McCarthy	Charlie Grimm
1937	**American,** 8-3	Washington (Griffith Stadium)	Joe McCarthy	Bill Terry
1938	National, 4-1	Cincinnati (Crosley Field)	Joe McCarthy	Bill Terry
1939	**American,** 3-1	New York (Yankee Stadium)	Joe McCarthy	Gabby Hartnett
1940	National, 4-0	St.Louis (Sportsman's Park)	Joe Cronin	Bill McKechnie
1941	**American,** 7-5	Detroit (Briggs Stadium)	Del Baker	Bill McKechnie
1942	**American,** 3-1	New York (Polo Grounds)	Joe McCarthy	Leo Durocher
1943	**American,** 5-3	Philadelphia (Shibe Park)	Joe McCarthy	Billy Southworth
1944	National, 7-1	Pittsburgh (Forbes Field)	Joe McCarthy	Billy Southworth
1945	No Game			
1946	**American,** 12-0	Boston (Fenway Park)	Steve O'Neill	Charlie Grimm
1947	**American,** 2-1	Chicago (Wrigley Field)	Joe Cronin	Eddie Dyer
1948	**American,** 5-2	St.Louis (Sportsman's Park)	Bucky Harris	Leo Durocher
1949	**American,** 11-7	Brooklyn (Ebbets Field)	Lou Boudreau	Billy Southworth
1950	National, 4-3 (14)	Chicago (Comiskey Park)	Casey Stengel	Burt Shotton
1951	National, 8-3	Detroit (Briggs Stadium)	Casey Stengel	Eddie Sawyer
1952	National, 3-2 (5, rain)	Philadelphia (Shibe Park)	Casey Stengel	Leo Durocher
1953	National, 5-1	Cincinnati (Crosley Field)	Casey Stengel	Charlie Dressen
1954	**American,** 11-9	Cleveland (Cleveland Stadium)	Casey Stengel	Walter Alston
1955	National, 6-5 (12)	Milwaukee (County Stadium)	Al Lopez	Leo Durocher
1956	National, 7-3	Washington (Griffith Stadium)	Casey Stengel	Walter Alston
1957	**American,** 6-5	St.Louis (Busch Stadium)	Casey Stengel	Walter Alston
1958	**American,** 4-3	Baltimore (Memorial Stadium)	Casey Stengel	Fred Haney
1959 Game 1	National, 5-4	Pittsburgh (Forbes Field)	Casey Stengel	Fred Haney
Game 2	**American,** 5-3	Los Angeles (Memorial Coliseum)	Casey Stengel	Fred Haney
1960 Game 1	National, 5-3	Kansas City (Municipal Stadium)	Al Lopez	Walter Alston
Game 2	National, 6-0	New York (Yankee Stadium)	Al Lopez	Walter Alston
1961 Game 1	National, 5-4 (10)	San Francisco (Candlestick Park)	Paul Richards	Danny Murtaugh
Game 2	TIE, 1-1 (9, rain)	Boston (Fenway Park)	Paul Richards	Danny Murtaugh
1962 Game 1	National, 3-1	Washington (D.C.Stadium)	Ralph Houk	Fred Hutchinson
Game 2	**American,** 9-4	Chicago (Wrigley Field)	Ralph Houk	Fred Hutchinson
1963	National, 5-3	Cleveland (Cleveland Stadium)	Ralph Houk	Alvin Dark
1964	National, 7-4	New York (Shea Stadium)	Al Lopez	Walter Alston
1965	National, 6-5	Minnesota (Metropolitan Stadium)	Al Lopez	Gene Mauch
1966	National, 2-1 (10)	St.Louis (Busch Memorial Stadium)	Sam Mele	Walter Alston
1967	National, 2-1 (15)	California (Anaheim Stadium)	Hank Bauer	Walter Alston
1968	National, 1-0	Houston (The Astrodome)	Dick Williams	Red Schoendienst
1969	National, 9-3	Washington (RFK Stadium)	Mayo Smith	Red Schoendienst
1970	National, 5-4 (12)	Cincinnati (Riverfront Stadium)	Earl Weaver	Gil Hodges
1971	**American,** 6-4	Detroit (Tiger Stadium)	Earl Weaver	Sparky Anderson
1972	National, 4-3 (10)	Atlanta (Atlanta Stadium)	Earl Weaver	Danny Murtaugh
1973	National, 7-1	Kansas City (Royals Stadium)	Dick Williams	Sparky Anderson
1974	National, 7-2	Pittsburgh (Three Rivers Stadium)	Dick Williams	Yogi Berra
1975	National, 6-3	Milwaukee (County Stadium)	Alvin Dark	Walter Alston
1976	National, 7-1	Philadelphia (Veterans Stadium)	Darrell Johnson	Sparky Anderson
1977	National, 7-5	New York (Yankee Stadium)	Billy Martin	Sparky Anderson
1978	National, 7-3	San Diego (San Diego Stadium)	Billy Martin	Tommy Lasorda
1979	National, 7-6	Seattle (The Kingdome)	Bob Lemon	Tommy Lasorda
1980	National, 4-2	Los Angeles (Dodger Stadium)	Earl Weaver	Chuck Tanner
1981	National, 5-4	Cleveland (Cleveland Stadium)	Jim Frey	Dallas Green
1982	National, 4-1	Montreal (Olympic Stadium)	Billy Martin	Tommy Lasorda
1983	**American,** 13-3	Chicago (Comiskey Park)	Harvey Kuenn	Whitey Herzog
1984	National, 3-1	San Francisco (Candlestick Park)	Joe Altobelli	Paul Owens
1985	National, 6-1	Minnesota (HHH Metrodome)	Sparky Anderson	Dick Williams
1986	**American,** 3-2	Houston (The Astrodome)	Dick Howser	Whitey Herzog
1987	National, 2-0 (13)	Oakland (Oakland Coliseum)	John McNamara	Davey Johnson
1988	**American,** 2-1	Cincinnati (Riverfront Stadium)	Tom Kelly	Whitey Herzog
1989	**American,** 5-3	California (Anaheim Stadium)	Tony La Russa	Tommy Lasorda
1990	**American,** 2-0	Chicago (Wrigley Field)	Tony La Russa	Roger Craig
1991	**American,** 4-2	Toronto (SkyDome)	Tony La Russa	Lou Piniella
1992	**American,** 13-6	San Diego (SD/Murphy Stadium)	Tom Kelly	Bobby Cox

Arch Ward Memorial Award

The All-Star Game MVP award is named after Arch Ward, the Chicago Tribune sports editor who founded the game in 1933. First given at the two All-Star games in 1962, the name of the award was changed to the Commissioner's Trophy in 1970 and back to the Ward Memorial Award in 1985.
Multiple winners: Gary Carter, Steve Garvey and Willie Mays (2).

Year		Year		Year	
1962-a	Maury Wills, LA (NL), SS	1972	Joe Morgan, Cin., 2B	1982	Dave Concepcion, Cin., SS
1962-b	Leon Wagner, LA (AL), OF	1973	Bobby Bonds, SF, OF	1983	Fred Lynn, Cal., OF
1963	Willie Mays, SF, OF	1974	Steve Garvey, LA, 1B	1984	Gary Carter, Mon., C
1964	Johnny Callison, Phi., OF	1975	Bill Madlock, Chi.(NL), 3B	1985	LaMarr Hoyt, SD, P
1965	Juan Marichal, SF, P		& Jon Matlock, NY (NL), P	1986	Roger Clemens, Bos., P
1966	Brooks Robinson, Bal., 3B	1976	George Foster, Cin., OF	1987	Tim Raines, Mon., OF
1967	Tony Perez, Cin., 3B	1977	Don Sutton, LA, P	1988	Terry Steinbach, Oak., C
1968	Willie Mays, SF, OF	1978	Steve Garvey, LA, 1B	1989	Bo Jackson, KC, OF
1969	Willie McCovey, SF, 1B	1979	Dave Parker, Pit, OF		
				1990	Julio Franco, Tex., 2B
1970	Carl Yastrzemski, Bos., OF-1B	1980	Ken Griffey, Cin., OF	1991	Cal Ripken, Bal., SS
1971	Frank Robinson, Bal., OF	1981	Gary Carter, Mon., C	1992	Ken Griffey, Sea., OF

All-Time Winningest Managers

Top 20 Major League career victories through the 1991 season. Career, regular season and postseason (playoffs and World Series) records are noted along with AL and NL pennants and World Series titles won. Managers active during 1991 season in **bold** type.

			Career			Regular Season			Postseason			
		Yrs	W	L	Pct	W	L	Pct	W	L	Pct	Titles
1	Connie Mack	53	**3755**	3967	.486	3731	3948	.486	24	19	.558	9 AL, 5 WS
2	John McGraw	33	**2810**	1987	.586	2784	1959	.587	26	28	.482	10 NL, 2 WS
3	Bucky Harris	29	**2168**	2228	.493	2157	2218	.493	11	10	.524	3 AL, 2 WS
4	Joe McCarthy	24	**2155**	1346	.616	2125	1333	.615	30	13	.698	1 NL, 8 AL, 7 WS
5	Walter Alston	23	**2063**	1634	.558	2040	1613	.558	23	21	.523	7 NL, 4 WS
6	**Sparky Anderson**	23	**2030**	1632	.554	1996	1611	.553	34	21	.618	4 NL, 1 AL, 3 WS
7	Leo Durocher	24	**2015**	1717	.540	2008	1709	.540	7	8	.467	3 NL, 1 WS
8	Casey Stengel	25	**1942**	1868	.510	1905	1842	.508	37	26	.587	10 AL, 7 WS
9	Gene Mauch	26	**1907**	2044	.483	1902	2037	.483	5	7	.417	—None—
10	Bill McKechnie	25	**1904**	1737	.523	1896	1723	.524	8	14	.364	4 NL, 2 WS
11	Ralph Houk	20	**1627**	1539	.514	1619	1531	.514	8	8	.500	3 AL, 2 WS
12	Fred Clarke	19	**1609**	1189	.575	1602	1181	.576	7	8	.467	2 NL, 1 WS
13	Dick Williams	21	**1592**	1474	.519	1571	1451	.520	21	23	.477	3 AL, 1 NL, 2 WS
14	Earl Weaver	17	**1506**	1080	.582	1480	1060	.583	26	20	.565	4 AL, 1 WS
15	Clark Griffith	20	**1491**	1367	.522	1491	1367	.522	0	0	.000	1 AL (1901)
16	Miller Huggins	17	**1431**	1149	.555	1413	1134	.555	18	15	.545	6 AL, 3 WS
17	Al Lopez	17	**1412**	1012	.583	1410	1004	.584	2	8	.200	2 AL
18	Jimmy Dykes	21	**1406**	1541	.477	1406	1541	.477	0	0	.000	—None—
19	Wilbert Robertson	19	**1402**	1407	.499	1399	1398	.500	3	9	.250	2 NL
20	**Tommy Lasorda**	17	**1372**	1228	.528	1341	1201	.528	31	27	.534	4 NL, 2 WS

Notes: John McGraw's postseason record also includes two World Series tie games (1912, '22); Miller Huggins postseason record also includes one World Series tie game (1922).

Where They Managed

Alston—Brooklyn/Los Angeles NL (1954-76); **Anderson**—Cincinnati NL (1970-78), Detroit AL (1979—); **Clarke**—Louisville NL (1897-99), Pittsburgh NL (1900-15); **Durocher**—Brooklyn NL (1939-46,48), New York NL (1948-55), Chicago NL (1966-72), Houston NL (1972-73); **Dykes**—Chicago AL (1934-46), Philadelphia AL (1951-53), Baltimore AL (1954), Cincinnati NL (1958), Detroit AL (1959-60), Cleveland AL (1960-61); **Griffith**—Chicago AL (1901-02), New York AL (1903-08), Cincinnati NL (1909-11), Washington AL (1912-20); **Harris**—Washington AL (1924-28,35-42,50-54), Detroit AL (1929-33,55-56), Boston AL (1934), Philadelphia NL (1943), New York AL (1947-48); **Houk**—New York AL (1961-63,66-73), Detroit AL (1974-78), Boston AL (1981-84); **Huggins**—St.Louis NL (1913-17), New York AL (1918-29); **Lasorda**—Los Angeles NL (1976—); **Lopez**—Cleveland AL (1951-56), Chicago AL (1957-65,68-69).

Mack—Pittsburgh NL (1894-96), Philadelphia AL (1901-50); **Mauch**—Philadelphia NL (1960-68), Montreal NL (1969-75), Minnesota AL (1976-80), California AL (1981-82,85-87); **McCarthy**—Chicago NL (1926-30), New York AL (1931-46), Boston AL (1948-50); **McGraw**—Baltimore AL (1899), Baltimore NL (1901-02), New York NL (1902-32); **McKechnie**—Newark FL (1915), Pittsburgh NL (1922-26), St.Louis NL (1928-29), Boston NL (1930-37), Cincinnati NL (1938-46); **Robertson**—Baltimore AL (1902), Brooklyn NL (1914-31); **Stengel**—Brooklyn NL (1934-36), Boston NL (1938-43), New York AL (1949-60), New York NL (1962-65); **Weaver**—Baltimore AL (1968-82,85-86); **Williams**—Boston AL (1967-69), Oakland AL (1971-73), California AL (1974-76), Montreal NL (1977-81), San Diego NL (1982-85), Seattle AL (1986-88).

All-Time Winningest Managers (Cont.)

Regular Season Winning Pct.
Minimum of 750 victories.

		Yrs	W	L	Pct	Pen
1	Joe McCarthy	24	2125	1333	.614	9
2	Charlie Comiskey	12	838	541	.608	4
3	Frank Selee	16	1284	862	.598	5
4	Billy Southworth	13	1044	704	.597	4
5	Frank Chance	11	946	648	.593	4
6	John McGraw	33	2784	1959	.587	9
7	Al Lopez	17	1410	1004	.584	2
8	Earl Weaver	17	1480	1060	.583	4
9	Harry Wright	23	1225	885	.581	6
10	Cap Anson	20	1296	947	.578	5
11	Fred Clarke	19	1602	1181	.576	2
12	Steve O'Neill	14	1040	821	.559	1
13	Walter Alston	23	2040	1613	.558	7
14	Bill Terry	10	823	661	.555	3
15	Miller Huggins	17	1413	1134	.555	6
16	**Sparky Anderson**	23	1996	1611	.554	5
17	Billy Martin	16	1253	1013	.553	2
18	Charlie Grimm	19	1287	1067	.547	3
19	**Tony La Russa**	14	1134	949	.544	3
20	Hugh Jennings	15	1163	984	.542	3

World Series Victories

		App	W	L	T	Pct	WS
1	Casey Stengel	10	37	26	0	.587	7
2	Joe McCarthy	9	30	13	0	.698	7
3	John McGraw	9	26	28	2	.482	2
4	Connie Mack	8	24	19	0	.558	5
5	Walter Alston	7	20	20	0	.523	4
6	Miller Huggins	6	18	15	1	.544	3
7	**Sparky Anderson**	5	16	12	0	.571	3
8	**Tommy Lasorda**	4	12	11	0	.522	2
	Dick Williams	4	12	14	0	.462	2
10	Frank Chance	4	11	9	1	.548	2
	Bucky Harris	3	11	10	0	.524	2
	Billy Southworth	4	11	11	0	.500	2
	Earl Weaver	4	11	13	0	.458	1
14	Whitey Herzog	3	10	11	0	.476	1
15	Bill Carrigan	2	8	2	0	.800	2
	Danny Murtaugh	2	8	6	0	.571	2
	Ralph Houk	2	8	8	0	.500	2
	Bill McKechnie	4	8	14	0	.364	2
	Tom Kelly	2	8	6	0	.571	2

Seven tied with 7 wins each.

Active Managers Records
Regular season games only; through 1992.

American League

		Yrs	W	L	Pct
1	Sparky Anderson, Det	23	**1996**	1611	.553
2	Tony La Russa, Oak	14	**1134**	949	.544
3	Buck Rodgers, Cal*	11	**696**	659	.514
4	Tom Kelly, Min	7	**527**	468	.530
5	Cito Gaston, Tor†	4	**323**	242	.572
6	Johnny Oates, Balt	2	**143**	144	.498
7	Hal McRae, KC	2	**138**	148	.483
8	Mike Hargrove, Cle	2	**108**	139	.437
9	Phil Garner, Mil	1	**92**	70	.568
10	Gene Lamont, Chi	1	**86**	76	.531
11	Buck Showalter, NY	1	**76**	86	.469
12	Butch Hobson, Bos	1	**73**	89	.451
13	Kevin Kennedy, Tex	0	**0**	0	.000

Seattle job vacant as of Oct. 30.

National League

		Yrs	W	L	Pct
1	Tommy Lasorda, LA	17	**1341**	1201	.528
2	Bobby Cox, Atl	11	**853**	804	.515
3	Roger Craig, SF	10	**738**	737	.500
4	Joe Torre, St.L	10	**734**	840	.466
5	Jim Leyland, Pit	8	**593**	541	.523
6	Jim Fregosi, Phi	9	**574**	641	.472
7	Jeff Torborg, NY	7	**479**	526	.477
8	Jim LeFebvre, Chi	4	**311**	337	.480
9	Art Howe, Hou	4	**307**	341	.474
10	Rene Lachemann, Fla	4	**207**	274	.430
11	Felipe Alou, Mon	1	**70**	55	.560
12	Jim Riggleman, SD	1	**4**	8	.333
13	Don Baylor, Colo	0	**0**	0	.000
14	Tony Perez, Cin	0	**0**	0	.000

*Rodgers' total does not include California's 39-50 record while he was on a medical leave from May 22 to Aug.28. Coach John Wathan gets credit for a 36-49 record and Marcel Lachemann gets credit for a 3-1 record.

†Gaston's total does not include Toronto's 19-14 record while he was on a 33-day medical leave from Aug.26-Sept.27. Coach and interim manager Gene Tenace gets credit for those 33 games.

Annual Awards
Most Valuable Player

There have been three different Most Valuable Player awards in baseball since 1911—the Chalmers Award (1911-14), presented by the Detroit-based automobile company; the League Award (1922-29), presented by the National and American Leagues; and the Baseball Writers' Award (since 1931), presented by the Baseball Writers' Association of America. Statistics for winning players are provided below. Stats for winning pitchers are listed separately.

Multiple winners: NL—Roy Campanella, Stan Musial and Mike Schmidt (3); Ernie Banks, Johnny Bench, Rogers Hornsby, Carl Hubbell, Willie Mays, Joe Morgan and Dale Murphy (2). **AL**—Yogi Berra, Joe DiMaggio, Jimmie Foxx and Mickey Mantle (3); Mickey Cochrane, Lou Gehrig, Hank Greenberg, Walter Johnson, Roger Maris, Hal Newhouser, Cal Ripken and Ted Williams (2). **NL & AL**—Frank Robinson (2, one in each).

Chalmers Award
Winning pitchers' statistics on next page.

National League

Year		Pos	HR	RBI	Avg
1911	Wildfire Schulte, Chi	OF	21	121	.300
1912	Larry Doyle, NY	2B	10	90	.330
1913	Jake Daubert, Bklyn	1B	2	52	.350
1914	Johnny Evers, Bos	2B	1	40	.279

American League

Year		Pos	HR	RBI	Avg
1911	Ty Cobb, Det	OF	8	144	.420
1912	Tris Speaker, Bos	OF	10	98	.383
1913	Walter Johnson, Wash	P	—	—	—
1914	Eddie Collins, Phi	2B	2	85	.344

League Award

Winning pitchers' statistics on next page.

National League

Year		Pos	HR	RBI	Avg
1922	No selection				
1923	No selection				
1924	Dazzy Vance, Bklyn	P	—	—	—
1925	Rogers Hornsby, St.L	2B-Mgr	29	143	.403
1926	Bob O'Farrell, St.L	C	7	68	.293
1927	Paul Waner, Pit	OF	9	131	.380
1928	Jim Bottomley, St.L	1B	31	136	.325
1929	Rogers Hornsby, Chi	2B	39	149	.380

American League

Year		Pos	HR	RBI	Avg
1922	George Sisler, St.L	1B	8	105	.420
1923	Babe Ruth, NY	OF	41	131	.393
1924	Walter Johnson, Wash.	P	—	—	—
1925	Roger Peckinpaugh, Wash	SS	4	64	.294
1926	George Burns, Cle	1B	4	114	.358
1927	Lou Gehrig, NY	1B	47	175	.373
1928	Mickey Cochrane, Phi	C	10	57	.293
1929	No selection				

Baseball Writers' Award

Winning pitchers' statistics on next page.

National League

Year		Pos	HR	RBI	Avg
1930	Hack Wilson, Chi	OF	56	190	.356
1931	Frankie Frisch, St.L	2B	4	82	.311
1932	Chuck Klein, Phi	OF	38	137	.348
1933	Carl Hubbell, NY	P	—	—	—
1934	Dizzy Dean, St.L	P	—	—	—
1935	Gabby Hartnett,	C	13	91	.344
1936	Carl Hubbell, NY	P	—	—	—
1937	Joe Medwick, St.L	OF	31	154	.374
1938	Ernie Lombardi, Cin	C	19	95	.342
1939	Bucky Walters, Cin.	P	—	—	—
1940	Frank McCormick, Cin	1B	19	127	.309
1941	Dolf Camilli, Bklyn.	1B	34	120	.285
1942	Mort Cooper, St.L	P	—	—	—
1943	Stan Musial, St.L	OF	13	81	.357
1944	Marty Marion, St.L	SS	6	63	.267
1945	Phil Cavarretta, Chi	1B	6	97	.355
1946	Stan Musial, St.L	1B-OF	16	103	.365
1947	Bob Elliott, Bos	3B	22	113	.317
1948	Stan Musial, St.L	OF	39	131	.376
1949	Jackie Robinson, Bklyn	2B	16	124	.342
1950	Jim Konstanty, Phi	P	—	—	—
1951	Roy Campanella, Bklyn	C	33	108	.325
1952	Hank Sauer, Chi	OF	37	121	.270
1953	Roy Campanella, Bklyn	C	41	142	.312
1954	Willie Mays, NY	OF	41	110	.345
1955	Roy Campanella, Bklyn	C	32	107	.318
1956	Don Newcombe, Bklyn	P	—	—	—
1957	Hank Aaron, Mil	OF	44	132	.322
1958	Ernie Banks, Chi.	SS	47	129	.313
1959	Ernie Banks, Chi.	SS	45	143	.304
1960	Dick Groat, Pit	SS	2	50	.325
1961	Frank Robinson, Cin.	OF	37	124	.323
1962	Maury Wills, LA	SS	6	48	.299
1963	Sandy Koufax, LA.	P	—	—	—
1964	Ken Boyer, St.L.	3B	24	119	.295
1965	Willie Mays, SF	OF	52	112	.317
1966	Roberto Clemente, Pit.	OF	29	119	.317
1967	Orlando Cepeda, St.L.	1B	25	111	.325
1968	Bob Gibson, St.L	P	—	—	—
1969	Willie McCovey, SF	1B	45	126	.320
1970	Johnny Bench, Cin	C	45	148	.293
1971	Joe Torre, St.L	3B	24	137	.363
1972	Johnny Bench, Cin	C	40	125	.270
1973	Pete Rose, Cin	OF	5	64	.338
1974	Steve Garvey, LA	1B	21	111	.312
1975	Joe Morgan, Cin	2B	17	94	.327
1976	Joe Morgan, Cin	2B	27	111	.320
1977	George Foster, Cin	OF	52	149	.320
1978	Dave Parker, Pit	OF	30	117	.334
1979	Keith Hernandez, St.L	1B	11	105	.344
	& Willie Stargell, Pit	1B	32	82	.281

American League

Year		Pos	HR	RBI	Avg
1930	Joe Cronin, Wash	SS	13	126	.346
1931	Lefty Grove, Phi	P	—	—	—
1932	Jimmie Foxx, Phi	1B	58	169	.364
1933	Jimmie Foxx, Phi	1B	48	163	.356
1934	Mickey Cochrane, Det	C-Mgr	2	76	.320
1935	Hank Greenberg, Det	1B	36	170	.328
1936	Lou Gehrig, NY	1B	49	152	.354
1937	Charlie Gehringer, Det	2B	14	96	.371
1938	Jimmie Foxx, Bos	1B	50	175	.349
1939	Joe DiMaggio, NY	OF	30	126	.381
1940	Hank Greenberg, Det	OF	41	150	.340
1941	Joe DiMaggio, NY	OF	30	125	.357
1942	Joe Gordon, NY	2B	18	103	.322
1943	Spud Chandler, NY	P	—	—	—
1944	Hal Newhouser, Det	P	—	—	—
1945	Hal Newhouser, Det	P	—	—	—
1946	Ted Williams, Bos	OF	38	123	.342
1947	Joe DiMaggio, NY	OF	20	97	.315
1948	Lou Boudreau, Cle	SS-Mgr	18	106	.355
1949	Ted Williams, Bos	OF	43	159	.343
1950	Phil Rizzuto, NY	SS	7	66	.324
1951	Yogi Berra, NY	C	27	88	.294
1952	Bobby Shantz, Phi	P	—	—	—
1953	Al Rosen, Cle	3B	43	145	.336
1954	Yogi Berra, NY	C	22	125	.307
1955	Yogi Berra, NY	C	27	108	.272
1956	Mickey Mantle, NY	OF	52	130	.353
1957	Mickey Mantle, NY	OF	34	94	.365
1958	Jackie Jensen, Bos	OF	35	122	.286
1959	Nellie Fox, Chi	2B	2	70	.306
1960	Roger Maris, NY	OF	39	112	.283
1961	Roger Maris, NY	OF	61	142	.269
1962	Mickey Mantle, NY	OF	30	89	.321
1963	Elston Howard, NY	C	28	85	.287
1964	Brooks Robinson, Bal	3B	28	118	.317
1965	Zoilo Versalles, Min	SS	19	77	.273
1966	Frank Robinson, Bal	OF	49	122	.316
1967	Carl Yastrzemski, Bos	OF	44	121	.326
1968	Denny McLain, Det	P	—	—	—
1969	Harmon Killebrew, Min	3B-1B	49	140	.276
1970	Boog Powell, Bal	1B	35	114	.297
1971	Vida Blue, Oak.	P	—	—	—
1972	Dick Allen, Chi	1B	37	113	.308
1973	Reggie Jackson, Oak	OF	32	117	.293
1974	Jeff Burroughs, Tex.	OF	25	118	.301
1975	Fred Lynn, Bos	OF	21	105	.331
1976	Thurman Munson, NY	C	17	105	.302
1977	Rod Carew, Min.	1B	14	100	.388
1978	Jim Rice, Bos	OF-DH	46	139	.315
1979	Don Baylor, Cal	OF-DH	36	139	.296

Annual Awards (Cont.)
Most Valuable Player

National League Year	Pos	HR	RBI	Avg	American League Year	Pos	HR	RBI	Avg
1980 Mike Schmidt, Phi	3B	48	121	.286	1980 George Brett, KC	3B	24	118	.390
1981 Mike Schmidt, Phi	3B	31	91	.316	1981 Rollie Fingers, Mil	P	—	—	—
1982 Dale Murphy, Atl	OF	36	109	.281	1982 Robin Yount, Mil	SS	29	114	.331
1983 Dale Murphy, Atl	OF	36	121	.302	1983 Cal Ripken, Bal	SS	27	102	.318
1984 Ryne Sandberg, Chi	2B	19	84	.314	1984 Willie Hernandez, Det	P	—	—	—
1985 Willie McGee, St.L	OF	10	82	.353	1985 Don Mattingly, NY	1B	35	145	.324
1986 Mike Schmidt, Phi	3B	37	119	.290	1986 Roger Clemens, Bos	P	—	—	—
1987 Andre Dawson, Chi	OF	49	137	.287	1987 George Bell, Tor	OF	47	134	.308
1988 Kirk Gibson, LA	OF	25	76	.290	1988 Jose Canseco, Oak	OF	42	124	.307
1989 Kevin Mitchell, SF	OF	47	125	.291	1989 Robin Yount, Mil	OF	21	103	.318
1990 Barry Bonds, Pit	OF	33	114	.301	1990 Rickey Henderson, Oak	OF	28	61	.325
1991 Terry Pendleton, Atl	3B	22	86	.319	1991 Cal Ripken, Bal	SS	34	114	.323

MVP Pitchers' Statistics

Pitchers have been named Most Valuable Player on 22 occasions, 10 times in the NL and 12 in the AL. Three have been relief pitchers—Jim Konstanty, Rollie Fingers and Willie Hernandez.

National League Year	Gm	W-L	SV	ERA	American League Year	Gm	W-L	SV	ERA
1924 Dazzy Vance, Bklyn	35	28-6	0	2.16	1913 Walter Johnson, Wash	47	36-7	2	1.09
1933 Carl Hubbell, NY	45	23-12	5	1.66	1924 Walter Johnson, Wash	38	23-7	0	2.72
1934 Dizzy Dean, St.L	50	30-7	7	2.65	1931 Lefty Grove, Phi	41	31-4	5	2.05
1936 Carl Hubbell, NY	42	26-6	3	2.31	1943 Spud Chandler, NY	30	20-4	0	1.64
1939 Bucky Walters, Cin	39	27-11	0	2.29	1944 Hal Newhouser, Det	47	29-9	2	2.22
1942 Mort Cooper, St.L	37	22-7	0	1.77	1945 Hal Newhouser, Det	40	25-9	0	1.81
1950 Jim Konstanty, Phi	74	16-7	22	2.66	1952 Bobby Shantz, Phi	33	24-7	0	2.48
1956 Don Newcombe, Bklyn	38	27-7	0	3.06	1968 Denny McLain, Det	41	31-6	0	1.96
1963 Sandy Koufax, LA	40	25-5	0	1.88	1971 Vida Blue, Oak	39	24-8	0	1.82
1968 Bob Gibson, St.L	34	22-9	0	1.12	1981 Rollie Fingers, Mil	47	6-3	28	1.04
					1984 Willie Hernandez, Det	80	9-3	32	1.92
					1986 Roger Clemens, Bos	33	24-4	0	2.48

Cy Young Award

Voted on by the Baseball Writers Association of America. One award was presented from 1956-66, two since 1967. Pitchers who won the MVP and Cy Young awards in the same season are in **bold** type.

Multiple winners: NL—Steve Carlton (4); Sandy Koufax and Tom Seaver (3); Bob Gibson (2). **AL**—Jim Palmer (3); Roger Clemens and Denny McLain (2). **NL & AL**—Gaylord Perry (2, one in each).

NL-AL Combined

Year	National League	Gm	W-L	SV	ERA	Year	American League	Gm	W-L	SV	ERA
1956	**Don Newcombe**, Bklyn	38	27-7	0	3.06	1958	Bob Turley, NY	33	21-7	1	2.97
1957	Warren Spahn, Mil	39	21-11	3	2.69	1959	Early Wynn, Chi	37	22-10	0	3.17
1960	Vernon Law, Pit	35	20-9	0	3.08	1961	Whitey Ford, NY	39	25-4	0	3.21
1962	Don Drysdale, LA	43	25-9	1	2.83	1964	Dean Chance, LA	46	20-9	4	1.65
1963	**Sandy Koufax**, LA	40	25-5	0	1.88						
1965	Sandy Koufax, LA	43	26-8	2	2.04						
1966	Sandy Koufax, LA	41	27-9	0	1.73						

Separate League Awards

National League Year	Gm	W-L	SV	ERA	American League Year	Gm	W-L	SV	ERA
1967 Mike McCormick, SF	40	22-10	0	2.85	1967 Jim Lonborg, Bos	39	22-9	0	3.16
1968 **Bob Gibson**, St.L	34	22-9	0	1.12	1968 **Denny McLain**, Det	41	31-6	0	1.96
1969 Tom Seaver, NY	36	25-7	0	2.21	1969 Denny McLain, Det	42	24-9	0	2.80
					& Mike Cuellar, Bal	39	23-11	0	2.38
1970 Bob Gibson, St.L	34	23-7	0	3.12	1970 Jim Perry, Min	40	24-12	0	3.03
1971 Ferguson Jenkins, Chi	39	24-13	0	2.77	1971 **Vida Blue**, Oak	39	24-8	0	1.82
1972 Steve Carlton, Phi	41	27-10	0	1.97	1972 Gaylord Perry, Cle	41	24-16	1	1.92
1973 Tom Seaver, NY	36	19-10	0	2.08	1973 Jim Palmer, Bal	38	22-9	1	2.40
1974 Mike Marshall, LA	106	15-12	21	2.42	1974 Catfish Hunter, Oak	41	25-12	0	2.49

	National League					American League			
Year		Gm	W-L	SV ERA	Year		Gm	W-L	SV ERA
1975	Tom Seaver, NY	36	22-9	0 2.38	1975	Jim Palmer, Bal	39	23-11	1 2.09
1976	Randy Jones, SD	40	22-14	0 2.74	1976	Jim Palmer, Bal	40	22-13	0 2.51
1977	Steve Carlton, Phi.	36	23-10	0 2.64	1977	Sparky Lyle, NY	72	13-5	26 2.17
1978	Gaylord Perry, SD	37	21-6	0 2.72	1978	Ron Guidry, NY	35	25-3	0 1.74
1979	Bruce Sutter, Chi	62	6-6	37 2.23	1979	Mike Flanagan, Bal	39	23-9	0 3.08
1980	Steve Carlton, Phi.	38	24-9	0 2.34	1980	Steve Stone, Bal	37	25-7	0 3.23
1981	Fernando Valenzuela, LA	25	13-7	0 2.48	1981	**Rollie Fingers**, Mil	47	6-3	28 1.04
1982	Steve Carlton, Phi.	38	23-11	0 3.10	1982	Pete Vuckovich, Mil	30	18-6	0 3.34
1983	John Denny, Phi.	36	19-6	0 2.37	1983	LaMarr Hoyt, Chi.	36	24-10	0 3.66
1984	Rick Sutcliffe, Chi	20*	16-1	0 2.69	1984	**Willie Hernandez**, Det	80	9-3	32 1.92
1985	Dwight Gooden, NY	35	24-4	0 1.53	1985	Bret Saberhagen, KC	32	20-6	0 2.87
1986	Mike Scott, Hou	37	18-10	0 2.22	1986	**Roger Clemens**, Bos	33	24-4	0 2.48
1987	Steve Bedrosian, Phi	65	5-3	40 2.83	1987	Roger Clemens, Bos	36	20-9	0 2.97
1988	Orel Hershiser, LA	35	23-8	1 2.26	1988	Frank Viola, Min	35	24-7	0 2.64
1989	Mark Davis, SD	70	4-3	44 1.85	1989	Bret Saberhagen, KC	36	23-6	0 2.16
1990	Doug Drabek, Pit	33	22-6	0 2.76	1990	Bob Welch, Oak	35	27-6	0 2.95
1991	Tom Glavine, Atl	34	20-11	0 2.55	1991	Roger Clemens, Bos	35	18-10	0 2.62

*NL games only, Sutcliffe pitched 15 games with Cleveland before being traded to the Cubs.

Rookie of the Year

Voted on by the Baseball Writers Assn. of America. One award was presented from 1947-48. Two awards (one for each league) have been presented since 1949.

AL and NL Combined

Year		Pos	Year		Pos
1947	Jackie Robinson, Brooklyn	1B	1948	Alvin Dark, Boston, NL	SS

National League

Year		Pos	Year		Pos	Year		Pos
1949	Don Newcombe, Bkln	P	1964	Richie Allen, Phi	3B	1978	Bob Horner, Atl	3B
1950	Sam Jethroe, Bos	OF	1965	Jim Lefebvre, LA	2B	1979	Rick Sutcliffe, LA	P
1951	Willie Mays, NY	OF	1966	Tommy Helms, Cin	3B	1980	Steve Howe, LA	P
1952	Joe Black, Bkln	P	1967	Tom Seaver, NY	P	1981	Fernando Valenzuela, LA	P
1953	Jim Gilliam, Bkln	2B	1968	Johnny Bench, Cin	C	1982	Steve Sax, LA	2B
1954	Wally Moon, St.L.	OF	1969	Ted Sizemore, LA.	2B	1983	Darryl Strawberry, NY	OF
1955	Bill Virdon, St.L.	OF	1970	Carl Morton, Mon	P	1984	Dwight Gooden, NY	P
1956	Frank Robinson, Cin.	OF	1971	Earl Williams, Atl	C	1985	Vince Coleman, St.L.	OF
1957	Jack Sanford, Phi	P	1972	Jon Matlack, NY.	P	1986	Todd Warrell, St.L	P
1958	Orlando Cepeda, SF.	1B	1973	Gary Matthews, SF	OF	1987	Benito Santiago, SD	C
1959	Willie McCovey, SF	1B	1974	Bake McBride, St.L	OF	1988	Chris Sabo, Cin	3B
1960	Frank Howard, LA	OF	1975	John Montefusco, SF	P	1989	Jerome Walton, Chi	OF
1961	Billy Williams, Chi	OF	1976	Butch Metzger, SD	P	1990	David Justice, Atl	OF
1962	Ken Hubbs, Chi	2B		& Pat Zachry, Cin.	P	1991	Jeff Bagwell, Hou	1B
1963	Pete Rose, Cin	2B	1977	Andre Dawson, Mon	OF			

American League

Year		Pos	Year		Pos	Year		Pos
1949	Roy Sievers, St.L	OF	1964	Tony Oliva, Min	OF	1979	John Castino, Min	3B
			1965	Curt Blefary, Bal	OF		& Alfredo Griffin, Tor	SS
1950	Walt Dropo, Bos	1B	1966	Tommie Agee, Chi	OF	1980	Joe Charboneau, Cle	OF-DH
1951	Gil McDougald, NY	3B	1967	Rod Carew, Min.	2B	1981	Dave Righetti, NY	P
1952	Harry Byrd, Phi	P	1968	Stan Bahnsen, NY	P	1982	Cal Ripken, Bal	SS-3B
1953	Harvey Kuenn, Det.	SS	1969	Lou Piniella, KC.	OF	1983	Ron Kittle, Chi	OF
1954	Bob Grim, NY	P	1970	Thurman Munson, NY	C	1984	Alvin Davis, Sea	1B
1955	Herb Score, Cle	P	1971	Chris Chambliss, Cle	1B	1985	Ozzie Guillen, Chi	SS
1956	Luis Aparicio, Chi	SS	1972	Carlton Fisk, Bos	C	1986	Jose Canseco, Oak	OF
1957	Tony Kubek, NY	INF-OF	1973	Al Bumbry, Bal	OF	1987	Mark McGwire, Oak	1B
1958	Albie Pearson, Wash	OF	1974	Mike Hargrove, Tex.	1B	1988	Walt Weiss, Oak	SS
1959	Bob Allison, Wash.	OF	1975	Fred Lynn, Bos	OF	1989	Gregg Olson, Bal.	P
1960	Ron Hansen, Bal	SS	1976	Mark Fidrych, Det.	P	1990	Sandy Alomar, Cle	C
1961	Don Schwall, Bos	P	1977	Eddie Murray, Bal	DH-1B	1991	Chuck Knoblauch, Min	2B
1962	Tom Tresh, NY.	SS-OF	1978	Lou Whitaker, Det	2B			
1963	Gary Peters, Chi	P						

Annual Awards (Cont.)
The Sporting News' MVP Awards

When the major leagues temporarily discontinued their Most Valuable Player awards in 1929 (AL) and 1930 (NL), The Sporting News stepped in to present its own league honors—for MVP from 1929-45 and for Player and Pitcher of the Year since 1948. There were no awards given in 1946 and '47.

National League

Multiple winners: Carl Hubbell and Chuck Klein (2).

Year	Pos	Year	Pos	Year	Pos
1929 No selection		1935 Arky Vaughan, Pit	SS	1941 Dolf Camilli, Bklyn	1B
1930 Bill Terry, NY	1B	1936 Carl Hubbell, NY	P	1942 Mort Cooper, St.L	P
1931 Chuck Klein, Phi	OF	1937 Joe Medwick, St.L	OF	1943 Stan Musial, St.L	OF
1932 Chuck Klein, Phi	OF	1938 Ernie Lombardi, Cin	C	1944 Marty Marion, St.L	SS
1933 Carl Hubbell, NY	P	1939 Bucky Walters, Cin	P	1945 Tommy Holmes, Bos	OF
1934 Dizzie Dean, St.L	P	1940 Frank McCormick, Cin	1B		

American League

Multiple winners: Jimmie Foxx and Lou Gehrig (3); Joe DiMaggio and Hank Greenberg (2).

Year	Pos	Year	Pos	Year	Pos
1929 Al Simmons, Phi	OF	1935 Hank Greenberg, Det	1B	1941 Joe DiMaggio, NY	OF
1930 Joe Cronin, Wash	SS	1936 Lou Gehrig, NY	1B	1942 Joe Gordon, NY	2B
1931 Lou Gehrig, NY	1B	1937 Charlie Gehringer, Det	2B	1943 Spud Chandler, NY	P
1932 Jimmie Foxx, Phi	1B	1938 Jimmie Foxx, Bos	1B	1944 Bobby Doerr, Bos	2B
1933 Jimmie Foxx, Phi	1B	1939 Joe DiMaggio, NY	OF	1945 Eddie Mayo, Det	2B
1934 Lou Gehrig, NY	1B	1940 Hank Greenberg, Det	OF		

The Sporting News' Players of the Year

National League

Multiple winners: Hank Aaron, Ernie Banks, Barry Bonds, Andre Dawson, George Foster, Willie Mays, Dale Murphy, Stan Musial and Mike Schmidt (2).

Year	Pos	Year	Pos	Year	Pos
1948 Stan Musial, St.L	OF-1B	1963 Hank Aaron, Mil	OF	1978 Dave Parker, Pit	OF
1949 Enos Slaughter, St.L	OF	1964 Ken Boyer, St.L	3B	1979 Keith Hernandez, St.L	1B
1950 Ralph Kiner, Pit	OF	1965 Willie Mays, SF	OF	1980 Mike Schmidt, Phi	3B
1951 Stan Musial, St.L	OF	1966 Roberto Clemente, Pit	OF	1981 Andre Dawson, Mon	OF
1952 Hank Sauer, Chi	OF	1967 Orlando Cepeda, St.L	1B	1982 Dale Murphy, Atl	OF
1953 Roy Campanella, Bklyn	C	1968 Pete Rose, Cin	OF	1983 Dale Murphy, Atl	OF
1954 Willie Mays, NY	OF	1969 Willie McCovey, SF	1B	1984 Ryne Sandberg, Chi	2B
1955 Duke Snider, Bklyn	OF	1970 Johnny Bench, Cin	C	1985 Willie McGee, St.L	OF
1956 Hank Aaron, Mil	OF	1971 Joe Torre, St.L	3B	1986 Mike Schmidt, Phi	3B
1957 Stan Musial, St.L	1B	1972 Billy Williams, Chi	OF	1987 Andre Dawson, Chi	OF
1958 Ernie Banks, Chi	SS	1973 Bobby Bonds, SF	OF	1988 Andy Van Slyke, Pit	OF
1959 Ernie Banks, Chi	SS	1974 Lou Brock, St.L	OF	1989 Kevin Mitchell, SF	OF
1960 Dick Groat, Pit	SS	1975 Joe Morgan, Cin	2B	1990 Barry Bonds, Pit	OF
1961 Frank Robinson, Cin	OF	1976 George Foster, Cin	OF	1991 Barry Bonds, Pit	OF
1962 Maury Wills, LA	SS	1977 George Foster, Cin	OF		

American League

Multiple winners: Don Mattingly (3); Al Kaline, Harmon Killebrew, Mickey Mantle, Roger Maris, Tony Oliva, Carl Ripken and Ted Williams (2).

Year	Pos	Year	Pos	Year	Pos
1948 Lou Boudreau, Cle	SS	1963 Al Kaline, Det	OF	1978 Jim Rice, Bos	OF
1949 Ted Williams, Bos	OF	1964 Brooks Robinson, Bal	3B	1979 Don Baylor, Cal	OF-DH
1950 Phil Rizzuto, NY	SS	1965 Tony Oliva, Min	OF	1980 George Brett, KC	3B
1951 Ferris Fain, Phi	1B	1966 Frank Robinson, Bal	OF	1981 Tony Armas, Oak	OF
1952 Luke Easter, Cle	1B	1967 Carl Yastrzemski, Bos	OF	1982 Robin Yount, Mil	SS
1953 Al Rosen, Cle	3B	1968 Ken Harrelson, Bos	OF	1983 Cal Ripken, Bal	SS
1954 Bobby Avila, Cle	2B	1969 Harmon Killebrew, Min	INF	1984 Don Mattingly, NY	1B
1955 Al Kaline, Det	OF	1970 Harmon Killebrew, Min	INF	1985 Don Mattingly, NY	1B
1956 Mickey Mantle, NY	OF	1971 Tony Oliva, Min	OF	1986 Don Mattingly, NY	1B
1957 Ted Williams, Bos	OF	1972 Dick Allen, Chi	1B	1987 George Bell, NY	OF
1958 Jackie Jensen, Bos	OF	1973 Reggie Jackson, Oak	OF	1988 Jose Canseco, Oak	OF
1959 Nellie Fox, Chi	2B	1974 Jeff Burroughs, Tex	OF	1989 Ruben Sierra, Tex	OF
1960 Roger Maris, NY	OF	1975 Fred Lynn, Bos	OF	1990 Cecil Fielder, Det	1B
1961 Roger Maris, NY	OF	1976 Thurman Munson, NY	C	1991 Cal Ripken, Bal	SS
1962 Mickey Mantle, NY	OF	1977 Rod Carew, Min	1B		

The Sporting News' Pitchers of the Year

National League

Multiple winners: Steve Carlton, Sandy Koufax and Warren Spahn (4); Bob Gibson, Robin Roberts, Tom Seaver and Rick Sutcliffe (2).

Year		Year		Year	
1948	Johnny Sain, Bos.	1963	Sandy Koufax, LA	1978	Vida Blue, SF
1949	Howie Pollet, St.L.	1964	Sandy Koufax, LA	1979	Joe Niekro, Hou.
		1965	Sandy Koufax, LA		
1950	Jim Konstanty, Phi.	1966	Sandy Koufax, LA	1980	Steve Carlton, Phi.
1951	Preacher Roe, Bklyn.	1967	Mike McCormick, SF	1981	Fernando Valenzuela, LA
1952	Robin Roberts, Phi.	1968	Bob Gibson, St.L.	1982	Steve Carlton, Phi.
1953	Warren Spahn, Mil.	1969	Tom Seaver, NY	1983	John Denny, Phi.
1954	Johnny Antonelli, NY			1984	Rick Sutcliffe, Chi.
1955	Robin Roberts, Phi.	1970	Bob Gibson, St.L.	1985	Dwight Gooden, NY
1956	Don Newcombe, Bklyn.	1971	Ferguson Jenkins, Chi.	1986	Mike Scott, Hou.
1957	Warren Spahn, Mil.	1972	Steve Carlton, Phi.	1987	Rick Sutcliffe, Chi.
1958	Warren Spahn, Mil.	1973	Ron Bryant, SF	1988	Orel Hershiser, LA
1959	Sam Jones, SF	1974	Mike Marshall, LA	1989	Mark Davis, SD
		1975	Tom Seaver, NY		
1960	Vernon Law, Pit.	1976	Randy Jones, SD	1990	Doug Drabek, Pit.
1961	Warren Spahn, Mil.	1977	Steve Carlton, Phi.	1991	Tom Glavine, Atl.
1962	Don Drysdale, LA				

American League

Multiple winners: Whitey Ford, Bob Lemon and Jim Palmer (3); Roger Clemens, Denny McLain, Billy Pierce and Bret Saberhagen (2).

Year		Year		Year	
1948	Bob Lemon, Cle.	1963	Whitey Ford, NY	1978	Ron Guidry, NY
1949	Ellis Kinder, Bos.	1964	Dean Chance, LA	1979	Mike Flanagan, Bal.
		1965	Mudcat Grant, Min.		
1950	Bob Leman, Cle.	1966	Jim Kaat, Min.	1980	Steve Stone, Bal.
1951	Bob Feller, Cle.	1967	Jim Lonborg, Bos.	1981	Jack Morris, Det.
1952	Bobby Shantz, Phi.	1968	Denny McLain, Det.	1982	Dave Stieb, Tor.
1953	Bob Porterfield, Wash.	1969	Denny McLain, Det.	1983	LaMarr Hoyt, Chi.
1954	Bob Lemon, Cle.			1984	Willie Hernandez, Det.
1955	Whitey Ford, NY.	1970	Sam McDowell, Cle	1985	Bret Saberhagen, KC
1956	Billy Pierce, Chi.	1971	Vida Blue, Oak.	1986	Roger Clemens, Bos.
1957	Billy Pierce, Chi.	1972	Wilbur Wood, Chi.	1987	Jimmy Key, Tor.
1958	Bob Turley, NY	1973	Jim Palmer, Bal.	1988	Frank Viola, Min.
1959	Early Wynn, Chi.	1974	Catfish Hunter, Oak.	1989	Bret Saberhagen, KC
		1975	Jim Palmer, Bal.		
1960	Chuck Estrada, Bal.	1976	Jim Palmer, Bal.	1990	Bob Welch, Oak.
1961	Whitey Ford, NY	1977	Nolan Ryan, Cal.	1991	Roger Clemens, Bos.
1962	Dick Donavan, Cle.				

The Sporting News' Rookies of the Year

One award was presented from 1946-48 and in 1950. Two awards (one for each league) were presented in 1949 and from 1951-62. And four awards (best rookie player and pitcher in each league) have been regularly presented since 1963.

AL and NL Combined

Year			Year		
1946	Del Ennis, Philadelphia, NL	OF	1948	Richie Ashburn, Philadelphia, NL	OF
1947	Jackie Robinson, Brooklyn	1B	1950	Whitey Ford, New York, AL	P

American League

Year		Pos	Year		Pos	Year		Pos
1949	Roy Sievers, St.L	OF	1962	Tom Tresh, NY.	OF-SS	1970	Roy Foster, Cle	OF
			1963	Pete Ward, Chi	3B		& Bert Blyleven, Min.	P
1950	Combined pick (see above)			& Gary Peters, Chi.	P	1971	Chris Chambliss, NY.	1B
1951	Minnie Minoso, Chi	OF	1964	Tony Oliva, Min	OF		& Bill Parsons, Mil.	P
1952	Clint Courtney, St.L	C		& Wally Bunker, Bal	P	1972	Carlton Fisk, Bos	C
1953	Harvey Kuenn, Det.	SS	1965	Curt Blefary, Bal	OF		& Dick Tidrow, Cle.	P
1954	Bob Grim, NY	P		& Marcelino Lopez	P	1973	Al Bumbry, Bal	OF
1955	Herb Score, Cle	P	1966	Tommie Agee, Chi	OF		& Steve Busby, KC	P
1956	Luis Aparicio, Chi.	SS		& Jim Nash, KC	P	1974	Mike Hargrove, Tex.	1B
1957	Tony Kubek, NY	INF-OF	1967	Rod Carew, Min.	2B		& Frank Tanana, Cal.	P
1958	Albie Pearson, Wash	OF		& Tom Phoebus, Bal	P	1975	Fred Lynn, Bos	OF
	& Ryne Duran, NY	P	1968	Del Unser, Wash.	OF		& Dennis Eckersley, Cle.	P
1959	Bob Allison, Wash.	OF		& Stan Bahnsen, NY	P	1976	Butch Wynegar, Min	C
1960	Ron Hansen, Bal	SS	1969	Carlos May, Chi	OF		& Mark Fidrych, Det.	P
1961	Dick Howser, KC	SS		& Mike Nagy, Bos	P	1977	Mitchell Page, Oak.	OF
	& Don Schwall, Bos	P					& Dave Rozema, Det	P

Annual Awards (Cont.)
The Sporting News' Rookies of the Year

American League

Year		Pos	Year		Pos	Year		Pos
1978	Paul Molitor, Mil.	2B	1983	Ron Kittle, Chi	OF	1988	Walt Weiss, Oak	SS
	& Rich Gale, KC	P		& Mike Boddicker, Bal	P		& Bryan Harvey, Cal	P
1979	Pat Putnam, Tex.	1B	1984	Alvin Davis, Sea	1B	1989	Craig Worthington, Bal	3b
	& Mark Clear, Cal	P		& Mark Langston, Sea	P		& Tom Gordon, KC	P
1980	Joe Charboneau, Cle.	OF	1985	Ozzie Guillen, Chi	SS	1990	Sandy Alomar, Jr., Cle	C
	& Britt Burns, Chi	P		& Teddy Higuera, Mil.	P		& Kevin Appier, KC	P
1981	Rich Gedman, Bos	C	1986	Jose Canseco, Oak	OF	1991	Chuck Knoblauch, Min	2B
	& Dave Righetti, NY	P		& Mark Eichhorn, Tor.	P		& Juan Guzman, Tor	P
1982	Cal Ripken, Bal.	SS-3B	1987	Mark McGwire, Oak.	1B			
	& Ed Vande Berg, Sea	P		& Mike Henneman, Det.	P			

National League

Year		Pos	Year		Pos	Year		Pos
1949	Don Newcombe, Bklyn.	P	1967	Lee May, Cin	1B	1980	Lonnie Smith, Phi	OF
				& Dick Hughes, St.L	P		& Bill Gullickson, Mon	P
1950	Combined pick (see above)		1968	Johnny Bench, Cin	C	1981	Tim Raines, MON.	OF
1951	Willie Mays, NY.	OF		Jerry Koosman, NY	P		& Fernando Valenzuela, LA.	P
1952	Joe Black, Bklyn	P	1969	Coco Laboy, Mon	3B	1982	Johnny Ray, Pit.	2B
1953	Jim Gilliam, Bklyn	2B		Tom Griffin, Hou	P		Steve Bedrosian, Atl	P
1954	Wally Moon, St.L.	OF	1970	Bernie Carbo, Cin	OF	1983	Darryl Strawberry, NY	OF
1955	Bill Virdon, St.L.	OF		& Carl Morton, Mon	P		Craig McMurty, Atl.	P
1956	Frank Robinson, Cin.	OF	1971	Earl Williams, Atl	C	1984	Juan Samuel, Phi.	2B
1957	Ed Bouchee, Phi.	1B		& Reggie Cleveland, St.L	P		& Dwight Gooden, NY	P
	& Jack Sanford, Phi	P	1972	Dave Rader, SF	C	1985	Vince Coleman, St.L.	OF
1958	Orlando Cepeda, SF.	1B		& Jon Matlack, NY	P		& Tom Browning, Cin	P
	& Carlton Willey, Mil	P	1973	Gary Matthews, SF	OF	1986	Robby Thompson, SF	2B
1959	Willie McCovey, SF	1B		& Steve Rogers, Mon	P		Todd Worrell, St.L	P
1960	Frank Howard, LA	OF	1974	Greg Gross, Hou	OF	1987	Benito Santiago, SD	C
1961	Billy Williams, Chi.	OF		& John D'Acquisto, SF	P		& Mike Dunne, Pit	P
	& Ken Hunt, Cin.	P	1975	Gary Carter, Mon.	OF-C	1988	Mark Grace, Chi	1B
1962	Ken Hubbs, Chi	2B		& John Montefusco, SF	P		Tim Belcher, LA	P
1963	Pete Rose, Cin	2B	1976	Larry Herndon, SF	OF	1989	Jerome Walton, Chi	OF
	& Ray Culp, Phi	P		Butch Metzger, SD	P		& Andy Benes, SD	P
1964	Richie Allen, Phi	3B	1977	Andre Dawson, Mon	OF	1990	David Justice, Atl.	OF
	& Billy McCool, Cin	P		Bob Owchinko, SD.	P		Mike Harkey, Chi	P
1965	Joe Morgan, Hou	2B	1978	Bob Horner, Atl	3B	1991	Jeff Bagwell, Hou.	1B
	& Frank Linzy, SF	P		& Don Robinson, Pit.	P		Al Osuna, Hou.	P
1966	Tommy Helms, Cin.	3B	1979	Jeff Leonard, Hou.	OF			
	& Don Sutton, LA	P		Rick Sutcliffe, LA	P			

The Sporting News' Manager of the Year

One award was presented from 1936-85. Two awards (one for each league) have been presented since 1986. Note that (*) indicates a league pennant (1936-68) or division championship (since 1969).

Multiple winners: Walter Alston, Leo Durocher, Joe McCarthy and Casey Stengel (3); Tony La Russa, Jim Leyland, Bill McKechnie, Danny Murtaugh, Billy Southworth, Bill Virdon and Earl Weaver (2).

AL and NL Combined

Year		Improvement			Year		Improvement		
1936	Joe McCarthy, NY (AL)	89-60	to	102-51*	1955	Walter Alston, Bklyn	92-62	to	98-55*
1937	Bill McKechnie, Bos.(NL)	71-83	to	79-73	1956	Birdie Tebbetts, Cin	75-79	to	91-63
1938	Joe McCarthy, NY (AL)	102-52*	to	99-53*	1957	Fred Hutchinson, St.L.	76-78	to	87-67
1939	Leo Durocher, Bklyn.(NL)	69-80	to	84-69	1958	Casey Stengel, NY (AL)	98-56*	to	92-62*
1940	Bill McKechnie, Cin	97-57*	to	100-53*	1959	Walter Alston, LA.	71-83	to	88-68*
1941	Billy Southworth, St.L.(NL)	84-69	to	97-56	1960	Danny Murtaugh, Pit.	78-76	to	95-59*
1942	Billy Southworth, St.L.(NL)	97-56	to	106-48*	1961	Ralph Houk, NY (AL)	97-57*	to	109-53*
1943	Joe McCarthy, NY (AL)	103-51*	to	98-56*	1962	Bill Rigney, LA (AL)	70-91	to	86-76
1944	Luke Sewell, St.L.(AL)	72-80	to	89-65*	1963	Walter Alston, LA.	102-63	to	99-63*
1945	Ossie Bluege, Wash.	64-90	to	87-67	1964	Johnny Keane, St.L.	93-69	to	93-69*
1946	Eddie Dyer, St.L.(NL)	95-59	to	98-58*	1965	Sam Mele, Min	79-83	to	102-60*
1947	Bucky Harris, NY (AL)	87-67	to	97-57*	1966	Hank Bauer, Bal	94-68	to	97-63*
1948	Bill Meyer, Pit.	62-92	to	83-71	1967	Dick Williams, Bos.	72-90	to	92-70*
1949	Casey Stengel, NY (AL)	94-60	to	97-57*	1968	Mayo Smith, Det	91-71	to	103-59*
1950	Red Rolfe, Det	87-67	to	95-59	1969	Gil Hodges, NY (NL)	73-89	to	100-62*
1951	Leo Durocher, NY (NL)	86-68	to	98-59*	1970	Danny Murtaugh, Pit.	88-74	to	89-73*
1952	Eddie Stanky, St.L.	81-73	to	88-66	1971	Charlie Fox, SF	86-76	to	90-72*
1953	Casey Stengel, NY (AL)	95-59*	to	99-52*	1972	Chuck Tanner, Chi. (AL)	79-83	to	87-67
1954	Leo Durocher, NY (NL)	70-84	to	97-57*	1973	Gene Mauch, Mon	70-86	to	79-83

Year		Improvement			Year		Improvement		
1974	Bill Virdon, NY (AL)	80-82	to	89-73	1980	Bill Virdon, Hou	89-73	to	93-70*
1975	Darrell Johnson, Bos.	84-78	to	95-65*	1981	Billy Martin, Oak	83-79	to	64-45*
1976	Danny Ozark, Phi	86-76	to	101-61*	1982	Whitey Herzog, St.L.	59-43	to	92-70*
1977	Earl Weaver, Bal	88-74	to	97-64	1983	Tony La Russa, Chi. (AL)	87-75	to	99-63*
1978	George Bamberger, Mil	67-95	to	93-69	1984	Jim Frey, Chi. (NL)	71-91	to	96-75*
1979	Earl Weaver, Bal	90-71	to	102-57*	1985	Bobby Cox, Tor	89-73	to	99-62*

Note: In 1981, both league seasons were reduced to 110 games or less due to a players' strike.

National League

Year		Improvement		
1986	Hal Lanier, Hou.	83-79	to	96-66*
1987	Buck Rogers, Mon	78-83	to	91-71
1988	Tommy Lasorda, LA	73-89	to	94-67*
	& Jim Leyland, Pit	80-82	to	85-75
1989	Don Zimmer, Chi	77-85	to	93-69*
1990	Jim Leyland, Pit	74-88	to	95-67
1991	Bobby Cox, Atl.	65-97	to	94-68*

American League

Year		Improvement		
1986	John McNamara, Bos.	81-81	to	95-66*
1987	Sparky Anderson, Det.	87-75	to	98-64*
1988	Tony La Russa, Oak	81-81	to	104-58*
1989	Frank Robinson, Bal	54-107	to	87-75
1990	Jeff Torborg, Chi.	69-92	to	94-68
1991	Tom Kelly, Min	74-88	to	95-67*

The Sporting News' Executive of the Year

Multiple winners: George Weiss (4); Branch Rickey (3); Ed Barrow, Harry Dalton, Bing Devine, Roland Hemond, Dick O'Connell, Gabe Paul, Hank Peters and Bill Veeck (2).

AL and NL Combined

Year			Year			Year		
1936	Branch Rickey, St.L	NL	1956	Gabe Paul, Cin	NL	1975	Dick O'Connell, Bos	AL
1937	Ed Barrow, NY	AL	1957	France Lane, St.L.	NL	1976	Joe Burke, KC	AL
1938	Warren Giles, Cin	NL	1958	Joe Brown, Pit	NL	1977	Bill Veeck, Chi	AL
1939	Larry MacPhail, Bklyn	NL	1959	Buzzie Barasi, LA	NL	1978	Spec Richardson, SF	NL
1940	W.O.Briggs Sr., Det.	AL	1960	George Weiss, NY	AL	1979	Hank Peters, Bal.	AL
1941	Ed Barrow, NY	AL	1961	Dan Topping, NY	AL	1980	Tal Smith, Hou.	NL
1942	Branch Rickey, St.L	NL	1962	Fred Haney, LA	NL	1981	John McHale, Mon	AL
1943	Clark Griffith, Wash	AL	1963	Bing Devine, St.L.	NL	1982	Harry Dalton, Mil.	AL
1944	William DeWitt, St.L.	AL	1964	Bing Devine, St.L.	NL	1983	Hank Peters, Bal.	AL
1945	Philip Wrigley, Chi.	NL	1965	Calvin Griffith, Min	AL	1984	Dallas Green, Chi.	NL
1946	Thomas Yawkey, Bos.	AL	1966	Lee MacPhail, Commissioner's Office		1985	John Schuerholz, KC	AL
1947	Branch Rickey, Bklyn	AL				1986	Frank Cashen, NY	NL
1948	Bill Veeck, Cle	AL	1967	Dick O'Connell, Bos	AL	1987	Al Rosen, SF.	NL
1949	Robert Carpenter, Phi	NL	1968	James Campbell, Det	AL	1988	Fred Claire, LA	NL
			1969	John Murphy, NY	NL	1989	Roland Hemond, Bal	AL
1950	George Weiss, NY.	AL	1970	Harry Dalton, Bal.	AL	1990	Bob Quinn, Cin	NL
1951	George Weiss, NY.	AL	1971	Cedric Tallis, KC	AL	1991	Andy MacPhail, Min.	AL
1952	George Weiss, NY.	AL	1972	Roland Hemond, Chi	AL			
1953	Louis Perini, Mil	NL	1973	Bob Howsam, Cin.	NL			
1954	Horace Stoneman, NY	NL	1974	Gabe Paul, NY.	AL			
1955	Walter O'Malley, Bklyn	NL						

College Baseball
College World Series

The NCAA Division I College World Series has been held in Kalamazoo, Mich. (1947-48), Wichita, Kan. (1949) and Omaha, Neb. (since 1950).

Multiple winners: USC (11); Arizona St. (5); Texas (4); Arizona and Minnesota (3); Cal State Fullerton, California, Miami-FL, Michigan and Stanford (2).

Year	Winner	Coach	Score	Loser	Year	Winner	Coach	Score	Loser
1947	California	Clint Evans	8-7	Yale	1960	Minnesota	Dick Siebert	2-1	USC
1948	USC	Sam Barry	9-2	Yale	1961	USC	Rod Dedeaux	1-0	Okla.St.
1949	Texas	Bibb Falk	10-3	W.Forest	1962	Michigan	Don Lund	5-4	S.Clara
1950	Texas	Bibb Falk	3-0	Wash.St.	1963	USC	Rod Dedeaux	5-2	Arizona
1951	Oklahoma	Jack Baer	3-2	Tennessee	1964	Minnesota	Dick Siebert	5-1	Missouri
1952	Holy Cross	Jack Barry	8-4	Missouri	1965	Arizona St.	Bobby Winkles	2-1	Ohio St.
1953	Michigan	Ray Fisher	7-5	Texas	1966	Ohio St.	Marty Karow	8-2	Okla.St.
1954	Missouri	Hi Simmons	4-1	Rollins	1967	Arizona St.	Bobby Winkles	11-2	Houston
1955	Wake Forest	Taylor Sanford	7-6	W.Mich.	1968	USC	Rod Dedeaux	4-3	So.Ill.
1956	Minnesota	Dick Siebert	12-1	Arizona	1969	Arizona St.	Bobby Winkles	10-1	Tulsa
1957	California	Geo. Wolfman	1-0	Penn St.	1970	USC	Rod Dedeaux	2-1	Fla.St.
1958	USC	Rod Dedeaux	8-7	Missouri	1971	USC	Rod Dedeaux	7-2	So.Ill.
1959	Oklahoma St.	Toby Greene	5-3	Arizona	1972	USC	Rod Dedeaux	1-0	Ariz.St.

College Baseball (Cont.)
College World Series

Year	Winner	Coach	Score	Loser	Year	Winner	Coach	Score	Loser
1973	USC	Rod Dedeaux	4-3	Ariz.St.	1983	Texas	Cliff Gustafson	4-3	Alabama
1974	USC	Rod Dedeaux	7-3	Miami,FL	1984	CS Fullerton	Augie Garrido	3-1	Texas
1975	Texas	Cliff Gustafson	5-1	S.Carolina	1985	Miami-FL	Ron Fraser	10-6	Texas
1976	Arizona	Jerry Kindall	7-1	E.Michigan	1986	Arizona	Jerry Kindall	10-2	Fla.St.
1977	Arizona St.	Jim Brock	2-1	S.Carolina	1987	Stanford	M.Marquess	9-5	Okla.St.
1978	USC	Rod Dedeaux	10-3	Ariz.St.	1988	Stanford	M.Marquess	9-4	Ariz.St.
1979	CS Fullerton	Augie Garrido	2-1	Arkansas	1989	Wichita St.	G.Stephenson	5-3	Texas
1980	Arizona	Jerry Kindall	5-3	Hawaii	1990	Georgia	Steve Webber	2-1	Okla.St.
1981	Arizona St.	Jim Brock	7-4	Okla.St.	1991	LSU	Skip Bertman	6-3	Wichita St.
1982	Miami-FL	Ron Fraser	9-3	Wichita St.	1992	Pepperdine	Andy Lopez	3-2	CS-Fullerton

Most Outstanding Players

The Most Outstanding Player has been selected every year of the College World Series since 1949. Winners who did not play for the CWS champion are listed in **bold** type. No player has won the award more than once.

Year		Year		Year	
1949	**Charles Teague,** W.Forest	1965	Sal Bando, Ariz.St.	1980	Terry Francona, Arizona
		1966	Steve Arlin, Ohio St.	1981	Stan Holmes, Ariz.St.
1950	**Ray VanCleef,** Rutgers	1967	Ron Davini, Ariz.St.	1982	Dan Smith, Miami-FL
1951	**Sidney Hatfield,** Tenn.	1968	Bill Seinsoth, USC	1983	Calvin Schiraldi, Texas
1952	James O'Neill, Holy Cross	1969	John Dolinsek, Ariz.St.	1984	John Fishel, CS-Fullerton
1953	**J.L. Smith,** Texas			1985	Greg Ellena, Miami-FL
1954	**Tom Yewcic,** Mich.St.	1970	**Gene Ammann,** Fla.St.	1986	Mike Senne, Arizona
1955	**Tom Borland,** Okla.St.	1971	**Jerry Tabb,** Tulsa	1987	Paul Carey, Stanford
1956	Jerry Thomas, Minn.	1972	Russ McQueen, USC	1988	Lee Plemel, Stanford
1957	**Cal Emery,** Penn St.	1973	**Dave Winfield,** Minn.	1989	Greg Brummett, Wich.St.
1958	Bill Thom, USC	1974	George Milke, USC		
1959	Jim Dobson, Okla.St.	1975	Mickey Reichenbach, Texas	1990	Mike Rebhan, Georgia
		1976	Steve Powers, Arizona	1991	Gary Hymel, LSU
1960	John Erickson, Minn.	1977	Bob Horner, Ariz. St.	1992	**Phil Nevin,** CS-Fullerton
1961	**Littleton Flower,** Okla.St.	1978	Rod Boxberger, USC		
1962	**Bob Garibaldi,** Santa Clara	1979	Tony Hudson, CS-Fullerton		
1963	Bud Hollowell, USC				
1964	**Joe Ferris,** Maine				

Golden Spikes Award

First presented in 1978 by the U.S. Baseball Federation, honoring the nation's best amateur player. Alex Fernandez, the 1990 winner, was the first junior college player chosen.

Year		Year		Year	
1978	Bob Horner, Ariz.St, 2B	1983	Dave Magadan, Alabama, 1B	1988	Robin Ventura, Okla.St., 3B
1979	Tim Wallach, CS-Fullerton, 1B	1984	Oddibe McDowell, Ariz.St., OF	1989	Ben McDonald, LSU, P
1980	Terry Francona, Arizona, OF	1985	Will Clark, Miss.St., 1B	1990	Alex Fernandez, Miami-Dade, P
1981	Mike Fuentes, Fla.St., OF	1986	Mike Loynd, Fla.St., P	1991	Mike Kelly, Ariz. St., OF
1982	Augie Schmidt, N.Orleans, SS	1987	Jim Abbott, Michigan, P		

Other NCAA Champions

Divison II

Multiple winners: Florida Southern (7); Cal Poly Pomona (3); CS-Northridge, Jacksonville St., Troy St., UC-Irvine and UC-Riverside (2).

Year		Year		Year		Year	
1968	Chapman, CA	1975	Florida Southern	1981	Florida Southern	1987	Troy St., AL
1969	Illinois St.	1976	Cal Poly Pomona	1982	UC-Riverside	1988	Florida Southern
		1977	UC-Riverside	1983	Cal Poly Pomona	1989	Cal Poly SLO
1970	CS-Northridge	1978	Florida Southern	1984	CS-Northridge		
1971	Florida Southern	1979	Valdosta St., GA	1985	Florida Southern	1990	Jacksonville St., AL
1972	Florida Southern			1986	Troy St., AL	1991	Jacksonville St., AL
1973	UC-Irvine	1980	Cal Poly Pomona			1992	Tampa
1974	UC-Irvine						

Divison III

Multiple winners: Marietta (3); CS-Stanislaus, Eastern Conn. St., Glassboro St. and Ithaca (2).

Year		Year		Year		Year	
1976	CS-Stanislaus	1981	Marietta, OH	1985	Wisconsin-Oshkosh	1989	NC-Wesleyan
1977	CS-Stanislaus	1982	Eastern Conn. St.	1986	Marietta, OH	1990	Eastern Conn. St.
1978	Glassboro St., NJ	1983	Marietta, OH	1987	Monclair St., NJ	1991	Southern Maine
1979	Glassboro St., NJ	1984	Ramapo, NJ	1988	Ithaca, NY	1992	Wm.Paterson, NJ
1980	Ithaca, NY						

Wide World Photos

Florida State defensive back **Kirk Carruthers** comes to grips with the agony of defeat after the top-ranked Seminoles' 17-16 loss to Miami.

COLLEGE FOOTBALL

Two For One

Miami beats Florida State, but ties Washington in the polls as national title is shared for the second consecutive year.

The 1991 college football season ended in a dead heat. Miami of Florida and Washington of Seattle each played 12 games and won them all. No other Division I-A team went undefeated, including preseason favorite Florida State, which fell to Miami by a point in the decade's first No. 1 vs No. 2 showdown.

Washington and Miami both had claims on the national championship and staked them New Year's Day—the Huskies beating Michigan by 20 in the Rose Bowl and then the Hurricanes shutting out Nebraska by 22 in the Orange.

Yet, on Jan. 2, when the Associated Press media poll gave Miami the national title in its closest vote ever (four points) and the new *USA Today*/CNN coaches' poll chose Washington (by nine points), the strangest thing happened—neither coach complained.

"It would have been an injustice if one team was shut out," said Miami's Dennis Erickson. "You had two great football teams. Both went undefeated, which is hard enough to do. I have no problems with a split championship. They're great; we're great. I'm happy."

So was Don James of Washington. "I don't mind sharing it," he said with tears in his eyes. "I'm emotional now, and it's so difficult to express the feelings I have for the kids. For them not to get a piece of this would have been a tragedy."

Normally, a disputed national championship triggers a venomfest between rival coaches that would make the producers of "Geraldo" drool.

Not this time. For one thing, the coaches had too much in common. James is a Miami graduate who set five passing records as a Hurricane quarterback in 1952 and '53, while Erickson grew up in Everett, Wash., coached at Washington State from 1987-88, and is best friends with former Huskies' offensive coordinator (now California head coach) Keith Gilbertson.

Furthermore, both teams had better years than expected. Miami was rebuilding after losing 12 starters and Washington entered the season with Rose Bowl MVP quarterback Mark Brunell sidelined with a serious knee injury.

For James, who came to Seattle as head coach in 1975 and has a record of 144-54-2 since then, the national title made up for the disappointment of 1984 when his Huskies went 11-1 and had to settle for No. 2 behind unbeaten BYU.

"It's very fulfilling, no question about it," he said. "I've watched this trophy go out the door to someone else every year."

Erickson, on the other hand, has now won the title twice since taking over for Jimmy Johnson in 1989.

Ivan Maisel is the national college football writer for *The Dallas Morning News* and a columnist for *The Sporting News*.

Wide World Photos

University of Washington coach **Don James** celebrates the Huskies' winning of the *USA Today*/CNN coaches' poll with quarterback **Billy Joe Hobert** (left) and tailback **Beno Bryant**. Miami won the Associated Press media poll.

"This means more to me than the first one," he said, "because we were unbeaten and because of where we were picked."

Miami not only continued its winning tradition (four titles since 1983), but also managed to break with its bad boy past, which had raised the Canes to public enemy status in the eyes of school officials and the NCAA after thrashing and trashing Texas in the 1991 Cotton Bowl.

The rest of the Top 5, according to both the media and the coaches, were Penn State (11-2), Florida State (11-2) and Alabama (11-1), respectively.

Penn State lost to Southern Cal and Miami on the road, but finished strong with a 42-17 rout of Tennessee in the Fiesta Bowl. Alabama was beaten, 35-0, by eventual Southeastern Conference champion Florida on Sept. 14, then ran off nine straight wins, including a five-point decision over defending national champ Colorado in the Blockbuster Bowl.

The last time PSU and Bama placed in the Top 5 they won national championships—the Nittany Lions in 1986 and the Crimson Tide in 1979. Florida State, however, came into the season with four straight Top 5 finishes (second only to Miami's five in a row) and no titles to show for it.

The preseason No. 1 choice of both the media and the coaches, FSU opened with lopsided wins over BYU, Tulane and Western Michigan, then blew past No. 3 Michigan, 51-31, in Ann Arbor and trounced No.10 Syracuse, 45-10, at home. But injuries on the offensive line and to quarterback Casey Weldon (knee) halted State's momentum.

Nevertheless, by November (and with the considerable help of ex-FSUer Deion Sanders and the Atlanta Braves) the Seminoles' drum-beating, arm-bending war chant ("Oooh-oh-ohoaaaaa. . .") had become America's sports mantra.

Then, on Nov. 16, after holding the top spot for 12 weeks, Florida State's national championship dreams collided with its annual regional nightmare—No. 2 Miami.

FSU, winners of 16 straight, came in as 3½-point favorites at home. Miami, winners of 14 in a row, had beaten the Seminoles five of the last six years and four times in its last five trips to Tallahassee.

Their showdown was expected to be an offensive fireworks display, but instead featured great defense. After allowing Miami to open the game with a touchdown march that covered 74 yards in less than two minutes, Florida State scored 16 unanswered points and led by nine early in the fourth quarter.

The Hurricanes then rallied for a touchdown and field goal to go ahead 17-16 with 3:01 left. FSU responded by mounting a last-minute drive that reached the Miami 17 with 0:25 left, but Gerry Thomas' 34-yard field goal attempt was wide right by less than a foot (see box).

"We choked," said Florida State senior linebacker Kirk Carruthers. "We knew we were the better team, but they knew they were going to win. If we had wanted to win the national championship bad enough, we would've found a way."

Seminoles' coach Bobby Bowden, whose teams have lost 11 of 16 games to Miami, tried to ease the hurt by making light of the so-called Miami curse on FSU.

"I think the curse is they're on our schedule," he said. "They're going to chisel on my tombstone, '. . . and he had to play Miami.' "

Two weeks later, the Seminoles fell to their other in-state rival, the Florida Gators, 14-9, but restored some luster to the season with a sloppy 10-2 victory over Texas A&M in the Cotton Bowl.

Miami took over the No. 1 position in the polls after the FSU game, but lost ground to Washington following a lackluster 19-14 victory at Boston College the following week. Not even Miami's season-ending 39-12 victory over San Diego State could stem the voters' rush to the Huskies. At the end of the regular season, AP ranked Miami first by 14 points but the coaches poll had them tied.

While the balloting for No.1 was the closest ever, Michigan wide receiver and kick return specialist Desmond Howard won the Heisman Trophy with the second largest winning margin in the history of the award.

Howard, a junior who caught 61 passes and scored 23 touchdowns in 11 regular season games, received 640 first place votes and 2,077 points. Florida State quarterback Weldon finished a distant second with 19 first place votes and 503 points. Howard's 1,574-point plurality is surpassed only by O.J. Simpson's 1,750-point cushion over LeRoy Keyes in 1968.

The Heisman race was pretty much decided on Sept. 14, when Howard insured Michigan's first victory over Notre Dame in five years with a spectacular 25-yard touchdown catch with 9:02 left in the game.

NCAA Puts Kickers In Their Place

As football fields go, four feet, 10 inches doesn't seem like much. It isn't even two yards.

Yet, that was all it took to change the identity of the national champion last season and produce the most noticeable change in the college game since scholarship limitations.

In 1991, the width of the goalposts was reduced from 23 feet, 4 inches, to 18 feet, 6 inches—the same as the National Football League.

Since 1959, when the NCAA Football Rules Committee voted to widen the goalposts and permit a two-inch kicking tee, the number of field goals per game had increased nearly sevenfold, from 0.34 to 2.16.

The idea had been to spur scoring, but it had gotten out of control. Once soccer-style kickers took over in the 1970s, field goal accuracy increased to the point where all practitioners were hitting on 67.3 percent of their combined attempts by 1988. John Lee of UCLA booted 29 field goals in 1984 alone and connected on 85.9 percent of his career kicks from 1982-85.

In 1989, the committee took action by taking away the two-inch kicking tee. No good. Overall accuracy increased to a record 69.2 percent.

If narrowing the goalposts had failed, the next logical step would have been to station a defender on the crossbar with a fish net.

"I guess they're going to blindfold us next," said Ole Miss kicker Brian Lee (no relation to John).

Squeezing the goalposts back to 18-6 did work, however, just as the committee hoped and coaches feared. And as if having less to aim at wasn't hard enough, the hash marks on the field remained the same—setting up angles unseen outside of a geometry classroom.

By itself, narrowing the goalposts may not have worked, just as removing the kicking tee didn't work. Together, however, the two changes proved devastating.

Accuracy fell below 60 percent. More important to the rules committee, the number of attempts from 40 yards or greater fell by about one in six.

But the statistics don't tell the story nearly as well as the vignettes:

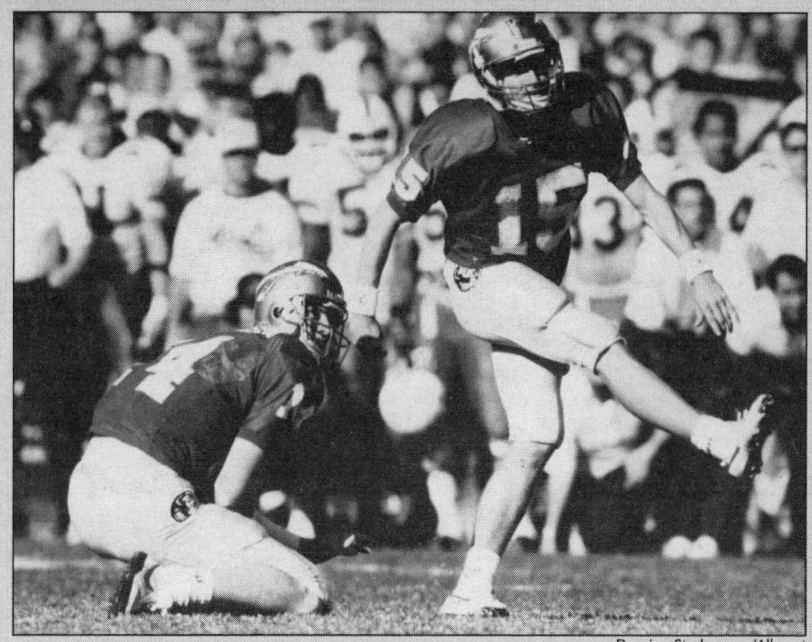

Damian Strohmeyer/Allsport

The most prominent victim of the NCAA decision to narrow the goalposts in 1991 was Florida State kicker **Gerry Thomas**, whose ill-fated 34-yard attempt to beat Miami would have been good in 1990.

Minnesota made two extra points—all year. Yet, a week after getting clobbered 58-0 by Colorado, the feeble Golden Gophers nearly beat Pittsburgh when Panthers' kicker Scott Kaplan missed four field goals.

Rice defeated Baylor, 20-17, after Bears' kicker Jeff Ireland missed three field goals in the second half. The same thing happened to Oklahoma kicker Scott Blanton in the Sooners' 10-7 loss to Texas.

Miami senior kicker Carlos Huerta missed the first extra point of his career, ending a four-year streak at 157.

Of the six most prolific kickers during the 1990 and '91 seasons, only one—Dan Eichloff of Kansas—was more accurate in 1991 than he had been the year before.

And then there was Florida State.

The top-ranked Seminoles roared out of preseason practice and dismantled everyone in sight, winning their first 10 games by an average score of 41-16. But a small problem nagged at coach Bobby Bowden. His kickers couldn't make extra points. On Sept. 28, Dan Mowrey missed three out of four PATs in the first half against Michigan

and at halftime Bowden sent punter John Wimberly onto the field to practice. Soon, however, sophomore walk-on Gerry Thomas won the job.

On Nov. 16, Thomas kicked field goals from 25, 31 and 20 yards to help the Seminoles build a 16-7 lead over No. 2 Miami. But after the Hurricanes rallied in the fourth quarter to go in front, 17-16, Thomas was called on again to win the game with 25 seconds left.

His 34-yard attempt had the distance, but drifted wide right and missed by less than a foot.

As The New York Times observed, "Florida State's Achilles heel was its kicking toe."

"It's amazing to me that it (the rule change) could cost us the national championship," Bowden said after the game. "I wasn't in favor of moving the goalposts. Very few coaches were in favor of it. Most of us don't like change."

Longtime rules committee secretary Dave Nelson, who wasn't afraid of change and led the fight to narrow the goalposts, died two weeks after the FSU-Miami game at age 71.

Wide World Photos

Heisman Trophy winner **Desmond Howard** of Michigan (right) with 1968 recipient **O.J. Simpson** at the Downtown Athletic Club in New York. They own the two largest winning margins in the history of the award.

Calling it merely spectacular may not do the catch justice. Howard snagged the ball at the back of the end zone on fourth down while diving through the air against double coverage. Oh, and he did it in South Bend and in front of a national television audience. Hello, Downtown Athletic Club?

The pass came from quarterback Elvis Grbac, a senior with junior eligibility who has been playing catch with Howard since the two were teammates at St.Joseph High in Cleveland. Grbac went on to have a decent year as well, leading the nation in passing efficiency.

The second most efficient quarterback in the country was 1990 Heisman winner Ty Detmer of Brigham Young, who fell out of contention for back-to-back trophies when the inexperienced Cougars lost their first three games of the season to Florida State, UCLA and Penn State by a combined score of 104-58.

Once out of the spotlight, Detmer, who entered the season in good health after

suffering two separated shoulders against Texas A&M in the '90 Holiday Bowl, proceeded to play better than he had when he won the Heisman. Colorado State coach Earle Bruce called him the best college quarterback he had ever seen, and mentioned that he had twice seen John Elway at Stanford.

As Detmer's teammates matured, his statistics soared. In his shining moment on Nov. 16, he brought BYU back from a 45-17 third-quarter deficit to tie San Diego State, 52-52, and secure the Western Athletic Conference championship. Detmer threw for 599 yards and six touchdowns in that game, while the Aztecs' David Lowery passed for 560 yards and five scores.

Detmer finished the season with 4,031 passing yards and 35 touchdown passes, while rallying BYU to eight wins and two ties in its last 10 games, including a 13-13 tie with Iowa in the Holiday Bowl. He also won his second consecutive Davey O'Brien National Quarterback Award, placed third in the Heisman vote and ended his collegiate career with all or part of 59 NCAA records.

David Klingler of Houston, the nation's other high-profile Cougar quarterback, wasn't so fortunate.

Entering the season with 33 NCAA passing records and enough magazine covers to make even a Sports Information Director blush, Klingler all but clinched the Heisman in the eyes of many on Aug. 31, when he passed for 510 yards and nine touchdowns as Houston trounced hapless Louisiana Tech, 73-3.

Twelve days later, the high-octane Houston run-and-shoot offense went down to Miami and crashed, 40-10.

Miami's defensive speed reduced the run-and-shoot to run-for-your-life. Klingler was sacked five times and could manage only one TD pass—on the final play from scrimmage.

"I was very tired of hearing about Klingler," Hurricanes' flanker Lamar Thomas said. "I thought he was going to line up at defensive back and cover me. I was kind of disappointed."

The Cougars finished at 4-7 and Klingler ended up with 3,388 yards in the air and 29 touchdown passes—down from 5,140 yards and 54 TDs the year before.

The defensive player of the year was junior tackle Steve Emtman of Washington, who won both the Outland Trophy and Lombardi Award. Emtman and Florida State junior defensive back Terrell Buckley were the only defensive players to crack the Top 10 in the Heisman vote, placing fourth and eighth.

They joined Heisman winner Howard and 31 other underclassmen in giving up their remaining eligibility and declaring for the April NFL Draft. Eleven were selected in the first round, led by Emtman, who went to Indianapolis as the first overall pick. (See page 213.)

Speaking of underclassmen, freshman tailback Marshall Faulk of San Diego State led the nation in both rushing with 158.8 yards per game and scoring with 140 points. He exploded onto the national scene Sept. 14 with an NCAA single-game rushing record of 386 yards against Pacific. On Nov. 23, Kansas senior Tony Sands, a 5-6, 175-pound fire hydrant, broke the record with 396 yards on a record 58 carries against Missouri.

When the 1991 season began, no one knew which Carolina it was that East Carolina belonged to. By the end of the season, everybody knew that Coach of the Year Bill Lewis' Pirates hailed from Greenville, N.C. Led by exciting quarterback Jeff Blake, East Carolina finished 10-1 and defeated archrival North Carolina State, 37-34, in the Peach Bowl.

Mississippi State took an unaccustomed position among the hierarchy of the Southeastern Conference as new coach Jackie Sherrill brought his winning football to Starkville. The Bulldogs went 7-4 before losing to Air Force in the Liberty Bowl.

Sherrill brought something else to Starkville—his checkered reputation. Before the season even began, Billy Brewer, the coach of archrival Mississippi, called Sherrill a "habitual liar." On Nov. 23, Sherrill returned the compliment as State beat Ole Miss, 24-9.

The last regular season SEC championship went to Florida, which had never won it before—officially, anyway. The Gators placed first in 1984 and '85, but due to NCAA and conference probation were not allowed to keep the titles.

[The SEC will add Arkansas and South Carolina and split into two six-team divisions in 1992 with a playoff game to decide the title on Dec. 5.]

Florida, which ended the regular season 10-1 and ranked third behind Miami and Washington, faced a seemingly overmatched Notre Dame team in the Sugar Bowl.

On Nov. 9, the Fighting Irish blew a 31-7 second-quarter lead at home against Tennessee, losing 35-34 in the final seconds. Coach Lou Holtz called the defeat the most difficult in his two decades of coaching. A week later, they lost again, this time at Penn State, 35-13. Two weeks after that, they barely beat Hawaii, 48-42.

Now 9-3, Notre Dame was written off by the pollsters, but not by the Sugar Bowl committee. ABC Sports wanted a television draw to compete against the Miami-Nebraska Orange Bowl game on NBC—and they got it.

The match-up quickly became a joke.

Q: What's the difference between Notre Dame and Cheerios?

A: Cheerios belong in a bowl.

Wide World Photos

Washington defensive tackle **Steve Emtman** not only won the Lombardi Award as the nation's top lineman, but was also the overall top pick in the NFL Draft.

But you make fun of Holtz at your own peril. With a fourth-quarter burst led by fullback Jerome Bettis, the Irish beat Florida, 39-28.

Such bowling shenanigans should be a thing of the past with the formalizing of the Bowl Alliance on Jan. 23. (See page 163 for details.)

One of the season's more seismic occurrences happened in the Pac-10, where Bay Area schools California and Stanford both swept Southern Cal and UCLA for the first time in 50 years.

The aftershock wasn't bad either— Bears' coach Bruce Snyder left for Arizona State and was replaced by Washington assistant Gilbertson, while Cardinal coach Dennis Green left for the NFL's Minnesota Vikings and was replaced by Bill Walsh, the three-time Super Bowl winner with the San Francisco 49ers.

Walsh coached the Cardinal to a 17-7 record from 1977-78. Returning to Palo Alto on Jan. 16, he quoted the late Joseph Campbell, the university professor made famous by the "The Power of Myth" television series. "Campbell said you should return to your bliss," Walsh said. "This is my bliss."

There were 16 coaching changes in Division I-A during the off-season, including the departure of Georgia Tech's Bobby Ross for San Diego of the NFL, and the arrival of ex-NFL and Alabama coach Ray Perkins at Arkansas State.

Texas, the Southwest Conference champion in 1990, fell to 5-6. Coach David McWilliams, a home-grown hero, was then sacked when he refused to clean out his coaching staff.

Auburn also fell to 5-6 and attracted the attention of the NCAA and "60 Minutes" after Eric Ramsey, a former Tigers' defensive back, produced audiotapes that implicated boosters and assistant coaches in a full-scale assault on the NCAA Rules Manual.

Hence the bumper sticker of an unsympathetic fan: "My son goes to Auburn and my money goes to Eric Ramsey."

Coach Pat Dye kept his football job but resigned as athletic director in the spring, saying the Ramsey affair had nothing to do with his decision. Uh-huh.

But there was one coaching change the NCAA could have done without. The number of black coaches went from three out of 107 to zero. Green left Stanford for the NFL, Northwestern fired Francis Peay after six years and a 13-51-2 record, and Willie Brown lost his job at Long Beach State when the athletic department solved its budget crunch by dropping football.

The demise of Long Beach State was one of three membership developments for the Big West in 1992. Fresno State moved to the WAC; Division I-AA Nevada-Reno moved over from the Big Sky, and the conference announced that independents Southwestern Louisiana, Louisiana Tech, Northern Illinois and Arkansas State will join the league for football only in 1993.

No word yet on a name change to reflect the new conference geography. □

THE 1993 SPORTS ALMANAC · INFORMATION PLEASE

COLLEGE FOOTBALL
S T A T I S T I C S

THE SEASON IN REVIEW
1991-1992
TOP 25 · BOWLS · STANDINGS

SEC
A

PAGE
135

Final AP Top 25 Poll

Voted on by panel of 60 sportswriters & broadcasters following Jan.1, 1992 bowl games: first place votes in parentheses, records, total points (based on 25 for 1st, 24 for 2nd, etc.) bowl game result, head coach and career record, preseason rank (Aug.24) and final regular season rank (Dec.2).

		Final Record	Points	Bowl Game	Head Coach	Aug.24 Rank	Dec.2 Rank
1	Miami-FL (32)	12-0-0	1472	Won Orange	Dennis Erickson (10 yrs: 83-34-1)	3	1
2	Washington (28)	12-0-0	1468	Won Rose	Don James (21 yrs: 167-75-3)	4	2
3	Penn St	11-2-0	1342	Won Fiesta	Joe Paterno (26 yrs: 240-62-3)	7	6
4	Florida St	11-2-0	1310	Won Cotton	Bobby Bowden (26 yrs: 216-76-3)	1	5
5	Alabama	11-1-0	1216	Won Blockbuster	Gene Stallings (9 yrs: 45-51-1)	22	8
6	Michigan	10-2-0	1151	Lost Rose	Gary Moeller (5 yrs: 25-29-3)	2	4
7	Florida	10-2-0	1119	Lost Sugar	Steve Spurrier (5 yrs: 39-17-1)	5	3
8	California	10-2-0	1039	Won Citrus	Bruce Snyder (12 yrs: 66-62-6)	32	14
9	East Carolina	11-1-0	1024	Won Peach	Bill Lewis (6 yrs: 34-33-2)	NR	12
10	Iowa	10-1-1	883	Tied Holiday	Hayden Fry (30 yrs: 189-140-9)	18	7
11	Syracuse	10-2-0	876	Won Hall of Fame	Paul Pasqualoni (6 yrs: 44-19-0)	25	16
12	Texas A&M	10-2-0	870	Lost Cotton	R.C.Slocum (3 yrs:127-9-1)	21	9
13	Notre Dame	10-3-0	848	Won Sugar	Lou Holtz (22 yrs: 172-82-5)	6	18
14	Tennessee	9-3-0	716	Lost Fiesta	Johnny Majors (24 yrs: 168-102-10)	11	10
15	Nebraska	9-2-1	666	Lost Orange	Tom Osborne (19 yrs: 186-43-3)	15	11
16	Oklahoma	9-3-0	629	Won Gator	Gary Gibbs (3 yrs: 24-10-0)	10	20
17	Georgia	9-3-0	428	Won Independence	Ray Goff (3 yrs: 19-16-0)	38	24
18	Clemson	9-2-1	410	Lost Citrus	Ken Hatfield (13 yrs: 100-53-3)	9	13
19	UCLA	9-3-0	406	Won Hancock	Terry Donahue (16 yrs: 125-54-8)	24	22
20	Colorado	8-3-1	383	Lost Blockbuster	Bill McCartney (10 yrs: 65-49-3)	13	15
21	Tulsa	10-2-0	348	Won Freedom	David Rader (4 yrs: 23-23-0)	NR	23
22	Stanford	8-4-0	262	Lost Aloha	Dennis Green (8 yrs: 26-63-0)	40	17
23	BYU	8-3-2	182	Tied Holiday	LaVell Edwards (20 yrs: 183-62-3)	19	NR
24	N.C.State	9-3-0	109	Lost Peach	Dick Sheridan (14 yrs, 112-49-4)	31	21
25	Air Force	10-3-0	87	Won Liberty	Fisher DeBerry (8 yrs: 65-33-1)	37	NR

Other teams receiving votes: 26. Georgia Tech (8-5-0, 70 points, won Aloha); **27.** Virginia (8-3-1, 63 pts, lost Gator); **28.** Indiana (7-4-1, 48 pts, won Copper); **29.** Ohio St.(8-4-0, 31 pts, lost Hall of Fame); **30.** Bowling Green (11-1-0, 27 pts, won California); **31.** Baylor (8-4-0, 5 pts, lost Copper) and San Diego St.(8-4-1, 5 pts, lost Freedom); **33.** Arkansas (6-6-0, 4 pts, lost Independence); **35.** Kansas St.(7-4-0, 3 pts, no bowl).

1991–92 Bowl Games

Date	Winner		Loser		Date	Winner		Loser
12/14	California	Bowl.Green 28	Fresno St. 21		12/31	Copper	Indiana 24	Baylor 0
12/25	Aloha	Ga.Tech 18	Stanford 17		1/1	Peach	E.Carolina 37	N.C.State 34
12/28	Blockbuster	Alabama 30	Colorado 25		1/1	Hall of Fame	Syracuse 24	Ohio St. 17
12/29	Independence	Georgia 24	Arkansas 15		1/1	Citrus	California 37	Clemson 13
12/29	Liberty	Air Force 38	Miss.St. 15		1/1	Cotton	Florida St. 10	Texas A&M 2
12/29	Gator	Oklahoma 48	Virginia 14		1/1	Fiesta	Penn St. 42	Tennessee 17
12/30	Holiday	13-13 Tie	Iowa vs BYU		1/1	Rose	Washington 34	Michigan 14
12/30	Freedom	Tulsa 28	S.Diego St. 17		1/1	Orange	Miami-FL 22	Nebraska 0
12/31	Hancock	UCLA 6	Illinois 3		1/1	Sugar	Notre Dame 39	Florida 28

Per Team Payouts

Rose ($6.5 million each); **Federal Express Orange** ($4.2 million); **USF&G Sugar** ($3.6 million); **Mobil Cotton** ($3.1 million); **Blockbuster** ($3 million); **Fiesta** ($2 million); **Florida Citrus** ($1.35 million); **Thrifty Car Rental Holiday** ($1.3 million); **Gator** ($1.2 million); **Hall of Fame** and **John Hancock** ($1 million); **Liberty** and **Peach** ($900,000); **Jeep Eagle Aloha, Domino's Copper, Freedom** and **Poulan/Weed Eater Independence** ($650,000); **California Raisin** ($250,000).

Other Division I-A Polls

USA Today/CNN Coaches Poll

Voted on by panel of 59 Division I-A head coaches: first place votes in parentheses with total points (based on 15 for 1st, 14 for 2nd, etc.).

	Points		Points
1 Washington (33½)	1449½	14 Oklahoma	694
2 Miami-FL (25½)	1440½	15 Tennessee	617
3 Penn St.	1321	16 Nebraska	608
4 Florida St.	1292	17 Clemson	450
5 Alabama	1191	18 UCLA	443
6 Michigan	1071	19 Georgia	407
7 California	1027	20 Colorado	366
8 Florida	1020	21 Tulsa	233
9 E.Carolina	1003	22 Stanford	216
10 Iowa	944	23 BYU	207
11 Syracuse	891	24 Air Force	165
12 Notre Dame	815	25 N.C.State	142
13 Texas A&M	799		

Other teams receiving votes: Indiana (83); Virginia (76); Ohio St.(61); Georgia Tech (47); Bowling Green (45); Illinois (17); Fresno St.(15); Mississippi St.(8); Baylor (5); New Mexico and San Diego St.(2); Arkansas and Louisiana Tech (1).

UPI/NFF Poll

Voted on by panel of 104 National Football Foundation members; winner receives NFF's MacArthur Bowl, given since 1959; first place votes in parentheses with total points (based on 25 for 1st, 14 for 2nd, etc.).

	Points		Points
1 Washington (71)	2279	14 Tennessee	1059
2 Miami-FL (21)	2224	15 Nebraska	964
3 Penn St.	2055	16 Oklahoma	961
4 Florida St.	1998	17 Clemson	681
5 Alabama	1850	18 Colorado	666
6 Michigan	1743	19 UCLA	655
7 Florida	1652	20 Georgia	565
8 California	1607	21 Tulsa	381
9 E.Carolina	1482	22 Stanford	325
10 Iowa	1439	23 N.C.State	303
11 Syracuse	1361	24 BYU	262
12 Notre Dame	1349	25 Ohio St.	181
13 Texas A&M	1236		

Other teams receiving votes (in alphabetical order)**:** Air Force, Arizona St., Baylor, Bowling Green, Georgia Tech, Holy Cross (I-AA), Illinois, Indiana, Mississippi St., San Diego St. and Virginia.
Teams on probation (and ineligible to receive votes)**:** Minnesota and Oklahoma St.

FWAA Poll

Voted on by 5-man panel including Bob Hammel, Bloomington (Ind.) Herald Times; Bill Lumpkin, Birmingham (Ala.) Post Herald; Bill McGrotha, Tallahassee (Fla.) Democrat; Volney Meece, Oklahoma City Daily Oklahoman; and Tom O'Toole, Scripps-Howard News Service in Washington, D.C. Each selector has one vote; winner receives Grantland Rice Award, given since 1954.

1 Washington (3)
2 Miami-FL (2)

NY Times Computer Ranking

Based on an analysis of each team's scores with emphasis on three factors: who won, by what margin, and against what quality opposition. Computer balances lop-sided scores, notes home field advantage and gives late season games more weight than those played earlier in the schedule. The top team is assigned a rating of 1.000, ratings of all other teams reflect their strength relative to strength of No.1 team.

	Rating		Rating
1 Miami-FL	1.000	14 Texas A&M	.783
2 Washington	.949	15 Oklahoma	.776
3 Penn St.	.882	16 Tennessee	.765
4 Florida St.	.873	17 Georgia	.745
5 Michigan	.848	18 BYU	.740
6 Alabama	.835	19 Virginia	.738
7 Florida	.831	20 Stanford	.737
8 Nebraska	.828	21 Colorado	.712
9 E.Carolina	.819	22 UCLA	.707
10 Syracuse	.816	23 Tulsa	.688
11 Notre Dame	.811	24 Georgia Tech	.686
12 California	.809	25 Indiana	.684
13 Iowa	.802		

Top 25 Teams Over Last 5 Years

Division I-A schools with the best overall winning percentage over the last five seasons (1987-91), through the bowl games of Jan. 1, 1992.
National Championships: 1987—Miami-FL; 1988—Notre Dame; 1989—Miami-FL; 1990—Colorado (AP,FWAA,NFF) and Georgia Tech (UPI); 1991—Miami-FL (AP) and Washington (FWAA,NFF, USA/CNN).

		Overall Record	Bowls W-L-T	Overall Win Pct.
1	Miami-FL	56- 4-0	5-0-0	.933
2	Florida St	53- 8-0	5-0-0	.869
3	Clemson	49-10-1	4-1-0	.825
4	Notre Dame	51-11-0	3-2-0	.823
5	Nebraska	49-11-1	0-5-0	.811
6	Fresno St	45-12-1	2-1-0	.784
7	Syracuse	46-12-3	4-0-1	.779
8	Michigan	46-13-1	3-2-0	.775
9	Colorado	45-13-2	1-3-0	.767
10	Oklahoma	44-14-0	1-2-0	.759
11	Tennessee	44-14-3	3-1-0	.746
12	Washington	43-15-1	4-0-0	.737
	Auburn	42-14-3	2-1-1	.737
14	Alabama	44-16-0	2-3-0	.733
15	Texas A&M	44-16-1	2-2-0	.730
16	BYU	46-17-2	1-3-1	.723
17	Penn St	41-18-1	2-2-0	.692
18	Virginia	41-18-2	1-3-0	.689
19	Iowa	39-18-4	1-2-1	.672
20	Florida	39-20-0	1-3-0	.661
21	USC	38-20-1	1-3-0	.653
22	Wyoming	39-21-1	0-3-0	.648
23	UCLA	37-20-1	3-0-0	.647
24	Arkansas	38-22-0	0-4-0	.633
25	Georgia	37-22-0	3-1-0	.627
	San Jose St	36-21-2	1-1-0	.627
	Air Force	39-23-1	2-2-0	.627

The Top Two

Listed records and AP rank of opponents are day of game.

Miami Hurricanes (12-0)

Date	AP Rank	Opponent	Result
Aug.31	#3	at Arkansas (0-0)	31- 3
Sept.12	#2	#10 Houston (1-0)	40-10
Sept.28	#2	at Tulsa (3-1)	34-10
Oct. 5	#2	Oklahoma St.(0-3)	40- 3
Oct.12	#2	#9 Penn St.(5-1)	26-20
Oct.19	#2	Long Beach St.(1-5)	55- 0
Oct.26	#2	at Arizona (2-4)	36- 9
Nov. 9	#2T	West Virginia (6-3)	27- 3
Nov.16	#2	at #1 Florida St.(10-0)	17-16
Nov.23	#1	at Boston College (4-6)	19-14
Nov.30	#1	San Diego St.(8-2-1)	39-12
Jan. 1	#1	#11 Nebraska (9-1-1)	22- 0

Regular Season Statistics

Passing	Att	Cmp	Pct	Yds	TD	Rate
Gino Torretta	371	205	55.3	3095	20	138.9
Frank Costa	25	18	72.0	149	0	98.1

Interceptions: Torretta 8, Costa 3.

Top Receivers	No	Yds	Avg	Long	TD
Lamar Thomas	39	623	16.0	71-td	6
Horace Copeland	31	592	19.1	99-td	4
Darryl Spencer	28	380	13.6	27	1
Coleman Bell	27	376	13.9	31	1
Martin Patton	26	428	16.5	69-td	3
Kevin Williams	21	330	15.7	51-td	3

Top Rushers	Car	Yds	Avg	Long	TD
Stephen McGuire	123	608	4.9	34	9
Larry Jones	65	326	15.0	32-td	3
Martin Patton	75	242	3.3	17	4
Kevin Williams	10	108	10.8	71	0

Most Touchdowns	TD	Run	Rec	Ret	Pts
Stephen McGuire	9	9	0	0	54
Martin Patton	7	4	3	0	42
Lamar Thomas	6	0	6	0	38*
Kevin Williams	6	0	3	3	36
Horace Copeland	4	0	4	0	24

*Includes one 2-point conversion.

Kicking	FG/Att	Lg	PAT/Att	Pts
Carlos Huerta	17/21	46	37/40	88

Punting	No	Yds	Long	Blk	Avg
Paul Snyder	36	1381	50	0	38.4

Most Interceptions		Most Sacks	
Ryan McNeil	5	Rusty Medearis	10

Washington Huskies (12-0)

Date	AP Rank	Opponent	Result
Sept. 7	#4	at Stanford (0-0)	42- 7
Sept.21	#4	at #9 Nebraska (2-0)	36-21
Sept.28	#4	Kansas St.(3-0)	56- 3
Oct. 5	#3	Arizona (2-2)	54- 0
Oct.12	#3	Toledo (1-1)	48- 0
Oct.19	#3	at #7 California (5-0)	24-17
Oct.26	#3	Oregon (3-3)	29- 7
Nov. 2	#3	Arizona St.(4-3)	44-16
Nov. 9	#2T	at USC (3-5)	14- 3
Nov.16	#3	at Oregon St.(0-9)	58- 6
Nov.23	#2	Washington St.(4-6)	56-21
Jan. 1	#2	#4 Michigan (10-2)	34-14

Regular Season Statistics

Passing	Att	Cmp	Pct	Yds	TD	Rate
Billy Joe Hobert	285	173	60.7	2271	22	146.1
Mark Brunell	44	26	59.1	333	4	143.6

Interceptions: Hobert 10, Brunell 2.

Top Receivers	No	Yds	Avg	Long	TD
Mario Bailey	62	1037	16.7	71-td	17
Orlando McKay	47	627	13.3	69-td	6
Aaron Pierce	23	280	12.2	30	0
Curtis Gaspard	18	201	11.2	18	0
Matt Jones	14	131	9.4	20	0

Top Rushers	Car	Yds	Avg	Long	TD
Beno Bryant	158	943	6.0	65-td	8
Jay Barry	146	718	4.9	82-td	10
Napoleon Kaufman	67	307	4.6	19	4
Matt Jones	43	222	5.2	36	2
Leif Johnson	17	100	5.9	23	1

Most Touchdowns	TD	Run	Rec	Ret	Pts
Mario Bailey	17	0	17	0	102
Jay Barry	11	10	1	0	68*
Beno Bryant	9	9	0	0	54
Orlando McKay	6	0	6	0	36
Billy Joe Hobert	5	5	0	0	30

*Includes one 2-point conversion.

Kicking	FG/Att	Lg	PAT/Att	Pts
Travis Hanson	8/15	44	40/44	64

Punting	No	Yds	Long	Blk	Avg
John Werdel	31	1266	58	1	40.8
Billy Joe Hobert	16	612	59	0	38.3

Most Interceptions		Most Sacks	
Walter Bailey	7	Donald Jones	8½

No.1 vs No.2: Miami Edges Florida St.

On Nov. 16 in Tallahassee, top-ranked Florida State's effort to win its first national championship sailed wide right when a 34-yard field goal attempt by Gerry Thomas barely missed with 25 seconds left to play in the game.

The failed kick allowed No.2 Miami of Florida to beat the Seminoles, 17-16, before a record crowd of 63,442 at Doak Campbell Stadium. Trailing 16-7 with 14:32 remaining in the fourth quarter, the Hurricanes rallied for 10 points, culminating with a Larry Jones touchdown from one yard out with 3:01 left.

The victory was Miami's sixth in the last seven meetings with FSU and sent the Canes to the Orange Bowl where they finished the season undefeated and clinched their fourth AP national title in nine years.

Scoring Summary

#2	Miami-FL (8-0)	7	0	0	10—**17**
#1	Florida St.(10-0)	3	7	3	3—**16**

1st Quarter: UM—Stephen McGuire 2-yd run (Carlos Huerta kick), 13:07 left; **FSU**—Gerry Thomas 25-yd FG, 5:15 left.

2nd Quarter: FSU—Paul Moore 1-yd run (Thomas kick), 13:26 left.

3rd Quarter: FSU—Thomas 31-yd FG, 8:29 left.

4th Quarter: FSU—Thomas 20-yd FG, 14:32 left; **UM**—Huerta 45-yd FG, 9:48 left; **UM**—Larry Jones 1-yd run (Huerta kick), 3:01 left.

Final NCAA Division I-A Standings

Overall records include postseason games.

Atlantic Coast Conference

	Conference					Overall				
	W	L	T	PF	PA	W	L	T	PF	PA
*Clemson........	6	0	1	180	90	9	2	1	317	185
*N.C.State.......	5	2	0	163	150	9	3	0	304	222
*Georgia Tech....	5	2	0	165	91	8	5	0	283	214
*Virginia........	4	2	1	185	90	8	3	1	327	167
N.Carolina......	3	4	0	131	118	7	4	0	282	199
Maryland.......	2	5	0	87	163	2	9	0	138	202
Duke...........	1	6	0	106	207	4	6	1	231	280
Wake Forest.....	1	6	0	86	194	3	8	0	195	300

*Bowls (1-3): Georgia Tech (won Aloha); Clemson (lost Citrus); N.C.State (lost Peach); Virginia (lost Gator).

Big East Conference

	Conference					Overall				
	W	L	T	PF	PA	W	L	T	PF	PA
*Miami-FL......	2	0	0	46	17	12	0	0	386	100
*Syracuse.......	5	0	0	133	66	10	2	0	321	200
Pittsburgh......	3	2	0	121	95	6	5	0	244	241
West Virginia...	3	4	0	99	133	6	5	0	187	224
Rutgers........	2	3	0	88	84	6	5	0	217	217
Virginia Tech....	1	0	0	20	14	5	6	0	275	229
Boston College...	2	4	0	138	133	4	7	0	247	246
Temple.........	0	5	0	35	137	2	9	0	145	290

Note: Miami-FL wins conference title by virtue of higher ranking in national coaches' poll. Conference schedule will not be fully integrated until 1993.
*Bowls (2-0): Miami-FL (won Orange); Syracuse (won Hall of Fame).

Big Eight Conference

	Conference					Overall				
	W	L	T	PF	PA	W	L	T	PF	PA
*Nebraska.......	6	0	1	285	121	9	2	1	454	230
*Colorado.......	6	0	1	181	93	8	3	1	329	180
*Oklahoma.....	5	2	0	206	93	9	3	0	383	157
Kansas St.......	4	3	0	159	121	7	4	0	263	226
Kansas........	3	4	0	187	175	6	5	0	313	244
Iowa St.........	1	5	1	71	190	3	7	1	157	266
Missouri.......	1	6	0	121	289	3	7	1	223	403
Oklahoma St....	0	6	1	72	200	0	10	1	106	307

Note: Nebraska and Colorado played to a 19-19 tie (Nov.2) and ended up sharing the conference title. The Orange Bowl committee invited the higher-ranked Huskers.
*Bowls (1-2): Oklahoma (won Gator); Nebraska (lost Orange); Colorado (lost Blockbuster).

Big Ten Conference

	Conference					Overall				
	W	L	T	PF	PA	W	L	T	PF	PA
*Michigan........	8	0	0	316	91	10	2	0	420	203
*Iowa	7	1	0	190	139	10	1	1	343	179
*Ohio St........	5	3	0	166	115	8	4	0	277	187
*Indiana........	5	3	0	214	138	7	4	1	305	224
*Illinois..........	4	4	0	153	118	6	6	0	264	188
Purdue.........	3	5	0	132	182	4	7	0	219	272
Michigan St.....	3	5	0	142	189	3	8	0	162	272
Wisconsin.......	2	6	0	113	169	5	6	0	172	194
Northwestern ...	2	6	0	94	234	3	8	0	160	306
Minnesota......	1	7	0	65	210	2	9	0	104	302

*Bowls (1-3-1): Indiana (won Cooper); Iowa (tied Holiday); Michigan (lost Rose); Ohio St.(lost Hall of Fame); Illinois (lost Hancock).

Big West Conference

	Conference					Overall				
	W	L	T	PF	PA	W	L	T	PF	PA
*Fresno St........	6	1	0	279	133	10	2	0	514	228
San Jose St	6	1	0	276	137	6	4	1	372	298
Utah St	5	2	0	153	101	5	6	0	219	265
Pacific	4	3	0	253	239	5	7	0	435	481
UNLV	2	5	0	153	239	4	7	0	220	360
Long Beach St....	2	5	0	159	215	2	9	0	207	412
New Mexico St ...	2	5	0	173	228	2	9	0	224	350
CS-Fullerton	1	6	0	97	251	2	9	0	138	376

Tiebreaker: Fresno St. beat San Jose St.(31-28, Nov.23).
*Bowl (0-1): Fresno St.(lost California).

Mid-American Conference

	Conference					Overall				
	W	L	T	PF	PA	W	L	T	PF	PA
*Bowling Green ..	8	0	0	192	88	11	1	0	279	168
Central Mich....	3	1	4	127	101	6	1	4	205	157
Miami-OH	4	3	1	145	94	6	4	1	214	140
Toledo..........	4	3	1	138	110	5	5	1	187	209
Ball St	4	4	0	96	108	6	5	0	159	150
Western Mich....	4	4	0	161	173	6	5	0	218	253
Eastern Mich....	3	4	1	121	145	3	7	1	144	232
Ohio Univ.......	1	6	1	114	211	2	8	1	176	308
Kent............	1	7	0	134	198	1	0	0	159	307

*Bowl (1-0): Bowling Green (won California).

Pacific-10 Conference

	Conference					Overall				
	W	L	T	PF	PA	W	L	T	PF	PA
*Washington	8	0	0	321	77	12	0	0	495	115
*California	6	2	0	237	164	10	2	0	443	239
*Stanford	6	2	0	241	159	8	4	0	368	246
*UCLA	6	2	0	237	122	9	3	0	323	190
Arizona St........	4	4	0	158	174	6	5	0	218	210
Arizona	3	5	0	180	266	6	4	1	248	361
Washington St ...	3	5	0	191	260	4	7	0	280	340
USC............	2	6	0	178	218	3	8	0	229	276
Oregon.........	1	7	0	112	205	3	8	0	186	248
Oregon St.......	1	7	0	86	296	1	0	0	125	365

*Bowls (3-1): Washington (won Rose); California (won Citrus); UCLA (won Hancock); Stanford (lost Aloha).

Southeastern Conference

	Conference					Overall				
	W	L	T	PF	PA	W	L	T	PF	PA
*Florida.........	7	0	0	226	74	10	2	0	389	191
*Alabama........	6	1	0	128	101	11	1	0	324	143
*Tennessee......	5	2	0	190	136	9	3	0	352	263
*Georgia	4	3	0	192	163	9	3	0	336	219
*Mississippi St.....	4	3	0	145	119	7	5	0	291	194
LSU	3	4	0	116	157	5	6	0	248	263
Vanderbilt.......	3	4	0	127	192	5	6	0	205	267
Auburn	2	5	0	128	170	5	6	0	233	214
Mississippi......	1	6	0	148	189	5	6	0	242	223
Kentucky.......	0	7	0	113	212	3	8	0	190	268

*Bowls (2-3): Alabama (won Blockbuster); Georgia (won Independence); Florida (lost Sugar); Tennessee (lost Fiesta); Mississippi St. (lost Liberty).

Southwest Conference

	Conference					Overall			
	W	L	T	PF	PA	W	L	T	PF	PA
*Texas A&M	8	0	0	289	95	10	2	0	404	154
*Baylor	5	3	0	192	138	8	4	0	282	204
*Arkansas	5	3	0	131	117	6	6	0	175	203
Texas Tech	5	3	0	244	215	6	5	0	315	272
TCU	4	4	0	173	223	7	4	0	279	267
Texas	4	4	0	169	111	5	6	0	195	145
Houston	3	5	0	260	250	4	7	0	353	344
Rice	2	6	0	148	233	4	7	0	239	287
SMU	0	8	0	73	297	1	10	0	141	359

Bowls (0-3): Texas A&M (lost Cotton); Baylor (lost Copper); Arkansas (lost Independence).

Western Athletic Conference

	Conference					Overall			
	W	L	T	PF	PA	W	L	T	PF	PA
*BYU	7	0	1	324	194	8	3	2	433	321
*San Diego St.	6	1	1	275	214	8	4	1	420	365
*Air Force	6	2	0	210	183	10	3	0	382	263
Utah	4	4	0	203	222	7	5	0	276	277
Hawaii	3	5	0	218	231	4	7	1	335	388
Wyoming	2	5	1	242	295	4	6	1	305	357
UTEP	2	5	1	194	183	4	7	1	254	252
Colorado St	2	6	0	206	241	3	8	0	265	375
New Mexico	2	6	0	177	286	3	9	0	240	473

Bowls (1-1-1): Air Force (won Liberty); BYU (tied Holiday); San Diego St.(lost Freedom).

I-A Independents

	W	L	T	PF	PA
*East Carolina	11	1	0	409	277
*Florida St	11	2	0	449	188
*Penn St	11	2	0	474	184
Louisiana Tech	8	1	2	280	194
*Tulsa	10	2	0	333	225
*Notre Dame	10	3	0	465	289
Akron	5	6	0	257	308
Memphis St.	5	6	0	228	229
Army	4	7	0	196	226
Cincinnati	4	7	0	201	323
South Carolina	3	6	2	250	268
Southern Mississippi	4	7	0	212	225
Southwestern Louisiana	2	8	1	148	269
Louisville	2	9	0	135	335
Northern Illinois	2	9	0	143	364
Navy	1	10	0	160	321
Tulane	1	10	0	146	384

Bowls (5-0): East Carolina (won Peach); Florida St.(won Cotton); Penn St.(won Fiesta); Tulsa (won Freedom); Notre Dame (won Sugar).

Conference Moves

After the 1991 season, **Arkansas** left the SWC for the SEC; **Fresno St.** left the Big West for the WAC; **Nevada** left the Big Sky (Div.I-AA) for the Big West; and independents **Akron** (MAC), **Florida St.**(ACC) and **South Carolina** (SEC) joined conferences.

Top 50 Rivalries

Top Division I series records, including games through the 1991 season. Note that the Boston College-Holy Cross series ended after the 1986 season, while Notre Dame and Miami-FL concluded their series in 1990. The series between Miami-FL and Florida was suspended after the 1987 season and formally cancelled in 1991. Penn St. and Pittsburgh, who have played each other annually since 1935 and 91 times since 1893, are scheduled to play in 1992 then not again until 1997.

	Gm	Series Leader
Air Force-Army	26	Air Force (14-11-1)
Air Force-Navy	24	Air Force (16-8-0)
Alabama-Auburn	56	Alabama (32-23-1)
Alabama-Tennessee	74	Alabama (40-27-7)
Arizona-Arizona St.	65	Arizona (37-27-1)
Arkansas-Texas	73	Texas (54-19-0)
Army-Navy	92	Navy (43-42-7)
Auburn-Georgia	95	Auburn (45-43-7)
Baylor-TCU	98	TCU (45-46-7)
Boston Col-Holy Cross	79	BC (48-31-0)
BYU-Utah	67	Utah (40-23-4)
California-Stanford	94	Stanford (46-37-11)
Cincinnati-Miami,OH	96	Miami 52-38-6)
Clemson-S.Carolina	89	Clemson (53-32-4)
Colorado-Colorado St.	66	Colorado (48-16-2)
Duke-North Carolina	77	N.Carolina (38-35-4)
Florida-Florida St.	34	Florida (23-10-1)
Florida-Miami,FL	49	Florida (25-24-0)
Florida-Georgia	69	Georgia (44-24-2)
Florida St.-Miami,FL	35	Miami (21-14-0)
Georgia-Georgia Tech	86	Georgia (46-35-5)
Harvard-Yale	108	Yale (59-41-8)
Indiana-Purdue	94	Purdue (57-31-6)
Iowa-Iowa St.	39	Iowa (27-12-0)
Kansas-Missouri	100	Missouri (47-44-9)
Kansas-Kansas St.	89	Kansas (60-24-5)
Kentucky-Tennessee	87	Tennessee (55-23-9)
Lafayette-Lehigh	127	Lafayette (69-53-5)
LSU-Tulane	89	LSU (60-22-7)
Miami,FL-Notre Dame	23	Notre Dame (15-7-1)
Michigan-Michigan St	84	Michigan (55-24-5)
Michigan-Notre Dame	23	Michigan (14-9-0)
Michigan-Ohio St.	88	Michigan (50-33-5)
Minnesota-Wisconsin	101	Minnesota (55-38-8)
Mississippi-Miss.St.	87	Mississippi (51-31-6)
Nebraska-Oklahoma	72	Oklahoma (39-30-3)
N.Carolina-N.C.State.	81	N.Carolina (52-23-6)
Notre Dame-Purdue	63	Notre Dame (40-21-2)
Notre Dame-USC	63	Notre Dame (36-23-4)
Oklahoma-Okla.St.	86	Oklahoma (69-11-6)
Oklahoma-Texas	86	Texas (50-32-4)
Oregon-Oregon St.	95	Oregon (46-39-10)
Penn St.-Pittsburgh	91	Penn St.(46-41-4)
Pittsburgh-West Va.	84	Pittsburgh (55-26-3)
Princeton-Yale	114	Yale (63-41-10)
Richmond-Wm.& Mary	101	Wm.& Mary (49-47-5)
Tennessee-Vanderbilt	85	Tennessee (54-26-5)
Texas-Texas A&M	98	Texas (64-29-5)
UCLA-USC	61	USC (34-20-7)
Washington-Wash.St.	84	Washington (54-24-6)

Annual Awards

Offensive Players of the Year

Heisman Trophy (Top Player)....... Desmond Howard
Maxwell Award (Top Player)....... Desmond Howard
Walter Camp Trophy (Top Player) .. Desmond Howard
Sporting News Player of Year ...... Desmond Howard
UPI Player of Year................. Desmond Howard
Davey O'Brien Award (Top QB)............ Ty Detmer
Johnny Unitas Award (Top Sr.QB)...... Casey Weldon
Doak Walker Award (Top RB)....... Trevor Cobb, Rice

Defensive Players of the Year

UPI Lineman of Year .... Steve Emtman
Outland Trophy (Top Int.Lineman)...... Steve Emtman
Lombardi Award (Top Lineman)........ Steve Emtman
Butkus Award (Top LB)...... Erick Anderson, Michigan
Thorpe Award (Top DB) .... Terrell Buckley

Coaches of the Year

FWAA Writers .... Don James, Washington
AFCA Coaches.............. Bill Lewis, East Carolina

Heisman Trophy Vote

Presented since 1935 by the Downtown Athletic Club of New York City and named after former college coach and DAC athletic director John W.Heisman. Voting done by national media and former Heisman winners. Each ballot allows for three names (points based on 3 for 1st, 2 for 2nd and 1 for 3rd).

TOP 10 VOTE-GETTERS

	Pos	1st	2nd	3rd	Pts
Desmond Howard, Mich ... WR	640	68	21	2077
Casey Weldon, Fla.St...... QB	19	175	96	503
Ty Detmer, BYU .... QB	19	129	130	445
Steve Emtman, Wash ...... DT	29	100	70	357
Shane Matthews, Fla ...... QB	11	72	69	246
Vaughn Dunbar, Ind .... RB	6	51	53	173
Jeff Blake, E.Car.......... QB	7	29	35	114
Terrell Buckley, Florida St.* .. DB	1	24	51	102
Marshall Faulk, S.D.St...... RB	0	10	32	52
B.Richardson, Tex.A&M .... QB	6	9	9	45

Note: Howard, Emtman, Matthews and Buckley were juniors, and Faulk was a freshman. All other players were seniors.

Consensus All-America Team

NCAA Division I-A players cited most frequently by the following five selectors: AFCA (Kodak), AP, FWAA, UPI and Walter Camp Foundation. Holdovers from 1990 All-America team are in **bold** type; (*) indicates unanimous selection.

Offense

Pos	Class	Hgt	Wgt
WR—Desmond Howard, Michigan*........	Jr.	5-9	176
WR—Mario Bailey, Washington...........	Sr.	5-9	167
TE—Kelly Blackwell, TCU...............	Sr.	6-2	242
L—Greg Skrepenak, Michigan*	Sr.	6-8	322
L—Bob Whitfield, Stanford	Jr.	6-7	300
L—Jeb Flesch, Clemson	Sr.	6-3	266
L—Jerry Ostroski, Tulsa................	Sr.	6-4	305
L—Mirko Jurkovic, Notre Dame	Sr.	6-4	289
C—Jay Leeuwenburg, Colorado*........	Sr.	6-3	265
QB—**Ty Detmer**, BYU...................	Sr.	6-0	175
RB—Vaughn Dunbar, Indiana*...........	Sr.	6-0	207
RB—Trevor Cobb, Rice................	Jr.	5-9	180
RB—Russell White, California	Jr.	6-0	210
K—Carlos Huerta, Miami-FL...........	Sr.	5-9	186

Defense

Pos	Class	Hgt	Wgt
L—Steve Emtman, Washington*..........	Jr.	6-4	280
L—Santana Dotson, Baylor*.............	Sr.	6-5	264
L—Brad Culpepper, Florida	Sr.	6-2	263
L—Leroy Smith, Iowa	Sr.	6-2	214
LB—Robert Jones, East Carolina*	Sr.	6-3	234
LB—Marvin Jones, Florida St............	So.	6-2	220
LB—Levon Kirkland, Clemson	Sr.	6-2	245
B—Terrell Buckley, Florida St.*.........	Jr.	5-10	175
B—Dale Carter, Tennessee	Sr.	6-2	182
B—Kevin Smith, Texas A&M.............	Sr.	6-0	180
B—Darryl Williams, Miami-FL...........	Jr.	6-2	190
P—Mark Bounds, Texas Tech*..........	Sr.	5-11	185

Underclassmen Selected in 1992 NFL Draft

Thirty-four players—all juniors except sophomore Tommy Maddox—forfeited the remainder of their college eligibility and declared for the NFL Draft in 1992. NFL teams drafted 22 underclassmen. (See NFL draft on page 213.)

First Round (11)

		Drafted by
1	Steve Emtman, Washington, DT........	Indianapolis
3	Sean Gilbert, Pitt, DE....................	LA Rams
4	Desmond Howard, Michigan, WR	Washington
5	Terrell Buckley, Florida St., DB	Green Bay
8	Bob Whitfield, Stanford, OT	Atlanta
12	Marco Coleman, Georgia Tech, LB..........	Miami
15	Johnny Mitchell, Nebraska, TE...........	NY Jets
16	Chester McGlockton, Clemson, DT	LA Raiders
22	Alonzo Spellman, Ohio St., DE	Chicago
25	Tommy Maddox, UCLA, QB...............	Denver
28	Darryl Williams, Miami-FL, DB...........	Cincinnati

Second Round (3)

31	Carl Pickens, Tennessee, WR.............	Cincinnati
45	Amp Lee, Florida St., RB..............	San Francisco
54	Shane Dronett, Texas, DE	Denver

Third Round

64	Todd Collins, Carson-Newman, LB.....	New England

Fourth Round

		Drafted by
99	Keith Hamilton, Pitt, DE	NY Giants

Sixth Round (2)

150	Michael Bates, Arizona, RB	Seattle
160	Jeff Sydner, Hawaii, WR...............	Philadelphia

Eighth Round

217	Reggie Dwight, Troy St., TE.................	Atlanta

Ninth Round

226	Ostell Miles, Houston, RB...............	Cincinnati

Eleventh Round

284	Mazio Royster, USC, RB	Tampa Bay

Twelfth Round

322	Joseph Randolph, Elon, WR.............	Minnesota

NCAA Division I-A Individual Leaders

REGULAR SEASON

Total Offense

	Rushing				Passing		Total Offense				
	Car	Gain	Loss	Net	Att	Yds	Plays	Yds	YdsPP	TDR	YdsPG
Ty Detmer, BYU	75	272	302	−30	403	4031	478	4001	8.37	39	333.42
David Klingler, Houston	92	212	374	−162	497	3388	589	3226	5.48	30	322.60
Troy Kopp, Pacific	47	114	195	−81	449	3767	496	3686	7.43	38	307.17
Jeff Blake, E.Carolina	77	286	177	109	368	3073	445	3182	7.15	31	289.27
Gino Torretta, Miami-FL	49	174	114	60	371	3095	420	3155	7.51	22	286.82
Shane Matthews, Florida.	50	149	139	10	361	3130	411	3140	7.64	29	285.45
Dave Brown, Duke.	90	334	277	57	437	2794	527	2851	5.41	25	259.18
Andy Kelly, Tennessee	57	170	110	60	361	2759	418	2819	6.74	18	256.27
Jason Verduzco, Illinois	47	137	181	−44	382	2825	429	2781	6.48	15	252.82
Alex Van Pelt, Pittsburgh	26	55	74	−19	398	2796	424	2777	6.55	16	252.45

Games: All played 11, except Kopp and Detmer (12); Klingler (10).

All-Purpose Running

	Gm	Rush	Rec	PR	KOR	Total Yds	YdsPG
Ryan Benjamin, Pacific	12	1581	612	4	798	2995	249.58
Vaughn Dunbar, Indiana	11	1699	252	0	262	2213	201.18
Marshall Faulk, San Diego St.	9	1429	201	0	33	1663	184.78
Trevor Cobb, Rice	11	1692	136	0	16	1844	167.64
Corey Harris, Vanderbilt.	11	1103	283	0	445	1831	166.45
Tony Smith, Southern Miss	9	998	97	115	271	1481	164.56
Desmond Howard, Michigan.	11	165	950	261	373	1749	159.00
Chris Hughley, Tulsa	10	1326	74	0	190	1590	159.00
Russell White, California.	11	1177	139	0	408	1724	156.73
Dion Johnson, E.Carolina	11	255	743	162	513	1673	152.09

Passing Efficiency
(Minimum 15 attempts per game)

	Gm	Att	Cmp	Cmp Pct	Int	Int Pct	Yds	Yds/ Att	TD	TD Pct	Rating Points
Elvis Grbac, Michigan.	11	228	152	66.67	5	2.19	1955	8.57	24	10.53	169.0
Ty Detmer, BYU	12	403	249	61.79	12	2.98	4031	10.00	33	8.68	168.5
Jeff Garcia, San Jose St	9	160	99	61.87	5	3.13	1519	9.49	12	7.50	160.1
Matt Blundin, Virginia	9	224	135	60.27	0	.00	1902	8.49	19	8.48	159.6
Troy Kopp, Pacific	12	449	275	61.25	16	3.56	3767	8.39	37	8.24	151.8
Steve Stenstrom, Stanford	9	197	119	60.41	7	3.55	1683	8.54	15	7.61	150.2
Tony Sacca, Penn St	12	292	169	57.88	5	1.71	2488	8.52	21	7.19	149.8
Rick Mirer, Notre Dame	12	234	132	56.41	10	4.27	2116	9.04	18	7.69	149.2
Shane Matthews, Florida	11	361	218	60.39	18	4.99	3130	8.67	28	7.76	148.8
Keithen McCant, Nebraska	11	168	97	57.74	8	4.76	1454	8.65	13	7.74	146.5

Scoring

Non-Kickers

	Gm	TD	Pts	P/Gm
Marshall Faulk, San Diego St.	9	23	140*	15.56
Desmond Howard, Michigan.	11	23	140	12.55
Tommy Vardell, Stanford	11	20	120	10.91
Jerome Bettis, Notre Dame	12	20	120	10.00
Aaron Turner, Pacific.	11	18	108	9.82

*Faulk also scored a 2-point conversion.

Kickers

	Gm	FG	XP	Pts	P/Gm
Doug Brien, California	11	19	41	98	8.91
Derek Mahoney, Fresno St	11	11	63	96	8.73
Carlos Huerta, Miami-FL	11	17	37	88	8.00
Terry Venetoulias, Tex.A&M	11	13	49	88	8.00
Craig Fayak, Penn St	12	17	42	93	7.75

Abbreviation Key

Att—Attempted passes; **Avg**—Average; **Cat**—Catches; **Car**—Carries; **CPG**—Catches Per Game; **Cmp**—Completions; **FG**—Field Goals; **FGA**—Field Goal Attempts; **FGPG**—Field Goals Per Game; **Gain**—yards Gained; **Gm**—Games played; **Int**—Interceptions; **IPG**—Interceptions Per Game; **KOR**—Kickoff Return yards; **Loss**—yards Lost; **Net**—Net yards gained; **No**—Number; **Pct**—Percentage; **Plays**—Plays from scrimmage; **PR**—Punt Return yards; **Pts**—points; **P/Gm**—Points Per Game; **Rec**—Receiving yards; **Rush**—Rushing yards; **TD**—Touchdowns; **TDR**—Touchdowns Responsible for; **XP**—Extra Points; **Yds**—Yards; **Yds/Att**—Yards per Attempt; **YdsPG**—Yards Per Game; **YdsPP**—Yards Per Play.

NCAA Division I-A Individual Leaders (Cont.)

Rushing

	Car	Yds	TD	YdsPG
Marshall Faulk, San Diego St.	201	1429	21	158.78
Vaughn Dunbar, Indiana	336	1699	11	154.45
Trevor Cobb, Rice	360	1692	14	153.82
Jason Davis, La.Tech	244	1351	14	135.10
Chris Hughley, Tulsa	267	1326	8	132.60
Ryan Benjamin, Pacific	226	1581	13	131.75
Tony Sands, Kansas	273	1442	9	131.09
Billy Smith, C.Michigan	374	1440	6	130.91
Derek Brown, Nebraska	230	1313	14	119.36
Mike Gaddis, Oklahoma	221	1240	14	112.73

Games: All played 11, except Benjamin (12); Davis and Hughley (10); Faulk (9).

Receiving

	Ct	Yds	TD	CPG
Fred Gilbert, Houston	106	957	7	9.64
Aaron Turner, Pacific	92	1604	18	8.36
Marcus Grant, Houston	78	1262	10	7.09
Wilbert Ursin, Tulane	70	969	9	6.36
Carl Winston, New Mexico	76	1177	7	6.33
Sean LaChapelle, UCLA	68	987	11	6.18
Greg Primus, Colorado St	67	1081	8	6.09
Chris Walsh, Stanford	66	934	6	6.00
Mark Szlachcic, Bowl.Green	65	943	8	5.91
Kelly Blackwell, TCU	64	762	6	5.82

Games: All played 11, except Winston (12).

Field Goals

	FGA	FG	Pct	FGPG
Doug Brien, California	28	19	.679	1.73
Dan Eichloff, Kansas	24	18	.750	1.64
Jason Elam, Hawaii	24	19	.792	1.58
Carlos Huerta, Miami-FL	21	17	.810	1.55
John Biskup, Syracuse	22	17	.773	1.55
Nelson Welch, Clemson	26	17	.654	1.55
Lin Elliott, Texas Tech	26	17	.654	1.55

Games: All played 11, except Elam (12).

Interceptions

	No	Yds	TD	IPG
Terrell Buckley, Florida.St	12	238	2	1.00
Carlton Gray, UCLA	10	119	1	0.91
Willie Clay, Georgia Tech	9	66	1	0.75
Ray Buchanan, Louisville	8	89	0	0.73
Tracy Saul, Texas Tech	8	79	0	0.73

Games: All played 11, except Buckley and Clay (12).

Punting
(Minimum of 3.6 per game)

	No	Yds	Avg
Mark Bounds, Texas Tech	53	2481	46.81
Jason Christ, Air Force	50	2283	45.66
Pete Raether, Arkansas	65	2836	43.63
Shayne Edge, Florida	46	1991	43.28
Charles Langston, Houston	52	2246	43.19
Eric Bruun, Purdue	59	2548	43.19

Punt Returns
(Minimum of 1.2 per game)

	No	Yds	TD	Avg
Bo Campbell, Va.Tech	15	273	0	18.20
Desmond Howard, Michigan	15	261	1	17.40
David Palmer, Alabama	24	386	3	16.08
Kevin Williams, Miami-FL	36	560	3	15.56
James McMillion, Iowa St	17	241	0	14.76

Kickoff Returns
(Minimum of 1.2 per game)

	No	Yds	TD	Avg
Fred Montgomery, N.Mex.St	25	734	1	29.36
Ronald Rice, E.Michigan	11	319	0	29.00
Jeff Sydner, Hawaii	18	495	0	27.50
Courtney Hawkins, Mich.St	20	548	0	27.40
Eric Blount, N.Carolina	25	679	1	27.16

NCAA Division I-A Team Leaders

REGULAR SEASON

Scoring Offense

	Gm	Record	Pts	Avg
Fresno St	11	10-1-0	486	44.2
Washington	11	11-0-0	461	41.9
Nebraska	11	9-1-1	454	41.3
California	11	9-2-0	406	36.9
Michigan	11	10-1-0	406	36.9
Florida St	12	10-2-0	439	36.6
Texas A&M	11	10-1-0	402	36.5
Pacific	12	5-7-0	435	36.3
Penn St	12	10-2-0	432	36.0
Notre Dame	12	9-3-0	426	35.5

Scoring Defense

	Gm	Record	Pts	Avg
Miami-FL	11	11-0-0	100	9.1
Washington	11	11-0-0	101	9.2
Alabama	11	10-1-0	118	10.7
Virginia	11	8-2-1	119	10.8
Miami-OH	11	6-4-1	140	12.7
Oklahoma	11	8-3-0	143	13.0
Texas A&M	11	10-1-0	144	13.1
Texas	11	5-6-0	145	13.2
Bowling Green	11	10-1-0	147	13.4
Clemson	11	9-1-1	148	13.5

Total Offense

	Gm	Plays	Yds	Avg	TD	YdsPG
Fresno St	11	922	5961	6.5	62	541.91
Pacific	12	871	6135	7.0	61	511.25
Nebraska	11	800	5571	7.0	60	506.45
San Jose St	11	813	5279	6.5	47	479.91
BYU	12	837	5754	6.9	54	479.50
San Diego St	12	955	5739	6.0	52	478.25
Washington	11	861	5191	6.0	60	471.91
Tennessee	11	878	5145	5.9	36	467.73
Florida	11	787	5028	6.4	45	457.09
UCLA	11	883	5019	6.0	39	456.27

Note: Touchdowns scored by rushing and passing only.

Total Defense

	Gm	Plays	Yds	Avg	TD	YdsPG
Texas A&M	11	683	2446	3.6	19	222.4
Washington	11	730	2608	3.6	12	237.1
Texas	11	769	2848	3.7	15	258.9
Clemson	11	718	2895	4.0	17	263.2
Miami-OH	11	747	2980	4.0	15	270.9
Iowa	11	712	2987	4.2	20	271.5
Central Mich	11	741	3001	4.0	16	272.8
Georgia Tech	12	831	3333	4.0	22	277.8
Penn St	12	805	3366	4.2	22	280.5
Florida St	12	776	3375	4.3	22	281.3

Note: Opponents' TDs scored by rushing and passing only.

Final NCAA Division I-AA Standings

Overall records include postseason games.

Big Sky Conference

	Conference					Overall				
	W	L	T	PF	PA	W	L	T	PF	PA
*Nevada	8	0	0	329	177	12	1	0	546	245
*Weber St	6	2	0	369	314	8	4	0	516	241
Montana	6	2	0	222	183	7	4	0	274	241
Boise St	4	4	0	234	162	7	4	0	355	197
Idaho	4	4	0	271	232	6	5	0	375	313
Eastern Wash	4	4	0	246	286	5	6	0	301	364
Idaho St	2	6	0	207	275	3	7	1	287	358
Northern Ariz	1	7	0	193	328	3	8	0	294	404
Montana St	1	7	0	127	241	2	9	0	197	300

Playoffs (1-2): Nevada (1-1, lost Quarterfinal); Weber St.(0-1, lost 1st Round).

Gateway Athletic Conference

	Conference					Overall				
	W	L	T	PF	PA	W	L	T	PF	PA
*Northern Iowa	5	1	0	150	90	11	2	0	417	220
*Western Ill	4	2	0	108	99	7	4	1	272	187
Southern Ill	4	2	0	129	122	7	4	0	238	271
SW Missouri St	3	3	0	156	121	6	4	1	295	199
Indiana St	2	4	0	89	174	5	6	0	229	242
Eastern Ill	2	4	0	149	138	4	7	0	307	264
Illinois St	1	5	0	77	114	5	6	0	218	176

Playoffs (1-2): Northern Iowa (1-1, lost Quarterfinal); Western Illinois (0-1, lost 1st Round).

Ivy League

	Conference					Overall				
	W	L	T	PF	PA	W	L	T	PF	PA
Dartmouth	6	0	1	215	140	7	2	1	283	209
Princeton	5	2	0	172	126	8	2	0	253	171
Harvard	4	2	1	163	160	4	5	1	203	223
Yale	4	3	0	172	135	6	4	0	241	190
Cornell	4	3	0	139	124	5	5	0	181	218
Penn	2	5	0	113	143	2	8	0	142	236
Brown	1	6	0	163	246	1	9	0	227	372
Columbia	1	6	0	114	177	1	9	0	154	249

Playoffs: league does not play postseason games.

Mid-Eastern Athletic Conference

	Conference					Overall				
	W	L	T	PF	PA	W	L	T	PF	PA
*N.Carolina A&T	5	1	0	207	111	9	3	0	394	199
Delaware St	4	2	0	162	110	8	3	0	300	220
Beth-Cookman	4	2	0	162	146	5	5	0	264	256
S.C.State	3	3	0	108	110	7	4	0	234	157
Florida A&M	3	3	0	168	134	6	5	0	325	238
Howard	1	5	0	96	170	2	9	0	208	318
Morgan St	1	5	0	72	194	1	10	0	127	425

Postseason (0-1): no teams qualified for I-AA playoffs, but North Carolina A&T lost to SWAC champion Alabama St. in inaugural Heritage Bowl (36-13, Dec.21).

Ohio Valley Conference

	Conference					Overall				
	W	L	T	PF	PA	W	L	T	PF	PA
*E.Kentucky	7	0	0	216	74	12	2	0	377	177
*Mid.Tenn.St.	6	1	0	218	47	9	4	0	345	193
Austin Peay	3	4	0	111	156	5	6	0	191	231
Morehead St	3	4	0	124	181	4	7	0	189	345
SE Missouri	3	4	0	126	220	3	8	0	213	374
Tennessee St	2	4	0	119	154	3	8	0	206	286
Tenn.Tech	2	5	0	161	130	2	9	0	221	244
Murray St	1	6	0	67	207	3	8	0	162	313

Playoffs (3-2): Eastern Kentucky (2-1, lost Semifinal); Middle Tennessee St.(1-1, lost Quarterfinal).

Patriot League

	Conference					Overall				
	W	L	T	PF	PA	W	L	T	PF	PA
Holy Cross	5	0	0	185	84	11	0	0	372	174
Lehigh	3	2	0	172	103	9	2	0	363	235
Lafayette	3	2	0	133	138	6	5	0	277	312
Colgate	3	2	0	119	115	4	7	0	224	311
Bucknell	1	4	0	62	155	1	9	0	99	326
Fordham	0	5	0	59	135	2	8	0	149	242

Playoffs: league does not play postseason games.

Southern Conference

	Conference					Overall				
	W	L	T	PF	PA	W	L	T	PF	PA
*Appalachian St	6	1	0	156	97	8	4	0	215	202
*Marshall	5	2	0	260	146	11	4	0	506	257
The Citadel	5	2	0	156	120	7	4	0	238	183
Furman	4	3	0	228	160	4	7	0	363	217
Tenn-Chatt	4	3	0	216	190	7	4	0	305	293
VMI	2	5	0	137	243	4	7	0	243	373
W.Carolina	2	5	0	146	197	2	9	0	179	345
E.Tenn St	0	7	0	114	260	0	10	0	140	384

Playoffs (3-2): Marshall (3-1, lost Final); Appalachian St.(0-1, lost 1st Round).

Southland Conference

	Conference					Overall				
	W	L	T	PF	PA	W	L	T	PF	PA
*Sam Houston St	5	2	0	122	89	8	3	1	241	165
*McNeese St	4	1	2	120	78	6	4	2	192	156
NE Louisiana	4	2	1	168	110	7	3	1	237	175
SW Texas	4	3	0	150	89	7	4	0	307	179
Northwestern St	4	3	0	124	84	6	5	0	192	169
Nicholls St	2	5	0	102	118	4	7	0	157	189
North Texas	2	5	0	90	192	3	7	1	137	325
S.F.Austin	1	5	1	69	185	2	8	1	151	279

Playoffs (0-2): Sam Houston St.(0-1, lost 1st Round); McNeese St.(0-1, lost 1st Round).

Southwestern Athletic Conference

	Conference					Overall				
	W	L	T	PF	PA	W	L	T	PF	PA
*Alabama St	6	0	1	279	104	11	0	1	489	183
Alcorn St	4	2	1	206	139	7	2	1	357	190
Southern-BR	4	3	0	191	178	4	7	0	255	286
Miss.Valley	3	3	1	176	159	7	3	1	307	182
Tex.Southern	3	3	1	164	130	5	5	1	270	208
Grambling	3	4	0	232	221	5	6	0	330	338
Jackson St	2	4	0	124	154	5	5	0	247	202
Prairie View	0	6	0	33	350	0	11	0	48	617

Postseason (1-0): no teams qualified for I-AA playoffs, but Alabama St. beat MEAC champion North Carolina A&T in inaugural Heritage Bowl (36-13, Dec.21).

Yankee Conference

	Conference					Overall				
	W	L	T	PF	PA	W	L	T	PF	PA
*Delaware	7	1	0	273	153	10	2	0	393	241
*Villanova	7	1	0	308	102	10	2	0	413	149
*New Hamp	7	1	0	267	186	9	3	0	369	281
Rhode Island	3	5	0	155	249	6	5	0	266	330
Boston Univ	3	5	0	177	209	4	7	0	232	292
Massachusetts	3	5	0	151	150	4	7	0	205	208
Connecticut	2	6	0	164	250	3	8	0	241	340
Maine	2	6	0	130	244	3	8	0	210	333
Richmond	2	6	0	134	216	2	9	0	210	350

Playoffs (0-3): Delaware (0-1, lost 1st Round); Villanova (0-1, lost 1st Round); New Hampshire (0-1, lost 1st Round).

Final NCAA Standings (Cont.)
I-AA Independents

	W	L	T	PF	PA
*Samford	12	2	0	385	198
*Youngstown St	12	3	0	413	256
*James Madison	9	4	0	414	343
Georgia Southern	7	4	0	257	160
Central Florida	6	5	0	278	230
William & Mary	5	6	0	343	320
Liberty	4	7	0	233	248
Northeastern	4	7	0	239	277
Western Kentucky	3	8	0	235	301
Towson St	1	10	0	212	378
Arkansas St	0	10	0	169	344

*Playoffs (7-2): Youngstown St.(4-0, won Final); Samford (2-1,lost Semifinal); James Madison (1-1, lost Quarterfinal).

NCAA Playoffs
Division I-AA
First Round (Nov.30)
Nevada 22 .... McNeese St. 16
Youngstown St. 17 .... Villanova 16
James Madison 42 .... 2 OT .... Delaware 35
Samford 29 .... New Hampshire 13
Eastern Kentucky 14 .... Appalachian St. 3
Middle Tenn.St. 20 .... OT ..... Sam Houston St. 19
Northern Iowa 38 .... Weber St. 21
Marshall 20 .... OT .... Western Illinois 17

Quarterfinals (Dec.7)
Youngstown St. 30 .... Nevada 28
Samford 24 .... James Madison 21
Eastern Kentucky 23 .... Middle Tenn.St. 13
Marshall 41 .... Northern Iowa 13

Semifinals (Dec.14)
Youngstown St. 10 .... Samford 0
Marshall 14 .... Eastern Kentucky 7

Championship Game
Dec.21 at Statesboro, Ga.
Youngstown St. 25 .... Marshall 17
(12-3)   (11-4)

Division II
First Round (Nov.23)
Indiana,PA 56 .... Virginia Union 7
Jacksonville St.,AL 49 .... Winston-Salem St.,NC 24
Pittsburg St.,KS 26 .... Butler,IN 16
Portland St.,OR 28 .... Northern Colorado 24
Mankato St.,MN 27 .... North Dakota St. 7
East Texas St. 36 .... Grand Valley St.,MI 15
Mississippi Col. 28 .... Wofford,SC 15
Shippensburg,PA 34 .... OT .... E.Stroudsburg,PA 33

Quarterfinals (Nov.30)
Indiana,PA 35 .... Shippensburg 7
Jacksonville St. 35 .... Mississippi Col. 7
Pittsburg St. 38 .... East Texas St. 28
Portland St. 37 .... Mankato St. 27

Semifinals (Dec.7)
Jacksonville St. 27 .... Indiana,PA 20
Pittsburg St. 53 .... Portland St. 21

Championship Game
Dec.14 at Florence, Ala.
Pittsburg St. 23 .... Jacksonville St. 6
(13-1-1)   (12-1-0)

Division III
First Round (Nov.23)
Ithaca,NY 31 .... Glassboro St.,NJ 10
Union,NY 55 .... Lowell,MA 16
Allegheny,PA 24 ...... OT .... Albion,MI 21
Dayton,OH 27 .... Baldwin-Wallace,OH 10
Lycoming,PA 18 .... Wash.& Jefferson,PA 14
Susquehanna,PA 21 .... Dickinson,PA 20
St.John's-MN 75 .... Coe,IA 2
Wisconsin-La Crosse 28 .... Simpson,IA 13

Quarterfinals (Nov.30)
Ithaca 35 .... Union 23
Dayton 28 .... OT .... Allegheny 25
Susquehanna 31 .... Lycoming 24
St.John's-MN 29 .... Wisconsin-La Crosse 10

Semifinals (Dec.7)
Ithaca 49 .... Susquehanna 13
Dayton 19 .... St.John's-MN 7

Amos Alonzo Stagg Bowl
Dec.14 at Bradenton, Fla.
Ithaca 34 .... Dayton 20
(12-1-0)   (13-1-0)

Division I-AA, II and III Awards
Players of the Year
Payton Award (Div.I-AA) .... Jamie Martin, QB
                                       Weber St.
Hill Trophy (Div.II) .... Ronnie West, WR
                                    Pittsburg St.

AFCA Coaches of the Year
NCAA Div.I-AA .... Mark Duffner, Holy Cross
College Div.I .... Frank Cignetti, Indiana-PA
College Div.II .... Mike Kelly, Dayton

NAIA Playoffs
Division I
First Round (Nov.23)—Central Arkansas 30, Northeastern St.,OK 14; Central St.,OH 34, Shepherd,WV 22; Western St.,CO 38, Carson-Newman,TN 21; Moorhead St.,MN 47, Iowa Wesleyan 16.
Semifinals (Dec.7)—Central St. 20, Western St. 13; Central Arkansas 38, Moorhead St. 18.
Championship (Dec.14)—Central Arkansas 19, Central St. 16. Final records: Central Arkansas (9-2-2), Central St.(11-2-0).

Division II
First Round (Nov.23)—Pacific Lutheran,WA 27, Central Washington 0; Georgetown-KY 42, Eureka,IL 14; Findlay,OH 9, Westminster,PA 8; Dickinson St.,ND 26, Minot St.,ND 21; Peru St.,NE 41, Nebraska Wesleyan 20; Hastings,NE 28, St.Mary of the Plains,KS 21; Linfield,OR 59, Lewis & Clark,OR 30; Midwestern St.,TX 29, Bethany,KS 0.
Quarterfinals (Dec.7)—Georgetown-KY 37, Findlay 19; Pacific Lutheran 23, Linfield 0; Dickinson St. 42, Hastings 10; Peru St. 28, Midwestern St. 24.
Semifinals (Dec.14)—Georgetown-KY 42, Peru St. 28; Pacific Lutheran 47, Dickinson St. 25.
Championship (Dec.21)—Georgetown-KY 28, Pacific Lutheran 20. Final records: Georgetown-KY (13-1-0), Pacific Lutheran (11-2-0).

COLLEGE FOOTBALL STATISTICS

THROUGH THE YEARS

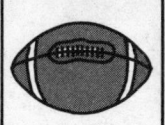

1883-1992

BOWLS • ALL-TIME LEADERS

SEC B

PAGE 145

National Champions

Over the years, 23 different national selectors have chosen college football's Number One team by way of polls (12), mathematical rating systems (10) and historical research (1). The list below has been culled from eight of those groups: the Helms Athletic Foundation (1883-1935), the Dickinson System (1924-40), Associated Press (since 1936), United Press (1950-57), International News Service (1952-57), United Press International (1958-90), the Football Writers Association of America (since 1954), the National Football Foundation and Hall of Fame (since 1959), and USA Today/CNN (since 1991). In 1991, the American Football Coaches Association switched its poll from UPI to USA Today/CNN, and UPI merged with the NFF-Hall of Fame poll.

Bowl game results were counted in the Helms selections but not in the Dickinson picks. The final AP sportswriters and broadcasters poll was taken following the bowl games for the first time in 1965. After returning to a pre-bowls final vote in 1966 and '67, the AP poll has been taken following the bowls since 1968. The FWAA has selected its champion after the bowl games since 1955, the NFF-Hall of Fame since 1971, UPI after 1974, and USA-Today/CNN since 1982.

The Football Writers' championship trophy is called the Grantland Rice Award (in honor of the legendary sportswriter) and the NFF-Hall of Fame trophy is called the MacArthur Bowl (in honor of Gen. Douglas MacArthur). Whenever more than one champion is listed in the chart below, the selector's initials are given.

Multiple champions (1883-1935): Yale (11); Princeton and Harvard (7); Michigan and Penn (4); Cornell, Notre Dame and USC (3); Alabama, Georgia Tech, Illinois, Minnesota and Pittsburgh (2).

Multiple champions (since 1936): Notre Dame (9); Alabama, Ohio St. and Oklahoma (6); USC (5); Miami-FL and Minnesota (4); Michigan St. and Texas (3); Nebraska, Penn St. and Pittsburgh (2).

Year		Record	Year		Record	Year		Record
1883	**Yale**	8–0–0	1889	**Princeton**	10–0–0	1895	**Penn**	14–0–0
1884	**Yale**	9–0–0	1890	**Harvard**	11–0–0	1896	**Princeton**	10–0–1
1885	**Princeton**	9–0–0	1891	**Yale**	13–0–0	1897	**Penn**	15–0–0
1886	**Yale**	9–0–1	1892	**Yale**	13–0–0	1898	**Harvard**	11–0–0
1887	**Yale**	9–0–0	1893	**Princeton**	11–0–0	1899	**Harvard**	10–0–1
1888	**Yale**	13–0–0	1894	**Yale**	16–0–0			

Year		Record	Bowl Game	Head Coach	Outstanding Player
1900	**Yale**	12–0–0	No bowl	Malcolm McBride	Perry Hale, HB
1901	**Michigan**	11–0–0	Won Rose	Hurry Up Yost	Willie Heston, HB
1902	**Michigan**	11–0–0	No bowl	Hurry Up Yost	Willie Heston, HB
1903	**Princeton**	11–0–0	No bowl	Art Hillebrand	John DeWitt, G
1904	**Penn**	12–0–0	No bowl	Carl Williams	Andy Smith, HB
1905	**Chicago**	11–0–0	No bowl	Amos Alonzo Stagg	Walter Eckersall, QB
1906	**Princeton**	9–0–1	No bowl	Bill Roper	Ed Dillon, HB
1907	**Yale**	9–0–1	No bowl	Bill Knox	T.A.D. Jones, HB
1908	**Penn**	11–0–1	No bowl	Sol Metzger	Hunter Scarlett, E
1909	**Yale**	10–0–0	No bowl	Howard Jones	Ted Coy, FB
1910	**Harvard**	8–0–1	No bowl	Percy Haughton	Percy Wendell, HB
1911	**Princeton**	8–0–2	No bowl	Bill Roper	Sanford White, E
1912	**Harvard**	9–0–0	No bowl	Percy Haughton	Charley Brickley, HB
1913	**Harvard**	9–0–0	No bowl	Percy Haughton	Eddie Mahan, FB
1914	**Army**	9–0–0	No bowl	Charley Daly	John McEwan, C
1915	**Cornell**	9–0–0	No bowl	Al Sharpe	Charley Barrett, HB
1916	**Pittsburgh**	8–0–0	No bowl	Pop Warner	Bob Peck, C
1917	**Georgia Tech**	9–0–0	No bowl	John Heisman	George Strupper, HB
1918	**Pittsburgh**	4–1–0	No bowl	Pop Warner	Tom Davies, HB
1919	**Harvard**	9–0–1	Won Rose	Bob Fisher	Ed Casey, HB
1920	**California**	9–0–0	Won Rose	Andy Smith	Brick Muller, E
1921	**Cornell**	8–0–0	No bowl	Gil Dobie	Eddie Kaw, HB
1922	**Cornell**	8–0–0	No bowl	Gil Dobie	George Pfann, QB
1923	**Illinois**	8–0–0	No bowl	Bob Zuppke	Red Grange, HB
1924	**Notre Dame**	10–0–0	Won Rose	Knute Rockne	"The Four Horsemen"*

*Notre Dame's **Four Horsemen** were Harry Stuhldreher (QB), Jim Crowley (HB), Don Miller (HB-P) and Elmer Layden (FB).

National Champions (Cont.)

Year		Record	Bowl Game	Head Coach	Outstanding Player
1925	**Alabama** (H)	10-0-0	Won Rose	Wallace Wade	Johnny Mack Brown, HB
	& **Dartmouth** (D)	8-0-0	No bowl	Jesse Hawley	Andy Oberlander, HB
1926	**Alabama** (H)	9-0-1	Tied Rose	Wallace Wade	Hoyt Winslett, E
	& **Stanford** (D)	10-0-1	Tied Rose	Pop Warner	Ted Shipkey, E
1927	**Illinois**	7-0-1	No bowl	Bob Zuppke	Russ Crane, G
1928	**Georgia Tech** (H)	10-0-0	Won Rose	Bill Alexander	Pete Pund, C
	& **USC** (D)	9-0-1	No bowl	Howard Jones	Lloyd Thomas, HB
1929	**Notre Dame**	9-0-0	No bowl	Knute Rockne	Frank Carideo, QB
1930	**Notre Dame**	10-0-0	No bowl	Knute Rockne	Frank Carideo, QB
1931	**USC**	10-1-0	Won Rose	Howard Jones	Ernie Pinckert, HB
1932	**USC** (H)	10-0-0	Won Rose	Howard Jones	Ernie Smith, T-K
	& **Michigan** (D)	8-0-0	No bowl	Harry Kipke	Harry Newman, QB
1933	**Michigan**	7-0-1	No bowl	Harry Kipke	Frank Wistert, T
1934	**Minnesota**	8-0-0	No bowl	Bernie Bierman	Pug Lund, HB
1935	**Minnesota** (H)	8-0-0	No bowl	Bernie Bierman	Dick Smith, T
	& **SMU** (D)	12-1-0	Lost Rose	Matty Bell	Bobby Wilson, HB
1936	**Minnesota**	7-1-0	No bowl	Bernie Bierman	Ed Widseth, T
1937	**Pittsburgh**	9-0-1	No bowl	Jock Sutherland	Marshall Goldberg, HB
1938	**TCU**	11-0-0	Won Sugar	Dutch Meyer	Davey O'Brien, QB
1939	**Texas A&M**	11-0-0	Won Sugar	Homer Norton	John Kimbrough, FB
1940	**Minnesota**	8-0-0	No Bowl	Bernie Bierman	George Franck, FB
1941	**Minnesota**	8-0-0	No bowl	Bernie Bierman	Bruce Smith, HB
1942	**Ohio St.**	9-1-0	No bowl	Paul Brown	Gene Fekete, FB
1943	**Notre Dame**	9-1-0	No bowl	Frank Leahy	Angelo Bertelli, QB
1944	**Army**	9-0-0	No bowl	Red Blaik	Glenn Davis, HB
1945	**Army**	9-0-0	No bowl	Red Blaik	Doc Blanchard, FB
1946	**Notre Dame**	8-0-1	No bowl	Frank Leahy	Johnny Lujack, QB
1947	**Notre Dame**	9-0-0	No bowl	Frank Leahy	Johnny Lujack, QB
	Michigan†	10-0-0	Won Rose	Fritz Crisler	Bob Chappuis, HB
1948	**Michigan**	9-0-0	No bowl	Bennie Oosterbaan	Dick Rifenburg, E
1949	**Notre Dame**	10-0-0	No bowl	Frank Leahy	Leon Hart, E
1950	**Oklahoma**	10-1-0	Lost Sugar	Bud Wilkinson	Leon Heath, FB
1951	**Tennessee**	10-0-0	Lost Sugar	Bob Neyland	Hank Lauricella, QB
1952	**Michigan St.** (AP, UP)	9-0-0	No bowl	Biggie Munn	Don McAuliffe, HB
	& **Georgia Tech** (INS)	12-0-0	Won Sugar	Bobby Dodd	Hal Miller, T
1953	**Maryland**	10-1-0	Lost Orange	Jim Tatum	Bernie Faloney, QB
1954	**Ohio St.** (AP, INS)	10-0-0	Won Rose	Woody Hayes	Howard Cassady, HB
	& **UCLA** (UP, FW)	9-0-0	No bowl	Red Sanders	Bob Davenport, FB
1955	**Oklahoma**	11-0-0	Won Orange	Bud Wilkinson	Jerry Tubbs, C
1956	**Oklahoma**	10-0-0	No bowl	Bud Wilkinson	Tommy McDonald, HB
1957	**Auburn** (AP)	10-0-0	No bowl	Shug Jordan	Jimmy Phillips, E
	& **Ohio St.** (UP, FW, INS)	9-1-0	Won Rose	Woody Hayes	Bob White, FB
1958	**LSU** (AP, UPI)	11-0-0	Won Sugar	Paul Dietzel	Billy Cannon, HB
	& **Iowa** (FW)	8-1-1	Won Rose	Forest Evashevski	Ranky Duncan, QB
1959	**Syracuse**	11-0-0	Won Cotton	Ben Schwartzwalder	Ernie Davis, HB
1960	**Minnesota** (AP, UPI, NFF)	8-2-0	Lost Rose	Murray Warmath	Tom Brown, G
	& **Mississippi** (FW)	10-0-1	Won Sugar	Johnny Vaught	Jake Gibbs, QB
1961	**Alabama** (AP, UPI, NFF)	11-0-0	Won Sugar	Bear Bryant	Billy Neighbors, T
	& **Ohio St.** (FW)	8-0-1	No bowl	Woody Hayes	Bob Ferguson, HB
1962	**USC**	11-0-0	Won Rose	John McKay	Hal Bedsole, E
1963	**Texas**	11-0-0	Won Cotton	Darrell Royal	Scott Appleton, T
1964	**Alabama** (AP, UPI)	10-1-0	Lost Orange	Bear Bryant	Joe Namath, QB
	Arkansas (FW)	11-0-0	Won Cotton	Frank Broyles	Ronnie Caveness, LB
	& **Notre Dame** (NFF)	9-1-0	No bowl	Ara Parseghian	John Huarte, QB
1965	**Alabama** (AP, FW-tie)	9-1-1	Won Orange	Bear Bryant	Paul Crane, C
	& **Michigan St.** (UPI, NFF, FW-tie)	10-1-0	Lost Rose	Duffy Daugherty	George Webster, LB
1966	**Notre Dame** (AP, UPI, FW, NFF-tie)	9-0-1	No bowl	Ara Parseghian	Jim Lynch, LB
	& **Michigan St.** (NFF-tie)	9-0-1	No bowl	Duffy Daugherty	Bubba Smith, DE
1967	**USC**	10-1-0	Won Rose	John McKay	O.J. Simpson, HB
1968	**Ohio St.**	10-0-0	Won Rose	Woody Hayes	Rex Kern, QB
1969	**Texas**	11-0-0	Won Cotton	Darrell Royal	James Street, QB
1970	**Nebraska** (AP, FW)	11-0-1	Won Orange	Bob Devaney	Jerry Tagge, QB
	Texas (UPI, NFF-tie)	10-1-0	Lost Cotton	Darrell Royal	Steve Worster, RB
	& **Ohio St.** (NFF-tie)	9-1-0	Lost Rose	Woody Hayes	Jim Stillwagon, MG
1971	**Nebraska**	13-0-0	Won Orange	Bob Devaney	Johnny Rodgers, WR

Year		Record	Bowl Game	Head Coach	Outstanding Player
1972	**USC**...............................	12-0-0	Won Rose	John McKay	Charles Young, TE
1973	**Notre Dame** (AP, FW, NFF)..........	11-0-0	Won Sugar	Ara Parseghian	Mike Townsend, DB
	& Alabama (UPI).................	11-1-0	Lost Sugar	Bear Bryant	Buddy Brown, OT
1974	**Oklahoma** (AP).....................	11-0-0	No bowl	Barry Switzer	Joe Washington, RB
	& USC (UPI, FW, NFF).............	10-1-1	Won Rose	John McKay	Anthony Davis, RB
1975	**Oklahoma**........................	11-1-0	Won Orange	Barry Switzer	Lee Roy Selmon, DT
1976	**Pittsburgh**......................	12-0-0	Won Sugar	Johnny Majors	Tony Dorsett, RB
1977	**Notre Dame**......................	11-1-0	Won Cotton	Dan Devine	Ross Browner, DE
1978	**Alabama** (AP, FW, NFF).............	11-1-0	Won Sugar	Bear Bryant	Marty Lyons, DT
	& USC (UPI)....................	12-1-0	Won Rose	John Robinson	Charles White, RB
1979	**Alabama**.........................	12-0-0	Won Sugar	Bear Bryant	Steadman Shealy, QB
1980	**Georgia**.........................	12-0-0	Won Sugar	Vince Dooley	Herschel Walker, RB
1981	**Clemson**.........................	12-0-0	Won Orange	Danny Ford	Jeff Davis, LB
1982	**Penn St.**........................	11-1-0	Won Sugar	Joe Paterno	Todd Blackledge, QB
1983	**Miami-FL**........................	11-1-0	Won Orange	H. Schnellenberger	Bernie Kosar, QB
1984	**BYU**.............................	13-0-0	Won Holiday	LaVell Edwards	Robbie Bosco, QB
1985	**Oklahoma**........................	11-1-0	Won Orange	Barry Switzer	Brian Bosworth, LB
1986	**Penn St.**........................	12-0-0	Won Fiesta	Joe Paterno	D.J. Dozier, RB
1987	**Miami-FL**........................	12-0-0	Won Orange	Jimmy Johnson	Steve Walsh, QB
1988	**Notre Dame**......................	12-0-0	Won Fiesta	Lou Holtz	Tony Rice, QB
1989	**Miami-FL**........................	11-1-0	Won Sugar	Dennis Erickson	Craig Erickson, QB
1990	**Colorado** (AP, FW, NFF).............	11-1-1	Won Orange	Bill McCartney	Eric Bieniemy, RB
	& Georgia Tech (UPI).............	11-0-1	Won Citrus	Bobby Ross	Shawn Jones, QB
1991	**Miami-FL** (AP)....................	12-0-0	Won Orange	Dennis Erickson	Gino Torretta, QB
	& Washington (USA, FW, NFF).......	12-0-0	Won Rose	Don James	Steve Emtman, DT

Number 1 vs Number 2

Since the Associated Press writers poll started keeping track of such things in 1936, the No.1 and No.2 ranked teams in the country have met 26 times; 18 during the regular season and eight in bowl games. Since the first showdown in 1943, the No.1 team has beaten the No.2 team 15 times, lost nine and there have been two ties. Notre Dame (3-3-2) has been involved in eight of these games, two more than Oklahoma (1-5).

Each showdown is listed below with the date, the match-up, each team's record going into the game, the final score, the stadium and site.

Date		Match-up		Stadium
Oct. 9	**#1**	Notre Dame (2-0)	 35	Michigan
1943	**#2**	Michigan (3-0)	 12	(Ann Arbor)
Nov. 20	**#1**	Notre Dame (8-0)	 14	Notre Dame
1943	**#2**	Iowa Pre-Flight (8-0)	.. 13	(South Bend)
Dec. 2	**#1**	Army (8-0)	 23	Municipal
1944	**#2**	Navy (6-2)	 7	(Baltimore)
Nov. 10	**#1**	Army (6-0)	 48	Yankee
1945	**#2**	Notre Dame (5-0-1)	... 0	(New York)
Dec. 1	**#1**	Army (8-0)	 32	Municipal
1945	**#2**	Navy (7-0-1)	 13	(Philadelphia)
Nov. 9	**#1**	Army (8-0)	 0	Yankee
1946	**#2**	Notre Dame (5-0)	 0	(New York)
		• • • • •		
Jan. 1	**#1**	USC (10-0)	 42	ROSE BOWL
1963	**#2**	Wisconsin (8-1)	 37	(Pasadena)
Oct. 12	**#2**	Texas (3-0)	 28	Cotton Bowl
1963	**#1**	Oklahoma (2-0)	 7	(Dallas)
Jan. 1	**#1**	Texas (10-0)	 28	COTTON BOWL
1964	**#2**	Navy (9-1)	 6	(Dallas)
Nov. 19	**#1**	Notre Dame (8-0)	 10	Spartan
1966	**#2**	Michigan St. (9-0)	 10	(East Lansing)
Sept. 28	**#1**	Purdue (1-0)	 37	Notre Dame
1968	**#2**	Notre Dame (1-0)	... 22	(South Bend)
Jan. 1	**#1**	Ohio St. (9-0)	 27	ROSE BOWL
1969	**#2**	USC (9-0-1)	 16	(Pasadena)
Dec. 6	**#1**	Texas (9-0)	 15	Razorback
1969	**#2**	Arkansas (9-0)	 14	(Fayetteville)

Date		Match-up		Stadium
Nov. 25	**#1**	Nebraska (10-0)	 35	Owen Field
1971	**#2**	Oklahoma (9-0)	 31	(Norman)
Jan. 1	**#1**	Nebraska (12-0)	 38	ORANGE BOWL
1972	**#2**	Alabama (11-0)	 6	(Miami)
Jan. 1	**#2**	Alabama (10-1)	 14	SUGAR BOWL
1979	**#1**	Penn St. (11-0)	 7	(New Orleans)
		• • • • •		
Sept. 26	**#1**	USC (2-0)	 28	Coliseum
1981	**#2**	Oklahoma (1-0)	 24	(Los Angeles)
Jan. 1	**#2**	Penn St. (10-1)	 27	SUGAR BOWL
1983	**#1**	Georgia (11-0)	 23	(New Orleans)
Oct. 19	**#1**	Iowa (5-0)	 12	Kinnick
1985	**#2**	Michigan (5-0)	 10	(Iowa City)
Sept. 27	**#2**	Miami-FL (3-0)	 28	Orange Bowl
1986	**#1**	Oklahoma (2-0)	 16	(Miami)
Jan. 2	**#2**	Penn St. (11-0)	 14	FIESTA BOWL
1987	**#1**	Miami-FL (11-0)	 10	(Tempe)
Nov. 21	**#1**	Oklahoma (10-0)	 17	Memorial
1987	**#2**	Nebraska (10-0)	 7	(Lincoln)
Jan. 1	**#2**	Miami-FL (11-0)	 20	ORANGE BOWL
1988	**#1**	Oklahoma (11-0)	 14	(Miami)
Nov. 26	**#1**	Notre Dame (10-0)	... 27	Coliseum
1988	**#2**	USC (10-0)	 10	(Los Angeles)
Sept. 16	**#1**	Notre Dame (1-0)	 24	Michigan
1989	**#1**	Michigan (0-0)	 19	(Ann Arbor)
		• • • • •		
Nov. 16	**#2**	Miami-FL (8-0)	 17	Doak Campbell
1991	**#1**	Florida St. (10-0)	 16	(Tallahassee)

Associated Press Final Polls

The Associated Press introduced its weekly college football poll of sportswriters (later, sportswriters and broadcasters) in 1936. The final AP poll was released at the end of the regular season until 1965, when bowl results were included for one year. After a two-year return to regular season games only, the final poll has come out after the bowls since 1968.

1936

Final poll released Nov. 30. Top 20 regular season results after that: **Dec.5**—#8 Notre Dame tied USC, 13-13; #17 Tennessee tied Ole Miss, 0-0; #18 Arkansas over Texas, 6-0. **Dec.12**—#16 TCU over #6 Santa Clara, 9-0.

	As of Nov. 30	Head Coach	After Bowls
1 Minnesota	7-1-0	Bernie Bierman	same
2 LSU	9-0-1	Bernie Moore	9-1-1
3 Pittsburgh	7-1-1	Jock Sutherland	8-1-1
4 Alabama	8-0-1	Frank Thomas	same
5 Washington	7-1-1	Jimmy Phelan	7-2-1
6 Santa Clara	7-0-0	Buck Shaw	8-1-0
7 Northwestern	7-1-0	Pappy Waldorf	same
8 Notre Dame	6-2-0	Elmer Layden	6-2-1
9 Nebraska	7-2-0	Dana X.Bible	same
10 Penn	7-1-0	Harvey Harman	same
11 Duke	9-1-0	Wallace Wade	same
12 Yale	7-1-0	Ducky Pond	same
13 Dartmouth	7-1-1	Red Blaik	same
14 Duquesne	7-2-0	John Smith	8-2-0
15 Fordham	5-1-2	Jim Crowley	same
16 TCU	7-2-2	Dutch Meyer	9-2-2
17 Tennessee	6-2-1	Bob Neyland	6-2-2
18 Arkansas	6-3-0	Fred Thomsen	7-3-0
Navy	6-3-0	Tom Hamilton	same
20 Marquette	7-1-0	Frank Murray	7-2-0

Key Bowl Games

Sugar—#6 Santa Clara over #2 LSU, 21-14; **Rose**—#3 Pitt over #5 Washington, 21-0; **Orange**—#14 Duquesne over Mississippi St., 13-12; **Cotton**—#16 TCU over #20 Marquette, 16-6.

1937

Final poll released Nov.29. Top 20 regular season results after that: **Dec.4**—#18 Rice over SMU, 15-7.

	As of Nov. 29	Head Coach	After Bowls
1 Pittsburgh	9-0-1	Jock Sutherland	same
2 California	9-0-1	Stub Allison	10-0-1
3 Fordham	7-0-1	Jim Crowley	same
4 Alabama	9-0-0	Frank Thomas	9-1-0
5 Minnesota	6-2-0	Bernie Bierman	same
6 Villanova	8-0-1	Clipper Smith	same
7 Dartmouth	7-0-2	Red Blaik	same
8 LSU	9-1-0	Bernie Moore	9-2-0
9 Notre Dame	6-2-1	Elmer Layden	same
Santa Clara	8-0-0	Buck Shaw	9-0-0
11 Nebraska	6-1-2	Biff Jones	same
12 Yale	6-1-1	Ducky Pond	same
13 Ohio St.	6-2-0	Francis Schmidt	same
14 Holy Cross	8-0-2	Eddie Anderson	same
Arkansas	6-2-2	Fred Thomsen	same
16 TCU	4-2-2	Dutch Meyer	same
17 Colorado	8-0-0	Bunnie Oakes	8-1-0
18 Rice	4-3-2	Jimmy Kitts	6-3-2
19 North Carolina	7-1-1	Ray Wolf	same
20 Duke	7-2-1	Wallace Wade	same

Key Bowl Games

Rose—#2 Cal over #4 Alabama, 13-0; **Sugar**—#9 Santa Clara over #8 LSU, 6-0; **Cotton**—#18 Rice over #17 Colorado, 28-14; **Orange**—Auburn over Michigan St., 6-0.

1938

Final poll released Dec.5. Top 20 regular season results after that: **Dec.26**—#14 Cal over Georgia Tech, 13-7.

	As of Dec. 5	Head Coach	After Bowls
1 TCU	10-0-0	Dutch Meyer	11-0-0
2 Tennessee	10-0-0	Bob Neyland	11-0-0
3 Duke	9-0-0	Wallace Wade	9-1-0
4 Oklahoma	10-0-0	Tom Stidham	10-1-0
5 Notre Dame	8-1-0	Elmer Layden	same
6 Carnegie Tech	7-1-0	Bill Kern	7-2-0
7 USC	8-2-0	Howard Jones	9-2-0
8 Pittsburgh	8-2-0	Jock Sutherland	same
9 Holy Cross	8-1-0	Eddie Anderson	same
10 Minnesota	6-2-0	Bernie Bierman	same
11 Texas Tech	10-0-0	Pete Cawthon	10-1-0
12 Cornell	5-1-1	Carl Snavely	same
13 Alabama	7-1-1	Frank Thomas	same
14 California	9-1-0	Stub Allison	10-1-0
15 Fordham	6-1-2	Jim Crowley	same
16 Michigan	6-1-1	Fritz Crisler	same
17 Northwestern	4-2-2	Pappy Waldorf	same
18 Villanova	8-0-1	Clipper Smith	same
19 Tulane	7-2-1	Red Dawson	same
20 Dartmouth	7-2-0	Red Blaik	same

Key Bowl Games

Sugar—#1 TCU over #6 Carnegie Tech, 15-7; **Orange**—#2 Tennessee over #4 Oklahoma, 17-0; **Rose**—#7 USC over #3 Duke, 7-3; **Cotton**—St.Mary's over #11 Texas Tech 20-13.

1939

Final poll released Dec.11. Top 20 regular season results after that: None.

	As of Dec. 11	Head Coach	After Bowls
1 Texas A&M	10-0-0	Homer Norton	11-0-0
2 Tennessee	10-0-0	Bob Neyland	10-1-0
3 USC	7-0-2	Howard Jones	8-0-2
4 Cornell	8-0-0	Carl Snavely	same
5 Tulane	8-0-1	Red Dawson	8-1-1
6 Missouri	8-1-0	Don Faurot	8-2-0
7 UCLA	6-0-4	Babe Horrell	same
8 Duke	8-1-0	Wallace Wade	same
9 Iowa	6-1-1	Eddie Anderson	same
10 Duquesne	8-0-1	Buff Donelli	same
11 Boston College	9-1-0	Frank Leahy	9-2-0
12 Clemson	8-1-0	Jess Neely	9-1-0
13 Notre Dame	7-2-0	Elmer Layden	same
14 Santa Clara	5-1-3	Buck Shaw	same
15 Ohio St.	6-2-0	Francis Schmidt	same
16 Georgia Tech	7-2-0	Bill Alexander	8-2-0
17 Fordham	6-2-0	Jim Crowley	same
18 Nebraska	7-1-1	Biff Jones	same
19 Oklahoma	6-2-1	Tom Stidham	same
20 Michigan	6-2-0	Fritz Crisler	same

Key Bowl Games

Sugar—#1 Texas A&M over #5 Tulane, 14-13; **Rose**—#3 USC over #2 Tennessee, 14-0; **Orange**—#16 Georgia Tech over #6 Missouri, 21-7; **Cotton**—#12 Clemson over #11 Boston College, 6-3.

1940

Final poll released Dec.2. Top 20 regular season results after that: **Dec.7**—#16 SMU over Rice, 7-6.

	As of Dec. 2	Head Coach	After Bowls
1 Minnesota	8-0-0	Bernie Bierman	same
2 Stanford	9-0-0	C.Shaughnessy	10-0-0
3 Michigan	7-1-0	Fritz Crisler	same
4 Tennessee	10-0-0	Bob Neyland	10-1-0
5 Boston College	10-0-0	Frank Leahy	11-0-0
6 Texas A&M	8-1-0	Homer Norton	9-1-0
7 Nebraska	8-1-0	Biff Jones	8-2-0
8 Northwestern	6-2-0	Pappy Waldorf	same
9 Mississippi St.	9-0-1	Allyn McKeen	10-0-1
10 Washington	7-2-0	Jimmy Phelan	same
11 Santa Clara	6-1-1	Buck Shaw	same
12 Fordham	7-1-0	Jim Crowley	7-2-0
13 Georgetown	8-1-0	Jack Hagerty	8-2-0
14 Penn	6-1-1	George Munger	same
15 Cornell	6-2-0	Carl Snavely	same
16 SMU	7-1-1	Matty Bell	8-1-1
17 Hardin-Simmons	9-0-0	Abe Woodson	same
18 Duke	7-2-0	Wallace Wade	same
19 Lafayette	9-0-0	Hooks Mylin	same
20 —			

Note: Only 19 teams ranked.

Key Bowl Games

Rose—#2 Stanford over #7 Nebraska, 21-13; **Sugar**—#5 Boston College over #4 Tennessee, 19-13; **Cotton**—#6 Texas A&M over #12 Fordham, 13-12; **Orange**—#9 Mississippi St. over #13 Georgetown, 14-7.

1941

Final poll released Dec.1. Top 20 regular season results after that: **Dec.6**—#4 Texas over Oregon, 71-7; #9 Texas A&M over #19 Washington St., 7-0; #16 Mississippi St. over San Francisco, 26-13.

	As of Dec. 1	Head Coach	After Bowls
1 Minnesota	8-0-0	Bernie Bierman	same
2 Duke	9-0-0	Wallace Wade	9-1-0
3 Notre Dame	8-0-1	Frank Leahy	same
4 Texas	7-1-1	Dana X.Bible	8-1-1
5 Michigan	6-1-1	Fritz Crisler	same
6 Fordham	7-1-0	Jim Crowley	8-1-0
7 Missouri	8-1-0	Don Faurot	8-2-0
8 Duquesne	8-0-0	Buff Donelli	same
9 Texas A&M	8-1-0	Homer Norton	9-2-0
10 Navy	7-1-1	Swede Larson	same
11 Northwestern	5-3-0	Pappy Waldorf	same
12 Oregon St.	7-2-0	Lon Stiner	8-2-0
13 Ohio St.	6-1-1	Paul Brown	same
14 Georgia	8-1-1	Wally Butts	9-1-1
15 Penn	7-1-1	George Munger	same
16 Mississippi St.	7-1-1	Allyn McKeen	8-1-1
17 Mississippi	6-2-1	Harry Mehre	same
18 Tennessee	8-2-0	John Barnhill	same
19 Washington St.	6-3-0	Babe Hollingbery	6-4-0
20 Alabama	8-2-0	Frank Thomas	9-2-0

Note: 1942 Rose Bowl moved to Durham, NC, for one year after outbreak of World War II.

Key Bowl Games

Rose—#12 Oregon St. over #2 Duke, 20-16; **Sugar**—#6 Fordham over #7 Missouri, 2-0; **Cotton**—#20 Alabama over #9 Texas A&M, 29-21; **Orange**—#14 Georgia over TCU, 40-26.

1942

Final poll released Nov.30. Top 20 regular season results after that: **Dec.5**—#6 Notre Dame tied Great Lakes Naval Station, 13-13; #13 UCLA over Idaho, 40-13; #14 William & Mary over Oklahoma, 14-7; #17 Washington St. lost to Texas A&M, 21-0; #18 Mississippi St. over San Francisco, 19-7. **Dec.12**—#13 UCLA over USC, 14-7.

	As of Nov. 30	Head Coach	After Bowls
1 Ohio St.	9-1-0	Paul Brown	same
2 Georgia	10-1-0	Wally Butts	11-1-0
3 Wisconsin	8-1-1	Harry Stuhldreher	same
4 Tulsa	10-0-0	Henry Frnka	10-1-0
5 Georgia Tech	9-1-0	Bill Alexander	9-2-0
6 Notre Dame	7-2-1	Frank Leahy	7-2-2
7 Tennessee	8-1-1	John Barnhill	9-1-1
8 Boston College	8-1-0	Denny Myers	8-2-0
9 Michigan	7-3-0	Fritz Crisler	same
10 Alabama	7-3-0	Frank Thomas	8-3-0
11 Texas	8-2-0	Dana X.Bible	9-2-0
12 Stanford	6-4-0	Marchie Schwartz	same
13 UCLA	5-3-0	Babe Horrell	7-4-0
14 William & Mary	8-1-1	Carl Voyles	9-1-1
15 Santa Clara	7-2-0	Buck Shaw	same
16 Auburn	6-4-1	Jack Meagher	same
17 Washington St.	6-1-2	Babe Hollingbery	6-2-2
18 Mississippi St.	7-2-0	Allyn McKeen	8-2-0
19 Minnesota	5-4-0	George Hauser	same
Holy Cross	5-4-1	Ank Scanlon	same
Penn St.	6-1-1	Bob Higgins	same

Key Bowl Games

Rose—#2 Georgia over #13 UCLA, 9-0; **Sugar**—#7 Tennessee over #4 Tulsa, 14-7; **Cotton**—#11 Texas over #5 Georgia Tech, 14-7; **Orange**—#10 Alabama over #8 Boston College, 37-21.

1943

Final poll released Nov.29. Top 20 regular season results after that: **Dec.11**—#10 March Field over #19 Pacific, 19-0.

	As of Nov. 29	Head Coach	After Bowls
1 Notre Dame	9-1-0	Frank Leahy	same
2 Iowa Pre-Flight	9-1-0	Don Faurot	same
3 Michigan	8-1-0	Fritz Crisler	same
4 Navy	8-1-0	Billick Whelchel	same
5 Purdue	9-0-0	Elmer Burnham	same
6 Great Lakes Naval Station	10-2-0	Tony Hinkle	same
7 Duke	8-1-0	Eddie Cameron	same
8 Del Monte Pre-Flight	7-1-0	Bill Kern	same
9 Northwestern	6-2-0	Pappy Waldorf	same
10 March Field	8-1-0	Paul Schissler	9-1-0
11 Army	7-2-1	Red Blaik	same
12 Washington	4-0-0	Ralph Welch	4-1-0
13 Georgia Tech	7-3-0	Bill Alexander	8-3-0
14 Texas	7-1-0	Dana X.Bible	7-1-1
15 Tulsa	6-0-1	Henry Frnka	6-1-1
16 Dartmouth	6-1-0	Earl Brown	same
17 Bainbridge Navy Training School	7-0-0	Joe Maniaci	same
18 Colorado College	7-0-0	Hal White	same
19 Pacific	7-1-0	Amos A.Stagg	7-2-0
20 Penn	6-2-1	George Munger	same

Key Bowl Games

Rose—USC over #12 Washington, 29-0; **Sugar**—#13 Georgia Tech over #15 Tulsa, 20-18; **Cotton**—#14 Texas tied Randolph Field, 7-7; **Orange**—LSU over Texas A&M, 19-14.

Associated Press Final Polls (Cont.)

1944

Final poll released Dec. 4. Top 20 regular season results after that: **Dec. 10**—#3 Randolph Field over #10 March Field, 20-7; #18 Fort Pierce over Kessler Field, 34-7; Morris Field over #20 Second Air Force, 14-7.

		As of Dec. 4	Head Coach	After Bowls
1	Army	9-0-0	Red Blaik	same
2	Ohio St.	9-0-0	Carroll Widdoes	same
3	Randolph Field	10-0-0	Frank Tritico	12-0-0
4	Navy	6-3-0	Oscar Hagberg	same
5	Bainbridge Navy Training School	10-0-0	Joe Maniaci	same
6	Iowa Pre-Flight	10-1-0	Jack Meagher	same
7	USC	7-0-2	Jeff Cravath	8-0-2
8	Michigan	8-2-0	Fritz Crisler	same
9	Notre Dame	8-2-0	Ed McKeever	same
10	March Field	7-0-2	Paul Schissler	7-1-2
11	Duke	5-4-0	Eddie Cameron	6-4-0
12	Tennessee	7-0-1	John Barnhill	7-1-1
13	Georgia Tech	8-2-0	Bill Alexander	8-3-0
14	Norman Pre-Flight	6-0-0	John Gregg	same
15	Illinois	5-4-1	Ray Eliot	same
16	El Toro Marines	8-1-0	Dick Hanley	same
17	Great Lakes Naval Station	9-2-1	Paul Brown	same
18	Fort Pierce	8-0-0	Hamp Pool	9-0-0
19	St.Mary's Pre-Flight	4-4-0	Jules Sikes	same
20	Second Air Force	10-2-1	Bill Reese	10-4-1

Key Bowl Games

Treasury—#3 Randolph Field over #20 Second Air Force, 13-6; **Rose**—#7 USC over #12 Tennessee, 25-0; **Sugar**—#11 Duke over Alabama, 29-26; **Orange**—Tulsa over #13 Georgia Tech, 26-12; **Cotton**—Oklahoma A&M over TCU, 34-0.

1946

Final poll released Dec. 2. Top 20 regular season results after that: None.

		As of Dec. 2	Head Coach	After Bowls
1	Notre Dame	8-0-1	Frank Leahy	same
2	Army	9-0-1	Red Blaik	same
3	Georgia	10-0-0	Wally Butts	11-0-0
4	UCLA	10-0-0	Bert LaBrucherie	10-1-0
5	Illinois	7-2-0	Ray Eliot	8-2-0
6	Michigan	6-2-1	Fritz Crisler	same
7	Tennessee	9-1-0	Bob Neyland	9-2-0
8	LSU	9-1-0	Bernie Moore	9-1-1
9	North Carolina	8-1-1	Carl Snavely	8-2-1
10	Rice	8-2-0	Jess Neely	9-2-0
11	Georgia Tech	8-2-0	Bobby Dodd	9-2-0
12	Yale	7-1-1	Howard Odell	same
13	Penn	6-2-0	George Munger	same
14	Oklahoma	7-3-0	Jim Tatum	8-3-0
15	Texas	8-2-0	Dana X.Bible	same
16	Arkansas	6-3-1	John Barnhill	6-3-2
17	Tulsa	9-1-0	J.O.Brothers	same
18	N.C.State	8-2-0	Beattie Feathers	8-3-0
19	Delaware	9-0-0	Bill Murray	10-0-0
20	Indiana	6-3-0	Bo McMillan	same

Key Bowl Games

Sugar—#3 Georgia over #9 N.Carolina, 20-10; **Rose**—#5 Illinois over #4 UCLA, 45-14; **Orange**—#10 Rice over #7 Tennessee, 8-0; **Cotton**—#8 LSU tied #16 Arkansas, 0-0.

1945

Final poll released Dec. 3. Top 20 regular season results after that: None.

		As of Dec. 3	Head Coach	After Bowls
1	Army	9-0-0	Red Blaik	same
2	Alabama	9-0-0	Frank Thomas	10-0-0
3	Navy	7-1-1	Oscar Hagberg	same
4	Indiana	9-0-1	Bo McMillan	same
5	Oklahoma A&M	8-0-0	Jim Lookabaugh	9-0-0
6	Michigan	7-3-0	Fritz Crisler	same
7	St.Mary's-CA	7-1-0	Jimmy Phelan	7-2-0
8	Penn	6-2-0	George Munger	same
9	Notre Dame	7-2-1	Hugh Devore	same
10	Texas	9-1-0	Dana X.Bible	10-1-0
11	USC	7-3-0	Jeff Cravath	7-4-0
12	Ohio St.	7-2-0	Carroll Widdoes	same
13	Duke	6-2-0	Eddie Cameron	same
14	Tennessee	8-1-0	John Barnhill	same
15	LSU	7-2-0	Bernie Moore	same
16	Holy Cross	8-1-0	John DeGrosa	8-2-0
17	Tulsa	8-2-0	Henry Frnka	8-3-0
18	Georgia	8-2-0	Wally Butts	9-2-0
19	Wake Forest	4-3-1	Peahead Walker	5-3-1
20	Columbia	8-1-0	Lou Little	same

Key Bowl Games

Rose—#2 Alabama over #11 USC, 34-14; **Sugar**—#5 Oklahoma A&M over #7 St.Mary's, 33-13; **Cotton**—#10 Texas over Missouri, 40-27; **Orange**—Miami-FL over #16 Holy Cross, 13-6.

1947

Final poll released Dec. 8. Top 20 regular season results after that: None.

		As of Dec. 8	Head Coach	After Bowls
1	Notre Dame	9-0-0	Frank Leahy	same
2	Michigan	9-0-0	Fritz Crisler	10-0-0
3	SMU	9-0-1	Matty Bell	9-0-2
4	Penn St.	9-0-0	Bob Higgins	9-0-1
5	Texas	9-1-0	Blair Cherry	10-1-0
6	Alabama	8-2-0	Red Drew	8-3-0
7	Penn	7-0-1	George Munger	same
8	USC	7-1-1	Jeff Cravath	7-2-1
9	North Carolina	8-2-0	Carl Snavely	same
10	Georgia Tech	9-1-0	Bobby Dodd	10-1-0
11	Army	5-2-2	Red Blaik	same
12	Kansas	8-0-2	George Sauer	8-1-2
13	Mississippi	8-2-0	Johnny Vaught	9-2-0
14	William & Mary	9-1-0	Rube McCray	9-2-0
15	California	9-1-0	Pappy Waldorf	same
16	Oklahoma	7-2-1	Bud Wilkinson	same
17	N.C.State	5-3-1	Beattie Feathers	same
18	Rice	6-3-1	Jess Neely	same
19	Duke	4-3-2	Wallace Wade	same
20	Columbia	7-2-0	Lou Little	same

Key Bowl Games

Rose—#2 Michigan over #8 USC, 49-0; **Cotton**—#3 SMU tied #4 Penn St., 13-13; **Sugar**—#5 Texas over #6 Alabama, 27-7; **Orange**—#10 Georgia Tech over #12 Kansas, 20-14.

1948

Final poll released Nov.29. Top 20 regular season results after that: **Dec.3**—#12 Vanderbilt over Miami-FL, 33-6. **Dec.4**—#2 Notre Dame tied USC, 14-14; #11 Clemson over The Citadel, 20-0.

		As of Nov.29	Head Coach	After Bowls
1	Michigan	9-0-0	Bennie Oosterbaan	same
2	Notre Dame	9-0-0	Frank Leahy	9-0-1
3	North Carolina	9-0-1	Carl Snavely	9-1-1
4	California	10-0-0	Pappy Waldorf	10-1-0
5	Oklahoma	9-1-0	Bud Wilkinson	10-1-0
6	Army	8-0-1	Red Blaik	same
7	Northwestern	7-2-0	Bob Voigts	8-2-0
8	Georgia	9-1-0	Wally Butts	9-2-0
9	Oregon	9-1-0	Jim Aiken	9-2-0
10	SMU	8-1-1	Matty Bell	9-1-1
11	Clemson	9-0-0	Frank Howard	11-0-0
12	Vanderbilt	7-2-1	Red Sanders	8-2-1
13	Tulane	9-1-0	Henry Frnka	same
14	Michigan St.	6-2-2	Biggie Munn	same
15	Mississippi	8-1-0	Johnny Vaught	same
16	Minnesota	7-2-0	Bernie Bierman	same
17	William & Mary	6-2-2	Rube McCray	7-2-2
18	Penn St.	7-1-1	Bob Higgins	same
19	Cornell	8-1-0	Lefty James	same
20	Wake Forest	6-3-0	Peahead Walker	6-4-0

Note: Big Nine "no-repeat" rule kept Michigan from Rose Bowl.

Key Bowl Games

Sugar—#5 Oklahoma over #3 North Carolina, 14-6; **Rose**—#7 Northwestern over #4 Cal, 20-14; **Orange**—Texas over #8 Georgia, 41-28; **Cotton**—#10 SMU over #9 Oregon, 21-13.

1949

Final poll released Nov.28. Top 20 regular season results after that: **Dec.2**—#14 Maryland over Miami-FL, 13-0. **Dec.3**—#1 Notre Dame over SMU, 27-20; #10 Pacific over Hawaii, 75-0.

		As of Nov.28	Head Coach	After Bowls
1	Notre Dame	9-0-0	Frank Leahy	10-0-0
2	Oklahoma	10-0-0	Bud Wilkinson	11-0-0
3	California	10-0-0	Pappy Waldorf	10-1-0
4	Army	9-0-0	Red Blaik	same
5	Rice	9-1-0	Jess Neely	10-1-0
6	Ohio St.	6-1-2	Wes Fesler	7-1-2
7	Michigan	6-2-1	Bennie Oosterbaan	same
8	Minnesota	7-2-0	Bernie Bierman	same
9	LSU	8-2-0	Gaynell Tinsley	8-3-0
10	Pacific	10-0-0	Larry Siemering	11-0-0
11	Kentucky	9-2-0	Bear Bryant	9-3-0
12	Cornell	8-1-0	Lefty James	same
13	Villanova	8-1-0	Jim Leonard	same
14	Maryland	7-1-0	Jim Tatum	9-1-0
15	Santa Clara	7-2-1	Len Casanova	8-2-1
16	North Carolina	7-3-0	Carl Snavely	7-4-0
17	Tennessee	7-2-1	Bob Neyland	same
18	Princeton	6-3-0	Charlie Caldwell	same
19	Michigan St.	6-3-0	Biggie Munn	same
20	Missouri	7-3-0	Don Faurot	7-4-0
	Baylor	7-3-0	Bob Woodruff	same

Key Bowl Games

Sugar—#2 Oklahoma over #9 LSU, 35-0; **Rose**—#6 Ohio St. over #3 Cal, 17-14; **Cotton**—#5 Rice over #16 North Carolina, 27-13; **Orange**—#15 Santa Clara over #11 Kentucky, 21-13.

1950

Final poll released Nov.27. Top 20 regular season results after that: **Nov.30**—#3 Texas over Texas A&M, 17-0. **Dec.1**—#15 Miami-FL over Missouri, 27—9. **Dec.2**—#1 Oklahoma over Okla. A&M, 41-14; Navy over #2 Army, 14-2; #4 Tennessee over Vanderbilt, 43-0; #16 Alabama over Auburn, 34-0; #19 Tulsa over Houston, 28-21; #20 Tulane tied LSU, 14-14. **Dec.9**—#3 Texas over LSU, 21-6.

		As of Nov. 27	Head Coach	After Bowls
1	Oklahoma	9-0-0	Bud Wilkinson	10-1-0
2	Army	8-0-0	Red Blaik	8-1-0
3	Texas	7-1-0	Blair Cherry	9-2-0
4	Tennessee	9-1-0	Bob Neyland	11-1-0
5	California	9-0-1	Pappy Waldorf	9-1-1
6	Princeton	9-0-0	Charlie Caldwell	same
7	Kentucky	10-1-0	Bear Bryant	11-1-0
8	Michigan St.	8-1-0	Biggie Munn	same
9	Michigan	5-3-1	Bennie Oosterbaan	6-3-1
10	Clemson	8-0-1	Frank Howard	9-0-1
11	Washington	8-2-0	Howard Odell	same
12	Wyoming	9-0-0	Bowden Wyatt	10-0-0
13	Illinois	7-2-0	Ray Eliot	same
14	Ohio St.	6-3-0	Wes Fesler	same
15	Miami-FL	8-0-1	Andy Gustafson	9-1-1
16	Alabama	8-2-0	Red Drew	9-2-0
17	Nebraska	6-2-1	Bill Glassford	same
18	Wash.& Lee	8-2-0	George Barclay	8-3-0
19	Tulsa	8-1-1	J.O.Brothers	9-1-1
20	Tulane	6-2-0	Henry Frnka	6-2-1

Key Bowl Games

Sugar—#7 Kentucky over #1 Oklahoma, 13-7; **Cotton**—#4 Tennessee over #3 Texas, 20-14; **Rose**—#9 Michigan over #5 Cal, 14-6; **Orange**—#10 Clemson over #15 Miami-FL, 15-14.

1951

Final poll released Dec.3. Top 20 regular season results after that: None.

		As of Dec. 3	Head Coach	After Bowls
1	Tennessee	10-0-0	Bob Neyland	10-1-0
2	Michigan St.	9-0-0	Biggie Munn	same
3	Maryland	9-0-0	Jim Tatum	10-0-0
4	Illinois	8-0-1	Ray Eliot	9-0-1
5	Georgia Tech	10-0-1	Bobby Dodd	11-0-1
6	Princeton	9-0-0	Charlie Caldwell	same
7	Stanford	9-1-0	Chuck Taylor	9-2-0
8	Wisconsin	7-1-1	Ivy Williamson	same
9	Baylor	8-1-1	George Sauer	8-2-1
10	Oklahoma	8-2-0	Bud Wilkinson	same
11	TCU	6-4-0	Dutch Meyer	6-5-0
12	California	8-2-0	Pappy Waldorf	same
13	Virginia	8-1-0	Art Guepe	same
14	San Francisco	9-0-0	Joe Kuharich	same
15	Kentucky	7-4-0	Bear Bryant	8-4-0
16	Boston University	6-4-0	Buff Donelli	same
17	UCLA	5-3-1	Red Sanders	same
18	Washington St.	7-3-0	Forest Evashevski	same
19	Holy Cross	8-2-0	Eddie Anderson	same
	Clemson	7-2-0	Frank Howard	7-3-0

Key Bowl Games

Sugar—#3 Maryland over #1 Tennessee, 28-13; **Rose**—#4 Illinois over #7 Stanford, 40-7; **Orange**—#5 Georgia Tech over #9 Baylor, 17-14; **Cotton**—#15 Kentucky over #11 TCU, 20-7.

Associated Press Final Polls (Cont.)

1952

Final poll released Dec.1. Top 20 regular season results after that: **Dec.6**—#15 Florida over #20 Kentucky, 27-20.

		As of Dec. 1	Head Coach	After Bowls
1	Michigan St.	9-0-0	Biggie Munn	same
2	Georgia Tech	11-0-0	Bobby Dodd	12-0-0
3	Notre Dame	7-2-1	Frank Leahy	same
4	Oklahoma	8-1-1	Bud Wilkinson	same
5	USC	9-1-0	Jess Hill	10-1-0
6	UCLA	8-1-0	Red Sanders	same
7	Mississippi	8-0-2	Johnny Vaught	8-1-2
8	Tennessee	8-1-1	Bob Neyland	8-2-1
9	Alabama	9-2-0	Red Drew	10-2-0
10	Texas	8-2-0	Ed Price	9-2-0
11	Wisconsin	6-2-1	Ivy Williamson	6-3-1
12	Tulsa	8-1-1	J.O.Brothers	8-2-1
13	Maryland	7-2-0	Jim Tatum	same
14	Syracuse	7-2-0	Ben Schwartzwalder	7-3-0
15	Florida	6-3-0	Bob Woodruff	8-3-0
16	Duke	8-2-0	Bill Murray	same
17	Ohio St.	6-3-0	Woody Hayes	same
18	Purdue	4-3-2	Stu Holcomb	same
19	Princeton	8-1-0	Charlie Caldwell	same
20	Kentucky	5-3-2	Bear Bryant	5-4-2

Note: Michigan St. would officially join Big Ten in 1953.

Key Bowl Games

Sugar—#2 Georgia Tech over #7 Ole Miss, 24-7; **Rose**—#5 USC over #11 Wisconsin, 7-0; **Cotton**—#10 Texas over #8 Tennessee, 16-0; **Orange**—#9 Alabama over #14 Syracuse, 61-6.

1954

Final poll released Nov.29. Top 20 regular season results after that: **Dec.4th**—#4 Notre Dame over SMU, 26-14.

		As of Nov. 29	Head Coach	After Bowls
1	Ohio St.	9-0-0	Woody Hayes	10-0-0
2	UCLA	9-0-0	Red Sanders	same
3	Oklahoma	10-0-0	Bud Wilkinson	same
4	Notre Dame	8-1-0	Terry Brennan	9-1-0
5	Navy	7-2-0	Eddie Erdelatz	8-2-0
6	Mississippi	9-1-0	Johnny Vaught	9-2-0
7	Army	7-2-0	Red Blaik	same
8	Maryland	7-2-1	Jim Tatum	same
9	Wisconsin	7-2-0	Ivy Williamson	same
10	Arkansas	8-2-0	Bowden Wyatt	8-3-0
11	Miami-FL	8-1-0	Andy Gustafson	same
12	West Virginia	8-1-0	Art Lewis	same
13	Auburn	7-3-0	Shug Jordan	8-3-0
14	Duke	7-2-1	Bill Murray	8-2-1
15	Michigan	6-3-0	Bennie Oosterbaan	same
16	Virginia Tech	8-0-1	Frank Moseley	same
17	USC	8-3-0	Jess Hill	8-4-0
18	Baylor	7-3-0	George Sauer	7-4-0
19	Rice	7-3-0	Jess Neely	same
20	Penn St.	7-2-0	Rip Engle	same

Note: PCC and Big Seven "no-repeat" rules kept UCLA and Oklahoma from Orange and Rose bowls, respectively.

Key Bowl Games

Rose—#1 Ohio St. over #17 USC, 20-7; **Sugar**—#5 Navy over #6 Ole Miss, 21-0; **Cotton**—Georgia Tech over #10 Arkansas, 14-6; **Orange**—#14 Duke over Nebraska, 34-7.

1953

Final poll released Nov.30. Top 20 regular season results after that: **Dec.5**—#2 Notre Dame over SMU, 40-14.

		As of Nov. 30	Head Coach	After Bowls
1	Maryland	10-0-0	Jim Tatum	10-1-0
2	Notre Dame	8-0-1	Frank Leahy	9-0-1
3	Michigan St.	8-1-0	Biggie Munn	9-1-0
4	Oklahoma	8-1-1	Bud Wilkinson	9-1-1
5	UCLA	8-1-0	Red Sanders	8-2-0
6	Rice	8-2-0	Jess Neely	9-2-0
7	Illinois	7-1-1	Ray Eliot	same
8	Georgia Tech	8-2-1	Bobby Dodd	9-2-1
9	Iowa	5-3-1	Forest Evashevski	same
10	West Virginia	8-1-0	Art Lewis	8-2-0
11	Texas	7-3-0	Ed Price	same
12	Texas Tech	10-1-0	DeWitt Weaver	11-1-0
13	Alabama	6-2-3	Red Drew	6-3-3
14	Army	7-1-1	Red Blaik	same
15	Wisconsin	6-2-1	Ivy Williamson	same
16	Kentucky	7-2-1	Bear Bryant	same
17	Auburn	7-2-1	Shug Jordan	7-3-1
18	Duke	7-2-1	Bill Murray	same
19	Stanford	6-3-1	Chuck Taylor	same
20	Michigan	6-3-0	Bennie Oosterbaan	same

Key Bowl Games

Orange—#4 Oklahoma over #1 Maryland, 7-0; **Rose**—#3 Michigan St. over #5 UCLA, 28-20; **Cotton**—#6 Rice over #13 Alabama, 28-6; **Sugar**—#8 Georgia Tech over #10 West Virginia, 42-19.

1955

Final poll released Nov.28. Top 20 regular season results after that: None.

		As of Nov. 28	Head Coach	After Bowls
1	Oklahoma	10-0-0	Bud Wilkinson	11-0-0
2	Michigan St.	8-1-0	Duffy Daugherty	9-1-0
3	Maryland	10-0-0	Jim Tatum	10-1-0
4	UCLA	9-1-0	Red Sanders	9-2-0
5	Ohio St.	7-2-0	Woody Hayes	same
6	TCU	9-1-0	Abe Martin	9-2-0
7	Georgia Tech	8-1-1	Bobby Dodd	9-1-1
8	Auburn	8-1-1	Shug Jordan	8-2-1
9	Notre Dame	8-2-0	Terry Brennan	same
10	Mississippi	9-1-0	Johnny Vaught	10-1-0
11	Pittsburgh	7-3-0	John Michelosen	7-4-0
12	Michigan	7-2-0	Bennie Oosterbaan	same
13	USC	6-4-0	Jess Hill	same
14	Miami-FL	6-3-0	Andy Gustafson	same
15	Miami-OH	9-0-0	Ara Parseghian	same
16	Stanford	6-3-1	Chuck Taylor	same
17	Texas A&M	7-2-1	Bear Bryant	same
18	Navy	6-2-1	Eddie Erdelatz	same
19	West Virginia	8-2-0	Art Lewis	same
20	Army	6-3-0	Red Blaik	same

Note: Big Ten "no-repeat" rule kept Ohio St. from Rose Bowl.

Key Bowl Games

Orange—#1 Oklahoma over #3 Maryland, 20-6; **Rose**—#2 Michigan St. over #4 UCLA, 17-14; **Cotton**—#10 Ole Miss over #6 TCU, 14-13; **Sugar**—#7 Georgia Tech over #11 Pitt, 7-0; **Gator**—Vanderbilt over #8 Auburn, 25-13.

1956

Final poll released Dec.3. Top 20 regular season results after that: **Dec.8**—#13 Pitt over #6 Miami-FL, 14-7.

		As of Dec. 3	Head Coach	After Bowls
1	Oklahoma	10-0-0	Bud Wilkinson	same
2	Tennessee	10-0-0	Bowden Wyatt	10-1-0
3	Iowa	8-1-0	Forest Evashevski	9-1-0
4	Georgia Tech	9-1-0	Bobby Dodd	10-1-0
5	Texas A&M	9-0-1	Bear Bryant	same
6	Miami-FL	8-0-1	Andy Gustafson	8-1-1
7	Michigan	7-2-0	Bennie Oosterbaan	same
8	Syracuse	7-1-0	Ben Schwartzwalder	7-2-0
9	Michigan St.	7-2-0	Duffy Daugherty	same
10	Oregon St.	7-2-1	Tommy Prothro	7-3-1
11	Baylor	8-2-0	Sam Boyd	9-2-0
12	Minnesota	6-1-2	Murray Warmath	same
13	Pittsburgh	6-2-1	John Michelosen	7-3-1
14	TCU	7-3-0	Abe Martin	8-3-0
15	Ohio St.	6-3-0	Woody Hayes	same
16	Navy	6-1-2	Eddie Erdelatz	same
17	G. Washington	7-1-1	Gene Sherman	8-1-1
18	USC	8-2-0	Jess Hill	same
19	Clemson	7-1-2	Frank Howard	7-2-2
20	Colorado	7-2-1	Dallas Ward	8-2-1

Note: Big Seven "no-repeat" rule kept Oklahoma from Orange Bowl and Texas A&M was on probation.

Key Bowl Games

Sugar—#11 Baylor over #2 Tennessee, 13-7; **Rose**—#3 Iowa over #10 Oregon St., 35-19; **Gator**—#4 Georgia Tech over #13 Pitt, 21-14; **Cotton**—#14 TCU over #8 Syracuse, 28-27; **Orange**—#20 Colorado over #19 Clemson, 27-21.

1957

Final poll released Dec.2. Top 20 regular season results after that: **Dec.7th**—#10 Notre Dame over SMU, 54-21.

		As of Dec. 2	Head Coach	After Bowls
1	Auburn	10-0-0	Shug Jordan	same
2	Ohio St.	8-1-0	Woody Hayes	9-1-0
3	Michigan St.	8-1-0	Duffy Daugherty	same
4	Oklahoma	9-1-0	Bud Wilkinson	10-1-0
5	Navy	8-1-1	Eddie Erdelatz	9-1-1
6	Iowa	7-1-1	Forest Evashevski	same
7	Mississippi	8-1-1	Johnny Vaught	9-1-1
8	Rice	7-3-0	Jess Neely	7-4-0
9	Texas A&M	8-2-0	Bear Bryant	8-3-0
10	Notre Dame	6-3-0	Terry Brennan	7-3-0
11	Texas	6-3-1	Darrell Royal	6-4-1
12	Arizona St.	10-0-0	Dan Devine	same
13	Tennessee	7-3-0	Bowden Wyatt	8-3-0
14	Mississippi St.	6-2-1	Wade Walker	same
15	N.C.State	7-1-2	Earle Edwards	same
16	Duke	6-2-2	Bill Murray	6-3-2
17	Florida	6-2-1	Bob Woodruff	same
18	Army	7-2-0	Red Blaik	same
19	Wisconsin	6-3-0	Milt Bruhn	same
20	VMI	9-0-1	John McKenna	same

Note: Auburn on probation, ineligible for bowl game.

Key Bowl Games

Rose—#2 Ohio St. over Oregon, 10-7; **Orange**—#4 Oklahoma over #16 Duke, 48-21; **Cotton**—#5 Navy over #8 Rice, 20-7; **Sugar**—#7 Ole Miss over #11 Texas, 39-7; **Gator**—#13 Tennessee over #9 Texas A&M, 3-0.

1958

Final poll released Dec.1. Top 20 regular season results after that: None.

		As of Dec. 1	Head Coach	After Bowls
1	LSU	10-0-0	Paul Dietzel	11-0-0
2	Iowa	7-1-1	Forest Evashevski	8-1-1
3	Army	8-0-1	Red Blaik	same
4	Auburn	9-0-1	Shug Jordan	same
5	Oklahoma	9-1-0	Bud Wilkinson	10-1-0
6	Air Force	9-0-1	Ben Martin	9-0-2
7	Wisconsin	7-1-1	Milt Bruhn	same
8	Ohio St.	6-1-2	Woody Hayes	same
9	Syracuse	8-1-0	Ben Schwartzwalder	8-2-0
10	TCU	8-2-0	Abe Martin	8-2-1
11	Mississippi	8-2-0	Johnny Vaught	9-2-0
12	Clemson	8-2-0	Frank Howard	8-3-0
13	Purdue	6-1-2	Jack Mollenkopf	same
14	Florida	6-3-1	Bob Woodruff	6-4-1
15	South Carolina	7-3-0	Warren Giese	same
16	California	7-3-0	Pete Elliott	7-4-0
17	Notre Dame	6-4-0	Terry Brennan	same
18	SMU	6-4-0	Bill Meek	same
19	Oklahoma St.	7-3-0	Cliff Speegle	8-3-0
20	Rutgers	8-1-0	John Stiegman	same

Key Bowl Games

Sugar—#1 LSU over #12 Clemson, 7-0; **Rose**—#2 Iowa over #16 Cal, 38-12; **Orange**—#5 Oklahoma over #9 Syracuse, 21-6; **Cotton**—#6 Air Force tied #10 TCU, 0-0.

1959

Final poll released Dec.7. Top 20 regular season results after that: None.

		As of Dec. 7	Head Coach	After Bowls
1	Syracuse	10-0-0	Ben Schwartzwalder	11-0-0
2	Mississippi	9-1-0	Johnny Vaught	10-1-0
3	LSU	9-1-0	Paul Dietzel	9-2-0
4	Texas	9-1-0	Darrell Royal	9-2-0
5	Georgia	9-1-0	Wally Butts	10-1-0
6	Wisconsin	7-2-0	Milt Bruhn	7-3-0
7	TCU	8-2-0	Abe Martin	8-3-0
8	Washington	9-1-0	Jim Owens	10-1-0
9	Arkansas	8-2-0	Frank Broyles	9-2-0
10	Alabama	7-1-2	Bear Bryant	7-2-2
11	Clemson	8-2-0	Frank Howard	9-2-0
12	Penn St.	8-2-0	Rip Engle	9-2-0
13	Illinois	5-3-1	Ray Eliot	same
14	USC	8-2-0	Don Clark	same
15	Oklahoma	7-3-0	Bud Wilkinson	same
16	Wyoming	9-1-0	Bob Devaney	same
17	Notre Dame	5-5-0	Joe Kuharich	same
18	Missouri	6-4-0	Dan Devine	6-5-0
19	Florida	5-4-1	Bob Woodruff	same
20	Pittsburgh	6-4-0	John Michelosen	same

Note: Big Seven "no-repeat" rule kept Oklahoma from Orange Bowl.

Key Bowl Games

Cotton—#1 Syracuse over #4 Texas, 23-14; **Sugar**—#2 Ole Miss over #3 LSU, 21-0; **Orange**—#5 Georgia over #18 Missouri, 14-0; **Rose**—#8 Washington over #6 Wisconsin, 44-8; **Bluebonnet**—#11 Clemson over #7 TCU, 23-7; **Gator**—#9 Arkansas over Georgia Tech, 14-7; **Liberty**—#12 Penn St. over #10 Alabama, 7-0.

Associated Press Final Polls (Cont.)

AP ranked only 10 teams from 1962-67.

1960

Final poll released Nov.28. Top 20 regular season results after that: **Dec.3**—UCLA over #10 Duke, 27-6.

		As of Nov. 28	Head Coach	After Bowls
1	Minnesota	8-1-0	Murray Warmath	8-2-0
2	Mississippi	9-0-1	Johnny Vaught	10-0-1
3	Iowa	8-1-0	Forest Evashevski	same
4	Navy	9-1-0	Wayne Hardin	9-2-0
5	Missouri	9-1-0	Dan Devine	10-1-0
6	Washington	9-1-0	Jim Owens	10-1-0
7	Arkansas	8-2-0	Frank Broyles	8-3-0
8	Ohio St.	7-2-0	Woody Hayes	same
9	Alabama	8-1-1	Bear Bryant	8-1-2
10	Duke	7-2-0	Bill Murray	8-3-0
11	Kansas	7-2-1	Jack Mitchell	same
12	Baylor	8-2-0	John Bridgers	8-3-0
13	Auburn	8-2-0	Shug Jordan	same
14	Yale	9-0-0	Jordan Olivar	same
15	Michigan St.	6-2-1	Duffy Daugherty	same
16	Penn St.	6-3-0	Rip Engle	7-3-0
17	New Mexico St.	10-0-0	Warren Woodson	11-0-0
18	Florida	8-2-0	Ray Graves	9-2-0
19	Syracuse	7-2-0	Ben Schwartzwalder	same
	Purdue	4-4-1	Jack Mollenkopf	same

Key Bowl Games

Rose—#6 Washington over #1 Minnesota, 17-7; **Sugar**—#2 Ole Miss over Rice, 14-6; **Orange**—#5 Missouri over #4 Navy, 21-14; **Cotton**—#10 Duke over #7 Arkansas, 7-6; **Bluebonnet**—#9 Alabama tied Texas, 3-3.

1961

Final poll released Dec.4. Top 20 regular season results after that: None.

		As of Dec. 4	Head Coach	After Bowls
1	Alabama	10-0-0	Bear Bryant	11-0-0
2	Ohio St.	8-0-1	Woody Hayes	same
3	Texas	9-1-0	Darrell Royal	10-1-0
4	LSU	9-1-0	Paul Dietzel	10-1-0
5	Mississippi	9-1-0	Johnny Vaught	9-2-0
6	Minnesota	7-2-0	Murray Warmath	8-2-0
7	Colorado	9-1-0	Sonny Grandelius	9-2-0
8	Michigan St.	7-2-0	Duffy Daugherty	same
9	Arkansas	8-2-0	Frank Broyles	8-3-0
10	Utah St.	9-0-1	John Ralston	9-1-1
11	Missouri	7-2-1	Dan Devine	same
12	Purdue	6-3-0	Jack Mollenkopf	same
13	Georgia Tech	7-3-0	Bobby Dodd	7-4-0
14	Syracuse	7-3-0	Ben Schwartzwalder	8-3-0
15	Rutgers	9-0-0	John Bateman	same
16	UCLA	7-3-0	Bill Barnes	7-4-0
17	Rice	7-3-0	Jess Neely	7-4-0
	Penn St.	7-3-0	Rip Engle	8-3-0
	Arizona	8-1-1	Jim LaRue	same
20	Duke	7-3-0	Bill Murray	same

Note: Ohio St. faculty council turned down Rose Bowl invitation citing concern with OSU's overemphasis on sports.

Key Bowl Games

Sugar—#1 Alabama over #9 Arkansas, 10-3; **Cotton**—#3 Texas over #5 Ole Miss, 12-7; **Orange**—#4 LSU over #7 Colorado, 25-7; **Rose**—#6 Minnesota over #16 UCLA, 21-3; **Gotham**—Baylor over #10 Utah St., 24-9.

1962

Final poll released Dec.3. Top 10 regular season results after that: None.

		As of Dec. 3	Head Coach	After Bowls
1	USC	10-0-0	John McKay	11-0-0
2	Wisconsin	8-1-0	Milt Bruhn	8-2-0
3	Mississippi	9-0-0	Johnny Vaught	10-0-0
4	Texas	9-0-1	Darrell Royal	9-1-1
5	Alabama	9-1-0	Bear Bryant	10-1-0
6	Arkansas	9-1-0	Frank Broyles	9-2-0
7	LSU	8-1-1	Charlie McClendon	9-1-1
8	Oklahoma	8-2-0	Bud Wilkinson	8-3-0
9	Penn St.	9-1-0	Rip Engle	9-2-0
10	Minnesota	6-2-1	Murray Warmath	same

Key Bowl Games

Rose—#1 USC over #2 Wisconsin, 42-37; **Sugar**—#3 Ole Miss over #6 Arkansas, 17-13; **Cotton**—#7 LSU over #4 Texas, 13-0; **Orange**—#5 Alabama over #8 Oklahoma, 17-0; **Gator**—Florida over #9 Penn St., 17-7.

1963

Final poll released Dec.9. Top 10 regular season results after that: **Dec.14**—#8 Alabama over Miami-FL, 17-12.

		As of Dec. 9	Head Coach	After Bowls
1	Texas	10-0-0	Darrell Royal	11-0-0
2	Navy	9-1-0	Wayne Hardin	9-2-0
3	Illinois	7-1-1	Pete Elliott	8-1-1
4	Pittsburgh	9-1-0	John Michelosen	same
5	Auburn	9-1-0	Shug Jordan	9-2-0
6	Nebraska	9-1-0	Bob Devaney	10-1-0
7	Mississippi	7-0-2	Johnny Vaught	7-1-2
8	Alabama	7-2-0	Bear Bryant	9-2-0
9	Michigan St.	6-2-1	Duffy Daugherty	same
10	Oklahoma	8-2-0	Bud Wilkinson	same

Key Bowl Games

Cotton—#1 Texas over #2 Navy, 28-6; **Rose**—#3 Illinois over Washington, 17-7; **Orange**—#6 Nebraska over #5 Auburn, 13-7; **Sugar**—#8 Alabama over #7 Ole Miss, 12-7.

1964

Final poll released Nov.30. Top 10 regular season results after that: **Dec.5th**—Florida over #7 LSU, 20-6.

		As of Nov. 30	Head Coach	After Bowls
1	Alabama	10-0-0	Bear Bryant	10-1-0
2	Arkansas	10-0-0	Frank Broyles	11-0-0
3	Notre Dame	9-1-0	Ara Parseghian	same
4	Michigan	8-1-0	Bump Elliott	9-1-0
5	Texas	9-1-0	Darrell Royal	10-1-0
6	Nebraska	9-1-0	Bob Devaney	9-2-0
7	LSU	7-1-1	Charlie McClendon	8-2-1
8	Oregon St.	8-2-0	Tommy Prothro	8-3-0
9	Ohio St.	7-2-0	Woody Hayes	same
10	USC	7-3-0	John McKay	same

Key Bowl Games

Orange—#5 Texas over #1 Alabama, 21-17; **Cotton**—#2 Arkansas over #6 Nebraska, 10-7; **Rose**—#4 Michigan over #8 Oregon St., 34-7; **Sugar**—#7 LSU over Syracuse, 13-10.

1965

Final poll taken after bowl games for the first time.

		After Bowls	Head Coach	Regular Season
1	Alabama	9-1-1	Bear Bryant	8-1-1
2	Michigan St.	10-1-0	Duffy Daugherty	10-0-0
3	Arkansas	10-1-0	Frank Broyles	10-0-0
4	UCLA	8-2-1	Tommy Prothro	7-1-1
5	Nebraska	10-1-0	Bob Devaney	10-0-0
6	Missouri	8-2-1	Dan Devine	7-2-1
7	Tennessee	8-1-2	Doug Dickey	6-1-2
8	LSU	8-3-0	Charlie McClendon	7-3-0
9	Notre Dame	7-2-1	Ara Parseghian	same
10	USC	7-2-1	John McKay	same

Key Bowl Games

Rankings below reflect final regular season poll, released Nov.29. No bowls for then #8 USC or #9 Notre Dame.
Rose—#5 UCLA over #1 Michigan St., 14-12; **Cotton**—LSU over #2 Arkansas, 14-7; **Orange**—#4 Alabama over #3 Nebraska, 39-28; **Sugar**—#6 Missouri over Florida, 20-18; **Bluebonnet**—#7 Tennessee over Tulsa, 27-6; **Gator**—Georgia Tech over #10 Texas Tech, 31-21.

1966

Final poll released Dec.5, returning to pre-bowl status. Top 10 regular season results after that: None.

		As of Dec. 5	Head Coach	After Bowls
1	Notre Dame	9-0-1	Ara Parseghian	same
2	Michigan St.	9-0-1	Duffy Daugherty	same
3	Alabama	10-0-0	Bear Bryant	11-0-0
4	Georgia	9-1-0	Vince Dooley	10-1-0
5	UCLA	9-1-0	Tommy Prothro	same
6	Nebraska	9-1-0	Bob Devaney	9-2-0
7	Purdue	8-2-0	Jack Mollenkopf	9-2-0
8	Georgia Tech	9-1-0	Bobby Dodd	9-2-0
9	Miami-FL	7-2-1	Charlie Tate	8-2-1
10	SMU	8-2-0	Hayden Fry	8-3-0

Key Bowl Games

Sugar—#3 Alabama over #6 Nebraska, 34-7; **Cotton**—#4 Georgia over #10 SMU, 24-9; **Rose**—#7 Purdue over USC, 14-13; **Orange**—Florida over #8 Georgia Tech, 27-12; **Liberty**—#9 Miami-FL over Virginia Tech, 14-7.

1967

Final poll released Nov.27. Top 10 regular season results after that: **Dec.2**—#2 Tennessee over Vanderbilt, 41-14; #3 Oklahoma over Oklahoma St., 38-14; #8 Alabama over Auburn, 7-3.

		As of Nov. 27	Head Coach	After Bowls
1	USC	9-1-0	John McKay	10-1-0
2	Tennessee	8-1-0	Doug Dickey	9-2-0
3	Oklahoma	8-1-0	Chuck Fairbanks	10-1-0
4	Indiana	9-1-0	John Pont	9-2-0
5	Notre Dame	8-2-0	Ara Parseghian	same
6	Wyoming	10-0-0	Lloyd Eaton	10-1-0
7	Oregon St.	7-2-1	Dee Andros	same
8	Alabama	7-1-1	Bear Bryant	8-2-1
9	Purdue	8-2-0	Jack Mollenkopf	same
10	Penn St.	8-2-0	Joe Paterno	8-2-1

Key Bowl Games

Rose—#1 USC over #4 Indiana, 14-3; **Orange**—#3 Oklahoma over #2 Tennessee, 26-24; **Sugar**—LSU over #6 Wyoming, 20-13; **Cotton**—Texas A&M over #8 Alabama, 20-16; **Gator**—#10 Penn St. tied Florida St. 17-17.

1968

Final poll taken after bowl games for first time since close of 1965 season.

		After Bowls	Head Coach	Regular Season
1	Ohio St.	10-0-0	Woody Hayes	9-0-0
2	Penn St.	11-0-0	Joe Paterno	10-0-0
3	Texas	9-1-1	Darrell Royal	8-1-1
4	USC	9-1-1	John McKay	9-0-1
5	Notre Dame	7-2-1	Ara Parseghian	same
6	Arkansas	10-1-0	Frank Broyles	9-1-0
7	Kansas	9-2-0	Pepper Rodgers	9-1-0
8	Georgia	8-1-2	Vince Dooley	8-0-2
9	Missouri	8-3-0	Dan Devine	7-3-0
10	Purdue	8-2-0	Jack Mollenkopf	same
11	Oklahoma	7-4-0	Chuck Fairbanks	7-3-0
12	Michigan	8-2-0	Bump Elliott	same
13	Tennessee	8-2-1	Doug Dickey	8-1-1
14	SMU	8-3-0	Hayden Fry	7-3-0
15	Oregon St.	7-3-0	Dee Andros	same
16	Auburn	7-4-0	Shug Jordan	6-4-0
17	Alabama	8-3-0	Bear Bryant	8-2-0
18	Houston	6-2-2	Bill Yeoman	same
19	LSU	8-3-0	Charlie McClendon	7-3-0
20	Ohio Univ.	10-1-0	Bill Hess	10-0-0

Key Bowl Games

Rankings below reflect final regular season poll, released Dec.2. No bowls for then #7 Notre Dame and #11 Purdue.
Rose—#1 Ohio St. over #2 USC, 27-16; **Orange**—#3 Penn St. over #6 Kansas, 15-14; **Sugar**—#9 Arkansas over #4 Georgia, 16-2; **Cotton**—#5 Texas over #8 Tennessee, 36-13; **Bluebonnet**—#20 SMU over #10 Oklahoma, 28-27; **Gator**—#16 Missouri over #12 Alabama, 35-10.

1969

Final poll taken after bowl games.

		After Bowls	Head Coach	Regular Season
1	Texas	11-0-0	Darrell Royal	10-0-0
2	Penn St.	11-0-0	Joe Paterno	10-0-0
3	USC	10-0-1	John McKay	9-0-1
4	Ohio St.	8-1-0	Woody Hayes	same
5	Notre Dame	8-2-1	Ara Parseghian	8-1-1
6	Missouri	9-2-0	Dan Devine	9-1-0
7	Arkansas	9-2-0	Frank Broyles	9-1-0
8	Mississippi	8-3-0	Johnny Vaught	7-3-0
9	Michigan	8-3-0	Bo Schembechler	8-2-0
10	LSU	9-1-0	Charlie McClendon	same
11	Nebraska	9-2-0	Bob Devaney	8-2-0
12	Houston	9-2-0	Bill Yeoman	8-2-0
13	UCLA	8-1-1	Tommy Prothro	same
14	Florida	9-1-1	Ray Graves	8-1-1
15	Tennessee	9-2-0	Doug Dickey	9-1-0
16	Colorado	8-3-0	Eddie Crowder	7-3-0
17	West Virginia	10-1-0	Jim Carlen	9-1-0
18	Purdue	8-2-0	Jack Mollenkopf	same
19	Stanford	7-2-1	John Ralston	same
20	Auburn	8-3-0	Shug Jordan	8-2-0

Key Bowl Games

Rankings below reflect final regular season poll, released Dec.8. No bowls for then #4 Ohio St., #8 LSU and #10 UCLA.
Cotton—#1 Texas over #9 Notre Dame, 21-17; **Orange**—#2 Penn St. over #6 Missouri, 10-3; **Sugar**—#13 Ole Miss over #3 Arkansas, 27-22; **Rose**—#5 USC over #7 Michigan, 10-3.

Associated Press Final Polls (Cont.)

1970

Final poll taken after bowl games.

		After Bowls	Head Coach	Regular Season
1	Nebraska	11-0-1	Bob Devaney	10-0-1
2	Notre Dame	10-1-0	Ara Parseghian	9-0-1
3	Texas	10-1-0	Darrell Royal	10-0-0
4	Tennessee	11-1-0	Bill Battle	10-1-0
5	Ohio St.*	9-1-0	Woody Hayes	9-0-0
6	Arizona St.	11-0-0	Frank Kush	10-0-0
7	LSU	9-3-0	Charlie McClendon	9-2-0
8	Stanford	9-3-0	John Ralston	8-3-0
9	Michigan	9-1-0	Bo Schembechler	same
10	Auburn	9-2-0	Shug Jordan	8-2-0
11	Arkansas	9-2-0	Frank Broyles	same
12	Toledo	12-0-0	Frank Lauterbur	11-0-0
13	Georgia Tech	9-3-0	Bud Carson	8-3-0
14	Dartmouth	9-0-0	Bob Blackman	same
15	USC	6-4-1	John McKay	same
16	Air Force	9-3-0	Ben Martin	9-2-0
17	Tulane	8-4-0	Jim Pittman	7-4-0
18	Penn St.	7-3-0	Joe Paterno	same
19	Houston	8-3-0	Bill Yeoman	same
20	Oklahoma	7-4-1	Chuck Fairbanks	7-4-0
	Mississippi	7-4-0	Johnny Vaught	7-3-0

Key Bowl Games

Rankings below reflect final regular season poll, released Dec.7. No bowls for then #4 Arkansas and #7 Michigan.

Cotton—#6 Notre Dame over #1 Texas, 24-11; **Rose**—#12 Stanford over #2 Ohio St., 27-17; **Orange**—#3 Nebraska over #8 LSU, 17-12; **Sugar**—#5 Tennessee over #11 Air Force, 34-13; **Peach**—#9 Ariz.St. over N.Carolina, 48-26;

1971

Final poll taken after bowl games.

		After Bowls	Head Coach	Regular Season
1	Nebraska	13-0-0	Bob Devaney	12-0-0
2	Oklahoma	11-1-0	Chuck Fairbanks	10-1-0
3	Colorado	10-2-0	Eddie Crowder	9-2-0
4	Alabama	11-1-0	Bear Bryant	11-0-0
5	Penn St.	11-1-0	Joe Paterno	10-1-0
6	Michigan	11-1-0	Bo Schembechler	11-0-0
7	Georgia	11-1-0	Vince Dooley	10-1-0
8	Arizona St.	11-1-0	Frank Kush	10-1-0
9	Tennessee	10-2-0	Bill Battle	9-2-0
10	Stanford	9-3-0	John Ralston	8-3-0
11	LSU	9-3-0	Charlie McClendon	8-3-0
12	Auburn	9-2-0	Shug Jordan	9-1-0
13	Notre Dame	8-2-0	Ara Parseghian	same
14	Toledo	12-0-0	John Murphy	11-0-0
15	Mississippi	10-2-0	Billy Kinard	9-2-0
16	Arkansas	8-3-1	Frank Broyles	8-2-1
17	Houston	9-3-0	Bill Yeoman	9-2-0
18	Texas	8-3-0	Darrell Royal	8-2-0
19	Washington	8-3-0	Jim Owens	same
20	USC	6-4-1	John McKay	same

Key Bowl Games

Rankings below reflect final regular season poll, released Dec.6.

Orange—#1 Nebraska over #2 Alabama, 38-6; **Sugar**—#3 Oklahoma over #5 Auburn, 40-22; **Rose**—#16 Stanford over #4 Michigan, 13-12; **Gator**—#6 Georgia over N.Carolina, 7-3; **Bluebonnet**—#7 Colorado over #15 Houston, 29-17; **Fiesta**—#8 Ariz. St. over Florida St., 45-38; 14-13; **Cotton**—#10 Penn St. over #12 Texas, 30-6.

1972

Final poll taken after bowl games.

		After Bowls	Head Coach	Regular Season
1	USC	12-0-0	John McKay	11-0-0
2	Oklahoma	11-1-0	Chuck Fairbanks	10-1-0
3	Texas	10-1-0	Darrell Royal	9-1-0
4	Nebraska	9-2-1	Bob Devaney	8-2-1
5	Auburn	10-1-0	Shug Jordan	9-1-0
6	Michigan	10-1-0	Bo Schembechler	same
7	Alabama	10-2-0	Bear Bryant	10-1-0
8	Tennessee	10-2-0	Bill Battle	9-2-0
9	Ohio St.	9-2-0	Woody Hayes	9-1-0
10	Penn St.	10-2-0	Joe Paterno	10-1-0
11	LSU	9-2-1	Charlie McClendon	9-1-1
12	North Carolina	11-1-0	Bill Dooley	10-1-0
13	Arizona St.	10-2-0	Frank Kush	9-2-0
14	Notre Dame	8-3-0	Ara Parseghian	8-2-0
15	UCLA	8-3-0	Pepper Rodgers	same
16	Colorado	8-4-0	Eddie Crowder	8-3-0
17	N.C.State	8-3-1	Lou Holtz	7-3-1
18	Louisville	9-1-0	Lee Corso	same
19	Washington St.	7-4-0	Jim Sweeney	same
20	Georgia Tech	7-4-1	Bill Fulcher	6-4-1

Key Bowl Games

Rankings below reflect final regular season poll, released Dec.4. No bowl for then #8 Michigan.

Rose—#1 USC over #3 Ohio St., 42-17; **Sugar**—#2 Oklahoma over #5 Penn St., 14-0; **Cotton**—#7 Texas over #4 Alabama, 17-13; **Orange**—#9 Nebraska over #12 Notre Dame, 40-6; **Gator**—#6 Auburn over #13 Colorado, 24-3; **Bluebonnet**—#11 Tennessee over #10 LSU, 24-17.

1973

Final poll taken after bowl games.

		After Bowls	Head Coach	Regular Season
1	Notre Dame	11-0-0	Ara Parseghian	10-0-0
2	Ohio St.	10-0-1	Woody Hayes	9-0-1
3	Oklahoma	10-0-1	Barry Switzer	same
4	Alabama	11-1-0	Bear Bryant	11-0-0
5	Penn St.	12-0-0	Joe Paterno	11-0-0
6	Michigan	10-0-1	Bo Schembechler	same
7	Nebraska	9-2-1	Tom Osborne	8-2-1
8	USC	9-2-1	John McKay	9-1-1
9	Arizona St.	11-1-0	Frank Kush	10-1-0
	Houston	11-1-0	Bill Yeoman	10-1-0
11	Texas Tech	11-1-0	Jim Carlen	10-1-0
12	UCLA	9-2-0	Pepper Rodgers	same
13	LSU	9-3-0	Charlie McClendon	9-2-0
14	Texas	8-3-0	Darrell Royal	8-2-0
15	Miami-OH	11-0-0	Bill Mallory	10-0-0
16	N.C.State	9-3-0	Lou Holtz	8-3-0
17	Missouri	8-4-0	Al Onofrio	7-4-0
18	Kansas	7-4-1	Don Fambrough	7-3-1
19	Tennessee	8-4-0	Bill Battle	8-3-0
20	Maryland	8-4-0	Jerry Claiborne	8-3-0
	Tulane	9-3-0	Bennie Ellender	9-2-0

Key Bowl Games

Rankings below reflect final regular season poll, released Dec.3. No bowls for then #2 Oklahoma (probation), #5 Michigan and #9 UCLA.

Sugar—#3 Notre Dame over #1 Alabama, 24-23; **Rose**—#4 Ohio St. over #7 USC, 42-21; **Orange**—#6 Penn St. over #13 LSU, 16-9; **Cotton**—#12 Nebraska over #8 Texas, 19-3; **Fiesta**—#10 Ariz.St. over Pitt, 28-7; **Bluebonnet**—#14 Houston over #17 Tulane, 47-7.

1974
Final poll taken after bowl games.

		After Bowls	Head Coach	Regular Season
1	Oklahoma	11-0-0	Barry Switzer	same
2	USC	10-1-1	John McKay	9-1-1
3	Michigan	10-1-0	Bo Schembechler	same
4	Ohio St.	10-2-0	Woody Hayes	10-1-0
5	Alabama	11-1-0	Bear Bryant	11-0-0
6	Notre Dame	10-2-0	Ara Parseghian	9-2-0
7	Penn St.	10-2-0	Joe Paterno	9-2-0
8	Auburn	10-2-0	Shug Jordan	9-2-0
9	Nebraska	9-3-0	Tom Osborne	8-3-0
10	Miami-OH	10-0-1	Dick Crum	9-0-1
11	N.C.State	9-2-1	Lou Holtz	9-2-0
12	Michigan St.	7-3-1	Denny Stolz	same
13	Maryland	8-4-0	Jerry Claiborne	8-3-0
14	Baylor	8-4-0	Grant Teaff	8-3-0
15	Florida	8-4-0	Doug Dickey	8-3-0
16	Texas A&M	8-3-0	Emory Ballard	same
17	Mississippi St.	9-3-0	Bob Tyler	8-3-0
	Texas	8-4-0	Darrell Royal	8-3-0
19	Houston	8-3-1	Bill Yeoman	8-3-0
20	Tennessee	7-3-2	Bill Battle	6-3-2

Key Bowl Games
Rankings below reflect final regular season poll, released Dec.2. No bowls for #1 Oklahoma (probation) and then #4 Michigan.
Orange—#9 Notre Dame over #2 Alabama, 13-11; **Rose**—#5 USC over #3 Ohio St., 18-17; **Gator**— #6 Auburn over #11 Texas, 27-3; **Cotton**—#7 Penn St. over #12 Baylor, 41-20; **Sugar**—#8 Nebraska over #18 Florida, 13-10; **Liberty**—Tennessee over #10 Maryland, 7-3.

1975
Final poll taken after bowl games.

		After Bowls	Head Coach	Regular Season
1	Oklahoma	11-1-0	Barry Switzer	10-1-0
2	Arizona St.	12-0-0	Frank Kush	11-0-0
3	Alabama	11-1-0	Bear Bryant	10-1-0
4	Ohio St.	11-1-0	Woody Hayes	11-0-0
5	UCLA	9-2-1	Dick Vermeil	8-2-1
6	Texas	10-2-0	Darrell Royal	9-2-0
7	Arkansas	10-2-0	Frank Broyles	9-2-0
8	Michigan	8-2-2	Bo Schembechler	8-1-2
9	Nebraska	10-2-0	Tom Osborne	10-1-0
10	Penn St.	9-3-0	Joe Paterno	9-2-0
11	Texas A&M	10-2-0	Emory Bellard	10-1-0
12	Miami-OH	11-1-0	Dick Crum	10-1-0
13	Maryland	9-2-1	Jerry Claiborne	8-2-1
14	California	8-3-0	Mike White	same
15	Pittsburgh	8-4-0	Johnny Majors	7-4-0
16	Colorado	9-3-0	Bill Mallory	9-2-0
17	USC	8-4-0	John McKay	7-4-0
18	Arizona	9-2-0	Jim Young	same
19	Georgia	9-3-0	Vince Dooley	9-2-0
20	West Virginia	9-3-0	Bobby Bowden	8-3-0

Key Bowl Games
Rankings below reflect final regular season poll, released Dec.1. Texas A&M was unbeaten and ranked 2nd in that poll, but lost to #18 Arkansas, 31-6, in its final regular season game on Dec.6.
Rose—#11 UCLA over #1 Ohio St., 23-10; **Liberty**— #17 USC over #2 Texas A&M, 20-0; **Orange**— #3 Oklahoma over #5 Michigan, 14-6; **Sugar**— #4 Alabama over #8 Penn St., 13-6; **Fiesta**—#7 Ariz. St. over #6 Nebraska, 17-14; **Bluebonnet**—#9 Texas over #10 Colorado, 38-21; **Cotton**—#18 Arkansas over #12 Georgia, 31-10.

1976
Final poll taken after bowl games.

		After Bowls	Head Coach	Regular Season
1	Pittsburgh	12-0-0	Johnny Majors	11-0-0
2	USC	11-1-0	John Robinson	10-1-0
3	Michigan	10-2-0	Bo Schembechler	10-1-0
4	Houston	10-2-0	Bill Yeoman	9-2-0
5	Oklahoma	9-2-1	Barry Switzer	8-2-1
6	Ohio St.	9-2-1	Woody Hayes	8-2-1
7	Texas A&M	10-2-0	Emory Bellard	9-2-0
8	Maryland	11-1-0	Jerry Claiborne	11-0-0
9	Nebraska	9-3-1	Tom Osborne	8-3-1
10	Georgia	10-2-0	Vince Dooley	10-1-0
11	Alabama	9-3-0	Bear Bryant	8-3-0
12	Notre Dame	9-3-0	Dan Devine	8-3-0
13	Texas Tech	10-2-0	Steve Sloan	10-1-0
14	Oklahoma St.	9-3-0	Jim Stanley	8-3-0
15	UCLA	9-2-1	Terry Donahue	9-1-1
16	Colorado	8-4-0	Bill Mallory	8-3-0
17	Rutgers	11-0-0	Frank Burns	same
18	Kentucky	8-4-0	Fran Curci	7-4-0
19	Iowa St.	8-3-0	Earle Bruce	same
20	Mississippi St.	9-2-0	Bob Tyler	same

Key Bowl Games
Rankings below reflect final regular season poll, released Nov.29. No bowl for then #20 Miss. St. (probation).
Sugar—#1 Pitt over #5 Georgia, 27-3; **Rose**—#3 USC over #2 Michigan, 14-6; **Cotton**—#6 Houston over #4 Maryland, 30-21; **Liberty**—#16 Alabama over #7 UCLA, 36-6; **Fiesta**—#8 Oklahoma over Wyoming, 41-7; **Bluebonnet**—#13 Nebraska over #9 Texas Tech, 27-24; **Sun**—#10 Texas A&M over Florida, 37-14; **Orange**—#11 Ohio St. over #12 Colorado, 27-10.

1977
Final poll taken after bowl games.

		After Bowls	Head Coach	Regular Season
1	Notre Dame	11-1-0	Dan Devine	10-1-0
2	Alabama	11-1-0	Bear Bryant	10-1-0
3	Arkansas	11-1-0	Lou Holtz	10-1-0
4	Texas	11-1-0	Fred Akers	11-0-0
5	Penn St.	11-1-0	Joe Paterno	10-1-0
6	Kentucky	10-1-0	Fran Curci	same
7	Oklahoma	10-2-0	Barry Switzer	10-1-0
8	Pittsburgh	9-2-1	Jackie Sherrill	8-2-1
9	Michigan	10-2-0	Bo Schembechler	10-1-0
10	Washington	8-4-0	Don James	7-4-0
11	Ohio St.	9-3-0	Woody Hayes	9-2-0
12	Nebraska	9-3-0	Tom Osborne	8-3-0
13	USC	8-4-0	John Robinson	7-4-0
14	Florida St.	10-2-0	Bobby Bowden	9-2-0
15	Stanford	9-3-0	Bill Walsh	8-3-0
16	San Diego St.	10-1-0	Claude Gilbert	same
17	North Carolina	8-3-1	Bill Dooley	8-2-1
18	Arizona St.	9-3-0	Frank Kush	9-2-0
19	Clemson	8-3-1	Charley Pell	8-2-1
20	BYU	9-2-0	LaVell Edwards	same

Key Bowl Games
Rankings below reflect final regular season poll, released Nov.28. No bowl for then #7 Kentucky (probation).
Cotton—#5 Notre Dame over #1 Texas, 38-10; **Orange**—#6 Arkansas over #2 Oklahoma, 31-6; **Sugar**—#3 Alabama over #9 Ohio St., 35-6; **Rose**—#13 Washington over #4 Michigan, 27-20; **Fiesta**—#8 Penn St. over #15 Ariz. St., 42-30; **Gator**—#10 Pitt over #11 Clemson, 34-3.

Associated Press Final Polls (Cont.)

1978
Final poll taken after bowl games.

		After Bowls	Head Coach	Regular Season
1	Alabama	11-1-0	Bear Bryant	10-1-0
2	USC	12-1-0	John Robinson	11-1-0
3	Oklahoma	11-1-0	Barry Switzer	10-1-0
4	Penn St.	11-1-0	Joe Paterno	11-0-0
5	Michigan	10-2-0	Bo Schembechler	10-1-0
6	Clemson	11-1-0	Charley Pell	10-1-0
7	Notre Dame	9-3-0	Dan Devine	8-3-0
8	Nebraska	9-3-0	Tom Osborne	9-2-0
9	Texas	9-3-0	Fred Akers	8-3-0
10	Houston	9-3-0	Bill Yeoman	9-2-0
11	Arkansas	9-2-1	Lou Holtz	9-2-0
12	Michigan St.	8-3-0	Darryl Rogers	same
13	Purdue	9-2-1	Jim Young	8-2-1
14	UCLA	8-3-1	Terry Donahue	8-3-0
15	Missouri	8-4-0	Warren Powers	7-4-0
16	Georgia	9-2-1	Vince Dooley	9-1-1
17	Stanford	8-4-0	Bill Walsh	7-4-0
18	N.C.State	9-3-0	Bo Rein	8-3-0
19	Texas A&M	8-4-0	E.Bellard (4-2) & T.Wilson (4-2)	7-4-0
20	Maryland	9-3-0	Jerry Claiborne	9-2-0

Key Bowl Games
Rankings below reflect final regular season poll, released Dec. 4. No bowl for then #12 Michigan St. (probation).
Sugar—#2 Alabama over #1 Penn St., 14-7; **Rose**—#3 USC over #5 Michigan, 17-10; **Orange**—#4 Oklahoma over #6 Nebraska, 31-24; **Gator**—#7 Clemson over #20 Ohio St., 17-15; **Fiesta**—#8 Arkansas tied #15 UCLA, 10-10; **Cotton**—#10 Notre Dame over #9 Houston, 35-34;

1980
Final poll taken after bowl games.

		After Bowls	Head Coach	Regular Season
1	Georgia	12-0-0	Vince Dooley	11-0-0
2	Pittsburgh	11-1-0	Jackie Sherrill	10-1-0
3	Oklahoma	10-2-0	Barry Switzer	9-2-0
4	Michigan	10-2-0	Bo Schembechler	9-2-0
5	Florida St.	10-2-0	Bobby Bowden	10-1-0
6	Alabama	10-2-0	Bear Bryant	9-2-0
7	Nebraska	10-2-0	Tom Osborne	9-2-0
8	Penn St.	10-2-0	Joe Paterno	9-2-0
9	Notre Dame	9-2-1	Dan Devine	9-1-1
10	North Carolina	11-1-0	Dick Crum	10-1-0
11	USC	8-2-1	John Robinson	same
12	BYU	12-1-0	LaVell Edwards	11-1-0
13	UCLA	9-2-0	Terry Donahue	same
14	Baylor	10-2-0	Grant Teaff	10-1-0
15	Ohio St.	9-3-0	Earle Bruce	9-2-0
16	Washington	9-3-0	Don James	9-2-0
17	Purdue	9-3-0	Jim Young	8-3-0
18	Miami-FL	9-3-0	H.Schnellenberger	8-3-0
19	Mississippi St.	9-3-0	Emory Bellard	9-2-0
20	SMU	8-4-0	Ron Meyer	8-3-0

Key Bowl Games
Rankings below reflect final regular season poll, released Dec.8.
Sugar—#1 Georgia over #7 Notre Dame, 17-10; **Orange**—#4 Oklahoma over #2 Florida St., 18-17; **Gator**—#3 Pitt over #18 S.Carolina, 37-9; **Rose**—#5 Michigan over #16 Washington, 23-6; **Cotton**—#9 Alabama over #6 Baylor, 30-2; **Sun**—#8 Nebraska over #17 Miss. St., 31-17; **Fiesta**—#10 Penn St. over #11 Ohio St., 31-19; **Bluebonnet**—#13 N.Carolina over Texas, 16-7.

1979
Final poll taken after bowl games.

		After Bowls	Head Coach	Regular Season
1	Alabama	12-0-0	Bear Bryant	11-0-0
2	USC	11-0-1	John Robinson	10-0-1
3	Oklahoma	11-1-0	Barry Switzer	10-1-0
4	Ohio St.	11-1-0	Earle Bruce	11-0-0
5	Houston	11-1-0	Bill Yeoman	10-1-0
6	Florida St.	11-1-0	Bobby Bowden	11-0-0
7	Pittsburgh	11-1-0	Jackie Sherrill	10-1-0
8	Arkansas	10-2-0	Lou Holtz	10-1-0
9	Nebraska	10-2-0	Tom Osborne	10-1-0
10	Purdue	10-2-0	Jim Young	9-2-0
11	Washington	9-3-0	Don James	8-3-0
12	Texas	9-3-0	Fred Akers	9-2-0
13	BYU	11-1-0	LaVell Edwards	11-0-0
14	Baylor	8-4-0	Grant Teaff	7-4-0
15	North Carolina	8-3-1	Dick Crum	7-3-1
16	Auburn	8-3-0	Doug Barfield	same
17	Temple	10-2-0	Wayne Hardin	9-2-0
18	Michigan	8-4-0	Bo Schembechler	8-3-0
19	Indiana	8-4-0	Lee Corso	7-4-0
20	Penn St.	8-4-0	Joe Paterno	7-4-0

Key Bowl Games
Rankings below reflect final regular season poll, released Dec.3. No bowl for then #17 Auburn (probation).
Sugar—#2 Alabama over #6 Arkansas, 24-9; **Rose**—#3 USC over #1 Ohio St., 17-16; **Orange**—#5 Oklahoma over #4 Florida St., 24-7; **Sun**—#13 Washington over #11 Texas, 14-7; **Cotton**—#8 Houston over #7 Nebraska, 17-14; **Fiesta**—#10 Pitt over Arizona, 16-10;

1981
Final poll taken after bowl games.

		After Bowls	Head Coach	Regular Season
1	Clemson	12-0-0	Danny Ford	11-0-0
2	Texas	10-1-1	Fred Akers	9-1-1
3	Penn St.	10-2-0	Joe Paterno	9-2-0
4	Pittsburgh	11-1-0	Jackie Sherrill	10-1-0
5	SMU	10-1-0	Ron Meyer	same
6	Georgia	10-2-0	Vince Dooley	10-1-0
7	Alabama	9-2-1	Bear Bryant	9-1-1
8	Miami-FL	9-2-0	H.Schnellenberger	same
9	North Carolina	10-2-0	Dick Crum	9-2-0
10	Washington	10-2-0	Don James	9-2-0
11	Nebraska	9-3-0	Tom Osborne	9-2-0
12	Michigan	9-3-0	Bo Schembechler	8-3-0
13	BYU	11-2-0	LaVell Edwards	10-2-0
14	USC	9-3-0	John Robinson	9-2-0
15	Ohio St.	9-3-0	Earle Bruce	8-3-0
16	Arizona St.	9-2-0	Darryl Rogers	same
17	West Virginia	9-3-0	Don Nehlen	8-3-0
18	Iowa	8-4-0	Hayden Fry	8-3-0
19	Missouri	8-4-0	Warren Powers	7-4-0
20	Oklahoma	7-4-1	Barry Switzer	6-4-1

Key Bowl Games
Rankings below reflect final regular season poll, released Nov.30. No bowl for then #5 SMU (probation), #9 Miami-FL (probation), and #17 Ariz. St. (probation).
Orange—#1 Clemson over #4 Nebraska, 22-15; **Sugar**—#10 Pitt over #2 Georgia, 24-20; **Cotton**—#6 Texas over #3 Alabama, 14-12; **Fiesta**—#2 Penn St. over #8 USC, 26-10; **Gator**—#11 N.Carolina over Arkansas, 31-27; **Rose**—#12 Washington over #13 Iowa, 28-0.

1982

Final poll taken after bowl games.

		After Bowls	Head Coach	Regular Season
1	Penn St.	11-1-0	Joe Paterno	10-1-0
2	SMU	11-0-1	Bobby Collins	10-0-1
3	Nebraska	12-1-0	Tom Osborne	11-1-0
4	Georgia	11-1-0	Vince Dooley	11-0-0
5	UCLA	10-1-1	Terry Donahue	9-1-1
6	Arizona St.	10-2-0	Darryl Rogers	9-2-0
7	Washington	10-2-0	Don James	9-2-0
8	Clemson	9-1-1	Danny Ford	same
9	Arkansas	9-2-1	Lou Holtz	8-2-1
10	Pittsburgh	9-3-0	Foge Fazio	9-2-0
11	LSU	8-3-1	Jerry Stovall	8-2-1
12	Ohio St.	9-3-0	Earle Bruce	8-3-0
13	Florida St.	9-3-0	Bobby Bowden	8-3-0
14	Auburn	9-3-0	Pat Dye	8-3-0
15	USC	8-3-0	John Robinson	same
16	Oklahoma	8-4-0	Barry Switzer	8-3-0
17	Texas	9-3-0	Fred Akers	9-2-0
18	North Carolina	8-4-0	Dick Crum	7-4-0
19	West Virginia	9-3-0	Don Nehlen	9-2-0
20	Maryland	8-4-0	Bobby Ross	8-3-0

Key Bowl Games

Rankings below reflect final regular season poll, released Dec.6. No bowl for then #7 Clemson (probation) and #15 USC (probation).

Sugar—#2 Penn St. over #1 Georgia, 27-23; **Orange**—#3 Nebraska over #13 LSU, 21-20; **Cotton**—#4 SMU over #6 Pitt, 7-3; **Rose**—#5 UCLA over #19 Michigan, 24-14; **Aloha**—#9 Washington over #16 Maryland, 21-20; **Fiesta**—#11 Ariz. St. over #12 Oklahoma, 32-21; **Bluebonnet**—#14 Arkansas over Florida, 28-24.

1983

Final poll taken after bowl games.

		After Bowls	Head Coach	Regular Season
1	Miami-FL	11-1-0	H.Schnellenberger	10-1-0
2	Nebraska	12-1-0	Tom Osborne	12-0-0
3	Auburn	11-1-0	Pat Dye	10-1-0
4	Georgia	10-1-1	Vince Dooley	9-1-1
5	Texas	11-1-0	Fred Akers	11-0-0
6	Florida	9-2-1	Charley Pell	8-2-1
7	BYU	11-1-0	LaVell Edwards	10-1-0
8	Michigan	9-3-0	Bo Schembechler	9-2-0
9	Ohio St.	9-3-0	Earle Bruce	8-3-0
10	Illinois	10-2-0	Mike White	10-1-0
11	Clemson	9-1-1	Danny Ford	same
12	SMU	10-2-0	Bobby Collins	10-1-0
13	Air Force	10-2-0	Ken Hatfield	9-2-0
14	Iowa	9-3-0	Hayden Fry	9-2-0
15	Alabama	8-4-0	Ray Perkins	7-4-0
16	West Virginia	9-3-0	Don Nehlen	8-3-0
17	UCLA	7-4-1	Terry Donahue	6-4-1
18	Pittsburgh	8-3-1	Foge Fazio	8-2-1
19	Boston College	9-3-0	Jack Bicknell	9-2-0
20	East Carolina	8-3-0	Ed Emory	same

Key Bowl Games

Rankings below reflect final regular season poll, released Dec.5. No bowl for then #12 Clemson (probation).

Orange—#5 Miami-FL over #1 Nebraska, 31-30; **Cotton**—#7 Georgia over #2 Texas, 10-9; **Sugar**—#3 Auburn over #8 Michigan, 9-7; **Rose**—UCLA over #4 Illinois, 45-9; **Holiday**—#9 BYU over Missouri, 21-17; **Gator**—#11 Florida over #10 Iowa, 14-6; **Fiesta**—#14 Ohio St. over #15 Pitt, 28-23.

1984

Final poll taken after bowl games.

		After Bowls	Head Coach	Regular Season
1	BYU	13-0-0	LaVell Edwards	12-0-0
2	Washington	11-1-0	Don James	10-1-0
3	Florida	9-1-1	C.Pell (0-1-1) & G.Hall (9-0)	same
4	Nebraska	10-2-0	Tom Osborne	9-2-0
5	Boston College	10-2-0	Jack Bicknell	9-2-0
6	Oklahoma	9-2-1	Barry Switzer	9-1-1
7	Oklahoma St.	10-2-0	Pat Jones	9-2-0
8	SMU	10-2-0	Bobby Collins	9-2-0
9	UCLA	9-3-0	Terry Donahue	8-3-0
10	USC	9-3-0	Ted Tollner	8-3-0
11	South Carolina	10-2-0	Joe Morrison	10-1-0
12	Maryland	9-3-0	Bobby Ross	8-3-0
13	Ohio St.	9-3-0	Earle Bruce	9-2-0
14	Auburn	9-4-0	Pat Dye	8-4-0
15	LSU	.8-3-1	Bill Arnsparger	8-2-1
16	Iowa	8-4-1	Hayden Fry	7-4-1
17	Florida St.	7-3-2	Bobby Bowden	7-3-1
18	Miami-FL	8-5-0	Jimmy Johnson	8-4-0
19	Kentucky	9-3-0	Jerry Claiborne	8-3-0
20	Virginia	8-2-2	George Welsh	7-2-2

Key Bowl Games

Rankings below reflect final regular season poll, released Dec.3. No bowl for then #3 Florida (probation).

Holiday—#1 BYU over Michigan, 24-17; **Orange**—#4 Washington over #2 Oklahoma, 28-17; **Sugar**—#5 Nebraska over #11 LSU, 28-10; **Rose**—#18 USC over #6 Ohio St., 20-17; **Gator**—#9 Okla. St. over #7 S. Carolina, 21-14; **Cotton**—#8 BC over Houston, 45-28; **Aloha**—#10 SMU over #17 Notre Dame, 27-20.

1985

Final poll taken after bowl games.

		After Bowls	Head Coach	Regular Season
1	Oklahoma	11-1-0	Barry Switzer	10-1-0
2	Michigan	10-1-1	Bo Schembechler	9-1-1
3	Penn St.	11-1-0	Joe Paterno	11-0-0
4	Tennessee	9-1-2	Johnny Majors	8-1-2
5	Florida	9-1-1	Galen Hall	same
6	Texas A&M	10-2-0	Jackie Sherrill	9-2-0
7	UCLA	9-2-1	Terry Donahue	8-2-1
8	Air Force	12-1-0	Fisher DeBerry	11-1-0
9	Miami-FL	10-2-0	Jimmy Johnson	10-1-0
10	Iowa	10-2-0	Hayden Fry	10-1-0
11	Nebraska	9-3-0	Tom Osborne	9-2-0
12	Arkansas	10-2-0	Ken Hatfield	9-2-0
13	Alabama	9-2-1	Ray Perkins	8-2-1
14	Ohio St.	9-3-0	Earle Bruce	8-3-0
15	Florida St.	9-3-0	Bobby Bowden	8-3-0
16	BYU	11-3-0	LaVell Edwards	11-2-0
17	Baylor	9-3-0	Grant Teaff	8-3-0
18	Maryland	9-3-0	Bobby Ross	8-3-0
19	Georgia Tech	9-2-1	Bill Curry	8-2-1
20	LSU	9-2-1	Bill Arnsparger	9-1-1

Key Bowl Games

Rankings below reflect final regular season poll, released Dec. 9. No bowl for then #6 Florida (probation).

Orange—#3 Oklahoma over #1 Penn St., 25-10; **Sugar**—#8 Tennessee over #2 Miami-FL, 35-7; **Rose**—#13 UCLA over #4 Iowa, 45-28; **Fiesta**—#5 Michigan over #7 Nebraska, 27-23; **Bluebonnet**—#10 Air Force over Texas, 24-16; **Cotton**—#11 Texas A&M over #16 Auburn, 36-16.

Associated Press Final Polls (Cont.)

1986

Final poll taken after bowl games.

		After Bowls	Head Coach	Regular Season
1	Penn St.	12-0-0	Joe Paterno	11-0-0
2	Miami-FL	11-1-0	Jimmy Johnson	11-0-0
3	Oklahoma	11-1-0	Barry Switzer	10-1-0
4	Arizona St.	10-1-1	John Cooper	9-1-1
5	Nebraska	10-2-0	Tom Osborne	9-2-0
6	Auburn	10-2-0	Pat Dye	9-2-0
7	Ohio St.	10-3-0	Earle Bruce	9-3-0
8	Michigan	11-2-0	Bo Schembechler	11-1-0
9	Alabama	10-3-0	Ray Perkins	9-3-0
10	LSU	9-3-0	Bill Arnsparger	9-2-0
11	Arizona	9-3-0	Larry Smith	8-3-0
12	Baylor	9-3-0	Grant Teaff	8-3-0
13	Texas A&M	9-3-0	Jackie Sherrill	9-2-0
14	UCLA	8-3-1	Terry Donahue	7-3-1
15	Arkansas	9-3-0	Ken Hatfield	9-2-0
16	Iowa	9-3-0	Hayden Fry	8-3-0
17	Clemson	8-2-2	Danny Ford	7-2-2
18	Washington	8-3-1	Don James	8-2-1
19	Boston College	9-3-0	Jack Bicknell	8-3-0
20	Virginia Tech	9-2-1	Bill Dooley	8-2-1

Key Bowl Games

Rankings below reflect final regular season poll, released Dec.1.

Fiesta—#2 Penn St. over #1 Miami-FL, 14-10; **Orange**—#3 Oklahoma over #9 Arkansas, 42-8; **Rose**—#7 Ariz. St. over #4 Michigan, 22-15; **Sugar**—#6 Nebraska over #5 LSU, 30-15; **Cotton**—#11 Ohio St. over #8 Texas A&M, 28-12; **Citrus**—#10 Auburn over USC, 16-7; **Sun**—#13 Alabama over #12 Washington, 28-6.

1987

Final poll taken after bowl games.

		After Bowls	Head Coach	Regular Season
1	Miami-FL	12-0-0	Jimmy Johnson	11-0-0
2	Florida St.	11-1-0	Bobby Bowden	10-1-0
3	Oklahoma	11-1-0	Barry Switzer	11-0-0
4	Syracuse	11-0-1	Dick MacPherson	11-0-0
5	LSU	10-1-1	Mike Archer	9-1-1
6	Nebraska	10-2-0	Tom Osborne	10-1-0
7	Auburn	9-1-2	Pat Dye	9-1-1
8	Michigan St.	9-2-1	George Perles	8-2-1
9	UCLA	10-2-0	Terry Donahue	9-2-0
10	Texas A&M	10-2-0	Jackie Sherrill	9-2-0
11	Oklahoma St.	10-2-0	Pat Jones	9-2-0
12	Clemson	10-2-0	Danny Ford	9-2-0
13	Georgia	9-3-0	Vince Dooley	8-3-0
14	Tennessee	10-2-1	Johnny Majors	9-2-1
15	South Carolina	8-4-0	Joe Morrison	8-3-0
16	Iowa	10-3-0	Hayden Fry	9-3-0
17	Notre Dame	8-4-0	Lou Holtz	8-3-0
18	USC	8-4-0	Larry Smith	8-3-0
19	Michigan	8-4-0	Bo Schembechler	7-4-0
20	Arizona St.	7-4-1	John Cooper	6-4-1

Key Bowl Games

Rankings below reflect final regular season poll, released Dec.7.

Orange—#2 Miami-FL over #1 Oklahoma, 20-14; **Fiesta**—#3 Florida St. over #5 Nebraska, 31-28; **Sugar**—#4 Syracuse tied #6 Auburn, 16-16; **Gator**—#7 LSU over #9 S.Carolina, 30-13; **Rose**—#8 Mich. St. over #16 USC, 20-17; **Aloha**—#10 UCLA over Florida, 20-16; **Cotton**—#13 Texas A&M over #12 Notre Dame, 35-10.

1988

Final poll taken after bowl games.

		After Bowls	Head Coach	Regular Season
1	Notre Dame	12-0-0	Lou Holtz	11-0-0
2	Miami-FL	11-1-0	Jimmy Johnson	10-1-0
3	Florida St.	11-1-0	Bobby Bowden	10-1-0
4	Michigan	9-2-1	Bo Schembechler	8-2-1
5	West Virginia	11-1-0	Don Nehlen	11-0-0
6	UCLA	10-2-0	Terry Donahue	9-2-0
7	USC	10-2-0	Larry Smith	10-1-0
8	Auburn	10-2-0	Pat Dye	10-1-0
9	Clemson	10-2-0	Danny Ford	9-2-0
10	Nebraska	11-2-0	Tom Osborne	11-1-0
11	Oklahoma St.	10-2-0	Pat Jones	9-2-0
12	Arkansas	10-2-0	Ken Hatfield	10-1-0
13	Syracuse	10-2-0	Dick MacPherson	9-2-0
14	Oklahoma	9-3-0	Barry Switzer	9-2-0
15	Georgia	9-3-0	Vince Dooley	8-3-0
16	Washington St.	9-3-0	Dennis Erickson	8-3-0
17	Alabama	9-3-0	Bill Curry	8-3-0
18	Houston	9-3-0	Jack Pardee	9-2-0
19	LSU	8-4-0	Mike Archer	8-3-0
20	Indiana	8-3-1	Bill Mallory	7-3-1

Key Bowl Games

Rankings below reflect final regular season poll, released Dec.5.

Fiesta—#1 Notre Dame over #3 West Va., 34-21; **Orange**—#2 Miami-FL over #6 Nebraska, 23-3; **Sugar**—#4 Florida St. over #7 Auburn, 13-7; **Rose**—#11 Michigan over #5 USC, 22-14; **Cotton**—#9 UCLA over #8 Arkansas, 17-3; **Citrus**—#13 Clemson over #10 Oklahoma, 13-6.

1989

Final poll taken after bowl games.

		After Bowls	Head Coach	Regular Season
1	Miami-FL	11-1-0	Dennis Erickson	10-1-0
2	Notre Dame	12-1-0	Lou Holtz	11-1-0
3	Florida St.	10-2-0	Bobby Bowden	9-2-0
4	Colorado	11-1-0	Bill McCartney	11-0-0
5	Tennessee	11-1-0	Johnny Majors	10-1-0
6	Auburn	10-2-0	Pat Dye	9-2-0
7	Michigan	10-2-0	Bo Schembechler	10-1-0
8	USC	9-2-1	Larry Smith	8-2-1
9	Alabama	10-2-0	Bill Curry	10-1-0
10	Illinois	10-2-0	John Mackovic	9-2-0
11	Nebraska	10-2-0	Tom Osborne	10-1-0
12	Clemson	10-2-0	Danny Ford	9-2-0
13	Arkansas	10-2-0	Ken Hatfield	10-1-0
14	Houston	9-2-0	Jack Pardee	same
15	Penn St.	8-3-1	Joe Paterno	7-3-1
16	Michigan St.	8-4-0	George Perles	7-4-0
17	Pittsburgh	8-3-1	M.Gottfried (7-3-1) & P.Hackett (1-0)	7-3-1
18	Virginia	10-3-0	George Welsh	10-2-0
19	Texas Tech	9-3-0	Spike Dykes	8-3-0
20	Texas A&M	8-4-0	R.C.Slocum	8-3-0

Key Bowl Games

Rankings below reflect final regular season poll, released Dec.11. No bowl for then #13 Houston (probation).

Orange—#4 Notre Dame over #1 Colorado, 21-6; **Sugar**—#2 Miami-FL over #7 Alabama, 33-25; **Rose**—#12 USC over #3 Michigan, 17-10; **Fiesta**—#5 Florida St. over #6 Nebraska, 41-17; **Cotton**—#8 Tennessee over #10 Arkansas, 31-27; **Hall of Fame**—#9 Auburn over #21 Ohio St., 31-14; **Citrus**—#11 Illinois over #15 Virginia, 31-21.

1990
Final poll taken after bowl games.

		After Bowls	Head Coach	Regular Season
1	Colorado	11-1-1	Bill McCartney	10-1-1
2	Georgia Tech	11-0-1	Bobby Ross	10-0-1
3	Miami-FL	10-2-0	Dennis Erickson	9-2-0
4	Florida St.	10-2-0	Bobby Bowden	9-2-0
5	Washington	10-2-0	Don James	9-2-0
6	Notre Dame	9-3-0	Lou Holtz	9-2-0
7	Michigan	9-3-0	Gary Moeller	8-3-0
8	Tennessee	9-2-2	Johnny Majors	8-2-2
9	Clemson	10-2-0	Ken Hatfield	9-2-0
10	Houston	10-1-0	John Jenkins	same
11	Penn St.	9-3-0	Joe Paterno	9-2-0
12	Texas	10-2-0	David McWilliams	10-1-0
13	Florida	9-2-0	Steve Spurrier	same
14	Louisville	10-1-1	H.Schnellenberger	9-1-1
15	Texas A&M	9-3-1	R.C.Slocum	8-3-1
16	Michigan St.	8-3-1	George Perles	7-3-1
17	Oklahoma	8-3-0	Gary Gibbs	same
18	Iowa	8-4-0	Hayden Fry	8-3-0
19	Auburn	8-3-1	Pat Dye	7-3-1
20	USC	8-4-1	Larry Smith	8-3-1

Key Bowl Games
Rankings below reflect final regular season poll, released Dec.3. No bowl for then #9 Houston (probation), #11 Florida (probation) and #20 Oklahoma (probation).

Orange—#1 Colorado over #5 Notre Dame, 10-9; **Citrus**—#2 Ga. Tech over #19 Nebraska, 45-21; **Cotton**—#4 Miami-FL over #3 Texas, 46-3; **Blockbuster**—#6 Florida St. over #7 Penn St., 24-17; **Rose**—#8 Washington over #17 Iowa, 46-34; **Sugar**—#10 Tennessee over Virginia, 23-22; **Gator**—#12 Michigan over #15 Ole Miss, 35-3.

1991
Final poll taken after bowl games.

		After Bowls	Head Coach	Regular Season
1	Miami-FL	12-0-0	Dennis Erickson	11-0-0
2	Washington	12-0-0	Don James	11-0-0
3	Penn St.	11-2-0	Joe Paterno	10-2-0
4	Florida St.	11-2-0	Bobby Bowden	10-2-0
5	Alabama	11-1-0	Gene Stallings	10-1-0
6	Michigan	10-2-0	Gary Moeller	10-1-0
7	Florida	10-2-0	Steve Spurrier	10-1-0
8	California	10-2-0	Bruce Snyder	9-2-0
9	East Carolina	11-1-0	Bill Lewis	10-1-0
10	Iowa	10-1-1	Hayden Fry	10-1-0
11	Syracuse	10-2-0	Paul Pasqualoni	9-2-0
12	Texas A&M	10-2-0	R.C.Slocum	10-1-0
13	Notre Dame	10-3-0	Lou Holtz	9-3-0
14	Tennessee	9-3-0	Johnny Majors	9-2-0
15	Nebraska	9-2-1	Tom Osborne	9-1-1
16	Oklahoma	9-3-0	Gary Gibbs	8-3-0
17	Georgia	9-3-0	Ray Goff	8-3-0
18	Clemson	9-2-1	Ken Hatfield	9-1-1
19	UCLA	9-3-0	Terry Donahue	8-3-0
20	Colorado	8-3-1	Bill McCartney	8-2-1

Key Bowl Games
Rankings below reflect final regular season poll, taken Dec.2nd.

Orange—#1 Miami-FL over #11 Nebraska, 22-0; **Rose**—#2 Washington over #4 Michigan, 34-14; **Sugar**—#18 Notre Dame over #3 Florida, 39-28; **Cotton**—#5 Florida St. over #9 Texas A&M, 10-2; **Fiesta**—#6 Penn St. over #10 Tennessee, 42-17; **Holiday**—#7 Iowa tied BYU, 13-13; **Blockbuster**—#8 Alabama over #15 Colorado, 30-25; **Citrus**—#14 California over #13 Clemson, 37-13; **Peach**—#12 East Carolina over #21 N.C.State, 37-34.

All-Time AP Top 20

The composite AP Top 20 from the 1936 season through the 1991 season, based on the final rankings of each year. The final AP poll has been taken after the bowl games in 1965 and since 1968. Team point totals are based on 20 points for all 1st place finishes, 19 for each 2nd, etc. Also listed are the number of times named national champion by AP, and times ranked in the final Top 10 and Top 20.

		Pts	No.1	Top 10	Top 20
1	Notre Dame	578	8	32	40
2	Oklahoma	554	6	29	40
3	Michigan	516	1	31	40
4	Alabama	498	5	28	37
5	Ohio St.	436	3	21	34
6	Nebraska	401	2	22	31
7	USC	397	3	20	34
8	Texas	393	2	19	30
9	Tennessee	339	1	17	29
10	Penn St.	330	2	18	28
11	UCLA	290	0	14	26
12	LSU	260	1	14	23
13	Arkansas	259	0	13	23
14	Auburn	242	1	12	23
15	Michigan St	238	1	12	19
16	Georgia	225	1	12	19
17	Miami-FL	217	4	11	16
18	Pittsburgh	194	2	10	16
19	Georgia Tech	188	1	9	17
	Mississippi	188	0	10	16

The Special Election That Didn't Count

There was one other No. 1 vs No. 2 confrontation, but it came in a special election or re-vote of AP selectors following the 1948 Rose Bowl. Here's what happened:

Unbeaten Notre Dame was declared 1947 national champion by AP on Dec. 8, two days after closing out an undefeated season with a 38-7 rout of then third-ranked USC in Los Angeles. Twenty-four days later, however, unbeaten Michigan, AP's final No. 2 team, clobbered now 8th-ranked USC, 49-0, in the Rose Bowl.

An immediate cry went up for an unprecedented two-team, "Who's No. 1" ballot and AP gave in. Michigan won the election, 226-119, with 12 voters calling it even, but AP ruled that the Dec. 8 final poll won by Notre Dame would be the vote of record.

All-Time Winningest Division I-A Teams

Schools classified as Divison I-A for at least 10 years; through 1991 season (including bowl games).

Top 25 Winning Percentage

		Years	Games	W	L	T	Pct	Bowls App	Bowls Record
1	Notre Dame	103	951	702	209	40	.759	17	11-6-0
2	Michigan	112	993	722	238	33	.744	23	10-13-0
3	Alabama	97	946	669	234	43	.730	44	24-17-3
4	Oklahoma	97	928	645	233	50	.722	30	19-10-1
5	Texas	99	970	676	263	31	.713	34	16-16-2
6	USC	99	911	616	244	51	.704	34	22-12-0
7	Ohio St.	102	953	641	261	51	.699	24	11-13-0
8	Penn St.	105	982	657	284	41	.690	28	17-9-2
9	Nebraska	102	979	653	286	40	.687	30	14-16-0
10	Tennessee	95	941	618	271	52	.684	32	17-15-0
11	Central Michigan	91	749	470	243	36	.652	4	3-1-0
12	LSU	98	922	566	310	46	.639	28	11-16-1
13	Army	102	943	577	316	50	.638	3	2-1-0
14	Miami-OH	103	874	536	297	41	.637	7	5-2-0
15	Washington	102	898	546	303	49	.635	20	12-7-1
16	Arizona St.	79	701	432	245	24	.633	15	9-5-1
17	Georgia	98	952	574	325	53	.631	30	14-13-3
18	Florida St	45	483	293	174	16	.623	21	12-7-2
19	Auburn	99	917	542	330	45	.616	23	12-9-2
20	Michigan St	95	869	510	316	43	.612	10	5-5-0
21	Minnesota	108	935	549	343	43	.610	5	2-3-0
22	Colorado	102	917	540	343	34	.607	16	5-11-0
23	UCLA	73	731	423	271	37	.604	18	10-7-1
24	Arkansas	98	929	542	349	38	.604	27	9-15-3
25	Bowling Green	73	661	373	238	50	.602	4	1-3-0

Top 50 Victories

		Wins			Wins			Wins
1	Michigan	722	18	Georgia Tech	544	35	Vanderbilt	494
2	Notre Dame	702	19	Arkansas	542	36	Virginia	487
3	Texas	676		Auburn	542	37	Illinois	485
4	Alabama	669	21	Navy	541	38	Boston College	480
5	Penn St	657		West Virginia	541		Kentucky	480
6	Nebraska	653	23	Colorado	540	40	Florida	471
7	Oklahoma	645	24	Miami-OH	536	41	Central Michigan	470
8	Ohio St	641	25	North Carolina	529	42	Purdue	466
9	Tennessee	618	26	Texas A&M	527		Stanford	466
10	USC	616	27	Rutgers	519		Tulsa	466
11	Army	577	28	California	517	45	Kansas	464
12	Georgia	574	29	Clemson	512	46	Wisconsin	463
13	Syracuse	567	30	Michigan St	510	47	Utah	460
14	LSU	566	31	Virginia Tech	502	48	Baylor	456
15	Pittsburgh	560	32	Missouri	501	49	Iowa	454
16	Minnesota	549	33	Maryland	500	50	Arizona	443
17	Washington	546	34	Mississippi	499			

Note: Division I-AA schools with over 500 wins through 1991: Yale (766), Harvard (695), Princeton (690), Penn (677), Dartmouth (576), Lafayette (551), Cornell (537) and Holy Cross (513).

Bowl Appearances

		Overall App	W	L	T	Big Four W	L	T			Overall App	W	L	T	Big Four W	L	T
1	Alabama	44	24	17	3	17	12	1	12	Mississippi	24	13	11	0	6	5	0
2	USC	34	22	12	0	19	8	0		Ohio St	24	11	13	0	7	8	0
	Texas	34	16	16	2	12	10	1	14	Auburn	23	12	9	2	2	4	1
4	Tennessee	32	17	15	0	7	9	0		Michigan	23	10	13	0	6	11	0
5	Oklahoma	30	19	10	1	15	6	0	16	Florida St	21	12	7	2	2	2	0
	Georgia	30	14	13	3	7	6	0	17	Washington	20	12	7	1	7	5	1
	Nebraska	30	14	16	0	9	11	0	18	Texas A&M	19	11	8	0	5	4	0
8	Penn St	28	17	9	2	6	5	1		Missouri	19	8	11	0	2	5	0
	LSU	28	11	16	1	7	10	1		Florida	19	8	11	0	1	3	0
10	Arkansas	27	9	15	3	4	10	1	21	Pittsburgh	18	8	10	0	3	5	0
11	Georgia Tech	25	17	8	0	9	3	0		Texas Tech	18	4	13	1	0	1	0

Note: The "Big Four" bowls are the Rose, Orange, Sugar and Cotton. Only Alabama, Georgia, Georgia Tech and Notre Dame have won all four.

Bowl Games
JAN. 1, 1902 — JAN. 1, 1992

Rose Bowl

City: Pasadena, CA; **Stadium:** Rose Bowl; **Capacity:** 104,091; **Playing surface:** Grass; **First year:** 1902; **Playing sites:** Tournament Park (1902, 1916-22), Rose Bowl (1923-41 and since 1943) and Duke Stadium in Durham, NC (1942).

Automatic berths: Pacific Coast Conference champion vs opponent selected by PCC (1925-46); Big 10 champion vs. Pac-10 champion (since 1947).

Multiple wins: USC (19); Michigan and Washington (6); Ohio St., Stanford and UCLA (5); 1Alabama (4); Illinois and Michigan St.(3); California1and Iowa (2).

Year*		Year		Year	
1902*	Michigan 49, Stanford 0	1942	Oregon St. 20, Duke 16	1968	USC 14, Indiana 3
1916	Washington St. 14, Brown 0	1943	Georgia 9, UCLA 0	1969	Ohio St. 27, USC 16
1917	Oregon 14, Penn 0	1944	USC 29, Washington 0		
1918	Mare Island 19, Camp Lewis 7	1945	USC 25, Tennessee 0	1970	USC 10, Michigan 3
1919	Great Lakes 17, Mare Is. 0	1946	Alabama 34, USC 14	1971	Stanford 27, Ohio St. 17
		1947	Illinois 45, UCLA 14	1972	Stanford 13, Michigan 12
1920	Harvard 7, Oregon 6	1948	Michigan 49, USC 0	1973	USC 42, Ohio St. 17
1921	California 28, Ohio St. 0	1949	N'western 20, California 14	1974	Ohio St. 42, USC 21
1922	0–0, California vs Wash.& Jeff.			1975	USC 18, Ohio St. 17
1923	USC 14, Penn St. 0	1950	Ohio St. 17, California 14	1976	UCLA 23, Ohio St. 10
1924	14–14, Navy vs Washington	1951	Michigan 14, California 6	1977	USC 14, Michigan 6
1925	Notre Dame 27, Stanford 10	1952	Illinois 40, Stanford 7	1978	Washington 27, Michigan 20
1926	Alabama 20, Washington 19	1953	USC 7, Wisconsin 0	1979	USC 17, Michigan 10
1927	7–7, Alabama vs Stanford	1954	Michigan St. 28, UCLA 20		
1928	Stanford 7, Pittsburgh 6	1955	Ohio St. 20, USC 7	1980	USC 17, Ohio St. 16
1929	Ga.Tech 8, California 7	1956	Michigan St. 17, UCLA 14	1981	Michigan 23, Washington 6
		1957	Iowa 35, Oregon St. 19	1982	Washington 28, Iowa 0
1930	USC 47, Pittsburgh 14	1958	Ohio St. 10, Oregon 7	1983	UCLA 24, Michigan 14
1931	Alabama 24, Wash.St. 0	1959	Iowa 38, California 12	1984	UCLA 45, Illinois 9
1932	USC 21, Tulane 0			1985	USC 20, Ohio St. 17
1933	USC 35, Pittsburgh 0	1960	Washington 44, Wisconsin 8	1986	UCLA 45, Iowa 28
1934	Columbia 7, Stanford 0	1961	Washington 17, Minnesota 7	1987	Arizona St. 22, Michigan 15
1935	Alabama 29, Stanford 13	1962	Minnesota 21, UCLA 3	1988	Michigan St. 20, USC 17
1936	Stanford 7, SMU 0	1963	USC 42, Wisconsin 37	1989	Michigan 22, USC 14
1937	Pitt 21, Washington 0	1964	Illinois 17, Washington 7		
1938	California 13, Alabama 0	1965	Michigan 34, Oregon St. 7	1990	USC 17, Michigan 10
1939	USC 7, Duke 3	1966	UCLA 14, Michigan St. 12	1991	Washington 46, Iowa 34
		1967	Purdue 14, USC 13	1992	Washington 34, Michigan 14
1940	USC 14, Tennessee 0				
1941	Stanford 21, Nebraska 13				

*January game since 1902.

The Bowl Alliance

Division I-A football is the only NCAA sport on any level that does not have a national championship playoff. Why? Because most coaches and administrators prefer the traditional postseason bowl system that yields nine winners in 18 games. Unfortunately, the bowls rarely provide a showdown between the two top-ranked teams in the country.

The Bowl Alliance is a coalition of seven bowl games, six conferences and independent Notre Dame that was formalized on Jan. 23, 1992, and promises to be college football's best shot at a national championship, short of a playoff.

Major bowls: Cotton, Fiesta, Orange and Sugar. **Secondary bowls:** Gator, Blockbuster and John Hancock. **Conferences:** ACC, Big East, Big Eight, and SWC (champions and runners-up); SEC (champion only, runner-up committed to Citrus Bowl); Pac-10 (runner-up only, champion committed to Rose Bowl). **Independents:** Notre Dame and Penn State (PSU for 1992 season only).

Selection date: Following SEC championship game in December.

How it works

1. Cotton, Orange and Sugar bowls select at-large opponents. The bowl with the highest-ranked automatic qualifier picks first. The ACC and Big East champions are guaranteed berths in one of these three bowls, but can refuse an invitation in order to play in the Fiesta.

2. If any combination of the ACC champion, the Big East champion and Notre Dame are ranked 1-2, then those two teams must play in the Fiesta.

3. A team can refuse an invitation to an allied bowl if it results in a rematch with a regular season opponent, if it can make significantly more money in another bowl, or if it has already played in that bowl the last two seasons.

4. Secondary bowls make selections from remaining member teams, most of whom are conference runners-up.

Missing Ingredients

The Rose Bowl, which pairs the Big Ten and Pac-10 champions.

Bowl Games (Cont.)

Orange Bowl

City: Miami, FL; **Stadium:** Orange Bowl; **Capacity:** 74,712; **Playing surface:** Grass; **First year:** 1935; **Playing site:** Orange Bowl (since 1935). **Corporate title sponsor:** Federal Express (since 1990).

Automatic berths: Big Eight champion vs at-large opponent (1954-64, 1976-92); Big Eight champion vs first level opponent from Bowl Alliance (starting in 1993).

Multiple wins: Oklahoma (11); Miami-FL and Nebraska (5); Alabama (4); Georgia Tech and Penn St.(3); Clemson, Colorado, Georgia, LSU, Notre Dame and Texas (2).

Year*		Year		Year	
1935*	Bucknell 26, Miami-FL 0	1955	Duke 34, Nebraska 7	1975	Notre Dame 13, Alabama 11
1936	Catholic U. 20, Mississippi 19	1956	Oklahoma 20, Maryland 6	1976	Oklahoma 14, Michigan 6
1937	Duquesne 13, Miss.St. 12	1957	Colorado 27, Clemson 21	1977	Ohio St. 27, Colorado 10
1938	Auburn 6, Michigan St. 0	1958	Oklahoma 48, Duke 21	1978	Arkansas 31, Oklahoma 6
1939	Tennessee 17, Oklahoma 0	1959	Oklahoma 21, Syracuse 6	1979	Oklahoma 31, Nebraska 24
1940	Georgia Tech 21, Missouri 7	1960	Georgia 14, Missouri 0	1980	Oklahoma 24, Florida St. 7
1941	Miss.St. 14, Georgetown 7	1961	Missouri 21, Navy 14	1981	Oklahoma 18, Florida St. 17
1942	Georgia 40, TCU 26	1962	LSU 25, Colorado 7	1982	Clemson 22, Nebraska 15
1943	Alabama 37, Boston Col. 21	1963	Alabama 17, Oklahoma 0	1983	Nebraska 21, LSU 20
1944	LSU 19, Texas A&M 14	1964	Nebraska 13, Auburn 7	1984	Miami-FL 31, Nebraska 30
1945	Tulsa 26, Georgia Tech 12	1965†	Texas 21, Alabama 17	1985	Washington 28, Oklahoma 17
1946	Miami-FL 13, Holy Cross 6	1966	Alabama 39, Nebraska 28	1986	Oklahoma 25, Penn St. 10
1947	Rice 8, Tennessee 0	1967	Florida 27, Georgia Tech 12	1987	Oklahoma 42, Arkansas 8
1948	Georgia Tech 20, Kansas 14	1968	Oklahoma 26, Tennessee 24	1988	Miami-FL 20, Oklahoma 14
1949	Texas 41, Georgia 28	1969	Penn St. 15, Kansas 14	1989	Miami-FL 23, Nebraska 3
1950	Santa Clara 21, Kentucky 13	1970	Penn St. 10, Missouri 3	1990	Notre Dame, 21, Colorado 6
1951	Clemson 15, Miami-FL 14	1971	Nebraska 17, LSU 12	1991	Colorado 10, Notre Dame 9
1952	Georgia Tech 17, Baylor 14	1972	Nebraska 38, Alabama 6	1992	Miami-FL 22, Nebraska 0
1953	Alabama 61, Syracuse 6	1973	Nebraska 40, Notre Dame 6		
1954	Oklahoma 7, Maryland 0	1974	Penn St. 16, LSU 9		

*January game since 1937.   †Night game since 1965.

Sugar Bowl

City: New Orleans, LA; **Stadium:** Louisiania Superdome; **Capacity:** 72,704; **Playing surface:** AstroTurf; **First year:** 1935; **Playing sites:** Tulane Stadium (1935-74) and Superdome (since 1975). **Corporate title sponsor:** USF&G Financial Services (since 1987).

Automatic berths: SEC champion vs at-large opponent (1977-92); SEC champion vs first level opponent from Bowl Alliance (starting in 1993).

Multiple wins: Alabama (7); Mississippi (5); Georgia Tech, Oklahoma and Tennessee (4); LSU and Nebraska (3); Georgia, Notre Dame, Pittsburgh, Santa Clara and TCU (2).

Year*		Year		Year	
1935*	Tulane 20, Temple 14	1955	Navy 21, Mississippi 0	1974	Nebraska 13, Florida 10
1936	TCU 3, LSU 2	1956	Georgia Tech 7, Pittsburgh 0	1975	Alabama 13, Penn St. 6
1937	Santa Clara 21, LSU 14	1957	Baylor 13, Tennessee 7	1977*	Pittsburgh 27, Georgia 3
1938	Santa Clara 6, LSU 0	1958	Mississippi 39, Texas 7	1978	Alabama 35, Ohio St. 6
1939	TCU 15, Carnegie Tech 7	1959	LSU 7, Clemson 0	1979	Alabama 14, Penn St. 7
1940	Texas A&M 14, Tulane 13	1960	Mississippi 21, LSU 0	1980	Alabama 24, Arkansas 9
1941	Boston Col. 19, Tennessee 13	1961	Mississippi 14, Rice 6	1981	Georgia 17, Notre Dame 10
1942	Fordham 2, Missouri 0	1962	Alabama 10, Arkansas 3	1982	Pittsburgh 24, Georgia 20
1943	Tennessee 14, Tulsa 7	1963	Mississippi 17, Arkansas 13	1983	Penn St. 27, Georgia 23
1944	Georgia Tech 20, Tulsa 18	1964	Alabama 12, Mississippi 7	1984	Auburn 9, Michigan 7
1945	Duke 29, Alabama 26	1965	LSU 13, Syracuse 10	1985	Nebraska 28, LSU 10
1946	Okla.A&M 33, St.Mary's 13	1966	Missouri 20, Florida 18	1986	Tennessee 35, Miami-FL 7
1947	Georgia 20, N.Carolina 10	1967	Alabama 34, Nebraska 7	1987	Nebraska 30, LSU 15
1948	Texas 27, Alabama 7	1968	LSU 20, Wyoming 13	1988	16–16, Syracuse vs Auburn
1949	Oklahoma 14, N.Carolina 6	1969	Arkansas 16, Georgia 2	1989	Florida St. 13, Auburn 7
1950	Oklahoma 35, LSU 0	1970	Mississippi 27, Arkansas 22	1990	Miami-FL 33, Alabama 25
1951	Kentucky 13, Oklahoma 7	1971	Tennessee 34, Air Force 13	1991	Tennessee 23, Virginia 22
1952	Maryland 28, Tennessee 13	1972†	Oklahoma 40, Auburn 22	1992	Notre Dame 39, Florida 28
1953	Georgia Tech 24, Mississippi 7	1972	Oklahoma 14, Penn St. 0		
1954	Georgia Tech 42, West Va. 19	1973	Notre Dame 24, Alabama 23		

*January game from 1935–72 and since 1977.   †Game played on Dec. 31 from 1972–75.

Cotton Bowl

City: Dallas, TX; **Stadium:** Cotton Bowl; **Capacity:** 72,032; **Playing surface:** Astroturf; **First year:** 1937; **Playing sites:** Fair Park Stadium (1937) and Cotton Bowl (since 1938). **Corporate title sponsor:** Mobil Corporation (since 1989).

Automatic berths: SWC champion vs at-large opponent (1942-92); SWC champion vs first level opponent from Bowl Alliance (starting in 1993).

Multiple wins: Texas (9); Texas A&M (4); Notre Dame and Rice (3); Alabama, Arkansas, Georgia, Houston, LSU, Penn St., SMU, Tennessee and TCU (2).

Year		Year		Year	
1937*	TCU 16, Marquette 6	1956	Mississippi 14, TCU 13	1975	Penn St. 41, Baylor 20
1938	Rice 28, Colorado 14	1957	TCU 28, Syracuse 17	1976	Arkansas 31, Georgia 10
1939	St.Mary's 20, Texas Tech 13	1958	Navy 20, Rice 7	1977	Houston 30, Maryland 21
1940	Clemson 6, Boston Col. 3	1959	0–0, TCU vs Air Force	1978	Notre Dame 38, Texas 10
1941	Texas A&M 13, Fordham 12	1960	Syracuse 23, Texas 14	1979	Notre Dame 35, Houston 34
1942	Alabama 29, Texas A&M 21	1961	Duke 7, Arkansas 6	1980	Houston 17, Nebraska 14
1943	Texas 14, Georgia Tech 7	1962	Texas 12, Mississippi 7	1981	Alabama 30, Baylor 2
1944	7–7, Texas vs Randolph Field	1963	LSU 13, Texas 0	1982	Texas 14, Alabama 12
1945	Oklahoma A&M 34, TCU 0	1964	Texas 28, Navy 6	1983	SMU 7, Pittsburgh 3
1946	Texas 40, Missouri 27	1965	Arkansas 10, Nebraska 7	1984	Georgia 10, Texas 9
1947	0–0, Arkansas vs LSU	1966	LSU 14, Arkansas 7	1985	Boston Col. 45, Houston 28
1948	13–13, SMU vs Penn St.	1966†	Georgia 24, SMU 9	1986	Texas A&M 36, Auburn 16
1949	SMU 21, Oregon 13	1968*	Texas A&M 20, Alabama 16	1987	Ohio St. 28, Texas A&M 12
1950	Rice 27, N.Carolina 13	1969	Texas 36, Tennessee 13	1988	Texas A&M 35, Notre Dame 10
1951	Tennessee 20, Texas 14	1970	Texas 21, Notre Dame 17	1989	UCLA 17, Arkansas 3
1952	Kentucky 20, TCU 7	1971	Notre Dame 24, Texas 11	1990	Tennessee 31, Arkansas 27
1953	Texas 16, Tennessee 0	1972	Penn St. 30, Texas 6	1991	Miami-FL 46, Texas 3
1954	Rice 28, Alabama 6	1973	Texas 17, Alabama 13	1992	Florida St. 10, Texas A&M 2
1955	Georgia Tech 14, Arkansas 6	1974	Nebraska 19, Texas 3		

*January game from 1937–66 and since 1968.   †Game played on Dec. 31, 1966.

John Hancock Bowl

City: El Paso, TX; **Stadium:** Sun Bowl; **Capacity:** 52,000; **Playing surface:** AstroTurf; **First year:** 1936; **Name changes:** Sun Bowl (1936-85), John Hancock Sun Bowl (1986-88) and John Hancock Bowl (since 1989); **Playing sites:** Kidd Field (1936-62) and Sun Bowl (since 1963). **Corporate title sponsor:** John Hancock Financial Services (since 1986).

Automatic berths: Match-up of second level Bowl Alliance teams (starting in 1992).

Multiple wins: Texas Western/UTEP (5); Alabama and Wyoming (3); Nebraska, New Mexico St., North Carolina, Pittsburgh, Southwestern-Texas, West Texas St. and West Virginia (2).

Year		Year		Year	
1936*	14–14, Hardin-Simmons vs New Mexico St.	1953	Pacific 26, Southern Miss. 7	1972	N.Carolina 32, Tex.Tech 28
1937	Hardin-Simmons 34, Texas Mines 6	1954	Tex.Western 37, Southern Miss. 14	1973	Missouri 34, Auburn 17
1938	West Va. 7, Texas Tech 6	1955	Tex.Western 47, Florida St. 20	1974	Miss.St. 26, N.Carolina 24
1939	Utah 26, New Mexico 0	1956	Wyoming 21, Texas Tech 14	1975	Pittsburgh 33, Kansas 19
1940	0–0, Catholic U. vs Arizona St.	1957	Geo.Wash. 13, Tex.Western 0	1977*	Texas A&M 37, Florida 14
1941	W.Reserve 26, Arizona St. 13	1958	Louisville 34, Drake 20	1977†	Stanford 24, LSU 14
1942	Tulsa 6, Texas Tech 0	1958*	Wyoming 14, Hard.-Simmons 6	1978	Texas 42, Maryland 0
1943	Second Air Force 13, Hardin-Simmons 7	1959	New Mex.St. 28, N.Texas 8	1979	Washington 14, Texas 7
1944	SW Texas 7, New Mexico 0	1960	New Mex.St. 20, Utah St. 13	1980	Nebraska 31, Miss.St. 17
1945	SW Texas 35, U.of Mexico 0	1961	Villanova 17, Wichita 9	1981	Oklahoma 40, Houston 14
1946	New Mexico 34, Denver 24	1962	West Texas 15, Ohio U. 14	1982	N.Carolina 26, Texas 10
1947	Cincinnati 18, Va.Tech 6	1963	Oregon 21, SMU 14	1983	Alabama 28, SMU 7
1948	Miami-OH 13, Texas Tech 12	1964	Georgia 7, Gergia Tech 0	1984	Maryland 28, Tennessee 27
1949	West Va. 21, Texas Mines 12	1965	Texas Western 13, TCU 12	1985	13–13, Georgia vs Arizona
1950	Tex.Western 33, Georgetown 20	1966	Wyoming 28, Florida St. 20	1986	Alabama 28, Washington 6
1951	West Texas 14, Cincinnati 13	1967	UTEP 14, Mississippi 7	1987	Okla.St. 35, West Va. 33
1952	Texas Tech 25, Pacific 14	1968	Auburn 34, Arizona 10	1988	Alabama 29, Army 28
		1969	Nebraska 45, Georgia 6	1989	Pittsburgh 31, Texas A&M 28
		1970	Georgia Tech 17, Texas Tech 9	1990	Michigan St. 17, USC 16
		1971	LSU 33, Iowa St. 15	1991	UCLA 6, Illinois 3

*January game from 1936–58 and in 1977.   †December game from 1958–75 and since 1977.

Bowl Games (Cont.)
Gator Bowl

City: Jacksonville, FL; **Stadium:** Gator Bowl; **Capacity:** 80,129; **Playing surface:** Grass; **First year:** 1946;
Playing site: Gator Bowl (since 1946). **Corporate title sponsor:** Mazda Motor of America, Inc. (1986-Jan.'91).
  Automatic berths: Match-up of second level Bowl Alliance teams (starting in 1993).
  Multiple wins: Florida (5); Auburn and Clemson (4); Florida St. and North Carolina (3); Georgia, Georgia Tech, Maryland, Oklahoma, Pittsburgh, Tennessee and Texas Tech (2).

Year		Year		Year	
1946*	Wake Forest 26, S.Carolina 14	1961	Penn St. 30, Georgia Tech 15	1977	Pittsburgh 34, Clemson 3
1947	Oklahoma 34, N.C.State 13	1962	Florida 17, Penn St. 7	1978	Clemson 17, Ohio St. 15
1948	20–20, Maryland vs Georgia	1963	N.Carolina 35, Air Force 0	1979	N.Carolina 17, Michigan 15
1949	Clemson 24, Missouri 23	1965*	Florida St. 36, Oklahoma 19		
		1965†	Georgia Tech 31, Texas Tech 21	1980	Pittsburgh 37, S.Carolina 9
1950	Maryland 20, Missouri 7	1966	Tennessee 18, Syracuse 12	1981	N.Carolina 31, Arkansas 27
1951	Wyoming 20, Wash.& Lee 7	1967	17–17, Florida St. vs Penn St.	1982	Florida St. 31, West Va. 12
1952	Miami-FL 14, Clemson 0	1968	Missouri 35, Alabama 10	1983	Florida 14, Iowa 6
1953	Florida 14, Tulsa 13	1969	Florida 14, Tennessee 13	1984	Okla.St. 21, S.Carolina 14
1954	Texas Tech 35, Auburn 13			1985	Florida St. 34, Okla.St. 23
1954†	Auburn 33, Baylor 13	1971*	Auburn 35, Mississippi 28	1986	Clemson 27, Stanford 21
1955	Vanderbilt 25, Auburn 13	1971†	Georgia 7, N.Carolina 3	1987	LSU 30, S.Carolina 13
1956	Georgia Tech 21, Pittsburgh 14	1972	Auburn 24, Colorado 3	1989*	Georgia 34, Michigan St. 27
1957	Tennessee 3, Texas A&M 0	1973	Texas Tech 28, Tennessee 19	1989†	Clemson 27, West Va. 7
1958	Mississippi 7, Florida 3	1974	Auburn 27, Texas 3		
		1975	Maryland 13, Florida 0	1991*	Michigan 35, Mississippi 3
1960*	Arkansas 14, Georgia Tech 7	1976	Notre Dame 20, Penn St. 9	1991†	Oklahoma 48, Virginia 14
1960†	Florida 13, Baylor 12				

*January game from 1946–54, 1960, 1965, 1971, 1989 and 1991.
†December game from 1954–58, 1960–63, 1965–69, 1971–87, 1989 and 1991.

Florida Citrus Bowl

City: Orlando, FL; **Stadium:** Florida Citrus Bowl; **Capacity:** 70,000; **Playing surface:** Grass; **First year:** 1947;
Name changes: Tangerine Bowl (1947-82) and Florida Citrus Bowl (since 1983); **Playing sites:** Tangerine Bowl
(1947-72, 1974-82), Florida Field in Gainesville (1973), Orlando Stadium (1983-85) and Florida Citrus Bowl (since
1986). The Tangerine Bowl, Orlando Stadium and Florida Citrus Bowl are all the same stadium. **Corporate title
sponsor:** Florida Department of Citrus (since 1983).
  Automatic berths: Championship game of Atlantic Coast Regional Conference (1964-67); Mid-American
Conference champion vs Southern Conference champion (1968-75); ACC champion vs at-large opponent (1988-
92); Big 10 runner-up vs SEC runner-up or a higher-ranked SEC also-ran (starting in 1993).
  Multiple wins: East Texas St., Miami-OH and Toledo (3); Auburn, Catawba, Clemson, East Carolina (2).

Year		Year		Year	
1947*	Catawba 31, Maryville 6	1962	Houston 49, Miami-OH 21	1978	N.C.State 30, Pittsburgh 17
1948	Catawba 7, Marshall 0	1963	West.Ky. 27, Coast Guard 0	1979	LSU 34, Wake Forest 10
1949	21–21, Murray St. vs. Sul Ross St.	1964	E.Carolina 14, Mass. 13		
		1965	E.Carolina 31, Maine 0	1980	Florida 35, Maryland 20
1950	St.Vincent 7, Emory & Henry 6	1966	Morgan St. 14, W.Chester 6	1981	Missouri 19, Southern Miss. 17
1951	M.Harvey 35, Emory & Henry 14	1967	Tenn.Martin 25, W.Chester 8	1982	Auburn 33, Boston Col. 26
1952	Stetson 35, Arkansas St. 20	1968	Richmond 49, Ohio U. 42	1983	Tennessee 30, Maryland 23
1953	E.Texas St. 33, Tenn. Tech 0	1969	Toledo 56, Davidson 33	1984	17–17, Florida St. vs Georgia
1954	7–7, E.Texas St. vs Ark.St.			1985	Ohio St. 10, BYU 7
1955	Neb.-Omaha 7, Eastern Ky. 6	1970	Toledo 40, Wm.& Mary 12	1987*	Auburn 16, USC 7
1956	6–6, Juniata vs Mo.Valley	1971	Toledo 28, Richmond 3	1988	Clemson 35, Penn St. 10
1957	W.Texas St. 20, So.Miss. 13	1972	Tampa 21, Kent St. 18	1989	Clemson 13, Oklahoma 6
1958	E.Texas St. 10, So.Miss. 9	1973	Miami-OH 16, Florida 7		
1958†	E.Texas St. 26, Mo.Valley 7	1974	Miami-OH 21, Georgia 10	1990	Illinois 31, Virginia 21
		1975	Miami-OH 20, S.Carolina 7	1991	Georgia Tech 45, Nebraska 21
1960*	Mid.Tenn. 21, Presbyterian 12	1976	Oklahoma 49, BYU 21	1992	California 37, Clemson 13
1960†	Citadel 27, Tenn. Tech 0	1977	Florida St. 40, Texas Tech 17		
1961	Lamar 21, Middle Tenn. 14				

*January game from 1947–58, in 1960 and since 1987.   †December game from 1958 and 1960–85.

Bowl Matchups of Unbeaten Teams, 1902-50

Date	Bowl	Winner	Head Coach	Score	Loser	Head Coach
1/1/21	Rose	California (8-0)	Andy Smith	28-0	Ohio St.(7-0)	John Wilce
1/2/22	Rose	Wash.& Jeff.(10-0)	Greasy Neale			
		& California (9-0)	Andy Smith	0-0		
1/1/27	Rose	Stanford (10-0)	Pop Warner			
		& Alabama (9-0)	Wallace Wade	7-7		
1/1/31	Rose	Alabama (9-0)	Wallace Wade	24-0	Washington St.(9-0)	Babe Hollingbery
1/2/39	Orange	Tennessee (10-0)	Bob Neyland	17-0	Oklahoma (10-0)	Tom Stidham
1/1/41	Sugar	Boston Coll.(10-0)	Frank Leahy	19-13	Tennessee (10-0)	Bob Neyland

Liberty Bowl

City: Memphis, TN; **Stadium:** Liberty Bowl Memorial; **Capacity:** 63,244; **Playing surface:** Grass; **First year:** 1959; **Playing sites:** Municipal Stadium in Philadelphia (1959-63); Convention Hall in Atlantic City, NJ (1964); Memphis Memorial Stadium (1965-75); Liberty Bowl Memorial Stadium (since 1976). Memphis Memorial Stadium renamed Liberty Bowl Memorial in 1976.

Automatic berths: Commander-in-Chief's Trophy winner (Army, Navy or Air Force) vs at-large opponent (since 1989). If Air Force wins C-in-C trophy but also wins WAC title, it must play in Holiday Bowl. Liberty Bowl committee must then decide between Army and Navy. Service academy representative must have .500 record or better to qualify.

Multiple wins: Mississippi, Penn St. and Tennessee (3); Air Force, Alabama and N.C.State (2).

Year		Year		Year	
1959†	Penn St. 7, Alabama 0	1970	Tulane 17, Colorado 3	1981	Ohio St. 31, Navy 28
1960	Penn St. 41, Oregon 12	1971	Tennessee 14, Arkansas 13	1982	Alabama 21, Illinois 15
1961	Syracuse 15, Miami-FL 14	1972	Georgia Tech 31, Iowa St. 30	1983	Notre Dame 19, Boston Col. 18
1962	Oregon St. 6, Villanova 0	1973	N.C.State 31, Kansas 18	1984	Auburn 21, Arkansas 15
1963	Mississippi St. 16, N.C.State 12	1974	Tennessee 7, Maryland 3	1985	Baylor 21, LSU 7
1964	Utah 32, West Virgina 6	1975	USC 20, Texas A&M 0	1986	Tennessee 21, Minnesota 14
1965	Mississippi 13, Auburn 7	1976	Alabama 36, UCLA 6	1987	Georgia 20, Arkansas 17
1966	Miami-FL 14, Va.Tech 7	1977	Nebraska 21, N.Carolina 17	1988	Indiana 34, S.Carolina 10
1967	N.C.State 14, Georgia 7	1978	Missouri 20, LSU 15	1989	Mississippi 42, Air Force 29
1968	Mississippi 34, Va.Tech 17	1979	Penn St. 9, Tulane 6	1990	Air Force 23, Ohio St. 11
1969	Colorado 47, Alabama 33	1980	Purdue 28, Missouri 25	1991	Air Force 38, Miss.St. 15

†December game since 1959.

Peach Bowl

City: Atlanta; GA; **Stadium:** Georgia Dome; **Capacity:** 70,500; **Playing surface:** AstroTurf; **First year:** 1968; **Playing sites:** Grant Field (1968-70); Atlanta Stadium (1971-92); Georgia Dome (starting in 1993).

Automatic berths: Highest-ranked ACC team not playing in first or second level Bowl Alliance game (starting in 1993).

Multiple wins: N.C.State and West Virginia (3).

Year		Year		Year	
1968†	LSU 31, Florida St. 27	1976	Kentucky 21, N.Carolina 0	1984	Virginia 27, Purdue 24
1969	West Va. 14, S.Carolina 3	1977	N.C.State 24, Iowa St. 14	1985	Army 31, Illinois 29
1970	Arizona St. 48, N.Carolina 26	1978	Purdue 41, Georgia Tech 21	1986	Va.Tech 25, N.C.State 24
1971	Mississippi 41, Georgia Tech 18	1979	Baylor 24, Clemson 18	1988*	Tennessee 27, Indiana 22
1972	N.C.State 49, West Va. 13	1981*	Miami-FL 20, Va.Tech 10	1988†	N.C.State 28, Iowa 23
1973	Georgia 17, Maryland 16	1981†	West Va. 26, Florida 6	1989	Syracuse 19, Georgia 18
1974	6–6, Vanderbilt vs Texas Tech	1982	Iowa 28, Tennessee 22	1990	Auburn 27, Indiana 23
1975	West Va. 13, N.C.State 10	1983	Florida St. 28, N.Carolina 3	1992	E.Carolina 37, N.C.State 34

†December game from 1968–79, 1981–86, and 1988–90.   *January game in 1981, 1988 and 1992.

Fiesta Bowl

City: Tempe, AZ; **Stadium:** Sun Devil; **Capacity:** 74,865; **Playing surface:** Grass; **First year:** 1971; **Playing site:** Sun Devil Stadium (since 1971). **Corporate title sponsor:** Sunkist Citrus Growers (1986-91).

Automatic berths: Two first level teams from Bowl Alliance (starting in 1993).

Multiple wins: Arizona St. and Penn St.(5); Florida St.(2).

Year		Year		Year	
1971†	Arizona St. 45, Florida St. 38	1979	Pittsburgh 16, Arizona 10	1987	Penn St. 14, Miami-FL 10
1972	Arizona St. 49, Missouri 35	1980	Penn St. 31, Ohio St. 19	1988	Florida St. 31, Nebraska 28
1973	Arizona St. 28, Pittsburgh 7	1982*	Penn St. 26, USC 10	1989	Notre Dame 34, West Va. 21
1974	Oklahoma St. 16, BYU 6	1983	Arizona St. 32, Oklahoma 21		
1975	Arizona St. 17, Nebraska 14	1984	Ohio St. 28, Pittsburgh 23	1990	Florida St. 41, Nebraska 17
1976	Oklahoma 41, Wyoming 7	1985	UCLA 39, Miami-FL 37	1991	Louisville 34, Alabama 7
1977	Penn St. 42, Arizona St. 30	1986	Michigan 27, Nebraska 23	1992	Penn St. 42, Tennessee 17
1978	10–10, Arkansas vs UCLA				

†December game from 1971–80.   *January game since 1982.

Bowl Matchups of Unbeaten Teams, Since 1951

Date	Bowl	Winner	Head Coach	Score	Loser	Head Coach
1/1/52	Sugar	Maryland (9-0)	Jim Tatum	28-13	Tennessee (10-0)	Bob Neyland
1/2/56	Orange	Oklahoma (10-0)	Bud Wilkinson	20-6	Maryland (10-0)	Jim Tatum
1/1/72	Orange	Nebraska (12-0)	Bob Devaney	38-6	Alabama (11-0)	Bear Bryant
12/31/73	Sugar	Notre Dame (10-0)	Ara Parseghian	24-23	Alabama (11-0)	Bear Bryant
1/2/87	Fiesta	Penn St.(11-0)	Joe Paterno	14-10	Miami-FL (11-0)	Jimmy Johnson
1/1/88	Orange	Miami-FL (11-0)	Jimmy Johnson	20-14	Oklahoma (11-0)	Barry Switzer
1/2/89	Fiesta	Notre Dame (11-0)	Lou Holtz	34-21	West Va.(11-0)	Don Nehlen

Bowl Games (Cont.)
Independence Bowl

City: Shreveport, LA; **Stadium:** Independence; **Capacity:** 50,459; **Playing surface:** Grass; **First year:** 1976; **Playing sites:** Independence Stadium (since 1976). **Corporate title sponsor:** Poulan/Weed Eater (since 1990).
    Automatic berths: None.
    Multiple wins: Air Force and Southern Miss.(2).

Year		Year		Year	
1976†	McNeese St. 20, Tulsa 16	1982	Wisconsin 14, Kansas St. 3	1988	So.Miss 38, UTEP 18
1977	La.Tech 24, Louisville 14	1983	Air Force 9, Mississippi 3	1989	Oregon 27, Tulsa 24
1978	E.Carolina 35, La.Tech 13	1984	Air Force 23, Va.Tech 7	1990	34-34, La.Tech vs Maryland
1979	Syracuse 31, McNeese St. 7	1985	Minnesota 20, Clemson 13	1991	Georgia 24, Arkansas 15
1980	So.Miss 16, McNeese St. 14	1986	Mississippi 20, Texas Tech 17		
1981	Texas A&M 33, Okla.St. 16	1987	Washington 24, Tulane 12		

†December game since 1976.

Holiday Bowl

City: San Diego, CA; **Stadium:** San Diego/Jack Murphy; **Capacity:** 60,000; **Playing surface:** Grass; **First year:** 1978; **Playing sites:** San Diego/Jack Murphy Stadium (since 1978). **Corporate title sponsors:** Sea World (1986-90); Thrifty Car Rental (since 1991).
    Automatic berths: WAC champion vs at-large opponent (1978-84, 1986-90); WAC champion vs Big 10 runner-up (1991); WAC champion vs Big 10 third place team, provided it has at least 8 wins or a Top 20 ranking (starting in 1992).
    Multiple wins: BYU (4); Iowa (2).

Year		Year		Year	
1978†	Navy 23, BYU 16	1983	BYU 21, Missouri 17	1988	Okla.St. 62, Wyoming 14
1979	Indiana 38, BYU 37	1984	BYU 24, Michigan 17	1989	Penn St. 50, BYU 39
1980	BYU 46, SMU 45	1985	Arkansas 18, Arizona St. 17	1990	Texas A&M 65, BYU 14
1981	BYU 38, Wash.St. 36	1986	Iowa 39, San Diego St. 38	1991	13-13, Iowa vs BYU
1982	Ohio St. 47, BYU 17	1987	Iowa 20, Wyoming 19		

†December game since 1978.

California Bowl

City: Fresno, CA; **Stadium:** Bulldog; **Capacity:** 40,541; **Playing surface:** Grass; **First year:** 1981; **Name change:** California Bowl (1981-88, 1992), Californina Raisin Bowl (1989-91); **Playing site:** Bulldog Stadium (since 1981); **Corporate title sponsor:** California Raisin Advisory Board (1988-91).
    Automatic berths: Mid-American champion vs Big West champion (1981-91); none (starting in 1992).
    Multiple wins: Fresno St.(4); San Jose St. and Toledo (2).

Year		Year		Year	
1981†	Toledo 27, San Jose St. 25	1985	Fresno St. 51, Bowling Green 7	1989	Fresno St. 27, Ball St. 6
1982	Fresno St. 29, Bowling Green 28	1986	San Jose St. 37, Miami-OH 7	1990	San Jose St. 48, C.Michigan 24
1983	Northern Ill. 20, CS-Fullerton 13	1987	E.Michigan 30, San Jose St. 27	1991	Bowling Green 28, Fresno St. 21
1984	UNLV 30, Toledo 13	1988	Fresno St. 35, W.Michigan 30		

†December game since 1981.
Note: Toledo later ruled winner of 1984 game by forfeit when UNLV was found to have used ineligible players.

Aloha Bowl

City: Honolulu, HI; **Stadium:** Aloha; **Capacity:** 50,000; **Playing surface:** AstroTurf; **First year:** 1982; **Playing site:** Aloha Stadium (since 1982). **Corporate title sponsor:** Jeep Eagle Division of Chrysler (since 1987).
    Automatic berths: None.
    Multiple wins: None.

Year		Year		Year	
1982†	Washington 21, Maryland 20	1986	Arizona 30, N.Carolina 21	1990	Syracuse 28, Arizona 0
1983	Penn St. 13, Washington 10	1987	UCLA 20, Florida 16	1991	Georgia Tech 18, Stanford 17
1984	SMU 27, Notre Dame 20	1988	Wash.St. 24, Houston 22		
1985	Alabama 24, USC 3	1989	Michigan St. 33, Hawaii 13		

†December game since 1982.

Freedom Bowl

City: Anaheim, CA; **Stadium:** Anaheim; **Capacity:** 69,001; **Playing surface:** Grass; **First year:** 1984; **Playing site:** Anaheim Stadium (since 1984).
    Automatic berths: Third-place team from Pac-10 (starting in 1992).
    Multiple wins: Washington (2).

Year		Year		Year	
1984†	Iowa 55, Texas 17	1987	Arizona St. 33, Air Force 28	1990	Colorado St. 32, Oregon 31
1985	Washington 20, Colorado 17	1988	BYU 20, Colorado 17	1991	Tulsa 28, San Diego St. 17
1986	UCLA 31, BYU 10	1989	Washington 34, Florida 7		

†December game since 1984.

Hall of Fame Bowl

City: Tampa, FL; **Stadium:** Tampa; **Capacity:** 74,314; **Playing surface:** Grass; **First year:** 1986; **Playing site:** Tampa Stadium (since 1986).
Automatic berths: None.
Multiple wins: Syracuse (2).

Year		Year		Year	
1986†	Boston College 27, Georgia 24	1989	Syracuse 23, LSU 10	1991	Clemson 30, Illinois 0
1988*	Michigan 28, Alabama 24	1990	Auburn 31, Ohio St. 14	1992	Syracuse 24, Ohio St. 17

†December game in 1986.   *January game since 1988.

Copper Bowl

City: Tucson, AZ; **Stadium:** Arizona; **Capacity:** 56,167; **Playing surface:** Grass; **First year:** 1989; **Playing site:** Arizona Stadium (since 1989). **Corporate title sponsor:** Domino's Pizza (since 1990).
Automatic berths: None.
Multiple wins: None.

Year		Year		Year	
1989†	Arizona 17, N.C.State 10	1990	California 17, Wyoming 15	1991	Indiana 24, Baylor 0

†December game since 1989.

Blockbuster Bowl

City: Miami, FL; **Stadium:** Joe Robbie; **Capacity:** 73,000; **Playing surface:** Grass; **First year:** 1990; **Playing site:** Joe Robbie Stadium (since 1990). **Corporate title sponsor:** Blockbuster Entertainment (since 1990).
Automatic berths: Independent Penn St. assured berth for 1992 season only, provided it wins at least six games (PSU joins Big Ten in 1993). Match-up of second level Bowl Alliance teams starting in 1993.
Multiple wins: None.

Year		Year	
1990†	Florida St. 24, Penn St. 17	1991	Alabama 30, Colorado 25

†December game 1990-91 (moves to Jan. 1 in 1993).

Discontinued Bowls
Bowls of five games or more.

Bluebonnet Bowl

Years: 1959-87; **City:** Houston, TX; **Name changes:** Bluebonnet Bowl (1959-67, 1977-87); Astro-Bluebonnet Bowl (1968-76); **Playing sites:** Rice Stadium(1959-67, 1985-86), Astrodome (1968-84, 1987); **Dates:** December game every year.
Automatic berths: None.
Multiple wins: Texas (3); Baylor, Colorado, Houston and Tennessee (2).

Year		Year		Year	
1959	Clemson 23, TCU 7	1969	Houston 36, Auburn 7	1979	Purdue 27, Tennessee 22
1960	3-3, Alabama vs Texas	1970	24-24, Alabama vs Oklahoma	1980	N.Carolina 16, Texas 7
1961	Kansas 33, Rice 7	1971	Colorado 29, Houston 17	1981	Michigan 33, UCLA 14
1962	Missouri 14, Georgia Tech 10	1972	Tennessee 24, LSU 17	1982	Arkansas 28, Florida 24
1963	Baylor 14, LSU 7	1973	Houston 47, Tulane 7	1983	Oklahoma St. 24, Baylor 14
1964	Tulsa 14, Mississippi 7	1974	31-31, Houston vs N.C.State	1984	West Va. 31, TCU 14
1965	Tennessee 27, Tulsa 6	1975	Texas 38, Colorado 21	1985	Air Force 24, Texas 16
1966	Texas 19, Mississippi 0	1976	Nebraska 27, Texas Tech 24	1986	Baylor 21, Colorado 9
1967	Colorado 31, Miami-FL 21	1977	USC 47, Texas A&M 28	1987	Texas 32, Pittsburgh 27
1968	SMU 28, Oklahoma 27	1978	Stanford 25, Georgia 22		

All-American Bowl

Years: 1977-90; **City:** Birmingham, AL; **Name changes:** Hall of Fame Classic (1977-84), All-American Bowl (1985-90); **Playing sites:** Legion Field (1977-90); **Dates:** December game each year.
Automatic berths: None.
Multiple wins: None.

Year		Year		Year	
1977	Maryland 17, Minnesota 7	1982	Air Force 36, Vanderbilt 28	1987	Virginia 22, BYU 16
1978	Texas A&M 28, Iowa St. 12	1983	West Va. 20, Kentucky 16	1988	Florida 14, Illinois 10
1979	Missouri 24, S.Carolina 14	1984	Kentucky 20, Wisconsin 19	1989	Texas Tech 49, Duke 21
1980	Arkansas 34, Tulane 15	1985	Georgia Tech 17, Mich.St. 14	1990	N.C.State 31, So.Miss 27
1981	Miss.St. 10, Kansas 0	1986	Florida St. 27, Indiana 13		

Major Conference Champions
Atlantic Coast Conference

Founded in 1953 when charter members all left Southern Conference to form ACC. **Charter members** (7): Clemson, Duke, Maryland, North Carolina, North Carolina St., South Carolina and Wake Forest. **Admitted later** (3): Virginia in 1953 (began play in '54), Georgia Tech in 1978 (began play in '83) Florida St.(began play in '92). **Withdrew later** (1): South Carolina in 1971.

    Current playing membership (9): Clemson, Duke, Florida St., Georgia Tech, Maryland, North Carolina, N.C.State, Virginia and Wake Forest.

    Multiple titles: Clemson (12); Maryland (8); Duke and N.C.State (7); North Carolina (5).

Year		Year		Year		Year	
1953	Duke (4-0)	1963	North Carolina (6-1)	1973	N.C.State (6-0)	1985	Clemson (7-0)†
	& Maryland (3-0)		& N.C.State (6-1)	1974	Maryland (6-0)		& Maryland (6-0)
1954	Duke (4-0)	1964	N.C.State (5-2)	1975	Maryland (5-0)	1986	Clemson (5-1-1)
1955	Maryland (4-0)	1965	Clemson (5-2)	1976	Maryland (5-0)	1987	Clemson (6-1)
	& Duke (4-0)		& N.C.State (5-2)	1977	North Carolina (5-0-1)	1988	Clemson (6-1)
1956	Clemson (4-0-1)	1966	Clemson (6-1)	1978	Clemson (6-0)	1989	Virginia (6-1)
1957	N.C.State (5-0-1)	1967	Clemson (6-0)	1979	N.C.State (5-1)		& Duke (6-1)
1958	Clemson (5-1)	1968	N.C.State (6-1)				
1959	Clemson (6-1)	1969	South Carolina (6-0)	1980	North Carolina (6-0)	1990	Georgia Tech (6-0-1)
				1981	Clemson (6-0)	1991	Clemson (6-0-1)
1960	Duke (5-1)	1970	Wake Forest (5-1)	1982	Clemson (6-0)		
1961	Duke (5-1)	1971	North Carolina (6-0)	1983	Maryland (5-0)		
1962	Duke (6-0)	1972	North Carolina (6-0)	1984	Maryland (5-0)		

†On probation, ineligible for championship.

Big East Conference

Founded in 1991 when charter members all gave up independent football status to form Big East. **Charter members** (8): Boston College, Miami of Florida, Pittsburgh, Rutgers, Syracuse, Temple, Virginia Tech and West Virginia. **Note:** Rutgers, Temple, Virginia Tech and West Virginia are Big East members in football only.

    Current playing membership (8): Boston College, Miami-FL, Pittsburgh, Rutgers, Syracuse, Temple, Virginia Tech and West Virginia.

    Conference champion: For 1991 and '92, team with highest ranking in final regular season USA Today/CNN Coaches poll wins title. Starting in 1993, the championship will be decided by full 7-game round robin schedule.

Year
1991 Miami-FL (2-0,#1)
    & Syracuse (5-0),#16)

Big Eight Conference

Originally founded in 1907 as Missouri Valley Intercollegiate Athletic Assn. **Charter members** (5): Iowa, Kansas, Missouri, Nebraska and Washington University of St.Louis. **Admitted later** (6): Drake and Iowa St.(then Ames College) in 1908; Kansas St. in 1913, Grinnell in 1919, Oklahoma in 1920 and Oklahoma St.(then Oklahoma A&M) in 1925. **Withdrew later** (1): Iowa in 1911. **Note:** Iowa belonged to both the MVIAA and Western Conference from 1907-10.

    Big Six founded in 1928 when charter members left MVIAA. **Charter members** (6): Iowa St., Kansas, Kansas St., Missouri, Nebraska and Oklahoma. **Admitted later** (2): Colorado in 1947 (began play in '48), Oklahoma St. in 1957 (began play in '60). Renamed **Big Seven** in 1948 and **Big Eight** in 1958.

    Current playing membership (8): Colorado, Iowa St., Kansas, Kansas St., Missouri, Nebraska, Oklahoma and Oklahoma St.

    Multiple titles: Nebraska (37); Oklahoma (33); Missouri (12); Kansas (6); Colorado (5); Iowa St. and Oklahoma St.(2).

Year		Year		Year		Year	
1907	Iowa (1-0)	1916	Nebraska (3-1)	1928	Nebraska (4-0)	1940	Nebraska (5-0)
	& Nebraska (1-0)	1917	Nebraska (2-0)	1929	Nebraska (3-0-2)	1941	Missouri (5-0)
1908	Kansas (4-0)	1918	Vacant (WW I)			1942	Missouri (4-0-1)
1909	Missouri (4-0-1)	1919	Missouri (4-0-1)	1930	Kansas (4-1)	1943	Oklahoma (5-0)
				1931	Nebraska (5-0)	1944	Oklahoma (4-0-1)
1910	Nebraska (2-0)	1920	Oklahoma (4-0-1)	1932	Nebraska (5-0)	1945	Missouri (5-0)
1911	Iowa St. (2-0-1)	1921	Nebraska (3-0)	1933	Nebraska (5-0)	1946	Oklahoma (4-1)
	& Nebraska (2-0-1)	1922	Nebraska (5-0)	1934	Kansas St. (5-0)		& Kansas (4-1)
1912	Iowa St. (2-0)	1923	Nebraska (3-0-2)	1935	Nebraska (4-0-1)	1947	Kansas (4-0-1)
	& Nebraska (2-0)		& Kansas (3-0-3)	1936	Nebraska (5-0)		& Oklahoma (4-0-1)
1913	Missouri (4-0)	1924	Missouri (5-1)	1937	Nebraska (3-0-2)	1948	Oklahoma (5-0)
	& Nebraska (3-0)	1925	Missouri (5-1)	1938	Oklahoma (5-0)	1949	Oklahoma (5-0)
1914	Nebraska (3-0)	1926	Oklahoma A&M (3-0-1)	1939	Missouri (5-0)		
1915	Nebraska (4-0)	1927	Missouri (5-1)				

Year			
1950 Oklahoma (6-0)	1963 Nebraska (7-0)	1974 Oklahoma (7-0)	1982 Nebraska (7-0)
1951 Oklahoma (6-0)	1964 Nebraska (6-1)	1975 Nebraska (6-1)	1983 Nebraska (7-0)
1952 Oklahoma (5-0-1)	1965 Nebraska (6-1)	& Oklahoma (6-1)	1984 Oklahoma (6-1)
1953 Oklahoma (6-0)	1966 Nebraska (6-1)	1976 Colorado (5-2),	& Nebraska (6-1)
1954 Oklahoma (6-0)	1967 Oklahoma (7-0)	Oklahoma (5-2)	1985 Oklahoma (7-0)
1955 Oklahoma (6-0)	1968 Kansas (6-1)	& Oklahoma St. (5-2)	1986 Oklahoma (7-0)
1956 Oklahoma (6-0)	& Oklahoma (6-1)	1977 Oklahoma (7-0)	1987 Oklahoma (7-0)
1957 Oklahoma (6-0)	1969 Missouri (6-1)	1978 Nebraska (6-1)	1988 Nebraska (7-0)
1958 Oklahoma (6-0)	& Nebraska (6-1)	& Oklahoma (6-1)	1989 Colorado (7-0)
1959 Oklahoma (5-1)	1970 Nebraska (7-0)	1979 Oklahoma (7-0)	1990 Colorado (7-0)
1960 Missouri (7-0)	1971 Nebraska (7-0)	1980 Oklahoma (7-0)	1991 Nebraska (6-0-1)
1961 Colorado (7-0)	1972 Nebraska (5-1-1)*	1981 · Nebraska (7-0)	& Colorado (6-0-1)
1962 Oklahoma (7-0)	1973 Oklahoma (7-0)		

*Oklahoma (6-1) forfeited title in 1972.

Big Ten Conference

Originally founded in 1895 as the Intercollegiate Conference of Faculty Representatives, better known as the Western Conference. **Charter members** (7): Chicago, Illinois, Michigan, Minnesota, Northwestern, Purdue and Wisconsin. **Admitted later** (5): Indiana and Iowa in 1899, Ohio St. in 1912, Michigan St. in 1950 (began play in '53) and Penn St. in 1990 (will begin play in 1993). **Withdrew later** (2): Michigan in 1907 (rejoined in '17), Chicago in 1940. **Note**: Iowa belonged to both the Western and Missouri Valley conferences from 1907-10.

Unofficially called **Big Ten** from 1912 until Chicago withdrew after 1939 season, then **Big Nine** from 1940 until Michigan St. began conference play in 1953. Formally renamed **Big Ten** in 1984 and will keep name with Penn St. as 11th member.

Current playing membership (10): Illinois, Indiana, Iowa, Michigan, Michigan St., Minnesota, Northwestern, Ohio St., Purdue and Wisconsin.

Multiple titles: Michigan (36); Ohio St.(25); Minnesota (18); Illinois (14); Iowa (9); Wisconsin (8); Purdue (7); Chicago and Michigan St.(6); Northwestern (5); Indiana (2).

Year			
1896 Wisconsin (2-0-1)	1920 Ohio St. (5-0)	1944 Ohio St. (6-0)	1972 Ohio St. (8-0)
1897 Wisconsin (3-0)	1921 Iowa (5-0)	1945 Indiana (5-0-1)	& Michigan (7-1)
1898 Michigan (3-0)	1922 Iowa (5-0)	1946 Illinois (6-1)	1973 Ohio St. (7-0-1)
1899 Chicago (4-0)	& Michigan (4-0)	1947 Michigan (6-0)	& Michigan (7-0-1)
1900 Iowa (3-0-1)	1923 Illinois (5-0)	1948 Michigan (6-0)	1974 Ohio St. (7-1)
& Minnesota (3-0-1)	& Michigan (4-0)	1949 Ohio St. (4-1-1)	& Michigan (7-1)
1901 Michigan (4-0)	1924 Chicago (3-0-3)	& Michigan (4-1-1)	1975 Ohio St. (8-0)
& Wisconsin (2-0)	1925 Michigan (5-1)	1950 Michigan (4-1-1)	1976 Michigan (7-1)
1902 Michigan (5-0)	1926 Michigan (5-0)	1951 Illinois (5-0-1)	& Ohio St. (7-1)
1903 Michigan (3-0-1),	& Northwestern (5-0)	1952 Wisconsin (4-1-1)	1977 Michigan (7-1)
Minnesota (3-0-1)	1927 Illinois (5-0)	& Purdue (4-1-1)	& Ohio St. (7-1)
& Northwestern (1-0-2)	& Minnesota (3-0-1)	1953 Michigan St. (5-1)	1978 Michigan (7-1)
1904 Minnesota (3-0)	1928 Illinois (4-1)	& Illinois (5-1)	& Michigan St. (7-1)
& Michigan (2-0)	1929 Purdue (5-0)	1954 Ohio St. (7-0)	1979 Ohio St. (8-0)
1905 Chicago (7-0)	1930 Michigan (5-0)	1955 Ohio St. (6-0)	1980 Michigan (8-0)
1906 Wisconsin (3-0),	& Northwestern (5-0)	1956 Iowa (5-1)	1981 Iowa (6-2)
Minnesota (2-0)	1931 Purdue (5-1),	1957 Ohio St. (7-0)	& Ohio St. (6-2)
& Michigan (1-0)	Michigan (5-1)	1958 Iowa (5-1)	1982 Michigan (8-1)
1907 Chicago (4-0)	& Northwestern (5-1)	1959 Wisconsin (5-2)	1983 Illinois (9-0)
1908 Chicago (5-0)	1932 Michigan (6-0)	1960 Minnesota (5-1)	1984 Ohio St. (7-2)
1909 Minnesota (3-0)	& Purdue (5-0-1)	& Iowa (5-1)	1985 Iowa (7-1)
1910 Illinois (4-0)	1933 Michigan (5-0-1)	1961 Ohio St. (6-0)	1986 Michigan (7-1)
& Minnesota (2-0)	& Minnesota (2-0-4)	1962 Wisconsin (6-1)	& Ohio St. (7-1)
1911 Minnesota (3-0-1)	1934 Minnesota (5-0)	1963 Illinois (5-1-1)	1987 Michigan St. (7-0-1)
1912 Wisconsin (6-0)	1935 Minnesota (5-0)	1964 Michigan (6-1)	1988 Michigan (7-0-1)
1913 Chicago (7-0)	& Ohio St. (5-0)	1965 Michigan St. (7-0)	1989 Michigan (8-0)
1914 Illinois (6-0)	1936 Northwestern (6-0)	1966 Michigan St. (7-0)	1990 Iowa (6-2),
1915 Minnesota (3-0-1)	1937 Minnesota (5-0)	1967 Indiana (6-1),	Michigan (6-2),
& Illinois (3-0-2)	1938 Minnesota (4-1)	Purdue (6-1)	Michigan St. (6-2)
1916 Ohio St. (4-0)	1939 Ohio St. (5-1)	& Minnesota (6-1)	& Illinois (6-2)
1917 Ohio St. (4-0)	1940 Minnesota (6-0)	1968 Ohio St. (7-0)	1991 Michigan (8-0)
1918 Illinois (4-0),	1941 Minnesota (5-0)	1969 Ohio St. (6-1)	
Michigan (2-0)	1942 Ohio St. (5-1)	& Michigan (6-1)	
& Purdue (1-0)	1943 Purdue (6-0)	1970 Ohio St. (7-0)	
1919 Illinois (6-1)	& Michigan (6-0)	1971 Michigan (8-0)	

Major Conference Champions (Cont.)
Big West Conference

Originally founded in 1969 as Pacific Coast Athletic Assn. **Charter members** (7): Cal-Santa Barbara, Cal St.-Los Angeles, Fresno St., Long Beach St., Pacific, San Diego St. and San Jose St. **Admitted later** (9): Cal St.-Fullerton in 1974, Utah St. in 1977 (began play in '78), Nevada-Las Vegas in 1982 and New Mexico St. in 1983 (began play in '84), Nevada-Reno in 1991 (began play in '92), Arkansas St., Louisiana Tech, Northern Illinois and SW Louisiana in 1992 (all four will begin play in '93 in football only). **Withdrew later** (5): UC-Santa Barbara in 1972, CS-Los Angeles in 1974, San Diego St. in 1976, Fresno St. in 1991 (left for WAC after '91 season), Long Beach St. in 1991 (dropped football as I-AA*sport after '91 season). Renamed **Big West** in 1988.

   Current playing membership (7): CS-Fullerton, Nevada-Reno, New Mexico St., Pacific, San Jose St. UNLV and Utah St.

   Multiple titles: San Jose St.(8); Fresno St.(6); San Diego St.(5); Long Beach St.(3); CS-Fullerton St. and Utah St.(2).

Year		Year		Year		Year	
1969	San Diego St. (6-0)	1975	San Jose St. (5-0)	1981	San Jose St. (5-0)	1988	Fresno St. (7-0)
1970	Long Beach St. (5-1)	1976	San Jose St. (4-0)	1982	Fresno St. (6-0)	1989	Fresno St. (7-0)
	& San Diego St. (5-1)	1977	Fresno St. (4-0)	1983	CS-Fullerton (5-1)	1990	San Jose St. (7-0)
1971	Long Beach St. (5-1)	1978	San Jose St. (4-1)	1984	CS-Fullerton (6-1)**	1991	Fresno St. (6-1)
1972	San Diego St. (4-0)		& Utah St. (4-1)	1985	Fresno St. (7-0)		& San Jose St. (6-1)
1973	San Diego St. (3-0-1)	1979	Utah St. (4-0-1)*	1986	San Jose St. (7-0)		
1974	San Diego St. (4-0)	1980	Long Beach St. (5-0)	1987	San Jose St. (7-0)		

*San Jose St. (4-0-1) forfeited share of title in 1979. **UNLV (7-0) forfeited title in 1984.

Mid-American Conference

Founded in 1946. **Charter members** (6): Butler, Cincinnati, Miami of Ohio, Ohio University, Western Michigan and Western Reserve (Miami and WMU began play in '48). **Admitted later** (9): Kent St. (now Kent) and Toledo in 1951 (Toledo began play in '52), Bowling Green in 1952, Marshall in 1954, Central Michigan and Eastern Michigan in 1972 (CMU began play in '75, EMU in '76), Ball St. and Northern Illinois in 1973 (both began play in '75), Akron in 1991 (began play in '92). **Withdrew later** (5): Butler in 1950, Cincinnati in 1953, Western Reserve in 1955, Marshall in 1969, Northern Ill. in 1986.

   Current playing membership (10): Akron, Ball St., Bowling Green, Central Michigan, Eastern Michigan, Kent, Miami-OH, Ohio University, Toledo and Western Michigan.

   Multiple titles: Miami-OH (15); Bowling Green (9); Toledo (7); Ohio University (5); Cincinnati (4); Ball St. and Central Michigan (3); Western Michigan (2).

Year		Year		Year		Year	
1947	Cincinnati (3-1)	1958	Miami-OH (5-0)	1968	Ohio Univ. (6-0)	1981	Toledo (8-1)
1948	Miami-OH (4-0)	1959	Bowling Green (6-0)	1969	Toledo (5-0)	1982	Bowling Green (7-2)
1949	Cincinnati (4-0)	1960	Ohio Univ. (6-0)	1970	Toledo (5-0)	1983	Northern Ill. (8-1)
1950	Miami-OH (4-0)	1961	Bowling Green (5-1)	1971	Toledo (5-0)	1984	Toledo (7-1-1)
1951	Cincinnati (3-0)	1962	Bowling Green (5-0-1)	1972	Kent St. (4-1)	1985	Bowling Green (9-0)
1952	Cincinnati (3-0)	1963	Ohio Univ. (5-1)	1973	Miami-OH (5-0)	1986	Miami-OH (6-2)
1953	Ohio Univ. (5-0-1)	1964	Bowling Green (5-1)	1974	Miami-OH (5-0)	1987	Eastern Mich. (7-1)
	& Miami-OH (3-0-1)	1965	Bowling Green (5-1)	1975	Miami-OH (6-0)	1988	Western Mich. (7-1)
1954	Miami-OH (4-0)		& Miami-OH (5-1)	1976	Ball St. (4-1)	1989	Ball St. (6-1-1)
1955	Miami-OH (5-0)	1966	Miami-OH (5-1)	1977	Miami-OH (5-0)	1990	Central Mich. (7-1)
1956	Bowling Green (5-0-1)		& Western Mich. (5-1)	1978	Ball St. (8-0)		& Toledo (7-1)
	& Miami-OH (4-0-1)	1967	Toledo (5-1)	1979	Central Mich. (8-0-1)	1991	Bowling Green (8-0)
1957	Miami-OH (5-0)		& Ohio Univ. (5-1)	1980	Central Mich. (7-2)		

Pacific-10 Conference

Originally founded in 1915 as Pacific Coast Conference. **Charter members** (4): California, Oregon, Oregon St. and Washington. **Admitted later** (6): Washington St. in 1917, Stanford in 1918, Idaho and USC (Southern Cal) in 1922, Montana in 1924, UCLA in 1928. **Withdrew later** (1): Montana in 1950.

   The **PCC** dissolved in 1959 and the **AAWU** (Athletic Assn. of Western Universities) was founded. **Charter members** (5): California, Stanford, UCLA, USC and Washington. **Admitted later** (5): Washington St. in 1962, Oregon and Oregon St. in 1964, Arizona and Arizona St. in 1978. Conference renamed **Pac-8** in 1968 and **Pac-10** in 1978.

   Current playing membership (10): Arizona, Arizona St., California, Oregon, Oregon St., Stanford, UCLA, USC, Washington and Washington St.

   Multiple titles: USC (29); UCLA (15); California (13); Washington (12); Stanford (10); Oregon and Oregon St. (4); Washington St.(2).

Year		Year		Year		Year	
1916	Washington (3-0-1)	1920	California (3-0)	1925	Washington (5-0)	1929	USC (6-1)
1917	Washington St. (3-0)	1921	California (5-0)	1926	Stanford (4-0)	1930	Washington St. (6-0)
1918	California (3-0)	1922	California (3-0)	1927	USC (4-0-1)	1931	USC (7-0)
1919	Oregon (2-1)	1923	California (5-0)		& Stanford (4-0-1)	1932	USC (6-0)
	& Washington (2-1)	1924	Stanford (3-0-1)	1928	USC (4-0-1)		

Year	Year	Year	Year
1933 Oregon (4-1) & Stanford (4-1)	1946 UCLA (7-0)	1960 Washington (4-0)	1976 USC (7-0)
1934 Stanford (5-0)	1947 USC (6-0)	1961 UCLA (3-1)	1977 Washington (6-1)
1935 California (4-1), Stanford (4-1) & UCLA (4-1)	1948 California (6-0) & Oregon (6-0)	1962 USC (4-0)	1978 USC (6-1)
	1949 California (7-0)	1963 Washington (4-1)	1979 USC (6-0-1)
1936 Washington (6-0-1)	1950 California (5-0-1)	1964 Oregon St. (3-1) & USC (3-1)	1980 Washington (6-1)
1937 California (6-0-1)	1951 Stanford (6-1)	1965 UCLA (4-0)	1981 Washington (6-2)
1938 USC (6-1) & California (6-1)	1952 USC (6-0)	1966 USC (4-1)	1982 UCLA (5-1-1)
1939 USC (5-0-2) & UCLA (5-0-3)	1953 UCLA (6-1)	1967 USC (6-1)	1983 UCLA (6-1-1)
	1954 UCLA (6-0)	1968 USC (6-0)	1984 USC (7-1)
	1955 UCLA (6-0)	1969 USC (6-0)	1985 UCLA (6-2)
1940 Stanford (7-0)	1956 Oregon St. (6-1-1)		1986 Arizona St. (5-1-1)
1941 Oregon St. (7-2)	1957 Oregon (6-2) & Oregon St. (6-2)	1970 Stanford (6-1)	1987 USC (7-1) & UCLA (7-1)
1942 UCLA (6-1)		1971 Stanford (6-1)	
1943 USC (4-0)	1958 California (6-1)	1972 USC (7-0)	1988 USC (8-0)
1944 USC (3-0-2)	1959 Washington (3-1), USC (3-1) & UCLA (3-1)	1973 USC (7-0)	1989 USC (6-0-1)
1945 USC (5-1)		1974 USC (6-0-1)	
		1975 UCLA (6-1) & California (6-1)	1990 Washington (7-1)
			1991 Washington (8-0)

Southeastern Conference

Founded in 1933 when charter members all left Southern Conference to form SEC. **Charter members** (13): Alabama, Auburn, Florida, Georgia, Georgia Tech, Kentucky, LSU (Louisiana St.), Mississippi, Mississippi St., Sewanee, Tennessee, Tulane and Vanderbilt. **Admitted later** (2): Arkansas and South Carolina in 1990 (both began play in '92). **Withdrew later** (3): Sewanee in 1940, Georgia Tech in 1964, Tulane in 1966.
   Current playing membership (12): Alabama, Arkansas, Auburn, Florida, Georgia, Kentucky, LSU, Mississippi, Mississippi St., South Carolina, Tennessee and Vanderbilt.
   Multiple titles: Alabama (19); Tennessee (11); Georgia (10); LSU (7); Mississippi (6); Auburn and Georgia Tech (5); Kentucky and Tulane (3); Florida (2, one vacated).

Year	Year	Year	Year
1933 Alabama (5-0-1)	1948 Georgia (6-0)	1965 Alabama (6-1-1)	1981 Georgia (6-0) & Alabama (6-0)
1934 Tulane (8-0) & Alabama (7-0)	1949 Tulane (5-1)	1966 Alabama (6-0) & Georgia (6-0)	1982 Georgia (6-0)
1935 LSU (5-0)	1950 Kentucky (5-1)	1967 Tennessee (6-0)	1983 Auburn (6-0)
1936 LSU (6-0)	1951 Georgia Tech (7-0) & Tennessee (5-0)	1968 Georgia (5-0-1)	1984 Florida (5-0-1)*
1937 Alabama (6-0)		1969 Tennessee (5-1)	1985 Florida (5-1)† & Tennessee (5-1)
1938 Tennessee (7-0)	1952 Georgia Tech (6-0)		
1939 Tennessee (6-0), Georgia Tech (6-0) & Tulane (5-0)	1953 Alabama (4-0-3)	1970 LSU (5-0)	1986 LSU (5-1)
	1954 Mississippi (5-1)	1971 Alabama (7-0)	1987 Auburn (5-0-1)
	1955 Mississippi (5-1)	1972 Alabama (7-1)	1988 Auburn (6-1) & LSU (6-1)
	1956 Tennessee (6-0)	1973 Alabama (8-0)	
1940 Tennessee (5-0)	1957 Auburn (7-0)	1974 Alabama (6-0)	1989 Alabama (6-1), Tennessee (6-1) & Auburn (6-1)
1941 Mississippi St. (4-0-1)	1958 LSU (6-0)	1975 Alabama (6-0)	
1942 Georgia (6-1)	1959 Georgia (7-0)	1976 Georgia (5-1) & Kentucky (5-1)	
1943 Georgia Tech (3-0)	1960 Mississippi (5-0-1)	1977 Alabama (7-0) & Kentucky (6-0)	1990 Florida (6-1)† & Tennessee (5-1-1)
1944 Georgia Tech (4-0)	1961 Alabama (7-0) & LSU (6-0)		
1945 Alabama (6-0)		1978 Alabama (6-0)	1991 Florida (7-0)
1946 Georgia (6-0) & Tennessee (5-0)	1962 Mississippi (6-0)	1979 Alabama (6-0)	
	1963 Mississippi (5-0-1)		
1947 Mississippi (6-1)	1964 Alabama (8-0)	1980 Georgia (6-0)	

*Title vacated   †On probation, ineligible for championship.

Southwest Conference

Founded in 1914 as Southwest Athletic Conference. **Charter members** (8): Arkansas, Baylor, Oklahoma, Oklahoma A&M (now Oklahoma St.), Rice, Southwestern, Texas, Texas A&M. **Admitted later** (5): SMU (Southern Methodist) in 1918, Phillips in 1920, TCU (Texas Christian) in 1923, Texas Tech in 1956 (began play in 1960), Houston in 1971 (began play in 1976). **Withdrew later** (5): Southwestern in 1917, Oklahoma in 1920, Phillips in 1921, Oklahoma A&M in 1925, Arkansas in 1990 (left for SEC after '91 season).
   Current playing membership (8): Baylor, Houston, Rice, SMU, Texas, Texas A&M, TCU and Texas Tech.
   Multiple titles: Texas (24); Texas A&M (15); Arkansas (14, one vacated); SMU (10); TCU (8); Rice (6); Baylor and Houston (4).

Year	Year	Year	Year
1914 No champion	1920 Texas (5-0)	1926 SMU (5-0)	1932 TCU (6-0)
1915 Oklahoma (3-0)	1921 Texas A&M (3-0-2)	1927 Texas A&M (4-0-1)	1933 Arkansas (4-1)*
1916 No champion	1922 Baylor (5-0)	1928 Texas (5-1)	1934 Rice (5-1)
1917 Texas A&M (2-0)	1923 SMU (5-0)	1929 TCU (4-0-1)	1935 SMU (6-0)
1918 No champion	1924 Baylor (4-0-1)	1930 Texas (4-1)	1936 Arkansas (5-1)
1919 Texas A&M (4-0)	1925 Texas A&M (4-1)	1931 SMU (5-0-1)	1937 Rice (4-1-1)

Major Conference Champions (Cont.)
Southwest Conference

Year		Year		Year		Year	
1938	TCU (6-0)	1953	Rice (5-1)	1967	Texas A&M (6-1)	1980	Baylor (8-0)
1939	Texas A&M (6-0)		& Texas (5-1)	1968	Arkansas (6-1)	1981	SMU (7-1)†
1940	Texas A&M (5-1)	1954	Arkansas (5-1)		& Texas (6-1)		& Texas (6-1-1)
	& SMU (5-1)	1955	TCU (5-1)	1969	Texas (7-0)	1982	SMU (7-0-1)
1941	Texas A&M (5-1)	1956	Texas A&M (6-0)			1983	Texas (8-0)
1942	Texas (5-1)	1957	Rice (5-1)	1970	Texas (7-0)	1984	SMU (6-2)
1943	Texas (5-0)	1958	TCU (5-1)	1971	Texas (6-1)		& Houston (6-2)
1944	TCU (3-1-1)	1959	Texas (5-1),	1972	Texas (7-0)	1985	Texas A&M (7-1)
1945	Texas (5-1)		TCU (5-1)	1973	Texas (7-0)	1986	Texas A&M (7-1)
1946	Rice (5-1)		& Arkansas (5-1)	1974	Baylor (6-1)	1987	Texas A&M (6-1)
	& Arkansas (5-1)	1960	Arkansas (6-1)	1975	Arkansas (6-1),	1988	Arkansas (7-0)
1947	SMU (5-0-1)	1961	Texas (6-1)		Texas (6-1)	1989	Arkansas (7-1)
1948	SMU (5-0-1)		& Arkansas (6-1)		& Texas A&M (6-1)		
1949	Rice (6-0)	1962	Texas (6-0-1)	1976	Houston (7-1)	1990	Texas (8-0)
		1963	Texas (7-0)		& Texas Tech (7-1)	1991	Texas A&M (8-0)
1950	Texas (6-0)	1964	Arkansas (7-0)	1977	Texas (8-0)		
1951	TCU (5-1)	1965	Arkansas (7-0)	1978	Houston (7-1)		
1952	Texas (6-0)	1966	SMU (6-1)	1979	Houston (7-1)		
					& Arkansas (7-1)		

*Title vacated.   †On probation, ineligible for championship.

Western Athletic Conference

Founded in 1962 when charter members left the Skyline and Border Conferences to form the WAC. **Charter members** (6): Arizona (independent); Arizona St.(from Border); BYU (Brigham Young), New Mexico, Utah and Wyoming (from Skyline). **Admitted later** (6): Colorado St. and UTEP (Texas-El Paso) in 1967 (both began play in '68), San Diego St. in 1978, Hawaii in 1979, Air Force in 1980, Fresno St. in 1991 (began play in '92). **Withdrew later** (2): Arizona and Arizona St. in 1978.

Current playing membership (10): Air Force, BYU, Colorado St., Fresno St., Hawaii, New Mexico, San Diego St., UTEP, Utah and Wyoming.

Multiple titles: BYU (15); Arizona St.(7); Wyoming (6); New Mexico (3); Arizona (2).

Year		Year		Year		Year	
1962	New Mexico (2-1-1)	1970	Arizona St.(7-0)	1977	Arizona St.(6-1)	1985	Air Force (7-1)
1963	New Mexico (3-1)	1971	Arizona St.(7-0)		& BYU (6-1)		& BYU (7-1)
1964	Utah (3-1),	1972	Arizona St.(5-1)	1978	BYU (5-1)	1986	San Diego St.(7-1)
	New Mexico (3-1)	1973	Arizona St.(6-1)	1979	BYU (7-0)	1987	Wyoming (8-0)
	& Arizona (3-1)		& Arizona (6-1)	1980	BYU (6-1)	1988	Wyoming (8-0)
1965	BYU (4-1)	1974	BYU (6-0-1)	1981	BYU (7-1)	1989	BYU (8-0)
1966	Wyoming (5-0)	1975	Arizona St.(7-0)	1982	BYU (7-1)		
1967	Wyoming (5-0)	1976	BYU (6-1)	1983	BYU (7-0)	1990	BYU (7-1)
1968	Wyoming (6-1)		& Wyoming (6-1)	1984	BYU (8-0)	1991	BYU (7-0-1)
1969	Arizona St.(6-1)						

Ivy League

First called the ''Ivy League'' in 1937 by sportswriter Caswell Adams of the *New York Herald Tribune*. Unofficial conference of 10 eastern teams was occasionally referred to as the ''Old 10'' and included: Army, Brown, Columbia, Cornell, Dartmouth, Harvard, Navy, Pennsylvania, Princeton and Yale. Army and Navy were dropped from the group after 1940. **League formalized** in 1954 for play beginning in 1956. **Charter members** (8): Brown, Columbia, Cornell, Dartmouth, Harvard, Pennsylvania, Princeton, and Yale. League downgraded from Division I to Division I-AA after 1977 season. **Current playing membership:** the same.

Multiple titles: Dartmouth (15); Yale (12); Harvard (8); Penn (7); Princeton (6); Cornell (3).

Year		Year		Year		Year	
1955	Princeton (6-1)	1966	Dartmouth (6-1),	1974	Harvard (6-1)	1983	Harvard (5-1-1)
1956	Yale (7-0)		Harvard (6-1)		& Yale (6-1)		& Penn (5-1-1)
1957	Princeton (6-1)		& Princeton (6-1)	1975	Harvard (6-1)	1984	Penn (7-0)
1958	Dartmouth (6-1)	1967	Yale (7-0)	1976	Brown (6-1)	1985	Penn (7-0)
1959	Penn (6-1)	1968	Harvard (6-0-1)		& Yale (6-1)	1986	Penn (7-0)
			& Yale (6-0-1)	1977	Yale (6-1)	1987	Harvard (6-1)
1960	Yale (7-0)	1969	Dartmouth (6-1),	1978	Dartmouth (6-1)	1988	Penn (7-0)
1961	Columbia (6-1)		Yale (6-1)	1979	Yale (6-1)		& Cornell (6-1)
	& Harvard (6-1)		& Princeton (6-1)			1989	Princeton (6-1)
1962	Dartmouth (7-0)	1970	Dartmouth (7-0)	1980	Yale (6-1)		& Yale (6-1)
1963	Dartmouth (5-2)	1971	Cornell (6-1)	1981	Yale (6-1)		
	& Princeton (5-2)		& Dartmouth (6-1)		& Dartmouth (6-1)	1990	Cornell (6-1)
1964	Princeton (7-0)	1972	Dartmouth (5-1-1)	1982	Harvard (5-2),		& Dartmouth (6-1)
1965	Dartmouth (7-0)	1973	Dartmouth (6-1)		Penn (5-2)	1991	Dartmouth (6-0-1)
					& Dartmouth (5-2)		

Annual NCAA Division I-A Leaders

Rushing

Individual championship decided on Rushing Yards (1937–69), and on Yards Per Game (since 1970).

Year		Car	Yards
1937	Byron (Whizzer) White, Colorado	181	1121
1938	Len Eshmont, Fordham	132	831
1939	John Polansky, Wake Forest	137	882
1940	Al Ghesquiere, Detroit	146	957
1941	Frank Sinkwich, Georgia	209	1103
1942	Rudy Mobley, Hardin-Simmons	187	1281
1943	Creighton Miller, Notre Dame	151	911
1944	Red Williams, Minnesota	136	911
1945	Bob Fenimore, Oklahoma A&M*	142	1048
1946	Rudy Mobley, Hardin-Simmons	227	1262
1947	Wilton Davis, Hardin-Simmons	193	1173
1948	Fred Wendt, Texas Mines*	184	1570
1949	John Dottley, Ole Miss	208	1312
1950	Wilford White, Arizona St	199	1502
1951	Ollie Matson, San Francisco	245	1566
1952	Howie Waugh, Tulsa	164	1372
1953	J.C.Caroline, Illinois	194	1256
1954	Art Luppino, Arizona	179	1359
1955	Art Luppino, Arizona	209	1313
1956	Jim Crawford, Wyoming	200	1104
1957	Leon Burton, Arizona St	117	1126
1958	Dick Bass, Pacific	205	1361
1959	Pervis Atkins, New Mexico St	130	971
1960	Bob Gaiters, New Mexico St	197	1338
1961	Jim Pilot, New Mexico St	191	1278
1962	Jim Pilot, New Mexico St	208	1247
1963	Dave Casinelli, Memphis St	219	1016
1964	Brian Piccolo, Wake Forest	252	1044

Year		Car	Yards
1965	Mike Garrett, USC	267	1440
1966	Ray McDonald, Idaho	259	1329
1967	O.J.Simpson, USC	266	1415
1968	O.J.Simpson, USC	355	1709
1969	Steve Owens, Oklahoma	358	1523

Year		Car	Yards	P/Gm
1970	Ed Marinaro, Cornell	285	1425	158.3
1971	Ed Marinaro, Cornell	356	1881	209.0
1972	Pete VanValkenburg, BYU	232	1386	138.6
1973	Mark Kellar, Northern Ill.	291	1719	156.3
1974	Louie Giammona, Utah St.	329	1534	153.4
1975	Ricky Bell, USC	357	1875	170.5
1976	Tony Dorsett, Pittsburgh	338	1948	177.1
1977	Earl Campbell, Texas	267	1744	158.5
1978	Billy Sims, Oklahoma	231	1762	160.2
1979	Charles White, USC	293	1803	180.3
1980	George Rogers, S.Carolina	297	1781	161.9
1981	Marcus Allen, USC	403	2342	212.9
1982	Ernest Anderson, Okla.St	353	1877	170.6
1983	Mike Rozier, Nebraska	275	2148	179.0
1984	Keith Byars, Ohio St	313	1655	150.5
1985	Lorenzo White, Mich.St	386	1908	173.5
1986	Paul Palmer, Temple	346	1866	169.6
1987	Ickey Woods, UNLV	259	1658	150.7
1988	Barry Sanders, Okla.St	344	2628	238.9
1989	Anthony Thompson, Ind	358	1793	163.0
1990	Gerald Hudson, Okla.St	279	1642	149.3
1991	Marshall Faulk, S.Diego St	201	1429	158.8

*Oklahoma A&M is now Oklahoma St. and Texas Mines is now UTEP.

All-Purpose Running

Championship decided on Running Yards Per Game.

Year		Yards	P/Gm
1937	Byron (Whizzer) White, Colorado	1970	246.3
1938	Parker Hall, Ole Miss	1420	129.1
1939	Tom Harmon, Michigan	1208	151.0
1940	Tom Harmon, Michigan	1312	164.0
1941	Bill Dudley, Virginia	1674	186.0
1942	Records not available		
1943	Stan Koslowski, Holy Cross	1411	176.4
1944	Red Williams, Minnesota	1467	163.0
1945	Bob Fenimore, Oklahoma A&M*	1577	197.1
1946	Rudy Mobley, Hardin-Simmons	1765	176.5
1947	Wilton Davis, Hardin-Simmons	1798	179.8
1948	Lou Kusserow, Columbia	1737	193.0
1949	Johnny Papit, Virginia	1611	179.0
1950	Wilford White, Arizona St	2065	206.5
1951	Ollie Matson, San Francisco	2037	226.3
1952	Billy Vessels, Oklahoma	1512	151.2
1953	J.C.Caroline, Illinois	1470	163.3
1954	Art Luppino, Arizona	2193	219.3
1955	Jim Swink, TCU	1702	170.2
	& Art Luppino, Arizona	1702	170.2
1956	Jack Hill, Utah St	1691	169.1
1957	Overton Curtis, Utah St	1608	160.8
1958	Dick Bass, Pacific	1878	187.8
1959	Pervis Atkins, New Mexico St	1800	180.0
1960	Pervis Atkins, New Mexico St	1613	161.3
1961	Jim Pilot, New Mexico St	1606	160.6
1962	Gary Wood, Cornell	1395	155.0
1963	Gary Wood, Cornell	1508	167.6

Year		Yards	P/Gm
1964	Donny Anderson, Texas Tech	1710	171.0
1965	Floyd Little, Syracuse	1990	199.0
1966	Frank Quayle, Virginia	1616	161.6
1967	O.J.Simpson, USC	1700	188.9
1968	O.J.Simpson, USC	1966	196.6
1969	Lynn Moore, Army	1795	179.5
1970	Don McCauley, North Carolina	2021	183.7
1971	Ed Marinaro, Cornell	1932	214.7
1972	Howard Stevens, Louisville	2132	213.2
1973	Willard Harrell, Pacific	1777	177.7
1974	Louie Giammona, Utah St	1984	198.4
1975	Louie Giammona, Utah St	2045	185.9
1976	Tony Dorsett, Pittsburgh	2021	183.7
1977	Earl Campbell, Texas	1855	168.6
1978	Charles White, USC	2096	174.7
1979	Charles White, USC	1941	194.1
1980	Marcus Allen, USC	1794	179.4
1981	Marcus Allen, USC	2559	232.6
1982	Carl Monroe, Utah	2036	185.1
1983	Napoleon McCallum, Navy	2385	216.8
1984	Keith Byars, Ohio St	2284	207.6
1985	Napoleon McCallum, Navy	2330	211.8
1986	Paul Palmer, Temple	2633	239.4
1987	Eric Wilkerson, Kent St	2074	188.6
1988	Barry Sanders, Oklahoma St.	3250	295.5
1989	Mike Pringle, CS-Fullerton	2690	244.6
1990	Glyn Milburn, Stanford	2222	202.0
1991	Ryan Benjamin, Pacific	2995	249.6

*Oklahoma A&M is now Oklahoma St.

Annual NCAA Division I-A Leaders (Cont.)

Total Offense

Individual championship decided on Total Yards (1937–69), and on Yards Per Game (since 1970).

Year		Plays	Yards
1937	Byron (Whizzer) White, Colorado	224	1596
1938	Davey O'Brien, TCU	291	1847
1939	Kenny Washington, UCLA	259	1370
1940	Johnny Knolla, Creighton	298	1420
1941	Bud Schwenk, Washington-MO	354	1928
1942	Frank Sinkwich, Georgia	341	2187
1943	Bob Hoernschemeyer, Indiana	355	1648
1944	Bob Fenimore, Oklahoma A&M*	241	1758
1945	Bob Fenimore, Oklahoma A&M	203	1641
1946	Travis Bidwell, Auburn	339	1715
1947	Fred Enke, Arizona	329	1941
1948	Stan Heath, Nevada-Reno	233	1992
1949	Johnny Bright, Drake	275	1950
1950	Johnny Bright, Drake	320	2400
1951	Dick Kazmaier, Princeton	272	1827
1952	Ted Marchibroda, Detroit	305	1813
1953	Paul Larson, California	262	1572
1954	George Shaw, Oregon	276	1536
1955	George Welsh, Navy	203	1348
1956	John Brodie, Stanford	295	1642
1957	Bob Newman, Washington St	263	1444
1958	Dick Bass, Pacific	218	1440
1959	Dick Norman, Stanford	319	2018
1960	Bill Kilmer, UCLA	292	1889
1961	Dave Hoppmann, Iowa St	320	1638
1962	Terry Baker, Oregon St	318	2276
1963	George Mira, Miami-FL	394	2318
1964	Jerry Rhome, Tulsa	470	3128

Year		Plays	Yards
1965	Bill Anderson, Tulsa	580	3343
1966	Virgil Carter, BYU	388	2545
1967	Sal Olivas, New Mexico St	368	2184
1968	Greg Cook Cincinnati	507	3210
1969	Dennis Shaw, San Diego St	388	3197

Year		Plays	Yards	P/Gm
1970	Pat Sullivan, Auburn	333	2856	285.6
1971	Gary Huff, Florida St	386	2653	241.2
1972	Don Strock, Va.Tech	480	3170	288.2
1973	Jesse Freitas, S.Diego St	410	2901	263.7
1974	Steve Joachim, Temple	331	2227	222.7
1975	Gene Swick, Toledo	490	2706	246.0
1976	Tommy Kramer, Rice	562	3272	297.5
1977	Doug Williams, Grambling	377	3229	293.5
1978	Mike Ford, SMU	459	2957	268.8
1979	Marc Wilson, BYU	488	3580	325.5
1980	Jim McMahon, BYU	540	4627	385.6
1981	Jim McMahon, BYU	487	3458	345.8
1982	Todd Dillon, L.Beach St	585	3587	326.1
1983	Steve Young, BYU	531	4346	395.1
1984	Robbie Bosco, BYU	543	3932	327.7
1985	Jim Everett, Purdue	518	3589	326.3
1986	Mike Perez, San Jose St	425	2969	329.9
1987	Todd Santos, S.Diego St	562	3688	307.3
1988	Scott Mitchell, Utah	589	4299	390.8
1989	Andre Ware, Houston	628	4661	423.7
1990	David Klingler, Houston	704	5221	474.6
1991	Ty Detmer, BYU	478	4001	333.4

*Oklahoma A&M is now Oklahoma St.

Passing

Individual championship decided on Completions (1937-69), on Completions Per Game (1970–78), and on Passing Efficiency rating points (since 1979).

Year		Cmp	Pct	TD	Yds
1937	Davey O'Brien, TCU	94	.402	—	969
1938	Davey O'Brien, TCU	93	.557	—	1457
1939	Kay Eakin, Arkansas	78	.404	—	962
1940	Billy Sewell, Wash.St	86	.494	—	1023
1941	Bud Schwenk, Wash.-MO	114	.487	—	1457
1942	Ray Evans, Kansas	101	.505	—	1117
1943	Johnny Cook, Georgia	73	.465	—	1007
1944	Paul Rickards, Pittsburgh	84	.472	—	997
1945	Al Dekdebrun, Cornell	90	.464	—	1227
1946	Travis Tidwell, Auburn	79	.500	5	943
1947	Charlie Conerly, Ole Miss	133	.571	18	1367
1948	Stan Heath, Nev-Reno	126	.568	22	2005
1949	Adrian Burk, Baylor	110	.576	14	1428
1950	Don Heinrich, Washington	134	.606	14	1846
1951	Don Klosterman, Loyola-CA	159	.505	9	1843
1952	Don Heinrich, Washington	137	.507	13	1647
1953	Bob Garrett, Stanford	118	.576	17	1637
1954	Paul Larson, California	125	.641	10	1537
1955	George Welsh, Navy	94	.627	8	1319
1956	John Brodie, Stanford	139	.579	12	1633
1957	Ken Ford, H-Simmons	115	.561	14	1254
1958	Buddy Humphrey, Baylor	112	.574	7	1316
1959	Dick Norman, Stanford	152	.578	11	1963
1960	Harold Stephens, H-Simm.	145	.566	3	1254
1961	Chon Gallegos, S.Jose St	117	.594	14	1480
1962	Don Trull, Baylor	125	.546	11	1627
1963	Don Trull, Baylor	174	.565	12	2157
1964	Jerry Rhome, Tulsa	224	.687	32	2870
1965	Bill Anderson, Tulsa	296	.582	30	3464

Year		Cmp	Pct	TD	Yds
1966	John Eckman, Wichita St	195	.426	7	2339
1967	Terry Stone, N.Mexico	160	.476	9	1946
1968	Chuck Hixon, SMU	265	.566	21	3103
1969	John Reaves, Florida	222	.561	24	2896

Year		Cmp	P/Gm	TD	Yds
1970	Sonny Sixkiller, Wash	186	18.6	15	2303
1971	Brian Sipe, S.Diego St.	196	17.8	17	2532
1972	Don Strock, Va.Tech	228	20.7	16	3243
1973	Jesse Freitas, S.Diego St	227	20.6	21	2993
1974	Steve Bartkowski, Cal	182	16.5	12	2580
1975	Craig Penrose, S.Diego St.	198	18.0	15	2660
1976	Tommy Kramer, Rice	269	24.5	21	3317
1977	Guy Benjamin, Stanford	208	20.8	19	2521
1978	Steve Dils, Stanford	247	22.5	22	2943

Year		Cmp	TD	Yds	Rating
1979	Turk Schonert, Stanford	148	19	1922	163.0
1980	Jim McMahon, BYU	284	47	4571	176.9
1981	Jim McMahon, BYU	272	30	3555	155.0
1982	Tom Ramsey, UCLA	191	21	2824	153.5
1983	Steve Young, BYU	306	33	3902	168.5
1984	Doug Flutie, BC	233	27	3454	152.9
1985	Jim Harbaugh, Michigan	139	18	1913	163.7
1986	V.Testaverde, Miami-FL	175	26	2557	165.8
1987	Don McPherson, Syracuse	129	22	2341	164.3
1988	Timm Rosenbach, Wash.St	199	23	2791	162.0
1989	Ty Detmer, BYU	265	32	4560	175.6
1990	Shawn Moore, Virginia	144	21	2262	160.7
1991	Elvis Grbac, Michigan	152	24	1955	169.0

Receiving

Championship decided on Passes Caught (1937–69), and on Catches Per Game (since 1970).

Year		No	TD	Yds
1937	Jim Benton, Arkansas	47	—	754
1938	Sam Boyd Baylor	32	—	537
1939	Ken Kavanaugh, LSU	30	—	467
1940	Eddie Bryant, Virginia	30	—	222
1941	Hank Stanton, Arizona	50	—	820
1942	Bill Rogers, Texas A&M	39	—	432
1943	Neil Armstrong, Okla.A&M*	39	—	317
1944	Reid Moseley, Georgia	32	—	506
1945	Reid Moseley, Georgia	31	—	662
1946	Neil Armstrong, Okla.A&M	32	1	479
1947	Barney Poole, Ole Miss	52	8	513
1948	Red O'Quinn, Wake Forest	39	7	605
1949	Art Weiner, N.Carolina	52	7	762
1950	Gordon Cooper, Denver	46	8	569
1951	Dewey McConnell, Wyoming	47	9	725
1952	Ed Brown, Fordham	57	6	774
1953	John Carson, Georgia	45	4	663
1954	Jim Hanifan, California	44	7	569
1955	Hank Burnine, Missouri	44	2	594
1956	Art Powell, San Jose St	40	5	583
1957	Stuart Vaughan, Utah	53	5	756
1958	Dave Hibbert, Arizona	61	4	606
1959	Chris Burford, Stanford	61	6	756
1960	Hugh Campbell, Wash.St.	66	10	881
1961	Hugh Campbell, Wash.St.	53	5	723
1962	Vern Burke, Oregon St	69	10	1007
1963	Lawrence Elkins, Baylor	70	8	873
1964	Howard Twilley, Tulsa	95	13	1178

*Oklahoma A&M now Oklahoma St.

Year		No	TD	Yds
1965	Howard Twilley, Tulsa	134	16	1779
1966	Glenn Meltzer, Wichita St	91	4	1115
1967	Bob Goodridge, Vanderbilt	79	6	1114
1968	Ron Sellers, Florida St	86	12	1496
1969	Jerry Hendren, Idaho	95	12	1452

Year		No	P/Gm	TD	Yds
1970	Mike Mikolayunas, Davidson	87	8.7	8	1128
1971	Tom Reynolds, S.Diego St	67	6.7	7	1070
1972	Tom Forzani, Utah St.	85	7.7	8	1169
1973	Jay Miller, BYU	100	9.1	8	1181
1974	Dwight McDonald, S.Diego St	86	7.8	7	1157
1975	Bob Farnham, Brown	56	6.2	2	701
1976	Billy Ryckman, La.Tech	77	7.0	10	1382
1977	Wayne Tolleson, W.Carolina	73	6.6	7	1101
1978	Dave Petzke, Northern Ill.	91	8.3	11	1217
1979	Rick Beasley, Appalach.St	74	6.7	12	1205
1980	Dave Young, Purdue	67	6.1	8	917
1981	Pete Harvey, N.Texas St.	57	6.3	3	743
1982	Vincent White, Stanford	68	6.8	8	677
1983	Keith Edwards, Vanderbilt	97	8.8	8	909
1984	David Williams, Illinois	101	9.2	8	1278
1985	Rodney Carter, Purdue	98	8.9	4	1099
1986	Mark Templeton, L.Beach St	99	9.0	2	688
1987	Jason Phillips, Houston	99	9.0	3	875
1988	Jason Phillips, Houston	108	9.8	15	1444
1989	Manny Hazard, Houston	142	12.9	22	1689
1990	Manny Hazard, Houston	78	7.8	9	946
1991	Fred Gilbert, Houston	106	9.6	7	957

Scoring

Championship decided on Total Points (1937–69), and on Points Per Game (since 1970).

Year		TD	XP	FG	Pts
1937	Byron (Whizzer) White, Colo	16	23	1	122
1938	Parker Hall, Ole Miss	11	7	0	73
1939	Tom Harmon, Michigan	14	15	1	102
1940	Tom Harmon, Michigan	16	18	1	117
1941	Bill Dudley, Virginia	18	23	1	134
1942	Bob Steuber, Missouri	18	13	0	121
1943	Steve Van Buren, LSU	14	14	0	98
1944	Glenn Davis, Army	20	0	0	120
1945	Doc Blanchard, Army	19	1	0	115
1946	Gene Roberts, Tenn-Chatt	18	9	0	117
1947	Lou Gambino, Maryland	16	0	0	96
1948	Fred Wendt, Texas Mines*	20	32	0	152
1949	George Thomas, Oklahoma	19	3	0	117
1950	Bobby Reynolds, Oklahoma	22	25	0	157
1951	Ollie Matson, San Francisco	21	0	0	126
1952	Jackie Parker, Miss.St.	16	24	0	120
1953	Earl Lindley, Utah St.	13	3	0	81
1954	Art Luppino, Arizona	24	22	0	166
1955	Jim Swink, TCU	20	5	0	125
1956	Clendon Thomas, Oklahoma	18	0	0	108
1957	Leon Burton, Ariz.St.	16	0	0	96
1958	Dick Bass, Pacific	18	8	0	116
1959	Pervis Atkins, N.Mexico St.	17	5	0	107
1960	Bob Gaiters, N.Mexico St.	23	7	0	145
1961	Jim Pilot, N.Mexico St.	21	12	0	138
1962	Jerry Logan, W.Texas St.	13	32	0	110
1963	Cosmo Iacavazzi, Princeton	14	0	0	84
	& Dave Casinelli, Memphis St.	14	0	0	84
1964	Brian Piccolo, Wake Forest	17	9	0	111

*Texas Mines is now UTEP.

Year		TD	XP	FG	Pts
1965	Howard Twilley, Tulsa	16	31	0	127
1966	Ken Hebert, Houston	11	41	2	113
1967	Leroy Keyes, Purdue	19	0	0	114
1968	Jim O'Brien, Cincinnati	12	31	13	142
1969	Steve Owens, Oklahoma	23	0	0	138

Year		TD	XP	FG	Pts	P/Gm
1970	Brian Bream, Air Force	20	0	0	120	12.0
	& Gary Kosins, Dayton	18	0	0	108	12.0
1971	Ed Marinaro, Cornell	24	4	0	148	16.4
1972	Harold Henson, Ohio St.	20	0	0	120	12.0
1973	Jim Jennings, Rutgers	21	2	0	128	11.6
1974	Bill Marek, Wisconsin	19	0	0	114	12.7
1975	Pete Johnson, Ohio St.	25	0	0	150	13.6
1976	Tony Dorsett, Pitt	22	2	0	134	12.2
1977	Earl Campbell, Texas	19	0	0	114	10.4
1978	Billy Sims, Oklahoma	20	0	0	120	10.9
1979	Billy Sims, Oklahoma	22	0	0	132	12.0
1980	Sammy Wilder, So.Miss	20	0	0	120	10.9
1981	Marcus Allen, USC	23	0	0	138	12.5
1982	Greg Allen, Fla.St	21	0	0	126	11.5
1983	Mike Rozier, Nebraska	29	0	0	174	14.5
1984	Keith Byars, Ohio St	24	0	0	144	13.1
1985	Bernard White, B.Green	19	0	0	114	10.4
1986	Steve Bartalo, Colo.St	19	0	0	114	10.4
1987	Paul Hewitt, S.Diego St	24	0	0	144	12.0
1988	Barry Sanders, Okla.St	39	0	0	234	21.3
1989	Anthony Thompson, Ind	25	4	0	154	14.0
1990	Stacey Robinson, No.Ill	19	6	0	120	10.9
1991	Marshall Faulk, S.D.St	23	2	0	140	15.6

All-Time NCAA Division I-A Individual Leaders

CAREER

Through the 1991 regular season. Players with eligibility remaining after the 1991 season in **bold** type. Note that the NCAA does not recognize active players among career Per Game leaders.

Total Offense

Yards Gained	Years	Yards
Ty Detmer, BYU	1988-91	14,665
Doug Flutie, Boston College	1981-84	11,317
Todd Santos, San Diego St	1984-87	10,513
Kevin Sweeney, Fresno St.	1983-86	10,252
Brian McClure, Bowling Green	1982-85	9,774

Yards Per Game	Years	Yards	P/Gm
Ty Detmer, BYU	1988-91	14,665	318.8
Mike Perez, San Jose St	1986-87	6,182	309.1
Doug Gaynor, L.Beach St	1984-85	6,710	305.0
Tony Eason, Illinois	1981-82	6,589	299.5
David Klingler, Houston	1988-91	9,327	291.5

Rushing

Yards Gained	Years	Yards
Tony Dorsett, Pitt	1973-76	6082
Charles White, USC	1976-79	5598
Herschel Walker, Georgia	1980-82	5259
Archie Griffin, Ohio St	1972-75	5177
Darren Lewis, Texas A&M	1987-90	5012

Yards Per Game	Years	Yards	P/Gm
Ed Marinaro, Cornell	1969-71	4715	174.6
O.J.Simpson, USC	1967-68	3124	164.4
Herschel Walker, Georgia	1980-82	5259	159.4
Tony Dorsett, Pitt	1973-76	6082	141.4
Mike Rozier, Nebraska	1981-83	4780	136.6

Passing

(Minimum 500 Completions)

Passing Efficiency	Years	Rating
Ty Detmer, BYU	1988-91	162.7
Jim McMahon, BYU	1977-78,80-81	156.9
Steve Young, BYU	1982,84-86	149.8
Troy Aikman, Okla-UCLA	1984-85,87-88	149.7
Robbie Bosco, BYU	1981-83	149.4

Yards Gained	Years	Yards
Ty Detmer, BYU	1988-91	15,031
Todd Santos, San Diego St	1984-87	11,425
Kevin Sweeney, Fresno St.	1983-86	10,623
Doug Flutie, Boston College	1981-84	10,579
Brian McClure, Bowling Green	1982-85	10,280

Completions	Years	No
Ty Detmer, BYU	1988-91	958
Todd Santos, San Diego St	1984-87	910
Brian McClure, Bowling Green	1982-85	900
Ben Bennett, Duke	1980-83	820
John Elway, Stanford	1979-82	774

Receiving

Catches	Years	No
Terance Mathis, New Mexico	1985-87,89	263
Mark Templeton, Long Beach St	1983-86	262
Howard Twilley, Tulsa	1963-65	261
David Williams, Illinois	1983-85	245
Marc Zeno, Tulane	1984-87	236

Catches Per Game	Years	No	P/Gm
Manny Hazard, Houston	1989-90	220	10.5
Howard Twilley, Tulsa	1963-65	261	10.0
Jason Phillips, Houston	1987-88	207	9.4
Neal Sweeney, Tulsa	1965-66	134	7.4
David Williams, Illinois	1983-85	245	7.4

Yards Gained	Years	No	Yards
Terance Mathis, New Mexico	1985-87,89	263	4254
Marc Zeno, Tulane	1984-87	236	3725
Ron Sellers, Florida St.	1966-68	212	3598
Elmo Wright, Houston	1968-70	153	3347
Howard Twilley, Tulsa	1963-65	261	3343
Gerald Harp, W.Carolina	1977-80	197	3305

Scoring

NON-KICKERS

Points	Years	TD	Xpt	FG	Pts
Anthony Thompson, Ind.	1986-89	65	4	0	394
Tony Dorsett, Pitt.	1973-76	59	2	0	356
Glenn Davis, Army	1943-46	59	0	0	354
Art Luppino, Ariz.	1953-56	48	49	0	337
Steve Owens, Okla.	1967-69	56	0	0	336

Points Per Game	Years	Pts	P/Gm
Bob Gaiters, N.Mexico St.	1959-60	203	11.9
Ed Marinaro, Cornell	1969-71	318	11.8
Bill Burnett, Arkansas	1968-70	294	11.3
Steve Owens, Oklahoma	1967-69	336	11.2
Eddie Talboom, Wyoming	1948-50	303	10.8

Touchdowns Rushing	Years	No
Steve Owens, Oklahoma	1967-69	56
Tony Dorsett, Pitt	1973-76	55
Anthony Thompson, Indiana	1986-89	54
Ed Marinaro, Cornell	1969-71	50
Mike Rozier, Nebraska	1981-83	50

Touchdowns Passing	Years	No
Ty Detmer, BYU	1988-91	121
David Klingler, Houston	1988-91	91
Jim McMahon, BYU	1977-78,80-81	84
Joe Adams, Tenn.St	1977-80	81
Troy Kopp, Pacific	1989-91	79
John Elway, Stanford	1979-82	77
Andre Ware, Houston	1987-89	75

Touchdown Catches	Years	No
Clarkston Hines, Duke	1986-89	38
Terance Mathis, N.Mexico	1985-87,89	36
Elmo Wright, Houston	1968-70	34
Aaron Turner, Pacific	1989-91	32
Howard Twilley, Tulsa	1963-65	32
Manny Hazard, Houston	1989-90	31

KICKERS

Points	Years	FG	XP	Pts
Roman Anderson, Hou	1988-91	70	213	423
Carlos Huerta, Mia.	1988-91	73	178	397
Derek Schmidt, Fla.St	1984-87	73	174	393
Luis Zendejas, Ariz.St	1981-84	78	134	368
Jeff Jaeger, Wash	1983-86	80	118	358
John Lee, UCLA	1982-85	79	116	353
Max Zendejas, Arizona	1982-85	77	122	353
Kevin Butler, Georgia	1981-84	77	122	353

Field Goals	Years	No
Jeff Jaeger, Wash	1983-86	80
John Lee, UCLA	1982-85	79
Philip Doyle, Alabama	1987-90	78
Luis Zendejas, Ariz.St	1981-84	78
Kevin Butler, Georgia	1981-84	77
Max Zendejas, Arizona	1982-85	77

All-Purpose Running

Yards Gained	Years	Yards		Yards Gained	Years	Yards	P/Gm
Napoleon McCallum, Navy	1981-85	7172		Sheldon Canley, S.Jose St	1988-90	5146	205.8
Darrin Nelson, Stanford	1977-78,80-81	6885		Howard Stevens, Louisville	1971-72	3873	193.7
Terance Mathis, N.Mexico	1985-87,89	6691		O.J.Simpson, USC	1967-68	3666	192.9
Tony Dorsett, Pitt	1973-76	6615		Ed Marinaro, Cornell	1969-71	4940	183.0
Paul Palmer, Temple	1983-86	6609		Herschel Walker, Georgia	1980-82	5749	174.2

Miscellaneous

Interceptions	Years	No		Punt Return Average*	Years	Avg
Al Brosky, Illinois	1950-52	29		Jack Mitchell, Oklahoma	1946-48	23.6
John Provost, Holy Cross	1972-74	27		Gene Gibson, Cincinnati	1949-50	20.5
Martin Bayless, Bowl.Green	1980-83	27		Eddie Macon, Pacific	1949-51	18.9
Tom Curtis, Michigan	1967-69	25		Jackie Robinson, UCLA	1939-40	18.8
Tony Thurman, Boston Col	1981-84	25		Two tied at 17.7 each.		

*At least 1.2 punt returns per game.

Punting Average*	Years	Avg		Kickoff Return Average*	Years	Avg
Reggie Roby, Iowa	1979-82	45.6		Forrest Hall, San Fran	1946-47	36.2
Greg Montgomery, Mich.St	1985-87	45.4		Anthony Davis, USC	1972-74	35.1
Tom Tupa, Ohio St	1984-87	45.2		Overton Curtis, Utah St	1957-58	31.0

*At least 150 punts kicked.

*At least 1.2 kickoff returns per game.

SINGLE SEASON

Through the 1991 regular season.

Total Offense

Yards Gained	Year	Gm	Plays	Yards
David Klingler, Hou	1990	11	704	5221
Ty Detmer, BYU	1990	12	635	5022
Andre Ware, Hou	1989	11	628	4661
Jim McMahon, BYU	1980	12	540	4627
Ty Detmer, BYU	1989	12	497	4433

Yards Per Game	Year	Gm	Yards	P/Gm
David Klingler, Hou	1990	11	5221	474.6
Andre Ware, Hou	1989	11	4661	423.7
Ty Detmer, BYU	1990	12	5022	418.5
Steve Young, BYU	1983	11	4346	395.1
Scott Mitchell, Utah	1988	11	4299	390.8

Rushing

Yards Gained	Year	Gm	Car	Yards
Barry Sanders, Okla.St	1988	11	344	2628
Marcus Allen, USC	1981	11	403	2342
Mike Rozier, Nebraska	1983	12	275	2148
Tony Dorsett, Pitt	1976	11	338	1948
Lorenzo White, Mich.St	1985	11	386	1908

Yards Per Game	Year	Gm	Yards	P/Gm
Barry Sanders, Okla.St	1988	11	2628	238.9
Marcus Allen, USC	1981	11	2342	212.9
Ed Marinaro, Cornell	1971	9	1881	209.0
Charles White, USC	1979	10	1803	180.3
Mike Rozier, Nebraska	1983	12	2148	179.0

All-Purpose Running

Yards Gained	Year	Yards
Barry Sanders, Okla.St	1988	3250
Ryan Benjamin, Pacific	1991	2995
Paul Palmer, Temple	1986	2633
Marcus Allen, USC	1981	2559
Mike Rozier, Nebraska	1983	2486

Yards Per Game	Year	Yards	P/Gm
Barry Sanders, Oklahoma St	1988	3250	295.5
Ryan Benjamin, Pacific	1991	2995	249.6
Byron (Whizzer) White, Colo	1937	1970	246.3
Mike Pringle, CS-Fullerton	1989	2690	244.6
Paul Palmer, Temple	1986	2633	239.4

Passing

(Minimum 15 Attempts Per Game)

Passing Efficiency	Year	Rating
Jim McMahon, BYU	1980	176.9
Ty Detmer, BYU	1989	175.6
Jerry Rhome, Tulsa	1964	172.6
Elvis Grbac, Michigan	1991	169.0
Steve Young, BYU	1983	168.5
Ty Detmer, BYU	1991	168.5

Yards Gained	Year	Yards
Ty Detmer, BYU	1990	5188
David Klingler, Houston	1990	5140
Andre Ware, Houston	1989	4699
Jim McMahon, BYU	1980	4571
Ty Detmer, BYU	1989	4560

Completions	Year	Att	No
David Klingler, Houston	1990	643	374
Andre Ware, Houston	1989	578	365
Ty Detmer, BYU	1990	562	361
Robbie Bosco, BYU	1985	511	338
Scott Mitchell, Utah	1988	533	323

Receiving

Catches	Year	Gm	No
Manny Hazard, Houston	1989	11	142
Howard Twilley, Tulsa	1965	10	134
Jason Phillips, Houston	1988	11	108
Fred Gilbert, Houston	1991	11	106
James Dixon, Houston	1988	11	102

Catches Per Game	Year	No	P/Gm
Howard Twilley, Tulsa	1965	134	13.4
Manny Hazard, Houston	1989	142	12.9
Jason Phillips, Houston	1988	108	9.8
Fred Gilbert, Houston	1991	106	9.6
Jerry Hendren, Idaho	1969	95	9.5
Howard Twilley, Tulsa	1964	95	9.5

Yards Gained	Year	No	Yards
Howard Twilley, Tulsa	1965	134	1779
Manny Hazard, Houston	1989	142	1689
Aaron Turner, Pacific	1991	92	1604
Chuck Hughes, UTEP*	1965	80	1519
Henry Ellard, Fresno St	1982	62	1510

*UTEP was Texas Western in 1965.

All-Time NCAA Division I-A Individual Leaders (Cont.)

Scoring

Points	Year	TD	Xpt	FG	Pts
Barry Sanders, Okla.St.	1988	39	0	0	234
Mike Rozier, Nebraska	1983	29	0	0	174
Lydell Mitchell, Penn St.	1971	29	0	0	174
Art Luppino, Arizona	1954	24	22	0	166
Bobby Reynolds, Nebraska	1950	22	25	0	157

Touchdowns Passing	Year	No
David Klingler, Houston	1990	54
Jim McMahon, BYU	1980	47
Andre Ware, Houston	1989	46
Ty Detmer, BYU	1990	41
Dennis Shaw, San Diego St	1969	39

Points Per Game	Year	Pts	P/Gm
Barry Sanders, Okla.St.	1988	234	21.3
Bobby Reynolds, Nebraska	1950	157	17.4
Art Luppino, Arizona	1954	166	16.6
Ed Marinaro, Cornell	1971	148	16.4
Lydell Mitchell, Penn St	1971	174	15.8

Touchdown Catches	Year	No
Manny Hazard, Houston	1989	22
Desmond Howard, Michigan	1991	19
Tom Reynolds, San Diego St	1969	18
Dennis Smith, Utah	1989	18
Aaron Turner, Pacific	1991	18

Touchdowns Rushing	Year	No
Barry Sanders, Okla.St.	1988	37
Mike Rozier, Nebraska	1983	29
Ed Marinaro, Cornell	1971	24
Anthony Thompson, Indiana	1988	24
Anthony Thompson, Indiana	1989	24

Field Goals	Year	No
John Lee, UCLA	1984	29
Paul Woodside, West Virginia	1982	28
Luis Zendejas, Arizona St	1983	28
Fuad Reveiz, Tennessee	1982	27
Three tied with 25 each.		

Miscellaneous

Interceptions	Year	No
Al Worley, Washington	1968	14
George Shaw, Oregon	1951	13
Eight tied with 12 each.		

Punt Return Average*	Year	Avg
Bill Blackstock, Tennessee	1951	25.9
George Sims, Baylor	1948	25.0
Gene Derricotte, Michigan	1947	24.8
Erroll Tucker, Utah	1985	24.3
George Hoey, Michigan	1967	24.3
*At least 1.2 returns per game.		

Punting Average*	Year	Avg
Reggie Roby, Iowa	1981	49.8
Kirk Wilson, UCLA	1956	49.3
Zack Jordan, Colorado	1950	48.2
Ricky Anderson, Vanderbilt	1984	48.2
Marv Bateman, Utah	1971	48.1
Reggie Roby, Iowa	1982	48.1
*Qualifiers for championship.		

Kickoff Return Average*	Year	Avg
Forrest Hall, San Francisco	1946	38.2
Tony Ball, Tenn-Chattanooga	1977	36.4
Rocket Ismail, Notre Dame	1988	36.1
George Marinkov, N.Carolina St	1954	35.8
Bob Baker, Cornell	1964	35.1
*At least 1.2 kickoff returns per game.		

SINGLE GAME

Through the 1991 regular season.

Total Offense

Yards Gained	Opponent	Year	Yds
David Klingler, Hou	Arizona St.	1990	732
Matt Vogler, TCU	Houston	1990	696
David Klingler, Hou	TCU	1990	625
Scott Mitchell, Utah	Air Force	1988	625
Ty Detmer, BYU	S.Diego St.	1991	603

Rushing

Yards Gained	Opponent	Year	Yds
Tony Sands, Kansas	Missouri	1991	396
Marshall Faulk, S.Diego St	Pacific	1991	386
Anthony Thompson, Ind	Wisconsin	1989	377
Rueben Mayes, Wash.St.	Oregon	1984	357
Mike Pringle, CS-Fullerton	N.Mex.St.	1989	357

Passing

Yards Gained	Opponent	Year	Yds
David Klingler, Hou	Arizona St.	1990	716
Matt Vogler, TCU	Houston	1990	690
Scott Mitchell, Utah	Air Force	1988	631
Jeremy Leach, N.Mex	Utah	1989	622
Dave Wilson, Illinois	Ohio St.	1980	621

Receiving

Catches	Opponent	Year	No
Jay Miller, BYU	New Mexico	1973	22
Rick Eber, Tulsa	Idaho St.	1967	20
Howard Twilley, Tulsa	Colo.St.	1965	19
Ron Fair, Ariz.St.	Wash.St.	1989	19
Manny Hazard, Hou	TCU	1989	19
Manny Hazard, Hou	Texas	1989	19

Completions	Opponent	Year	No
David Klingler, Hou	SMU	1990	48
Sandy Schwab, Northwestern	Michigan	1982	45
Chuck Hartlieb, Iowa	Indiana	1988	44
Jim McMahon, BYU	Colo.St.	1981	44
Matt Vogler, TCU	Houston	1990	44

Yards Gained	Opponent	Year	Yds
Chuck Hughes, UTEP*	N.Texas St.	1965	349
Rick Eber, Tulsa	Idaho St.	1967	322
Harry Wood, Tulsa	Idaho St.	1967	318
Jeff Evans, N.Mexico St	So.Ill.	1978	316
Tom Reynolds, S.Diego St	Utah St.	1971	290
*UTEP was Texas Western in 1965.			

Scoring

Points

	Opponent	Year	Pts
Howard Griffith, Illinois	So.Ill.	1990	48
Marshall Faulk, S.Diego St	Pacific	1991	44
Jim Brown, Syracuse	Colgate	1956	43
Showboat Boykin, Miss	Miss.St.	1951	42
Fred Wendt, UTEP*	N.Mex.St.	1948	42
Dick Bass, Pacific	S.Diego St.	1958	38

*UTEP was Texas Mines in 1948

Touchdowns Rushing

	Opponent	Year	No
Howard Griffith, Illinois	So.Ill	1990	8
Showboat Boykin, Miss	Miss.St.	1951	7

Note: Griffith's TD runs (5-51-7-41-5-18-5-3).

Touchdowns Passing

	Opponent	Year	No
David Klingler, Houston	E.Wash.	1990	11
Dennis Shaw, S.Diego St	N.Mex.St.	1969	9

Note: Klingler's TD passes (5-48-29-7-3-7-40-8-7-8-51).

Touchdown Catches

	Opponent	Year	No
Tim Delaney, S.Diego St	N.Mex.St.	1969	6

Note: Delaney TD catches (2-22-34-31-30-9).

Field Goals

	Opponent	Year	No
Dale Klein, Nebraska	Missouri	1985	7
Mike Prindle, W.Mich	Marshall	1984	7

Note: Klein's FGs (32-22-43-44-29-43-43);
Prindle's FGs (32-44-42-23-48-41-27).

Extra Points (Kick)

	Opponent	Year	No
Terry Leiweke, Houston	Tulsa	1968	13
Derek Mahoney, Fresno St	New Mexico	1991	13

Extra Points (2-Pts)

	Opponent	Year	No
Jim Pilot, N.Mexico St	H-Simmons	1961	6

Longest Plays (since 1941)

Rushing

	Opponent	Year	Yds
Gale Sayers, Kansas	Nebraska	1963	99
Max Anderson, Ariz.St	Wyoming	1967	99
Ralph Thompson, W.Texas St	Wich.St.	1970	99
Kelsey Finch, Tennessee	Florida	1977	99

Passing

	Opponent	Year	Yds
Fred Owens			
to Jack Ford, Portland	St.Mary's	1947	99
Bo Burris			
to Warren McVea, Houston	Wash.St.	1966	99
Colin Clapton			
to Eddie Jenkins, Holy Cross	Boston U.	1970	99
Terry Peel			
to Robert Ford, Houston	Syracuse	1970	99
Terry Peel			
to Robert Ford, Houston	S.Diego St.	1972	99
Cris Collinsworth			
to Derrick Gaffney, Florida	Rice	1977	99
Scott Ankrom			
to James Maness, TCU	Rice	1984	99
Gino Torretta			
to Horace Copeland, Miami-FL	Arkansas	1991	99

Field Goals

	Opponent	Year	Yds
Steve Little, Arkansas	Texas	1977	67
Russell Erxleben, Texas	Rice	1977	67
Joe Williams, Wichita St	So.Ill.	1978	67

Punts

	Opponent	Year	Yds
Pat Brady, Nevada-Reno	Loyola-CA	1950	99
George O'Brien, Wisconsin	Iowa	1952	98

Punt Returns
100-yd punt returns since 1941: 7 players.

Kickoff Returns
100-yd kickoff returns since 1941: 163 players.

Interception Returns
100-yd interception returns since 1941: 56 players.

Longest Division I Streaks

Winning Streaks
(Including bowl games)

No		Seasons	Spoiler	Score
47	Oklahoma	1953–57	Notre Dame	7–0
39	Washington	1908–14	Oregon St.	0–0
37	Yale	1890–93	Princeton	6–0
37	Yale	1887–89	Princeton	10–0
35	Toledo	1969–71	Tampa	21–0
34	Penn	1894–96	Lafayette	6–4
31	Oklahoma	1948–50	Kentucky	13–7*
31	Pittsburgh	1914–18	Cleve. Naval	10–9
31	Penn	1896–98	Harvard	10–0
30	Texas	1968–70	Notre Dame	24–11*
29	Michigan	1901–03	Minnesota	6–6
28	Alabama	1978–80	Miss.St.	6–3
28	Oklahoma	1973–75	Kansas	23–3
28	Mich.St.	1950–53	Purdue	6–0
27	Nebraska	1901–04	Colorado	6–0
26	Cornell	1921–24	Williams	14–7
26	Michigan	1903–05	Chicago	2–0
25	BYU	1983–85	UCLA	27–24
25	Michigan	1946–49	Army	21–7
25	Army	1944–46	Notre Dame	0–0
25	USC	1931–33	Oregon St.	0–0

*Note: Kentucky beat Oklahoma in 1951 Sugar Bowl and Notre Dame beat Texas in 1971 Cotton Bowl.

Unbeaten Streaks
(Including bowl games)

No	W–T		Seasons	Spoiler	Score
63	59-4	Washington	1907–17	California	27–0
56	55-1	Michigan	1901–05	Chicago	2–0
50	46-4	California	1920–25	Olympic	15–0
48	47-1	Oklahoma	1953–57	N. Dame	7–0
48	47-1	Yale	1885–89	Princeton	10–0
47	42-5	Yale	1879–85	Princeton	6–5
44	42-2	Yale	1894–96	Princeton	24–6
42	39-3	Yale	1904–08	Harvard	4–0
39	37-2	N. Dame	1946–50	Purdue	28–14
37	36-1	Oklahoma	1972–75	Kansas	23–3
37	37-0	Yale	1890-93	Princeton	6-0
35	34-1	Minnesota	1903–05	Wisconsin	16–12

Losing Streaks

No		Seasons	Victim	Score
44	Columbia	1983–88	Princeton	16–14
34	Northwestern	1979–82	No.Illinois	31–6
28	Virginia	1958–60	Wm.&Mary	21–6*
28	Kansas St	1945–48	Arkansas St.	37–6
27	E.Michigan	1980–82	Kent St.	9–7

*Note: Virginia ended its losing streak in the opening game of the 1961 season.

Annual Awards

Heisman Trophy

Originally presented in 1935 as the DAC Trophy by the Downtown Athletic Club of New York City to the best college football player east of the Mississippi. In 1936, players across the country were eligible and the award was renamed the Heisman Trophy following the death of former college coach and DAC athletic director John W. Heisman. Top three vote getters for each year are listed with point totals.

Multiple winner: Archie Griffin (2).

Winners in junior year (11): Doc Blanchard (1945), Ty Detmer (1990); Archie Griffin (1974), Desmond Howard (1991), Vic Janowicz (1950), Barry Sanders (1988), Billy Sims (1978), Roger Staubach (1963), Doak Walker (1948), Herschel Walker (1982), Andre Ware (1989).

Winners on AP national champions (7): Angelo Bertelli (Notre Dame, 1943); Doc Blanchard (Army, 1945); Tony Dorsett (Pittsburgh, 1976); Leon Hart (Notre Dame, 1949); Johnny Lujack (Notre Dame, 1947); Davey O'Brien (TCU, 1938); Bruce Smith (Minnesota, 1941).

Year		Points
1935	**Jay Berwanger**, Chicago, HB	84
	2nd—Monk Meyer, Army, HB	29
	3rd—Bill Shakespeare, Notre Dame, HB	23
	4th—Pepper Constable, Princeton, FB	20
1936	**Larry Kelley**, Yale, E	219
	2nd—Sam Francis, Nebraska, FB	47
	3rd—Ray Buivid, Marquette, HB	43
	4th—Sammy Baugh, TCU, HB	39
1937	**Clint Frank**, Yale, HB	524
	2nd—Byron (Whizzer) White, Colo., HB	264
	3rd—Marshall Goldberg, Pitt, HB	211
	4th—Alex Wojciechowicz, Fordham, C	85
1938	**Davey O'Brien**, TCU, QB	519
	2nd—Marshall Goldberg, Pitt, HB	294
	3rd—Sid Luckman, Columbia, QB	154
	4th—Bob MacLeod, Dartmouth, HB	78
1939	**Nile Kinnick**, Iowa, HB	651
	2nd—Tom Harmon, Michigan, HB	405
	3rd—Paul Christman, Missouri, QB	391
	4th—George Cafego, Tennessee, QB	296
1940	**Tom Harmon**, Michigan, HB	1303
	2nd—John Kimbrough, Texas A&M, FB	841
	3rd—George Franck, Minnesota, HB	102
	4th—Frankie Albert, Stanford, QB	90
1941	**Bruce Smith**, Minnesota, HB	554
	2nd—Angelo Bertelli, N.Dame, QB	345
	3rd—Frankie Albert, Stanford, QB	336
	4th—Frank Sinkwich, Georgia, HB	249
1942	**Frank Sinkwich**, Georgia, TB	1059
	2nd—Paul Governali, Columbia, QB	218
	3rd—Clint Castleberry, Ga.Tech, HB	99
	4th—Mike Holovak, Boston College, FB	95
1943	**Angelo Bertelli**, Notre Dame, QB	648
	2nd—Bob Odell, Penn, HB	177
	3rd—Otto Graham, Northwestern, QB	140
	4th—Creighton Miller, Notre Dame, HB	134
1944	**Les Horvath**, Ohio St., TB-QB	412
	2nd—Glenn Davis, Army, HB	287
	3rd—Doc Blanchard, Army, FB	237
	4th—Don Whitmore, Navy, T	115
1945	**Doc Blanchard**, Army, FB	860
	2nd—Glenn Davis, Army, HB	638
	3rd—Bob Fenimore, Oklahoma A&M, HB	187
	4th—Herman Wedermeyer, St.Mary's, HB	152
1946	**Glenn Davis**, Army, HB	792
	2nd—Charlie Trippi, Georgia, HB	435
	3rd—Johnny Lujack, N.Dame, QB	379
	4th—Doc Blanchard, Army, FB	267
1947	**Johnny Lujack**, Notre Dame, QB	742
	2nd—Bob Chappius, Michigan, HB	555
	3rd—Doak Walker, SMU, HB	196
	4th—Charlie Conerly, Mississippi, QB	186
1948	**Doak Walker**, SMU, HB	778
	2nd—Charlie Justice, N.Carolina, HB	443
	3rd—Chuck Bednarik, Penn, C	336
	4th—Jackie Jensen, California, HB	143

Year		Points
1949	**Leon Hart**, Notre Dame, E	995
	2nd—Charlie Justice, N.Carolina, HB	272
	3rd—Doak Walker, SMU, HB	229
	4th—Arnold Galiffa, Army QB	196
1950	**Vic Janowicz**, Ohio St., HB	633
	2nd—Kyle Rote, SMU, HB	280
	3rd—Reds Bagnell, Penn, HB	231
	4th—Babe Parilli, Kentucky, QB	214
1951	**Dick Kazmaier**, Princeton, TB	1777
	2nd—Hank Lauricella, Tennessee, HB	424
	3rd—Babe Parilli, Kentucky, QB	344
	4th—Bill McColl, Stanford, E	313
1952	**Billy Vessels**, Oklahoma, HB	525
	2nd—Jack Scarbath, Maryland, QB	367
	3rd—Paul Giel, Minnesota, HB	329
	4th—Donn Moomaw, UCLA, C	257
1953	**Johnny Lattner**, Notre Dame, HB	1850
	2nd—Paul Giel, Minnesota, HB	1794
	3rd—Paul Cameron, UCLA, HB	444
	4th—Bernie Faloney, Maryland, QB	258
1954	**Alan Ameche**, Wisconsin, FB	1068
	2nd—Kurt Burris, Oklahoma, C	838
	3rd—Howard Cassady, Ohio St., HB	810
	4th—Ralph Guglielmi, Notre Dame, QB	691
1955	**Howard Cassady**, Ohio St., HB	2219
	2nd—Jim Swink, TCU, HB	742
	3rd—George Welsh, Navy, QB	383
	4th—Earl Morrall, Michigan St., QB	323
1956	**Paul Hornung**, Notre Dame, QB	1066
	2nd—Johnny Majors, Tennessee, HB	994
	3rd—Tommy McDonald, Oklahoma, HB	973
	4th—Jerry Tubbs, Oklahoma, C	724
1957	**John David Crow**, Texas A&M, HB	1183
	2nd—Alex Karras, Iowa, T	693
	3rd—Walt Kowalczyk, Mich.St., HB	630
	4th—Lou Michaels, Kentucky, T	330
1958	**Pete Dawkins**, Army, HB	1394
	2nd—Randy Duncan, Iowa, QB	1021
	3rd—Billy Cannon, LSU, HB	975
	4th—Bob White, Ohio St., HB	365
1959	**Billy Cannon**, LSU, HB	1929
	2nd—Richie Lucas, Penn St., QB	613
	3rd—Don Meredith, SMU, QB	286
	4th—Bill Burrell, Illinois, G	196
1960	**Joe Bellino**, Navy, HB	1793
	2nd—Tom Brown, Minnesota, G	731
	3rd—Jake Gibbs, Mississippi, QB	453
	4th—Ed Dyas, Auburn, HB	319
1961	**Ernie Davis**, Syracuse, HB	824
	2nd—Bob Ferguson, Ohio St., HB	771
	3rd—Jimmy Saxton, Texas, HB	551
	4th—Sandy Stephens, Minnesota, QB	543
1962	**Terry Baker**, Oregon St., QB	707
	2nd—Jerry Stovall, LSU, HB	618
	3rd—Bobby Bell, Minnesota, T	429
	4th—Lee Roy Jordan, Alabama, C	321

Year		Points
1963	**Roger Staubach**, Navy, QB	1860
	2nd—Billy Lothridge, Ga.Tech, QB	504
	3rd—Sherman Lewis, Mich.St., HB	369
	4th—Don Trull, Baylor, QB	253
1964	**John Huarte**, Notre Dame, QB	1026
	2nd—Jerry Rhome, Tulsa, QB	952
	3rd—Dick Butkus, Illinois, C	505
	4th—Bob Timberlake, Michigan, QB	361
1965	**Mike Garrett**, USC, HB	926
	2nd—Howard Twilley, Tulsa, E	528
	3rd—Jim Grabowsky, Illinois, FB	481
	4th—Donny Anderson, Texas Tech, HB	408
1966	**Steve Spurrier**, Florida, QB	1679
	2nd—Bob Griese, Purdue, QB	816
	3rd—Nick Eddy, Notre Dame, HB	456
	4th—Gary Beban, UCLA, QB	318
1967	**Gary Beban**, UCLA, QB	1968
	2nd—O.J.Simpson, USC, HB	1722
	3rd—Leroy Keyes, Purdue, HB	1366
	4th—Larry Csonka, Syracuse, FB	136
1968	**O.J.Simpson**, USC, HB	2853
	2nd—Leroy Keyes, Purdue, HB	1103
	3rd—Terry Hanratty, Notre Dame, QB	387
	4th—Ted Kwalick, Penn St., TE	254
1969	**Steve Owens**, Oklahoma, HB	1488
	2nd—Mike Phipps, Purdue, QB	1344
	3rd—Rex Kern, Ohio St., QB	856
	4th—Archie Manning, Mississippi, QB	582
1970	**Jim Plunkett**, Stanford, QB	2229
	2nd—Joe Theismann, Notre Dame, QB	1410
	3rd—Archie Manning, Mississippi, QB	849
	4th—Steve Worster, Texas, RB	398
1971	**Pat Sullivan**, Auburn, QB	1597
	2nd—Ed Marinaro, Cornell, RB	1445
	3rd—Greg Pruitt, Oklahoma, RB	586
	4th—Johnny Musso, Alabama, RB	365
1972	**Johnny Rodgers**, Nebraska, FL	1310
	2nd—Greg Pruitt, Oklahoma, RB	966
	3rd—Rich Glover, Nebraska, MG	652
	4th—Bert Jones, LSU, QB	351
1973	**John Cappelletti**, Penn St., RB	1057
	2nd—John Hicks, Ohio St., OT	524
	3rd—Roosevelt Leaks, Texas, RB	482
	4th—David Jaynes, Kansas, QB	394
1974	**Archie Griffin**, Ohio St., RB	1920
	2nd—Anthony Davis, USC, RB	819
	3rd—Joe Washington, Oklahoma, RB	661
	4th—Tom Clements, Notre Dame, QB	244
1975	**Archie Griffin**, Ohio St., RB	1800
	2nd—Chuck Muncie, California, RB	730
	3rd—Ricky Bell, USC, RB	708
	4th—Tony Dorsett, Pitt, RB	616
1976	**Tony Dorsett**, Pittsburgh, RB	2357
	2nd—Ricky Bell, USC, RB	1346
	3rd—Rob Lytle, Michigan, RB	413
	4th—Terry Miller, Oklahoma St., RB	197
1977	**Earl Campbell**, Texas, RB	1547
	2nd—Terry Miller, Oklahoma, RB	812
	3rd—Ken MacAfee, Notre Dame, TE	343
	4th—Doug Williams, Grambling, QB	266

Year		Points
1978	**Billy Sims**, Oklahoma, RB	827
	2nd—Chuck Fusina, Penn St., QB	750
	3rd—Rick Leach, Michigan, QB	435
	4th—Charles White, USC, RB	354
1979	**Charles White**, USC, RB	1695
	2nd—Billy Sims, Oklahoma, RB	773
	3rd—Marc Wilson, BYU, QB	589
	4th—Art Schlichter, Ohio St., QB	251
1980	**George Rogers**, South Carolina, RB	1128
	2nd—Hugh Green, Pittsburgh, DE	861
	3rd—Herschel Walker, Georgia, RB	683
	4th—Mark Herrmann, Purdue, QB	405
1981	**Marcus Allen**, USC, RB	1797
	2nd—Herschel Walker, Georgia, RB	1199
	3rd—Jim McMahon, BYU, QB	706
	4th—Dan Marino, Pitt, QB	256
1982	**Herschel Walker**, Georgia, RB	1926
	2nd—John Elway, Stanford, QB	1231
	3rd—Eric Dickerson, SMU, RB	465
	4th—Anthony Carter, Michigan, WR	142
1983	**Mike Rozier**, Nebraska, RB	1801
	2nd—Steve Young, BYU, QB	1172
	3rd—Doug Flutie, Boston College, QB	253
	4th—Turner Gill, Nebraska, QB	190
1984	**Doug Flutie**, Boston College, QB	2240
	2nd—Keith Byers, Ohio St., RB	1251
	3rd—Robbie Bosco, BYU, QB	443
	4th—Bernie Kosar, Miami-FL, QB	320
1985	**Bo Jackson**, Auburn, RB	1509
	2nd—Chuck Long, Iowa, QB	1464
	3rd—Robbie Bosco, BYU, QB	459
	4th—Lorenzo White, Michigan St., RB	391
1986	**Vinny Testaverde**, Miami-FL, QB	2213
	2nd—Paul Palmer, Temple, RB	672
	3rd—Jim Harbaugh, Michigan, QB	458
	4th—Brian Bosworth, Oklahoma, LB	395
1987	**Tim Brown**, Notre Dame, WR	1442
	2nd—Don McPherson, Syracuse, QB	831
	3rd—Gordie Lockbaum, Holy Cross, WR-DB	657
	4th—Lorenzo White, Michigan St., RB	632
1988	**Barry Sanders**, Oklahoma St., RB	1878
	2nd—Rodney Peete, USC, QB	912
	3rd—Troy Aikman, UCLA, QB	582
	4th—Steve Walsh, Miami-FL, QB	341
1989	**Andre Ware**, Houston, QB	1073
	2nd—Anthony Thompson, Ind., RB	1003
	3rd—Major Harris, West Va., QB	709
	4th—Tony Rice, Notre Dame, QB	523
1990	**Ty Detmer**, BYU, QB	1482
	2nd—Rocket Ismail, Notre Dame, FL	1177
	3rd—Eric Bieniemy, Colorado, RB	798
	4th—Shawn Moore, Virginia, QB	465
1991	**Desmond Howard**, Michigan, WR	2077
	2nd—Casey Weldon, Florida St., QB	503
	3rd—Ty Detmer, BYU, QB	445
	4th—Steve Emtman, Washington, DT	357

Colleges With More Than One Winner

Notre Dame (7)—Bertelli (1943), Brown (1987), Hart (1949), Hornung (1956), Huarte (1964), Lattner (1953) and Lujack (1947). **Ohio St.** (5)—Cassady (1955), Griffin (1974-75), Horvath (1944) and Janowicz (1950). **USC** (4)—Allen (1981), Garrett (1965), Simpson (1968) and White (1979). **Army** (3)—Blanchard (1945), Davis (1946) and Dawkins (1958).

Oklahoma (3)—Owens (1969), Sims (1978) and Vessels (1952). **Auburn** (2)—Jackson (1985) and Sullivan (1971). **Georgia** (2)—Sinkwich (1942) and Walker (1982). **Michigan** (2)—Harmon (1940) and Howard (1991). **Navy** (2)—Bellino (1960) and Staubach (1963). **Nebraska** (2)—Rodgers (1972) and Rozier (1983). **Yale** (2)—Frank (1937) and Kelley (1936).

Annual Awards (Cont.)

Maxwell Award

First presented in 1937 by the Maxwell Memorial Football Club of Philadelphia, the award is named after Robert "Tiny" Maxwell, a Philadelphia native who was a standout lineman at the University of Chicago at the turn of the century.

Like the Heisman, the Maxwell is given to the outstanding college player in the nation. Both awards have gone to the same player in the same season 28 times. Those players are preceded by (#). Glenn Davis of Army and Doak Walker of SMU won both but in different years.

Multiple winner: Johnny Lattner (1952-53).

Year		Year		Year	
1937	#Clint Frank, Yale, HB	1956	Tommy McDonald, Okla., HB	1975	#Archie Griffin, Ohio St., RB
1938	#Davey O'Brien, TCU, QB	1957	Bob Reifsnyder, Navy, T	1976	#Tony Dorsett, Pitt, RB
1939	#Nile Kinnick, Iowa, HB	1958	#Pete Dawkins, Army, HB	1977	Ross Browner, Notre Dame, DE
		1959	Rich Lucas, Penn St., QB	1978	Chuck Fusina, Penn St., QB
1940	#Tom Harmon, Michigan, HB			1979	#Charles White, USC, RB
1941	Bill Dudley, Virginia, HB	1960	#Joe Bellino, Navy, HB		
1942	Paul Governali, Columbia, QB	1961	Bob Ferguson, Ohio St., HB	1980	Hugh Green, Pitt, DE
1943	Bob Odell, Penn, HB	1962	#Terry Baker, Oregon St., QB	1981	#Marcus Allen, USC, RB
1944	Glenn Davis, Army, HB	1963	#Roger Staubach, Navy, QB	1982	#Herschel Walker, Georgia, RB
1945	#Doc Blanchard, Army, FB	1964	Glenn Ressler, Penn St., G	1983	#Mike Rozier, Nebraska, RB
1946	Charley Trippi, Georgia, HB	1965	Tommy Nobis, Texas, LB	1984	#Doug Flutie, Boston Col., QB
1947	Doak Walker, SMU, HB	1966	Jim Lynch, Notre Dame, LB	1985	Chuck Long, Iowa, QB
1948	Chuck Bednarik, Penn, C	1967	#Gary Beban, UCLA, QB	1986	#V. Testaverde, Miami-FL, QB
1949	#Leon Hart, Notre Dame, E	1968	#O.J.Simpson, USC, HB	1987	Don McPherson, Syracuse, QB
		1969	Mike Reid, Penn St., DT	1988	#Barry Sanders, Okla.St., RB
1950	Reds Bagnell, Penn, HB			1989	Anthony Thompson, Indiana, RB
1951	#Dick Kazmaier, Princeton, TB	1970	#Jim Plunkett, Stanford, QB		
1952	Johnny Lattner, Notre Dame, HB	1971	Ed Marinaro, Cornell, RB	1990	#Ty Detmer, BYU, QB
1953	#Johnny Lattner, N. Dame, HB	1972	Brad VanPelt, Michigan St., DB	1991	#Desmond Howard, Michigan, WR
1954	Ron Beagle, Navy, E	1973	#John Cappelletti, Penn St., RB		
1955	#Howard Cassady, Ohio St., HB	1974	Steve Joachim, Temple, QB		

Outland Trophy

First presented in 1946 by the Football Writers Association of America, honoring the the nation's outstanding interior lineman. The award is named after its benefactor, Dr. John H. Outland (Kansas, Class of 1898). Players listed in **bold** type helped lead their team to a national championship (according to AP).

Multiple winner: Dave Rimmington (1981-82). **Winners in junior year:** Ross Browner (1976), Steve Emtman (1991) and Rimmington (1981).

Year		Year		Year	
1946	**George Connor,** Notre Dame, T	1962	Bobby Bell, Minnesota, T	1978	Greg Roberts, Oklahoma, G
1947	Joe Steffy, Army, G	1963	**Scott Appleton,** Texas, T	1979	Jim Richter, N.C.State, C
1948	Bill Fischer, Notre Dame, G	1964	Steve DeLong, Tennessee, T		
1949	Ed Bagdon, Michigan St., G	1965	Tommy Nobis, Texas, G	1980	Mark May, Pittsburgh, OT
		1966	Loyd Phillips, Arkansas, T	1981	Dave Rimmington, Nebraska, C
1950	Bob Gain, Kentucky, T	1967	**Ron Yary,** USC, T	1982	Dave Rimmington, Nebraska, C
1951	Jim Weatherall, Oklahoma, T	1968	Bill Stanfill, Georgia, T	1983	Dean Steinkuhler, Nebraska, G
1952	Dick Modzelewski, Maryland, T	1969	Mike Reid, Penn St., DT	1984	Bruce Smith, Virginia Tech, DT
1953	J.D.Roberts, Oklahoma, G			1985	Mike Ruth, Boston College, NG
1954	Bill Brooks, Arkansas, G	1970	Jim Stillwagon, Ohio St., MG	1986	Jason Buck, BYU, DT
1955	Calvin Jones, Iowa, G	1971	**Larry Jacobson,** Neb., DT	1987	Chad Hennings, Air Force, DT
1956	Jim Parker, Ohio St., G	1972	Rich Glover, Nebraska, MG	1988	Tracy Rocker, Auburn, DT
1957	Alex Karras, Iowa, T	1973	John Hicks, Ohio St., OT	1989	Mohammed Elewonibi, BYU, G
1958	Zeke Smith, Auburn, G	1974	Randy White, Maryland, DT		
1959	Mike McGee, Duke, T	1975	**Lee Roy Selmon,** Okla., DT	1990	Russell Maryland, Miami-FL, NT
		1976	Ross Browner, Notre Dame, DE	1991	Steve Emtman, Washington, DT
1960	**Tom Brown,** Minnesota, G	1977	Brad Shearer, Texas, DT		
1961	Merlin Olsen, Utah St., T				

Butkus Award

First presented in 1985 by the Downtown Athletic Club of Orlando, Fla., to honor the nation's outstanding linebacker. The award is named after Dick Butkus, two-time consensus All-America at Illinois and six-time All-Pro with the Chicago Bears.

Multiple winner: Brian Bosworth (1985-86).

Year		Year		Year	
1985	Brian Bosworth, Oklahoma	1988	Derrick Thomas, Alabama	1990	Alfred Williams, Colorado
1986	Brian Bosworth, Oklahoma	1989	Percy Snow, Michigan St.	1991	Erick Anderson, Michigan
1987	Paul McGowan, Florida St.				

Lombardi Award

First presented in 1970 by the Rotary Club of Houston, honoring the nation's best lineman. The award is named after pro football coach Vince Lombardi, who, as a guard, was a member of the famous "Seven Blocks of Granite" at Fordham in the 1930s. The Lombardi and Outland awards have gone to the same player in the same year nine times. Those players are preceded by (#). Ross Browner of Notre Dame won both, but in different years.

Year		Year		Year	
1970	#Jim Stillwagon, Ohio St., MG	1978	Bruce Clark, Penn St., DT	1986	Cornelius Bennett, Alabama, LB
1971	Walt Patulski, Notre Dame, DE	1979	Brad Budde, USC, G	1987	Chris Spielman, Ohio St., LB
1972	#Rich Glover, Nebraska, MG			1988	#Tracy Rocker, Auburn, DT
1973	#John Hicks, Ohio St., OT	1980	Hugh Green, Pitt, DE	1989	Percy Snow, Michigan St., LB
1974	#Randy White, Maryland, DT	1981	Kenneth Sims, Texas, DT		
1975	#Lee Roy Selmon, Okla., DT	1982	#Dave Rimmington, Neb., C	1990	Chris Zorich, Notre Dame, NT
1976	Wilson Whitley, Houston, DT	1983	#Dean Steinkuhler, Neb., G	1991	#Steve Emtman, Washington, DT
1977	Ross Browner, Notre Dame, DE	1984	Tony Degrate, Texas, DT		
		1985	Tony Casillas, Oklahoma, NG		

O'Brien Quarterback Award

First presented in 1977 as the O'Brien Memorial Trophy, the award went to the outstanding player in the Southwest. In 1981, however, the Davey O'Brien Educational and Charitable Trust of Ft. Worth renamed the prize the O'Brien National Quarterback Award and now honors the nation's best quarterback. The award is named after 1938 Heisman Trophy-winning QB Davey O'Brien of Texas Christian.

Multiple winners: Ty Detmer (1990-91), Mike Singletary (1979-80).

Memorial Trophy

Year		Year		Year	
1977	Earl Campbell, Texas, RB	1979	Mike Singletary, Baylor, LB	1980	Mike Singletary, Baylor, LB
1978	Billy Sims, Oklahoma, RB				

National QB Award

Year		Year		Year	
1981	Jim McMahon, BYU	1985	Chuck Long, Iowa	1989	Andre Ware, Houston
1982	Todd Blackledge, Penn St.	1986	Vinny Testaverde, Miami,FL	1990	Ty Detmer, BYU
1983	Steve Young, BYU	1987	Don McPherson, Syracuse	1991	Ty Detmer, BYU
1984	Doug Flutie, Boston College	1988	Troy Aikman, UCLA		

Thorpe Award

First presented in 1986 by the Jim Thorpe Athletic Club of Oklahoma City to honor the nation's outstanding defensive back. The award is named after Jim Thorpe—Olympic champion, two-time consensus All-America HB at Carlisle, and pro football pioneer.

Year		Year		Year	
1986	Thomas Everett, Baylor	1988	Deion Sanders, Florida St.	1990	Darryl Lewis, Arizona
1987	Bennie Blades, Miami-FL & Rickey Dixon, Oklahoma	1989	Mike Carrier, USC	1991	Terrell Buckley, Florida St.

Payton Award

First presented in 1987 by the Sports Network and Division I-AA sports information directors to honor the nation's outstanding Division I-AA player. The award is named after Walter Payton, the NFL's all-time leading rusher who was an All-America RB at Jackson St.

Year		Year		Year	
1987	Kenny Gamble, Colgate, RB	1989	John Friesz, Idaho, QB	1991	Jamie Martin, Weber St., QB
1988	Dave Meggett, Towson St., RB	1990	Walter Dean, Grambling, RB		

Hill Trophy

First presented in 1986 by the Harlon Hill Awards Committee in Florence, AL, to honor the nation's outstanding Division II player. The award is named after three-time NFL All-Pro Harlon Hill who played college ball at North Alabama.

Multiple winner: Johnny Bailey (1987-88-89).

Year		Year		Year	
1986	Jeff Bentrim, N.Dakota St., QB	1988	Johnny Bailey, Texas A&I,RB	1990	Chris Simdorn, N.Dakota St.,QB
1987	Johnny Bailey, Texas A&I,RB	1989	Johnny Bailey, Texas A&I,RB	1991	Ronnie West, Pittsburg St., WR

All-Time Winningest Division I-A Coaches

Minimum of 10 years in Division I-A through 1991 season. Regular season and bowl games included. Coaches active in 1991 in **bold** type.

Top 25 Winning Percentage

		Yrs	W	L	T	Pct
1	Knute Rockne	13	105	12	5	.881
2	Frank Leahy	13	107	13	9	.864
3	George Woodruff	12	142	25	2	.846
4	Barry Switzer	16	157	29	4	.837
5	Percy Haughton	13	96	17	6	.832
6	Bob Neyland	21	173	31	12	.829
7	Hurry Up Yost	29	196	36	12	.828
8	Bud Wilkinson	17	145	29	4	.826
9	Jock Sutherland	20	144	28	14	.812
10	**Tom Osborne**	19	186	43	3	.808
11	Bob Devaney	16	136	30	7	.806
12	Frank Thomas	19	141	33	9	.795
13	**Joe Paterno**	26	240	62	3	.792
14	Henry Williams	23	139	34	10	.787
15	Gil Dobie	33	180	45	15	.781
16	Bear Bryant	38	323	85	17	.780
17	Fred Folsom	19	106	28	6	.779
18	Bo Schembechler	27	234	65	8	.775
19	Fritz Crisler	18	116	32	9	.768
20	Charley Moran	18	122	33	12	.766
21	Wallace Wade	24	171	49	10	.765
22	Frank Kush	22	176	54	1	.764
23	Dan McGugin	30	197	55	19	.762
24	Andy Smith	17	116	32	13	.761
	Jim Crowley	13	78	21	10	.761

Top 25 Victories

		Yrs	W	L	T	Pct
1	Bear Bryant	38	323	85	17	.780
2	Amos Alonzo Stagg	57	314	199	35	.605
3	Pop Warner	44	313	106	32	.729
4	**Joe Paterno**	26	240	62	3	.792
5	Woody Hayes	33	238	72	10	.759
6	Bo Schembechler	27	234	65	8	.775
7	**Bobby Bowden**	26	216	76	3	.737
8	Jess Neely	40	207	176	19	.539
9	Warren Woodson	31	203	95	14	.673
10	Vince Dooley	25	201	77	10	.715
	Eddie Anderson	39	201	128	15	.606
12	Dana X. Bible	33	198	72	23	.715
13	Dan McGugin	30	197	55	19	.762
14	Hurry Up Yost	29	196	36	12	.828
15	Howard Jones	29	194	64	21	.733
16	Johnny Vaught	25	190	61	12	.745
17	**Hayden Fry**	30	189	140	9	.572
18	**Tom Osborne**	19	186	43	3	.808
19	John Heisman	36	185	70	17	.711
20	Darrell Royal	23	184	60	5	.749
21	**LaVell Edwards**	20	183	62	3	.744
22	Gil Dobie	33	180	45	15	.781
	Carl Snavely	32	180	96	16	.644
24	Jerry Claiborne	28	179	122	8	.592
25	Ben Schwartzwalder	28	178	96	3	.648

Note: Eddie Robinson of Division I-AA Grambling (1941-42, 1945—) is the all-time NCAA leader in coaching wins with a 371-134-15 record and .728 winning pct. over 49 seasons.

Where They Coached

Anderson—Loras (1922-24), DePaul (1925-31), Holy Cross (1933-38), Iowa (1939-42), Holy Cross (1950-64); **Bible**—Mississippi Col.(1913-15), LSU (1916), Texas A&M (1917, 1919-28), Nebraska (1929-36), Texas (1937-46); **Bowden**—Samford (1959-62), West Va.(1970-75), Florida St.(1976—); **Bryant**—Maryland (1945), Kentucky (1946-53), Texas A&M (1954-57), Alabama (1958-82); **Claiborne**—Va.Tech (1961-70), Maryland (1972-81), Kentucky (1982-89); **Crisler**—Minnesota (1930-31), Princeton (1932-37), Michigan (1938-47); **Crowley**—Michigan St.(1929-32), Fordham (1933-41); **Devaney**—Wyoming (1957-61), Nebraska (1962-72); **Dobie**—N.Dakota St.(1906-07), Washington (1908-16), Navy (1917-19), Cornell (1920-35), Boston Col.(1936-38); **V.Dooley**—Georgia (1964-88).

Edwards—BYU (1972—); **Folsom**—Colorado (1895-99, 1901-02), Dartmouth (1903-06), Colorado (1908-15); **Fry**—SMU (1962-72), North Texas (1973-78), Iowa (1979—); **Haughton**—Cornell (1899-1900), Harvard (1908-16), Columbia (1923-24); **Hayes**—Denison (1946-48), Miami-OH (1949-50), Ohio St.(1951-78); **Heisman**—Oberlin (1892), Akron (1893), Oberlin (1894), Auburn (1895-99), Clemson (1900-03), Ga.Tech (1904-19), Penn (1920-22), Wash.& Jeff.(1923), Rice (1924-27); **Jones**—Syracuse (1908), Yale (1909), Ohio St.(1910), Yale (1913), Iowa (1916-23), Duke (1924), USC (1925-40); **Kush**—Arizona St.(1958-79); **Leahy**—Boston Col.(1939-40), Notre Dame (1941-43, 1946-53); **McGugin**—Vanderbilt (1904-17, 1919-34); **Moran**—Texas A&M (1909-14), Centre (1919-23), Bucknell (1924-26), Catawba (1930-33).

Neely—Rhodes (1924-27), Clemson (1931-39), Rice (1940-66); **Neyland**—Tennessee (1926-34, 1936-40, 1946-52); **Osborne**—Nebraska (1973—); **Paterno**—Penn St.(1966—); **Rockne**—Notre Dame (1918-30); **Royal**—Mississippi St.(1954-55), Washington (1956), Texas (1957-76); **Schembechler**—Miami-OH (1963-68), Michigan (1969-89); **Schwartzwalder**—Muhlenberg (1946-48), Syracuse (1949-73); **Smith**—Penn (1909-12), Purdue (1913-15), California (1916-25); **Snavely**—Bucknell (1927-33), N.Carolina (1934-35), Cornell (1936-44), N.Carolina (1945-52), Washington-MO (1953-58); **Stagg**—Springfield (1890-91), Chicago (1892-1932), Pacific (1933-46); **Sutherland**—Lafayette (1919-23), Pittsburgh (1924-38); **Switzer**—Oklahoma (1973-88).

Thomas—Chattanooga (1925-28), Alabama (1931-42, 1944-46); **Vaught**—Mississippi (1947-70); **Wade**—Alabama (1923-30), Duke (1931-41, 1946-50); **Warner**—Georgia (1895-96), Cornell (1897-98), Carlisle (1899-1903), Cornell (1904-06), Carlisle (1907-13), Pittsburgh (1915-23), Stanford (1924-32), Temple (1933-38); **Wilkinson**—Oklahoma (1947-63); **Williams**—Army (1891), Minnesota (1900-21); **Woodruff**—Penn (1892-1901), Illinois (1903), Carlisle (1905); **Woodson**—Cen.Ark.(1935-39), Hardin-Simmons (1941-42, 1946-51), Arizona (1952-56), N.Mexico St.(1958-67), Trinity-TX (1972-73); **Yost**—Ohio Wesleyan (1897), Nebraska (1898), Kansas (1899), Stanford (1900), Michigan (1901-23, 1925-26).

All-Time Bowl Appearances

Active coaches in **bold** type.

		—Overall—			Big Four		
		App	W	L	T	W	L	T
1	Bear Bryant	29	15	12	2	12	8	0
2	**Joe Paterno**	22	14	7	1	6	4	0
3	Vince Dooley	20	8	10	2	3	5	0
4	**Tom Osborne**	19	8	11	0	5	7	0
5	Johnny Vaught	18	10	8	0	6	4	0
6	Bo Schembechler	17	5	12	0	2	10	0
7	**Johnny Majors**	16	9	7	0	4	0	0
	Lou Holtz	16	8	6	2	3	3	0
	Darrell Royal	16	8	7	1	6	6	0
	LaVell Edwards	16	5	10	1	0	0	0
11	**Bobby Bowden**	15	11	3	1	3	2	0
12	**Don James**	14	10	4	0	5	1	0
13	Bobby Dodd	13	9	4	0	6	1	0
	Barry Switzer	13	8	5	0	6	3	0
	Charlie McClendon	13	7	6	0	4	2	0
	Hayden Fry	13	5	7	1	0	4	0
17	**Earle Bruce**	12	7	5	0	1	2	0
	Woody Hayes	12	6	6	0	5	5	0
	Shug Jordan	12	5	7	0	0	2	0
20	Three tied at 11 each.							

Active Coaches' Victories

Minimum 5 years in Division I-A.

		Yrs	W	L	T	Pct
1	Joe Paterno, Penn St	26	240	62	3	.792
2	Bobby Bowden, Fla.St	26	216	76	3	.737
3	Hayden Fry, Iowa	30	189	140	9	.572
4	Tom Osborne, Nebraska	19	186	43	3	.808
5	LaVell Edwards, BYU	20	183	62	3	.744
6	Lou Holtz, Notre Dame	22	172	82	5	.674
7	Jim Sweeney, Fresno St.	27	169	125	4	.574
8	Johnny Majors, Tenn.	24	168	102	10	.618
9	Don James, Washington	21	167	75	3	.688
10	Grant Teaff, Baylor	29	163	146	8	.527
11	Bill Dooley, Wake Forest	25	153	123	5	.553
12	Earle Bruce, Colorado St	20	149	83	2	.641
13	Pat Dye, Auburn	18	148	57	4	.718
14	Jim Wacker, TCU	21	144	91	3	.611
15	Bill Mallory, Indiana	22	143	98	4	.592
16	Don Nehlen, West Va.	21	140	86	6	.616
17	Terry Donahue, UCLA	16	125	54	8	.690
18	George Welsh, Virginia	19	121	93	4	.564
19	Dick Sheridan, N.C.State	14	112	49	4	.690
	Jackie Sherrill, Miss.St	14	112	50	2	.689

Note: The "Big Four" bowls are the Rose, Orange, Sugar and Cotton. Only three coaches—Bill Alexander, Ga.Tech (1920-44); Bob Neyland, Tenn.(1926-34,36-40,46-52); and Frank Thomas, Ala.(1931-42,44-46)—have taken teams to all four. Alexander and Thomas won three of the Big Four, Neyland two.

AFCA Coach of the Year

First presented in 1935 by the American Football Coaches Association.
Multiple winners: Joe Paterno (4), Bear Bryant (3), John McKay and Darrell Royal (2).

Year		Year		Year	
1935	Pappy Waldorf, Northwestern	1955	Duffy Daugherty, Michigan St.	1973	Bear Bryant, Alabama
1936	Dick Harlow, Harvard	1956	Bowden Wyatt, Tennessee	1974	Grant Teaff, Baylor
1937	Hooks Mylin, Lafayette	1957	Woody Hayes, Ohio St.	1975	Frank Kush, Arizona St.
1938	Bill Kern, Carnegie Tech	1958	Paul Dietzel, LSU	1976	Johnny Majors, Pittsburgh
1939	Eddie Anderson, Iowa	1959	Ben Schwartzwalder, Syracuse	1977	Don James, Washington
1940	Clark Shaughnessy, Stanford	1960	Murray Warmath, Minnesota	1978	Joe Paterno, Penn St.
1941	Frank Leahy, Notre Dame	1961	Bear Bryant, Alabama	1979	Earle Bruce, Ohio St.
1942	Bill Alexander, Georgia Tech	1962	John McKay, USC	1980	Vince Dooley, Georgia
1943	Amos Alonzo Stagg, Pacific	1963	Darrell Royal, Texas	1981	Danny Ford, Clemson
1944	Carroll Widdoes, Ohio St.	1964	Frank Broyles, Arkansas	1982	Joe Paterno, Penn St.
1945	Bo McMillin, Indiana		& Ara Parseghian, Notre Dame	1983	Ken Hatfield, Air Force
1946	Red Blaik, Army	1965	Tommy Prothro, UCLA	1984	LaVell Edwards, BYU
1947	Fritz Crisler, Michigan	1966	Tom Cahill, Army	1985	Fisher DeBerry, Air Force
1948	Bennie Oosterbaan, Michigan	1967	John Pont, Indiana	1986	Joe Paterno, Penn St.
1949	Bud Wilkinson, Oklahoma	1968	Joe Paterno, Penn St.	1987	Dick MacPherson, Syracuse
1950	Charlie Caldwell, Princeton	1969	Bo Schembechler, Michigan	1988	Don Nehlen, West Virginia
1951	Chuck Taylor, Stanford	1970	Charlie McClendon, LSU	1989	Bill McCartney, Colorado
1952	Biggie Munn, Michigan St.		& Darrell Royal, Texas	1990	Bobby Ross, Georgia Tech
1953	Jim Tatum, Maryland	1971	Bear Bryant, Alabama	1991	Bill Lewis, East Carolina
1954	Red Sanders, UCLA	1972	John McKay, USC		

FWAA Coach of the Year

First presented in 1957 by the Football Writers Association of America. The FWAA and AFCA awards have both gone to the same coach in the same season 24 times. Those double winners are preceded by (#).
Multiple winners: Woody Hayes and Joe Paterno (3); Lou Holtz, Johnny Majors and John McKay (2).

Year		Year		Year	
1957	#Woody Hayes, Ohio St.	1969	#Bo Schembechler, Michigan	1980	#Vince Dooley, Georgia
1958	#Paul Dietzel, LSU	1970	Alex Agase, Northwestern	1981	#Danny Ford, Clemson
1959	#Ben Schwartzwalder, Syracuse	1971	Bob Devaney, Nebraska	1982	#Joe Paterno, Penn St.
1960	#Murray Warmath, Minnesota	1972	#John McKay, USC	1983	Howard Schnellenberger, Miami-FL
1961	Darrell Royal, Texas	1973	Johnny Majors, Pitt	1984	#LaVell Edwards, BYU
1962	#John McKay, USC	1974	#Grant Teaff, Baylor	1985	#Fisher DeBerry, Air Force
1963	#Darrell Royal, Texas	1975	Woody Hayes, Ohio St.	1986	#Joe Paterno, Penn St.
1964	#Ara Parseghian, Notre Dame	1976	#Johnny Majors, Pitt	1987	#Dick MacPherson, Syracuse
1965	Duffy Daugherty, Michigan St.	1977	Lou Holtz, Arkansas	1988	Lou Holtz, Notre Dame
1966	#Tom Cahill, Army	1978	#Joe Paterno, Penn St.	1989	#Bill McCartney, Colorado
1967	#John Pont, Indiana	1979	#Earle Bruce, Ohio St.	1990	#Bobby Ross, Georgia Tech
1968	Woody Hayes, Ohio St.			1991	Don James, Washington

Divisional Playoffs

The NCAA has decided its Division I-AA champion with a postseason playoff since 1978. Divisions II and III have had playoffs since 1973.

The NAIA has used playoffs since 1956 for Division I and since 1970 for Division II.

NCAA Champions
Division I-AA

Year	Winner	Score	Loser
1978	Florida A&M	35-28	Massachusetts
1979	Eastern Kentucky	30-7	Lehigh,PA
1980	Boise St., ID	31-29	Eastern Kentucky
1981	Idaho St.	34-23	Eastern Kentucky
1982	Eastern Kentucky	17-14	Delaware
1983	Southern Illinois	43-7	Western Carolina
1984	Montana St.	19-6	Louisiana Tech
1985	Georgia Southern	44-42	Furman, SC
1986	Georgia Southern	48-21	Arkansas St.
1987	NE Louisiana	43-42	Marshall,WV
1988	Furman, SC	17-12	Georgia Southern
1989	Georgia Southern	37-34	S.F.Austin St.
1990	Georgia Southern	36-13	Nevada-Reno
1991	Youngstown St.	25-17	Marshall

Division II

Year	Winner	Score	Loser
1973	Louisiana Tech	34-0	Western Kentucky
1974	Central Michigan	54-14	Delaware
1975	Northern Michigan	16-14	Western Kentucky
1976	Montana St.	24-13	Akron,OH
1977	Lehigh,PA	33-0	Jacksonville,AL
1978	Eastern Illinois	10-9	Delaware
1979	Delaware	38-21	Youngstown St.,OH
1980	Cal Poly-SLO	21-13	Eastern Illinois
1981	SW Texas St.	42-13	North Dakota St.
1982	SW Texas St.	34-9	UC-Davis
1983	North Dakota St.	41-21	Central St.,OH
1984	Troy St.,AL	18-17	North Dakota St.
1985	North Dakota St.	35-7	North Alabama
1986	North Dakota St.	27-7	South Dakota
1987	Troy St.,AL	31-17	Portland St.,OR
1988	North Dakota St.	35-21	Portland St.,OR
1989	Mississippi Col.	3-0	Jacksonville St.
1990	North Dakota St.	51-11	Indiana, PA
1991	Pittsburg St., KS	23-6	Jacksonville St.

Division III

Year	Winner	Score	Loser
1973	Wittenberg,OH	41-0	Juniata,PA
1974	Central, IA	10-8	Ithaca,NY
1975	Wittenberg,OH	28-0	Ithaca,NY
1976	St.John's,MN	31-28	Towson St.,MD
1977	Widener,PA	39-36	Wabash,IN
1978	Baldwin-Wallace	24-10	Wittenberg,OH
1979	Ithaca,NY	14-10	Wittenberg,OH
1980	Dayton,OH	63-0	Ithaca,NY
1981	Widener,PA	17-10	Dayton,OH
1982	West Georgia	14-0	Augustana,IL
1983	Augustana,IL	21-17	Union,NY
1984	Augustana,IL	21-12	Central,IA
1985	Augustana,IL	20-7	Ithaca,NY
1986	Augustana,IL	31-3	Salisbury St.,MD
1987	Wagner,NY	19-3	Dayton,OH
1988	Ithaca,NY	39-24	Central,IA
1989	Dayton,OH	17-7	Union,NY
1990	Allegheny, PA	21-14	Lycoming, PA
1991	Ithaca, NY	34-20	Dayton, OH

NAIA Champions
Division I

Year	Winner	Score	Loser
1956	Montana St. & St.Joseph's,IN	0-0	—
1957	Pittsburg St.,KS	27-26	Hillsdale,MI
1958	NE Oklahoma	19-13	Northern Arizona
1959	Texas A&I	20-7	Lenoir-Rhyne,NC
1960	Lenoir-Rhyne,NC	15-14	Humboldt St.,CA
1961	Pittsburg St.,KS	12-7	Linfield,OR
1962	Central St.,OK	28-13	Lenoir-Rhyne,NC
1963	St.John's,MN	33-27	Prairie View,TX
1964	Concordia,MN & Sam Houston,TX	7-7	—
1965	St.John's,MN	33-0	Linfield,OR
1966	Waynesburg,PA	42-21	WI-Whitewater
1967	Fairmont St.,WV	28-21	Eastern Wash.
1968	Troy St.,AL	43-35	Texas A&I
1969	Texas A&I	32-7	Concordia,MN
1970	Texas A&I	48-7	Wofford,SC
1971	Livingston,AL	14-12	Arkansas Tech
1972	East Texas St.	21-18	Car-Newman,TN
1973	Abilene Christian	42-14	Elon,NC
1974	Texas A&I	34-23	Henderson St.,AR
1975	Texas A&I	37-0	Salem, WV
1976	Texas A&I	26-0	Central Arkansas
1977	Abilene Christian	24-7	SW Oklahoma
1978	Angelo St.,TX	24-14	Elon,NC
1979	Texas A&I	20-14	Central St.,OK
1980	Elon,NC	17-10	NE Oklahoma
1981	Elon,NC	3-0	Pittsburg St.,KS
1982	Central St.,OK	14-11	Mesa,CO
1983	Carson-Newman,TN	36-28	Mesa,CO
1984	Carson-Newman,TN & Central Arkansas	19-19	—
1985	Hillsdale,MI & Central Arkansas	10-10	—
1986	Carson-Newman,TN	17-0	Cameron,OK
1987	Cameron,OK	30-2	Car-Newman,TN
1988	Carson-Newman,TN	56-21	Adams St.,CO
1989	Carson-Newman,TN	34-20	Emporia St.,KS
1990	Central St., OH	38-16	Mesa, CO
1991	Central Arkansas	19-16	Central St., OH

Division II

Year	Winner	Score	Loser
1970	Westminster,PA	21-16	Anderson,IN
1971	Calif.Lutheran	30-14	Westminster,PA
1972	Missouri Southern	21-14	Northwestern,IA
1973	Northwestern,IA	10-3	Clenville St.,WV
1974	Texas Lutheran	42-0	Missouri Valley
1975	Texas Lutheran	34-8	Calif.Lutheran
1976	Westminster,PA	20-13	Redlands,CA
1977	Westminster,PA	27-9	Calif.Lutheran
1978	Concordia,MN	7-0	Findlay,OH
1979	Findlay,OH	51-6	Northwestern,IA
1981	Austin College,TX & Concordia,MN	24-24	—
1982	Linfield,OR	33-15	Wm. Jewell, MO
1983	Northwestern,IA	25-21	Pacific Lutheran
1984	Linfield, OR	33-22	Northwestern,IA
1985	WI-La Crosse	24-7	Pacific Lutheran
1986	Linfield,OR	17-0	Baker,KS
1987	Pacific Lutheran & WI-Stevens Pt.*	16-16	—
1988	Westminster,PA	21-14	WI-La Crosse
1989	Westminster,PA	51-30	WI-La Crosse
1990	Peru St.,NE	17-7	Westminster, PA
1991	Georgetown-KY	28-20	Pacific Lutheran

*Wisconsin-Stevens Point forfeited its entire 1987 schedule due to its use of an ineligible player.

Wide World Photos

Washington Redskins owner **Jack Kent Cooke** (right) congratulates coach **Joe Gibbs** after beating Buffalo, 37-24, in Super Bowl XXVI.

PRO FOOTBALL

Hog Heaven

Capital punishment is alive and well in Washington, D.C. as the Redskins claim their third Super Bowl in 10 years.

They say that nothing ever gets done in Washington. That the corridors of power in the nation's capital are hopelessly gridlocked. That there are no men of action inside the Beltway.

Well, that may hold true in Congress or at the White House, but it was definitely not the case at RFK Stadium. In a city without a compass, the Washington Redskins knew exactly where they were going.

To Minneapolis. And when they got there on Jan. 26, they won their third Super Bowl in 10 years, trouncing the Buffalo Bills, 37-24.

You want men of action? How about Mark Rypien, Art Monk, Gary Clark, Earnest Byner and Chip Lohmiller? And Jim Lachey, Darrell Green and Wilber Marshall?

And how about Joe Gibbs? In his 11 years as head coach of the Redskins, he has 10 winning seasons, an overall record of 130-55 and three Super Bowl championships with three different quarterbacks—Joe Theismann, Doug Williams and now Rypien.

The victory moved the low-key Gibbs into the official NFL genius category along with Chuck Noll, who won four Vince Lombardi Trophies in Pittsburgh in the 1970s, and Bill Walsh, who won three times with San Francisco in the '80s.

Gary Myers is the national pro football columnist for the *New York Daily News* and a reporter on HBO's "Inside the NFL."

"I think I'm on the lower end of the genius scale," Gibbs said after Super Bowl XXVI. "Anyone who has been around the Redskins for a long time knows where I stand there."

Nevertheless, it was unfair to give him two weeks to prepare for the Bills. And then at the NFL Draft in April, general manager Charley Casserly traded up and got him the one player he really wanted— game-breaking wide receiver and Heisman Trophy winner Desmond Howard.

Gibbs had his team focused for a Super Bowl run right from the start, steam-rolling Detroit, 45-0, before the RFK faithful on opening night. Sure, the Lions played without the mercurial Barry Sanders, but it didn't matter. The Redskins proved that 19 weeks later when they surprisingly met up with Detroit again in the NFC Championship Game. This time, even with Sanders, the Lions couldn't come any closer than 41-17.

The Skins won their first 11 games of the regular season before losing twice in the final five weeks to familiar NFC East foes. Dallas ended the dream of going 16-0 on Nov. 24, with a 24-21 upset at RFK. A month later, the Eagles beat them, 24-22, in Philadelphia.

But Washington was the class of the league—winning more games (14) and scoring more points (485) than anybody else and giving up fewer points (224) than everyone else except New Orleans.

Wide World Photos

Redskins quarterback **Mark Rypien** preparing to throw against Buffalo during the first quarter of Super Bowl XXVI. Rypien passed for 292 yards and two touchdowns and was named the game's Most Valuable Player.

The Redskins also outscored their opponents by a punishing 261 points. The next biggest point spread, belonging to Buffalo, was only 140.

Individually, Rypien ranked second in the NFC in passing, Byner was fourth in rushing, Monk and Clark were fifth and sixth in receiving, and Lohmiller kicked his way to the league scoring title with 149 points.

Then came the playoffs and the dispatching of Atlanta, Detroit and Buffalo by a combined score of 102-41.

"This team had great chemistry," said Gibbs when it was all over. "There was a great feeling among the players for each other from Day One. There was nobody in it for their own personal goals. I think it was truly an exceptional team from the chemistry standpoint."

And at the center of the science project was Rypien, the Super Bowl Most Valuable Player. Protected by the Hogs—Washington's heavy duty offensive line that averaged 6 feet, 4 inches and 275 pounds—and locked on to the Posse—the fleet Redskin receiving corps—Rypien

electrified the Metrodome crowd with two touchdown passes and 292 yards.

"I'm looking forward to putting together four or five years of consistency," said Rypien, looking down the road. "I think if I can do that—become a quarterback like a Joe Montana or a Terry Bradshaw—then as a team we'll be all right."

Meanwhile, Buffalo left Minneapolis as the third team to lose back-to-back Super Bowls and the eighth straight loser from the AFC. A year ago in Tampa, only a missed field goal in the final seconds kept the Bills from beating the New York Giants. This time, however, they fell behind 17-0 at the half and trailed by 27 early in the fourth quarter.

Buffalo's difficulties surfaced on its first offensive series when running back Thurman Thomas, the NFL's consensus regular season MVP, was on the sidelines searching for his helmet as the Bills ran their first two plays from scrimmage.

Thomas, who led the AFC in rushing with 1,407 yards and the entire NFL in all-purpose running with 2,038, could manage just 40 overall yards against

Washington, including an embarrassing 13 yards on 10 carries.

Bills' quarterback Jim Kelly, who was the AFC's top passer in 1991, also suffered at the hands of the Redskin defense. He threw for 275 yards and two touchdowns, but four of his 58 passes were intercepted and he was sacked five times.

The 1991 regular season saw Dallas, Atlanta and Detroit return to their winning ways after long absences.

The Cowboys, in the third year of the Jerry Jones-Jimmy Johnson regime, went 11-5 and made the playoffs for the first time since 1985 (see box). The Falcons, losers of 46 games in the last four seasons, jumped to 10-6 in Jerry Glanville's second season—including two wins over San Francisco for the first time since 1982. And the Lions went from 6-10 to 11-5 to win the NFC Central, reach the playoffs for the first time since 1983 and gain consensus Coach of the Year honors for Wayne Fontes.

Detroit's new-found success, however, was tempered by the season's cruelest story. On Nov. 17, in a game with the Los Angeles Rams at the Pontiac Silverdome, Mike Utley, the Lions' 6-6, 290-pound guard, suffered a neck injury that left him a paraplegic. Utley was an inspiration in the upbeat manner he handled the tragedy. He even offered a "thumbs up" to his teammates as he was carried off the field on a stretcher—a gesture his teammates used as a rallying point all the way to the NFC Championship Game.

Despite his misfortune, Utley said football was a way of life for him and he would recommend it to anybody. "Most definitely I would," he said. "It's what I've done since I was a little rug rat." And he refused to feel sorry for himself, saying, "I've always been a positive guy. It happened. I'm not going to give up my life just because I can't walk."

Elsewhere, the New York Jets (8-8) returned to postseason play for the first time since 1986, while AFC West champion Denver (12-4) was back after a one-year absence.

The Broncos, a dismal 5-11 in 1990, almost made it all the way back to the Super Bowl, losing 10-7 to Buffalo in the AFC title game. Their 26-24, come-from-behind victory over Houston in the semifinals was the most exciting game of the

Wheeling And Dealing In Dallas

Three years ago, Tom Landry sat in his office packing 29 years of memories into boxes and loading them into the trunk of his car.

An Arkansas businessman named Jerry Jones had just bought the Dallas Cowboys for $140 million and his first move was to unceremoniously dump the man the team's public relations staff had always pompously billed as, "the only coach the Cowboys have ever had."

Dallas was coming off a 3-13 season and Landry's popularity was at an all-time low. But when Jones, an outsider, came in and fired him, Landry became a martyr. The town immediately turned on the new boss and his hand-picked new coach Jimmy Johnson. No matter that Johnson had been 52-9 and won a national championship in five years at the University of Miami.

Jones and Johnson had been roommates in college, but this was no case of cronyism. Johnson knew how to organize. Knew how to coach, too—although it was hard to tell that first season when the Cowboys went 1-15 with one of the poorest collections of talent the NFL had ever seen.

Fast forward three years and it's like old times. The Cowboys are good enough to hate again. Maybe not quite the cocksure "America's Team" of the 1970s, but getting there.

Johnson has done a quick and very impressive rebuilding job, but he had help. It helped that Landry's last team earned the first pick of the 1989 Draft and thus the right to select franchise quarterback Troy Aikman of UCLA. It also helped that Johnson was able to pick the pockets of Minnesota GM Mike Lynn on Oct. 12, 1989, dealing running back Herschel Walker to the Vikings for five players and a total of six first, second and third round draft picks over three years. Johnson then became the Monty Hall of the NFL, making league bookkeepers' heads spin with all his wheeling and dealing.

The result was an 11-5 season in 1991, a return to the playoffs for the first time since 1985, and expectations greater than any in Dallas since the early '80s. Johnson has assembled a potential powerhouse—a team capable of winning multiple Super Bowls.

Three years after riding into town and firing Tom Landry, Dallas owner **Jerry Jones** (left) and coach **Jimmy Johnson** have the Cowboys back in the saddle again.

Allan Kaye/Allsport

A large part of Johnson's success stems from his not being afraid to make trades—he made 41 of them in his first 37 months on the job. He is also one of the game's more astute judges of personnel.

His philosophy is simple: you've got to be willing to take a shot. "The only people who are going to succeed at something are the ones who try something," he says. "You've got to be aggressive."

Last season, the Cowboys had the NFL's leading rusher in Emmitt Smith (1,563 yards) and the NFC's leading receiver in Michael Irvin (93 catches). Smith was acquired with the help of one of the Walker picks, while Irvin, who was Landry's final No. 1 draft pick in 1988, played for Johnson at Miami.

Johnson has put together a young offensive line to protect Aikman and brought in sure-handed tight end Jay Novacek to give Aikman a keep-the-drive-alive target. He also acquired a reliable backup quarterback from the Raiders in Steve Beuerlein, who took the Cowboys on a 5-0 stretch run when Aikman hurt his knee. He then moved to upgrade the defense in the '92 Draft by taking cornerback Kevin Smith and middle linebacker Robert Jones with Dallas' two first round picks.

There is an easy explanation as to why the Cowboys have been so active making moves. Johnson and Jones are the full extent of the team's chain of command. There is hardly any red tape.

"It's very difficult to make a trade in this league," Johnson says. "That may sound like a foolish statement because we've made so many of them. But I've probably discussed a couple of hundred. Most clubs have so many people involved in the decisions that there's always going to be someone playing devil's advocate and someone who is going to kill the trade. Most clubs have a very difficult time pulling the trigger."

This is a new and much different era in Dallas. The first championship phase of the organization was built around Landry and players like Staubach, Pearson, Lilly and Dorsett. Now it's Johnson and players like Aikman, Smith and Irvin.

By the time this current bunch is through, maybe they will own a couple of Super Bowl trophies, too.

playoffs. Quarterback John Elway, who has done this sort of thing before, directed an 87-yard scoring drive with less than two minutes to go and no timeouts. David Treadwell kicked the winning 28-yard field goal with 16 seconds left to beat the Oilers, then went 0-for-3 the next week in the three-point loss to the Bills.

Five 1990 playoff teams, including the defending Super Bowl champion New York Giants (8-8), failed to make the cut in '91. It marked the second time the Giants have been unable to qualify the year after winning it all.

Miami (8-8) and Cincinnati (3-13) also had lackluster seasons, but San Francisco and Philadelphia each won 10 games and they couldn't get in either.

The 49ers finished with six straight victories and may have been the league's second-best team behind the Redskins by the end of the season. It was an impressive performance considering they went the whole way without Joe Montana, who had elbow surgery as the result of a training camp injury. His backups, Steve Young and Steve Bono, finished first and third, respectively, in the NFC passing ratings.

Even more impressive were the Eagles, who lost quarterback and top rusher Randall Cunningham for the season when his knee was injured in the second quarter of the first game of the year. Somehow, Jim McMahon, Brad Goebel and Jeff Kemp managed to provide enough offense to win 10 games, and the NFL's No. 1 defense, anchored by linemen Reggie White and Jerome Brown, did the rest.

Houston quarterback Warren Moon led the league in passing yardage for the second straight year and set a record for single season completions with 404. The Oilers had four receivers with over 50 catches, led by Haywood Jeffires (100) and Drew Hill (90).

We have probably seen the last of Bo Jackson in an NFL uniform. The hip injury he suffered in a 1991 playoff victory over Cincinnati eventually forced hip replacement surgery. Jackson, nevertheless, left his mark on the NFL during four abbreviated seasons with the Raiders. He quit the game as the only rusher in league history with two 90-yard plus runs from scrimmage.

Jackson's position as pro football's best baseball player was taken by corner-back Deion Sanders, who made All-Pro as a cornerback with the Atlanta Falcons in 1991 and was the Opening Day centerfielder for the Atlanta Braves in 1992.

A record 10 head coaches were either fired, pressured to quit or eased into retirement between the opening of the 1991 season and the '92 Draft.

Of the 11 teams that finished the season with losing records, nine changed coaches. The Indianapolis Colts, in fact, got rid of two—firing Ron Meyer after an 0-5 start and then busting interim replacement Rick Venturi back to defensive coordinator after he went 1-10.

Things got so confusing at the Hoosier Dome that when former Colts coach Ted Marchibroda (1975-79) was hired away from Buffalo after the Super Bowl he opened his first press conference by saying it was great to be back with the *Baltimore* Colts.

Marchibroda planned to bring the no-huddle offense with him to Indy and teach it to Jeff George, who led the NFL in times sacked with 56. The Colts also had the first two picks of the draft and selected University of Washington defensive tackle Steve Emtman and Texas A&M linebacker Quintin Coryatt. Between them, Emtman and Coryatt signed contracts totalling almost $18 million. (The Colts saved $2.1 million when they shipped Eric Dickerson to the Raiders for picks in the fourth and eighth rounds.)

Another former Baltimore coach, Don Shula, won his 300th game on Sept. 22, when Miami beat Green Bay, 16-13. He entered the 1992 season only 19 wins behind George Halas, the NFL's all-time winningest coach.

Shula, now 62, was only 33 when he took his first head coaching job with Baltimore in 1963. Two days after Christmas, the Cincinnati Bengals made his son David a head coach at age 32. David's appointment brightened an otherwise grim year for Don, who had to deal with the deaths of three close friends—his wife Dorothy, his team owner Joe Robbie and his first pro coach and mentor Paul Brown.

Brown, the innovative Hall of Famer and founder of both the Bengals and Cleveland Browns, died during training camp at 82.

Chuck Noll, another of Brown's disciples, stepped down in Pittsburgh after 23 years, 209 victories and the aforemen-

Wide World Photos

Detroit offensive lineman **Lomas Brown** (center) leads Lions' "thumbs up" tribute to fallen teammate **Mike Utley** before the start of their Thanksgiving game with Chicago on Nov. 28.

tioned four Super Bowl wins (although none since the 1979 season). Of the Super Bowl era coaches, only Tom Landry's 29-year reign in Dallas lasted longer than Noll's stretch with the Steelers. He was replaced by Kansas City defensive coordinator Bill Cowher, who at 35 is two years younger than Noll was when he got the job in 1969.

The only two losing teams to keep their heads were New England and Cleveland, who each went 6-10 with rookie coaches. And why not? Dick MacPherson of the Patriots and Bill Belichick of the Browns turned around two teams that were a combined 4-28 in 1990.

The Los Angeles Rams and Tampa Bay Buccaneers were both 3-13 and each hired veterans to lead them back to respectability.

The Rams welcomed home old coach Chuck Knox, who left Seattle after nine years. Home actually may not be the right word—the Rams played at Memorial Coliseum in L.A. when Knox was there in 1973-77, but they moved to Anaheim in 1980. Back in Seattle, the Seahawks replaced Knox with team president and GM Tom Flores, the former Raiders coach and two-time Super Bowl winner.

Meanwhile, the Buccaneers turned to recently fired Cincinnati coach Sam Wyche to break a losing streak of nine consecutive 10-defeat seasons. Wyche's Bengals lost 13 games in 1991, but he did get them to the Super Bowl in 1988.

Minnesota (8-8) and San Diego (4-12) opted for successful college coaches—the Vikings making Stanford's Dennis Green the second black coach in the NFL and the Chargers naming Bobby Ross, who led Georgia Tech to a piece of the national championship in 1990. The last time San Diego general manager Bobby Beathard hired a head coach it was for Washington in 1981. His choice was Joe Gibbs.

San Francisco passing game maven Mike Holmgren, who removed himself from consideration by both Phoenix and the New York Jets two years ago, surfaced as the new coach in Green Bay, where the Packers have qualified for the playoffs only once since 1972. Unfortunately, he couldn't bring Montana along with him.

Green Bay and Tampa Bay were both originally interested in Bill Parcells, the mastermind-turned-TV-analyst who had resigned from the New York Giants on

195

May 15, 1991, less than four months after winning his second Super Bowl.

The Bucs had the inside track, but on Dec. 28, Parcells surprised everybody by rejecting a five-year, $6.5 million Tampa Bay contract that would have made him coach and head of football operations.

A stunned and embarrassed Bucs' owner Hugh Culverhouse called a hurry-up press conference the next day to say Parcells had in fact agreed to the deal on Dec. 26 and was now backing out.

"We feel we've been jilted at the altar," Culverhouse said. "I thought we had a deal."

Parcells disagreed. "I never said I would take the job at Tampa Bay," he said from his analyst's chair at NBC. "What I had agreed to do is consider the job on the basis of a number of things that we enumerated in writing, for me to take a look at them and then make a decision. I considered it on that basis and in the end, I had to say no."

Eleven days later, Culverhouse got to say no.

On Jan. 4, Parcells told longtime friend and Packers GM Ron Wolf that he really wasn't interested in returning to coaching in Green Bay or anywhere else. Then on Jan. 8, he met with Culverhouse outside Washington, D.C., and asked to be reconsidered. Culverhouse passed.

"It's just a personal thing," Bucs' attorney Steve Story told the Associated Press. "(Culverhouse) couldn't reach that comfort level to get over the rejection."

So ended the year's strangest story. Culverhouse hired Wyche on Jan. 10 and Parcells returned to NBC.

Also coming to Tampa in the offseason was Plan B free agent Steve DeBerg. the one-time Bucs quarterback (1984-87) who became expendable in Kansas City when the Chiefs signed Seattle's Dave Krieg off Plan B.

Other prominent Plan B signings included Houston wide receiver Drew Hill by Atlanta; Cincinnati running back James Brooks by Cleveland, L.A. Rams cornerback Jerry Gray by Houston, and L.A. Raiders running back Roger Craig by Minnesota.

On March 18, at the owners' meeting in Phoenix, Instant Replay went the way of the leather helmet after six seasons. Despite the backing of commissioner Paul

Wide World Photos

Tampa Bay owner **Hugh Culverhouse** holds up the five-year, $6.5 million contract he said former Giants coach **Bill Parcells** agreed to on Dec. 26 then rejected on Dec. 28.

Tagliabue and competition committee chairman Jim Finks, pro-Replay owners could only come up with 17 out of 28 votes in favor and they needed 21.

One of the happiest owners in Phoenix was Al Davis of the Raiders, who was finally elected to the Pro Football Hall of Fame in January. The Class of '92 also included John Mackey, Lem Barney and John Riggins.

Finally, Raghib (Rocket) Ismail, the Notre Dame running back, receiver and kick return specialist who spurned the NFL for a four-year, $18 million contract with Toronto of the Canadian Football League, led the Argonauts to the CFL championship in 1991.

Ismail was the CFL's leading all-purpose runner with 2,959 yards and was named the Most Outstanding Player in Toronto's 36-21 Grey Cup victory over Calgary. The regular season Most Outstanding Player was NFL reject Doug Flutie of the B.C.Lions, who passed for 6,619 yards and 38 touchdowns. □

PRO FOOTBALL
STATISTICS
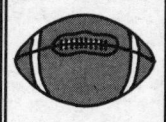

THE SEASON IN REVIEW

1991-1992

STANDINGS • PLAYOFFS • DRAFT

SEC **A**

PAGE **197**

Final NFL Standings

Division champions (*) and Wild Card playoff qualifiers (†) are noted; division champions with two best records received first round byes. Number of seasons listed after each head coach refers to tenure with club through 1991 season.

American Football Conference

Eastern Division

	W	L	T	PF	PA	vs Div	vs AFC
*Buffalo	13	3	0	458	318	7-1-0	10-2-0
†NY Jets	8	8	0	314	293	4-4-0	6-6-0
Miami	8	8	0	343	349	4-4-0	5-7-0
New England	6	10	0	211	305	4-4-0	5-9-0
Indianapolis	1	15	0	143	381	1-7-0	1-11-0

1991 Head Coaches: Buf—Marv Levy (6th season); **NY**—Bruce Coslet (2nd); **Mia**—Don Shula (22nd); **NE**—Dick MacPherson (1st); **Ind**—replaced Ron Meyer (6th, 0-5) with assistant Rick Venturi (1-10) on Oct.1.
1990 Standings: 1.Buffalo (13-3); 2.Miami (12-4); 3.Indianapolis (7-9); 4.NY Jets (6-10); 5.New England (1-15).

Central Division

	W	L	T	PF	PA	vs Div	vs AFC
*Houston	11	5	0	386	251	5-1-0	10-2-0
Pittsburgh	7	9	0	292	344	4-2-0	7-5-0
Cleveland	6	10	0	293	298	2-4-0	6-6-0
Cincinnati	3	13	0	263	435	1-5-0	2-10-0

1991 Head Coaches: Hou—Jack Pardee (2nd season); **Pit**—Chuck Noll (23rd); **Cle**—Bill Belichick (1st); **Cin**—Sam Wyche (8th).
1990 Standings: 1.Cincinnati (9-7); 2.Houston (9-7); 3.Pittsburgh (9-7); 4.Cleveland (3-13).

Western Division

	W	L	T	PF	PA	vs Div	vs AFC
*Denver	12	4	0	304	235	5-3-0	10-4-0
†Kansas City	10	6	0	322	252	6-2-0	8-4-0
†LA Raiders	9	7	0	298	297	5-3-0	7-5-0
Seattle	7	9	0	276	261	2-6-0	6-6-0
San Diego	4	12	0	274	342	2-6-0	3-9-0

1991 Head Coaches: Den—Dan Reeves (11th season); **KC**—Marty Schottenheimer (3rd); **LA**—Art Shell (3rd); **Sea**—Chuck Knox (9th); **SD**—Dan Henning (3rd).
1990 Standings: 1.LA Raiders (12-4); 2.Kansas City (11-5); 3.Seattle (9-7); 4.San Diego (6-10); 5.Denver (5-11).

National Football Conference

Eastern Division

	W	L	T	PF	PA	vs Div	vs NFC
*Washington	14	2	0	485	224	6-2-0	10-2-0
†Dallas	11	5	0	342	310	5-3-0	8-4-0
Philadelphia	10	6	0	285	244	5-3-0	6-6-0
NY Giants	8	8	0	281	297	3-5-0	5-7-0
Phoenix	4	12	0	196	344	1-7-0	3-11-0

1991 Head Coaches: Wash—Joe Gibbs (11th season); **Dal**—Jimmy Johnson (3rd); **Phi**—Rich Kotite (1st); **NY**—Ray Handley (1st); **Pho**—Joe Bugel (2nd).
1990 Standings: 1.NY Giants (13-3); 2.Philadelphia (10-6); 3.Washington (10-6); 4.Dallas (7-9); 5.Phoenix (5-11).

Central Division

	W	L	T	PF	PA	vs Div	vs NFC
*Detroit	12	4	0	339	295	6-2-0	8-4-0
†Chicago	11	5	0	299	269	7-1-0	9-3-0
Minnesota	8	8	0	301	306	3-5-0	8-6-0
Green Bay	4	12	0	273	313	3-5-0	3-9-0
Tampa Bay	3	13	0	199	365	1-7-0	2-10-0

1991 Head Coaches: Det—Wayne Fontes (4th season); **Chi**—Mike Ditka (10th); **Min**—Jerry Burns (6th); **GB**—Lindy Infante (4th); **TB**—Richard Williamson (2nd).
1990 Standings: 1.Chicago (11-5); 2.Tampa Bay (6-10); 3.Detroit (6-10); 4.Green Bay (6-10); 5.Minnesota (6-10).

Western Division

	W	L	T	PF	PA	vs Div	vs NFC
*New Orleans	11	5	0	341	211	4-2-0	8-4-0
†Atlanta	10	6	0	361	338	5-1-0	7-5-0
San Francisco	10	6	0	393	239	3-3-0	7-5-0
LA Rams	3	13	0	234	390	0-6-0	2-10-0

1991 Head Coaches: NO—Jim Mora (6th season); **Atl**—Jerry Glanville (2nd); **SF**—George Seifert (3rd); **LA**—John Robinson (9th).
1990 Standings: 1.San Francisco (14-2); 2.New Orleans (8-8); 3.LA Rams (5-11); 4.Atlanta (5-11).

Tiebreakers to Qualify for Playoffs
Wild Cards
AFC—NY Jets finished ahead of Miami by sweeping head-to-head series (41-23 and 23-20 in OT).
NFC—Atlanta finished ahead of San Francisco by sweeping head-to-head series (39-34 and 17-14).

NFL Regular Season Individual Leaders
(*) indicates rookies.

Passing Efficiency
(Minimum of 224 attempts)

AFC	Att	Cmp	Cmp Pct	Yds	Avg Gain	TD	Long	Int	Sack	Yds Lost	Rating
Jim Kelly, Buf	474	304	64.1	3844	8.11	33	77-td	17	31	227	97.6
Bernie Kosar, Cle	494	307	62.1	3487	7.06	18	71-td	9	41	232	87.8
Dan Marino, Mia	549	318	57.9	3970	7.23	25	54	13	27	182	85.8
Dave Krieg, Sea	285	187	65.6	2080	7.30	11	60	12	32	216	82.5
Warren Moon, Hou	655	404	61.7	4690	7.16	23	61-td	21	23	174	81.7
Steve DeBerg, KC	434	256	59.0	2965	6.83	17	63	14	19	161	79.3
Neil O'Donnell, Pit	286	156	54.5	1963	6.86	11	89-td	7	30	214	78.8
Ken O'Brien, NY	489	287	58.7	3300	6.75	10	53	11	33	273	76.6
John Elway, Den	451	242	53.7	3253	7.21	13	71	12	45	305	75.4
Jeff George, Ind	485	292	60.2	2910	6.00	10	49-td	12	56	481	73.8

NFC	Att	Cmp	Cmp Pct	Yds	Avg Gain	TD	Long	Int	Sack	Yds Lost	Rating
Steve Young, SF	279	180	64.5	2517	9.02	17	97-td	8	13	79	101.8
Mark Rypien, Wash	421	249	59.1	3564	8.47	28	82-td	11	7	59	97.9
Steve Bono, SF	237	141	59.5	1617	6.82	11	78	4	11	91	88.5
Troy Aikman, Dal	363	237	65.3	2754	7.59	11	61	10	32	224	86.7
Jeff Hostetler, NY	285	179	62.8	2032	7.13	5	55	4	20	100	84.1
Rich Gannon, Min	354	211	59.6	2166	6.12	12	50	6	19	91	81.5
Chris Miller, Atl	413	220	53.3	3103	7.51	26	80-td	18	23	145	80.6
Jim McMahon, Phi	311	187	60.1	2239	7.20	12	75-td	11	21	128	80.3
Steve Walsh, NO	255	149	55.3	1638	6.42	11	41	6	3	26	79.5
Bobby Hebert, NO	248	149	60.1	1676	6.76	9	65-td	8	16	134	79.0

Receiving

AFC	No	Yds	Avg	Long	TD
Haywood Jeffires, Hou	100	1181	11.8	44	7
Drew Hill, Hou	90	1109	12.3	61-td	4
Marv Cook, NE	82	808	9.9	49	3
Andre Reed, Buf	81	1113	13.7	55	10
Al Toon, NY	74	963	13.0	32	0
Bill Brooks, Ind	72	888	12.3	46	4
Mark Duper, Mia	70	1085	15.5	43-td	5
Mark Clayton, Mia	70	1053	15.0	43-td	12
Brian Blades, Sea	70	1003	14.3	52	2
Ernest Givins, Hou	70	996	14.2	49	5
Rob Moore, NY	70	963	13.0	32	0

NFC	No	Yds	Avg	Long	TD
Michael Irvin, Dal	93	1523	16.4	66-td	8
Andre Rison, Atl	81	976	12.0	39-td	12
Jerry Rice, SF	80	1206	15.1	73-td	14
Cris Carter, Min	72	962	13.4	50	5
Art Monk, Wash	71	1049	14.8	64-td	8
Gary Clark, Wash	70	1340	19.1	82-td	10
Sterling Sharpe, GB	69	961	13.9	58-td	4
Eric Martin, NO	66	803	12.2	30	4
Henry Ellard, LA	64	1052	16.4	38	3
John Taylor, SF	64	1011	15.8	97-td	9
Floyd Turner, NO	64	927	14.5	65-td	8

Rushing

AFC	Att	Yds	Avg	Long	TD
Thurman Thomas, Buf	288	1407	4.9	33	7
Gaston Green, Den	261	1037	4.0	63-td	4
Christian Okoye, KC	225	1031	4.6	48	9
Leonard Russell, NE*	266	959	3.6	24	4
Mark Higgs, Mia	231	905	3.9	24	4
Marion Butts, SD	193	834	4.3	44	6
Rod Bernstine, SD	159	766	4.8	63-td	8
John L.Williams, Sea	188	741	3.9	42	4
Harold Green, Cin	158	731	4.6	75-td	2
Blair Thomas, NY	189	728	3.9	25	3

NFC	Att	Yds	Avg	Long	TD
Emmitt Smith, Dal	365	1563	4.3	75-td	12
Barry Sanders, Det	342	1548	4.5	69-td	16
Rodney Hampton, NY	256	1059	4.1	44	10
Earnst Byner, Wash	274	1048	3.8	32	5
Herschel Walker, Min	198	825	4.2	71-td	10
Reggie Cobb, TB	196	752	3.8	59-td	7
Neal Anderson, Chi	210	747	3.6	42-td	6
Robert Delpino, LA	214	688	3.2	36	9
Ricky Ervins, Wash*	145	680	4.7	65-td	3
Johnny Johnson, Pho	196	666	3.4	21	4

All-Purpose Running

AFC	Rush	Rec	Ret	Total
Thurman Thomas, Buf	1407	631	0	2038
Allen Pinkett, Hou	720	228	508	1456
Rod Woodson, Pit	0	0	1272	1272
Andre Reed, Buf	136	1113	0	1249
John L.Williams, Sea	741	499	0	1240
Nate Lewis, SD	10	554	637	1201
Haywood Jeffires, Hou	0	1181	0	1181
Ernest Givins, Hou	30	996	107	1133
Ronnie Harmon, SD	544	555	25	1124
Gaston Green, Den	1037	78	0	1115
Drew Hill, Hou	1	1109	0	1110
Terance Mathis, NY	19	329	756	1104

NFC	Rush	Rec	Ret	Total
Barry Sanders, Det	1548	307	0	1855
Emmitt Smith, Dal	1563	258	0	1821
Rodney Hampton, NY	1059	283	204	1546
Michael Irvin, Dal	0	1523	0	1523
Dexter Carter, SF	379	253	839	1471
Mel Gray, Det	11	42	1314	1367
Dave Meggett, NY	153	412	801	1366
Robert Delpino, LA	688	617	54	1359
Earnest Byner, Wash	1048	308	0	1356
Gary Clark, Wash	0	1340	0	1340
John Taylor, SF	0	1011	267	1278
Jerry Rice, SF	2	1206	0	1208

Note: Returns (Ret) includes kickoffs, punts, fumbles and interceptions returned.

Scoring

Kickers

AFC	PAT	FG	Long	Pts
Pete Stoyanovich, Mia	28/29	31/37	53	121
Jeff Jaeger, LA	29/30	29/34	53	116
David Treadwell, Den	31/32	27/36	47	112
Nick Lowery, KC	35/35	25/30	48	110
Scott Norwood, Buf	56/58	18/29	52	110
Pat Leahy, NY	30/30	26/37	40	108
John Kasay, Sea*	27/28	25/31	54	102
Gary Anderson, Pit	31/31	23/33	54*	100
Jim Breech, Cin	27/27	23/29	50	96
John Carney, SD	31/31	19/29	54	88

NFC	PAT	FG	Long	Pts
Chip Lohmiller, Wash	56/56	31/43	53	149
Ken Willis, Dal	37/37	27/39	54	118
Morten Andersen, NO	38/38	25/32	60	113
Roger Ruzek, Phi	27/29	28/33	51	111
Eddie Murray, Det	40/40	19/28	50	97
Norm Johnson, Atl	38/39	19/23	50	95
Mike Cofer, SF	49/50	14/28	50	91
Matt Bahr, NY	24/25	22/29	54	90
Kevin Butler, Chi	32/34	19/29	50	89
Chris Jacke, GB	31/31	18/24	53	85
Fuad Reveiz, Min	34/35	17/24	50	85

Touchdowns

AFC	TD	Rush	Rec	Ret	Pts
Mark Clayton, Mia	12	0	12	0	72
Thurman Thomas, Buf	12	7	5	0	72
Brad Baxter, NY	11	11	0	0	66
Leroy Hoard, Cle	11	2	9	0	66
Kevin Mack, Cle	10	8	2	0	60
Allen Pinkett, Hou	10	9	1	0	60
Andre Reed, Buf	10	0	10	0	60
Christian Okoye, KC	9	9	0	0	54
Rod Bernstine, SD	8	8	0	0	48
James Lofton, Buf	8	0	8	0	48

NFC	TD	Rush	Rec	Ret	Pts
Barry Sanders, Det	17	16	1	0	102
Jerry Rice, SF	14	0	14	0	84
Emmitt Smith, Dal	13	12	1	0	78
Andre Rison, Atl	12	0	12	0	72
Michael Haynes, Atl	11	0	11	0	66
Gerald Riggs, Wash	11	11	0	0	66
Vince Workman, GB	11	7	4	0	66
Gary Clark, Wash	10	0	10	0	60
Robert Delpino, LA	10	9	1	0	60
Rodney Hampton, NY	10	10	0	0	60
Herschel Walker, Min	10	10	0	0	60

Interceptions

AFC	No	Yds	Long	TD
Ronnie Lott, LA	8	52	27	0
Cris Dishman, Hou	6	61	43	0
Gill Byrd, SD	6	48	22	0
Seven tied with 5 each.				

NFC	No	Yds	Long	TD
Ray Crockett, Det	6	141	96-td	1
Deion Sanders, Atl.	6	119	55-td	1
Aeneas Williams, Pho*	6	60	32	0
Tim McKyer, Atl	6	24	24	0
Eight tied with 5 each.				

Sacks

AFC	No
William Fuller, Houston	15
Simon Fletcher, Denver	13½
Derrick Thomas, Kansas City	13½
Greg Townsend, Los Angeles	13
Anthony Smith, Los Angeles	10½

NFC	No
Pat Swilling, New Orleans	17
Reggie White, Philadelphia	15
Tony Bennett, Green Bay	13
Clyde Simmons, Philadelphia	13
Rickey Jackson, New Orleans	11½
Charles Mann, Washington	11½

Punting

AFC	No	Yds	Long	Avg	In 20
Reggie Roby, Mia	54	2466	64	45.7	17
Jeff Gossett, LA	67	2961	61	44.2	26
Greg Montgomery, Hou	48	2105	60	43.9	13
Lee Johnson, Cin	64	2795	62	43.7	15
Rick Tuten, Sea	49	2106	60	43.0	8

NFC	No	Yds	Long	Avg	In 20
Harry Newsome, Min	68	3095	65	45.5	17
Rich Camarillo, Pho	76	3445	60	45.3	19
Tommy Barnhardt, NO	86	3743	61	43.5	20
Sean Landeta, NY	64	2768	61	43.3	16
Scott Fulhage, Atl	81	3470	60	42.8	21

Punt Returns

AFC	No	Yds	Avg	Long	TD
Rod Woodson, Pit	28	320	11.4	40	0
Tim Brown, LA	29	330	11.4	75-td	1
Kitrick Taylor, SD	28	269	9.6	48	0
Chris Warren, Sea	32	298	9.3	59-td	1
Scott Miller, Mia	28	248	8.9	32	0

NFC	No	Yds	Avg	Long	TD
Mel Gray, Det	25	385	15.4	78-td	1
Brian Mitchell, Wash	45	600	13.3	69-td	2
Kelvin Martin, Dal	21	244	11.6	85-td	1
Dave Meggett, NY	28	287	10.3	70-td	1
Willie Drewrey, TB	38	360	9.5	33	0

Kickoff Returns

AFC	No	Yds	Avg	Long	TD
Nate Lewis, SD	23	578	25.1	95-td	1
Sammy Martin, NE-Ind	20	483	24.2	38	1
Chris Warren, Sea	35	792	22.6	55	0
Harvey Williams, KC	24	524	21.8	76	0
Jon Vaughn, NE*	34	717	21.1	99-td	1

NFC	No	Yds	Avg	Long	TD
Mel Gray, Det	36	929	25.8	71	0
Alexander Wright, Dal	21	514	24.5	102-td	1
Charles Wilson, GB	23	522	22.7	82-td	1
Dexter Carter, SF	37	839	22.7	98-td	1
Deion Sanders, Atl	26	576	22.2	100-td	1

NFL Regular Season Team Leaders

Offense

AFC	Points For	Avg	Yardage Rush	Pass	Total	Avg
Buffalo	458	28.6	2381	3871	6252	390.8
Houston	386	24.1	1366	4621	5987	374.2
Kansas City	322	20.1	2217	3104	5321	332.6
New York	314	19.6	2160	3156	5316	332.3
Miami	343	21.4	1352	3889	5241	327.6
Denver	304	19.0	2018	2994	5012	313.3
San Diego	274	17.1	2248	2747	4995	312.2
Cincinnati	263	16.4	1811	3158	4969	310.6
Cleveland	293	18.3	1360	3304	4664	291.5
Pittsburgh	292	18.3	1627	2954	4581	286.3
Seattle	276	17.3	1426	3108	4534	283.4
New England	211	13.2	1467	3006	4473	279.6
Los Angeles	298	18.6	1706	2719	4425	276.6
Indianapolis	143	8.9	1169	2579	3748	234.3

NFC	Points For	Avg	Yardage Rush	Pass	Total	Avg
San Francisco	393	24.6	1861	3997	5858	366.1
Washington	485	30.3	2049	3692	5741	358.8
Atlanta	361	22.6	1664	3449	5113	319.6
Dallas	342	21.4	1711	3390	5101	318.8
Minnesota	301	18.8	2201	2883	5084	317.8
Chicago	299	18.7	1949	3120	5069	316.8
New Orleans	341	21.3	1709	3259	4968	310.5
New York	281	17.6	2064	2844	4908	306.8
Detroit	339	21.2	1930	2858	4788	299.3
Los Angeles	234	14.6	1285	3410	4695	293.4
Green Bay	273	17.1	1389	2943	4332	270.8
Philadelphia	285	17.8	1396	2906	4302	268.9
Tampa Bay	199	12.4	1429	2572	4001	250.1
Phoenix	196	12.3	1295	2667	3962	247.6

Defense

AFC	Points Opp	Avg	Yardage Rush	Pass	Total	Avg
Denver	235	14.7	1794	2755	4549	284.3
Seattle	261	16.3	1684	3019	4703	293.9
Houston	251	15.7	1540	3208	4748	296.8
New York	293	18.3	1442	3539	4981	311.3
Kansas City	252	15.8	1770	3228	4998	312.4
Cleveland	298	18.6	1875	3209	5084	317.8
San Diego	342	21.4	1669	3442	5111	319.4
Indianapolis	381	23.8	2327	2800	5127	320.4
Los Angeles	297	18.6	1889	3276	5165	322.8
Pittsburgh	344	21.5	1582	3586	5168	323.0
Miami	349	21.8	2301	3105	5406	337.9
New England	305	19.1	1579	3852	5431	339.4
Buffalo	318	19.9	2044	3414	5458	341.1
Cincinnati	435	27.2	1662	3990	5652	353.3

NFC	Points Opp	Avg	Yardage Rush	Pass	Total	Avg
Philadelphia	244	15.3	1136	2413	3549	221.8
New Orleans	211	13.2	1213	2720	3933	245.8
Washington	224	14.0	1346	2947	4293	268.3
Chicago	269	16.8	1580	2927	4507	281.7
San Francisco	239	14.9	1512	3042	4554	284.6
New York	297	18.6	1726	2874	4600	287.5
Green Bay	313	19.6	1546	3266	4812	300.8
Tampa Bay	365	22.8	2107	2872	4979	311.2
Minnesota	306	19.1	1837	3179	5016	313.5
Detroit	295	18.4	1760	3286	5046	315.4
Phoenix	344	21.5	2136	2916	5052	315.8
Dallas	310	19.4	1571	3495	5066	316.6
Los Angeles	390	24.4	1659	3545	5204	325.3
Atlanta	338	21.1	1953	3295	5248	328.0

Takeaways / Giveaways

AFC	Takeaways Int	Fum	Tot	Giveaways Int	Fum	Tot	Net Diff
Cleveland	15	18	33	10	8	18	+15
New York	18	19	37	12	13	25	+12
Kansas City	15	18	33	14	8	22	+11
Denver	23	10	33	12	13	25	+8
Buffalo	23	14	37	19	16	35	+2
Pittsburgh	19	11	30	16	14	30	0
Los Angeles	18	13	31	18	13	31	0
San Diego	19	9	28	16	12	28	0
Houston	20	18	38	21	19	40	-2
Indianapolis	15	13	28	16	15	31	-3
Seattle	18	21	39	26	17	43	-4
Miami	12	9	21	14	14	28	-7
Cincinnati	17	14	31	22	20	42	-11
New England	12	19	31	22	20	42	-11

NFC	Takeaways Int	Fum	Tot	Giveaways Int	Fum	Tot	Net Diff
New Orleans	29	19	48	15	15	30	+18
Washington	27	14	41	11	12	23	+18
Detroit	19	17	36	17	13	30	+6
Philadelphia	26	22	48	27	16	43	+5
Minnesota	17	11	28	16	10	26	+2
Atlanta	19	16	35	22	14	36	-1
Dallas	12	11	23	12	12	24	-1
Phoenix	17	21	38	25	14	39	-1
New York	12	9	21	8	15	23	-2
Chicago	17	13	30	17	16	33	-3
San Francisco	12	16	28	12	19	31	-3
Green Bay	15	14	29	19	17	36	-7
Tampa Bay	11	16	27	29	18	47	-20
Los Angeles	11	8	19	20	20	40	-21

Overall Club Rankings

Combined AFC and NFC rankings by yards gained on offense and yards given up on defense.

	Offense Rush	Pass	Rank	Defense Rush	Pass	Rank
Atlanta	16	6	8	23	20	24
Buffalo	1	4	1	24	21	27
Chicago	9	13	11	10	8	4
Cincinnati	12	11	14	13	28	28
Cleveland	24	9	19	21	15	18
Dallas	13	8	9	8	23	17
Denver	8	17	12	19	3	5
Detroit	10	22	17	17	19	15
Green Bay	22	19	24	7	17	10
Houston	23	1	2	6	14	9
Indianapolis	28	27	28	28	4	20
Kansas City	3	15	5	18	16	13
LA Raiders	15	25	23	22	18	21
LA Rams	27	7	18	12	25	23
Miami	25	3	7	27	12	25
Minnesota	4	21	10	20	13	14
N.England	18	16	22	9	27	26
N.Orleans	14	10	15	2	2	2
NY Giants	6	23	16	16	6	7
NY Jets	5	12	6	4	24	12
Philadelphia	21	20	25	1	1	1
Phoenix	26	26	27	26	7	16
Pittsburgh	17	18	20	11	26	22
San Diego	2	24	13	14	22	19
San Fran	11	2	3	5	11	6
Seattle	20	14	21	15	10	8
Tampa Bay	19	28	26	25	5	11
Washington	7	5	4	3	9	3

AFC Team by Team Statistics

Players with more than one team during the regular season are listed with second club; (*) denotes rookies.

Buffalo Bills

Passing (5 Att)	Att	Cmp	Pct	Yds	TD	Rate
Jim Kelly	474	304	64.1	3844	33	97.6
Frank Reich	41	27	65.9	305	6	107.2

Interceptions: Kelly 17, Reich 2.

Top Receivers	No	Yds	Avg	Long	TD
Andre Reed	81	1113	13.7	55	10
Thurman Thomas	62	631	10.2	50-td	5
James Lofton	57	1072	18.8	77-td	8
Keith McKeller	44	434	9.9	29-td	3
Don Beebe	32	414	12.9	34-td	6

Top Rushers	Car	Yds	Avg	Long	TD
Thurman Thomas	288	1407	4.9	33	7
Kenneth Davis	129	624	4.8	78-td	4
Carwell Gardner	42	146	3.5	18	4
Andre Reed	12	136	11.3	46	0
Jim Kelly	20	45	2.3	12	1

Most Touchdowns	TD	Run	Rec	Ret	Pts
Thurman Thomas	12	7	5	0	72
Andre Reed	10	0	10	0	60
James Lofton	8	0	8	0	48
Don Beebe	6	0	6	0	36
Kenneth Davis	5	4	1	0	30

Kicking	PAT/Att	FG/Att	Lg	Pts
Scott Norwood	56/58	18/29	52	110

Punts (15 or more)	No	Yds	Long	Avg	In 20
Chris Mohr	54	2085	58	38.6	12

Most Interceptions		Most Sacks	
Nate Odomes	5	Cornelius Bennett	9
Darryl Talley	5		

Cleveland Browns

Passing (5 Att)	Att	Cmp	Pct	Yds	TD	Rate
Bernie Kosar	494	307	62.1	3487	18	87.8
Todd Philcox	8	4	50.0	49	0	29.7

Interceptions: Kosar 9, Philcox 1.
Also threw TD pass: Brian Hansen 1.

Top Receivers	No	Yds	Avg	Long	TD
Webster Slaughter	64	906	14.2	62-td	3
Leroy Hoard	48	567	11.8	71-td	9
Kevin Mack	40	255	6.4	22	2
Reggie Langhorne	39	505	12.9	40-td	2
Brian Brennan	31	325	10.5	30	1

Top Rushers	Car	Yds	Avg	Long	TD
Kevin Mack	197	726	3.7	51-td	8
Joe Morris	93	289	3.1	15	2
Leroy Hoard	37	154	4.2	52	2
Eric Metcalf	30	107	3.6	15	0
Bernie Kosar	26	74	2.8	14	0

Most Touchdowns	TD	Run	Rec	Ret	Pts
Leroy Hoard	11	2	9	0	66
Kevin Mack	10	8	2	0	60
Webster Slaughter	3	0	3	0	18

Three tied with 2 TDs each.

Kicking	PAT/Att	FG/Att	Lg	Pts
Matt Stover	33/34	16/22	55	81

Punts (15 or more)	No	Yds	Long	Avg	In 20
Brian Hansen	80	3397	65	42.5	20

Most Interceptions		Most Sacks	
Stephen Braggs	3	Michael Dean Perry	8½

Cincinnati Bengals

Passing (5 Att)	Att	Cmp	Pct	Yds	TD	Rate
Boomer Esiason	413	233	56.4	2883	13	72.5
Donald Hollas*	55	32	58.2	310	1	49.8
Erik Wilhelm	42	24	57.1	217	9	51.4

Interceptions: Esiason 14, Hollas 4, Wilhelm 2.

Top Receivers	No	Yds	Avg	Long	TD
Eddie Brown	59	827	14.0	53	2
Tim McGee	51	802	15.7	52-td	4
James Brooks	40	348	8.7	40	2
Rodney Holman	31	445	14.4	39	2
Mike Barber	23	255	11.1	42-td	1

Top Rushers	Car	Yds	Avg	Long	TD
Harold Green	158	731	4.6	75-td	2
James Brooks	152	571	3.8	25	2
Craig Taylor	33	153	4.6	34-td	2
Ickey Woods	36	97	2.7	12	4
Mike Dingle*	21	91	4.3	21	0

Most Touchdowns	TD	Run	Rec	Ret	Pts
James Brooks	4	2	2	0	24
Tim McGee	4	0	4	0	24
Ickey Woods	4	4	0	0	24

Four tied with 2 TDs each.

Kicking	PAT/Att	FG/Att	Lg	Pts
Jim Breech	27/27	23/29	50	96

Punts (15 or more)	No	Yds	Long	Avg	In 20
Lee Johnson	64	2795	62	43.7	15

Most Interceptions		Most Sacks	
David Fulcher	4	Tim Krumrie	4
		Danny Stubbs	4

Signed: Stubbs (Nov.5) after release by Dallas (Nov.4).

Denver Broncos

Passing (5 Att)	Att	Cmp	Pct	Yds	TD	Rate
John Elway	451	242	53.7	3253	13	75.4
Gary Kubiak	5	3	60.0	33	0	79.6

Interceptions: Elway 12.

Top Receivers	No	Yds	Avg	Long	TD
Mike Young	44	629	14.3	52-td	2
Steve Sewell	38	436	11.5	60	2
Mark Jackson	33	603	18.3	71	1
Shannon Sharpe	22	322	14.6	37	1

Two tied with 21 catches each.

Top Rushers	Car	Yds	Avg	Long	TD
Gaston Green	261	1037	4.0	63-td	4
Greg Lewis*	99	376	3.8	27	4
John Elway	54	255	4.6	17-td	6
Steve Sewell	50	211	4.2	26	2
Bob Perryman	21	45	2.1	6	0

Most Touchdowns	TD	Run	Rec	Ret	Pts
John Elway	6	6	0	0	36
Gaston Green	4	4	0	0	24
Greg Lewis*	4	4	0	0	24
Steve Sewell	4	2	2	0	24
Vance Johnson	3	0	3	0	18

Kicking	PAT/Att	FG/Att	Lg	Pts
David Treadwell	31/32	27/36	47	112

Punts (15 or more)	No	Yds	Long	Avg	In 20
Mike Horan	72	3012	71	41.8	24

Most Interceptions		Most Sacks	
Steve Atwater	5	Simon Fletcher	13½
Dennis Smith	5		

Houston Oilers

Passing (5 Att)	Att	Cmp	Pct	Yds	TD	Rate
Warren Moon	655	404	61.7	4690	23	81.7
Cody Carlson	12	7	58.3	114	1	118.1

Interceptions: Moon 21.

Top Receivers	No	Yds	Avg	Long	TD
Haywood Jeffries..........	100	1181	11.8	44	7
Drew Hill	90	1109	12.3	61-td	5
Ernest Givins	70	996	14.2	49	5
Curtis Duncan	55	588	10.7	42	4
Allen Pinkett	29	228	7.9	36-td	1

Top Rushers	Car	Yds	Avg	Long	TD
Allen Pinkett	171	720	4.2	32	9
Lorenzo White	110	465	4.2	20	4
Gary Brown*	8	85	10.6	39-td	1
Warren Moon	33	68	2.1	12	2
Ernest Givins	4	30	7.5	23	0

Most Touchdowns	TD	Run	Rec	Ret	Pts
Allen Pinkett	10	9	1	0	60
Haywood Jeffries..........	7	0	7	0	42
Ernest Givins	5	0	5	0	30
Curtis Duncan	4	0	4	0	24
Drew Hill	4	0	4	0	24
Lorenzo White	4	4	0	0	24

Kicking	PAT/Att	FG/Att	Lg	Pts
Ian Howfield	25/29	13/18	46	64
Al Del Greco	16/16	10/13	52	46

Released: Howfield (Nov.4).
Signed: De Greco (Nov.5).

Punts (15 or more)	No	Yds	Long	Avg	In 20
Greg Montgomery	48	2105	60	43.9	13

Most Interceptions		Most Sacks	
Cris Dishman...........	6	William Fuller..........	15

Indianapolis Colts

Passing (5 Att)	Att	Cmp	Pct	Yds	TD	Rate
Jeff George	485	292	60.2	2910	10	73.8
Mark Herrmann ...	19	11	57.9	137	0	40.8
Jack Trudeau	7	2	28.6	19	0	0.0

Interceptions: George 12, Herrmann 3, Trudeau 1.

Top Receivers	No	Yds	Avg	Long	TD
Bill Brooks	72	888	12.3	46	4
Jessie Hester	60	753	12.6	49-td	5
Anthony Johnson	42	344	8.2	24	0
Eric Dickerson	41	269	6.6	26	1
Ken Clark.................	33	245	7.4	23	0

Top Rushers	Car	Yds	Avg	Long	TD
Eric Dickerson	167	536	3.2	28	2
Ken Clark.................	114	366	3.2	25	0
Tim Manoa	27	144	5.3	44	1
Anthony Johnson	22	94	4.3	15	0
Jeff George	16	36	2.3	13	0

Most Touchdowns	TD	Run	Rec	Ret	Pts
Jessie Hester................	5	0	5	0	30
Bill Brooks.................	4	0	4	0	24
Eric Dickerson	3	2	1	0	18

Two tied with 1 TD each.

Kicking	PAT/Att	FG/Att	Lg	Pts
Dean Biasucci	14/14	15/26	54	59

Punts (15 or more)	No	Yds	Long	Avg	In 20
Rohn Stark...............	82	3492	65	42.6	14

Most Interceptions		Most Sacks	
John Baylor	4	Duane Bickett...........	5
		Jon Hand..............	5
		Donnell Thompson	5

Kansas City Chiefs

Passing (5 Att)	Att	Cmp	Pct	Yds	TD	Rate
Steve DeBerg......	434	256	59.0	2965	17	79.3
Mark Vlasic	44	28	63.6	316	2	100.2

Interceptions: DeBerg 14.

Top Receivers	No	Yds	Avg	Long	TD
Robb Thomas	43	495	11.5	39	1
Tim Barnett*.............	41	564	13.8	63	5
Todd McNair	37	342	9.2	36	1
Emile Harry	35	431	12.3	36	3
J.J.Birden	27	465	17.2	57-td	2

Top Rushers	Car	Yds	Avg	Long	TD
Christian Okoye	225	1031	4.6	48	9
Barry Word	160	684	4.3	37	4
Harvey Williams*..........	87	447	4.6	21	1
Todd McNair	10	51	5.1	11	0
James Saxon	6	13	2.2	8	0

Most Touchdowns	TD	Run	Rec	Ret	Pts
Christian Okoye	9	9	0	0	54
Tim Barnett*..............	5	0	5	0	30
Barry Word...............	4	4	0	0	24
Emile Harry	3	0	3	0	18
Harvey Williams*...........	3	1	2	0	18

Kicking	PAT/Att	FG/Att	Lg	Pts
Nick Lowery...........	35/35	25/30	48	110

Punts (15 or more)	No	Yds	Long	Avg	In 20
Bryan Barker	57	2303	57	40.4	11

Most Interceptions		Most Sacks	
Deron Cherry...........	4	Derrick Thomas......	13½

Los Angeles Raiders

Passing (5 Att)	Att	Cmp	Pct	Yds	TD	Rate
Jay Schroeder	357	189	52.9	2562	15	71.4
Todd Marinovich* ...	40	23	57.5	243	3	100.3
Vince Evans	14	6	42.9	127	1	59.8

Interceptions: Schroeder 16, Evans 2.
Also threw TD pass: Marcus Allen 1.

Top Receivers	No	Yds	Avg	Long	TD
Ethan Horton	53	650	12.3	52	5
Mervyn Fernandez..........	46	694	15.1	59	1
Tim Brown	36	554	15.4	78-td	5
Willie Gault	20	346	17.3	59-td	4
Roger Craig	17	136	8.0	20	0

Top Rushers	Car	Yds	Avg	Long	TD
Roger Craig	162	590	3.6	15	1
Nick Bell*	78	307	3.9	15	3
Marcus Allen	63	287	4.6	26	2
Steve Smith	62	265	4.3	19	1
Napoleon McCallum ...	31	110	3.5	9	1

Most Touchdowns	TD	Run	Rec	Ret	Pts
Tim Brown	6	0	5	1	36
Ethan Horton	5	0	5	0	30
Willie Gault	4	0	4	0	24
Nick Bell*	3	3	0	0	18
Andrew Glover*.............	3	0	3	0	18

Kicking	PAT/Att	FG/Att	Lg	Pts
Jeff Jaeger	29/30	29/34	53	116

Punts (15 or more)	No	Yds	Long	Avg	In 20
Jeff Gossett	67	2961	61	44.2	26

Most Interceptions		Most Sacks	
Ronnie Lott	8	Greg Townsend........	13

Miami Dolphins

Passing (5 Att)	Att	Cmp	Pct	Yds	TD	Rate
Dan Marino	549	318	57.9	3970	25	85.8
Scott Secules	13	8	61.5	90	1	75.8

Interceptions: Marino 13, Secules 1.

Top Receivers	No	Yds	Avg	Long	TD
Mark Duper	70	1085	15.5	43-td	5
Mark Clayton	70	1053	15.0	43-td	12
Tony Paige	57	469	8.2	26	1
Tony Martin	27	434	16.1	54	2
Jim Jensen	21	183	8.7	19	2

Top Rushers	Car	Yds	Avg	Long	TD
Mark Higgs	231	905	3.9	24	4
Sammie Smith	83	297	3.6	18	1
Aaron Craver*	20	58	2.9	7-td	1
Dan Marino	27	32	1.2	11	1
Scott Secules	4	30	7.5	12	1

Most Touchdowns	TD	Run	Rec	Ret	Pts
Mark Clayton	12	0	12	0	72
Mark Duper	5	0	5	0	30
Mark Higgs	4	4	0	0	24

Three tied with 2 TDs each.

Kicking	PAT/Att	FG/Att	Lg	Pts
Pete Stoyanovich	28/29	31/37	53	121

Signed: Stoyanovich (Sept.6) after holdout.
Released: Charlie Bauman (Sept.13).

Punts (15 or more)	No	Yds	Long	Avg	In 20
Reggie Roby	54	2466	64	45.7	17

Most Interceptions		Most Sacks	
Louis Oliver	5	Jeff Cross	7

New York Jets

Passing (5 Att)	Att	Cmp	Pct	Yds	TD	Rate
Ken O'Brien	489	287	58.7	3300	10	76.6
Troy Taylor	10	5	50.0	76	1	69.2

Interceptions: O'Brien 11, Taylor 1.
Also threw TD pass: Blair Thomas 1.

Top Receivers	No	Yds	Avg	Long	TD
Al Toon	74	963	13.0	32	0
Rob Moore	70	987	14.1	53	5
Blair Thomas	30	195	6.5	18	1
Terance Mathis	28	329	11.8	39	1
Chris Burkett	23	327	14.2	50-td	4

Top Rushers	Car	Yds	Avg	Long	TD
Blair Thomas	189	728	3.9	25	3
Brad Baxter	184	666	3.6	31	11
Johnny Hector	62	345	5.6	47	0
Freeman McNeill	51	300	5.9	58	2

Most Touchdowns	TD	Run	Rec	Ret	Pts
Brad Baxter	11	11	0	0	66
Chris Burkett	5	0	4	1	30
Rob Moore	5	0	5	0	30
Blair Thomas	4	3	1	0	24

Kicking	PAT/Att	FG/Att	Lg	Pts
Pat Leahy	30/30	26/37	40	108
Raul Allegre	7/7	5/6	44	22
NYG	5/5	2/2	36	11
NYJ	2/2	3/4	44	11

Signed: Allegre (Dec.17) after release by NY Giants (Nov.29).

Punts (15 or more)	No	Yds	Long	Avg	In 20
Louie Aguiar	64	2521	61	39.4	14

Most Interceptions		Most Sacks	
Mike Brim	4	Jeff Lageman	10

New England Patriots

Passing (5 Att)	Att	Cmp	Pct	Yds	TD	Rate
Hugh Millen	409	246	60.1	3073	9	72.5
Tom Hodson	68	36	52.9	345	1	47.7

Interceptions: Millen 18, Hodson 4.
Also threw TD pass: Jon Vaughn 1.

Top Receivers	No	Yds	Avg	Long	TD
Marv Cook	82	808	9.9	49	3
Irving Fryar	68	1014	14.9	56-td	3
Greg McMurtry	41	614	15.0	40	2
Michael Timpson	25	471	18.8	60-td	2
Leonard Russell*	18	81	4.5	18	0

Top Rushers	Car	Yds	Avg	Long	TD
Leonard Russell*	266	959	3.6	24	4
John Stephens	63	163	2.6	13	2
Jon Vaughn*	31	146	4.7	23	2
Hugh Millen	31	92	3.0	14	1

Most Touchdowns	TD	Run	Rec	Ret	Pts
Leonard Russell*	4	4	0	0	24
Marv Cook	3	0	3	0	18
Irving Fryar	3	0	3	0	18
Jon Vaughn*	3	2	0	1	18

Kicking	PAT/Att	FG/Att	Lg	Pts
Jason Staurovsky	10/11	13/19	42	49
Charlie Baumann	15/16	9/12	48	42
MIA	6/6	2/2	48	12
NE	9/10	7/10	46	30

Signed: Bauman (Nov.6) after release by Miami (Sept.13).

Punts (15 or more)	No	Yds	Long	Avg	In 20
Shawn McCarthy	66	2650	93	40.2	17

Most Interceptions		Most Sacks	
Maurice Hurst	3	Andre Tippett	8½

Pittsburgh Steelers

Passing (5 Att)	Att	Cmp	Pct	Yds	TD	Rate
Neil O'Donnell	286	156	54.5	1963	11	78.8
Bubby Brister	190	103	54.2	1350	9	72.9

Interceptions: Brister 9, O'Donnell 7.

Top Receivers	No	Yds	Avg	Long	TD
Louis Lipps	55	671	12.2	35	2
Merril Hoge	49	379	7.7	25	1
Eric Green	41	582	14.2	49	6
Dwight Stone	32	649	20.3	89-td	5

Two tied with 15 catches each.

Top Rushers	Car	Yds	Avg	Long	TD
Merril Hoge	165	610	3.7	24	1
Barry Foster	96	488	5.1	56-td	1
Warren Williams	57	262	4.6	21	4
Tim Worley	22	117	5.3	16	0
Neil O'Donnell	18	82	4.6	22	1

Most Touchdowns	TD	Run	Rec	Ret	Pts
Eric Green	6	0	6	0	36
Dwight Stone	5	0	5	0	30
Warren Williams	4	4	0	0	24
Merril Hoge	3	2	1	0	18

Four tied with 2 TDs each.

Kicking	PAT/Att	FG/Att	Lg	Pts
Gary Anderson	31/31	23/33	54	100

Punts (15 or more)	No	Yds	Long	Avg	In 20
Dan Stryzinski	74	2996	63	40.5	10

Most Interceptions		Most Sacks	
Thomas Everett	4	Jerrol Williams	9

San Diego Chargers

Passing (5 Att)	Att	Cmp	Pct	Yds	TD	Rate
John Friesz	487	262	53.8	2896	12	67.1
Bob Gagliano	23	9	39.1	76	0	30.3

Interceptions: Friesz 15, Gagliano 1.
Also threw TD pass: Rod Bernstine 1.

Top Receivers	No	Yds	Avg	Long	TD
Ronnie Harmon	59	555	9.4	36	1
Anthony Miller	44	649	14.8	58	3
Nate Lewis	42	554	13.2	49-td	3
Craig McEwen	37	399	10.8	30	3
Kitrick Taylor	24	218	9.1	27	0

Top Rushers	Car	Yds	Avg	Long	TD
Marion Butts	193	834	4.3	44	6
Rod Bernstine	159	766	4.8	63-td	8
Ronnie Harmon	89	544	6.1	33	1

Most Touchdowns	TD	Run	Rec	Ret	Pts
Rod Bernstine*	8	8	0	0	48
Marion Butts	7	6	1	0	42
Nate Lewis	4	0	3	1	24
Craig McEwen	3	0	3	0	18
Anthony Miller	3	0	3	0	18

Kicking	PAT/Att	FG/Att	Lg	Pts
John Carney	31/31	19/29	54	88

Punts (15 or more)	No	Yds	Long	Avg	In 20
John Kidd	76	3064	60	40.3	22

Most Interceptions		Most Sacks	
Gill Byrd	6	Leslie O'Neal	9

Seattle Seahawks

Passing (5 Att)	Att	Cmp	Pct	Yds	TD	Rate
Dave Krieg	285	187	65.6	2080	11	82.5
Kelly Stouffer	15	6	40.0	57	0	23.5
Dan McGwire*	7	3	42.9	27	0	14.3

Interceptions: Krieg 12, McGwire 1.
Released: QB Jeff Kemp (Oct.15).

Top Receivers	No	Yds	Avg	Long	TD
Brian Blades	70	1003	14.3	52	2
John L.Williams	61	499	8.2	35	1
Tommy Kane	50	763	15.3	60	2
Jeff Chadwick	22	255	11.6	29	3
Louis Clark	21	228	10.9	24-td	2

Top Rushers	Car	Yds	Avg	Long	TD
John L.Williams	188	741	3.9	42	4
Derrick Fenner	91	267	2.9	15	4
James Jones	45	154	3.4	22	3
Derek Loville	22	69	3.1	22	0
Dave Krieg	13	59	4.5	24	0

Most Touchdowns	TD	Run	Rec	Ret	Pts
John L.Williams	5	4	1	0	30
Derrick Fenner	4	4	0	0	24
Mike Tice	4	0	4	0	24

Two tied with 3 TDs each.

Kicking	PAT/Att	FG/Att	Lg	Pts
John Kasay*	27/28	25/31	54	102

Punts (15 or more)	No	Yds	Long	Avg	In 20
Rick Tuten	49	2106	60	43.0	8

Signed: Tuten (Oct.9) after preseason release by Green Bay.

Most Interceptions		Most Sacks	
Eugene Robinson	5	Rufus Porter	10

NFC Team by Team Statistics

Players with more than one team during the regular season are listed with second club; (*) denotes rookies.

Atlanta Falcons

Passing (5 Att)	Att	Cmp	Pct	Yds	TD	Rate
Chris Miller	413	220	53.3	3103	26	80.6
Billy Joe Tolliver	82	40	48.8	531	4	75.8
Brett Favre*	5	0	00.0	0	0	00.0

Interceptions: Miller 18, Tolliver 2, Favre 2.

Top Receivers	No	Yds	Avg	Long	TD
Andre Rison	81	976	12.0	39-td	12
Michael Haynes	50	1122	22.4	80-td	11
Mike Pritchard*	50	624	12.5	29	2
George Thomas	28	365	13.0	37	2
Floyd Dixon	12	146	12.2	23	1

Top Rushers	Car	Yds	Avg	Long	TD
Steve Broussard	99	449	4.5	36	4
Mike Rozier	96	361	3.8	19	0
Erric Pegram*	101	349	3.5	34	1
Chris Miller	32	229	7.2	20	0
Pat Chaffey	29	127	4.4	27	1

Most Touchdowns	TD	Run	Rec	Ret	Pts
Andre Rison	12	0	12	0	72
Michael Haynes	11	0	11	0	66
Steve Broussard	5	4	1	0	30

Three tied with 2 TDs each.

Kicking	PAT/Att	FG/Att	Lg	Pts
Norm Johnson	38/39	19/23	50	95

Punts (15 or more)	No	Yds	Long	Avg	In 20
Scott Fulhage	81	3470	60	42.8	21

Most Interceptions		Most Sacks	
Tim McKyer	6	Tim Green	5
Deion Sanders	6		

Chicago Bears

Passing (5 Att)	Att	Cmp	Pct	Yds	TD	Rate
Jim Harbaugh	478	275	57.5	3121	15	73.7
Peter Tom Willis	11	61.1	171	1	88.0

Interceptions: Harbaugh 16, Willis 1.

Top Receivers	No	Yds	Avg	Long	TD
Wendell Davis	61	945	15.5	75-td	6
Tom Waddle	55	599	10.9	37-td	3
Neal Anderson	47	368	7.8	26-td	3
Brad Muster	35	287	8.2	21	1
James Thornton	17	278	16.4	33	1

Top Rushers	Car	Yds	Avg	Long	TD
Neal Anderson	210	747	3.6	42-td	6
Brad Muster	90	412	4.6	24	6
Jim Harbaugh	70	338	4.8	20	2
Mark Green	61	217	3.6	18	3
James Rouse	27	74	2.7	10	0

Most Touchdowns	TD	Run	Rec	Ret	Pts
Neal Anderson	9	6	3	0	54
Brad Muster	7	6	1	0	42
Wendell Davis	6	0	6	0	36
Mark Green	3	3	0	0	18
Tom Waddle	3	0	3	0	18

Kicking	PAT/Att	FG/Att	Lg	Pts
Kevin Butler	32/34	19/29	50	89

Punts (15 or more)	No	Yds	Long	Avg	In 20
Maury Buford	69	2814	64	40.8	13

Most Interceptions		Most Sacks	
Lemuel Stinson	4	Richard Dent	10½

Dallas Cowboys

Passing (5 Att)

	Att	Cmp	Pct	Yds	TD	Rate
Troy Aikman	363	237	65.3	2754	11	86.7
Steve Beuerlein	137	68	49.6	909	5	77.2

Interceptions: Aikman 10, Beuerlein 2.

Top Receivers

	No	Yds	Avg	Long	TD
Michael Irvin	93	1523	16.4	66-td	8
Jay Novacek	59	664	11.3	49	4
Emmitt Smith	49	258	5.3	14	1
Daryl Johnston	28	244	8.7	22	1
Alvin Harper*	20	326	16.3	39	1

Top Rushers

	Car	Yds	Avg	Long	TD
Emmitt Smith	365	1563	4.3	75-td	12
Ricky Blake	15	80	5.3	30-td	1
Daryl Johnston	17	54	3.2	10	0
Tommie Agee	9	20	2.2	8	1
Troy Aikman	16	5	0.3	9	1

Most Touchdowns

	TD	Run	Rec	Ret	Pts
Emmitt Smith	13	12	1	0	78
Michael Irvin	8	0	8	0	48
Jay Novacek	4	0	4	0	24
Ray Horton	2	0	0	2	12

Ten tied with 1 TD each.

Kicking

	PAT/Att	FG/Att	Lg	Pts
Ken Willis	37/37	27/39	54	118

Punts (15 or more)

	No	Yds	Long	Avg	In 20
Mike Saxon	57	2426	64	42.6	16

Most Interceptions
Issiac Holt 4

Most Sacks
Tony Tolbert 7

Detroit Lions

Passing (5 Att)

	Att	Cmp	Pct	Yds	TD	Rate
Erik Kramer	265	136	51.3	1635	11	71.8
Rodney Peete	194	116	59.8	1339	5	69.9

Interceptions: Peete 9, Kramer 8.

Top Receivers

	No	Yds	Avg	Long	TD
Brett Perriman	52	668	12.8	42	1
Robert Clark	47	640	13.6	68-td	6
Mike Farr	42	431	10.3	34-td	1
Barry Sanders	41	307	7.5	34	1
Willie Green	39	592	15.2	73-td	7

Top Rushers

	Car	Yds	Avg	Long	TD
Barry Sanders	342	1548	4.5	69-td	16
Rodney Peete	25	125	5.0	26	2
Don Overton	14	59	4.2	9	0
Cedric Jackson*	17	55	3.2	10	0
D.J.Dozier	9	48	5.3	29	0

Most Touchdowns

	TD	Run	Rec	Ret	Pts
Barry Sanders	17	16	1	0	102
Willie Green	7	0	7	0	42
Robert Clark	6	0	6	0	36
Rodney Peete	2	2	0	0	12

Eight tied with 1 TD each.

Kicking

	PAT/Att	FG/Att	Lg	Pts
Eddie Murray	40/40	19/28	50	97

Punts (15 or more)

	No	Yds	Long	Avg	In 20
Jim Arnold	75	3092	63	41.2	27

Most Interceptions
Ray Crockett 6

Most Sacks
Jeff Hunter 6

Green Bay Packers

Passing (5 Att)

	Att	Cmp	Pct	Yds	TD	Rate
Mike Tomczak	238	128	53.8	1490	11	72.6
Don Majkowski	226	115	50.9	1362	3	59.3
Blair Kiel	50	29	58.0	361	3	83.8

Interceptions: Tomczak 9, Majkowski 8, Kiel 2.

Top Receivers

	No	Yds	Avg	Long	TD
Sterling Sharpe	69	961	13.9	58-td	4
Vince Workman	46	371	8.1	25	4
Perry Kemp	42	583	13.9	39	2
Jackie Harris	24	264	11.0	35	3
Keith Woodside	22	185	8.4	28	0

Top Rushers

	Car	Yds	Avg	Long	TD
Darrell Thompson	141	471	3.3	40-td	1
Keith Woodside	84	326	3.9	29	1
Vince Workman	71	237	3.3	30-td	1
Don Majkowski	25	108	4.3	15	2
Allen Rice	30	100	3.3	21	0

Most Touchdowns

	TD	Run	Rec	Ret	Pts
Vince Workman	11	7	4	0	66
Sterling Sharpe	4	0	4	0	24
Jackie Harris	3	0	3	0	18
Ed West	3	0	3	0	18

Three tied with 2 TDs each.

Kicking

	PAT/Att	FG/Att	Lg	Pts
Chris Jacke	31/31	18/24	53	85

Punts (15 or more)

	No	Yds	Long	Avg	In 20
Paul McJulien	86	3473	62	40.4	22

Most Interceptions
LeRoy Butler 3
Chuck Cecil 3
Mark Murphy 3

Most Sacks
Tony Bennett 13

Los Angeles Rams

Passing (5 Att)

	Att	Cmp	Pct	Yds	TD	Rate
Jim Everett	490	277	56.5	3438	11	68.9
Mike Pagel	27	11	40.7	150	2	83.9

Interceptions: Everett 20.

Top Receivers

	No	Yds	Avg	Long	TD
Henry Ellard	64	1052	16.4	38	3
Robert Delpino	55	617	11.2	78	1
Jim Price	35	410	11.7	27	2
Willie Anderson	32	530	16.6	54	1
Damone Johnson	32	253	7.9	27	2

Top Rushers

	Car	Yds	Avg	Long	TD
Robert Delpino	214	688	3.2	36	9
Cleveland Gary	68	245	3.6	14	1
Marcus Dupree	49	179	3.7	24	1
Buford McGee	19	65	3.4	9	0
Jim Everett	27	44	1.6	10	0

Most Touchdowns

	TD	Run	Rec	Ret	Pts
Robert Delpino	10	9	1	0	60
Henry Ellard	3	0	3	0	18
Pat Carter	2	0	2	0	12
Damone Johnson	2	0	2	0	12
Jim Price	2	0	2	0	12

Kicking

	PAT/Att	FG/Att	Lg	Pts
Tony Zendejas	25/26	17/17	50	76

Punts (15 or more)

	No	Yds	Long	Avg	In 20
Dale Hatcher	63	2403	52	38.1	16

Released: Hatcher (Dec.4).

Most Interceptions
Jerry Gray 3
Darryl Henley 3

Most Sacks
Kevin Greene 3
Gerald Robinson 3

Minnesota Vikings

Passing (5 Att)	Att	Cmp	Pct	Yds	TD	Rate
Rich Gannon	354	211	59.6	2166	12	81.5
Wade Wilson	122	72	59.0	825	3	53.5

Interceptions: Wilson 10, Gannon 6.
Also threw TD pass: Darrin Nelson 1.

Top Receivers	No	Yds	Avg	Long	TD
Cris Carter	72	962	13.4	50	5
Steve Jordan	57	638	11.2	25	2
Anthony Carter	51	553	10.8	46-td	5
Herschel Walker	33	204	6.2	19	0
Hassan Jones	32	384	12.0	43	1

Top Rushers	Car	Yds	Avg	Long	TD
Herschel Walker	198	825	4.2	71-td	10
Terry Allen	120	563	4.7	55-td	2
Rich Gannon	43	236	5.5	42	2
Darrin Nelson	28	210	7.5	29	2
Alfred Anderson	26	118	4.5	19	1

Most Touchdowns	TD	Run	Rec	Ret	Pts
Herschel Walker	10	10	0	0	60
Anthony Carter	6	1	5	0	36
Cris Carter	5	0	5	0	30
Terry Allen	3	2	1	0	18

Four tied with 2 TDs each.

Kicking	PAT/Att	FG/Att	Lg	Pts
Fuad Reveiz	34/35	17/24	50	85

Punts (15 or more)	No	Yds	Long	Avg	In 20
Harry Newsome	68	3095	65	45.5	17

Most Interceptions		Most Sacks	
Joey Browner	5	John Randle	9½

New Orleans Saints

Passing (5 Att)	Att	Cmp	Pct	Yds	TD	Rate
Steve Walsh	255	141	55.3	1638	11	79.5
Bobby Hebert	248	149	60.1	1676	9	79.0

Interceptions: Hebert 8, Walsh 6.

Top Receivers	No	Yds	Avg	Long	TD
Eric Martin	66	803	12.2	30	4
Floyd Turner	64	927	14.5	65-td	8
Quinn Early	32	541	16.9	52	2
Gill Fenerty	26	235	9.0	50-td	2
John Tice	22	230	10.5	22	0

Top Rushers	Car	Yds	Avg	Long	TD
Fred McAfee*	109	494	4.5	34	2
Gill Fenerty	139	477	3.4	54	3
Craig Heyward	76	260	3.4	15	4
Dalton Hilliard	79	252	3.2	65-td	4
Buford Jordan	47	150	3.2	25	2

Most Touchdowns	TD	Run	Rec	Ret	Pts
Floyd Turner	8	0	8	0	48
Gill Fenerty	5	3	2	0	30
Craig Heyward	5	4	1	0	30
Dalton Hilliard	5	4	1	0	30
Eric Martin	4	0	4	0	24

Kicking	PAT/Att	FG/Att	Lg	Pts
Morten Andersen	38/38	25/32	60	113

Punts (15 or more)	No	Yds	Long	Avg	In 20
Tommy Barnhardt	86	3743	64	43.5	20

Most Interceptions		Most Sacks	
Gene Atkins	5	Pat Swilling	17
Vince Buck	5		

New York Giants

Passing (5 Att)	Att	Cmp	Pct	Yds	TD	Rate
Jeff Hostetler	285	179	62.8	2032	5	84.1
Phil Simms	141	82	58.2	993	8	87.0

Interceptions: Hostetler 4, Simms 4.

Top Receivers	No	Yds	Avg	Long	TD
Mark Ingram	51	824	16.2	41	3
Dave Meggett	50	412	8.2	22	3
Rodney Hampton	43	283	6.6	19	0
Stephen Baker	30	525	17.5	52	4
Odessa Turner	21	356	17.0	55	0

Top Rushers	Car	Yds	Avg	Long	TD
Rodney Hampton	256	1059	4.1	44	10
Lewis Tillman	65	287	4.4	17	1
Jeff Hostetler	42	273	6.5	47-td	2
Dave Meggett	29	153	5.3	30-td	1
Ottis Anderson	53	141	2.7	9	1

Most Touchdowns	TD	Run	Rec	Ret	Pts
Rodney Hampton	10	10	0	0	60
Dave Meggett	5	1	3	1	30
Stephen Baker	4	0	4	0	24
Mark Ingram	3	0	3	0	18

Kicking	PAT/Att	FG/Att	Lg	Pts
Matt Bahr	24/25	22/29	54	90

Signed: Raul Allegre (Oct.25).
Released: Allegre (Nov.29).

Punts (15 or more)	No	Yds	Long	Avg	In 20
Sean Landeta	64	2768	61	43.3	16

Most Interceptions		Most Sacks	
Mark Collins	4	Leonard Marshall	11
Everson Walls	4		

Philadelphia Eagles

Passing (5 Att)	Att	Cmp	Pct	Yds	TD	Rate
Jim McMahon	311	187	60.1	2239	12	80.3
Jeff Kemp	295	151	51.2	1753	9	55.7
SEA	181	94	51.9	1207	4	52.9
PHI	114	57	50.0	546	5	60.1
Brad Goebel*	56	30	53.6	267	0	27.0
Pat Ryan	26	10	38.5	98	0	10.3

Interceptions: Kemp 17 (12/5), McMahon 11, Goebel 6, Ryan 4.
Signed: Kemp (Oct.16) after release by Seattle (Oct.15).

Top Receivers	No	Yds	Avg	Long	TD
Fred Barnett	62	948	15.3	75-td	4
Keith Byars	62	564	9.1	37	3
Keith Jackson	48	569	11.9	73-td	5
Calvin Williams	33	326	9.9	30	3

Top Rushers	Car	Yds	Avg	Long	TD
James Joseph*	135	440	3.3	24	3
Keith Byars	94	383	4.1	28	1
Heath Sherman	106	279	2.6	12	0
Jeff Kemp	38	179	4.7	18	0
SEA	22	106	4.8	18	0
PHI	16	73	4.6	18	0

Most Touchdowns	TD	Run	Rec	Ret	Pts
Keith Jackson	5	0	5	0	30
Fred Barnett	4	0	4	0	24
Keith Byars	4	1	3	0	24

Two tied with 3 TDs each.

Kicking	PAT/Att	FG/Att	Lg	Pts
Roger Ruzek	27/29	28/33	51	111

Punts (15 or more)	No	Yds	Long	Avg	In 20
Jeff Feagles	87	3640	77	41.8	29

Most Interceptions		Most Sacks	
Eric Allen	5	Reggie White	15
Wes Hopkins	5		

Phoenix Cardinals

Passing (5 Att)

	Att	Cmp	Pct	Yds	TD	Rate
Tom Tupa	315	165	52.4	2053	6	62.0
Chris Chandler	154	78	50.6	846	5	50.9
TB	104	53	51.0	557	4	47.6
PHO	50	25	50.0	289	1	57.8
Stan Gelbaugh	118	61	51.7	674	3	42.1
Craig Kupp	7	3	42.9	23	0	51.5

Interceptions: Tupa 13, Chandler 10.
Signed: QB Chandler (Nov.6) after being waived by Tampa Bay (Nov.5).

Top Receivers

	No	Yds	Avg	Long	TD
Ernie Jones	61	957	15.7	53	4
Ricky Proehl	55	766	13.9	62-td	2
Randal Hill*	43	495	11.5	31-td	1
Johnny Johnson	29	225	7.8	51-td	2

Acquired: Hill from Miami (Sept.3) for 1992 1st Rd draft pick.

Top Rushers

	Car	Yds	Avg	Long	TD
Johnny Johnson	196	666	3.4	21	4
Anthony Thompson	126	376	3.0	22	1
Chris Chandler	26	111	4.3	12	0
TB	18	79	4.4	12	0
PHO	8	32	4.0	12	0

Most Touchdowns

	TD	Run	Rec	Ret	Pts
Johnny Johnson	6	4	2	0	36
Ernie Jones	4	0	4	0	24

Kicking

	PAT/Att	FG/Att	Lg	Pts
Greg Davis	19/19	21/30	52	82

Punts (15 or more)

	No	Yds	Long	Avg	In 20
Rich Camarillo	76	3445	60	45.3	19

Most Interceptions
Aeneas Williams* 6

Most Sacks
Ken Harvey 9

Tampa Bay Buccaneers

Passing (5 Att)

	Att	Cmp	Pct	Yds	TD	Rate
Vinny Testaverde	326	166	50.9	1994	8	59.0
Jeff Carlson	65	31	47.7	404	1	34.4

Interceptions: Testaverde 15, Carlson 6.
Released: Chris Chandler (Nov.5).

Top Receivers

	No	Yds	Avg	Long	TD
Lawrence Dawsey*	55	818	14.9	65-td	3
Mark Carrier	47	698	14.9	35	2
Ron Hall	31	284	9.2	24	0
Willie Drewrey	26	375	14.4	87-td	2
Gary Anderson	25	184	7.4	21	0

Top Rushers

	Car	Yds	Avg	Long	TD
Reggie Cobb	196	752	3.8	59-td	7
Gary Anderson	72	263	3.7	64-td	1
Robert Wilson*	42	179	4.3	20	0
Vinny Testaverde	32	101	3.2	19	0
Jeff Carlson	5	25	5.0	11	0

Most Touchdowns

	TD	Run	Rec	Ret	Pts
Reggie Cobb	7	7	0	0	42
Lawrence Dawsey*	4	1	3	0	24

Five tied with 2 TDs each.

Kicking

	PAT/Att	FG/Att	Lg	Pts
Steve Christie	22/22	15/20	49	67

Punts (15 or more)

	No	Yds	Long	Avg	In 20
Mark Royals	84	3389	56	40.3	22

Most Interceptions
Tony Covington* 3

Most Sacks
Broderick Thomas 11

San Francisco 49ers

Passing (5 Att)

	Att	Cmp	Pct	Yds	TD	Rate
Steve Young	279	180	64.5	2517	17	101.8
Steve Bono	237	141	59.5	1617	11	88.5
Bill Musgrave*	5	4	80.0	33	1	133.8

Interceptions: Young 8, Bono 4.

Top Receivers

	No	Yds	Avg	Long	TD
Jerry Rice	80	1206	15.1	73-td	14
John Taylor	64	1011	15.8	97-td	9
Tom Rathman	34	286	8.4	32	0
Keith Henderson	30	303	10.1	23	0
Brent Jones	27	417	15.4	41	0

Top Rushers

	Car	Yds	Avg	Long	TD
Keith Henderson	137	561	4.1	25	2
Steve Young	66	415	6.3	21	4
Dexter Carter	85	379	4.5	53-td	2
Harry Sydney	57	245	4.3	32	5
Tom Rathman	63	183	2.9	16	6

Most Touchdowns

	TD	Run	Rec	Ret	Pts
Jerry Rice	14	0	14	0	84
John Taylor	9	0	9	0	54
Harry Sydney	7	5	2	0	42
Tom Rathman	6	6	0	0	36

Two tied with 4 TDs each.

Kicking

	PAT/Att	FG/Att	Lg	Pts
Mike Cofer	49/50	14/28	50	91

Punts (15 or more)

	No	Yds	Long	Avg	In 20
Joe Prokop	40	1541	58	38.5	8
Ralf Mojsiejenko	16	656	55	41.0	0

Signed: Prokop (Oct.7) after preseason release by NY Jets.

Most Interceptions
Dave Waymer 4

Most Sacks
Charles Haley 7
Larry Roberts 7

Washington Redskins

Passing (5 Att)

	Att	Cmp	Pct	Yds	TD	Rate
Mark Rypien	421	249	59.1	3564	28	97.9
Jeff Rutledge	22	11	50.0	189	1	94.7

Interceptions: Rypien 11.
Also threw TD pass: Earnest Byner 1.

Top Receivers

	No	Yds	Avg	Long	TD
Art Monk	71	1049	14.8	64-td	8
Gary Clark	70	1340	19.1	82-td	10
Ricky Sanders	45	580	12.9	45	5
Earnest Byner	34	308	9.1	31	0
Ricky Ervins*	16	181	11.3	28	1

Top Rushers

	Car	Yds	Avg	Long	TD
Earnest Byner	274	1048	3.8	32	5
Ricky Ervins*	145	680	4.7	65-td	3
Gerald Riggs	78	248	3.2	32	11
Ricky Sanders	7	47	6.7	17	1
Art Monk	9	19	2.1	14	0

Most Touchdowns

	TD	Run	Rec	Ret	Pts
Gerald Riggs	11	11	0	0	66
Gary Clark	10	0	10	0	60
Art Monk	8	0	8	0	48
Ricky Sanders	6	1	5	0	36
Earnest Byner	5	5	0	0	30

Kicking

	PAT/Att	FG/Att	Lg	Pts
Chip Lohmiller	56/56	31/43	53	149

Punts (15 or more)

	No	Yds	Long	Avg	In 20
Kelly Goodburn	52	2070	61	39.8	16

Most Interceptions
Darrell Green 5
Wilber Marshall 5

Most Sacks
Charles Mann 11½

1991–1992 NFL PLAYOFFS

WILD CARD	SEMIFINAL	FINAL		FINAL	SEMIFINAL	WILD CARD

NY Jets 10
Houston 17
Houston 24
Denver 7
Denver 26
LA Raiders 6
Kansas City 10
Kansas City 14
Buffalo 10
Buffalo 37
AFC

Atlanta 7
Washington 41
Washington 24
Washington 37
Buffalo 24
NFC
Detroit 10
Dallas 6
Detroit 38

Atlanta 27
New Orleans 20
Dallas 17
Chicago 13

Jan. 26, 1992
Metrodome, Minneapolis

Playoff Summaries
Team records listed in parentheses indicate records before game.

WILD CARD GAMES

AFC

Chiefs 10, Raiders 6

LA Raiders (9-7)	0	3	3	0	**6**
Kansas City (10-6)	0	7	0	3	**10**

Date—Dec.28. **Att**—75,827. **Time**—2:44.

2nd Quarter
KC—Fred Jones 11-yd pass from Steve DeBerg (Nick Lowery kick), 9:53. **LA**—Jeff Jaeger 32-yd FG, 14:34.

3rd Quarter
LA—Jaeger 26-yd FG, 6:41.

4th Quarter
KC—Lowery 18-yd FG, 4:34.

Oilers 17, Jets 10

NY Jets (8-8)	0	10	0	0	**10**
Houston (11-5)	7	7	0	3	**17**

Date—Dec.29. **Att**—61,485. **Time**—2:49.

1st Quarter
Hou—Ernest Givens 5-yd pass from Warren Moon (Al Del Groco kick), 9:19.

2nd Quarter
NY—Al Toon 10-yd pass from Ken O'Brien (Raul Allegre kick), 2:44. **Hou**—Givins 20-yd pass from Moon (Del Groco kick), 11:04. **NY**—Allegre 33-yd FG, 14:56.

4th Quarter
Hou—Del Groco 53-yd FG, 1:31.

NFC

Falcons 27, Saints 20

Atlanta (10-6)	0	10	7	10	**27**
New Orleans (11-5)	7	6	0	7	**20**

Date—Dec.28. **Att**—68,794. **Time**—3:23.

1st Quarter
NO—Floyd Turner 26-yd pass from Bobby Hebert (Morten Andersen kick), 6:03.

2nd Quarter
NO—Andersen 45-yd FG, 3:23. **Atl**—Andre Rison 24-yd pass from Miller (Norm Johnson kick), 9:34. **Atl**—Johnson 45-yd FG, 14:23. **NO**—Andersen 35-yd FG, 14:57.

3rd Quarter
Atl—Michael Haynes 20-yd pass from Miller (Johnson kick), 5:01.

4th Quarter
NO—Dalton Hilliard 1-yd run (Andersen kick), 0:50. **Atl**—Johnson 36-yd FG, 7:17. **Atl**—Haynes 61-yd pass from Miller (Johnson kick), 12:19.

Cowboys 17, Bears 13

Dallas (11-5)	10	0	7	0	**17**
Chicago (11-5)	0	3	3	7	**13**

Date—Dec.29. **Att**—62,594. **Time**—3:04.

1st Quarter
Dal—Ken Willis 27-yd FG, 7:55. **Dal**—Emmitt Smith 1-yd run (Willis kick), 12:10.

2nd Quarter
Chi—Kevin Butler 19-yd FG, 14:45.

3rd Quarter
Chi—Butler 43-yd FG, 6:34. **Dal**—Jay Novacek 3-yd pass from Steve Beuerlein (Willis kick), 14:37.

4th Quarter
Chi—Tom Waddle 6-yd pass from Jim Harbaugh (Butler kick), 12:18.

SEMIFINAL GAMES

AFC

Broncos 26, Oilers 24

Houston (12-5)	14	7	0	3	—24
Denver (12-4)	6	7	3	10	—26

Date—Jan.4. **Att**—75,301. **Time**—3:09.

1st Quarter
Hou—Haywood Jeffires 15-yd pass from Warren Moon (Al-Del Greco kick), 1:46. **Hou**—Drew Hill 9-yd pass from Moon (Del Greco kick), 9:44. **Den**—Vance Johnson 10-yd pass from John Elway (kick failed), 13:4.

2nd Quarter
Hou—Curtis Duncan 6-yd pass from Moon (Del Greco kick), 4:05. **Den**—Greg Lewis 1-yd run (David Treadwell kick), 14:21.

3rd Quarter
Den—Treadwell 49-yd FG, 13:02.

4th Quarter
Hou—Del Greco 25-yd FG, 1:35. **Den**—Lewis 1-yd run (Treadwell kick), 8:07. **Den**—Treadwell 28-yd FG, 14:44.

Bills 37, Chiefs 14

Kansas City (11-6)	0	0	7	7	—14
Buffalo (13-3)	7	10	7	13	—37

Date—Jan.5. **Att**—80,182 (49). **Time**—3:11.

1st Quarter
Buf—Andre Reed 25-yd pass from Jim Kelly (Scott Norwood kick), 14:08.

2nd Quarter
Buf—Reed 53-yd pass from Kelly (Norwood kick), 4:25. **Buf**—Norwood 33-yd FG, 14:58.

3rd Quarter
Buf—James Lofton 10-yd pass from Kelly (Norwood kick), 3:07. **KC**—Barry Word 3-yd run (Nick Lowery kick), 11:52.

4th Quarter
Buf—Norwood 20-yd FG, 4:06. **Buf**—Norwood 47-yd FG, 5:52. **Buf**—Kenneth Davis 5-yd run (Norwood kick), 10:03. **KC**—Fred Jones 20-yd pass from Mark Vlasic (Lowery kick), 12:53.

NFC

Redskins 24, Falcons 7

Atlanta (11-6)	0	7	0	0	— 7
Washington (14-2)	0	14	3	7	—24

Date—Jan.4. **Att**—55,181. **Time**—3:05

2nd Quarter
Wash—Ricky Ervins 17-yd run (Chip Lohmiller kick), 2:24. **Wash**—Gerald Riggs 2-yd run (Lohmiller kick), 5:35. **Atl**—Tracy Johnson 1-yd run (Norm Johnson kick), 14:03.

3rd Quarter
Wash—Lohmiller 24-yd FG, 8:06.

4th Quarter
Wash—Riggs 1-yd run (Lohmiller kick), 8:28.

Lions 38, Cowboys 6

Dallas (12-5)	3	3	0	0	— 6
Detroit (12-4)	7	10	14	7	—38

Date—Jan.5. **Att**—79,835. **Time**—2:56.

1st Quarter
Det—Willie Green 31-yd pass from Erik Kramer (Eddie Murray kick), 3:31. **Dal**—Ken Willis 28-yd FG, 14:50.

2nd Quarter
Det—Melvin Jenkins 41-yd interception return (Murray kick), 8:18. **Dal**—Willis 28-yd FG, 12:02. **Det**—Murray 36-yd FG, 14:33.

3rd Quarter
Det—Green 9-yd pass from Kramer (Murray kick), 13:41. **Det**—Herman Moore 7-yd pass from Kramer (Murray kick), 14:46.

4th Quarter
Det—Barry Sanders 47-yd run (Murray kick), 7:04.

CHAMPIONSHIP GAMES

AFC

Bills 10, Broncos 7

Denver (13-4)	0	0	0	7	— 7
Buffalo (14-3)	0	0	7	3	—10

Date—Jan.12. **Att**—80,272. **Time**—2:59.

3rd Quarter
Buf—Carlton Bailey 11-yd interception return (Scott Norwood kick), 9:32.

4th Quarter
Buf—Norwood 44-yd FG, 10:42. **Den**—Gary Kubiak 3-yd run (David Treadwell kick), 13:17.

NFC

Redskins 41, Lions 10

Detroit (13-4)	0	10	0	0	—10
Washington (15-2)	10	7	10	14	—41

Date—Jan.12. **Att**—55,585. **Time**—3:00.

1st Quarter
Wash—Gerald Riggs 2-yd run (Chip Lohmiller kick), 1:06. **Wash**—Lohmiller 20-yd FG, 4:02.

2nd Quarter
Det—Willie Green 18-yd pass from Kramer (Murray kick), 2:25. **Wash**—Riggs 3-yd run (Lohmiller kick), 7:16. **Det**—Murray 30-yd FG, 14:23.

3rd Quarter
Wash—Lohmiller 28-yd FG, 3:08. **Wash**—Gary Clark 45-yd pass from Mark Rypien (Lohmiller kick), 12:37.

4th Quarter
Wash—Art Monk 21-yard pass from Rypien (Lohmiller kick), 4:15. **Wash**—Darrell Green 32-yd interception return (Lohmiller kick), 4:49.

Super Bowl XXVI

Sunday, Jan.26 at Hubert Humphrey Metrodome, Minneapolis

Washington (16-2)............	0	17	14	6—**37**
Buffalo (15-3)	0	0	10	14—**24**

2nd Quarter: Wash—Chip Lohmiller 34-yd FG, 1:58 (Drive: 64 yards in 7 plays). **Wash**—Earnest Byner 10-yd pass from Mark Rypien (Lohmiller kick), 5:06 (Drive: 51 yards in 5 plays). **Wash**—Gerald Riggs 1-yd run (Lohmiller kick), 7:43 (Drive: 55 yards in 5 plays).
3rd Quarter: Wash—Riggs 2-yd run (Lohmiller kick), 0:16 (Drive: 2 yards in 1 play after 23-yd Kurt Gouveia interception return). **Buf**—Scott Norwood 21-yd FG, 3:01 (Drive: 77 yards in 11 plays). **Buf**—Thurman Thomas 1-yd run (Norwood kick), 9:02 (Drive: 56 yards in 6 plays). **Wash**—Gary Clark 30-yd pass from Rypien (Lohmiller kick), 13:36 (Drive: 79 yards in 11 plays).
4th Quarter: Wash—Lohmiller 25-yd FG, 0:06 (Drive: 7 yards in 4 plays after Fred Stokes recovery of Jim Kelly fumble at Bills' 14). **Wash**—Lohmiller 39-yd FG, 3:24 (Drive: 11 yards in 5 plays after 35-yd Brad Edwards interception return). **Buf**—Pete Metzelaars 2-yd pass from Kelly (Norwood kick), 9:01 (Drive: 79 yards in 15 plays). **Buf**—Don Beebe 4-yd pass from Kelly (Norwood kick), 11:05 (Drive: 50 yards in 9 plays after Carlton Bailey recovered onside kick at 50).

Favorite: Redskins by 7 **Attendance:** 63,130
Field: AstroTurf **Time:** 3:43
Weather: Indoors **TV Rating:** 40.3/61 share (CBS)

MVP—Mark Rypien, Washington, QB

Team Statistics

	Redskins	Bills
Touchdowns............................	4	3
Rushing............................	2	1
Passing............................	2	2
Returns	0	0
Time of possession	33:43	26:17
First downs............................	24	25
Rushing............................	10	4
Passing............................	12	18
Penalties	2	3
3rd down efficiency	6/16	7/17
4th down efficiency	0/1	2/2
Total offense (net yards)....................	417	283
Plays	73	82
Average gain	5.7	3.5
Rushes/yards.........................	40/125	18/43
Passing yards........................	292	240
Completions/attempts	18/33	29/59
Times intercepted.....................	1	4
Times sacked-yards lost	0/0	5/46
Return yardage	95	90
Punts/return yards	0/0	3/9
Kickoffs/return yards	1/16	4/77
Interceptions/return yds	4/79	1/4
Fumbles/lost...........................	1/0	6/1
Penalties/yards	5/82	6/50
Punts/Average	4/37.5	6/35.0
Punts blocked..........................	0	0

Individual Statistics

Washington Redskins

Passing	Att	Cmp	Pct	Yds	TD	Int
Mark Rypien...........	33	18	54.5	292	2	1

Receiving	No	Yds	Avg	Long	TD
Gary Clark..................	7	114	16.3	34	1
Art Monk..................	7	113	16.1	31	0
Earnest Byner.............	3	24	8.0	10-td	1
Ricky Sanders..............	1	41	41.0	41	0
TOTAL	18	292	16.2	41	2

Rushing	Car	Yds	Avg	Long	TD
Ricky Ervins.............	13	72	5.5	21	0
Earnest Byner.............	14	49	3.5	19	0
Gerald Riggs.............	5	7	1.4	4	2
Ricky Sanders.............	1	1	1.0	1	0
Jeff Rutledge.............	1	0	0.0	0	0
Mark Rypien.............	6	−4	−0.7	2	0
TOTAL	40	125	3.1	21	2

Field Goals	20-29	30-39	40-49	Total
Chip Lohmiller	1-1	2-2	0-0	3-3

Punting	No	Yds	Long	Avg	In 20
Kelly Goodburn.............	4	150	45	37.5	

Punt Returns	FC	Ret	Yds	Long	Avg	TD
Brian Mitchell.............	2	0	0	—	0.0	0

Kickoff Returns	No	Yds	Long	Avg	TD
Brian Mitchell.............	1	16	16	16.0	0

Interceptions	No	Yds	Long	Avg	TD
Brad Edwards................	2	56	35	28.0	0
Kurt Gouveia.............	1	23	23	23.0	0
Darrell Green.............	1	0	—	0.0	0
TOTAL	4	79	35	19.8	0

Fumble Recoveries	No	Sacks
Fred Stokes.............	1	Five tied with one each.

Buffalo Bills

Passing	Att	Cmp	Pct	Yds	TD	Int
Jim Kelly...............	58	28	48.3	275	2	4
Frank Reich	1	1	100.0	11	0	0
TOTAL	59	29	49.2	286	2	4

Receiving	No	Yds	Avg	Long	TD
James Lofton.............	7	92	13.1	18	0
Andre Reed	5	34	6.8	12	0
Don Beebe.............	4	61	15.3	43	1
Kenneth Davis	4	38	9.5	12	0
Thurman Thomas	4	27	6.8	8	0
Keith McKeller	2	29	14.5	21	0
Al Edwards..................	1	11	11.0	11	0
Pete Metzelaars	2	2	2.0	2-td	1
Jim Kelly..................	1	−8	−8.0	−8	0
TOTAL	29	286	9.7	43	2

Rushing	Car	Yds	Avg	Long	TD
Kenneth Davis	4	17	4.3	13	0
Jim Kelly.............	3	16	5.3	9	0
Thurman Thomas	10	13	1.3	6	1
James Lofton.............	1	−3	−3.0	−3	0
TOTAL	18	43	2.4	13	1

Field Goals	20-29	30-39	40-49	Total
Scott Norwood.............	1-1	0-0	0-0	1-1

Punting	No	Yds	Long	Avg	In 20
Chris Mohr.................	6	210	53	35.0	4

Punt Returns	FC	Ret	Yds	Long	Avg	TD
Clifford Hicks.............	0	3	9	7	3.0	0

Kickoff Returns	No	Yds	Long	Avg	TD
Al Edwards..................	4	77	24	19.3	0

Interceptions	No	Yds	Long	Avg	TD
Kirby Jackson.............	1	4	4	4.0	0

Super Bowl Finalists' Playoff Statistics

Washington (3-0)

Passing	Att	Cmp	Pct	Yds	TD	Int
Mark Rypien	79	44	55.7	690	4	2

Receiving	No	Yds	Avg	Long	TD
Gary Clark	17	255	15.0	45-td	2
Art Monk	15	252	16.8	31	1
Ricky Sanders	4	79	19.8	41	0
Earnest Byner	4	35	8.8	11	1
Ricky Ervins	3	24	8.0	11	0
Terry Orr	1	45	45.0	45	0
TOTAL	44	690	15.7	45-td	4

Rushing	Car	Yds	Avg	Long	TD
Ricky Ervins	49	229	4.7	21	1
Earnest Byner	45	168	3.7	19	0
Gerald Riggs	11	19	1.7	4	6
Ricky Sanders	1	1	1.0	1	0
Art Monk	1	−2	−2.0	−2	0
Jeff Rutledge	4	−3	−0.8	−1	0
Mark Rypien	9	−8	−0.9	2	0
TOTAL	120	404	3.4	21	7

Touchdowns	TD	Run	Rec	Ret	Pts
Gerald Riggs	6	6	0	0	36
Gary Clark	2	0	2	0	12
Earnest Byner	1	0	1	0	6
Ricky Ervins	1	1	0	0	6
Darrell Green	1	0	0	1*	6
Art Monk	1	0	1	0	6
TOTAL	12	7	4	1	72

*Interception return.

Kicking	PAT/Att	FG/Att	Long	Pts
Chip Lohmiller	12/12	6/10	39	30

Punting	No	Yds	Long	Avg	In 20
Kelly Goodburn	11	412	45	37.5	2

Most Interceptions		Most Sacks	
Kurt Gouveia	3	Wilber Marshall	4
Darrell Green	2	Fred Stokes	3
Brad Edwards	2		

Buffalo (2-1)

Passing	Att	Cmp	Pct	Yds	TD	Int
Jim Kelly	118	64	54.2	665	5	9
Frank Reich	1	1	100.0	11	0	0
TOTAL	119	65	54.6	676	5	9

Receiving	No	Yds	Avg	Long	TD
Andre Reed	11	153	13.9	53-td	2
Don Beebe	11	144	13.1	43	1
James Lofton	11	137	12.5	18	1
Thurman Thomas	11	63	5.7	8	0
Keith McKeller	10	102	10.2	25	0
Others	11	77	7.0	14	1
TOTAL	65	676	10.4	53-td	5

Rushing	Car	Yds	Avg	Long	TD
Thurman Thomas	58	185	3.2	19	1
Kenneth Davis	29	99	3.4	13	1
Jim Kelly	6	27	4.5	10	0
Andre Reed	2	22	11.0	16	0
Frank Reich	3	−3	−1.0	−1	0
James Lofton	1	−3	−3.0	−3	0
TOTAL	99	327	3.3	19	2

Touchdowns	TD	Run	Rec	Ret	Pts
Andre Reed	2	0	2	0	12
Carlton Bailey	1	0	0	1*	6
Don Beebe	1	0	1	0	6
Kenneth Davis	1	1	0	0	6
James Lofton	1	0	1	0	6
Pete Metzelaars	1	0	1	0	6
Thurman Thomas	1	1	0	0	6
TOTAL	8	2	5	1	48

*Interception return.

Kicking	PAT/Att	FG/Att	Long	Pts
Scott Norwood	7/7	4/4	47	19

Punting	No	Yds	Long	Avg	In 20
Chris Mohr	17	614	53	36.1	5

Most Interceptions		Most Sacks	
Kirby Jackson	3	Leonard Smith	1½

Redskins' 1991 Schedule

(*) indicates Monday Night game; listed records of opponents are day of game.

Date	Regular Season	Result	W-L
Sept. 1	Detroit (0-0)	W, 45-0	1-0
Sept. 9*	at Dallas (1-0)	W, 33-31	2-0
Sept.15	Phoenix (2-0)	W, 34-0	3-0
Sept.22	at Cincinnati (0-3)	W, 34-27	4-0
Sept.30*	Philadelphia (3-1)	W, 23-0	5-0
Oct. 6	at Chicago (4-1)	W, 20-7	6-0
Oct.13	Cleveland (2-3)	W, 42-17	7-0
Oct.20	OPEN DATE	—	—
Oct.27	at NY Giants (4-3)	W, 17-13	8-0
Nov. 3	Houston (7-1)	W, 16-13 OT	9-0
Nov.10	Atlanta (5-4)	W, 56-17	10-0
Nov.17	at Pittsburgh (4-6)	W, 41-14	11-0
Nov.24	Dallas (6-5)	L, 21-24	11-1
Dec. 1	at LA Rams (3-9)	W, 27-6	12-1
Dec. 8	at Phoenix (4-9)	W, 20-14	13-1
Dec.15	NY Giants (7-7)	W, 34-17	14-1
Dec.22	at Philadelphia (9-6)	L, 22-24	14-2

Date	Playoffs	Result	W-L
1st Rd.	BYE	—	—
Jan. 4	Atlanta (11-6)	W, 24-7	15-2
Jan.12	Detroit (13-4)	W, 41-10	16-2
Jan.26	Buffalo (15-3)	W, 37-24	17-2

Bills' 1991 Schedule

(*) indicates Monday Night game; listed records of opponents are day of game.

Date	Regular Season	Result	W-L
Sept. 1	Miami (0-0)	W, 35-31	1-0
Sept. 8	Pittsburgh (1-0)	W, 52-34	2-0
Sept.15	at NY Jets (1-1)	W, 23-20	3-0
Sept.22	at Tampa Bay (0-3)	W, 17-10	4-0
Sept.29	Chicago (4-0)	W, 35-20	5-0
Oct. 7*	at Kansas City (3-2)	L, 6-33	5-1
Oct.13	Indianapolis (0-6)	W, 42-6	6-1
Oct.21*	Cincinnati (0-6)	W, 35-16	7-1
Oct.27	OPEN DATE	—	—
Nov. 3	New England (3-5)	W, 22-17	8-1
Nov.10	vs Green Bay (2-7)†	W, 34-24	9-1
Nov.18*	at Miami (5-5)	W, 41-27	10-1
Nov.24	at New England (3-8)	L, 13-16	10-2
Dec. 1	NY Jets (7-5)	W, 24-13	11-2
Dec. 8	at LA Raiders (9-4)	W, 30-27 OT	12-2
Dec.15	at Indianapolis (1-13)	W, 35-7	13-2
Dec.22	Detroit (11-4)	L, 14-17 OT	13-3

Date	Playoffs	Result	W-L
1st Rd.	BYE	—	—
Jan. 5	Kansas City (11-6)	W, 37-14	14-3
Jan.12	Denver (13-4)	W, 10-7	15-3
Jan.26	Washington (16-2)	L, 24-37	15-4

†at Milwaukee.

NFL Pro Bowl

42nd NFL Pro Bowl Game and 22nd AFC-NFC contest (NFC leads series, 13-9). **Date:** Feb.2 at Aloha Stadium in Honolulu; **Coaches:** Wayne Fontes of Detroit (NFC) and Dan Reeves of Denver (AFC); **MVP:** WR Michael Irvin of Dallas, who set a Pro Bowl record of 8 catches for 125 yards and one TD.
Attendance—50,209; **Time**—3:18; **TV Rating**—7.3/11 share (ESPN).

National	7	7	0	7—21
American	7	5	0	3—15

1st Quarter

AFC—Mark Clayton 4-yd pass from Jim Kelly (Jeff Jaeger kick), 9:00; **NFC**—Michael Irvin 13-yd pass from Mark Rypien (Chip Lohmiller kick), 12:18.

2nd Quarter

AFC—Safety, RB Earnest Byner tackled in end zone, 0:25; **AFC**—Jaeger 48-yd FG, 11:07; **NFC**—Gary Clark 35-yd pass from Rypien (Lohmiller kick), 14:34.

4th Quarter

AFC—Jaeger 27-yd FG, 1:49; **NFC**—Jerry Rice 11-yd pass from Chris Miller (Lohmiller kick), 10:56.

STARTING LINEUPS
As voted on by NFL players and coaches.

NFC

Pos Offense	Pos Defense
WR—Michael Irvin, Dal.	E—Reggie White, Phi.
WR—Jerry Rice, SF	E—Clyde Simmons, Phi.
TE—Jay Novacek, Dal.	NT—Jerome Brown, Phi.
T—Jim Lachey, Wash.	OLB—Pat Swilling, NO
T—Lomas Brown, Det.	OLB—Seth Joyner, Phi.
G—Randall McDaniel, Min.	ILB—Vaughn Johnson, NO
G—Guy McIntyre, SF	ILB—Sam Mills, NO
C—Jay Hilgenberg, Chi.	CB—Darrell Green, Wash.
QB—Mark Rypien, Wash.	CB—Deion Sanders, Atl.
RB—Barry Sanders, Det.	S—Tim McDonald, Pho.
RB—Emmitt Smith, Dal.	S—Mark Carrier, Chi.
K—Chip Lohmiller, Wash.	P—Rich Camarillo, Pho.

Note: S McDonald was injured (fractured left ankle) and unable to play.

AFC

Pos Offense	Pos Defense
WR—Haywood Jeffires, Hou.	E—William Fuller, Hou.
WR—Andre Reed, Buf.	E—Greg Townsend, LA
TE—Marv Cook, NE	NT—Michael D.Perry, Cle.
T—Anthony Munoz, Cin.	OLB—Cornelius Bennett, Buf.
T—Bruce Armstrong, NE	OLB—Derrick Thomas, KC
G—Mike Munchak, Hou.	ILB—Al Smith, Hou.
G—Steve Wisniewski, LA	ILB—Junior Seau, SD
C—Bruce Matthews, Hou.	CB—Cris Dishman, Hou.
QB—Jim Kelly, Buf.	CB—Gill Byrd, SD
RB—Thurman Thomas, Buf.	S—Ronnie Lott, LA
RB—Christian Okoye, KC	S—Steve Atwater, Den.
K—Jeff Jaeger, LA	P—Jeff Gossett, LA

Note: RB Okoye was injured (right knee sprain) and unable to play.

Reserves

Offense: WR—Gary Clark, Wash., and Andre Rison, Atl.; **TE**—Steve Jordan, Min.; **T**—Chris Hinton, Atl.; **G**—Mark Schlereth, Wash.; **C**—Bart Oates, NY; **QB**—Troy Aikman, Dal. and Chris Miller, Atl.; **RB**—Earnest Byner, Wash. and Neal Anderson, Chi.

Defense: E—Charles Mann, Wash.; **NT**—Jerry Ball, Det.; **LB**—Charles Haley, SF and Mike Singletary, Chi.; **CB**—Eric Allen, Phi.; **S**—Bennie Blades, Det.

Specialists: KR—Mel Gray, Det.; **Teams**—Bennie Thompson, NO.

Replacements: S Shaun Gayle, Chi. for McDonald.

Reserves

Offense: WR—Mark Clayton, Mia. and James Lofton, Buf.; **TE**—Ethan Horton, LA; **T**—Richmond Webb, Mia; **G**—Jim Ritcher, Buf.; **C**—Don Mosebar, LA; **QB**—Dan Marino, Mia. and Warren Moon, Hou.; **RB**—Marion Butts, SD and Gaston Green, Den.

Defense: E—Neil Smith, KC; **NT**—Ray Childress, Hou.; **LB**—Karl Mecklenburg, Den. and Darryl Talley, Buf.; **CB**—Rod Woodson, Pit.; **S**—Dennis Smith, Den.

Specialists: KR—Tim Brown, LA; **Teams**—Steve Tasker, Buf.

Replacements: QB John Elway, Den. for Marino; QB Bernie Kosar, Cle. for Elway; QB Ken O'Brien, NY for Kosar; RB John L.Williams, Sea. for Okoye; NT Cortez Kennedy, Sea. for Childress.

Annual Awards

The NFL does not sanction any postseason awards for players or coaches, but many are given out. Among the presenters for the 1991 regular season were AP, UPI, *The Sporting News* and the Pro Football Writers of America. MVP awards are also given out by the Maxwell Club of Philadelphia (Bert Bell Award) and the NFL Players Assn.(Jim Thorpe Trophy).

Most Valuable Player / Selectors

Thurman Thomas, Buffalo, RB	AP,PFWA,TSN and NFLPA
Barry Sanders, Detroit, RB	Maxwell

Offensive Players of the Year

NFL Thurman Thomas, Buffalo, RB	AP
AFC Thurman Thomas, Buffalo, RB	UPI
NFC Mark Rypien, Washington, QB	UPI

Defensive Players of the Year

NFL Pat Swilling, New Orleans, LB	AP
AFC Cornelius Bennett, Buffalo, DE	UPI
NFC Reggie White, Philadelphia, DE	UPI

Rookies of the Year / Selectors

NFL Mike Croel, Denver, LB	PFWA,TSN
AFC Mike Croel, Denver, LB	UPI
NFC Lawrence Dawsey, Tampa Bay, WR	UPI
Offense Leonard Russell, New England, RB	AP
Defense Mike Croel, Denver, LB	AP

Coaches of the Year

NFL Wayne Fontes, Detroit	AP,PFWA
NFL Joe Gibbs, Washington	TSN
AFC Dan Reeves, Denver	UPI
NFC Wayne Fontes, Detroit	UPI

All-NFL Team

The 1991 All-NFL team combining the All-Pro selections of the Associated Press and the Pro Football Writers of America (PFWA). Holdovers from the 1990 All-NFL team in **bold** type.

Offense

Pos	Selectors
WR—Michael Irvin, Dallas	AP,PFWA
WR—Haywood Jeffires, Houston	AP,PFWA
TE—Marv Cook, New England	AP,PFWA
T—**Jim Lachey**, Washington	AP,PFWA
T—Mike Kenn, Atlanta	AP,PFWA
G—**Steve Wisniewski**, LA Raiders	AP,PFWA
G—Mike Munchak, Houston	AP,PFWA
C—**Kent Hull**, Buffalo	AP,PFWA
QB—Jim Kelly, Buffalo	AP,PFWA
RB—**Thurman Thomas**, Buffalo	AP,PFWA
RB—**Barry Sanders**, Detroit	AP,PFWA

Specialists

Pos	Selectors
K—Jeff Jaeger, LA Raiders	AP,PFWA
P—Jeff Gossett, LA Raiders	AP,PFWA
KR—**Mel Gray**, Detroit	AP,PFWA

Defense

Pos	Selectors
DE—**Reggie White**, Philadelphia	AP,PFWA
DE—Clyde Simmons, Philadelphia	AP,PFWA
DT—**Jerome Brown**, Philadelphia	AP,PFWA
DT—Jerry Ball, Detroit	AP,PFWA
OLB—Pat Swilling, New Orleans	AP,PFWA
OLB—**Derrick Thomas**, Kansas City	AP
OLB—Seth Joyner, Philadelphia	PFWA
ILB—Mike Singletary, Chicago	AP
ILB—Chris Spielman, Detroit	AP
ILB—Sam Mills, New Orleans	PFWA
ILB—Al Smith, Houston	PFWA
CB—Darrell Green, Washington	AP,PFWA
CB—Cris Dishman, Houston	AP
CB—Deion Sanders, Atlanta	PFWA
S—**Ronnie Lott**, LA Raiders	AP,PFWA
S—Steve Atwater, Denver	AP,PFWA

NFL College Draft

First and second round selections at the 61st annual NFL College Draft held April 26-27, 1992, in New York City. Fourteen underclassmen were among the first 56 players chosen and are listed in CAPITAL letters.

First Round

No	Team		Pos
1	Indianapolis	STEVE EMTMAN, Washington	DT
2	a-Indianapolis	Quentin Coryatt, Tex.A&M	LB
3	LA Rams	SEAN GILBERT, Pitt	DE
4	b-Washington	DESMOND HOWARD, Michigan	WR
5	Green Bay	TERRELL BUCKLEY, Fla.St.	DB
6	c-Cincinnati	David Klingler, Houston	QB
7	d-Miami	Troy Vincent, Wisconsin	DB
8	e-Atlanta	BOB WHITFIELD, Stanford	OT
9	Cleveland	Tommy Vardell, Stanford	FB
10	Seattle	Ray Roberts, Virginia	OT
11	Pittsburgh	Leon Searcy, Miami-FL	OT
12	Miami	MARCO COLEMAN, Ga.Tech	LB
13	f-New England	Eugene Chung, Va.Tech	OT
14	NY Giants	Derek Brown, Notre Dame	TE
15	NY Jets	JOHNNY MITCHELL, Nebraska	TE
16	LA Raiders	CHESTER McGLOCKTON, Clem.	DT
17	g-Dallas	Kevin Smith, Texas A&M	DB
18	San Francisco	Dana Hall, Washington	DB
19	h-Atlanta	Tony Smith, So.Miss.	RB
20	Kansas City	Dale Carter, Tennessee	DB
21	New Orleans	Vaughn Dunbar, Indiana	RB
22	Chicago	ALONZO SPELLMAN, Ohio St.	DE
23	i-San Diego	Chris Mims, Tennessee	DE
24	Dallas	Robert Jones, E.Carolina	LB
25	Denver	TOMMY MADDOX, UCLA	QB
26	Detroit	Robert Porcher, S.Car.St.	DT
27	Buffalo	John Fina, Arizona	OT
28	j-Cincinnati	DARRYL WILLIAMS, Miami-FL	DB

Acquired picks: a—from Tampa Bay; **b**—from Cincinnati; **c**—from Washington thru San Diego; **d**—from Phoenix; **e**—from New England; **f**—from Minnesota thru Dallas; **g**—from Philadelphia thru Green Bay and Atlanta; **h**—from Atlanta thru Dallas and New England; **i**—from Houston; **j**—from Washington.

Second Round

No	Team		Pos
29	Indianapolis	Ashley Ambrose, Miss.Valley	DB
30	LA Rams	Steve Israel, Pitt	DB
31	Cincinnati	CARL PICKENS, Tennessee	WR
32	k-LA Raiders	Greg Skrepenak, Michigan	OT
33	San Diego	Marquez Pope, Fresno St.	DB
34	Green Bay	Mark D'Onofrio, Penn St.	LB
35	l-New England	Rodney Smith, Notre Dame	DB
36	m-Dallas	Jimmy Smith, Jackson St.	WR
37	n-Dallas	Darren Woodson, Ariz.St.	DB
38	Pittsburgh	Levon Kirkland, Clemson	LB
39	o-Minnesota	Robert Harris, Southern	DE
40	p-Kansas City	Matt Blundin, Virginia	QB
41	NY Giants	Phillippi Sparks, Ariz.St.	DB
42	NY Jets	Kurt Barber, USC	LB
43	Miami	Eddie Blake, Auburn	DT
44	q-Tampa Bay	Courtney Hawkins, Mich.St.	WR
45	San Francisco	AMP LEE, Florida St.	RB
46	r-Phoenix	Tony Sacca, Penn St.	QB
47	s-Washington	Shane Collins, Ariz.St.	DE
48	Philadelphia	Siran Stacy, Alabama	RB
49	Chicago	Troy Auzenne, California	OT
50	Houston	Eddie Robinson, Ala.St.	LB
51	t-Atlanta	Chuck Smith, Tennessee	DE
52	u-Cleveland	Patrick Rowe, S.Diego St.	WR
53	Detroit	Tracy Scroggins, Tulsa	LB
54	Denver	SHANE DRONETT, Texas	DE
55	Buffalo	James Patton, Texas	NT
56	v-Detroit	Jason Hanson, Wash.St.	PK

Acquired Picks: k—from Tampa Bay; **l**—from Phoenix; **m**—from Cleveland; **n**—from New England; **o**—from Seattle; **p**—from Minnesota thru Dallas; **q**—from LA Raiders; **r**—from Atlanta thru New England; **s**—from Kansas City thru Dallas; **t**—from Dallas; **u**—from New Orleans thru Dallas; **v**—from Washington thru Dallas.

Notables Drafted in Later Rounds

Craig Erickson, Miami-FL QB (4th Rd/86th pick, Tampa Bay); Casey Weldon, Fla.St., QB (4th/102, Philadelphia); Mario Bailey, Washington, WR (6th/162, Houston); Jeff Blake, E.Carolina, QB (6th/166, NY Jets); Erick Anderson, Michigan, LB (7th/186, Kansas City); Bucky Richardson, Texas A&M, QB (8th/220, Houston); Ty Detmer, BYU, QB (9th/230, Green Bay); Darian Hagan, Colorado, QB (9th/242, San Francisco); Carlos Huerta, Miami-FL, PK (12th/315, San Diego).

Canadian Football League
Final 1991 Standings

Division champions (*) and other playoff qualifiers (+) are noted. Number of seasons listed after each head coach refers to current tenure with club.

Western Division

	W	L	T	Pts	PF	PA	vs Div
*Edmonton	12	6	0	24	671	569	6-4-0
†Calgary	11	7	0	22	596	552	6-4-0
†B.C.Lions	11	7	0	22	661	587	5-5-0
Saskatchewan	6	12	0	12	606	710	3-7-0

1991 Head Coaches: Edm—Ron Lancaster (1st season); **Calg**—Wally Buono (2nd); **BC**—Bob O'Billovich (2nd); **Sask**—replaced John Gregory (5th, 1-6) with Don Matthews (5-6) on Aug.22.
1990 Standings: 1.Calgary (11-6-1); 2.Edmonton (10-8); 3.Saskatchewan (9-9); 4.B.C.Lions (6-11-1).

Eastern Division

	W	L	T	Pts	PF	PA	vs Div
*Toronto	13	5	0	26	647	526	8-2-0
†Winnipeg	9	9	0	18	516	499	6-4-0
†Ottawa	7	11	0	14	522	577	5-5-0
Hamilton	3	15	0	6	400	599	1-9-0

1991 Head Coaches: Tor—Adam Rita (1st season); **Win**—Darryl Rogers (1st); **Ott**—replaced Steve Goldman (3rd, 0-4) with Joe Faragalli (7-7) on Aug.5; **Ham**—replaced David Beckman (2nd, 0-8) with John Gregory (3-7) on Aug.31.
1990 Standings: 1.Winnipeg (12-6); 2.Toronto (10-8); 3.Ottawa (7-11); 4.Hamilton (6-12).

1991 CFL Playoffs

Division Semifinals (Nov.10)
Eastern: at Winnipeg 26 . . . . Ottawa 8
Western: at Calgary 43 . . . . B.C.Lions 41

Division Championships (Nov.17)
Eastern: at Toronto 42 . . . . Winnipeg 3
Western: Calgary 38 . . . . at Edmonton 36

79th Grey Cup Championship
Nov.24 at Winnipeg Stadium, Manitoba
(Att: 51,985)

Calgary (13-7)	7	3	4	7	21
Toronto (14-5)	8	3	8	17	36

Most Outstanding Player
Rocket Ismail, Toronto, WR-KR
(Ran back 4 kickoffs for 183 yards, including an 87-yd TD return in the 4th quarter; also ran back 5 punts for 70 yards and caught 2 passes for 7 yards.)

All-CFL Team

Selected by a Football Writers of Canada panel. Holdovers from the 1990 All-CFL team in **bold** type.

Pos	Offense	Pos	Defense
WR—	Ray Alexander, BC	E—	Will Johnson, Calg.
WR—	Rocket Ismail, Tor.	E—	Mike Campbell, Tor.
T—	**Jim Mills**, BC	T—	**Harold Hallman**, Tor.
T—	**Chris Walby**, Win.	T—	Brett Williams, Edm.
G—	Leo Groenewegen, BC	LB—	**Willie Pless**, Edm.
G—	**Dan Ferrone**, Tor.	LB—	Greg Battle, Win.
C—	**Rod Connop**, Edm.	LB—	Darryl Ford, Tor.
QB—	Doug Flutie, BC	CB—	**Less Browne**, Win.
FB—	**Blake Marshall**, Edm.	CB—	Junior Thurman, Calg.
RB—	**Robert Mimbs**, Win.	HB—	Darryl Hall, Calg.
SB—	Matt Clark, BC	HB—	**Don Wilson**, BC
SB—	Allen Pitts, Calg.	S—	Glen Suitor, Sask.

Specialists: Kicker—Lance Chomyc, Tor.; Punter—Hank Ilesic, Tor.; Kick Returns—Henry Williams, Edm.

CFL Regular Season Individual Leaders
Passing Efficiency
(Minimum of 400 attempts)

	Att	Cmp	Cmp Pct	Yds	Avg Gain	TD	Long	Int	Sack	Yds Lost	Rating
Doug Flutie, BC	730	466	63.8	6619	9.07	38	89-td	24	29	N/A	96.6
Danny Barrett, Calg	438	249	56.8	3453	7.88	19	83	5	42	N/A	92.0
Tracy Ham, Edm	454	242	53.3	3862	8.51	31	66	16	43	281	90.0
Kent Austin, Sask	554	302	54.5	4137	7.47	32	99-td	18	12	88	84.2
Tom Burgess, Win	525	261	49.7	4212	8.02	27	104-td	29	27	181	71.0

All-Purpose Running

	Rush	Rec	Ret	Total
Rocket Ismail, Tor	271	1300	1388	2959
Willis Jacox, Sask	93	392	2294	2779
Henry Williams, Edm	1	233	2033	2267
Robert Mimbs, Win	1769	438	0	2207
Jon Volpe, BC	1395	459	118	1972
Anthony Drawhorn, Ott	0	0	1900	1900
Peewee Smith, Calg	-6	467	1413	1874
Reggie Barnes, Ott	1486	246	135	1867

Note: Returns (Ret) includes kickoffs, punts, fumbles, and interceptions returned.

Touchdowns

	TD	Rush	Rec	Ret	Pts
Blake Marshall, Edm	20	16	4	0	120
Jon Volpe, BC	20	16	4	0	120
Robert Mimbs, Win	16	15	1	0	98*
Allen Pitts, Calg	15	0	15	0	90
David Williams, Edm-Tor	15	0	15	0	90
Doug Flutie, BC	14	14	0	0	86*
Reggie Barnes, Ott	13	10	3	0	80*
Rocket Ismail, Tor	13	3	9	1	80*

*Total includes one 2-point conversion.

Other Individual Leaders

Points (Kicking)	236	Lance Chomyc, Tor.
Rushing Yards	1769	Robert Mimbs, Win.
Passing Yards	6619	Doug Flutie, BC
Receptions	118	Allen Pitts, Calg.
Interceptions	10	Less Browne, Win.
Sacks	15	Will Johnson, Calg.
Punting Average	44.4	Hank Ilesic, Tor.

Most Outstanding Players

Top Player	Doug Flutie, B.C.Lions, QB
Canadian	Blake Marshall, Edmonton, FB
Offensive Lineman	Jim Mills, B.C.Lions, T
Defensive Player	Greg Battle, Winnipeg, LB
Rookie	Jon Volpe, B.C.Lions, RB
Coach	Adam Rita, Toronto

PRO FOOTBALL

S T A T I S T I C S

THE 1993 | INFORMATION PLEASE | SPORTS ALMANAC

THROUGH THE YEARS
1920-1992
SUPER BOWLS • NFL LEADERS

SEC B

PAGE 215

The Super Bowl

The first AFL-NFL World Championship Game, as it was originally called, was played seven months after the two leagues agreed to merge in June of 1966. It became the Super Bowl (complete with roman numerals) by the third game in 1969. The Super Bowl winner has been presented the Vince Lombardi Trophy since 1971. Lombardi, whose Green Bay teams won the first two title games, died in 1970. NFL champions (1966-69) and NFC champions (since 1970) are listed in CAPITAL letters.

Multiple winners: Pittsburgh and San Francisco (4); Oakland-LA Raiders and Washington (3); Dallas, Green Bay, Miami, and NY Giants (2).

Bowl	Date	Winner	Head Coach	Score	Loser	Head Coach	Site
I	1/15/67	GREEN BAY	Vince Lombardi	35-21	Kansas City	Hank Stram	Los Angeles
II	1/14/68	GREEN BAY	Vince Lombardi	33-14	Oakland	John Rauch	Miami
III	1/12/69	NY Jets	Weeb Ewbank	16- 7	BALTIMORE	Don Shula	Miami
IV	1/11/70	Kansas City	Hank Stram	23- 7	MINNESOTA	Bud Grant	New Orleans
V	1/17/71	Baltimore	Don McCafferty	16-13	DALLAS	Tom Landry	Miami
VI	1/16/72	DALLAS	Tom Landry	24- 3	Miami	Don Shula	New Orleans
VII	1/14/73	Miami	Don Shula	14- 7	WASHINGTON	George Allen	Los Angeles
VIII	1/13/74	Miami	Don Shula	24- 7	MINNESOTA	Bud Grant	Houston
IX	1/12/75	Pittsburgh	Chuck Noll	16- 6	MINNESOTA	Bud Grant	New Orleans
X	1/18/76	Pittsburgh	Chuck Noll	21-17	DALLAS	Tom Landry	Miami
XI	1/ 9/77	Oakland	John Madden	32-14	MINNESOTA	Bud Grant	Pasadena
XII	1/15/78	DALLAS	Tom Landry	27-10	Denver	Red Miller	New Orleans
XIII	1/21/79	Pittsburgh	Chuck Noll	35-31	DALLAS	Tom Landry	Miami
XIV	1/20/80	Pittsburgh	Chuck Noll	31-19	LA RAMS	Ray Malavasi	Pasadena
XV	1/25/81	Oakland	Tom Flores	27-10	PHILADELPHIA	Dick Vermeil	New Orleans
XVI	1/24/82	SAN FRANCISCO	Bill Walsh	26-21	Cincinnati	Forrest Gregg	Pontiac, MI
XVII	1/30/83	WASHINGTON	Joe Gibbs	27-17	Miami	Don Shula	Pasadena
XVIII	1/22/84	LA Raiders	Tom Flores	38- 9	WASHINGTON	Joe Gibbs	Tampa
XIX	1/20/85	SAN FRANCISCO	Bill Walsh	38-16	Miami	Don Shula	Stanford
XX	1/26/86	CHICAGO	Mike Ditka	46-10	New England	Raymond Berry	New Orleans
XXI	1/25/87	NY GIANTS	Bill Parcells	39-20	Denver	Dan Reeves	Pasadena
XXII	1/31/88	WASHINGTON	Joe Gibbs	42-10	Denver	Dan Reeves	San Diego
XXIII	1/22/89	SAN FRANCISCO	Bill Walsh	20-16	Cincinnati	Sam Wyche	Miami
XXIV	1/28/90	SAN FRANCISCO	George Seifert	55-10	Denver	Dan Reeves	New Orleans
XXV	1/27/91	NY GIANTS	Bill Parcells	20-19	Buffalo	Marv Levy	Tampa
XXVI	1/26/92	WASHINGTON	Joe Gibbs	37-24	Buffalo	Marv Levy	Minneapolis

Pete Rozelle Award (MVP)

The Most Valuable Player in the Super Bowl. Currently selected by an 11-member panel made up of national pro football writers and broadcasters chosen by the NFL. Presented by *Sport* magazine from 1967-89 and by the NFL since 1990. Named after former NFL commissioner Pete Rozelle in 1990. Winners who did not play for Super Bowl champions are in **bold** type.

Multiple winners: Joe Montana (3); Terry Bradshaw and Bart Starr (2).

Bowl		Bowl		Bowl	
I	Bart Starr, Green Bay, QB	XI	Fred Biletnikoff, Oakland, WR	XIX	Joe Montana, San Francisco, QB
II	Bart Starr, Green Bay, QB	XII	Harvey Martin, Dallas, DE	XX	Richard Dent, Chicago, DE
III	Joe Namath, NY Jets, QB		& Randy White, Dallas, DT	XXI	Phil Simms, NY Giants, QB
IV	Len Dawson, Kansas City, QB	XIII	Terry Bradshaw, Pittsburgh, QB	XXII	Doug Williams, Washington, QB
V	**Chuck Howley**, Dallas, LB	XIV	Terry Bradshaw, Pittsburgh, QB	XXIII	Jerry Rice, San Francisco, WR
VI	Roger Staubach, Dallas, QB	XV	Jim Plunkett, Oakland, QB	XXIV	Joe Montana, San Francisco, QB
VII	Jake Scott, Miami, S	XVI	Joe Montana, San Francisco, QB	XXV	Ottis Anderson, NY Giants, RB
VIII	Larry Csonka, Miami, RB	XVII	John Riggins, Washington, RB	XXVI	Mark Rypien, Washington, QB
IX	Franco Harris, Pittsburgh, RB	XVIII	Marcus Allen, LA Raiders, RB		
X	Lynn Swann, Pittsburgh, WR				

All-Time Super Bowl Leaders
Through Super Bowl XXVI, Jan. 26, 1992.

CAREER
Passing Efficiency

Ratings based on performance standards established for completion percentage, average gain, touchdown percentage and interception percentage. Quarterbacks are allocated points according to how their statistics measure up to those standards. Minimum 40 passing attempts.

		Gm	Att	Comp	Comp%	Yards	Avg Gain	TD	TD%	Int	Int%	Rating
1	Joe Montana, SF	4	122	83	68.0	1142	9.36	11	9.0	0	0.0	127.8
2	Jim Plunkett, Raiders	2	46	29	63.0	433	9.41	4	8.7	0	0.0	122.8
3	Terry Bradshaw, Pit	4	84	49	58.3	932	11.10	9	10.7	4	4.8	112.6
4	Roger Staubach, Dal	4	98	61	62.2	734	7.49	8	8.2	4	4.1	95.4
5	Bart Starr, GB	2	47	29	61.7	452	9.62	3	6.4	1	2.1	95.1
6	Len Dawson, KC	2	44	28	63.6	353	8.02	2	4.5	2	4.5	84.8
7	Bob Griese, Mia.	3	41	26	63.4	295	7.20	1	2.4	2	4.9	72.5
8	Dan Marino, Mia.	1	50	29	58.0	318	6.36	1	2.0	2	4.0	66.9
9	Jim Kelly, Buf	2	88	46	52.3	487	5.53	2	2.3	4	4.5	57.3
10	Joe Theismann, Wash.	2	58	31	53.4	386	6.66	2	3.4	4	6.9	56.9

Passing Yardage

		Gm	Att	Cmp	Pct	Yds
1	Joe Montana, SF	4	122	83	68.0	1142
2	Terry Bradshaw, Pit	4	84	49	58.3	932
3	Roger Staubach, Dal	4	98	61	62.2	734
4	John Elway, Den	3	101	46	45.5	669
5	Fran Tarkenton, Min	3	89	46	51.7	489
6	Jim Kelly, Buf	2	88	46	52.3	487
7	Bart Starr, GB	2	47	29	61.7	452
8	Jim Plunkett, Raiders	2	46	29	63.0	433
9	Joe Theismann, Wash	2	58	31	53.4	386
10	Len Dawson, KC	2	44	28	63.6	353
11	Doug Williams, Wash	1	29	18	62.1	340
12	Dan Marino, Mia.	1	50	29	58.0	318
13	Ken Anderson, Cin	1	34	25	73.5	300
14	Bob Griese, Mia.	3	41	26	63.4	295
15	Mark Rypien, Wash	1	33	18	54.5	292

Receiving

		Gm	No	Yds	Avg	TD
1	Roger Craig, SF	3	20	212	10.6	3
2	Jerry Rice, SF	2	18	363	20.2	4
3	Lynn Swann, Pit	4	16	364	22.8	3
4	Chuck Foreman, Min	3	15	139	9.3	0
5	Cliff Branch, Raiders	3	14	181	12.9	3
6	Andre Reed, Buf.	2	13	96	7.4	0
7	Preston Pearson, Bal-Pit-Dal	5	12	105	8.8	0
8	John Stallworth, Pit	4	11	268	24.4	3
9	Dan Ross, Cin	1	11	104	9.5	2
10	Gary Clark, Wash	2	10	169	16.9	2
	Otis Taylor, KC	2	10	138	13.8	1
	Dwight Clark, SF	2	10	122	12.2	0
	Tony Nathan, Mia	2	10	83	8.3	0
	Ricky Sanders, Wash	2	10	234	23.4	2
15	Six tied with 9 each.					

Rushing

		Gm	Car	Yds	Avg	TD
1	Franco Harris, Pit	4	101	354	3.5	4
2	Larry Csonka, Mia	3	57	297	5.2	2
3	John Riggins, Wash	2	64	230	3.6	2
4	Timmy Smith, Wash.	1	22	204	9.3	2
5	Roger Craig, SF	3	52	201	3.9	2
6	Marcus Allen, Raiders	1	20	191	9.5	2
7	Tony Dorsett, Dal	2	31	162	5.2	1
8	Mark van Eeghen, Raiders	2	37	153	4.1	0
9	Thurman Thomas, Buf	2	25	148	5.9	2
10	Rocky Bleier, Pit	4	44	144	3.3	0
11	Walt Garrison, Dal	2	26	139	5.3	0
12	Clarence Davis, Raiders	1	16	137	8.6	0
13	Duane Thomas, Dal	2	37	130	3.5	1
14	Wendell Tyler, Rams-SF	2	30	125	4.2	0
15	Matt Snell, NYJ	1	30	121	4.0	1

All-Purpose Running

		Gm	Rush	Rec	Ret	Total
1	Franco Harris, Pit	4	354	114	0	468
2	Roger Craig, SF	3	201	212	0	413
3	Lynn Swann, Pit	4	−7	364	34	391
4	Jerry Rice, SF	2	5	363	0	368
5	Larry Csonka, Mia	3	297	17	0	314
6	Fulton Walker, Mia	2	0	0	298	298
7	Ricky Sanders, Wash	2	−3	234	46	277
8	Preston Pearson, Balt-Pit-Dal	5	31	105	122	258
9	John Riggins, Wash	2	230	16	0	246
10	Thurman Thomas, Buf	2	148	82	0	230

Super Bowl Appearances

Through Super Bowl XXVI, nine NFL teams have yet to play for the Vince Lombardi Trophy. In alphabetical order: Atlanta, Cleveland, Detroit, Houston, New Orleans, Phoenix, San Diego, Seattle and Tampa Bay. Of the 19 teams that have made the trip, Dallas, Miami and Washington have the most appearances (5), while Pittsburgh and San Francisco have the most titles (4).

App		W	L	Pct	PF	PA
5	Washington	3	2	.600	122	103
5	Dallas	2	3	.400	112	85
5	Miami	2	3	.400	74	103
4	Pittsburgh	4	0	1.000	103	73
4	San Francisco	4	0	1.000	139	63
4	Oak/LA Raiders	3	1	.750	111	66
4	Denver	0	4	.000	50	163
4	Minnesota	0	4	.000	34	95
2	Green Bay	2	0	1.000	68	24
2	NY Giants	2	0	1.000	59	39
2	Baltimore Colts	1	1	.500	23	29
2	Kansas City	1	1	.500	33	42
2	Buffalo	0	2	.000	43	57
2	Cincinnati	0	2	.000	37	46
1	Chicago	1	0	1.000	46	10
1	NY Jets	1	0	1.000	16	7
1	LA Rams	0	1	.000	19	31
1	New England	0	1	.000	10	46
1	Philadelphia	0	1	.000	10	27

Scoring

Points

		Gm	TD	FG	PAT	Pts
1	Roger Craig, SF	3	4	0	0	24
	Franco Harris, Pit	4	4	0	0	24
	Jerry Rice, SF	2	4	0	0	24
4	Ray Wersching, SF	2	0	5	7	22
5	Don Chandler, GB	2	0	4	8	20
6	Cliff Branch, Raiders	3	3	0	0	18
	John Stallworth, Pit	4	3	0	0	18
	Lynn Swann, Pit	4	3	0	0	18
9	Chris Bahr, Raiders	2	0	3	8	17
10	Matt Bahr, Pit-NYG	2	0	3	6	15
	Mike Cofer, SF	2	0	2	9	15
	Uwe von Schamann, Mia	2	0	4	3	15
13	Kevin Butler, Chi	1	0	3	5	14
	Ray Gerela, Pit	3	0	2	8	14
	Jim Turner, NYJ-Den	2	0	4	2	14
16	Jim Breech, Cin	2	0	3	4	13
	Mike Clark, Dal	2	0	3	4	13
	Chip Lohmiller, Wash	1	0	3	4	13

Touchdowns

		Gm	Rush	Rec	Ret	TD
1	Roger Craig, SF	3	2	2	0	4
	Franco Harris, Pit	4	4	0	0	4
	Jerry Rice, SF	4	0	4	4	4
4	Cliff Branch, Raiders	3	0	3	0	3
	John Stallworth, Pit	4	0	3	0	3
	Lynn Swann, Pit	4	0	3	0	3
7	Twenty-two tied with 2 TDs each.					

(Marcus Allen, Raiders; Ottis Anderson, NYG; Pete Banaszak, Raiders; Gary Clark, Wash.; Larry Csonka, Mia.; John Elway, Den.; Butch Johnson, Dal.; Jim Kiick, Mia.; Max McGee, GB; Jim McMahon, Chi.; Bill Miller, Raiders; Joe Montana, SF; Elijah Pitts, GB; Tom Rathman, SF; John Riggins, Wash.; Gerald Riggs, Wash.; Dan Ross, Cin.; Ricky Sanders, Wash.; Timmy Smith, Wash.; John Taylor, SF; Thurman Thomas, Buf. and Duane Thomas, Dal.)

SINGLE GAME

Passing

Yards Gained	Year	Att/Cmp	Yds
Joe Montana, SF vs Cin	1989	36/23	357
Doug Williams, Wash vs Den	1988	29/18	340
Joe Montana, SF vs Mia	1985	35/24	331
Terry Bradshaw, Pit vs Dal	1979	30/17	318
Dan Marino, Mia vs SF	1985	50/29	318
Terry Bradshaw, Pit vs Rams	1980	21/14	309
John Elway, Den vs NYG	1987	37/22	304
Ken Anderson, Cin vs SF	1982	34/25	300
Joe Montana, SF vs Den	1990	29/22	297
Mark Rypien, Wash vs Buf	1992	33/18	292

Touchdown Passes	Year	TD	Int
Joe Montana, SF vs Den	1990	5	0
Terry Bradshaw, Pit vs Dal	1979	4	1
Doug Williams, Wash vs Den	1988	4	1
Roger Staubach, Dal vs Pit	1979	3	1
Jim Plunkett, Raiders vs Phi	1981	3	0
Joe Montana, SF vs Mia	1985	3	0
Phil Simms, NYG vs Den	1987	3	0

Eleven tied with 2 TD passes each.

Scoring

Points	Year	TD	FG	PAT	Pts
Roger Craig, SF vs Mia	1985	3	0	0	18
Jerry Rice, SF vs Den	1990	3	0	0	18
Don Chandler, GB vs Raiders . .	1968	0	4	3	15
Ray Wersching, SF vs Cin	1982	0	4	2	14
Kevin Butler, Chi vs NE	1986	0	3	5	14
Chip Lohmiller, Wash vs Buf . . .	1992	0	3	4	13

Fifteen tied with 12 points each.

Touchdowns	Year	TD	Rush	Rec
Roger Craig, SF vs Mia	1985	3	1	2
Jerry Rice, SF vs Den	1990	3	0	3
Max McGee, GB vs KC	1967	2	0	2
Bill Miller, Raiders vs GB	1968	2	0	2
Larry Csonka, Mia vs Min	1974	2	2	0
Pete Banaszak, Raiders vs Min.	1977	2	2	0
John Stallworth, Pit vs Dal	1979	2	0	2
Franco Harris, Pit vs Rams	1980	2	2	0
Cliff Branch, Raiders vs Phi	1981	2	0	2
Dan Ross, Cin vs SF	1982	2	0	2
Marcus Allen, Raiders vs Wash	1984	2	2	0
Jim McMahon, Chi vs NE	1986	2	2	0
Ricky Sanders, Wash vs Den	1988	2	0	2
Timmy Smith, Wash vs Den	1988	2	2	0
Tom Rathman, SF vs Den	1990	2	2	0
Gerald Riggs, Wash vs Buf	1992	2	2	0

Receiving

Catches	Year	No	Yds	TD
Dan Ross, Cin vs SF	1982	11	104	2
Jerry Rice, SF vs Cin	1989	11	215	1
Ricky Sanders, Wash vs Den	1988	9	193	2
George Sauer, NYJ vs Bal	1969	8	133	0
Roger Craig, SF vs Cin	1989	8	101	0
Andre Reed, Buf vs NYG	1991	8	62	0
Max McGee, GB vs KC	1967	7	138	2
John Henderson, Min vs KC	1970	7	111	0
Lynn Swann, Pit vs Dal	1979	7	124	1
Stanley Morgan, NE vs Chi	1986	7	70	0
Jerry Rice, SF vs Den	1990	7	148	3
Gary Clark, Wash vs Buf	1992	7	114	1
James Lofton, Buf vs Wash	1992	7	92	0
Art Monk, Wash vs Buf	1992	7	113	0

Rushing

Yards Gained	Year	Car	Yds	TD
Timmy Smith, Wash vs Den	1988	22	204	2
Marcus Allen, Raiders vs Wash	1984	20	191	2
John Riggins, Wash vs Mia	1983	38	166	1
Franco Harris, Pit vs Min	1975	34	158	1
Larry Csonka, Mia vs Min	1974	33	145	2
Clarence Davis, Raiders vs Min.	1977	16	137	0
Thurman Thomas, Buf vs NYG	1991	15	135	1
Matt Snell, NYJ vs Bal	1969	30	121	1
Tom Matte, Bal vs NYJ	1969	11	116	0
Larry Csonka, Mia vs Wash	1973	15	112	1
Ottis Anderson, NYG vs Buf	1991	21	102	1

All-Purpose Running

Yards Gained	Year	Yds
Ricky Sanders, Wash vs Den	1988	235
Jerry Rice, SF vs Cin	1989	220
Marcus Allen, Raiders vs Wash	1984	209
Stephen Starring, NE vs Chi	1986	192
Fulton Walker, Mia vs Wash	1983	190
Thurman Thomas, Buf vs NYG	1991	190

Interceptions

	Year	No	Yds	TD
Rod Martin, Raiders vs Phi	1981	3	44	0
Randy Beverly, NYJ vs Bal	1969	2	0	0
Chuck Howley, Dal vs Bal	1971	2	22	0
Jake Scott, Mia vs Wash	1973	2	63	0
Barry Wilburn, Wash vs Den	1988	2	11	0
Brad Edwards, Wash vs Buf	1992	2	56	0

Super Bowl Playoffs

The Super Bowl created pro football's first guaranteed multiple-game playoff format. Only four teams qualified for the playoffs in 1966, but by the time the 10 AFL teams joined the NFL in 1970, the field had doubled. Since 1978, 10 teams (out of 28) have made the postseason cut.

In the strike year of 1982, when the regular season was shortened to just nine games, playoff berths were extended to 16 teams and a 15-game tournament was played.

Throughout the following year-by-year playoff summary, home teams are listed in CAPITAL letters and records of the finalists include all games leading up to the Super Bowl; (*) indicates Wild Card teams.

1966 Season

AFL Playoffs

Championship.......... Kansas City 31, BUFFALO 7

NFL Playoffs

Championship .... Green Bay 34, DALLAS 27

Super Bowl I

Jan. 15, 1967
Memorial Coliseum, Los Angeles
(Favorite: Packers by 14)

Kansas City (12-2-1) .... 0 10   0   0—**10**
Green Bay (13-2) 7   7 14   7—**35**
MVP: Green Bay QB Bart Starr (16 for 23, 250 yds, 2 TD, 1 Int)

1967 Season

AFL Playoffs

Championship............. OAKLAND 40, Houston 7

NFL Playoffs

Eastern Conf .... DALLAS 52, Cleveland 14
Western Conf .... GREEN BAY 28, LA Rams 7
Championship .... GREEN BAY 21, Dallas 17

Super Bowl II

Jan. 14, 1968
Orange Bowl, Miami
(Favorite: Packers by 13½)

Green Bay (11-4-1) .... 3 13 10   7—**33**
Oakland (14-1) 0   7   0   7—**14**
MVP: Green Bay QB Bart Starr (13 for 24, 202 yds, 1 TD)

1968 Season

AFL Playoffs

Western Div.Playoff .... OAKLAND 41, Kan.City 6
AFL Championship .... NY JETS 27, Oakland 23

NFL Playoffs

Eastern Conf.............. CLEVELAND 31, Dallas 20
Western Conf......... BALTIMORE 24, Minnesota 14
NFL Championship..... Baltimore 34, CLEVELAND 0

Super Bowl III

Jan. 12, 1969
Orange Bowl, Miami
(Favorite: Colts by 18)

NY Jets (12-3) 0   7   6   3—**16**
Baltimore (15-1) 0   0   0   7— **7**
MVP: NY Jets QB Joe Namath (17 for 28, 206 yds)

1969 Season

AFL Playoffs

Inter-Division.............. Kansas City 13, NY JETS 6
.... OAKLAND 56, Houston 7
AFL Championship...... Kansas City 17, OAKLAND 7

NFL Playoffs

Eastern Conf .... Cleveland 38, DALLAS 14
Western Conf .... MINNESOTA 23, LA Rams 20
NFL Championship..... MINNESOTA 27, Cleveland 7

Super Bowl IV

Jan. 11, 1970
Tulane Stadium, New Orleans
(Favorite: Vikings by 12)

Minnesota (14-2) 0   0   7   0— **7**
Kansas City (13-3) .... 3 13   7   0—**23**
MVP: Kansas City QB Len Dawson (12 for 17, 142 yds, 1 TD, 1 Int)

1970 Season

AFC Playoffs

First Round.............. BALTIMORE 17, Cincinnati 0
.... OAKLAND 21, Miami* 14
Championship .... BALTIMORE 27, Oakland 17

NFC Playoffs

First Round..................... DALLAS 5, Detroit* 0
.... San Francisco 17, MINNESOTA 14
Championship....... Dallas 17, SAN FRANCISCO 10

Super Bowl V

Jan. 17, 1971
Orange Bowl, Miami
(Favorite: Cowboys by 2½)

Baltimore (13-2-1) 0   6   0 10—**16**
Dallas (12-4) .... 3 10   0   0—**13**
MVP: Dallas LB Chuck Howley (2 Interceptions for 22 yds)

1971 Season

AFC Playoffs

First Round .... Miami 27, KANSAS CITY 24 (OT)
.... Baltimore* 20, CLEVELAND 3
Championship................ MIAMI 21, Baltimore 0

NFC Playoffs

First Round................ Dallas 20, MINNESOTA 12
.... SAN FRANCISCO 24, Washington* 20
Championship .... DALLAS 14, San Francisco 3

Super Bowl VI

Jan. 16, 1972
Tulane Stadium, New Orleans
(Favorite: Cowboys by 6)

Dallas (13-3) 3   7   7   7—**24**
Miami (12-3-1) 0   3   0   0— **3**
MVP: Dallas QB Roger Staubach (12 for 19, 119 yds, 2 TD)

1972 Season

AFC Playoffs
First Round............. PITTSBURGH 13, Oakland 7
.... MIAMI 20, Cleveland* 14
Championship .... Miami 21, PITTSBURGH 17

NFC Playoffs
First Round .... Dallas* 30, SAN FRANCISCO 28
.... WASHINGTON 16, Green Bay 3
Championship .... WASHINGTON 26, Dallas 3

Super Bowl VII
Jan. 14, 1973
Memorial Coliseum, Los Angeles
(Favorite: Redskins by 1½)

Miami (16-0) 7   7   0   0—**14**
Washington (13-3) 0   0   0   7—**7**
MVP: Miami safety Jake Scott (2 Interceptions for 63 yds)

1973 Season

AFC Playoffs
First Round .... OAKLAND 33, Pittsburgh* 14
.... MIAMI 34, Cincinnati 16
Championship .... MIAMI 27, Oakland 10

NFC Playoffs
First Round .... MINNESOTA 27, Washington* 20
.... DALLAS 27, LA Rams 16
Championship .... Minnesota 27, DALLAS 10

Super Bowl VIII
Jan. 13, 1974
Rice Stadium, Houston
(Favorite: Dolphins by 6½)

Minnesota (14-2) 0   0   0   7—**7**
Miami (12-4) 14   3   7   0—**24**
MVP: Miami FB Larry Csonka (33 carries, 145 yds, 2 TD)

1974 Season

AFC Playoffs
First Round .... OAKLAND 28, Miami 26
.... PITTSBURGH 32, Buffalo* 14
Championship .... Pittsburgh 24, OAKLAND 13

NFC Playoffs
First Round............. MINNESOTA 30, St.Louis 14
.... LA RAMS 19, Washington* 10
Championship .... MINNESOTA 14, LA Rams 10

Super Bowl IX
Jan. 12, 1975
Tulane Stadium, New Orleans
(Favorite: Steelers by 3)

Pittsburgh (12-3-1) 0   2   7   7—**16**
Minnesota (12-4) 0   0   0   6—**6**
MVP: Pittsburgh RB Franco Harris (34 carries, 158 yds, 1 TD)

1975 Season

AFC Playoffs
First Round .... PITTSBURGH 28, Baltimore 10
.... OAKLAND 31, Cincinnati* 28
Championship .... PITTSBURGH 16, Oakland 10

NFC Playoffs
First Round .... LA RAMS 35, St.Louis 23
.... Dallas* 17, MINNESOTA 14
Championship .... Dallas 37, LA RAMS 7

Super Bowl X
Jan. 18, 1976
Orange Bowl, Miami
(Favorite: Steelers by 6½)

Dallas (12-4) 7   3   0   7—**17**
Pittsburgh (14-2) 7   0   0   14—**21**
MVP: Pittsburgh WR Lynn Swan (4 catches, 161 yds, 1 TD)

1976 Season

AFC Playoffs
First Round .... OAKLAND 24, New England* 21
.... Pittsburgh 40, BALTIMORE 14
Championship .... OAKLAND 24, Pittsburgh 7

NFC Playoffs
First Round........ MINNESOTA 35, Washington* 20
.... LA Rams 14, DALLAS 12
Championship .... MINNESOTA 24, LA Rams 13

Super Bowl XI
Jan. 9, 1977
Rose Bowl, Pasadena
(Favorite: Raiders by 4½)

Oakland (15-1) 0   16   3   13—**32**
Minnesota (13-2-1) 0   0   7   7—**14**
MVP: Oakland WR Fred Biletnikoff (4 catches, 79 yds)

1977 Season

AFC Playoffs
First Round................ DENVER 34, Pittsburgh 21
.... Oakland* 37, BALTIMORE 31 (OT)
Championship .... DENVER 20, Oakland 17

NFC Playoffs
First Round.................. DALLAS 37, Chicago* 7
.... Minnesota 14, LA RAMS 7
Championship.............. DALLAS 23, Minnesota 6

Super Bowl XII
Jan. 15, 1978
Louisiana Superdome, New Orleans
(Favorite: Cowboys by 6)

Dallas (14-2) 10   3   7   7—**27**
Denver (14-2) 0   0   10   0—**10**
MVPs: Dallas DE Harvey Martin and DT Randy White
(Cowboys' defense forced 8 turnovers)

A Year Later. . .
Super Bowl champions who did not qualify for playoffs the following season.

Season		Record	Finish	Season		Record	Finish
1968	Green Bay	6-7-1	3rd in NFL Central	1982	San Francisco	3-6-0*	11th in overall NFC
1970	Kansas City	7-5-2	2nd in AFC Western	1987	NY Giants	6-9-0*	5th in NFC East
1980	Pittsburgh	9-7-0	3rd in AFC Central	1988	Washington	7-9-0	3rd in NFC Eastern
1981	Oakland	7-9-0	4th in AFC Western	1991	NY Giants	8-8-0	4th in NFC Eastern

*Seasons when player strikes interrupted schedule.

Super Bowl Playoffs (Cont.)

1978 Season

AFC Playoffs

Wild Cards .... Houston 17, MIAMI 9
Second Round ...... Houston 31, NEW ENGLAND 14
.... PITTSBURGH 33, Denver 10
Championship ...... PITTSBURGH 34, Houston 5

NFC Playoffs

Wild Cards .... ATLANTA 14, Philadelphia 13
Second Round .... DALLAS 27, Atlanta 20
.... LA RAMS 34, Minnesota 10
Championship .... Dallas 28, LA RAMS 0

Super Bowl XIII
Jan. 21, 1979
Orange Bowl, Miami
(Favorite: Steelers by 3½)

Pittsburgh (16-2) .... 7 14 0 14—**35**
Dallas (14-4) .... 7 7 3 14—**31**
MVP: Pittsburgh QB Terry Bradshaw (17 for 30, 318 yds, 4 TD, 1 Int)

1979 Season

AFC Playoffs

Wild Cards................. HOUSTON 13, Denver 7
Second Round .... Houston 17, SAN DIEGO 14
.... PITTSBURGH 34, Miami 14
Championship.......... PITTSBURGH 27, Houston 13

NFC Playoffs

Wild Cards .... PHILADELPHIA 27, Chicago 17
Second Round .... TAMPA BAY 24, Philadelphia 17
.... LA Rams 21, DALLAS 19
Championship .... LA Rams 9, TAMPA BAY 0

Super Bowl XIV
Jan. 20, 1980
Rose Bowl, Pasadena
(Favorite: Steelers by 10½)

LA Rams (11-7) .... 7 6 6 0—**19**
Pittsburgh (14-4) .... 3 7 7 14—**31**
MVP: Pittsburgh QB Terry Bradshaw (14 for 21, 309 yds, 2 TD, 3 Int)

1980 Season

AFC Playoffs

Wild Cards .... OAKLAND 27, Houston 7
Second Round .... SAN DIEGO 20, Buffalo 14
.... Oakland 14, CLEVELAND 12
Championship .... Oakland 34, SAN DIEGO 27

NFC Playoffs

Wild Cards .... DALLAS 34, LA Rams 13
Second Round ...... PHILADELPHIA 31, Minnesota 16
.... Dallas 30, ATLANTA 27
Championship:......... PHILADELPHIA 20, Dallas 7

Super Bowl XV
Jan. 25, 1981
Louisiana Superdome, New Orleans
(Favorite: Eagles by 3)

Oakland (14-5) .... 14 0 10 3—**27**
Philadelphia (14-4) .... 0 3 0 7—**10**
MVP: Oakland QB Jim Plunkett (13 for 21, 261 yds, 3 TD)

1981 Season

AFC Playoffs

Wild Cards................... Buffalo 31, NY JETS 27
Second Round .... San Diego 41, MIAMI 38 (OT)
.... CINCINNATI 28, Buffalo 21
Championship......... CINCINNATI 27, San Diego 7

NFC Playoffs

Wild Cards .... NY Giants 27, PHILADELPHIA 21
Second Round .... DALLAS 38, Tampa Bay 0
... SAN FRANCISCO 38, NY Giants 24
Championship....... SAN FRANCISCO 28, Dallas 27

Super Bowl XVI
Jan. 24, 1982
Pontiac Silverdome, Pontiac,MI
(Favorite: Pick'em)

San Francisco (15-3) .... 7 13 0 6—**26**
Cincinnati (14-4) .... 0 0 7 14—**21**
MVP: San Francisco QB Joe Montana (14 for 22, 157 yds, 1 TD; 6 carries, 18 yds, 1 TD)

1982 Season

A 57-day players' strike shortened the regular season from 16 games to nine. The playoff format was changed to a 16-team tournament open to the top eight teams in each conference.

AFC Playoffs

First Round .... LA RAIDERS 27, Cleveland 10
.... MIAMI 28, New England 3
..............NY Jets 44, CINCINNATI 17
.... San Diego 31, PITTSBURGH 28
Second Round .... NY Jets 17, LA RAIDERS 14,
.... MIAMI 34, San Diego 13,
Championship.................. MIAMI 14, NY Jets 0

NFC Playoffs

First Round .... WASHINGTON 31, Detroit 7
.... DALLAS 30, Tampa Bay 17
..............GREEN BAY 41, St.Louis 16
.... MINNESOTA 30, Atlanta 24
Second Round....... WASHINGTON 21, Minnesota 7
.... DALLAS 37, Green Bay 26
Championship .... WASHINGTON 31, Dallas 17

Super Bowl XVII
Jan. 30, 1983
Rose Bowl, Pasadena
(Favorite: Dolphins by 3)

Miami (10-2) .... 7 10 0 0—**17**
Washington (11-1) .... 0 10 3 14—**27**
MVP: Washington RB John Riggins (38 carries, 166 yds, 1 TD; 1 catch, 15 yds)

Most Popular Playing Sites
Stadiums hosting more than one Super Bowl.

No	Stadium	Years
5	Orange Bowl (Miami)	1968-69, 71, 76, 79
4	Rose Bowl (Pasadena)	1977, 80, 83, 87
	Superdome (New Orleans)	1978, 81, 86, 90
3	Tulane Stadium (New Orleans)	1970, 72, 75
2	LA Memorial Coliseum	1967, 73
	Tampa Stadium	1984, 91

1983 Season
AFC Playoffs
Wild Cards.................... SEATTLE 31, Denver 7
Second Round................... Seattle 27, MIAMI 20
.... LA RAIDERS 38, Pittsburgh 10
Championship .... RAIDERS 30, Seattle 14

NFC Playoffs
Wild Cards .... LA Rams 24, DALLAS 17
Second Round....... SAN FRANCISCO 24, Detroit 23
.... WASHINGTON 51, LA Rams 7
Championship .. WASHINGTON 24, San Francisco 21

Super Bowl XVIII
Jan. 22, 1984
Tampa Stadium, Tampa
(Favorite: Redskins by 3)

Washington (16-2)	......	0	3	6 0—	**9**
LA Raiders (14-4)	......	7	14	14 3—	**38**

MVP: LA Raiders RB Marcus Allen (20 carries, 191 yds, 2 TD; 2 catches, 18 yds)

1984 Season
AFC Playoffs
Wild Cards .... SEATTLE 13, LA Raiders 7
Second Round.................. MIAMI 31, Seattle 10
.... Pittsburgh 24, DENVER 17
Championship .... MIAMI 45, Pittsburgh 28

NFC Playoffs
Wild Cards................ NY Giants 16, LA RAMS 13
Second Round ... SAN FRANCISCO 21, NY Giants 10
.... Chicago 23, WASHINGTON 19
Championship ...... SAN FRANCISCO 23, Chicago 0

Super Bowl XIX
Jan. 20, 1985
Stanford Stadium, Stanford,CA
(Favorite: 49ers by 3)

Miami (16-2)	......	10	6	0 0—	**16**
San Francisco (17-1)	......	7	21	10 0—	**38**

MVP: San Francisco QB Joe Montana (24 for 35, 331 yds, 2 TD; 5 carries, 59 yards, 1 TD)

1985 Season
AFC Playoffs
Wild Cards .... New England 26, NY JETS 14
Second Round .... MIAMI 24, Cleveland 21
...... New England 27, LA RAIDERS 20
Championship .... New England 31, MIAMI 14

NFC Playoffs
Wild Cards .... NY GIANTS 17, San Francisco 3
Second Round................. LA RAMS 20, Dallas 0
.... CHICAGO 21, NY Giants 0
Championship .... CHICAGO 24, LA Rams 0

Super Bowl XX
Jan. 26, 1986
Louisiana Superdome, New Orleans
(Favorite: Bears by 10)

Chicago Bears (17-1)	......	13	10	21 2—	**46**
New England (14-5)	......	3	0	0 7—	**10**

MVP: Chicago DE Richard Dent (Bears defense: 7 sacks, 6 turnovers, 1 safety and gave up just 123 total yards)

1986 Season
AFC Playoffs
Wild Cards .... NY JETS 35, Kansas City 15
Second Round ...... CLEVELAND 23, NY Jets 20 (OT)
.... DENVER 22, New England 17
Championship...... Denver 23, CLEVELAND 20 (OT)

NFC Playoffs
Wild Cards .... WASHINGTON 19, LA Rams 7
Second Round .... Washington 27, CHICAGO 13
.... NY GIANTS 49, San Francisco 3
Championship .... NY GIANTS 17, Washington 0

Super Bowl XXI
Jan. 25, 1987
Rose Bowl, Pasadena
(Favorite: Giants by 9½)

Denver (13-5)	......	10	0	0 10—	**20**
NY Giants (16-2)	......	7	2	17 13—	**39**

MVP: NY Giants QB Phil Simms (22 for 25, 268 yds, 3 TD; 3 carries, 25 yds)

1987 Season
A 24-day players' strike shortened the regular season from 16 games to 15 with replacement teams playing for three weeks. The playoffs proceeded as usual.

AFC Playoffs
Wild Cards .... HOUSTON 23, Seattle 20 (OT)
Second Round ...... CLEVELAND 38, Indianapolis 21
.... DENVER 34, Houston 10
Championship .... DENVER 38, Cleveland 33

NFC Playoffs
Wild Cards .... Minnesota 44, NEW ORLEANS 10
Second Round ... Minnesota 36, SAN FRANCISCO 24
.... Washington 21, CHICAGO 17
Championship ..... WASHINGTON 17, Minnesota 10

Super Bowl XXII
Jan. 31, 1988
San Diego/Jack Murphy Stadium
(Favorite: Broncos by 3½)

Washington (13-4)	......	0	35	0 7—	**42**
Denver (12-4-1)	......	10	0	0 0—	**10**

MVP: Washington QB Doug Williams (18 for 29, 340 yds, 4 TD, 1 Int)

1988 Season
AFC Playoffs
Wild Cards .... Houston 24, CLEVELAND 23
Second Round............. BUFFALO 17, Houston 10
.... CINCINNATI 21, Seattle 13
Championship........... CINCINNATI 21, Buffalo 10

NFC Playoffs
Wild Cards .... MINNESOTA 28, LA Rams 17
Second Round..... SAN FRANCISCO 34, Minnesota 9
.... CHICAGO 20, Philadelphia 12
Championship........ San Francisco 28, CHICAGO 3

Super Bowl XXIII
Jan. 22, 1989
Joe Robbie Stadium, Miami
(Favorite: 49ers by 7)

Cincinnati (17-1)	......	0	3	10 3—	**16**
San Francisco (14-5)	......	3	0	3 14—	**20**

MVP: San Francisco WR Jerry Rice (11 catches, 215 yds, 1 TD; 1 carry, 5 yds)

Super Bowl Playoffs (Cont.)

1989 Season
AFC Playoffs
Wild Cards............ Pittsburgh 26, HOUSTON 23
Second Round........... CLEVELAND 34, Buffalo 30
.... DENVER 24, Pittsburgh 23
Championship .... DENVER 37, Cleveland 21

NFC Playoffs
Wild Cards .... LA Rams 21, PHILADELPHIA 7
Second Round...... LA Rams 19, NY GIANTS 13 (OT)
... SAN FRANCISCO 41, Minnesota 13
Championship ...... SAN FRANCISCO 30, LA Rams 3

Super Bowl XXIV
Jan. 28, 1990
Louisiana Superdome, New Orleans
(Favorite: 49ers by 12½)

San Francisco (17-2) .... 13 14 14 14—**55**
Denver (13-6) .... 3 0 7 0—**10**
MVP: San Francisco QB Joe Montana (22 for 29, 297 yds, 5 TD, 0 Int)

1990 Season
AFC Playoffs
First Round.............. MIAMI* 17, Kansas City* 16
.... CINCINNATI 41, Houston* 14
Second Round.............. BUFFALO 44, Miami 34
.... LA RAIDERS 20, Cincinnati 10
Championship........... BUFFALO 51, LA Raiders 3

NFC Playoffs
First Round....... Washington* 20, PHILADELPHIA* 6
.... CHICAGO 16, New Orleans* 6
Second Round.. SAN FRANCISCO 28, Washington 10
.... NY GIANTS 31, Chicago 3
Championship .. NY Giants 15, SAN FRANCISCO 13

Super Bowl XXV
Jan. 27, 1991
Tampa Stadium, Tampa
(Favorite: Bills by 7)

Buffalo (15-4) .... 3 9 0 7—**19**
NY Giants (16-3) .... 3 7 7 3—**20**
MVP: NY Giants RB Ottis Anderson (21 carries, 102 yds, 1 TD; 1 catch, 7 yds)

1991 Season
AFC Playoffs
First Round.......... KANSAS CITY* 10, LA Raiders* 6
.... HOUSTON 17, NY Jets* 10
Second Round .... DENVER 26, Houston 24
.... BUFFALO 37, Kansas City 14
Championship .... BUFFALO 10, Denver 7

NFC Playoffs
First Round........... Atlanta* 27, NEW ORLEANS 20
.... Dallas* 17, CHICAGO* 13
Second Round .... WASHINGTON 24, Atlanta 7
.... DETROIT 38, Dallas 6
Championship........ WASHINGTON 41, Detroit 10

Super Bowl XXVI
Jan. 26, 1992
Hubert Humphrey Metrodome, Minneapolis
(Favorite: Redskins by 7)

Washington (16-2).................. 0 17 14 6—**37**
Buffalo (15-3) .... 0 0 10 14—**24**
MVP: Washington QB Mark Rypien (18 for 33, 292 yds, 2 TD, 1 Int)

FOUR-TIME WINNERS

Through the 1991 season, the Pittsburgh Steelers and San Francisco 49ers are the only two NFL teams with four Super Bowl victories.

Pittsburgh

The Steelers won four Super Bowls in as many appearances and finished on top of the AFC's Central Division seven times in the 1970's. In that decade, the Steelers posted an overall record (regular season and playoffs) of 113-48-1 for a winning percentage of .701.

(*) indicates AFC Central Division title.

Year	Regular Season	Playoffs	Comment
1970	5-9	None	7th losing year in row
1971	6-8	None	8th losing year in row
1972	11-3*	1-1	Lost AFC title game
1973	10-4	0-1	Lost AFC 1st round
1974	10-3-1*	3-0	**Won Super Bowl IX**
1975	12-2*	3-0	**Won Super Bowl X**
1976	10-4*	1-1	Lost AFC title game
1977	9-5*	0-1	Lost AFC 1st round
1978	14-2*	3-0	**Won Super Bowl XIII**
1979	12-4*	3-0	**Won Super Bowl XIV**
Total	99-44-1	14-4	4 Super Bowl wins

Twenty players played on all four Steeler Super Bowl winners: Rocky Bleier, RB; Mel Blount, CB; Terry Bradshaw, QB; Larry Brown, TE-T; Sam Davis, G; Steve Furness, DT-DE; Joe Greene, DT; L.C.Greenwood, DE; Randy Grossman, TE; Jack Ham, LB; Franco Harris, RB; Jon Kolb, T; Jack Lambert, LB; Gerry Mullins, G; Donnie Shell, S-CB; John Stallworth, WR; Lynn Swann, WR; Loren Toews, LB; Mike Webster, C; Dwight White, DE.

San Francisco

The 49ers won four Super Bowls in as many appearances and finished on top of the NFC's Western Division seven times in the 1980's. In that decade, the Niners posted an overall record (regular season and playoffs) of 117-51-1 for a winning percentage of .695.

(*) indicates NFC Western Division title.

Year	Regular Season	Playoffs	Comment
1980	6-10	None	4th losing year in row
1981	13-3*	3-0	**Won Super Bowl XVI**
1982	3-6	None	Strike season
1983	10-6*	1-1	Lost NFC title game
1984	15-1*	3-0	**Won Super Bowl XIX**
1985	10-6	0-1	Lost NFC wildcard game
1986	10-5-1*	0-1	Lost NFC 2nd round
1987	13-2*	0-1	Lost NFC 2nd round
1988	10-6*	3-0	**Won Super Bowl XXIII**
1989	14-2*	3-0	**Won Super Bowl XXIV**
Total	104-47-1	13-4	4 Super Bowl wins

Five players played on all four 49er Super Bowl winners: Ronnie Lott, CB-S; Joe Montana, QB; Keena Turner, LB; Mike Wilson, WR; Eric Wright, CB.

Before the Super Bowl

Time did not begin with the Super Bowl, it only seems that way. The first NFL champion was the Akron Pros in 1920, when the league was called the American Professional Football Association (APFA) and the title went to the team with the best regular season record.

The first playoff game with the championship at stake came in 1932, when the Chicago Bears beat the Portsmouth, Ohio, Spartans, 9-0. Due to a snowstorm and bitter cold weather, the game was moved from Wrigley Field to an improvised 80-yard dirt field at Chicago Stadium, making it the first indoor title game as well.

The NFL Championship Game decided the league title until the NFL merged with the AFL and the first Super Bowl was played following the 1966 season.

NFL Champions, 1920-32

Multiple winners: Green Bay (3); Canton (2).

Year	Champion	Head Coach
1920	Akron Pros	Fritz Pollard, HB & Elgie Tobin, QB
1921	Chicago Staleys (Renamed Bears in 1922)	George Halas, E
1922	Canton Bulldogs	Guy Chamberlin, E
1923	Canton Bulldogs	Guy Chamberlin, E
1924	Cleveland Bulldogs	Guy Chamberlin, E
1925	Chicago Cardinals	Norm Barry
1926	Frankford Yellow Jackets	Guy Chamberlin, E
1927	New York Giants	Earl Potteiger, QB
1928	Providence Steam Roller	Jimmy Conzelman, HB
1929	Green Bay Packers	Curly Lambeau, QB
1930	Green Bay Packers	Curly Lambeau
1931	Green Bay Packers	Curly Lambeau
1932	Chicago Bears (beat Portsmouth-OH in playoff, 9-0)	Ralph Jones

NFL-NFC Championship Game

NFL Championship games from 1933-69 and NFC Championship games since the completion of the NFL-AFL merger following the 1969 season.

Multiple winners: Green Bay (8); Chicago Bears and Washington (7); Dallas and NY Giants (5); Cleveland Browns, Detroit, Minnesota, Philadelphia and San Francisco (4); Baltimore and Los Angeles Rams (2).

Season	Winner	Head Coach	Score	Loser	Head Coach	Site
1933	Chicago Bears	George Halas	23-21	New York	Steve Owen	Chicago
1934	New York	Steve Owen	30-13	Chicago Bears	George Halas	New York
1935	Detroit	Potsy Clark	26- 7	New York	Steve Owen	Detroit
1936	Green Bay	Curly Lambeau	21- 6	Boston Redskins	Ray Flaherty	New York
1937	Washington Redskins	Ray Flaherty	28-21	Chicago Bears	George Halas	Chicago
1938	New York	Steve Owen	23-17	Green Bay	Curly Lambeau	New York
1939	Green Bay	Curly Lambeau	27- 0	New York	Steve Owen	Milwaukee
1940	Chicago Bears	George Halas	73- 0	Washington	Ray Flaherty	Washington
1941	Chicago Bears	George Halas	37- 9	New York	Steve Owen	Chicago
1942	Washington	Ray Flaherty	14- 6	Chicago Bears	Hunk Anderson & Luke Johnsos	Washington
1943	Chicago Bears	Hunk Anderson & Luke Johnsos	41-21	Washington	Arthur Bergman	Chicago
1944	Green Bay	Curly Lambeau	14- 7	New York	Steve Owen	New York
1945	Cleveland Rams	Adam Walsh	15-14	Washington	Dudley DeGroot	Cleveland
1946	Chicago Bears	George Halas	24-14	New York	Steve Owen	New York
1947	Chicago Cards	Jimmy Conzelman	28-21	Philadelphia	Greasy Neale	Chicago
1948	Philadelphia	Greasy Neale	7- 0	Chicago Cards	Jimmy Conzelman	Philadelphia
1949	Philadelphia	Greasy Neale	14- 0	LA Rams	Clark Shaughnessy	Los Angeles
1950	Cleveland Browns	Paul Brown	30-28	Los Angeles	Joe Stydahar	Cleveland
1951	Los Angeles	Joe Stydahar	24-17	Cleveland	Paul Brown	Los Angeles
1952	Detroit	Buddy Parker	17- 7	Cleveland	Paul Brown	Cleveland
1953	Detroit	Buddy Parker	17-16	Cleveland	Paul Brown	Detroit
1954	Cleveland	Paul Brown	56-10	Detroit	Buddy Parker	Cleveland
1955	Cleveland	Paul Brown	38-14	Los Angeles	Sid Gillman	Los Angeles
1956	New York	Jim Lee Howell	47- 7	Chicago Bears	Paddy Driscoll	New York
1957	Detroit	George Wilson	59-14	Cleveland	Paul Brown	Detroit
1958	Baltimore	Weeb Ewbank	23-17*	New York	Jim Lee Howell	New York
1959	Baltimore	Weeb Ewbank	31-16	New York	Jim Lee Howell	Baltimore
1960	Philadelphia	Buck Shaw	17-13	Green Bay	Vince Lombardi	Philadelphia
1961	Green Bay	Vince Lombardi	37- 0	New York	Allie Sherman	Green Bay
1962	Green Bay	Vince Lombardi	16- 7	New York	Allie Sherman	New York
1963	Chicago	George Halas	14-10	New York	Allie Sherman	Chicago
1964	Cleveland	Blanton Collier	27- 0	Baltimore	Don Shula	Cleveland
1965	Green Bay	Vince Lombardi	23-12	Cleveland	Blanton Collier	Green Bay
1966	Green Bay	Vince Lombardi	34-27	Dallas	Tom Landry	Dallas
1967	Green Bay	Vince Lombardi	21-17	Dallas	Tom Landry	Green Bay
1968	Baltimore	Don Shula	34- 0	Cleveland	Blanton Collier	Cleveland
1969	Minnesota	Bud Grant	27- 7	Cleveland	Blanton Collier	Minnesota
1970	Dallas	Tom Landry	17-10	San Francisco	Dick Nolan	San Francisco
1971	Dallas	Tom Landry	14- 3	San Francisco	Dick Nolan	Dallas
1972	Washington	George Allen	26- 3	Dallas	Tom Landry	Washington

NFL-NFC Championship Game (Cont.)

Season	Winner	Head Coach	Score	Loser	Head Coach	Site
1973	Minnesota	Bud Grant	27-10	Dallas	Tom Landry	Dallas
1974	Minnesota	Bud Grant	14-10	Los Angeles	Chuck Knox	Minnesota
1975	Dallas	Tom Landry	37- 7	Los Angeles	Chuck Knox	Los Angeles
1976	Minnesota	Bud Grant	24-13	Los Angeles	Chuck Knox	Minnesota
1977	Dallas	Tom Landry	23- 6	Minnesota	Bud Grant	Dallas
1978	Dallas	Tom Landry	28- 0	Los Angeles	Ray Malavasi	Los Angeles
1979	Los Angeles	Ray Malavasi	9- 0	Tampa Bay	John McKay	Tampa Bay
1980	Philadelphia	Dick Vermeil	20- 7	Dallas	Tom Landry	Philadelphia
1981	San Francisco	Bill Walsh	28-27	Dallas	Tom Landry	San Francisco
1982	Washington	Joe Gibbs	31-17	Dallas	Tom Landry	Washington
1983	Washington	Joe Gibbs	24-21	San Francisco	Bill Walsh	Washington
1984	San Francisco	Bill Walsh	23- 0	Chicago	Mike Ditka	San Francisco
1985	Chicago	Mike Ditka	24- 0	Los Angeles	John Robinson	Chicago
1986	New York	Bill Parcells	17- 0	Washington	Joe Gibbs	New York
1987	Washington	Joe Gibbs	17-10	Minnesota	Jerry Burns	Washington
1988	San Francisco	Bill Walsh	28- 3	Chicago	Mike Ditka	Chicago
1989	San Francisco	George Seifert	30- 3	Los Angeles	John Robinson	San Francisco
1990	New York	Bill Parcells	15-13	San Francisco	George Seifert	San Francisco
1991	Washington	Joe Gibbs	41-10	Detroit	Wayne Fontes	Washington

*Sudden death overtime

NFL-NFC Championship Game Appearances

App		W	L	Pct	PF	PA	App		W	L	Pct	PF	PA
16	NY Giants	5	11	.313	240	322	8	San Francisco	4	4	.500	156	103
13	Chicago Bears	7	6	.538	286	245	6	Minnesota	4	2	.667	108	80
12	Boston-Wash.Redskins	7	5	.583	222	255	6	Detroit	4	2	.667	139	141
12	Dallas Cowboys	5	7	.417	227	213	5	Philadelphia	4	1	.800	79	48
12	Cleveland-LA Rams	3	9	.250	123	270	4	Baltimore Colts	3	1	.750	88	60
11	Cleveland Browns	4	7	.364	224	253	2	Chicago Cardinals	1	1	.500	28	28
10	Green Bay	8	2	.800	223	116	1	Tampa Bay	0	1	.000	0	9

AFL-AFC Championship Game

AFL Championship games from 1960-69 and AFC Championship games since the completion of the NFL-AFL merger following the 1969 season.

Multiple winners: Miami (5); Buffalo, Denver, Oakland-LA Raiders and Pittsburgh (4); Dallas Texans-KC Chiefs (3); Cincinnati and Houston (2).

Season	Winner	Head Coach	Score	Loser	Head Coach	Site
1960	Houston	Lou Rymkus	24-16	LA Chargers	Sid Gillman	Houston
1961	Houston	Wally Lemm	10- 3	SD Chargers	Sid Gillman	San Diego
1962	Dallas	Hank Stram	20-17*	Houston	Pop Ivy	Houston
1963	San Diego	Sid Gillman	51-10	Boston Patriots	Mike Holovak	San Diego
1964	Buffalo	Lou Saban	20- 7	San Diego	Sid Gillman	Buffalo
1965	Buffalo	Lou Saban	23- 0	San Diego	Sid Gillman	San Diego
1966	Kansas City	Hank Stram	31- 7	Buffalo	Joel Collier	Buffalo
1967	Oakland	John Rauch	40- 7	Houston	Wally Lemm	Oakland
1968	NY Jets	Webb Ewbank	27-23	Oakland	John Rauch	New York
1969	Kansas City	Hank Stram	17- 7	Oakland	John Madden	Oakland
1970	Baltimore	Don McCafferty	27-17	Oakland	John Madden	Baltimore
1971	Miami	Don Shula	21- 0	Baltimore	Don McCafferty	Miami
1972	Miami	Don Shula	21-17	Pittsburgh	Chuck Noll	Pittsburgh
1973	Miami	Don Shula	27-10	Oakland	John Madden	Miami
1974	Pittsburgh	Chuck Noll	24-13	Oakland	John Madden	Oakland
1975	Pittsburgh	Chuck Noll	16-10	Oakland	John Madden	Pittsburgh
1976	Oakland	John Madden	24- 7	Pittsburgh	Chuck Noll	Oakland
1977	Denver	Red Miller	20-17	Oakland	John Madden	Denver
1978	Pittsburgh	Chuck Noll	34- 5	Houston	Bum Phillips	Pittsburgh
1979	Pittsburgh	Chuck Noll	27-13	Houston	Bum Phillips	Pittsburgh
1980	Oakland	Tom Flores	34-27	San Diego	Don Coryell	San Diego
1981	Cincinnati	Forrest Gregg	27- 7	San Diego	Don Coryell	Cincinnati
1982	Miami	Don Shula	14- 0	NY Jets	Walt Michaels	Miami
1983	LA Raiders	Tom Flores	30-14	Seattle	Chuck Knox	Los Angeles
1984	Miami	Don Shula	45-28	Pittsburgh	Chuck Noll	Miami
1985	NE Patriots	Raymond Berry	31-14	Miami	Don Shula	Miami
1986	Denver	Dan Reeves	23-20*	Cleveland	Marty Schottenheimer	Cleveland

*Sudden death overtime

Season	Winner	Head Coach	Score	Loser	Head Coach	Site
1987	Denver	Dan Reeves	38-33	Cleveland	Marty Schottenheimer	Denver
1988	Cincinnati	Sam Wyche	21-10	Buffalo	Marv Levy	Cincinnati
1989	Denver	Dan Reeves	37-21	Cleveland	Bud Carson	Denver
1990	Buffalo	Marv Levy	51- 3	LA Raiders	Art Shell	Buffalo
1991	Buffalo	Marv Levy	10- 7	Denver	Dan Reeves	Buffalo

AFL-AFC Championship Game Appearances

App		W	L	Pct	PF	PA	App		W	L	Pct	PF	PA
12	Oakland-LA Raiders	4	8	.333	228	264	3	Dallas Texans/ KC Chiefs	3	0	1.000	68	31
7	Pittsburgh	4	3	.571	153	131	3	Cleveland	0	3	.000	74	98
7	LA-San Diego Chargers	1	6	.143	111	148	2	Cincinnati	2	0	1.000	48	17
6	Miami	5	1	.833	142	86	2	Baltimore Colts	1	1	.500	27	38
6	Buffalo	4	2	.667	121	69	2	Boston-NE Patriots	1	1	.500	41	65
6	Houston	2	4	.333	76	140	2	NY Jets	1	1	.500	27	37
5	Denver	4	1	.800	125	101	1	Seattle	0	1	.000	14	30

NFL Playoff Bowl

The NFL staged a postseason exhibition game between its Eastern and Western Conference runners-up from the 1960 season through 1969. Called the Bert Bell Benefit Bowl (Bell was league commissioner from 1946 until his death in 1959) and referred to as the Playoff Bowl, it gave the winner little more than bragging rights to third place in the NFL. All 10 Playoff Bowls were played in Miami and game statistics do not count in career player and coaching records. Western Division teams won eight of the 10 games, losing only to St.Louis in 1965 and Dallas in 1969.
   Multiple winners: Detroit (3); Baltimore (2); LA Rams (2).

Season	Winner	Head Coach	Score	Loser	Head Coach	Site
1960	Detroit	George Wilson	17-16	Cleveland	Paul Brown	Miami
1961	Detroit	George Wilson	38-10	Philadelphia	Nick Skorich	Miami
1962	Detroit	George Wilson	17-10	Pittsburgh	Buddy Parker	Miami
1963	Green Bay	Vince Lombardi	40-23	Cleveland	Blanton Collier	Miami
1964	St.Louis	Wally Lemm	24-17	Green Bay	Vince Lombardi	Miami
1965	Baltimore	Don Shula	35- 3	Dallas	Tom Landry	Miami
1966	Baltimore	Don Shula	20-14	Philadelphia	Joe Kuharich	Miami
1967	LA Rams	George Allen	30- 6	Cleveland	Blanton Collier	Miami
1968	Dallas	Tom Landry	17-13	Minnesota	Bud Grant	Miami
1969	LA Rams	George Allen	31- 0	Dallas	Tom Landry	Miami

Champions Of Leagues That No Longer Exist

No professional league in American sports has had to contend with more pretenders to the throne than the NFL. Seven times in as many decades a rival league has risen up to challenge the NFL and six of them went under in less than five seasons. Only the fourth American Football League (1960-69) succeeded, forcing the older league to sue for peace and a full partnership in 1966.
   Of the six leagues that didn't make it, only the All-America Football Conference (1946-49) lives on—the Cleveland Browns and San Francisco 49ers joined the NFL after the AAFC folded in 1949.
   The champions of leagues past are listed below.

American Football League I

Year		Head Coach
1926	Philadelphia Quakers	Bob Folwell

American Football League II

Year		Head Coach
1936	Boston Shamrocks	George Kennealy
1937	Los Angeles Bulldogs	Gus Henderson

American Football League III

Year		Head Coach
1940	Columbus Bullies	Phil Bucklew
1941	Columbus Bullies	Phil Bucklew

All-America Football Conference

Year	Championship Game	Head Coach
1946	At Cleve.Browns 14, NY Yankees 9	Paul Brown
1947	Cleve.Browns 14, at NY Yankees 3	Paul Brown
1948	At Cleve.Browns 49, Buffalo 7	Paul Brown
1949	At Cleve.Browns 21, S.F.49ers 7	Paul Brown

World Football League

Year	World Bowl	Head Coach
1974	At Birmingham 22, Florida 21	Jack Gotta
1975	Folded mid-season	

United States Football League

Year	Championship Game	Head Coach
1983	Michigan 24, Philadelphia Stars 22	Jim Stanley
1984	Philadelphia Stars 23, Arizona 3	Jim Mora
1985	Baltimore Stars 28, Oakland 24	Jim Mora

USFL Championship Game sites: Denver (1983), Tampa (1984), East Rutherford, N.J. (1985).

NFL Franchise Origins

Here is what the current 28 teams in the National Football League have to show for the years they have put in as members of the American Professional Football Association (APFA), the NFL, the All-America Football Conference (AAFC) and the American Football League (AFL).

American Football Conference

	First Season		League Titles	Franchise Stops
Buffalo Bills	1960	(AFL)	2 AFL (1964-65)	Buffalo (1960-72) Orchard Park, NY (1973—)
Cincinnati Bengals	1968	(AFL)	None	Cincinnati (1968—)
Cleveland Browns	1946	(AAFC)	4 AAFC (1946-49) 4 NFL (1950,54-55,64)	Cleveland (1946—)
Denver Broncos	1960	(AFL)	None	Denver (1960—)
Houston Oilers	1960	(AFL)	2 AFL (1960-61)	Houston (1960—)
Indianapolis Colts	1953	(NFL)	3 NFL (1958-59,68) 1 Super Bowl (1970)	Baltimore (1953-83) Indianapolis (1984—)
Kansas City Chiefs	1960	(AFL)	3 AFL (1962,66,69) 1 Super Bowl (1969)	Dallas (1960-62) Kansas City (1963—)
Los Angeles Raiders	1960	(AFL)	1 AFL (1967) 3 Super Bowls (1976,80,83)	Oakland (1960-81) Los Angeles (1982—)
Miami Dolphins	1966	(AFL)	2 Super Bowls (1972-73)	Miami (1966—)
New England Patriots	1960	(AFL)	None	Boston (1960-70) Foxboro, MA (1971—)
New York Jets	1960	(AFL)	1 AFL (1968) 1 Super Bowl (1968)	New York (1960-83) E.Rutherford, NJ (1984—)
Pittsburgh Steelers	1933	(NFL)	4 Super Bowls (1974-75,78-79)	Pittsburgh (1933—)
San Diego Chargers	1960	(AFL)	1 AFL (1963)	Los Angeles (1960) San Diego (1961—)
Seattle Seahawks	1976	(NFL)	None	Seattle (1976—)

National Football Conference

	First Season		League Titles	Franchise Stops
Atlanta Falcons	1966	(NFL)	None	Atlanta (1966—)
Chicago Bears	1920	(APFA)	7 NFL (1932-33,40-41,43,46,63) 1 Super Bowl (1985)	Decatur,IL (1920) Chicago (1921—)
Dallas Cowboys	1960	(NFL)	2 Super Bowls (1971,77)	Dallas (1960-70) Irving,TX (1971—)
Detroit Lions	1930	(NFL)	4 NFL (1935,52-53,57)	Portsmouth,OH (1930-33) Detroit (1934-74) Pontiac,MI (1975—)
Green Bay Packers	1921	(APFA)	8 NFL (1936,39,44,61-62,65-67) 2 Super Bowls (1966-67)	Green Bay (1921—)
Los Angeles Rams	1937	(NFL)	2 NFL (1945,51)	Cleveland (1937-45) Los Angeles (1946-79) Anaheim (1980—)
Minnesota Vikings	1961	(NFL)	1 NFL (1969)	Bloomington, MN (1961-81) Minneapolis,MN (1982—)
New Orleans Saints	1967	(NFL)	None	New Orleans (1967—)
New York Giants	1925	(NFL)	3 NFL (1934,38,56) 2 Super Bowls (1986,90)	New York (1925-73,75) New Haven,CT (1973-74) E.Rutherford,NJ (1976—)
Philadelphia Eagles	1933	(NFL)	3 NFL (1948-49,60)	Philadelphia (1933—)
Phoenix Cardinals	1920	(APFA)	1 NFL (1947)	Chicago (1920-59) St.Louis (1960-87) Phoenix (1988—)
San Francisco 49ers	1946	(AAFC)	4 Super Bowls (1981,84,88-89)	San Francisco (1946—)
Tampa Bay Buccaneers	1976	(NFL)	None	Tampa,FL (1976—)
Washington Redskins	1932	(NFL)	2 NFL (1937,42) 3 Super Bowls (1982,87,91)	Boston (1932-36) Washington,DC (1937—)

The Growth of the NFL

Of the 14 franchises that comprised the American Professional Football Association in 1920, only two remain—the Chicago Bears (originally the Decatur-IL Staleys) and the Phoenix Cardinals (then the Chicago Cardinals). Green Bay joined the APFC in 1921 and the league changed its name to the NFL in 1922. Since then, 52 NFL clubs have come and gone, five rival leagues have expired and two other leagues have been swallowed up.

The NFL merged with the **All-American Football Conference** (1946-49) following the 1949 season and adopted three of its seven clubs—the Baltimore Colts, Cleveland Browns and San Francisco 49ers. The four remaining AAFC teams—the Brooklyn/NY Yankees, Buffalo Bills, Chicago Hornets and Los Angeles Dons—did not survive.

After the 1950 season, the financially troubled Colts were sold back to the NFL. The league folded the team and added its players to the 1951 college draft pool. A new Baltimore franchise, also named the Colts, joined the NFL in 1953.

The formation of the **American Football League** (1960-69) was announced in 1959 with ownership lined up in eight cities—Boston, Buffalo, Dallas, Denver, Houston, Los Angeles, Minneapolis and New York.

Set to begin play in the autumn of 1960, the AFL was stunned early that year when Minneapolis withdrew to accept an offer to join the NFL as an expansion team in 1961. The new league responded by choosing Oakland to replace Minneapolis and inherit the departed team's draft picks. Since no AFL team actually played in Minneapolis, it is not considered the original home of the Oakland (now Los Angeles) Raiders.

In 1966, the NFL and AFL agreed to a merger that resulted in the first Super Bowl (originally called the AFL-NFL World Championship Game) following the 1966 season. In 1970, the now 10-member AFL officially joined the NFL, forming a 26-team league made up of two conferences of three divisions each.

Expansion/Merger Timetable
For teams currently in NFL.

1921—Green Bay Packers; **1925**—New York Giants ; **1930**—Portsmouth-OH Spartans (now Detroit Lions); **1932**—Boston Braves (now Washington Redskins); **1933**—Philadelphia Eagles and Pittsburgh Pirates (now Steelers); **1937**—Cleveland Rams (now Los Angeles); **1950**—added AAFC's Cleveland Browns and San Francisco 49ers; **1953**—Baltimore Colts (now Indianapolis).

1960—Dallas Cowboys; **1961**—Minnesota Vikings; **1966**—Atlanta Falcons; **1967**—New Orleans Saints; **1970**—added AFL's Boston Patriots (now New England), Buffalo Bills, Cincinnati Bengals (1968 expansion team), Denver Broncos, Houston Oilers, Kansas City Chiefs, Miami Dolphins (1966 expansion team), New York Jets, Oakland Raiders (now Los Angeles) and San Diego Chargers (the AFL-NFL merger divided the league into two 13-team conferences with old-line NFL clubs Baltimore, Cleveland and Pittsburgh moving to the AFC); **1976**—Seattle Seahawks and Tampa Bay Buccaneers (Seattle was originally in the NFC West and Tampa Bay in the AFC West, but were switched to their current divisions in 1977).

City and Nickname Changes

1921—Decatur Staleys move to Chicago; **1922**—Chicago Staleys renamed Bears; **1933**—Boston Braves renamed Redskins; **1934**—Boston Redskins move to Washington; **1937**—Portsmouth (Ohio) Spartans move to Detroit and become Lions; **1941**—Pittsburgh Pirates renamed Steelers; **1943**—Philadelphia and Pittsburgh merge for one season and become Phil-Pitt, or the "Steagles"; **1944**—Chicago Cardinals and Pittsburgh merge for one season and become Card-Pitt; **1946**—Cleveland Rams move to Los Angeles.

1960—Chicago Cardinals move to St.Louis; **1961**—Los Angeles Chargers (AFL) move to San Diego; **1963**—New York Titans (AFL) renamed Jets and Dallas Texans (AFL) move to Kansas City and become Chiefs; **1971**—Boston Patriots become New England Patriots; **1982**—Oakland Raiders move to Los Angeles; **1984**—Baltimore Colts move to Indianapolis; **1988**—St.Louis Cardinals move to Phoenix.

Defunct NFL Teams
Teams that once played in the APFA and NFL, but no longer exist.

Akron-OH—Pros (1920-25) and Indians (1926); **Baltimore**—Colts (1950); **Boston**—Bulldogs (1926) and Yanks (1944-48); **Brooklyn**—Lions (1926), Dodgers (1930-43) and Tigers (1944); **Buffalo**—All-Americans (1921-23), Bisons (1924-25), Rangers (1926), Bisons (1927,1929); **Canton-OH**—Bulldogs (1920-23,1925-26); **Chicago**—Tigers (1920); **Cincinnati**—Celts (1921) and Reds (1933-34); **Cleveland**—Tigers (1920), Indians (1921), Indians (1923), Bulldogs (1924-25,1927) and Indians (1931); **Columbus-OH**—Panhandles (1920-22) and Tigers (1923-26); **Dallas**—Texans (1952); **Dayton-OH**—Triangles (1920-29).

Detroit—Heralds (1920-21), Panthers (1925-26) and Wolverines (1928); **Duluth-MN**—Kelleys (1923-25) and Eskimos (1926-27); **Evansville-IN**—Crimson Giants (1921-22); **Frankford-PA**—Yellow Jackets (1924-31); **Hammond-IN**—Pros (1920-26); **Hartford**—Blues (1926); **Kansas City**—Blues (1924) and Cowboys (1925-26); **Kenosha-WI**—Maroons (1924); **Los Angeles**—Buccaneers (1926); **Louisville**—Brecks (1921-23) and Colonels (1926); **Marion-OH**—Oorang Indians (1922-23); **Milwaukee**—Badgers (1922-26); **Minneapolis**—Marines (1922-24) and Red Jackets (1929-30); **Muncie-IN**—Flyers (1920-21).

New York—Giants (1921), Yankees (1927-28), Bulldogs (1949) and Yankees (1950-51); **Newark-NJ**—Tornadoes (1930); **Orange-NJ**—Tornadoes (1929); **Pottsville-PA**—Maroons (1925-28); **Providence-RI**—Steam Roller (1925-31); **Racine-WI**—Legion (1922-24) and Tornadoes (1926); **Rochester-NY**—Jeffersons (1920-25); **Rock Island-IL**—Independents (1920-26); **Staten Island-NY**—Stapletons (1929-32); **St.Louis**—All-Stars (1923) and Gunners (1934); **Toledo-OH**—Maroons (1922-23); **Tonawanda-NY**—Kardex (1921), also called Lumbermen; **Washington**—Senators (1921).

Annual NFL Leaders

Individual leaders in NFL (1932-69), NFC (since 1970), AFL (1960-69) and AFC (since 1970).

Passing

NFL-NFC

Since 1932, the NFL has used several formulas to determine passing leadership, from Total Yards alone (1932-37), to the current rating system—adopted in 1973—that takes Completions, Completion Pct., Yards Gained, TD Passes, Interceptions, Interception Pct. and other factors into account. The quarterbacks listed below all led the league according to the system in use at the time.

Multiple winners: Sammy Baugh (6); Joe Montana and Roger Staubach (5); Arnie Herber, Sonny Jurgensen, Bart Starr and Norm Van Brocklin (3); Otto Graham, Cecil Isbell, Milt Plum and Bob Waterfield (2).

Year		Att	Cmp	Yds	TD	Year		Att	Cmp	Yds	TD
1932	Arnie Herber, GB	101	37	639	9	1962	Bart Starr, GB	285	178	2438	12
1933	Harry Newman, NY	136	53	973	11	1963	Y.A.Tittle, NY	367	221	3145	36
1934	Arnie Herber, GB	115	42	799	8	1964	Bart Starr, GB	272	163	2144	15
1935	Ed Danowski, NY	113	57	794	10	1965	Rudy Bukich, Chi	312	176	2641	20
1936	Arnie Herber, GB	173	77	1239	11	1966	Bart Starr, GB	251	156	2257	14
1937	Sammy Baugh, Wash	171	81	1127	8	1967	Sonny Jurgensen, Wash	508	288	3747	31
1938	Ed Danowski, NY	129	70	848	7	1968	Earl Morrall, Bal	317	182	2909	26
1939	Parker Hall, Cle.Rams	208	106	1227	9	1969	Sonny Jurgensen, Wash	442	274	3102	22
1940	Sammy Baugh, Wash	177	111	1367	12	1970	John Brodie, SF	378	223	2941	24
1941	Cecil Isbell, GB	206	117	1479	15	1971	Roger Staubach, Dal	211	126	1882	15
1942	Cecil Isbell, GB	268	146	2021	24	1972	Norm Snead, NY	325	196	2307	17
1943	Sammy Baugh, Wash	239	133	1754	23	1973	Roger Staubach, Dal	286	179	2428	23
1944	Frank Filchock, Wash	147	84	1139	13	1974	Sonny Jurgensen, Wash	167	107	1185	11
1945	Sammy Baugh, Wash	182	128	1669	11	1975	Fran Tarkenton, Min	425	273	2994	25
	& Sid Luckman, Chi. Bears	217	117	1725	14	1976	James Harris, LA	158	91	1460	8
1946	Bob Waterfield, LA	251	127	1747	18	1977	Roger Staubach, Dal	361	210	2620	18
1947	Sammy Baugh, Wash	354	210	2938	25	1978	Roger Staubach, Dal	413	231	3190	25
1948	Tommy Thompson, Phi	246	141	1965	25	1979	Roger Staubach, Dal	461	267	3586	27
1949	Sammy Baugh, Wash	255	145	1903	18	1980	Ron Jaworski, Phi	451	257	3529	27
1950	Norm Van Brocklin, LA	233	127	2061	18	1981	Joe Montana, SF	488	311	3565	19
1951	Bob Waterfield, LA	176	88	1566	13	1982	Joe Theismann, Wash	252	161	2033	13
1952	Norm Van Brocklin, LA	205	113	1736	14	1983	Steve Bartkowski, Atl	432	274	3167	22
1953	Otto Graham, Cle	258	167	2722	11	1984	Joe Montana, SF	432	279	3630	28
1954	Norm Van Brocklin, LA	260	139	2637	13	1985	Joe Montana, SF	494	303	3653	27
1955	Otto Graham, Cle	185	98	1721	15	1986	Tommy Kramer, Min	372	208	3000	24
1956	Ed Brown, Chi. Bears	168	96	1667	11	1987	Joe Montana, SF	398	266	3054	31
1957	Tommy O'Connell, Cle	110	63	1229	9	1988	Wade Wilson, Min	332	204	2746	15
1958	Eddie LeBaron, Wash	145	79	1365	11	1989	Don Majkowski, GB	599	353	4318	27
1959	Charlie Conerly, NY	194	113	1706	14	1990	Joe Montana, SF	520	321	3944	26
1960	Milt Plum, Cle	250	151	2297	21	1991	Steve Young, SF	279	180	2517	17
1961	Milt Plum, Cle	302	177	2416	16						

Note: In 1945, Baugh and Luckman tied with 8 points on an inverse rating system.

AFL-AFC

Multiple winners: Ken Anderson, Len Dawson, Dan Marino (4); Bob Griese, Daryle Lamonica and Ken Stabler (2).

Year		Att	Cmp	Yds	TD	Year		Att	Cmp	Yds	TD
1960	Jack Kemp, LA	406	211	3018	20	1977	Bob Griese, Mia	307	180	2252	22
1961	George Blanda, Hou	362	187	3330	36	1978	Terry Bradshaw, Pit	368	207	2915	28
1962	Len Dawson, Dal	310	189	2759	29	1979	Dan Fouts, SD	530	332	4082	24
1963	Tobin Rote, SD	286	170	2510	20	1980	Brian Sipe, Cle	554	337	4132	30
1964	Len Dawson, KC	354	199	2879	30	1981	Ken Anderson, Cin	479	300	3753	29
1965	John Hadl, SD	348	174	2798	20	1982	Ken Anderson, Cin	309	218	2495	12
1966	Len Dawson, KC	284	159	2527	26	1983	Dan Marino, Mia	296	173	2210	20
1967	Daryle Lamonica, Oak	425	220	3228	30	1984	Dan Marino, Mia	564	362	5084	48
1968	Len Dawson, KC	224	131	2109	17	1985	Ken O'Brien, NY	488	297	3888	25
1969	Greg Cook, Cin	197	106	1854	15	1986	Dan Marino, Mia	623	378	4746	44
1970	Daryle Lamonica, Oak	356	179	2516	22	1987	Bernie Kosar, Cle	389	241	3033	22
1971	Bob Griese, Mia	263	145	2089	19	1988	Boomer Esiason, Cin	388	223	3572	28
1972	Earl Morrall, Mia	150	83	1360	11	1989	Dan Marino, Mia	550	308	3997	24
1973	Ken Stabler, Oak	260	163	1997	14	1990	Warren Moon, Hou	584	362	4689	33
1974	Ken Anderson, Cin	328	213	2667	18	1991	Jim Kelly, Buf	474	304	3844	33
1975	Ken Anderson, Cin	377	228	3169	21						
1976	Ken Stabler, Oak	291	194	2737	27						

Receiving
NFL-NFC

Multiple winners: Don Hutson (8); Raymond Berry, Tom Fears, Pete Pihos and Billy Wilson (3); Dwight Clark, Ahmad Rashad, Jerry Rice and Charley Taylor (2).

Year		No	Yds	Avg	TD	Year		No	Yds	Avg	TD
1932	Ray Flaherty, NY	21	350	16.7	3	1962	Bobby Mitchell, Wash	72	1384	19.2	11
1933	Shipwreck Kelly, Bklyn.	22	246	11.2	3	1963	Bobby Joe Conrad, St.L	73	967	13.2	10
1934	Joe Carter, Phi	16	238	14.9	4	1964	Johnny Morris, Chi. Bears	93	1200	12.9	10
	& Red Badgro, NY	16	206	12.9	1	1965	Dave Parks, SF	80	1344	16.8	12
1935	Tod Goodwin, NY	26	432	16.6	4	1966	Charley Taylor, Wash	72	1119	15.5	12
1936	Don Hutson, GB	34	536	15.8	8	1967	Charley Taylor, Wash	70	990	14.1	9
1937	Don Hutson, GB	41	552	13.5	7	1968	Clifton McNeil, SF	71	994	14.0	7
1938	Gaynell Tinsley, Chi. Cards	41	516	12.6	1	1969	Dan Abramowicz, NO	73	1015	13.9	7
1939	Don Hutson, GB	34	846	24.9	6						
1940	Don Looney, Phi	58	707	12.2	4	1970	Dick Gordon, Chi	71	1026	14.5	13
1941	Don Hutson, GB	58	739	12.7	10	1971	Bob Tucker, NY	59	791	13.4	4
1942	Don Hutson, GB	74	1211	16.4	17	1972	Harold Jackson, Phi	62	1048	16.9	4
1943	Don Hutson, GB	47	776	16.5	11	1973	Harold Carmichael, Phi	67	1116	16.7	9
1944	Don Hutson, GB	58	866	14.9	9	1974	Charle Young, Phi.	63	696	11.0	3
1945	Don Hutson, GB	47	834	17.7	9	1975	Chuck Foreman, Min	73	691	9.5	9
1946	Jim Benton, LA	63	981	15.6	6	1976	Drew Pearson, Dal	58	806	13.9	6
1947	Jim Keane, Chi. Bears	64	910	14.2	10	1977	Ahmad Rashad, Min	51	681	13.4	2
1948	Tom Fears, LA	51	698	13.7	4	1978	Rickey Young, Min.	88	704	8.0	5
1949	Tom Fears, LA	77	1013	13.2	9	1979	Ahmad Rashad, Min	80	1156	14.5	9
1950	Tom Fears, LA	84	1116	13.3	7	1980	Earl Cooper, SF	83	567	6.8	4
1951	Elroy Hirsch, LA	66	1495	22.7	17	1981	Dwight Clark, SF	85	1105	13.0	4
1952	Mac Speedie, Cle	62	911	14.7	5	1982	Dwight Clark, SF	60	913	12.2	5
1953	Pete Pihos, Phi	63	1049	16.7	10	1983	Roy Green, St.L	78	1227	15.7	14
1954	Pete Pihos, Phi	60	872	14.5	10		Charlie Brown, Wash	78	1225	15.7	8
	& Billy Wilson, SF	60	830	13.8	5		& Earnest Gray, NY	78	1139	14.6	5
1955	Pete Pihos, Phi	62	864	13.9	7	1984	Art Monk, Wash	106	1372	12.9	7
1956	Billy Wilson, SF	60	889	14.8	5	1985	Roger Craig, SF	92	1016	11.0	6
1957	Billy Wilson, SF	52	757	14.6	6	1986	Jerry Rice, SF	86	1570	18.3	15
1958	Raymond Berry, Bal.	56	794	14.2	9	1987	J.T.Smith, St.L	91	1117	12.3	8
	& Pete Retzlaff, Phi.	56	766	13.7	2	1988	Henry Ellard, LA	86	1414	16.4	10
1959	Raymond Berry, Bal.	66	959	14.5	14	1989	Sterling Sharpe, GB.	90	1423	15.8	12
1960	Raymond Berry, Bal.	74	1298	17.5	10	1990	Jerry Rice, SF	100	1502	15.0	13
1961	Red Phillips, LA	78	1092	14.0	5	1991	Michael Irvin, Dal	93	1523	16.4	8

AFL-AFC

Multiple winners: Lionel Taylor (5); Lance Alworth and Kellen Winslow (3); Fred Biletnikoff, Todd Christensen, Haywood Jeffires, Lydell Mitchell and Al Toon (2).

Year		No	Yds	Avg	TD	Year		No	Yds	Avg	TD
1960	Lionel Taylor, Den.	92	1235	13.4	12	1977	Lydell Mitchell, Bal.	71	620	8.7	4
1961	Lionel Taylor, Den.	100	1176	11.8	4	1978	Steve Largent, Sea.	71	1168	16.5	8
1962	Lionel Taylor, Den.	77	908	11.8	4	1979	Joe Washington, Bal.	82	750	9.1	3
1963	Lionel Taylor, Den.	78	1101	14.1	10	1980	Kellen Winslow, S.D	89	1290	14.5	9
1964	Charley Hennigan, Hou	101	1546	15.3	8	1981	Kellen Winslow, S.D	88	1075	12.2	10
1965	Lionel Taylor, Den.	85	1131	13.3	6	1982	Kellen Winslow, S.D	54	721	13.4	6
1966	Lance Alworth, SD.	73	1383	18.9	13	1983	Todd Christensen, LA	92	1247	13.6	12
1967	George Sauer, NY	75	1189	15.9	6	1984	Ozzie Newsome, Cle	89	1001	11.2	5
1968	Lance Alworth, SD.	68	1312	19.3	10	1985	Lionel James, SD.	86	1027	11.9	6
1969	Lance Alworth, SD.	64	1003	15.7	4	1986	Todd Christensen, LA	95	1153	12.1	8
1970	Marlin Briscoe, Buf	57	1036	18.2	8	1987	Al Toon, NY	68	976	14.4	5
1971	Fred Biletnikoff, Oak.	61	929	15.2	9	1988	Al Toon, NY	93	1067	11.5	5
1972	Fred Biletnikoff, Oak.	58	802	13.8	7	1989	Andre Reed, Buf	88	1312	14.9	9
1973	Fred Willis, Hou.	57	371	6.5	1	1990	Haywood Jeffires, Hou	74	1048	14.2	8
1974	Lydell Mitchell, Bal.	72	544	7.6	2	1991	Haywood Jeffires, Hou	100	1181	11.8	7
1975	Reggie Rucker, Cle	60	770	12.8	3						
1976	MacArthur Lane, KC	66	686	10.4	1						

Annual NFL Leaders (Cont.)

Rushing
NFL-NFC

Multiple winners: Jim Brown (8); Walter Payton (5); Steve Van Buren (4); Eric Dickerson (3); Cliff Battles, John Brockington, Larry Brown, Bill Dudley, Leroy Kelly, Bill Paschal, Joe Perry, Barry Sanders, Gale Sayers and Whizzer White (2).

Year		Att	Yds	Avg	Year		Att	Yds	Avg
1932	Cliff Battles, Bos	148	576	3.9	1962	Jim Taylor, GB	272	1474	5.4
1933	Jim Musick, Bos	173	809	4.7	1963	Jim Brown, Cle	291	1863	6.4
1934	Beattie Feathers, Chi. Bears	101	1004	9.9	1964	Jim Brown, Cle	280	1446	5.1
1935	Doug Russell, Chi. Cards	140	499	3.6	1965	Jim Brown, Cle	289	1544	5.3
1936	Tuffy Leemans, NY	206	830	4.0	1966	Gale Sayers, Chi	229	1231	5.4
1937	Cliff Battles, Wash	216	874	4.0	1967	Leroy Kelly, Cle	235	1205	5.1
1938	Byron (Whizzer) White, Pit	152	567	3.7	1968	Leroy Kelly, Cle	248	1239	5.0
1939	Bill Osmanski, Chi. Bears	121	699	5.9	1969	Gale Sayers, Chi	236	1032	4.4
1940	Byron (Whizzer) White, Det	146	514	3.5	1970	Larry Brown, Wash	237	1125	4.7
1941	Pug Manders, Bklyn	111	486	4.4	1971	John Brockington, GB	216	1105	5.1
1942	Bill Dudley, Pit	162	697	4.3	1972	Larry Brown, Wash	285	1216	4.3
1943	Bill Paschal, NY	147	572	3.9	1973	John Brockington, GB	265	1144	4.3
1944	Bill Paschal, NY	196	737	3.8	1974	Lawrence McCutcheon, LA	236	1109	4.7
1945	Steve Van Buren, Phi	143	832	5.8	1975	Jim Otis, St.L	269	1076	4.0
1946	Bill Dudley, Pit	146	604	4.1	1976	Walter Payton, Chi	311	1390	4.5
1947	Steve Van Buren, Phi	217	1008	4.6	1977	Walter Payton, Chi	339	1852	5.5
1948	Steve Van Buren, Phi	201	945	4.7	1978	Walter Payton, Chi	333	1395	4.2
1949	Steve Van Buren, Phi	263	1146	4.4	1979	Walter Payton, Chi	369	1610	4.4
1950	Marion Motley, Cle	140	810	5.8	1980	Walter Payton, Chi	317	1460	4.6
1951	Eddie Price, NY Giants	271	971	3.6	1981	George Rogers, NO	378	1674	4.4
1952	Dan Towler, LA	156	894	5.7	1982	Tony Dorsett, Dal	177	745	4.2
1953	Joe Perry, SF	192	1018	5.3	1983	Eric Dickerson, LA	390	1808	4.6
1954	Joe Perry, SF	173	1049	6.1	1984	Eric Dickerson, LA	379	2105	5.6
1955	Alan Ameche, Bal	213	961	4.5	1985	Gerald Riggs, Atl	397	1719	4.3
1956	Rick Casares, Chi. Bears	234	1126	4.8	1986	Eric Dickerson, LA	404	1821	4.5
1957	Jim Brown, Cle	202	942	4.7	1987	Charles White, LA	324	1374	4.2
1958	Jim Brown, Cle	257	1527	5.9	1988	Herschel Walker, Dal	361	1514	4.2
1959	Jim Brown, Cle	290	1329	4.6	1989	Barry Sanders, Det	280	1470	5.3
1960	Jim Brown, Cle	215	1257	5.8	1990	Barry Sanders, Det	255	1304	5.1
1961	Jim Brown, Cle	305	1408	4.6	1991	Emmitt Smith, Dal	365	1563	4.3

Note: Jim Brown led the NFL in rushing eight of his nine years in the league. The one season he didn't win (1962) he finished fourth (996 yds) behind Taylor, John Henry Johnson of Pittsburgh (1141 yds) and Dick Bass of the LA Rams (1033 yds).

AFL-AFC

Multiple winners: Earl Campbell and O.J. Simpson (4); Cookie Gilchrist, Eric Dickerson, Floyd Little, Jim Nance, Thurman Thomas and Curt Warner (2).

Year		Att	Yds	Avg	Year		Att	Yds	Avg
1960	Abner Haynes, Dal.	157	875	5.6	1977	Mark van Eeghen, Oak	324	1273	3.9
1961	Billy Cannon, Hou.	200	948	4.7	1978	Earl Campbell, Hou	302	1450	4.8
1962	Cookie Gilchrist, Buf.	214	1096	5.1	1979	Earl Campbell, Hou	368	1697	4.6
1963	Clem Daniels, Oak.	215	1099	5.1	1980	Earl Campbell, Hou	373	1934	5.2
1964	Cookie Gilchrist, Buf.	230	981	4.3	1981	Earl Campbell, Hou	361	1376	3.9
1965	Paul Lowe, SD	222	1121	5.0	1982	Freeman McNeil, NY	151	786	5.2
1966	Jim Nance, Bos	299	1458	4.9	1983	Curt Warner, Sea	335	1449	4.3
1967	Jim Nance, Bos	269	1216	4.5	1984	Earnest Jackson, SD	296	1179	4.0
1968	Paul Robinson, Cin	238	1023	4.3	1985	Marcus Allen, LA	380	1759	4.6
1969	Dickie Post, SD	182	873	4.8	1986	Curt Warner, Sea	319	1481	4.6
1970	Floyd Little, Den.	209	901	4.3	1987	Eric Dickerson, LA Rams-Ind	283	1288	4.6
1971	Floyd Little, Den.	284	1133	4.0	1988	Eric Dickerson, Ind	388	1659	4.3
1972	O.J.Simpson, Buf	292	1251	4.3	1989	Christian Okoye, KC	370	1480	4.0
1973	O.J.Simpson, Buf	332	2003	6.0	1990	Thurman Thomas, Buf	271	1297	4.8
1974	Otis Armstrong, Den.	263	1407	5.4	1991	Thurman Thomas, Buf	288	1407	4.9
1975	O.J.Simpson, Buf	329	1817	5.5					
1976	O.J.Simpson, Buf	290	1503	5.2					

Scoring
NFL-NFC

Multiple winners: Don Hutson (5); Dutch Clark, Pat Harder, Paul Hornung and Mark Moseley (3); Kevin Butler, Mike Cofer, Fred Cox, Chip Lohmiller, Jack Manders, Chester Marcol, Eddie Murray, Gordy Soltau and Doak Walker (2).

Year		TD	FG	PAT	Pts	Year		TD	FG	PAT	Pts
1932	Dutch Clark, Portsmouth	6	3	10	55	1961	Paul Hornung, GB	10	15	41	146
1933	Glenn Presnell, Portsmouth	6	6	10	64	1962	Jim Taylor, GB	19	0	0	114
	& Ken Strong, NY	6	5	13	64	1963	Don Chandler, NY	0	18	52	106
1934	Jack Manders, Chi. Bears	3	10	31	79	1964	Lenny Moore, Bal	20	0	0	120
1935	Dutch Clark, Det	6	1	16	55	1965	Gale Sayers, Chi	22	0	0	132
1936	Dutch Clark, Det	7	4	19	73	1966	Bruce Gossett, LA	0	28	29	113
1937	Jack Manders, Chi. Bears	5	8	15	69	1967	Jim Bakken, St.L	0	27	36	117
1938	Clarke Hinkle, GB	7	3	7	58	1968	Leroy Kelly, Cle	20	0	0	120
1939	Andy Farkas, Wash	11	0	2	68	1969	Fred Cox, Min	0	26	43	121
1940	Don Hutson, GB	7	0	15	57	1970	Fred Cox, Min	0	30	35	125
1941	Don Hutson, GB	12	1	20	95	1971	Curt Knight, Wash	0	29	27	114
1942	Don Hutson, GB	17	1	33	138	1972	Chester Marcol, GB	0	33	29	128
1943	Don Hutson, GB	12	3	26	117	1973	David Ray, LA	0	30	40	130
1944	Don Hutson, GB	9	0	31	85	1974	Chester Marcol, GB	0	25	19	94
1945	Steve Van Buren, Phi	18	0	2	110	1975	Chuck Foreman, Min	22	0	0	132
1946	Ted Fritsch, GB	10	9	13	100	1976	Mark Moseley, Wash.	0	22	31	97
1947	Pat Harder, Chi. Cards	7	7	39	102	1977	Walter Payton, Chi	16	0	0	96
1948	Pat Harder, Chi. Cards	6	7	53	110	1978	Frank Corral, LA	0	29	31	118
1949	Gene Roberts, NY Giants	17	0	0	102	1979	Mark Moseley, Wash.	0	25	39	114
	& Pat Harder, Chi. Cards	8	3	45	102	1980	Eddie Murray, Det	0	27	35	116
1950	Doak Walker, Det	11	8	38	128	1981	Rafael Septien, Dal	0	27	40	121
1951	Elroy Hirsch, LA	17	0	0	102		& Eddie Murray, Det	0	25	46	121
1952	Gordy Soltau, SF	7	6	34	94	1982	Wendell Tyler, LA	13	0	0	78
1953	Gordy Soltau, SF	6	10	48	114	1983	Mark Moseley, Wash.	0	33	62	161
1954	Bobby Walston, Phi	11	4	36	114	1984	Ray Wersching, SF	0	25	56	131
1955	Doak Walker, Det	7	9	27	96	1985	Kevin Butler, Chi	0	31	51	144
1956	Bobby Layne, Det	5	12	33	99	1986	Kevin Butler, Chi	0	28	36	120
1957	Sam Baker, Wash	1	14	29	77	1987	Jerry Rice, SF	23	0	0	138
	& Lou Groza, Cle	0	15	32	77	1988	Mike Cofer, SF.	0	27	40	121
1958	Jim Brown, Cle	18	0	0	108	1989	Mike Cofer, SF.	0	29	49	136
1959	Paul Hornung, GB.	7	7	31	94	1990	Chip Lohmiller, Wash	0	30	41	131
1960	Paul Hornung, GB.	15	15	41	176	1991	Chip Lohmiller, Wash	0	31	56	149

AFL-AFC

Multiple winners: Gino Cappelletti (5); Gary Anderson (3); Jim Breech, Roy Gerela, Gene Mingo, Nick Lowery, John Smith and Jim Turner (2).

Year		TD	FG	PAT	Pts	Year		TD	FG	PAT	Pts
1960	Gene Mingo, Den	6	18	33	123	1977	Errol Mann, Oak	0	20	39	99
1961	Gino Cappelletti, Bos	8	17	48	147	1978	Pat Leahy, NY	0	22	41	107
1962	Gene Mingo, Den	4	27	32	137	1979	John Smith, NE	0	23	46	115
1963	Gino Cappelletti, Bos	2	22	35	113	1980	John Smith, NE	0	26	51	129
1964	Gino Cappelletti, Bos	7	25	36	155	1981	Nick Lowery, KC	0	26	37	115
1965	Gino Cappelletti, Bos	9	17	27	132		& Jim Breech, Cin	0	22	49	115
1966	Gino Cappelletti, Bos	6	16	35	119	1982	Marcus Allen, LA	14	0	0	84
1967	George Blanda, Oak	0	20	56	116	1983	Gary Anderson, Pit	0	27	38	119
1968	Jim Turner, NY.	0	34	43	145	1984	Gary Anderson, Pit	0	24	45	117
1969	Jim Turner, NY.	0	32	33	129	1985	Gary Anderson, Pit	0	33	40	139
1970	Jan Stenerud, KC	0	30	26	116	1986	Tony Franklin, NE	0	32	44	140
1971	Garo Yepremian, Mia	0	28	33	117	1987	Jim Breech, Cin	0	24	25	97
1972	Bobby Howfield, NY	0	27	40	121	1988	Scott Norwood, Buf	0	32	33	129
1973	Roy Gerela, Pit	0	29	36	123	1989	David Treadwell, Den	0	27	39	120
1974	Roy Gerela, Pit	0	20	33	93	1990	Nick Lowery, KC	0	34	37	139
1975	O.J.Simpson, Buf	23	0	0	138	1991	Pete Stoyanovich, Mia	0	31	28	121
1976	Toni Linhart, Bal.	0	20	49	109						

All-Time NFL Leaders
Through 1991 regular season.

CAREER
Players active in 1991 in **bold** type.

Passing Efficiency

Ratings based on performance standards established for completion percentage, average gain, touchdown percentage and interception percentage. Quarterbacks are allocated points according to how their statistics measure up to those standards. Minimum 1500 passing attempts.

		Yrs	Att	Comp	Comp%	Yards	Avg Gain	TD	TD%	Int	Int%	Rating
1	Joe Montana	12	4579	2914	63.6	34,998	7.64	242	5.3	123	2.7	93.4
2	**Dan Marino**	9	4730	2798	59.2	35,386	7.48	266	5.6	149	3.2	88.2
3	**Jim Kelly**	6	2562	1555	60.7	19,574	7.64	138	5.4	89	3.5	88.0
4	**Boomer Esiason**	8	3100	1753	56.5	24,264	7.83	163	5.3	114	3.7	84.0
5	Roger Staubach	11	2958	1685	57.0	22,700	7.67	153	5.2	109	3.7	83.4
6	Neil Lomax	8	3153	1817	57.6	22,771	7.22	136	4.3	90	2.9	82.7
7	Sonny Jurgensen	18	4262	2433	57.1	32,224	7.56	255	6.0	189	4.4	82.6
	Len Dawson	19	3741	2136	57.1	28,711	7.67	239	6.4	183	4.9	82.6
9	**Dave Krieg**	12	3576	2096	58.6	26,132	7.31	195	5.5	148	4.1	82.3
10	Ken Anderson	16	4475	2654	59.3	32,838	7.34	197	4.4	160	3.6	81.9
11	Danny White	13	2950	1761	59.7	21,959	7.44	155	5.3	132	4.5	81.7
12	**Bernie Kosar**	7	2857	1671	58.5	19,937	6.98	103	3.6	71	2.5	81.6
13	**Ken O'Brien**	8	3367	1984	58.9	23,744	7.05	119	3.5	89	2.6	81.3
14	Bart Starr	16	3149	1808	57.4	24,718	7.85	152	4.8	138	4.4	80.5
15	Fran Tarkenton	18	6467	3686	57.0	47,003	7.27	342	5.3	266	4.1	80.4
16	**Warren Moon**	8	3680	2105	57.2	27,679	7.52	157	4.3	133	3.6	80.3
17	Dan Fouts	15	5604	3297	58.8	43,040	7.68	254	4.5	242	4.3	80.2
18	**Jim Everett**	6	2528	1431	56.6	18,783	7.43	112	4.4	93	3.7	79.7
	Tony Eason	8	1564	911	58.2	11,142	7.12	61	3.9	51	3.3	79.7
20	**Jim McMahon**	10	2151	1243	57.8	15,637	7.27	89	4.1	77	3.6	79.4
21	**Randall Cunningham**	7	2257	1231	54.6	15,418	6.83	107	4.7	71	3.1	78.7
22	Bert Jones	10	2551	1430	56.1	18,190	7.13	124	4.9	101	4.0	78.2
23	Johnny Unitas	18	5186	2830	54.6	40,239	7.76	290	5.6	253	4.9	78.2
24	Otto Graham	6	1565	872	55.7	13,499	8.63	88	5.6	94	6.0	78.2
25	Bobby Hebert	6	1633	953	58.4	11,343	6.95	66	4.0	59	3.6	78.1

Note: The NFL does not recognize records from the All-American Football Conference (1946-49). If it did, **Otto Graham** would rank 4th (after Kelly) with the following stats: 10 Yrs; 2,626 Att; 1,464 Comp; 55.8 Comp Pct; 23,584 Yards; 8.98 Avg Gain; 174 TD; 6.6 TD Pct; 135 Int; 5.1 Int Pct; and 86.6 Rating Pts.

Touchdown Passes

		No
1	Fran Tarkenton	342
2	Johnny Unitas	290
3	**Dan Marino**	266
4	Sonny Jurgensen	255
5	Dan Fouts	254
6	John Hadl	244
7	Joe Montana	242
8	Len Dawson	239
9	George Blanda	236
10	John Brodie	214
11	Terry Bradshaw	212
	Y.A. Tittle	212
13	Jim Hart	209
14	Roman Gabriel	201
15	Ken Anderson	197
16	Joe Ferguson	196
	Bobby Layne	196
	Norm Snead	196

		No
19	**Dave Krieg**	195
20	Ken Stabler	194
21	Bob Griese	192
22	Sammy Baugh	187
23	**Steve DeBerg**	183
	Craig Morton	183
25	Steve Grogan	182
26	Ron Jaworski	179
	Phil Simms	179
28	Babe Parilli	178
29	Charlie Conerly	173
	Joe Namath	173
	Norm Van Brocklin	173
32	Charley Johnson	170
33	Daryle Lamonica	164
	Jim Plunkett	164

		No
35	**Boomer Esiason**	163
36	Earl Morrall	161
37	Joe Theismann	160
38	Tommy Kramer	159
39	**Warren Moon**	157
40	Steve Bartkowski	156
41	Danny White	155
42	Brian Sipe	154
43	Roger Staubach	153
44	Billy Kilmer	152
	Bart Starr	152
46	Frank Ryan	149
47	**John Elway**	148
	Tobin Rote	148
49	Lynn Dickey	141
50	**Jim Kelly**	138

Note: The NFL does not recognize records from the All-American Football Conference (1946-49). If it did, **Y.A. Tittle** would rank 7th (tied with Montana) with 242 TDs and **Otto Graham** would rank 29th (after Parilli) with 174 TDs.

Passes Intercepted

		No
1	George Blanda	277
2	John Hadl	268
3	Fran Tarkenton	266
4	Norm Snead	253
	Johnny Unitas	253
6	Jim Hart	247
7	Bobby Layne	243

		No
8	Dan Fouts	242
9	John Brodie	224
10	Ken Stabler	222
11	Y.A. Tittle	221
12	Joe Namath	220
	Babe Parilli	220
14	Terry Bradshaw	210

		No
15	Joe Ferguson	209
16	Steve Grogan	208
17	Sammy Baugh	203
18	Jim Plunkett	198
19	Tobin Rote	191
20	**Steve DeBerg**	189
	Sonny Jurgensen	189

Passing Yardage

		Yrs	Att	Comp	Pct	Yards
1	Fran Tarkenton	18	6467	3686	57.0	47,003
2	Dan Fouts	15	5604	3297	58.8	43,040
3	Johnny Unitas	18	5186	2830	54.6	40,239
4	**Dan Marino**	9	4730	2798	59.2	35,386
5	Joe Montana	12	4579	2914	63.6	34,998
6	Jim Hart	19	5076	2593	51.1	34,665
7	John Hadl	16	4687	2363	50.4	33,513
8	Ken Anderson	16	4475	2654	59.3	32,838
9	Sonny Jurgensen	18	4262	2433	57.1	32,224
10	John Brodie	17	4491	2469	55.0	31,548
11	**Steve DeBerg**	15	4613	2632	57.1	31,455
12	Norm Snead	15	4353	2276	52.3	30,797
13	Joe Ferguson	18	4519	2369	52.4	29,817
14	**Phil Simms**	12	4110	2246	54.6	29,512
15	Roman Gabriel	16	4498	2366	52.6	29,444
16	Len Dawson	19	3741	2136	57.1	28,711
17	Y.A.Tittle	15	3817	2118	55.5	28,339
18	Ron Jaworski	16	4117	2187	53.1	28,190
19	Terry Bradshaw	14	3901	2025	51.9	27,989
20	**John Elway**	9	4023	2201	54.7	27,974
21	Ken Stabler	15	3793	2270	59.8	27,938
22	Craig Morton	18	3786	2053	54.2	27,908
23	**Warren Moon**	8	3680	2105	57.2	27,679
24	Joe Namath	13	3762	1886	50.1	27,663
25	George Blanda	26	4007	1911	47.7	26,920

Note: The NFL does not recognize records from the All-American Football Conference (1946-49). If it did, **Y.A.Tittle** would rank 8th (after Hadl) with the following stats: 17 Yrs; 4,395 Att; 2,427 Comp; 55.2 Pct; and 33,070 Yards.

Receiving

		Yrs	No	Yards	Avg	TD
1	Steve Largent	14	819	13,089	16.0	100
2	**Art Monk**	12	801	10,984	13.7	60
3	Charlie Joiner	18	750	12,146	16.2	65
4	**James Lofton**	14	699	13,035	18.6	69
5	Ozzie Newsome	13	662	7,980	12.1	47
6	Charley Taylor	13	649	9,110	14.0	79
7	Don Maynard	15	633	11,834	18.7	88
8	Raymond Berry	13	631	9,275	14.7	68
9	Harold Carmichael	14	590	8,985	15.2	79
10	Fred Biletnikoff	14	589	8,974	15.2	76
11	Harold Jackson	16	579	10,372	17.9	76
12	Lionel Taylor	10	567	7,195	12.7	45
13	Wes Chandler	11	559	8,966	16.0	56
14	Stanley Morgan	14	557	10,716	19.2	72
15	**Roy Green**	13	551	8,860	16.1	66
16	J.T.Smith	13	544	6,974	12.8	35
17	Lance Alworth	11	542	10,266	18.9	85
18	Kellen Winslow	10	541	6,741	12.5	45
19	**Drew Hill**	12	540	8,824	16.3	57
20	John Stallworth	14	537	8,723	16.2	63
21	**Jerry Rice**	7	526	9,072	17.2	93
22	**Roger Craig**	9	525	4,478	8.7	16
23	Bobby Mitchell	11	521	7,954	15.3	65
24	Nat Moore	13	510	7,546	14.8	74
25	**Mark Clayton**	9	507	8,024	15.8	78

Rushing

		Yrs	Car	Yards	Avg	TD
1	Walter Payton	13	3838	16,726	4.4	110
2	Tony Dorsett	12	2936	12,739	4.3	77
3	**Eric Dickerson**	9	2783	12,439	4.5	88
4	Jim Brown	9	2359	12,312	5.2	106
5	Franco Harris	13	2949	12,120	4.1	91
6	John Riggins	14	2916	11,352	3.9	104
7	O.J.Simpson	11	2404	11,236	4.7	61
8	**Ottis Anderson**	13	2552	10,242	4.0	81
9	Earl Campbell	8	2187	9,407	4.3	74
10	Jim Taylor	10	1941	8,597	4.4	83
11	Joe Perry	14	1737	8,378	4.8	53
12	**Marcus Allen**	10	2023	8,244	4.1	77
13	**Gerald Riggs**	10	1989	8,188	4.1	69
14	Larry Csonka	11	1891	8,081	4.3	64
15	**James Brooks**	11	1667	7,918	4.7	49
16	**Freeman McNeil**	11	1755	7,904	4.5	38
17	**Roger Craig**	9	1848	7,654	4.1	51
18	Mike Pruitt	11	1844	7,378	4.0	51
19	Leroy Kelly	10	1727	7,274	4.2	74
20	George Rogers	7	1692	7,176	4.2	54
21	Curt Warner	8	1698	6,844	4.0	56
22	John H.Johnson	13	1571	6,803	4.3	48
23	Wilbert Montgomery	9	1540	6,789	4.4	45
24	Chuck Muncie	9	1561	6,702	4.3	71
25	Mark van Eeghen	10	1652	6,651	4.0	36

Note: The NFL does not recognize records from the All-American Football Conference (1946-49). If it did, **Joe Perry** would rank 9th (after Anderson) with the following stats: 16 Yrs; 1,929 Att; 9,723 Yards; 5.0 Avg; and 71 TD.

All-Purpose Running

		Rush	Rec	Ret	Total
1	Walter Payton	16,726	4,538	539	21,803
2	Tony Dorsett	12,739	3,554	33	16,326
3	Jim Brown	12,312	2,499	648	15,459
4	**James Brooks**	7,918	3,622	3,278	14,818
5	Franco Harris	12,120	2,287	215	14,622
6	**Eric Dickerson**	12,439	1,994	15	14,448
7	O.J.Simpson	11,236	2,142	990	14,368
8	Bobby Mitchell	2,735	7,954	3,389	14,078
9	John Riggins	11,352	2,090	-7	13,435
10	Steve Largent	83	13,089	224	13,396
11	**Ottis Anderson**	10,242	3,062	29	13,333
12	**James Lofton**	246	13,035	27	13,308
13	Greg Pruitt	5,672	3,069	4,521	13,262
14	Ollie Matson	5,173	3,285	4,426	12,884
15	Tim Brown	3,862	3,399	5,423	12,684
16	Lenny Moore	5,174	6,039	1,238	12,451
17	Don Maynard	70	11,834	475	12,379
18	Charlie Joyner	22	12,146	199	12,367
19	Leroy Kelly	7,274	2,281	2,775	12,330
	Drew Hill	19	8,824	3,482	12,330
21	**Roger Craig**	7,654	4,578	32	12,264
22	**Marcus Allen**	8,244	3,981	0	12,225
23	Floyd Little	6,323	2,418	3,432	12,173
24	Abner Haynes	4,630	3,535	3,900	12,065
25	Stump Mitchell	4,649	1,955	5,381	11,985

Note: The NFL does not recognize records from the All-American Football Conference (1946-49). If it did, **Joe Perry** would rank 16th (after Tim Brown) with the following stats: 9,723 Rush; 2,021 Rec; 788 Ret; 12,532 Total in 16 years.

Years played: Allen (10); Anderson (13); Brooks (11); J.Brown (9); T.Brown (10); Craig (9); Dickerson (9); Dorsett (12); Harris (13); Haynes (8); Hill (12); Joiner (18); Kelly (10); Largent (14); Little (9); Lofton (14); Matson (14); Maynard (15); B.Mitchell (11); S.Mitchell (9); Moore (12); Payton (13); Pruitt (12); Riggins (14); Simpson (11).

All-Time NFL Leaders (Cont.)
Scoring

	Points	Yrs	TD	FG	PAT	Total
1	George Blanda	26	9	335	943	2002
2	Jan Stenerud	19	0	373	580	1699
3	Pat Leahy	18	0	304	558	1470
4	Jim Turner	16	1	304	521	1439
5	Mark Moseley	16	0	300	482	1382
6	Jim Bakken	17	0	282	534	1380
7	Fred Cox	15	0	282	519	1365
8	Lou Groza	17	1	234	641	1349
9	Nick Lowery	13	0	284	410	1262
10	Chris Bahr	14	0	241	490	1213
11	Jim Breech	13	0	224	486	1158
12	Gino Cappelletti	11	42	176	350	1130†
13	Ray Wersching	15	0	222	456	1122
14	Eddie Murray	12	0	244	381	1113
15	Don Cockroft	13	0	216	432	1080
16	Garo Yepremian	14	0	210	444	1074
17	Matt Bahr	13	0	221	402	1065
18	Bruce Gossett	11	0	219	374	1031
19	Gary Anderson	10	0	229	323	1010
20	Sam Baker	15	2	179	428	977
21	Morten Andersen	10	0	217	314	965
22	Rafael Septien	10	0	180	420	960
23	Lou Michaels	13	1	187	386	955†
24	Norm Johnson	10	0	178	371	905
25	Roy Gerela	11	0	184	351	903

†Cappelletti's total includes four 2-point conversions, and Michaels' total includes one safety.

Note: The NFL does not recognize records from the All-American Football Conference (1946-49). If it did, Lou Groza would move up to 3rd (after Stenerud) with the following stats: 21 Yrs; 1 TD; 264 FG, 810 PAT, 1,608 Pts.

	Touchdowns	Yrs	Rush	Rec	Ret	Total
1	Jim Brown	9	106	20	0	126
2	Walter Payton	13	110	15	0	125
3	John Riggins	14	104	12	0	116
4	Lenny Moore	12	63	48	2	113
5	Don Hutson	11	3	99	3	105
6	Steve Largent	14	1	100	0	101
7	Franco Harris	13	91	9	0	100
8	Jerry Rice	7	4	93	0	97
9	Marcus Allen	10	77	17	1	95
10	Eric Dickerson	9	88	5	0	93
	Jim Taylor	10	83	10	0	93
12	Tony Dorsett	12	77	13	1	91
	Bobby Mitchell	11	18	65	8	91
14	Leroy Kelly	10	74	13	3	90
	Charley Taylor	13	11	79	0	90
16	Don Maynard	15	0	88	0	88
17	Lance Alworth	11	2	85	0	87
18	Ottis Anderson	13	81	5	0	86
	Paul Warfield	13	1	85	0	86
20	Tommy McDonald	12	0	84	1	85
21	Pete Johnson	8	76	6	0	82
22	Art Powell	10	0	81	1	82
23	Mark Clayton	9	0	78	1	79
	Harold Carmichael	14	0	79	0	79
25	Frank Gifford	12	34	43	1	78

Note: The NFL does not recognize records from the All-American Football Conference (1946-49). If it did, Joe Perry would rank 21st (after McDonald) with the following stats: 16 Yrs; 71 Rush; 12 Rec; 1 Ret; 84 TDs.

Miscellaneous

Interceptions

		Yrs	No	Yards	TD
1	Paul Krause	16	81	1185	3
2	Emlen Tunnell	14	79	1282	4
3	Dick "Night Train" Lane	14	68	1207	5
4	Ken Riley	15	65	596	5
5	Dick LeBeau	13	62	762	3
	Dave Brown	15	62	698	5

Punting
Minimum 300 punts.

		Yrs	No	Yards	Avg
1	Sammy Baugh	16	338	15,245	45.1
2	Tommy Davis	11	511	22,833	44.7
3	Yale Lary	11	503	22,279	44.3
4	Rohn Stark	10	746	32,757	43.9
5	Horace Gillom	7	385	16,872	43.8
	Jerry Norton	11	358	15,671	43.8

Kickoff Returns
Minimum 75 returns.

		Yrs	No	Yards	Avg	TD
1	Gale Sayers	7	91	2781	30.6	6
2	Lynn Chandnois	7	92	2720	29.6	3
3	Abe Woodson	9	193	5538	28.7	5
4	Buddy Young	6	90	2514	27.9	2
5	Travis Williams	5	102	2801	27.5	6

Punt Returns
Minimum 75 returns.

		Yrs	No	Yards	Avg	TD
1	George McAfee	8	112	1431	12.8	2
	Jack Christiansen	8	85	1084	12.8	8
3	Claude Gibson	5	110	1381	12.6	3
4	Mel Grey	6	119	1479	12.4	2
5	Bill Dudley	9	124	1515	12.2	3

Sacks
Records compiled since 1982.

		Yrs	No
1	Lawrence Taylor	11	121½
2	Reggie White	7	110
3	Richard Dent	9	103½

Safeties

		Yrs	No
1	Ted Hendricks	15	4
	Doug English	10	4

Eleven players tied with three.

Long-Playing Records

Seasons

		No
1	George Blanda, QB-K	26
2	Earl Morrall, QB	21
3	Jim Marshall, DE	20

Games

		No
1	George Blanda, QB-K	340
2	Jim Marshall, DE	282
3	Jan Stenerud, K	263

Consecutive Games

		No
1	Jim Marshall, DE	282
2	Mick Tingelhoff, C	240
3	Jim Bakken, K	234

SINGLE SEASON

Passing

Yards Gained	Year	Att	Cmp	Pct	Yds
Dan Marino, Mia	1984	564	362	64.2	5084
Dan Fouts, SD	1981	609	360	59.1	4802
Dan Marino, Mia	1986	623	378	60.7	4746
Dan Fouts, SD	1980	589	348	59.1	4715
Warren Moon, Hou	1991	655	404	61.7	4690
Warren Moon, Hou	1990	584	362	62.0	4689
Neil Lomax, St.L	1984	560	345	61.6	4614
Lynn Dickey, GB	1983	484	289	59.7	4458
Dan Marino, Mia	1988	606	354	58.4	4434
Bill Kenney, KC	1983	603	346	57.4	4348

Rushing

Yards Gained	Year	Att	Yds	Avg
Eric Dickerson, Rams	1984	379	2105	5.6
O.J.Simpson, Buf	1973	332	2003	6.0
Earl Campbell, Hou	1980	373	1934	5.2
Jim Brown, Cle	1963	291	1863	6.4
Walter Payton, Chi	1977	339	1852	5.5
Eric Dickerson, Rams	1986	404	1821	4.5
O.J.Simpson, Buf	1975	329	1817	5.5
Eric Dickerson, Rams	1983	390	1808	4.6
Marcus Allen, Raiders	1985	390	1759	4.6
Gerald Riggs, Atl.	1985	397	1719	4.3

Receiving

Catches	Year	No	Yds
Art Monk, Wash	1984	106	1372
Charley Hennigan, Hou	1964	101	1546
Jerry Rice, SF	1990	100	1502
Haywood Jeffires, Hou	1991	100	1181
Lionel Taylor, Den	1961	100	1176
Todd Christensen, Raiders	1986	95	1153
Michael Irvin, Dal	1991	93	1523
Johnny Morris, Chi	1964	93	1200
Al Toon, Jets	1988	93	1067
Todd Christensen, Raiders	1983	92	1247
Lionel Taylor, Den	1960	92	1235
Roger Craig, SF	1985	92	1016

All-Purpose Running

	Year	Run	Rec	Ret	Total
Lionel James, SD	1985	516	1027	992	2535
Terry Metcalf, StL	1975	816	378	1268	2462
Mack Herron, NE	1974	824	474	1146	2444
Gale Sayers, Chi.	1966	1231	447	762	2440
Timmy Brown, Phi.	1963	841	487	1100	2428
Tim Brown, Raid	1988	50	725	1542	2317
Marcus Allen, Rad.	1985	1759	555	-6	2308
Timmy Brown, Phi.	1962	545	849	912	2306
Gale Sayers, Chi.	1965	867	507	898	2272
Eric Dickerson, Rams	1984	2105	139	15	2259
O.J.Simpson, Buf	1975	1817	426	0	2243

Scoring

Points

	Year	TD	PAT	FG	Pts
Paul Hornung, GB	1960	15	41	15	176
Mark Moseley, Wash	1983	0	62	33	161
Gino Cappelletti, Bos	1964	7	38	25	155
Chip Lohmiller, Wash.	1991	0	56	31	149
Gino Cappelletti, Bos	1961	8	48	17	147
Paul Hornung, GB	1961	10	41	15	146
Jim Turner, Jets	1968	0	43	34	145
John Riggins, Wash	1983	24	0	0	144
Kevin Butler, Chi.	1985	0	51	31	144
Tony Franklin, NE	1986	0	44	32	140

Touchdowns

	Year	Rush	Rec	Ret	Total
John Riggins, Wash	1983	24	0	0	24
O.J.Simpson, Buf	1975	16	7	0	23
Jerry Rice, SF	1987	1	22	0	23
Gale Sayers, Chi.	1966	14	6	2	22
Chuck Foreman, Min	1975	13	9	0	22
Jim Brown, Cle	1965	17	4	0	21
Joe Morris, NY Giants	1985	21	0	0	21
Lenny Moore, Bal	1964	16	3	1	20
Leroy Kelly, Cle.	1968	16	4	0	20
Eric Dickerson, LA Rams	1983	18	2	0	20

Note: The NFL regular season schedule grew from 12 games (1947-60) to 14 (1961-77) to 16 (1978-present). The AFL regular season schedule was always 14 games (1960-69).

Touchdowns Rushing

	Year	No
John Riggins, Washington	1983	24
Joe Morris, NY Giants	1985	21
Jim Taylor, Green Bay	1962	19
Earl Campbell, Houston	1979	19
Chuck Muncie, San Diego	1981	19
Eric Dickerson, LA Rams	1983	18
George Rogers, Washington	1986	18
Jim Brown, Cleveland	1958	17
Jim Brown, Cleveland	1965	17

Touchdowns Receiving

	Year	No
Jerry Rice, San Francisco	1987	22
Mark Clayton, Miami	1984	18
Don Hutson, Green Bay	1942	17
Elroy "Crazylegs" Hirsch, LA Rams	1951	17
Bill Groman, Houston	1961	17
Jerry Rice, San Francisco	1989	17
Art Powell, Oakland	1963	16
Jerry Rice, San Francisco	1986	15

Touchdowns Passing

	Year	No
Dan Marino, Miami	1984	48
Dan Marino, Miami	1986	44
George Blanda, Houston	1961	36
Y.A.Tittle, NY Giants	1963	36
Y.A.Tittle, NY Giants	1962	33
Dan Fouts, San Diego	1981	33
Warren Moon, Houston	1990	33
Jim Kelly, Buffalo	1991	33
Johnny Unitas, Baltimore	1959	32
Sonny Jurgensen, Philadelphia	1961	32
Lynn Dickey, Green Bay	1983	32
Dave Krieg, Seattle	1984	32

Field Goals

	Year	Att	No
Ali Haji-Sheikh, NY Giants	1983	42	35
Nick Lowery, Kansas City	1990	37	34
Jim Turner, NY Jets*	1968	46	34
Gary Anderson, Pittsburgh	1985	42	33
Mark Moseley, Washington*	1983	47	33
Chester Marcol, Green Bay	1972	48	33
Scott Norwood, Buffalo	1988	37	32
Tony Franklin, New England	1986	41	32
Jim Turner, NY Jets*	1969	47	32

Five tied with 31 each.

*Old-style, straight ahead kicker

All-Time NFL Leaders (Cont.)

Miscellaneous

Interceptions

	Year	No
Dick "Night Train" Lane, Detroit	1952	14
Dan Sandifer, Washington	1948	13
Spec Sanders, NY Yanks	1950	13
Lester Hayes, Oakland	1980	13

Punting

Qualifiers	Year	Avg
Sammy Baugh, Washington	1940	51.4
Yale Lary, Detroit	1963	48.9
Sammy Baugh, Washington	1941	48.7

Kickoff Returns

	Year	Avg
Travis Williams, Green Bay	1967	41.1
Gale Sayers, Chicago	1967	37.7
Ollie Matson, Chicago Cards:	1958	35.5

Punt Returns

	Year	Avg
Herb Rich, Baltimore	1950	23.0
Jack Christiansen, Detroit	1952	21.5
Dick Christy, NY Titans	1961	21.3
Bob Hayes, Dallas	1968	20.8

Sacks

	Year	No		Year	No
Mark Gastineau, NY Jets	1984	22	Chris Doleman, Minnesota	1989	21
Reggie White, Philadelphia	1987	21	Lawrence Taylor, NY Giants	1986	20½

SINGLE GAME

Passing

Yards Gained

	Date	Yds
Norm Van Brocklin, LA vs NY Yanks	9/28/51	554
Warren Moon, Hou at KC	12/16/90	527
Dan Marino, Mia vs NYJ	10/23/88	521
Phil Simms, NYG vs Cin	10/13/85	513
Vince Ferragamo, Rams vs Chi	12/26/82	509

Completions

	Date	No
Richard Todd, NYJ vs SF	9/21/80	42
Warren Moon, Hou vs Dal	11/10/91	41
Ken Anderson, Cin vs SD	12/20/82	40
Phil Simms, NYG vs Cin	10/13/85	40
Dan Marino, Mia vs Buf	11/16/86	39

Receiving

Catches

	Date	No
Tom Fears, LA vs GB	12/3/50	18
Clark Gaines, NYJ vs SF	9/21/80	17
Sonny Randle, St.L vs NYG	11/4/62	16
Five tied with 15 each.		

Yards Gained

	Date	Yds
Flipper Anderson, LA Rams vs NO	11/26/89	336
Stephone Paige, KC vs SD	12/22/85	309
Jim Benton, Cle vs Det	11/22/45	303
Cloyce Box, Det vs Bal	12/3/50	302
John Taylor, SF vs LA Rams	12/11/89	286

Rushing

Yards Gained

	Date	Yds
Walter Payton, Chi vs Min	11/20/77	275
O.J.Simpson, Buf vs Det	11/25/76	273
O.J.Simpson, Buf vs NE	9/16/73	250
Willie Ellison, LA Rams vs NO	12/5/71	247
Cookie Gilchrist, Buf vs NYJ	12/8/63	243

All-Purpose Running

	Date	Yds
Billy Cannon, Hou vs NY Titans	12/10/61	373
Lionel James, SD vs Raiders	11/10/85	345
Timmy Brown, Phi vs St.L	12/16/62	341
Gale Sayers, Chi vs Min	12/18/66	339
Gale Sayers, Chi vs SF	12/12/65	336

Scoring

Points

	Date	Pts
Ernie Nevers, Chi. Cards vs Chi. Bears	11/28/29	40
Dub Jones, Cle vs Chi. Bears	11/25/51	36
Gale Sayers, Chi vs SF	12/12/65	36
Paul Hornung, GB vs Bal	10/8/61	33
Bob Shaw, Chi. Cards vs Bal	10/2/50	30
Jim Brown, Cle vs Bal	11/1/59	30
Abner Haynes, Dal.Texans vs Oak	11/26/61	30
Billy Cannon, Hou vs NY Titans	12/10/61	30
Cookie Gilchrist, Buf vs NY Jets	12/8/63	30
Kellen Winslow, SD vs Oak	11/22/81	30
Jerry Rice, SF at Atl	10/14/90	30

Note: Nevers celebrated Thanksgiving, 1929, by scoring all the Chicago Cardinals' points on six rushing TDs and four PATs. The Cards beat Red Grange and the Chicago Bears, 40-6.

Touchdowns Rushing

	Date	No
Ernie Nevers, Chi. Cards vs Chi. Bears	11/28/29	6
Dub Jones, Cle vs Chi. Bears	11/25/51	6
Gale Sayers, Chi vs SF	12/12/65	6
Eight players tied with five TDs.		

Touchdowns Passing

	Date	No
Sid Luckman, Chi Bears vs NYG	11/14/43	7
Adrian Burk, Phi vs Wash	10/17/54	7
George Blanda, Hou vs NY Titans	11/19/61	7
Y.A.Tittle, NYG vs Wash	10/28/62	7
Joe Kapp, Min vs Bal	9/28/69	7

Touchdowns Receiving

	Date	No
Bob Shaw, Chi. Cards vs Bal	10/2/50	5
Kellen Winslow, SD vs Oak	11/22/81	5
Jerry Rice, SF at Atl	10/14/90	5

Field Goals

	Date	No
Jim Bakken, St.L vs Pit	9/24/67	7
Rich Karlis, Min vs Rams	11/5/89	7
Eight players tied with 6 FGs.		

Note: Bakken was 7-for-9, Karlis 7-for-7.

Extra Point Kicks

	Date	No
Pat Harder, Cards vs NYG	10/17/48	9
Bob Waterfield, LA vs Bal	10/22/50	9
Charlie Gogolak, Wash vs NYG	11/27/66	9

LONGEST PLAYS

Passing (all for TDs)	Date	Yds
Frank Filchock to Andy Farkas, Wash vs Pit	10/15/39	99
George Izo to Bobby Mitchell, Wash vs Cle	9/15/63	99
Karl Sweetan to Pat Studstill, Det vs Bal	10/16/66	99
Sonny Jurgensen to Gerry Allen, Wash vs Chi	9/15/68	99
Jim Plunkett to Cliff Branch, LA Raiders vs Wash	10/2/83	99
Ron Jaworski to Mike Quick, Phi vs Atl	11/10/85	99

Runs from Scrimmage (all for TDs)	Date	Yds
Tony Dorsett, Dal vs Min	1/3/83	99
Andy Uram, GB vs Chi. Cards	10/8/39	97
Bob Gage, Pit vs Bears	12/4/49	97

Field Goals	Date	Yds
Tom Dempsey, NO vs Det	11/8/70	63
Steve Cox, Cle vs Cin	10/21/84	60
Morten Andersen, NO vs Chi	10/27/91	60

Punt Returns (all for TDs)	Date	Yds
Gil LeFebvre, Cin vs Bklyn	12/3/33	98
Charlie West, Min vs Wash	11/3/68	98
Dennis Morgan, Dal vs St.L	10/13/74	98
Terance Mathis, NYJ vs Dal	11/4/90	98

Kickoff Returns (all for TDs)	Date	Yds
Al Carmichael, GB vs Chi. Bears	10/7/56	106
Noland Smith, KC vs Den	12/17/67	106
Roy Green, St.L vs Dal	10/21/79	106

Interception Returns (for TDs)	Date	Yds
Vencie Glenn, SD vs Den	11/29/87	103
Four players tied with 102-yd returns.		

NFL Pro Bowl

A postseason All-Star game between the new league champion and a team of professional all-stars was added to the NFL schedule in 1939. In the first game at Wrigley Field in Los Angeles, the NY Giants beat a team made up of players from NFL teams and two independent clubs in Los Angeles (the LA Bulldogs and Hollywood Stars). An all-NFL All-Star team provided the opposition over the next four seasons, but the game was cancelled in 1943.

The Pro Bowl was revived in 1951 as a contest between conference all-star teams: American vs National (1951-53), Eastern vs Western (1954-70), and AFC vs NFC (since 1971). The NFC leads the current series with the AFC, 13-9.

The MVP trophy was named the Dan McGuire Award in 1984 after the late SF 49ers publicist and *Honolulu Advertiser* sports columnist.

Year	Winner	Score	Loser
1939	NY Giants	13-10	All-Stars
1940	Green Bay	16- 7	All-Stars
1940	Chi.Bears	28-14	All-Stars
1942	Chi.Bears	35-24	All-Stars
1942	All-Stars	17-14	Washington
1943-50	No game		

Year	Winner	MVP
1951	American, 28-27	Otto Graham, Cle., QB
1952	National, 30-13	Dan Towler, LA, HB
1953	National, 27-7	Don Doll, Det., DB
1954	East, 20-9	Chuck Bednarik, Phi., LB
1955	West, 26-19	Billy Wilson, SF, E
1956	East, 31-30	Ollie Matson, Cards, HB
1957	West, 19-10	Back—Bert Rechicahr, Bal.
		Line—Ernie Stautner, Pit.
1958	West, 26-7	Back—Hugh McElhenny, SF
		Line—Gene Brito, Wash.
1959	East, 28-21	Back—Frank Gifford, NY
		Line—Doug Atkins, Chi
1960	West, 38-21	Back—Johnny Unitas, Bal.
		Line—Big Daddy Lipscomb, Pit.
1961	West, 35-31	Back—Johnny Unitas, Bal.
		Line—Sam Huff, NY
1962	West, 31-30	Back—Jim Brown, Cle.
		Line—Henry Jordan, GB
1963	East, 30-20	Back—Jim Brown, Cle,
		Line—Big Daddy Lipscomb, Pit.
1964	West, 31-17	Back—Johnny Unitas, Bal.
		Line—Gino Marchetti, Bal
1965	West, 34-14	Back—Fran Tarkenton, Min
		Line—Terry Barr, Det.
1966	East, 36-7	Back—Jim Brown, Cle.
		Line—Dale Meinhart, St.L.
1967	East, 20-10	Back—Gale Sayers, Chi.
		Line—Floyd Peters, Phi.

Year	Winner	MVP
1968	West, 38-20	Back—Gale Sayers, Chi.
		Line—Dave Robinson, GB
1969	West, 10-7	Back—Roman Gabriel, LA
		Line—Merlin Olsen, LA
1970	West, 16-13	Back—Gale Sayers, Chi.
		Line—George Andrie, Dal.
1971	NFC, 27-6	Back—Mel Renfro, Dal.
		Line—Fred Carr, GB
1972	AFC, 26-13	Off—Jan Stenerud, KC
		Def—Willie Lanier, KC
1973	AFC, 33-28	O.J. Simpson, Buf., RB
1974	AFC, 15-13	Garo Yepremian, Mia, PK
1975	NFC, 17-10	James Harris, LA Rams, QB
1976	NFC, 23-20	Billy Johnson, Hou., KR
1977	AFC, 24-14	Mel Blount, Pit., CB
1978	NFC, 14-13	Walter Payton, Chi., RB
1979	NFC, 13-7	Ahmad Rashad, Min., WR
1980	NFC, 37-27	Chuck Muncie, NO, RB
1981	NFC, 21-7	Eddie Murray, Det., PK
1982	AFC, 16-13	Kellen Winslow, SD, WR
		& Lee Roy Selmon, TB, DE
1983	NFC, 20-19	Dan Fouts, SD, QB
		& John Jefferson, GB, WR
1984	NFC, 45-3	Joe Theismann, Wash., QB
1985	AFC, 22-14	Mark Gastineau, NYJ, DE
1986	NFC, 28-24	Phil Simms, NYG, QB
1987	AFC, 10-6	Reggie White, Phi., DE
1988	AFC, 15-6	Bruce Smith, Buf., DE
1989	NFC, 34-3	Randall Cunningham, Phi., QB
1990	NFC, 27-21	Jerry Gray, LA Rams, CB
1991	AFC, 23-21	Jim Kelly, Buf., QB
1992	NFC, 21-15	Michael Irvin, Dal., WR

Playing sites: Wrigley Field in Los Angeles (1939); Gilmore Stadium in Los Angeles (both games); Polo Grounds in New York (Jan., 1942); Shibe Park in Philadelphia (Dec., 1942); Memorial Coliseum in Los Angeles (1951-72 and 1979); Texas Stadium in Irving,TX (1973); Arrowhead Stadium in Kansas City (1974); Orange Bowl in Miami (1975); Superdome in New Orleans (1976); Kingdome in Seattle (1977); Tampa Stadium in Tampa (1978) and Aloha Stadium in Honolulu (since 1980).

AFL All-Star Game

The AFL did not play an All-Star game after its first season in 1960 but did stage All-Star games from 1962-70. All-Star teams from the Eastern and Western divisions played each other every year except 1966 with the West winning the series, 6-2. In 1966, the league champion Buffalo Bills met an elite squad made up of the best players from the league's other eight clubs and lost, 30-19.

Year	Winner	MVP
1962	West, 47-27	Cotton Davidson, Oak., QB
1963	West, 21-14	Off—Curtis McClinton, Dal.
		Def—Earl Faison, SD
1964	West, 27-24	Off—Keith Lincoln, SD
		Def—Archie Matsos, Oak.
1965	West, 38-14	Off—Keith Lincoln, SD
		Def—Willie Brown, Den.
1966	All-Stars 30	Off—Joe Namath, NY
	Buffalo 19	Def—Frank Buncom, SD

Year	Winner	MVP
1967	East, 30-23	Off—Babe Parilli, Bos.
		Def—Verlon Biggs, NY
1968	East, 25-24	Off—Joe Namath, NY
		& Don Maynard, NY
		Def—Speedy Duncan, SD
1969	West, 38-25	Off—Len Dawson, KC
		Def—George Webster, Hou.
1970	West, 26-3	John Hadl, SD, QB

Playing sites: Balboa Stadium in San Diego (1962-64); Jeppesen Stadium in Houston (1965); Rice Stadium in Houston (1966); Oakland Coliseum (1967); Gator Bowl in Jacksonville (1968-69) and Astrodome in Houston (1970).

Chicago College All-Star Game

On Aug.31, 1934, a year after sponsoring Major League Baseball's first All-Star Game, the Chicago Tribune and sports editor Arch Ward presented the first Chicago College All-Star Game at Soldier Field. A crowd of 79,432 turned out to see an all-star team of graduated college seniors battle the 1933 NFL champion Chicago Bears to a scoreless tie. The preseason game was played annually at Soldier Field until it was cancelled in 1977.

Year		Year		Year	
1934	Chi.Bears 0, All-Stars 0	1950	All-Stars 17, Philadelphia 7	1965	Cleveland 24, All-Stars 16
1935	Chi.Bears 5, All-Stars 0	1951	Cleveland 33, All-Stars 0	1966	Green Bay 38, All-Stars 0
1936	Detroit 7, All-Stars 0	1952	LA Rams 10, All-Stars 7	1967	Green Bay 27, All-Stars 0
1937	All-Stars 6, Green Bay 0	1953	Detroit 24, All-Stars 10	1968	Green Bay 34, All-Stars 17
1938	All-Stars 28, Washington 16	1954	Detroit 31, All-Stars 6	1969	NY Jets 26, All-Stars 24
1939	NY Giants 9, All-Stars 0	1955	All-Stars 30, Cleveland 27		
		1956	Cleveland 26, All-Stars 0	1970	Kansas City 24, All-Stars 3
1940	Green Bay 45, All-Stars 28	1957	NY Giants 22, All-Stars 12	1971	Baltimore 24, All-Stars 17
1941	Chi.Bears 37, All-Stars 13	1958	All-Stars 35, Detroit 19	1972	Dallas 20, All-Stars 7
1942	Chi.Bears 21, All-Stars 0	1959	Baltimore 29, All-Stars 0	1973	Miami 14, All-Stars 3
1943	All-Stars 27, Washington 7			1974	No Game (NFLPA Strike)
1944	Chi.Bears 24, All-Stars 21	1960	Baltimore 32, All-Stars 7	1975	Pittsburgh 21, All-Stars 14
1945	Green Bay 19, All-Stars 7	1961	Philadelphia 28, All-Stars 14	1976	Pittsburgh 24, All-Stars 0*
1946	All-Stars 16, LA Rams 0	1962	Green Bay 42, All-Stars 20		
1947	All-Stars 16, Chi.Bears 0	1963	All-Stars 20, Green Bay 17	*Downpour flooded field, game called with
1948	Chi.Cards 28, All-Stars 0	1964	Chi.Bears 28, All-Stars 17	1:22 left in 3rd quarter.
1949	Philadelphia 38, All-Stars 0				

Number One Draft Choices

In an effort to blunt the dominance of the Chicago Bears and New York Giants in the 1930s and distribute talent more evenly throughout the league, the NFL established the college draft in 1936. The first player chosen in the first draft was Jay Berwanger, who was also college football's Heisman Trophy winner. In all, 16 Heisman winners have also been the NFL's No.1 draft choice. They are noted in **bold** type.

The American Football League (formed in 1960) held its own draft for six years before agreeing to merge with the NFL and select players in a common draft starting in 1967.

Year	Team	
1936	Philadelphia	**Jay Berwanger**, HB, Chicago
1937	Philadelphia	Sam Francis, FB, Nebraska
1938	Cleve.Rams	Corbett Davis, FB, Indiana
1939	Chicago Cards	Ki Aldrich, C, TCU
1940	Chicago Cards	George Cafego, HB, Tennessee
1941	Chicago Bears	**Tom Harmon**, HB, Michigan
1942	Pittsburgh	Bill Dudley, HB, Viginia
1943	Detroit	**Frank Sinkwich**, HB, Georgia
1944	Boston Yanks	**Angelo Bertelli**, QB, N.Dame
1945	Chicago Cards	Charley Trippi, HB, Georgia
1946	Boston Yanks	Frank Dancewicz, QB, N.Dame
1947	Chicago Bears	Bob Fenimore, HB, Okla.A&M
1948	Washington	Harry Gilmer, QB, Alabama
1949	Philadelphia	Chuck Bednarik, C, Penn
1950	Detroit	**Leon Hart**, E, Notre Dame
1951	NY Giants	Kyle Rote, HB, SMU
1952	LA Rams	Bill Wade, QB, Vanderbilt

Year	Team	
1953	San Francisco	Harry Babcock, E, Georgia
1954	Cleveland	Bobby Garrett, QB, Stanford
1955	Baltimore	George Shaw, QB, Oregon
1956	Pittsburgh	Gary Glick, DB, Colo.A&M
1957	Green Bay	**Paul Hornung**, QB, N.Dame
1958	Chicago Cards	King Hill, QB, Rice
1959	Green Bay	Randy Duncan, QB, Iowa
1960	NFL—LA Rams	**Billy Cannon**, HB, LSU
	AFL—No choice	
1961	NFL—Minnesota	Tommy Mason, HB, Tulane
	AFL—Buffalo	Ken Rice, G, Auburn
1962	NFL—Washington	**Ernie Davis**, HB, Syracuse
	AFL—Oakland	Roman Gabriel, QB, N.C.State
1963	NFL—LA Rams	**Terry Baker**, QB, Oregon St.
	AFL—Kan.City	Buck Buchanan, DT, Grambling
1964	NFL—San Fran	Dave Parks, E, Texas Tech
	AFL—Boston	Jack Concannon, QB, Boston Col.

Year	Team		Year	Team	
1965	NFL—NY Giants	Tucker Frederickson, HB, Auburn	1980	Detroit	**Billy Sims**, RB, Oklahoma
	AFL—Houston	Lawrence Elkins, E, Baylor	1981	New Orleans	**George Rogers**, RB, S.Carolina
1966	NFL—Atlanta	Tommy Nobis, LB, Texas	1982	New England	Kenneth Sims, DT, Texas
	AFL—Miami	Jim Grabowski, FB, Illinois	1983	Baltimore	John Elway, QB, Stanford
1967	Baltimore	Bubba Smith, DT, Michigan St.	1984	New England	Irving Fryar, WR, Nebraska
1968	Minnesota	Ron Yary, T, USC	1985	Buffalo	Bruce Smith, DE, Va.Tech
1969	Buffalo	**O.J.Simpson**, RB, USC	1986	Tampa Bay	**Bo Jackson**, RB, Auburn
			1987	Tampa Bay	**V. Testaverde**, QB, Miami-FL
1970	Pittsburgh	Terry Bradshaw, QB, La.Tech	1988	Atlanta	Aundray Bruce, LB, Auburn
1971	New England	**Jim Plunkett**, QB, Stanford	1989	Dallas	Troy Aikman, QB, UCLA
1972	Buffalo	Walt Patulski, DE, Notre Dame			
1973	Houston	John Matuszak, DE, Tampa	1990	Indianapolis	Jeff George, QB, Illinois
1974	Dallas	Ed "Too Tall" Jones, Tenn.St.	1991	Dallas	Russell Maryland, DL, Miami-FL
1975	Atlanta	Steve Bartkowski, QB, Calif.	1992	Indianapolis	Steve Emtman, DL, Washington
1976	Tampa Bay	Lee Roy Selmon, DE, Oklahoma			
1977	Tampa Bay	Ricky Bell, RB, USC			
1978	Houston	**Earl Campbell**, RB, Texas			
1979	Buffalo	Tom Cousineau, LB, Ohio St.			

All-Time Winningest NFL Coaches

Top 20 NFL career victories through the 1991 season. Career, regular season and playoff records are noted along with NFL, AFL and Super Bowl titles won. Active coaches in **bold** type.

		Career				Regular Season				Playoffs			
		Yrs	W	L	T	Pct	W	L	T	Pct	W	L	Pct	League Titles
1	George Halas	40	**325**	151	31	.672	319	148	31	.692	6	3	.667	5 NFL
2	**Don Shula**	29	**306**	145	6	.676	289	131	6	.685	17	14	.548	2 Super Bowls and 1 NFL
3	Tom Landry	29	**270**	178	6	.601	250	162	6	.605	20	16	.556	2 Super Bowls
4	Curly Lambeau	33	**229**	134	22	.623	226	132	22	.624	3	2	.600	6 NFL
5	**Chuck Noll**	23	**209**	156	1	.572	193	148	1	.566	16	8	.667	4 Super Bowls
6	**Chuck Knox**	19	**178**	125	1	.587	171	114	1	.600	7	11	.389	—None—
7	Paul Brown	21	**170**	108	6	.609	166	100	6	.621	4	8	.333	3 NFL
8	Bud Grant	18	**168**	108	5	.607	158	96	5	.620	10	12	.455	1 NFL
9	Steve Owen	23	**153**	108	17	.581	151	100	17	.595	2	8	.200	2 NFL
10	Hank Stram	17	**136**	100	10	.573	131	97	10	.571	5	3	.625	1 Super Bowl, and 3 AFL
11	Webb Ewbank	20	**134**	130	7	.507	130	129	7	.502	4	1	.800	1 Super Bowl, 2 NFL & 1 AFL
12	**Joe Gibbs**	11	**130**	57	0	.695	115	53	0	.685	15	4	.789	3 Super Bowls
13	Sid Gillman	18	**123**	104	7	.541	122	99	7	.550	1	5	.167	1 AFL
14	George Allen	12	**118**	54	5	.681	116	47	5	.705	2	7	.222	—None—
15	Don Coryell	14	**114**	89	1	.561	111	83	1	.572	3	6	.333	—None—
16	John Madden	10	**112**	39	7	.731	103	32	7	.750	9	7	.563	1 Super Bowl
17	**Dan Reeves**	11	**109**	71	1	.605	102	65	1	.610	7	6	.538	—None—
18	**Mike Ditka**	10	**107**	57	0	.652	101	51	0	.664	6	6	.500	1 Super Bowl
19	Buddy Parker	15	**107**	76	9	.581	104	75	9	.577	3	1	.750	2 NFL
20	Vince Lombardi	10	**105**	35	6	.740	96	34	6	.728	9	1	.900	2 Super Bowls and 5 NFL
21	Bill Walsh	10	**102**	63	1	.617	92	59	1	.609	10	4	.714	3 Super Bowls
22	Lou Saban	16	**97**	101	7	.490	95	100	7	.488	2	1	.667	2 AFL
23	**Marv Levy**	11	**92**	76	0	.548	87	72	0	.547	5	4	.556	—None—
24	Jimmy Conzelman	16	**92**	69	17	.565	91	68	17	.565	1	1	.500	2 NFL
25	Tom Flores	9	**91**	56	0	.619	83	53	0	.610	8	3	.727	2 Super Bowls

Notes: The NFL does not recognize records from the All-American Football Conference (1946-49). If it did, Paul Brown (52-4-3 in four AAFC seasons) would move up to 6th on the all-time list with the following career stats—25 Yrs; 222 Wins; 112 Losses; 9 Ties; .660 Pct; 9-8 playoff record; and 4 AAFC titles.

Where They Coached

Allen—LA Rams (1966-70), Washington (1971-77); **Brown**—Cleveland (1950-62), Cincinnati (1968-75); **Conzelman**—Rock Island (1920-21), Milwaukee (1923-24), Detroit Panthers (1925-26), Providence (1927-30), Chicago Cards (1940-42,46-48); **Coryell**—St.Louis (1973-77), San Diego (1978-86); **Ditka**—Chicago (1982—); **Ewbank**—Baltimore (1954-62), NY Jets (1963-73); **Flores**—Oakland-LA Raiders (1979-87); **Gibbs**—Washington (1981—).

Gillman—LA Rams (1955-59), LA-San Diego Chargers (1960-69), Houston (1973-74); **Grant**—Minnesota (1967-83,1985); **Halas**—Chicago Bears (1920-29,33-42,46-55,58-67); **Knox**—LA Rams (1973-77), Buffalo (1978-82), Seattle (1983—); **Lambeau**—Green Bay (1921-49), Chicago Cards (1950-51), Washington (1952-53); **Landry**—Dallas (1960-88); **Levy**—Kansas City (1978-82), Buffalo (1986—); **Lombardi**—Green Bay (1959-67), Washington (1969).

Madden—Oakland (1969-78); **Noll**—Pittsburgh (1969—); **Owen**—NY Giants (1931-53); **Parker**—Chicago Cards (1949), Detroit (1951-56), Pittsburgh (1957-64); **Reeves**—Denver (1981—); **Saban**—Boston Patriots (1960-61), Buffalo (1962-65,72-76), Denver (1967-71); **Shula**—Baltimore (1963-69), Miami (1970—); **Stram**—Dallas-Kansas City (1960-74), New Orleans (1976-77); **Walsh**—San Francisco (1979-88).

All-Time Winningest NFL Coaches (Cont.)

Top Winning Percentages
Minimum of 85 NFL victories, including playoffs.

		Yrs	W	L	T	Pct
1	Vince Lombardi	10	105	35	6	.740
2	John Madden	10	112	39	7	.731
3	**Joe Gibbs**	11	130	57	0	.695
4	George Allen	12	118	54	5	.681
5	**Don Shula**	29	306	145	6	.676
6	George Halas	40	325	151	31	.672
7	**Mike Ditka**	10	107	57	0	.652
8	Curly Lambeau	33	229	134	22	.623
9	Bill Parcells	8	85	52	1	.620
10	Tom Flores	9	91	56	0	.619
11	Bill Walsh	10	102	63	1	.617
12	Paul Brown	21	170	108	6	.609
13	Bud Grant	18	168	108	5	.607
14	**Dan Reeves**	11	109	71	1	.605
15	Tom Landry	29	270	178	6	.601
16	**Chuck Knox**	19	178	125	1	.587
17	Steve Owen	23	153	108	17	.581
	Buddy Parker	15	107	76	9	.581
19	Hank Stram	17	136	100	10	.573
20	**Chuck Noll**	23	209	156	1	.572
21	Jimmy Conzelman	15	88	64	18	.571
22	Don Coryell	14	114	89	1	.561
23	**Marv Levy**	11	92	76	0	.548
24	Sid Gillman	18	123	104	7	.541
25	Bum Phillips	11	86	80	0	.518

Note: If AAFC records are included, Paul Brown moves to 7th with a percentage of .660 (25 yrs, 222-112-9) and Buck Shaw ties for 10th at .619 (8 yrs, 91-55-5).

Active Coaches' Victories
Through 1991 season, including playoffs.

		Yrs	W	L	T	Pct
1	Don Shula, Miami	29	306	145	6	.676
2	Chuck Knox, LA Rams	19	178	125	1	.587
3	Joe Gibbs, Washington	11	130	57	0	.695
4	Dan Reeves, Denver	11	109	71	1	.605
5	Mike Ditka, Chicago	10	107	57	0	.652
6	Marv Levy, Buffalo	11	92	76	0	.548
7	Tom Flores, Seattle	9	91	56	0	.619
8	Marty Schottenheimer, KC	8	76	51	1	.598
9	Jack Pardee, Houston	8	65	61	0	.516
10	Sam Wyche, Tampa Bay	8	64	68	0	.485
11	Jim Mora, New Orleans	6	57	41	0	.582
12	Jerry Glanville, Atlanta	7	51	53	0	.490
13	George Seifert, San Fran.	3	42	11	0	.792
14	Ted Marchibroda, Ind.	5	41	36	0	.532
15	Art Shell, LA Raiders	3	29	18	0	.617
16	Wayne Fontes, Detroit	4	28	27	0	.509
17	Jimmy Johnson, Dallas	3	20	30	0	.400
18	Bruce Coslet, NY Jets	2	14	19	0	.424
19	Rich Kotite, Philadelphia	1	10	6	0	.625
20	Joe Bugel, Phoenix	2	9	23	0	.281
21	Ray Handley, NY Giants	1	8	8	0	.500
22	Bill Belichick, Cleveland	1	6	10	0	.375
	Dick MacPherson, New Eng.	1	6	10	0	.375
24	Bill Cowher, Pittsburgh	0	0	0	0	.000
	Dennis Green, Minnesota	0	0	0	0	.000
	Mike Holmgren, Green Bay	0	0	0	0	.000
	Bobby Ross, San Diego	0	0	0	0	.000
	David Shula, Cincinnati	0	0	0	0	.000

Annual Awards
NFL Player of the Year

Unlike the other major pro team sports, the NFL no longer sanctions a Most Valuable Player award. The league gave out the Joe F. Carr Trophy (Carr was NFL president from 1921-39) for nine years but discontinued it in 1947. Since then, four principal MVP awards have been given out: UPI (1953-69), AP (since 1957), the Maxwell Club of Philadelphia's Bert Bell Trophy (since 1959) and the Pro Football Writers Assn.(since 1976). UPI switched to AFC and NFC Player of the Year awards in 1970.

Multiple winners (named in more than one season): Jim Brown (4); Johnny Unitas and Y.A.Tittle (3); Earl Campbell, Randall Cunningham, Otto Graham, Don Hutson, Joe Montana, Walter Payton and Joe Theismann (2).

Year		Awards
1938	Mel Hein, NY Giants, C	Carr
1939	Parker Hall, Cleveland Rams, HB	Carr
1940	Ace Parker, Brooklyn, HB	Carr
1941	Don Hutson, Green Bay, E	Carr
1942	Don Hutson, Green Bay, E	Carr
1943	Sid Luckman, Chicago Bears, QB	Carr
1944	Frank Sinkwich, Detroit, HB	Carr
1945	Bob Waterfield, Cleveland Rams, QB	Carr
1946	Bill Dudley, Pittsburgh, HB	Carr
1947-49 No award		
1950-52 No award		
1953	Otto Graham, Cleveland Browns, QB	UPI
1954	Joe Perry, San Francisco, FB	UPI
1955	Otto Graham, Cleveland, QB	UPI
1956	Frank Gifford, NY Giants, HB	UPI
1957	Y.A.Tittle, San Francisco, QB	UPI
	& Jim Brown, Cleveland, FB	AP
1958	Jim Brown, Cleveland, FB	UPI
	& Gino Marchetti, Baltimore, DE	AP
1959	Johnny Unitas, Baltimore, QB	UPI-Bell
	& Charley Conerly, NY Giants, QB	AP
1960	Norm Van Brocklin, Phi., QB	UPI-AP(tie)-Bell
	& Joe Schmidt, Detroit, LB	AP (tie)
1961	Paul Hornung, Green Bay, HB	UPI-AP-Bell

Year		Awards
1962	Y.A.Tittle, NY Giants, QB	UPI
	Jim Taylor, Green Bay, FB	AP
	& Andy Robustelli, NY Giants, DE	Bell
1963	Jim Brown, Cleveland, FB	UPI-Bell
	& Y.A.Tittle, NY Giants, QB	AP
1964	Johnny Unitas, Baltimore, QB	UPI-AP
1965	Jim Brown, Cleveland, FB	UPI-AP
	& Pete Retzlaff, Philadelphia, TE	Bell
1966	Bart Starr, Green Bay, QB	UPI-AP
	& Don Meredith, Dallas, QB	Bell
1967	Johnny Unitas, Baltimore, QB	UPI-AP-Bell
1968	Earl Morrall, Baltimore, QB	UPI-AP
	& Leroy Kelly, Cleveland, RB	Bell
1969	Roman Gabriel, LA Rams, QB	UPI-AP-Bell
1970	John Brodie, San Francisco, QB	AP
	& George Blanda, Oakland, QB-PK	Bell
1971	Alan Page, Minnesota, DT	AP
	& Roger Staubach, Dallas, QB	Bell
1972	Larry Brown, Washington, RB	AP-Bell
1973	O.J.Simpson, Buffalo, RB	AP-Bell
1974	Ken Stabler, Oakland, QB	AP
	& Merlin Olsen, LA Rams, DT	Bell
1975	Fran Tarkenton, Minnesota, QB	AP-Bell
1976	Bert Jones, Baltimore, QB	AP-PFWA
	& Ken Stabler, Oakland, QB	Bell

Year		Awards	Year		Awards
1977	Walter Payton, Chicago, RB	AP-PFWA	1984	Dan Marino, Miami, QB	AP-Bell-PFWA
	& Bob Griese, Miami, QB	Bell	1985	Marcus Allen, LA Raiders, RB	AP-PFWA
1978	Terry Bradshaw, Pittsburgh, QB	AP-Bell		& Walter Payton, Chicago, RB	Bell
	& Earl Campbell, Houston, RB	PFWA	1986	Lawrence Taylor, NY Giants, LB	AP-Bell-PFWA
1979	Earl Campbell, Houston, RB	AP-Bell-PFWA	1987	Jerry Rice, San Francisco, WR	Bell-PFWA
				& John Elway, Denver, QB	AP
1980	Brian Sipe, Cleveland, QB	AP-PFWA	1988	Boomer Esiason, Cincinnati, QB	AP-PFWA
	& Ron Jaworski, Philadelphia, QB	Bell		& Randall Cunningham, Phila, QB	Bell
1981	Ken Anderson, Cincinnati, QB	AP-Bell-PFWA	1989	Joe Montana, San Francisco, QB	AP-Bell-PFWA
1982	Mark Moseley, Washington, PK	AP			
	Joe Theismann, Washington, QB	Bell	1990	Randall Cunningham, Phila., QB	Bell-PFWA
	& Dan Fouts, San Diego, QB	PFWA		& Joe Montana, San Francisco, QB	AP
1983	Joe Theismann, Washington, QB	AP-PFWA	1991	Thurman Thomas, Buffalo, RB	AP,PFWA
	& John Riggins, Washington, RB	Bell		& Barry Sanders, Detroit, RB	Bell

NFC Player of the Year

Given out by UPI since 1970. Offensive and defensive players have been honored since 1983. Rookie winners are in **bold** type.

Multiple winners: Eric Dickerson and Mike Singletary (3); Walter Payton and Lawrence Taylor (2).

Year		Pos	Year		Pos
1970	John Brodie, San Francisco	QB	1985	Off—Walter Payton, Chicago	RB
1971	Alan Page, Minnesota	DT		Def—Mike Singletary, Chicago	LB
1972	Larry Brown, Washington	RB	1986	Off—Eric Dickerson, Los Angeles	RB
1973	John Hadl, Los Angeles	QB		Def—Lawrence Taylor, New York	LB
1974	Jim Hart, St.Louis	QB	1987	Off—Jerry Rice, San Francisco	WR
1975	Fran Tarkenton, Minnesota	QB		Def—Reggie White, Philadelphia	DE
1976	Chuck Foreman, Minnesota	RB	1988	Off—Roger Craig, San Francisco	RB
1977	Walter Payton, Chicago	RB		Def—Mike Singletary, Chicago	LB
1978	Archie Manning, New Orleans	QB	1989	Off—Joe Montana, San Francisco	QB
1979	**Ottis Anderson**, St.Louis	RB		Def—Keith Millard, Minnesota	DT
1980	Ron Jaworski, Philadelphia	QB	1990	Off—Randall Cunningham, Philadelphia	QB
1981	Tony Dorsett, Dallas	RB		Def—Charles Haley, San Francisco	LB
1982	Mark Moseley, Washington	PK	1991	Off—Mark Rypien, Washington	QB
1983	Off—**Eric Dickerson**, Los Angeles	RB		Def—Reggie White, Philadelphia	DE
	Def—Lawrence Taylor, New York	LB			
1984	Off—Eric Dickerson, Los Angeles	RB			
	Def—Mike Singletary, Chicago	LB			

AFL-AFC Player of the Year

Presented by UPI to the top player in the AFL (1960-69) and AFC (since 1970). Offensive and defensive players have been honored since 1983. Rookie winners are in **bold** type.

Multiple winners: O.J.Simpson and Bruce Smith (3); Cornelius Bennett, George Blanda, Dan Fouts, Daryle Lamonica and Curt Warner (2).

Year		Pos	Year		Pos
1960	**Abner Haynes**, Dallas Texans	HB	1982	Dan Fouts, San Diego	QB
1961	George Blanda, Houston	QB	1983	Off—**Curt Warner**, Seattle	RB
1962	Cookie Gilchrist, Buffalo	FB		Def—Rod Martin, Los Angeles	LB
1963	Lance Alworth, San Diego	FL	1984	Off—Dan Marino, Miami	QB
1964	Gino Cappelletti, Boston	FL-PK		Def—Mark Gastineau, New York	DE
1965	Paul Lowe, San Diego	HB	1985	Off—Marcus Allen, Los Angeles	RB
1966	Jim Nance, Boston	FB		Def—Andre Tippett, New England	LB
1967	Daryle Lamonica, Oakland	QB	1986	Off—Curt Warner, Seattle	RB
1968	Joe Namath, New York	QB		Def—Rulon Jones, Denver	DE
1969	Daryle Lamonica, Oakland	QB	1987	Off—John Elway, Denver	QB
				Def—Bruce Smith, Buffalo	DE
1970	George Blanda, Oakland	QB-PK	1988	Off—Boomer Esiason, Cincinnatti	QB
1971	Otis Taylor, Kansas City	WR		Def—Bruce Smith, Buffalo	DE
1972	O.J.Simpson, Buffalo	RB		& Cornelius Bennett, Buffalo	LB
1973	O.J.Simpson, Buffalo	RB	1989	Off—Christian Okoye, Kansas City	RB
1974	Ken Stabler, Oakland	QB		Def—Michael Dean Perry, Cleveland	NT
1975	O.J.Simpson, Buffalo	RB			
1976	Bert Jones, Baltimore	QB	1990	Off—Warren Moon, Houston	QB
1977	Craig Morton, Denver	QB		Def—Bruce Smith, Buffalo	DE
1978	**Earl Campbell**, Houston	RB	1991	Off—Thurman Thomas, Buffalo	RB
1979	Dan Fouts, San Diego	QB		Def—Cornelius Bennett, Buffalo	LB
1980	Brian Sipe, Cleveland	QB			
1981	Ken Anderson, Cincinnati	QB			

NFL-NFC Rookie of the Year

Presented by UPI to the top rookie in the NFL (1955-69) and NFC (since 1970). Players who were the overall first pick in the NFL draft are in **bold** type.

Year		Pos	Year		Pos	Year		Pos
1955	Alan Ameche, Bal	FB	1970	Bruce Taylor, SF	DB	1982	Jim McMahon, Chi	QB
1956	Lenny Moore, Bal	HB	1971	John Brockington, GB	RB	1983	Eric Dickerson, LA	RB
1957	Jim Brown, Cle.	FB	1972	Chester Marcol, GB.	PK	1984	Paul McFadden, Phi.	PK
1958	Jimmy Orr, Pit.	FL	1973	Charle Young, Phi	TE	1985	Jerry Rice, SF.	WR
1959	Boyd Dowler, GB	FL	1974	John Hicks, NY	G	1986	Reuben Mayes, NO.	RB
			1975	Mike Thomas, Wash	RB	1987	Robert Awalt, St.L.	TE
1960	Gail Cogdill, Det	FL	1976	Sammy White, Min.	WR	1988	Keith Jackson, Phi	TE
1961	Mike Ditka, Chi	TE	1977	Tony Dorsett, Dal.	RB	1989	Barry Sanders, Det.	RB
1962	Ronnie Bull, Chi	FB	1978	Bubba Baker, Det	DE			
1963	Paul Flatley, Min.	FL	1979	Ottis Anderson, St.L.	RB	1990	Mark Carrier, Chi	S
1964	Charley Taylor, Wash.	HB				1991	Lawrence Dawsey, TB	WR
1965	Gale Sayers, Chi.	HB	1980	**Billy Sims,** Det	RB			
1966	Johnny Roland, St.L	HB	1981	**George Rogers,** NO	RB			
1967	Mel Farr, Det	RB						
1968	Earl McCullough, Det	FL						
1969	Calvin Hill, Dal.	RB						

AFL-AFC Rookie of the Year

Presented by UPI to the top rookie in the AFL (1960-69) and AFC (since 1970). Players who were the overall first pick in the AFL or NFL draft are in **bold** type.

Year		Pos	Year		Pos	Year		Pos
1960	Abner Haynes, Dal	HB	1972	Franco Harris, Pit.	RB	1984	Louis Lipps, Pit	WR
1961	Earl Faison, SD	DE	1973	Boobie Clark, Cin	RB	1985	Kevin Mack, Cle.	RB
1962	Curtis McClinton, Dal	FB	1974	Don Woods, SD.	RB	1986	Leslie O'Neal, SD	DE
1963	Billy Joe, Den	FB	1975	Robert Brazile, Hou	LB	1987	Shane Conlan, Buf.	LB
1964	Matt Snell, NY	FB	1976	Mike Haynes, NE	DB	1988	John Stephens, NE.	RB
1965	Joe Namath, NY	QB	1977	A.J.Duhe, Mia	DE	1989	Derrick Thomas, KC	LB
1966	Bobby Burnett, Buf	HB	1978	**Earl Campbell,** Hou	RB			
1967	George Webster, Hou	LB	1979	Jerry Butler, Buf	WR	1990	Richmond Webb, Mia	OT
1968	Paul Robinson, Cin	RB				1991	Mike Croel, Den.	LB
1969	Greg Cook, Cin	QB	1980	Joe Cribbs, Buf	RB			
			1981	Joe Delaney, KC	RB			
1970	Dennis Shaw, Buf	QB	1982	Marcus Allen, LA	RB			
1971	**Jim Plunkett,** NE	QB	1983	Curt Warner, Sea.	RB			

NFL-NFC Coach of the Year

Presented by UPI to the top coach in the NFL (1955-69) and NFC (since 1970). Records indicate how much coach's team improved over one season.

Multiple winners: George Allen, Leeman Bennett, Mike Ditka, George Halas, Tom Landry, Jack Pardee, Allie Sherman, Don Shula and Bill Walsh (2).

Year		Improvement	Year		Improvement
1955	Joe Kuharich, Washington	3-9 to 8-4	1976	Jack Pardee, Chicago	4-10 to 7-7
1956	Buddy Parker, Detroit	3-9 to 9-3	1977	Leeman Bennett, Atlanta	4-10 to 7-7
1957	Paul Brown, Cleveland	5-7 to 9-2-1	1978	Dick Vermeil, Philadelphia	5-9 to 9-7
1958	Weeb Ewbank, Baltimore	7-5 to 9-3	1979	Jack Pardee, Washington	8-8 to 10-6
1959	Vince Lombardi, Green Bay	1-10-1 to 7-5			
1960	Buck Shaw, Philadelphia	7-5 to 10-2	1980	Leeman Bennett, Atlanta	6-10 to 12-4
1961	Allie Sherman, New York	6-4-2 to 10-3-1	1981	Bill Walsh, San Francisco	6-10 to 13-3
1962	Allie Sherman, New York	10-3-1 to 12-2	1982	Joe Gibbs, Washington	8-8 to 8-1
1963	George Halas, Chicago	9-5 to 11-1-2	1983	John Robinson, Los Angeles	2-7 to 9-7
1964	Don Shula, Baltimore	8-6 to 12-2	1984	Bill Walsh, San Francisco	10-6 to 15-1
1965	George Halas, Chicago	5-9 to 9-5	1985	Mike Ditka, Chicago	10-6 to 15-1
1966	Tom Landry, Dallas	7-7 to 10-3-1	1986	Bill Parcells, New York	10-6 to 14-2
1967	George Allen, Los Angeles	8-6 to 11-1-2	1987	Jim Mora, New Orleans	7-9 to 12-3
1968	Don Shula, Baltimore	11-1-2 to 13-1	1988	Mike Ditka, Chicago	11-4 to 12-4
1969	Bud Grant, Minnesota	8-6 to 12-2	1989	Lindy Infante, Green Bay	4-12 to 10-6
1970	Alex Webster, New York	6-8 to 9-5	1990	Jimmy Johnson, Dallas	1-15 to 7-9
1971	George Allen, Washington	6-8 to 9-4-1	1991	Wayne Fontes, Detroit	6-10 to 12-4
1972	Dan Devine, Green Bay	4-8-2 to 10-4			
1973	Chuck Knox, Los Angeles	6-7-1 to 12-2			
1974	Don Coryell, St.Louis	4-9-1 to 10-4			
1975	Tom Landry, Dallas	8-6 to 10-4			

AFL-AFC Coach of the Year

Presented by UPI to the top coach in the AFL (1960-69) and AFC (since 1970). Records indicate how much coach's team improved over one season. The AFC began play in 1960.
Multiple winners: Chuck Knox, Sam Rutigliano, Lou Saban, Dan Reeves and Don Shula (2)

Year		Improvement	Year		Improvement
1960	Lou Rymkus, Houston	10-4	1976	Chuck Fairbanks, New England	3-11 to 11-3
1961	Wally Lemm, Houston	10-4 to 10-3-1	1977	Red Miller, Denver	9-5 to 12-2
1962	Jack Faulkner, Denver	3-11 to 7-7	1978	Walt Michaels, New York	3-11 to 8-8
1963	Al Davis, Oakland	1-13 to 10-4	1979	Sam Rutigliano, Cleveland	8-8 to 9-7
1964	Lou Saban, Buffalo	7-6-1 to 12-2			
1965	Lou Saban, Buffalo	12-2 to 10-3-1	1980	Sam Rutigliano, Cleveland	9-7 to 11-5
1966	Mike Holovak, Boston	4-8-2 to 8-4-2	1981	Forrest Gregg, Cincinnati	6-10 to 12-4
1967	John Rauch, Oakland	8-5-1 to 13-1	1982	Tom Flores, Los Angeles	7-9 to 8-1
1968	Hank Stram, Kansas City	9-5 to 12-2	1983	Chuck Knox, Seattle	4-5 to 9-7
1969	Paul Brown, Cincinnati	3-11 to 4-9-1	1984	Chuck Knox, Seattle	9-7 to 12-4
			1985	Raymond Berry, New England	9-7 to 11-5
1970	Don Shula, Miami	3-10-1 to 10-4	1986	Marty Schottenheimer, Cleveland	8-8 to 12-4
1971	Don Shula, Miami	10-4 to 10-3-1	1987	Ron Meyer, Indianapolis	3-13 to 9-6
1972	Chuck Noll, Pittsburgh	6-8 to 11-3	1988	Marv Levy, Buffalo	7-8 to 12-4
1973	John Ralston, Denver	5-9 to 7-5-2	1989	Dan Reeves, Denver	8-8 to 11-5
1974	Sid Gillman, Houston	1-13 to 7-7			
1975	Ted Marchibroda, Baltimore	2-12 to 10-4	1990	Art Shell, Los Angeles	8-8 to 12-4
			1991	Dan Reeves, Denver	5-11 to 12-4

Canadian Football
The Grey Cup

Earl Grey, the Governor-General of Canada (1904-11) donated a trophy in 1909 for the Rugby Football Championship of Canada. The trophy, which later became known as the Grey Cup, was originally open to competition for teams registered with the Canada Rugby Union. Since 1954, the Cup has gone to the champion of the Canadian Football League (CFL).
Multiple winners: Toronto Argonauts (12); Edmonton Eskimos (10); Winnipeg Blue Bombers (9); Hamilton Tiger-Cats and Ottawa Rough Riders (7); Hamilton Tigers (5); Montreal Alouettes and University of Toronto (4); Queen's University (3); B.C. Lions, Calgary Stampeders, Ottawa Senators, Sarnia Imperials, Saskatchewan Roughriders and Toronto Balmy Beach (2).
CFL multiple winners (since 1954): Edmonton (10); Winnipeg (7); Hamilton (6); Ottawa (5); Montreal (3); B.C. Lions, Saskatchewan and Toronto (2).

Year	Cup Final	Year	Cup Final
1909	Univ.of Toronto 26, Toronto Parkdale 6	1934	Sarnia Imperials 20, Regina Roughriders 12
1910	Univ.of Toronto 16, Hamilton Tigers 7	1935	Winnipegs 18, Hamilton Tigers 12
1911	Univ.of Toronto 14, Toronto Argonauts 7	1936	Sarnia Imperials 26, Ottawa Rough Riders 20
1912	Hamilton Alerts 11, Toronto Argonauts 4	1937	Toronto Argonauts 4, Winnipeg Blue Bombers 3
1913	Hamilton Tigers 44, Toronto Parkdale 2	1938	Toronto Argonauts 30, Winnipeg Blue Bombers 7
1914	Toronto Argonauts 14, Univ.of Toronto 2	1939	Winnipeg Blue Bombers 8, Ottawa Rough Riders 7
1915	Hamilton Tigers 13, Toronto Rowing 7		
1916-19	Not held (WWI)	1940	Gm 1: Ottawa Rough Riders 8, Toronto B-Beach 2
			Gm 2: Ottawa Rough Riders 12, Toronto B-Beach 5
1920	Univ.of Toronto 16, Toronto Argonauts 3	1941	Winnipeg Blue Bombers 18, Ottawa Rough Riders 16
1921	Toronto Argonauts 23, Edmonton Eskimos 0	1942	Toronto RACF 8, Winnipeg RACF 5
1922	Queens Univ. 13, Edmonton Elks 1	1943	Hamilton Wildcats 23, Winnipeg RACF 14
1923	Queens Univ. 54, Regina Roughriders 0	1944	Montreal HMCS 7, Hamilton Wildcats 6
1924	Queens Univ. 11, Toronto Balmy Beach 3	1945	Toronto Argonauts 35, Winnipeg Blue Bombers 0
1925	Ottawa Senators 24, Winnipeg Tigers 1	1946	Toronto Argonauts 28, Winnipeg Blue Bombers 6
1926	Ottawa Senators 10, Univ.of Toronto 7	1947	Toronto Argonauts 10, Winnipeg Blue Bombers 9
1927	Toronto Balmy Beach 9, Hamilton Tigers 6	1948	Calgary Stampeders 12, Ottawa Rough Riders 7
1928	Hamilton Tigers 30, Regina Roughriders 0	1949	Montreal Alouettes 28, Calgary Stampeders 15
1929	Hamilton Tigers 14, Regina Roughriders 3		
		1950	Toronto Argonauts 13, Winnipeg Blue Bombers 0
1930	Toronto Balmy Beach 11, Regina Roughriders 6	1951	Ottawa Rough Riders 21, Saskatch.Roughriders 14
1931	Montreal AAA 22, Regina Roughriders 0	1952	Toronto Argonauts 21, Edmonton Eskimos 11
1932	Hamilton Tigers 25, Regina Roughriders 6	1953	Hamilton Tiger-Cats 12, Winnipeg Blue Bombers 6
1933	Toronto Argonauts 4, Sarnia Imperials 3		

Year	Winner	Head Coach	Score	Loser	Head Coach	Site
1954	Edmonton	Frank (Pop) Ivy	26-25	Montreal	Doug Walker	Toronto
1955	Edmonton	Frank (Pop) Ivy	34-19	Montreal	Doug Walker	Vancouver
1956	Edmonton	Frank (Pop) Ivy	50-27	Montreal	Doug Walker	Toronto
1957	Hamilton	Jim Trimble	32- 7	Winnipeg	Bud Grant	Toronto
1958	Winnipeg	Bud Grant	35-28	Hamilton	Jim Trimble	Vancouver
1959	Winnipeg	Bud Grant	21- 7	Hamilton	Jim Trimble	Toronto

Canadian Football (Cont.)
The Grey Cup

Year	Winner	Head Coach	Score	Loser	Head Coach	Site
1960	Ottawa	Frank Clair	16- 6	Edmonton	Eagle Keys	Vancouver
1961	Winnipeg	Bud Grant	21-14*	Hamilton	Jim Trimble	Toronto
1962	Winnipeg	Bud Grant	28-27**	Hamilton	Jim Trimble	Toronto
1963	Hamilton	Ralph Sazio	21-10	B.C. Lions	Dave Skrien	Vancouver
1964	B.C. Lions	Dave Skrien	34-24	Hamilton	Ralph Sazio	Toronto
1965	Hamilton	Ralph Sazio	22-16	Winnipeg	Bud Grant	Toronto
1966	Saskatchewan	Eagle Keys	29-14	Ottawa	Frank Clair	Vancouver
1967	Hamilton	Ralph Sazio	24- 1	Saskatchewan	Eagle Keys	Ottawa
1968	Ottawa	Frank Clair	24-21	Calgary	Jerry Williams	Toronto
1969	Ottawa	Frank Clair	29-11	Saskatchewan	Eagle Keys	Montreal
1970	Montreal	Sam Etcheverry	23-10	Calgary	Jim Duncan	Toronto
1971	Calgary	Jim Duncan	14-11	Toronto	Leo Cahill	Vancouver
1972	Hamilton	Jerry Williams	13-10	Saskatchewan	Dave Skrien	Hamilton
1973	Ottawa	Jack Gotta	22-18	Edmonton	Ray Jauch	Toronto
1974	Montreal	Marv Levy	20- 7	Edmonton	Ray Jauch	Vancouver
1975	Edmonton	Ray Jauch	9- 8	Montreal	Marv Levy	Calgary
1976	Ottawa	George Brancato	23-20	Saskatchewan	John Payne	Toronto
1977	Montreal	Marv Levy	41- 6	Edmonton	Hugh Campbell	Montreal
1978	Edmonton	Hugh Campbell	20-13	Montreal	Joe Scannella	Toronto
1979	Edmonton	Hugh Campbell	17- 9	Montreal	Joe Scannella	Montreal
1980	Edmonton	Hugh Campbell	48-10	Hamilton	John Payne	Toronto
1981	Edmonton	Hugh Campbell	26-23	Ottawa	George Brancato	Montreal
1982	Edmonton	Hugh Campbell	32-16	Toronto	Bob O'Billovich	Toronto
1983	Toronto	Bob O'Billovich	18-17	B.C. Lions	Don Matthews	Vancouver
1984	Winnipeg	Cal Murphy	47-17	Hamilton	Al Bruno	Edmonton
1985	B.C. Lions	Don Matthews	37-24	Hamilton	Al Bruno	Montreal
1986	Hamilton	Al Bruno	39-15	Edmonton	Jack Parker	Vancouver
1987	Edmonton	Joe Faragalli	38-36	Toronto	Bob O'Billovich	Vancouver
1988	Winnipeg	Mike Riley	22-21	B.C. Lions	Larry Donovan	Ottawa
1989	Saskatchewan	John Gregory	43-40	Hamilton	Al Bruno	Toronto
1990	Winnipeg	Mike Riley	50-11	Edmonton	Joe Faragalli	Vancouver
1991	Toronto	Adam Rita	36-21	Calgary	Wally Buono	Winnipeg

*Overtime.
**Halted by fog in 4th quarter, final 9:29 played the following day.

CFL Most Outstanding Player

Regular season Player of the Year as selected by The Football Reporters of Canada since 1953.
Multiple winners: Russ Jackson and Jackie Parker (3); Dieter Brock and Ron Lancaster (2).

Year		Year		Year	
1953	Billy Vessels, Edmonton, RB	1966	Russ Jackson, Ottawa, QB	1980	Dieter Brock, Winnipeg, QB
1954	Sam Etcheverry, Montreal, QB	1967	Peter Liske, Calgary, QB	1981	Dieter Brock, Winnipeg, QB
1955	Pat Abbruzzi, Montreal, RB	1968	Bill Symons, Toronto, RB	1982	Condredge Holloway, Tor., QB
1956	Hal Patterson, Montreal, E-DB	1969	Russ Jackson, Ottawa, QB	1983	Warren Moon, Edmonton, QB
1957	Jackie Parker, Edmonton, RB			1984	Willard Reaves, Winnipeg, RB
1958	Jackie Parker, Edmonton, QB	1970	Ron Lancaster, Saskatchewan, QB	1985	Merv Fernandez, B.C. Lions, WR
1959	Johnny Bright, Edmonton, RB	1971	Don Jonas, Winnipeg, QB	1986	James Murphy, Winnipeg, WR
		1973	Geo. McGowan, Edmonton, WR	1987	Tom Clements, Winnipeg, QB
1960	Jackie Parker, Edmonton, QB	1974	Tom Wilkinson, Edmonton, QB	1988	David Williams, B.C. Lions, WR
1961	Bernie Faloney, Hamilton, QB	1975	Willie Burden, Calgary, RB	1989	Tracy Ham, Edmonton, QB
1962	George Dixon, Montreal, RB	1976	Ron Lancaster, Saskatchewan, QB		
1963	Russ Jackson, Ottawa, QB	1977	Jimmy Edwards, Hamilton, RB	1990	Mike Clemons, Toronto, RB
1964	Lovell Coleman, Calgary, RB	1978	Tony Gabriel, Ottawa, TE	1991	Doug Flutie, B.C. Lions, QB
1965	George Reed, Saskatchewan, RB	1979	David Green, Montreal, RB		

CFL Most Outstanding Rookie

Regular season Rookie of the Year as selected by The Football Reporters of Canada since 1972.

Year		Year		Year	
1972	Chuck Ealey, Hamilton, QB	1980	William Miller, Winnipeg, RB	1988	Orville Lee, Ottawa, RB
1973	Johnny Rodgers, Montreal, WR	1981	Vince Goldsmith, Saskatchewan, LB	1989	Stephen Jordan, Hamilton, DB
1974	Sam Cvijanovich, Toronto, LB	1982	Chris Issac, Ottawa, QB		
1975	Tom Clements, Ottawa, QB	1983	Johnny Shepherd, Hamilton, RB	1990	Reggie Barnes, Ottawa, RB
1976	John Sciarra, B.C. Lions, QB	1984	Dwaine Wilson, Montreal, RB	1991	Jon Volpe, B.C. Lions, RB
1977	Leon Bright, B.C. Lions, WR	1985	Mike Gray, B.C. Lions, DT		
1978	Joe Poplawski, Winnipeg, WR	1986	Harold Hallman, Calgary, DT		
1979	Brian Kelly, Edmonton, WR	1987	Gill Fenerty, Toronto, RB		

Wide World Photos

Duke center **Christian Laettner** lets go of the overtime buzzer-beater that defeated Kentucky, 104-103, in the NCAA East Regional final.

COLLEGE BASKETBALL

Devils' Food

Duke downs Michigan's Fab Five in the NCAA Final, 71-51, becoming the first repeat national champion in 19 years.

The way Duke coach Mike Krzyzewski looked at it, the Blue Devils had nothing to defend in 1991-92. The national championship trophy won a season earlier at Indianapolis was safely stored. The ink in the NCAA record books was completely dry. And the memories of upsetting mighty UNLV in the Final Four semifinals were appropriately cherished.

If anything, Krzyzewski tried to distance himself and his team from that NCAA trophy. After all, this was a new season, a new schedule and a new set of dynamics.

"We don't look at defending anything because it is a different team, even though we have a lot of guys back," Krzyzewski said at the season's beginning. "Each year is different, just like it has been in the past."

As it turned out, Krzyzewski was right—Duke, ranked No. 1 from start to finish, defended nothing. Instead, the Blue Devils (34-2) earned every bit of a second consecutive national championship, the first team to do so since John Wooden-led UCLA accomplished the feat in 1973.

This time, in the billowy confines of the Minneapolis Metrodome, Duke beat Michigan and the Fabulous Five (the Wolverines' remarkable all-freshmen starting lineup), 71-51, in front of 50,379 fans.

Gene Wojciechowski is the national college basketball writer for the *Los Angeles Times* and a columnist for *The Sporting News*.

To do so, the Blue Devils had to overcome a one-point Wolverine lead at halftime, an ankle injury to starting senior swingman Brian Davis, a so-so first half performance by All-America center Christian Laettner, and the growing suspicion that maybe Duke wasn't so invincible, after all.

Yes, well, tell it to the Maize and Blue, who were outscored 23-6 in the final 6:51 of the game. Michigan (25-9) couldn't do much of anything in the second half, except miss shot after shot and watch as Duke took advantage of nearly every mistake.

In all, the Wolverines converted only 29% of their field goals in the final period and a slightly less miserable 37.9% for the game. NCAA history buffs will also note that Michigan's 51 points was the second-lowest total in a championship game since 1949.

The Fab Five, consisting of center Chris Webber, guards Jalen Rose and Jimmy King, and forwards Juwan Howard and Ray Jackson, reacted to the loss—their second of the season to Duke—with varying degrees of emotion. Many of the players cried and at one point, Webber cursed and berated a cameraman who recorded his postgame tears. A more composed Webber later apologized for his actions.

"Cry, that's part of it," Michigan coach Steve Fisher told his team in the locker room. "Feel awful, but proud of what you've done

Colleen Fitzgerald/The Ann Arbor News

Michigan's Fab Five starting freshmen (from left to right): **Jimmy King, Juwan Howard, Chris Webber, Jalen Rose,** and **Ray Jackson.**

and be determined you're going to learn from this game. And set your sights next year as high as they were this year."

To the assembled media, Fisher was more succinct. "We're crushed and we should be," he said.

Responsible for many of Michigan's tears was Duke sophomore swingman Grant Hill, who seems to save his finest performances for the Final Four. Last year against Kansas in the championship game, Hill provided the Blue Devils with 10 points, eight rebounds, three assists, two blocks and two steals. Against Michigan, he scored 18 points and finished with 10 rebounds, five assists, three steals and two blocks. Ten of those 18 points came in the final 5:41 of the game, when the Wolverines still threatened.

Junior point guard Bobby Hurley, who was named the Final Four's Most Outstanding Player, scored only nine points but he had seven assists, played with four fouls during the final nine minutes and calmed the Blue Devils during the Wolverines' early runs.

And then there was Laettner, who made just two of eight shots while committing an unsightly seven turnovers in the

first half. He finished with 19 points, seven rebounds and a second championship ring in four trips to the Final Four.

"It wasn't the prettiest game, but we were resilient out there," Hurley said. "We got the job done."

The same could be said of Duke's entire season. It won its first 17 games before losing to North Carolina by two points, 75-73, at Chapel Hill on Feb. 5. More disturbing than the loss itself was a foot injury to Hurley. A broken bone caused him to miss five games, including a four-point loss to Wake Forest on Feb. 23.

"I think they need Bobby Hurley to make another run at the national championship," said Georgia Tech's Bobby Cremins at the time.

Meanwhile, North Carolina's Dean Smith suggested that Duke might actually benefit from Hurley's forced departure.

They were both correct. Without Hurley, the Blue Devils lacked perhaps the best point guard in college. But because of his absence, other players—most notably Grant Hill—found themselves in different or expanded roles. By the time Hurley returned to the lineup on Feb. 26, Krzyzewski had a deeper, more capable team.

247

Duke didn't lose another game after Hurley's return. It beat an improved UCLA team at Pauley Pavilion. It avenged the loss to North Carolina. It swept through the ACC Tournament—one of the few titles to elude Coach K and company in recent years—and beat the Tar Heels by 20 in the final. They were seeded first in the East Regional of the NCAAs and proceeded to defeat Campbell University, Iowa and Seton Hall before facing Kentucky for the right to advance to the Final Four.

As usual, Duke was favored. But the undersized and overmatched Wildcats weren't interested in pregame spreads. Using its two favorite weapons—the press and the three-point shot—Kentucky overcame double-digit Duke leads in the second half, pushed the game into overtime and, with 2.1 seconds remaining, led, 103-102.

Down by that single point with a scant few seconds left on the clock and his team moments away from elimination, Krzyzewski diagrammed a final play. That done, he said, "We're going to get a good shot. We can win."

Moments later, Hill heaved the ball 77 feet to a double-teamed Laettner, who caught the pass near the Duke free throw line, took one dribble, faked right, pivoted left and then, as the buzzer was ready to sound, released a 17-foot jump shot that touched nothing but the bottom of the net.

NCAA basketball observers called it the greatest college game ever played and for once, the hyperbole might be justified. The praise certainly applied to Laettner, who made each of his 10 field goal attempts and each of his 10 free throws. He played 43 of the 45 minutes, scored 31 points and added seven rebounds. Except for any ugly moment when he stepped on the chest of Wildcat Aminu Timberlake, Laettner was near perfect on the court.

"I felt like I was watching Robert Redford in 'The Natural,'" Hill said.

Added Krzyzewski: "I think we've all been part of one of the great games ever."

For Kentucky (29-7), the loss was both painful and, in a strange way, encouraging. In fact, as several players fought back tears in the Wildcat locker room, coach Rick Pitino reminded his team how

Wide World Photos

No stranger to controversy, Indiana coach **Bob Knight** prospered in the NCAAs, but drew some heat from the NAACP for cracking the whip in practice at the West Regionals.

far the once-disgraced program had come since NCAA sanctions were imposed in 1989.

"We are not losers," Pitino told reporters. "I told the guys, 'Don't let two seconds determine your basketball life because it's worth more than that.' And I showed them an article, a front-page story from *Sports Illustrated* three years ago that said, 'Kentucky's Shame.' From three years to now, I couldn't be any more proud of a basketball team."

Duke joined Michigan, Indiana and Cincinnati in the Final Four. It was the Blue Devils' fifth appearance in as many years, a streak surpassed only by UCLA.

Meanwhile, Bob Knight's Hoosiers were making their first Final Four appearance since 1987, the year they beat Syracuse for the championship. Along the way to Minneapolis, Knight managed to attract controversy with his sometimes bizarre press conferences and an incident in which he was photographed playfully wielding a bullwhip over junior forward Calbert Cheaney during a practice at the West Regionals.

The local chapter of the NAACP decried Knight's actions, however innocent they might have been, and said the coach was racially insensitive.

"Don't bother me with that [bleep]," said Knight.

Cheaney insisted he wasn't offended and that the whip was a present from the players themselves. To prove his point, Cheaney later snapped a towel at Knight during the waning moments of the West Regional final against UCLA.

The bullwhip imbroglio partially overshadowed a season in which the Hoosiers almost won another national title. As it was, Indiana (27-7) came within three points of upsetting Duke in the semifinals. Equally compelling was the confrontation of sorts between the two Coach Ks. Knight coached Krzyzewski at Army and Krzyzewski was later a Knight assistant at Indiana.

The other semifinal wasn't quite as dramatic, but it did have its share of subplots.

For Michigan, it was another chance at the improbable. In 1989, the Wolverines shocked everyone, including themselves, by winning the tournament. Three years later, led by the most heralded freshman recruiting class of recent memory, Michigan needed two more victories to earn a second championship.

The Wolverines beat Cincinnati, 76-72, but it wasn't easy. The surprising Bearcats, whose lineup included eight former junior college players and two Division I transfers, finished 29-5 and confirmed what insiders already knew—that Bob Huggins was a coach worth watching.

In fact, the entire Great Midwest Conference was worth another look. In only its first year of existence, the league was represented by Cincinnati in the Final Four, Memphis State in the Regional Finals and DePaul in the first round.

Several more-established conferences were not as successful. For the third consecutive season and fourth out of the last five, no Big East team advanced to the Final Four. The Southeastern Conference hasn't had a representative since 1986 (newcomer Arkansas doesn't count). As for the Southwest Conference, with Arkansas gone, the less said the better.

Also struggling was the Big West, which had to make do without talented but troubled UNLV (see box). NCAA-imposed sanctions prevented the Runnin' Rebels,

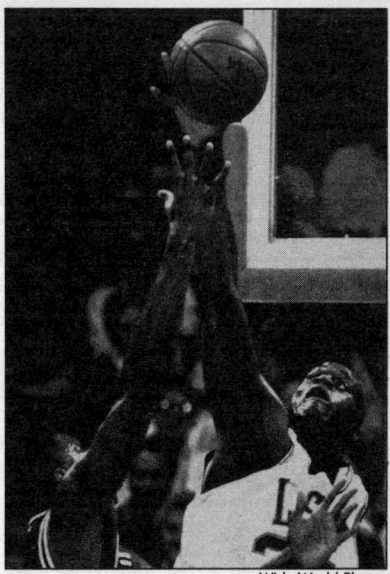

Wide World Photos

LSU center **Shaquille O'Neal** led the nation in blocked shots with over five a game, then led the parade of juniors declaring for the NBA Draft.

national champions as recently as 1990, from playing any postseason games. If not for the unexpected success of New Mexico State, which advanced to the Sweet 16, the Big West's season would have been a disaster.

Despite the many controversies surrounding the program, UNLV finished at 26-2 and No. 7 in the final regular season Associated Press media poll. The 26 wins were even more remarkable in light of the almost daily developments at Vegas. The short list: coach Jerry Tarkanian rescinded his resignation; the *Las Vegas Review-Journal* published a story saying that a federal task force was investigating allegations of point shaving; Tarkanian and school officials traded verbal shots; and Tarkanian threatened to run for the state's Board of Regents.

All that ended on Apr. 15, when Tarkanian accepted an offer to coach the NBA's San Antonio Spurs.

Tarkanian's departure sparked a nationwide search by UNLV athletic director Jim Weaver. In a bit of a shock, Weaver chose Villanova's Rollie Massimino, who immediately vowed to clean and buff the

Rebels' tainted national image. For his trouble, Massimino received a five-year, $2-million contract. With outside income, the figure could reach $3.5 million.

The 57-year old Massimino felt unappreciated at Villanova, where he won an NCAA title in 1985. At Vegas, he inherited a program that is currently facing nearly 40 NCAA violations and the distinct possibility of more sanctions.

Massimino and Tarkanian weren't the only Division I coaches on the move during the off-season. In all, 27 changes were made before June, including 1992 Hall of Fame inductee Lou Carnesecca's decision to step down at St. John's. Carnesecca, 66, was the second oldest coach in Division I and departed with 526 victories and 24 postseason appearances.

Elsewhere, Manhattan's Steve Lappas, a former Villanova assistant, took Massimino's place; Carnesecca assistant Brian Mahoney was promoted at St.John's; Baylor fired Gene Iba; Scott Thompson left Rice for Wichita State; Rob Evans became the first black basketball head coach at Ole Miss; and Stu Jackson, the NBA's Director of Basketball Operations, was named at Wisconsin. Jackson thus became the third straight ex-New York Knicks coach to take a college job, following Pitino and Notre Dame's John MacLeod.

George Raveling, tempted by an offer to become executive director of the National Association of Basketball Coaches, decided to stay at Southern Cal, where he has helped energize the Trojan program. His decision was made easier by a five-year contract extension. UCLA's Jim Harrick also received a raise for his efforts to move the Bruins back into national prominence.

But at Alabama, Wimp Sanderson was pressured to resign in May after 12 years and 10 NCAA tournament appearances when his longtime secretary Nancy Watts filed sex discrimination charges against him for striking her in the face during an argument in March.

In other postseason activity, a handful of star juniors, led by LSU center Shaquille O'Neal, left school early for the NBA Draft. Also opting for the pros were UPI Player of the Year Jim Jackson of Ohio State, Harold Miner of USC and Tracy Murray of UCLA.

Cantankerous Tark Bids Vegas Adieu

No matter how hard anyone tries, the legacy of Jerry Tarkanian won't soon be forgotten at UNLV.

How could it? Tarkanian won 509 games at Vegas and a national title in 1990. His overall record of 625-122 and career winning percentage of .837 make him the winningest coach in the history of the college game. His players adored him. His fans were as loyal as house pets. His peers respected his on-court tactics and teachings.

But Tarkanian's 19-year tenure at the school, which ended amidst acrimony and threats of lawsuits, was just as famous for his battles with the NCAA and later, with his own administration.

In April, when he left UNLV for the NBA's San Antonio Spurs, Tarkanian was the only college coach to have been placed on NCAA probation three times—a lasting reminder of his excesses.

Tarkanian made mistakes, some he admitted, some not. He said he should have never recruited the infamous Lloyd Daniels, a New York City high school star who had academic and drug problems. (Not surprisingly, thanks mostly to violations related to Daniels' recruitment, UNLV is a likely candidate for more sanctions.) But that was about it for *mea culpas*. He rarely apologized for indiscretions, no matter how obvious. He protected his team, his family and his friends. To Tarkanian, loyalty, no matter the costs, was a person's most important virtue.

Perhaps that is what made his final season at UNLV the strangest of all. It began with the Runnin' Rebels on probation (again), banned from television and postseason play. But the sanctions, part of a final resolution to the 14-year skirmish between Tarkanian and his most hated foe, the NCAA, were only part of the story.

Tarkanian himself had announced on June 7, 1991, his decision to resign after the 1991-92 season. "I love this university and I do not want to cause it any harm," he said at the time . But nine months later, in front of a packed audience at nearby Zion Methodist Church, Tarkanian said he was rescinding his resignation and would fight any efforts

Wide World Photos

Former UNLV coach **Jerry Tarkanian** answers questions at an April 15th press conference after being named the new head coach of the NBA's San Antonio Spurs.

by the UNLV administration to force him out.

At issue were allegations of UNLV point-shaving during the 1990-91 season, allegations which were supposedly being investigated by the Internal Revenue Service and the Organized Crime Strike Force.

"I bet you in a month's time you won't hear another thing about the [investigation]," Tarkanian angrily predicted.

Tarkanian immediately blamed UNLV legal counsel Brad Booke for somehow initiating the inquiry and leaking the rumors to the *Las Vegas Review-Journal*, which reported the story. "You don't have to be an FBI agent or Dick Tracy to know where it came from," Tarkanian said. "I've taken a lot through the years, but this is the worst." He also criticized school president Robert Maxson and vowed not to leave until "the truth is out."

Within weeks of the point-shaving rumors, federal authorities announced that no such investigation had ever taken place. It was sweet vindication for Tarkanian.

But this wasn't the only controversy involving the UNLV program. Booke ordered the installation of video cameras in a gym air-conditioning duct to secretly record alleged illegal Rebel workouts. Attendance was down about 7,000 fans per game and morale was shot.

Despite the upheaval, the Rebels managed to win 26 of their 28 games, an impressive feat considering that UNLV was without its five 1990-91 starters, including Larry Johnson, Stacey Augmon and Greg Anthony.

Tarkanian couldn't hide his emotions during the season finale against Utah State on March 3. For the first time all season, the 18,500-seat Thomas & Mack Center was sold out. Many of the fans wore "Keep Tark, Fire Maxson" T-shirts or carried signs to the same effect.

When Tarkanian walked onto the court during pregame warmups, he was greeted with a standing ovation. Some fans dabbed away tears. As for Tarkanian, he barely acknowledged the crowd.

But later, after UNLV had beaten Utah State, 63-53, and the lights were dimmed for the postgame ceremony, Tarkanian could be seen sipping continuously from a glass of water. It was a favorite Tarkanian ploy, one that he used whenever he tried to fight back tears. It didn't work. During a brief speech, Tarkanian had to stop and walk away from the microphone.

A month later, UNLV hired Villanova coach Rollie Massimino, whose commitment to academics and integrity was considered even more important than his ability to win games.

O'Neal, Jackson and Miner were all members of the consensus All-America team along with seniors Laettner and Alonzo Mourning of Georgetown.

While O'Neal and Mourning might have been considered the best pro prospects, it was Duke's Laettner who earned most of the Player of the Year nods—taking home the Wooden, Rupp, Eastman, Naismith and U.S. Basketball Writers awards—and was named as the only collegian on the U.S. Olympic team.

The consensus Coach of the Year was Tulane's Perry Clark, who was honored for reviving a program that went 21-8 during the regular season after being left for dead several years ago.

Elsewhere, the NCAA may have to examine its decision to allow television to dictate the starting times of its men's and women's tournament games. A Southeast Regional semifinal between Oklahoma State and Michigan at Lexington's Rupp Arena didn't begin until 10:20 P.M. and didn't finish until nearly 1 A.M.

A week later, the Southwest Missouri State-Western Kentucky semifinal of the Women's Final Four began at 9:30 A.M. at the Los Angeles Sports Arena. This was the tradeoff for the women: national television exposure in exchange for a gawdawful tipoff time. In a game that featured 63 fouls and seven players fouling out, Western Kentucky won, 84-72. A textbook piece of basketball it wasn't.

Not to worry. The game that followed between No. 1 Virginia and No. 3 Stanford more than compensated for the earlier foulfest. As a near-sellout crowd of 12,241 looked on, Stanford (30-3) rallied in the closing minutes and then survived not one, but two last-chance shots by the Cavaliers (32-2).

The 66-65 Stanford victory ended the remarkable career of Virginia's All-America guard and two-time Player of the Year Dawn Staley, whose 26-foot shot at the buzzer bounced off the backboard and away from the rim.

Stanford had little trouble defeating Western Kentucky, 78-62, for its second title in three years. Cardinal junior guard Molly Goodenbour was the tournament Most Outstanding Player.

The Virginia men won the National Invitation Tournament in New York, beating Notre Dame, 81-76, in overtime. Con-

Jim Gund/Allsport

Stanford won its second NCAA Division I women's title in three years and junior guard **Molly Goodenbour** was named the tournament's Most Outstanding Player.

sidering the brutal independent schedule the Fighting Irish had to play—Indiana, Kentucky, USC, North Carolina, Missouri, DePaul, Michigan, Syracuse, UCLA and St. John's among others—it's a good thing they had ex-NBA coach MacLeod at the helm.

Meanwhile, down in Durham another NCAA banner will hang from the rafters at Cameron Indoor Stadium.

Of course, with Duke's success comes higher expectations. The chant last heard by the Cameron Crazies who attended the Final Four? "Three-peat . . . Three-peat."

Speaking of high expectations, the fans of Division II Troy (Ala.) State could be chanting "Three-hundred . . . Three hundred" next season when the Trojans play DeVry Institute.

On Jan. 12, Troy State became the first team in NCAA history to score 200 points in a game, beating DeVry, 258-141. In all, 13 NCAA records were set, including 51 three point-baskets in 102 attempts by the winners.

In case you're wondering, the old record for points in a game also belonged to Troy State. In 1991, the Trojans beat (you guessed it) DeVry, 187-116.□

COLLEGE BASKETBALL
S T A T I S T I C S

THE SEASON IN REVIEW
1991-1992
TOP 25 • NCAA'S • STANDINGS

THE 1993 SPORTS ALMANAC — INFORMATION PLEASE

SEC **A**

PAGE **253**

Final Regular Season AP Men's Top 25 Poll

Taken before start of NCAA tournament.

The sportswriters & broadcasters poll: first place votes in parentheses; records through March 15; total points (based on 25 for 1st, 24 for 2nd, etc.); record in NCAA tourney and team lost to; head coach (career years and record, including NCAA tourney), and preseason ranking. Teams in **bold** type went on to reach NCAA Final Four.

	Mar. 15 Record	Points	NCAA Recap	Head Coach	Preseason Rank
1 **Duke**(64)	28-2	1624	6-0	Mike Krzyzewski (17th: 370-169)	1
2 Kansas	26-4	1543	1-1 (UTEP)	Roy Williams (4th: 103-30)	12
3 Ohio St	23-5	1461	3-1 (Michigan)	Randy Ayers (3rd: 70-23)	7
4 UCLA	25-4	1390	3-1 (Indiana)	Jim Harrick (13th: 261-132)	11
5 **Indiana**	23-6	1266	4-1 (Duke)	Bob Knight (27th: 588-210)	2
6 Kentucky	26-6	1242	3-1 (Duke)	Rick Pitino (10th: 198-101)	4
7 UNLV (1)	26-2	1182	0-0 Ineligible	Jerry Tarkanian (24th: 625-122)	31
8 USC	23-5	1164	1-1 (Ga. Tech)	George Raveling (20th: 302-268)	42t
9 Arkansas	25-7	1081	1-1 (Memphis St.)	Nolan Richardson (12th: 286-100)	3
10 Arizona	24-6	1045	1-1 (E. Tenn.St.)	Lute Olson (19th: 405-169)	5
11 Oklahoma St	26-7	957	2-1 (Michigan)	Eddie Sutton (22nd: 482-180)	13
12 **Cincinnati**	25-4	908	4-1 (Michigan)	Bob Huggins (11th: 235-103)	68t
13 Alabama	25-8	685	1-1 (N.Carolina)	Wimp Sanderson (12th: 265-118)	17
14 Michigan St	21-7	640	1-1 (Cincinnati)	Jud Heathcote (21st: 360-244)	36t
15 **Michigan**	20-8	634	5-1 (Duke)	Steve Fisher (4th: 68-32)	20
16 Missouri	20-8	557	1-1 (Seton Hall)	Norm Stewart (31st: 593-292)	32
17 Massachusetts	28-4	533	2-1 (Kentucky)	John Calipari (4th: 77-50)	48t
18 North Carolina	21-9	486	2-1 (Ohio St.)	Dean Smith (31st: 740-219)	8
19 Seton Hall	21-8	471	2-1 (Duke)	P.J.Carlesimo (17th: 246-250)	9
20 Florida St	20-9	427	2-1 (Indiana)	Pat Kennedy (12th: 243-126)	30
21 Syracuse	21-9	363	1-1 (UMass)	Jim Boeheim (16th: 391-124)	28
22 Georgetown	21-9	328	1-1 (Florida St.)	John Thompson (20th: 464-165)	16
23 Oklahoma	21-8	243	0-1 (SW La.)	Billy Tubbs (18th: 404-177)	19
24 DePaul	20-8	189	0-1 (N.Mexico St.)	Joey Meyer (8th: 168-79)	18
25 LSU	20-9	161	1-1 (Indiana)	Dale Brown (21st: 381-222)	6

Note: In a violations settlement with the NCAA in 1991, UNLV was given the option of defending its title in 1991 and sitting out the '92 tournament, or passing up the 1991 tourney and playing in '92. The Rebels chose to defend in 1991 and then sit in '92.

Others receiving votes: 26. Houston (25-5, 122 pts); **27.** Tulane (21-8, 68); **28.** NC-Charlotte (23-8, 63); **29.** BYU (25-6, 53); **30.** St.John's (19-10, 50); **31.** UTEP (25-6, 42); **32.** Pepperdine (24-6, 35); **33.** Evansville (24-5, 24); **34.** Princeton (22-5, 17); **35.** Memphis St.(20-10, 16); **36.** Nebraska (19-10, 11); **37.** WI-Green Bay (25-4, 9); **38.** Georgia Tech (21-11, 8); **39.** Texas (23-11, 7); **40.** Wake Forest (17-11, 4); **41.** Delaware (27-3, 3), Montana (27-3, 3) and New Mexico St.(23-7, 3); **44.** East Tenn.St.(23-6, 2), Iowa St.(20-12, 2) and Miami-OH (23-7, 2); **47.** Washington St.(21-10, 1).

NCAA Men's Division I Tournament Seeds

WEST	MIDWEST	SOUTHEAST	EAST
1 UCLA (25-4)	1 Kansas (25-3)	1 Ohio St. (23-5)	1 **Duke** (28-2)
2 **Indiana** (23-6)	2 USC (23-5)	2 Oklahoma St. (26-7)	2 Kentucky 926-6)
3 Florida St.	3 Arkansas (25-7)	3 Arizona (24-6)	3 Massachusetts (28-4)
4 Oklahoma (21-8)	4 **Cincinnati** (25-4)	4 North Carolina (21-9)	4 Seton Hall (21-8)
5 DePaul (20-8)	5 Michigan St. (21-7)	5 Alabama (25-8)	5 Missouri (20-8)
6 Georgetown (21-9)	6 Memphis St. (20-10)	6 **Michigan** (20-8)	6 Syracuse (21-9)
7 LSU (20-9)	7 Georgia Tech (21-11)	7 St. John's (19-10)	7 NC-Charlotte (23-9)
8 Louisville (18-10)	8 Evansville (24-5)	8 Nebraska (19-10)	8 Texas (23-11)
9 Wake Forest (17-11)	9 UTEP (25-6)	9 Connecticut (19-9)	9 Iowa (18-10)
10 BYU (25-6)	10 Houston (25-5)	10 Tulane (21-8)	10 Iowa St.(20-12)
11 South Florida (19-9)	11 Pepperdine (24-6)	11 Temple (17-12)	11 Princeton (22-5)
12 New Mexico St. (23-7)	12 SW Missouri St. (23-7)	12 Stanford (18-10)	12 West Virginia (20-11)
13 Southwestern La. (20-10)	13 Delaware (27-3)	13 Miami-OH (23-7)	13 La Salle (20-10)
14 Montana (27-3)	14 Murray St. (17-12)	14 East Tennessee St. (23-6)	14 Fordham (18-12)
15 Eastern Illinois (17-13)	15 NE Louisiana (19-9)	15 Georgia Southern (25-5)	15 Old Dominion (15-14)
16 Robert Morris (19-11)	16 Howard (17-13)	16 Miss.Valley St. (16-13)	16 Campbell (19-11)

1992 NCAA BASKETBALL MEN'S DIVISION I

FINAL FOUR
at the Metrodome
TWIN CITIES
* * *
Semifinals: April 4
Final: April 6

NATIONAL CHAMPIONSHIP
Duke 71
Michigan 51

SOUTHEAST — LEXINGTON, KY

1st ROUND March 19–20	2nd ROUND March 21–22	REGIONALS March 27–29
1 Ohio St. 83	Ohio St. 78	Ohio St. 80
16 Miss. Valley St. 56		
9 Nebraska 65	Connecticut 55	
8 Connecticut 86		
5 Alabama 80	Alabama 55	N. Carolina 73
12 Stanford 75		
4 N. Carolina 68	N. Carolina 64	
13 Miami-OH 63		
6 Michigan 73	Michigan 102	Michigan 75
11 Temple 66		
3 Arizona 80	East Tenn. St. 90	
14 East Tenn. St. 87		
7 St. John's 57	Tulane 71	Oklahoma St. 72
10 Tulane 61		
2 Oklahoma St. 100	Oklahoma St. 87	
15 Ga. Southern 73		

Ohio St. 71 (OT)
Michigan 75
Southeast final: **Michigan 76**

MIDWEST — KANSAS CITY, MO

1st ROUND March 19–20	2nd ROUND March 21–22	REGIONALS March 27–29
1 Kansas 100	Kansas 60	UTEP 67
16 Howard 67		
8 Evansville 50	UTEP 66	
9 UTEP 55		
5 Michigan St. 61	Michigan St. 65	Cincinnati 69
12 SW Missouri St. 54		
4 Cincinnati 85	Cincinnati 77	
13 Delaware 47		
6 Memphis St. 80	Memphis St. 82	Memphis St. 83
11 Pepperdine 70		
3 Arkansas 80	Arkansas 80	
14 Murray St. 69		
7 Georgia Tech 65	Georgia Tech 79	Georgia Tech 79
10 Houston 60		
2 USC 84	USC 78	
15 NE Louisiana 54		

Cincinnati 88
Memphis St. 57
Midwest final: **Cincinnati 72**

EAST — PHILADELPHIA, PA

1st ROUND March 19–20	2nd ROUND March 21–22	REGIONALS March 26–28
1 Duke 82	Duke 75	Duke 81
16 Campbell 56		
8 Iowa 92	Iowa 62	
9 Texas 98		
5 Missouri 89	Missouri 71	Seton Hall 69
12 West Virginia 78		
4 Seton Hall 78	Seton Hall 88	
13 La Salle 76		
6 Syracuse 51	Syracuse 71 (OT)	UMass 77
11 Princeton 43		
3 Massachusetts 85	UMass 77	
14 Fordham 58		
7 NC-Charlotte 74	Iowa St. 98	Kentucky 87
10 Iowa St. 76		
2 Kentucky 88	Kentucky 106	
15 Old Dominion 69		

Duke 104 (OT)
Kentucky 103
East final: **Duke 81**

WEST — ALBUQUERQUE, NM

1st ROUND March 19–20	2nd ROUND March 21–22	REGIONALS March 26–28
1 UCLA 73	UCLA 85	UCLA 85
16 Robert Morris 53		
8 Louisville 81	Louisville 69	
9 Wake Forest 58		
5 DePaul 73	N. Mexico St. 81	N. Mexico St. 78
12 New Mexico St. 81		
4 Oklahoma 83	SW Louisiana 73	
13 SW Louisiana 87		
6 Georgetown 75	Georgetown 68	Florida St. 74
11 South Florida 60		
3 Florida St. 78	Florida St. 78	
14 Montana 68		
7 LSU 94	LSU 79	Indiana 85
10 BYU 83		
2 Indiana 94	Indiana 89	
15 Eastern Ill. 55		

UCLA 79
Indiana 106
West final: **Indiana 78**

Duke 81 (Final Four)
Michigan 51 (National Championship)

1992 NCAA FINAL FOUR

NCAA Men's Championship Game

54th NCAA Division I Championship Game. **Date:** Monday, April 6 at the Hubert Humphrey Metrodome in Minneapolis. **Coaches:** Steve Fisher of Michigan and Mike Krzyzewski of Duke. **Favorite:** Duke by 6.

Attendance—50,379; **Officials**—Gerry Donaghy, Tom Harrington and Dave Libbey; **TV Rating**—22.7/35 share (CBS).

Michigan 51

	Min	FG M-A	FT M-A	Pts	Reb O-T	A	F
Chris Webber	30	6-12	2-5	14	4-11	1	4
Ray Jackson	16	0-1	0-0	0	1-1	2	1
Juwan Howard	29	4-9	1-3	9	1-3	0	3
Jalen Rose	37	5-12	1-2	11	2-5	4	4
Jimmy King	40	3-10	0-0	7	1-2	1	1
Eric Riley	19	2-6	0-0	4	2-4	1	2
James Voskuil	14	1-2	2-2	4	0-3	3	2
Rob Pelinka	9	1-2	0-0	2	1-2	1	0
Freddie Hunter	2	0-1	0-0	0	0-0	0	0
Michael Talley	1	0-1	0-0	0	1-1	0	0
Jason Bossard	1	0-1	0-0	0	0-0	0	0
Chris Seter	1	0-1	0-0	0	1-1	0	0
Chip Armer	1	0-0	0-0	0	0-0	0	0
TOTALS	200	22-58	6-12	51	15-35	13	17

Three-point FG: 1-11 (King 1-2, Bossard 0-1, Howard 0-1, Talley 0-1, Voskuil 0-1, Webber 0-2, Rose 0-3); **Team Rebounds:** 1 (not listed above); **Blocked Shots:** 3 (Jackson 2, King); **Turnovers:** 20 (Howard 4, Rose 4, Voskuil 3, Riley 2, Webber 2, Bossard, Hunter, Jackson, King, Talley); **Steals:** 8 (King 2, Rose 2, Webber 2, Jackson, Voskuil). **Percentages:** 2-Pt FG (.447), 3-Pt FG (.091), Total FG (.379), Free Throws (.500).

Duke 71

	Min	FG M-A	FT M-A	Pts	Reb O-T	A	F
Antonio Lang	32	2-3	1-2	5	2-3	0	1
Grant Hill	36	8-14	2-2	18	5-10	5	2
Christian Laettner	36	6-13	5-6	19	1-7	0	1
Bobby Hurley	37	3-12	2-2	9	0-3	7	4
Thomas Hill	34	5-10	5-8	16	3-7	0	2
Cherokee Parks	12	1-3	2-2	4	2-3	0	3
Brian Davis	9	0-2	0-0	0	0-0	0	0
Christian Ast.	1	0-0	0-0	0	0-1	0	0
Marty Clark	1	0-0	0-0	0	0-0	0	0
Kenny Blakeney	1	0-0	0-0	0	0-0	0	0
Ron Burt	1	0-0	0-0	0	0-0	0	0
TOTALS	200	25-57	17-22	71	13-35	12	13

Three-point FG: 4-9 (Laettner 2-4, T.Hill 1-2, Hurley 1-3); **Team Rebounds:** 2 (not listed above); **Blocked Shots:** 4 (G.Hill 2, Laettner, Parks); **Turnovers:** 14 (Laettner 7, G.Hill 3, Hurley 3, Parks); **Steals:** 9 (G.Hill 3, T.Hill 2, Davis, Hurley, Laettner, Lang). **Percentages:** 2-Pt FG (.438), 3-Pt FG (.444), Total FG (.439), Free Throws (.773).

Michigan (Big 10)	31	20—51	
Duke (ACC)	30	41—71	

THE FINAL FOUR
At Minneapolis (April 4-6)

Most Outstanding Player
Bobby Hurley, Duke junior guard. Semifinal—37 minutes, 26 points (6-for-9 from 3-point line), 4 assists and 2 steals; Final—37 minutes, 9 points and 7 assists.

All-Tournament Team
Hurley, center Christian Laettner and forward/guard Grant Hill of Duke; guard Jalen Rose and forward Chris Webber of Michigan.

Semifinal—Game One
Southeast Regional champion Michigan vs Midwest Regional champion Cincinnati. **Date:** Saturday, April 4 (5:30 p.m. tipoff). **Coaches:** Steve Fisher of Michigan and Bob Huggins of Cincinnati. **Favorite:** Michigan by 2½.
Attendance—50,379. **TV Rating**—13.7/29 share (CBS).

Michigan (Big Ten)	38	38—76
Cincinnati (Great Midwest)	41	31—72

High scorers: Michigan—guard Jimmy King (17); Cincinnati—guard Nick Van Exel (21).

Semifinal—Game Two
East Regional champion Duke vs West Regional champion Indiana. **Date:** Saturday, April 4 (8:30 p.m. tipoff). **Coaches:** Mike Krzyzewski of Duke and Bob Knight of Indiana. **Favorite:** Duke by 2½.
Attendance—50,379. **TV Rating**—16.8/30 share (CBS).

Indiana (Big Ten)	42	36—78
Duke (ACC)	37	44—81

High scorers: Indiana—guard Greg Graham (18); Duke—guard Bobby Hurley (26).

Final USA Today/CNN Coaches Poll
Taken **after** NCAA Tournament.

Voted on by a panel of 34 Division I head coaches following the NCAA tournament; first place votes in parentheses with total points (based on 25 for 1st, 24 for 2nd, etc.).

		Overall W-L	Pts	Reg Season W-L	Rank	NCAAs W-L
1	Duke (34)	34-2	850	28-2	1	6-0
2	Indiana	27-7	804	23-6	4	4-1
3	Michigan	25-9	768	20-8	16	5-1
4	Ohio St.	26-6	712	23-5	3	3-1
5	Cincinnati	29-5	692	25-4	11	4-1
6	Kentucky	29-7	661	26-6	9	3-1
7	Kansas	27-5	654	26-4	2	1-1
8	UCLA	28-5	596	25-4	5	3-1
9	Oklahoma St.	28-8	544	26-7	10	2-1
10	Arkansas	26-8	472	25-7	8	1-1
11	USC	24-6	466	23-5	6	1-1
12	N.Carolina	23-10	416	21-9	14	2-1
13	Seton Hall	23-9	397	21-8	19	2-1
14	Florida St.	22-10	388	20-9	17	2-1
15	UMass	30-5	339	28-4	21	1-1
16	Arizona	24-7	305	24-6	7	0-1
17	Memphis St	23-11	261	20-10	36	3-1
18	Missouri	21-9	251	20-8	13	1-1
19	Alabama	26-9	209	25-8	12	1-1
20	Michigan St	22-8	198	21-7	15	1-1
21	Georgia Tech	23-12	181	21-11	35	2-1
22	UTEP	27-7	167	25-6	27	2-1
23	Georgetown	22-10	122	21-9	18	1-1
24	Syracuse	22-10	112	21-9	20	1-1
25	LSU	21-10	69	20-9	26	1-1

Teams on probation or excluded from postseason play (and unable to receive votes): Maryland, Texas A&M and UNLV.

NCAA Finalists' Tournament and Season Statistics

Duke (34-2)

| | NCAA Tournament | | | | | | Overall | | | | | |
| | | | | Per Game | | | | | | | Per Game | | |
	Gm	FG%	TPts	Pts	Reb	Ast	Gm	FG%	TPts	Pts	Reb	Ast
Christian Laettner	6	.557	115	19.2	7.8	1.7	35	.575	751	21.5	7.9	2.0
Thomas Hill	6	.500	89	14.8	4.5	1.0	36	.534	525	14.6	3.4	1.5
Bobby Hurley	6	.417	83	13.8	2.3	7.8	31	.433	410	13.2	2.0	7.6
Grant Hill	6	.528	72	12.0	6.5	4.2	33	.611	463	14.0	5.7	4.1
Brian Davis	6	.395	61	10.2	4.3	1.0	36	.481	402	11.2	4.5	1.9
Antonio Lang	6	.591	37	6.2	4.7	0.0	34	.562	219	6.4	4.1	0.7
Cherokee Parks	6	.600	22	3.7	1.7	0.0	34	.571	170	5.0	2.4	0.4
Marty Clark	6	.500	9	1.5	0.7	0.2	34	.541	99	2.9	0.8	0.6
Eric Meek	3	.667	4	1.3	0.7	0.3	25	.579	62	2.5	1.2	0.2
Christian Ast.	3	.500	2	0.7	0.7	0.0	14	.417	16	1.1	1.0	0.1
Ron Burt	4	.000	0	0.0	0.3	0.3	19	.273	10	0.5	0.1	0.4
Kenny Blakeney	4	.000	0	0.0	0.0	0.0	29	.565	40	1.4	0.8	0.6
DUKE	6	.497	494	82.3	36.3	16.3	36	.536	3167	88.0	34.1	18.1
OPPONENTS	6	.430	419	69.8	34.2	15.7	36	.467	2615	72.6	31.4	15.5

Three-pointers: NCAA TOURNEY—Hurley (15-for-31), Laettner (7-15), T.Hill (6-12), Davis (2-11), Clark (0-1), G.Hill (0-1), Team (30-71 for .423 Pct.); OVERALL—Hurley (59-for-140), Laettner (54-97), T.Hill (37-91), Clark (12-18), Davis (8-39), Blakeney (1-4), G.Hill (0-1), Ast (0-4), Team (171-394 for .434 Pct.).

Michigan (25-9)

| | NCAA Tournament | | | | | | Overall | | | | | |
| | | | | Per Game | | | | | | | Per Game | | |
	Gm	FG%	TPts	Pts	Reb	Ast	Gm	FG%	TPts	Pts	Reb	Ast
Jalen Rose	6	.486	107	17.8	5.8	5.0	34	.486	597	17.6	4.3	4.0
Chris Webber	6	.612	98	16.3	9.7	2.3	34	.556	528	15.5	10.0	2.2
Jimmy King	6	.500	83	13.8	3.7	3.0	34	.496	337	9.9	3.3	2.3
Juwan Howard	6	.477	82	13.7	5.2	2.2	34	.450	377	11.1	6.2	1.8
Eric Riley	6	.522	28	4.7	4.2	0.0	32	.590	201	6.3	4.3	0.7
Ray Jackson	6	.412	19	3.2	3.3	1.8	34	.545	155	4.6	3.0	1.7
James Voskuil	6	.444	16	2.7	1.7	0.5	31	.481	137	4.4	2.0	1.0
Rob Pelinka	5	.429	10	2.0	1.2	1.0	28	.404	77	2.8	1.6	0.7
Michael Talley	4	.143	7	1.8	0.5	1.0	29	.386	152	5.2	1.0	1.9
Chris Seter	2	.000	2	1.0	1.5	0.0	6	.333	5	0.8	1.3	0.3
Chip Armer	2	.000	0	0.0	0.0	0.0	6	.667	4	0.7	0.0	0.0
Freddie Hunter	5	.000	0	0.0	0.8	0.2	29	.529	25	0.9	2.0	0.7
Jason Bossard	2	.000	0	0.0	0.0	0.0	6	.300	8	1.3	0.0	0.0
MICHIGAN	6	.495	452	75.3	38.8	17.0	34	.496	2647	77.9	40.4	16.6
OPPONENTS	6	.414	442	73.7	33.0	12.0	34	.415	2426	71.4	33.0	13.4

Three-pointers: NCAA TOURNEY—King (10-for-17), Rose (7-19), Pelinka (2-4), Voskuil (2-5), Webber (2-8), Jackson (1-2), Howard (0-1), Talley (0-1), Bossard (0-2), Team (24-59 for .407 Pct.); OVERALL—Rose (36-for 111), King (28-60), Voskuil (14-54), Webber (14-54), Talley (11-38), Pelinka (8-25), Bossard (2-7), Jackson (2-10), Howard (0-2), Team (118-360 for .328 Pct.).

Duke's Schedule

Regular Season (25-2)

W	E.Carolina	103-75
W	Harvard	118-65
W	vs St.John's*	91-81
W	at Canisius	96-60
W	at Michigan .. (OT)	88-85
W	Wm.& Mary	97-61
W	at Virginia	68-62
W	Florida St.	86-70
W	at Maryland	83-66
W	Georgia Tech	97-84
W	N.C.State	110-75
W	NC-Charlotte	104-82
W	at Boston Univ	95-85
W	Wake Forest	84-68
W	Clemson	112-73
W	at Florida St	75-62
W	Notre Dame	100-71
L	at N.Carolina	73-75
W	at LSU	77-67
W	at Georgia Tech	71-62
W	at N.C.State	71-63
W	Maryland	91-89
L	at Wake Forest	68-72
W	Virginia	76-67
W	at UCLA	75-65
W	at Clemson	98-97
W	N.Carolina	89-77

*at Greensboro, NC.

ACC Tournament (3-0)

W	Maryland	94-87
W	Georgia Tech	89-76
W	N.Carolina	94-74

NCAA Tournament (6-0)

W	Campbell	82-56
W	Iowa	75-62
W	Seton Hall	81-69
W	Kentucky . (OT)	104-103
W	Indiana	81-78
W	Michigan	71-51

Michigan's Schedule

Regular Season (20-8)

W	at Detroit	100-74
W	at Cleveland St.	80-61
W	Chicago St	112-62
W	Eastern Mich.	91-77
L	Duke	(OT) 85-88
W	Central Mich.	86-70
W	Rice	87-70
W	vs BYU*	86-83
W	vs Va. Tech*	63-51
W	at Iowa	(OT) 80-77
L	at Minnesota	64-73
L	Purdue	60-65
W	at Illinois	68-61
L	at Indiana	74-89
W	Wisconsin	98-83
W	at Mich.St.	(OT) 89-79
L	Ohio St	58-68
W	Northwestern	81-58
W	at Notre Dame	74-65
W	Iowa	79-74
L	Michigan St.	59-70
W	Minnesota	95-70
W	at Northwestern	76-63
L	at Wisconsin	78-96
L	at Ohio St	66-77
W	Indiana	68-60
W	at Purdue	70-61
W	Illinois	68-59

*Citrus Bowl Classic in Orlando.

Note: There is no postseason tournament in the Big 10.

NCAA Tournament (5-1)

W	Temple	73-66
W	East Tenn.St	102-90
W	Oklahoma St	75-72
W	Ohio St	(OT) 75-71
W	Cincinnati	76-72
L	Duke	51-71

Final NCAA Men's Division I Standings

Conference records include regular season games only. Overall records include all postseason games.

Atlantic Coast Conference

	Conference			Overall		
	W	L	Pct	W	L	Pct
*Duke	14	2	.875	34	2	.944
*Florida St	11	5	.688	22	10	.688
*North Carolina	9	7	.563	23	10	.697
*Georgia Tech	8	8	.500	23	12	.657
†Virginia	8	8	.500	20	13	.606
*Wake Forest	7	9	.438	17	12	.586
N.C.State	6	10	.375	12	18	.400
Maryland	5	11	.313	14	15	.483
Clemson	4	12	.250	14	14	.500

Note: New member Florida St. moved from Metro.
Probation: Maryland ineligible for postseason.
Conf. Tournament Final: Duke 94, N.Carolina 74.
***NCAA Tournament (12-4):** Duke (6-0), Fla.St. (2-1), Ga. Tech (2-1), N.Carolina (2-1), Wake Forest (0-1).
†NIT Tournament (5-0): Virginia (5-0).

Atlantic 10 Conference

	Conference			Overall		
	W	L	Pct	W	L	Pct
*Massachusetts	13	3	.813	30	5	.857
*Temple	11	5	.688	17	13	.567
*West Virginia	10	6	.625	20	12	.625
†Rhode Island	9	7	.563	22	10	.688
George Washington	8	8	.500	16	12	.571
†Rutgers	6	10	.375	16	15	.516
Duquesne	6	10	.375	13	15	.464
St.Joseph's	6	10	.375	13	15	.464
St.Bonaventure	3	13	.188	9	19	.321

Conf. Tournament Final: UMass 97, West Va. 91.
***NCAA Tournament (2-3):** UMass (2-1), Temple (0-1), West Va. (0-1).
†NIT Tournament (3-2): Rhode Is. (2-1), Rutgers (1-1).

Big East Conference

	Conference			Overall		
	W	L	Pct	W	L	Pct
*Seton Hall	12	6	.667	23	9	.719
*Georgetown	12	6	.667	22	10	.688
*St. John's	12	6	.667	19	11	.633
Villanova	11	7	.611	14	15	.483
*Syracuse	10	8	.556	22	10	.688
*Connecticut	10	8	.556	20	10	.667
†Pittsburgh	9	9	.500	18	16	.529
†Boston College	7	11	.389	17	14	.548
Providence	6	12	.333	14	17	.452
Miami-FL	1	17	.056	8	24	.250

Note: New member Miami-FL was an independent.
Conf. Tournament Final: Syracuse 56, Georgetown 54.
***NCAA Tournament (5-5):** Seton Hall (2-1), UConn (1-1), Georgetown (1-1), Syracuse (1-1), St.John's (0-1).
†NIT Tournament (2-3): BC (1-1), Pitt (1-1), Villanova (0-1).

Big Eight Conference

	Conference			Overall		
	W	L	Pct	W	L	Pct
*Kansas	11	3	.786	27	5	.844
*Oklahoma St	8	6	.571	28	8	.778
*Oklahoma	8	6	.571	21	9	.700
*Missouri	8	6	.571	21	9	.700
*Nebraska	7	7	.500	19	10	.655
*Iowa St	5	9	.357	21	13	.618
†Kansas St	5	9	.357	16	14	.533
Colorado	4	10	.286	13	15	.464

Conf. Tournament Final: Kansas 66, Oklahoma St. 57.
***NCAA Tournament (5-6):** Okla.St. (2-1), Kansas (1-1), Iowa St. (1-1), Missouri (1-1), Nebraska (0-1), Oklahoma (0-1).
†NIT Tournament (1-1): Kansas St. (1-1).

Big Sky Conference

	Conference			Overall		
	W	L	Pct	W	L	Pct
*Montana	14	2	.875	27	4	.871
Nevada	13	3	.813	19	10	.655
Idaho	10	6	.625	18	14	.563
Weber St	10	6	.625	16	13	.552
Boise St	7	9	.438	16	13	.552
Montana St	6	10	.375	14	14	.500
Idaho St	6	10	.375	9	21	.300
Northern Arizona	3	13	.188	7	20	.259
Eastern Washington	3	13	.188	6	21	.222

Conf. Tournament Final: Montana 73, Nevada 68.
***NCAA Tournament (0-1):** Montana (0-1).

Big South Conference

	Conference			Overall		
	W	L	Pct	W	L	Pct
Radford	12	2	.857	20	9	.659
Liberty	10	4	.714	22	7	.759
*Campbell	7	7	.500	19	12	.613
Charleston Southern	7	7	.500	16	14	.533
Davidson	6	8	.429	11	17	.393
Coast Carolina	6	8	.429	19	11	.387
NC-Asheville	6	8	.429	9	19	.321
Winthrop	2	12	.143	6	22	.214

Note: New member Liberty was an independent.
Conf. Tournament Final: Campbell 67, Charleston 53.
***NCAA Tournament (0-1):** Campbell (0-1).

Big Ten Conference

	Conference			Overall		
	W	L	Pct	W	L	Pct
*Ohio St	15	3	.833	26	6	.813
*Indiana	14	4	.778	27	7	.794
*Michigan St	11	7	.611	22	8	.733
*Michigan	11	7	.611	25	9	.735
*Iowa	10	8	.556	19	11	.633
†Purdue	8	10	.444	18	15	.545
†Minnesota	8	10	.444	16	16	.500
Illinois	7	11	.389	13	15	.464
Wisconsin	4	14	.222	13	18	.419
Northwestern	2	16	.111	9	19	.321

Conf. Tournament Final: Big Ten has no tournament.
***NCAA Tournament (14-5):** Michigan (5-1), Indiana (4-1), Ohio St. (3-1), Iowa (1-1), Mich.St. (1-1).
†NIT Tournament (2-2): Purdue (2-1), Minnesota (0-1).

Big West Conference

	Conference			Overall		
	W	L	Pct	W	L	Pct
UNLV	18	0	1.000	26	2	.929
†UC-Santa Barbara	13	5	.722	20	9	.690
*New Mexico St	12	6	.667	25	8	.758
†Long Beach St	11	7	.611	18	12	.600
Utah St	10	8	.556	16	12	.571
Pacific	8	10	.444	14	16	.467
CS-Fullerton	8	10	.444	16	14	.429
Fresno St	6	12	.333	15	16	.484
UC-Irvine	3	15	.167	7	22	.241
San Jose St	1	17	.056	2	24	.077

Barred: UNLV ineligible for postseason play in agreement with NCAA.
Conf. Tournament Final: N.Mexico St. 74, Pacific 73.
***NCAA Tournament (2-1):** N.Mexico St. (2-1).
†NIT Tournament (0-2): L.Beach St. (0-1), UCSB (0-1).

Final NCAA Men's Division I Standings (Cont.)

Colonial Athletic Association

	Conference			Overall		
	W	L	Pct	W	L	Pct
†Richmond	12	2	.857	22	8	.733
†James Madison	12	2	.857	21	11	.656
*Old Dominion	8	6	.571	15	15	.500
American	8	6	.571	11	18	.379
NC-Wilmington	6	8	.429	13	15	.464
East Carolina	4	10	.286	10	18	.357
William & Mary	3	11	.214	10	19	.345
George Mason	3	11	.214	7	21	.250

Note: New member Old Dominion moved from Sun Belt.
Conf. Tournament Final: Old Dominion 78, J.Madison 73.
*NCAA Tournament (0-1): Old Dominion (0-1).
†NIT Tournament (0-2): J.Madison (0-1), Richmond (0-1).

East Coast Conference

	Conference			Overall		
	W	L	Pct	W	L	Pct
Hofstra	10	2	.833	20	9	.690
Towson St	9	3	.750	17	13	.567
Rider	9	3	.750	16	13	.552
MD-Baltimore County	8	4	.667	10	19	.345
Central Conn. St	3	9	.250	7	21	.250
Brooklyn	3	9	.250	5	23	.179
Buffalo	0	12	.000	2	26	.071

Note: New members Buffalo moved up from Division II and Brooklyn was an independent.
Conf. Tournament Final: Towson St. 69, Hofstra 61.
NCAA Tournament: No automatic berth and no member invited.

Great Midwest Conference

	Conference			Overall		
	W	L	Pct	W	L	Pct
*Cincinnati	8	2	.800	29	5	.853
*DePaul	8	2	.800	20	9	.690
Memphis St.	5	5	.500	23	11	.676
Marquette	5	5	.500	16	13	.552
†Ala-Birmingham	4	6	.400	20	9	.690
St. Louis	0	10	.000	5	23	.179

Note: New conference. Cincinnati and Memphis St. moved from Metro, Marquette and St.Louis from Midwestern, Alabama-Birmingham from Sun Belt, and DePaul was an independent.
Conf. Tournament Final: Cincinnati 75, Memphis St. 63.
*NCAA Tournament (7-3): Cincinnati (4-1), Memphis St. (3-1), DePaul (0-1).
†NIT Tournament (0-1): Ala-Birm. (0-1).

Ivy League

	Conference			Overall		
	W	L	Pct	W	L	Pct
*Princeton	12	2	.857	22	6	.786
Penn	9	5	.643	16	10	.615
Columbia	8	6	.571	10	16	.385
Yale	7	7	.500	17	9	.654
Brown	5	9	.357	11	15	.423
Dartmouth	5	9	.357	10	16	.385
Cornell	5	9	.357	7	19	.269
Harvard	5	9	.357	6	20	.231

Conf. Tournament Final: Ivy League has no tournament.
*NCAA Tournament (0-1): Princeton (0-1).

Metro Conference

	Conference			Overall		
	W	L	Pct	W	L	Pct
*Tulane	8	4	.667	22	9	.710
*NC-Charlotte	7	5	.583	23	9	.719
*South Florida	7	5	.583	19	10	.655
*Louisville	7	5	.583	19	11	.633
VCU	5	7	.417	14	15	.483
Southern Miss	5	7	.417	13	16	.448
Virginia Tech	3	9	.250	10	18	.357

Note: New members NC-Charlotte, South Florida and VCU all moved from Sun Belt.
Conf. Tournament Final: NC-Charlotte 64, Tulane 63.
*NCAA Tournament (2-4): Louisville (1-1), Tulane (1-1), NC-Char. (0- 1), So.Fla. (0-1).

Metro Atlantic Conference

	Conference			Overall		
	W	L	Pct	W	L	Pct
†Manhattan	13	3	.813	25	9	.735
*La Salle	12	4	.750	20	11	.645
Siena	11	5	.688	19	10	.655
Loyola-MD	10	6	.625	14	14	.500
Niagara	8	8	.500	14	14	.500
Iona	8	8	.500	14	15	.483
Fairfield	4	12	.250	8	20	.286
St. Peter's	3	13	.188	8	21	.276
Canisius	3	13	.188	8	22	.267

Conf. Tournament Final: La Salle 77, Manhattan 76.
*NCAA Tournament (0-1): La Salle (0-1).
†NIT Tournament (2-1): Manhattan (2-1).

Mid-American Conference

	Conference			Overall		
	W	L	Pct	W	L	Pct
*Miami-OH	13	3	.813	23	8	.766
†Ball St	11	5	.688	24	9	.750
†Western Michigan	11	5	.688	21	9	.724
Ohio Univ.	10	6	.625	18	10	.643
Bowling Green	8	8	.500	14	15	.483
Central Michigan	6	10	.375	12	16	.429
Kent	6	10	.375	9	19	.321
Eastern Michigan	4	12	.250	9	22	.290
Toledo	3	13	.188	7	20	.259

Conf. Tournament Final: Miami-OH 58, Ball St. 57.
*NCAA Tournament (0-1): Miami-OH (0-1).
†NIT Tournament (0-2): Ball St. (0-1), W.Mich. (0-1).

Mid-Continent Conference

	Conference			Overall		
	W	L	Pct	W	L	Pct
†Wisconsin-Green Bay	14	2	.875	25	5	.833
Akron	10	6	.625	16	12	.571
IL-Chicago	10	6	.625	16	14	.533
*Eastern Illinois	9	7	.563	17	14	.548
Wright St	9	7	.563	15	13	.536
Cleveland St	7	9	.438	16	13	.552
Northern Illinois	7	9	.438	11	17	.393
Western Illinois	4	12	.250	10	18	.357
Valparaiso	2	14	.125	5	22	.185

Note: New member Wright St. was an independent.
Conf. Tournament Final: Eastern Ill. 83, IL-Chicago 68.
*NCAA Tournament (0-1): Eastern Ill. (0-1).
†NIT Tournament (0-1): WI-Green Bay (0-1).

Mid-Eastern Athletic Conference

	Conference			Overall		
	W	L	Pct	W	L	Pct
†Howard	12	4	.750	17	14	.548
N. Carolina A&T	12	4	.750	17	9	.654
Florida A&M	11	5	.688	16	14	.533
Coppin St	9	7	.563	15	13	.536
S. Carolina St	9	7	.563	14	15	.483
Delaware St	9	7	.563	12	16	.429
Morgan St	5	11	.313	6	23	.207
Bethune-Cookman	3	13	.188	4	25	.138
MD-Eastern Shore	2	14	.125	3	25	.107

Conf. Tournament Final: Howard 67, Florida A&M 65.
*NCAA Tournament (0-1): Howard (0-1).

Northeast Conference

	Conference			Overall		
	W	L	Pct	W	L	Pct
*Robert Morris	12	4	.750	19	12	.613
Monmouth	11	5	.688	20	9	.690
Fairleigh Dickinson	11	5	.688	14	14	.500
Wagner	9	7	.563	16	12	.571
St. Francis-NY	8	8	.500	15	14	.517
Long Island	7	9	.438	11	19	.367
Marist	6	10	.375	10	20	.333
St. Francis-PA	5	11	.313	13	16	.448
Mount St. Mary's	3	13	.188	6	22	.214

Conf. Tournament Final: Robt.Morris 85, Marist 81.
*NCAA Tournament (0-1): Robt.Morris (0-1).

Midwestern Collegiate Conference

	Conference			Overall		
	W	L	Pct	W	L	Pct
*Evansville	8	2	.800	24	6	.800
†Butler	7	3	.700	21	10	.677
Xavier-OH	7	3	.700	15	12	.556
Dayton	5	5	.500	15	15	.500
Loyola-IL	2	8	.200	13	16	.448
Detroit	1	9	.100	12	17	.414

Conf. Tournament Final: Evansville 95, Butler 76.
*NCAA Tournament (0-1): Evansville (0-1).
†NIT Tournament (0-1): Butler (0-1).

Ohio Valley Conference

	Conference			Overall		
	W	L	Pct	W	L	Pct
*Murray St	11	3	.786	17	13	.567
Middle Tenn. St	9	5	.643	16	11	.593
Eastern Kentucky	9	5	.643	19	14	.576
Tennessee Tech	8	6	.571	14	15	.483
Morehead St	6	8	.429	14	15	.483
Austin Peay St	6	8	.429	11	17	.393
SE Missouri St	5	9	.357	12	16	.429
Tennessee St	2	12	.143	4	24	.143

Note: New member SE Missouri St. moved up from Div.II.
Conf. Tournament Final: Murray St.81, Eastern Ky.60.
*NCAA Tournament (0-1): Murray St. (0-1).

Missouri Valley Conference

	Conference			Overall		
	W	L	Pct	W	L	Pct
†Southern Illinois	14	4	.778	22	8	.733
Illinois St	14	4	.778	18	11	.621
*SW Missouri St	13	5	.722	23	8	.742
Tulsa	12	6	.667	17	13	.567
Indiana St	12	6	.667	13	15	.464
Creighton	7	11	.389	9	19	.321
Northern Iowa	6	12	.333	10	18	.357
Wichita St	6	12	.333	8	20	.286
Bradley	3	15	.167	7	23	.233
Drake	3	15	.167	6	21	.222

Note: New member Northern Iowa moved from Mid-Continent.
Conf. Tournament Final: SW Missouri St. 71, Tulsa 68.
*NCAA Tournament (0-1): SW Missouri St. (0-1).
†NIT Tournament (0-1): Southern Ill. (0-1).

Pacific-10 Conference

	Conference			Overall		
	W	L	Pct	W	L	Pct
*UCLA	16	2	.889	28	5	.848
*USC	15	3	.833	24	6	.800
*Arizona	13	5	.722	24	7	.774
*Stanford	10	8	.556	18	11	.621
†Washington St	9	9	.500	22	11	.667
†Arizona St	9	9	.500	19	14	.576
Oregon St	7	11	.389	15	16	.484
Washington	5	13	.278	12	17	.414
California	4	14	.222	10	18	.357
Oregon	2	16	.111	6	21	.222

Conf. Tournament Final: Pac-10 has no tournament.
*NCAA Tournament (4-4): UCLA (3-1), USC (1-1), Arizona (0-1), Stanford (0-1).
†NIT Tournament (2-2): Ariz.St. (1-1), Wash.St. (1-1).

North Atlantic Conference

	Conference			Overall		
	W	L	Pct	W	L	Pct
*Delaware	14	0	1.000	27	4	.871
Drexel	9	5	.643	16	14	.533
Maine	8	6	.571	17	15	.531
Vermont	7	7	.500	16	13	.552
Boston Univ	5	9	.357	10	18	.357
Northeastern	5	9	.357	9	19	.321
New Hampshire	5	9	.357	7	21	.250
Hartford	3	11	.214	6	21	.222

Note: New members Delaware and Drexel moved from East Coast.
Conf. Tournament Final: Delaware 92, Drexel 68.
*NCAA Tournament (0-1): Delaware (0-1).

Patriot League

	Conference			Overall		
	W	L	Pct	W	L	Pct
*Fordham	11	3	.786	18	13	.581
Bucknell	11	3	.786	21	9	.700
Holy Cross	10	4	.714	18	11	.621
Lehigh	8	6	.571	14	15	.483
Colgate	7	7	.500	14	14	.500
Lafayette	6	8	.429	8	20	.286
Army	2	12	.142	4	24	.142
Navy	1	13	.071	6	22	.214

Note: New member Navy moved from Colonial.
Conf. Tournament Final: Fordham 70, Bucknell 65.
*NCAA Tournament (0-1): Fordham (0-1).

Final NCAA Men's Division I Standings (Cont.)

Southeastern Conference

Eastern Div.	Conference			Overall		
	W	L	Pct	W	L	Pct
*Kentucky	12	4	.750	29	7	.806
†Florida	9	7	.563	19	14	.576
†Tennessee	8	8	.500	19	15	.559
Georgia	7	9	.438	15	14	.517
†Vanderbilt	6	10	.375	15	15	.500
South Carolina	3	13	.188	11	17	.393

Western Div.	Conference			Overall		
	W	L	Pct	W	L	Pct
*Arkansas	13	3	.813	26	8	.765
*LSU	12	4	.750	21	10	.677
*Alabama	10	6	.625	26	9	.743
Mississippi St.	7	9	.438	15	13	.536
Auburn	5	11	.313	12	15	.444
Mississippi	4	12	.250	11	17	.393

Note: New members Arkansas moved from SWC and South Carolina from Metro. Twelve-team SEC split into two divisions in 1991-92.
Conf. Tournament Final: Kentucky 80, Alabama 54.
*NCAA Tournament (6-4): Kentucky (3-1), Alabama (1-1), Arkansas (1-1), LSU (1-1).
†NIT Tournament (4-4): Florida (3-2), Tennessee (1-1), Vanderbilt (0-1).

Southern Conference

	Conference			Overall		
	W	L	Pct	W	L	Pct
*East Tennessee St.	12	2	.857	24	7	.774
Tenn-Chattanooga	12	2	.857	23	7	.767
Furman	9	5	.643	17	11	.607
Appalachian St.	9	5	.643	15	14	.517
Western Carolina	5	9	.357	11	17	.393
The Citadel	3	11	.214	10	18	.357
VMI	3	11	.214	10	18	.357
Marshall	3	11	.214	7	22	.241

Conf. Tournament Final: E. Tenn.St.74, Tenn-Chatt.62.
*NCAA Tournament (1-1): E. Tenn.St. (1-1).

Southland Conference

	Conference			Overall		
	W	L	Pct	W	L	Pct
Texas-San Antonio	15	3	.833	21	8	.724
*NE Louisiana	12	6	.667	19	10	.655
Nicholls St.	12	6	.667	15	13	.536
North Texas	12	6	.667	15	14	.517
Texas-Arlington	11	7	.611	16	13	.552
Stephen F. Austin	10	8	.556	15	13	.536
Northwestern St	9	9	.500	15	13	.536
SW Texas St	4	14	.222	72	0	.259
McNeese St.	4	14	.222	7	22	.241
Sam Houston St	1	17	.056	2	25	.074

Note: New members Texas-San Antonio moved from Trans America and Nicholls St. was an independent.
Probation: Northwestern St. ineligible for postseason.
Conf. Tournament Final: NE Louisiana 81, TX-San Antonio 77.
*NCAA Tournament (0-1): NE Louisiana (0-1).

Best In Show

Conferences with at least five victories in 1992 NCAA tournament.

	W-L		W-L
Big Ten	14-5	SEC	6-4
ACC	12-4	Big East	5-5
Great Midwest	7-3	Big Eight	5-6

Southwest Conference

	Conference			Overall		
	W	L	Pct	W	L	Pct
*Texas	11	3	.786	23	12	.657
*Houston	11	3	.786	25	6	.806
†TCU	9	5	.643	23	11	.676
Rice	8	6	.571	20	11	.645
Texas Tech	6	8	.429	15	14	.517
Baylor	5	9	.357	13	15	.464
SMU	4	10	.286	10	18	.357
Texas A&M	2	12	.143	6	22	.214

Probation: Texas A&M ineligible for postseason.
Conf. Tournament Final: Houston 91, Texas 72.
*NCAA Tournament (0-2): Houston (0-1), Texas (0-1).
†NIT Tournament (1-1): TCU (1-1).

Southwestern Athletic Conference

	Conference			Overall		
	W	L	Pct	W	L	Pct
*Miss. Valley St.	11	3	.786	16	14	.533
Texas Southern	11	3	.786	15	14	.517
Southern-BR	9	5	.643	18	12	.600
Alcorn St	8	6	.571	15	14	.517
Alabama St.	8	6	.571	14	14	.500
Jackson St.	7	7	.500	12	16	.429
Grambling St	2	12	.143	4	24	.143
Prairie View A&M	0	14	.000	0	28	.000

Conf. Tournament Final: Miss.Valley St. 85, Southern 77.
*NCAA Tournament (0-1): Miss.Valley St. (0-1).

Sun Belt Conference

	Conference			Overall		
	W	L	Pct	W	L	Pct
†Louisiana Tech	13	3	.813	23	8	.742
*SW Louisiana	12	4	.750	21	11	.656
Arkansas St.	11	5	.688	17	11	.607
†Western Kentucky	10	6	.625	21	11	.656
South Alabama	9	7	.563	14	14	.500
Ark-Little Rock	8	8	.500	17	13	.567
New Orleans	8	8	.500	17	15	.531
Lamar	7	9	.438	12	19	.387
Jacksonville	6	10	.375	12	17	.414
Central Florida	3	13	.188	10	18	.357
Texas-Pan American	1	15	.063	3	26	.103

Note: Formerly the American South. Absorbed old Sun Belt members Jacksonville, South Alabama and Western Kentucky, and added Ark-Little Rock from Trans America.
Also: On Feb. 27, New Orleans beat La. Tech, 54-53, but had to forfeit win because of an ineligible player.
Conf. Tournament Final: SW Louisiana 75, La. Tech 71.
*NCAA Tournament (1-1): SW Louisiana (1-1).
†NIT Tournament (0-2): La. Tech (0-1), Western Ky. (0-1).

Trans America Athletic Conference

	Conference			Overall		
	W	L	Pct	W	L	Pct
*Georgia Southern	13	1	.929	25	6	.806
Georgia St	8	6	.571	16	14	.533
Florida Int'l	7	7	.500	11	17	.393
Stamford	7	7	.500	11	18	.379
Stetson	6	8	.429	11	17	.393
Mercer	6	8	.429	11	18	.379
Centenary	5	9	.357	10	18	.357
SE Louisiana	4	10	.286	6	22	.214

Note: New members Fla.International and SE Louisiana were independents. Ex-members Texas-San Antonio left for Southland and Ark-Little Rock for Sun Belt.
Conf. Tournament Final: Ga.Southern 95, Georgia St.82.
*NCAA Tournament (0-1): Ga.Southern (0-1).

West Coast Conference

	Conference			Overall		
	W	L	Pct	W	L	Pct
*Pepperdine	14	0	1.000	24	7	.774
Santa Clara	9	5	.643	14	15	.483
Gonzaga	8	6	.571	20	10	.667
Loyola-CA	8	6	.571	15	13	.536
San Diego	6	8	.429	14	14	.500
San Francisco	4	10	.286	13	16	.448
St. Mary's	4	10	.286	13	17	.433
Portland	3	11	.214	10	18	.357

Conf. Tournament Final: Pepperdine 73, Gonzaga 70.
*NCAA Tournament (0-1): Pepperdine (0-1).

Western Athletic Conference

	Conference			Overall		
	W	L	Pct	W	L	Pct
*BYU	12	4	.750	25	7	.781
*UTEP	12	4	.750	27	7	.794
†New Mexico	11	5	.688	20	13	.606
†Utah	9	7	.563	24	11	.686
Hawaii	9	7	.563	16	12	.571
Wyoming	8	8	.500	16	13	.552
Colorado St	8	8	.500	14	17	.452
Air Force	3	13	.188	9	20	.310
San Diego St.	0	16	.000	2	26	.071

Conf. Tournament Final: BYU 73, UTEP 71.
*NCAA Tournament (2-2): UTEP (2-1), BYU (0-1).
†NIT Tournament (6-2): Utah (4-1), N.Mexico (2-1).

Division I Independents

	W	L	Pct
†Penn St.	21	8	.724
Missouri-Kansas City	20	8	.714
Southern Utah	20	8	.714
Wisconsin-Milwaukee	20	8	.714
College of Charleston	19	8	.704
†Notre Dame	18	15	.545
CS-Northridge	11	17	.393
NE Illinois	8	20	.286
Chicago St.	7	21	.250
NC-Greensboro	7	21	.250
Youngstown St.	6	22	.214
CS-Sacramento	4	24	.143

Note: New independents Penn St. left Atlantic 10; CS-Sacramento, College of Charleston and NC-Greensboro moved up from Div.II. Ex-independents include Brooklyn (East Coast), DePaul (Great Midwest), Fla.International (Trans America), Liberty (Big South), Miami-FL (Big East), Nicholls St. (Southland) SE Louisiana (Trans America), US International (school folded), and Wright St. (Mid-Continent).
†NIT Tournament (4-2): Notre Dame (4-1), Penn St. (0-1).

Conference Moves

After the 1991-92 season, 22 Division I schools either changed conferences, left the independent ranks to join a conference or left a conference to become independent.

The East Coast conference lost four of its seven members and ceased to be a viable league. See "College Sports" for further details.

Annual Awards

Players of the Year

Christian Laettner, Duke.... Eastman, Naismith, Rupp, USBWA and Wooden
Jim Jackson, Ohio St .... UPI

Wooden Award Voting

Presented since 1977 by the Los Angeles Athletic Club and named after the former Purdue All-America and UCLA coach John Wooden. Voting done by 1000-member panel of national media; candidates must have a minimum grade point average of 2.0 (out of 4.0).

		Class	Pos	Points
1	Christian Laettner, Duke	Sr.	C	4560
2	Shaquille O'Neal, LSU	Jr.	C	3964
3	Jim Jackson, Ohio St	Jr.	G/F	3381
4	Harold Miner, USC	Jr.	G	2916
5	Alonzo Mourning, Georgetown	Sr.	C/F	2710

Coaches of the Year

Perry Clark, Tulane .... UPI and USBWA
Roy Williams, Kansas .... AP
George Raveling, USC .... NABC
Mike Krzyzewski, Duke .... Naismith

AP Coach of the Year Voting

Presented by the Associated Press since 1967. Voting done by national panel of AP sportswriters and broadcasters. First place votes in parentheses.

		Pts
1	Roy Williams, Kansas (21)	129
2	Jerry Tarkanian, UNLV (20)	117
3	Mike Krzyzewski, Duke (14)	116
4	George Raveling, USC (14)	111
5	Perry Clark, Tulane (14)	110

Consensus All-America Team

The NCAA Division I players cited most frequently by the following All-America selectors: AP, US Basketball Writers Association, National Association of Basketball Coaches, and UPI.

First Team

	Class	Hgt	Pos
Jim Jackson, Ohio St	Jr.	6-6	F
Christian Laettner, Duke	Sr.	6-11	C
Harold Miner, USC	Jr.	6-5	G
Alonzo Mourning, Georgetown	Sr.	6-10	C
Shaquille O'Neal, LSU	Jr.	7-1	C

Second Team

	Class	Hgt	Pos
Byron Houston, Oklahoma St.	Sr.	6-7	F
Bobby Hurley, Duke	Jr.	6-1	G
Don MacLean, UCLA	Sr.	6-10	F
Anthony Peeler, Missouri	Sr.	6-4	G
Malik Sealy, St.John's	Sr.	6-8	F
Walt Williams, Maryland	Sr.	6-8	G

Third Team

	Class	Hgt	Pos
Calbert Cheaney, Indiana	Jr.	6-6	F
Todd Day, Arkansas	Sr.	6-9	F
Adam Keefe, Stanford	Sr.	6-9	F
Lee Mayberry, Arkansas	Sr.	6-2	G
Grant Hill, Duke	So.	6-8	F/G

Defensive Player of the Year

The Henry Iba Corinthian Award, presented by the Rotary Club of River Oakes in Houston since 1987 and named after the former Oklahoma St. and U.S. Olympic coach. Voting done by NABC.

Alonzo Mourning, Georgetown

NCAA Men's Division I Leaders
Includes games through NCAA and NIT tournaments.

INDIVIDUAL

Scoring

	Cl	Gm	Pts	Avg
Brett Roberts, Morehead St	Sr.	29	815	28.1
Vin Baker, Hartford	Jr.	27	745	27.6
Alphonso Ford, Miss.Valley St.	Jr.	26	714	27.5
Randy Woods, La Salle	Sr.	31	847	27.3
Steve Rogers, Alabama St	Sr.	28	764	27.3
Walt Williams, Maryland	Sr.	29	776	26.8
Harold Miner, USC	Jr.	30	789	26.3
Terrell Lowery, Loyola-CA	Sr.	26	675	26.0
Reggie Cunningham, Beth-Cook	Sr.	29	744	25.7
Parrish Casebier, Evansville	So.	25	634	25.4
Adam Keefe, Stanford	Sr.	29	734	25.3
Joe Harvell, Mississippi	Jr.	28	699	25.0
Darin Archbold, Butler	Sr.	31	770	24.8
Lindsey Hunter, Jackson St	Jr.	28	693	24.8
Shaquille O'Neal, LSU	Jr.	30	722	24.1
Davor Marcelic, So.Utah	Sr.	28	659	23.5
Anthony Peeler, Missouri	Sr.	29	678	23.4
Terrance Jacobs, Towson St.	Sr.	30	692	23.1
Terry Boyd, W.Carolina	Sr.	23	525	22.8
Darrick Suber, Rider	Jr.	29	660	22.8

Rebounds

	Cl	Gm	No	Avg
Popeye Jones, Murray St.	Sr.	30	431	14.4
Shaquille O'Neal, LSU	Jr.	30	421	14.0
Tim Burroughs, Jacksonville	Sr.	28	370	13.2
Adam Keefe, Stanford	Sr.	29	355	12.2
Leonard White, Southern-BR.	Sr.	30	367	12.2
Jerome Sims, Youngstown St	Jr.	28	327	11.7
LaPhonso Ellis, Notre Dame	Sr.	33	385	11.7
Marcus Stokes, SW Louisiana	Sr.	32	370	11.6
Darryl Johnson, San Francisco	Sr.	27	309	11.4
Drew Henderson, Fairfield	Jr.	28	318	11.4
Reggie Smith, TCU	Sr.	34	386	11.4

Blocked Shots

	Cl	Gm	No	Avg
Shaquille O'Neal, LSU	Jr.	30	157	5.2
Alonzo Mourning, Georgetown	Sr.	32	160	5.0
Kevin Roberson, Vermont	Sr.	28	139	5.0
Acie Earl, Iowa	Jr.	30	121	4.0
Vin Baker, Hartford	Jr.	27	100	3.7
David Van Dyke, UTEP	Sr.	33	116	3.5
Robert Horry, Alabama	Sr.	35	121	3.5
Khari Jaxon, New Mexico	Jr.	33	109	3.3
Derrick Chandler, Nebraska	Jr.	29	91	3.1
Charles Outlaw, Houston	Jr.	31	97	3.1

Assists

	Cl	Gm	No	Avg
Van Usher, Tenn. Tech	Sr.	29	254	8.8
Sam Crawford, N.Mexico St	Jr.	33	282	8.5
Orlando Smart, San Fran	So.	29	241	8.3
Kevin Soares, Nevada	Sr.	29	227	7.8
Chuck Evans, Miss.St	Jr.	28	219	7.8
Tony Walker, Loyola-CA	Sr.	28	218	7.8
Dallas Dale, Southern Miss.	Sr.	29	222	7.7
Bobby Hurley, Duke	Jr.	31	237	7.6
Tony Miller, Marquette	Fr.	29	221	7.6
Cedric Yelding, So.Alabama	Jr.	26	184	7.1

Steals

	Cl	Gm	No	Avg
Victor Snipes, NE Illinois	So.	25	86	3.4
Reggie Burcy, Chicago St	Sr.	26	85	3.3
David Corbitt, Central Conn St	So.	28	88	3.1
Marc Mitchell, WI-Milwaukee	Jr.	25	78	3.1
Kevin Soares, Nevada	Sr.	29	90	3.1
Leonard White, Southern BR.	Jr.	30	92	3.1

Field Goal Percentage
Minimum 5 Field Goals made per game.

	Cl	Gm	FG	FGA	Pct
Charles Outlaw, Houston	Jr.	31	156	228	.684
Warren Kidd, Mid.Tenn.St	Jr.	27	156	235	.664
Matt Fish, NC-Wilmington	Sr.	28	206	319	.646
Johnny McDowell, TX-Arlington	Jr.	29	184	287	.641
Elmore Spencer, UNLV	Sr.	28	174	273	.637

Free Throw Percentage
Minimum 2.5 Free Throws made per game.

	Cl	Gm	FT	FTA	Pct
Don MacLean, UCLA	Sr.	32	197	214	.921
Keith Adkins, NC-Wilmington	Jr.	27	78	85	.918
Scott Shreffler, Evansville	Jr.	24	78	85	.918
Matt Hildebrand, Liberty	So.	29	114	125	.912
Jeff Lauritzen, Indiana St.	Sr.	28	82	91	.901

3-Pt Field Goal Percentage
Minimum 1.5 Three-Point FG made per game.

	Cl	Gm	FG	FGA	Pct
Sean Wightman, Western Mich	Jr.	30	48	76	.632
Christian Laettner, Duke	Sr.	35	54	97	.557
Lance Barker, Valparaiso	Fr.	26	61	117	.521
Ronnie Battle, Auburn	Jr.	27	71	139	.511
Tony Bennett, WI-Green Bay	Sr.	30	95	186	.511

3-Pt Field Goals Per Game

	Cl	Gm	No	Avg
Doug Day, Radford	Jr.	29	117	4.0
Mark Alberts, Akron	Jr.	28	110	3.9
Randy Woods, La Salle	Sr.	31	121	3.9
Peter McKelvey, Portland	Jr.	28	106	3.8
Jack Hurd, La Salle	Sr.	31	113	3.6
Derek Turner, So.Alabama	Sr.	26	93	3.6

TEAM

Scoring Offense

	Gm	W-L	Pts	Avg
Northwestern St	28	15-13	2660	95.0
Oklahoma	30	21-9	2838	94.6
Southern-BR.	30	18-12	2809	93.6
Georgia Southern	31	25-6	2836	91.5
Loyola-CA	28	15-13	2552	91.1
Texas	35	23-12	3175	90.7
Arkansas	34	26-8	3053	89.8
Southern Utah	28	20-8	2489	88.9
Morehead St	29	14-15	2564	88.4
Alabama St	28	14-14	2471	88.3

Scoring Defense

	Gm	W-L	Pts	Avg
Princeton	28	22-6	1349	48.2
Wisconsin-Green Bay	30	25-5	1659	55.3
SW Missouri St	31	23-8	1761	56.8
Monmouth	29	20-9	1701	58.7
Ball St	33	24-9	1959	59.4
Miami-OH	31	23-8	1887	60.9
Marquette	29	16-13	1777	61.3
Utah	35	24-11	2157	61.6
Dartmouth	26	10-16	1604	61.7
Yale	26	17-9	1610	61.9

Scoring Margin

	Off	Def	Margin
Indiana	83.4	65.8	+17.6
Kansas	84.5	68.1	+16.4
Arizona	84.8	68.8	+16.0
Cincinnati	79.0	63.1	+15.9
Duke	88.0	72.6	+15.4

Other Men's Tournaments

NIT Tournament

The 55th annual National Invitational Tournament had a 32-team field. First three rounds played on home courts of higher seeded teams. Semifinal, Third Place and Championship games played March 30-April 1 at Madison Square Garden in New York.

First Round

at Tennessee 71	Ala-Birmingham	68
at Notre Dame 63	Western Mich.	56
Virginia 83	at Villanova	80
at Kansas St. 85	Western Ky.	74
Pittsburgh 67	at Penn St.	65
at Washington St. 72	Minnesota	70
at Manhattan 67	WI-Green Bay	65
at Purdue 82	Butler	56
at Florida 66	Richmond	52
at Boston College 78	Southern Ill.	69
Rhode Island 68	at Vanderbilt	63
at TCU 73	Long Beach St.	61
at New Mexico 90	Louisiana Tech	84
at Utah 57	Ball St.	57
Arizona St. 71	at UC-Santa Barbara	65
at Rutgers 73	James Madison	69

Second Round

at Purdue 67		TCU	51
at Notre Dame 64		Kansas St.	47
at Virginia 77		Tennessee	52
Manhattan 62		at Rutgers	61
Florida 77		at Pittsburgh	74
at New Mexico 79		Washington St.	71
Rhode Island 81	2OT	at Boston College	80
Utah 60		Arizona St.	58

Quarterfinals

at Notre Dame 74	Manhattan	58
Florida 74	at Purdue	67
at Virginia 76	New Mexico	71
at Utah 84	Rhode Island	72

Semifinals

Virginia 62	Florida	56
Notre Dame 58	Utah	55

Third Place

Utah 81	Florida 78

Championship

Virginia 81	OT	Notre Dame	76

Final NY Times Computer Top 30
Taken **before** NCAA Tournament.

Based on an analysis of each team's scores with emphasis on three factors: who won, by what margin, and against what quality opposition.

	Rating			Rating
1 Duke	1.000	16	Houston	.865
2 Kansas	.992	17	Nebraska	.854
3 UNLV	.949	18	Michigan St	.852
4 UCLA	.936	19	Michigan	.847
5 Indiana	.925	20	Alabama	.846
6 Kentucky	.924	21	Seton Hall	.841
7 UMass	.923	22	LSU	.836
8 Cincinnati	.914	23	N.Carolina	.831
9 Ohio St	.911	24	St.John's	.815
Oklahoma St	.911	25	Georgia Tech	.814
11 Arkansas	.893		NC-Charlotte	.814
12 USC	.891	27	Memphis St	.813
13 Arizona	.890	28	Iowa St	.811
14 Oklahoma	.884	29	Florida St	.807
15 Missouri	.873	30	Rhode Island	.797

NCAA Division II

The eight regional winners of the 32-team Division II tournament: NEW ENGLAND—Bridgeport,CT (26-6); EAST—California-PA (30-1); SOUTH ATLANTIC—Virginia Union (27-3); SOUTH—Jacksonville St.,AL (28-1); SOUTH CENTRAL—Central Oklahoma (25-6); GREAT LAKES—Kentucky Wesleyan (23-7); NORTH CENTRAL—South Dakota St. (24-8); WEST—CS-Bakersfield (25-6).

The Elite Eight played for the Division II championship, March 26-28, in Springfield, MA. There was no Third Place game.

Quarterfinals

Bridgeport 127	OT	Central Okla. 124
California-PA 84		S.Dakota St. 73
CS-Bakersfield 89		Jacksonville St. 59
Virginia Union 81		Ky.Wesleyan 69

Semifinals

Bridgeport 76	California-PA 75
Virginia Union 69	CS-Bakersfield 66

Championship

Virginia Union 100	Bridgeport 75

NCAA Division III

The four sectional winners of the 40-team Division III tournament: ATLANTIC/NORTHEAST—Jersey City St. (27-3); MID-ATLANTIC/EAST—Rochester,NY (27-2); MIDWEST/SOUTH—Wisconsin-Platteville (26-3); GREAT LAKES/WEST—Calvin,MI (29-1).

The Final Four played for the Division III championship, March 20-21, in Springfield, OH.

Semifinals

Rochester 61	WI-Platteville 48
Calvin 81	Jersey City St. 40

Third Place

WI-Platteville 72	Jersey City St. 61

Championship

Calvin 62	Rochester 49

NAIA Division I

The quarterfinalists, in alphabetical order, after two rounds of the 32-team NAIA tournament: Biola,CA (33-3); BYU-Hawaii (28-6); Central Arkansas (26-4); Cumberland,KY (24-8); Erskine,SC (27-6); Georgetown-KY (34-1); Oklahoma City (35-0); Pfeiffer,NC (29-4).

All tournament games played, March 17-23, at Kemper Arena in Kansas City. There was no Third Place game.

Quarterfinals: Oklahoma City 97, Cumberland 63; Pfeiffer 99, Biola 83; BYU-Hawaii 72, Georgetown-KY 70; Central Arkansas 74, Erskine 62.

Semifinals: Oklahoma City 102, Pfeiffer 92; Central Arkansas 72, BYU-Hawaii 65.

Championship: Oklahoma City 82, Central Arkansas 73 (OT).

NAIA Division II

The semifinalists, in alphabetical order, after two rounds of the 20-team NAIA tournament: Concordia,NE (27-9); Dakota St. (19-15); Grace,IN (30-5); Northwestern-IA (24-7).

All tournament games played, March 12-17, at Stephenville, Texas. There was no Third Place game.

Semifinals: Northwestern-IA 91, Dakota St. 68; Grace 95, Concordia 89. **Championship:** Grace 85, Northwestern-IA 79 (OT).

Final Regular Season AP Women's Top 25 Poll

Taken before start of NCAA tournament.

Compiled by Mel Greenberg of the *Philadelphia Inquirer*: first place votes in parentheses; records through March 15; total points (based on 25 for 1st, 24 for 2nd, etc.); record in NCAA tourney and team lost to; head coach (career years and record, including NCAA tourney), and preseason ranking. Teams in **bold** type went on to reach NCAA Final Four.

	Mar.15 Record	Points	NCAA Recap	Head Coach	Preseason Rank
1 **Virginia** (65)	29-1	1745	3-1 (Stanford)	Debbie Ryan (15th: 333-124)	2
2 Tennessee (5)	27-2	1685	1-1 (Western Ky.)	Pat Summitt (18th: 470-121)	1
3 **Stanford**	25-3	1561	5-0	Tara VanDerveer (13th: 296-92)	7
4 S.F.Austin St	27-2	1490	1-1 (USC)	Gary Blair (7th: 182-39)	14
5 Mississippi	27-2	1441	2-1 (SW Mo.St.)	Van Chancellor (14th: 341-105)	23
6 Miami-FL	29-1	1384	1-1 (Vanderbilt)	Ferne Labati (13th: 232-147)	47t
7 Iowa	25-3	1381	0-1 (SW Mo.St.)	Vivian Stringer (20th: 461-107)	9
8 Maryland	23-5	1271	2-1 (Western Ky.)	Chris Weller (17th: 353-145)	15
9 Penn St	23-6	1185	1-1 (Mississippi)	Rene Portland (16th: 362-126)	3
10 **SW Missouri St**	27-2	1054	4-1 (Western Ky.)	Cheryl Burnett (5th: 92-53)	30
11 Purdue	22-6	1044	1-1 (Maryland)	Lin Dunn (21st: 358-222)	10
12 Texas Tech	26-4	916	1-1 (Stanford)	Marsha Sharp (10th: 210-94)	26
13 Vanderbilt	20-8	848	2-1 (Virginia)	Jim Foster (14th: 270-135)	8
14 West Virginia	25-3	786	1-1 (Virginia)	*Kittie Blakemore (19th: 301-214) & Scott Harrelson (4th: 86-34)	61t
15 **Western Ky.**	23-7	760	4-1 (Stanford)	Paul Sanderford (10th: 248-77)	5
16 George Washington	24-6	633	1-1 (Virginia)	Joe McKeown (6th: 130-48)	25
17 Kansas	25-5	600	1-1 (SW Mo.St.)	Marian Washington (19th: 347-216)	34
18 Alabama	22-6	494	1-1 (Western Ky.)	Rick Moody (3rd: 56-31)	38
19 Texas	21-9	389	0-1 (UCLA)	Jody Conradt (23rd: 598-145)	12
20 Clemson	20-9	375	1-1 (West Va.)	Jim Davis (5th: 125-59)	20
21 Creighton	27-3	311	1-1 (S.F.Austin)	Bruce Rasmussen (12th: 196-147)	47t
22 Houston	22-7	261	0-1 (UCSB)	Jessie Kenlaw (2nd: 42-20)	NR
23 USC	21-7	177	2-1 (Stanford)	Marianne Stanley (15th: 329-139)	19
24 Colorado	22-8	143	0-1 (So.Ill.)	Ceal Barry (13th: 239-151)	45
25 UC-Santa Barbara	26-4	107	1-1 (Stanford)	Mark French (13th: 175-183)	59
Vermont	29-0	107	0-1 (Geo.Wash.)	Cathy Inglese (6th: 92-73)	NR

*Co-coaches.

Others receiving votes: 26. Hawaii (22-6, 95 pts) **27.** Georgia (19-11, 78) **28.** Wisconsin (20-8, 76) **29.** California (20-8, 54) **30.** North Carolina (21-8, 45) **31.** Connecticut (22-10, 29) **32.** UCLA (20-9, 28) **33.** DePaul (21-10, 25) **34.** Toledo (25-5, 22) **35.** Long Beach St. (21-9, 19) **36.** Arizona St. (20-8, 16) **37.** Louisiana Tech (20-9, 12), Northwestern (17-10, 12) and Rutgers (20-10, 12) **40.** Providence (21-8, 11) **41.** Ala-Birmingham (21-6, 9) and Lamar (21-7, 9) **43.** Montana (22-6, 8) and Nebraska (20-9, 8) **45.** Northern Ill. (17-13, 6) and St.Peter's (24-6, 6) **47.** Arkansas (23-6, 3), Auburn (17-12, 3), La Salle (25-5, 3) and Southern Ill. (22-7, 3) **52.** Bowling Green (24-5, 1), Florida Int'l (22-8, 1), Fordham (21-8, 1), Georgia Tech (17-13, 1) and Old Dominion (20-10, 1).

NCAA Women's Division I

Individual Leaders

Includes games through NCAA tournament.

Scoring

	Cl.	Gm	Pts	Avg
Andrea Congreavers, Mercer	Jr.	28	925	33.0
Martha Sheldon, Portland	Sr.	27	721	26.7
Sarah Behn, Boston College	Jr.	28	743	26.5
Tracy Lis, Providence	Sr.	30	767	25.6
Karen Jennings, Nebraska	Jr.	32	810	25.3
Rosemary Kosiorek, West Va	Sr.	30	730	24.3
Shannon Cate, Montana	Sr.	25	583	23.3
Frances Savage, Miami-FL	Sr.	32	742	23.2
Trisha Stafford, California	Sr.	29	647	22.3
MaChelle Joseph, Purdue	Sr.	30	665	22.2

Rebounds

	Cl.	Gm	No	Avg
Christy Greis, Evansville	Jr.	28	383	13.7
Belinda Strong, LIU-Bklyn	Sr.	29	394	13.6
Angel Webb, MD-Balt.County	Sr.	28	370	13.2
Lanette Taylor, Cleveland St	Sr.	27	352	13.0
Chanta Powell, So.Alabama	Sr.	28	335	12.0

Assists

	Cl.	Gm	No	Avg
Mimi Harris, La Salle	Sr.	33	320	9.7
Tine Freil, Pacific	Jr.	28	251	9.0
Andrea Nagy, Fla Int'l	Fr.	33	282	8.5
Stephany Raines, Mercer	Sr.	27	223	8.3
Kim Kawamoto, Army	Sr.	29	234	8.1

Tournament Seeds

WEST

1 **Stanford** (25-3)
2 S.F.Austin (27-2)
3 USC (21-7)
4 Texas Tech (26-4)
5 California (20-8)
6 Wisconsin (20-8)
7 Creighton (27-3)
8 Houston (22-7)
9 UC-S.Barbara (26-4)
10 Long Beach St. (21-9)
11 Montana (22-6)
12 Santa Clara (20-9)

MIDEAST

1 Tennessee (27-2)
2 Maryland (23-5)
3 Purdue (22-6)
4 **Western Ky.** (23-7)
5 Alabama (22-6)
6 La. Tech (20-9)
7 Providence (21-8)
8 Rutgers (20-10)
9 Southern Miss. (21-9)
10 Toledo (25-5)
11 Northern Ill. (17-13)
12 Tenn. Tech (21-8)

MIDWEST

1 Iowa (25-3)
2 Mississippi (27-2)
3 Penn St. (20-9)
4 Texas (21-9)
5 UCLA (19-9)
6 Arizona St. (20-8)
7 Colorado (22-8)
8 **SW Missouri St.** (27-2)
9 Kansas (25-5)
10 Southern Ill. (22-7)
11 DePaul (20-9)
12 Notre Dame (14-16)

EAST

1 **Virginia** (29-1)
2 Miami-FL (29-1)
3 Vanderbilt (20-8)
4 W.Virginia (25-3)
5 Clemson (20-9)
6 Connecticut (22-10)
7 N.Carolina (21-8)
8 G.Washington (24-6)
9 Vermont (29-0)
10 Old Dominion (20-10)
11 St.Peter's (24-6)
12 Tenn-Chatt. (18-11)

1992 NCAA BASKETBALL WOMEN'S DIVISION I

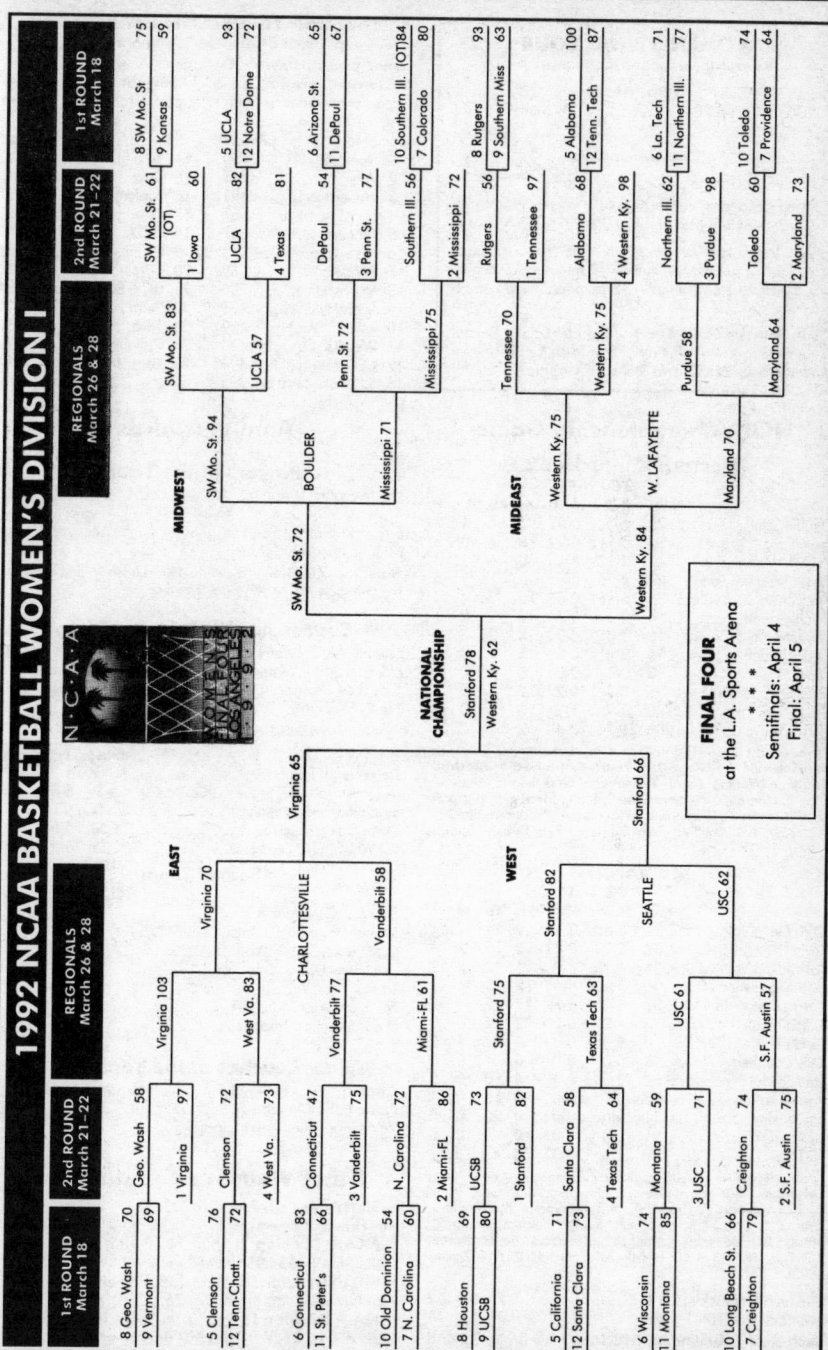

N·C·A·A

1992 FINAL FOUR
LOS ANGELES
1·9·9·2

FINAL FOUR
at the L.A. Sports Arena
* * *
Semifinals: April 4
Final: April 5

NATIONAL CHAMPIONSHIP
Stanford 78
Western Ky. 62

NATIONAL CHAMPIONSHIP
Stanford 66

MIDWEST

1st ROUND March 18	2nd ROUND March 21-22	REGIONALS March 26 & 28
8 SW Mo. St. 75		
9 Kansas 59	SW Mo. St. 61 (OT)	
	1 Iowa 60	SW Mo. St. 83
5 UCLA 93		
12 Notre Dame 72	UCLA 82	
	4 Texas 81	UCLA 57
6 Arizona St. 65		
11 DePaul 67	DePaul 54	
	3 Penn St. 77	Penn St. 72
10 Southern Ill. (OT)84		
7 Colorado 80	Southern Ill. 56	
	2 Mississippi 72	Mississippi 75

SW Mo. St. 94
BOULDER
Mississippi 71

SW Mo. St. 72

MIDEAST

1st ROUND March 18	2nd ROUND March 21-22	REGIONALS March 26 & 28
8 Rutgers 93		
9 Southern Miss 63	Rutgers 56	
	1 Tennessee 97	Tennessee 70
5 Alabama 100		
12 Tenn. Tech 87	Alabama 68	
	4 Western Ky. 98	Western Ky. 75
6 La. Tech 71		
11 Northern Ill. 77	Northern Ill. 62	
	3 Purdue 98	Purdue 58
10 Toledo 74		
7 Providence 64	Toledo 60	
	2 Maryland 73	Maryland 64

Western Ky. 75
W. LAFAYETTE
Maryland 70

Western Ky. 84

EAST

1st ROUND March 18	2nd ROUND March 21-22	REGIONALS March 26 & 28
8 Geo. Wash 70		
9 Vermont 69	Geo. Wash 58	
	1 Virginia 97	Virginia 103
5 Clemson 76		
12 Tenn.-Chatt. 72	Clemson 72	
	4 West Va. 73	West Va. 83
6 Connecticut 83		
11 St. Peter's 66	Connecticut 47	
	3 Vanderbilt 75	Vanderbilt 77
10 Old Dominion 54		
7 N. Carolina 60	N. Carolina 72	
	2 Miami-FL 86	Miami-FL 61

Virginia 70
CHARLOTTESVILLE
Vanderbilt 58

Virginia 65

WEST

1st ROUND March 18	2nd ROUND March 21-22	REGIONALS March 26 & 28
8 Houston 69		
9 UCSB 80	UCSB 73	
	1 Stanford 82	Stanford 75
5 California 71		
12 Santa Clara 73	Santa Clara 58	
	4 Texas Tech 64	Texas Tech 63
6 Wisconsin 74		
11 Montana 85	Montana 59	
	3 USC 71	USC 61
10 Long Beach St. 66		
7 Creighton 79	Creighton 74	
	2 S.F. Austin 75	S.F. Austin 57

Stanford 82
SEATTLE
USC 62

Stanford 66

WOMEN'S FINAL FOUR

At Los Angeles Sports Arena (April 4-5)

Semifinals

Western Kentucky 84 . . . . SW Missouri St. 72
Stanford 66 . . . . Virginia 65

Championship

Stanford 78 . . . . Western Kentucky 62

Final records: Stanford (30-3), Western Kentucky (27-8), Virginia (32-2), SW Missouri St. (31-3).

Outstanding Player: Molly Goodenbour, Stanford junior guard. Semifinal—39 minutes, 16 points, 6 assists, 5 steals. Final—36 minutes, 12 points, 6 assists.

All-Tournament Team: Goodenbour, Rachel Hemmer and Val Whiting of Stanford; Kim Pehlke of Western Ky. and Dawn Staley of Virginia.

Final USA Today/CNN Coaches Poll

Taken **after** NCAA Tournament.

Voted on by panel of 30 women's basketball coaches and media following the NCAA tournament: first place votes in parentheses with total points (based on 25 for 1st, 24 for 2nd, etc.).

		Points			Points
1	Stanford (30)	750	14	Penn St	393
2	Virginia	711	15	Texas Tech	345
3	Western Ky	699	16	Purdue	313
4	SW Missouri St.	657	17	Alabama	236
5	Tennessee	607	18	UCLA	217
6	Mississippi	577	19	Clemson	201
7	Vanderbilt	539	20	G.Washington	179
8	Maryland	503	21	UC-S.Barbara	125
9	Miami-FL	496	22	Vermont	119
10	Iowa	459	23	Texas	98
11	West Va	410	24	Creighton	95
12	USC	404	25	Kansas	89
13	S.F.Austin	395			

NCAA Championship Game

Western Kentucky 62

	Min	FG M-A	FT M-A	Pts	Rb	A	F
Debbie Scott	25	1-7	0-0	**2**	4	4	3
Liesa Lang	32	5-11	8-12	**18**	12	0	5
Paulette Monroe	17	3-12	2-2	**8**	6	0	3
Renee Westmoreland	29	2-10	0-0	**6**	1	1	5
Kim Pehlke	38	6-16	0-0	**16**	3	4	3
Debbie Houk	6	0-1	0-0	**0**	1	0	1
Trina Wilson	18	1-3	0-2	**2**	3	0	1
Kristie Jordan	16	2-4	0-0	**5**	4	1	2
Lea Robinson	3	0-1	0-0	**0**	0	0	1
Jennifer Berryman	6	0-2	2-2	**2**	1	0	2
Veronica Cook	10	1-4	1-2	**3**	3	0	1
TOTALS	200	21-71	13-20	**62**	38	10	27

Three-point FG: 7-19 (Pehlke 4-8, Westmoreland 2-5, Jordan 1-3, Robinson 0-1, Cook 0-2); **Team Rebounds:** 4; **Blocked Shots:** 1 (Westmoreland); **Turnovers:** 14 (Pehlke 5, Houk 2, Lang 2, Monroe 2, Westmoreland 2, Scott); **Steals:** 11 (Lang 3, Scott 3, Jordan 2, Westmoreland 2, Wilson). **Percentages:** 2-pt FG (.269); 3-Pt FG (.368); Total FG (.296); Free Throws (.650).

Stanford 78

	Min	FG M-A	FT M-A	Pts	Rb	A	F
Chris MacMurdo	31	3-5	3-4	**9**	11	1	1
Rachel Hemmer	37	5-12	8-11	**18**	15	2	3
Val Whiting	36	4-10	8-9	**16**	13	2	1
Molly Goodenbour	36	3-10	5-6	**12**	3	6	2
Christy Hedgpeth	33	6-15	3-3	**17**	2	1	2
Anita Kaplan	3	1-3	0-0	**2**	1	0	1
Tanda Rucker	8	0-0	0-0	**0**	1	1	0
Kelly Daugherty	5	0-0	0-0	**0**	1	0	0
Kate Paye	7	0-0	4-4	**4**	0	0	2
Angela Taylor	2	0-0	0-0	**0**	0	0	1
Ann Adkins	1	0-0	0-0	**0**	0	0	0
Niki Sevillian	1	0-0	0-0	**0**	0	0	0
TOTALS	200	22-55	31-37	**78**	47	13	13

Three-point FG: 3-14 (Hedgpeth 2-7, Goodenbour 1-7); **Team Rebounds:** 4; **Blocked Shots:** 3 (Dougherty, MacMurdo, Whiting); **Turnovers:** 20 (Goodenbour 5, Hemmer 4, MacMurdo 3, Whiting 2, Dougherty, Hedgpeth, Rucker, Sevillian, Team 2); **Steals:** 3 (Goodenbour, Hedgpeth, Hemmer). **Percentages:** 2-Pt FG (.463); 3-Pt FG (.214); Total FG (.400); Free Throws (.838).

Western Kentucky (Sun Belt) . . . . 27 35—**62**
Stanford (Pac-10) . . . . 37 41—**78**

Technical Fouls: none. **Officials:** Patty Broderick and Bill Stokes. **Attendance:** 12,072. **TV Rating:** 4.1/11 share (CBS).

Annual Awards

Players of the Year

Dawn Staley, Virginia . . . . Naismith,WBCA
and USBWA
Susan Robinson, Penn St . . . . Wade
MaChelle Joseph, Purdue . . . . WBNS
Note: The Wade Trophy is awarded for academics and community service as well as player performance.

Consensus All-America Team

The NCAA Division I players cited most frequently by the US Basketball Writers Association, Women's Basketball Coaches Association, and the Women's Basketball News Service.

First Team

	Class	Hgt	Pos
Dena Head, Tennessee	Sr.	5-10	G
MaChelle Joseph, Purdue	Sr.	5-8	G
Susan Robinson, Penn St.	Sr.	6-1	F
Dawn Staley, Virginia	Sr.	5-5	G
Val Whiting, Stanford	Jr.	6-2	C

Second Team

	Class	Hgt	Pos
Shannon Cate, Montana	Sr.	6-1	F
Shantel Hardison, La. Tech.	Sr.	5-8	G
Rosemary Kosiorek, West Va	Sr.	5-5	G
Lisa Leslie, USC	So.	6-5	C
Tammi Reiss, Virginia	Sr.	5-5	G
Frances Savage, Miami-FL	Sr.	5-10	F
Sheryl Swoopes, Texas Tech	Jr.	6-0	F

Coaches of the Year

Chris Weller, Maryland . . . . Naismith and USBWA
Ferne Labati, Miami-FL . . . . WBCA
Van Chancellor, Mississippi . . . . WBNS

Other Women's Tournaments

NWIT (Mar.28, Amarillo, TX): Final—Georgia Tech 90, Hawaii 72.
NCAA Division II (Mar.28, Fargo, ND): Final—Delta St.(MS) 65, North Dakota St. 63.
NCAA Division III (Mar.21, Bethlehem, PA): Final—Alma (MI) 79, Moravian (PA) 75.
NAIA Division I (Mar.10, Jackson, TN): Final—Arkansas Tech 84, Wayland (TX) Baptist 68.
NAIA Division II (Mar.17, Monmouth, OR): Final—Northern St.(SD) 73, Tarleton St.(TX) 56.

COLLEGE BASKETBALL
S T A T I S T I C S

THROUGH THE YEARS
1901-1992

NCAA'S • ALL-TIME LEADERS

THE 1993 INFORMATION PLEASE SPORTS ALMANAC

SEC B

PAGE 267

National Champions

The Helms Foundation of Los Angeles, under the direction of founder Bill Schroeder, selected national college basketball champions from 1942-82 and researched retroactive picks from 1901-41. The first NIT tournament and then the NCAA tournament have settled the national championship since 1938, but there are four years (1939,'40,'44 and '54) where the Helms selections differ.

Multiple champions (1901-37): Chicago, Columbia and Wisconsin (3); Kansas, Minnesota, Notre Dame, Penn, Pittsburgh, Syracuse and Yale (2).

Multiple champions (since 1938): UCLA (10); Kentucky (6); Indiana (5); Cincinnati, Duke, Kansas, Louisville, North Carolina, N.C.State, Oklahoma A&M and San Francisco (2).

Year		Record	Head Coach	Outstanding Player
1901	**Yale**	10-4	No coach	G.M.Clark, F
1902	**Minnesota**	11-0	Louis Cooke	W.C.Deering, F
1903	**Yale**	15-1	W.H.Murphy	R.B.Hyatt, F
1904	**Columbia**	17-1	No coach	Harry Fisher, F
1905	**Columbia**	19-1	No coach	Harry Fisher, F
1906	**Dartmouth**	16-2	No coach	George Grebenstein, F
1907	**Chicago**	22-2	Joseph Raycroft	John Schommer, C
1908	**Chicago**	21-2	Joseph Raycroft	John Schommer, C
1909	**Chicago**	12-0	Joseph Raycroft	John Schommer, C
1910	**Columbia**	11-1	Harry Fisher	Ted Kiendl, F
1911	**St.John's-NY**	14-0	Claude Allen	John Keenan, F/C
1912	**Wisconsin**	15-0	Doc Meanwell	Otto Stangel, F
1913	**Navy**	9-0	Louis Wenzel	Laurence Wild, F
1914	**Wisconsin**	15-0	Doc Meanwell	Gene Van Gent, C
1915	**Illinois**	16-0	Ralph Jones	Ray Woods, G
1916	**Wisconsin**	20-1	Doc Meanwell	George Levis, F
1917	**Washington St**	25-1	Doc Bohler	Roy Bohler, G
1918	**Syracuse**	16-1	Edmund Dollard	Joe Schwarzer, G
1919	**Minnesota**	13-0	Louis Cooke	Arnold Oss, F
1920	**Pennsylvania**	22-1	Lon Jourdet	George Sweeney, F
1921	**Pennsylvania**	21-2	Edward McNichol	Danny McNichol, G
1922	**Kansas**	16-2	Phog Allen	Paul Endacott, G
1923	**Kansas**	17-1	Phog Allen	Paul Endacott, G
1924	**North Carolina**	25-0	Bo Shepard	Jack Cobb, F
1925	**Princeton**	21-2	Al Wittmer	Art Loeb, G
1926	**Syracuse**	19-1	Lew Andreas	Vic Hanson, F
1927	**Notre Dame**	19-1	George Keogan	John Nyikos, C
1928	**Pittsburgh**	21-0	Doc Carlson	Chuck Hyatt, F
1929	**Montana St.**	36-2	Schubert Dyche	John (Cat) Thompson, F
1930	**Pittsburgh**	23-2	Doc Carlson	Chuck Hyatt, F
1931	**Northwestern**	16-1	Dutch Lonborg	Joe Reiff, C
1932	**Purdue**	17-1	Piggy Lambert	John Wooden, G
1933	**Kentucky**	20-3	Adolph Rupp	Forest Sale, F
1934	**Wyoming**	26-3	Willard Witte	Les Witte, G
1935	**NYU**	19-1	Howard Cann	Sid Gross, F
1936	**Notre Dame**	22-2-1	George Keogan	John Moir, F
1937	**Stanford**	25-2	John Bunn	Hank Luisetti, F

Year		Record	Winner	Head Coach	Outstanding Player
1938	**Temple**	23-2	NIT	James Usilton	Meyer Bloom, G
1939	**Oregon**	29-5	NCAA	Howard Hobson	Slim Wintermute, C
	LIU-Brooklyn (Helms)	24-0	NIT	Clair Bee	Irv Torgoff, F
1940	**Indiana**	20-3	NCAA	Branch McCracken	Marv Huffman, G
	USC (Helms)	20-3	*	Sam Barry	Ralph Vaughn, F

*USC was beaten by Kansas in the West regional of the NCAA tournament.

National Champions (Cont.)

Year		Record	Winner	Head Coach	Outstanding Player
1941	Wisconsin	20-3	NCAA	Bud Foster	Gene Englund, F
1942	Stanford	27-4	NCAA	Everett Dean	Jim Pollard, F
1943	Wyoming	31-2	NCAA	Everett Shelton	Kenny Sailors, G
1944	Utah	21-4	NCAA	Vadal Peterson	Arnie Ferrin, F
	Army (Helms)	15-0	**	Ed Kelleher	Dale Hall, F
1945	Oklahoma A&M	27-4	NCAA	Hank Iba	Bob Kurland, C
1946	Oklahoma A&M	31-2	NCAA	Hank Iba	Bob Kurland, C
1947	Holy Cross	27-3	NCAA	Doggie Julian	George Kaftan, F
1948	Kentucky	36-3	NCAA	Adolph Rupp	Ralph Beard, G
1949	Kentucky	32-2	NCAA	Adolph Rupp	Alex Groza, C
1950	CCNY	24-5	NCAA & NIT	Nat Holman	Irwin Dambrot, G
1951	Kentucky	32-2	NCAA	Adolph Rupp	Bill Spivey, C
1952	Kansas	28-3	NCAA	Phog Allen	Clyde Lovellette, C
1953	Indiana	23-3	NCAA	Branch McCracken	Don Schlundt, C
1954	La Salle	26-4	NCAA	Ken Loeffler	Tom Gola, F
	Kentucky (Helms)	25-0	***	Adolph Rupp	Cliff Hagan, G
1955	San Francisco	28-1	NCAA	Phil Woolpert	Bill Russell, C
1956	San Francisco	29-0	NCAA	Phil Woolpert	Bill Russell, C
1957	North Carolina	32-0	NCAA	Frank McGuire	Lennie Rosenbluth, F
1958	Kentucky	23-6	NCAA	Adolph Rupp	Vern Hatton, G
1959	California	24-4	NCAA	Pete Newell	Darrall Imhoff, C
1960	Ohio St	25-3	NCAA	Fred Taylor	Jerry Lucas, C
1961	Cincinnati	27-3	NCAA	Ed Jucker	Bob Wiesenhahn, F
1962	Cincinnati	29-2	NCAA	Ed Jucker	Paul Hogue, C
1963	Loyola-IL	29-2	NCAA	George Ireland	Jerry Harkness, F
1964	UCLA	30-0	NCAA	John Wooden	Walt Hazzard, G
1965	UCLA	28-2	NCAA	John Wooden	Gail Goodrich, G
1966	Texas Western	28-1	NCAA	Don Haskins	Bobby Joe Hill, G
1967	UCLA	30-0	NCAA	John Wooden	Lew Alcindor, C
1968	UCLA	29-1	NCAA	John Wooden	Lew Alcindor, C
1969	UCLA	29-1	NCAA	John Wooden	Lew Alcindor, C
1970	UCLA	28-2	NCAA	John Wooden	Sidney Wicks, F
1971	UCLA	29-1	NCAA	John Wooden	Sidney Wicks, F
1972	UCLA	30-0	NCAA	John Wooden	Bill Walton, C
1973	UCLA	30-0	NCAA	John Wooden	Bill Walton, C
1974	N.C.State	30-1	NCAA	Norm Sloan	David Thompson, F
1975	UCLA	28-3	NCAA	John Wooden	Dave Meyers, F
1976	Indiana	32-0	NCAA	Bob Knight	Scott May, F
1977	Marquette	25-7	NCAA	Al McGuire	Butch Lee, G
1978	Kentucky	30-2	NCAA	Joe B.Hall	Jack Givens, F
1979	Michigan St	26-6	NCAA	Jud Heathcote	Magic Johnson, G
1980	Louisville	33-3	NCAA	Denny Crum	Darrell Griffith, G
1981	Indiana	26-9	NCAA	Bob Knight	Isiah Thomas, G
1982	North Carolina	32-2	NCAA	Dean Smith	James Worthy, F
1983	N.C.State	28-8	NCAA	Jim Valvano	Sidney Lowe, G
1984	Georgetown	34-3	NCAA	John Thompson	Patrick Ewing, C
1985	Villanova	25-10	NCAA	Rollie Massimino	Ed Pinckney, C
1986	Louisville	32-7	NCAA	Denny Crum	Pervis Ellison, C
1987	Indiana	30-4	NCAA	Bob Knight	Steve Alford, G
1988	Kansas	27-11	NCAA	Larry Brown	Danny Manning, C
1989	Michigan	30-7	NCAA	Steve Fisher	Glen Rice, F
1990	UNLV	35-5	NCAA	Jerry Tarkanian	Larry Johnson, F
1991	Duke	32-7	NCAA	Mike Krzyzewski	Christian Laettner, F/C
1992	Duke	34-2	NCAA	Mike Krzyzewski	Christian Laettner, C

**Army did not lift its policy against postseason play until accepting a bid to the 1961 NIT.
***Unbeaten Kentucky turned down a bid to the NCAA tournament after the NCAA declared seniors Cliff Hagan, Frank Ramsey and Lou Tsioropoulos ineligible for postseason play.

The Red Cross Benefit Games, 1943-45

	Year	Winner	Score	Loser
For three seasons during World War II, the NCAA and NIT champions met in a benefit game at Madison Square Garden in New York to raise money for the Red Cross. The NCAA champs won all three games.	1943	Wyoming (NCAA)	52-47	St.John's (NIT)
	1944	Utah (NCAA)	43-36	St.John's (NIT)
	1945	Oklahoma A&M (NCAA)	52-44	DePaul (NIT)

NCAA Final Four

The NCAA basketball tournament began in 1939 under the sponsorship of the National Association of Basketball Coaches, but was taken over by the NCAA in 1940. From 1939-51, the winners of the Eastern and Western Regionals played for the national championship, while regional runners-up shared third place. The concept of a Final Four originated in 1952 when four teams qualified for the first national semifinals. Consolation games to determine overall third place were held between regional finalists from 1946-51 and then national semifinalists from 1952-81. Consolation games were discontinued in 1982.

Multiple winners: UCLA (10); Indiana and Kentucky (5); Cincinnati, Duke, Kansas, Louisville, North Carolina, N.C. State, Oklahoma A&M (now Okla.St.) and San Francisco (2).

Year	Champion	Runner-up	Score	Final Two	Third Place	
1939	Oregon	Ohio St.	46-33	@ Evanston,IL	Oklahoma	Villanova
1940	Indiana	Kansas	60-42	@ Kansas City	Duquesne	USC
1941	Wisconsin	Washington St.	39-34	@ Kansas City	Arkansas	Pittsburgh
1942	Stanford	Dartmouth	53-38	@ Kansas City	Colorado	Kentucky
1943	Wyoming	Georgetown	46-34	@ New York	DePaul	Texas
1944	Utah	Dartmouth	42-40	@ New York	Iowa St.	Ohio St.
1945	Oklahoma A&M	NYU	49-45	@ New York	Arkansas	Ohio St.

Year	Champion	Runner-up	Score	Final Two	Third Place	Fourth Place
1946	Oklahoma A&M	North Carolina	43-40 (OT)	@ New York	Ohio St.	California
1947	Holy Cross	Oklahoma	58-47	@ New York	Texas	CCNY
1948	Kentucky	Baylor	58-42	@ New York	Holy Cross	Kansas St.
1949	Kentucky	Oklahoma A&M	46-36	@ Seattle	Illinois	Oregon St.
1950	CCNY	Bradley	71-68	@ New York	N.C.State	Baylor
1951	Kentucky	Kansas St.	68-58	@ Minneapolis	Illinois	Oklahoma A&M

Year	Champion	Runner-up	Score	Third Place	Fourth Place	Final Four
1952	Kansas	St.John's	80-63	Illinois	Santa Clara	@ Seattle
1953	Indiana	Kansas	69-68	Washington	LSU	@ Kansas City
1954	La Salle	Bradley	92-76	Penn St.	USC	@ Kansas City
1955	San Francisco	La Salle	77-63	Colorado	Iowa	@ Kansas City
1956	San Francisco	Iowa	83-71	Temple	SMU	@ Evanston,IL
1957	North Carolina	Kansas	54-53 (3OT)	San Francisco	Michigan St.	@ Kansas City
1958	Kentucky	Seattle	84-72	Temple	Kansas St.	@ Louisville
1959	California	West Virginia	71-70	Cincinnati	Louisville	@ Louisville
1960	Ohio St.	California	75-55	Cincinnati	NYU	@ San Francisco
1961	Cincinnati	Ohio St.	70-65 (OT)	St.Joseph's-PA	Utah	@ Kansas City
1962	Cincinnati	Ohio St.	71-59	Wake Forest	UCLA	@ Louisville
1963	Loyola-IL	Cincinnati	60-58 (OT)	Duke	Oregon St.	@ Louisville
1964	UCLA	Duke	98-83	Michigan	Kansas St.	@ Kansas City
1965	UCLA	Michigan	91-80	Princeton	Wichita St.	@ Portland,OR
1966	Texas Western	Kentucky	72-65	Duke	Utah	@ College Park,MD
1967	UCLA	Dayton	79-64	Houston	North Carolina	@ Louisville
1968	UCLA	North Carolina	78-55	Ohio St.	Houston	@ Los Angeles
1969	UCLA	Purdue	92-72	Drake	North Carolina	@ Louisville
1970	UCLA	Jacksonville	80-69	New Mexico St.	St.Bonaventure	@ College Park,MD
1971	UCLA	Villanova	68-62	Western Ky.	Kansas	@ Houston
1972	UCLA	Florida St.	81-76	North Carolina	Louisville	@ Los Angeles
1973	UCLA	Memphis St.	87-66	Indiana	Providence	@ St.Louis
1974	N.C.State	Marquette	76-64	UCLA	Kansas	@ Greensboro,NC
1975	UCLA	Kentucky	92-85	Louisville	Syracuse	@ San Diego
1976	Indiana	Michigan	86-68	UCLA	Rutgers	@ Philadelphia
1977	Marquette	North Carolina	67-59	UNLV	NC-Charlotte	@ Atlanta
1978	Kentucky	Duke	94-88	Arkansas	Notre Dame	@ St.Louis
1979	Michigan St.	Indiana St.	75-64	DePaul	Penn	@ Salt Lake City
1980	Louisville	UCLA	59-54	Purdue	Iowa	@ Indianapolis
1981	Indiana	North Carolina	63-50	Virginia	LSU	@ Philadelphia

Year	Champion	Runner-up	Score	Third Place		Final Four
1982	North Carolina	Georgetown	63-62	Houston	Louisville	@ New Orleans
1983	N.C.State	Houston	54-52	Georgia	Louisville	@ Albuquerque
1984	Georgetown	Houston	84-75	Kentucky	Virginia	@ Seattle
1985	Villanova	Georgetown	66-64	Memphis St.	St.John's	@ Lexington
1986	Louisville	Duke	72-69	Kansas	LSU	@ Dallas
1987	Indiana	Syracuse	74-73	Providence	UNLV	@ New Orleans
1988	Kansas	Oklahoma	83-79	Arizona	Duke	@ Kansas City
1989	Michigan	Seton Hall	80-79 (OT)	Duke	Illinois	@ Seattle
1990	UNLV	Duke	103-73	Arkansas	Georgia Tech	@ Denver
1991	Duke	Kansas	72-65	North Carolina	UNLV	@ Indianapolis
1992	Duke	Michigan	71-51	Cincinnati	Indiana	@ Minneapolis

Note: Five teams have had their standing in the Final Four vacated for using ineligible players: **1961**—St.Joseph's-PA (3rd place); **1971**—Villanova (Runner-up) and Western Kentucky (3rd place); **1980**—UCLA (Runner-up); **1985**—Memphis St.(3rd place).

Most Outstanding Player

A Most Outstanding Player has been selected every year of the NCAA tournament. Winners who did not play for the tournament champion are listed in **bold** type. The 1939 and 1951 winners are unofficial and not recognized by the NCAA.

Multiple winners: Lew Alcindor (3); Alex Groza, Bob Kurland, Jerry Lucas and Bill Walton (2).

Year		Year		Year	
1939	**Jimmy Hull**, Ohio St.	1957	**Wilt Chamberlain**, Kansas	1975	Richard Washington, UCLA
		1958	**Elgin Baylor**, Seattle	1976	Kent Benson, Indiana
1940	Marv Huffman, Indiana	1959	**Jerry West**, West Virginia	1977	Butch Lee, Marquette
1941	John Kotz, Wisconsin			1978	Jack Givens, Kentucky
1942	Howie Dallmar, Stanford	1960	Jerry Lucas, Ohio St.	1979	Magic Johnson, Michigan St.
1943	Kenny Sailors, Wyoming	1961	**Jerry Lucas**, Ohio St.		
1944	Arnie Ferrin, Utah	1962	Paul Hogue, Cincinnati	1980	Darrell Griffith, Louisville
1945	Bob Kurland, Okla.A&M	1963	**Art Heyman**, Duke	1981	Isiah Thomas, Indiana
1946	Bob Kurland, Okla.A&M	1964	Walt Hazzard, UCLA	1982	James Worthy, N.Carolina
1947	George Kaftan, Holy Cross	1965	**Bill Bradley**, Princeton	1983	**Akeem Olajuwon**, Houston
1948	Alex Groza, Kentucky	1966	**Jerry Chambers**, Utah	1984	Patrick Ewing, Georgetown
1949	Alex Groza, Kentucky	1967	Lew Alcindor, UCLA	1985	Ed Pinckney, Villanova
		1968	Lew Alcindor, UCLA	1986	Pervis Ellison, Louisville
1950	Irwin Dambrot, CCNY	1969	Lew Alcindor, UCLA	1987	Keith Smart, Indiana
1951	Bill Spivey, Kentucky			1988	Danny Manning, Kansas
1952	Clyde Lovellette, Kansas	1970	Sidney Wicks, UCLA	1989	Glen Rice, Michigan
1953	**B.H.Born**, Kansas	1971	**Howard Porter**, Villanova		
1954	Tom Gola, La Salle	1972	Bill Walton, UCLA	1990	Anderson Hunt, UNLV
1955	Bill Russell, San Francisco	1973	Bill Walton, UCLA	1991	Christian Laettner, Duke
1956	**Hal Lear**, Temple	1974	David Thompson, N.C.State	1992	Bobby Hurley, Duke

Note: Howard Porter (1971) was declared ineligible by the NCAA after the tournament and his award was vacated.

Final Four All-Decade Teams

To celebrate the 50th anniversary of the NCAA tournament in 1989, five All-Decade teams were selected by a blue ribbon panel of coaches and administrators. An All-Time Final Four team was also chosen.

Selection panel: Vic Bubas, Denny Crum, Wayne Duke, Dave Gavitt, Joe B. Hall, Jud Heathcote, Hank Iba, Pete Newell, Dean Smith, John Thompson and John Wooden.

All-Time Team
	Years
Lew Alcindor, UCLA	1967–69
Larry Bird, Indiana St.	1979
Wilt Chamberlain, Kansas	1957
Magic Johnson, Mich.St	1979
Michael Jordan, N.Carolina	1982

All-1950s
	Years
Elgin Baylor, Seattle	1958
Wilt Chamberlain, Kansas	1957
Tom Gola, La Salle	1954
K.C. Jones, San Francisco	1955
Clyde Lovellette, Kansas	1952
Oscar Robertson, Cincinnati	1959–60
Guy Rodgers, Temple	1958
Lennie Rosenbluth, N.Carolina	1957
Bill Russell, San Francisco	1955–56
Jerry West, West Virginia	1959

All-1970s
	Years
Kent Benson, Indiana	1976
Larry Bird, Indiana St	1979
Jack Givens, Kentucky	1978
Magic Johnson, Mich.St	1979
Marques Johnson, UCLA	1975–76
Scott May, Indiana	1976
David Thompson, N.C. State	1974
Bill Walton, UCLA	1972–74
Sidney Wicks, UCLA	1969–71
Keith Wilkes, UCLA	1972–74

All-1940s
	Years
Ralph Beard, Kentucky	1948–49
Howie Dallmar, Stanford	1942
Dwight Eddleman, Illinois	1949
Arnie Ferrin, Utah	1944
Alex Groza, Kentucky	1948–49
George Kaftan, Holy Cross	1947
Bob Kurland, Okla A&M	1945–46
Jim Pollard, Stanford	1942
Kenny Sailors, Wyoming	1943
Gerry Tucker, Oklahoma	1947

All-1960s
	Years
Lew Alcindor, UCLA	1967–69
Bill Bradley, Princeton	1965
Gail Goodrich, UCLA	1964–65
John Havlicek, Ohio St	1961–62
Elvin Hayes, Houston	1967
Walt Hazzard, UCLA	1964
Jerry Lucas, Ohio St.	1960–61
Jeff Mullins, Duke	1964
Cazzie Russell, Michigan	1965
Charlie Scott, N.Carolina	1968–69

All-1980s
	Years
Steve Alford, Indiana	1987
Johnny Dawkins, Duke	1986
Patrick Ewing, Georgetown	1982–84
Darrell Griffith, Louisville	1980
Michael Jordan, N.Carolina	1982
Rodney McCray, Louisville	1980
Akeem Olajuwon, Houston	1983–84
Ed Pinckney, Villanova	1985
Isiah Thomas, Indiana	1981
James Worthy, N.Carolina	1982

Note: Lew Alcindor later changed his name to Kareem Abdul-Jabbar; Keith Wilkes later changed his first name to Jamaal; and Akeem Olajuwon later changed the spelling of his first name to Hakeem.

Collegiate Commissioners Association Tournament

The Collegiate Commissioners Association staged an eight-team tournament for teams that didn't make the NCAA tournament in 1974 and '75.

Most Valuable Players: 1974—Kent Benson, Indiana; 1975—Bob Elliot, Arizona.

Year	Winner	Score	Loser	Site	Year	Winner	Score	Loser	Site
1974	Indiana	85-60	USC	St.Louis	1975	Drake	83-76	Arizona	Louisville

NCAA Tournament Appearances

Through 1992; listed are schools with most appearances, overall tournament records, times reaching Final Four, and number of NCAA championships.

App		W-L	F4	Championships	App		W-L	F4	Championships
34	Kentucky	58-31	9	5 (1948-49, 51,58,78)	18	Ohio St.	31-17	8	1 (1960)
28	UCLA	67-22	14	10 (1964-65, 67-73,75)	18	Arkansas	22-19	4	None
26	N.Carolina	56-27	10	2 (1957,82)	18	Houston	26-23	5	None
24	Notre Dame	25-28	1	None	18	Princeton	11-22	1	None
22	Louisville	39-24	7	2 (1980,86)	17	Duke	50-15	10	2 (1991-92)
22	St.John's	22-24	2	None	17	Georgetown	30-16	4	1 (1984)
21	Indiana	45-16	7	5 (1940,53, 76,81,87)	17	N.C.State	27-16	3	2 (1974,83)
21	Kansas	43-21	9	2 (1952,88)	17	Marquette	25-18	2	1 (1977)
21	Villanova	35-21	3	1 (1985)	17	West Va	11-17	1	None
20	Syracuse	27-21	2	None	16	Temple	18-16	2	None
20	Kansas St	27-24	4	None	16	Oregon St	12-19	2	None
20	DePaul	20-23	2	None	16	Connecticut	10-17	0	None
					16	BYU	10-19	0	None

Note: Although all NCAA tournament appearances are included above, the NCAA has officially voided the records of 1971 runner-up Villanova (4-1) and 1980 runner-up UCLA (5-1) for using ineligible players.

All-Time NCAA Division I Tournament Leaders
CAREER

Scoring

Points

	Years	Gm	Pts
Christian Laettner, Duke	1989-92	23	407
Elvin Hayes, Houston	1966-68	13	358
Danny Manning, Kansas	1985-88	16	328
Oscar Robertson, Cincinnati	1958-60	10	324
Glen Rice, Michigan	1986-89	13	308
Lew Alcindor, UCLA	1967-69	12	304
Bill Bradley, Princeton	1963-65	9	303
Austin Carr, Notre Dame	1969-71	7	289
Jerry West, West Virginia	1958-60	9	275
Danny Ferry, Duke	1986-89	19	269

Average

	Years	Pts	Avg
Austin Carr, Notre Dame	1969-71	289	41.3
Bill Bradley, Princeton	1963-65	303	33.7
Oscar Robertson, Cincinnati	1958-60	324	32.4
Jerry West, W.Virginia	1958-60	275	30.6
Bob Pettit, LSU	1953-54	183	30.5
Bo Kimble, Loyola-CA	1988-90	204	29.1
Len Chappell, Wake Forest	1961-62	221	27.6
Elvin Hayes, Houston	1966-68	358	27.5
Kenny Anderson, Ga.Tech	1990-91	180	25.7
Lew Alcindor, UCLA	1967-69	304	25.3

Rebounds

Total

	Years	Gm	No
Elvin Hayes, Houston	1966-68	13	222
Lew Alcindor, UCLA	1967-69	12	201
Jerry Lucas, Ohio St	1960-62	12	197
Bill Walton, UCLA	1972-74	12	176
Christian Laettner, Duke	1989-92	23	169
Paul Hogue, Cincinnati	1960-62	12	160
Sam Lacey, New Mexico St.	1968-70	11	157
Akeem Olajuwon, Houston	1982-84	15	153
Patrick Ewing, Georgetown	1982-85	18	144
Marques Johnson, UCLA	1974-77	16	138

Average

	Years	Reb	Avg
Johnny Green, Mich.St	1957-59	118	19.7
Artis Gilmore, Jacksonville	1970-71	115	19.2
Paul Silas, Creighton	1962-64	111	18.5
Len Chappell, Wake Forest	1961-62	137	17.1
Elvin Hayes, Houston	1966-68	222	17.1
Lew Alcindor, UCLA	1967-69	201	16.8
Jerry Lucas, Ohio St	1960-61	197	16.4
Bill Walton, UCLA	1972-74	176	14.7
Sam Lacey, New Mexico St.	1968-70	157	14.3
Mel Counts, Oregon St.	1962-64	127	14.1

SINGLE TOURNAMENT
Scoring

Points

	Year	Gm	Pts
Glen Rice, Michigan	1989	6	184
Bill Bradley, Princeton	1965	5	177
Elvin Hayes, Houston	1968	5	167
Danny Manning, Kansas	1988	6	163
Hal Lear, Temple	1956	5	160
Jerry West, W.Virginia	1959	5	160

Average

	Year	Gm	Pts	Avg
Austin Carr, Notre Dame	1970	3	158	52.7
Austin Carr, Notre Dame	1971	3	125	41.7
Jerry Chambers, Utah	1966	4	143	35.8
Bo Kimble, Loyola-CA	1990	4	143	35.8
Bill Bradley, Princeton	1965	5	177	35.4
Clyde Lovellette, Kansas	1952	4	141	35.3

SINGLE GAME
Scoring

Points

	Year	Pts
Austin Carr, N.Dame vs Ohio U.	1970	61
Bill Bradley, Princeton vs Wich.St.	1965	58
Oscar Robertson, Cinn.vs Arkansas	1958	56
Austin Carr, N.Dame vs Kentucky	1970	52
Austin Carr, N.Dame vs TCU	1971	52
David Robinson, Navy vs Michigan	1987	50
Elvin Hayes, Houston vs Loyola-IL	1968	49
Hal Lear, Temple vs SMU	1956	48
Austin Carr, N.Dame vs Houston	1971	47
Dave Corzine, DePaul vs Louisville	1978	46
Bob Houbregs, Wash.vs Seattle	1956	45
Austin Carr, N.Dame vs Iowa	1970	45
Bo Kimble, Loyola-CA vs N.Mex.St	1990	45

Rebounds

Total

	Year	Gm	No	Avg
Elvin Hayes, Houston	1968	5	97	19.4
Artis Gilmore, Jacksonville	1970	5	93	18.6
Elgin Baylor, Seattle	1958	5	91	18.2
Sam Lacey, New Mexico St.	1970	5	90	18.0
Clarence Glover, Western Ky	1971	5	89	17.8

Rebounds

Total

	Year	No
Fred Cohen, Temple vs UConn.	1956	34
Nate Thurmond, B.Green vs Miss.St	1963	31
Jerry Lucas, Ohio St.vs Kentucky	1961	30
Toby Kimball, UConn vs St.Joe's-PA	1965	29
Elvin Hayes, Houston vs Pacific	1966	28

NIT Championship

The National Invitation Tournament began under the sponsorship of the Metropolitan New York Basketball Writers Association in 1938. The NIT is now administered by the Metropolitan Intercollegiate Basketball Association. All championship games have been played at Madison Square Garden; (*) indicates overtime.
Multiple winners: St.John's (5); Bradley (4); BYU, Dayton, Kentucky, LIU-Brooklyn, Providence, Temple and Virginia (2).

Year	Winner	Score	Loser		Year	Winner	Score	Loser
1938	Temple	60-36	Colorado		1966	BYU	97-84	NYU
1939	LIU-Brooklyn	44-32	Loyola-IL		1967	So.Illinois	71-56	Marquette
					1968	Dayton	61-48	Kansas
1940	Colorado	51-40	Duquesne		1969	Temple	89-76	Boston College
1941	LIU-Brooklyn	56-42	Ohio Univ.					
1942	West Virginia	47-45	Western Ky.		1970	Marquette	65-53	St.John's
1943	St.John's	48-27	Toledo		1971	North Carolina	84-66	Georgia Tech
1944	St.John's	47-39	DePaul		1972	Maryland	100-69	Niagara
1945	DePaul	71-54	Bowling Green		1973	Virginia Tech	92-91*	Notre Dame
1946	Kentucky	46-45	Rhode Island		1974	Purdue	97-81	Utah
1947	Utah	49-45	Kentucky		1975	Princeton	80-69	Providence
1948	St.Louis	65-52	NYU		1976	Kentucky	71-67	NC-Charlotte
1949	San Francisco	48-47	Loyola-IL		1977	St.Bonaventure	94-91	Houston
					1978	Texas	101-93	N.C.State
1950	CCNY	69-61	Bradley		1979	Indiana	53-52	Purdue
1951	BYU	62-43	Dayton					
1952	La Salle	75-64	Dayton		1980	Virginia	58-55	Minnesota
1953	Seton Hall	58-46	St.John's		1981	Tulsa	86-84*	Syracuse
1954	Holy Cross	71-62	Duquesne		1982	Bradley	67-58	Purdue
1955	Duquesne	70-58	Dayton		1983	Fresno St.	69-60	DePaul
1956	Louisville	93-80	Dayton		1984	Michigan	83-63	Notre Dame
1957	Bradley	84-83	Memphis St.		1985	UCLA	65-62	Indiana
1958	Xavier-OH	78-74*	Dayton		1986	Ohio St.	73-63	Wyoming
1959	St.John's	76-71*	Bradley		1987	Southern Miss.	84-80	La Salle
					1988	Connecticut	72-67	Ohio St.
1960	Bradley	88-72	Providence		1989	St.John's	73-65	St.Louis
1961	Providence	62-59	St.Louis					
1962	Dayton	73-67	St.John's		1990	Vanderbilt	74-72	St.Louis
1963	Providence	81-66	Canisius		1991	Stanford	78-72	Oklahoma
1964	Bradley	86-54	New Mexico		1992	Virginia	81-76*	Notre Dame
1965	St.John's	55-51	Villanova					

Most Valuable Player

A Most Valuable Player has been selected every year of the NIT tournament. Winners who did not play for the tournament champion are listed in **bold** type.
Multiple winners: None. However, Tom Gola is the only player to be named MVP in both the NIT (1952) and NCAA (1954) tournaments.

Year		Year		Year	
1938	Don Shields, Temple	1957	**Win Wilfong**, Memphis St.	1977	Greg Sanders, St. Bonaventure
1939	**Bill Lloyd**, St.John's	1958	Hank Stein, Xavier-OH	1978	Ron Baxter, Texas
		1959	Tony Jackson, St.John's		& Jim Krivacs, Texas
1940	Bob Doll, Colorado			1979	Clarence Carter, Indiana
1941	**Frank Baumholtz**, Ohio U.	1960	**Len Wilkens**, Providence		& Ray Tolbert, Indiana
1942	Rudy Baric, West Virginia	1961	Vin Ernst, Providence		
1943	Harry Boykoff, St.John's	1962	Bill Chmielewski, Dayton	1980	Ralph Sampson, Virginia
1944	Bill Kotsores, St.John's	1963	Ray Flynn, Providence	1981	Greg Stewart, Tulsa
1945	George Mikan, DePaul	1964	Lavern Tart, Bradley	1982	Mitchell Anderson, Bradley
1946	**Ernie Calverley**, Rhode Island	1965	Ken McIntyre, St.John's	1983	Ron Anderson, Fresno St.
1947	Vern Gardner, Utah	1966	**Bill Melchionni**, Villanova	1984	Tim McCormick, Michigan
1948	Ed Macauley, St.Louis	1967	Walt Frazier, So.Illinois	1985	Reggie Miller, UCLA
1949	Don Lofgran, San Francisco	1968	Don May, Dayton	1986	Brad Sellers, Ohio St.
		1969	**Terry Driscoll**, Boston College	1987	Randolph Keys, So.Miss.
1950	Ed Warner, CCNY			1988	Phil Gamble, Connecticut
1951	Roland Minson, BYU	1970	Dean Meminger, Marquette	1989	Jayson Williams, St.John's
1952	Tom Gola, La Salle	1971	Bill Chamberlain, N.Carolina		
	& Norm Grekin, La Salle	1972	Tom McMillen, Maryland	1990	Scott Draud, Vanderbilt
1953	Walter Dukes, Seton Hall	1973	**John Shumate**, Notre Dame	1991	Adam Keefe, Stanford
1954	Togo Palazzi, Holy Cross	1974	**Mike Sojourner**, Utah	1992	Bryant Stith, Virginia
1955	**Maurice Stokes**, St.Francis-PA	1975	**Ron Lee**, Oregon		
1956	Charlie Tyra, Louisville	1976	**Cedric Maxwell**, NC-Charlotte		

Associated Press Final Polls

The Associated Press introduced its weekly college basketball poll of sportswriters (later, sportswriters and broadcasters) during the 1948-49 season.

Since the NCAA Division I tournament has determined the national champion since 1939, the final AP poll ranks the nation's best teams through the regular season and conference tournaments.

Except for 1974 and '75, the final AP poll has always been released prior to the NCAA and NIT tournaments and has gone from a Top 10 (1949 and 1963-67) to a Top 20 (1950-62 and 1968-89) to a Top 25 (since 1990).

Tournament champions are in **bold** type.

1949

		Before Tourns	Head Coach	Final Record
1	**Kentucky**	29-1	Adolph Rupp	32-2
2	Oklahoma A&M	21-4	Hank Iba	23-5
3	St.Louis	22-3	Eddie Hickey	22-4
4	Illinois	19-3	Harry Combes	21-4
5	Western Ky.	25-3	Ed Diddle	25-4
6	Minnesota	18-3	Ozzie Cowles	same
7	Bradley	25-6	Forddy Anderson	27-8
8	**San Francisco**	21-5	Pete Newell	25-5
9	Tulane	24-4	Cliff Wells	same
10	Bowling Green	21-6	Harold Anderson	24-7

NCAA Final Four (at Edmundson Pavilion, Seattle): **Third Place**—Illinois 57, Oregon St.53. **Championship**—Kentucky 46, Oklahoma A&M 36.

NIT Final Four (at Madison Sq.Garden): **Semifinals**—San Francisco 49, Bowling Green 39; Loyola-IL 55, Bradley 50. **Third Place**—Bowling Green 82, Bradley 77. **Championship**—San Francisco 48, Loyola-IL 47.

1950

		Before Tourns	Head Coach	Final Record
1	Bradley	28-3	Forddy Anderson	32-5
2	Ohio St.	21-3	Tippy Dye	22-4
3	Kentucky	25-4	Adolph Rupp	25-5
4	Holy Cross	27-2	Buster Sheary	27-4
5	N.C.State	25-5	Everett Case	27-6
6	Duquesne	22-5	Dudey Moore	23-6
7	UCLA	24-5	John Wooden	24-7
8	Western Ky.	24-5	Ed Diddle	25-6
9	St.John's	23-4	Frank McGuire	24-5
10	La Salle	20-3	Ken Loeffler	21-4
11	Villanova	25-4	Al Severance	same
12	San Francisco	19-6	Pete Newell	19-7
13	LIU-Brooklyn	20-4	Clair Bee	20-5
14	Kansas St.	17-7	Jack Gardner	same
15	Arizona	26-4	Fred Enke	26-5
16	Wisconsin	17-5	Bud Foster	same
17	San Jose St.	21-7	Walter McPherson	same
18	Washington St.	19-13	Jack Friel	same
19	Kansas	14-11	Phog Allen	same
20	Indiana	17-5	Branch McCracken	same

Note: Unranked CCNY, coached by Nat Holman, won both the NCAAs and NIT. The Beavers entered the postseason at 17-5 and had a final record of 24-5.

NCAA Final Four (at Madison Square Garden): **Third Place**—N.Carolina 53, Baylor 41. **Championship**—CCNY 71, Bradley 68.

NIT Final Four (at Madison Sq.Garden): **Semifinals**—Bradley 83, St.John's 72; CCNY 62, Duquesne 52. **Third Place**—St.John's 69, Duquesne 67 (OT). **Championship**—CCNY 69, Bradley 61.

1951

		Before Tourns	Head Coach	Final Record
1	**Kentucky**	28-2	Adolph Rupp	32-2
2	Oklahoma A&M	27-4	Hank Iba	29-6
3	Columbia	22-0	Lou Rossini	22-1
4	Kansas St.	22-3	Jack Gardner	25-4
5	Illinois	19-4	Harry Combes	22-5
6	Bradley	32-6	Forddy Anderson	same
7	Indiana	19-3	Branch McCracken	same
8	N.C.State	29-4	Everett Case	30-7
9	St.John's	22-3	Frank McGuire	26-5
10	St.Louis	21-7	Eddie Hickey	22-8
11	**BYU**	22-8	Stan Watts	26-10
12	Arizona	24-4	Fred Enke	24-6
13	Dayton	24-4	Tom Blackburn	27-5
14	Toledo	23-8	Jerry Bush	same
15	Washington	22-5	Tippy Dye	24-6
16	Murray St.	21-6	Harlan Hodges	same
17	Cincinnati	18-3	John Wiethe	18-4
18	Siena	19-8	Dan Cunha	same
19	USC	21-6	Forrest Twogood	same
20	Villanova	25-6	Al Severance	25-7

NCAA Final Four (at Williams Arena, Minneapolis): **Third Place**—Illinois 61, Oklahoma St.46. **Championship**—Kentucky 68, Kansas St.58.

NIT Final Four (at Madison Sq.Garden): **Semifinals**—Dayton 69, St.John's 62 (OT); BYU 69, Seton Hall 59. **Third Place**—St.John's 70, Seton Hall 68 (2 OT). **Championship**—BYU 62, Dayton 43.

1952

		Before Tourns	Head Coach	Final Record
1	Kentucky	28-2	Adolph Rupp	29-3
2	Illinois	19-3	Harry Combes	22-4
3	Kansas St.	19-5	Jack Gardner	same
4	Duquesne	21-1	Dudey Moore	23-4
5	St.Louis	22-6	Eddie Hickey	23-8
6	Washington	25-6	Tippy Dye	same
7	Iowa	19-3	Bucky O'Connor	same
8	**Kansas**	24-3	Phog Allen	28-3
9	West Virginia	23-4	Red Brown	same
10	St.John's	22-3	Frank McGuire	25-5
11	Dayton	24-3	Tom Blackburn	28-5
12	Duke	24-6	Harold Bradley	same
13	Holy Cross	23-3	Buster Sheary	24-4
14	Seton Hall	25-2	Honey Russell	25-3
15	St.Bonaventure	19-5	Ed Melvin	21-6
16	Wyoming	27-6	Everett Shelton	28-7
17	Louisville	20-5	Peck Hickman	20-6
18	Seattle	29-7	Al Brightman	29-8
19	UCLA	19-10	John Wooden	19-12
20	SW Texas St.	30-1	Milton Jowers	same

Note: Unranked La Salle, coached by Ken Loefler, won the NIT. The Explorers entered the postseason at 21-7 and had a final record of 25-7.

NCAA Final Four (at U.of Wash.Pavilion, Seattle): **Semifinals**—St.John's 61, Illinois 59; Kansas 74, Santa Clara 59. **Third Place**—Illinois 67, Santa Clara 64. **Championship**—Kansas 80, St.John's 63.

NIT Final Four (at Madison Sq.Garden): **Semifinals**—La Salle 59, Duquesne 46; Dayton 69, St.Bonaventure 62. **Third Place**—St.Bonaventure 48, Duquesne 34. **Championship**—La Salle 75, Dayton 64.

Associated Press Final Polls (Cont.)

Taken before NCAA and NIT tournaments

1953

		Before Tourns	Head Coach	Final Record
1	Indiana	19-3	Branch McCracken	23-3
2	Seton Hall	28-2	Honey Russell	31-2
3	Kansas	16-5	Phog Allen	19-6
4	Washington	27-2	Tippy Dye	30-3
5	LSU	22-1	Harry Rabenhorst	24-3
6	La Salle	25-2	Ken Loeffler	25-3
7	St.John's	14-5	Al DeStefano	17-6
8	Oklahoma A&M	22-6	Hank Iba	23-7
9	Duquesne	18-7	Dudey Moore	21-8
10	Notre Dame	17-4	John Jordan	19-5
11	Illinois	18-4	Harry Combes	same
12	Kansas St.	17-4	Jack Gardner	same
13	Holy Cross	18-5	Buster Sheary	20-6
14	Seattle	27-3	Al Brightman	29-4
15	Wake Forest	21-6	Murray Greason	22-7
16	Santa Clara	18-6	Bob Feerick	20-7
17	Western Ky.	25-5	Ed Diddle	25-6
18	N.C.State	26-6	Everett Case	same
19	DePaul	18-7	Ray Meyer	19-9
20	SW Missouri St.	19-4	Bob Vanatta	24-4

NCAA Final Four (at Municipal Auditorium, Kansas City): **Semifinals**—Indiana 80, LSU 67; Kansas 79, Washington 53. **Third Place**—Washington 88, LSU 69. **Championship**—Indiana 69, Kansas 68.

NIT Final Four (at Madison Sq.Garden): **Semifinals**—Seton Hall 74, Manhattan 56; St.John's 64, Duquesne 55. **Third Place**—Duquesne 81, Manhattan 67. **Championship**—Seton Hall 58, St.John's 46.

1955

		Before Tourns	Head Coach	Final Record
1	San Francisco	23-1	Phil Woolpert	28-1
2	Kentucky	22-2	Adolph Rupp	23-3
3	La Salle	22-4	Ken Loeffler	26-5
4	N.C.State	28-4	Everett Case	same
5	Iowa	17-5	Bucky O'Connor	19-7
6	Duquesne	19-4	Dudey Moore	22-4
7	Utah	23-3	Jack Gardner	24-4
8	Marquette	22-2	Jack Nagle	24-3
9	Dayton	23-3	Tom Blackburn	25-4
10	Oregon St.	21-7	Slats Gill	22-8
11	Minnesota	15-7	Ozzie Cowles	same
12	Alabama	19-5	Johnny Dee	same
13	UCLA	21-5	John Wooden	same
14	G. Washington	24-6	Bill Reinhart	same
15	Colorado	16-5	Bebe Lee	19-6
16	Tulsa	20-6	Clarence Iba	21-7
17	Vanderbilt	16-6	Bob Polk	same
18	Illinois	17-5	Harry Combes	same
19	West Virginia	19-10	Fred Schaus	19-11
20	St.Louis	19-7	Eddie Hickey	20-8

NCAA Final Four (at Municipal Auditorium, Kansas City): **Semifinals**—La Salle 76, Iowa 73; San Francisco 62, Colorado 50. **Third Place**—Colorado 75, Iowa 74. **Championship**—San Francisco 77, La Salle 63.

NIT Final Four (at Madison Sq.Garden): **Semifinals**—Dayton 79, St.Francis-PA 73 (OT); Duquesne 65, Cincinnati 51. **Third Place**—Cincinnati 96, St.Francis-PA 91 (OT). **Championship**—Duquesne 70, Dayton 58.

1954

		Before Tourns	Head Coach	Final Record
1	Kentucky	25-0	Adolph Rupp	same
2	La Salle	21-4	Ken Loeffler	26-4
3	Holy Cross	23-2	Buster Sheary	26-2
4	Indiana	19-3	Branch McCracken	20-4
5	Duquesne	24-2	Dudey Moore	26-3
6	Notre Dame	20-2	John Jordan	22-3
7	Bradley	15-12	Forddy Anderson	19-13
8	Western Ky.	28-1	Ed Diddle	29-3
9	Penn St.	14-5	Elmer Gross	18-6
10	Oklahoma A&M	23-4	Hank Iba	24-5
11	USC	17-12	Forrest Twogood	19-14
12	G. Washington	23-2	Bill Reinhart	23-3
13	Iowa	17-5	Bucky O'Connor	same
14	LSU	21-3	Harry Rabenhorst	21-5
15	Duke	22-6	Harold Bradley	same
16	Niagara	22-5	Taps Gallagher	24-6
17	Seattle	26-1	Al Brightman	26-2
18	Kansas	16-5	Phog Allen	same
19	Illinois	17-5	Harry Combes	17-5
20	Maryland	23-7	Bud Millikan	same

NCAA Final Four (at Municipal Auditorium, Kansas City): **Semifinals**—La Salle 69, Penn St. 54; Bradley 74, USC 72. **Third Place**—Penn St. 70, USC 61. **Championship**—La Salle 92, Bradley 76.

NIT Final Four (at Madison Sq.Garden): **Semifinals**—Duquesne 66, Niagara 51; Holy Cross 75, Western Ky. 69. **Third Place**—Niagara 71, Western Ky. 65. **Championship**—Holy Cross 71, Duquesne 62.

1956

		Before Tourns	Head Coach	Final Record
1	San Francisco	25-0	Phil Woolpert	29-0
2	N.C.State	24-3	Everett Case	24-4
3	Dayton	23-3	Tom Blackburn	25-4
4	Iowa	17-5	Bucky O'Connor	20-6
5	Alabama	21-3	Johnny Dee	same
6	Louisville	23-3	Peck Hickman	26-3
7	SMU	22-2	Doc Hayes	25-4
8	UCLA	21-5	John Wooden	22-6
9	Kentucky	19-5	Adolph Rupp	20-6
10	Illinois	18-4	Harry Combes	same
11	Oklahoma City	18-6	Abe Lemons	20-7
12	Vanderbilt	19-4	Bob Polk	same
13	North Carolina	18-5	Frank McGuire	same
14	Holy Cross	22-4	Roy Leenig	22-5
15	Temple	23-3	Harry Litwack	27-4
16	Wake Forest	19-9	Murray Greason	same
17	Duke	19-7	Harold Bradley	same
18	Utah	21-5	Jack Gardner	22-6
19	Oklahoma A&M	18-8	Hank Iba	18-9
20	West Virginia	21-8	Fred Schaus	21-9

NCAA Final Four (at McGaw Hall, Evanston,IL): **Semifinals**—Iowa 83, Temple 76; San Francisco 76, SMU 68. **Third Place**—Temple 90, SMU 81. **Championship**—San Francisco 83, Iowa 71.

NIT Final Four (at Madison Sq.Garden): **Semifinals**—Dayton 89, St.Francis-NY 58; Louisville 89, St.Joseph's-PA 79. **Third Place**—St.Joseph's-PA 93, St.Francis-NY 82. **Championship**—Louisville 93, Dayton 80.

1957

		Before Tourns	Head Coach	Final Record
1	**North Carolina**	27-0	Frank McGuire	32-0
2	Kansas	21-2	Dick Harp	24-3
3	Kentucky	22-4	Adolph Rupp	23-5
4	SMU	21-3	Doc Hayes	22-4
5	Seattle	24-2	John Castellani	24-3
6	Louisville	21-5	Peck Hickman	same
7	West Va.	25-4	Fred Schaus	25-5
8	Vanderbilt	17-5	Bob Polk	same
9	Oklahoma City	17-8	Abe Lemons	19-9
10	St. Louis	19-7	Eddie Hickey	19-9
11	Michigan St.	14-8	Forddy Anderson	16-10
12	Memphis St.	21-5	Bob Vanatta	24-6
13	California	20-4	Pete Newell	21-5
14	UCLA	22-4	John Wooden	same
15	Mississippi St.	17-8	Babe McCarthy	same
16	Idaho St.	24-2	John Grayson	25-4
17	Notre Dame	18-7	John Jordan	20-8
18	Wake Forest	19-9	Murray Greason	same
19	Canisius	22-4	Joe Curran	22-6
20	Oklahoma A&M	17-9	Hank Iba	same

Note: Unranked Bradley, coached by Chuck Orsborn, won the NIT. The Braves entered the tourney at 19-7 and had a final record of 22-7.

NCAA Final Four (at Municipal Auditorium, Kansas City): **Semifinals**—North Carolina 74, Michigan St. 70 (3 OT); Kansas 80, San Francisco 56. **Third Place**—San Francisco 67, Michigan St. 60. **Championship**—North Carolina 54, Kansas 53 (3 OT).

NIT Final Four (at Madison Sq.Garden): **Semifinals**—Memphis St. 80, St.Bonaventure 78; Bradley 78, Temple 66. **Third Place**—Temple 67, St.Bonaventure 50. **Championship**—Bradley 84, Memphis St. 83.

1958

		Before Tourns	Head Coach	Final Record
1	West Virginia	26-1	Fred Schaus	26-2
2	Cincinnati	24-2	George Smith	25-3
3	Kansas St.	20-3	Tex Winter	22-5
4	San Francisco	24-1	Phil Woolpert	25-2
5	Temple	24-2	Harry Litwack	27-3
6	Maryland	20-6	Bud Millikan	22-7
7	Kansas	18-5	Dick Harp	same
8	Notre Dame	22-4	John Jordan	24-5
9	**Kentucky**	19-6	Adolph Rupp	23-6
10	Duke	18-7	Harold Bradley	same
11	Dayton	23-3	Tom Blackburn	25-4
12	Indiana	12-10	Branch McCracken	13-11
13	North Carolina	19-7	Frank McGuire	same
14	Bradley	20-6	Chuck Orsborn	20-7
15	Mississippi St.	20-5	Babe McCarthy	same
16	Auburn	16-6	Joel Eaves	same
17	Michigan St.	16-6	Forddy Anderson	same
18	Seattle	20-6	John Castellani	24-7
19	Oklahoma St.	19-7	Hank Iba	21-8
20	N.C.State	18-6	Everett Case	same

Note: Unranked Xavier-OH, coached by Jim McCafferty, won the NIT. The Musketeers entered the tourney at 15-11 and had a final record of 19-11.

NCAA Final Four (at Freedom Hall, Louisville): **Semifinals**—Kentucky 61, Temple 60; Seattle 73, Kansas St. 51. **Third Place**—Temple 67, Kansas St. 57. **Championship**—Kentucky 84, Seattle 72.

NIT Final Four (at Madison Sq.Garden): **Semifinals**—Dayton 80, St.John's 56; Xavier-OH 72, St.Bonaventure 53. **Third Place**—St.Bonaventure 84, St.John's 69. **Championship**—Xavier-OH 78, Dayton 74 (OT).

1959

		Before Tourns	Head Coach	Final Record
1	Kansas St.	24-1	Tex Winter	25-2
2	Kentucky	23-2	Adolph Rupp	24-3
3	Mississippi St.	24-1	Babe McCarthy	same*
4	Bradley	23-3	Chuck Orsborn	25-4
5	Cincinnati	23-3	George Smith	26-4
6	N.C.State	22-4	Everett Case	same
7	Michigan St.	18-3	Forddy Anderson	19-4
8	Auburn	20-2	Joel Eaves	same
9	North Carolina	20-4	Frank McGuire	20-5
10	West Virginia	25-4	Fred Schaus	29-5
11	**California**	20-4	Pete Newell	24-4
12	St. Louis	20-5	John Benington	20-6
13	Seattle	23-6	Vince Cazzetta	same
14	St.Joseph's-PA	22-3	Jack Ramsay	22-5
15	St.Mary's-CA	18-5	Jim Weaver	19-6
16	TCU	19-5	Buster Brannon	20-6
17	Oklahoma City	20-6	Abe Lemons	20-7
18	Utah	21-5	Jack Gardner	21-7
19	St.Bonaventure	20-2	Eddie Donovan	20-3
20	Marquette	22-4	Eddie Hickey	23-6

Note: Unranked St.John's, coached by Joe Lapchick, won the NIT. The Redmen entered the tourney at 16-6 and had a final record of 20-6.

NCAA Final Four (at Freedom Hall, Louisville): **Semifinals**—West Virginia 94, Louisville 79; California 64, Cincinnati 58. **Third Place**—Cincinnati 98, Louisville 85. **Championship**—California 71, West Virginia 70.

NIT Final Four (at Madison Sq.Garden): **Semifinals**—Bradley 59, NYU 57; St.John's 76, Providence 55. **Third Place**—NYU 71, Providence 57. **Championship**—St.John's 76, Bradley 71 (OT).

1960

		Before Tourns	Head Coach	Final Record
1	Cincinnati	25-1	George Smith	28-2
2	California	24-1	Pete Newell	28-2
3	**Ohio St.**	21-3	Fred Taylor	25-3
4	**Bradley**	24-2	Chuck Orsborn	27-2
5	West Virginia	24-4	Fred Schaus	26-5
6	Utah	24-2	Jack Gardner	26-3
7	Indiana	20-4	Branch McCracken	same
8	Utah St.	22-4	Cecil Baker	24-5
9	St.Bonaventure	19-3	Eddie Donovan	21-5
10	Miami-FL	23-3	Bruce Hale	23-4
11	Auburn	19-3	Joel Eaves	same
12	NYU	19-4	Lou Rossini	22-5
13	Georgia Tech	21-5	Whack Hyder	22-6
14	Providence	21-4	Joe Mullaney	24-5
15	St.Louis	19-7	John Benington	19-8
16	Holy Cross	20-5	Roy Leenig	20-6
17	Villanova	19-5	Al Severance	20-6
18	Duke	15-10	Vic Bubas	17-11
19	Wake Forest	21-7	Bones McKinney	same
20	St.John's	17-7	Joe Lapchick	17-8

NCAA Final Four (at the Cow Palace, San Fran.): **Semifinals**—Ohio St.76, NYU 54; California 77, Cincinnati 69. **Third Place**—Cincinnati 95, NYU 71. **Championship**—Ohio St.75, California 55.

NIT Final Four (at Madison Sq.Garden): **Semifinals**—Bradley 82, St.Bonaventure 71; Providence 68, Utah St.62. **Third Place**—Utah St.99, St.Bonaventure 93. **Championship**—Bradley 88, Providence 72.

Associated Press Final Polls (Cont.)

Taken before NCAA and NIT tournaments

1961

		Before Tourns	Head Coach	Final Record
1	Ohio St.	24-0	Fred Taylor	27-1
2	**Cincinnati**	23-3	Ed Jucker	27-3
3	St.Bonaventure	22-3	Eddie Donovan	24-4
4	Kansas St.	22-3	Tex Winter	23-4
5	North Carolina	19-4	Frank McGuire	same
6	Bradley	21-5	Chuck Orsborn	21-8
7	USC	20-6	Forrest Twogood	21-8
8	Iowa	18-6	S. Scheuerman	same
9	West Virginia	23-4	George King	same
10	Duke	22-6	Vic Bubas	same
11	Utah	21-6	Jack Gardner	23-8
12	Texas Tech	14-9	Polk Robison	15-10
13	Niagara	16-4	Taps Gallagher	16-5
14	Memphis St.	20-2	Bob Vanatta	20-3
15	Wake Forest	17-10	Bones McKinney	19-11
16	St.John's	20-4	Joe Lapchick	20-5
17	St.Joseph's-PA	22-4	Jack Ramsay	25-5
18	Drake	19-7	Maury John	same
19	Holy Cross	19-4	Roy Leenig	22-5
20	Kentucky	18-8	Adolph Rupp	19-9

Note: Unranked Providence, coached by Joe Mullaney, won the NIT. The Friars entered the tourney at 20-5 and had a final record of 24-5.

NCAA Final Four (at Municipal Auditorium, Kansas City): **Semifinals**—Ohio St. 95, St. Joseph's-PA 69; Cincinnati 82, Utah 67. **Third Place**—St. Joseph's-PA 127, Utah 120 (4 OT). **Championship**—Cincinnati 70, Ohio St. 65 (OT).
NIT Final Four (at Madison Sq.Garden) **Semifinals**—St.Louis 67, Dayton 60; Providence 90, Holy Cross 83 (OT). **Third Place**—Holy Cross 85, Dayton 67. **Championship**—Providence 62, St.Louis 59.

1962

		Before Tourns	Head Coach	Final Record
1	Ohio St.	23-1	Fred Taylor	26-2
2	**Cincinnati**	25-2	Ed Jucker	29-2
3	Kentucky	22-2	Adolph Rupp	23-3
4	Mississippi St.	19-6	Babe McCarthy	same
5	Bradley	21-6	Chuck Orsborn	21-7
6	Kansas St.	22-3	Tex Winter	same
7	Utah	23-3	Jack Gardner	same
8	Bowling Green	21-3	Harold Anderson	same
9	Colorado	18-6	Sox Walseth	19-7
10	Duke	20-5	Vic Bubas	same
11	Loyola-IL	21-3	George Ireland	23-4
12	St.John's	19-4	Joe Lapchick	21-5
13	Wake Forest	18-8	Bones McKinney	22-9
14	Oregon St.	22-4	Slats Gill	24-5
15	West Virginia	24-5	George King	24-6
16	Arizona St.	23-3	Ned Wulk	23-4
17	Duquesne	20-5	Red Manning	22-7
18	Utah St.	21-5	Ladell Andersen	22-7
19	UCLA	16-9	John Wooden	18-11
20	Villanova	19-6	Jack Kraft	21-7

Note: Unranked Dayton, coached by Tom Blackburn, won the NIT. The Flyers entered the tourney at 20-6 and had a final record of 24-6.

NCAA Final Four (at Freedom Hall, Louisville): **Semifinals**—Ohio St. 84, Wake Forest 68; Cincinnati 72, UCLA 70. **Third Place**—Wake Forest 82, UCLA 80. **Championship**—Cincinnati 71, Ohio St. 59.
NIT Final Four (at Madison Sq.Garden): **Semifinals**—Dayton 98, Loyola-IL 82; St.John's 76, Duquesne 65. **Third Place**—Loyola-IL 95, Duquesne 84. **Championship**—Dayton 73, St.John's 67.

1963

AP ranked only 10 teams from the 1962-63 season through 1967-68.

		Before Tourns	Head Coach	Final Record
1	Cincinnati	23-1	Ed Jucker	26-2
2	Duke	24-2	Vic Bubas	27-3
3	**Loyola-IL**	24-2	George Ireland	29-2
4	Arizona St.	24-2	Ned Wulk	26-3
5	Wichita	19-7	Ralph Miller	19-8
6	Mississippi St.	21-5	Babe McCarthy	22-6
7	Ohio St.	20-4	Fred Taylor	same
8	Illinois	19-5	Harry Combes	20-6
9	NYU	17-3	Lou Rossini	18-5
10	Colorado	18-6	Sox Walseth	19-7

Note: Unranked Providence, coached by Joe Mullaney, won the NIT. The Friars entered the tourney at 21-4 and had a final record of 24-4.

NCAA Final Four (at Freedom Hall, Louisville): **Semifinals**—Loyola-IL 94, Duke 75; Cincinnati 80, Oregon St. 46. **Third Place**—Duke 85, Oregon St. 63. **Championship**—Loyola-IL 60, Cincinnati 58 (OT).
NIT Final Four (at Madison Sq.Garden): **Semifinals**—Providence 70, Marquette 64; Canisius 61, Villanova 46. **Third Place**—Marquette 66, Villanova 58. **Championship**—Providence 81, Canisius 66.

1964

AP ranked only 10 teams from the 1962-63 season through 1967-68.

		Before Tourns	Head Coach	Final Record
1	UCLA	26-0	John Wooden	30-0
2	Michigan	20-4	Dave Strack	23-5
3	Duke	23-4	Vic Bubas	26-5
4	Kentucky	21-4	Adolph Rupp	21-6
5	Wichita St.	22-5	Ralph Miller	23-6
6	Oregon St.	25-3	Slats Gill	25-4
7	Villanova	22-3	Jack Kraft	24-4
8	Loyola-IL	20-5	George Ireland	22-6
9	DePaul	21-3	Ray Meyer	21-4
10	Davidson	22-4	Lefty Driesell	same

Note: Unranked Bradley, coached by Chuck Orsborn, won the NIT. The Braves entered the tourney at 20-6 and finished with a record of 23-6.

NCAA Final Four (at Municipal Auditorium, Kansas City): **Semifinals**—Duke 91, Michigan 80; UCLA 90, Kansas St. 84. **Third Place**—Michigan 100, Kansas St. 90. **Championship**—UCLA 98, Duke 83.
NIT Final Four (at Madison Sq.Garden): **Semifinals**—New Mexico 72, NYU 65; Bradley 67, Army 52. **Third Place**—Army 60, NYU 59. **Championship**—Bradley 86, New Mexico 54.

Undefeated National Champions

The 1964 UCLA team is one of only seven NCAA champions to win the title with an undefeated record.

Year		W-L	Year		W-L
1956	San Francisco	29-0	1972	UCLA	30-0
1957	North Carolina	32-0	1973	UCLA	30-0
1964	UCLA	30-0	1976	Indiana	32-0
1967	UCLA	30-0			

1965

AP ranked only 10 teams from the 1962-63 season through 1967-68.

	Before Tourns	Head Coach	Final Record
1 Michigan	21-3	Dave Strack	24-4
2 **UCLA**	24-2	John Wooden	28-2
3 St.Joseph's-PA	25-1	Jack Ramsay	26-3
4 Providence	22-1	Joe Mullaney	24-2
5 Vanderbilt	23-3	Roy Skinner	24-4
6 Davidson	24-2	Lefty Driesell	same
7 Minnesota	19-5	John Kundla	same
8 Villanova	21-4	Jack Kraft	23-5
9 BYU	21-5	Stan Watts	21-7
10 Duke	20-5	Vic Bubas	same

Note: Unranked St.John's, coached by Joe Lapchick, won the NIT. The Redmen entered the tourney at 17-8 and finished with a record of 21-8.

NCAA Final Four (at Memorial Coliseum, Portland,OR): **Semifinals**—Michigan 93, Princeton 76; UCLA 108, Wichita St. 89. **Third Place**—Princeton 118, Wichita St. 82. **Championship**—UCLA 91, Michigan 80.

NIT Final Four (at Madison Sq.Garden): **Semifinals**—Villanova 91, NYU 69; St.John's 67, Army 60. **Third Place**—Army 75, NYU 74. **Championship**—St.John's 55, Villanova 51.

1966

AP ranked only 10 teams from the 1962-63 season through 1967-68.

	Before Tourns	Head Coach	Final Record
1 Kentucky	24-1	Adolph Rupp	27-2
2 Duke	23-3	Vic Bubas	26-4
3 **Texas Western**	23-1	Don Haskins	28-1
4 Kansas	22-3	Ted Owens	23-4
5 St.Joseph's-PA	22-4	Jack Ramsay	24-5
6 Loyola-IL	22-2	George Ireland	22-3
7 Cincinnati	21-5	Tay Baker	21-7
8 Vanderbilt	22-4	Roy Skinner	same
9 Michigan	17-7	Dave Strack	18-8
10 Western Ky.	23-2	Johnny Oldham	25-3

Note: Unranked BYU, coached by Stan Watts, won the NIT. The Cougars entered the tourney at 17-5 and had a final record of 20-5.

NCAA Final Four (at Cole Fieldhouse, College Park,MD): **Semifinals**—Kentucky 83, Duke 79; Texas Western 85, Utah 78. **Third Place**—Duke 79, Utah 77. **Championship**—Texas Western 72, Kentucky 65.

NIT Final Four (at Madison Sq.Garden): **Semifinals**—BYU 66, Army 60; NYU 69, Villanova 63. **Third Place**—Villanova 76, Army 65. **Championship**—BYU 97, NYU 84.

1967

AP ranked only 10 teams from the 1962-63 season through 1967-68.

	Before Tourns	Head Coach	Final Record
1 **UCLA**	26-0	John Wooden	30-0
2 Louisville	23-3	Peck Hickman	23-5
3 Kansas	22-3	Ted Owens	23-4
4 North Carolina	24-4	Dean Smith	26-6
5 Princeton	23-2	B.vanBreda Kolff	25-3
6 Western Ky.	23-2	Johnny Oldham	23-3
7 Houston	23-3	Guy Lewis	27-4
8 Tennessee	21-5	Ray Mears	21-7
9 Boston College	19-2	Bob Cousy	21-3
10 Texas Western	20-5	Don Haskins	22-6

Note: Unranked Southern Illinois, coached by Jack Hartman, won the NIT. The Salukis entered the tourney at 20-2 and had a final record of 24-2.

NCAA Final Four (at Freedom Hall, Louisville): **Semifinals**—Dayton 76, N.Carolina 62; UCLA 73, Houston 58. **Third Place**—Houston 84, N.Carolina 62. **Championship**—UCLA 79, Dayton 64.

NIT Final Four (at Madison Sq.Garden): **Semifinals**—Marquette 83, Marshall 78; Southern Ill.79, Rutgers 70. **Third Place**—Rutgers 93, Marshall 76. **Championship**—Southern Ill.71, Marquette 56.

1968

AP ranked only 10 teams from the 1962-63 season through 1967-68.

	Before Tourns	Head Coach	Final Record
1 Houston	28-0	Guy Lewis	31-2
2 **UCLA**	25-1	John Wooden	29-1
3 St.Bonaventure	22-0	Larry Weise	23-2
4 North Carolina	25-3	Dean Smith	28-4
5 Kentucky	21-4	Adolph Rupp	22-5
6 New Mexico	23-3	Bob King	23-5
7 Columbia	21-4	Jack Rohan	23-5
8 Davidson	22-4	Lefty Driesell	24-5
9 Louisville	20-6	John Dromo	21-7
10 Duke	21-5	Vic Bubas	22-6

Note: Unranked Dayton, coached by Don Donoher, won the NIT. The Flyers entered the tourney at 17-9 and had a final record of 21-9.

NCAA Final Four (at the Sports Arena, Los Angeles): **Semifinals**—N.Carolina 80, Ohio St. 66; UCLA 101, Houston 69. **Third Place**—Ohio St. 89, Houston 85. **Championship**—UCLA 78, N.Carolina 55.

NIT Final Four (at Madison Sq.Garden): **Semifinals**—Dayton 76, Notre Dame 74 (OT), St.Peter's 46. **Third Place**—Notre Dame 81, St.Peter's 78. **Championship**—Dayton 61, Kansas 48.

Highest-Rated College Games on TV

The dozen highest-rated college basketball games seen on U.S. television have been NCAA tournament championship games, led by the 1979 Michigan State-Indiana State final that featured Magic Johnson and Larry Bird. The 1992 final between Duke and Michigan is third.

Listed below are the finalists (winning team first), date of game, TV network, and TV rating and audience share (according to Nielson Media Research).

	Date	Net	Rtg/Sh			Date	Net	Rtg/Sh
1 Michigan St.-Indiana St.	3/26/79	NBC	24.1/38		7 Michigan-Seton Hall	4/3/89	CBS	21.3/33
2 Villanova-Georgetown	4/1/85	CBS	23.3/33		8 Louisville-Duke	3/32/86	CBS	20.7/31
3 Duke-Michigan	4/6/92	CBS	22.7/35		9 Indiana-N.Carolina	3/30/81	NBC	20.7/29
4 N.C.State-Houston	4/4/83	CBS	22.3/32		10 UCLA-Memphis St.	3/26/73	NBC	20.5/32
5 N.Carolina-Georgetown	3/29/82	CBS	21.6/31		11 Indiana-Michigan	3/29/76	NBC	20.4/31
6 UCLA-Kentucky	3/31/75	NBC	21.3/33		12 UNLV-Duke	4/2/90	CBS	20.0/31

Associated Press Final Polls (Cont.)

Taken before NCAA, NIT and Collegiate Commissioner's Assn. (1974-75) tournaments; (*) indicates on probation.

1969

		Before Tourns	Head Coach	Final Record
1	UCLA	25-1	John Wooden	29-1
2	La Salle	23-1	Tom Gola	same*
3	Santa Clara	26-1	Dick Garibaldi	27-2
4	North Carolina	25-3	Dean Smith	27-5
5	Davidson	24-2	Lefty Driesell	26-3
6	Purdue	20-4	George King	23-5
7	Kentucky	22-4	Adolph Rupp	23-5
8	St.John's	22-4	Lou Carnesecca	23-6
9	Duquesne	19-4	Red Manning	21-5
10	Villanova	21-4	Jack Kraft	21-5
11	Drake	23-4	Maury John	26-5
12	New Mexico St.	23-3	Lou Henson	24-5
13	South Carolina	20-6	Frank McGuire	21-7
14	Marquette	22-4	Al McGuire	24-5
15	Louisville	20-5	John Dromo	21-6
16	Boston College	21-3	Bob Cousy	24-4
17	Notre Dame	20-6	Johnny Dee	20-7
18	Colorado	20-6	Sox Walseth	21-7
19	Kansas	20-6	Ted Owens	20-7
20	Illinois	19-5	Harvey Schmidt	same

Note: NIT champ Temple, coached by Harry Litwak, entered the tourney unranked at 18-8 and had a final record of 22-8.

NCAA Final Four (at Freedom Hall, Louisville): **Semifinals**—Purdue 92, N.Carolina 65; UCLA 85, Drake 82. **Third Place**—Drake 104, N.Carolina 84. **Championship**—UCLA 92, Purdue 72. †
NIT Final Four (at Madison Sq.Garden): **Semifinals**—Temple 63, Tennessee 58; Boston College 73, Army 61. **Third Place**—Tennessee 64, Army 52. **Championship**—Temple 89, Boston College 76.

1970

		Before Tourns	Head Coach	Final Record
1	Kentucky	25-1	Adolph Rupp	26-2
2	UCLA	24-2	John Wooden	28-2
3	St.Bonaventure	22-1	Larry Weise	25-3
4	Jacksonville	23-1	Joe Williams	27-2
5	New Mexico.St.	23-2	Lou Henson	27-3
6	South Carolina	25-3	Frank McGuire	25-3
7	Iowa	19-4	Ralph Miller	20-5
8	Marquette	22-3	Al McGuire	26-3
9	Notre Dame	20-6	Johnny Dee	21-8
10	N.C.State	22-6	Norm Sloan	23-7
11	Florida St.	23-3	Hugh Durham	23-3
12	Houston	24-3	Guy Lewis	25-5
13	Penn	25-1	Dick Harter	25-2
14	Drake	21-6	Maury John	22-7
15	Davidson	22-4	Terry Holland	22-5
16	Utah St.	20-6	Ladell Andersen	22-7
17	Niagara	21-5	Frank Layden	22-7
18	Western Ky.	22-2	John Oldham	22-3
19	Long Beach St.	23-3	Jerry Tarkanian	24-5
20	USC	18-8	Bob Boyd	18-8

NCAA Final Four (at Cole Fieldhouse, College Park,MD): **Semifinals**—Jacksonville 91, St.Bonaventure 83; UCLA 93, New Mexico St.77. **Third Place**—N.Mexico St.79, St.Bonaventure 73. **Championship**—UCLA 80, Jacksonville 69.
NIT Final Four (at Madison Sq.Garden): **Semifinals**—St.John's 60, Army 59; Marquette 101, LSU 79. **Third Place**—Army 75, LSU 68. **Championship**—Marquette 65, St.John's 53.

1971

		Before Tourns	Head Coach	Final Record
1	UCLA	25-1	John Wooden	29-1
2	Marquette	26-0	Al McGuire	28-1
3	Penn	26-0	Dick Harter	28-1
4	Kansas	25-1	Ted Owens	27-3
5	USC	24-2	Bob Boyd	24-2
6	South Carolina	23-4	Frank McGuire	23-6
7	Western Ky.	20-5	John Oldham	24-6
8	Kentucky	22-4	Adolph Rupp	22-6
9	Fordham	25-1	Digger Phelps	26-3
10	Ohio St.	19-5	Fred Taylor	20-6
11	Jacksonville	22-3	Tom Wasdin	22-4
12	Notre Dame	19-7	Johnny Dee	20-9
13	North Carolina	22-6	Dean Smith	26-6
14	Houston	20-6	Guy Lewis	22-7
15	Duquesne	21-3	Red Manning	21-4
16	Long Beach St.	21-4	Jerry Tarkanian	23-5
17	Tennessee	20-6	Ray Mears	21-7
18	Villanova	19-5	Jack Kraft	23-6
19	Drake	20-7	Maury John	21-8
20	BYU	18-9	Stan Watts	18-11

NCAA Final Four (at The Astrodome, Houston): **Semifinals**—Villanova 92, Western Ky.89 (2 OT); UCLA 68, Kansas 60. **Third Place**—Western Ky.77, Kansas 75. **Championship**—UCLA 68, Villanova 62.
NIT Final Four (at Madison Sq.Garden): **Semifinals**—N.Carolina 73, Duke 69; Ga.Tech 76, St. Bonaventure 71 (2 OT). **Third Place**—St.Bonaventure 92, Duke 88 (OT). **Championship**—N.Carolina 84, Ga.Tech 66.

1972

		Before Tourns	Head Coach	Final Record
1	UCLA	26-0	John Wooden	30-0
2	North Carolina	23-4	Dean Smith	26-5
3	Penn	23-2	Chuck Daly	25-3
4	Louisville	23-4	Denny Crum	26-5
5	Long Beach St.	23-3	Jerry Tarkanian	25-4
6	South Carolina	22-4	Frank McGuire	24-5
7	Marquette	24-2	Al McGuire	25-4
8	SW Louisiana	23-3	Beryl Shipley	25-4
9	BYU	21-4	Stan Watts	21-5
10	Florida St.	23-5	Hugh Durham	27-6
11	Minnesota	17-6	Bill Musselman	18-7
12	Marshall	23-3	Carl Tacy	23-4
13	Memphis St.	21-6	Gene Bartow	21-7
14	Maryland	23-5	Lefty Driesell	27-5
15	Villanova	19-6	Jack Kraft	20-8
16	Oral Roberts	25-1	Ken Trickey	26-2
17	Indiana	17-7	Bob Knight	17-8
18	Kentucky	20-6	Adolph Rupp	21-7
19	Ohio St.	18-6	Fred Taylor	same
20	Virginia	21-6	Bill Gibson	21-7

NCAA Final Four (at the Sports Arena, Los Angeles): **Semifinals**—Florida St.79, N.Carolina 75; UCLA 96, Louisville 77. **Third Place**—N.Carolina 105, Louisville 91. **Championship**—UCLA 81, Florida St.76.
NIT Final Four (at Madison Sq.Garden): **Semifinals**—Maryland 91, Jacksonville 77; Niagara 69, St.John's 67. **Third Place**—Jacksonville 83, St.John's 80. **Championship**—Maryland 100, Niagara 69.

1973

		Before Tourns	Head Coach	Final Record
1	UCLA	26-0	John Wooden	30-0
2	N.C.State	27-0	Norm Sloan	same*
3	Long Beach St.	24-2	Jerry Tarkanian	26-3
4	Providence	24-2	Dave Gavitt	27-4
5	Marquette	23-3	Al McGuire	25-4
6	Indiana	19-5	Bob Knight	22-6
7	SW Louisiana	23-2	Beryl Shipley	24-5
8	Maryland	22-6	Lefty Driesell	23-7
9	Kansas St.	22-4	Jack Hartman	23-5
10	Minnesota	20-4	Bill Musselman	21-5
11	North Carolina	22-7	Dean Smith	25-8
12	Memphis St.	21-5	Gene Bartow	24-6
13	Houston	23-3	Guy Lewis	23-4
14	Syracuse	22-4	Roy Danforth	24-5
15	Missouri	21-5	Norm Stewart	21-6
16	Arizona St.	18-7	Ned Wulk	19-9
17	Kentucky	19-7	Joe B.Hall	20-8
18	Penn	20-5	Chuck Daly	21-7
19	Austin Peay	21-5	Lake Kelly	22-7
20	San Francisco	22-4	Bob Gaillard	23-5

Note: NIT champ Va.Tech, coached by Don DeVoe, entered the tourney unranked at 18-5 and had a final record of 22-5.

NCAA Final Four (At The Arena, St.Louis): **Semifinals**—Memphis St.98, Providence 85; UCLA 70, Indiana 59. **Third Place**—Indiana 97, Providence 79. **Championship**—UCLA 87, Memphis St. 66.
NIT Final Four (at Madison Sq.Garden): **Semifinals**—Va.Tech 74, Alabama 73; Notre Dame 78, N.Carolina 71. **Third Place**—N.Carolina 88, Alabama 69. **Championship**—Va.Tech 92, Notre Dame 91 (OT).

1974

		Before Tourns	Head Coach	Final Record
1	N.C.State	26-1	Norm Sloan	30-1
2	UCLA	23-3	John Wooden	26-4
3	Notre Dame	24-2	Digger Phelps	26-3
4	Maryland	23-5	Lefty Driesell	same
5	Providence	26-3	Dave Gavitt	28-4
6	Vanderbilt	23-3	Roy Skinner	23-5
7	Marquette	22-4	Al McGuire	26-5
8	North Carolina	22-5	Dean Smith	22-6
9	Long Beach St.	24-2	Lute Olson	same
10	Indiana	20-5	Bob Knight	23-5
11	Alabama	22-4	C.M.Newton	same
12	Michigan	21-4	Johnny Orr	22-5
13	Pittsburgh	23-3	Buzz Ridl	25-4
14	Kansas	21-5	Ted Owens	23-7
15	USC	22-4	Bob Boyd	24-5
16	Louisville	21-6	Denny Crum	21-7
17	New Mexico	21-6	Norm Ellenberger	22-7
18	South Carolina	22-4	Frank McGuire	22-5
19	Creighton	22-6	Eddie Sutton	23-7
20	Dayton	19-7	Don Donoher	20-9

NCAA Final Four (at Greensboro,NC Coliseum): **Semifinals**—N.C.State 80, UCLA 77 (2 OT); Marquette 64, Kansas 51. **Third Place**—UCLA 78, Kansas 61. **Championship**—N.C.State 76, Marquette 64.
NIT Final Four (at Madison Sq.Garden): **Semifinals**—Purdue 78, Jacksonville 63; Utah 117, Boston Col.93. **Third Place**—Boston Col.87, Jacksonville 77. **Championship**—Purdue 87, Utah 81.
CCA Final Four (at The Arena, St.Louis): **Semifinals**—Indiana 73, Toledo 72; USC 74, Bradley 73. **Championship**—Indiana 85, USC 60.

1975

		Before Tourns	Head Coach	Final Record
1	Indiana	29-0	Bob Knight	31-1
2	UCLA	23-3	John Wooden	28-3
3	Louisville	24-2	Denny Crum	28-3
4	Maryland	22-4	Lefty Driesell	24-5
5	Kentucky	22-4	Joe B.Hall	26-5
6	North Carolina	21-7	Dean Smith	23-8
7	Arizona St.	23-3	Ned Wulk	25-4
8	N.C.State	22-6	Norm Sloan	22-6
9	Notre Dame	18-8	Digger Phelps	19-10
10	Marquette	23-3	Al McGuire	23-4
11	Alabama	22-4	C.M.Newton	22-5
12	Cincinnati	21-5	Gale Catlett	23-6
13	Oregon St.	18-10	Ralph Miller	19-12
14	**Drake**	16-10	Bob Ortegel	19-10
15	Penn	23-4	Chuck Daly	23-5
16	UNLV	22-4	Jerry Tarkanian	24-5
17	Kansas St.	18-8	Jack Hartman	20-9
18	USC	18-7	Bob Boyd	18-8
19	Centenary	25-4	Larry Little	same
20	Syracuse	20-7	Roy Danforth	23-9

NCAA Final Four (at San Diego Sports Arena): **Semifinals**—Kentucky 95, Syracuse 79; UCLA 75, Louisville 74 (OT). **Third Place**—Louisville 96, Syracuse 88 (OT). **Championship**—UCLA 92, Kentucky 85.
NIT Championship (at Madison Sq.Garden): Princeton 80, Providence 69. No Top 20 teams played in NIT.
CCA Championship (at Freedom Hall, Louisville): Drake 83, Arizona 76. No.14 Drake and No.18 USC were only Top 20 teams in CCA.

Post-Tournament Polls

The final AP Top 20 poll has been released after the postseason tournaments only twice—in 1974 and '75. Those two polls are listed below; teams not included in the last regular season poll are in CAPITAL *italic* letters.

	1974	Final Record		1975	Final Record
1	N.C.State	30-1	1	UCLA	28-3
2	UCLA	26-4	2	Kentucky	26-5
3	Marquette	26-5	3	Indiana	31-1
4	Maryland	23-5	4	Louisville	28-3
5	Notre Dame	26-3	5	Maryland	24-5
6	Michigan	22-5	6	Syracuse	23-9
7	Kansas	23-7	7	N.C.State	22-6
8	Providence	28-4	8	Arizona St.	25-4
9	Indiana	23-5	9	N.Carolina	23-8
10	Long Beach St.	24-2	10	Alabama	22-5
11	*PURDUE*	22-8	11	Marquette	23-4
12	N.Carolina	22-6	12	*PRINCETON*	22-8
13	Vanderbilt	23-5	13	Cincinnati	23-6
14	Alabama	22-4	14	Notre Dame	19-10
15	*UTAH*	22-8	15	Kansas St.	20-9
16	Pittsburgh	25-4	16	Drake	19-10
17	USC	24-5	17	UNLV	24-5
18	*ORAL ROBERTS*	23-6	18	Oregon St.	19-12
19	S.Carolina	22-5	19	*MICHIGAN*	19-8
20	Dayton	20-9	20	Penn	23-5

Pre-Tournament Records
1974—Purdue (Fred Schaus, 18-8), Utah (Bill Foster, 19-7), Oral Roberts (Ken Trickey, 21-5).
1975—Princeton (Pete Carril, 18-8), Michigan (Johnny Orr, 19-7).

Associated Press Final Polls (Cont.)

Taken before NCAA and NIT Tournaments; (*) indicates on probation.

1976

		Before Tourns	Head Coach	Final Record
1	Indiana	27-0	Bob Knight	32-0
2	Marquette	25-1	Al McGuire	27-2
3	UNLV	28-1	Jerry Tarkanian	29-2
4	Rutgers	28-0	Tom Young	31-2
5	UCLA	24-3	Gene Bartow	28-4
6	Alabama	22-4	C.M.Newton	23-5
7	Notre Dame	22-5	Digger Phelps	23-6
8	North Carolina	25-3	Dean Smith	25-4
9	Michigan	21-6	Johnny Orr	25-7
10	Western Mich.	24-2	Eldon Miller	25-3
11	Maryland	22-6	Lefty Driesell	same
12	Cincinnati	25-5	Gale Catlett	25-6
13	Tennessee	21-5	Ray Mears	21-6
14	Missouri	24-4	Norm Stewart	26-5
15	Arizona	22-8	Fred Snowden	24-9
16	Texas Tech	24-5	Gerald Myers	25-6
17	DePaul	19-8	Ray Meyer	20-9
18	Virginia	18-11	Terry Holland	18-12
19	Centenary	22-5	Larry Little	same
20	Pepperdine	21-5	Gary Colson	22-6

NCAA Final Four (at The Spectrum, Phila.); **Semifinals**—Michigan 86, Rutgers 70; Indiana 65, UCLA 51. **Third Place**—UCLA 106, Rutgers 92. **Championship**—Indiana 86, Michigan 68.
NIT Championship (at Madison Sq.Garden): Kentucky 71, NC-Charlotte 67. No Top 20 teams played in NIT.

1977

		Before Tourns	Head Coach	Final Record
1	Michigan	24-3	Johnny Orr	26-4
2	UCLA	24-3	Gene Bartow	26-4
3	Kentucky	24-3	Joe B.Hall	26-4
4	UNLV	25-2	Jerry Tarkanian	29-3
5	North Carolina	24-4	Dean Smith	28-5
6	Syracuse	25-3	Jim Boeheim	26-4
7	Marquette	20-7	Al McGuire	25-7
8	San Francisco	29-1	Bob Gaillard	29-2
9	Wake Forest	20-7	Carl Tacy	22-8
10	Notre Dame	21-6	Digger Phelps	22-7
11	Alabama	23-4	C.M.Newton	25-6
12	Detroit	24-3	Dick Vitale	25-4
13	Minnesota	24-3	Jim Dutcher	same*
14	Utah	22-6	Jerry Pimm	23-7
15	Tennessee	22-5	Ray Mears	22-6
16	Kansas St.	23-6	Jack Hartman	24-7
17	NC-Charlotte	25-3	Lee Rose	28-5
18	Arkansas	26-1	Eddie Sutton	26-2
19	Louisville	21-6	Denny Crum	21-7
20	VMI	25-3	Charlie Schmaus	26-4

NCAA Final Four (at The Omni, Atlanta): **Semifinals**—Marquette 51, NC-Charlotte, 49; N.Carolina 84, UNLV 83. **Third Place**—UNLV 106, NC-Charlotte 94. **Championship**—Marquette 67, N.Carolina 59.
NIT Championship (at Madison Square Garden): St.Bonaventure 94, Houston 91. No.11 Alabama was only Top 20 team in NIT.

1978

		Before Tourns	Head Coach	Final Record
1	Kentucky	25-2	Joe B.Hall	30-2
2	UCLA	24-2	Gary Cunningham	25-3
3	DePaul	25-2	Ray Meyer	27-3
4	Michigan St.	23-4	Jud Heathcote	25-5
5	Arkansas	28-3	Eddie Sutton	32-3
6	Notre Dame	20-6	Digger Phelps	23-8
7	Duke	23-6	Bill Foster	27-7
8	Marquette	24-3	Hank Raymonds	24-4
9	Louisville	22-6	Denny Crum	23-7
10	Kansas	24-4	Ted Owens	24-5
11	San Francisco	22-5	Bob Gaillard	23-6
12	New Mexico	24-3	Norm Ellenberger	24-4
13	Indiana	20-7	Bob Knight	21-8
14	Utah	22-5	Jerry Pimm	23-6
15	Florida St.	23-5	Hugh Durham	23-6
16	North Carolina	23-7	Dean Smith	23-8
17	Texas	22-5	Abe Lemons	26-5
18	Detroit	24-3	Dave Gaines	25-4
19	Miami-OH	18-8	Darrell Hedric	19-9
20	Penn	19-7	Bob Weinhauer	20-8

NCAA Final Four (at The Checkerdome, St.Louis): **Semifinals**—Kentucky 64, Arkansas 59; Duke 90, Notre Dame 86. **Third Place**—Arkansas 71, Notre Dame 69. **Championship**—Kentucky 94, Duke 88.
NIT Championship (at Madison Square Garden): Texas 101, N.C.State 93. No.17 Texas and No.18 Detroit were only Top 20 teams in NIT.

1979

		Before Tourns	Head Coach	Final Record
1	Indiana St.	29-0	Bill Hodges	33-1
2	UCLA	23-4	Gary Cunningham	25-5
3	Michigan St.	21-6	Jud Heathcote	26-6
4	Notre Dame	22-5	Digger Phelps	24-6
5	Arkansas	23-4	Eddie Sutton	25-5
6	DePaul	22-5	Ray Meyer	26-6
7	LSU	22-5	Dale Brown	23-6
8	Syracuse	25-3	Jim Boeheim	26-4
9	North Carolina	23-5	Dean Smith	23-6
10	Marquette	21-6	Hank Raymonds	22-7
11	Duke	22-7	Bill Foster	22-8
12	San Francisco	21-6	Dan Belluomini	22-7
13	Louisville	23-7	Denny Crum	24-8
14	Penn	21-5	Bob Weinhauer	25-7
15	Purdue	23-7	Lee Rose	27-8
16	Oklahoma	20-9	Dave Bliss	21-10
17	St.John's	18-10	Lou Carnesecca	21-11
18	Rutgers	21-8	Tom Young	22-9
19	Toledo	21-6	Bob Nichols	22-7
20	Iowa	20-7	Lute Olson	20-8

NCAA Final Four (at Special Events Center, Salt Lake City): **Semifinals**—Michigan St. 101, Penn 67; Indiana St.76, DePaul 74. **Third Place**—DePaul 96, Penn 93. **Championship**—Michigan St.75, Indiana St.64.
NIT Championship (at Madison Square Garden): Indiana 53, Purdue 52. No.15 Purdue was only Top 20 team in NIT.

1980

		Before Tourns	Head Coach	Final Record
1	DePaul	26-1	Ray Meyer	26-2
2	**Louisville**	28-3	Denny Crum	33-3
3	LSU	24-5	Dale Brown	26-6
4	Kentucky	28-5	Joe B.Hall	29-6
5	Oregon St.	26-3	Ralph Miller	26-4
6	Syracuse	25-3	Jim Boeheim	26-4
7	Indiana	20-7	Bob Knight	21-8
8	Maryland	23-6	Lefty Driesell	24-7
9	Notre Dame	20-7	Digger Phelps	20-8
10	Ohio St.	24-5	Eldon Miller	21-8
11	Georgetown	24-5	John Thompson	26-6
12	BYU	24-4	Frank Arnold	24-5
13	St.John's	24-4	Lou Carnesecca	24-5
14	Duke	22-8	Bill Foster	24-9
15	North Carolina	21-7	Dean Smith	21-8
16	Missouri	23-5	Norm Stewart	25-6
17	Weber St.	26-2	Neil McCarthy	26-3
18	Arizona St.	21-6	Ned Wulk	22-7
19	Iona	28-4	Jim Valvano	29-5
20	Purdue	19-9	Lee Rose	23-10

NCAA Final Four (at Market Sq.Arena, Indianapolis): **Semifinals**—Louisville 80, Iowa 72; UCLA 67, Purdue 62; **Championship**—Louisville 59, UCLA 54.
NIT Championship (at Madison Sq.Garden): Virginia 58, Minnesota 55. No Top 20 teams played in NIT.

1981

		Before Tourns	Head Coach	Final Record
1	DePaul	27-1	Ray Meyer	27-2
2	Oregon St.	26-1	Ralph Miller	26-2
3	Arizona St.	24-3	Ned Wulk	24-4
4	LSU	28-3	Dale Brown	31-5
5	Virginia	25-3	Terry Holland	29-4
6	North Carolina	25-7	Dean Smith	29-8
7	Notre Dame	22-5	Digger Phelps	23-6
8	Kentucky	22-5	Joe B.Hall	22-6
9	**Indiana**	21-9	Bob Knight	26-9
10	UCLA	20-6	Larry Brown	20-7
11	Wake Forest	22-6	Carl Tacy	22-7
12	Louisville	21-8	Denny Crum	21-9
13	Iowa	21-6	Lute Olson	21-7
14	Utah	24-4	Jerry Pimm	25-5
15	Tennessee	20-7	Don DeVoe	21-8
16	BYU	22-6	Frank Arnold	25-7
17	Wyoming	23-5	Jim Brandenburg	24-6
18	Maryland	20-9	Lefty Driesell	21-10
19	Illinois	20-7	Lou Henson	21-8
20	Arkansas	22-7	Eddie Sutton	24-8

NCAA Final Four (at The Spectrum, Phila.): **Semifinals**—N.Carolina 78, Virginia 65; Indiana 67, LSU 49. **Third Place**—Virginia 78, LSU 74. **Championship**—Indiana 63, N.Carolina 50.
NIT Championship (at Madison Sq.Garden): Tulsa 86, Syracuse 84. No Top 20 teams played in NIT.

1982

		Before Tourns	Head Coach	Final Record
1	**North Carolina**	27-2	Dean Smith	32-2
2	DePaul	26-1	Ray Meyer	26-2
3	Virginia	29-3	Terry Holland	30-4
4	Oregon St.	23-4	Ralph Miller	25-5
5	Missouri	26-3	Norm Stewart	27-4
6	Georgetown	26-6	John Thompson	30-7
7	Minnesota	22-5	Jim Dutcher	23-6
8	Idaho	26-2	Don Monson	27-3
9	Memphis St.	23-4	Dana Kirk	24-5
10	Tulsa	24-5	Nolan Richardson	24-6
11	Fresno St.	26-2	Boyd Grant	27-3
12	Arkansas	23-5	Eddie Sutton	23-6
13	Alabama	23-6	Wimp Sanderson	24-7
14	West Virginia	26-3	Gale Catlett	27-4
15	Kentucky	22-7	Joe B.Hall	22-8
16	Iowa	20-7	Lute Olson	21-8
17	Alabama-Birm.	23-5	Gene Bartow	25-6
18	Wake Forest	20-8	Carl Tacy	21-9
19	UCLA	21-6	Larry Farmer	21-6
20	Louisville	20-9	Denny Crum	23-10

NCAA Final Four (at The Superdome, New Orleans): **Semifinals**—N.Carolina 68, Houston 63; Georgetown 50, Louisville 46. **Championship**—N.Carolina 63, Georgetown 62.
NIT Championship (at Madison Sq.Garden): Bradley 67, Purdue 58. No Top 20 teams played in NIT.

1983

		Before Tourns	Head Coach	Final Record
1	Houston	27-2	Guy Lewis	31-3
2	Louisville	29-3	Denny Crum	32-4
3	St.John's	27-4	Lou Carnesecca	28-5
4	Virginia	27-4	Terry Holland	29-5
5	Indiana	23-5	Bob Knight	24-6
6	UNLV	28-2	Jerry Tarkanian	28-3
7	UCLA	23-5	Larry Farmer	23-6
8	North Carolina	26-7	Dean Smith	28-8
9	Arkansas	25-3	Eddie Sutton	26-4
10	Missouri	26-7	Norm Stewart	26-8
11	Boston College	24-6	Gary Williams	25-7
12	Kentucky	22-7	Joe B.Hall	23-8
13	Villanova	22-7	Rollie Massimino	24-8
14	Wichita St.	25-3	Gene Smithson	same*
15	Tenn-Chatt.	26-3	Murray Arnold	26-4
16	**N.C.State**	20-10	Jim Valvano	26-10
17	Memphis St.	22-7	Dana Kirk	23-8
18	Georgia	21-9	Hugh Durham	24-10
19	Oklahoma St.	24-6	Paul Hansen	24-7
20	Georgetown	21-9	John Thompson	22-10

NCAA Final Four (at The Pit, Albuquerque,NM): **Semifinals**—N.C.State 67, Georgia 60; Houston 94, Louisville 81. **Championship**—N.C.State 54, Houston 52.
NIT Championship (at Madison Sq.Garden): Fresno St.69, DePaul 60. No Top 20 teams played in NIT.

Associated Press Final Polls (Cont.)

Taken before NCAA and NIT Tournaments; (*) indicates on probation.

1984

		Before Tourns	Head Coach	Final Record
1	North Carolina	27-2	Dean Smith	28-3
2	**Georgetown**	29-3	John Thompson	34-3
3	Kentucky	26-4	Joe B.Hall	29-5
4	DePaul	26-2	Ray Meyer	27-3
5	Houston	28-4	Guy Lewis	32-5
6	Illinois	24-4	Lou Henson	26-5
7	Oklahoma	29-4	Billy Tubbs	29-5
8	Arkansas	25-6	Eddie Sutton	25-7
9	UTEP	27-3	Don Haskins	27-4
10	Purdue	22-6	Gene Keady	22-7
11	Maryland	23-7	Lefty Driesell	24-8
12	Tulsa	27-3	Nolan Richardson	27-4
13	UNLV	27-5	Jerry Tarkanian	29-6
14	Duke	24-9	Mike Krzyzewski	24-10
15	Washington	22-6	Marv Harshman	24-7
16	Memphis St.	24-6	Dana Kirk	26-7
17	Oregon St.	22-6	Ralph Miller	22-7
18	Syracuse	22-8	Jim Boeheim	23-9
19	Wake Forest	21-8	Carl Tacy	23-9
20	Temple	25-4	John Chaney	26-5

NCAA Final Four (at The Kingdome, Seattle): **Semifinals**—Houston 49, Virginia 47 (OT); Georgetown 53, Kentucky 40. **Championship**—Georgetown 84, Houston 75.

NIT Championship (at Madison Sq.Garden): Michigan 83, Notre Dame 63. No Top 20 teams played in NIT.

1985

		Before Tourns	Head Coach	Final Record
1	Georgetown	30-2	John Thompson	35-3
2	Michigan	25-3	Bill Frieder	26-4
3	St.John's	27-3	Lou Carnesecca	31-4
4	Oklahoma	28-5	Billy Tubbs	31-6
5	Memphis St.	27-3	Dana Kirk	31-4
6	Georgia Tech	24-7	Bobby Cremins	27-8
7	North Carolina	24-8	Dean Smith	27-9
8	Louisiana Tech	27-2	Andy Russo	29-3
9	UNLV	27-3	Jerry Tarkanian	28-4
10	Duke	22-7	Mike Krzyzewski	23-8
11	VCU	25-5	J.D.Barnett	26-6
12	Illinois	24-8	Lou Henson	26-9
13	Kansas	25-7	Larry Brown	26-8
14	Loyola-IL	25-5	Gene Sullivan	27-6
15	Syracuse	21-8	Jim Boeheim	22-9
16	N.C.State	20-9	Jim Valvano	23-10
17	Texas Tech	23-7	Gerald Myers	23-8
18	Tulsa	23-7	Nolan Richardson	23-8
19	Georgia	21-8	Hugh Durham	22-9
20	LSU	19-9	Dale Brown	19-10

Note: Unranked Villanova, coached by Rollie Massimino, won the NCAAs. The Wildcats entered the tourney at 19-10 and had a final record of 25-10.

NCAA Final Four (at Rupp Arena, Lexington, KY): **Semifinals**— Georgetown 77, St.John's 59; Villanova 52, Memphis St.45. **Championship**—Villanova 66, Georgetown 64.

NIT Championship (at Madison Sq.Garden): UCLA 65, Indiana 62. No Top 20 teams played in NIT.

1986

		Before Tourns	Head Coach	Final Record
1	Duke	32-2	Mike Krzyzewski	37-3
2	Kansas	31-3	Larry Brown	35-4
3	Kentucky	29-3	Eddie Sutton	32-4
4	St.John's	30-4	Lou Carnesecca	31-5
5	Michigan	27-4	Bill Frieder	28-5
6	Georgia Tech	25-6	Bobby Cremins	27-7
7	**Louisville**	26-7	Denny Crum	32-7
8	North Carolina	26-5	Dean Smith	28-6
9	Syracuse	25-5	Jim Boeheim	26-6
10	Notre Dame	23-5	Digger Phelps	23-6
11	UNLV	31-4	Jerry Tarkanian	33-5
12	Memphis St.	27-5	Dana Kirk	28-6
13	Georgetown	23-7	John Thompson	24-8
14	Bradley	31-2	Dick Versace	32-3
15	Oklahoma	25-8	Billy Tubbs	26-9
16	Indiana	21-7	Bob Knight	21-8
17	Navy	27-4	Paul Evans	30-5
18	Michigan St.	21-7	Jud Heathcote	23-8
19	Illinois	21-9	Lou Henson	22-10
20	UTEP	27-5	Don Haskins	27-6

NCAA Final Four (at Reunion Arena, Dallas): **Semifinals**—Duke 71, Kansas 67; Louisville 88, LSU 77. **Championship**—Louisville 72, Duke 69.

NIT Championship (at Madison Sq.Garden): Ohio St.73, Wyoming 63. No Top 20 teams played in NIT.

1987

		Before Tourns	Head Coach	Final Record
1	UNLV	33-1	Jerry Tarkanian	37-2
2	North Carolina	29-3	Dean Smith	32-4
3	**Indiana**	24-4	Bob Knight	30-4
4	Georgetown	26-4	John Thompson	29-5
5	DePaul	26-2	Joey Meyer	28-3
6	Iowa	27-4	Tom Davis	30-5
7	Purdue	24-4	Gene Keady	25-5
8	Temple	31-3	John Chaney	32-4
9	Alabama	26-4	Wimp Sanderson	28-5
10	Syracuse	26-6	Jim Boeheim	31-7
11	Illinois	23-7	Lou Henson	23-8
12	Pittsburgh	24-7	Paul Evans	25-8
13	Clemson	25-5	Cliff Ellis	25-6
14	Missouri	24-9	Norm Stewart	24-10
15	UCLA	24-6	Walt Hazzard	25-7
16	New Orleans	25-3	Benny Dees	26-4
17	Duke	22-8	Mike Krzyzewski	24-9
18	Notre Dame	22-7	Digger Phelps	24-8
19	TCU	23-6	Jim Killingsworth	24-7
20	Kansas	23-10	Larry Brown	25-11

NCAA Final Four (at The Superdome, New Orleans): **Semifinals**—Syracuse 77, Providence 63; Indiana 97, UNLV 93. **Championship**—Indiana 74, Syracuse 73.

NIT Championship (at Madison Sq. Garden): Southern Miss 84, La Salle 80. No Top 20 teams played in NIT.

1988

		Before Tourns	Head Coach	Final Record
1	Temple	29-1	John Chaney	32-2
2	Arizona	31-2	Lute Olson	35-3
3	Purdue	27-3	Gene Keady	29-4
4	Oklahoma	30-3	Billy Tubbs	35-4
5	Duke	24-6	Mike Krzyzewski	28-7
6	Kentucky	25-5	Eddie Sutton	27-6
7	North Carolina	24-6	Dean Smith	27-7
8	Pittsburgh	23-6	Paul Evans	24-7
9	Syracuse	25-8	Jim Boeheim	26-9
10	Michigan	24-7	Bill Frieder	26-8
11	Bradley	26-4	Stan Albeck	26-5
12	UNLV	27-5	Jerry Tarkanian	28-6
13	Wyoming	26-5	Benny Dees	26-6
14	N.C.State	24-7	Jim Valvano	24-8
15	Loyola-CA	27-3	Paul Westhead	28-4
16	Illinois	22-9	Lou Henson	23-10
17	Iowa	22-9	Tom Davis	24-10
18	Xavier-OH	26-3	Pete Gillen	26-4
19	BYU	25-5	Ladell Andersen	26-6
20	Kansas St.	22-8	Lon Kruger	25-9

Note: Unranked Kansas, coached by Larry Brown, won the NCAAs. The Jayhawks entered the tourney at 21-11 and had a final record of 27-11.

NCAA Final Four (at Kemper Arena, Kansas City): **Semifinals**—Kansas 66, Duke 59; Oklahoma 86, Arizona 78. **Championship**—Kansas 83, Oklahoma 79.
NIT Championship (at Madison Sq. Garden): Connecticut 72, Ohio St.67. No Top 20 team played in NIT.

1990

		Before Tourns	Head Coach	Final Record
1	Oklahoma	26-4	Billy Tubbs	27-5
2	**UNLV**	29-5	Jerry Tarkanian	35-5
3	Connecticut	28-5	Jim Calhoun	31-6
4	Michigan St.	26-5	Jud Heathcote	28-6
5	Kansas	29-4	Roy Williams	30-5
6	Syracuse	24-6	Jim Boeheim	26-7
7	Arkansas	26-4	Nolan Richardson	30-5
8	Georgetown	23-6	John Thompson	24-7
9	Georgia Tech	24-6	Bobby Cremins	28-7
10	Purdue	21-7	Gene Keady	22-8
11	Missouri	26-5	Norm Stewart	26-6
12	La Salle	29-1	Speedy Morris	30-2
13	Michigan	22-7	Steve Fisher	23-8
14	Arizona	24-6	Lute Olson	25-7
15	Duke	24-8	Mike Krzyzewski	29-9
16	Louisville	26-7	Denny Crum	27-8
17	Clemson	24-8	Cliff Ellis	26-9
18	Illinois	21-7	Lou Henson	21-8
19	LSU	22-8	Dale Brown	23-9
20	Minnesota	20-8	Clem Haskins	23-9
21	Loyola-CA	23-5	Paul Westhead	26-6
22	Oregon St.	22-6	Jim Anderson	22-7
23	Alabama	24-8	Wimp Sanderson	26-9
24	New Mexico St.	26-4	Neil McCarthy	26-5
25	Xavier-OH	26-4	Pete Gillen	28-5

NCAA Final Four (at McNichols Sports Arena, Denver): **Semifinals**—Duke 97, Arkansas 83; UNLV 90, Georgia Tech 81. **Championship**—UNLV 103, Duke 73.
NIT Championship (at Madison Sq.Garden): Vanderbilt 74, St.Louis 72. No Top 20 teams played in NIT.

1989

		Before Tourns	Head Coach	Final Record
1	Arizona	27-3	Lute Olson	29-4
2	Georgetown	26-4	John Thompson	29-5
3	Illinois	27-4	Lou Henson	31-5
4	Oklahoma	28-5	Billy Tubbs	30-6
5	North Carolina	27-7	Dean Smith	29-8
6	Missouri	27-7	Norm Stewart & Rich Daly	29-8
7	Syracuse	27-7	Jim Boeheim	30-8
8	Indiana	25-7	Bob Knight	27-8
9	Duke	24-7	Mike Krzyzewski	28-8
10	**Michigan**	24-7	Bill Frieder & Steve Fisher	30-7
11	Seton Hall	26-6	P.J.Carlesimo	31-7
12	Louisville	22-8	Denny Crum	24-9
13	Stanford	26-6	Mike Montgomery	26-7
14	Iowa	22-9	Tom Davis	23-10
15	UNLV	26-7	Jerry Tarkanian	29-8
16	Florida St.	22-7	Pat Kennedy	22-8
17	West Virginia	25-4	Gale Catlett	26-5
18	Ball State	28-2	Rick Majerus	29-3
19	N.C.State	20-8	Jim Valvano	22-9
20	Alabama	23-7	Wimp Sanderson	23-8

NCAA Final Four (at The Kingdome, Seattle): **Semifinals**—Seton Hall 95, Duke 78; Michigan 83, Illinois 81. **Championship**—Michigan 80, Seton Hall 79 (OT).
NIT Championship (at Madison Sq. Garden): St.John's 73, St.Louis 65. No Top 20 teams played in NIT.

1991

		Before Tourns	Head Coach	Final Record
1	UNLV	30-0	Jerry Tarkanian	34-1
2	Arkansas	31-3	Nolan Richardson	34-4
3	Indiana	27-4	Bob Knight	29-5
4	North Carolina	25-5	Dean Smith	29-6
5	Ohio St.	25-3	Randy Ayers	27-4
6	**Duke**	26-7	Mike Krzyzewski	32-7
7	Syracuse	26-5	Jim Boeheim	26-6
8	Arizona	26-6	Lute Olson	28-7
9	Kentucky	22-6	Rick Pitino	same*
10	Utah	28-3	Rick Majerus	30-4
11	Nebraska	26-7	Danny Nee	26-8
12	Kansas	22-7	Roy Williams	27-8
13	Seton Hall	22-8	P.J.Carlesimo	25-9
14	Oklahoma St.	22-7	Eddie Sutton	24-8
15	New Mexico St.	23-5	Neil McCarthy	23-6
16	UCLA	23-8	Jim Harrick	23-9
17	E.Tennessee St.	28-4	Alan LaForce	28-5
18	Princeton	24-2	Pete Carril	24-3
19	Alabama	21-9	Wimp Sanderson	23-10
20	St.John's	20-8	Lou Carnesecca	23-9
21	Mississippi St.	20-8	Richard Williams	20-9
22	LSU	20-9	Dale Brown	20-10
23	Texas	22-8	Tom Penders	23-9
24	DePaul	20-8	Joey Meyer	20-9
25	So.Mississippi	21-7	M.K.Turk	21-8

NCAA Final Four (at the Hoosier Dome, Indianapolis): **Semifinals**—Kansas 79, North Carolina 73; Duke 79, UNLV 77. **Championship**—Duke 72, Kansas 65.
NIT Championship (at Madison Sq.Garden): Stanford 78, Oklahoma 72. No Top 20 teams played in NIT.

Associated Press Final Polls (Cont.)
Taken before NCAA and NIT Tournaments; (*) indicates on probation.

1992

		Before Tourns	Head Coach	Final Record
1	**Duke**	28-2	Mike Krzyzewski	34-2
2	Kansas	26-4	Roy Williams	27-5
3	Ohio St.	23-5	Randy Ayers	26-6
4	UCLA	25-4	Jim Harrick	28-5
5	Indiana	23-6	Bob Knight	27-7
6	Kentucky	26-6	Rick Pitino	29-7
7	UNLV	26-2	Jerry Tarkanian	same*
8	USC	23-5	George Raveling	24-6
9	Arkansas	25-7	Nolan Richardson	26-8
10	Arizona	24-6	Lute Olson	24-7
11	Oklahoma St.	26-7	Eddie Sutton	28-8
12	Cincinnati	25-4	Bob Huggins	29-5
13	Alabama	25-8	Wimp Sanderson	26-9
14	Michigan St.	21-7	Jud Heathcote	22-8
15	Michigan	20-8	Steve Fisher	25-9
16	Missouri	20-8	Norm Stewart	21-9
17	Massachusetts	28-4	John Calipari	30-5
18	North Carolina	21-9	Dean Smith	23-10
19	Seton Hall	21-8	P.J.Carlesimo	23-9
20	Florida St.	20-9	Pat Kennedy	22-10
21	Syracuse	21-9	Jim Boeheim	22-10
22	Georgetown	21-9	John Thompson	22-10
23	Oklahoma	21-8	Billy Tubbs	21-9
24	DePaul	20-8	Joey Meyer	20-9
25	LSU	20-9	Dale Brown	21-10

NCAA Final Four (at Metrodome in Minneapolis): **Semifinals**—Michigan 76, Cincinnati 72; Duke 81, Indiana 78. **Championship**—Duke 71, Michigan 51.
NIT Championship (at Madison Sq.Garden): Virginia 81, Notre Dame 76 (OT). No Top 20 teams played in NIT.

All-Time AP Top 20

The composite AP Top 20 from the 1948-49 season through 1991-92, based on the final **regular season** rankings of each year. Team point totals are based on 20 points for all 1st place finishes, 19 for each 2nd, etc. Also listed are the number of times ranked No.1 by AP going into the tournaments, and times ranked in the pre-tournament Top 10 and Top 20.

		Pts	No. 1	Top 10	Top 20
1	Kentucky	481	7	27	32
2	North Carolina	396	3	22	29
3	UCLA	389	6	20	27
4	Duke	275	2	15	24
5	Indiana	265	3	15	20
6	Kansas	213	0	11	18
7	Louisville	209	0	10	19
8	Notre Dame	195	0	13	17
9	UNLV	173	2	8	13
10	N.C.State	166	1	9	15
11	Marquette	165	0	11	13
12	Michigan	163	2	9	12
13	Cincinnati	158	2	7	11
14	Illinois	156	0	7	17
15	Bradley	152	1	8	11
16	Ohio St	149	2	9	10
17	DePaul	143	2	8	10
	Kansas St.	143	1	7	12
	St.John's	143	0	8	14
20	Syracuse	138	0	9	13

All-Time Winningest Division I Teams

Division I schools with best winning percentages through 1991-92 season (including tournament games). Years in Division I only; minimum 25 years. **NCAA Tourney** columns indicate years in tournament, record and number of championships.

Top 20 Winning Percentage

		First Year	Yrs	Games	Won	Lost	Tied	Pct	NCAA Tourney Yrs	W-L	Titles
1	UNLV	1959	32	945	726	219	0	.768	12	30-11	1
2	Kentucky	1903	89	2036	1532	503	1	.753	34	58-31	5
3	North Carolina	1911	82	2096	1536	560	0	.733	26	56-27	2
4	St.John's	1908	85	2087	1463	624	0	.701	22	22-24	0
5	UCLA	1920	73	1844	1277	567	0	.693	28	67-22	10
6	Kansas	1899	94	2168	1486	682	0	.685	21	43-21	2
7	Syracuse	1901	91	1975	1340	635	0	.678	20	27-21	0
	Western Kentucky	1915	73	1862	1262	600	0	.678	13	12-14	0
9	DePaul	1924	69	1660	1118	542	0	.673	20	20-23	0
10	Duke	1906	87	2106	1411	695	0	.670	17	50-15	2
11	Notre Dame	1898	87	2037	1353	683	1	.664	24	25-28	0
12	La Salle	1931	62	1577	1031	546	0	.654	11	11-10	1
13	Louisville	1912	78	1852	1207	645	0	.652	22	39-24	2
14	Houston	1946	47	1304	846	458	0	.649	18	26-23	0
15	Indiana	1901	92	2005	1298	707	0	.647	21	45-16	5
	Temple	1895	96	2121	1373	748	0	.647	16	18-16	0
	North Carolina St	1913	80	1927	1246	681	0	.647	17	27-16	2
18	Arkansas	1924	69	1733	1119	614	0	.646	18	22-19	0
19	Illinois	1906	87	1903	1226	677	0	.644	14	20-15	0
	Weber St.	1963	30	845	544	301	0	.644	10	4-11	0

Top 30 Victories

Division I schools with most victories through 1991-92 (including postseason tournaments). Totals reflect games won in Division I only.

		Wins			Wins			Wins
1	North Carolina	1536	11	Washington	1305	21	Bradley	1225
2	Kentucky	1532	12	Indiana	1298	22	Utah	1224
3	Kansas	1486	13	UCLA	1277	23	Washington St	1217
4	St.John's	1463	14	Princeton	1264	24	Louisville	1207
5	Duke	1411	15	Western Ky	1262	25	Texas	1203
6	Oregon St	1404	16	Fordham	1260	26	Montana St	1183
7	Temple	1373	17	N.C.State	1246	27	Villanova	1157
8	Notre Dame	1353	18	West Virginia	1245	28	St.Joseph's-PA	1152
9	Penn	1340	19	Purdue	1239	29	Arkansas	1119
	Syracuse	1340	20	Illinois	1226	30	DePaul	1118

Top 50 Single-Season Victories

Division I schools with most victories in a single season through 1991–92 (including postseason tournaments). NCAA champions in **bold** type.

		Year	Record			Year	Record			Year	Record
1	UNLV	1987	37-2	17	**N.Carolina**	1957	32-0	35	Indiana	1975	31-1
	Duke	1986	37-3		**Indiana**	1976	32-0		**Wyoming**	1943	31-2
3	**Kentucky**	1948	36-3		**Kentucky**	1949	32-2		**Okla. A&M**	1946	31-2
4	Georgetown	1985	35-3		**Kentucky**	1951	32-2		Seton Hall	1953	31-2
	Arizona	1988	35-3		**N.Carolina**	1982	32-2		Houston	1968	31-2
	Kansas	1986	35-4		Temple	1988	32-2		Rutgers	1976	31-2
	Oklahoma	1988	35-4		Arkansas	1978	32-3		Houston	1983	31-3
	UNLV	1990	35-5		Bradley	1986	32-3		Memphis St	1985	31-4
9	UNLV	1991	34-1		Louisville	1983	32-4		St.John's	1985	31-4
	Duke	1992	34-2		Kentucky	1986	32-4		LSU	1981	31-5
	Kentucky	1947	34-3		N.Carolina	1987	32-4		St.John's	1986	31-5
	Georgetown	1984	34-3		Temple	1987	32-4		Illinois	1989	31-5
	Arkansas	1991	34-4		Bradley	1950	32-5		Oklahoma	1985	31-6
14	Indiana St.	1979	33-1		Marshall	1947	32-5		Connecticut	1990	31-6
	Louisville	1980	33-3		Houston	1984	32-5		Syracuse	1987	31-7
	UNLV	1986	33-5		Bradley	1951	32-6		Seton Hall	1989	31-7
					Louisville	1986	32-7				
					Duke	1991	32-7				

Winning Streaks

Full Season
(Including tournaments)

No		Seasons	Broken by	Score
88	UCLA	1971-74	Notre Dame	71-70
60	San Francisco	1955-57	Illinois	62-33
47	UCLA	1966-68	Houston	71-69
45	UNLV	1990-91	Duke	79-77
44	Texas	1913-17	Rice	24-18
43	Seton Hall	1939-41	LIU-Bklyn	49-26
43	LIU-Brooklyn	1935-37	Stanford	45-31
41	UCLA	1968-69	USC	46-44
39	Marquette	1970-71	Ohio St.	60-59
37	Cincinnati	1962-63	Wichita St.	65-64
37	North Carolina	1957-58	West Virginia	75-64
36	N.C.State	1974-75	Wake Forest	83-78
35	Arkansas	1927-29	Texas	26-25

Regular Season
(Not including tournaments)

No		Seasons	Broken by	Score
76	UCLA	1971-74	Notre Dame	71-70
57	Indiana	1975-77	Toledo	59-57
56	Marquette	1970-72	Detroit	70-49
54	Kentucky	1952-55	Georgia Tech	59-58
51	San Francisco	1955-57	Illinois	62-33
48	Penn	1970-72	Temple	57-52
47	Ohio St	1960-62	Wisconsin	86-67
44	Texas	1913-17	Rice	24-18
43	UCLA	1966-68	Houston	71-69
43	LIU-Brooklyn	1935-37	Stanford	45-31
42	Seton Hall	1939-41	LIU-Bklyn	49-26

All-Time Highest Scoring Teams

SINGLE SEASON
Scoring

	Year	Gm	Pts	Avg
Loyola-CA	1990	32	3918	122.4
Loyola-CA	1989	31	3486	112.5
UNLV	1976	31	3426	110.5
Loyola-CA	1988	32	3528	110.3
UNLV	1977	32	3426	107.1

SINGLE GAME
Scoring

	Score	Opponent	Date
Loyola-CA	186-140	US Int'l	1/5/91
Loyola-CA	181-150	US Int'l	1/31/89
Oklahoma	173-101	US Int'l	11/29/89
Oklahoma	172-112	Loyola-CA	12/15/90
Arkansas	166-101	US Int'l	12/9/89

Annual NCAA Division I Leaders

Scoring

The NCAA did not begin keeping individual scoring records until the 1947-48 season. All averages include postseason games where applicable.

Multiple winners: Pete Maravich, Oscar Robertson (3); Darrell Floyd, Harry Kelly, Frank Selvy and Freeman Williams (2).

Year		Gm	Pts	Avg	Year		Gm	Pts	Avg
1948	Murray Wier, Iowa	19	399	21.0	1972	Dwight Lamar, SW La	29	1054	36.3
1949	Tony Lavelli, Yale	30	671	22.4	1973	William Averitt, Pepperdine	25	848	33.9
					1974	Larry Fogle, Canisius	25	835	33.4
1950	Paul Arizin, Villanova	29	735	25.3	1975	Bob McCurdy, Richmond	26	855	32.9
1951	Bill Mlkvy, Temple	25	731	29.2	1976	Marshall Rodgers, Pan Am	25	919	36.8
1952	Clyde Lovellette, Kansas	28	795	28.4	1977	Freeman Williams, Portland St.	26	1010	38.8
1953	Frank Selvy, Furman	25	738	29.5	1978	Freeman Williams, Portland St.	27	969	35.9
1954	Frank Selvy, Furman	29	1209	41.7	1979	Lawrence Butler, Idaho St	27	812	30.1
1955	Darrell Floyd, Furman	25	897	35.9					
1956	Darrell Floyd, Furman	28	946	33.8	1980	Tony Murphy, Southern-BR	29	932	32.1
1957	Grady Wallace, S.Carolina	29	906	31.2	1981	Zam Fredrick, S.Carolina	27	781	28.9
1958	Oscar Robertson, Cinncinati	28	984	35.1	1982	Harry Kelly, TX-Southern	29	862	29.7
1959	Oscar Robertson, Cinncinati	30	978	32.6	1983	Harry Kelly, TX-Southern	29	835	28.8
					1984	Joe Jakubick, Akron	27	814	30.1
1960	Oscar Robertson, Cincinnati	30	1011	33.7	1985	Xavier McDaniel, Wichita St.	31	844	27.2
1961	Frank Burgess, Gonzaga	26	842	32.4	1986	Terrance Bailey, Wagner	29	854	29.4
1962	Billy McGill, Utah	26	1009	38.8	1987	Kevin Houston, Army	29	953	32.9
1963	Nick Werkman, Seton Hall	22	650	29.5	1988	Hersey Hawkins, Bradley	31	1125	36.3
1964	Howie Komives, Bowl.Green	23	844	36.7	1989	Hank Gathers, Loyola-CA	31	1015	32.7
1965	Rick Barry, Miami-FL	26	973	37.4					
1966	Dave Schellhase, Purdue	24	781	32.5	1990	Bo Kimble, Loyola-CA	32	1131	35.3
1967	Jimmy Walker, Providence	28	851	30.4	1991	Kevin Bradshaw, US Int'l	28	1054	37.6
1968	Pete Maravich, LSU	26	1138	43.8	1992	Brett Roberts, Morehead St	29	815	28.1
1969	Pete Maravich, LSU	26	1148	44.2					
1970	Pete Maravich, LSU	31	1381	44.5					
1971	Johnny Neumann, Ole Miss	23	923	40.1					

Note: Fourteen underclassmen have won the title: **Sophomores** (4)—Robertson (1958), Maravich (1968), Neumann (1971), Fogle (1974); **Juniors** (10)—Selvy (1953), Floyd (1955), Robertson (1959), Werkman (1963), Maravich (1969), Lamar (1972), Williams (1977), Kelly (1982), Bailey (1986), Gathers (1989).

Rebounds

The NCAA did not begin keeping individual rebounding records until the 1950-51 season. From 1956-62, the championship was decided on highest percentage of recoveries out of all rebounds made by both teams in all games. All averages include postseason games where applicable; (*) indicates also led nation in scoring.

Multiple winners: Artis Gilmore, Jerry Lucas, Xavier McDaniel, Kermit Washington and Leroy Wright (2).

Year		Gm	No	Avg	Year		Gm	No	Avg
1951	Ernie Beck, Penn	27	556	20.6	1974	Marvin Barnes, Providence	32	597	18.7
1952	Bill Hannon, Army	17	355	20.9	1975	John Irving, Hofstra	21	323	15.4
1953	Ed Conlin, Fordham	26	612	23.5	1976	Sam Pellom, Buffalo	26	420	16.2
1954	Art Quimby, Connecticut	26	588	22.6	1977	Glenn Moseley, Seton Hall	29	473	16.3
1955	Charlie Slack, Marshall	21	538	25.6	1978	Ken Williams, N. Texas	28	411	14.7
1956	Joe Holup, G. Washington	26	604	.256	1979	Monti Davis, Tennessee St.	26	421	16.2
1957	Elgin Baylor, Seattle	25	508	.235					
1958	Alex Ellis, Niagara	25	536	.262	1980	Larry Smith, Alcorn State	26	392	15.1
1959	Leroy Wright, Pacific	26	652	.238	1981	Darryl Watson, Miss. Valley St.	27	379	14.0
1960	Leroy Wright, Pacific	17	380	.234	1982	LaSalle Thompson, Texas	27	365	13.5
1961	Jerry Lucas, Ohio St.	27	470	.198	1983	Xavier McDaniel, Wichita St.	28	403	14.4
1962	Jerry Lucas, Ohio St.	28	499	.211	1984	Akeem Olajuwon, Houston	37	500	13.5
1963	Paul Silas, Creighton	27	557	20.6	1985	Xavier McDaniel, Wichita St.*	31	460	14.8
1964	Bob Pelkington, Xavier-OH	26	567	21.8	1986	David Robinson, Navy	35	455	13.0
1965	Toby Kimball, Connecticut	23	483	21.0	1987	Jerome Lane, Pittsburgh	33	444	13.5
1966	Jim Ware, Oklahoma City	29	607	20.9	1988	Kenny Miller, Loyola-IL	29	395	13.6
1967	Dick Cunningham, Murray St	22	479	21.8	1989	Hank Gathers, Loyola-CA*	31	426	13.7
1968	Neal Walk, Florida	25	494	19.8					
1969	Spencer Haywood, Detroit	22	472	21.5	1990	Anthony Bonner, St. Louis	33	456	13.8
1970	Artis Gilmore, Jacksonville	28	621	22.2	1991	Shaquille O'Neal, LSU	28	411	14.7
1971	Artis Gilmore, Jacksonville	26	603	23.2	1992	Popeye Jones, Murray St.	30	431	14.4
1972	Kermit Washington, American	23	455	19.8					
1973	Kermit Washington, American	22	439	20.0					

All-Time NCAA Division I Individual Leaders
Through 1991-92; includes regular season and tournament games.

CAREER
Scoring

Points	Years	Gm	Pts		Average	Years	No	Avg
Pete Maravich, LSU	1968-70	83	3667		Pete Maravich, LSU	1968-70	3667	44.2
Freeman Williams, Portland St	1975-78	106	3249		Austin Carr, Notre Dame	1969-71	2560	34.6
Lionel Simmons, La Salle	1987-90	131	3217		Oscar Robertson, Cincinnati	1958-60	2973	33.8
Harry Kelly, Tex-Southern	1980-83	110	3066		Calvin Murphy, Niagara	1968-70	2548	33.1
Hersey Hawkins, Bradley	1985-88	125	3008		Dwight Lamar, SW La	1972-73	1862	32.7
Oscar Robertson, Cincinnati	1958-60	88	2973		Frank Selvy, Furman	1952-54	2538	32.5
Danny Manning, Kansas	1985-88	147	2951		Rick Mount, Purdue	1968-70	2323	32.3
Alfredrick Hughes, Loyola-IL	1982-85	120	2914		Darrell Floyd, Furman	1954-56	2281	32.1
Elvin Hayes, Houston	1966-68	93	2884		Nick Werkman, Seton Hall	1962-64	2273	32.0
Larry Bird, Indiana St	1977-79	94	2850		Willie Humes, Idaho St	1970-71	1510	31.5

Field Goal Pct.	Years	FG	FGA	Pct	Free Throw Pct.	Years	FT	FTA	Pct
Stephen Scheffler, Purdue	1987-90	408	596	68.5	Greg Starrick, Ky/So.Ill.	1969-72	341	375	90.9
Steve Johnson, Ore.St	1978-81	828	1222	67.8	Jack Moore, Nebraska	1979-82	446	495	90.1
Murray Brown, Fla.St	1977-80	566	847	66.8	Steve Henson, Kansas St	1986-90	361	401	90.0
Lee Campbell, SW Mo.St	1987-90	411	618	66.5	Steve Alford, Indiana	1984-87	535	596	89.8
Joe Senser, W.Chester	1976-79	476	719	66.2	Bob Lloyd, Rutgers	1965-67	543	605	89.8

Note: Minimum 400 FGs scored.
Note: Minimum 250 FTs scored.

Rebounds

Total (before 1973)	Years	Gm	No		Total (since 1973)	Years	Gm	No
Tom Gola, La Salle	1952-55	118	2201		Derrick Coleman, Syracuse	1987-90	143	1537
Joe Holup, G.Washington	1953-56	104	2030		Ralph Sampson, Virginia	1980-83	132	1511
Charlie Slack, Marshall	1953-56	88	1916		Pete Padgett, NV-Reno	1973-76	104	1464
Ed Conlin, Fordham	1951-55	102	1884		Lionel Simmons, La Salle	1987-90	131	1429
Dickie Hemric, W.Forest	1952-55	104	1802		Anthony Bonner, St.Louis	1987-90	133	1424

Note: Minimum 650 rebounds.

2000 Points/1000 Rebounds

For a combined total of 4000 or more.

	Gm	Pts	Reb	Total		Gm	Pts	Reb	Total
Tom Gola, La Salle	118	2462	2201	4663	Harry Kelly, TX-Southern	110	3066	1085	4151
Lionel Simmons, La Salle	131	3217	1429	4646	Danny Manning, Kansas	147	2951	1187	4138
Elvin Hayes, Houston	93	2884	1602	4486	Larry Bird, Indiana St	94	2850	1247	4097
Dickie Hemric, W.Forest	104	2587	1802	4389	Elgin Baylor, Col. Idaho/Seattle	80	2500	1559	4059
Oscar Robertson, Cinn	88	2973	1338	4311	Michael Brooks, La Salle	114	2628	1372	4000
Joe Holup, Geo.Wash	104	2226	2030	4256					

Years Played—Baylor (1956-58); **Bird** (1977-79); **Brooks** (1977-80); **Gola** (1952-55); **Hayes** (1966-68); **Hemric** (1952-55); **Holup** (1953-56); **Kelly** (1980-83); **Manning** (1985-88); **Robertson** (1958-60); **Simmons** (1987-90).

Assists

Total	Years	Gm	No		Average	Years	No	Avg
Chris Corchiani, N.C.State	1988-91	124	1038		Avery Johnson, Cameron/South.-BR.	1986-88	838	8.91
Keith Jennings, E.Tennessee St	1988-91	127	983		Mark Wade, Okla/UNLV	1985-87	693	8.77
Sherman Douglas, Syracuse	1986-89	138	960		Chris Corchiani, N.C.State	1988-91	1038	8.37
Gary Payton, Oregon St.	1987-90	120	938		Taurence Chisholm, Delaware	1985-88	877	7.97
Andre LaFleur, N'eastern	1984-87	128	894		Van Usher, Tenn. Tech.	1990-92	676	7.95

Note: Minimum 550 assists.

SINGLE SEASON
Scoring

Points	Year	Gm	Pts		Average	Year	Pts	Avg
Pete Maravich, LSU	1970	31	1381		Pete Maravich, LSU	1970	1381	44.5
Elvin Hayes, Houston	1968	33	1214		Pete Maravich, LSU	1969	1148	44.2
Frank Selvy, Furman	1954	29	1209		Pete Maravich, LSU	1968	1138	43.8
Pete Maravich, LSU	1969	26	1148		Frank Selvy, Furman	1954	1209	41.7
Pete Maravich, LSU	1968	26	1138		Johnny Neumann, Ole Miss	1971	923	40.1
Bo Kimble, Loyola-CA	1990	32	1131		Freeman Williams, Port.St	1977	1010	38.8
Hersey Hawkins, Bradley	1988	31	1125		Billy McGill, Utah	1962	1009	38.8
Austin Carr, Notre Dame	1970	29	1106		Calvin Murphy, Niagara	1968	916	38.2
Austin Carr, Notre Dame	1971	29	1101		Austin Carr, Notre Dame	1970	1106	38.1
Otis Birdsong, Houston	1977	36	1090		Austin Carr, Notre Dame	1971	1101	38.0

All-Time NCAA Division I Individual Leaders (Cont.)

Scoring

Field Goal Pct.

	Year	FG	FGA	Pct
Steve Johnson, Oregon St.	1981	235	315	.746
Dwayne Davis, Florida	1989	179	248	.722
Keith Walker, Utica	1985	154	216	.713
Steve Johnson, Oregon St.	1980	211	297	.710
Oliver Miller, Arkansas	1991	254	361	.704

Free Throw Pct.

	Year	FG	FGA	Pct
Craig Collins, Penn St	1985	94	98	.959
Rod Foster, UCLA	1982	95	100	.950
Carlos Gibson, Marshall	1978	84	89	.944
Jim Barton, Dartmouth	1986	65	69	.942
Jack Moore, Nebraska	1982	123	131	.939

3-Pt Field Goal Pct.

	Year	FG	FGA	Pct
Glenn Tropf, Holy Cross	1988	52	82	.634
Sean Wightman, Western Mich.	1992	48	76	.632
Keith Jennings, E.Tennessee St.	1991	84	142	.592
Dave Calloway, Monmouth	1989	48	82	.585
Steve Kerr, Arizona	1988	114	199	.573

3-Pt FGs Per Game

	Year	Gm	No	Avg
Darrin Fitzgerald, Butler	1987	28	158	5.64
Tim Pollard, Miss.Valley St.	1988	28	132	4.71
Dave Jamerson, Ohio U	1990	28	131	4.68
Sydney Grider, SW La	1990	29	131	4.52
Tim Pollard, Miss.Valley St.	1989	28	124	4.43

Assists

Average

	Year	Gm	No	Avg
Avery Johnson, Southern-BR	1988	30	399	13.3
Anthony Manuel, Bradley	1988	31	373	12.0
Avery Johnson, Southern-BR	1987	31	333	10.7
Mark Wade, UNLV	1987	38	406	10.7
Glenn Williams, Holy Cross	1989	28	278	9.9

Rebounds

Average (before 1973)

	Year	No	Avg
Charlie Slack, Marshall	1955	538	25.6
Leroy Wright, Pacific	1959	652	25.1
Art Quimby, Connecticut	1955	611	24.4
Charlie Slack, Marshall	1956	520	23.6
Ed Conlin, Fordham	1953	612	23.5

Average (since 1973)

	Year	No	Avg
Kermit Washington, American	1973	439	20.0
Marvin Barnes, Providence	1973	571	19.0
Marvin Barnes, Providence	1974	597	18.7
Pete Padgett, NV-Reno	1973	462	17.8
Jim Bradley, Northern.Ill	1973	426	17.8

Blocked Shots

Average

	Year	Gm	No	Avg
David Robinson, Navy	1986	35	207	5.91
Shaquille O'Neal, LSU	1992	30	157	5.23
Shawn Bradley, BYU	1991	34	177	5.21
Cedric Lewis, Maryland	1991	28	143	5.11
Shaquille O'Neal, LSU	1991	28	140	5.00
Alonzo Mourning, G'town	1992	32	160	5.00

Steals

Average

	Year	Gm	No	Avg
Darron Bittman, Chicago St.	1986	28	139	4.96
Aldwin Ware, Fla.A&M	1988	29	142	4.90
Ronn McMahon, E.Wash	1990	29	130	4.48
Jim Paguaga, St.Fran-NY	1986	28	120	4.29
Marty Johnson, Towson St	1988	30	124	4.13

SINGLE GAME

Scoring

Points vs Div.I Team

	Year	Pts
Kevin Bradshaw, US Int'l vs Loyola-CA	1991	72
Pete Maravich, LSU vs Alabama	1970	69
Calvin Murphy, Niagara vs Syracuse	1969	68
Jay Handlan, Wash.& Lee vs Furman	1951	66
Pete Maravich, LSU vs Tulane	1969	66
Anthony Roberts, O.Roberts vs N.C.A&T	1977	66
Scott Haffner, Evansville vs Dayton	1989	65
Anthony Roberts, O.Roberts vs Oregon	1977	65
Pete Maravich, LSU vs Kentucky	1970	64
Hersey Hawkins, Bradley vs Detroit	1988	63
Johnny Neumann, Ole Miss vs LSU	1971	63

Points vs Non-Div.I Team

	Year	Pts
Frank Selvy, Furman vs Newberry	1954	100
Paul Arizin, Villanova vs Phi.NAMC	1949	85
Freeman Williams, Portland St.vs Rocky Mt	1978	81
Bill Mlkvy, Temple vs Wilkes	1951	73
Freeman Williams, Portland St.vs So.Ore	1977	71

3-Pt Field Goals

	Year	No
Dave Jamerson, Ohio U. vs Charleston	1989	14

Eight tied with 11 each.

Assists

	Year	No
Tony Fairley, Charleston So. vs Armstrong St.	1987	22
Avery Johnson, Southern-BR vs Texas So	1988	22
Sherman Douglas, Syracuse vs Providence	1989	22

Four tied with 21 each.

Rebounds

Total (before 1973)

	Year	No
Bill Chambers, Wm.& Mary vs Virginia	1953	51
Charlie Slack, Marshall vs M.Harvey	1954	43
Tom Heinsohn, Holy Cross vs BC	1955	42
Art Quimby, UConn vs BU	1955	40
Maurice Stokes, St.Fran-PA vs J.Carroll	1955	39
Dave DeBusschere, Detroit vs Central Mich.	1960	39
Keith Swagerty, Pacific vs UCSB	1965	39

Total (since 1973)

	Year	No
David Vaughn, O.Roberts vs Brandeis	1973	34
Robert Parish, Centenary vs So.Miss	1973	33
Jim Bradley, No.Ill vs WI-Milwaukee	1973	31
Calvin Natt, NE La. vs Ga.Southern	1976	31
Eddie Woods, O.Roberts vs Lamar	1972	30
Eddie Woods, O.Roberts vs La.Tech	1972	30
Brad Robinson, Kent St.vs Central Mich.	1974	30

Blocked Shots

	Year	No
David Robinson, Navy vs NC-Wilmington	1986	14
Shawn Bradley, BYU vs Eastern Ky.	1990	14
Kevin Roberson, Vermont vs N.Hampshire	1992	13

Eight tied with 11 each.

Steals

	Year	No
Mookie Blaylock, Oklahoma vs Centenary	1987	13
Mookie Blaylock, Oklahoma vs Loyola-CA	1988	13
Kenny Robertson, Cleve.St. vs Wagner	1988	12

Six tied with 11 each.

Annual Awards

UPI picked the first national Division I Player of the Year in 1955. Since then, The U.S.Basketball Writers Assn.(1959), the Commonwealth Athletic Club of Kentucky's Adolph Rupp Trophy (1961), the Atlanta Tip-Off Club (1969), the National Assn. of Basketball Coaches (1975), and the LA Athletic Club's John Wooden Award (1977) have joined in.

Since 1977, the first year all six awards were given out, the same player has won all of them in the same season seven times: Marques Johnson in 1977, Larry Bird in 1979, Ralph Sampson in both 1982 and '83, Michael Jordan in 1984, David Robinson in 1987 and Lionel Simmons in 1990.

United Press International

Voted on by a panel of UPI college basketball writers and first presented in 1955.
Multiple winners: Oscar Robertson, Ralph Sampson and Bill Walton (3); Lew Alcindor and Jerry Lucas (2).

Year		Year		Year	
1955	Tom Gola, La Salle	1968	Elvin Hayes, Houston	1980	Mark Aguirre, DePaul
1956	Bill Russell, San Francisco	1969	Lew Alcindor, UCLA	1981	Ralph Sampson, Virginia
1957	Chet Forte, Columbia			1982	Ralph Sampson, Virginia
1958	Oscar Robertson, Cincinnati	1970	Pete Maravich, LSU	1983	Ralph Sampson, Virginia
1959	Oscar Robertson, Cincinnati	1971	Austin Carr, Notre Dame	1984	Michael Jordan, North Carolina
		1972	Bill Walton, UCLA	1985	Chris Mullin, St.John's
1960	Oscar Robertson, Cincinnati	1973	Bill Walton, UCLA	1986	Walter Berry St.John's
1961	Jerry Lucas, Ohio St.	1974	Bill Walton, UCLA	1987	David Robinson, Navy
1962	Jerry Lucas, Ohio St.	1975	David Thompson, N.C.State	1988	Hersey Hawkins, Bradley
1963	Art Heyman, Duke	1976	Scott May, Indiana	1989	Danny Ferry, Duke
1964	Gary Bradds, Ohio St.	1977	Marques Johnson, UCLA		
1965	Bill Bradley, Princeton	1978	Butch Lee, Marquette	1990	Lionel Simmons, La Salle
1966	Cazzie Russell, Michigan	1979	Larry Bird, Indiana St.	1991	Shaquille O'Neal, LSU
1967	Lew Alcindor, UCLA			1992	Jim Jackson, Ohio St.

U.S. Basketball Writers Association

Voted on by the USBWA and first presented in 1959.
Multiple winners: Ralph Sampson and Bill Walton (3); Lew Alcindor, Jerry Lucas, Oscar Robertson (2).

Year		Year		Year	
1959	Oscar Robertson, Cincinnati	1972	Bill Walton, UCLA	1985	Chris Mullin, St.John's
		1973	Bill Walton, UCLA	1986	Walter Berry St.John's
1960	Oscar Robertson, Cincinnati	1974	Bill Walton, UCLA	1987	David Robinson, Navy
1961	Jerry Lucas, Ohio St.	1975	David Thompson, N.C.State	1988	Hersey Hawkins, Bradley
1962	Jerry Lucas, Ohio St.	1976	Adrian Dantley, Notre Dame	1989	Danny Ferry, Duke
1963	Art Heyman, Duke	1977	Marques Johnson, UCLA		
1964	Walt Hazzard, UCLA	1978	Phil Ford, North Carolina	1990	Lionel Simmons, La Salle
1965	Bill Bradley, Princeton	1979	Larry Bird, Indiana St.	1991	Larry Johnson, UNLV
1966	Cazzie Russell, Michigan			1992	Christian Laettner, Duke
1967	Lew Alcindor, UCLA	1980	Mark Aguirre, DePaul		
1968	Elvin Hayes, Houston	1981	Ralph Sampson, Virginia		
1969	Lew Alcindor, UCLA	1982	Ralph Sampson, Virginia		
		1983	Ralph Sampson, Virginia		
1970	Pete Maravich, LSU	1984	Michael Jordan, North Carolina		
1971	Sidney Wicks, UCLA				

Rupp Trophy

Voted on by AP sportswriters and broadcasters and first presented in 1961 by the Commonwealth Athletic Club of Kentucky in the name of former Univ.of Kentucky coach Adolph Rupp.
Multiple winners: Ralph Sampson (3); Lew Alcindor, Jerry Lucas, David Thompson and Bill Walton (2).

Year		Year		Year	
1961	Jerry Lucas, Ohio St.	1972	Bill Walton, UCLA	1983	Ralph Sampson, Virginia
1962	Jerry Lucas, Ohio St.	1973	Bill Walton, UCLA	1984	Michael Jordan, North Carolina
1963	Art Heyman, Duke	1974	David Thompson, N.C.State	1985	Patrick Ewing, Georgetown
1964	Gary Bradds, Ohio St.	1975	David Thompson, N.C.State	1986	Walter Berry, St.John's
1965	Bill Bradley, Princeton	1976	Scott May, Indiana	1987	David Robinson, Navy
1966	Cazzie Russell, Michigan	1977	Marques Johnson, UCLA	1988	Hersey Hawkins, Bradley
1967	Lew Alcindor, UCLA	1978	Butch Lee, Marquette	1989	Sean Elliott, Arizona
1968	Elvin Hayes, Houston	1979	Larry Bird, Indiana St.		
1969	Lew Alcindor, UCLA			1990	Lionel Simmons, La Salle
		1980	Mark Aguirre, DePaul	1991	Shaquille O'Neal, LSU
1970	Pete Maravich, LSU	1981	Ralph Sampson, Virginia	1992	Christian Laettner, Duke
1971	Austin Carr, Notre Dame	1982	Ralph Sampson, Virginia		

Annual Awards (Cont.)
Naismith Award

Voted on by a panel of coaches, sportswriters and broadcasters and first presented in 1969 by the Atlanta Tip-Off Club in 1969 in the name of the inventor of basketball, Dr. James Naismith.

Multiple winners: Ralph Sampson and Bill Walton (3).

Year		Year		Year	
1969	Lew Alcindor, UCLA	1977	Marques Johnson, UCLA	1985	Patrick Ewing, Georgetown
		1978	Butch Lee, Marquette	1986	Johnny Dawkins, Duke
1970	Pete Maravich, LSU	1979	Larry Bird, Indiana St.	1987	David Robinson, Navy
1971	Austin Carr, Notre Dame			1988	Danny Manning, Kansas
1972	Bill Walton, UCLA	1980	Mark Aguirre, DePaul	1989	Danny Ferry, Duke
1973	Bill Walton, UCLA	1981	Ralph Sampson, Virginia		
1974	Bill Walton, UCLA	1982	Ralph Sampson, Virginia	1990	Lionel Simmons, La Salle
1975	David Thompson, N.C.State	1983	Ralph Sampson, Virginia	1991	Larry Johnson, UNLV
1976	Scott May, Indiana	1984	Michael Jordan, North Carolina	1992	Christian Laettner, Duke

Eastman Award

Voted on by the National Assn. of Basketball Coaches and first presented by the Eastman Kodak Co. in 1975.

Multiple winner: Ralph Sampson (2).

Year		Year		Year	
1975	David Thompson, N.C.State	1981	Danny Ainge, BYU	1987	David Robinson, Navy
1976	Scott May, Indiana	1982	Ralph Sampson, Virginia	1988	Danny Manning, Kansas
1977	Marques Johnson, UCLA	1983	Ralph Sampson, Virginia	1989	Sean Elliott, Arizona
1978	Phil Ford, North Carolina	1984	Michael Jordan, North Carolina		
1979	Larry Bird, Indiana St.	1985	Patrick Ewing, Georgetown	1990	Lionel Simmons, La Salle
		1986	Walter Berry St.John's	1991	Larry Johnson, UNLV
1980	Michael Brooks, La Salle			1992	Christian Laettner, Duke

Wooden Award

Voted on by a panel of coaches, sportswriters and broadcasters and first presented in 1977 by the Los Angeles Athletic Club in the name of former Purdue All-America and UCLA coach John Wooden. Unlike the other five Player of the Year awards, candidates for the Wooden must have a minimum grade point average of 2.00 (out of 4.00).

Multiple winner: Ralph Sampson (2).

Year		Year		Year	
1977	Marques Johnson, UCLA	1982	Ralph Sampson, Virginia	1988	Danny Manning, Kansas
1978	Phil Ford, North Carolina	1983	Ralph Sampson, Virginia	1989	Sean Elliott, Arizona
1979	Larry Bird, Indiana St.	1984	Michael Jordan, North Carolina		
		1985	Chris Mullin, St.John's	1990	Lionel Simmons, La Salle
1980	Darrell Griffith, Louisville	1986	Walter Berry St.John's	1991	Larry Johnson, UNLV
1981	Danny Ainge, BYU	1987	David Robinson, Navy	1992	Christian Laettner, Duke

Iba Defensive Player Award

Officially, the Henry Iba Corinthian Award and given to the outstanding defensive player in the nation. Voted on by the National Association of Basketball Coaches and first presented in 1987 by the Rotary Club of River Oakes in Houston in the name of former Oklahoma State and US Olympic coach Hank Iba.

Multiple winner: Stacey Augmon (3).

Year		Year		Year	
1987	Tommy Amaker, Duke	1989	Stacey Augmon, UNLV	1991	Stacey Augmon, UNLV
1988	Billy King, Duke	1990	Stacey Augmon, UNLV	1992	Alonzo Mourning, Georgetown

---

Player of the Year and NBA MVP

College Players of the Year who have gone on to win Most Valuable Player award (the Maurice Podoloff Trophy) in the NBA.

Bill Russell: COLLEGE—San Francisco (1956); PROS—Boston Celtics (1988, 1961, 1962, 1963 and 1965).
Oscar Robertson: COLLEGE—Cincinnati (1958, 1959 and 1960); PROS—Cincinnati Royals (1964).
Kareem Abdul-Jabbar: COLLEGE—UCLA (1967 and 1968); PROS—Milwaukee Bucks (1971 and 1972) & LA Lakers (1974, 1976, 1977 and 1980).
Bill Walton: COLLEGE—UCLA (1972, 1873 and 1974); PROS—Portland Trail Blazers (1978).
Larry Bird: COLLEGE—Indiana St. (1979); PROS—Boston Celtics (1984, 1985, and 1986).
Michael Jordan: COLLEGE—North Carolina (1984); PROS—Chicago Bulls (1988, 1991 and 1992).

All-Time Winningest Division I Coaches

Minimum of 10 seasons as Division I head coach; regular season and tournament games included; coaches active during 1991-92 in **bold** type.

Top 30 Winning Percentage

		Yrs	Won	Lost	Pct
1	**Jerry Tarkanian**	24	625	122	**.837**
2	Clair Bee	21	412	87	**.826**
3	Adolph Rupp	41	875	190	**.822**
4	John Wooden	29	664	162	**.804**
5	**Dean Smith**	31	740	219	**.772**
6	Harry Fisher	13	147	44	**.770**
7	Frank Keaney	27	387	117	**.768**
8	George Keogan	24	385	117	**.767**
9	Jack Ramsay	11	231	71	**.765**
10	John Chaney	20	458	143	**.762**
11	Vic Bubas	10	213	67	**.761**
12	**Jim Boeheim**	16	391	124	**.759**
13	Chick Davies	21	314	106	**.748**
14	Ray Mears	21	399	135	**.747**
15	**Nolan Richardson**	12	286	100	**.741**
16	Al McGuire	20	405	143	**.739**
	Everett Case	18	376	133	**.739**
	Phog Allen	48	746	264	**.739**
19	John Thompson	20	464	165	**.738**
20	**Bob Knight**	27	588	210	**.737**
21	Walter Meanwell	22	280	101	**.735**
22	**Denny Crum**	21	496	183	**.730**
	Cam Henderson	35	583	216	**.730**
24	**Eddie Sutton**	22	482	180	**.728**
25	Lew Andreas	25	355	134	**.726**
26	**Lou Carnesecca**	24	526	200	**.725**
27	Fred Schaus	12	251	96	**.723**
28	Hugh Greer	17	290	112	**.721**
29	Joe Lapchick	20	335	130	**.720**
30	Dudey Moore	15	270	107	**.716**

Top 30 Victories

		Yrs	Won	Lost	Pct
1	Adolph Rupp	41	875	190	.822
2	Hank Iba	41	767	338	.694
3	Ed Diddle	42	759	302	.715
4	Phog Allen	48	746	264	.739
5	**Dean Smith**	31	740	219	.772
6	Ray Meyer	42	724	354	.672
7	John Wooden	29	664	162	.804
8	Ralph Miller	38	657	382	.632
9	Marv Harshman	40	642	448	.589
10	**Jerry Tarkanian**	24	625	122	.837
11	Norm Sloan	37	624	393	.614
12	**Don Haskins**	31	606	263	.697
13	**Lefty Driesell**	30	600	270	.690
14	Slats Gill	36	599	392	.604
15	Abe Lemons	34	597	344	.634
16	**Norm Stewart**	31	593	292	.670
17	Guy Lewis	30	592	279	.680
18	**Lou Henson**	30	590	282	.677
19	**Bob Knight**	27	588	210	.737
20	Cam Henderson	35	583	216	.730
21	**Gene Bartow**	30	574	301	.656
22	Tony Hinkle	41	560	392	.588
23	Frank McGuire	30	550	235	.701
24	**Glenn Wilkes**	35	538	422	.560
25	Harry Miller	34	534	374	.588
26	**Lou Carnesecca**	24	526	200	.725
27	Fred Enke	38	525	341	.606
28	Tom Young	31	524	328	.615
29	**Gary Colson**	31	516	344	.600
30	C.M.Newton	32	509	375	.576

Note: Clarence "Bighouse" Gaines of Division II Winston-Salem St.(1947—) is No.2 on the all-time NCAA list of all coaches regardless of division. His record is 822-429 for a .657 winning percentage over 46 seasons.

Where They Coached

Allen—Kansas & Baker (1908-09), & Haskell (1909), Central Mo.St.(1913-19), Kansas (1920-56); **Andreas**—Syracuse (1925-43; 45-50); **Bartow**—Central Mo.St.(1962-64), Valparaiso (1965-70), Memphis St.(1971-74), Illinois (1975), UCLA (1976-77), UAB (1979—); **Bee**—Rider (1929-31), LIU-Brooklyn (1932-45, 46-51); **Boeheim**—Syracuse (1977—); **Bubas**—Duke (1960-69); **Carnesecca**—St.John's (1966-70,74-92); **Case**—N.C.-State (1947-64); **Colson**—Valdosta St.(1959-68), Pepperdine (1969-79), New Mexico (1981-88), Fresno St.(1991—); **Crum**—Louisville (1972—); **Davies**—Duquesne (1925-43, 47-48); **Diddle**—Western Ky.(1923-64); **Driesell**—Davidson (1961-69), Maryland (1970-86), J.Madison (1989—); **Enke**—Louisville (1924-25), Arizona (1926-61); **Fisher**—Columbia (1907-16), Army (1922-23,25).

Gill—Oregon St.(1929-64); **Greer**—Connecticut (1947-63); **Harshman**—Pacific Lutheran (1946-58), Wash.St.(1959-71), Washington (1972-85); **Haskins**—UTEP (1962—); **Henderson**—Muskingum (1920-22), Davis & Elkins (1923-35), Marshall (1936-55); **Henson**—Hardin-Simmons (1963-66), N.Mexico St.(1967-75), Illinois (1976—); **Hinkle**—Butler (1927-42, 46-70); **Iba**—NW Missouri St.(1930-33), Colorado (1934), Oklahoma St.(1935-70); **Keaney**— Rhode Island (1921-48); **Knight**—Army (1966-71), Indiana (1972—); **Koegan**—St.Louis (1916), Allegheny (1919), Valparaiso (1920-21), Notre Dame (1924-43).

Lapchick—St.John's (1937-47,57-65); **Lemons**—Okla.City (1956-73), Pan American (1974-76), Texas (1977-82), Okla.City (1984-90); **Lewis**— Houston (1957-86); **A.McGuire**—Belmont Abbey (1958-64), Marquette (1965-77); **F.McGuire**—St.John's (1948-52), North Carolina (1953-61), South Carolina (1965-80); **Meanwell**—Wisconsin (1912-17,21-34), Missouri (1918-20); **Mears**—Wittenberg (1957-62), Tennessee (1963-77); **R.Meyer**—DePaul (1943-84); **H.Miller**—Western St.(1953-58), Fresno St.(1961-65), E.New Mexico (1966-70), North Texas (1971), Wichita St.(1972-78), S.F.Austin (1979-88); **R.Miller**—Wichita St.(1952-64), Iowa (1965-70), Oregon St.(1971-89) **Moore**—Duquesne (1949-58), La Salle (1959-63); **Newton**—Transylvania (1956-64,66-68), Alabama (1969-80), Vanderbilt (1982-89).

Ramsay—St.Joseph's-PA (1956-66); **Richardson**—Tulsa (1981-85), Arkansas (1986—); **Rupp**—Kentucky (1931-72); **Schaus**—West Va. (1955-60), Purdue (1973-78); **Sloan**—Presbyterian (1952-55), Citadel (1957-60), Florida (1961-66), N.C.State (1967-80), Florida (1981-89); **Smith**—North Carolina (1962—); **Stewart**—No.Iowa (1962-67), Missouri (1968—); **Sutton**—Creighton (1970-74), Arkansas (1975-85), Kentucky (1986-89); Oklahoma St.(1991—); **Tarkanian**—Long Beach St.(1969-73), UNLV (1974-92); **Thompson**—Georgetown (1973—); **Wilkes**—Stetson (1958—); **Wooden**— Indiana St.(1947-48), UCLA (1949-75); **Young**—Catholic (1959-67), American (1970-73), Rutgers (1974-85), Old Dominion (1986-91).

All-Time Winningest Division I Coaches (Cont.)

Most NCAA Tournaments

Through 1992; listed are number of appearances, overall tournament record, times reaching Final Four, and number of NCAA championships. Coaches with teams in 1992 tournament in bold type.

App		W-L	F4	Championships
22	**Dean Smith**	49-23	8	1 (1982)
20	Adolph Rupp	30-18	6	4 (1948-49, 51, 58)
18	**Lou Carnesecca**	17-20	1	None
16	John Wooden	47-10	12	10 (1964-65, 67-73, 75)
16	Jerry Tarkanian	37-16	4	1 (1990)
16	**Bob Knight**	35-13	5	3 (1976,81,87)
16	**Denny Crum**	33-16	6	2 (1980,86)
16	**John Thompson**	28-15	3	1 (1984)
15	**Eddie Sutton**	21-15	1	None
15	Lou Henson	18-16	2	None
15	Digger Phelps	17-17	1	None
14	Guy Lewis	26-18	5	None
14	**Jim Boeheim**	19-14	1	None
14	**Don Haskins**	14-13	1	1 (1966)
13	**Lute Olson**	16-14	2	None
13	Ray Meyer	14-16	2	None

Active Coaches' Victories

Minimum five seasons in Division I.

		Yrs	W	L	Pct
1	Dean Smith, N.Carolina	31	**740**	219	.772
2	Don Haskins, UTEP	31	**606**	263	.697
3	Lefty Driesell, J.Madison	30	**600**	270	.690
4	Norm Stewart, Missouri	31	**593**	292	.670
5	Lou Henson, Illinois	30	**590**	282	.677
6	Bob Knight, Indiana	27	**588**	210	.737
7	Gene Bartow, UAB	30	**574**	301	.656
8	Glenn Wilkes, Stetson	35	**538**	422	.560
9	Gary Colson, Fresno St	31	**516**	344	.600
10	Denny Crum, Louisville	21	**496**	183	.730
11	Eldon Miller, No.Iowa	30	**492**	329	.599
12	Eddie Sutton, Oklahoma St.	22	**482**	180	.728
13	Hugh Durham, Georgia	26	**480**	270	.640
14	John Thompson, Georgetown	20	**464**	165	.738
	B.van Breda Kolff, Hofstra	26	**464**	234	.665
16	Bill Foster, Northwestern	32	**459**	390	.541
17	John Chaney, Temple	20	**458**	143	.762
18	Pete Carril, Princeton	26	**454**	237	.657
19	Bill Foster, Va.Tech	25	**441**	265	.625
20	Johnny Orr, Iowa St.	27	**432**	322	.573

Annual Awards

UPI picked the first national Division I Coach of the Year in 1955. Since then, The U.S.Basketball Writers Assn. (1959), AP (1967), the National Assn. of Basketball Coaches (1969), and the Atlanta Tip-Off Club (1987) have joined in. Since 1987, the first year all five awards were given out, no coach has won all of them in the same season.

United Press International

Voted on by a panel of UPI college basketball writers and first presented in 1955.
Multiple winners: John Wooden (6); Bob Knight, Ray Meyer, Adolph Rupp, Fred Taylor and Phil Woopert (2).

Year		Year		Year	
1955	Phil Woolpert, San Francisco	1970	John Wooden, UCLA	1985	Lou Carnesecca, St.John's
1956	Phil Woolpert, San Francisco	1971	Al McGuire, Marquette	1986	Mike Krzyzewski, Duke
1957	Frank McGuire, North Carolina	1972	John Wooden, UCLA	1987	John Thompson, Georgetown
1958	Tex Winter, Kansas St.	1973	John Wooden, UCLA	1988	John Chaney, Temple
1959	Adolph Rupp, Kentucky	1974	Digger Phelps, Notre Dame	1989	Bob Knight, Indiana
1960	Pete Newell, California	1975	Bob Knight, Indiana	1990	Jim Calhoun, Connecticut
1961	Fred Taylor, Ohio St.	1976	Tom Young, Rutgers	1991	Rick Majerus, Utah
1962	Fred Taylor, Ohio St.	1977	Bob Gaillard, San Francisco	1992	Perry Clark, Tulane
1963	Ed Jucker, Cincinnati	1978	Eddie Sutton, Arkansas		
1964	John Wooden, UCLA	1979	Bill Hodges, Indiana St.		
1965	Dave Strack, Michigan	1980	Ray Meyer, DePaul		
1966	Adolph Rupp, Kentucky	1981	Ralph Miller, Oregon St.		
1967	John Wooden, UCLA	1982	Norm Stewart, Missouri		
1968	Guy Lewis, Houston	1983	Jerry Tarkanian, UNLV		
1969	John Wooden, UCLA	1984	Ray Meyer, DePaul		

U.S. Basketball Writers Association

Voted on by the USBWA and first presented in 1959.
Multiple winners: John Wooden (5); Bob Knight (3); Lou Carnesecca, John Chaney and Ray Meyer (2).

Year		Year		Year	
1959	Eddie Hickey, Marquette	1970	John Wooden, UCLA	1982	John Thompson, Georgetown
1960	Pete Newell, California	1971	Al McGuire, Marquette	1983	Lou Carnesecca, St. John's
1961	Fred Taylor, Ohio St.	1972	John Wooden, UCLA	1984	Gene Keady, Purdue
1962	Fred Taylor, Ohio St.	1973	John Wooden, UCLA	1985	Lou Carnesecca, St. John's
1963	Ed Jucker, Cincinnati	1974	Norm Sloan, N.C.State	1986	Dick Versace, Bradley
1964	John Wooden, UCLA	1975	Bob Knight, Indiana	1987	John Chaney, Temple
1965	Butch van Breda Kolff, Princeton	1976	Bob Knight, Indiana	1988	John Chaney, Temple
1966	Adolph Rupp, Kentucky	1977	Eddie Sutton, Arkansas	1989	Bob Knight, Indiana
1967	John Wooden, UCLA	1978	Ray Meyer, DePaul	1990	Roy Williams, Kansas
1968	Guy Lewis, Houston	1979	Dean Smith, North Carolina	1991	Randy Ayers, Ohio St.
1969	Maury John, Drake	1980	Ray Meyer, DePaul	1992	Perry Clark, Tulane
		1981	Ralph Miller, Oregon St.		

Associated Press

Voted on by AP sportswriters and broadcasters and first presented in 1967.
Multiple winners: John Wooden (5); Bob Knight (3); Guy Lewis, Ray Meyer, Ralph Miller and Eddie Sutton (2).

Year		Year		Year	
1967	John Wooden, UCLA	1976	Bob Knight, Indiana	1985	Bill Frieder, Michigan
1968	Guy Lewis, Houston	1977	Bob Gailliard, San Francisco	1986	Eddie Sutton, Kentucky
1969	John Wooden, UCLA	1978	Eddie Sutton, Arkansas	1987	Tom Davis, Iowa
		1979	Bill Hodges, Indiana St.	1988	John Chaney, Temple
1970	John Wooden, UCLA			1989	Bob Knight, Indiana
1971	Al McGuire, Marquette	1980	Ray Meyer, DePaul		
1972	John Wooden, UCLA	1981	Ralph Miller, Oregon St.	1990	Jim Calhoun, Connecticut
1973	John Wooden, UCLA	1982	Ralph Miller, Oregon St.	1991	Randy Ayers, Ohio St.
1974	Norm Sloan, N.C.State	1983	Guy Lewis, Houston	1992	Roy Williams, Kansas
1975	Bob Knight, Indiana	1984	Ray Meyer, DePaul		

National Association of Basketball Coaches

Voted on by NABC membership and first presented in 1969.
Multiple winner: John Wooden (3).

Year		Year		Year	
1969	John Wooden, UCLA	1978	Bill Foster, Duke	1985	John Thompson, Georgetown
			& Abe Lemons, Texas	1986	Eddie Sutton, Kentucky
1970	John Wooden, UCLA	1979	Ray Meyer, DePaul	1987	Rick Pitino, Providence
1971	Jack Kraft, Villanova			1988	John Chaney, Temple
1972	John Wooden, UCLA	1980	Lute Olson, Iowa	1989	P.J.Carlesimo, Seton Hall
1973	Gene Bartow, Memphis St.	1981	Ralph Miller, Oregon St.		
1974	Al McGuire, Marquette		& Jack Hartman, Kansas St.	1990	Jud Heathcote, Michigan St.
1975	Bob Knight, Indiana	1982	Don Monson, Idaho	1991	Mike Krzyzewski, Duke
1976	Johnny Orr, Michigan	1983	Lou Carnesecca, St.John's	1992	George Raveling, USC
1977	Dean Smith, North Carolina	1984	Marv Harshman, Washington		

Naismith Award

Voted on by a panel of coaches, sportswriters and broadcasters and first presented by the Atlanta Tip-Off Club in 1987 in the name of the inventor of basketball, Dr.James Naismith.
Multiple winner: Mike Krzyzewski (2).

Year		Year		Year	
1987	Bob Knight, Indiana	1989	Mike Krzyzewski, Duke	1991	Randy Ayers, Ohio St.
1988	Larry Brown, Kansas	1990	Bobby Cremins, Georgia Tech.	1992	Mike Krzyzewski, Duke

---

Other Men's Champions
NCAA Div. II Finals

Year	Winner	Score	Loser	Year	Winner	Score	Loser
1957	Wheaton,IL	89-65	Ky.Wesleyan	1975	Old Dominion,VA	76-74	New Orleans,LA
1958	South Dakota	75-53	St.Michaels,VT	1976	Puget Sound, WA	83-74	Tennessee-Chatt.
1959	Evansville,IN	83-67	SW Missouri St.	1977	Tennessee-Chatt.	71-62	Randolph-Macon
1960	Evansville,IN	90-69	Chapman,CA	1978	Cheyney,PA	47-40	WI-Green Bay
1961	Wittenberg,OH	42-38	SE Missouri St.	1979	North Alabama	64-50	WI-Green Bay
1962	Mt.St.Mary's, MD	58-57*	CS-Sacramento	1980	Virginia Union	80-74	New York Tech
1963	South Dakota St.	42-40	Wittenberg,OH	1981	Florida Southern	73-68	Mt.St.Mary's,MD
1964	Evansville,IN	72-59	Akron,OH	1982	Dist.of Columbia	73-63	Florida Southern
1965	Evansville,IN	85-82*	Southern Illinois	1983	Wright St.,OH	92-73	Dist.of Columbia
1966	Ky.Wesleyan	54-51	Southern Illinois	1984	Central Mo.St.	81-77	St.Augustine's,NC
1967	Winston-Salem,NC	77-74	SW Missouri St.	1985	Jacksonville St.	74-73	South Dakota St.
1968	Ky.Wesleyan	63-52	Indiana St.	1986	Sacred Heart,CT	93-87	SE Missouri St.
1969	Ky.Wesleyan	75-71	SW Missouri St.	1987	Ky.Wesleyan	92-74	Gannon,PA
1970	Phila.Textile	76-65	Tennessee St.	1988	Lowell,MA	75-72	AK-Anchorage
1971	Evansville,IN	97-82	Old Dominion,VA	1989	N.C.Central	73-46	SE Missouri St.
1972	Roanoke,VA	84-72	Akron,OH	1990	Ky.Wesleyan	93-79	CS-Bakersfield
1973	Ky.Wesleyan	78-76*	Tennessee St.	1991	North Alabama	79-72	Bridgeport, CT
1974	Morgan St.,MD	67-52	SW Missouri St.	1992	Virginia Union	100-75	Bridgeport, CT

*Overtime

Other Men's Champions (Cont.)
NCAA Div. III Finals

Year	Winner	Score	Loser	Year	Winner	Score	Loser
1975	LeMoyne-Owen,TN	57-54	Glassboro St.,NJ	1984	WI-Whitewater	103-86	Clark,MA
1976	Scranton,PA	60-57	Wittenberg,OH	1985	North Park,IL	72-71	Potsdam St.,NY
1977	Wittenberg,OH	79-66	Oneonta St.,NY	1986	Potsdam St.,NY	76-73	LeMoyne-Owen,TN
1978	North Park,IL	69-57	Widener,PA	1987	North Park,IL	106-100	Clark,MA
1979	North Park,IL	66-62	Potsdam St.,NY	1988	Ohio Wesleyan	92-70	Scranton,PA
				1989	WI-Whitewater	94-86	Trenton St.,NJ
1980	North Park,IL	83-76	Upsala,NJ				
1981	Potsdam St.,NY	67-65*	Augustana,IL	1990	Rochester, NY	43-42	DePauw, IN
1982	Wabash,IN	83-62	Potsdam St.,NY	1991	WI-Platteville	81-74	Franklin Marshall
1983	Scranton,PA	64-63	Wittenberg,OH	1992	Calvin, MI	62-49	Rochester, NY

*Overtime

NAIA Finals, 1937-91

Year	Winner	Score	Loser	Year	Winner	Score	Loser
1937	Central Missouri	35-24	Morningside,IA	1965	Central St.,OH	85-51	Oklahoma Baptist
1938	Central Missouri	45-30	Roanoke,VA	1966	Oklahoma Baptist	88-59	Georgia Southern
1939	Southwestern,KS	32-31	San Diego St.	1967	St.Benedict's,KS	71-65	Oklahoma Baptist
1940	Tarkio,MO	52-31	San Diego St.	1968	Central St.,OH	51-48	Fairmont St.,WV
1941	San Diego St.	36-32	Murray St.,KY	1969	Eastern New Mexico	99-76	MD-Eastern Shore
1942	Hamline,MN	33-31	S'eastern Okla.	1970	Kentucky St.	79-71	Central Wash.
1943	SE Missouri St.	34-32	NW Missouri St.	1971	Kentucky St.	102-82	Eastern Michigan
1944	Not held			1972	Kentucky St.	71-62	WI-Eau Claire
1945	Loyola-LA	49-36	Pepperdine,CA	1973	Guilford,NC	99-96	MD-Eastern Shore
1946	Southern Illinois	49-40	Indiana St.	1974	West Georgia	97-79	Alcorn St.,MS
1947	Marshall,WV	73-59	Mankato St.,MN	1975	Grand Canyon,AZ	65-54	M'western St.,TX
1948	Louisville,KY	82-70	Indiana St.	1976	Coppin St.,MD	96-91	Henderson St.,AR
1949	Hamline,MN	57-46	Regis,CO	1977	Texas Southern	71-44	Campbell,NC
1950	Indiana St.	61-47	East Central,OK	1978	Grand Canyon,AZ	79-75	Kearney St.,NE
1951	Hamline,MN	69-61	Millikin,IL	1979	Drury,MO	60-54	Henderson St.,AR
1952	SW Missouri St.	73-64	Murray St.,KY	1980	Cameron,OK	84-77	Alabama St.
1953	SW Missouri St.	79-71	Hamline,MN	1981	Beth.Nazarene,OK	86-85*	AL-Huntsville
1954	St.Benedict's,KS	62-56	Western Illinois	1982	SC-Spartanburg	51-38	Biola,CA
1955	East Texas St.	71-54	S'eastern Okla.	1983	Charleston,SC	57-53	WV-Wesleyan
1956	McNeese St.,LA	60-55	Texas Southern	1984	Fort Hays St.,KS	48-46*	WI-Stevens Pt.
1957	Tennessee St.	92-73	S'eastern Okla.	1985	Fort Hays St.,KS	82-80*	Wayland Bapt.,TX
1958	Tennessee St.	85-73	Western Illinois	1986	David Lipscomb,TN	67-54	AR-Monticello
1959	Tennessee St.	97-87	Pacific-Luth., WA	1987	Washburn,KS	79-77	West Virginia St.
1960	SW Texas St.	66-44	Westminster,PA	1988	Grand Canyon,AZ	88-86*	Auburn-Montg,AL
1961	Grambling,LA	95-75	Georgetown,KY	1989	St.Mary's,TX	61-58	East Central,OK
1962	Prairie View,TX	62-53	Westminster,PA	1990	Birm-Southern,AL	88-80	WI-Eau Claire
1963	Pan American,TX	73-62	Western Carolina	1991	Oklahoma City	77-74	Central Arkansas
1964	Rockhurst,MO	66-56	Pan American,TX				

*Overtime

NAIA Div. I Finals
NAIA split tournament into two divisions in 1992.

Year	Winner	Score	Loser
1992	Oklahoma City	82-73*	Central Arkansas

*Overtime

NAIA Div.II Finals
NAIA split tournament into two divisions in 1992.

Year	Winner	Score	Loser
1992	Grace,IN	85-79*	Northwestern-IA

NCAA WOMEN'S FINAL FOUR

Replaced the Association of Intercollegiate Athletics for Women (AIAW) tournament in 1982 as the official playoff for the national championship; (*) indicates overtime.

Multiple winners: Tennessee (3); Louisiana Tech, Stanford and USC (2)

Year	Champion	Head Coach	Score	Runner-up	Third Place	
1982	Louisiana Tech	Sonya Hogg	76-62	Cheyney	Maryland	Tennessee
1983	USC	Linda Sharp	69-67	Louisiana Tech	Georgia	Old Dominion
1984	USC	Linda Sharp	72-61	Tennessee	Cheyney	Louisiana Tech
1985	Old Dominion	Marianne Stanley	70-65	Georgia	NE Louisiana	Western Ky.
1986	Texas	Jody Conradt	97-81	USC	Tennessee	Western Ky.
1987	Tennessee	Pat Summitt	67-44	Louisiana Tech	Long Beach St.	Texas
1988	Louisiana Tech	Leon Barmore	56-54	Auburn	Long Beach St.	Tennessee
1989	Tennessee	Pat Summitt	76-60	Auburn	Louisiana Tech	Maryland
1990	Stanford	Tara VanDerveer	88-81	Auburn	Louisiana Tech	Virginia
1991	Tennessee	Pat Summitt	70-67*	Virginia	Connecticut	Stanford
1992	Stanford	Tara Van Derveer	78-62	Western Kentucky	SW Missouri St.	Virginia

Most Outstanding Player

A Most Outstanding Player has been selected every year of the NCAA tournament. Winners who did not play for the tournament champion are listed in **bold** type.
   Multiple winner: Cheryl Miller (2).

Year	Year	Year
1982 Janice Lawrence, La.Tech	1986 Clarissa Davis, Texas	1990 Jennifer Azzi, Stanford
1983 Cheryl Miller, USC	1987 Tonya Edwards, Tennessee	1991 **Dawn Staley**, Virginia
1984 Cheryl Miller, USC	1988 Erica Westbrooks, La.Tech	1992 Molly Goodenbour, Stanford
1985 Tracy Claxton, Old Dominion	1989 Bridgette Gordon, Tennessee	

All-Time Winningest Division I Women's Teams

Top 10 Winning Percentage

		Yrs	W	L	T	Pct
1	Louisiana Tech	18	498	92	0	.844
2	Texas	18	519	100	0	.838
3	Tennessee	18	470	121	0	.795
4	Long Beach St	30	555	154	0	.783
5	Stephen F. Austin St.	20	473	155	0	.753
6	UNLV	18	380	128	0	.748
7	Mississippi	18	419	144	0	.744
8	Rutgers	18	384	134	0	.741
9	Montana	18	368	130	0	.739
10	N.C.State	18	394	140	0	.738

Top 10 Victories

		Yrs	W	L	T	Pct
1	Long Beach St	30	555	154	0	.783
2	James Madison	70	522	280	5	.650
3	Texas	18	519	100	0	.838
4	Louisiana Tech	18	498	92	0	.844
5	Tennessee Tech	22	497	185	0	.729
6	Stephen F. Austin St.	20	473	155	0	.753
7	Tennessee	18	470	121	0	.795
8	Old Dominion	23	456	185	0	.711
9	Kansas St	24	452	243	0	.650
10	Ohio St.	27	451	176	0	.719

All-Time Leading Scorers

CAREER

	Years	Pts	Avg
Patricia Hoskins, Miss.Valley St.	1985-89	3122	28.4
Sandra Hodge, New Orleans	1981-84	2860	26.7
Lorri Bauman, Drake	1981-84	3115	26.0
Valorie Whiteside, Appalach.St	1984-88	2944	25.4
Joyce Walker, LSU	1981-84	2906	24.8
Tarcha Hollis, Grambling	1988-91	2058	24.2
Karen Pelphrey, Marshall	1983-86	2746	24.1
Erma Jones, Bethune-Cookman	1982-84	2095	24.1
Cheryl Miller, USC	1983-86	3018	23.6
Chris Starr, Nevada-Reno	1983-86	2356	23.3

SINGLE SEASON

	Year	Gm	Pts	Avg
Patricia Hoskins, Miss.Valley St.	1989	27	908	33.6
Adrea Congreaves, Mercer	1992	28	925	33.0
Deborah Temple, Delta St	1984	28	873	31.2
Wanda Ford, Drake	1986	30	919	30.6
Anucha Browne, Northwestern	1985	28	855	30.5
LeChandra LeDay, Grambling	1988	28	850	30.4
Kim Perrot, SW Louisiana	1990	28	839	30.0
Tina Hutchinson, San Diego St	1984	30	898	29.9
Jan Jensen, Drake	1991	30	888	29.6
Genia Miller, CS-Fullerton	1991	33	969	29.4

Annual Awards

The Broderick Award was first given out to the Women's Division I or Large School Player of the Year in 1977. Since then, the National Assn. for Girls and Women in Sports (1978), the Women's Basketball Coaches Assn. (1983) and the Atlanta Tip-Off Club (1983) have joined in.

   Since 1983, the first year all four awards were given out, the same player has won all of them in the same season once: Cheryl Miller of USC in 1985.

Broderick Award

Voted on by a national panel of women's collegiate athletic directors and first presented by the late Thomas Broderick, an athletic outfitter, in 1976. Honda has presented the award since 1987. Basketball Player of the Year is one of 10 nominated for Collegiate Woman Athlete of the Year; (*) indicates player also won Athlete of the Year.
   Multiple winners: Nancy Lieberman and Cheryl Miller (2).

Year	Year	Year
1977 Lucy Harris, Delta St.*	1983 Anne Donovan, Old Dominion	1988 Teresa Weatherspoon, La.Tech*
1978 Anne Meyers, UCLA*	1984 Cheryl Miller, USC*	1989 Bridgette Gordon, Tennessee
1979 Nancy Lieberman, Old Dominion*	1985 Cheryl Miller, USC	1990 Jennifer Azzi, Stanford
1980 Nancy Lieberman, Old Dominion*	1986 Kamie Ethridge, Texas*	1991 Dawn Staley, Virginia
1981 Lynette Woodward, Kansas	1987 Katrina McClain, Georgia	1992 TBA in fall
1982 Pam Kelly, La.Tech.		

Wade Trophy

Voted on by the National Assn. for Girls and Women in Sports (NAGWS) and awarded for academics and community service as well as player performance. First presented in 1978 in the name of former Delta St. coach Margaret Wade.
   Multiple winner: Nancy Lieberman (2).

Year	Year	Year
1978 Carol Blazejowski, Montclair St.	1983 LaTaunya Pollard, L.Beach St.	1988 Teresa Weatherspoon, La.Tech.
1979 Nancy Lieberman, Old Dominion	1984 Janice Lawrence, La.Tech.	1989 Clarissa Davis, Texas
1980 Nancy Lieberman, Old Dominion	1985 Cheryl Miller, USC	1990 Jennifer Azzi, Stanford
1981 Lynette Woodward, Kansas	1986 Kamie Ethridge, Texas	1991 Daedra Charles, Tennessee
1982 Pam Kelly, La.Tech.	1987 Shelly Pennefather, Villanova	1992 Susan Robinson, Penn St.

Naismith Trophy

Voted on by a panel of coaches, sportwriters and broadcasters and first presented in 1983 by the Atlanta Tip-Off Club in the name of the inventor of basketball, Dr. James Naismith.

Multiple winners: Cheryl Miller (3); Clarissa Davis and Dawn Staley (2).

Year		Year		Year	
1983	Anne Donovan, Old Dominion	1987	Clarissa Davis, Texas	1990	Jennifer Azzi, Stanford
1984	Cheryl Miller, USC	1988	Sue Wicks, Rutgers	1991	Dawn Staley, Virginia
1985	Cheryl Miller, USC	1989	Clarissa Davis, Texas	1992	Dawn Staley, Virginia
1986	Cheryl Miller, USC				

Women's Basketball Coaches Association

Voted on by the WBCA and first presented by Champion athletic outfitters in 1983.

Multiple winners: Cheryl Miller and Dawn Staley (2).

Year		Year		Year	
1983	Anne Donovan, Old Dominion	1987	Katrina McClain, Georgia	1990	Venus Lacey, La.Tech
1984	Janice Lawrence, La.Tech.	1988	Michelle Edwards, Iowa	1991	Dawn Staley, Virgina
1985	Cheryl Miller, USC	1989	Clarissa Davis, Texas	1992	Dawn Staley, Virginia
1986	Cheryl Miller, USC				

Coach of the Year Award

Voted on by the Women's Basketball Coaches Assn. and first presented by Converse athletic outfitters in 1983.

Multiple winner: Jody Conradt (2).

Year		Year		Year	
1983	Pat Summitt, Tennessee	1987	Theresa Grentz, Rutgers	1990	Kay Yow, N.C.State
1984	Jody Conradt, Texas	1988	Vivian Stringer, Iowa	1991	Rene Portland, Penn St.
1985	Jim Foster, St. Joseph's-PA	1989	Tara VanDerveer, Stanford	1992	Ferne Labati, Miami-Fl
1986	Jody Conradt, Texas				

Other Women's Champions

AIAW Finals

The Association of Intercollegiate Athletics for Women Large College tournament determined the women's national champion for 10 years until supplanted by the NCAA. In 1982, most Division I teams entered the first NCAA tournament rather than the last one staged by the AIAW.

Year	Winner	Score	Loser
1972	Immaculata,PA	52-48	West Chester,PA
1973	Immaculata,PA	59-52	Queens College,NY
1974	Immaculata,PA	68-53	Mississippi College
1975	Delta St.,MS	90-81	Immaculata,PA
1976	Delta St.,MS	69-64	Immaculata,PA
1977	Delta St.,MS	68-55	LSU
1978	UCLA	90-74	Maryland
1979	Old Dominion	75-65	Louisiana Tech
1980	Old Dominion	68-53	Tennessee
1981	Louisiana Tech	79-59	Tennessee
1982	Rutgers	83-77	Texas

NCAA Div. III Finals

Year	Winner	Score	Loser
1982	Elizabethtown,PA	67-66*	NC-Greensboro
1983	North Central,IL	83-71	Elizabethtown,PA
1984	Rust College,MS	51-49	Elizabethtown,PA
1985	Scranton,PA	68-59	New Rochelle,NY
1986	Salem St.,MA	89-85	Bishop,TX
1987	WI-Stevens Pt.	81-74	Concordia,MN
1988	Concordia,MN	65-57	St.John Fisher,NY
1989	Elizabethtown,PA	66-65	CS-Stanislaus
1990	Hope, MI	65-63	St. John Fisher
1991	St. Thomas, MN	73-55	Muskingum, OH
1992	Alma, MI	79-75	Moravian, PA

*Overtime

Note: Concordia,MN is Concordia College in Moorhead,MN, not Concordia College in St.Paul,MN.

NCAA Div. II Finals

Year	Winner	Score	Loser
1982	Cal Poly Pomona	93-74	Tuskegee,AL
1983	Virginia Union	73-60	Cal Poly Pomona
1984	Central Mo.St.	80-73	Virginia Union
1985	Cal Poly Pomona	80-69	Central Mo.St.
1986	Cal Poly Pomona	70-63	North Dakota St.
1987	New Haven,CT	77-75	Cal Poly Pomona
1988	Hampton,VA	65-48	West Texas St.
1989	Delta St.,MS	88-58	Cal Poly Pomona
1990	Delta St.,MS	77-43	Bentley,MA
1991	North Dakota St.	81-74	SE Missouri St.
1992	Delta St., MS	65–63	North Dakota St.

NAIA Finals

Year	Winner	Score	Loser
1981	Kentucky St.	73-67	Texas Southern
1982	S'western Okla.	80-45	Mo.Southern
1983	S'western Okla.	80-68	AL-Huntsville
1984	NC-Asheville	72-70*	Portland,OR
1985	S'western Okla.	55-54	Saginaw Val.,MI
1986	Francis Marion,SC	75-65	Wayland Baptist,TX
1987	S'western Okla.	60-58	North Georgia
1988	Oklahoma City	113-95	Claflin,SC
1989	So.Nazarene	98-96	Claflin,SC
1990	SW Oklahoma	82-75	AR-Monticello
1991	Ft. Hays St., KS	57-53	SW Oklahoma
1992	(Division I)		
	Arkansas Tech	84-68	Wayland Baptist,TX
	(Division II)		
	Northern St.	73-56	Tarleton St.,TX

*Overtime

Wide World Photos

Three months after testing HIV-positive and announcing his retirement,
Magic Johnson was the Most Valuable Player in the NBA All-Star Game

PRO
BASKETBALL

PRO BASKETBALL
By Bob Ryan

Mike & Magic

Jordan and the Bulls repeat, but the talk of the NBA season is Johnson's AIDS-related retirement and All-Star comeback.

The only question left following the 1991-92 season is "Who's Number 2?" Player, that is. Portland is still the second-best team.

But the Trail Blazers' Clyde Drexler was going to use the NBA Finals as a showcase to demonstrate his proximity to Michael Jordan as the Planet's Best Player.

Not!

No offense, Clyde, but after Jordan and Da Bulls dispatched the Blazers in six games, many observers were reminded of something Sparky Anderson said during the 1976 World Series. With Yankee catcher Thurman Munson standing nearby, Sparky instructed the media: "Don't ever embarrass anyone by comparing him to Johnny Bench."

Same here. His Airness is so far ahead of the pack individually these days the truth is there may not be a No. 2.

Any other year and it would have been Magic Johnson. After all, he and Michael have each won three Most Valuable Player awards in the last six seasons. In fact, from 1987-91, Johnson and Jordan placed either 1-2 or 1-3 in every MVP vote.

But on Nov. 7, 1991, only seven days into the season, Magic ended the rivalry when he announced at a crowded Los Angeles press conference that he was re-

tiring on the spot due to the discovery that he was HIV-positive.

No off-the-court event in NBA history (and very few in the chronology of all sports) stunned fans and non-fans alike as did Magic's bombshell. Here was one of the game's two or three all-time greatest players, and still one of the premier forces in the league at age 32, stepping aside for an almost unimaginable reason. The real world of AIDS collided with the fantasy world of sports in a story that had international repercussions. Only a month before, Magic had added to the NBA's enormous popularity in Europe by leading the Lakers to victory in the McDonald's Open in Paris. Shortly after returning home, he told team doctors he wasn't feeling well.

Tributes came from all corners of society. "It's a tragedy," said President Bush. "He's a hero to me and to everyone who loves sports."

"No one has contributed more to the success of the NBA than Earvin "Magic" Johnson," said commissioner David Stern. "I know his fans around the world, myself included, will miss the thrill of watching him compete."

But Stern was wrong. Magic wasn't through competing. When fans voted him on to the Western Conference starting team for the NBA All-Star Game in February, Magic not only played but scored 25 points, led the West to a 153-113 victory,

Bob Ryan is a columnist for *The Boston Globe* and has covered the NBA for 18 years. He is also a regular on ESPN's "Sports Reporters."

Wide World Photos

All attempts by Portland's **Clyde Drexler** (left) to grab the spotlight in the NBA Finals were kept at arm's length by **Michael Jordan** of the Bulls. Drexler finished a distant second to Jordan in the regular season MVP voting.

and was named MVP. Then, during the summer he was in the backcourt for the victorious U.S Olympic team (see box).

Of all Magic's NBA colleagues, the one hardest hit by his decision to quit as an everyday player may have been arch-rival Larry Bird of the Boston Celtics.

"These are probably the toughest days I've had since my father passed away," Bird said after Magic's announcement. "I was hoping I'd never have to go through anything like that again."

In his autobiography, *Drive: The Story of My Life*, Bird said of Magic: "I have always admired the way Magic handles himself. I feel he's the greatest all-around team player in basketball. I have always looked up to him because *he knows how to win*. I've always put him a step ahead of me. . . . Magic plays basketball the way I think you *should* play the game."

On Feb. 16, Bird and the Celtics were on hand at the Forum when the Lakers retired Magic's number 32.

Four months later, Jordan and the Bulls joined the Lakers, Celtics and Detroit Pistons as the NBA's only repeat champions.

Jordan put his stamp on the Finals in the first half of Game One, when he erupted for a record 35 points, fueled by six three-pointers. That was the spring-

board for Chicago's second NBA championship in a row and Michael's second straight Finals' MVP award. Coupled with his MVP selection during the regular season, Jordan became the first player to win both honors consecutively. And since he won't turn 30 until four days before the '93 All-Star Game and is clearly at his physical peak, would anyone dare bet against his making it three in a row in 1992-93?

The coming season will be easier on Jordan, if only because he won't be burdened with the fallout from Chicago sportswriter Sam Smith's controversial best-seller, *The Jordan Rules*—the essential premise of which was that Michael was a tyrannical figure to whom everyone in the organization catered in terror.

Basically, the book revealed Jordan to be a flawed human. Horrors. Here's a guy who toys with the best basketball players in the world, who makes many millions more outside the game than he does to play it, who receives countless requests a year to visit sick and dying children who idolize him, and who is one of the most recognizable personalities in the entire country. People should not have been surprised to discover he is not what you would call normal.

Rather than dwell on the unaccustomed negative press, Jordan lost himself in Chicago's season-long quest to repeat as champions. From Opening Night there was little doubt that the Bulls would, at the very least, be given an opportunity to defend their title in the Finals. Enjoying excellent health—center Bill Cartwright was the only one of coach Phil Jackson's top seven to miss more than three games—the Bulls jumped out to a 20-4 start. By the All-Star Break they were 39-9 and finished the season with a franchise-record 67 victories (up six wins from the year before).

Jordan won his sixth straight scoring crown with a 30.1 average. Fellow Olympian Scottie Pippen scored 21 points a game while leading the team in assists from the forward position. Power forward Horace Grant made a strong bid for an All-Star berth. And Jackson, the actual hero of the Smith book, coached magnificently.

In the playoffs, however, the Bulls encountered far more difficulty than they had a year previous, when they romped through four rounds with a 15-2 record. This time they went 15-7: struggling a bit against Miami (they trailed by 18 at one point in Game Three), huffing and puffing mightily to eliminate New York in seven, wheezing some in a six-game conquest of Cleveland and then recovering to flatten Portland in a six-game series that could easily have ended in four.

The Bulls capped their season in Game Six of the Finals before the usual full house at Chicago Stadium, coming from 15 points down at the start of the fourth quarter to win, 97-93.

Said Jordan: "I feel very joyous. It was an unbelievable season for me, and for us as a team. We went through a long test of adversity; it might not have all been pretty, but today, we stand tall."

Meanwhile, Magic's retirement was only the beginning of a bizarre journey for the Lakers, who, after a brief adrenalin rush, began spinning wildly up and down until the last day of the season, when a jump shot by guard Sedale Threatt lifted them into the playoffs with a victory over the cross-town Clippers.

The Lakers not only lost Magic for the entire year, but also had to do without James Worthy for 28 games, Sam Perkins for 19 and Vlade Divac for 46. Yet coach

The Best Team Ever Assembled

They came. They dunked. They posed.

The world mandated they do these things. The international basketball community did not simply allow a fox known as the United States Olympic Basketball Team into their hen house. Indeed, they express-mailed a golden engraved invitation to the Americans, gleefully forfeiting the 1992 gold medal to the Dream Team in the hopes that better days for them would lie ahead (2004? 2008? To them, it does not matter).

"Only playing against the best teams can people improve," explained FIBA (Federation Internationale de Basketball) Secretary-General Boris Stankovic, the man more responsible than anyone else for the presence of the celebrated Dream Team in Barcelona. "Open competition is absolutely necessary to bring new blood into international basketball."

This particular squad was more than just a collection of superb athletes. "This team has a mystique of quality built up over 15 years," said coach Chuck Daly. "You have Magic (Johnson), Michael (Jordan) and Larry (Bird). It won't be like this again."

So while uncomprehending Americans whined about the bullying nature of the routs—the Dream Team would win its 14 summer games by an average score of 122-72—or moaned about the heavy-handed marketing of the American squad (an irrelevant issue to opponents awed to be on the same slice of real estate as the Americans) the rest of the world lined up gleefully for the honor of being thrashed about by the Dream Teamers.

Hence the theme of the summer competition: Beat Me, Whip Me, Take My Picture.

An Argentine guard named Marcelo Milanesio ordered a teammate on the bench to get a Camcorder shot of him being posted up by Magic Johnson. Lithuanian forward Arturas Karnisovas snapped photos as he sat, in uniform, on the sidelines. There were the obligatory pre-game joint team photos.

With outcomes being no issue, simply being there was all the fun. "I loved it," said Brazil's Oscar Schmidt after his team lost to the USA by 44 and he had seen five of his shots rejected. "They are my idols. I will remember this game for the rest of my life."

NBA Photos

The Dream Team may have beaten all comers at the Summer Olympics by 50 points a game, but none of the losers seemed to mind.

The Dream Team proved to be every bit as potent in real life as it was on paper. "On your regular team," explained Magic Johnson, "when you're running a fast break, you're always thinking about how you'll distribute the ball: 'I can't give it to *him*.' Or, 'I can't give it to *him*.' On this team you can give it to *anybody*."

Or, as Charles Barkley put it, "This is the best team ever assembled. That's a nobrainer. I get amazed every day at the things I see. Whatever you want or need, we've got. We've got speed, quickness—me."

He was entitled to his braggadocio. Including an exhibition game against France, he averaged a point a minute. Michael Jordan is the greatest player in the world, as everyone knows, but when it comes to an international game the surest thing that could be said is that no one can stop Charles Barkley.

Coach Daly, who proved to have the perfect temperament to guide this team, likened the experience to "traveling with 12 rock stars." Fans were ceaselessly curious and solicitous, from La Jolla to Portland to Monte Carlo to Barcelona. In a march of some 10,000 athletes at Barcelona's Opening Ceremony, the object of the most affection and interest was Magic Johnson. Small wonder, therefore, that the gold medal meant more to him than to anyone else.

"I feel just tremendous," he said after the team's 117-85 victory over noble Croatia. "It's the most awesome feeling I've ever had winning anything. I've got goose bumps all over my body."

It was the greatest, and strangest, athletic unit ever assembled in any sport, at any time. There was so much talent that no one individual mattered. At one time or another, Patrick Ewing, David Robinson, Larry Bird, John Stockton, Magic Johnson, Clyde Drexler and Scotty Pippen were injured to some degree, and yet the average victory margin for 14 games was 50 points; the smallest margin was 32. "We have a saying in Cuba," observed coach Miguel Calderon Gomez after his team's 79-point (136-59) loss. " One finger cannot cover the whole sun."

That sun shone from Portland's Tournament of the Americas right through to the gold medal game.

Jim Gund/Allsport

Six-foot, eight-inch forward **Dennis Rodman** of Detroit was the 1991-92 season's top rebounder, pulling down 18.7 a game. The Pistons however, were eliminated from the playoffs in the opening round.

Mike Dunleavy somehow kept the team together and got them into the playoffs. At the season's end, they also lost Dunleavy, who grabbed an offer he couldn't refuse (eight years for $10 million-plus) and fled to Milwaukee, where he had been an assistant from 1987-90.

Dunleavy was one of the lucky ones. Six teams unloaded head coaches during the regular season and nine more changes were made in the off-season. When the dust had cleared, no fewer than 12 of the league's 27 franchises had changed scoutmasters (some more than once). In all, 15 coaches were replaced but only three—Dunleavy, Larry Brown and Chuck Daly—managed to find another NBA top job.

Does it not stand to reason that the first man in NBA history to coach two teams in a season would be the peripatetic Larry Brown? And was it not predictable that he would have a salutary effect on his new club? The Clippers went 23-12 after dropping Mike Schuler in February and hiring Brown, whose exit from San Antonio two weeks earlier had been somewhat peculiar in that it was never made clear whether he jumped ship or walked the plank. At any rate, the Clippers finished with 45 wins (up 14 from the year before) and made the playoffs for the first time since 1976, when the franchise was still known as the Buffalo Braves.

Daly bowed out in Detroit after a nine-year run and back-to-back NBA titles in 1989 and '90. The Pistons won 48, but fell to New York in the first round of the playoffs (their earliest exit since 1986). Although Dennis Rodman raised his game to new heights by leading the NBA with a spectacular 18.7 rebounds a game, Daly had to contend with two major controversies—Isiah Thomas being left off the Olympic team, and GM Jack McCloskey allowing both James Edwards and Vinnie Johnson to go elsewhere.

After summering with the Dream Team in Barcelona, Daly returned to take the reins of a New Jersey franchise that has always been weirdness personified.

During a tumultuous 1991-92, Nets' coach Bill Fitch knocked management early on for releasing players he liked in order to make financial room for first draft pick Kenny Anderson. He then refused to play Anderson very much, saying he wasn't ready for the NBA after missing training camp. Temperamental and talented forward Derrick Coleman mixed All-Star play with petulant behavior, even refusing to re-enter a game because he was upset with Fitch. Through it all, the Nets played some of their best basketball in eight years, winning 40 times (a 14-game improvement) and making it back to the playoffs for the first time since 1986.

Four other clubs—Cleveland, Miami, New York and Golden State—improved their records by at least 11 victories.

While no one ever challenged Chicago in the Central Division, the Cavaliers tied Portland for the league's second-best record at 57-25. The 24-game turn-around under sixth-year coach Lenny Wilkins was directly attributable to the return to good health of point guard Mark

Tim Defrisco/Allsport

Utah guard **John Stockton** led the NBA in assists for the fifth season in a row with 13.7 a game. The Jazz won 55 games and took the Midwest Division by eight games over San Antionio.

Price, who missed 66 games in 1990-91 with a knee injury.

Miami's 1988 expansion team master plan to go with kids continued to pay off handsomely as the Heat became the first of the league's four newest teams to reach the playoffs. In four seasons their victory progression is 15-18-24-38. And with Rony Seikaly, Glen Rice and Steve Smith, they have three of the NBA's top young players.

Don Nelson of Golden State and Pat Riley of New York finished a close 1-2 in the Coach of the Year vote, making Nelson the first three-time winner of the award.

The Warriors led the league in both points scored and points allowed, winning 55 games without anything resembling a center. Chris Mullin again led the league in minutes played (3,346), while Tim Hardaway moved into the upper echelon of both point guards and players in general with a spectacular season (23.4 points and 10 assists a game). Nelson fretted all season that the team's lack of an inside game would be a problem in the playoffs, and he was correct—Seattle beat them in the first round, three games to one.

Riley's defensive-minded Knickerbockers, on the other hand, thrived in the postseason. After winning 51 regular season games, the Knicks met Detroit in the opening round and beat the Pistons in five, then badgered Chicago for seven punishing games in the conference semifinals. In those 12 games, the Knicks gave up only 89 points a game, but they scored just 90—a problem they hope to have remedied in the off-season by acquiring Dallas sniper Rolando Blackman (18.3 points a game) to supplement ironman center Patrick Ewing (24.0)

New York was unable to win the Atlantic Division because Boston stole it from them by winning 15 of their last 16. But even the Celtics' staunchest backers know they are yesterday's news. Bird missed 37 games with a bad back. Ankle woes sidelined Kevin McHale for 26 games. And even though Robert Parish played 79 games, he was the league's oldest player at 38.

The season's top rookie was Charlotte's Larry Johnson, the Number One pick in the 1991 Draft. Thought by some to be a risk at the time, Johnson made his employers look smart by putting up 19 points and 11 rebounds a game while running away with the Rookie of the Year vote. Guard Kendall Gill also progressed, and now with the addition of Georgetown ace Alonzo Mourning, the Hornets are ready to make a move up the standings ladder.

Atlanta, Houston and Milwaukee all fell out of the playoffs for various reasons. The Hawks lost All-Star forward Dominique Wilkins for the final two and a half months with a ruptured Achilles tendon. The Rockets won 10 fewer games, fired coach Don Chaney in February and then had to deal with an unhappy Hakeem Olajuwon, who wound up the season insulted (the team suggested he had faked an injury) and on the trading block. And the aging Bucks slipped 17 games (48 wins to 31) and missed the playoffs for the first time since 1979.

Then there was Philadelphia—another also-ran whose three-year victory regression now reads: 53-44-35. Little wonder the 76ers shook themselves up in the off-season by promoting Jim Lynam to general manager, bringing in Doug Moe as head coach, and trading disgruntled star Charles Barkley to Phoenix for Suns' starters Jeff Hornacek, Andrew Lang and Tim Perry.

It was the culmination of a long season for the outspoken Barkley—who saw his scoring average dip to 23.1, was charged and later acquitted of battery and disorderly conduct after punching out an obnoxious fan in Milwaukee, and claimed to have been misquoted in his own autobiography (appropriately entitled *Outrageous*.)

Barkley joined Kevin Johnson, Dan Majerle and Tom Chambers in Phoenix where Cotton Fitzsimmons decided to step aside after four straight seasons of 53 wins or more to give assistant Paul Westphal a chance to coach the Suns to the next level.

The Pacific was the NBA's most competitive division in 1991-92, sending six teams to the playoffs and three to the second round. Front runners Portland, Golden State and Phoenix all finished within four games of each other, while Seattle and the L.A. Clippers came close to 50 wins.

Fifty-win seasons are nothing new in Utah, where the Jazz have a progression of 51-55-54-55 going since 1988-89. Along the way, John Stockton won his fifth straight assist title, Karl Malone made first team All-NBA for the fourth year in a row and the Jazz had the league's best home record (37-4) at the brand new Delta Center.

Defending Midwest Division champion San Antonio finished eight games behind Utah, but All-NBA first team center David Robinson distinguished himself by finishing in the Top 10 in five categories—scoring (7th), rebounds (4th), field goal percentage (7th), steals (5th) and blocked shots (1st). The Spurs, however, seemed to be in constant turmoil: guard Rod Strickland missed the first 24 games of the season as a holdout; Brown exited under mysterious circumstances on Jan. 21; Robinson tore ligaments in his left thumb on March 16 and missed 14 of the last 17 regular season games and all of the playoffs; and former UNLV legend

Wide World Photos

Don Nelson of Golden State became the NBA's first three-time Coach of the Year winner after leading the Warriors to a 55-27 record and a second-place finish in the Pacific Division.

Jerry Tarkanian was named coach for 1992-93 while the 1991-92 season was still going on.

It could have been worse. Midwest member Minnesota was 8-38 at the All-Star break and went downhill from there. Seriously. The Timberwolves were 1-15 in March and finished with the worst record in the league at 15-67.

Orlando, a 31-game winner in the Midwest in 1990-91, moved to the Atlantic Division and won only 21. Unlucky? Hardly. The Magic came up big in the Draft Lottery and picked LSU junior Shaquille O'Neal. Then all they had to do was get the 7-1, 303-pound center in under the salary cap.

"I'm not promising we'll win the championship in the first year," O'Neal told *USA Today* after his selection. "But I'll learn the ropes, get my feet wet, and after that, I think I'll be pretty hard to stop."

The Sacramento Kings finally stopped an NBA record 45-game road losing streak on Nov. 23, 1991, beating the Magic, 95-93, at Orlando Arena. Said a relieved Wayman Tisdale of the Kings, "We're going to Disney World!" □

THE 1993 INFORMATION PLEASE SPORTS ALMANAC

PRO BASKETBALL STATISTICS

THE SEASON IN REVIEW
1991-1992
STANDINGS • PLAYOFFS • DRAFT

SEC A
PAGE 305

Final NBA Standings

Division champions (*) and playoff qualifiers (†) are noted. Number of seasons listed after each head coach refers to current tenure with club through the 1991-92 season.

Western Conference

Midwest Division

	W	L	Pct	GB	Per Game—For	Opp
*Utah	55	27	.671	—	108.3	101.9
†San Antonio	47	35	.573	8	104.0	100.6
Houston	42	40	.512	13	102.0	103.7
Denver	24	58	.293	31	99.7	107.6
Dallas	22	60	.268	33	97.6	105.3
Minnesota	15	67	.183	40	100.5	107.5

Head Coaches: Utah—Jerry Sloan (4th season); **SA**—replaced Larry Brown (4th, 21-17) with Bob Bass (26-18) on Jan.21; **Hou**—replaced Don Chaney (4th, 26-26) with Rudy Tomjanovich (16-14) on Feb. 18; **Den**—Paul Westhead (2nd); **Dal**—Richie Adubato (3rd); **Min**—Jimmy Rodgers (1st).
1990-91 Standings: 1.San Antonio (55-27); 2.Utah (54-28); 3.Houston (52-30); 4.Orlando (31-51); 5.Minnesota (29-53); 6.Dallas (28-54); 7.Denver (20-62).

Pacific Division

	W	L	Pct	GB	Per Game—For	Opp
*Portland	57	25	.695	—	111.4	104.1
†Golden St	55	27	.671	2	118.7	114.8
†Phoenix	53	29	.646	4	112.1	106.2
†Seattle	47	35	.573	10	106.5	104.7
†LA Clippers	45	37	.549	12	102.9	101.9
†LA Lakers	43	39	.524	14	100.4	101.5
Sacramento	29	53	.354	28	104.3	110.3

Head Coaches: Por—Rick Adelman (4th season); **GS**—Don Nelson (4th); **Pho**—Cotton Fitzsimmons (4th); **Sea**—replaced K.C.Jones (2nd, 18-18) with Bob Kloppenburg (2-2) on Jan.15, then named George Karl (27-15) on Jan.23; **LAC**—replaced Mike Schuler (2nd, 21-24) with Mack Calvin (1-1) on Feb. 2, then named Larry Brown (23-12) on Feb.6; **LAL**—Mike Dunleavy (2nd); **Sac**—replaced Dick Motta (3rd, 7-18) with Rex Hughes (22-35) on Dec.24.
1990-91 Standings: 1.Portland (63-19); 2.Lakers (58-24); 3.Phoenix (55-27); 4.Golden St.(44-38); 5.Seattle (41-41); 6.Clippers (31-51); 7.Sacramento (25-57).

Eastern Conference

Atlantic Division

	W	L	Pct	GB	Per Game—For	Opp
*Boston	51	31	.622	—	106.6	103.0
†New York	51	31	.622	—	101.6	97.7
†New Jersey	40	42	.488	11	105.4	107.1
†Miami	38	44	.463	13	105.0	109.2
Philadelphia	35	47	.427	16	101.9	103.2
Washington	25	57	.305	26	102.4	106.8
Orlando	21	61	.256	30	101.6	108.5

Head Coaches: Bos—Chris Ford (2nd season); **NY**—Pat Riley (1st); **NJ**—Bill Fitch (3rd); **Mia**—Kevin Loughery (1st); **Phi**—Jim Lynam (5th); **Wash**—Wes Unseld (5th); **Orl**—Matt Guokas (3rd).
1990-91 Standings: 1.Boston (56-26); 2.Philadelphia (44-38); 3.New York (39-43); 4.Washington (30-52); 5.New Jersey (26-56); 6.Miami (24-58).

Central Division

	W	L	Pct	GB	Per Game—For	Opp
*Chicago	67	15	.817	—	109.9	99.5
†Cleveland	57	25	.695	10	108.9	103.4
†Detroit	48	34	.585	19	98.9	96.9
†Indiana	40	42	.488	27	112.2	110.3
Atlanta	38	44	.463	29	106.2	107.7
Charlotte	31	51	.378	36	109.5	113.4
Milwaukee	31	51	.378	36	105.0	106.7

Head Coaches: Chi—Phil Jackson (3rd season); **Det**—Chuck Daly (9th); **Mil**—replaced Del Harris (5th, 8-9) with Frank Hamblen (23-42) on Dec. 4; **Atl**—Bob Weiss (2nd); **Ind**—Bob Hill (2nd); **Cle**—Lenny Wilkens (6th); **Char**—Allan Bristow (1st).
1990-91 Standings: 1.Chicago (61-21); 2.Detroit (50-32); 3.Milwaukee (48-34); 4.Atlanta (43-39); 5.Indiana (41-41); 6.Cleveland (33-49); 7.Charlotte (26-5.

Overall Conference Standings

Sixteen teams—eight from each conference—qualify for the NBA Playoffs; (*) indicates division champions.

Western Conference

		W	L	Home	Away	Conf
1	Portland*	57	25	33-8	24-17	37-17
2	Utah*	55	27	37-4	18-23	37-17
3	Golden St	55	27	31-10	24-17	36-18
4	Phoenix	53	29	36-5	17-24	34-20
5	San Antonio	47	35	31-10	16-25	34-20
6	Seattle	47	35	28-13	19-22	34-20
7	LA Clippers	45	37	29-12	16-25	29-25
8	LA Lakers	43	39	24-17	19-22	27-27
	Houston	42	40	28-13	14-27	26-28
	Sacramento	29	53	21-20	8-33	17-37
	Denver	24	58	18-23	6-35	14-40
	Dallas	22	60	15-26	7-34	15-39
	Minnesota	15	67	9-32	6-35	11-43

Eastern Conference

		W	L	Home	Away	Conf
1	Chicago*	67	15	36-5	31-10	47-9
2	Cleveland	57	25	35-6	22-19	42-14
3	Boston*	51	31	34-7	17-24	35-21
4	New York	51	31	30-11	21-20	34-22
5	Detroit	48	34	25-16	23-18	31-25
6	Indiana	40	42	26-15	14-27	27-29
7	New Jersey	40	42	25-16	15-26	29-27
8	Miami	38	44	28-13	10-31	27-29
	Atlanta	38	44	23-18	15-26	23-33
	Philadelphia	35	47	23-18	12-29	23-33
	Charlotte	31	51	22-19	9-32	21-35
	Milwaukee	31	51	25-16	6-35	22-34
	Washington	25	57	14-27	11-30	15-41
	Orlando	21	61	13-28	8-33	16-40

NBA Regular Season Individual Leaders
Scoring
(Minimum 70 games or 1400 points)

	Gm	Min	FG	FG%	3Pt/Att	FT	FT%	Reb	Ast	Stl	Blk	Pts	Avg	Hi
Michael Jordan, Chi	80	3102	943	.519	27/100	491	.832	511	489	182	75	2404	30.1	51
Karl Malone, Utah	81	3054	798	.526	3/17	673	.778	909	241	108	51	2272	28.0	44
Chris Mullin, GS	81	3346	830	.524	64/175	350	.833	450	286	173	62	2074	25.6	40
Clyde Drexler, Por	76	2751	694	.470	114/338	401	.794	500	512	138	70	1903	25.0	40
Patrick Ewing, NY	82	3150	796	.522	1/6	377	.738	921	156	88	245	1970	24.0	45
Tim Hardaway, GS	81	3332	734	.461	127/376	298	.766	310	807	164	13	1893	23.4	43
David Robinson, SA	68	2564	592	.551	1/8	393	.701	829	181	158	305	1578	23.2	39
Charles Barkley, Phi	75	2881	622	.552	32/137	454	.695	830	308	136	44	1730	23.1	38
Mitch Richmond, Sac	80	3095	685	.468	103/268	330	.813	319	411	92	34	1803	22.5	37
Glen Rice, Mia	79	3007	672	.469	155/396	266	.836	394	184	90	35	1765	22.3	46
Ricky Pierce, Sea	78	2658	620	.475	33/123	417	.916	233	241	86	20	1690	21.7	34
Hakeem Olajuwon, Hou	70	2636	591	.502	0/1	328	.766	845	157	127	304	1510	21.6	40
Brad Daugherty, Cle	73	2643	576	.570	0/2	414	.777	760	262	65	78	1566	21.5	32
Scottie Pippen, Chi	82	3164	687	.506	16/80	330	.760	630	572	155	93	1720	21.0	41
Reggie Lewis, Bos	82	3070	703	.503	5/21	292	.851	394	185	125	105	1703	20.8	38
Reggie Miller, Ind	82	3120	562	.501	129/341	442	.858	318	314	105	26	1695	20.7	31
Drazen Petrovic, NJ	82	3027	668	.508	123/277	232	.808	258	252	105	11	1691	20.6	39
Kendall Gill, Char	79	2906	666	.467	6/25	284	.745	402	329	154	46	1622	20.5	32
Jeff Malone, Utah	81	2922	691	.511	1/12	256	.898	233	180	56	5	1639	20.2	35
Jeff Hornacek, Pho	81	3078	635	.512	83/189	279	.886	407	411	158	31	1632	20.1	35

Rebounds

	Gm	Off	Def	Total	Avg
Dennis Rodman, Det	82	523	1007	1530	18.7
Kevin Willis, Atl	81	418	840	1258	15.5
Dikembe Mutombo, Den*	71	316	554	870	12.3
David Robinson, SA	68	261	568	829	12.2
Hakeem Olajuwon, Hou	70	246	599	845	12.1
Rony Seikaly, Mia	79	307	627	934	11.8
Greg Anderson, Den	82	337	604	941	11.5
Patrick Ewing, NY	82	228	693	921	11.2
Karl Malone, Utah	81	225	684	909	11.2
Charles Barkley, Phi	75	271	559	830	11.1
Larry Johnson, Char*	82	323	576	899	11.0
Otis Thorpe, Hou	82	285	577	862	10.5
Brad Daugherty, Cle	73	191	569	760	10.4
Horace Grant, Chi	81	344	463	807	10.0
Detlef Schrempf, Ind	80	202	568	770	9.6

Assists

	Gm	No	Avg
John Stockton, Utah	82	1126	13.7
Kevin Johnson, Pho	78	836	10.7
Tim Hardaway, GS	81	807	10.0
Muggsy Bogues, Char	82	743	9.1
Rod Strickland, SA	57	491	8.6
Mark Jackson, NY	81	694	8.6
Pooh Richardson, Min	82	685	8.4
Micheal Williams, Ind	79	647	8.2
Michael Adams, Wash	78	594	7.6
Mark Price, Cle	72	535	7.4
Scott Skiles, Orl	75	544	7.3
Sedale Threatt, LAL	82	593	7.2
Isiah Thomas, Det	78	560	7.2
Spud Webb, Sac	77	547	7.1
Scottie Pippen, Chi	82	572	7.0

Blocked Shots

	Gm	No	Avg
David Robinson, SA	68	305	4.49
Hakeem Olajuwon, Hou	70	304	4.34
Larry Nance, Cle	81	243	3.00
Patrick Ewing, NY	82	245	2.99
Dikembe Mutombo, Den	71	210	2.96
Manute Bol, Phi	71	205	2.89
Duane Causwell, Sac	80	215	2.69
Pervis Ellison, Wash	66	177	2.68
Mark Eaton, Utah	81	205	2.53
Andrew Lang, Pho	81	201	2.48

Field Goals

	Gm	FG	Att	Pct
Buck Williams, Port	80	340	563	.604
Otis Thorpe, Hou	82	558	943	.592
Horace Grant, Chi	81	457	790	.578
Brad Daugherty, Cle	73	576	1010	.570
Michael Cage, Sea	82	307	542	.566
Charles Barkley, Phi	75	622	1126	.552
David Robinson, SA	68	592	1074	.551
Danny Manning, LAC	82	650	1199	.542
Pervis Ellison, Wash	66	547	1014	.539
Larry Nance, Cle	81	556	1032	.539
Dennis Rodman, Det	82	342	635	.539

Steals

	Gm	No	Avg
John Stockton, Utah	82	244	2.98
Micheal Williams. Ind	79	233	2.95
Alvin Robertson, Mil	82	210	2.56
Mookie Blaylock, NJ	72	170	2.36
David Robinson, SA	68	158	2.32
Michael Jordan, Chi	80	182	2.28
Chris Mullin, GS	81	173	2.14
Muggsy Bogues, Char	82	170	2.07
Sedale Threatt, LAL	82	168	2.05
Mark Macon, Den*	76	154	2.03

Free Throws

	Gm	FT	Att	Pct
Mark Price, Cle	72	270	285	.947
Larry Bird, Bos	45	150	162	.926
Ricky Pierce, Sea	78	417	455	.916
Rolando Blackman, Dal	75	239	266	.898
Jeff Malone, Utah	81	256	285	.898
Scott Skiles, Orl	75	248	277	.895
Jeff Hornacek, Pho	81	279	315	.886
Kevin Gamble, Bos	82	139	157	.885
Johnny Dawkins, Phi	82	164	186	.882
Ron Anderson, Phi	82	143	163	.877

3-Point Field Goals

	Gm	FG	Att	Pct
Dana Barros, Sea	75	83	186	.446
Drazen Petrovic, NJ	82	123	277	.444
Jeff Hornacek, Pho	81	83	189	.439
Mike Iuzzolino, Dal	52	59	136	.434
Dale Ellis, Mil	81	138	329	.419
Craig Ehlo, Cle	63	69	167	.413
John Stockton, Utah	82	83	204	.407
Larry Bird, Bos	45	52	128	.406
Dell Curry, Char	77	74	183	.404
Hersey Hawkins, Phi	81	91	229	.397

Game High Points

	Opp	Date	FG-FT —Pts
Dominique Wilkins, Atl	vs NY	12/7	17-16 —52*
Michael Jordan, Chi	at Wash	3/19	19-12 —51
Michael Jordan, Chi	vs Den	3/24	18-12 —50
Larry Bird, Bos	vs Port	3/15	19- 9 —49*
Clyde Drexler, Port	vs SA	11/24	17-11 —48
Michael Jordan, Chi	at Mil	11/2	19- 7 —46
Michael Jordan, Chi	vs Cle	2/17	21- 4 —46
Glen Rice, Mia	vs Orl	4/11	19- 4 —46
Patrick Ewing, NY	vs Det	11/30	17-11 —45
Joe Dumars, Det	at GS	3/12	17- 9 —45

*Double overtime.

Rookie Leaders

Scoring

	Gm	FG	FT	Pts	Avg
Larry Johnson, Char	82	616	339	1576	19.2
Dikembe Mutombo, Den	71	428	321	1177	16.6
Billy Owens, GS	80	468	204	1141	14.3
Stacey Augmon, Atl	82	440	213	1094	13.3
Mark Macon, Den	76	333	135	805	10.6

Field Goals

	Gm	FG	Att	Pct
Victor Alexander, GS	80	243	459	.529
Billy Owens, GS	80	468	891	.525
Dikembo Mutombo, Den	71	438	869	.493
Larry Johnson, Char	82	616	1258	.490
Stacey Augmon, Atl	82	440	899	.489

Rebounds

	Gm	Off	Def	Tot	Avg
Dikembe Mutombo, Den	71	316	554	870	12.3
Larry Johnson, Char	82	323	576	899	11.0
Billy Owens, GS	80	243	396	639	8.0
Larry Stewart, Wash	76	186	263	449	5.9
Doug Smith, Dal	76	129	262	391	5.1

Assists

	Gm	No	Avg
Terrell Brandon, Cle	82	316	3.9
Greg Anthony, NY	82	314	3.8
Larry Johnson, Char	82	292	3.6
Stacey Augmon, Atl	82	201	2.5
Billy Owens, GS	80	188	2.4

Personal Fouls

Tyrone Hill, GS	315
Otis Thorpe, Hou	307
Andrew Lang, Pho	306
Danny Manning, LAC	293
Detlef Schrempf, Ind	286

Disqualifications

Shawn Kemp, Sea	13
Frank Brickowski, Mil	11
Cliff Robinson, Port	11
Andrew Lang, Pho	8
Six tied with 7 each.	

Turnovers

John Stockton, Utah	286
Kevin Johnson, Pho	272
Tim Hardaway, GS	267
Scottie Pippen, Chi	253
Three tied with 252 each.	

NBA Regular Season Team Leaders

Offense

WEST	Pts	Reb	Ast	FG%	3Pt%	FT%
Golden St	118.7	42.8	25.2	.507	.333	.746
Phoenix	112.1	44.5	26.9	.492	.381	.776
Portland	111.4	46.9	25.2	.473	.344	.754
Utah	108.3	44.4	26.7	.492	.345	.788
Seattle	106.5	43.2	22.9	.474	.317	.783
Sacramento	104.3	41.6	23.9	.466	.353	.747
San Antonio	104.0	46.1	24.5	.476	.292	.736
LA Clippers	102.9	43.0	25.0	.473	.289	.720
Houston	102.0	42.8	25.1	.475	.343	.738
Minnesota	100.5	40.7	24.7	.458	.320	.743
LA Lakers	100.4	40.9	22.0	.456	.267	.766
Denver	99.7	45.1	18.9	.442	.301	.738
Dallas	97.6	44.3	19.9	.439	.336	.750

EAST	Pts	Reb	Ast	FG%	3Pt%	FT%
Indiana	112.2	44.5	29.2	.494	.354	.790
Chicago	109.9	44.0	27.8	.508	.304	.744
Charlotte	109.5	43.1	27.7	.477	.317	.755
Cleveland	108.9	42.6	27.6	.488	.357	.805
Boston	106.6	44.9	25.3	.492	.306	.808
Atlanta	106.2	46.2	25.9	.467	.313	.731
New Jersey	105.4	47.6	23.6	.458	.334	.732
Milwaukee	105.0	42.3	24.6	.460	.369	.759
Miami	105.0	43.3	21.3	.461	.342	.790
Washington	102.4	41.6	24.5	.461	.272	.778
Philadelphia	101.9	41.1	21.4	.471	.334	.775
Orlando	101.6	42.7	21.9	.453	.324	.746
New York	101.6	44.8	26.0	.477	.325	.734
Detroit	98.9	44.3	23.2	.465	.314	.743

Defense

WEST	Pts	Reb	Ast	FG%	3Pt%	FT%
San Antonio	100.6	42.3	23.0	.452	.347	.770
LA Lakers	101.5	44.1	26.5	.480	.292	.762
LA Clippers	101.9	43.9	21.8	.459	.346	.759
Utah	101.9	41.5	23.5	.459	.337	.747
Houston	103.7	44.4	26.0	.463	.341	.770
Portland	104.1	41.9	24.1	.454	.303	.759
Seattle	104.7	40.9	22.3	.475	.337	.751
Dallas	105.3	46.2	23.6	.470	.306	.770
Phoenix	106.2	43.5	23.3	.459	.307	.756
Minnesota	107.5	46.9	25.5	.485	.354	.744
Denver	107.6	44.4	22.1	.480	.350	.773
Sacramento	110.3	48.2	26.0	.479	.331	.752
Golden St	114.8	45.9	25.9	.482	.331	.750

EAST	Pts	Reb	Ast	FG%	3Pt%	FT%
Detroit	96.9	41.1	23.1	.453	.338	.762
New York	97.7	39.7	21.7	.458	.295	.767
Chicago	99.5	39.7	22.5	.460	.332	.768
Boston	103.0	42.8	23.5	.456	.308	.768
Philadelphia	103.2	43.1	27.1	.483	.307	.776
Cleveland	103.4	44.0	26.3	.470	.332	.769
Milwaukee	106.7	42.5	25.8	.498	.367	.746
Washington	106.8	46.7	23.2	.478	.353	.753
New Jersey	107.1	43.5	21.8	.477	.317	.766
Atlanta	107.7	45.2	26.4	.480	.343	.766
Orlando	108.5	43.3	25.5	.486	.353	.751
Miami	109.2	43.3	25.2	.493	.347	.752
Indiana	110.3	43.5	26.4	.468	.338	.752
Charlotte	113.4	46.8	28.9	.496	.324	.741

Team by Team Statistics

At least 20 games played. Players who competed for more than one team during the regular season are listed with their final club; (*) indicates rookies.

Atlanta Hawks

	Gm	FG%	TPts	Pts	Reb	Ast
				—Per Game—		
Dominique Wilkins	42	.464	1179	28.1	7.0	3.8
Kevin Willis	81	.483	1480	18.3	15.5	2.1
Stacey Augmon*	82	.489	1094	13.3	5.1	2.5
Rumeal Robinson	81	.456	1055	13.0	2.7	5.5
Duane Ferrell	66	.524	839	12.7	3.2	1.4
Paul Graham	78	.447	791	10.1	3.0	2.2
Blair Rasmussen	81	.478	729	9.0	4.9	1.3
Alexander Volkov	77	.441	662	8.6	3.4	3.2
Maurice Cheeks	56	.462	259	4.6	1.7	3.3
Morlon Wiley	53	.430	204	3.8	1.5	3.4
ORL	9	.321	21	2.3	0.8	1.4
SA	3	.600	6	2.0	0.3	0.3
ATL	41	.444	177	4.3	1.8	4.0
Rodney Monroe*	38	.368	131	3.4	0.9	0.7
Jon Koncak	77	.391	241	3.1	3.4	1.7

Triple Doubles: none.
Steals leader: Augmon (124). **Blocks leader:** Koncak (67).
Signed: G Wiley as free agent (Jan.2).

Boston Celtics

	Gm	FG%	TPts	Pts	Reb	Ast
				—Per Game—		
Reggie Lewis	82	.503	1703	20.8	4.8	2.3
Larry Bird	45	.466	908	20.2	9.6	6.8
Robert Parish	79	.535	1115	14.1	8.9	0.9
Kevin McHale	56	.509	780	13.9	5.9	1.5
Kevin Gamble	82	.529	1108	13.5	3.5	2.7
Dee Brown	31	.426	363	11.7	2.5	5.3
Rick Fox*	81	.459	644	8.0	2.7	1.6
Ed Pinckney	81	.537	613	7.6	7.0	0.8
Sherman Douglas	42	.462	308	7.3	1.5	4.1
MIA	5	.516	37	7.4	1.2	3.8
BOS	37	.455	271	7.3	1.5	4.1
John Bagley	73	.441	524	7.2	2.2	6.6
Joe Kleine	70	.491	326	4.7	4.2	0.5
Rickey Green	26	.447	106	4.1	0.9	2.6

Triple Double: Bird.
Steals leader: Lewis (125). **Blocks leader:** Lewis (105).
Acquired: G Douglas from Miami for G Brian Shaw (Jan.10).

Charlotte Hornets

	Gm	FG%	TPts	Pts	Reb	Ast
				—Per Game—		
Kendall Gill	79	.467	1622	20.5	5.1	4.2
Larry Johnson*	82	.490	1576	19.2	11.0	3.6
Dell Curry	77	.486	1209	15.7	3.4	2.3
Johnny Newman	55	.477	839	15.3	3.3	2.7
Kenny Gattison	82	.529	1042	12.7	7.1	1.6
Tom Hammonds	37	.488	440	11.9	5.0	1.0
WASH	37	.488	440	11.9	5.0	1.0
CHAR	0	.000	0	0.0	0.0	0.0
J.R.Reid	51	.490	560	11.0	6.2	1.6
Muggsy Bogues	82	.472	730	8.9	2.9	9.1
Anthony Frederick	66	.435	389	5.9	2.2	1.1
Mike Gminski	35	.452	202	5.8	3.4	0.9
Kevin Lynch*	55	.417	224	4.1	1.5	1.5
Eric Leckner	59	.513	196	3.3	3.5	0.5
Elliot Perry*	50	.380	126	2.5	0.8	1.6
LAC	10	.400	13	1.3	0.7	1.4
CHAR	40	.377	113	2.8	0.8	1.6

Triple Doubles: none.
Steals leader: Bogues (170). **Blocks leader:** Gattison (69).
Acquired: F Hammonds from Washington for G Rex Chapman (Feb.19).
Signed: G Perry as free agent (Dec.9).

Chicago Bulls

	Gm	FG%	TPts	Pts	Reb	Ast
				—Per Game—		
Michael Jordan	80	.519	2404	30.1	6.4	6.1
Scottie Pippen	82	.506	1720	21.0	7.7	7.0
Horace Grant	81	.578	1149	14.2	10.0	2.7
B.J.Armstrong	82	.481	809	9.9	1.8	3.2
Bill Cartwright	64	.497	512	8.0	5.1	1.4
John Paxson	79	.528	555	7.0	1.2	3.1
Stacey King	79	.506	551	7.0	2.6	1.0
Will Perdue	77	.547	350	4.5	4.1	1.0
Craig Hodges	56	.384	238	4.3	0.4	1.0
Cliff Levingston	79	.498	311	3.9	2.9	0.8
Scott Williams	63	.483	214	3.4	3.9	0.8
Bobby Hansen	68	.444	173	2.5	1.1	1.0
SAC	2	.444	8	4.0	2.0	0.5
CHI	66	.444	165	2.5	1.1	1.0

Triple Doubles: Jordan and Pippen (2).
Steals leader: Jordan (182). **Blocks leader:** Grant (131).
Acquired: G Hansen from Sacramento for G Dennis Hopson (Nov.4).

Cleveland Cavaliers

	Gm	FG%	TPts	Pts	Reb	Ast
				—Per Game—		
Brad Daugherty	73	.570	1566	21.5	10.4	3.6
Mark Price	72	.488	1247	17.3	2.4	7.4
Larry Nance	81	.539	1375	17.0	8.3	2.9
Craig Ehlo	63	.453	776	12.3	4.9	3.8
Hot Rod Williams	80	.503	952	11.9	7.6	2.5
John Battle	76	.480	779	10.3	1.5	2.1
Terrell Brandon*	82	.479	605	7.4	2.0	3.9
Mike Sanders	31	.571	221	7.1	3.1	1.7
IND	10	.500	27	2.7	0.8	1.1
CLE	21	.583	194	9.2	4.2	2.0
Steve Kerr	48	.511	319	6.6	1.6	2.3
Henry James	65	.407	418	6.4	1.7	0.4
Danny Ferry	68	.409	346	5.1	3.1	1.1
Jimmy Oliver*	27	.398	96	3.6	1.0	0.7

Triple Doubles: Daugherty and Nance.
Steals leader: Price (94). **Blocks leader:** Nance (243).
Signed: F Sanders as free agent (Mar.12).

Dallas Mavericks

	Gm	FG%	TPts	Pts	Reb	Ast
				—Per Game—		
Rolando Blackman	75	.461	1374	18.3	3.2	2.7
Derek Harper	65	.443	1152	17.7	2.6	5.7
Herb Williams	75	.431	859	11.5	6.1	1.3
Fat Lever	31	.387	347	11.2	5.2	3.5
Terry Davis	68	.482	693	10.2	9.9	0.8
Mike Iuzzolino*	52	.451	486	9.3	1.9	3.7
Rodney McCray	75	.436	677	9.0	6.2	2.9
Doug Smith*	76	.415	671	8.8	5.1	1.7
Tracy Moore	42	.400	355	8.5	2.0	1.1
Donald Hodge*	51	.497	426	8.4	5.4	0.8
Randy White	65	.380	418	6.4	3.6	0.5
Brian Howard	27	.519	131	4.9	1.9	0.5
Tom Garrick	40	.413	137	3.4	1.4	2.5
MIN	15	.333	29	1.9	0.6	1.2
SA	19	.453	98	5.2	2.2	3.3
DAL	6	.235	10	1.7	1.0	0.8
Brian Quinnett	39	.347	115	2.9	1.3	0.3
NY	24	.384	74	3.1	1.0	0.3
DAL	15	.294	41	2.7	1.8	0.3
Brad Davis	33	.442	92	2.8	1.0	2.0

Triple Double: McCray.
Steals leader: Harper (101). **Blocks leader:** Williams (98).
Acquired: Quinnett from New York for James Donaldson (Feb.20).
Signed: G Garrick as free agent (Mar.21).

Denver Nuggets

	Gm	FG%	TPts	Pts	Reb	Ast
Reggie Williams........	81	.471	1474	18.2	5.0	2.9
Dikembe Mutombo*....	71	.493	1177	16.6	12.3	2.2
Greg Anderson........	82	.456	945	11.5	11.5	1.0
Winston Garland.......	78	.444	846	10.8	2.4	5.3
Mark Macon*.........	76	.375	805	10.6	2.9	2.2
Chris Jackson.........	81	.421	837	10.3	1.4	2.4
Walter Davis	46	.459	457	9.9	1.5	1.5
Marcus Liberty	75	.443	698	9.3	4.1	0.8
Todd Lichti	68	.460	446	6.6	1.7	1.1
Joe Wolf..............	67	.361	254	3.8	3.6	0.9
Kevin Brooks*	37	.443	105	2.8	1.1	0.3
Anthony Cook	22	.600	34	1.5	1.5	0.1
Scott Hastings	40	.340	58	1.5	2.5	0.7

Triple Doubles: none.
Steals leader: Macon (154). **Blocks leader:** Mutombo (210).

Houston Rockets

	Gm	FG%	TPts	Pts	Reb	Ast
Hakeem Olajuwon	70	.502	1510	21.6	12.1	2.2
Otis Thorpe	82	.592	1420	17.3	10.5	3.0
Vernon Maxwell........	80	.413	1372	17.2	3.0	4.1
Kenny Smith*.........	81	.475	1137	14.0	2.2	6.9
Sleepy Floyd.........	82	.406	744	9.1	1.8	2.9
Buck Johnson.........	80	.458	685	8.6	3.9	2.0
Matt Bullard..........	80	.459	512	6.4	2.8	0.9
Avery Johnson	69	.479	386	5.6	1.2	3.9
SA..................	20	.509	135	6.8	1.8	5.0
HOU..............	49	.464	251	5.1	0.9	3.4
Carl Herrera*.........	43	.516	191	4.4	2.3	0.6
Dave Jamerson	48	.414	191	4.0	0.9	0.7
John Turner*.........	42	.439	117	2.8	1.9	0.3
Larry Smith..........	45	.543	104	2.3	5.7	0.7
Tree Rollins...........	59	.535	118	2.0	2.9	0.3

Triple Double: Thorpe.
Steals leader: Olajuwon (127). **Blocks leader:** Olajuwon (304).
Signed: G Avery Johnson as free agent (Jan.10).

Detroit Pistons

	Gm	FG%	TPts	Pts	Reb	Ast
Joe Dumars	82	.448	1635	19.9	2.3	4.6
Isiah Thomas	78	.446	1445	18.5	3.2	7.2
Orlando Woolridge	82	.498	1146	14.0	3.2	1.1
Mark Aguirre	75	.431	851	11.3	3.1	1.7
Dennis Rodman	82	.539	800	9.8	18.7	2.3
Bill Laimbeer	81	.470	783	9.7	5.6	2.0
John Salley...........	72	.512	684	9.5	4.1	1.6
Darrell Walker	74	.423	387	5.2	3.2	2.8
William Bedford	32	.413	114	3.6	2.0	0.4
Brad Sellers	43	.466	102	2.4	1.0	0.3
Lance Blanks	43	.455	64	1.5	0.5	0.4
Charles Thomas*......	37	.353	48	1.3	0.6	0.6
Bob McCann	26	.394	30	1.2	1.2	0.2

Triple Doubles: none.
Steals leader: I.Thomas (118). **Blocks leader:** Salley (110).

Indiana Pacers

	Gm	FG%	TPts	Pts	Reb	Ast
Reggie Miller	82	.501	1695	20.7	3.9	3.8
Chuck Person.........	81	.480	1497	18.5	5.3	4.7
Detlef Schrempf	80	.536	1380	17.3	9.6	3.9
Micheal Williams......	79	.490	1188	15.0	3.6	8.2
Rik Smits.............	74	.510	1024	13.8	5.6	1.6
Vern Fleming	82	.482	726	8.9	2.5	3.2
George McCloud	51	.409	338	6.6	2.6	2.3
Dale Davis*..........	64	.552	395	6.2	6.4	0.5
LaSalle Thompson.....	80	.468	394	4.9	4.8	1.3
Ken Williams.........	60	.518	252	4.2	2.2	0.7
Sean Green*	35	.390	141	4.0	1.2	0.6
Greg Dreiling	60	.494	117	2.0	1.6	0.4
Randy Wittman	24	.421	17	0.7	0.4	0.5

Triple Doubles: Schrempf and M.Williams.
Steals leader: M.Williams (233). **Blocks leader:** Smits (100).

Golden State Warriors

	Gm	FG%	TPts	Pts	Reb	Ast
Chris Mullin	81	.524	2074	25.6	5.6	3.5
Tim Hardaway........	81	.461	1893	23.4	3.8	10.0
Sarunas Marciulionis ..	72	.538	1361	18.9	2.9	3.4
Billy Owens*.........	80	.525	1141	14.3	8.0	2.4
Rod Higgins	25	.412	255	10.2	3.4	0.9
Tyrone Hill	82	.522	671	8.2	7.2	0.6
Mario Elie............	79	.521	620	7.8	2.9	2.2
Victor Alexander*......	80	.529	589	7.4	4.2	0.4
Vincent Askew	80	.509	498	6.2	2.9	2.4
Chris Gatling*	54	.568	306	5.7	3.4	0.3
Alton Lister	26	.557	102	3.9	3.5	0.5
Tom Tolbert	35	.384	90	2.6	1.6	0.6
Jud Buechler	28	.408	70	2.5	1.9	0.8
NJ	2	.500	8	4.0	1.0	1.0
SA	11	.500	33	3.0	2.0	1.0
GS	15	.303	29	1.9	1.9	0.7
Jim Petersen.........	27	.450	43	1.6	1.7	0.3

Triple Double: Hardaway.
Steals leader: Mullin (173). **Blocks leader:** Owens (65).
Signed: F Buechler as free agent (Dec.23).

Los Angeles Clippers

	Gm	FG%	TPts	Pts	Reb	Ast
Danny Manning	82	.542	1579	19.3	6.9	3.5
Ron Harper	82	.440	1495	18.2	5.5	5.1
Charles Smith	49	.466	714	14.6	6.1	1.1
Ken Norman	77	.490	929	12.1	5.8	1.6
Doc Rivers	59	.424	641	10.9	2.5	3.9
James Edwards	72	.465	698	9.7	2.8	0.7
Olden Polynice	76	.519	613	8.1	7.1	0.6
Gary Grant	78	.462	609	7.8	2.4	6.9
Loy Vaught..........	79	.492	601	7.6	6.5	0.9
Danny Young	62	.392	280	4.5	1.2	2.8
PORT	18	.400	45	2.5	0.5	1.1
LAC................	44	.391	235	5.3	1.5	3.5
Tharon Mayes*	24	.303	99	4.1	0.7	1.5
PHI	21	.298	90	4.3	0.7	1.5
LAC................	3	.400	9	3.0	0.3	1.0
Bo Kimble	34	.396	112	3.3	0.9	0.5
LeRon Ellis*	29	.340	43	1.5	0.8	0.0

Triple Double: Harper.
Steals leader: Harper (152). **Blocks leader:** Manning (122).
Signed: G Mayes (Mar.3) and G Young (Jan.11) as free agents.

Team by Team Statistics (Cont.)

Los Angeles Lakers

	Gm	FG%	TPts	Pts	Reb	Ast
				—Per Game—		
James Worthy	54	.447	1075	19.9	5.6	4.7
Sam Perkins	63	.450	1041	16.5	8.8	2.2
Sedale Threatt	82	.489	1240	15.1	3.1	7.2
Byron Scott	82	.458	1218	14.9	3.8	2.8
A.C. Green	82	.476	1116	13.6	9.3	1.4
Vlade Divac	36	.495	405	11.3	6.9	1.7
Terry Teagle	82	.452	880	10.7	2.2	1.4
Elden Campbell	81	.448	578	7.1	5.2	0.7
Tony Smith	63	.399	275	4.4	1.2	1.7
Chucky Brown	42	.469	150	3.6	2.0	0.6
CLE	6	.500	15	2.5	1.0	0.5
LAL	36	.466	135	3.8	2.1	0.6
Rory Sparrow	46	.384	127	2.8	0.6	1.8
CHI	4	.125	3	0.8	0.3	1.0
LAL	42	.399	124	3.0	0.6	1.9
Jack Haley	49	.369	76	1.6	1.9	0.1
Keith Owens*	20	.281	26	1.3	0.8	0.2

Triple Doubles: none.
Steals leader: Threatt (168). **Blocks leader:** Campbell (159).
Signed: F Brown (Dec.5) and G Sparrow (Dec.6) as free agents.

Minnesota Timberwolves

	Gm	FG%	TPts	Pts	Reb	Ast
				—Per Game—		
Tony Campbell	78	.464	1307	16.8	3.7	2.9
Pooh Richardson	82	.466	1350	16.5	3.7	8.4
Doug West	80	.518	1116	14.0	3.2	3.5
Gerald Glass	75	.440	859	11.5	3.5	2.3
Thurl Bailey	84	.440	951	11.3	5.8	0.9
UTAH	13	.386	122	9.4	6.0	1.5
MIN	71	.448	829	11.7	5.7	0.8
Sam Mitchell	82	.423	825	10.1	5.8	1.1
Felton Spencer	61	.426	405	6.6	7.1	0.9
Randy Breuer	67	.468	363	5.4	4.2	1.3
Scott Brooks	82	.447	417	5.1	1.2	2.5
Luc Longley*	66	.458	281	4.3	3.9	0.8
Mark Randall*	54	.456	171	3.2	1.3	0.6
CHI	15	.455	26	1.7	0.6	0.5
MIN	39	.457	145	3.7	1.6	0.7
Tod Murphy	47	.488	98	2.1	2.3	0.2

Triple Doubles: none.
Steals leader: Richardson (119). **Blocks leader:** Bailey (117).
Acquired: F Bailey and 2nd round pick in 1992 Draft from Utah for F Tyrone Corbin (Nov.25).
Signed: F Randall as free agent (Jan.2).

Miami Heat

	Gm	FG%	TPts	Pts	Reb	Ast
				—Per Game—		
Glen Rice	79	.469	1765	22.3	5.0	2.3
Rony Seikaly	79	.489	1296	16.4	11.8	1.4
Grant Long	82	.494	1212	14.8	8.4	2.7
Steve Smith*	61	.454	729	12.0	3.1	4.6
Willie Burton	68	.450	762	11.2	3.6	1.8
Kevin Edwards	81	.454	819	10.1	2.6	2.1
Vernell Coles	81	.455	816	10.1	2.3	4.5
Brian Shaw	63	.407	495	7.9	3.2	4.0
BOS	17	.427	175	0.3	4.1	5.2
MIA	46	.398	320	7.0	2.9	3.5
Alec Kessler	77	.413	410	5.3	4.1	0.4
John Morton	25	.387	106	4.2	1.0	1.3
CLE	4	.250	14	3.5	1.8	1.3
MIA	21	.407	92	4.4	0.9	1.3
Keith Askins	59	.410	219	3.7	2.4	0.6
Winston Bennett	54	.379	195	3.6	3.0	0.7
CLE	52	.378	193	3.7	3.1	0.7
MIA	2	.500	2	1.0	0.5	0.0
Alan Ogg	43	.548	108	2.5	1.7	0.2

Triple Doubles: none.
Steals leader: Long (139). **Blocks leader:** Seikaly (121).
Acquired: G Shaw from Boston for G Sherman Douglas (Jan.10).
Signed: F Bennett (Apr.10) and G Morton (Nov.22) as free agents.

Milwaukee Bucks

	Gm	FG%	TPts	Pts	Reb	Ast
				—Per Game—		
Dale Ellis	81	.469	1272	15.7	3.1	1.3
Moses Malone	82	.474	1279	15.6	9.1	1.1
Jay Humphries	71	.469	991	14.0	2.6	6.6
Alvin Robertson	82	.430	1010	12.3	4.3	4.4
Frank Brickowski	65	.524	740	11.4	5.3	1.9
Fred Roberts	80	.482	769	9.6	3.2	1.5
Larry Krystkowiak	79	.444	714	9.0	5.4	1.4
Jeff Grayer	82	.448	739	9.0	3.1	1.8
Brad Lohaus	70	.450	408	5.8	3.6	1.1
Dan Schayes	43	.417	240	5.6	3.9	0.8
Lester Conner	81	.431	287	3.5	2.3	3.6
Steve Henson	50	.361	150	3.0	0.8	1.6

Triple Doubles: none.
Steals leader: Robertson (210). **Blocks leader:** Lohaus (71).

New Jersey Nets

	Gm	FG%	TPts	Pts	Reb	Ast
				—Per Game—		
Drazen Petrovic	82	.508	1691	20.6	3.1	3.1
Derrick Coleman	65	.504	1289	19.8	9.5	3.2
Sam Bowie	71	.445	1062	15.0	8.1	2.6
Mookie Blaylock	72	.432	996	13.8	3.7	6.8
Chris Morris	77	.477	879	11.4	6.4	2.6
Terry Mills	82	.463	742	9.0	5.5	1.0
Kenny Anderson*	64	.390	450	7.0	2.0	3.2
Tate George	70	.427	418	6.0	1.5	2.3
Rafael Addison	76	.433	444	5.8	2.2	0.9
Chris Dudley	82	.403	460	5.6	9.0	0.7
Doug Lee	46	.431	120	2.6	0.8	0.5
Dave Feitl	34	.429	82	2.4	1.8	0.2

Triple Double: Coleman.
Steals leader: Blaylock (170). **Blocks leader:** Dudley (179).

New York Knickerbockers

	Gm	FG%	TPts	Pts	Reb	Ast
				—Per Game—		
Patrick Ewing	82	.522	1970	24.0	11.2	1.9
John Starks	82	.449	1139	13.9	2.3	3.4
Xavier McDaniel	82	.478	1125	13.7	5.6	1.8
Gerald Wilkins	82	.447	1016	12.4	2.5	2.7
Mark Jackson	81	.491	916	11.3	3.8	8.6
Anthony Mason	82	.509	573	7.0	7.0	1.3
Kiki Vandeweghe	67	.491	467	7.0	1.3	0.9
Charles Oakley	82	.522	506	6.2	8.5	1.6
Greg Anthony*	82	.370	447	5.5	1.7	3.8
James Donaldson	58	.457	285	4.9	5.0	0.6
DAL	44	.471	273	6.2	6.1	0.7
NY	14	.278	12	0.9	1.4	0.1
Tim McCormick	22	.424	42	1.9	1.5	0.4

Triple Double: Jackson.
Steals leader: Jackson (112). **Blocks leader:** Ewing (245).
Acquired: C Donaldson from Dallas for F Brian Quinnett (Feb.20).

Orlando Magic

	Gm	FG%	TPts	Pts	Reb	Ast
Nick Anderson	60	.463	1196	19.9	6.4	2.7
Terry Catledge	78	.496	1154	14.8	7.0	1.4
Anthony Bowie	52	.493	758	14.6	4.7	3.1
Scott Skiles	75	.414	1057	14.1	2.7	7.3
Jerry Reynolds	46	.380	555	12.1	3.2	3.3
Sam Vincent	39	.430	411	10.5	2.6	3.8
Stanley Roberts*	55	.529	573	10.4	6.1	0.7
Brian Williams*	48	.528	437	9.1	5.7	0.7
Sean Higgins	38	.458	291	7.7	2.7	1.1
SA	6	.267	15	2.5	1.3	0.7
ORL	32	.469	276	8.6	2.9	1.2
Jeff Turner	75	.451	530	7.1	3.3	1.2
Otis Smith	55	.365	310	5.6	2.1	1.0
Chris Corchiani*	51	.399	255	5.0	1.5	2.8
Greg Kite	72	.437	228	3.2	5.6	0.6
Mark Acres	68	.517	208	3.1	3.7	0.3

Note: Dennis Scott averaged 19.9 points a game in 18 games.
Triple Double: Anderson.
Steals leader: Anderson (97). **Blocks leader:** Roberts (83).
Signed: F Higgins as free agent (Jan.10).

Portland Trail Blazers

	Gm	FG%	TPts	Pts	Reb	Ast
Clyde Drexler	76	.470	1903	25.0	6.6	6.7
Terry Porter	82	.461	1485	18.1	3.1	5.8
Jerome Kersey	77	.467	971	12.6	8.2	3.2
Cliff Robinson	82	.466	1016	12.4	5.1	1.7
Buck Williams	80	.604	901	11.3	8.8	1.4
Kevin Duckworth	82	.461	880	10.7	6.1	1.2
Danny Ainge	81	.442	784	9.7	1.8	2.5
Alaa Abdelnaby	71	.493	432	6.1	3.7	0.4
Robert Pack*	72	.423	332	4.6	1.3	1.9
Mark Bryant	56	.480	230	4.1	3.6	0.7
Ennis Whatley	23	.412	69	3.0	0.9	1.5
Wayne Cooper	35	.427	77	2.2	2.9	0.6

Triple Doubles: none.
Steals leader: Drexler (138). **Blocks leader:** Robinson (107).

Philadelphia 76ers

	Gm	FG%	TPts	Pts	Reb	Ast
Charles Barkley	75	.552	1730	23.1	11.1	4.1
Hersey Hawkins	81	.462	1536	19.0	3.3	3.1
Armon Gilliam	81	.511	1367	16.9	8.1	1.5
Ron Anderson	82	.465	1123	13.7	3.4	1.6
Johnny Dawkins	82	.437	988	12.0	2.8	6.9
Charles Shackleford	72	.486	473	6.6	5.8	0.6
Mitchell Wiggins	49	.384	211	4.3	1.9	0.4
Jayson Williams	50	.364	206	4.1	2.9	0.2
Greg Grant	68	.440	225	3.3	1.0	3.2
CHAR	13	.000	1	0.1	0.3	1.4
PHI	55	.456	224	4.1	1.2	3.6
Kenny Payne	49	.448	144	2.9	1.1	0.3
Brian Oliver	34	.330	81	2.4	0.9	0.6
Manute Bol	71	.383	110	1.5	3.1	0.3

Triple Doubles: none.
Steals leader: Hawkins (157). **Blocks leader:** Bol (205).
Signed: G Grant as free agent (Dec.22).
Comeback: Jeff Ruland, who retired at 27 with a damaged left knee in 1986, returned (Jan.8) for 13 games, recording 51 points, 47 rebounds and a .526 FG%. He missed 85 games, however, with an Achilles tendon injury.

Sacramento Kings

	Gm	FG%	TPts	Pts	Reb	Ast
Mitch Richmond	80	.468	1803	22.5	4.0	5.1
Lionel Simmons	78	.454	1336	17.1	8.1	4.3
Wayman Tisdale	72	.500	1195	16.6	6.5	1.5
Spud Webb	77	.454	1231	16.0	2.9	7.1
Dennis Hopson	71	.465	743	10.5	2.9	1.4
CHI	2	.500	2	1.0	0.0	0.0
SAC	69	.465	741	10.7	3.0	1.5
Anthony Bonner	79	.447	740	9.4	6.1	1.6
Duane Causwell	80	.549	636	8.0	7.3	0.7
Jim Les	62	.385	231	3.7	1.0	2.3
Pete Chilcutt*	69	.452	251	3.6	2.7	0.6
Randy Brown*	56	.456	192	3.4	1.2	1.1
Dwayne Schintzius	33	.427	110	3.3	3.6	0.6
Les Jepsen	31	.375	25	0.8	1.0	0.0

Triple Doubles: Richmond and Simmons.
Steals leader: Simmons (135). **Blocks leader:** Causwell (215).
Acquired: G Hopson from Chicago for G Bob Hansen (Nov.4).

Phoenix Suns

	Gm	FG%	TPts	Pts	Reb	Ast
Jeff Hornacek	81	.512	1632	20.1	5.0	5.1
Kevin Johnson	78	.479	1536	19.7	3.7	10.7
Dan Majerle	82	.478	1418	17.3	5.9	3.3
Tom Chambers	69	.431	1128	16.3	5.8	2.1
Tim Perry	80	.523	982	12.3	6.9	1.7
Andrew Lang	81	.522	622	7.7	6.7	0.5
Cedric Ceballos	64	.482	462	7.2	2.4	0.8
Mark West	82	.632	501	6.1	4.5	0.3
Steve Burtt	31	.463	187	6.0	1.1	1.9
Negele Knight	42	.475	243	5.8	1.1	2.7
Jerrod Mustaf	52	.477	233	4.5	2.8	0.9
Kurt Rambis	28	.463	90	3.2	3.8	1.3
Ed Nealy	52	.512	160	3.1	2.1	0.7

Triple Doubles: Hornacek and Johnson.
Steals leader: Hornacek (158). **Blocks leader:** Lang (201).

San Antonio Spurs

	Gm	FG%	TPts	Pts	Reb	Ast
David Robinson	68	.551	1578	23.2	12.2	2.7
Terry Cummings	70	.488	1210	17.3	9.0	1.5
Sean Elliott	82	.494	1338	16.3	5.4	2.6
Rod Strickland	57	.455	787	13.8	4.6	8.6
Willie Anderson	57	.455	744	13.1	5.3	5.3
Antoine Carr	81	.490	881	10.9	4.3	0.8
Vinnie Johnson	60	.405	478	8.0	3.0	2.4
Trent Tucker	24	.465	155	6.5	1.5	1.1
Sidney Green	80	.427	367	4.6	4.3	0.5
Donald Royal	60	.449	252	4.2	2.1	0.6
Greg Sutton*	67	.388	246	3.7	0.7	1.4
Paul Pressey	56	.373	151	2.7	1.7	2.5
Thomas Copa	33	.550	48	1.5	1.1	0.1

Triple Doubles: Robinson (2) and Anderson.
Steals leader: Robinson (158). **Blocks leader:** Robinson (305).

Team by Team Statistics (Cont.)

Seattle Supersonics

	Gm	FG%	TPts	—Per Game— Pts	Reb	Ast
Ricky Pierce	78	.475	1690	21.7	3.0	3.1
Eddie Johnson	81	.459	1386	17.1	3.6	2.0
Shawn Kemp	64	.504	994	15.5	10.4	1.3
Derrick McKey	52	.472	777	14.9	5.2	2.3
Benoit Benjamin	63	.478	879	14.0	8.1	1.2
Gary Payton	81	.451	764	9.4	3.6	6.2
Michael Cage	82	.566	720	8.8	8.9	1.1
Dana Barros	75	.483	619	8.3	1.1	1.7
Nate McMillan	72	.437	435	6.0	3.5	5.0
Tony Brown	57	.410	271	4.8	1.5	0.8
LAC	22	.438	103	4.7	1.3	0.7
SEA	35	.394	168	4.8	1.6	0.9
Marty Conlon	45	.475	120	2.7	1.5	0.3
Rich King*	40	.380	88	2.2	1.2	0.3
Bart Kofoed	44	.472	66	1.5	0.6	1.2

Triple Doubles: Payton (2).
Steals leader: Payton (147). **Blocks leader:** Kemp (124).
Signed: F Brown as free agent (Jan.28).

Utah Jazz

	Gm	FG%	TPts	—Per Game— Pts	Reb	Ast
Karl Malone	81	.526	2272	28.0	11.2	3.0
Jeff Malone	81	.511	1639	20.2	2.9	2.2
John Stockton	82	.482	1297	15.8	3.3	13.7
Blue Edwards	81	.522	1018	12.6	3.7	1.7
Tyrone Corbin	80	.481	780	9.8	5.9	1.8
MIN	11	.401	158	14.4	6.3	3.0
UTAH	69	.504	622	9.0	5.8	1.6
Mike Brown	82	.453	632	7.7	5.8	1.0
David Benoit*	77	.467	434	5.6	3.8	0.4
Eric Murdock*	50	.415	203	4.1	1.1	1.8
Mark Eaton	81	.446	266	3.3	6.1	0.5
Delaney Rudd	65	.399	193	3.0	0.8	1.7
Corey Crowder*	51	.384	114	2.2	0.8	0.3
Isaac Austin*	31	.457	61	2.0	1.1	0.2

Triple Doubles: none.
Steals leader: Stockton (244). **Blocks leader:** Eaton (205).
Acquired: F Corbin from Minnesota for F Thurl Bailey and 2nd round pick in 1992 Draft (Nov.25).

Washington Bullets

	Gm	FG%	TPts	—Per Game— Pts	Reb	Ast
Pervis Ellison	66	.539	1322	20.0	11.2	2.9
Michael Adams	78	.393	1408	18.1	4.0	7.6
Harvey Grant	64	.478	1155	18.0	6.8	2.7
Ledell Eackles	65	.448	856	13.2	2.7	1.9
Rex Chapman	22	.448	270	12.3	2.6	4.0
CHAR	21	.450	260	12.4	2.6	4.1
WASH	1	.417	10	10.0	4.0	3.0
A.J.English	81	.433	886	10.9	2.1	1.8
Larry Stewart*	76	.514	794	10.4	5.9	1.6
David Wingate	81	.465	638	7.9	3.3	3.4
LaBradford Smith*	48	.407	247	5.1	1.7	2.1
Greg Foster	49	.461	213	4.3	3.0	0.7
Andre Turner	70	.425	284	4.1	1.3	2.5
Charles Jones	75	.367	86	1.1	4.2	0.8

Triple Doubles: none.
Steals leader: Adams (145). **Blocks leader:** Ellison (177).
Acquired: G Chapman from Charlotte for F Tom Hammonds (Feb.19).
Note: Bernard King underwent knee surgery and missed the entire season.

1992 NBA All-Star Game
West 153, East 113

42nd NBA All-Star Game. **Date:** Feb.9, at Orlando Arena; **Coaches:** Don Nelson, Golden St.(West) and Phil Jackson, Chicago (East); **MVP:** Magic Johnson, LA Lakers (ret.)—25 points, 9 assists, 5 rebounds.

Starters chosen by fan vote; bench chosen by conference coaches vote; East starter Larry Bird of Boston (back) and reserve Dominique Wilkins of Atlanta (ruptured right Achilles tendon) replaced by Scottie Pippen and Kevin Willis. NBA commissioner David Stern allowed West 13 players in light of fans' voting in Johnson (who retired on Nov.7, 1991).

Western Conference

Pos	Starters	Min	FG M-A	Pts	Rb	A
G	Magic Johnson, LAL	29	9-12	25	5	9
G	Clyde Drexler, Port	28	10-15	22	9	6
C	David Robinson, SA	18	7-9	19	5	2
F	Chris Mullin, GS	24	6-7	13	1	3
F	Karl Malone, Utah	19	5-7	11	7	3
	Bench					
G	Tim Hardaway, GS	20	5-10	14	0	7
G	John Stockton, Utah	18	5-8	12	1	5
G	Jeff Hornacek, Pho	24	5-7	11	2	3
F	James Worthy, LAL	14	4-7	9	4	1
C	Hakeem Olajuwon, Hou	20	3-6	7	4	2
F	Dan Majerle, Pho	12	2-5	4	3	2
C	Dikembe Mutombo, Den	10	2-4	4	2	1
F	Otis Thorpe, Hou	4	1-1	2	0	0
	Totals	240	64-98	153	43	44

Three-Point FG: 11-20 (Johnson 3-3, Stockton 2-3, Drexler 2-4, Hardaway 2-5, Mullin 1-1, Hornacek 1-2, Majerle 0-2); **Free Throws:** 14-20 (Robinson 5-8, Johnson 4-4, Hardaway 2-2, Malone 1-2, Olajuwon 1-2, Worthy 1-2); **Percentages:** FG (.653), Three-Pt FG (.550), Free Throws (.700); **Turnovers:** 21 (Johnson 7, Olajuwon 3, Stockton 3, Hardaway 2, Mutombo 2, Drexler, Majerle, Malone, Mullin); **Steals:** 15 (Robinson 3, Stockton 3, Johnson 2, Olajuwon 2, Hardaway, Hornacek, Malone, Mutombo, Worthy); **Blocked Shots:** 5 (Drexler 2, Malone, Olajuwon, Robinson); **Fouls:** 13 (Olajuwon 3, Robinson 3, Drexler 2, Hardaway 2, Stockton 2, Malone); **Team Rebounds:** 13.

Eastern Conference

Pos	Starters	Min	FG M-A	Pts	Rb	A
G	Michael Jordan, Chi	31	9-17	18	1	5
G	Isiah Thomas, Det	28	7-14	15	1	5
F	Scottie Pippen, Chi	21	6-13	14	4	1
F	Charles Barkley, Phi	28	6-14	12	9	1
C	Patrick Ewing, NY	17	4-7	10	4	0
	Bench					
G	Michael Adams, Wash	14	4-8	9	1	1
F	Kevin Johnson, Atl	14	4-10	8	4	0
F	Reggie Lewis, Bos	15	3-7	7	4	2
C	Brad Daugherty, Cle	15	3-8	6	6	1
G	Mark Price, Cle	15	1-5	6	0	3
G	Joe Dumars, Det	17	2-7	4	1	3
F	Dennis Rodman, Det	25	2-7	4	13	0
	Totals	240	51-117	113	48	22

Three-Point FG: 2-13 (Adams 1-3, Thomas 1-3, Dumars 0-2, Barkley 0-2, Ewing 0-2, Price 0-3); **Free Throws:** 9-14 (Price 4-4, Pippen 2-3, Ewing 2-5, Lewis 1-2); **Percentages:** FG (.436), Three-Pt FG (.154), Free Throws (.643); **Turnovers:** 22 (Barkley 3, Daugherty 3, Price 3, Thomas 3, Dumars 2, Ewing 2, Rodman 2, Adams, Jordan, Lewis, Pippen); **Steals:** 16 (Adams 4, Thomas 3, Ewing 2, Jordan 2, Pippen 2, Daugherty, Price, Rodman); **Blocked Shots:** 3 (Ewing, Lewis, Pippen); **Fouls:** 15 (Barkley 3, Ewing 3, Lewis 3, Jordan 2, Adams, Price, Rodman, Willis); **Team Rebounds:** 7.

West						153
	44	35	36	38	—	153
East	31	24	28	30	—	113

Halftime—West, 79-55; **Third Quarter**—West, 115-83; **Technical Fouls**—None; **Illegal Defense**—None; **Officials**—Darell Garretson, Joe Crawford, Tommy Nunez; **Attendance**—14,272; **Time**—2:01; **TV Rating**—12.8/26 share (NBC).

1992 NBA PLAYOFFS

| FIRST ROUND | SEMI-FINALS | FINAL | *The* **1992 NBA** *Finals* | FINAL | SEMI-FINALS | FIRST ROUND |

Portland 3
LA Lakers 1
Portland 4
Phoenix 3
San Antonio 0
Phoenix 1
Portland 4
Utah 3
LA Clippers 2
Utah 4
Golden St. 1
Seattle 3
Seattle 1
Utah 2

WESTERN CONFERENCE

Chicago 4
Portland 2

Chicago 3
Miami 0
Chicago 4
New York 3
Detroit 2
New York 3
Chicago 4
Boston 3
Indiana 0
Boston 3
Cleveland 2
Cleveland 3
New Jersey 1
Cleveland 4

EASTERN CONFERENCE

Series Summaries
Western Conference
FIRST ROUND (Best of 5)

	W	L	Avg.	Leading Scorer
Portland	3	1	109.3	Drexler (26.3)
LA Lakers	1	3	94.5	Scott (18.8)

Date	Winner	Home Court
Apr.23	Blazers, 115-102	at Portland
Apr.25	Blazers, 101-79	at Portland
Apr.29	Lakers, 121-119 (OT)	at Los Angeles
May 3	Blazers, 102-76	at Las Vegas*
*Game moved after Apr.29 riots in L.A.

	W	L	Avg.	Leading Scorer
Seattle	3	1	116.5	Kemp (22.0)
Golden St.	1	3	117.0	Hardaway (24.5)

Date	Winner	Home Court
Apr.23	Sonics, 117-109	at Golden St.
Apr.25	Warriors, 115-101	at Golden St.
Apr.28	Sonics, 129-128	at Seattle
Apr.30	Sonics, 119-116	at Seattle

	W	L	Avg.	Leading Scorer
Utah	3	2	102.2	K.Malone (29.8)
LA Clippers	2	3	98.2	Manning (22.6)

Date	Winner	Home Court
Apr.24	Jazz, 115-97	at Utah
Apr.26	Jazz, 103-92	at Utah
Apr.28	Clippers, 98-88	at Los Angeles
May 3	Clippers, 115-107	at Anaheim*
May 4	Jazz, 98-89	at Utah
*Game moved after Apr.29 riots in L.A.

	W	L	Avg.	Leading Scorer
Phoenix	3	0	112.3	Hornacek (24.7)
San Antonio	0	3	103.3	Cummings (26.0)

Date	Winner	Home Court
Apr.24	Suns, 117-111	at Phoenix
Apr.26	Suns, 119-107	at Phoenix
Apr.29	Suns, 101-92	at San Antonio

SEMIFINALS (Best of 7)

	W	L	Avg.	Leading Scorer
Portland	4	1	125.4	Drexler (31.4)
Phoenix	1	4	122.2	K.Johnson (24.4)

Date	Winner	Home Court
May 5	Blazers, 113-111	at Portland
May 7	Blazers, 126-119	at Portland
May 9	Suns, 124-117	at Phoenix
May 11	Blazers, 153-151 (2 OT)	at Phoenix
May 14	Blazers, 118-106	at Portland

	W	L	Avg.	Leading Scorer
Utah	4	1	101.8	K.Malone (29.4)
Seattle	1	4	96.8	Pierce (18.4)

Date	Winner	Home Court
May 6	Jazz, 108-100	at Utah
May 8	Jazz, 103-97	at Utah
May 10	Sonics, 104-98	at Seattle
May 12	Jazz, 89-83	at Seattle
May 14	Jazz, 111-100	at Utah

CHAMPIONSHIP (Best of 7)

	W	L	Avg	Leading Scorer
Portland	4	2	110.8	Porter (26.0)
Utah	2	4	104.3	K. Malone (28.2)

Date	Winner	Home Court	Date	Winner	Home Court
May 16	Blazers, 113-88	at Portland	May 24	Jazz, 121-112	at Utah
May 19	Blazers, 119-102	at Portland	May 26	Blazers, 127-121 (OT)	at Portland
May 22	Jazz, 97-89	at Utah	May 28	Blazers, 105-97	at Utah

NBA Playoffs (Cont.)
Eastern Conference
FIRST ROUND (Best of 5)

	W	L	Avg.	Leading Scorer
Chicago	3	0	117.3	Jordan (45.0)
Miami	0	3	99.3	Seikaly (20.7)

Date	Winner	Home Court
Apr.24	Bulls, 113-94	at Chicago
Apr.26	Bulls, 120-90	at Chicago
Apr.29	Bulls, 119-114	at Miami

	W	L	Avg	Leading Scorer
Boston	3	0	115.0	Lewis (27.7)
Indiana	0	3	107.7	Miller (27.0)

Date	Winner	Home Court
Apr.23	Celtics, 124-113	at Boston
Apr.25	Celtics, 119-112 (OT)	at Boston
Apr.27	Celtics, 102-98	at Indiana

	W	L	Avg	Leading Scorer
Cleveland	3	1	110.0	Daugherty (25.5)
New Jersey	1	3	101.8	Petrovic (24.3)

Date	Winner	Home Court
Apr.23	Cavs, 120-113	at Cleveland
Apr.25	Cavs, 118-96	at Cleveland
Apr.28	Nets, 109-104	at New Jersey
Apr.30	Cavs, 98-89	at New Jersey

	W	L	Avg	Leading Scorer
New York	3	2	92.6	Ewing (23.4)
Detroit	2	3	84.8	Dumars (16.8)

Date	Winner	Home Court
Apr.24	Knicks, 109-75	at New York
Apr.26	Pistons, 89-88	at New York
Apr.28	Knicks, 90-87 (OT)	at Detroit
May 1	Pistons, 86-82	at Detroit
May 3	Knicks, 94-87	at New York

SEMIFINALS (Best of 7)

	W	L	Avg	Leading Scorer
Chicago	4	3	92.4	Jordan (31.3)
New York	3	4	88.6	Ewing (22.1)

Date	Winner	Home Court
May 5	Knicks, 94-89	at Chicago
May 7	Bulls, 86-78	at Chicago
May 9	Bulls, 94-86	at New York
May 10	Knicks, 93-86	at New York
May 12	Bulls, 96-88	at Chicago
May 14	Knicks, 100-86	at New York
May 17	Bulls, 110-81	at Chicago

	W	L	Avg	Leading Scorer
Cleveland	4	3	106.7	Daugherty (22.6)
Boston	3	4	103.7	Lewis (28.1)

Date	Winner	Home Court
May 2	Cavs, 101-76	at Cleveland
May 4	Celtics, 104-98	at Cleveland
May 8	Celtics, 110-107	at Boston
May 10	Cavs, 114-112 (OT)	at Boston
May 13	Cavs, 114-98	at Cleveland
May 15	Celtics, 122-91	at Boston
May 17	Cavs, 122-104	at Cleveland

CHAMPIONSHIP (Best of 7)

	W	L	Avg	Leading Scorer
Chicago	4	2	97.5	Jordan (31.7)
Cleveland	2	4	95.7	Price (18.5)

Date	Winner	Home Court
May 19	Bulls, 103-89	at Chicago
May 21	Cavs, 107-81	at Chicago
May 23	Bulls, 105-96	at Cleveland
May 25	Cavs, 99-85	at Cleveland
May 27	Bulls, 112-89	at Chicago
May 29	Bulls, 99-94	at Cleveland

NBA FINALS
(Best of 7)

	W	L	Avg	Leading Scorer
Chicago	4	2	104.0	Jordan (35.8)
Portland	2	4	96.7	Drexler (24.8)

Date	Winner	Home Court
June 3	Bulls, 122-89	at Chicago
June 5	Blazers, 115-104 (OT)	at Chicago
June 7	Bulls, 94-84	at Portland
June 10	Blazers, 93-88	at Portland
June 12	Bulls, 119-106	at Portland
June 14	Bulls, 97-93	at Chicago

Most Valuable Player
Michael Jordan, Chicago, guard
35.8 pts, 6.5 asts, 4.8 rebs, 1.7 steals

Final Standings

	Gm	W	L	Pct	—Per Game—	
					For	Opp
Chicago	22	15	7	.682	100.4	94.2
Portland	21	13	8	.619	110.0	106.6
Utah	16	9	7	.563	102.9	102.5
Cleveland	17	9	8	.529	103.6	101.1
Boston	10	6	4	.600	107.1	107.0
New York	12	6	6	.500	90.3	89.3
Phoenix	8	4	4	.500	118.5	117.1
Seattle	9	4	5	.444	105.6	108.6
Detroit	5	2	3	.400	84.8	92.6
LA Clippers	5	2	3	.400	98.2	102.2
Golden St.	4	1	3	.250	117.0	116.5
LA Lakers	4	1	3	.250	94.5	109.3
New Jersey	4	1	3	.250	101.8	110.0
Indiana	3	0	3	.000	107.7	115.0
San Antonio	3	0	3	.000	103.3	112.3
Miami	3	0	3	.000	99.3	117.3

Scoring Leaders

	Gm	FG	FT	Pts	Avg
Michael Jordan, Chi	22	290	162	759	34.5
Karl Malone, Utah	16	148	169	465	29.1
Reggie Lewis, Bos	10	115	48	280	28.0
Reggie Miller, Ind.	3	25	24	81	27.0
Clyde Drexler, Port	21	198	138	553	26.3
Terry Cummings, SA	3	34	10	78	26.0
Tim Hardaway, GS	4	32	24	98	24.5
Drazen Petrovic, NJ	4	41	11	97	24.3
Kevin Johnson, Pho	8	62	62	189	23.6
Patrick Ewing, NY	12	109	54	272	22.7

NBA Finalists' Composite Box Scores
Chicago Bulls (15-7)

	Finals vs Portland						Overall Playoffs				
				Per Game						Per Game		
	Gm	FG%	TPts	Pts	Reb	Ast	Gm	FG%	TPts	Pts	Reb	Ast
Michael Jordan	6	.526	215	35.8	4.8	6.5	22	.499	759	34.5	6.2	5.8
Scottie Pippen	6	.484	125	20.8	8.3	7.7	22	.468	428	19.5	8.8	6.7
John Paxson	6	.520	62	10.3	0.8	2.7	22	.525	174	7.9	1.0	2.8
Horace Grant	6	.561	55	9.2	7.8	4.0	22	.541	249	11.3	8.8	3.0
Bill Cartwright	6	.500	38	6.3	4.0	1.5	22	.474	123	5.6	4.5	1.7
B.J. Armstrong	6	.429	35	5.8	0.8	2.3	22	.453	161	7.3	1.1	2.1
Scott Williams	6	.542	33	5.5	6.2	1.0	22	.486	88	4.0	4.3	0.3
Stacey King	4	.333	18	4.5	2.5	0.0	14	.450	53	3.8	1.4	0.4
Cliff Levingston	6	.450	23	3.8	2.2	0.7	22	.439	64	2.9	1.9	0.4
Bobby Hansen	5	.600	16	3.2	0.4	0.6	9	.409	22	2.4	1.0	1.1
Craig Hodges	2	1.000	2	1.0	0.0	0.0	17	.390	42	2.5	0.2	0.3
Will Perdue	3	.333	2	0.7	1.0	0.0	18	.486	45	2.5	2.2	0.5
BULLS	6	.504	624	104.0	37.5	26.8	22	.487	2208	100.4	39.9	24.1
OPPONENTS	6	.443	580	96.7	41.8	20.8	22	.449	2072	94.2	39.3	22.8

Three-pointers: FINALS—Jordan (12-for-28), Paxson (7-18), Hansen (3-4), Pippen (2-9), Armstrong (1-4), Grant (0-1), Levingston (0-1), Team (25-65 for .385 Pct.); PLAYOFFS—Jordan (17-for-44), Paxson (12-27), Hodges (9-20), Pippen (6-24), Armstrong (5-17), King (2-2), Hansen (3-6), Levingston (0-1), Perdue (0-2), Williams (0-1), Grant (0-2), Team (54-145 for .372 Pct.).

Portland Trail Blazers (13-8)

	Finals vs Chicago						Overall Playoffs				
				Per Game						Per Game		
	Gm	FG%	TPts	Pts	Reb	Ast	Gm	FG%	TPts	Pts	Reb	Ast
Clyde Drexler	6	.407	149	24.8	7.8	5.3	21	.466	553	26.3	7.4	7.0
Terry Porter	6	.471	97	16.2	4.3	4.7	21	.516	450	21.4	4.6	6.7
Jerome Kersey	6	.481	89	14.8	8.7	3.3	21	.510	341	16.2	7.7	3.6
Cliff Robinson	6	.442	62	10.3	3.0	2.2	21	.462	227	10.8	4.2	2.0
Danny Ainge	6	.434	60	10.0	2.0	2.5	21	.479	222	10.6	1.9	2.3
Mark Bryant	1	.625	10	10.0	5.0	0.0	12	.345	23	1.9	2.4	0.1
Kevin Duckworth	6	.431	56	9.3	6.8	1.5	21	.495	249	11.9	5.6	2.0
Buck Williams	6	.500	47	7.8	7.3	1.0	21	.508	201	9.6	8.5	1.0
Robert Pack	2	.167	5	2.5	0.5	0.5	14	.222	11	0.8	0.4	0.5
Alaa Abdelnaby	1	.000	1	1.0	0.0	0.0	8	.500	12	1.5	0.5	0.3
Ennis Whatley	5	.286	4	0.8	0.2	0.2	15	.300	16	1.1	0.7	0.9
Wayne Cooper	1	—	0	0.0	2.0	0.0	3	.500	4	1.3	2.7	0.0
TRAIL BLAZERS	6	.443	580	96.7	41.8	20.8	21	.482	2309	110.0	42.6	25.8
OPPONENTS	6	.504	624	104.0	37.5	26.8	21	.472	2239	106.6	38.0	24.9

Three-pointers: FINALS—Ainge (4-for-17), Porter (3-13), Drexler (3-20), Kersey (0-1), Robinson (0-1), Team (10-52 for .192 Pct.); PLAYOFFS—Porter (37-for-78), Ainge (21-52), Drexler (19-81), Robinson (1-6), Whatley (0-1), Kersey (0-3), Team (78-221 for .353 Pct.).

Annual Awards

Most Valuable Player

The Maurice Podoloff Trophy; voting by a 96-member panel of local and national pro basketball writers and broadcasters. Each ballot has five entries; points awarded on 10-7-5-3-1 basis.

	1st	2nd	3rd	4th	5th	Pts
Michael Jordan, Chi	80	12	3	0	1	900
Clyde Drexler, Port	12	46	18	8	5	561
David Robinson, SA	2	17	26	19	11	337
Karl Malone, Utah	1	13	19	19	9	262
Patrick Ewing, NY	0	2	8	10	16	100
Chris Mullin, GS	0	2	7	6	14	81
Mark Price, Cle	0	1	4	10	9	66
Tim Hardaway, GS	0	1	4	10	7	64
Scottie Pippen, Chi	1	0	2	2	6	32
Dennis Rodman, Det	0	0	1	5	6	26

Rookie of the Year

The Eddie Gottlieb Trophy; voting by a 96-member panel of local and national pro basketball writers and broadcasters. Each ballot has one entry.

	Pos	Votes
Larry Johnson, Charlotte	F	90½
Dikembe Mutombo, Denver	C	3½
Billy Owens, Golden St	F/G	2

All-NBA Teams

Voting by a 96-member panel of local and national pro basketball writers and broadcasters. Each ballot has entries for three teams; points awarded on 5-3-1 basis. First Team repeaters from 1990-91 are in **bold** type.

Pos	First Team	1st	Pts
G	**Michael Jordan**, Chicago	95	478
G	Clyde Drexler, Portland	65	408
C	**David Robinson**, San Antonio	62	397
F	**Karl Malone**, Utah	91	466
F	Chris Mullin, Golden St.	53	379

Pos	Second Team	1st	Pts
G	Tim Hardaway, Golden St	15	288
G	John Stockton, Utah	14	269
C	Patrick Ewing, New York	31	309
F	Scottie Pippen, Chicago	37	341
F	Charles Barkley, Philadelphia	6	196

Pos	Third Team	1st	Pts
G	Mark Price, Cleveland	0	81
G	Kevin Johnson, Phoenix	2	78
C	Brad Daugherty, Cleveland	3	70
F	Dennis Rodman, Detroit	5	179
F	Kevin Willis, Atlanta	0	38

Annual Awards (Cont.)

Coach of the Year

The Red Auerbach Trophy; voting by a 96-member panel of local and national pro basketball writers and broadcasters. Each ballot has one entry. Vote totals followed by 1991-92 record and division standing.

	Votes	Record	Div
Don Nelson, Golden St.	26	55-27	2nd
Pat Riley, New York	21	51-31	1st-T
Phil Jackson, Chicago	17	67-15	1st
Larry Brown, LA Clippers	7	23-12	5th
Lenny Wilkens, Cleveland	6	57-25	2nd
Bill Fitch, New Jersey	4	40-42	3rd
Mike Dunleavy, LA Lakers	3	43-39	6th
Chris Ford, Boston	3	51-31	1st-T

Note: Brown was fired by San Antonio (21-17) on Jan.21 and hired by the Clippers, who were 22-25 on Feb.6.

All-Rookie Team

Voting by NBA head coaches, who cannot vote for players on their team. Each ballot has entries for two teams, regardless of position; two points given for 1st team, one for 2nd. First team votes in parentheses.

First Team	College	Pts
Larry Johnson, Charlotte (26)	UNLV	52
Dikembe Mutombo, Denver (26)	Georgetown	52
Billy Owens, Golden St. (26)	Syracuse	52
Steve Smith, Miami (25)	Michigan St.	51
Stacey Augmon, Atlanta (24)	UNLV	50

All-Defensive Teams

Voting by NBA head coaches. Each ballot has entries for two teams; two points given for 1st team, one for 2nd. Coaches cannot vote for their own players. First Team repeaters from 1990-91 are in **bold** type.

Pos	First Team	1st	Pts
F	**Dennis Rodman**, Detroit	24	50
F	Scottie Pippen, Chicago	13	31
C	**David Robinson**, San Antonio	22	47
G	**Michael Jordan**, Chicago	23	49
G	Joe Dumars, Detroit	17	39

Pos	Second Team	1st	Pts
F	Larry Nance, Cleveland	8	25
F	Buck Williams, Portland	6	21
C	Patrick Ewing, New York	4	18
G	John Stockton, Utah	3	15
G	Micheal Williams, Indiana	2	9

Other Awards

Defensive Player of the Year—David Robinson, San Antonio; **Most Improved Player**—Pervis Ellison, Washington; **Sixth Man Award**—Detlef Schrempf, Indiana; **Schick Award** (for contributing most to team's success)—Dennis Rodman, Detroit; **Kennedy Citizenship Award**—Magic Johnson; **Executive of the Year** (chosen by The Sporting News)—Wayne Embry, Cleveland.

NBA Draft

First and second round picks at the 46th annual NBA College Draft held June 24, 1992, at Memorial Coliseum in Portland. The order of the first 11 positions determined by a Draft Lottery held May 17, in Secaucus, N.J. Positions 12-27 reflect regular season records in reverse order. Underclassmen selected are noted in CAPITAL letters.

First Round

	Team		Pos
1	Orlando	SHAQUILLE O'NEAL, LSU	C
2	Charlotte	Alonzo Mourning, G'town	C
3	Minnesota	Christian Laettner, Duke	F/C
4	Dallas	JIM JACKSON, Ohio St.	G
5	Denver	LaPhonso Ellis, Notre Dame	F
6	Washington	Tom Gugliotta, N.C.State	F
7	Sacramento	Walt Williams, Maryland	G
8	Milwaukee	Todd Day, Arkansas	G/F
9	Philadelphia	Clarence Weatherspoon, So.Miss	F
10	Atlanta	Adam Keefe, Stanford	F
11	Houston	Robert Horry, Alabama	F
12	Miami	HAROLD MINER, USC	G
13	a-Denver	Bryant Stith, Virginia	G/F
14	Indiana	Malik Sealy, St.John's	F
15	LA Lakers	Anthony Peeler, Missouri	G
16	LA Clippers	Randy Woods, La Salle	G
17	Seattle	Doug Christie, Pepperdine	G
18	San Antonio	TRACY MURRAY, UCLA	F
19	Detroit	Don MacLean, UCLA	F
20	New York	Hubert Davis, N.Carolina	G
21	Boston	Jon Barry, Ga.Tech	G
22	Phoenix	Oliver Miller, Arkansas	C/F
23	b-Milwaukee	Lee Mayberry, Arkansas	G
24	Golden St	Latrell Sprewell, Alabama	G
25	c-LA Clippers	Elmore Spencer, UNLV	C
26	Portland	Dave Johnson, Syracuse	G/F
27	Chicago	Byron Houston, Okla.St.	F

Second Round

	Team		Pos
28	Minnesota	Marlon Maxey, UTEP	F
29	d-New Jersey	P.J.Brown, La.Tech	C
30	Dallas	Sean Rooks, Arizona	F
31	e-Portland	Reggie Smith, TCU	G
32	Washington	Brent Price, Oklahoma	G
33	f-Chicago	Corey Williams, Okla.St.	G
34	g-Minnesota	Chris Smith, UConn	G
35	Charlotte	Tony Bennett, WI-Green Bay	G
36	h-LA Lakers	Duane Cooper, USC	G
37	Miami	Isiah Morris, Arkansas	F
38	Atlanta	Elmer Bennett, Notre Dame	G
39	i-Chicago	Litterial Green, Georgia	G
40	New Jersey	Steve Rogers, Alabama St.	G
41	Houston	Popeye Jones, Murray St.	F
42	j-Miami	Matt Geiger, Ga.Tech	C
43	k-Golden St	Pedrag Danilovic, Belgrade*	G
44	San Antonio	Henry Williams, NC-Charlotte	G
45	Seattle	Chris King, Wake Forest	F
46	l-Denver	Robert Werdann, St.John's	C
47	Boston	Darren Morningstar, Pitt	C
48	m-Phoenix	Brian Davis, Duke	F
49	Phoenix	Ron Ellis, La.Tech	F
50	Golden St	Matt Fish, NC-Wilmington	C
51	n-Minnesota	Tom Burroughs, Jacksonville	F
52	o-Chicago	Matt Steigenga, Mich.St.	F
53	p-Houston	Curtis Blair, Richmond	G
54	q-Sacramento	Brett Roberts, Morehead St.	F

*Yugoslavia.

Acquired Picks

First Round: a-from New Jersey; **b**-from Utah; **c**-from Cleveland.
Second Round: d-from Orlando thru Chicago; **e**-from Denver; **f**- from Sacramento; **g**-from Milwaukee; **h**-from Philadelphia thru Minnesota and Milwaukee; **i**-from Indiana; **j**-from LA Lakers; **k**-from LA Clippers; **l**-from Detroit; **m**-from New York; **n**-from Utah; **o**-from Portland; **p**-from Cleveland; **q**-from Chicago thru Portland.

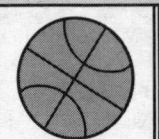

THE 1993 — INFORMATION PLEASE SPORTS ALMANAC

PRO BASKETBALL STATISTICS

THROUGH THE YEARS 1947-1992
CHAMPIONS • NBA LEADERS

SEC B

PAGE 317

The NBA Finals

Although the National Basketball Association traces its first championship back to the 1946-47 season, the league was then called the Basketball Association of America (BAA). It did not become the NBA until after the 1948-49 season when the BAA and the National Basketball League (NBL) agreed to merge.

In the chart below, the Eastern finalists (representing the NBA Eastern Division from 1947-70, and the NBA Eastern Conference since 1971) are listed in CAPITAL letters. Also, each NBA champion's wins and losses are noted in parentheses after the series score.

Multiple winners: Boston (16); Minneapolis-LA Lakers (11); Phi-SF-Golden St. Warriors and Syracuse Nats-Phi. 76ers (3); Chicago Bulls, Detroit and New York (2).

Year	Winner	Head Coach	Series	Loser	Head Coach
1947	PHILADELPHIA WARRIORS	Eddie Gottlieb	4-1 (WWWLW)	Chicago Stags	Harold Olsen
1948	Baltimore Bullets	Buddy Jeannette	4-2 (LWWWLW)	PHILA.WARRIORS	Eddie Gottlieb
1949	Minneapolis Lakers	John Kundla	4-2 (WWWLLW)	WASH.CAPITOLS	Red Auerbach
1950	Minneapolis Lakers	John Kundla	4-2 (WLWLW)	SYRACUSE	Al Cervi
1951	Rochester	Les Harrison	4-3 (WWWLLLW)	NEW YORK	Joe Lapchick
1952	Minneapolis Lakers	John Kundla	4-3 (LWWLWLW)	NEW YORK	Joe Lapchick
1953	Minneapolis Lakers	John Kundla	4-1 (LWWWW)	NEW YORK	Joe Lapchick
1954	Minneapolis Lakers	John Kundla	4-3 (WLWLWLW)	SYRACUSE	Al Cervi
1955	SYRACUSE	Al Cervi	4-3 (WWLLLWW)	Ft.Wayne Pistons	Charles Eckman
1956	PHILADELPHIA WARRIORS	George Senesky	4-1 (WLWWW)	Ft.Wayne Pistons	Charles Eckman
1957	BOSTON	Red Auerbach	4-3 (LWLWWLW)	St.Louis Hawks	Alex Hannum
1958	St.Louis Hawks	Alex Hannum	4-2 (WLWLWW)	BOSTON	Red Auerbach
1959	BOSTON	Red Auerbach	4-0	Minn.Lakers	John Kundla
1960	BOSTON	Red Auerbach	4-3 (WLWLWLW)	St.Louis Hawks	Ed Macauley
1961	BOSTON	Red Auerbach	4-1 (WLWWW)	St.Louis Hawks	Paul Seymour
1962	BOSTON	Red Auerbach	4-3 (WLLWLWW)	LA Lakers	Fred Schaus
1963	BOSTON	Red Auerbach	4-2 (WWLWLW)	LA Lakers	Fred Schaus
1964	BOSTON	Red Auerbach	4-1 (WWLWW)	SF Warriors	Alex Hannum
1965	BOSTON	Red Auerbach	4-1 (WWLWW)	LA Lakers	Fred Schaus
1966	BOSTON	Red Auerbach	4-3 (LWWWLLW)	LA Lakers	Fred Schaus
1967	PHILADELPHIA 76ERS	Alex Hannum	4-2 (WWLWLW)	SF Warriors	Bill Sharman
1968	BOSTON	Bill Russell	4-2 (WLWLWW)	LA Lakers	B.van Breda Kolff
1969	BOSTON	Bill Russell	4-3 (LLWWLWW)	LA Lakers	B.van Breda Kolff
1970	NEW YORK	Red Holzman	4-3 (WLWLWLW)	LA Lakers	Joe Mullaney
1971	Milwaukee	Larry Costello	4-0	BALT.BULLETS	Gene Shue
1972	LA Lakers	Bill Sharman	4-1 (LWWWW)	NEW YORK	Red Holzman
1973	NEW YORK	Red Holzman	4-1 (LWWWW)	LA Lakers	Bill Sharman
1974	BOSTON	Tommy Heinsohn	4-3 (WLWLWLW)	Milwaukee	Larry Costello
1975	Golden St.Warriors	Al Attles	4-0	WASH.BULLETS	K.C. Jones
1976	BOSTON	Tommy Heinsohn	4-2 (WWLLWW)	Phoenix	John MacLeod
1977	Portland	Jack Ramsay	4-2 (LLWWWW)	PHILA.76ERS	Gene Shue
1978	WASHINGTON BULLETS	Dick Motta	4-3 (LWLWLWW)	Seattle	Lenny Wilkens
1979	Seattle	Lenny Wilkens	4-1 (LWWWW)	WASH.BULLETS	Dick Motta
1980	LA Lakers	Paul Westhead	4-2 (WLWLWW)	PHILA.76ERS	Billy Cunningham
1981	BOSTON	Bill Fitch	4-2 (WLWLWW)	Houston	Del Harris
1982	LA Lakers	Pat Riley	4-2 (WLWLWLW)	PHILA 76ERS	Billy Cunningham
1983	PHILADELPHIA 76ERS	Billy Cunningham	4-0	LA Lakers	Pat Riley
1984	BOSTON	K.C. Jones	4-3 (LWWLWWLW)	LA Lakers	Pat Riley
1985	LA Lakers	Pat Riley	4-2 (LWWWLW)	BOSTON	K.C. Jones
1986	BOSTON	K.C. Jones	4-2 (WWLWLW)	Houston	Bill Fitch
1987	LA Lakers	Pat Riley	4-2 (WWLWLW)	BOSTON	K.C. Jones
1988	LA Lakers	Pat Riley	4-3 (LWWLLWW)	DETROIT PISTONS	Chuck Daly
1989	DETROIT PISTONS	Chuck Daly	4-0	LA Lakers	Pat Riley

NBA Finals (Cont.)

Year	Winner	Head Coach	Series	Loser	Head Coach
1990	DETROIT	Chuck Daly	4-1 (WLWWW)	Portland	Rick Adelman
1991	CHICAGO	Phil Jackson	4-1 (LWWWW)	LA Lakers	Mike Dunleavy
1992	CHICAGO	Phil Jackson	4-2 (WLWLWW)	Portland	Rick Adelman

Note: Four Finalists were led by player-coaches: **1948**—Buddy Jeannette (guard) of Baltimore; **1950**—Al Cervi (guard) of Syracuse; **1968**—Bill Russell (center) of Boston; **1969**—Bill Russell (center) of Boston.

Most Valuable Players

Selected by an 11-member media panel. Winners who did not play for the NBA champion are in **bold** type.
Multiple winners: Magic Johnson (3); Kareem Abdul-Jabbar, Larry Bird and Michael Jordan (2).

Year		Year		Year	
1969	**Jerry West**, LA Lakers, G	1977	Bill Walton, Portland, C	1985	K. Abdul-Jabbar, LA Lakers, C
1970	Willis Reed, New York, C	1978	Wes Unseld, Washington, C	1986	Larry Bird, Boston, F
1971	Lew Alcindor, Milwaukee, C	1979	Dennis Johnson, Seattle, G	1987	Magic Johnson, LA Lakers, G
1972	Wilt Chamberlain, LA Lakers, C	1980	Magic Johnson, LA Lakers, G/C	1988	James Worthy, LA Lakers, F
1973	Willis Reed, New York, C	1981	Cedric Maxwell, Boston, F	1989	Joe Dumars, Detroit, G
1974	John Havlicek, Boston, F	1982	Magic Johnson, LA Lakers, G	1990	Isiah Thomas, Detroit, G
1975	Rick Barry, Golden State, F	1983	Moses Malone, Philadelphia, C	1991	Michael Jordan, Chicago, G
1976	Jo Jo White, Boston, G	1984	Larry Bird, Boston, F	1992	Michael Jordan, Chicago, G

Note: Alcindor changed his name to Kareem Abdul-Jabbar after the 1970-71 season.

All-Time NBA Playoff Leaders

Through 1992 playoffs.

CAREER

Years listed indicate number of playoff appearances. Players active in 1992 in **bold** type.

Points

		Yrs	Gm	Pts	Avg
1	Kareem Abdul-Jabbar	18	237	5762	24.3
2	Jerry West	13	153	4457	29.1
3	**Larry Bird**	12	164	3897	23.8
4	John Havlicek	13	172	3776	22.0
5	**Magic Johnson**	12	186	3640	19.6
6	Elgin Baylor	12	134	3623	27.0
7	Wilt Chamberlain	13	160	3607	22.5
8	**Michael Jordan**	8	92	3184	34.6
9	Dennis Johnson	13	180	3116	17.3
10	**Kevin McHale**	12	165	3106	18.8
11	Julius Erving	11	141	3088	21.9
12	**James Worthy** (DNP)	8	138	2953	21.4
13	Sam Jones	12	154	2909	18.9
14	**Robert Parish**	13	174	2736	15.7
15	Bill Russell	13	165	2673	16.2
16	**Isiah Thomas**	9	111	2261	20.4
17	Bob Pettit	9	88	2240	25.5
18	Elvin Hayes	10	96	2194	22.9
19	George Mikan	9	91	2141	23.5
20	**Byron Scott**	9	137	2104	15.4

DNP (Did not play)—Worthy was injured and missed '92 Playoffs.

Scoring Average

Minimum of 25 games or 700 points.

		Yrs	Gm	Pts	Avg
1	**Michael Jordan**	8	92	3184	34.6
2	Jerry West	13	153	4457	29.1
3	**Karl Malone**	7	53	1464	27.6
4	Bernard King	4	25	679	27.2
5	Elgin Baylor	12	134	3623	27.0
	George Gervin	9	59	1592	27.0
7	**Hakeem Olajuwon** (DNP)	7	50	1326	26.5
8	**Dominique Wilkins** (DNP)	7	48	1255	26.1
9	Bob Pettit	9	88	2240	25.5
10	Rick Barry	7	74	1833	24.8
11	Alex English	10	68	1661	24.4
12	Kareem Abdul-Jabbar	18	237	5762	24.3
13	Paul Arizin	8	49	1186	24.2
14	**Larry Bird**	12	164	3897	23.8
15	George Mikan	9	91	2141	23.5
16	**Patrick Ewing**	5	38	870	22.9
	Bob Love	6	47	1076	22.9
	Elvin Hayes	10	96	2194	22.9
19	Wilt Chamberlain	13	160	3607	22.5
20	**Terry Cummings**	8	61	1369	22.4
	Charles Barkley (DNP)	6	51	1144	22.4

DNP (Did not play)—The teams of Barkley (Philadelphia), Olajuwon (Houston) and Wilkins (Atlanta) did not qualify for '92 Playoffs.

Field Goals

		Yrs	FG	Att	Pct
1	Kareem Abdul-Jabbar	18	2356	4422	.533
2	Jerry West	13	1622	3460	.469
3	**Larry Bird**	12	1458	3090	.472
4	John Havlicek	13	1451	3329	.436
5	Wilt Chamberlain	13	1425	2728	.522
6	Elgin Baylor	12	1388	3161	.439
7	Magic Johnson	12	1276	2513	.508
8	**James Worthy** (DNP)	8	1235	2243	.551
9	Julius Erving	11	1187	2441	.486
10	**Kevin McHale**	12	1172	2090	.561

DNP (Did not play)—Worthy was injured and missed '92 Playoffs.

Free Throws

		Yrs	FT	Att	Pct
1	Jerry West	13	1213	1507	.805
2	Kareem Abdul-Jabbar	18	1050	1419	.740
3	Magic Johnson	12	1040	1241	.838
4	**Larry Bird**	12	901	1012	.891
5	John Havlicek	13	874	1046	.836
6	Elgin Baylor	12	847	1101	.769
7	**Michael Jordan**	8	806	960	.840
8	Wilt Chamberlain	13	757	1627	.465
9	Dennis Johnson	13	756	943	.802
10	Dolph Schayes	15	755	918	.822

Assists

		Yrs	Gm	No	Avg
1	Magic Johnson	12	186	2320	12.5
2	**Larry Bird**	12	164	1062	6.5
3	Dennis Johnson	13	180	1006	5.6
4	**Isiah Thomas**	9	111	987	8.9
5	Jerry West	13	153	970	6.3

Rebounds

		Yrs	Gm	Reb	Avg
1	Bill Russell	13	165	4104	24.9
2	Wilt Chamberlain	13	160	3913	24.5
3	Kareem Abdul-Jabbar	18	237	2481	10.5
4	Wes Unseld	12	119	1777	14.9
5	Elgin Baylor	12	134	1725	12.9

Appearances

	No		No
Kareem Abdul-Jabbar	18	John Havlicek	13
Dolph Schayes	15	Dennis Johnson	13
Paul Silas	14	**Robert Parish**	13
Wilt Chamberlain	13	Bill Russell	13
Bob Cousy	13	Chet Walker	13
Hal Greer	13	Jerry West	13

Games Played

	No		No
K.Abdul-Jabbar	237	**Kevin McHale**	165
Magic Johnson	186	Bill Russell	165
Dennis Johnson	180	**Larry Bird**	164
Robert Parish	174	Paul Silas	163
John Havlicek	172	Wilt Chamberlain	160
Michael Cooper	168	Sam Jones	154

SINGLE GAME

Points

	Date	FG-FT—Pts
Michael Jordan, Chi.at Bos.*	4/20/86	22-19—63
Elgin Baylor, LA at Bos	4/14/62	22-17—61
Wilt Chamberlain, Phi.vs Syr	3/22/62	22-12—56
Michael Jordan, Chi.at Mia	4/29/92	20-16—56
Rick Barry, SF vs Phi	4/18/67	22-11—55
Michael Jordan, Chi.vs Cle.	5/1/88	24- 7—55

*Double overtime.

Field Goals

	Date	FG	Att
Wilt Chamberlain, Phi.vs Syr	3/14/60	24	42
Michael Jordan, Chi.vs Cle.	5/1/88	24	36
John Havlicek, Bos.vs Atl.	4/1/73	24	45

Seven players tied with 22 each.

Free Throws

	Date	FT	Att
Bob Cousy, Bos.vs Syr.*	3/21/53	30	32
Michael Jordan, Chi.vs NY	5/14/89	23	28
Michael Jordan, Chi.vs Cle.	5/5/89	22	27
Oscar Robertson, Cin.at Bos	4/10/63	21	22

Three players tied with 20 each.

*Four overtimes.

Others

3-Pt Field Goals

	Date	No
Chuck Person, Ind.at Bos	4/28/91	7

Eight players tied with 6 each.

Assists

	Date	No
Magic Johnson, LA Lakers vs Pho	5/15/84	24
John Stockton, Utah at LA Lakers	5/17/88	24
Magic Johnson, LA Lakers at Port	5/3/85	23

Rebounds

	Date	No
Wilt Chamberlain, Phi.vs Bos	4/5/67	41
Bill Russell, Bos.vs Phi	3/23/58	40
Bill Russell, Bos.vs St.L.	3/29/60	40
Bill Russell, Bos.vs LA*	4/18/62	40

*Overtime

Blocked Shots

	Date	No
Mark Eaton, Utah vs.Hou.	4/26/85	10
Hakeem Olajuwon, Hou.at LA Lakers	4/29/90	10

Steals

	Date	No
Rick Barry, GS vs Sea	4/14/75	8
Lionel Hollins, Port.at LA	5/8/77	8
Maurice Cheeks, Phi.vs NJ	4/11/79	8
Craig Hodges, Mil. at Phi	5/9/86	8

Appearances in NBA Finals

Standings of all NBA teams that have reached the NBA Finals since 1947.

App		Titles	Last Won
24	Minneapolis-LA Lakers	11	1988
19	Boston Celtics	16	1986
8	Syracuse Nats-Phila.76ers	3	1983
6	Phila-SF-Golden St.Warriors	3	1975
6	New York Knicks	2	1973
4	Ft.Wayne-Detroit Pistons	2	1990
4	St.Louis Hawks	1	1958
4	Baltimore-Washington Bullets	1	1978
3	Portland Trail Blazers	1	1977
2	Chicago Bulls	2	1992
2	Milwaukee Bucks	1	1971
2	Seattle SuperSonics	1	1979
2	Houston Rockets	0	—
1	Baltimore Bullets	1	1948
1	Chicago Stags	0	—
1	Phoenix Suns	0	—
1	Rochester Royals	1	1951
1	Washington Capitols	0	—

Change of address: The St.Louis Hawks now play in Atlanta and the Rochester Royals are now the Sacramento Kings.

Teams now defunct: Baltimnore Bullets (1947-55), Chicago Stags (1946-50) and Washington Capitols (1946-51).

SINGLE NBA FINALS

Points

Series		Year	Pts
4-Gm	Rick Barry, GS vs Wash	1975	118
5-Gm	Jerry West, LA vs Bos	1965	169
6-Gm	Rick Barry, SF vs Phi	1967	245
7-Gm	Elgin Baylor, LA vs Bos	1962	284

Field Goals

Series		Year	No
4-Gm	K.Abdul-Jabbar, Mil.vs Bal.	1971	46
5-Gm	Michael Jordan, Chi.vs LAL	1991	63
6-Gm	Rick Barry, SF vs Phi	1967	94
7-Gm	Elgin Baylor, LA vs Bos	1962	101

Assists

Series		Year	No
4-Gm	Bob Cousy, Bos.vs Mpls	1959	51
5-Gm	Magic Johnson, LAL vs Chi	1991	62
6-Gm	Magic Johnson, LAL vs Bos	1985	84
7-Gm	Magic Johnson, LA vs Bos	1984	95

Rebounds

Series		Year	No
4-Gm	Bill Russell, Bos.vs Mpls	1959	118
5-Gm	Bill Russell, Bos.vs St.L	1961	144
6-Gm	Wilt Chamberlain, Phi.vs SF	1967	171
7-Gm	Bill Russell, Bos.vs LA	1962	189

NBA Franchise Origins

Here is what the current 27 teams in the National Basketball Association have to show for the years they have put in as members of the National Basketball League (NBL), Basketball Association of America (BAA), the NBA, and the American Basketball Association (ABA). League titles are noted by year won.

Western Conference

	First Season		League Titles	Franchise Stops
Dallas Mavericks	1980-81	(NBA)	None	Dallas (1980—)
Denver Nuggets	1967-68	(ABA)	None	Denver (1967—)
Golden St. Warriors	1946-47	(BAA)	1 BAA (1947)	Philadelphia (1946-62)
			2 NBA (1956,75)	San Francisco (1962-71)
				Oakland (1971—)
Houston Rockets	1967-68	(NBA)	None	San Diego (1967-71)
				Houston (1971—)
LA Clippers	1970-71	(NBA)	None	Buffalo (1970-78)
				San Diego (1978-84)
				Los Angeles (1984—)
LA Lakers	1947-48	(NBL)	1 NBL (1947)	Minneapolis (1947-60)
			1 BAA (1949)	Los Angeles (1960-67)
			10 NBA (1950,52-54,72,	Inglewood,CA (1967—)
			80,82,85,87-88)	
Minnesota Timberwolves	1989-90	(NBA)	None	Minneapolis (1989—)
Phoenix Suns	1968-69	(NBA)	None	Phoenix (1968—)
Portland Trail Blazers	1970-71	(NBA)	1 NBA (1977)	Portland (1970—)
Sacramento Kings	1945-46	(NBL)	1 NBL (1946)	Rochester,NY (1945-58)
			1 NBA (1951)	Cincinnati (1958-72)
				KC-Omaha (1972-75)
				Kansas City (1975-85)
				Sacramento (1985—)
San Antonio Spurs	1967-68	(ABA)	None	Dallas (1967-73)
				San Antonio (1973—)
Seattle SuperSonics	1967-68	(NBA)	1 NBA (1979)	Seattle (1967—)
Utah Jazz	1974-75	(NBA)	None	New Orleans (1974-79)
				Salt Lake City (1979—)

Eastern Conference

	First Season		League Titles	Franchise Stops
Atlanta Hawks	1946-47	(NBL)	1 NBA (1958)	Tri-Cities (1946-51)
				Milwaukee (1951-55)
				St.Louis (1955-68)
				Atlanta (1968—)
Boston Celtics	1946-47	(BAA)	16 NBA (1957,59-66,68-69	Boston (1946—)
			74,76,81,84,86)	
Charlotte Hornets	1988-89	(NBA)	None	Charlotte (1988—)
Chicago Bulls	1966-67	(NBA)	2 NBA (1991-92)	Chicago (1966—)
Cleveland Cavaliers	1970-71	(NBA)	None	Cleveland (1970-74)
				Richfield, OH (1974—)
Detroit Pistons	1941-42	(NBL)	2 NBL (1944-45)	Ft.Wayne,IN (1941-57)
			2 NBA (1989-90)	Detroit (1957-78)
				Pontiac,MI (1978-88)
				Auburn Hills,MI (1988—)
Indiana Pacers	1967-68	(ABA)	3 ABA (1970,72-73)	Indianapolis (1967—)
Miami Heat	1988-89	(NBA)	None	Miami (1988—)
Milwaukee Bucks	1968-69	(NBA)	1 NBA (1971)	Milwaukee (1968—)
New Jersey Nets	1967-68	(ABA)	2 ABA (1974,76)	Paramus,NJ (1967-68)
				Commack,NY (1968-69)
				W.Hempstead,NY (1969-71)
				Uniondale,NY (1971-77)
				Piscataway,NJ (1977-81)
				E.Rutherford,NJ (1981—)
New York Knicks	1946-47	(BAA)	2 NBA (1970,73)	New York (1946—)
Orlando Magic	1989-90	(NBA)	None	Orlando,FL (1989—)
Philadelphia 76ers	1949-50	(NBA)	3 NBA (1955,67,83)	Syracuse,NY (1949-63)
				Philadelphia (1963—)
Washington Bullets	1961-62	(NBA)	1 NBA (1978)	Chicago (1961-63)
				Baltimore (1963-73)
				Landover,MD (1973—)

Note: The Tri-Cities Blackhawks represented Moline and Rock Island, Ill., and Davenport, Iowa.

The Growth of the NBA

Of the 11 franchises that comprised the **Basketball Association of America** (BAA) at the start of the 1946-47 season, only three remain—the Boston Celtics, New York Knickerbockers and Golden State Warriors (originally Philadelphia Warriors).

Just before the start of the 1948-49 season, four teams from the more established **National Basketball League** (NBL)—the Ft. Wayne Pistons (now Detroit), Indianapolis Jets, Minneapolis Lakers (now Los Angeles) and Rochester Royals (now Sacramento Kings)—joined the BAA.

A year later, the six remaining NBL franchises—Anderson (Ind.), Denver, Sheboygan (Wisc.), the Syracuse Nationals (now Philadelphia 76ers), Tri-Cities Blackhawks (now Atlanta Hawks) and Waterloo (Iowa)—joined along with the new Indianapolis Olympians and the BAA became the 17-team **National Basketball Association.**

The NBA was down to 10 teams by the 1950-51 season and slipped to eight by 1954-55 with Boston, New York, Philadelphia and Syracuse in the Eastern Division, and Ft.Wayne, Milwaukee (formerly Tri-Cities), Minneapolis and Rochester in the West.

By 1960, five of those surviving eight teams had moved to other cities but by the end of the decade the NBA was a 14-team league. It also had a rival, the **American Basketball Association**, which began play in 1967 with a red, white and blue ball, a three-point line and 11 teams.

The NBA added four expansion teams in the 1970s and absorbed four ABA clubs—the Denver Nuggets, Indiana Pacers, New York Nets and San Antonio Spurs—when the two leagues sued for peace. Five more teams were added in the 1980s, giving the NBA its current 27-team roster.

Expansion/Merger Timetable
For teams currently in NBA.

1948—Added NBL's Ft.Wayne Pistons (now Detroit), Minneapolis Lakers (now Los Angeles) and Rochester Royals (now Sacramento Kings); **1949**—Syracuse Nationals (now Philadelphia 76ers) and Tri-Cities Blackhawks (now Atlanta Hawks).

1961—Chicago Packers (now Washington Bullets); **1966**—Chicago Bulls; **1967**—San Diego Rockets (now Houston) and Seattle SuperSonics; **1968**—Milwaukee Bucks and Phoenix Suns.

1970—Buffalo Braves (now Los Angeles Clippers), Cleveland Cavaliers and Portland Trail Blazers; **1974**—New Orleans Jazz (now Utah); **1976**—added ABA's Denver Nuggets, Indiana Pacers, New York Nets (now New Jersey) and San Antonio Spurs.

1980—Dallas Mavericks; **1988**—Charlotte Hornets and Miami Heat; **1989**—Minnesota Timberwolves and Orlando Magic.

City and Nickname Changes

1951—Tri-Cities Blackhawks, who divided home games between Moline and Rock Island, Ill., and Davenport, Iowa, move to Milwaukee and become the Hawks; **1955**—Milwaukee Hawks move to St.Louis; **1957**—Ft.Wayne Pistons move to Detroit, while Rochester Royals move to Cincinnati.

1960—Minneapolis Lakers move to Los Angeles; **1962**—Chicago Packers renamed Zephyrs, while Philadelphia Warriors move to San Francisco; **1963**—Chicago Zephyrs move to Baltimore and become Bullets, while Syracuse Nationals move to Philadelphia and become 76ers; **1968**—St.Louis Hawks move to Atlanta.

1971—San Diego Rockets move to Houston, while San Francisco Warriors move to Oakland and become Golden State Warriors; **1972**—Cincinnati Royals move to Midwest, divide home games between Kansas City, Mo., and Omaha, Neb., and become Kings; **1973**—Baltimore Bullets move to Landover, Md., outside Washington and become Capital Bullets; **1974**—Capital Bullets renamed Washington Bullets; **1975**—KC-Omaha Kings settle in Kansas City; **1977**—New York Nets move from Uniondale, N.Y., to Piscataway, N.J. (later East Rutherford) and become New Jersey Nets; **1978**—Buffalo Braves move to San Diego and become Clippers.

1980—New Orleans Jazz move to Salt Lake City and become Utah Jazz; **1984**—San Diego Clippers move to Los Angeles; **1985**—Kansas City Kings move to Sacramento.

Defunct NBA Teams
Teams that once played in the BAA and NBA, but no longer exist.

Anderson (Ind.)—Packers (1949-50); **Baltimore**—Bullets (1947-55); **Chicago**—Stags (1946-50); **Cleveland**—Rebels (1946-47); **Denver**—Nuggets (1949-50); **Detroit**—Falcons (1946-47); **Indianapolis**—Jets (1948-49) and Olympians (1949-53). **Pittsburgh**—Ironmen (1946-47); **Providence**—Steamrollers (1946-49); **St.Louis**—Bombers (1946-50); **Sheboygan (Wisc.)**—Redskins (1949-50); **Toronto**—Huskies (1946-47); **Washington**—Capitols (1946-51); **Waterloo (Iowa)**—Hawks (1949-50).

ABA Teams (1967-76)

Anaheim—Amigos (1967-68, moved to LA); **Baltimore**—Claws (1975, never played); **Carolina**—Cougars (1969-74, moved to St. Louis); **Dallas**—Chaparrals (1967-73, called Texas Chaparrals in 1970-71, moved to San Antonio); **Denver**—Rockets (1967-76, renamed Nuggets in 1974-76); **Miami**—Floridians (1968-72, called simply Floridians from 1970-72).

Houston—Mavericks (1967-69, moved to North Carolina); **Indiana**—Pacers (1967-76); **Kentucky**—Colonels (1967-76); **Los Angeles**—Stars (1968-70, moved to Utah); **Memphis**—Pros (1970-75, renamed Tams in 1972 and Sounds in 1974, moved to Baltimore); **Minnesota**—Muskies (1967-68, moved to Miami) and Pipers (1968-69, moved back to Pittsburgh); **New Jersey**—Americans (1967-68, moved to New York).

New Orleans—Buccaneers (1967-70, moved to Memphis); **New York**—Nets (1968-76); **Oakland**—Oaks (1967-69, moved to Washington); **Pittsburgh**—Pipers (1967-68, moved to Minnesota, Pipers (1969-72, renamed Condors in 1970); **St. Louis**—Spirits of St. Louis (1974-76); **San Antonio**—Spurs (1973-76); **San Diego**—Conquistadors (1972-75, renamed Sails in 1975); **Utah**—Stars (1970-75); **Virginia**—Squires (1970-76); **Washington**—Caps (1969-70, moved to Virginia).

Annual NBA Leaders
Scoring

Championship decided by total points from 1947-69, and per game average since 1970.

Multiple winners: Wilt Chamberlain (7); Michael Jordan (6); George Gervin (4); Neil Johnston, Bob McAdoo and George Mikan (3); Kareem Abdul-Jabbar, Paul Arizin, Adrian Dantley and Bob Pettit (2).

Year		Gm	Pts	Avg	Year		Gm	Pts	Avg
1947	Joe Fulks, Phi	60	1389	23.2	1970	Jerry West, LA	74	2309	31.2
1948	Max Zaslofsky, Chi	48	1007	21.0	1971	Lew Alcindor, Mil	82	2596	31.7
1949	George Mikan, Mpls	60	1698	28.3	1972	Kareem Abdul-Jabbar, Mil	81	2822	34.8
					1973	Nate Archibald, KC-Oma	80	2719	34.0
1950	George Mikan, Mpls	68	1865	27.4	1974	Bob McAdoo, Buf	74	2261	30.6
1951	George Mikan, Mpls	68	1932	28.4	1975	Bob McAdoo, Buf	82	2831	34.5
1952	Paul Arizin, Phi	66	1674	25.4	1976	Bob McAdoo, Buf	78	2427	31.1
1953	Neil Johnston, Phi	70	1564	22.3	1977	Pete Maravich, NO	73	2273	31.1
1954	Neil Johnston, Phi	72	1759	24.4	1978	George Gervin, SA	82	2232	27.2
1955	Neil Johnston, Phi	72	1631	22.7	1979	George Gervin, SA	80	2365	29.6
1956	Bob Pettit, St.L	72	1849	25.7					
1957	Paul Arizin, Phi	71	1817	25.6	1980	George Gervin, SA	78	2585	33.1
1958	George Yardley, Det	72	2001	27.8	1981	Adrian Dantley, Utah	80	2452	30.7
1959	Bob Pettit, St.L	72	2105	29.2	1982	George Gervin, SA	79	2551	32.3
					1983	Alex English, Den.	82	2326	28.4
1960	Wilt Chamberlain, Phi	72	2707	37.6	1984	Adrian Dantley, Utah	79	2418	30.6
1961	Wilt Chamberlain, Phi	79	3033	38.4	1985	Bernard King, NY	55	1809	32.9
1962	Wilt Chamberlain, Phi	80	4029	50.4	1986	Dominique Wilkins, Atl	78	2366	30.3
1963	Wilt Chamberlain, SF	80	3586	44.8	1987	Michael Jordan, Chi	82	3041	37.1
1964	Wilt Chamberlain, SF	80	2948	36.9	1988	Michael Jordan, Chi	82	2868	35.0
1965	Wilt Chamberlain, SF-Phi	73	2534	34.7	1989	Michael Jordan, Chi	81	2633	32.5
1966	Wilt Chamberlain, Phi	79	2649	33.5					
1967	Rick Barry, SF	78	2775	35.6	1990	Michael Jordan, Chi	82	2753	33.6
1968	Dave Bing, Det	79	2142	27.1	1991	Michael Jordan, Chi	82	2580	31.5
1969	Elvin Hayes, SD	82	2327	28.4	1992	Michael Jordan, Chi	80	2404	30.1

Note: Alcindor changed his name to Kareem Abdul-Jabbar after the 1970-71 season.

Assists

NBA assist championship was decided by Total Assists from 1952-69 and Per Game Average since 1970.

Multiple winners: Bob Cousy (8); Oscar Robertson (6); John Stockton (5); Magic Johnson and Kevin Porter (4); Andy Phillip and Guy Rodgers (2).

Year		Gm	No	Avg	Year		Gm	No	Avg
1947	Ernie Calverley, Prov	59	202	3.4	1970	Lenny Wilkens, Sea	75	683	9.1
1948	Howie Dallmar, Phi	48	120	2.5	1971	Norm Van Lier, Chi	82	832	10.1
1949	Bob Davies, Roch	60	321	5.4	1972	Jerry West, LA	77	747	9.7
					1973	Nate Archibald, KC-Oma	80	910	11.4
1950	Dick McGuire, NY	68	386	5.7	1974	Ernie DiGregorio, Buf	81	663	8.2
1951	Andy Phillip, Phi	66	414	6.3	1975	Kevin Porter, Wash	81	650	8.0
1952	Andy Phillip, Phi	66	539	8.2	1976	Slick Watts, Sea	82	661	8.1
1953	Bob Cousy, Bos	71	547	7.7	1977	Don Buse, Ind	81	685	8.5
1954	Bob Cousy, Bos	72	518	7.2	1978	Kevin Porter, Det-NJ	82	837	10.2
1955	Bob Cousy, Bos	71	557	7.8	1979	Kevin Porter, Det	82	1099	13.4
1956	Bob Cousy, Bos	72	642	8.9					
1957	Bob Cousy, Bos	64	478	7.5	1980	Micheal Ray Richardson, NY	82	832	10.1
1958	Bob Cousy, Bos	65	463	7.1	1981	Kevin Porter, Wash	81	734	9.1
1959	Bob Cousy, Bos	65	557	8.6	1982	Johnny Moore, SA	79	762	9.6
					1983	Magic Johnson, LA	79	829	10.5
1960	Bob Cousy, Bos	75	715	9.5	1984	Magic Johnson, LA	67	875	13.1
1961	Oscar Robertson, Cin	71	690	9.7	1985	Isiah Thomas, Det	81	1123	13.9
1962	Oscar Robertson, Cin	79	899	11.4	1986	Magic Johnson, LA Lakers	72	907	12.6
1963	Guy Rodgers, SF	79	825	10.4	1987	Magic Johnson, LA Lakers	80	977	12.2
1964	Oscar Robertson, Cin	79	868	11.0	1988	John Stockton, Utah	82	1128	13.8
1965	Oscar Robertson, Cin	75	861	11.5	1989	John Stockton, Utah	82	1118	13.6
1966	Oscar Robertson, Cin	76	847	11.1					
1967	Guy Rodgers, Chi	81	908	11.2	1990	John Stockton, Utah	78	1134	14.5
1968	Wilt Chamberlain, Phi	82	702	8.6	1991	John Stockton, Utah	82	1164	14.2
1969	Oscar Robertson, Cin	79	772	9.8	1992	John Stockton, Utah	82	1126	13.7

Rebounds

Championship was decided by total rebounds from 1951-69 and per game average since 1970.

Multiple winners: Wilt Chamberlain (11); Moses Malone (6); Bill Russell (4); Elvin Hayes and Hakeem Olajuwon (2).

Year		Gm	No	Avg	Year		Gm	No	Avg
1951	Dolph Schayes, Syr	66	1080	16.4	1973	Wilt Chamberlain, LA	82	1526	18.6
1952	Larry Foust, Ft.Wayne	66	880	13.3	1974	Elvin Hayes, Cap*	81	1463	18.1
	& Mel Hutchins, Mil	66	880	13.3	1975	Wes Unseld, Wash	73	1077	14.8
1953	George Mikan, Mpls.	70	1007	14.4	1976	Kareem Abdul-Jabbar. LA	82	1383	16.9
1954	Harry Gallatin, NY	72	1098	15.3	1977	Bill Walton, Port	65	934	14.4
1955	Neil Johnston, Phi	72	1085	15.1	1978	Len Robinson, NO.	82	1288	15.7
1956	Bob Pettit, St.L	72	1164	16.2	1979	Moses Malone, Hou	82	1444	17.6
1957	Maurice Stokes, Roch	72	1256	17.4					
1958	Bill Russell, Bos.	69	1564	22.7	1980	Swen Nater, SD	81	1216	15.0
1959	Bill Russell, Bos.	70	1612	23.0	1981	Moses Malone, Hou	80	1180	14.8
					1982	Moses Malone, Hou	81	1188	14.7
1960	Wilt Chamberlain, Phi.	72	1941	27.0	1983	Moses Malone, Phi	78	1194	15.3
1961	Wilt Chamberlain, Phi.	79	2149	27.2	1984	Moses Malone, Phi	71	950	13.4
1962	Wilt Chamberlain, Phi.	80	2052	25.7	1985	Moses Malone, Phi	79	1031	13.1
1963	Wilt Chamberlain, SF	80	1946	24.3	1986	Bill Laimbeer, Det	82	1075	13.1
1964	Bill Russell, Bos.	78	1930	24.7	1987	Charles Barkley, Phi	68	994	14.6
1965	Bill Russell, Bos.	78	1878	24.1	1988	Michael Cage, LA Clippers.	72	938	13.0
1966	Wilt Chamberlain, Phi.	79	1943	24.6	1989	Hakeem Olajuwon, Hou	82	1105	13.5
1967	Wilt Chamberlain, Phi.	81	1957	24.2					
1968	Wilt Chamberlain, Phi.	82	1952	23.8	1990	Hakeem Olajuwon, Hou	82	1149	14.0
1969	Wilt Chamberlain, LA	81	1712	21.1	1991	David Robinson, SA.	82	1063	13.0
					1992	Dennis Rodman, Det.	82	1530	18.7
1970	Elvin Hayes, SD	82	1386	16.9					
1971	Wilt Chamberlain, LA	82	1493	18.2					
1972	Wilt Chamberlain, LA	82	1572	19.2					

*The Baltimore Bullets moved to Landover,MD for the 1973-74 season and became first the Capital Bullets, then the Washington Bullets in 1974-75.

All-Time NBA Leaders

Through the 1991-92 regular season.

CAREER

Players active in 1991-92 in **bold** type.

Points

		Yrs	Gm	Pts	Avg
1	Kareem Abdul-Jabbar	20	1560	38,387	24.6
2	Wilt Chamberlain	14	1045	31,419	30.1
3	Elvin Hayes	16	1303	27,313	21.0
4	**Moses Malone**	16	1246	27,016	21.7
5	Oscar Robertson	14	1040	26,710	25.7
6	John Havlicek	16	1270	26,395	20.8
7	Alex English	15	1193	25,613	21.5
8	Jerry West	14	932	25,192	27.0
9	Adrian Dantley	15	955	23,177	24.3
10	Elgin Baylor	14	846	23,149	27.4
11	**Larry Bird**	13	897	21,791	24.3
12	Hal Greer	15	1122	21,586	19.2
13	Walt Bellamy	14	1043	20,941	20.1
14	Bob Pettit	11	792	20,880	26.4
15	George Gervin	10	791	20,708	26.2
16	**Robert Parish**	16	1260	20,634	16.4
17	**Dominique Wilkins**	10	762	19,975	26.2
18	**Walter Davis**	15	1033	19,521	18.9
19	Bernard King	13	842	19,432	23.1
20	Dolph Schayes	16	1059	19,249	18.2
21	Bob Lanier	14	959	19,248	20.1
22	Gail Goodrich	14	1031	19,181	18.6
23	Reggie Theus	13	1026	19,015	18.5
24	**Michael Jordan**	8	589	19,000	32.3
25	Chet Walker	13	1032	18,831	18.2
26	Bob McAdoo	14	852	18,787	22.1
27	Rick Barry	10	794	18,395	23.2
28	Julius Erving	11	836	18,364	22.0
29	Dave Bing	12	901	18,327	20.3
30	World B.Free	13	886	17,955	20.3

Scoring Average

Minimum of 400 games or 10,000 points.

		Yrs	Gm	Pts	Avg
1	**Michael Jordan**	8	589	19,000	32.3
2	Wilt Chamberlain	14	1045	31,419	30.1
3	Elgin Baylor	14	846	23,149	27.4
4	Jerry West	14	932	25,192	27.0
5	Bob Pettit	11	792	20,880	26.4
6	**Dominique Wilkins**	10	762	19,975	26.2
	George Gervin	10	791	20,708	26.2
8	**Karl Malone**	7	570	14,770	25.9
9	Oscar Robertson	14	1040	26,710	25.7
10	Kareem Abdul-Jabbar	20	1560	38,387	24.6
11	**Larry Bird**	13	897	21,791	24.3
	Adrian Dantley	15	955	23,177	24.3
13	Pete Maravich	10	658	15,948	24.2
14	**Patrick Ewing**	7	520	12,293	23.6
15	**Charles Barkley**	8	610	14,184	23.3
16	Rick Barry	10	794	18,395	23.2
17	Bernard King	13	842	19,432	23.1
18	**Hakeem Olajuwon**	8	594	13,575	22.9
19	Paul Arizin	10	713	16,266	22.8
20	George Mikan	9	520	11,764	22.6
21	**Chris Mullin**	7	520	11,536	22.2
22	David Thompson	8	509	11,264	22.1
	Bob McAdoo	14	852	18,787	22.1
24	Julius Erving	11	836	18,364	22.0
25	**Moses Malone**	16	1246	27,016	21.7
26	Alex English	15	1193	25,613	21.5
27	**Terry Cummings**	10	768	16,364	21.3
28	**Mark Aguirre**	11	833	17,542	21.1
29	Elvin Hayes	16	1303	27,313	21.0
	Clyde Drexler	9	709	14,857	21.0

All-Time NBA Leaders (Cont.)

NBA-ABA Top 20
Points

All-Time combined regular season scoring leaders, including ABA service (1968-76). NBA players with ABA experience are listed in CAPITAL letters. Players active during 1991-92 are in **bold** type.

		Yrs	Gm	Pts	Avg
1	Kareem Abdul-Jabbar...	20	1560	38,387	24.6
2	Wilt Chamberlain.......	14	1045	31,419	30.1
3	JULIUS ERVING	16	1243	30,026	24.2
4	**MOSES MALONE**	18	1372	29,187	21.3
5	DAN ISSEL	15	1218	27,482	22.6
6	Elvin Hayes	16	1303	27,313	21.0
7	Oscar Robertson	14	1040	26,710	25.7
8	GEORGE GERVIN	14	1060	26,595	25.1
9	John Havlicek..........	16	1270	26,395	20.8
10	Alex English	15	1193	25,613	21.5
11	RICK BARRY	14	1020	25,279	24.8
12	Jerry West	14	932	25,192	27.0
13	ARTIS GILMORE	17	1329	24,941	18.8
14	Adrian Dantley........	15	955	23,177	24.3
15	Elgin Baylor...........	14	846	23,149	27.4
16	**Larry Bird**.........	13	897	21,791	24.3
17	Hal Greer............	15	1122	21,586	19.2
18	Walt Bellamy	14	1043	20,941	20.1
19	Bob Pettit...........	11	792	20,880	26.4
20	**Robert Parish**	16	1260	20,634	16.4

ABA Totals: BARRY (4 yrs, 226 gm, 6884 pts, 30.5 avg); ERVING (5 yrs, 407 gm, 11,662 pts, 28.7 avg); GERVIN (4 yrs, 269 gm, 5887 pts, 21.9 avg); GILMORE (5 yrs, 420 gm, 9362 pts, 22.3 avg); ISSEL (6 yrs, 500 gm, 12,823 pts, 25.6 avg); MALONE (2 yrs, 126 gm, 2171 pts, 17.2 avg).

Field Goals

		Yrs	FG	Att	Pct
1	Kareem Abdul-Jabbar.....	20	15,837	28,307	.559
2	Wilt Chamberlain.........	14	12,681	23,497	.540
3	Elvin Hayes	16	10,976	24,272	.452
4	Alex English	15	10,659	21,036	.507
5	John Havlicek..........	16	10,513	23,930	.439
6	Oscar Robertson	14	9,508	19,620	.485
7	**Moses Malone**	16	9,307	18,916	.492
8	Jerry West............	14	9,016	19,032	.474
9	Elgin Baylor...........	14	8,693	20,171	.431
10	**Larry Bird**.............	13	8,591	17,334	.496

Note: If field goals made in the ABA are included, consider these NBA-ABA totals: Julius Erving (11,818), Dan Issel (10,431), George Gervin (10,368), Moses Malone (10,149), Rick Barry (9,695) and Artis Gilmore (9,403).

Free Throws

		Yrs	FT	Att	Pct
1	**Moses Malone**	16	8395	10,910	.769
2	Oscar Robertson	14	7694	9,185	.838
3	Jerry West	14	7160	8,801	.814
4	Dolph Schayes	16	6979	8,273	.844
5	Adrian Dantley.........	15	6832	8,351	.818
6	Kareem Abdul-Jabbar...	20	6712	9,304	.721
7	Bob Pettit............	11	6182	8,119	.761
8	Wilt Chamberlain.......	14	6057	11,862	.511
9	Elgin Baylor...........	14	5763	7,391	.780
10	Lenny Wilkens	15	5394	6,973	.774

Note: If free throws made in the ABA are included, consider these totals: Moses Malone (8,882), Dan Issel (6,591), Julius Erving (6,256) and Artis Gilmore (6,132).

Assists

		Yrs	Gm	Ast	Avg
1	Magic Johnson................	12	874	9921	11.4
2	Oscar Robertson	14	1040	9887	9.5
3	**Isiah Thomas**	11	842	7991	9.5
4	**John Stockton**	8	652	7365	11.3
5	**Maurice Cheeks**	14	1066	7285	6.8
6	Lenny Wilkens	15	1077	7211	6.7
7	Bob Cousy	14	924	6955	7.5
8	Guy Rodgers	12	892	6917	7.8
9	Nate Archibald	13	876	6476	7.4
10	John Lucas	14	928	6454	7.0

Rebounds

		Yrs	Gm	Reb	Avg
1	Wilt Chamberlain.............	14	1045	23,924	22.9
2	Bill Russell	13	963	21,620	22.5
3	Kareem Abdul-Jabbar.........	20	1560	17,440	11.2
4	Elvin Hayes	16	1303	16,279	12.5
5	**Moses Malone**	16	1246	15,894	12.8
6	Nate Thurmond	14	964	14,464	15.0
7	Walt Bellamy	14	1043	14,241	13.7
8	Wes Unseld	13	984	13,769	14.0
9	Jerry Lucas	11	829	12,942	15.6
10	Bob Pettit	11	792	12,849	16.2

Note: If rebounds pulled down in the ABA are included, consider the following totals: Moses Malone (17,516) and Artis Gilmore (16,330).

Years Played

		Yrs	Career	Gm
1	Kareem Abdul-Jabbar...........	20	1970-89	1560
2	Elvin Hayes	16	1969-84	1303
	John Havlicek...............	16	1963-78	1270
	Robert Parish	16	1977—	1260
	Paul Silas	16	1965-80	1254
	Moses Malone..............	16	1977—	1246
	Dolph Schayes	16	1949-64	1059

Note: If ABA records are included, consider the following year totals: Moses Malone (18, 1975—); Artis Gilmore (17, 1972-88); Caldwell Jones (17, 1974-90); Julius Erving (16, 1972-87); Dan Issel (15, 1971-85); Billy Paultz (15, 1971-85).

Games Played

		Yrs	Career	No
1	Kareem Abdul-Jabbar...........	20	1970-89	1560
2	Elvin Hayes...................	16	1969-84	1303
3	John Havlicek	16	1963-78	1270
4	**Robert Parish**	16	1977—	1260
5	Paul Silas	16	1965-80	1254

Note: If ABA records are included, consider the following game totals: Moses Malone (1,372); Artis Gilmore (1,329); Caldwell Jones (1,299); Julius Erving (1,243); Dan Issel (1,218); Billy Paultz (1,124).

Personal Fouls

		Yrs	Gm	Fouls	DQ
1	Kareem Abdul-Jabbar........	20	1560	4657	48
2	Elvin Hayes	16	1303	4193	53
3	Jack Sikma	14	1107	3879	80
4	Hal Greer	15	1122	3855	72
5	**Robert Parish**	16	1260	3800	80

Note: If ABA records are included, consider the following personal foul totals: Artis Gilmore (4,529) and Caldwell Jones (4,436).

Disqualifications

		Yrs	Gm	No
1	Vern Mikkelsen	10	699	127
2	Walter Dukes	8	553	121
3	Charlie Share	8	555	105
4	Paul Arizin	10	713	101
5	Darryl Dawkins	14	726	100

SINGLE SEASON

Scoring Average

		Season	Avg
1	Wilt Chamberlain, Phi	1961-62	50.4
2	Wilt Chamberlain, SF	1962-63	44.8
3	Wilt Chamberlain, Phi	1960-61	38.4
4	Elgin Baylor, LA	1961-62	38.3
5	Wilt Chamberlain, Phi	1959-60	37.6
6	Michael Jordan, Chi	1986-87	37.1
7	Wilt Chamberlain, SF	1963-64	36.9
8	Rick Barry, SF	1966-67	35.6
9	Michael Jordan, Chi	1987-88	35.0
10	Elgin Baylor, LA	1960-61	34.8
	Kareem Abdul-Jabbar, Mil	1971-72	34.8

Field Goals

		Season	Pct
1	Wilt Chamberlain, LA	1972-73	.727
2	Wilt Chamberlain, SF	1966-67	.683
3	Artis Gilmore, Chi	1980-81	.670
4	Artis Gilmore, Chi	1981-82	.652
5	Wilt Chamberlain, LA	1971-72	.649

Free Throws

		Season	Pct
1	Calvin Murphy, Hou	1980-81	.958
2	Mark Price, Cle	1991-92	.947
	Rick Barry, Hou	1978-79	.947
3	Ernie DiGregorio, Buf	1976-77	.945
5	Ricky Sobers, Chi	1980-81	.935
	Rick Barry, Hou	1979-80	.935

3-Pt Field Goals

		Season	Pct
1	Jon Sundvold, Mia	1988-89	.522
2	Steve Kerr, Cle	1989-90	.507
3	Craig Hodges, Mil-Pho	1987-88	.491
4	Mark Price, Cle	1987-88	.486
5	Kiki Vandeweghe, Port	1986-87	.481
	Craig Hodges, Chi	1989-90	.481

Assists

		Season	Avg
1	John Stockton, Utah	1989-90	14.5
2	John Stockton, Utah	1990-91	14.2
3	Isiah Thomas, Det	1984-85	13.9
4	John Stockton, Utah	1987-88	13.8
5	John Stockton, Utah	1991-92	13.7
6	John Stockton, Utah	1988-89	13.6
7	Kevin Porter, Det	1978-79	13.4
8	Magic Johnson, LA Lakers	1983-84	13.1
9	Magic Johnson, LA Lakers	1988-89	12.8
10	Magic Johnson, LA Lakers	1984-85	12.6

Rebounds

		Season	Avg
1	Wilt Chamberlain, Phi	1960-61	27.2
2	Wilt Chamberlain, Phi	1959-60	27.0
3	Wilt Chamberlain, Phi	1961-62	25.7
4	Bill Russell, Bos	1963-64	24.7
5	Wilt Chamberlain, Phi	1965-66	24.6

Blocked Shots

		Season	Avg
1	Mark Eaton, Utah	1984-85	5.56
2	Manute Bol, Wash	1985-86	4.96
3	Elmore Smith, LA	1973-74	4.85
4	Mark Eaton, Utah	1985-86	4.61
5	Hakeem Olajuwon, Hou	1989-90	4.59

Steals

		Season	Avg
1	Alvin Robertson, SA	1985-86	3.67
2	Don Buse, Ind	1976-77	3.47
3	Magic Johnson, LA Lakers	1980-81	3.43
4	Micheal Ray Richardson, NY	1979-80	3.23
5	Alvin Robertson, SA	1986-87	3.21

SINGLE GAME

Points

	Date	Pts
Wilt Chamberlain, Phi.vs NY	3/2/62	100
Wilt Chamberlain, Phi.vs LA*	12/8/61	78
Wilt Chamberlain, Phi.vs Chi	1/13/62	73
Wilt Chamberlain, SF at NY	11/16/62	73
David Thompson, Den.at Det	4/9/78	73
Wilt Chamberlain, SF at LA	11/3/62	72
Elgin Baylor, LA at NY	11/15/60	71
Wilt Chamberlain, SF at Syr	3/10/63	70

*Triple overtime.
Note: Chamberlain's 100-point game vs New York was played at Hershey, PA.

Field Goals

	Date	FG	Att
Wilt Chamberlain, Phi.vs NY	3/2/62	36	63
Wilt Chamberlain, Phi.vs LA*	12/8/61	31	62
Wilt Chamberlain, Phi.at Chi	12/16/67	30	40
Rick Barry, GS vs Port	2/26/74	30	45
Four players tied with 29 each.			

*Triple overtime.

Free Throws

	Date	FT	Att
Wilt Chamberlain, Phi.vs NY	3/2/62	28	32
Adrian Dantley, Utah vs Hou	1/4/84	28	29
Adrian Dantley, Utah vs Den	11/25/83	27	31
Adrian Dantley, Utah vs Dal	10/31/80	26	29
Michael Jordan, Chi.vs NJ	2/26/87	26	27

3-Pt Field Goals

	Date	No
Dale Ellis, Sea.vs LA Clippers	4/20/90	9
Michael Adams, Den.at LA Clippers	4/12/91	9
Five players tied with 8 each.		

Assists

	Date	No
Scott Skiles, Orl.vs Den	12/30/90	30
Kevin Porter, NJ vs Hou	2/24/78	29
Three players tied with 28 each.		

Rebounds

	Date	No
Wilt Chamberlain, Phi.vs Bos	11/24/60	55
Bill Russell, Bos.vs Syr	2/5/60	51
Bill Russell, Bos.vs Phi	11/16/57	49
Bill Russell, Bos.vs Det	3/11/65	49

Blocked Shots

	Date	No
Elmore Smith, LA vs Port	10/28/73	17
Manute Bol, Wash.vs Atl	1/25/86	15
Manute Bol, Wash.vs Ind	2/26/87	15
Four players tied with 14 each.		

Steals

	Date	No
Larry Kenon, San Antonio vs KC	2/9/80	11

10 players tied with 10 steals each, including Alvin Robertson (4 times).

Number One Draft Choices

Overall first choices in the NBA Draft since the abolition of the Territorial Draft in 1966. Players who became Rookie of the Year are in **bold** type.

Year	Overall 1st Pick	Year	Overall 1st Pick
1966	New York........Cazzie Russell, Michigan	1980	Golden St........Joe Barry Carroll, Purdue
1967	Detroit........Jimmy Walker, Providence	1981	Dallas........Mark Aguirre, DePaul
1968	Houston........Elvin Hayes, Houston	1982	LA Lakers........James Worthy, N.Carolina
1969	Milwaukee........**Lew Alcindor,** UCLA	1983	Houston........**Ralph Sampson,** Virginia
		1984	Houston........Akeem Olajuwon, Houston
1970	Detroit........Bob Lanier, St.Bonaventure	1985	New York........**Patrick Ewing,** Georgetown
1971	Cleveland........Austin Carr, Notre Dame	1986	Cleveland........Brad Daugherty, N.Carolina
1972	Portland........LaRue Martin, Loyola-Chicago	1987	San Antonio........**David Robinson,** Navy
1973	Philadelphia........Doug Collins, Illinois St.	1988	LA Clippers........Danny Manning, Kansas
1974	Portland........Bill Walton, UCLA	1989	Sacramento........Pervis Ellison, Louisville
1975	Atlanta........David Thompson, N.C.State		
1976	Houston........John Lucas, Maryland	1990	New Jersey........**Derrick Coleman,** Syracuse
1977	Milwaukee........Kent Benson, Indiana	1991	Charlotte........**Larry Johnson,** UNLV
1978	Portland........Mychal Thompson, Minnesota	1992	Orlando........Shaquille O'Neal, LSU
1979	LA Lakers........Magic Johnson, Michigan St.		

Notes: Alcindor changed his name to Kareem Abdul-Jabbar after the 1970-71 season; Olajuwon changed his first name to Hakeem in 1991; and Robinson joined NBA for 1989-90 season after fulfilling military obligation.

NBA All-Star Game

The NBA staged its first All-Star Game before 10,094 at Boston Garden on March 2, 1951. From that year on, the All-Star game has matched the best players in the East against the best in the West. Winning coaches are listed first.
　　Series: East leads, 27-15.
　　Multiple MVP winners: Bob Pettit (4); Oscar Roberston (3); Bob Cousy, Julius Erving, Magic Johnson and Isiah Thomas (2).

Year		Host	Coaches	Most Valuable Player
1951	East 111, West 94	Boston	Joe Lapchick, John Kundla	Ed Macauley, Boston
1952	East 108, West 91	Boston	Al Cervi, John Kundla	Paul Arizin, Philadelphia
1953	West 79, East 75	Ft.Wayne	John Kundla, Joe Lapchick	George Mikan, Minneapolis
1954	East 98, West 93 (OT)	New York	Joe Lapchick, John Kundla	Bob Cousy, Boston
1955	East 100, West 91	New York	Al Cervi, Charley Eckman	Bill Sharman, Boston
1956	West 108, East 94	Rochester	Charley Eckman, George Senesky	Bob Pettit, St.Louis
1957	East 109, West 97	Boston	Red Auerbach, Bobby Wanzer	Bob Cousy, Boston
1958	East 130, West 118	St.Louis	Red Auerbach, Alex Hannum	Bob Pettit, St.Louis
1959	West 124, East 108	Detroit	Ed Macauley, Red Auerbach	Bob Pettit, St.Louis & Elgin Baylor, Minneapolis
1960	East 125, West 115	Philadelphia	Red Auerbach, Ed Macauley	Wilt Chamberlain, Philadelphia
1961	West 153, East 131	Syracuse	Paul Seymour, Red Auerbach	Oscar Robertson, Cincinnati
1962	West 150, East 130	St.Louis	Fred Schaus, Red Auerbach	Bob Pettit, St.Louis
1963	East 115, West 108	Los Angeles	Red Auerbach, Fred Schaus	Bill Russell, Boston
1964	East 111, West 107	Boston	Red Auerbach, Fred Schaus	Oscar Robertson, Cincinnati
1965	East 124, West 123	St.Louis	Red Auerbach, Alex Hannum	Jerry Lucas, Cincinnati
1966	East 137, West 94	Cincinnati	Red Auerbach, Fred Schaus	Adrian Smith, Cincinnati
1967	West 135, East 120	San Francisco	Fred Schaus, Red Auerbach	Rick Barry, San Francisco
1968	East 144, West 124	New York	Alex Hannum, Bill Sharman	Hal Greer, Philadelphia
1969	East 123, West 112	Baltimore	Gene Shue, Richie Guerin	Oscar Robertson, Cincinnati
1970	East 142, West 135	Philadelphia	Red Holzman, Richie Guerin	Willis Reed, New York
1971	West 108, East 107	San Diego	Larry Costello, Red Holzman	Lenny Wilkens, Seattle
1972	West 112, East 110	Los Angeles	Bill Sharman, Tom Heinsohn	Jerry West, Los Angeles
1973	East 104, West 84	Chicago	Tom Heinsohn, Bill Sharman	Dave Cowens, Boston
1974	West 134, East 123	Seattle	Larry Costello, Tom Heinsohn	Bob Lanier, Detroit
1975	East 108, West 102	Phoenix	K.C.Jones, Al Attles	Walt Frazier, New York
1976	East 123, West 109	Philadelphia	Tom Heinsohn, Al Attles	Dave Bing, Washington
1977	West 125, East 124	Milwaukee	Larry Brown, Gene Shue	Julius Erving, Philadelphia
1978	East 133, West 125	Atlanta	Billy Cunningham, Jack Ramsay	Randy Smith, Buffalo
1979	West 134, East 129	Detroit	Lenny Wilkens, Dick Motta	David Thompson, Denver
1980	East 144, West 135 (OT)	Washington	Billy Cunningham, Len Wilkens	George Gervin, San Antonio
1981	East 123, West 120	Cleveland	Billy Cunningham, John MacLeod	Nate Archibald, Boston
1982	East 120, West 118	New Jersey	Bill Fitch, Pat Riley	Larry Bird, Boston
1983	East 132, West 123	Los Angeles	Billy Cunningham, Pat Riley	Julius Erving, Philadelphia

Year		Host	Coaches	Most Valuable Player
1984	East 154, West 145 (OT)	Denver	K.C.Jones, Frank Layden	Isiah Thomas, Detroit
1985	West 140, East 129	Indiana	Pat Riley, K.C.Jones	Ralph Sampson, Houston
1986	East 139, West 132	Dallas	K.C.Jones, Pat Riley	Isiah Thomas, Detroit
1987	West 154, East 149 (OT)	Seattle	Pat Riley, K.C.Jones	Tom Chambers, Seattle
1988	East 138, West 133	Chicago	Mike Fratello, Pat Riley	Michael Jordan, Chicago
1989	West 143, East 134	Houston	Pat Riley, Lenny Wilkens	Karl Malone, Utah
1990	East 130, West 113	Miami	Chuck Daly, Pat Riley	Magic Johnson, LA Lakers
1991	East 116, West 114	Charlotte	Chris Ford, Rick Adelman	Charles Barkley, Philadelphia
1992	West 153, East 113	Orlando	Don Nelson, Phil Jackson	Magic Johnson, LA Lakers

All-Time Winningest NBA Coaches

Top 25 NBA career victories through the 1991-92 season. Career, regular season and playoff records are noted along with NBA titles won. Coaches active during 1991-92 season in **bold** type.

		Yrs	Career W	L	Pct	Reg. W	Season L	Pct	Playoffs W	L	Pct	NBA Titles
1	Red Auerbach	20	**1037**	548	.654	938	479	.662	99	69	.589	9 (1957,59-66)
2	**Dick Motta**	22	**912**	933	.494	856	863	.498	56	70	.444	1 (1978)
3	Jack Ramsay	21	**908**	841	.519	864	783	.525	44	58	.431	1 (1977)
4	**Bill Fitch**	21	**900**	928	.492	845	877	.491	55	51	.519	1 (1981)
5	**Lenny Wilkens**	19	**867**	770	.530	815	721	.531	52	49	.515	1 (1979)
6	**Cotton Fitzsimmons**	19	**839**	791	.515	805	745	.519	34	46	.425	—None—
7	Gene Shue	22	**814**	908	.473	784	861	.477	30	47	.390	—None—
8	**Don Nelson**	15	**770**	581	.583	719	493	.593	51	58	.468	—None—
9	Red Holzman	18	**754**	651	.537	696	604	.535	58	47	.552	2 (1970,73)
	John MacLeod	18	**754**	711	.515	707	657	.518	47	54	.465	—None—
11	**Pat Riley**	10	**692**	278	.713	584	225	.722	108	53	.671	4 (1982,85,87-88)
12	Doug Moe	14	**642**	542	.542	609	492	.549	33	50	.398	—None—
13	**K.C.Jones**	10	**603**	309	.661	522	252	.674	81	57	.587	2 (1984,86)
14	Al Attles	14	**588**	548	.518	557	518	.518	31	30	.508	1 (1975)
15	**Chuck Daly**	10	**547**	345	.613	476	303	.611	71	42	.628	2 (1989-90)
16	Billy Cunningham	8	**520**	235	.689	454	196	.698	66	39	.629	1 (1983)
17	Alex Hannum	12	**516**	446	.536	471	412	.533	45	34	.570	2 (1958,67)
18	John Kundla	11	**483**	337	.589	423	302	.583	60	35	.632	5 (1949-50,52-54)
19	Tommy Heinsohn	9	**474**	296	.616	427	263	.619	47	33	.588	2 (1974,76)
20	Larry Costello	10	**467**	323	.591	430	300	.589	37	23	.617	1 (1971)
21	**Larry Brown**	9	**410**	324	.559	393	301	.566	17	23	.425	—None—
22	**Kevin Loughery**	14	**383**	565	.404	379	547	.409	4	18	.182	—None—
23	Bill Russell	8	**375**	317	.542	341	290	.540	34	27	.557	2 (1968-69)
24	Bill Sharman	7	**368**	267	.580	333	240	.581	35	27	.565	1 (1972)
25	Al Cervi	9	**359**	267	.573	326	241	.575	33	26	.559	1 (1955)

Note: The NBA does not recognize records from the National Basketball League (1937-49), the American Basketball League (1961-62) or the American Basketball Assn.(1968-76), so the following NBL, ABL and ABA overall coaching records are not included above: NBL—**Kundla** (51-19 and a title in 1 year). ABL—**Sharman** (48-28 in 1 yr). ABA—**Brown** (249-129 in 4 yrs), **Hannum** (194-164 and one title in 4 yrs), **Jones** (30-58 in 1 yr) **Loughery** (189-95 and one title in 3 yrs); **Sharman** (155-126 and one title in 3 yrs).

Where They Coached

Attles—Golden St.(1970-80,80-83); **Auerbach**—Washington (1946-49); Tri-Cities (1949-50); Boston (1950-66); **Brown**—Denver (1976-79), New Jersey (1981-83), San Antonio (1988-92), LA Clippers (1992—); **Cervi**—Syracuse (1949-56), Phila.Warriors (1958-59); **Costello**—Milwaukee (1968-76), Chicago (1978-79); **Cunningham**—Philadelphia (1977-85); **Daly**—Cleveland (1981-82), Detroit (1983-92), New Jersey (1992—); **Fitch**—Cleveland (1970-79), Boston (1979-83), Houston (1983-88), New Jersey (1989-92); **Fitzsimmons**—Phoenix (1970-72), Atlanta (1972-76), Buffalo (1977-78), Kansas City (1978-84), San Antonio (1984-86), Phoenix (1988-92).

Hannum—St.Louis (1957-58), Syracuse (1960-63), San Francisco (1963-66), Phila.76ers (1966-68), Houston (1970-71); **Heinsohn**—Boston (1969-77); **Holzman**—Milwaukee-St.Louis Hawks (1954-57), NY Knicks (1968-77,78-82); **Jones**—Washington (1973-76), Boston (1983-88), Seattle (1990-92); **Kundla**—Minneapolis (1948-57,58-59); **Loughery**—Philadelphia (1972-73), NY-NJ Nets (1976-81), Atlanta (1981-83), Chicago (1983-85), Washington (1985-88), Miami (1991—); **MacLeod**—Phoenix (1973-87), Dallas (1987-89), NY Knicks (1990-91); **Moe**—San Antonio (1976-80), Denver (1981-90), Philadelphia (1992—).

Motta—Chicago (1968-76), Washington (1976-80), Dallas (1980-87), Sacramento (1990-91); **Nelson**—Milwaukee (1976-87), Golden St.(1988—); **Ramsay**—Philadelphia (1968-72), Buffalo (1972-76), Portland (1976-86), Indiana (1986-89); **Riley**—LA Lakers (1981-90), New York (1991—); **Russell**—Boston (1966-68), Seattle (1973-77), Sacramento (1987-88); **Sharman**—SF Warriors (1966-68), LA Lakers (1971-76); **Shue**—Baltimore (1967-73), Philadelphia (1973-77), San Diego Clippers (1978-80), Washington (1980-86), LA Clippers (1987-89); **Wilkens**—Seattle (1969-72), Portland (1974-76), Seattle (1977-85), Cleveland (1986—).

All-Time Winningest NBA Coaches (Cont.)

Top Winning Percentages

Minimum of 350 victories, including playoffs; coaches active during 1991-92 season in **bold** type.

		Yrs	W	L	Pct
1	**Pat Riley**	10	692	278	**.713**
2	Billy Cunningham	8	520	235	**.689**
3	**K.C.Jones**	10	603	309	**.661**
4	Red Auerbach	20	1037	548	**.654**
5	Tommy Heinsohn	9	474	296	**.616**
6	**Chuck Daly**	10	547	345	**.613**
7	Larry Costello	10	467	323	**.591**
8	John Kundla	11	483	337	**.589**
9	**Don Nelson**	15	770	551	**.583**
10	Bill Sharman	7	368	267	**.580**
11	Al Cervi	9	359	267	**.573**
12	Joe Lapchick	9	356	277	**.562**
13	**Larry Brown**	9	410	324	**.559**
14	Doug Moe	14	642	542	**.542**
	Bill Russell	8	375	317	**.542**
16	Red Holzman	18	754	651	**.537**
17	Alex Hannum	12	516	446	**.536**
18	**Lenny Wilkens**	19	867	770	**.530**
19	Jack Ramsay	21	908	841	**.519**
20	Al Attles	14	588	548	**.518**
21	**Cotton Fitzsimmons**	19	839	791	**.515**
	John MacLeod	18	754	711	**.515**
23	Dick Motta	22	912	933	**.494**
24	**Bill Fitch**	21	900	928	**.492**
25	**Del Harris**	9	353	372	**.487**

Active Coaches' Victories

Through 1991-92 season, including playoffs.

		Yrs	W	L	Pct
1	Lenny Wilkens, Cleveland	19	**867**	770	.530
2	Don Nelson, Golden St	15	**770**	551	.583
3	Pat Riley, New York	10	**692**	278	.713
4	Doug Moe, Philadelphia	14	**642**	542	.542
5	Chuck Daly, New Jersey	10	**547**	345	.613
6	Larry Brown, LA Clippers	9	**410**	324	.559
7	Kevin Loughery, Miami	14	**383**	565	.404
8	Jerry Sloan, Utah	7	**315**	250	.558
9	Rick Adelman, Portland	4	**227**	115	.664
10	Phil Jackson, Chicago	3	**223**	78	.740
11	Matt Guokas, Orlando	6	**197**	273	.419
12	Wes Unseld, Washington	5	**158**	230	.407
13	George Karl, Seattle	5	**155**	205	.431
14	Bob Weiss, Atlanta	4	**142**	194	.423
15	Chris Ford, Boston	2	**118**	67	.638
16	Mike Dunleavy, Milwaukee	2	**114**	73	.610
17	Jimmy Rodgers, Minnesota	3	**111**	143	.437
18	Richie Adubato, Dallas	3	**104**	204	.338
19	Bob Hill, Indiana	3	**94**	119	.441
20	Ron Rothstein, Detroit	3	**57**	189	.232
21	Allan Bristow, Charlotte	1	**31**	51	.378
22	Rudy Tomjanovich, Houston	1	**16**	14	.533
23	Dan Issel, Denver	0	**0**	0	.000
	Randy Pfund, LA Lakers	0	**0**	0	.000
	Garry St.Jean, Sacramento	0	**0**	0	.000
	Jerry Tarkanian, San Antonio	0	**0**	0	.000
	Paul Westphal, Phoenix	0	**0**	0	.000

Annual Awards

Most Valuable Player

The Maurice Podoloff Trophy for regular season MVP. Named after the first commissioner (then president) of the NBA. Winners first selected by the NBA players (1956-80) then a national panel of pro basketball writers and broadcasters (since 1981). Winners' scoring averages are provided; (*) indicates led league.

Multiple winners: Kareem Abdul-Jabbar (6); Bill Russell (5); Wilt Chamberlain (4); Larry Bird, Magic Johnson, Michael Jordan and Moses Malone (3); Bob Pettit (2).

Year		Pts	Year		Pts
1956	Bob Pettit, St. Louis, F	25.7*	1975	Bob McAdoo, Buffalo, F	34.5*
1957	Bob Cousy, Boston, G	20.6	1976	Kareem Abdul-Jabbar, LA, C	27.7
1958	Bill Russell, Boston, C	16.6	1977	Kareem Abdul-Jabbar, LA, C	26.2
1959	Bob Pettit, St. Louis, F	29.2*	1978	Bill Walton, Portland, C	18.9
			1979	Moses Malone, Houston, C	24.8
1960	Wilt Chamberlain, Philadelphia, C	37.6*			
1961	Bill Russell, Boston, C	16.9	1980	Kareem Abdul-Jabbar, LA, C	24.8
1962	Bill Russell, Boston, C	18.9	1981	Julius Erving, Philadelphia, F	24.6
1963	Bill Russell, Boston, C	16.8	1982	Moses Malone, Houston, C	31.1
1964	Oscar Robertson, Cincinnati, G	31.4	1983	Moses Malone, Philadelphia, C	24.5
1965	Bill Russell, Boston, C	14.1	1984	Larry Bird, Boston, F	24.2
1966	Wilt Chamberlain, Philadelphia, C	33.5*	1985	Larry Bird, Boston, F	28.7
1967	Wilt Chamberlain, Philadelphia, C	24.1	1986	Larry Bird, Boston, F	25.8
1968	Wilt Chamberlain, Philadelphia, C	24.3	1987	Magic Johnson, LA Lakers, G	23.9
1969	Wes Unseld, Baltimore, C	13.8	1988	Michael Jordan, Chicago, G	35.0*
			1989	Magic Johnson, LA Lakers, G	22.5
1970	Willis Reed, New York, C	21.7			
1971	Lew Alcindor, Milwaukee, C	31.7*	1990	Magic Johnson, LA Lakers, G	22.3
1972	Kareem Abdul-Jabbar, Milwaukee, C	34.8*	1991	Michael Jordan, Chicago, G	31.5*
1973	Dave Cowens, Boston, C	20.5	1992	Michael Jordan, Chicago, G	30.1*
1974	Kareem Abdul-Jabbar, LA, C	27.0			

Note: Alcindor changed his name to Kareem Abdul-Jabbar after the 1970-71 season.

Rookie of the Year

The Eddie Gottlieb Trophy for outstanding rookie of the regular season. Named after the pro basketball pioneer and owner-coach of the first NBA champion Philadelphia Warriors. Winners selected by a national panel of pro basketball writers and broadcasters. Winners' scoring averages provided; (*) indicates led league; winners who were also named MVP are in **bold** type.

Year		Pts	Year		Pts
1953	Don Meineke, Ft.Wayne, F	10.8	1973	Bob McAdoo, Buffalo, C/F	18.0
1954	Ray Felix, Baltimore, C.	17.6	1974	Ernie DiGregorio, Buffalo, G	15.2
1955	Bob Pettit, Mil. Hawks, F	20.4	1975	Keith Wilkes, Golden St., F	14.2
1956	Maurice Stokes, Rochester., F/C	16.8	1976	Alvan Adams, Phoenix, C	19.0
1957	Tommy Heinsohn, Boston, F	16.2	1977	Adrian Dantley, Buffalo, F	20.3
1958	Woody Sauldsberry, Philadelphia, F/C	12.8	1978	Walter Davis, Phoenix, G	24.2
1959	Elgin Baylor, Minneapolis, F	24.9	1979	Phil Ford, Kansas City, G	15.9
1960	**Wilt Chamberlain**, Philadelphia	37.6*	1980	Larry Bird, Boston, F	21.3
1961	Oscar Robertson, Cincinnati, G	30.5	1981	Darrell Griffith, Utah, G	20.6
1962	Walt Bellamy, Chi. Packers, C.	31.6	1982	Buck Williams, New Jersey, F	15.5
1963	Terry Dischinger, Chi. Zephyrs, F	25.5	1983	Terry Cummings, San Diego, F	23.7
1964	Jerry Lucas, Cincinnati, F/C	17.7	1984	Ralph Sampson, Houston, C	21.0
1965	Willis Reed, New York, C.	19.5	1985	Michael Jordan, Chicago, G	28.2
1966	Rick Barry, San Francisco, F	25.7	1986	Patrick Ewing, New York, C	20.0
1967	Dave Bing, Detroit, G	20.0	1987	Chuck Person, Indiana, F	18.8
1968	Earl Monroe, Baltimore, G	24.3	1988	Mark Jackson, New York, G	13.6
1969	**Wes Unseld**, Baltimore, C	13.8	1989	Mitch Richmond, Golden St., G	22.0
1970	Lew Alcindor, Mil. Bucks, C	28.8	1990	David Robinson, San Antonio, C	24.3
1971	Dave Cowens, Boston, C	17.0	1991	Derrick Coleman, New Jersey, F	18.4
	& Geoff Petrie, Portland, F	24.8	1992	Larry Johnson, Charlotte, F	19.2
1972	Sidney Wicks, Portland, F	24.5			

Note: Alcindor changed his name to Kareem Abdul-Jabbar after the 1970-71 season.

Defensive Player of the Year

Awarded to the Best Defensive Player for the regular season. Winners selected by a national panel of pro basketball writers and broadcasters.
   Multiple winners: Mark Eaton, Sidney Moncrief and Dennis Rodman (2).

Year		Year		Year	
1983	Sidney Moncrief, Mil., G	1987	Michael Cooper, LAL, F	1990	Dennis Rodman, Det., F
1984	Sidney Moncrief, Mil., G	1988	Michael Jordan, Chi., G	1991	Dennis Rodman, Det., F
1985	Mark Eaton, Utah, C	1989	Mark Eaton, Utah, C	1992	David Robinson, SA, C
1986	Alvin Robertson, SA, G				

Sixth Man Award

Awarded to the Best Player Off the Bench for the regular season. Winners selected by a national panel of pro basketball writers and broadcasters.
   Multiple winners: Kevin McHale, Ricky Pierce and Detlef Schrempf (2).

Year		Year		Year	
1983	Bobby Jones, Phi., F	1987	Ricky Pierce, Mil., G/F	1990	Ricky Pierce, Mil., G/F
1984	Kevin McHale, Bos., F	1988	Roy Tarpley, Dal., F	1991	Detlef Schrempf, Ind., F
1985	Kevin McHale, Bos., F	1989	Eddie Johnson, Pho., F	1992	Detlef Schrempf, Ind., F
1986	Bill Walton, Bos., C/F				

Coach of the Year

The Red Auerbach Trophy for outstanding coach of the year. Renamed in 1967 for the former Boston coach who led the Celtics to nine NBA titles. Winners selected by a national panel of pro basketball writers and broadcasters. Previous season and winning season records are provided; (*) indicates division title.
   Multiple winners: Don Nelson (3); Bill Fitch, Cotton Fitzsimmons and Gene Shue (2).

Year		Improvement			Year		Improvement		
1963	Harry Gallatin, St.L	29-51	to	48-32	1978	Hubie Brown, Atl	31-51	to	41-41
1964	Alex Hannum, SF	31-49	to	48-32*	1979	Cotton Fitzsimmons, KC	31-51	to	48-34*
1965	Red Auerbach, Bos	59-21*	to	61-18*	1980	Bill Fitch, Bos	29-53	to	61-21*
1966	Dolph Schayes, Phi	40-40	to	55-25*	1981	Jack McKinney, Ind	37-45	to	44-38
1967	Johnny Kerr, Chi	Expan.	to	33-48	1982	Gene Shue, Wash	39-43	to	43-39
1968	Richie Guerin, St.L	39-42	to	56-26*	1983	Don Nelson, Mil	55-27*	to	51-31*
1969	Gene Shue, Balt	36-46	to	57-25*	1984	Frank Layden, Utah	30-52	to	45-37*
1970	Red Holzman, NY	54-28	to	60-22*	1985	Don Nelson, Mil	50-32*	to	59-23*
1971	Dick Motta, Chi	39-43	to	51-31	1986	Mike Fratello, Atl	34-48	to	50-32
1972	Bill Sharman, LA	48-34*	to	69-13*	1987	Mike Schuler, Port	40-42	to	49-33
1973	Tommy Heinsohn, Bos	56-26*	to	68-14*	1988	Doug Moe, Den	37-45	to	54-28*
1974	Ray Scott, Det	40-42	to	52-30	1989	Cotton Fitzsimmons, Pho	28-54	to	55-27
1975	Phil Johnson, KC-Oma	33-49	to	44-38	1990	Pat Riley, LA Lakers	57-25*	to	63-19*
1976	Bill Fitch, Cle	40-42	to	49-33*	1991	Don Chaney, Hou	41-41	to	52-30
1977	Tom Nissalke, Hou	40-42	to	49-33*	1992	Don Nelson, GS	44-38	to	55-27

American Basketball Association
ABA Finals

The American Basketball Assn. began play in 1967-68 as a 10-team rival of the 21 year-old NBA. The ABA, which introduced the three-point basket, a multi-colored ball and the All-Star Game Slam Dunk Contest, lasted nine seasons before folding following the 1975-76 season. Four ABA teams—Denver, Indiana, New York and San Antonio—survived to enter the NBA in 1976-77. The NBA also adopted the 3-pt basket (in 1979-80) and the All-Star Game Slam Dunk Contest. The older league, however, refused to take in the ABA ball.

Multiple winners: Indiana (3); New York (2).

Year	Winner	Head Coach	Series	Loser	Head Coach
1968	Pittsburgh Pipers	Vince Cazetta	4-2 (WLLWLWW)	New Orleans Bucs	Babe McCarthy
1969	Oakland Oaks	Alex Hannum	4-1 (WLWWW)	Indiana Pacers	Bob Leonard
1970	Indiana Pacers	Bob Leonard	4-2 (WWLWLW)	Los Angeles Stars	Bill Sharman
1971	Utah Stars	Bill Sharman	4-3 (WWLLWLW)	Kentucky Colonels	Frank Ramsey
1972	Indiana Pacers	Bob Leonard	4-2 (WLWLWW)	New York Nets	Lou Carnesecca
1973	Indiana Pacers	Bob Leonard	4-3 (WLLWLWL)	Kentucky Colonels	Joe Mullaney
1974	New York Nets	Kevin Loughery	4-1 (WWWLW)	Utah Stars	Joe Mullaney
1975	Kentucky Colonels	Hubie Brown	4-1 (WWWLW)	Indiana Pacers	Bob Leonard
1976	New York Nets	Kevin Loughery	4-2 (WLWWLW)	Denver Nuggets	Larry Brown

Most Valuable Player

Winners' scoring averages provided; (*) indicates led league.

Multiple winners: Julius Erving (3); Mel Daniels (2).

Year		Pts
1968	Connie Hawkins, Pittsburgh, C	26.8*
1969	Mel Daniels, Indiana, C	24.0
1970	Spencer Haywood, Denver, C	30.0*
1971	Mel Daniels, Indiana, C	21.0
1972	Artis Gilmore, Kentucky, C	23.8
1973	Billy Cunningham, Carolina, F	24.1
1974	Julius Erving, New York, F	27.4*
1975	George McGinnis, Indiana, F	29.8*
	& Julius Erving, New York, F	27.9
1976	Julius Erving, New York, F	29.3*

Rookie of the Year

Winners' scoring averages provided; (*) indicates led league. Rookies who were also named Most Valuable Player are in **bold** type.

Year		Pts
1968	Mel Daniels, Minnesota, C	22.2
1969	Warren Armstrong†, Oakland, G	21.5
1970	**Spencer Haywood**, Denver, C	30.0*
1971	Dan Issel, Kentucky, C	29.8*
	& Charlie Scott, Virginia, G	27.1
1972	**Artis Gilmore**, Kentucky, C	23.8
1973	Brian Taylor, New York, G	15.3
1974	Swen Nater, Virginia-SA, C	14.1
1975	Marvin Barnes, St. Louis, C	24.0
1976	David Thompson, Denver, F	26.0

†Armstrong changed his name to Warren Jabali after the 1970-71 season.

Coach of the Year

Previous season and winning season records are provided; (*) indicates division title.

Multiple winner: Larry Brown (3).

Year		Improvement
1968	Vince Cazetta, Pittsburgh	54-24*
1969	Alex Hannum, Oakland	22-56 to 60-18*
1970	Joe Belmont, Denver	44-34 to 51-33*
	& Bill Sharman, LA Stars	33-45 to 43-41
1971	Al Bianchi, Virginia	44-40 to 55-29*
1972	Tom Nissalke, Dallas	30-54 to 42-42
1973	Larry Brown, Carolina	35-49 to 57-27*
1974	Babe McCarthy, Kentucky	56-28 to 53-31
	& Joe Mullaney, Utah	55-29* to 51-33*
1975	Larry Brown, Denver	37-47 to 65-19*
1976	Larry Brown, Denver	65-19* to 60-24*

Scoring Leaders

Scoring championship decided by per game point average.

Multiple winner: Julius Erving (3).

Year		Gm	Avg	Pts
1968	Connie Hawkins, Pittsburgh	70	1875	26.8
1969	Rick Barry, Oakland	35	1190	34.0
1970	Spencer Haywood, Denver	84	2519	30.0
1971	Dan Issel, Kentucky	83	2480	29.8
1972	Charlie Scott, Virginia	73	2524	34.6
1973	Julius Erving, Virginia	71	2268	31.9
1974	Julius Erving, NY Mets	84	2299	27.4
1975	George McGinnis, Indiana	79	2353	29.8
1976	Julius Erving, NY Nets	84	2462	29.3

ABA All-Star Game

The ABA All-Star Game was an Eastern Division vs Western Division contest from 1968-75. League membership had dropped to seven teams by 1976, the ABA's last season, so the team in first place at the break (Denver) played an All-Star team made up from the other six clubs.

Series: East won 5, West 3 and Denver 1.

Year	Result	Host	Coaches	Most Valuable Player
1968	East 126, West 120	Indiana	Jim Pollard, Babe McCarthy	Larry Brown, New Orleans
1969	West 133, East 127	Louisville	Alex Hannum, Gene Rhodes	John Beasley, Dallas
1970	West 128, East 98	Indiana	Babe McCarthy, Bob Leonard	Spencer Haywood, Denver
1971	East 126, West 122	Carolina	Al Bianchi, Bill Sharman	Mel Daniels, Indiana
1972	East 142, West 115	Louisville	Joe Mullaney, Ladell Andersen	Dan Issel, Kentucky
1973	West 123, East 111	Utah	Ladell Andersen, Larry Brown	Warren Jabali, Denver
1974	East 128, West 112	Virginia	Babe McCarthy, Joe Mullaney	Artis Gilmore, Kentucky
1975	East 151, West 124	San Antonio	Kevin Loughery, Larry Brown	Freddie Lewis, St.Louis
1976	Denver 144, ABA 138	Denver	Larry Brown, Kevin Loughery	David Thompson, Denver

Bruce Bennett/BBS

The Pittsburgh Penguins held on to the Stanley Cup in 1992, thanks to the inspired performances of **Mario Lemieux** (left) and **Jaromir Jagr**, among others.

HOCKEY

Back-to-Back

*Penguins mourn Badger Bob, win another Stanley Cup
and find that J-A-R-O-M-I-R spells M-A-R-I-O J-R.*

The computer programmers at Nintendo are already up to Super Mario 3, with Dr. Mario and Mario World thrown in for good measure. But they had nothing on the Pittsburgh Penguins in 1991-92. Not when the Pens could boast of Super Mario 2 (Stanley Cups), Super Mario 3 (Art Ross Trophies) and Mario Jr. (Jaromir Jagr).

In a trying season that began with the death of popular coach Bob Johnson and almost ended with the first players' strike in the 75-year history of the National Hockey League, Mario Lemieux saved the day.

Despite missing 16 regular season games with a bad back and six playoff games with a sore shoulder and a broken left hand, Lemieux led the Penguins to their second straight Stanley Cup championship (and picked up his second Conn Smythe Trophy as MVP), won his third Ross Trophy as the NHL's leading scorer (131 points), and watched his 20-year-old Czechoslovakian protégé Jagr become a budding superstar and successor-in-waiting.

But while the end was sweet, the beginning was not. Johnson, who had guided the Pens to their first title in 1991, died of brain cancer on Nov. 26, three months after collapsing on the eve of the Canada Cup tournament.

***

Eric Duhatschek has covered the NHL for the *Calgary Herald* since 1980. He is also a columnist for *The Hockey News*.

Luckily, Pittsburgh had a highly qualified replacement waiting in the wings—Scotty Bowman. The team's director of player development since 1990, Bowman was also the NHL's all-time winningest coach with 853 career wins and a winning percentage of .655 in 17 years with St. Louis, Montreal and Buffalo.

But Bowman's style was diametrically opposed to Johnson's. That's not just hearsay, either. That was Johnson's view. "There are two ways to coach," the Badger once said. "From the point of fear and from the point of pride. I coached mainly from pride. Pride in your performance. Pride in the team's performance. Pride in getting the job done. Now, Scotty Bowman didn't use that approach. He coached from fear. He sat a guy out, wouldn't talk to him, played mind games with him. I don't believe in that. I never will."

In memory of Johnson's positive influence on the team, all the players wore a "Badger, 1931-1991" patch on the left sleeve of their sweaters and the Civic Arena ice surface carried his signature greeting, "It's A Great Day For Hockey." And on April 10, Johnson was named to the Hockey Hall of Fame in the builders' category.

Off the ice, the Penguins' ownership situation was finally resolved on Nov. 18, 1991, when the DeBartolo family sold the team and the lease to the Civic Arena to a group that included Howard Baldwin, a

Bruce Bennett/BBS

New York Rangers' captain **Mark Messier** (right) on maneuvers in front of Montreal goaltender **Patrick Roy.** Messier led the Rangers to their first 50-win season ever and won his second Hart Trophy in three years. Roy was the Vezina Trophy winner for the third time in four years.

founder of the defunct WHA and former part-owner of both the Hartford Whalers and Minnesota North Stars. Announced as a $65 million transaction, of which $31 million was for the team, the sale took several months to complete and (given rumors that the new owners were economy-minded) proved to be a major distraction to the team.

Then there was the question of Lemieux's health. While still only 26, he has a chronic back problem that the Pens know will never go away. Accordingly, they go into each season knowing that their captain will not play 80 games. If he gets into 60, plus the majority of the playoff schedule, that's great. Complicating matters in the 1992 playoffs were a minor shoulder injury that kept Lemieux out of the first game of the opening round and a broken left hand—courtesy of an Adam Graves slash in the second round against the New York Rangers—that cost him five more games.

An unexpected uphill battle to secure a playoff berth prepared Pittsburgh for the rough and tumble of the postseason. As late as March 1st, they were clinging to fourth place in the powerful Patrick Division, one game over .500 and just three points ahead of the resurgent New York Islanders. But an 11-5-1 run over the last 17 games moved them out of danger and into third place.

The turnaround began two weeks after a blockbuster, three-team trade that saw the Pens surrender two of their key supporting personnel—high-scoring winger Mark Recchi and defenseman Paul Coffey—to Philadelphia and Los Angeles, respectively. In return, they received right wing Rick Tocchet, defenseman Kjell Samuelsson and backup goaltender Ken Wregget from the Flyers and defenseman Jeff Chychrun from the Kings.

With power forwards Tocchet and Kevin Stevens flanking Lemieux, the most skilled player in the game, the Penguins now had a classic hockey line. Stevens, the 27-year-old left wing, was also the NHL's No. 2 scorer with 123 points—a single-season record for an American-born player.

The Penguins started slowly in the play-offs, losing three of their first four games against Washington before winning three in a row to set up the Patrick showdown that everybody wanted to see—the defending champions against the New York Rangers, the regular season's top team with a record of 50-25-5.

However, Graves' slashing of Lemieux, a season-ending knee injury to the Pens' Joe Mullen, and a back injury to Rangers' captain and regular season MVP Mark Messier took much of the glitter out of the series. Down two games to one, the talent-rich Penguins pulled out the series in six with huge assists from Ron Francis and Jagr. Francis supplied the strength down the middle (and 12 points) while Jagr, the human highlight film, scored several pivotal goals that proved to be fatal for the New Yorkers.

By the time Lemieux returned—in Game Two of the Wales Conference final against Boston—the Penguins were on a roll that never stopped. They swept the Bruins and then did the same to Campbell Conference champion Chicago in the Cup Finals to finish with a record-tying 11 wins in a row. The Blackhawks had set the mark earlier in the playoffs by routing St. Louis, Detroit and Edmonton in the first three rounds.

Afterward, amid talk of "three-peat" and dynasty in the winners' locker room, Lemieux said, "That's a pretty strong word, dynasty, but I like our chances the next few years. I'd say our future is very bright." Meanwhile, Bowman toasted his predecessor, saying, "This one's for you, Bob."

But it was also for Bowman, who won his sixth Stanley Cup as a coach and his first since 1979. And for 35-year-old Bryan Trottier, who has now won the Cup six times as a player—the first four with the New York Islanders and the last two with Pittsburgh after being released by the Isles. And don't forget goaltender Tom Barrasso (2.82 goals per game) and the Pens' underrated defensemen, who contributed solid, two-way play throughout.

Pittsburgh won the Cup on June 1st, capping the longest (243 days) and most celebrated (Happy 75th!) season ever in

NHL Decides It's Time To Clean House

Imagine a National Hockey League game that lasts less than two-and-a-half hours, thus fitting snugly into a national prime time TV schedule.

Imagine a national prime time TV schedule.

Imagine a game without fighting, that minimizes stick fouls and cracks down on holding and hooking, thus enabling Mario Lemieux, Wayne Gretzky and company to really show what they can do.

It could happen—and sooner than you think.

Two days after holding its 1992 Entry Draft, the NHL started cleaning house. After 15 years in office, president John Ziegler stepped down voluntarily when it became clear his removal was imminent.

Ziegler's long-time ally, Chicago Black-hawks' president Bill Wirtz, also gave up his position as chairman of the board after 18 years.

"There is a momentum (in the league) to remove the establishment," said Ziegler. "And I'm the establishment."

Ziegler resigned on June 12 and was replaced 10 days later on an interim basis by 64-year-old NHL chief counsel, Gil Stein. A search committee was also formed to find a permanent replacement before the year is out.

Perhaps more significantly, Wirtz, the hard-liner from the old school, was replaced by Los Angeles Kings' owner Bruce McNall, one of the league's most progressive thinkers. McNall is the man who brought Gretzky to L.A. and turned one of the NHL's weakest franchises into one of its strongest.

McNall believes that hockey is on the verge of a new golden era and that all it will take to turn things around is an innovative approach to marketing the game.

Fifteen years ago, major-league hockey and basketball were on parallel roads to ruin. Franchises in both leagues were in danger of folding. Network TV shunned them and salaries, thanks to competition from the ABA and WHA, were out of control.

Since then, the NBA has merged with the ABA, expanded to 27 teams, made peace with its players' union, acquired the services of players like Magic Johnson, Larry Bird and Michael Jordan and signed a recent

NHL president **John Ziegler** (left) and Players' Association executive director **Bob Goodenow** at a joint press conference after ending the 10-day players' strike with a new collective bargaining agreement.

three-year network TV deal with NBC for $600 million.

The NHL's progress, on the other hand, has been more modest—merger with the WHA and expansion to 24 teams. Despite the arrival of Gretzky and Lemieux, the success of the 1980 U.S. Olympic team and powerhouse American Stanley Cup winners like the Islanders and Penguins, the NHL has failed to catch fire. The league has no U.S. TV contract to speak of and the international (and artistic) success of its five Canada Cup tournaments (since 1976) pales in comparison to the worldwide attention paid this summer to the exploits of the NBA's Olympic Dream Team.

Perhaps the most sensitive issue the NHL must address in retooling itself for wider public acceptance is fighting—hockey's black eye. For two years now, Gretzky has been outspoken in his belief that while fighting may attract some fans to the game, it keeps far greater numbers away.

"We need to showcase our stars, not beat them up," McNall says. "What sickens me is that the rules are there to prohibit it, but the referees won't make the calls because they're not being told to."

As for Ziegler, it's ironic that the momentum for his removal came after what was arguably his shining moment as league president—helping to settle the 10-day players' strike in April. Some NHL owners believe they surrendered too much in an attempt to achieve short-term labor peace and blame Ziegler, the peacemaker.

They overlook the fact that a prolonged strike would have created chaos in the NHL. No playoffs, no set schedule for the 1992-93 season and no chance at a decent TV contract. And what about the two expansion teams in Ottawa and Tampa Bay? With no players to stock their rosters, might they have asked for their $50 million entry fees back?

By negotiating a settlement, Ziegler gave the NHL season a much-needed resolution. Vancouver fans learned their team wasn't as good as they thought, Pittsburgh fans realized the Penguins were better than ever, and those long-suffering New York Ranger fans found out the Cup wasn't coming home after all.

the NHL. It was also the most disruptive, resulting in the league's first player strike (see box), which threatened to cancel the playoffs. The collective bargaining agreement between the NHL Players' Association and team owners had actually expired on Sept. 15, but play continued without a contract until the final week of the regular season. Appropriately, on April Fool's Day, eight days before the scheduled start of the playoffs, the NHLPA voted 560-4 to go out on strike. The key issues: less restrictive free agency, a shorter entry draft and a larger share of the league's licensing and marketing revenues.

On April 10th, NHL president John Ziegler and players' union executive director Bob Goodenow hammered out a short-term deal that will expire on Sept. 15, 1993. In the interim, the two sides plan to address some of the larger issues facing hockey.

"We did not solve industry issues," said Goodenow. "We negotiated a contract." Both sides also agreed to increase the regular season by two games to 84 starting in 1992-93.

No one benefited more from the strike than eventual Stanley Cup finalist Chicago, which got a badly needed 10-day rest. Playing general manager and coach Mike Keenan's aggressive, hit'em-hard-and-often style eventually takes its toll on any team. In two previous trips to the Finals with Philadelphia, Keenan's teams came up short partly because they were beat-up, run-down and understaffed due to injuries.

The Blackhawks' regular season had been disappointing. The NHL's winningest team in 1990-91 (106 points), the Hawks slipped 19 points in the overall standings despite the acquisition of two former Cup winners—defenseman Steve Smith of Edmonton and forward Brent Sutter of the New York Islanders. Meanwhile, the unconventional Keenan decided to bench his star center, Jeremy Roenick for long stretches during select playoff games. This followed a season-long pattern of trying to extract more from Roenick, who finished with 53 goals.

Other than the strike, the NHL's top regular season story was the New York Rangers, who started the campaign by trading Bernie Nicholls and two prospects to Edmonton for Messier and ended it by winning the Prince of Wales Trophy with the league's best record. Messier scored 35 goals and 107 points and won his second Hart Trophy as MVP (the first Ranger winner since Andy Bathgate in 1959). Brian Leetch, the league's top-scoring defenseman with 102 points, won the Norris Trophy (the first Ranger winner since Harry Howell in 1967).

But New York could not keep it going in the playoffs, struggling to beat New Jersey in seven games and then falling to the Penguins in six. As the curtain came down in Pittsburgh, the Igloo crowd gleefully chanted "1940, 1940, 1940," reminding the Rangers that it was now 52 years since they last sipped from Lord Stanley's Cup.

"It's like a poison arrow has hit you in the heart," said Rangers' goaltender John Vanbiesbrouck. "Now we have to start back at square one and that's such a long road."

Washington, the team with the regular season's second-best record (45-27-8), gave the Penguins their best test before bowing out in seven games. Long known for their defensive style, the Capitals went on the offensive with 330 goals (second only to Pittsburgh's 343) and did it with a lot of European firepower. Four of the Caps' top eight scorers were Europeans, led by Michal Pivonka of Czechoslovakia.

Detroit made huge strides as well, finishing with 98 points (up 22 from the year before) and winning the Norris Division. The Red Wings' rise could also be traced to European immigrants, namely, second-year center Sergei Fedorov, plus rookie defensemen Vladimir Konstantinov and Niklas Lidstrom.

Vancouver ended one of pro sports' most miserable streaks—a run of 15 consecutive losing seasons—by finishing with a club record 96 points and a Smythe Division title. The Canucks were aided and abetted by imported Russian forwards Igor Larionov and Pavel Bure. Contract problems with his Red Army team kept the 21-year-old Bure out of the Canucks' first 16 games, but he finished with 60 points in 65 games and won the Calder Trophy as Rookie of the Year.

There was very little to cheer about in Calgary, where the Flames flickered out and missed the playoffs for the first time since 1975. After averaging 47 wins and 103 points over the last five seasons, the

Ken Levine/Allsport

St. Louis right wing **Brett Hull** reached the 70-goal plateau for the third straight season and was named the Most Valuable Player of the NHL All-Star Game.

back in the Canada Cup and played hurt most of the season. On top of that, his father fell ill with a brain aneurism in October and he took some time off to be with him in the hospital. When the Great One returned, he couldn't shake himself out of the doldrums. By almost anybody else's standards, Gretzky's 121 points in 74 games would have been a career year. But this is Wayne Gretzky we're talking about and 121 points was his lowest total since coming to the league in 1979-80.

Less than thrilled with the performance of the Kings, whose $13.5 million payroll is the league's highest, owner Bruce McNall shook up his braintrust in the off-season, removing GM Rogie Vachon, promoting assistant GM Nick Beverley, firing third-year coach Tom Webster, and plucking replacement Barry Melrose out of the Detroit farm system.

Job security among NHL head coaches is roughly the same as in other team sports, and the 1991-92 regular season was about normal with four—Risebrough, Buffalo's Rick Dudley, Quebec's Dave Chambers and Philadelphia's Paul Holmgren—getting the gate. The off-season, on the other hand, was unusually harsh as nine changes were made. And six of those coaches—Keenan, Webster, Pat Burns of Montreal, Brian Sutter of St. Louis, Rick Bowness of Boston and Tom McVie of New Jersey—had winning records! Keenan stepped aside in Chicago and promoted associate coach Darryl Sutter. Burns jumped from Montreal to Toronto, but the other four were fired—some for dubious reasons at best.

Bowness, the first-year coach in Boston, was without his best forward, Cam Neely, for all but nine games. In addition, the Bruins were almost completely remade following the Winter Olympics when six new faces were added. For all that, Bowness still got them into the Wales Conference finals, sweeping Montreal along the way. So why was he canned? According to Boston GM Harry Sinden, it was because Bowness lacked some "intangibles."

In McVie's case, the New Jersey Devils had the best regular season in franchise history (38-31-11) and came within a whisker of upsetting the Rangers in the first round. Nevertheless, McVie was sent packing because, according to GM Lou Lamoriello, incoming coach (and 1980

1989 Stanley Cup champs plunged to just 31 wins and 74 points. The telling blow came on Jan. 2 with an NHL-record 10-player trade with Toronto.

The deal was a disaster for the Flames, who basically sent center Doug Gilmour and defenseman Jamie Macoun to the Maple Leafs for right winger Gary Leeman and defenseman Michel Petit. Gilmour prospered in Toronto and almost carried the woeful Leafs to a playoff spot. Leeman, meanwhile, scored only two goals in 29 games. The trade undermined player confidence in GM-coach Doug Risebrough, but when he finally got around to replacing himself as coach with Guy Charron on Mar. 3, it was too late.

Almost as disappointing were the Los Angeles Kings, who finished second in the Smythe and were then bounced from the first round of the playoffs by Edmonton. Former Oiler Wayne Gretzky injured his

John Giammundo/BBS

After refusing to play for Quebec and sitting out the entire 1991-92 NHL season, 19-year-old **Eric Lindros** signed a six-year contract with Philadelphia on July 14.

Olympic legend) Herb Brooks was better suited to the changing face of hockey. "It's very simple to say you'll do nothing and everyone will agree with you," said Lamoriello. "I did not feel it was time to wait."

Sutter's last year in St. Louis was also frustrating. Before the season even started, the Blues lost captain and defenseman Scott Stevens to New Jersey as compensation for signing free agent forward Brendan Shanahan. Then, center Adam Oates began feuding with GM Ron Caron over money, which led to Caron trading Oates to Boston for Craig Janney on Feb. 7, which, in turn, upset star right winger and All-Star Game MVP Brett Hull. Hull and Oates were close friends as well as linemates and even though Hull reached the 70-goal plateau for the second consecutive year, he did it in a less than giddy environment. "I play the game to have fun," he said, "and this sure took the fun right out of it."

Speaking of unhappy campers, there was the unresolved NHL status of 19-year-old phenom Eric Lindros, the top selection of the 1991 Draft, who refused to sign with the small-market, French-speaking Quebec Nordiques. Instead, he went to Albertville with the Canadian Olympic Team and came back with a silver medal.

After conducting a spirited eight-team auction for the rights to Lindros in the week leading up to the '92 Draft, Quebec president Marcel Aubut couldn't decide between the offers made by Philadelphia and the Rangers. So he said yes to both. Needless to say, the Flyers and Rangers were not amused and both filed grievances with the league. Normally, Ziegler would have arbitrated the dispute, but since he had become a lame duck in the wake of the strike settlement, the NHL turned to an independent arbitrator—Toronto lawyer Larry Bertuzzi.

Bertuzzi spent almost a week trying to reconstruct the 24-hour period leading up to the double deal. After hearing testimony from all three parties, he ruled on June 30 that the Flyers and Nordiques made an "enforceable" deal some 90 minutes before the entry draft began. Accordingly, that agreement superseded any subsequent deal—namely, the one the Rangers and Quebec agreed to later that morning.

Gaining the rights to Lindros cost the Flyers plenty: goaltender Ron Hextall, defensemen Steve Duchesne and Kerry Huffman, forwards Mike Ricci, Peter Forsberg and Chris Simon, No. 1 draft choices in 1993 and '94 and $15 million.

Flyers' general manager Russ Farwell, perhaps aware of what a gamble he was taking, was unusually circumspect afterward. "You seldom get a chance to trade for this type of player," he said. "They only come along once every 10 years, so we wanted to pursue it as far as we could."

On July 14, the Flyers made Lindros one of the highest-paid players in the NHL with a six-year contract worth over $2.5 million a year.

Why was interest in Lindros so high? Just ask them in Pittsburgh, where the Penguins finished third in the Patrick with 87 points and still won their second straight Stanley Cup.

With Ottawa and Tampa Bay making the NHL a 24-team league in 1992-93, the conventional wisdom is that a superstar can take an 87-point team to the next level.

Philadelphia is confident that Lindros is such a player. Now all the Flyers have to do is get 87 points.   □

Final NHL Standings

Division champions (*) and playoff qualifiers (†) are noted. Number of seasons listed after each head coach refers to current tenure with club through 1991-92 season. Note that San Jose of the Smythe Division is an expansion team. Two more expansion teams will join the league for the 1992-93 season—Ottawa in the Adams Division and Tampa Bay in the Norris.

Campbell Conference

Norris Division

	W	L	T	Pts	For	Opp	Dif
*Detroit	43	25	12	**98**	320	256	+64
†Chicago	36	29	15	**87**	257	236	+21
†St.Louis	36	33	11	**83**	279	263	+16
Minnesota	32	42	6	**70**	246	278	−32
Toronto	30	43	7	**67**	234	294	−60

Head Coaches: Det—Bryan Murray (2nd season); **Chi**—Mike Keenan (4th); **St.L**—Brian Sutter (4th); **Min**—Bob Gainey (2nd); **Tor**—Tom Watt (2nd).

1990—91 Standings: 1.Chicago (49−23−8, 106 points); 2.St.Louis (47−22−11, 105 pts); 3.Detroit (34−38−8, 76 pts); 4.Minnesota (27−39−14, 68 pts); 5.Toronto (23−46−11, 57 pts).

Smythe Division

	W	L	T	Pts	For	Opp	Dif
*Vancouver	42	26	12	**96**	285	250	+35
†Los Angeles	35	31	14	**84**	287	296	−9
†Edmonton	36	34	10	**82**	295	297	−2
†Winnipeg	33	32	15	**81**	251	244	+7
Calgary	31	37	12	**74**	296	305	−9
San Jose	17	58	5	**39**	219	359	−140

Head Coaches: Van—Pat Quinn (2nd season); **LA**—Tom Webster (3rd); **Edm**—Ted Green (1st); **Win**—John Paddock (1st); **Calg**—replaced Doug Risebrough (2nd, 25-31-9) with Guy Charron (6-6-3) on Mar. 3; **SJ**—George Kingston (1st).

1990-91 Standings: 1.Los Angeles (46-24-10, 102 points); 2.Calgary (46-26-8, 100 pts); 3.Edmonton (37-37-6, 80 pts); 4.Vancouver (28-43-9, 65 pts); 5.Winnipeg (26-43-11, 63 pts).

Wales Conference

Adams Division

	W	L	T	Pts	For	Opp	Dif
*Montreal	41	28	11	**93**	267	207	+60
†Boston	36	32	12	**84**	270	275	−5
†Buffalo	31	37	12	**74**	289	299	−10
†Hartford	26	41	13	**65**	247	283	−36
Quebec	20	48	12	**52**	255	318	−63

Head Coaches: Mon—Pat Burns (4th season); **Bos**—Rick Bowness (1st); **Buf**—replaced Rick Dudley (3rd, 9-15-4) with John Muckler (22-22-8) on Dec. 11; **Hart**—Jim Roberts (1st); **Que**—replaced Dave Chambers (2nd, 3-14-1) with GM Pierre Page (17-34-11) on Nov.17.

1990-91 Standings: 1.Boston (44-24-12, 100 points); 2.Montreal (39-30-11, 89 pts); 3.Buffalo (31-30-19, 81 pts); 4.Hartford (31-38-11, 73 pts); 5.Quebec (16-50-14, 46 pts).

Patrick Division

	W	L	T	Pts	For	Opp	Dif
*NY Rangers	50	25	5	**105**	321	246	+75
†Washington	45	27	8	**98**	330	275	+55
†Pittsburgh	39	32	9	**87**	343	308	+35
†New Jersey	38	31	11	**87**	289	259	+30
NY Islanders	34	35	11	**79**	291	299	−8
Philadelphia	32	37	11	**75**	252	273	−21

Head Coaches: NYR—Roger Neilson (3rd season); **Wash**—Terry Murray (3rd); **Pit**—Scotty Bowman (1st); **NJ**—Tom McVie (2nd); **NYI**—Al Arbour (4th); **Phi**—replaced Paul Holmgren (3rd, 8-14-2) with Bill Dineen (24-23-9) on Dec. 4.

1990-91 Standings: 1.Pittsburgh (41-33-6, 88 points); 2.NY Rangers (36-31-13, 85 pts); 3.Washington (37-36-7, 81 pts); 4.New Jersey (32-33-15, 79 pts); 5.Philadelphia (33-37-10, 76 pts); 6.NY Islanders (25-45-10, 60 pts).

Home & Away, Division Records

Sixteen teams qualify for the Stanley Cup Playoffs with the two divisions in each conference represented by their top four clubs. Qualifying teams below are preceded by the first letter of their division: N—Norris and S—Smythe in the Campbell Conference, and A—Adams and P—Patrick in the Wales; (*) indicates division champions.

Campbell Conference

	Pts	Home	Away	Div
N—Detroit*	98	24-12-4	19-13-8	19-10-3
S—Vancouver*	96	23-10-7	19-16-5	20-10-5
N—Chicago	87	23- 9-8	13-20-7	15-12-5
S—Los Angeles	84	20-11-9	15-20-5	16-13-6
N—St.Louis	83	25-13-3	11-21-8	11-17-4
S—Edmonton	82	22-13-5	14-21-5	15-14-6
S—Winnipeg	81	20-14-6	13-18-9	15-14-6
Calgary	74	19-14-7	12-23-5	16-15-4
N—Minnesota	70	20-16-4	12-26-2	12-16-4
Toronto	67	21-16-3	9-27-4	14-16-2
San Jose	39	14-23-3	3-35-2	8-24-3

Wales Conference

	Pts	Home	Away	Div
P—NY Rangers*	105	28- 8- 4	22-17-1	19-15-1
P—Washington	98	25-12- 3	20-15-5	22-12-1
A—Montreal*	93	27- 8- 5	14-20-6	16-10-6
P—Pittsburgh	87	21-13- 6	18-19-3	16-16-3
P—New Jersey	87	24-12- 4	14-19-7	14-16-5
A—Boston	84	23-11- 6	13-21-6	16-10-6
NY Islanders	79	20-15- 5	14-20-6	13-15-7
Philadelphia	75	22-11- 7	10-26-4	10-20-5
A—Buffalo	74	22-13- 5	9-24-7	12-14-6
A—Hartford	65	13-17-10	13-24-3	10-16-6
Quebec	52	18-19- 3	2-29-9	11-15-6

NHL Regular Season Individual Leaders
Scoring

	Pos	Gm	G	A	Pts	PM	+/−	PP	SH	GW	GT	Shots	Pct
Mario Lemieux, Pittsburgh	C	64	44	87	**131**	94	+27	12	4	5	1	249	17.7
Kevin Stevens, Pittsburgh	L	80	54	69	**123**	252	+8	19	0	4	0	325	16.6
Wayne Gretzky, Los Angeles	C	74	31	90	**121**	34	−12	12	2	2	1	215	14.4
Brett Hull, St.Louis	R	73	70	39	**109**	48	−2	20	5	9	1	408	17.2
Luc Robitaille, Los Angeles	L	80	44	63	**107**	95	−4	26	0	6	1	240	18.3
Mark Messier, NY Rangers	C	79	35	72	**107**	76	+31	12	4	6	0	212	16.5
Jeremy Roenick, Chicago	C	80	53	50	**103**	98	+23	22	3	13	0	234	22.6
Steve Yzerman, Detroit	C	79	45	58	**103**	64	+26	9	8	9	0	295	15.3
Brian Leetch, NY Rangers	D	80	22	80	**102**	26	+25	10	1	3	1	245	9.0
Adam Oates, St.Louis-Boston	C	80	20	79	**99**	22	−9	6	0	4	2	191	10.5
Dale Hawerchuk, Buffalo	C	77	23	75	**98**	27	−22	13	0	4	0	242	9.5
Mark Recchi, Pittsburgh-Philadelphia	R	80	43	54	**97**	96	−21	20	1	5	1	210	20.5
Pierre Turgeon, Buffalo-NY Islanders	C	77	40	55	**95**	20	+7	13	0	6	0	207	19.3
Joe Sakic, Quebec	C	69	29	65	**94**	20	+5	6	3	1	1	217	13.4
Pat LaFontaine, Buffalo	C	57	46	47	**93**	98	+10	23	0	5	1	203	22.7
Dave Andreychuk, Buffalo	L	80	41	50	**91**	71	−9	28	0	2	2	337	12.2
Gary Roberts, Calgary	L	76	53	37	**90**	219	+32	15	0	2	3	196	27.0
Vincent Damphousse, Edmonton	L	80	38	51	**89**	53	+10	12	1	8	1	247	15.4
Joe Mullen, Pittsburgh	R	77	42	45	**87**	30	+12	14	0	4	1	226	18.6
Doug Gilmour, Calgary-Toronto	C	78	26	61	**87**	78	+25	10	1	4	1	168	15.5
Craig Janney, Boston-St.Louis	C	78	18	69	**87**	22	+6	6	0	2	0	127	14.2

Note: LaFontaine was a holdout with the NY Islanders and did not play until he was traded to Buffalo on Oct.25.

Goals
Hull, St.L ... 70
Stevens, Pit ... 54
Roberts, Calg ... 53
Roenick, Chi ... 53
LaFontaine, Buf ... 46
Yzerman, Det ... 45
Lemieux, Pit ... 44
Robitaille, LA ... 44
Recchi, Pit-Phi ... 43
Nolan, Que ... 42
Mullen, Pit ... 42

Assists
Gretzky, LA ... 90
Lemieux, Pit ... 87
Leetch, NYR ... 80
Oates, St.L-Bos ... 79
Hawerchuk, Buf ... 75
Messier, NYR ... 72
Janney, Bos-St.L ... 69
Stevens, Pit ... 69
Sakic, Que ... 65
Housley, Win ... 63
Robitaille, LA ... 63

Defensemen Points
Leetch, NYR ... 102
Housley, Win ... 86
Bourque, Bos ... 81
Murphy, Pit ... 77
MacInnis, Calg ... 77
Patrick, NYR ... 71
Coffey, Pit-LA ... 69
Olausson, Win ... 62
Lidstrom, Det* ... 60
Stevens, NJ ... 59

Rookie Points
Amonte, NYR ... 69
Todd, NJ ... 63
Bure, Van ... 60
Lidstrom, Det ... 60
Falloon, SJ ... 59
Emerson, St.L ... 59
Audette, Buf ... 48
Borsato, Win ... 36
Dionne, Mon ... 34
Lapointe, Que ... 33
Konstantinov, Det ... 33

Power Play Goals
Andreychuk, Buf ... 28
Robitaille, LA ... 26
LaFontaine, Buf ... 23
Roenick, Chi ... 22
King, NYI ... 21

Short-Handed Goals
Yzerman, Det ... 8
Hull, St.L ... 5
Ridley, Wash ... 5
Nine tied with 4 each.

Plus/Minus
Ysebaert, Det ... +44
McCrimmon, Det ... +39
Lidstrom, Det* ... +36
Patrick, NYR ... +34
Hardy, NYR ... +33
Murphy, Pit ... +33

Penalty Minutes
Peluso, Chi ... 408
Ray, Buf ... 354
Odjick, Van ... 348
Stern, Calg ... 338
Gaetz, SJ* ... 324

Goaltending
(Minimum 40 games)

	Gm	Min	Avg	GA	Saves	Pct	EN	SO	Record	Offense			
										G	A	Pts	PM
Patrick Roy, Montreal	67	3935	**2.36**	155	1806	.914	7	5	36-22-8	0	5	5	4
Ed Belfour, Chicago	52	2928	**2.70**	132	1241	.894	4	5	21-18-10	0	2	2	40
Kirk McLean, Vancouver	65	3852	**2.74**	176	1780	.901	1	5	38-17-9	0	4	4	0
John Vanbiesbrouck, NY Rangers	45	2526	**2.85**	120	1331	.910	4	2	27-13-3	0	3	3	23
Bob Essensa, Winnipeg	47	2627	**2.88**	126	1407	.910	2	5	21-17-6	0	2	2	2
Curtis Joseph, St.Louis	60	3494	**3.01**	175	1953	.910	5	2	27-20-10	0	9	9	12
Mike Richter, NY Rangers	41	2298	**3.11**	119	1205	.901	3	3	23-12-2	0	0	0	6
Tim Cheveldae, Detroit	72	4236	**3.20**	226	1978	.886	1	2	38-23-9	0	4	4	6
Chris Terreri, New Jersey	54	3169	**3.20**	169	1511	.888	0	1	22-22-10	0	1	1	13
Don Beaupre, Washington	54	3108	**3.20**	166	1435	.884	2	1	29-17-6	0	0	0	30

Wins
Cheveldae, Det ... 38
McLean, Van ... 38
Roy, Mon ... 36
Beaupre, Wash ... 29
Moog, Bos ... 28

Shutouts
Belfour, Chi ... 5
Essensa, Win ... 5
McLean, Van ... 5
Roy, Mon ... 5
Three tied with 3 each.

Save Pct.
Roy, Mon ... .914
Essensa, Win ... .910
Joseph, St.L ... .910
Van'brouck, NYR ... .910
Three tied at .901.

Losses
Fuhr, Tor ... 33
Vernon, Calg ... 30
Hackett, SJ ... 27
Ranford, Edm ... 26
Casey, Min ... 23
Cheveldae, Det ... 23

Team by Team Statistics

High scorers and goaltenders with at least 10 games played. Players who competed for more than one team during the regular season are listed with their final club; (*) indicates rookies.

Boston Bruins

Top Scorers	Pos	Gm	G	A	Pts	+/-	PM
Adam Oates	C	80	20	79	99	−9	22
STL.		54	10	59	69	−4	12
BOS.		26	10	20	30	−5	10
Ray Bourque	D	80	21	60	81	+11	56
Vladimir Ruzicka	C	77	39	36	75	−10	48
Stephen Leach	R	78	31	29	60	−8	147
Bob Carpenter	L	60	25	23	48	−3	46
Glen Wesley	D	78	9	37	46	−9	54
Brent Ashton	L	68	18	22	40	−7	51
WIN.		7	1	0	1	−3	4
BOS.		61	17	22	39	−4	47
Andy Brickley	L	23	10	17	27	+6	2
Peter Douris	R	54	10	13	23	+9	10
Bob Sweeney	C	63	6	14	20	−9	103
Joe Juneau*	C	14	5	14	19	+6	4
Gordon Murphy	D	73	5	14	19	−2	84
PHI.		31	2	8	10	−4	33
BOS.		42	3	6	9	2	51
Ken Hodge	C	42	6	11	17	−8	10

Acquired: Ashton from Win.(Oct.29); Murphy from Phi.(Jan.2); Oates from St.L.(Feb.7).

Goalies (10 Gm)	Gm	Min	Avg	SO	Record
Andy Moog	62	3640	3.23	1	28-22-9
Daniel Berthiaume	27	1378	3.79	0	8-14-3
LA.	19	979	4.04	0	7-10-1
BOS	8	399	3.16	0	1-4-2
Matt Delguidice*	10	424	3.96	0	2-5-1
BOSTON	80	4880	3.38	1	36-32-12

Assists: Moog (3); **PM:** Moog (52), Delguidice (2).
Acquired: Berthiaume from LA (Jan.20).

Calgary Flames

Top Scorers	Pos	Gm	G	A	Pts	+/-	PM
Gary Roberts	L	76	53	37	90	+32	219
Al MacInnis	D	72	20	57	77	+13	83
Theoren Fleury	C	80	33	40	73	0	133
Sergei Makarov	R	68	22	48	70	+14	60
Joe Nieuwendyk	C	69	22	34	56	−1	55
Gary Suter	D	70	12	43	55	+1	126
Robert Reichel	C	77	20	34	54	+1	34
Paul Ranheim	L	80	23	20	43	+16	32
Joel Otto	C	78	13	21	34	−10	163
Gary Leeman	R	63	9	19	28	−12	81
TOR.		34	7	12	19	−1	54
CALG		29	2	7	9	−11	27
Michel Petit.	D	70	4	23	27	−15	164
TOR.		34	1	13	14	−17	85
CALG		36	3	10	13	+2	79
Carey Wilson	C	42	11	12	23	−6	37
Ronnie Stern	R	72	13	9	22	0	338
Marc Habscheid	C	46	7	11	18	−11	42
Craig Berube	L	76	6	11	17	−5	264
TOR.		40	5	7	12	−2	109
CALG		36	1	4	5	−3	155

Acquired: Berube, Leeman, Petit and goalie Reese from Tor. (Jan.2).

Goalies (10 Gm)	Gm	Min	Avg	SO	Record
Jeff Reese	20	1000	3.42	1	4-7-3
TOR.	8	413	2.91	1	1-5-1
CALG	12	587	3.78	0	3-2-2
Mike Vernon	63	3460	3.58	0	24-30-9
CALGARY.	80	4879	3.75	0	31-37-12

Assists: Vernon (7), Reese (1); **PM:** Reese (12), Vernon (8).
Acquired: Reese from Tor. (Jan. 2).

Buffalo Sabres

Top Scorers	Pos	Gm	G	A	Pts	+/-	PM
Dale Hawerchuk	C	77	23	75	98	−22	27
Pat LaFontaine.	C	57	46	47	93	+10	98
Dave Andreychuk	L	80	41	50	91	−9	71
Alexander Mogilny	R	67	39	45	84	+7	73
Donald Audette*	R	63	31	17	48	−1	75
Doug Bodger	D	73	11	35	46	−1	108
Randy Wood	L	78	22	18	40	−12	86
NYI		8	2	2	4	−3	21
BUF		70	20	16	36	−9	65
Tony Tanti	R	70	15	16	31	−4	100
Petr Svoboda	D	71	6	22	28	+1	146
MON.		58	5	16	21	+9	94
BUF		13	1	6	7	+8	52
Wayne Presley	R	59	10	16	26	−27	133
SJ		47	8	14	22	−29	76
BUF		12	2	2	4	+2	57
Christian Ruutu	C	70	4	21	25	−7	76
Grant Ledyard	D	50	5	16	21	−4	45
Ken Sutton*	D	64	2	18	20	+5	71
Brad May*	L	69	11	6	17	−12	309
Mike Ramsey	D	66	3	14	17	+8	67

Acquired: Wood from NYI (Oct.25, in LaFontaine deal); Presley from SJ (Mar.9); Svoboda from Mon.(Mar.10).

Goalies (10 Gm)	Gm	Min	Avg	SO	Record
Tom Draper*	26	1403	3.21	1	10-9-5
Clint Malarchuk	29	1639	3.73	0	10-13-3
Daren Puppa	33	1757	3.89	0	11-14-4
BUFFALO	80	4869	3.68	1	31-37-12

Assists: Draper (2); **PM:** Malarchuk (6), Draper and Puppa (2).

Chicago Blackhawks

Top Scorers	Pos	Gm	G	A	Pts	+/-	PM
Jeremy Roenick	C	80	53	50	103	+23	98
Steve Larmer	R	80	29	45	74	+10	65
Michel Goulet	L	75	22	41	63	+20	69
Brent Sutter	C	69	22	38	60	−10	36
NYI		8	4	6	10	−5	6
CHI		61	18	32	50	−5	30
Chris Chelios	D	80	9	47	56	+24	245
Rob Brown	R	67	21	26	47	−15	71
HART.		42	16	15	31	−14	39
CHI		25	5	11	16	−1	32
Dirk Graham	R	80	17	30	47	−5	89
Brian Noonan	R	65	19	12	31	+9	81
Steve Smith	D	76	9	21	30	+23	304
Mike Hudson	C	76	14	15	29	−11	92
Keith Brown	D	57	6	10	16	+7	69
Jocelyn Lemieux	L	78	6	10	16	−2	80
Bryan Marchment	D	58	5	10	15	−4	168
Tony Hrkac	C	40	3	12	15	+2	10
SJ		22	2	10	12	−2	4
CHI		18	1	2	3	+4	6

Acquired: Sutter from NYI (Oct.25); R.Brown from Hart.(Jan.24); Hrkac from SJ (Feb.7).

Goalies (10 Gm)	Gm	Min	Avg	SO	Record
Dominik Hasek*	20	1014	2.60	1	10-4-1
Ed Belfour	52	2928	2.70	5	21-18-10
Jim Waite*	17	877	3.69	0	4-7-4
CHICAGO	80	4884	2.90	6	36-29-15

Assists: Belfour (2), Waite (1); **PM:** Belfour (40), Hasek (8).

Team by Team Statistics (Cont.)

Detroit Red Wings

Top Scorers	Pos	Gm	G	A	Pts	+/−	PM
Steve Yzerman	C	79	45	58	103	+26	64
Sergei Fedorov	C	80	32	54	86	+26	72
Paul Ysebaert	L	79	35	40	75	+44	55
Jimmy Carson	C	80	34	35	69	+17	30
Ray Sheppard	R	74	36	26	62	+7	27
Nicklas Lidstrom*	D	80	11	49	60	+36	22
Shawn Burr	L	79	19	32	51	+26	118
Kevin Miller	L	80	20	26	46	+6	53
Bob Probert	R	63	20	24	44	+16	276
Gerard Gallant	L	69	14	22	36	+16	187
Steve Chiasson	D	62	10	24	34	22	136
Vlad. Konstantinov*	D	79	8	25	33	+25	172
Brad McCrimmon	D	79	7	22	29	+39	118
Yves Racine	D	61	2	22	24	−6	94
Keith Primeau	C	35	6	10	16	+9	83
Brent Fedyk	R	61	5	8	13	−5	42
Sheldon Kennedy	R	27	3	8	11	−2	24
Alan Kerr	R	58	3	8	11	+1	133
Brad Marsh	D	55	3	5	8	+8	53
Doug Crossman	D	26	0	8	8	+8	14
Brian MacLellan	L	23	1	5	6	+4	38

Goalies (10 Gm)	Gm	Min	Avg	SO	Record
Greg Millen	10	487	2.71	0	3-2-3
NYR	0	0	0.00	0	0-0-0
DET	10	487	2.71	0	3-2-3
Tim Cheveldae	72	4236	3.20	2	38-23-9
DETROIT	80	4870	3.15	3	43-25-12

Note: Cheveldae shared a third shutout with Vincent Riendeau.
Assists: Cheveldae (4); **PM:** Cheveldae (6).
Acquired: Millen from NYR (Dec.26).

Hartford Whalers

Top Scorers	Pos	Gm	G	A	Pts	+/−	PM
John Cullen	C	77	26	51	77	−28	141
Murray Craven	L	73	24	30	60	−2	46
PHI.		12	3	3	6	+2	8
HART.		61	24	30	54	−4	38
Pat Verbeek	R	76	22	35	57	−16	243
Zarley Zalapski	D	79	20	37	57	−7	116
Mikael Anderson	L	74	18	29	47	+18	14
Bobby Holik	L	76	21	24	45	+4	44
Andrew Cassels	C	67	11	30	41	+3	18
Geoff Sanderson*	C	64	13	18	31	+5	18
Steve Konroyd	D	82	4	24	28	−1	97
CHI.		49	2	14	16	+4	65
HART.		33	2	10	8	−5	32
Brad Shaw	D	62	3	22	25	+1	44
Adam Burt	D	66	9	15	24	−16	93
Marc Bergevin	D	75	7	17	24	−13	64
Mark Hunter	R	63	10	13	23	−8	159
Yvon Corriveau	L	38	12	8	20	+5	36
Randy Cunneyworth	L	39	7	10	17	−5	71

Acquired: Craven from Phi.(Nov.13); Konroyd from Chi.(Jan.24).

Goalies (10 Gm)	Gm	Min	Avg	SO	Record
Peter Sidorkiewicz	35	1995	3.34	2	9-19-6
Frank Pietrangelo	10	531	3.62	0	5-2-1
PIT.	5	225	5.33	0	2-1-0
HART.	5	306	2.35	0	3-1-1
Kay Whitmore	45	2567	3.62	3	14-21-6
HARTFORD	80	4878	3.48	5	26-41-13

Assists: Sidorkiewicz and Whitmore (1); **PM:** Whitmore (16), Sidorkiewicz (2).
Acquired: Pietrangelo from Pit.(Mar.10).

Edmonton Oilers

Top Scorers	Pos	Gm	G	A	Pts	+/−	PM
Vincent Damphousse	L	80	38	51	89	+10	53
Joe Murphy	R	80	35	47	82	+17	52
Craig Simpson	L	79	24	37	61	+8	80
Scott Mellanby	R	80	23	27	50	+5	197
Bernie Nicholls	C	50	20	29	49	+4	40
NYR		1	0	0	0	−1	0
EDM		49	20	29	49	+5	40
Dave Manson	D	79	15	32	47	+9	220
Kelly Buchberger	L	79	20	24	44	+9	157
Anatoli Semenov	C	59	20	22	42	+12	16
Norm Maciver	D	57	6	34	40	+20	38
Petr Klima	L	57	21	13	34	−18	52
Craig MacTavish	C	80	12	18	30	−1	98
Martin Gelinas	L	68	11	18	29	+14	62
Esa Tikkanen	L	40	12	16	28	−8	44
Josef Beranek*	C	58	12	16	28	−2	18
Mark Lamb	C	59	6	22	28	+4	46
David Maley	L	60	10	17	27	+8	104
NJ		37	7	11	18	0	58
EDM		23	3	6	9	+8	46

Acquired: Nicholls from NYR (Oct.4 in Messier deal); Maley from NJ (Jan.12).

Goalies (10 Gm)	Gm	Min	Avg	SO	Record
Norm Foster	10	439	2.73	0	5-3-0
Bill Ranford	67	3822	3.58	1	27-26-10
Ron Tugnutt	33	1707	4.08	1	7-18-3
QUE	30	1583	4.02	1	6-17-3
EDM	3	124	4.84	0	1-1-0
Peter Ing	12	463	4.28	0	1-3-0
EDMONTON	80	4858	3.67	1	36-34-10

Assists: Ing and Ranford (3); **PM:** Ranford (4), Foster and Tugnutt (2).
Acquired: Tugnutt from Que.(Mar.10).

Los Angeles Kings

Top Scorers	Pos	Gm	G	A	Pts	+/−	PM
Wayne Gretzky	C	74	31	90	121	−12	34
Luc Robitaille	L	80	44	63	107	−4	95
Paul Coffey	D	64	11	58	69	+1	87
PIT		54	10	54	64	+4	62
LA		10	1	4	5	−3	25
Tony Granato	L	80	39	29	68	+4	187
Jari Kurri	R	73	23	37	60	−24	24
Corey Millen	C	57	21	25	46	+2	66
NYR		11	1	4	5	−1	10
LA		46	20	21	41	+3	56
Mike Donnelly	L	80	29	16	45	+5	50
Bob Kudelski	L	80	22	21	43	−15	42
Tomas Sandstrom	R	49	17	22	39	−2	70
Dave Taylor	R	77	10	19	29	+10	63
Marty McSorley	D	71	7	22	29	−13	268
John McIntyre	C	73	5	19	24	0	100
Charlie Huddy	D	56	4	19	23	−10	43
Rob Blake	D	57	7	13	20	−5	102
Peter Ahola*	D	71	7	12	19	+12	101
Larry Robinson	D	56	3	10	13	+1	37
Jay Miller	L	67	4	7	11	−8	237
Kyosti Karjalainen*	L	28	1	8	9	+4	12
Tim Watters	D	37	0	7	7	−2	92

Acquired: Millen from NYR (Dec.23); Coffey from Pit.(Feb.19).

Goalies (10 Gm)	Gm	Min	Avg	SO	Record
Kelly Hrudey	60	3509	3.37	1	26-17-13
Steve Weeks	30	1284	3.69	0	10-7-2
NYI		23	1032	3.60	0	9-4-2
LA		7	252	4.05	0	1-3-0
LOS ANGELES	80	4874	3.64	1	35-31-14

Assists: Hrudey and Weeks (1); **PM:** Hrudey (12), Weeks (2).
Acquired: Weeks from NYI (Feb.18).

Minnesota North Stars

Top Scorers	Pos	Gm	G	A	Pts	+/-	PM
Mike Modano	C	76	33	44	77	-9	46
Brian Bellows	L	80	30	45	75	-20	41
Dave Gagner	C	78	31	40	71	-4	107
Ulf Dahlen	R	79	36	30	66	-5	10
Todd Elik	C	62	15	31	46	0	125
Bobby Smith	C	68	9	37	46	-24	111
Brian Propp	L	51	12	23	35	-3	49
Neal Broten	C	76	8	26	34	-15	16
Mike Craig	R	67	15	16	31	-12	155
Mark Tinordi	D	63	4	24	28	-13	177
Gaetan Duchesne	L	73	8	15	23	+6	102
Kip Miller*	C	39	6	12	18	-22	14
QUE		36	5	10	15	-21	12
MIN		3	1	2	3	-1	2
Jim Johnson	D	71	4	10	14	+11	102
Chris Dahlquist	D	74	1	13	14	-10	68
Basil McRae	L	59	5	8	13	-14	245
Derian Hatcher*	D	43	7	5	12	+7	88
Craig Ludwig	D	73	2	9	11	0	54
Marc Bureau*	C	46	6	4	10	-5	50
David Shaw	D	59	1	9	10	-12	72
NYR		10	0	1	1	+1	15
EDM		12	1	1	2	-8	8
MIN		37	0	7	7	-5	49
Stewart Gavin	R	35	5	4	9	0	27
Rob Ramage	D	34	4	5	9	-4	69

Acquired: Shaw from Edm. (Jan.21); Miller from Que.(Mar.8)

Goalies (10 Gm)	Gm	Min	Avg	SO	Record
Darcy Wakaluk	36	1905	3.28	1	13-19-1
Jon Casey	52	2911	3.40	2	19-23-5
MINNESOTA	80	4835	3.45	3	32-42-6

Assists: Casey (2); **PM:** Casey (26), Wakaluk (20).

Montreal Canadiens

Top Scorers	Pos	Gm	G	A	Pts	+/-	PM
Kirk Muller	L	78	36	41	77	+15	86
Denis Savard	C	77	28	42	70	+6	73
Stephan Lebeau	C	77	27	31	58	+18	14
Shayne Corson	L	64	17	36	53	+15	118
Brent Gilchrist	C	79	23	27	50	+29	57
Mike Keane	R	67	11	30	41	+16	64
Guy Carbonneau	C	72	18	21	39	+2	39
Eric Desjardins	D	77	6	32	38	+17	50
Gilbert Dionne*	L	39	21	13	34	+7	10
Matt Schneider	D	78	8	24	32	+10	72
Mike McPhee	L	78	16	15	31	+6	63
Kevin Haller*	D	66	8	17	25	-9	92
BUF		58	6	15	21	-13	75
MON		8	2	2	4	+4	17
Russ Courtnall	R	27	7	14	21	+6	6
Sylvain Turgeon	L	56	9	11	20	-4	39
John LeClair*	C	59	8	11	19	+5	14
J.J. Daigneault	D	79	4	14	18	+16	36
Sylvain Lefebvre	D	69	3	14	17	+9	91
Chris Nilan	R	56	6	8	14	-6	260
BOS		39	5	5	10	-5	186
MON		17	1	3	4	-1	74
Benoit Brunet*	L	18	4	6	10	+4	14
Paul DiPietro*	C	33	4	6	10	+5	25
Patrice Brisebois*	D	26	2	8	10	+9	20

Acquired: Haller from Buf.(Mar.10). **Claimed:** Nilan on waivers from Bos.(Feb.12).

Goalies (10 Gm)	Gm	Min	Avg	SO	Record
Patrick Roy	67	3935	2.36	5	36-22-8
MONTREAL	80	4877	2.55	7	41-28-11

Assists: Roy (5); **PM:** Roy (4).

New Jersey Devils

Top Scorers	Pos	Gm	G	A	Pts	+/-	PM
Claude LeMieux	R	74	41	27	68	+9	109
Stephane Richer	R	74	29	35	64	-1	25
Kevin Todd*	C	80	21	42	63	+8	69
Peter Stastny	C	66	24	38	62	+6	42
Scott Stevens	D	68	17	42	59	+24	124
Claude Vilgrain	L	71	19	27	46	+27	74
Bruce Driver	D	78	7	35	42	+5	66
Alexi Kasatonov	D	76	12	28	40	+14	70
Tom Chorske	L	76	19	17	36	+8	32
Randy McKay	R	80	17	16	33	+6	246
Eric Weinrich	D	76	7	25	32	+10	55
Valeri Zelepukin*	L	44	13	18	31	+11	28
Doug Brown	R	71	11	17	28	+17	27
Laurie Boschman	C	75	8	20	28	+9	121
Viacheslav Fetisov	D	70	3	23	26	+11	108
Dave Barr	R	41	6	12	18	+9	32
Zdeno Ciger	L	20	6	5	11	-2	10
Alexander Semak*	C	25	5	6	11	+5	0
Troy Mallette	L	32	4	7	11	+6	79
EDM		15	1	3	4	-1	36
NJ		17	3	4	7	+7	43
Pat Conacher	L	44	7	3	10	0	16
Ken Daneyko	D	80	1	7	8	+7	170
Jarrod Skalde*	C	15	2	4	6	-1	4

Acquired: Mallette from Edm. (Jan.12).

Goalies (10 Gm)	Gm	Min	Avg	SO	Record
Craig Billington	26	1363	3.04	2	13-7-1
Chris Terreri	54	3169	3.20	1	22-22-10
NEW JERSEY	80	4868	3.19	3	38-31-11

Assists: Billington and Terreri (1); **PM:** Terreri (13), Billington (2).

New York Islanders

Top Scorers	Pos	Gm	G	A	Pts	+/-	PM
Pierre Turgeon	C	77	40	55	95	+7	20
BUF		8	2	6	8	-1	4
NYI		69	38	49	87	+8	16
Ray Ferraro	C	80	40	40	80	+25	92
Derek King	L	80	40	38	78	-10	46
Steve Thomas	L	82	30	48	78	+8	97
CHI		11	2	6	8	-3	26
NYI		71	28	42	70	+11	71
Benoit Hogue	C	75	30	46	76	+30	67
BUF		3	0	1	1	0	0
NYI		72	30	45	75	+30	67
Dave Volek	L	74	18	42	60	0	35
Tom Kurvers	D	74	9	47	56	-18	30
Uwe Krupp*	D	67	8	29	37	+13	49
BUF		8	2	0	2	0	6
NYI		59	6	29	35	+13	43
Adam Creighton	C	77	21	15	36	-5	118
CHI		11	6	6	12	-1	16
NYI		66	15	9	24	-4	102
Patrick Flatley	R	38	8	28	36	+14	31
Dan Marois	R	75	17	16	33	-34	94
TOR		63	15	11	26	-36	76
NYI		12	2	5	7	+2	18
Jeff Norton	D	28	1	18	19	+2	18

Acquired: Creighton and Thomas from Chi.(Oct.25); Hogue, Krupp and Turgeon from Buf.(Oct.25 in LaFontaine deal); Marois from Tor.(Mar.10).

Goalies (10 Gm)	Gm	Min	Avg	SO	Record
Mark Fitzpatrick	30	1743	3.20	0	11-13-5
Glenn Healy	37	1960	3.80	1	14-16-4
NY ISLANDERS	80	4868	3.69	1	34-35-11

Assists: Fitzpatrick (2), Healy (1); **PM:** Healy (18), Fitzpatrick (8).

Team by Team Statistics (Cont.)

New York Rangers

Top Scorers	Pos	Gm	G	A	Pts	+/-	PM
Mark Messier.........	C	79	35	72	107	+31	76
Brian Leetch........	D	80	22	80	102	+25	26
Mike Gartner........	R	76	40	41	81	+11	55
James Patrick........	C	80	14	57	71	+34	54
Tony Amonte*........	R	79	35	34	69	+12	55
Adam Graves........	C	80	26	33	59	+19	139
Sergei Nemchinov......	C	73	30	28	58	+19	15
Darren Turcotte.......	C	71	30	23	53	+11	57
John Ogrodnick......	L	55	17	13	30	+6	22
Doug Weight*........	C	53	8	22	30	−3	23
Paul Broten..........	R	74	13	15	28	+14	102
Randy Gilhen........	C	73	10	13	23	+2	28
LA............		33	3	6	9	−3	14
NYR............		40	7	7	14	+5	14
Kris King..........	L	79	10	9	19	+13	224
Per Djoos...........	D	50	1	18	19	+7	40
Tim Kerr...........	R	32	7	11	18	−5	12
Jan Erixon..........	L	46	8	9	17	+13	4
Jeff Beukeboom.......	D	74	1	15	16	+23	200
EDM............		18	0	5	5	+4	78
NYR............		56	1	10	11	+19	122
Joe Cirella.........	D	67	3	12	15	+11	121
Joey Kocur.........	R	51	7	4	11	−4	121
Jay Wells..........	D	52	2	9	11	−1	181
BUF............		41	2	9	11	−3	157
NYR............		11	0	0	0	+2	24

Acquired: Beukeboom from Edm.(Nov.11); Gilhen from LA (Dec.23); Wells from Buf.(Mar.9).

Goalies (10 Gm)	Gm	Min	Avg	SO	Record
John Vanbiesbrouck ...	45	2526	2.85	2	27-13-3
Mike Richter........	41	2298	3.11	3	23-12-2
NY RANGERS	80	4836	3.05	5	50-25-5

Assists: Vanbiesbrouck (3); **PM:** Vanbiesbrouck (23), Richter (6).

Philadelphia Flyers

Top Scorers	Pos	Gm	G	A	Pts	+/-	PM
Mark Recchi..........	R	80	43	54	97	−21	96
PIT................		58	33	37	70	−16	78
PHI................		22	10	17	27	−5	18
Rob Brind'Amour	C	80	33	44	77	−3	100
Kevin Dineen........	R	80	30	32	62	−5	143
HART............		16	4	2	6	−6	23
PHI............		64	26	30	56	+1	120
Mike Ricci..........	C	78	20	36	56	−10	93
Steve Duchesne.......	D	78	18	38	56	−7	86
Brian Benning.......	D	75	4	42	46	−5	134
LA................		53	2	30	32	+4	99
PHI................		22	2	12	14	−9	35
Mark Pederson.......	L	58	15	25	40	+14	22
Dan Quinn..........	C	67	11	26	37	−13	26
Kerry Huffman.......	D	60	14	18	32	+1	41
Garry Galley........	D	77	5	27	32	−2	117
BOS............		38	2	12	14	−3	83
PHI............		39	3	15	18	+1	34
Andrei Lomakin.......	L	57	14	16	30	−6	26
Mark Howe..........	D	42	7	18	25	+18	18
Per-Erik Eklund	C	51	7	16	23	0	4
Claude Boivin*.......	L	58	5	13	18	−2	187
Brad Jones..........	L	48	7	10	17	−2	44

Acquired: Dineen from Hart.(Nov.13); Galley from Bos.(Jan.2); Benning from LA and Recchi from Pit.(Feb.19).

Goalies (10 Gm)	Gm	Min	Avg	SO	Record
Dominic Roussel*	17	922	2.60	1	7-8-2
Ron Hextall........	45	2668	3.40	3	16-21-6
PHILADELPHIA.........	80	4866	3.37	4	32-37-11

Assists: Hextall (4), Roussel (1); **PM:** Hextall (35), Roussel (2).

Pittsburgh Penguins

Top Scorers	Pos	Gm	G	A	Pts	+/-	PM
Mario Lemieux.........	C	64	44	87	131	+27	94
Kevin Stevens	L	80	54	69	123	+8	252
Joe Mullen	R	77	42	45	87	+12	30
Larry Murphy..........	D	77	21	56	77	+33	50
Jaromir Jagr..........	R	70	32	37	69	+12	34
Rick Tocchet..........	R	61	27	32	59	+15	151
PHI..............		42	13	16	29	+3	102
PIT..............		19	14	16	30	+12	49
Ron Francis	C	70	21	33	54	−7	30
Bob Errey	L	78	19	16	35	+1	119
Bryan Trottier........	C	63	11	18	29	−11	54
Phil Bourque	L	58	10	16	26	−6	58
Troy Loney	L	76	10	16	26	−5	127
Gordie Roberts	D	73	2	22	24	+19	87
Kjell Samuelsson	D	74	5	11	16	+1	110
PHI..............		54	4	9	13	+1	76
PIT..............		20	1	2	3	0	34
Jiri Hrdina	C	56	3	13	16	+4	16
Ulf Samuelsson	D	62	1	14	15	+2	206
Ken Priestlay	C	50	2	8	10	+5	4
Paul Stanton	D	54	2	8	10	−8	62

Acquired: K.Samuelsson, Tocchet and goalie Wregget from Phi.(Feb.19).

Goalies (10 Gm)	Gm	Min	Avg	SO	Record
Tom Barrasso	57	3329	3.53	1	25-22-9
Ken Wregget	32	1707	3.73	0	14-11-3
PHI..............	23	1259	3.57	0	9-8-3
PIT..............	9	448	4.15	0	5-3-0
Wendell Young	18	838	3.79	0	7-6-0
PITTSBURGH...........	80	4854	3.81	1	39-32-9

Assists: Barrasso (4), Wregget (2); **PM:** Barrasso (30), Wregget (2).
Acquired: Wregget from Phi.(Feb.19).

Quebec Nordiques

Top Scorers	Pos	Gm	G	A	Pts	+/-	PM
Joe Sakic	C	69	29	65	94	+5	20
Mats Sundin	R	80	33	43	76	−19	105
Owen Nolan	R	75	42	31	73	−9	181
Greg Paslawski	R	80	28	17	45	−12	18
Mike Hough	L	61	16	22	38	−1	77
Mikhail Tatarinov	D	66	11	27	38	+8	72
Claude Lapointe*.....	C	78	13	20	33	−8	86
Doug Smail..........	L	46	10	18	28	−11	47
Gino Cavallini	L	66	10	14	24	−9	44
STL..............		48	9	7	16	−8	40
QUE..............		18	1	7	8	−1	4
Alexei Gusarov	D	68	5	18	23	−9	12
Valeri Kamensky*......	L	23	7	14	21	−1	14
Herb Raglan	R	62	6	14	20	−5	120
Jamie Baker*.........	C	52	7	10	17	−5	32
Curtis Leschyshyn	D	42	5	12	17	−28	42
Dan Lambert*........	D	28	6	9	15	−5	22
Bryan Fogarty	D	20	3	12	15	−15	16
Marc Fortier	C	39	5	9	14	−7	33
John Tonelli	L	52	3	11	14	−5	51
CHI..............		33	1	7	8	+2	37
QUE..............		19	2	4	6	−7	14

Acquired: Tonelli from Chi.(Feb.17).
Claimed: Cavallini on waivers from St.L.(Feb.27).

Goalies (10 Gm)	Gm	Min	Avg	SO	Record
John Tanner*..........	14	796	3.47	1	1-7-4
Stephane Fiset*	23	1133	3.76	1	7-10-2
Jacques Cloutier	26	1345	3.93	0	6-14-3
QUEBEC	80	4876	3.91	3	20-48-12

Assists: none; **PM:** Fiset (8), Cloutier (6), Tanner (4).

St. Louis Blues

Top Scorers	Pos	Gm	G	A	Pts	+/-	PM
Brett Hull..............	R	73	70	39	109	-2	48
Craig Janney..........	C	78	18	69	87	+6	22
BOS.................		53	12	39	51	+1	20
STL.................		25	6	30	36	+5	2
Brendan Shanahan.....	R	80	33	36	69	-3	171
Nelson Emerson*......	C	79	23	36	59	-5	66
Jeff Brown............	D	80	20	38	58	+8	38
Ron Sutter............	C	68	19	27	46	+9	91
Dave Christian........	R	78	20	24	44	+2	41
Paul Cavallini.........	D	66	10	25	35	+7	95
Bob Bassen...........	C	79	7	25	32	+12	167
Ron Wilson...........	C	64	12	17	29	+10	46
Rich Sutter...........	R	77	9	16	25	+7	107
Dave Lowry...........	L	75	7	13	20	-11	77
Garth Butcher.........	D	68	5	15	20	+5	189
Stephane Quintal......	D	75	4	16	20	-11	109
BOS.................		49	4	10	14	-8	77
STL.................		26	0	6	6	-3	32
Rick Zombo...........	D	67	3	15	18	+1	61
DET.................		3	0	0	0	-3	15
STL.................		64	3	15	18	+4	46
Michel Mongeau.......	C	36	3	12	15	-2	6
Lee Norwood..........	D	50	3	11	14	+14	110
HART.................		6	0	0	0	0	16
STL.................		44	3	11	14	+14	94

Acquired: Zombo from Det.(Oct.18); Norwood from Hart.(Nov.13); Janney and Quintal from Bos.(Feb.7).

Goalies (10 Gm)	Gm	Min	Avg	SO	Record
Guy Hebert*..........	13	738	2.93	0	5-5-1
Curtis Joseph.........	60	3494	3.01	2	27-20-10
Pat Jablonski*..........	10	468	4.87	0	3-6-0
ST.LOUIS.............	80	4868	3.28	2	36-33-11

Assists: Joseph (9), Hebert (1); **PM:** Joseph (12), Jablonski (4).

Toronto Maple Leafs

Top Scorers	Pos	Gm	G	A	Pts	+/-	PM
Doug Gilmour.........	C	78	26	61	87	+25	78
CALG...............		38	11	27	38	+12	46
TOR.................		40	15	34	49	+13	32
Glenn Anderson.......	R	72	24	33	57	-13	100
Dave Ellett...........	D	79	18	33	51	-13	95
Peter Zezel...........	C	64	16	33	49	-22	26
Wendel Clark.........	L	43	19	21	40	-14	123
Brian Bradley.........	C	59	10	21	31	-3	48
Jamie Macoun........	D	76	5	25	30	+10	71
CALG...............		37	2	12	14	+10	53
TOR.................		39	3	13	16	0	18
Mike Bullard	C	65	14	14	28	-19	42
Dave McLlwain........	C	73	10	18	28	-9	36
WIN.................		3	1	1	2	+1	2
BUF.................		5	0	0	0	-3	2
NYI.................		54	8	15	23	-8	28
TOR.................		11	1	2	3	+1	4
Rob Pearson*..........	R	47	14	10	24	-16	58
Mike Krushelnyski......	C	72	9	15	24	-5	72
Bob Rouse	D	79	3	19	22	-20	97
Rick Nattress	D	54	2	19	21	-1	63
CALG...............		18	0	5	5	0	31
TOR.................		36	2	14	16	-1	32

Acquired: Gilmour, Macoun, Nattress and goalie Wamsley from Calg.(Jan.2); McLlwain from NYI (Mar.10).

Goalies (10 Gm)	Gm	Min	Avg	SO	Record
Grant Fuhr...........	65	3774	3.66	2	25-33-5
Rick Wamsley...........	17	885	4.14	0	7-7-0
CALG...............	9	457	4.46	0	3-4-0
TOR.................	8	428	3.79	0	4-3-0
TORONTO	80	4843	3.64	3	30-43-7

Assists: Fuhr (1); **PM:** Fuhr (4).
Acquired: Wamsley from Calg.(Jan.2).

San Jose Sharks

Top Scorers	Pos	Gm	G	A	Pts	+/-	PM
Pat Falloon*..........	R	79	25	34	59	-32	16
Brian Mullen..........	R	72	18	28	46	-14	66
David Bruce..........	R	60	22	16	38	-20	46
Brian Lawton..........	C	59	15	22	37	-25	42
Kelly Kisio............	C	48	11	26	37	-7	54
Doug Wilson..........	D	44	9	19	28	-38	26
David Williams*........	D	56	3	25	28	-13	40
Dean Evason..........	C	74	11	15	26	-22	94
Perry Berezan........	C	66	12	7	19	-26	30
Mike Sullivan*.........	C	64	8	11	19	-18	15
Neil Wilkinson........	D	60	4	15	19	-11	97
Dave Snuggerud	L	66	3	16	19	-15	45
BUF.................		55	3	15	18	-3	36
SJ.................		11	0	1	1	-12	9
Jay More*............	D	46	4	13	17	-32	85
Steve Bozek...........	L	58	8	8	16	-30	27
Dale Craigwell*........	C	32	5	11	16	-3	8
Pat MacLeod*.........	D	37	5	11	16	-32	4
Paul Fenton...........	L	60	11	4	15	-39	33
Ken Hammond.........	D	46	5	10	15	-17	82

Acquired: Snuggerud from Buf.(Mar.9).

Goalies (10 Gm)	Gm	Min	Avg	SO	Record
Jeff Hackett	42	2314	3.84	0	11-27-1
Arturs Irbe*.............	13	645	4.47	0	2-6-3
Jarmo Myllys	27	1374	5.02	0	3-18-1
SAN JOSE	80	4829	4.46	0	17-58-5

Assists: Hackett (2), Irbe and Myllys (1); **PM:** Hackett (8), Myllys (2).

Vancouver Canucks

Top Scorers	Pos	Gm	G	A	Pts	+/-	PM
Trevor Linden.........	R	80	31	44	75	+3	99
Cliff Ronning.........	C	80	24	47	71	+18	42
Igor Larionov.........	C	72	21	44	65	+7	56
Pavel Bure*..........	R	65	34	26	60	0	30
Greg Adams..........	L	76	30	27	57	+8	26
Geoff Courtnall.......	L	70	23	34	57	-6	118
Jyrki Lumme	D	75	12	32	44	+25	65
Sergio Momesso......	L	58	20	23	43	+16	198
Jim Sandlak	R	66	16	24	40	+22	176
Tom Fergus	C	55	15	23	38	-10	21
TOR.................		11	1	3	4	-11	4
VAN.................		44	14	20	34	+1	17
Petr Nedved..........	C	77	15	22	37	-3	36
Doug Lidster	D	66	6	23	29	+9	39
Dave Babych.........	D	75	5	24	29	-2	63
Gerald Diduck........	D	77	6	21	27	-3	224
Garry Valk...........	L	65	8	17	25	+3	56
Ryan Walter	C	67	6	11	17	+6	49
Dana Murzyn.........	D	70	3	12	15	+15	145
Gino Odjick..........	L	65	4	6	10	-1	348
Adrien Plavsic........	D	16	1	9	10	+4	14
Robert Dirk	D	72	2	7	9	+6	126
Randy Gregg	D	21	1	4	5	-3	24

Acquired: Fergus from Tor.(Dec.18).

Goalies (10 Gm)	Gm	Min	Avg	SO	Record
Kirk McLean...........	65	3852	2.74	5	38-17-9
Troy Gamble..........	19	1009	4.34	0	4-9-3
VANCOUVER...........	80	4874	3.08	5	42-26-12

Assists: McLean (4); **PM:** Gamble (8).

Team by Team Statistics (Cont.)

Washington Capitals

Top Scorers	Pos	Gm	G	A	Pts	+/−	PM
Michal Pivonka	C	80	23	57	80	+10	47
Dale Hunter	C	80	28	50	78	−2	205
Dino Ciccarelli	R	78	38	38	76	−10	78
Dimitri Khristich	C	80	36	37	73	+24	35
Mike Ridley	C	80	29	40	69	+3	38
Randy Burridge	L	66	23	44	67	−4	50
Peter Bondra	R	71	28	28	56	+16	42
Calle Johansson	D	80	14	42	56	+2	49
Kevin Hatcher	D	79	17	37	54	+18	105
Kelly Miller	L	78	14	38	52	+20	49
Al Iafrate	D	78	17	34	51	+1	180
Sylvain Cote	D	78	11	29	40	+7	31
John Druce	R	67	19	18	37	+14	39
Todd Krygier	L	37	13	17	30	−1	107
Paul MacDermid	R	74	12	16	28	−6	194
WIN		59	10	11	21	−8	151
WASH		15	2	5	7	+2	43
Alan May	L	75	6	9	15	−7	221
Rod Langway	D	64	0	13	13	+11	22
Dave Tippett	L	30	2	10	12	+2	16
Nick Kypreos	L	65	4	6	10	−3	206
Tim Bergland	R	22	1	4	5	−3	2

Acquired: MacDermid from Win.(Mar.2).

Goalies (10 Gm)	Gm	Min	Avg	SO	Record
Don Beaupre	54	3108	3.20	1	29-17-6
Jim Hrivnak	12	605	3.47	0	6-3-0
Mike Liut	21	1123	3.74	1	10-7-2
WASHINGTON	80	4846	3.40	2	45-27-8

Assists: Liut (1); **PM:** Beaupre (30), Liut (2).

Winnipeg Jets

Top Scorers	Pos	Gm	G	A	Pts	+/−	PM
Phil Housley	D	74	23	63	86	−5	92
Ed Olczyk	C	64	32	33	65	+11	67
Frederik Olausson	D	77	20	42	62	−31	34
Pat Elynuik	R	60	25	25	50	−2	65
Troy Murray	C	74	17	30	47	−13	69
Darrin Shannon	L	69	13	27	40	+6	41
BUF		1	0	1	1	+1	0
WIN		68	13	26	39	+5	41
Teppo Numminen	D	80	5	34	39	+15	32
Thomas Steen	C	38	13	25	38	+5	29
Luciano Borsato*	C	56	15	21	36	−6	45
Lucien DeBlois	C	65	9	13	22	−2	41
TOR		54	8	11	19	−3	39
WIN		11	1	2	3	+1	2
Stu Barnes*	C	46	8	9	17	−2	26
Mike Eagles	C	65	7	10	17	−17	118
Mike Lalor	D	79	7	10	17	+25	78
WASH		64	5	7	12	+14	64
WIN		15	2	3	5	+11	14
Doug Evans	L	30	7	7	14	+2	68
Danton Cole	R	52	7	5	12	−15	32
Igof Ulanov*	D	27	2	9	11	+5	67
Randy Carlyle	D	66	1	9	10	+4	54
Aaron Broten	C	25	4	5	9	+2	14

Acquired: Shannon from Buf.(Oct.10); Lalor from Wash.(Mar.2); DeBlois from Tor.(Mar.11).

Goaltending	Gm	Min	Avg	SO	Record
Bob Essensa	47	2627	2.88	5	21-17-6
Steph Beauregard	26	1267	2.89	2	6-8-6
Rick Tabaracci*	18	966	3.23	0	6-7-3
WINNIPEG	80	4888	3.00	7	33-32-15

Assists: Essensa (2), Tabaracci (1); **PM:** Tabaracci (4), Essensa (2).

1992 NHL All-Star Game
Campbell 10, Wales 6

43rd NHL All-Star Game. **Date:** Jan.18, at the Spectrum in Philadelphia; **Coaches:** Bob Gainey, Minnesota (Campbell) and Scotty Bowman, Pittsburgh (Wales); **MVP:** Brett Hull, St.Louis (Campbell)—2 goals, 1 assist.

Campbell Conference

Pos	Starters	G	A	Pts	PM
RW	Brett Hull, St.Louis	2	1	3	0
C	Wayne Gretzky, Los Angeles	1	2	3	0
LW	Luc Robitaille, Los Angeles	0	3	3	0
D	Al MacInnis, Calgary	0	1	1	0
D	Chris Chelios, Chicago	0	0	0	0
G	Ed Belfour, Chicago	0	0	0	0
	Bench				
W	Brian Bellows, Minnesota	2	0	2	0
W	Theo Fleury, Calgary	2	0	2	0
W	Trevor Linden, Vancouver	1	1	2	0
C	Jeremy Roenick, Chicago	1	1	2	0
C	Sergei Fedorov, Detroit	0	2	2	0
W	Gary Roberts, Calgary	1	0	1	0
W	Vincent Damphousse, Edmonton	0	1	1	0
D	Dave Ellett, Toronto	0	1	1	0
C	Adam Oates, St.Louis	0	1	1	0
D	Larry Robinson, Los Angeles	0	1	1	0
D	Mark Tinordi, Minnesota	0	1	1	0
D	Phil Housley, Winnipeg	0	0	0	0
D	Doug Wilson, San Jose	0	0	0	0
C	Steve Yzerman, Detroit	0	0	0	0
	TOTALS	10	16	26	0

Goaltenders	Mins	Shots	Saves	GA
Ed Belfour, Chi	20:00	14	13	1
Kirk McLean, Van.(W)	20:00	9	7	2
Tim Cheveldae, Det	20:00	18	15	3
TOTALS	60:00	41	35	6

Wales Conference

Pos	Starters	G	A	Pts	PM
LW	Kevin Stevens, Pittsburgh	1	0	1	0
D	Ray Bourque, Boston	0	1	1	0
RW	Jaromir Jagr, Pittsburgh	0	1	1	0
C	Mario Lemieux, Pittsburgh	0	1	1	0
D	Paul Coffey, Pittsburgh	0	0	0	0
G	Patrick Roy, Montreal	0	0	0	0
	Bench				
W	Alexander Mogilny, Buffalo	1	1	2	0
W	Owen Nolan, Quebec	1	1	2	0
C	Joe Sakic, Quebec	0	2	2	0
W	Randy Burridge, Washington	1	0	1	0
D	Scott Stevens, New Jersey	0	1	1	0
C	Bryan Trottier, Pittsburgh	1	0	1	0
D	Eric Desjardins, Montreal	0	1	1	0
C	Mark Messier, NY Rangers	0	1	1	0
W	Rod Brind'Amour, Philadelphia	0	0	0	0
C	John Cullen, Hartford	0	0	0	0
W	Ray Ferraro, NY Islanders	0	0	0	0
D	Brian Leetch, NY Rangers	0	0	0	0
W	Kirk Muller, Montreal	0	0	0	0
	TOTALS	6	10	16	0

Goaltenders	Mins	Shots	Saves	GA
Patrick Roy, Mon	20:00	15	13	2
Don Beaupre, Wash.(L)	20:00	12	6	6
Mike Richter, NYR	20:00	15	13	2
TOTALS	60:00	42	32	10

Score by Periods

Campbell (West)	2	6	2	—10
Wales (East)	1	2	3	—6

Power plays—Wales (0 for 0), Campbell (0 for 0); **Officials**—Don Koharski (Referee), Mark Vines and Mark Pare (Linesmen).
Attendance—17,380; **TV Rating**—2.3/7 share (NBC).

1992 STANLEY CUP PLAYOFFS

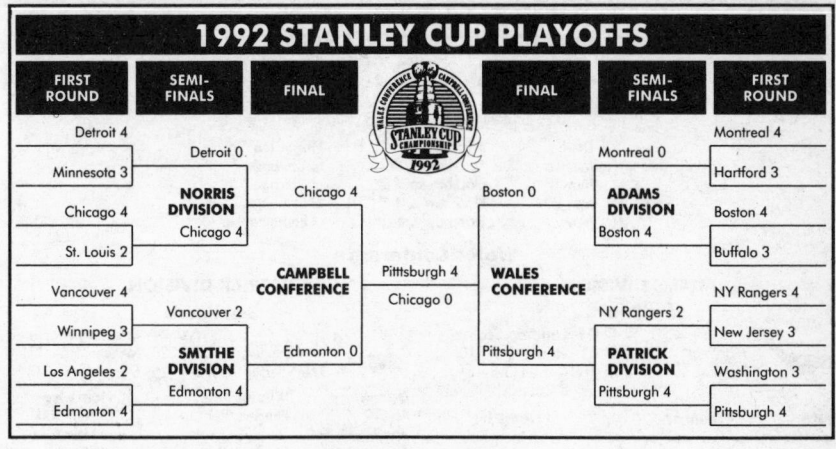

FIRST ROUND	SEMI-FINALS	FINAL			FINAL	SEMI-FINALS	FIRST ROUND

Detroit 4 — Minnesota 3 → Detroit 0

Chicago 4 — St. Louis 2 → Chicago 4

NORRIS DIVISION — Chicago 4

Chicago 4 — **CAMPBELL CONFERENCE** — Pittsburgh 4 — Chicago 0

Vancouver 4 — Winnipeg 3 → Vancouver 2

Los Angeles 2 — Edmonton 4 → Edmonton 4

SMYTHE DIVISION — Edmonton 0

STANLEY CUP CHAMPIONSHIP 1992

Montreal 4 — Hartford 3 → Montreal 0

Boston 4 — Buffalo 3 → Boston 4

ADAMS DIVISION — Boston 4

Boston 0 — **WALES CONFERENCE** — Pittsburgh 4

NY Rangers 4 — New Jersey 3 → NY Rangers 2

Washington 3 — Pittsburgh 4 → Pittsburgh 4

PATRICK DIVISION — Pittsburgh 4

Series Summaries
All series Best-of-7 games.
Campbell Conference

NORRIS DIVISION

Semifinals

	W-L	GF	Leading Scorers
Detroit	4-3	23	Fedorov (5-3—8)
Minnesota	3-4	19	Bellows (4-4—8)

Date	Winner	Home Ice
Apr.18	North Stars, 4-3	at Detroit
Apr.20	North Stars, 4-2	at Detroit
Apr.22	Red Wings, 5-4	at Minnesota
Apr.24	North Stars, 5-4	at Minnesota
Apr.26	Red Wings, 3-0	at Detroit
Apr.28	Red Wings, 1-0 (OT)	at Minnesota
Apr.30	Red Wings, 5-2	at Detroit

	W-L	GF	Leading Scorer
Chicago	4-2	23	K.Brown (0-8—8)
St.Louis	2-4	19	Hull (4-4—8)

Date	Winner	Home Ice
Apr.18	Blackhawks, 3-1	at Chicago
Apr.20	Blues, 5-3	at Chicago
Apr.22	Blues, 5-4 (2 OT)	at St.Louis
Apr.24	Blackhawks, 5-3	at St.Louis
Apr.26	Blackhawks, 6-4	at Chicago
Apr.28	Blackhawks, 2-1	at St.Louis

Finals

	W-L	GF	Leading Scorer
Chicago	4-0	11	Roenick (2-3—5)
Detroit	0-4	6	Yzerman (1-2—3)

Date	Winner	Home Ice
May 3	Blackhawks, 2-1	at Detroit
May 4	Blackhawks, 3-1	at Detroit
May 6	Blackhawks, 5-4	at Chicago
May 8	Blackhawks, 1-0	at Chicago

SMYTHE DIVISION

Semifinals

	W-L	GF	Leading Scorer
Vancouver	4-3	29	Bure (5-3—8) & Fergus (5-3—8)
Winnipeg	3-4	17	Steen (2-4—6) & Olausson (1-5—6)

Date	Winner	Home Ice
Apr.18	Jets, 3-2	at Vancouver
Apr.20	Canucks, 3-2	at Vancouver
Apr.22	Jets, 4-2	at Winnipeg
Apr.24	Jets, 3-1	at Winnipeg
Apr.26	Canucks, 8-2	at Vancouver
Apr.28	Canucks, 8-3	at Winnipeg
Apr.30	Canucks, 5-0	at Vancouver

	W-L	GF	Leading Scorer
Edmonton	4-2	23	Nicholls (5-8—13)
Los Angeles	2-4	18	Coffey (4-3—7), Robitaille (3-4—7) & Gretzky (2-5—7)

Date	Winner	Home Ice
Apr.18	Oilers, 3-1	at Los Angeles
Apr.20	Kings, 8-5	at Los Angeles
Apr.22	Oilers, 4-3	at Edmonton
Apr.24	Kings, 4-3	at Edmonton
Apr.26	Oilers, 5-2	at Los Angeles
Apr.28	Oilers, 3-0	at Edmonton

Finals

	W-L	GF	Leading Scorer
Edmonton	4-2	18	Murphy (5-6—11)
Vancouver	2-4	15	Courtnall (2-6—8)

Date	Winner	Home Ice
May 3	Oilers, 4-3 (OT)	at Vancouver
May 4	Canucks, 4-0	at Vancouver
May 6	Oilers, 5-2	at Edmonton
May 8	Oilers, 3-2	at Edmonton
May 10	Canucks, 4-3	at Vancouver
May 12	Oilers, 3-0	at Edmonton

Stanley Cup Playoffs (Cont.)

CAMPBELL CONFERENCE FINAL

	W-L	GF	Leading Scorer
Chicago	4-0	21	Larmer (4-4—8)
			& Roenick (4-4—8)
Edmonton	0-4	8	Buchberger (1-2—3)

Date	Winner	Home Ice
May 16	Blackhawks, 8-2	at Chicago
May 18	Blackhawks, 4-2	at Chicago
May 20	Blackhawks, 4-3 (OT)	at Edmonton
May 22	Blackhawks, 5-1	at Edmonton

Wales Conference

ADAMS DIVISION

Semifinals

	W-L	GF	Leading Scorer
Montreal	4-3	21	Savard (1-9—10)
Hartford	3-4	18	Craven (3-3—6)
			& Cassels (2-4—6)

Date	Winner	Home Ice
Apr.19	Canadiens, 2-0	at Montreal
Apr.21	Canadiens, 5-2	at Montreal
Apr.23	Whalers, 5-2	at Hartford
Apr.25	Whalers, 3-1	at Hartford
Apr.27	Canadiens, 7-4	at Montreal
Apr.29	Whalers, 2-1 (OT)	at Hartford
May 1	Canadiens, 3-2 (2 OT)	at Montreal

	W-L	GF	Leading Scorers
Boston	4-3	19	Oates (4-6—10)
Buffalo	3-4	24	LaFontaine (8-3—11)

Date	Winner	Home Ice
Apr.19	Sabres, 3-2	at Boston
Apr.21	Bruins, 3-2 (OT)	at Boston
Apr.23	Bruins, 3-2	at Buffalo
Apr.25	Bruins, 5-4 (OT)	at Buffalo
Apr.27	Sabres, 2-0	at Boston
Apr.29	Sabres, 9-3	at Buffalo
May 1	Bruins, 3-2	at Boston

Finals

	W-L	GF	Leading Scorer
Boston	4-0	14	Poulin (3-2—5)
			& Reid (0-5—5)
Montreal	0-4	8	Desjardin (2-1—3)

Date	Winner	Home Ice
May 3	Bruins, 6-4	at Montreal
May 5	Bruins, 3-2 (OT)	at Montreal
May 7	Bruins, 3-2	at Boston
May 9	Bruins, 2-0	at Boston

PATRICK DIVISION

Semifinals

	W-L	GF	Leading Scorer
NY Rangers	4-3	28	Messier (5-6—11)
New Jersey	3-4	25	Stastny (3-7—10)

Date	Winner	Home Ice
Apr.19	Rangers, 2-1	at New York
Apr.21	Devils, 7-3	at New York
Apr.23	Devils, 3-1	at New Jersey
Apr.25	Rangers, 3-0	at New Jersey
Apr.27	Rangers, 8-5	at New Jersey
Apr.29	Devils, 5-3	at New Jersey
May 1	Rangers, 8-4	at New York

	W-L	GF	Leading Scorer
Pittsburgh	4-3	25	Lemieux (7-10—17)
Washington	3-4	27	Ridley (0-11—11)

Date	Winner	Home Ice
Apr.19	Capitals, 3-1	at Washington
Apr.21	Capitals, 6-2	at Washington
Apr.23	Penguins, 6-4	at Pittsburgh
Apr.25	Capitals, 7-2	at Pittsburgh
Apr.27	Penguins, 5-2	at Washington
Apr.29	Penguins, 6-4	at Pittsburgh
May 1	Penguins, 3-1	at Washington

Finals

	W-L	GF	Leading Scorer
Pittsburgh	4-2	24	Francis (8-4—12)
NY Rangers	2-4	19	Gartner (2-5—7)
			& Leetch (1-6—7)

Date	Winner	Home Ice
May 3	Penguins, 4-2	at New York
May 5	Rangers, 4-2	at New York
May 7	Rangers, 6-5 (OT)	at Pittsburgh
May 9	Penguins, 5-4 (OT)	at Pittsburgh
May 11	Penguins, 3-2	at New York
May 13	Penguins, 5-1	at Pittsburgh

WALES CONFERENCE FINAL

	W-L	GF	Leading Scorer
Pittsburgh	4-0	19	Lemieux (4-4—8)
			& Jagr (3-5—8)
Boston	0-4	7	Oates (1-4—5)

Date	Winner	Home Ice
May 17	Penguins, 4-3 (OT)	at Pittsburgh
May 19	Penguins, 5-2	at Pittsburgh
May 21	Penguins, 5-1	at Boston
May 23	Penguins, 5-1	at Boston

STANLEY CUP FINAL

	W-L	GF	Leading Scorer
Pittsburgh	4-0	15	Tocchet (2-6—8)
Chicago	0-4	10	Chelios (1-4—5)

Date	Winner	Home Ice
May 26	Penguins, 5-4	at Pittsburgh
May 28	Penguins, 3-1	at Pittsburgh
May 30	Penguins, 1-0	at Chicago
June 1	Penguins, 6-5	at Chicago

Conn Smythe Trophy
Mario Lemieux, Pittsburgh, C
15 games, 16 goals, 18 assists, 34 points.

Stanley Cup Individual Leaders

Scoring

	Pos	Gm	G	A	Pts	+/-	PM
Mario Lemieux, Pit	C	15	16	18	34	+6	2
Kevin Stevens, Pit	L	21	13	15	28	+2	28
Ron Francis, Pit	C	21	8	19	27	+8	6
Jaromir Jagr, Pit	R	21	11	13	24	+4	6
Joe Murphy, Edm	R	16	8	16	24	+2	12
Jeremy Roenick, Chi	C	18	12	10	22	+11	12
Chris Chelios, Chi	D	18	6	15	21	+19	37
Bernie Nicholls, Edm	C	16	8	11	19	+2	25
Rick Tocchet, Pit	R	14	6	13	19	0	24
Adam Oates, Bos	C	15	5	14	19	-6	4
Mike Gartner, NYR	R	13	8	8	16	+3	4
Larry Murphy, Pit	D	21	6	10	16	-4	19
Steve Larmer, Chi	R	18	8	7	15	+9	6
Brian Noonan, Chi	R	18	6	9	15	-3	30
Brian Leetch, NYR	D	13	4	11	15	-5	4

Goals
Lemieux, Pit	16
Stevens, Pit	13
Roenick, Chi	12
Jagr, Pit	11
Seven tied with 8 each.	

Assists
Francis, Pit	19
Lemieux, Pit	18
Murphy, Edm	16
Chelios, Chi	15
Stevens, Pit	15

Power Play Goals
Lemieux, Pit	8
LaFontaine, Buf	5
Murphy, Edm	4
Nicholls, Edm	4
Roenick, Chi	4
Stevens, Pit	4

Short-Handed Goals
Fedorov, Det	2
Lemieux, Pit	2
Messier, NYR	2
17 tied with 1 each.	

Plus/Minus
Chelios, Chi	+19
Smith, Chi	+12
Roenick, Chi	+11
Paek, Pit*	+10
Graham, Chi	+9
Larmer, Chi	+9

Penalty Minutes
Beukeboom, NYR	47
Richardson, Edm	45
Manson, Edm	44
Stanton, Pit	42
U.Samuelsson, Pit	39
Ulanov, Win	39

Goaltending
(Minimum 450 minutes)

	Gm	Min	GA	SO	Avg
Ed Belfour, Chi	18	949	39	1	2.47
Tim Cheveldae, Det	11	597	25	2	2.51
Kirk McLean, Van	13	785	33	2	2.52
Patrick Roy, Mon	11	686	30	1	2.62
Tom Barrasso, Pit	21	1233	58	1	2.82
Andy Moog, Bos	15	866	46	1	3.19
Bill Ranford, Edm	16	909	51	2	3.37

Wins
Barrasso, Pit	16-5
Belfour, Chi	12-4
Moog, Bos	8-7
Ranford, Edm	8-8
McLean, Van	6-7

Save Pct.
Pietrangelo, Hart	.922
Cheveldae, Det	.910
McLean, Van	.909
Barrasso, Pit	.907
Draper, Buf*	.905

Final Standings

	Gm	W	L	Pts	Goals For	Goals Opp	Goals Dif
Pittsburgh	21	16	5	32	83	63	+20
Chicago	18	12	6	24	65	48	+17
Boston	15	8	7	16	40	51	-11
Edmonton	16	8	8	16	49	54	-5
Vancouver	13	6	7	12	44	35	+9
NY Rangers	13	6	7	12	47	49	-2
Detroit	11	4	7	8	29	30	-1
Montreal	11	4	7	8	29	32	-3
Buffalo	7	3	4	6	24	19	+5
Washington	7	3	4	6	27	25	+2
Hartford	7	3	4	6	18	21	-3
New Jersey	7	3	4	6	25	28	-3
Minnesota	7	3	4	6	19	23	-4
Winnipeg	7	3	4	6	17	29	-12
St.Louis	6	2	4	4	19	23	-4
Los Angeles	6	2	4	4	18	23	-5

Finalists' Composite Box Scores
Pittsburgh Penguins (16-5)

		Overall Playoffs							Finals vs Chicago					
Top Scorers	Pos	Gm	G	A	Pts	+/-	PM	PP	TS	Gm	G	A	Pts	+/-	PM	PP	TS
Mario Lemieux	C	15	16	18	34	+6	2	8	69	4	5	2	7	0	0	3	23
Kevin Stevens	L	21	13	15	28	+2	28	4	86	4	3	5	8	+2	0	0	12
Ron Francis	C	21	8	19	27	+8	6	2	58	4	1	2	3	-1	0	0	4
Jaromir Jagr	R	21	11	13	24	+4	6	2	59	4	2	0	2	-2	2	0	9
Rick Tocchet	R	14	6	13	19	0	24	3	30	4	2	6	8	+3	2	0	6
Larry Murphy	D	21	6	10	16	-4	19	3	59	4	1	2	3	-3	2	0	12
Troy Loney	L	21	4	5	9	+1	32	0	32	4	0	1	1	0	0	0	7
Shawn McEachern*	C	19	2	7	9	+6	4	0	36	4	0	2	2	+3	0	0	9
Paul Stanton	D	21	1	7	8	+6	42	0	24	4	0	1	1	+1	18	0	5
Bryan Trottier	C	21	4	3	7	0	8	0	30	4	0	0	0	0	2	0	13
Phil Bourque	L	21	3	4	7	-1	25	2	32	4	1	0	1	-1	0	1	5
Joe Mullen	R	9	3	1	4	-4	4	1	21	—	—	—	—	—	—	—	—
Jock Callander	R	12	1	3	4	0	2	0	9	4	0	0	0	0	0	0	0
Jim Paek*	D	19	0	4	4	+10	6	0	7	4	0	3	3	+4	2	0	2
Bob Errey	L	14	3	0	3	0	10	0	16	3	1	0	1	+1	0	0	1
Kjell Samuelsson	D	15	0	3	3	+6	12	0	7	4	0	1	1	+4	2	0	1

Shorthanded goals: OVERALL (Lemieux 2, Errey 1); FINALS (Errey 1).

Goaltending	Gm	Min	Avg	GA	SA	Pct	W-L	Gm	Min	Avg	GA	SA	Pct	W-L
Tom Barrasso	21	1233	2.82	58	622	.907	16-5	4	240	2.50	10	109	.908	4-0
Ken Wregget	1	40	6.00	4	16	.750	0-0	0	0	0.00	0	0	.000	0-0
TOTAL	21	1274	2.97	63	639	.901	16-5	4	240	2.50	10	109	.908	4-0

Empty Net Goals: OVERALL (1), FINALS (0); **Shutouts:** OVERALL (Barrasso 1), FINALS (Barrasso 1); **Assists:** OVERALL (Barrasso 2), FINALS (none); **Penalty minutes:** OVERALL (Barrasso 4), FINALS (none).

Stanley Cup Playoffs (Cont.)
Chicago Blackhawks (12-6)

Top Scorers	Pos	Overall Playoffs								Finals vs Chicago							
		Gm	G	A	Pts	+/−	PM	PP	TS	Gm	G	A	Pts	+/−	PM	PP	TS
Jeremy Roenick	C	18	12	10	22	+11	12	4	56	4	2	0	2	0	0	0	6
Chris Chelios	D	18	6	15	21	+19	37	3	54	4	1	4	5	+2	9	1	12
Steve Larmer	R	18	8	7	15	+9	6	3	69	4	0	1	1	+1	2	0	13
Brian Noonan	R	18	6	9	15	−3	30	3	37	4	0	3	3	−1	2	0	8
Dirk Graham	R	18	7	5	12	+9	8	0	45	4	4	0	4	+2	0	0	11
Steve Smith	D	18	1	11	12	+12	16	1	37	4	0	0	0	−2	4	0	5
Stephane Matteau	L	18	4	6	10	+5	24	1	32	4	0	1	1	−1	0	0	4
Mike Hudson	C	16	3	5	8	+1	26	0	26	4	0	0	0	−1	2	0	6
Brent Sutter	C	18	3	5	8	−2	22	1	41	4	1	1	2	0	0	0	12
Igor Kravchuk*	D	18	2	6	8	−2	8	1	48	4	0	0	0	+1	2	0	13
Keith Brown	D	14	0	8	8	−3	18	0	20	—	—	—	—	—	—	—	—
Michel Goulet	L	9	3	4	7	+4	6	0	19	4	1	0	1	−2	2	0	6
Rob Brown	R	8	2	4	6	+1	4	1	8	3	0	0	0	−1	2	0	2
Jocelyn Lemieux	L	18	3	1	4	0	33	0	32	4	0	1	1	−2	0	0	3
Greg Gilbert	L	10	1	3	4	1	16	0	9	3	0	2	2	+2	10	0	2
Mike Peluso	L	17	1	2	3	−3	8	0	4	3	0	0	0	−2	4	0	0

Shorthanded goals: OVERALL (Matteau 1); FINALS (none).

Goaltending	Gm	Min	Avg	GA	SA	Pct	W-L	Gm	Min	Avg	GA	SA	Pct	W-L
Ed Belfour	18	949	2.47	39	398	.902	12-4	4	187	3.53	11	88	.875	0-3
Dominik Hasek*	3	158	3.04	8	70	.886	0-2	1	53	4.55	4	25	.840	0-1
TOTAL	18	1106	2.60	48	469	.898	12-6	4	240	3.75	15	113	.867	0-4

Empty Net Goals: OVERALL (1), FINALS (0); **Shutouts:** OVERALL (Belfour, 1), FINALS (none); **Assists:** OVERALL (none), FINALS (none); **Penalty minutes:** OVERALL (Belfour 6), FINALS (none).

Annual Awards

Field of candidates for each award narrowed to three before final vote. Except for Vezina Trophy and Adams Award, voting done by members of the Pro Hockey Writers' Assn. The Vezina Trophy is voted on by the NHL's 22 general managers and the Adams Award is decided by NHL broadcasters. Points awarded on 5-3-1 basis.

Hart Trophy
For Most Valuable Player.

	Pos	1st	2nd	3rd	Pts
Mark Messier, NY Rangers	C	67	2	0	—341
Patrick Roy, Montreal	G	1	27	19	—105
Brett Hull, St.Louis	RW	1	12	8	— 49
Kirk McLean, Vancouver	G	0	11	4	— 37
Mario Lemieux, Pittsburgh	C	0	7	8	— 29
Jeremy Roenick, Chicago	C	0	5	14	— 29

Calder Trophy
For Rookie of the Year.

	Pos	1st	2nd	3rd	Pts
Pavel Bure, Vancouver	LW	26	27	11	—222
Nicklas Lidstrom, Detroit	D	23	16	20	—183
Tony Amonte, NY Rangers	RW	18	22	27	—183

Norris Trophy
For Best Defenseman.

	1st	2nd	3rd	Pts
Brian Leetch, NY Rangers	65	3	1	—335
Ray Bourque, Boston	3	25	22	—112
Phil Housley, Winnipeg	0	21	19	— 82

Vezina Trophy
For Outstanding Goaltender.

	1st	2nd	3rd	Pts
Patrick Roy, Montreal	17	3	3	— 95
Kirk McLean, Vancouver	5	12	1	— 62
Bob Essensa, Winnipeg	0	3	4	— 13

Adams Award
For Coach of the Year.

	1st	2nd	3rd	Pts
Pat Quinn, Vancouver	34	8	6	—200
Roger Neilson, NY Rangers	11	13	10	—104
Pat Burns, Montreal	2	9	11	— 48

Other Awards

Lady Byng Trophy (gentlemanly play and ability)— Wayne Gretzky, Los Angeles; **Lester Pearson Award** (NHL Players Assn. MVP)—Mark Messier, NY Rangers, C; **Selke Trophy** (best defensive forward)—Guy Carbonneau, Montreal, C; **Jennings Trophy** (fewest team goals against)—Patrick Roy and 2 other goalies, Montreal; **Masterton Trophy** (for perseverance and dedication to hockey)—Mark Fitzpatrick, NY Islanders, G; **King Clancy Trophy** (for humanitarian contribution)— Ray Bourque, Boston, D.

All-NHL

Voting done by Pro Hockey Writers' Association (PHWA). Holdovers from 1990-91 All-NHL first team in **bold** type.

	First Team	1st	2nd	3rd	Pts
G	Patrick Roy, Montreal	54	11	0	—303
D	Brian Leetch, NY Rangers	64	1	0	—323
D	**Ray Bourque**, Boston	29	27	6	—232
C	Mark Messier, NY Rangers	38	11	10	—233
R	**Brett Hull**, St.Louis	65	0	0	—325
L	Kevin Stevens, Pittsburgh	62	2	0	—316

	Second Team	1st	2nd	3rd	Pts
G	Kirk McLean, Vancouver	10	41	11	—184
D	Phil Housley, Winnipeg	17	29	9	—181
D	Scott Stevens, New Jersey	9	18	22	—121
C	Mario Lemieux, Pittsburgh	20	26	14	—192
R	Mark Recchi, Pit-Phi	0	29	9	— 96
L	Luc Robitaille, Los Angeles	2	41	18	—151

All-Rookie Team

Voting done by Pro Hockey Writers' Assn. Vote totals not released.

Top Rookie: Pavel Bure, Vancouver, RW

G	Dominik Hasek, Chi.	C	Kevin Todd, NJ
D	Nicklas Lidstrom, Det.	R	Tony Amonte, NYR
D	Vladimir Konstantinov, Det.	L	Gilbert Dionne, Mont.

NHL Drafts

Expansion Draft

On June 18, 1992, the Ottawa Senators and Tampa Bay Lightning participated in the NHL Expansion Draft, picking 21 players each from a pool of unprotected players provided by the league's other 22 clubs. Players were picked by position and are listed in the order picked; no more than two players per established team could be chosen from the pool.

Ottawa

Goaltenders
1 Peter Sidorkiewicz, Hart.
2 Mark LaForest, NYR

Defensemen
3 Brad Shaw, NJ
4 Darren Rumble, Phi.
5 Dominic Lavoie, St.L.
6 Brad Miller, Buf.
7 Ken Hammond, Van.
8 Kent Paynter, Win.
9 John Van Kessel, LA

Forwards
10 Sylvain Turgeon, Mon.
11 Mike Peluso, Chi.
12 Rob Murphy, Van.
13 Mark Lamb, Edm.
14 Laurie Boschman, NJ
15 Jim Thomson, LA
16 Lonnie Loach, Det.
17 Mark Freer, Phi.
18 Chris Lindberg, Calg.
19 Jeff Lazaro, Bos.
20 Darcy Loewen, Buf.
21 Blair Atcheynum, Hart.

Tampa Bay

Goaltenders
1 Wendall Young, Pit.
2 Frederic Chabot, Mon.

Defensemen
3 Joe Reekie, NYI
4 Shawn Chambers, Wash.
5 Peter Taglianetti, Pit.
6 Bob McGill, Det.
7 Jeff Bloemberg, NYR
8 Doug Crossman, Que.
9 Rob Ramage, Min.

Forwards
10 Michel Mongeau, St.L.
11 Anatoli Semenov, Edm.
12 Mike Hartman, Win.
13 Basil McRae, Min.
14 Rob DiMaio, NYI
15 Steve Maltais, Que.
16 Dan Vincelette, Chi.
17 Tim Bergland, Wash.
18 Brian Bradley, Tor.
19 Keith Osborne, Tor.
20 Shayne Stevenson, Bos.
21 Tim Hunter, Calg.

Entry Draft

30th annual draft held June 20, 1992, in Montreal.

First Round

	Team		Pos
1	Tampa Bay	Roman Hamrlik, ZPS Zin	D
2	Ottawa	Alexei Yashin, Dynamo Moscow	C
3	San Jose	Mike Rathje, Medicine Hat	D
4	Quebec	Todd Warriner, Windsor	L
5	a-NY Isles	Darius Kasparaitis, Dynamo Mos.	D
6	Calgary	Corey Stillman, Windsor	L
7	Philadelphia ...	Ryan Sittler, Nichols HS	L
8	b-Toronto	Brandon Convery, Sudbury	C
9	Hartford	Robert Petrovicky, Dukla Trecin	C
10	c-San Jose	Andrei Nazarov, Dynamo Moscow	L
11	Buffalo	David Cooper, Medicine Hat	D
12	d-Chicago	Sergei Krivokrasov, Red Army	R
13	Edmonton	Joe Hulbig, St.Sebastian HS	L
14	e-Washington ..	Sergei Gonchar, Dynamo Moscow	D
15	f-Phila	Jason Bowen, Tri-City	L
16	Boston	Dmitri Kvartainov, San Diego	L
17	g-Winnipeg	Sergei Bautin, Dynamo Moscow	D
18	New Jersey	Jason Smith, Regina	D
19	Pittsburgh......	Martin Straka, Skoda Pizen	C
20	Montreal	David Wilkie, Kamloops	D
21	Vancouver	Libor Polasek, TJ Vikovice	C
22	Detroit	Curtis Bowen, Ottawa	L
23	h-Toronto	Grant Marshall, Ottawa	R
24	NY Rangers	Peter Ferraro, Waterloo	C

Acquired picks: a—from Toronto; **b**—from NY Islanders; **c**—from Minnesota; **d**—from Winnipeg; **e**—from St.Louis; **f**—from Los Angeles thru Pittsburgh; **g**—from Chicago; **h**—from Washington.

Affiliations: Czechoslovakia—Dukla Trecin, Skoda Pizen, TJ Vikovice, ZPS Zin; **IHL** (International Hockey League)—San Diego; **OHL** (Ontario Hockey League)—Ottawa, Sudbury, Windsor; **Russia**—Central Red Army, Dynamo Moscow; **US High Schools**—Nichols (Buffalo, NY), St.Sebastian (Needham, MA); **USHL** (US Hockey League)—Waterloo; **WHL** (Western Hockey League)—Kamloops, Medicine Hat, Regina, Tri-City.

World Championship

The 45th World Hockey Championships, held in Prague and Bratislava, Czechoslovakia, Apr.28-May 10, 1992. Top four teams in Groups A and B after preliminary round-robin advanced to quarterfinals. Rosters for Canada and USA were limited to players not participating in Stanley Cup playoffs. (*) indicates teams advancing to medal round.

Final Round Robin Standings

Group A	Gm	W-L-T	Pts	GF	GA
*Finland	5	5-0-0	10	32	8
*Germany	5	4-1-0	8	30	14
*United States	5	2-2-1	5	14	15
*Sweden	5	1-2-2	4	14	12
Italy	5	1-3-1	3	10	18
Poland........................	5	0-5-0	0	8	41

Group B	Gm	W-L-T	Pts	GF	GA
*Russia	5	4-0-1	9	23	10
*Czechoslovakia	5	4-1-0	8	18	7
*Switzerland	5	2-1-2	6	12	11
*Canada	5	2-2-1	5	15	18
Norway	5	1-4-0	2	8	16
France........................	5	0-5-0	0	8	22

Quarterfinals

Finland 4, Canada 3 Switzerland 3, Germany 1
Sweden 2, Russia 0   Czechoslovakia 8, USA 1

Semifinals

Sweden 4................................. Switzerland 1
Finland 2 .... (OT) .... Czechoslovakia 2
(Finland won shootout after 10-minute OT)

Third Place

Czechoslovakia 5 .... Switzerland 2

Championship Game

Sweden 5 .... Finland 2

Leading Scorers

	Gm	G	A	Pts
Jarkko Varvio, Finland	8	9	1	10
Mikko Makela, Finland	8	2	8	10
Tomas Jelinek, Czechoslovakia	8	4	5	9
Dieter Hegen, Germany....................	6	7	2	9
Robert Svehla, Czechoslovakia..............	8	4	4	8
Mats Sundin, Sweden	8	2	6	8

All-Tournament Team

First Team (picked by media): **Goal**—Markus Ketterer, Finland; **Defense**—Timo Jutila, Finland and Frantisek Musil; **Forwards**—Mats Sundin, Sweden, Petr Hrbek, Czechoslovakia, and Jarkko Varvio, Finland.

Top Position Players (picked by tournament officials): **Goalie**—Tommy Soderstrom, Sweden; **Defenseman**—Robert Svehla, Czechoslovakia; **Forward**—Mats Sundin, Sweden.

Lake State Proves It's Superior
by Mike Lucas

Each had All-America goaltenders, a blue collar work ethic on defense and balanced scoring from four lines. Each was making its fifth straight appearance in the NCAA Division I hockey tournament. And now, Lake Superior State, the 1988 NCAA champion, and Wisconsin, the 1990 NCAA champion, were meeting on April 4, in the title game at Knickerbocker Arena in Albany, N.Y.

It was supposed to have been a rebuilding year for both programs.

Lakers' coach Jeff Jackson had to replace eight seniors and the top five scorers from his 1991 team that had won a school record 36 games. Badgers' coach Jeff Sauer had to replace seven seniors from the winningest class in school history and five defensemen from his '91 team that had won 26 games.

Fittingly for the two evenly-matched opponents, the score was tied with less than five minutes to play in the title game. Wisconsin had taken a 2-0 first period lead on a pair of goals from Jason Zent, the second most famous graduate of Nichols School in Buffalo, N.Y., to star in an NCAA Final Four (Duke's Christian Laettner was the other). Lake Superior had drawn even on second period goals from Paul Constantin, who would be named the tourney MVP, and Tim Hanley, who had scored with six seconds remaining.

The teams traded goals early in the third period (with Zent scoring his third) before freshman Brian Rolston tallied the game-winner at 15:08 on Badger goaltender Duane Derksen. Darrin Madeley, who led the nation in goals-against average and save percentage, protected the lead for the Lakers, who added an empty net goal with two seconds left to punctuate their 5-3 win in front of 12,891.

"We came in with the feeling that we were the underdog," said Madeley, "and it's nice for a small school like us to win."

Lake Superior State (enrollment: 3,200) is based in Sault Ste. Marie, Mich., and is the smallest university in the state. Nonetheless, the Lakers have had the best winning percentage in Division I college hockey over the last five years—better than Maine, Michigan

Wide World Photos

Lake Superior St. forward **Dean Hulett** hoists the NCAA Division I trophy after the Lakers' 5-3 victory over Wisconsin.

and Minnesota, who were arguably the three best teams during the 1991-92 regular season. But all three struggled in the tournament as the NCAA unveiled its new format, a one-game knockout at two regional sites (Detroit and Providence).

Only Michigan and Maine's Scott Pellerin made it to the Final Four. None of the six Eastern teams got past the quarterfinals, including top-seeded Maine, a 3-2 loser to Michigan State, and No. 2 St. Lawrence, a 5-2 victim of Wisconsin.

In Albany, Michigan and Michigan State both went out in the semifinals by identical 4-2 scores, the Wolverines getting upset by Wisconsin and the Spartans falling to Lake Superior.

Pellerin, the first player in Maine history to score 100 goals and 100 assists in his career, received the Hobey Baker Award as Player of the Year the day before the championship game. The Black Bears, led by Pellerin and Jean-Yves Roy, were ranked No. 1 most of the year.

In the end, however, Lake State and Madeley proved superior.

Mike Lucas is a columnist for *The Capital Times* in Madison, Wisc., and has covered college hockey for 21 years.

U.S. Division I College Hockey

Final regular season standings; overall records, including league tournament and NCAA tournament games, in parentheses.

Central Collegiate Hockey Assn. (CCHA)

	W	L	T	Pts	GF	GA
*Michigan (32-9-3)	22	7	3	47	150	104
*Lake Superior St. (29-9-4)	20	8	4	44	141	78
*Michigan St. (24-11-8)	18	7	7	43	149	105
Western Mich.(16-14-6)	14	12	6	34	119	114
Miami-OH (17-17-6)	12	14	6	30	124	145
Ferris St.(13-18-7)	11	15	6	28	102	127
IL-Chicago (10-20-6)	8	18	6	22	101	132
Ohio St.(12-21-5)	8	19	5	21	134	182
Bowling Green (8-21-5)	7	20	5	19	123	156

Conf.Tourney Final: Lake Superior St. 3, Michigan 1.
***NCAA Tournament (7-2):** Lake Superior St.(4-0), Michigan St.(2-1), Michigan (1-1).

Western Collegiate Hockey Assn. (WCHA)

	W	L	T	Pts	GF	GA
*Minnesota (33-11-0)	26	6	0	52	163	89
*Wisconsin (27-14-2)	19	11	2	40	129	106
*Northern Mich.(25-14-3)	17	12	3	37	184	133
Colorado Col.(18-18-5)	14	14	4	32	138	141
Minn-Duluth (15-20-2)	14	16	2	30	124	137
Michigan Tech (15-22-1)	14	17	1	29	114	137
St.Cloud St.(14-21-2)	12	19	1	25	120	138
North Dakota (17-21-1)	12	19	1	25	137	172
Denver (9-25-2)	8	22	2	18	110	166

Conf.Tourney Final: Northern Mich. 4, Minnesota 2.
***NCAA Tournament (4-3):** Wisconsin (3-1), No.Michigan (1-1), Minnesota (0-1).

Eastern Collegiate Athletic Assn. (ECAC)

	W	L	T	Pts	GF	GA
Harvard (14-7-6)	13	3	6	32	90	59
*St. Lawrence (22-10-2)	15	6	1	31	104	66
*Clarkson (22-10-1)	15	6	1	31	101	63
Yale (13-7-7)	11	4	7	29	103	90
Cornell (14-11-4)	10	8	4	24	70	59
Brown (10-16-4)	10	8	4	24	93	86
Vermont (16-12-3)	10	9	3	23	78	84
Colgate (14-16-1)	11	11	0	22	105	108
Princeton (12-14-1)	9	12	1	19	85	92
RPI (14-15-4)	6	12	4	16	70	89
Dartmouth (3-21-2)	3	17	2	8	60	116
Union (3-21-1)	2	19	1	5	61	118

Conf.Tourney Final: St.Lawrence 4, Cornell 2.
***NCAA Tournament (0-2):** St.Lawrence (0-1), Clarkson (0-1).

Hockey East Association (HEA)

	W	L	T	Pts	GF	GA
*Maine (29-4-2)	17	2	2	36	115	54
*New Hampshire (22-13-2)	13	6	2	28	94	75
Providence (21-13-2)	11	8	2	24	99	79
*Boston University (22-9-4)	10	7	4	24	92	88
Boston College (20-18-3)	9	10	2	20	68	76
UMass-Lowell (11-19-4)	6	11	4	16	75	91
Northeastern (6-15-0)	6	15	0	12	70	103
Merrimack (13-21-0)	4	17	0	8	60	102

Conf.Tourney Final: Maine 4, New Hampshire 1.
***NCAA Tournament (0-3):** Maine (0-1), New Hampshire (0-1), Boston University (0-1).

NCAA Top 15

Taken before NCAA Tournament.

Final weekly Top 15 NCAA Poll determined by the four-man NCAA Division I Hockey Committee of Boston University coach Jack Parker, Cornell AD Laing Kennedy, Bowling Green AD Jack Gregory and Northern Michigan coach and AD Rick Comley with the assistance of two regional advisory committees. Records through March 15, 1992. First place votes in parentheses.

	League	W	L	T	Pts
1 Maine (4)	HEA	29	3	2	60
2 Michigan	CCHA	30	7	3	55
3 Minnesota	WCHA	32	9	0	53
4 Lake Superior St.	CCHA	23	9	4	48
5 Michigan St	CCHA	21	9	8	44
6 Wisconsin	WCHA	23	12	2	40
7 St.Lawrence	ECAC	22	8	1	33
8 Northern Michigan	WCHA	23	13	3	30
9 Boston University	HEA	21	8	4	29
10 New Hampshire	HEA	22	12	2	28
11 Alaska-Anchorage	Indep	21	7	1	19
12 Clarkson	ECAC	20	9	1	16
13 Providence	HEA	21	13	2	12
14 Miami-OH	CCHA	17	15	6	5
15 Colorado College	WCHA	18	16	5	4
Harvard	ECAC	14	7	6	4

Leading Scorers

Including all postseason games.

West	Cl	Pos	Gm	G	A	Pts
Denny Felsner, Mich	Sr.	R	44	42	52	94
Jim Hiller, No.Mich	Jr.	L	41	31	55	86
Dwayne Norris, Mich.St	Sr.	R	44	44	39	83
Dallas Drake, No.Mich	Sr.	C	40	39	44	83
Mark Beaufait, No.Mich	Sr.	C	41	31	50	81
Larry Olimb, Minn	Jr.	C	44	24	56	80
Peter White, Mich.St.	Sr.	L	44	26	51	77
Scott Beattie, No.Mich	Jr.	C	40	28	46	74
Greg Johnson, N.Dak	Jr.	C	39	20	54	74
Brian Wiseman, Mich	So.	C	44	27	44	71

East	Cl	Pos	Gm	G	A	Pts
Mike Boback, Prov	Sr.	C	36	24	48	72
Domenic Amodeo, N.Hamp	Sr.	C	37	26	42	68
Jim Montgomery, Maine	Jr.	C	37	21	44	65
Mike Iappin, St.Law	Sr.	C	33	25	37	62
Joe Flanagan, N.Hamp	Sr.	C	37	26	34	60
Scott Pellerin, Maine	Sr.	L	37	32	25	57
Savo Mitrovic, N.Hamp	Sr.	R	37	15	42	57
Jean-Yves Roy, Maine	Jr.	R	35	32	24	56
Steve Dubinsky, Clark	Sr.	C	33	21	34	55
Rob Gaudreau, Prov	Sr.	D	36	21	34	55

Leading Goaltenders

Including all postseason games; minimum 15 games.

West	Cl	Record	GA	Avg
Darrin Madeley, Lk.Super	Jr.	25- 6-4	74	2.07
Steve Shields, Mich	So.	27- 7-2	100	2.87
Jeff Stolp, Minn	Sr.	26- 9-0	98	2.92
Duane Derksen, Wisc	Sr.	24-12-2	118	3.07
Nike Gilmore, Mich.St.	Sr.	16-10-7	103	3.07

East	Cl	Record	GA	Avg
Garth Snow, Maine	Jr.	25- 4-2	73	2.44
Allain Roy, Harv	Sr.	9- 4-2	39	2.55
Parris Duffus, Cor	So.	14-11-3	74	2.65
Christian Soucy, Ver	Fr.	15-11-3	84	2.80
Jason Currie, Clark	So.	11- 7-1	48	2.88

NCAA Division I Tournament
Tournament Seeds

East	West
1 Maine (29-3-2)	1 **Michigan** (31-8-3)
2 St.Lawrence (22-8-1)	2 Minnesota (33-10)
3 **Michigan St.**(23-10-8)	3 **Lake Superior** (25-9-4)
4 **Wisconsin** (24-13-2)	4 Northern Mich.(24-13-3)
5 New Hamp.(22-12-2)	5 Clarkson (20-9-1)
6 Boston U.(22-8-4)	6 AK-Anchorage (25-7-1)

East Regional

At Providence (RI) Civic Center, March 26-28. Single elimination, two second round winners advance to Final Four.

First Round

Michigan St. 4 . . . . Boston Univ. 2
Wisconsin 4 . . . . New Hampshire 2
(Byes: Maine and St.Lawrence)

Second Round

Wisconsin 5 . . . . St.Lawrence 2
Michigan St. 3 . . . . Maine 2

West Regional

At Joe Louis Arena in Detroit, March 27-28. Single elimination, two second round winners advance to Final Four.

First Round

Northern Michigan 8 . . . . Clarkson 4
Lake Superior St. 7 . . . . Alaska-Anchorage 4
(Byes: Michigan and Minnesota)

Second Round

Lake Superior St. 8 . . . . Minnesota 3
Michigan 7 . . . . Northern Michigan 6

FINAL FOUR

At Knickerbocker Arena in Albany, NY, April 2-4. Single elimination.

Semifinals

Lake Superior St. 4 . . . . Michigan St. 2
Wisconsin 4 . . . . Michigan 2

Championship

Lake Superior St. 5 . . . . Wisconsin 3
Final records: Lake Superior St.(30-9-4), Wisconsin (27-14-2), Michigan (32-9-3), Michigan St.(25-11-8).
Outstanding Player: Paul Constantin, forward, Lake Superior St., (Semifinal—2 goals, Final—1 goal).
All-Tournament Team: Constantin, forward Brian Rolston, defenseman Mark Astley and goalie Darrin Madeley of Lake Superior St.; forward Jason Zent and defenseman Barry Richter of Wisconsin.

Championship Game
Lake Superior St. 5, Wisconsin 3

Saturday, April 4, 1992, at Knickerbocker Arena in Albany, N.Y.; Attendance: 12,891.

Wisconsin (27-13-2)	2	0	1—**3**
Lake Superior St.(29-9-4)	0	2	3—**5**

Scoring

1st Period: WI—Jason Zent (Doug MacDonald, Barry Richter), 9:45; WI—Zent (Richter), power play, 18:58.
2nd Period: LSS—Paul Constantin (John Hendry, Steven Barnes), power play, 11:40; LSS—Tim Hanley (Vince Faucher), 19:54.
3rd Period: LSS—Michael Smith (unassisted), power play, 4:16; WI—Zent (Dan Plante, Richter), power play, 8:24; LSS—Brian Rolston (Hendry, Dean Hulett), 15:08; LSS—Jay Ness (unassisted), empty net goal, 19:58.

Goaltenders

Saves: WI—Duane Derksen (32); LSS—Darrin Madeley (24).

Annual Awards
Hobey Baker Award

For College Player of the Year. National coaches' vote determines 10 finalists. Winner then selected by 16-member panel of writers, broadcasters, coaches and pro scouts. First presented in 1981 by the Decathlon Athletic Club of Bloomington, MN, in the name of the late Princeton collegiate hockey and football star.

Top Vote Getters

Vote totals not released.
Winner: Scott Pellerin, Maine, Sr., LW.
Runner-up: Daniel Laperriere, St.Lawrence, Sr., D.
Other finalists (8): Scott Beattie, Northern Mich., Jr., C; Duane Derksen, Wisconsin, Sr., G; Denny Felsner, Michigan, Sr., RW; Rob Gaudreau, Providence, Sr., D; Greg Johnson, North Dakota, Jr., C; Darrin Madeley, Lake Superior St., Jr., G; Larry Olimb, Minnesota, Jr., C.; Jean-Yves Roy, Maine, Jr., RW.

Division I All-America

Regional First Team selections as chosen by the American Hockey Coaches Association. Holdovers from 1990-91 All-America first teams are in **bold** type.

West Team

Pos		Cl	Hgt	Wgt
G	**Darrin Madeley**, Lake Superior St . . . Jr.	5-11	165
D	Mark Astley, Lake Superior St. . . . . Sr.	6-0	180
D	Joby Messier, Michigan St. . . . . Sr.	6-1	215
F	Dwayne Norris, Michigan St. . . . . Sr.	5-10	178
F	Dallas Drake, Northern Mich . . . . Sr.	6-1	181
F	Denny Felsner, Michigan . . . . Sr.	6-0	185

East Team

Pos		Cl	Hgt	Wgt
G	Parris Duffus, Cornell . . . . So.	6-1	193
D	Mike Brewer, Brown . . . . Sr.	5-10	175
D	Daniel LaPerriere, St.Lawrence . . . . Sr.	6-1	190
F	Scott Pellerin, Maine . . . . Sr.	5-11	200
F	**Jean-Yves Roy**, Maine . . . . Jr.	5-10	175
F	David Sacco, Boston University . . . . Jr.	5-10	185

NCAA Division III Tournament

All rounds decided in two games with mini-game (one 20-minute period), if necessary; winning teams in CAPITAL letters. There was no Division II tournament in 1992.

First Round

PLATTSBURGH ST. over Elmira (3-1, 8-1); SALEM ST. over Babson (6-4, 3-4, 3-0 minigame); WISCONSIN-STEVENS POINT over St.Thomas-MN (3-4, 4-2, 1-0 minigame); WISCONSIN-SUPERIOR over Mankato St. (8-7, 4-3).

Final Four

March 20-21 at Plattsburgh, NY.

Semifinals—WI-STEVENS POINT. 12, Salem St. 7; PLATTSBURGH ST. 8, WI-Superior 5. **Third Place**—SALEM ST. 7, WI-Superior 6. **Championship**—PLATTSBURGH ST. 7, WI-Stevens Point 3.
Final records: Plattsburgh St.(32-2-2), WI-Stevens Point (25-7-4), Salem St.(18-10), WI-Superior (22-8-1).

THE 1993 INFORMATION PLEASE SPORTS ALMANAC

HOCKEY STATISTICS

THROUGH THE YEARS
1893-1992
STANLEY CUP • NHL LEADERS

SEC B

PAGE 355

The Stanley Cup

The Stanley Cup was originally donated to the Canadian Amateur Hockey Assn. by Sir Frederick Arthur Stanley, Lord Stanley of Preston and 16th Earl of Derby, who had become interested in the sport while Governor General of Canada from 1888 to 1893. Stanley wanted the trophy to be a challenge cup, contested for each year by the best amateur hockey teams in Canada.

In 1893, the Cup was presented without a challenge to the AHA champion Montreal Amateur Athletic Assn. team. Every year since, however, there has been a playoff. In 1914, Cup trustees limited the field challenging for the trophy to the champion of the eastern professional National Hockey Assn.(NHA, organized in 1910) and the western professional Pacific Coast Hockey Assn.(PCHA, organized in 1912).

The NHA disbanded in 1917 and the National Hockey League (NHL) was formed. From 1918 to 1926, the NHL and PCHL champions played for the Cup with the Western Canada Hockey League (WCHL) champion joining in a three-way challenge in 1923 and '24. The PCHA disbanded in 1924, the WCHL became the Western Hockey League (WHL) for the 1925-26 season and folded the following year. The NHL playoffs have decided the winner of the Stanley Cup ever since.

Champions, 1893-1917

Multiple winners: Montreal Victorias and Montreal Wanderers (4); Montreal Amateur Athletic Association and Ottawa Silver Seven (3); Montreal Shamrocks, Ottawa Senators, Quebec Bulldogs and Winnipeg Victorias (2).

Year		Year		Year	
1893	Montreal AAA	1901	Winnipeg Victorias	1909	Ottawa Senators
1894	Montreal AAA	1902	Montreal AAA	1910	Montreal Wanderers
1895	Montreal Victorias	1903	Ottawa Silver Seven	1911	Ottawa Senators
1896	(Feb.) Winnipeg Victorias	1904	Ottawa Silver Seven	1912	Quebec Bulldogs
	(Dec.) Montreal Victorias	1905	Ottawa Silver Seven	1913	Quebec Bulldogs
1897	Montreal Victorias	1906	Montreal Wanderers	1914	Toronto Blueshirts (NHA)
1898	Montreal Victorias	1907	(Jan.) Kenora Thistles	1915	Vancouver Millionaires (PCHA)
1899	Montreal Shamrocks		(Mar.) Mon.Wanderers	1916	Montreal Canadiens (NHA)
1900	Montreal Shamrocks	1908	Montreal Wanderers	1917	Seattle Metropolitans (PCHA)

Champions since 1918

Multiple winners: Montreal Canadiens (22); Toronto Arenas-St.Pats-Maple Leafs (13); Detroit Red Wings (7); Boston Bruins and Edmonton Oilers (5); NY Islanders and Ottawa Senators (4); Chicago Blackhawks and NY Rangers (3); Philadelphia Flyers, Pittsburgh Penguins and Montreal Maroons (2).

Year	Winner	Head Coach	Series	Loser	Head Coach
1918	Toronto Arenas	Dick Carroll	3-2 (WLWLW)	Vancouver (PCHA)	Frank Patrick
1919	No Decision: (see below).				
1920	Ottawa	Pete Green	3-2 (WWLLW)	Seattle (PCHA)	Pete Muldoon
1921	Ottawa	Pete Green	3-2 (LWWLW)	Vancouver (PCHA)	Frank Patrick
1922	Toronto St.Pats	Eddie Powers	3-2 (LWLWW)	Vancouver (PCHA)	Frank Patrick
1923	Ottawa	Pete Green	3-1 (WLWW)	Vancouver (PCHA)	Frank Patrick
			2-0	Edmonton (WCHL)	K.C.McKenzie
1924	Montreal	Leo Dandurand	2-0	Vancouver (PCHA)	Frank Patrick
			2-0	Calgary (WCHL)	Eddie Oatman
1925	Victoria (WCHL)	Lester Patrick	3-1 (WWLW)	Montreal	Leo Dandurand
1926	Montreal Maroons	Eddie Gerard	3-1 (WWLW)	Victoria (WHL)	Lester Patrick
1927	Ottawa	Dave Gil	2-0 (TWTW)	Boston	Art Ross
1928	NY Rangers	Lester Patrick	3-2 (LWLWW)	Montreal Maroons	Eddie Gerard
1929	Boston	Art Ross	2-0	NY Rangers	Lester Patrick
1930	Montreal	Cecil Hart	2-0	Boston	Art Ross
1931	Montreal	Cecil Hart	3-2 (WLLWW)	Chicago	Art Duncan
1932	Toronto	Dick Irvin	3-0	NY Rangers	Lester Patrick
1933	NY Rangers	Lester Patrick	3-1 (WWLW)	Toronto	Dick Irvin
1934	Chicago	Tommy Gorman	3-1 (WWLW)	Detroit	Jack Adams

Note: The 1919 Finals were cancelled after five games due to an influenza epidemic with Montreal and Seattle (PCHA) tied at 2-2-1.

Stanley Cup Champions since 1918 (Cont.)

Year	Winner	Head Coach	Series	Loser	Head Coach
1935	Montreal Maroons	Lionel Conacher	3-0	Toronto	Dick Irvin
1936	Detroit	Jack Adams	3-1 (WWLW)	Toronto	Dick Irvin
1937	Detroit	Jack Adams	3-2 (LWLWW)	NY Rangers	Lester Patrick
1938	Chicago	Bill Stewart	3-1 (WLWW)	Toronto	Dick Irvin
1939	Boston	Art Ross	4-1 (WLWWW)	Toronto	Dick Irvin
1940	NY Rangers	Frank Boucher	4-2 (WWLLWW)	Toronto	Dick Irvin
1941	Boston	Cooney Weiland	4-0	Detroit	Jack Adams
1942	Toronto	Hap Day	4-3 (LLLWWWW)	Detroit	Jack Adams
1943	Detroit	Jack Adams	4-0	Boston	Art Ross
1944	Montreal	Dick Irvin	4-0	Chicago	Paul Thompson
1945	Toronto	Hap Day	4-3 (WWWLLLW)	Detroit	Jack Adams
1946	Montreal	Dick Irvin	4-1 (WWWLW)	Boston	Dit Clapper
1947	Toronto	Hap Day	4-2 (LWWWLW)	Montreal	Dick Irvin
1948	Toronto	Hap Day	4-0	Detroit	Tommy Ivan
1949	Toronto	Hap Day	4-0	Detroit	Tommy Ivan
1950	Detroit	Tommy Ivan	4-3 (WLWLLWW)	NY Rangers	Lynn Patrick
1951	Toronto	Joe Primeau	4-1 (WLWWW)	Montreal	Dick Irvin
1952	Detroit	Tommy Ivan	4-0	Montreal	Dick Irvin
1953	Montreal	Dick Irvin	4-1 (WLWWW)	Boston	Lynn Patrick
1954	Detroit	Tommy Ivan	4-3 (WLWWLLW)	Montreal	Dick Irvin
1955	Detroit	Jimmy Skinner	4-3 (WWLLWW)	Montreal	Dick Irvin
1956	Montreal	Toe Blake	4-1 (WWLWW)	Detroit	Jimmy Skinner
1957	Montreal	Toe Blake	4-1 (WWLW)	Boston	Milt Schmidt
1958	Montreal	Toe Blake	4-2 (WLWLW)	Boston	Milt Schmidt
1959	Montreal	Toe Blake	4-1 (WWLWW)	Toronto	Punch Imlach
1960	Montreal	Toe Blake	4-0	Toronto	Punch Imlach
1961	Chicago	Rudy Pilous	4-2 (WLWLW)	Detroit	Sid Abel
1962	Toronto	Punch Imlach	4-2 (WWLLWW)	Chicago	Rudy Pilous
1963	Toronto	Punch Imlach	4-1 (WWLWW)	Detroit	Sid Abel
1964	Toronto	Punch Imlach	4-3 (WLLWLWW)	Detroit	Sid Abel
1965	Montreal	Toe Blake	4-3 (WWLLWLW)	Chicago	Billy Reay
1966	Montreal	Toe Blake	4-2 (LLWWWW)	Detroit	Sid Abel
1967	Toronto	Punch Imlach	4-2 (LWWLWW)	Montreal	Toe Blake
1968	Montreal	Toe Blake	4-0	St. Louis	Scotty Bowman
1969	Montreal	Claude Ruel	4-0	St. Louis	Scotty Bowman
1970	Boston	Harry Sinden	4-0	St. Louis	Scotty Bowman
1971	Montreal	Al MacNeil	4-3 (LLWLWLW)	Chicago	Billy Reay
1972	Boston	Tom Johnson	4-2 (WWLWLW)	NY Rangers	Emile Francis
1973	Montreal	Scotty Bowman	4-2 (WWLWLW)	Chicago	Billy Reay
1974	Philadelphia	Fred Shero	4-2 (LWWWLW)	Boston	Bep Guidolin
1975	Philadelphia	Fred Shero	4-2 (WWLLWW)	Buffalo	Floyd Smith
1976	Montreal	Scotty Bowman	4-0	Philadelphia	Fred Shero
1977	Montreal	Scotty Bowman	4-0	Boston	Don Cherry
1978	Montreal	Scotty Bowman	4-2 (WWLLWW)	Boston	Don Cherry
1979	Montreal	Scotty Bowman	4-1 (LWWWW)	NY Rangers	Fred Shero
1980	NY Islanders	Al Arbour	4-2 (WLWLWW)	Philadelphia	Pat Quinn
1981	NY Islanders	Al Arbour	4-1 (WWWLW)	Minnesota	Glen Sonmor
1982	NY Islanders	Al Arbour	4-0	Vancouver	Roger Neilson
1983	NY Islanders	Al Arbour	4-0	Edmonton	Glen Sather
1984	Edmonton	Glen Sather	4-1 (WLWWW)	NY Islanders	Al Arbour
1985	Edmonton	Glen Sather	4-1 (LWWWW)	Philadelphia	Mike Keenan
1986	Montreal	Jean Perron	4-1 (LWWWW)	Calgary	Bob Johnson
1987	Edmonton	Glen Sather	4-3 (WWLWLLW)	Philadelphia	Mike Keenan
1988	Edmonton	Glen Sather	4-0	Boston	Terry O'Reilly
1989	Calgary	Terry Crisp	4-2 (WLLWWW)	Montreal	Pat Burns
1990	Edmonton	John Muckler	4-1 (WLWWW)	Boston	Mike Milbury
1991	Pittsburgh	Bob Johnson	4-2 (LWLWWW)	Minnesota	Bob Gainey
1992	Pittsburgh	Scotty Bowman	4-0	Chicago	Mike Keenan

M. J. O'Brien Trophy

Donated by Canadian mining magnate M. J. O'Brien, whose son Ambrose founded the National Hockey Assn. in 1910. Originally presented to the NHA champion until the league's demise in 1917, the trophy then passed to the NHL champion through 1927. It was awarded to the NHL's Canadian Division winner from 1927-38 and the Stanley Cup runner-up from 1939-50 before being retired in 1950.

    NHA winners included the Montreal Wanderers (1910), Ottawa Senators (1911 and '15), Quebec Bulldogs (1912 and '13), Toronto Blueshirts (1914) and Montreal Canadiens (1916 and '17).

Conn Smythe Trophy

The Most Valuable Player of the Stanley Cup Playoffs, as selected by the Pro Hockey Writers Assn. Presented since 1965 by Maple Leaf Gardens Limited in the name of the former Toronto coach, GM and owner, Conn Smythe. Winners who did not play for the Cup champion are in **bold** type.

Multiple winners: Wayne Gretzky, Mario Lemieux, Bobby Orr and Bernie Parent (2).

Year		Year		Year	
1965	Jean Beliveau, Mon., C	1975	Bernie Parent, Phi., G	1984	Mark Messier, Edm., LW
1966	**Roger Crozier,** Det., G	1976	**Reggie Leach,** Phi., RW	1985	Wayne Gretzky, Edm., C
1967	Dave Keon, Tor., C	1977	Guy Lafleur, Mon., RW	1986	Patrick Roy, Mon., G
1968	**Glenn Hall,** St.L., G	1978	Larry Robinson, Mon., D	1987	**Ron Hextall,** Phi., G
1969	Serge Savard, Mon., D	1979	Bob Gainey, Mon., LW	1988	Wayne Gretzky, Edm., C
				1989	Al MacInnis, Calg., D
1970	Bobby Orr, Bos., D	1980	Bryan Trottier, NYI, C		
1971	Ken Dryden, Mon., G	1981	Butch Goring, NYI, C	1990	Bill Ranford, Edm., G
1972	Bobby Orr, Bos., D	1982	Mike Bossy, NYI, RW	1991	Mario Lemieux, Pit., C
1973	Yvan Cournoyer, Mon., RW	1983	Billy Smith, NYI, G	1992	Mario Lemieux, Pit., C
1974	Bernie Parent, Phi., G				

Note: Ken Dryden (1971) and Patrick Roy (1986) are the only players to win as rookies.

All-Time Stanley Cup Playoff Leaders
CAREER

Stanley Cup Playoff leaders through 1992. Years listed indicate number of playoff appearances. Players active in 1992 in **bold** type.

Scoring

Points

		Yrs	Gm	G	A	Pts
1	**Wayne Gretzky**	13	156	95	211	306
2	**Mark Messier**	13	177	87	142	229
3	**Jari Kurri**	11	150	93	112	205
4	**Bryan Trottier**	16	219	71	113	184
5	**Glenn Anderson** (DNP)	11	164	81	102	183
6	Jean Beliveau	17	162	79	97	176
7	Denis Potvin	14	185	56	108	164
8	Mike Bossy	10	129	85	75	160
	Gordie Howe	20	157	68	92	160
	Bobby Smith	13	184	64	96	160
11	Stan Mikita	18	155	59	91	150
12	**Brian Propp**	14	160	64	84	148
13	**Denis Savard**	12	123	58	89	147
14	**Larry Robinson**	20	227	28	116	144
15	Jacques Lemaire	11	145	61	78	139
16	Phil Esposito	15	130	61	76	137
17	**Paul Coffey**	10	123	44	92	136
18	Guy Lafleur	14	128	58	76	134
19	Bobby Hull	14	119	62	67	129
	Henri Richard	18	180	49	80	129

DNP (Did not play)—Anderson's Toronto team did not qualify for the '92 playoffs.

Assists

		Yrs	Gm	No
1	**Wayne Gretzky**	13	156	211
2	**Mark Messier**	13	177	142
3	**Larry Robinson**	20	227	116
4	**Bryan Trottier**	16	219	113
5	**Jari Kurri**	11	150	112
6	Denis Potvin	14	185	108
7	**Glenn Anderson** (DNP)	11	164	102
8	Jean Beliveau	17	162	97
9	**Bobby Smith**	13	184	96
10	**Ray Bourque**	13	135	95

DNP (Did not play)—Anderson's Toronto team did not qualify for the '92 playoffs.

Miscellaneous
Championships

		Yrs	Cups
1	Henri Richard, Montreal	18	11
2	Yvan Cournoyer, Montreal	15	10
3	Jean Beliveau, Montreal	17	10
4	Claude Provost, Montreal	14	9
5	Jacques Lemaire, Montreal	11	8
	Maurice Richard, Montreal	17	8
	Red Kelly, Detroit-Toronto	19	8

Goals

		Yrs	Gm	No
1	**Wayne Gretzky**	13	156	95
2	**Jari Kurri**	11	150	93
3	**Mark Messier**	13	177	87
4	Mike Bossy	10	129	85
5	Maurice Richard	17	133	82
6	**Glenn Anderson** (DNP)	11	164	81
7	Jean Beliveau	17	162	79
8	**Bryan Trottier**	16	219	71
9	Gordie Howe	20	157	68
10	Yvon Cornoyer	12	147	64
	Brian Propp	13	159	64
	Bobby Smith	13	184	64
13	Bobby Hull	14	119	62
14	Phil Esposito	15	130	61
	Jacques Lemaire	11	145	61

DNP (Did not play)—Anderson's Toronto team did not qualify for the '92 playoffs.

Appearances

		Yrs	Gm
1	Gordie Howe, Detroit-Hartford	20	157
	Larry Robinson, Montreal-Los Angeles	20	227
3	Red Kelly, Detroit-Toronto	19	164
4	Henri Richard, Montreal	18	180
	Stan Mikita, Chicago	18	155

Games Played

		Yrs	Gm
1	**Larry Robinson**, Montreal-Los Angeles	20	227
2	**Bryan Trottier**, NY Isles-Pittsburgh	16	219
3	Denis Potvin, NY Islanders	14	185
4	**Bobby Smith**, Min-Mon-Min	13	184
5	Bob Gainey, Montreal	16	182

Penalty Minutes

		Yrs	Gm	PM
1	**Dale Hunter**	12	120	564
2	**Chris Nilan**	12	111	541
3	Willi Plett	10	83	466
4	Tiger Williams	12	83	455
5	Dave Schultz	6	73	412

All-Time Stanley Cup Playoff Leaders (Cont.)
Goaltending

Wins

		Gm	Min	W-L	SO	Avg
1	Billy Smith	132	7645	88-36	5	2.73
2	Ken Dryden	112	6846	80-32	10	2.40
3	**Grant Fuhr**(DNP)	111	6528	74-32	2	3.03
4	Jacques Plante	112	6651	71-37	15	2.17
5	**Andy Moog**	104	5845	59-38	3	2.98
6	Turk Broda	101	6389	58-42	13	1.98
7	Terry Sawchuk	106	6291	54-48	12	2.64
8	**Patrick Roy**	88	5296	51-35	5	2.53
9	Glenn Hall	115	6899	49-65	6	2.79
10	Gerry Cheevers	88	5396	47-35	8	2.69
11	Tony Esposito	99	6017	45-53	6	3.09
12	Gump Worsley	70	4079	41-25	5	2.82
13	**Mike Vernon** (DNP)	70	4157	39-28	0	2.92
14	**Tom Barrasso**	64	3702	38-24	2	3.16
	Bernie Parent	71	4302	38-33	6	2.43

DNP (Did not play)—Fuhr's Toronto team and Vernon's Calgary team did not qualify for the '92 playoffs.

Shutouts

		Gm	No
1	Clint Benedict	48	15
	Jacques Plante	112	15
3	Turk Broda	102	13
4	Terry Sawchuck	106	12
5	Ken Dryden	112	10

Appearances in Cup Final

Standings of all teams that have reached the Stanley Cup championship round, since 1918.

App		Cups	Last Won
31	Montreal Canadiens	22*	1986
21	Toronto Maple Leafs	13†	1967
18	Detroit Red Wings	7	1955
17	Boston Bruins	5	1972
10	Chicago Blackhawks	3	1961
9	New York Rangers	3	1940
6	Edmonton Oilers	5	1990
6	Philadelphia Flyers	2	1975
5	New York Islanders	4	1983
5	Vancouver Millionaires (PCHA)	0	—
4	Ottawa Senators	4	1927
3	Montreal Maroons	2	1935
3	St.Louis Blues	0	—
2	Pittsburgh Penguins	2	1992
2	Calgary Flames	1	1989
2	Victoria Cougars (WCHL-WHL)	1	1925
2	Minnesota North Stars	0	—
2	Seattle Metropolitans (PCHA)	0	—
1	Buffalo Sabres	0	—
1	Calgary Tigers (WCHL)	0	—
1	Edmonton Eskimos (WCHL)	0	—
1	Vancouver Canucks	0	—

*Montreal Canadiens also won the Cup in 1916 for a total of 32 appearances and 23 titles. Also, their final with Seattle in 1919 was cancelled due to an influenza epidemic that claimed the life of the Habs' Joe Hall.

†Toronto won the Cup under three nicknames—Arenas (1918), St.Pats (1922) and Maple Leafs (1932,42,45,47-49,51,62-64,67).

Teams now defunct (6): Calgary Tigers, Edmonton Eskimos, Montreal Maroons, Ottawa, Seattle, Vancouver Millionaires and Victoria. Edmonton, Calgary and Victoria (1925-26) represented the WCHL and later the WHL, while Vancouver (1918,1921-24) and Seattle (1919-20) played out of the PCHA.

Goals Against Average
Minimum of 50 games played.

		Gm	Min	GA	Avg
1	George Hainsworth	52	3486	112	1.93
2	Turk Broda	101	6389	211	1.98
3	Jacques Plante	112	6651	241	2.17
4	Ken Dryden	112	6846	274	2.40
5	Bernie Parent	71	4302	174	2.43

Note: Clint Benedict had an average of 1.80 but played in only 48 games.

Games Played

		Yrs	Gm
1	Billy Smith, NY Islanders	13	132
2	Glenn Hall, Det-Chi-StL	17	115
3	Jacques Plante, Mon-StL-Tor-Bos	16	112
4	Ken Dryden, Montreal	8	112
5	**Grant Fuhr**, Edmonton	9	111

SINGLE SEASON
Scoring
Points

		Year	Gm	G	A	Pts
1	Wayne Gretzky, Edm	1985	18	17	30	47
2	Mario Lemieux, Pit	1991	23	16	28	44
3	Wayne Gretzky, Edm	1988	19	12	31	43
4	Wayne Gretzky, Edm	1983	16	12	26	38
5	Paul Coffey, Edm	1985	18	12	25	37
6	Mike Bossy, NYI	1981	18	17	18	35
	Wayne Gretzky, Edm	1984	19	13	22	35
8	Mark Messier, Edm	1988	19	11	23	34
	Mario Lemieux, Pit	1992	15	16	18	34
	Mark Recchi, Pit	1991	24	10	24	34
	Wayne Gretzky, Edm	1987	21	5	29	34

Goals

		Year	Gm	No
1	Reggie Leach, Philadelphia	1976	16	19
	Jari Kurri, Edmonton	1985	18	19
3	Newsy Lalonde, Montreal	1919	10	17
	Mike Bossy, NY Islanders	1981	18	17
	Wayne Gretzky, Edmonton	1985	18	17
	Steve Payne, Minnesota	1981	19	17
	Mike Bossy, NY Islanders	1982	19	17
	Mike Bossy, NY Islanders	1983	19	17
	Kevin Stevens, Pittsburgh	1991	24	17
10	Five tied with 16 goals each.			

Assists

		Year	Gm	No
1	Wayne Gretzky, Edmonton	1988	19	31
2	Wayne Gretzky, Edmonton	1985	18	30
3	Wayne Gretzky, Edmonton	1987	21	29
4	Mario Lemieux, Pittsburgh	1991	23	28
5	Wayne Gretzky, Edmonton	1983	16	26

Goaltending
Wins

		Year	Gm	Min	W-L
1	Grant Fuhr, Edm	1988	19	1136	16- 2
	Mike Vernon, Calg	1989	22	1381	16- 5
	Tom Barrasso, Pit	1992	21	1233	16- 5
	Bill Ranford, Edm	1990	22	1401	16- 6
5	Billy Smith, NYI	1982	18	1120	15- 3
	Grant Fuhr, Edm	1985	18	1064	15- 3
	Billy Smith, NYI	1980	20	1198	15- 4
	Patrick Roy, Mon	1986	20	1218	15- 5
	Ron Hextall, Phi	1987	26	1540	15-11
10	Three tied with 14 wins each.				

Shutouts

		Year	Gm	No
1	Clint Benedict, Mon.Maroons	1926	8	4
	Terry Sawchuk, Detroit	1952	8	4
	Clint Benedict, Mon.Maroons	1928	9	4
	Dave Kerr, NY Rangers	1937	9	4
	Frank McCool, Toronto	1945	13	4
	Ken Dryden, Montreal	1977	14	4
	Bernie Parent, Philadelphia	1975	17	4

Goals Against Average

Minimum of eight games played.

		Year	Gm	Min	GA	Avg
1	Terry Sawchuk, Det	1952	8	480	5	0.63
2	Turk Broda, Tor	1951	9	509	9	1.06
3	Dave Kerr, NYR	1937	9	553	10	1.08
4	Jacques Plante, Mon	1960	8	488	11	1.35
5	Jacques Plante, StL	1969	10	589	14	1.43

SINGLE GAME

Scoring

Points

	Date	G	A	Pts
Patrik Sundstrom, NJ vs Wash	4/22/88	3	5	8
Mario Lemieux, Pit.vs Phi	4/25/89	5	3	8
Wayne Gretzky, Edm.at Calg	4/17/83	4	3	7
Wayne Gretzky, Edm.at Win	4/25/85	3	4	7
Wayne Gretzky, Edm.vs LA	4/9/87	1	6	7

Goals

	Date	No
Newsy Lalonde, Mon.vs Ott	3/1/19	5
Maurice Richard, Mon.vs Tor	3/23/44	5
Darryl Sittler, Tor.vs Phi	4/22/76	5
Reggie Leach, Phi.vs Bos	5/6/76	5
Mario Lemieux, Pit.vs Phi	4/25/89	5

NHL Franchise Origins

Here is what the current 24 teams in the National Hockey League have to show for the years they have put in as members of the NHL and World Hockey Association (WHA). League titles are noted by year won. Conferences named after Clarence Campbell, the NHL's third president (1946-77); and Edward VIII, who, while Prince of Wales, donated a trophy to the league in 1924. Edward became king of England in 1936 and abdicated the same year to marry American divorcée Wallis Simpson.

Clarence Campbell Conference

	First Season	League Titles	Franchise Stops
Calgary Flames	1972-73 (NHL)	1 NHL (1989)	Atlanta (1972-80)
			Calgary (1980—)
Chicago Blackhawks	1926-27 (NHL)	3 NHL (1934,38,61)	Chicago (1926—)
Detroit Red Wings	1926-27 (NHL)	7 NHL (1936-37,43,50,	Detroit (1926—)
		52,54-55)	
Edmonton Oilers	1973-74 (WHA)	5 NHL (1984-85,87-88, 90)	Edmonton (1972—)
Los Angeles Kings	1967-68 (NHL)	None	Los Angeles (1967—)
Minnesota North Stars	1967-68 (NHL)	None	Bloomington,MN (1967—)
St.Louis Blues	1967-68 (NHL)	None	St.Louis (1967—)
San Jose Sharks	1991-92 (NHL)	None	San Jose, CA (1991—)
Tampa Bay Lightning	1992-93 (NHL)	None	Tampa, FL (1992—)
Toronto Maple Leafs	1917-18 (NHL)	13 NHL (1918,22,32,42,45 47-49,51,62-64,67)	Toronto (1917—)
Vancouver Canucks	1970-71 (NHL)	None	Vancouver (1970—)
Winnipeg Jets	1972-73 (WHA)	3 WHA (1976,78-79)	Winnipeg (1972—)

Prince of Wales Conference

	First Season	League Titles	Franchise Stops
Boston Bruins	1924-25 (NHL)	5 NHL (1929,39,41,70,72)	Boston (1924—)
Buffalo Sabres	1970-71 (NHL)	None	Buffalo (1970—)
Hartford Whalers	1972-73 (WHA)	1 WHA (1973)	Boston (1972-74)
			W.Springfield,MA (1974-75)
			Hartford,CT (1975-78)
			Springfield,MA (1978-80)
			Hartford (1980—)
Montreal Canadiens	1917-18 (NHL)	22 NHL (1924,30-31,44,46,53, 56-60,65-66,68-69, 71,73,76-79,86)	Montreal (1917—)
New Jersey Devils	1974-75 (NHL)	None	Kansas City (1974-76)
			Denver (1976-82)
			E.Rutherford,NJ (1982—)
New York Islanders	1972-73 (NHL)	4 NHL (1980-83)	Uniondale,NY (1972—)
New York Rangers	1926-27 (NHL)	3 NHL (1928,33,40)	New York (1926—)
Ottawa Senators	1992-93 (NHL)	None	Ottawa (1992—)
Philadelphia Flyers	1967-68 (NHL)	2 NHL (1974-75)	Philadelphia (1967—)
Pittsburgh Penguins	1967-68 (NHL)	2 NHL (1991-92)	Pittsburgh (1967—)
Quebec Nordiques	1972-73 (WHA)	1 WHA (1977)	Quebec City (1972—)
Washington Capitals	1974-75 (NHL)	None	Landover,MD (1974—)

Note: The Hartford Civic Center roof caved in Jan,1978, forcing the Whalers to move home games to Springfield, MA, for two years.

The Growth of the NHL

Of the four franchises that comprised the **National Hockey League** (NHL) at the start of the 1917-18 season, only two remain—the Montreal Canadiens and the Toronto Maple Leafs (originally the Toronto Arenas). From 1919-26, eight new teams joined the league, but only four—the Boston Bruins, Chicago Blackhawks (originally Black Hawks), Detroit Red Wings (originally Cougars) and New York Rangers—survived.

It was 41 years before the NHL expanded again, doubling in size for the 1967-68 season with new teams in Los Angeles, Minnesota, Oakland, Philadelphia, Pittsburgh and St.Louis. The league had 16 clubs by the start of the 1972-73 season, but it also had a rival in the **World Hockey Association**, which debuted that year with 12 teams.

The NHL added two more teams in 1974 and merged the struggling Cleveland Barons (originally the Oakland Seals) and Minnesota North Stars in 1978, before absorbing four WHA clubs—the Edmonton Oilers, Hartford Whalers, Quebec Nordiques and Winnipeg Jets—in time for the 1979-80 season. Three expansion teams have joined the league so far in the 1990s, giving the NHL its current 24-team roster.

Expansion/Merger Timetable
For teams currently in NHL.

1919—Quebec Bulldogs finally take the ice after sitting out NHL's first two seasons; **1924**—Boston Bruins and Montreal Maroons; **1925**—New York Americans and Pittsburgh Pirates; **1926**—Chicago Black Hawks (now Blackhawks), Detroit Cougars (now Red Wings) and New York Rangers; **1932**—Ottawa Senators return after sitting out 1931-32 season.

1967—California Seals (later Cleveland Barons), Los Angeles Kings, Minnesota North Stars, Philadelphia Flyers, Pittsburgh Penguins and St.Louis Blues.

1970—Buffalo Sabres and Vancouver Canucks; **1972**—Atlanta Flames (now Calgary) and New York Islanders; **1974**—Kansas City Scouts (now New Jersey Devils) and Washington Capitals; **1978**—Cleveland Barons merge with Minnesota North Stars and team remains in Minnesota; **1979**—added WHA's Edmonton Oilers, Hartford Whalers, Quebec Nordiques and Winnipeg Jets.

1991—San Jose Sharks; **1992**—Ottawa Senators and Tampa Bay Lightning.

City and Nickname Changes

1919—Toronto Arenas renamed St.Pats; **1920**—Quebec moves to Hamilton and becomes Tigers (will fold in 1925); **1927**—Toronto St.Pats renamed Maple Leafs; **1929**—Detroit Cougars renamed Falcons.

1930—Pittsburgh Pirates move to Philadelphia and become Quakers (will fold in 1931); **1932**—Detroit Falcons renamed Red Wings; **1934**—Ottawa Senators move to St.Louis and become Eagles (will fold in 1935); **1941**—New York Americans renamed Brooklyn Americans (will fold in 1942).

1967—California Seals renamed Oakland Seals three months into first season; **1970**—Oakland Seals renamed California Golden Seals; **1975**—California Golden Seals renamed Seals; **1976**—California Seals move to Cleveland and become Barons, while Kansas City Scouts move to Denver and become Colorado Rockies; **1978**—Cleveland Barons merge with Minnesota North Stars and become Minnesota North Stars.

1980—Atlanta Flames move to Calgary; **1982**—Colorado Rockies move to East Rutherford, N.J., and become New Jersey Devils; **1986**—Chicago Black Hawks renamed Blackhawks.

Defunct NHL Teams
Teams that once played in the NHL, but no longer exist.

Brooklyn—Americans (1941-42, formerly NY Americans from 1925-41); **Cleveland**—Barons (1976-78, originally California-Oakland Seals from 1967-76); **Hamilton (Ont.)**—Tigers (1920-25, originally Quebec Bulldogs from 1919-20); **Montreal**—Maroons (1924-38) and Wanderers (1917-18); **New York**—Americans (1925-42, later Brooklyn Americans for 1941-42); **Oakland**—Seals (1967-76, also known as California Seals and Golden Seals and later Cleveland Barons from 1976-78); **Ottawa**—Senators (1917-31 and 1932-34, later St.Louis Eagles for 1934-35); **Philadelphia**—Quakers (1930-31, originally Pittsburgh Pirates from 1925-30); **Pittsburgh**—Pirates (1925-30, later Philadelphia Quakers for 1930-31); **Quebec**—Bulldogs (1919-20, later Hamilton Tigers from 1920-25); **St.Louis**—Eagles (1934-35), originally Ottawa Senators (1917-31 and 1932-34).

WHA Teams (1972–79)

Baltimore—Blades (1975); **Birmingham**—Bulls (1976-78); **Calgary**—Cowboys (1975-77); **Chicago**—Cougars (1972-75); **Cincinnati**—Stingers (1975-79); **Cleveland**—Crusaders (1972-76, moved to Minnesota); **Denver**—Spurs (1975-76, moved to Ottawa); **Edmonton**—Oilers (1972-79, originally called Alberta Oilers in 1972-73); **Houston**—Aeros (1972-78); **Indianapolis**—Racers (1974-78).

Los Angeles—Sharks (1972-74, moved to Michigan); **Michigan**—Stags (1974-75, moved to Baltimore); **Minnesota**—Fighting Saints (1972-76) and New Fighting Saints (1976-77); **New England**—Whalers (1972-79, played in Boston from 1972-74, West Springfield-MA from 1974-75, Hartford from 1975-78 and Springfield-MA in 1979); **New Jersey**—Knights (1973-74, moved to San Diego); **New York**—Raiders (1972-73, renamed Golden Blades in 1973, moved to New Jersey).

Ottawa—Nationals (1972-73, moved to Toronto) and Civics (1976); **Philadelphia**—Blazers (1972-73, moved to Vancouver); **Phoenix**—Roadrunners (1974-77); **Quebec**—Nordiques (1972-79); **San Diego**—Mariners (1974-77); **Toronto**—Toros (1973-76, moved to Birmingham, AL); **Vancouver**—Blazers (1973-75, moved to Calgary); **Winnipeg**—Jets (1972-79).

All-Time NHL Regular Season Leaders

Through the 1991-92 regular season.

CAREER

Players active during 1991-92 in **bold** type.

Scoring

Points

		Yrs	Gm	G	A	Pts
1	**Wayne Gretzky**	13	999	749	1514	2263
2	Gordie Howe	26	1767	801	1049	1850
3	Marcel Dionne	18	1348	731	1040	1771
4	Phil Esposito	18	1282	717	873	1590
5	Stan Mikita	22	1394	541	926	1467
6	**Bryan Trottier**	17	1238	520	890	1410
7	John Bucyk	23	1540	556	813	1369
8	Guy Lafleur	17	1126	560	793	1353
9	Gilbert Perreault	17	1191	512	814	1326
10	Alex Delvecchio	24	1549	456	825	1281
11	Jean Ratelle	21	1281	491	776	1267
12	Norm Ullman	20	1410	490	739	1229
13	Jean Beliveau	20	1125	507	712	1219
14	Bobby Clarke	15	1144	358	852	1210
15	**Peter Stastny**	12	892	427	754	1181
16	Bobby Hull	16	1063	610	560	1170
17	**Denis Savard**	12	883	407	735	1142
18	**Mark Messier**	13	930	427	714	1141
19	Bernie Federko	14	1000	369	761	1130
20	Mike Bossy	10	752	573	553	1126
21	Darryl Sittler	15	1096	484	637	1121
22	**Dale Hawerchuk**	11	870	433	683	1116
23	**Paul Coffey**	12	873	318	796	1114
24	Frank Mahovlich	18	1181	533	570	1103
	Jari Kurri	11	827	497	606	1103
26	**Michel Goulet**	13	970	509	569	1078
27	Denis Potvin	15	1060	310	742	1052
28	**Dave Taylor**	15	1030	421	626	1047
29	Henri Richard	20	1256	358	688	1046
30	**Mike Gartner**	13	1005	538	501	1039

Assists

		Yrs	Gm	No
1	**Wayne Gretzky**	13	999	1514
2	Gordie Howe	26	1767	1049
3	Marcel Dionne	18	1348	1040
4	Stan Mikita	22	1394	926
5	**Bryan Trottier**	17	1238	890
6	Phil Esposito	18	1282	873
7	Bobby Clarke	15	1144	852
8	Alex Delvecchio	24	1549	825
9	Gilbert Perreault	17	1191	814
10	John Bucyk	23	1540	813
11	**Paul Coffey**	12	873	796
12	Guy Lafleur	17	1126	793
13	Jean Ratelle	21	1281	776
14	Bernie Federko	14	1000	761
15	**Peter Stastny**	12	892	754
16	**Larry Robinson**	20	1384	750
17	**Ray Bourque**	13	950	743
18	Denis Potvin	15	1060	742
19	Norm Ullman	20	1410	739
20	**Denis Savard**	12	883	735

Penalty Minutes

		Yrs	Gm	PM
1	Tiger Williams	13	962	3966
2	**Chris Nilan**	13	688	3043
3	**Dale Hunter**	11	918	2676
4	Willi Plett	12	834	2572
5	**Tim Hunter**	10	545	2404
6	Dave Schultz	9	535	2294
7	Bryan Watson	16	878	2212
8	Laurie Boschman	13	939	2164
9	Terry O'Reilly	14	891	2095
10	Al Secord	11	766	2093

Goals

		Yrs	Gm	No
1	Gordie Howe	26	1767	801
2	**Wayne Gretzky**	13	999	749
3	Marcel Dionne	18	1348	731
4	Phil Esposito	18	1282	717
5	Bobby Hull	16	1063	610
6	Mike Bossy	10	752	573
7	Guy Lafleur	17	1126	560
8	John Bucyk	23	1540	556
9	Maurice Richard	18	978	544
10	Stan Mikita	22	1394	541
11	**Mike Gartner**	13	1005	538
12	Frank Mahovlich	18	1181	533
13	**Bryan Trottier**	17	1238	520
14	Gilbert Perreault	17	1191	512
15	**Michel Goulet**	13	970	509
16	Jean Beliveau	20	1125	507
17	Lanny McDonald	16	1111	500
18	**Jari Kurri**	11	827	497
19	Jean Ratelle	21	1281	491
20	Norm Ullman	20	1410	490
21	Darryl Sittler	15	1096	484
22	Alex Delvecchio	24	1549	456
23	Rick Middleton	14	1005	448
24	**Dino Ciccarelli**	12	825	444
25	**Rick Vaive**	13	877	441
26	**Glenn Anderson**	12	900	437
27	**Dale Hawerchuk**	11	870	433
28	Yvan Cournoyer	16	968	428
29	**Peter Stastny**	12	892	427
	Mark Messier	13	930	427

NHL-WHA Top 15

All-Time regular season scoring leaders, including games played in World Hockey Assn. (1972-79). NHL players with WHA experience are listed in CAPITAL letters. Players active during 1991-92 are in **bold** type.

Points

		Yrs	Gm	G	A	Pts
1	**WAYNE GRETZKY**	14	1079	795	1578	2373
2	GORDIE HOWE	32	2186	975	1383	2358
3	BOBBY HULL	23	1474	913	895	1808
4	Marcel Dionne	18	1348	731	1040	1771
5	Phil Esposito	18	1282	717	873	1590
6	Stan Mikita	22	1394	541	926	1467
7	**Bryan Trottier**	17	1238	520	890	1410
8	John Bucyk	23	1540	556	813	1369
9	NORM ULLMAN	22	1554	537	822	1359
10	Guy Lafleur	17	1126	560	793	1353
11	FRANK MAHOVLICH	22	1418	622	713	1335
12	Gilbert Perreault	17	1191	512	814	1326
13	Alex Delvecchio	24	1549	456	825	1281
14	DAVE KEON	22	1597	498	779	1277
15	Jean Ratelle	21	1281	491	776	1267

WHA Totals: GRETZKY (1 yr, 80 gm, 46-64—110); HOWE (6 yrs, 419 gm, 174-334—508); HULL (7 yrs, 411 gm, 303-335—638); KEON (4 yrs, 301 gm, 102-189—291); MAHOVLICH (4 yrs, 237 gm, 89-143—232); ULLMAN (2 yrs, 144 gm, 47-83—130).

All-Time NHL Regular Season Leaders (Cont.)

Years Played

		Yrs	Career	Gm
1	Gordie Howe	26	1946-71,79-80	1767
2	Alex Delvecchio	24	1950-74	1549
	Tim Horton	24	1949-50,51-74	1446
4	John Bucyk	23	1955-78	1540
5	Stan Mikita	22	1958-80	1394
	Doug Mohns	22	1953-75	1390
	Dean Prentice	22	1952-74	1378
8	Harry Howell	21	1952-73	1411
	Ron Stewart	21	1952-73	1353
	Jean Ratelle	21	1960-81	1281
	Allan Stanley	21	1948-69	1244
	Eric Nesterenko	21	1951-72	1219
	George Armstrong	21	1949-50,51-71	1187
	Terry Sawchuk	21	1949-70	971
	Gump Worsley	21	1952-53,54-74	862

Note: Combined NHL-WHA years played: Howe (32); Howell (24); Bobby Hull (23); Nesterenko, Norm Ullman, Frank Mahovlich and Dave Keon (22).

Games Played

		Yrs	Career	No
1	Gordie Howe	26	1946-71,79-80	1767
2	Alex Delvecchio	24	1950-74	1549
3	John Bucyk	23	1955-78	1540
4	Tim Horton	24	1949-50,51-74	1446
5	Harry Howell	21	1952-73	1411
6	Norm Ullman	20	1955-75	1410
7	Stan Mikita	22	1958-80	1394
8	Doug Mohns	22	1953-75	1390
9	Larry Robinson	20	1972—	1384
10	Dean Prentice	22	1952-74	1378
11	Ron Stewart	21	1952-73	1353
12	Marcel Dionne	18	1971-89	1348
13	Red Kelly	20	1947-67	1316
14	Dave Keon	18	1960-75,79-82	1296
15	Phil Esposito	18	1963-81	1282

Note: Combined NHL-WHA games played: Howe (2,186), Keon (1,597), Howell (1,581), Ullman (1,554), Bobby Hull (1,474) and Frank Mahovlich (1,418).

Goaltending

Wins

		Yrs	Gm	W	L	T	Pct
1	Terry Sawchuk	21	971	435	337	188	.551
2	Jacques Plante	18	837	434	246	137	.615
3	Tony Esposito	16	886	423	307	151	.566
4	Glenn Hall	18	906	407	327	165	.544
5	Rogie Vachon	16	795	355	291	115	.542
6	Gump Worsley	21	862	335	353	150	.489
7	Harry Lumley	16	804	332	324	143	.505
8	Billy Smith	18	680	305	233	105	.556
9	Turk Broda	12	629	302	224	101	.562
10	**Mike Liut**	13	663	293	271	74	.517
11	Ed Giacomin	13	610	289	206	97	.570
12	Dan Bouchard	14	655	286	232	113	.543
13	Tiny Thompson	12	553	284	194	75	.581
14	Bernie Parent	13	608	270	197	121	.562
	Gilles Meloche	18	788	270	351	131	.446
16	Ken Dryden	8	397	258	57	74	.758
17	Frankie Brimsek	10	514	252	182	80	.568
18	**Grant Fuhr**	11	488	251	150	59	.610
	Johnny Bower	15	549	251	196	90	.551
20	George Hainsworth	11	465	247	146	74	.608

Losses

		Yrs	Gm	W	L	T	Pct
1	Gump Worsley	21	862	335	353	150	.489
2	Gilles Meloche	18	788	270	351	131	.446
3	Terry Sawchuk	21	971	435	337	188	.551
4	Glenn Hall	18	906	407	327	165	.544
5	Harry Lumley	16	804	332	324	143	.505

Goals Against Average
Minimum of 300 games played.

Before 1950

		Gm	Min	GA	Avg
1	George Hainsworth	465	29,415	937	1.91
2	Alex Connell	417	26,030	830	1.91
3	Chuck Gardiner	316	19,687	664	2.02
4	Lorne Chabot	411	25,309	861	2.04
5	Tiny Thompson	553	34,174	1183	2.08

Since 1950

		Gm	Min	GA	Avg
1	Ken Dryden	397	23,352	870	2.24
2	Jacques Plante	837	49,533	1965	2.38
3	Glenn Hall	906	53,484	2239	2.51
4	Terry Sawchuk	971	57,205	2401	2.52
5	Johnny Bower	552	32,077	1347	2.52

Shutouts

		Yrs	Games	No
1	Terry Sawchuk	21	971	103
2	George Hainsworth	11	465	94
3	Glenn Hall	18	906	84
4	Jacques Plante	18	837	82
5	Alex Connell	12	417	81
	Tiny Thompson	12	553	81
7	Tony Esposito	16	886	76
8	Lorne Chabot	11	411	73
9	Harry Lumley	16	804	71
10	Roy Worters	12	484	66
11	Turk Broda	14	629	62
12	John Roach	14	491	58
13	Clint Benedict	13	362	57
14	Bernie Parent	13	608	55
15	Ed Giacomin	13	610	54

NHL-WHA Top 15

All-Time regular season wins leaders, including games played in World Hockey Assn.(1972-79). NHL goaltenders with WHA experience are listed in CAPITAL letters. Players active during 1991-92 are in **bold** type.

Wins

		Yrs	Gm	W	L	T	Pct
1	JACQUES PLANTE	19	868	449	260	138	.612
2	Terry Sawchuk	21	971	435	337	188	.551
3	Tony Esposito	16	886	423	307	151	.566
4	Glenn Hall	18	906	407	327	165	.544
5	Rogie Vachon	16	795	355	291	115	.542
6	Gump Worsley	21	862	335	353	150	.489
7	Harry Lumley	16	804	332	324	143	.505
8	GERRY CHEEVERS	16	609	329	172	83	.634
9	**MIKE LIUT**	15	744	324	310	78	.510
10	Billy Smith	18	680	305	233	105	.556
11	BERNIE PARENT	14	671	303	225	121	.560
12	Turk Broda	12	629	302	224	101	.562
13	Ed Giacomin	13	610	289	206	97	.570
14	Dan Bouchard	14	655	286	232	113	.543
15	Tiny Thompson	12	553	284	194	75	.581

WHA Totals: CHEEVERS (4 yrs, 191 gm, 99-78-9); LIUT (2 yrs, 81 gm, 31-39-4); PARENT (1 yr, 63 gm, 33-28-0); PLANTE (1 yr, 31 gm, 15-14-1).

SINGLE SEASON

Scoring

Points

		Season	G	A	Pts
1	Wayne Gretzky, Edm	1985-86	52	163	215
2	Wayne Gretzky, Edm	1981-82	92	120	212
3	Wayne Gretzky, Edm	1984-85	73	135	208
4	Wayne Gretzky, Edm	1983-84	87	118	205
5	Mario Lemieux, Pit	1988-89	85	114	199
6	Wayne Gretzky, Edm	1982-83	71	125	196
7	Wayne Gretzky, Edm	1986-87	62	121	183
8	Mario Lemieux, Pit	1987-88	70	98	168
	Wayne Gretzky, LA	1988-89	54	114	168
10	Wayne Gretzky, Edm	1980-81	55	109	164
11	Wayne Gretzky, LA	1990-91	41	122	163
12	Steve Yzerman, Det	1988-89	65	90	155
13	Phil Esposito, Bos	1970-71	76	76	152
14	Bernie Nicholls, LA	1988-89	70	80	150
15	Wayne Gretzky, Edm	1987-88	40	109	149
16	Mike Bossy, NYI	1981-82	64	83	147
17	Phil Esposito, Bos	1973-74	68	77	145
18	Wayne Gretzky, LA	1989-90	40	102	142
19	Mario Lemieux, Pit	1985-86	48	93	141
20	Peter Stastny, Que	1981-82	46	93	139
	Bobby Orr, Bos	1970-71	37	102	139

WHA 150 points or more: 154—Marc Tardif, Que.(1977-78).

Goals

		Season	Gm	No
1	Wayne Gretzky, Edm	1981-82	80	92
2	Wayne Gretzky, Edm	1983-84	74	87
3	Brett Hull, St.L	1990-91	78	86
4	Mario Lemieux, Pit	1988-89	76	85
5	Phil Esposito, Bos	1970-71	78	76
6	Wayne Gretzky, Edm	1984-85	80	73
7	Brett Hull, St.L	1989-90	80	72
8	Jari Kurri, Edm	1984-85	73	71
	Wayne Gretzky, Edm	1982-83	80	71
10	Brett Hull, St.L	1991-92	73	70
	Mario Lemieux, Pit	1987-88	77	70
	Bernie Nicholls, LA	1988-89	79	70
13	Mike Bossy, NYI	1978-79	80	69
14	Phil Esposito, Bos	1973-74	78	68
	Jari Kurri, Edm	1985-86	78	68
	Mike Bossy, NYI	1980-81	79	68
17	Phil Esposito, Bos	1971-72	76	66
	Lanny McDonald, Calg	1982-83	80	66
19	Steve Yzerman, Det	1988-89	80	65
20	Mike Bossy, NYI	1981-82	80	64

WHA 70 goals or more: 77—Bobby Hull, Win.(1974-75); **75**—Real Cloutier, Que.(1978-79); **71**—Marc Tardif, Que.(1975-76); **70**—Anders Hedberg, Win.(1976-77).

Assists

		Season	Gm	No
1	Wayne Gretzky, Edm	1985-86	80	163
2	Wayne Gretzky, Edm	1984-85	80	135
3	Wayne Gretzky, Edm	1982-83	80	125
4	Wayne Gretzky, LA	1990-91	78	122
5	Wayne Gretzky, Edm	1986-87	79	121
6	Wayne Gretzky, Edm	1981-82	80	120
7	Wayne Gretzky, Edm	1983-84	74	118
8	Mario Lemieux, Pit	1988-89	76	114
	Wayne Gretzky, LA	1988-89	78	114
10	Wayne Gretzky, Edm	1987-88	64	109
	Wayne Gretzky, Edm	1980-81	80	109
12	Wayne Gretzky, LA	1989-90	73	102
	Bobby Orr, Bos	1970-71	78	102
14	Mario Lemieux, Pit	1987-88	77	98
15	Mario Lemieux, Pit	1985-86	79	93
	Peter Stastny, Que	1981-82	80	93

WHA 95 assists or more: 106—Andre Lacroix, S.Diego (1974-75).

Goaltending

Wins

		Season	Record
1	Bernie Parent, Phi	1973-74	47-13-12
2	Bernie Parent, Phi	1974-75	44-14- 9
	Terry Sawchuk, Det	1950-51	44-13-13
	Terry Sawchuk, Det	1951-52	44-14-12
5	Ed Belfour, Chi	1990-91	43-19- 7
6	Jacques Plante, Mon	1955-56	42-12-10
	Jacques Plante, Mon	1961-62	42-14-14
	Ken Dryden, Mon	1975-76	42-10- 8
9	Ken Dryden, Mon	1976-77	41- 6- 8
10	Six tied with 40 wins each.		

WHA 40 wins or more: 44—Richard Brodeur, Que.(1975-76); **41**—Joe Daley, Win.(1975-76) and Dave Dryden, Edm.(1978-79).

Losses

		Season	Record
1	Gary Smith, Cal	1970-71	19-48- 4
2	Al Rollins, Chi	1953-54	12-47- 7
3	Harry Lumley, Chi	1951-52	17-44- 9
4	Harry Lumley, Chi	1950-51	12-41- 1
5	Eddie Johnston, Bos	1963-64	18-40-12

Most WHA losses in one season: 36—Don McLeod, Van.(1974-75) and Andy Brown, Ind.(1974-75).

Shutouts

		Season	Gm	No
1	George Hainsworth, Mon	1928-29	44	22
2	Alex Connell, Ott	1925-26	36	15
	Alex Connell, Ott	1927-28	44	15
	Hal Winkler, Bos	1927-28	44	15
	Tony Esposito, Chi	1969-70	63	15

Most WHA shutouts in one season: 5—Gerry Cheevers, Cle.(1972-73) and Joe Daly, Win.(1975-76).

Goals Against Average

Before 1950

		Season	Gm	Avg
1	George Hainsworth, Mon	1928-29	44	0.92
2	George Hainsworth, Mon	1927-28	44	1.05
3	Alex Connell, Ott	1925-26	36	1.12
4	Tiny Thompson, Bos	1928-29	44	1.15
	Roy Worters, NY Americans	1928-29	38	1.15

Since 1950

		Season	Gm	Avg
1	Tony Esposito, Chi	1971-72	48	1.77
	Al Rollins, Tor	1950-51	40	1.77
3	Harry Lumley, Tor	1953-54	69	1.86
	Jacques Plante, Mon	1955-56	64	1.86
5	Jacques Plante, Tor	1970-71	40	1.88

Penalty Minutes

		Season	PM
1	Dave Schultz, Phi	1974-75	472
2	Paul Baxter, Pit	1981-82	409
3	Mike Peluso, Chi	1991-92	408
4	Dave Schultz, LA	1977-78	405
5	Bob Probert, Det	1987-88	398
6	Basil McRae, Min	1987-88	382
7	Joey Kocur, Det	1985-86	377
8	Tim Hunter, Calg	1988-89	375
9	Steve Durbano, Pit-KC	1975-76	370
10	Basil McRae, Min	1988-89	365

WHA 355 minutes or more: 365—Curt Brackenbury, Min-Que. (1975-76).

All-Time NHL Regular Season Leaders (Cont.)
SINGLE GAME
Scoring

	Date	G	A	Pts
Darryl Sittler, Tor.vs Bos	2/7/76	6	4	10
Maurice Richard, Mon.vs Det.	12/28/44	5	3	8
Bert Olmstead, Mon.vs Chi	1/9/54	4	4	8
Tom Bladon, Phi.vs Cle	12/11/77	4	4	8
Bryan Trottier, NYI vs NYR	12/23/78	5	3	8
Peter Stastny, Que.at Wash	2/22/81	4	4	8
Anton Stastny, Que.at Wash	2/22/81	3	5	8
Wayne Gretzky, Edm. vs NJ	11/19/83	3	5	8
Wayne Gretzky, Edm.vs Min.	1/4/84	4	4	8
Paul Coffey, Edm.vs Det.	3/14/86	2	6	8
Mario Lemieux, Pit.vs StL	10/15/88	2	6	8
Bernie Nicholls, LA vs Tor	12/1/88	2	6	8
Mario Lemieux, Pit.vs NJ	12/31/88	5	3	8

NHL All-Star Game

The NHL All-Star Game began at the start of the 1947-48 season as an exhibition contest between the defending league champion and a squad of star players from the other five teams. Two All-Star teams played each other in 1951 and '52, but 1953 saw a return to the original format. The game moved to mid-season in 1967, became an East Division vs West Division contest in 1969, and finally a Wales Conference vs Campbell Conference contest in 1975. Winning coaches are listed first. **Campbell-Wales series:** Wales (East), 11-5.

Multiple MVP winners: Mario Lemieux (3); Wayne Gretzky, Bobby Hull and Frank Mahovlich (2).

Year		Host	Coaches	Most Valuable Player
1947	All-Stars 4, Toronto 3	Toronto	Dick Irvin, Hap Day	No award
1948	All-Stars 3, Toronto 1	Chicago	Tommy Ivan, Hap Day	No award
1949	All-Stars 3, Toronto 1	Toronto	Tommy Ivan, Hap Day	No award
1950	Detroit 7, All-Stars 1	Detroit	Tommy Ivan, Lynn Patrick	No award
1951	1st Team 2, 2nd Team 2	Toronto	Joe Primeau, Hap Day	No award
1952	1st Team 1, 2nd Team 1	Detroit	Tommy Ivan, Dick Irvin	No award
1953	All-Stars 3, Montreal 1	Montreal	Lynn Patrick, Dick Irvin	No award
1954	All-Stars 2, Detroit 2	Detroit	King Clancy, Jim Skinner	No award
1955	Detroit 3, All-Stars 1	Detroit	Jim Skinner, Dick Irvin	No award
1956	All-Stars 1, Montreal 1	Montreal	Jim Skinner, Toe Blake	No award
1957	All-Stars 5, Montreal 3	Montreal	Milt Schmidt, Toe Blake	No award
1958	Montreal 6, All-Stars 3	Montreal	Toe Blake, Milt Schmidt	No award
1959	Montreal 6, All-Stars 1	Montreal	Toe Blake, Punch Imlach	No award
1960	All-Stars 2, Montreal 1	Montreal	Punch Imlach, Toe Blake	No award
1961	All-Stars 3, Chicago 1	Chicago	Sid Abel, Rudy Pilous	No award
1962	Toronto 4, All-Stars 1	Toronto	Punch Imlach, Rudy Pilous	Eddie Shack, Tor.
1963	All-Stars 3, Toronto 3	Toronto	Sid Abel, Punch Imlach	Frank Mahovlich, Tor.
1964	All-Stars 3, Toronto 2	Toronto	Sid Abel, Punch Imlach	Jean Beliveau, Mon.
1965	All-Stars 5, Montreal 2	Montreal	Billy Reay, Toe Blake	Gordie Howe, Det.
1966	No Game (see below)			
1967	Montreal 3, All-Stars 0	Montreal	Toe Blake, Sid Abel	Henri Richard, Mon.
1968	Toronto 4, All-Stars 3	Toronto	Punch Imlach, Toe Blake	Bruce Gamble, Tor.
1969	West 3, East 3	Montreal	Scotty Bowman, Toe Blake	Frank Mahovlich, Det.
1970	East 4, West 1	St.Louis	Claude Ruel, Scotty Bowman	Bobby Hull, Chi.
1971	West 2, East 1	Boston	Scotty Bowman, Harry Sinden	Bobby Hull, Chi.
1972	East 3, West 2	Minnesota	Al MacNeil, Billy Reay	Bobby Orr, Bos.
1973	East 5, West 4	NY Rangers	Tom Johnson, Billy Reay	Greg Polis, Pit.
1974	West 6, East 4	Chicago	Billy Reay, Scotty Bowman	Garry Unger, St.L.
1975	Wales 7, Campbell 1	Montreal	Bep Guidolin, Fred Shero	Syl Apps,Jr.,Pit.
1976	Wales 7, Campbell 5	Philadelphia	Floyd Smith, Fred Shero	Peter Mahovlich, Mon.
1977	Wales 4, Campbell 3	Vancouver	Scotty Bowman, Fred Shero	Rick Martin, Buf.
1978	Wales 3, Campbell 2 (OT)	Buffalo	Scotty Bowman, Fred Shero	Billy Smith, NYI
1979	No Game (see below)			
1980	Wales 6, Campbell 3	Detroit	Scotty Bowman, Al Arbour	Reggie Leach, Phi.
1981	Campbell 4, Wales 1	Los Angeles	Pat Quinn, Scotty Bowman	Mike Liut, St.L.
1982	Wales 4, Campbell 2	Washington	Al Arbour, Glen Sonmor	Mike Bossy, NYI
1983	Campbell 9, Wales 3	NY Islanders	Roger Neilson, Al Arbour	Wayne Gretzky, Edm.
1984	Wales 7, Campbell 6	New Jersey	Al Arbour, Glen Sather	Don Maloney, NYR
1985	Wales 6, Campbell 4	Calgary	Al Arbour, Glen Sather	Mario Lemieux, Pit.
1986	Wales 4, Campbell 3 (OT)	Hartford	Mike Keenan, Glen Sather	Grant Fuhr, Edm.
1987	No Game (see below)			
1988	Wales 6, Campbell 5 (OT)	St.Louis	Mike Keenan, Glen Sather	Mario Lemieux, Pit.
1989	Campbell 9, Wales 5	Edmonton	Glen Sather, Terry O'Reilly	Wayne Gretzky, LA
1990	Wales 12, Campbell 7	Pittsburgh	Pat Burns, Terry Crisp	Mario Lemieux, Pit.
1991	Campbell 11, Wales 5	Chicago	John Muckler, Mike Milbury	Vincent Damphousse, Tor.
1992	Campbell 10, Wales 6	Philadelphia	Bob Gainey, Scotty Bowman	Brett Hull, St.L.

No All-Star Game: in 1966 (moved from start of season to mid-season); in 1979 (replaced by Challenge Cup series with USSR); in 1987 (replaced by Rendez-Vous '87 series with USSR). See page 371.

All-Time Winningest NHL Coaches

Top 25 NHL career victories through the 1991-92 season. Career, regular season and playoff records are noted along with NHL titles won. Coaches active during 1991-92 season in **bold** type.

		Career				Regular Season				Playoffs				
		Yrs	W	L	T	Pct	W	L	T	Pct	W	L	T	Pct Stanley Cups
1	**Scotty Bowman**	18	**908**	436	219	.651	778	359	219	.654	130	77	0	.628 6 (1973,76-79,92)
2	**Al Arbour**	20	**819**	577	229	.574	705	504	229	.570	114	73	0	.610 4 (1980-83)
3	Dick Irvin	26	790	609	228	.556	690	521	226	.559	100	88	2	.532 4 (1932,44,46,53)
4	Billy Reay	16	599	445	175	.563	542	385	175	.571	57	60	0	.487 —None—
5	Toe Blake	13	582	292	159	.640	500	255	159	.634	82	37	0	.689 8 (1956-60,65-66,68)
6	Glen Sather	10	531	278	99	.639	442	241	99	.629	89	37	0	.706 4 (1984-85,87-88)
7	Jack Adams	21	475	449	163	.512	423	397	162	.513	52	52	1	.500 3 (1936-37,43)
8	Punch Imlach	15	467	421	163	.522	423	373	163	.526	44	48	0	.478 4 (1962-64,67)
9	Fred Shero	10	451	272	120	.606	390	225	120	.612	61	47	0	.565 2 (1974-75)
	Bryan Murray	11	451	349	103	.556	420	309	103	.567	31	40	0	.437 —None—
11	Emile Francis	13	433	326	112	.561	393	273	112	.556	40	53	0	.430 —None—
12	Sid Abel	16	414	470	155	.473	382	426	155	.477	32	44	0	.421 —None—
13	**Mike Keenan**	8	408	280	69	.585	343	228	69	.590	65	52	0	.556 —None—
14	Art Ross	18	395	333	95	.538	368	300	90	.545	27	33	5	.454 1 (1939)
15	Michel Bergeron	10	369	387	104	.490	338	350	104	.492	31	37	0	.456 —None—
16	Bob Pulford	14	364	348	130	.510	336	305	130	.520	28	43	0	.394 —None—
17	**Roger Neilson**	10	346	293	105	.536	309	253	105	.542	37	40	0	.481 —None—
18	Tommy Ivan	9	324	205	111	.593	288	174	111	.599	36	31	0	.537 3 (1950,52,54)
19	Bob Berry	9	315	306	100	.506	311	292	100	.514	4	14	0	.222 —None—
20	Lester Patrick	13	312	242	115	.552	281	216	107	.554	31	26	8	.538 2 (1928,33)

Note: The NHL does not recognize records from the Pacific Coast Hockey Assn. (1912-25), the Western Canada Hockey League (1922-26), or the World Hockey Assn.(1972-79), so the following PCHA, WCHL and WHA overall coaching records are not included above: PCHL & WCHL—**Patrick** (15-year record unavailable, but won 1925 Stanley Cup); WHA—**Sather** (103-97-1 in 3 yrs).

Where They Coached

Abel—Chicago (1952-54), Detroit (1957-68,69-70), St.Louis (1971-72), Kansas City (1975-76); **Adams**—Toronto (1922-23), Detroit (1927-47); **Arbour**—St.Louis (1970-73), NY Islanders (1973-86,88—); **Bergeron**—Quebec (1980-87), NY Rangers (1987-89), Quebec (1989-90); **Berry**—Los Angeles (1978-81), Montreal (1981-84), Pittsburgh (1984-87); **Blake**—Montreal (1955-68); **Bowman**—St.Louis (1967-71), Montreal (1971-79), Buffalo (1979-87), Pittsburgh (1991—).

Francis—NY Rangers (1965-75), St.Louis (1976-77,81-83); **Imlach**—Toronto (1958-69), Buffalo (1970-72), Toronto (1979-81); **Irvin**—Chicago (1930-31,55-56), Toronto (1931-40), Montreal (1940-55); **Ivan**—Detroit (1947-54), Chicago (1956-58); **Keenan**—Philadelphia (1984-88), Chicago (1988-92); **B.Murray**—Washington (1982-90), Detroit (1990—).

Neilson—Toronto (1977-79), Buffalo (1979-81), Vancouver (1982-83), Los Angeles (1984), NY Rangers (1989—); **Patrick**—NY Rangers (1926-39); **Pulford**—Los Angeles (1972-77), Chicago (1977-79,81-82,85-87); **Reay**—Toronto (1957-59), Chicago (1963-77); **Ross**—Mont.Wanderers (1917-18), Hamilton (1922-23), Boston (1924-28,29-34,36-39,41-45); **Sather**—Edmonton (1979-89); **Shero**—Philadelphia (1971-78), NY Rangers (1978-81).

Top Winning Percentages

Minimum of 275 victories, including playoffs.

		Yrs	W	L	T	Pct
1	Scotty Bowman	18	908	436	219	**.651**
2	Toe Blake	13	582	292	159	**.640**
3	Glen Sather	10	531	278	99	**.639**
4	Fred Shero	10	451	272	120	**.606**
5	Don Cherry	6	281	177	77	**.597**
6	Tommy Ivan	9	324	205	111	**.593**
7	**Mike Keenan**	8	408	280	69	**.585**
8	**Al Arbour**	20	819	577	229	**.574**
9	Billy Reay	16	599	445	175	**.563**
10	Emile Francis	13	433	326	112	**.561**
11	Hap Day	10	308	237	81	**.557**
12	**Bryan Murray**	11	451	349	103	**.556**
	Dick Irvin	26	790	609	228	**.556**
14	Lester Patrick	13	312	242	115	**.552**
15	Bob Johnson	6	275	223	98	**.547**
16	**Pat Quinn**	9	297	244	90	**.542**
17	Art Ross	18	395	333	95	**.538**
18	**Roger Neilson**	10	346	293	105	**.536**
19	Punch Imlach	15	467	421	163	**.522**
20	Jack Adams	17	465	442	164	**.512**
21	Bob Pulford	14	364	348	130	**.510**
22	Bob Berry	9	315	306	100	**.506**
23	Michel Bergeron	10	369	387	104	**.490**
24	Jacques Demers	8	304	321	86	**.488**
25	Sid Abel	15	414	470	155	**.473**

Active Coaches' Victories

Through 1991-92 season, including playoffs.

		Yrs	W	L	T	Pct
1	Scotty Bowman, Pit	18	**908**	436	219	.651
2	Al Arbour, NYI	20	**819**	577	229	.574
3	Bryan Murray, Det	11	**451**	349	103	.556
4	Roger Neilson, NYR	10	**346**	293	105	.536
5	Jacques Demers, Mon	8	**304**	321	86	.488
6	Pat Quinn, Van	9	**297**	244	90	.542
7	Pat Burns, Tor	4	**204**	130	42	.598
8	Brian Sutter, Bos	4	**173**	145	43	.539
9	Terry Crisp, T.Bay	3	**166**	78	33	.659
10	Herb Brooks, NJ	5	**162**	173	54	.486
11	John Muckler, Buf	4	**131**	129	34	.503
12	Paul Holmgren, Hart	4	**117**	135	31	.468
13	Terry Murray, Wash	3	**116**	94	17	.548
14	Pierre Page, Que	3	**84**	119	31	.425
15	Bob Gainey, Min	2	**76**	94	20	.453
16	Rick Bowness, Ott	2	**52**	56	15	.484
17	Ted Green, Edm	1	**44**	42	10	.510
18	John Paddock, Win	1	**36**	36	15	.500
19	Bill Dineen, Phi	1	**24**	23	9	.509
20	George Kingston, SJ	1	**17**	58	5	.244
21	Dave King, Calg	0	**0**	0	0	.000
	Barry Melrose, LA	0	**0**	0	0	.000
	Bob Plager, St.L	0	**0**	0	0	.000
	Darryl Sutter, Chi	0	**0**	0	0	.000

Annual Awards
Hart Memorial Trophy

Awarded to the player "adjudged to be the most valuable to his team" and named after Cecil Hart, the former manager-coach of the Montreal Canadiens. Winners selected by Pro Hockey Writers Assn. (PHWA). Winners' scoring statistics or goaltender W-L records and goals against average are provided; (*) indicates led league in scoring.

Multiple winners: Wayne Gretzky (9); Gordie Howe (6); Eddie Shore (4); Bobby Clarke, Howie Morenz and Bobby Orr (3); Jean Beliveau, Bill Cowley, Phil Esposito, Bobby Hull, Guy Lafleur, Mark Messier, Stan Mikita, and Nels Stewart (2).

Year		G	A	Pts	Year		G	A	Pts
1924	Frank Nighbor, Ottawa., C	10	3	13	1960	Gordie Howe, Det., RW	28	45	73
1925	Billy Burch, Hamilton, C	20	4	24	1961	Bernie Geoffrion, Mon., RW	50	45	95*
1926	Nels Stewart, Maroons, C	34	8	42*	1962	Jacques Plante, Mon., G	42-14-14;		2.37*
1927	Herb Gardiner, Mon., D	6	6	12	1963	Gordie Howe, Det., RW	38	48	86*
1928	Howie Morenz, Mon., C	33	18	51*	1964	Jean Beliveau, Mon., C	28	50	78
1929	Roy Worters, NYA, G	16-13-9;		1.21	1965	Bobby Hull, Chi., LW	39	32	71
					1966	Bobby Hull, Chi., LW	54	43	97*
1930	Nels Stewart, Maroons, C	39	16	55	1967	Stan Mikita, Chi., C	35	62	97*
1931	Howie Morenz, Mon., C	28	23	51*	1968	Stan Mikita, Chi., C	40	47	87*
1932	Howie Morenz, Mon., C	24	25	49	1969	Phil Esposito, Bos., C	49	77	126*
1933	Eddie Shore, Bos., D	8	27	35					
1934	Aurel Joliat, Mon., LW	22	15	37	1970	Bobby Orr, Bos., D	33	87	120*
1935	Eddie Shore, Bos., D	7	26	33	1971	Bobby Orr, Bos., D	37	102	139
1936	Eddie Shore, Bos., D	3	16	19	1972	Bobby Orr, Bos., D	37	80	117
1937	Babe Siebert, Mon., D	8	20	28	1973	Bobby Clarke, Phi., C	37	67	104
1938	Eddie Shore, Bos., D	3	14	17	1974	Phil Esposito, Bos., C	68	77	145*
1939	Toe Blake, Mon., LW	24	23	47*	1975	Bobby Clarke, Phi., C	27	89	116
					1976	Bobby Clarke, Phi., C	30	89	119
1940	Ebbie Goodfellow, Det.,D	11	17	28	1977	Guy Lafleur, Mon., RW	56	80	136*
1941	Bill Cowley, Bos., C	17	45	62*	1978	Guy Lafleur, Mon., RW	60	72	132*
1942	Tommy Anderson, NYA, D	12	29	41	1979	Bryan Trottier, NYI., C	47	87	134*
1943	Bill Cowley, Bos, C	27	45	72					
1944	Babe Pratt, Tor., D	17	40	57	1980	Wayne Gretzky, Edm., C	51	86	137
1945	Elmer Lach, Mon., C	26	54	80*	1981	Wayne Gretzky, Edm., C	55	109	164*
1946	Max Bentley, Chi., C	31	30	61*	1982	Wayne Gretzky, Edm., C	92	120	212*
1947	Maurice Richard, Mon., RW	45	26	71	1983	Wayne Gretzky, Edm., C	71	125	196*
1948	Buddy O'Connor, NYR, C	24	36	60	1984	Wayne Gretzky, Edm., C	87	118	205*
1949	Sid Abel, Det., C	28	26	54	1985	Wayne Gretzky, Edm., C	73	135	208*
					1986	Wayne Gretzky, Edm., C	52	163	215*
1950	Chuck Rayner, NYR, G	28-30-11;		2.62	1987	Wayne Gretzky, Edm., C	62	121	183*
1951	Milt Schmidt, Bos., C	22	39	61	1988	Mario Lemieux, Pit., C	70	98	168*
1952	Gordie Howe, Det., RW	47	39	86*	1989	Wayne Gretzky, LA, C	54	114	168
1953	Gordie Howe, Det., RW	49	46	95*					
1954	Al Rollins, Chi., G	12-47-7;		3.23	1990	Mark Messier, Edm., C	45	84	129
1955	Ted Kennedy, Tor., C	10	42	52	1991	Brett Hull, St. L., RW	86	45	131
1956	Jean Beliveau, Mon., C	47	41	88*	1992	Mark Messier, NYR, C	35	72	107
1957	Gordie Howe, Det., RW	44	45	89*					
1958	Gordie Howe, Det., RW	33	44	77					
1959	Andy Bathgate, NYR, RW	40	48	88					

Art Ross Trophy

Given to the player who leads the league in points scored and named after the former Boston Bruins general manager-coach. First presented in 1947, names of prior leading scorers have been added retroactively. A tie for the scoring championship is broken three ways: 1. total goals; 2. fewest games played; 3. first goal scored.

Multiple winners: Wayne Gretzky (9); Gordie Howe (6); Phil Esposito (5); Stan Mikita (4); Guy Lafleur and Mario Lemieux (3); Max Bentley, Charlie Conacher, Bill Cook, Babe Dye, Bernie Geoffrion, Bobby Hull, Elmer Lach, Newsy Lalonde, Joe Malone, Dickie Moore, Howie Morenz, Bobby Orr and Sweeney Schriner (2).

Year		Gm	G	A	Pts	Year		Gm	G	A	Pts
1918	Joe Malone, Mon	20	44	0	44	1930	Cooney Weiland, Bos	44	43	30	73
1919	Newsy Lalonde, Mon	17	23	9	32	1931	Howie Morenz, Mon	39	28	23	51
						1932	Busher Jackson, Tor	48	28	25	53
1920	Joe Malone, Que	24	39	6	45	1933	Bill Cook, NYR	48	28	22	50
1921	Newsy Lalonde, Mon	24	33	8	41	1934	Charlie Conacher, Tor	42	32	20	52
1922	Punch Broadbent, Ott	24	32	14	46	1935	Charlie Conacher, Tor	47	36	21	57
1923	Babe Dye, Tor	22	26	11	37	1936	Sweeney Schriner, NYA	48	19	26	45
1924	Cy Denneny, Ott	21	22	1	23	1937	Sweeney Schriner, NYA	48	21	25	46
1925	Babe Dye, Tor	29	38	6	44	1938	Gordie Drillon, Tor	48	26	26	52
1926	Nels Stewart, Maroons	36	34	8	42	1939	Toe Blake, Mon	48	24	23	47
1927	Bill Cook, NYR	44	33	4	37						
1928	Howie Morenz, Mon	43	33	18	51	1940	Milt Schmidt, Bos	48	22	30	52
1929	Ace Bailey, Tor	44	22	10	32	1941	Bill Cowley, Bos	46	17	45	62

Year		Gm	G	A	Pts
1942	Bryan Hextall, NYR	48	24	32	56
1943	Doug Bentley, Chi	50	33	40	73
1944	Herbie Cain, Bos	48	36	46	82
1945	Elmer Lach, Mon	50	26	54	80
1946	Max Bentley, Chi	47	31	30	61
1947	Max Bentley, Chi	60	29	43	72
1948	Elmer Lach, Mon	60	30	31	61
1949	Roy Conacher, Chi	60	26	42	68
1950	Ted Lindsay, Det	69	23	55	78
1951	Gordie Howe, Det	70	43	43	86
1952	Gordie Howe, Det	70	47	39	86
1953	Gordie Howe, Det	70	49	46	95
1954	Gordie Howe, Det	70	33	48	81
1955	Bernie Geoffrion, Mon	70	38	37	75
1956	Jean Beliveau, Mon	70	47	41	88
1957	Gordie Howe, Det	70	44	45	89
1958	Dickie Moore, Mon	70	36	48	84
1959	Dickie Moore, Mon	70	41	55	96
1960	Bobby Hull, Chi	70	39	42	81
1961	Bernie Geoffrion, Mon	64	50	45	95
1962	Bobby Hull, Chi.*	70	50	34	84
1963	Gordie Howe, Det	70	38	48	86
1964	Stan Mikita, Chi	70	39	50	89
1965	Stan Mikita, Chi	70	28	59	87
1966	Bobby Hull, Chi	65	54	43	97
1967	Stan Mikita, Chi	70	35	62	97
1968	Stan Mikita, Chi	72	40	47	87
1969	Phil Esposito, Bos	74	49	77	126
1970	Bobby Orr, Bos	76	33	87	120
1971	Phil Esposito, Bos	78	76	76	152
1972	Phil Esposito, Bos	76	66	67	133
1973	Phil Esposito, Bos	78	55	75	130
1974	Phil Esposito, Bos	78	68	77	145
1975	Bobby Orr, Bos	80	46	89	135
1976	Guy Lafleur, Mon	80	56	59	125
1977	Guy Lafleur, Mon	80	56	80	136
1978	Guy Lafleur, Mon	79	60	72	132
1979	Bryan Trottier, NYI	76	47	87	134
1980	Marcel Dionne, LA*	80	53	84	137
1981	Wayne Gretzky, Edm	80	55	109	164
1982	Wayne Gretzky, Edm	80	92	120	212
1983	Wayne Gretzky, Edm	80	71	125	196
1984	Wayne Gretzky, Edm	74	87	118	205
1985	Wayne Gretzky, Edm	80	73	135	208
1986	Wayne Gretzky, Edm	80	52	163	215
1987	Wayne Gretzky, Edm	79	62	121	183
1988	Mario Lemieux, Pit	77	70	98	168
1989	Mario Lemieux, Pit	76	85	114	199
1990	Wayne Gretzky, LA	73	40	102	142
1991	Wayne Gretzky, LA	78	41	122	163
1992	Mario Lemieux, Pit	64	44	87	131

Note: The two times players have tied for total points in one season the player with more goals has won the trophy. In 1961-62, Hull outscored Andy Bathgate of NY Rangers, 50 goals to 28. In 1979-80, Dionne outscored Wayne Gretzky of Edmonton, 53-51.

Calder Memorial Trophy

Awarded to the most outstanding rookie of the year and named after Frank Calder, the late NHL president (1917-43). Since the 1990-91 season, all eligible candidates must not have attained their 26th birthday by Sept. 15 of their rookie year. Winners selected by PHWA. Winners' scoring statistics or goaltender W-L record & goals against average are provided.

Year		G	A	Pts
1933	Carl Voss, NYR-Det., C	8	15	23
1934	Russ Blinco, M.Maroons, C	14	9	23
1935	Sweeney Schriner, NYA., LW	18	22	40
1936	Mike Karakas, Chi., G	21-19-8;		1.92
1937	Syl Apps, Tor., C	16	29	45
1938	Cully Dahlstrom, Chi., C	10	9	19
1939	Frank Brimsek, Bos, G	33-9-1;		1.58
1940	Kilby MacDonald, NYR, LW	15	13	28
1941	John Quilty, Mon., C	18	16	34
1942	Knobby Warwick, NYR, RW	16	17	33
1943	Gaye Stewart, Tor., LW	24	23	47
1944	Gus Bodnar, Tor., C	22	40	62
1945	Frank McCool, Tor., G	24-22-2;		3.22
1946	Edgar Laprade, NYR, C	15	19	34
1947	Howie Meeker, Tor., RW	27	18	45
1948	Jim McFadden, Det., C	24	24	48
1949	Penny Lund, NYR, RW	14	16	30
1950	Jack Gelineau, Bos., G	22-30-15;		3.28
1951	Terry Sawchuk, Det., G	44-13-13;		1.99
1952	Bernie Geoffrion, Mon., RW	30	24	54
1953	Gump Worsley, NYR, G	13-29-13;		3.06
1954	Camille Henry, NYR, LW	24	15	39
1955	Ed Litzenberger, Mon-Chi., RW	16	24	40
1956	Glenn Hall, Det., G	30-24-16;		2.11
1957	Larry Regan, Bos., RW	14	19	33
1958	Frank Mahovlich, Tor., LW	20	16	36
1959	Ralph Backstrom, Mon., C	18	22	40
1960	Billy Hay, Chi., C	18	37	55
1961	Dave Keon, Tor., C	20	25	45
1962	Bobby Rousseau, Mon., RW	21	24	45
1963	Kent Douglas, Tor., D	7	15	22
1964	Jacques Laperriere, Mon., D	2	28	30
1965	Roger Crozier, Det., G	40-23-7;		2.42
1966	Brit Selby, Tor., LW	14	13	27
1967	Bobby Orr, Bos., D	13	28	41
1968	Derek Sanderson, Bos., C	24	25	49
1969	Danny Grant, Min., LW	34	31	65
1970	Tony Esposito, Chi., G	38-17-8;		2.17
1971	Gilbert Perreault, Buf., C	38	34	72
1972	Ken Dryden, Mon., G	39-8-15;		2.24
1973	Steve Vickers, NYR, LW	30	23	53
1974	Denis Potvin, NYI, D	17	37	54
1975	Eric Vail, Atl., LW	39	21	60
1976	Bryan Trottier, NYI, C	32	63	95
1977	Willi Plett, Atl., RW	33	23	56
1978	Mike Bossy, NYI, RW	53	38	91
1979	Bobby Smith, Min., C	30	44	74
1980	Ray Bourque, Bos., D	17	48	65
1981	Peter Stastny, Que., C	39	70	109
1982	Dale Hawerchuk, Win., C	45	58	103
1983	Steve Larmer, Chi., RW	43	47	90
1984	Tom Barrasso, Buf., G	26-12-3;		2.84
1985	Mario Lemieux, Pit., C	43	57	100
1986	Gary Suter, Calg., D	18	50	68
1987	Luc Robitaille, LA, LW	45	39	84
1988	Joe Nieuwendyk, Calg., C	51	41	92
1989	Brian Leetch, NYR, D	23	48	71
1990	Sergei Makarov, Calg., RW	24	62	86
1991	Ed Belfour, Chi., G	43-19-7;		2.47
1992	Pavel Bure, Van., RW	34	26	60

Annual Awards (Cont.)
Vezina Trophy

From 1926-80, given to the principal goaltender(s) on the team allowing the fewest goals during the regular season and named after 1920's goalie Georges Vezina of the Montreal Canadiens, who died of tuberculosis in 1926.

Since the 1980-81 season, the trophy has been awarded to the most outstanding goaltender of the year as selected by the league's general managers.

Multiple winners: Jacques Plante (7, one of them shared); Bill Durnan (6); Ken Dryden (5, three shared); Bunny Larocque (4, all shared); Tiny Thompson (4); Terry Sawchuk (4, one shared); Tony Esposito (3, one shared); George Hainsworth (3); Glenn Hall (3, two shared); Patrick Roy (3); Frank Brimsek (2); Turk Broda (2); Johnny Bower (2, one shared); Chuck Gardiner (2); Charlie Hodge (2, one shared); Bernie Parent (2); Gump Worsley (2, both shared).

Year		Record	Avg	Year		Record	Avg
1927	George Hainsworth, Mon	28-14-2	1.52	1966	Gump Worsley, Mon	29-14-6	2.36
1928	George Hainsworth, Mon	26-11-7	1.09		& Charlie Hodge, Mon	12-7-2	2.58
1929	George Hainsworth, Mon	22-7-15	0.98	1967	Glenn Hall, Chi	19-5-5	2.38
					& Denis Dejordy, Chi	22-12-7	2.46
1930	Tiny Thompson, Bos	38-5-1	2.23	1968	Gump Worsley, Mon	19-9-8	1.98
1931	Roy Worters, NYA	18-16-10	1.68		& Rogie Vachon, Mon	23-13-2	2.48
1932	Chuck Gardiner, Chi	18-19-11	2.10	1969	Jacques Plante, St.L	18-12-6	1.96
1933	Tiny Thompson, Bos	25-15-8	1.83		& Glenn Hall, St.L	19-12-8	2.17
1934	Chuck Gardiner, Chi	20-17-11	1.73				
1935	Lorne Chabot, Chi	26-17-5	1.83	1970	Tony Esposito, Chi	38-17-8	2.17
1936	Tiny Thompson, Bos	22-20-6	1.73	1971	Ed Giacomin, NYR	27-10-7	2.16
1937	Norm Smith, Det	25-14-9	2.13		& Gilles Villemure, NYR	22-8-4	2.30
1938	Tiny Thompson, Bos	30-11-7	1.85	1972	Tony Esposito, Chi	31-10-6	1.77
1939	Frank Brimsek, Bos	33-9-1	1.59		& Gary Smith, Chi	14-5-6	2.42
				1973	Ken Dryden, Mon	33-7-13	2.26
1940	Dave Kerr, NYR	27-11-10	1.60	1974	(Tie) Bernie Parent, Phi	47-13-12	1.89
1941	Turk Broda, Tor	28-14-6	2.06		Tony Esposito, Chi	34-14-21	2.04
1942	Frank Brimsek, Bos	24-17-6	2.44	1975	Bernie Parent, Phi	44-14-10	2.03
1943	Johnny Mowers, Det	25-14-11	2.48	1976	Ken Dryden, Mon	42-10-8	2.03
1944	Bill Durnan, Mon	38-5-7	2.18	1977	Ken Dryden, Mon	41-6-8	2.14
1945	Bill Durnan, Mon	38-8-4	2.42		& Bunny Larocque, Mon	19-2-4	2.09
1946	Bill Durnan, Mon	24-11-5	2.60	1978	Ken Dryden, Mon	37-7-7	2.05
1947	Bill Durnan, Mon	34-16-10	2.30		& Bunny Larocque, Mon	22-3-4	2.67
1948	Turk Broda, Tor	32-15-13	2.38	1979	Ken Dryden, Mon	30-10-7	2.30
1949	Bill Durnan, Mon	28-23-9	2.10		& Bunny Larocque, Mon	22-7-4	2.84
1950	Bill Durnan, Mon	26-21-17	2.20	1980	Bob Sauve, Buf	20-8-4	2.36
1951	Al Rollins, Tor	27-5-8	1.75		& Don Edwards, Buf	27-9-12	2.57
1952	Terry Sawchuk, Det	44-14-12	1.90	1981	Richard Sevigny, Mon	20-4-3	2.40
1953	Terry Sawchuk, Det	32-15-16	1.90		Denis Herron, Mon	6-9-6	3.50
1954	Harry Lumley, Tor	32-24-13	1.85		& Bunny Larocque, Mon	16-9-3	3.03
1955	Terry Sawchuk, Det	40-17-11	1.94	1982	Billy Smith, NYI	32-9-4	2.97
1956	Jacques Plante, Mon	42-12-10	1.86	1983	Pete Peeters, Bos	40-11-9	2.36
1957	Jacques Plante, Mon	31-18-12	2.02	1984	Tom Barrasso, Buf	26-12-3	2.84
1958	Jacques Plante, Mon	34-14-8	2.11	1985	Pelle Lindbergh, Phi	40-17-7	3.02
1959	Jacques Plante, Mon	38-16-13	2.18	1986	John Vanbiesbrouck, NYR	31-21-5	3.32
1960	Jacques Plante, Mon	40-17-12	2.54	1987	Ron Hextall, Phi	37-21-6	3.00
1961	Johnny Bower, Tor	33-15-10	2.50	1988	Grant Fuhr, Edm	40-24-9	3.43
1962	Jacques Plante, Mon	42-14-14	2.37	1989	Patrick Roy, Mon	33-5-6	2.47
1963	Glenn Hall, Chi	30-20-16	2.51				
1964	Charlie Hodge, Mon	33-18-11	2.26	1990	Patrick Roy, Mon	31-16-5	2.53
1965	Johnny Bower, Tor	13-13-8	2.38	1991	Ed Belfour, Chi	43-19-7	2.47
	& Terry Sawchuk, Tor	17-13-6	2.56	1992	Patrick Roy, Mon	36-22-8	2.36

Lady Byng Memorial Trophy

Awarded to the player "adjudged to have exhibited the best type of sportsmanship and gentlemanly conduct combined with a high standard of playing ability" and named after Lady Evelyn Byng, the wife of former Canadian Governor General (1921-26) Baron Byng of Vimy. Winners selected by PHWA.

Multiple winners: Frank Boucher (7); Red Kelly (4); Bobby Bauer, Mike Bossy, Alex Delvecchio and Wayne Gretzky (3); Johnny Bucyk, Marcel Dionne, Dave Keon, Stan Mikita, Joey Mullen, Frank Nighbor, Jean Ratelle, Clint Smith and Sid Smith (2).

Year		Year		Year	
1925	Frank Nighbor, Ott., C	1933	Frank Boucher, NYR, C	1940	Bobby Bauer, Bos., RW
1926	Frank Nighbor, Ott., C	1934	Frank Boucher, NYR, C	1941	Bobby Bauer, Bos., RW
1927	Billy Burch, NYA, C	1935	Frank Boucher, NYR, C	1942	Syl Apps, Tor., C
1928	Frank Boucher, NYR, C	1936	Doc Romnes, Chi., F	1943	Max Bentley, Chi., C
1929	Frank Boucher, NYR, C	1937	Marty Barry, Det., C	1944	Clint Smith, Chi., C
1930	Frank Boucher, NYR, C	1938	Gordie Drillon, Tor., RW	1945	Bill Mosienko, Chi., RW
1931	Frank Boucher, NYR, C	1939	Clint Smith, NYR, C	1946	Toe Blake, Mon., LW
1932	Joe Primeau, Tor., C			1947	Bobby Bauer, Bos., RW

Year		Year		Year	
1948	Buddy O'Connor, NYR, C	1963	Dave Keon, Tor., C	1978	Butch Goring, LA, C
1949	Bill Quackenbush, Det., D	1964	Ken Wharram, Chi., RW	1979	Bob MacMillan, Atl., RW
1950	Edgar Laprade, NYR,	1965	Bobby Hull, Chi., LW	1980	Wayne Gretzky, Edm., C
1951	Red Kelly, Det., D	1966	Alex Delvecchio, Det., LW	1981	Rick Kehoe, Pit., RW
1952	Sid Smith, Tor., LW	1967	Stan Mikita, Chi., C	1982	Rick Middleton, Bos., RW
1953	Red Kelly, Det., D	1968	Stan Mikita, Chi., C	1983	Mike Bossy, NYI, RW
1954	Red Kelly, Det., D	1969	Alex Delvecchio, Det., LW	1984	Mike Bossy, NYI, RW
1955	Sid Smith, Tor., LW			1985	Jari Kurri, Edm., RW
1956	Earl Reibel, Det., C	1970	Phil Goyette, St.L., C	1986	Mike Bossy, NYI, RW
1957	Andy Hebenton, NYR, RW	1971	Johnny Bucyk, Bos., LW	1987	Joey Mullen, Calg., RW
1958	Camille Henry, NYR, LW	1972	Jean Ratelle, NYR, C	1988	Mats Naslund, Mon., LW
1959	Alex Delvecchio, Det., LW	1973	Gilbert Perreault, Buf., C	1989	Joey Mullen, Calg., RW
		1974	Johnny Bucyk, Bos., LW		
1960	Don McKenney, Bos., C	1975	Marcel Dionne, Det., C	1990	Brett Hull, St.L., RW
1961	Red Kelly, Tor., C	1976	Jean Ratelle, NY-Bos., C	1991	Wayne Gretzky, LA, C
1962	Dave Keon, Tor., C	1977	Marcel Dionne, LA, C	1992	Wayne Gretzky, LA, C

Note: Quackenbush and Kelly are the only defensemen to win the Lady Byng.

James Norris Memorial Trophy

Awarded to the most outstanding defenseman of the year and named after James Norris, the late Detroit Red Wings owner-president. Winners selected by PHWA.

Multiple winners: Bobby Orr (8); Doug Harvey (7); Ray Bourque (4); Pierre Pilote and Denis Potvin (3); Paul Coffey, Rod Langway and Larry Robinson (2).

Year		Year		Year	
1954	Red Kelly, Detroit	1967	Harry Howell, NY Rangers	1980	Larry Robinson, Montreal
1955	Doug Harvey, Montreal	1968	Bobby Orr, Boston	1981	Randy Carlyle, Pittsburgh
1956	Doug Harvey, Montreal	1969	Bobby Orr, Boston	1982	Doug Wilson, Chicago
1957	Doug Harvey, Montreal			1983	Rod Langway, Washington
1958	Doug Harvey, Montreal	1970	Bobby Orr, Boston	1984	Rod Langway, Washington
1959	Tom Johnson, Montreal	1971	Bobby Orr, Boston	1985	Paul Coffey, Edmonton
		1972	Bobby Orr, Boston	1986	Paul Coffey, Edmonton
1960	Doug Harvey, Montreal	1973	Bobby Orr, Boston	1987	Ray Bourque, Boston
1961	Doug Harvey, Montreal	1974	Bobby Orr, Boston	1988	Ray Bourque, Boston
1962	Doug Harvey, NY Rangers	1975	Bobby Orr, Boston	1989	Chris Chelios, Montreal
1963	Pierre Pilote, Chicago	1976	Denis Potvin, NY Islanders		
1964	Pierre Pilote, Chicago	1977	Larry Robinson, Montreal	1990	Ray Bourque, Boston
1965	Pierre Pilote, Chicago	1978	Denis Potvin, NY Islanders	1991	Ray Bourque, Boston
1966	Jacques Laperriere, Mon.	1979	Denis Potvin, NY Islanders	1992	Brian Leetch, NY Rangers

Jack Adams Award

Awarded to the coach "adjudged to have contributed the most to his team's success" and named after the late Detroit Red Wings coach and general manager. Winners selected by NHL Broadcasters' Assn.; (*) indicates division champion.

Multiple winners: Jacques Demers and Pat Quinn (2).

Year		Improvement		Year		Improvement	
1974	Fred Shero, Phi.	37-30-11	to	50-16-12*	1984	Bryan Murray, Wash	39-25-16	to	48-27- 5
1975	Bob Pulford, Chi.	41-14-23	to	37-35- 8	1985	Mike Keenan, Phi	44-26-10	to	53-20- 7*
1976	Don Cherry, Bos	40-26-14	to	48-15-17*	1986	Glen Sather, Edm	49-20-11*	to	56-17- 7*
1977	Scotty Bowman, Mon.	58-11-11*	to	60- 8-12*	1987	Jacques Demers, Det.	17-57- 6	to	34-36-10
1978	Bobby Kromm, Det	16-55- 9	to	32-34-14	1988	Jacques Demers, Det.	34-36-10	to	41-28-11*
1979	Al Arbour, NYI	48-17-15*	to	51-15-14*	1989	Pat Burns, Mon.	45-22-13	to	53-18- 9*
1980	Pat Quinn, Phi	40-25-15	to	48-12-20*	1990	Bob Murdoch, Win.	26-42-12	to	37-32-11
1981	Red Berenson, StL	34-34-12	to	45-18-17*	1991	Brian Sutter, St. L	37-34- 9	to	47-22-11
1982	Tom Watt, Win	9-57-14	to	33-33-14	1992	Pat Quinn, Van	28-43- 9	to	42-26-12*
1983	Orval Tessier, Chi	30-38-12	to	47-23-10*					

Number One Draft Choices

Overall first choices in the NHL Draft since the league staged its first universal amateur draft in 1969. Players are listed with team that selected them; those who became Rookie of the Year are in **bold** type.

Year		Year		Year	
1969	Rejean Houle, Mon.	1977	Dale McCourt, Det.	1985	Wendel Clark, Tor.
1970	**Gilbert Perreault**, Buf.	1978	**Bobby Smith**, Min.	1986	Joe Murphy, Det.
1971	Guy Lafleur, Mon.	1979	Rob Ramage, Colo.	1987	Pierre Turgeon, Buf.
1972	Billy Harris, NYI			1988	Mike Modano, Min.
1973	**Denis Potvin**, NYI	1980	Doug Wickenheiser, Mon.	1989	Mats Sundin, Que.
1974	Greg Joly, Wash.	1981	**Dale Hawerchuk**, Win.		
1975	Mel Bridgman, Phi.	1982	Gord Kluzak, Bos.	1990	Owen Nolan, Que.
1976	Rick Green, Wash.	1983	Brian Lawton, Min.	1991	Eric Lindros, Que.
		1984	**Mario Lemieux**, Pit.	1992	Roman Hamrlik, T.Bay

World Hockey Association
WHA Finals

The World Hockey Association began play in 1972-73 as a 12-team rival of the 56-year-old NHL. The WHA played for the Avco World Trophy in its seven playoff finals (Avco Financial Services underwrote the playoffs).
Multiple winners: Winnipeg (3); Houston (2).

Year	Winner	Head Coach	Series	Loser	Head Coach
1973	New England Whalers	Jack Kelley	4-1 (WWLWW)	Winnipeg Jets	Bobby Hull
1974	Houston Aeros	Bill Dineen	4-0	Chicago Cougars	Pat Stapleton
1975	Houston Aeros	Bill Dineen	4-0	Que.Nordiques	Jean-Guy Gendron
1976	Winnipeg Jets	Bobby Kromm	4-0	Houston Aeros	Bill Dineen
1977	Quebec Nordiques	Marc Boileau	4-3 (LWLWWLW)	Winnipeg Jets	Bobby Kromm
1978	Winnipeg Jets	Larry Hillman	4-0	NE Whalers	Harry Neale
1979	Winnipeg Jets	Larry Hillman	4-2 (WWLWLW)	Edmonton Oilers	Glen Sather

Playoff MVPs—1973—No award; **1974**—No award; **1975**—Ron Grahame, Houston, G; **1976**—Ulf Nilsson, Winnipeg, C; **1977**—Serg Bernier, Quebec, C; **1978**—Bobby Guindon, Winnipeg, C; **1979**—Rich Preston, Winnipeg, RW.

Most Valuable Player
(Gordie Howe Trophy, 1976-79)

Year		G	A	Pts
1973	Bobby Hull, Win., LW	51	52	103
1974	Gordie Howe, Hou., RW	31	69	100
1975	Bobby Hull, Win., LW	77	65	142
1976	Marc Tardif, Que., LW	71	77	148
1977	Robbie Ftorek, Pho., C	46	71	117
1978	Marc Tardif, Que., LW	65	89	154
1979	Dave Dryden, Edm., G	41-17-2;		2.89

Rookie of the Year

Year		G	A	Pts
1973	Terry Caffery, N.Eng., C	39	41	100
1974	Mark Howe, Hou., LW	38	41	79
1975	Anders Hedberg, Win., RW	53	47	100
1976	Mark Napier, Tor., RW	43	50	93
1977	George Lyle, N.Eng., LW	39	33	72
1978	Kent Nilsson, Win., C	42	65	107
1979	Wayne Gretzky, Edm., C	46	64	110

Best Defenseman

Year	
1973	J.C.Tremblay, Quebec
1974	Pat Stapleton, Chicago
1975	J.C.Tremblay, Quebec
1976	Paul Shmyr, Cleveland
1977	Ron Plumb, Cincinnati
1978	Lars-Erik Sjoberg, Winnipeg
1979	Rick Ley, New England

Scoring Leaders

Year		Gm	G	A	Pts
1973	Andre Lacroix, Phi	78	50	74	124
1974	Mike Walton, Min	78	57	60	117
1975	Andre Lacroix, S.Diego	78	41	106	147
1976	Marc Tardif, Que.	81	71	77	148
1977	Real Cloutier, Que.	76	66	75	141
1978	Marc Tardif, Que.	78	65	89	154
1979	Real Cloutier, Que.	77	75	54	129

Note: In 1979, 18 year-old Rookie of the Year Wayne Gretzky finished third in scoring (46-64—110).

Best Goaltender

Year		Record	Avg
1973	Gerry Cheevers, Cleveland	32-20-0	2.84
1974	Don MacLeod, Houston	33-13-3	2.56
1975	Ron Grahame, Houston	33-10-0	3.03
1976	Michel Dion, Indianapolis	14-15-1	2.74
1977	Ron Grahame, Houston	27-10-2	2.74
1978	Al Smith, New England	30-20-3	3.22
1979	Dave Dryden, Edmonton	41-17-2	2.89

Coach of the Year

Year		Improvement	
1973	Jack Kelley, N.Eng		46-30-2*
1974	Billy Harris, Tor	35-39-4	to 41-33-4
1975	Sandy Hucul, Pho	Expan.	to 39-31-8
1976	Bobby Kromm, Win	38-35-5	to 52-27-2*
1977	Bill Dineen, Hou	53-27-0*	to 50-24-6*
1978	Bill Dineen, Hou	50-24-6*	to 42-34-4
1979	John Brophy, Birm	36-41-3	to 32-42-6

*Won Division.

WHA All-Star Game

The WHA All-Star Game was an Eastern Division vs Western Division contest from 1973-75. In 1976, the league's five Canadian-based teams played the nine teams in the US. Over the final three seasons—East played West in 1977; AVCO Cup champion Quebec played a WHA All-Star team in 1978; and in 1979, a full WHA All-Star team played a three-game series with Moscow Dynamo of the Soviet Union.

Year	Result	Host	Coaches	Most Valuable Player
1973	East 6, West 2	Quebec	Jack Kelley, Bobby Hull	Wayne Carleton, Ottawa
1974	East 8, West 4	St.Paul,MN	Jack Kelley, Bobby Hull	Mike Walton, Minnesota
1975	West 6, East 4	Edmonton	Bill Dineen, Ron Ryan	Rejean Houle, Quebec
1976	Canada 6, USA 1	Cleveland	Jean-Guy Gendron, Bill Dineen	Can—Real Cloutier, Que. USA—Paul Shmyr, Cleve.
1977	East 4, West 2	Hartford	Jacques Demers, Bobby Kromm	East—L.Levasseur, Min. West—W.Lindstrom, Win.
1978	Quebec 5, WHA 4	Quebec	Marc Boileau, Bill Dineen	Quebec—Marc Tardif WHA—Mark Howe, NE
1979	WHA def. Moscow Dynamo 4-2, 4-2 and 4-3	Edmonton	Larry Hillman, P.Iburtovich	No awards

World Championship

The World Hockey Championship tournament has been played regularly since 1930. The International Ice Hockey Federation (IIHF), which governs both the World and Winter Olympic tournaments, considers the Olympic champions from 1920-68 to also be the World champions. However the IIHF has not recognized an Olympic champion as World champion since 1968. The IIHF has sanctioned separate World Championships in Olympic years three times—in 1972, 1976 and again in 1992. The World championship is officially vacant for the three Olympic years from 1980-88.

Multiple winners: Soviet Union (22); Canada (19); Czechoslovakia and Sweden (6); USA (2).

Year		Year		Year		Year	
1920	Canada	1948	Canada	1963	Soviet Union	1978	Soviet Union
1924	Canada	1949	Czechoslovakia	1964	Soviet Union	1979	Soviet Union
1928	Canada			1965	Soviet Union		
		1950	Canada	1966	Soviet Union	1980	Not held
1930	Canada	1951	Canada	1967	Soviet Union	1981	Soviet Union
1931	Canada	1952	Canada	1968	Soviet Union	1982	Soviet Union
1932	Canada	1953	Sweden	1969	Soviet Union	1983	Soviet Union
1933	United States	1954	Soviet Union			1984	Not held
1934	Canada	1955	Canada	1970	Soviet Union	1985	Czechoslovakia
1935	Canada	1956	Soviet Union	1971	Soviet Union	1986	Soviet Union
1936	Great Britain	1957	Sweden	1972	Czechoslovakia	1987	Sweden
1937	Canada	1958	Canada	1973	Soviet Union	1988	Not held
1938	Canada	1959	Canada	1974	Soviet Union	1989	Soviet Union
1939	Canada			1975	Soviet Union		
		1960	United States	1976	Czechoslovakia	1990	Soviet Union
1940-46	Not held	1961	Canada	1977	Czechoslovakia	1991	Sweden
1947	Czechoslovakia	1962	Sweden			1992	Sweden

Canada vs USSR Summits

The first competition between the Soviet National Team and the NHL took place Sept.2-28, 1972. A team of NHL All-Stars emerged as the winner of the heralded 8-game series, but just barely—winning with a record of 4-3-1 after trailing 1-3-1.

Two years later a WHA All-Star team played the Soviet Nationals and could win only one game and tie three others in eight contests. Two other Canada vs USSR series took place during NHL All-Star breaks: the three-game Challenge Cup at New York in 1979, and the two-game Rendez-Vous '87 in Quebec City in 1987.

The NHL All-Stars played the USSR in a three-game Challenge Cup series in 1979.

1972 Team Canada vs USSR
NHL All-Stars vs Soviet National Team.

Date	City	Result	Goaltenders
9/2	Montreal	USSR, 7-3	Tretiak/Dryden
9/4	Toronto	Canada, 4-1	Esposito/Tretiak
9/6	Winnipeg	Tie, 4-4	Tretiak/Esposito
9/8	Vancouver	USSR, 5-4	Tretiak/Dryden
9/22	Moscow	USSR, 5-4	Tretiak/Esposito
9/24	Moscow	Canada, 3-2	Dryden/Tretiak
9/26	Moscow	Canada, 4-3	Esposito/Tretiak
9/28	Moscow	Canada, 6-5	Dryden/Tretiak

Standings

	W	L	T	Pts	GF	GA
Team Canada (NHL)	4	3	1	9	32	32
Soviet Union	3	4	1	7	32	32

Leading Scorers
1. Phil Esposito, Canada, (7-6—13); **2.** Aleksandr Yakushev, USSR (7-4—11); **3.** Paul Henderson, Canada (7-2—9); **4.** Boris Shadrin, USSR (3-5—8); **5.** Valeri Kharlamov, USSR (3-4—7) and Vladimir Petrov, USSR (3-4—7); **7.** Bobby Clarke, Canada (2-4—6).

1974 Team Canada vs USSR
WHA All-Stars vs Soviet National Team.

Date	City	Result	Goaltenders
9/17	Quebec	Tie, 3-3	Tretiak/Cheevers
9/19	Toronto	Canada, 4-1	Cheevers/Tretiak
9/21	Winnipeg	USSR, 8-5	Tretiak/McLeod
9/23	Vancouver	Tie, 5-5	Tretiak/Cheevers
10/1	Moscow	USSR, 3-2	Tretiak/Cheevers
10/3	Moscow	USSR, 5-2	Tretiak/Cheevers
10/5	Moscow	Tie, 4-4	Cheevers/Tretiak
10/6	Moscow	USSR, 3-2	Sdn'kov/Cheevers

Standings

	W	L	T	Pts	GF	GA
Soviet Union	4	1	3	11	32	27
Team Canada (WHA)	1	4	3	5	27	32

Leading Scorers
1. Bobby Hull, Canada (7-2—9); **2.** Aleksandr Yakushev, USSR (6-2—8), Ralph Backstrom, Canada (4-4—8) and Valeri Kharlamov, USSR (2-6—8); **5.** Gordie Howe, Canada (3-4—7), Andre Lacroix, Canada (1-6—7) and Vladimir Petrov, USSR (1-6—7).

1979 Challenge Cup Series
NHL All-Stars vs Soviet National Team

Date	City	Result	Goaltenders
2/8	New York	NHL, 4-2	K.Dryden/Tretiak
2/10	New York	USSR, 5-4	Tretiak/K.Dryden
2/11	New York	USSR, 6-0	Myshkin/Cheevers

Rendez-Vous '87
NHL All-Stars vs Soviet National Team

Date	City	Result	Goaltenders
2/11	Quebec	NHL, 4-3	Fuhr/Belosheykhin
2/13	Quebec	USSR, 5-3	Belosheykhin/Fuhr

The Canada Cup

After organizing the historic 8-game Team Canada-Soviet Union series of 1972, NHL Players Association executive director Alan Eagleson and the NHL created the Canada Cup in 1976. For the first time, the best players from the world's six major hockey powers—Canada, Czechoslovakia, Finland, Russia, Sweden and the USA competed together in one tournament.

1976

Round Robin Standings

	W	L	T	Pts	GF	GA
Canada	4	1	0	8	22	6
Czechoslovakia	3	1	1	7	19	9
Soviet Union	2	2	1	5	23	14
Sweden	2	2	1	5	16	18
United States	1	3	1	3	14	21
Finland	1	4	0	2	16	42

Finals (Best of 3 Games)

Date	City	Score
9/13	Toronto	Canada 6, Czechoslovakia 0
9/15	Montreal	Canada 5, Czechoslovakia 4 (OT)

Note: Darryl Sittler scored the winning goal for Canada at 11:33 in overtime to clinch the Cup, 2 games to none.

Team MVPs

Canada—Rogie Vachon	Sweden—Borje Salming
Czech.—Milan Novy	USA—Robbie Ftorek
USSR—Alexandr Maltsev	Finland—Matti Hagman

Tournament MVP—Bobby Orr, Canada

1981

Round Robin Standings

	W	L	T	Pts	GF	GA
Canada	4	0	1	9	32	13
Soviet Union	3	1	1	7	20	13
Czechoslovakia	2	1	2	6	21	13
United States	2	2	1	5	17	19
Sweden	1	4	0	2	13	20
Finland	0	4	1	1	6	31

Semifinals

Date	City	Score
9/11	Ottawa	USSR 4, Czechoslovakia 1
9/15	Montreal	Canada 4, United States 1

Finals

Date	City	Score
9/13	Montreal	USSR 8, Canada 1

Leading Scorers

1. Wayne Gretzky, Canada (5-7—12); **2.** Mike Bossy, Canada (8-3—11), Bryan Trottier, Canada (3-8—11), Guy Lafleur, Canada (2-9—11), Alexei Kasatonov, USSR (1-10—11).

All-Star Team

Goal—Vladislav Tretiak, USSR; **Defense**—Arnold Kadlec, Czech. and Alexei Kasatonov, USSR; **Forwards**—Mike Bossy, Canada, Gil Perreault, Canada, and Sergei Shepelev, USSR. **Tournament MVP**—Tretiak.

1984

Round Robin Standings

	W	L	T	Pts	GF	GA
Soviet Union	5	0	0	10	22	7
United States	3	1	1	7	21	13
Sweden	3	2	0	6	15	16
Canada	2	2	1	5	23	18
West Germany	0	4	1	1	13	29
Czechoslovakia	0	4	1	1	10	21

Semifinals

Date	City	Score
9/12	Edmonton	Sweden 9, United States 2
9/15	Montreal	Canada 3, USSR 2 (OT)

Note: Mike Bossy scored the winning goal for Canada at 12:29 in overtime.

Finals (Best of 3 Games)

Date	City	Score
9/16	Calgary	Canada 5, Sweden 2
9/18	Edmonton	Canada 6, Sweden 5

Leading Scorers

1. Wayne Gretzky, Canada (5-7—12); **2.** Michel Goulet, Canada (5-6—11), Kent Nilsson, Sweden (3-8—11), Paul Coffey, Canada (3-8—11); **5.** Hakan Loob, Sweden (6-4—10).

All-Star Team

Goal—Vladimir Myshkin, USSR; **Defense**—Paul Coffey, Canada and Rod Langway, Canada; **Forwards**—Wayne Gretzky, Canada, John Tonelli, Canada, and Sergei Makarov, USSR. **Tournament MVP**—Tonelli.

1987

Round Robin Standings

	W	L	T	Pts	GF	GA
Canada	3	0	2	8	19	13
Soviet Union	3	1	1	7	22	13
Sweden	3	2	0	6	17	14
Czechoslovakia	2	2	1	5	12	15
United States	2	3	0	4	13	14
Finland	0	5	0	0	9	23

Semifinals

Date	City	Score
9/8	Hamilton	USSR 4, Sweden 2
9/9	Montreal	Canada 5, Czechoslovakia 3

Finals (Best of 3 Games)

Date	City	Score
9/11	Montreal	USSR 6, Canada 5 (OT)
9/13	Hamilton	Canada 6, USSR 5 (2 OT)
9/15	Hamilton	Canada 6, USSR 5

Note: In Game 1, Alexander Semak of USSR scored at 5:33 in overtime. In Game 2, Mario Lemieux of Canada scored at 10:07 in the second overtime period. Lemieux also won Game 3 on a goal with 1:26 left in regulation time.

Leading Scorers

1. Wayne Gretzky, Canada (3-18—21); **2.** Mario Lemieux, Canada (11-7—18); **3.** Sergei Makarov, USSR (7-8—15); **4.** Vladimir Krutov, USSR (7-7—14); **5.** Viacheslav Bykov, USSR (2-7—9); **6.** Ray Bourque, Canada (2-6—8).

All-Star Team

Goal—Grant Fuhr, Canada; **Defense**—Ray Bourque, Canada and Viacheslav Fetisov, USSR; **Forwards**—Wayne Gretzky, Canada, Mario Lemieux, Canada, and Vladimir Krutov, USSR. **Tournament MVP**—Gretzky.

1991

Round Robin Standings

	W	L	T	Pts	GF	GA
Canada	3	0	2	8	21	11
United States	4	1	0	8	19	15
Finland	2	2	1	5	10	13
Sweden	2	3	0	4	13	17
Soviet Union	1	3	1	3	14	14
Czechoslovakia	1	4	0	2	11	18

Leading Scorers

1. Wayne Gretzky, Canada (4-8—12); **2.** Steve Larmer, Canada (6-5—11); **3.** Brett Hull, USA (2-7—9); **4.** Mike Modano, USA (2-7—9); **5.** Mark Messier, Canada (2-6—8).

Semifinals

Date	City	Score
9/11	Hamilton	United States 7, Finland 3
9/12	Toronto	Canada 4, Sweden 0

Finals (Best of 3)

Date	City	Score
9/14	Montreal	Canada 4, United States 1
9/16	Hamilton	Canada 4, United States 2

All-Star Team

Goal—Bill Ranford, Canada; **Defense**—Al MacInnis, Canada and Chris Chelios, USA; **Forwards**—Wayne Gretzky, Canada, Jeremy Roenick, USA and Mats Sundin, Sweden. **Tournament MVP**—Bill Ranford.

U.S. Division I College Hockey

NCAA Final Four

The NCAA Division I hockey tournament began in 1948 and was played at the Broadmoor Ice Palace in Colorado Springs from 1948-57. Since 1958, the tournament has moved around the country, stopping for consecutive years only at Boston Garden from 1972-74. Consolation games to determine third place were played from 1949-89 and discontinued in 1990.

Multiple Winners: Michigan (7); Denver, North Dakota and Wisconsin (5); Boston University, Michigan Tech and Minnesota (3); Colorado College, Cornell, Lake Superior St., Michigan St. and RPI (2).

Year	Champion	Head Coach	Score	Runner-up	Third Place		
1948	Michigan	Vic Heyliger	8-4	Dartmouth	Colorado Col. and Boston Col.		

Year	Champion	Head Coach	Score	Runner-up	Third Place	Score	Fourth Place
1949	Boston College	Snooks Kelley	4-3	Dartmouth	Michigan	8-4	Colorado Col.
1950	Colorado College	Cheddy Thompson	13-4	Boston Univ.	Michigan	10-6	Boston Col.
1951	Michigan	Vic Heyliger	7-1	Brown	Boston U.	7-4	Colorado Col.
1952	Michigan	Vic Heyliger	4-1	Colorado Col.	Yale	4-1	St.Lawrence
1953	Michigan	Vic Heyliger	7-3	Minnesota	RPI	6-3	Boston Univ.
1954	RPI	Ned Harkness	5-4*	Minnesota	Michigan	7-2	Boston Col.
1955	Michigan	Vic Heyliger	5-3	Colorado Col.	Harvard	6-3	St.Lawrence
1956	Michigan	Vic Heyliger	7-5	Michigan Tech	St.Lawrence	6-2	Boston Col.
1957	Colorado College	Tom Bedecki	13-6	Michigan	Clarkson	2-1†	Harvard
1958	Denver	Murray Armstrong	6-2	North Dakota	Clarkson	5-1	Harvard
1959	North Dakota	Bob May	4-3*	Michigan St.	Boston Col.	7-6†	St. Lawrence
1960	Denver	Murray Armstrong	5-3	Michigan Tech	Boston Univ.	7-6	St.Lawrence
1961	Denver	Murray Armstrong	12-2	St.Lawrence	Minnesota	4-3	RPI
1962	Michigan Tech	John MacInnes	7-1	Clarkson	Michigan	5-1	St.Lawrence
1963	North Dakota	Barry Thorndycraft	6-5	Denver	Clarkson	5-3	Boston Col.
1964	Michigan	Allen Renfrew	6-3	Denver	RPI	2-1	Providence
1965	Michigan Tech	John MacInnes	8-2	Boston Col.	North Dakota	9-0	Brown
1966	Michigan St.	Amo Bessone	6-1	Clarkson	Denver	4-3	Boston Univ.
1967	Cornell	Ned Harkness	4-1	Boston Univ.	Michigan St.	6-1	North Dakota
1968	Denver	Murray Armstrong	4-0	North Dakota	Cornell	6-1	Boston Col.
1969	Denver	Murray Armstrong	4-3	Cornell	Harvard	6-5†	Michigan Tech
1970	Cornell	Ned Harkness	6-4	Clarkson	Wisconsin	6-5	Michigan Tech
1971	Boston Univ.	Jack Kelley	4-2	Minnesota	Denver	1-0	Harvard
1972	Boston Univ.	Jack Kelley	4-0	Cornell	Wisconsin	5-2	Denver
1973	Wisconsin	Bob Johnson	4-2	Denver	Boston Col.	3-1	Cornell
1974	Minnesota	Herb Brooks	4-2	Michigan Tech	Boston Univ.	7-5	Harvard
1975	Michigan Tech	John MacInnes	6-1	Minnesota	Boston Univ.	10-5	Harvard
1976	Minnesota	Herb Brooks	6-4	Michigan Tech	Brown	8-7	Boston Univ.
1977	Wisconsin	Bob Johnson	6-5*	Michigan	Boston Univ.	6-5	New Hampshire
1978	Boston Univ.	Jack Parker	5-3	Boston Col.	Bowling Green	4-3	Wisconsin
1979	Minnesota	Herb Brooks	4-3	North Dakota	Dartmouth	7-3	New Hampshire
1980	North Dakota	Gino Gasparini	5-2	Northern Mich.	Dartmouth	8-4	Cornell
1981	Wisconsin	Bob Johnson	6-3	Minnesota	Michigan Tech	5-2	Northern Mich.
1982	North Dakota	Gino Gasparini	5-2	Wisconsin	Northeastern	10-4	New Hampshire
1983	Wisconsin	Jeff Sauer	6-2	Harvard	Providence	4-3	Minnesota
1984	Bowling Green	Jerry York	5-4*	Minn-Duluth	North Dakota	6-5†	Michigan St.
1985	RPI	Mike Addesa	2-1	Providence	Minn-Duluth	7-6†	Boston Col.
1986	Michigan St.	Ron Mason	6-5	Harvard	Minnesota	6-4	Denver
1987	North Dakota	Gino Gasparini	5-3	Michigan St.	Minnesota	6-3	Harvard
1988	Lake Superior St.	Frank Anzalone	4-3*	St.Lawrence	Maine	5-2	Minnesota
1989	Harvard	Billy Cleary	4-3*	Minnesota	Michigan St.	7-4	Maine

U.S. Division I College Hockey (Cont.)
NCAA Final Four

Year	Champion	Head Coach	Score	Runner-up	Third Place
1990	Wisconsin	Jeff Sauer	7-3	Colgate	Boston Col. and Boston Univ.
1991	Northern Michigan	Rick Comley	8-7*	Boston Univ.	Maine and Clarkson
1992	Lake Superior St.	Jeff Jackson	5-3	Wisconsin	Michigan and Michigan St.

*Championship game overtime goals: **1954**—1:54; **1959**—4:22; **1977**—0: 23; **1984**—7:11 in 4th OT; **1988**—4:46; **1989**—4:16; **1991**—1:57 in 3rd OT.

†Consolation game overtimes ended in 1st OT except in 1957, '59 and '69, which all ended in 2nd OT.

Most Outstanding Player

The Most Outstanding Players of each NCAA Div.I tournament since 1948. Winners of the award who did not play for the tournament champion are in **bold** type. In 1960, three players, none on the winning team, shared the award.
Multiple winners: Lou Angotti and Marc Behrend (2).

Year		Year		Year	
1948	**Joe Riley,** Dartmouth, F	1962	Lou Angotti, Mich. Tech.	1978	Jack O'Callahan, Boston U., D
1949	**Dick Desmond,** Dart., G	1963	Al McLean, N.Dakota, F	1979	Steve Janaszak, Minn., G
1950	**Ralph Bevins,** Boston U., G	1964	Bob Gray, Michigan, G	1980	Doug Smail, N.Dakota, F
1951	**Ed Whiston,** Brown, G	1965	Gary Milroy, Mich. Tech, F	1981	Marc Behrend, Wisc., G
1952	**Ken Kinsley,** Colo. Col., G	1966	Gaye Cooley, Mich. St., G	1982	Phil Sykes, N.Dakota, F
1953	John Matchefts, Mich., F	1967	Walt Stanowski, Cornell, D	1983	Marc Behrend, Wisc., G
1954	Abbie Moore, RPI, F	1968	Gerry Powers, Denver, G	1984	Gary Kruzich, Bowl.Green, G
1955	**Phil Hilton,** Colo. Col., D	1969	Keith Magnuson, Denver, D	1985	**Chris Terreri,** Prov., G
1956	Lorne Howes, Mich., G	1970	Dan Lodboa, Cornell, D	1986	Mike Donnelly, Mich.St., F
1957	Bob McCusker, Colo.Col., F	1971	Dan Brady, Boston U., G	1987	Tony Hrkac, N.Dakota, F
1958	Murray Massier, Denver, F	1972	Tim Regan, Boston U., G	1988	Bruce Hoffort, Lk.Superior, G
1959	Reg Morelli, N.Dakota, F	1973	Dean Talafous, Wisc., F	1989	Ted Donato, Harvard, F
1960	**Lou Angotti,**Mich.Tech, F;	1974	Brad Shelstad, Minn., G	1990	Chris Tancill, Wisconsin, F
	Bob Marquis, Boston U., F;	1975	Jim Warden, Mich. Tech, G	1991	Scott Beattie, No. Mich., F
	& **Barry Urbanski,** Bos.U., G	1976	Tom Vanelli, Minn., F	1992	Paul Constantin, Lk. Superior, F
1961	Bill Masterton, Denver, F	1977	Julian Baretta, Wisc., G		

Hobey Baker Award

College hockey's Player of the Year award; voted on by a national panel of sportswriters, broadcasters, college coaches and pro scouts. First presented in 1981 by the Decathlon Athletic Club of Bloomington,MN, in the name of the Princeton collegiate hockey and football star who was killed in World War I.

Year		Class	Year		Class
1981	Neal Broten, Minnesota, F	So.	1988	Robb Stauber, Minnesota, G	So.
1982	George McPhee, Bowling Green, F	Sr.	1989	Lane MacDonald, Harvard, F	Sr.
1983	Mark Fusco, Harvard, D	Sr.	1990	Kip Miller, Michigan St., F	Sr.
1984	Tom Kurvers, Minnesota-Duluth, D	Sr.	1991	Dave Emma, Boston College, F	Sr.
1985	Bill Watson, Minnesota-Duluth, F	Jr.	1992	Scott Pellerin, Maine, F	Sr.
1986	Scott Fusco, Harvard, F	Sr.			
1987	Tony Hrkac, North Dakota, F	So.			

Other NCAA Champions

Division II-III, 1978-84

NCAA College Division tournament was discontinued in 1984 in favor of separate playoffs for Divisions II and III.

Year	Winner	Score	Loser
1978	Merrimack,MA	12-2	Lake Forest,IL
1979	Lowell,MA	6-4	Mankato St.,MN
1980	Mankato St.,MN	5-2	Elmira,NY
1981	Lowell,MA	5-4	Plattsburgh St.,NY
1982	Lowell, MA	6-1	Plattsburgh St.,NY
1983	Rochester Inst.,NY	4-2	Bemidji St.,MN

Division II, 1984

Tournament discontinued after one year because there were not enough Division II schools sponsoring hockey to warrant a sanctioned national playoff. In 1985, participating programs either moved up to Division I or down to Division III.

Year	Winner	Score	Loser
1984	Bemidji St.,MN	14-4*	Merrimack,MA

*Two Games/Total Goals: Bemidji St. won both games—6-3,8-1.

Division III

In effect, the old NCAA Division II-III tournament.

Year	Winner	Score	Loser
1984	Babson,MA	8-0	Union,NY
1985	Rochester Inst.,NY	5-1	Bemidji St.,MN
1986	Bemidji St.,MN	8-5	Plattsburgh St.,NY
1987	Plattsburgh St., NY	8-3	Oswego St.,NY
1988	WI-River Falls	3 Gms†	Elmira,NY
1989	WI-Stevens Pt.	2 Gms†	Rochester Inst.,NY
1990	WI-Stevens Pt.	3 Gms†	Plattsburgh St.,NY
1991	WI-Stevens Pt.	6-2	Mankato St., MN
1992	Plattsburgh St,NY	7-3	WI-Stevens Pt.

†Two-Game Championship Series (1988-90)
1988: Game 1—River Falls, 7-1; Game 2—Elmira, 5-3; Mini-Game—River Falls, 3-0. **1989:** Game 1—3-3 tie; Game 2—Stevens Pt., 3-2. **1990:** Game 1—Stevens Pt., 10-1; Game 2—Plattsburgh, 6-3; Mini-Game—Stevens Pt., 1-0.

Rod Searcey

In the lifetime of basketball star **Molly Goodenbour** of NCAA champion Stanford, Title IX has made women's sports a force to be reckoned with in college.

COLLEGE SPORTS

COLLEGE SPORTS
by David Davidson

Gender Equity

Twenty years after Title IX, women are demanding equal treatment and the NCAA is scrambling to make it happen.

A classic battle of the sexes is brewing that will likely revolutionize college athletics.

Traditionally a domain funded by revenues from big-time football and basketball—and big-time boosters—college athletic departments nationwide are under increasing pressure to provide equal opportunity for women.

The 20th anniversary on June 23, 1992, of the implementation of Title IX has provided a rallying point for activists campaigning for a better deal for women in college athletics.

"There's a pervasive attitude that participation in college athletics is a right for boys, but a privilege for girls," says Donna Lopiano, the former women's athletic director at the University of Texas, who resigned earlier this year to become executive director of the Women's Sports Foundation in New York.

"Women should have the same opportunity to play college sports as men. Period."

"Gender equity" has replaced "Proposition 48" as the NCAA's newest buzzword.

There are signs the NCAA is moving in that direction:

—At the 1992 convention at Los Angeles in January, Judy Sweet became the

first female president to preside over the organization's legislative body.

—Elaine Dreidame, associate athletic director at Dayton, was elected Division I vice president, where a strong performance could boost her into an even more prominent role.

—In May of 1991, Barbara Hedges was named AD at the University of Washington, becoming the first woman to control an athletics department at a big-time football school. After New Year's Day, she celebrated the school's first national football championship.

—On April 3, 1992, Michigan State University president John DiBiaggio appointed Merrily Dean Baker, formerly the NCAA's assistant executive director for administration, to replace head football coach George Perles as AD.

—At the Los Angles convention, delegates postponed for one year legislation that would have reduced women's scholarships by 10 percent, a move many feel is a precursor to gender equity.

Nevertheless, the NCAA itself is guilty of discrimination. For example, it allows a $150 per diem with a traveling party of 75 for the first round of the Division I men's basketball tournament. But for the women, the per diem is $125 with a traveling party of only 28.

Lopiano sees the appointment of Hedges and Baker as a dawning of a new era in the NCAA.

David Davidson is an assistant sports editor at the *Atlanta Journal and Constitution*, where he has been covering college sports since 1973.

Wide World Photos

Since her appointment in March as executive director of the Women's Sports Foundation, former University of Texas women's athletic director **Donna Lopiano** has become the most visible leader of the push for gender equity.

"(Male) athletic directors have lost their credibility and their control of intercollegiate athletics," says Lopiano, who built a nationally-prominent women's program in her 18 years at Texas. "The presidents are in charge now and they're saying, 'We don't trust you guys any more. You run deficit programs. You get us in deep trouble with the press. And now with gender equity, we're going to have all these lawsuits. Get outta here.'"

Obviously, women are gaining a greater share of power within the NCAA structure. The next goal is to reach parity with men in participation opportunities and funding.

"Ultimately, this argument is not about what is legal, but what is fair," says Dr. Christine Grant, women's AD at Iowa. "That should be our focus."

There is no doubt among those on all sides of the importance of gender equity.

"I think this will quite likely be the most prominent and potentially the most volatile issue that we will face for the next couple of years," says University of Georgia president Charles Knapp. "It's a question whose time has come."

Like most of the male athletics directors and football coaches at Division I-A institutions, Georgia AD Vince Dooley isn't opposed to equity—as long as football is exempt from the equation.

"Football aside," Dooley says, "if you went across the board and made sure that sport for sport there were equal percentages of money spent, most reasonable women would feel good about that."

What Lopiano and thousands of other activists want, however, is complete equality—nothing less than scholarships allotted in direct proportion to the student population. And that formula would include football, which offers 95 grants-in-aid at Division I-A institutions—a number that will shrink to 85 by 1994 under legislation now on the books. Such a plan would almost certainly entail reducing the scholarship limits for men's sports. Women also want equality in areas such as recruiting dollars and the availability of facilities and services.

377

"There is absolutely no way football needs 85 guys on scholarship," argues Ellen Vargyas of the National Women's Law Center. "The NFL gets by with 45 players. I think 50 or 55 scholarships would be just fine."

That argument isn't valid according to Georgia football coach Ray Goff, voicing the opinion of virtually all his peers.

"This isn't the NFL," Goff counters. "In the pros, if a player gets hurt, they simply go out and sign another one. We can't do that. And if we make a mistake in recruiting and a guy can't play, we can't run him off (like the pros do). He stays on scholarship."

In the minds of male football coaches and ADs, gender equity means taking money away from football and giving it to women's programs.

"They (the forces pushing gender equity) are coming after men's sports, especially football," says Georgia Tech AD Homer Rice. "Football is going to be the hot spot in this discussion."

Counters Lopiano, "Football coaches and athletic directors seem to think there are three sexes in the world—men, women and football. Those days are over."

A task force set up by the NCAA to study the gender equity issue with an eye toward legislative relief has reiterated that the position of Congress is clear: Football will be included in the Title IX formula.

As was the case when Title IX was enacted back in 1972, athletic directors and football coaches are crying gloom and doom. They maintain that cutting back scholarships in football and men's basketball will lower the level of talent in both and result in not only reducing fan interest, but forcing television to divert money away from the college game and into professional sports.

"It's something I see coming and snowballing," says Goff. "It's going to get political, too, and that scares me."

Although the male-to-female ratio on college campuses is approximately 50-50, the average Division I-A institution spends $1.3 million per year on scholarships for men and $505,000 on scholarships for women.

That imbalance has not escaped the notice of Congress.

"If schools had a special program for male scientists only, or if they designated two-thirds of their academic scholarship for men, we would be outraged," says Rep. Cardiss Collins, a black congresswoman from Illinois. "We should have similar outrage with respect to sports."

Other legislators, like Sen. Bill Bradley (D-N.J.) and Rep. Tom McMilland (D-Md.), have threatened to take action and that has created a sense of urgency within the leadership of the NCAA.

Collins is chairman of the sub committee on Commerce, Consumer Protection and Competitiveness. She held a congressional hearing on April 9 on the subject of gender equity and has insisted that if the NCAA does not act, Congress will.

The Big Ten Conference already has a plan. It intends to allocate resources on a 60-40 male-female ratio by 1997, and a ratio reflecting the student body by 2002.

"That's the standard we all should be pointing toward and that's why we are taking the lead," said Iowa's Grant. Iowa unilaterally has announced its intention to achieve equity in five years.

The NCAA's gender equity task force, which is co-chaired by Big Ten assistant commissioner Phyllis Howlett, will not put forward any legislative proposals to be voted upon by the membership until the organization's 1994 convention. No one ever accused the NCAA of moving too fast. However, the task force will make non-binding recommendations at the Jan. '93 convention in Dallas that will no doubt underscore a wide financial gulf between men's and women's sports. Consider these items:

Title IX

"No person in the United States shall, on the basis of sex, be excluded from participation in, be denied the benefits of, or be subjected to discrimination under any education program or activity receiving Federal financial assistance."

—United States Congress, June 23, 1972

University of Georgia

Like most of their colleagues, University of Georgia athletic director **Vince Dooley** (left) and football coach **Ray Goff** aren't opposed to the mathematics of gender equity, as long as football isn't part of the equation.

—Of the average athletic department operations budget of $1.31 million, only $262,570—that's 20 percent—is spent on women's athletics.

—Of the average recruiting budget of $318,402, only $49,406—15 percent—is spent on recruiting female athletes.

—Of the $1,346,106 the average Division I school pays in coaching salaries, only $325,003—31.8 percent—goes to coaches of women's sports.

—In 1972, 90 percent of women's teams were coached by women, but in 1991-92 only 48.3 percent of women's teams were coached by women.

Preliminary indications were that the task force would recommend an increase in participation opportunities for women rather than a reduction of opportunities for men. For example, the committee suggested the addition of sports such as synchronized swimming or badminton for women. NCAA grants to conferences could be used as seed money for such sports.

The women's movement in sports began in earnest with the implementation of Title IX, the 37-word act of Congress states: "No person in the United States shall, on the basis of sex, be excluded from participation in, be denied the benefits of, or be subjected to discrimination under any education program or activity receiving Federal financial assistance."

The key question in athletic departments around the country immediately after Title IX's passage was: Does it apply to non-federally funded athletic programs at institutions that receive federal aid? The U.S. Supreme Court ultimately ruled that no, it did not apply to such institutions in its decision on Grove City (Pa.) College v. Bell in 1984 (Terrel Bell was Secretary of Education from 1981-85).

However, in 1988 Congress passed the Civil Rights Restoration Act, which applied Title IX to all education programs at institutions that received federal aid, effectively reversing Grove City v. Bell. Therefore, any school found to be in violation of Title IX risks having its federal funds cut off—a devastating prospect for most major research universities.

The NCAA's task force has also discussed many cost factors—such as scholarship reductions, state appropriations (illegal in California, Georgia and some other states), federal grants, U.S. Olympic Committee sponsorship, and common sense cost reductions in areas such as travel. However, an idea being discussed more and more is need-based scholarships pioneered by the Ivy League.

Meanwhile, the NCAA has not only been facing Congressional pressure, but catching heat from the judicial branch as well:

—In 1979, the Supreme Court decided that private parties could file suit to seek relief from Title IX violations.

—In 1987, the State Supreme Court in Washington ruled that Washington State University would have to equalize its athletics scholarships. As a result, the school added two women's sports and made other adjustments to make revenue distribution reflect the male-female ratio of the student body.

—Oklahoma, South Carolina, William & Mary and New Hampshire announced plans to disband certain women's sports at one time or another over the last two school years, but were forced to reconsider under threat of lawsuits.

—In Feb., 1992, the U.S. Supreme Court ruled in a Georgia high school case that those who file Title IX suits are eligible for monetary damages, paving the way for suits against college athletics departments, which might have to pay punitive damages in the millions of dollars if found in willful violation.

—Arthur Bryant, executive director of the Trial Lawyers for Public Justice, has sued Temple and Brown universities and threatened Oklahoma, William & Mary and New Hampshire over the question of sex discrimination in athletics.

Another key figure in the debate is Vargyas of the National Women's Law Center, who played a major role in the lawsuit against Temple—the first to find a school guilty of widespread sexual discrimination in athletics. Vargyas and her organization are very active in fighting sex discrimination on many fronts.

The last person an athletic director or college president wants to hear from is an attorney representing a female athlete in a Title IX case.

"Let's face it," says Vargyas, "when there is an opportunity to win substantial financial judgments, the legal community is going to get more involved in an issue."

For a typical large state university, the price tag for equalizing scholarships alone could run as high as $1 million. Already in a financial bind—70 percent of all Division I athletic departments lost money last year—most ADs say those funds simply are not available.

Prop 48: The NCAA's Tough Love

Steve Davis, a splendid running back from Spartanburg, S.C., is the latest in a long line of southern schoolboy running backs billed as the "next Herschel Walker."

Only this one might be the real thing. At 6-1, 220 pounds, Davis is similar to Walker in stature and his running style also is similar—with a distinct forward lean.

Davis' numbers are also Herschelesque: he gained 2,400 yards and scored 30 touchdowns while leading his team to the 1991 South Carolina Class AAAA state championship.

There's only one problem: Davis failed to make the 700 cutoff score on the Scholastic Aptitude Test (SAT) mandated by the NCAA's Proposition 48 and, therefore, is ineligible to compete at Auburn as a freshman. No one will ever know if he could have matched the 1,616 rushing yards Walker gained in 1980, which remains an NCAA record for freshmen.

Instead, Davis—if he can pass his course work—will begin his collegiate career in 1993.

As Prop 48 reads now, prospects must score at least 700 on the SAT or a 17 on the American College Test (ACT). They must also earn at least a 2.0 grade-point average (GPA) in a core curriculum of 11 college preparatory academic courses, if they want to be eligible for an athletics scholarship and compete as freshmen.

Although research concerning the effects of Prop 48, which was implemented in 1986, has not yet been compiled, the NCAA Presidents Commission—under pressure by the reform-minded Knight Commission—pushed through legislation at the NCAA's 1992 convention in Los Angeles which will drastically strengthen academic requirements.

The new legislation increases the core curriculum from 11 to 13, the required high school GPA from 2.0 to 2.5 and the required SAT cutoff score from 700 to 750.

It also introduces a sliding index under which a prospect could be eligible to play as a freshman with a 700 SAT score, if it was offset by a 2.9 grade-point average, or retain eligibility with a 2.0 grade-point average, if it was offset by a 790 SAT score.

The new requirements, which won't go

Thomas E. McCarver/Spartanburg Herald-Journal

Star running back **Steve Davis** (48) gained 2,400 yards for state champion Spartanburg (S.C.) High in 1991, but he was tackled by Prop 48 on his way to Auburn.

into effect until 1996 (to allow freshmen entering high school this year time to gear up for the tougher standards), reopened conflict between academicians and coaches, and between administrators at major football-playing institutions and historically black institutions.

Coaches like Auburn's Pat Dye have decried the tougher academic standards, but others such as Penn State's Joe Paterno applaud the NCAA's effort to reemphasize the fact that athletes should be students first and foremost.

Mississippi State assistant athletic director David Boles predicted the new standards "could affect 77 percent of the minority athletes we're currently certifying—if the students don't react and do their school work in high school."

One study showed that 61 of 100 black athletes would have been ineligible had the new standards been in effect last year.

Roy Hudson, vice president for administration at Mississippi Valley State University, points out that the new NCAA standards exceed those of his school's general student population.

"I think athletic eligibility at a particular institution should be in parallel and based on the general academic requirements of that institution," Hudson argues. "The new standard is much higher than is required of our general student body and we see that as not fair. An athlete below 2.5 might have trouble at Notre Dame or Penn State or Southern Cal, but he would be right in line to have a good opportunity for success at Valley, Grambling, Jackson State and a lot of predominantly white institutions."

Not only did delegates at the January convention toughen the standards up front, they approved legislation that will virtually force athletes to be on track to graduate to remain eligible to play.

"The Dukes and Vanderbilts may be better off than the traditional powers," says Boles. "They're already there."

"Coaches will get the message," he adds, "when that first group hits its junior year (in 1994) and they start losing athletes."

Michigan State

Former NCAA official **Merrily Dean Baker** replaced football coach George Perles as Michigan State athletic director in April.

The spectre of gender equality threatens to force many Division I schools to swallow their pride and consider stepping down to another, more affordable division.

The issue could also lead to an even greater dilemma for traditionally black schools. At Division II Clark Atlanta University in Georgia, for instance, the student body is 69 percent female.

"There's no way a poor school could survive," says Clark athletic director and football coach Willie Hunter. "If they're talking gender equity for Division I schools, where they have the money to support those programs, I think it should be done. But black schools can just barely survive with the way things are now."

"If they go to gender equity," Hunter continues, "basically all we'll have is girls' basketball and girls' track. Our football program would either have to be stopped or turned into an intramural sport."

Of 2,739 female students enrolled at Clark during the 1991-92 school year, only 39 participated in athletics. For the male students, it was 81 of 1,257. The school spent $470,000 on men's athletics and $140,000 for women with 48 of 53 total scholarships going to men's sports—and 35 of them to football.

If gender equity is mandated by the NCAA, Clark likely would have to drop to Division III—a non-scholarship division—to continue to compete in football. On the Division III level, Clark athletes would have to compete for whatever financial aid is available to the general student body.

Achieving gender equity would involve a different set of numbers at virtually every NCAA institution. At the University of Georgia during the 1991-92 school year, with a male-female student body ratio of approximately 50-50, men received 156 scholarships, women only 78. Take football out of the mix and women received 17 more athletic scholarships than men (78 to 61).

One possible solution would be to add soccer, softball and field hockey as women's sports and give three additional scholarships to each of the existing women's programs. That, combined with scholarship reductions in men's sports already scheduled to take full effect by 1994, would bring about scholarship parity. The price tag would be approximately $850,000 per year, according to school officials.

The new model might include reducing football scholarships on the Division I level and revamping the recruiting process. Georgia and Georgia Tech, for instance, combined to spend $890,000 last year on football recruiting alone.

"You can drop the numbers to whatever you want," argues Georgia's Goff, "but if you do, you won't be as good a football team. I don't think fans and advertisers are going to be as willing to pay the money if the product drops in quality. You could start losing money and then you'd have to start cutting back on other sports. This thing (gender equity) could kill the goose that lays the golden eggs."

Goff's point is echoed by the rest of the football fraternity, but the facts don't support their argument. According to NCAA studies, approximately 89 percent of all football programs lose money, much less fund other sports.

Says Lopiano, "If everybody disarms at once and sticks to the new standard, then the pecking order will stay the same and everybody will be happy."

Maybe. In any case, there are going to be some changes made and soon.

"I would never hurt my football program because it means too much to the people of our state," says Iowa's Grant. "But we have got to find a new model."□

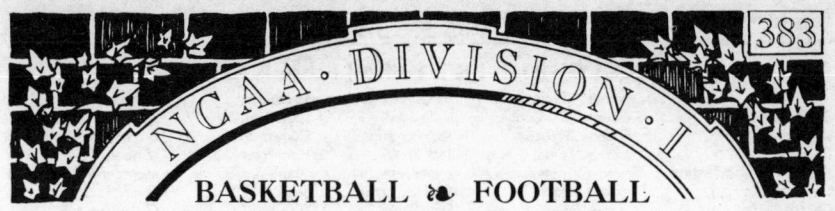

NCAA Division I Basketball Schools
Conferences and coaches as of Sept. 1, 1992.

Switching conferences in 1992-93 (11): **1.** AKRON from Mid-Continent to MAC; **2.** CENTRAL FLORIDA from Sun Belt to Trans America; **3.** DAVIDSON from Big South to Southern; **4.** DUQUESNE from Atlantic 10 to Midwestern; **5.** FRESNO ST. from Big West to WAC; **6.** GEORGIA SOUTHERN from Trans America to Southern; **7.** LA SALLE from Metro Atlantic to Midwestern; **8.** MD-BALTIMORE COUNTY from East Coast to Big South; **9.** NEVADA from Big Sky to Big West; **10.** RIDER from East Coast to Northeast; **11.** TOWSON ST. from East Coast to Big South.

Conference breaking up in 1992: EAST COAST (Brooklyn eliminated program; MD-Baltimore County and Towson St. moved to Big South; Rider moved to Northeast; and Buffalo, Central Conn. St. and Hofstra went independent).

Joining Div. I in 1992-93: TENNESSEE-MARTIN from Gulf South Conference (Div. II) to Ohio Valley.

Leaving Div. I in 1992-93: BROOKLYN eliminated its entire athletic program.

Independents joining conferences in 1992-93 (3): **1.** COLLEGE OF CHARLESTON to Trans America; **2.** NC-GREENSBORO to Big South; **3.** PENN ST. to Big 10.

Conference members becoming Independents in 1992-93 (3): **1.** BUFFALO, **2.** CENTRAL CONN. ST. and **3.** HOFSTRA , all from dissolved East Coast Conference.

Independent joining conference in 1993-94: WI-MILWAUKEE to Mid-Continent.

	Nickname	Conference	Head Coach	Location	Colors
Air Force	Falcons	WAC	Reggie Minton	Colo.Springs,CO	Blue/Silver
Akron	Zips	MAC	Coleman Crawford	Akron,OH	Blue/Gold
Alabama	Crimson Tide	SEC-West	David Hobbs	Tuscaloosa,AL	Crimson/White
Alabama St	Hornets	Southwestern	James Oliver	Montgomery,AL	Black/Gold
Ala-Birmingham	Blazers	Great Midwest	Gene Bartow	Birmingham,AL	Green/Gold
Alcorn St	Braves	Southwestern	Lonnie Walker	Lorman,MS	Purple/Gold
American	Eagles	Colonial	Chris Knoche	Washington,DC	Red/White/Blue
Appalachian St	Mountaineers	Southern	Tom Apke	Boone,NC	Black/Gold
Arizona	Wildcats	Pac-10	Lute Olson	Tucson,AZ	Cardinal/Navy
Arizona St	Sun Devils	Pac-10	Bill Frieder	Tempe,AZ	Maroon/Gold
Arkansas	Razorbacks	SEC-West	Nolan Richardson	Fayetteville,AR	Cardinal/White
Arkansas-Little Rock	Trojans	Sun Belt	Jim Platt	Little Rock,AR	Maroon/White
Arkansas St	Indians	Sun Belt	Nelson Catalina	State University,AR	Scarlet/Black
Army	Cadets	Patriot	Tom Miller	West Point,NY	Black/Gold/Gray
Auburn	Tigers	SEC-West	Tommy Joe Eagles	Auburn,AL	Orange/Blue
Austin Peay	Governors	Ohio Valley	Dave Loos	Clarksville,TN	Red/White
Ball St	Cardinals	MAC	Dick Hunsaker	Muncie,IN	Cardinal/White
Baylor	Bears	SWC	Darrel Johnson	Waco,TX	Green/Gold
Bethune-Cookman	Wildcats	Mid-Eastern	Cy McClairen	Daytona Beach,FL	Maroon/Gold
Boise St	Broncos	Big Sky	Bobby Dye	Boise,ID	Orange/Blue
Boston College	Eagles	Big East	Jim O'Brien	Chestnut Hill,MA	Maroon/Gold
Boston University	Terriers	North Atlantic	Bob Brown	Boston,MA	Scarlet/White
Bowling Green	Falcons	MAC	Jim Larranaga	Bowling Green,OH	Orange/Brown
Bradley	Braves	Mo.Valley	Jim Molinari	Peoria,IL	Red/White
BYU	Cougars	WAC	Roger Reid	Provo,UT	Royal Blue/White
Brown	Bears	Ivy	Frank Dobbs	Providence,RI	Brown/Red/White
Bucknell	Bison	Patriot	Charlie Woollum	Lewisburg,PA	Orange/Blue
Buffalo	Bulls	Independent	Dan Bazzani	Buffalo,NY	Blue/Red/White
Butler	Bulldogs	Midwestern	Barry Collier	Indianapolis,IN	Blue/White
California	Golden Bears	Pac-10	Lou Campanelli	Berkeley,CA	Blue/Gold
CS-Fullerton	Titans	Big West	Brad Holland	Fullerton,CA	Blue/Orange/White
CS-Northridge	Matadors	Independent	Pete Cassidy	Northridge,CA	Red/White
CS-Sacramento	Hornets	Independent	Don Newman	Sacramento,CA	Green/Gold
Campbell	Fighting Camels	Big South	Billy Lee	Buies Creek,NC	Orange/Black
Canisius	Golden Griffins	Metro Atlantic	John Beilein	Buffalo,NY	Blue/Gold
Centenary	Gentlemen	Trans Am.	Tommy Vardeman	Shreveport,LA	Maroon/White
Central Conn.St	Blue Devils	Independent	Mark Adams	New Britain,CT	Blue/White
Central Florida	Knights	Trans Am.	Joe Dean Jr.	Orlando,FL	Black/Gold
Central Michigan	Chippewas	MAC	Keith Dambrot	Mt.Pleasant,MI	Maroon/Gold
Charleston Southern	Buccaneers	Big South	Gary Edwards	Charleston,SC	Blue/Gold
Chicago St	Cougars	Independent	Rick Pryor	Chicago,IL	Green/White
Cincinnati	Bearcats	Great Midwest	Bob Huggins	Cincinnati,OH	Red/Black
The Citadel	Bulldogs	Southern	Pat Dennis	Charleston,SC	Blue/White
Clemson	Tigers	ACC	Cliff Ellis	Clemson,SC	Purple/Orange

NCAA Division I Basketball Schools (Cont.)

	Nickname	Conference	Head Coach	Location	Colors
Cleveland St	Vikings	Mid-Cont.	Mike Boyd	Cleveland,OH	Green/White
Coastal Carolina	Chanticleers	Big South	Russ Bergman	Conway,SC	Scarlet/Black
Colgate	Red Raiders	Patriot	Jack Bruen	Hamilton,NY	Maroon/White
College of Charleston	Cougars	Trans Am.	John Kresse	Charleston,SC	Maroon/White
Colorado	Buffaloes	Big 8	Joe Harrington	Boulder,CO	Silver/Gold/Black
Colorado St	Rams	WAC	Stew Morrill	Ft.Collins,CO	Green/Gold
Columbia	Lions	Ivy	Jack Rohan	New York,NY	Lt.Blue/White
Connecticut	Huskies	Big East	Jim Calhoun	Storrs,CT	Blue/White
Coppin St	Eagles	Mid-Eastern	Ron Mitchell	Baltimore,MD	Royal Blue/Gold
Cornell	Big Red	Ivy	J.van Breda Kolff	Ithaca,NY	Red/White
Creighton	Bluejays	Mo.Valley	Rick Johnson	Omaha,NE	Blue/White
Dartmouth	Big Green	Ivy	Dave Faucher	Hanover,NH	Green/White
Davidson	Wildcats	Southern	Bob McKillop	Davidson,NC	Red/Black
Dayton	Flyers	Midwestern	Jim O'Brien	Dayton,OH	Red/Blue
DePaul	Blue Demons	Great Midwest	Joey Meyer	Chicago,IL	Scarlet/Blue
Delaware	Blue Hens	North Atlantic	Steve Steinwedel	Newark,DE	Blue/Gold
Delaware St	Hornets	Mid-Eastern	Jeff Jones	Dover,DE	Red/Blue
Detroit Mercy	Titans	Midwestern	Ricky Byrdsong	Detroit,MI	Red/White/Blue
Drake	Bulldogs	Mo.Valley	Rudy Washington	Des Moines,IA	Blue/White
Drexel	Dragons	North Atlantic	Bill Herrion	Philadelphia,PA	Navy Blue/Gold
Duke	Blue Devils	ACC	Mike Krzyzewski	Durham,NC	Royal Blue/White
Duquesne	Dukes	Midwestern	John Carroll	Pittsburgh,PA	Red/Blue
East Carolina	Pirates	Colonial	Eddie Payne	Greenville,NC	Purple/Gold
East Tenn.St	Buccaneers	Southern	Alan LeForce	Johnson City,TN	Blue/Gold
Eastern Illinois	Panthers	Mid-Cont.	Rick Samuels	Charleston,IL	Blue/Gray
Eastern Kentucky	Colonels	Ohio Valley	Mike Calhoun	Richmond,KY	Maroon/White
Eastern Michigan	Eagles	MAC	Ben Braun	Ypsilanti,MI	Green/White
Eastern Washington	Eagles	Big Sky	John H.Wade II	Cheney,WA	Red/White
Evansville	Purple Aces	Midwestern	Jim Crews	Evansville,IN	Purple/White
Fairfield	Stags	Metro Atlantic	Paul Cormier	Fairfield,CT	Cardinal Red
Fairleigh Dickinson	Knights	Northeast	Tom Green	Teaneck,NJ	Maroon/White/Blue
Florida	Gators	SEC-East	Lon Kruger	Gainesville,FL	Orange/Blue
Florida A&M	Rattlers	Mid-Eastern	Willie Booker	Tallahassee,FL	Orange/Green
Florida Int'l	Golden Panthers	Trans Am.	Bob Weltlich	Miami,FL	Blue/Yellow
Florida St	Seminoles	ACC	Pat Kennedy	Tallahassee,FL	Garnet/Gold
Fordham	Rams	Patriot	Nick Macarchuk	Bronx,NY	Maroon/White
Fresno St	Bulldogs	WAC	Gary Colson	Fresno,CA	Cardinal/Blue
Furman	Paladins	Southern	Butch Estes	Greenville,SC	Purple/White
George Mason	Patriots	Colonial	Ernie Nestor	Fairfax,VA	Green/Gold
George Washington	Colonials	Atlantic 10	Mike Jarvis	Washington,DC	Buff/Blue
Georgetown	Hoyas	Big East	John Thompson	Washington,DC	Blue/Gray
Georgia	Bulldogs, 'Dawgs	SEC-East	Hugh Durham	Athens,GA	Red/Black
Georgia Southern	Eagles	Southern	Frank Kerns	Statesboro,GA	Blue/White
Georgia St	Panthers	Trans Am.	Bob Reinhart	Atlanta,GA	Royal Blue/Crimson
Georgia Tech	Yellow Jackets	ACC	Bobby Cremins	Atlanta,GA	Old Gold/White
Gonzaga	Bulldogs, Zags	West Coast	Dan Fitzgerald	Spokane,WA	Blue/White/Red
Grambling St	Tigers	Southwestern	Aaron James	Grambling,LA	Black/Gold
Hartford	Hawks	North Atlantic	Paul Brazeau	West Hartford,CT	Scarlet/White
Harvard	Crimson	Ivy	Frank Sullivan	Cambridge,MA	Crimson/Black/White
Hawaii	Rainbows	WAC	Riley Wallace	Honolulu,HI	Green/White
Hofstra	Flying Dutchmen	Independent	B.van Breda Kolff	Hempstead,NY	Blue/White/Gold
Holy Cross	Crusaders	Patriot	George Blaney	Worcester,MA	Royal Purple
Houston	Cougars	SWC	Pat Foster	Houston,TX	Scarlet/White
Howard	Bison	Mid-Eastern	Butch Beard	Washington,DC	Blue/White
Idaho	Vandals	Big Sky	Larry Eustachy	Moscow,ID	Silver/Gold
Idaho St	Bengals	Big Sky	Herb Williams	Pocatello,ID	Orange/Black
Illinois	Fighting Illini	Big 10	Lou Henson	Champaign,IL	Orange/Blue
Illinois-Chicago	Flames	Mid-Cont.	Bob Hallberg	Chicago,IL	Indigo/Flame
Illinois St	Redbirds	Mo.Valley	Bob Bender	Normal,IL	Red/White
Indiana	Hoosiers	Big 10	Bob Knight	Bloomington,IN	Cream/Crimson
Indiana St	Sycamores	Mo.Valley	Tates Locke	Terre Haute,IN	Blue/White
Iona	Gaels	Metro Atlantic	Jerry Welsh	New Rochelle,NY	Maroon/Gold
Iowa	Hawkeyes	Big 10	Tom Davis	Iowa City,IA	Old Gold/Black
Iowa St	Cyclones	Big 8	Johnny Orr	Ames,IA	Cardinal/Gold
Jackson St	Tigers	Southwestern	Andrew Stoglin	Jackson,MS	Blue/White
Jacksonville	Dolphins	Sun Belt	Matt Kilcullen	Jacksonville,FL	Green/Gold
James Madison	Dukes	Colonial	Lefty Driesell	Harrisonburg,VA	Purple/Gold

	Nickname	Conference	Head Coach	Location	Colors
Kansas	Jayhawks	Big 8	Roy Williams	Lawrence,KS	Crimson/Blue
Kansas St	Wildcats	Big 8	Dana Altman	Manhattan,KS	Purple/White
Kent	Golden Flashes	MAC	Dave Grube	Kent,OH	Navy Blue/Gold
Kentucky	Wildcats	SEC-East	Rick Pitino	Lexington,KY	Blue/White
La Salle	Explorers	Midwestern	Bill Morris	Philadelphia,PA	Blue/Gold
Lafayette	Leopards	Patriot	John Leone	Easton,PA	Maroon/White
Lamar	Cardinals	Sun Belt	Mike Newell	Beaumont,TX	Red/White
Lehigh	Engineers	Patriot	Dave Duke	Bethlehem,PA	Brown/White
Liberty	Flames	Big South	Jeff Meyer	Lynchburg,VA	Red/White/Blue
Long Beach St	49ers	Big West	Seth Greenberg	Long Beach,CA	Black/Gold
LIU-Brooklyn	Blackbirds	Northeast	Paul Lizzo	Brooklyn,NY	Blue/White
LSU	Fighting Tigers	SEC-West	Dale Brown	Baton Rouge,LA	Purple/Gold
Louisiana Tech	Bulldogs	Sun Belt	Jerry Loyd	Ruston,LA	Red/Blue
Louisville	Cardinals	Metro	Denny Crum	Louisville,KY	Red/Black/White
Loyola-CA	Lions	West Coast	John Olive	Los Angeles,CA	Crimson/Gray/Lt.Blue
Loyola-IL	Ramblers	Midwestern	Will Rey	Chicago,IL	Maroon/Gold
Loyola-MD	Greyhounds	Metro Atlantic	Tom Schneider	Baltimore,MD	Green/Gray
Maine	Black Bears	North Atlantic	Rudy Keeling	Orono,ME	Blue/White
Manhattan	Jaspers	Metro Atlantic	Fran Fraschilla	Riverdale,NY	Green/White
Marist	Red Foxes	Northeast	Dave Magarity	Poughkeepsie,NY	Red/White
Marquette	Warriors	Great Midwest	Kevin O'Neill	Milwaukee,WI	Blue/Gold
Marshall	Thundering Herd	Southern	Dwight Freeman	Huntington,WV	Green/White
Maryland	Terrapins, Terps	ACC	Gary Williams	College Park,MD	Red/White/Black/Gold
MD-Balt.County	Retrievers	Big South	Earl Hawkins	Baltimore,MD	Black/Old Gold
MD-Eastern Shore	Hawks	Mid-Eastern	Rob Chavez	Princess Anne,MD	Maroon/Gray
Massachusetts	Minutemen	Atlantic 10	John Calipari	Amherst,MA	Maroon/White
McNeese St	Cowboys	Southland	Steve Welch	Lake Charles,LA	Blue/Gold
Memphis St	Tigers	Great Midwest	Larry Finch	Memphis,TN	Blue/Gray
Mercer	Bears	Trans Am.	Bill Hodges	Macon,GA	Orange/Black
Miami-FL	Hurricanes	Big East	Leonard Hamilton	Miami,FL	Orange/Green/White
Miami-OH	Redskins	MAC	Joby Wright	Oxford,OH	Red/White
Michigan	Wolverines	Big 10	Steve Fisher	Ann Arbor,MI	Maize/Blue
Michigan St	Spartans	Big 10	Jud Heathcote	East Lansing,MI	Green/White
Middle Tenn.St	Blue Raiders	Ohio Valley	Dave Farrar	Murfreesboro,TN	Blue/White
Minnesota	Golden Gophers	Big 10	Clem Haskins	Minneapolis,MN	Maroon/Gold
Mississippi	Ole Miss, Rebels	SEC-West	Rob Evans	Oxford,MS	Red/Blue
Mississippi St	Bulldogs	SEC-West	Richard Williams	Starkville,MS	Maroon/White
Miss.Valley St	Delta Devils	Southwestern	Lafayette Stribling	Itta Bena,MS	Green/White
Missouri	Tigers	Big 8	Norm Stewart	Columbia,MO	Old Gold/Black
Missouri-KC	Kangaroos	Independent	Lee Hunt	Kansas City,MO	Blue/Gold
Monmouth	Hawks	Northeast	Wayne Szoke	W.Long Branch,NJ	Royal Blue/White
Montana	Grizzlies	Big Sky	Blaine Taylor	Missoula,MT	Copper/Silver/Gold
Montana St	Bobcats	Big Sky	Mick Durham	Bozeman,MT	Blue/Gold
Morehead St	Eagles	Ohio Valley	Dick Fick	Morehead,KY	Blue/Gold
Morgan St	Bears	Mid-Eastern	Michael Holmes	Baltimore,MD	Blue/Orange
Mt.St.Mary's	Mountaineers	Northeast	Jim Phelan	Emmitsburg,MD	Blue/White
Murray St	Racers	Ohio Valley	Scott Edgar	Murray,KY	Blue/Gold
Navy	Midshipmen	Patriot	Don DeVoe	Annapolis,MD	Navy Blue/Gold
Nebraska	Cornhuskers	Big 8	Danny Nee	Lincoln,ME	Scarlet/Cream
Nevada	Wolf Pack	Big West	Len Stevens	Reno,NV	Silver/Blue
New Hampshire	Wildcats	North Atlantic	Gib Chapman	Durham,NH	Blue/White
New Mexico	Lobos	WAC	Dave Bliss	Albuquerque,NM	Cherry/Silver
New Mexico St	Aggies	Big West	Neil McCarthy	Las Cruces,NM	Crimson/White
New Orleans	Privateers	Sun Belt	Tim Floyd	New Orleans,LA	Royal Blue/Silver
Niagara	Purple Eagles	Metro Atlantic	Jack Armstrong	Niagara,NY	Purple/White/Gold
Nicholls St	Colonels	Southland	Rickey Broussard	Thibodaux,LA	Red/Gray
North Carolina	Tar Heels	ACC	Dean Smith	Chapel Hill,NC	Carolina Blue/White
North Carolina A&T	Aggies	Mid-Eastern	Don Corbett	Greensboro,NC	Blue/Gold
North Carolina St	Wolfpack	ACC	Les Robinson	Raleigh,NC	Red/White
NC-Asheville	Bulldogs	Big South	Don Doucette	Asheville,NC	Royal Blue/White
NC-Charlotte	49ers	Metro	Jeff Mullins	Charlotte,NC	Green/White
NC-Greensboro	Spartans	Big South	Mike Dement	Greensboro,NC	Gold/White/Navy
NC-Wilmington	Seahawks	Colonial	Kevin Eastman	Wilmington,NC	Green/Gold
North Texas	Mean Green	Southland	Jimmy Gales	Denton,TX	Green/White
NE Illinois	Golden Eagles	Independent	Rees Johnson	Chicago,IL	Royal Blue/Gold
NE Louisiana	Indians	Southland	Mike Vining	Monroe,LA	Maroon/Gold
Northeastern	Huskies	North Atlantic	Karl Fogel	Boston,MA	Red/Black
Northern Arizona	Lumberjacks	Big Sky	Harold Merritt	Flagstaff,AZ	Blue/Gold
Northern Illinois	Huskies	Mid-Cont.	Brian Hammel	De Kalb,IL	Cardinal/Black
Northern Iowa	Panthers	Mo.Valley	Eldon Miller	Cedar Falls,IA	Purple/Old Gold
Northwestern	Wildcats	Big 10	Bill Foster	Evanston,IL	Purple/White

NCAA Division I Basketball Schools (Cont.)

	Nickname	Conference	Head Coach	Location	Colors
Northwestern St	Demons	Southland	Dan Bell	Natchitoches,LA	Burnt Orange/Purple
Notre Dame	Fighting Irish	Independent	John MacLeod	South Bend,IN	Gold/Blue
Ohio St	Buckeyes	Big 10	Randy Ayers	Columbus,OH	Scarlet/Gray
Ohio University	Bobcats	MAC	Larry Hunter	Athens,OH	Kelly Green/White
Oklahoma	Sooners	Big 8	Billy Tubbs	Norman,OK	Crimson/Cream
Oklahoma St	Cowboys	Big 8	Eddie Sutton	Stillwater,OK	Orange/Black
Old Dominion	Monarchs	Colonial	Oliver Purnell	Norfolk,VA	Slate Blue/Silver
Oregon	Ducks	Pac-10	Jerry Green	Eugene,OR	Green/Yellow
Oregon St	Beavers	Pac-10	Jim Anderson	Corvallis,OR	Orange/Black
Pacific	Tigers	Big West	Bob Thomason	Stockton,CA	Orange/Black
Pennsylvania	Quakers	Ivy	Fran Dunphy	Philadelphia,PA	Red/Blue
Penn St	Nittany Lions	Big 10	Bruce Parkhill	University Park,PA	Blue/White
Pepperdine	Waves	West Coast	Tom Asbury	Malibu,CA	Blue/Orange
Pittsburgh	Panthers	Big East	Paul Evans	Pittsburgh,PA	Gold/Blue
Portland	Pilots	West Coast	Larry Steele	Portland,OR	Purple/White
Prairie View A&M	Panthers	Southwestern	Elwood Plummer	Prairie View,TX	Purple/Gold
Princeton	Tigers	Ivy	Pete Carril	Princeton,NJ	Orange/Black
Providence	Friars	Big East	Rick Barnes	Providence,RI	Black/White
Purdue	Boilermakers	Big 10	Gene Keady	West Lafayette,IN	Old Gold/Black
Radford	Highlanders	Big South	Ron Bradley	Radford,VA	Blue/Red/Green
Rhode Island	Rams	Atlantic 10	Al Skinner	Kingston,RI	Blue/White
Rice	Owls	SWC	Willis Wilson	Houston,TX	Blue/Gray
Richmond	Spiders	Colonial	Dick Tarrant	Richmond,VA	Red/Blue
Rider	Broncs	Northeast	Kevin Bannon	Lawrenceville,NJ	Cranberry/White
Robert Morris	Colonials	Northeast	Jarrett Durham	Coraopolis,PA	Blue/White
Rutgers	Scarlet Knights	Atlantic 10	Bob Wenzel	New Brunswick,NJ	Scarlet
St.Bonaventure	Bonnies	Atlantic 10	Jim Baron	St.Bonaventure,NY	Brown/White
St.Francis-NY	Terriers	Northeast	Ron Ganulin	Brooklyn,NY	Red/Royal Blue
St.Francis-PA	Red Flash	Northeast	TBA	Loretto,PA	Red/White
St.John's	Redmen	Big East	Brian Mahoney	Jamaica,NY	Red/White
St.Joseph's-PA	Hawks	Atlantic 10	John Griffin	Philadelphia,PA	Crimson/Gray
St.Louis	Billikens	Great Midwest	Charlie Spoonhour	St. Louis,MO	Blue/White
St.Mary's-CA	Gaels	West Coast	Ernie Kent	Moraga,CA	Red/Blue
St.Peter's	Peacocks	Metro Atlantic	Ted Fiore	Jersey City,NJ	Blue/White
Sam Houston St	Bearkats	Southland	Jerry Hopkins	Huntsville,TX	Orange/White
Samford	Bulldogs	Trans Am.	John Brady	Birmingham,AL	Red/Blue
San Diego	Toreros	West Coast	Hank Egan	San Diego,CA	Lt.Blue/Navy/White
San Diego St	Aztecs	WAC	Tony Fuller	San Diego, CA	Scarlet/Black
San Francisco	Dons	West Coast	Jim Brovelli	San Francisco,CA	Green/Gold
San Jose St	Spartans	Big West	Stan Morrison	San Jose,CA	Gold/White/Blue
Santa Clara	Broncos	West Coast	Carroll Williams	Santa Clara,CA	Bronco Red/White
Seton Hall	Pirates	Big East	P.J.Carlesimo	South Orange,NJ	Blue/White
Siena	Saints	Metro Atlantic	Mike Deane	Loudonville,NY	Green/Gold
South Alabama	Jaguars	Sun Belt	Ronnie Arrow	Mobile,AL	Red/White/Blue
South Carolina	Gamecocks	SEC-East	Steve Newton	Columbia,SC	Garnet/Black
South Carolina St	Bulldogs	Mid-Eastern	Cy Alexander	Orangeburg,SC	Garnet/Blue
South Florida	Bulls	Metro	Bobby Paschal	Tampa,FL	Green/Gold
SE Louisiana	Lions	Trans Am.	Norm Picou	Hammond,LA	Green/Gold
SE Missouri St	Indians	Ohio Valley	Ron Shumate	Cape Girardeau,MO	Red/Black
Southern Illinois	Salukis	Mo.Valley	Rich Herrin	Carbondale,IL	Maroon/White
SMU	Mustangs	Southwest	John Shumate	Dallas,TX	Red/Blue
Southern Miss	Golden Eagles	Metro	M.K.Turk	Hattiesburg,MS	Black/Gold
Southern Utah St	Thunderbirds	Independent	Bill Evans	Cedar City,UT	Scarlet/Royal Blue
Southern-BR	Jaguars	Southwestern	Ben Jobe	Baton Rouge,LA	Blue/Gold
SW Missouri St	Bears	Mo.Valley	Mark Bernsen	Springfield,MO	Maroon/White
SW Texas St	Bobcats	Southland	Jim Wooldridge	San Marcos,TX	Maroon/Gold
SW Louisiana	Ragin' Cajuns	Sun Belt	Marty Fletcher	Lafayette,LA	Vermilion/White
Stanford	Cardinal	Pac 10	Mike Montgomery	Stanford,CA	Cardinal/White
S.F.Austin St	Lumberjacks	Southland	Ned Fowler	Nacogdoches,TX	Purple/White
Stetson	Hatters	Trans Am.	Glenn Wilkes	De Land,FL	Green/White
Syracuse	Orangemen	Big East	Jim Boeheim	Syracuse, NY	Orange
Temple	Owls	Atlantic 10	John Chaney	Philadelphia,PA	Cherry/White
Tennessee	Volunteers	SEC-East	Wade Houston	Knoxville,TN	Orange/White
Tenn-Chattanooga	Moccasins	Southern	Mack McCarthy	Chattanooga,TN	Navy Blue/Gold
Tenn-Martin	Pacers	Ohio Valley	Calvin Luther	Martin,TN	Orange/White/Blue
Tennessee St	Tigers	Ohio Valley	Frankie Allen	Nashville,TN	Blue/White
Tennessee Tech	Golden Eagles	Ohio Valley	Frank Harrell	Cookville,TN	Purple/Gold
Texas	Longhorns	SWC	Tom Penders	Austin,TX	Burnt Orange/White
Texas A&M	Aggies	SWC	Tony Barone	College Station,TX	Maroon/White

	Nickname	Conference	Head Coach	Location	Colors
TCU	Horned Frogs	SWC	Moe Iba	Ft. Worth,TX	Purple/White
Texas Southern	Tigers	Southwestern	Robert Moreland	Houston,TX	Maroon/Gray
Texas Tech	Red Raiders	SW	James Dickey	Lubbock,TX	Scarlet/Black
TX-Arlington	Mavericks	Southland	Mark Nixon	Arlington,TX	Royal Blue/White
TX-Pan American	Broncs	Sun Belt	Mark Adams	Edinburg,TX	Green/White
TX-San Antonio	Roadrunners	Southland	Stu Starner	San Antonio,TX	Orange/Navy Blue
Toledo	Rockets	MAC	Larry Gipson	Toledo,OH	Blue/Gold
Towson St	Tigers	Big South	Terry Truax	Towson,MD	Gold/White/Black
Tulane	Green Wave	Metro	Perry Clark	New Orleans,LA	Olive Green/Sky Blue
Tulsa	Golden Hurricane	Mo.Valley	Tubby Smith	Tulsa,OK	Blue/Red/Gold
UC-Irvine	Anteaters	Big West	Rod Baker	Irvine,CA	Blue/Gold
UCLA	Bruins	Pac-10	Jim Harrick	Los Angeles,CA	Blue/Gold
UC-Santa Barbara	Gauchos	Big West	Jerry Pimm	Santa Barbara,CA	Blue/Gold
UNLV	Runnin' Rebels	Big West	Rollie Massimino	Las Vegas,NV	Scarlet/Gray
USC	Trojans	Pac-10	George Raveling	Los Angeles,CA	Cardinal/Gold
Utah	Utes	WAC	Rick Majerus	Salt Lake City,UT	Crimson/White
Utah St	Aggies	Big West	Kohn Smith	Logan,UT	Navy Blue/White
UTEP	Miners	WAC	Don Haskins	El Paso,TX	Orange/White/Blue
Valparaiso	Crusaders	Mid-Cont.	Homer Drew	Valparaiso,IN	Brown/Gold
Vanderbilt	Commodores	SEC-East	Eddie Fogler	Nashville,TN	Black/Gold
Vermont	Catamounts	North Atlantic	Tom Brennan	Burlington,VT	Green/Gold
Villanova	Wildcats	Big East	Steve Lappas	Villanova,PA	Blue/White
Virginia	Cavaliers	ACC	Jeff Jones	Charlottesville, VA	Orange/Blue
VCU	Rams	Metro	Sonny Smith	Richmond,VA	Black/Gold
VMI	Keydets	Southern	Joe Cantafio	Lexington,VA	Red/White/Yellow
Virginia Tech	Hokies, Gobblers	Metro	Bill Foster	Blacksburg,VA	Orange/Maroon
Wagner	Seahawks	Northeast	Tim Capstraw	Staten Island,NY	Green/White
Wake Forest	Demon Deacons	ACC	Dave Odom	Winston-Salem,NC	Old Gold/Black
Washington	Huskies	Pac-10	Lynn Nance	Seattle,WA	Purple/Gold
Washington St	Cougars	Pac-10	Kelvin Sampson	Pullman,WA	Crimson/Gray
Weber St	Wildcats	Big Sky	Ron Abegglen	Ogden,UT	Royal Purple/White
West Virginia	Mountaineers	Atlantic 10	Gale Catlett	Morgantown,WV	Old Gold/Blue
Western Carolina	Catamounts	Southern	Greg Blatt	Cullowhee,NC	Purple/Gold
Western Illinois	Leathernecks	Mid-Cont.	Jim Kerwin	Macomb,IL	Purple/Gold
Western Kentucky	Hilltoppers	Sun Belt	Ralph Willard	Bowling Green,KY	Red/White
Western Michigan	Broncos	MAC	Bob Donewald	Kalamazoo,MI	Brown/Gold
Wichita St	Shockers	Mo.Valley	Scott Thompson	Wichita,KS	Yellow/Black
William & Mary	Tribe	Colonial	Chuck Swenson	Williamsburg,VA	Green/Gold/Silver
Winthrop	Eagles	Big South	Dan Kenney	Rock Hill,SC	Garnet/Gold
Wisconsin	Badgers	Big 10	Stu Jackson	Madison,WI	Cardinal/White
WI-Green Bay	Phoenix	Mid-Cont.	Dick Bennett	Green Bay,WI	Green/White/Red
WI-Milwaukee	Panthers	Mid-Cont.('93)	Steve Antrim	Milwaukee,WI	Black/Gold
Wright St	Raiders	Mid-Cont.	Ralph Underhill	Dayton,OH	Green/Gold
Wyoming	Cowboys	WAC	Benny Dees	Laramie,WY	Brown/Yellow
Xavier	Musketeers	Midwestern	Pete Gillen	Cincinnati,OH	Blue/White
Yale	Bulldogs, Elis	Ivy	Dick Kuchen	New Haven,CT	Yale Blue/White
Youngstown St	Penguins	Mid-Cont.	John Stroia	Youngstown,OH	Scarlet/White

NCAA Division I-A Football Schools

Conferences and coaches as of Aug. 15, 1992.

Switching conferences in 1992 (2): **1.** ARKANSAS from SWC to SEC; **2.** FRESNO ST. from Big West to WAC.

Conference moving to divisional play in 1992: SEC added Arkansas from SWC and independent South Carolina and split into two divisions—WESTERN (Alabama, Arkansas, Auburn, LSU, Mississippi and Miss.St.) and EASTERN (Florida, Georgia, Kentucky, South Carolina, Tennessee and Vanderbilt).

Joining Div. I-A in 1992 (2): **1.** Independent ARKANSAS ST. (Div. I-AA Independent); **2.** NEVADA from Big Sky (Div. I-AA) to Big West.

Independents joining conferences in 1992 (3): **1.** AKRON to MAC; **2.** FLORIDA ST. to ACC; **3.** SOUTH CAROLINA to SEC-East.

Independents joining conferences in 1993 (5): **1.** ARKANSAS ST., **2.** LOUISIANA TECH, **3.** NORTHERN ILLINOIS and **4.** SW LOUISIANA all to Big West; **5.** PENN ST. to Big 10.

	Nickname	Conference	Head Coach	Location	Colors
Air Force	Falcons	WAC	Fisher DeBerry	Colo.Springs,CO	Blue/Silver
Akron	Zips	MAC	Gerry Faust	Akron,OH	Blue/Gold
Alabama	Crimson Tide	SEC-West	Gene Stallings	Tuscaloosa,AL	Crimson/White
Arizona	Wildcats	Pac-10	Dick Tomey	Tucson,AZ	Cardinal/Navy
Arizona St	Sun Devils	Pac-10	Bruce Snyder	Tempe,AZ	Maroon/Gold
Arkansas	Razorbacks	SEC-West	Jack Crowe	Fayetteville,AR	Cardinal/White
Arkansas St	Indians	Big West ('93)	Ray Perkins	State University,AR	Scarlet/Black

NCAA Division I-A Football Schools (Cont.)

	Nickname	Conference	Head Coach	Location	Colors
Army	Cadets	Independent	Bob Sutton	West Point,NY	Black/Gold/Gray
Auburn	Tigers	SEC-West	Pat Dye	Auburn,AL	Orange/Blue
Ball St	Cardinals	MAC	Paul Schudel	Muncie,IN	Cardinal/White
Baylor	Bears	SWC	Grant Teaff	Waco,TX	Green/Gold
Boston College	Eagles	Big East	Tom Coughlin	Chestnut Hill,MA	Maroon/Gold
Bowling Green	Falcons	MAC	Gary Blackney	Bowling Green,OH	Orange/Brown
BYU	Cougars	WAC	LaVell Edwards	Provo,UT	Royal Blue/White
California	Golden Bears	Pac-10	Keith Gilbertson	Berkeley,CA	Blue/Gold
CS-Fullerton	Titans	Big West	Gene Murphy	Fullerton,CA	Blue/Orange/White
Central Michigan	Chippewas	MAC	Herb Deromedi	Mt.Pleasant,MI	Maroon/Gold
Cincinnati	Bearcats	Independent	Tim Murphy	Cincinnati,OH	Red/Black
Clemson	Tigers	ACC	Ken Hatfield	Clemson,SC	Purple/Orange
Colorado	Buffaloes	Big 8	Bill McCartney	Boulder,CO	Silver/Gold/Black
Colorado St	Rams	WAC	Earle Bruce	Ft.Collins,CO	Green/Gold
Duke	Blue Devils	ACC	Barry Wilson	Durham,NC	Royal Blue/White
East Carolina	Pirates	Independent	Steve Logan	Greenville,NC	Purple/Gold
Eastern Michigan	Eagles	MAC	Jim Harkema	Ypsilanti,MI	Green/White
Florida	Gators	SEC-East	Steve Spurrier	Gainesville,FL	Orange/Blue
Florida St	Seminoles	AAC	Bobby Bowden	Tallahassee,FL	Garnet/Gold
Fresno St	Bulldogs	WAC	Jim Sweeney	Fresno,CA	Cardinal/Blue
Georgia	Bulldogs, 'Dawgs	SEC-East	Ray Goff	Athens,GA	Red/Black
Georgia Tech	Yellow Jackets	ACC	Bill Lewis	Atlanta,GA	Old Gold/White
Hawaii	Rainbows	WAC	Bob Wagner	Honolulu,HI	Green/White
Houston	Cougars	SWC	John Jenkins	Houston,TX	Scarlet/White
Illinois	Fighting Illini	Big 10	Lou Tepper	Champaign,IL	Orange/Blue
Indiana	Hoosiers	Big 10	Bill Mallory	Bloomington,IN	Cream/Crimson
Iowa	Hawkeyes	Big 10	Hayden Fry	Iowa City,IA	Old Gold/Black
Iowa St	Cyclones	Big 8	Jim Walden	Ames,IA	Cardinal/Gold
Kansas	Jayhawks	Big 8	Glen Mason	Lawrence,KS	Cimson/Blue
Kansas St	Wildcats	Big 8	Bill Snyder	Manhattan,KS	Purple/White
Kent	Golden Flashes	MaC	Pete Cordelli	Kent,OH	Navy Blue/Gold
Kentucky	Wildcats	SEC-East	Bill Curry	Lexington,KY	Blue/White
LSU	Fighting Tigers	SEC-West	Curley Hallman	Baton Rouge,LA	Purple/Gold
Louisiana Tech	Bulldogs	Big West ('93)	Joe Raymond Peace	Ruston,LA	Red/Blue
Louisville	Cardinals	Independent	H.Schnellenberger	Louisville,KY	Red/Black/White
Maryland	Terrapins, Terps	ACC	Mark Duffner	College Park,MD	Red/White/Black/Gold
Memphis St	Tigers	Independent	Chuck Stobart	Memphis,TN	Blue/Gray
Miami-FL	Hurricanes	Big East	Dennis Erickson	Miami,FL	Orange/Green/White
Miami-OH	Redskins	MAC	Randy Walker	Oxford,OH	Red/White
Michigan	Wolverines	Big 10	Gary Moeller	Ann Arbor,MI	Maize/Blue
Michigan St	Spartans	Big 10	George Perles	East Lansing,MI	Green/White
Minnesota	Golden Gophers	Big 10	Jim Wacker	Minneapolis,MN	Maroon/Gold
Mississippi	Ole Miss, Rebels	SEC-West	Billy Brewer	Oxford,MS	Cardinal/Navy Blue
Mississippi St	Bulldogs	SEC-West	Jackie Sherrill	Starkville,MS	Maroon/White
Missouri	Tigers	Big 8	Bob Stull	Columbia,MO	Old Gold/Black
Navy	Midshipmen	Independent	George Chaump	Annapolis,MD	Navy Blue/Gold
Nebraska	Cornhuskers	Big 8	Tom Osborne	Lincoln,NE	Scarlet/Cream
Nevada	Wolf Pack	Big West	Chris Ault	Reno,NV	Silver/Blue
New Mexico	Lobos	WAC	Dennis Franchione	Albuquerque,NM	Cherry/Silver
New Mexico St	Aggies	Big West	Jim Hess	Las Cruces,NM	Crimson/White
North Carolina	Tar Heels	ACC	Mark Brown	Chapel Hill,NC	Carolina Blue/White
North Carolina St	Wolfpack	ACC	Dick Sheridan	Raleigh,NC	Red/White
Northern Illinois	Huskies	Big West ('93)	Charlie Sadler	De Kalb,IL	Cardinal/Black
Northwestern	Wildcats	Big 10	Gary Barnett	Evanston,IL	Purple/White
Notre Dame	Fighting Irish	Independent	Lou Holtz	South Bend,IN	Gold/Blue
Ohio St	Buckeyes	Big 10	John Cooper	Columbus,OH	Scarlet/Gray
Ohio University	Bobcats	MAC	Tom Lichtenberg	Athens,OH	Kelly Green/White
Oklahoma	Sooners	Big 8	Gary Gibbs	Norman,OK	Crimson/Cream
Oklahoma St	Cowboys	Big 8	Pat Jones	Stillwater,OK	Orange/Black
Oregon	Ducks	Pac-10	Rich Brooks	Eugene,OR	Green/Yellow
Oregon St	Beavers	Pac-10	Jerry Pettibone	Corvallis,OR	Orange/Black
Pacific	Tigers	Big West	Chuck Shelton	Stockton,CA	Orange/Black
Penn St	Nittany Lions	Big 10 ('93)	Joe Paterno	University Park,PA	Blue/White
Pittsburgh	Panthers	Big East	Paul Hackett	Pittsburgh,PA	Blue/Gold
Purdue	Boilermakers	Big 10	Jim Colletto	West Lafayette,IN	Old Gold/Black

	Nickname	Conference	Head Coach	Location	Colors
Rice	Owls	SWC	Fred Goldsmith	Houston,TX	Blue/Gray
Rutgers	Scarlet Knights	Big East	Doug Graber	New Brunswick,NJ	Scarlet
San Diego St	Aztecs	WAC	Al Luginbill	San Diego, CA	Scarlet/Black
San Jose St	Spartans	Big West	Ron Turner	San Jose, CA	Gold/White/Blue
South Carolina	Gamecocks	SEC-East	Sparky Woods	Columbia, SC	Garnet/Black
SMU	Mustangs	SWC	Tom Rossley	Dallas, TX	Red/Blue
Southern Miss	Golden Eagles	Independent	Jeff Bower	Hattiesburg, MS	Black/Gold
SW Louisiana	Ragin' Cajuns	Big West ('93)	Nelson Stokley	Lafayette, LA	Vermilion/White
Stanford	Cardinal	Pac-10	Bill Walsh	Stanford, CA	Cardinal/White
Syracuse	Orangemen	Big East	Paul Pasqualoni	Syracuse, NY	Orange
Temple	Owls	Big East	Jerry Berndt	Philadelphia,PA	Cherry/White
Tennessee	Volunteers	SEC-East	Johnny Majors	Knoxville,TN	Orange/White
Texas	Longhorns	SWC	John Mackovic	Austin,TX	Burnt Orange/White
Texas A&M	Aggies	SWC	R.C.Slocum	College Station,TX	Maroon/White
TCU	Horned Frogs	SWC	Pat Sullivan	Ft.Worth,TX	Purple/White
Texas Tech	Red Raiders	SWC	Spike Dykes	Lubbock,TX	Scarlet/Black
Toledo	Rockets	MAC	Gary Pinkel	Toledo,OH	Blue/Gold
Tulane	Green Wave	Independent	Buddy Teevens	New Orleans,LA	Olive Green/Sky Blue
Tulsa	Golden Hurricane	Independent	Dave Rader	Tulsa,OK	Blue/Gold
UCLA	Bruins	Pac-10	Terry Donahue	Los Angeles,CA	Blue/Gold
UNLV	Runnin' Rebels	Big West	Jim Strong	Las Vegas,NV	Scarlet/Gray
USC	Trojans	Pac-10	Larry Smith	Los Angeles,CA	Cardinal/Gold
Utah	Utes	WAC	Ron McBride	Salt Lake City,UT	Crimson/White
Utah St	Aggies	Big West	Charlie Weatherbie	Logan,UT	Navy Blue/White
UTEP	Miners	WAC	David Lee	El Paso,TX	Orange/White/Blue
Vanderbilt	Commodores	SEC-East	Gerry DiNardo	Nashville,TN	Black/Gold
Virginia	Cavaliers	ACC	George Welsh	Charlottesville,VA	Orange/Blue
Virginia Tech	Hokies, Gobblers	Big East	Frank Beamer	Blacksburg,VA	Orange/Maroon
Wake Forest	Demon Deacons	ACC	Bill Dooley	Winston-Salem,NC	Old Gold/Black
Washington	Huskies	Pac-10	Don James	Seattle,WA	Purple/Gold
Washington St	Cougars	Pac-10	Mike Price	Pullman,WA	Crimson/Gray
West Virginia	Mountaineers	Big East	Don Nehle	Morgantown,WV	Old Gold/Blue
Western Michigan	Broncos	MAC	Al Molde	Kalamazoo,MI	Brown/Gold
Wisconsin	Badgers	Big 10	Barry Alvarez	Madison,WI	Cardinal/White
Wyoming	Cowboys	WAC	Joe Tiller	Laramie,WY	Brown/Yellow

NCAA Division I-AA Football Schools
Conferences and coaches as of Aug. 15, 1992.

Leaving Div. I-AA in 1992 (2): **1.** Independent ARKANSAS ST. to Div. I-A; **2.** NEVADA from Big Sky to Big West (Div. I-A).

Joining Div. I-AA in 1992: TENNESSEE-MARTIN from Gulf South (Div. II) to Ohio Valley.

Independent joining conference in 1992: GEORGIA SOUTHERN to Southern.

Independents joining conference in 1993 (3): **1.** JAMES MADISON, **2.** NORTHEASTERN and **3.** WILLIAM & MARY all to Yankee.

	Nickname	Conference	Head Coach	Location	Colors
Alabama St	Hornets	Southwestern	Houston Markham	Montgomery,AL	Black/Gold
Alcorn St	Braves	Southwestern	Cardell Jones	Lorman,MS	Purple/Gold
Appalachian St	Mountaineers	Southern	Jerry Moore	Boone,NC	Black/Gold
Austin Peay St	Governors	Ohio Valley	Roy Gregory	Clarksville,TN	Red/White
Bethune-Cookman	Wildcats	Mid-Eastern	Sylvester Collins	Daytona Beach,FL	Maroon/Gold
Boise St	Broncos	Big Sky	Skip Hall	Boise,ID	Orange/Blue
Boston University	Terriers	Yankee	Dan Allen	Boston,MA	Scarlet/White
Brown	Bears	Ivy	Mickey Kwiatkowski	Providence,RI	Brown/Red/White
Bucknell	Bison	Patriot	Lou Maranzana	Lewisburg,PA	Orange/Blue
Central Florida	Knights	Independent	Gene McDowell	Orlando,FL	Black/Gold
The Citadel	Bulldogs	Southern	Charlie Taaffe	Charleston SC	Blue/White
Colgate	Red Raiders	Patriot	Mike Foley	Hamilton,NY	Maroon/White
Columbia	Lions	Ivy	Ray Tellier	New York,NY	Lt.Blue/White
Connecticut	Huskies	Yankee	Tom Jackson	Storrs,CT	Blue/White
Cornell	Big Red	Ivy	Jim Hofher	Ithaca,NY	Red/White
Dartmouth	Big Green	Ivy	John Lyons	Hanover,NH	Green/White
Delaware	Blue Hens	Yankee	Tubby Raymond	Newark,DE	Blue/Gold
Delaware St	Hornets	Mid-Eastern	Bill Collick	Dover,DE	Red/Blue
East Tenn.St	Buccaneers	Southern	Mike Cavan	Johnson City,TN	Blue/Gold
Eastern Illinois	Panthers	Gateway	Bob Spoo	Charleston,IL	Blue/Gray
Eastern Kentucky	Colonels	Ohio Valley	Roy Kidd	Richmond,KY	Maroon/White
Eastern Washington	Eagles	Big Sky	Dick Zornes	Cheney,WA	Red/White

NCAA Division I-AA Football Schools (Cont.)

	Nickname	Conference	Head Coach	Location	Colors
Florida A&M	Rattlers	Mid-Eastern	Ken Riley	Tallahassee,FL	Orange/Green
Fordham	Rams	Patriot	Larry Glueck	New York,NY	Maroon/White
Furman	Paladins	Southern	Jim Satterfield	Greenville,SC	Purple/White
Georgia Southern	Eagles	Southern	Tim Stowers	Statesboro,GA	Blue/White
Grambling St	Tigers	Southwestern	Eddie Robinson	Grambling,LA	Black/Gold
Harvard	Crimson	Ivy	Joe Restic	Cambridge,MA	Crimson/Black/White
Holy Cross	Crusaders	Patriot	Peter Vaas	Worcester,MA	Royal Purple
Howard	Bison	Mid-Eastern	Steve Wilson	Washington,DC	Blue/White
Idaho	Vandals	Big Sky	John L.Smith	Moscow,ID	Silver/Gold
Idaho St.	Bengals	Big Sky	Brian McNeely	Pocatello,ID	Orange/Black
Illinois St	Redbirds	Gateway	Jim Heacock	Normal,IL	Red/White
Indiana St	Sycamores	Gateway	Dennis Raetz	Terre Haute,IN	Blue/White
Jackson St	Tigers	Southwestern	James Carson	Jackson,MS	Blue/White
James Madison	Dukes	Yankee ('93)	Rip Scherer	Harrisonburg,VA	Purple/Gold
Lafayette	Leopards	Patriot	Bill Russo	Easton,PA	Maroon/White
Lehigh	Engineers	Patriot	Hank Small	Bethlehem,PA	Brown/White
Liberty	Flames	Independent	Sam Rutigliano	Lynchburg,VA	Red/White/Blue
Maine	Black Bears	Yankee	Kirk Ferentz	Orono,ME	Blue/White
Marshall	Thundering Herd	Southern	Jim Donnan	Huntington,WV	Green/White
Massachusetts	Minutemen	Yankee	Mike Hodges	Amherst,MA	Maroon/White
McNeese St	Cowboys	Southland	Bobby Keasler	Lake Charles,LA	Blue/Gold
Middle Tenn.St.	Blue Raiders	Ohio Valley	Boots Donnelly	Murfreesboro,TN	Blue/White
Miss.Valley St	Delta Devils	Southwestern	Larry Dorsey	Itta Bena,MS	Green/White
Montana	Grizzlies	Big Sky	Don Read	Missoula,MT	Copper/Silver/Gold
Montana St.	Bobcats	Big Sky	Cliff Hysell	Bozeman,MT	Blue/Gold
Morehead St	Eagles	Ohio Valley	Cole Proctor	Morehead,KY	Blue/Gold
Morgan St	Bears	Mid-Eastern	Ricky Diggs	Baltimore,MD	Blue/Orange
Murray St	Racers	Ohio Valley	Mike Mahoney	Murray,KY	Blue/Gold
New Hampshire	Wildcats	Yankee	Bill Bowes	Durham,NH	Blue/White
Nicholls St	Colonels	Southland	Phil Greco	Thibodaux,LA	Red/Gray
North Carolina A&T	Aggies	Mid-Eastern	Bill Hayes	Greensboro,NC	Blue/Gold
North Texas	Mean Green	Southland	Dennis Parker	Denton,TX	Green/White
NE Louisiana	Indians	Southland	Dave Roberts	Monroe,LA	Maroon/Gold
Northeastern	Huskies	Yankee ('93)	Barry Gallup	Boston,MA	Red/Black
Northern Arizona	Lumberjacks	Big Sky	Steve Axman	Flagstaff,AZ	Blue/Gold
Northern Iowa	Panthers	Gateway	Terry Allen	Cedar Falls,IA	Purple/Old Gold
Northwestern St	Demons	Southland	Sam Goodwin	Natchitoches LA	Purple/White
Pennsylvania	Quakers	Ivy	Al Bagnoli	Philadelphia,PA	Red/Blue
Prairie View A&M	Panthers	Southwestern	Ron Beard	Prairie View,TX	Purple/Gold
Princeton	Tigers	Ivy	Steve Tosches	Ptinceton,NJ	Orange/Black
Rhode Island	Rams	Yankee	Bob Griffin	Kingston,RI	Blue/White
Richmond	Spiders	Yankee	Jim Marshall	Richmond,VA	Red/Blue
Sam Houston St	Bearkats	Southland	Ron Randleman	Huntsville, TX	Orange/White/Blue
Samford	Bulldogs	Independent	Terry Bowden	Birmingham,AL	Crimson/Blue
South Carolina St	Bulldogs	Mid Eastern	Willie Jeffries	Orangeburg,SC	Garnet/Blue
SE Missouri St	Indians	Ohio Valley	John Mumford	Cape Girardeau,MO	Red/Black
Southern Illinois	Salukis	Gateway	Bob Smith	Cardondale,IL	Maroon/White
Southern-BR	Jaguars	Southwestern	Marino Casem	Baton Rouge,LA	Blue/Gold
SW Missouri St.	Bears	Gateway	Jesse Branch	Springfield,MO	Maroon/White
SW Texas St	Bobcats	Southland	Jim Bob Helduser	San Marcos,TX	Maroon/Gold
S.F.Austin St	Lumberjacks	Southland	John Pearce	Nacogdoches,TX	Purple/White
Tenn-Chattanooga	Moccasins	Southern	Buddy Nix	Chattanooga,TN	Navy Blue/Gold
Tenn-Martin	Pacers	Ohio Valley	Don McLeary	Martin,TN	Orange/White/Blue
Tennessee St	Tigers	Ohio Valley	Joe Gilliam,Sr.	Nashville,TN	Blue/White
Tennessee Tech	Golden Eagles	Ohio Valley	Jim Ragland	Cookeville,TN	Purple/Gold
Texas Southern	Tigers	Southwestern	Walter Highsmith	Houston,TX	Maroon/Gray
Towson St	Tigers	Independent	Gordy Combs	Towson,MD	Gold/White
Villanova	Wildcats	Yankee	Andy Talley	Villanova,PA	Blue/White
VMI	Keydets	Southern	Jim Shuck	Lexington,VA	Red/White/Yellow
Weber St	Wildcats	Big Sky	Dave Arslanian	Ogden,UT	Royal Purple/White
Western Carolina	Catamounts	Southern	Steve Hodgin	Cullowhee,NC	Purple/Gold
Western Illinois	Leathernecks	Gateway	Randy Ball	Macomb,IL	Purple/Gold
Western Kentucky	Hilltoppers	Independent	Jack Harbaugh	Bowling Green,KY	Red/White
William & Mary	Tribe	Yankee ('93)	Jimmye Laycock	Williamsburg,VA	Green/Gold
Yale	Bulldogs, Elis	Ivy	Carmen Cozza	New Haven,CT	Yale Blue/White
Youngstown St	Penguins	Independent	Jim Tressel	Youngstown,OH	Scarlet/White

USA Today Division I All-Sports Rankings

Unofficial men's and women's national rankings, compiled by Steve Williams for *USA Today* and released June 18, 1992. NCAA Division I athletic programs are ranked according to 1991-92 performance in 10 leading sports (based on participation). Points based on 20 for a national championship, 19 for runner-up, etc. Where Top 20 finishers in any sport were unavailable (football, basketball, tennis, etc.) CNN/*USA Today* coaches' final polls were used.

MEN

		Conf.	Cross-country	Soccer	Football	Wrestling	Swimming	Basketball	Tennis	Outdoor Track	Golf	Baseball	TOTAL
1	UCLA	Pac-10	0	16	3	0	18	14½	17½	12½	0	0	**81½**
2	Arkansas	SEC	20	0	0	0	0	10	4	20	13	0	**67**
	Texas	SWC	14	0	0	0	19	0	2	0	15	17	**67**
4	Florida	SEC	0	0	13	0	12	0	9	10½	14	8	**66½**
5	Arizona	Pac-10	16½	0	0	0	16	4	0	0	20	4	**60½**
6	Michigan	Big 10	15	0	15	0	11	19	0	0	0	0	**60**
7	USC	Pac-10	0	0	0	0	14	9	17½	18	0	0	**58½**
8	Oklahoma St	Big 8	0	0	0	19	0	11	0	0	18	10	**58**
	Stanford	Pac-10	0	0	0	0	20	0	20	0	12	6	**58**
10	Wisconsin	Big 10	18	11	0	14	0	0	0	7	3	0	**53**

Others in Top 30 standings: 11. Miami-FL (52 points); **12.** Ohio St.(50½); **13.** California (47½); **14.** Penn St.(47); **15.** Indiana (44); **16.** N.C.State (43); **17.** Arizona St.(41); **18.** Iowa (39); **19.** Florida St.(38½); **20.** Tennessee (38); **21.** Oklahoma (37½); **22.** LSU (37); **23.** Iowa St.(36); **24.** Notre Dame (35); **25.** Clemson (34); **26.** Georgia Tech (30½); **27.** Pepperdine (30); **28.** Kentucky (29½); **29.** Alabama (29); **30.** Georgia (28½).

WOMEN

		Conf.	Field Hockey	Soccer	Cross-country	Volleyball	Swimming	Basketball	Tennis	Golf	Softball	Outdoor Track	TOTAL
1	Stanford	Pac-10	0	16	0	16	20	20	17½	0	17	17	**123½**
2	UCLA	Pac-10	0	0	0	20	15	3	14	20	16	0	**88**
3	Arizona	Pac-10	0	0	10	0	16	0	12	19	19	7½	**83½**
4	Texas	SWC	0	0	0	8	19	0	19	0	15	11	**72**
5	Florida	SEC	0	0	0	13	18	0	20	0	0	19	**70**
6	North Carolina	ACC	19	20	0	0	7	0	0	0	13	9	**68**
7	Georgia	SEC	0	0	1	7	12	0	16	0	18	0	**54**
8	Wisconsin	Big 10	0	19	14½	0	0	0	0	0	0	11	**44½**
9	Virginia	ACC	5½	17½	3	0	0	17½	0	0	0	0	**43½**
10	California	Pac-10	0	0	0	0	10	0	15	15½	0	0	**40½**
	Massachusetts	Atl.10	12	11	0	0	0	0	0	17½	0	0	**40½**

Others in Top 30 standings: 12. Nebraska (39 points); **13.** Arizona St. and LSU (37½); **15.** Penn St.(37); **16.** Tennessee (35½); **17.** Miami-FL (35); **18.** Long Beach St. and USC (34½); **20.** Iowa and Maryland (32½); **22.** Duke (30½); **23.** BYU and SMU (30); **25.** N.C.State (28); **26.** San Jose St. and Villanova (26); **28.** UNLV (25½); **29.** Oklahoma St.(24½); **30.** Indiana (24).

1991-92 NCAA Team Champions

Stanford won a total of five Division I national championships during the 1991-92 season, the most since fellow Pac-10 member UCLA won five in 1981-82. The Cardinal won its fourth men's tennis title in five years and 12th overall, while also taking men's gymnastics, women's basketball and sweeping men's and women's swimming.

Arkansas and Division III **Trenton State** of New Jersey won three national titles apiece. The running Razorbacks won in men's cross-country, indoor track and outdoor track, while the Lions took titles in women's field hockey, lacrosse and softball.

The state of California brought home 18 championships, led by Stanford, **Pepperdine** (baseball and men's volleyball) and **UCLA** (softball and women's volleyball). New York State was runner-up with seven overall titles. Otherwise, **Iowa** and **Kenyon** claimed their 13th titles in Div. I wrestling and Div. III men's swimming, respectively.

FALL

Overall titles in parentheses.

Cross-country

Men's Division I .... Arkansas (5)
Division II .... Lowell, MA (1)
Division III.................. Rochester, NY (1)

Women's Division I .... Villanova (3)
Division II .... Cal Poly-SLO (10)
Division III .... Wisconsin-Oshkosh (3)

1991-92 NCAA Team Champions (Cont.)

FALL

Field Hockey

Women's Division I .... Old Dominion (6)
      Division III .... Trenton St., NJ (6)

Football

Men's Division I-A .... AP: Miami-FL (4)
      Coaches: Washington (1)
      Division I-AA .... Youngstown St., OH (1)
      Division II .... Pittsburg St., KS (1)
      Division III .... Ithaca, NY (3)
Note: There is no official NCAA Div.I-A playoff.

Soccer

Men's Division I .... Virginia (2)
      Division II .... Florida Tech (2)
      Division III .... UC-San Diego (2)

Women's Division I .... North Carolina (9)
      Division II ...... Cal St-Dominguez Hills (1)
      Division III .... Ithaca, NY (2)

Volleyball

Women's Division I .... UCLA (3)
      Division II .... West Texas St. (2)
      Division III .... Washington, MO (2)

Water Polo

Men's Champion .... California (10)

WINTER
Overall titles in parentheses.

Basketball

Men's Division I .... Duke (2)
      Division II .... Virginia Union (2)
      Division III .... Calvin, MI (1)

Women's Division I .... Stanford (2)
      Division II .... Delta St., MS (3)
      Division III .... Alma, MI (1)

Fencing

Men/Women Combined .... Columbia-Barnard (1)

Gymnastics

Men's Champion....................... Stanford (1)

Women's Champion........................ Utah (7)

Ice Hockey

Men's Division I .... Lake Superior St. (2)
      Division III .... Plattsburgh St., NY (2)

Rifle

Men/Women Combined............ West Virginia (8)

Skiing

Men/Women Combined .... Vermont (4)

Swimming & Diving

Men's Division I .... Stanford (5)
      Division II .... Cal St-Bakersfield (7)
      Division III .... Kenyon, OH (13)

Women's Division I .... Stanford (3)
      Division II .... Oakland, MI (3)
      Division III .... Kenyon, OH (9)

Indoor Track

Men's Division I .... Arkansas (9)
      Division II .... St.Augustine's, NC (6)
      Division III .... Wisconsin-La Crosse (4)

Women's Division I .... Florida (1)
      Division II .... Alabama A&M (1)
      Division III ..... Christopher Newport, VA (4)

Wrestling

Men's Division I .... Iowa (13)
      Division II .... Central Oklahoma (1)
      Division III .... Brockport St., NY (5)

SPRING
Overall titles in parentheses.

Baseball

Men's Division I .... Pepperdine (1)
      Division II .... Tampa, FL (1)
      Division III .... William Paterson, NJ (1)

Golf

Men's Division I .... Arizona (1)
      Division II .... Columbus, GA (4)
      Division III .... Methodist, NC (3)

Women's Champion .... San Jose St. (3)

Lacrosse

Men's Division I .... Princeton (1)
      Division III .... Nazareth, NY (1)

Women's Division I .... Maryland (2)
      Division III............... Trenton St., NJ (5)

Softball

Women's Division I .... UCLA (7)
      Division II .... Missouri Southern St. (1)
      Division III............... Trenton St., NJ (4)

Tennis

Men's Division I .... Stanford (12)
      Division II .... UC-Davis (7)
      Division III............... Kalamazoo, MI (6)

Women's Division I .... Florida (1)
      Division II .... Cal Poly-Pomona (2)
      Division III........... Pomona-Pitzer, CA (1)

Outdoor Track

Men's Division I .... Arkansas (2)
      Division II .... St.Augustine's, NC (4)
      Division III .... Wisconsin-La Crosse (3)

Women's Division I .... LSU (6)
      Division II .... Alabama A&M (1)
      Division III ..... Christopher Newport, VA (4)

Volleyball

Men's Champion .... Pepperdine (4)

NCAA Schools on Probation

As of Aug. 1, 1992, there were 22 member institutions serving NCAA probations.

School (Division)	Sport	Yrs	Penalty To End	School (Division)	Sport	Yrs	Penalty To End
Florida (I)	Football	2	9/24/92	Maryland (I)	Basketball	3	8/3/93
	& Basketball	2	9/24/92	Tulane (1)	Tennis	2	8/23/93
Missouri (I)	Basketball	2	11/7/92	Tennessee (I-A)	Football	2	9/23/93
Oklahoma St.(I-A)	Football	4	1/9/93	Northwestern St.(I)	Basketball	3	10/5/93
	& Wrestling	4	1/9/93	Texas A&M (I)	Basketball	2	11/11/93
Miami-OH (I)	Basketball	2	1/17/93	Illinois (I)	Basketball	3	11/12/93
Hampton (II)	Football	2	2/1/93	Auburn (I)	Basketball	2	11/22/93
Lowell (I)	Ice Hockey	2	3/21/93		& Tennis	2	11/22/93
Michigan (I)	Baseball	2	3/26/93	Howard (I)	Football	2	12/25/93
Minnesota (I)	Basketball	2	3/29/93	Dist.of Columbia (II)	Football	3	9/25/94
	Football	2	3/29/93		& W.Basketball	3	9/25/94
	& Wrestling	2	3/29/93	SE Louisiana (I)	Basketball	5	10/2/94
Houston Baptist (I)	M/W Gymnastics	3	4/2/93	UTEP (I)	Basketball	3	10/30/94
Pacific (I)	Basketball	2	4/3/93	Upsala (III)	Basketball	5	9/7/95

Violations & Sanctions

In alphabetical order.

Auburn—VIOLATIONS: improper transportation; extra benefits; improper recruiting contacts; entertainment and inducements; coaching staff limitations; unethical conduct; certification of compliance. SANCTIONS: 2-year probations for both men's basketball and men's tennis; no 1992 postseason for basketball and no 1991 postseason for tennis; maximum 14 grants for 1990-91 and 12 grants for 1992-93 for basketball; maximum 4 grants for both 1990-91 and 1991-92 for tennis; maximum one coaching staff member may recruit off-campus for basketball in 1992; head basketball coach may not recruit off-campus during 1992 signing period; maximum 7 official visits for basketball in 1992; no official visits for tennis in 1992; assistant basketball coach's salary frozen for 16 months, he was reassigned for one year and cannot be replaced; reprimanded head basketball coach and another assistant coach; institution prohibited from employing volunteer or graduate assistant coaches in 1991-92 or restricted earnings coaches in 1992-93 for basketball; recertification; annual compliance reports; show cause why disciplinary action should not be taken if any member institution hires former assistant basketball coach during next 2 years and former head tennis coach during next 5 years; disassociated two representatives.

District of Columbia—VIOLATIONS: improper financial aid and transportation; extra benefits; eligibility; institutional control. SANCTIONS: 3-year probation for men's football and women's basketball; accepted institutional action to suspend football program for 1990 and '91 seasons and women's basketball during 1989-90 and for 1990-91 seasons; recertification; annual compliance reports; forfeited all contests and deleted team and individual records in which ineligible student-athletes participated.

Florida—VIOLATIONS: improper transportation; extra benefits; improper recruiting transportation; eligibility; unethical conduct; certification of compliance. SANCTIONS: 2-year probation for both programs; no 1990-91 postseason for football; maximum 13 grants for 1991-92 and 14 grants for 1992-93 in basketball; returned revenue from 1988 basketball championship; deleted team and individual records for 1987 and '88 basketball championships; recertification; annual compliance reports; show cause why disciplinary action should not be taken if any member institution hires former head football and basketball coaches during next 5 years.

Hampton—VIOLATIONS: eligibility; institutional control. SANCTIONS: 2-year probation; no 1991 postseason; forfeited all victories for 1986 and '87; recertification.

Houston Baptist—VIOLATIONS: improper transportation; improper recruiting entertainment and lodging; tryouts; unethical conduct; institutional control. SANCTIONS: 3-year probation for both men's and women's teams; no 1989-90 and 1990-91 postseason for men; no initial grants for 1990-91 and 1991-92 and no increase in percentage of aid for 1990-91 and 1991-92 for men; deleted team and individual records for 1987,'88,'89 men's championships; annual audits; no participation in or support for participation in outside club competition for 1990-91 and 1991-92 for men; show cause why more penalties should not be imposed if institution does not prohibit head coach from all coaching and athletically related responsibilities until July 1, 1991 and off-campus recruiting until Dec. 15, 1991.

Howard—VIOLATIONS: improper financial aid; improper administration of financial aid; eligibility; institutional control. SANCTIONS: 2-year probation for football; no 1992 postseason; maximum 65 grants to 88 individuals in 1992-93 and 63 grants to 88 individuals in for 1993-94; maximum 60 official visits in 1992-93; recertification; annual compliance reports; show cause why disciplinary action should not be taken if the former head coach's present institution does not take action against the coach.

Illinois—VIOLATIONS: improper financial aid; extra benefits; complimentary tickets; improper recruiting contacts, inducements and lodging; institutional control. SANCTIONS: 3-year probation; no 1990-91 postseason; maximum 2 initial grants for 1991-92 and 1992-93; no off-campus recruiting for 1991, and only head coach and one assistant coach may recruit for 1992; no official visits for 1991; recertification; annual compliance reports; show cause why more penalties should not be imposed if institution does not disassociate one representative; head coach and 2 assistant coaches salaries frozen until May 1, 1991, and they may not receive bonuses; placed one assistant coach on probation for 2 years; one assistant coach prohibited from recruiting for 2 years.

Lowell—VIOLATIONS: improper financial aid and lodging; extra benefits; improper recruiting contact, entertainment, inducements, lodging and transportation;

NCAA Schools on Probation (Cont.)
Violations & Sanctions

unethical conduct; institutional control. SANCTIONS: 2-year probation; no 1991-92 postseason; recertification; annual compliance reports; required self-study; show cause why disciplinary action should not be taken if any member institution hires former head coach during next 5 years.

Maryland—VIOLATIONS: improper transportation; extra benefits; complimentary tickets; improper recruiting contacts, inducements and transportation; unethical conduct; institutional control. SANCTIONS: 3-year probation; no 1990-91 and 1991-92 postseason; no 1990-91 TV games; maximum 13 grants for 1990-91 and 1991-92; returned revenue from 1988 championship; deleted team and individual records from '88 championship; recertification; annual compliance reports; show cause why more penalties should not be imposed if institution does not disassociate 2 representatives; show cause why disciplinary action should not be taken if any member institution hires former head coach, graduate assistant and part-time assistant coaches and administrative assistant during next 5 years.

Miami-OH—VIOLATIONS: academic fraud; eligibility; unethical conduct. SANCTIONS: 2-year probation; deleted team and individual records and forfeited all contests in which ineligibile student-athlete participated; recertification; annual compliance reports; show cause why disciplinary action should not be taken if any member institution hires former head coach during next 3 years.

Michigan—VIOLATIONS: improper employment; entertainment, financial aid and transportation; extra benefits; improper recruiting contact, entertainment, inducements, lodging and transportation; tryouts; excessive number of official visits; unethical conduct; institutional control. SANCTIONS: 2-year probation; no 1990-91 and 1991-92 postseason; no 1990-91 and 1991-92 TV games; no initial grants for 1990-91; maximum 10 total grants for 1991-92 and 11 for 1992-93; no off-campus recruiting through Aug.31, 1990; no expense-paid visits for 1989-90; eliminated one coaching position; returned revenue from 6 championships (1984-89); deleted team and individual records for those championships; recertification; show cause why disciplinary action should not be taken if any member institution hires former head coach during next 5 years.

Minnesota—VIOLATIONS: improper employment, entertainment, financial aid and transportation; extra benefits; improper recruiting contacts, employment, lodging and inducements; tryouts; eligibility; institutional control. SANCTIONS: 2-year probation for all 3 programs; no 1991-92 postseason for football; maximum 14 grants for 1991-92 basketball; no initial grants for 1990-91 wrestling; no off-campus recruiting by head basketball coach during January, 1991, evaluation period; no off-campus recruiting in wrestling until after 1990-91 championship; head basketball and wrestling coaches placed on probation through 1990-91; head wrestling coach's salary frozen for 1990-91; recertification; annual compliance reports; wrestling team shall operate separately from outside wrestling club involved in case.

Missouri—VIOLATIONS: improper entertainment, lodging and transportation; extra benefits; improper recruiting contacts, employment, entertainment, inducements, lodging and transportation; eligibility; unethical conduct; institutional control. SANCTIONS: 2-year probation; no 1990-91 postseason; maximum one initial grant for 1991-92 and 2 for 1992-93; maximum one coach may recruit off campus in 1991; no official visits in 1991; annual compliance reports.

Northwestern St.—VIOLATIONS: improper employment, financial aid and transportation; extra benefits;

improper recruiting contacts, entertainment, inducements and transportation; tryouts; academic fraud; eligibility; unethical conduct; institutional control; certification of compliance. SANCTIONS: 3-year probation; no 1990-91 and 1991-92 postseason; no 1990-91 TV games; maximum 13 grants for 1990-91; maximum 2 initial grants for 1991-92 and 3 for 1992-93; maximum 8 official visits for 1990-91 and 12 for 1991-92; limit coaching staff to head coach, one assistant coach and one graduate assistant coach for probationary period; recertification; annual compliance reports; show cause why disciplinary action should not be taken if any member institution hires former head coach during next 15 years, former volunteer coach during next 7 years and 2 former assistant coaches during next 5 years.

Oklahoma St.—VIOLATIONS: improper financial aid and transportation; extra benefits; improper recruiting contacts, employment, entertainment, inducements, lodging and transportation; eligibility; improper administration of financial aid; unethical conduct; institutional control; certification of compliance. SANCTIONS: 4-year probation; no 1989-90, 1990-91 and 1991-92 postseason; no 1989-90 and 1990-91 TV games; maximum 20 initial grants for 1989-90, 1990-91 and 1991-92; maximum 50 official visits for 1989-90 and 1990-91; recertification; annual compliance reports; show cause why more penalties should not be imposed if institution does not disassociate 14 representatives; show cause why disciplinary action should not be taken if any member institution hires one former assistant coach during next 12 years.

Pacific—VIOLATIONS: improper transportation; extra benefits; improper recruiting transportation; unethical conduct. SANCTIONS: 2-year probation; maximum 14 total grants for 1991-92 and 13 for 1992-93; recertification; show cause why disciplinary action should not be taken if any member institution hires former assistant coach, former director of athletics or former business manager during next 5 years.

SE Louisiana—VIOLATIONS: improper employment; extra benefits; improper recruiting entertainment, inducements and transportation; tryouts; unethical conduct; institutional control; certification of compliance. SANCTIONS: 5-year probation; accepted action to suspend program until at least 1990-91; annual compliance reports; required self-study; show cause why disciplinary action should not be taken if any member institution hires one former assistant coach during next 5 years.

Tennessee—VIOLATIONS: improper recruiting contacts and transportation; unethical conduct; certification of compliance. SANCTIONS: 2-year probation for football; maximum 85 grants for both 1992-93 and 1993-94; recertification; annual compliance reports; show cause why disciplinary action should not be taken if any member institution hires former assistant coach during next 3 years.

Texas A&M—VIOLATIONS: improper recruiting contacts, inducement and transportation; unethical conduct. SANCTIONS: 2-year probation for men's basketball; no postseason for 1992; maximum 2 initial grants for 1992-93; no off-campus recruiting for spring of 1992; maximum 8 official visits for 1992; recertification; annual compliance reports; show cause why disciplinary action should not be taken if any member institution hires former head coach or former assistant coach during next 2 years.

Upsala—VIOLATIONS: improper employment, entertainment and financial aid; extra benefits; out-of-season practice; improper recruiting inducements; institutional control; certification of compliance.

SANCTIONS: 5-year probation; no 1990-91, 1991-92 and 1992-93 postseasons; maximum 22 contests for 1990-91; no representative may recruit; deleted team and individual records for 1986 championship; annual compliance reports; disassociated one representative; show cause why more penalties should not be imposed if institution does not disassociate another representative.

UTEP—VIOLATIONS: improper lodging and transportation (to enroll); improper recruiting contacts, inducements, lodging and transportation; extra benefits; institutional control. SANCTIONS: 3-year probation for men's basketball; maximum 2 initial grants for both 1992-93 and 1993-94; maximum 8 official visits for 1992; recertification; annual compliance reports.

Major Coaching Changes

New head coaches were named at 31 Division I basketball schools after the 1991-92 season and at 17 Division I-A football schools following the 1991 season. Coaching changes listed below are as of Aug. 15, 1992.

Division I Basketball

School	Old Coach	Record	Why Left?	New Coach	Old Job
Alabama	Wimp Sanderson	26- 9	Resigned	David Hobbs	Asst., Alabama
Baylor	Gene Iba	13-15	Fired	Darrel Johnson	Coach, Okla.City
CS-Fullerton	John Sneed	12-16	Fired	Brad Holland	Asst., UCLA
CS-Sacramento	Joe Anders	4-24	Fired	Don Newman	Asst., Wash.St.
Canisius	Marty Marbach	8-22	Fired	John Beilein	Coach, Le Moyne
The Citadel	Randy Nesbit	10-18	Fired	Pat Dennis	Asst., Richmond
Eastern Kentucky	Mike Pollio	19-14	Resigned	Mike Calhoun	Asst., Eastern Ky.
Hartford	Jack Phelan	6-21	Resigned	Paul Brazeau	Asst., Ohio St.
Kent	Jim McDonald	9-19	Resigned	Dave Grube	Asst., Kent
Loyola-CA	Jay Hillock	15-13	Fired	John Olive	Asst., Villanova
Manhattan	Steve Lappas	25- 9	to Villanova	Fran Fraschilla	Asst., Providence
MD-Eastern Shore	Robert Hopkins & Bobby Wilkerson	3-25	Interim	Rob Chavez	Coach, Chemeketa Jr.C.
Mississippi	Ed Murphy	11-17	Resigned	Rob Evans	Asst., Oklahoma St.
Navy	Pete Herrmann	6-22	Fired	Don DeVoe	Coach, Florida (1989-90)
New Hampshire	Jim Boylan	7-21	Fired	Gib Chapman	AD, New Hampshire
Oregon	Don Monson	6-21	Fired	Jerry Green	Asst., Kansas
Rice	Scott Thompson	20-11	to Wichita St.	Willis Wilson	Asst., Stanford
St.Bonaventure	Tom Chapman	9-19	Fired	Jim Baron	Coach, St.Francis-PA
St.Francis-PA	Jim Baron	13-16	to St.Bonaventure	TBA	—
St.John's	Lou Carnesecca	19-11	Retired	Brian Mahoney	Asst., St.John's
St.Louis	Rich Grawer	5-23	Fired	Charlie Spoonhour	Coach, SW Missouri St.
San Diego St	Jim Brandenburg & Jim Harrick, Jr.	2-26	Interim	Tony Fuller	Asst., UCLA
SE Louisiana	Don Wilson	6-22	Fired	Norm Picou	Asst., SE Louisiana
Southern Utah St	Neil Roberts	20- 8	Resigned	Bill Evans	Interim, So.Utah St.
SW Missouri St	Charlie Spoonhour	23- 8	to St.Louis	Mark Bernsen	Asst., SW Missouri St.
Texas-Pan American	Kevin Wall	3-26	Fired	Mark Adams	Coach, W.Texas St.
UNLV	Jerry Tarkanian	26- 2	Resigned	Rollie Massimino	Coach, Villanova
Villanova	Rollie Massimino	14-15	to UNLV	Steve Lappas	Coach, Manhattan
Western Illinois	Jack Margenthaler	10-18	Fired	Jim Kerwin	Asst., Kansas St.
Wichita St	Mike Cohen	8-20	Resigned	Scott Thompson	Coach, Rice
Winthrop	Steve Vacendak	6-22	Retired	Dan Kenney	Coach, Pembroke St.
Wisconsin	Steve Yoder	13-18	Resigned	Stu Jackson	NBA Operations Dir.

Note: At San Diego St., interim coach Harrick replaced Brandenburg on Feb. 11, 1992; at Southern Utah St., Evans replaced Roberts on Feb. 8, 1992.

Division I-A Football

School	Old Coach	Record	Why Left?	New Coach	Old Job
Arizona St	Larry Marmie	6-5-0	Fired	Bruce Snyder	Coach, California
Arkansas St	Al Kincaid	0-10-0	Fired	Ray Perkins	Coach, NFL Tampa Bay (1987-90)
California	Bruce Snyder	10-2-0	to Arizona St.	Keith Gilbertson	Asst., Washington
East Carolina	Bill Lewis	11-1-0	to Georgia Tech	Steve Logan	Asst., East Carolina
Georgia Tech	Bobby Ross	8-5-0	to NFL Chargers*	Bill Lewis	Coach, East Carolina
Illinois	John Mackovic	6-6-0	to Texas	Lou Tepper	Asst., Illinois
Long Beach St	Willie Brown	2-9-0	Program dropped	—	—
Maryland	Joe Krivak	2-9-0	Fired	Mark Duffner	Coach, Holy Cross
Minnesota	John Gutekunst	2-9-0	Fired	Jim Wacker	Coach, TCU
New Mexico	Mike Sheppard	3-9-0	Fired	Dennis Franchione	Coach, SW Texas St.
Northwestern	Francis Peay	3-8-0	Fired	Gary Barnett	Asst., Colorado
Pacific	Walt Harris	5-7-0	to NFL Jets†	Chuck Shelton	Coach, Utah St.
San Jose St	Terry Shea	6-4-1	Resigned	Ron Turner	Asst., Stanford
Stanford	Dennis Green	8-4-0	to NFL Vikings*	Bill Walsh	NBC-TV commentator
Texas	David McWilliams	5-6-0	Fired	John Mackovic	Coach, Illinois
TCU	Jim Wacker	7-4-0	to Minnesota	Pat Sullivan	Asst., Auburn
Tulane	Greg Davis	1-10-0	Fired	Buddy Teevens	Coach, Dartmouth
Utah St	Chuck Shelton	5-6-0	to Pacific	Charlie Weatherbie	Asst., Arkansas

Note: Arkansas St. was a Division I-AA program in 1991.
*NFL head coach.
†NFL assistant coach.

Annual NCAA Division I Team Champions

Men's and Women's NCAA Division I team champions from Cross-country to Wrestling. Rowing is included, although the NCAA does not sanction championships in the sport. Team champions in baseball, basketball, football, golf, ice hockey, soccer and tennis can be found in appropriate chapters throughout the almanac.

CROSS-COUNTRY

Men

Arkansas placed four runners among the first 10 finishers to win its second straight title Nov. 25, 1991, in Tucson, Ariz. The Razorbacks beat second place Iowa St. by 62 points, 52-to-114. Sean Dollman of Western Kentucky was the individual winner, covering the 10,000-meter course in 30:17.1. Niall Bruton of Arkansas was second (30:35.3).

Multiple winners: Michigan St. (8); UTEP (7); Arkansas (5); Oregon and Villanova (4); Drake, Indiana, Penn St. and Wisconsin (3); San Jose St. and Western Mich. (2).

Year		Year		Year		Year		Year	
1938	Indiana	1948	Michigan St.	1959	Michigan St.	1970	Villanova	1981	UTEP
1939	Michigan St.	1949	Michigan St.	1960	Houston	1971	Oregon	1982	Wisconsin
1940	Indiana	1950	Penn St.	1961	Oregon St.	1972	Tennessee	1983	Vacated
1941	Rhode Island	1951	Syracuse	1962	San Jose St.	1973	Oregon	1984	Arkansas
1942	Indiana	1952	Michigan St.	1963	San Jose St.	1974	Oregon	1985	Wisconsin
	& Penn St.	1953	Kansas	1964	Western Mich.	1975	UTEP	1986	Arkansas
1943	Not held	1954	Oklahoma St.	1965	Western Mich.	1976	UTEP	1987	Arkansas
1944	Drake	1955	Michigan St.	1966	Villanova	1977	Oregon	1988	Wisconsin
1945	Drake	1956	Michigan St.	1967	Villanova	1978	UTEP	1989	Iowa St.
1946	Drake	1957	Notre Dame	1968	Villanova	1979	UTEP	1990	Arkansas
1947	Penn St.	1958	Michigan St.	1969	UTEP	1980	UTEP	1991	Arkansas

Women

With Sonia O'Sullivan successfully defending her individual title, Villanova ran off with its third consecutive team championship Nov. 25, 1991, in Tucson. O'Sullivan's time of 16:30.3 over the 5000-meter course was 4.6 seconds better than teammate Carole Zajac. The Wildcats outdistanced runner-up Arkansas in the team standings, 85-to-168.

Multiple winners: Villanova (3); Oregon, Virginia and Wisconsin (2).

Year		Year		Year		Year		Year	
1981	Virginia	1984	Wisconsin	1986	Texas	1988	Kentucky	1990	Villanova
1982	Virginia	1985	Wisconsin	1987	Oregon	1989	Villanova	1991	Villanova
1983	Oregon								

FENCING

Men & Women

Columbia-Barnard broke Penn State's two-year hold on the combined men's and women's title, beating the defending champs, 4,150 points to 3,646, March 20-24, 1992, at Notre Dame. The New Yorkers finished among the top five in every team event. Individual winners included Tom Strzalkowski of Penn St. in men's sabre, Nick Bravin of Stanford in men's foil, Harald Bauder of Wayne St. in men's épée, and Olga Chernyak of Penn St. in women's foil.

Multiple winner: Penn St.(2)

Note: Prior to 1990, men and women held separate championships. Men's multiple winners included: NYU (12); Columbia (11); Wayne St.(7); Navy, Notre Dame and Penn (3); Illinois (2).Women's multiple winners included: Wayne St.(3); Yale (2).

Year		Year		Year	
1990	Penn St.	1991	Penn St.	1992	Columbia-Barnard

FIELD HOCKEY

Women

Defending champion Old Dominion defeated two ACC opponents in the Final Four to win its sixth overall championship since 1982. Playing at Villanova, the Monarchs beat Maryland 3-1 in the semifinals then shut out North Carolina 2-0 in the final on goals by Jill Reeve and Maike Hilbrand on Nov. 24, 1991. The Tar Heels reached the final after downing Penn St., 2-1, in overtime.

Multiple winners: Old Dominion (6); Connecticut (2).

Year		Year		Year		Year		Year	
1981	Connecticut	1984	Old Dominion	1986	Iowa	1988	Old Dominion	1990	Old Dominion
1982	Old Dominion	1985	Connecticut	1987	Maryland	1989	North Carolina	1991	Old Dominion
1983	Old Dominion								

GYMNASTICS

Men

Top-ranked Stanford won its first national gymnastics title, beating runner-up Nebraska 289.575 points to 288.400 in Lincoln, Neb., April 23-25, 1992. The Cardinal's point total bettered its own national meet record of 288.400 set on March 7. Minnesota's John Roethlisberger repeated as individual all-around champion, beating Scott Keswick of UCLA for the honor for the second straight year.

Multiple winners: Illinois and Penn St.(9); Nebraska (7); So.Illinois (4); Iowa St. and Oklahoma (3); California, Florida St., Michigan and UCLA (2).

Year		Year		Year		Year		Year	
1938	Chicago	1953	Penn St.	1963	Michigan	1972	So.Illinois	1982	Nebraska
1939	Illinois	1954	Penn St.	1964	So.Illinois	1973	Iowa St.	1983	Nebraska
1940	Illinois	1955	Illinois	1965	Penn St.	1974	Iowa St.	1984	UCLA
1941	Illinois	1956	Illinois	1966	So.Illinois	1975	California	1985	Ohio St.
1942	Illinois	1957	Penn St.	1967	So.Illinois	1976	Penn St.	1986	Arizona St.
1943-47	Not held	1958	Michigan St.	1968	California	1977	Indiana St.	1987	UCLA
1948	Penn St.		& Illinois	1969	Iowa		& Oklahoma	1988	Nebrasksa
1949	Temple	1959	Penn St.		& Michigan (T)	1978	Oklahoma	1989	Illinois
		1960	Penn St.			1979	Nebraska		
1950	Illinois	1961	Penn St.	1970	Michigan			1990	Nebraska
1951	Florida St.	1962	USC		& Michigan (T)	1980	Nebraska	1991	Oklahoma
1952	Florida St.			1971	Iowa St.	1981	Nebraska	1992	Stanford

(T) indicates won trampoline competition (1969 and '70).

Women

Utah's Missy Marlowe won individual titles in the uneven bars, floor exercise and all-around events and tied for first with Alabama's Dana Dobranskey in the balance beam to lead the Utes to their seventh NCAA title, April 24-25, 1992 in St.Paul, Minn. Scoring a team record 195.650 points, Utah has now finished first or second in 10 of the championship's 11 years.

Multiple winners: Utah (7); Georgia and Alabama (2).

Year		Year		Year		Year		Year	
1982	Utah	1985	Utah	1987	Georgia	1989	Georgia	1991	Alabama
1983	Utah	1986	Utah	1988	Alabama	1990	Utah	1992	Utah
1984	Utah								

LACROSSE

Men

Princeton, which didn't get an invitation to its first national lacrosse tournament until 1990, upset traditional powers North Carolina and Syracuse to win the title, May 25, 1992, at Franklin Field in Philadelphia. The Tigers beat the defending champion Tar Heels, 16-14, in the semifinals, then took the Orangemen into double overtime before winning it all, 10-9. Princeton's Andy Moe led all scorers with four goals, including the game-winner nine seconds into the second extra period.

Multiple winners: Johns Hopkins (7); North Carolina and Syracuse (4); Cornell (3); Maryland (2).

Year		Year		Year		Year		Year	
1971	Cornell	1976	Cornell	1981	North Carolina	1986	North Carolina	1990	Syracuse
1972	Virginia	1977	Cornell	1982	North Carolina	1987	Johns Hopkins	1991	North Carolina
1973	Maryland	1978	Johns Hopkins	1983	Syracuse	1988	Syracuse	1992	Princeton
1974	Johns Hopkins	1979	Johns Hopkins	1984	Johns Hopkins	1989	Syracuse		
1975	Maryland	1980	Johns Hopkins	1985	Johns Hopkins				

Women

After losing the championship game in both 1990 and '91, Maryland returned to win its first national title with an 11-10 overtime victory over Harvard, May 17, 1992, at Lehigh. The Terps won despite trailing by three goals in the second half and one goal in overtime. Senior Leigh Frendberg scored the winning goal with 1:15 left in the first extra period.

Multiple winners: Maryland, Penn St. and Temple (2).

Year		Year		Year		Year		Year	
1982	Massachusetts	1985	New Hampshire	1987	Penn St.	1989	Penn St.	1991	Virginia
1983	Delaware	1986	Maryland	1988	Temple	1990	Harvard	1992	Maryland
1984	Temple								

Annual NCAA Division I Team Champions (Cont.)

RIFLE

Men & Women

Ann-Marie Pfiffner repeated as individual air-rifle champion and teammate Tim Manges captured the smallbore title to lead West Virginia to its fifth straight championship and eighth in the last 10 years, March 6-7, 1992, at Murray, Ky. Pfiffner is only the second marksman to win two air-rifle titles. The Mountaineers scored an aggregate 6,214 points to win by 48 points over runner-up Alaska Fairbanks.

Multiple winners: West Virginia (8); Tennessee Tech (3); Murray St.(2).

Year		Year		Year		Year		Year	
1980	Tenn. Tech	1983	West Virginia	1986	West Virginia	1989	West Virginia	1991	West Virginia
1981	Tenn. Tech	1984	West Virginia	1987	Murray St.	1990	West Virginia	1992	West Virginia
1982	Tenn. Tech	1985	Murray St.	1988	West Virginia				

ROWING

Intercollegiate Rowing Association Regatta
VARSITY EIGHTS
Men

The first dead heat in the 97-year history of the Intercollegiate Rowing Association (IRA) Regatta resulted on June 6, 1992, when Dartmouth and Navy crossed the finish line together in the time of 5 minutes, 52.1 seconds. The race, which covered 2000 meters across Onondaga Lake in Syracuse, N.Y., was further complicated when third place finisher Penn protested that a wake created by an officials' launch slowed the Quakers' closing drive and knocked them out of contention. Race officials upheld the Penn protest and declared the championship a three-way tie.

The IRA was formed in 1895 by several northeastern schools, shortly after Harvard and Yale quit the Rowing Association (established in 1871) to stage an annual race of their own. Since then the IRA Regatta has been contested over courses of varying lengths in Poughkeepsie, N.Y., Marietta, Ohio,and Onondaga Lake in Syracuse, N.Y. The race has been over a 2000-meter course in Syracuse since 1968.

Distances: 4 miles (1895-97,1899-1916,1925-41); 3 miles (1898,1921-24,1947-49,1952-63,1965-67); 2 miles (1920,1950-51); 2000 meters (1964, since 1968).

Multiple winners: Cornell (24); Navy (13); California and Washington (10); Penn (9); Wisconsin (7); Syracuse (6); Brown and Columbia (4); Northwestern (2).

Year		Year		Year		Year		Year	
1895	Columbia	1915	Cornell	1936	Washington	1959	Wisconsin	1978	Syracuse
1896	Cornell	1916	Syracuse	1937	Washington	1960	California	1979	Brown
1897	Cornell	1917–19	Not held	1938	Navy	1961	California	1980	Navy
1898	Penn	1920	Syracuse	1939	California	1962	Cornell	1981	Cornell
1899	Penn	1921	Navy			1963	Cornell	1982	Cornell
1900	Penn	1922	Navy	1940	Washington	1964	California	1983	Brown
1901	Cornell	1923	Washington	1941	Washington	1965	Navy	1984	Navy
1902	Cornell	1924	Washington	1942–46	Not held	1966	Wisconsin	1985	Princeton
1903	Cornell	1925	Navy	1947	Navy	1967	Penn	1986	Brown
1904	Syracuse	1926	Washington	1948	Washington	1968	Penn	1987	Brown
1905	Cornell	1927	Columbia	1949	California	1969	Penn	1988	Northeastern
1906	Cornell	1928	California					1989	Penn
1907	Cornell	1929	Columbia	1950	Washington	1970	Washington		
1908	Syracuse			1951	Wisconsin	1971	Cornell	1990	Wisconsin
1909	Cornell	1930	Cornell	1952	Navy	1972	Penn	1991	Northeastern
1910	Cornell	1931	Navy	1953	Navy	1973	Wisconsin	1992	Dartmouth,
1911	Cornell	1932	California	1954	Navy*	1974	Wisconsin		Navy
1912	Cornell	1933	Not held	1955	Cornell	1975	Wisconsin		& Penn
1913	Syracuse	1934	California	1956	Cornell	1976	California		
1914	Columbia	1935	California	1957	Cornell	1977	Cornell		
				1958	Cornell				

*In 1954, Navy was disqualified because of an ineligible coxwain; no trophies were given.

The Harvard-Yale Regatta

Harvard won the 127th Harvard-Yale Regatta for varsity eights for the eighth year in a row, June 6, 1992, beating Yale over the four-mile Thames River course with a time of 19 minutes, 8.3 seconds at New London, Conn. The Harvard-Yale Regatta is the country's oldest intercollegiate sporting event and Harvard holds a 76-51 edge.

National Championships

VARSITY EIGHTS

The Harvard men's crew and the Boston University women won the varsity eights titles at the 1992 National Collegiate Rowing Championships, June 13, 1992, at Harsha Lake in Bantam, Ohio. Harvard edged Dartmouth by less than a foot to win the Herschede Cup for the sixth time, covering the 2000-meter course in a record 5 minutes, 33.97 seconds. Meanwhile, BU took its second straight Ferguson Bowl, beating runner-up Cornell by four seconds with a time of 6:28.79.

Men

National championship determined at Cincinnati Regatta over a 2000-meter course on Harsha Lake since 1982. Winner receives Herschede Cup.
Multiple winners: Harvard (6); Wisconsin (2).

Year	Champion	Time	Runner-up	Time	Year	Champion	Time	Runner-up	Time
1982	Yale	5:50.8	Cornell	5:54.15	1988	Harvard	5:35.98	Northeastern	5:37.07
1983	Harvard	5:59.6	Washington	6:00.0	1989	Harvard	5:36.6	Washington	5:38.93
1984	Washington	5:51.1	Yale	5:55.6	1990	Wisconsin	5:52.5	Harvard	5:56.84
1985	Harvard	5:44.4	Princeton	5:44.87	1991	Penn	5:58.21	Northeastern	5:58.48
1986	Wisconsin	5:57.8	Brown	5:59.9	1992	Harvard	5:33.97	Dartmouth	5:34.28
1987	Harvard	5:35.17	Brown	5:35.63					

Women

National championship held over various distances at 10 different venues since 1979. Distances—1000 meters (1979-81); 1500 meters (1982-83); 1000 meters (1984); 1750 meters (1985); 2000 meters (1986-88, since 1991); 1852 meters (1989-90). Winner receives Ferguson Bowl.
Multiple winners: Washington (7); Boston U.(2).

Year	Champion	Time	Runner-up	Time	Year	Champion	Time	Runner-up	Time
1979	Yale	3:06	California	3:08.6	1986	Wisconsin	6:53.28	Radcliffe	6:53.34
1980	California	3:05.4	Oregon St.	3:05.8	1987	Washington	6:33.8	Yale	6:37.4
1981	Washington	3:20.6	Yale	3:22.9	1988	Washington	6:41.0	Yale	6:42.37
1982	Washington	4:56.4	Wisconsin	4:59.83	1989	Cornell	5:34.9	Wisconsin	5:37.5
1983	Washington	4:57.5	Dartmouth	5:03.02	1990	Princeton	5:52.2	Radcliffe	5:54.2
1984	Washington	3:29.48	Radcliffe	3:31.08	1991	Boston Univ.	7:03.2	Cornell	7:06.21
1985	Washington	5:28.4	Wisconsin	5:32.0	1992	Boston Univ.	6:28.79	Cornell	6:32.79

SKIING

Men & Women

Trailing New Mexico by 10 points going into the last day at Waterville Valley, N.H., Vermont came up with a solid showing in the diagonal cross-country events to win its third title in the last four years on March 7, 1992. Trond Nystad's victory in the men's diagonal was one of three individual titles for the Catamounts. Sally Knight (women's giant slalom) and Einar Bohmer (men's slalom) were the others.
Multiple winners: Denver (14); Colorado (12); Utah (6); Vermont (4); Dartmouth and Wyoming (2).

Year		Year		Year		Year		Year	
1954	Denver	1963	Denver	1972	Colorado	1980	Vermont	1987	Utah
1955	Denver	1964	Denver	1973	Colorado	1981	Utah	1988	Utah
1956	Denver	1965	Denver	1974	Colorado	1982	Colorado	1989	Vermont
1957	Denver	1966	Denver	1975	Colorado	1983	Utah	1990	Vermont
1958	Dartmouth	1967	Denver	1976	Colorado	1984	Utah	1991	Colorado
1959	Colorado	1968	Wyoming		& Dartmouth	1985	Wyoming	1992	Vermont
1960	Colorado	1969	Denver	1977	Colorado	1986	Utah		
1961	Denver	1970	Denver	1978	Colorado				
1962	Denver	1971	Denver	1979	Colorado				

SOFTBALL

Women

Freshman Jennifer Brewster's two-run homer in the bottom of the seventh inning was all the offense UCLA needed to beat defending champion Arizona, 2-0, May 25, 1992, at Oklahoma City. Winning pitcher Lisa Fernandez struck out six and scattered four hits for her fourth win of the tournament and 29th of the season. It was the Bruins' third title in four years and their seventh in the last 11.
Multiple winners: UCLA (7); Texas A&M (2).

Year		Year		Year		Year		Year	
1982	UCLA	1985	UCLA	1987	Texas A&M	1989	UCLA	1991	Arizona
1983	Texas A&M	1986	CS-Fullerton	1988	UCLA	1990	UCLA	1992	UCLA
1984	UCLA								

Annual NCAA Division I Team Champions (Cont.)

SWIMMING & DIVING

Men

A week after the Stanford women dethroned Texas to win their title, the Cardinal men's team toppled the Longhorns March 26-28, 1992, in Bloomington, Ind., to complete the sweep. Jeff Rouse led the way, setting American backstroke records at 100 yards (46.12) and 200 yards (1:40.64) and swimming on three winning relay teams. In all, Stanford set five American marks and won all five relay races for a meet-record 632 points. Second place Texas had 356 points.

Multiple winners: Ohio St.(11); Michigan (10); USC (9); Indiana (6); Stanford and Texas (5); Yale (4); California and Florida (2).

Year		Year		Year		Year		Year	
1937	Michigan	1949	Ohio St.	1960	USC	1971	Indiana	1982	UCLA
1938	Michigan	1950	Ohio St.	1961	Michigan	1972	Indiana	1983	Florida
1939	Michigan	1951	Yale	1962	Ohio St.	1973	Indiana	1984	Florida
1940	Michigan	1952	Ohio St.	1963	USC	1974	USC	1985	Stanford
1941	Michigan	1953	Yale	1964	USC	1975	USC	1986	Stanford
1942	Yale	1954	Ohio St.	1965	USC	1976	USC	1987	Stanford
1943	Ohio St.	1955	Ohio St.	1966	USC	1977	USC	1988	Texas
1944	Yale	1956	Ohio St.	1967	Stanford	1978	Tennessee	1989	Texas
1945	Ohio St.	1957	Michigan	1968	Indiana	1979	California	1990	Texas
1946	Ohio St.	1958	Michigan	1969	Indiana	1980	California	1991	Texas
1947	Ohio St.	1959	Michigan	1970	Indiana	1981	Texas	1992	Stanford
1948	Michigan								

Women

Stanford's Summer Sanders won three individual events and swam on three winning relay teams to pace the Cardinal to its third national championship, March 19-21, 1992, in Austin, Texas. Along the way, she set American records in the 200-yard Individual Medley (1:55.54) and 400-yard IM (4:02.28) and was named the Most Outstanding Swimmer of the meet for the second year in a row. Runner-up behind Texas in 1990 and '91, Stanford beat the host Longhorns this time, 735½ points to 651.

Multiple winners: Texas (7); Stanford (3).

Year		Year		Year		Year		Year	
1982	Florida	1985	Texas	1987	Texas	1989	Stanford	1991	Texas
1983	Stanford	1986	Texas	1988	Texas	1990	Texas	1992	Stanford
1984	Texas								

INDOOR TRACK

Men

Paced by Erick Walder's double victory in the long and triple jumps, Arkansas claimed its ninth straight indoor track title at the Hoosier Dome, March 13-14, 1992. Walder, whose winning leaps were 55-4¾ in the triple jump and 26-3½ in the long jump, joins Mike Conley of Arkansas (1984 and '85) and Bob Beamon of UTEP (1968) as the only three winners of the triple/long jump double.

Multiple winners: Arkansas (9); UTEP (7); Kansas and Villanova (3); USC (2).

Year		Year		Year		Year		Year	
1965	Missouri	1971	Villanova	1977	Washington St.	1983	SMU	1988	Arkansas
1966	Kansas	1972	USC	1978	UTEP	1984	Arkansas	1989	Arkansas
1967	USC	1973	Manhattan	1979	Villanova	1985	Arkansas	1990	Arkansas
1968	Villanova	1974	UTEP	1980	UTEP	1986	Arkansas	1991	Arkansas
1969	Kansas	1975	UTEP	1981	UTEP	1987	Arkansas	1992	Arkansas
1970	Kansas	1976	UTEP	1982	UTEP				

Women

Despite a disappointing fourth in the 55-meter hurdles by world-record-holder Michelle Freeman, Florida won its first national indoor crown by a mile at the Hoosier Dome, March 13-14, 1992. Led by a victorious 4 × 400-meter relay team and Leah Kiklin's win in the triple jump, the Gators scored 50 points and beat runner-up Stanford by 24 points.

Multiple winners: LSU and Texas (3); Nebraska (2).

Year		Year		Year		Year		Year	
1983	Nebraska	1985	Florida St.	1987	LSU	1989	LSU	1991	LSU
1984	Nebraska	1986	Texas	1988	Texas	1990	Texas	1992	Florida

OUTDOOR TRACK

Men

Led by winners Erick Walder in the long jump (a meet-record 27-9½) and Brian Wellman in the triple jump (56-9¼), Arkansas edged defending champion Tennessee, 60 points to 46½, June 3-6, 1992, in Austin, Texas. The win enabled the Razorbacks to become just the second team to sweep the cross-country, indoor track and outdoor track titles in the same year. UTEP has done it four times.

Multiple winners: USC (26); UCLA (8); UTEP (6); Illinois and Oregon (5); Kansas, LSU and Stanford (3); Arkansas, SMU and Tennessee (2).

Year		Year		Year		Year		Year	
1921	Illinois	1937	USC	1952	USC	1966	UCLA	1979	UTEP
1922	California	1938	USC	1953	USC	1967	USC	1980	UTEP
1923	Michigan	1939	USC	1954	USC	1968	USC	1981	UTEP
1924	Not held	1940	USC	1955	USC	1969	San Jose St.	1982	UTEP
1925	Stanford*	1941	USC	1956	UCLA	1970	BYU, Kansas	1983	SMU
1926	USC*	1942	USC	1957	Villanova		& Oregon	1984	Oregon
1927	Illinois*	1943	USC	1958	USC	1971	UCLA	1985	Arkansas
1928	Stanford	1944	Illinois	1959	Kansas	1972	UCLA	1986	SMU
1929	Ohio St.	1945	Navy	1960	Kansas	1973	UCLA	1987	UCLA
1930	USC	1946	Illinois	1961	USC	1974	Tennessee	1988	UCLA
1931	USC	1947	Illinois	1962	Oregon	1975	UTEP	1989	LSU
1932	Indiana	1948	Minnesota	1963	USC	1976	USC	1990	LSU
1933	LSU	1949	USC	1964	Oregon	1977	Arizona St.	1991	Tennessee
1934	Stanford	1950	USC	1965	Oregon	1978	UCLA	1992	Arkansas
1935	USC	1951	USC		& USC		& UTEP		
1936	USC								

(*) indicates unofficial championship.

Women

Florida won five events, but it didn't have the depth to hold off five-time defending champion LSU, losing 87 points to 81, June 3-6, 1992, in Austin, Texas. Dahlia Duhaney paced LSU, winning the 200 meters in 22.80 seconds and placing second to Stanford's Chryste Gaines in the 100 meters. LSU scored in nine events, including 28 points in the two dashes.

Multiple winners: LSU (6); UCLA (2).

Year		Year		Year		Year		Year	
1982	UCLA	1985	Oregon	1987	LSU	1989	LSU	1991	LSU
1983	UCLA	1986	Texas	1988	LSU	1990	LSU	1992	LSU
1984	Florida St.								

VOLLEYBALL

Men

Appearing in the tournament for the first time since winning back-to-back titles in 1986, Pepperdine returned to the college volleyball summit on April 25, 1992, at Muncie, Ind., sweeping Stanford by 15-7, 15-13, 16-14. The Waves were led by Tom Sorenson and Alon Grinberg, who combined for 54 kills, and Chip McCaw, who contributed 77 assists.

Multiple winners: UCLA (13); Pepperdine and USC (4).

Year		Year		Year		Year		Year	
1970	UCLA	1975	UCLA	1980	USC	1985	Pepperdine	1990	USC
1971	UCLA	1976	UCLA	1981	UCLA	1986	Pepperdine	1991	Long Beach St.
1972	USC	1977	USC	1982	UCLA	1987	UCLA	1992	Pepperdine
1973	San Diego St.	1978	Pepperdine	1983	UCLA	1988	USC		
1974	UCLA	1979	UCLA	1984	UCLA	1989	UCLA		

Women

Helped by the familiar surroundings of Pauley Pavilion, UCLA was able to successfully defend its national title, Dec. 21, 1991, coming from behind to defeat Long Beach State in five games, 12-15, 13-15, 15-12, 15-6, 15-11. The Bruins were led by junior Natalie Williams, who had 32 kills and three service aces in the match.

Multiple winners: Hawaii and UCLA (3); Pacific (2).

Year		Year		Year		Year		Year	
1981	USC	1984	UCLA	1986	Pacific	1988	Texas	1990	UCLA
1982	Hawaii	1985	Pacific	1987	Hawaii	1989	Long Beach St.	1991	UCLA
1983	Hawaii								

Annual NCAA Division I Team Champions (Cont.)

WATER POLO

Men

Defending champion California rallied for three goals in the fourth period to beat UCLA, 7-6, Dec. 1, 1991, in Long Beach. Dirk Zeien and Chris Oeding each had two goals for the winners. The Bears, who only lost once in 27 matches, have now won five of the last eight championships and 10 in all.
Multiple winners: California (10); Stanford (6); UC-Irvine and UCLA (3).

Year		Year		Year		Year		Year	
1969	UCLA	1974	California	1979	UC-S.Barbara	1984	California	1988	California
1970	UC-Irvine	1975	California	1980	Stanford	1985	Stanford	1989	UC-Irvine
1971	UCLA	1976	Stanford	1981	Stanford	1986	Stanford	1990	California
1972	UCLA	1977	California	1982	UC-Irvine	1987	California	1991	California
1973	California	1978	Stanford	1983	California				

WRESTLING

Men

Perennial powerhouse and defending champion Iowa scored 149 points, won three individual titles and earned nine All-America honors on the way to a smashing 48½-point victory, March 19-21, 1992, in Oklahoma City. Hawkeye champions included twin brothers Terry and Tom Brands at 126 and 134 pounds, respectively, and Troy Steiner at 142. It was the second title in three years for Terry Brands and the third straight for Tom Brands, who was named the meet's Most Outstanding Wrestler.
Multiple winners: Oklahoma St.(29); Iowa (13); Iowa St.(8); Oklahoma (7).

Year		Year		Year		Year		Year	
1928	Okla.A&M*	1940	Okla.A&M	1955	Okla.A&M	1968	Okla.St.	1980	Iowa
1929	Okla.A&M	1941	Okla.A&M	1956	Okla.A&M	1969	Iowa St.	1981	Iowa
1930	Okla.A&M*	1942	Okla.A&M	1957	Oklahoma	1970	Iowa St.	1982	Iowa
1931	Okla.A&M*	1943-45	Not held	1958	Okla.St.	1971	Okla.St.	1983	Iowa
1932	Indiana*	1946	Okla.A&M	1959	Okla.St.	1972	Iowa St.	1984	Iowa
1933	Okla.A&M* & Iowa St.*	1947	Cornell Col.	1960	Oklahoma	1973	Iowa St.	1985	Iowa
		1948	Okla.A&M	1961	Okla.St.	1974	Oklahoma	1986	Iowa
1934	Okla.A&M	1949	Okla.A&M	1962	Okla.St.	1975	Iowa	1987	Iowa St.
1935	Okla.A&M	1950	Northern Iowa	1963	Oklahoma	1976	Iowa	1988	Arizona St.
1936	Oklahoma	1951	Oklahoma	1964	Okla.St.	1977	Iowa St.	1989	Okla.St.
1937	Okla.A&M	1952	Oklahoma	1965	Iowa St.	1978	Iowa	1990	Okla.St.
1938	Okla.A&M	1953	Penn St.	1966	Okla.St.	1979	Iowa	1991	Iowa
1939	Okla.A&M	1954	Okla.A&M	1967	Michigan St.			1992	Iowa

(*) indicates unofficial champions.
Note: Oklahoma A&M became Oklahoma St. in 1958.

1991-92 NAIA Team Champions

Adams State of Colorado, Drury College of Missouri and Pacific Lutheran of Washington State each won two of the NAIA's 23 team championships during the 1991-92 school year. Adams State took home titles in women's cross-country and men's indoor track, while Drury swept men's and women's swimming, and Pacific Lutheran won in women's soccer and softball. The NAIA added two new championships by creating a second division in both the men's and women's basketball tournaments.

Note that numbers in parentheses indicate overall championships won in that sport.

FALL

Cross Country: MEN'S—Lubbock Christian, TX (2); WOMEN'S—Adams St., CO (3); **Football**: MEN'S—Division I: Central Arkansas (1); Division II: Georgetown, KY (1). **Soccer**: MEN'S—Lynn, FL (2); WOMEN'S—Pacific Lutheran, WA (3). **Volleyball**: WOMEN'S—BYU-Hawaii (3).

WINTER

Basketball: MEN'S—Division I: Oklahoma City (2); Division II: Grace, IN (1). WOMEN'S—Division I: Arkansas Tech (1); Division II: Northern St., SD (1). **Swimming & Diving**: MEN'S—Drury, MO (8); WOMEN'S—Drury, MO (1). **Indoor Track**: MEN'S—Adams St., CO (1); WOMEN'S—Simon Fraser, BC (2). **Wrestling**: MEN'S—Northern Montana (2).

SPRING

Baseball: MEN'S—Lewis-Clark St., ID (9). **Golf**: MEN'S—Huntingdon, AL (5). **Softball**: WOMEN'S—Pacific Lutheran, WA (2). **Tennis**: MEN'S—Lander, SC (4); WOMEN'S—Auburn-Montgomery, AL (1). **Outdoor Track**: MEN'S—Azusa Pacific, CA (9); WOMEN'S—Central St., OH (2).

Wide World Photos

Winning the 1992 U.S. Women's Open in an 18-hole playoff on July 27 put golfer **Patty Sheehan** within one victory of the LPGA Hall of Fame.

HALLS OF FAME & AWARDS

AUTO RACING

Indianapolis Motor Speedway Hall of Fame

Originally the Auto Racing Hall of Fame. Established by the American Automobile Association Contest Board in 1952, disbanded in 1955, and revived by the Indianapolis Speedway Foundation in 1962. **Address:** 4790 West 16th Street, Indianapolis, IN 46222. **Telephone:** (317) 248-6747.

Eligibility: Candidates cannot be nominated until at least 20 years after the date of first active participation in auto racing. Voting done by 100-member panel made up of racing officials, Hall of Fame members and media representatives.

Class of 1992 (2): Drivers—**Bill Holland** and **Troy Ruttman**.

Members are listed with year of induction; (+) indicates deceased members.

Drivers

+Aitken, Johnny	1981	+Foyt, A.J	1978
+Anderson, Gil	1983	+Frame, Fred	1984
Andretti, Mario	1986	+Goux, Jules	1989
+Baker, Cannonball	1981	+Grant, Harry	1982
Banks, Henry	1985	Gurney, Dan	1988
+Bergere, Cliff	1976	Hanks, Sam	1981
+Bettenhausen, Tony	1968	+Harroun, Ray	1952
+Boyer, Joe	1985	+Hartz, Harry	1963
+Bruce-Brown, David	1980	+Hearne, Eddie	1964
+Burman, Bob	1953-54	+Hepburn, Ralph	1970
+Bryan, Jimmy	1973	Holland, Bill	1992
+Chevrolet, Gaston	1964	+Horn, Ted	1964
+Chevrolet, Louis	1952	Jones, Parnelli	1985
+Clark, Jimmy	1988	+Keech, Ray	1984
+Cooper, Earl	1953-54	+Lockhart, Frank	1965
+Cummings, Bill	1970	+Mays, Rex	1963
+Dawson, Joe	1976	+McGrath, Jack	1987
+DePalma, Ralph	1953-54	Meyer, Louis	1963
+DePaolo, Peter	1963	+Milton, Tommy	1953-54
+Durant, Cliff	1983	+Moore, Lou	1969
+Fengler, Harlan	1983	+Mulford, Ralph	1953-54

+Murphy, Jimmy	1964
Nalon, Dennis (Duke)	1983
+Oldfield, Barney	1952
+Parsons, Johnnie	1986
+Resta, Dario	1953-54
+Rickenbacker, Eddie	1954
+Roberts, Floyd	1985
+Rose, Mauri	1967
Ruby, Lloyd	1991
Rutherford, Johnny	1987
Ruttman, Troy	1992
+Shaw, Wilbur	1963
+Snyder, Jimmy	1981
+Stevens, Myron	1983
+Strang, Lewis	1982
Unser, Al	1986
Unser, Bobby	1990
+Vukovich, Bill	1972
Ward, Rodger	1981
+Wilcox, Howard	1963

Contributors

+Agajanian, J.C.	1990	+Firestone, Harvey, Sr	1952
+Allison, James A	1964	+Fisher, Carl	1952
Bignotti, George	1975	+Ford, Henry	1952
+Brawner, Clint	1984	+Gilmore, Earl	1987
+Christie, Walter	1980	+Goossen, Leo	1978
+Cloutier, Joe	1989	+Henning, Harry (Cotton)	1969
+Dingley, Bert	1952	+Hulman, Tony	1967
+Drake, Darrell	1991	+Kurtis, Frank	1983
+Duesenberg, Augie	1963	+Marcenac, Jean	1968
+Duesenberg, Fred	1962	+Miller, Harry	1963
+Edenburn, Eddie	1986	+Myers, T.E.(Pop)	1952

+Offenhauser, Fred	1982
+Pillsbury, Art	1981
+Ricker, Chester	1989
+Robertson, George	1980
+Sparks, Art	1987
+Stutz, Henry	1963
+Vanderbilt, William K	1952
+Wagner, Fred	1952
Watson, A.J.	1981
+Welch, Lew	1986
+Winfield, Ed	1983

Motorsports Hall of Fame of America

Established in 1989. **Address:** P.O.Box 194, Novi, MI 48050. **Telephone:** (313) 349-7223.

Eligibility: Nominees must be retired at least three years or engaged in their area of motor sports for at least 20 years. Areas include: open wheel, stock car, dragster, sports car, motorcycle, off road, power boat, air racing and land speed records.

Class of 1992 (10): Auto drivers—**Bobby Allison**, **Ralph DePalma** and **Bill Vukovich, Sr.**; Drag racer—**Connie Kalitta**; Motorcyclist—**Joe Petrali**; Power Boat driver—**Bill Cantrell**; Air racing pilot—**Amelia Earhart**; At Large driver—**Parnelli Jones**; Contributors—**J.C. Agajanian** and **Carroll Shelby**,

Members are listed with year of induction; (+) indicates deceased members.

Drivers

Allison, Bobby	1992	Johnson, Junior	1991
Andretti, Mario	1990	Jones, Parnelli	1992
Arfons, Art	1991	Kalitta, Connie	1992
+Baker, Cannonball	1989	Leonard, Joe	1991
Cantrell, Bill	1992	Muldowney, Shirley	1990
+Chenoweth, Dean	1991	+Muncy, Bill	1989
+Clark, Jim	1990	+Oldfield, Barney	1989
+DePalma, Ralph	1992	+Petrali, Joe	1992
+Donahue, Mark	1990	Petty, Richard	1989
Foyt, A.J.	1989	Prudhomme, Don	1991
Garlits, Don	1989	Roberts, Kenny	1990
Gurney, Dan	1991	+Shaw, Wilbur	1991
Hill, Phil	1989	+Thompson, Mickey	1990

+Turner, Roscoe	1991
+Vukovich, Bill Sr.	1992
+Wood, Gar	1990

Pilots

+Curtiss, Glenn	1990
Doolittle, Jimmy	1989
+Earhart, Amelia	1992

Contributors

+Agajanian, J.C	1992
+France, Bill Sr.	1990
+Hulman, Tony	1991
Shelby, Carroll	1992

International Motorsports Hall of Fame

Established in 1990 by the International Motorsports Hall of Fame Commission. **Address:** P.O.Box 1018, Talladega, AL, 35160. **Telephone:** (205) 362-5002.

Eligibility: Nominees must be retired from their specialty in motor sports for five years. Voting done by 150-member panel made up of the world-wide auto racing media.

Class of 1992 (10): Indy Car drivers—**Louis Meyer** and **Rodger Ward**; Stock Car driver—**Curtis Turner**; Grand Prix driver—**Alberto Ascari**; Endurance driver—**Peter Gregg**; Motorcyclist—**Kenny Roberts**; Contributors—**Louis Chevrolet**, **Andy Granatelli**, **Wally Parks** and **Eddie Rickenbacker**.

Members are listed with year of induction; (+) indicates deceased members.

Drivers

+Ascari, Alberto	1992	Jarrett, Ned	1991	Unser, Bobby	1990
Baker, Buck	1990	Johnson, Junior	1990	+Vukovich, Bill	1991
+Bettenhausen, Tony	1991	Jones, Parnelli	1990	Ward Rodger	1992
Brabham, Jack	1990	Lorenzen, Fred	1991		
+Campbell, Sir Malcolm	1990	+McLaren, Bruce	1991		

Contributors

+Clark, Jim	1990	Meyer, Louis	1992	+Chevrolet, Louis	1992
+DePalma, Ralph	1991	Moss, Stirling	1990	+France, Bill, Sr.	1990
+Donahue, Mark	1990	+Oldfield, Barney	1990	Andy Granatelli	1992
+Fangio, Juan Manuel	1990	Petty, Lee	1990	+Hulman, Tony	1990
Flock, Tim	1991	Roberts, Fireball	1990	Parks, Wally	1992
+Gregg, Peter	1992	Roberts, Kenny	1992	+Rickenbacker, Eddie	1992
Gurney, Dan	1990	+Shaw, Wilbur	1991	Shelby, Carroll	1991
+Hill, Graham	1990	Stewart, Jackie	1990	+Thompson, Mickey	1990
+Hill, Phil	1991	+Turner, Curtis	1992	Yunick, Smokey	1990

BASEBALL

National Baseball Hall of Fame & Museum

Established in 1935 by Major League Baseball to celebrate the game's 100th anniversary. **Address:** P.O.Box 590, Cooperstown, NY 13326. **Telephone:** (607) 547-9988.

Eligibility: Nominated players must have played at least part of 10 seasons in the Major Leagues and be retired for five years. Voting done by Baseball Writers' Association of America. Any nominated player not elected after 15 years on the writers' ballot becomes eligible for consideration by the Veterans' Committee after a three-year wait. The Hall of Fame board of directors voted unanimously on Feb. 4, 1991, to exclude players on baseball's permanently ineligible list from consideration. Pete Rose is the only living ex-player on that list.

Class of 1992 (4): PITCHERS—**Rollie Fingers**, Oakland (1968-76), San Diego (1977-80) and Milwaukee (1981-85); **Hal Newhouser**, Detroit (1939-53), Cleveland (1954-55); **Tom Seaver**, N.Y.Mets (1967-77, 1983), Cincinnati (1977-82), Chicago White Sox (1984-86) and Boston (1986). UMPIRE—**Bill McGowan**, American League (1925-54). **Note:** Seaver and Fingers were voted in by BBWAA; Newhouser and McGowan by Veterans' Committee.

1992 Top 10 vote-getters (323 votes to elect): **1.** Tom Seaver (425); **2.** Rollie Fingers (349); **3.** Orlando Cepeda (246); **4.** Tony Perez (215); **5.** Bill Mazeroski (182); **6.** Tony Oliva (175); **7.** Ron Santo (136); **8.** Jim Kaat (114); **9.** Maury Wills (110); **10.** Ken Boyer (71). Pete Rose received 41 write-in votes.

Elected first year on ballot (23): Hank Aaron, Ernie Banks, Johnny Bench, Lou Brock, Rod Carew, Bob Feller, Bob Gibson, Al Kaline, Sandy Koufax, Mickey Mantle, Willie Mays, Willie McCovey, Joe Morgan, Stan Musial, Jim Palmer, Brooks Robinson, Frank Robinson, Jackie Robinson, **Tom Seaver**, Warren Spahn, Willie Stargell, Ted Williams and Carl Yastrzemski.

Members are listed with years of induction; (+) indicates deceased members.

1st Basemen

+Anson, Cap	1939	+Connor, Roger	1976	Killebrew, Harmon	1984
+Beckley, Jake	1971	+Foxx, Jimmie	1951	McCovey, Willie	1986
+Bottomley, Jim	1974	+Gehrig, Lou	1939	Mize, Johnny	1981
+Brouthers, Dan	1945	+Greenberg, Hank	1956	+Sisler, George	1939
+Chance, Frank	1946	+Kelly, George	1973	+Terry, Bill	1954

2nd Basemen

Carew, Rod	1991	Gehringer, Charlie	1949	Morgan, Joe	1990
+Collins, Eddie	1939	Herman, Billy	1975	+Robinson, Jackie	1962
Doerr, Bobby	1986	+Hornsby, Rogers	1942	Schoendienst, Red	1989
+Evers, Johnny	1946	+Lajoie, Nap	1937		
+Frisch, Frankie	1947	+Lazzeri, Tony	1991		

Shortstops

Aparicio, Luis	1984	+Jackson, Travis	1982	+Tinker, Joe	1946
+Appling, Luke	1964	+Jennings, Hugh	1945	+Vaughan, Arky	1985
+Bancroft, Dave	1971	+Maranville, Rabbit	1954	+Wagner, Honus	1936
Banks, Ernie	1977	Reese, Pee Wee	1984	+Wallace, Bobby	1953
Boudreau, Lou	1970	+Sewell, Joe	1977	+Ward, Monte	1964
+Cronin, Joe	1956				

Baseball Hall of Fame (Cont.)

3rd Basemen

+Baker, Frank 1955
+Collins, Jimmy. 1945
Kell, George 1983

+Lindstrom, Fred. 1976
Mathews, Eddie. 1978

Robinson, Brooks 1983
+Traynor, Pie. 1948

Brock, Lou 1985
+Burkett, Jesse. 1946
+Clarke, Fred 1945
+Delahanty, Ed 1945
+Goslin, Goose. 1968
+Hafey, Chick 1971

Left Fielders

+Kelley, Joe 1971
Kiner, Ralph. 1975
+Manush, Heinie. 1964
+Medwick, Joe 1968
Musial, Stan 1969
+O'Rourke, Jim. 1945

+Simmons, Al 1953
Stargell, Willie 1988
+Wheat, Zack 1959
Williams, Billy 1987
Williams, Ted 1966
Yastrzemski, Carl 1989

+Averill, Earl 1975
+Carey, Max 1961
+Cobb, Ty 1936
+Combs, Earle 1970
DiMaggio, Joe 1955

Center Fielders

+Duffy, Hugh. 1945
+Hamilton, Billy. 1961
Mantle, Mickey 1974
Mays, Willie. 1979
+Roush, Edd 1962

Snider, Duke 1980
+Speaker, Tris 1937
+Waner, Lloyd. 1967
+Wilson, Hack. 1979

Aaron, Hank 1982
+Clemente, Roberto 1973
+Crawford, Sam 1957
+Cuyler, Kiki 1968
+Flick, Elmer 1963
+Heilmann, Harry. 1952
+Hooper, Harry. 1971

Right Fielders

Kaline, Al 1980
+Keeler, Willie 1939
+Kelly, King 1945
+Klein, Chuck 1980
+McCarthy, Tommy 1946
+Ott, Mel 1951
+Rice, Sam. 1963

Robinson, Frank 1982
+Ruth, Babe. 1936
Slaughter, Enos. 1985
+Thompson, Sam 1974
+Waner, Paul 1952
+Youngs, Ross. 1972

Catchers

Bench, Johnny. 1989
Berra, Yogi 1972
+Bresnahan, Roger. 1945
Campanella, Roy 1969

+Cochrane, Mickey. 1947
Dickey, Bill. 1954
+Ewing, Buck. 1939
Ferrell, Rick 1984

+Hartnett, Gabby 1955
+Lombardi, Ernie 1986
+Schalk, Ray 1955

Pitchers

+Alexander, Grover 1938
+Bender, Chief 1953
+Brown, Mordecai 1949
+Chesbro, Jack 1946
+Clarkson, John 1963
+Coveleski, Stan 1969
+Dean, Dizzy 1953
Drysdale, Don. 1984
+Faber, Red. 1964
Feller, Bob. 1962
Fingers, Rollie 1992
Ford, Whitey 1974
+Galvin, Pud 1965
Gibson, Bob 1981
+Gomez, Lefty. 1972
+Grimes, Burleigh. 1964
+Grove, Lefty. 1947
+Haines, Jess. 1970

+Hoyt, Waite 1969
+Hubbell, Carl 1947
Hunter, Catfish 1987
Jenkins, Ferguson 1991
+Johnson, Walter 1936
+Joss, Addie 1978
+Keefe, Tim 1964
Koufax, Sandy. 1972
Lemon, Bob. 1976
+Lyons, Ted 1955
+Marichal, Juan 1983
+Marquard, Rube. 1971
+Mathewson, Christy 1936
+McGinnity, Joe 1946
Newhouser, Hal 1992
+Nichols, Kid 1949
Palmer, Jim 1990

+Pennock, Herb 1948
Perry, Gaylord. 1991
+Plank, Eddie 1946
+Radbourne, Old Hoss 1939
+Rixey, Eppa 1963
Roberts, Robin 1976
+Ruffing, Red. 1967
+Rusie, Amos. 1977
Seaver, Tom 1992
Spahn, Warren 1973
+Vance, Dazzy 1955
+Waddell, Rube 1946
+Walsh, Ed 1946
+Welch, Mickey. 1973
Wilhelm, Hoyt 1985
Wynn, Early. 1972
+Young, Cy. 1937

From Negro Leagues

+Bell, Cool Papa (OF) 1974
+Charleston, Oscar (1B-OF) 1976
Dandridge, Ray (3B). 1987
+Dihigo, Martin (P-OF). 1977

+Foster, Rube (P-Mgr). 1981
+Gibson, Josh (C). 1972
Irvin, Monte (OF) 1973
+Johnson, Judy (3B) 1975

Leonard, Buck (1B). 1972
+Lloyd, Pop (SS) 1977
+Paige, Satchel (P) 1971

Managers

+Alston, Walter 1983
+Harris, Bucky. 1975
+Huggins, Miller 1964
Lopez, Al 1977

+Mack, Connie 1937
+McCarthy, Joe 1957
+McGraw, John 1937

+McKechnie, Bill 1962
+Robinson, Wilbert 1945
+Stengel, Casey 1966

Umpires

Barlick, Al 1989
+Conlan, Jocko. 1974
+Connolly, Tom 1953

+Evans, Billy. 1973
+Hubbard, Cal. 1976

+Klem, Bill 1953
+McGowan, Bill. 1992

Pioneers and Executives

+Barrow, Ed. 1953	+Frick, Ford 1970	+Rickey, Branch. 1967
+Bulkeley, Morgan 1937	+Giles, Warren 1979	+Spalding, Al. 1939
+Cartwright, Alexander 1938	+Griffith, Clark 1946	+Veeck, Bill 1991
+Chadwick, Henry 1938	+Harridge, Will 1972	+Weiss, George 1971
+Chandler, Happy 1982	+Johnson, Ban 1937	+Wright, George. 1937
+Comiskey, Charles 1939	+Landis, Kenesaw 1944	+Wright, Harry 1953
+Cummings, Candy 1939	+MacPhail, Larry 1978	+Yawkey, Tom. 1980

J.G.Taylor Spink Award

First presented in 1962 by the Baseball Writers' Association of America for meritorious contributions by members of the BBWAA. Named in honor of the late publisher of *The Sporting News*, the Spink Award does not constitute induction into the Hall of Fame. Winners are honored in the year following their selection.

Year	Year	Year
1962 J.G.Taylor Spink	1974 John Carmichael	1982 Si Burick
1963 Ring Lardner	& James Isaminger	1983 Ken Smith
1964 Hugh Fullerton	1975 Tom Meaney	1984 Joe McGuff
1965 Charley Dryden	& Shirley Povich	1985 Earl Lawson
1966 Grantland Rice	1976 Harold Kaese	1986 Jack Lang
1967 Damon Runyon	& Red Smith	1987 Jim Murray
1968 H.G.Salsinger	1977 Gordon Cobbledick	1988 Bob Hunter & Ray Kelly
1969 Sid Mercer	& Edgar Munzel	1989 Jerome Holtzman
1970 Heywood C. Broun	1978 Tim Murnane	1990 Phil Collier
1971 Frank Graham	& Dick Young	1991 Ritter Collett
1972 Dan Daniel, Fred Lieb	1979 Bob Broeg & Tommy Holmes	
& J.Roy Stockton	1980 Joe Reichler & Milt Richman	
1973 Warren Brown, John Drebinger	1981 Bob Addie & Allen Lewis	
& John F. Kieran		

Ford Frick Award

First presented in 1978 by Hall of Fame for meritorious contributions by baseball broadcasters. Named in honor of the late broadcaster, National League president and commissioner, the Frick Award does not constitute induction into the Hall of Fame.

Year	Year	Year
1978 Mel Allen & Red Barber	1983 Jack Brickhouse	1988 Lindsey Nelson
1979 Bob Elson	1984 Curt Gowdy	1989 Harry Caray
1980 Russ Hodges	1985 Buck Canel	1990 Byrum Saam
1981 Ernie Harwell	1986 Bob Prince	1991 Joe Garagiola
1982 Vin Scully	1987 Jack Buck	1992 Milo Hamilton

BASKETBALL

Naismith Memorial Basketball Hall of Fame

Established in 1949 by the National Association of Basketball Coaches in memory of the sport's inventor, Dr.James Naismith. Original Hall opened in 1968 and current Hall in 1985. **Address:** 1150 West Columbus Avenue, Springfield, MA 01105. **Telephone:** (413) 781-6500.

Eligibility: Nominated players and referees must be retired for five years, coaches must have coached 25 years or be retired for five, and contributors must have already completed their noteworthy service to the game. Voting done by 24-member honors committee made up of media representatives, Hall of Fame members and trustees. Any nominee not elected after five years becomes eligible for consideration by the Veterans' Committee after a five-year wait.

Class of 1992 (9)**:** PLAYERS—forward **Connie Hawkins**, ABA (Pit-Min, 1967-69), NBA (Pho-LA-Atl, 1969-76); center **Bob Lanier**, college (St.Bonaventure, 1968-70), NBA (Det-Mil, 1970-84). COACHES—**Lou Carnesecca**, college (St.John's, 1966-70,73-92), ABA (NY, 1970-73); **Al McGuire**, college (Belmont Abbey, 1957-64 and Marquette, 1964-77); **Jack Ramsay**, college (St.Joseph's-PA, 1955-66), NBA (Phi-Buf-Port-Ind, 1968-89); **Phil Woolpert**, college (San Francisco, 1950-59 and San Diego, 1962-69). WOMEN—**Lucy Harris**, college (Delta St., 1974-77), U.S. Olympic team (1976); **Nera White** AAU (Nashville Business College, 1955-69). INTERNATIONAL— **Sergei Belov**, USSR National team (1968-80), USSR Olympic team (1968,72,76,80).

Members are listed with years of induction; (+) indicates deceased members.

Men

Archibald, Nate 1991	Bing, Dave. 1990	Cousy, Bob 1970
Arizin, Paul 1977	+Borgmann, Benny. 1961	Cowens, Dave. 1991
+Barlow, Thomas (Babe) 1980	Bradley, Bill 1982	Cunningham, Billy 1986
Barry, Rick 1987	+Brennan, Joe 1974	+Davies, Bob. 1969
Baylor, Elgin 1976	Cervi, Al. 1984	+DeBernardi, Forrest 1961
+Beckman, John 1972	Chamberlain, Wilt 1978	DeBusschere, Dave. 1982
Belov, Sergei 1992	+Cooper, Charles (Tarzan) 1976	+Dehnert, Dutch 1968

A Hawk Lands in Springfield

by Terry Pluto

If anyone invented the dunk shot—that exclamation point of today's NBA—it was Connie Hawkins. The Hawk dunked when such activity was frowned upon in basketball.

"When I did it, it was called hot-dogging," says Hawkins. "Now, they call it 'Showtime.' People associated those kinds of plays with blacks, and they didn't want to see it as part of the game."

If there is a family tree of Slamma Jamma, Hawkins is the grandfather, Julius Erving the father, and Michael Jordan the favorite son.

Some would trace the dunk back to Elgin Baylor, but Baylor's style was different. "When I played, you just didn't dunk on a guy," says Baylor. "It was considered showing him up. And the next time you went to the basket, your butt was going down."

Hawkins didn't care. He dunked anytime, anywhere and against anyone.

"One summer, I saw Connie play Wilt Chamberlain when Connie was in high school and Wilt was averaging 40-some in the NBA," recalls former Indiana Pacers forward Jerry Harkness. "Believe me, Connie more than held his own. He had the biggest hands and he'd hold the ball like a grapefruit, waving it around. He was doing all the Doctor J moves 15 years before anyone ever heard of Julius Erving."

Hawkins was a schoolboy sensation at Boys High in Brooklyn, leading his team to a pair of New York City titles in the late 1950's. But a promising college career at Iowa vanished when he was linked to a convicted game fixer his freshman year. Though no charges were ever proven, the NCAA and NBA banished him.

Cast into the darkness at age 19, Hawkins took work where he could find it, most notably with the Pittsburgh Rens of the American Basketball League and the Harlem Globetrotters. He was the ABL's leading scorer and MVP during the 1961-62 season, but the league soon folded. With the Trotters, his flamboyance should have made him a natural, but his artistic side was insulted by their haphazard approach to the game and he quit.

That might have been the end of the story, but when the American Basketball Associa-

Basketball Hall of Fame

Hall of Famer **Connie Hawkins** (right) gets a hug from fellow inductee **Bob Lanier** at their investiture on May 11, 1992.

tion opened for business in 1967-68, Hawkins returned to repeat his leading scorer-MVP double and carry the Pittsburgh Pipers to the first ABA championship.

His years of exile, however, continued to weigh on him. In 1969, after two seasons in the ABA, Hawkins sued the NBA for blackballing him. He won the case, received a million-dollar settlement and got a contract to play for the Phoenix Suns.

Hawkins was 27 when he joined the Suns and he had the knees of a 40-year-old, the price of being a legend on the unforgiving pavement of the playgrounds. Still, he managed to average 16.5 points a game in seven NBA seasons and made four All-Star teams.

"In the ABA, the feeling among the players was that they were ignored, starving artists, but one day—probably after they were dead—their work would hang in the Louvre," says NBC's Bob Costas, the one and only voice of the ABA's Spirits of St. Louis.

For Hawkins, that day came on May 11, when he was inducted into the Basketball Hall of Fame.

Terry Pluto covers the NBA for the *Akron Beacon Journal* and is the author of *Loose Balls*, an oral history of the ABA.

Basketball Hall of Fame (Cont.)

Endacott, Paul	1971	Jones, K. C	1989	Ramsey, Frank	1981
Foster, Bud	1964	Jones, Sam	1983	Reed, Willis	1981
Frazier, Walt	1987	Krause, Edward (Moose)	1975	Robertson, Oscar	1979
+Friedman, Marty	1971	Kurland, Bob	1961	+Roosma, John	1961
+Fulks, Joe	1977	Lanier, Bob	1992	+Russell, John (Honey)	1964
Gale, Laddie	1976	+Lapchick, Joe	1966	Russell, Bill	1974
Gallatin, Harry	1991	Lovellette, Clyde	1988	Schayes, Dolph	1972
Gates, William (Pop)	1989	Lucas, Jerry	1979	+Schmidt, Ernest J.	1973
Gola, Tom	1975	Luisetti, Hank	1959	+Schommer, John	1959
Greer, Hal	1981	Macauley, Ed	1960	+Sedran, Barney	1962
+Gruenig, Robert	1963	+Maravich, Pete	1987	Sharman, Bill	1975
Hagan, Cliff	1977	Martin, Slater	1981	+Steinmetz, Christian	1961
+Hanson, Victor	1960	+McCracken, Branch	1960	+Thompson, John (Cat)	1962
Havlicek, John	1983	+McCracken, Jack	1962	Thurmond, Nate	1984
Hawkins, Connie	1992	McDermott, Bobby	1988	Twyman, Jack	1982
Hayes, Elvin	1990	Mikan, George	1959	Unseld, Wes	1988
Heinsohn, Tom	1986	Monroe, Earl	1990	+Vandivier, Robert (Fuzzy)	1974
Holman, Nat	1964	Murphy, Charles (Stretch)	1960	+Wachter, Ed.	1961
Houbregs, Bob	1987	+Page, Harlan (Pat)	1962	Wanzer, Bobby	1987
+Hyatt, Chuck	1959	Pettit, Bob	1970	West, Jerry	1979
+Johnson, Bill (Skinny)	1976	Phillip, Andy	1961	Wilkens, Lenny	1989
+Johnston, Neil	1990	Pollard, Jim	1977	Wooden, John	1960

Women

Harris, Lucy	1992	White, Nera	1992

Coaches

+Anderson, Harold (Andy)	1984	Harshman, Marv	1984	McGuire, Frank	1976
+Auerbach, Red	1968	+Hickey, Eddie	1978	+Meanwell, Walter (Doc)	1959
+Barry, Sam	1978	+Hobson, Howard (Hobby)	1965	Meyer, Ray	1978
+Blood, Ernest (Prof)	1960	Holzman, Red	1986	Miller, Ralph	1988
Cann, Howard	1967	Iba, Hank	1968	Ramsay, Jack	1992
+Carlson, Henry (Doc)	1959	+Julian, Alvin (Doggie)	1967	+Rupp, Adolph	1968
Carnesecca, Lou	1992	+Keaney, Frank	1960	+Sachs, Leonard	1961
Carnevale, Ben	1969	+Keogan, George	1961	+Shelton, Everett	1979
+Case, Everett	1981	Knight, Bob	1991	Smith, Dean	1982
Dean, Everett	1966	+Lambert, Ward (Piggy)	1960	Taylor, Fred	1985
+Diddle, Ed	1971	Litwack, Harry	1975	Wade, Margaret	1984
+Drake, Bruce	1972	+Leoffler, Ken	1964	Watts, Stan	1985
Gaines, Clarence	1981	+Lonborg, Dutch	1972	Wooden, John	1972
Gardner, Jack	1983	McCutchan, Arad	1980	+Woolpert, Phil	1992
+Gill, Amory (Slats)	1967	McGuire, Al	1992	

Teams

Buffalo Germans	1961	New York Renaissance	1963	Original Celtics	1959
First Team	1959		

Referees

+Enright, Jim	1978	+Leith, Lloyd	1982	Shirley, J. Dallas	1979
+Hepbron, George	1960	Mihalik, Red	1986	Tobey, Dave	1961
+Hoyt, George	1961	Nucatola, John	1977	+Walsh, David	1961
+Kennedy, Pat	1959	+Quigley, Ernest (Quig)	1961	

Contributors

+Abbott, Senda Berenson	1984	Hinkle, Tony	1965	+Porter, Henry (H.V.)	1960
+Allen, Forrest (Phog)	1959	+Irish, Ned	1964	+Reid, William A	1963
+Bee, Clair	1967	+Jones, R. William	1964	+Ripley, Elmer	1972
+Brown, Walter A	1965	+Kennedy, Walter	1980	+St. John, Lynn W	1962
+Bunn, John	1964	+Liston, Emil (Liz)	1974	+Saperstein, Abe	1970
+Douglas, Bob	1971	McLendon, John	1978	+Schabinger, Arthur	1961
+Duer, Al	1981	+Mokray, Bill	1965	+Stagg, Amos Alonzo	1959
Fagen, Clifford B	1983	+Morgan, Ralph	1959	Stankovic, Boris	1991
+Fisher, Harry	1973	+Morgenweck, Frank (Pop)	1962	+Steitz, Ed	1983
+Fleisher, Larry	1991	+Naismith, James	1959	+Taylor, Chuck	1968
+Gottlieb, Eddie	1971	Newell, Pete	1978	+Teague, Bertha	1984
+Gulick, Luther	1959	+O'Brien, John J. (Jack)	1961	+Tower, Oswald	1959
Harrison, Les	1979	+O'Brien, Larry	1991	+Trester, Ather (A.L.)	1961
+Hepp, Ferenc	1980	+Olsen, Harold G.	1959	+Wells, Cliff	1971
+Hickox, Ed	1959	+Podoloff, Maurice	1973	+Wilke, Lou	1982

Basketball Hall of Fame (Cont.)
Curt Gowdy Award

First presented in 1990 by the Hall of Fame Board of Trustees for meritorious contributions by the media. Named in honor of the former NBC sportscaster, the Gowdy Award does not constitute induction into the Hall of Fame.

Year	Year	Year
1990 Curt Gowdy and Dick Herbert	1991 Dave Dorr and Marty Glickman	1992 Sam Goldaper and Chick Hearn

BOWLING

National Hall of Fame

The National Bowling Hall is one museum with separate wings for honorees of the American Bowling Congress (ABC), Professional Bowlers' Association (PBA) and Women's International Bowling Congress (WIBC). **Address:** 111 Stadium Plaza, St.Louis, MO 63102. **Telephone:** (314) 231-6340.

American Bowling Congress

Established in 1941 and open to professional and amateur bowlers. **Eligibility:** Nominated bowlers must have competed in at least 20 years of ABC tournaments. Voting done by 170-member panel made up of ABC officials, Hall of Fame members and media representatives.

Class of 1992 (4)**:** Performance—**Gary Dickinson** and **Bud Horn**; Meritorious Service—**Dick Evans** and **Bill Franklin**.

Members are listed with years of induction; (+) indicates deceased members.

Performance

Allison, Glenn	1979	Godman, Jim	1987	O'Donnell, Chuck	1968
Anthony, Earl	1986	Golembiewski, Billy	1979	Pappas, George	1989
+Asplund, Harold	1978	Guenther, Johnny	1988	+Patterson, Pat	1974
Baer, Gordy	1987	Hardwick, Billy	1985	Ritger, Dick	1984
Beach, Bill	1991	Hennessey, Tom	1976	Salvino, Carmen	1979
Benkovic, Frank	1958	Hoover, Dick	1974	Schissler, Les	1991
Billick, George	1982	Horn, Bud	1992	Schroeder, Jim	1990
+Blouin, Jimmy	1953	Howard, George	1986	+Schwoegler, Connie	1968
Bluth, Ray	1973	Jackson, Eddie	1988	Semiz, Teata	1991
+Bodis, Joe	1941	Johnson, Don	1982	+Sielaff, Lou	1968
+Bomar, Buddy	1966	Johnson, Earl	1987	+Sinke, Joe	1977
+Brandt, Allie	1960	+Joseph, Joe	1969	+Sixty, Billy	1961
+Brosius, Eddie	1976	+Jouglard, Lee	1979	Smith, Harry	1978
+Bujack, Fred	1967	+Kartheiser, Frank	1967	+Smith, Jimmy	1941
Bunetta, Bill	1968	+Kawolics, Ed	1968	Soutar, Dave	1985
Burton, Nelson, Sr	1964	+Kissoff, Joe	1976	+Sparando, Tony	1968
Burton, Nelson, Jr	1981	Klares, John	1982	+Spinella, Barney	1968
+Campi, Lou	1968	+Knox, Billy	1954	+Steers, Harry	1941
+Carlson, Adolph	1941	+Koster, John	1941	Stefanich, Jim	1983
Carter, Don	1970	+Krems, Eddie	1973	+Stein, Otto, Jr	1971
+Caruana, Frank	1977	Kristof, Joe	1968	Stoudt, Bud	1991
+Cassio, Marty	1972	+Krumske, Paul	1968	Strampe, Bob	1977
+Castellano, Graz	1976	+Lange, Herb	1941	+Thoma, Sykes	1971
+Clause, Frank	1980	Lauman, Hank	1976	Toft, Rod	1991
Cohn, Alfred	1985	Lillard, Bill	1972	Tountas, Pete	1989
+Crimmins, Johnny	1962	Lindenman, Tony	1979	Tucker, Bill	1988
Davis, Dave	1990	+Lindsey, Mort	1941	+Varipapa, Andy	1957
+Daw, Charlie	1941	Lippe, Harry	1989	+Ward, Walter	1959
+Day, Ned	1952	Lubanski, Ed	1971	Weber, Dick	1970
Dickinson, Gary	1992	Lucci, Vince, Sr	1978	+Welu, Billy	1975
+Easter, Sarge	1963	+Marino, Hank	1941	+Wilman, Joe	1951
Ellis, Don	1981	+Martino, John	1969	+Wolf, Phil	1961
+Falcaro, Joe	1968	+McMahon, Junie	1967	Wonders, Rich	1990
Faragalli, Lindy	1968	+Mercurio, Skang	1967	+Young, George	1959
Fazio, Buzz	1963	+Meyers, Norm	1984	Zahn, Wayne	1980
+Gersonde, Russ	1968	+Nagy, Steve	1963	Zikes, Les	1983
+Gibson, Therm	1965	Norris, Joe	1954	+Zunker, Gil	1941

Meritorious Service

+Allen, Harold	1966	+Coker, John	1980	Evans, Dick	1992
Baker, Frank	1975	+Collier, Chuck	1963	Franklin, Bill	1992
+Baumgarten, Elmer	1963	+Cruchon, Steve	1983	+Hagerty, Jack	1963
+Bellisimo, Lou	1986	+Ditzen, Walt	1973	+Hattstrom, H.A.(Doc)	1980
+Bensinger, Bob	1969	+Doehrman, Bill	1968	+Hermann, Cone	1968
+Chase, LeRoy	1972	Elias, Eddie	1985	+Howley, Pete	1941

+Kennedy, Bob 1981
+Langtry, Abe 1963
+Levine, Sam. 1971
+Luby, David. 1969
Luby, Mort, Jr. 1988
+Luby, Mort, Sr. 1974
+McCullough, Howard. 1971

+Patterson, Morehead 1985
+Petersen, Louie 1963
Pezzano, Chuck 1982
Pluckhahn, Bruce 1989
+Raymer, Milt 1972
+Reed, Elmer. 1978
Rudo, Milt 1984

Schenkel, Chris. 1988
+Sweeney, Dennis. 1974
+Thum, Joe 1980
Weinstein, Sam. 1970
+Whitney, Eli 1975
Wolf, Fred 1976

Professional Bowlers Association

Established in 1975. **Eligibility:** Nominees must be PBA members and at least 35 years old. Voting done by 50-member panel that includes writers who have covered bowling for at least 12 years.

Class of 1992 (3): Performance—**Roy Buckley**; Veteran—**Skee Foremsky**; Meritorious Service—**Jack Reichert**.

Members are listed with years of induction; (+) indicates deceased members.

Performance

+Allen, Bill 1983
Anthony, Earl. 1986
Berardi, Joe. 1990
Bluth, Ray 1975
Buckley, Roy 1992
Burton, Nelson, Jr. 1979
Carter, Don. 1975
Colwell, Paul. 1991
Davis, Dave 1978
Dickinson, Gary 1988

Durbin, Mike. 1984
Fazio, Buzz 1976
Godman, Jim 1987
Hardwick, Billy 1977
Holman, Marshall. 1990
Hudson, Tommy. 1989
Johnson, Don 1977
Laub, Larry 1985
Pappas, George 1986
Petraglia, John 1982

Ritger, Dick 1978
Roth, Mark. 1987
Salvino, Carmen 1975
Smith, Harry 1975
Soutar, Dave 1979
Stefanich, Jim 1980
Weber, Dick 1975
+Welu, Billy 1975
Zahn, Wayne 1981

Veterans

Allison, Glenn. 1984
Asher, Barry. 1988
Foremsky, Skee. 1992
Guenther, Johnny. 1986

+Joseph, Joe 1985
Marzich, Andy. 1990
McCune, Don 1991

McGrath, Mike 1988
+St.John, Jim. 1989
Strampe, Bob 1987

Meritorious Service

Archibald, John. 1989
Elias, Eddie 1976
Esposito, Frank 1975
Evans, Dick 1986
Firestone, Raymond 1987
Fisher, E.A.(Bud) 1984

+Frantz, Lou 1978
Golden, Harry. 1983
Hoffman, Ted, Jr. 1985
Jowdy, John 1988
Kelley, Joe 1989
+Nagy, Steve. 1977

Pezzano, Chuck 1975
Reichert, Jack 1992
+Richards, Joe. 1976
Schenkel, Chris. 1976
Stitzlein, Lorraine 1980
Thompson, Al 1991

Women's International Bowling Congress

Established in 1953. **Eligibility:** Performance nominees must have won at least one WIBC Championship Tournament title, a WIBC Queens tournament title or an international competition title and have bowled in at least 15 national WIBC Championship Tournaments (unless injury or illness cut career short).

Class of 1992 (3): Performance—**Linda Graham**; Meritorious Service—**Clover Bayley** and **Billie O'Connor**.

Members are listed with years of induction; (+) indicates deceased members.

Performance

Abel, Joy 1984
Bolt, Mae. 1978
Bouvia, Gloria. 1987
Boxberger, Loa 1984
Buckner, Pam 1990
Burling, Catherine 1958
+Burns, Nina. 1977
Cantaline, Anita 1979
Carter, LaVerne 1977
Coburn, Doris. 1976
Costello, Pat 1986
Costello, Patty 1989
Dryer, Pat 1978
Duval, Helen 1970
Fellmeth, Catherine 1970
Fothergill, Dotty. 1980
+Fritz, Deane. 1966
Garms, Shirley 1971
Gloor, Olga 1976
Graham, Linda 1992
Graham, Mary Lou 1989
+Greenwald, Goldie. 1953
Grinfelds, Vesma 1991

+Harman, Janet 1985
+Hartrick, Stella. 1972
+Hatch, Grayce. 1953
Havlish, Jean. 1987
Hoffman, Martha 1979
Holm, Joan 1974
+Humphreys, Birdie 1979
Jacobson, D.D 1981
+Jaeger, Emma. 1953
Kelly, Annesse 1985
+Knechtges, Doris. 1983
Kuczynski, Betty. 1981
Ladewig, Marion. 1964
Martin, Sylvia Wene 1966
Martorella, Millie. 1975
+Matthews, Merle 1974
+McCutcheon, Floretta 1956
Merrick, Marge. 1980
+Mikiel, Val 1979
+Miller, Dorothy 1954
Mivelaz, Betty 1991
Morris, Betty 1983
Nichols, Lorrie 1989

Norton, Virginia 1988
Notaro, Phyllis. 1979
Ortner, Bev 1972
Powers, Connie. 1973
+Robinson, Leona 1969
+Rump, Anita 1962
+Ruschmeyer, Addie. 1961
+Ryan, Esther. 1963
+Sablatnik, Ethel. 1979
+Schulte, Myrtle. 1965
+Shablis, Helen 1977
+Simon, Violet (Billy) 1960
+Small, Tess 1971
+Smith, Grace. 1968
Soutar, Judy 1976
+Stockdale, Louise 1953
Toepfer, Elvira 1976
+Twyford, Sally 1964
+Warmbier, Marie 1953
Wilkinson, Dorothy 1990
+Winandy, Cecelia 1975
Zimmerman, Donna 1982

WIBC Hall of Fame (Cont.)
Meritorious Service

Baetz, Helen 1977
+Baker, Helen 1989
+Bayley, Clover 1992
Berger, Winifred 1976
+Bohlen, Philena 1955
Borschuk, Lo 1988
Botkin, Freda 1986
+Chapman, Emily 1957
+Crowe, Alberta 1982
+Dornblaser, Gertrude 1979
Duffy, Agnes 1987
Finke, Gertrude 1990
+Fisk, Rae 1983

+Haas, Dorothy 1977
+Higley, Margaret 1969
+Hochstadter, Bee 1967
+Kay, Nora 1964
+Kelly, Ellen 1979
Kelone, Theresa 1978
+Knepprath, Jeannette 1963
+Lasher, Iolia 1967
Marrs, Mabel 1979
+McBride, Bertha 1968
+Menne, Catherine 1979
+Mraz, Jo 1959
O'Connor, Billie 1992

+Phaler, Emma 1965
+Porter, Cora 1986
+Quinn, Zoe 1979
+Rishling, Gertrude 1972
Simone, Anne 1991
Sloan, Catherine 1985
+Speck, Berdie 1966
+Spring, Alma 1979
+Switzer, Pearl 1973
+Veatch, Georgia 1974
+White, Mildred 1975
+Wood, Ann 1970

BOXING

International Boxing Hall of Fame

Established in 1989 and opened in 1990. **Address:** 1 Hall of Fame Drive, Canastota, NY 13032. **Telephone:** (315) 697-7095.

Eligibility: All nominees must be retired for five years. Voting done by 115-member panel made up of Boxing Writers' Association members and world-wide boxing historians.

Class of 1992: 29 third-year members (see below).

Members are listed with year of induction; (+) indicates deceased members.

Modern Era

Ali, Muhammad 1990
Arguello, Alexis 1992
+Armstrong, Henry 1990
Basilio, Carmen 1990
Benvenuti, Nino 1992
Burley, Charley 1992
+Cerdan, Marcel 1991
+Charles, Ezzard 1990
Conn, Billy 1990
Foster, Bob 1990
Frazier, Joe 1990
Fullmer, Gene 1991
Gavilan, Kid 1990

+Graham, Billy 1992
+Graziano, Rocky 1991
Griffith, Emile 1990
Jack, Beau 1991
Jofre, Eder 1992
LaMotta, Jake 1990
+Liston, Sonny 1991
+Louis, Joe 1990
+Marciano, Rocky 1990
Monzon, Carlos 1990
Moore, Archie 1990
Napoles, Jose 1990
Norton, Ken 1992

Olivares, Ruben 1991
Ortiz, Carlos 1991
Patterson, Floyd 1991
Pep, Willie 1990
+Robinson, Sugar Ray 1990
Saddler, Sandy 1990
+Sanchez, Salvadore 1991
Schmeling, Max 1992
+Tiger, Dick 1991
+Walcott, Jersey Joe 1990
Williams, Ike 1990
Zale, Tony 1991

Old-Timers

Ambers, Lou 1992
+Attell, Abe 1990
+Britton, Jack 1990
+Brown, Panama Al 1992
+Canzoneri, Tony 1990
+Carpentier, Georges 1991
+Chocolate, Kid 1991
+Corbett, James J 1990
+Dempsey, Jack 1990
+Dempsey, Jack (the Nonpareil) . 1992
+Dixon, George 1990
+Driscoll, Jim 1990
+Dundee, Johnny 1991

+Fitzsimmons, Bob 1990
+Gans, Joe 1990
+Gibbons, Mike 1992
+Greb, Harry 1990
+Griffo, Young 1991
+Jackson, Peter 1990
+Jeffries, James J 1990
+Johnson, Jack 1990
+Ketchel, Stanley 1990
+Langford, Sam 1990
+Leonard, Benny 1990
+Lewis, Ted (Kid) 1992
+Loughran, Tommy 1991

+McCoy, Charles (Kid) 1991
+McFarland, Packey 1992
+McGovern, Terry 1990
McLarnin, Jimmy 1991
+Nelson, Battling 1992
+Ross, Barney 1990
+Ryan, Tommy 1991
+Tunney, Gene 1990
+Walker, Mickey 1990
+Walcott, Joe 1991
+Wilde, Jimmy 1990
+Wills, Harry 1992

Pioneers

+Belcher, Jem 1992
+Broughton, Jack 1990
+Burke, James 1992
+Cribb, Tom 1991
+Figg, James 1992

+Jackson, John 1992
+King, Tom 1992
+Langham, Nat 1992
+Mace, Jem 1990
+Mendoza, Daniel 1990

+Sayers, Tom 1990
Spring, Tom 1992
+Sullivan, John L 1990
+Thompson, William 1991

Non-Participants

+Andrews, Thomas S 1992
Arcel, Ray 1991
+Blackburn, Jack 1992
+Chambers, John Graham 1990
+Coffroth, James W 1991
Dundee, Angelo 1992

+Egan, Pierce 1991
+Fleischer, Nat 1990
+Goldman, Charley 1992
+Jacobs, Mike 1990
+Kearns, Jack (Doc) 1990
+Liebling, A.J. 1992

+Lonsdale, Lord 1990
Markson, Harry 1992
+Parnassus, George 1991
+Queensberry, Marquis of 1990
+Rickard, Tex 1990
+Walker, James J.(Jimmy) 1992

FOOTBALL

College Football Hall of Fame

Established in 1955 by the National Football Foundation. **Address:** 5440 Kings Island Drive, Kings Island, OH 45034 (currently closed to visitors, but is moving to South Bend, Ind., and will reopen in the spring of 1994.) **Telephone:** (513)-398-5410.

Eligibility: Nominated players must be out of college 10 years and a first team All-America pick by a major selector during career; coaches must be retired three years. Voting done by 12-member panel of athletic directors, conference and bowl officials and media representatives.

Class of 1992 (13): PLAYERS—HB **Ron Johnson**, Michigan (1966-68); LB **Jim Lynch**, Notre Dame (1964-66); T **Lou Michaels**, Kentucky (1954-57); C-LB **Larry Morris**, Georgia Tech (1951-54); QB **Craig Morton**, California (1962-64); HB **Bob Odell**, Penn (1941-43); T **Loyd Phillips**, Arkansas (1964-66); E **Howard Twilley**, Tulsa (1963-65); T **Jim Weatherall**, Oklahoma (1949-51); E **Art Weiner**, North Carolina (1946-49); DL **Jack Youngblood**, Florida (1968-70). COACHES—**Earl Banks**, Morgan St.(1960-73); **John Ralston**, Utah St.(1959-62), Stanford (1963-71).

Players are listed with final year they played in college and coaches are listed with year of induction; (+) indicates deceased members.

Players

+Abell, Earl–Colgate 1915
+Agase, Alex–Purdue/Ill. 1946
+Agganis, Harry–Boston U 1952
Albert, Frank–Stanford 1941
+Aldrich, Ki–TCU 1938
+Aldrich, Malcolm–Yale 1921
+Alexander, Joe–Syracuse 1920
Alworth, Lance–Arkansas 1961
+Ames, Knowlton–Princeton 1889
+Ameche, Alan–Wisconsin 1954
Amling, Warren–Ohio St 1946
Anderson, Donny–Tex.Tech. 1966
+Anderson, Hunk–N.Dame. 1921
Atkins, Doug–Tennessee 1952

Bacon, Everett–Wesleyan 1912
Bagnell, Reds–Penn 1950
+Baker, Hobey–Princeton 1913
+Baker, John–USC 1931
+Baker, Moon–N'western 1926
Baker, Terry–Oregon St 1962
+Ballin, Harold–Princeton 1914
+Banker, Bill–Tulane 1929
Banonis, Vince–Detroit 1941
+Barnes, Stan–California 1921
+Barrett, Charles–Cornell 1915
+Baston, Bert–Minnesota 1916
+Battles, Cliff–WV Wesleyan 1931
Baugh, Sammy–TCU 1936
Baughan, Maxie–Ga.Tech. 1959
+Bausch, James–Kansas 1930
Beagle, Ron–Navy 1955
Beban, Gary–UCLA 1967
Bechtol, Hub–Texas 1946
+Beckett, John–Oregon 1916
Bednarik, Chuck–Penn. 1948
Behm, Forrest–Nebraska 1940
Bell, Bobby–Minnesota. 1962
Bellino, Joe–Navy. 1960
Below, Marty–Wisconsin 1923
+Benbrook, Al–Michigan 1910
Bertelli, Angelo–N.Dame. 1943
+Berry, Charlie–Lafayette. 1924
Berwanger, Jay–Chicago. 1935
+Bettencourt, L.–St.Mary's 1927
Biletnikoff, Fred–Fla.St. 1964
Blanchard, Doc–Army 1946
+Blozis, Al–Georgetown. 1942
Bock, Ed–Iowa St 1938
Bomar, Lynn–Vanderbilt 1924
+Bomeisler, Bo–Yale 1913
+Booth, Albie–Yale. 1931

+Borries, Fred–Navy. 1934
Bosely, Bruce–West Va. 1955
Bosseler, Don–Miami,FL 1956
Bottari, Vic–California 1938
+Boynton, Ben–Williams 1920
+Brewer, Charles–Harvard 1895
+Bright, Johnny–Drake. 1951
Brodie, John–Stanford 1956
+Brooke, George–Penn 1895
Brown, Geo–Navy/S.Diego St . . 1947
+Brown, Gordon–Yale 1900
+Brown, John, Jr.–Navy. 1913
+Brown, Johnny Mack–Ala 1925
Brown, Tay–USC 1932
+Bunker, Paul–Army. 1902
Burton, Ron–N'western 1959
+Butkus, Dick–Illinois 1964
+Butler, Robert–Wisconsin 1912

Cafego, George–Tenn. 1939
+Cagle, Red–SWLa/Army 1929
+Cain, John–Alabama. 1932
Cameron, Ed–Wash.& Lee 1924
+Campbell, David–Harvard 1901
Campbell, Earl–Texas 1977
+Cannon, Jack–N.Dame. 1929
+Carideo, Frank–N.Dame. 1930
Caroline, J.C.–Illinois. 1954
+Carney, Charles–Illinois. 1921
Carpenter, Bill–Army 1959
+Carpenter, Hunter–Va.Tech. 1905
Carroll, Chas.–Washington. 1928
+Casey, Edward–Harvard 1919
Cassady, Howard–Ohio St 1955
+Chamberlin, Guy–Neb. 1915
Chapman, Sam–California 1938
Chappuis, Bob–Michigan 1947
+Christman, Paul–Missouri 1940
+Clark, Dutch–Colo. Col. 1929
Cleary, Paul–USC. 1947
+Clevenger, Zora–Indiana. 1903
Cloud, Jack–Wm&Mary. 1948
+Cochran, Gary–Princeton 1897
+Cody, Josh–Vanderbilt 1919
Coleman, Don–Mich.St 1951
Conerly, Charlie–Miss 1947
Connor, George–HC/ND 1947
+Corbin, William–Yale. 1888
Corbus, William–Stanford 1933
+Cowan, Hector–Princeton 1889
+Coy, Edward (Tad)–Yale 1909
+Crawford, Fred–Duke 1933

Crow, John David–Tex.A&M 1957
+Crowley, Jim–Notre Dame 1924
Csonka, Larry–Syracuse. 1967
Cutter, Slade–Navy 1934
+Czarobski, Ziggie–N.Dame. 1947

Dale, Carroll–Va.Tech 1959
+Dalrymple, Gerald–Tulane 1931
Daniell, Averell–Pitt. 1936
+Daniell, James–Ohio St 1941
Dalton, John–Navy. 1911
Daly, Chas.–Harvard/Army. 1902
+Davies, Tom–Pittsburgh 1921
+Davis, Ernie–Syracuse 1961
Davis, Glenn–Army 1946
Davis, Robert–Ga.Tech 1947
Dawkins, Pete–Army. 1958
DeRogatis, Al–Duke 1948
+DesJardien, Paul–Chicago 1914
+Devine, Aubrey–Iowa 1921
+DeWitt, John–Princeton 1903
Ditka, Mike–Pittsburgh. 1960
Dobbs, Glenn–Tulsa 1942
+Dodd, Bobby–Tennessee 1930
Donan, Holland–Princeton 1950
+Donchess, Joseph–Pitt 1929
+Dougherty, Nathan–Tenn 1909
Drahos, Nick–Cornell 1940
+Driscoll, Paddy–N'western. 1917
+Drury, Morley–USC 1927
Dudley, Bill–Virginia. 1941

Easley, Kenny–UCLA 1980
+Eckersall, Walter–Chicago. 1906
+Edwards, Turk–Wash.St 1931
Edwards, Wm.–Princeton 1899
+Eichenlaub, Ray–N.Dame 1914
Elliott, Bump–Mich/Purdue 1947
Evans, Ray–Kansas. 1947
+Exendine, Albert–Carlisle 1907

Falaschi, Nello–S.Clara. 1936
Fears, Tom–S.Clara/UCLA 1947
+Feathers, Beattie–Tenn. 1933
Fenimore, Bob–Okla.St 1946
+Fenton, Doc–LSU 1909
Ferraro, John–USC 1944
Fesler, Wes–Ohio St. 1930
+Fincher, Bill–Ga.Tech. 1920
Fischer, Bill–Notre Dame 1948
+Fish, Hamilton–Harvard. 1909
+Fisher, Robert–Harvard 1911
+Flowers, Allen–Ga.Tech. 1920

College Football Hall of Fame (Cont.)

Fortmann Danny–Colgate.... 1935
Francis, Sam–Nebraska...... 1936
Franco, Ed–Fordham......... 1937
+Frank, Clint–Yale 1937
Franz, Rodney–California 1949
+Friedman, Benny–Michigan ... 1926

Gabriel, Roman–N.C.State ... 1961
Gain, Bob–Kentucky......... 1950
+Galiffa, Arnold–Army........ 1949
Gallarneau, Hugh–Stanford ... 1940
+Garbisch, Edgar–W.& J./Army . 1924
Garrett, Mike–USC........... 1965
+Gelbert, Charles–Penn....... 1896
Geyer, Forest–Oklahoma 1915
Giel, Paul–Minnesota......... 1953
Gifford, Frank–USC.......... 1951
+Gilbert, Walter–Auburn 1936
+Gipp, George–N.Dame....... 1920
+Gladchuk, Chet–Boston Col ... 1940
Glass, Bill–Baylor 1956
Goldberg, Marshall–Pitt....... 1938
Goodreault, Gene–BC........ 1940
+Gordon, Walter–Calif 1918
+Governali, Paul–Columbia 1942
Graham, Otto–N'western 1943
+Grange, Red–Illinois......... 1925
+Grayson, Bobby–Stanford 1935
+Green, Jack–Tulane/Army..... 1945
+Green, Joe–N.Texas St....... 1968
Griese, Bob–Purdue.......... 1966
Griffin, Archie–Ohio St....... 1975
+Gulick, Merle–Toledo/Hobart . 1929
+Guyon, Joe–Ga.Tech........ 1918

+Hale, Edwin–Miss.College ... 1921
Hall, Parker–Miss 1938
Ham, Jack–Penn.St 1970
Hamilton, Bob–Stanford 1935
Hamilton, Tom–Navy........ 1926
+Hanson, Vic–Syracuse 1926
+Hardwick, Tack–Harvard..... 1914
+Hare, T.Truxton–Penn 1900
+Harley, Chick–Ohio St....... 1919
+Harmon, Tom–Michigan 1940
+Harpster, Howard–Carnegie.. 1928
+Hart, Edward–Princeton 1911
Hart, Leon–Notre Dame 1949
Hartman, Bill–Georgia........ 1937
+Hazel, Homer–Rutgers....... 1924
+Hazeltine, Matt–Calif 1954
+Healey, Ed.–Dartmouth...... 1916
+Heffelfinger, Pudge–Yale..... 1891
Hein, Mel–Washington St 1930
+Heinrich, Don–Washington ... 1952
Hendricks, Ted–Miami,FL 1968
+Henry, Wilbur–Wash&Jeff 1919
+Herschberger, C.–Chicago ... 1898
+Herwig, Robert–Calif 1937
+Heston, Willie–Michigan 1904
+Hickman, Herman–Tenn 1931
+Hickok, William–Yale........ 1894
Hill, Dan–Duke.............. 1938
+Hillebrand, Art–Princeton..... 1899
+Hinkey, Frank–Yale 1894
Hinkle, Carl–Vanderbilt....... 1937
Hinkle, Clarke–Bucknell...... 1931
Hirsch, Elroy–Wisc./Mich 1943
+Hitchcock, James–Auburn 1932
Hoffmann, Frank–N.Dame..... 1931
+Hogan, James J.–Yale........ 1904
+Holland, Brud–Cornell....... 1938

+Holleder, Don–Army 1955
+Hollenback, Bill–Penn 1908
Holovak, Mike–Boston Col 1942
Holub, E.J.–Texas Tech 1960
Hornung, Paul–N.Dame...... 1956
Horrell, Edwin–California 1924
Horvath, Les–Ohio St........ 1944
+Howe, Arthur–Yale........... 1911
+Howell, Dixie–Alabama 1934
+Hubbard, Cal–Centenary 1926
+Hubbard, John–Amherst 1906
+Hubert, Pooley–Ala.......... 1925
Huff, Sam–West Virginia 1955
Humble, Weldon–Rice 1946
+Hunt, Joe–Texas A&M 1927
Huntington, Ellery–Colgate ... 1914
Hutson, Don–Alabama 1934

+Ingram, Jonas–Navy 1906
+Isbell, Cecil–Purdue......... 1937

+Jablonsky, J.–Army/Wash ... 1933
Janowicz, Vic–Ohio St....... 1951
+Jenkins, Darold–Missouri..... 1941
+Jensen, Jackie–California 1948
+Joesting, Herbert–Minn...... 1927
Johnson, Bob–Tennessee...... 1967
+Johnson, Jimmie–Carlisle/
                        N'western ... 1903
Johnson, Ron–Michigan...... 1968
+Jones, Calvin–Iowa 1955
+Jones, Gomer–Ohio St 1935
Jordan, Lee Roy–Alabama 1962
+Juhan, Frank–U.of South..... 1910
Justice, Charlie–N.Car....... 1949

+Kaer, Mort–USC............ 1926
Karras, Alex–Iowa 1957
Kavanaugh, Ken–LSU 1939
+Kaw, Edgar–Cornell......... 1922
Kazmaier, Dick–Princeton 1951
+Keck, James–Princeton...... 1921
Kelley, Larry–Yale........... 1936
+Kelly, Wild Bill–Montana 1926
Kenna, Doug–Army.......... 1944
+Kerr, George–Boston Col 1941
+Ketcham, Henry–Yale 1913
Keyes, Leroy–Purdue 1968
+Killinger, Glenn–Penn St 1921
+Kilpatrick, John–Yale 1910
Kimbrough, John–TexA&M 1940
+Kinard, Frank–Mississippi 1937
+King, Phillip–Princeton 1893
+Kinnick, Nile–Iowa 1939
+Kipke, Harry–Michigan 1923
+Kirkpatrick, John–Yale 1910
+Kitzmiller, John–Oregon 1930
+Koch, Barton–Baylor........ 1931
+Koppisch, Walt–Columbia.... 1924
Kramer, Ron–Michigan 1956
Krueger, Charlie–Tex.A&M 1957
Kutner, Malcolm–Texas 1941
Kwalick, Ted–Penn St 1968

+Lach, Steve–Duke........... 1941
+Lane, Myles–Dartmouth..... 1927
Lattner, Johnny–N.Dame...... 1953
Lauricella, Hank–Tenn....... 1952
+Lautenschlaeger–Tulane 1925
+Layden, Elmer–N.Dame 1924
+Layne, Bobby–Texas........ 1947
+Lea, Langdon–Princeton 1895
LeBaron, Eddie–Pacific....... 1949

+Leech, James–VMI 1920
Lester, Darrell–TCU 1935
Lilly, Bob–TCU 1960
Little, Floyd–Syracuse 1966
+Lio, Augie–Georgetown...... 1940
+Locke, Gordon–Iowa 1922
+Lourie, Don–Princeton 1921
Lucas, Richie–Penn St....... 1959
Luckman, Sid–Columbia 1938
Lujack, Johnny–N.Dame...... 1947
Lund, Pug–Minnesota 1934
Lynch, Jim–Notre Dame 1966

+Macomber, Bart–Illinois...... 1915
MacLeod, Robert–Dart....... 1938
Maegle, Dick–Rice 1954
+Mahan, Eddie–Harvard...... 1915
Majors, John–Tennessee 1956
+Mallory, William–Yale 1923
Mancha, Vaughn–Ala 1947
+Mann, Gerald–SMU......... 1927
Manning, Archie–Miss 1970
Manske, Edgar–N'western.... 1933
Marinaro, Ed–Cornell 1971
Markov, Vic–Washington...... 1937
+Marshall, Bobby–Minn....... 1906
Matson, Ollie–San Fran....... 1952
Matthews, Ray–TCU.......... 1927
+Maulbetsch, John–Mich 1914
+Mauthe, Pete–Penn St....... 1912
+Maxwell, Robert–Chicago/
                        Swarthmore .. 1906
McAfee, George–Duke 1939
+McClung, Thomas–Yale....... 1891
McColl, Bill–Stanford 1951
+McCormick, Jim–Princeton ... 1907
McDonald, Tommy–Okla 1956
+McDowall, Jack–N.C.State 1927
McElhenny, Hugh–Wash 1951
+McEver, Gene–Tennessee 1931
+McEwan, John–Army 1916
McFadden, Banks–Clemson ... 1939
McFadin, Bud–Texas 1950
McGee, Mike–Duke 1959
+McGinley, Edward–Penn 1924
+McGovern, John–Minn 1910
McGraw, Thurman–Colo.St.... 1949
+McKeever, Mike–USC........ 1960
+McLaren, George–Pitt 1918
+McMillan, Dan–USC/Calif..... 1922
+McMillin, Bo–Centre........ 1921
+McWhorter, Bob–Georgia 1913
+Mercer, LeRoy–Penn........ 1912
Meredith,Don–SMU 1959
+Metzger, Bert–N.Dame 1930
+Meylan, Wayne–Nebraska ... 1967
Michaels, Lou–Kentucky...... 1957
Mickal, Abe–LSU 1935
Miller, Creighton–N.Dame 1943
+Miller, Don–Notre Dame 1924
Miller, Rip–Notre Dame....... 1924
+Miller, Eugene–Penn St 1913
+Miller, Fred–Notre Dame..... 1928
Millner, Wayne–N.Dame...... 1935
+Milstead, C.A.–Wabash/Yale .. 1923
+Minds, John–Penn 1897
Minisi, Skip–Penn/Navy 1947
+Moffat, Alex–Princeton....... 1883
+Molinski, Ed–Tenn 1940
Montgomery, Cliff–Columbia .. 1933
Moomaw, Donn–UCLA....... 1952

+Morley, William–Columbia 1902
Morris, George–Ga.Tech...... 1952
Morris, Larry–Ga.Tech........ 1954
Morton, Craig–California...... 1964
+Morton, Bill–Dartmouth....... 1931
+Moscrip, Monk–Stanford...... 1935
+Muller, Brick–California....... 1922

+Nagurski, Bronko–Minn....... 1929
+Nevers, Ernie–Stanford 1925
+Newell, Marshall–Harvard..... 1893
Newman, Harry–Michigan 1932
Nobis, Tommy–Texas......... 1965
Nomellini, Leo–Minnesota 1949

+Oberlander, Andrew–Dart. 1925
+O'Brien, Davey–TCU 1938
+O'Dea, Pat–Wisconsin 1899
Odell, Bob–Penn 1943
+O'Hearn, Jack–Cornell 1915
Olds, Robin–Army 1942
+Oliphant, Elmer–Army/Pur 1917
Olsen, Merlin–Utah St 1961
+Oosterbaan, Bennie–Mich..... 1927
O'Rourke, Charles–BC 1940
+Orsi, John–Colgate 1931
+Osgood, Win–Cornell 1892
Osmanski, Bill–Holy Cross 1938
+Owen, George–Harvard 1922
Owens, Jim–Oklahoma...... 1949
Owens, Steve–Oklahoma 1969

Pardee, Jack–Texas A&M...... 1956
Parilli, Babe–Kentucky 1951
Parker, Ace–Duke............ 1936
Parker, Jackie–Miss.St 1953
Parker, Jim–Ohio St......... 1956
+Pazzetti, Vince–Lehigh 1912
+Peabody, Chub–Harvard...... 1941
+Peck, Robert–Pittsburgh 1916
+Pennock, Stan–Harvard....... 1914
Pfann, George–Cornell 1923
+Phillips, H.D.–U.of South 1904
Phillips, Loyd–Arkansas 1966
Pingel, John–Michigan St...... 1938
Pihos, Pete–Indiana 1946
+Pinckert, Erny–USC.......... 1931
Plunkett, Jim–Stanford 1970
+Poe, Arthur–Princeton........ 1899
+Pollard, Fritz–Brown 1916
Poole, B.–Miss/NC/Army..... 1947
Pregulman, Merv–Michigan 1943
+Price, Eddie–Tulane 1949
+Pund, Peter–Georgia Tech..... 1928

Ramsey, G.–Wm&Mary 1942
+Reeds, Claude–Oklahoma 1913
Reid, Mike–Penn St.......... 1969
Reid, Steve–Northwestern 1936
+Reid, William–Harvard........ 1899
Renfro, Mel–Oregon 1963
+Rentner, Pug–N'western...... 1932
+Reynolds, Bobby–Nebraska.... 1952
Reynolds, Bob–Stanford...... 1935
Richter, Les–California 1951
Riley, Jack–Northwestern..... 1931
+Rinehart, Chas.–Lafayette 1897
+Rodgers, Ira–West Va........ 1919
+Rogers, Ed–Carlisle/Minn..... 1903
Romig, Joe–Colorado 1961
+Rosenberg, Aaron–USC....... 1933
Rote, Kyle–SMU 1950
+Routt, Joe–Texas A&M 1937

+Salmon, Red–N.Dame........ 1903
Sauer, George–Nebraska..... 1933

Savitsky, George–Penn 1947
Sayers, Gale–Kansas 1964
Scarbath, Jack–Maryland 1952
+Scarlett, Hunter–Penn........ 1908
Schloredt, Bob–Wash......... 1960
+Schoonover, Wear–Ark....... 1929
Schreiner, Dave–Wisconsin ... 1942
+Schultz, Germany–Mich....... 1908
+Schwab, Dutch–Lafayette...... 1922
+Schwartz, Marchy–N.Dame.... 1931
+Schwegler, Paul–Wash........ 1931
Scott, Clyde–Arkansas 1948
Scott, Richard–Navy 1947
Scott, Tom–Virginia 1953
+Seibels, Henry–Sewanee 1899
Sellers, Ron–Florida St 1968
Selmon, Lee Roy–Okla....... 1975
+Shakespeare, Bill–N.Dame 1935
+Shelton, Murray–Cornell 1915
+Shevlin, Tom–Yale 1905
+Shively, Bernie–Illinois 1926
+Simons, Monk–Tulane 1934
Simpson, O.J.–USC.......... 1968
+Sington, Fred–Alabama....... 1930
+Sinkwich, Frank–Georgia 1942
+Sitko, Emil–Notre Dame 1949
+Skladany, Joe–Pittsburgh..... 1933
+Slater, Duke–Iowa 1921
+Smith, Bruce–Minnesota 1941
Smith, Bubba–Michigan St.... 1966
+Smith, Ernie–USC........... 1932
Smith, Harry–USC 1939
Smith, Jim Ray–Baylor 1954
+Smith, Clipper–N.Dame 1927
Smith, Riley–Alabama 1935
+Smith, Vernon–Georgia 1931
+Snow, Neil–Michigan 1901
Sparlis, Al–UCLA 1945
+Spears, Clarence–Dart....... 1915
Spears, W.D.–Vanderbilt 1927
+Sprackling, Wm.–Brown 1911
+Sprague, Bud–Army/Texas 1928
Spurrier, Steve–Florida...... 1966
Stafford, Harrison–Texas 1932
+Stagg, Amos Alonzo–Yale 1889
+Starcevich, Max–Wash....... 1936
Staubach, Roger–Navy 1964
+Steffen, Walter–Chicago 1908
Steffy, Joe–Tenn/Army....... 1947
+Stein, Herbert–Pitt........... 1921
Steuber, Bob–Missouri 1943
+Stevens, Mal–Yale 1923
Stillwagon, Jim–Ohio St...... 1970
+Stinchcomb, Pete–Ohio St 1920
+Stevenson, Vincent–Penn..... 1905
Strom, Brock–Air Force 1959
+Strong, Ken–NYU........... 1928
+Strupper, George–Ga.Tech.... 1917
+Stuhldreher, Harry–N.Dame ... 1924
+Sturhan, Herb–Yale 1926
+Stydahar, Joe–West Va....... 1935
+Suffridge, Bob–Tennessee 1940
+Suhey, Steve–Penn St 1947
Sullivan, Pat–Auburn 1971
+Sundstrom, Frank–Cornell..... 1923
+Swanson, Clarence–Neb...... 1921
+Swiacki, Bill–Columbia/HC.... 1947
Swink, Jim–TCU 1956

Taliaferro, Geo.–Indiana...... 1948
Tarkenton, Fran–Georgia 1960
Tavener, John–Indiana 1944
Taylor, Chuck–Stanford....... 1942
Thomas, Aurelius–Ohio St..... 1957

+Thompson, Joe–Pittsburgh..... 1907
+Thorne, Samuel–Yale......... 1895
+Thorpe, Jim–Carlisle 1912
+Ticknor, Ben–Harvard 1930
+Tigert, John–Vanderbilt 1904
Tinsley, Gaynell–LSU 1936
Tipton, Eric–Duke 1938
Tonnemaker, Clayton–Minn ... 1949
+Torrey, Bob–Pennsylvania 1905
+Travis, Brick–Missouri 1920
Trippi, Charley–Georgia 1946
+Tryon, Edward–Colgate 1925
Turner, Bulldog–H.Simmons .. 1939
Twilley, Howard–Tulsa 1965

+Utay, Joe–Texas A&M 1907

+Van Brocklin, Norm–Ore...... 1948
+Van Sickel, Dale–Florida 1929
+Van Surdam, H.–Wesleyan 1905
+Very, Dexter–Penn St 1912
Vessels, Billy–Oklahoma 1952
+Vick, Ernie–Michigan 1921

+Wagner, Hube–Pittsburgh..... 1913
Walker, Doak–SMU 1949
Wallace, Bill–Rice 1935
+Walsh, Adam–N.Dame....... 1924
+Warburton, Cotton, USC 1934
Ward, Bob–Maryland........ 1951
+Warner, William–Cornell..... 1904
+Washington, Kenny–UCLA 1939
+Weatherall, Jim–Okla........ 1951
Webster, George–Mich.St 1966
Wedemeyer, H.–St.Mary's.... 1947
+Weekes, Harold–Columbia.... 1902
Weiner, Art–N.Carolina....... 1949
+Weir, Ed–Nebraska 1925
+Welch, Gus–Carlisle......... 1914
+Weller, John–Princeton...... 1935
+Wendell, Percy–Harvard 1912
+West, Belford–Colgate 1919
+Westfall, Bob–Michigan 1941
+Weyand, Babe–Army........ 1915
+Wharton, Buck–Penn 1896
+Wheeler, Arthur–Princeton.... 1894
White, Byron–Colorado 1938
Whitmire, Don–Navy/Ala 1944
+Wickhorst, Frank–Navy 1926
Widseth, Ed–Minnesota 1936
+Wildung, Dick–Minnesota 1942
Williams, Bob–N.Dame....... 1950
Williams, Froggie–Rice....... 1949
Willis, Bill–Ohio St 1944
Wilson, Bobby–SMU........ 1935
+Wilson, George–Wash....... 1925
+Wilson, Harry–Army/Penn St .. 1926
Wilson, Mike–Lafayette 1928
Wistert, Albert–Michigan 1942
Wistert, Alvin–Michigan 1949
+Wistert, Whitey–Michigan 1933
+Wood, Barry–Harvard 1931
+Wojciechowicz, Alex–Ford 1937
+Wyant, Andy–Chicago....... 1894
+Wyatt, Bowden–Tenn 1938
+Wyckoff, Clint–Cornell....... 1895

+Yarr, Tommy–N.Dame 1931
Yary, Ron–USC............ 1967
+Yoder, Lloyd–Carnegie 1926
+Young, Buddy–Illinois....... 1946
+Young, Harry–Wash.& Lee ... 1916
+Young, Waddy–Okla........ 1938
Youngblood, Jack–Florida..... 1970

Zarnas, Gust–Ohio State...... 1937

College Football Hall of Fame (Cont.)
Coaches

+Aillet, Joe	1989	
+Alexander, Bill	1951	
+Anderson, Ed	1971	
+Armstrong, Ike	1957	
+Bachman, Charlie	1978	
Banks, Earl	1992	
+Baujan, Harry	1990	
+Bell, Matty	1955	
+Bezdek, Hugo	1954	
+Bible, Dana X	1951	
+Bierman, Bernie	1955	
Blackman, Bob	1987	
+Blaik, Earl (Red)	1965	
Broyles, Frank	1983	
+Bryant, Paul (Bear)	1986	
+Caldwell, Charlie	1961	
+Camp, Walter	1951	
Casanova, Len	1977	
+Cavanaugh, Frank	1954	
+Colman, Dick	1990	
+Crisler, Fritz	1954	
+Daugherty, Duffy	1984	
Devaney, Bob	1981	
Devine, Dan	1985	
+Dobie, Gil	1951	
+Donohue, Michael	1951	
+Dorais, Gus	1954	
+Edwards, Bill	1986	
+Engle, Rip	1973	
Faurot, Don	1961	
Gaither, Jake	1973	
Gillman, Sid	1989	
+Godfrey, Ernest	1972	
Graves, Ray	1990	
+Gustafson, Andy	1985	
+Hall, Edward	1951	
+Harding, Jack	1980	
+Harlow, Richard	1954	
+Harman, Harvey	1981	

+Harper, Jesse	1971	
+Haughton, Percy	1951	
+Hayes, Woody	1983	
+Heisman, John W	1954	
+Higgins, Robert	1954	
+Hollingberry, Babe	1979	
Howard, Frank	1989	
+Ingram, Bill	1973	
+Jennings, Morley	1973	
+Jones, Howard	1951	
+Jones, Biff	1954	
+Jones, Tad	1958	
+Jordan, Lloyd	1978	
+Jordan, Ralph (Shug)	1982	
+Kerr, Andy	1951	
+Leahy, Frank	1970	
+Little, George	1955	
+Little, Lou	1960	
+Madigan, Slip	1974	
Maurer, Dave	1991	
McClendon, Charley	1986	
McCracken, Herb	1973	
+McGugin, Dan	1951	
McKay, John	1988	
+McKeen, Allyn	1991	
+McLaughry, Tuss	1962	
+Meyer, Dutch	1956	
+Mollenkopf, Jack	1988	
+Moore, Bernie	1954	
+Moore, Scrappy	1980	
+Morrison, Ray	1954	
+Munger, George	1976	
+Munn, Clarence (Biggie)	1959	
+Murray, Bill	1974	
+Murray, Frank	1983	
+Mylin, Ed (Hooks)	1974	
+Neale, Earle (Greasy)	1967	
+Neely, Jess	1971	
+Nelson, David	1987	

+Neyland, Robert	1956	
+Norton, Homer	1971	
+O'Neill, Frank (Buck)	1951	
+Owen, Bennie	1951	
Parseghian, Ara	1980	
+Perry, Doyt	1988	
+Phelan, Jimmy	1973	
Prothro, Tommy	1991	
Ralston, John	1992	
+Robinson, E.N.	1955	
+Rockne, Knute	1951	
+Romney, Dick	1954	
+Roper, Bill	1951	
Royal, Darrell	1983	
+Sanford, George	1971	
+Schmidt, Francis	1971	
Schwartzwalder, Ben	1982	
+Shaughnessy, Clark	1968	
+Shaw, Buck	1972	
+Smith, Andy	1951	
+Snavely, Carl	1965	
+Stagg, Amos Alonzo	1951	
+Sutherland, Jock	1951	
+Tatum, Jim	1984	
+Thomas, Frank	1951	
+Vann, Thad	1987	
Vaught, Johnny	1979	
+Wade, Wallace	1955	
+Waldorf, Lynn (Pappy)	1966	
+Warner, Glenn (Pop)	1951	
+Wieman, E.E.(Tad)	1956	
+Wilce, John	1954	
Wilkinson, Bud	1969	
+Williams, Henry	1951	
+Woodruff, George	1963	
Woodson, Warren	1989	
+Yost, Fielding (Hurry Up)	1951	
+Zuppke, Bob	1951	

Wide World Photos

The Pro Football Hall of Fame's newest members with Miss America **Carolyn Sapp** of Hawaii at the 1992 Pro Bowl. From left to right: **Al Davis**, **John Riggins**, Sapp, **John Mackey** and **Lem Barney**.

Pro Football Hall of Fame

Established in 1963 by National Football League to commemorate the sport's professional origins. **Address:** 2121 George Halas Drive NW, Canton, OH 44708. **Telephone:** (216) 456-8207.

Eligibility: Nominated players must be retired five years, coaches must be retired, and contributors can still be active. Voting done by 34-member panel made up of media representatives from all 28 NFL cities, one PFWA representative and five selectors-at-large.

Class of 1992 (4): PLAYERS—CB-KR **Lem Barney**, Detroit (1967-77); TE **John Mackey**, Baltimore (1963-71), San Diego (1972); RB **John Riggins**, NY Jets (1971-75), Washington (1976-79, 81-85). CONTRIBUTOR—**Al Davis**, Oakland head coach (1963-65), AFL commissioner (1966), Oakland managing general partner (since 1967).

1992 Finalists (nominated, but not elected): Players—Bob Brown, Dan Dierdorf, Carl Eller, Willie Galimore, Ray Guy, Charlie Joiner, Tom Mack and Lynn Swann; Coaches—Bud Grant and Bill Walsh; Contributor—Wellington Mara. Members are listed with year of induction; (+) indicates deceased members.

Quarterbacks

Baugh, Sammy	1963	Griese, Bob	1990	Starr, Bart	1977
Blanda, George (also PK)	1981	+Herber, Arnie	1966	Staubach, Roger	1985
Bradshaw, Terry	1989	Jurgensen, Sonny	1983	Tarkenton, Fran	1986
+Clark, Dutch	1963	+Layne, Bobby	1967	Tittle, Y.A.	1971
+Conzelman, Jimmy	1964	Luckman, Sid	1965	Unitas, Johnny	1979
Dawson, Len	1987	Namath, Joe	1985	+Van Brocklin, Norm	1971
+Driscoll, Paddy	1965	Parker, Clarence (Ace)	1972	+Waterfield, Bob	1965
Graham, Otto	1965				

Running Backs

+Battles, Cliff	1968	Hornung, Paul	1986	Perry, Joe	1969
Brown, Jim	1971	Johnson, John Henry	1987	Riggins, John	1992
Campbell, Earl	1991	+Leemans, Tuffy	1978	Sayers, Gale	1977
Canadeo, Tony	1974	Matson, Ollie	1972	Simpson, O.J	1985
Csonka, Larry	1987	McAfee, George	1966	+Strong, Ken	1967
Dudley, Bill	1966	McElhenny, Hugh	1970	Taylor, Jim	1976
Gifford, Frank	1977	+McNally, Johnny (Blood)	1963	+Thorpe, Jim	1963
+Grange, Red	1963	Moore, Lenny	1975	Trippi, Charley	1968
+Guyon, Joe	1966	Motley, Marion	1968	Van Buren, Steve	1965
Harris, Franco	1990	+Nagurski, Bronko	1963	Walker, Doak	1986
+Hinkle, Clarke	1964	+Nevers, Ernie	1963		

Ends & Wide Receivers

Alworth, Lance	1978	Fears, Tom	1970	Maynard, Don	1987
Badgro, Red	1981	+Hewitt, Bill	1971	+Millner, Wayne	1968
Berry, Raymond	1973	Hirsch, Elroy (Crazylegs)	1968	Mitchell, Bobby	1983
Biletnikoff, Fred	1988	Hutson, Don	1963	Pihos, Pete	1970
+Chamberlin, Guy	1965	Lavelli, Dante	1975	Taylor, Charley	1984
Ditka, Mike	1988	Mackey, John	1992	Warfield, Paul	1983

Linemen (pre-World War II)

+Edwards, Turk (T)	1969	+Hubbard, Cal (T)	1963	Musso, George (T-G)	1982
Fortmann, Dan (G)	1985	Kiesling, Walt (G)	1966	+Stydahar, Joe (T)	1967
+Healey, Ed (T)	1964	+Kinard, Bruiser (T)	1971	+Trafton, George (C)	1964
+Hein, Mel (C)	1963	+Lyman, Link (T)	1964	Turner, Bulldog (C)	1966
+Henry, Pete (T)	1963	+Michalske, Mike (G)	1964	+Wojciechowicz, Alex (C)	1968

Offensive Linemen

Bednarik, Chuck (C-LB)	1967	Jones, Stan (T-G-DT)	1991	Parker, Jim (G)	1973
Brown, Roosevelt (T)	1975	Langer, Jim (C)	1987	Ringo, Jim (C)	1981
Gatski, Frank (C)	1985	McCormack, Mike (T)	1984	St.Clair, Bob (T)	1990
Gregg, Forrest (T-G)	1977	Mix, Ron (T-G)	1979	Shell, Art	1989
Groza, Lou (T-PK)	1974	Otto, Jim (C)	1980	Upshaw, Gene	1987
Hannah, John (G)	1991				

Defensive Linemen

Atkins, Doug	1982	Jones, Deacon	1980	Page, Alan	1988
+Buchanan, Buck	1990	Lilly, Bob	1980	Robustelli, Andy	1971
Davis, Willie	1981	Marchetti, Gino	1972	Stautner, Ernie	1969
Donovan, Art	1968	Nomellini, Leo	1969	Weinmeister, Arnie	1984
+Ford, Len	1976	Olsen, Merlin	1982	Willis, Bill	1977
Greene, Joe	1987				

Linebackers

Bell, Bobby	1983	Ham, Jack	1988	Lanier, Willie	1986
Butkus, Dick	1979	Hendricks, Ted	1990	Nitschke, Ray	1978
Connor, George (DT-OT)	1975	Huff, Sam	1982	Schmidt, Joe	1973
+George, Bill	1974	Lambert, Jack	1990		

Pro Football Hall of Fame (Cont.)

Defensive Backs

Adderley, Herb 1980	+Christiansen, Jack. 1970	+Tunnell, Emlen 1967
Barney, Lem 1992	Houston, Ken 1986	Wilson, Larry. 1978
Blount, Mel 1989	Lane, Dick (Night Train) 1974	Wood, Willie 1989
Brown, Willie. 1984	Lary, Yale 1979	

Placekicker

Stenerud, Jan 1991

Founder–Coaches

+Halas George 1963	+Lambeau, Curly 1963

Coaches

Brown, Paul. 1967	Gillman, Sid 1983	+Neale, Earle (Greasy). 1969
Ewbank, Weeb 1978	Landry, Tom 1990	+Owen, Steve 1966
Flaherty, Ray 1976	+Lombardi, Vince 1971	

Contributors

+Bell, Bert 1963	Hunt, Lamar 1972	+Reeves, Dan 1967
+Bidwill, Charles 1967	+Mara, Tim 1963	+Rooney, Art 1964
+Carr, Joe 1963	+Marshall, George 1963	Rozelle, Pete 1985
Davis, Al 1992	+Ray, Hugh (Shorty) 1966	Schramm, Tex. 1991

Dick McCann Award

First presented in 1969 by the Pro Football Writers of America for long and distinguished reporting on pro football. Named in honor of the first director of the Hall, the McCann Award does not constitute induction into the Hall of Fame.

Year	**Year**	**Year**
1969 George Strickler	1977 Art Daley	1985 Cooper Rollow
1970 Arthur Daley	1978 Murray Olderman	1986 Bill Wallace
1971 Joe King	1979 Pat Livingston	1987 Jerry Magee
1972 Lewis Atchison		1988 Gordon Forbes
1973 Dave Brady	1980 Chuck Heaton	1989 Vito Stellino
1974 Bob Oates	1981 Norm Miller	
1975 John Steadman	1982 Cameron Snyder	1990 Will McDonough
1976 Jack Hand	1983 Hugh Brown	1991 Dick Connor
	1984 Larry Felser	1992 Frank Luska

Pete Rozelle Award

First presented in 1989 by the Hall of Fame for exceptional longtime contributions to radio and TV in pro football. Named in honor of the former NFL commissioner, who was also a publicist and GM for the LA Rams, the Rozelle Award does not constitute induction into the Hall of Fame.

Year	**Year**	**Year**
1989 Bill McPhail	1991 Ed Sabol	1992 Chris Schenkel
1990 Lindsey Nelson		

Canadian Football Hall of Fame

Established in 1963. Current Hall opened in 1972. **Address:** 58 Jackson Street West, Hamilton, Ontario, L8P 1L4. **Telephone:** (416) 528-7566.

   Eligibility: Nominated players must be retired three years, but coaches and builders can still be active. Voting done by 15-member panel of Canadian pro and amateur football officials.

   Class of 1992 (4): PLAYERS—RB-P **Ken Charlton**, Regina (1941, 48-54), Winnipeg (1942), All-Service Rough-riders (1943), Ottawa (1945-47); OL **Ellison Kelly**, Hamilton (1960-70), Toronto (1971-72); DB-K **Don Southern**, Hamilton (1958,60-66), Ottawa (1967-69), Toronto (1970). BUILDER—**Ralph Cooper**, former Hamilton president-owner who was prominent in amalgamation of Hamilton's Tigers and Wildcats into the Tiger-Cats in 1950.

   Members are listed with year of induction; (+) indicates deceased members.

Players

Atchison, Ron 1978	+Conacher, Lionel 1963	Faloney, Bernie. 1974
Bailey, Byron 1975	Copeland, Royal 1988	+Fear, A.H. (Cap) 1967
Barrow, John 1976	Corrigall, Jim 1990	Fennell, Dave 1990
+Batstone, Harry 1963	+Cox, Ernest 1963	+Ferraro, John 1966
+Beach, Ormond 1963	+Craig, Ross 1964	Fieldgate, Norm 1979
Box, Ab 1965	+Cronin, Carl 1967	Fleming, Willie 1982
+Breen, Joseph 1963	+Cutler, Wes 1968	Gabriel, Tony 1985
+Bright, Johnny. 1970	+Dixon, George 1974	+Gall, Hugh 1963
Brown, Tom. 1984	+Eliowitz, Abe 1969	Golab, Tony 1964
Casey, Tom. 1964	+Emerson, Eddie 1963	Gray, Herbert 1983
Charlton, Ken 1992	Etcheverry, Sam 1969	Griffing, Dean. 1965
Coffey, Tommy Joe 1977	Evanshen, Terry 1984	Hanson, Fritz. 1963

Harris, Wayne	1976	+McCance, Ches	1976	+Russel, Jeff	1963
Helton, John	1986	+McGill, Frank	1965	+Scott, Vince	1982
Henley, Garney	1979	McQuarters, Ed.	1988	Shatto, Dick	1975
Hinton, Tom	1991	Miles, Rollie	1980	+Simpson, Ben	1963
+Huffman, Dick	1987	+Molson, Percy	1963	Simpson, Bob	1976
+Isbister, Bob Sr	1965	Morris, Frank	1983	Southern, Don	1992
Jackson, Russ	1973	+Morris, Ted	1964	+Sprague, David	1963
+Jacobs, Jack	1963	Mosca, Angelo	1987	Stevenson, Art	1969
+James, Eddie	1963	Nelson, Roger	1986	Stewart, Ron	1977
James, Gerry	1981	Neumann, Peter	1979	Stirling, Hugh (Bummer)	1966
+Kabat, Greg	1966	O'Quinn, John Red	1981	Thelen, Dave	1989
Kapp, Joe	1984	Pajaczkowski, Tony	1988	+Timmis, Brian	1963
Keeling, Jerry	1989	Parker, Jackie	1971	Tinsley, Bud	1982
Kelly, Brian	1991	Patterson, Hal	1971	+Tommy, Andy	1989
Kelly, Ellison	1992	Perry, Gordon	1970	+Trawick, Herb	1975
Krol, Joe	1963	+Perry, Norm.	1963	+Tubman, Joe	1968
Kwong, Normie	1969	Ploen, Ken	1975	Urness, Ted	1989
Lancaster, Ron	1982	+Quilty, S.P.(Silver)	1966	Vaughan, Kaye	1978
+Lawson, Smirle	1963	Rebholz, Russ	1963	Wagner, Virgil	1980
+Leadlay, Frank	1963	Reed, George	1979	+Welch, Hawley (Huck)	1964
+Lear, Les	1974	+Reeve, Ted.	1963	Wilkinson, Tom	1987
Lewis, Leo	1973	Rigney, Frank	1985	Wylie, Harvey	1980
Lunsford, Earl	1983	+Rodden, Michael	1964	Young, Jim	1991
Luster, Marv	1990	+Rowe, Paul.	1964	+Zock, William	1984
Luzzi, Don	1986	Ruby, Martin	1974		

Builders

+Back, Leonard	1971	Grant, Bud	1983	+Newton, Jack	1964
+Bailey, Harold	1965	+Grey, Lord Earl	1963	+Preston, Ken	1990
+Ballard, Harold	1987	+Griffith, Harry	1963	+Ritchie, Alvin	1963
+Brook, Tom	1975	+Halter, Sydney.	1966	+Ryan, Joe B.	1968
+Brown, D.Wes	1963	+Hannibal, Frank	1963	Sazio, Ralph	1988
Chipman, Arthur	1969	+Hayman, Lew	1975	+Shaughnessy, Frank (Shag)	1963
Clair, Frank	1981	+Hughes, W.P.(Billy)	1974	+Shouldice, W.T.(Hap)	1977
Cooper, Ralph	1992	Keys, Eagle	1990	+Simpson, Jimmy	1985
+Crighton, Hec	1986	Kimball, Norman	1991	+Slocomb, Karl	1989
+Currie, Andrew	1974	+Kramer, R.A. (Bob)	1987	+Spring, Harry	1976
+Davies, Dr. Andrew	1969	+Lieberman, M.I.(Moe)	1973	Stukus, Annis	1974
+DeGruchy, John	1963	+McBrien, Harry	1978	+Taylor, N.J.(Piffles)	1963
Dojack, Paul	1978	+McCaffrey, Jimmy	1967	Tindall, Frank	1985
+Duggan, Eck	1981	+McCann, Dave	1966	+Warner, Clair	1965
+DuMoulin, Seppi	1963	+McPherson, Don	1983	+Warwick, Bert	1964
+Foulds, Willliam	1963	+Metras, Johnny	1980	+Wilson, Seymour	1984
Gaudaur, J.G.(Jake)	1984	+Montgomery, Ken	1970		

GOLF

There are two principal golf halls of fame: the PGA/World Golf Hall of Fame in Pinehurst, NC, and the LPGA Hall of Fame in Daytona Beach, FL. A third museum, the old PGA Hall, was abandoned in 1983 when the PGA of America took over the running of the World Golf Hall of Fame. Plans call for all members of the old PGA Hall to be included in a separate wing of the PGA/World Hall.

PGA/World Golf Hall of Fame

Established in 1974 and taken over by PGA of America in 1983. **Address:** PGA Boulevard, P.O.Box 1908, Pinehurst, NC 28374. **Telephone:** (919) 295-6651.

Eligibility: Nominees must have played 10 years of major competition and can still be active. Voting done by Golf Writers' Association of America.

Class of 1992 (4): Players—**Hale Irwin** and **Lighthorse Harry Cooper**; Contributors—**Chi Chi Rodriguez** and **Richard Tufts**.

Members are listed with year of induction; (+) indicates deceased members.

Men

+Anderson, Willie	1975	DeVicenzo, Roberto	1989	Littler, Gene	1990
+Armour, Tommy	1976	+Evans, Chick	1975	+Locke, Bobby	1977
+Ball, John, Jr	1977	Floyd, Ray	1989	Middlecoff, Cary	1986
+Barnes, Jim	1989	+Guldahl, Ralph	1981	+Morris, Tom, Sr	1976
Boros, Julius	1982	+Hagen, Walter	1974	+Morris, Tom, Jr	1975
+Braid, James	1976	+Hilton, Harold	1978	Nelson, Byron	1974
Casper, Billy	1978	Hogan, Ben	1974	Nicklaus, Jack	1974
Cooper, Lighthorse Harry	1992	Irwin, Hale	1992	+Ouimet, Francis	1974
+Cotton, Thomas	1980	+Jones, Bobby	1974	Palmer, Arnold	1974
+Demaret, Jimmy	1983	+Little, Lawson	1980	Player, Gary	1974

PGA/World Golf Hall of Fame (Cont.)

Men

Runyan, Paul	1990	+Taylor, John H.	1975	Trevino, Lee	1981
Sarazen, Gene	1974	Thomson, Peter	1988	+Vardon, Harry	1974
+Smith, Horton	1990	+Travers, Jerry	1976	Watson, Tom	1988
Snead, Sam	1974	+Travis, Walter	1979		

Women

Berg, Patty	1974	Rawls, Betsy	1987	Whitworth, Kathy	1982
+Howe, Dorothy C.H	1978	Suggs, Louise	1979	Wright, Mickey	1976
Carner, JoAnne	1985	+Vare, Glenna Collett	1975	+Zaharias, Babe Didrikson	1974
Lopez, Nancy	1989	+Wethered, Joyce	1975		

Contributors

Campbell, William	1990	+Graffis, Herb	1977	+Roberts, Clifford	1978
+Corcoran, Fred	1975	+Harlow, Robert	1988	Rodriguez, Chi Chi	1992
+Crosby, Bing	1978	Hope, Bob	1983	+Ross, Donald	1977
+Dey, Joe	1975	Jones, Robert Trent	1987	+Tufts, Richard	1992

Old PGA Hall Members Not in PGA/World Hall

The original PGA Hall of Fame was established in 1940 by the PGA of America, but abandoned after the 1982 inductions in favor of the PGA/World Hall of Fame. Twenty-seven members of the old PGA Hall have since been elected to the PGA/World Hall. Players yet to make the cut are listed below with year of induction into old PGA Hall.

+Brady, Mike	1960	Ford, Doug	1975	+McLeod, Fred	1960
+Burke, Billy	1966	+Ghezzi, Vic	1965	+Picard, Henry	1961
Burke, Jack, Jr.	1975	Harbert, Chick	1968	+Revolta, Johnny	1963
+Cruickshank, Bobby	1967	Harper, Chandler	1969	+Shute, Denny	1957
+Diegel, Leo	1955	+Harrison, Dutch	1962	+Smith, Alex	1940
+Dudley, Ed.	1964	+Hutchison, Jock, Sr	1959	+Smith, Macdonald	1954
+Dutra, Olin	1962	+McDermott, John	1940	+Wood, Craig	1956
+Farroll, Johnny	1961	+Mangrum, Lloyd	1964		

LPGA Hall of Fame

Established in 1967 by the LPGA to replace the old Women's Golf Hall of Fame (founded in 1950). Originally located in Augusta, GA (1967-77), the Hall has been moved to Pinehurst, NC (1977-83), Sugar Land, TX (1983-89) and Daytona Beach, FL (since 1990). There is currently no museum to visit, but a new building is scheduled to open in October of 1992. **Address:** LPGA Headquarters, 2570 Volusia Ave., Suite B, Daytona Beach, FL, 32114. **Telephone:** (904) 254-8800.

Eligibility: Nominees must have played 10 years on the LPGA tour and won 30 official events, including two major championships; 35 official events and one major; or 40 official events and no majors.

Last inductee: Pat Bradley on Sept. 29, 1991 (18 years, 30 wins, 6 majors).

Leading candidates (through Aug. 1, 1992)**:** Amy Alcott (29 wins, 5 majors), Patty Sheehan (29 wins, 3 majors), Beth Daniel (27 wins, 1 major) and Betsy King (27 wins, 5 majors).

Members are listed with year of induction; (+) indicates deceased members.

Berg, Patty	1951	Jameson, Betty	1951	Suggs, Louise	1951
Bradley, Pat	1991	Lopez, Nancy	1987	Whitworth, Kathy	1975
Carner, JoAnne	1982	Mann, Carol	1977	Wright, Mickey	1964
Haynie, Sandra	1977	Rawls, Betsy	1960	+Zaharias, Babe Didrikson	1951

HOCKEY

Hockey Hall of Fame

Established in 1945 by the National Hockey League and opened in 1961. **Current Address:** Exhibition Place, Toronto, Ontario, M6K 3C3. **New Address:** BCE Place in downtown Toronto by June, 1993. **Current Telephone:** (416) 595-1345.

Eligibility: Nominated players and referees must be retired three years. Voting done by 12-member panel made up of pro and amateur hockey personalities and media representatives.

Class of 1992 (7): PLAYERS—C **Marcel Dionne**, Detroit (1971-75), Los Angeles (1975-87), NY Rangers (1987-89); LW **Bob Gainey**, Montreal 1973-89; RW **Lanny McDonald**, Toronto (1973-79), Colorado (1980-81), Calgary (1981-89). VETERAN—LW **Woody Dumart**, Boston (1936-42,45-54). BUILDERS—**Keith Allen**, Philadelphia-NHL coach (1967-69) and GM (1970-83); **Bob Johnson**, University of Wisconsin coach (1966-75,76-82), U.S. Olympic team coach (1976), Calgary-NHL coach (1982-87), Pittsburgh-NHL (1990-91); **Frank Mathers**, coach and GM with AHL Hershey Bears.

Members are listed with year of induction; (+) indicates deceased members.

Forwards

Abel, Sid	1969	+Bailey, Ace	1975	+Barry, Marty	1965
+Adams, Jack	1959	+Bain, Dan	1945	Bathgate, Andy	1978
Apps, Syl	1961	Baker, Hobey	1945	Beliveau, Jean	1972
Armstrong, George	1975	Barber, Bill	1990	+Bentley, Doug	1964

+Bentley, Max 1966
Blake, Toe 1966
Bossy, Mike 1991
+Boucher, Frank 1958
+Bowie, Dubbie 1945
+Broadbent, Punch 1962
Bucyk, John (Chief) 1981
Burch, Billy 1974
Clarke, Bobby 1987
Colville, Neil 1967
Conacher, Charlie 1961
+Cook, Bill 1952
Cournoyer, Yvan 1982
Cowley, Bill 1968
+Crawford, Rusty 1962
+Darragh, Jack 1962
+Davidson, Scotty 1950
Day, Hap 1961
Delvecchio, Alex 1977
+Denneny, Cy 1959
Dionne, Marcel 1992
+Drillon, Gordie 1975
+Drinkwater, Graham 1950
Dumart, Woody 1992
+Dunderdale, Tommy 1974
+Dye, Babe 1970
Esposito, Phil 1984
+Farrell, Arthur 1965
+Foyston, Frank 1958
+Frederickson, Frank 1958
Gainey, Bob 1992
+Gardner, Jimmy 1962
Geoffrion, Bernie 1972
+Gerard, Eddie 1945
Gilbert, Rod 1982
+Gilmour, Billy 1962
+Griffis, Si 1950

+Hay, George 1958
+Hextall, Bryan 1969
+Hooper, Tom 1962
Howe, Gordie 1972
+Howe, Syd 1965
Hull, Bobby 1983
+Hyland, Harry 1962
+Irvin, Dick 1958
+Jackson, Busher 1971
+Joliat, Aurel 1947
+Keats, Duke 1958
Kennedy, Ted (Teeder) 1966
Keon, Dave 1986
Lach, Elmer 1966
Lafleur, Guy 1988
+Lalonde, Newsy 1950
Lemaire, Jacques 1984
+Lewis, Herbie 1989
Lindsay, Ted 1966
+MacKay, Mickey 1952
Mahovlich, Frank 1981
+Malone, Joe 1950
+Marshall, Jack 1965
+Maxwell, Fred 1962
McDonald, Lanny 1992
+McGee, Frank 1945
+McGimsie, Billy 1962
Mikita, Stan 1983
Moore, Dickie 1974
+Morenz, Howie 1945
+Mosienko, Bill 1965
+Nighbor, Frank 1947
+Noble, Reg 1962
+O'Connor, Buddy 1988
+Oliver, Harry 1967
Olmstead, Bert 1985
+Patrick, Lynn 1980

Perreault, Gilbert 1990
+Phillips, Tom 1945
+Primeau, Joe 1963
Pulford, Bob 1991
+Rankin, Frank 1961
Ratelle, Jean 1985
Richard, Henri 1979
Richard, Maurice (Rocket) .. 1961
+Richardson, George 1950
+Roberts, Gordie 1971
+Russel, Blair 1965
+Russell, Ernie 1965
+Ruttan, Jack 1962
+Scanlan, Fred 1965
Schmidt, Milt 1961
+Schriner, Sweeney 1962
+Seibert, Oliver 1961
+Siebert, Babe 1964
Sittler, Darryl 1989
+Smith, Alf 1962
Smith, Clint 1991
+Smith, Hooley 1972
+Smith, Tommy 1973
+Stanley, Barney 1962
+Stewart, Nels 1962
+Stuart, Bruce 1961
+Taylor, Fred (Cyclone) 1947
+Trihey, Harry 1950
Ullman, Norm 1982
+Walker, Jack 1960
+Walsh, Marty 1962
+Watson, Harry (Moose) 1962
+Weiland, Cooney 1971
+Westwick, Harry (Rat) 1962
+Whitcroft, Fred 1962

Defensemen

Boivin, Leo 1986
+Boon, Dickie 1952
Bouchard, Butch 1966
+Boucher, George 1960
+Cameron, Harry 1962
+Clancy, King 1958
+Clapper, Dit 1947
+Cleghorn, Sprague 1958
Coulter, Art 1974
+Dutton, Red 1958
Flaman, Fern 1990
Gadsby, Bill 1970
+Gardiner, Herb 1958
+Goheen, F.X.(Moose) 1952
+Goodfellow, Ebbie 1963
+Grant, Mike 1950
+Green, Wilf (Shorty) 1962

Hall, Joe 1961
Harvey, Doug 1973
Horner, Red 1965
+Horton, Tim 1977
Howell, Harry 1979
+Johnson, Ching 1958
+Johnson, Ernie 1952
Johnson, Tom 1970
Kelly, Red 1969
+Laviolette, Jack 1962
Laperrière, Jacques 1987
+Mantha, Sylvio 1960
+McNamara, George 1958
Orr, Bobby 1979
Park, Brad 1988
+Patrick, Lester 1947
Pilote, Pierre 1975

+Pitre, Didier 1962
Potvin, Denis 1991
+Pratt, Babe 1966
Pronovost, Marcel 1978
+Pulford, Harvey 1945
Quackenbush, Bill 1976
Reardon, Kenny 1966
+Ross, Art 1945
Savard, Serge 1986
Seibert, Earl 1963
+Shore, Eddie 1947
+Simpson, Joe 1962
Stanley, Allan 1981
+Stewart, Jack 1964
+Stuart, Hod 1945
+Wilson, Gordon (Phat) 1962

Goaltenders

+Benedict, Clint 1965
Bower, Johnny 1976
Brimsek, Frankie 1966
+Broda, Turk 1967
Cheevers, Gerry 1985
+Connell, Alex 1958
Dryden, Ken 1983
+Durnan, Bill 1964
Esposito, Tony 1988
+Gardiner, Chuck 1945

Giacomin, Eddie 1987
+Hainsworth, George 1961
Hall, Glenn 1975
+Hern, Riley 1962
+Holmes, Hap 1972
+Hutton, J.B.(Bouse) 1962
+Lehman, Hughie 1958
+LeSueur, Percy 1961
Lumley, Harry 1980
+Moran, Paddy 1958

Parent, Bernie 1984
+Plante, Jacques 1978
Rayner, Chuck 1973
+Sawchuk, Terry 1971
+Thompson, Tiny 1959
Tretiak, Vladislav 1989
+Vezina, Georges 1945
Worsley, Gump 1980
Worters, Roy 1969

Referees & Linesmen

Armstrong, Neil 1991
Ashley, John 1981
Chadwick, Bill 1964
+Elliott, Chaucer 1961

+Hayes, George 1988
+Hewitson, Bobby 1963
+Ion, Mickey 1961
Pavelich, Matt 1987

Rodden, Mike 1962
+Smeaton, J. Cooper 1961
Storey, Red 1967
Udvari, Frank 1973

Hockey Hall of Fame (Cont.)

Builders

+Adams, Charles 1960	+Hay, Charles 1984	+Patrick, Frank 1958
+Adams, Weston W.,Sr 1972	+Hendy, Jim 1968	+Pickard, Allan 1958
+Ahearn, Frank 1962	+Hewitt, Foster 1965	Pilous, Rudy 1985
+Ahearn, J.F.(Bunny) 1977	+Hewitt, W.A. 1945	Poile, Bud 1990
+Allan, Sir Montagu 1945	+Hume, Fred 1962	Pollock, Sam 1978
Allen, Keith 1992	+Imlach, Punch 1984	+Raymond, Donat 1958
+Ballard, Harold 1977	Ivan, Tommy 1964	+Robertson, John Ross 1945
+Bauer, Fr. David 1989	+Jennings, William 1975	+Robinson, Claude 1945
+Bickell, J.P. 1978	+Johnson, Bob 1992	+Ross, Philip 1976
+Brown, George 1961	Juckes, Gordon. 1979	+Selke, Frank 1960
+Brown, Walter 1962	+Kilpatrick, John 1960	Sinden, Harry 1983
+Buckland, Frank 1975	+Leader, Al 1969	+Smith, Frank 1962
Butterfield, Jack. 1980	LeBel, Bob 1970	+Smythe, Conn 1958
+Calder, Frank 1945	+Lockhart, Thomas 1965	Snider, Ed 1988
+Campbell, Angus 1964	+Loicq, Paul 1961	+Stanley, Lord of Preston 1945
+Campbell, Clarence 1966	+Mariucci, John. 1985	+Sutherland, James 1945
+Cattarinich, Joseph. 1977	Mathers, Frank 1992	Tarasov, Anatoli 1974
+Dandurand, Leo 1963	+McLaughlin, Frederic 1963	+Turner, Lloyd 1958
Dilio, Frank 1964	+Milford, Jake 1984	+Tutt, William Thayer 1978
+Dudley, George 1958	Molson, Hartland 1973	Voss, Carl 1974
+Dunn, James. 1968	+Nelson, Francis 1945	+Waghorne, Fred 1961
Eagleson, Alan 1989	+Norris, Bruce. 1969	+Wirtz, Arthur 1971
Francis, Emile 1982	+Norris, James D 1962	Wirtz, Bill. 1976
+Gibson, Jack 1976	+Norris, James, Sr 1958	Ziegler, John. 1987
+Gorman, Tommy 1963	+Northey, William. 1945	
+Hanley, Bill 1986	+O'Brien, J.A. 1962	

Elmer Ferguson Award

First presented in 1984 by the Professional Hockey Writers' Association for meritorious contributions by members of the PHWA. Named in honor of the late Montreal newspaper reporter, the Ferguson Award does not constitute induction into the Hall of Fame and is not necessarily an annual presentation.

1984—Jacques Beauchamp, Jim Burchard, Red Burnett, Dink Carroll, Jim Coleman, Ted Damata, Marcel Desjardins, Jack Dulmage, Milt Dunnell, Elmer Ferguson, Tom Fitzgerald, Trent Frayne, Al Laney, Joe Nichols, Basil O'Meara, Jim Vipond and Lewis Walter

1985—Charlie Barton, Red Fisher, George Gross, Zotique L'Esperance, Charles Mayer and Andy O'Brien

1986—Dick Johnston, Leo Monahan and Tim Moriarty

1987—Bill Brennan, Rex MacLeod, Ben Olan and Fran Rosa

1988—Jim Proudfoot and Scott Young

1989—Claude Larochelle and Frank Orr

1990—Bertrand Raymond

1991—Hugh Delano

Foster Hewitt Award

First presented in 1984 by the NHL Broadcasters' Association for meritorious contributions by members of the NHLBA. Named in honor of Canada's legendary "Voice of Hockey," the Hewitt Award does not constitute induction into the Hall of Fame and is not necessarily an annual presentation.

1984—Fred Cusick, Danny Gallivan, Foster Hewitt & Rene Lecavelier
1985—Budd Lynch & Doug Smith
1986—Wes McKnight & Lloyd Petit
1987—Bob Wilson
1988—Dick Irvin
1989—Dan Kelly
1990—Jiggs McDonald
1991—Bruce Martyn
1992—Jim Robson

U.S. Hockey Hall of Fame

Established in 1968 by the Eveleth (Minn.) Civic Association Project H Committee and opened in 1973. **Address:** 801 Hat Trick Ave., Eveleth, MN 55734. **Telephone:** (218) 744-5167.

Eligibility: Nominated players and referees must be American-born and retired five years; coaches must be American-born and must have coached predominantly American teams. Voting done by 12-member panel made up of Hall of Fame members and U.S. hockey officials.

Class of 1992 (3): Coaches—**Amo Bessone, Len Ceglarski** and **James Fullerton**.
Members are listed with year of induction; (+) indicates deceased members.

Players

+Abel, Clarence (Taffy). 1973	Brimsek, Frankie 1973	Cleary, Bob. 1981
+Baker, Hobey 1973	+Chaisson, Ray. 1974	Cleary, Bill. 1976
Bartholome, Earl. 1977	Chase, John 1973	+Conroy, Tony 1975
Bessone, Peter. 1978	Christian, Bill. 1984	Dahlstrom, Carl (Cully) 1973
Blake, Bob. 1985	Christian, Roger 1989	+DesJardins, Vic 1974

+ Desmond, Richard 1988
+ Dill, Bob 1979
Everett, Doug 1974
Ftorek, Robbie 1991
+ Garrison, John 1974
Garrity, Jack 1986
+ Goheen, Frank (Moose) 1973
+ Harding, Austie 1975
Iglehart, Stewart 1975
Ikola, Willard 1990
Johnson, Virgil 1974
+ Karakas, Mike 1973

Kirrane, Jack 1987
Lane, Myles 1973
+ Linder, Joe 1975
+ LoPresti, Sam 1973
+ Mariucci, John 1973
Matchefts, John 1991
Mayasich, John 1976
McCartan, Jack 1983
Moe, Bill 1974
Moseley, Fred 1975
+ Murray, Hugh (Muzz) Sr 1987
+ Nelson, Hub 1978

Olson, Eddie 1977
+ Owen, George 1973
+ Palmer, Winthrop 1973
Paradise, Bob 1989
Purpur, Clifford (Fido) 1974
Riley, Bill 1977
+ Romnes, Elwin (Doc) 1973
Rondeau, Dick 1985
+ Williams, Tom 1981
+ Winters, Frank (Coddy) 1973
+ Yackel, Ken 1986

Coaches

+ Almquist, Oscar 1983
Bessone, Amo 1992
Brooks, Herb 1990
Ceglarski, Len 1992
+ Fullerton, James 1992
+ Gordon, Malcolm 1973

Heyliger, Vic 1974
Ikola, Willard 1990
+ Jeremiah, Eddie 1973
+ Johnson, Bob 1991
+ Kelley, John (Snooks) 1974
Pleban, Connie 1990

Riley, Jack 1979
Ross, Larry 1988
+ Thompson, Cliff 1973
+ Stewart, Bill 1982
+ Winsor, Ralph 1973

Referee
Chadwick, Bill 1974

Administrators

+ Brown, George 1973
+ Brown, Walter 1973
Bush, Walter 1980
Clark, Don 1978
+ Gibson, J.C. (Doc) 1973

+ Jennings, William 1981
+ Kahler, Nick 1980
+ Lockhart, Tom 1973
Marvin, Cal 1982
Ridder, Bob 1976

Trumble, Hal 1970
+ Tutt, Thayer 1973
Wirtz, William 1967
+ Wright, Lyle 1973

HORSE RACING

National Horse Racing Hall of Fame

Established in 1950 by the Saratoga Springs Racing Association and opened in 1955. **Address:** National Museum of Racing and Hall of Fame, Union Ave., Saratoga Springs, NY 12866. **Telephone:** (518) 584-0400.

Eligibility: Nominated horses must be retired five years; jockeys must be active at least 15 years; trainers must be active at least 25 years. Voting done by 100-member panel of horse racing media.

Class of 1992 (6): Jockeys—**Jery Fishback** (steeplechase) and **Sandy Hawley**; Trainer—**Scotty Schulhofer**; Horses—**Johnstown**, **Lady's Secret** and **Slew o'Gold**.

Members are listed with year of induction; (+) indicates deceased members.

Exemplars of Racing

+ Hanes, John W 1982

+ Jeffords, Walter M 1973
Mellon, Paul 1989

+ Widener, George D 1971

Jockeys

+ Adams, Frank (Dooley)* 1970
+ Adams, John 1965
+ Aitcheson, Joe Jr.* 1978
Arcaro, Eddie 1958
Atkinson, Ted 1957
Baeza, Braulio 1976
+ Bassett, Carroll* 1972
+ Blum, Walter 1987
+ Bostwick, George H.* 1968
+ Boulmetis, Sam 1973
+ Brooks, Steve 1963
+ Burns, Tommy 1983
+ Butwell, Jimmy 1984
Day, Pat 1991
+ Coltiletti, Frank 1970
Cordero, Angel Jr. 1988
+ Crawford, Robert (Specs)* 1973
+ Ensor, Lavelle (Buddy) 1962
+ Fator, Laverne 1955
Fishback, Jerry* 1992
+ Garner, Andrew (Mack) 1969
+ Garrison, Snapper 1955
+ Griffin, Henry 1956

Guerin, Eric 1972
Hartack, Bill 1959
Hawley, Sandy 1992
+ Johnson, Albert 1971
+ Knapp, Willie 1969
+ Kummer, Clarence 1972
+ Kurtsinger, Charles 1967
+ Loftus, John 1959
Longden, Johnny 1958
Maher, Danny 1955
+ McAtee, Linus 1956
McCarron, Chris 1989
+ McCreary, Conn 1974
+ McKinney, Rigan 1968
+ McLaughlin, James 1955
+ Miller, Walter 1955
+ Murphy, Isaac 1955
+ Neves, Ralph 1960
+ Notter, Joe 1963
+ Odom, George 1955
+ O'Connor, Winnie 1956
+ O'Neill, Frank 1956
+ Parke, Ivan 1978

+ Patrick, Gil 1970
Pincay, Laffit Jr. 1975
+ Purdy, Sam 1970
+ Reiff, John 1956
+ Robertson, Alfred 1971
Rotz, John L. 1983
+ Sande, Earl 1955
+ Schilling, Carroll 1970
Shoemaker, Bill 1958
+ Simms, Willie 1977
+ Sloan, Todhunter 1955
+ Smithwick, A. Patrick* 1973
+ Stout, James 1968
+ Taral, Fred 1955
+ Tuckman, Bayard Jr.* 1973
Turcotte, Ron 1979
+ Turner, Nash 1955
Ussery, Robert 1980
Velasquez, Jorge 1990
+ Woolfe, George 1955
+ Workman, Raymond 1956
Ycaza, Manuel 1977

*Steeplechase jockey

National Horse Racing Hall of Fame (Cont.)

Trainers

+Barrera, Laz................ 1979
+Bedwell, H.Guy............. 1971
+Brown, Edward D.......... 1984
  Burch, Elliot 1980
+Burch, Preston M. 1963
+Burch, W.P. 1955
+Burlew, Fred 1973
+Byers, J.D. (Dilly)......... 1967
+Childs, Frank E. 1968
  Cocks, W. Burling........ 1985
+Duke, William............. 1956
+Feustel, Louis.............. 1964
+Fitzsimmons, J.(Sunny Jim)..... 1958
+Gaver, John M............. 1966
+Healey, Thomas 1955
+Hildreth, Samuel........... 1955
+Hirsch, Max 1959
+Hirsch, W.J.(Buddy) 1982
+Hitchcock, Thomas Sr........ 1973
+Hughes, Hollie 1973
+Hyland, John.............. 1956

+Jacobs, Hirsch............. 1958
  Jerkens, H.Allen 1975
+Johnson, William R. 1986
+Jolley, LeRoy 1987
+Jones, Ben A. 1958
  Jones, H.A.(Jimmy)........ 1959
+Joyner, Andrew............. 1955
  Laurin, Lucien 1977
+Lewis, J.Howard 1969
+Luro, Horatio.............. 1980
+Madden, John............. 1983
+Maloney, Jim.............. 1989
  Martin, Frank (Pancho)........ 1981
  McAnally, Ron............. 1990
+McDaniel, Henry........... 1956
+Miller, MacKenzie 1987
+Molter, William, Jr. 1960
+Mulholland, Winbert........ 1967
+Neloy, Eddie 1983
  Nerud, John 1972
+Parke, Burley.............. 1986

+Penna, Angel Sr........... 1988
+Pincus, Jacob.............. 1988
+Rogers, John 1955
+Rowe, James Sr............ 1955
  Schulhofer, Scotty 1992
  Sheppard, Jonathan........ 1990
+Smith, Robert A. 1976
+Smithwick, Mike 1976
  Stephens, Woody 1976
+Thompson, H.J. 1969
+Trotsek, Harry 1984
  Van Berg, Jack 1985
+Van Berg, Marion 1970
+Veitch, Sylvester........... 1977
+Walden, Robert............ 1970
+Ward, Sherrill 1978
  Whiteley, Frank Jr. 1978
  Whittingham, Charlie........ 1974
+Winfrey, W.C.(Bill) 1971

Horses
Year foaled in parentheses.

+Ack Ack (1966)............ 1986
  Affectionately (1960) 1989
  Affirmed (1975) 1980
  All-Along (1979)........... 1990
+Alsab (1939).............. 1976
+Alydar (1975) 1989
+American Eclipse (1814) 1970
+Armed (1941)............. 1963
+Artful (1902) 1956
+Assault (1943)............. 1964

+Battleship (1927) 1969
+Bed O'Roses(1947) 1976
+Beldame (1901) 1956
+Ben Brush (1893) 1955
+Bewitch (1945) 1977
+Bimelech (1937).......... 1990
+Black Gold (1919) 1989
+Black Helen 1939
+Blue Larkspur (1926) 1957
+Bold Ruler (1954) 1973
+Bon Nouvel (1960)........ 1976
+Boston (1833)............. 1955
+Broomstick (1901) 1956
+Buckpasser (1963)......... 1970
+Busher (1942).............. 1964
+Bushranger (1930)......... 1967

+Cafe Prince (1970)......... 1985
+Carry Back (1958) 1975
+Challendon (1936)......... 1977
+Chris Evert (1988)......... 1971
+Cicada (1959)............. 1967
+Citation (1945)............ 1959
+Coaltown (1945) 1983
+Colin (1905) 1956
+Commando (1898) 1956
+Count Fleet (1940)......... 1961

+Dahlia (1971)............. 1981
+Damascus (1964).......... 1974
+Dark Mirage (1965)........ 1974
+Davona Dale (1976)........ 1985
+Desert Vixen (1970)........ 1979
+Devil Diver (1939)......... 1980
+Discovery (1931).......... 1969
+Domino (1891)............ 1955
+Dr. Fager (1964) 1971

+Elkridge (1938)........... 1966
+Emperor of Norfolk (1885) 1988
+Equipoise (1928) 1957
+Exterminator (1915)....... 1957

+Fairmount (1921) 1985
+Fair Play (1905) 1956
+Firenze (1885)............. 1981
+Forego (1971)............ 1979

+Gallant Bloom (1966) 1977
+Gallant Fox (1927)......... 1957
+Gallant Man (1954)........ 1987
+Gallorette (1942) 1962
+Gamely (1964)............ 1980
  Genuine Risk (1977) 1986
+Good and Plenty (1900) 1956
+Grey Lag (1918)........... 1957

+Hamburg (1895)........... 1986
+Hanover (1884) 1955
+Henry of Navarre (1891)..... 1985
+Hill Prince 1947
+Hindoo (1878) 1955

+Imp (1894) 1965

+Jay Trump (1957).......... 1971
  John Henry (1975) 1990
+Johnstown (1936)......... 1992
+Jolly Roger (1922) 1965

+Kingston (1884) 1955
+Kelso (1957).............. 1967
+Kentucky (1861) 1983

  Lady's Secret (1982).......... 1992
+L'Escargot (1963) 1977
+Lexington (1850) 1955
+Longfellow (1867) 1971
+Luke Blackburn (1877)...... 1956

+Majestic Prince (1966) 1988
+Man o'War (1917)......... 1957
+Miss Woodford (1880)....... 1967
+Myrtlewood (1933)......... 1979

+Nashua (1952)............. 1965
+Native Dancer (1950)....... 1963
+Native Diver (1959)........ 1978
+Northern Dancer (1961) 1976

+Neji (1950) 1966

+Oedipus (1941)........... 1978
+Old Rosebud (1911) 1968
+Omaha (1932)............. 1965

+Pan Zareta (1910) 1972
+Parole (1873) 1984
+Peter Pan (1904)......... 1956
  Princess Rooney 1980

+Real Delight (1949) 1987
+Regret (1912) 1957
+Reigh Count (1925) 1978
+Roamer (1911)............ 1981
+Roseben (1901)........... 1956
+Round Table (1954)........ 1972
+Ruffian (1972)............ 1976
+Ruthless (1864)............ 1975

+Salvator (1886)............ 1955
+Sarazen (1921)............ 1957
+Seabiscuit (1933)......... 1958
+Searching (1952)......... 1978
  Seattle Slew (1974)......... 1981
+Secretariat (1970)........ 1974
+Shuvee (1966)............. 1975
+Silver Spoon (1956) 1978
+Sir Archy (1805) 1955
+Sir Barton (1916) 1957
  Slew o'Gold (1980) 1992
+Stymie (1941)............. 1975
+Susan's Girl (1969) 1976
+Swaps (1952).............. 1966
+Sword Dancer (1956)....... 1977
+Sysonby (1902)............ 1956

+Tim Tam (1955)........... 1985
+Tom Fool (1949).......... 1960
+Top Flight (1929) 1966
+Tosmah (1961)............ 1984
+Twenty Grand (1928)....... 1957
+Twilight Tear (1941) 1963

+War Admiral (1934)....... 1958
+Whirlaway (1938).......... 1959
+Whisk Broom II (1907)...... 1979

  Zaccio (1976).............. 1990
+Zev (1920)................ 1983

OLYMPICS

U.S. Olympic Hall of Fame

Established in 1983 by the United States Olympic Committee. **Current Address:** U.S. Olympic Committee, 1750 East Boulder Street, Colorado Springs, CO 80909. A permanent museum site is in the planning stages. **Telephone:** (719) 578-4529.

Eligibility: Nominated athletes must be five years removed from active competition. Voting done by National Sportscasters and Sportswriters Association, Hall of Fame members and the USOC board members of directors.

Class of 1991 (7)**:** ATHLETES—**Lee Calhoun** (track & field), **Bart Connor** (gymnastics), **Willie Davenport** (track & field), **Dorothy Hamill** (figure skating), **Peter Vidmar** (gymnastics) and **Charley Paddock** (track & field). CONTRIBUTOR—**William Simon** (USOC president, 1981-84).

Class of 1992: to be announced in the fall.

Members are listed with year of induction; (+) indicates deceased members.

Bobsled

+Eagan, Eddie (see Boxing) 1983

Boxing

Clay, Cassius* 1983
+Eagan, Eddie (see Bobsled) 1983
Foreman, George. 1990
Frazier, Joe 1989
Leonard, Sugar Ray 1985
Patterson, Floyd 1987

*Clay changed name to Muhammad Ali in 1964.

Diving

Lee, Sammy 1990
Louganis, Greg. 1985
McCormick, Pat 1985

Figure Skating

Albright, Tenley. 1988
Button, Dick. 1983
Fleming, Peggy. 1983
Hamill, Dorothy 1991
Hamilton, Scott 1990

Gymnastics

Conner, Bart 1991
Retton, Mary Lou. 1985
Vidmar, Peter 1991

Rowing

+Kelly, Jack, Sr. 1990

Speed Skating

Heiden, Eric. 1983

Swimming

Babashoff, Shirley. 1987
Caulkins, Tracy 1990
+Daniels, Charles 1988
de Varona, Donna 1987
+Kahanamoku, Duke. 1984
Meyer, Debbie 1986
Naber, John 1984
Schollander, Don 1983
Spitz, Mark 1983
+Weissmuller, Johnny. 1983

Track & Field

Beamon, Bob 1983
Boston, Ralph 1985
+Calhoun, Lee 1991
Davenport, Willie 1991
Davis, Glenn 1986
+Didrikson, Babe 1983
Dillard, Harrison 1983
Evans, Lee 1989
+Ewry, Ray. 1983
Jenner, Bruce 1986
Johnson, Rafer 1983
+Kraenzlein, Alvin 1985
Lewis, Carl. 1985
Mathias, Bob. 1983
Mills, Billy. 1984
Morrow, Bobby 1989

Moses, Edwin 1985
O'Brien, Parry. 1984
Oerter, Al 1983
+Owens, Jesse 1983
+Paddock, Charley. 1991
Richards, Bob 1983
Rudolph, Wilma 1983
+Sheppard, Mel 1989
Shorter, Frank 1984
+Thorpe, Jim. 1983
Toomey, Bill. 1984
Tyus, Wyomia 1985
Whitfield, Mal 1988
+Wykoff, Frank 1984

Weight Lifting

+Davis, John 1989
Kono, Tommy 1990

Wrestling

Gable, Dan 1985

Contributors

Arledge, Roone. 1989
+Brundage, Avery. 1983
+Bushnell, Asa. 1990
Iba, Hank 1985
+Kane, Robert 1986
McKay, Jim 1988
Miller, Don 1984
Simon, William 1991
Walker, Leroy 1987

Teams

1956 Basketball—Dick Boushka, Carl Cain, Chuck Darling, Bill Evans, Gib Ford, Burdy Haldorson, Bill Hougland, Bob Jeangerard, K.C.Jones, Bill Russell, Ron Tomsic, +Jim Walsh and coach +Gerald Tucker.

1960 Basketball—Jay Arnette, Walt Bellamy, Bob Boozer, Terry Dischinger, Burdy Haldorson, Darrall Imhoff, Allen Kelley, +Lester Lane, Jerry Lucas, Oscar Robertson, Adrian Smith, Jerry West and coach Pete Newell.

1964 Basketball—Jim Barnes, Bill Bradley, Larry Brown, Joe Caldwell, Mel Counts, Richard Davies, Walt Hazzard, Luke Jackson, John McCaffrey, Jeff Mullins, Jerry Shipp, George Wilson and coach Hank Iba.

1960 Ice Hockey—Billy Christian, Roger Christian, Billy Cleary, Bob Cleary, Gene Grazia, Paul Johnson, Jack Kirrane, John Mayasich, Jack McCartan, Bob McKay, Dick Meredith, Weldon Olson, Ed Owen, Rod Paavola, Larry Palmer, Dick Rodenheiser, +Tom Williams and coach Jack Riley.

1980 Ice Hockey—Bill Baker, Neal Broten, Dave Christian, Steve Christoff, Jim Craig, Mike Eruzione, John Harrington, Steve Janaszak, Mark Johnson, Ken Morrow, Rob McClanahan, Jack O'Callahan, Mark Pavelich, Mike Ramsey, Buzz Schneider, Dave Silk, Eric Strobel, Bob Suter, Phil Verchota, Mark Wells and coach Herb Brooks.

The Olympic Order

Established in 1974 by the International Olympic Committee (IOC) to honor athletes, officials and media members who have made remarkable contributions to the Olympic movement. The IOC's Council of the Olympic Order is presided over by the IOC president and active IOC members are not eligible for consideration. Through 1992, only two American officials have received the Order's highest commendation—the gold medal:

Avery Brundage, past president of USOC (1928-53) and IOC (1982-72), was given the award posthumously in 1975.

Peter Ueberroth, president of LA Olympic Organizing Committee, was given the award in 1984.

MEDIA

National Sportscasters and Sportswriters Hall of Fame

Established in 1959 by the National Sportscasters' and Sportswriters' Association. **Temporary Address:** 322 East Innes Street, P.O. Box 559, Salisbury, NC 28144. A permanent museum is scheduled to open in the spring of 1993. **Telephone:** (704) 633-4275.

Eligibility: Nominees must be active for at least 25 years. Voting done by NSSA membership and other media representatives.

Class of 1992 (2): sportscaster **Marty Glickman** and sportswriter **Dick Connor**.

Members are listed with year of induction; (+) indicates deceased members.

Sportscasters

Allen, Mel	1972	Glickman, Marty	1992	+McNamee, Graham	1964
Barber, Walter (Red)	1973	Gowdy, Curt	1981	Nelson, Lindsey	1979
Brickhouse, Jack	1983	Harwell, Ernie	1989	+Prince, Bob	1986
Buck, Jack	1990	+Hodges, Russ	1975	Schenkel, Chris	1981
Caray, Harry	1989	+Husing, Ted	1963	Scott, Ray	1982
+Dean, Dizzy	1976	+McCarthy, Clem	1970	Scully, Vin	1991
Dunphy, Don	1986	McKay, Jim	1987	+Stern, Bill	1974

Sportswriters

Anderson, Dave	1990	+Grimsley, Will	1987	+Runyon, Damon	1964
Bisher, Furman	1989	+Kieran, John	1971	Russell, Fred	1988
Burick, Si	1985	+Lardner, Ring	1967	Sherrod, Blackie	1991
+Cannon, Jimmy	1986	+Murphy, Jack	1988	+Smith, Walter (Red)	1977
Connor, Dick	1992	Murray, Jim	1978	+Spink, J.G.Taylor	1969
+Considine, Bob	1980	+Parker, Dan	1975	+Ward, Arch	1973
+Daley, Arthur	1976	Povich, Shirley	1984	+Woodward, Stanley	1974
Gould, Alan	1990	+Rice, Grantland	1962		

Contributors

Ronald Reagan	1989	+John Wayne	1979

American Sportscasters Hall of Fame

Established in 1984 by the American Sportscasters' Association. **Address:** 5 Beekman Street, New York, NY 10038. A permanent museum site is planned for late 1992. **Telephone:** (212) 227-8080.

Eligibility: Nominations made by 12-member selection committee, voting by ASA membership.

Class of 1992: to be announced in the fall.

Members are listed with year of induction; (+) indicates deceased members.

Allen, Mel	1985	Dunphy, Don	1984	McKay, Jim	1987
Barber, Walter (Red)	1984	Gowdy, Curt	1985	+McNamee, Graham	1984
Brickhouse, Jack	1985	Harwell, Ernie	1991	Nelson, Lindsey	1986
Buck, Jack	1990	+Husing, Ted	1984	+Stern, Bill	1984
Caray, Harry	1989	+McCarthy, Clem	1987		

The 40 Who Changed Sports, 1946-86

Selected by the editors of *Sport* magazine for their 40th Anniversary Issue (December, 1986).

Auto Racing
Bill France, Sr.

Baseball
Hank Aaron
Curt Flood
Mickey Mantle
Willie Mays
Marvin Miller
Branch Rickey
Jackie Robinson
Pete Rose
Casey Stengel
Ted Williams

Basketball
Red Auerbach
Wilt Chamberlain
Bob Cousy
Bill Russell
John Wooden

Boxing
Muhammad Ali
James D. Norris
Sugar Ray Robinson

Football
Jim Brown
Paul Brown
Bear Bryant
Al Davis
Vince Lombardi
Joe Namath
Pete Rozelle

Golf
Jack Nicklaus
Arnold Palmer

Hockey
Wayne Gretzky
Bobby Orr

Horse Racing
Willie Shoemaker

Literature
Jim Bouton

Olympics
Abebe Bikila
Avery Brundage

Soccer
Pelé

Television
Roone Arledge
Howard Cosell

Tennis
Chris Evert
Billie Jean King
Martina Navratilova

TENNIS

International Tennis Hall of Fame

Originally the National Tennis Hall of Fame. Established in 1953 by James Van Alen and sanctioned by the U.S. Tennis Association in 1954. Renamed the International Tennis Hall of Fame in 1976. **Address:** 194 Bellevue Ave., Newport, RI 02840. **Telephone:** (401) 846-4567.

Eligibility: Nominated players must be five years removed from being a "significant factor" in competitive tennis. Voting done by members of the international tennis media.

Class of 1992 (4): Players—American **Tracy Austin** and the South African doubles team of **Bob Hewitt** and **Frew McMillan**; Contributor—**Philippe Chatrier**, former president of International Tennis Federation (1977-91). Members are listed with year of induction; (+) indicates deceased members.

Men

+Adee, George	1964	
+Alexander, Fred	1961	
+Allison, Wilmer	1963	
+Alonso, Manuel	1977	
Ashe, Arthur	1985	
+Behr, Karl	1969	
Borg, Bjorn	1987	
Borotra, Jean	1976	
Bromwich, John	1984	
+Brookes, Norman	1977	
+Brugnon, Jacques	1976	
Budge, Don	1964	
+Campbell, Oliver	1955	
+Chace, Malcolm	1961	
+Clark, Clarence	1983	
+Clark, Joseph	1955	
+Clothier, William	1956	
+Cochet, Henri	1976	
Cooper, Ashley	1991	
+Crawford, Jack	1979	
+Doeg, John	1962	
+Doherty, Lawrence	1980	
+Doherty, Reginald	1980	
Drobny, Jaroslav	1983	
+Dwight, James	1955	
Emerson, Roy	1982	
+Etchebaster, Pierre	1978	
Falkenburg, Bob	1974	
Fraser, Neale	1984	
+Garland, Chuck	1969	
Gonzales, Pancho	1968	
+Grant, Bryan (Bitsy)	1972	
+Griffin, Clarence	1970	
+Hackett, Harold	1961	

Hewitt, Bob	1992	
Hoad, Lew	1980	
+Hovey, Fred	1974	
+Hunt, Joe	1966	
Hunter, Frank	1961	
+Johnston, Bill	1958	
+Jones, Perry	1970	
Kodes, Jan	1990	
Kramer, Jack	1968	
Lacoste, Rene	1976	
+Larned, William	1956	
Larsen, Art	1969	
Laver, Rod	1981	
+Lott, George	1964	
Mako, Gene	1973	
+McKinley, Chuck	1986	
+McLoughlin, Maurice	1957	
McMillan, Frew	1992	
McNeill, Don	1965	
Mulloy, Gardnar	1972	
+Murray, Lindley	1958	
+Myrick, Julian	1963	
Nastase, Ilie	1991	
Newcombe, John	1986	
+Nielsen, Arthur	1971	
Olmedo, Alex	1987	
+Osuna, Rafael	1979	
Parker, Frank	1966	
+Patterson, Gerald	1989	
Patty, Budge	1977	
Perry, Fred	1975	
+Pettitt, Tom	1982	
Peitrangeli, Nicola	1986	
+Quist, Adrian	1984	

Ralston, Dennis	1987	
+Renshaw, Ernest	1983	
+Renshaw, William	1983	
+Richards, Vincent	1961	
Riggs, Bobby	1967	
Roche, Tony	1986	
Rosewall, Ken	1980	
Santana, Manuel	1984	
Savitt, Dick	1976	
Schroeder, Ted	1966	
+Sears, Richard	1955	
Sedgman, Frank	1979	
Segura, Pancho	1984	
Seixas, Vic	1971	
+Shields, Frank	1964	
+Slocum, Henry	1955	
Smith, Stan	1987	
Stolle, Fred	1985	
Talbert, Bill	1967	
+Tilden, Bill	1959	
Trabert, Tony	1970	
Van Ryn, John	1963	
Vilas, Guillermo	1991	
Vines, Ellsworth	1962	
+von Cramm, Gottfried	1977	
+Ward, Holcombe	1956	
+Washburn, Watson	1965	
+Whitman, Malcolm	1955	
+Wilding, Anthony	1978	
+Williams, Richard 2nd	1957	
Wood, Sidney	1964	
+Wrenn, Robert	1955	
+Wright, Beals	1956	

Women

+Atkinson, Juliette	1974	
Austin, Tracy	1992	
+Barger-Wallach, Maud	1958	
Betz Addie, Pauline	1965	
Brough Clapp, Louise	1967	
+Browne, Mary	1957	
Bueno, Maria	1978	
+Bjurstedt Mallory, Molla	1958	
+Cahill, Mabel	1976	
+Connolly Brinker, Maureen	1968	
+Dod, Charlotte (Lottie)	1983	
+Douglass Chambers, Dorothy	1981	
Fry Irvin, Shirley	1970	

Gibson, Althea	1971	
+Hansell, Ellen	1965	
Hard, Darlene	1973	
Hart, Doris	1969	
Hayden Jones, Ann	1985	
Heldman, Gladys	1979	
+Hotchkiss Wightman, Hazel	1957	
Jacobs, Helen Hull	1962	
King, Billie Jean	1987	
+Lenglen, Suzanne	1978	
+Marble, Alice	1964	
+McKane Godfree, Kitty	1978	
+Moore, Elisabeth	1971	

+Nuthall Shoemaker, Betty	1977	
Osborne duPont, Margaret	1967	
Palfrey Danzig, Sarah	1963	
+Roosevelt, Ellen	1975	
+Round Little, Dorothy	1986	
+Ryan, Elizabeth	1972	
+Sears, Eleanora	1968	
Smith Court, Margaret	1979	
+Sutton Bundy, May	1956	
+Townsend Toulmin, Bertha	1974	
Wade, Virginia	1989	
+Wagner, Marie	1969	
Wills Moody Roark, Helen	1959	

Contributors

+Baker, Lawrence, Sr	1975	
Chatrier, Philippe	1992	
Cullman, Joseph F.3rd	1990	
+Danzig, Allison	1968	
+Davis, Dwight	1956	
+Gray, David	1985	

+Gustaf, V (King of Sweden)	1980	
+Hester, W.E.(Slew)	1981	
+Hopman, Harry	1978	
+Laney, Al	1979	
Martin, Alastair	1973	
Martin, William McC	1982	

+Outerbridge, Mary	1981	
+Pell, Theodore	1966	
+Tingay, Lance	1982	
+Tinling, Ted	1986	
+Van Alen, James	1965	

TRACK & FIELD

National Track & Field Hall of Fame

Established in 1974 by the The Athletics Congress. Originally located in Charleston, WV, the Hall moved to Indianapolis in 1983 and reopened at the Hoosier Dome in 1986. **Address:** One Hoosier Dome, Indianapolis, IN 46225. **Telephone:** 317-261-0483.

Eligibility: Nominated athletes must be retired three years and coaches must have coached at least 20 years, if retired, or 35 years, if still coaching. Voting done by 800-member panel made up of Hall of Fame and TAC officials, Hall of Famer members, current U.S. champions and members of the Track & Field Writers of America.

Class of 1992: to be announced in the fall.

Members are listed with year of induction; (+) indicates deceased members.

Men

Albritton, Dave	1980	Held, Bud	1987	Richards, Bob	1975
Ashenfelter, Horace	1975	Hines, Jim	1979	+Rose, Ralph	1976
+Bausch, James	1979	Houser, Bud	1979	Ryun, Jim	1980
Beamon, Bob	1977	+Hubbard, DeHart	1979	+Scholz, Jackson	1977
Beatty, Jim	1990	Jenner, Bruce	1980	Schul, Bob	1991
Bell, Greg	1988	Johnson, Rafer	1974	Seagren, Bob	1986
+Boeckmann, Dee	1976	Jones, Hayes	1976	+Sheppard, Mel	1976
Boston, Ralph	1974	Kelley, John	1980	+Sheridan, Martin	1988
+Calhoun, Lee	1974	Kiviat, Abel	1985	Shorter, Frank	1989
Campbell, Milt	1989	+Kraenzlein, Alvin	1974	Sime, Dave	1981
+Clark, Ellery	1991	Laird, Ron	1986	+Simpson, Robert	1974
Connolly, Harold	1984	Mathias, Bob	1974	Smith, Tommie	1978
Courtney, Tom	1978	Matson, Randy	1984	+Stanfield, Andy	1977
+Cunningham, Glenn	1974	+Meredith, Ted	1982	Steers, Les	1974
+Curtis, William	1979	+Metcalfe, Ralph	1975	Thomas, John	1985
Davenport, Willie	1982	Mills, Billy	1976	+Thomson, Earl	1977
Davis, Glenn	1974	Moore, Tom	1988	+Thorpe, Jim	1975
Davis, Harold	1974	Morrow, Bobby	1975	+Tolan, Eddie	1982
Dillard, Harrison	1974	+Myers, Lawrence	1974	Toomey, Bill	1975
Dumas, Charley	1990	O'Brien, Parry	1974	+Towns, Forrest (Spec)	1976
Evans, Lee	1983	Oerter, Al	1974	Warmerdam, Cornelius	1974
Ewell, Barney	1986	+Osborn, Harold	1974	White, Willye	1981
+Ewry, Ray	1974	+Owens, Jesse	1974	Whitfield, Mal	1974
+Flanagan, John	1975	+Paddock, Charley	1976	Wohlhuter, Rick	1990
Fosbury, Dick	1981	Patton, Mel	1985	Woodruff, John	1978
+Gordien, Fortune	1979	Peacock, Eulace	1987	Wottle, Dave	1982
+Hahn, Archie	1983	+Prefontaine, Steve	1976	+Wykoff, Frank	1977
+Hardin, Glenn	1978	+Ray, Joie	1976	Young, George	1981
Hayes, Bob	1976	+Rice, Greg	1977		

Women

Coachman, Alice	1975	+Jackson, Nell	1989	Rudolph, Wilma	1974
+Didrikson, Babe	1974	Manning, Madeline	1984	Stephens, Helen	1975
Faggs, Mae	1976	McDaniel, Mildred	1983	Tyus, Wyomia	1980
Ferrell, Barbara	1988	McGuire, Edith	1979	+Walsh, Stella	1975
Hall, Evelyne	1988	Robinson, Betty	1977	Watson, Martha	1987
Heritage, Doris Brown	1990				

Coaches

Baskin, Weems	1982	+Hamilton, Brutus	1974	+Littlefield, Clyde	1981
Beard, Percy	1981	+Haydon, Ted	1975	+Moakley, Jack	1988
Botts, Tom	1983	+Hayes, Billy	1976	+Murphy, Michael	1974
Bowerman, Bill	1981	Haylett, Ward	1979	+Snyder, Larry	1978
Bush, Jim	1987	Higgins, Ralph	1982	Temple, Ed	1989
+Cromwell, Dean	1974	+Hillman, Harry	1976	+Templeton, Dink	1976
Doherty, Ken	1976	+Hurt, Edward	1975	Walker, LeRoy	1983
Easton, Bill	1975	+Hutsell, Wilbur	1977	Wilt, Fred	1981
+Elliott, Jumbo	1981	+Jones, Thomas	1977	+Winter, Bud	1985
+Giegengack, Bob	1978	Jordan, Payton	1982	+Yancy, Joseph	1984

Contributors

+Abramson, Jesse	1981	+Brundage, Avery	1974	Nelson, Cordner	1988
Andersen, Roxanne	1991	+Ferris, Dan	1974	Nelson, Bert	1991
+Bakjian, Andy	1986	+Griffith, John	1979	+Sullivan, James	1977

OTHER

B'nai B'rith Sports Hall of Fame

Established in 1991 by B'nai B'rith to recognize the achievements and contributions of Jewish athletes and sportsmen in America. **Address:** 1640 Rhode Island Ave. NW, Washington, DC 20036. A permanent museum was scheduled to open in October, 1992. **Telephone:** (202) 857-6580.

Eligibility: Nominees must be prominent Jewish athletes, coaches, administrators or media figures. Voting done every other year by 7-member panel of B'nai B'rith lay persons.

Class of 1993: To be announced in the fall.

Members are listed with year of induction; (+) indicates deceased members.

Allen, Mel 1991	+Leonard, Benny 1991	Rosen, Al 1991
Auerbach, Red 1991	Luckman, Sid 1991	Savitt, Dick 1991
+Gottlieb, Eddie 1991	Pollin, Abe 1991	Schayes, Dolph 1991
+Greenberg, Hank 1991	Povich, Shirley 1991	Spitz, Mark 1991
Koufax, Sandy 1991		

International Women's Sports Hall of Fame

Established in 1980 by the Women's Sports Foundation. **Current Address:** Women's Sports Foundation, 342 Madison Avenue, Suite 728, New York, NY 10173. A permanent museum site is in the planning stages. **Telephone:** (212) 972-9170.

Eligibility: Nominees' achievements and commitment to the development of women's sports must be internationally recognized. Athletes are elected in two categories—Pioneer (before 1960) and Contemporary (since 1960). Members are divided below by sport for the sake of easy reference; (*) indicates member inducted in Pioneer category. Coaching nominees must have coached at least 10 years.

Class of 1992 (5): PIONEERS—**Bessie Coleman**, aviation; **Carol Heiss Jenkins**, figure skating. CONTEMPORARY—**Ludmila Protopopov**, figure skating; **Irena Kirszenstein Szewinska**, track & field. COACH—**Margaret Wade**, basketball.

Members are listed with year of induction; (+) indicates deceased members.

Alpine Skiing
Cranz, Christl* 1991
Lawrence, Andrea Mead* 1983
Moser-Proell, Annemarie 1982

Auto Racing
Guthrie, Janet 1980

Aviation
+Coleman, Bessie* 1992
+Earhart, Amelia* 1980
+Marvingt, Marie* 1987

Basketball
Meyers, Ann 1985
Miller, Cheryl 1991

Bowling
Ladewig, Marion* 1984

Cycling
Carpenter Phinney, Connie 1990

Diving
King Hogue, Micki 1983
McCormick, Pat* 1984
Riggin, Aileen* 1988

Fencing
Schacherer-Elek, Ilona* 1989

Figure Skating
Albright, Tenley* 1983
+Blanchard, Theresa Weld* 1989
Fleming, Peggy 1981
Heiss Jenkins, Carol 1992
+Henie, Sonja* 1982
Protopopov, Ludmila 1992
Rodnina, Irena 1988

Golf
Berg, Patty* 1980
Carner, JoAnne 1987
Mann, Carol 1982
Rawls, Betsy* 1986
Suggs, Louise* 1987
+Vare, Glenna Collett* 1981
Whitworth, Kathy 1984
Wright, Mickey 1981

Golf/Track & Field
+Zaharias, Babe Didrikson* 1980

Gymnastics
Caslavska, Vera 1991
Comaneci, Nadia 1990
Korbut, Olga 1982
Latynina, Larissa* 1985
Tourischeva, Lyudmila 1987

Shooting
Murdock, Margaret 1988

Softball
Joyce, Joan 1989

Speed Skating
Young, Sheila 1981

Swimming
Caulkins, Tracy 1986
Curtis Cuneo, Ann* 1985
de Varona, Donna 1983
Ederle, Gertrude* 1980
Fraser, Dawn 1985
Holm, Eleanor* 1980
Meyer-Reyes, Debbie 1987

Tennis
+Connelly, Maureen* 1987
+Dod, Charlotte (Lottie)* 1986
Evert, Chris 1981
Gibson, Althea* 1980
Goolagong Cawley, Evonne ... 1989
+Hotchkiss Wightman, Hazel* ... 1986
King, Billie Jean 1980
+Lenglen, Suzanne* 1984
Navratilova, Martina 1984
+Sears, Eleanora* 1984
Smith Court, Margaret 1986

Track & Field
Blankers-Koen, Fanny* 1982
Coachman Davis, Alice* 1991
Manning Mims, Madeline 1987
Rudolph, Wilma 1980
Stephens, Helen* 1983
Szewinska, Irena 1992
Tyus, Wyomia 1981
White, Willye 1988

Volleyball
+Hyman, Flo 1986

Water Skiing
McGuire, Willa Worthington* .. 1990

Coaches
Applebee, Constance 1991
Grossfeld, Muriel 1991
+Jackson, Nell 1990
Summit, Pat Head 1990
Wade, Margaret 1992

RETIRED NUMBERS

Major League Baseball

The New York Yankees have retired the most uniform numbers (12) in the Major Leagues; followed by Pittsburgh and the Brooklyn-Los Angeles Dodgers (8), the Chicago White Sox (7), the New York-San Francisco Giants (6) and the St.Louis Cardinals (5). Three players and a manager have had their numbers retired by two teams: **Hank Aaron**— #44 by the Boston-Milwaukee-Atlanta Braves and the Milwaukee Brewers; **Rod Carew**—#29 by Minnesota and California; **Frank Robinson**—#20 by Cincinnati and Baltimore; and **Casey Stengel**—#37 by the New York Yankees and New York Mets.

    Numbers retired in 1992 (2): California #30, worn by pitcher **Nolan Ryan** (1972-79); Milwaukee #34, worn by pitcher **Rollie Fingers** (1981-85).

AMERICAN LEAGUE

Three AL teams—the Seattle Mariners, Texas Rangers and Toronto Blue Jays—have not retired any numbers.

Baltimore
4 Earl Weaver
5 Brooks Robinson
20 Frank Robinson
22 Jim Palmer
33 Eddie Murray

Boston Red Sox
1 Bobby Doerr
4 Joe Cronin
8 Carl Yastrzemski
9 Ted Williams

California Angels
26 Gene Autry
29 Rod Carew
30 Nolan Ryan

Chicago White Sox
2 Nellie Fox
3 Harold Baines
4 Luke Appling
9 Minnie Minoso
11 Luis Aparicio
16 Ted Lyons
19 Billy Pierce

Cleveland Indians
3 Earl Averill
5 Lou Boudreau
18 Mel Harder
19 Bob Feller

Detroit Tigers
2 Charlie Gehringer
5 Hank Greenberg
6 Al Kaline

Kansas City Royals
10 Dick Howser

Milwaukee Brewers
34 Rollie Fingers
44 Hank Aaron

Minnesota Twins
3 Harmon Killebrew
6 Tony Oliva
29 Rod Carew

New York Yankees
1 Billy Martin
3 Babe Ruth
4 Lou Gehrig
5 Joe DiMaggio
7 Mickey Mantle
8 Yogi Berra & Bill Dickey
9 Roger Maris
10 Phil Rizzuto
15 Thurman Munson
16 Whitey Ford
32 Elston Howard
37 Casey Stengel

Oakland Athletics
27 Catfish Hunter

NATIONAL LEAGUE

One NL team—the Montreal Expos—has not retired a number. Also, San Francisco has honored former N.Y.Giants Christy Mathewson and John McGraw even though they played before numbers were worn.

Atlanta Braves
21 Warren Spahn
35 Phil Niekro
41 Eddie Mathews
44 Hank Aaron

Chicago Cubs
14 Ernie Banks
26 Billy Williams

Cincinnati Reds
1 Fred Hutchinson
5 Johnny Bench

Houston Astros
32 Jim Umbricht
40 Don Wilson

Los Angeles Dodgers
1 Pee Wee Reese
4 Duke Snider
19 Jim Gilliam
24 Walter Alston
32 Sandy Koufax
39 Roy Campanella
42 Jackie Robinson
53 Don Drysdale

New York Mets
14 Gil Hodges
37 Casey Stengel
41 Tom Seaver

Philadelphia Phillies
1 Richie Ashburn
20 Mike Schmidt
32 Steve Carlton
36 Robin Roberts

Pittsburgh Pirates
1 Billy Meyer
4 Ralph Kiner
8 Willie Stargell
9 Bill Mazeroski
20 Pie Traynor
21 Roberto Clemente
33 Honus Wagner
40 Danny Murtaugh

St.Louis Cardinals
6 Stan Musial
14 Ken Boyer
17 Dizzy Dean
20 Lou Brock
45 Bob Gibson
85 August (Gussie) Busch

San Diego Padres
6 Steve Garvey

San Francisco Giants
3 Bill Terry
4 Mel Ott
11 Carl Hubbell
24 Willie Mays
27 Juan Marichal
44 Willie McCovey

National Basketball Association

Boston has retired the most numbers (16) in the NBA; followed by the New York Knicks (7); Milwaukee, Portland and the Rochester-Cincinnati Royals/Kansas City-Omaha-Sacramento Kings (6); and the Los Angeles Lakers and Syracuse Nats/Philadelphia 76ers (5). Four players have had their numbers retired by two teams: **Wilt Chamberlain**— #13 by the Los Angeles Lakers and Philadelphia; **Julius Erving**—#6 by Philadelphia and #32 by New Jersey; **Oscar Robertson**—#1 by Milwaukee and #14 by Sacramento; and **Nate Thurmond**—#42 by Cleveland and Golden State.

    Numbers retired in 1991-92 (3): Boston #3 worn by **Dennis Johnson** (1983-90); Los Angeles Lakers #32, worn by **Magic Johnson** (1979-91); New York #15, worn by **Dick McGuire** (1949-57).

WESTERN CONFERENCE

Three Western teams—the Dallas Mavericks, Los Angeles Clippers and Minnesota Timberwolves—have not retired any numbers.

Denver Nuggets
40 Byron Beck
44 Dan Issel

Golden St. Warriors
14 Tom Meschery
16 Al Attles
24 Rick Barry
42 Nate Thurmond

Houston Rockets
23 Calvin Murphy
45 Rudy Tomjanovich

Los Angeles Lakers
13 Wilt Chamberlain
22 Elgin Baylor
32 Magic Johnson
33 Kareem Abdul-Jabbar
44 Jerry West

Phoenix Suns
5 Dick Van Arsdale
33 Alvan Adams
42 Connie Hawkins
44 Paul Westphal

Portland Trail Blazers
13 Dave Twardzik
15 Larry Steele
20 Maurice Lucas
32 Bill Walton
36 Lloyd Neal
45 Geoff Petrie

Sacramento Kings
6 Fans ("Sixth Man")
11 Bob Davies
12 Maurice Stokes
14 Oscar Robertson
27 Jack Twyman
44 Sam Lacey

San Antonio Spurs
13 James Silas
44 George Gervin

Seattle SuperSonics
19 Lenny Wilkens
32 Fred Brown

Utah Jazz
1 Frank Layden
7 Pete Maravich

EASTERN CONFERENCE

Three Eastern teams—the Charlotte Hornets, Miami Heat, and Orlando Magic—have not retired any numbers. Also, Philadelphia's Charles Barkley asked for and received permission from Billy Cunningham to wear No.32 during the 1991-92 season in tribute to Magic Johnson.

Atlanta Hawks
9 Bob Pettit
23 Lou Hudson

Boston Celtics
1 Walter A.Brown
2 Red Auerbach
3 Dennis Johnson
6 Bill Russell
10 Jo Jo White
14 Bob Cousy
16 Tom Heinsohn
16 Tom (Satch) Sanders
17 John Havlicek
18 Dave Cowens
19 Don Nelson
21 Bill Sharman
22 Ed Macauley
23 Frank Ramsey
24 Sam Jones
25 K.C.Jones
Loscy Jim Loscutoff
Radio mike Johnny Most

Chicago Bulls
4 Jerry Sloan

Cleveland Cavaliers
7 Bingo Smith
34 Austin Carr
42 Nate Thurmond

Detroit Pistons
21 Dave Bing

Indiana Pacers
30 George McGinnis
34 Mel Daniels
35 Roger Brown

Milwaukee Bucks
1 Oscar Robertson
2 Junior Bridgeman
4 Sidney Moncrief
14 Jon McGlocklin
16 Bob Lanier
32 Brian Winters

New York Knicks
10 Walt Frazier
12 Dick Barnett
15 Dick McGuire
& Earl Monroe
19 Willis Reed
22 Dave DeBusschere
24 Bill Bradley
613 Red Holzman

New Jersey Nets
4 Wendell Ladner
23 John Williamson
25 Bill Melchionni
32 Julius Erving

Philadelphia 76ers
6 Julius Erving
13 Wilt Chamberlain
15 Hal Greer
24 Bobby Jones
32 Billy Cunningham
P.A. mike Dave Zinkoff

Washington Bullets
11 Elvin Hayes
25 Gus Johnson
41 Wes Unseld

National Football League

The Chicago Bears have retired the most uniform numbers (10) in the NFL; followed by the Dallas Texans/Kansas City Chiefs (8); the Baltimore-Indianapolis Colts, New York Giants and San Francisco (7); Detroit (6); and the Boston-New England Patriots, Cleveland and Philadelphia (5). No player has ever had his number retired by more than one NFL team.

Numbers retired in 1992 (4): Three by Kansas City—#3 worn by **Jan Stenerud** (1967-79), #63 worn by **Willie Lanier** (1967-77) and #86 worn by **Buck Buchanan** (1963-75); Philadelphia #99 worn by **Jerome Brown** (1987-91).

AFC

Three AFC teams—the Buffalo Bills, Los Angeles Raiders and Pittsburgh Steelers—have not retired any numbers.

Cincinnati Bengals
54 Bob Johnson

Cleveland Browns
14 Otto Graham
32 Jim Brown
45 Ernie Davis
46 Don Fleming
76 Lou Groza

Denver Broncos
18 Frank Tripucka
44 Floyd Little

Houston Oilers
34 Earl Campbell
43 Jim Norton
65 Elvin Bethea

Indianapolis Colts
19 Johnny Unitas
22 Buddy Young
24 Lenny Moore
70 Art Donovan
77 Jim Parker
82 Raymond Berry
89 Gino Marchetti

Kansas City Chiefs
3 Jan Stenerud
16 Len Dawson
28 Abner Haynes
33 Stone Johnson
36 Mack Lee Hill
63 Willie Lanier
78 Bobby Bell
86 Buck Buchanan

Miami Dolphins
12 Bob Griese

New England Patriots
20 Gino Cappelletti
57 Steve Nelson
73 John Hannah
79 Jim Hunt
89 Bob Dee

New York Jets
12 Joe Namath
13 Don Maynard

San Diego Chargers
14 Dan Fouts

Seattle Seahawks
12 Fans ("12th Man")

National Football League (Cont.)
NFC

Dallas is the only NFC team that hasn't retired a number. Instead, the Cowboys have a "Ring of Honor" at Texas Stadium that includes seven players—Chuck Howley, Lee Roy Jordan, Bob Lilly, Don Meredith, Don Perkins, Mel Renfro and Roger Staubach.

Atlanta Falcons
10 Steve Bartkowski
31 William Andrews
57 Jeff Van Note
60 Tommy Nobis

Chicago Bears
3   Bronko Nagurski
5   George McAfee
28 Willie Galimore
34 Walter Payton
41 Brian Piccolo
42 Sid Luckman
56 Bill Hewitt
61 Bill George
66 Bulldog Turner
77 Red Grange
GSH George Halas

Detroit Lions
7   Dutch Clark
22 Bobby Layne
37 Doak Walker
56 Joe Schmidt
85 Chuck Hughes
88 Charlie Sanders

Green Bay Packers
3   Tony Canadeo
14 Don Hutson
15 Bart Starr
66 Ray Nitschke

Los Angeles Rams
7   Bob Waterfield
74 Merlin Olsen

Minnesota Vikings
10 Fran Tarkenton
88 Alan Page

New Orleans Saints
31 Jim Taylor
81 Doug Atkins

New York Giants
1   Ray Flaherty
7   Mel Hein
14 Y.A.Tittle
32 Al Blozis
40 Joe Morrison
42 Charlie Conerly
50 Ken Strong

Philadelphia Eagles
15 Steve Van Buren
40 Tom Brookshier
44 Pete Retzlaff
60 Chuck Bednarik
70 Al Wistert
99 Jerome Brown

Phoenix Cardinals
8   Larry Wilson
77 Stan Mauldin
88 J.V.Cain
99 Marshall Goldberg

San Francisco 49ers
12 John Brodie
34 Joe Perry
37 Jimmy Johnson
39 Hugh McElhenny
70 Charlie Krueger
73 Lou Nomellini
87 Dwight Clark

Tampa Bay Bucs
63 Lee Roy Selmon

Wash. Redskins
33 Sammy Baugh

National Hockey League

The Boston Bruins have retired the most uniform numbers (7) in the NHL; followed by Montreal (6); Chicago, Detroit, St.Louis and Philadelphia (4); and the Boston-New England-Hartford Whalers (3). Two players have had their numbers retired by two teams: **Gordie Howe**—#9 by Detroit and Hartford; and **Bobby Hull**—#9 by Chicago and Winnipeg.

Numbers retired in 1991-92 (5): Two by Detroit—#7 worn by **Ted Lindsay** and #10 worn by **Alex Delvecchio**; two by the New York Islanders—#5 worn by **Denis Potvin** and #22 worn by **Mike Bossy**; and Minnesota #8, worn by **Bill Goldsworthy**.

CAMPBELL CONFERENCE

The San Jose Sharks and expansion Tampa Bay Lightning are the only Campbell teams that have not retired a number.

Calgary Flames
9   Lanny McDonald

Chicago Blackhawks
1   Glenn Hall
9   Bobby Hull
21 Stan Mikita
35 Tony Esposito

Detroit Red Wings
6   Larry Aurie
7   Ted Lindsay
9   Gordie Howe
10 Alex Delvecchio

Edmonton Oilers
3   Al Hamilton

Los Angeles Kings
16 Marcel Dionne
30 Rogie Vachon

Minnesota North Stars
8   Bill Goldsworthy
19 Bill Masterton

St.Louis Blues
3   Bob Gassoff
8   Barclay Plager
11 Brian Sutter
24 Bernie Federko

Toronto Maple Leafs
5   Bill Barilko
6   Ace Bailey

Vancouver Canucks
11 Wayne Maki
12 Stan Smyl

Winnipeg Jets
9   Bobby Hull

WALES CONFERENCE

The New Jersey Devils and expansion Ottawa Senators are the only Wales teams that have not retired a number.

Boston Bruins
2   Eddie Shore
3   Lionel Hitchman
4   Bobby Orr
5   Dit Clapper
7   Phil Esposito
9   John Bucyk
15 Milt Schmidt

Buffalo Sabres
11 Gilbert Perreault

Hartford Whalers
2   Rick Ley
9   Gordie Howe
19 John McKenzie

Montreal Canadiens
2   Doug Harvey
4   Jean Beliveau
    & Aurele Joliat
7   Howie Morenz
9   Maurice Richard
10 Guy Lafleur
16 Henri Richard
    & Elmer Lach

New York Islanders
5   Denis Potvin
22 Mike Bossy

New York Rangers
1   Eddie Giacomin
7   Rod Gilbert

Philadelphia Flyers
1   Bernie Parent
4   Barry Ashbee
7   Bill Barber
16 Bobby Clarke

Pittsburgh Penguins
21 Michel Briere

Quebec Nordiques
3   J.C.Tremblay
8   Marc Tardif

Washington Capitals
7   Yvon Labre

Wide World Photos

Ted Williams (center) chats with **President Bush** while **Barbara Bush** ties the Presidential Medal of Freedom around his neck on Nov. 19, 1991. Williams is only the seventh sports figure to receive the nation's highest civilian honor.

AWARDS

Presidential Medal of Freedom

Since President John F. Kennedy established the Medal of Freedom as America's highest civilian honor in 1963, only seven sports figures have won the award. Note that (*) indicates the presentation was made posthumously.

Year		President	Year		President
1963	**Bob Kiphuth**, swimming	Kennedy	1984	**Jackie Robinson**, baseball	Reagan
1976	**Jesse Owens**, track & field	Ford	1986	**Earl (Red) Blaik**, football	Reagan
1977	**Joe DiMaggio**, baseball	Ford	1991	**Ted Williams**, baseball	Bush
1983	**Paul (Bear) Bryant***, football	Reagan			

Sports Illustrated Sportsman of the Year

Selected annually by the editors of *Sports Illustrated* magazine since 1954.

Year		Year		Year	
1954	**Roger Bannister**, track	1972	**Billie Jean King**, tennis	1987	**"8 Athletes Who Care"**
1955	**Johnny Podres**, baseball		& **John Wooden**, basketball		**Bob Bourne**, hockey
1956	**Bobby Morrow**, track	1973	**Jackie Stewart**, auto racing		**Kip Keino**, track
1957	**Stan Musial**, baseball	1974	**Muhammad Ali**, boxing		**Judi Brown King**, track
1958	**Rafer Johnson**, track	1975	**Pete Rose**, baseball		**Dale Murphy**, baseball
1959	**Ingemar Johansson**, boxing	1976	**Chris Evert**, tennis		**Chip Rives**, football
1960	**Arnold Palmer**, golf	1977	**Steve Cauthen**, horse racing		**Patty Sheehan**, golf
1961	**Jerry Lucas**, basketball	1978	**Jack Nicklaus**, golf		**Rory Sparrow**, basketball
1962	**Terry Baker**, football	1979	**Terry Bradshaw**, football		**Reggie Williams**, football
1963	**Pete Rozelle**, pro football		& **Willie Stargell**, baseball	1988	**Orel Hershiser**, baseball
1964	**Ken Venturi**, golf	1980	**US Olympic hockey team**	1989	**Greg LeMond**, cycling
1965	**Sandy Koufax**, baseball	1981	**Sugar Ray Leonard**, boxing	1990	**Joe Montana**, football
1966	**Jim Ryun**, track	1982	**Wayne Gretzky**, hockey	1991	**Michael Jordan**, basketball
1967	**Carl Yastrzemski**, baseball	1983	**Mary Decker**, track		
1968	**Bill Russell**, basketball	1984	**Mary Lou Retton**, gymnastics		
1969	**Tom Seaver**, baseball		& **Edwin Moses**, track		
1970	**Bobby Orr**, hockey	1985	**K.Abdul-Jabbar**, basketball		
1971	**Lee Trevino**, golf	1986	**Joe Paterno**, football		

Associated Press Athletes of the Year

Selected annually by AP newspaper sports editors since 1931.

Male

NBA regular season and playoff MVP Michael Jordan of the Chicago Bulls outpolled world record-breaking long jumper Mike Powell, 46-to-22 in first place votes to win the AP Male Athlete of the Year award for 1991.

The Top 10 vote-getters of 1991 are as follows; numbers in parentheses indicate first place votes: **1.** Jordan, pro basketball (46), 348 points; **2.** Powell, track & field (22), 134 pts; **3.** Carl Lewis, track & field (8), 80 pts; **4.** Nolan Ryan, baseball (10), 76 pts; **5.** Cal Ripken, baseball (8), 68 pts; **6.** Magic Johnson, pro basketball (8), 48 pts; **7.** Jimmy Connors, tennis (4), 40 pts; **8.** Sergei Bubka, track & field (4), 36 pts; **9.** Desmond Howard, college football (2), 26 pts; **10.** George Foreman, boxing (4), 24 pts.

Multiple winners: Don Budge, Sandy Koufax, Carl Lewis, Joe Montana and Byron Nelson (2).

Year		Year		Year	
1931	**Pepper Martin**, baseball	1952	**Bob Mathias**, track	1973	**O.J.Simpson**, pro football
1932	**Gene Sarazen**, golf	1953	**Ben Hogan**, golf	1974	**Muhammad Ali**, boxing
1933	**Carl Hubbell**, baseball	1954	**Willie Mays**, baseball	1975	**Fred Lynn**, baseball
1934	**Dizzy Dean**, baseball	1955	**Hopalong Cassady**, col.football	1976	**Bruce Jenner**, track
1935	**Joe Louis**, boxing	1956	**Mickey Mantle**, baseball	1977	**Steve Cauthen**, horse racing
1936	**Jesse Owens**, track	1957	**Ted Williams**, baseball	1978	**Ron Guidry**, baseball
1937	**Don Budge**, tennis	1958	**Herb Elliot**, track	1979	**Willie Stargell**, baseball
1938	**Don Budge**, tennis	1959	**Ingemar Johansson**, boxing		
1939	**Nile Kinnick**, college football			1980	**US Olympic hockey team**
		1960	**Rafer Johnson**, track	1981	**John McEnroe**, tennis
1940	**Tom Harmon**, college football	1961	**Roger Maris**, baseball	1982	**Wayne Gretzky**, hockey
1941	**Joe DiMaggio**, baseball	1962	**Maury Wills**, baseball	1983	**Carl Lewis**, track
1942	**Frank Sinkwich**, college football	1963	**Sandy Koufax**, baseball	1984	**Carl Lewis**, track
1943	**Gunder Haegg**, track	1964	**Don Schollander**, swimming	1985	**Dwight Gooden**, baseball
1944	**Byron Nelson**, golf	1965	**Sandy Koufax**, baseball	1986	**Larry Bird**, pro basketball
1945	**Byron Nelson**, golf	1966	**Frank Robinson**, baseball	1987	**Ben Johnson**, track
1946	**Glenn Davis**, college football	1967	**Carl Yastrzemski**, baseball	1988	**Orel Hershiser**, baseball
1947	**Johnny Lujack**, college football	1968	**Denny McLain**, baseball	1989	**Joe Montana**, pro football
1948	**Lou Boudreau**, baseball	1969	**Tom Seaver**, baseball		
1949	**Leon Hart**, college football			1990	**Joe Montana**, pro football
		1970	**George Blanda**, pro football	1991	**Michael Jordan**, pro basketball
1950	**Jim Konstanty**, baseball	1971	**Lee Trevino**, golf		
1951	**Dick Kazmaier**, college football	1972	**Mark Spitz**, swimming		

Female

Seventeen-year-old tennis champion Monica Seles, who won three Grand Slam tournaments in 1991 and skipped the fourth (Wimbledon), was the landslide winner of the '91 AP Female Athlete of the Year award.

The Top 10 vote-getters of 1991 are as follows; numbers in parentheses indicate first place votes: **1.** Seles, tennis (72), 432 points; **2.** (tie) Pat Bradley, golf (6) and Martina Navratilova (6), 114 pts; **4.** Meg Mallon, golf (6), 104 pts; **5.** Debbie Doom, softball (6), 96 pts; **6.** Kim Zmeskal, gymnastics (10), 72 pts; **7.** Gabriela Sabatini, tennis (2), 42 pts; **8.** Steffi Graf, tennis (2), 38 pts; **9.** Jennifer Capriati, tennis (4), 34 pts; **10.** Diane Dixon, track & field (2), 30 pts.

Multiple winners: Babe Didrikson Zaharias (6); Chris Evert (4); Patty Berg and Maureen Connolly (3); Tracy Austin, Althea Gibson, Billie Jean King, Nancy Lopez, Alice Marble, Martina Navratilova, Wilma Rudolph, Kathy Whitworth and Mickey Wright (2).

Year		Year		Year	
1931	**Helene Madison**, swimming	1952	**Maureen Connolly**, tennis	1973	**Billie Jean King**, tennis
1932	**Babe Didrikson**, track	1953	**Maureen Connolly**, tennis	1974	**Chris Evert**, tennis
1933	**Helen Jacobs**, tennis	1954	**Babe Didrikson Zaharias**, golf	1975	**Chris Evert**, tennis
1934	**Virginia Van Wie**, golf	1955	**Patty Berg**, golf	1976	**Nadia Comaneci**, gymnastics
1935	**Helen Wills Moody**, tennis	1956	**Pat McCormick**, diving	1977	**Chris Evert**, tennis
1936	**Helen Stephens**, track	1957	**Althea Gibson**, tennis	1978	**Nancy Lopez**, golf
1937	**Katherine Rawls**, swimming	1958	**Althea Gibson**, tennis	1979	**Tracy Austin**, tennis
1938	**Patty Berg**, golf	1959	**Maria Bueno**, tennis		
1939	**Alice Marble**, tennis			1980	**Chris Evert Lloyd**, tennis
		1960	**Wilma Rudolph**, track	1981	**Tracy Austin**, tennis
1940	**Alice Marble**, tennis	1961	**Wilma Rudolph**, track	1982	**Mary Decker Tabb**, track
1941	**Betty Hicks Newell**, golf	1962	**Dawn Fraser**, swimming	1983	**Martina Navratilova**, tennis
1942	**Gloria Callen**, swimming	1963	**Mickey Wright**, golf	1984	**Mary Lou Retton**, gymnastics
1943	**Patty Berg**, golf	1964	**Mickey Wright**, golf	1985	**Nancy Lopez**, golf
1944	**Ann Curtis**, swimming	1965	**Kathy Whitworth**, golf	1986	**Martina Navratilova**, tennis
1945	**Babe Didrikson Zaharias**, golf	1966	**Kathy Whitworth**, golf	1987	**Jackie Joyner-Kersee**, track
1946	**Babe Didrikson Zaharias**, golf	1967	**Billie Jean King**, tennis	1988	**Florence Griffith Joyner**, track
1947	**Babe Didrikson Zaharias**, golf	1968	**Peggy Fleming**, skating	1989	**Steffi Graf**, tennis
1948	**Fanny Blankers-Koen**, track	1969	**Debbie Meyer**, swimming		
1949	**Marlene Bauer**, golf			1990	**Beth Daniel**, golf
		1970	**Chi Cheng**, track	1991	**Monica Seles**, tennis
1950	**Babe Didrikson Zaharias**, golf	1971	**Evonne Goolagong**, tennis		
1951	**Maureen Connolly**, tennis	1972	**Olga Korbut**, gymnastics		

UPI International Athletes of the Year

Selected annually by United Press International's European newspaper sports editors since 1974.

Male

Multiple winners: Sebastian Coe, Alberto Juantorena and Carl Lewis (2).

Year	Year	Year
1974 **Muhammad Ali,** boxing	1980 **Eric Heiden,** speed skating	1986 **Diego Maradona,** soccer
1975 **Joao Oliveira,** track	1981 **Sebastian Coe,** track	1987 **Ben Johnson,** track
1976 **Alberto Juantorena,** track	1982 **Daley Thompson,** track	1988 **Matt Biondi,** swimming
1977 **Alberto Juantorena,** track	1983 **Carl Lewis,** track	1989 **Boris Becker,** tennis
1978 **Henry Rono,** track	1984 **Carl Lewis,** track	1990 **Stefan Edberg,** tennis
1979 **Sebastian Coe,** track	1985 **Steve Cram,** track	1991 **Sergei Bubka,** track

Female

Multiple winners: Nadia Comaneci, Steffi Graf and Marita Koch (2).

Year	Year	Year
1974 **Irena Szewinska,** track	1980 **Hanni Wenzel,** alpine skiing	1986 **Heike Drechsler,** track
1975 **Nadia Comaneci,** gymnastics	1981 **Chris Evert Lloyd,** tennis	1987 **Steffi Graf,** tennis
1976 **Nadia Comaneci,** gymnastics	1982 **Marita Koch,** track	1988 **Florence Griffith Joyner,** track
1977 **Rosie Ackermann,** track	1983 **Jarmila Kratochvilova,** track	1989 **Steffi Graf,** tennis
1978 **Track Caulkins,** swimming	1984 **Martina Navratilova,** tennis	1990 **Merlene Ottey,** track
1979 **Marita Koch,** track	1985 **Mary Docker Slaney,** track	1991 **Monica Seles,** tennis

Jesse Owens International Trophy

Presented annually by the International Amateur Athletic Association since 1981 and selected by a worldwide panel of electors. The Jesse Owens International Trophy is named after the late American Olympic champion, who won four gold medals at the 1936 Summer Games in Berlin.

Year	Year	Year
1981 **Eric Heiden,** speed skating	1985 **Carl Lewis,** track	1990 **Roger Kingdom,** track
1982 **Sebastian Coe,** track	1986 **Said Aouita,** track	1991 **Greg LeMond,** cycling
1983 **Mary Decker,** track	1987 **Greg Louganis,** diving	1992 **Mike Powell,** track
1984 **Edwin Moses,** track	1988 **Ben Johnson,** track	

James E. Sullivan Memorial Award

Presented annually by the Amateur Athletic Union since 1930. The Sullivan Award is named after the former AAU president and given to the athlete who, ''by his or her performance, example and influence as an amateur, has done the most during the year to advance the cause of sportsmanship.'' An athlete cannot win the award more than once.
 1991 winner: Mike Powell, track & field. **Other 1991 finalists (9):** Mike Barrowman, swimming; Kent Ferguson, diving; Eric Griffin, boxing; Sarah Josephson, synchronized swimming; Michael Johnson, track & field; Christian Laettner, basketball; Donna Weinbrecht, freestyle skiing; Kristi Yamaguchi, figure skating; and Kim Zmeskal, gymnastics. Vote totals not released.

Year	Year	Year
1930 **Bobby Jones,** golf	1952 **Horace Ashenfelter,** track	1974 **Rich Wohlhuter,** track
1931 **Barney Berlinger,** track	1953 **Sammy Lee,** diving	1975 **Tim Shaw,** swimming
1932 **Jim Bausch,** track	1954 **Mal Whitfield,** track	1976 **Bruce Jenner,** track
1933 **Glenn Cunningham,** track	1955 **Harrison Dillard,** track	1977 **John Naber,** swimming
1934 **Bill Bonthron,** track	1956 **Pat McCormick,** diving	1978 **Tracy Caulkins,** swimming
1935 **Lawson Little,** golf	1957 **Bobby Morrow,** track	1979 **Kurt Thomas,** gymnastics
1936 **Glenn Morris,** track	1958 **Glenn Davis,** track	
1937 **Don Budge,** tennis	1959 **Parry O'Brien,** track	1980 **Eric Heiden,** speed skating
1938 **Don Lash,** track		1981 **Carl Lewis,** track
1939 **Joe Burk,** rowing	1960 **Rafer Johnson,** track	1982 **Mary Decker,** track
	1961 **Wilma Rudolph,** track	1983 **Edwin Moses,** track
1940 **Greg Rice,** track	1963 **John Pennel,** track	1984 **Greg Louganis,** diving
1941 **Leslie MacMitchell,** track	1964 **Don Schollander,** swimming	1985 **Joan B. Samuelson,** track
1942 **Cornelius Warmerdam,** track	1965 **Bill Bradley,** basketball	1986 **Jackie Joyner-Kersee,** track
1943 **Gilbert Dodds,** track	1966 **Jim Ryun,** track	1987 **Jim Abbott,** baseball
1944 **Ann Curtis,** swimming	1967 **Randy Matson,** track	1988 **Florence Griffith Joyner,** track
1945 **Doc Blanchard,** football	1968 **Debbie Meyer,** swimming	1989 **Janet Evans,** swimming
1946 **Arnold Tucker,** football	1969 **Bill Toomey,** track	
1947 **John B. Kelly, Jr.,** rowing		1990 **John Smith,** wrestling
1948 **Bob Mathias,** track	1970 **John Kinsella,** swimming	1991 **Mike Powell,** track
1949 **Dick Button,** skating	1971 **Mark Spitz,** swimming	
	1972 **Frank Shorter,** track	
1950 **Fred Wilt,** track	1973 **Bill Walton,** basketball	
1951 **Bob Richards,** track		

The Sporting News Man of the Year

Selected annually by the editors of The Sporting News since 1968.

Year		Year		Year	
1968	**Denny McLain**, baseball	1976	**Larry O'Brien**, basketball	1984	**Peter Ueberroth**, LA Olympics
1969	**Tom Seaver**, baseball	1977	**Steve Cauthen**, horse racing	1985	**Pete Rose**, baseball
1970	**John Wooden**, basketball	1978	**Ron Guidry**, baseball	1986	**Larry Bird**, pro basketball
1971	**Lee Trevino**, golf	1979	**Willie Stargell**, baseball	1987	No award
1972	**Charles O.Finley**, baseball	1980	**George Brett**, baseball	1988	**Jackie Joyner-Kersee**, track
1973	**O.J.Simpson**, pro football	1981	**Wayne Gretzky**, hockey	1989	**Joe Montana**, football
1974	**Lou Brock**, baseball	1982	**Whitey Herzog**, baseball	1990	**Nolan Ryan**, baseball
1975	**Archie Griffin**, football	1983	**Bowie Kuhn**, baseball	1991	**Michael Jordan,** basketball

Time Man of the Year

Since Charles Lindbergh was named Time magazine's first Man of the Year for 1927, two individuals with significant sports credentials have won the honor.

Year
1984 **Peter Ueberroth**, president LA Olympic Organizing Committee.
1991 **Ted Turner**, owner-president Turner Broadcasting System, founder of CNN cable news network, owner of the Atlanta Braves (NL) and Atlanta Hawks (NBA), and former winning America's Cup skipper.

Honda Broderick Cup

To the outstanding collegiate woman athlete of the year in NCAA competition. Winner is chosen from nominees in each of the NCAA's 10 competitive sports. Final voting is done by member athletic directors. Award is named after founder and sportswear manufacturer Thomas Broderick.
Multiple winner: Tracy Caulkins (2).

Year			Year		
1977	**Lucy Harris**, Delta St	basketball	1985	**Jackie Joyner**, UCLA	track & field
1978	**Ann Meyers**, UCLA	basketball	1986	**Kamie Ethridge**, Texas	basketball
1979	**Nancy Lieberman**, Old Dominion	basketball	1988	**Teresa Weatherspoon**, La.Tech	basketball
1980	**Julie Shea**, N.C.State	track & field	1989	**Vicki Huber**, Villanova	track
1981	**Jill Sterkel**, Texas	swimming	1990	**Suzy Favor**, Wisconsin	track
1982	**Tracy Caulkins**, Florida	swimming	1991	**Dawn Staley**, Virginia	basketball
1983	**Deitre Collins**, Hawaii	volleyball			
1984	**Tracy Caulkins**, Florida	swimming			
	& **Cheryl Miller**, USC	basketball			

Flo Hyman Award

Presented annually since 1987 by the Women's Sports Foundation for "exemplifying dignity, spirit and commitment to excellence" and named in honor of the late captain of the 1984 U.S. Women's Volleyball team. Voting is done by WSF members.

Year		Year		Year	
1987	**Martina Navratilova**, tennis	1989	**Evelyn Ashford**, track	1991	**Diana Golden,** skiing
1988	**Jackie Joyner-Kersee**, track	1990	**Chris Evert**, tennis	1992	**Nancy Lopez**, golf

Theodore Roosevelt Award

First presented in 1967 by the NCAA, "to honor a distinguished citizen of national reputation and outstanding accomplishment who earned a varsity athletic award in college and has demonstrated a continuing interest in physical fitness and intercollegiate sports." The Teddy Award is the highest honor the NCAA confers on an individual and is named after the 26th President of the United States, who boxed at Harvard (Class of 1880) and played an instrumental role in the formation of the NCAA in 1906.

Year		College Class	Year		College Class
1967	**Gen.Dwight Eisenhower**	Army, 1915	1980	**Dr.Denton Cooley**	Texas, 1941
1968	**Leverett Saltonstall**	Harvard, 1914	1981	**Art Linkletter**	San Diego St., 1934
1969	**Byron (Whizzer) White**	Colorado, 1938	1982	**Bill Cosby**	Temple, 1977
			1983	**Arnold Palmer**	Wake Forest, 1951
1970	**Frederick Hovde**	Minnesota, 1929	1984	**Vice Adm.William Lawrence**	Navy, 1951
1971	**Christopher Kraft**	VPI, 1944	1985	**Robben Fleming**	Beloit, 1938
1972	**Jerome Holland**	Cornell, 1939	1986	**George Bush**	Yale, 1948
1973	**Gen.Omar Bradley**	Army, 1915	1987	**Walter Zable**	Wm.& Mary, 1937
1974	**Jesse Owens**	Ohio St., 1937	1988	**Walter Byers**	Iowa, 1943
1975	**Gerald Ford**	Michigan, 1935	1989	**Dr.Paul Ebert**	Ohio St., 1954
1976	**Adm.Tom Hamilton**	Navy, 1927			
1977	**Tom Bradley**	UCLA, 1941	1990	**Ronald Reagan**	Eureka, 1932
1978	**Gerald Zornow**	Rochester, 1937	1991	**Althea Gibson**	Florida A&M, 1953
1979	**Otis Chandler**	Stanford, 1950	1992	**Jack Kemp**	Occidental, 1957

Note: The NCAA recognized retiring executive director Walter Byers with a special Teddy Award in 1988 after 37 years of leadership.

Jeff MacNelly

TROPHIES

First Prize

*From Coroebus to Al Davis, the principle hasn't changed;
the thrill of victory isn't quite the same without a trophy.*

They've been awarding trophies, cups, medals and wreaths to winners in sport since the Greek Coroebus of Elis was crowned with wild olive for winning the 200-yard dash in the stadium at Olympia in 776 B.C. But there's rarely been a more electric award ceremony or one more flushed with irony and loathing than Pete Rozelle's presentation of the Vince Lombardi Trophy to Al Davis at the Superdome on the banks of the Mississippi in 1981 A.D.

Rozelle and Davis, of course, hated each other—and with good reason. They had been rival commissioners at the height of hostilities between the National and American football leagues in 1966 and now, 15 years later, Davis' intention to transfer his rowdy Raiders from Oakland to Los Angeles had not only produced an epic law suit, but had shaken the foundations of the NFL in the view of the supremely corporate Mr. Rozelle. More to the point, Mr. Davis wore his Brooklyn tough guy image like a suit of armor. There are diabolical linebackers in this game who would not dare cross Al Davis, which is why the commissioner was somewhat concerned as he approached the Raiders' locker room in the final moments of their thrashing of the Philadelphia Eagles in Super Bowl XV.

"It had been a perfect day," recalls Will McDonough, the network analyst and football elder, who was there. "The Iranian hostages had just been released and there was a huge yellow ribbon tied around the entire dome. The bow was right over the entrance, and all day long people were singing that crazy song. It was great. But when it got down near the end of the game with the Raiders way ahead, Pete didn't know what to expect."

Add to that an audience of roughly 80 million Americans, inert before their TV sets but fully aware of the dynamics of the situation. "A lot of the players were hooting and cursing Pete as they came off the field," says McDonough. "But when he walked into the room, one of the veterans winked at him and said, 'Don't worry, it'll be okay.'"

In the end, the cagey Davis charmed the fretful Rozelle, beating the former PR man at his own game. He was exceedingly gracious and took no shots. "As usual," McDonough notes, "Al had a fine sense of the moment."

The crowning of the moment with gestures that are elegant and gracious; the adorning of achievement with prizes that are symbolically rich. That is what this trophy business is all about. Some 2,700 years of history, more than even H.G. Wells could comprehend, span the age of Coroebus with that of Al Davis. But the principle hasn't changed. To the victor belongs the laurel wreath, trophy, chalice,

Clark Booth is the special projects reporter at WCVB-TV in Boston and has covered sports and politics in the city since 1962.

Wide World Photos

NFL Commissioner **Pete Rozelle** (right) presents the Vince Lombardi Trophy to **Al Davis** after the Raiders' 27-10 victory over Philadelphia in Super Bowl XV. Sportscaster **Bryant Gumble** presides.

plaque, plate, pennant, banner, belt, bowl, bell, brooch, watch, ring, jacket, medallion or sports car.

In the ancient Olympic games, before they were ruined by greed and corruption and finally banned by Theodosius in 393 A.D., the Greeks would build a statue of a chap if he won an event three times. We do roughly the same thing today by elevating our most storied athletes into Halls of Fame—over 20 national pantheons honoring some 3,500 greats in a dozen different games. We yearn, godlike, to confer immortality by crafting graven images of our heroes and hanging them on walls like museum artwork. Or preserving their heroic aura at home by lifting revered uniform numbers and championship banners to the rafters for all to see and remember.

Few are the arena attics with a more celebrated clothesline than the one saluting the Celtics at Boston Garden, but in truth even 16 pennants and 16 retired numbers are only so much laundry. Precious metal is the real coin of the trophy realm

and the most prized of those possessions these days is the Lombardi Trophy—the stunning talisman Rozelle handed to Davis that giddy day in New Orleans. There are XXVI in existence and there are folks out there who would kill for one. Designed by Tiffany and Co., it consists of seven pounds of sterling silver forming a regulation-sized football mounted on a pyramid-shaped stand. It is new as these relics go, having been minted for the inaugural Super Bowl in 1967 and then christened three years later in the rush to canonize pro football's favorite benevolent despot after his untimely death at age 57.

In 1992 dollars, the Lombardi Trophy (not to be confused, by the way, with the Lombardi Award, which has gone to college football's best lineman since 1970) is worth about $12,500. In effective terms, however, the price for winning one is actually closer to a quarter of a billion dollars—roughly the cost of purchasing and developing an NFL champion. Aside from the Olympic rings, it may be the emblem corporate America most admires

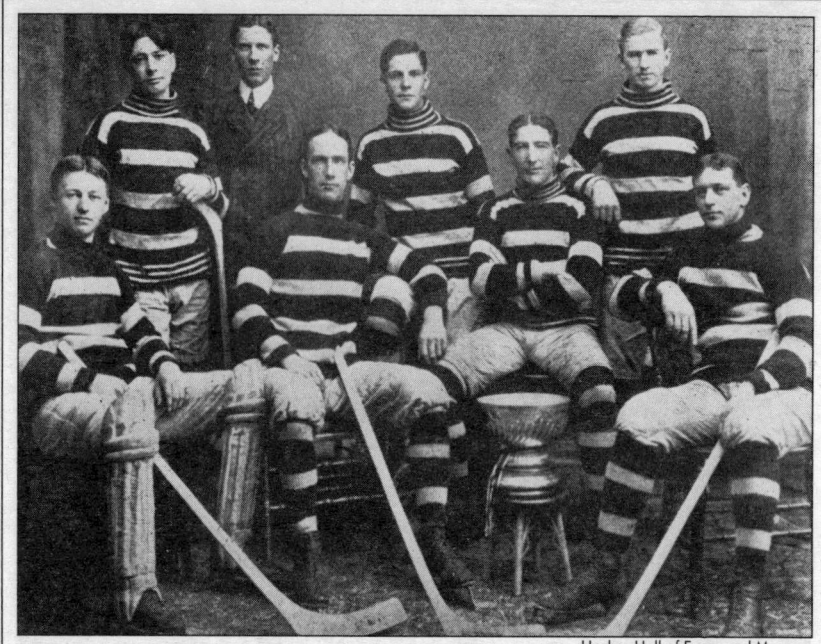

Hockey Hall of Fame and Museum

The Stanley Cup was still a mere bowl at the turn of the century when the **Ottawa Silver Seven** won it for three consecutive years from 1903-05. Even then, players put it on a pedestal.

these days. If it isn't, the honor goes to the oldest sporting prize still up for grabs at regular intervals, yachting's America's Cup. The Auld Mug is the trophy of choice for snobs, although a lot less so since 1983 when the Australians separated it from the clutches of the New York Yacht Club after 132 years.

The contesting of the America's Cup began in 1851, when the 101-foot schooner America beat 14 British boats of various sizes in a spin around the Isle of Wight as Queen Victoria looked on. Faithfully, every few years since, except when wars have intervened, the idle rich have gleefully squandered millions in the vainglorious pursuit of a rather ugly silver ewer shaped like a pelican.

That it should have become so coveted is amazing in its own right. Originally called the One Hundred Guinea Cup (that's what it cost a London silversmith to hammer out the prize), it was almost melted down into commemorative medals after the first race. Spared by mere whim, it eventually became yachting's Holy Grail. The American Civil War delayed the first challenge until 1870, but

ever since, folks who are smart enough to be rich have been making fools of themselves over the thing. And never more so than in 1992 when a fleet of dreamers from Europe, the U.S. and the Antipodes budgeted $278 million for the trials alone, according to Yachting magazine. Even the initiates say the fever is out of control with masts costing $650,000, keels going for $100,000 and top skippers commanding salaries of a million dollars, plus perks.

After successfully defending the Cup in May against the Italian challenger Il Moro di Venezia, skipper Bill Koch of America[3] let all within earshot know he wasn't thrilled about the bottom line. "It's gotten obscene and wasteful," Koch told The New York Times, adding, "Like an arms race or anything else, it will only escalate." Hardly a piker, the Kansan Koch, billionaire heir of an oil fortune, put up some $10 million of his own dough. But the cost of the enterprise mushroomed from the $20 million he projected to $64 million.

Which is just about what it would have cost Koch to win hockey's Stanley Cup.

The Pittsburgh Penguins, who bestride the National Hockey League like a Colossus, have won two straight NHL championships, yet were sold last November along with their lease on the Civic Arena for $65 million.

There's no trophy in any other North American team sport that is prized more highly than the Stanley Cup. No players in any other game care as much for a piece of hardware or attach more importance to its mystique. Hockey players, whatever their flaws, are intensely loyal to their game and devoutly subscribe to its scripture and ritual. At the center of the hockey player's devotions, much like a tabernacle in the middle of an altar, is "the Cup."

Lord Stanley of Preston, the Earl of Derby and Governor General of Canada in the good old days of the Commonwealth, purchased the original silver bowl for 10 guineas ($48.67) in 1893 and decreed that it should be "a challenge cup" to be contested "from year to year." It is not true, as has been too often written, that Lord Stanley was not a hockey fan; far from it. It is true, however, that he never saw a Stanley Cup match. Just weeks after he donated the Cup he was called home by the Queen.

After 99 years, the Cup has become one of the most enduring symbols in all of sport. And one of the largest. With every winning team's roster stamped on it somewhere, the Cup, which was originally 7½ inches high and 10 pounds, has grown into a long-neck drum of silver nickel alloy that measures 35¼ inches from top to bottom and weighs in at 32 pounds.

But there's a limit to how much engraving you can cram on to one surface and it was reached in 1992. With the usual sentimental pangs, it was resolved to alter the Cup by removing the highest of the five bands, the one bearing the rosters of the Cup winners from 1928 through 1942. "It wasn't an easy decision to make," says Philip Pritchard of the Hockey Hall of Fame, the custodian of the Cup. "We finally decided we didn't want to make it any bigger, so from now on we'll just retire another band every 16 years or so." Boffy, Inc., the prestigious Montreal silversmith that has lovingly ministered to the Cup for three generations, will do the alterations.

It's hardly the first time modifications to hockey's grail have been necessary. Indeed, the Cup itself—the actual bowl that Lord Stanley donated which sits atop the trophy—was retired to the Hall of Fame in 1970 after it was deemed to have become too fragile. The replacement is exact in every detail, but it's not the real thing.

Much as it's treasured, the Cup has been bounced around by the rollicking lads who have won it. Already legend is the tale of its sinking to the bottom of Mario Lemieux' swimming pool the night after the Penguins won it for the first time in 1991.

Among other misadventures, dating back to the turn of the century—it has been left in an Ottawa graveyard; tossed into Ottawa's Rideau Canal where it might have drifted to oblivion had the canal not frozen overnight; tumbled from a rumble seat while being borne through the streets of Montreal; and as recently as 1968, stolen from the Hall of Fame and held for ransom (the thieves returned it unscathed three weeks later, having heard, no doubt, that a lynch mob was forming).

I once sipped from the Cup myself, in 1970, then watched with delight as the victorious Bruins tossed it through the ranks like a volleyball with champagne spilling all over the place. The Cup took a real pounding that night.

The National Basketball Association has many things to recommend it these days, but a strong sense of tradition is not one of them. Even though it's been around since 1947, the NBA didn't have a definitive championship trophy until it instructed Tiffany to create one in 1978. The two-foot high trophy, which depicts a regulation-size basketball over the rim of a basket, was originally named in honor of Walter A. Brown, the late NBA pioneer and owner of the Boston Celtics. Six years later, however, the league renamed the award as a going-away present to retiring commissioner Larry O'Brien.

Nevertheless, to the game's more intense players the symbolism of the Brown/O'Brien Trophy is precious. I have the vivid memory of a 24-year-old Larry Bird lugging it home to Boston from Houston after the Celtics won the 1981 title. So tight was Bird's grip on the thing, even as he slept on the plane, you would have needed a crowbar to pry it loose. Ten years later, Chicago's Michael Jordan wept as he hugged it after the Bulls won their first title in his seventh season.

But overall, trophies are not a major feature of the NBA style. More to the point, the assiduous marketing of the league's properties under the shrewd leadership of commissioner David Stern has resulted in the outright selling of the individual player awards to corporate high-rollers. The Rookie of the Year award, to cite one example, was sponsored by Minute Maid Orange Soda in 1990-91 and then by Coca-Cola Classic in 1991-92. Little mention was made either year of NBA pioneer Eddie Gottlieb for whom the original award was named in 1952-53. Should this be viewed as egregious huckstering, Mr. Stern's apologists are pleased to point out that his league, unlike most others, is awash in black ink.

Outrageous commercialism offends few these days. We've come to realize that corporate sponsors not only help foot the bills, but in many cases pay the freight entirely. Hence, the Federal Express Orange Bowl and the Poulan/Weed Eater Independence Bowl in college football, the Ford Australian Open in tennis and the Daytona 500 by STP in auto racing.

It all has to do with the new first commandment of sport: expanded revenues must exceed increased costs. Nothing is sacred, and to the creative go the spoils. As a result, horse racing, the so-called sport of kings, has become the sport of shills. The Kentucky Derby, Preakness Stakes and Belmont Stakes are no longer simply the Triple Crown, but the "Chrysler Triple Crown Challenge." Even the English Derby, raced at Epsom since 1780, has a sponsor—Eveready batteries.

On the surface, the grueling 2,200-mile Tour de France bike race that stretches from Paris to the Alps and back while a billion people watch on TV, is waged, in all of its suffering, for a very simple winner's cup. But beyond the surface, the subsidies are enormous and if you are a three-time winner like Greg LeMond, a French merchant will gladly pay you $5 million to wear his shirt on your back.

For almost a century, spartans ran the Boston Marathon for a laurel wreath and a bowl of beef stew. Now they also carve up $418,000 from the John Hancock in-

What Is It About The Heisman?

The Heisman Trophy is college football's premier prize. It is also one of the more mystical in all of sport and the question persists: Why?

It may be hard to believe now, but the Maxwell Award, which also anoints the top collegiate player, ranked with the Heisman stride for stride through the 1950's. The trophies were near equally valued, got equal attention and often went to the same fellow. But the Maxwell is presented by a Philadelphia boosters club whereas the Heisman is the concoction of the high-powered Downtown Athletic Club on Manhattan's West Side. It is choice establishment turf and costs $2,200 a year to belong, that is if you can come up with two members to sponsor you.

That, combined with lots of free publicity from the New York media and a gimmicky, if highly suspect, voting process have made the Heisman *the* trophy of trophies.

At the core of this marvelous promotion is the very curious John William Heisman. Although he has been immortalized by the trophy that was quite incidentally named for him, it's debatable whether he is deserving or really represents what college sport is or ought to be all about.

Heisman was a notable and very innovative coach whose teams won 185 games from 1892 to 1927. Those were the days when top college coaches had the status of eminent divines and darn well knew it. In terms of skill and color he was the peer of contemporary giants Amos Alonzo Stagg, Pop Warner, Hurry Up Yost and Knute Rockne. But he didn't have their charm. Heisman was actually a colossal eccentric and an early gridiron crank. He was a stumpy and verbose thespian who liked to call the football, "a prolate spheroid." In his stock address to his players, he would say things like: "Better to have died as a small boy than ever fumble this football." He made his team eat raw meat because he liked it and banned soup from the training table because he didn't like it. His practices were long and arduous, and not to be followed by hot showers with soap because he considered both 'debilitating.'

In Heisman's most celebrated victory, his

UPI/Bettmann

John W. Heisman (right), seen here with assistant **Harold Gaston** while at Penn in the early 1920s, coached at eight different colleges from 1892-1927 and won 185 games.

mighty Georgia Tech team massacred poor Cumberland College, 222-0, in 1916. Seems he was annoyed at some sportswriter who, he believed, made too much of comparative scores. So, anxious to prove that he could run up the score at will against a lesser opponent, Heisman picked luckless little Cumberland to be the unwitting pigeon.

His arrogance seems to have been boundless. He once wrote: "The Coach should be masterful and commanding, even dictatorial. He has not the time to say 'please' or 'Mister.' He must be severe, arbitrary and little short of a czar." It was clear he lived what he preached.

A twist of fate led to the trophy being named for Heisman in 1936. He had been the Downtown Athletic Club's athletic director during his last years and when he died just a few months after the DAC inaugurated the award, the club deemed it fitting that the prize be named after him even though Rockne, among others, would have been more worthy.

The voting process is the key to the Heisman's grip. All those rather anonymous sportswriters and sportscasters who are asked to vote on it inevitably feel obliged also to promote it. It's ingenious. But it's also flawed. Many electors openly scorn the process and several have admitted ruefully that they vote without having seen a single college game in the flesh all season. That's why image-making, tub-thumping and outright, unabashed campaigning, usually mounted by hustling college SID's, plays such a big role in deciding who wins. In 1992, there were 919 electors; 145 from each of six regions of the country plus the 49 living Heisman winners. Selecting the electors is done quietly and there are only two conditions for the chosen: vote and keep your vote secret.

There is this last Heisman footnote. In 1935, an NYU halfback named Ed Smith posed for the making of the trophy by 23-year-old sculptor Frank Eliscu, who would go on to gain fame in the field. Smith neither knew nor cared why he was posing, believing he was simply doing Eliscu a favor. It wasn't until 1982, 47 years after the fact, that Smith learned he had been the model for the determined, straight-arming chap with the firm grip on the prolate spheroid.

surance folks. For 90 years, the old smoothies at Wimbledon gave "the gentleman" who won their tennis title a handsome chalice while "the lady" champion got a shiny, silver tray. They still do. But since the arrival of open tennis in 1968, they've also received a handsome paycheck which has grown to $501,514 for the men's winner and $421,584 for the women's.

Even if the assault of money has diluted them as a priority, some of the great trophies of sport still exert a powerful visceral sway. Is there a more noble tribute than the Amateur Athletic Union's James E. Sullivan Memorial Award, which is conferred each year upon America's best amateur athlete, male or female? It has a wonderful classic look and you can only win it once, no matter how good you are. It's sponsored, of course, but at least the Mars candy folks haven't renamed it the Snickers Award.

Well over half of the Sullivan Award's 62 winners are former Olympic champions. Olympic medals, be they for win, place or show, symbolize the pinnacle of personal achievement and you should weep for the kid who finishes fourth in anything. When the Games were revived in Athens in 1896, officials gave out a few medals and a lot of wreaths. Four years later they awarded "valuable artifacts," according to the record book, and finally settled on the three-medal (gold, silver and bronze) concept in 1908.

Early on, before they became standardized, there were some brilliant variations in the medals, and through the years the informal prizes have been even more fascinating. At the Stockholm Games of 1912, America's Jim Thorpe not only won gold medals in the pentathlon and decathlon, but also received a bejeweled model of a Viking ship and a bronze bust of the King of Sweden. "You, sir," said Gustav V at the awards ceremony, "are the greatest athlete in the world." Not one to argue with the truth, Thorpe replied, "Thanks, King."

In 1913, it came to light that Thorpe had unknowingly forfeited his amateur standing in 1910 by playing some semi-pro baseball. An unforgiving International Olympic Committee struck his name from the record books and ordered him to return both the medals and the gifts.

Years later, a nearly-destitute Thorpe told reporters: "In the twilight of my life, the one thing I dream of constantly is that the American people will try to get back for me the Olympic trophies I won in 1912. I'd be the happiest man in the world if I could just get my medals back." The honors were finally returned in 1982—30 years after Thorpe's death.

Two years before Thorpe was covered in glory in Stockholm, an avid American baseball fan and car manufacturer named Hugh Chalmers announced that he would give the National and American League batting champions one of his Chalmers Thirty roadsters.

Back then, motor cars were a phenomenon. More to the point, the Chalmers Thirty was a top-of-the-line buggy, the equal of today's 500 SL Mercedes, and worth several times the average player's salary. Hugh Chalmers was a regular Gatsby. But he was also unlucky.

The first year he and his lovely car got caught in the middle of the mean scandal over the alleged fixing of the AL batting race between Ty Cobb of Detroit and Nap Lajoie of Cleveland. The St. Louis Browns apparently disliked Cobb so much they made it easy for Lajoie to go 8-for-8 in a season-ending doubleheader. Cobb, who had sat out the last two games, won the title by less than a point—.38507 to .38409. Great sport that he was, Chalmers, with nary a blink, gave cars to both men and decreed that henceforth they would go to a player in each league who was judged "the most useful player to his club and to the league at large in point of deportment and value of services rendered."

In other words, the Most Valuable Player. This is where and how the concept was established and the choices were superb, including Cobb, Tris Speaker, Walter Johnson and such subtle picks as Larry Doyle and Johnny Evers. Then came the troubles with the Federal League from 1914-15, followed by America's involvement in World War I from 1917-18. By the time things returned to normal, the Chalmers Motor Co. was on its way out of business.

The two leagues revived the MVP awards in the 1920s, but gave way in 1930 to the deliberations of the baseball writers, who have handed out the postseason bouquets ever since.

National Baseball Library, Cooperstown, NY

That's **Hugh Chalmers** (right) enjoying himself in the back seat of **Ty Cobb's** new car the day he presented matching roadsters to Cobb and 1910 American League batting championship runner-up **Nap Lajoie.** Back then, steering wheels were still on the right side of American automobiles.

Chalmers' automotive generosity was revived in 1955, when *Sport,* the most popular and influential sporting magazine of the day, gave Brooklyn pitcher Johnny Podres a shiny new Corvette for being the MVP of the World Series. It was deemed a very big deal at the time, there being little difference between the price of a Corvette and an average player's salary. It is not such a big deal today, nor is *Sport,* for that matter.

Curiously, for a game bold enough in 1903 to call its year-end championship the "World Series," baseball didn't come up with a formal World Series trophy until 1967. That's the year the largely forgotten William (Spike) Eckert presented the first Commissioner's Trophy to the St. Louis Cardinals, conquerors of the Boston Red Sox in seven games. Four commissioners have done the honors in the intervening 25 years and six flags have been added to the 30-pound trophy that features a pennant for every major league team.

Elsewhere in sport, there are trophies that men and women would still die for (or at least risk their necks for) as the 33 qualifiers of the Indianapolis 500 prove every Memorial Day weekend. But then,

Indy's Borg-Warner Trophy (named after the Chicago automotive components company) is a true gem—80 pounds of silver stretched over four feet with a likeness of every winner since 1936 engraved upon it in low relief.

Not nearly as stunning, but much more coveted on a global scale, is soccer's World Cup. Trophies mesmerize soccer fans and the tradition is rich. The World Cup, which was established in 1930, descends from the English Football Association Cup (established in 1871), which, in turn, is akin to the British Rugby Union's fabulous Calcutta Cup (established in 1822). The current World Cup, an 11-pound globe of solid 18 karat gold, was commissioned for $20,000 in time for the 1974 tournament. Brazil retired the first Cup—the Jules Rimet Trophy—by winning it for a third time in 1970. Rimet was president of FIFA, soccer's international governing body, from 1920-54.

True international competitions have the most intriguing hardware. The best of the tennis prizes is the Davis Cup for men's team play. Donated in 1900 by collegiate champion Dwight Davis, who would later serve as Calvin Coolidge's Secretary of War, the Davis Cup is certainly the heaviest major trophy—weighing 400 pounds, thanks to a two-tiered base large enough to accommodate the names of 81 winning team rosters this century.

Golf's Ryder Cup, donated by English seed merchant Samuel Ryder to promote biennial competition between British and American professionals in 1927, is one of the smallest trophies in sport. It measures only 16½ inches high and weighs a mere three pounds. Nevertheless, it attracts the heaviest hitters on the American and European PGA Tours, who eagerly participate despite the fact that the competition offers no prize money whatsoever.

Other than that, the most treasured trinket in golf's vast trophy case is not made of silver or gold, but of a woolen blend—the Green Jacket of the Masters, tailored these days by Hamilton Brothers of Cincinnati. While everything seems a bit too calculated at Augusta, this tradition sprang from mere whim. Sam Snead took a shine to the blazers worn by the folks who worked the tourney, so in 1949, when he won the event for the first time, they gave him one. It's been sport's most celebrated fashion statement ever since.

The custom of giving boxing champions those gaudy, jewel-studded belts seems to have begun in 1860 with the heavyweight title bout between elegant roughnecks Tom Heenan and Tom Sayers, which ended in a draw when a mob, fired up by gamblers, charged the ring. The heavyweight belt won by John L. Sullivan for his bare-knuckle joust with Jake Kilraine is a work of art worthy of the Louvre. Boxing belts are the sum total of what passes for class in this grueling dodge, but even they have been cheapened in the last 15 years by a glut of boxing organizations and alphabet soup championships that rarely have meaning.

College football's Heisman Trophy may be the country's most celebrated sports award, thanks to a public relations strategy that belongs in the Madison Avenue Hall of Fame (see box). But there remain some terrific gridiron traditions that have been maintained for the sheer sport of it.

In the days when Boston College and Holy Cross College annually renewed their ancient football dispute, the game's MVP received a trophy named for Captain Eddie O'Melia, a Holy Cross star of

Wide World Photos

Three-time champion **Sam Snead** got the blazer tradition started at the Masters.

the thirties who died heroically at Schwanpanavel Dam in Holland in World War II. At one time, it was a bigger deal than the Heisman in New England because it seemed to epitomize what this business is all about. Then in '86, B.C. and Holy Cross stopped playing, consigning Capt. O'Melia's memorial to certain obscurity.

Many ancient college rivals still compete for wonderfully wacky relics, ranging from beer barrels and wagon wheels to spittoons and megaphones. It should come as no surprise then that the oldest conference in the land, the Big Ten, has some of the oldest and wackiest trophies. Michigan and Minnesota, for instance, have feuded over the Little Brown Jug since 1909, while Indiana and Purdue have been playing for the Old Oaken Bucket for nearly 70 years.

Then there's Floyd of Rosedale, the full-blooded champion pig originally fought over by Minnesota and Iowa in 1935. Fifty-seven years later, Floyd's likeness graces the trophy that goes to the winner of the annual meeting between the Gophers and Hawkeyes at the end of the regular season. Such traditions still strike chords with old grads, but the younger generation would rather go to a bowl game. □

TROPHY CASE

From the first organized track meet at Olympia in 776 B.C., to the Summer Games of the XXVth Olympiad in Barcelona over 2,700 years later, championships have been officially recognized with prizes that are symbolically rich and eagerly pursued.

Here are 15 of the most coveted trophies in America, beginning with the 141-year-old America's Cup.

(Illustrations by Lynn Mercer Michaud.)

America's Cup

First presented by England's Royal Yacht Squadron to the winner of an invitational race around the Isle of Wight on Aug. 22, 1851 .... originally called the Hundred Guinea Cup .... renamed after the U.S. boat *America*, winner of the first race .... made of sterling silver and designed by London jewelers R. & G. Garrard .... measures 2 feet, 3 inches high and weighs 16 lbs .... originally cost 100 guineas ($500), now valued at $250,000 .... bell-shaped base added in 1958 .... challenged for every three to four years .... trophy held by yacht club sponsoring winning boat.

Vince Lombardi Trophy

First presented at the AFL-NFL World Championship Game (now Super Bowl) on Jan. 15, 1967 .... originally called the World Championship Game Trophy .... renamed in 1971 in honor of former Green Bay Packers GM-coach and two-time Super Bowl winner Vince Lombardi, who died in 1970 as coach of Washington .... made of sterling silver and designed by Tiffany & Co. of New York .... measures 21 inches high and weighs 7 lbs (football depicted is regulation size) .... valued at $12,500 .... competed for annually .... winning team keeps trophy.

Olympic Gold Medal

First presented by International Olympic Committee in 1908 (until then winners received silver medals) .... second and third place finishers also got medals of silver and bronze for first time in 1908 .... each medal must be at least 2.4 inches in diameter and 0.12 inches thick .... the gold medal is actually made of silver, but must be gilded with at least 6 grams (0.21 ounces) of pure gold .... the Barcelona gold medal, designed by local sculptor Xavier Corbero, contained 13.5 grams (0.47 oz.) of pure gold .... 613 were made for approximately $195 each .... competed for every four years .... winners keep medals.

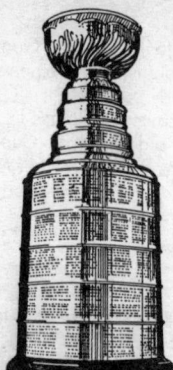

Stanley Cup

Donated by Lord Stanley of Preston, the Governor General of Canada and first presented in 1893 .... original cup was made of sterling silver by an unknown London silversmith and measured 7½ inches high with an 11¼-inch diameter .... in order to accommodate all the rosters of winning teams, the cup now measures 35¼ inches high with a base 54¼ inches around and weighs 32 lbs .... originally bought for 10 guineas ($48.67), it is now insured for $75,000 .... actual cup retired to Hall of Fame and replaced in 1970 .... presented to NHL playoff champion since 1918 .... trophy loaned to winning team for one year.

World Cup

First presented by the Federation Internationale de Football Association (FIFA) .... originally called the World Cup Trophy .... renamed the Jules Rimet Cup (after the then FIFA president) in 1946, but retired by Brazil after that country's third title in 1970 .... new World Cup trophy created in 1974 .... designed by Italian sculptor Silvio Gazzaniga and made of solid 18 carat gold with two malachite rings inlaid at the base .... measures 14.2 inches high and weighs 11 lbs .... insured for $200,000 (U.S.) .... competed for every four years .... winning team gets gold-plated replica.

Commissioner's Trophy

First presented by the Commissioner of baseball to the winner of the 1967 World Series .... also known as the World Championship Trophy .... made of brass and gold plate with an ebony base and a baseball in the center made of pewter with a silver finish .... designed by Balfour & Co. of Attleboro, Mass .... 26 pennants represent 14 AL and 12 NL teams (two more will be added in 1993 when the NL expands) .... measures 30 inches high and 36 inches around at the base and weighs 30 lbs .... valued at $15,000 .... competed for annually .... winning team keeps trophy.

Larry O'Brien Trophy

First presented in 1978 to winner of NBA Finals .... originally called the Walter A. Brown Trophy after the league pioneer and Boston Celtics owner (an earlier NBA championship bowl was also named after Brown) .... renamed in 1984 in honor of outgoing commissioner O'Brien, who served from 1975-84 .... made of sterling silver with 24 carat gold overlay and designed by Tiffany & Co. of New York .... measures 2 feet high and weighs 14½ lbs (basketball depicted is regulation size) .... valued at $13,500 .... competed for annually .... winning team keeps trophy.

Heisman Trophy

First presented in 1935 to the best college football player east of the Mississippi by the Downtown Athletic Club of New York . . . . players across the entire country eligible since 1936 . . . . originally called the DAC Trophy . . . . renamed in 1936 following the death of DAC athletic director and former college coach John W. Heisman . . . . made of bronze and designed by New York sculptor Frank Eliscu, it measures 13½ in. high, 6½ in. wide and 14 in. long at the base and weighs 25 lbs . . . . valued at $2,000 . . . . voting done by national media and former Heisman winners . . . . awarded annually . . . . winner keeps trophy.

James E. Sullivan Memorial Award

First presented by the Amateur Athletic Union (AAU) in 1930 as a gold medal and given to the nation's outstanding amateur athlete . . . . trophy given since 1933 . . . . named after the amateur sports movement pioneer, who was a founder and past president of AAU and the director of the 1904 Olympic Games in St. Louis . . . . made of bronze with a marble base, it measures 17½ in. high and 11 in. wide at the base and weighs 13½ lbs . . . . valued at $2,500 . . . . voting done by AAU and USOC officials, former winners and selected media . . . . awarded annually . . . . winner keeps trophy.

Ryder Cup

Donated in 1927 by English seed merchant Samuel Ryder, who offered the gold cup for a biennial match between teams of golfing pros from Great Britain and the United States . . . . the format changed in 1977 to include the best players on the European PGA Tour . . . . made of 14 carat gold on a wood base and designed by Mappin and Webb of London . . . . the golfer depicted on the top of the trophy is Ryder's friend and teaching pro Abe Mitchell . . . . the cup measures 16½ in. high and weighs 4 lbs . . . . insured for $50,000 . . . . competed for every two years at alternating British and U.S. sites . . . . the cup is held by the PGA headquarters of the winning side.

Davis Cup

Donated by American college student and U.S. doubles champion Dwight F. Davis in 1900 and presented by the International Tennis Federation (ITF) to the winner of the annual 16-team men's competition . . . . officially called the International Lawn Tennis Challenge Trophy . . . . made of sterling silver and designed by Shreve, Crump and Low of Boston, the cup has a matching tray (added in 1921) and a very heavy two-tiered base containing rosters of past winning teams . . . . it stands 34¼ in. high and 108 in. around at the base and weighs 400 lbs . . . . insured for $150,000 . . . . competed for annually . . . . trophy loaned to winning country for one year.

Borg-Warner Trophy

First presented by the Borg-Warner Automotive Co. of Chicago in 1936 to the winner of the Indianapolis 500 . . . . replaced the Wheeler-Schebler Trophy which went to the 400-mile leader from 1911-32 . . . . made of sterling silver with bas-relief sculptured heads of each winning driver and a gold bas-relief head of Tony Hulman, the owner of the Indy Speedway from 1945-77 . . . . designed by Robert J. Hill and made by Gorham, Inc. of Rhode Island . . . . measures 51½ in. high and weighs over 80 lbs . . . . new base added in 1988 and the entire trophy restored in 1991 . . . . competed for annually . . . . insured for $1 million . . . . trophy stays at Speedway Hall of Fame . . . . winner gets a 14-in. high replica valued at $30,000.

NCAA Championship Trophy

First presented in 1952 by the NCAA to all 1st, 2nd and 3rd place teams in sports with sanctioned tournaments . . . . 1st place teams receive gold-plated awards, 2nd place award is silver-plated and 3rd is bronze . . . . replaced silver cup given to championship teams from 1939-1951 . . . . made of walnut, the trophy stands 24¾ in. high, 14½ in. wide and 4⅛ in. deep at the base and weighs 15 lbs . . . . designed by Medallic Art Co. of Danbury, Conn. and made by House of Usher of Kansas City since 1990 . . . . valued at $500 . . . . competed for annually . . . . winning teams keep trophies.

WBA Championship Belt

First presented in 1921 by the World Boxing Association, one of the three organizations (the World Boxing Council and International Boxing Federation are the others) generally accepted as sanctioning legitimate world championship fights . . . . belt weighs 8 lbs. and is made of hand tanned leather . . . . the outsized buckle measures 10½ in. high and 8 in. wide, is made of pewter with 24 carat gold plate and contains crystal and semi-precious stones . . . . side panels of polished brass are for engraving title bout results . . . . currently made by Phil Valentino Originals of Jersey City, N.J. . . . . champions keep belts even if they lose their title.

Floyd of Rosedale

Floyd of Rosedale was a full-blooded champion pig whose brother Blue Boy appeared in the 1933 Will Rogers' film "State Fair" . . . . the prize porker was presented by Gov. Clyde Herring of Iowa to Gov. Floyd Olson of Minnesota to pay off a friendly wager on the 1935 Iowa-Minnesota football game (won by the Gophers, 13-6) . . . . the bet, arranged to calm tensions between the two neighboring state universities, became a trophy in 1936 when Olson commissioned St. Paul sculptor Charles Brioschi to create a 25-lb. bronze statue which measures 15½ in. high and 21 in. across and is mounted on a wood and metal base . . . . winning team keeps Floyd for one year.

Tom Herde/The Boston Globe

1992 Boston Marathon champion **Ibrahim Hussein** (right) of Kenya greets **Johnny Kelley** after the 84-year-old race legend completed his 58th and final Boston in 61 starts. Between them, Kelley and Hussein have won the race five times.

WHO'S WHO

Sports Personalities

Six hundred ninety noteworthy names dating back to the turn of the century.

Hank Aaron (b.2/5/1934): Baseball OF; led NL in HRs and RBI 4 times each and batting twice; MVP in 1957; played in 24 All-Star Games, all-time leader in HRs (755) and RBI (2,297), 3rd in hits (3,771).

Kareem Abdul-Jabbar (b.Lew Alcindor,4/16/1947): Basketball C; led UCLA to 3 NCAA titles (1967-69); tourney MVP 3 times; Player of Year twice; led Milwaukee (1) and LA Lakers (5) to 6 NBA titles; playoff MVP twice (1971,85), reg.season MVP 6 times (1971-72, 74,76-77, 80); retired after 20 seasons as all-time leader in over 20 categories.

Andre Agassi (b.4/29/1970): Tennis; entered 1992 with 14 career tournament wins; helped U.S. win Davis Cup final (1990); won 1st Grand Slam title at Wimbledon in 1992; Nick Bollettieri Academy classmate of Jim Courier.

Tenley Albright (b.7/18/1935): Figure skater; 2-time world champion (1953,55), won Olympic silver (1952) and gold (1956) medals.

Grover Cleveland Alexander (1887-1950): Baseball RHP; won 20 or more games 9 times; 373 career wins and 90 shutouts.

Vasily Alexeyev (b.1942): Soviet weightlifter; 1st man to lift 500 lbs.; 8-time world champion; 2-time Olympic super-heavyweight champ (1972,76); set 80 world records between 1970-77.

Muhammad Ali (b.Cassius Clay, 1/17/1942): Boxer; 1960 Olympic light-heavyweight champion; only 3-time world heavyweight champ (1964-67,1974-78,1978-79); defeated Sonny Liston (1964), George Foreman (1974) and Leon Spinks (1978) for title; fought Joe Frazier in 3 memorable bouts (1971-75), winning twice; adopted Black Muslim faith in 1964 and changed name; stripped of title in 1967 after conviction for refusing induction into U.S. Army; verdict reversed by Supreme Court in 1971; career record of 56-5 with 37 KOs and 19 successful title defenses.

Forrest (Phog) Allen (1885-74): Basketball; college coach 48 years; directed Kansas to NCAA title (1952), 746 career wins.

Bobby Allison (b.12/3/1937): Auto racer; 3-time winner of Daytona 500 (1978,82,88); NASCAR national champ in 1983; father of Davey.

Davey Allison (b.2/25/1961): Auto racer; entered 1992 with 13 NASCAR victories; won 1992 Daytona 500, giving Allison family 4 overall titles; son of Bobby.

Walter Alston (1911-84): Baseball; managed Brooklyn-LA Dodgers 23 years, won 7 pennants and 4 World Series (1955,59,63,65).

Sparky Anderson (b.2/22/1934): Baseball; only manager to win World Series in each league—Cincinnati in NL (1975-76) and Detroit in AL (1984); entered 1992 ranked 7th on all-time career list with 1,955 wins (1,921 regular season and 34 postseason).

Willie Anderson (1880-1910): Scottish golfer, who became an American citizen and won 4 U.S. Open titles, including an unmatched 3 straight from 1903-05; also won four Western Opens from 1902-09.

Mario Andretti (b.2/28/1940): Auto racer; 4-time USAC/CART national champion (1965-66,69,84); only driver to win Daytona 500 (1967), Indy 500 (1969) and Formula One world championship (1978); Indy 500 Rookie of Year (1965); entered 1992 ranked 2nd on all-time IndyCar list with 51 wins; father of Michael and Jeff, uncle of John.

Michael Andretti (b.10/5/1962): Auto racer; 1992 CART national champion setting single-season records for wins (8) and money won ($2,461,734); Indy 500 Rookie of Year (1984); entered 1992 with 22 IndyCar wins; son of Mario.

Earl Anthony (b.4/27/1938): Bowler; 6-time PBA Bowler of Year; 41 career titles; first to earn $100,000 in 1 season (1975); first to earn $1 million in career.

Said Aouita (b.11/2/1959): Moroccan runner; won gold (5000m) and bronze (800m) in 1984 Olympics; won 5000m at 1987 World Championship; entered 1992 holding 4 world records recognized by IAAF—1500m, 2000m, 3000m and 5000m.

Luis Aparicio (b.4/29/1934), Baseball SS; all-time leader in most games, assists, chances and double plays by shortstop; led AL in stolen bases 9 times (1956-64); 506 career steals.

Al Arbour (b.11/1/1932): Hockey; coached NY Islanders to 4 straight Stanley Cup titles (1980-83); entered 1992-92 season 2nd on all-time career list with 819 wins.

Eddie Arcaro (b.2/19/1916): Jockey; 2-time Triple Crown winner (Whirlaway in 1941, Citation in '48); won Kentucky Derby 5 times, Preakness and Belmont 6 times each.

Roone Arledge (b.7/8/1931): Sports TV innovator of live events, anthology shows, Olympic coverage and "Monday Night Football;" ran ABC Sports from 1968-86; has run ABC News since 1977.

Henry Armstrong (1912-88): Boxer; held feather-, light- and welterweight titles simultaneously in 1938; pro record 145-20-9 with 98 KOs.

Arthur Ashe (b.7/10/1943): Tennis; first black man to win U.S. Championship (1968) and Wimbledon (1975); 1st U.S. player to earn $100,000 in 1 year (1970); won Davis Cup as player (1968-70) and captain (1981-82); wrote black sports history, Hard Road to Glory; announced on Apr.8, 1992, that he was infected with AIDS virus from a blood transfusion during 1983 heart surgery.

Evelyn Ashford (b.4/16/1957): Track & Field; winner of 4 olympic gold medals—including 100m in 1984, and 4 × 100m in 1984, '88 and '92; also won silver medal in 100m in 1988; member of 5 U.S. Olympic teams (1976-92).

Red Auerbach (b.9/20/1917): Basketball; winningest coach in NBA history; won 1,037 times (including playoffs) in 20 years; as coach-GM, led Boston to 9 NBA titles, including 8 in a row (1959-66); also coached defunct Wash. Capitols (1946-49); NBA Coach of the Year award named after him; retired as Celtics' coach in 1966 and as GM in '84; club president since 1970.

Tracy Austin (b.12/12/1962): Tennis; youngest player ever to win U.S. Open (age 16 in 1979); won 2nd U.S. Open in '81; named AP Female Athlete of Year twice before she was 20; recurring neck and back injuries shortened her career after June, 1983; youngest player ever inducted into Tennis Hall of Fame (age 29 in 1992).

Hobey Baker (1892-1918): Football and hockey star at Princeton (1911-14); member of college football and pro hockey halls of fame; college hockey Player of the Year award named after him; killed in WWI plane crash.

Seve Ballesteros (b.4/9/1957): Spanish golfer; has won British Open 3 times (1979,84,88) and Masters twice (1980,83); 3-time European Golfer of Year (1986,88,91); entered 1992 with 66 world-wide victories.

Ernie Banks (b.1/31/1931): Baseball SS-1B; led NL in home runs and RBI twice each; 2-time MVP (1958-59) with Chicago Cubs; 512 career HRs.

Roger Bannister (b.3/23/1929): British runner; first to run mile in less than 4 minutes (3:59.4 on May 6, 1954).

Walter (Red) Barber (b.2/17/1908): Radio-TV; renowned baseball play-by-play broadcaster for Cincinnati, Brooklyn and N.Y. Yankees from 1937-64; won Peabody Award for commentary in 1991.

Rick Barry (b.3/28/1944): Basketball F; only player to lead both NBA and ABA in scoring; 5-time All-NBA 1st team; playoff MVP with Golden St. in 1975.

Sammy Baugh (b.3/17/1914): Football QB; led Washington to NFL titles in 1937 (his rookie year) and '42; led league in passing 6 times, punting 4 times and interceptions once.

Elgin Baylor (b.9/16/1934): Basketball F; MVP of NCAA tournament in 1958; led Minn.-LA Lakers to 8 NBA Finals; 10-time All-NBA 1st team (1959-65,67-69).

Bob Beamon (b.8/29/1946): Track & Field; won 1968 Olympic gold medal in long jump with world record (29- ft, 2½ in.) that shattered old mark by nearly 2 feet; record finally broken by 2 inches in 1991 by Mike Powell.

Franz Beckenbauer (b.9/11/1945): Soccer; captain of West German World Cup champions in 1974 then coached West Germany to World Cup title in 1990; invented sweeper position; played in U.S. for NY Cosmos (1977-80,83).

Boris Becker (b.11/22/1967): German tennis player; 3-time Wimbledon champ (1985-86,89); youngest male (17) to win Wimbledon; led country to 1st Davis Cup win in 1988; has also won U.S. (1989) and Australian (1991) opens.

Chuck Bednarik (b.5/1/1925): Football C-LB; 2-time All-America at Penn and 7-time All-Pro with NFL Philadelphia Eagles as both center (1950) and linebacker (1951-56); knocked NY Giants' Frank Gifford out of commission for over a year with epic 1960 tackle; missed only 3 games in 14 seasons; led Eagles to 1959 NFL title as a 35-year-old two-way player.

Clair Bee (1896-1983); Basketball coach who led LIU to 10 undefeated seasons (1936,39) and 2 NIT titles (1939,41); his teams won 95 percent of their games between 1931-51, including 43 in a row from 1935-37; coached NBA Baltimore Bullets from 1952-54, but was only 34-116; contributions to game include 1-3-1 zone defense, 3-second rule and NBA 24-second clock; also authored sports manuals and fictional Chip Hilton sports books for kids.

Jean Beliveau (b.8/31/1931): Hockey C; led Montreal to 10 Stanley Cups in 17 playoffs; playoff MVP (1965); 2-time regular season MVP (1956,64).

Bert Bell (1895-1959): Football; team owner and 2nd NFL commissioner (1946-59); proposed college draft in 1935 and instituted TV blackout rule.

Deane Beman (b.4/22/1938): Golf; PGA commissioner since 1974; introduced "stadium golf"; as player, won U.S. Amateur twice and British Amateur once.

Johnny Bench (b.12/7/1947): Baseball C; led NL in HRs twice and RBI 3 times; 2-time regular season MVP (1970,72) with Cincinnati, World Series MVP in 1976; 389 career HRs.

Patty Berg (b.2/13/1918): Golfer; 57 career pro wins including 15 Majors; 3-time AP Female Athlete of Year (1938,43,55).

Yogi Berra (b.5/12/1925): Baseball C; played on 10 World Series winners with NY Yankees; 3-time AL MVP (1951,54-55); managed both Yankees (1964) and NY Mets (1973) to pennants.

Jay Berwanger (b.3/19/1914): Football HB; U.of Chicago star; won 1st Heisman Trophy in 1935.

Abebe Bikila (1932-1973): Ethiopian runner; 1st to win consecutive Olympic marathons (1960,64).

Matt Biondi (b.10/8/1965): Swimmer; won 7 medals in 1988 Olympics, including 5 gold (2 individual, 3 relay); has won a total of 11 medals (8 gold, 2 silver and a bronze) in 3 Olympics (1984,88,92).

Larry Bird (b.12/7/1956): Basketball F; college Player of Year (1979); 9-time All-NBA 1st team; 3-time regular season MVP (1984-86); led Boston to 3 NBA titles; 2-time playoff MVP (1984,86).

The Black Sox—Eight Chicago White Sox players who were banned from baseball for life in 1921 for allegedly throwing the 1919 World Series: RHP **Eddie Cicotte** (1884-1969), OF **Happy Felsch** (1891-1964), 1B **Chick Gandil** (1887-1970), OF **Shoeless Joe Jackson** (1887-1951), INF **Fred McMullan** (1891-1952), SS **Swede Risberg** (1894-1975), 3B-SS **Buck Weaver** (1890-1956), and LHP **Lefty Williams** (1893-1959).

Earl (Red) Blaik (1897-89): Football; coached Army to consecutive national titles in 1944-45; 166 career wins and 3 Heisman Trophy winners (Blanchard, Davis, Dawkins).

Bonnie Blair (b.3/18/1964): Speedskater; won 500m gold medal at 1988 Winter Olympics; World Sprint champion in 1989; won 500m and 1000m gold medals at 1992 Olympics.

Toe Blake (b.8/21/1912): Hockey LW; led Montreal to 2 Stanley Cups as a player and 8 more as coach; regular season MVP in 1939.

Felix (Doc) Blanchard (b12/11/1924): Football FB; 3-time All-America; led Army to national titles in 1944-45; Glenn Davis' running mate; won Heisman Trophy and Sullivan Award in 1945.

George Blanda (b.9/17/1927): Football QB-PK; NFL's all-time leading scorer (2,002 points); led Houston to 2 AFL titles (1960-61); played 26 pro seasons; retired at 48.

Fanny Blankers-Koen (b.4/26/1918): Dutch sprinter; 30 year-old mother of two, who won 4 gold medals (100m, 200m,800m hurdles and 4x100m relay) at 1948 Olympics.

Bert Blyleven (b.4/6/1951): Baseball RHP; entered 1992 season with 279 career victories in 21 years and ranked 4th on all-time strikeout list with 3,631; missed entire 1991 season with torn rotator cuff; threw no-hitter vs California (1977); holds major league record for HRs allowed in one season (50 in 1986).

Wade Boggs (b.6/15/1958): Baseball 3B; entered 1992 season with 5 AL batting titles (1983,85-88) at Boston and .345 career average.

Bjorn Borg (b. 6/6/1956): Swedish tennis player; 2-time Player of Year (1979-80); won 6 French Opens and 5 straight Wimbledons (1976-80); led Sweden to 1st Davis Cup win in 1975; retired in 1983 at age 26; came out of retirement in 1991.

Mike Bossy (b.1/22/1957): Hockey RW; led NY Islanders to 4 Stanley Cups; playoff MVP in 1982; scored 50 goals or more 9 straight years; 573 career goals.

Ralph Boston (b.5/9/1939): Track & Field; medaled in 3 consecutive Olympic long jumps—gold (1960), silver (1964), bronze (1968).

Ray Bourque (b.12/28/1960): Hockey D; 9-time All-NHL 1st team, has won Norris Trophy 4 times (1987-88,1990-91) with Boston.

Bobby Bowden (b.11/8/1929): Football; entered 1992 regular season with 216 career wins and 11-3-1 bowl record in 26 years as coach at Samford, West Va. and Florida St.

Scotty Bowman (b.9/8/1933): Hockey; all-time winningest NHL coach with 908 career wins in 18 years; led Montreal to 5 Stanley Cups (1973,76-79) and Pittsburgh to another (1992); also coached St.Louis and Buffalo.

Jack Brabham (b.1926): Australian auto racer; 3-time Formula One champion (1959-60,66); 14 career wins.

Bill Bradley (b.7/28/1943): Basketball F; 3-time All-America at Princeton, Player of Year and NCAA tourney MVP in 1965; captain of gold medal-winning 1964 U.S. Olympic team; Sullivan Award winner (1965); led NY Knicks to 2 NBA titles (1970,73); U.S. Senator (D,NJ) since 1979.

Pat Bradley (b.3/24/1951): Golfer; 2-time LPGA Player of Year (1986,91); has won all four majors on LPGA tour, including 3 du Maurier Classics; entered 1992 as all-time LPGA money leader and 11th in wins (30).

Terry Bradshaw (b.9/2/1948): Football QB; led Pittsburgh to 4 Super Bowl titles (1975-76,79-80); 2-time Super Bowl MVP (1979-80).

George Brett (b. 5/15/1953): Baseball 3B-1B; has led AL in batting in 3 different decades (1976,80,90); MVP in 1980; led KC to World Series title in 1985; entered 1992 season with 2,836 hits.

Lou Brock (b.6/18/1939): Baseball OF; former all-time stolen base leader (938); led NL in steals 8 times; led St.Louis to 2 World Series titles (1964,67); had 3,023 career hits.

Herb Brooks (b.8/5/1937): Hockey; former U.S. Olympic player (1964,68) who coached 1980 team to gold medal; coached Minnesota to 3 NCAA titles (1974,76,78); also coached NY Rangers and Minnesota in NHL; entered 1992-93 NHL season as coach of New Jersey.

Dr.Bobby Brown (b.10/25/1924): Baseball; cardiologist and AL president since 1983; as player, hit .279 in 8 years as NY Yankees; hit .439 with 3 pinch hits in 41 World Series at bats (1947-51).

Jim Brown (b.2/17/1936): Football FB; led NFL in rushing 8 times; 8-time All-Pro (1957-61,63-65); 3-time MVP (1958,63,65) with Cleveland; ran for 12,312 yards and scored 756 points in just 9 seasons.

Larry Brown (b.9/14/1940): Basketball; played in ACC, AAU, 1964 Olympics and ABA; coached in college at UCLA and Kansas and pros with ABA's Carolina and Denver and NBA's Denver, New Jersey, San Antonio and LA Clippers; 3-time assist leader (1968-70) and 3-time Coach of Year (1973,75-76) in ABA; led UCLA to Final Four (1980) and Kansas to NCAA title (1988).

Paul Brown (1908-91): Football innovator; coached Ohio St. to national title in 1942; in pros, directed Cleveland Browns to 4 straight AAFC titles (1946-49) and 3 NFL titles (1950,54-55); formed Cincinnati Bengals in 1968 (reached playoffs in '70).

Walter A. Brown (1905-64): member of both basketball and hockey halls of fame; succeeded father George as GM of Boston Garden in 1937; later became president of Garden and co-owner of both Bruins and Celtics.

Valery Brumel (b.1942): Soviet high jumper; dominated event from 1961-64; broke world record 5 times; won silver medal in 1960 Olympics and gold in 1964; highest jump 7-5¾.

Avery Brundage (1887-1975): Amateur sports czar for over 40 years as president of AAU (1928-35), U.S. Olympic Committee (1929-53) and Int'l Olympic Committee (1952-72).

Paul (Bear) Bryant (1913-1983): Football; coached at 4 colleges over 38 years; directed Alabama to 5 national titles (1961,64-65,78-79); 323 career wins; 15 bowl wins including 8 Sugar Bowls.

Sergei Bubka (b.12/4/1963): Ukrainian pole vaulter; 1st man to clear 20 feet both indoors and out (1991); holder of indoor (20-1¼) and outdoor (20-½) world records as of Sept. 1, 1992; 3-time world champion (1983, 87, 91); won Olympic gold medal in 1988, but failed to clear any height in 1992 Games.

Don Budge (b.6/13/1915): Tennis; in 1938 became 1st player to win the Grand Slam—the French, Wimbledon, U.S. and Australian titles in 1 year; led U.S. to 2 Davis Cups (1937-38); turned pro in late '38.

Maria Bueno (b.10/11/1939): Brazilian tennis player; won 4 U.S. Championships (1959,63-64,66) and 3 Wimbledons (1959-60,64).

George Bush (b.6/12/1924): 41st President of U.S. (1989–) and avid sportsman; played 1B on 1947 and '48 Yale baseball teams that placed 2nd in College World Series; captain of 1948 team.

Susan Butcher (b.12/26/1956): Sled Dog racer; 4-time winner of Iditarod Trail race (1986-88,90).

Dick Butkus (b.12/9/1942): Football LB; 2-time All-America at Illinois (1963-64); All-Pro 7 of 9 NFL seasons with Chicago.

Dick Button (b.7/18/1929): Figure skater; 5-time world champion (1948-52); 2-time Olympic champ (1948,52); Sullivan Award winner (1949); won Emmy Award as Best Analyst for 1980-81 TV season.

Walter Byers (b.3/13/1922): College athletics; 1st executive director of NCAA, serving from 1951-88.

Frank Calder (1877-1943): Hockey; 1st NHL president (1917-43); guided league through its formative years; NHL's rookie of the year award named after him.

Lee Calhoun (1933-89): Track & Field: won consecutive Olympic gold medals in the 110m hurdles (1956,60).

Walter Camp (1859-1925): Football coach and innovator; established scrimmage line, center snap, downs, 11 players per side; named 1st All-America team (1889).

Roy Campanella (b.11/19/1921): Baseball C; 3-time NL MVP (1951,53,55); led Brooklyn to 5 pennants and 1st World Series title (1955).

Clarence Campbell (1905-84): Hockey; 3rd NHL president (1946-77); league tripled in size from 6 to 18 teams during his tenure; NHL's western conference named after him.

Earl Campbell (b.3/29/1955): Football RB; won Heisman Trophy in 1977; led NFL in rushing 3 times; 3-time All-Pro; 2-time MVP (1978-80) at Houston.

Milt Campbell (b.12/9/1933): Track & field; won silver medal in 1952 Olympic decathlon and gold medal in '56.

Jimmy Cannon (1910-73): Tough, opinionated New York sportswriter and essayist who viewed sports as an extension of show business; protege of Damon Runyon; covered World War II for *Stars & Stripes*.

Tony Canzoneri (1908-59): Boxer; 2-time world lightweight champion (1930-33,35-36); pro record 141-24-10 with 44 KOs.

Jennifer Capriati (b.3/29/1976): Tennis; youngest Grand Slam semifinalist ever (age 14 in 1990 French Open); also youngest to win a match at Wimbledon (1990); entered 1992 with 3 career tournament wins; upset Steffi Graf to win gold medal in 1992 Olympics.

Harry Caray (b.3/1/1917): Radio-TV; baseball play-by-play broadcaster for St.Louis Cardinals, Oakland, Chicago White Sox and Cubs since 1945; father of sportscaster Skip and grandfather of sportscaster Chip.

Rod Carew (b.10/1/1945): Baseball 2B-1B; led AL in batting 7 times (1969,72-75,77-78) with Minnesota; MVP in 1977; had 3,053 career hits.

Steve Carlton (b.12/22/1944): Baseball LHP; won 20 or more games 6 times; 4-time Cy Young winner (1972,77, 80,82) with Philadelphia; 329 career wins.

JoAnn Carner (b.4/4/1939): Golfer; 5-time U.S. Amateur champion; 2-time U.S. Open champ; 3-time LPGA Player of Year (1974,81-82).

Don Carter (b.7/29/1926): Bowler; 6-time Bowler of Year (1953-54,57-58,60-61); voted Greatest of All-Time in 1970.

Alexander Cartwright (1820-92): Baseball; engineer and draftsman who is widely regarded as father of modern game; his guidelines set bases 90 feet apart, 3 outs per side, 9 innings per game, 9 men per team, unalterable batting order and ended practice of throwing ball at runner to retire him; also organized 1st team—the NY Knickerbockers (1845).

Billy Casper (b. 6/24/1931): Golfer; 2-time PGA Player of Year (1966,70); has won U.S. Open (1959,66), Masters (1970), U.S. Sr.Open (1983); entered 1992 with 51 PGA wins and 9 on Senior Tour.

Tracy Caulkins (b. 1/11/1963): Swimmer; won 3 gold medals (2 individual) at 1984 Olympics; set 5 world records and won 48 U.S. national titles from 1978-84; Sullivan Award winner (1978); 2-time Honda Broderick Cup winner (1982,84).

Evonne Goolagong Cawley (b.7/31/1951): Australian tennis player; won Australian Open 4 times, Wimbledon twice (1971-72), French once.

Florence Chadwick (b.11/9/1917): Dominant distance swimmer of 1950s; set English Channel records from France to England (1950) and England to France (1951 and '55).

Wilt Chamberlain (b.8/21/1936): Basketball C; led NBA in scoring 7 times and rebounding 11 times; 7-time All-NBA first team; 4-time MVP (1960,66-68) in Philadelphia; scored 100 pts vs. NY Knicks in Hershey, Pa., Mar. 2, 1962; led Phila. 76ers (1967) and LA Lakers (1972) to NBA titles; playoff MVP in 1972.

A.B. (Happy) Chandler (1898-1991); Baseball; former Kentucky governor and U.S. Senator who became commissioner when Judge Landis died in 1945; backed Branch Rickey's move in 1947 to make Jackie Robinson 1st black player in major leagues; deemed pro-player and ousted by owners in 1951.

Julio Cesar Chavez (b.7/12/1962): Boxing; world junior welterweight champion; also held titles as junior lightweight (1984-87) and lightweight (1987-89); entered 1992 undefeated in 78 fights with 64 KOs.

Jim Clark (1936-68): Scottish auto racer; 2-time Formula One world champion (1963,65); won Indy 500 in 1965; killed in car crash.

Bobby Clarke (b.8/13/1949): Hockey C; led Philadelphia to consecutive Stanley Cups in 1974-75; 3-time regular season MVP (1973,75-76).

Ron Clarke (b.1937): Australian runner; from 1963-70 set 17 world records in races from 2 miles to 20,000 meters; never won Olympic gold medal.

Roger Clemens (b.8/4/1962): Baseball RHP; fanned record 20 batters in 9-inning game (1986); 3 Cy Young Awards (1986-87,91) with Boston; AL MVP in 1986; entered 1992 season with 134 wins; nicknamed "Rocket" and born on same day as hockey's Maurice (Rocket) Richard.

Roberto Clemente (1934-72): Baseball OF; hit .300 or better 13 times with Pittsburgh; led NL in batting 4 times; World Series MVP in 1971; regular season MVP in 1966; had 3,000 career hits; killed in plane crash.

Ty Cobb (1886-1961): Baseball OF; all-time highest career batting average (.367); hit .400 or better 3 times; led AL in batting 12 times and stolen bases 6 times with Detroit; MVP in 1911; had 4,191 career hits and 892 steals.

Mickey Cochrane (1903-62): Baseball C; led Phila.A's (1929-30) and Detroit (1935) to 3 World Series titles; 2-time AL MVP (1928,34).

Sebastian Coe (b.9/29/1956): British runner; won gold medal in 1500m and silver medal in 800m at both 1980 and '84 Olympics; although retired, still holds world records in 800m and 1000m; elected to Parliament as Conservative in 1992.

Eddie Collins (1887-1951): Baseball 2B; led Phila.A's (1910-11) and Chicago White Sox (1917) to 3 World Series titles; AL MVP in 1914; had 3,311 career hits and 743 stolen bases.

Nadia Comaneci (b.11/12/1961): Romanian gymnast; 1st to record perfect 10 in Olympics; won 3 individual gold medals at 1976 Olympics and 2 more in '80.

Lionel Conacher (1902-54): Canada's greatest all-around athlete; NHL hockey (2 Stanley Cups), CFL football (1 Grey Cup), minor league baseball, soccer, lacrosse, track, amateur boxing champion; also member of Parliament (1949-54).

Billy Conn (b.10/8/1917): Boxer; world light heavyweight champion (1939-41); pro record 63-11-1 with 14 KOs.

Dennis Conner (b.9/16/1942): Sailing; 3-time America's Cup-winning skipper aboard *Freedom* (1980), *Stars & Stripes* (1987) and the *Stars & Stripes* catamaran (1988); became first and only American skipper to lose Cup in 1983 when *Australia II* beat *Liberty*.

Maureen Connolly (1934-69): Tennis; in 1953 1st woman to win Grand Slam (at age 18); riding accident ended her career in '54; won both Wimbledon and U.S. titles 3 times (1951-53); 3-time AP Female Athlete of Year (1951-53).

Jimmy Connors (b.9/2/1952): Tennis; No.1 player in world 5 times (1974-78); has won 5 U.S. Opens, 2 Wimbledons and 1 Australian; rose from No. 936 at the close of 1990 to U.S.Open semifinals in 1991 at age 39; NCAA singles champ (1971); entered 1992 as all-time leader in pro singles titles (109) and matches won at U.S.Open (97) and Wimbledon (84).

Jack Kent Cooke (b.10/25/1912): Football; sole owner of NFL Washington Redskins since 1985; teams have won 2 Super Bowls (1987,91); also owned NBA Lakers and NHL Kings in LA; built LA Forum for $12 million in 1967.

Angel Cordero, Jr. (b.11/8/1942): Jockey; retired on doctor's orders in 1992 after 4-horse collision on Jan. 12th left him with a broken arm, 3 broken ribs and a damaged kidney and spleen; won 7,057 races in 38,646 starts; won Kentucky Derby 3 times, Preakness twice and Belmont once; 2-time Eclipse winner (1982-83).

Howard Cosell (b.3/25/1920): Radio-TV; former ABC commentator on "Monday Night Football" and "Wide World of Sports," who energized TV sports journalism with "Tell it like it is" style.

James (Doc) Counsilman (b. 12/28/1920): coached Indiana men's swim team to 6 NCAA championships (1968-73); coached the 1964 and '76 U.S. Men's Olympic teams that won a combined 21 of 24 gold medals (the Hoosiers' Mark Spitz won 7 in 1976); in 1979 became oldest person (59) to swim English Channel; retired in 1990 with dual meet record of 287-36-1.

Jim Courier (b.8/17/1970): Tennis; No. 2 player in the world in 1991, who opened '92 by capturing Australian Open then winning his 2nd straight French Open (1991-92); Nick Bollettieri Academy classmate of Andre Agassi.

Margaret Smith Court (b.7/16/1942): Australian tennis player; won Grand Slam in both singles (1970) and mixed doubles (1963 with Ken Fletcher); 26 Grand Slam singles titles—11 Australian, 7 U.S., 5 French and 3 Wimbledon.

Bob Cousy (b.8/9/1928): Basketball G; led NBA in assists 8 times; 10-time All-NBA 1st team (1952-61); MVP in 1957; led Boston to 6 NBA titles (1957,59-63).

Joe Cronin (1906-84): Baseball SS; hit over .300 and drove in over 100 runs 8 times each, MVP in 1930; player-manager in Washington and Boston (1933-47); AL president (1959-73).

Glenn Cunningham (1910-88): Track & Field; dominant U.S. miler of 1930s; ran sub-4:10 mile 12 times; lost Olympic 1,500m to Jack Lovelock in 1936.

Ann Curtis (b.3/6/1926): Swimming; won 2 gold medals and 1 silver in 1948 Olympics; set 4 world and 18 U.S. records during career; 1st woman and swimmer to win Sullivan Award (1944).

Chuck Daly (b.7/20/1930): Basketball; coached Detroit to two NBA titles (1989-90) before quitting after 1991-92 season to coach New Jersey; entered 1992-93 season with 547 career wins (including playoffs) in 10 years; coached NBA "Dream Team" to gold medal in 1992 Olympics.

Stanley Dancer (b.7/25/1927): Harness racing; winner of 4 Hambletonians; trainer-driver of Triple Crown winners in Trotting (Nevele Pride in 1968 and Super Bowl in '72) and Pacing (Most Happy Fella in 1970); entered 1992 with 3,762 career wins.

Tamas Darnyi (b. 6/3/1967): Hungarian swimmer; 2-time double gold medal winner in 200m and 400m individual medley at 1988 and '92 Olympics; also won both events in 1986 and '91 world championships; set world records in both at '91 worlds; only swimmer to break 2 minutes in 200m IM (1:59:36).

Al Davis (b.7/4/1929): Football; GM-coach of Oakland 1963-66; helped force AFL-NFL merger as AFL commissioner (April-July,1966); returned to Oakland as managing general partner and directed club to 3 Super Bowl wins (1977,81,84); moved Raiders to LA in 1982.

Dwight Davis (1879-1945): Tennis; donor of Davis Cup; played for winning U.S. team in 1st two Cup finals (1900,02); won U.S. and Wimbledon doubles titles in 1901; Secretary of War (1925-29) under Coolidge.

Glenn Davis (b.12/26/1924): Football HB; 3-time All-America; led Army to national titles in 1944-45; Doc Blanchard's running mate; won Heisman Trophy in 1946.

John Davis (1921-84): Weightlifting; 6-time world champion; 2-time Olympic super-heavyweight champ (1948,52), undefeated 1938-53.

Dizzy Dean (1911-74): Baseball RHP; led NL in strikeouts and complete games 4 times; last NL pitcher to win 30 games (30-7 in 1934); MVP in 1934 with St. Louis; 150 career wins.

Dave DeBusschere (b.10/16/1940): Basketball F; 3-time All-America at Detroit; youngest coach in NBA history (24 in 1964); player-coach of Detroit Pistons (1964-67); played in 8 All-Star games; won 2 NBA titles as player with NY Knicks; ABA commissioner (1975-76); also pitched 2 seasons for Chicago White Sox (1962-63) with 3-4 record.

Pierre de Coubertin (1863-1937): French educator; father of the Modern Olympic Games; IOC president from 1896-1925.

Anita DeFrantz (b.10/4/1952): Olympics; attorney who entered 1992 as only American delegate to International Olympic Committee; (other position vacant); first woman to represent U.S. on IOC; member of USOC Executive Committee; member of bronze medal U.S. women's eight-oared shell at Montreal in 1976.

Jack Dempsey (1895-1983): Boxer; world heavyweight champion from 1919-26; lost title and rematch to Gene Tunney; pro record 62-6-10 with 49 KOs.

Donna de Varona (b.4/26/1947): Swimming; won gold medals in 400 IM and 400 freestyle relay at 1964 Olympics; set 18 world records during career; co-founder of Women's Sports Foundation in 1974.

Klaus Dibiasi (b.10/6/1947): Italian diver; won 3 consecutive Olympic gold medals in Platform Diving (1968,72,76).

Eric Dickerson (b.9/2/1960): Football RB; has led NFL in rushing 4 times (1983-84,86,88); NFC Rookie of Year in 1983; All-Pro 5 times, traded from LA Rams to Indianapolis (Oct.31,1987) in 3-team, 10-player (including draft picks) deal that also involved Buffalo; released after 1992 season and signed by LA Raiders; entered 1992 season 3rd on all-time career rushing list with 12,439 yards.

Harrison Dillard (b.7/8/1923): Track & Field; only man to win Olympic gold medals in both sprints (100m in 1948) and hurdles (110m in 1952).

Joe DiMaggio (b.11/25/1914): Baseball OF; hit safely in 56 straight games (1941), led AL in batting, HRs and RBI twice each; 3-time MVP (1939,41,47); led NY Yankees to 10 World Series titles in 13 seasons.

Marcel Dionne (b.8/3/1951): Hockey C; scored 50 or more goals 6 times; led NHL in scoring in 1980, 2nd in all-time goals (731); 3rd in assists (1,348) and 3rd in points (1,771).

Charlotte (Lottie) Dod (1871-1962): British athlete, who was 5-time Wimbledon singles champion (1887-88,91-93); youngest player ever to win Wimbledon (15 in 1887), archery silver medalist at 1908 Olympics, member of national field hockey team in 1899, and British Amateur golf champ in 1904.

Tony Dorsett (b.4/7/1954): Football RB; last Heisman Trophy winner to lead team to national championship (Pitt in 1976); all-time NCAA Div. I-A rushing leader with 6,082 yards; led Dallas to Super Bowl championship as NFC Rookie of Year (1977); NFC Player of Year (1981); ranks 2nd on all-time NFL list with 12,739 yards gained in 12 years; holds NFL record for run from scrimmage (99 yards vs Min. in 1983).

James (Buster) Douglas (b. 4/7/1960): Boxing; 50-1 shot who knocked out undefeated Mike Tyson in 10th round on Feb.10, 1990 to win heavyweight title in Tokyo; 10 months later, lost 1st title defense to Evander Holyfield by KO in 3rd round.

The Dream Team—Head coach **Chuck Daly's** "Best Ever" 12-member NBA All-Star squad that easily won the basketball gold medal in 1992 Olympics: co-captains **Magic Johnson** and **Larry Bird**, veterans **Charles Barkley** (b.2/20/1963), **Clyde Drexler** (6/22/1962), **Patrick Ewing, Michael Jordan, Karl Malone** (b.7/24/1963), **Chris Mullin** (b.7/30/1963), **Scottie Pippen** (b.9/25/1965), **David Robinson** (b.8/6/1965), **John Stockton** (b.3/26/1962) and rookie **Christian Laettner** (b.8/17/1969).

Ken Dryden (b.8/8/1947): Hockey G; led Montreal to 6 Stanley Cup titles; playoff MVP as rookie in 1971; won or shared 5 Vezina Trophies.

Charley Dumas (b.2/12/1937): U.S. high jumper; first man to clear 7 feet (7-0½) on June 29, 1956; won gold medal at 1956 Olympics.

Margaret Osborne du Pont (b.3/4/1918): Tennis; won 5 French, 7 Wimbledon and an unprecedented 24 U.S. national titles in singles, doubles and mixed doubles from 1941-62.

Roberto Duran (b.6/16/1951): Panamanian boxer; one of only 3 fighters to hold 4 different world titles—lightweight (1972-79); welterweight (1980) junior middleweight (1983) and middleweight (1989-90); lost famous "No Mas" welterweight title bout when he quit in 8th round against Sugar Ray Leonard (1980); finished with pro record of 86-9-0 and 60 KOs.

Leo Durocher (1905-91): Baseball; managed in NL 24 years; won 2,015 games, including postseason; 3 pennants with Brooklyn (1941) and NY Giants (1951,54); won World Series in 1954.

Eddie Eagan (1898-1967): Only U.S. athlete to win gold medals in Summer and Winter Olympics (Boxing in 1920, Bobsled in 1932).

Alan Eagleson (b.4/24/1933): Hockey; executive director of NHL players union 1967-90, arranged Team Canada vs Soviet series (1972) and Canada Cup.

Dale Earnhardt (b.4/29/1952): Auto racer; 5-time NASCAR national champion (1980,86-87,90-91); Rookie of Year in 1979; entered 1992 as all-time NASCAR money leader with $15,244,319 and 7th in career wins list with 52; in 18 years, has never won Daytona 500.

Stefan Edberg (b.1/19/1966): Swedish tennis player; 2-time No.1 player (1990-91); 2-time winner of Australian Open (1985, 87), Wimbledon (1988, 90) and U.S. Open (1991-92); French Open finalist in '89.

Gertrude Ederle (b.10/23/1906): Swimmer; 1st woman to swim English Channel, breaking men's record by 2 hours in 1926; won 3 medals in 1924 Olympics.

Krisztina Egerszegi (b. 1974): Hungarian swimmer; 3-time gold medal winner (100m and 200m backstroke and 400m IM) in 1992 Olympics; also won a gold (200m back) and silver (100m back) in 1988 Games; youngest (age 14) ever to win swimming gold.

Bill Elliott (b.10/8/1955): Auto racer; 2-time winner of Daytona 500 (1985,87); NASCAR national champ in 1988; entered 1992 with 34 NASCAR wins.

Herb Elliott (b.2/25/1938): Australian runner; undefeated from 1958-60; ran 17 sub-4:00 miles; 3 world records; won gold medal in 1,500m of 1960 Olympics; retired at 22.

Roy Emerson (b.11/3/1936): Australian tennis player; won 12 Majors in singles—6 Australian, 2 French, 2 Wimbledon and 2 U.S. from 1961-67.

Kornelia Ender (b.10/25/1958): East German swimmer; 1st woman to win 4 gold medals at one Olympics (1976), all in world record time.

Julius Erving (b.2/22/1950): Basketball F; in ABA (1972-76)—3-time MVP, 2-time playoff MVP, led NY Nets to 2 titles (1974-76); in NBA (1977-87)—5-time All-NBA 1st team, MVP in 1981, led Phila.76ers to title in 1983.

Phil Esposito (b.2/20/1942): Hockey C; 1st NHL player to score 100 points in a season (126 in 1969); 6-time All-NHL 1st team with Boston; 2-time MVP (1969,74); 5-time scoring champ; star of 1972 Canada-Soviet series; president-GM of new Tampa Bay entry in NHL.

Janet Evans (b.8/28/1971): Swimmer; won 3 individual gold medals (400m & 800m freestyle,400m IM) at 1988 Olympics; 1989 Sullivan Award winner; entered 1992 as world record-holder in 400m, 800m and 1500m freestyles; won 1 goal (800m) and 1 silver (400m) at 1992 Olympics.

Lee Evans (b.2/25/1947): Track & Field; dominant quarter-miler from 1966-72; world record in 400m at 1968 Olympics stood 20 years.

Chris Evert (b.12/21/1954): Tennis; No.1 player in world 5 times (1975-77,80-81); won at least 1 Grand Slam singles title every year from 1974-86; 18 Majors in all—7 French, 6 U.S., 3 Wimbledon and 2 Australian.

Weeb Ewbank (b.5/6/1907): Football; only coach to win NFL and AFL titles; led Baltimore to 2 NFL titles (1958-59) and NY Jets to Super Bowl III win.

Patrick Ewing (b.8/5/1962): Basketball C; 3-time All-America; led Georgetown to 3 NCAA Finals and 1984 title; tourney MVP in '84; NBA Rookie of Year with New York in 1986; has led U.S. Olympic team to gold medals in 1984 and '92.

Ray Ewry (1873-1937): Track & Field; won 10 gold medals over 4 consecutive Olympics (1900,04,06,08); all events he won (Standing HJ,LJ and TJ) were discontinued in 1912.

Nick Faldo (b.7/18/1957): British golfer; 3-time winner of British Open (1987,90,92) and 2-time winner of Masters (1989-90); 2-time European Golfer of Year (1989-90); PGA Player of Year in 1990.

Juan Manuel Fangio (b.6/24/1911): Argentine auto racer; 5-time Formula One world champion (1951,54-57); 24 career wins, retired in 1958.

Donald Fehr (b.7/18/1948): Baseball; executive director and general counsel of Major League Players Assn. since 1983.

Bob Feller (b.11/3/1918): Baseball RHP; led AL in strikeouts 7 times and wins 6 times with Cleveland; threw 3 no-hitters and 12 one-hitters; 266 career wins.

Tom Ferguson (b.12/20/1950): Rodeo; 6-time All-Around champion (1974-79); 1st cowboy to win $100,000 in one season (1978); 1st to win $1 million in career (1986).

Cecil Fielder (b. 9/21/1963): Baseball 1B; returned from one season with Hanshin Tigers in Japan to hit 51 HRs for Detroit Tigers in 1990; hit 44 more in '91 and led AL in RBI both years; AL MVP runner-up in 1990 and '91.

Herve Filion (b.2/1/1940): Harness racing; 10-time Driver of the Year; entered 1992 season as all-time leader in races won with 13,313 in 31 years.

Rollie Fingers (b.8/25/1946): Baseball RHP; all-time save leader with 341; won AL MVP and Cy Young awards in 1981 with Milwaukee; World Series MVP in 1974 with Oakland.

Charles O. Finley (b.2/22/1918): Baseball owner; moved KC A's to Oakland in 1968; won 3 straight World Series from 1972-74; also owned teams in NHL and ABA.

Bobby Fischer (b.3/9/1943): Chess; only American to hold world championship (1972-75); resigned title in 1975 and became recluse; re-emerged to play old foe and former world champion Boris Spassky in 1992.

Carlton Fisk (b.12/26/1947): Baseball C; entered 23rd season in 1992 as all-time HR leader among catchers (347) and AL leader in games caught (2,147); AL Rookie of Year (1972); has played in 10 All-Star Games; in all, has played 11 seasons for Boston Red Sox and 12 for Chicago White Sox.

Emerson Fittipaldi (b.12/12/1946): Brazilian auto racer; 2-time Formula One world champion (1972,74); won Indy 500 and overall CART title in 1989.

Bob Fitzsimmons (1863-1917): British boxer; held three world titles—middleweight (1981-97), heavyweight (1897-99) and light heavyweight (1903-05); pro record 40-11 with 32 KOs.

James (Sunny Jim) Fitzsimmons (1874-1966): Horse racing; trained horses that won over 2,275 races, including 2 Triple Crown winners—Gallant Fox in 1930 and Omaha in '35.

Larry Fleisher (1930-89): Basketball; led NBA players union from 1961-89; in that time, increased average yearly salary from $9,400 in 1967 to $600,000 without a strike.

Peggy Fleming (b.7/27/1948): Figure skating; 3-time world champion (1966-68); won Olympic gold medal in 1968.

Curt Flood (b.1/18/1938): Baseball OF; played 15 years (1956-71); lost challenge to MLB's reserve clause in Supreme Court in 1972 (see Peter Seitz).

Gerald Ford (b.7/14/1913): 38th President of the U.S.: lettered as center on undefeated Michigan football teams in 1932 and '33; team MVP of 1934 squad.

Whitey Ford (b.10/21/1928): Baseball LHP; all-time leader in World Series wins (10); led AL in wins 3 times; won both Cy Young and World Series MVP in 1961 with NY Yankees.

George Foreman (b.1/10/1948): Boxer; Olympic heavyweight champ (1968); world heavyweight champ (1973-74); lost title to Muhammad Ali (KO-8th) in '74; lost comeback bid for title at age 42 to Evander Holyfield (D-12) in 1991; entered 1992 with pro record of 70-3-0 and 66 KOs.

Dick Fosbury (b.3/6/1947): Track & Field; revolutioned high jump with back-first "Fosbury Flop;" won gold medal at 1968 Olympics.

The Four Horsemen—Senior backfield that led Notre Dame to national collegiate football championship in 1924: HB **Jim Crowley** (1902-86), FB **Elmer Layden** (1903-73), HB **Don Miller** (1902-79) and QB **Harry Stuhldreher** (1901-65).

The Four Musketeers—French quartet that dominated men's world tennis in 1920s and '30s, winning 8 straight French singles titles (1925-32), 6 Wimbledons in a row (1924-29) and 6 consecutive Davis Cups (1927-32): **Jean Borotra** (b.8/13/1898), **Jacques Brugnon** (1895-1978), **Henri Cochet** (1901-1987), **Rene Lacoste** (b.7/2/1905).

Jimmie Foxx (1907-67): Baseball 1B; led`AL in HRs 4 times and batting twice; won Triple Crown in 1933; 3-time MVP (1932-33,38) with Phila. and Boston; hit 30 HRs or more 12 years in a row; 534 career HRs.

A.J.Foyt (b.1/16/1935): Auto racer; 7-time USAC/ CART national champion (1960-61,63-64,67,75,79); 4-time Indy 500 winner (1961,64,67,77); only driver in history to win Indy 500, Daytona 500 (1972) and 24 Hours of LeMans (1967 with Dan Gurney); entered 1992 as all-time IndyCar wins leader with 67.

Bill France, Sr. (1909-92): stock car pioneer and promoter; founded NASCAR in 1948; guided race circuit through formative years; built both Daytona (Fla.) International Speedway and Talladega (Ala.) Super- speedway.

Dawn Fraser (b.9/4/1937): Australian swimmer; won gold medals in 100m freestyle at 3 consecutive Olympics (1956,60,64).

Joe Frazier (b.1/12/1944): Boxer; 1964 Olympic heavyweight champion; world heavyweight champ (1970-73); fought Muhammad Ali 3 times; pro record 32-4-1 with 27 KOs.

Ford Frick (1894-78): Baseball; sportswriter and radio announcer who served as NL president (1934-51) and commissioner (1951-65); put asterisk back on Roger Maris' 61 homers in 162 games in 1961; major leagues moved to west coast and expanded from 16 to 20 teams during his tenure.

Frankie Frisch (1898-1973): Baseball 2B; played on 8 NL pennant winners in 19 years with NY· and St.Louis; hit .300 or better 11 years in a row (1921-31); MVP in 1931; player-manager from 1933-37.

Dan Gable (b.10/25/1948): Wrestling; career college wrestling record of 118-1 at Iowa St., where he was a 2-time NCAA champ (1968,69) and tourney MVP in 1969 (137 lbs.); won gold medal (149 lbs) at 1972 Olympics; coach U.S. freestyle team in 1988; coached Iowa to 9 straight NCAA titles (1978-86) and added two more in 1991 and '92.

Eddie Gaedel (1925-61): Baseball PH; St.Louis Browns' midget whose career lasted one at bat (he walked) on Aug.19,1951 (see Bill Veeck).

Clarence (Bighouse) Gaines (b.5/21/1924): Basketball; entered 1992-93 season ranked 2nd on all-time college wins list with 822; trails Adolph Rupp by 53; has coached at Div.II Winston-Salem since 1947.

Alonzo (Jake) Gaither (b.4/11/1903): Football; head coach at Florida A&M for 25 years; led Rattlers to 6 national black college titles; retired after 1969 season with record of 203-36-4 and a winning percentage of .844; coined phrase, "I like my boys agile, mobile and hostile."

Lou Gehrig (1903-41): Baseball 1B; played in 2,130 consecutive games from 1923-39; led AL in RBI 5 times and HRs 3 times; drove in 100 runs or more 13 years in a row; 2-time MVP (1927,36); led NY Yankees to 7 World Series titles.

Charlie Gehringer (b.6/11/1903): Baseball 2B; hit .300 or better 13 times; AL batting champion and MVP with Detroit in 1937.

A.Bartlett Giamatti (1938-89): Scholar and 7th commissioner of baseball; banned Pete Rose for life for betting on Major League games and associating with known gamblers and drug dealers; also served as president of Yale (1978-86) and National League (1986-89).

Joe Gibbs (b.11/25/1940): Football; in 11 seasons, has led Washington to 3 Super Bowl titles (1983,88,92); entered 1992 regular season ranked 12th on all-time NFL list with 130 wins and 3rd in winning percentage at .695.

Althea Gibson (b.8/25/1927): Tennis; won both Wimbledon and U.S. championships in 1957 and '58; 1st black to play in either tourney and 1st to win each title.

Bob Gibson (b.11/9/1935): Baseball RHP; won 20 or more games 5 times; won 2 NL Cy Young Awards (1968,70); winner in 1968; led St. Louis to 2 World Series titles; Series MVP twice (1964,67); 251 career wins.

Josh Gibson (1911-47): Baseball C; the "Babe Ruth of the Negro Leagues;" Satchel Paige's battery mate with Pittsburgh Crawfords.

Kirk Gibson (b.5/28/1957): All-America flanker at Mich.St. in 1978; chose baseball career and was AL playoff MVP with Detroit in 1984 and NL regular season MVP with Los Angeles in 1988.

Frank Gifford (b.8/16/1930): Football HB; 4-time All-Pro (1955-57,59); MVP in 1956; led NY Giants to 3 NFL title games; TV sportscaster since 1958 (while still player).

Sid Gillman (b.10/26/1911): Football innovator; coached LA Rams (1955-59) in NFL, then led LA-SD Chargers of AFL to 5 Western titles and 1 championship in the league's 1st six years.

George Gipp (1895-1920): Football FB; died of throat infection (Dec.14) 2 weeks before he made All-America (Notre Dame's 1st); rushed for 2,341 yards, scored 156 points and averaged 38 yards a punt in 4 years (1917-20).

Tom Gola (b.1/13/1933): Basketball F; 4-time All-America and 1955 Player of the Year at La Salle; MVP in 1952 NIT and '54 NCAA tournaments, leading Pioneers to both titles; won NBA title as rookie with Phila.Warriors in 1956; 4-time NBA All-Star.

Marshall Goldberg (b.10/24/1917): Football HB; 2-time consensus All-America at Pittsburgh (1937-38); led Pitt to national championship in 1937; played with NFL champion Chicago Cardinals 10 years later.

Lefty Gomez (1908-89): Baseball LHP, 4-time 20-game winner with NY Yankees; holds World Series record for most wins (6) without a defeat; pitched on 5 world championship clubs in 1930s.

Pancho Gonzales (b.5/9/1928): Tennis; won consecutive U.S. Championships in 1947-48 before turning pro at 21; dominated pro tour from 1950-61; in 1969 at age 41, played longest Wimbledon match ever (5:12) beating Charlie Pasarell 22-24,1-6,16-14,6-3,11-9.

Shane Gould (b.11/23/1956): Australian swimmer; set world records in 5 different freestyle events between July,1971 and Jan,1972; won 3 gold medals, a silver and bronze in 1972 Olympics then retired at age 16.

Alf Goullet (b.4/5/1891): Cycling; Australian who gained fame and fortune in U.S. early in century as premier performer on U.S. 6-day bike race circuit; won 8 annual races at Madison Square Garden with 6 different partners from 1913-23.

Curt Gowdy (b.7/31/1919): Radio-TV; former radio voice of NY Yankees and then Boston Red Sox from 1949-66; TV play-by-play man for both AFL and major league baseball; has broadcast World Series, All-Star Games, Rose Bowls, Super Bowls, Olympics and NCAA Final Fours for all 3 networks; also hosted "The American Sportsman."

Steffi Graf (b.6/14/1969): German tennis player; won Grand Slam and Olympic gold medal in 1988 at age 19; has won Wimbledon 4 times and Australian 3 times and French and U.S. Opens twice each; No.1 player in world 4 times (1987-90).

Gillis Grafstrom (1894-1938): Swedish figure skater; 3-time world champ; won 3 straight gold medals then a silver in 4 Olympics (1920,24,28,32).

Otto Graham (b.12/6/1921): Football QB and basketball All-America at Northwestern; in pro ball, led Cleve. Browns to 7 league titles in 10 years, winning 4 AAFC championships (1946-50) and 3 NFL (1950,54-55); 5- time All-Pro; 2-time NFL MVP (1953,55).

Red Grange (1903-91): Football HB; 3-time All-America at Illinois who brought 1st huge crowds to pro football when he signed with Chicago in 1925; formed 1st AFL with manager C.C.Pyle in 1926, but league folded and he returned to NFL.

Rocky Graziano (1921-90): Boxer; world middleweight champion (1946-47); fought Tony Zale for title 3 times in 21 months, losing twice; pro record 67-10-6 with 52 KOs; movie "Somebody Up There Likes Me" based on his life.

Hank Greenberg (1911-86): Baseball 1B; led AL in HRs and RBI 4 times each; 2-time MVP (1935,40) with Detroit; 331 career HRs.

Joe Greene (b.9/24/1946): Football DT; 5-time All-Pro (1972-74,77,79); led Pittsburgh to 4 Super Bowl titles.

Wayne Gretzky (b.1/26/1961): Hockey C; 9-time regular season MVP (1979-87,89); 8-time All-NHL first team; 9-time scoring champ; has scored 200 points or more in a season 4 times; led Edmonton to 4 Stanley Cups (1984-85,87-88); 2-time playoff MVP (1985,88); traded to LA Kings (Aug.9, 1988); entered 1992-93 regular season as all-time NHL leader in points (2,263) and assists (1,514) and trails all-time goals leader Gordie Howe by only 51 (801 to 749); also all-time Stanley Cup leader in points (306), goals (95) and assists (211).

Bob Griese (b.2/3/1945): Football QB; 2-time All-Pro (1971,77); led Miami to undefeated season (17-0) in 1972 and consecutive Super Bowl titles (1973-74).

Archie Griffin (b.8/21/1954): Football RB; only college player to win two Heisman Trophies (1974-75); rushed for 5,177 yards in career at Ohio St.

Emile Griffith (b.2/3/1938): Boxer; world welterweight champion (1961,62-63,63-65); world middleweight champ (1966-67,67-68); pro record 85-24-2 with 23 KOs.

Dick Groat (b.11/41930): Two-time basketball All-America at Duke and college Player of the Year in 1951; chose baseball career and won NL MVP award as shortstop with Pittsburgh in 1960; won World Series with Pirates (1960) and St.Louis (1964).

Lefty Grove (1900-75): Baseball LHP; won 20 or more games 8 times; led AL in ERA 9 times and strikeouts 7 times; 31-4 record and MVP in 1931 with Phila.; 300 career wins.

Lou Groza (b.1/25/1924): Football T-PK; 6-time All-Pro; played in 13 championship games for Cleveland from 1946-67; kicked winning field goal in 1950 NFL title game; 1,608 career points (1,349 in NFL).

Janet Guthrie (b.3/7/1938): Auto racer; in 1977, became 1st woman to race in Indianapolis 500; placed 9th at Indy in 1978.

Tony Gwynn (b.5/7/1960): Baseball OF; entered 1992 season with 4 NL batting titles (1984,87-89) at San Diego and .328 career average.

Harvey Haddix (b.9/18/1925): Baseball LHP; pitched 12 perfect innings for Pittsburgh, but lost to Milwaukee in the 13th, 1-0 (May 26,1959).

Walter Hagen (1892-1969): Pro golf pioneer; won 2 U.S. Opens (1914,19), 4 British Opens (1922,24,28-29), 5 PGA Championships (1921,24-27) and 5 Western Opens; retired with 40 PGA wins; 6-time U.S. Ryder Cup captain.

Marvin Hagler (b.5/23/1954): Boxer; world middleweight champion 1980-87; pro record 62-3-2 with 52 KOs.

George Halas (1895-1983): Football pioneer; MVP in 1919 Rose Bowl; player-coach-owner of Chicago Bears from 1920-83; signed Red Grange in 1925; coached Bears for 40 seasons and won 7 NFL titles (1932-33,40-41,43,46,63); all-time leader in career wins (325).

Dorothy Hamill (b.7/26/1956): Figure skater; won Olympic gold medal and world championship in 1976.

Scott Hamilton (b.8/28/1958): Figure skater; 4-time world champion (1981-84); won gold medal at 1984 Olympics.

Tom Harmon (1919-90): Football HB; 2-time All-America at Michigan; won Heisman Trophy in 1940; played with AFL NY Americans in 1941 and NFL LA Rams (1946-47); World War II fighter pilot who won Silver Star and Purple Heart; became radio-TV commentator.

Franco Harris (b.3/7/1950): Football RB; ran for over 1,000 yards a season 8 times; rushed for 12,120 yards in 13 years; led Pittsburgh to 4 Super Bowl titles.

Leon Hart (b.11/2/1928); Football E; only player to win 3 national championships in college and 3 more in the NFL; won his titles at Notre Dame (1946-47,49) and with Detroit Lions (1952-53,57); 3-time All-America and last lineman to win Heisman Trophy (1949); All-Pro on both offense and defense in 1951.

Bill Hartack (b.12/9/1932): Jockey; won Kentucky Derby 5 times (1957,60,62,64,69), Preakness 3 times (1956,64,69), but the Belmont only once (1960).

Doug Harvey (1924-90): Hockey D; 10-time All-NHL 1st team; won Norris Trophy 7 times (1955-58,60-62); led Montreal to 6 Stanley Cups.

Billy Haughton (1923-86): Harness racing; 4-time winner of Hambletonian; trainer-driver of one Pacing Triple Crown winner (1968); winner of 4,910 races in career.

John Havlicek (b.4/8/1940): Basketball; played in 3 NCAA finals at Ohio St. (1960-62); led Boston to 8 NBA titles (1963-66,68-69,74,76); playoff MVP in 1974; 4-time All-NBA 1st team.

Bob Hayes (b.12/20/1942): Track & Field/Football; won gold medal in 100m at 1964 Olympics; All-Pro SE for Dallas in 1966; convicted of drug trafficking in 1979 and served 18 months of a 5-year sentence.

Woody Hayes (1913-87): Football; coached Ohio St. to 3 national titles (1954,57,68) and 4 Rose Bowl victories; 238 career wins.

Thomas Hearns (b. 10/15/1958): Boxer; claimed 5th different world title in 1991, winning WBA light heavyweight crown at age 32; lost crown by split decision to Iran Barkley on Mar. 20, 1992, dropping pro record to 50-4-1 with 40 KOs.

Eric Heiden (b. 6/14/1958): Speedskater; 3-time overall world champion (1977-79), won all 5 men's gold medals at 1980 Olympics setting new records in each; Sullivan Award winner (1980).

Mel Hein (1909-92): Football C; NFL All-Pro 8 straight years (1933-40); MVP in 1938 with NY Giants; didn't miss a game in 15 seasons.

John W.Heisman (1869-1936): Football; coached at 9 colleges from 1892-1927; won 185 games; Dir.of Athletics at Downtown Athletic Club in NYC (1928-36); DAC named Heisman Trophy after him.

Carol Heiss (b.1/20/1940): Figure skater; 5-time world champion (1956-60); won Olympic silver medal in 1956 and gold in '60; married 1956 men's gold medalist Hayes Jenkins.

Rickey Henderson (b. 12/25/1958): Baseball OF; AL playoff MVP (1989) and AL regular season MVP (1990); set single season base stealing record of 130 in 1982; has led AL in steals 11 times; broke Lou Brock's all-time record of 938 on May 1, 1991; entered 1992 season as all-time leader in steals (994) and HRs as leadoff batter (50).

Sonja Henie (1912-69): Norwegian figure skater; 10-time world champion (1927-36); won 3 consecutive Olympic gold medals (1928,32,36); became movie star.

Foster Hewitt (1902-85): Radio-TV; Canada's premier hockey play-by-play broadcaster from 1923-81; coined phrase, "He shoots. . . . he scores!"

Graham Hill (1929-75): British auto racer; 2-time Formula One world champion (1962,68); won Indy 500 in 1966; killed in plane crash.

Phil Hill (b.4/20/1927): Auto racer; first U.S. driver to win Formula One championship (1961); 3 career wins (1958-64).

Max Hirsch (1880-1969): Horse racing; trained 1,933 winners from 1908-68; won Triple Crown with Assault in 1946.

Tommy Hitchcock (1900-44): Polo; world class player at 20; achieved 10-goal rating 18 times from 1922-40.

Ben Hogan (b.8/13/1912): Golfer; 4-time PGA Player of Year; won 4 U.S. Opens, 2 Masters, 2 PGA and 1 British Open between 1946-53; won 3 of 4 Majors (Masters, U.S. Open, British Open) in 1953; 62 career wins.

Eleanor Holm (b.12/6/1913): Swimmer; won gold medal in 100m backstroke at 1932 Olympics; thrown off '36 U.S. team for drinking champagne in public and shooting craps on boat to Germany.

Nat Holman (b.10/18/1896): Basketball pioneer; played pro with Original Celtics (1920-28); coached CCNY to both NCAA and NIT titles in 1950 (a year later, several of his players were caught up in a point-shaving scandal); 423 career wins.

Larry Holmes (b.11/3/1949): Boxer; heavyweight champion (WBC or IBF) from 1978-85; successfully defended title 20 times before losing to Michael Spinks; returned from first retirement in 1988 and was KO'd in 4th by then champ Mike Tyson; launched second comeback in 1991; was 42 years and 7 months old when he fought 29-year-old Evander Holyfield on June 19, 1992, and lost a 12-round decision; defeat dropped pro record to 54-4-0 and 37 KOs.

Evander Holyfield (b.10/19/1962): Boxer; knocked out Buster Douglas to become world heavyweight champion in 1990; lost shot at Olympic gold medal in 1984 when he lost controversial light heavy semifinal after knocking his opponent out (referee ruled it was a late hit); 3 title defenses include decisions over 42-year-old ex-champs George Foreman and Larry Holmes; Holmes victory improved pro record to 28-0 with 22 KOs.

Red Holzman (b.8/10/1920): Basketball; played for NBL and NBA champions at Rochester (1946,51); coached NY Knicks to 2 NBA titles (1970,73); Coach of Year (1970); ranks 9th on all-time NBA list with 754 wins (including playoffs).

Rogers Hornsby (1896-1963): Baseball 2B; hit .400 three times, including .424 in 1924; led NL in batting 7 times; 2-time MVP (1925,29) with St. Louis; career average of .358 over 23 years is all-time highest.

Paul Hornung (b.12/23/1935): Football HB-PK; only Heisman Trophy winner to play for losing team (2-8 Notre Dame in 1956); 3-time NFL scoring leader (1959-61) at Green Bay; 176 points in 1960 all-time record; MVP in 1961.

Gordie Howe (b.3/31/1928): Hockey RW; played 32 seasons in NHL and WHA from 1946-80; led NHL in scoring 6 times; All-NHL 1st team 12 times; MVP 6 times in NHL (1952-53,57-58,60,63) with Detroit and once in WHA (1974) with Houston; all-time NHL leader in goals (801) and 2nd in points (1,850) to Wayne Gretzky; played with sons Mark and Marty at Houston (1973-77) and New England-Hartford (1977-80).

Cal Hubbard (1900-77): Member of college football, pro football and baseball halls of fame; 9 years in NFL; 4-time All-Pro at end and tackle; AL umpire for 15 years (1936-51).

Carl Hubbell (1903-88): Baseball LHP; led NL in wins and ERA 3 times each; 2-time MVP (1933,36) with NY Giants; fanned Ruth, Gehrig, Foxx, Simmons and Cronin in succession in 1934 All-Star Game; 253 career wins.

Miller Huggins (1880-1929): Baseball; managed NY Yankees to 6 pennants and 3 World Series titles from 1921-27.

Bobby Hull (b.1/3/1939): Hockey LW; led NHL in scoring 3 times; 2-time MVP (1965-66) with Chicago; All-NHL first team 10 times; jumped to WHA in 1972, 2-time MVP there (1973,75) with Winnipeg; scored 913 goals in both leagues; father of Brett.

Brett Hull (b. 8/9/1964): Hockey RW; named NHL MVP in 1991 with St.Louis; holds RW scoring record with 86 goals; he and father Bobby have both won Hart (MVP), Lady Byng (sportsmanship) and All-Star Game MVP trophies; entered 1992-93 with three straight seasons of 70 goals or more (72,86,70).

Jim (Catfish) Hunter (b.4/8/1946): Baseball RHP; won 20 games or more 5 times (1971-75); played on 5 World Series winners with Oakland, NY Yankees; threw perfect game in 1968; won Cy Young Award in '74.

Ibrahim Hussein (b. 6/3/1958): Kenyan distance runner; 3-time winner of Boston Marathon (1988,91-92) and 1st African runner to win in Boston; won New York Marathon in 1987.

Don Hutson (b.1/31/1913): Football E-PK; led NFL in receptions 8 times and interceptions once; 9-time All-Pro (1936, 38-45) for Green Bay.

Flo Hyman (1954-86): Volleyball; 3-time All-America spiker at Houston and captain of 1984 U.S. Women's Olympic team; died of heart attack caused by Marfan Syndrome during a match in Japan in 1986; Women's Sports Foundation's Hyman Award for excellence and dedication named after her.

Hank Iba (b.8/6/1904): Basketball; coached Oklahoma A&M to 2 straight NCAA titles (1945-46); 767 career wins in 41 years; coached U.S. Olympic team to 2 gold medals (1964,68), but lost to Soviets in controversial '72 final.

Punch Imlach (1918-1987): Hockey; directed Toronto to 4 Stanley Cups (1962-64,67) in 11 seasons as GM-coach.

Hale Irwin (b. 6/3/1945): Golf; oldest player ever to win U.S. Open (45 in 1990); NCAA champion in 1967; entered 1992 with 19 PGA victories, including 3 U.S. Opens (1974,79,90).

Bo Jackson (b. 11/30/1962): Baseball OF and Football RB; won Heisman Trophy in 1985 and MVP of baseball All-Star Game in 1989; starter for both baseball's KC Royals and NFL's LA Raiders in 1988 and '89; severely injured left hip Jan. 13, 1991, in NFL playoffs; waived by Royals in March, 1991, but signed by Chi. White Sox a month later and returned to line-up on Sept. 2, 1991; missed entire 1992 baseball season recovering from hip surgery.

Joe Jackson (1887-1951): Baseball OF; hit .300 or better 11 times; career average of .356 (see Black Sox).

Reggie Jackson (b.5/18/1946): Baseball OF; led AL in HRs 4 times; MVP in 1973; played on 5 World Series winners with Oakland, NY Yankees; 1977 Series MVP with 5 HRs; 563 career HRs; all-time strikeout leader (2,597).

Helen Jacobs (b.8/8/1908): Tennis; 4-time winner of U.S. Championship (1932-35); Wimbledon winner in 1936; lost 4 Wimbledon finals to arch-rival Helen Wills Moody.

Jim Jacobs (1930-88): Handball/Boxing; won 12 U.S. Handball titles (6 singles and 6 doubles) from 1955-68; also managed 4 world champion boxers, including Mike Tyson (from 1985-88).

James J.Jeffries (1875-1953): Boxer; world heavyweight champion (1899-1905); retired undefeated but came back to fight Jack Johnson in 1910 and lost (KO,15th).

David Jenkins (b.6/29/1936): Figure skater; brother of Hayes; 3-time world champion (1957-59); won gold medal at 1960 Olympics.

Hayes Jenkins (b.3/23/1933): Figure skater; 4-time world champion (1953-56), won gold medal at 1956 Olympics; married 1960 women's gold medalist Carol Heiss.

Bruce Jenner (b.10/28/1949): Track & Field; won gold medal in 1976 Olympic decathlon.

Ben Johnson (b. 12/30/1961): Canadian sprinter; set 100m world record (9.83) at 1987 World Championships; won 100m at 1988 Olympics, but flunked drug test and forfeited gold medal; 1987 world record revoked in '89 for admitted steroid use; returned drug-free in 1991, but performed poorly; made Canadian Olympic team in 1992, but did not qualify for 100m final.

Earvin (Magic) Johnson (b. 8/14/1959): Basketball G; led Michigan St. to NCAA title in 1979 and was tourney MVP; All-NBA 1st team 9 times; all-time NBA assist leader with 9,921; 3-time MVP (1987,89-90); led LA Lakers to 5 NBA titles; 3-time playoff MVP (1980,82,87); stunned world with retirement announcement on Nov. 7, 1991, stating he was HIV-positive for AIDS; returned on Feb. 9, 1992, to score 25 points in NBA All-Star game and win 2nd MVP award; also led NBA "Dream Team" to gold medal in 1992 Olympics.

Jack Johnson (1878-1946): Boxer; 1st black world heavyweight champion (1908-15); pro record 78-8-12 with 45 KOs.

Rafer Johnson (b.8/18/1935): Track & Field; won silver medal in 1956 Olympic decathlon and gold medal in 1960.

Walter Johnson (1887-1946): Baseball RHP; won 20 games or more 10 straight years; led AL in ERA 5 times, wins 6 times and strikeouts 12 times; twice MVP (1913, 24) with Washington; all-time leader in shutouts (113) and 2nd in wins (416).

Ben A. Jones (1882-1961): Horse racing; Calumet Farm trainer (1939-47); saddled 6 Kentucky Derby champions and 2 Triple Crown winners—Whirlaway in 1941 and Citation in '48.

Bobby Jones (1902-71): Won U.S. and British Opens plus U.S. and British Amateurs in 1930 to become golf's only Grand Slam winner ever; from 1922-30, won 4 U.S. Opens, 5 U.S. Amateurs, 3 British Opens, and played in 6 Walker Cups; founded Masters tournament in 1934.

Deacon Jones (b.12/9/1938): Football DE; 5-time All-Pro (1965-69) with LA Rams.

Michael Jordan (b. 2/17/1963): Basketball G; College Player of Year in 1984; has led NBA in scoring 6 years in a row (1987-92); 6-time All-NBA 1st team; 3-time regular season MVP (1988,91-92) and 2-time MVP of NBA Finals (1991-92); has led U.S. Olympic team to gold medals in 1984 and '92.

Florence Griffith Joyner (b. 12/21/1959): Track & Field; set world records in 100 and 200 meters in 1988; won 3 gold medals at '88 Olympics (100m, 200m, 4x100 relay); Sullivan Award winner (1988); retired in 1989; designed NBA Indiana Pacers uniforms (1990).

Jackie Joyner-Kersee (b. 3/3/1962): Track & Field; in Olympic Games, has won a silver (1984) and 2 gold medals (1988,92) in heptathlon, and a gold (1988) and bronze (1992) in long jump; Sullivan Award winner (1986), entered 1992 as world record holder in heptathlon (7,291 pts).

Alberto Juantorena (b.3/12/1951): Cuban runner; won both 400m and 800m gold medals at 1976 Olympics.

Sonny Jurgensen (b.8/23/1934): Football QB; played 18 seasons with Phila. and Wash.; led NFL in passing twice (1967,69); All-Pro in 1961; 255 career TD passes.

Duke Kahanamoku (1890-1968): Swimmer; won 3 gold medals and 2 silver over 3 Olympics (1912, 20, 24); also surfing pioneer.

Al Kaline (b.12/19/1934): Baseball; youngest player (20) to win batting title (led AL with .340 in 1955); had 3,007 hits, 399 HRs in 22 years with Detroit.

Anatoly Karpov (b.5/23/1951): Chess; Soviet world champion, 1975-85.

Gary Kasparov (b.4/13/1963): Chess; Soviet world champion since 1985; defeated Karpov for title.

Kip Keino (b.1/17/1940): Kenyan runner; won one gold medal in 1,500m at 1968 Olympics and another in steeplechase at 1972 Games.

Johnny Kelley (b. 9/6/1907): Distance runner, ran in his 61st and final Boston Marathon at age 84 on April 20, 1992, finishing in 5:58:36; has won Boston twice (1935,45) and been 2nd 7 times.

Walter Kennedy (1912-77): Basketball; 2nd NBA commissioner (1963-75), league doubled in size to 18 teams during his term of office.

Stanley Ketchel (1886-1910): Boxer; claimed 3 world titles—welterweight (1908,08-10), middleweight (1908-10) and light heavyweight (1909-10); murdered at age 24; pro record 53-4-5 with 50 KOs.

Harmon Killebrew (b.6/29/1936): Baseball 3B-1B; led AL in HRs 6 times and RBI 4 times; MVP in 1969 with Minnesota; 573 career HRs.

Jean-Claude Killy (b.8/30/1943): French alpine skier; 2-time World Cup champion (1967-68); won 3 gold medals 1968 Olympics; co-president of 1992 Winter Games in Albertville.

Ralph Kiner (b.10/27/1922): Baseball OF; led NL in home runs 7 straight years (1946-52) with Pittsburgh; 369 career HRs.

Billie Jean King (b.11/22/1943): Tennis; Wimbledon singles champ 6 times; U.S. champ 4 times; first woman athlete to earn $100,000 in one year (1971); beat 55-year-old Bobby Riggs 6-4, 6-3, 6-3, to win $100,000 in 1973.

Don King (b.8/20/1931): Boxing promoter; controlled heavyweight title from 1978-90 while Larry Holmes and Mike Tyson were champions; 1st major bout Muhammad Ali's comeback fight in 1970; former numbers operator who served 4 years for manslaughter (1967–70); acquitted of tax evasion and fraud in 1984.

Tom Kite (b.12/9/1949): Golfer; entered 1992 as all-time PGA Tour money leader with over $6.6 million; finally won 1st major with victory in 1992 U.S. Open at Pebble Beach; NCAA champion (1972); PGA Rookie of Year (1973): PGA Player of Year (1989).

Gene Klein (1921-1990): Horseman; won 3 Eclipse awards as top owner (1985-87); filly Winning Colors won 1988 Kentucky Derby; also owned San Diego Chargers football team (1966-84).

Bob Knight (b.10/25/1940): Basketball; has coached Indiana to 3 NCAA titles (1976,81,87); 3-time Coach of Year (1975-76,89); 588 career wins; coached 1984 U.S. Olympic team to gold medal.

Olga Korbut (b.5/16/1955): Soviet gymnast; 3 gold medals 1972 Olympics; first to perform back somersault on balance beam.

Sandy Koufax (b.12/30/1935): Baseball LHP; led NL in strikeouts 4 times and ERA 5 straight years; won 3 Cy Young Awards (1963,65,66) with LA Dodgers; MVP in 1963; 2-time World Series MVP (1963,65); pitched 1 perfect game and 3 other no-hitters.

Alvin Kraenzlein (1876-1928): Track & Field; won 4 individual gold medals in 1900 Olympics (60m,long jump, and 110m & 200m hurdles).

Jack Kramer (b.8/1/1921): Tennis; Wimbledon singles champ 1947; U.S. champ 1946-47; promoter and Open pioneer.

Ingrid Kristiansen (b. 3/21/1956): Norwegian runner; 2-time Boston Marathon winner (1986,89); won New York City Marathon in 1989; entered 1992 holding 3 world records recognized by IAAF—5,000m, 10,000m and marathon.

Bob Kurland (b.12/23/1924): Basketball C; 3-time All-America (1944-46); led Okla.A&M to 2 NCAA titles (1945-46) and U.S. to 2 Olympic gold medals (1948, 52); did not turn pro.

Marion Ladewig (b.10/30/1914): named Woman Bowler of the Year 9 times, (1950-54,57-59,63).

Guy Lafleur (b.9/20/1951): Hockey RW; has led NHL in scoring 3 times (1975-78); 2-time MVP (1977-78), played for 5 Stanley Cup winners in Montreal; playoff MVP in 1977; returned to NHL as player in 1988 after election to Hall of Fame; retired again in 1991.

Napoleon Lajoie (1875-1959): Baseball 2B; led AL in batting 4 times (1901-04); hit .422 in 1901; had 3,251 career hits.

Jack Lambert (b.7/8/1952): Football LB; 6-time All-Pro (1975-76,79-82); led Pittsburgh to 4 Super Bowl titles.

Kenesaw Mountain Landis (1866-1944): Baseball's first commissioner (1920-44); banned Black Sox for life.

Tom Landry (b.9/11/1924): Football; coached Dallas for 29 years (1960-88); won 2 Super Bowls (1972,78); 271 career wins.

Steve Largent (b.9/28/1954): Football WR; retired in 1989 after 14 years with Seattle as all-time NFL leader in passes caught (819) and TD passes caught (100).

Don Larsen (b.8/7/1929): Baseball RHP; pitched only perfect game in World Series history—NY Yankees 2, Brooklyn 0 (Oct.8,1956); Series MVP that year.

Tommy Lasorda (b.9/22/1927): Baseball; managed LA Dodgers to 2 World Series titles (1981,88) in 4 appearances; entered 1992 season with 1,278 regular-season wins in 16 years.

Larissa Latynina (b.1934): Soviet gymnast; won total of 18 medals, (9 gold) in 3 Olympics (1956,60,64).

Nikki Lauda (b.2/22/1949): Austrian auto racer; 3-time world Formula One champion (1975,77,84), 25 career wins from 1971-85.

Rod Laver (b.8/9/1938): Australian tennis player; only player to win Grand Slam twice (1962,69); Wimbledon champion 4 times; 1st to earn $1 million in prize money.

Andrea Mead Lawrence (b.4/19/1932): Alpine skier; won 2 gold medals at 1952 Olympics.

Bobby Layne (1926-86): Football QB; college star at Texas; led Detroit to 2 straight NFL titles (1952-53).

Frank Leahy (1908-73): Football; coached Notre Dame to four national titles (1943,46-47,49); career record of 107-13-9.

Mario Lemieux (b.10/5/1965): Hockey C; 3-time NHL scoring leader (1988-89,92); Rookie of Year (1985); 2-time All-NHL 1st team (1988-89); regular season MVP (1988); 3-time All-Star Game MVP; has led Pittsburgh to consecutive Stanley Cup titles (1991-92) and was playoff MVP both years.

Greg LeMond (b.6/26/1961): Cyclist; 3-time Tour de France winner (1986,89-90); only American to win the event.

Ivan Lendl (b.3/7/1960): Tennis; No.1 player in world 4 times (1985-87,89); has won both French and U.S. Opens 3 times and Australian twice; entered 1992 with 91 career tournament wins.

Suzanne Lenglen (1899-1938): French tennis player; dominated women's tennis from 1919-26; won both Wimbledon and French singles titles 6 times.

Sugar Ray Leonard (b.5/17/1956): Boxer; light welterweight Olympic champ (1976); won world welterweight title 1979 and four more titles; retired after losing to Terry Norris on Feb. 9, 1991, with record of 36-2-1 and 25 KOs.

Carl Lewis (b.7/1/1961): Track & Field; won 4 Olympic gold medals in 1984 (100m, 200m, 4 × 100m, LJ), 2 more in '88 (100m, LJ) and 2 more in '92 (4 × 100m, LJ) for a career total of 8; has record 7 World Championship titles and 9 medals in all; Sullivan Award winner in 1981; entered 1992 as world record-holder in 100m (9.86) and with 62 long jumps over 28 feet.

Nancy Lieberman-Cline (b.7/1/1958): Basketball; 3-time All-America and 2-time Player of Year (1979-80); led Old Dominion to consecutive AIAW titles in 1979 and '80; played in defunct WPBL and WABA and became 1st woman to play in men's pro league (USBL) in 1986.

Sonny Liston (1932-70): Boxer; heavyweight champ (1962-64); lost title to Muhammad Ali (then Cassius Clay) in 1964; pro record 50-4 with 39 KOs.

Vince Lombardi (1913-70): Football; coached Green Bay to 5 NFL titles; won first 2 Super Bowls (1967-68).

Johnny Longden (b.2/14/1907): Jockey; first to win 6,000 races; rode Count Fleet to Triple Crown in 1943.

Nancy Lopez (b.1/6/1957): Golfer; 4-time LPGA Player of the Year (1978-79,85,88); Rookie of Year (1977); 3-time winner of LPGA Championship; reached Hall of Fame by age 30 with 35 victories; entered 1992 with 44 career wins.

Greg Louganis (b.1/29/1960): U.S. diver; won platform and springboard gold medals at both 1984 and '88 Olympics.

Joe Louis (1914-81): Boxer; world heavyweight champion (1937-49); reign of 11 years, 8 months longest in division history; pro record 63-3 with 49 KOs.

Sid Luckman (b.11/21/1916): Football QB; 6-time All-Pro; led Chicago Bears to 4 NFL titles (1940-41,43,46); MVP in 1943.

Hank Luisetti (b.6/16/1916): Basketball F; 3-time All-America at Stanford (1935-38); revolutionized game with one-handed shot.

Johnny Lujack (b.1/4/1925): Football QB; led Notre Dame to three national titles (1943,46-47); won Heisman Trophy in 1947.

Gen.Douglas MacArthur (1880-1964): Leading U.S. general in World War II and Korea; president of U.S. Olympic Committee (1927-28); college football devotee, National Football Foundation MacArthur Bowl (for No.1 team) named after him.

Connie Mack (1862-1956): Baseball owner; managed Phila.A's until he was 87 (1901-50); all-time major league wins leader with 3,755, including postseason; won 9 AL pennants and 5 World Series (1910-11,13,29-30); also finished last 18 times.

Andy MacPhail (b.4/5/1953): Baseball; general manager of 2 World Series champions in Minnesota (1987,91), the first title coming at age 34; son of Lee and grandson of Larry.

Larry MacPhail (1890-1975): Baseball executive and innovator; introduced major leagues to night games at Cincinnati (May 24, 1935); won pennant in Brooklyn (1948) and World Series with NY Yankees (1947); father of Lee.

Lee MacPhail (b.10/25/1917): Baseball; AL president (1974-83); president of owners' Player Relations Committee (1984-85); also GM of Baltimore (1959-65) and NY Yankees (1967-74); father of Andy, current Minnesota GM.

John Madden (b.4/10/1936): Football; won 112 games and a Super Bowl (1976 season) as coach of the Oakland Raiders; has won 9 Emmy Awards since since 1981-82 season as television analyst with CBS.

Larry Mahan (b.11/21/1943): Rodeo; 6-time All-Around Cowboy (1966-70,73).

Phil Mahre (b.5/10/1957): Alpine skier; 3-time World Cup overall champ (1981-83); finished 1-2 with twin brother Steve in 1984 Olympic slalom.

Moses Malone (b.3/23/1955): Basketball C; signed with Utah of ABA at age 19; has led NBA in rebounding 6 times; 4-time All-NBA 1st team; 3-time NBA MVP (1979,82-83); playoff MVP with Philadelphia in 1983.

Mickey Mantle (b.10/20/1931): Baseball OF; led AL in home runs 4 times; won Triple Crown in 1956; 3-time MVP (1956-57,62); 536 career HRs; played on 7 World Series winners with NY Yankees.

Diego Maradona (b.10/30/1960): Soccer F; captain and MVP of 1986 World Cup champion Argentina; also led national team to 1990 World Cup final; consensus Player of Decade in 1980s; led Napoli to 2 Italian League titles (1987,90) and UEFA Cup (1989); tested positive for cocaine and suspended 15 months by FIFA and Italian Soccer Federation in March, 1991.

Pete Maravich (1948-88): Basketball; NCAA scoring leader 3 times (1968-70); averaged 44.2 points a game over career; Player of Year in 1970; NBA scoring champ in 1977.

Alice Marble (1913-90): Tennis; 4-time U.S. champion (1936,38-40); won Wimbledon in 1939; swept U.S. singles, doubles and mixed doubles from 1938-40.

Gino Marchetti (b.1/2/1927): Football DE; 8-time NFL All-Pro (1957-64) with Baltimore Colts.

Rocky Marciano (1923-69): Boxer; heavyweight champion (1952-56); retired undefeated; pro record of 49-0 with 43 KOs; killed in plane crash.

Juan Marichal (b.10/24/1937): Baseball RHP; won 21 or more games 6 times with S.F. Giants; 243 career wins.

Dan Marino (b.9/15/1961): Football QB; 4-time leading passer in AFC (1983-84,86,89); set NFL single-season records for TD passes (48) and passing yards (5,084) with Miami in 1984; entered 1992 season ranked 3rd in career TD passes (266) and 4th in passing yards (35,386).

Roger Maris (1934-85): Baseball OF; broke Babe Ruth's single-season HR record with 61 in 1961; 2-time AL MVP (1960-61) with NY Yankees.

Billy Martin (1928-1989): Baseball; 5-time manager of NY Yankees; won 2 pennants and 1 World Series (1977); also managed Minnesota, Detroit, Texas and Oakland; played 2B on 4 Yankee world champions in 1950s.

Eddie Mathews (b.10/13/1931): Baseball 3B; led NL in HRs twice (1953,59); hit 30 or more home runs 9 straight years; 512 career HRs.

Christy Mathewson (1880-1925): Baseball RHP; won 22 or more games 12 straight years (1903-14); 373 career wins; pitched 3 shutouts in 1905 World Series.

Bob Mathias (b.11/17/1930): Track & Field; youngest winner of decathlon with gold medal in 1948 Olympics at age 17; first to repeat as decathlon champ in 1952; Sullivan Award winner (1948); 4-term member of U.S. Congress (R,Calif.) from 1967-74.

Ollie Matson (b.5/1/1930): Football HB; All-America at San Francisco (1951); bronze medal winner in 400m at 1952 Olympics; 4-time All-Pro for NFL Chicago Cardinals (1954-57); traded to LA Rams for 9 players in 1959; accounted for 12,884 all-purpose yards and scored 73 TDs in 14 seasons.

Willie Mays (b.5/6/1931): Baseball OF; led NL in HRs and stolen bases 4 times each; 2-time MVP (1954,65) with NY-SF Giants; played in 24 All-Star Games; 660 HRs and 3,283 hits in career.

Bill Mazeroski (b.9/5/1936): Baseball 2B; career .260 hitter who won the 1960 World Series for Pittsburgh with a lead-off HR in the bottom of the 9th inning of Game 7; the pitcher was Ralph Terry of the NY Yankees, the count was 1-0 and the score was tied 9-9; also sure-fielder, Maz won 8 gold gloves in 17 seasons.

Joe McCarthy (1887-1978): Baseball; managed NY Yankees to 8 pennants and 7 World Series titles (1931-46).

Mark McCormack (b.11/6/1930): founder and CEO of International Management Group, the sports management conglomerate.

Pat McCormick (b.5/12/1930): U.S. diver; won women's platform and springboard gold medals in both 1952 and '56 Olympics.

Willie McCovey (b.1/10/1938): Baseball 1B; led NL in HRs 3 times and RBI twice; MVP in 1969 with SF; 521 career HRs.

John McEnroe (b.2/16/1959): Tennis; No.1 player in the world 4 times (1981-84); 4-time U.S. Open singles champ (1979-81,84); 3-time Wimbledon champ (1981,83-84); has played on 4 Davis Cup winners (1978-79,81-82); won NCAA singles title (1978); entered 1992 with 77 championships in singles, 74 more in doubles (including 9 Grand Slam titles), and American Davis Cup records for years played (12) and singles matches won (41).

John McGraw (1873-1934): Baseball; managed NY Giants to 10 NL pennants and 3 World Series titles in 30 years; 2,810 career wins, including postseason.

Jim McKay (b.9/24/1921): Radio-TV; host and commentator of ABC's Olympic coverage and "Wide World of Sports" show since 1961; 12-time Emmy winner; also given Peabody Award in 1988 and Life Achievement Emmy in 1990.

John McKay (b.7/5/1923): Football; coached USC to 3 national titles (1962,67,72); won Rose Bowl 5 times; reached NFL playoffs 3 times with Tampa Bay.

Denny McLain (b.3/29/1944): Baseball RHP; last pitcher to win 30 games (1968); 2-time Cy Young winner (1968-69) with Detroit; convicted of racketeering, extortion and drug possession in 1985, served 29 months of 25-year jail term, sentence overturned when court ruled he had not received a fair trial.

Bruce McNall (b. 4/17/1950): Owner; bought NHL LA Kings in 1988; sent 5 players and $15 million to Edmonton for Wayne Gretzky (Aug.8,1988); bought CFL Toronto Argonauts in 1990; signed Notre Dame's Rocket Ismail for $18.2 million (Apr.21,1991); became chairman of NHL board of governors in 1992.

Rick Mears (b.12/3/1951): Auto racer; 3-time CART national champ (1979,81-82); 4-time winner of Indianapolis 500 (1979,84,88,91) and only driver to win 6 Indy 500 poles; Indy 500 Rookie of Year (1978); entered 1992 with 29 IndyCar wins and 40 poles.

Debbie Meyer (b.8/14/1952): Swimmer; 1st swimmer to win 3 individual gold medals at one Olympics (1968).

George Mikan (b.6/18/1924): Basketball C; 3-time All-America (1944-46); led DePaul to NIT title (1945); led Minneapolis Lakers to 5 NBA titles in 6 years (1949-54); Commissioner of ABA (1967-69).

Stan Mikita (b.5/20/1940): Hockey C; led NHL in scoring 4 times; won both MVP and Lady Byng awards in 1967 and '68 with Chicago.

Cheryl Miller (b.1/3/1964): Basketball; 3-time college Player of Year (1984-86); led USC to NCAA title and U.S. to Olympic gold medal in 1984.

Del Miller (b.7/5/1913): Harness racing; driver, trainer, owner, breeder, seller and track owner; has driven over 2,400 winners since 1939.

Marvin Miller (b.4/14/1917): Baseball; executive director of Players' Assn. from 1966-82; increased average salary from $19,000 to over $240,000; led 13-day strike in 1972 and 50-day walkout in '81.

Shannon Miller (b.3/10/1977): Gymnast; won 5 medals in 1992 Olympics, including a silver in the All-Around, another in the floor exercise and 3 bronzes.

Billy Mills (b.6/30/1938): Track & Field; upset winner of 10,000m gold medal at 1964 Olympics.

Joe Montana (b.6/11/1956): Football QB; led Notre Dame to national title in 1977; has since led San Francisco to 4 Super Bowls (1982,85,89-90); 2-time NFL MVP (1989-90); only 3-time Super Bowl MVP; led NFC in passing 5 times (1981,84-85,87,90); sat out entire 1991 season after elbow surgery; entered 1992 ranked 1st in all-time passing efficiency (93.4), 5th in yards passing (34,998) and 7th in TD passes (242).

Helen Wills Moody (b.10/6/1905): Tennis; won 8 Wimbledon singles titles, 7 U.S. and 4 French from 1923-38.

Archie Moore (b.12/13/1913): Boxer; world light-heavyweight champion (1952-60); pro record 199-26-8 with 145 KOs.

Howie Morenz (1902-37): Hockey C; 3-time NHL MVP (1928,31-32); led Montreal Canadiens to 3 Stanley Cups; voted Outstanding Player of the Half-Century in 1950.

Joe Morgan (b.9/19/1943): Baseball 2B; led NL in walks 4 times; regular season MVP both years he led Cincinnati to World Series titles (1975-76).

Bobby Morrow (b.10/15/1935): Track & Field; won 3 gold medals at 1956 Olympics (100m,200m and 4x400m relay).

Willie Mosconi (b.6/27/1913), Pocket Billiards; 14-time world champion from 1941-57.

Annemarie Moser-Pröll (b.3/27/1953): Austrian alpine skier; won World Cup overall title 6 times (1971-75,79); won Downhill in 1980 Olympics.

Edwin Moses (b.8/31/1955): Track & Field; won 400m hurdles at 1976 and '84 Olympics, bronze medal in '88; also winner of 122 consecutive races from 1977-87.

Stirling Moss (b.9/17/1929): Auto racer; won 194 of 466 career races and 16 Formula One events, but was never world champion.

Marion Motley (b.6/5/1920): Football FB; all-time leading AAFC rusher; rushed for over 4,700 yards and 31 TDs for Cleveland Browns (1946-53).

Dale Murphy (b.3/12/1956): Baseball OF; led NL in RBI 3 times and HRs twice; 2-time MVP (1982-83) with Atlanta; traded to Philadelphia in 1990; entered 1992 with 396 HRs.

Jim Murray (b.12/29/1919): sports columnist for LA Times since 1961; 14-time Sportswriter of the Year; won Pulitzer Prize for commentary in 1990.

Stan Musial (b.11/21/1920): Baseball OF-1B; led NL in batting 7 times; 3-time MVP (1943,46,48) with St. Louis; played in 24 All-Star Games; had 3,630 career hits and .331 average.

John Naber (b.1/20/1956): Swimmer; won 4 gold medals and a silver in 1976 Olympics.

Bronko Nagurski (1908-90): Football FB-T; All-America at Minnesota (1929); All-Pro with Chicago Bears (1932-34); charter member of both college and pro halls of fame.

James Naismith (1861-1939): Canadian physical education instructor who invented basketball in 1891 at the YMCA Training School (now Springfield College) in Springfield, Mass.

Joe Namath (b.5/31/1943): Football QB; signed for unheard of $400,000 as rookie with AFL's NY Jets in 1965; 2-time All-AFL (1968-69) and All-NFL (1972); led Jets to Super Bowl title as MVP in '69.

Ilie Nastase (b.7/19/1946): Rumanian tennis player; No.1 in the world twice (1972-73); won U.S. (1972) and French (1973) Opens.

Martina Navratilova (b.10/18/1956): Tennis; No.1 player in the world 7 times (1978-79,82-86); won her record 9th Wimbledon singles title in 1990; has also won 4 U.S. Opens, 3 Australian and 2 French; in all, has won 18 Grand Slam singles titles and 36 Grand Slam doubles titles; had 86-1 match record in singles in 1983; entered 1992 as all-time women's money leader with over $17.6 million and tied with Chris Evert for all-time lead in singles titles won (157).

Earle (Greasy) Neale (1891-1973): Hit .357 for Cincinnati in 1919 World Series; also played with pre-NFL Canton Bulldogs; later coached Philadelphia Eagles to 2 NFL titles (1948-49).

Byron Nelson (b.2/14/1912): Golfer; won Masters and PGA twice, U.S. Open once; also won 11 consecutive tournaments (19 overall) in 1945.

Lindsey Nelson (b.5/25/1919): Radio-TV; all-purpose play-by-play broadcaster for CBS, NBC and others; 4-time Sportscaster of the Year (1959-62); voice of Cotton Bowl for 25 years and NY Mets from 1962-78; given Life Achievement Emmy Award in 1991.

Ernie Nevers (1903-76): Football FB; earned 11 letters in four sports at Stanford; played pro football, baseball and basketball; scored 40 points for Chicago Cardinals in one NFL game (1929).

John Newcombe (b.5/23/1943): Australian tennis player; No.1 player in world 3 times (1967,70-71); won Wimbledon 3 times and U.S. and Australian championships twice each.

Bob Neyland (1892-1962): Football; 3-time coach at Tennessee; had 173-31-12 record in 21 years; won national title in 1951; Vols' stadium named for him; also Army general who won Distinguished Service Cross as supply officer in World War II.

Jack Nicklaus (b.1/21/1940): Golfer; all-time leader in major tournament wins with 20—including 6 Masters, 5 PGAs, 4 U.S. Opens and 3 British Opens; oldest player to win Masters (46 in 1986); PGA Player of Year 5 times (1967,72-73,75-76); named Golfer of Century by PGA in 1988; 6-time Ryder Cup player and 2-time captain (1983,87); won NCAA title (1961) and 2 U.S. Amateurs (1959,61); entered 1992 with 70 PGA Tour wins (2nd to Sam Snead's 81) and 5 Senior Tour wins.

Chuck Noll (b.1/5/1932): Football; coached Pittsburgh to 4 Super Bowl titles (1975-76,79-80); retired after 1991 season ranked 5th on all-time list with 209 wins (including playoffs) in 23 years.

Leo Nomellini (b.6/19/1924): Football DT; played in 174 consecutive regular season games over 14 seasons with San Francisco (1950-63).

Greg Norman (b.2/10/1955): Australian golfer; 2-time leading money winner on PGA Tour (1986,90); entered 1992 with 58 tournament wins world-wide, but only one major—the 1986 British Open; lost Masters by a stroke in both 1986 (to Jack Nicklaus) and '87 (to Larry Mizo in sudden death).

James D. Norris (1906-66): boxing promoter and NHL owner; president of International Boxing Club from 1949 until US Supreme Court ordered its break-up (for anti-trust violations) in 1958; only NHL owner to win Stanley Cups in two cities—Detroit (1936-37,43) and Chicago (1961).

Paavo Nurmi (1897-1973): Finnish runner; won 9 gold medals (6 individual) in 1920,'24 and '28 Olympics; from 1921-31 broke 23 world outdoor records in events ranging from 1,500 to 20,000 meters.

Larry O'Brien (1917-90): Basketball; former U.S. Postmaster General and 3rd NBA commissioner (1975-84); league absorbed 4 ABA teams and created salary cap during his term in office.

Parry O'Brien (b.1/28/1932): Track & field; in 4 consecutive Olympics, won two gold medals, a silver and placed 4th in the shot put (1952-64).

Al Oerter (b.8/19/1936): Track & Field; his 4 discus gold medals in consecutive Olympics from 1956-68 is an unmatched Olympic record.

Sadaharu Oh (b.5/20/1940): Baseball 1B; led Japan League in HRs 15 times; 9-time MVP for Tokyo Giants; hit 868 HRs in 22 years.

Barney Oldfield (1878-1946): Auto racing pioneer; drove cars built by Henry Ford; first man to drive car a mile per minute (1903).

Walter O'Malley (1903-79): Baseball owner; moved Brooklyn Dodgers to Los Angeles after 1957 season; won 4 World Series (1955,59,63,65).

Bobby Orr (b.3/20/1948) Hockey D; 8-time Norris Trophy winner as best defenseman; led NHL in scoring twice and assists 5 times; All-NHL 1st team 8 times; regular season MVP 3 times (1970-72); playoff MVP twice (1970,72) with Boston.

Mel Ott (1909-58): Baseball OF; joined NY Giants at age 16; led NL in HRs 6 times; had 511 HRs and 1,860 RBI in 22 years.

Kristin Otto (b.1966): East German swimmer; 1st woman to win 6 gold medals (4 individual) at one Olympics (1988).

Francis Ouimet (1893-1967): Golfer; won 1913 U.S. Open as 20-year-old amateur playing on Brookline, Mass. course where he used to caddie; won U.S. Amateur twice; 8-time Walker Cup player.

Jesse Owens (1913-80): Track & Field; broke 5 world records at Big 10 Championships (May 25, 1935); a year later, won 4 gold medals (100m, 200m, 4 × 100 relay and long jump) at Berlin Olympics.

Satchel Paige (1906-82): Baseball RHP; pitched 55 career no-hitters in Negro Leagues, entered Major Leagues in 1948 at age 42.

Arnold Palmer (b.9/10/1929): Golfer; winner of 4 Masters, 2 British Opens and 1 U.S. Open; PGA Player of the Year twice (1960,62); first player to earn over $1 million in career (1968).

Jim Palmer (b.10/15/1945): Baseball RHP; 3-time Cy Young Award winner (1973,75-76); won 20 or more games 8 times with Baltimore; 1991 comeback attempt at age 45 scrubbed in spring training.

Bill Parcells (b. 8/22/1941): Football; coached NY Giants to 2 Super Bowl titles (1986,90); won 85 games in 8 seasons for winning percentage of .620.

Bernie Parent (b.4/3/1945): Hockey G; led Philadelphia Flyers to 2 Stanley Cups as playoff MVP (1974,75); 2-time Vezina Trophy winner.

Joe Paterno (b.12/21/1926): Football; has coached Penn State to 2 national titles (1982,86) and 14-7-1 bowl record in 26 years; 4-time Coach of Year (1968,78,82,86); entered 1992 season with 240 career wins (including bowls).

Craig Patrick (b.5/20/1946): Hockey; 3rd generation Patrick to have name inscribed on Stanley Cup; GM of 2-time Cup champion Pittsburgh Penguins (1991-92); also captain of 1969 NCAA champion at Denver, assistant coach/GM of 1980 gold medalwinning U.S. Olympic team; scored 72 goals in 8 NHL seasons and won 69 games in 3 years as coach; grandson of Lester.

Lester Patrick (1883-1960): Pro hockey pioneer as player, coach and manager for 43 years; managed NY Rangers to their only Stanley Cups (1928,33,40).

Floyd Patterson (b.1/4/1935): Boxer; Olympic middleweight champ in 1952; world heavyweight champion (1956-59,60-62); 1st to regain heavyweight crown; pro record 55-8-1 with 40 KOs.

Walter Payton (b.7/25/1954): Football RB; NFL's all-time leading rusher with 16,726 yards; scored 109 TDs; All-Pro 7 times with Chicago; MVP in 1977.

Pelé (b.10/23/1940) Brazilian soccer F; given name—Edson Arantes do Nascimento; led Brazil to 3 World Cup titles (1958,62,70); came to U.S. in 1975 to play for NY Cosmos in NASL; scored 1,281 goals in 22 years.

Roger Penske (b.2/20/1937): Auto racing; national sports car driving champion (1964); established racing team in 1961; co-founder of Championship Auto Racing Teams (CART); Penske Racing entered 1992 with a record 67 IndyCar victories, including 8 Indianapolis 500s and 7 IndyCar points championships.

Willie Pep (b.9/19/1922): Boxer; 2-time world featherweight champion (1942-48,49-50); pro record 230-11-1 with 65 KOs.

Fred Perry (b.5/18/1909): British tennis player; 3-time Wimbledon champ (1934-36); last native to win All-England men's title.

Gaylord Perry (b.9/15/1938): Baseball RHP; won Cy Young Awards in each league; 314 wins and 3,534 strikeouts in 22 years.

Bob Pettit (b.12/12/1932): Basketball F; All-NBA 1st team 10 times (1955-64); 2-time MVP (1956,59) with St. Louis Hawks; first player to score 20,000 points.

Richard Petty (b. 7/2/1937): Auto racer; 7-time winner of Daytona 500; 7-time NASCAR national champ (1964, 67,71-72,74-75,79); first stock car driver to win $1 million in career; entered 1992 as all-time NASCAR leader in races won (200), poles (127) and wins in a single season (27 in 1967); will retire at end of year; son of Lee (54 career wins) and father of Kyle (4 wins entering 1992).

Laffit Pincay, Jr. (b.12/29/1946): Jockey; 5-time Eclipse award winner (1971,73-74,79,85); trails only Bill Shoemaker in career wins; winner of 3 Belmonts and 1 Kentucky Derby (aboard Swale in 1984).

Nelson Piquet (b.8/17/1952): Brazilian auto racer; 3-time Formula One world champion (1981,83,87); entered 1990 won 20 career wins.

Jacques Plante (1929-86): Hockey G; led Montreal to 6 Stanley Cups (1953,56-60); won 7 Vezina Trophies; MVP in 1962; first goalie to regularly wear a mask.

Gary Player (b.11/1/1936): South African golfer; 3-time winner of Masters and British Open; also won 2 PGAs, U.S. Open and 2 U.S. Senior Opens.

Jim Plunkett (b.12/5/1947): Football QB; Heisman Trophy winner in 1970; led Oakland-LA Raiders to Super Bowl wins in 1981 and '84; MVP in '81.

Maurice Podoloff (1890-85): Basketball; engineered merger of Basketball Assn. of America and National Basketball League into NBA in 1949; NBA commissioner (1949-63); league MVP trophy named after him.

Sam Pollack (b.12/15/1925): Hockey GM; managed NHL Montreal Canadiens to 9 Stanley Cups in 14 years (1965-78).

Fritz Pollard (1894-1986): Football; 1st black All-America RB (1916 at Brown); 1st black to play in Rose Bowl; 7-year NFL pro (1920-26); 1st black NFL coach, at Milwaukee and Hammond, Ind.

Denis Potvin (b.10/29/1953): Hockey D; won Norris Trophy 3 times (1976,78-79); 5-time All-NHL 1st-team; led NY Islanders to 4 Stanley Cups.

Mike Powell (b. 11/10/1963): Track and Field; broke Bob Beamon's 23-year-old long jump world record by 2 inches with leap of 29-ft., 4-1/2 in., on Aug. 30, 1991, at the World Championships in Tokyo; Sullivan Award winner (1991); won long jump silver medals in 1988 and '92 Olympics.

Alain Prost (b.2/24/1955): French auto racer; 3-time Formula One world champion (1985-86,89), entered 1991 with 44 career wins.

Kirby Puckett (b.3/14/1961): Baseball OF; led Minnesota to 2 World Series titles (1987,'91); entered 1992 season with a batting title (1989) and .320 career average.

C.C.Pyle (1884-1939): Promoter; known as "Cash and Carry"; hyped Red Grange's pro football debut by arranging 1925 barnstorming tour with Chicago Bears; had Grange bolt NFL for new AFL in 1926 (AFL folded in '27); also staged 2 Transcontinental Races (1928-29), known as "Bunion Derbies."

Willis Reed (b.6/25/1942): Basketball C; led NY Knicks to NBA titles in 1970 and '73, playoff MVP both years; regular season MVP 1970.

Mary Lou Retton (b.1/24/1968): Gymnast; won gold medal in women's All-Around at the 1984 Olympics, also won 2 silvers and 2 bronzes.

Willy T.Ribbs (b.1/3/1956): Auto racer; successful IMSA driver; 1st black to race in Indianapolis 500 (1991).

Grantland Rice (1880-54): first celebrated American sportswriter; chronicled the Golden Age of Sport in 1920s; immortalized Notre Dame's "Four Horsemen."

Jerry Rice (b.10/13/1962): Football WR; 5-time All-Pro, regular season MVP in 1987 and Super Bowl MVP in 1989 with San Francisco; entered 1992 season with 526 catches and 93 TD receptions in only 7 seasons.

Henri Richard (b. 2/29/1936): Hockey C; leap year baby, who played on more Stanley Cup championship teams (11) than anybody else; at 5-foot-7, known as the "Pocket Rocket"; brother of Maurice.

Maurice Richard (b.8/4/1921): Hockey RW; the "Rocket"; 8-time NHL 1st team All-Star; MVP in 1947; 1st to score 50 goals in one season (1945); 544 career goals; played on 8 Stanley Cup winners in Montreal.

Bob Richards (b.2/2/1926): Track & Field; only 2-time Olympic gold medalist in pole vault (1952,56).

Tex Rickard (1870-1929): Promoter who handled boxing's first $1 million gate (Dempsey vs Carpentier in 1921); built Madison Square Garden in 1925.

Eddie Rickenbacher (1890-1973): Mechanic and auto racer; became America's top flying ace (22 kills) in World War I; owned Indianapolis Speedway (1927-45) and ran Eastern Air Lines (1938-59).

Branch Rickey (1881-1965): In baseball 59 years as player, manager and GM; made Jackie Robinson 1st black player in Major Leagues (1947).

Bobby Riggs (b.2/25/1918): Tennis; won Wimbledon once (1939) and U.S. title twice (1939,41) before turning pro in 1941; beat Margaret Court Smith but lost to Billie Jean King in 1973 exhibition matches.

Pat Riley (b.3/20/1945): Basketball; coached LA Lakers to 4 of their 5 NBA titles in 1980s (1982,85,87-88); quit after 1989-90 season, then returned to coach NY Knicks in 1991; entered 1992-93 season as all-time leader in playoff wins (108) and overall winning percentage (.713).

Cal Ripken, Jr. (b.8/24/1961): Baseball SS; 2-time AL MVP (1983,91) for Baltimore; AL Rookie of Year (1982); AL starting SS in All-Star Game since 1984; entered 1992 season with 259 HRs in 11 seasons and with consecutive game playing streak at 1,573 (it began May 30, 1982); the streak is 2nd only to Gehrig's 2,130.

Joe Robbie (1916-90): Football; original owner of Miami Dolphins (1965-90); won 2 Super Bowls (1972-73); built $115 Robbie Stadium with private funds in 1987.

Oscar Robertson (b.11/24/1938): Basketball G; 3-time college Player of Year (1958-60) at Cincinnati; led 1960 U.S. Olympic team to gold medal; NBA Rookie of Year (1961); 9-time All-NBA 1st team; MVP in 1964 with Cincinnati Royals; NBA champion in 1971 with Milwaukee Bucks; 2nd in career assists with 9,887.

Paul Robeson (1898-1976): Black 4-sport star and 2-time football All-America (1917-18) at Rutgers; 3-year NFL pro; also scholar, lawyer, singer, actor and political activist.

Brooks Robinson (b.5/18/1937): Baseball 3B; led AL in fielding 12 times from 1960-72 with Baltimore; regular season MVP in 1964; World Series MVP in 1970.

Eddie Robinson (b.2/13/1919): Football; head coach at Div. I-AA Grambling State for 49 years; winningest coach in college history; has led Tigers to 8 national black college titles; entered 1992 regular season (his 50th) with 371 career wins.

Frank Robinson (b.8/31/1935): Baseball OF; won MVP in NL (1961) and AL (1966); Triple Crown winner and World Series MVP in 1966 with Baltimore; 1st black manager in Major Leagues with Cleveland in 1975; also managed in SF and Baltimore.

Jackie Robinson (1919-72): Baseball 2B; 4-sport athlete at UCLA; 1st black player in Majors with Brooklyn in 1947; Rookie of the Year in 1947; NL MVP in 1949.

Sugar Ray Robinson (1921-89): Boxer; world welterweight champion (1946-51); 5-time middleweight champ; retired at age 45 after 25 years in the ring; pro record 174-19-6 with 109 KOs.

Knute Rockne (1888-1931): Football; coached Notre Dame to 3 consensus national titles (1924,29,30), career record of 105-12-5 in 13 years; killed in plane crash.

Bill Rodgers (b.12/23/1947): Track & Field; won Boston and New York City marathons 4 times each from 1975-80.

Irina Rodnina (b.1953): Soviet figure skater; won 10 world championships and 3 Olympic gold medals in pairs competiton from 1971-80.

Art Rooney (1901-1988): Sportsman, race track legend and pro football pioneer; bought Pittsburgh Steelers franchise in 1933 for $2,500; finally won NFL championship with 1st of 4 Super Bowl titles in 1974 season.

Theodore Roosevelt (1838-1919): 26th President of the U.S.; physical fitness buff who boxed as undergraduate at Harvard; credited with presidential assist in forming of Intercollegiate Athletic Assn. (now NCAA) in 1905-06.

Mauri Rose (1906-81): Auto racer; 3-time winner of Indy 500 (1941,47-48).

Murray Rose (b.1/6/1939): Australian swimmer; won 3 gold medals at 1956 Olympics; added a gold, silver and bronze in 1960.

Pete Rose (b.4/14/1941): Baseball OF-Inf.; all-time hits leader with 4,256; led NL in batting 3 times; regular season MVP in 1973; World Series MVP in 1975; had 44-game hitting streak in '78; managed Cincinnati (1984- 89); banned for life in '89 for betting on baseball and associating with known gamblers and drug dealers; convicted of tax evasion in 1990 and sentenced to 5 months in prison; released Jan. 7, 1991.

Ken Rosewall (b.11/2/1934): Tennis; won French and Australian singles titles at age 18; U.S. champ twice, but never won Wimbledon.

Mark Roth (b.4/10/1951): Bowler; 4-time PBA Player of the Year (1977-79,84); entered 1991 season with 33 tournament wins, including 1984 U.S. Open.

Pete Rozelle (b.3/1/1926): Football; NFL Commissioner from 1960-89; presided over growth of league from 12 to 28 teams, merger with AFL, creation of Super Bowl and advent of huge TV rights fees.

Wilma Rudolph (b.6/23/1940): Track & Field; won 3 gold medals (100m,200m and 4x400m relay) at 1960 Olympics.

Damon Runyon (1880-1946): Kansas native who gained fame as New York journalist, sports columnist and short-story writer; best known for 1932 story collection, "Guys and Dolls."

Adolph Rupp (1901-77) Basketball; all-time college wins leader with 875; coached Kentucky to 4 NCAA titles (1948-49,51,58).

Bill Russell (b.2/12/1934): Basketball C; won titles in college, Olympics and pros; 5-time NBA MVP; led Boston to 11 titles, also became first big league black head coach in 1966.

Babe Ruth (1895-1948): Baseball LHP-OF; 2-time 20-game winner with Boston Red Sox (1916-17); had a 94-46 regular season record with a 2.28 ERA, while he was 3-0 in the World Series with an ERA of 0.87; sold to NY Yankees for $100,000 in 1920; AL MVP in 1923; led AL in slugging average 13 times, HRs 12 times, RBI 6 times and batting once (.378 in 1924); hit 60 HRs in 1927 and 50 or more 3 other times; ended career with Boston Braves in 1935 with 714 HRs, 2,211 RBI and a batting average of .342; remains all-time leader in times walked (2,056) and slugging average (.692).

Johnny Rutherford (b.3/12/1938): Auto racer; 3-time winner of Indy 500 (1974,76,80); CART national champion in 1980.

Nolan Ryan (b.1/31/1947): Baseball RHP; author of record 7 no-hitters against Kansas City A's and Detroit (1973), Minnesota (1974), Baltimore (1975), LA Dodgers (1981), Oakland A's (1990) and Toronto (1991 at age 44); 2-time 20-game winner (1973-74); 2-time NL leader in ERA (1981,87); has led AL in strikeouts 9 times and NL twice; entered 1992 season with 314 wins and an all-time record 5,511 strikeouts.

Toni Sailer (b.11/17/1935); Austrian skier; 1st to win 3 alpine gold medals in Winter Olympics—taking downhill, slalom and giant slalom events in 1956.

Juan Antonio Samaranch (b.7/17/1920): of Spain, President of International Olympic Committee since 1980.

Joan Benoit Samuelson (b.5/16/1957): Track & Field; has won Boston marathon twice (1979,83); winner of first women's Olympic marathon in 1984.

Earl Sande (1889-1968): Jockey; rode Gallant Fox to Triple Crown in 1930; won 5 Belmonts and 3 Kentucky Derbys.

Barry Sanders (b.7/16/1968): Football RB; won 1988 Heisman Trophy as junior at Oklahoma St.; all-time NCAA single season leader in rushing (2,628 yards), scoring (234 points) and TDs (39); 2-time NFC rushing leader with Detroit (1989-90); NFC Rookie of Year (1988); NFL Player of Year (1991).

Deion Sanders (b.8/9/1967): Baseball OF and Football DB; 2-time consensus All-America at Florida St. in football (1987, 88); NFL All-Pro with Atlanta Falcons (1991); Opening Day CF for NL Atlanta Braves (1992).

Abe Saperstein (1902-66): Basketball; founded all-black, Harlem Globetrotters barnstorming team in 1927; coached sharpshooting comedians to 1940 world pro title in Chicago and established troop as game's foremost goodwill ambassadors; also served as 1st commissioner of American Basketball League (1961-62).

Gene Sarazen (b.2/27/1902): Golfer; won Masters, British Open, 2 U.S. Opens and 3 PGA titles between 1922-35; invented sand wedge in 1930.

Glen Sather (b.9/2/1943): Hockey; GM-coach of 4 Stanley Cup winners in Edmonton (1984-85,87-88) and GM-only for another in 1990.

Terry Sawchuk (1929-1970): Hockey G; recorded 103 shutouts in 21 NHL seasons; 4-time Vezina Trophy winner; played on 4 Stanley Cup winners at Detroit and Toronto.

Gale Sayers (b.5/30/1943): Football HB; 2-time All-America at Kansas; NFL Rookie of Year (1965) and 5-time All-Pro with Chicago; scored then-record 22 TDs in rookie year.

Bo Schembechler (b.9/1/1929): Football; retired in 1989 as 5th winningest Div.I college coach ever; 234-65-8 record in 27 years; coached Michigan from 1969-89; 13 Rose Bowls but only 2 wins; president of AL Detroit Tigers from 1990-92.

Vitaly Scherbo (b.1973): Russian gymnast; winner of unprecedented 6 gymnastics' gold medals, including men's All-Around, for Unified Team in 1992 Olympics.

Mike Schmidt (b.9/27/1949): Baseball 3B; led NL in HRs 8 times; 3-time MVP (1980,81,86) with Phila.; 548 career HRs; 10 gold gloves.

Don Schollander (b.4/30/1946): Swimming; won 4 gold medals at 1964 Olympics, plus one gold and one silver in 1968.

Dick Schultz (b.9/5/1929): executive director of NCAA since 1988; head coach of baseball (1964-70) and basketball (1970-74) at Iowa; athletic director at Cornell (1976-81) and Virginia (1981-87).

Bob Seagren (b.10/17/1946): Track & Field; won gold medal in pole vault at 1968 Olympics; broke world outdoor record 5 times.

Tom Seaver (b.11/17/1944): Baseball RHP; won 3 Cy Young Awards (1969,73,75); had 311 wins and 3,640 strikeouts over 20 years.

Peter Seitz (b.1905): Baseball arbitrator; ruled in 1975 (Dec.23) that players who perform for one season without a signed contract can become free agents; decision ushered in big money era for players.

Monica Seles (b.12/2/1973): Yugoslavian tennis player; No.1 in the world in 1991 after winning Australian, French and U.S. Opens (didn't play Wimbledon); youngest to win Grand Slam title this century when she won French in 1990 at age 16; entered 1992 with 20 singles titles in just 4 years; in '92, repeated Australian-French-U.S. Open triple, but lost Wimbledon final to Graf.

Frank Selke (1893-1985): Hockey; GM of 6 Stanley Cup champions in Montreal (1953,56-60).

Wilbur Shaw (1902-54): Auto racer; 3-time winner and 3-time runner-up of Indy 500 from 1933-1940.

Fred Shero (1925-90): Hockey; former NY Rangers defenseman who led Philadelphia Flyers to consecutive Stanley Cup titles (1974-75); also took Rangers to Cup final in 1979; ranks 9th on all-time NHL list with 451 wins (including playoffs).

Bill Shoemaker (b. 8/19/1931): Jockey; all-time career wins leader with 8,833; 3-time Eclipse Award winner as Jockey (1981) and special award recipient (1976,81); won Belmont 5 times, Kentucky Derby 4 times and Preakness twice; oldest jockey to win Kentucky Derby (age 54, aboard Ferdinand in 1986); retired in 1990 to become trainer; paralyzed in 1991 auto accident but continues to train horses.

Eddie Shore (1902-85): Hockey D; only NHL defenseman (including Bobby Orr) to win MVP trophy 4 times (1933,35- 36,38), all with Boston.

Frank Shorter (b.10/31/1947): Track & Field; won gold medal in marathon at 1972 Olympics, 1st U.S. marathoner to win in 64 years.

Don Shula (b.1/4/1930): Football; one of only two NFL coaches with 300 wins (George Halas is the other); has taken 6 teams to Super Bowls and won twice with Miami (1973-74); 4-time Coach of Year, twice with Baltimore (1964,68) and twice with Miami (1970-71); entered 1992 regular season with 306 career wins (including playoffs) and a winning percentage of .676; father of Cincinnati head coach David.

Al Simmons (1902-56): Baseball OF; led AL in batting twice (1930-31) and knocked in 100 runs or more 11 straight years (1924-34).

O.J.Simpson (b.7/9/1947): Football RB; won Heisman Trophy in 1968 at USC; ran for 2,003 yards in NFL in 1973; All-Pro 5 times; MVP in 1973; rushed for 11,236 career yards.

Harry Sinden (b.9/14/1932): Hockey; in 1970, coached Boston to 1st Stanley Cup title since 1941; came out of retirement in 1972 to coach victorious Team Canada in landmark, 8-game summit with USSR; Boston GM since 1972.

George Sisler (1893-73): Baseball 1B; hit over .400 twice (1920,22); 257 hits in 1920 still a major league record.

Mary Decker Slaney (b.8/4/1958): US middle distance runner; has held 7 separate American track & field records from the 800 to 10,000 meters; won both 1,500 and 3,000 meters at 1983 World Championships in Helsinki, but no Olympic medals.

Raisa Smetanina (b.1953): Russian Nordic skiier; all-time Winter Olympics medalist with 10 cross-country medals (4 gold, 5 silver and a bronze) in 5 appearances (1976,80,84,88,92) for USSR and Unified Team.

Billy Smith (b.12/12/1950): Hockey G; led NY Islanders to 4 consecutive Stanley Cups (1979-83); won Vezina Trophy in 1982 and was Stanley Cup MVP in 1983.

Dean Smith (b.2/28/1931): Basketball; has coached North Carolina to 22 NCAA tournaments in 31 years, reaching Final Four 8 times and winning championship in 1982; has also led Tar Heels to 12 ACC tourney titles; coached U.S. Olympic team to gold medal in 1976; entered 1992-93 season ranked 5th on all-time victory list with 740.

John Smith (b.8/9/1965): Wrestler; 2-time NCAA champion for Oklahoma State at 134 lbs.(1987-88) and Most Outstanding Wrestler of '88 championships; 3-time world champion; 2-time gold medal winner at 1988 and '92 Olympics at 137 lbs; only wrestler ever to win Sullivan Award (1990).

Ozzie Smith (b.12/26/1954): Baseball SS; entered 1992 with 12 straight gold gloves (1980-91); 9-time starter for NL in All-Star Game.

Walter (Red) Smith (1905-82): Sportswriter for newspapers in Philadelphia and New York from 1936-82; won Pulitzer Prize for commentary in 1976.

Conn Smythe (1895-1980): Hockey pioneer; built Maple Leaf Gardens in 1931; managed Toronto to 7 Stanley Cups before retiring in 1961.

Sam Snead (b.5/27/1912): Golfer; won both Masters and PGA 3 times, British Open once; runner-up in U.S. Open 4 times but never won; PGA Player of Year in 1949; PGA career victory leader with 84.

Peter Snell (b.12/17/1939): New Zealander who won gold medal in 800m at 1960 Olympics, then won both the 800m and 1,500m at 1964 Games.

Javier Sotomayor (b.10/13/1967): Cuban high jumper; first man to clear 8 feet (8-0) on July 29, 1989; won gold medal at 1992 Olympics with jump of only 7-ft, 8-in.

Warren Spahn (b.4/23/1921): Baseball LHP; led NL in wins 8 times; won 20 or more games 13 times; Cy Young winner in 1957; most career wins (363) by a left-hander.

Tris Speaker (1888-1958): Baseball OF; all-time leader in outfield assists (449) and doubles (793); had .344 career batting average and 3,515 hits.

J.G. Taylor Spink (1888-1962): Publisher of *The Sporting News* from 1914-62; Baseball Writers' Assn. annual meritorious service award named after him.

Mark Spitz (b.2/10/1950): set 23 world and 35 U.S. records; won all-time record 7 gold medals (4 individual, 3 relay) in 1972 Olympics; also won 4 medals (2 gold, a silver and a bronze) in 1968 Games for a total of 11; comeback attempt at age 41 foundered in 1991.

Amos Alonzo Stagg (1862-1965): Football innovator; coached at U.of Chicago for 41 seasons and College of the Pacific for 14 more; won 314 games; elected to both college football and basketball halls of fame.

Willie Stargell (b.3/6/1940): Baseball OF-1B; led NL in home runs twice (1971,73); 475 career HRs; regular season and World Series MVP in 1979.

Bart Starr (b.1/9/1934): Football QB; led Green Bay to 5 NFL titles and 2 Super Bowl wins from 1961-67; reg.season MVP in 1966; 2-time Super Bowl MVP (1967,68).

Roger Staubach (b.2/5/1942): Football QB; Heisman Trophy winner as Navy junior in 1963; led Dallas to 2 Super Bowl titles (1972,78) and was Super Bowl MVP in 1972; 5-time leading passer in NFC (1971,73,77-79); ranks 5th in all-time passing efficiency (83.4).

George Steinbrenner (b.7/4/1930): principal owner of NY Yankees since 1973; teams have won 4 pennants and 2 World Series (1977-78); has changed managers 18 times, pitching coaches 15 times and GMs 10 times in 20 years; ordered by baseball commissioner Fay Vincent on July 30, 1990, to surrender control of club for dealings with small-time gambler Howard Spira; will be reinstated on Mar. 1, 1993; also serves as one of 3 VPs of U.S. Olympic Committee.

Casey Stengel (1890-1975): Baseball; player for 14 years and manager for 25; outfielder and lifetime .284 hitter with 5 clubs (1912-25); guided NY Yankees to 10 AL pennants and 7 World Series titles from 1949-60; 1st NY Mets skipper from 1962-65.

Ingemar Stenmark (b.3/18/1956): Swedish alpine skier; 3-time World Cup overall champ (1976-78); 86 World Cup wins in 16 years; won 2 gold medals at 1980 Olympics.

Woody Stephens (b.9/1/1913): Horse racing; trainer who saddled an unprecedented 5 straight winners in Belmont Stakes (1982-86); also had two Kentucky Derby winners (1974,84); trained 1982 Horse of Year Conquistador Cielo.

David Stern (b.9/22/1942): Basketball; marketing expert and NBA commissioner since 1984, has presided over growth of league from 23 to 27 teams, received unprecedented 5-year, $27.5 million contract extension in 1990.

Teofilo Stevenson (b.1951): Cuban boxer; won 3 consecutive gold medals as Olympic heavyweight (1972,76,80); did not turn pro.

Jackie Stewart (b.6/11/1939): Auto racer; won 27 Formula One races and 3 world driving titles from 1965-73.

Curtis Strange (b.1/30/1955): Golfer; won consecutive U.S. Open titles (1988-89); 3-time leading money winner on PGA Tour (1985,87-88); first PGA player to win $1 million in one year (1988).

Louise Suggs (b.9/7/1923): Golfer; won 11 Majors and 50 LPGA events overall from 1949-62.

John L. Sullivan (1858-1918): Boxer; world heavyweight champion (1882-92); last of bare-knuckle champions.

Barry Switzer (b.10/5/1937): Football; coached Oklahoma to 3 national titles (1974-75,85); 157 career wins in 16 years.

Paul Tagliabue (b.11/24/1940): Football; NFL attorney who was elected league's 4th commissioner in 1989.

Anatoli Tarasov (b.1918): Hockey; coached USSR to 9 straight world championships and 3 Olympic gold medals (1964,68,72).

Jerry Tarkanian (b.8/30/1930): Basketball; all-time winningest college coach with .837 winning percentage; had record 625-122 over 24 years at Long Beach State and UNLV; led UNLV to 4 Final Fours and one national championship (1990); fought 16-year battle with NCAA over purity of UNLV program; quit as coach after going 26-2 in 1991-92; named to coach San Antonio Spurs of NBA in 1992.

Fran Tarkenton (b.2/3/1940): Football QB; 2-time All-Pro (1973,75); Player of the Year (1975); threw for 47,003 yards and 342 TDs (both NFL records) in 18 seasons with Minnesota and NY Giants.

Chuck Taylor (1901-69): Converse traveling salesman whose name came to grace the classic, high-top canvas basketball sneakers known as "Chucks"; over 500 million pairs have been sold since 1917; he also ran clinics worldwide and edited Converse Basketball Yearbook from 1922-68.

Lawrence Taylor (b.2/4/1959): Football LB; All-America at North Carolina (1980); only defensive player in NFL history to be consensus Player of Year (1986); led NY Giants to NFL titles in Super Bowls XXI and XXV; has played in a record 10 Pro Bowls (1981-90); entered 1992 season as all-time NFL sacks leader (121½).

Gustave Thoeni (b.2/28/1951): Italian alpine skier; 4-time World Cup overall champion (1971-73,75); won Giant Slalom at 1972 Olympics.

Daley Thompson (b.7/30/1958): British track & field; won consecutive gold medals in decathlon at 1980 and '84 Olympics.

Bobby Thomson (b.10/25/1923); Baseball OF; career .270 hitter who won the 1951 NL pennant for the NY Giants with a 1-out, 3-run HR in the bottom of the 9th inning of Game 3 of a best-of-3 playoff with Brooklyn; the pitcher was Ralph Branca, the count was 1-1 and the Dodgers were ahead 4-2; the Giants had trailed Brooklyn by 13½ games on Aug. 11th.

Jim Thorpe (1888-1953): 2-time All-America in football; won both pentathlon and decathlon at 1912 Olympics; played major league baseball (1913-19) and pro football (1920- 26,28); chosen "Athlete of the Half Century" by AP in 1950.

Bill Tilden (1893-1953): Tennis; won 7 U.S. and 3 Wimbledon titles in 1920s; led U.S. to 7 straight Davis Cup victories (1920-26).

Tinker to Evers to Chance—Chicago Cubs double play combination from 1903-08; immortalized in poem by New York sportswriter Franklin P. Adams: SS **Joe Tinker** (1880-1948), 2B **Johnny Evers** (1883-1947) and 1B **Frank Chance** (1877-1924); all 3 managed the Cubs and made the Hall of Fame.

Y.A.Tittle (b.10/24/1926): Football QB; played 17 years in AFC and NFL; All-Pro 4 times; league MVP with San Francisco (1957) and NY Giants (1962); passed for 28,339 career yards.

Pie Traynor (1899-1972): Baseball 3B; hit .300 or better 10 times; led Pittsburgh to World Series title in 1925.

Vladislav Tretiak (b.4/25/1952): Hockey G; led USSR to Olympic gold medals in 1972 and '76; starred for Soviets against Team Canada in 1972, and again in 2 Canada Cups (1976,81).

Lee Trevino (b.12/1/1939): Golfer; 2-time winner of 3 Majors—U.S. Open (1968,71), British Open (1971-72) and PGA (1974,84); joined Seniors Tour in late 1990; won 7 titles, including the U.S. Senior Open, and over $1 million in 1st full year on tour in 1991.

Bryan Trottier (b.7/17/1956): Hockey C; led NY Islanders to 4 straight Stanley Cups (1980-83); Rookie of Year (1976); scoring champion (134 points) and regular season MVP in 1979; playoff MVP (1980); added 5th and 6th Cups with Pittsburgh in 1991 and '92.

Gene Tunney (b.1897-78): Boxer; world heavyweight champion (1926-28); defeated Jack Dempsey twice on points; pro record 65-2-1 with 43 KOs.

Ted Turner (b.11/19/1938): Sportsman and TV mogul, skippered Courageous to America's Cup win in 1977; owner of both Atlanta Braves and Hawks; owner of superstation WTBS, and cable stations CNN and TNT; founder of Goodwill Games; 1991 *Time* Man of Year.

Mike Tyson (b.6/30/1965): Boxer; youngest (age 19) to win heavyweight title (WBC in 1986); undisputed champ from 1987 until upset loss to 50-1 shot Buster Douglas on Feb. 10, 1990, in Tokyo; pro record of 41-1-0 with 36 KOs through 1991; found guilty on Feb. 10, 1992, of raping 18-year-old Miss Black America contestant Desiree Washington in Indianapolis on July 19, 1991; sentenced to 6 years in prison.

Wyomia Tyus (b.8/29/1945): Track & Field; 1st woman to win consecutive Olympic gold medals in 100m (1964-68).

Peter Ueberroth (b.9/2/1937): Organizer of 1984 Summer Olympics in LA; 1984 *Time* Man of the Year; baseball commissioner from 1984-89; named to head *Rebuild Los Angeles* after 1992 riots.

Johnny Unitas (b.5/7/1933): Football QB; led Baltimore Colts to 2 NFL titles (1958-59) and a Super Bowl win (1971); All-Pro 5 times; 3-time MVP (1959,64,67); passed for 40,239 career yards and 290 TDs.

Al Unser, Jr. (b.4/19/1962): Auto racer; won unprecedented four straight races and CART title in 1990; entered 1992 with 17 IndyCar victories; won 1992 Indy 500, giving Unser family 8 overall titles at the Brickyard; son of Al and nephew of Bobby.

Al Unser, Sr. (b.5/29/1939): Auto racer; 3-time USAC/CART national champion (1970,83,85); 4-time winner of Indy 500 (1970-71,78,87); entered 1992 ranked 3rd on all-time IndyCar list with 39 wins; younger brother of Bobby and father of Little Al.

Bobby Unser (b.2/20/1934): Auto racer; 2-time USAC/CART national champion (1968,74); 3-time winner of Indy 500 (1968,75,81); retired after 1981 season; ranks 4th on all-time IndyCar list with 35 wins.

Norm Van Brocklin (1926-83): Football QB; led NFL in passing 3 times and punting twice; led LA Rams (1951) and Philadelphia (1960) to NFL titles; MVP in 1960.

Steve Van Buren (b.12/28/1920): Football HB; led Philadelphia to 2 NFL titles (1948-49); league's top rusher 4 times.

Johnny Vander Meer (b.11/2/1914): Baseball LHP; only major leaguer to pitch consecutive no-hitters (June 11 & 15, 1938).

Harold S. Vanderbilt (1884-70): Sportsman; successfully defended America's Cup 3 times (1930, 34,37); also invented contract bridge in 1926.

Glenna Collett Vare (1903-89): Golfer; won record 6 U.S. Women's Amateur titles from 1922-35; known as "the female Bobby Jones."

Andy Varipapa (1891-1984): Bowler; trick-shot artist; won consecutive All-Star match game titles (1947-48) at age 53.

Bill Veeck (1914-86): Maverick baseball executive; owned American League teams in Cleveland, St.Louis and Chicago from 1946-80; introduced ballpark giveaways, exploding scoreboards, and midget Eddie Gaedel; won World Series with Indians (1948) and pennant with White Sox (1959).

Fay Vincent (b.5/29/1938): Baseball; became 8th commissioner after death of A.Bartlett Giamatti in 1989; presided over World Series earthquake, owners' lockout and banishment of NY Yankees' owner George Steinbrenner in his first year on the job; in 1991, ordered NL to give AL $42 million of its $190 million expansion money; in 1992, reinstated Steinbrenner (as of Mar. 1, 1993) and ordered Chicago and St.Louis to move to NL West, prompting Cubs' lawsuit; resigned on Sept. 7, 1992, four days after 18-9 "no confidence" vote by owners.

Lasse Viren (b.7/22/1949): Finnish runner; won gold medals in 5,000m and 10,000m at both the 1972 and '76 Olympics.

Honus Wagner (1874-1955): Baseball SS; hit .300 for 17 consecutive seasons (1897-1913) with Pittsburgh; led NL in batting 8 times; ended career with 3,430 career hits, a .329 average and 720 stolen bases.

Grete Waitz (b.10/1/1953): Norwegian runner; 9-time winner of New York City Marathon from 1978-88.

Doak Walker (b.1/1/1927): Football HB; won Heisman Trophy as SMU junior in 1948; led Detroit to 2 NFL titles (1952-53); All-Pro 4 times in 6 years.

Herschel Walker (b.3/3/1962): Football RB; led Georgia to national title as freshman in 1980; won Heisman as junior in 1982 then jumped to USFL in '83; signed by Dallas of NFL after USFL folded; led NFL in rushing in 1988; traded by Cowboys to Minnesota in 1989 for 5 players and 6 draft picks; released by Vikings in 1992 and signed by Philadelphia.

Bill Walsh (b.11/30/1931): Football; coached San Francisco to 3 Super Bowl titles (1982,85,89); retired after 1988 season with 102 wins in 10 seasons; entered autumn of 1992 in 2nd term as coach at Stanford where he was from 1977-78.

Bill Walton (b.11/5/1950): Basketball C; 3-time college Player of Year (1972-74); led UCLA to 2 national titles (1972-73); led Portland to NBA title as MVP in 1977, regular season MVP in 1978.

Darrell Waltrip (b.2/5/1947): Auto racer; 3-time NASCAR national champion (1981-82,85); won 1989 Daytona 500 after 17 tries; entered 1992 ranked 5th on the all-time NASCAR list with 81 wins.

Paul Waner (1903-65): Baseball OF; led NL in batting 3 times; MVP in 1927 with Pittsburgh; had 3,152 hits and .333 career average; brother of Lloyd.

Arch Ward (1896-55): Promoter and sports editor of Chicago Tribune from 1930-55; founder of baseball All-Star Game (1933), Chicago College All-Star Football Game (1934) and the All-America Football Conference (1946-49).

Glenn (Pop) Warner (1871-1954): Football innovator; coached at 7 colleges over 49 years; 313 career wins; produced 47 All-Americas, including Jim Thorpe and Ernie Nevers.

Tom Watson (b.9/4/1949): Golfer; 6-time PGA player of the Year (1977-80,82,84); has won 5 British Opens, 2 Masters and a U.S. Open; 4-time Ryder Cup member who will serve as captain of 1993 team; entered 1992 with 32 tour wins.

Dick Weber (b.12/23/1929): Bowler; 3-time PBA Bowler of the Year (1961,63,65); won 30 PBA titles in 4 decades.

Johnny Weismuller (1904-84): Swimmer; won 3 gold medals at 1924 Olympics and 2 more at 1928 Games; became Hollywood's most famous Tarzan.

Jerry West (b.5/28/1938): Basketball G; 2-time All-America and NCAA tourney MVP (1959) at West Virginia; led 1960 U.S. Olympic team to gold medal; 10-time All-NBA 1st-team; NBA finals MVP (1969); led LA Lakers to NBA title once as player (1972) and 5 times as GM in 1980s.

Bill White (b./18/1934): Baseball; NL president since 1989; highest ranking black executive in sports; as 1st baseman, won 7 gold gloves and hit .286 with 202 HRs.

Byron (Whizzer) White (b.6/8/1918): Football; All-America HB at Colorado (1935-37); signed with Pittsburgh in 1938 for the then largest contract in pro history ($15,800); took Rhodes scholarship in 1939; returned to NFL in 1940 to lead league in rushing and retired in 1941; named to US Supreme Court in 1962.

Kathy Whitworth (b.9/27/1939): Golf; 7-time LPGA Player of the Year (1966-69,71-73); won 6 Majors; 88 tour wins most on LPGA or PGA tour.

Hazel Hotchkiss Wightman (1886-1974): Tennis; won 16 U.S. national titles; 4-time U.S. Women's champion (1909-11,19); donor of Wightman Cup.

Mats Wilander (b.8/22/1964): Swedish tennis player; 1988 Player of the Year; has won Australian and French Opens 3 times each and U.S. Open in 1988.

Hoyt Wilhelm (b.7/26/1923): Baseball RHP; 1st relief pitcher inducted into Hall of Fame (1985); knuckleballer and all-time leader in games pitched (1,070), games finished (651) and games won in relief (124); had career ERA of 2.52 and 227 saves; threw no-hitter vs NY Yankees (1958); also hit one and only HR of career in first major league at bat (1952).

Bud Wilkinson (b.4/23/1916): Football; played on 1936 national championship team at Minnesota; coached Oklahoma to 3 national titles (1950,55,56); won 4 Orange and 2 Sugar Bowls; teams had winning streaks of 47 (1953-57) and 31 (1948-50); retired after 1963 season with 145-29-4 record in 17 years; also coached St.Louis of NFL to 9-20 record in 1978-79.

Ted Williams (b.8/30/1918): Baseball OF; led AL in batting 6 times; won Triple Crown twice (1942,47); MVP twice (1946,49); last player to hit .400 (1941); hit .344 with 521 HRs in 19 years.

Dave Winfield (b.10/3/1951): Baseball OF; selected in 4 major sports league drafts in 1973—NFL, NBA, ABA and MLB; chose baseball and has played in 12 All-Star Games over 19-year career; entered 1992 season as leading active player in HRs (406) and RBI (1,602).

Katarina Witt (b.12/3/1965): East German figure skater; 4-time world champion (1984-85,87-88); won consecutive Olympic gold medals (1984,88).

John Wooden (b.10/14/1910): Basketball; college Player of Year at Purdue in 1932; coached UCLA to 10 national titles (1964-65,67-73,75); only member of Basketball Hall of Fame inducted as player and coach.

Mickey Wright (b.2/14/1935): Golfer; won 3 of 4 Majors (LPGA, U.S. Open, Titleholders) in 1961; 4-time winner of both U.S. Open and LPGA titles; 82 career wins including 13 Majors.

Early Wynn (b.1/6/1920): Baseball RHP; won 20 games 5 times; Cy Young winner in 1959; 300 career wins in 23 years.

Cale Yarborough (b.3/20/1939): Auto racer; 3-time NASCAR national champion (1976-78); 4-time winner of Daytona 500 (1968,77,83-84); ranks 4th on NASCAR all-time list with 83 wins.

Carl Yastrzemski (b.8/22/1939): Baseball OF; led AL in batting 3 times; won Triple Crown and MVP in 1967; had 3,419 hits and 452 HRs in 23 years with Boston.

Cy Young (1867-1955): Baseball RHP; all-time leader in wins (511), losses (315), complete games (750) and innings pitched (7,355); had career 2.63 ERA in 22 years (1890-1911); 30-game winner 5 times and 20 game winner 10 other times; threw 3 no-hitters and perfect game (1904); AL and NL pitching awards named after him.

Dick Young (1917-87): confrontational sportswriter for 44 years with New York tabloids; as baseball beat writer and columnist, he spearheaded change in daily coverage from flowery prose to hard-nosed reporting.

Sheila Young (b.10/14/1950): Speed skater-cyclist; 1st U.S. athlete to win 3 medals at Winter Olympics (1976); won speed skating overall and sprint cycling world titles in 1976.

Robin Yount (b.9/16/1955): Baseball SS-OF; 2-time AL MVP (1982,89) for Milwaukee; entered 1992 season with 2,878 hits at age 36.

Mario Zagalo (b.8/9/1931): Soccer; Brazilian forward who is one of only two men (Franz Beckenbauer is the other) to serve as both captain (1962) and coach (1970) of World Cup champion.

Babe Didrikson Zaharias (1914-56): won 2 gold medals and a silver at 1932 Olympics; took up golf in 1935; won 55 pro & amateur events; helped found LPGA in 1949; won 10 Majors including 3 U.S. Opens (1948,50,54); chosen female "Athlete of the Half Century" by AP in 1950.

Tony Zale (b.5/29/1913): Boxer; world middleweight champion (1941-47,48); pro record 67-18-2 with 44 KOs.

Frank Zamboni (1901-88): mechanic, ice salesman and skating rink owner in Paramount, Calif.; invented 1st ice-resurfacing machine in 1949; 4,000 sold in over 33 countries since then.

Emile Zatopek (b.9/19/1922): Czech runner; won total of 4 Olympic gold medals, including unprecedented triple (5,000m, 10,000m and marathon), in 1952.

John Ziegler (b.2/9/1934): Hockey; NHL president from 1977-92; negotiated settlement with rival WHA in 1979 that led to inviting four WHA teams (Edmonton, Hartford, Quebec and Winnipeg) to join NHL; stepped down June 12, 1992, 2 months after settling 10-day players' strike.

Pirmin Zurbriggen (b.1963): Swiss alpine skier; 4-time World Cup overall champ (1984,87,88,90) and 3-time runner-up; 40 World Cup wins in 10 years; won gold and bronze medals at 1988 Olympics.

© Wachter Sports Photo

Stadium architecture took a crowd-pleasing step backward in 1992 and downtown Baltimore got a new landmark with the opening of **Camden Yards.**

ARENAS & BALLPARKS

Birds' Nest

The opening of Oriole Park at Camden Yards in Baltimore marks baseball's overdue return to traditional ballparks.

The Opening Day wind blew nostalgic over Baltimore's brand new Oriole Park at Camden Yards on April 6. It rippled the patriotic bunting that festooned the box-seat gates, spun the eight-foot-high aluminum Oriole-shaped weather vanes that straddled the scoreboard, hung up a fly ball to deep center so Oriole centerfielder Mike Devereaux could make an over-the-shoulder catch like Willie Mays in the '54 Series, and carried a whiff of crab cakes and barbequed beef through the stands.

The President was there. He may have bounced the ceremonial first pitch to the plate, but the crowd of 44,568 didn't seem to mind as it savored the timelessness of the Birds' new $105 million nest, securely in touch with Babe Ruth's ghost. After all, Ruth's Cafe, run by the Babe's dad, once stood in right-center.

Of course, it is all a beautiful, architectural illusion. For Oriole Park—with its grassy asymmetry, short home run porch down the right field line, and brick-and-steel construction—resembles the classic yards of childhood memory much more than adulthood's concrete cereal bowls.

Who deserves our thanks? Head architect Janet Marie Smith and graphic designer David Ashton, for starters. Also,

the architect firm of Hellmuth Obata & Kassbaum of Kansas City. The ballpark, built near Baltimore's rejuvenated Inner Harbor, is owned by the Maryland Stadium Authority but all design decisions were approved by the Orioles.

Team President Larry Lucchino said he wanted a ballpark that reflected "traditional baseball values" and that's just what he got. Boston ivy grows on a wall beyond the centerfield fence. Hand-forged steel letters glimmer in the sun as they spell the park's name above the main entrance, where fans get their first glimpse of green through iron gates and brick arches. It is the first big-league park in 22 years (Connie Mack Stadium in Philadelphia was the last) to feature advertising on the outfield walls and there's an old-fashioned manually-operated auxiliary scoreboard in right.

The old B&O Railroad Warehouse—once the longest building on the East Coast (1,016 ft.)—overlooks right field, with only Eutaw Street—a walking mall lined with concessions—in between. The warehouse, which influenced the stadium's brick pattern, sits 432 feet from home plate and has been converted into stores, restaurants and office space. The stadium's rightfield lights are also mounted on the warehouse roof.

It should be a hitter's park. Foul territory is sparse. The dimensions are LF 333, LCF 410, CF 400, RCF 373, and RF

Michael Benson is a magazine editor, freelance writer and author of *Ballparks of North America* (McFarland, 1989).

© Wachter Sports Photo

Built in the shadow of the old B&O Railroad Warehouse at Camden Yards, Oriole Park is in sync with Baltimore and its industrial past.

319. The left-field fence, though 25 feet high, is an inviting target for lefty power. Fences elsewhere are seven feet high. Former Oriole great Frank Robinson (now the Orioles' assistant GM) said before the season that the big wall in left and the funny angle in left-center provide "a chance to put the triple back in the game." Prophetic words. As of Labor Day, Orioles Devereaux and Brady Anderson led the AL in triples.

Even the site of the new park is rich in history. During the Revolutionary War, southbound French General Jean Rochambeau camped here on his way to join George Washington at the decisive Battle of Yorktown. In 1828, the B&O railroad was built, stimulating Baltimore's industrial economy by linking the city with the Ohio Valley. In 1857, the B&O Camden Station was built, then the world's largest rail depot. It was here that the first casualties of the Civil War were suffered. After the war, Camden Yards developed into an industrial hub. In the early 1900's, Babe Ruth's father opened Ruth's Cafe at 406 Conway St. (now right-center field) where the young Babe lived when he wasn't attending St. Mary's Industrial School in West Baltimore.

Not everything about Oriole Park is old-fashioned. Many things are state of the art: the Diamond Vision megaboard in center, the sound system, fan accommodations, the lights and the press facilities. The Orioles' clubhouse is the largest in baseball, with 50 changing stalls, several meeting rooms, a video room, exercise room and artificially-turfed tunnels for hitting, pitching and loosening up. The trainer's room is bigger than the entire clubhouse at the club's previous home, Memorial Stadium.

While Camden Yards was the year's most talked-about new major league playpen, three other buildings—basketball arenas in Salt Lake City and Phoenix and a domed football stadium in Atlanta—opened for business in 1992.

The NBA's Utah Jazz actually baptised their new $80 million, 19,911-seat Delta Center on Nov. 7, 1991, with a 103-95 loss to Seattle. By the end of the 1991-92 season, however, the Jazz enjoyed the league's best home record (37-4), sold out every game and led the Western Conference in attendance. The Jazz had played at the 12,616-seat Salt Palace since moving from New Orleans in 1979.

Delta Airlines paid an undisclosed

473

Cleveland Gateway Project

Among the big league's current works in progress are a neighboring ballpark and arena (foreground) in downtown Cleveland where the American League Indians and NBA Cavaliers will open for business in 1994.

amount of money to be the corporate sponsor and namesake of the new Jazz arena. Another airline, America West, struck the same kind of deal in Phoenix, agreeing to pay the city's Arena Development Limited Partnership $20 million over 30 years. Unlike Delta, however, America West has been operating under Bankruptcy Court protection since June 27, 1991. It was able to make its first vanity payment of $500,000 in June, but it appears the 19,000-seat facility will have a new name before long. The Phoenix Suns, who played at the 14,487-seat Arizona Veterans Memorial Coliseum since joining the NBA in 1968, were scheduled to officially open their new home on Nov. 7 against the L.A. Clippers.

The Atlanta Falcons of the NFL officially opened the 71,594-seat Georgia Dome on Sept. 6, with a 20-17 victory over the New York Jets. The Dome, which cost $210 million and took three years to build, was designed by Heery Architects and Engineers, Inc. It is only the second home for the Falcons, who played at 59,643-seat Atlanta-Fulton County Stadium from 1966-91. While Georgia Tech elected to continue its football schedule on campus, the Peach Bowl will join the Falcons indoors on Jan. 2, 1993.

The National Hockey League introduced new (but not brand new) home rinks in October as the expansion Ottawa Senators and Tampa Bay Lightning set up shop for the 1992-93 season. The Senators will play at the Ottawa Civic Center and the Lightning at Expo Hall in Tampa. Both buildings hold 10,500 and both teams hope to be playing in larger new arenas within three years.

Baseball's National League will also expand in 1993 as the Colorado Rockies and Florida Marlins move into two reconfigured NFL stadiums—the Rockies at 76,100-seat Mile High Stadium in Denver and the Marlins at 48,000-seat Joe Robbie Stadium in Miami.

The Rockies plan to call Mile High home for two seasons then move downtown in 1995 to new 45,000-seat Coors Field, named after the brewer and part-owner of the team. Groundbreaking was set for the fall of '92. Home run distances have not yet been determined, as tests are still underway to quantify the effect of altitude on fly-ball distance.

Soccer's World Cup tournament will be held in the United States for the first time in 1994 and on March 23, FIFA announced the nine playing sites (see page 486 for complete list).

Since all World Cup matches must be

played on real grass, the selection of the Pontiac Silverdome as the tournament's first-ever indoor venue was a surprise. For the first time since the Astrodome opened in Houston back in 1965, a serious attempt is underway to grow grass indoors. Dr. Trey Rogers, a turf-grass management professor at Michigan State University in Lansing, is conducting experiments in the Silverdome, as well as in a research facility built specifically for the project on the MSU campus.

"We're experimenting with different grass species and supplemental lighting," says Dr. Rogers. "Success is the only answer, here. They're playing a World Cup exhibition game in the Silverdome in 1993 and we hope to have the field ready for that."

If the experiments turn out as successful as hoped, the last non-monetary argument for artificial turf will be gone forever. □

Coming Attractions

New ballparks and arenas either under construction or in the advanced planning stages as of Sept. 1, 1992.

Major League Baseball

AL

Cleveland: Construction underway on 42,500-seat park on downtown Gateway Project site; plans include possibility of adding 29,000 seats for football, if necessary; will be adjacent to new basketball arena, which is also under construction; Indians' opener scheduled for April, 1994.

Milwaukee: On the drawing boards; park to be built across centerfield fence from County Stadium; figures to seat 50,000 for baseball and be expandable to 60,000 seats for football; Brewers' opener planned for April, 1996.

Texas: Construction underway on 48,100-seat park being built a half mile south of current Arlington Stadium; Rangers' opener scheduled for April, 1994.

NL

Atlanta: On the drawing boards; plans call for moving into as yet unbuilt main Olympic stadium after 1996 Summer Games; immediately after the Games, the 85,000-seat main stadium will be converted into a 45,000-seat ballpark with Braves' opener planned for April, 1997.

Colorado: On the drawing boards; plans call for construction of 45,000-seat Coors Field to begin in late 1992; Rockies' opener planned for April, 1995.

NBA Basketball

Western Conference

San Antonio: Construction on Alamodome expected to be completed in April of 1993, although Spurs won't move in until November; will seat 32,500 for basketball and 65,000 for football; suspended Dome roof is cable-supported.

Eastern Conference

Boston: Construction set to begin in mid-1993 on New Boston Garden on a site 100 yards behind the current Garden; it will seat 18,400 for basketball and 17,200 for hockey; Celtics' opener scheduled for November, 1995.

Chicago: Ground broken Apr. 6, 1992, on New Chicago Stadium on a site across the street from the current Stadium; it will seat 21,000 for basketball and 20,000 for hockey; Bulls' opener scheduled for November, 1994.

Cleveland: Construction underway on 21,000-seat facility on downtown Gateway Project site; will be adjacent to new baseball park, which is also under construction; Cavaliers' opener scheduled for November, 1994.

Philadelphia: On the drawing boards; plans call for New Spectrum to be built on site of razed JFK Stadium near current Spectrum; it will seat 21,000 for

basketball and 20,000 for hockey; construction set to begin in late 1992, with 76ers opener scheduled for November, 1994.

NFL Football

AFC
None

NFC

Washington: Redskins' owner Jack Kent Cooke unveiled plans on July, 9, 1992, to build a 78,000-seat field named after himself across the Potomac River in Alexandria, Va.; opener planned for September, 1994.

NHL Hockey

Campbell Conference

Chicago: Ground broken Apr. 6, 1992, on New Chicago Stadium on a site across the street from the current Stadium; it will seat 20,000 for hockey and 21,000 for basketball; Blackhawks' opener scheduled for October, 1994.

San Jose: Construction underway on 18,000-seat facility as yet unnamed; Sharks' opener scheduled for October, 1993.

Tampa Bay: Construction set to begin in early 1993 on site next to Tampa Stadium; arena to hold 18,500 for hockey and 20,000 for basketball; currently referred to as Tampa Coliseum, but ought to be called the Thunderdome; Lightning opener scheduled for October, 1994.

Vancouver: Plans announced on Aug. 13, 1992, to build new 20,000-seat downtown facility near B.C. Place; Canucks' opener planned for October, 1995.

Eastern Conference

Boston: Construction set to begin in mid-1993 on New Boston Garden on a site 100 yards behind the current Garden; it will seat 18,400 for basketball and 17,200 for hockey; Bruins' opener scheduled for October, 1995.

Buffalo: On the drawing boards; plans call for 20,000-seat New Memorial Auditorium several blocks from the old Aud; Sabres' opener planned for October, 1995.

Montreal: On the drawing boards; plans call for 20,000-seat New Forum near current Forum; Canadiens' opener planned for October, 1995.

Ottawa: Ground broken June 29, 1992, for the 18,500-seat Palladium; Senators' opener scheduled for October, 1994.

Philadelphia: On the drawing boards; plans call for New Spectrum to be built on site of razed JFK Stadium near current Spectrum; it will seat 20,000 for hockey and 21,000 for basketball; construction set to begin in late 1992, with Flyers' opener scheduled for October, 1994.

Home, Sweet Home

The home fields, home courts and home ice of the AL, NL, NBA, NFL, CFL, NHL, NCAA Division I-A college football and Division I basketball. Also, selected Auto Racing and Horse Racing tracks and Grand Slam Tennis center courts.

Attendance figures for the 1991 NFL regular season and the 1991-92 NBA and NHL regular seasons are provided. See Baseball chapter for 1992 AL and NL attendance figures.

MAJOR LEAGUE BASEBALL

American League

		Built	Capacity	LF	LCF	CF	RCF	RF	Field
Baltimore Orioles	**Oriole Park at Camden Yards**	1992	**48,041**	333	410	400	373	318	Grass
Boston Red Sox	**Fenway Park**	1912	**34,142**	315	379	390	380	302	Grass
California Angels	**Anaheim Stadium**	1966	**64,593**	333	386	404	386	333	Grass
Chicago White Sox	**Comiskey Park**	1991	**44,702**	347	383	400	383	347	Grass
Cleveland Indians	**Cleveland Stadium**	1931	**74,483**	320	375	404	370	320	Grass
Detroit Tigers	**Tiger Stadium**	1912	**52,416**	340	365	440	370	325	Grass
Kansas City Royals	**Royals Stadium**	1973	**40,625**	330	385	410	385	330	Turf
Milwaukee Brewers	**County Stadium**	1953	**53,192**	315	392	402	392	315	Grass
Minnesota Twins	**Hubert H.Humphrey Metrodome**	1982	**55,883**	343	385	408	367	327	Turf
New York Yankees	**Yankee Stadium**	1923	**57,545**	318	399	408	385	314	Grass
Oakland Athletics	**Oakland-Alameda County Coliseum**	1966	**47,313**	330	375	400	375	330	Grass
Seattle Mariners	**The Kingdome**	1976	**59,702**	331	372	405	349	312	Turf
Texas Rangers	**Arlington Stadium**	1965	**43,521**	330	380	400	380	330	Grass
Toronto Blue Jays	**SkyDome**	1989	**50,516**	328	375	400	375	328	Turf

National League

		Built	Capacity	LF	LCF	CF	RCF	RF	Field
Atlanta Braves	**Atlanta-Fulton County Stadium**	1965	**52,007**	330	385	402	385	330	Grass
Chicago Cubs	**Wrigley Field**	1914	**38,710**	355	368	400	368	353	Grass
Cincinnati Reds	**Riverfront Stadium**	1970	**52,952**	330	375	404	375	330	Turf
Colorado Rockies	**Mile High Stadium**	1948	**76,100**	335	375	423	390	370	Grass
Florida Marlins	**Joe Robbie Stadium**	1987	**48,000**	335	380	410	380	345	Grass
Houston Astros	**The Astrodome**	1965	**54,816**	330	380	400	380	330	Turf
Los Angeles Dodgers	**Dodger Stadium**	1962	**56,000**	330	385	395	385	330	Grass
Montreal Expos	**Olympic Stadium**	1976	**43,739**	325	375	404	375	325	Turf
New York Mets	**Shea Stadium**	1964	**55,601**	338	371	410	371	338	Grass
Philadelphia Phillies	**Veterans Stadium**	1971	**62,382**	330	371	408	371	330	Turf
Pittsburgh Pirates	**Three Rivers Stadium**	1970	**58,729**	335	375	400	375	335	Turf
St.Louis Cardinals	**Busch Stadium**	1966	**56,227**	330	375	402	375	330	Turf
San Diego Padres	**San Diego/ Jack Murphy Stadium**	1967	**59,700**	327	370	405	370	327	Grass
San Francisco Giants	**Candlestick Park**	1960	**62,000**	335	365	400	365	335	Grass
or									
Tampa Bay Giants	**Florida Suncoast Dome**	1990	**43,000**	335	385	410	385	335	Turf

Note: The Giants announced on Aug. 4, 1992, that, pending approval of both leagues and the commissioner, the club would be sold and moved to St.Petersburg, Fla., in time for the 1993 season.

Rank by Capacity

AL		NL	
Cleveland	74,483	Mile High	76,100
Anaheim	64,593	Veterans	62,382
Kingdome	59,702	Candlestick	62,000
Yankee	57,545	SD/Murphy	59,700
Metrodome	55,883	Three Rivers	58,729
County	53,192	Busch	56,227
Tiger	52,416	Dodger	56,000
SkyDome	50,516	Shea	55,601
Camden Yards	48,041	Astrodome	54,816
Oakland	47,313	Riverfront	52,952
Comiskey	44,702	Atlanta	52,007
Arlington	43,521	Joe Robbie	48,000
Royals	40,625	Olympic	43,739
Fenway	34,142	Wrigley	38,710

Note: If the SF Giants move to St.Petersburg, Fla., the Suncoast Dome (43,000) would rank behind Olympic Stadium in the NL.

Rank by Age

AL		NL	
Fenway	1912	Wrigley	1914
Tiger	1912	Mile High	1948
Yankee	1923	Candlestick	1960
Cleveland	1931	Dodger	1962
County	1953	Shea	1964
Arlington	1965	Astrodome	1965
Anaheim	1966	Atlanta	1965
Oakland	1966	Busch	1966
Royals	1973	SD/Murphy	1967
Kingdome	1977	Riverfront	1970
Metrodome	1982	Three Rivers	1970
SkyDome	1989	Veterans	1971
Comiskey	1991	Olympic	1976
Camden Yards	1992	Joe Robbie	1987

Note: If the SF Giants move to St.Petersburg, Fla., the Suncoast Dome (1990) would rank behind Joe Robbie Stadium.

Home Fields

Listed below are the principal home fields used through the years by current American and National League teams. The NL became a major league in 1876, the AL in 1901.

The capacity figures in the right-hand column indicate the largest seating capacity of the ballpark while the club played there. Capacity figures before 1915 (and the introduction of concrete grandstands) are sketchy at best and have been left blank.

American League

Baltimore Orioles

1901	Lloyd Street Grounds (Milwaukee)	—
1902-53	Sportsman's Park II (St. Louis)	30,500
1954-91	Memorial Stadium (Baltimore)	53,371
1992–	Camden Yards	48,041

Boston Red Sox

1901-11	Huntington Ave. Grounds	—
1912–	Fenway Park	34,142
	(1934 capacity—27,000)	

California Angels

1961	Wrigley Field (Los Angeles)	20,457
1962-65	Dodger Stadium	56,000
1966–	Anaheim Stadium	64,593
	(1966 capacity—43,250)	

Chicago White Sox

1901-10	Southside Park	—
1910-90	Comiskey Park I	43,931
1991–	Comiskey Park II	44,702

Cleveland Indians

1901-09	League Park I	—
1910-46	League Park II	21,414
1932–	Cleveland Stadium	74,483
	(1932 capacity—77,797)	

Detroit Tigers

1901-11	Bennett Park	—
1912–	Tiger Stadium	52,416
	(1912 capacity—23,000)	

Kansas City Royals

1969-72	Municipal Stadium	35,020
1973–	Royals Stadium	40,625
	(1973 capacity—40,762)	

Milwaukee Brewers

1969	Sick's Stadium (Seattle)	25,420
1970–	County Stadium (Milwaukee)	53,192
	(1970 capacity—46,62)	

Minnesota Twins

1901-02	American League Park (Washington, DC)	—
1903-60	Griffith Stadium	27,410
1960-81	Metropolitan Stadium (Bloomington, MN)	45,919
1982–	HHH Metrodome (Minneapolis)	55,883
	(1982 capacity—54,000)	

New York Yankees

1901-02	Oriole Park (Baltimore)	—
1903-12	Hilltop Park (New York)	—
1913-22	Polo Grounds II	38,000
1923-73	Yankee Stadium I	67,224
1974-75	Shea Stadium	55,101
1976–	Yankee Stadium II	57,545
	(1976 capacity—57,145)	

Oakland Athletics

1901-08	Columbia Park (Philadelphia)	—
1909-54	Shibe Park	33,608
1955-67	Municipal Stadium (Kansas City)	35,020
1968–	Oakland Alameda County Coliseum	47,313
	(1968 capacity—48,621)	

Seattle Mariners

1977–	The Kingdome	59,702
	(1977 capacity—59,438)	

Texas Rangers

1961	Griffith Stadium (Washington, DC)	27,410
1962-71	RFK Stadium	45,016
1972–	Arlington Stadium (Texas)	43,521
	(1972 capacity—35,698)	

Toronto Blue Jays

1977-89	Exhibition Stadium	43,737
1989–	SkyDome	50,516
	(1989 capacity—49,500)	

Ballpark Name Changes: CHICAGO—**Comiskey Park I** originally White Sox Park (1910-12), then Comiskey Park in 1913, then White Sox Park again in 1962, then Comiskey Park again in 1976; CLEVELAND—**League Park** renamed Dunn Field in 1920, then League Park again in 1928; **Cleveland Stadium** originally Municipal Stadium (1932-74); DETROIT—**Tiger Stadium** originally Navin Field (1912-37), then Briggs Stadium (1938-60); LOS ANGELES—**Dodger Stadium** referred to as Chavez Ravine by AL while Angels played there (1962-65); PHILADELPHIA—**Shibe Park** renamed Connie Mack Stadium in 1953; ST.LOUIS—**Sportsman's Park** renamed Busch Stadium in 1953; WASHINGTON—**Griffith Stadium** originally National Park (1892-20), **RFK Stadium** originally D.C. Stadium (1961-68).

National League

Atlanta Braves

1876-94	South End Grounds I (Boston)	—
1894-1914	South End Grounds II	—
1915-52	Braves Field	40,000
1953-65	County Stadium (Milwaukee)	43,394
1966–	Atlanta-Fulton County Stadium	52,007
	(1966 capacity—50,000)	

Chicago Cubs

1876-77	State Street Grounds	—
1878-84	Lakefront Park	—
1885-91	West Side Park	—
1891-93	Brotherhood Park	—
1893-1915	West Side Grounds	—
1916–	Wrigley Field	38,710
	(1916 capacity—16,000)	

Major League Baseball (Cont.)
Home Fields

Cincinnati Reds

1876-79	Avenue Grounds	—
1880	Bank Street Grounds	—
1890-1901	Redland Field I	—
1902-11	Palace of the Fans	—
1912-70	Crosley Field	29,603
1970–	Riverfront Stadium	52,952
	(1970 capacity—52,000)	

Colorado Rockies

1993–	Mile High Stadium (Denver)	76,100

Florida Marlins

1993–	Joe Robbie Stadium (Miami)	48,000

Houston Astros

1962-64	Colt Stadium	32,601
1965–	The Astrodome	54,816
	(1965 capacity—45,011)	

Los Angeles Dodgers

1890	Washington Park I (Brooklyn)	—
1891-97	Eastern Park	—
1898-1912	Washington Park II	—
1913-56	Ebbets Field	31,497
1957	Ebbets Field	31,497
	& Roosevelt Stadium (Jersey City)	24,167
1958-61	Memorial Coliseum (Los Angeles)	93,600
1962–	Dodger Stadium	56,000

Montreal Expos

1969-76	Jarry Park	28,000
1977–	Olympic Stadium	43,739
	(1977 capacity—58,500)	

New York Mets

1962-63	Polo Grounds	55,987
1964–	Shea Stadium	55,601
	(1964 capacity—55,101)	

Philadelphia Phillies

1883-86	Recreation Park	—
1887-94	Huntingdon Ave.Grounds	—
1895-1938	Baker Bowl	18,800
1938-70	Shibe Park	33,608
1971–	Veterans Stadium	62,382
	(1971 capacity—56,371)	

Pittsburgh Pirates

1887-90	Recreation Park	—
1891-1909	Exposition Park	—
1909-70	Forbes Field	35,000
1970–	Three Rivers Stadium	58,729
	(1970 capacity—50,235)	

St.Louis Cardinals

1876-77	Sportsman's Park I	—
1885-86	Vandeventer Lot	—
1892-1920	Robison Field	18,000
1920-66	Sportsman's Park II	30,500
1966–	Busch Stadium	56,227
	(1966 capacity—50,126)	

San Diego Padres

1969–	San Diego/Jack Murphy Stadium	59,700
	(1969 capacity—47,634)	

San Francisco Giants

1876	Union Grounds (Brooklyn)	—
1883-88	Polo Grounds I (New York)	—
1889-90	Manhattan Field	—
1891-1957	Polo Grounds II	55,987
1958-59	Seals Stadium (San Francisco)	22,900
1960–	Candlestick Park	62,000
	(1960 capacity—42,553)	

Note: If the Giants move to Tampa Bay in 1993, they will play at the Florida Suncoast Dome in St. Petersburg (capacity: 43,000).

Ballpark Name Changes: ATLANTA—**Atlanta-Fulton County Stadium** originally Atlanta Stadium (1966-1974); CHICAGO—**Wrigley Field** originally Weeghman Park (1914-17), then Cubs Park (1918-25); CINCINNATI—**Redland Field** originally League Park (1890-93) and **Crosley Field** originally Redland Field II (1912-33); HOUSTON—**Astrodome** originally Harris County Domed Stadium before it opened in 1965; PHILADELPHIA—**Shibe Park** renamed Connie Mack Stadium in 1953; ST.LOUIS—**Robison Field** originally Vandeventer Lot, then League Park, then Cardinal Park all before becoming Robison Field in 1901, **Sportsman's Park** renamed Busch Stadium in 1953, and **Busch Stadium** originally Busch Memorial Stadium (1966-82); SAN DIEGO—**San Diego/Jack Murphy Stadium** originally San Diego Stadium (1967-81).

NATIONAL BASKETBALL ASSOCIATION

Western Conference

		Location	Built	Capacity
Dallas Mavericks	**Reunion Arena**	Dallas, TX	1980	**17,502**
Denver Nuggets	**McNichols Arena**	Denver, CO	1975	**17,022**
Golden State Warriors	**Oakland Coliseum Arena**	Oakland, CA	1966	**15,025**
Houston Rockets	**The Summit**	Houston, TX	1975	**16,279**
Los Angeles Clippers	**Los Angeles Sports Arena**	Los Angeles, CA	1959	**15,800**
Los Angeles Lakers	**Great Western Forum**	Inglewood, CA	1967	**17,505**
Minnesota Timberwolves	**Target Center**	Minneapolis, MN	1990	**19,006**
Phoenix Suns	**America West Arena**	Phoenix, AZ	1992	**19,000**
Portland Trail Blazers	**Memorial Coliseum**	Portland, OR	1960	**12,888**
Sacramento Kings	**ARCO Arena**	Sacramento, CA	1988	**17,280**
San Antonio Spurs	**HemisFair Arena**	San Antonio, TX	1968	**16,057**
Seattle SuperSonics	**The Coliseum**	Seattle, WA	1962	**14,250**
	& The Kingdome	Seattle, WA	1976	**38,000**
Utah Jazz	**Delta Center**	Salt Lake City, UT	1991	**19,911**

Note: Seattle is scheduled to play four of 41 regular season games at the Kingdome in 1992-93.

Eastern Conference

	Location	Built	Capacity
Atlanta Hawks . . . . **The Omni**	Atlanta, GA	1972	**16,510**
Boston Celtics . . . . **Boston Garden**	Boston, MA	1928	**14,890**
& Hartford Civic Center	Hartford, CT	1975	**15,239**
Charlotte Hornets . . . . **Charlotte Coliseum**	Charlotte, NC	1988	**23,698**
Chicago Bulls. . . . . **Chicago Stadium**	Chicago, IL	1929	**17,339**
Cleveland Cavaliers . . . . **The Coliseum**	Richfield, OH	1974	**20,273**
Detroit Pistons . . . . **The Palace of Auburn Hills**	Auburn Hills, MI	1988	**21,454**
Indiana Pacers. . . . . **Market Square Arena**	Indianapolis, IN	1974	**16,530**
Miami Heat . . . . **Miami Arena**	Miami, FL	1988	**15,008**
Milwaukee Bucks. **Bradley Center**	Milwaukee, WI	1988	**18,633**
New Jersey Nets . . . . **Meadowlands Arena**	E.Rutherford, NJ	1981	**20,039**
New York Knicks . . . . **Madison Square Garden**	New York, NY	1968	**19,763**
Orlando Magic . . . . **Orlando Arena**	Orlando, FL	1989	**15,077**
Philadelphia 76ers . . . . **The Spectrum**	Philadelphia	1967	**18,168**
Washington Bullets . . . . **Capital Centre**	Landover, MD	1973	**18,756**
& Baltimore Arena	Baltimore, MD	1962	**12,654**

Note: Boston is scheduled to play three of 41 regular season games at Hartford Civic Center and Washington is scheduled to play four of 41 regular season games at Baltimore Arena in 1992-93.

Rank by Capacity

West		East	
Delta Center	19,911	Charlotte	23,698
Target Center	19,006	Palace	21,454
America West	19,000	Cleveland	20,273
GW Forum	17,505	Meadowlands	20,039
Reunion	17,502	Mad.Sq.Garden	19,763
ARCO	17,280	Capital Centre	18,756
McNichols	17,022	Bradley Center	18,633
Summit	16,279	Spectrum	18,168
HemisFair	16,057	Chicago Stadium	17,339
LA Sports	15,800	Market Square	16,530
Oakland	15,025	Omni	16,510
Seattle	14,250	Orlando	15,077
Portland	12,888	Miami	15,008
		Boston Garden	14,890

Note: Figures do not include Standing Room.

Rank by Age

West		East	
LA Sports	1959	Boston Garden.	1928
Portland	1960	Chicago Stadium	1929
Seattle	1962	Spectrum.	1967
Oakland	1966	Mad.Sq.Garden	1968
GW Forum	1967	Omni	1972
HemisFair	1968	Capital Centre	1973
McNichols.	1975	Cleveland	1974
Summit	1975	Market Square	1974
Reunion.	1980	Meadowlands.	1981
ARCO	1988	Bradley Center	1988
Target Center	1990	Charlotte.	1988
Delta Center	1991	Miami	1988
America West	1992	Palace	1988
		Orlando	1989

1991-92 NBA Attendance

Overall attendance in the NBA was 17,367,239 in 1107 games for an average per game crowd of 15,689. Teams in each conference are ranked by attendance over 41 home games; **S/O** heading indicates number of sellouts. Figures provided by NBA league office. Numbers in parentheses indicate rank in 1990-91.

Western Conference

		Attendance	S/O	Average
1	Utah (12)	806,663	41	19,675
2	Minnesota (1).	769,035	23	18,757
3	LA Lakers (3)	699,240	13	17,055
4	Sacramento (2)	697,574	41	17,014
5	San Antonio (5)	658,337	41	16,057
6	Dallas (4)	649,741	6	15,847
7	Golden St.(7)	616,025	41	15,025
8	Phoenix (9)	594,336	41	14,496
9	Houston (8)	592,790	3	14,458
10	Seattle (13).	586,929	5	14,315
11	Denver (14)	534,323	6	13,032
12	Portland (10)	528,408	41	12,888
13	LA Clippers (11).	500,200	9	12,200
	TOTAL.	8,233,601	311	15,448

Note: Seattle played 37 games at Seattle Coliseum (3 sellouts, 11,952 avg.) and four at the Kingdome (2 sellouts, 36,174 avg.).

Eastern Conference

		Attendance	S/O	Average
1	Charlotte (1).	971,618	41	23,698
2	Detroit (2).	879,614	41	21,454
3	Chicago (3)	759,968	41	18,536
4	New York (5)	731,371	16	17,838
5	Cleveland (7)	677,408	6	16,522
6	Milwaukee (4)	635,514	3	15,500
7	Orlando*	621,191	41	15,151
8	Miami (8)	613,583	37	14,965
9	Boston (9).	610,976	41	14,902
10	Philadelphia (6)	574,128	6	14,003
11	New Jersey (11).	517,356	5	12,618
12	Indiana (13)	517,352	5	12,618
13	Atlanta (10)	511,903	0	12,485
14	Washington (15)	511,655	15	12,479
	TOTAL.	9,133,637	298	15,912

*Orlando ranked 6th in attendance in the Western Conference in 1990-91.

Note: Boston played 38 games at Boston Garden (38 sellouts, 14,890 avg.) and three at Hartford Civic Center (3 sellouts, 15,052 avg.); Washington played 37 games at Capital Centre (11 sellouts, 12,525 avg.) and four at Baltimore Arena (4 sellouts, 12,054 avg.).

National Basketball Association (Cont.)
Home Courts

Listed below are the principal home courts used through the years by current NBA teams. The largest capacity of each arena is noted in the right-hand column. ABA arenas (1972-76) are included for Denver, Indiana, New Jersey and San Antonio.

Western Conference

Dallas Mavericks
1980–	Reunion Arena	17,502
	(1980 capacity—17,828)	

Denver Nuggets
1967-75	Auditorium Arena	6,841
1975–	McNichols Sports Arena	17,022
	(1975 capacity—16,700)	

Golden State Warriors
1946-52	Philadelphia Arena	7,777
1952-62	Convention Hall (Philadelphia)	9,200
	& Philadelphia Arena	7,777
1962-64	Cow Palace (San Francisco)	13,862
1964-66	Civic Auditorium	7,500
	& (USF Memorial Gym)	6,000
1966-67	Cow Palace, Civic Auditorium	
	& Oakland Coliseum Arena	15,000
1967-71	Cow Palace	14,500
1971–	Oakland Coliseum Arena	15,025
	(1971 capacity—12,905)	

Houston Rockets
1967-71	San Diego Sports Arena	14,000
1971-72	Hofheinz Pavilion (Houston)	10,218
	& six other sites	
1972-73	Hofheinz Pavilion	10,218
	& HemisFair Arena (San Antonio)	10,446
1973-75	Hofheinz Pavilion	10,218
1975–	The Summit	16,279
	(1975 capacity—15,600)	

Note: During the 1971-72 season, the Rockets played 21 games at Hofheinz, 8 at Astrohall and 6 at the Astrodome in Houston, as well as 3 games in San Antonio, 2 in Waco and 1 in El Paso. In 1972-73, they played 28 games at Hofheinz and 13 at the HemisFair in San Antonio.

Los Angeles Clippers
1970-78	Memorial Auditorium (Buffalo)	17,300
1978-84	San Diego Sports Arena	12,167
1985–	Los Angeles Sports Arena	15,800
	(1985 capacity—15,300)	

Los Angeles Lakers
1948-60	Minneapolis Auditorium	10,000
1960-67	Los Angeles Sports Arena	14,781
1967–	Great Western Forum (Inglewood, CA)	17,505
	(1967 capacity—17,086)	

Minnesota Timberwolves
1989-90	Hubert H. Humphrey Metrodome	23,000
1990–	Target Center	19,006

Phoenix Suns
1968-92	Arizona Veterans' Memorial Coliseum	14,487
1992–	America West Arena	19,000

Portland Trail Blazers
1970–	Memorial Coliseum	12,888
	(1970 capacity—12,366)	

Sacramento Kings
1948-55	Edgarton Park Arena (Rochester, NY)	5,000
1955-58	Rochester War Memorial	10,000
1958-72	Cincinnati Gardens	11,438
1972-74	Municipal Auditorium (Kansas City)	9,929
	& Omaha (NE) Civic Auditorium	9,136
1974-78	Kemper Arena (Kansas City)	16,785
	& Omaha Civic Auditorium	9,136
1978-85	Kemper Arena	16,785
1985-88	ARCO Arena I	10,333
1988–	ARCO Arena II	17,280
	(1988 capacity—16,517)	

San Antonio Spurs
1967-70	Memorial Auditorium (Dallas)	8,088
	& Moody Coliseum (Dallas)	8,500
1970-71	Three courts—Moody Coliseum	8,500
	Tarrant Convention Center (Ft. Worth)	13,500
	& Municipal Coliseum (Lubbock)	10,400
1971-73	Two courts—Moody Coliseum	9,500
	& Memorial Auditorium	8,088
1973–	HemisFair Arena (San Antonio)	16,057
	(1973 capacity—10,446)	

Seattle SuperSonics
1967-78	Seattle Center Coliseum	14,098
1978-85	Kingdome	40,192
1985–	The Coliseum	14,250
	(1985 capacity—14,000)	

Utah Jazz
1974-75	Municipal Auditorium	7,853
	& Louisiana Superdome	47,284
1975-79	Superdome	47,284
1979-83	Salt Palace (Salt Lake City)	12,519
1983-84	Salt Palace	12,519
	& Thomas-Mack Center (Las Vegas)	18,500
1985-91	Salt Palace	12,616
1991–	Delta Center	19,911

Eastern Conference

Atlanta Hawks
1949-51	Wheaton Field House (Moline, IL)	6,000
1951-55	Milwaukee Arena	11,000
1955-68	Kiel Auditorium (St.Louis)	10,000
1968-72	Alexander Mem. Coliseum (Atlanta)	7,166
1972–	The Omni	16,510
	(1972 capacity—16,818)	

Boston Celtics
1946–	Boston Garden	14,890
	(1946 capacity—13,909)	

Note: Since 1975-76, the Celtics have played some regular season games at the Hartford Civic Center (16,344).

Charlotte Hornets

1988–	Charlotte Coliseum	23,698
	(1988 capacity—23,500)	

Chicago Bulls

1966-67	Chicago Amphitheater	11,002
1967–	Chicago Stadium	17,339
	(1967 capacity—17,374)	

Cleveland Cavaliers

1970-74	Cleveland Arena	11,000
1974–	The Coliseum (Richfield, OH)	20,273
	(1974 capacity—19,500)	

Detroit Pistons

1948-52	North Side H.S.Gym (Ft.Wayne, IN)	3,800
1952-57	Memorial Coliseum (Ft.Wayne)	9,306
1957-61	Olympia Stadium (Detroit)	14,000
1961-78	Cobo Arena	11,147
1978-88	Silverdome (Pontiac, MI)	22,366
1988–	The Palace (Auburn Hills, MI)	21,454

Indiana Pacers

1967-74	State Fairgrounds (Indianapolis)	9,479
1974–	Market Square Arena	16,530
	(1974 capacity—17,287)	

Miami Heat

1988–	Miami Arena	15,008
	(1988 capacity—15,362)	

Milwaukee Bucks

1968-88	Milwaukee Arena (The Mecca)	11,052
1988–	Bradley Center	18,633

New Jersey Nets

1967-68	Teaneck (NJ) Armory	3,500
1968-69	Long Island Arena (Commack, NY)	6,500
1969-71	Island Garden (W.Hempstead, NY)	5,200
1971-77	Nassau Coliseum (Uniondale, NY)	15,500
1977-81	Rutgers Ath.Center (Piscataway, NJ)	9,050
1981–	Meadowlands Arena (E.Rutherford, NJ)	20,039

New York Knicks

1946-68	Madison Sq. Garden III (50th St)	18,496
1968–	Madison Sq. Garden IV (33rd St.)	19,763
	(1968 capacity—19,694)	

Orlando Magic

1989–	Orlando Arena	15,077

Philadelphia 76ers

1949-51	State Fair Coliseum (Syracuse, NY)	7,500
1951-63	Onondaga County (NY)	
	War Memorial	8,000
1963-67	Convention Hall (Philadelphia)	12,000
	& Philadelphia Arena	7,777
1967–	The Spectrum	18,168
	(1967 capacity—15,205)	

Washington Bullets

1961-62	Chicago Amphitheater	11,000
1962-63	Chicago Coliseum	7,100
1963-73	Baltimore Civic Center	12,289
1973–	Capital Centre (Landover, MD)	18,756
	(1973 capacity—17,500)	

Note: Since 1988-89, the Bullets have played four regular season games at Baltimore Arena.

NATIONAL FOOTBALL LEAGUE

American Conference

		Location	Built	Capacity	Field
Buffalo Bills	**Rich Stadium**	Orchard Park, NY	1973	80,290	Turf
Cincinnati Bengals	**Riverfront Stadium**	Cincinnati, OH	1970	60,389	Turf
Cleveland Browns	**Cleveland Stadium**	Cleveland, OH	1931	78,512	Grass
Denver Broncos	**Mile High Stadium**	Denver, CO	1948	76,273	Grass
Houston Oilers	**The Astrodome**	Houston, TX	1965	62,021	Turf
Indianapolis Colts	**The Hoosier Dome**	Indianapolis, IN	1984	60,389	Turf
Kansas City Chiefs	**Arrowhead Stadium**	Kansas City, MO	1972	77,872	Turf
Los Angeles Raiders	**LA Memorial Coliseum**	Los Angeles, CA	1923	92,488	Grass
Miami Dolphins	**Joe Robbie Stadium**	Miami, FL	1987	73,000	Grass
New England Patriots	**Foxboro Stadium**	Foxboro, MA	1971	60,300	Grass
New York Jets	**Giants Stadium**	E.Rutherford, NJ	1976	76,891	Turf
Pittsburgh Steelers	**Three Rivers Stadium**	Pittsburgh, PA	1970	59,030	Turf
San Diego Chargers	**San Diego/Jack Murphy Stadium**	San Diego, CA	1967	60,750	Grass
Seattle Seahawks	**The Kingdome**	Seattle, WA	1976	66,000	Turf

National Conference

		Location	Built	Capacity	Field
Atlanta Falcons	**Georgia Dome**	Atlanta, GA	1992	71,594	Turf
Chicago Bears	**Soldier Field**	Chicago, IL	1924	66,946	Grass
Dallas Cowboys	**Texas Stadium**	Irving, TX	1971	65,024	Turf
Detroit Lions	**Pontiac Silverdome**	Pontiac, MI	1975	80,494	Turf
Green Bay Packers	**Lambeau Field**	Green Bay, WI	1957	59,543	Grass
	& County Stadium	Milwaukee, WI	1953	56,051	Grass
Los Angeles Rams	**Anaheim Stadium**	Anaheim, CA	1966	69,008	Grass
Minnesota Vikings	**Hubert H. Humphrey Metrodome**	Minneapolis, MN	1982	63,000	Turf
New Orleans Saints	**Louisiana Superdome**	New Orleans, LA	1975	69,065	Turf
New York Giants	**Giants Stadium**	E.Rutherford, NJ	1976	76,891	Turf
Philadelphia Eagles	**Veterans Stadium**	Philadelphia, PA	1971	65,356	Turf
Phoenix Cardinals	**Sun Devil Stadium**	Tempe, AZ	1958	73,473	Grass
San Francisco 49ers	**Candlestick Park**	San Francisco, CA	1960	66,503	Grass
Tampa Bay Buccaneers	**Tampa Stadium**	Tampa, FL	1967	74,315	Grass
Washington Redskins	**Robert F. Kennedy Stadium**	Washington, DC	1961	55,672	Grass

Note: Green Bay was scheduled to play three of eight home games in Milwaukee in 1992.

National Football League (Cont.)

Rank by Capacity		Rank by Age	
AFC	**NFC**	**AFC**	**NFC**
LA Coliseum 92,488	Silverdome 80,494	LA Coliseum 1923	Soldier Field 1924
Rich 80,290	Giants 76,891	Cleveland 1931	County 1953
Cleveland 78,512	Tampa 74,315	Mile High 1948	Lambeau Field 1957
Arrowhead 77,872	Sun Devil 73,473	Astrodome 1965	Sun Devil 1958
Giants 76,891	Georgia Dome 71,594	SD/Murphy 1967	Candlestick 1960
Mile High 76,273	Superdome 69,065	Riverfront 1970	RFK 1961
Joe Robbie 73,000	Anaheim 69,008	Three Rivers 1970	Anaheim 1966
Kingdome 66,000	Soldier Field 66,946	Foxboro 1971	Tampa 1967
Astrodome 62,021	Candlestick 66,503	Arrowhead 1972	Texas 1971
SD/Murphy 60,750	Veterans 65,356	Rich 1973	Veterans 1971
Hoosier Dome 60,389	Texas 65,024	Giants 1976	Silverdome 1975
Riverfront 60,389	HHH Metrodome 63,000	Kingdome 1976	Superdome 1975
Foxboro 60,300	Lambeau Field 59,543	Hoosier Dome 1984	Giants 1976
Three Rivers 59,030	County 56,051	Joe Robbie 1987	HHH Metrodome 1982
	RFK 55,672		Georgia Dome 1992

1991 NFL Attendance

The official overall attendance figure released by the NFL for the 224-game 1991 regular season was 13,481,459, putting the official average per game crowd at 61,792.

Since the NFL does not release team-by-team attendance figures, the totals below were taken from published newspaper game summaries compiled by *The Sporting News* for its 1992 *Pro Football Guide*. The *TSN* figures show overall attendance at 13,187,478 with an average per game crowd of 58,873. Teams in each conference are ranked by attendance over eight home games; numbers in parentheses indicate rank in 1991 (based on published attendance figures).

	AFC				NFC		
	Attendance	**Gm**	**Average**		**Attendance**	**Gm**	**Average**
1 Buffalo (1).	635,889	8	79,486	1 NY Giants (1).	597,199	8	74,650
2 Kansas City (4).	598,094	8	74,762	2 New Orleans (2)	548,655	8	68,582
3 Denver (3)	584,214	8	73,027	3 Philadelphia (3)	513,196	8	64,150
4 Cleveland (2).	571,752	8	71,469	4 Dallas (8)	501,901	8	62,738
5 LA Raiders (7).	507,781	8	63,473	5 Chicago (6)	491,778	8	61,472
6 NY Jets (8)	495,562	8	61,945	6 Detroit (4)	491,492	8	61,437
7 Houston (10)	482,726	8	60,341	7 San Francisco (5).	478,570	8	59,821
8 Miami (5)	475,858	8	59,482	8 Washington (12)	438,266	8	54,783
9 Seattle (9)	466,880	8	58,360	9 Green Bay (11)	425,037	8	53,130
10 Indianapolis (11)	434,008	8	54,251	10 LA Rams (7)	412,685	8	51,586
11 Cincinnati (6)	422,592	8	52,824	11 Minnesota (10).	410,762	8	51,345
12 Pittsburgh (12)	406,935	8	50,867	12 Atlanta (13)	402,931	8	50,366
13 San Diego (13)	386,128	8	48,266	13 Tampa Bay (9)	371,800	8	46,475
14 New England (14)	308,442	8	38,555	14 Phoenix (14).	326,345	8	40,793
TOTAL.	6,776,861	112	60,508	TOTAL.	6,410,617	112	57,238

Note: Green Bay played 5 games at Lambeau Field (55,407 avg.) and 3 at County Stadium (49,334 avg.).

Home Fields

Listed below are the principal home fields used through the years by current NFL teams. The largest capacity of each stadium is noted in the right-hand column. All-America Football Conference stadiums (1946-49) are included for Cleveland and San Francisco; and American Football League stadiums (1960-69) are included for Buffalo, Cincinnati, Denver, Houston, Kansas City, LA (Oakland) Raiders, Miami, New England (Boston), NY Jets and San Diego.

AFC

Buffalo Bills

1960-72	War Memorial Stadium.	45,748
1973–	Rich Stadium (Orchard Park, NY).	80,290
	(1973 capacity—80,020)	

Cincinnati Bengals

1968-69	Nippert Stadium (Univ. of Cincinnati)	26,500
1970–	Riverfront Stadium	60,389
	(1970 capacity—56,200)	

Cleveland Browns

1946–	Cleveland Stadium	78,512
	(1946 capacity—85,703)	

Denver Broncos

1960–	Mile High Stadium	76,273
	(1960 capacity—34,000)	

Houston Oilers

1960-64	Jeppesen Stadium	23,500
1965-67	Rice Stadium (Rice Univ.).	70,000
1968–	Astrodome	62,021
	(1968 capacity—52,000)	

Indianapolis Colts

1953-83	Memorial Stadium (Baltimore)	60,020
1984–	Hoosier Dome (Indianapolis)	60,389
	(1984 capacity—60,127)	

Kansas City Chiefs

1960-62	Cotton Bowl (Dallas)	72,000
1963-71	Municipal Stadium (Kansas City)	47,000
1972–	Arrowhead Stadium	77,872
	(1972 capacity—78,097)	

Los Angeles Raiders

1960	Kesar Stadium (San Francisco)	59,636
1961	Candlestick Park	42,500
1962-65	Frank Youell Field (Oakland)	20,000
1666-81	Oakland-Alameda County Coliseum	54,587
1982–	Memorial Coliseum (Los Angeles)	92,488
	(1982 capacity—92,604)	

Miami Dolphins

1966-86	Orange Bowl	75,206
1987–	Joe Robbie Stadium	73,000
	(1987 capacity—75,500)	

New England Patriots

1960-62	Nickerson Field (Boston Univ.)	17,369
1963-68	Fenway Park	33,379
1969	Alumni Stadium (Boston College)	26,000
1970	Harvard Stadium	37,300
1971–	Foxboro Stadium	60,300
	(1971 capacity—61,114)	

New York Jets

1960-63	Polo Grounds	55,987
1964-83	Shea Stadium	60,372
1984–	Giants Stadium (E.Rutherford, NJ)	76,891

Pittsburgh Steelers

1933-57	Forbes Field	35,000
1958-63	Forbes Field	35,000
	& Pitt Stadium	54,500
1964-69	Pitt Stadium	54,500
1970–	Three Rivers Stadium	59,030
	(1970 capacity—49,000)	

San Diego Chargers

1960	Memorial Coliseum (Los Angeles)	92,604
1961-66	Balboa Stadium (San Diego)	34,000
1967–	San Diego/Jack Murphy Stadium	60,750
	(1967 capacity—54,000)	

Seattle Seahawks

1976–	Kingdome	66,400
	(1976 capacity—65,000)	

Ballpark Name Changes: CLEVELAND—**Cleveland Stadium** originally Municipal Stadium (1932-74); DENVER—**Mile High Stadium** originally Bears Stadium (1948-66); NEW ENGLAND—**Foxboro Stadium** originally Schaefer Stadium (1971-82), then Sullivan Stadium (1983-89); SAN DIEGO—**San Diego/Jack Murphy Stadium** originally San Diego Stadium (1967-81).

NFC

Atlanta Falcons

1966-91	Atlanta-Fulton County Stadium	59,643
1992–	Georgia Dome	71,594

Chicago Bears

1920	Staley Field (Decatur, IL)	—
1921-70	Wrigley Field (Chicago)	37,741
1971–	Soldier Field	66,946
	(1971 capacity—55,049)	

Dallas Cowboys

1960-70	Cotton Bowl	72,132
1971–	Texas Stadium (Irving, TX)	65,024
	(1971 capacity—65,101)	

Detroit Lions

1930-33	Spartan Stadium (Portsmouth, OH)	8,200
1934-37	Univ.of Detroit Stadium	25,000
1938-74	Tiger Stadium	54,468
1975–	Pontiac Silverdome	80,494
	(1975 capacity—80,638)	

Green Bay Packers

1921-22	Hagemeister Brewery Park	—
1923-24	Bellevue Park	—
1925-56	City Stadium I	24,800
1957–	Lambeau Field	59,543
	(1957 capacity—32,150)	

Note: The Packers have played some games in Milwaukee each season since 1933: at Borchert Field, State Fair Park and Marquette Stadium (1933-52), and County Stadium (56,051) since 1953.

Los Angeles Rams

1937-42	Municipal Stadium (Cleveland)	85,703
1945	Suspended operations for one year	
1944-45	Municipal Stadium	85,703
1946-79	Memorial Coliseum (Los Angeles)	92,604
1980–	Anaheim Stadium	69,008

Minnesota Vikings

1961-81	Metropolitan Stadium (Bloomington)	48,446
1982–	HHH Metrodome (Minneapolis)	63,000
	(1982 capacity—62,220)	

New Orleans Saints

1967-74	Tulane Stadium	80,997
1975–	Louisiana Superdome	69,065
	(1975 capacity—74,472)	

New York Giants

1925-55	Polo Grounds II	55,200
1956-73	Yankee Stadium I	63,800
1973-74	Yale Bowl (New Haven, CT)	70,896
1975	Shea Stadium	60,372
1976–	Giants Stadium (E.Rutherford, NJ)	76,891
	(1976 capacity—76,800)	

Philadelphia Eagles

1933-35	Baker Bowl	18,800
1936-39	Municipal Stadium	73,702
1940	Shibe Park	33,608
1941	Municipal Stadium	73,702
1942	Shibe Park	33,608
1943	Forbes Field (Pittsburgh)	34,528
1944-57	Shibe Park	33,608
1958-70	Franklin Field (Univ.of Penn.)	60,546
1971–	Veterans Stadium	65,356
	(1971 capacity—65,000)	

Phoenix Cardinals

1920-21	Normal Field (Chicago)	7,500
1922-25	Comiskey Park	28,000
1926-28	Normal Field	7,500
1929-59	Comiskey Park	52,000
1960-65	Busch Stadium (St.Louis)	34,000
1966-87	Busch Memorial Stadium	54,392
1988–	Sun Devil Stadium (Tempe, AZ)	73,473

National Football League (Cont.)
Home Fields

San Francisco 49ers

1946-70	Kezar Stadium	59,636
1971–	Candlestick Park	66,503
	(1971 capacity—61,246)	

Tampa Bay Buccaneers

1976–	Tampa Stadium	74,315
	(1976 capacity—71,951)	

Washington Redskins

1932	Braves Field (Boston)	40,000
1933-36	Fenway Park	27,000
1937-60	Griffith Stadium (Washington, DC)	35,000
1961–	RFK Stadium	55,672
	(1961 capacity—55,004)	

Ballpark Name Changes: ATLANTA—**Atlanta-Fulton County Stadium** originally Atlanta Stadium (1966-74); CHICAGO—**Wrigley Field** originally Cubs Park (1916-25), also, **Comiskey Park** originally White Sox Park (1910-12); DETROIT— **Tiger Stadium** originally Navin Field (1912-37), then Briggs Stadium (1938-60), also, **Pontiac Silverdome** originally Pontiac Metropolitan Stadium (1975); GREEN BAY—**Lambeau Field** originally City Stadium II (1957-64); PHILADELPHIA—**Shibe Park** renamed Connie Mack Stadium in 1953; ST. LOUIS—**Busch Memorial Stadium** renamed Busch Stadium in 1983; WASHINGTON—**RFK Stadium** originally D.C.Stadium (1961-68).

NATIONAL HOCKEY LEAGUE

Campbell Conference

		Location	Built	Capacity
Calgary Flames	**Olympic Saddledome**	Calgary, Alb.	1983	20,214
Chicago Blackhawks	**Chicago Stadium**	Chicago, IL	1929	17,317
Detroit Red Wings	**Joe Louis Arena**	Detroit, MI	1979	19,275
Edmonton Oilers	**Northlands Coliseum**	Edmonton, Alb.	1974	17,503
Los Angeles Kings	**Great Western Forum**	Inglewood, CA	1967	16,005
Minnesota North Stars	**Met Center**	Bloomington, MN	1967	15,274
St.Louis Blues	**St.Louis Arena**	St.Louis, MO	1929	17,188
San Jose Sharks	**Cow Palace**	Daly City, CA	1941	11,100
Tampa Bay Lightning	**Expo Hall**	Tampa, FL	1977	10,500
Toronto Maple Leafs	**Maple Leaf Gardens**	Toronto, Ont.	1931	16,382
Vancouver Canucks	**Pacific Coliseum**	Vancouver, B.C.	1968	16,123
Winnipeg Jets	**Winnipeg Arena**	Winnipeg, Man.	1954	15,393

Wales Conference

		Location	Built	Capacity
Boston Bruins	**Boston Garden**	Boston, MA	1928	14,448
Buffalo Sabres	**Memorial Auditorium**	Buffalo, NY	1940	16,325
Hartford Whalers	**Civic Center Coliseum**	Hartford, CT	1975	15,635
Montreal Canadiens	**Montreal Forum**	Montreal, Que.	1924	16,197
New Jersey Devils	**Meadowlands Arena**	E.Rutherford, NJ	1981	19,040
New York Islanders	**Veterans' Coliseum**	Uniondale, NY	1971	16,297
New York Rangers	**Madison Sqare Garden**	New York, NY	1968	18,200
Ottawa Senators	**Ottawa Civic Center**	Ottawa, Ont.	1967	10,500
Philadelphia Flyers	**The Spectrum**	Philadelphia, PA	1967	17,380
Pittsburgh Penguins	**Civic Arena**	Pittsburgh, PA	1961	16,164
Quebec Nordiques	**Colisée de Quebec**	Quebec City, Que.	1951	15,399
Washington Capitals	**Capital Centre**	Landover, MD	1973	18,130

Rank by Capacity

Campbell		Wales	
Saddledome	20,214	Meadowlands	19,040
Joe Louis	19,275	Mad.Sq.Garden	18,200
Northlands	17,503	Capital Centre	18,130
Chicago Stadium	17,317	Spectrum	17,380
St.Louis	17,188	Buffalo Aud.	16,325
M.Leaf Gardens	16,382	Veterans'	16,297
Pacific	16,123	Montreal Forum	16,197
GW Forum	16,005	Pittsburgh	16,164
Winnipeg	15,393	Hartford	15,635
Met Center	15,274	Le Colisée	15,399
Cow Palace	11,100	Boston Garden	14,448
Expo Hall	10,500	Ottawa	10,500

Note: Figures do not include Standing Room.

Rank by Age

Campbell		Wales	
Chicago Stadium	1929	Montreal Forum	1924
St.Louis	1929	Boston Garden	1928
M.Leaf Gardens	1931	Buffalo Aud.	1940
Cow Palace	1941	Le Colisée	1951
Winnipeg	1954	Pittsburgh	1961
Met Center	1967	Ottawa	1967
GW Forum	1967	Spectrum	1967
Pacific	1968	Mad.Sq.Garden	1968
Northlands	1974	Veterans'	1971
Expo Hall	1977	Capital Centre	1973
Joe Louis	1979	Hartford	1975
Saddledome	1983	Meadowlands	1981

Note: The Montreal Forum was rebuilt in 1968; the Hartford Civic Center in 1980.

1991-92 NHL Attendance

The official overall paid attendance figure released by the NHL for the 880-game 1991-92 regular season was 12,769,676 for an official average per game crowd of 14,511.

Since the NHL does not release team-by-team attendance figures, the totals below were taken from the May, 8, 1992 issue of *The Hockey News*. The figures show overall attendance at 13,413,275 with an average per game crowd of 15,242. Teams in each conference are ranked by attendance over 40 home games; **S/O** heading indicates number of sellouts; numbers in parentheses indicate rank in 1990-91 (based on published attendance figures).

Campbell Conference

		Attendance	S/O	Average
1	Detroit (2)	788,920	40	19,723
2	Calgary (1)	788,760	17	19,719
3	St.Louis (4)	700,724	29	17,518
4	Chicago (3)	700,360	39	17,509
5	Edmonton (5)	647,170	7	16,179
6	Los Angeles (7)	640,200	40	16,005
7	Vancouver (8)	630,755	25	15,769
8	Toronto (6)	623,439	33	15,586
9	Minnesota (10)	538,860	13	13,471
10	Winnipeg (9)	491,640	5	12,291
11	San Jose*	435,520	40	10,888
	TOTAL	6,986,348	288	15,878

*San Jose was an expansion team in 1991-92.

Wales Conference

		Attendance	S/O	Average
1	Philadelphia (1)	685,604	11	17,140
2	Montreal (2)	680,203	40	17,005
3	NY Rangers (5)	676,141	11	16,903
4	Washington (3)	663,591	13	16,590
5	Pittsburgh (4)	639,736	31	15,993
6	Buffalo (6)	615,699	16	15,392
7	Boston (7)	570,957	18	14,274
8	Quebec (8)	546,654	4	13,666
9	New Jersey (9)	513,499	5	12,837
10	Hartford (10)	433,289	2	10,832
11	NY Islanders (11)	401,554	4	10,038
	TOTAL	6,426,927	155	14,607

Home Ice

Listed below are the principal home buildings used through the years by current NHL teams. The largest capacity of each arena is noted in the right hand column. World Hockey Association arenas (1972-76) are included for Edmonton, Hartford, Quebec and Winnipeg.

Campbell Conference

Calgary Flames
1972-80	The Omni (Atlanta)	15,278
1980-83	Calgary Corral	7,424
1983–	Olympic Saddledome	20,214
	(1983 capacity—16,674)	

Chicago Stadium
1926-29	Chicago Coliseum	5,000
1929–	Chicago Stadium	17,317
	(1929 capacity—16,500)	

Detroit Red Wings
1926-27	Border Cities Arena (Windsor, Ont.)	3,200
1927-79	Olympia Stadium (Detroit)	16,700
1979–	Joe Louis Arena	19,275
	(1979 capacity—19,275)	

Edmonton Oilers
1972-74	Edmonton Gardens	7,200
1974–	Northlands Coliseum	17,503
	(1974 capacity—15,513)	

Los Angeles Kings
1967–	Great Western Forum	16,005
	(1967 capacity—15,651)	

Note: The Kings played 17 games at Long Beach Sports Arena and LA Sports Arena at the start of the 1967-68 season.

Minnesota North Stars
1967–	Met Center	15,274
	(1967 capacity—14,400)	

St.Louis Blues
1967–	St.Louis Arena	17,188
	(1967 capacity—14,200)	

San Jose Sharks
1991–	Cow Palace	11,100

Tampa Bay Lightning
1992–	Expo Hall (Tampa)	10,500

Toronto Maple Leafs
1917-31	Mutual Street Arena	8,000
1931–	Maple Leaf Gardens	16,382
	(1931 capacity—13,542)	

Vancouver Canucks
1970–	Pacific Coliseum	16,123
	(1970 capacity—15,760)	

Winnipeg Jets
1972–	Winnipeg Arena	15,393
	(1972 capacity—10,177)	

Building Name Changes: LOS ANGELES—**Great Western Forum** originally The Forum (1967-88); MINNESOTA—**Met Center** originally Metropolitan Sports Center (1967-82); ST.LOUIS—**St.Louis Arena** renamed The Checkerdome in 1977, then St.Louis Arena again in 1982.

Wales Conference

Boston Bruins
1924-28	Boston Arena	6,200
1928–	Boston Garden	14,448
	(1928 capacity—14,500)	

Buffalo Sabres
1970–	Memorial Auditorium	16,325
	(1970 capacity—10,429)	

National Hockey League (Cont.)
Home Ice

Hartford Whalers

1972-73	Boston Garden	14,442
1973-74	Boston Garden (regular season)	14,442
	W.Springfield, MA Big E (playoffs)	5,513
1974-75	West Springfield Big E	5,513
	& Hartford (CT) Civic Center	10,507
1975-77	Hartford Civic Center	10,507
1977-78	Hartford Civic Center	10,507
	& Springfield (MA) Civic Center	7,725
1978-79	Springfield Civic Center	7,725
1979-80	Springfield Civic Center	7,725
	& Hartford Civic Center II	14,250
1980–	Hartford Civic Center II	15,635
	(1980 capacity—14,460)	

Note: The Hartford Civic Center roof caved in Jan, 1978, forcing the Whalers to move their home games to Springfield,MA, for two years.

Montreal Canadiens

1910-20	Jubilee Arena	3,200
1913-18	Montreal Arena (Westmount)	6,000
1918-26	Mount Royal Arena	6,750
1926-68	Montreal Forum I	15,500
1968–	Montreal Forum II	16,197
	(1968 capacity—16,074)	

Note: The Forum (original capacity: 9,200) was built in 1924 for Montreal's other NHL team, the Maroons, who were its only tenant from 1924-26. The Maroons, who folded after the 1937-38 season, shared the Forum with the Canadiens from 1924-38.

New Jersey Devils

1974-76	Kemper Arena (Kansas City)	16,300
1976-82	McNichols Arena (Denver)	15,900
1982–	Meadowlands Arena	
	(E.Rutherford, NJ)	19,040
	(1982 capacity—19,023)	

New York Islanders

1972–	Nassau Veterans' Mem.Coliseum	16,297
	(1972 capacity—14,500)	

New York Rangers

1925-68	Madison Square Garden III	15,925
1968–	Madison Square Garden IV	18,200
	(1968 capacity—17,250)	

Ottawa Senators

1992–	Ottawa Civic Center	10,500

Philadelphia Flyers

1967–	The Spectrum	17,382
	(1967 capacity—14,558)	

Note: A section of Spectrum roof blew off in March,1968, forcing the Flyers to play their last seven regular season home games at Madison Sq.Garden (1 game), Maple Leaf Gardens (1) and Le Colisée in Quebec (5). The roof was fixed by the playoffs.

Pittsburgh Penguins

1967–	Civic Arena	16,164
	(1967 capacity—12,508)	

Quebec Nordiques

1972–	Le Colisée de Québec	15,399
	(1972 capacity—10,004)	

Washington Capitals

1974–	Capital Centre (Landover, MD)	18,130

CANADIAN FOOTBALL LEAGUE

Western Division

		Location	Built	Capacity	Field
British Columbia Lions	B.C. Place	Vancouver, B.C.	1983	59,478	Turf
Calgary Stampeders	McMahon Stadium	Calgary, Alb.	1960	38,200	Turf
Edmonton Eskimos	Commonwealth Stadium	Edmonton, Alb.	1978	60,081	Grass
Saskatchewan Roughriders	Taylor Field	Regina, Sask.	1948	27,637	Turf

Eastern Division

		Location	Built	Capacity	Field
Hamilton Tiger-Cats	Ivor Wynne Stadium	Hamilton, Ont.	1932	29,161	Turf
Ottawa Rough Riders	Lansdowne Stadium	Ottawa, Ont.	1967	30,927	Turf
Toronto Argos	SkyDome	Toronto, Ont.	1989	53,595	Turf
Winnipeg Blue Bombers	Winnipeg Stadium	Winnipeg, Man.	1953	32,648	Turf

WORLD CUP SOCCER

On Mar. 23, 1992, nine playing sites were chosen by the Federation Internationale de Football Association (FIFA) for the 1994 World Cup soccer tournament to be held in the United States from June 17 through July, 17. The Rose Bowl will be the site of the Cup final.

	Location	Built	Seats	Field
Cotton Bowl	Dallas, TX	1932	72,032	Turf
Florida Citrus Bowl	Orlando, FL	1936	70,000	Grass
Foxboro Stadium	Foxboro, MA	1975	69,065	Grass
Giants Stadium	E.Rutherford, NJ	1976	77,152	Turf
Pontiac Silverdome	Pontiac, MI	1975	80,494	Turf
RFK Stadium	Washington, DC	1961	55,672	Grass
Rose Bowl	Pasadena, CA	1922	102,083	Grass
Soldier Field	Chicago, IL	1924	66,946	Grass
Stanford Stadium	Stanford, CA	1921	86,019	Grass

Note: All turf playing fields will have to be replaced by grass, even the indoor Silverdome.

MISCELLANEOUS

Auto Racing's two biggest 500-mile races—the Daytona 500 and Indianapolis 500; the Tennis Grand Slam—Wimbledon and the Australian, French and U.S. Opens; Horse Racing's Triple Crown—the Kentucky Derby, Preakness Stakes and Belmont Stakes; are all held annually at the same sites. Note that seating does not include standing room, and infield capacity for auto and horse racing is estimated.

Auto Racing

Oval	Seats	Infield
Daytona International Speedway	94,500	55,000
Indianapolis Motor Speedway	265,000	135,000

Tennis

Event	Main Stadium	Seats
Australian Open	National Tennis Centre	15,000
French Open	Stade Roland Garros	16,500
Wimbledon	Centre Court	13,107
U.S.Open	Louis Armstrong Stadium	20,000

Horse Racing

Race	Racetrack	Seats	Infield
Kentucky Derby	Churchill Downs	51,500	100,000
Preakness	Pimlico Race Course	40,000	50,000
Belmont Stakes	Belmont Park	32,491	50,000

Record crowds: Kentucky Derby—163,628 (1974, 100th running, won by Cannonade); Preakness—90,14 (1989, 114th running, won by Sunday Silence); Belmont Stakes—82,694 (1971, 103rd running, Canonero II loses bid to win Triple Crown).

COLLEGE BASKETBALL

The 50 Largest Arenas

The 50 largest arenas in Division I college basketball. Note that (*) indicates part-time home court.

#	Arena	Seats	Home Team
1	Carrier Dome	33,000	Syracuse
2	Thompson-Boling Center	24,535	Tennessee
3	Charlotte Coliseum	23,698	NC-Charlotte
4	Rupp Arena	23,000	Kentucky
5	Marriott Center	22,700	BYU
6	Dean Smith Center	21,572	N.Carolina
7	Meadowlands Arena	20,039	Seton Hall*
8	The Pyramid	20,000	Memphis St.
9	Madison Square Garden	19,763	St.John's*
10	Freedom Hall	18,865	Louisville
11	Capital Centre	18,756	Georgetown
12	Bradley Center	18,633	Marquette
13	Thomas & Mack Center	18,500	UNLV
14	The Spectrum	18,168	Villanova*
15	Rosemont Horizon	17,500	DePaul* & Loyola-IL*
16	Assembly Hall	17,357	Indiana
17	University Arena (The Pit)	17,126	New Mexico
18	Pittsburgh Civic Arena	16,798	Pittsburgh*
19	Memorial Auditorium	16,564	Canisius*
20	Williams Arena	16,426	Minnesota
21	Assembly Hall	16,321	Illinois
22	Erwin Center	16,231	Texas
23	Allen Field House	15,800	Kansas
	LA Sports Arena	15,800	USC
25	Carver-Hawkeye	15,550	Iowa
26	LA Sports Arena	15,509	USC
27	Knickerbocker Arena	15,500	Siena*
28	Memorial Gymnasium	15,378	Vanderbilt
29	Hartford Civic Center	15,239	UConn*
30	Breslin Student Events Center	15,138	Mich.St.
31	Coleman Coliseum	15,043	Alabama
32	Arena-Auditorium	15,028	Wyoming
33	Oakland Coliseum Arena	15,025	California*
34	Miami Arena	15,008	Miami-FL
35	Huntsman Center	15,000	Utah
36	Cole Fieldhouse	14,500	Maryland
37	Joel Coliseum	14,407	W.Forest
38	Devaney Sports Center	14,302	Nebraska
39	University Center	14,287	Arizona St.
40	Maravich Center	14,164	LSU
41	Mackey Arena	14,123	Purdue
42	Hilton Coliseum	14,020	Iowa St.
43	WVU Coliseum	14,000	West Va.
44	San Diego Sports Arena	13,741	S.Diego.St.
45	Crisler Arena	13,609	Michigan
46	Bramlage Coliseum	13,500	Kansas St.
47	CSU Convention Center	13,500	Cleveland St.
48	McKale Center	13,477	Arizona
49	Univ. of Dayton Arena	13,455	Dayton
50	Hearnes Center	13,300	Missouri

Conference Home Courts

Division I conference by conference listing includes member teams for 1992-93 season. Teams with home games in more than one arena are noted.

Atlantic Coast

	Home Floor	Seats
Clemson	Littlejohn Coliseum	11,020
Duke	Cameron Indoor Stadium	9,314
Florida St	Tallahassee Civic Center	12,500
Georgia Tech	Alexander Mem. Coliseum	10,300
Maryland	Cole Field House	14,500
North Carolina	Dean Smith Center	21,572
N.C.State	Reynolds Coliseum	12,400
Virginia	University Hall	8,864
Wake Forest	Joel Coliseum	14,407

Atlantic 10

	Home Floor	Seats
G.Washington	Charles E.Smith Center	5,000
Massachusetts	Curry Hicks Cage	4,058
	& Wm. D. Mullins Center	9,493
Rhode Island	Keaney Gymnasium	5,000
	& Providence Civic Center	13,203
Rutgers	Louis Brown Athletic Center	9,000
St.Joseph's-PA	Alumni Mem. Fieldhouse	3,200
St.Bonaventure	Reilly Center	6,000
Temple	McGonigle Hall	3,900
West Virginia	WVU Coliseum	14,000

Note: There are only eight teams in the Atlantic 10.

College Basketball (Cont.)
Conference Home Courts

Big East

Home Floor		Seats
Boston College.....	Conte Forum	8,624
Connecticut	Gampel Pavilion	8,302
	& Hartford Civic Center	15,239
Georgetown.......	Capital Centre	18,756
Miami-FL	Miami Arena	15,008
Pittsburgh	Fitzgerald Field House	6,798
	& Pittsburgh Civic Arena	16,798
Providence	Providence Civic Center	13,203
St.John's	Alumni Hall	6,008
	& Madison Sq.Garden	19,763
Seton Hall........	Walsh Gymnasium	3,200
	& Meadowlands Arena	20,039
Syracuse	Carrier Dome	33,000
Villanova..........	duPont Pavilion	6,500
	& The Spectrum	18,168

Big Eight

Home Floor		Seats
Colorado	Coors Events Center	11,196
Iowa St	Hilton Coliseum	14,020
Kansas	Allen Fieldhouse	15,800
Kansas St	Bramlage Coliseum	13,500
Missouri	Hearnes Center	13,300
Nebraska	Devaney Sports Center	14,302
Oklahoma	Lloyd Noble Center	10,861
Okla.St	Gallagher-Iba Arena	6,381

Big Sky

Home Floor		Seats
Boise St	BSU Pavilion	12,200
Eastern Wash......	Reese Court	5,000
Idaho	Kibbie Dome	10,000
Idaho St	Holt Arena	7,938
Montana..........	Dahlberg Arena	9,057
Montana St.......	Brick Breeden Fieldhouse	7,848
Northern Arizona...	Walkup Skydome	7,500
Weber St..........	Dee Events Center	12,000

Big South

Home Floor		Seats
Campbell	Carter Gym	1,500
	& Cumberland County CC	5,500
Charleston	Charleston Southern FH	2,500
Coastal Carolina ...	Kimbel Gym	2,000
Liberty	Vines Center	9,000
MD-Balt.County	UMBC Fieldhouse	4,024
NC-Asheville	Justice Center	2,500
	& Asheville Civic Center	6,800
NC-Greensboro....	Spectator Gymnasium	2,500
Radford...........	Dedmon Center	5,000
Towson St	Towson Center	5,000
Winthrop..........	Winthrop Coliseum	6,100

Note: Maryland-Baltimore Country and Towson St. moved from East Coast after 1991-92 season.

Big Ten

Home Floor		Seats
Illinois	Assembly Hall	16,153
Indiana	Assembly Hall	17,357
Iowa	Carver-Hawkeye Arena	15,550
Michigan..........	Crisler Arena	13,609
Michigan St........	Breslin Events Center	15,138
Minnesota........	Williams Arena	16,426
Northwestern......	Welsh-Ryan Arena	8,117
Ohio St	St.John Arena	13,276
Penn St	Rec Hall	6,846
Purdue	Mackey Arena	14,123
Wisconsin	Wisconsin Field House	11,886

Note: Penn St., an independent during the 1991-92 season, makes the Big Ten an 11-team league.

Big West

Home Floor		Seats
CS-Fullerton	Titan Gym	4,000
Long Beach St	University Gym	2,200
	& Long Beach Arena	12,000
Nevada...........	Lawler Event Center	11,200
New Mexico St	Pan American Center	13,222
Pacific	Alex G.Spanos Center	6,000
San Jose St	The Event Center	4,600
UC-Irvine	Donald Bren Events Center	5,000
UC-Santa Barbara..	Campus Events Center	6,000
UNLV	Thomas & Mack Center	18,500
Utah St	The Spectrum	10,270

Note: Nevada moved from Big Sky after 1991-92 season.

Colonial

Home Floor		Seats
American	Bender Arena	5,000
East Carolina	Minges Coliseum	6,500
George Mason.....	Patriot Center	10,000
James Madison	JMU Convocation Center	7,612
NC-Wilmington	Trask Coliseum	6,100
Old Dominion	Norfolk Scope	10,253
Richmond	Robins Center	9,171
Wm.& Mary	William & Mary Hall	10,000

Great Midwest

Home Floor		Seats
Ala-Birmingham....	UAB Arena	8,500
	& Birmingham Civic Center	17,500
Cincinnati	Shoemaker Center	13,176
DePaul	Rosemont Horizon	17,500
	& Alumni Hall	5,229
Marquette.........	Bradley Center	18,633
Memphis St........	The Pyramid	20,000
St.Louis	The Arena	11,200

Ivy League

Home Floor		Seats
Brown	Pizzitola Sports Center	2,800
Columbia	Levien Gymnasium	3,408
Cornell	Alberding Field House	4,750
Dartmouth	Leede Arena	2,100
Harvard	Briggs Athletic Center	3,000
Penn	The Palestra	8,722
Princeton..........	Jadwin Gymnasium	7,442
Yale..............	Payne Whitney Gymnasium	3,100

Metro

Home Floor		Seats
Louisville..........	Freedom Hall	18,865
NC-Charlotte......	Charlotte Coliseum	23,698
South Florida	Sun Dome	10,347
Southern Miss......	Reed Green Coliseum	8,053
Tulane............	Fogelman Arena	3,500
VCU	Richmond Coliseum	10,716
Virginia Tech	Cassell Coliseum	9,971

Metro Atlantic

Home Floor		Seats
Canisius	The Aud	15,564
	& Koessler Athletic Center	1,800
Fairfield...........	Alumni Hall	3,022
Iona..............	Mulcahy Center	3,200
Loyola-MD	Reitz Arena	3,000
Manhattan	Draddy Gymnasium	3,000
Niagara	Niagara Falls Conv.Center	6,000
	& Gallagher Center	3,200
St.Peter's	Yanitelli Center	3,200
Siena.............	Alumni Recreation Center	4,000
	& Knickerbocker Arena	15,500

Mid-American

Home Floor		Seats
Akron	James A. Rhodes Arena	6,250
Ball St	Activities Complex	12,000
Bowling Green	Anderson Arena	5,000
Central Mich.	Rose Arena	6,000
Eastern Mich.	Bowen Field House	5,600
Kent	Memorial Gym	6,034
Miami-OH	Millett Hall	9,200
Ohio Univ.	Convocation Center	13,080
Toledo	John F.Savage Hall	9,000
Western Mich	Read Fieldhouse	8,250

Note: Akron moved from Mid-Continent after 1991-92 season.

Mid-Continent

Home Floor		Seats
Cleveland St	Convocation Center	13,500
Eastern Ill	Lantz Gym	6,500
IL-Chicago	UIC Pavillion	10,000
Northern Ill.	Chick Evans Field House	6,044
Valparaiso	Athletics-Rec. Center	4,500
Western Ill.	Western Hall	5,139
WI-Green Bay	Veterans' Memorial	5,600
Wright St.	Ervin Nutter Center	10,632
Youngstown St	Beeghly Center	7,200

Note: Independent Wisconsin-Milwaukee will join conference in 1993-94.

Mid-Eastern

Home Floor		Seats
Bethune-Cookman	Moore Gym	2,000
Coppin St	Pullen Gym	3,000
Delaware St	Memorial Hall	4,000
Florida A&M.	Gaither Gym	6,000
Howard.	Burr Gym	3,900
MD-East.Shore.	Tawes Gym	3,500
Morgan St.	T.L.Hill Field House	7,500
N.Carolina A&T.	Corbett Sports Center	7,500
S.Carolina St	Smith-Hammond-Middleton	3,200

Midwestern

Home Floor		Seats
Butler.	Hinkle Fieldhouse	10,800
Dayton	Univ.of Dayton Arena	13,455
Detroit.	Cobo Arena	11,143
Duquesne	A.J.Palumbo Center	6,200
Evansville	Roberts Stadium	12,300
La Salle.	Philadelphia Civic Center	10,000
Loyola-IL.	Rosemont Horizon	17,500
	& Alumni Gym	1,500
Xavier-OH	Cincinnati Gardens	10,400

Note: Duquesne moved from Atlantic 10 and La Salle from Metro Atlantic after 1991-92 season.

Missouri Valley

Home Floor		Seats
Bradley	Carver Arena	10,470
Creighton	Omaha Civic Auditorium	9,481
Drake	Veterans Mem. Auditorium	11,679
Illinois St	Redbird Arena	10,125
Indiana St	Hulman Center	10,200
Northern Iowa	UNI-Dome	10,000
Southern Ill	SIU Arena	10,014
SW Missouri St	Hammons Student Center	8,858
Tulsa	Maxwell Convention Center	9,200
Wichita St	Levitt Arena	10,656

North Atlantic

Home Floor		Seats
Boston University	Walter Brown Arena	4,400
Delaware	Delaware Field House	3,000
Drexel	Phys.Education Center	2,500
Hartford	The Sports Center	4,475
Maine	Alfond Arena	6,000
New Hampshire	Lundholm Gym	3,500
Northeastern	Matthews Arena	6,500
Vermont	Patrick Gym	3,200

Northeast

Home Floor		Seats
FDU-Teaneck	Rothman Center	5,000
LIU-Brooklyn.	Schwartz Athletic Center	1,700
Marist	McCann Center	3,944
Monmouth	Alumni Memorial Gym	2,800
Mt.St.Mary's	Knott Arena	3,500
Rider	Alumni Gymnasium	2,200
Robert Morris	Charles Sewall Center	3,056
St.Francis-NY	Physical Ed. Center	1,400
St.Francis-PA.	Maurice Stokes Center	4,000
Wagner	Sutter Gym	1,650

Note: Rider moved from East Coast after 1991-92 season.

Ohio Valley

Home Floor		Seats
Austin Peay	Dunn Center	9,000
Eastern Ky.	McBrayer Arena	6,500
Middle Tenn.St	Murphy Athletic Center	11,520
Morehead St.	Ellis Johnson Arena	6,500
Murray St	Racer Arena	5,550
SE Missouri St	Show Me Center	7,000
Tennessee-Martin	Pacer Arena	6,400
Tennessee St.	Gentry Center	10,500
Tennessee Tech	Eblen Center	10,150

Note: Tennessee-Martin moved from Gulf South (Div.II) after 1991-92 season.

Pacific-10

Home Floor		Seats
Arizona	McKale Center	13,477
Arizona St	University Activity Center	14,287
California	Harmon Arena	6,578
	& Oakland Coliseum	15,025
Oregon	McArthur Court	10,063
Oregon St.	Gill Coliseum	10,400
Stanford	Maples Pavilion	7,500
UCLA	Pauley Pavilion	12,543
USC.	LA Sports Arena	15,800
Washington	Hec Edmundson Pavilion	8,000
Wash.St.	Friel Court	12,058

Patriot League

Home Floor		Seats
Army	Cristl Arena	5,043
Bucknell	Davis Gym	2,100
Colgate	Cotterell Court	3,000
Fordham.	Rose Hill Gymnasium	3,470
Holy Cross	Hart Center	4,000
Lafayette	Kirby Field House	3,500
Lehigh.	Stabler Center	5,600
Navy	Alumni Hall	5,710

Future NCAA Final Four Sites

Year	Arena	Seats	Location	Year	Arena	Seats	Location
1993	Superdome	65,000	New Orleans	1996	Meadowlands	20,039	E.Rutherford
1994	Charlotte Coliseum	23,698	Charlotte	1997	Hoosier Dome	38,000	Indianapolis
1995	Kingdome	38,000	Seattle				

College Basketball (Cont.)
Conference Home Courts

Southeastern

EASTERN	Home Floor	Seats
Florida	O'Connell Center	12,000
Georgia	Georgia Coliseum	10,400
Kentucky	Rupp Arena	23,000
South Carolina	Carolina Coliseum	12,401
Tennessee	Thompson-Boling Arena	24,535
Vanderbilt	Memorial Gymnasium	15,378

WESTERN	Home Floor	Seats
Alabama	Coleman Coliseum	15,043
Arkansas	Barnhill Arena	9,000
	Barton Coliseum	8,303
	& Convention Center	7,473
Auburn	Eaves Memorial Coliseum	12,500
LSU	Maravich Assembly Center	14,164
Mississippi	Tad Smith Coliseum	8,135
Mississippi St.	Humphrey Coliseum	10,000

Southern

	Home Floor	Seats
Appalachian St.	Varsity Gymnasium	8,000
The Citadel	McAlister Field House	6,200
Davidson	Belk Arena	6,000
E.Tenn.St.	Memorial Center	12,000
Furman	Greenville Memorial Aud.	6,000
Ga.Southern	Hanner Fieldhouse	5,500
Marshall	Henderson Center	10,250
Tenn-Chatt	UTC Arena	11,218
VMI	Cameron Hall	5,029
W.Carolina	Ramsey Center	7,826

Note: Davidson moved from Big South and Georgia Southern from Trans America after 1991-92 season.

Southland

	Home Floor	Seats
McNeese St.	Burton Coliseum	8,000
Nicholls St.	Stopher Gym	3,800
North Texas	UNT Super Pit	10,000
NE Louisiana	Ewing Coliseum	8,000
N'western St.	Prather Coliseum	3,900
Sam Houston St.	Johnson Coliseum	6,172
SW Texas St	Strahan Coliseum	7,200
S.F.Austin	SFA Coliseum	7,050
TX-Arlington	Texas Hall	4,200
TX-San Antonio	Convocation Center	5,100

Southwest

	Home Floor	Seats
Baylor	Ferrell Center	10,084
Houston	Hofheinz Pavilion	10,060
Rice	Autry Court	5,400
SMU	Moody Coliseum	9,007
Texas	Erwin Center	16,231
Texas A&M	G. Rollie White Coliseum	7,500
TCU	Daniel-Meyer Coliseum	7,166
Texas Tech	Lubbock Municipal Coliseum	8,174

Southwestern

	Home Floor	Seats
Alabama St.	C.J. Dunn Arena	3,200
Alcorn St	Scalpin' Grounds Arena	7,000
Grambling	Memorial Gym	5,000
Jackson St.	Williams Assembly Center	8,000
Miss.Valley St	Harrison Athletic Complex	6,000
Prairie View	Baby Dome	6,600
Southern-BR	F.G. Clark Activity Center	7,500
TX Southern	Health & P.E. Building	7,500

Sun Belt

	Home Floor	Seats
Ark-Little Rock	Barton Coliseum	8,303
Arkansas St.	Convocation Center	10,563
Jacksonville	Jacksonville Coliseum	10,000
Lamar	Montagne Center	10,080
Louisiana Tech	Thomas Assembly Center	8,000
New Orleans	Kiefer Lakefront Arena	10,000
South Alabama	Mobile Civic Center	10,000
SW Louisiana	Cajundome	12,000
Texas-Pan Am	UTPA Field House	5,000
Western Ky	E.A. Diddle Arena	12,000

Trans America

	Home Floor	Seats
Centenary	Gold Dome	4,000
Central Fla	UCF Arena	5,100
Charleston	F. Mitchell Johnson Center	3,052
Florida Int'l	Golden Panther Arena	4,661
Georgia St	GSU Athletic Complex	5,500
Mercer	Macon Coliseum	8,500
Samford	Seibert Hall	4,000
SE Louisiana	University Center	6,500
Stetson	Edmunds Center	5,000

Note: Central Florida moved from Sun Belt after 1991-92 season.

West Coast

	Home Floor	Seats
Gonzaga	Charlotte Martin Centre	4,000
Loyola-CA	Albert Gersten Pavilion	4,500
Pepperdine	Firestone Fieldhouse	3,104
Portland	Earle Chiles Center	5,000
St.Mary's-CA	McKeon Pavilion	3,500
San Diego	USD Sports Center	2,500
San Francisco	Memorial Gymnasium	5,300
Santa Clara	Toso Pavilion	5,000

Western Athletic

	Home Floor	Seats
Air Force	Cadet Fieldhouse	6,000
BYU	Marriott Center	22,700
Colorado St	Moby Arena	9,001
Fresno St.	Selland Arena	10,159
Hawaii	Blaisdell Center	7,575
New Mexico	University Arena (The Pit)	17,126
San Diego St	San Diego Sports Arena	13,741
UTEP	Special Events Center	12,222
Utah	Jon Huntsman Center	15,000
Wyoming	Arena-Auditorium	15,028

Note: Fresno St. moved from Big West after 1991-92 season.

Independents

	Home Floor	Seats
Buffalo	Alumni Arena	10,000
Cent.Conn.St	Wm. Detrick Gymnasium	4,000
CS-Northridge	Matador Gymnasium	3,000
CS-Sacramento	Hornet Gym	1,800
Chicago St	Phys. Ed. & Athletics Building	2,500
Hofstra	Physical Fitness Center	3,500
Missouri-KC	Municipal Auditorium	10,000
NE Illinois	Chick Evans Field House	6,076
Notre Dame	Joyce Center	11,418
So.Utah St.	The Centrum	5,300
WI-Milwaukee	Klotsche Center	4,000
	& The Mecca	11,052

COLLEGE FOOTBALL

The 30 Largest Stadiums

The 30 largest stadiums in Division I college football. Note that (*) indicates part-time home field.

		Location	Seats	Home Team	Conference	Built	Field
1	Michigan Stadium	Ann Arbor, MI	102,501	Michigan	Big Ten	1927	Grass
2	Rose Bowl	Pasadena, CA	102,083	UCLA	Pac-10	1922	Grass
3	Beaver Stadium	University Park, PA	93,713	Penn St.	Big Ten	1960	Grass
4	Memorial Coliseum	Los Angeles, CA	92,516	USC	Pac-10	1923	Grass
5	Neyland Stadium	Knoxville, TN	91,902	Tennessee	SEC-East	1921	Turf
6	Ohio Stadium	Columbus, OH	91,470	Ohio St.	Big Ten	1922	Grass
7	Stanford Stadium	Stanford, CA	86,019	Stanford	Pac-10	1921	Grass
8	Sanford Stadium	Athens, GA	85,434	Georgia	SEC-East	1929	Grass
9	Jordan-Hare Stadium	Auburn, AL	85,214	Auburn	SEC-West	1939	Grass
10	Legion Field	Birmingham, AL	83,071	Alabama*	SEC-West	1927	Turf
11	Florida Field	Gainesville, FL	83,000	Florida	SEC-East	1929	Turf
12	Tiger Stadium	Baton Rouge, LA	80,140	LSU	SEC-West	1924	Grass
13	Memorial Stadium	Clemson, SC	79,854	Clemson	ACC	1942	Grass
14	Memorial Stadium	Austin, TX	77,809	Texas	SWC	1924	Turf
15	Camp Randall Stadium	Madison, WI	77,745	Wisconsin	Big Ten	1917	Turf
16	Giants Stadium	E.Rutherford, NJ	76,891	Rutgers*	Big East	1976	Turf
17	Spartan Stadium	East Lansing, MI	76,000	Michigan St.	Big Ten	1957	Turf
18	Memorial Stadium	Berkeley, CA	75,662	California	Pac-10	1923	Turf
19	Owen Field	Norman, OK	75,004	Oklahoma	Big Eight	1923	Turf
20	Orange Bowl	Miami, FL	74,712	Miami-FL	Big East	1935	Grass
21	Sun Devil Stadium	Tempe, AZ	73,656	Arizona St.	Pac-10	1958	Grass
22	Memorial Stadium	Lincoln, NE	73,650	Nebraska	Big Eight	1923	Turf
23	Husky Stadium	Seattle, WA	72,500	Washington	Pac-10	1920	Turf
24	Williams-Brice Stadium	Columbia, SC	72,400	South Carolina	SEC	1934	Grass
25	Cotton Bowl	Dallas, TX	72,032	SMU*	SWC	1932	Turf
26	Yale Bowl	New Haven, CT	70,896	Yale	Ivy League	1914	Grass
27	Kinnick Stadium	Iowa City, IA	70,311	Iowa	Big Ten	1929	Grass
28	Kyle Field	College Station, TX	70,210	Texas A&M	SWC	1925	Turf
29	Bryant-Denny Stadium	Tuscaloosa, AL	70,123	Alabama	SEC	1929	Turf
	Doak Campbell	Tallahassee, FL	70,123	Florida St.	ACC	1950	Grass

Conference Home Fields

Division I-A conference by conference listing includes member teams for 1993 season, but reflects 1992 seating capacities.

ACC

	Stadium	Built	Seats	Field
Clemson	Memorial	1942	79,854	Grass
Duke	Wallace Wade	1929	33,941	Grass
Florida St	Doak Campbell	1950	70,123	Grass
Ga. Tech	Dodd/Grant	1914	46,000	Turf
Maryland	Byrd	1950	45,000	Grass
North Carolina	Kenan	1927	52,000	Grass
N.C. State	Carter-Finley	1966	47,000	Grass
Virginia	Scott	1931	42,000	Turf
Wake Forest	Groves	1968	31,500	Grass

Big East

	Stadium	Built	Seats	Field
Boston Col	Alumni	1957	32,000	Turf
Miami-FL	Orange Bowl	1935	74,712	Grass
Pittsburgh	Pitt	1925	56,500	Turf
Rutgers	Rutgers & Giants	1938 / 1976	23,000 / 76,891	Grass / Turf
Syracuse	Carrier Dome	1980	50,000	Turf
Temple	Veterans	1971	66,592	Turf
Va. Tech	Lane	1965	51,000	Grass
West Va.	Mountaineer Field	1980	63,500	Grass

Big Eight

	Stadium	Built	Seats	Field
Colorado	Folsom Field	1924	51,748	Turf
Iowa St	Trice Field	1975	50,000	Turf
Kansas	Memorial	1927	50,250	Turf
Kansas St	KSU	1968	42,000	Turf
Missouri	Faurot Field	1926	62,000	Turf
Nebraska	Memorial	1923	73,650	Turf
Oklahoma	Owen Field	1923	75,004	Turf
Oklahoma St	Lewis Field	1920	50,440	Turf

Big Ten

	Stadium	Built	Seats	Field
Illinois	Memorial	1923	69,000	Turf
Indiana	Memorial	1960	52,354	Turf
Iowa	Kinnick	1929	70,311	Grass
Michigan	Michigan	1927	102,501	Grass
Michigan St.	Spartan	1957	76,000	Turf
Minnesota	HHH Metrodome	1982	63,699	Turf
Northwestern	Dyche	1926	49,256	Turf
Ohio St	Ohio	1922	91,470	Grass
Penn St	Beaver	1960	93,713	Grass
Purdue	Ross-Ade	1924	67,861	Grass
Wisconsin	Camp Randall	1917	77,745	Turf

Note: Penn St. begins play in 1993.

College Football (Cont.)
Home Fields

Big West

Stadium		Built	Seats	Field
Arkansas St.	Indiana	1974	33,410	Grass
CS-Fullerton	Titan	1992	10,000	Grass
Louisiana Tech	Joe Aillet	1968	30,200	Grass
Nevada	Mackay	1966	30,485	Grass
New Mexico St	Aggie Memorial	1978	30,343	Grass
Northern Ill.	Huskie	1965	30,998	Turf
Pacific	Stagg Memorial	1950	30,153	Grass
San Jose St	Spartan	1933	31,218	Grass
SW Louisiana	Cajun Field	1971	31,000	Grass
UNLV	Silver Bowl	1971	32,000	Turf
Utah St	Dick Romney	1968	30,257	Grass

Note: Arkansas St., Louisiana Tech, Northern Illinois and SW Louisiana all begin play in 1993.

Mid-American

Stadium		Built	Seats	Field
Akron	Rubber Bowl	1940	35,202	Turf
Ball St	Ball State	1967	16,319	Grass
Bowling Green	Doyt Perry	1966	30,599	Grass
Central Mich.	Kelly/Shorts	1972	20,086	Turf
Eastern Mich.	Rynearson	1969	30,000	Turf
Kent	Dix	1969	30,520	Grass
Miami-OH	Fred Yager	1983	25,183	Grass
Ohio Univ.	Peden	1929	20,000	Grass
Toledo	Glass Bowl	1937	26,248	Turf
Western Mich	Waldo	1939	30,000	Turf

Pacific-10

Stadium		Built	Seats	Field
Arizona	Arizona	1928	56,167	Grass
Arizona St	Sun Devil	1958	73,656	Grass
California	Memorial	1923	75,662	Turf
Oregon	Autzen	1967	41,678	Turf
Oregon St.	Parker	1953	35,362	Turf
Stanford	Stanford	1921	86,019	Grass
UCLA	Rose Bowl	1922	102,083	Grass
USC	LA Coliseum	1923	92,516	Grass
Washington	Husky	1920	72,500	Turf
Washington St.	Martin	1972	40,000	Grass

Southeastern

EASTERN	Stadium	Built	Seats	Field
Florida	Florida Field	1930	83,000	Grass
Georgia	Sanford	1929	85,434	Grass
Kentucky	Commonwealth	1973	57,800	Grass
South Carolina	Williams-Brice	1934	72,400	Grass
Tennessee	Neyland	1921	91,902	Turf
Vanderbilt	Vanderbilt	1981	41,000	Turf

WESTERN	Stadium	Built	Seats	Field
Alabama	Bryant-Denny	1929	70,123	Grass
	& Legion Field	1927	83,091	Turf
Arkansas	Razorback	1938	52,968	Turf
	& War Memorial	1948	53,645	Grass
Auburn	Jordan-Hare	1939	85,214	Grass
LSU	Tiger	1924	80,140	Grass
Mississippi	Vaught-Hem'way	1941	42,577	Grass
	& Memorial	1953	60,549	Grass
Mississippi St.	Scott Field	1920	41,200	Grass

Note: At Alabama, Bryant-Denny Stadium is in Tuscaloosa and Legion Field is in Birmingham; at Mississippi, Vaught-Hemingway Stadium is in Oxford and Memorial Stadium is in Jackson.

Southwest

Stadium		Built	Seats	Field
Baylor	Casey	1950	48,500	Turf
Houston	Astrodome	1965	62,021	Turf
Rice	Rice	1950	70,000	Turf
SMU	Ownby	1926	23,783	Turf
Texas	Memorial	1924	77,809	Turf
Texas A&M	Kyle Field	1925	70,210	Turf
TCU	Carter	1929	46,000	Turf
Texas Tech	Jones	1947	50,500	Turf

WAC

Stadium		Built	Seats	Field
Air Force	Falcon	1962	53,333	Grass
BYU	Cougar	1964	65,000	Grass
Colorado St	Hughes	1968	30,000	Grass
Fresno St.	Bulldog	1980	40,513	Grass
Hawaii	Aloha	1975	50,000	Turf
New Mexico	University	1960	30,646	Grass
San Diego St	SD/Murphy	1967	60,409	Grass
Utah	Rice	1927	35,000	Turf
UTEP	Sun Bowl	1963	52,000	Turf
Wyoming	War Memorial	1950	33,500	Grass

I-A Independents

Stadium		Built	Seats	Field
Army	Michie	1924	39,929	Turf
Cincinnati	Nippert	1924	35,000	Turf
E. Carolina	Ficklin	1963	35,000	Grass
Louisville	Cardinal	1956	35,500	Turf
Memphis St.	Liberty Bowl	1965	62,380	Grass
Navy	Navy-Marine Corps Memorial	1959	30,000	Grass
Notre Dame	Notre Dame	1930	59,075	Grass
So. Miss	Roberts	1976	33,000	Grass
Tulane	Superdome	1975	69,065	Turf
Tulsa	Skelly	1930	40,385	Turf

1992-93 Bowl Games

Stadium		Built	Seats	Field
Aloha	Aloha	1975	50,000	Grass
Blockbuster	Joe Robbie	1986	73,000	Grass
Copper	Arizona	1928	56,167	Grass
Cotton	Cotton	1932	72,032	Turf
Fiesta	Sun Devil	1958	73,656	Grass
Fla.Citrus	Fla.Citrus Bowl	1936	70,000	Grass
Freedom	Anaheim	1966	69,008	Grass
Gator	Gator Bowl	1949	80,129	Grass
Hall of Fame	Tampa	1967	74,315	Grass
Holiday	SD/Jack Murphy	1967	60,750	Grass
Independence	Independence	1936	50,459	Grass
John Hancock	Sun Bowl	1863	52,000	Turf
Las Vegas	Silver Bowl	1971	32,000	Turf
Liberty	Liberty Bowl	1965	62,380	Grass
Orange	Orange Bowl	1935	74,712	Grass
Peach	Georgia Dome	1992	71,594	Turf
Rose	Rose Bowl	1922	102,083	Grass
Sugar	Superdome	1975	69,065	Turf

Playing Sites

Aloha—Honolulu; **Blockbuster**—Miami; **Copper**—Tucson, AZ; **Cotton**—Dallas; **Fiesta**—Tempe, AZ; **Florida Citrus**—Orlando; **Freedom**—Anaheim, CA; **Gator**—Jacksonville, FL; **Hall of Fame**—Tampa; **Holiday**—San Diego; **Independence**—Shreveport, LA; **John Hancock**—El Paso, TX; **Las Vegas**—Las Vegas; **Liberty**—Memphis; **Orange**—Miami; **Peach**—Atlanta; **Rose**—Pasadena; **Sugar**—New Orleans.

Wide World Photos

All-Star second baseman **Ryne Sandberg** meets the press March 2, after the Chicago Cubs agreed to make him baseball's first $7 million-a-year player.

BUSINESS & MEDIA

Fix-It Time

The split personality of big time sports finds networks determined to spend less while teams keep spending more.

Have Dr. Jekyll and Mr. Hyde been named SportsBiz Inc.'s co-CEOs, or has the face of sports finance turned so blatantly sane and insane that the prospect of spending more and taking in less seems normal?

After a spendthrift decade in which the TV networks wrote checks with all the restraint of a wealthy yachtsman in pursuit of the America's Cup—bidding $3.6 billion for the National Football League, $1.46 billion for Major League Baseball and $401 million for the Summer Olympics in Barcelona—recent deals have resuscitated the forgotten concept of common sense and set up a dilemma for profligate team owners who will soon wonder how to meet their exorbitant current and future salary commitments. Consider:

—The Mobil Cotton Bowl will get $2.75 million for each of the next three years from NBC; down from its previous $4.1 million a year deal with CBS. Along with the extra cash went network coverage of the annual Cotton Bowl parade (which was subsequently cancelled).

—Coverage of the World Gymnastics Championships tumbled from $2.5 million to $300,000 on ABC; the Tour de France skidded from $1 million on ABC

to zero on ESPN; the U.S. Olympic Trials fell 50 percent to $2 million on NBC, and the New York City Marathon went from $1.5 million in 1986 to $50,000 in 1992.

—The ratings orphan World League of springtime football was tackled for a $13 million loss when ABC slashed its annual rights fee from $12 million to $3 million and USA Network did likewise, from $14 million to $10 million. Cheaper, however, wasn't better and viewership was worse in 1992 than in '91.

But the most significant proof of the downward spiral in TV rights fees came from the commissioner's offices of Major League Baseball and the NFL. Late in 1991, Fay Vincent warned baseball owners that their network and cable annuities would fall by up to 50 percent after 1993. Meanwhile, this spring, Paul Tagliabue was unsuccessful in his attempt to convince football owners to rebate $210 million to the networks to help stem their losses.

The state of sports rights can be viewed in the balance sheet at CBS, where, over the past two years, the network has written off the value of $604 million from its baseball and football contracts.

At the same time, NBC is believed to have lost more than $100 million on its NFL deal.

"With the state of the economy and the TV market, they need our help," says Cleveland Browns owner Art Modell, who

Richard Sandomir writes the television sports column for *The New York Times*.

Wide World Photos

Despite the lobbying efforts of commissioner **Paul Tagliabue** (left) and Cleveland Browns' owner **Art Modell**, NFL owners refused to back Modell's plan to help the struggling TV networks with a $210 million rebate.

crafted the NFL's give-back offering. The plan would have reduced 1993 network payouts from $41 million per team to $32.5 million while extending the current deal with ABC, CBS and NBC for two seasons through 1995. Twenty-one teams needed to approve, but only 18 agreed. The megarollback was replaced by a $1 million-per-team rebate for '93 and another sop—delaying indefinitely a plan to extend the season from 17 to 18 weeks.

Tagliabue was disappointed. So were the network chieftains who asked aloud if the NFL was now willing to chance negotiating post-1993 contracts in an economy that is pointing in only one direction—down, perhaps below the level Tagliabue offered through 1995. As ABC Sports President Dennis Swanson told *USA Today*, "Maybe we should take our lumps in the fourth year of the contract and take our chances on a new deal that really offers us the least risk."

Continued interest will focus on how far baseball rights fees fall. CBS and ESPN have amassed huge losses on their national contracts, and while they may want to retain a piece of the action beyond 1993, they want less risk. Baseball has voiced a desire to revive the Saturday

Game of the Week with either a network or a syndicator (bet on one of the networks). And ESPN may seek a reduction in its six-games-a-week schedule.

In the meantime, ESPN and the National Hockey League agreed in September to a five-year contract worth $80 million. The deal, which also provides for limited NHL exposure on ABC (ESPN's owner), is a three-fold improvement over the $5.5 million pittance SportsChannel America paid for the 1991-92 season.

On the Olympics front, Atlanta Organizing Committee president Billy Payne wants $600 million for the TV rights to the 1996 Summer Games. That's 50 percent more than any network has ever paid for the Olympics, but comes on the heels of an estimated $40 million to $100 million loss by NBC on its coverage of the 1992 Barcelona Olympics.

"Billy's engaging in a perfectly acceptable practice of pre-negotiating chatter," says CBS Sports president Neal Pilson, who has laid out a combined $543 million for the 1992 and 1994 Winter Olympics. "The number will be what any network decides it wants to bid, not what he may be looking for."

The wild card in bidding for the Atlanta

Games will be hometown cable mogul Ted Turner. Will the International Olympic Committee offer him a place at the negotiating table in hopes of a blockbuster bid? Will the powerful Turner Broadcasting board allow him to bid much more than the $30 million he has paid CBS for the cable rights to the 1994 Winter Games? Stay tuned: the mixture of Turner and Atlanta is potent and unpredictable.

The Winter Olympics may not have made money for CBS, but then, the network insists that it did not lose any, either. In fact, the telecasts from Albertville exceeded expectations, and along with the Super Bowl, World Series and NCAA Final Four helped CBS win the 1991-92 season ratings race after finishing third in 1990-91. The Dream Season, at last.

Five nights of Winter Olympics coverage made it into the Nielsen Top 20 of the year's highest-rated sports events, despite the presence of miscast anchors Paula Zahn and Tim McCarver. The former was a morning news host with no sports experience, the latter a baseball analyst with no hosting background. Tethered to a studio set that could have been a dentist's waiting room in Phoenix, they seemed utterly cut off from the flow of events in the French Alps.

Bob Costas hosted NBC's prime time coverage of the Summer Olympics in Barcelona and proved to be the equal of ABC's perennial Olympic guide, Jim McKay. NBC's ratings were also better than expected, thanks to a savvy production that leaned heavily on storytelling and gymnastics (the better to woo women). Unfortunately, NBC, which paid $401 million to air the Games, saw its ballyhooed pay-per-view Triplecast fall flatter than Sergei Bubka in the pole vault (see box).

"Much as I'd like to read about how well we produced this," NBC Sports President Dick Ebersol said later, "we lost money. But I wasn't around to make this deal—and I wouldn't have."

Tough talk? Of course. But it is a sign of a troubled market righting itself. The networks have lost money on nearly every major property in recent years—except for NBC's contract with the NBA—and falling advertising revenues will probably never return to their dizzy old highs.

The networks are now so averse to risk

that they are creating their own no-fee properties (beach volleyball on NBC, for instance) and welcoming producers who create programs and buy time to show them—an instant boon for the networks. Two examples are the Blockbuster Bowl on CBS, for which Raycom will pay $900,000 a year, and college basketball on ABC.

If only team owners had the intelligence to look at what lies ahead financially in order to determine their spending on players. Instead, they continue to be improvident spendaholics, who can't stop themselves from signing mediocre free agents to eight-figure contracts.

The onslaught of incredible salaries continued unabated in 1992. The average baseball salary zoomed past $1 million a year, while 269 players made more than that—some, a lot more.

In December, the New York Mets signed free agent outfielder Bobby Bonilla for nearly $6 million a year (actually, $29 million over five years). Then in March, the Chicago Cubs made Ryne Sandberg baseball's first $7 Million Man, inking this All-Star second baseman to a four-year deal worth $28.4 million. In August, Baltimore held on to ironman shortstop and two-time MVP Cal Ripken, Jr., for $30.5 million over five years.

At those prices, Minnesota's Kirby Puckett, who signed baseball's first $3 million-a-year contract in November, 1989, will be looking to double his salary when he becomes a free agent after the 1992 season.

"If we continue to increase player payrolls at the rate of over 20 percent a year," says Philadelphia Phillies owner Bill Giles, "we're headed for a collision beginning in either 1993 or 1994. This has got to change."

Unlike baseball, where first-year pro players rarely make it to the big leagues, rookies continued to command enormous salaries in hockey, basketball and football.

In hockey, the NHL's Philadelphia Flyers sent six players, two draft picks and $15 million (U.S.) to Quebec for 19-year-old junior league sensation Eric Lindros, who sat out 1991-92 rather than play for the Nordiques. Estimates on what it cost the Flyers to sign Lindros range from $2.5 million to over $3.5 million a year for six

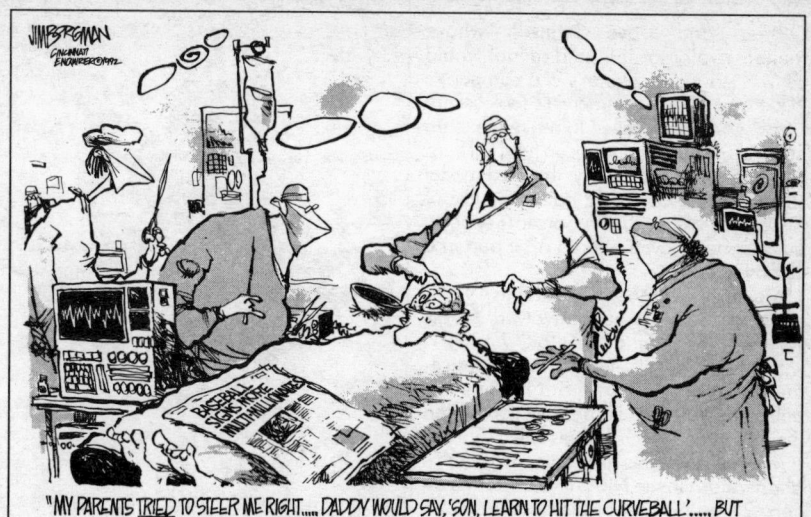

"MY PARENTS TRIED TO STEER ME RIGHT..... DADDY WOULD SAY, 'SON, LEARN TO HIT THE CURVEBALL'..... BUT NOOOOOO, I HAD TO GO OFF AND BECOME A BRAIN SURGEON!"

King Features Syndicate

years. Whatever the figure is, it's more than either Wayne Gretzky or Mario Lemieux make and they've won six Stanley Cups between them.

The NBA's Orlando Magic saw enough of Shaquille O'Neal after three seasons at LSU to figure the 20-year-old, All-America center was a franchise player worth $40 million over seven years. O'Neal's deal is the most lucrative in team sports history and more than the Chicago Bulls pay Michael Jordan, whose $3 million salary is augmented considerably by about $17 million in endorsement income.

Being a rookie in football isn't a bad business, either. The Indianapolis Colts signed defensive end Steve Emtman and linebacker Quentin Coryett, the No.1 and No. 2 picks of the NFL Draft, to a pair of very lucrative four-year contracts. Emtman's was for $9.2 million and Coryett's for $8.9 million. Both got $4.16 million signing bonuses.

One could detect a glimmer of good sense when the Super Bowl champion Washington Redskins did not cave in to quarterback Mark Rypien's demands for a multi-year deal at $4.4 million per—more than Miami QB Dan Marino's $4.3 million paycheck—or his threat to bolt to Toronto of the CFL. Instead, the Skins

sprang for a miserly $3 million a year through 1995.

More athletes are making more money than ever, even if the imprisoned former heavyweight champion Mike Tyson has gone from making millions to an hourly wage in a federal prison where he's doing six years for rape. Those who made *Forbes* magazine's 1992 list of sport's top 40 moneymakers can be found in the "Updates" chapter.

Two of the most commercialized athletes on TV in '92 were Michael Jordan and Magic Johnson. Jordan played basketball with Bugs Bunny in Nike ads, swigged Gatorade in "Be Like Mike" spots, and led the Chicago Bulls to their second straight NBA on NBC title.

His Airness also got into a flap about whether he would allow his image to be used on "Dream Team" T-shirts for the Summer Olympics (he eventually relented), and into an even bigger brouhaha over his refusal to wear Reebok's medal-ceremony sweatsuit when the Dreamers accepted their gold medals. Touched by Michael's loyalty, Nike said "Just do it," but Jordan was appeased only when he was allowed to open the jacket and fold the collar over the Reebok logo.

Reebok had other problems at the Olympics. After spending $25 million to promote American decathletes Dan

O'Brien and Dave Johnson—whose friendly rivalry for the gold medal would be "settled in Barcelona"—the company's "Dan and Dave" commercials took severe hits when O'Brien failed to make the team at the U.S. Trials and Johnson finished third in Barcelona. Interestingly, the gold medal winner turned out to be Robert Zmelic of Czechoslovakia, who endorsed Reeboks, but was never even offered a bit part in a commercial.

Many of the most remarkable TV images of the past year involved Magic Johnson, beginning on Nov. 7, 1991, with the nationally-televised announcement of his retirement from the Los Angeles Lakers because he had contracted the HIV virus, which causes AIDS. Subsequently, the images graduated to a triumphant return in the NBA All-Star Game on Feb. 9, the retiring of his number 32 in L.A. a week later, and his starring role with the Dream Team in Barcelona during the summer (see the "Olympics" chapter).

Somewhat problematical for Magic was the reaction of his corporate sponsors to his illness. Nestle dropped him from a campaign, Pepsi vacillated, and Kentucky Fried Chicken has not run anything new featuring Johnson since the HIV announcement. Only Sky Box International, a card company, signed Johnson to endorse their product after his illness was made public.

Even as Magic mulled a possible return to the Lakers (pending the consent of his wife and doctors), he was also thinking of pursuing a full-time business career and a long-time desire to own an NBA team.

There aren't many NBA teams on the market, but baseball clubs were a different story in 1992:

—John McMullen ended his long quest for a buyer by selling his Houston Astros to Drayton McLane Jr., for $115 million.

—The Detroit Tigers were sold for $85 million by Domino's Pizza baron Tom Monaghan to Little Caesars Pizza man Mike Ilitch who already owned the local Red Wings of the NHL.

—Bob Lurie, frustrated by politicans and voters alike and four separate attempts since 1989 to find a new Bay Area home for the San Francisco Giants, finally gave up and made a deal to sell the club for $110 million to investors in St. Petersburg, Fla. Barring a miracle, the Tampa

The Triplecast was a fiasco, but the real blow to PPV in 1992 came in March when boxing superstar **Mike Tyson** was sentenced to six years for rape.

Jeff Atteberry/The Indianapolis Star

Triplecast + Tyson = Trouble

They were told to slash the price and offer free previews. They were told that marketing pay-per-view eight months in advance was folly. They were told that too few viewers would pay for three channels of commercial-free coverage of the Summer Olympics—not when 161 hours were available free on NBC.

No, shouted the brains behind the Triplecast, we will draw two million buyers! We will hold to the price! We have an irresistible concept that will revolutionize sports viewing forever! We will market the bejesus out of America because, if we offer it, they will buy!

In the end, it was a bust—the New Coke of sports TV—drawing a tip-top estimate of 250,000 buyers to the $125 15-day subscription and the $29.95 (later, discounted to $19.95) one-day purchase. "We were 1.75 million short," admits Jim Dolan, the executive in charge. "We expected two million buys before the Olympics began."

Depending upon the accounting, NBC will lose at least $50 million thanks to the venture. Partner Cablevision will likely lose its $50 million commitment.

The Triplecast will taint pay-per-view only if the industry doesn't return to its roots: attractive, competitive events that are exclusive to cable viewers with access to PPV technology.

What hurt pay-per-view more than the Triplecast fiasco, however, was former heavyweight champion Mike Tyson's imprisonment for rape on March 26. Tyson's two 1991 PPV bouts with Razor Ruddoch were worth a combined $75 million and his scheduled Nov. 8, 1991, showdown with unbeaten champ Evander Holyfield expected to clear $100 million. An injured rib cage forced Tyson to call off the fight temporarily last October. But his six-year jail sentence has probably made the cancellation permanent.

One victim of the post-Tyson landscape was TVKO, which was launched with high hopes in April, 1991, by Time Warner. Its match-up of Holyfield and 42-year-old ex-champ Larry Holmes on June 19, lost $2.75 million, causing TVKO to lay off 10 workers and cut its roster of shows from 10 to 6 per year. TVKO lost $7 million to $10 million in its first year-plus in business.

Part of the future may be visible in an ABC venture that ran through November in which regional college football games were distributed to cable systems for $8.95 each ($1 more for each additional game). ABC affiliates still aired the game of greatest local interest, while matchups from other regions filled the pay menu.

Expectations were decidedly lower for this undertaking than the Triplecast: perhaps 20,000 to 30,000 per week out of 17 million addressable cable homes. Depending on channel capacity, systems carried from one to four games.

The experiment may be a model for the National Football League's pay-per-view future, which has been delayed until its current network contract ends after the 1993 season. The NFL has regional games to package for PPV, which would enable an expatriate Washington Redskins fan in Kansas City to pay a fee to watch a game he would not otherwise see on his CBS affiliate.

"The NFL can take its time," says Rick Kulis, president of Event Entertainment, a pay-per-view distributor. "They have a strong broadcast product. It's wise for them to wait."

Wait for what? Well, the next wave of technology for one thing. There is the promise of direct broadcast satellites, which would bring 18-inch dishes into homes and immediately create a new market to service uncabled homes and even replace cable in some areas. Then there is digital compression, which, when perfected, can transform one cable channel into three or more.

To Kulis, a multi-channel environment can bring a plethora of low-cost pay-per-view events. "With a lot of events, showing the full array of all kinds of sports, you'd have a sort of multiplex," he says.

Unfortunately, the industry has not improved much beyond major boxing fights and wrestling extravaganzas. Last spring's one-on-one basketball match between Julius Erving and Kareem Abdul-Jabbar flopped badly.

The future will see a continued search for more major fights, events that are competitive and compelling (with a good story hook) and programming that offers something the networks can't.

"I believe in simulcasting," says Scott Kurnit, president of SET Pay-Per-View. "Take the Super Bowl or the Indy 500, for instance. You don't displace the network, you just charge, say, $9.95, and get rid of the commercials."

Nike/Warner Bros.

Loyal Nike pitchman **Michael Jordan** played hoops with **Bugs Bunny,** but wouldn't play ball with Reebok at the Olympics.

Bay Giants will open up shop at the Suncoast Dome in 1993—36 years after abandoning New York for the West Coast. The Giants' pending migration upset the carefully-laid plans of Blockbuster Video tycoon H. Wayne Huizenga, who had been led to believe that he would have Florida all to himself when he shelled out $95 million for the right to bring the Florida Marlins into the National League in 1993.

—The on-again, off-again sale of the Seattle Mariners finally ended as Nintendo acquired the team for $125 million from Jeff Smulyan, who bought the club for $75 million in 1989. The action surrounding Nintendo's offer made the company's Super Mario Brothers video game look inert, with charges of racism against commissioner Vincent coupled with Americans' fears of a Japanese investment in the national pastime. In the end, baseball agreed to let Nintendo own a majority share of the Mariners, but mandated that voting power rest with the minority ownership of local executives.

Elsewhere, Victor Kiam sold his 51 percent share of the New England Patriots to St. Louis investor James Orthwein, who repaid $28.5 million in debts owed by Kiam. It was no secret that Orthwein stepped in as a favor to the NFL, but the team he really wants to own is an expansion club in his hometown.

Edward DeBartolo Sr., whose son Eddie owns the San Francisco 49ers, sold the Pittsburgh Penguins in November, 1991, to a group headed by former Hartford Whalers owner Howard Baldwin and partners for $30 million plus other considerations. The change at the top didn't keep the Penguins from winning their second straight Stanley Cup.

According to *Financial World* magazine's second annual survey of big league franchises, the 102 teams in baseball, basketball, football and hockey slipped in value by 2.3 percent between 1991 and '92, thanks to rising player costs and the prospect of falling TV revenues.

Asked by *Mediaweek* magazine to comment on the situation teams currently find themselves in, ABC Sports' Swanson issued this warning: "Some teams say they're losing money and a number of them have. But they're tied to a marketplace that dictates certain salaries. Instead of looking at (cutting) costs, they're all looking for new revenue sources. Forget it. Adding games and new teams isn't the answer. That's what got us into this mess. Now it's fix-it time." □

Wide World Photos

New Houston Astros' owner **Drayton McLane Jr.** addresses the media after buying the club for $115 million in July.

500

1991-92 Top 30 Prime Time TV Series

Final 1991-92 prime time network television ratings, according to Nielsen Media Research. Covers period from Sept.16, 1991 through April 12, 1992, and includes all series of 12 episodes or more. Events are listed with ratings points and audience share; each ratings point represents 921,000 households and shares indicate percentage of TV sets in use.

Overall network ratings: 1. CBS (13.8); **2.** NBC (12.3); **3.** ABC (12.2) **4.** Fox (8.0).

	Series	Net	Rating	Share		Series	Net	Rating	Share
1	60 Minutes	CBS	21.9	36	16	A Different World	NBC	15.2	24
2	Roseanne	ABC	20.2	31	17	The Cosby Show	NBC	14.8	24
3	Murphy Brown	CBS	18.6	27	18	Wings	NBC	14.6	23
4	Cheers	NBC	17.6	27	19	Amer.Funniest Home Videos	ABC	14.5	22
5	Home Improvement	ABC	17.5	27		Fresh Prince of Bel Air	NBC	14.5	23
6	Designing Women	CBS	17.3	26	21	20/20	ABC	14.4	26
7	Coach	ABC	17.2	27	22	Empty Nest	NBC	14.3	25
8	Full House	ABC	17.0	27	23	NBC Monday Night Movies	NBC	13.9	22
9	Murder, She Wrote	CBS	16.9	25	24	America's Funniest People	ABC	13.8	20
	Unsolved Mysteries	NBC	16.9	27	25	Family Matters	ABC	13.5	24
11	Major Dad	CBS	16.8	25		Rescue 911	CBS	13.5	22
12	**Monday Night Football**	ABC	16.6	28	27	In the Heat of the Night	NBC	13.3	21
13	CBS Sunday Movie	CBS	15.9	25		L.A. Law	NBC	13.3	23
14	Evening Shade	CBS	15.8	25	29	48 Hours	CBS	13.1	23
15	Northern Exposure	CBS	15.5	25		Golden Girls	NBC	13.1	23

1991-92 Top 75 TV Sports Events

Final 1991-92 network television ratings for nationally-telecast sports events, including 15 Monday Night Football games but not including pre- and post-game shows, according to Nielsen Media Research. Covers period from Sept.16, 1991 through Aug. 31, 1992. Events are listed with ratings points and audience share; each ratings point represents 921,000 households and shares indicate percentage of TV sets in use.

Multiple entries: NFL football (32); Winter Olympics and Summer Olympics (18 each); Major League baseball (14); NBA basketball (10); NCAA basketball (5); College bowl games (3). **Top 20:** NFL (7); Baseball (6); Winter Olympics (5); Summer Olympics and NCAA basketball (1 each). **Nos. 21-50:** NFL (13); Summer Olympics (7); Winter Olympics (6); Baseball (3); NCAA basketball (1). **Nos. 51-75:** NFL (8); Summer Olympics (7); Winter Olympics (4); Baseball (3); NBA basketball (2); College bowl game (1).

		Date	Net	Rtg/Sh			Date	Net	Rtg/Sh
1	**Super Bowl XXVI** (Redskins vs Bills)	1/26	CBS	40.3/61	16	**AFC Semifinal** (Chiefs at Bills)	1/5	NBC	22.0/48
2	**World Series Game 7** (Braves at Twins)	10/27	CBS	32.2/49	17	**World Series Game 2** (Braves at Twins)	10/20	CBS	21.7/34
3	**NFC Championship** (Lions at Redskins)	1/12	CBS	29.5/53		**Winter Olympics** (Ice Dance final/ USA-Sweden/Nordic)	2/17	CBS	21.7/32
4	**AFC Championship** (Broncos at Bills)	1/12	NBC	27.4/58	19	**Winter Olympics** (Pairs Fig.Skate final/ Alpine/Hockey/Luge)	2/11	CBS	21.5/32
	NFC Semifinal (Cowboys at Lions)	1/5	CBS	27.4/50	20	**AFC Semifinal** (Oilers at Broncos)	1/4	NBC	21.3/43
6	**World Series Game 6** (Braves at Twins)	10/26	CBS	25.4/44	21	**AFC Wild Card** (Jets at Oilers)	12/29	NBC	21.2/41
7	**Winter Olympics** (Women's Fig.Skate final/ Hockey/Bobsled)	2/21	CBS	25.0/40	22	**Winter Olympics** (Ice Dance/Alpine/ Ski Jump/Bobsled)	2/16	CBS	21.2/32
8	**World Series Game 3** (Twins at Braves)	10/22	CBS	23.5/39	23	**NFC Wild Card** (Falcons at Saints)	12/28	ABC	21.1/45
	Winter Olympics (Pairs Fig.Skate short/ Men's Downhill)	2/9	CBS	23.5/33	24	**NFC Semifinal** (Falcons at Redskins)	1/4	CBS	20.5/48
10	**NFC Wild Card** (Cowboys at Bears)	12/29	CBS	23.3/52		**Summer Olympics** (W-Gym Team final/ Swim/Dive/Box)	7/28	NBC	20.5/37
11	**World Series Game 5** (Twins at Braves)	10/24	CBS	22.9/37	26	**Baseball NLCS Game 7** (Braves at Pirates)	10/17	CBS	19.9/32
	World Series Game 4 (Twins at Braves)	10/23	CBS	22.9/36	27	**Summer Olympics** (M-Gym Team 1st day/ Swim/Dive/Hoop)	7/27	NBC	19.7/36
13	**Winter Olympics** (Women's Fig.Skate short/ W-Alpine/Hockey)	2/19	CBS	22.8/35	28	**Winter Olympics** (Men's Fig.Skate short/ Alpine/Hockey/Free)	2/13	CBS	19.2/29
14	**NCAA Basketball Championship** (Duke vs Michigan)	4/6	CBS	22.7/35	29	**Winter Olympics** (Alpine/Hockey/Luge/ Freestyle)	2/10	CBS	19.1/29
15	**Summer Olympics** (W-Gym All-Around final/ Swim/Eques/Box)	7/30	NBC	22.2/40					

1991-92 Top 75 TV Sports Events (Cont.)

		Date	Net	Rtg/Sh
30	**Summer Olympics** (M-Gym Team final/Swim/ Dive/Hoop/Eques/Box)	7/29	NBC	18.9/35
31	**Monday Night Football** (Raiders at Saints)	12/16	ABC	19.0/32
32	**Baseball NLCS Game 6** (Braves at Pirates)	10/16	CBS	18.3/31
	Summer Olympics (W-Gym Individual finals/ Track/Dive/Canoe)	8/1	NBC	18.3/39
34	**Winter Olympics** (Men's Fig.Skate final/ Alpine/M-SpSkate)	2/15	CBS	18.1/31
	Summer Olympics (W-Gym Team 1st day/ Swim/Dive/Bike)	7/26	NBC	18.1/33
	Summer Olympics (M-Gym Individual finals/ Track/Dive/Bike/Canoe)	8/2	NBC	18.1/34
37	**Monday Night Football** (Eagles at Oilers)	12/2	ABC	17.9/30
38	**Monday Night Football** (Bills at Chiefs)	10/7	ABC	17.7/30
39	**World Series Game 1** (Braves at Twins)	10/19	CBS	17.6/32
	Monday Night Football (Bears at Vikings)	11/11	ABC	17.6/29
41	**AFC Wild Card Game** (Raiders at Chiefs)	12/28	ABC	17.3/45
42	**Monday Night Football** (Eagles at Redskins)	9/30	ABC	17.1/29
43	**Monday Night Football** (Bengals at Bills)	10/21	ABC	17.0/29
44	**Summer Olympics** (M-Gym All-Around final/ Swim/Track/Hoop)	7/31	NBC	16.9/34
45	**Monday Night Football** (Jets at Bears)	9/23	ABC	16.8/30
	NCAA Basketball Semifinal (Duke vs Indiana)	4/4	CBS	16.8/30
	NFL Thanksgiving (Bears at Lions)	11/28	CBS	16.8/44
	Winter Olympics (Ice Dance/W-SpSkate/ Ski Jump)	2/14	CBS	16.8/30
49	**Monday Night Football** (Bears at 49ers)	12/23	ABC	16.7/31
	Winter Olympics (W-SpSkate/W-Alpine/ Luge/Freestyle)	2/12	CBS	16.7/26
51	**Summer Olympics** (Track: Decath & LJ/Hoop/ Box/Volley/Sync)	8/6	NBC	16.6/32
	Summer Olympics (Track/Diving/ Volley/Tennis)	8/3	NBC	16.6/31

		Date	Net	Rtg/Sh
53	**Monday Night Football** (Bills at Dolphins)	11/18	ABC	16.3/27
	Monday Night Football (Giants at Steelers)	10/14	ABC	16.3/26
	Monday Night Football (Giants at Eagles)	11/4	ABC	16.3/26
	Monday Night Football (Raiders at Chiefs)	10/28	ABC	16.2/28
57	**Winter Olympics** (Fig.Skate Exhibition/ Alpine/Bobsled)	2/22	CBS	16.1/28
	NBA Finals Game 4 (Bulls at Blazers)	6/10	NBC	16.0/29
59	**Winter Olympics** (Hockey quarterfinals/ Alpine/M-SpSkate)	2/18	CBS	15.9/24
60	**Summer Olympics** (Track: Decathalon/ Volley/Wrest)	8/5	NBC	15.8/31
	Monday Night Football (Chiefs at Oilers)	9/16	ABC	15.8/30
62	**Summer Olympics** (Hoop: USA-P.Rico/Dive/ Box/Wgt.Lift/Eques)	8/4	NBC	15.4/29
	Rose Bowl (Washington vs Michigan)	1/1	ABC	15.4/26
	Winter Olympics (Women's Fig.Skate preview/ Alpine/SpSkate/Biath)	2/20	CBS	15.4/24
65	**Baseball All-Star Game** (at San Diego)	7/14	CBS	14.9/27
66	**NBA Finals Game 6** (Blazers at Bulls)	6/14	NBC	14.7/29
67	**Baseball NLCS Game 2** (Braves at Pirates)	10/10	CBS	14.5/24
	Winter Olympics (Opening ceremonies)	2/8	CBS	14.5/24
69	**NFL Thanksgiving** (Steelers at Cowboys)	11/28	NBC	14.4/40
	NFL Regular Season Early Game (Various teams)	Season	CBS	14.4/35
71	**Monday Night Football** (49ers at Rams)	11/25	ABC	14.3/24
72	**Summer Olympics** (Track/Box/Volley/ Tennis/Wres/Sync)	8/7	NBC	14.2/30
	Summer Olympics (Closing ceremonies)	8/9	NBC	14.2/26
74	**Summer Olympics** (12 pm: Gym/Swim/Box/ Dive/Hoop/Wgt.Lift/)	7/26	NBC	14.1/37
	Baseball NLCS Game 1 (Braves at Pirates)	10/9	CBS	14.1/25

1991-92 Top-Rated Cable TV Sports Events

Final 1991-92 cable television ratings for sports events, according to ESPN, Turner Sports and USA Network research. Covers period from Sept. 1, 1991 through Aug. 31, 1992.

NFL Telecasts

		Date	Net	Rtg
1	Atlanta at New Orleans	11/24	ESPN	11.2
2	Cleveland at Houston	11/17	ESPN	10.5
3	Pittsburgh at Denver	11/3	ESPN	10.3
4	Washington at NY Giants	10/27	ESPN	10.0*
5	LA Raiders at San Diego	12/1	ESPN	9.7

*Aired opposite World Series Game 7 on CBS.

Non-NFL Telecasts

		Date	Net	Rtg
1	CFA: Houston at U. of Miami	9/12	ESPN	6.5
2	U.S. Open: Conners-Haarhuis	9/5	USA	5.9
	NBA: Knicks-Bulls Game 5	5/12	TNT	5.9
	Holiday Bowl: BYU-Iowa	12/30	ESPN	5.9
5	CFA: Nebraska at Colorado	11/2	ESPN	5.1

All-Time Top-Rated TV Programs

NFL Football dominates television's All-Time Top-Rated 50 Programs with 18 Super Bowls and the 1981 NFC Championship Game making the list. Rankings based on surveys taken from July, 1960 through July, 1992; include only sponsored programs seen on individual networks; and programs under 30 minutes scheduled duration are excluded. Programs are listed with ratings points, audience share and number of households watching, according to Nielsen Media Research.

Multiple entries: The Super Bowl (18); ''The Beverly Hillbillies'' and ''Roots'' (7); ''The Thorn Birds'' (3); ''The Bob Hope Christmas Show,'' ''The Ed Sullivan Show'' and ''Gone With The Wind'' (2).

	Program	Episode/Game	Net	Date	Rating	Share	Households
1	M*A*S*H (series)	Final episode	CBS	2/28/83	60.2	77	50,150,000
2	Dallas (series)	''Who Shot J.R.?''	CBS	11/21/80	53.3	76	41,470,000
3	Roots (mini-series)	Part 8	ABC	1/30/77	51.1	71	36,380,000
4	**Super Bowl XVI**	49ers 26, Bengals 21	CBS	1/24/82	49.1	73	40,020,000
5	**Super Bowl XVII**	Redskins 27, Dolphins 17	NBC	1/30/83	48.6	69	40,480,000
6	**Super Bowl XX**	Bears 46, Patriots 10	NBC	1/26/86	48.3	70	41,490,000
7	Gone With the Wind (movie)	Part 1	NBC	11/7/76	47.7	65	33,960,000
8	Gone with the Wind (movie)	Part 2	NBC	11/8/76	47.4	64	33,750,000
9	**Super Bowl XII**	Cowboys 27, Broncos 10	CBS	1/15/78	47.2	67	34,410,000
10	**Super Bowl XIII**	Steelers 35, Cowboys 31	NBC	1/21/79	47.1	74	35,090,000
11	Bob Hope Special	Christmas Show	NBC	1/15/70	46.6	64	27,260,000
12	**Super Bowl XVIII**	Raiders 38, Redskins 9	CBS	1/22/84	46.4	71	38,800,000
	Super Bowl XIX	49ers 38, Dolphins 16	ABC	1/20/85	46.4	63	39,390,000
14	**Super Bowl XIV**	Steelers 31, Rams 19	CBS	1/20/80	46.3	67	35,330,000
15	ABC Theater (special)	''The Day After''	ABC	11/20/83	46.0	62	38,550,000
16	Roots (mini-series)	Part 6	ABC	1/28/77	45.9	66	32,680,000
	The Fugitive (series)	Final episode	ABC	8/29/67	45.9	72	25,700,000
18	**Super Bowl XXI**	Giants 39, Broncos 20	CBS	1/25/87	45.8	66	40,030,000
19	Roots (mini-series)	Part 5	ABC	1/27/77	45.7	71	32,540,000
20	The Ed Sullivan Show	Beatles' 1st appearence	CBS	2/9/64	45.3	60	23,240,000
21	Bob Hope Special	Christmas Show	NBC	1/14/71	45.0	61	27,050,000
22	Roots (mini-series)	Part 3	ABC	1/25/77	44.8	68	31,900,000
23	**Super Bowl XI**	Raiders 32, Vikings 14	NBC	1/9/77	44.4	73	31,610,000
	Super Bowl XV	Raiders 27, Eagles 10	NBC	1/25/81	44.4	63	34,540,000
25	**Super Bowl VI**	Cowboys 24, Dolphins 3	CBS	1/16/72	44.2	74	27,450,000
26	Roots (mini-series)	Part 2	ABC	1/24/77	44.1	62	31,400,000
27	The Beverly Hillbillies	Regular episode	CBS	1/8/64	44.0	65	22,570,000
28	Roots (mini-series)	Part 4	ABC	1/26/77	43.8	66	31,190,000
	The Ed Sullivan Show	Beatles' 2nd appearence	CBS	2/16/64	43.8	60	22,445,000
30	**Super Bowl XXIII**	49ers 20, Bengals 16	NBC	1/22/89	43.5	68	39,320,000
31	The Academy Awards	John Wayne wins Oscar	ABC	4/7/70	43.4	78	25,390,000
32	Thorn Birds (mini-series)	Part 3	ABC	3/29/83	43.2	62	35,990,000
33	Thorn Birds (mini-series)	Part 4	ABC	3/30/83	43.1	62	35,900,000
34	**NFC Championship Game**	49ers 28, Cowboys 27	CBS	1/10/82	42.9	62	34,940,000
35	The Beverly Hillbillies	Regular episode	CBS	1/15/64	42.8	62	21,960,000
36	**Super Bowl VII**	Dolphins 14, Redskins 7	NBC	1/14/73	42.7	72	27,670,000
37	Thorn Birds (mini-series)	Part 2	ABC	3/28/83	42.5	59	35,400,000
38	**Super Bowl IX**	Steelers 16, Vikings 6	NBC	1/12/75	42.4	72	29,040,000
	The Beverly Hillbillies	Regular episode	CBS	2/26/64	42.4	60	21,750,000
40	**Super Bowl X**	Steelers 21, Cowboys 17	CBS	1/18/76	42.3	78	29,440,000
	ABC Sunday Night Movie	''Airport''	ABC	11/11/73	42.3	63	28,000,000
	ABC Sunday Night Movie	''Love Story''	ABC	10/1/72	42.3	62	27,410,000
	Cinderella	Musical special	CBS	2/22/65	42.3	59	22,250,000
	Roots (mini-series)	Part 7	ABC	1/29/77	42.3	65	30,120,000
45	The Beverly Hillbillies	Regular episode	CBS	3/25/64	42.2	59	21,650,000
46	The Beverly Hillbillies	Regular episode	CBS	2/6/64	42.0	61	21,550,000
47	**Super Bowl XXV**	Giants 20, Bills 19	ABC	1/27/91	41.9	63	39,010,000
	The Beverly Hillbillies	Regular episode	CBS	1/29/64	41.9	62	21,490,000
	Super Bowl XXII	Redskins 42, Broncos 10	ABC	1/31/88	41.9	62	37,120,000
50	Miss America Pageant	Miss Michigan wins	CBS	9/9/61	41.8	75	19,600,000
	The Beverly Hillbillies	Regular episode	CBS	1/1/64	41.8	59	21,440,000

All-Time Top-Rated Cable TV Sports Events

All-time cable television ratings for sports events, according to ESPN and Turner Sports research. Covers period from Sept. 1, 1980 through Aug. 31, 1992.

NFL Telecasts	Date	Net	Rtg	Non-NFL Telecasts	Date	Net	Rtg
1 Chicago at Minnesota	12/6/87	ESPN	17.6	1 NBA: Detroit-Boston	6/1/88	TBS	8.8
2 Chicago at Minnesota	12/3/89	ESPN	14.7	2 NBA: Chicago-Detroit	5/31/89	TBS	8.2
3 Cleveland at San Fran	11/29/87	ESPN	14.2	3 NBA: Detroit-Boston	5/26/88	TBS	8.1
4 Pittsburgh at Houston	12/30/90	ESPN	13.8	4 NCAA: G'town-St.John's	2/27/85	ESPN	8.0
5 Three games tied		ESPN	13.1	5 MLB: SF-Atlanta	9/27/83	TBS	7.7

The Rights Stuff

The network-by-network roster of 1992-93 television rights on network and cable TV as of Sept.15, 1992.

ABC

Auto Racing—Indianapolis 500.
College Basketball—Regular season and conference tournaments.
Bowling—PBA Winter and Spring Tours.
College Football—Big 10/Pac-10 regular season; CFA (except Notre Dame home games); Army-Navy Game, SEC Championship Game; Rose and Sugar bowls.
NFL Football—Monday Night Football; two Wild Card Playoff games.
Golf—US Open; British Open; Senior Open; US Women's Open; PGA Skins; Seniors Skins; LPGA Skins.
Hockey—Selected NHL regular season games.
Horse Racing—Kentucky Derby; Preakness; Belmont Stakes.
Soccer—1994 World Cup Final (and 10 other World Cup weekend games)

CBS

Auto Racing—Daytona 500.
Major League Baseball—Regular season, All-Star Game, AL and NL Playoffs and World Series.
College Basketball—Regular season, conference tournaments, NCAA Tournament, Men's and Women's Final Fours.
College Football—Blockbuster and John Hancock bowls.
NFL Football—NFC regular season and NFC Playoffs.
Golf—PGA Tour; Masters; PGA Championship.
Olympics—1994 (Lillehammer) Winter Games.
Tennis—U.S. Open.

NBC

NBA Basketball—Regular season, All-Star Game, Playoffs and NBA Finals.
Bowling—PBA Fall Tour.
Figure Skating—World and European Championships.
College Football—Notre Dame home games; Heisman Trophy Show; Bayou Classic (Grambling-Southern); Cotton, Fiesta and Orange bowls.
NFL Football—AFC regular season, AFC playoffs and 1993 Super Bowl.
Golf—Ryder Cup; Players Championship; LPGA Championship; PGA Seniors Championship.
Horse Racing—Breeders' Cup.
Tennis—French Open and Wimbledon.
Track & Field—World Championships.
Volleyball—AVP Beach Pro Tour.

ESPN

Alpine Skiing—World Cup.
Auto Racing—IndyCar, NASCAR and Formula One.
Major League Baseball—Regular season.
College Basketball—Regular season.
Bowling—PBA and LPBT tours.
Boxing—Top Rank series.
Cycling—Tour de France (probable)
NFL Football—Sunday Night Football (2nd half of season), Pro Bowl and NFL Draft.
College Football—CFA and Big 10/Pac 10 regular season (except Notre Dame home games); Copper, Hall of Fame, Holiday, Independence, Las Vegas, Liberty and Peach bowls.
Golf—U.S. Open and British Open (early rounds); PGA, Senior and LPGA tour events
NHL Hockey—Regular season and Stanley Cup Playoffs.
Soccer—1994 World Cup: 41 games.
Tennis—ATP Tour; Australian Open; French Open (early rounds); Davis Cup; Grand Slam Cup.

HBO

Boxing—Championship fights.
NFL Football—"Inside the NFL" (series).
Tennis—Wimbledon (early rounds).

Turner

Auto Racing—NASCAR on TBS.
Major League Baseball—Atlanta Braves on TBS.
NBA Basketball—Regular season, Playoffs and NBA Draft on TNT; Atlanta Hawks on TBS.
College Football—Gator Bowl on TBS.
NFL Football—Sunday Night Football (1st half of season) on TNT.
Golf—PGA Championship (early rounds, partial 3rd and 4th) and Grand Slam of Golf on TBS.
Goodwill Games—1994 (St.Petersburg, Russia) on TBS.
Olympics—cable coverage of 1994 (Lillehammer) Winter Games on TNT.

USA Network

Boxing—Tuesday Night Fights.
Dog Shows—Westminster Dog Show.
Golf—Ryder Cup (early rounds), Masters (early rounds).
Tennis—U.S. Open (early rounds).

Olympics TV Rights

The reported cost of securing exclusive U.S. television rights for the Olympic Games has skyrocketed over the last 30 years. In 1960, CBS paid $50,000 for the Winter Olympics. In 1989, CBS agreed to pay $300 million for the 1994 Winter Games—an increase of 6,000 percent. In the same time, the cost of the Summer Games has gone from just under $400,000 to just over $400 million.

Year	Games	Location	Rights Fee	Net	TV Hrs
1960	Winter	Squaw Valley. .	$ 50,000	CBS	15
	Summer	Rome	$394,000	CBS	20
1964	Winter	Innsbruck . . .	$597,000	ABC	17¼
	Summer	Tokyo	1.5 mil.	NBC	14
1968	Winter	Grenoble	$2.5 mil.	ABC	27
	Summer	Mexico City	4.5 mil.	ABC	43¾
1972	Winter	Sapporo	$6.4 mil.	NBC	37
	Summer	Munich	7.5 mil.	ABC	62¾
1976	Winter	Innsbruck . . .	$10 mil.	ABC	43½
	Summer	Montreal	25 mil.	ABC	76½
1980	Winter	Lake Placid . .	$15.5 mil.	ABC	53¼
	Summer	Moscow	87 mil.	NBC	150*
1984	Winter	Sarajevo	$91.5 mil.	ABC	63
	Summer	Los Angeles . . .	225 mil.	ABC	180
1988	Winter	Calgary	$309 mil.	ABC	94½
	Summer	Seoul	300 mil.	NBC	179½
1992	Winter	Albertville . . .	$243 mil.	CBS	116
	Summer	Barcelona	401 mil.	NBC	161
1994	Winter	Lillehammer . . .	$300 mil.	CBS	120
1996	Summer	Atlanta.	To be determined		
1998	Winter	Nagano	To be determined		

*NBC planned 150 hours of coverage for the 1980 Summer Olympics, but since the U.S. boycotted the Games, NBC did not cover them and did not pay the rights fee.
Cable TV: CBS sold TNT the cable TV rights to the 1992 and '94 Winter Games for $20 million and $30 million, respectively. TNT televised 45 hours of 1992 coverage and plans 50 hours for '94.
Pay Per View: In 1992, NBC and Cablevision offered viewers the "Olympic Triplecast," presenting 12 hours of uninterrupted live events (and 12 hours taped) on three different channels every day of the Games. The venture lost an estimated $100 million.

What Major League Teams Are Worth

The estimated total market value of the 102 major league baseball, basketball, football and hockey franchises in the U.S. and Canada, according to *Financial World* magazine's second annual survey released June 16, 1992. The 1992 values listed below show a 2.3 decline in overall worth from the year before with 33 teams losing money.

Value is based on gate receipts, media revenues, stadium revenues, operating income, player salaries and other expenses. Figures are in millions of dollars. Teams are listed by sport.

	Value 1992	1991		Value 1992	1991		Value 1992	1991		Value 1992	1991
NY Yankees...	$200	$225	LA Lakers.....	$150	$200	Miami	$150	$205	Detroit	$70	$44
LA Dodgers....	180	200	Detroit	120	150	NY Giants	150	150	Boston	67	57
NY Mets.......	170	200	Boston	110	180	Dallas.........	146	180	NY Rangers	62	54
Toronto.......	160	178	Chicago.......	200	200	Philadelphia....	146	141	Montreal........	62	60
Boston	160	180	New York......	83	100	Chicago.......	139	126	Chicago........	61	45
Baltimore.....	140	200	Cleveland.....	81	61	San Francisco ..	134	150	Los Angeles	60	45
Chi.White Sox ..	140	125	Phoenix........	80	99	Seattle.......	130	130	Calgary.......	55	52
St.Louis.......	132	128	Portland.......	78	60	Houston.......	128	119	Edmonton	55	52
Chicago Cubs..	132	125	Charlotte.....	74	59	LA Raiders.....	128	135	Toronto........	54	45
Texas.........	123	101	Sacramento.....	63	49	LA Rams.......	126	135	NY Islanders	53	52
Kansas City....	117	122	Philadelphia....	63	75	Buffalo	125	126	Philadelphia....	51	43
Philadelphia....	115	130	Golden St.......	63	51	Cleveland.....	125	145	Hartford.......	49	45
Oakland.......	115	116	San Antonio....	63	47	New Orleans...	123	124	Quebec	45	45
California......	103	102	Orlando........	62	61	Kansas City....	123	122	Vancouver	45	42
San Francisco ..	99	105	Minnesota	62	51	Pittsburgh......	121	112	New Jersey.....	41	35
Cincinnati......	98	102	Houston........	61	58	Indianapolis....	121	116	Pittsburgh.......	41	42
San Diego.....	96	99	Dallas.........	60	54	Minnesota	120	119	Washington....	40	38
Houston.......	95	92	Miami........	60	59	Phoenix.......	120	120	Buffalo	39	37
Pittsburgh......	87	82	Atlanta	57	53	Atlanta........	120	113	St. Louis	39	32
Detroit	85	84	Milwaukee.....	56	53	Washington....	117	125	Minnesota	34	30
Atlanta.......	83	74	New Jersey....	54	43	NY Jets.......	117	125	Winnipeg	30	30
Minnesota	83	81	LA Clippers	54	43	Green Bay.....	115	200			
Seattle..........	79	71	Utah.........	52	45	Cincinnati	115	125			
Milwaukee.....	77	81	Denver	46	41	San Diego.....	115	113			
Cleveland......	77	75	Washington	46	38	Denver........	114	113			
Montreal........	75	75	Seattle..........	45	37	Tampa Bay	113	114			
			Indiana.........	43	33	Detroit........	110	116			
						New England...	103	100			

AWARDS

The Peabody Award

Presented annually since 1940 for outstanding achievement in radio and television broadcasting. Only 13 Peabodys have been given for sports programming.

Named after Georgia banker and philanthropist George Foster Peabody, the awards are administered by the Henry W. Grady College of Journalism and Mass Communication at the University of Georgia.

Television

Year
1960 **CBS** for coverage of 1960 Winter and Summer Olympic Games (for Outstanding Contribution to International Understanding).
1966 ABC's "**Wide World of Sports**" (for Outstanding Achievement in Promotion of International Understanding).
1968 **ABC Sports** coverage of both the 1968 Winter and Summer Olympic Games.
1972 **ABC Sports** coverage of the 1972 Summer Olympics in Munich.
1973 **Joe Garagiola** of NBC Sports (for "The Baseball World of Joe Garagiola").
1976 **ABC Sports** coverage of both the 1976 Winter and Summer Olympic Games.
1984 **Roone Arledge**, president of ABC News & Sports (for significant contributions to television news and sports programming).
1986 **WFAA-TV**, Dallas for its investigation of the Southern Methodist University football program.
1988 **Jim McKay** of ABC Sports (for pioneering efforts and career accomplishments in the world of TV sports).
1991 **CBS Sports** coverage of the 1991 Masters golf tournament
    & **HBO Sports** and **Black Canyon Productions** for the baseball special "When It Was A Game."

Radio

Year
1974 **WSB** radio in Atlanta for "Henry Aaron: A Man with a Mission."
1991 **Red Barber** of National Public Radio (for his six decades as a broadcaster and his 10 years as a commentator on NPR's "Morning Edition").

National Emmy Awards
Sports Programs

Presented by the Academy of Television Arts and Sciences since 1948. Eligibility period covered the calendar year from 1948-57 and since 1988.

Multiple Major Award Winners: ABC "Wide World of Sports" (18); ABC Olympic Coverage (9); CBS NFL Coverage (7); NFL Films Football Coverage (5); ABC "Monday Night Football" (4); ABC "The American Sportsman," ABC Indianapolis 500 Coverage, and CBS NCAA Basketball Coverage (3); ABC Kentucky Derby Coverage, and NBC World Series Coverage (2).

1949
Coverage—"Wrestling"(KTLA, Los Angeles)

1950
Program—"Rams Football" (KNBH-TV, Los Angeles)

1954
Program—"Gillette Cavalcade of Sports" (NBC)

1965-66
Programs—"Wide World of Sports" (ABC), "Shell's Wonderful World of Golf" (NBC) and "CBS Golf Classic" (CBS)

1966-67
Program—"Wide World of Sports" (ABC)

1967-68
Program—"Wide World of Sports" (ABC)

1968-69
Program—"1968 Summer Olympics" (ABC)

1969-70
Programs—"NFL Football" (CBS) and "Wide World of Sports" (ABC)

1970-71
Program—"Wide World of Sports" (ABC)

1971-72
Program—"Wide World of Sports" (ABC)

1972-73
News Special—"Coverage of Munich Olympic Tragedy" (ABC)
Sports Programs—"1972 Summer Olympics" (ABC) and "Wide World of Sports" (ABC)

1973-74
Program—"Wide World of Sports" (ABC)

1974-75
Non-Edited—"Jimmy Connors vs Rod Laver Tennis Challenge" (CBS)
Edited—"Wide World of Sports" (ABC)

1975-76
Live Special—"1975 World Series: Cincinnati vs Boston" (NBC)
Live Series—"NFL Monday Night Football" (ABC)
Edited Specials—"1976 Winter Olympics" (ABC) and "Triumph and Tragedy: The Olympic Experience" (ABC)
Edited Series—"Wide World of Sports" (ABC)

1976-77
Live Special—"1976 Summer Olympics" (ABC)
Live Series—"The NFL Today/NFL Football" (CBS)
Edited Special—"1976 Summer Olympics Preview" (ABC)
Edited Series—"The Olympiad" (PBS)

1977-78
Live Special—"Muhammad Ali vs Leon Spinks Heavyweight Championship Fight (CBS)
Live Series—"The NFL Today/NFL Football" (CBS)
Edited Special—"The Impossible Dream: Ballooning Across the Atlantic" (CBS)
Edited Series—"The Way It Was" (PBS)

1978-79
Live Special—"Super Bowl XIII: Pittsburgh vs Dallas" (NBC)
Live Series—"NFL Monday Night Football" (ABC)
Edited Special—"Spirit of '78: The Flight of Double Eagle II" (ABC)
Edited Series—"The American Sportsman" (ABC)

1979-80
Live Special—"1980 Winter Olympics" (ABC)
Live Series—"NCAA College Football" (ABC)
Edited Special—"Gossamer Albatross: Flight of Imagination" (CBS)
Edited Series—"NFL Game of the Week" (NFL Films)

1980-81
Live Special—"1981 Kentucky Derby" (ABC)
Live Series—"PGA Golf Tour" (CBS)
Edited Special—"Wide World of Sports 20th Anniversary Show" (ABC)
Edited Series—"The American Sportsman" (ABC)

1981-82
Live Special—"1982 NCAA Basketball Final: North Carolina vs Georgetown" (CBS)
Live Series—"NFL Football" (ABC)
Edited Special—"1982 Indianapolis 500" (ABC)
Edited Series—"Wide World of Sports" (ABC)

1982-83
Live Special—"1982 World Series: St. Louis vs Milwaukee" (NBC)
Live Series—"NFL Football" (CBS)
Edited Special—"Wimbledon '83" (NBC)
Edited Series—"Wide World of Sports" (ABC)

1983-84
No awards given

1984-85
Live Special—"1984 Summer Olympics" (ABC)
Live Series—No award given
Edited Special—"Road to the Super Bowl '85" (NFL Films)
Edited Series—"The American Sportsman" (ABC)

1985-86
No awards given

1986-87
Live Special—"1987 Daytona 500" (CBS)
Live Series—"NFL Football" (CBS)
Edited Special—"Wide World of Sports 25th Anniversary Special" (ABC)
Edited Series—"Wide World of Sports" (ABC)

1987-88
Live Special—"1987 Kentucky Derby" (ABC)
Live Series—"NFL Monday Night Football" (ABC)
Edited Special—"Paris-Roubaix Bike Race" (CBS)
Edited Series—"Wide World of Sports" (ABC)

1988
Live Special—"1988 Summer Olympics" (NBC)
Live Series—"1988 NCAA Basketball" (CBS)
Edited Special—"Road to the Super Bowl '88" (NFL Films)
Edited Series—"Wide World of Sports" (ABC)
Studio Show—"NFL GameDay" (ESPN)

He Told It Like It Was

by Howard Rosenberg

He is arrogant, narcissistic, pedantic, condescending, quarrelsome, overbearing, insufferable and a general pain—as he might pretentiously say—in either of the two fleshy rounded parts at the back of the hips.

So why do we miss the 72-year-old Howard Cosell?

Because until retiring this year, he was that refreshingly shrill note in the bland, monotonal Muzak of sportscasting. Cosell's absence has cost sports broadcasting its intellectual and journalistic center, creating a void that won't be soon filled, given the inclination of nearly all of today's sportscasters to speak volumes while saying nothing.

None could command a stage or stimulate and outrage us like Cosell. The voice, the fat cigar, the narrow eyes, the supercilious grin, the slick . . . uh . . . hair. It was inevitable that such a package would become a favorite target of impressionists.

An attorney who spent nearly four decades in broadcasting, Cosell withdrew from the airwaves in stages, leaving television's ABC Sports in 1985, then last January ending his daily sportscasts and weekly interview programs on ABC Radio.

Had he been more genteel and not left behind a legacy of bitter criticism aimed at some of his former colleagues, Cosell might have been remembered as the Edward R. Murrow of sportscasting. Both men were pioneers who elevated broadcast journalism and gained early fame by taking courageously controversial stands, Murrow against notorious Commie-hunter Sen. Joseph McCarthy, and Cosell in support of Muhammad Ali's resistance to the draft during the Vietnam War.

But unlike Murrow, who spawned a whole generation of newsmen and has become an enduring icon, Cosell's influence has proved fleeting. He left no protégés—only his reputation as sportscasting's tart tongue you loved to hate.

Cosell gained fame as a charter member of ABC's "Monday Night Football" in 1969. The series made him a superstar and prime time sports a part of mainstream entertainment. With Frank Gifford playing straight man to the parrying Cosell and Don Meredith, the banter in the booth often over-

Wide World Photos

Sportscaster **Howard Cosell** at his perch in the early days of ABC's Monday Night Football telecast.

shadowed the battle on the field. Meanwhile, Cosell used his pulpit to break the sportscasters' code of never criticizing the NFL or its players on the air.

Critical evaluation—that is to say, flat-out tongue-lashing—was Cosell's forte. After helping define the contemporary image of professional boxing as ABC's primary fight announcer, he became one of the sport's severest critics, saying he could no longer tolerate the sleaze.

He also spewed contempt for sports reporting, in particular TV's "jockocracy," those former athletes hired as sportscasters regardless of their rudimentary skills. Unlike most of them, Cosell regarded sports as merely one thread in the complex weave of society. In his twilight years on the air, he campaigned against the very industry that he had so closely associated with, charging in his book, *I Never Played the Game*, that sports is an "ever-spinning spiral of deceit, immorality, absence of ethics, and defiance of the public interest."

His words are like his personality: indelible.

Howard Rosenberg, the TV critic of the *Los Angeles Times*, won the Pulitzer Prize for criticism in 1985.

National Emmy Awards (Cont.)
Sports Programs

1989

Live Special—"1989 Indianapolis 500" (ABC)
Live Series—"NFL Monday Night Football" (ABC)
Edited Special—"Trans-Antarctica! The International
   Expedition" (ABC)
Edited Series—"This is the NFL" (NFL Films)
Studio Show—"NFL Today" (CBS)

1990

Live Special—"1990 Indianapolis 500" (ABC)
Live Series—"1990 NCAA Basketball Tournament" (CBS)
Edited Special—"Road to Super Bowl XXIV" (NFL Films)
Edited Series—"Wide World of Sports" (ABC)
Studio Show—"SportsCenter" (ESPN)

1991

Live Special—"1991 NBA Finals: Chicago vs LA Lakers"
   (NBC)
Live Series—"1991 NCAA Basketball Tournament" (CBS)
Edited Special—"Wide World of Sports 30th Anniversary
   Special" (ABC)

Edited Series—"This is the NFL" (NFL Films)
Studio Show—"NFL Game Day" (ESPN) and "NFL Live"
   (NBC)

Sportscasters

First presented as Outstanding Host/Commentator award for the 1967-68 TV season and given annually since 1972-73 (except in 1983-84 and 1985-86). Split into Host and Analyst awards for the 1980-81 season. Eligibility period has covered calendar year since 1988.

Multiple winners: John Madden and Jim McKay (9); Bob Costas and Dick Enberg (3); Al Michaels (2).

Season	Host/Commentator	Season	Host/Play-by-Play	Season	Analyst
1967-68	Jim McKay, ABC	1980-81	Dick Enberg, NBC	1980-81	Dick Button, ABC
1968-69	No award	1981-82	Jim McKay, ABC	1981-82	John Madden, CBS
1969-70	No award	1982-83	Dick Enberg, NBC	1982-83	John Madden, CBS
1970-71	Jim McKay, ABC	1983-84	No award	1983-84	No award
	& Don Meredith, ABC	1984-85	George Michael, NBC	1984-85	John Madden, CBS
1971-72	No award	1985-86	No award	1985-86	No award
1972-73	Jim McKay, ABC	1986-87	Al Michaels, ABC	1986-87	John Madden, CBS
1973-74	Jim McKay, ABC	1987-88	Bob Costas, NBC	1987-88	John Madden, CBS
1974-75	Jim McKay, ABC	1988	Bob Costas, NBC	1988	John Madden, CBS
1975-76	Jim McKay, ABC	1989	Al Michaels, ABC	1989	John Madden, CBS
1976-77	Frank Gifford, ABC	1990	Dick Enberg, NBC	1990	John Madden, CBS
1977-78	Jack Whitaker, CBS	1991	Bob Costas, NBC	1991	John Madden, CBS
1978-79	Jim McKay, ABC				
1979-80	Jim McKay, ABC				

Note: Jim McKay has won a total of 12 Emmy awards: 9 for Host/ Commentator, two for Sports Writing, and one for News Commentary.

Life Achievement Award

For outstanding work as an exemplary television sportscaster over many years.

Year		Year		Year	
1989	Jim McKay	1990	Lindsey Nelson	1991	Curt Gowdy

Sportscaster of the Year
NSSA Award

Presented annually since 1959 by the National Sportscasters and Sportswriters Association, based in Salisbury, N.C. Voting is done by NSSA members and selected national media.

Multiple winners: Keith Jackson (5); Bob Costas, Lindsey Nelson and Chris Schenkel (4); Dick Enberg, Al Michaels and Vin Scully (3); Chris Berman, Curt Gowdy and Ray Scott (2).

Year		Year		Year		Year	
1959	Lindsey Nelson	1968	Ray Scott	1977	Pat Summerall	1984	John Madden
1960	Lindsey Nelson	1969	Curt Gowdy	1978	Vin Scully	1985	Bob Costas
1961	Lindsey Nelson	1970	Chris Schenkel	1979	Dick Enberg	1986	Al Michaels
1962	Lindsey Nelson	1971	Ray Scott	1980	Dick Enberg	1987	Bob Costas
1963	Chris Schenkel	1972	Keith Jackson		& Al Michaels	1988	Bob Costas
1964	Chris Schenkel	1973	Keith Jackson	1981	Dick Enberg	1989	Chris Berman
1965	Vin Scully	1974	Keith Jackson	1982	Vin Scully	1990	Chris Berman
1966	Curt Gowdy	1975	Keith Jackson	1983	Al Michaels	1991	Bob Costas
1967	Chris Schenkel	1976	Keith Jackson				

ASA Award

Presented annually since 1984 by the American Sportscasters Association, based in New York. Voting is done by ASA members and officials.

Multiple winners: Dick Enberg (4); Bob Costas (3).

Year		Year		Year		Year		Year	
1984	Dick Enberg	1986	Dick Enberg	1988	No award	1990	Dick Enberg	1992	Bob Costas
1985	Vin Scully	1987	Dick Enberg	1989	Bob Costas	1991	Bob Costas		

The Pulitzer Prize

The Pulitzer Prizes for journalism, letters and music have been presented annually since 1917 in the name of Joseph Pulitzer (1847-1911), the publisher of the New York *World*. Prizes are awarded by the president of Columbia University on the recommendation of a board of review.

Since 1917, eight Pulitzers have been awarded for newspaper sportswriting or reporting on sports-related general news.

Commentary

1976 **Red Smith,** NY *Times,* for his 1975 columns.
1981 **Dave Anderson,** NY *Times,* for his 1980 columns.
1990 **Jim Murray,** LA *Times,* for his 1989 columns.

General Reporting

1956 **Arthur Daley,** NY *Times,* for his 1955 "Sports of the Times" columns.

Investigative Reporting

1986 **Jeffrey Marx & Michael York,** Lexington (Ky.) *Herald-Leader,* for their 1985 investigation of the basketball program at the University of Kentucky and other major colleges.

News Coverage

1935 **Bill Taylor,** NY *Herald Tribune,* for reporting on the 1934 America's Cup yacht races.

Special Citation

1952 **Max Kase,** NY *Journal-American,* for his reporting on the 1951 college basketball point-shaving scandal.

Specialized Reporting

1985 **Randall Savage & Jackie Crosby,** Macon (Ga.) *Telegraph and News,* for their 1984 investigation of athletics and academics at the University of Georgia and Georgia Tech.

Sportswriter of the Year

NSSA Award

Presented annually since 1959 by the National Sportscasters and Sportswriters Association, based in Salisbury, N.C. Voting is done by NSSA members and selected national media.

Multiple winners: Jim Murray (14); Frank Deford (6); Red Smith (5); Will Grimsley (4); Peter Gammons (2).

Year	Year	Year
1959 Red Smith, NY *Herald-Tribune*	1970 Jim Murray, LA *Times*	1981 Will Grimsley, AP
1960 Red Smith, NY *Herald-Tribune*	1971 Jim Murray, LA *Times*	1982 Frank Deford, *Sports Ill.*
1961 Red Smith, NY *Herald-Tribune*	1972 Jim Murray, LA *Times*	1983 Will Grimsley, AP
1962 Red Smith, NY *Herald-Tribune*	1973 Jim Murray, LA *Times*	1984 Frank Deford, *Sports Ill.*
1963 Arthur Daley, NY *Times*	1974 Jim Murray, LA *Times*	1985 Frank Deford, *Sports Ill.*
1964 Jim Murray, LA *Times*	1975 Jim Murray, LA *Times*	1986 Frank Deford, *Sports Ill.*
1965 Red Smith, NY *Herald-Tribune*	1976 Jim Murray, LA *Times*	1987 Frank Deford, *Sports Ill.*
1966 Jim Murray, LA *Times*	1977 Jim Murray, LA *Times*	1988 Frank Deford, *Sports Ill.*
1967 Jim Murray, LA *Times*	1978 Will Grimsley, AP	1989 Peter Gammons, *Sports Ill.*
1968 Jim Murray, LA *Times*	1979 Jim Murray, LA *Times*	1990 Peter Gammons, *Boston Globe*
1969 Jim Murray, LA *Times*	1980 Will Grimsley, AP	1991 Rick Reilly, *Sports Ill.*

Red Smith Award

Presented annually since 1981 by the Associated Press Sports Editors for "extended meritorious labor in the art of sports writing" and named in honor of the late newspaper columnist for the *New York Herald-Tribune* and *New York Times.* Voting is done by AP sports editors across the country.

Year	Year
1981 Red Smith, New York Times	1987 Will Grimsley, Associated Press
1982 Jim Murray, Los Angeles Times	1988 Furman Bisher, Atlanta Journal
1983 Shirley Povich, Washington Post	1989 Edwin Pope, Miami Herald
1984 Fred Russell, Nashville Banner	1990 Dave Smith, Dallas Morning News
1985 Blackie Sherrod, Dallas Morning News	1991 Dave Kindred, The National
1986 Si Burdick, Dayton Daily News	1992 Ed Storin, Miami Herald (ret.)

Best Newspaper Sports Sections of 1991

Winners of the annual Associated Press Sports Editors' contest for best daily and Sunday sports sections in newspapers of 175,000 circulation or more. Selections made by a committee of APSE members and released on March 1, 1992.

Top 10 Dailies

Atlanta Journal-Constitution Detroit News
Boston Globe Ft. Lauderdale Sun-Sentinel
Chicago Tribune Orange County Register
Dallas Morning News USA Today
Detroit Free Press Washington Post

Honorable mention: Chicago Sun-Times; Denver Post; Ft. Worth Star-Telegram; Los Angeles Daily News; Los Angeles Times; Miami Herald; Newsday; Orlando Sentinel; St. Paul Pioneer Press; St. Petersburg Times.

Top 10 Sunday

Atlanta Journal-Constitution Ft. Lauderdale Sun-Sentinel
Boston Globe Miami Herald
Chicago Sun-Times Newsday
Chicago Tribune Orange County Register
Dallas Morning News Washington Post

Honorable mention: Baltimore Sun; Detroit News; Ft. Worth Star-Telegram; Hartford Courant; Los Angeles Daily News; Los Angeles Times; Orlando Sentinel; Philadelphia Inquirer; St. Paul Pioneer Press; St. Petersburg Times.

Directory of Organizations

Listing of the major sports organizations, teams and media addresses and officials as of Sept. 15, 1992.

AUTO RACING

IndyCar
(Championship Auto Racing Teams, Inc.)
390 Enterprise Court, Bloomfield Hills, MI 48302
(313) 334-8500
Chairman-CEO .... William Stokkan
Director of Publicity.................... David Elshoff

FISA—Formula One
(Federation Internationale de Sport Automobile)
8 Place de la Concorde, 75008 Paris, France
TEL: 011-33-1-4265-9951
President................................ Max Mosley
Director of Public Relations ...... Francesco Longanesi

NASCAR
(National Assn. of Stock Car Auto Racing)
P.O. Box 2875, Daytona Beach, FL 32120
(904) 253-0611
President .... Bill France, Jr.
Director of Public Relations................ Andy Hall

MAJOR LEAGUE BASEBALL

Office of the Commissioner
350 Park Ave., New York, NY 10022
(212) 339-7800
Commissioner .... vacant
        (Fay Vincent resigned Sept. 7, 1992)
Chairman, Executive Council .... Bud Selig
        (interim commissioner)
Deputy Commissioner .... Steve Greenberg
Executive Dir. of Public Relations .... Rich Levin

Player Relations Committee
350 Park Ave., New York, NY 10022
(212) 339-7400
President & CEO .... Richard Ravitch
General Counsel .... Charles O'Connor

Major League Baseball Players Association
805 Third Ave., New York, NY 10022
(212) 826-0808
Exec. Director & General Counsel........ Donald Fehr
Special Assistant...................... Mark Belanger

AL

American League Office
350 Park Ave., New York, NY 10022
(212) 339-7600
President (until Dec. 31, 1993)......... Bobby Brown
Director of Public Relations........... Phyllis Merhige

Baltimore Orioles
333 West Camden St., Baltimore, MD 21201
(410) 685-9800
Chairman .... Eli Jacobs
President & CEO..................... Larry Lucchino
Exec. V.P. & General Manager .... Roland Hemond
Director of Public Relations .... Rick Vaughn

Boston Red Sox
Fenway Park, 4 Yawkey Way, Boston MA 02215
(617) 267-9440
General Partners.................... JRY Corporation
        and Haywood Sullivan
President .... John Harrington
Executive V.P. & General Manager....... Lou Gorman
Director of Public Relations............. Dick Bresciani

California Angels
P. O. Box 2000, Anaheim, CA 92803
(714) 937-7200 or (213) 625-1123
Owner .... Gene Autry
President .... Richard Brown
Senior V.P., Baseball Operations .... Dan O'Brien
Senior V.P., Player Personnel .... Whitey Herzog
Asst. V.P., Media Relations................ Tim Mead

Chicago White Sox
Comiskey Park, 333 W. 35th St., Chicago, IL 60616
(312) 924-1000
Chairman............................ Jerry Reinsdorf
Vice Chairman .... Eddie Einhorn
General Manager .... Ron Schueler
Director of Public Relations................ Doug Abel

Cleveland Indians
Cleveland Stadium, Cleveland, OH 44114
(216) 861-1200
Chairman-CEO .... Richard Jacobs
Vice Chairman........................ David Jacobs
President-COO............................ Rick Bay
V.P., Baseball Operations.................. John Hart
V.P., Media Relations.................... John Maroon

Detroit Tigers
Tiger Stadium, Detroit, MI 48216
(313) 962-4000
Owner-President....................... Mike Ilitch
Senior V.P., Player Personnel .... Jerry Walker
V.P., Media and Public Relations.......... Dan Ewald

Kansas City Royals
P O Box 419969, Kansas City, MO 64141
(816) 921-2200
Chairman .... Ewing Kauffman
Exec. V.P. & General Manager......... Herk Robinson
V.P., Director of Public Relations....... Dean Vogelaar

Milwaukee Brewers
County Stadium, 201 S. 46th St., Milwaukee, WI 53214
(414) 933-4114
President-CEO............................ Bud Selig
Senior V.P., Baseball Operations........... Sal Bando
Director of Media Relations .... Tom Skibosh

Minnesota Twins
Hubert H. Humphrey Metrodome
501 Chicago Ave. South, Minneapolis, MN 55415
(612) 375-1366
Owner .... Carl Pohlad
President .... Jerry Bell
General Manager .... Andy MacPhail
Director of Media Relations.............. Rob Antony

New York Yankees
Yankee Stadium, Bronx, NY 10451
(718) 293-4300
Principal Owner .... George Steinbrenner
Managing General Partner................ Joe Malloy
General Manager .... Gene Michael
Director of Media Relations.............. Jeff Idelson

Oakland Athletics
Oakland-Alameda County Coliseum
Oakland, CA 94621
(510) 638-4900
Owner............................ Walter A. Haas, Jr.
President-CEO .... Walter J. Haas
General Manager .... Sandy Alderson
Director of Media Relations........... Kathy Jacobson

Seattle Mariners
P.O. Box 4100, Seattle, WA 98104
(206) 628-3555
Chairman-CEO............................. John Ellis
President .... Chuck Armstrong
V.P., Baseball Operations .... Woody Woodward
Director of Public Relations .... Dave Aust

Texas Rangers
P.O. Box 90111, Arlington, TX 76004
(817) 273-5222
General Partners .. George W. Bush and Edward Rose
President.............................. Tom Schieffer
V.P., General Manager .... Tom Grieve
V.P., Public Relations .... John Blake

Toronto Blue Jays
SkyDome, 300 Bremner Blvd., Suite 3200
Toronto, Ontario M5V 3B3
(416) 341-1000
Chairman........................ P.N.T. Widdrington
President-CEO .... Paul Beeston
Exec. V.P. & General Manager .... Pat Gillick
Director of Public Relations .... Howie Starkman

NL

National League Office
350 Park Ave., New York, NY 10022
(212) 339-7700
President (until Mar. 1, 1993)............... Bill White
Director of Public Relations............... Katy Feeney

Atlanta Braves
P.O. Box 4064, Atlanta, GA 30302
(404) 522-7630
Owner....................... Ted Turner
President................................. Stan Kasten
Exec. V.P. & General Manager .... John Schuerholz
Director of Public Relations............... Jim Schultz

Chicago Cubs
1060 West Addison St., Chicago, IL 60613
(312) 404-2827
Owner....................... The Tribune Company
Chairman.............................. Stanton Cook
Exec. V.P., Baseball Operations .... Larry Himes
Director of Public Relations .... Sharon Pannozzo

Cincinnati Reds
100 Riverfront Stadium, Cincinnati, OH 45202
(513) 421-4510
Owner-President....................... Marge Schott
V.P. & General Manager.................. Bob Quinn
Director of Public Relations .... Jon Braude

Colorado Rockies
1700 Broadway, Suite 2100, Denver, CO 80290
(303) 292-0200
Chairman-CEO....................... John Antonucci
President-COO .... Steve Ehrhart
Senior V.P. & General Manager .... Bob Gebhard
Director of Public Relations .... Mike Swanson

Florida Marlins
100 NE 3rd Ave., 3rd Floor, Ft. Lauderdale, FL 33301
(305) 779-7070
Owner....................... H. Wayne Huizenga
President................................. Carl Barger
Exec. V.P. & General Manager ..... Dave Dombrowski
Director of Media Relations............... Chuck Pool

Houston Astros
P.O. Box 288, Houston, TX 77001
(713) 799-9600
Owner .... Drayton McLane
President .... TBA
General Manager .... Bill Wood
Director of Public Relations .... Rob Matwick

Los Angeles Dodgers
1000 Elysian Park Ave., Los Angeles, CA 90012
(213) 224-1500
Owner-President .... Peter O'Malley
Exec. V.P., Player Personnel............... Fred Claire
Director of Public Relations .... Jay Lucas

Montreal Expos
P.O. Box 500, Station M, Montreal, Quebec H1V 3P2
(514) 253-3434
General Partner-President............. Claude Brochu
V.P. & General Manger................ Dan Duquette
Director of Public Relations .... Richard Morency

New York Mets
Shea Stadium, Flushing, NY 11368
(718) 507-6387
Chairman........................ Nelson Doubleday
President-CEO........................... Fred Wilpon
Sr. Exec. V.P. & COO.................. Frank Cashen
Exec. V.P. & General Manager .... Al Harazin
Director of Public Relations .... Jay Horwitz

Philadelphia Phillies
P.O. Box 7575, Philadelphia, PA 19101
(215) 463-6000
General Partner-President-CEO .... Bill Giles
Senior V.P. & General Manager......... Lee Thomas
V.P., Public Relations..................... Larry Shenk

Pittsburgh Pirates
P.O. Box 7000, Pittsburgh, PA 15212
(412) 323-5000
Chairman........................ Douglas Danforth
President-CEO .... Mark Sauer
General Manager .... Ted Simmons
V.P., Public Relations.................... Rick Cerrone

St. Louis Cardinals
250 Stadium Plaza, St. Louis, MO 63102
(314) 421-3060
Chairman .... August A. Busch III
Vice Chairman....................... Fred Kuhlmann
President-CEO .... Stuart Meyer
V.P. & General Manager .... Dal Maxvill
Director of Public Relations .... Jeff Wehling

San Diego Padres
P.O. Box 2000, San Diego, CA 92112
(619) 283-7294
Chairman............................... Tom Werner
President................................. Dick Freeman
Exec. V.P. & General Manager.......... Joe McIlvaine
Director, Media Relations............... Jim Ferguson

San Francisco Giants
Candlestick Park, San Francisco, CA 94124
(415) 468-3700
Chairman................................. Bob Lurie
President & General Manager.............. Al Rosen
Exec. V.P., Administration .... Corey Busch
V.P., Public Relations.................. Duffy Jennings

PRO BASKETBALL

NBA

League Office
Olympic Tower, 645 Fifth Ave., New York, NY 10022
(212) 826-7000
Commissioner........................... David Stern
Deputy Commissioner................ Russell Granik
V.P., Public Relations .... Brian McIntyre
Director of Media Relations............... Terry Lyons

NBA Players Association
1775 Broadway, Suite 2401, New York, NY 10019
(212) 333-7510
Executive Director................. Charles Grantham
General Counsel .... Simon Gourdine

Atlanta Hawks
One CNN Center, South Tower, Suite 405
Atlanta, GA 30303
(404) 827-3800
Owner....................................... Ted Turner
President................................. Stan Kasten
General Manager...................... Pete Babcock
Director of Public Relations.............. Arthur Triche

Boston Celtics
151 Merrimac St., 5th Floor, Boston, MA 02114
(617) 523-6050
Owners ...... Don Gaston, Paul Dupee & Alan Cohen
President............................... Red Auerbach
Sr. Executive V.P......................... Dave Gavitt
Exec. V.P. & General Manager .... Jan Volk
Director of Public Relations .... Jeff Twiss

Charlotte Hornets
One Hive Drive, Charlotte, NC 28217
(704) 357-0252
Owner................................... George Shinn
President............................. Spencer Stolpen
Player Personnel Director.............. Dave Twardzik
Director of Media Relations.......... Harold Kaufman

Chicago Bulls
One Magnificent Mile, 980 N. Michigan Ave.
Suite 1600, Chicago, IL 60611
(312) 943-5800
Chairman............................. Jerry Reinsdorf
V.P., Basketball Operations.............. Jerry Krause
Director of Media Services .... Tim Hallam

Cleveland Cavaliers
2923 Streetsboro Rd., Richfield, OH 44286
(216) 659-9100
Chairman .... Gordon Gund
President............................. Tom Chestnut
V.P. & General Manager............... Wayne Embry
Director of Public Relations .... Bob Price

Dallas Mavericks
Reunion Arena, 777 Sports St., Dallas, TX 75207
(214) 988-0117
Owner-President...................... Donald Carter
COO-General Manager................. Norm Sonju
V.P., Basketball Operations .... Rick Sund
Director of Public Relations............ Kevin Sullivan

Denver Nuggets
1635 Clay St., Denver, CO 80204
(303) 893-6700
Managing General Partner.............. Peter Bynoe
General Manager.................... Bernie Bickerstaff
Director of Media Services.................. Jay Clark

Detroit Pistons
The Palace of Auburn Hills
Two Championship Dr., Auburn Hills, MI 48326
(313) 377-0100
Managing Partner .... William Davidson
President............................... Tom Wilson
Director of Player Personnel........... Billy McKinney
Director of Public Relations............... Matt Dobek

Golden State Warriors
Oakland Coliseum Arena, Oakland, CA 94621
(510) 638-6300
Chairman........................... James Fitzgerald
General Manager & Head Coach .... Don Nelson
Director of Public Relations............... Julie Marvel

Houston Rockets
The Summit, 10 Greenway Plaza, Houston, TX 77277
(713) 627-0600
Chairman............................ Charlie Thomas
President .... Ed Schmidt
General Manager .... Steve Patterson
Director of Media Information .... Jay Goldberg

Indiana Pacers
300 East Market St., Indianapolis, IN 46204
(317) 263-2100
Owners .... Melvin Simon & Herb Simon
President & General Manager.......... Donnie Walsh
V.P., Media Relations................ Dale Ratermann

Los Angeles Clippers
L.A. Sports Arena
3939 S. Figueroa St., Los Angeles, CA 90037
(213) 748-8000
Chairman........................... Donald Sterling
Exec. V.P. & General Manager .... Elgin Baylor
VP, Public Relations.................... Mike Williams

Los Angeles Lakers
Great Western Forum
3900 W. Manchester Blvd., Inglewood, CA 90306
(310) 419-3100
Owner .... Jerry Buss
General Manager........................ Jerry West
Director of Public Relations................. John Black

Miami Heat
Miami Arena, Miami, FL 33136
(305) 577-4328
Partners .... Ted Arison, Zev Bufman
                  Billy Cunningham & Lewis Schaffel
Director of Player Personnel .... Stu Inman
Director of Public Relations .... Mark Pray

Milwaukee Bucks
Bradley Center, 1001 N. Fourth St., Milwaukee, WI 53203
(414) 227-0500
President .... Herb Kohl
General Manager & Head Coach ..... Mike Dunleavy
Director of Public Relations .... Bill King II

Minnesota Timberwolves
Target Center, 600 First Ave. North, Minneapolis, MN 55403
(612) 673-1600
Owners .... Harvey Ratner and Marv Wolfenson
President.................................. Bob Stein
General Manager .... Jack McCloskey
Director of Public Relations .... Bill Robertson

New Jersey Nets
Meadowlands Arena, East Rutherford, NJ 07073
(201) 935-8888
Chairman-CEO .... Alan Aufzien
President-COO .... Jerry Cohen
Sr. V.P., Basketball Operations .... Willis Reed
Director of Public Relations................ John Mertz

New York Knickerbockers
Madison Square Garden
2 Penn Plaza, 3rd Floor, New York, NY 10121
(212) 465-6499
Owner.................. Paramount Communications
President .... David Checketts
V.P., Player Personnel .... Ernie Grunfeld
V.P., Public Relations .... John Cirillo

Orlando Magic
Orlando Arena, 1 Magic Place, Orlando, FL 32801
(407) 649-3200
Owner................................. Rich DeVos
President-CEO............................ Dick DeVos
General Manager....................... Pat Williams
Director of Public Relations .... Alex Martins

Philadelphia 76ers
Veterans Stadium
Broad St. and Pattison Ave., Philadelphia, PA 19148
(215) 339-7600
Owner-President .... Harold Katz
General Manager .... Jim Lynam
Director of Public Relations................. Zack Hill

Phoenix Suns
P.O. Box 1369, Phoenix, AZ 85001
(602) 379-7900
President-CEO .... Jerry Colangelo
V.P., Basketball Operations .... Dick Van Arsdale
Director of Public Relations .... Julie Fie

Portland Trail Blazers
Suite 600, Lloyd Building
700 N.E. Multnomah St., Portland, OR 97232
(503) 234-9291
Owner .... Paul Allen
President.......................... Harry Glickman
Sr. V.P. & General Manager.............. Geoff Petrie
Director of Public Relations............. John Lashway

Sacramento Kings
One Sports Parkway, Sacramento, CA 95834
(916) 928-0000
Owner .... Jim Thomas
President................................ Rick Benner
Director of Player Personnel............ Jerry Reynolds
Director of Public Relations .... TBA

San Antonio Spurs
600 East Market St., Suite 102, San Antonio TX 78205
(512) 554-7787
Chairman........................... Red McCombs
President................................ Gary Woods
V.P., Basketball Operations................. Bob Bass
Director of Public Relations.............. Dave Senko

Seattle Supersonics
190 Queene Anne Ave. North, Suite 200
Seattle, WA 98109
(206) 281-5800
Chairman........................... Barry Ackerley
President................................ Bob Whitsitt
Director of Public Relations .... Jim Rupp

Utah Jazz
Delta Center, 301 West South Temple,
Salt Lake City, UT 84101
(801) 325-2500
Owner .... Larry Miller
President.............................. Frank Layden
General Manager....................... Tim Howells
Director of Public Relations .... Kim Turner

Washington Bullets
One Harry S. Truman Dr., Landover, MD 20785
(301) 773-2255
Chairman................................. Abe Pollin
President........................... Susan O'Malley
V.P. & General Manager.................... John Nash
Director of Public Relations .... Matt Williams

BOWLING

ABC
(American Bowling Congress)
5301 South 76th St., Greendale, WI 53129
(414) 421-6400
Executive Director .... Darold Dobs
Public Relations Manager........... Dave DeLorenzo

BPAA
(Bowling Proprietors' Assn. of America)
P.O. Box 5802, Arlington, TX 76011
(817) 649-5105
Chief Executive Officer .... William Blue
President .... John LaSpina
Director of Public Relations.............. Rosie Crews

LPBT
(Ladies Professional Bowlers Tour)
7171 Cherryvale Blvd., Rockford, IL 61112
(815) 332-5756
President .... John Falzone
Media Director .... Dave Schroeder

PBA
(Professional Bowlers Association)
1720 Merriman Road, P.O. Box 5118
Akron, OH 44334
(216) 836-5568
Commissioner .... Mike Connor
Public Relations Director .... Kevin Shippy

WIBC
(Women's International Bowling Congress)
5301 South 76th St., Greendale, WI 53129
(414) 421-9000
President .... Gladys Banker
Director of Public Relations .... Jerry Topczewski

BOXING

IBF
(International Boxing Federation)
134 Evergreen Place, 9th Floor
East Orange, NJ 07018
(201) 414-0300
President......................... Robert (Bobby) Lee
Executive Secretary .... Marian Muhammad
Ratings Chairman .... Douglas Beavers
              1601 Holiday St., Portsmouth, VA 23704
                                      (804) 399-4503

WBA
(World Boxing Association)
Centro Comercial Ciudad Turmero, Local #21, Piso #2
Calle Petion Cruce Con Urdaneta
Turmero, 2115 Estado Aragua, Venezuela
TEL: 011-58-44-61645
President......................... Gilberto Mendoza
General Counsel/U.S. Spokesman....... Jimmy Binns
              300 Walnut St., Philadelphia, PA 19106
                                      (215) 922-4000
Ratings Chairman .... Alberto Sarmiento
              P.O. Box 69675, Caracas 1060A, Venezuela
                                   TEL: 011-58-2-682-3353

WBC
(World Boxing Council)
Genova 33-503, Col. Juarez
Delegacion Cuauhtemoc, MEXICO, 06600, D.F.
TEL: 011-525-755-7738
President .... Jose Sulaiman
Executive Secretary .... Eduardo Lamazon
Press Information/U.S. Spokesman .... John Brister
      402 Ocean View Ave., Santa Cruz, CA 95062
                            (408) 423-2631
Ratings Chairman .... Robert Busse
    1711 San Jacinto, P.O. Box 13047, Austin, TX 78711
                         (512) 345-4761

COLLEGE SPORTS

NAIA
(Natonal Assn. of Intercollegiate Athletics)
1221 Baltimore Ave., Kansas City, MO 64105
(816) 842-5050
President-CEO .... James Chasteen
Director of Communications .... John Mulvihill

NCAA
(National Collegiate Athletic Association)
6201 College Blvd., Overland Park, KS 66211
(913) 339-1906
President .... Judy Sweet
              (term expires Jan. 16, 1993)
Executive Director .... Dick Schultz
Asst Exec. Dir. for Enforcement........... David Berst
Director of Communications .... Jim Marchiony

WSF
Women's Sports Foundation
342 Madison Ave., Suite 728, New York, NY 10173
(212) 972-9170
Executive Director .... Donna Lopiano
Communications Director .... Kathryn Reith

🍂

Major NCAA Conferences

See pages 383-390 for basketball coaches, football
coaches, nicknames and colors of all Division I basketball schools and Division I-A and I-AA football schools.

ATLANTIC COAST CONFERENCE
P.O.Drawer ACC
Greensboro, NC 27419
(919) 854-8787   Founded: 1953
Commissioner .... Gene Corrigan
Director of Information................ Brian Morrison
   1993 Members: BASKETBALL & FOOTBALL (9)—
Clemson, Duke, Florida St., Georgia Tech, Maryland,
North Carolina, North Carolina St., Virginia and Wake
Forest.

Clemson University
Clemson, SC 29633   Founded: 1889
SID: (803) 656-2114   Enrollment: 16,300
President .... Max Lennon
Athletic Director .... Bobby Robinson
Sports Information Director .... Tim Bourret

Duke University
Durham, NC 27706   Founded: 1838
SID: (919) 684-2633   Enrollment: 6,300
President .... H.Keith H.Brodie
Athletic Director .... Tom Butters
Sports Information Director .... Mike Cragg

Florida State University
Tallahassee, FL 32316   Founded: 1857
SID: (904) 644-1403   Enrollment: 28,100
President............................. Dale W. Lick
Athletic Director .... Bob Goin
Sports Information Director .... Wayne Hogan

Georgia Tech
Atlanta, GA 30332   Founded: 1885
SID: (404) 894-5445   Enrollment: 11,900
President .... John Patrick Crecine
Athletic Director .... Homer Rice
Sports Information Director .... Mike Finn

University of Maryland
College Park, MD 20740   Founded: 1807
SID: (301) 314-7064   Enrollment: 26,900
President .... William E. Kirwan
Athletic Director .... Andy Geiger
Sports Information Director............. Herb Hartnett

University of North Carolina
Chapel Hill, NC 27514   Founded: 1789
SID: (919) 962-2123   Enrollment: 23,900
Chancellor............................. Paul Hardin
Athletic Director...................... John Swofford
Sports Information Director.............. Rick Brewer

North Carolina State University
Raleigh, NC 27695   Founded: 1887
SID: (919) 515-2102   Enrollment: 24,300
President .... Larry Monteith
Athletic Director......................... Todd Turner
Sports Information Director.......... Mark Bockelman

University of Virginia
Charlottesville, VA 22903   Founded: 1819
SID: (804) 982-5500   Enrollment: 18,100
President .... John T. Casteen III
Athletic Director .... Jim Copeland
Sports Information Director .... Rich Murray

Wake Forest University
Winston-Salem, NC 27109   Founded: 1834
SID: (919) 759-5640   Enrollment: 3,400
President....................... Thomas K. Hearn, Jr.
Athletic Director .... Gene Hooks
Sports Information Director.............. John Justus

🍂

BIG EAST CONFERENCE
56 Exchange Terrace
Providence, RI 02903
(401) 272-9108   Founded: 1979
Commissioner...................... Mike Tranghese
Director of Information .... John Paquette
   1993 Members: BASKETBALL (10)—Boston
College, Connecticut, Georgetown, Miami-FL,
Pittsburgh, Providence, St.John's, Seton Hall, Syracuse
and Villanova; FOOTBALL (8)—Boston College,
Miami-FL, Pittsburgh, Rutgers, Syracuse, Temple,
Virginia Tech and West Virginia.

Boston College
Chestnut Hill, MA 02167   Founded: 1863
SID: (617) 552-3004   Enrollment: 9,000
President.................... Rev.J.Donald Monan, SJ
Athletic Director....................... Chet Gladchuk
Sports Information Director................ Reid Oslin

University of Connecticut
Storrs, CT 06268   Founded: 1881
SID: (203) 486-3531   Enrollment: 12,600
President............................. Harry J. Hartley
Athletic Director .... Lew Perkins
Sports Information Director.............. Tim Tolokan

Georgetown University
Washington, DC 20057 Founded: 1798
SID: (202) 687-2492 Enrollment: 5,800
President.................. Rev. Leo J. O'Donovan, SJ
Athletic Director .... Francis X. Rienzo
Sports Information Director .... Bill Shapland

University of Miami
Coral Cables, FL 33124 Founded: 1926
SID: (305) 284-3244 Enrollment: 13,200
President.......................... Edward T. Foote II
Athletic Director .... Dave Maggard
Sports Information Director .... Linda Venzon

University of Pittsburgh
Pittsburgh, PA 15213 Founded: 1787
SID: (412) 648-8240 Enrollment: 13,500
President........................ J. Dennis O'Connor
Athletic Director......................... Oval Jaynes
Sports Information Director .... Larry Eldridge

Providence College
Providence, RI 02918 Founded: 1917
SID: (401) 865-2272 Enrollment: 3,800
President .... Rev. John F. Cunningham, OP
Athletic Director .... John Marinatto
Sports Information Director .... Gregg Burke

Rutgers University
New Brunswick, NJ 08903 Founded: 1766
SID: (908) 932-4200 Enrollment: 22,000
President .... Francis L. Lawrence
Athletic Director...................... Fred Gruninger
Sports Information Director............. Pete Kowalski

St. John's University
Jamaica, NY 11439 Founded: 1870
SID: (718) 990-6367 Enrollment: 19,500
President .... Rev. Donald J. Harrington, CM
Athletic Director .... John Kaiser
Sports Information Director .... Frank Racaniello

Seton Hall University
South Orange, NJ 07079 Founded: 1856
SID: (201) 761-9493 Enrollment: 8,500
President .... Rev. Thomas R. Peterson, OP
Athletic Director........................ Larry Keating
Sports Information Director .... John Wooding

Syracuse University
Syracuse, NY 13244 Founded: 1870
SID: (315) 443-2608 Enrollment: 12,000
President .... Kenneth Shaw
Athletic Director .... Jake Crouthamel
Sports Information Director .... Larry Kimball

Temple University
Philadelphia, PA 19122 Founded: 1884
SID: (215) 787-7445 Enrollment: 30,000
President .... Peter J. Liacouras
Athletic Director..................... Charlie Theokas
Sports Information Director.................. Al Shrier

Villanova University
Villanova, PA 19085 Founded: 1842
SID: (215) 645-4120 Enrollment: 6,500
President .... Rev. Edmund Dobbin, OSA
Athletic Director........................... Ted Aceto
Sports Information Director........... Jim DeLorenzo

Virginia Tech
Blacksburg, VA 24061 Founded: 1872
SID: (703) 231-6726 Enrollment: 23,400
President........................ James D. McComas
Athletic Director......................... Dave Braine
Sports Information Director.............. Dave Smith

West Virginia University
Morgantown, WV 26507 Founded: 1867
SID: (304) 293-2821 Enrollment: 20,000
President............................... Neil Bucklew
Athletic Director........................ Ed Pastilong
Sports Information Director .... Shelly Poe

BIG EIGHT CONFERENCE
104 West 9th Street, Suite 408
Kansas City, MO 64105-1755
(816) 471-5088 Founded: 1907
Commissioner........................... Carl James
Director of Information .... Jeff Bollig
  1993 Members: BASKETBALL & FOOTBALL
(8)—Colorado, Iowa St., Kansas, Kansas St., Missouri,
Nebraska, Oklahoma and Oklahoma St.,

University of Colorado
Boulder, CO 80309 Founded: 1876
SID: (303) 492-5626 Enrollment: 25,200
President......................... Judith E.N. Albino
Athletic Director........................... Bill Marolt
Sports Information Director .... Dave Plati

Iowa State University
Ames, IA 50011 Founded: 1868
SID: (515) 294-3372 Enrollment: 25,500
President .... Martin Jischke
Athletic Director........................... Max Urick
Sports Information Director............... Dave Starr

University of Kansas
Lawrence, KS 66045 Founded: 1866
SID: (913) 864-3417 Enrollment: 28,900
President .... Gene Budig
Athletic Director .... Bob Frederick
Sports Information Director............. Doug Vance

Kansas State University
Manhattan, KS 66506 Founded: 1863
SID: (913) 532-6735 Enrollment: 21,100
President .... Jon Wefald
Athletic Director .... Milt Richards
Sports Information Director .... Ben Boyle

University of Missouri
Columbia, MO 65205 Founded: 1839
SID: (314) 882-3241 Enrollment: 25,000
Interim President..................... Gerald Brouder
Athletic Director .... Dan Devine
Sports Information Director .... Bob Brendel

University of Nebraska
Lincoln, NE 68588 Founded: 1869
SID: (402) 472-2263 Enrollment: 24,000
President........................... Graham Spanier
Athletic Director............................ Bill Byrne
Sports Information Director .... Don Bryant

University of Oklahoma
Norman, OK 73019 Founded: 1890
SID: (405) 325-8225 Enrollment: 23,000
President...................... Richard L. Van Horn
Athletic Director .... Donnie Duncan
Sports Information Director .... Mike Prusinski

Oklahoma State University
Stillwater, OK 74078 Founded: 1890
SID: (405) 744-5749 Enrollment: 18,500
President........................... John R. Campbell
Athletic Director......................... Jim Garner
Sports Information Director............ Steve Buzzard

BIG TEN CONFERENCE
1500 West Higgins Road
Park Ridge, IL 60068-6300
(708) 696-1010 Founded: 1895
Commissioner .... Jim Delany
Director of Information .... Mark Rudner
1993 Members: BASKETBALL & FOOTBALL (11)—
Illinois, Indiana, Iowa, Michigan, Michigan St.,
Minnesota, Northwestern, Ohio St., Penn St., Purdue
and Wisconsin.

University of Illinois
Champaign, IL 61820 Founded: 1867
SID: (217) 333-1390 Enrollment: 35,800
President .... Stanley O.Ikenberry
Athletic Director .... Ron Guenther
Sports Information Director .... Mike Pearson

Indiana University
Bloomington, IN 47405 Founded: 1820
SID: (812) 855-2421 Enrollment: 34,000
President .... Thomas Ehrlich
Athletic Director .... Clarence Doninger
Sports Information Director........... Kit Klingelhoffer

University of Iowa
Iowa City, IA 52242 Founded: 1847
SID: (319) 335-9411 Enrollment: 28,000
President .... Hunter Rawlings III
Athletic Director .... Bob Bowlsby
Sports Information Director .... George Wine

University of Michigan
Ann Arbor, MI 48109 Founded: 1817
SID: (313) 763-1381 Enrollment: 36,300
President....................... James J. Duderstadt
Interim Athletic Director .... Jack Weidenbach
Sports Information Director............. Bruce Madej

Michigan State University
East Lansing, MI 48824 Founded: 1855
SID: (517) 355-2271 Enrollment: 42,800
President............................. Gordon Guyer
Athletic Director .... Merrily Dean Baker
Sports Information Director .... Ken Hoffman

University of Minnesota
Minneapolis, MN 55455 Founded: 1851
SID: (612) 625-4090 Enrollment: 42,000
President .... Nils Hasselmo
Athletic Director..................... McKinley Boston
Sports Information Director .... Bob Peterson

Northwestern University
Evanston, IL 60201 Founded: 1851
SID: (708) 491-7503 Enrollment: 15,700
President............................. Arnold Weber
Athletic Director .... Bruce Corrie
Sports Information Director .... Rob Grady

Ohio State University
Columbus, OH 43210 Founded: 1870
SID: (614) 292-6861 Enrollment: 54,000
President .... E. Gordon Gee
Athletic Director .... Jim Jones
Sports Information Director .... Steve Snapp

Penn State University
University Park, PA 16802 Founded: 1855
SID: (814) 865-1757 Enrollment: 30,500
President............................. Joab Thomas
Athletic Director .... Jim Tarman
Sports Information Director............ Budd Thalman

Purdue University
West Lafayette, IN 47907 Founded: 1869
SID: (317) 494-3200 Enrollment: 36,200
President.......................... Steven C. Beering
Interim Athletic Director.................. John Hicks
Sports Information Director .... Mark Adams

University of Wisconsin
Madison, WI 53711 Founded: 1848
SID: (608) 262-1811 Enrollment: 43,000
Chancellor.......................... Donna Shalala
Athletic Director .... Pat Richter
Sports Information Director............ Steve Malchow

BIG WEST CONFERENCE
2 Corporate Park, Suite 206
Irvine, CA 92714
(714) 261-2525 Founded: 1969
Commissioner .... Dennis Farrell
Director of Information .... Jacqueline Myrick
1993 Members: BASKETBALL (10)—CS-Fullerton,
Long Beach St., Nevada, New Mexico St., Pacific, San
Jose St., UC-Irvine, UC-Santa Barbara, UNLV and
Utah St.; FOOTBALL (11)—Arkansas St., CS-Fullerton,
Louisiana Tech, Nevada, New Mexico St., Northern
Illinois, Pacific, San Jose St., SW Louisiana, UNLV and
Utah St.

Arkansas State University
State University AK 72467 Founded: 1909
SID: (501) 972-2541 Enrollment: 9,800
President............................. Eugene Smith
Athletic Director.................... Charles Thornton
Sports Information Director........... Jerry Schaeffer

Cal State-Fullerton
Fullerton, CA 92634 Founded: 1957
SID: (714) 773-3970 Enrollment: 24,500
President.......................... Milton A. Gordon
Athletic Director .... Bill Shumard
Sports Information Director .... Mel Franks

Long Beach State
Long Beach, CA 90840 Founded: 1949
SID: (310) 985-7978 Enrollment: 31,000
President .... Curtis McCray
Interim Athletic Director................ David O'Brien
Sports Information Director .... Becca Wholt

Louisiana Tech
Ruston, LA 71272 Founded: 1894
SID: (318) 257-3144 Enrollment: 10,200
President .... Dan Reneau
Athletic Director .... Jerry Stovall
Sports Information Director.............. Keith Prince

University of Nevada
Reno, NV 89557 Founded: 1874
SID: (702) 784-4600 Enrollment: 12,000
President........................... Joseph Crowley
Athletic Director .... Chris Ault
Sports Information Director .... Paul Stewart

New Mexico State University
Las Cruces, NM 88003 Founded: 1888
SID: (505) 646-3929 Enrollment: 14,800
President......................... James E. Halligan
Athletic Director........................ Al Gonzales
Sports Information Director .... Steve Shutt

Northern Illinois University
De Kalb, IL 60115 Founded: 1895
SID: (815) 753-1706 Enrollment: 24,900
President........................ John E. La Tourette
Athletic Director........................ Gerald Odell
Sports Information Director .... Mike Korcek

University of the Pacific
Stockton, CA 95211 — Founded: 1851
SID: (209) 946-2479 — Enrollment: 3,600
President................................... Bill Atchley
Athletic Director............................ Bob Lee
Sports Information Director.......... Kevin Messenger

San Jose State University
San Jose, CA 95192 — Founded: 1857
SID: (408) 924-1217 — Enrollment: 30,000
Interim President .... J. Handel Evans
Athletic Director......................... Tom Brennan
Sports Information Director............ Lawrence Fan

University of Southwestern Louisiana
Lafayette, LA 70506 — Founded: 1898
SID: (318) 231-6331 — Enrollment: 16,500
President............................. Ray Authement
Athletic Director .... Nelson Stokley
Sports Information Director .... Dan McDonald

University of California, Irvine
Irvine, CA 92717 — Founded: 1962
SID: (714) 856-5814 — Enrollment: 16,700
Acting Chancellor.................... L. Dennis Smith
Interim Athletic Director.............. Barbara Camp
Sports Information Director............... Bob Olson

University of California, Santa Barbara
Santa Barbara, CA 93106 — Founded: 1944
SID: (805) 893-3428 — Enrollment: 18,700
Chancellor .... Barbara Uehling
Athletic Director........................ John Kasser
Sports Information Director .... Bill Mahoney

UNLV—University of Nevada, Las Vegas
Las Vegas, NV 89154 — Founded: 1957
SID: (702) 739-3207 — Enrollment: 18,200
President............................. Robert Maxson
Athletic Director .... Jim Weaver
Sports Information Director .... Joe Hawk

Utah State University
Logan, UT 84322 — Founded: 1888
SID: (801) 750-1361 — Enrollment: 15,600
President............................ Stanford Cazier
Athletic Director......................... Rod Tueller
Sports Information Director.............. Craig Hislop

ð▲

MID-AMERICAN CONFERENCE
Four SeaGate, Suite 102
Toledo, OH 43604
(419) 249-7177 — Founded: 1946
Commissioner .... Karl Benson
Director of Communications............. Sue Brague
   1993 Members: BASKETBALL & FOOTBALL (10)—
Akron, Ball St., Bowling Green, Central Michigan,
Eastern Michigan, Kent, Miami-OH, Ohio University,
Toledo and Western Michigan.

University of Akron
Akron, OH 44325 — Founded: 1870
SID: (216) 972-7468 — Enrollment: 29,000
President ..../..... Peggy Gordon Elliott
Athletic Director .... Jim Dennison
Sports Information Director............... Mac Yates

Ball State University
Muncie, IN 47306 — Founded: 1918
SID: (317) 285-8242 — Enrollment: 20,500
President............................ John Worthen
Athletic Director .... Don Purvis
Sports Information Director .... Joe Hernandez

Bowling Green State University
Bowling Green, OH 43403 — Founded: 1910
SID: (419) 372-7075 — Enrollment: 18,000
President .... Paul Olscamp
Athletic Director......................... Jack Gregory
Sports Information Director .... Steve Barr

Central Michigan University
Mt. Pleasant, MI 48859 — Founded: 1892
SID: (517) 774-3277 — Enrollment: 16,600
Interim President .... Leonard Plachta
Athletic Director .... Dave Keilitz
Sports Information Director .... Fred Stabley

Eastern Michigan University
Ypsilanti, MI 48197 — Founded: 1849
SID: (313) 487-0318 — Enrollment: 25,000
President............................ William Shelton
Athletic Director .... Gene Smith
Sports Information Director.............. Jim Streeter

Kent State University
Kent, OH 44242 — Founded: 1910
SID: (216) 672-2110 — Enrollment: 33,500
President........................... Carol Cartwright
Athletic Director .... Paul Amodio
Sports Information Director .... John Wagner

Miami University
Oxford, OH 45056 — Founded: 1809
SID: (513) 529-4327 — Enrollment: 16,000
President .... Paul Pearson
Athletic Director........................ R.C. Johnson
Sports Information Director .... Brian Teter

Ohio University
Athens, OH 45701 — Founded: 1804
SID: (614) 593-1298 — Enrollment: 18,300
President............................... Charles Ping
Athletic Director................... Harold McElhaney
Sports Information Director .... Glenn Coble

University of Toledo
Toledo, OH 43606 — Founded: 1872
SID: (419) 537-3790 — Enrollment: 25,000
President .... Frank Horton
Athletic Director............................... Al Bohl
Sports Information Director .... Rod Brandt

Western Michigan University
Kalamazoo, MI 49008 — Founded: 1903
SID: (616) 387-4104 — Enrollment: 27,700
President .... Diether Haenicke
Athletic Director .... Leland Byrd
Sports Information Director.............. John Beatty

ð▲

PACIFIC-10 CONFERENCE
800 South Broadway, Suite 400
Walnut Creek, CA 94596
(510) 932-4411 — Founded: 1915
Commissioner .... Thomas Hansen
Director of Information .... Jim Muldoon
   1993 Members: BASKETBALL & FOOTBALL (10)—
Arizona, Arizona St., California, Oregon, Oregon St.,
Stanford, UCLA, USC, Washington and Washington St.

University of Arizona
Tucson, AZ 85721 — Founded: 1885
SID: (602) 621-4163 — Enrollment: 34,000
President .... Manuel Pacheco
Athletic Director...................... Cedric Dempsey
Sports Information Director .... Butch Henry

Arizona State University
Tempe, AZ 85287   Founded: 1885
SID: (602) 965-6592   Enrollment: 43,400
President.............................. Lattie F. Coor
Athletic Director........................ Charles Harris
Sports Information Director .... Mark Brand

University of California
Berkeley, CA 94720   Founded: 1868
SID: (510) 642-5363   Enrollment: 31,000
Chancellor .... Chang-Lin Tien
Athletic Director .... Robert Bockrath
Sports Information Director............ Kevin Reneau

University of Oregon
Eugene, OR 97403   Founded: 1872
SID: (503) 346-5488   Enrollment: 16,400
President .... Myles Brand
Athletic Director .... Rich Brooks
Sports Information Director .... Steve Hellyer

Oregon State University
Corvallis, OR 97331   Founded: 1868
SID: (503) 737-3720   Enrollment: 14,000
President .... John Byrne
Athletic Director .... Dutch Bauchman
Sports Information Director.............. Hal Cowan

Stanford University
Stanford, CA 94305   Founded: 1891
SID: (415) 723-4418   Enrollment: 6,600
President .... Casper Gerhard
Athletic Director........................ Ted Leyland
Sports Information Director .... Bob Vazquez

UCLA—Univ. of California, Los Angeles
Los Angeles, CA 90024   Founded: 1919
SID: (310) 206-6831   Enrollment: 34,000
Chancellor........................... Charles Young
Athletic Director .... Pete Dalis
Sports Information Director............. Marc Dellins

USC—Univ. of Southern California
Los Angeles, CA 90089   Founded: 1880
SID: (213) 740-8480   Enrollment: 28,000
President.............................. Steven Sample
Athletic Director .... Mike McGee
Sports Information Director .... Tim Tessalone

University of Washington
Seattle, WA 98195   Founded: 1861
SID: (206) 543-2230   Enrollment: 34,000
President...................... William P. Gerberding
Athletic Director.................... Barbara Hedges
Sports Information Director................ Jim Daves

Washington State University
Pullman, WA.99164   Founded: 1890
SID: (509) 335-0270   Enrollment: 17,500
President............................. Samuel Smith
Athletic Director........................ Jim Livengood
Sports Information Director .... Rod Commons

≷

SOUTHEASTERN CONFERENCE
2201 Civic Center Blvd.
Birmingham, AL 35203
(205) 458-3010   Founded: 1933
Commissioner.......................... Roy Kramer
Director of Information .... Mark Whitworth
   1993 Members: BASKETBALL & FOOTBALL (12)—
Alabama, Arkansas, Auburn, Florida, Georgia, Kentucky, LSU, Mississippi, Mississippi St., South Carolina, Tennessee and Vanderbilt.

University of Alabama
Tuscaloosa, AL 35487   Founded: 1831
SID: (205) 348-6084   Enrollment: 20,000
President .... Roger Sayers
Athletic Director....................... Hootie Ingram
Sports Information Director.............. Larry White

University of Arkansas
Fayetteville, AR 72701   Founded: 1871
SID: (501) 575-2751   Enrollment: 14,000
President............................. Daniel Ferritor
Athletic Director........................ Frank Broyles
Sports Information Director .... Rick Schaeffer

Auburn University
Auburn, AL 36831   Founded: 1856
SID: (205) 844-9807   Enrollment: 21,800
President .... William V. Muse
Athletic Director.......................... Mike Lude
Sports Information Director .... David Housel

University of Florida
Gainesville, FL 32604   Founded: 1853
SID: (904) 375-4683   Enrollment: 34,500
President .... Nicholas Cassisi
Athletic Director .... Jeremy Foley
Sports Information Director .... John Humenik

University of Georgia
Athens, GA 30613   Founded: 1785
SID: (706) 542-1621   Enrollment: 28,300
President .... William Powell
Athletic Director .... Vince Dooley
Sports Information Director .... Claude Felton

University of Kentucky
Lexington, KY 40506   Founded: 1865
SID: (606) 257-3838   Enrollment: 23,000
President....................... Charles Wethington
Athletic Director....................... C.M. Newton
Sports Information Director .... Joey Howard

LSU—Louisiana State University
Baton Rouge, LA 70894   Founded: 1860
SID: (504) 388-8226   Enrollment: 26,100
Chancellor .... William (Bud) Davis
Athletic Director .... Joe Dean
Sports Information Director .... Herb Vincent

University of Mississippi
University, MS 38677   Founded: 1848
SID: (601) 232-7522   Enrollment: 11,000
Chancellor......................... R. Gerald Turner
Athletic Director....................... Warner Alford
Sports Information Director .... Langston Rogers

Mississippi State University
Starkville, MS 39762   Founded: 1878
SID: (601) 325-2703   Enrollment: 13,600
President........................... Donald Zecharias
Athletic Director..................... Larry Templeton
Sports Information Director.................. Joe Dier

University of South Carolina
Columbia, SC 29208   Founded: 1801
SID: (803) 777-5204   Enrollment: 26,600
President .... John Palms
Athletic Director .... King Dixon
Sports Information Director.............. Kerry Tharp

University of Tennessee
Knoxville, TN 37901   Founded: 1794
SID: (615) 974-1212   Enrollment: 25,600
President .... Joe Johnson
Athletic Director........................ Doug Dickie
Sports Information Director .... Bud Ford

Vanderbilt University

Nashville, TN 37212   Founded: 1873
SID: (615) 322-4121   Enrollment: 8,900
Chancellor .... Joe B. Wyatt
Athletic Director .... Paul Hoolahan
Sports Information Director .... Tony Neeley

ॐ

SOUTHWEST CONFERENCE

P.O.Box 569420
Dallas, TX 75356
(214) 634-7353   Founded: 1914
Commissioner .... Fred Jacoby
Director of Information .... Bo Carter
1993 Members: BASKETBALL & FOOTBALL (8)—
Baylor, Houston, Rice, SMU, TCU, Texas, Texas A&M
and Texas Tech.

Baylor University

Waco, TX 76711   Founded: 1845
SID: (817) 755-1222   Enrollment: 12,100
President........................ Herbert H. Reynolds
Athletic Director .... Grant Teaff
Sports Information Director .... Maxey Parrish

University of Houston

Houston, TX 77204   Founded: 1927
SID: (713) 749-2180   Enrollment: 33,000
President........................ James H. Pickering
Athletic Director .... Rudy Davalos
Sports Information Director .... Ted Nance

Rice University

Houston, TX 77251   Founded: 1912
SID: (713) 527-4034   Enrollment: 3,600
President............................. George Rupp
Athletic Director.......................... Bobby May
Sports Information Director............... Bill Cousins

SMU—Southern Methodist University

Dallas, TX 75275   Founded: 1911
SID: (214) 692-2883   Enrollment: 5,400
President .... Kenneth Pye
Athletic Director .... Forrest Gregg
Sports Information Director .... Ed Wisneski

TCU—Texas Christian University

Fort Worth, TX 76129   Founded: 1873
SID: (817) 921-7969   Enrollment: 7,000
Chancellor.......................... William Tucker
Athletic Director.................... Frank Windegger
Sports Information Director .... Glen Stone

University of Texas

Austin, TX 78713   Founded: 1883
SID: (512) 471-7437   Enrollment: 50,000
Chancellor.................... William Cunningham
Athletic Director....................... DeLoss Dodds
Sports Information Director .... Bill Little

Texas A&M University

College Station, TX 77843   Founded: 1876
SID: (409) 845-0563   Enrollment: 41,000
President........................... William Mobley
Athletic Director.................... John David Crow
Sports Information Director .... Alan Cannon

Texas Tech University

Lubbock, TX 79409   Founded: 1923
SID: (806) 742-2770   Enrollment: 25,500
President........................... Robert Lawless
Athletic Director.............................. T. Jones
Sports Information Director .... Joe Hornaday

WESTERN ATHLETIC CONFERENCE

14 West Dry Creek Circle, Littleton, CO 80120
(303) 795-1962   Founded: 1962
Commissioner .... Joe Kearney
Director of Information .... Jeff Hurd
1993 Members: BASKETBALL & FOOTBALL (10)—
Air Force, BYU, Colorado St., Fresno St., Hawaii, New
Mexico, San Diego St., Utah, UTEP and Wyoming.

Air Force—U.S. Air Force Academy

Colorado Springs, CO 80840   Founded: 1959
SID: (719) 472-2313   Enrollment: 4,400
Superintendent.............. Lt. Gen. Bradley Hosmer
Athletic Director.............. Col. Kenneth Schweitzer
Sports Information Director......,..... Dave Kellogg

BYU—Brigham Young University

Provo, UT 84602   Founded: 1875
SID: (801) 378-4911   Enrollment: 26,000
President .... Rex E. Lee
Athletic Director .... Glen Tuckett
Sports Information Director............. Ralph Zobell

Colorado State University

Fort Collins, CO 80523   Founded: 1870
SID: (303) 491-5067   Enrollment: 20,600
President .... Albert Yates
Athletic Director .... Corey Johnson
Sports Information Director .... Gary Ozzello

Fresno State University

Fresno, CA 93740   Founded: 1911
SID: (209) 278-2509   Enrollment: 19,600
President .... John Welty
Athletic Director .... Gary Cunningham
Sports Information Director............. Scott Johnson

University of Hawaii

Honolulu, HI 96822   Founded: 1907
SID: (808) 956-7523   Enrollment: 19,400
Interim President .... Paul Yuen
Athletic Director......................... Stan Sheriff
Sports Information Director .... Eddie Inouye

University of New Mexico

Albuquerque, NM 87131   Founded: 1889
SID: (505) 277-2026   Enrollment: 24,600
President............................... Richard Peck
Athletic Director .... Gary Ness
Sports Information Director .... Greg Remington

San Diego State University

San Diego, CA 92182   Founded: 1897
SID: (619) 594-5547   Enrollment: 34,800
President................................ Thomas Day
Athletic Director .... Fred Miller
Sports Information Director .... John Rosenthal

University of Utah

Salt Lake City, UT 84112   Founded: 1850
SID: (801) 581-3510   Enrollment: 26,000
President .... Arthur Smith
Athletic Director............................ Chris Hill
Sports Information Director .... Bruce Woodbury

UTEP—University of Texas at El Paso

El Paso, TX 79968   Founded: 1913
SID: (915) 747-5330   Enrollment: 15,800
President............................. Diana Natalicio
Athletic Director......................... Brad Hovious
Sports Information Director .... Eddie Mullens

University of Wyoming

Laramie, WY 82071   Founded: 1886
SID: (307) 766-2256   Enrollment: 11,000
President.................................. Terry Roark
Athletic Director........................... Paul Roach
Sports Information Director........... Kevin McKinney

MAJOR INDEPENDENTS

Ten schools with a Division I basketball program also fielded a Division I-A football team in 1992. Five other I-A football independents will join conferences in 1993. Accordingly, Penn St. is listed with the Big Ten; while Arkansas St., Louisiana Tech, Northern Illinois and SW Louisiana can all be found with the Big West.

Army—U.S. Military Academy

West Point, NY 10996	Founded: 1802
SID: (914) 938-3303	Enrollment: 4,300
Superintendent	Lt. Gen. Howard D. Graves
Athletic Director	Al Vanderbush
Sports Information Director	Bob Kinney

University of Cincinnati

Cincinnati, OH 45221	Founded: 1819
SID: (513) 556-5191	Enrollment: 36,000
President	Joseph A. Steger
Athletic Director	Rick Taylor
Sports Information Director	Tom Hathaway

East Carolina University

Greenville, NC 27858	Founded: 1907
SID: (919) 757-4522	Enrollment: 16,000
Chancellor	Richard Eakin
Athletic Director	Dave Hart, Jr.
Sports Information Director	Charles Bloom

University of Louisville

Louisville, KY 40292	Founded: 1798
SID: (502) 588-6581	Enrollment: 23,500
President	Donald C. Swain
Athletic Director	Bill Olsen
Sports Information Director	Kenny Klein

Memphis State University

Memphis, TN 38152	Founded: 1912
SID: (901) 678-2337	Enrollment: 21,500
President	V. Lane Rawlins
Athletic Director	Charles Cavagnaro
Sports Information Director	Bob Winn

Navy—U.S. Naval Academy

Annapolis, MD 21402	Founded: 1845
SID: (301) 268-6226	Enrollment: 4,300
Superintendent	Rear Adm. Thomas C. Lynch
Athletic Director	Jack Lengyel
Sports Information Director	Tom Bates

University of Notre Dame

Notre Dame, IN 46556	Founded: 1842
SID: (219) 239-7516	Enrollment: 10,000
President	Rev. Edward A. (Monk) Malloy
Athletic Director	Dick Rosenthal
Sports Information Director	John Heisler

University of Southern Mississippi

Hattiesburg, MS 39406	Founded: 1910
SID: (601) 266-4503	Enrollment: 13,900
President	Aubrey K. Lucas
Athletic Director	Bill McLellan
Sports Information Director	Regiel Napier

Tulane University

New Orleans, LA 70118	Founded: 1834
SID: (504) 865-5506	Enrollment: 11,400
President	Eamon M. Kelly
Athletic Director	Kevin White
Sports Information Director	Lenny Vangilder

University of Tulsa

Tulsa, OK 74104	Founded: 1894
SID: (918) 631-2395	Enrollment: 4,600
President	Robert Donaldson
Athletic Director	Rick Dickson
Sports Information Director	Don Tomkalski

OTHER MAJOR DIVISION I CONFERENCES

Conferences that play either Division I basketball or Division I-AA football, or both.

Atlantic 10 Conference

10 Woodbridge Center Drive, Suite 660

Woodbridge, NJ 07095	Founded: 1976
(908) 634-6900	
Commissioner	Ron Bertovich
Director of Information	Ray Cella

1993 Members: BASKETBALL (8)—George Washington, Massachusetts, Rhode Island, Rutgers, St.Bonaventure, St.Joseph's-PA, Temple and West Virginia.

Big Sky Conference

P.O. Box 1736, Boise, ID 83701

(208) 345-0281	Founded: 1963
Commissioner	Ron Stephenson
Director of Information	Arnie Sgalio

1993 Members: BASKETBALL & FOOTBALL (8)—Boise St., Eastern Washington, Idaho, Idaho St., Montana, Montana St., Northern Arizona and Weber St.

Big South Conference

1551 21st Avenue North, Suite 11
Myrtle Beach, SC 29577

(803) 448-9998	Founded: 1983
Commissioner	Buddy Sasser
Director of Information	Karen Clark

1993 Members: BASKETBALL (10)—Campbell, Charleston Southern, Coastal Carolina, Liberty, MD-Baltimore County, NC-Asheville, NC-Greensboro, Radford, Towson St. and Winthrop.

Note: NC-Greensboro will not compete for conference title until the 1994-95 season.

Colonial Athletic Association

2550 Professional Road, Suite 16
Richmond, VA 23235

(804) 272-1616	Founded: 1985
Commissioner	Tom Yeager
Director of Information	Tripp Sheppard

1993 Members: BASKETBALL (8)—American, East Carolina, George Mason, James Madison, NC-Wilmington, Old Dominion, Richmond and William & Mary.

Gateway Football Conference

100 North Broadway, Suite 1135,
St.Louis, MO 63102

(314) 421-2268	Founded: 1982
Commissioner	Patty Viverito
Director of Information	Mike Kern

1993 Members (7): Eastern Illinois, Illinois St., Indiana St., Northern Iowa, Southern Illinois, SW Missouri St. and Western Illinois.

Great Midwest Conference

35 East Wacker Drive, Suite 650,
Chicago, IL 60601

(312) 553-0483	Founded: 1990
Commissioner	Mike Slive
Director of Media Relations	Tim Stephens

1993 Members: BASKETBALL (6)—Ala-Birmingham, Cincinnati, DePaul, Marquette, Memphis St. and St.Louis.

Ivy League

120 Alexander Street, Princeton, NJ 08544

(609) 258-6426	Founded: 1954
Executive Director	Jeffrey Orleans
Director of Information	Chuck Yrigoyen

1993 Members: BASKETBALL & FOOTBALL (8)—Brown, Columbia, Cornell, Dartmouth, Harvard, Pennsylvania, Princeton and Yale.

Metro Conference
Two Ravinia Drive, Suite 210
Atlanta, GA 30346
(404) 395-6444 Founded: 1975
Commissioner........................ Ralph McFillen
Director of Communications........ Jamie Kimbrough
1993 Members: BASKETBALL (7)—Louisville, NC-Charlotte, South Florida, Southern Mississippi, Tulane, VCU and Virginia Tech.

Metro Atlantic Athletic Conference
1099 Wall Street West, Suite 242
Lyndhurst, NJ 07071
(201) 896-8443 Founded: 1980
Commissioner......................... Richard Ensor
Director of Media Relations ...... Carolanne McAuliffe
1993 Members: BASKETBALL (8)—Canisius, Fairfield, Iona, Loyola-MD, Manhattan, Niagara, St.Peter's and Siena.

Mid-Continent Conference
40 Shuman Blvd., Suite 118,
Naperville, IL 60563
(708) 416-7560 Founded: 1982
Commissioner......................... Jerry Ippoliti
Director pf Publicity........................ Tom Lessig
1993 Members: BASKETBALL (10)—Cleveland St., Eastern Illinois, Illinois-Chicago, Northern Illinois, Valparaiso, Western Illinois, Wisconsin-Green Bay, Wisconsin-Milwaukee, Wright St. and Youngstown St.
Note: WI-Milwaukee will not compete for conference title until the 1993-94 season.

Mid-Eastern Athletic Conference
P.O. Box 21205
Greensboro, NC 27420
(919) 275-9961 Founded:1970
Commissioner .... Ken Free
Director of Service Bureau .... Larry Barber
1993 Members: BASKETBALL (9)—Bethune-Cookman, Coppin St., Delaware St., Florida A&M, Howard, MD-Eastern Shore, Morgan St., North Carolina A&T and South Carolina St.; FOOTBALL (7)—all but Coppin St. and MD-Eastern Shore.

Midwestern Collegiate Conference
201 South Capitol Ave., Suite 500
Indianapolis, IN 46225
(317) 237-5622 Founded: 1979
Commissioner .... Jonathon LeCrone
Director of Information .... Mike Hermann
1993 Members: BASKETBALL (8)—Butler, Dayton, Detroit, Duquesne, Evansville, La Salle, Loyola-IL and Xavier-OH.

Missouri Valley Conference
100 North Broadway, Suite 1135
St.Louis, MO 63102
(314) 421-0339 Founded: 1907
Commissioner .... Doug Elgin
Dir.of Information .... Jack Watkins
1993 Members: BASKETBALL (10)—Bradley, Creighton, Drake, Illinois St., Indiana St., Northern Iowa, Southern Illinois, SW Missouri St., Tulsa and Wichita St.

North Atlantic Conference
P.O.Box 69 —28 Main Street
Orono, ME 04473
(207) 866-2383 Founded: 1979
Commissioner........................ Stuart Haskell
Director of Information................... Len Harlow
1993 Members: BASKETBALL (8)—Boston University, Delaware, Drexel, Hartford, Maine, New Hampshire, Northeastern and Vermont.

Northeast Conference
900 Route 9, Suite 120
Woodbridge, NJ 07095
(908) 636-9119 Founded: 1979
Commissioner .... Chris Monasch
Director of Information................... Dave Siroty
1993 Members: BASKETBALL (10)—Fairleigh Dickinson, LIU-Brooklyn, Marist, Monmouth, Mount St.Mary's, Rider, Robert Morris, St.Francis-NY, St.Francis-PA and Wagner.

Ohio Valley Conference
278 Franklin Road, Suite 103
Brentwood, TN 37027
(615) 371-1698 Founded: 1948
Commissioner .... Dan Beebe
Director of Information .... Angela Hazel
1993 Members: BASKETBALL & FOOTBALL (9)—Austin Peay St., Eastern Kentucky, Middle Tennessee St., Morehead St., Murray St., SE Missouri St., Tennessee-Martin, Tennessee St. and Tennessee Tech.
Note: Tenn-Martin will not compete for conference title in basketball until the 2000-2001 season.

Patriot League
3897 Adler Place, Building C, Suite 310
Bethlehem, PA 18017
(215) 691-2414 Founded: 1984
Executive Director........................ Carl Ullrich
Director of Information .... Todd Newcomb
1993 Members: BASKETBALL (8)—Army, Bucknell, Colgate, Fordham, Holy Cross, Lafayette, Lehigh and Navy; FOOTBALL (6)—all except Army and Navy, who play independent Div.I-A schedules.

Southern Conference
1 West Pack Square, Suite 1508
Asheville, NC 28801
(704) 255-7872 Founded: 1921
Commissioner .... Wright Waters
Director of Information .... Geoff Cabe
1993 Members: BASKETBALL (10)—Appalachian St., The Citadel, Davidson, East Tennessee St., Furman, Georgia Southern, Marshall, Tennessee-Chattanooga, VMI and Western Carolina; FOOTBALL (9)—all except Davidson.

Southland Conference
1309 West 15th Street, Suite 303
Plano, TX 75075
(214) 424-4833 Founded: 1963
Executive Director........................ Bill Belknap
Director of Information.................. Tammy Broz
1993 Members: BASKETBALL (10)—McNeese St., Nicholls St., North Texas, NE Louisiana, Northwestern St., Sam Houston St., Southwest Texas St., Stephen F.Austin St., Texas-Arlington and Texas-San Antonio; FOOTBALL (8)—all except Texas-Arlington and Texas-San Antonio.

Southwestern Athletic Conference
1500 Sugar Bowl Drive, Superdome
New Orleans, LA 70112
(504) 523-7574 Founded: 1920
Commissioner........................... James Frank
Director of Publicity .... Lonza Hardy, Jr.
1993 Members: BASKETBALL & FOOTBALL (8)—Alabama St., Alcorn St., Grambling St., Jackson St., Mississippi Valley St., Prairie View A&M, Southern-Baton Rouge and Texas Southern.

Sun Belt Conference
One Galleria Boulevard, Suite 2115
Metairie, LA 70001
(504) 834-6600   Founded: 1976
Commissioner...................... Craig Thompson
Director of Communications .... Tom Burnett
   1993 Members: BASKETBALL (10)—Arkansas-Little
Rock, Arkansas St., Jacksonville, Lamar, Louisiana
Tech, New Orleans, South Alabama, SW Louisiana,
Texas-Pan American and Western Kentucky.

Trans America Conference
The Commons, 3370 Vineville Ave., Suite 108-B,
Macon, GA 31204
(912) 474-3394   Founded: 1978
Commissioner............................. Bill Bibb
Director of Information................ Ted Gumbart
   1993 Members: BASKETBALL (10)—Centenary,
Central Florida, College of Charleston, Florida A&M,
Florida International, Georgia St., Mercer, Samford,
SE Louisiana and Stetson. **Note:** Central Fla. and
Charleston will not compete for conference title until
the 1993-94 season.

West Coast Conference
400 Oyster Point Blvd., Suite 221
South San Francisco, CA 94080
(415) 873-8622   Founded: 1952
Commissioner...................... Michael Gilleran
Director of Information..................... Don Ott
   1993 Members: BASKETBALL (8)—Gonzaga,
Loyola Marymount, Pepperdine, Portland, St.Mary's,
San Diego, San Francisco and Santa Clara.

Yankee Conference
MBE—Suite 400, 1600 Falmouth Road,
Centerville, MA 02632
(508) 778-4110   Founded: 1946
Commissioner............................. Al Benson
Director of Information.................. Bruce Hack
   1993 Members: FOOTBALL (12)—Boston University,
Connecticut, Delaware, James Madison, Maine,
Massachusetts, New Hampshire, Northeastern, Rhode
Island, Richmond, Villanova and William & Mary.

PRO FOOTBALL

National Football League

League Office
410 Park Ave., New York, NY 10022
(212) 758-1500
Commissioner........................ Paul Tagliabue
President .... Neil Austrian
Director of Information .... Pete Abitante

NFL Players Association
2021 L Street NW, Suite 600, Washington, DC 20036
(202) 463-2200
Executive Director .... Gene Upshaw
Assistant Director .... Doug Allen
General Counsel.................. Richard Berthelsen
Director of Public Relations........... Frank Woschitz

AFC

Buffalo Bills
One Bills Drive, Orchard Park, NY 14127
(716) 648-1800
Owner-President.................... Ralph Wilson, Jr.
V.P. & General Manager................... Bill Polian
Director of Public Relations............. Denny Lynch

Cincinnati Bengals
200 Riverfront Stadium, Cincinnati, OH 45202
(513) 621-3550
Chairman........................... Austin Knowlton
President .... John Sawyer
V.P. & General Manager................. Mike Brown
Director of Public Relations .... Al Heim

Cleveland Browns
80 First Avenue, Berea, OH 44017
(216) 891-5000
Owner-President.......................... Art Modell
V.P. & Assistant to President............. David Modell
V.P., Public Relations..................... Kevin Byrne

Denver Broncos
13655 Broncos Parkway, Englewood, CO 80112
(303) 649-9000
Owner-President .... Pat Bowden
V.P. & Head Coach...................... Dan Reeves
General Manager .... John Beake
Director of Public Relations .... Jim Saccomano

Houston Oilers
6910 Fannin St., Houston, TX 77030
(713) 797-9111
Owner-President .... Bud Adams, Jr.
Exec. V.P. & General Manager .... Mike Holovak
Director of Public Relations .... Chip Namias

Indianapolis Colts
P.O. Box 535000, Indianapolis, IN 46253
(317) 297-2658
Owner-President .... Robert Irsay
V.P. & General Manager.................... Jim Irsay
Director of Public Relations .... Craig Kelley

Kansas City Chiefs
One Arrowhead Drive, Kansas City, MO 64129
(816) 924-9300
Owner .... Lamar Hunt
President & General Manager .... Carl Peterson
Director of Public Relations .... Bob Moore

Los Angeles Raiders
332 Center St., El Segundo, CA 90245
(310) 322-3451
Managing General Partner .... Al Davis
Executive Assistant....................... Al LoCasale
Publications Director .... Mike Taylor

Miami Dolphins
Joe Robbie Stadium
2269 NW 199th Street, Miami, FL 33056
(305) 620-5000
President .... Tim Robbie
Exec. V.P. & General Manager .... Eddie Jones
Director of Media Relations .... Harvey Greene

New England Patriots
Foxboro Stadium, Route 1, Foxboro, MA 02035
(508) 543-8200
Owner............................. James B. Orthwein
President .... Fran Murray
CEO & General Manager............. Sam Jankovich
V.P., Public Relations .... Pat Hanlon

New York Jets
1000 Fulton Ave., Hempstead, NY 11550
(516) 538-6600
Chairman............................... Leon Hess
President .... Steve Gutman
V.P. & General Manager .... Dick Steinberg
Director of Public Relations............. Frank Ramos

Pittsburgh Steelers
300 Stadium Circle, Pittsburgh, PA 15212
(412) 323-1200
Owner-President . . . . Dan Rooney
Director of Public Relations . . . . Dan Edwards

San Diego Chargers
Box 609609, San Diegeo, CA 92160
(619) 280-2111
Chairman-President . . . . Alex Spanos
General Manager . . . . Bobby Beathard
Director of Public Relations . . . . Bill Johnston

Seattle Seahawks
11220 NE 53rd Street, Kirkland, WA 98033
(206) 827-9777
Owner . . . . Ken Behring
President-GM-Head Coach . . . . Tom Flores
V.P., Public Relations . . . . Gary Wright

NFC

Atlanta Falcons
2745 Burnett Road., Suwanee, GA 30174
(404) 945-1111
Chairman. . . . . Rankin Smith, Sr.
President . . . . Taylor Smith
Director of Public Relations. . . . . Charlie Taylor

Chicago Bears
Halas Hall, 250 N. Washington, Lake Forest, IL 60045
(708) 295-6600
Chairman . . . . Edward McCaskey
President-CEO . . . . Michael McCaskey
V.P., Player Personnel . . . . Bill Tobin
Director of Public Relations . . . . Bryan Harlan

Dallas Cowboys
Cowboys Center
One Cowboys Parkway, Irving, TX 75063
(214) 556-9900
Owner-President-GM. . . . . Jerry Jones
Director of Public Relations. . . . . Rich Dalrymple

Detroit Lions
Pontiac Silverdome
1200 Featherstone Rd., Pontiac, MI 48342
(313) 335-4131
Owner-President . . . . William Clay Ford
Exec. V.P. & COO . . . . Chuck Schmidt
Media Relations Coordinator . . . . Mike Murray

Green Bay Packers
P.O. Box 10628, Green Bay, WI 54307
(414) 496-5700
Chairman . . . . Robert Parins
President-CEO . . . . Bob Harlan
Exec. V.P. & General Manager . . . . Ron Wolf
Director of Public Relations . . . . Lee Remmel

Los Angeles Rams
2327 West Lincoln Ave., Anaheim, CA 92801
(714) 535-7267
Owner-President. . . . . Georgia Frontiere
Executive V.P . . . . John Shaw
General Manager . . . . Jack Faulkner
Director of Public Relations . . . . Rick Smith

Minnesota Vikings
9520 Viking Drive., Eden Prairie, MN 55344
(612) 828-6500
Chairman . . . . John Skoglund
President-CEO. Roger Headrick
Director of Public Relations . . . . Merrill Swanson

New Orleans Saints
6928 Saints Drive, Metairie, LA 70003
(504) 733-0255
Owner-General Partner . . . . Tom Benson
President & General Manager . . . . Jim Finks
Director of Public Relations . . . . Rusty Kasmiersky

New York Giants
Giants Stadium, East Rutherford, NJ 07073
(201) 935-8111
President/Co-CEO . . . . Wellington Mara
Chairman/Co-CEO. . . . . Preston Robert Tisch
V.P. & General Manager . . . . George Young
Director of Media Services. . . . . Ed Croke

Philadelphia Eagles
Veterans Stadium, Broad St. & Pattison Ave.
Philadelphia, PA 19148
(215) 463-2500
Owner. . . . . Norman Braman
President & General Manager . . . . Harry Gamble
Director of Public Relations . . . . Ron Howard

Phoenix Cardinals
P.O. Box 888, Phoenix, AZ 85001
(602) 379-0101
Owner-President . . . . Bill Bidwill
V.P. & General Manager . . . . Larry Wilson
Director of Public Relations . . . . Paul Jensen

San Francisco 49ers
4949 Centennial Blvd., Santa Clara, CA 95054
(408) 562-4949
Owner . . . . Edward DeBartolo, Jr.
President . . . . Carmen Policy
V.P. & General Manager. . . . . John McVay
Director of Public Relations . . . . Jerry Walker

Tampa Bay Buccanners
1 Buccaneer Place, Tampa, FL 33607
(813) 870-2700
Owner . . . . Hugh Culverhouse
President . . . . Gay Culverhouse
Director of Public Relations. . . . . Rick Odioso

Washington Redskins
21300 Redskin Park Drive., Ashburn, VA 22011
(703) 478-8900
Chairman-CEO . . . . Jack Kent Cooke
Executive V.P . . . . John Kent Cooke
General Manager . . . . Charley Casserly
V.P., Communications . . . . Charlie Dayton

World League
(formerly **World League of American Football**)
540 Madison Avenue, New York, NY 10022
(212) 838-9400
Chief Operating Officer . . . . Joe Bailey
Director of Information . . . . Vince Casey

Canadian Football League

League Office
CFL Building, 110 Eglinton Avenue West, 5th Floor
Toronto, Ontario M4R 1A3
(416) 322-9650
Commissioner . . . . Larry Smith
Chairman . . . . John Tory
Communications Co-ordinators . . . . Diane Milhalek
and Norm Miller

B.C. Lions
10605 135th St., Surrey, B.C. V3T 4C8
(604) 585-3323
Owner. . . . . Murray Pezim
President . . . . Frank Gigliotti
General Manager & Head Coach . . . . . Bob O'Billovich
Director of Communications . . . . Roger Kelly

Calgary Stampeders
McMahon Stadium, 1817 Crowchild Trail NW
Calgary, Alberta T2M 4R6
(403) 289-0205
Owner................................. Larry Ryckman
General Manager & Head Coach .... Wally Buono
Dir. of Public/Media Relations .... Kevin Gallant

Edmonton Eskimos
9023—11th Ave., Edmonton, Alberta T5B 0C3
(403) 448-1525
Owner............................. Community-owned
President............................. Gary Campbell
General Manager .... Hugh Campbell
Dir. of Public/Media Relations .... Allan Watt

Hamilton Tiger-Cats
14 Hughson Street South, Hamilton, Ontario L8N 4H3
(416) 547-2418
Owner............................. Community-owned
President............................. John Michaluk
General Manager........................ Joe Zuger
Communications Director............. Chris Dowhun

Ottawa Rough Riders
Coliseum Building, Lansdowne Park
Ottawa, Ontario K1S 3W7
(613) 563-4551
Owner-Chairman............... Bernard Glieberman
President........................... Lonie Glieberman
V.P & General Manager .... Dan Rambo
Director of Communications .... Sal De Meo

Saskatchewan Roughriders
2940—10th Avenue, P.O. Box 1277
Regina, Saskatchewan S4P 3B8
(306) 569-2323
Owner............................. Community-owned
President............................. Phil Kershaw
COO & General Manager................. Alan Ford
Director of Media/Marketing .... Barry Taman

Toronto Argos
Exhibition Place, Toronto, Ontario M6K 3C3
(416) 595-9600
Owners................ Bruce McNall, Wayne Gretzky
and John Candy
Exec. V.P. & COO .... Brian Cooper
V.P. & General Manager.............. Mike McCarthy
Director of Communications........... David Watkins

Winnipeg Blue Bombers
1465 Maroons Road, Winnipeg, Manitoba R3G 0L6
(204) 784-2583
Owner............................. Community-owned
President............................. Bruce Robinson
General Manager & Head Coach .... Cal Murphy
Dir. of Public/Media Relations ...... Kevin O'Donovan

GOLF

LPGA Tour
(Ladies Professional Golf Association)
2570 Volusia Ave., Daytona Beach, FL 32114
(904) 254-8800
Commissioner...................... Charles Mechem
Director of Public Relations .... Elaine Scott

PGA of America
100 Avenue of the Champions
Palm Beach Gardens, FL 33418
(407) 624-8400
President................................. Dick Smith
Executive Director .... Jim Awtrey
Director of Public Relations........... Terry McSweeney

PGA European Tour
Wentworth Club, Wentworth Drive
Virginia Water, Surrey, England GU25 4LS
TEL: 011-44-344-842881
Executive Director...................... Ken Schofield
Director of Communications......... Scott MacCallum

PGA Tour
(Professional Golfer's Association)
Sawgrass, Ponte Vedra, FL 32082
(904) 285-3700
Commissioner .... Deane Beman
Director of Information.................... Tom Place

Royal & Ancient Golf Club of St. Andrews
St. Andrews, Fife, Scotland KY16 9JD
TEL: 011-44-334-72112
Secretary .... Michael Bonallack

USGA
(United States Golf Association)
P.O. Box 708, Liberty Corner Road, Far Hills, NJ 07931
(908) 234-2300
President .... Stewart Block
Executive Director .... David Fay
Director of Communications............ Mark Carlson

PRO HOCKEY
NHL
President................................... Gil Stein
Exec. Director, Communications .... Gary Meagher

League Offices
Montreal: 1155 Metcalfe St., Suite 960
Montreal, Quebec H3B 2W2
(514) 871-9220

New York: 650 Fifth Ave., 33rd Floor
New York, NY 10019
(212) 398-1100

Toronto: 75 International Blvd., Suite 300
Rexdale, Ontario M9W 6L9
(416) 798-0820

NHL Players' Association
1 Dundas St. West, Suite 2406
Toronto, Ontario M5G 1Z3
(416) 408-4040
Executive Director..................... Bob Goodenow
Director of Operations .... Sam Simpson

Boston Bruins
Boston Garden, 150 Causeway St., Boston, MA 02114
(617) 227-3206
Owner .... Jeremy Jacobs
President & General Manager.......... Harry Sinden
Director of Media Relations .... Heidi Holland

Buffalo Sabres
Memorial Auditorium, 140 Main St., Buffalo, NY
14202
(716) 856-7300
Chairman-President................ Seymour Knox, III
V.P. & General Manager .... Gerry Meehan
Director of Public Relations................ Steve Rossi

Calgary Flames
Olympic Saddledome, P.O. Box 1540, Station M
Calgary, Alberta T2P 3B9
(403) 261-0475
Owners .... Harley Hotchkiss, Norman Kwong,
Sonia Scurfield, Byron and Daryl Seamen
President................................. W.C. (Bill) Hay
General Manager................... Doug Risebrough
Director of Public Relations............... Rick Skaggs

Chicago Blackhawks
Chicago Stadium, 1800 West Madison St., Chicago, IL 60612
(312) 733-5300
Owner-President...................... William Wirtz
General Manager...................... Mike Keenan
Director of Public Relations............. Jim DeMaria

Detroit Red Wings
Joe Louis Arena
600 Civic Center Drive, Detroit, MI 48226
(313) 567-7333
Owner-President...................... Mike Ilitch
General Manager & Head Coach...... Bryan Murray
Director of Public Relations............. Bill Jamieson

Edmonton Oilers
Northlands Coliseum, 7424 118th Ave.
Edmonton, Alberta, T5B 4M9
(403) 474-8561
Owner.......................... Peter Pocklington
President & General Manager........... Glen Sather
Director of Public Relations .... Bill Tuele

Hartford Whalers
242 Trumbull St., 8th Floor, Hartford, CT 06103
(203) 728-3366
Managing General Partner........... Richard Gordon
General Manager .... Brian Burke
Director of Public Relations............. John Forslund

Los Angeles Kings
Great Western Forum, 3900 West Manchester Blvd.
Inglewood, CA 90306
(310) 419-3160
Owner............................... Bruce McNall
President.............................. Roy Mlakar
General Manager...................... Nick Beverley
Director of Public Relations .... Adam Fell

Minnesota North Stars
Metropolitan Sports Center
7901 Cedar Ave. South, Bloomington, MN 55425
(612) 853-9333
Owner-President..................... Norman Green
General Manager & Head Coach .... Bob Gainey
Director of Public Relations .... Joanie St. Peter

Montreal Canadiens
Montreal Forum, 2313 St. Catherine St. West
Montreal, Quebec H3H 1N2
(514) 932-2582
Owner...................... Molson Companies, Ltd.
Chairman-President .... Ronald Corey
V.P., Managing Director...!............ Serge Savard
Director of Public Relations .... Michele Lapointe

New Jersey Devils
Meadowlands Arena
P.O. Box 504, East Rutherford, NJ 07073
(201) 935-6050
Chairman .... John McMullen
President & General Manager......... Lou Lamoriello
Director of Public Relations .... Dave Freed

New York Islanders
Nassau Veterans' Memorial Coliseum
Uniondale, NY 11553
(516) 794-4100
Partner-President-CEO .... Jerome Grossman
Executive Assistant .... Bryan Trottier
General Manager .... Don Maloney
Director of Public Relations.............. Greg Bouris

New York Rangers
4 Penn Plaza, 4th Floor, New York, NY 10001
(212) 465-6486
Owner................. Paramount Communications
President & General Manager .... Neil Smith
Director of Public Relations............. Barry Watkins

Ottawa Senators
301 Moodie Dr., Suite 200, Nepean, Ontario, K2H 9C4
(613) 721-0115
Owner .... Terrace Investments, Ltd.
President-CEO........................ Randy Sexton
General Manager..................... Mel Bridgman
Director of Public Relations .... Laurent Benoit

Philadelphia Flyers
The Spectrum, Pattison Place, Philadelphia, PA 19148
(215) 465-4500
Owner................................ Ed Snider
President .... Jay Snider
Senior V.P .... Bob Clarke
General Manager...................... Russ Farwell
Director of Public Relations .... Mark Piazza

Pittsburgh Penguins
Civic Arena, Pittsburgh, PA 15219
(412) 642-1800
Owners .... Howard Baldwin, Morris Belzberg
                                       and Thomas Ruta
General Manager .... Craig Patrick
Director of Public Relations.............. Cindy Himes

Quebec Nordiques
Colisée de Quebec, 2205 Avenue du Colisée
Quebec City, Quebec G1L 4W7
(418) 529-8441
Owner-President...................... Marcel Aubut
General Manager & Head Coach......... Pierre Page
Director of Press Relations .... Jean Martineau

St. Louis Blues
St. Louis Arena, 5700 Oakland Ave., St. Louis, MO 63110
(314) 781-5300
Chairman .... Michael Shanahan
President .... Jack Quinn
V.P. & General Manager.................. Ron Caron
Director of Public Relations............. Susie Mathieu

San Jose Sharks
10 Almaden Blvd., Suite 600, San Jose, CA 95113
(408) 287-7070
Owner-Chairman.................... George Gund III
Owner-Vice Chairman .... Gordon Gund
President-CEO .... Art Savage
V.P., Player Personnel................... Chuck Grillo
Director of Media Relations .... Tim Bryant

Tampa Bay Lightning
501 East Kennedy Blvd., Suite 175, Tampa, FL 33602
(813) 229-2658
Owners .... Lightning Partners, Inc.
President & General Manager .... Phil Esposito
V.P., Communications .... Gerry Helper

Toronto Maple Leafs
Maple Leaf Gardens
60 Carlton Street, Toronto, Ontario M5B 1L1
(416) 977-1641
Chairman-CEO......................... Steve Stavro
President & General Manager .... Cliff Fletcher
Public Relations Coordinator................ Pat Park

Vancouver Canucks
Pacific Coliseum, 100 North Renfrew St.
Vancouver, British Columbia V5K 3N7
(604) 254-5141
Chairman .... Frank Griffiths
President-GM-Head Coach .... Pat Quinn
Director of Public Relations.......... Steve Tambellini

Washington Capitals
Capitol Centre, Landover, MD 20785
(301) 386-7000
Chairman .... Abe Pollin
President.................................. Dick Patrick
V.P. & General Manager.................. Dave Poile
Director of Public Relations .... Lou Corletto

Winnipeg Jets
Winnipeg Arena, 15-1430 Maroons Road,
Winnipeg, Manitoba R3G 0L5
(204) 783-5387
Owner-President .... Barry Shenkarow
V.P. & General Manager............... Michael Smith
Director of Public Relations .... Mike O'Hearn

HORSE RACING

Breeders' Cup Limited
2525 Harrodsburg Road, Suite 500
Lexington, KY 40504
(606) 223-5444
President.................... James E. (Ted) Bassett III
Executive Director .... D.G. Van Clief, Jr.
Director of Communications .... Dan Metzger

The Jockeys' Guild
250 West Main Street, Lexington, KY 40507
(606) 259-3211
President .... Jerry Bailey
National Manager .... John Giovanni

**TRA
(Thoroughbred Racing Associations)**
420 Fair Hill Drive, Suite 1, Elkton, MD 21921
(301) 392-9200
President............................... Tom Meeker
Executive V.P............................ Chris Scherf
Director of Services .... Ken Knelly

**TRC
(Thoroughbred Racing Communications)**
40 East 52nd Street, New York, NY 10022
(212) 371-5910
Executive Director........................ Tom Merritt
Director of Media Relations .... Bob Curran

**USTA
(United States Trotting Association)**
750 Michigan Ave., Columbus, OH 43215
(614) 224-2291
President........................... Corwin M. Nixon
Executive V.P........................ Francis X. Ready
Director of Public Relations .... John Pawlak

MEDIA

DAILY NEWSPAPER

USA Today
1000 Wilson Blvd. Arlington, VA 22229
(703) 276-3400
Owner .... Gannett Company
Publisher .... Thomas Curley
Managing Editor/Sports .... Gene Policinski

WEEKLY MAGAZINES

Sports Illustrated
Time & Life Bldg., Rockefeller Center
New York, NY 10020
(212) 586-1212
President-Publisher .... Donald M. Elliman, Jr.
Managing Editor .... Mark Mulvoy

The Sporting News
1212 N.Lindbergh Blvd., St. Louis, MO 63132
(314) 997-7111
Publisher .... Thomas Osenton
Editor .... John Rawlings

TELEVISION

ABC Sports
47 West 66th St., 13th Floor, New York, NY 10023
(212) 456-4867
President .... Dennis Swanson
Senior V.P., Administration .... Stephen Solomon
Senior V.P., Production .... Dennis Lewin
Executive Producer...................... Jack O'Hara
Director of Information .... Mark Mandel

CBS Sports
51 West 52nd St., 30th Floor, New York, NY 10019
(212) 975-5230
President .... Neal Pilson
Senior VP, Production.................... Rick Gentile
V.P., Programming.................... Jay Rosenstein
Director of Information .... Susan Kerr

ESPN
ESPN Plaza, Bristol, CT 06010
(203) 585-2000
President .... Steve Bornstein
Exec. V.P., Operations.................... Jim Allegro
Executive Editor...................... John Walsh
Managing Editor...................... Steve Anderson
Director of Communications .... Mike Soltys

HBO Sports
1100 Ave. of the Americas, New York, NY 10036
(212) 512-1000
President .... Seth Abraham
V.P., Executive Producer.............. Ross Greenburg
V.P., Programming .... Bob Greenway
Director of Publicity.................... Ross Levinsohn

NBC Sports
30 Rockefeller Plaza, New York, NY 10112
(212) 664-4444
President .... Dick Ebersol
Executive V.P............................ Ken Schanzer
Executive Producer...................... Terry O'Neil
Director of Public Relations .... Ed Markey

Prime Network
600 East Lascolinas Blvd., Suite 2200, Irving, TX 75039
(214) 401-0099
President-CEO............................ Ed Frazier
Executive V.P. .... Matt Tinley
Director of Media Relations .... Bob Wheeler

SportsChannel America
3 Crossways Park West, Woodbury, NY 11797
(516) 921-3764
President .... Jeff Ruhe
V.P., Programming..................... Mike Lardner
Director of Information............... Carole Shander

Turner Sports
One CNN Center, 13th Floor, Atlanta, GA 30303
(404) 827-1735
President . . . . Terry McGuirk
Sr. V.P., Executive Producer . . . . Don McGuire
Sr. V.P., Programming . . . . Kevin O'Malley
Director of Media Relations . . . . Mark Parkman

USA Network
1230 Ave. of the Americas, New York, NY 10020
(212) 408-8895
Executive Producer . . . . Gordon Beck
Director of Public Relations . . . . Leslie Anne Wade

OLYMPICS

IOC
(International Olympic Committee)
Chateau de Vidy, CH-1007 Lausanne, Switzerland
TEL: 011-41-21-253-271
President . . . . Juan Antonio Samaranch
Director General . . . . Francois Carrard
Director of Information . . . . Michele Verdier

1994 WINTER GAMES

Lillehammer Olympic Organizing Committee
Elve Gaten 19, P.O. Box 106
N-2601 Lillehammer, Norway
TEL: 011-47-62-7-1994
President-CEO . . . . Gerhard Heiberg
Director General . . . . Petter Ronningen
Director of Information . . . . Aage Enghaug
(XVIIth Olympic Winter Games, Feb. 12-27, 1994)

1996 SUMMER GAMES

Atlanta Committee for the Olympic Games
250 Williams St., Suite 6000,
Atlanta, GA 30303
(404) 224-1996
President-CEO . . . . Billy Payne
Sr. Exec. V.P. & COO . . . . A.D. Frazier, Jr.
Director of Information . . . . Harry Shuman
(Games of XXVIth Olympiad, July 20-Aug. 4, 1996)

1998 WINTER GAMES

Nagano Olympic Organizing Committee
Fuginkaitan Building, 6882 Minami Ajata Machi
Nagano City 380, Japan
TEL: 011-81-262-32-1998
President . . . . Eishiro Saito
Secretary General . . . . Tadashi Tsuda
(XVIIIth Olympic Winter Games, Dates TBA)

2002 WINTER GAMES

Salt Lake City Organizing Committee (U.S. Bid City)
420 East South Temple, Suite 340,
Salt Lake City, UT 84111
(801) 322-1998
President . . . . Tom Welch
V.P., Public Information . . . . Mickey Gallivan

COA
(Canadian Olympic Association)
1600 James Naismith Dr., Ottawa Ontario K1B 5N4
(613) 748-5647
President . . . . Carol Anne Letheren
Chief Operating Officer . . . . Sherif Alaily
IOC members . . . . Carol Anne Letheren
& Richard Pound
Director of Communications . . . . Frank Ratcliffe

USOC
(United States Olympic Committee)
1750 East Boulder St., Colorado Springs, CO 80909
(719) 578-4529
President . . . . William Hybl
(term expires Dec. 31, 1992)
Executive Director . . . . Harvey Schiller
Treasurer . . . . LeRoy Walker
IOC member . . . . Anita DeFrantz
Director of Public/Media Relations . . . . Mike Moran

U.S. OLYMPIC FESTIVALS

1993—San Antonio Organizing Committee
P.O. Box 830386, San Antonio, TX 78283
President . . . . Robert Marbut, Jr.
Director of Public Relations . . . . Rick Pych

1994—St. Louis Organizing Committee
1395 North Highway Drive, Fenton, MO 63099
President . . . . Denny Bond
V.P., Marketing . . . . Earl Wilson

1995—Denver Organizing Committee
Colorado Sports Council,
1700 Lincoln, Suite 3750, Denver, CO 80203
President-CEO . . . . Edmond F. Noel Jr.

U.S. OLYMPIC TRAINING CENTERS

Colorado Springs Training Center
1776 East Boulder Street
Colorado Springs, CO 80909
(719) 578-4500
Director . . . . Charles Davis

Lake Placid Training Center
421 Old Military Road
Lake Placid, NY 12946
(518) 523-2600
Director . . . . Gloria Chadwick

San Diego Training Center
c/o San Diego National Sports Training Foundation
1904 Hotel Circle N., San Diego, CA 92108
(619) 291-8802
Executive V.P. . . . . Dave Nielsen

U.S. OLYMPIC ORGANIZATIONS

National Archery Association (NAA)
1750 East Boulder St., Colorado Springs, CO 80909
(719) 578-4576
President . . . . Don Marcure
Executive Director . . . . Christine McCartney

U.S. Baseball Federation (USBF)
2160 Greenwood Avenue, Trenton, NJ 08609
(609) 586-2381
President . . . . Mark Marquess
Executive Director & CEO . . . . Richard Case
Communications Director . . . . Bob Bensch

USA Basketball
1750 East Boulder Street, Colorado Springs, CO 80909
(719) 632-7687
President . . . . Dave Gavitt
Exeutive Director . . . . Bill Wall
Director of Public relations . . . . Craig Miller

U.S. Biathlon Association (USBA)
P.O. Box 5515, Essex Junction, VT 05453
(802) 655-4524
President . . . . Howard Buxton
Executive Director . . . . Jed Williamson
Marketing and Public Relations . . . . Ted Fay

U.S. Bobsled and Skeleton Federation
P.O. Box 828, 421 Old Military Road
Lake Placid, NY 12946
(518) 523-1842
President............................. Neil Richardson
Program Director .... James Hickey

USA Boxing
1750 East Boulder Street, Colorado Springs, CO 80909
(719) 578-4506
President .... Billy Dove
Executive Director .... Jim Fox
Communications Director .... Jay Miller

U.S. Canoe and Kayak Team
201 South Capitol Avenue, Indianapolis, IN 46225
(317) 237-5690
Chairman................................. Eric Haught
Executive Director .... Chuck Wielgus
Communications Director .... Craig Bohnert

U.S. Cycling Federation (USCF)
1750 East Boulder Street, Colorado Springs, CO 80909
(719) 578-4581
President .... Richard DeGarmo
Executive Director .... Jerry Lace
Dir. of Media/Public Relations............ Steve Penny

United States Diving, Inc. (USD)
201 South Capitol Avenue, Indianapolis, IN 46225
(317) 237-5252
President .... Micki King Hogue
Executive Director......................... Todd Smith
Director of Communications......... Dave Shatkowski

U.S. Equestrian Team (USET)
Pottersville Road, Gladstone, NJ 07934
(908) 234-1251
President............................. Finn Casperson
Executive Director .... Bob Standish
Director of Public Relations .... Marty Bauman

U.S. Fencing Association (USFA)
1750 East Boulder Street, Colorado Springs, CO 80909
(719) 578-4511
President............................. Michel Mamlouk
Executive Director................ Carla-Mae Richards
Media Relations Director .... Colleen Walker

U.S. Field Hockey Assocation (USFHA)
1750 East Boulder Street, Colorado Springs, CO 80909
(719) 578-4567
President............................. Judith Davidson
Executive Director .... Carolyn Moody
Director of Public Relations .... Kinda Asher

U.S. Figure Skating Association
20 First Street, Colorado Springs, CO 80906
(719) 635-5200
President .... Franklin S. Nelson
Executive Director...................... Ian Anderson
Director of Communications............. Kristin Matta

U.S. Gymnastics Federation (USGF)
201 South Capitol Avenue, Indianapolis, IN 46225
(317) 237-5050
President............................. Mike Donahue
Executive Director........................ Mike Jacki
Media Contact..................... Susan Baughman

USA Hockey
2997 Broadmoor Valley Road, Colorado Springs, CO 80906
(719) 599-5500
President .... Walter Bush
Executive Director................... Baaron Pittenger
Public Relations Coordinator .... Tom Douglis

U.S. Luge Association (USLA)
P.O. Box 651, Lake Placid, NY 12946
(518) 523-2071
President .... Dwight Bell
Executive Director........................... Ron Rossi
Media Coordinator .... Christina Compeau

United States Rowing Association (USRowing)
201 South Capitol Avenue, Indianapolis, IN 46225
(317) 237-5656
President .... Peter Zandbergen
Acting Executive Director .... Anita Metzger
Director of Communications .... Maureen Merhoff

U.S. Shooting Team
1750 East Boulder Street, Colorado Springs, CO 80909
(719) 578-4670
Team Director......................... Lones Wigger
Public Relations Director .... Karen Mutka

U.S. Skiing Team (USST)
P.O. Box 100, 1500 Kearns Blvd., Park City, UT 84060
(801) 649-9090
Chairman .... Thomas Weisel
President & CEO .... Howard Peterson
Director of Communications .... Tom Kelly

Amateur Softball Association (ASA)
2801 N.E. 50th Street, Oklahoma City, OK 73111
(405) 424-5266
President .... G. Pat Adkinson
Executive Director .... Don Porter
Public Relations/Media Director .... Bill Plummer

U.S. International Speedskating Assn. (USIA)
P.O. Box 100, Park City, UT 84060
(801) 649-0903, -0920
President .... Bill Cushman
Executive Director .... Katie Class
Director of Publicity................... Sean Callahan

U.S. Swimming, Inc. (USS)
1750 East Boulder Street, Colorado Springs, CO 80909
(719) 578-4578
President............................... Bill Maxson
Executive Director .... Ray Essick
Director, Information Services............ Jeff Dimond

U.S. Synchronized Swimming, Inc. (USSS)
201 South Capitol Avenue, Indianapolis, IN 46225
(317) 237-5700
President........................ Barbara McNamee
Executive Director.................... Betty Watanabe
Communications Coordinator .... Laura La Marca

U.S. Team Handball Federation (USTHF)
1750 East Boulder Street, Colorado Springs, CO 80909
(719) 578-4582
President............................. Peter Buehning
Executive Director .... Michael Cavanaugh
Media Contact...................... Evelyn Anderson

U.S. Volleyball Association (USVBA)
3595 East Fountain Blvd., Suite I-2
Colorado Springs, CO 80910
(719) 637-8300
President .... William Baird
Senior Director.................... Kerry Klostermann
Coordinator of Media Relations ...... Rich Wanninger

United States Water Polo (USWP)
201 South Capitol Avenue, Indianapolis, IN 46225
(317) 237-5599
President .... Richard Foster
Executive Director......................... Bruce Wigo
Dir. of Media/Public Relations........... Eileen Sexton

U.S. Weightlifting Federation (USWF)
1750 East Boulder Street, Colorado Springs, CO 80909
(719) 578-4508
President.................................. Jim Schmitz
Executive Director .... George Greenway
Communications Director .... Mary Ann Rinehart

USA Wrestling
225 South Academy Blvd.
Colorado Springs, CO 80910
(719) 597-8333
President .... Terry McCann
Executive Director.......................... Jim Scherr
Dir. of Communications .... Gary Abbott

Yachting—U.S. Sailing Assn. (U.S. Sailing)
P O Box 209, Newport, RI 02840
(401) 849-5200
President............................. William Martin
Executive Director .... John B. Bonds
Olympic Yachting Director.......... Jonathan Harley
Public Relations Director................ Connie Smith

SOCCER

FIFA
(Federation Internationale de Football Assn.)
Hitzigweg 11, 8032 Zurich, Switzerland
TEL: 011-41-1-384-9595
President .... Joao Havelange
General Secretary .... Joseph Blatter
Director of Information .... Guido Tognoni

1994 WORLD CUP

World Cup USA 1994
Executive Offices: 2049 Century Park East, Suite 4400
          Los Angeles, CA 90067
          (310) 552-1994
Public Relations: 1270 Ave. of the Americas, Suite 220
          New York, NY 10020
          (212) 332-1994
President-CEO .... Alan Rothenberg
Managing Director.................... Charles Kenny
Director of Public Relations .... Jim Trecker
(15th World Cup, June 17-July 17, 1994)

1998 WORLD CUP

French Organizing Committee
Federation Francaise de Football
60 BIS Avenue d'Iena
F-75783 Paris CEDEX 16 France
TEL: 011-33-1-44-31-7300
President .... Jean Fournet-Fayard
General Secretary .... Michel Cagnion
(16th World Cup, June/July, 1998)

CONCACAF
(Confederation of North, Central American & Caribbean Association Football)
717 Fifth Avenue, 13th Floor, New York, NY 10022
(212) 308-1851
President........................ Jack Austin Warner
General Secretary....:................ Chuck Blazer

U.S. Soccer
(United States Soccer Federation)
Soccer House, 1801-1811 South Prairie Ave.
Chicago, IL 60616
(312) 808-1300
President........................... Alan Rothenberg
Secretary General................. Hank Steinbrecher
Director of Public Relations................ John Polis

APSL
(American Professional Soccer League)
League Office: 4300 Fair Lakes Court, Suite 300-B
          Fairfax, VA 22033
          (703) 222-2403
Media Relations: P.O. Box 92861, Pasadena, CA 91109
          (818) 791-3076
Commissioner .... Bill Sage
Operations Director .... Emily Ballus
Director of Media Relations .... Donn Risolo
  Member teams (6): Colorado Foxes, Ft. Lauderdale Strikers, Los Angeles Salsa, Miami Freedom, San Francisco Blackhawks, Tampa Bay Rowdies.

TENNIS

ATP
(Association of Tennis Professionals)
200 ATP Tour Blvd., Ponte Vedra Beach, FL 32082
(904) 285-8000
Chief Executive Officer.................... Mark Miles
V.P., Communications .... Jay Beck

ITF
(International Tennis Federation)
Pallisert Road, Barons Court
London, England W14 9EN
TEL: 011-44-71- 3818060
President................................. Brian Tobin
Media Administrator...................... Ian Barnes

USTA
(United States Tennis Association)
1212 Ave. of the Americas, 12th Floor
New York, NY 10036
(212) 302-3322
Executive Director.................... Marshall Happer
Director of Communications .... Edwin Fabricius

WTA
(Women's Tennis Association)
133 First Street NE, St. Petersburg, FL 33701
(813) 895-5000
Executive Director & CEO .... Gerard Smith
Director of Public Relations................ Ana Leaird

TRACK & FIELD

AAU
(Amateur Athletic Union)
3400 W.86th St., Indianapolis, IN 46268
(317) 872-2900
President........................... Gussie Crawford
Executive Director .... Stan Hooley
Director of Communications........... David Morton

IAAF
(International Amateur Athletics Federation)
3 Hans Crescent, Knightsbridge
London, England SWIX 0LN
TEL: 011-44-71- 581-8771
President............................ Primo Nebiolo
General Secretary .... Istvan Gyulai
Director of Information .... Jayne Pearce

TAC
(The Athletics Congress)
One Hoosier Dome, Suite 140
Indianapolis, IN 46225
(317) 261-0500
Executive Director...................... Ollan Cassell
Director of Information .... Pete Cava

YACHTING

1995 America's Cup

America's Cup '95 Defense Committee
San Diego Yacht Club
1011 Anchorage Lane, San Diego, CA 92106
(619) 222-1103
Chairman........................ H.P. (Sandy) Purdon
Public Information Officer................ Tom Wilson

MISCELLANEOUS

All-American Soap Box Derby
P.O. Box 7233, Akron, OH 44306
(216) 733-8723
President .... G.A. Dietrich
Director of Public Relations .... Joyce Lagios

Amateur Softball Association
2801 Northeast 50th Street
Oklahoma City, OK 73111
(405) 424-5266
Executive Director .... Don Porter
Director of Public Relations .... Bill Plummer

Arena Football League
2200 East Devon, Suite 247, Des Plaines, IL 60018
(708) 297-7600
Founder & Consultant .... Jim Foster
President .... Joseph O'Hara
Director of Public Relations .... Bob Hillman

CBA
(Continental Basketball League)
425 South Cherry St., Suite 230, Denver, CO 80222
(303) 331-0404
Commissioner .... Terdema Ussery
Director of Public Relations .... Greg Anderson

International Game Fish Association
1301 East Atlantic Blvd., Pompano Beach, FL 33060
(305) 941-3474
Chairman........................ George Matthews
President .... Mike Leach
Editor.................................. Ray Crawford

1994 Goodwill Games
U.S. Offices
One CNN Center, Box 105366, Atlanta, GA 30348
(404) 827-3400
President.................................. Jack Kelly
Director of Public Relations................ Leslie King
(3rd Goodwill Games, July 23-Aug. 7, 1994,
in St.Petersburg, Russia)

National Hot Rod Association
2035 Financial Way, Glendora, CA 91740
(818) 914-4761
President .... Dallas Gardner
Director of Communications .... Rick Lalor

Little League Baseball Incorporated
P.O. Box 3485, Williamsport, PA 17701
(717) 326-1921
President/CEO .... C.J. Hale
Director of Public Relations.............. Steve Keener

Professional Rodeo Cowboys Association
101 Pro Rodeo Drive, Colorado Springs, CO 80919
(719) 593-8840
Commissioner........................... Lewis Cryer
Director of Public Relations............ Steve Fleming

Association of Volleyball Professionals
100 Corporate Pointe, #195, Culver City, CA 90230
(213) 337-4842
President .... Jon Stevenson
Director of Public Relations .... Debbie Rubio

Commissioners & Presidents
Chief executives of established major sports organizations since 1876.

Major League Baseball

Commissioner	Tenure
Kanesaw Mountain Landis*	1920-44
Albert B. (Happy) Chandler	1945-51
Ford Frick	1951-65
William Eckert	1965-68
Bowie Kuhn	1964-84
Peter Ueberroth	1984-89
A.Bartlett Giamatti*	1989
Fay Vincent	1989-92
Bud Selig†	1992–

*Died in office.
†Chairman of Executive Committee.

National League

President	Tenure
Morgan G.Bulkeley	1876
William A.Hulbart*	1877-82
A.G.Mills	1883-84
Nicholas Young	1885-1902
Henry Pulliam*	1903-09
Thomas J.Lynch	1910-13
John K.Tener	1914-18
John A.Heydler	1918-34
Ford Frick	1935-51
Warren Giles	1951-69
Charles (Chub) Feeney	1970-86
A.Bartlett Giamatti	1987-89
Bill White	1989–

*Died in office.

American League

President	Tenure
Bancroft (Ban) Johnson	1901-27
Ernest S.Barnard*	1927-31
William Harridge	1931-59
Joe Cronin	1959-73
Lee McPhail	1974-83
Bobby Brown	1984–

*Died in office.

NBA

Commissioner	Tenure
Maurice Podoloff	1949-63
J.Walter Kennedy	1963-75
Larry O'Brien	1975-84
David Stern	1984–

NFL

President	Tenure
Jim Thorpe	1920
Joe Carr	1921-39
Carl Storck	1939-31

Commissioner	
Elmer Layden	1941-46
Bert Bell*	1946-59
Austin Gunsel†	1959-60
Pete Rozelle	1960-89
Paul Tagliabue	1989–

*Died in office.   †Acting Commissioner.

NHL

President	Tenure
Frank Calder*	1917-43
Mervyn (Red) Dutton	1943-34
Clarence Campbell	1946-77
John Ziegler	1977-92
Gil Stein	1992–

*Died in office.

NCAA

Executive Director	Tenure
Walter Byers	1951-88
Richard (Dick) Schultz	1988–

IOC

President	Tenure
Demetrius Vikelas Greece	1894-96
Baron Pierre de Coubertin, France	1896-1925
Count Henri de Baillet-Latour, Belgium	1925-42
Vacant	1942-46
J.Sigfried Edstrom, Sweden	1946-52
Avery Brundage, USA	1952-72
Lord Michael Killanin, Ireland	1972-80
Juan Antonio Samaranch, Spain	1980–

Greg Mortimore/Allsport

When native son **Juan Antonio Samaranch** opened the Summer Olympic Games in Barcelona on July 25, he ended the most hectic four years of his IOC presidency.

OLYMPICS OVERVIEW

Out of Order

*If nothing else, the four years of the XXVth Olympiad
will be remembered as a time of chaotic worldwide change.*

In the lexicon of the Olympic movement, an Olympiad is the four-year period that begins at the end of one Summer Games and continues through the end of the next. Each Olympiad is identified with a set of Roman numerals, but few are remembered for anything more than the actual Games played out during them.

Not so the XXVth Olympiad of the modern era. It was a period of such stunning geopolitical change that it will forever be known as the Olympiad of the New World Disorder. It was also the last in which the Winter and Summer Games were held in the same year.

The same confusion that besets politicians, economists and mapmakers left the International Olympic Committee ill-equipped to govern an Olympic world whose globe is on a constantly shifting axis. "Every day, the situation takes a new, unpredictable turn," says IOC president Juan Antonio Samaranch.

Within days of the Feb. 8 opening of the 1992 Winter Olympics in Albertville, the IOC was granting recognition to the former Yugoslav republics of Croatia and Slovenia and letting a Ukrainian born in Russia and a Lithuanian who had trained in Russia compete as a couple in ice dancing for the former Soviet republic of Lithuania.

Not until one day before the Summer Games began in Barcelona on July 24 was the latest piece of a fragmenting Europe fit into the puzzle of 172 nations, former nations, soon-to-be former nations, about-to-be-nations and want-to-be nations that sent athletes to the first Olympics held in Spain.

It was so much simpler four years ago, a continuation of the pattern that had basically applied since the Soviet Union made its first Olympic appearance in 1952. Back then, the Olympics pitted the state-supported amateurs of the Soviet Bloc, notably the Soviet Union and East Germany, against the ever-more-professional amateurs of the West.

Since the 1988 Olympics, the two Germanies became one, and the whole turned out to be less than its East German part. Meanwhile, the Soviet Union became 15 uneasy pieces—12 of them patched together to be called, ironically, the Unified Team. The other three, Estonia, Latvia and Lithuania, regained the Olympic (and political) independence they had enjoyed between the two world wars.

In Albertville, athletes of the Unified Team were an amorphous lump, many of them dressed in training uniforms with the familiar CCCP and hammer-and-sickle, as if they were back in the USSR. But they were saluted in victory with the Olympic hymn and Olympic flag.

Phil Hersh covers international sports for the *Chicago Tribune* and has been the *Tribune's* full-time Olympics writer since 1986.

Wide World Photos

Eight years after hosting the 1984 Winter Olympics, the Bosnian capital of Sarajevo was reduced to rubble as civil war tore apart the former nation of Yugoslavia.

In Barcelona, the Unifieds were able to wear the colors of their republics and see those flags raised—except in team events, where the Olympic flag was used once again. On Jan. 1, 1993, all 12 republics were to gain individual Olympic recognition.

The four years after Seoul also saw Cuba and Albania return from years of Olympic boycotts. And South Africa, the former pariah, returned to the Games for the first time since 1960—and with an integrated team for first time since the turn of the century.

The Koreas remained two, while the Yemens became one. Czechoslovakia voted to split into Czechs and Slovaks too late for Barcelona, but in plenty of time for the next Winter Games at Lillehammer, Norway, in 1994. The tenuous federation that used to be Yugoslavia continued tearing itself apart during the Summer Games in late July and early August, despite a plea by IOC members that the ancient tradition of an Olympic truce be observed.

While the Winter Olympics remained manageable, since the ice-or-snow dictate necessarily limits the number of nations that compete, the Summer Games lurched toward the brink of gigantism.

Barcelona attracted a record number of 10,160 athletes, from a record number of nations and shards of nations. By the centennial Summer Olympics at Atlanta in 1996, there could be 200 national teams, although Samaranch has vowed not to let the number of athletes grow any more.

Samaranch, 72, has been IOC president since 1980 and during the summer he announced his intention to run for a fourth term in 1993. That election will be held at the same autumn meeting in Monte Carlo that will decide the host city for the 2000 Olympics. Under Samaranch, the Games recovered from successive superpower boycotts in 1980 and 1984 to achieve virtual universality in 1992. In fact, Samaranch's desire to have maximum participation in the Games of his hometown, Barcelona, became a near obsession.

He realized his objective after dealing with a rebuff by the United Nations, which rejected an IOC proposal that Yugoslav athletes all be allowed to compete as the "Independent Team." The U.N. decided the concept of a team that could in any way be construed as representing Yugoslavia ran counter to the spirit of its sanctions against Yugoslavia for alleged aggression in Bosnia.

That aggression has destroyed nearly all of the 1984 Winter Olympic venues in the Bosnian capital of Sarajevo. By sad coincidence, April rioting in South Central Los Angeles resulted in burning neighborhoods bordering some of the sites of the '84 Summer Olympics.

Despite some theatrical indignation about the intrusion of politics into sports (they have long been bedfellows) the IOC wound up accepting an 11th-hour compromise that allowed Yugoslav athletes to enter in individual events but not team sports. That eliminated the powerful Yugoslav water polo team, but permitted doubles teams in table tennis. If the terms of the U.N.'s decision were not clear, its point was: The IOC's power stretches only so far.

What remained of the nation that two years ago was Yugoslavia came to Barcelona as several entities: the full-fledged Olympic Committees of Croatia and Slovenia; the provisional Olympic Committee of Bosnia-Herzegovena; and two groups of athletes listed as "Independent Olympic Participants." One group was from Macedonia, the other from Serbia and Montenegro, which still claims the name Yugoslavia.

Less than 10 hours after the July 25 Opening Ceremonies, a woman from Serbia was standing next to a woman from Bosnia on the firing line of the air rifle final. The Yugoslav, Aranka Binder, won the bronze medal, for which the Olympic flag was raised. "At least," said another competitor, Suzana Skoko of Croatia, "they weren't shooting at each other."

A special flag was also raised to honor the medalists—two white tennis players and a white runner—from South Africa. Its recently-formed, non-racial Olympic Committee sought unity under a banner that carried none of the emblems that symbolized the country's former system of legal segregation.

Despite a population that is overwhelmingly black, there were only 11 non-whites on South Africa's 97-member 1992 Olympic team—an imbalance that will change slowly until the effects of continuing de facto segregation can be eliminated.

Cuba's rainbow coalition of athletes

Wide World Photos

Namibian sprinter **Frankie Fredericks** (right) with gold medalist **Linford Christie** of Britain after they finished 1-2 in the 100 meters.

returned to the Olympics after successive boycotts and showed expected strength in boxing and baseball. Namibia, once part of South Africa, won IOC recognition two years ago and its first two medals in Barcelona, thanks to American-educated sprinter Frankie Fredericks. Albania showed up for the first time since 1972, after two decades of unexplained absences.

Even the Dream Team dropped by, shot a few hoops and snagged the gold medal in basketball. Some thought it was shortsighted to let the cream of the NBA compete in the Olympics. Instead, those who voted for their presence should be commended for taking the long view, that excellence is contagious, even if not immediately.

Such a perspective was also necessary to sort out the XXVth Olympiad. Seen day-to-day over four years, it was a constant swirl of confusing change. "Much madness," wrote Emily Dickinson, "makes divinest sense to the discerning eye."

What else are you going to say about a millennium arriving eight years early? ☐

Pascal Rondeau/Allsport

American speedskater **Bonnie Blair** waves to the crowd in Albertville after winning the 500 meters for the first of her two gold medals.

WINTER OLYMPICS

Homecoming

The Winter Games return to the French Alps, but while much has changed, the Germans and Russians still win big.

ALBERTVILLE, France—Sixty-eight years after the first Winter Olympics were staged in nearby Chamonix, the Games returned to the snow-capped French Savoie in February for 16 days of international competition in mountain towns and tiny villages that succeeded in recapturing the essence of the Olympics.

A record cold-weather turnout of 65 nations attended the Albertville Games, up from 16 that first year in Chamonix, and 37 the last time France hosted the Games in 1964 at Grenoble. Another record was set when 20 different nations medaled (one better than Lake Placid in 1980).

While East and West Germany had reunited and the Soviet Union had come unglued since the last quadrennial get-together at Calgary in 1988, the Germans and Russians still sent the two best teams—even if referring to the old USSR as the new Unified Team took some getting used to.

Germany won the most overall medals (26) and the most gold (10), while the Unified Team gathered in 23 medals (nine gold), Austria had 20 (six gold) and Norway had 20 (nine gold). Italy, the United States and France rounded out the top seven with 14, 11 and nine medals, respectively.

Women carried the U.S. team, winning nine medals (see box). Speedskater Bonnie Blair led the way with two gold medals, while figure skater Kristi Yamaguchi, freestyle skier Donna Weinbrecht and short track speedskater Cathy Turner won one each.

The Norwegians, who will host the next Winter Games in Lillehammer when the four-year cycle is moved up to 1994, improved their gold-silver-bronze medal count from 0-3-2 in Calgary to 9-6-5 in Albertville. But it was the host French who showed the most dramatic four-year improvement. France went from a medal count of 1-0-0 in 1988 to 3-5-1 in '92—its best performance since going 4-3-2 at Grenoble in 1968, the year Jean-Claude Killy swept the men's alpine events. In fact, in the five Olympics between Grenoble and Albertville the French had won a total of only nine medals.

Besides the friendly surroundings of the Savoie, the common denominator between 1968 and '92 was Killy, who organized and ran these Games along with his politically well-connected partner Michel Barnier. While the 16-day carnival ultimately ran upwards of $60 million in the red, Killy and Barnier won universal praise for pulling it off.

Albertville was a harbinger of future Winter Olympics: far-flung, relying on temporary bleachers and stadiums, and using numerous athletes' villages, not

---

Christine Brennan has covered international sports and the Olympics for *The Washington Post* since 1988.

Wide World Photos

Finland's **Toni Nieminen** soars to a gold medal in the 120-meter ski jump. He also won a bronze at 90 meters and another gold in the team jump.

one big international gathering spot. While the International Olympic Committee has discussed having more than one country host an Olympics someday, Albertville, with 131 competitions spread out over 10 towns and across 640 square miles, was pretty much the same thing.

The frostbite fortnight got off to a dazzling start for the French, who raised the curtain on the 16th Winter Games with a new-wave, circus-style opening ceremony, then proceeded to win six of their nine medals in the first week. On the opening day of competition, Franck Piccard, the country's lone medalist in 1988 (a gold in the super giant slalom) won a surprising silver in the men's downhill. Before the week was out, Fabrice Guy and Sylvain Guillaume placed 1-2 in the Nordic Combined; Edgar Grospiron and Olivier Allamand did the same in men's freestyle moguls, and the French team won the women's biathlon relay.

On the other hand, none of the new nations in attendance—Croatia, Estonia, Latvia, Lithuania and Slovenia—won a medal.

Figure Skating. What was unforgettable about the figure skating competition was that almost everyone fell. And

fell. And fell. Yamaguchi had to put her hand down to avoid slipping to the ice during her long program, yet she still won the gold medal, the only gold not won by the Unified Team. Ukrainian Viktor Petrenko fell once and was wobbly throughout his long program, but still held off American Paul Wylie for the men's gold. It was the first individual figure skating gold medal ever won by the former Soviet Union, and Petrenko did it by beating one of the sport's few surprises in Wylie, who had never finished better than ninth in a world championship. The 27-year-old Harvard graduate was the only skater in the top six who did not either fall or touch the ice with his hand during the men's long program.

Spills took the excitement out of one of the most anticipated battles of the Games—the women's duel between Yamaguchi and Japan's Midori Ito. Ito, nervous about her vaunted triple Axel, took it out of her short program and replaced it with a triple lutz. When she fell on that jump, the gold medal was gone two days before it was awarded.

Ito, 22, the world champion in 1989, was skating under tremendous pressure. She arrived in Albertville as Japan's most famous athlete and nearly left in disgrace. After falling to fourth in the short program, she issued a formal apology to her country. Then, in the last minute of her long program, she became the first woman to land a triple Axel in Olympic competition and leaped past Nancy Kerrigan of the U.S. to win the silver medal.

Within two months, Ito had retired from the sport. "The mental pressure was the biggest reason," she said. "I became tense as the Olympics came closer and I wasn't able to give my best showing."

Experts explained all the falls in several ways—without the compulsory school figures, skaters now feel they have to go for broke in the short and long programs; like other sports, skating is becoming more competitive and athletes are trying to execute harder, more spectacular moves; and, finally, the financial stakes are higher than ever.

Alpine Skiing. Norwegians Finn Christian Jagge (slalom) and Kjetil Andre Aamodt (super giant slalom) won their country's first Alpine gold medals in 40 years—since Stein Eriksen won the GS in the Oslo Games of 1952. Marc Girardelli, the Austrian-born superstar who races for Luxembourg and has won the World Cup Overall title four times, finally overcame his Olympic jinx by winning silvers in the giant slalom and Super G. Patrick Ortlieb, the first man down the mountain at Val d'Isere on the opening day of the Games, won the downhill and the first of Austria's six gold medals.

But the big winner, for a second consecutive Olympics, was the irrepressible Alberto Tomba. The Italian playboy might have been overly optimistic when he said the site of the Games was going to have to be renamed "Alberto-ville," but he was close. He put together two masterful runs to win the giant slalom, then almost caught Jagge on his second run in the slalom to finish second.

The only double-gold medalist on the slopes was Austria's Petra Kronberger, the women's top all-around skier of the 1990's. She won both the combined and the slalom as the Austrians schussed off with five women's medals, while Switzerland, surprisingly, was shut out.

The American men's and women's teams, which failed to place higher than ninth at Calgary in 1988, won two silver

U.S. Women Go Stompin' In The Savoie

When the Winter Olympics ended, an American official was asked to summarize the Games. "It was," he said, "a U.S. Women's Olympics."

Perhaps it was the 20th anniversary of Title IX. Or just the coincidental emergence of some very talented U.S. Olympians. Whatever the reason, of the 11 medals won by U.S. athletes in Albertville, nine were won by women. What's more, the United States won five gold medals and women won them all.

Veteran speedskater Bonnie Blair of Champaign, Ill., led the way with two gold medals in her favorite events, the 500 and 1,000 meters. Kristi Yamaguchi of Fremont, Calif., the reigning world champion, elegantly combined six triple jumps with near-flawless artistry to become the first U.S. woman to win the Olympic figure skating gold since Dorothy Hamill in 1976. Cathy Turner of Rochester, N.Y., won a gold in 500-meter short-track speed skating and Donna Weinbrecht of West Milford, N.J., won in mogul skiing, two events that were new Olympic medal events at Albertville.

The U.S. "Golden Girls," as they came to be called, were joined by silver medalists Hilary Lindh of Juneau, Alaska, in downhill skiing; Diann Roffe (after the Games, she added her married name, Steinrotter) of Potsdam, N.Y. in giant slalom; and the U.S. 3,000-meter relay team in short-track speed skating. Stately figure skater Nancy Kerrigan of Stoneham, Mass., added a bronze.

Why were the U.S. women so strong?

"We don't have professional football, baseball or basketball teams," said Blair, whose three career gold medals rank behind only Eric Heiden's five on the all-time American Winter Games list. "For us, the Olympics are the highest you can get in athletic achievement."

But it was individual performances rather than across-the-board brilliance that propelled the United States to equal its best performance in a Winter Olympics on foreign ice and snow. Yes, Blair was spectacular in a sport in which athletes race only against the clock with no margin for error. But the entire speedskating team recorded

Peggy Fleming (left), the only U.S. gold medalist in 1968, with fellow figure skater **Kristi Yamaguchi**, one of four American women to strike gold in Albertville.

Wide World Photos

an average finish of 21st place—an abysmal showing.

"I don't think there's any way any of us could have trained any harder," Blair said. "There's such a fine line between first and 20th. Look at the time differences (hundredths of seconds). The skaters are closer than people think. It's hard to explain why. We're still at a point where we're learning."

In figure skating, it was no secret that the United States had its strongest women's team in history. Yamaguchi, Tonya Harding of Portland, Ore., and Kerrigan had swept the medals at the 1991 World Championships in Munich and only a dramatic free skating performance by Japan's Midori Ito prevented another hat trick in Albertville. The unpredictable Harding, the only U.S. woman ever to complete the difficult triple Axel in competition, finished fourth—but it still marked the first time three U.S. women were in the top four in Olympic figure skating.

Turner and Weinbrecht won their medals in sports that had been added to the Olympic program in 1992. Weinbrecht, the 1991 world champion, was expected to win. Turner, a former hotel lounge singer, was a pleasant surprise.

In 1988, after winning just six medals in Calgary, the U.S. Olympic Committee formed a commission to figure out ways to get more money to athletes and bring home more medals. At first glance, it looked as if their efforts worked. But four of the 11 medals—two in short-track speedskating and two in mogul skiing—were won in sports that were not even contested in 1988. That means that in sports held at both Games, the United States improved by just one medal, going from six to seven (with six being won by the women).

There is also the theory that the women looked so good because the men looked so bad. Only a surprising silver medal by figure skater Paul Wylie of Boston and a bronze in mogul skiing by Nelson Carmichael of Steamboat Springs, Colo., prevented a shutout. It was the worst U.S. men's showing since 1972, when only the U.S. ice hockey team managed a silver, while the women won seven medals in Sapporo.

No one had a specific answer as to why the men performed so poorly, except to say, as did Blair, that the top male athletes in the United States gravitate to more lucrative sports like baseball, basketball and football, not toward skiing and speedskating as many European men do.

"It is clear that Albertville is a step along the way," said USOC executive director Harvey Schiller. "You're not going to make dramatic changes to the American sports system in a couple years. It will be Lillehammer (in 1994) and beyond."

medals—Hilary Lindh in the downhill and Diann Roffe, who tied Austria's Anita Wachter in the GS.

Nordic Skiing. Norway and the Unified Team dominated in cross-country, winning all but two gold medals. Norwegians Vegard Ulvang and Bjorn Dählie each won three golds and one silver to lead their nation's sweep of the five men's events. Interestingly, Norway won just one nordic medal in 1988.

Among the women, Unified Teammates Lyubov Egorova (three gold and two silver) and Elena Valbe (one gold and four bronze) won 10 medals between them. Joining those two on the winners' platform after the 4x5-kilometer relay was 39-year-old Raisa Smetanina, who became the Winter Olympics' all-time leading medal winner with 10—four golds, five silvers and one bronze in five consecutive trips to the Games.

Sixteen-year-old Toni Nieminen of Finland was the airborne hero in Albertville, winning a gold medal in the 120-meter ski jump to go along with his bronze in the 90-meter and gold in the team competition. The ski jump was the Games' most tactical event, as most of the top skiers, including Nieminen, spread or "V-ed" their skis in flight—a technically illegal move that provided 28 percent more lift. Practitioners were clearly willing to trade style points for distance.

Ice Hockey. The Unified Team won the hockey gold medal for the eighth time in the last 10 Olympics, defeating Canada, 3-1, in the final. The team was made up entirely of Russians, as was a vast majority of the entire Unified Olympic squad. The Unifieds lost only once in the first round, a 4-3 defeat at the hands of Czechoslovakia, then went through the medal round undefeated.

Canada barely made it to the gold-medal game, having to survive a sudden-death shootout with underdog Germany to reach the semifinals. Eric Lindros, the 18-year-old superstar-in-waiting who chose to sit out the entire NHL season rather than toil for the lowly Quebec Nordiques, scored the winning goal against the Germans.

The United States, inspired by 27-year-old minor league goalie Ray LeBlanc, was undefeated in five first round games—including a 3-3 tie with Sweden—but lost, 5-2, to the Unified Team in the medal-round semifinals. It was the first time the two teams had met in Olympic competition since the Americans' "Miracle on Ice" in Lake Placid 12 years earlier. Lake Placid had also been Viktor Tikhonov's first trip to the Games as Russian coach—a nightmare he has recovered from with three straight gold medals.

Led by fiery coach Dave Peterson, several U.S. players complained about the officiating after losing to the Russians and were blistered with criticism from the international media. Their shot at redemption went for the boards in the bronze-medal game, where they bowed to the Czechs, 6-1.

Speed Skating. As expected, Germans, Norwegians and Bonnie Blair outraced the field, with the Germans winning five of the 10 races. Former East German Uwe-Jens Mey won the gold in his 500-meter showdown with friend and rival Dan Jansen of the U.S. Although Jansen finished a disappointing fourth, it turned out to be the highest finish by an American men's speedskater.

Blair won gold at 500 and 1,000 meters, becoming the first woman ever to win the Olympic 500 back-to-back. Hard-luck Ye Qiaobo of China finished second to Blair twice—losing by a combined fifth of a second. Germany's Gunda Niemann equalled Blair with a pair of golds at 3,000 and 5,000 meters, but missed a third when she placed second to teammate Jacqueline Borner in the 1,500 (Blair was a distant 21st).

Bobsled and Luge. Veteran Gustav Weder drove Switzerland I to victory in the two-man bobsled and Ingo Appelt led Austria I to a come-from-behind win over Germany I in four-man. The story of the four-man competition, however, was the controversial ouster of Herschel Walker from USA I by driver Randy Will. Will replaced the NFL football star and former Heisman Trophy winner with brakeman Chris Coleman and the team finished the two-day event in ninth place, a full second behind the winners. Six days earlier, Walker had teamed with driver Brian Shimer for a seventh in two-man.

In the luge, Germans won the men's singles and doubles. The U.S. didn't medal, but Cammy Myler (5th) and Duncan Kennedy (10th) registered the best American performances ever in the two singles events. □

OLYMPICS
STATISTICS

THE 1993 SPORTS ALMANAC · INFORMATION PLEASE

THE GAMES IN REVIEW
1992
ALBERTVILLE

SEC A

PAGE 541

Final Medal Standings

National medal standings are not recognized by the IOC. The unofficial point totals are based on three points for every gold medal, two for each silver and one for each bronze. Demonstration sport medals not included.

		G	S	B	Total	Pts			G	S	B	Total	Pts
1	Germany	10	10	6	26	56	11	South Korea	2	1	1	4	9
2	Unified Team*	9	6	8	23	47	12	Holland	1	1	2	4	7
3	Norway	9	6	5	20	44	13	Sweden	1	0	3	4	6
4	Austria	6	7	8	21	40		China	0	3	0	3	6
5	Italy	4	6	4	14	28	15	Switzerland	1	0	2	3	5
6	**United States**	5	4	2	11	25		Luxembourg	0	2	0	2	4
7	France	3	5	1	9	20	17	Czechoslovakia	0	0	3	3	3
8	Finland	3	1	3	7	14		New Zealand	0	1	0	1	2
	Canada	2	3	2	7	14	19	North Korea	0	0	1	1	1
10	Japan	1	2	4	7	11		Spain	0	0	1	1	1

*The Unified Team included former Soviet Union republics of Belarus, Kazakhstan, Russia, Ukraine and Uzbekistan.

Leading Medal Winners

Number of individual medals won on the left; gold, silver and bronze medal breakdown to the right. Demonstra- tion sport medals not included.

MEN

No		Sport	G-S-B		No		Sport	G-S-B
4	Bjorn Dählie, NOR	Cross-country	3-1-0		2	Ricco Gross, GER	Biathlon	1-1-0
4	Vegard Ulvang, NOR	Cross-country	3-1-0		2	Johann Koss, NOR	Speed Skating	1-1-0
3	Mark Kirchner, GER	Biathlon	2-1-0		2	Alberto Tomba, ITA.	Alpine	1-1-0
3	Toni Nieminen, FIN	Ski Jump	2-0-1		2	Ernst Vettori, AUT	Ski Jump	1-1-0
3	Martin Höllwarth, AUT	Ski Jump	0-3-0		2	Kjetil Andre Aamodt, NOR	Alpine	1-0-1
3	Giorgio Vanzetta, ITA.	Cross-country	0-1-2		2	Donat Acklin, SWI.	Bobsled	1-0-1
2	Kim Ki-Hoon, S.KOR	ST Speed Skate	2-0-0		2	Geir Karlstad, NOR	Speed Skating	1-0-1
					2	Terje Langli, NOR.	Cross-country	1-0-1
					2	Gustav Weder, SWI	Bobsled	1-0-1
					2	Lee Joon Ho, S.KOR	ST Speed Skate	1-0-1
					2	Marco Albarello, ITA.	Cross-country	0-2-0
					2	Frederick Blackburn, CAN	ST Speed Skate	0-2-0
					2	Marc Girardeli, LUX	Alpine	0-2-0
					2	Heinz Kuttin, AUT	Ski Jump	0-1-1
					2	Mikael Lofgren, SWE	Biathlon	0-0-2
					2	Klaus Sulzenbacher, AUT	Nordic Comb.	0-0-2
					2	Leo Visser, HOL	Speed Skating	0-0-2

WOMEN

No		Sport	G-S-B
5	Lyubov Egorova, UT	Cross-country	3-2-0
5	Elena Valbe, UT	Cross-country	1-0-4
3	Gunda Niemann, GER	Speed Skating	2-1-0
3	Antje Misersky, GER	Biathlon	1-2-0
3	Stefania Belmondo, ITA	Cross-country	1-1-1
2	**Bonnie Blair, USA**	Speed Skating	2-0-0
2	Petra Kronberger, AUT	Alpine	2-0-0
2	Marjut Lukkarinen, FIN	Cross-country	1-1-0
2	**Cathy Turner, USA**	ST Speed Skate	1-1-0
2	Anfisa Reztsova, UT	Biathlon	1-0-1
2	Ye Qiaobo, CHN.	Speed Skating	0-2-0
2	Anita Wachter, AUT	Alpine	0-2-0
2	Heike Warnicke, GER	Speed Skating	0-2-0
2	Elena Belova, UT	Biathlon	0-0-2

Lee Farrant/Allsport

Top women's medalists **Lyubov Egorova** (left) and **Elena Valbe** of the Unified Team.

MEDAL SPORTS

Medal winners in individual and team sports at Albertville, France, from Feb. 9-22, 1992. Demonstration sports are not included.

ALPINE SKIING

MEN

Downhill

		Time
1	Patrick Ortlieb, AUT	1:50.37
2	Franck Piccard, FRA	1:50:42
3	Günther Mader, AUT	1:50:47

Top 10 USA: 9th—AJ Kitt (1:51.98).

Slalom

		Time
1	Finn Christian Jagge, NOR	1:44.39
2	Alberto Tomba, ITA	1:44.67
3	Michael Tritscher, AUT	1:44.85

Top 10 USA: 10th—Matthew Grosjean (1:46.94).

Giant Slalom

		Time
1	Alberto Tomba, ITA	2:06.98
2	Marc Girardelli, LUX	2:07.30
3	Kjetil Andre Aamodt, NOR	2:07.82

Super Giant Slalom

		Time
1	Kjetil Andre Aamodt, NOR	1:13.04
2	Marc Girardelli, LUX	1:13.77
3	Jan Einar Thorsen, NOR	1:13.83

Combined

		Points
1	Josef Polig, ITA.	14.58
2	Gianfranco Martin, ITA	14.90
3	Steve Locher, SWI	18.16

WOMEN

Downhill

		Time
1	Kerrin Lee-Gartner, CAN	1:52.55
2	Hilary Lindh, USA	1:52.61
3	Veronika Wallinger, AUT	1:52.64

Slalom

		Time
1	Petra Kronberger, AUT	1:32.68
2	Annelise Coberger, NZE	1:33.10
3	Blanca Fernández Ochoa, SPA.	1:33.35

Top 10 USA: 4th—Julie Parisien (1:33.40).

Giant Slalom

		Time
1	Pernilla Wiberg, SWE	2:12.74
2	(TIE) Diann Roffe, USA.	2:13.71
	& Anita Wachter, AUT	2:13.71

Other Top 10 USA: 5th—Julie Parisien (2:14.10).

Super Giant Slalom

		Time
1	Deborah Compagnoni, ITA	1:21.22
2	Carole Merle, FRA	1:22.63
3	Katja Seizinger, GER	1:23.19

Top 10 USA: 8th—Eva Twardokens (1:24.19).

Combined

		Points
1	Petra Kronberger, AUT	2.55
2	Anita Wachter, AUT.	19.39
3	Florence Masnada, FRA	21.38

BIATHLON

MT indicates Missed Targets.

MEN

10 kilometers

		MT	Time
1	Mark Kirchner, GER	0	26:02.3
2	Ricco Gross, GER	1	26:18.0
3	Harri Eloranta, FIN.	0	26:26.6

20 kilometers

		MT	Time
1	Yevgeny Redkine, UT	0	57:34.4
2	Mark Kirchner, GER	3	57:40.8
3	Mikael Lofgren, SWE	2	57:59.4

4 x 7.5-kilometer Relay

		MT	Time
1	Germany	0	1:24:43.5
2	Unified Team	0	1:25:06.3
3	Sweden	0	1:25:38.2

GER—Ricco Gross, Jens Steinigen, Mark Kirchner, Fritz Fischer; **UT**—Valeri Medvedtzev, Alexander Popov, Valeri Kirienko, Sergei Tchepikov; **SWE**—Ulf Johansson, Leif Andersson, Tord Wiksten, Mikael Lofgren.
  USA Entry: 13th—Joh Engen, Duncan Douglas, Josh Thompson, Curt Schreiner; (1:30:44.0).

WOMEN

7.5 kilometers

		MT	Time
1	Anfisa Reztsova, UT	3	24:29.2
2	Antje Misersky, GER	2	24:45.1
3	Elena Belova, UT	2	24:50.8

15 kilometers

		MT	Time
1	Antje Misersky, GER	1	51:47.2
2	Svetlana Pecherskaia, UT	1	51:58.5
3	Myriam Bedard, CAN	2	52:15.0

3 x 7.5-kilometer Relay

		MT	Time
1	France.	0	1:15:55.6
2	Germany	0	1:16:18.4
3	Unified Team	0	1:16:54.6

FRA—Corinne Niogret, Veronique Claudel, Anne Briand; **GER**—Uschi Disl, Antje Misersky, Petra Schaaf; **UT**—Elena Belova, Anfisa Reztsova, Elena Melnikova.
  USA Entry: 15th—Nancy Bell, Joan Smith, Mary Ostergren (1:24.36.9).

BOBSLED

Two-Man

	Time
1 Switzerland I	4:03.26
2 Germany I	4:03.55
3 Germany II	4:03.63

SWI I—Gustav Weder & Donat Acklin; **GER I**— Rudi Lochner & Markus Zimmerman; **GER II**—Christoph Langen & Gunther Eger.
  Top 10 USA: 7th—Brian Shimer & Herschel Walker (4:03.95).

Four-Man

	Time
1 Austria I	3:53.90
2 Germany I	3:53.92
3 Switzerland I	3:54.13

AUT I—Ingo Appelt (driver), Harald Winkler, Gerhard Haidacher, Thomas Schroll; **GER I**—Wolfgang Hoppe (driver), Bogdan Musiol, Axel Kuhn, Rene Hannemann; **SWI I**—Gustav Weder (driver), Donat Acklin, Lorenz Schindelholz, Curdin Morell.
  Top 10 USA: 9th—USA I—Randy Will (driver), Joseph Sawyer, Karlos Kirby, Chris Coleman (3:54.92).

CROSS-COUNTRY SKIING

MEN

10 kilometers

	Time
1 Vegard Ulvang, NOR	27:36.0
2 Marco Albarello, ITA	27:55.2
3 Christer Majbäck, SWE	27:56.4

15 kilometers

	Time
1 Bjorn Dählie, NOR	38:01.9
2 Vegard Ulvang, NOR	38:55.3
3 Giorgio Vanzetta, ITA	38:56.2

30 kilometers

	Time
1 Vegard Ulvang, NOR	1:22:27.8
2 Bjorn Dählie, NOR	1:23:14.0
3 Terje Langli, NOR	1:23:42.5

50 kilometers

	Time
1 Bjorn Dählie, NOR	2:03:41.5
2 Maurilio De Zolt, ITA	2:04:39.1
3 Giorgio Vanzetta, ITA	2:06:42.1

Note: Norway's Vegard Ulvang finished 9th (2:08: 21.5).

4 x 10-kilometer Relay

	Time
1 Norway	1:39:26.0
2 Italy	1:40:52.7
3 Finland	1:41:22.9

NOR—Terje Langli, Vegard Ulvang, Kristen Skjeldal, Bjorn Dählie; **ITA**—Giuseppe Pulie, Marco Albarello, Giorgio Vanzetta, Silvio Fauner; **FIN**—Mika Kuusisto, Harri Kirvesniemi, Jari Rasanen, Jari Isometsa.
  USA Entry: 12th—John Aalberg, Ben Husaby, John Bauer, Luke Bodensteiner (1:48:15.8).

WOMEN

5 kilometers

	Time
1 Marjut Lukkarinen, FIN	14:13.8
2 Lyubov Egorova, UT	14:14.7
3 Elena Valbe, UT	14:22.7

10 kilometers

	Time
1 Lyubov Egorova, UT	25:53.7
2 Stefania Belmondo, ITA	26:17.8
3 Elena Valbe, UT	26:37.7

15 kilometers

	Time
1 Lyubov Egorova, UT	42:20.8
2 Marjut Lukkarinen, FIN	43:29.9
3 Elena Valbe, UT	43:42.3

30 kilometers

	Time
1 Stefania Belmondo, ITA	1:22:30.1
2 Lyubov Egorova, UT	1:22:52.0
3 Elena Valbe, UT	1:24:13.9

4 x 5-kilometer Relay

	Time
1 Unified Team	59:34.8
2 Norway	59:56.4
3 Italy	1:00:25.9

UT—Elena Valbe, Raisa Smetanina, Larisa Lasutina, Lyubov Egorova; **NOR**—Solveig Pedersen, Inger Helene Nybraten, Trude Dybendahl, Elin Nilsen; **ITA**—Bice Vanzetta, Manuela Di Centra, Gabriella Paruzzi, Stefania Belmondo.
  USA Entry: 13th—Nancy Fiddler, Ingrid Butts, Leslie Thompson, Elizabeth Youngman (1:04:48.5).

Shaun Botterill/Allsport

Norwegian cross-country skiers (from left to right) **Vegard Ulvang, Bjorn Däblie** and **Terje Langli** after sweeping the Men's 30-kilometer race on Feb. 10 at Les Saises.

FIGURE SKATING

FP indicates Factored Placements.

MEN

		FP
1 Viktor Petrenko, UT		1.5
2 Paul Wylie, USA		3.5
3 Petr Barna, CZE		4.0

Other Top 10 USA: 4th—Christopher Bowman (7.5); 10th—Todd Eldredge (15.5).

WOMEN

		FP
1 Kristi Yamaguchi, USA		1.5
2 Midori Ito, JPN		4.0*
3 Nancy Kerrigan, USA		4.0

*Ito takes silver based on superior free program.
Other Top 10 USA: 4th—Tonya Harding (7.0).

PAIRS

		FP
1 Natalya Mishkutienok & Artur Dmitriev, UT		1.5
2 Elena Bechke & Denis Petrov, UT		3.0
3 Isabelle Brasseur & Lloyd Eisler, CAN		4.5

Top 10 USA: 10th—Calla Urbanski & Rocky Marval (14.5).

ICE DANCING

		FP
1 Marina Klimova & Sergei Ponomarenko, UT		1.0
2 Isabelle & Paul Duchesnay, FRA		2.0
3 Maia Usova & Alexander Zhulin, UT		3.0

FREESTYLE SKIING

MEN

Moguls

		Pts
1 Edgar Grospiron, FRA		25.81
2 Olivier Allamand, FRA		24.87
3 Nelson Carmichael, USA		24.82

WOMEN

Moguls

		Pts
1 Donna Weinbrecht, USA		23.69
2 Elizaveta Kojevnikova, UT		23.50
3 Stine Hattestad, NOR		23.04

Other Top 10 USA: 6th—Liz McIntyre (21.24).

Rick Stewart/Allsport

Unified Team hockey coach **Viktor Tikhonov** with his third straight gold medal.

ICE HOCKEY

Round Robin Standings

First four teams in each group advance to medal round.

Group A	Gm	W-L-T	Pts	GF	GA
*United States	5	4-0-1	9	18	7
*Sweden	5	3-0-2	8	22	11
*Finland	5	3-1-1	7	22	11
*Germany	5	2-3-0	4	11	12
Italy	5	1-4-0	2	18	24
Poland	5	0-5-0	0	4	30

Group B	Gm	W-L-T	Pts	GF	GA
*Canada	5	4-1-0	8	28	9
*Unified Team	5	4-1-0	8	32	10
*Czechoslovakia	5	4-1-0	8	25	15
*France	5	2-3-0	4	14	22
Switzerland	5	1-4-0	2	13	25
Norway	5	0-5-0	0	7	38

Quarterfinals

Canada 3	Germany 3

(Canada wins shootout, 3-2)

USA 4	France 1
Czechoslovakia 3	Sweden 1
Unified Team 6	Finland 1

Semifinals

Unified Team 5	USA 2
Canada 4	Czechoslovakia 2

Bronze Medal

Czechoslovakia 6	USA 1

Gold Medal

Unified Team 3	Canada 1

Leading Scorers

Includes all games; goals scored in Canada-Germany quarterfinal shootout not included.

	Gm	G	A	Pts
Joe Juneau, CAN	8	6	9	15
Andrei Khomoutov, UT	8	7	7	14
Robert Lang, CZH	8	5	8	13
Teemu Selanne, FIN	8	7	4	11
Hannu Jarvenpaa, FIN	8	5	6	11
Eric Lindros, CAN	8	5	6	11
Viatcheslav Bykov, UT	8	4	7	11
Yuri Khmylev, UT	8	4	6	10
Mika Nieminen, FIN	8	4	6	10
Nikolai Borstchevski, UT	8	7	2	9
David Archibald, CAN	8	7	1	8
Petr Resol, CZE	7	6	2	8
Hakan Loob, SWE	8	4	4	8
Dave Hannan, CAN	8	3	5	8
Igor Boldin, UT	8	2	6	8
Randy Smith, CAN	8	1	7	8

Top US scorers: Marty McInnis (8 gms, 5-2—7 pts); Ted Donato (8 gms, 4-3—7); Tim Sweeney (8 gm, 3-4—7).

Leading Goaltenders

Minimum 150 minutes.

	Gm	Min	GA	Avg	Record
Mikhail Shtalenkov, UT	8	441	12	1.63	7-1-0
Helmut DeRaaf, GER	4	250	8	1.92	2-2-0
Roger Nordstrom, SWE	3	179	6	2.01	2-0-1
Ray LeBlanc, USA	8	463	17	2.20	5-2-1
Sean Burke, CAN	7	429	17	2.37	5-2-0
Tommy Soderstrom, SWE	5	291	13	2.61	3-1-1
Jukka Tammi, FIN	5	299	13	2.61	2-2-1
Markus Ketterer, FIN	3	180	8	2.67	2-1-0
Petr Briza, CZE	7	419	19	2.72	5-2-0

LUGE

MEN

Singles: 1. Georg Hackl, GER (3:02.363); **2.** Markus Prock, AUT (3:02.669); **3.** Markus Schmidt, AUT (3:02.942).

Top 10 USA: 10th—Duncan Kennedy (3:03.852).

Doubles: 1. Stefan Krausse & Jan Behrendt, GER (1:32.053); **2.** Yves Mankel & Thomas Rudolph, GER (1:32.239); **3.** Hansjorg Raffl & Norbert Huber, ITA (1:32.298).

Top 10 USA: 9th—Wendl Suckow & Bill Tavares (1:33.451).

WOMEN

Singles: 1. Doris Neuner, AUT (3:06.696); **2.** Angelika Neuner, AUT (3:06.769); **3.** Susi Erdmann, GER (3:07.115).

Top 10 USA: 5th—Cammy Myler (3:07.973); 9th—Erica Terwillegar (3:08.547).

NORDIC COMBINED

Three jumps off Normal Hill (70 meters) and a 15-kilometer cross-country race.

Individual: 1. Fabrice Guy, FRA (426.470 points); **2.** Sylvain Guillaume, FRA (419.205); **3.** Klaus Sulzenbacher, AUT (416.520).

Team: 1. Japan (1,247.180 points); **2.** Norway (1,229.900); **3.** Austria (1,227.060).

USA entry: 8th—Tim Tetreault, Ryan Heckman, Joe Holland (1,137.520 pts).

SKI JUMPING

Normal Hill (90 meters)

		Points
1	Ernst Vettori, AUT	222.8
2	Martin Höllwarth, AUT	218.1
3	Toni Nieminen, FIN	217.0

Large Hill (120 meters)

		Points
1	Toni Nieminen, FIN	239.5
2	Martin Höllwarth, AUT	227.3
3	Heinz Kuttin, AUT	214.8

Team Large Hill (120 meters)

		Points
1	Finland	644.4
2	Austria	642.9
3	Czechoslovakia	620.1

FIN—Ari-Pekka Nikkola, Mika Laitinen, Risto Laakkoneen, Toni Nieminen; **AUT**—Heinz Kuttin, Ernst Vettori, Martin Höllwarth, Andreas Felder; **CZE**—Tomas Goder, Frantisek Jez, Jaroslav Sakala, Jiri Parma.

USA Entry: 12th—Robert Holme, Tad Langlois, Bryan Sanders, Jim Holland (482.4 pts).

SPEED SKATING

MEN

500 Meters

		Time
1	Uwe-Jens Mey, GER	37.14
2	Toshiyuki Kuroiwa, JPN	37.18
3	Junichi Inoue, JPN	37.26

Top 10 USA: 4th—Dan Jansen (37.46).

1000 Meters

		Time
1	Olaf Zinke, GER	1:14.85
2	Kim Yoon Man, S.Kor	1:14.86
3	Yukinori Miyabe, JPN	1:14.92

1500 Meters

		Time
1	Johann Koss, NOR	1:54.81
2	Adne Sondral, NOR	1:54.85
3	Leo Visser, HOL	1:54.90

5000 Meters

		Time
1	Geir Karlstad, NOR	6:59.97
2	Falco Zandstra, HOL	7:02.28
3	Leo Visser, HOL	7:04.96

Top 10 USA: 6th—Eric Flaim (7:11.15).

10,000 Meters

		Time
1	Bart Veldkamp, HOL	14:12.12
2	Johann Koss, NOR	14:14.58
3	Geir Karlstad, NOR	14:18.13

WOMEN

500 Meters

		Time
1	Bonnie Blair, USA	40.33
2	Ye Qiaobo, CHN	40.51
3	Christa Luding, GER	40.57

1000 Meters

		Time
1	Bonnie Blair, USA	1:21.90
2	Ye Qiaobo, CHN	1:21.92
3	Monique Garbrecht, GER	1:22.10

1500 Meters

		Time
1	Jacqueline Börner, GER	2:05.87
2	Gunda Niemann, GER	2:05.92
3	Seiko Hashimoto, JPN	2:06.88

Note: Bonnie Blair of USA finished 21st (2:10.89).

3000 Meters

		Time
1	Gunda Niemann, GER	4:19.90
2	Heike Warnicke, GER	4:22.88
3	Emese Hunyady, AUT	4:24.64

5000 Meters

		Time
1	Gunda Niemann, GER	7:31.57
2	Heike Warnicke, GER	7:37.59
3	Claudia Pechstein, GER	7:39.80

SHORT TRACK SPEED SKATING

MEN

1000 meters: 1. Kim Ki Hoon, S.KOR (1:30.76/**WR**); **2.** Frederic Blackburn, CAN (1:31.11); **3.** Lee Joon Ho, S.KOR (1:31.16).

5000-meter Relay: 1. South Korea (7:14.02/**WR**); **2.** Canada (7:14.06); **3.** Japan (7:18.18).

WOMEN

500 meters: 1. Cathy Turner, USA (47.04); **2.** Li Yan, CHN (47.08); **3.** Hwang Ok Sil, N.KOR (47.23).

3000-meter Relay: 1. Canada (4:36.62); **2.** United States (4:37.85); 3. Unified Team (4:42.69).

USA entry: Cathy Turner, Amy Peterson, Darci Dohnal, Nikki Ziegelmeyer.

THE 1993 INFORMATION PLEASE SPORTS ALMANAC

OLYMPICS STATISTICS

THROUGH THE YEARS
1924-1992
WINTER GAMES

SEC B

PAGE 546

The Winter Olympics

The move toward a winter version of the Olympics began in 1908 when figure skating made an appearance at the Summer Games in London.

Ten-time world champion Ulrich Salchow of Sweden, who originated the backwards, one-revolution jump that bears his name, and Madge Syers of Great Britain were the first singles champions. Germans Anna Hubler and Heinrich Berger won the pairs competition.

Figure skating returned in 1920 at Antwerp where ice hockey was added as a medal event. Sweden's Gillis Grafström and Magda Julin took individual honors, while Ludovika and Walter Jakobsson were the top pair. In hockey, Canada won the gold medal, with the United States second and Czechoslovakia third.

Although resisted at first by the Scandinavian countries, which had their own Nordic championships, the IOC successfully inaugurated the Winter Games in 1924 at Chamonix in the French Alps, 60 miles northeast of Grenoble. The first Winter Olympic Games were actually called "The International Winter Sports Week" and went on for 11 days.

Seventy years after those first cold weather Games, the 17th edition of the Winter Olympics will take place in Lillehammer, Norway, in 1994. The event will end the four-year Olympic cycle of staging both Winter and Summer Games in the same year and begin a new schedule that calls for the two Games to alternate every two years.

Year	No.	Location	Dates	Nations	Most medals	USA Medals
1924	I	Chamonix, FRA	Jan. 25-Feb. 4	16	Norway (4-7-6—17)	1-2-1— 4 (3th)
1928	II	St. Moritz, SWI	Feb. 11-19	25	Norway (6-4-5—15)	3-2-2— 7 (2nd)
1932	III	Lake Placid, NY	Feb. 4-15	17	USA (6-4-2—12)	6-4-2—12 (1st)
1936	IV	Garmisch-Partenkirchen, GER	Feb. 6-16	28	Norway (7-5-3—15)	1-0-3— 4 (T-5th)
1940-a	—	Sapporo, JPN	Cancelled (WWII)			
1944	—	Cortina d'Ampezzo, ITA	Cancelled (WWII)			
1948	V	St. Moritz, SWI	Jan. 30-Feb. 8	28	Norway (4-3-3—10), Sweden (4-3-3—10 & Switzerland (3-4-3—10)	3-4-2— 9 (4th)
1952-b	VI	Oslo, NOR	Feb. 14-25	30	Norway (7-3-6—16)	4-6-1—11 (2nd)
1956-c	VII	Cortina d'Ampezzo, ITA	Jan. 26-Feb. 5	32	USSR (7-3-6—16)	2-3-2— 7 (T-4th)
1960	VIII	Squaw Valley, CA	Feb. 18-28	30	USSR (7-5-9—21)	3-4-3—10 (2nd)
1964	IX	Innsbruck, AUT	Jan. 29-Feb. 9	36	USSR (11-8-6—25)	1-2-3— 6 (7th)
1968-d	X	Grenoble, FRA	Feb. 6-18	37	Norway (6-6-2—14)	1-5-1— 7 (T-7th)
1972	XI	Sapporo, JPN	Feb. 3-13	35	USSR (8-5-3—16)	3-2-3— 8 (6th)
1976-e	XII	Innsbruck, AUT	Feb. 4-15	37	USSR (13-6-8—27)	3-3-4—10 (T-3rd)
1980	XIII	Lake Placid, NY	Feb. 14-24	37	E. Germany (9-7-7—23)	6-4-2—12 (3rd)
1984	XIV	Sarajevo, YUG	Feb. 8-19	49	USSR (6-10-9—25)	4-4-0— 8 (T-5th)
1988	XV	Calgary, CAN	Feb. 13-28	57	USSR (11-9-9—29)	2-1-3— 6 (T-8th)
1992-f	XVI	Albertville, FRA	Feb. 8-23	64	Germany (10-10-6—26)	5-4-2—11 (6th)
1994-g	XVII	Lillehammer, NOR	Feb.12-27			
1998	XVIII	Nagano, JPN	TBA			

a—The 1940 Winter Games are originally scheduled for Sapporo, but Japan resigns as host in 1937 after the Sino-Japanese war breaks out. St. Moritz is the next choice, but the Swiss feel that ski instructors should not be considered as professionals and the IOC withdraws its offer. Finally, Garmisch-Partenkirchen is asked to serve again as host, but the Germans invade Poland in 1939 and the games are eventually cancelled.

b—Germany and Japan are allowed to rejoin the Olympic community for the first time since World War II. Though a divided country, the Germans send a joint East-West team.

c—The Soviet Union (USSR) participates in its first Winter Olympics, and takes home the most medals, including its first gold medal in ice hockey.

d—East Germany and West Germany send separate teams for the first time and will continue to do so through 1988.

e—The IOC originally grants the 1976 Winter Games to Denver, but in 1972 Colorado voters reject a $5 million bond issue to finance the undertaking. Denver immediately withdraws as host and the IOC selects Innsbruck, the site of the 1964 Games, to take over.

f—Germany sends a single team after East and West German reunification in 1990 and the USSR competes as the Unified Team after the breakup of the Soviet Union in 1991.

g—In 1988, the IOC votes to move the Winter Games' four-year cycle ahead two years in order to separate them from the Summer Games and alternate between the two Olympics every two years.

Event-by-Event

Gold medal winners from 1924-92 in the following events: Alpine Skiing, Biathlon, Bobsled, Cross-country Skiing, Figure Skating, Ice Hockey, Luge, Nordic Combined, Ski Jumping, and Speed Skating.

ALPINE SKIING

MEN

Multiple goal medals: Jean-Claude Killy, Toni Sailer and Alberto Tomba (3); Henri Oreiller and Ingemar Stenmark (2).

Downhill

Year		Time	Year		Time
1948	Henri Oreiller, FRA	2:55.0	1972	Bernhard Russi, SWI	1:51.43
1952	Zeno Colo, ITA	2:30.8	1976	Franz Klammer AUT	1:45.73
1956	Toni Sailer, AUT	2:52.2	1980	Leonhard Stock, AUT	1:45.50
1960	Jean Vuarnet, FRA	2:06.0	1984	Bill Johnson, USA	1:45.59
1964	Egon Zimmermann, AUT	2:18.16	1988	Pirmin Zurbriggen, SWI	1:59.63
1968	Jean-Claude Killy, FRA	1:59.85	1992	Patrick Ortlieb, AUT	1:50.37

Slalom

Year		Time	Year		Time
1948	Edi Reinalter, SWI	2:10.3	1972	Francisco Ochoa, SPA	1:49.27
1952	Othmar Schneider, AUT	2:00.0	1976	Piero Gros, ITA	2:03.29
1956	Toni Sailer, AUT	3:14.7	1980	Ingemar Stenmark, SWE	1:44.26
1960	Ernst Hinterseer, AUT	2:08.9	1984	Phil Mahre, USA	1:39.41
1964	Pepi Stiegler, AUT	2:11.13	1988	Alberto Tomba, ITA	1:39.47
1968	Jean-Claude Killy, FRA	1:39.73	1992	Finn-Christian Jagge, NOR	1:44.39

Giant Slalom

Year		Time	Year		Time
1952	Stein Eriksen, NOR	2:25.0	1976	Heini Hemmi, SWI	3:26.97
1956	Toni Sailer, AUT	3:00.1	1980	Ingemar Stenmark, SWE	2:40.74
1960	Roger Staub, SWI	1:48.3	1984	Max Julen, SWI	2:41.18
1964	Francois Bonlieu, FRA	1:46.71	1988	Alberto Tomba, ITA	2:06.37
1968	Jean-Claude Killy, FRA	3:29.28	1992	Alberto Tomba, ITA	2:06.98
1972	Gustav Thöni, ITA	3:09.62			

Super Giant Slalom

Year		Time	Year		Time
1988	Franck Piccard, FRA	1:39.66	1992	Kjetil Andre Aamodt, NOR	1:13.04

Alpine Combined

Year		Points	Year		Points
1936	Franz Pfnür, GER	99.25	1988	Hubert Strolz, AUT	36.55
1948	Henri Oreiller, FRA	3.27	1992	Josef Polig, ITA	14.58

WOMEN

Multiple gold medals: Marielle Goitschel, Trude Jochum-Beiser, Petra Kronberger, Andrea Mead Lawrence, Rosi Mittermaier, Marie-Theres Nadig, Vreni Schneider and Hanni Wenzel (2).

Downhill

Year		Time	Year		Time
1948	Hedy Schlunegger, SWI	2:28.3	1972	Marie-Theres Nadig, SWI	1:36.68
1952	Trude Jochum-Beiser, AUT	1:47.1	1976	Rosi Mittermaier, W.Ger	1:46.16
1956	Madeleine Berthod, SWI	1:40.7	1980	Annemarie Moser-Pröll, AUT	1:37.52
1960	Heidi Biebl, GER	1:37.6	1984	Michela Figini, SWI	1:13.36
1964	Christl Haas, AUT	1:55.39	1988	Marina Kiehl, W.Ger	1:25.86
1968	Olga Pall, AUT	1:40.87	1992	Kerrin Lee-Gartner, CAN	1:52:55

Slalom

Year		Time	Year		Time
1948	Gretchen Fraser, USA	1:57.2	1972	Barbara Cochran, USA	1:31.24
1952	Andrea Mead Lawrence, USA	2:10.6	1976	Rosi Mittermaier, W.Ger	1:30.54
1956	Renée Colliard, SWI	1:52.3	1980	Hanni Wenzel, LIE	1:25.09
1960	Anne Heggtveit, CAN	1:49.6	1984	Paoletta Magoni, ITA	1:36.47
1964	Christine Goitschel, FRA	1:29.86	1988	Vreni Schneider, SWI	1:36.69
1968	Marielle Goitschel, FRA	1:25.86	1992	Petra Kronberger, AUT	1:32.68

Giant Slalom

Year		Time	Year		Time
1952	Andrea Mead Lawrence, USA	2:06.8	1976	Kathy Kreiner, CAN	1:29.13
1956	Ossi Reichert, GER	1:56.5	1980	Hanni Wenzel, LIE	2:41.66
1960	Yvonne Rüegg, SWI	1:39.9	1984	Debbie Armstrong, USA	2:20.98
1964	Marielle Goitschel, FRA	1:52.24	1988	Vreni Schneider, SWI	2:06.49
1968	Nancy Greene, CAN	1:51.97	1992	Pernilla Wiberg, SWE	2:12.74
1972	Marie-Theres Nadig, SWI	1:29.90			

Alpine Skiing (Cont.)
WOMEN
Super Giant Slalom

Year	Time	Year	Time
1988 Sigrid Wolf, AUT	1:19.03	1992 Deborah Compagnoni, ITA	1:21.22

Alpine Combined

Year	Points	Year	Points
1936 Christl Cranz, GER	97.06	1988 Anita Wachter, AUT	29.25
1948 Trude Beiser, AUT	6.58	1992 Petra Kronberger, AUT	2.55

BIATHLON

MEN

Multiple gold medals (including relays): Aleksandr Tikhonov (3); Anatoly Alyabyev, Mark Kirchner, Viktor Mamatov, Frank-Peter Roetsch, Magnar Solberg and Dmitri Vasilyev (2).

10 kilometers

Year	Time	Year	Time
1980 Frank Ullrich, E.Ger	32:10.69	1988 Frank-Peter Roetsch, E.Ger	25:08.1
1984 Eirik Kvalfoss, NOR	30:53.8	1992 Mark Kirchner, GER	26:02.3

20 kilometers

Year	Time	Year	Time
1960 Klas Lestander, SWE	1:33:21.6	1980 Anatoly Alyabyev, USSR	1:08:16.31
1964 Vladimir Melanin, USSR	1:20:26.8	1984 Peter Angerer, W.Ger	1:11:52.7
1968 Magnar Solberg, NOR	1:13:45.9	1988 Frank-Peter Roetsch, E.Ger	56:33.3
1972 Magnar Solberg, NOR	1:15:55.50	1992 Yevgeny Redkine, UT	57:34.4
1976 Nikolai Kruglov, USSR	1:14:12.26		

4x7.5-kilometer Relay

Year	Time	Year	Time	Year	Time
1968 Soviet Union	2:13:02.4	1980 Soviet Union	1:34:03.27	1988 Soviet Union	1:22:30.0
1972 Soviet Union	1:51:44.92	1984 Soviet Union	1:38:51.7	1992 Germany	1:24:43.5
1976 Soviet Union	1:57:55.64				

WOMEN

7.5 kilometers		15 kilometers		3 × 7.5-kilometer Relay	
Year	Time	Year	Time	Year	Time
1992 Anfisa Reztsova, UT	24:29.2	1992 Antje Misersky, GER	51:47.2	1992 France	1:15:55.6

BOBSLED

Multiple gold medals: DRIVERS—Meinhard Nehmer (3); Billy Fiske, Wolfgang Hoppe, Eugenio Monti, Andreas Ostler (2). CREW—Bernard Germeshausen (3), Cliff Gray, Lorenz Nieberl and Dietmar Schauerhammer (2).

Two-Man

Year	Time	Year	Time
1932 United States I (Hubert Stevens)	8:14.74	1968 Italy I (Eugenio Monti)	4:41.54
1936 United States I (Ivan Brown)	5:29.29	1972 West Germany II (Wolfgang Zimmerer)	4:57.07
1948 Switzerland II (Felix Endrich)	5:29.2	1976 East Germany I (Meinhard Nehmer)	3:44.42
1952 Germany I (Andreas Ostler)	5:24.54	1980 Switzerland II (Erich Schärer)	4:09.36
1956 Italy I (Lamberto Dalla Costa)	5:30.14	1984 East Germany II (Wolfgang Hoppe)	3:25.56
1960 Not held		1988 Soviet Union I (Jānis Kipurs)	3:53.48
1964 Great Britain I (Anthony Nash)	4:21.90	1992 Switzerland I (Gustav Weder)	4:03.26

Four-Man

Year	Time	Year	Time
1924 Switzerland I (Eduard Scherrer)	5:45.54	1964 Canada I (Vic Emery)	4:14.46
1928 United States II (Billy Fiske)	3:20.5	1968 Italy I (Eugenio Monti)	2:17.39
1932 United States I (Billy Fiske)	7:53.68	1972 Switzerland I (Jean Wicki)	4:43.07
1936 Switzerland II (Pierre Musy)	5:19.85	1976 East Germany I (Meinhard Nehmer)	3:40.43
1948 United States II (Francis Tyler)	5:20.1	1980 East Germany I (Meinhard Nehmer)	3:59.92
1952 Germany I (Andreas Ostler)	5:07.84	1984 East Germany I (Wolfgang Hoppe)	3:20.22
1956 Switzerland I (Franz Kapus)	5:10.44	1988 Switzerland I (Ekkehard Fasser)	3:47.51
1960 Not held		1992 Austria I (Ingo Appelt)	3:53.90

Note: Five-man sleds were used in 1928.

CROSS-COUNTRY SKIING

MEN

Multiple gold medals (including relays): Sixten Jernberg, Gunde Svan, Thomas Wassberg and Nikolai Zimyatov (4); Bjorn Dählie, Veikko Hakulinen, Eero Mäntyranta and Vegard Ulvang (3); Hallgeir Brenden, Harald Grönningen, Thorlief Haug, Jan Ottoson, Pål Tyldum and Vyacheslav Vedenine (2).
Multiple gold medals (including Nordic Combined): Johan Gröttumsbråten and Thorlief Haug (3).

10 kilometers

Year		Time
1992	Vegard Ulvang, NOR	27:36.0

15 kilometers

Year		Time	Year		Time
1924	Thorleif Haug, NOR	1:14:31.0	1964	Eero Mäntyranta, FIN	50:54.1
1928	Johan Grüttumsbråten, NOR	1:37:01.0	1968	Harald Grönningen, NOR	47:54.2
1932	Sven Utterstråm, SWE	1:23:07.0	1972	Sven-Ake Lundbäck, SWE	45:28.24
1936	Erik-August Larsson, SWE	1:14:38.0	1976	Nikolai Bazhukov, USSR	43:58.47
1948	Martin Lundström, SWE	1:13:50.0	1980	Thomas Wassberg, SWE	41:57.63
1952	Hallgeir Brenden, NOR	1:01:34.0	1984	Gunde Svan, SWE	41:25.6
1956	Hallgeir Brenden, NOR	49:39.0	1988	Mikhail Devyatyarov, USSR	41:18.9
1960	Håkon Brusveen NOR	51:55.5	1992	Bjorn Dählie, NOR	38:01.9

Note: Event was held over 18 kilometers from 1924-52.

30 kilometers

Year		Time	Year		Time
1956	Veikko Hakulinen, FIN	1:44:06.0	1976	Sergei Saveliev, USSR	1:30:29.38
1960	Sixten Jernberg, SWE	1:51:03.9	1980	Nikolai Zimyatov, USSR	1:27:02.80
1964	Eero Mäntyranta, FIN	1:30:50.7	1984	Nikolai Zimyatov, USSR	1:28:56.3
1968	Franco Nones, ITA	1:35:39.2	1988	Alexi Prokurorov, USSR	1:24:26.3
1972	Vyacheslav Vedenine, USSR	1:36:31.15	1992	Vegard Ulvang, NOR	1:22:27.8

50 kilometers

Year		Time	Year		Time
1924	Thorleif Haug, NOR	3:44:32.0	1964	Sixten Jernberg, SWE	2:43:52.6
1928	Per Erik Hedlund, SWE	4:52:03.0	1968	Ole Ellefsaeter, NOR	2:28:45.8
1932	Veli Saarinen, FIN	4:28:00.0	1972	Pål Tyldum, NOR	2:43:14.75
1936	Elis Wiklund, SWE	3:30:11.0	1976	Ivar Formo, NOR	2:37:30.05
1948	Nils Karlsson, SWE	3:47:48.0	1980	Nikolai Zimyatov, USSR	2:27:24.60
1952	Veikko Hakulinen, FIN	3:33:33.0	1984	Thomas Wassberg, SWE	2:15:55.8
1956	Sixten Jernberg, SWE	2:50:27.0	1988	Gunde Svan, SWE	2:04:30.9
1960	Kalevi Hämäläinen, FIN	2:59:06.3	1992	Bjorn Dählie, NOR	2:03:41.5

4x10-kilometer Relay

Year		Time	Year		Time	Year		Time
1936	Finland	2:41:33.0	1964	Sweden	2:18:34.6	1980	Soviet Union	1:57.03.46
1948	Sweden	2:32:08.0	1968	Norway	2:08:33.5	1984	Sweden	1:55:06.3
1952	Finland	2:20:16.0	1972	Soviet Union	2:04:47.94	1988	Sweden	1:43:58.6
1956	Soviet Union	2:15.30.0	1976	Finland	2:07:59.72	1992	Norway	1:39:26.0
1960	Finland	2:18.45.6						

WOMEN

Multiple gold medals (including relays): Galina Kulakova and Raisa Smetanina (4); Claudia Boyarskikh, Lyubov Egorova and Marja-Liisa Hämäläinen (3); Toini Gustafsson and Barbara Petzold (2).
Multiple gold medals (including relays and Biathlon): Anfisa Reztsova (2).

5 kilometers

Year		Time	Year		Time
1964	Claudia Boyarskikh, USSR	17:50.5	1980	Raisa Smetanina, USSR	15:06.92
1968	Toini Gustafsson, SWE	16:45.2	1984	Marja-Liisa Hämäläinen, FIN	17:04.0
1972	Galina Kulakova, USSR	17:00.50	1988	Marjo Matikainen, FIN	15:04.0
1976	Helena Takalo, FIN	15:48.69	1992	Marjut Lukkarinen, FIN	14:13.8

10 kilometers

Year		Time	Year		Time
1952	Lydia Wideman, FIN	41:40.0	1976	Raisa Smetanina, USSR	30:13.41
1956	Lyubov Kosyreva, USSR	38:11.0	1980	Barbara Petzold, E.Ger	30:31.54
1960	Maria Gusakova, USSR	39:46.6	1984	Marja-Liisa Hämäläinen, FIN	31:44.2
1964	Claudia Boyarskikh, USSR	40:24.3	1988	Vida Venciene, USSR	30:08.3
1968	Toini Gustafsson, SWE	36:46.5	1992	Lyubov Egorova, UT	25:53.7
1972	Galina Kulakova, USSR	34:17.82			

15 kilometers

Year		Time
1992	Lyubov Egorova, UT	42:20.8

Cross-country Skiing (Cont.)

30 kilometers

Year		Time	Year		Time
1984	Marja-Liisa Hämäläinen, FIN	1:01:45.0	1992	Stefania Belmondo, ITA	1:22:30.1
1988	Tamara Tikhonova, USSR	55:53.6			

Note: Event was held over 20 kilometers from 1984–88.

4x5-kilometer Relay

Year		Time	Year		Time	Year		Time
1956	Finland	1:09:01.0	1972	Soviet Union	48:46.15	1984	Norway	1:06:49.7
1960	Sweden	1:04:21.4	1976	Soviet Union	1:07:49.75	1988	Soviet Union	59:51.1
1964	Soviet Union	59:20.2	1980	East Germany	1:02:11.10	1992	Unified Team	1:00:25.9
1968	Norway	57:30.0						

Note: Event featured three skiers per team from 1956–72.

FIGURE SKATING

Part of Summer Games in 1908 and 1920.

MEN

Multiple gold medals: Gillis Grafström (3); Dick Button and Karl Schäfer (2).

Year			Year			Year		
1908	Ulrich Salchow	SWE	1948	Dick Button	USA	1972	Ondrej Nepela	CZE
1920	Gillis Grafström	SWE	1952	Dick Button	USA	1976	John Curry	GBR
1924	Gillis Grafström	SWE	1956	Hayes Alan Jenkins	USA	1980	Robin Cousins	GBR
1928	Gillis Grafström	SWE	1960	David Jenkins	USA	1984	Scott Hamilton	USA
1932	Karl Schäfer	AUT	1964	Manfred Schnelldorfer	GER	1988	Brian Boitano	USA
1936	Karl Schäfer	AUT	1968	Wolfgang Schwarz	AUT	1992	Victor Petrenko	UT

WOMEN

Multiple gold medals: Sonja Henie (3); Katarina Witt (2).

Year			Year			Year		
1908	Madge Syers	GBR	1948	Barbara Ann Scott	CAN	1972	Beatrix Schuba	AUT
1920	Magda Julin	SWE	1952	Jeanette Altwegg	GBR	1976	Dorothy Hamill	USA
1924	Herma Planck-Szabó	AUT	1956	Tenley Albright	USA	1980	Anett Pötzsch	E. GER
1928	Sonja Henie	NOR	1960	Carol Heiss	USA	1984	Katarina Witt	E. GER
1932	Sonja Henie	NOR	1964	Sjoukje Dijkstra	HOL	1988	Katarina Witt	E. GER
1936	Sonja Henie	NOR	1968	Peggy Fleming	USA	1992	Kristi Yamaguchi	USA

PAIRS

Multiple gold medals: MEN—Pierre Brunet, Oleg Protopopov and Aleksandr Zaitsev (2). WOMEN—Irina Rodnina (3); Ludmila Belousova and Andrée Joly Brunet (2).

Year			Year		
1908	Anna Hübler & Heinrich Burger	Germany	1960	Barbara Wagner & Robert Paul	Canada
1920	Ludovika & Walter Jakobsson	Finland	1964	Ludmila Belousova & Oleg Protopopov	USSR
1924	Helene Engelmann & Alfred Berger	Austria	1968	Ludmila Belousova & Oleg Protopopov	USSR
1928	Andrée Joly & Pierre Brunet	France	1972	Irina Rodnina & Aleksei Ulanov	USSR
1932	Andrée & Pierre Brunet	France	1976	Irina Rodnina & Aleksandr Zaitsev	USSR
1936	Maxi Herber & Ernst Baier	Germany	1980	Irina Rodnina & Aleksandr Zaitsev	USSR
1948	Micheline Lannoy & Pierre Baugniet	Belgium	1984	Elena Valova & Oleg Vasiliev	USSR
1952	Ria & Paul Falk	Germany	1988	Ekaterina Gordeeva & Sergei Grinkov	USSR
1956	Elisabeth Schwartz & Kurt Oppelt	Austria	1992	Natalya Mishkutienok & Arthur Dmitriev	UT

ICE DANCING

Year			Year		
1976	Lyudmila Pakhomova & Aleksandr Gorshkov	USSR	1988	Natalia Bestemianova & Andrei Bukin	USSR
1980	Natalia Linichuk & Gennady Karponosov	USSR	1992	Marina Klimova & Sergei Ponomarenko	UT
1984	Jayne Torvill & Christopher Dean	Great Britain			

ICE HOCKEY

Part of Summer Games in 1920. Listed are gold, silver and bronze medal-winning teams.

Multiple gold medals: Soviet Union/Unified Team (8); Canada (6); United States (2).

Year		Year	
1920	**Canada**, United States Czechoslovakia	1964	**Soviet Union**, Sweden, Czechoslovakia
1924	**Canada**, United States, Great Britain	1968	**Soviet Union**, Czechoslovakia, Canada
1928	**Canada**, Sweden, Switzerland	1972	**Soviet Union**, United States, Czechoslovakia
1932	**Canada**, United States, Germany	1976	**Soviet Union**, Czechoslovakia, West Germany
1936	**Great Britain**, Canada, United States	1980	**United States**, Soviet Union, Sweden
1948	**Canada**, Czechoslovakia, Switzerland	1984	**Soviet Union**, Czechoslovakia, Sweden
1952	**Canada**, United States, Sweden	1988	**Soviet Union**, Finland, Sweden
1956	**Soviet Union**, United States, Canada	1992	**Unified Team**, Canada, Czechoslovakia
1960	**United States**, Canada, Soviet Union		

U.S. Gold Medal Hockey Teams

1960

Forwards: Billy Christian, Roger Christian, Billy Cleary, Gene Grazia, Paul Johnson, Bob McVey, Dick Meredith, Weldy Olson, Dick Rodenheiser and Tom Williams. **Defensemen:** Bob Cleary, Jack Kirrane (captain), John Mayasich, Bob Owen and Rod Paavola. **Goaltenders:** Jack McCartan and Larry Palmer. **Coach:** Jack Riley.

1980

Forwards: Neal Broten, Steve Christoff, Mike Eruzione (captain), John Harrington, Mark Johnson, Rob McClanahan, Mark Pavelich, Buzz Schneider, Eric Strobel, Phil Verchota and Mark Wells. **Defensemen:** Bill Baker, Dave Christian, Ken Morrow, Jack O'Callahan, Mike Ramsey and Bob Suter. **Goaltenders:** Jim Craig and Steve Janaszak. **Coach:** Herb Brooks.

LUGE

MEN

Multiple gold medals: (including doubles): Norbert Hahn, Paul Hildgartner, Thomas Köhler and Hans Rinn (2).

Singles

Year		Time	Year		Time
1964	Thomas Köhler, GER	3:26.77	1980	Bernhard Glass, E.Ger	2:54.796
1968	Manfred Schmid, AUT	2:52.48	1984	Paul Hildgartner, ITA	3:04.258
1972	Wolfgang Scheidel, E.Ger	3:27.58	1988	Jens Müller, E.Ger	3:05.548
1976	Dettlef Günther, E.Ger	3:27.688	1992	Georg Hackl, GER	3:02.363

Doubles

Year		Time	Year		Time	Year		Time
1964	Austria	1:41.62	1976	East Germany	1:25.604	1988	East Germany	1:31.940
1968	East Germany	1:35.85	1980	East Germany	1:19.331	1992	Germany	1:32.053
1972	(TIE) East Germany	1:28.35	1984	West Germany	1:23.620			
	& Italy	1.28.35						

WOMEN

Multiple gold medals: Steffi Martin Walter (2).

Singles

Year		Time	Year		Time
1964	Ortrun Enderlein, GER	3:24.67	1980	Vera Zozulya, USSR	2:36.537
1968	Erica Lechner, ITA	2:28.66	1984	Steffi Martin, E.Ger	2:46.570
1972	Anna-Maria Müller, E.Ger	2:59.18	1988	Steffi Martin Walter, E.Ger	3:03.973
1976	Margit Schumann, E.Ger	2:50.621	1992	Doris Neuner, AUT	3:06.696

NORDIC COMBINED

Multiple gold medals: Ulrich Wehling (3); Johan Gröttumsbråten (2).

Individual

Year		Points	Year		Points
1924	Thorleif Haug, NOR	18.906	1964	Tormod Knutsen, NOR	469.28
1928	Johan Gröttumsbråten, NOR	17.833	1968	Franz Keller, W.Ger	449.04
1932	Johan Gröttumsbråten, NOR	446.00	1972	Ulrich Wehling, E.Ger	413.340
1936	Oddbjörn Hagen, NOR	430.3	1976	Ulrich Wehling, E.Ger	423.39
1948	Heikki Hasu, FIN	448.80	1980	Ulrich Wehling, E.Ger	432.200
1952	Simon Slattvik, NOR	451.621	1984	Tom Sandberg, NOR	422.595
1956	Sverre Stenersen, NOR	455.000	1988	Hippolyt Kempf, SWI	432.230
1960	Georg Thoma, GER	457.952	1992	Fabrice Guy, FRA	426.470

Team

Year		Points	Year		Points
1988	West Germany	792.08	1992	Japan	1247.180

SKI JUMPING

Multiple gold medals (including team jumping): Matti Nykänen (4); Birger Ruud and Toni Nieminen (2).

Normal Hill—70 Meters

Year		Points	Year		Points
1964	Veikko Kankkonen, FIN	229.9	1980	Anton Innauer, AUT	266.3
1968	Jiří Raška, CZE	216.5	1984	Jens Weissflog, E.Ger	215.2
1972	Yukio Kasaya, JPN	244.2	1988	Matti Nykänen, FIN	229.1
1976	Hans-Georg Aschenbach, E.Ger	252.0	1992	Ernst Vettori, AUT	222.8

Ski Jumping (Cont.)
Large Hill—90 Meters

Year	Points	Year	Points
1924 Jacob Tullin Thams, NOR	18.960	1964 Toralf Engan, NOR	230.7
1928 Alf Andersen, NOR	19.208	1968 Vladimir Beloussov, USSR	231.3
1932 Birger Ruud, NOR	228.1	1972 Wojciech Fortuna, POL	219.9
1936 Birger Ruud, NOR	232.0	1976 Karl Schnabl, AUT	234.8
1948 Petter Hugsted, NOR	228.1	1980 Jouko Törmänen, FIN	271.0
1952 Arnfinn Bergmann, NOR	226.0	1984 Matti Nykänen, FIN	231.2
1956 Antti Hyvärinen, FIN	227.0	1988 Matti Nykänen, FIN	224.0
1960 Helmut Recknagel, GER	227.2	1992 Toni Nieminen, FIN	239.5

Note: Jump held at various lengths from 1924–56; at 80 meters from 1960–64; at 90 meters from 1968–88; and at 120 meters in 1992.

Team Large Hill

Year	Points	Year	Points
1988 Finland	634.4	1992 Finland	644.4

SPEED SKATING
MEN

Multiple gold medals: Eric Heiden and Clas Thunberg (5); Ivar Ballangrud and Yevgeny Grishin (4); Hjallis Andersen, Tomas Gustafson, Irving Jaffee and Ard Schenk (3); Gaétan Boucher, Knut Johannesen, Erhard Keller, Uwe-Jens Mey and Jack Shea (2).
Note: Thunberg's total includes the All-Around, which was contested for the only time in 1924.

500 meters

Year	Time		Year	Time	
1924 Charles Jewtraw, USA	44.0		1964 Terry McDermott, USA	40.1	**OR**
1928 (TIE) Bernt Evensen, NOR	43.4	**OR**	1968 Erhard Keller, W.Ger	40.3	
& Clas Thunberg, FIN	43.4	**OR**	1972 Erhard Keller, W.Ger	39.44	**OR**
1932 Jack Shea, USA	43.4	=**OR**	1976 Yevgeny Kulikov, USSR	39.17	**OR**
1936 Ivar Ballangrud, NOR	43.4	=**OR**	1980 Eric Heiden, USA	38.03	**OR**
1948 Finn Helgesen, NOR	43.1	**OR**	1984 Sergei Fokichev, USSR	38.19	
1952 Ken Henry, USA	43.2		1988 Uwe-Jens Mey, E.Ger	36.45	**WR**
1956 Yevgeny Grishin, USSR	40.2	=**WR**	1992 Uwe-Jens Mey, GER	37.14	
1960 Yevgeny Grishin, USSR	40.2	=**WR**			

1000 meters

Year	Time		Year	Time	
1976 Peter Mueller, USA	1:19.32		1988 Nikolai Gulyaev, USSR	1:13.03	**OR**
1980 Eric Heiden, USA	1:15.18	**OR**	1992 Olaf Zinke, GER	1:14.85	
1984 Gaétan Boucher, CAN	1:15.80				

1500 meters

Year	Time		Year	Time	
1924 Clas Thunberg, FIN	2:20.8		1964 Ants Antson, USSR	2:10.3	
1928 Clas Thunberg, FIN	2:21.1		1968 Kees Verkerk, HOL	2:03.4	**OR**
1932 Jack Shea, USA	2:57.5		1972 Ard Schenk, HOL	2:02.96	**OR**
1936 Charles Mathisen, NOR	2:19.2	**OR**	1976 Jan Egil Storholt, NOR	1:59.38	**OR**
1948 Sverre Farstad, NOR	2:17.6	**OR**	1980 Eric Heiden, USA	1:55.44	**OR**
1952 Hjallis Andersen, NOR	2:20.4		1984 Gaétan Boucher, CAN	1:58.36	
1956 (TIE) Yevgeny Grishin, USSR	2:08.6	**WR**	1988 André Hoffman, E.Ger	1:52.06	**WR**
&Yuri Mikhailov, USSR	2:08.6	**WR**	1992 Johann Koss, NOR	1:54.81	
1960 (TIE) Roald Aas, NOR	2:10.4				
&Yevgeny Grishin, USSR	2:10.4				

5000 meters

Year	Time		Year	Time	
1924 Clas Thunberg, FIN	8:39.0		1964 Knut Johannesen, NOR	7:38.4	**OR**
1928 Ivar Ballangrud, NOR	8:50.5		1968 Fred Anton Maier, NOR	7:22.4	**WR**
1932 Irving Jaffee, USA	9:40.8		1972 Ard Schenk, HOL	7:23.61	
1936 Ivar Ballangrud, NOR	8:19.6	**OR**	1976 Sten Stensen, NOR	7:24.48	
1948 Reidar Liaklev, NOR	8:29.4		1980 Eric Heiden, USA	7:02.29	**OR**
1952 Hjallis Andersen, NOR	8:10.6	**OR**	1984 Tomas Gustafson, SWE	7:12.28	
1956 Boris Shilkov, USSR	7:48.7	**OR**	1988 Tomas Gustafson, SWE	6:44.63	**WR**
1960 Viktor Kosichkin, USSR	7:51.3		1992 Geir Karlstad, NOR	6:59.97	

10,000 meters

Year		Time	Year		Time
1924	Julius Skutnabb, FIN	18:04.8	1964	Jonny Nilsson, SWE	15:50.1
1928	Irving Jaffee, USA*	18:36.5	1968	Johnny Höglin, SWE	15:23.6 **OR**
1932	Irving Jaffee, USA.	19:13.6	1972	Ard Schenk, HOL.	15:01.35 **OR**
1936	Ivar Ballangrud, NOR.	17:24.3 **OR**	1976	Piet Kleine, HOL.	14:50.59 **OR**
1948	Ake Seyffarth, SWE.	17:26.3	1980	Eric Heiden, USA	14:28.13 **WR**
1952	Hjallis Andersen, NOR.	16:45.8 **OR**	1984	Igor Malkov, USSR.	14:39.90
1956	Sigvard Ericsson, SWE	16:35.9 **OR**	1988	Tomas Gustafson, SWE	13:48.20 **WR**
1960	Knut Johannesen, NOR.	15:46.6 **WR**	1992	Bart Veldkamp, HOL.	14:12.12

*Unofficial, according to the IOC. Jaffee recorded the fastest time, but the event was called off in progress due to thawing ice.

WOMEN

Multiple gold medals: Lydia Skoblikova (6); Bonnie Blair, Karin Enke and Yvonne van Gennip (3); Tatiana Averina, Gunda Niemann and Christa Rothenburger (2).

500 meters

Year		Time	Year		Time
1960	Helga Haase, GER.	45.9	1980	Karin Enke, E.Ger	41.78 **OR**
1964	Lydia Skoblikova, USSR.	45.0 **OR**	1984	Christa Rothenburger, E.Ger	41.02 **OR**
1968	Lyudmila Titova, USSR.	46.1	1988	Bonnie Blair, USA	39.10 **WR**
1972	Anne Henning, USA.	43.33 **OR**	1992	Bonnie Blair, USA	40.33
1976	Sheila Young, USA.	42.76 **OR**			

1000 meters

Year		Time	Year		Time
1960	Klara Guseva, USSR	1:34.1	1980	Natalia Petruseva, USSR	1:24.10 **OR**
1964	Lydia Skoblikova, USSR.	1:33.2 **OR**	1984	Karin Enke, E.Ger	1:21.61 **OR**
1968	Carolina Geijssen, HOL	1:32.6 **OR**	1988	Christa Rothenburger, E.Ger.	1:17.65 **WR**
1972	Monika Pflug, W.Ger.	1:31.40 **OR**	1992	Bonnie Blair, USA.	1:21.90
1976	Tatiana Averina, USSR.	1:28.43 **OR**			

1500 meters

Year		Time	Year		Time
1960	Lydia Skoblikova, USSR.	2:25.2 **WR**	1980	Annie Borckink, HOL.	2:10.95 **OR**
1964	Lydia Skoblikova, USSR.	2:22.6 **OR**	1984	Karin Enke, E.Ger	2:03.42 **WR**
1968	Kaija Mustonen, FIN	2:22.4 **OR**	1988	Yvonne van Gennip, HOL.	2:00.68 **OR**
1972	Dianne Holum, USA	2:20.85 **OR**	1992	Jacqueline Börner, GER.	2:05.87
1976	Galina Stepanskaya, USSR	2:16.58 **OR**			

3000 meters

Year		Time	Year		Time
1960	Lydia Skoblikova, USSR.	5:14.3	1980	Bjorg Eva Jensen, NOR.	4:32.13 **OR**
1964	Lydia Skoblikova, USSR.	5:14.9	1984	Andrea Schöne, E.Ger.	4:24.79 **OR**
1968	Johanna Schut, HOL.	4:56.2 **OR**	1988	Yvonne van Gennip, HOL.	4:11.94 **WR**
1972	Christina Baas-Kaiser, HOL.	4:52.14 **OR**	1992	Gunda Niemann, GER.	4:19.90
1976	Tatiana Averina, USSR.	4:45.19 **OR**			

5000 meters

Year		Time	Year		Time
1988	Yvonne van Gennip, HOL.	7:14.13 **WR**	1992	Gunda Niemann, GER	7:31.57

All-Time Top 20 Medal Standings, 1924–92

National medal standings for the Winter Olympics are not recognized by the IOC. The unofficial point totals are based on three points for each gold medal, two for each silver and one for each bronze. Demonstration sport medals are not included.

		G	S	B	Total	Pts			G	S	B	Total	Pts
1	USSR/Unified Team*	88	63	67	218	457	11	Canada	16	14	21	51	97
2	Norway	63	66	59	188	380	12	France	16	15	16	47	94
3	**United States**	48	50	34	132	278	13	Holland	14	18	14	46	92
4	Finland	36	44	37	117	233	14	West Germany†	11	15	13	39	76
5	Austria	34	45	40	119	232	15	Great Britain	7	5	10	22	41
6	East Germany†	39	36	35	110	224	16	Czechoslovakia	2	8	16	26	38
7	Sweden	37	25	34	96	195	17	Japan	2	6	6	14	24
8	Switzerland	24	25	27	76	149	18	Lichtenstein	2	2	5	9	15
9	Germany†	25	20	16	61	131	19	South Korea	2	1	1	4	9
10	Italy	18	16	13	47	99	20	Hungary	0	2	4	6	8

*The USSR first participated in the Winter Games in 1956 and became the Unified Team after the breakup of the Soviet Union in 1991. Medal total includes one gold won by Russia in figure skating (Special Figures) at 1908 Summer Games in London.

†After World War II, West Germany competed in the Winter Games as Germany in 1952 and formed a combined German team with East Germany from 1956-64. East and West Germany sent separate teams from 1968-88. Germany was reunified as a nation in 1990. Germany medal total includes one silver won in women's figure skating at 1908 Summer Games in London.

All-Time Leading Medal Winners
MEN

No		Sport	G-S-B
9	Sixten Jernberg, SWE	Cross-country	4-3-2
7	Clas Thunberg, FIN	Speed Skating	5-1-1
7	Ivar Ballangrud, NOR	Speed Skating	4-2-1
7	Veikko Hakulinen, FIN	Cross-country	3-3-1
7	Eero Mäntyranta, FIN	Cross-country	3-2-2
7	Bogdan Musiol, E.Ger/GER	Bobsled	1-5-1
6	Gunde Svan, SWE	Cross-country	4-1-1
6	Johan Gröttumsbråten, NOR	Nordic	3-1-2
6	Eugenio Monti, ITA	Bobsled	2-2-2
6	Roald Larsen, NOR	Speed Skating	0-2-4
5	**Eric Heiden, USA**	Speed Skating	5-0-0
5	Yevgeny Grishin, USSR	Speed Skating	4-1-0
5	Matti Nykänen, FIN	Ski Jumping	4-1-0
5	Aleksandr Tikhonov, USSR	Biathlon	4-1-0
5	Nikolai Zimyatov, USSR	Cross-country	4-1-0
5	Vegard Ulvang, NOR	Cross-country	3-1-1
5	Harald Grönningen, NOR	Cross-country	2-3-0
5	Wolfgang Hoppe, E.Ger/GER	Bobsled	2-3-0
5	Pål Tyldum, NOR	Cross-country	2-3-0

No		Sport	G-S-B
5	Knut Johannesen, NOR	Speed Skating	2-2-1
5	Peter Angerer, W.Ger/GER	Biathlon	1-2-2
5	Juha Mieto, FIN	Cross-country	1-2-2
5	Fritz Feierabend, SWI	Bobsled	0-3-2

WOMEN

No		Sport	G-S-B
10	Raisa Smetanina, USSR/UT	Cross-country	4-5-1
8	Galina Kulakova, USSR	Cross-country	4-2-2
8	Karin (Enke) Kania, E.Ger	Speed Skating	3-4-1
7	Andrea (Mitscherlich, Schöne) Ehrig, E.Ger	Speed Skating	1-5-1
6	Lydia Skoblikova, USSR	Speed Skating	6-0-0
5	Lyubov Egorova, UT	Cross-country	3-2-0
5	Marja-Liisa Hämäläinen, FIN	Cross-country	3-0-2
5	Helena Takalo, FIN	Cross-country	1-3-1
5	Alevtina Kolchina, USSR	Cross-country	1-1-3
5	Elena Valbe, UT	Cross-country	1-0-4

Gold Medals
MEN

No		Sport	G-S-B
5	Clas Thunberg, FIN	Speed Skating	5-1-1
5	**Eric Heiden, USA**	Speed Skating	5-0-0
4	Sixten Jernberg, SWE	Cross-country	4-3-2
4	Ivar Ballangrud, NOR	Speed Skating	4-2-1
4	Gunde Svan, SWE	Cross-country	4-1-1
4	Yevgeny Grishin, USSR	Speed Skating	4-1-0
4	Matti Nykänen, FIN	Ski Jumping	4-1-0
4	Aleksandr Tikhonov, USSR	Biathlon	4-1-0
4	Nikolai Zimyatov, USSR	Cross-country	4-1-0
4	Thomas Wassberg, SWE	Cross-country	4-0-0
3	Veikko Hakulinen, FIN	Cross-country	3-3-1
3	Eero Mäntyranta, FIN	Cross-country	3-2-2
3	Johan Gröttumsbråten, NOR	Nordic	3-1-2
3	Vegard Ulvang, NOR	Cross-country	3-1-1
3	Bjorn Dählie, NOR	Cross-country	3-1-0
3	Bernhard Germeshausen, E.Ger	Bobsled	3-1-0
3	Gillis Grafström, SWE	Figure Skating	3-1-0
3	Tomas Gustafson, SWE	Speed Skating	3-1-0
3	Alberto Tomba, ITA	Alpine	3-1-0
3	Vladislav Tretiak, USSR	Ice Hockey	3-1-0
3	Meinhard Nehmer, E.Ger	Bobsled	3-0-1
3	Hjallis Andersen, NOR	Speed Skating	3-0-0
3	Vitaly Davydov, USSR	Ice Hockey	3-0-0
3	Anatoly Firsov, USSR	Ice Hockey	3-0-0
3	Thorleif Haug, NOR	Nordic	3-0-0
3	**Irving Jaffee, USA**	Speed Skating	3-0-0
3	Andrei Khomoutov, USSR/UT	Ice Hockey	3-0-0
3	Jean-Claude Killy, FRA	Alpine	3-0-0
3	Viktor Kuzkin, USSR	Ice Hockey	3-0-0
3	Aleksandr Ragulin, USSR	Ice Hockey	3-0-0
3	Toni Sailer, AUT	Alpine	3-0-0
3	Ard Schenk, HOL	Speed Skating	3-0-0
3	Ulrich Wehling, E.Ger	Ski Jumping	3-0-0

WOMEN

No		Sport	G-S-B
6	Lydia Skoblikova, USSR	Speed Skating	6-0-0
4	Raisa Smetanina, USSR/UT	Cross-country	4-5-1
4	Galina Kulakova, USSR	Cross-country	4-2-2
3	Karin (Enke) Kania, E.GER	Speed Skating	3-4-1
3	Lyubov Egorova, UT	Cross-country	3-2-0
3	Marja-Liisa Hämäläinen, FIN	Cross-country	3-0-2
3	**Bonnie Blair, USA**	Speed Skating	3-0-1
3	Claudia Boyarskikh, USSR	Cross-country	3-0-0
3	Sonja Henie, NOR	Figure Skating	3-0-0
3	Irina Rodnina, USSR	Figure Skating	3-0-0
3	Yvonne van Gennip, HOL	Speed Skating	3-0-0

Top USA Medalists
MEN

No		Sport	G-S-B
5	Eric Heiden	Speed Skating	5-0-0
3†	Irving Jaffee	Speed Skating	3-0-0
3	Pat Martin	Bobsled	1-2-0
3	John Heaton	Bobsled/Cresta	0-2-1
2	Dick Button	Figure Skating	2-0-0
2*	Eddie Eagan	Boxing/Bobsled	2-0-0
2	Billy Fiske	Bobsled	2-0-0
2	Cliff Gray	Bobsled	2-0-0
2	Jack Shea	Speed Skating	2-0-0
2	Billy Cleary	Ice Hockey	1-1-0
2	Jennison Heaton	Bobsled/Cresta	1-1-0
2	John Mayasich	Ice Hockey	1-1-0
2	Terry McDermott	Speed Skating	1-1-0
2	Dick Meredith	Ice Hockey	1-1-0
2	Weldy Olson	Ice Hockey	1-1-0
2	Dick Rodenheiser	Ice Hockey	1-1-0
2	David Jenkins	Figure Skating	1-1-0
2	Stan Benham	Bobsled	0-2-0
2	Herb Drury	Ice Hockey	0-2-0
2	Frank Synott	Ice Hockey	0-2-0
2	John Garrison	Ice Hockey	0-1-1

*Eagan won the Light Heavyweight boxing title at the 1920 Summer Games in Antwerp and the four-man Bobsled at the 1932 Winter Games in Lake Placid. He is the only athlete ever to win gold medals in both the Winter and Summer Olympics.
†Jaffee is given credit for a third gold medal in the 10,000-meter Speed Skating race of 1928. He had the fastest time before the race was cancelled due to thawing ice. The IOC considers the race unofficial.

WOMEN

No		Sport	G-S-B
4	Bonnie Blair	Speed Skating	3-0-1
4	Dianne Holum	Speed Skating	1-2-1
3	Sheila Young	Speed Skating	1-1-1
3	Leah Poulos Mueller	Speed Skating	0-3-0
3	Beatrix Loughran	Figure Skating	0-2-1
2	Andrea Mead Lawrence	Alpine	2-0-0
2	Tenley Albright	Figure Skating	1-1-0
2	Gretchen Fraser	Alpine	1-1-0
2	Carol Heiss	Figure Skating	1-1-0
2	Cathy Turner	Short Track Sp. Skating	1-1-0
2	Anne Henning	Speed Skating	1-0-1
2	Penny Pitou	Alpine	0-2-0
2	Jean Saubert	Alpine	0-1-1

Wide World Photos

Spanish archer **Antonio Rebello** gets the Summer Games off to a sensational start as he lets go of the blazing arrow that will touch off the Olympic flame.

SUMMER OLYMPICS

Bull's Eye!

Barcelona welcomes 172 nations and turns the Summer Games into the universal festival they were always intended to be.

BARCELONA, Spain—Night after night they came, tens of thousands, hundreds of thousands, even a million in the space of the middle weekend of the 1992 Summer Olympics. Some had gone to the many events on the summit of Montjuic, site of the Olympic Stadium and several of the other major sports venues that were the heart of these Games. But others just came—some arriving on the last subway at 1 A.M.—to stroll on the boulevard leading to Montjuic, to stop by the magnificent fountains in front of the Palau Nacional.

Some were tourists, but most were Barcelonans. Well into the wee hours, well after spectators had come down from the stadium and the pools and the Palau Sant Jordi arena, they would still be climbing Montjuic on the newly installed escalators.

They sang and talked and sat and walked, infusing the 1992 Olympics with a joy and passion that left a striking impression no matter how many times one saw it. These people and their 2,000-year-old city were the stars of these Games, pouring out their soul for the world to share.

Barcelona was, in the words of University of Chicago anthropologist and Olympic historian John MacAloon, "a public,

popular festival, the most extraordinary Olympics I've ever been associated with."

It was perhaps the closest thing to a universal festival the world has ever known. A record 172 nations or cobbled-together remnants of nations sent teams, and a record 64 won medals, which is 12 more than won medals four years ago in Seoul.

Among the first-time winners was Israel, which saw its silver and bronze in judo as crucial in changing its relationship with the Olympics. Now Israelis can remember the Games for more than the killing of 11 Israeli athletes and coaches by Palestinian terrorists at Munich in 1972.

Other historic triumphs included the first gold medal for Lithuania, the former Soviet republic which regained its Olympic independence in 1991; the first medals for Namibia, formerly part of South Africa and independent only since 1990; and the first medals since 1960 for South Africa, the pariah nation readmitted to the Olympic movement only after revoking its legal racial discrimination in 1991.

One of those two South African medals was won by white distance runner Elana Meyer in the 10,000 meters, where she finished second to Derartu Tulu of Ethiopia, the first black woman from Africa ever to win an Olympic medal. Their embrace and hand-in-hand victory lap provided one of those moments when the Olympic ideal of peace through sports seemed stunningly real.

Phil Hersh covers international sports for the *Chicago Tribune* and has been the *Tribune's* full-time Olympics writer since 1986.

Mike Powell/Allsport

Gold medal winner **Derartu Tulu** (left) of Ethiopia and silver medalist **Elana Meyer** of South Africa share the victory lap after their historic 10,000 meters.

Meanwhile, the (dis)Unified Team, a patchwork of 12 former Soviet republics, led the counts of gold and total medals. Gymnast Vitaly Scherbo of Belarus was responsible for a sizeable chunk, winning six golds, including the individual all-around.

The United States was second in both medal counts, having amassed its biggest total (108) since the essentially intramural Olympics in St. Louis 88 years ago. U.S. gymnast Shannon Miller of Edmond, Okla., was the leading medalist among the women, with two silver and three bronze.

Germany was third in the medal standings, although its 82 medals were 20 fewer than East Germany alone won at Seoul four years ago. The big gainers were China, which went from 28 medals in 1988 to 54 in 1992; and Spain, which went from 25 medals in the previous 92 years to 22 in Barcelona alone.

Beginning with the host country, this was an Olympics in which nations more than individuals were the standouts.

Swimmer Krisztina Egerszegi of Hungary, the youngest-ever (14) Olympic champion in her sport four years ago in Seoul, became the biggest individual-event winner among women in any sport this time, with three golds. Yet the shy Egerszegi could not draw the spotlight.

Carl Lewis of the U.S. wound up with as much acclaim as anyone after winning two golds in an Olympics where it had seemed doubtful he might win anything. In three Olympics, Lewis now has eight gold medals, one short of the recognized record.

While the "Dream Team" of NBA stars won the gold medal in men's basketball and commanded much of the world's media attention, these remained an Olympics without a compelling star, a Mark Spitz of 1972, Nadia Comaneci of 1976 or Lewis of 1984. They also avoided the stigma of being remembered for an anti-hero, like Ben Johnson in 1988.

Canada's Johnson, suspended for two years and stripped of his 100-meter gold medal after a positive steroid test, returned in a smaller and slower embodiment. He made the semifinals of the 100, but left in shame again after a fight with an official in the Olympic village.

Ten athletes tested positive in Seoul, including three gold medalists. The count in Barcelona was five, including four from track and field and three from the U.S.

Drugs were still a much-discussed topic in Barcelona, largely because of allegations and insinuations made by U.S. sprinters

Gwen Torrence (two gold, one silver in track) and Jenny Thompson (two gold, one silver in swimming). Torrence indicted most of her 100-meter rivals before later issuing an apology. Thompson cast doubt on the Chinese women swimmers. Sadly, both will be remembered more for their words than their achievements.

A man who finished his semifinal heat of the 400 meters on one leg and the arms of his father, Great Britain's Derek Redmond, became an Olympian figure of determination. Redmond, denied an Olympic appearance in 1988 because of injury, just wanted to complete the race, and his will was both exhilarating and excruciating to watch.

In a way, he was a symbol of an Olympics in which taking part and being part seemed the essential matters. For the 16 days and nights after the Olympic cauldron was lit by a disabled archer firing a flaming arrow into a wall of gas, the Olympics took on a warmth and liveliness no future Games may be able to match.

Hours after the flame went out, the crowds were still there on Montjuic. In our minds, they always will be.

Track & Field. There are several ways to look at the Olympic track meet. It can be seen as a triumph for the United States, which won more medals (30) than it had in any Olympics since 1956. Or it can be seen as a world games—one in which there were no double individual-event winners for the first Olympics since 1968; one in which Spain, Algeria and Lithuania won their first-ever track and field golds; in which the Bahamas, Qatar, Colombia and Namibia all won their first medals ever, in which there were first-ever golds for women from Greece and Ethiopia; and in which South Africa won its first medal in the sport since it was ostracized in 1960.

Or, it can be seen as the apotheosis of Carl Lewis (see box), whose third straight Olympic long jump title was accompanied by a brilliant anchor leg on the 4x100-meter relay. Those performances left no doubt that the 100-meter victory by Great Britain's Linford Christie—his 9.96 time made him at age 32 the oldest Olympic champion in the event—was diminished somewhat by Lewis' absence (because he was sixth in the U.S. Olympic trials' 100).

Carl Lewis Removes All Doubts

This was to be the Olympics of Gotterdammerung for Carl Lewis, a track and field god who seemed headed into his twilight.

No such Sturm und Drang.

With a gold medal in the long jump and another as anchor on a world record-setting relay team, Lewis was overshadowed by no one in his third Olympic Games.

Few would argue that he was the best athlete in Barcelona—just as he had been eight years earlier in Los Angeles, where his four gold medals matched event-by-event the 1936 achievement of the legendary Jesse Owens in Berlin.

More significantly, few would now argue that Lewis is the biggest star in the history of the Olympics; his total of eight gold medals (three straight in the long jump, two in the 100 meters, two in the 4 x 100 relay and one in the 200 meters) bettered by only four other athletes.

The all-time gold standard of 10 was set by America's Ray Ewry at the turn of the century, but those titles all came in standing jumps that are no longer held. Behind him are three athletes with nine gold medals each—Paavo Nurmi, track's legendary "Flying Finn" of the 1920s, who won in only four distance events that are still contested; U.S. swimmer Mark Spitz; and Soviet gymnast Larissa Latynina.

"I've said it all along: Carl is the greatest athlete I have ever seen, and he proves it time and time again," says Mel Rosen, head coach of the U.S. Olympic men's track and field team.

Of the 39 individual-event track and field gold medalists from 1988, only Lewis and heptathlete Jackie Joyner-Kersee of the U.S. also won individual golds in 1992.

"I don't know whether I'll make it back in 1996 or not," says Lewis, "but I sure would like to."

Why should there be any doubt? After all, at 31, an age when few athletes have been able to maintain their speed, Lewis added two more golds in events where running fast is a prerequisite—the long jump and 4 x 100-meter relay. And that was after coming to Barcelona as the underdog to world record-holder Mike Powell in the long jump

Wide World Photos

Carl Lewis wraps himself in the American flag after anchoring a world record run in the men's 4x100-meter relay for his eighth gold medal in three Olympics.

and a long-shot to make the relay after finishing sixth in the 100 meters at the U.S. Olympic Trials. At the trials, he had also placed a non-qualifying fourth in the 200 and was beaten for the second straight time by Powell in the long jump.

Those performances at the trials, which were partly the result of a month-long virus, made it easy to doubt Lewis. Why, he hadn't even qualified for a track race.

The long jump still augured to be the ultimate confrontation of the Games, since Powell had broken Bob Beamon's 23-year-old world record in 1991 with a jump of 29 feet, 4½ inches, and Lewis was the greatest long jumper of all time.

Swirling winds reduced both the effectiveness of each jumper and the drama of their showdown. Lewis reached a relatively modest 28-5½ inches on his first jump and did not get to 28 feet again. Powell finally hit exactly 28 on his fifth jump and then 28-4¼ on his last. It wasn't enough.

"That was my toughest gold medal of all," Lewis said afterward. He had won the event in Los Angeles by 11¾ inches and again in Seoul—where Powell was also second—by 9¼.

The relay gold came a lot easier, once Lewis had made the team after Mark Witherspoon's injury. Yet it was far more stunning, even though Mike Marsh, Leroy Burrell and Dennis Mitchell gave Lewis a comfortable lead before he began the anchor leg. Running like the Lewis of old, he took command of the sprint at 50 meters and drove to a world record of 37.40 seconds—exactly .1 faster than the Lewis-anchored relay at the 1991 World Championships.

This was the fifth time since 1983 that Lewis has anchored a world-record sprint relay, and he was on a sixth that tied the record. Eleven other men have run on those relays.

"I almost slowed up, I was so excited to get the baton," Lewis said. "I wanted to concentrate on breaking the record to show everyone I might have been ready to run the 100."

He showed even more than that, displaying a greatness that transcends one race or one Olympics. In Europe, they have long called Carl Lewis, "the son of the wind." In events as elemental as nature, running and jumping, he has outraced everything else, including the twilight.

The sprint relay record of 37.40 seconds, by Mike Marsh, Leroy Burrell, Dennis Mitchell and Lewis, was one of three world marks that fell in the Games, all to U.S. men. The most impressive was Kevin Young's 46.78 in the 400-meter hurdles, breaking Edwin Moses' 9-year-old mark of 47.02. The sport's oldest record, that set in 1968 for the 4x400-meter relay (2:56.16), also fell after it had been tied in 1988. This time, the quartet of Andrew Valmon, Quincy Watts, Michael Johnson and Steve Lewis clocked 2:55.74. Three days earlier, converted sprinter Watts had won the open 400 by the largest margin (.71 seconds) in 68 years with the second-fastest time (43.50) in the history of the race.

Few results were predictable. The meet's most overwhelming favorite, pole vaulter Sergei Bubka of Ukraine, failed to clear any height at all. Another solid favorite, Michael Johnson of the U.S., failed to make the final in the 200 meters. Lewis, 31, and Jackie Joyner-Kersee, 30, were the only 1988 Olympic champions to repeat. In winning her second heptathlon gold after a silver in 1984, Joyner-Kersee became both the first woman to win successive Olympic multi-event titles and the first athlete of either sex to win a multi-event medal in three Olympics. Joyner-Kersee, who also won the bronze medal in the long jump (the winner was Heike Drechsler of Germany), was the only athlete to win individual medals in both track and field.

Other highlights:

► Gail Devers of the U.S., who was close to having her feet amputated two years ago because of complications from originally misdiagnosed Graves Disease, won the women's 100.

► Devers, better known as a high hurdler, was on her way to victory in that event when she stumbled and fell over the last hurdle, finishing fifth behind Paraskevi Patoulidou, Greece's first track and field champion since 1912.

► In the absence of world champion Dan O'Brien, who failed to qualify for the U.S. team, Czechoslovakia's Robert Zmelik won the decathlon. Dave Johnson of the U.S. finished third, competing with a painful stress fracture in the foot.

► All three medalists in the shotput, Mike Stulce and Jim Doehring of the U.S.

Wide World Photos

Airborne **Jackie Joyner-Kersee** of the U.S. successfully defended her heptathlon title and picked up a bronze in the long jump.

and Vyacheslav Lykho of the Unified Team, had served suspensions for use of performance-enhancing drugs.

► Spain's Fermin Cacho won the slowest metric mile final (3:40.12) in the Olympics since 1956.

► Hwang Young Cho of South Korea corrected a historic wrong by winning the men's marathon. The only other Korean to win the event, Sohn Kee-Chung, was forced to represent his homeland's Japanese occupiers at Berlin in 1936.

Baseball. The Cuban juggernaut was every bit as successful as anticipated. Cuba went 9-0, outscored its opponents 95-16, had a .404 team batting average and a 1.27 ERA. The hastily-assembled U.S. team, together barely two months, lost the bronze, 8-3, to Japan.

Men's Basketball. While the NBA Dream Team dominated the competition and the scene as completely as expected (see box and page 300), the tournament took on another dimension for newly independent Lithuania. Its bronze-medal victory was especially significant, for it came against the Unified Team, the group of athletes from a country—the Soviet Union—that had first absorbed and then oppressed Lithuania for a half-century.

"This is Lithuania's victory, not our victory," said the team's star, Sarunas Marciulionis of the Golden State Warriors. "It is payback for the bad things, for things like Siberia."

The Dreamers beat Croatia, 117-85, in the final, a winning margin less than its average (43.8 points per game) throughout the tournament.

Women's Basketball. Using the same strategy his brother Aleksandr had in an upset of the U.S. men four years ago, Unified Team coach Yevgeny Gomelski and his women beat the U.S. women 79-73 in the semifinals and went on to win the gold with a 76-66 victory over China. The U.S. women, who had looked unbeatable until the semis, finished with a hollow bronze-medal triumph over Cuba.

Boxing. Allowed one entry in each of 12 weight classes, Cuba won seven golds, two silvers and 46 of 51 bouts. The U.S. managed just three medals and only one gold—by Oscar de la Hoya in the lightweight class. It was the fewest overall boxing medals for the U.S. since winning three in 1956 and the worst overall showing since 1948. Four-time world champion Eric Griffin had the biggest disappointment, losing a second-round bout in a controversial decision involving the sport's new computerized scoring system.

Canoe/Kayak. Greg Barton, the double gold medalist in Seoul, returned from a brief retirement to win a bronze in the 1,000-meter kayak singles. Barton, who won another bronze in 1984, thus became only the second singles kayaker to win medals in more than two Olympics.

In white water competition, revived after a 20-year absence since its Olympic debut at the 1972 Games in Munich, heavily favored Jon Lugbill of the U.S., a five-time world champion, was fourth in canoe singles, while Joe Jacobi and Scott Strausburgh of the U.S. won the doubles.

Cycling. German athletes were the big winners with seven (four gold), but rewards were justly doled out, especially for the women. France's Jeannie Longo, the greatest woman cyclist in history, finally won the Olympic medal (silver in road race) that had been missing from

Mike Powell/Allsport

American **Dave Johnson** (foreground) had to settle for a bronze medal in the decathlon, while Czechoslovakia's **Robert Zmelik** was the surprise winner.

her resumé. Erika Salumae, who won the 1988 match sprint title for the Soviet Union, did it again, but this time for her homeland of Estonia, the newly independent former Soviet republic.

Diving. Led by 13-year-old Fu Mingxia, the women's platform champion, the Chinese were runaway gold medalists in three of the four events. Mark Lenzi of the U.S. prevented a sweep by rallying on his seventh of 11 dives to beat China's Tan Liangde, who had been runner-up to the incomparable Greg Louganis four years ago. The U.S. performance, with just one gold and three medals, equalled its worst ever. For the first time since the event was introduced in 1920, the U.S. won no medal in women's springboard.

Gymnastics. The greatest gymnastics program ever created, that of the former USSR, passed into history with another series of brilliant performances. The former Soviets won the men's and women's team and individual all-around events, and their star, Vitaly Scherbo, was the biggest medal-winner of the Olympics.

Richard Martin/Allsport

Aleksandr Popov (left) of the Unified Team accepts the congratulations of runner-up **Matt Biondi** of the U.S. after winning the men's 50-meter freestyle.

Scherbo set an Olympic gymnastics record with six gold medals, including the individual all-around, in which athletes from three different ex-Soviet republics swept the medals.

Meanwhile, Trent Dimas of Albuquerque (high bar) got in just under the wire to earn, quite unexpectedly, the distinction as the only U.S. gymnast to win a gold medal in Olympic competition where the Soviets (or a reasonable facsimile) were present.

Equally surprising was the performance of 15-year-old Shannon Miller, who finished second in the all-around and balance beam and picked up three bronze medals as well.

The expected all-around battle between reigning world champion Kim Zmeskal of Houston and 1989 world champion Svetlana Boguinskaya of Belorus never developed. Zmeskal made a costly mistake on her first routine and wound up 10th, while the harshly-judged Boguinskaya, 19 and a young woman among munchkins, took fifth.

The all-around winner was 15-year-old Tatiana Gutsu of Ukraine, who had not qualified for the all-around but wound up competing after a convenient injury to one of the three Unified Team women who did. It came down to Gutsu's final vault, her last event in the competi-

tion, after which the winning margin over Miller was .012 points—the closest in Olympic history.

Swimming. There was something vaguely unsettling about the entire Olympic swimming competition. The U.S. team won 27 medals, nearly tripling the total of runner-up Germany, yet that somehow didn't seem like enough. Summer Sanders' performance was emblematic: she set U.S. records in the 200- and 400-meter individual medleys, winning silver and bronze medals, but was perceived as a failure until she added a gold in the 200 butterfly.

The Chinese women, whose pre-Olympic performances had been below ordinary, won four gold and five silver medals, prompting unfounded accusations of doping that led the International Swimming Federation to change its testing policy midway through the meet so that all winners were guaranteed to be sampled. The Chinese seem heiresses to East Germany, whose once-unbeatable women's program crumbled beyond recognition two years after unification.

Two ex-Soviet men, Aleksandr Popov (50 and 100 meters) and Yevgeny Sadovyi (200 and 400 meters), won four of the five men's freestyle gold medals. Their four golds equalled the total by all Soviet swimmers from 1956-88 (excluding the

The Beatle Of Barcelona

From the moment Magic Johnson established his position in the front row of the Olympic Stadium infield during the opening ceremonies, the Games of the XXVth Olympiad were his.

On the world stage, he was the one the whole world was watching. What he did on the basketball floor for the gold-medal-winning Dream Team was incidental. What he did for a world terrified by AIDS—among other things—was to show how much fun it is to be alive.

He may be HIV positive. He may have retired from the NBA because of the disease. He may have hurt his knee in the Dream Team's second game and gimped about for an average of only 20 minutes per game in the tournament. But none of that mattered to the Spanish fans who worshipped him or the hundreds of other athletes for whom the high point of the opening ceremonies was to steal a Magic moment.

Johnson's megawatt smile, as bright as the Barcelona sun, attracted athletes as a light would moths. Rather than swat at them, as many superstars would have done, he obliged autograph seekers and picture-takers from as many countries as could get close to him on the stadium infield.

It was as if there were two reviewing stands during the parade of nations. One, draped in regal trappings, merely held King Juan Carlos of Spain. The other, the one commanding all the attention, had no formal designation. Just one 6-foot, 9-inch man, towering above the 65,000 in Olympic Stadium.

"This wasn't a basketball player," wrote Mike Downey of the *Los Angeles Times*, assessing Johnson's celebrity, "this was a Beatle."

Brazilians swarmed him. Chinese women sought pictures. American women squeezed their way from the back of the delegation to touch him. Athletes climbed onto each other's shoulders to photograph him. The entire Puerto Rican delegation stopped to take pictures as they marched past him. Several Spanish athletes lagged 15 meters behind the rest of the team to get their photos taken in front of him.

While most of the Dream Teamers holed up between games in their $900-a-night luxury hotel, Johnson was out experienc-

Wide World Photos

While many of his Dream Team mates remained in their luxury hotel, **Magic Johnson** ventured out often to enjoy the entire Olympic experience.

ing the fun and Games—checking out the competition in gymnastics, boxing, track and women's basketball. He walked two-month-old Earvin Jr. along the Rambla, attracting happy followers like the Pied Piper. He bought $5,000 worth of toys for Barcelona Olympic officials to distribute to needy children at Christmas.

And he enlisted the help of IOC president Juan Antonio Samaranch in the fight against AIDS. Asked if that meant financial help, Johnson replied, "No, but when he (Samaranch) speaks, people listen. That's what we need."

The Dream Team barely had to work up a sweat on its way to the gold medal. Yet Magic, who came to Barcelona with an NCAA title and five world championship rings already in his trophy case, placed the Olympic victory above them all.

"It was," he said, "the most awesome feeling I ever had winning anything. The most exciting thing I've ever been through. I got goosebumps all over my body."

He wasn't alone.

1980 Games boycotted by the U.S.). When Kieren Perkins of Australia won the 1,500 free in world-record time, it marked the first time since 1960 that the U.S. men had failed to win at least one Olympic freestyle race. Moreover, the American men lost the 4x200 freestyle relay for the first time since 1956.

There were nine world records set and one tied in the meet's 31 events—four (plus the tie) by the U.S., two each by China and the ex-Soviets, and one by Australia.

Krisztina Egerszegi of Hungary, youngest swimming gold medalist ever in 1988, won three more golds this time, in the 100- and 200-meter backstroke and 400-meter individual medley.

Victory in the 800-meter freestyle gave beleaguered Janet Evans of Placentia, Calif., a well-earned gold medal after enduring four years in which she had struggled, usually in vain, to match the expectations created by her three-gold-medal performance of Seoul. Evans, a world-weary 21, also had a silver medal in the 400 free.

Mike Barrowman, who had spent four years being driven by bad memories of his fourth-place finish in the 200-meter breaststroke in Seoul, won in Barcelona by setting his sixth world record in four years at the distance.

Matt Biondi, winner of seven medals in 1988, added three more to his collection, a silver in the 50 free, a gold in the 4x100 freestyle relay, and another gold for swimming the preliminary for the 4x100 medley relay team that went on to win the finals. His career medal count of 11 (8 gold, 2 silver, 1 bronze) ties shooter Carl Osburn (1912 and '20) and swimmer Mark Spitz (1968-72) for most ever by a U.S. athlete.

For another U.S. swimmer, Ron Karnaugh, the Olympic experience was a sadly eerie sequel to what happened to speedskater Dan Jansen in 1988, when his sister died the morning of his first competition. Karnaugh's father died after suffering a heart attack in the Olympic Stadium during Opening Ceremonies. Karnaugh, a medal favorite in the 200 IM, wound up sixth.

The most popular victories were those of a pair of Latino-Americans, Martin Lopez-Zubero of Jacksonville, Fla., and Pablo Morales of Stanford, Calif. Lopez-Zubero, a dual citizen who competed for Spain, became his country's first swimming gold medalist ever with a victory in the 200 backstroke. Morales, a Cuban-American competing for the U.S. after a three-year retirement from the sport, won the 100 butterfly to become, at 27, the oldest gold medalist in swimming history.

Volleyball. After struggling nearly four years to approach the level at which they won the 1984 and 1988 golds, the U.S. men regrouped when several '88 veterans, including Steve Timmons, returned in the spring. The team came home with a bronze medal, making Timmons the second person (joining Japan's Masayuki Minami) to win volleyball medals in three Olympics.

The U.S. women were the only team to extend gold-medal-winning Cuba beyond four sets, but they lost that semifinal match before beating Brazil for the bronze medal.

Weightlifting. Lifters from five different former Soviet republics won medals for the Unified Team, while the remaining five golds went to athletes from five more countries. One of them was Turkey's Naim Suleymanoglu, who reprised his Seoul triumph by lifting far less than his world-record performances of five years ago. Stricter drug testing has obviously had a major effect on this sport, which had two gold and one silver medalist disqualified in Seoul, where 15 world and 24 Olympic records were set. In Barcelona, there were no world records and just two Olympic marks.

Wrestling. The best U.S. freestyle wrestling team ever won three gold medals: heavyweight Bruce Baumgartner, 31, who reversed the 1988 final decision against David Gobedjishvili of Georgia (the ex-Soviet republic); Kevin Jackson at 180.5 lbs.; and John Smith, who won a second straight gold at 136.5.

Drugs. There were five positive drug tests among nearly 1,900 samples analyzed at the Olympics, four from track and field and two involving U.S. athletes. The highest finisher busted was fourth-place hammer thrower Jud Logan of Canton, Ohio, who was positive for clenbuterol, a drug with stimulant and steroidal qualities. ☐

THE 1993 INFORMATION PLEASE SPORTS ALMANAC

OLYMPICS STATISTICS

THE GAMES IN REVIEW

1992

BARCELONA

SEC A

PAGE 565

Final Medal Standings

National medal standings are not recognized by the IOC. The unofficial point totals are based on three points for every gold medal, two for each silver and one for each bronze. Demonstration sport medals not included.

		G	S	B	Total	Points			G	S	B	Total	Points
1	Unified Team	45	38	29	112	240	34	Ireland	1	1	0	2	5
2	**United States**	37	34	37	108	216		Ethiopia	1	0	2	3	5
3	Germany	33	21	28	82	169		Latvia	0	2	1	3	5
4	China	16	22	16	54	108	37	Algeria	1	0	1	2	4
5	Cuba	14	6	11	31	65		Estonia	1	0	1	2	4
6	Hungary	11	12	7	30	64		Lithuania	1	0	1	2	4
7	South Korea	12	5	12	29	58		Belgium	0	1	2	3	4
8	Spain	13	7	2	22	55		Croatia	0	1	2	3	4
9	France	8	5	16	29	50		Iran	0	1	2	3	4
	Australia	7	9	11	27	50		Yugoslavs	0	1	2	3	4
11	Italy	6	5	8	19	36		Austria	0	2	0	2	4
	Japan	3	8	11	22	36		Namibia	0	2	0	2	4
13	Canada	6	5	7	18	35		South Africa	0	2	0	2	4
14	Great Britain	5	3	12	20	33	47	Israel	0	1	1	2	3
15	Romania	4	6	8	18	32		Switzerland	1	0	0	1	3
16	Poland	3	6	10	19	31	49	Mongolia	0	0	2	2	2
17	Bulgaria	3	7	6	16	29		Slovenia	0	0	2	2	2
18	Holland	2	6	7	15	25		Mexico	0	1	0	1	2
19	Sweden	1	7	4	12	21		Peru	0	1	0	1	2
20	Czechoslovakia	4	2	1	7	17		Taiwan	0	1	0	1	2
	North Korea	4	0	5	9	17		Argentina	0	0	1	1	1
22	Kenya	2	4	2	8	16	55	Bahamas	0	0	1	1	1
	New Zealand	1	4	5	10	16		Colombia	0	0	1	1	1
24	Norway	2	4	1	7	15		Ghana	0	0	1	1	1
25	Turkey	2	2	2	6	12		Malaysia	0	0	1	1	1
26	Indonesia	2	2	1	5	11		Pakistan	0	0	1	1	1
27	Finland	1	2	2	5	9		Philippines	0	0	1	1	1
	Denmark	1	1	4	6	9		Puerto Rico	0	0	1	1	1
29	Brazil	2	1	0	3	8		Qatar	0	0	1	1	1
30	Jamaica	0	3	1	4	7		Suriname	0	0	1	1	1
	Nigeria	0	3	1	4	7		Thailand	0	0	1	1	1
32	Greece	2	0	0	2	6							
	Morocco	1	1	1	3	6							

Note: The Unified Team included former Soviet Union republics of Belarus, Kazakhstan, Russia, Ukraine and Uzbekistan.

Leading Medal Winners

(*) Indicates at least one medal earned as preliminary member of eventual medal-winning relay team.

MEN

No		Sport	G-S-B	No		Sport	G-S-B
6	Vitaly Scherbo, UT	Gymnastics	6-0-0	2	Kay Bluhm, GER	Kayaking	2-0-0
5	Grigory Misiutin, UT	Gymnastics	1-4-0	2	Nikolai Boukhalov, BUL	Canoeing	2-0-0
4	Aleksandr Popov, UT	Gymnastics	2-2-0	2	Tamás Darnyi, HUN	Swimming	2-0-0
3	Yevgeny Sadovyi, UT	Swimming	3-0-0	2	**Nelson Diebel**, USA	Swimming	2-0-0
3*	**Matt Biondi**, USA	Swimming	2-1-0	2	Torsten Gutsche, GER	Kayaking	2-0-0
3	**Jon Olsen**, USA	Swimming	2-0-1	2	**Carl Lewis**, USA	Track/Field	2-0-0
3*	**Mel Stewart**, USA	Swimming	2-0-1	2	**Mike Marsh**, USA	Track/Field	2-0-0
3*	Vladimir Pychnenko, UT	Swimming	1-2-0	2	**Pablo Morales**, USA	Swimming	2-0-0
3	Li Xiaoshuang, CHN	Gymnastics	1-1-1	2	Matthew Ryan, AUS	Equestrian	2-0-0
3	Li Jing, CHN	Gymnastics	0-3-0	2	Arkadiusz Skrzypaszek, POL	M.Pentath	2-0-0
3	Anders Holmertz, SWE	Swimming	0-2-1	2	**Quincy Watts**, USA	Track/Field	2-0-0
3	Andreas Wecker, GER	Gymnastics	0-1-2				

Leading Medal Winners (Cont.)

No		Sport	G-S-B
2	Jens Lehmann, GER	Cycling	1-1-0
2	**Steve Lewis**, USA	Track/Field	1-1-0
2	Ulrich Papke, GER.	Canoeing	1-1-0
2	Kieren Perkins, AUS	Swimming	1-1-0
2	Piet Raymakers, HOL	Equestrian	1-1-0
2	**Jeff Rouse**, USA	Swimming	1-1-0
2	Ingo Spelly, GER	Canoeing	1-1-0
2	Bence Szabo, HUN.	Fencing	1-1-0
2*	Veniamin Taianovitch, UT	Swimming	1-1-0
2	Wang Yifu, CHN.	Shooting	1-1-0
2	Klaus Balkenhol, GER	Equestrian	1-0-1
2	Valery Belenki, UT	Gymnastics	1-0-1
2*	**David Berkoff**, USA	Swimming	1-0-1
2	**Joe Hudepohl**, USA	Swimming	1-0-1
2	**Tom Jager**, USA.	Swimming	1-0-1
2	Igor Korobchinski, UT.	Gymnastics	1-0-1
2	**Dennis Mitchell**, USA	Track/Field	1-0-1
2	Mark Tewksbury, CAN	Swimming	1-0-1

No		Sport	G-S-B
2	Frankie Fredericks, NAM	Track/Field	0-2-0
2	Pavel Khnykine, UT.	Swimming	0-2-0
2	Norbert Rozsa, HUN	Swimming	0-2-0
2	Vladimir Selkov, UT	Swimming	0-2-0
2	Herbert Blocker, GER.	Equestrian	0-1-1
2	Knut Holmann, NOR.	Kayaking	0-1-1
2	Pavel Kolobkov, UT.	Fencing	0-1-1
2	Guo Linyao, CHN.	Gymnastics	0-1-1
2	Robert Tait, NZE	Equestrian	0-1-1
2	Edouard Zenovka, UT.	Mod.Pentathlon	0-1-1
2	Yukio Iketani, JPN.	Gymnastics	0-0-2
2	Goran Ivanisevic, CRO.	Tennis	0-0-2
2	Jean-Francois Lamour, FRA.	Fencing	0-0-2
2	Masayuki Matsunaga, JPN	Gymnastics	0-0-2
2	Kim Taek-Soo, S.KOR	Table Tennis	0-0-2
2	Simon Terry, GBR	Archery	0-0-2

Richard Martin/Allsport
Egerszegi

Yahn Guichaoua/Allsport
Scherbo

Bob Martin/Allsport
Sanders

Wide World Photos
Miller

WOMEN

No		Sport	G-S-B
5	**Shannon Miller**, USA	Gymnastics	0-2-3
4	Tatiana Gutsu, UT	Gymnastics	2-1-1
4	Lavinia Milosovici, ROM.	Gymnastics	2-1-1
4*	**Summer Sanders**, USA	Swimming	2-1-1
4	Franziska van Almsick, GER	Swimming	0-2-2
3	Krisztina Egerszegi, HUN.	Swimming	3-0-0
3*	**Nicole Haislett**, USA.	Swimming	3-0-0
3*	**Crissy Ahmann-Leighton**, USA	Swimming	2-1-0
3	**Jenny Thompson**, USA.	Swimming	2-1-0
3	**Gwen Torrence**, USA.	Track/Field	2-1-0
3	Tatiana Lysenko, UT.	Gymnastics	2-0-1
3	Lin Li, CHN.	Swimming	1-2-0
3	Dagmar Hase, GER.	Swimming	1-2-0
3	Zhuang Yong, CHN.	Swimming	1-2-0
3	Rita Koban, HUN.	Kayaking	1-1-1
3	**Anita Nall**, USA	Swimming	1-1-1
3	Daniela Hunger, GER.	Swimming	0-1-2
2	Cho Youn-Jeong, S.KOR	Archery	2-0-0
2	Marina Logvinenko, UT	Shooting	2-0-0
2	Giovanna Trillini, ITA	Fencing	2-0-0
2	Deng Yaping, CHN.	Table Tennis	2-0-0
2	Olga Bryzgina, UT	Track/Field	1-1-0
2	**Janet Evans**, USA	Swimming	1-1-0
2	Qiao Hong, CHN.	Table Tennis	1-1-0
2	Lu Li, CHN.	Gymnastics	1-1-0

No		Sport	G-S-B
2	Elisabeta Lipa, ROM	Rowing	1-1-0
2	Kim Soo-Nyung, S.KOR	Archery	1-1-0
2	Henrietta Onodi, HUN.	Gymnastics	1-1-0
2	Ramona Portwich, GER	Kayaking	1-1-0
2	Birgit Schmidt, GER	Kayaking	1-1-0
2	Anke Von Seck, GER	Kayaking	1-1-0
2	Yang Wenyi, CHN	Swimming	1-1-0
2	Isabelle Werth, GER.	Equestrian	1-1-0
2	Eva Donusz, HUN	Kayaking	1-0-1
2	**Mary Joe Fernandez**, USA	Tennis	1-0-1
2	Sally Gunnell, GBR	Track/Field	1-0-1
2	**Jackie Joyner-Kersee**, USA	Track/Field	1-0-1
2	**Lea Loveless**, USA.	Swimming	1-0-1
2	**Angel Martino**, USA.	Swimming	1-0-1
2	Yelena Rudkovskaya, UT.	Swimming	1-0-1
2	Veronica Cochelea, ROM.	Rowing	0-2-0
2	Juliet Cuthbert, JAM	Track/Field	0-2-0
2	Agneta Andersson, SWE	Kayaking	0-1-1
2	Cristina Bontas, ROM.	Gymnastics	0-1-1
2	Hayley Lewis, AUS	Swimming	0-1-1
2	Irina Privalova, UT.	Track/Field	0-1-1
2	Aranxta Sanchez Vicario, SPA	Tennis	0-1-1
2	Li Bun Hui, N.KOR	Table Tennis	0-0-2
2	Hyun Jung-Hwa, S.KOR	Table Tennis	0-0-2
2*	Kerstin Kielgass, GER.	Swimming	0-0-2
2	Natalia Valveeva, UT	Archery	0-0-2

MEDAL SPORTS

Medal winners in individual sports contested at Barcelona, Spain, from July 25-Aug. 9, 1992. Team sport summaries from Baseball to Water Polo begin on page 576. Demonstration sports are not included.

ARCHERY
(70 meters)

MEN

Individual: 1. Sebastian Flute, FRA, def. **2.** Chung Jae-Hun, S.KOR (110-107); **3.** Simon Terry, GBR, def. Bertil Martinus Grov, NOR (109-103).
Team: 1. Spain def. **2.** Finland (238-236); **3.** Great Britain def. France (233-231).

WOMEN

Individual: 1. Cho Youn-Jeong, S.KOR, def. **2.** Kim Soo-Nyung, S.KOR (112-105); **3.** Natalia Valeeva, UT, def. Wang Xiaozhu, CHN (104-102).
Team: 1. South Korea def. **2.** China (236-228); **3.** Unified Team def. France (240-222).

BADMINTON

MEN

Singles: 1. Alan Budi Kusuma, INA, def **2.** Ardy Wiranata, INA (15-12, 18-13); **3.** Thomas Stuer-Lauridsen, DEN, and Hermawan Susanto, INA.
Doubles: 1. Kim Moon-Soo & Park Joo-Bong, S.KOR, def. **2.** Eddy Hartono & Rudy Gunawan, INA (15-11, 15-7); **3.** Li Yongbo & Tian Bingyi, CHN, and Sidek Razif & Sidek Jalani, MAL.

WOMEN

Singles: 1. Susi Susanti, INA, def. **2.** Bang Soo Hyun, S.KOR (5-11, 11-5, 11-3); **3.** Huang Hua, CHN, and Tang Jiuhong, CHN.
Doubles: 1. Hwang Hye Young & Chung So-Young, S.KOR def **2.** Guan Weizhen & Nong Qunhua, CHN (18-16, 12-15, 15-13); **3.** Gil Young-Ah & Shim Eun-Jung, S. KOR, and Lin Yanfen & Yao Fen, CHN.

BOXING

Light Flyweight (106 lbs): **1.** Rogelio Marcelo, CUB, dec. **2.** Daniel Bojinov, BUL (24-10); **3.** Jan Quast, GER, and Roel Velasco, PHI.
Flyweight (112 lbs): **1.** Su Choi-Chol, N.KOR, dec. **2.** Raul Gonzalez, CUB (12-2); **3.** Timothy Austin, USA, and Istvan Kovacs, HUN.
Bantamweight (119 lbs): **1.** Joel Casamayor, CUB, dec. **2.** Wayne McCullough, IRE (14-8); **3.** Li Gwang Sik, N.KOR, and Mohamed Achik, MOR.
Featherweight (125 lbs): **1.** Andreas Tews, GER, dec. **2.** Faustino Reyes, SPA (16-7); **3.** Hocine Soltani, ALG and Ramazi Paliani, UT.
Lightweight (132 lbs): **1.** Oscar De La Hoya, USA, dec. **2.** Marco Rudolph, GER (7-2); **3.** Hong Sung-Sik, N.KOR and Namjil Bayarsaikhan, MON.
Light Welterweight (139 lbs): **1.** Hector Vinent, CUB, dec. **2.** Mark Leduc, CAN (11-1); **3.** Jyri Kjall, FIN and Leonard Doroftei, ROM.
Welterweight (147 lbs): **1.** Michael Carruth, IRE, dec. **2.** Juan Hernandez, CUB (13-10); **3.** Anibal Acevedo, PUR, and Arkom Chenglai, THA.
Light Middleweight (156 lbs): **1.** Juan Lemus, CUB, dec. **2.** Orhan Delibas, HOL (6-1); **3.** Gyorgy Mizsei, HUN, and Robin Reid, GBR.
Middleweight (165 lbs): **1.** Ariel Hernandez, CUB, dec. **2.** Chris Byrd, USA (12-7); **3.** Chris Johnson, CAN, and Lee Seung-Bae, S.KOR.

Light Heavyweight (178 lbs): **1.** Torsten May, GER, dec. **2.** Rostislav Zaoulitchnyi, UT (8-3); **3.** Zoltan Beres, HUN, and Wojciech Bartnik, POL.
Heavyweight (201 lbs): **1.** Felix Savon, CUB, dec. **2.** David Izonritei, NIG (14-1); **3.** Arnold van der Lijde, HOL, and David Tua, NZE.
Super Heavyweight (over 201 lbs): **1.** Roberto Balado, CUB, dec. **2.** Richard Igbineghu, NIG (13-2); **3.** Brian Nielsen, DEN, and Svilen Roussinov, BUL.

CANOE/KAYAK

MEN

Canoe 500m Singles: 1. Nikolai Boukhalov, BUL (1:51.15); **2.** Mikhail Slivinski, UT (1:51.40); **3.** Olaf Heukrodt, GER (1:53.00).
Canoe 1000m Singles: 1. Nikolai Boukhalov, BUL (4:05.92); **2.** Ivan Klementiev, LAT (4:06.60); **3.** Gyorgy Zala, HUN (4:07.53).
Canoe 500m Doubles: 1. Aleksandr Masseikov & Dmitri Dovgalenok, UT (1:41.54); **2.** Ulrich Papke & Ingo Spelly, GER (1:41.68); **3.** Martin Marinov & Blagovest Stoyanov, BUL (1:41.94).
Canoe 1000m Doubles: 1. Ulrich Papke & Ingo Spelly, GER (3:37.42); **2.** Arne Nielsson & Christian Frederiksen, DEN (3:39.26); **3.** Didier Hoyer & Olivier Boivin, FRA (3:39.51).
Canoe Slalom Singles: 1. Lukas Pollert, CZE (113.69 pts); **2.** Gareth Marriott, GBR (116.48); **3.** Jacky Avril, FRA (117.18).
Canoe Slalom Doubles: 1. Scott Strausbaugh & Joe Jacobi, USA (122.41 pts); **2.** Miroslva Simek & Jiri Rohan, CZE (124.25); **3.** Franck Adisson & Wilfrid Forgues, FRA (124.38).
Kayak 500m Singles: 1. Mikko Kolehmainen, FIN (1:40.34); **2.** Zsolt Gyulay, HUN (1:40.64); **3.** Knut Holmann, NOR (1:40.71).
Kayak 1000m Singles: 1. Clint Robinson, AUS (3:37.26); **2.** Knut Holmann, NOR (3:37.50); **3.** Greg Barton, USA (3:37.93).
Kayak 500m Doubles: 1. Kay Bluhm & Torsten Gutsche, GER (1:28.27); **2.** Maciej Freimut & Wojciech Kurpiewski, POL (1:29.84); **3.** Antonio Rossi & Bruno Dreossi, ITA (1:30.00).
Kayak 1000m Doubles: 1. Kay Bluhm & Torsten Gutsche, GER (3:16.10); **2.** Gunnar Olsson & Karl Sundqvist, SWE (3:17.70); **3.** Grzegorz Kotowicz & Dariusz Bialkowski, POL (3:18.86).
Kayak 1000m Fours: 1. Germany (2:54.18); **2.** Hungary (2:54.82); **3.** Australia (2:56.97).
Kayak Slalom Singles: 1. Pierpaolo Ferrazzi, ITA (106.89 pts); **2.** Sylvain Curinier, FRA (107.06); **3.** Jochen Lettmann, GER (108.52).

WOMEN

Kayak 500m Singles: 1. Birgit Schmidt, GER (1:51.60); **2.** Rita Koban, HUN (1:51.96); **3.** Izabella Dylewska, POL (1:52.36).
Kayak 500m Doubles: 1. Ramona Portwich & Anke von Seck, GER (1:40.29); **2.** Susanne Gunnarsson & Agneta Andersson, SWE (1:40.41); **3.** Rita Koban & Eva Donusz, HUN (1:40.81).
Kayak 500m Fours: 1. Hungary (1:38.32); **2.** Germany (1:38.47); **3.** Sweden (1:39.79).
Kayak Slalom Singles: 1. Elisabeth Micheler, GER (126.41 pts); **2.** Danielle Woodward, AUS (128.27); **3.** Dana Chladek, USA (131.75).

CYCLING

MEN

Time Trial (1km): **1.** Jose Moreno, SPA (1:03.342, OR); **2.** Shane Kelly, AUS (1:04.288); **3.** Erin Hartwell, USA (1:04.753).

Individual Match Sprint (3 laps): **1.** Jens Fiedler, GER; **2.** Garry Neiwand, AUS; **3.** Curtis Harnett, CAN.

Individual Points Race: 1. Giovanni Lombardi, ITA (44 pts); **2.** Leon Van Bon, HOL (43); **3.** Cedric Mathy, BEL (41).

Individual Pursuit (4000m): **1.** Chris Boardman, GBR (4:24.496, WR); **2.** Jens Lehmann, GER (overtaken); **3.** Gary Anderson, NZE (4:31.061).

Team Pursuit (4000m): **1.** Germany (4:08.791, WR); **2.** Australia (4:10.218); **3.** Denmark (4:15.860).

Individual Road Race: 1. Fabio Casartelli, ITA (4:35.21.00); **2.** Erik Dekker, HOL (4:35.22); **3.** Dainis Ozols, LAT (4:35.24).

Team Road Race (100km): **1.** Germany (2:01.39); **2.** Italy (2:02:39.00); **3.** France (2:05:25.00).

WOMEN

Individual Match Sprint (3 laps): **1.** Erika Salumae, EST; **2.** Annett Newmann, GER; **3.** Ingrid Haringa, HOL.

Individual Pursuit (3000m): **1.** Petra Rossner, GER (3:41.753); **2.** Kathryn Watt, AUS (3:43.438); **3.** Rebecca Twigg, USA (3:52.429).

Individual Road Race (83km): **1.** Kathryn Watt, AUS (2:04:42); **2.** Jeannie Longo, FRA (2:05:02); **3.** Monique Knol, HOL (2:05:03).

DIVING

MEN

Springboard: 1. Mark Lenzi, USA (676.53 pts); **2.** Tan Liangde, CHN (645.57); **3.** Dmitri Sautine, UT (627.78).

Platform: 1. Sun Shuewi, CHN (677.31 pts); **2.** Scott Donie, USA (633.63); **3.** Xiong Ni, CHN (600.15).

WOMEN

Springboard: 1. Gao Min, CHN (572.40 pts); **2.** Irina Lashko, UT (514.14); **3.** Brita Pia Baldus, GER (503.07).

Platform: 1. Fu Mingxia, CHN (461.43 pts); **2.** Elena Mirochina, UT (411.63); **3.** Mary Ellen Clark, USA (401.91).

EQUESTRIAN

Horses in parentheses.

Individual Dressage: 1. Nicole Uphoff (Rembrandt), GER (1,626 pts); **2.** Isabelle Werth (Gigolo), GER (1,551); **3.** Klaus Balkenhol (Goldstern), GER (1,515).

Team Dressage: 1. Germany (5,224 pts);**2.**Holland (4,742);**3.** USA (4,643).

Individual Jumping: 1. Ludger Beerbaum (Classic Touch), GER (0 pts); **2.** Piet Raymakers (Ratina Z), HOL (0.25); **3.** Norman Dello Joio (Irish), USA (4.75).

Team Jumping: 1. Holland (12.00 pts); **2.** Austria (16.75); **3.** France (24.75).

Individual 3-Day Event: 1. Matthew Ryan (Kibah Tic Toc), AUS (70.0 pts); **2.** Herbert Blocker (Feine Dame), GER (81.30); **3.** Robert Tait (Messiah), NZE (87.60).

Team 3-Day Event: 1. Australia (288.60 pts); **2.** New Zealand (290.80); **3.** Germany (300.30).

FENCING

MEN

Individual Foil: 1. Philippe Omnes, FRA, def. **2.** Sergei Goloubitski, UT (6-5, 3-5, 5-2); **3.** Elvis Gregory Gil, CUB, def. Udo Wagner, GER (5-3, 2-5, 5-3).

Team Foil: 1. Germany def. **2.** Cuba (8-8, 65-53 on touches); **3.** Poland def. Hungary (9-4).

Individual Sabre: 1. Bence Szabo, HUN, def. **2.** Marco Marin, ITA (5-1, 5-1); **3.** Jean-Francois Lamour, FRA, def. Giovanni Scalzo, ITA (3-5, 6-5, 5-1).

Team Sabre: 1. Unified Team def. **2.** Hungary (9-5); **3.** France def. Romania (9-4).

Individual Epee: 1. Eric Srecki, FRA, def. **2.** Pavel Kolobkov, UT (6-5, 5-2); **3.** Jean-Michel Henry, FRA, def. Kaido Kaaberma, EST (5-1, 5-2, 5-3).

Team Epee: 1. Germany def. **2.** Hungary (8-4); **3.** Unified Team def. France (8-8, 70-66 on touches).

WOMEN

Individual Foil: 1. Giovanna Trillini, ITA, def. **2.** Wang Huifeng, CHN (5-6, 5-3, 6-5); **3.** Tatiana Sadovskaya, UT, def. Laurence Modaine, FRA (5-1, 1-5, 5-3).

Team Foil: 1. Italy def. **2.** Germany (9-6); **3.** Romania def. Unified Team (8-8, 60-55 on touches).

GYMNASTICS

MEN

All-Around

		Points
1	Vitaly Scherbo, UT.	59.025
2	Grigory Misiutin, UT	58.925
3	Valery Belenki, UT.	58.625

Floor Exercise

		Points
1	Li Xiaosahuang, CHN.	9.925
2	(Tie) Grigory Misiutin, UT	9.787
	Yukio Iketani, JPN	9.787

Horizontal Bar

		Points
1	Trent Dimas, USA	9.875
2	(Tie) Andreas Wecker, GER.	9.837
	Grigory Misiutin, UT	9.837

Parallel Bars

		Points
1	Vitaly Scherbo, UT.	9.900
2	Li Jing, CHN	9.812
3	(Tie) Igor Korobchinski, UT	9.800
	Guo Linyao, CHN	9.800
	Masayuki Matsunaga, JPN	9.800

Top 10 USA: 6th—Jari Lynch (9.712).

Pommel Horse

		Points
1	(Tie) Vitaly Scherbo, UT.	9.925
	Pae Gil-Su, N.KOR	9.925
3	Andreas Wecker, GER.	9.887

Top 10 USA: 5th—Chris Waller (9.825).

Rings

		Points
1	Vitaly Scherbo, UT.	9.937
2	Li Jing, CHN	9.875
3	(Tie) Andreas Wecker, GER.	9.862
	Li Xiaosahuang, CHN.	9.862

Vault

		Points
1	Vitaly Scherbo, UT.	9.856
2	Grigory Misiutin, UT	9.781
3	Yoo Ok Ryul, S.KOR	9.762

Team

		Points
1	Unified Team	585.450
2	China	580.375
3	Japan	578.250

USA entry: 6th—Trent Dimas, Scott Keswick, Jair Lynch, Dominick Minicucci, John Roethlisberger, Chris Waller (571.725).

WOMEN
All-Around

		Points
1	Tatiana Gutsou, UT	39.737
2	Shannon Miller, USA	39.725
3	Laviana Milosovici, ROM	39.687

Other Top 10 USA: 10th—Kim Zmeskal (39.412)

Floor Exercise

		Points
1	Lavinia Milosovici, ROM	10.000
2	Henrietta Onodi, HUN	9.950
3	(Tie) Cristina Bontas, ROM	9.912
	Tatiana Gutsu, UT	9.912
	Shannon Miller, USA	9.912

Balance Beam

		Points
1	Tatiana Lysenko, UT	9.975
2	(Tie) Lü Li, CHN	9.912
	Shannon Miller, USA	9.912

Other Top 10 USA: 6th—Betty Okino (9.837).

Uneven Bars

		Points
1	Lu Li, CHN	10.000
2	Tatiana Gutsu, UT	9.975
3	Shannon Miller, USA	9.962

Vault

		Points
1	(Tie) Henrietta Onodi, HUN	9.925
	Lavinia Milosovici, ROM	9.925
3	Tatiana Lysenko, UT	9.912

Top 10 USA: 8th—Kim Zmeskal (9.593).

Team

		Points
1	Unified Team	395.666
2	Romania	395.079
3	United States	394.704

USA entry: Wendy Bruce, Dominique Dawes, Shannon Miller, Betty Okino, Kerri Strug, Kim Zmeskal.

Rhythmic All-Around

		Points
1	Aleksandra Timoshenko, UT	59.037
2	Carolina Pascual, SPA	58.100
3	Oksana Skaldina, UT	57.912

JUDO

MEN

Extra Lightweight (132 lbs): **1.** Nazim Gousseinov, UT; **2.** Yoon Hyun, S.KOR; **3.** Tadanori Koshino, JPN, and Richard Trautmann, GER.

Half-Lightweight (143 lbs): **1.** Rogerio Sampaio, BRA; **2.** Josef Csak, HUN; **3.** Udo Quellmalz, GER, and Israel Hernandez, CUB.

Lightweight (157 lbs): **1.** Toshihiko Koga, JPN; **2.** Bertalan Hajtos, HUN; **3.** Chung Hoon, S.KOR, and Shay Oren Smadga, ISR.

Half-Middleweight (172 lbs): **1.** Hidehiko Yoshida, JPN; **2.** Jason Morris, USA; **3.** Bertrand Damaisin, FRA, and Kim Byung-Joo, S.KOR.

Middleweight (190 lbs): **1.** Waldemar Legien, POL; **2.** Pascal Tayot, FRA; **3.** Hirotaka Okada, JPN, and Nicholas Gill, CAN.

Half-Heavyweight (209 lbs): **1.** Antal Kovacs, HUN; **2.** Raymond Stevens, GBR; **3.** Dmitri Sergeev, UT, and Theo Meijer, HOL.

Heavyweight (over 209 lbs): **1.** David Khakhaleichvili, UT; **2.** Naoya Ogawa, JPN; **3.** David Douillet, FRA, and Imre Csosz, HUN.

WOMEN

Extra Lightweight (106 lbs): **1.** Cecile Nowak, FRA; **2.** Ryoko Tamura, JPN; **3.** Hulya Senyurt, TUR, and Amarilis Savon, CUB.

Half-Lightweight (115 lbs): **1.** Almudena Munoz, SPA; **2.** Noriko Mizoguchi, JPN; **3.** Li Zhongyoun, CHN, and Sharon Rendle, GBR.

Lightweight (123 lbs): **1.** Miriam Blasco, SPA; **2.** Nicola Kim Fairbrother, GBR; **3.** Chiyori Tateno, JPN, and Driulis Gonzalez, CUB.

Half-Middleweight (134 lbs): **1.** Catherine Fleury, FRA; **2.** Yael Arad, ISR; **3.** Zhang Di, CHN, and Elena Petrova, UT.

Middleweight (146 lbs): **1.** Odalis Reve, CUB; **2.** Emanuela Pierantozzi, ITA; **3.** Kate Howey, GBR, and Heidi Rakels, BEL.

Half-Heavyweight (159 lbs): **1.** Kim Mi-Jung, S.KOR; **2.** Yoko Tanabe, JPN; **3.** Irene De Kok, HOL, and Laetitia Meignan, FRA.

Heavyweight (over 159 lbs): **1.** Zhuang Xiaoyan, CHN; **2.** Estela Rodriguez, CUB; **3.** Natalia Lupino, FRA, and Yoko Sakaue, JPN.

MODERN PENTATHLON

(Five events in four days—fencing, swimming, shooting, running and riding.)

Individual: 1. Arkadiusz Skrzypaszek, POL (5,559 pts.); **2.** Attila Mizser, HUN (5,446); **3.** Edouard Zenovka, UT (5,361).

Team: 1. Poland (16,018 pts.); **2.** Unified Team (15,924); **3.** Italy (15,760). **USA entry:** 4th—Michael Gostigian, James Haley, Rob Stull (15,649).

ROWING

MEN
(2000-meter course)

Single Sculls: 1. Thomas Lange, GER (6:51.40); **2.** Vaclav Chalupa, CZE (6:52.93); **3.** Kajetan Broniewski, POL (6:56.82).

Double Sculls: 1. Stephen Hawkins & Peter Antonie, AUS (6:17.32); **2.** Arnold Jonke & Christoph Zerbst, AUT (6:18.42); **3.** Henk-Jan Zwolle & Nico Rienks, HOL (6:22.82).

Quadruple Sculls: 1. Germany (5:45.17); **2.** Norway (5:47.09); **3.** Italy (5:47.33).

Coxless Pairs: 1. Steven Redgrave & Matthew Pinsent, GBR (6:27.72); **2.** Peter Hoeltzenbein & Colin Von Ettingshausen, GER (6:32.68); **3.** Iztok Cop & Denis Zvegelj, SLO (6:33.42).

Coxless Fours: 1. Australia (5:55.04); **2.** United States (5:56.68); **3.** Slovenia (5:58.24). **USA entry:** Doug Burden, Jeff McLaughlin, Thomas Bohrer, Patrick Manning.

Coxed Pairs: 1. Great Britain (6:49.83); **2.** Italy (6:50.98) 3. Romania (6:51.58).

Rowing (Cont.)
MEN

Coxed Fours: 1. Romania (5:59.37); **2.** Germany (6:00.34); **3.** Poland (6:03.27). **USA entry:** 4th—James Neil, Teo Bielefeld, Sean Hall, Jack Rusher, Timothy Evans (6:06.03).

Coxed Eights: 1. Canada (5:29.53); **2.** Romania (5:29.67); **3.** Germany (5:31.00). **USA entry:** 4th—Michael Teti, Chris Sahs, James Munn, Jeff Klepacki, Robert Shepherd, Malcolm Baker, Richard Kennelly, John Parker, Mike Moore (5:33.18).

WOMEN
(1000-meter course)

Single Sculls: 1. Elisabeta Lipa, ROM (7:25.54); **2.** Annelies Bredael, BEL (7:26.64); **3.** Silken Laumann, CAN (7:28.85). **Top 5 USA:** 4th—Anne Marden (7:29.84).

Double Sculls: 1. Kerstin Koeppen & Kathrin Boron, GER (6:49.00); **2.** Vernoic Cochelea & Elisabeta Lipa, ROM (6:51.47); **3.** Gu Xiaoli & Lu Huali, CHN (6:55.16).

Quadruple Sculls: 1. Germany (6:20.18); **2.** Romania (6:24.34); **3.** Unified Team (6:25.07). **Top 5 USA:** 5th—Kristine Karlson, Alison Townley, Serena Eddy-Moulton, Michelle Knox-Zaloom (6:32.65).

Coxless Pairs: 1. Marnie McBean & Kathleen Heddle, CAN (7:06.22); **2.** Stefani Werremeier & Ingeburg Schwerzmann, GER (7:07.96); **3.** Anna Seaton & Stephanie Pierson, USA (7:08.11).

Coxless Four: 1. Canada (7:06.22); **2.** Germany (7:07.96); **3.** United States (7:08.11). **USA entry:** Shelagh Donohoe, Cindy Eckert, Amy Fuller, Carol Feeney.

Coxed Eights: 1. Canada (6:02.62); **2.** Romania (6:06.26); **3.** Germany (6:07.80). **USA entry:** 6th—Tina Brown, Shannon Day, Betsy McCagg, Mary McCagg, Sarah Gengler, Tracy Rude, Kelley Jones, Diana Olson (6:12.25).

SHOOTING

MEN

Free Rifle/3 Positions: **1.** Gratchia Petikiane, UT (1,267.4 pts); **2.** Bob Foth, USA (1,266.6); **3.** Ryohei Koba, JPN (1,265.9).

Free Rifle/Prone: 1. Lee Eun-Chul, S.KOR (702.5 pts); **2.** Harald Stenvaag, NOR (701.4); **3.** Stevan Pletikosic, YUG (701.1).

Rapid Fire Pistol: 1. Ralf Schumann, GER (885 pts); **2.** Afanasij Kuzmin, LAT (882); **3.** Vladimir Vokhmianin, UT (882).

Free pistol: 1. Konstantine Loukachik, UT (658 pts); **2.** Wang Yifu, CHN (657); **3.** Ragnar Skanaker, SWE (657).

Running Game Target: 1. Michael Jakosits, GER (637 pts); **2.** Anatoly Asrabaev, UT (672); **3.** Lubos Racansky, CZE (670).

Air Pistol: 1. Wang Yifu, CHN (684.8 pts); **2.** Sergei Pyjianov, UT (684.1); **3.** Sorin Babii, ROM (684.1).

Air Rifle: 1. Yuri Fedkine, UT (695.3 pts); **2.** Franck Badiou, FRA (691.9); **3.** Johann Riederer, GER (691.7).

WOMEN

Free Rifle/3 Positions: **1.** Launi Meili, USA (684.3 pts); **2.** Nonka Matova, BUL (682.7); **3.** Malgorzata Ksiazkiewicz, POL (681.5).

Air Pistol:1. Marina Logvinenko, UT (486.4 pts); **2.** Jasna Sekaric, YUG (486.4); **3.** Maria Grousdeva, BUL (481.6).

Air Rifle: 1. Yeo Kab-Soon, S.KOR (498.2 pts); **2.** Vesela Letcheva, BUL (495.3); **3.** Aranka Binder, YUG (495.1).

Sport Pistol: 1. Marina Logvinenko, UT (684 pts); **2.** Li Duihong, CHN (680); **3.** Dorzhsuren Munkhbayar, MON (679).

MIXED

Open Trap (200 targets): **1.** Petr Hrdlicka, CZE (219 pts, won shootoff); **2.** Kazumi Watanabe, JPN (219); **3.** Marco Venturini, ITA (218).

Skeet (200 targets): **1.** Zhang Shan, CHN (223 pts); **2.** Juan Giha, PER (222, won shootoff); **3.** Bruno Rossetti, ITA (222).

SWIMMING

MEN
50-meter Freestyle

		Time	
1	Aleksandr Popov, UT	21.91	**OR**
2	Matt Biondi, USA	22.09	
3	Tom Jager, USA	22.30	

100-meter Freestyle

		Time
1	Aleksandr Popov, UT	49.02
2	Gustavo Borges, BRA	49.43
3	Stephan Caron, FRA	49.50

Top 10 USA: 4th—Jon Olsen (49.51); 5th—Matt Biondi (49.53).

200-meter Freestyle

		Time	
1	Yevgeny Sadovyi, UT	1:46.70	**OR**
2	Anders Holmertz, SWE	1:46.86	
3	Alexander Kasvio, FIN	1:47.63	

Top 10 USA: 6th—Joe Hudepohl (1:48.32); 8th—Doug Gjertsen (1:50.57).

400-meter Freestyle

		Time	
1	Yevgeny Sadovyi, UT	3:45.00	**WR**
2	Kieren Perkins, AUS	3:45.16	
3	Anders Holmertz, SWE	3:46.77	

1500-meter Freestyle

		Time	
1	Kieren Perkins, AUS	14:43.48	**WR**
2	Glen Housman, AUS	14:55.29	
3	Jörg Hoffman, GER	15:02.29	

Top 10 USA: 7th—Lawrence Frostad (15:19.41).

100-meter Backstroke

		Time	
1	Mark Tewksbury, CAN	53.98	**OR**
2	Jeff Rouse, USA	54.04	
3	David Berkoff, USA	54.78	

200-meter Backstroke

		Time	
1	Martin Lopez-Zubero, SPA	1:58.47	**OR**
2	Vladimir Selkov, UT	1:58.87	
3	Stefano Battistelli, ITA	1:59.40	

Top 10 USA: 5th—Tripp Schwenk (1:59.73).

100-meter Breaststroke

		Time	
1	Nelson Diebel, USA	1:01.50	**OR**
2	Norbert Rozsa, HUN	1:01.68	
3	Philip Rogers, AUS	1:01.76	

Other Top 10 USA: 10th—Hans Dersch (1:02.39).

200-meter Breaststroke

		Time	
1	Mike Barrowman, USA	2:10.16	WR
2	Norbert Rozsa, HUN	2:11.23	
3	Nick Gillingham, GBR	2:11.29	

100-meter Butterfly

		Time	
1	Pablo Morales, USA	53:32	
2	Rafal Szukala, POL	53.35	
3	Anthony Nesty, SUR.	53.41	

Other Top 10 USA: 5th—Mel Stewart (54.04).

200-meter Butterfly

		Time	
1	Mel Stewart, USA	1:56.26	OR
2	Danyon Loader, NZE	1:57.93	
3	Franck Esposito, FRA	1:58.51	

Other Top 10 USA: 10th—David Wharton (2:01.08).

200-meter Individual Medley

		Time
1	Tamas Darnyi, HUN	2:00.76
2	Greg Burgess, USA	2:00.97
3	Attila Czene, HUN	2:01.00

Other Top 10 USA: 6th—Ron Karnaugh (2:02.18).

400-meter Individual Medley

		Time	
1	Tamas Darnyi, HUN	4:14.23	OR
2	Eric Namesnik, USA	4:15.57	
3	Luca Sacchi, ITA	4:16.34	

Other Top 10 USA: 4th—David Wharton (4:17.26).

4 × 100-meter Freestyle Relay

		Time
1	United States	3:16.74
2	Unified Team	3:17.56
3	Germany	3:17.90

USA—Joe Hudepohl, Matt Biondi, Tom Jager, Jon Olsen; **UT**—Pavel Khnykine, Guennadi Prigoda, Yuri Bashkatov, Aleksandr Popov; **GER**—Christian Troeger, Dirk Richter, Steffen Zesner, Mark Pinger.

4 × 200-meter Freestyle Relay

		Time	
1	Unified Team	7:11.95	WR
2	Sweden	7:15.51	
3	United States	7:16.23	

UT—Dmitri Lepikov, Vladimir Pychnenko, Veniamin Taianovitch, Yevgeny Sadovyi; **SWE**—Christer Wallin, Anders Holmertz, Tommy Werner, Lars Frolander; **USA**—Joseph Hudepohl, Mel Stewart, Jon Olsen, Doug Gjertsen.

4 × 100-meter Medley Relay

		Time	
1	United States	3:36.93	=WR
2	Unified Team	3:38.56	
3	Canada	3:39.66	

USA—Jeff Rouse, Nelson Diebel, Pablo Morales, Jon Olsen; **UT**—Vladimir Selkov, Vassili Ivanov, Pavel Khnykine, Aleksandr Popov; **CAN**—Mark Tewksbury, Jonathan Cleveland, Marcel Gery, Stephen Clarke.

WOMEN

50-meter Freestyle

		Time	
1	Yang Wenyi, CHN	24.79	WR
2	Zhuang Yong, CHN	25.08	
3	Angel Martino, USA	25.23	

Other Top 10 USA: 5th—Jenny Thompson (25.37).

100-meter Freestyle

		Time	
1	Zhuang Yong, CHN	54.64	OR
2	Jenny Thompson, USA	54.84	
3	Franziska van Almsick, GER	54.94	

Other Top 10 USA: 4th—Nicole Haislett (55.19).

200-meter Freestyle

		Time
1	Nicole Haislett, USA	1:57.90
2	Franziska van Almsick, GER	1:58.00
3	Kerstin Kielgass, GER	1:59.67

400-meter Freestyle

		Time
1	Dagmar Hase, GER	4:07.18
2	Janet Evans, USA	4:07.37
3	Hayley Lewis, AUS	4:11.22

Other Top 10 USA: 4th—Erika Hansen (4:11.50).

800-meter Freestyle

		Time
1	Janet Evans, USA	8:25.52
2	Hayley Lewis, AUS	8:30.34
3	Jana Henke, GER	8:30.99

Other Top 10 USA: 7th—Erika Hansen (8:39.25).

100-meter Backstroke

		Time	
1	Krisztina Egerszegi, HUN	1:00.68	OR
2	Tunde Szabo, HUN	1:01.14	
3	Lea Loveless, USA	1:01.43	

Other Top 10 USA: 5th—Janie Wagstaff (1:01.81).

200-meter Backstroke

		Time	
1	Krisztina Egerszegi, HUN	2:07.06	OR
2	Dagmar Hase, GER	2:09.46	
3	Nicole Stevenson, AUS	2:10.20	

Top 10 USA: 4th—Lea Loveless (2:11.54).

100-meter Breaststroke

		Time
1	Yelena Rudkovskaya, UT	1:08.00
2	Anita Nall, USA	1:08.17
3	Samantha Riley, AUS	1:09.25

200-meter Breaststroke

		Time	
1	Kyoko Iwasaki, JPN	2:26.65	OR
2	Lin Li, CHN	2:26.85	
3	Anita Nall, USA	2:26.88	

100-meter Butterfly

		Time	
1	Qian Hong, CHN	58.62	OR
2	Crissy Ahmann-Leighton, USA	58.74	
3	Catherine Plewinski, FRA.	59.01	

Other Top 10 USA: 6th—Summer Sanders (59.82).

200-meter Butterfly

		Time
1	Summer Sanders, USA	2:08.67
2	Wang Xiaohong, CHN	2:09.01
3	Susan O'Neill, AUS	2:09.03

Other Top 10 USA: 7th—Angie Wester (2:11.46).

200-meter Individual Medley

		Time	
1	Lin Li, CHN	2:11.65	WR
2	Summer Sanders, USA	2:11.91	
3	Daniela Hunger, GER	2:13.92	

Swimming (Cont.)

WOMEN

400-meter Individual Medley

		Time
1	Krisztina Egerszegi, HUN.	4:36.54
2	Lin Li, CHN.	4:36.73
3	Summer Sanders, USA	4:37.58

Other Top 10 USA: 10th—Erika Hansen (4:48.37).

4×100-meter Freestyle Relay

		Time
1	United States.	3:39.46 **WR**
2	China	3:40.12
3	Germany	4:41.60

USA—Nicole Haislett, Dara Torres, Angel Martino, Jenny Thompson; **CHN**—Zhuang Yong, Lu Bin, Yang Wenyi, Li Jingyi; **GER**—Franziska van Almsick, Simone Osygus, Daniela Hunger, Manuela Stellmach.

4×100-meter Medley Relay

		Time
1	United States.	4:02.54 **WR**
2	Germany	4:05.19
3	Unified Team	4:06.44

USA—Lea Loveless, Anita Nall, Crissy Ahmann-Leighton, Jenny Thompson; **GER**—Dagmar Hase, Jana Doerries, Franziska van Almsick, Daniela Hunger; **UT**—Nina Jivanevskaia, Yelena Rudkovskaya, Olga Kiritchenko, Natalia Mechtcheriakova.

Synchronized Swimming

Solo: 1. Kristen Babb-Sprague, USA (191.848 pts); **2.** Sylvie Frechette, CAN (191.717); **3.** Fumiko Okuno, JPN (187.056).

Duet: 1. Karen & Sarah Josephson, USA (192.175 pts); **2.** Penny & Vicky Vilagos, CAN (189.394); **3.** Fumiko Okuno & Aki Takayama, JPN (186.868)

TABLE TENNIS

MEN

Singles: 1. Jan Ove Waldner, SWE, def. **2.** Jean Philippe Gatien, FRA (21-10, 21-18, 25-23); **3.** Kim Taek-Soo, S.KOR, and Ma Wenge, CHN.

Doubles:1. Lu Lin & Wang Tao, CHN, def. **2.** Steffen Fetzner & Jorg Rosskopf, GER (26-24, 18-21, 13-21, 21-14); **3.** Kang Hee-Chan & Lee Chul-Seung, S.KOR, and Kim Taek-Soo & Yoo Nam-Kyu, S.KOR.

WOMEN

Singles: 1. Deng Yaping, CHN, def. **2.** Qiao Hong, CHN (21-6, 21-8, 15-21, 23-21); **3.** Hyun Jung-Hwa, S.KOR, and Li Bun-Hui, N.KOR.

Doubles: 1. Deng Yaping & Qiao Hong, CHN, def. **2.** Chen Zihe & Gao Jun, CHN (21-13, 14-21, 21-14, 21-19). **3.** Li Bun-Hui & Yu Sun-Bok, N.KOR, and Hong Cha-Ok & Hyun Jung-Hwa, S.KOR.

TENNIS

MEN

Singles: 1. Marc Rosset, SWI, def. **2.** Jordi Arrese, SPA (7-6, 6-4, 3-6, 4-6, 8-6); **3.** Goran Ivanisevic, CRO, and Andrei Cherkasov, UT.

Doubles: 1. Boris Becker & Michael Stich, GER def. **2.** Wayne Ferreira & Piet Norval, SAF (7-6, 4-6, 7-6, 6-3); **3.** Goran Ivanisevic & Goran Prpic, CRO, and Javier Frana & Christian Carlos Miniussi, ARG.

WOMEN

Singles: 1. Jennifer Capriati, USA, def. **2.** Steffi Graf, GER (3-6, 6-3, 6-4); **3.** Aranxta Sanchez Vicario, SPA, and Mary Joe Fernandez, USA.

Doubles: 1. Gigi Fernandez & Mary Joe Fernandez, USA, def. **2.** Conchita Martinez & Arantxa Sanchez Vicario, SPA (7-5, 2-6, 6-2); **3.** Natalia Zvereva & Leila Meskhi, UT, and Rachel McQuillan & Nicole Provis, AUS.

TRACK & FIELD

MEN

100 meters

		Time
1	Linford Christie, GBR.	9.96
2	Frankie Fredericks, NAM	10.02
3	Dennis Mitchell, USA.	10.04

Other Top 10 USA: 5th—Leroy Burrell (10.10).

200 meters

		Time
1	Mike Marsh, USA.	20:01
2	Frankie Fredericks, NAM	20.13
3	Michael Bates, USA.	20.38

400 meters

		Time
1	Quincy Watts, USA	43.50 **OR**
2	Steve Lewis, USA	44.21
3	Samson Kitur, KEN	44.24

800 meters

		Time
1	William Tanui, KEN	1:43.66
2	Nixon Kiprotich, KEN	1:43.70
3	Johnny Gray, USA	1:43.97

1500 meters

		Time
1	Fermin Cacho, SPA	3:40.12
2	Rachid El-Basir, MOR.	3:40.62
3	Mohamed Sulaiman, QAT	3:40.69

Top 10 USA: 8th—Jim Spivey (3:41.74).

5000 meters

		Time
1	Dieter Baumann, GER.	13:12.52
2	Paul Bitok, KEN	13:12.71
3	Fita Bayissa, ETH	13:13.03

10,000 meters

		Time
1	Khalid Skah, MOR.	27:46.70
2	Richard Chelimo, KEN	27:47.72
3	Addis Abebe, ETH	28:00.07

Top 10 USA: 10th—Todd Williams (28:29.38)

Marathon

		Time
1	Hwang Young-Cho, S.KOR	2:13:23
2	Koichi Morishita, JPN.	2:13:45
3	Stephan Freigang, GER.	2:14:00

4×100-meter Relay

		Time
1	United States	37.40 **WR**
2	Nigeria	37.98
3	Cuba	38.00

USA—Mike Marsh, Leroy Burrell, Dennis Mitchell, Carl Lewis; **NGR**—Oluyemi Kayode, Chidi Imoh, Olapade Adeniken, Davidson Ezinwa; **CUB**—Andres Simon, Joel Lamela, Joel Isasi, Jorge Aguilera.

4×400-meter Relay

		Time
1	United States.	2:55.74 **WR**
2	Cuba	2:59.51
3	Great Britain.	2:59.73

USA—Andrew Valmon, Quincy Watts, Michael Johnson, Steve Lewis; **CUB**—Lazaro Martinez, Hector Herrera, Norberto Tellez, Roberto Hernandez; **GBR**—Roger Black, David Grinley, Kriss Akabusi, John Regis.

Wide World Photos

The United States' world record-breaking 4x100-meter relay team (from left to right):
Dennis Mitchell, **Leroy Burrell**, **Mike Marsh** and **Carl Lewis**.

110-meter Hurdles

		Time	
1	Mark McKoy, CAN	13.12	
2	Tony Dees, USA	13.24	
3	Jack Pierce, USA	13.26	

400-meter Hurdles

		Time	
1	Kevin Young, USA	46.78	WR
2	Winthrop Graham, JAM	47.66	
3	Kriss Akabusi, GBR	47.82	

Other Top 10 USA: 8th—David Patrick (49.26).

3000-meter Steeplechase

		Time
1	Matthew Birir, KEN	8:08.84
2	Patrick Sang, KEN	8:09.55
3	William Mutwol, KEN	8:10.74

Top 10 USA: 7th—Brian Diemer (8:18.77).

20-kilometer Walk

		Time
1	Daniel Plaza Montero, SPA	1:21:45
2	Guillaume LeBlanc, CAN	1:22:25
3	Giovanni De Benedictis, ITA	1:23:11

50-kilometer Walk

		Time
1	Andrei Perlov, UT	3:50:13
2	Carlos Mercenario MEX	3:52:09
3	Ronald Weigel, GER	3:53:45

High Jump

		Height
1	Javier Sotomayor, CUB	7-8
2	Patrik Sjoeberg, SWE	7-8
3	Hollis Conway, USA	7-8
	Timothy Forsythe, AUS	7-8
	Artur Partyka, POL	7-8

Other Top 10 USA: 8th(T)—Charles Austin (7-5¾).

Pole Vault

		Height
1	Maksim Tarasov, UT	19- 0¼
2	Igor Trandenkov, UT	19- 0¼
3	Javier Garcia, SPA	18-10¼

Top 10 USA: 4th—Kory Tapenning (18–10¼); 5th—Dave Volz (18-6½).
Note: Heavy favorite Sergei Bubka of UT no-heighted.

Long Jump

		Distance
1	Carl Lewis, USA	28- 5½
2	Mike Powell, USA	28- 4¼
3	Joe Greene, USA	27- 4½

Triple Jump

		Distance
1	Mike Conley, USA	59- 7½*
2	Charlie Simpkins, USA	57- 9
3	Frank Rutherford, BAH	56-11½

*Wind-aided (Conley set new OR with earlier jump of 57-10½).

Shot Put

		Distance
1	Michael Stulce, USA	71- 2½
2	Jim Doehring, USA	68- 9¼
3	Viacheslav Lykho, UT	68- 8½

Other Top 10 USA: 10th—Ron Backes (64–9¾).

Discus

		Distance
1	Romas Ubartas, LIT	213- 8
2	Jurgen Schult, GER	213- 1
3	Roberto Moya, CUB	210- 4

Hammer Throw

		Distance
1	Andrei Abduvaliyev, UT	270- 9
2	Igor Astapkovich, UT	268-11
3	Igor Nikulin, UT	267- 0

Top 10 USA: 7th—Lance Deal (252-1).

Javelin

		Distance	
1	Jan Zelezny, CZE	294- 2	OR
2	Seppo Raty, FIN	284- 1	
3	Steve Backley, GBR	273- 3	

Top 10 USA: 7th—Mike Barnett (258-4); 10th—Tom Pukstys (251-8).

Decathlon

(Ten events in two days: DAY 1—100m, 400m, LJ, Shot, HJ; DAY 2—100m H, Discus, PV, Javelin, 1500m.)

		Points
1	Robert Zmelik, CZE	8,611
2	Antonio Penalver, SPA	8,412
3	Dave Johnson, USA	8,309

Other Top 10 USA: 5th—Rob Muzzio (8,195).

Track & Field (Cont.)

WOMEN

100 meters

		Time
1	Gail Devers, USA	10.82
2	Juliet Cuthbert, JAM	10.83
3	Irina Privalova, UT	10.84

Other Top 10 USA: 4th—Gwen Torrence (10.86).

200 meters

		Time
1	Gwen Torrence, USA	21.81
2	Juliet Cuthbert, JAM	22.02
3	Merlene Ottey, JAM	22.09

Other Top 10 USA: 5th-Carlette Guidry-White (22.30); 7th—Michelle Finn (22.61).

400 meters

		Time
1	Marie-Jose Perec, FRA	48.83
2	Olga Bryzgina, UT	49.05
3	Ximena Restrepo, COL	49.64

Top 10 USA: 6th—Rochelle Stevens (50.11).

800 meters

		Time
1	Ellen van Langen, HOL	1:55.54
2	Lilia Nurutdinova, UT	1:55.99
3	Ana Quirot, CUB	1:56.80

Top 10 USA: 7th—Joetta Clark (1:58.06).

1500 meters

		Time
1	Hassiba Boulmerka, ALG	3:55.30
2	Lyudmila Rogacheva, UT	3:56.91
3	Qu Yunxia, CHN	3:57.08

Top 10 USA: 10th—PattiSue Plumer (4:03.42).

3000 meters

		Time
1	Elena Romanova, UT	8:46.04
2	Tatiana Dorovskikh, UT	8:46.85
3	Angela Chalmers, CAN	8:47.22

Top 10 USA: 5th—PattiSue Plumer (8:48.29); 7th—Shelly Steely (8:52.67).

10,000 meters

		Time
1	Derartu Tulu, ETH	31:06.02
2	Elana Meyer, SAF	31:11.75
3	Lynn Jennings, USA	31:19.89

Other Top 10 USA: 8th—Judi St. Hilare (31:38.4).

Marathon

		Time
1	Valentina Yegorova, UT	2:32:41
2	Yuko Arimori, JPN	2:32:49
3	Lorraine Moller, NZE	2:33:59

Top 10 USA: 10th—Cathy O'Brien (2:40:10).

4×100-meter Relay

		Time
1	United States	42.11
2	Unified Team	42.16
3	Nigeria	42.81

USA—Evelyn Ashford, Esther Jones, Carlette Guidry-White, Gwen Torrence; **UT**—Olga Bogoslovskaya, Galina Malchugina, Marina Trandenkova, Irina Privalova; **NGR**—Beatrice Utondu, Faith Idehen, Christy Opara Thompson, Mary Onyali.

4×400-meter Relay

		Time
1	Unified Team	3:20.20
2	United States	3:20.92
3	Great Britain	3:24.23

UT—Yelena Ruzina, Lyudmila Dzhigalova, Olga Nazarova, Olga Bryzgina; **USA**—Natasha Kaiser, Gwen Torrence, Jearl Miles, Rochelle Stevens. **GBR**—Phylis Smith, Sandra Douglas, Jennifer Stoute, Sally Gunnell.

100-meter Hurdles

		Time
1	Paraskevi Patoulidou, GRE	12.64
2	LaVonna Martin, USA	12.69
3	Yordanka Donkova, BUL	12.70

Other Top 10 USA: 4th—Lynda Tolbert (12.75); 5th—Gail Devers (12.75).

400-meter Hurdles

		Time
1	Sally Gunnell, GBR	53.23
2	Sandra Farmer-Patrick, USA	53.69
3	Janeene Vickers, USA	54.31

10-kilometer Walk

		Time
1	Chen Yueling, CHN	44.32*
2	Elena Nikolaeva, UT	44.33
3	Li Chunxiu, CHN	44.41

*First time event run.

High Jump

		Distance
1	Heike Henkel, GER	6- 7½
2	Galina Astafei, ROM	6- 6¾
3	Joanet Quintero, CUB	6- 5½

Long Jump

		Distance
1	Heike Drechsler, GER	23- 5¼
2	Inessa Kravets, UT	23- 4½
3	Jackie Joyner-Kersee, USA	23- 2½

Other Top 10 USA: 7th-Sharon Couch (21-10¼); 8th—Sheila Echols (21-8¾).

Shot Put

		Distance
1	Svetlana Krivaleva, UT	69- 1¼
2	Huang Zhihong, CHN	67- 2
3	Kathrin Neimke, GER	64-10¾

Discus

		Distance
1	Maritza Marten, CUB	229-10
2	Tsvetanka Khristova, BUL	222- 4
3	Daniela Costian, AUS	217- 4

Javelin

		Distance
1	Silke Renk, GER	224- 2
2	Natalia Shikolenko, UT	223-11
3	Karen Forkel, GER	219- 4

Heptathlon

(Seven events in two days: DAY 1—100m H, HJ, 200m, Shot; DAY 2—LJ, Javelin, 800m.)

		Points
1	Jackie Joyner-Kersee, USA	7,044
2	Irina Belova, UT	6,845
3	Sabine Braun, GER	6,649

Other Top 10 USA: 9th—Cindy Greiner (6,300).

Joyner-Kersee's numbers & points: 100m H—12.85 (1,147 pts); **HJ**— 6-3¼ (1,119); **200m**—23.12 (1,067); **Shot**—46-4¼ (803); **LJ**—23-3½ (1,206); **Javelin**—147-6¾ (763); **800m**—2:11.78 (939).

WEIGHTLIFTING

Flyweight (114 lbs): **1.** Ivan Ivanov, BUL (584 lbs); **2.** Lin Qisheng, CHN (579); **3.** Traian Ciharean, ROM (557).

Bantamweight (123 lbs): **1.** Chun Byung-Kwan, S.KOR (634 lbs); **2.** Liu Shoubin, CHN (611.12); **3.** Luo Jianming, CHN (611.12).

Featherweight (132 lbs): **1.** Naim Suleymanoglu, TUR (705 lbs); **2.** Nikolai Peshalov, BUL (672); **3.** He Yingqiang, CHN (650).

Lightweight (148 lbs): **1.** Israel Militossian, UT (744 lbs); **2.** Yoto Yotov, BUL (722); **3.** Andreas Behm, GER (706).

Middleweight (165 lbs): **1.** Fedor Kassapu, UT (788 lbs); **2.** Pablo Lara, CUB (788); **3.** Kim Myong-Nam, N.KOR (777).

Light Heavyweight (182 lbs): **1.** Pyrros Dimas, GRE (816 lbs); **2.** Krzysztof Siemion, POL (816); **3.** Ibragim Samadov, UT (816).

Middle Heavyweight (198 lbs): **1.** Kakhi Kakhiachvili, UT (909¼ lbs, equals OR); **2.** Sergei Syrtsov, UT (909); **3.** Sergiusz Wolczeniecki, POL (865).

100 KG (220 lbs): **1.** Viktor Tregoubov, UT (904 lbs, OR); **2.** Timour Taimazov, UT (887); **3.** Waldemar Malak, POL (882).

Heavyweight (243 lbs): **1.** Ronny Weller, GER (953 lbs; **2.** Artour Akoev, UT (948); **3.** Stefan Botev, BUL (921).

Super Heavyweight (over 243 lbs): **1.** Aleksandr Kourlovitch, UT (992 lbs); **2.** Leonid Taranenko, UT (937); **3.** Manfred Nerlinger, GER (910).

WRESTLING

Greco-Roman

Light Flyweight (106 lbs): **1.** Oleg Koutcherenko, UT, dec. **2.** Vincenzo Maenza, ITA (3-0); **3.** Wilber Sanchez, CUB, dec. Fuat Yildiz, GER (5-0).

Flyweight (115 lbs): **1.** Jon Ronningen, NOR, dec. **2.** Alfred Ter-Mkrttchian, UT; (2-1); **3.** Min Kyung-Kap, S.KOR. dec. Shawn Sheldon, USA (default).

Bantamweight (126 lbs): **1.** An Han-Bong, S.KOR, dec. **2.** Rifat Yildiz, GER (6-5); **3.** Sheng Zetian, CHN, dec. Aleksandr Ignatenko, UT (5-4).

Featherweight (137 lbs): **1.** Akif Pirim, TUR, dec. **2.** Sergei Martynov, UT (13-2); **3.** Juan Maren, CUB, dec. Wlodzimierz Zawadzki, POL (5-0).

Lightweight (150 lbs): **1.** Attila Repka, HUN, dec. **2.** Islam Dougoutchiev, UT (1-0); **3.** Rodney Smith, USA, dec. Cecilio Rodriguez, CUB (6-3).

Welterweight (163 lbs): **1.** Mnatsakan Iskandarian, UT, dec. **2.** Jozef Tracz, POL (6-3); **3.** Torbjoern Kornbakk, SWE, dec. Nestor Almanza, CUB (5-1).

Middleweight (181 lbs): **1.** Peter Farkas, HUN, dec. **2.** Piotr Stepien, POL (6-1); **3.** Daoulet Tourlykhanov, UT, dec. Magnus Fredriksson, SWE (2-0).

Light Heavyweight (198 lbs): **1.** Maik Bullman, GER, dec. **2.** Hakki Basar, TUR (5-0); **3.** Gogui Kogouachvili, UT, dec. Mikael Ljungberg, SWE (2-0).

Heavyweight (220 lbs): **1.** Hector Milian, CUB, dec. **2.** Dennis Koslowski, USA (2-1); **3.** Sergei Demiachkievitch, UT, dec. Andrzej Wronski, POL (1-0).

Super Heavyweight (286 lbs): **1.** Aleksandr Karelin, UT, dec. Tomas Johansson, SWE (6-0, touch); **3.** Ioan Grigoras, ROM, dec. Laslo Klauz, HUN (1-0).

Freestyle

Light Flyweight (106 lbs): **1.** Kim Il, N.KOR, dec. **2.** Kim Jong-Shin, S. KOR (4-1); **3.** Vougar Oroudjov, UT, dec. Romica Rasovan, ROM (2-1).

Flyweight (115 lbs): **1.** Li Hak-Son, S.KOR, dec. **2.** Zeke Jones, USA (8-1); **3.** Valentin Jordanov, BUL, dec. Kim Sun-Hak, S.KOR (9-3).

Bantamweight (126 lbs): **1.** Alejandro Puerto, CUB, dec. **2.** Sergei Smal, UT (5-0); **3.** Kim Yong-Sik, N.KOR, dec. Remzi Musaoglu, TUR (3-2).

Featherweight (137 lbs): **1.** John Smith, USA, dec. **2.** Asgari Mohammadian, IRA (6-0); **3.** Lazaro Reinoso, CUB, dec. Rossen Vassilev, BUL (4-0).

Lightweight (150 lbs): **1.** Arsen Fadzaev, UT, dec. **2.** Valentin Getzov, BUL (13-1, superiority); **3.** Kosei Akaishi, JPN, dec. Ali Akbarnejad, IRA (4-0).

Welterweight (163 lbs): **1.** Park Jang-Soon, S.KOR, dec. **2.** Kenny Monday, USA (1-0); **3.** Amir Khadem, IRA, dec. Magomedsalam Gadjiev, UT (1-0).

Middleweight (181 lbs): **1.** Kevin Jackson, USA, dec. **2.** Elmadi Jabraijlov, UT (1-0); **3.** Rasul Khadem, IRA, dec. Hans Gstoettner, GER (6-0).

Light Heavyweight (198 lbs): **1.** Makharbek Khadartsev, UT, dec. **2.** Kenan Simsek, TUR (1-0); **3.** Chris Campbell, USA, dec. Puntsag Sukhbat, MON (3-1).

Heavyweight (220 lbs): **1.** Leri Khabelov, UT, dec. **2.** Heiko Balz, GER (2-1); **3.** Ali Kayali, TUR, dec. Kim Tae-Woo, S.KOR (2-0).

Super Heavyweight (286 lbs): **1.** Bruce Baumgartner, USA, def. **2.** Jeff Thue, CAN (8-0); **3.** David Gobedjichvili, UT, dec. Mahmut Demir, TUR (4-0).

YACHTING

MEN

Finn Class: 1. Jose van der Ploeg, SPA (33.4 pts); **2.** Brian Ledbetter, USA (54.7); **3.** Craig Monk, NZE (64.7).

470 Class: 1. Jordi Calafat & Francisco Sanchez, SPA (50.0pts); **2.** Morgan Reeser & Kevin Burnham, USA (66.7); **3.** Tonu Toniste & Toomas Toniste, EST (68.7).

Sailboard: 1. Franck David, FRA (70.7 pts); **2.** Mike Gebhardt, USA (71.1); **3.** Lars Kleppich, AUS (98.7).

WOMEN

Europe Class: 1. Linda Andersend, NOR (48.7 pts); **2.** Natalia Via Dufresne, SPA (57.4); **3.** Julia Trotman, USA (62.7).

470 Class: 1. Theresa Zabell & Patricia Guerra, SPA (29.7 pts); **2.** Leslie Jean Egnot & Janet Shearer, NZE (36.7); **3.** J.J. Isler & Pamela Healy, USA (40.7).

Sailboard: 1. Barbara Kendall, NZE (47.8 pts); **2.** Zhang Ziaodong, CHN (65.8); **3.** Dorien De Vries, HOL (68.7).

MIXED

Flying Dutchman Class: 1. Luis Doreste & Domingo Manrique, SPA (29.7 pts); **2.** Paul Foerster & Stephen Bourdow, USA (32.7); **3.** Jorgen Bojsen & Jens Bojsen, DEN (37.7).

Soling Class: 1. Jesper Bank, Steen Secher & Jesper Seier, DEN def. **2.** Kevin Mahaney, James Brady & Doug Kern, USA (2-0); **3.** Lawrence Smith, Robert Cruikshank & Ossie Stewart, GBR def. Jochen Schumann, Thomas Flach & Bernd Jakel, GER (2-1).

Star Class: 1. Mark Reyonlds & Hal Haenel, USA (31.4 pts); **2.** Roderick Davis & Donald John Cowie, NZE (58.4); **3.** Ross MacDonald & Eric Jespersen, CAN (62.7).

Tornado: 1. Yves Loday & Nicolas Henard, FRA (40.4 pts); **2.** Randy Smyth & Keith Notary, USA (42.0); **3.** Mitch Booth & John Forbes, AUS (44.4).

TEAM SPORTS

BASEBALL

Round Robin Standings

First four teams advance to medal round.

	Gm	W	L	Pts	RF	RA	Medal Round
*Cuba	7	7	0	14	78	14	2-0
*Japan	7	5	2	10	61	15	1-1
*Taiwan	7	5	2	10	61	21	1-1
*United States	7	5	2	10	49	28	0-2
Puerto Rico	7	2	5	4	22	48	—
Dominican Republic	7	2	5	4	23	61	—
Italy	7	1	6	2	25	62	—
Spain	7	1	6	2	15	85	—

Semifinals

Cuba 6 .... United States 1
Taiwan 5 .... Japan 2

Bronze Medal

Japan 8 .... United States 3

Gold Medal

Cuba 11 .... Taiwan 1

Team USA Statistics

Batting

	Pos	Avg	AB	R	H	HR	RBI
Jeffrey Hammonds	OF	.432	37	8	16	1	8
Calvin Murray	OF	.368	38	5	14	0	5
Chad McConnell	OF	.300	30	5	10	1	8
Jason Giambi	1B	.296	27	9	8	0	1
Charles Johnson	C	.294	17	1	5	0	1
Jason Varitek	C	.286	14	3	4	0	3
Michael Tucker	DH	.276	29	7	8	2	8
Phil Nevin	3B	.219	32	4	7	2	6
Nomar Garciaparra	SS	.200	20	3	4	0	0
Craig Wilson	INF	.200	10	2	2	0	0
Chris Wimmer	2B	.156	32	6	5	0	5
Chris Roberts	OF/P	.000	1	0	0	0	0
TOTALS		.289	287	53	83	6	45

Pitching

	ERA	Gm	W-L	SV	IP	BB	SO
Jeff Alkire	1.93	3	2-0	0	18.2	7	18
B.J. Wallace	2.87	3	1-1	0	15.2	3	22
Chris Roberts	3.00	2	0-0	0	3.0	0	1
Willie Adams	3.86	2	0-0	0	2.1	1	1
Daron Kirkreit	4.50	2	0-1	1	2.0	0	0
Rick Greene	4.76	5	1-0	0	5.2	5	6
Darren Dreifort	5.19	5	0-0	2	8.2	5	3
Rick Helling	8.00	2	0-1	0	9.0	1	7
Ron Villone	8.18	3	1-1	0	11.0	5	11
TOTALS	4.50	9	5-4	3	76.0	27	69

BASKETBALL

Round Robin Standings

First four teams in each group advance to medal round.

MEN

Group A	Gm	W	L	Pts	Per Game For	Opp	Medal Round
*United States	5	5	0	10	115.8	70.0	3-0
*Croatia	5	4	1	8	84.6	80.0	2-1
*Brazil	5	2	3	4	84.0	92.6	0-1
*Germany	5	2	3	4	73.8	86.4	0-1
Angola	5	1	4	2	64.8	78.4	—
Spain	5	1	4	2	79.6	95.2	—

Group B	Gm	W	L	Pts	Per Game For	Opp	Medal Round
*Unified Team	5	4	1	8	85.0	74.6	1-2
*Lithuania	5	4	1	8	96.2	84.8	2-1
*Australia	5	3	2	6	86.4	79.2	0-1
*Puerto Rico	5	3	2	6	89.0	88.0	0-1
Venezuela	5	1	4	2	78.4	85.4	—
China	5	0	5	0	76.2	99.2	—

Quarterfinals

United States 115 .... Puerto Rico 77
Croatia 98 .... Australia 65
Lithuania 114 .... Brazil 96
Unified Team 83 .... Germany 76

Semifinals

United States 127 .... Lithuania 76
Croatia 75 .... Unified Team 74

Bronze Medal

Lithuania 82 .... Unified Team 78

Gold Medal

United States 117 .... Croatia 85

Team USA Scoring

	Gm	FG%	TPts	Per Game Pts	Reb	Ast
Charles Barkley	8	.711	144	18.0	4.1	2.4
Michael Jordan	8	.451	119	14.9	2.4	4.8
Karl Malone	8	.645	104	13.0	5.3	1.1
Chris Mullin	8	.619	103	12.9	1.6	3.6
Clyde Drexler	8	.578	84	10.5	3.0	3.6
Patrick Ewing	8	.623	76	9.5	5.3	0.4
Scottie Pippen	8	.596	72	9.0	2.1	5.9
David Robinson	8	.574	72	9.0	4.1	0.9
Larry Bird	8	.521	67	8.4	3.8	1.8
Magic Johnson	6	.567	48	8.0	2.3	5.5
Christian Laettner	8	.450	38	4.8	2.5	0.4
John Stockton	4	.500	11	2.8	0.3	2.0
USA TOTALS	8	.578	938	117.3	36.0	29.9
Opp TOTALS	8	.365	588	73.5	22.5	13.6

Minutes per game: Jordan (23); Mullin (22); Drexler and Pippen (22); Barkley (19); Bird, Ewing and Johnson (18); Malone and Robinson (17); Laettner (8); Stockton (7).

WOMEN

Group A	Gm	W	L	Pts	Per Game For	Opp	Medal Round
*Cuba	3	3	0	6	82.0	76.7	0-2
*Unified Team	3	2	1	4	81.3	74.0	2-0
Brazil	3	1	2	2	79.0	80.3	—
Italy	3	0	3	0	63.3	74.7	—

Group B	Gm	W	L	Pts	Per Game For	Opp	Medal Round
*United States	3	3	0	6	106.0	60.3	1-1
*China	3	2	1	4	68.3	75.3	1-1
Spain	3	1	2	2	60.3	79.3	—
Czechoslovakia	3	0	3	0	61.0	80.7	—

Semifinals

Unified Team 79 .... United States 73
China 109 .... Cuba 70

Bronze Medal

United States 88 .... Cuba 74

Gold medal

Unified Team 76 .... China 66

FIELD HOCKEY

Round Robin Standings

First two teams in each group advance to medal round.

MEN

Group A	Gm	W	L	T	Pts	GF	GA	Medal Round
*Australia	5	4	0	1	9	20	2	1-1
*Germany	5	4	0	1	9	16	4	2-0
Great Britain	5	3	2	0	6	7	10	—
India	5	2	3	0	4	3	6	—
Argentina	5	1	4	0	2	3	12	—
Egypt	5	0	5	0	0	4	18	—

Group B	Gm	W	L	T	Pts	GF	GA	Medal Round
*Pakistan	5	5	0	0	10	20	6	1-1
*Holland	5	4	1	0	8	20	10	0-2
Spain	5	3	2	0	6	15	11	—
Unified Team	5	1	4	0	2	12	20	—
Malaysia	5	1	4	0	2	9	24	—
New Zealand	5	1	4	0	2	7	12	—

Semifinals

Australia 3 .... Holland 2
Germany 2 .... Pakistan 1

Bronze Medal

Pakistan 4 .... Holland 3

Gold Medal

Germany 2 .... Australia 1

WOMEN

Group A	Gm	W	L	T	Pts	GF	GA	Medal Round
*Germany	3	2	0	1	5	7	2	1-1
*Spain	3	2	0	1	5	5	3	2-0
Australia	3	1	2	0	2	2	2	—
Canada	3	0	3	0	0	0	7	—

Group B	Gm	W	L	T	Pts	GF	GA	Medal Round
*South Korea	3	2	1	0	4	8	3	0-2
Great Britain	3	2	1	0	4	7	5	1-1
Holland	3	2	1	0	4	4	3	—
New Zealand	3	0	3	0	0	2	10	—

Semifinals

Germany 2 .... Great Britain 1
Spain 2 .... OT .... South Korea 1

Bronze Medal

Great Britain 4 .... OT .... South Korea 3

Gold Medal

Spain 2 .... OT .... Germany 1

SOCCER

Round Robin Standings

First two teams in each group advance to medal round.

MEN

Group A	Gm	W	L	T	Pts	GF	GA	Medal Round
*Poland	3	2	0	1	5	7	2	2-1
*Italy	3	2	1	0	4	3	4	0-1
United States	3	1	1	1	3	6	5	—
Kuwait	3	0	3	0	0	1	6	—

Group B	Gm	W	L	T	Pts	GF	GA	Medal Round
*Spain	3	3	0	0	6	8	0	3-0
*Qatar	3	1	1	1	3	2	3	0-1
Egypt	3	1	2	0	2	4	6	—
Colombia	3	0	2	1	1	4	9	—

Group C	Gm	W	L	T	Pts	GF	GA	Medal Round
*Sweden	3	1	0	2	4	5	1	0-1
*Paraguay	3	1	0	2	4	3	0	0-1
South Korea	3	0	0	3	3	2	2	—
Morocco	3	0	2	1	1	1	8	—

Group D	Gm	W	L	T	Pts	GF	GA	Medal Round
*Ghana	3	1	0	2	4	4	2	2-1
*Australia	3	1	1	1	3	5	4	1-2
Mexico	3	0	0	3	3	3	3	—
Denmark	3	0	1	2	2	1	4	—

Quarterfinals

Spain 1 .... Italy 0
Poland 2 .... Qatar 0
Ghana 4 .... Paraguay 2
Australia 2 .... Sweden 1

Semifinals

Poland 6 .... Australia 1
Spain 2 .... Ghana 0

Bronze Medal

Ghana 1 .... Australia 0

Gold Medal

Spain 3 .... Poland 2

TEAM HANDBALL

Round Robin Standings

First two teams in each group advance to medal round.

MEN

Group A	Gm	W	L	T	Pts	Medal Round
*Sweden	5	5	0	0	10	1-1
*Iceland	5	3	1	1	7	0-2
South Korea	5	3	2	0	6	—
Hungary	5	2	3	0	4	—
Czechoslovakia	5	1	3	1	3	—
Brazil	5	0	5	0	0	—

Group B	Gm	W	L	T	Pts	Medal Round
*Unified Team	5	5	0	0	10	2-0
*France	5	4	1	0	8	1-1
Spain	5	3	2	0	6	—
Romania	5	1	3	1	3	—
Germany	5	1	3	1	3	—
Egypt	5	0	5	0	0	—

Semifinals

Sweden 25 .... France 22
Unified Team 23 .... Iceland 19

Bronze Medal

France 24 .... Iceland 20

Gold Medal

Unified Team 22 .... Sweden 20

Handball (Cont.)

WOMEN

Group A	Gm	W	L	T	Pts	Medal Round
*Unified Team	3	3	0	0	6	1-1
*Germany	3	2	1	0	4	0-2
United States	3	1	2	0	2	—
Nigeria	3	0	3	0	0	—

Group B	Gm	W	L	T	Pts	Medal Round
*South Korea	3	2	0	1	5	2-0
*Norway	3	2	1	0	4	1-1
Austria	3	1	1	1	3	—
Spain	3	0	3	0	0	—

Semifinals

Norway 24 .... Unified Team 23
South Korea 26 .... Germany 25

Bronze Medal

Unified Team 24 .... Germany 20

Gold Medal

South Korea 28 .... Norway 21

VOLLEYBALL

Round Robin Standings

First four teams in each advance to medal round.

MEN

Group A	Gm	W	L	Pts	Medal Round
*Italy	5	4	1	8	0-1
*United States	5	4	1	8	2-1
*Spain	5	3	2	6	0-1
*Japan	5	2	3	4	0-1
Canada	5	1	4	2	—
France	5	1	4	2	—

Group B	Gm	W	L	Pts	Medal Round
*Brazil	5	5	0	10	3-0
*Cuba	5	4	1	8	1-2
*Unified Team	5	3	2	6	0-1
*Holland	5	2	3	4	2-1
South Korea	5	1	4	2	—
Algeria	5	0	5	0	—

Quarterfinals

United States 3 .... Unified Team 1
(12-15, 15-10, 15-4, 15-11)
Brazil 3 .... Japan 0
(15-12, 15-5, 15-12)
Holland 3 .... Italy 2
(15-9, 12-15, 8-15, 15-2, 17-16)
Cuba 3 .... Spain 0
(16-14, 15-9, 15-6)

Semifinals

Brazil 3 .... United States 1
(12-15, 15-8, 15-9, 15-12)
Holland 3 .... Cuba 0
(15-11, 15-13, 15-9)

Bronze Medal

United States 3 .... Cuba 1
(12-15, 15-13, 15-7, 15-11)

Gold Medal

Brazil 3 .... Holland 0
(15-12, 15-8, 15-5)

WOMEN

Group A	Gm	W	L	Pts	Medal Round
*Unified Team	3	2	1	4	1-1
*United States	3	2	1	4	2-1
Japan	3	2	1	4	0-1
Spain	3	0	3	0	—

Group B	Gm	W	L	Pts	Medal Round
*Cuba	3	3	0	6	2-0
*Brazil	3	2	1	4	1-2
Holland	3	1	2	1	0-1
China	3	0	3	0	—

Quarterfinals

Byes: Unified Team and Cuba

United States 3 .... Holland 1
(15-11, 11-15, 15-8, 15-7)
Brazil 3 .... Japan 1
(14-16, 15-13, 15-13, 15-9)

Semifinals

Cuba 3 .... United States 2
(8-15, 15-9, 6-15, 15-5, 15-11)
Unified Team 3 .... Brazil 1
(15-10, 13-15, 15-5, 15-5)

Bronze Medal

United States 3 .... Brazil 0
(15-8, 15-6, 15-13)

Gold Medal

Cuba 3 .... Unified Team 1
(16-14, 12-15, 15-12, 15-13)

WATER POLO

Round Robin Standings

First two teams in each group advance to medal round.

Group A	Gm	W	L	T	Pts	GF	GA	Medal Round
*Unified Team	5	5	0	0	10	50	32	1-1
*United States	5	4	1	0	8	40	24	0-2
Australia	5	2	2	1	5	44	41	—
Germany	5	1	2	2	4	38	41	—
France	5	1	3	1	3	38	42	—
Czechoslovakia	5	0	5	0	0	29	63	—

Group B	Gm	W	L	T	Pts	GF	GA	Medal Round
*Spain	5	4	0	1	9	52	36	1-1
*Italy	5	3	0	2	8	41	34	2-0
Hungary	5	2	1	2	6	49	46	—
Cuba	5	2	3	0	4	50	52	—
Holland	5	0	3	2	2	36	42	—
Greece	5	0	4	1	1	32	45	—

Semifinals

Spain 6 .... United States 4
Italy 9 .... Unified Team 8

Bronze Medal

Unified Team 8 .... United States 4

Gold Medal

Italy 9 .... 3 OT .... Spain 8

THE 1993 INFORMATION PLEASE SPORTS ALMANAC

O L Y M P I C S
S T A T I S T I C S

THROUGH THE YEARS
1896-1992
SUMMER GAMES

SEC B

PAGE 579

The Summer Olympics

The original Olympic Games were celebrated as a religious festival from 776 B.C. to 393 A.D., when Roman emperor Theodosius I banned all pagan festivals (the Olympics celebrated the Greek god Zeus).

On June 23, 1894, French educator Baron Pierre de Coubertin, speaking at the Sorbonne in Paris to a gathering of international sports leaders, proposed that the ancient games be revived on an international scale. The idea was enthusiastically received and the Modern Olympics were born.

The first Olympics were held two years later in Athens, where 311 athletes from 13 nations competed in the ancient Panathenaic stadium to large and enthusiastic crowds. Americans swept the track and field events, but Greece won the most medals with 47.

Year	No	Location	Dates	Nations	Most Medals	USA Medals
1896	I	Athens, GRE	Apr. 6-15	13	Greece (10-19-18—47)	11- 6- 2— 19 (2nd)
1900	II	Paris, FRA	May 20-Oct. 28	22	France (29-41-32—102)	20-14-19— 53 (2nd)
1904	III	St. Louis, Mo.	July 1-Nov. 23	12	USA (80-86-72—238)	80-86-72—238 (1st)
1906-a	—	Athens, GRE	Apr. 22-May 2	20	France (15-9-16—40)	12- 6- 5— 23 (4th)
1908	IV	London, GBR	Apr. 27-Oct .31	23	Britain (56-50-39—145)	23-12-12— 47 (2nd)
1912	V	Stockholm, SWE	May 5-July 22	28	Sweden (24-24-17—65)	23-19-19— 61 (2nd)
1916	VI	Berlin, GER	Cancelled (WWI)			
1920	VII	Antwerp, BEL	Apr. 20-Sept .12	29	USA (41-27-28—96)	41-27-28— 96 (1st)
1924	VIII	Paris, FRA	May 4-July 27	44	USA (45-27-27—99)	45-27-27— 99 (1st)
1928	IX	Amsterdam, HOL	May 17-Aug. 12	46	USA (22-18-16—56)	22-18-16— 56 (1st)
1932	X	Los Angeles, Calif.	July 30-Aug. 14	37	USA (41-32-31—104)	41-32-31—104 (1st)
1936	XI	Berlin, GER	Aug. 1-16	49	Germany (33-26-30-89)	24-20-12— 56 (2nd)
1940-b	XII	Tokyo, JPN	Cancelled (WWII)			
1944	XIII	London, GBR	Cancelled (WWII)			
1948	XIV	London, GBR	July 29-Aug. 14	59	USA (38-27-19—84)	38-27-19— 84 (1st)
1952-cd	XV	Helsinki, FIN	July 19-Aug. 3	69	USA (40-19-17—76)	40-19-17— 76 (1st)
1956-e	XVI	Melbourne, AUS	Nov. 22-Dec .8	67	USSR (37-29-32—98)	32-25-17— 74 (2nd)
1960	XVII	Rome, ITA	Aug. 25-Sept. 11	83	USSR (43-29-31—103)	34-21-16— 71 (2nd)
1964	XVIII	Tokyo, JPN	Oct. 10-24	93	USSR (36-26-28—90)	36-26-28— 90 (1st)
1968-f	XIX	Mexico City, MEX	Oct. 12-27	112	USA (45-28-34—107)	45-28-34—107 (1st)
1972	XX	Munich, W.GER	Aug. 26-Sept. 10	122	USSR (50-27-22-99)	33-31-30— 94 (2nd)
1976-g	XXI	Montreal, CAN	July 17-Aug. 1	92	USSR (49-41-35—125)	34-35-25— 94 (3rd)
1980-h	XXII	Moscow, USSR	July 19-Aug. 3	81	USSR (80-69-46—195)	Boycotted Games
1984-i	XXIII	Los Angeles, Calif.	July 28-Aug. 12	141	USA (83-61-30—174)	83-61-30—174 (1st)
1988	XXIV	Seoul, S.KOR	Sept. 17-Oct. 2	159	USSR (55-31-46—132)	36-31-27— 94 (3rd)
1992-j	XXV	Barcelona, SPA	July 25-Aug. 9	172	UT (45-38-29—112)	37-34-37—108 (2nd)
1996	XXVI	Atlanta, GA	July 20-Aug. 4			
2000-k	XXVII	TBA				

a—The 1906 Intercalated Games in Athens are considered unofficial by the IOC because they did not take place in the four-year cycle established in 1896. However, most record books include these interim games with the others.

b—The 1940 Summer Games are originally scheduled for Tokyo, but Japan resigns as host after the outbreak of the Sino-Japanese war in 1937. Helsinki is the next choice, but the IOC cancels the Games after Russian troops invade Finland in 1939.

c—Germany and Japan are allowed to rejoin Olympic community for first Summer Games since 1936. Though a divided country, the Germans send a joint East-West team.

d—The Soviet Union (USSR) participates in its first Olympics, Winter or Summer, since the Russian revolution in 1917 and takes home the second most medals (22-30-19—71).

e—Due to Australian quarantine laws, the equestrian events for the 1956 Games are held in Stockholm, June 10-17.

f—East Germany and West Germany send separate teams for the first time and will continue to do so through 1988.

g—The 1976 Games are boycotted by 32 nations, most of them from black Africa, because the IOC will not ban New Zealand. Earlier that year, a rugby team from New Zealand had toured racially-segregated South Africa.

h—The 1980 Games are boycotted by 64 nations, led by the USA, to protest the Russian invasion of Afghanistan on Dec.27, 1979.

i—The 1984 Games are boycotted by 14 Eastern Bloc nations, led by the USSR, to protest America's overcommercialization of the Games, inadequate security and an anti-Soviet attitude by the U.S. government. Most believe, however, the communist walkout is simply revenge for 1980.

j—Germany sends a single team after East and West German reunification in 1990 and the USSR competes as the Unified Team after the breakup of the Soviet Union in 1991.

k—As of September 1, 1992, the eight contending cities include Beijing, China; Berlin, Germany; Brazilia, Bazil; Istanbul, Turkey; Manchester, England; Milan, Italy; Sydney, Australia; and Tashkent, Uzbekistan.

Event-by-Event

Gold medal winners from 1896-1992 in the following events: baseball, basketball, boxing, diving, field hockey, gymnastics, soccer, swimming, tennis, and track & field.

BASEBALL

Year
1992 **Cuba**, Taiwan, Japan

BASKETBALL
MEN

Multiple gold medals: USA (10); USSR (2).

Year	
1936 **United States**, Canada, Mexico	
1948 **United States**, France, Brazil	
1952 **United States**, Soviet Union, Uruguay	
1956 **United States**, Soviet Union, Uruguay	
1960 **United States**, Soviet Union, Brazil	
1964 **United States**, Soviet Union, Brazil	
1968 **United States**, Yugoslavia, Soviet Union	

Year
1972 **Soviet Union**, United States, Cuba
1976 **United States**, Yugoslavia, Soviet Union
1980 **Yugoslavia**, Italy, Soviet Union
1984 **United States**, Spain, Yugoslavia
1988 **Soviet Union**, Yugoslavia, United States
1992 **United States**, Croatia, Lithuania

U.S. Medal-Winning Men's Basketball Teams

1936 (gold medal): Sam Balter, Ralph Bishop, Joe Fortenberry, Tex Gibbons, Francis Johnson, Carl Knowles, Frank Lubin, Art Mollner, Don Piper, Jack Ragland, Carl Shy, Willard Schmidt, Duane Swanson and William Wheatley. Coach—Jim Needles; Assistant—Gene Johnson. Final: USA over Canada, 19-8.

1948 (gold medal): Cliff Barker, Don Barksdale, Ralph Beard, Louis Beck, Vince Boryla, Gordon Carpenter, Alex Groza, Wallace Jones, Bob Kurland, Ray Lumpp, R.C. Pitts, Jesse Renick, Jackie Robinson and Ken Rollins. Coach—Omar Browning; Assistant—Adolph Rupp. Final: USA over France, 65-21.

1952 (gold medal): Ron Bontemps, Mark Freiberger, Wayne Glasgow, Charlie Hoag, Bill Hougland, John Keller, Dean Kelley, Bob Kenney, Bob Kurland, Bill Lienhard, Clyde Lovellette, Frank McCabe, Dan Pippen and Howie Williams. Coach—Warren Womble; Assistant—Forrest (Phog) Allen. Final: USA over USSR, 36-25.

1956 (gold medal): Dick Boushka, Carl Cain, Chuck Darling, Bill Evans, Gib Ford, Burdy Haldorson, Bill Hougland, Bob Jeangerard, K.C. Jones, Bill Russell, Ron Tomsic, Jim Walsh. Coach—Gerald Tucker; Assistant—Bruce Drake. Final: USA over USSR, 89-55.

1960 (gold medal): Jay Arnette, Walt Bellamy, Bob Boozer, Terry Dischinger, Jerry Lucas, Oscar Robertson, Adrian Smith, Burdy Haldorson, Darrall Imhoff, Allen Kelley, Lester Lane and Jerry West. Coach—Pete Newell; Assistant—Warren Womble. Final: USA over Brazil, 90-63.

1964 (gold medal): Jim (Bad News) Barnes, Bill Bradley, Larry Brown, Joe Caldwell, Mel Counts, Dick Davies, Walt Hazzard, Lucius Jackson, Pete McCaffrey, Jeff Mullins, Jerry Shipp and George Wilson. Coach—Hank Iba; Assistant—Henry Vaughn. Final: USA over USSR, 73-59.

1968 (gold medal): Mike Barnett, John Clawson, Don Dee, Cal Fowler, Spencer Haywood, Bill Hosket, Jim King, Glynn Saulters, Charlie Scott, Mike Silliman, Ken Spain, and JoJo White. Coach—Hank Iba; Assistant—Henry Vaughn. USA over Yugoslavia, 65-50.

1972 (silver medal/refused): Mike Bantom, Jim Brewer, Tom Burleson, Doug Collins, Kenny Davis, Jim Forbes, Tom Henderson, Bobby Jones, Dwight Jones, Kevin Joyce, Tom McMillen and Ed Ratleff. Coach—Hank Iba; Assistants— John Bach and Don Haskins. Final: USSR over USA, 51-50.

1976 (gold medal): Tate Armstrong, Quinn Buckner, Kenny Carr, Adrian Dantley, Walter Davis, Phil Ford, Ernie Grunfeld, Phil Hubbard, Mitch Kupchak, Tommy LaGarde, Scott May and Steve Sheppard. Coach—Dean Smith; Assistants—Bill Guthridge and John Thompson. Final: USA over Yugoslavia, 95-74.

1980 (no medal): USA boycotted Moscow Games. Final: Yugoslavia over Italy, 86-77.

1984 (gold medal): Steve Alford, Patrick Ewing, Vern Fleming, Michael Jordan; Joe Kleine, Jon Koncak, Chris Mullin, Sam Perkins, Alvin Robertson, Wayman Tisdale, Jeff Turner and Leon Wood. Coach—Bobby Knight; Assistants— Don Donoher and George Raveling. Final: USA over Spain, 96-65.

1988 (bronze medal): Stacey Augmon, Willie Anderson, Bimbo Coles, Jeff Grayer, Hersey Hawkins, Dan Magerle, Danny Manning, Mitch Richmond, J.R. Reid, David Robinson, Charles D. Smith and Charles E. Smith. Coach—John Thompson; Assistants—George Raveling and Mary Fenlon. Final: USSR over Yugoslavia, 76-63.

1992 (gold medal): Charles Barkley, Larry Bird, Clyde Drexler, Petrick Ewing, Magic Johnson, Michael Jordan, Christian Laettner, Karl Malone, Chris Mullin, Scottie Pippen, David Robinson and John Stockton. Coach—Chuck sxzDaly; Assistants—Lenny Wilkens, Mike Krzyzewski and P.J. Carlesimo. Final: USA over Croatia, 117-85.

WOMEN

Multiple gold medals: USSR/UT (3); USA (2).

Year
1976 **Soviet Union**, United States, Bulgaria
1980 **Soviet Union**, Bulgaria, Yugoslavia
1984 **United States**, South Korea, China

Year
1988 **United States**, Yugoslavia, Soviet Union
1992 **Unified Team**, China, United States

BOXING

Multiple gold medals: László Papp and Teofilo Stevenson (3); Angel Herrera, Oliver Kirk, Jerzy Kulej, Boris Lagutin and Harry Mallin (2). All fighters won titles in consecutive Olympics, except Kirk, who won both the Bantam and Featherweight titles in 1904 (he only had to fight once in each division).

Light Flyweight (106 lbs)

Year		Final Match	Year		Final Match
1968	Francisco Rodriguez, VEN.	Decision, 3-2	1984	Paul Gonzales, USA	Default
1972	György Gedó, HUN	Decision, 5-0	1988	Ivailo Hristov, BUL.	Decision, 5-0
1976	Jorge Hernandez, CUB.	Decision, 4-1	1992	Rogelio Marcelo, CUB	Decision, 24-10
1980	Shamil Sabyrov, USSR.	Decision, 3-2			

Flyweight (112 lbs)

Year		Final Match	Year		Final Match
1904	George Finnegan, USA.	Stopped, 1st	1960	Gyula Török, HUN	Decision, 3-2
1920	Frank Di Gennara, USA.	Decision	1964	Fernando Atzori, ITA.	Decision, 4-1
1924	Fidel LaBarba, USA.	Decision	1968	Ricardo Delgado, MEX	Decision, 5-0
1928	Antal Kocsis, HUN.	Decision	1972	Georgi Kostadinov, BUL.	Decision, 5-0
1932	István Énekes, HUN.	Decision	1976	Leo Randolph, USA	Decision, 3-2
1936	Willi Kaiser, GER.	Decision	1980	Peter Lessov, BUL.	Stopped, 2nd
1948	Pascual Perez, ARG.	Decision	1984	Steven McCrory, USA.	Decision, 4-1
1952	Nathan Brooks, USA.	Decision, 3-0	1988	Kim Swang-Sun, KOR.	Decision, 4-1
1956	Terence Spinks, GBR.	Decision	1992	Su Choi-Chol, N.Kor	Decision, 12-2

Bantamweight (119 lbs)

Year		Final Match	Year		Final Match
1904	Oliver Kirk, USA.	Stopped, 3rd	1960	Oleg Grigoryev, USSR	Decision
1908	Henry Thomas, GBR.	Decision	1964	Takao Sakurai, JPN	Stopped, 2nd
1920	Clarence Walker, SAF.	Decision	1968	Valery Sokolov, USSR	Stopped, 2nd
1924	William Smith, SAF.	Decision	1972	Orlando Martinez, CUB.	Decision, 5-0
1928	Vittorio Tamagnini, ITA.	Decision	1976	Gu Yong-Ju, N.Kor.	Decision, 5-0
1932	Horace Gwynne, CAN.	Decision	1980	Juan Hernandez, CUB	Decision, 5-0
1936	Ulderico Sergo, ITA.	Decision	1984	Maurizio Stecca, ITA.	Decision, 4-1
1948	Tibor Csik, HUN.	Decision	1988	Kennedy McKinney, USA	Decision, 5-0
1952	Pentti Hämäläinen, FIN.	Decision, 2-1	1992	Joel Casamayor, CUB	Decision, 14-8
1956	Wolfgang Behrendt, GER.	Decision			

Featherweight (125 lbs)

Year		Final Match	Year		Final Match
1904	Oliver Kirk, USA.	Decision	1960	Francesco Musso, ITA.	Decision, 4-1
1908	Richard Gunn, GBR.	Decision	1964	Stanislav Stepashkin, USSR	Decision, 3-2
1920	Paul Fritsch, FRA.	Decision	1968	Antonio Roldan, MEX	Won on Disq.
1924	John Fields, USA.	Decision	1972	Boris Kousnetsov, USSR	Decision, 3-2
1928	Lambertus van Klaveren, HOL.	Decision	1976	Angel Herrera, CUB	KO, 2nd
1932	Carmelo Robledo, ARG.	Decision	1980	Rudi Fink, E.Ger.	Decision, 4-1
1936	Oscar Casanovas, ARG.	Decision	1984	Meldrick Taylor, USA	Decision, 5-0
1948	Ernesto Formenti, ITA.	Decision	1988	Giovanni Parisi, ITA	Stopped, 1st
1952	Jan Zachara, CZE.	Decision, 2-1	1992	Andreas Tews, GER	Decision, 16-7
1956	Vladimir Safronov, USSR.	Decision			

Lightweight (132 lbs)

Year		Final Match	Year		Final Match
1904	Harry Spanger, USA	Decision	1960	Kazimierz Paździor, POL	Decision, 4-1
1908	Frederick Grace, GBR.	Decision	1964	Józef Grudzień, POL.	Decision
1920	Samuel Mosberg, USA.	Decision	1968	Ronnie Harris, USA.	Decision, 5-0
1924	Hans Nielsen, DEN.	Decision	1972	Jan Szczepański, POL.	Decision, 5-0
1928	Carlo Orlandi, ITA.	Decision	1976	Howard Davis, USA	Decision, 5-0
1932	Lawrence Stevens, SAF.	Decision	1980	Angel Herrera, CUB.	Stopped, 3rd
1936	Imre Harangi, HUN	Decision	1984	Pernell Whitaker, USA	Foe quit, 2nd
1948	Gerald Dreyer, SAF.	Decision	1988	Andreas Zuelow, E.Ger	Decision, 5-0
1952	Aureliano Bolognesi, ITA.	Decision, 2-1	1992	Oscar De La Hoya, USA	Decision, 7-2
1956	Richard McTaggart, GBR.	Decision			

Light Welterweight (139 lbs)

Year		Final Match	Year		Final Match
1952	Charles Adkins, USA.	Decision, 2-1	1976	Ray Leonard, USA.	Decision, 5-0
1956	Vladimir Yengibaryan, USSR	Decision	1980	Patrizio Oliva, ITA.	Decision, 4-1
1960	Bohumil Nemeček CZE.	Decision, 5-0	1984	Jerry Page, USA.	Decision, 5-0
1964	Jerzy Kulej, POL.	Decision, 5-0	1988	Vyacheslav Janovski, USSR	Decision, 5-0
1968	Jerzy Kulej, POL.	Decision, 3-2	1992	Hector Vinent, CUB.	Decision, 11-1
1972	Ray Seales, USA	Decision, 3-2			

Boxing (Cont.)

Welterweight (147 lbs)

Year		Final Match	Year		Final Match
1904	Albert Young, USA	Decision	1960	Nino Benvenuti, ITA	Decision, 4-1
1920	Albert Schneider, CAN	Decision	1964	Marian Kasprzyk, POL	Decision, 4-1
1924	Jean Delarge, BEL	Decision	1968	Manfred Wolke, E.Ger	Decision, 4-1
1928	Edward Morgan, NZE	Decision	1972	Emilio Correa, CUB	Decision, 5-0
1932	Edward Flynn, USA	Decision	1976	Jochen Bachfeld, E.Ger	Decision, 3-2
1936	Sten Suvio, FIN	Decision	1980	Andrés Aldama, CUB	Decision, 4-1
1948	Julius Torma, CZE	Decision	1984	Mark Breland, USA	Decision, 5-0
1952	Zygmunt Chychla, POL	Decision, 3-0	1988	Robert Wangila, KEN	KO, 2nd
1956	Nicolae Linca, ROM	Decision, 3-2	1992	Michael Carruth, IRE	Decision, 13-10

Light Middleweight (156 lbs)

Year		Final Match	Year		Final Match
1952	László Papp, HUN	Decision, 3-0	1976	Jerzy Rybicki, POL	Decision, 5-0
1956	László Papp, HUN	Decision	1980	Armando Martinez, CUB	Decision, 4-1
1960	Skeeter McClure, USA	Decision, 4-1	1984	Frank Tate, USA	Decision, 5-0
1964	Boris Lagutin, USSR	Decision, 4-1	1988	Park Si-Hun, S.Kor	Decision, 3-2
1968	Boris Lagutin, USSR	Decision, 5-0	1992	Juan Lemus, CUB	Decision, 6-1
1972	Dieter Kottysch, W.Ger	Decision, 3-2			

Middleweight (165 lbs)

Year		Final Match	Year		Final Match
1904	Charles Mayer, USA	Stopped, 3rd	1960	Edward Crook, USA	Decision, 3-2
1908	John Douglas, GBR	Decision	1964	Valery Popenchenko, USSR	Stopped, 1st
1920	Harry Mallin, GBR	Decision	1968	Christopher Finnegan, GBR	Decision, 3-2
1924	Harry Mallin, GBR	Decision	1972	Vyacheslav Lemechev, USSR	KO, 1st
1928	Piero Toscani, ITA	Decision	1976	Michael Spinks, USA	Stopped, 3rd
1932	Carmen Barth, USA	Decision	1980	José Gomez, CUB	Decision, 4-1
1936	Jean Despeaux, FRA	Decision	1984	Shin Joon-Sup, S.Kor	Decision, 3-2
1948	László Papp, HUN	Decision	1988	Henry Maske, E.Ger	Decision, 5-0
1952	Floyd Patterson, USA	KO, 1st	1992	Arie Hernandez, CUB	Decision, 12-7
1956	Gennady Schatkov, USSR	KO, 1st			

Light Heavyweight (178 lbs)

Year		Final Match	Year		Final Match
1920	Eddie Eagan, USA	Decision	1964	Cosimo Pinto, ITA	Decision, 3-2
1924	Harry Mitchell, GBR	Decision	1968	Dan Poznjak, USSR	Default
1928	Victor Avendaño, ARG	Decision	1972	Mate Parlov, YUG	Stopped, 2nd
1932	David Carstens, SAF	Decision	1976	Leon Spinks, USA	Stopped, 3rd
1936	Roger Michelot, FRA	Decision	1980	Slobodan Kacar, YUG	Decision, 4-1
1948	George Hunter, SAF	Decision	1984	Anton Josipović, YUG	Default
1952	Norvel Lee, USA	Decision, 3-0	1988	Andrew Maynard, USA	Decision, 5-0
1956	James Boyd, USA	Decision	1992	Torsten May, GER	Decision, 8-3
1960	Cassius Clay, USA	Decision, 5-0			

Note: Cassius Clay changed his name to Muhammad Ali after winning the world heavyweight championship in 1964.

Heavyweight (201 lbs)

Year		Final Match	Year		Final Match
1984	Henry Tillman, USA	Decision, 5-0	1992	Felix Savon, CUB	Decision, 14-1
1988	Ray Mercer, USA	KO, 1st			

Super Heavyweight (Unlimited)

Year		Final Match	Year		Final Match
1904	Samuel Berger, USA	Decision	1960	Franco De Piccoli, ITA	KO, 1st
1908	Albert Oldham, GBR	KO, 1st	1964	Joe Frazier, USA	Decision, 3-2
1920	Ronald Rawson, GBR	Decision	1968	George Foreman, USA	Stopped, 2nd
1924	Otto von Porat, NOR	Decision	1972	Teófilo Stevenson, CUB	Default
1928	Arturo Rodriguez Jurado, ARG	Stopped, 1st	1976	Teófilo Stevenson, CUB	KO, 3rd
1932	Santiago Lovell, ARG	Decision	1980	Teófilo Stevenson, CUB	Decision, 4-1
1936	Herbert Runge, GER	Decision	1984	Tyrell Biggs, USA	Decision, 4-1
1948	Rafael Iglesias, ARG	KO, 2nd	1988	Lennox Lewis, CAN	Stopped, 2nd
1952	Ed Sanders, USA	Won on Disq.	1992	Roberto Balado, CUB	Decision, 13-2
1956	Pete Rademacher, USA	Stopped, 1st			

Note: Heavyweight division until 1984.

Future World Heavyweight Champions

Six Olympic gold medal winners eventually went on to become heavyweight champion of the world.

Middleweights	Light Heavyweights	Heavyweights
Floyd Patterson	Cassius Clay	Joe Frazier
Michael Spinks	Leon Spinks	George Foreman

DIVING

MEN

Multiple gold medals: Greg Louganis (4); Klaus Dibiasi (3); Pete Desjardins, Sammy Lee, Bob Webster and Albert White (2).

Springboard

Year		Points	Year		Points
1908	Albert Zürner, GER	85.5	1960	Gary Tobian, USA	170.00
1912	Paul Günther, GER	79.23	1964	Ken Sitzberger, USA	159.90
1920	Louis Kuehn, USA	675.4	1968	Bernie Wrightson, USA	170.15
1924	Albert White, USA	696.4	1972	Vladimir Vasin, USSR	594.09
1928	Pete Desjardins, USA	185.04	1976	Phil Boggs, USA	619.05
1932	Michael Galitzen, USA	161.38	1980	Aleksandr Portnov, USSR	905.03
1936	Richard Degener, USA	163.57	1984	Greg Louganis, USA	754.41
1948	Bruce Harlan, USA	163.64	1988	Greg Louganis, USA	730.80
1952	David Browning, USA	205.29	1992	Mark Lenzi, USA	676.53
1956	Bob Clotworthy, USA	159.56			

Platform

Year		Points	Year		Points
1904	George Sheldon, USA	12.66	1956	Joaquin Capilla, MEX	152.44
1906	Gottlob Walz, GER	156.0	1960	Bob Webster, USA	165.56
1908	Hjalmar Johansson, SWE	83.75	1964	Bob Webster, USA	148.58
1912	Erik Adlerz, SWE	73.94	1968	Klaus Dibiasi, ITA	164.18
1920	Clarence Pinkston, USA	100.67	1972	Klaus Dibiasi, ITA	504.12
1924	Albert White, USA	97.46	1976	Klaus Dibiasi, ITA	600.51
1928	Pete Desjardins, USA	98.74	1980	Falk Hoffmann, E.Ger	835.65
1932	Harold Smith, USA	124.80	1984	Greg Louganis, USA	710.91
1936	Marshall Wayne, USA	113.58	1988	Greg Louganis, USA	638.61
1948	Sammy Lee, USA	130.05	1992	Sun Shuwei, CHN	677.31
1952	Sammy Lee, USA	156.28			

WOMEN

Multiple gold medals: Pat McCormick (4); Ingrid Engel-Krämer (3); Vicki Draves, Dorothy Poynton Hill and Gao Min (2).

Springboard

Year		Points	Year		Points
1920	Aileen Riggin, USA	539.9	1964	Ingrid Engel-Krämer, GER	145.00
1924	Elizabeth Becker, USA	474.5	1968	Sue Gossick, USA	150.77
1928	Helen Meany, USA	78.62	1972	Micki King, USA	450.03
1932	Georgia Coleman, USA	87.52	1976	Jennifer Chandler, USA	506.19
1936	Marjorie Gestring, USA	89.27	1980	Irina Kalinina, USSR	725.91
1948	Vicki Draves, USA	108.74	1984	Sylvie Bernier, CAN	530.70
1952	Pat McCormick, USA	147.30	1988	Gao Min, CHN	580.23
1956	Pat McCormick, USA	142.36	1992	Gao Min, CHN	572.40
1960	Ingrid Krämer, GER	155.81			

Platform

Year		Points	Year		Points
1912	Greta Johansson, SWE	39.9	1960	Ingrid Krämer, GER	91.28
1920	Stefani Fryland-Clausen, DEN	34.6	1964	Lesley Bush, USA	99.80
1924	Caroline Smith, USA	33.2	1968	Milena Duchková, CZE	109.59
1928	Elizabeth Becker Pinkston, USA	31.6	1972	Ulrika Knape, SWE	390.00
1932	Dorothy Poynton, USA	40.26	1976	Elena Vaytsekhovskaya, USSR	406.59
1936	Dorothy Poynton Hill, USA	33.93	1980	Martina Jäschke, E.Ger	596.25
1948	Vicki Draves, USA	68.87	1984	Zhou Jihong, CHN	435.51
1952	Pat McCormick, USA	79.37	1988	Xu Yanmei, CHN	445.20
1956	Pat McCormick, USA	84.85	1992	Fu Mingxia, CHN	461.43

FIELD HOCKEY

MEN

Multiple gold medals: India (8); Great Britain and Pakistan (3); West Germany/Germany (2).

Year		Year	
1908	**Great Britain**, Ireland, Scotland	1964	**India**, Pakistan, Australia
1920	**Great Britain**, Denmark, Belgium	1968	**Pakistan**, Australia, India
1928	**India**, Holland, Germany	1972	**West Germany**, Pakistan, India
1932	**India**, Japan, United States	1976	**New Zealand**, Australia, Pakistan
1936	**India**, Germany, Holland	1980	**India**, Spain, Soviet Union
1948	**India**, Great Britain, Holland	1984	**Pakistan**, West Germany, Great Britain
1952	**India**, Holland, Great Britain	1988	**Great Britain**, West Germany, Holland
1956	**India**, Pakistan, Germany	1992	**Germany**, Australia, Parkistan
1960	**Pakistan**, India, Spain		

Field Hockey (Cont.)

WOMEN

Year	
1980	**Zimbabwe**, Czechoslovakia, Soviet Union
1984	**Holland**, West Germany, United States

Year	
1988	**Australia**, South Korea, Holland
1992	**Spain**, Germany, Great Britain

GYMNASTICS

MEN

At least 4 gold medals (including team events): Sawao Kato (8); Nikolai Andrianov, Viktor Chukarin and Boris Shakhlin (7); Akinori Nakayama and Vitaly Scherbo (6); Anton Heida, Mitsuo Tsukahara and Takashi Ono (5); Vladimir Artemov, Yukio Endo, Georges Miez and Valentin Muratov (4).

All-Around

Year		Points	Year		Points
1900	Gustave Sandras, FRA	302	1952	Viktor Chukarin, USSR	115.7
1904	Julius Lenhart, AUT	69.80	1956	Viktor Chukarin, USSR	114.25
1906	Pierre Payssé, FRA	116	1960	Boris Shakhlin, USSR	115.95
1908	Alberto Braglia, ITA	317.0	1964	Yukio Endo, JPN	115.95
1912	Alberto Braglia, ITA	135.0	1968	Sawao Kato, JPN	115.9
1920	Giorgio Zampori, ITA	88.35	1972	Sawao Kato, JPN	114.650
1924	Leon Stukelj, YUG	110.340	1976	Nikolai Andrianov, USSR	116.65
1928	Georges Miez, SWI	247.500	1980	Aleksandr Dityatin, USSR	118.65
1932	Romeo Neri, ITA	140.625	1984	Koji Gushiken, JPN	118.7
1936	Alfred Schwarzmann, GER	113.100	1988	Vladimir Artemov, USSR	119.125
1948	Veikko Huhtanen, FIN	229.7	1992	Vitaly Scherbo, UT	59.025

Horizontal Bar

Year		Points	Year		Points
1896	Hermann Weingartner, GER	—	1964	Boris Shakhlin, USSR	19.625
1904	(TIE) Anton Heida, USA	40	1968	(TIE) Akinori Nakayama, JPN	19.55
	& Edward Hennig, USA	40		& Mikhail Voronin, USSR	19.55
1924	Leon Stukelj, YUG	19.73	1972	Mitsuo Tsukahara, JPN	19.725
1928	Georges Miez, SWI	19.17	1976	Mitsuo Tsukahara, JPN	19.675
1932	Dallas Bixler, USA	18.33	1980	Stoyan Deltchev, BUL	19.825
1936	Aleksanteri Saarvala, FIN	19.367	1984	Shinji Morisue, JPN	20.00
1948	Josef Stalder, SWI	19.85	1988	(TIE) Vladimir Artemov, USSR	19.900
1952	Jack Günthard, SWI	19.55		& Valeri Lyukin, USSR	19.900
1956	Takashi Ono, JPN	19.60	1992	Trent Dimas, USA	9.875
1960	Takashi Ono, JPN	19.60			

Parallel Bars

Year		Points	Year		Points
1896	Alfred Flatow, GER	—	1960	Boris Shakhlin, USSR	19.40
1904	George Eyser, USA	44	1964	Yukio Endo, JPN	19.675
1924	August Güttinger, SWI	21.63	1968	Akinori Nakayama, JPN	19.475
1928	Ladislav Vácha, CZE	18.83	1972	Sawao Kato, JPN	19.475
1932	Romeo Neri, ITA	18.97	1976	Sawao Kato, JPN	19.675
1936	Konrad Frey, GER	19.067	1980	Aleksandr Tkachyov, USSR	19.775
1948	Michael Reusch, SWI	19.75	1984	Bart Conner, USA	19.95
1952	Hans Eugster, SWI	19.65	1988	Vladimir Artemov, USSR	19.925
1956	Viktor Chukarin, USSR	19.20	1992	Vitaly Scherbo, UT	9.900

Vault

Year		Points	Year		Points
1896	Karl Schumann, GER	—	1960	(TIE) Takashi Ono, JPN	19.35
1904	(TIE) George Eyser, USA	36		& Boris Shakhlin, USSR	19.35
	& Anton Heida, USA	36	1964	Haruhiro Yamashita, JPN	19.60
1924	Frank Kriz, USA	9.98	1968	Mikhail Voronin, USSR	19.00
1928	Eugen Mack, SWI	9.58	1972	Klaus Köste, E.Ger	18.85
1932	Savino Guglielmetti, ITA	18.03	1976	Nikolai Andrianov, USSR	19.45
1936	Alfred Schwarzmann, GER	19.20	1980	Nikolai Andrianov, USSR	19.825
1948	Paavo Aaltonen, FIN	19.55	1984	Lou Yun, CHN	19.95
1952	Viktor Chukarin, USSR	19.20	1988	Lou Yun, CHN	19.875
1956	(TIE) Helmut Bantz, GER	18.85	1992	Vitaly Scherbo, UT	9.856
	& Valentin Muratov, USSR	18.85			

Pommel Horse

Year		Points	Year		Points
1896	Louis Zutter, SWI	—	1964	Miroslav Cerar, YUG	19.525
1904	Anton Heida, USA	42	1968	Miroslav Cerar, YUG	19.325
1924	Josef Wilhelm, SWI	21.23	1972	Viktor Klimenko, SOV	19.125
1928	Hermann Hänggi, SWI	19.75	1976	Zoltán Magyar, HUN	19.70
1932	István Pelle, HUN	19.07	1980	Zoltán Magyar, HUN	19.925
1936	Konr. J Frey, GER	19.333	1984	(TIE) Li Ning, CHN	19.95
1948	(TIE) Paavo Aaltonen, FIN	19.35		& Peter Vidmar, USA	19.95
	Veikko Huhtanen, FIN	19.35	1988	(TIE) Dmitri Bilozerchev, USSR	19.95
	& Heikki Savolainen, FIN	19.35		Zsolt Borkai, HUN	19.95
1952	Viktor Chukarin, USSR	19.50		& Lyubomir Gueraskov, BUL	19.95
1956	Boris Shakhlin, USSR	19.25	1992	(TIE) Pae Gil-Su, N.Kor	9.925
1960	(TIE) Eugen Ekman, FIN	19.375		& Vitaly Scherbo, UT	9.925
	& Boris Shakhlin, USSR	19.375			

Rings

Year		Points	Year		Points
1896	Ioannis Mitropoulos, GRE	—	1968	Akinori Nakayama, JPN	19.45
1904	Hermann Glass, USA	45	1972	Akinori Nakayama, JPN	19.35
1924	Francesco Martino, ITA	21.553	1976	Nikolai Andrianov, USSR	19.65
1928	Leon Štukelj, YUG	19.25	1980	Aleksandr Dityatin, USSR	19.875
1932	George Gulack, USA	18.97	1984	(TIE) Koji Gushiken, JPN	19.85
1936	Alois Hudec, CZE	19.433		& Li Ning, CHN	19.85
1948	Karl Frei, SWI	19.80	1988	(TIE) Holger Behrendt, E.Ger	19.85
1952	Grant Shaginyan, USSR	19.75		& Dmitri Bilozerchev, USSR	19.925
1956	Albert Azaryan, USSR	19.35	1992	Vitaly Scherbo, UT	9.862
1960	Albert Azaryan, USSR	19.725			
1964	Takuji Haytta, JPN	19.475			

Floor Exercise

Year		Points	Year		Points
1932	István Pelle, HUN	9.60	1968	Sawao Kato, JPN	19.475
1936	Georges Miez, SWI	18.666	1972	Nikolai Andrianov, USSR	19.175
1948	Ferenc Pataki, HUN	19.35	1976	Nikolai Andrianov, USSR	19.45
1952	William Thoresson, SWE	19.25	1980	Roland Brückner, E.Ger	19.75
1956	Valentin Muratov, USSR	19.20	1984	Li Ning, CHN	19.925
1960	Nobuyuki Aihara, JPN	19.45	1988	Sergei Kharkov, USSR	19.925
1964	Franco Menichelli, ITA	19.45	1992	Li Xiaosahuang, CHN	9.925

Team Combined Exercises

Year		Points	Year		Points
1904	United States	374.43	1956	Soviet Union	568.25
1906	Norway	19.00	1960	Japan	575.20
1908	Sweden	438	1964	Japan	577.95
1912	Italy	265.75	1968	Japan	575.90
1920	Italy	359.855	1972	Japan	571.25
1924	Italy	839.058	1976	Japan	576.85
1928	Switzerland	1718.625	1980	Soviet Union	598.60
1932	Italy	541.850	1984	United States	591.40
1936	Germany	657.430	1988	Soviet Union	593.35
1948	Finland	1358.30	1992	Unified Team	585.45
1952	Soviet Union	574.40			

WOMEN

At least 4 gold medals (including team events)**:** Larissa Latynina (9); Vera Cáslavská (7); Polina Astakhova, Nadia Comaneci, Agnes Keleti and Nelli Kim (5); Olga Korbut, Ecaterina Szabó and Lyudmila Tourischeva (4).

All-Around

Year		Points	Year		Points
1952	Maria Gorokhovskaya, USSR	76.78	1976	Nadia Comaneci, ROM	79.275
1956	Larissa Latynina, USSR	74.933	1980	Yelena Davydova, USSR	79.15
1960	Larissa Latynina, USSR	77.031	1984	Mary Lou Retton, USA	79.175
1964	Vera Cáslavská, CZE	77.564	1988	Yelena Shushunova, USSR	79.662
1968	Vera Cáslavská, CZE	78.25	1992	Tatiana Gutsu, UT	39.737
1972	Lyudmila Tourischeva, USSR	77.025			

Vault

Year		Points	Year		Points
1952	Yekaterina Kalinchuk, USSR	19.20	1976	Nelli Kim, USSR	19.80
1956	Larissa Latynina, USSR	18.833	1980	Natalia Shaposhnikova, USSR	19.725
1960	Margarita Nikolayeva, USSR	19.316	1984	Ecaterina Szabó, ROM	19.875
1964	Vera Cáslavská, CZE	19.483	1988	Svetlana Boginskaya, USSR	19.905
1968	Vera Cáslavská, CZE	19.775	1992	(TIE) Henrietta Onodi, HUN	9.925
1972	Karin Janz, E.Ger	19.525		& Lavinia Milosovici, ROM	9.925

Gymnastics (Cont.)
WOMEN
Uneven Bars

Year		Points	Year		Points
1952	Margit Korondi, HUN	19.40	1976	Nadia Comaneci, ROM	20.00
1956	Agnes Keleti, HUN	18.966	1980	Maxi Gnauck, E.Ger.	19.875
1960	Polina Astakhova, USSR	19.616	1984	Ma Yanhong, CHN.	19.95
1964	Polina Astakhova, USSR	19.332	1988	Daniela Silivas, ROM	20.00
1968	Vera Cáslavská, CZE	19.65	1992	Lu Li, CHN.	10.00
1972	Karin Janz, E.Ger	19.675			

Balance Beam

Year		Points	Year		Points
1952	Nina Bocharova, USSR.	19.22	1976	Nadia Comaneci, ROM	19.95
1956	Agnes Keleti, HUN	18.80	1980	Nadia Comaneci, ROM	19.80
1960	Eva Bosáková, CZE.	19.283	1984	(TIE) Simona Pauca, ROM	19.80
1964	Vera Cáslavská, CZE	19.449		& Ecaterina Szabó, ROM	19.80
1968	Natalya Kuchinskaya, USSR.	19.65	1988	Daniela Silivas, ROM	19.924
1972	Olga Korbut, USSR.	19.40	1992	Tatiana Lysenko, UT	9.975

Floor Exercise

Year		Points	Year		Points
1952	Agnes Keleti, HUN	19.36	1972	Olga Korbut, USSR	19.575
1956	(TIE) Agnes Keleti, HUN	18.733	1976	Nelli Kim, USSR.	19.85
	& Larissa Latynina, USSR.	18.733	1980	(TIE) Nadia Comaneci, ROM	19.875
1960	Larissa Latynina, USSR.	19.583		& Nelli Kim, USSR.	19.875
1964	Larissa Latynina, USSR.	19.599	1984	Ecaterina Szabó, ROM	19.975
1968	(TIE) Vera Cáslavská, CZE	19.675	1988	Daniela Silivas, ROM	19.937
	& Larissa Petrik, USSR.	19.675	1992	Lavinia Milosovici, ROM	10.000

Team Combined Exercises

Year		Points	Year		Points
1928	Holland	316.75	1968	Soviet Union	382.85
1936	Germany	506.50	1972	Soviet Union	380.50
1948	Czechoslovakia	445.45	1976	Soviet Union	466.00
1952	Soviet Union	527.03	1980	Soviet Union	394.90
1956	Soviet Union	444.800	1984	Romania	392.02
1960	Soviet Union	382.320	1988	Soviet Union	395.475
1964	Soviet Union	280.890	1992	Unified Team.	395.666

SOCCER

Multiple gold medals: Great Britain and Hungary (3); Uruguay and USSR (2).

Year		Year	
1900	**Great Britain**, France, Belgium	1956	**Soviet Union**, Yugoslavia, Bulgaria
1904	**Canada**, USA I, USA II	1960	**Yugoslavia**, Denmark, Hungary
1906	**Denmark**, Smyrna (Int'l entry), Greece	1964	**Hungary**, Czechoslovakia, Germany
1908	**Great Britain**, Denmark, Holland	1968	**Hungary**, Bulgaria, Japan
1912	**Great Britain**, Denmark, Holland	1972	**Poland**, Hungary, East Germany
1920	**Belgium**, Spain, Holland	1976	**East Germany**, Poland, Soviet Union
1924	**Uruguay**, Switzerland, Sweden	1980	**Czechoslovakia**, East Germany, Soviet Union
1928	**Uruguay**, Argentina, Italy	1984	**France**, Brazil, Yugoslavia
1936	**Italy**, Austria, Norway	1988	**Soviet Union**, Brazil, West Germany
1948	**Sweden**, Yugoslavia, Denmark	1992	**Spain**, Poland, Ghana
1952	**Hungary**, Yugoslavia, Sweden		

SWIMMING

World and Olympic records below that appear to be broken or equalled by winning times, heights and distances in susequent years, but are not so indicated, were all broken in preliminary races and field events leading up to the finals.

MEN
At least 4 gold medals (including relays): Mark Spitz (9); Matt Biondi (8); Charles Daniels, Don Schollander, and Johnny Weissmuller (5); Tamás Darnyi, Roland Matthes, John Naber, Murray Rose, Vladimir Salnikov and Henry Taylor (4). Note that Weissmuller's total includes a Water Polo gold medal.

50-meter Freestyle

Year		Time	Year		Time	
1904	Zoltán Halmay, HUN.	28.0	1988	Matt Biondi, USA.	22.14	**WR**
1906–84	Not held		1992	Aleksandr Popov, UT.	21.91	**OR**

100-meter Freestyle

Year		Time		Year		Time	
1896	Alfréd Hajós, HUN	1:22.2	OR	1952	Clarke Scholes, USA	57.4	
1904	Zoltán Halmay, HUN	1:02.8		1956	Jon Henricks, AUS	55.4	OR
1906	Charles Daniels, USA	1:13.4		1960	John Devitt, AUS	55.2	OR
1908	Charles Daniels, USA	1:05.6	WR	1964	Don Schollander, USA	53.4	OR
1912	Duke Kahanamoku, USA	1:03.4		1968	Michael Wenden, AUS	52.2	OR
1920	Duke Kahanamoku, USA	1:00.4	WR	1972	Mark Spitz, USA	51.22	WR
1924	Johnny Weissmuller, USA	59.0	OR	1976	Jim Montgomery, USA	49.99	WR
1928	Johnny Weissmuller, USA	58.6	OR	1980	Jorg Woithe, E.Ger	50:40	
1932	Yasuji Miyazaki, JPN	58.2		1984	Rowdy Gaines, USA	49.80	OR
1936	Ferenc Csik, HUN	57.6		1988	Matt Biondi, USA	48.63	OR
1948	Wally Ris, USA	57.3	OR	1992	Aleksandr Popov, UT	49.02	

200-meter Freestyle

Year		Time		Year		Time	
1900	Frederick Lane, AUS	2:25.2	OR	1980	Sergei Kopliakov, USSR	1:49.81	OR
1904	Charles Daniels, USA	2:44.2		1984	Michael Gross, W.Ger	1:47.44	WR
1968	Michael Wenden, AUS	1:55.2	OR	1988	Duncan Armstrong, AUS	1:47.25	WR
1972	Mark Spitz, USA	1:52.78	WR	1992	Yevgeny Sadovyi, UT	1:46.70	OR
1976	Bruce Furniss, USA	1:50.29	WR				

400-meter Freestyle

Year		Time		Year		Time	
1896	Paul Neumann, AUT	8:12.6		1952	Jean Boiteux, FRA	4:30.7	OR
1904	Charles Daniels, USA	6:16.2		1956	Murray Rose, AUS	4:27.3	OR
1906	Otto Scheff, AUT	6:23.8		1960	Murray Rose, AUS	4:18.3	OR
1908	Henry Taylor, GBR	5:36.8		1964	Don Schollander, USA	4:12.2	WR
1912	George Hodgson, CAN	5:24.4		1968	Mike Burton, USA	4:09.0	OR
1920	Norman Ross, USA	5:26.8		1972	Bradford Cooper, USA*	4:00.27	OR
1924	Johnny Weissmuller, USA	5:04.2	OR	1976	Brian Goodell, USA	3:51.93	WR
1928	Alberto Zorilla, ARG	5:01.6	OR	1980	Vladimir Salnikov, USSR	3:51.31	OR
1932	Buster Crabbe, USA	4:48.4	OR	1984	George DiCarlo, USA	3:51.23	OR
1936	Jack Medica, USA	4:44.5	OR	1988	Uwe Dassler, E.Ger	3:46.95	WR
1948	Bill Smith, USA	4:41.0	OR	1992	Yevgeny Sadovyi, UT	3:45.00	WR

*Cooper finished second to Rick DeMont of the U.S. who was disqualified when he flunked the post-race drug test (his asthma medication was on the IOC's banned list).

1500-meter Freestyle

Year		Time		Year		Time	
1896	Alfréd Hajós, HUN	18:22.2	OR	1952	Ford Konno, USA	18:30.3	OR
1900	John Arthur Jarvis, GBR	13:40.2		1956	Murray Rose, AUS	17:58.9	
1904	Emil Rausch, GER	27:18.2		1960	John Konrads, AUS	17:19.6	OR
1906	Henry Taylor, GBR	28:28.0		1964	Robert Windle, AUS	17:01.7	OR
1908	Henry Taylor, GBR	22:48.4	WR	1968	Mike Burton, USA	16:38.9	OR
1912	George Hodgson, CAN	22:00.0	WR	1972	Mike Burton, USA	15:52.58	WR
1920	Norman Ross, USA	22:23.2		1976	Brian Goodell, USA	15:02.40	WR
1924	Andrew (Boy) Charlton, AUS	20:06.6	WR	1980	Vladimir Salnikov, USSR	14:58.27	WR
1928	Arne Borge, SWE	19:51.8		1984	Mike O'Brien, USA	15:05.20	
1932	Kusuo Kitamura, JPN	19:12.4	OR	1988	Vladimir Salnikov, USSR	15:00.40	
1936	Noboru Terada, JPN	19:13.7		1992	Kieren Perkins, AUS	14:43.48	WR
1948	James McLane, USA	19:18.5					

100-meter Backstroke

Year		Time		Year		Time	
1904	Walter Brack, GER	1:16.8		1956	David Theile, AUS	1:02.2	OR
1908	Arno Bieberstein, GER	1:24.6	WR	1960	David Theile, AUS	1:01.9	OR
1912	Harry Hebner, USA	1:21.2		1968	Roland Matthes, E.Ger	58.7	OR
1920	Warren Kealoha, USA	1:15.2		1972	Roland Matthes, E.Ger	56.58	OR
1924	Warren Kealoha, USA	1:13.2	OR	1976	John Naber, USA	55.49	WR
1928	George Kojac, USA	1:08.2	WR	1980	Bengt Baron, SWE	56.33	
1932	Masaji Kiyokawa, JPN	1:08.6		1984	Rick Carey, USA	55.79	
1936	Adolf Kiefer, USA	1:05.9	OR	1988	Daichi Suzuki, JPN	55.05	
1948	Allen Stack, USA	1:06.4		1992	Mark Tewksbury, CAN	53.98	OR
1952	Yoshinobu Oyakawa, USA	1:05.4	OR				

Note: Event covered 100 yards in 1904.

200-meter Backstroke

Year		Time		Year		Time	
1900	Ernst Hoppenberg, GER	2:47.0		1980	Sándor Wladár, HUN	2:01.93	
1964	Jed Graef, USA	2:10.3	WR	1984	Rick Carey, USA	2:00.23	
1968	Roland Matthes, E.Ger	2:09.6	OR	1988	Igor Poliansky, USSR	1:59.37	
1972	Roland Matthes, E.Ger	2:02.82	=WR	1992	Martin Lopez-Zubero, SPA	1:58.47	OR
1976	John Naber, USA	1:59.19	WR				

Swimming (Cont.)
MEN
100-meter Breaststroke

Year		Time		Year		Time
1968	Don McKenzie, USA	1:07.7	OR	1984	Steve Lundquist, USA	1:01.65 WR
1972	Nobutaka Taguchi, JPN	1:04.94 WR		1988	Adrian Moorhouse, GBR	1:02.04
1976	John Hencken, USA	1:03.11 WR		1992	Nelson Diebel, USA	1:01.50 OR
1980	Duncan Goodhew, GBR	1:03.44				

200-meter Breaststroke

Year		Time		Year		Time
1908	Frederick Holman, GBR	3:09.2 WR		1960	Bill Mulliken, USA	2:37.4
1912	Walter Bathe, GER	3:01.8	OR	1964	Ian O'Brien, AUS	2:27.8 WR
1920	Hakan Malmroth, SWE	3:04.4		1968	Felipe Múñoz, MEX	2:28.7
1924	Robert Skelton, USA	2:56.6		1972	John Hencken, USA	2:21.55 WR
1928	Yoshiyuki Tsuruta, JPN	2:48.8	OR	1976	David Wilkie, GBR	2:15.11 WR
1932	Yoshiyuki Tsuruta, JPN	2:45.4		1980	Robertas Zhulpa, USSR	2:15.85
1936	Tetsuo Hamuro, JPN	2:41.5	OR	1984	Victor Davis, CAN	2:13.34 WR
1948	Joseph Verdeur, USA	2:39.3	OR	1988	József Szabó, HUN	2:13.52
1952	John Davies, AUS	2:34.4	OR	1992	Mike Barrowman, USA	2:10.16 WR
1956	Masaru Furukawa, JPN	2:34.7*	OR			

*In 1956, the butterfly stroke and breaststroke were separated into two different events.

100-meter Butterfly

Year		Time		Year		Time
1968	Doug Russell, USA	55.9	OR	1984	Michael Gross, W.Ger	53.08 WR
1972	Mark Spitz, USA	54.27 WR		1988	Anthony Nesty, SUR	53.0 OR
1976	Matt Vogel, USA	54.35		1992	Pablo Morales, USA	53.32
1980	Pär Arvidsson, SWE	54.92				

200-meter Butterfly

Year		Time		Year		Time
1956	Bill Yorzyk, USA	2:19.3	OR	1976	Mike Bruner, USA	1:59.23 WR
1960	Mike Troy, USA	2:12.8 WR		1980	Sergei Fesenko, USSR	1:59.76
1964	Kevin Berry, AUS	2:06.6 WR		1984	Jon Sieben, AUS	1:57.04 WR
1968	Carl Robie, USA	2:08.7		1988	Michael Gross, W.Ger	1:56.94 OR
1972	Mark Spitz, USA	2:00.70 WR		1992	Mel Stewart, USA	1:56.26 OR

200-meter Individual Medley

Year		Time		Year		Time
1968	Charles Hickcox, USA	2:12.0	OR	1988	Tamás Darnyi, HUN	2:00.17 WR
1972	Gunnar Larsson, SWE	2:07.17 WR		1992	Tamás Darnyi, HUN	2:00.76
1984	Alex Baumann, CAN	2:01.42 WR				

400-meter Individual Medley

Year		Time		Year		Time
1964	Richard Roth, USA	4:45.4 WR		1980	Aleksandr Sidorenko, USSR	4:22.89 OR
1968	Charles Hickcox, USA	4:48.4		1984	Alex Baumann, CAN	4:17.41 WR
1972	Gunnar Larsson, SWE	4:31.98 OR		1988	Tamás Darnyi, HUN	4:14.75 WR
1976	Rod Strachan, USA	4:23.68 WR		1992	Tamás Darnyi, HUN	4:14.23 OR

4x100-meter Freestyle Relay

Year		Time		Year		Time
1964	United States	3:32.2 WR		1984	United States	3:19.03 WR
1968	United States	3:31.7 WR		1988	United States	3:16.53 WR
1972	United States	3:26.42 WR		1992	United States	3:16.74
1976–80 Not held						

4x200-meter Freestyle Relay

Year		Time		Year		Time
1906	Hungary	16:52.4		1956	Australia	8:23.6 WR
1908	Great Britain	10:55.6 WR		1960	United States	8:10.2 WR
1912	Australia/New Zealand	10:11.6 WR		1964	United States	7:52.1 WR
1920	United States	10:04.4 WR		1968	United States	7:52.33
1924	United States	9:53.4 WR		1972	United States	7:35.78 WR
1928	United States	9:36.2 WR		1976	United States	7:23.22 WR
1932	Japan	8:58.4 WR		1980	Soviet Union	7:23.50
1936	Japan	8:51.5 WR		1984	United States	7:15.69 WR
1948	United States	8:46.0 WR		1988	United States	7:12.51 WR
1952	United States	8:31.1 OR		1992	Unified Team	7:11.95 WR

Note: Event was a 4x250-meter competition in 1906.

4x100-meter Medley Relay

Year		Time		Year		Time	
1960	United States	4:05.4	WR	1980	Australia	3:45.70	
1964	United States	3:58.4	WR	1984	United States	3:39.30	WR
1968	United States	3:54.9	WR	1988	United States	3:36.93	WR
1972	United States	3:48.16	WR	1992	United States	3:36.93	=WR
1976	United States	3:42.22	WR				

WOMEN

At least 4 gold medals (including relays): Kristin Otto (6); Krisztina Egerszegi, Kornelia Ender, Janet Evans and Dawn Fraser (4).

50-meter Freestyle

Year		Time		Year		Time	
1988	Kristin Otto, E.Ger	25.49	OR	1992	Yang Wenyi, CHN	24.79	WR

100-meter Freestyle

Year		Time		Year		Time	
1912	Fanny Durack, AUS	1:22.2		1964	Dawn Fraser, AUS	59.5	OR
1920	Ethelda Bleibtrey, USA	1:13.6	WR	1968	Jan Henne, USA	1:00.0	
1924	Ethel Lackie, USA	1:12.4		1972	Sandra Neilson, USA	58.59	OR
1928	Albina Osipowich, USA	1:11.0	OR	1976	Kornelia Ender, E.Ger	55.65	WR
1932	Helene Madison, USA	1:06.8	OR	1980	Barbara Krause, E.Ger	54.79	WR
1936	Rie Mastenbroek, HOL	1:05.9	OR	1984	(TIE) Nancy Hogshead, USA	55.92	
1948	Greta Andersen, DEN	1:06.3			& Carrie Steinseifer, USA	55.92	
1952	Katalin Szöke, HUN	1:06.8		1988	Kristin Otto, E.Ger	54.93	
1956	Dawn Fraser, AUS	1:02.0	WR	1992	Zhuang Yong, CHN	54.64	OR
1960	Dawn Fraser, AUS	1:01.2	OR				

200-meter Freestyle

Year		Time		Year		Time	
1968	Debbie Meyer, USA	2:10.5	OR	1984	Mary Wayte, USA	1:59.23	
1972	Shane Gould, AUS	2:03.56	WR	1988	Heike Friedrich, E.Ger	1:57.65	OR
1976	Kornelia Ender, E.Ger	1:59.26	WR	1992	Nicole Haislett, USA	1:57.90	
1980	Barbara Krause, E.Ger	1:58.33	OR				

400-meter Freestyle

Year		Time		Year		Time	
1920	Ethelda Bleibtrey, USA	4:34.0	WR	1964	Ginny Duenkel, USA	4:43.3	OR
1924	Martha Norelius, USA	6:02.2	OR	1968	Debbie Meyer, USA	4:31.8	OR
1928	Martha Norelius, USA	5:42.8	WR	1972	Shane Gould, AUS	4:19.44	WR
1932	Helene Madison, USA	5:28.5	WR	1976	Petra Thümer, E.Ger	4:09.89	WR
1936	Rie Mastenbroek, HOL	5:26.4	OR	1980	Ines Diers, E.Ger	4:08.76	OR
1948	Ann Curtis, USA	5:17.8	OR	1984	Tiffany Cohen, USA	4:07.10	OR
1952	Valéria Gyenge, HUN	5:12.1	OR	1988	Janet Evans, USA	4:03.85	WR
1956	Lorraine Crapp, AUS	4:54.6	OR	1992	Dagmar Hase, GER	4:07.18	
1960	Chris von Saltza, USA	4:50.6	OR				

Note: Event covered 300 meters in 1920.

800-meter Freestyle

Year		Time		Year		Time	
1968	Debbie Meyer, USA	9:24.0	OR	1984	Tiffany Cohen, USA	8:24.95	OR
1972	Keena Rothhammer, USA	8:53.68	WR	1988	Janet Evans, USA	8:20.20	OR
1976	Petra Thümer, E.Ger	8:37.14	WR	1992	Janet Evans, USA	8:25.52	
1980	Michelle Ford, AUS	8:28.90	OR				

100-meter Backstroke

Year		Time		Year		Time	
1924	Sybil Bauer, USA	1:23.2	OR	1964	Cathy Ferguson, USA	1:07.7	WR
1928	Maria Braun, HOL	1:22.0		1968	Kaye Hall, USA	1:06.2	WR
1932	Eleanor Holm, USA	1:19.4		1972	Melissa Belote, USA	1:05.78	OR
1936	Nida Senff, HOL	1:18.9		1976	Ulrike Richter, E.Ger	1:01.83	OR
1948	Karen-Margrete Harup, DEN	1:14.4	OR	1980	Rica Reinisch, E.Ger	1:00.86	WR
1952	Joan Harrison, SAF	1:14.3		1984	Theresa Andrews, USA	1:02.55	
1956	Judy Grinham, GBR	1:12.9	OR	1988	Kristin Otto, E.Ger	1:00.89	
1960	Lynn Burke, USA	1:09.3	WR	1992	Krisztina Egerszegi, HUN	1:00.68	OR

200-meter Backstroke

Year		Time		Year		Time	
1968	Pokey Watson, USA	2:24.8	OR	1984	Jolanda de Rover, HOL	2:12.38	
1972	Melissa Belote, USA	2:19.19	WR	1988	Krisztina Egerszegi, HUN	2:09.29	OR
1976	Ulrike Richter, E.Ger	2:13.43	OR	1992	Krisztina Egerszegi, HUN	2:07.06	OR
1980	Rica Reinisch, E.Ger	2:11.77	WR				

Swimming (Cont.)

100-meter Breaststroke

Year		Time		Year		Time	
1968	Djurdjica Bjedov, YUG.	1:15.8	OR	1984	Petra van Staveren, HOL	1:09.88	OR
1972	Cathy Carr, USA	1:13.58	WR	1988	Tania Dangalakova, BUL.	1:07.95	OR
1976	Hannelore Anke, E.Ger.	1:11.16		1992	Yelena Rudkovskaya, UT	1:08.00	
1980	Ute Geweniger, E.Ger	1:10.22					

WOMEN

200-meter Breaststroke

Year		Time		Year		Time	
1924	Lucy Morton, GBR	3:33.2	OR	1964	Galina Prozumenshikova, USSR	2:46.4	OR
1928	Hilde Schrader, GER	3:12.6		1968	Sharon Wichman, USA	2:44.4	OR
1932	Clare Dennis, AUS.	3:06.3	OR	1972	Beverley Whitfield, AUS	2:41.71	OR
1936	Hideko Maehata, JPN	3:03.6		1976	Marina Koshevaia, USSR	2:33.35	WR
1948	Petronella van Vliet, HOL	2:57.2		1980	Lina Kaciusyte, USSR	2:29.54	OR
1952	Éva Székely, HUN	2:51.7	OR	1984	Anne Ottenbrite, CAN	2:30.38	
1956	Ursula Happe, GER	2:53.1	OR	1988	Silke Hörner, E.Ger.	2:26.71	WR
1960	Anita Lonsbrough, GBR.	2:49.5	WR	1992	Kyoko Iwasaki, JPN	2:26.65	OR

100-meter Butterfly

Year		Time		Year		Time	
1956	Shelly Mann, USA	1:11.0	OR	1976	Kornelia Ender, E.Ger	1:00.13	=WR
1960	Carolyn Schuler, USA	1:09.5	OR	1980	Caren Metschuck, E.Ger	1:00.42	
1964	Sharon Stouder, USA.	1:04.7	WR	1984	Mary T. Meagher, USA	59.26	
1968	Lyn McClements, AUS	1:05.5		1988	Kristin Otto, E.Ger	59.00	OR
1972	Mayumi Aoki, JPN	1:03.34	WR	1992	Qian Hong, CHN	58.62	OR

200-meter Butterfly

Year		Time		Year		Time	
1968	Ada Kok, HOL.	2:24.7	OR	1984	Mary T. Meagher, USA.	2:06.90	OR
1972	Karen Moe, USA	2:15.57	WR	1988	Kathleen Nord, E.Ger.	2:09.51	
1976	Andrea Pollack, E.Ger.	2:11.41	OR	1992	Summer Sanders, USA.	2:08.67	
1980	Ines Geissler, E.Ger.	2:10.44	OR				

200-meter Individual Medley

Year		Time		Year		Time	
1968	Claudia Kolb, USA.	2:24.7	OR	1988	Daniela Hunger, E.Ger	2:12.59	OR
1972	Shane Gould, AUS.	2:23.07	WR	1992	Lin Li, CHN	2:11.65	WR
1984	Tracy Caulkins, USA	2:12.64	OR				

400-meter Individual Medley

Year		Time		Year		Time	
1964	Donna de Varona, USA.	5:18.7	OR	1980	Petra Schneider, E.Ger.	4:36.29	WR
1968	Claudia Kolb, USA.	5:08.5	OR	1984	Tracy Caulkins, USA.	4:39.24	
1972	Gail Neall, AUS.	5:02.97	WR	1988	Janet Evans, USA	4:37.76	
1976	Ulrike Tauber, E.Ger.	4:42.77	WR	1992	Krisztina Egerszegi, HUN	4:36.54	

4x100-meter Freestyle Relay

Year		Time		Year		Time	
1912	Great Britain.	5:52.8	WR	1960	United States.	4:08.9	WR
1920	United States.	5:11.6	WR	1964	United States.	4:03.8	WR
1924	United States.	4:58.8	WR	1968	United States.	4:02.5	OR
1928	United States.	4:47.6	WR	1972	United States.	3:55.19	WR
1932	United States.	4:38.0	WR	1976	United States.	3:44.82	WR
1936	Holland.	4:36.0	OR	1980	East Germany.	3:42.71	WR
1948	United States.	4:29.2	WR	1984	United States .	3:43.43	
1952	Hungary	4:24.4	WR	1988	East Germany.	3:40.63	OR
1956	Australia	4:17.1	WR	1992	United States.	3:39.46	WR

4x100-meter Medley Relay

Year		Time		Year		Time	
1960	United States.	4:41.1	WR	1980	East Germany.	4:06.67	WR
1964	United States.	4:33.9	WR	1984	United States.	4:08.34	
1968	United States.	4:28.3	OR	1988	East Germany.	4:03.74	OR
1972	United States.	4:20.75	WR	1992	United States.	4:02.54	WR
1976	East Germany.	4:07.95	WR				

TENNIS
MEN

Multiple gold medals (including doubles): John Boland, Max Decugis, Laurie Doherty, Reggie Doherty, Arthur Gore, Andre Grobert, Vincent Richards, Charles Winslow and Beals Wright (2).

Singles

Year			Year		
1896	John Boland	Great Britain/Ireland	1920	Louis Raymond	South Africa
1900	Laurie Doherty,	Great Britain	1924	Vincent Richards	United States
1904	Beals Wright	United States	1928–84	Not held	
1906	Max Decugis	France	1988	Miloslav Mecir	Czechoslovakia
1908	Josiah Ritchie	Great Britain	1992	Marc Rosset	Switzerland
	(Indoor) Arthur Gore	Great Britain			
1912	Charles Winslow	South Africa			
	(Indoor) André Gobert	France			

Doubles

Year		Year	
1896	John Boland, IRL & Fritz Traun, GER	1920	Noel Turnbull & Max Woosnam, GBR
1900	Laurie and Reggie Doherty, GBR	1924	Vincent Richards & Frank Hunter, USA
1904	Edgar Leonard & Beals Wright, USA	1928–84	Not held
1906	Max Decugis & Maurice Germot, FRA	1988	Ken Flach & Robert Seguso, USA
1908	George Hillyard & Reggie Doherty, GRB	1992	Boris Becker & Michael Stich, GER
	(Indoor) Arthur Gore & Herbert Barrett, GBR		
1912	Charles Winslow & Harold Kitson, SAF		
	(Indoor) André Gobert & Maurice Germot, FRA		

WOMEN

Multiple gold medals (including doubles): Helen Wills (2).

Singles

Year			Year		
1900	Charlotte Cooper	Great Britain	1920	Suzanne Lenglen	France
1906	Esmee Simiriotou	Greece	1924	Helen Wills	United States
1908	Dorothea Chambers	Great Britain	1928–84	Not held	
	(Indoor) Gwen Eastlake-Smith	Great Britain	1988	Steffi Graf	West Germany
1912	Marguerite Broquedis	France	1992	Jennifer Capriati	USA
	(Indoor) Edith Hannam	Great Britain			

Doubles

Year		Year	
1920	Winifred McNair & Kitty McKane, GBR	1988	Pam Shriver & Zina Garrison, USA
1924	Hazel Wightman & Helen Wills, USA	1992	Gigi Fernandez & Mary Joe Fernandez, USA
1928–84	Not held		

TRACK & FIELD

World and Olympic records below that appear to be broken or equalled by winning times, heights and distances in subsequent years, but are not so indicated, were all broken in preliminary races and field events leading up to the finals.

MEN

At least 4 gold medals (including relays and discontinued events): Ray Ewry (10); Paavo Nurmi (9); Carl Lewis (8); Ville Ritola and Martin Sheridan (5); Harrison Dillard, Archie Hahn, Hannes Kolehmainen, Alvin Kraenzlein, Eric Lemming, Jim Lightbody, Al Oerter, Jesse Owens, Meyer Prinstein, Mel Sheppard, Lasse Viren and Emil Zátopek (4). Note that all of Ewry's gold medals came before 1912, in the Standing High, Long and Triple jumps.

100 meters

Year		Time		Year		Time	
1896	Tom Burke, USA	12.0		1952	Lindy Remigino, USA	10.4	
1900	Frank Jarvis, USA	11.0		1956	Bobby Morrow, USA	10.5	
1904	Archie Hahn, USA	11.0		1960	Armin Hary, GER	10.2	OR
1906	Archie Hahn, USA	11.2		1964	Bob Hayes, USA	10.0	=WR
1908	Reggie Walker, SAF	10.8	=OR	1968	Jim Hines, USA	9.95	WR
1912	Ralph Craig, USA	10.8		1972	Valery Borzov, USSR	10.14	
1920	Charley Paddock, USA	10.8		1976	Hasely Crawford, TRI	10.06	
1924	Harold Abrahams, GBR	10.6	=OR	1980	Allan Wells, GBR	10.25	
1928	Percy Williams, CAN	10.8		1984	Carl Lewis, USA	9.99	
1932	Eddie Tolan, USA	10.3	OR	1988	Carl Lewis, USA*	9.92	WR
1936	Jesse Owens, USA	10.3ʷ		1992	Linford Christie, GBR	9.96	
1948	Harrison Dillard, USA	10.3	=OR				

ʷ indicates wind-aided.

*Lewis finished second to Ben Johnson of Canada, who set a world record of 9.79 seconds. A day later, Johnson was stripped of his gold medal and his record when he tested positive for steroid use in a post-race drug test.

Track & Field (Cont.)
MEN
200 meters

Year		Time		Year		Time	
1900	John Walter Tewksbury, USA	22.2		1956	Bobby Morrow, USA	20.6	OR
1904	Archie Hahn, USA	21.6		1960	Livio Berruti, ITA	20.5	=WR
1908	Bobby Kerr, CAN	22.6		1964	Henry Carr, USA	20.3	OR
1912	Ralph Craig, USA	21.7		1968	Tommie Smith, USA	19.83	WR
1920	Allen Woodring, USA	22.0		1972	Valery Borzov, USSR	20.00	
1924	Jackson Scholz, USA	21.6		1976	Donald Quarrie, JAM	20.23	
1928	Percy Williams, CAN	21.8		1980	Pietro Mennea, ITA	20.19	
1932	Eddie Tolan, USA	21.2	OR	1984	Carl Lewis, USA	19.80	OR
1936	Jesse Owens, USA	20.7	OR	1988	Joe DeLoach, USA	19.75	OR
1948	Mel Patton, USA	21.1		1992	Mike Marsh, USA	20:01	
1952	Andy Stanfield, USA	20.7					

400 meters

Year		Time		Year		Time	
1896	Tom Burke, USA	54.2		1952	George Rhoden, JAM	45.9	OR
1890	Maxey Long, USA	49.4	OR	1956	Charley Jenkins, USA	46.7	
1904	Harry Hillman, USA	49.2	OR	1960	Otis Davis, USA	44.9	WR
1906	Paul Pilgrim, USA	53.2		1964	Mike Larrabee, USA	45.1	
1908	Wyndham Halswelle, GBR	50.0		1968	Lee Evans, USA	43.86	WR
1912	Charlie Reidpath, USA	48.2	OR	1972	Vince Matthews, USA	44.66	
1920	Bevil Rudd, SAF	49.6		1976	Alberto Juantorena, CUB	44.26	
1924	Eric Liddell, GBR	47.6	OR	1980	Viktor Markin, USSR	44.60	
1928	Ray Barbuti, USA	47.8		1984	Alonzo Babers, USA	44.27	
1932	Bill Carr, USA	46.2	WR	1988	Steve Lewis, USA	43.87	
1936	Archie Williams, USA	46.5		1992	Quincy Watts, USA	43.50	OR
1948	Arthur Wint, JAM	46.2					

800 meters

Year		Time		Year		Time	
1896	Teddy Flack, AUS	2:11.0		1952	Mal Whittfield, USA	1:49.2	=OR
1900	Alfred Tysoe, GBR	2:01.2		1956	Tom Courtney, USA	1:47.7	OR
1904	Jim Lightbody, USA	1:56.0	OR	1960	Peter Snell, NZE	1:46.3	OR
1906	Paul Pilgrim, USA	2:01.5		1964	Peter Snell, NZE	1:45.1	OR
1908	Mel Sheppard, USA	1:52.8	OR	1968	Ralph Doubell, AUS	1:44.3	=WR
1912	Ted Meredith, USA	1:51.9	WR	1972	Dave Wottle, USA	1:45.9	
1920	Albert Hill, GBR	1:53.4		1976	Alberto Juantorena, CUB	1:43.50	WR
1924	Douglas Lowe, GBR	1:52.4		1980	Steve Ovett, GBR	1:45.4	
1928	Douglas Lowe, GBR	1:51.8	OR	1984	Joaquim Cruz, BRA	1:43.00	OR
1932	Tommy Hampson, GBR	1:49.7	WR	1988	Paul Ereng, KEN	1:43.45	
1936	John Woodruff, USA	1:52.9		1992	William Tanui, KEN	1:43.66	
1948	Mal Whittfield, USA	1:49.2	OR				

1500 meters

Year		Time		Year		Time	
1896	Teddy Flack, AUS	4:33.2		1952	Josy Barthel, LUX	3:45.1	OR
1900	Charles Bennett, GBR	4:06.2	WR	1956	Ron Delany, IRL	3:41.2	OR
1904	Jim Lightbody, USA	4:05.4	WR	1960	Herb Elliott, AUS	3:35.6	WR
1906	Jim Lightbody, USA	4:12.0		1964	Peter Snell, NZE	3:38.1	
1908	Mel Sheppard, USA	4:03.4	OR	1968	Kip Keino, KEN	3:34.9	OR
1912	Arnold Jackson, GBR	3:56.8	OR	1972	Pekkha Vasala, FIN	3:36.3	
1920	Albert Hill, GBR	4:01.8		1976	John Walker, NZE	3:39.17	
1924	Paavo Nurmi, FIN	3:53.6	OR	1980	Sebastian Coe, GBR	3:38.4	
1928	Harry Larva, FIN	3:53.2	OR	1984	Sebastian Coe, GBR	3:32.53	OR
1932	Luigi Beccali, ITA	3:51.2	OR	1988	Peter Rono, KEN	3:35.96	
1936	John Lovelock, NZE	3:47.8	WR	1992	Fermin Cacho, SPA	3:40.12	
1948	Henry Eriksson, SWE	3:49.8					

5000 meters

Year		Time		Year		Time	
1912	Hannes Kolehmainen, FIN	14:36.6	WR	1960	Murray Halberg, NZE	13:43.4	
1920	Joseph Guillemot, FRA	14:55.6		1964	Bob Schul, USA	13:48.8	
1924	Paavo Nurmi, FIN	14:31.2	OR	1968	Mohamed Gammoudi, TUN	14:05.0	
1928	Ville Ritola, FIN	14:38.0		1972	Lasse Viren, FIN	13:26.4	OR
1932	Lauri Lehtinen, FIN	14:30.0	OR	1976	Lasse Viren, FIN	13:24.76	
1936	Gunnar Höckert, FIN	14:22.2	OR	1980	Miruts Yifter, ETH	13:21.0	
1948	Gaston Reiff, BEL	14:17.6	OR	1984	Said Aouita, MOR	13:05.59	OR
1952	Emil Zátopek, CZE	14:06.6	OR	1988	John Ngugi, KEN	13:11.70	
1956	Vladimir Kuts, USSR	13:39.6	OR	1992	Dieter Baumann, GER	13:12.52	

10,000 meters

Year		Time		Year		Time	
1912	Hannes Kolehmainen, FIN	31:20.8		1960	Pyotr Bolotnikov, USSR	28:32.2	OR
1920	Paavo Nurmi, FIN	31:45.8		1964	Billy Mills, USA	28:24.4	OR
1924	Ville Ritola, FIN	30:23.2	WR	1968	Naftali Temu, KEN	29:27.4	
1928	Paavo Nurmi, FIN	30:18.8	OR	1972	Lasse Viren, FIN	27:38.4	WR
1932	Janusz Kusocinski, POL	30:11.4	OR	1976	Lasse Viren, FIN	27:40.38	
1936	Ilmari Salminen, FIN	30:15.4		1980	Miruts Yifter, ETH	27:42.7	
1948	Emil Zátopek, CZE	29:59.6	OR	1984	Alberto Cova, ITA	27:47.54	
1952	Emil Zátopek, CZE	29:17.0	OR	1988	Brahim Boutaib, MOR	27:21.46	OR
1956	Vladimir Kuts, USSR	28:45.6	OR	1992	Khalid Skah, MOR	27:46.70	

Marathon

Year		Time		Year		Time	
1896	Spiridon Louis, GRE	2:58:50		1952	Emil Zátopek, CZE	2:23:03.2	OR
1900	Michel Thqeato, FRA	2:59:45		1956	Alain Mimoun, FRA	2:25:00.0	
1904	Thomas Hicks, USA	3:28:53		1960	Abebe Bikila, ETH	2:15:16.2	WB
1906	Billy Sherring, CAN	2:51:23.6		1964	Abebe Bikila, ETH	2:12:11.2	WB
1908	Johnny Hayes, USA*	2:55:18.4	WR	1968	Mamo Wolde, ETH	2:20:26.4	
1912	Kenneth McArthur, SAF	2:36:54.8		1972	Frank Shorter, USA	2:12:19.8	
1920	Hannes Kolehmainen, FIN	2:32:35.8	WB	1976	Waldemar Cierpinski, E.Ger	2:09:55.0	OR
1924	Albin Stenroos, FIN	2:41:22.6		1980	Waldemar Cierpinski, E.Ger	2:11:03.0	
1928	Boughêra El Ouafi, FRA	2:32:57.0		1984	Carlos Lopes, POR	2:09:21.0	OR
1932	Juan Carlos Zabala, ARG	2:31:36.0	OR	1988	Gelindo Bordin, ITA	2:10:32	
1936	Sohn Kee-Chung, JPN†	2:29:19.2	OR	1992	Hwang Young-Cho, S.Kor	2:13:23	
1948	Delfo Cabrera, ARG	2:34:51.6					

*Dorando Pietri of Italy placed first, but was disqualified for being helped across the finish line.
†Sohn was a Korean, but he was forced to compete under the name Kitei Son by Japan, which occupied Korea at the time.
Note: Marathon distances—40,000 meters (1896,1904); 40,260 meters (1900); 41,860 meters (1906); 42,195 meters (1908 and since 1924); 40,200 meters (1912); 42,750 meters (1920). Current distance of 42,195 meters measures 26 miles, 385 yards.

110-meter Hurdles

Year		Time		Year		Time	
1896	Tom Curtis, USA	17.6		1952	Harrison Dillard, USA	13.7	OR
1900	Alvin Kraenzlein, USA	15.4	OR	1956	Lee Calhoun, USA	13.5	OR
1904	Frederick Schule, USA	16.0		1960	Lee Calhoun, USA	13.8	
1906	Robert Leavitt, USA	16.2		1964	Hayes Jones, USA	13.6	
1908	Forrest Smithson, USA	15.0	WR	1968	Willie Davenport, USA	13.3	OR
1912	Frederick Kelly, USA	15.1		1972	Rod Milburn, USA	13.24	=WR
1920	Earl Thomson, CAN	14.8	WR	1976	Guy Drut, FRA	13.30	
1924	Daniel Kinsey, USA	15.0		1980	Thomas Munkelt, E.Ger	13.39	
1928	Syd Atkinson, SAF	14.8		1984	Roger Kingdom, USA	13.20	OR
1932	George Saling, USA	14.6		1988	Roger Kingdom, USA	12.98	OR
1936	Forrest (Spec) Towns, USA	14.2		1992	Mark McKoy, USA	13.12	
1948	William Porter, USA	13.9	OR				

400-meter Hurdles

Year		Time		Year		Time	
1900	John Walter Tewksbury, USA	57.6		1956	Glenn Davis, USA	50.1	=OR
1904	Harry Hillman, USA	53.0		1960	Glenn Davis, USA	49.3	OR
1908	Charley Bacon, USA	55.0	WR	1964	Rex Cawley, USA	49.6	
1920	Frank Loomis, USA	54.0	WR	1968	David Hemery, GBR	48.12	WR
1924	Morgan Taylor, USA	52.6		1972	John Akii-Bua, UGA	47.82	WR
1928	David Burghley, GBR	53.4	OR	1976	Edwin Moses, USA	47.64	WR
1932	Bob Tisdall, IRL	51.7		1980	Volker Beck, E.Ger	48.70	
1936	Glenn Hardin, USA	52.4		1984	Edwin Moses, USA	47.75	
1948	Roy Cochran, USA	51.1	OR	1988	Andre Phillips, USA	47.19	OR
1952	Charley Moore, USA	50.8	OR	1992	Kevin Young, USA	46.78	WR

3000-meter Steeplechase

Year		Time		Year		Time	
1900	George Orton, CAN/USA	7:34.4		1956	Chris Brasher, GBR	8:41.2	OR
1904	Jim Lightbody, USA	7:39.6		1960	Zdzislaw Krzyszkowiak, POL	8:34.2	OR
1908	Arthur Russell, GBR	10:47.8		1964	Gaston Roelants, BEL	8:30.8	OR
1920	Percy Hodge, GBR	10:00.4	OR	1968	Amos Biwott, KEN	8:51.0	
1924	Ville Ritola, FIN	9:33.6	OR	1972	Kip Keino, KEN	8:23.6	OR
1928	Toivo Loukola, FIN	9:21.8	WR	1976	Anders Gärderud, SWE	8:08.2	WR
1932	Volmari Iso-Hollo, FIN*	10:33.4		1980	Bronislaw Malinowski, POL	8:09.7	
1936	Volmari Iso-Hollo, FIN	9:03.8	WR	1984	Julius Korir, KEN	8:11.80	
1948	Thore Sjöstrand, SWE	9:04.6		1988	Julius Kariuki, KEN	8:05.51	OR
1952	Horace Ashenfelter, USA	8:45.4	WR	1992	Matthew Birir, KEN	8:08.84	

*Iso-Hollo ran one extra lap due to lap counter's mistake.
Note: Other steeplechase distances—2500 meters (1900); 2590 meters (1904); 3200 meters (1908) and 3460 meters (1936).

Track & Field (Cont.)
MEN
4x100-meter Relay

Year		Time		Year		Time	
1912	Great Britain	42.4		1960	Germany	39.5	=WR
1920	United States	42.2	WR	1964	United States	39.0	WR
1924	United States	41.0	=WR	1968	United States	38.2	WR
1928	United States	41.0	=WR	1972	United States	38.19	WR
1932	United States	40.0	WR	1976	United States	38.33	WR
1936	United States	39.8	WR	1980	Soviet Union	38.26	
1948	United States	40.6		1984	United States	37.83	WR
1952	United States	40.1		1988	Soviet Union	38.19	
1956	United States	39.5	WR	1992	United States	37.40	WR

4x400-meter Relay

Year		Time		Year		Time	
1908	United States	3:29.4		1960	United States	3:02.2	WR
1912	United States	3:16.6	WR	1964	United States	3:00.7	WR
1920	Great Britain	3:22.2		1968	United States	2:56.16	WR
1924	United States	3:16.0	WR	1972	Kenya	2:59.8	
1928	United States	3:14.2	WR	1976	United States	2:58.65	
1932	United States	3:08.2	WR	1980	Soviet Union	3:01.1	
1936	Great Britain	3:09.0		1984	United States	2:57.91	
1948	United States	3:10.4		1988	United States	2:56.16	=WR
1952	Jamaica	3:03.9	WR	1992	United States	2:55.74	WR
1956	United States	3:04.8					

20-kilometer Walk

Year		Time		Year		Time	
1956	Leonid Spirin, USSR	1:31:27.4		1976	Daniel Bautista, MEX	1:24:40.6	OR
1960	Vladimir Golubnichiy, USSR	1:34:07.2		1980	Maurizio Damilano, ITA	1:23:35.5	OR
1964	Ken Matthews, GBR	1:29:34.0		1984	Ernesto Canto, MEX	1:23:13	OR
1968	Vladimir Golubnichiy, USSR	1:33:58.4		1988	Jozef Pribilinec, CZE	1:19:57	OR
1972	Peter Frenkel, E.Ger	1:26:42.4	OR	1992	Daniel Plaza Montero, SPA	1:21:45	

50-kilometer Walk

Year		Time		Year		Time	
1932	Thomas Green, GBR	4:50:10		1968	Christoph Höhne, E.Ger	4:20:13.6	
1936	Harold Whitlock, GBR	4:30:41.4	OR	1972	Bernd Kannenberg, W.Ger	3:56:11.6	OR
1948	John Ljunggren, SWE	4:41:52		1976	Not held		
1952	Giuseppe Dordoni, ITA	4:28:07.8	OR	1980	Hartwig Gauder, E.Ger	3:49:24.0	OR
1956	Norman Read, NZE	4:30:42.8		1984	Raúl González, MEX	3:47:26	OR
1960	Don Thompson, GBR	4:25:30.0	OR	1988	Vyacheslav Ivanenko, USSR	3:38:29	OR
1964	Abdon Pamich, ITA	4:11:12.4	OR	1992	Andrei Perlov, UT	3:50:13	

High Jump

Year		Height		Year		Height	
1896	Ellery Clark, USA	5-11¼		1952	Walt Davis, USA	6- 8½	OR
1900	Irving Baxter, USA	6- 2¾	OR	1956	Charley Dumas, USA	6-11½	OR
1904	Sam Jones, USA	5-11		1960	Robert Shavlakadze, USSR	7- 1	OR
1906	Cornelius Leahy, GBR/IRL	5-10		1964	Valery Brumel, USSR	7- 1¾	OR
1908	Harry Porter, USA	6- 3	OR	1968	Dick Fosbury, USA	7- 4¼	OR
1912	Alma Richards, USA	6- 4	OR	1972	Yuri Tarmak, USSR	7- 3¾	
1920	Richmond Landon, USA	6- 4	=OR	1976	Jacek Wszola, POL	7- 4½	OR
1924	Harold Osborn, USA	6- 6	OR	1980	Gerd Wessig, E.Ger	7- 8¾	WR
1928	Bob King, USA	6- 4½		1984	Dietmar Mögenburg, W.Ger	7- 8½	
1932	Duncan McNaughton, CAN	6- 5½		1988	Gennady Avdeyenko, USSR	7- 9¾	OR
1936	Cornelius Johnson, USA	6- 8	OR	1992	Javier Sotomayor, CUB	7- 8	
1948	John Winter, AUS	6- 6					

Pole Vault

Year		Height		Year		Height	
1896	William Hoyt, USA	10-10		1948	Guinn Smith, USA	14-1¼	
1900	Irving Baxter, USA	10-10		1952	Bob Richards, USA	14-11	
1904	Charles Dvorak, USA	11- 5¾		1956	Bob Richards, USA	14-11½	OR
1906	Fernand Gonder, FRA	11- 5¾		1960	Don Bragg, USA	15- 5	OR
1908	(TIE) Edward Cooke, USA	12- 2		1964	Fred Hansen, USA	16- 8¾	OR
	& Alfred Gilbert, USA	12- 2	OR	1968	Bob Seagren, USA	17- 8½	OR
1912	Harry Babcock, USA	12-11½	OR	1972	Wolfgang Nordwig, E.Ger	18- 0½	OR
1920	Frank Foss, USA	13- 5	WR	1976	Tadeusz Slusarski, POL	18- 0½	=OR
1924	Lee Barnes, USA	12-11½		1980	Wladyslaw Kozakiewicz, POL	18-11½	WR
1928	Sabin Carr, USA	13- 9¼	OR	1984	Pierre Quinon, FRA	18-10¼	
1932	Bill Miller, USA	14- 1¾	OR	1988	Sergei Bubka, USSR	19- 9¼	OR
1936	Earle Meadows, USA	14- 3¼	OR	1992	Maksim Tarasov, UT	19- 0¼	

Long Jump

Year		Distance		Year		Distance	
1896	Ellery Clark, USA	20-10		1952	Jerome Biffle, USA	24-10	
1900	Alvin Kraenzlein, USA	23- 6¼	OR	1956	Greg Bell, USA	25- 8¼	
1904	Meyer Prinstein, USA	24- 1	OR	1960	Ralph Boston, USA	26- 7¾	OR
1906	Meyer Prinstein, USA	23- 7½		1964	Lynn Davies, GBR	26- 5¾	
1908	Frank Irons, USA	24- 6½	OR	1968	Bob Beamon, USA	29- 2½	WR
1912	Albert Gutterson, USA	24-11¼	OR	1972	Randy Williams, USA	27- 0½	
1920	William Petersson, SWE	23- 5½		1976	Arnie Robinson, USA	27- 4¾	
1924	De Hart Hubbard, USA	24- 5		1980	Lutz Dombrowski, E.Ger	28- 0¼	
1928	Ed Hamm, USA	25- 4½	OR	1984	Carl Lewis, USA	28- 0¼	
1932	Ed Gordon, USA	25- 0¾		1988	Carl Lewis, USA	28- 7¼	
1936	Jesse Owens, USA	26- 5½	OR	1992	Carl Lewis, USA	28- 5½	
1948	Willie Steele, USA	25- 8					

Triple Jump

Year		Distance		Year		Distance	
1896	James Connolly, USA	44-11¾		1952	Adhemar da Silva, BRA	53- 2¾	WR
1900	Meyer Prinstein, USA	47- 5¾	OR	1956	Adhemar da Silva, BRA	53- 7¾	OR
1904	Meyer Prinstein, USA	47- 1		1960	Józef Schmidt, POL	55- 2	
1906	Peter O'Connor, GBR/IRL	46- 2¼		1964	Józef Schmidt, POL	55- 3½	OR
1908	Timothy Ahearne, GBR/IRL	48-11¼	OR	1968	Viktor Saneyev, USSR	57- 0¾	WR
1912	Gustaf Lindblom, SWE	48- 5¼		1972	Viktor Saneyev, USSR	56-11¼	
1920	Vilho Tuulos, FIN	47- 7		1976	Viktor Saneyev, USSR	56- 8¾	
1924	Nick Winter, AUS	50-11¼	WR	1980	Jaak Uudmäe, USSR	56-11¼	
1928	Mikio Oda, JPN	49-11		1984	Al Joyner, USA	56- 7½	
1932	Chuhei Nambu, JPN	51- 7	WR	1988	Khristo Markov, BUL	57- 9¼	OR
1936	Naoto Tajima, JPN	52- 6	WR	1992	Mike Conley, USA	59- 7½ʷ	
1948	Arne Ahman, SWE	50- 6¼					

ʷ indicates wind-aided

Shot Put

Year		Distance		Year		Distance	
1896	Bob Garrett, USA	36- 9¾		1952	Parry O'Brien, USA	57- 1½	OR
1900	Richard Sheldon, USA	46- 3¼		1956	Parry O'Brien, USA	60-11¼	OR
1904	Ralph Rose, USA	48- 7	WR	1960	Bill Nieder, USA	64- 6¾	OR
1906	Martin Sheridan, USA	40- 5¼		1964	Dallas Long, USA	66- 8½	OR
1908	Ralph Rose, USA	46- 7½		1968	Randy Matson, USA	67- 4¾	OR
1912	Patrick McDonald, USA	50- 4	OR	1972	Wladyslaw Komar, POL	69- 6	OR
1920	Ville Pörhölä, FIN	48- 7¼		1976	Udo Beyer, E.Ger	69- 0¾	
1924	Bud Houser, USA	49- 2¼		1980	Vladimir Kiselyov, USSR	70- 0½	OR
1928	John Kuck, USA	52- 0¾	WR	1984	Alessandro Andrei, ITA	69- 9	
1932	Leo Sexton, USA	52- 6	OR	1988	Ulf Timmermann, E.Ger	73- 8¾	OR
1936	Hans Woellke, GER	53- 1¾		1992	Mike Stulce, USA	71- 2½	
1948	Wilbur Thompson, USA	56- 2	OR				

Discus Throw

Year		Distance		Year		Distance	
1896	Bob Garrett, USA	95- 7½		1952	Sim Iness, USA	180- 6	OR
1900	Rudolf Bauer, HUN	118- 3	OR	1956	Al Oerter, USA	184-11	OR
1904	Martin Sheridan, USA	128-10½	OR	1960	Al Oerter, USA	194- 2	OR
1906	Martin Sheridan, USA	136- 0		1964	Al Oerter, USA	200- 1	OR
1908	Martin Sheridan, USA	134- 2	OR	1968	Al Oerter, USA	212- 6	OR
1912	Armas Taipale, FIN	148- 3	OR	1972	Ludvik Daněk, CZE	211- 3	
1920	Elmer Niklander, FIN	146- 7		1976	Mac Wilkins, USA	221- 5	
1924	Bud Houser, USA	151- 4	OR	1980	Viktor Rashchupkin, USSR	218- 8	
1928	Bud Houser, USA	155- 3	OR	1984	Rolf Danneberg, W.Ger	218- 6	
1932	John Anderson, USA	162- 4	OR	1988	Jürgen Schult, E.Ger	225- 9	OR
1936	Ken Carpenter, USA	165- 7	OR	1992	Romas Ubartas, LIT	213- 8	
1948	Adolfo Consolini, ITA	173- 2	OR				

Hammer Throw

Year		Distance		Year		Distance	
1900	John Flanagan, USA	163- 1		1956	Harold Connolly, USA	207- 3	OR
1904	John Flanagan, USA	168- 1	OR	1960	Vasily Rudenkov, USSR	220- 2	OR
1908	John Flanagan, USA	170- 4	OR	1964	Romuald Klim, USSR	228-10	OR
1912	Matt McGrath, USA	179- 7	OR	1968	Gyula Zsivótzky, HUN	240- 8	OR
1920	Pat Ryan, USA	173- 5		1972	Anatoly Bondarchuk, USSR	247- 8	OR
1924	Fred Tootell, USA	174-10		1976	Yuri Sedykh, USSR	254- 4	OR
1928	Pat O'Callaghan, IRL	168- 7		1980	Yuri Sedykh, USSR	268- 4	WR
1932	Pat O'Callaghan, IRL	176-11		1984	Juha Tiainen, FIN	256- 2	
1936	Karl Hein, GER	185- 4	OR	1988	Sergei Litvinov, USSR	278- 2½	OR
1948	Imre Németh, HUN	183-11		1992	Andrei Abduvaliyev, UT	270- 9	
1952	József Csérmák, HUN	197-11	WR				

Track & Field (Cont.)
MEN
Javelin Throw

Year		Distance		Year		Distance	
1908	Eric Lemming, SWE	179-10	WR	1960	Viktor Tsibulenko, USSR	277- 8	
1912	Eric Lemming, SWE	198-11	WR	1964	Pauli Nevala, FIN	271- 2	
1920	Jonni Myyrä, FIN	215-10	OR	1968	Jänis Lüsis, USSR	295- 7	OR
1924	Jonni Myyrä, FIN	206- 7		1972	Klaus Wolfermann, W.Ger	296-10	OR
1928	Erik Lundkvist, SWE	218- 6	OR	1976	Miklos Németh, HUN	310- 4	WR
1932	Matti Järvinen, FIN	238- 6	OR	1980	Dainis Kūla, USSR	299- 2	
1936	Gerhard Stöck, GER	235- 8		1984	Arto Härkönen, FIN	284- 8	
1948	Kai Tapio Rautavaara, FIN	228-10		1988	Tapio Korjus, FIN	276- 6	
1952	Cy Young, USA	242- 1	OR	1992	Jan Železný, CZE	294- 2*	OR
1956	Egil Danielson, NOR	281- 2	WR				

*In 1986 the balance point of the javelin was modified and new records have been kept since.

Decathlon

Year		Points		Year		Points	
1904	Thomas Kiely, IRL	6036		1956	Milt Campbell, USA	7937	OR
1906-08 Not held				1960	Rafer Johnson, USA	8392	OR
1912	Jim Thrope, USA	8412	WR	1964	Willi Holdorf, GER	7887	
1920	Helge Lövland, NOR	6803		1968	Bill Toomey, USA	8193	OR
1924	Harold Osborn, USA	7711	WR	1972	Nikolai Avilov, USSR	8454	WR
1928	Paavo Yrjölä, FIN	8053	WR	1976	Bruce Jenner, USA	8617	WR
1932	Jim Bausch, USA	8462	WR	1980	Daley Thompson, GBR	8495	
1936	Glenn Morris, USA	7900	WR	1984	Daley Thompson, GBR	8798	=WR
1948	Bob Mathias, USA	7139		1988	Christian Schenk, E.Ger	8488	
1952	Bob Mathias, USA	7887	WR	1992	Robert Zmelik, CZE	8611	

WOMEN

At least 3 gold medals (including relays): Evelyn Ashford, Fanny Blankers-Koen, Betty Cuthbert and Bärbel Eckert Wöckel (4); Olga Bryzgina, Florence Griffith Joyner Jackie Joyner-Kersee, Tamara Press, Wilma Rudolph, Renate Stecher, Shirley Strickland, Irena Kirszenstein Szewińska and Wyomia Tyus (3).

100 meters

Year		Time		Year		Time	
1928	Betty Robinson, USA	12.2	=WR	1968	Wyomia Tyus, USA	11.0	WR
1932	Stella Walsh, POL*	11.9	=WR	1972	Renate Stecher, E.Ger	11.07	
1936	Helen Stephens, USA	11.5w		1976	Annegret Richter, W.Ger	11.08	
1948	Fanny Blankers-Koen, HOL	11.9		1980	Lyudmila Kondratyeva, USSR	11.06	
1952	Marjorie Jackson, AUS	11.5	=WR	1984	Evelyn Ashford, USA	10.97	OR
1956	Betty Cuthbert, AUS	11.5		1988	Florence Griffith Joyner, USA	10.54w	
1960	Wilma Rudolph, USA	11.0w		1992	Gail Devers, USA	10.82	OR
1964	Wyomia Tyus, USA	11.4					

*An autopsy performed after Walsh's death in 1980 revealed that she was a man.
w indicates wind-aided.

200 meters

Year		Time		Year		Time	
1948	Fanny Blankers-Koen, HOL	24.4		1972	Renate Stecher, E.Ger	22.40	=WR
1952	Marjorie Jackson, AUS	23.7	OR	1976	Bärbel Eckert, E.Ger	22.37	OR
1956	Betty Cuthbert, AUS	23.4	=OR	1980	Bärbel Eckert Wöckel, E.Ger	22.03	OR
1960	Wilma Rudolph, USA	24.0		1984	Valerie Brisco-Hooks, USA	21.81	OR
1964	Edith McGuire, USA	23.0	OR	1988	Florence Griffith Joyner, USA	21.34	WR
1968	Irena Szewińska, POL	22.5	WR	1992	Gwen Torrence, USA	21.81	

400 meters

Year		Time		Year		Time	
1964	Betty Cuthbert, AUS	52.0		1980	Marita Koch, E.Ger	48.88	OR
1968	Colette Besson, FRA	52.0	=OR	1984	Valerie Brisco-Hooks, USA	48.83	OR
1972	Monika Zehrt, E.Ger	51.08	OR	1988	Olga Bryzgina, USSR	48.65	OR
1976	Irena Szewińska, POL	49.29	WR	1992	Marie-Jose Perec, FRA	48.83	

800 meters

Year		Time		Year		Time	
1928	Lina Radke, GER	2:16.8	WR	1976	Tatyana Kazankina, USSR	1:54.94	WR
1960	Lyudmila Shevtsova, USSR	2:04.3	=WR	1980	Nadezhda Olizarenko, USSR	1:53.42	WR
1964	Ann Packer, GBR	2:01.1	OR	1984	Doina Melinte, ROM	1:57.60	
1968	Madeline Manning, USA	2:00.9	OR	1988	Sigrun Wodars, E.Ger	1:56.10	
1972	Hildegard Falck, W.Ger	1:58.55	OR	1992	Ellen van Langen, HOL	1:55.54	

1500 meters

Year		Time		Year		Time	
1972	Lyudmila Bragina, USSR	4:01.4	WR	1984	Gabriella Dorio, ITA	4:03.25	
1976	Tatiana Kazankina, USSR	4:05.48		1988	Paula Ivan, ROM	3:53.96	OR
1980	Tatiana Kazankina, USSR	3:56.6	OR	1992	Hassiba Boulmerka, ALG	3:55.30	

3000 meters

Year		Time		Year		Time	
1984	Maricica Puică, ROM	8:35.96		1992	Elena Romanova, UT	8:46.04	
1988	Tatiana Samolenko, USSR	8:26.53	OR				

10,000 meters

Year		Time		Year		Time	
1988	Olga Boldarenko, USSR	31:05.21	OR	1992	Derartu Tulu, ETH	31:06.02	

Marathon

Year		Time	Year		Time
1984	Joan Benoit, USA	2:24:52	1992	Valentina Yegorova, UT	2:32:41
1988	Rosa Mota, POR	2:25:40			

100-meter Hurdles

Year		Time		Year		Time	
1932	Babe Didrikson, USA	11.7	WR	1968	Maureen Caird, AUS	10.3	OR
1936	Trebisonda Valla, ITA	11.7		1972	Annelie Ehrhardt, E.Ger	12.59	WR
1948	Fanny Blankers-Koen, HOL	11.2	OR	1976	Johanna Schaller, E.Ger	12.77	
1952	Shirley Strickland, AUS	10.9	WR	1980	Vera Komisova, USSR	12.56	OR
1956	Shirley Strickland, AUS	10.7	OR	1984	Benita Fitzgerald-Brown, USA	12.84	
1960	Irina Press, USSR	10.8		1988	Jordanka Donkova, BUL	12.38	OR
1964	Karin Balzer, GER	10.5ʷ		1992	Paraskevi Patoulidou, GRE	12.64	

ʷ Wind-aided.
Note: Event held over 80 meters from 1932-68.

400-meter Hurdles

Year		Time		Year		Time
1984	Nawal El Moutawakel, MOR	54.61	OR	1992	Sally Gunnell, GBR	53.23
1988	Debra Flintoff-King, AUS	53.17	OR			

4x100-meter Relay

Year		Time		Year		Time	
1928	Canada	48.4	WR	1968	United States	42.87	WR
1932	United States	46.9	WR	1972	West Germany	42.81	WR
1936	United States	46.9		1976	East Germany	42.55	WR
1948	Holland	47.5		1980	East Germany	41.60	WR
1952	United States	45.9	WR	1984	United States	41.65	
1956	Australia	44.5	WR	1988	United States	41.98	
1960	United States	44.5		1992	United States	42.11	
1964	Poland	43.6					

4x400-meter Relay

Year		Time		Year		Time	
1972	East Germany	3:23.0	WR	1984	United States	3:18.29	OR
1976	East Germany	3:19.23	WR	1988	Soviet Union	3:15.18	WR
1980	Soviet Union	3:20.2		1992	Unified Team	3:20.20	

10-kilometer Walk

Year		Time
1992	Chen Yueling, CHN	44.32

High Jump

Year		Height		Year		Height	
1928	Ethel Catherwood, CAN	5- 2½		1968	Miloslava Režková, CZE	5-11½	
1932	Jean Shiley, USA	5- 5¼	WR	1972	Ulrike Meyfarth, W.Ger	6- 3½	=WR
1936	Ibolya Csák, HUN	5- 3		1976	Rosemarie Ackermann, E.Ger	6- 4	OR
1948	Alice Coachman, USA	5- 6	OR	1980	Sara Simeoni, ITA	6- 5½	OR
1952	Esther Brand, SAF	5- 5¾		1984	Ulrike Meyfarth, W.Ger	6- 7½	OR
1956	Mildred McDaniel, USA	5- 9¼	WR	1988	Louise Ritter, USA	6- 8	OR
1960	Iolanda Balas, ROM	6- 0¾	OR	1992	Heike Henkel, GER	6- 7½	
1964	Iolanda Balas, ROM	6- 2¾	OR				

Long Jump

Year		Distance		Year		Distance	
1948	Olga Gyarmati, HUN	18- 8¼		1972	Heidemarie Rosendahl, W.Ger	22- 3	
1952	Yvette Williams, NZE	20- 5¾	OR	1976	Angela Voigt, E.Ger	22- 0¾	
1956	Elzbieta Krzesińska, POL	20-10	=WR	1980	Tatiana Kolpakova, USSR	23- 2	OR
1960	Vyera Krepkina, USSR	20-10¾	OR	1984	Anisoara Cusmir-Stanciu, ROM	22-10	
1964	Mary Rand, GBR	22- 2¼	WR	1988	Jackie Joyner-Kersee, USA	24- 3½	OR
1968	Viorica Viscopoleanu, ROM	22- 4½	WR	1992	Heike Drechsler, GER	23- 5¼	

Track & Field (Cont.)
WOMEN
Shot Put

Year		Distance		Year		Distance	
1948	Micheline Ostermeyer, FRA	45- 1½		1972	Nadezhda Chizhova, USSR	69- 0	WR
1952	Galina Zybina, USSR	50- 1¾	WR	1976	Ivanka Hristova, BUL	69- 5¼	OR
1956	Tamara Tyshkevich, USSR	54- 5		1980	Ilona Slupianek, E.Ger	73- 6¼	OR
1960	Tamara Press, USSR	56-10	OR	1984	Claudia Losch, W.Ger	67- 2¼	
1964	Tamara Press, USSR	59- 6¼	OR	1988	Natalia Lisovskaya, USSR	72-11¾	
1968	Margitta Gummel, E.Ger	64- 4	WR	1992	Svetlana Krivaleva, UT	69- 1¼	

Discus Throw

Year		Distance		Year		Distance	
1928	Halina Konopacka, POL	129-11¾	WR	1968	Lia Manoliu, ROM	191- 2	OR
1932	Lillian Copeland, USA	133- 2	OR	1972	Faina Meinik, USSR	218- 7	OR
1936	Gisela Mauermayer, GER	156- 3	OR	1976	Evelin Schlaak, E.Ger	226- 4	OR
1948	Micheline Ostermeyer, FRA	137- 6		1980	Evelin Schlaak Jahl, E.Ger	229- 6	OR
1952	Nina Romaschkova, USSR	168- 8	OR	1984	Ria Stalman, HOL	214- 5	
1956	Olga Fikotová, CZE	176- 1	OR	1988	Martina Hellmann, E.Ger	237- 2½	OR
1960	Nina Ponomaryeva, USSR	180- 9	OR	1992	Maritz Marten, CUB	229-10	
1964	Tamara Press, USSR	187-10	OR				

Javelin Throw

Year		Distance		Year		Distance	
1932	Babe Didrikson, USA	143- 4		1968	Angéla Németh, HUN	198- 0	
1936	Tilly Fleischer, GER	148- 3	OR	1972	Ruth Fuchs, E.Ger	209- 7	OR
1948	Herma Bauma, AUT	149- 6	OR	1976	Ruth Fuchs, E.Ger	216- 4	OR
1952	Dana Zátopková, CZE	165- 7	OR	1980	Maria Colon Rueñes, CUB	224- 5	OR
1956	Inese Jaunzeme, USSR	176- 8	OR	1984	Tessa Sanderson, GBR	228- 2	OR
1960	Elvira Ozolina, USSR	183- 8	OR	1988	Petra Felke, E.Ger	245- 0	OR
1964	Mihaela Penes, ROM	198- 7	OR	1992	Silke Renk, GER	224- 2	

Heptathlon

Year		Points		Year		Points	
1964	Irina Press, USSR	5246	WR	1980	Nadezhda Tkachenko, USSR	5083	WR
1968	Ingrid Becker, W.Ger	5098		1984	Glynis Nunn, AUS	6390	OR
1972	Mary Peters, GBR	4801	WR	1988	Jackie Joyner-Kersee, USA	7291	WR
1976	Siegrun Siegl, E.Ger	4745		1992	Jackie Joyner Kersee, USA	7044	

Note: Seven-event Heptathlon replaced five-event Pentathlon in 1984.

All-Time Top 35 Medal Standings, 1986–1992

National medal standings for the Summer Olympics are not recognized by the IOC. The unofficial point totals are based on three points for every gold medal, two for each silver and one for each bronze. Demonstration sport medals are not included.

		G	S	B	Total	Points			G	S	B	Total	Points
1	**United States**	790	605	523	1918	4103	19	Holland	45	52	71	168	310
2	USSR/UT*	441	361	318	1120	2363	20	Czechoslovakia	49	49	45	143	290
3	Great Britain	177	226	221	624	1204	21	Denmark	34	59	57	150	277
4	France	163	175	191	529	1030	22	Norway	44	37	34	115	240
5	Germany†	136	165	161	462	899	23	Belgium	35	43	42	120	233
6	Sweden	135	150	172	457	877	24	China	36	41	37	114	227
7	Italy	154	126	132	412	846	25	Cuba	37	28	26	91	193
8	East Germany†	153	129	127	409	844	26	Greece	24	39	40	103	190
9	Hungary	135	125	144	404	799	27	South Korea	31	27	41	99	188
10	Finland	99	77	112	288	563	28	Yugoslavia	26	30	30	86	168
11	Japan	90	83	93	266	529	29	Austria	18	29	33	80	145
12	Australia	80	76	100	256	492	30	New Zealand	26	10	26	62	124
13	Romania	59	70	90	219	407	31	Turkey	26	15	12	53	120
14	West Germany†	56	67	81	204	383	32	South Africa	16	17	21	54	103
15	Poland	43	62	105	210	358	33	Spain	17	20	11	48	102
16	Canada	46	67	83	196	355	34	Kenya	13	13	13	39	78
17	Bulgaria	40	69	58	167	316	35	Mexico	9	13	18	40	71
18	Switzerland	42	64	58	164	312							

*The USSR first participated in the Summer Games in 1952 and became the Unified Team after the breakup of the Soviet Union in 1991. Medal total includes eight medals (1-4-8) won by Russia between 1908–12.
†After World War II, West Germany competed in the Summer Games as Germany in 1952–64. East and West Germany sent separate teams from 1968–88. Germany was reunified as a nation in 1990.

All-Time Leading Medal Winners
All Nations

Most Overall Medals
MEN

No		Sport	G-S-B
15	Nikolai Andrianov, USSR	Gymnastics	7-5-3
13	Boris Shakhlin, USSR	Gymnastics	7-4-2
13	Edoardo Mangiarotti, ITA.	Fencing	6-5-2
12	Takashi Ono, JPN	Gymnastics	5-4-4
12	Paavo Nurmi, FIN	Track/Field	9-3-0
12	Sawao Kato, JPN	Gymnastics	8-3-1
11	**Mark Spitz**, USA	Swimming	9-1-1
11*	**Matt Biondi**, USA	Swimming	8-2-1
11	Viktor Chukarin, USSR	Gymnastics	7-3-1
11	**Carl Osburn**, USA	Shooting	5-4-2
10	**Ray Ewry**, USA	Track/Field	10-0-0
10	Aladar Gerevich, HUN	Fencing	8-1-2
10	Akinori Nakayama, JPN	Gymnastics	6-2-2
10	Aleksandr Dityatin, USSR	Gymnastics	3-6-1
9	**Carl Lewis**, USA	Track/Field	8-1-0
9	**Martin Sheridan**, USA	Track/Field	5-3-1
9	Zoltán Halmay, HUN	Swimming	3-5-1
9	Giulio Gaudini, ITA.	Fencing	3-4-2
9	Mikhail Voronin, USSR	Gymnastics	2-6-1
9	Heikki Savolainen, FIN.	Gymnastics	2-1-6
9	Yuri Titov, USSR	Gymnastics	1-5-3

Games Participated In
Andrianov (1972,76,80); **Biondi** (1984,88,92); **Chukarin** (1952,56); **Dityatin** (1976,80); **Ewry** (1900,04,06,08); **Gerevich** (1932,36,48,52,56,60); **Gaudini** (1928,32,36); **Halmay** (1900,04,06,08); **Kato** (1968,72,76); **Lewis** (1984,88,92); **Mangiarotti** (1936,48,52,56,60); **Nakayama** (1968,72); **Nurmi** (1920,24,28); **Ono** (1952,56,60,64); **Osburn** (1912,20,24); **Savolainen** (1928,32,36,48,52); **Shakhlin** (1956,60,64); **Sheridan** (1904,06,08); **Spitz** (1968,72); **Titov** (1956,60,64); **Voronin** (1968,72).

WOMEN

No		Sport	G-S-B
18	Larissa Latynina, USSR	Gymnastics	9-5-4
11	Vera Cáslavská, CZE	Gymnastics	7-4-0
10	Agnes Keleti, HUN	Gymnastics	5-3-2
10	Polina Astaknova, USSR	Gymnastics	5-2-3
9	Nadia Comaneci, ROM.	Gymnastics	5-3-1
9	Lyudmila Tourischeva, USSR	Gymnastics	4-3-2
8	Kornelia Ender, E.Ger	Swimming	4-4-0
8	Dawn Fraser, AUS	Swimming	4-4-0
8	**Shirley Babashoff**, USA	Swimming	2-6-0
8	Sofia Muratova, USSR	Gymnastics	2-2-4
7	Irena Kirszenstein Szewińska, POL	Track/Field	3-2-2
7	Shirley Strickland, AUS	Track/Field	3-1-3
7	Maria Gorokhovskaya, USSR	Gymnastics	2-5-0
7	Ildikó Ságiné-Ujlaki-Rejtö, HUN	Fencing	2-3-2

Games Participated In
Astaknova (1956,60,64); **Babashoff** (1972,76); **Cáslavská** (1960,64,68); **Comaneci** (1976,80); **Ender** (1972,76); **Fraser** (1956,60,64); **Gorokhovskaya** (1952); **Keleti** (1952,56); **Latynina** (1956,60,64); **Muratova** (1956,60); **Ságiné-Ujlaki-Rejtö** (1960,64,68, 72,76); **Strickland** (1948,52,56); **Szewińska** (1964,68, 72,76,80); **Tourischeva** (1968, 72,76).

Most Medals—Single Games

	Medals
Men: Aleksandr Dityatin, USSR (1980)	8 (3-4-1)
Women: Maria Gorokhovskaya, USSR (1952).	7 (2-5-0)

Most Gold Medals
MEN

No		Sport	G-S-B
10	**Ray Ewry**, USA.	Track/Field	10-0-0
9	Paavo Nurmi, FIN	Track/Field	9-3-0
9	**Mark Spitz**, USA	Swimming	9-1-1
8	Sawao Kato, JPN	Gymnastics	8-3-1
8*	**Matt Biondi**, USA.	Swimming	8-2-1
8	**Carl Lewis**, USA	Track/Field	8-1-0
7	Nikolai Andrianov, USSR	Gymnastics	7-5-3
7	Boris Shakhlin, USSR	Gymnastics	7-4-2
7	Viktor Chukarin, USSR	Gymnastics	7-3-1
7	Aladar Gerevich, HUN	Fencing	7-1-2

*Includes one gold medal as preliminary member of 1st-place relay team.

WOMEN

No		Sport	G-S-B
9	Larissa Latynina, USSR	Gymnastics	9-5-4
7	Vera Caslavska, CZE	Gymnastics	7-4-0
6	Kristin Otto, E.Ger	Swimming	6-0-0
5	Agnes Keleti, HUN	Gymnastics	5-3-2
5	Nadia Comaneci, ROM.	Gymnastics	5-3-1
5	Polina Astaknova, USSR	Gymnastics	5-2-3
4	Kornelia Ender, E.Ger	Swimming	4-4-0
4	Dawn Fraser, AUS	Swimming	4-4-0
4	Lyudmila Tourischeva, USSR	Gymnastics	4-3-2
4	**Evelyn Ashford**, USA.	Track/Field	4-1-0
4	Krisztina Egerszegi, HUN	Swimming	4-1-0
4	**Janet Evans**, USA	Swimming	4-1-0
4	Fanny Blankers-Koen, HOL	Track/Field	4-0-0
4	Betty Cuthbert, AUS.	Track/Field	4-0-0
4	**Pat McCormick**, USA.	Diving	4-0-0
4	Bärbel Eckert Wöckel, E.Ger.	Track/Field	4-0-0

Most Silver Medals
MEN

No		Sport	G-S-B
6	Alexandr Dityatin, USSR	Gymnastics	3-6-1
6	Mikhail Voronin, USSR	Gymnastics	2-6-1
5	Nikolai Andrianov, USSR	Gymnastics	7-5-3
5	Edoardo Mangiarotti, ITA.	Fencing	6-5-2
5	Zoltán Halmay, HUN	Swimming	3-5-1
5	Philippe Cattiau, FRA	Fencing	3-5-0
5	Gustavo Marzi, ITA.	Fencing	2-5-0
5	Yuri Titov, USSR	Gymnastics	1-5-3
5	Viktor Lisitsky, USSR	Gymnastics	0-5-0

WOMEN

No		Sport	G-S-B
6	**Shirley Babashoff**, USA.	Swimming	2-6-0
5	Larissa Latynina, USSR	Gymnastics	9-5-4
5	Maria Gorokhovskaya, USSR	Gymnastics	2-5-0
4	Vera Cáslavská, CZE	Gymnastics	7-4-0
4	Kornelia Ender, E.Ger	Swimming	4-4-0
4	Dawn Fraser, AUS	Swimming	4-4-0
4	Erica Zuchold, E.Ger	Gymnastics	0-4-1

Most Bronze Medals
MEN

No		Sport	G-S-B
6	Heikki Savolainen, FIN.	Gymnastics	2-1-6
5	Daniel Revenu, FRA	Fencing	1-0-5
5	Philip Edwards, CAN.	Track/Field	0-0-5
5	Adrianus Jong, HOL.	Fencing	0-0-5

WOMEN

No		Sport	G-S-B
4	Larissa Latynina, USSR.	Gymnastics	9-5-4
4	Sofia Muratova, USSR	Gymnastics	2-2-4
4	Merlene Page Ottey, JAM.	Track/Field	0-0-4

All-Time Leading Medal Winners
USA

Most Overall Medals
MEN

No		Sport	G-S-B
11	Mark Spitz	Swimming	9-1-1
11*	Matt Biondi	Swimming	8-2-1
11	Carl Osburn	Shooting	5-4-2
10	Ray Ewry	Track/Field	10-0-0
9	Carl Lewis	Track/Field	8-1-0
9	Martin Sheridan	Track/Field	5-3-1
8	Charles Daniels	Swimming	5-1-2
7†	Tom Jager	Swimming	5-1-1
7	Willis Lee	Shooting	5-1-1
7	Lloyd Spooner	Shooting	4-1-2
6	Anton Heida	Gymnastics	5-1-0
6	Don Schollander	Swimming	5-1-0
6	Johnny Weissmuller	Swim/Water Polo	5-0-1
6	Alfred Lane	Shooting	5-0-1
6	Jim Lightbody	Track/Field	4-2-0
6	George Eyser	Gymnastics	3-2-1
6	Michael Plumb	Equestrian	2-4-0
6	Burton Downing	Cycling	2-3-1
6	Bob Garrett	Track/Field	2-2-2

*Includes one gold medal as preliminary member of 1st-place relay team.
†Includes three gold medals as preliminary member of 1st-place relay teams.

Games Participated In
Biondi (1984,88,92); **Daniels** (1904,06,08); **Downing** (1904); **Ewry** (1900,04,06,08); **Eyser** (1904); **Garrett** (1896,1900); **Heida** (1904); **Jager** (1984, 88,92,); **Lane** (1912-20); **Lee** (1920); **Lewis** (1984, 88,92); **Lightbody** (1904,06); **Osburn** (1912,20,24); **Plumb** (1960, 64,68,72,76,84); **Schollander** (1964, 68); **Sheridan** (1904,06,08); **Spitz** (1968,72); **Spooner** (1920); **Weissmuller** (1924-28).

WOMEN

No		Sport	G-S-B
8	Shirley Babashoff	Swimming	2-6-0
5	Evelyn Ashford	Track/Field	4-1-0
5	Janet Evans	Swimming	4-1-0
5	Florence Griffith Joyner	Track/Field	3-2-0
5	Jackie Joyner-Kersee	Track/Field	3-1-1
5	Mary Lou Retton	Gymnastics	1-2-2
5	Shannon Miller	Gymnastics	0-2-3
4	Pat McCormick	Diving	4-0-0
4	Valerie Brisco-Hooks	Track/Field	3-1-0
4	Nancy Hogshead	Swimming	3-1-0
4*	Mary T. Meagher	Swimming	3-1-0
4	Sharon Stouder	Swimming	3-1-0
4	Wyomia Tyus	Track/Field	3-1-0
4	Chris von Saltza	Swimming	3-1-0
4	Sue Pederson	Swimming	2-2-0
4	Jan Henne	Swimming	2-1-1
4	Dorothy Poynton Hill	Diving	2-1-1
4*	Dara Torres	Swimming	2-1-1
4	Kathy Ellis	Swimming	2-0-2
4	Georgia Coleman	Diving	1-2-1

*Includes one silver medal as preliminary member of 2nd-place relay team.

Games Participated In
Ashford (1976,84,88,92); **Babashoff** (1972,76); **Brisco-Hooks** (1984,88); **Coleman** (1928,32); **Ellis** (1964); **Evans** (1988,92); **Griffith Joyner** (1984,88); **Henne** (1968); **Hogshead** (1984); **Joyner-Kersee** (1984,88,92); **McCormick** (1952,56); **Meagher** (1984,88); **Miller** (1992); **Pederson** (1968); **Poynton Hill** (1928-32,36); **Retton** (1984); **Stouter** (1964); **Torres** (1984,88,92); **Tyus** (1964,68); **von Saltza** (1960).

Most Gold Medals
MEN

No		Sport	G-S-B
10	Raymond Ewry	Track/Field	10-0-0
9	Mark Spitz	Swimming	9-1-1
8	Carl Lewis	Track/Field	8-1-0
8*	Matt Biondi	Swimming	8-2-1
5	Carl Osburn	Shooting	5-4-2
5	Martin Sheridan	Track/Field	5-3-1
5	Charles Daniels	Swimming	5-1-2
5†	Tom Jager	Swimming	5-1-1
5	Willis Lee	Shooting	5-1-1
5	Anton Heida	Gymnastics	5-1-0
5	Don Schollander	Swimming	5-1-0
5	Johnny Weissmuller	Swim/Water Polo	5-0-1
5	Alfred Lane	Shooting	5-0-1
5	Morris Fisher	Shooting	5-0-0
4	Jim Lightbody	Track/Field	4-2-0
4	Lloyd Spooner	Shooting	4-1-2
4	Greg Louganis	Diving	4-1-0
4	John Naber	Swimming	4-1-0
4	Meyer Prinstein	Track/Field	4-1-0
4	Mel Sheppard	Track/Field	4-1-0
4	Marcus Hurley	Cycling	4-0-1
4	Harrison Dillard	Track/Field	4-0-0
4	Archie Hahn	Track/Field	4-0-0
4	Alvin Kraenzlein	Track/Field	4-0-0
4	Al Oerter	Track/Field	4-0-0
4	Jesse Owens	Track/Field	4-0-0

*Includes one gold medal as preliminary member of 1st-place relay team.
†Includes three gold medals as preliminary member of 1st-place relay teams.

WOMEN

No		Sport	G-S-B
4	Evelyn Ashford	Track/Field	4-1-0
4	Janet Evans	Swimming	4-1-0
4	Pat McCormick	Diving	4-0-0
3	Florence Griffith Joyner	Track/Field	3-2-0
3	Jackie Joyner-Kersee	Track/Field	3-1-1
3	Valerie Brisco-Hooks	Track/Field	3-1-0
3	Nancy Hogshead	Swimming	3-1-0
3	Sharon Stouder	Swimming	3-1-0
3	Wyomia Tyus	Track/Field	3-1-0
3	Chris von Saltza	Swimming	3-1-0
3*	Nicole Haislett	Swimming	3-0-0

*Includes one gold medal as preliminary member of 1st-place relay team.

Most Silver Medals
MEN

No		Sport	G-S-B
4	Carl Osburn	Shooting	5-4-2
4	Michael Plumb	Equestrian	2-4-0
3	Martin Sheridan	Track/Field	5-3-1
3	Burton Downing	Cycling	2-3-1
3	Irving Baxter	Track/Field	2-3-0
3	Earl Thomson	Equestrian	2-3-0

WOMEN

No		Sport	G-S-B
6	Shirley Babashoff	Swimming	2-6-0

Most Bronze Medals
MEN

No		Sport	G-S-B
4	William Merz	Gym/Track/Field	0-1-4

WOMEN

No		Sport	G-S-B
3	Shannon Miller	Gymnastics	0-2-3

Wide World Photos

Six weeks after failing to clear any height in Barcelona, pole vaulter **Sergei Bubka** of Ukraine sets a world record of 20 feet 1½ inches at a track meet in Tokyo.

INTERNATIONAL SPORTS

The Non-Olympic News

Three champions set late season world records,
make amends for missing medals in Barcelona.

Three reigning track and field world champions who suffered major Olympic disappointments in Barcelona redeemed themselves before the end of the outdoor season. American decathlete Dan O'Brien, Algerian distance runner Noureddine Morceli and Ukranian pole vaulter Sergei Bubka all wound up feeling better when each broke world records.

O'Brien, who did not make the U.S. Olympic team when he failed to clear any height in the pole vault, can still claim the title of World's Greatest Athlete after his 8,891-point performance Sept. 4-5 at Talence, France. His total was 44 better than the record set by Daley Thompson of Great Britain when he won the event at the 1984 Olympics. In the process, O'Brien easily defeated 1992 Olympic champion Robert Zmelik of Czechoslovakia and improved his own record first-day score to 4,720.

A day after O'Brien's record came Morceli's in the 1,500 meters at Rieti, Italy. Morceli, who had finished seventh in the race at the Olympics, covered the distance in 3 minutes, 28.86 seconds, knocking .60 off the mark set by Said Aouita of Morocco in 1985.

Bubka, the bust of Barcelona after no-heighting twice at 18 feet, 8½ inches and once at 18-10, salvaged his summer with a pair of world records in the event—first clearing 20-1 in Padua, Italy, on Aug. 30,

and then 20-1½ on Sept. 19 in Tokyo. That made him the sport's biggest record-setter for the second year in a row, with one world mark indoors (20-1¼) and two outdoors, bringing his career total to an unprecedented 32.

The U.S. Olympic Trials, as expected, dominated the scene leading into the Olympics. Performances after the Games, during the second half of the European Circuit, produced five notable world records.

The Trials' only double winners were three women—Jackie Joyner-Kersee in the long jump and heptathlon; Gwen Torrence in the 100 and 200; and Connie Price-Smith in the shotput and discus. Both JJK and Torrence went on to Olympic gold.

The long-running story in New Orleans was Butch Reynolds' fight to enter the 400 meters despite his international disqualification for alleged steroid use in 1990. After the U.S. Supreme Court granted that permission to Reynolds, the 400-meter heats were postponed three times and four days while the International Amateur Athletics Federation issued vague threats against anyone who would run against Reynolds. The IAAF eventually backed down, and Reynolds ran three strong heats (44.58, 44.68, 44.14) before finishing an exhausted fifth (44.65) in the final behind Danny Everett, whose winning time (43.81) was then the third fastest ever.

Kenya's Moses Kiptanui finished fourth in the steeplechase in his country's Olympic trials and then graciously declined the opportunity to bump eventual bronze medal-

Phil Hersh covers international sports for the *Chicago Tribune* and has been the *Tribune's* full-time Olympics writer since 1986.

Richard Martin/Allsport

American **Dan O'Brien** (center) leaves Olympic gold medalist **Robert Zmelik** (right) of Czechoslovakia in his wake as he wins the 100 meters on the way to setting a new decathlon world record, Sept. 4-5, in Talance, France.

ist William Mutwol from the team that would sweep the event in Barcelona. After the Games, however, Kiptanui was being hailed as the "next Henry Rono" after breaking the world records for the 3,000-meter run and 3,000-meter steeplechase during four days in August (Rono set world records at four different distances within three months in 1978). Kiptanui, 22, ran the 3,000 in 7:28.96, which is equivalent to back-to-back 4-minute miles. Then he lopped nearly four seconds off the steeple mark with an 8:02.08.

Drugs. While the Butch Reynolds case generated enough attention in the United States to merit the attention of "Nightline," it was just a worldwide footnote compared to the long-running saga of German sprinter Katrin Krabbe and two of her club teammates, Grit Breuer and Silke Moeller. Krabbe, the 1991 world champion in the 100 and 200 meters and the sport's designated Golden Girl, was first found to have manipulated a urine sample given during a training trip to South Africa. The German track federation suspended the three former East German athletes for four years, but that decision was

first overturned by the federation's legal commission and then supported by an arbitration panel of the IAAF in June.

Krabbe announced she would not try to compete in the Olympics because she had been too distracted to prepare properly, leading to suggestions that was part of an IAAF deal not to ban her. During the Olympics, though, came the news that she had twice tested positive for the banned drug clenbuterol, which has both steroidal and stimulant effects. Krabbe was given another four-year ban, pending further appeal.

Cycling. Miguel Induráin of Spain was utterly dominant in the season's two major stage races, the Tour de France and the Tour of Italy. Induráin, 28, won both with stunning performances in the individual time trials and solid riding everywhere else. He became the sixth man ever to win both Tours in the same season, and the first since Stephen Roche of Ireland in 1987. Three-time Tour de France champion Greg LeMond of the U.S. dropped out with apparent chronic fatigue early in the 15th stage of the race. Earlier in the year, LeMond won the Tour

Wide World Photos

Failed drug tests landed Germany's
Katrin Krabbe a four-year suspension
and kept her far from Barcelona.

exercise and balance beam. Vitaly Scherbo of Belorus won pommel horse outright and tied in rings.

Of the 10 titlists in this first world meet under the new format, only Scherbo and Henrietta Onodi (vault) went on to win individual apparatus Olympic golds.

Marathons. With Muhammad Ali-like brashness, Liz McColgan of Scotland turned her marathon debut into an impressive victory Nov. 3, 1991, in New York. Her time of 2 hours, 27 minutes, 23 seconds, was more than a minute faster than Olga Markova of Russia. On the men's side, Salvador Garcia improved on his second-place finish of 1990 to become the first Mexican winner in New York (2:09:28).

In 1992, Kenya's Ibrahim Hussein won the Boston Marathon for the second straight time and third in the past five years. Hussein's winning time, 2:08.14, was second only to Rob de Castella's 6-year-old course record of 2:07.51.

The women's winner in Boston was Markova, who upset heavily-favored defending champion Wanda Panfil, who wound up 6th. The winning time of 2:23:43 was the second fastest ever for a woman at Boston (fastest: Joan Benoit, 2:22:43, in 1983).

Swimming. After a relatively poor Olympic showing in 1988, U.S. Swimming decided to move its trials from the traditional spot on the calendar—approximately one month before the Games—to the first week in March. The result may have been overinflated expectations for the U.S. team in Barcelona, since so many world-leading times were produced at the trials.

Best efforts were world-record swims by Jenny Thompson in the 100-meter freestyle (54.73 seconds) and Anita Nall, then 15, in the 200-meter breaststroke (2:25.35). Both broke records held by former East Germans, but neither Thompson nor Nall would win an individual-event Olympic gold.

Australian teenager Kieren Perkins was the season's biggest star going into the Olympics, setting world records in the 400, 800 and 1,500 freestyles from February to April. He went on to win a gold in the Olympic 1,500—lowering the record by another five seconds, to 14:43.48—and a silver in the 400 (the 800 is not a men's championship distance).

de Pont (his first win since 1990), but he struggled with health problems throughout the summer and withdrew from the World Championships because of a urinary tract infection.

Induráin tried for the cycling "triple crown" at September's World Championships in Spain, but defending champion Gianni Bugno of Italy became the first back-to-back winner of the pro road race since Belgium's Rik Van Steenbergen in 1956-57. Induráin was sixth.

Also at the worlds, Janie Eickhoff of the U.S. won her third bronze medal (her others came in 1989 and '91) in the points race; and time trialers Bunki Bankaitis-Davis, Eve Stephenson, Jan Bolland and Jeanne Golay won the 50-km event, becoming the first American cyclists to win a team event in World Championship history.

Gymnastics. The inaugural World Individual Apparatus Championships, held in Paris in mid-April, became a triumph for Kim Zmeskal of Houston but a generally inaccurate preview of what would happen 3½ months later at the Olympics.

Zmeskal was the meet's only clear-cut double winner, taking the titles in floor

Winter Sports

Alpine Skiing. While Paul Accola of Switzerland won the World Cup overall title, Alberto Tomba of Italy was once again the dominant figure on the White Circus. Tomba, who competes only in gated events, was second overall while winning nine races for the second time in four years, including six of nine slaloms (in which his worst finish was third) and three of seven giant slaloms.

On the women's side, Petra Kronberger of Austria won a third straight overall title, while Carole Merle of France, second overall, had seven individual race wins. Diann Roffe of Potsdam, N.Y., was 10th overall but third in giant slalom, the first seasonal World Cup medalist from the U.S. (men or women) since Tamara McKinney in 1987.

Figure Skating. All four Olympic champions also won world titles. Kristi Yamaguchi, 21, of Fremont, Calif., became the first U.S. woman to win back-to-back world titles since Peggy Fleming in 1967-68. Yamaguchi's path to the title was eased somewhat by the post-Olympic retirement of silver medalist Midori Ito of Japan, who admitted to having been overwhelmed by national pressure.

Other world champions: Viktor Petrenko of Ukraine, who ended the three-year reign of Canada's Kurt Browning; Natalia Mishkuteniok and Artur Dmitriev of Russia in pairs; and Marina Klimova and Sergei Ponomorenko of Russia in ice dancing.

In the 1992 U.S. nationals, Yamaguchi won her first title with performances of surpassing beauty and skill, while injured defending champion Tonya Harding staggered in third. Among the men, unrepentant bad boy Christopher Bowman regained a title he had won in 1989, thanks to the absence of 1990-91 winner Todd Eldredge, a last-minute withdrawal with a bad back. Eldredge was still named to the Olympic team.

Hockey. There was no fitting farewell for the Unified Team version of the former Soviet Big Red Machine, which had won 22 world championships since 1954. The Unifieds breezed through the prelims with a 4-0-1 record, then lost to Sweden 2-0 in the quarterfinals of the May tournament in Prague. Sweden went on to win its sixth title, while the U.S. was routed, 8-1, by Czechoslovakia in the quarters.

Wide World Photos

Swiss skier **Paul Accola** was shut out in Albertville, but still won his first World Cup overall title.

Luge. Duncan Kennedy and Cammy Myler had historic second-place overall finishes in the World Cup circuit, the best-ever for U.S. sliders, although neither won an Olympic medal. Early in the season, Kennedy became the first U.S. man to win a World Cup luge race.

Speedskating. Making up for her Olympic disappointment, where she twice lost gold medals to Bonnie Blair (one by .02 seconds), Ye Qiaobo became the first Chinese woman to win a world sprint title. Blair was second in the four-race, post-Olympic event in Oslo. Men's champion Igor Zhelezovski of Belorus became the first to win all four sprint races since Eric Heiden of the U.S. in 1979. Dan Jansen of the U.S. was second.

Roberto Sighel became the first Italian to win a speedskating world title, taking the World All-Around Championships at Calgary. Sighel won none of the four races but set a world record for total points in the sport's Samalog system. Gunda Niemann of Germany won her second straight world all-around title. □

INT'L SPORTS
STATISTICS

1991-1992

CHAMPIONS • RECORDS

THE 1993

SEC A

PAGE 606

World Records Set in 1992

World outdoor records set between Oct. 1, 1991 and Oct. 1, 1992.

Outdoor Track & Field

MEN

Event		Record	Old Mark	Former Holder
1500 meters	**Noureddine Morceli**, ALG	3:28.86	3:29.46	Said Aouita, MOR (1985)
3000 meters	**Moses Kiptanui**, KEN	7:28.96	7:29.45	Said Aouita, MOR (1989)
400m Hurdles	**Kevin Young**, USA	46.78	47.02	Edwin Moses, USA (1983)
3000m Steeplechase	**Moses Kiptanui**, KEN	8:02.08	8:05.35	Peter Koech, KEN (1989)
20 kilometer Walk	**Stefan Johansson**, SWE	1:18:35.2	1:18:40.0	Ernesto Canto, MEX (1984)
4 × 100-meter Relay	**USA Olympic Team** (Mike Marsh, Leroy Burrell, Dennis Mitchell, Carl Lewis)	37.40	37.50	USA (Andre Cason, Leroy Burrell, Dennis Mitchell, Carl Lewis), 1991
4 × 200-meter Relay	**Santa Monica Track Club** (Mike Marsh, Leroy Burrell, Floyd Heard, Carl Lewis)	1:19.11	1:19.38	USA (Danny Everett, Leroy Burrell, Floyd Heard, Carl Lewis), 1989
4 × 400-meter Relay	**USA Olympic Team** (Andrew Valmon, Quincy Watts, Michael Johnson, Steve Lewis)	2:55.74	2:56.16	USA Olympic Teams of 1968 and 1988
Javelin	**Steve Backley**, GBR	300-1	298-6	Steve Backley, GBR (1990)
Pole Vault	**Sergei Bubka**, CIS	20-0½	20-0	Sergei Bubka, USSR (1991)
Pole Vault	**Sergei Bubka**, CIS	20-1	20-0½	Sergei Bubka, CIS (1992)
Pole Vault	**Sergei Bubka**, CIS	20-1½	20-1	Sergei Bubka, CIS (1992)
Decathlon	**Dan O'Brien**, USA	8891 pts	8847 pts	Daley Thompson, GBR (1984)

Swimming

MEN

Event		Record	Old Mark	Former Holder
400m free	**Yevgeny Sadovyi**, UT	3:45.00	3:46.95	Uwe Dassler, E.Ger. (1988)
1500m free	**Kiren Perkins**, AUS	14:43.48	14:50.36	Joerg Hofman, GER (1991)
100m back	**Jeff Rouse**, USA	53.86	53.93	Jeff Rouse, USA (1991)
200m back	**Martin Zubero**, SPA	1:56.57	1:57.30	Martin Zubero, SPA (1991)
200m breast	**Mike Barrowman**, USA	2:10.16	2:10.60	Mike Barrowman, USA (1991)
4 × 200m free relay	**Unified Olympic Team** (Dmitri Lepikov, Vladimir Pychnenko, Veniamin Taianovitch, Yevgeny Sadovyi)	7:11.95	7:12.51	USA Olympic Team (Troy Dalbey, Matt Cetlinski, Doug Gjertsen, Matt Biondi), 1988
4 × 100m medley relay	**USA Olympic Team** (Jeff Rouse, Nelson Diebel, Pablo Morales, Jon Olsen)	3:36.93	3:36.93 (tied)	USA Olympic Team (David Berkoff, Rich Schroeder, Matt Biondi, Chris Jacobs), 1988

WOMEN

Event		Record	Old Mark	Former Holder
50m free	**Yang Wenyi**, CHN	24.79	24.98	Yang Wenyi, CHN (1990)
100m free	**Jenny Thompson**, USA	54.48	54.73	Kristin Otto, E.Ger.(1986)
200m breast	**Anita Nall**, USA	2:25.35	2:26.71	Silke Hoerner, E.Ger.(1988)
200m I.M	**Lin Li**, CHN	2:11.65	2:11.73	Uta Geweniger, E.Ger.(1981)
4 × 100m free relay	**USA Olympic Team** (Nicole Haislett, Dara Torres, Angel Martino, Jenny Thompson)	3:39.46	3:40.57	E.Germany (Kristin Otto, Manuella Stellmach, Sabine Schulze, Heike Friedrich), 1986
4 × 100m medley relay	**USA Olympic Team** (Lea Loveless, Anita Nall, Crissy Ahmann-Leighton, Jenny Thompson)	4:02.54	4:03.69	East German Olympic Team (Ina Kleber, Sylvia Gerasch, Ines Geissler, Birgit Meineke)

TRACK & FIELD

World, Olympic and American Records

As of Oct. 1, 1992.

World outdoor records officially recognized by the International Amateur Athletics Federation (IAAF).

MEN

Running

Event		Time		Date Set	Location
100 meters:	**World**	9.86	**Carl Lewis**, USA	Aug. 25, 1991	Tokyo
	Olympic	9.92	Carl Lewis, USA	Sept.24, 1988	Seoul
	American	9.86	Lewis (same as World)	—	—
200 meters:	**World**	19.72	**Pietro Mennea**, Italy	Sept.12, 1979	Mexico City
	Olympic	19.75	Joe DeLoach, USA	Sept.28, 1988	Seoul
	American	19.73	Mike Marsh	Aug. 5, 1992	Barcelona
400 meters:	**World**	43.29	**Butch Reynolds**, USA	Aug. 16, 1988	Zurich
	Olympic	43.86	Lee Evans, USA	Oct. 18, 1968	Mexico City
	American	43.29	Reynolds (same as World)	—	—
800 meters:	**World**	1:41.73	**Sebastian Coe**, Great Britain	June 10, 1981	Florence
	Olympic	1:43.00	Joaquim Cruz, Brazil	Aug. 6, 1984	Los Angeles
	American	1:42.60	Johnny Gray	Aug. 28, 1985	Koblenz
1000 meters:	**World**	2:12.18	**Sebastian Coe**, Great Britain	July 11, 1981	Oslo
	Olympic		Not an event	—	—
	American	2:13.9	Rick Wohlhuter	July 30, 1974	Oslo
1500 meters:	**World**	3:28.86	**Noureddine Morceli**, Algeria	Sept. 6, 1992	Rieti, ITA
	Olympic	3:32.53	Sebastian Coe, Great Britain	Aug. 1, 1980	Moscow
	American	3:29.77	Sydney Maree	Aug. 25, 1985	Cologne
Mile:	**World**	3:46.32	**Steve Cram**, Great Britain	July 27, 1985	Oslo, NOR
	Olympic		Not an event	—	—
	American	3:47.69	Steve Scott	July 7, 1982	Oslo
2000 meters:	**World**	4:50.81	**Said Aouita**, Morocco	July 16, 1987	Paris
	Olympic		Not an event	—	—
	American	4:52.44	Jim Spivey	Sept.15, 1987	Lausanne
3000 meters:	**World**	7:28.96	**Moses Kiptanui**, Kenya	Aug. 16, 1992	Cologne
	Olympic		Not an event	—	—
	American	7:33.37	Sydney Maree	July 17, 1982	London
5000 meters:	**World**	12:58.39	**Said Aouita**, Morocco	July 22, 1987	Rome
	Olympic	13:05.59	Said Aouita, Morocco	Aug. 11, 1984	Los Angeles
	American	13:01.15	Sydney Maree	July 27, 1985	Oslo
10,000 meters:	**World**	27:08.23	**Arturo Barrios**, Mexico	Aug. 18, 1989	West Berlin
	Olympic	27:21.46	Brahim Boutaib, Morocco	Sept.26, 1988	Seoul
	American	27:20.56	Mark Nenow	Sept. 5, 1986	Brussels
20,000 meters:	**World**	56:55.6	**Arturo Barrios**, Mexico	Mar. 30, 1991	La Fleche
	Olympic		Not an event	—	—
	American	58:25.0	Bill Rodgers	Aug. 9, 1977	Boston
25,000 meters:	**World**	1:13:55.8	**Toshihiko Seko**, Japan	Mar. 22, 1981	Christchurch
	Olympic		Not an event	—	—
	American	1:14:11.8	Bill Rodgers	Feb. 21, 1979	Saratoga
30,000 meters:	**World**	1:29:18.8	**Toshihiko Seko**, Japan	Mar. 22, 1991	Christchurch
	Olympic		Not an event	—	—
	American	1:31:49	Bill Rodgers	Feb. 21, 1979	Saratoga
Marathon:	**World**	2:06:50	**Belayneh Densimo**, Ethiopia	Apr. 17, 1988	Rotterdam
	Olympic	2:09:21	Carlos Lopes, Portugal	Aug. 12, 1984	Los Angeles
	American	2:08:52	Alberto Salazar	Apr. 19, 1982	Boston

Note: The **Mile** run is 1,609.344 meters and the **Marathon** is 42,194.988 meters (26 miles, 385 yards).

Hurdles

Event		Time		Date Set	Location
110 meters:	**World**	12.92	**Roger Kingdom**, USA	Aug. 16, 1989	Zurich
	Olympic	12.98	Roger Kingdom, USA	Sept.26, 1988	Seoul
	American	12.92	Kingdom (same as World)	—	—
400 meters:	**World**	46.78	**Kevin Young**, USA	Aug. 6, 1992	Barcelona
	Olympic	46.78	Young (same as World)	—	—
	American	46.78	Young (same as World)	—	—

Note: The hurdles at 110 meters are 3 feet, 6 inches high and the hurdles at 400 meters are 3 feet. There are 10 hurdles in both races.

Steeplechase

Event		Time		Date Set	Location
3000 meters:	**World**	8:02.08	**Moses Kiptanui**, Kenya	Aug. 19, 1992	Zurich
	Olympic	8:05.51	Julius Kariuki, Kenya	Sept.30, 1988	Seoul
	American	8:09.17	Henry Marsh	Aug. 28, 1985	Koblenz

Note: A steeplechase course consists of 28 hurdles (3 feet high) and seven water jumps (12 feet long).

Track & Field (Cont.)
World, Olympic and American Records
MEN
Walking

Event		Time		Date Set	Location
20 kilometers:	**World**	1:18:35.2	**Stefan Johansson**, Sweden	May 15, 1992	Fana
	Olympic	1:19:57	Jozef Pribilinec, Czechoslovakia	Sept.23, 1988	Seoul
	American	1:24:50	Tim Lewis	May 7, 1988	Seattle
30 kilometers:	**World**	2:03:56.5	**Thierry Toutain**, Spain	Mar. 24, 1991	Hericourt
	Olympic		Not an event	—	—
	American	2:21:40	Herm Nelson	Sept. 7, 1991	Bellevue
50 kilometers:	**World**	3:41:38.4	**Raul Gonzalez**, Mexico	May 25, 1979	Bergen
	Olympic	3:38:29	Vyacheslav Ivanenko, USSR	Sept.30, 1988	Seoul
	American	3:56:55	Marco Evoniuk	Sept.30, 1988	Seoul

Relays

Event		Time		Date Set	Location
4×100 meters:	**World**	37.40	**USA** (Marsh, Burrell, Mitchell, C.Lewis)	Aug. 8, 1992	Barcelona
	Olympic	37.40	USA (same as World)	—	—
	American	37.40	USA (same as World)	—	—
4×200 meters:	**World**	1:19.11	**USA** (Marsh, Burrell, Heard, C.Lewis)	Apr. 25, 1992	Philadelphia
	Olympic		Not an event	—	—
	American	1:19.11	USA (same as World)	—	—
4×400 meters:	**World**	2:55.74	**USA** (Valmon, Watts, Johnson, S.Lewis)	Aug. 8, 1992	Barcelona
	Olympic	2:55.74	USA (same as World)	—	—
	American	2:55.74	USA (same as World)	—	—
4×800 meters:	**World**	7:03.89	**Great Britain** (Elliott, Cook, Cram, Coe)	Aug. 30, 1982	London
	Olympic		Not an event	—	—
	American	7:06.5	SMTC (J.Robinson, Mack, E.Jones, Gray)	Apr. 26, 1986	Walnut, CA
4×1500 meters:	**World**	14:38.8	**West Germany** (Wessinghage, Hudak, Lederer, Fleschen)	Aug. 17, 1977	Cologne
	Olympic		Not an event	—	—
	American	14:46.3	USA (Aldridge, Clifford, Harbour, Duits)	June 23, 1979	Bourges, FRA

Field Events

Event		Mark		Date Set	Location
High Jump:	**World**	8- 0	**Javier Sotomayor**, Cuba	July 29, 1989	San Juan
	Olympic	7- 9¾	Gennady Avdeyenko, USSR	Sept.25, 1988	Seoul
	American	7-10½	Charles Austin	Aug. 7, 1991	Zurich
Pole Vault:	**World**	20- 1½	**Sergei Bubka**, CIS	Sept. 19, 1992	Tokyo
	Olympic	19- 4¼	Sergei Bubka, USSR	Sept.28, 1988	Seoul
	American	19- 6½	Joe Dial	June 18, 1987	Norman, OK
Long Jump:	**World**	29- 4½	**Mike Powell**, USA	Aug. 30, 1991	Tokyo
	Olympic	29- 2½	Bob Beamon, USA	Oct. 18, 1968	Mexico City
	American	29- 4½	Powell (same as World)	—	—
Triple Jump:	**World**	58-11½	**Willie Banks**, USA	June 16, 1985	Indianapolis
	Olympic	57-10½	Mike Conley, USA	Aug. 3, 1992	Barcelona
	American	58-11½	Banks (same as World)	—	—
Shot Put:	**World**	75-10¼	**Randy Barnes**, USA	May 20, 1990	Los Angeles
	Olympic	73- 8¾	Ulf Timmermann, East Germany	Sept.23, 1988	Seoul
	American	75-10¼	Barnes (same as World)	—	—
Discus:	**World**	243- 0	**Jurgen Schult**, East Germany	June 6, 1986	Neubrandenburg
	Olympic	225- 9	Jurgen Schult, East Germany	Oct. 1, 1988	Seoul
	American	237- 4	Ben Plucknett	July 7, 1981	Stockholm
Javelin:	**World**	300- 1	**Steve Backley**, Great Britain	Jan. 25, 1992	Auckland
	Olympic	281-10	Jan Zelezny, Czechoslovakia	Sept.23, 1988	Seoul
	American	280- 1	Tom Petranoff	July 7, 1986	Helsinki
Hammer:	**World**	284- 7	**Yuri Sedykh**, USSR	Aug. 30, 1986	Stuttgart
	Olympic	278- 2	Sergei Litvinov, USSR	Sept.26, 1988	Seoul
	American	268- 8	Jud Logan	Apr. 22, 1988	Univ.Park, PA

Note: The international weights for men—**Shot** (16 lbs); **Discus** (4 lbs/6.55 oz); **Hammer** (16 lbs); **Javelin** (minimum 1 lb/12¼ oz).

Decathlon

	Points			Date Set	Location
Ten Events:	**World** 8891	**Dave O'Brien**, USA		Sept.4-5, 1992	Talence, FRA
	Olympic 8847	Daley Thompson, Great Britain		Aug.8-9, 1984	Los Angeles
	American 8891	O'Brien (same as World)		—	—

Note: O'Brien's WR times and distances, in order over two days—**100m** (10.43); **LJ** (26-6); **SP** (54-9½); **HJ** (6-9½); **400m** (48.51); **110m H** (13.98); **Discus** (159-4); **PV** (16-4¾); **Jav** (206-4); **1500m** (4:42.10).

WOMEN

Running

Event	Time			Date Set	Location
100 meters:	**World** 10.49	**Florence Griffith Joyner**, USA		July 16, 1988	Indianapolis
	Olympic 10.62	Florence Griffith Joyner, USA		Sept.24, 1988	Seoul
	American 10.49	Griffith Joyner (same as World)		—	—
200 meters:	**World** 21.34	**Florence Griffith Joyner**, USA		Sept.29, 1988	Seoul
	Olympic 19.75	Griffith Joyner (same as World)		—	—
	American 19.73	Griffith Joyner (same as World)		—	—
400 meters:	**World** 47.60	**Marita Koch**, East Germany		Oct. 6, 1985	Canberra
	Olympic 48.65	Olga Bryzgina, USSR		Sept.26, 1988	Seoul
	American 48.83	Valerie Brisco		Aug. 6, 1984	Los Angeles
800 meters:	**World** 1:53.28	**Jarmila Kratochvilova**, Czech.		July 26, 1983	Munich
	Olympic 1:53.43	Nadezhda Olizarenko, USSR		July 27, 1980	Moscow
	American 1:56.90	Mary Decker Slaney		Aug. 16, 1985	Bern
1000 meters:	**World** 2:30.6	**Tatiana Providokhina**, USSR		Aug. 20, 1978	Pololsk, USSR
	Olympic	Not an event		—	—
	American 2:34.04	Julie Jenkins		Aug. 17, 1990	Berlin
1500 meters:	**World** 3:52.47	**Tatiana Kazankina**, USSR		Aug. 13, 1980	Zurich
	Olympic 3:53.96	Paula Ivan, Romania		Oct. 1, 1988	Seoul
	American 3:57.12	Mary Decker		July 26, 1983	Stockholm
Mile:	**World** 4:15.61	**Paula Ivan**, Romania		July 10, 1989	Nice
	Olympic	Not an event		—	—
	American 4:16.71	Mary Decker Slaney		Aug. 21, 1985	Zurich
2000 meters:	**World** 5:28.69	**Maricica Puica**, Romania		July 11, 1986	London
	Olympic	Not an event		—	—
	American 5:32.7	Mary Decker		Aug. 3, 1984	Eugene
3000 meters:	**World** 8:22.62	**Tatiana Kazankina**, USSR		Aug. 26, 1984	Leningrad
	Olympic 8:26.53	Tatiana Samolenko, USSR		Sept.25, 1988	Seoul
	American 8:25.83	Mary Decker Slaney		Sept. 7, 1985	Rome
5000 meters:	**World** 14:33.33	**Ingrid Kristiansen**, Norway		Aug. 5, 1986	Stockholm
	Olympic	Not an event		—	—
	American 15:00.00	PattiSue Plumer		July 3, 1989	Stockholm
10,000 meters:	**World** 27:08.23	**Ingrid Kristiansen**, Norway		July 5, 1986	Oslo
	Olympic 31:05.21	Olga Bondarenko, USSR		Sept.30, 1988	Seoul
	American 31:19.89	Lynn Jennings		Aug. 7, 1992	Barcelona
Marathon:	**World** 2:21:06	**Ingrid Kristiansen**, Norway		Apr. 21, 1985	London
	Olympic 2:24:52	Joan Benoit, USA		Aug. 5, 1984	Los Angeles
	American 2:21.21	Joan Benoit Samuelson		Oct. 20, 1985	Chicago

Note: The **Mile** run is 1,609.344 meters and the **Marathon** is 42,194.988 meters (26 miles, 385 yards).

Hurdles

Event	Time			Date Set	Location
100 meters:	**World** 12.21	**Yordanka Donkova**, Bulgaria		Aug. 20, 1988	Stara Zagora, BUL
	Olympic 12.38	Yordanka Donkova, Bulgaria		Sept.30, 1988	Seoul
	American 12.48	Gail Devers-Roberts		Sept.10, 1991	Berlin
400 meters:	**World** 52.94	**Marina Stepanova**, USSR		Sept.17, 1986	Tashkent
	Olympic	Not an event		—	—
	American 53.37	Sandra Farmer-Patrick		July 22, 1989	New York City

Note: The hurdles at 110 meters are 3 feet, 6 inches high and the hurdles at 400 meters are 3 feet. There are 10 hurdles in both races.

Walking

Event	Time			Date Set	Location
5 kilometers:	**World** 20:07.52	**Beate Anders**, East Germany		June 23, 1990	Rostock, E.Ger.
	Olympic	Not an event		—	—
	American 21:32.00	Debbi Lawrence¹		Apr. 25, 1992	Philadelphia
10 kilometers:	**World** 41:46.21	**Nadezhda Ryashkina**, USSR		July 24, 1990	Seattle
	Olympic 44:32	Yueling Chen, China		Aug. 3, 1992	Barcelona
	American 44:42	Debbi Lawrence		May 16, 1992	Kenosha, WI

Track & Field (Cont.)
World, Olympic and American Records
WOMEN
Relays

Event		Time		Date Set	Location
4 × 100 meters:	**World**	41.37	**East Germany** (Gladisch, Rieger, Auerswald, Gohr)	Oct. 6, 1985	Canberra
	Olympic	41.60	East Germany (Muller, Wockel, Auerswald, Gohr)	Aug. 1, 1980	Moscow
	American	41.55	USA (Brown, Williams Griffith, Marshall)	Aug. 21, 1987	W.Berlin
4 × 200 meters:	**World**	1:28.15	**East Germany** (Gohr, Muller, Wockel, Koch)	Aug. 9, 1980	Jena, E.Ger.
	Olympic		Not an event	—	—
	American	1:32.57	LSU (Stanley, Brydson, Jones, Sowell)	Apr. 28, 1989	Des Moines
4 × 400 meters:	**World**	3:15.18	**USSR** (Ledovskaya, Nazarova, Pinigina, Bryzgina)	Oct. 1, 1988	Seoul
	Olympic	3:15.18	USSR (same as World)	—	—
	American	3:15.51	USA (Howard, Dixon, Brisco, Griffith Joyner)	Oct. 1, 1988	Seoul
4 × 800 meters:	**World**	7:50.17	**USSR** (Olizarenko, Gurina, Borisova, Podyalovskaya)	Aug. 5, 1984	Moscow
	Olympic		Not an event	—	—
	American	8:17.09	Athletics West (Addison, Arbojast, Decker, Mullen)	Apr. 24, 1983	Walnut, CA

Field Events

Event		Mark		Date Set	Location
High Jump:	**World**	6-10¼	**Stefka Kostadinova**, Bulgaria	Aug. 30, 1987	Rome
	Olympic	6- 8	Louise Ritter, USA	Sept.30, 1988	Seoul
	American	6- 8	Louise Ritter	July 8, 1988	Austin
		6- 8	Ritter (see Olympic)		
Long Jump:	**World**	24- 8¼	**Galina Chistyakova**, USSR	June 11, 1988	Leningrad
	Olympic	24- 3¼	Jackie Joyner-Kersee, USA	Sept.29, 1988	Seoul
	American	24- 5½	Jackie Joyner-Kersee	Aug. 13, 1987	Indianapolis
Triple Jump:	**World**	49- 0¾	**Inessa Kravets**, USSR	June 10, 1991	Moscow
	Olympic		Not an event	—	—
	American	46- 0¾	Sheila Hudson	June 2, 1990	Durham, NC
Shot Put:	**World**	74- 3	**Natalia Lisovskaya**, USSR	June 7, 1987	Moscow
	Olympic	73- 6¼	Ilona Slupianek, E.Germany	July 24, 1980	Moscow
	American	66- 2½	Ramona Pagel	June 25, 1988	San Diego
Discus:	**World**	252- 0	**Gabriele Reinsch**, E.Germany	July 9, 1988	Neubrandenburg
	Olympic	237- 2½	Martina Hellmann, E.Germany	Sept.29, 1988	Seoul
	American	216-10	Carol Cady	May 31, 1986	San Jose
Javelin:	**World**	262- 5	**Petra Felke**, East Germany	Sept. 9, 1988	West Berlin
	Olympic	245- 0	Petra Felke, East Germany	Sept.26, 1988	Seoul
	American	227- 5	Kate Schmidt	Sept.10, 1977	Furth, W.Ger.

Note: The international weights for women—**Shot** (8 lbs/13 oz); **Discus** (2 lbs/3.27 oz); **Javelin** (minimum 1 lb/5.16 oz).

Heptathlon

Event		Points		Date Set	Location
Seven Events:	**World**	7291	**Jackie Joyner-Kersee**, USA	Sept.23-24, 1988	Seoul
	Olympic	7291	Joyner-Kersee (same as World)	—	—
	American	7291	Joyner-Kersee (same as World)	—	—

Note: Joyner-Kersee's WR times and distances, in order over two days—**100m H** (12.69); **HJ** (6-1¼); **SP** (51-10); **200m** (22.56); **LJ** (23-10¼); **Jav** (149-10); **800m** (2:08.51).

Indoor World and American Records
As of Oct. 1, 1992.
World indoor track and field records officially recognized by the International Amateur Athletics Federation (IAAF).

MEN
Running

Event		Time		Date Set	Location
50 meters:	**World**	5.61	**Manfred Kokot**, East Germany	Feb. 4, 1973	East Berlin
		5.61	**James Sanford**, USA	Feb. 20, 1981	San Diego
	American	5.61	Sanford (same as World)	—	—
60 meters:	**World**	6.41	**Andre Cason**, USA	Feb. 14, 1992	Madrid
	American	6.41	Cason (same as World)	—	—

Event		Time		Date Set	Location
200 meters:	World	20.36	**Bruno Marie-Rose**, France	Feb. 22, 1987	Lievin, FRA
	American	20.55	Michael Johnson	Jan. 26, 1991	Lievin, FRA
400 meters:	World	45.02	**Danny Everett**, USA	Feb. 2, 1992	Stuttgart
	American	45.02	Everett (same as World)	—	—
800 meters:	World	1:44.84	**Paul Ereng**, Kenya	Mar. 4, 1989	Budapest
	American	1:45.00	Johnny Gray	Mar. 8, 1992	Sindelfingen, GER
1000 meters:	World	2:15.26	**Noureddine Morceli**, Algeria	Feb. 22, 1992	Birmingham, GBR
	American	2:18.19	Ocky Clark	Feb. 12, 1989	Stuttgart
1500 meters:	World	3:34.16	**Noureddine Morceli**, Algeria	Feb. 28, 1991	Seville
	American	3:36.0	Steve Scott	Feb. 20, 1981	San Diego
Mile:	World	3:49.78	**Eammon Coghlan**, Ireland	Feb. 27, 1983	E.Rutherford
	American	3:51.8	Steve Scott	Feb. 20, 1981	San Diego
3000 meters:	World	7:37.31	**Moses Kiptanui**, Kenya	Feb. 20, 1992	Seville
	American	7:39.94	Steve Scott	Feb. 10, 1989	E.Rutherford
5000 meters:	World	13:20.40	**Suleiman Nyambui**, Tanzania	Feb. 6, 1981	New York City
	American	13:20.55	Doug Padilla	Feb. 12, 1982	New York City

Note: The **Mile** run is 1,609.344 meters.

Hurdles

Event		Time		Date Set	Location
50 meters:	World	6.25	**Mark McKoy**, Canada	Jan. 27, 1985	Rosemont, IL
	American	6.35	Greg Foster	Jan. 27, 1985	Rosemont, IL
		6.35	Greg Foster	Jan. 31, 1987	Ottawa
60 meters:	World	7.36	**Greg Foster**, USA	Jan. 16, 1987	Los Angeles
	American	7.36	Foster (same as World)	—	—

Note: The hurdles for both distances are 3 feet, 6 inches high. There are four hurdles in the 50 meters and five in the 60.

Walking

Event		Time		Date Set	Location
5000 meters:	World	18:15.25	**Grigory Kornev**, CIS	Feb. 7, 1992	Moscow
	American	19:18.40	Tim Lewis	Mar. 7, 1987	Indianapolis

Relays

Event		Time		Date Set	Location
4 × 200 meters:	World	1:22.11	**Great Britain**	Mar. 3, 1991	Glasgow
	American	1:22.71	National Team	Mar. 3, 1991	Glasgow
4 × 400 meters:	World	3:03.05	**Germany**	Mar. 10, 1991	Seville
	American	3:03.24	National Team	Mar. 10, 1991	Seville

Field Events

Event		Mark		Date Set	Location
High Jump:	World	7-11½	**Javier Sotomayor**, Cuba	Mar. 4, 1989	Budapest
	American	7-10½	Hollis Conway	Mar. 10, 1991	Seville
Pole Vault:	World	20- 1¼	**Sergei Bubka**, CIS	Feb. 21, 1992	Berlin
	American	19- 3¾	Billy Olson	Jan. 25, 1986	Albuquerque
Long Jump:	World	28-10¼	**Carl Lewis**, USA	Jan. 27, 1984	New York City
	American	28-10¼	Lewis (same as World)	—	—
Triple Jump:	World	58- 3¼	**Mike Conley**, USA	Feb. 27, 1987	New York City
	American	58- 3¼	Conley (same as World)	—	—
Shot Put:	World	74- 4¼	**Randy Barnes**, USA	Jan. 20, 1989	Los Angeles
	American	74- 4¼	Barnes (same as World)	—	—

Note: The international shotput weight for men is 16 lbs.

WOMEN
Running

Event		Time		Date Set	Location
50 meters:	World	6.06	**Angella Issajenko**, Canada	Feb. 2, 1980	Grenoble
	American	6.13	Jeanette Bolden	Feb. 21, 1981	Edmonton
		6:13	Michelle Finn	Feb. 15, 1992	Los Angeles
60 meters:	World	6.96	**Merlene Ottey**, Jamaica	Feb. 14, 1992	Madrid
	American	7.07	Gwen Torrence	Mar. 3, 1989	Budapest
		7.07	Michelle Finn	Feb. 28, 1992	New York City
200 meters:	World	22.24	**Merlene Ottey**, Jamaica	Mar. 10, 1991	Seville
	American	22.87	Dawn Sowell	Feb. 27, 1989	Baton Rouge
400 meters:	World	49.59	**Jarmila Kratochvilova**, Czech.	Mar. 7, 1982	Milan
	American	50.64	Diane Dixon	Mar. 10, 1991	Seville
800 meters:	World	1:56.40	**Christine Wachtel**, E.Germany	Feb. 14, 1988	Vienna
	American	1:58.9	Mary Decker	Feb. 22, 1980	San Diego
1000 meters:	World	2:34.67	**Lilia Nurutdinova**, CIS	Feb. 7, 1992	Moscow
	American	2:37.6	Mary Decker Slaney	Jan. 21, 1989	Portland
1500 meters:	World	4:00.27	**Doina Melinte**, Romania	Feb. 9, 1990	E.Rutherford
	American	4:00.8	Mary Decker	Feb. 8, 1980	New York City
Mile:	World	4:17.13	**Doina Melinte**, Romania	Feb. 9, 1990	E.Rutherford
	American	4:20.5	Mary Decker	Feb. 19, 1982	San Diego

Track & Field (Cont.)
Indoor World and American Records
WOMEN
Running

Event		Time		Date Set	Location
3000 meters:	**World**	8:33.82	**Elly van Hulst**, Holland	Feb. 8, 1986	Cosford, GBR
	American	8:40.45	Lynn Jennings	Feb. 23, 1990	New York City
5000 meters:	**World**	15:03.17	**Liz McGolgan**, Great Britain	Feb. 22, 1992	Birmingham, GBR
	American	15:22.64	Lynn Jennings	Jan. 7, 1990	Hanover, NH

Note: The **Mile** run is 1,609.344 meters.

Hurdles

Event		Time		Date Set	Location
50 meters:	**World**	6.58	**Cornelia Oschkenat**, E.Germany	Feb. 20, 1988	East BerlinL
	American	6.84	Kim McKenzie	Jan. 20, 1989	Ottawa
60 meters:	**World**	7.69	**Lyudmila Narozhilenko**, USSR	Feb. 4, 1990	Chelyabinsk, USSR
	American	7.81	Jackie Joyner-Kersee	Feb. 5, 1989	Fairfax, VA

Note: The hurdles for both distances are 2 feet, 9 inches high. There are four hurdles in the 50 meters and five in the 60.

Walking

Event		Time		Date Set	Location
3000 meters:	**World**	11:44.00	**Yelena Ivanova**, CIS	Feb. 7, 1992	Moscow
	American	12:45.38	Maryanne Torrellas	Feb. 26, 1988	New York City

Relays

Event		Time		Date Set	Location
4 × 200 meters:	**World**	1:32.55	**West Germany**	Feb. 20, 1988	Dortmund, W.Ger.
	American	1:36.8	Morgan St.	Mar. 7, 1981	Allston
4 × 400 meters:	**World**	3:27.22	**Germany**	Mar. 10, 1991	Seville
	American	3:32.46	Arizona St.	Mar. 9, 1991	Indianapolis
4 × 800 meters:	**World**	8:25.5	**Villanova**	Feb. 7, 1987	Gainesville
	American	8:25.5	Villanova (same as World)	—	—

Field Events

Event		Mark		Date Set	Location
High Jump:	**World**	6- 9½	**Heike Henkel**, Germany	Feb. 8, 1992	Karlstruhe, GER
	American	6- 6¾	Coleen Sommer	Feb. 13, 1882	Ottawa
Long Jump:	**World**	24- 2¼	**Heike Drechsler**, E.Germany	Feb. 14, 1988	Vienna
	American	23- 1¼	Jackie Joyner-Kersee	Mar. 7, 1992	Yokohama
Triple Jump:	**World**	47- 4½	**Inessa Kravets**, USSR	Mar. 9, 1991	Seville
	American	45- 9	Sheila Hudson	Mar. 10, 1990	Indianapolis
Shot Put:	**World**	73-10	**Helena Fibingerova**, Czech.	Feb. 19, 1977	Jablonec, CZE
	American	65- 0¾	Ramona Pagel	Feb. 20, 1987	Inglewood

Note: The international shotput weight for women is 8 lbs. and 13 oz.

SWIMMING

World, Olympic and American Records
As of Oct. 1, 1992.
World records officially recognized by the Federation Internationale de Natation Amateur (FINA).

MEN
Freestyle

Distance		Time		Date Set	Location
50 meters:	**World**	21.81	**Tom Jager**, USA	Mar. 24, 1990	Nashville
	Olympic	21.91	Aleksandr Popov, UT	July 30, 1992	Barcelona
	American	21.81	Jager (see World)	—	—
100 meters:	**World**	48.42	**Matt Biondi**, USA	Aug. 10, 1988	Austin, TX
	Olympic	48.42	Biondi (same as World)	—	—
	American	48.42	Biondi (same as World)	—	—
200 meters:	**World**	1:46.69	**Giorgio Lamberti**, Italy	Aug. 15, 1989	Bonn, W.Ger.
	Olympic	1:46.70	Yevgeny Sadovyi, UT	July 26, 1992	Barcelona
	American	1:47.72p	Matt Biondi	Aug. 8, 1988	Austin, TX
400 meters:	**World**	3:45.00	**Yevgeny Sadovyi**, UT	July 29, 1992	Barcelona
	Olympic	3:45.00	Sadovyi (same as World)	—	—
	American	3:48.06	Matt Cetlinski	Aug. 11, 1988	Austin, TX
800 meters:	**World**	7:47.85s	**Kieren Perkins**, AUS	Aug. 25, 1991	Edmonton
	Olympic		Not an event	—	—
	American	7:52.45	Sean Killion	July 27, 1987	Clovis, CA
1500 meters:	**World**	14:43.48	**Kieren Perkins**, AUS	July 31, 1992	Barcelona
	Olympic	14:43.48	Perkins (same as World)	—	—
	American	15:01.51	George DiCarlo	June 30, 1984	Indianapolis

Backstroke

Distance		Time		Date Set	Location
100 meters:	World	53.86r	**Jeff Rouse**, USA	July 31, 1992	Barcelona
	Olympic	53.98	Mark Tewksbury, CAN	July 30, 1992	Barcelona
	American	53.86r	Rouse (same as World)	—	—
200 meters:	World	1:56.57	**Martin Zubero**, Spain	Nov. 23, 1991	Tuscaloosa, AL
	Olympic	1:58.47	Martin Zubero, Spain	July 28, 1992	Barcelona
	American	1:58.66	Royce Sharp	Mar. 3, 1992	Indianapolis

Breaststroke

Distance		Time		Date Set	Location
100 meters:	World	1:01.29p	**Norbert Rosza**, Hungary	Aug. 20, 1991	Athens
	Olympic	1:01.50	Nelson Diebel, USA	July 26, 1992	Barcelona
	American	1:01.40	Nelson Diebel, USA	Mar. 1, 1992	Indianapolis
200 meters:	World	2:10.16	**Mike Barrowman**, USA	July 29, 1992	Barcelona
	Olympic	2:10.16	Barrowman (same as World)	—	—
	American	2:10.16	Barrowman (same as World)	—	—

Butterfly

Distance		Time		Date Set	Location
100 meters:	World	52.84	**Pablo Morales**, USA	June 23, 1986	Orlando
	Olympic	53.00	Anthony Nesty, Suriname	Sept. 21, 1988	Seoul
	American	52.84	Morales (same as World)	—	—
200 meters:	World	1:55.69	**Mel Stewart**, USA	Jan. 12, 1991	Perth
	Olympic	1:56.26	Mel Stewart, USA	July 30, 1992	Barcelona
	American	1:55.69	Stewart (same as World)	—	—

Individual Medley

Distance		Time		Date Set	Location
200 meters:	World	1:59.36	**Tamás Darnyi**, Hungary	Jan. 13, 1991	Perth
	Olympic	2:00.17	Tamás Darnyi, Hungary	Sept. 25, 1988	Seoul
	American	2:00.11	David Wharton	Aug. 20, 1989	Tokyo
400 meters:	World	4:12.36	**Tamás Darnyi**, Hungary	Jan. 8, 1991	Perth
	Olympic	4:14.23	Tamas Darnyi, Hungary	July 27, 1992	Barcelona
	American	4:15.21	Eric Namesnik	Jan. 8, 1991	Perth

Relays

Distance		Time		Date Set	Location
4 × 100m free:	World	3:16.53	**USA** (Jacobs, Dalbey, Jager, Biondi)	Sept. 23, 1988	Seoul
	Olympic	3:16.53	USA (same as World)	—	—
	American	3:16.53	USA (same as World)	—	—
4 × 200m free:	World	7:11.95	**Unified Team** (Lepikov, Pychnenko, Taianovitch, Sadovyi)	July 27, 1992	Barcelona
	Olympic	7:11.95	Unified Team (same as World)	—	—
	American	7:12.51	USA (Dalbey, Cetlinski, Gjertsen, Biondi)	Sept. 21, 1988	Seoul
4 × 100m medley:	World	3:36.93	**USA** (Berkoff, Schroeder, Biondi, Jacobs)	Sept. 25, 1988	Seoul
			USA (Rouse, Diebel, Morales, Olsen)	July 31, 1992	Barcelona
	Olympic	3:36.93	USA (same as World)	—	—
	American	3:36.93	USA (same as World)	—	—

Note: (p) indicates preliminary heat swim; (r) relay lead-off split; and (s) split time.

WOMEN

Freestyle

Distance		Time		Date Set	Location
50 meters:	World	24.79	**Yang Wenyi**, China	July 31, 1992	Barcelona
	Olympic	24.79	Wenyi (same as World)	—	—
	American	25.20	**Jenny Thompson**	Mar. 6, 1992	Indianapolis
100 meters:	World	54.48p	**Jenny Thompson**, USA	Mar. 1, 1992	Indianapolis
	Olympic	54.65	Zhaung Yong, China	July 26, 1992	Barcelona
	American	54.48p	Thompson (same as World)	—	—
200 meters:	World	1:57.55	**Heike Friedrich**, East Germany	June 18, 1986	Berlin
	Olympic	1:57.65	Heike Friedrich, East Germany	Sept. 21, 1988	Seoul
	American	1:57.90	Nicole Haislett	July 27, 1992	Barcelona
400 meters:	World	4:03.85	**Janet Evans**, USA	Sept. 22, 1988	Seoul
	Olympic	4:03.85	Evans (same as World)	—	—
	American	4:03.85	Evans (same as World)	—	—
800 meters:	World	8:16.22	**Janet Evans**, USA	Aug. 20, 1989	Tokyo
	Olympic	8:20.20	Janet Evans, USA	Sept. 24, 1988	Seoul
	American	8:16.22	Evans (same as World)	—	—
1500 meters:	World	15:52.10	**Janet Evans**, USA	Mar. 26, 1988	Orlando
	Olympic		Not an event		
	American	15:52.10	Evans (same as World)	—	—

Swimming (Cont.)
World, Olympic and American Records
WOMEN
Backstroke

Distance		Time		Date Set	Location
100 meters:	**World**	1:00.31	**Krisztina Egerszegi**, Hungary	Aug. 22, 1991	Athens
	Olympic	1:00.68	Krisztina Egerszegi, Hungary	July 28, 1992	Barcelona
	American	1:00.82r	Lea Loveless	July 30, 1992	Barcelona
200 meters:	**World**	2:06.62	**Krisztina Egerszegi**, Hungary	Aug. 25, 1991	Athens
	Olympic	2:07.06	Krisztina Egerszegi, Hungary	July 31, 1992	Barcelona
	American	2:08.60	Betsy Mitchell	June 27, 1986	Orlando

Breaststroke

Distance		Time		Date Set	Location
100 meters:	**World**	1:07.91	**Silke Horner**, East Germany	Aug. 21, 1987	Strasbourg, FRA
	Olympic	1:07.95	Tania Dangalakova, Bulgaria	Sept. 23, 1988	Seoul
	American	1:08.17	Anita Nall	July 29, 1992	Barcelona
200 meters:	**World**	2:25.35	**Anita Nall**, USA	Mar. 2, 1992	Indianapolis
	Olympic	2:26.65	Kyoko Iwasaki, Japan	July 27, 1992	Barcelona
	American	2:25.35	Nall (same as World)	—	—

Butterfly

Distance		Time		Date Set	Location
100 meters:	**World**	57.93	**Mary T. Meagher**, USA	Aug. 16, 1981	Brown Deer, WI
	Olympic	58.62	Hong Qian, China	July 29, 1992	Barcelona
	American	57.93	Meagher (same as World)	—	—
200 meters:	**World**	2:05.96	**Mary T. Meagher**, USA	Aug. 13, 1981	Brown Deer, WI
	Olympic	2:06.90	Mary T. Meagher, USA	Aug. 4, 1984	Los Angeles
	American	2:05.96	Meagher (same as World)	—	—

Individual Medley

Distance		Time		Date Set	Location
200 meters:	**World**	2:11.65	**Lin Li**, China	July 30, 1992	Barcelona
	Olympic	2:11.65	Li (same as World)	—	—
	American	2:11.91	Summer Sanders	July 30, 1992	Barcelona
400 meters:	**World**	4:36.10	**Petra Schneider**, East Germany	Aug. 1, 1982	Guayaquil, EQU
	Olympic	4:36.29	Petra Schneider, East Germany	July 26, 1980	Moscow
	American	4:37.58	Summer Sanders	July 26, 1992	Barcelona

Relays

Distance		Time		Date Set	Location
4 × 100m free:	**World**	3:39.46	**USA** (Haislett, Torres, Martino, Thompson)	July 28, 1992	Barcelona
	Olympic	3:39.46	USA (same as World)	—	—
	American	3:39.46	USA (same as World)	—	—
4 × 100m medley:	**World**	4:02.54	**USA** (Loveless, Nall, Ahmann-Leighton, Thompson)	July 30, 1992	Barcelona
	Olympic	4:02.54	USA (same as World)	—	—
	American	4:02.54	USA (same as World)	—	—

Note: (p) indicates preliminary heat swim; and (r) relay lead-off split.

WINTER SPORTS

Alpine Skiing

World Cup Champions

MEN

Overall	Paul Accola, SWI
Downhill	Franz Heinzer, SWI
Slalom	Alberto Tomba, ITA
Giant Slalom	Alberto Tomba, ITA
Super Giant Slalom	Paul Accola, SWI
Nation's Cup	Switzerland

WOMEN

Overall	Petra Kronberger, AUT
Downhill	Katja Seizinger, GER
Slalom	Vreni Schneider, SWI
Giant Slalom	Carole Merle, FRA
Super Giant Slalom	Carole Merle, FRA
Nation's Cup	Austria

U.S. Alpine Championships
at Winter Park, CO (Mar. 25-30)

MEN

Combined	Toni Standteiner, Olympic Valley, CA
Downhill	Jeff Olson, Park City, UT
Slalom	Matthew Grosjean, Steamboat Springs CO
Giant Slalom	Erik Schlopy, Stowe, VT
Super Giant Slalom	Erik Schlopy

WOMEN

Combined	Hilary Lindh, Juneau, AK
Downhill	Kate Pace, Canada
Slalom	Diann Roffe-Steinrotter, Potsdam, NY
Giant Slalom	Diann Roffe-Steinrotter
Super Giant Slalom	Diann Roffe-Steinrotter

Biathlon

World Cup Champions

Men's Overall . . . . Jon Age Tyldum, NOR
Women's Overall . . . . Anfisa Reztsova, CIS

U.S. National Champions

Men's Overall . . . . Josh Thompson, Gunnison, CO
Women's Overall . . Joan Guetschow, Minnetonka, MN

Bobsled

World Cup Champion Drivers

Two-Man . . . . Gunther Huber, Italy I
Four-Man . . . . Wolfgang Hoppe, Germany I
Combined . . . . Wolfgang Hoope

Best USA Drivers in World Cup

Two-Man . . . . Brian Shimer, Naples, FL
Four-Man . . . . Randy Will, Binghamton, NY

Figure Skating

World Championships
at Oakland (Mar. 24-29)

Men's . . . . Viktor Petrenko, CIS
Women's . . . . Kristi Yamaguchi, USA
Pairs . . . . . . Natalia Mishkuteniok & Artur Dmitriev, CIS
Ice Dance. Marina Klimova & Sergei Ponomarenko, CIS

U.S. Championships
at Orlando (Jan. 4-12)

Men's . . . . Christopher Bowman, Los Angeles
Women's . . . . Kristi Yamaguchi, Fremont, CA
Pairs . . . . Calla Urbanski, Chicago,
& Rocky Marval, New Egypt, NJ
Ice Dance . . . . April Sargent-Thomas, Ogdensburg, NY
& Russ Witherby, Cincinnati

Freestyle Skiing

World Cup Champions

MEN

Combined . . . . Trace Worthington, USA
Aerials . . . . Philippe LaRoche, CAN
Ballet . . . . Rune Kristiansen, NOR
Moguls . . . . Edgar Grospiron, FRA

WOMEN

Combined . . . . Conny Kissling, SWI
Aerials . . . . Kirstie Marshall, AUS
Ballet . . . . Conny Kissling, SWI
Moguls . . . . Donna Weinbrecht, USA

Luge

Overall World Cup Champions

MEN

Singles . . . . Marcus Prock, AUT
Doubles . . . . Norbert Huber & Yorg Ruffle, ITA

WOMEN

Singles . . . . Susi Erdman, GER

U.S. Champions

MEN

Singles . . . . Duncan Kennedy, Lake Placid, NY
Doubles . . . . Chris Thorpe, Marquette, MI
& Gordy Sheer, Croton, NY

WOMEN

Singles . . . . Cammy Myler, Lake Placid, NY

Nordic Skiing

World Cup Champions

MEN

Cross-country . . . . Bjorn Dahlie, NOR
Jumping . . . . Toni Nieminen, FIN
Combined . . . . Fabrice Guy, FRA

WOMEN

Cross-country . . . . Elena Valbe, CIS

U.S. Championships
Giants Ridge, MN (Jan. 4-11)

Cross-country

MEN

10-km classic . . . . John Aalberg, Salt Lake City
15-km freestyle . . . . John Aalberg
30-km classic . . . . John Aalberg
50-km freestyle . . . . John Bauer, Champlin, MN
(at Royal Gorge, CA, Mar. 15)

WOMEN

5-km classic . . . . Nancy Fiddler, Crowley Lake, CA
10-km freestyle . . . . Leslie Thompson, Stowe, VT
15-km classic . . . . Nancy Fiddler
30-km freestyle . . . . Leslie Thompson

Ski Jumping

Large Hill . . . . Jim Holland, Norwich, VT
(at Lake Placid, NY, Jan. 26)
Normal Hill . . . . Jim Holland
(at Brattleboro, VT, Feb. 1)

Nordic Combined

Individual . . . . Tim Tetreault, Norwich, VT

Speed Skating

World All-Around Championships

MEN
at Calgary (Mar. 21-22)

500 meters . . . . Peter Adeberg, GER
1500 meters . . . . Falko Zandstra, HOL
5000 meters . . . . Johann Koss, NOR
10,000 meters . . . . Falko Zandrsta, HOL
Overall . . . . Roberto Sighel, ITA

WOMEN
at Heerenveen, Holland (Mar. 7-8)

500 meters . . . . Qiaobo Ye, CHN
1500 meters . . . . Emese Hunyady, AUT
3000 meters . . . . Gunda Neimann, GER
5000 meters . . . . Gunda Neimann, GER
Overall . . . . Gunda Neimann, GER

World Sprint Championships
at Oslo (Feb. 29-Mar. 1)

(500-meter and 1000-meters Combined)

MEN

Overall . . . . Igor Zhelezovski, USSR

WOMEN

Overall . . . . Qiaobo Ye, CHN

SUMMER SPORTS

Basketball

CBA......................... La Crosse (WI) Catbirds
European.................... Partizan Belgrade (YUG)
Tournament of the Americas............ United States
Olympics: Men......................... United States
Women..................... Unified Team
French League......................... Pau-Orthez
Italian League...................... Benetton Treviso
Spanish League................... Joventud Badalona
1991 McDonalds Cup.................... LA Lakers

Cross-country

World Championships
at Boston (March 21)

Men............................. John Ngugi, KEN
Women......................... Lynn Jennings, USA

Cycling

Tour de France
79th Tour de France (July 4-26); 21 stages plus pro-
logue covering 2,490 miles from San Sebastian, Spain,
to Paris; 130 out of 197 riders finished the race.
  Winning time: 100 hours, 49 minutes, 30 seconds.
Winner's share: two million francs (about $400,000).

		Team	Behind
1	Miguel Indurain, SPA	Banesto	—
2	Claudio Chiappucci, ITA	Carrera	4:45
3	Gianni Bugno, ITA	Gatorade	10:49
4	Andy Hampsten, USA	Motorola	13:40
5	Pascal Lino, FRA	RMO	14:37
6	Pedro Delgado, SPA	Banesto	15:16
7	Erik Breukink, HOL	PDM	18:51
8	Giancarlo Perini, ITA	Carrera	19:16
9	Stephen Roche, IRE	Carrera	20:23
10	Jens Heppner, GER	Telekom	25:30

Note: Three-time winner Greg LeMond dropped out of the race
early in the 14th stage.

Worldwide Champions
MEN

Tour de France................. Miguel Indurain, SPA
Giro d'Italia (Italy).............. Miguel Indurain, SPA
Vuelta de Espana (Spain)........ Tony Rominger, SWI
World Pro Road Race............. Gianni Bugno, ITA
Olympic Road Race............. Fabio Casartelli, ITA
Tour du Pont (USA)...... Greg LeMond, Wayzata, MN

WOMEN

Ore-ida Challenge..... Eve Stephenson, Boulder, CO
Tour Cycliste Feminin..... Leontien Van Moorsel, HOL
Olympic Road Race.................. Kathy Watt, AUS

Gymnastics

World Championships
Apparatus Events Only, at Paris (Apr. 15-19)

MEN

Horizontal Bar.................. Grigory Misiutin, CIS
Parallel Bars............................ Li Jing, CHN
Vault...................... You Ok-Ryul, S.Kor
Pommel Horse.................... Pae Gil-Su, N.Kor
Rings............................. Vitaly Scherbo, CIS
Floor Exercise................. Igor Korobchinski, CIS

WOMEN

Vault...................... Henrietta Onodi, HUN
Uneven Bars................ Lavinia Milosovici, ROM
Balance Beam..................... Kim Zmeskal, USA
Floor Exercise..................... Kim Zmeskal, USA

U.S. Championships
at Columbus, OH (May 14-17)

MEN

All-Around.......... John Roethlisberger, Afton, MN
Horizontal Bar........... Jair Lynch, Washington, DC
Parallel Bars............. Jair Lynch, Washington, DC
Vault............... Trent Dimas, Albuquerque, NM
Pommel Horse.......... Chris Waller, Mt.Prospect, IL
Rings................... Tim Ryan, Coopersburg, PA
Floor Exercise............. Gregg Curtis, Carmel, NY

WOMEN

All-Around.................... Kim Zmeskal, Houston
Vault....................... Kerri Strug, Tucson, AZ
Uneven Bars.... Dominique Dawes, Silver Spring, MD
Balance Beam................. Kim Zmeskal, Houston
Floor Exercise................. Kim Zmeskal, Houston
Note: Shannon Miller was injured (elbow) and did not participate.

Marathons

1992 Winners

Boston: Men.................... Ibrahim Hussein, KEN
    Women.................. Olga Markova, CIS
London: Men..................... Antonio Pinto, POR
    Women.................. Katrin Dorre, GER
Los Angeles: Men.................... John Treacy, IRE
    Women..... Madina Biktagirova, CIS
U.S. Olympic Trials: Men............... Steve Spence
    Women.... Francie Larrieu Smith
Osaka (Women only)............. Yuki Kokamo, JPN
Rotterdam: Men............... Salvador Garcia, MEX
    Women.............. Aurora Cunha, POR

Late 1991

Chicago: Men..................... Joseildo Silva, BRA
    Women....... Midde Hamrin-Senorski, SWE
Fukuoka (Men only).............. Shuichi Morita, JPN
New York City: Men........... Salvador Garcia, MEX
    Women......... Liz McColgan, SCOT

Rowing

World Championships
at Montreal (Aug. 15-16)

MEN

Lightweight Single Sculls........ Jens Mohr Ernst, DEN
Lightweight Eight........................... Denmark
Junior Eight............................ United States

WOMEN

Lightweight Single Sculls..... Mette Bloch Jensen, DEN
Lightweight Four without Coxswain.......... Australia
Junior Eight................................ Germany

U.S. Nationals
at Indianapolis (June 25-28)

MEN

Single Sculls.................... Greg Walker, NYAC
Lightweight Single Sculls..... Brian Sweenor, OARS/RI
Lightweight Eights........................... Canada
Eights....................................... Canada

WOMEN

Single Sculls....................... Linda Mun, MIT
Lightweight Single Sculls........ Wendy Wiebe, CAN
Lightweight Eights.............. Boston Rowing Center
Eights............................. Vesper Boat Club

THE 1993 SPORTS ALMANAC — INFORMATION PLEASE

INT'L SPORTS STATISTICS

THROUGH THE YEARS
1896-1992
WINNERS • RECORDS

SEC B

PAGE 617

Track & Field World Championships

While the Summer Olympics have served as the unofficial world outdoor championships for track and field throughout the century, a separate World Championship meet was started in 1983 by the International Amateur Athletic Federation (IAAF). The meet was held every four years from 1983-91, but will begin an every-other-year cycle in 1993. World Championship sites have included Helsinki (1983), Rome (1987) and Tokyo (1991) with Stuttgart, Germany, scheduled to host the meet in 1993.

MEN

Multiple titles (including relays): Carl Lewis (8); Sergei Bubka, Greg Foster and Calvin Smith (3); Maurizio Damilano, Werner Gunthor, Billy Konchellah, Sergei Litvinov and Edwin Moses (2).

100 meters

Year		Time
1983	Carl Lewis, USA	10.07
1987	Carl Lewis, USA	9.93
1991	Carl Lewis, USA	9.86 **WR**

Note: Ben Johnson was the original winner in 1987, but was stripped of his title and world record time (9.83) following his 1989 admission of drug taking.

200 meters

Year		Time
1983	Calvin Smith, USA	20.14
1987	Calvin Smith, USA	20.16
1991	Michael Johnson, USA	20.01

400 meters

Year		Time
1983	Bert Cameron, JAM	45.05
1987	Thomas Schonlebe, E.Ger	44.33
1991	Antonio Pettigrew, USA	44.57

800 meters

Year		Time
1983	Willi Wubeck, W.Ger	1:43.65
1987	Billy Konchellah, KEN	1:43.06
1991	Billy Konchellah, KEN	1:43.99

1500 meters

Year		Time
1983	Steve Cram, GBR	3:41.59
1987	Abdi Bile, SOM	3:36.80
1991	Noureddine Morceli, ALG	3:32.84

5000 meters

Year		Time
1983	Eammon Coghlan, IRE	13:28.53
1987	Said Aoutia, MOR	13:26.44
1991	Yobes Ondieki, KEN	13:14.45

10,000 meters

Year		Time
1983	Alberto Cova, ITA	28:01.04
1987	Paul Kipkoech, KEN	27:38.63
1991	Moses Tanui, KEN	27:38.74

Marathon

Year		Time
1983	Rob de Castella, AUS	2:10:03
1987	Douglas Wakiihuri, KEN	2:11:48
1991	Hiromi Taniguchi, JPN	2:14:57

3000-meter Steeplechase

Year		Time
1983	Patriz Ilg, W.Ger	8:15.06
1987	Francesco Panetta, ITA	8:08.57
1991	Moses Kiptanui, KEN	8:12.59

110-meter Hurdles

Year		Time
1983	Greg Foster, USA	13.42
1987	Greg Foster, USA	13.21
1991	Greg Foster, USA	13.06

400-meter Hurdles

Year		Time
1983	Edwin Moses, USA	47.50
1987	Edwin Moses, USA	47.46
1991	Samuel Matete, ZAM	47.64

4 × 100-meter Relay

Year		Time
1983	United States	37.86 **WR**
1987	United States	37.90
1991	United States	37.50 **WR**

Note: Carl Lewis has run the anchor leg on all three winning U.S. 4 × 100-meter relay teams.

All-time Olympic Track & Field Champions can be found starting on page 591.

Track & Field World Championships (Cont.)

MEN

4×400-meter Relay

Year		Time
1983	Soviet Union	3:00.79
1987	United States	2:57.29
1991	Great Britain	2:57.53

20-kilometer Walk

Year		Time
1983	Ernesto Canto, MEX	1:20:49
1987	Maurizio Damilano, ITA	1:20:45
1991	Maurizio Damilano, ITA	1:19:37

50-kilometer Walk

Year		Time
1983	Ronald Weigel, E.Ger	3:43:08
1987	Hartwig Gauder, E.Ger	3:40:53
1991	Aleksandr Potashov, USSR	3:53:09

High Jump

Year		Height
1983	Gennedy Avdeyenko, USSR	7-7¼
1987	Patrik Sjoberg, SWE	7-9¾
1991	Charles Austin, USA	7-9¾

Pole Vault

Year		Height
1983	Sergei Bubka, USSR	18-8¼
1987	Sergei Bubka, USSR	19-2¼
1991	Sergei Bubka, USSR	19-6¼

Long Jump

Year		Distance
1983	Carl Lewis, USA	28-0¾
1987	Carl Lewis, USA	28-5¼
1991	Mike Powell, USA	29-4½ **WR**

Triple Jump

Year		Distance
1983	Zdzislaw Hoffmann, POL	57-2
1987	Khristo Markov, BUL	58-9½
1991	Kenny Harrison, USA	58-4

Shot Put

Year		Distance
1983	Edward Sarul, POL	70- 2¼
1987	Werner Gunthor, SWI	72-11¼
1991	Werner Gunthor, SWI	71- 1¾

Discus

Year		Distance
1983	Imrich Bugar, CZE	222-2
1987	Jurgen Schult, E.Ger	225-6
1991	Lars Riedel, GER	217-2

Hammer Throw

Year		Distance
1983	Sergei Litvinov, USSR	271-3
1987	Sergei Litvinov, USSR	272-6
1991	Yuri Sedykh, USSR	268-0

Javelin

Year		Distance
1983	Detlef Michel, E.Ger	293- 7 **OLD**
1987	Seppo Raty, FIN	274- 1 **NEW**
1991	Kimmo Kinnunen, FIN	297-11

Decathlon

Year		Points
1983	Daley Thompson, GBR	8714
1987	Torsten Voss, E.Ger	8680
1991	Dan O'Brien, USA	8812

WOMEN

Multiple titles (including relays): Tatiana Samolenko Dorovskikh, Silke Gladisch, Jackie Joyner-Kersee, and Marita Koch (3); Olga Bryzgina, Mary Decker, Martina Optiz Hellmann, Katrin Krabbe and Jarmila Kratochvilova (2).

100 meters

Year		Time
1983	Marlies Gohr, E.Ger	10.97
1987	Silke Gladisch, E.Ger	10.90
1991	Katrin Krabbe, GER	10.99

200 meters

Year		Time
1983	Marita Koch, E.Ger	22.13
1987	Silke Gladisch, E.Ger	21.74
1991	Katrin Krabbe, GER	22.09

400 meters

Year		Time
1983	Jarmila Kratochvilova, CZE	47.99 **WR**
1987	Olga Bryzgina, USSR	49.38
1991	Marie-Jose Perec, FRA	49.13

800 meters

Year		Time
1983	Jarmila Kratochvilova, CZE	1:54.68
1987	Sigrun Wodars, E.Ger	1:55.26
1991	Lilia Nurutdinova, USSR	1:57.50

1500 meters

Year		Time
1983	Mary Decker, USA	4:00.90
1987	Tatiana Samolenko, USSR	3:58.56
1991	Hassiba Boulmerka, ALG	4:02.21

3000 meters

Year		Time
1983	Mary Decker, USA	8:34.62
1987	Tatiana Samolenko, USSR	8:38.73
1991	Tatiana Samolenko Dorovskikh, USSR	8:35.82

10,000 meters

Year		Time
1983	Not held	
1987	Ingrid Kristiansen, NOR	31:05.85
1991	Liz McColgan, GBR	31:14.31

Marathon

Year		Time
1983	Grete Waitz, NOR	2:28:09
1987	Rose Mota, POR	2:25:17
1991	Wanda Panfil, POL	2:29:53

100-meter Hurdles

Year		Time
1983	Bettine Jahn, E.Ger	12.35
1987	Ginka Zagorcheva, BUL	12.34
1991	Lyudmila Narozhilenko, USSR	12.59

400-meter Hurdles

Year		Time
1983	Yekaterina Fesenko, USSR	54.14
1987	Sabine Busch, E.Ger	53.62
1991	Tatiana Ledovskaya, USSR	53.11

4 × 100-meter Relay

Year		Time
1983	East Germany	41.76
1987	United States	41.58
1991	Jamaica	41.94

4 × 400-meter Relay

Year		Time
1983	East Germany	3:19.73
1987	East Germany	3:18.63
1991	Soviet Union	3:18.43

10-kilometer Walk

Year		Time
1983	Not held	
1987	Irina Strakhova, USSR	44:12
1991	Alina Ivanova, USSR	42:57

High Jump

Year		Height	
1983	Tamara Bykova, USSR	6- 7	
1987	Stefka Kostadinova, BUL	6-10¼	**WR**
1991	Heike Henkel, GER	6- 8¾	

Long Jump

Year		Distance
1983	Heike Daute, E.Ger	23-10¼ʷ
1987	Jackie Joyner-Kersee, USA	24- 1¾
1991	Jackie Joyner-Kersee, USA	24- 0¼

ʷ indicates wind-aided.

Shot Put

Year		Distance
1983	Helena Fibingerova, CZE	69-0¾
1987	Natalia Lisovskaya, USSR	69-8¼
1991	Huang Zhihong, CHN	68-4¼

Discus

Year		Distance
1983	Martina Opitz, E.Ger	226-2
1987	Martina Opitz Hellmann, E.Ger	235-0
1991	Tsvetanka Khristova, BUL	233-0

Javelin

Year		Distance
1983	Tiina Lillak, FIN	232-4
1987	Fatima Whitbread, GBR	251-5
1991	Xu Demei, CHN	225-8

Heptathlon

Year		Points
1983	Ramona Neubert, E.Ger	6770
1987	Jackie Joyner-Kersee, USA	7128
1991	Sabine Braun, GER	6672

Boston Marathon

America's oldest regularly contested foot race, the Boston Marathon is held on Patriots' Day every April. It has been run at four different distances: 24 miles, 1232 yards (1897-1923); 26 miles, 209 yards (1924-26); 26 miles, 385 yards (1927-52); 25 miles, 958 yards (1953-56); and 26 miles, 385 yards (since 1957).

Men

Multiple winners: Clarence DeMar (7); Gerard Cote and Bill Rodgers (4); Ibrahim Hussein and Leslie Pawson (3); Tarzan Brown, Jim Caffery, John A. Kelley, John Miles, Eino Oksanen, Toshihiko Seko, Geoff Smith and Aurele Vandendriessche (2).

Year		Time
1897	John McDermott, New York	2:55:10
1898	Ronald McDonald, Massachusetts	2:42:00
1899	Lawrence Brignolia, Massachusetts	2:54:38
1900	Jim Caffrey, Canada	2:39:44
1901	Jim Caffrey, Canada	2:29:23
1902	Sam Mellor, New York	2:43:12
1903	J.C. Lorden, Massachusetts	2:41:29
1904	Mike Spring, New York	2:38:04
1905	Fred Lorz, New York	2:38:25
1906	Tim Ford, Massachusetts	2:45:45
1907	Tom Longboat, Canada	2:24:24
1908	Tom Morrissey, New York	2:25:43
1909	Henri Renaud, New Hampshire	2:53:36
1910	Fred Cameron, Nova Scotia	2:28:52
1911	Clarence DeMar, Massachusetts	2:21:39
1912	Mike Ryan, Illinois	2:21:18
1913	Fritz Carlson, Minnesota	2:25:14
1914	James Duffy, Canada	2:25:01

Year		Time
1915	Edouard Fabre, Canada	2:31:41
1916	Arthur Roth, Massachusetts	2:27:16
1917	Bill Kennedy, New York	2:28:37
1918	World War relay race	
1919	Carl Linder, Massachusetts	2:29:13
1920	Peter Trivoulidas, New York	2:29:31
1921	Frank Zuna, New Jersey	2:18:57
1922	Clarence DeMar, Massachusetts	2:18:10
1923	Clarence DeMar, Massachusetts	2:23:37
1924	Clarence DeMar, Massachusetts	2:29:40
1925	Charles Mellor, Illinois	2:33:00
1926	John Miles, Nova Scotia	2:25:40
1927	Clarence DeMar, Massachusetts	2:40:22
1928	Clarence DeMar, Massachusetts	2:37:07
1929	John Miles, Nova Scotia	2:33:08
1930	Clarence DeMar, Massachusetts	2:34:48
1931	James Henigan, Massachusetts	2:46:45
1932	Paul deBruyn, Germany	2:33:36

Boston Marathon (Cont.)

Year		Time	Year		Time
1933	Leslie Pawson, Rhode Island	2:31:01	1963	Aurele Vandendriessche, Belgium	2:18:58
1934	Dave Komonen, Canada	2:32:53	1964	Aurele Vandendriessche, Belgium	2:19:59
1935	John A. Kelley, Massachusetts	2:32:07	1965	Morio Shigematsu, Japan	2:16:33
1936	Ellison (Tarzan) Brown, Rhode Island	2:33:40	1966	Kenji Kimihara, Japan	2:17:11
1937	Walter Young, Canada	2:33:20	1967	David McKenzie, New Zealand	2:15:45
1938	Leslie Pawson, Rhode Island	2:35:34	1968	Amby Burfoot, Connecticut	2:22:17
1939	Ellison (Tarzan) Brown, Rhode Island	2:28:51	1969	Yoshiaki Unetani, Japan	2:13:49
1940	Gerard Cote, Canada	2:28:28	1970	Ron Hill, England	2:10:30
1941	Leslie Pawson, Rhode Island	2:30:38	1971	Alvaro Mejia, Colombia	2:18:45
1942	Joe Smith, Massachusetts	2:26:51	1972	Olavi Suomalainen, Finland	2:15:39
1943	Gerard Cote, Canada	2:28:25	1973	Jon Anderson, Oregon	2:16:03
1944	Gerard Cote, Canada	2:31:50	1974	Neil Cusack, Ireland	2:13:39
1945	John A.Kelley, Massachusetts	2:30:40	1975	Bill Rodgers, Massachusetts	2:09:55
1946	Stylianos Kyriakides, Greece	2:29:27	1976	Jack Fultz, Pennsylvania	2:20:19
1947	Yun Bok Suh, Korea	2:25:39	1977	Jerome Drayton, Canada	2:14:46
1948	Gerard Cote, Canada	2:31:02	1978	Bill Rodgers, Massachusetts	2:10:13
1949	Karle Leandersson, Sweden	2:31:50	1979	Bill Rodgers, Massachusetts	2:09:27
1950	Kee Yonh Ham, Korea	2:32:39	1980	Bill Rodgers, Massachusetts	2:12:11
1951	Shigeki Tanaka, Japan	2:27:45	1981	Toshihiko Seko, Japan	2:09:26
1952	Doroteo Flores, Guatemala	2:31:53	1982	Alberto Salazar, Massachusetts	2:08:52
1953	Keizo Yamada, Japan	2:18:51	1983	Greg Meyer, New Jersey	2:09:00
1954	Veiko Karvonen, Finland	2:20:39	1984	Geoff Smith, England	2:10:34
1955	Hideo Hamamura, Japan	2:18:22	1985	Geoff Smith, England	2:14:05
1956	Antti Viskari, Finland	2:14:14	1986	Rob de Castella, Australia	2:07:51*
1957	John J.Kelley, Connecticut	2:20:05	1987	Toshihiko Seko, Japan	2:11:50
1958	Franjo Mihalic, Yugoslavia	2:25:54	1988	Ibrahim Hussein, Kenya	2:08:43
1959	Eino Oksanen, Finland	2:22:42	1989	Abebe Mekonnen, Ethiopia	2:09:06
1960	Paavo Kotila, Finland	2:20:54	1990	Gelindo Bordin, Italy	2:08:19
1961	Eino Oksanen, Finland	2:23:39	1991	Ibrahim Hussein, Kenya	2:11:06
1962	Eino Oksanen, Finland	2:23:48	1992	Ibrahim Hussein, Kenya	2:08:14

*Record for distance.

WOMEN

Multiple winners: Rosa Mota (3); Joan Benoit, Miki Gorman and Ingrid Kristiansen (2).

Year		Time	Year		Time
1972	Nina Kuscsik, New York	3:08:58	1983	Joan Benoit, Maine	2:22:43*
1973	Jacqueline Hansen, California	3:05:59	1984	Lorraine Moller, New Zealand	2:29:28
1974	Miki Gorman, California	2:47:11	1985	Lisa Larsen Weidenbach, Mass	2:34:06
1975	Liane Winter, West Germany	2:42:24	1986	Ingrid Kristiansen, Norway	2:24:55
1976	Kim Merritt, Wisconsin	2:47:10	1987	Rosa Mota, Portugal	2:25:21
1977	Miki Gorman, California	2:48:33	1988	Rosa Mota, Portugal	2:24:30
1978	Gayle Barron, Georgia	2:44:52	1989	Ingrid Kristiansen, Norway	2:24:33
1979	Joan Benoit, Maine	2:35:15	1990	Rosa Mota, Portugal	2:25:23
1980	Jacqueline Gareau, Canada	2:34:28	1991	Wanda Panfil, Poland	2:24:18
1981	Allison Roe, New Zealand	2:26:46	1992	Olga Markova, CIS	2:23:43
1982	Charlotte Teske, West Germany	2:29:33			

*Record for distance.

New York City Marathon

Started in 1970, the New York City Marathon is run in the fall, usually on the first Sunday in November. The route winds through all of the city's five boroughs and finishes in Central Park.

MEN

Multiple winners: Bill Rodgers (4); Alberto Salazar (3); Tom Fleming and Orlando Pizzolato (2).

Year		Time	Year		Time
1970	Gary Muhrcke, USA	2:31:38	1975	Tom Fleming, USA	2:19:27
1971	Norman Higgins, USA	2:22:54	1976	Bill Rodgers, USA	2:10:09
1972	Sheldon Karlin, USA	2:27:52	1977	Bill Rodgers, USA	2:11:28
1973	Tom Fleming, USA	2:21:54	1978	Bill Rodgers, USA	2:12:12
1974	Norbert Sander, USA	2:26:30	1979	Bill Rodgers, USA	2:11:42

Year		Time	Year		Time
1980	Alberto Salazar, USA	2:09:41	1987	Ibrahim Hussein, Kenya	2:11:01
1981	Alberto Salazar, USA	2:08:13	1988	Steve Jones, Wales	2:08:20
1982	Alberto Salazar, USA	2:09:29	1989	Juma Ikangaa, Tanzania	2:08:01
1983	Rod Dixon, New Zealand	2:08:59			
1984	Orlando Pizzolato, Italy	2:14:53	1990	Douglas Wakiihuri, Kenya	2:12:39
1985	Orlando Pizzolato, Italy	2:11:34	1991	Salvador Garcia, Mexico	2:09:28
1986	Gianni Poli, Italy	2:11:06			

WOMEN

Multiple winners: Greta Waitz (9); Miki Gorman and Nina Kuscsik (2).

Year		Time	Year		Time
1970	No Finisher		1982	Greta Waitz, Norway	2:27:14
1971	Beth Bonner, USA	2:55:22	1983	Greta Waitz, Norway	2:27:00
1972	Nina Kuscsik, USA	3:08:41	1984	Greta Waitz, Norway	2:29:30
1973	Nina Kuscsik, USA	2:57:07	1985	Greta Waitz, Norway	2:28:34
1974	Katherine Switzer, USA	3:07:29	1986	Greta Waitz, Norway	2:28:06
1975	Kim Merritt, USA	2:46:14	1987	Priscilla Welch, Britain	2:30:17
1976	Miki Gorman, USA	2:39:11	1988	Greta Waitz, Norway	2:28:07
1977	Miki Gorman, USA	2:43:10	1989	Ingrid Kristiansen, Norway	2:25:30
1978	Greta Waitz, Norway	2:32:30			
1979	Greta Waitz, Norway	2:27:33	1990	Wanda Panfil, Poland	2:30:45
1980	Greta Waitz, Norway	2:25:41	1991	Liz McColgan, Scotland	2:27:23
1981	Allison Roe, New Zealand	2:25:29			

Annual Awards
Track & Field News Athletes of the Year

Voted on by an international panel of track and field experts and presented since 1959 (men) and 1974 (women) by *Track & Field News.*

MEN

Multiple winners: Carl Lewis (3); Sergei Bubka, Sebastian Coe, Alberto Juantorena, Jim Ryun, Peter Snell (2).

Year		Event	Year		Event
1959	Martin Lauer, W.Germany	110H/Decathlon	1976	Alberto Juantorena, Cuba	400/800
			1977	Alberto Juantorena, Cuba	400/800
1960	Rafer Johnson, USA	Decathlon	1978	Henry Rono, Kenya	5000/10,000/Steeplechase
1961	Ralph Boston, USA	Long Jump/110 Hurdles	1979	Sebastian Coe, Great Britain	800/1500
1962	Peter Snell, New Zealand	800/1500			
1963	C.K. Yang, Taiwan	Decathlon/Pole Vault	1980	Edwin Moses, USA	400 Hurdles
1964	Peter Snell, New Zealand	800/1500	1981	Sebastian Coe, Great Britain	800/1500
1965	Ron Clarke, Australia	5000/10,000	1982	Carl Lewis, USA	100/200/Long Jump
1966	Jim Ryun, USA	800/1500	1983	Carl Lewis, USA	100/200/Long Jump
1967	Jim Ryun, USA	1500	1984	Carl Lewis, USA	100/200/Long Jump
1968	Bob Beamon, USA	Long Jump	1985	Said Aouita, Morocco	1500/5000
1969	Bill Toomey, USA	Decathlon	1986	Yuri Sedykh, USSR	Hammer Throw
1970	Randy Matson, USA	Shot Put	1987	Ben Johnson, Canada	100
1971	Rod Milburn, USA	110 Hurdles	1988	Sergei Bubka, USSR	Pole Vault
1972	Lasse Viren, Finland	5000/10,000	1989	Roger Kingdom, USA	110 Hurdles
1973	Ben Jipcho, Kenya	1500/5000/Steeplechase			
1974	Rick Wohlhuter, USA	800/1500	1990	Michael Johnson, USA	200/400
1975	John Walker, New Zealand	800/1500	1991	Sergei Bubka, USSR	Pole Vault

WOMEN

Multiple winners: Marita Koch (4); Evelyn Ashford and Jackie Joyner-Kersee (2).

Year		Event	Year		Event
1974	Irena Szewinska, Poland	100/200/400	1983	Jarmila Kratochvilova, Czech	200/400/800
1975	Faina Melnik, USSR	Shot Put/Discus	1984	Evelyn Ashford, USA	100
1976	Tatiana Kazankina, USSR	800/1500	1985	Marita Koch, E.Germany	100/200/400
1977	Rosemarie Ackermann, E.Germany	High Jump	1986	Jackie Joyner-Kersee, USA	Heptahlon/Long Jump
1978	Marita Koch, E.Germany	100/200/400	1987	Jackie Joyner-Kersee, USA	100h/Heptahlon/LJ
1979	Marita Koch, E.Germany	100/200/400	1988	Florence Griffith Joyner, USA	100/200
1980	Ilona Briesenick, E.Germany	Shot Put	1989	Ana Quirot, Cuba	400/800
1981	Evelyn Ashford, USA	100/200			
1982	Marita Koch, E.Germany	100/200/400	1990	Merlene Ottey, Jamaica	100/200
			1991	Heike Henkel, Germany	High Jump

Cycling
Tour de France

The world's premier cycling event, the Tour de France is staged throughout the country (sometimes passing through neighboring countries) over four weeks. The 1946 Tour, however, the first after World War II, was only a five-day race.

Multiple winners: Jacques Anquetil, Bernard Hinault and Eddy Merckx (5); Louison Bobet, Gred LeMond and Philippe Thys (3); Gino Bartali, Ottavio Bottecchia, Fausto Coppi, Laurent Fignon, Nicholas Frantz, Miguel Induráin, Firmin Lambot, Andre Leducq, Sylvere Maes, Antonin Magne, Lucien Petit-Breton and Bernard Thevenet (2).

Year		Year		Year	
1903	Maurice Garin, France	1934	Antonin Magne, France	1967	Roger Pingeon, France
1904	Henri Cornet, France	1935	Romain Maes, Belgium	1968	Jan Janssen, Holland
1905	Louis Trousselier, France	1936	Sylvere Maes, Belgium	1969	Eddy Merckx, Belgium
1906	René Pottier, France	1937	Roger Lapebie, France		
1907	Lucien Petit-Breton, France	1938	Gino Bartali, Italy	1970	Eddy Merckx, Belgium
1908	Lucien Petit-Breton, France	1939	Sylvere Maes, Belgium	1971	Eddy Merckx, Belgium
1909	Francois Faber, Luxembourg			1972	Eddy Merckx, Belgium
		1940–45	Not held	1973	Luis Ocana, Spain
1910	Octave Lapize, France	1946	Jean Lazarides, France	1974	Eddy Merckx, Belgium
1911	Gustave Garrigou, France	1947	Jean Robic, France	1975	Bernard Thevenet, France
1912	Odile Defraye, Belgium	1948	Gino Bartali, Italy	1976	Lucien van Impe, Belgium
1913	Philippe Thys, Belgium	1949	Fausto Coppi, Italy	1977	Bernard Thevenet, France
1914	Philippe Thys, Belgium	1950	Ferdinand Kubler, Switzerland	1978	Bernard Hinault, France
1915–18	Not held	1951	Hugo Koblet, Switzerland	1979	Bernard Hinault, France
1919	Firmin Lambot, Belgium	1952	Fausto Coppi, Italy		
1920	Philippe Thys, Belgium	1953	Louison Bobet, France	1980	Joop Zoetemelk, Holland
1921	Léon Scieur, Belgium	1954	Louison Bobet, France	1981	Bernard Hinault, France
1922	Firmin Lambot, Belgium	1955	Louison Bobet, France	1982	Bernard Hinault, France
1923	Henri Pelissier, France	1956	Roger Walkowiak, France	1983	Laurent Fignon, France
1924	Ottavio Bottecchia, Italy	1957	Jacques Anquetil, France	1984	Laurent Fignon, France
1925	Ottavio Bottecchia, Italy	1958	Charly Gaul, Luxembourg	1985	Bernard Hinault, France
1926	Lucien Buysse, Belgium	1959	Federico Bahamontes, Spain	1986	Greg LeMond, USA
1927	Nicholas Frantz, Luxembourg			1987	Stephen Roche, Ireland
1928	Nicholas Frantz, Luxembourg	1960	Gastone Nencini, Italy	1988	Pedro Delgado, Spain
1929	Maurice Dewaele, Belgium	1961	Jacques Anquetil, France	1989	Greg LeMond, USA
		1962	Jacques Anquetil, France		
1930	André Leducq, France	1963	Jacques Anquetil, France	1990	Greg LeMond, USA
1931	Antonin Magne, France	1964	Jacques Anquetil, France	1991	Miguel Induráin, Spain
1932	André Leducq, France	1965	Felice Gimondi, Italy	1992	Miguel Induráin, Spain
1933	Georges Speicher, France	1966	Lucien Aimar, France		

Alpine Skiing
World Cup Overall Champions

World Cup Overall Champions (downhill and slalom events combined) since the tour was organized in 1967.

MEN

Multiple winners: Marc Girardelli, Gustavo Thoem and Pirmin Zurbrigger (4); Phil Mahre, and Ingemar Stenmark (3); Jean-Claude Killy and Karl Schranz (2).

Year		Year		Year	
1967	Jean-Claude Killy, France	1976	Ingemar Stenmark, Sweden	1985	Marc Girardelli, Luxembourg
1968	Jean Claude Killy, France	1977	Ingemar Stenmark, Sweden	1986	Marc Girardelli, Luxembourg
1969	Karl Schranz, Austria	1978	Ingemar Stenmark, Sweden	1987	Pirmin Zurbriggen, Switzerland
		1979	Peter Luescher, Switzerland	1988	Pirmin Zurbriggen, Switzerland
1970	Karl Schranz, Austria			1989	Marc Girardelli, Luxembourg
1971	Gustavo Thoeni, Italy	1980	Andreas Wenzel, Lichtenstein		
1972	Gustavo Thoeni, Italy	1981	Phil Mahre, USA	1990	Pirmin Zurbriggen, Switzerland
1973	Gustavo Thoeni, Italy	1982	Phil Mahre, USA	1991	Marc Girardelli, Luxembourg
1974	Piero Gros, Italy	1983	Phil Mahre, USA	1992	Paul Accola, Switzerland
1975	Gustavo Thoeni, Italy	1984	Pirmin Zurbriggen, Switzerland		

WOMEN

Multiple winners: Annemarie Moser-Proell (6); Petra Kronberger (3); Michela Figini, Nancy Greene, Erika Hess, Maria Walliser and Hanni Wenzel (2).

Year		Year		Year	
1967	Nancy Greene, Canada	1976	Rosi Mittermaier, W.Germany	1985	Michela Figini, Switzerland
1968	Nancy Greene, Canada	1977	Lise-Marie Morerod, Switzerland	1986	Maria Walliser, Switzerland
1969	Gertrud Gabi, Austria	1978	Hanni Wenzel, Lichtenstein	1987	Maria Walliser, Switzerland
		1979	Annemarie Moser-Proell, Austria	1988	Michela Figini, Switzerland
1970	Michele Jacot, France			1989	Vreni Schneider, Switzerland
1971	Annemarie Proell, Austria	1980	Hanni Wenzel, Lichtenstein		
1972	Annemarie Proell, Austria	1981	Marie-Theres Nadig, Switzerland	1990	Petra Kronberger, Austria
1973	Annemarie Proell, Austria	1982	Erika Hess, Switzerland	1991	Petra Kronberger, Austria
1974	Annemarie Proell, Austria	1983	Tamara McKinney, USA	1992	Petra Kronberger, Austria
1975	Annemarie Moser-Proell, Austria	1984	Erika Hess, Switzerland		

Figure Skating
World Champions

Skaters who won World and Olympic championships in the same year are listed in **bold** type.

MEN

Multiple winners: Ulrich Salchow (10); Karl Schafer (7); Dick Button (5); Willy Bockl, Scott Hamilton and Hayes Jenkins (4); Kurt Browning, Emmerich Danzor, Gillis Grafstrom, Gustav Hugel, David Jenkins, Fritz Kachler and Ondrej Nepela (3); Brian Boitano, Gilbert Fuchs, Jan Hoffmann, Felix Kaspar, Vladimir Kovalev and Tim Wood (2).

Year		Year		Year	
1896	Gilbert Fuchs, Germany	1932	**Karl Schafer**, Austria	1966	Emmerich Danzer, Austria
1897	Gustav Hugel, Austria	1933	Karl Schafer, Austria	1967	Emmerich Danzer, Austria
1898	Henning Grenander, Sweden	1934	Karl Schafer, Austria	1968	Emmerich Danzer, Austria
1899	Gustav Hugel, Austria	1935	Karl Schafer, Austria	1969	Tim Wood, USA
1900	Gustav Hugel, Austria	1936	**Karl Schafer**, Austria	1970	Tim Wood, USA
1901	Ulrich Salchow, Sweden	1937	Felix Kaspar, Austria	1971	Ondrej Nepela, Czechoslovakia
1902	Ulrich Salchow, Sweden	1938	Felix Kaspar, Austria	1972	**Ondrej Nepela**, Czechoslovakia
1903	Ulrich Salchow, Sweden	1939	Graham Sharp, Britain	1973	Ondrej Nepela, Czechoslovakia
1904	Ulrich Salchow, Sweden			1974	Jan Hoffmann, E.Germany
1905	Ulrich Salchow, Sweden	1940-46	Not held	1975	Sergie Volkov, USSR
1906	Gilbert Fuchs, Germany	1947	Hans Gerschwiler, Switzerland	1976	**John Curry**, Britain
1907	Ulrich Salchow, Sweden	1948	**Dick Button**, USA	1977	Vladimir Kovalev, USSR
1908	**Ulrich Salchow**, Sweden	1949	Dick Button, USA	1978	Charles Tickner, USA
1909	Ulrich Salchow, Sweden			1979	Vladimir Kovalev, USSR
1910	Ulrich Salchow, Sweden	1950	Dick Button, USA		
1911	Ulrich Salchow, Sweden	1951	Dick Button, USA	1980	Jan Hoffmann, E.Germany
1912	Fritz Kachler, Austria	1952	**Dick Button**, USA	1981	Scott Hamilton, USA
1913	Fritz Kachler, Austria	1953	Hayes Jenkins, USA	1982	Scott Hamilton, USA
1914	Gosta Sandhal, Sweden	1954	Hayes Jenkins, USA	1983	Scott Hamilton, USA
1915-21	Not held	1955	Hayes Jenkins, USA	1984	**Scott Hamilton**, USA
		1956	**Hayes Jenkins**, USA	1985	Alexander Fadeev, USSR
1922	Gillis Grafstrom, Sweden	1957	David Jenkins, USA	1986	Brian Boitano, USA
1923	Fritz Kachler, Austria	1958	David Jenkins, USA	1987	Brian Orser, Canada
1924	**Gillis Grafstrom**, Sweden	1959	David Jenkins, USA	1988	**Brian Boitano**, USA
1925	Willy Bockl, Austria			1989	Kurt Browning, Canada
1926	Willy Bockl, Austria	1960	Alan Giletti, France		
1927	Willy Bockl, Austria	1961	Not held	1990	Kurt Browning, Canada
1928	Willy Bockl, Austria	1962	Donald Jackson, Canada	1991	Kurt Browning, Canada
1929	Gillis Grafstrom, Sweden	1963	Donald McPherson, Canada	1992	**Viktor Petrenko**, CIS
		1964	**Manfred Schneldorfer**, W.Ger		
1930	Karl Schafer, Austria	1965	Alain Calmat, France		
1931	Karl Schafer, Austria				

WOMEN

Multiple winners: Sonja Henie (10); Carol Heiss and Herma Planck Szabo (5); Lily Kronberger and Katarina Witt (4); Sjoukje Dijkstra, Peggy Fleming, Meray Horvath (3); Tenley Albright, Linda Fratianne, Anett Poetzsch, Beatrix Schuba, Barbara Ann Scott, Gabriele Seyfert, Megan Taylor, Alena Vrzanova, and Kristi Yamaguchi (2).

Year		Year		Year	
1906	Madge Syers, Britain	1932	**Sonja Henie**, Norway	1958	Carol Heiss, USA
1907	Madge Syers, Britian	1933	Sonja Henie, Norway	1959	Carol Heiss, USA
1908	Lily Kronberger, Hungary	1934	Sonja Henie, Norway		
1909	Lily Kronberger, Hungary	1935	Sonja Henie, Norway	1960	**Carol Heiss**, USA
		1936	**Sonja Henie**, Norway	1961	Not held
1910	Lily Kronberger, Hungary	1937	Cecilia Colledge, Britain	1962	Sjoukje Dijkstra, Holland
1911	Lily Kronberger, Hungary	1938	Megan Taylor, Britain	1963	Sjoukje Dijkstra, Holland
1912	Meray Horvath, Hungary	1939	Megan Taylor, Britain	1964	**Sjoukje Dijkstra**, Holland
1913	Meray Horvath, Hungary			1965	Petra Burka, Canada
1914	Meray Horvath, Hungary	1940-46	Not held	1966	Peggy Fleming, USA
1915-21	Not held	1947	Barbara Ann Scott, Canada	1967	Peggy Fleming, USA
		1948	**Barbara Ann Scott**, Canada	1968	**Peggy Fleming**, USA
1922	Herma Planck-Szabo, Austria	1949	Alena Vrzanova, Czechoslovakia	1969	Gabriele Seyfert, E.Germany
1923	Herma Planck-Szabo, Austria				
1924	**Herma Planck-Szabo**, Austria	1950	Alena Vrzanova, Czechoslovakia	1970	Gabriele Seyfert, E.Germany
1925	Herma Planck-Szabo, Austria	1951	Jeannette Altwegg, Britain	1971	Beatrix Schuba, Austria
1926	Herma Planck-Szabo, Austria	1952	Jacqueline Du Bief, France	1972	**Beatrix Schuba**, Austria
1927	Sonja Henie, Norway	1953	Tenley Albright, USA	1973	Karen Magnussen, Canada
1928	**Sonja Henie**, Norway	1954	Gundi Busch, W.Germany	1974	Christine Errath, E.Germany
1929	Sonja Henie, Norway	1955	Tenley Albright, USA	1975	Dianne DeLeeuw, Holland
		1956	Carol Heiss, USA	1976	**Dorothy Hamill**, USA
1930	Sonja Henie, Norway	1957	Carol Heiss, USA	1977	Linda Fratianne, USA
1931	Sonja Henie, Norway				

Figure Skating (Cont.)
World Champions
WOMEN

Year		Year		Year	
1978	Anett Poetzsch, E.Germany	1983	Rosalyn Sumners, USA	1988	**Katarina Witt**, E.Germany
1979	Linda Fratianne, USA	1984	**Katarina Witt**, E.Germany	1989	Midori Ito, Japan
1980	**Anett Poetzsch**, E.Germany	1985	Katarina Witt, E.Germany	1990	Jill Trenary, USA
1981	Denise Biellmann, Switzerland	1986	Debi Thomas, USA	1991	Kristi Yamaguchi, USA
1982	Elaine Zayak, USA	1987	Katarina Witt, E.Germany	1992	**Kristi Yamaguchi**, USA

U.S. Champions

Skaters who won U.S., World and Olympic championships in same year are in **bold** type.

MEN

Multiple winners: Dick Button and Roger Turner (7); Sherwin Badger, Robin Lee (5); Brian Boitano, Scott Hamilton, David Jenkins, Hayes Jenkins and Charles Tickner (4); Gordon McKellen, Nathaniel Niles and Tim Wood (3); Scott Allen, Christopher Bowman, Todd Eldredge, Eugene Turner and Gary Visconti (2).

Year		Year		Year		Year	
1914	Norman Scott	1934	Roger Turner	1954	Hayes Jenkins	1974	Gordon McKellen
1915	Not held	1935	Robin Lee	1955	Hayes Jenkins	1975	Gordon McKellen
1916	Not held	1936	Robin Lee	1956	**Hayes Jenkins**	1976	Terry Kubicka
1917	Not held	1937	Robin Lee	1957	David Jenkins	1977	Charles Tickner
1918	Nathaniel Niles	1938	Robin Lee	1958	David Jenkins	1978	Charles Tickner
1919	Not held	1939	Robin Lee	1959	David Jenkins	1979	Charles Tickner
1920	Sherwin Badger	1940	Eugene Turner	1960	David Jenkins	1980	Charles Tickner
1921	Sherwin Badger	1941	Eugene Turner	1961	Bradley Lord	1981	Scott Hamilton
1922	Sherwin Badger	1942	Robert Specht	1962	Monty Hoyt	1982	Scott Hamilton
1923	Sherwin Badger	1943	Arthur Vaughn	1963	Thomas Litz	1983	Scott Hamilton
1924	Sherwin Badger	1944	Not held	1964	Scott Allen	1984	**Scott Hamilton**
1925	Nathaniel Niles	1945	Not held	1965	Gary Visconti	1985	Brian Boitano
1926	Chris Christenson	1946	Dick Button	1966	Scott Allen	1986	Brian Boitano
1927	Nathaniel Niles	1947	Dick Button	1967	Gary Visconti	1987	Brian Boitano
1928	Roger Turner	1948	**Dick Button**	1968	Tim Wood	1988	**Brian Boitano**
1929	Roger Turner	1949	Dick Button	1969	Tim Wood	1989	Christopher Bowman
1930	Roger Turner	1950	Dick Button	1970	Tim Wood	1990	Todd Eldredge
1931	Roger Turner	1951	Dick Button	1971	John (Misha) Petkevich	1991	Todd Eldredge
1932	Roger Turner	1952	**Dick Button**	1972	Ken Shelley	1992	Christopher Bowman
1933	Roger Turner	1953	Hayes Jenkins	1973	Gordon McKellen		

WOMEN

Multiple winners: Maribel Vinson (9); Theresa Weld Blanchard and Gretchen Merrill (6); Tenley Albright, Peggy Fleming, and Janet Lynn (5); Linda Fratianne and Carol Heiss (4); Dorothy Hamill, Beatrix Loughran, Rosalyn Summers, Joan Tozzer and Jill Trenary (3); Yvonne Sherman and Debi Thomas (2).

Year		Year		Year		Year	
1914	Theresa Weld	1936	Maribel Vinson	1956	Tenley Albright	1976	**Dorothy Hamill**
1915–17	Not held	1937	Maribel Vinson	1957	Carol Heiss	1977	Linda Fratianne
1918	Rosemary Beresford	1938	Joan Tozzer	1958	Carol Heiss	1978	Linda Fratianne
1919	Not held	1939	Joan Tozzer	1959	Carol Heiss	1979	Linda Fratianne
1920	Theresa Weld	1940	Joan Tozzer	1960	**Carol Heiss**	1980	Linda Fratianne
1921	Theresa Blanchard	1941	Jane Vaughn	1961	Laurence Owen	1981	Elaine Zayak
1922	Theresa Blanchard	1942	Jane Sullivan	1962	Barbara Pursley	1982	Rosalyn Sumners
1923	Theresa Blanchard	1943	Gretchen Merrill	1963	Lorraine Hanlon	1983	Rosalyn Sumners
1924	Theresa Blanchard	1944	Gretchen Merrill	1964	Peggy Fleming	1984	Rosalyn Sumners
1925	Beatrix Loughran	1945	Gretchen Merrill	1965	Peggy Fleming	1985	Tiffany Chin
1926	Beatrix Loughran	1946	Gretchen Merrill	1966	Peggy Fleming	1986	Debi Thomas
1927	Beatrix Loughran	1947	Gretchen Merrill	1967	Peggy Fleming	1987	Jill Trenary
1928	Maribel Vinson	1948	Gretchen Merrill	1968	**Peggy Fleming**	1988	Debi Thomas
1929	Maribel Vinson	1949	Yvonne Sherman	1969	Janet Lynn	1989	Jill Trenary
1930	Maribel Vinson	1950	Yvonne Sherman	1970	Janet Lynn	1990	Jill Trenary
1931	Maribel Vinson	1951	Sonya Klopfer	1971	Janet Lynn	1991	Tanya Harding
1932	Maribel Vinson	1952	Tenley Albright	1972	Janet Lynn	1992	**Kristi Yamaguchi**
1933	Maribel Vinson	1953	Tenley Albright	1973	Janet Lynn		
1934	Suzanne Davis	1954	Tenley Albright	1974	Dorothy Hamill		
1935	Maribel Vinson	1955	Tenley Albright	1975	Dorothy Hamill		

Simon Bruty/Allsport

Midfielder **Biran Laudrup** lifts the European Championship trophy after unheralded Denmark upset Germany, 2-0, to win the tournament in Gothenberg, Sweden.

SOCCER

Great Danes

Tiny Denmark accepts a last-minute invitation to Euro '92 and surprises World Cup champion Germany in the final.

Germany, crowned as World Champions in Italy in 1990, were hoping to do what no team has yet done: follow up the World Cup title with success in the European Championship two years later. And why not? For, despite the loss of its captain Lothar Matthaus to injury, the team had been strengthened by the addition of several stars from the former East Germany.

They almost made it, but not quite. At the 1992 European tournament, staged in Sweden, the Germans came a cropper at the last hurdle, falling 2-0 to Denmark in the final.

Denmark? Yes, little Denmark—which hadn't qualified for the 1990 World Cup, and which didn't even qualify for the European Championship! The Danes snuck into Sweden only because Yugoslavia—which had qualified ahead of them—had been thrown out of the tournament by the Union of European Football Associations (UEFA) in the wake of the violent breakup of that country.

Just 11 days before the opening game, the Danes were officially told they were in. With less preparation than any of the other seven teams, they got off to a wob-

bly start with a scoreless tie against England and 1-0 loss to the host Swedes.

One game away from elimination and under no pressure, Denmark then righted itself and proceeded to beat the last three European champions—France (1984), the Netherlands (1988) and Germany (1990)—one after another in their improbable march to the Euro '92 crown.

In the June 26 final at Gothenburg against a heavily-favored German side, the Danes scored first on a goal by midfielder John (Faxe) Jensen in the 19th minute. Backed by the acrobatic goalkeeping of Peter Schmeichel, they then held off the Germans until a Kim Vilfort goal 35 minutes into the second half put the game away.

"[The result] didn't surprise me," said German coach Berti Vogts. "What I saw here and knew in my heart of hearts was that Denmark was acting upon a wave of enthusiasm, and that's very hard to offset."

It was the first major soccer title for Denmark, and an appropriate fairy tale ending for the country that gave the world Hans Christian Andersen.

Overall, the tournament left much to be desired. A sluggish start saw only eight goals scored in the first eight games, which featured three 0-0 ties. Preben Elkjaer, a great Danish player during the 1980s, commented: "If they don't change something, football won't be Europe's number one sport much longer. I wouldn't pay to watch this."

Paul Gardner has been a columnist for *Soccer America* since 1982. He has covered international soccer as a writer and broadcaster in Europe and the United States since 1964 and has written three books on the sport.

Shaun Botterill/Allsport

Teammates mob Danish midfielder **Kim Vilfort** (hidden) after Vilfort's goal late in the second half gave Denmark an insurmountable two-goal lead over Germany.

Panic struck the organizers, who talked openly of changing the regulations in the middle of the tournament in an effort to make teams more adventurous. No changes were made, but the second round proved more entertaining, mostly thanks to the unlikely Danes.

FIFA, the governing body of international soccer, continued its search for rule changes the would encourage more attacking play. Its own Football 2000 Task Force came up with ten suggestions, but only one was quickly approved: A rule banning the goalkeeper from picking up a ball kicked to him by one of his teammates came into force in time for the Olympic Games in July.

The rule change was generally welcomed—but the Olympic soccer tournament was anything but a success. Soccer has, for years, been the Olympic Games' biggest money-maker. But the first-round crowds in Spain were poor. Recriminations filled the Barcelona air. FIFA President Joao Havelange accused the International Olympic Committee of not doing anything to publicize the tournament. The IOC made it clear that it felt that FIFA's insistence that the tournament

be limited to players under the age of 23 had led to a lack of interest. They also hinted that maybe soccer didn't have much of an Olympic future.

It that was bluff, it was quickly called by Havelange, who replied that FIFA was quite capable of organizing its own under-23 tournament, adding "The Olympic competition costs us $4 million, and we're getting nothing in return."

Things got better as the Barcelona tournament unfolded—thanks to the success of the host country Spain. On Aug. 8, over 95,000 fans turned out to see Spanish midfielder Quico Narvaez score twice in the second half—his second with just seconds left to play—to beat Poland, 3-2, and win the gold medal.

"We have written a new page in the history of Spanish soccer," said winning coach Vicente Miera. "They will talk about our gold medal for years to come."

The IOC-FIFA Olympic wrangle ended in the classic do-nothing compromise. Soccer would stay in the Games for Atlanta in 1996 and it would remain an under-23 event.

Another Olympic tiff blew up between the United States coach Lothar Osiander

Jonathan Daniel/Allsport

Back from Europe, **John Harkes** led the national team to a 1-1 draw with Italy and a U.S. Cup '92 championship.

and his star forward Steve Snow. After a highly convincing performance in the qualifying round (an 8-1-1 record with 35 goals for and 12 goals against) the Americans had gone to Barcelona with medal expectations.

Alas, a 2-1 loss to Italy in the opening game ruined the script. And the awful truth was that Snow, who had scored 19 goals in 18 games for the Olympians, had spent the game on the bench. Snow, a fiery character not known for keeping his mouth shut, spoke out: "We had no one out there who could score goals. This team cannot play without me. You can't have the best player on your team sit."

The exchanges continued. Osiander justified his move, saying he needed speed against Italy and Snow wasn't the fastest guy around. Replied Snow: "The coach's idea of a perfect soccer player is a track guy." Countered Osiander: "If he wants to play, he can apologize." Rejoined Snow: "I'm not kissing up to him just so I can get into a game."

But Snow did apologize, started the next two games against Kuwait and Poland, and continued his goal-a-game pace by scoring against both opponents. The Kuwaitis were beaten 3-1, but a 2-2 tie with Poland meant the USA was eliminated.

At least the U.S. men got to play in the Olympics. For the women there was no such chance, as women's soccer is not an Olympic sport—something that the United States Soccer Federation, led by its President Alan Rothenberg, is pushing to change. He should. The U.S. women are the current world champions, a title they won at the first-ever Women's World Cup in China in November, 1991. A pair of goals by the tournament's leading scorer Michelle Akers-Stahl led the Americans to a 2-1 victory over Norway in the final.

FIFA has said women's soccer might be added to the Olympics, perhaps by the Summer Games of 2000. But Rothenberg's dream is to have the sport introduced in 1996, in Atlanta.

No doubt FIFA feels it has more pressing problems to deal with. Not least, the matter of deciding which countries are members and which are not. Or, for that matter, which countries are still countries. Yugoslavia? The Soviet Union? Gone—but replaced by whom? FIFA's annual Congress acknowledged the changing world—and upped its membership to 178 countries—by admitting Armenia, Belorus, Croatia, Estonia, Georgia, Latvia, Lithuania, Russia, Slovenia, and Ukraine.

Meanwhile, South Africa—expelled from FIFA in 1976 because of its apartheid racial policies—was welcomed back, allowing it to enter the qualifying round for the 1994 World Cup.

Another of FIFA's important decisions was to decide which country would stage the 1998 World Cup. The candidates were France, Morocco and Switzerland, but the Swiss were forced to withdraw shortly before the vote—as the result of events on the island of Corsica. Shortly before the kick-off of a European Cup tie between Bastia and Marseille, a temporary stand collapsed, causing 15 deaths and hundreds of injuries. FIFA's response was to ban all such stands from its tournaments, which torpedoed the 1998 hopes of the Swiss, who were planning to enlarge their small stadiums with temporary seating.

Wide World Photos

Brazilian legend and former NASL star **Pele** (left), with World Cup USA 1994 chairman **Alan Rothenberg** and FIFA officials **Joao Havelange** and **Sepp Blatter** in Zurich.

France got the nod for '98, and Morocco—which had lost out to the United States in the voting for the 1994 World Cup—again came up empty. Looking as head, Havelange predicted that the 2000 World Cup would be staged in Asia. Sweet music for Japan, already well along in preparing its bid for that tournament.

The 1992 edition of the African Nations Cup was won by Ivory Coast, whose government declared a two-day national holiday. But in reality it was a far from convincing victory. Scoring just four goals in five games, Ivory Coast won both the semi-final and the final games on penalty kicks after 0-0 overtime ties.

The first real soccer event of the 1994 World Cup—the qualifying round draw—was staged in New York on Dec. 8, 1991. It was a smoothly run affair that succeeded precisely because of its low-key approach. It convinced many of the skeptics that the Americans could organize a soccer event without drowning it in brassy showbiz razzmatazz.

In March, the World Cup USA-94 organizers announced the cities where games would be played. Previous World Cups have employed 12 playing sites, but the U.S. reduced that number to nine—including the tournament's first indoor arena, the Detroit Silverdome. The other eight venues are: Giants Stadium (East Rutherford, N.J.), Foxboro Stadium (Mass.), RFK Stadium (Washington, DC), the Citrus Bowl (Orlando, Fla.), the Cotton Bowl (Dallas), Soldier Field (Chicago), plus two California sites: Stanford Stadium, and the Rose Bowl.

One tricky point was glossed over. Giants Stadium does not meet the 75-yard sideline-to-sideline requirement that has long been the standard for the World Cup Final. "You can be certain," said FIFA's General Secretary Sepp Blatter, "that all fields will meet the requirements for international games." Quite so, but the minimum width requirement for international games, at 70 yards, is five yards less than that for World Cup games.

The opening game of the '94 tournament—which will feature title-holder Germany against a yet-to-be-decided opponent—will be played in Chicago. One semifinal will be played in Giants Stadium, while the other goes to the Rose Bowl, which will also be the site of the World Cup Final.

A television deal was announced under which ABC-TV and its cable affiliate ESPN will televise all 52 tournament games in the U.S. All but a handful will be broadcast live, with ABC transmitting 11 games on weekends, and ESPN taking the rest. The deal included an agreement that play would not be interrupted by commercials.

ABC/ESPN will not actually produce the telecasts. That will be done by a team of technicians from the European Broadcasting Union, working out of the International Broadcasting Center in Dallas. The rights fee paid by ABC/ESPN—reportedly $14 million—will be used to pay for production costs.

Money was not exactly pouring into the coffers of World Cup USA 1994. A total of nine sponsors (or marketing partners) was sought, but by mid-1992, only four had been signed up. Ticket sales awaited an agreement with FIFA over pricing policies. Rumors had it that prices would range from a low of $25 for first-round games up to a massive high of $3,000 for the best seats at the final.

The Coin Bill, after several unsuccessful tries, was finally approved by Congress. It is calculated that the special World Cup coins, to be minted in 1994, could bring the World Cup '94 organizers as much as $50 million.

The United States national team, under coach Bora Milutinovic, continued its strange dual existence. For most of the year, the top players—engaged with European clubs—were unavailable to Bora. Only in the summer did the team begin to look like the one that will play in the 1994 World Cup. That roster included John Harkes (back from England) and Tab Ramos (Spain), plus three important newcomers who are First Division veterans—Roy Wegerle (England), Thomas Dooley (Germany) and Ernie Stewart (Netherlands). None was born in the U.S., but Wegerle has an American wife, while Dooley, like Stewart, has an American father. Enough to give them citizenship.

The reinforced team showed considerable promise in winning the U.S. Cup '92 in June, with wins over Ireland (3-1) and Portugal (1-0), and a 1-1 tie with Italy.

Argentine star Diego Maradona continued to command the headlines—without doing much in the way of playing. A tangled mass of rumors arose about his intentions after his suspension for drug offenses ended on June 30. He would

Curtain Falls On MSL After 14-Year Run

It had become an annual summer rite in American soccer. Every year the Major (Indoor) Soccer League would lose a club or two, threaten to go out of business, and then be saved by the arrival of a new franchise and some last-minute maneuvering.

But in 1992, the death-defying heroics never materialized. Down to just five franchises in early July, the MSL pulled the plug when it was unable to find a sixth team for the 1992-93 season. "At this time," said commissioner Earl Foreman, who helped found the league in 1978, "we probably have the strongest group of owners we've ever had. We just don't have enough of them."

So disappeared "the oldest active professional soccer league in the United States." Those were the MSL's own words, but they disguise a fierce conflict within the soccer community. For many—particularly soccer purists—the indoor game was an unholy bastardization of the sport, unworthy to be viewed as a form of soccer.

None of that worried the promoters who launched the Major Indoor Soccer League in 1978. They were not all unhappy to see their sport pictured as something different, something new. They tarred outdoor soccer with a "foreign" brush, pointing out that its rules were strictly controlled by the sport's international governing body, FIFA. (Indeed, even in the outdoor North American Soccer League there were owners who resented FIFA's dictatorial control.)

Indoor soccer already existed, in various forms, all over the world. But it was not, at that time, an area of great interest to FIFA. So there was much freedom to invent new rules, to "Americanize" soccer. Much of the MSL's publicity was based on comparing the two versions of soccer—with the outdoor game coming off second best. Indoor soccer, said the MSL, was designed for the American fan. It was faster and it featured more scoring than outdoor soccer. "This is the game Americans want," crowed Earl Foreman.

In that context, the San Diego Sockers were America's soccer team—winning 10 indoor championships, including eight MSL titles since joining the league in 1982. They won their 10th crown for coach Ron Newman

Essy Ghavameddini

In the 14-year history of the MSL, the **San Diego Sockers** won eight titles, including the 1992 final against Dallas. Two months after they celebrated, the league died.

in May, defeating Dallas in six games.

Those who felt that outdoor soccer (played in the summer) and indoor (played in the winter) could live happily together were disabused quickly. When the outdoor North American Soccer League began to run into serious financial difficulties, it was the MSL that helped to drive it to the wall.

As the NASL tried to reduce its salary bill, the MSL jumped in to lure away the better players with offers of more money. The NASL folded in 1984, a time when the MSL was enjoying its biggest success, with a league of 14 teams and an average attendance of over 8,500 per game.

But that was as good as it got. The league lost its flagship franchise, the New York Arrows, in that same year. In 1988 the MSL issued an ultimatum to the Players' Association: Agree to an immediate salary-cap reduction—down to $900,000 per club—or we go out of business. The reduction was agreed to, but the cash crisis persisted, and later that same year the cap was further lowered to $750,000.

Short-term TV contracts with ESPN in 1990, and SportsChannel in 1991 did not help. The salary cap was lowered again in 1991, by which time the number of teams had dropped to seven.

Then came a desperate effort at survival, which saw the league undergo an ironic change. Where once it had fought and scorned the outdoor game, it now attempted to embrace it. The league dropped the word "indoor" from its title, and talked of fielding outdoor teams. It was the last, cynical gesture of a dying league—an attempt to cash in on the perceived bonanza of the upcoming (and very outdoor . except in Pontiac, Mich.) 1994 World Cup.

It fooled no one.

While the MSL has disappeared, the sport of indoor soccer remains—represented by the minor-league National Professional Soccer League, which operates only in the East and the Midwest. Two former MSL clubs, the Baltimore Blast and the Cleveland Crunch, have decided to join the NPSL.

But other indoor activity is stirring. Not one, but two new indoor leagues are planned, both threatening to start in the summer of 1993. The Continental Indoor Soccer League hopes to convince National Basketball Association owners that they can get extra use out of their arenas by staging soccer games in the summer. While the Arena Soccer League, also planning to play in the summer, envisages a 12-team East Coast league run by the arena owners.

Wide World Photos

Argentine star **Diego Maradona** waves to Spanish fans shortly after his move from Naples to Seville on Sept. 22.

pionship in '89 with Maradona taking the Golden Ball as Most Valuable Player.

Italian clubs continued to spend vast sums of money importing foreign stars. The country's severe economic crisis seemed to have no effect on the billions of lire available for soccer deals. In an astonishing development, the top clubs started to engage four or more foreign players—even though Italian league regulations say that only three can play at any one time. These were top, expensive players, not used to sitting on the bench. "This is the way to go," said Milan president Silvio Berlusconi, "We will always have a strong bench, and it is better for the players, they will not be worn out by playing too many games."

The point was duly made when Milan's highly-paid Dutch trio of Ruud Gullit, Marco Van Basten and Frank Rijkaard were joined by Frenchman Jean-Pierre Papin (the European Player of the Year) plus former Yugoslav stars Dejan Savicevic and Zvonimir Boban. But Berlusconi delivered his biggest shock when he paid a world record $25 million for a young Italian player, Gianluigi Lentini.

Television money—the basis of Berlusconi's wealth—made its power felt in England, too. Twenty-two of the country's top clubs broke away from the 92-team Football League to form their own Premier League. The motivation was clearly to shed the burden of the other 70 second, third and fourth division clubs, and to sign its own TV deal. Sure enough, the Premier League soon signed a five-year, $600 million deal with the BBC and BSkyB satellite television.

The ubiquitous television cameras were not much help to Real Madrid's midfielder Miguel "Michel" Gonzalez. During a game against Valladolid, he was caught grabbing hold of opponent Carlos Valderrama—below the waist, you understand. The incident was gleefully played over and over on television. The Spanish Soccer Federation jumped in and fined Michel $5,000 for "lack of decorum." The Federation's report contained this rather airy description of a very earthy incident: Michel had "placed himself to the left of Valderrama and, with innocence shining from his face but not from his right hand, on two occasions had squeezed Valderrama's secret intimacy."

return to his old club Naples in Italy, which still owned his contract. No, he would never return to Naples. He would play in France, he would play in Spain, he would join his younger brother Hugo playing in Japan, he would retire and live in Florida.

In April, after the tragic death of a popular Argentine player, Maradona was invited to play in a benefit game for the player's family. FIFA, foolishly, warned him not to play. Maradona ignored his ban, and FIFA's warning, and played anyway, announcing that "No-one in Argentina will shed any tears when [FIFA president] Havelange dies." FIFA, wisely, took no action. The showdown came in August, at a special summit at FIFA's headquarters in Switzerland. Maradona's representative met with Napoli club officials to try to sort out the mess.

It wasn't until Sept. 22, however, that Napoli finally agreed to sell its disgruntled star to Seville of Spain for $7.5 million. The Spanish club is coached by Carlos Bilardo, who directed Argentina to consecutive World Cup finals against West Germany in 1986 and 1990. Argentina won the cham-

National Team Competition
WORLDWIDE CHAMPIONS

1991 Women's World Championship: United States   **1992 African Nations' Cup:** Ivory Coast
1992 European Championship: Denmark   **1992 Summer Olympics:** Spain
1992 Five-a-Side Championship: at Hong Kong (Nov. 15-29)

Women's World Championship
(Nov. 16-30, 1991, in China)
Quarterfinals

United States 7 .... Chinese Taipei 0
Sweden 1 .... China 0
Norway 3 .... OT .... Italy 2
Germany 2 .... OT .... Denmark 1

Semifinals

United States 5 .... Germany 2
Norway 4 .... Sweden 1

Third Place

Sweden 4 .... Germany 0

Final
(at Guangzhou; Att—60,000)

United States 2 .... Norway 1
Golden Ball (MVP)—Carin Jennings, USA; **Golden Boot** (leading scorer)—Michelle Akers-Stahl, USA (10).

African Nations' Cup
(Jan. 12-26, in Senegal)
Quarterfinals

Cameroon 1.............................. Senegal 0
Nigeria 1 .... Zaire 0
Ivory Coast 1 .... OT .... Zambia 0
Ghana 2 .... Congo 1

Semifinals

Ghana 2.................................. Nigeria 1
Ivory Coast 0.............................. Cameroon 0
(Ivory Coast wins on penalty kicks, 3-1)

Third Place

Nigeria 2 .... Cameroon 1

Final
(at Dakar; Att—47,500)

Ivory Coast 0 .... Ghana 0
(Ivory Coast wins on penalty kicks, 11-10)
Leading tournament scorers: Rashid Yekini, Nigeria (4) and Abedi Pele, Ghana (3).

European Championship
(June 10-16 in Sweden)

First Round

GROUP A	Gm	W	L	T	Pts	GF	GA
*Sweden	3	2	0	1	5	4	2
*Denmark	3	1	1	1	3	2	2
France	3	0	1	2	2	2	3
England	3	0	1	2	2	1	2

Results
June 10—Sweden 1, France 1. **June 11**—England 0, Denmark 0. **June 14**—France 0, England 0; Sweden 1, Denmark 0. **June 17**—Sweden 2, England 1; Denmark 2, France 1.

GROUP B	Gm	W	L	T	Pts	GF	GA
*Holland	3	2	0	1	5	4	1
*Germany	3	1	1	1	3	4	4
Scotland	3	1	2	0	2	3	3
CIS (ex-USSR)	3	0	1	2	2	1	4

Results
June 10—Holland 1, Scotland 0; CIS 1, Germany 1. **June 15**—Germany 2, Scotland 0; Holland 0, CIS 0. **June 18**—Holland 3, Germany 1; Scotland 3, CIS 0.

Semifinals

June 21—Germany 3 .... Sweden 2
June 22—Denmark 2 .... Holland 2
(Denmark wins on penalty kicks, 5-4)

Final
(June 26, at Gothenburg; Att—37,800)

Denmark 2.............................. Germany 0
Leading scorers: Tomas Brolin, SWE, Lars Eriksson, SWE, Henrik Larsen, DEN and Karlheinz Riedle, GER (3).

All-Tournament Team
(as chosen by Soccer America)

Goalkeeper—Peter Schmeichel, DEN; **Sweeper**—Lars Olsen, DEN; **Man-Marker**—Jan Eriksson, SWE and Des Walker, ENG; **Midfielder**—Thomas Haessler, GER, Tomas Brolin, SWE, Frank Rijkaard, HOL and Brian Laudrup, DEN; **Forwards**—Flemming Povlsen, DEN, Dennis Bergkamp, HOL and Karlheinz Riedle, GER; **Coach**—Rinus Michels, HOL.

Club Team Competition

1991 Toyota Cup: (European Cup winner vs. Copa Libertadores winner)
Red Star (YUG) 3, Colo Colo (CHI) 0

EUROPE

All sanctioned by the Union of European Football Associations (UEFA). The **European Cup** (officially, the Champions' Cup) is a knockout contest between national league champions; the **Cup Winners' Cup** is between winners of domestic cup competitions (a double winner—league and cup titles—would play for the European Cup and be placed by the team it defeated in the domestic cup final); and the **UEFA Cup** is between the so-called "best of the rest," usually the national league runners-up. Note that home teams are listed first.

European Cup

Six-game double round-robin in two 4-team groups (Nov.27-Apr.15); Group winners meet in one-game final.

ROUND ROBIN STANDINGS

GROUP A	Gm	W	L	T	Pts	GF	GA
Sampdoria (ITA)	6	3	1	2	8	10	5
Red Star (YUG)	6	3	3	0	6	9	10
Anderlecht (BEL)	6	2	2	2	6	8	9
Panathinaikos (GRE)	6	0	2	4	4	1	4

GROUP B	Gm	W	L	T	Pts	GF	GA
Barcelona (SPA)	6	4	1	1	9	10	4
Sparta Prague (CZE)	6	2	2	2	6	7	7
Benfica (POR)	6	1	2	3	5	8	5
Dinamo Kiev (CIS)	6	2	4	0	4	3	12

FINAL
(May 20 at London)

Barcelona 1 . . . . Sampdoria 0

Cup Winners' Cup

Two-leg Semifinals; one-game Final; home teams listed first.

SEMIFINALS

AS Monaco (FRA) vs. **Feyenoord** (HOL)
Apr. 1—AS Monaco 1 . . . . Feyenoord 1
Apr.15—Feyenoord 2 . . . . AS Monaco 2
(Aggregate 3-3, Monaco wins on away goals)

Werder Bremen (GER) vs. **FC Brugge** (BEL)
Apr. 1—FC Brugge 1 . . . . Werder Bremen 0
Apr.15—Werder Bremen 2 . . . . FC Brugge 0
(Werder Bremen wins, 2-1)

FINAL
(May 16 at Lisbon)

Werder Bremen 2 . . . . AS Monaco 0

UEFA Cup

Two-leg Semifinals and Final; home teams listed first.

SEMIFINALS

Torino (ITA) vs. **Real Madrid** (SPA)
Apr. 1—Real Madrid 2 . . . . Torino 1
Apr.15—Torino 2 . . . . Real Madrid 0
(Torino wins, 3-2)

Ajax Amsterdam (HOL) vs. **Genoa** (ITA)
Apr. 1—Genoa 2 . . . . Ajax Amsterdam 3
Apr.15—Ajax Amsterdam 1 . . . . Genoa 1
(Ajax wins, 4-3)

FINAL
Apr.29—Torino 2 . . . . Ajax Amsterdam 2
May 13—Ajax Amsterdam 0 . . . . Torino 0
(Aggregate 2-2, Ajax wins on away goals)

National Champions

Country	League Champion	Cup Winner
Belgium	FC Antwerp	Brugge
Bulgaria	CSKA Sofia	Levski Sofia
Czech	Slovan Bratislava	Sparta Prague
England	Leeds United	Liverpool
France	Marseille	Postponed*
Germany	VFB Stuttgart	Hanover
Greece	AEK Athens	Olympiakos
Holland	PSV Eindhoven	Feyenoord
Hungary	Ferencvaros	Ujpesti Budapest
Ireland	Shelbourne	Bohemians
Italy	AC Milan	Parma
No.Ireland	Glentoran	Glenavon
Poland	Lech Poznan	Miedz Legnica
Portugal	FC Porto	FC Porto
Romania	Dinamo Bucharest	Steaua Bucharest
Scotland	Glasgow Rangers	Glasgow Rangers
Spain	Barcelona	Atletico Madrid

*French Cup semifinal between Bastia and Marseille postponed after portable stands collapsed May 5, killing 13 and injuring 700.

SOUTH AMERICA

Copa Libertadores

Contested by the league champions of South America's football union. Two-leg Semifinals and Final; home teams listed first.

SEMIFINALS

Sao Paulo (BRA) vs. **Barcelona** (ECU)
May 27—Sao Paulo 3 . . . . Barcelona 0
June 3—Barcelona 2 . . . . Sao Paulo 0
(Sao Paulo wins, 3-2)

Newell's Old Boys (ARG) vs. **America Cali** (COL)
May 27—Newell's OB 1 . . . . America Cali 0
June 3—America Cali 1 . . . . Newell's OB 1
(Aggregate 2-2, Newell's wins on PKs, 11-10)

FINAL

June 10—Newell's OB 1 . . . . Sao Paulo 0
June 17—Sao Paulo 1 . . . . Newell's OB 0
(Aggregate 1-1, Sao Paulo wins on PKs, 3-2)

U.S. National Teams

1992 Men's National Team

The United States national team roster for the U.S. Cup '92 tournament, May 30-June 7.

Goalkeepers	Birthdate	Club
Mark Dodd	9/14/65	Colorado (APSL)
Kasey Keller	11/29/69	Millwall (ENG)
Tony Meola	2/21/69	National Team

Defenders	Birthdate	Club
Desmond Armstrong	11/2/64	National Team
Marcelo Balboa	8/8/67	Colorado (APSL)
Fernando Clavijo	1/23/57	National Team
Thomas Dooley	5/12/61	FC Kaiserslautern (GER)
John Doyle	3/16/66	S.F. Bay (APSL)
Zak Ibsen	6/2/72	UCLA

Midfielders	Birthdate	Club
Paul Caligiuri	3/9/64	National Team
Mark Chung	6/18/70	U. of South Fla.
John Harkes	3/8/67	Sheffield (ENG)
Chris Henderson	12/11/70	National Team
Dominic Kinnear	7/26/67	S.F. Bay (APSL)
Janusz Michallik	4/22/66	National Team
Bruce Murray	1/25/66	National Team
Hugo Perez	11/8/63	National Team
Brian Quinn	5/24/60	National Team
Tab Ramos	9/21/66	Figueras (SPA)

Forwards	Birthdate	Club
Ernie Stewart	3/28/69	Willem II (HOL)
Peter Vermes	11/21/66	National Team
Roy Wegerle	3/19/64	Blackburn (ENG)

Head Coach: Bora Milutinovic
Assistant Coaches: John Kowalski, Ralph Perez

U.S. Cup '92

ROUND ROBIN STANDINGS

	Gm	W	L	T	Pts	GF	GA
United States	3	2	0	1	5	5	2
Italy	3	1	0	2	4	3	1
Ireland	3	1	2	0	2	3	5
Portugal	3	0	2	1	1	0	3

May 30 (Washington, DC)—USA 3, Ireland 1; **May 31** (New Haven)—Italy 0, Portugal 0; **June 3** (Chicago)—USA 1, Portugal 0; **June 4** (Foxboro)—Italy 2, Ireland 0; **June 6** (Chicago)—USA 1, Italy 1; **June 7** (Foxboro)—Ireland 2, Portugal 1.

USA goals: John Harkes (2); Marcelo Balboa, Tab Ramos, Roy Wegerle.

Rest of 1992 Schedule

(Through Oct. 1)

Date		Score	Site	Crowd
1/25	CIS (ex-USSR)	L, 1-0	Miami	30,386
2/2	CIS	W, 2-1	Pontiac	35,248
2/12	Costa Rica	T, 0-0	Costa Rica	22,000
2/18	El Salvador	L, 2-0	El Salvador	45,000
2/26	Brazil	L, 3-0	Brazil	40,000
3/11	Spain	L, 2-0	Spain	35,000
3/18	Morocco	L, 3-1	Morocco	20,000
4/4	China	W, 5-0	Stanford	31,815
4/29	Ireland	L, 4-1	Ireland	27,000
5/17	Scotland	L, 1-0	Denver	24,157
6/13	Australia	L, 1-0	Orlando	17,309
6/27	Ukraine	T, 0-0	Piscataway	11,815
7/31	Colombia	L, 1-0	Los Angeles	28,651
8/2	Brazil	L, 1-0	Los Angeles	41,815
8/21	Fiorentina	L, 4-0	Italy	32,000
8/24	Juventus	L, 3-0	Italy	32,000
9/3	Canada	W, 2-0	St. John, N.B.	3,500

Record: 5-12-3.

1991 U.S. Women's National Team

Winners of the first FIFA World Championship for Women, held Nov. 16-30, 1991, in the People's Republic of China.

Goalkeepers	Age	School/Club
Amy Allmann	25	California Tremors
Mary Harvey	26	SSV Frankfurt
Kim Maslin-Kammerdeiner	27	Annandale Wildfire

Defenders	Age	School/Club
Debbie Belkin	25	Opus County
Joy Biefeld	24	California Tremors
Julie Foudy	20	Stanford
Linda Hamilton	22	North Carolina
Lori Henry	25	Texas Challenge
Carla Werden	23	Texas Challenge

Midfielders	Age	School/Club
Tracey Bates	24	Texas Challenge
Mia Hamm	19	North Carolina
Shannon Higgins	23	North Carolina
Kristine Lilly	20	North Carolina

Forwards	Age	School/Club
Michelle Akers-Stahl	25	Tyreso (SWE)
Brandi Chastain	23	Santa Clara
Wendy Gebauer	24	North Carolina
April Heinrichs	27	Fairfax Wildfire
Carin Jennings	26	California Tremors

Head Coach: Anson Dorrance
Assistant Coach: Lauren Gregg.

1992 U.S. Olympic (U-23) Team

The United States national team roster for the Summer Olympics in Barcelona, July 25-Aug. 9.

Goalkeepers	Birthdate	School/Club
Brad Friedel	5/18/71	UCLA
Ian Feuer	5/20/71	RWD Molenbeek (BEL)

Defenders	Birthdate	School/Club
Michael Burns	9/14/70	Hartwick
Troy Dayak	1/29/71	S.F. Bay (APSL)
Alexi Lalas	6/1/70	Rutgers
Curt Onalfo	11/19/69	Virginia
Cam Rast	1/16/70	Santa Clara

Midfielders	Birthdate	School/Club
Dario Brose	1/27/71	N.C. State
Chris Henderson	12/11/70	National Team
Mike Huwiler	1/4/72	Virginia
Erik Imler	6/1/71	Virginia
Cobi Jones	6/16/70	UCLA
Manny Lagos	6/11/71	UE Lleida (SPA)
Joe-Max Moore	2/23/71	UCLA
Claudio Reyna	7/20/73	Virginia

Forwards	Birthdate	School/Club
Yari Allnutt	2/17/70	U. of Portland
Zak Ibsen	6/2/72	UCLA
Steve Snow	2/2/71	Standard Liege (BEL)
Dante Washington	11/21/70	Radford

Head Coach: Lothar Osiander.
Assistant Coach: Colin Lindores.

U.S. Pro Leagues

1991-92 MSL (Indoor)

	W	L	Pct	GB	GF	GA
San Diego Sockers	26	14	.650	—	243	186
Dallas Sidekicks	22	18	.550	4	231	229
Cleveland Crunch	20	20	.500	6	249	229
Baltimore Blast	19	21	.475	7	213	230
Wichita Wings	18	22	.450	8	223	235
Tacoma Stars	18	22	.450	8	198	236
St.Louis Storm	17	23	.425	9	241	251

Playoffs

Semifinals (Best of 7): San Diego over Baltimore (4-1); Dallas over Cleveland (4-2); **Final** (Best of 7): San Diego over Dallas (4-2).

1992 APSL (Outdoor)

	W	L	Pct	Pts	GF	GA
Colorado Foxes	11	5	.688	89	27	18
Tampa Bay Rowdies	10	6	.625	87	35	26
S.F. Bay Blackhawks	8	8	.500	73	29	27
Ft. Lauderdale Strikers	7	9	.438	61	26	24
Miami Freedom	4	12	.250	43	17	39

Teams earn six points for a win and one point per goal up to a maximum of three per game. No points are given for goals scored in overtime. In shootout tie-breakers, the winning team earns three points and the loser gets two.

Playoffs

Semifinals: Tampa Bay 2, S.F. Bay 1; Colorado 3, Ft. Lauderdale 2 (Shootout). **Final:** Colorado 1, Tampa Bay 0.

Colleges

1991 NCAA Division I Men's Tournament

First Round

Byes: Indiana, St. Louis, UCLA and Virginia.

Hartford 2 .... at Columbia 1
at Yale 3 .... Boston University 2
Seton Hall 1 ..... 4 OT .... at Adelphi 1
(Seton Hall wins on PKs, 5-4)
at North Carolina 1 .... OT .... NC-Charlotte 0
Furman 1 .... 2 OT .... at Wake Forest 0
at N.C. State 3 .... Clemson 1
at Wisconsin 1 .... Evansville 0
at Rutgers 2 .... Old Dominion 1
at SMU 5 .... Tulsa 3
at Portland 1 .... 4 OT .... Florida Int'l 0
at Fresno St. 1 .... OT ... San Francisco 0
at Santa Clara 2 ..... 2 OT .... Stanford 0

Second Round

at Virginia 2 .... 4 OT .... Hartford 1
at Yale 4 .... 2 OT .... Seton Hall 3
at St. Louis 4 .... North Carolina 1
at N.C. State 4 .... Furman 1
at Indiana 2 .... 2 OT .... Wisconsin 1
SMU 3 .... at Rutgers 2
at UCLA 3 .... Portland 1
at Santa Clara 3 .... Fresno St. 0

Quarterfinals

at Virginia 2 .... Yale 1
at St. Louis 3 .... N.C. State 0
at Indiana 2 .... 4 OT .... SMU 2
(Indiana won on PKs, 5-4)
Santa Clara 2 .... at UCLA 1

FINAL FOUR
(at Tampa, Dec. 6-8)

Semifinals

Virginia 3 .... 3 OT .... St. Louis 2
Santa Clara 2 .... Indiana 0

Championship

Virginia 0 .... 4 OT .... Santa Clara 0
(Virginia wins on PKs, 3-1)

Final records: Virginia (20-1-1); Santa Clara (20-2-1); St. Louis (20-2-2); Indiana (19-3-2).

Soccer America Top 15

Final 1991 poll conducted by the national weekly Soccer America and released in the Nov. 25 issue. Listing includes records through conference playoffs as well as NCAA tournament record and team lost to. Teams in **bold** type went on to reach NCAA Final Four.

		W L T	NCAA Recap
1	**Virginia**	16-1-1	4-0
2	**Santa Clara**	16-1-1	4-1 (Virginia)
3	**St. Louis**	18-1-2	2-1 (Virginia)
4	Rutgers	18-2-1	1-1 (SMU)
5	San Francisco	17-3-0	0-1 (Fresno St.)
6	**Indiana**	17-2-2	2-1 (Santa Clara)
7	N.C. State	11-4-2	2-1 (St.Louis)
8	Wake Forest	13-4-3	0-1 (Furman)
9	SMU	14-4-0	2-1 (Indiana)
10	Old Dominion	18-1-2	0-1 (Rutgers)
11	UCLA	17-3-0	1-1 (Santa Clara)
12	Wisconsin	16-3-1	1-1 (Indiana)
13	Furman	14-4-1	1-1 (N.C.State)
14	North Carolina	14-5-1	1-1 (St.Louis)
15	Fresno St	13-3-4	1-1 (Santa Clara)

1991 NCAA Division I Women's Tournament

FINAL FOUR
(at Chapel Hill, Va., Nov. 23-24)

Semifinals

Wisconsin 1 .... Colorado College 0
North Carolina 5 .... Virginia 1

Championship

North Carolina 3 .... Wisconsin 1

Final records: North Carolina (24-0); Wisconsin (17-3); Colorado College (17-3); Virginia (14-5-1).

1991 Division I All-America Team
Selected by Soccer America

Pos		Class	Hgt	Wgt
G	Tim Deck, Wisconsin	So.	6-1	180
D	Erik Imler, Virginia	Jr.	5-10	155
D	Alexi Lalas, Rutgers	Sr.	6-3	185
D	Cam Rast, Santa Clara	Sr.	5-11	160
D	Matt Rast, Santa Clara	Sr.	5-11	160
M	Henry Gutierrez, N.C.State	Sr.	5-8	145
M	Joe-Max Moore, UCLA	So.	5-8	145
M	Claudio Reyna, Virginia	Fr.	5-10	160
F	Gerell Elliott, Fresno St	Sr.	5-11	153
F	Brian McBride, St. Louis	So.	6-1	170
F	Alan Prampin, SMU	So.	5-7	150

The World Cup

The Federation Internationale de Football Association (FIFA) began the World Cup championship tournament in 1930 with a 13-team field in Uruguay. Sixty years later, the 1990 World Cup in Italy marked the eighth time the competition has been held in Europe. Countries in South and Central America have hosted the Cup six times and the United States will host the tournament for the first time in 1994.

Brazil retired the first World Cup (called the Jules Rimet Trophy for FIFA's first president) in 1970 after winning it for the third time. Since 1974, the award has been known as simply the World Cup.

The 1942 and '46 World Cup tournaments were cancelled because of World War II. (*) indicates score after extra time.

Multiple winners: Brazil, Italy and West Germany (3); Argentina and Uruguay (2).

Year	Champion	Manager	Score	Runner-up	Host Country	Third Place
1930	Uruguay	Alberto Supicci	4-2	Argentina	Uruguay	No game
1934	Italy	Vittorio Pozzo	2-1*	Czechoslovakia	Italy	Germany 3, Austria 2
1938	Italy	Vittorio Pozzo	4-2	Hungary	France	Brazil 4, Sweden 2
1942– 46	Not held					
1950	Uruguay	Juan Lopez	2-1	Brazil	Brazil	No game
1954	W.Germany	Sepp Herberger	3-2	Hungary	Switzerland	Austria 3, Uruguay 1
1958	Brazil	Vicente Feola	5-2	Sweden	Sweden	France 6, W.Germany 3
1962	Brazil	Aymore Moreira	3-1	Czechoslovakia	Chile	Chile 1, Yugoslavia 0
1966	England	Alf Ramsey	4-2*	W.Germany	England	Portugal 2, USSR 1
1970	Brazil	Mario Zagalo	4-1	Italy	Mexico	W.Ger. 1, Uruguay 0
1974	W.Germany	Helmut Schoen	2-1	Holland	W.Germany	Poland 1, Brazil 0
1978	Argentina	Cesar Menotti	3-1*	Holland	Argentina	Brazil 2, Italy 1
1982	Italy	Enzo Bearzot	3-1	W.Germany	Spain	Poland 3, France 2
1986	Argentina	Carlos Bilardo	3-2	W.Germany	Mexico	France 4, Belgium 2*
1990	W.Germany	Franz Beckenbauer	1-0	Argentina	Italy	Italy 2, England 1

The United States in the World Cup

While the United States has fielded a national team every year of the World Cup, only four of those teams have been able to make it past the preliminary competition and qualify for the final World Cup tournament. The U.S. played in three of the first four World Cups (1930, '34 and '50) then not again until 1990.

The U.S. has won only three World Cup tournament matches—two opening round games in 1930 (which enabled the Americans to reach the semifinals) and a stunning first round, 1-0, upset of England in 1950. Center forward Joe Gaetjens scored the goal and goalkeeper Frank Borghi had the shutout against the English.

1930

1st Round Matches

United States 3 . . . . Belgium 0
United States 3 . . . . Paraguay 0

Semifinals

Argentina 6 . . . . United States 1
US Scoring—Bert Patenaude (3), Bart McGhee (2), James Brown, Ed Florie.

1934

1st Round Match

Italy 7 . . . . United States 1
US Scoring—Buff Donelli (who later became a noted college and NFL football coach).

1950

1st Round Matches

Spain 3 . . . . United States 1
United States 1 . . . . England 0
Chile 5 . . . . United States 2
US Scoring—John Souza (2), Joe Gaetjens, Gino Pariani.

1990

1st Round Matches

Czechoslovakia 5 . . . . United States 1
Italy 1 . . . . United States 0
Austria 2 . . . . United States 1
US Scoring—Paul Caligiuri, Bruce Murray.

All-Time World Cup Leaders

Career Goals

World Cup scoring leaders through 1990. Years listed are years played in World Cup.

	No
Gerd Mueller, West Germany (1970,74)	14
Just Fontaine, France (1958)	13
Pele, Brazil (1958,70)	12
Sandor Kocsis, Hungary (1954)	11
Teofilo Cubillas, Peru (1970, 78)	10
Gregorz Lato, Poland (1974, 78, 82)	10
Gary Lineker, England (1986,90)	10
Helmut Rahn, West Germany (1954,58)	10

Most Valuable Player

Officially, the Golden Ball Award, the Most Valuable Player of the World Cup tournament has been selected since 1982 by a panel of international soccer journalists.

Year		Year	
1982	Paolo Rossi, Italy	1990	Toto Schillaci, Italy
1986	Diego Maradona, Arg.		

Single Tournament Goals

World Cup tournament scoring leaders through 1990.

Year		Gm	No
1930	Guillermo Stabile, Argentina	4	8
1934	Angelo Schiavio, Italy	3	4
	Oldrich Nejedly, Czechoslovakia	4	4
	& Edmund Conen, Germany	4	4
1938	Leonidas, Brazil	3	8
1950	Ademir, Brazil	6	7
1954	Sandor Kocsis, Hungary	5	11
1958	Just Fontaine, France	6	13
1962	Drazen Jerkovic, Yugoslavia	6	5
1966	Eusebio, Portugal	6	9
1970	Gerd Mueller, West Germany	6	10
1974	Grzegorz Lato, Poland	7	7
1978	Mario Kempes, Argentina	7	6
1982	Paolo Rossi, Italy	7	6
1986	Gary Lineker, England	5	6
1990	Toto Schillaci, Italy	7	6

World Cup Appearances

The World Cup tournament field has grown from 13 (1930) to 16 (1934-78) to 24 (since 1982). Brazil is the only team to have played in every World Cup tournament, but eight other countries have qualified teams at least nine times.

The following FIFA Table ranks all national teams by total points earned in World Cup play through 1990. Note that West Germany's appearances include two by Germany in 1934 and 1938.

		App	Gm	W	L	T	Pts
1	Brazil	14	66	44	11	11	99
2	West Germany	12	68	39	14	15	93
3	Italy	12	54	31	11	12	74
4	Argentina	10	48	24	15	9	57
5	England	9	41	18	11	12	48
6	Uruguay	9	37	15	14	8	38
7	Soviet Union	7	31	15	10	6	36
8	France	9	34	15	14	5	35
	Yugoslavia	8	33	14	12	7	35
10	Hungary	9	32	15	14	3	33
	Spain	8	32	13	12	7	33
12	Poland	5	25	13	7	5	31
13	Sweden	8	31	11	14	6	28
14	Czechoslovakia	8	30	11	14	5	27
15	Austria	6	26	12	12	2	26

		App	Gm	W	L	T	Pts
16	Holland	5	20	8	6	6	22
17	Belgium	8	25	7	14	4	18
	Mexico	9	29	6	17	6	18
19	Chile	6	21	7	11	3	17
20	Scotland	7	20	4	10	6	14
21	Portugal	2	9	6	3	0	12
	Switzerland	6	18	5	11	2	12
24	Peru	4	15	4	8	3	11
	Northern Ireland	3	13	3	5	5	11
25	Paraguay	4	11	3	4	4	10
26	Cameroon	2	8	3	2	3	9
	Romania	5	12	3	6	3	9
28	Denmark	1	4	3	1	0	6
	United States	4	10	3	7	0	6
	East Germany	1	6	2	2	2	6

World Cup Finals

West Germany has appeared in the most World Cup championship games (6), winning three. Brazil (3-1), Italy (3-1) and Argentina (2-2) have each appeared in four finals. A four-team round robin decided the 1950 World Cup—fortunately, the deciding game turned out to be the last one of the tournament between Uruguay and Brazil.

1930

Uruguay 4, Argentina 2
(at Montevideo, Uruguay)

		1	2—T
July 30	Uruguay (4-0)	1	3—4
	Argentina (4-1)	2	0—2

Goals: Uruguay—Pablo Dorado (12th minute), Pedro Cea (54th), Santos Iriarte (68th), Castro (89th); Argentina—Carlos Peucelle (20th), Guillermo Stabile (37th).

Uruguay—Ballestrero, Nasazzi, Mascheroni, Andrade, Fernandez, Gestido, Dorado, Scarone, Castro, Cea, Iriarte.

Argentina—Botasso, Della Torre, Paternoster, J.Evaristo, Monti, Suarez, Peucelle, Varallo, Stabile, M.Ferreyra, M.Evaristo.

Attendance: 90,000. **Referee:** Langenus (Belgium).

1934

Italy 2, Czechoslovakia 1 (OT)
(at Rome)

		1	2	OT—T
June 10	Italy (4-0-1)	1	2	1—2
	Czechoslovakia (3-1)	1	2	0—1

Goals: Italy—Raimondo Orsi (80th minute), Angelo Schiavio (95th); Czechoslovakia—Puc (70th).

Italy—Combi, Monzeglio, Allemandi, Ferraris IV, Monti, Bertolini, Guaita, Meazza, Schiavio, Ferrari, Orsi.

Czechoslovakia—Planicka, Zenisek, Ctyroky, Kostalek, Cambal, Krcil, Junek, Svoboda, Sobotka, Nejedly, Puc.

Attendance: 55,000. **Referee:** Eklind (Sweden).

1938
Italy 4, Hungary 2
(at Paris)

	1	2—T
June 19 Italy (4-0)	3	1—4
Hungary (3-1)	1	1—2

Goals: Italy—Gino Colaussi (5th minute), Silvio Piola (16th), Colassi (35th), Piola (82nd); Hungary—Titkos (7th), Georges Sarosi (70th).

Italy—Olivieri, Foni, Rava, Serantoni, Andreolo, Locatelli, Biavati, Meazza, Piola, Ferrari, Colaussi.

Hungary—Szabo, Polgar, Biro, Szalay, Szucs, Lazar, Sas, Vincze, G.Sarosi, Szengeller, Titkos.

Attendance: 65,000. **Referee:** Capdeville (France)

1950
Uruguay 2, Brazil 1
(at Rio de Janeiro)

	1	2—T
July 16 Uruguay (3-0-1)	0	2—2
Brazil (4-1-1)	0	1—1

Goals: Uruguay—Juan Schiaffino (66th minute), Chico Ghiggia (79th); Brazil—Friaca (47th).

Uruguay—Maspoli, M.Gonzales, Tejera, Gambetta, Varela, Andrade, Ghiggia, Perez, Miguez, Schiaffino, Moran.

Brazil—Barbosa, Augusto, Juvenal, Bauer, Danilo, Bigode, Friaca, Zizinho, Ademir, Jair, Chico.

Attendance: 199,854. **Referee:** Reader (England)

1954
West Germany 3, Hungary 2
(at Berne, Switzerland)

	1	2—T
July 4 West Germany (5-1)	2	1—3
Hungary (4-1)	2	0—2

Goals: West Germany—Max Morlock (10th minute), Helmut Rahn (18th), Rahn (84th); Hungary—Ferenc Puskas (4th), Zoltan Czibor (9th).

West Germany—Turek, Posipal, Liebrich, Kohlmeyer, Eckel, Mai, Rahn, Morlock, O.Walter, F.Walter, Schaeffer.

Hungary—Grosics, Buzansky, Lorant, Lantos, Bozsik, Zakarias, Csibor, Kocsis, Higegkuti, Puskas, J.Toth.

Attendance: 60,000. **Referee:** Ling (England).

1958
Brazil 5, Sweden 2
(at Stockholm)

	1	2—T
June 29 Brazil (5-0-1)	2	3—5
Sweden (4-1-1)	1	1—2

Goals: Brazil—Vava (9th minute), Vava (32nd), Pele (55th), Mario Zagalo (68th), Pele (90th); Sweden—Nils Liedholm (3rd), Agne Simonsson (80th).

Brazil—Gilmar, D.Santos, N.Santos, Zito, Bellini, Orlando, Garrincha, Didi, Vava, Pele, Zagalo.

Sweden—Svensson, Bergmark, Axbom, Boerjesson, Gustavsson, Parling, Hamrin, Gren, Simonsson, Liedholm, Skoglund.

Attendance: 49,737. **Referee:** Guigue (France).

1962
Brazil 3, Czechoslovakia 1
(at Santiago, Chile)

	1	2—T
June 17 Brazil (5-0-1)	1	2—3
Czechoslovakia (3-2-1)	1	0—1

Goals: Brazil—Amarildo (17th minute), Zito (68th), Vava (77th); Czechoslovakia—Josef Masopust (15th).

Brazil—Gilmar, D.Santos, N.Santos, Zito, Mauro, Zozimo, Garrincha, Didi, Vava, Amarildo, Zagalo.

Czechoslovakia—Schroiff, Tichy, Novak, Pluskal, Popluhar, Masopust, Pospichal, Scherer, Kvasniak, Kadraba, Jelinek.

Attendance: 68,679. **Referee:** Latishev (USSR).

1966
England 4, West Germany 2 (OT)
(at London)

	1	2	OT—T
July 30 England (5-0-1)	1	1	2—4
West Germany (4-1-1)	1	1	0—2

Goals: England—Geoff Hurst (18th minute), Martin Peters (78th), Hurst (101st), Hurst (120th); West Germany—Helmut Haller (12th), Wolfgang Weber (90th).

England—Banks, Cohen, Wilson, Stiles, J.Charlton, Moore, Ball, Hurst, B.Charlton, Hunt, Peters.

West Germany—Tilkowski, Hottges, Schnellinger, Beckenbauer, Schulz, Weber, Haller, Seeler, Held, Overath, Emmerich.

Attendance: 93,802. **Referee:** Dienst (Switzerland).

1970
Brazil 4, Italy 1
(at Mexico City)

	1	2—T
June 20 Brazil (6-0)	1	3—4
Italy (3-1-2)	1	0—1

Goals: Brazil—Pele (18th minute), Gerson (65th), Jairzinho (70th), Carlos Alberto (86th); Italy—Roberto Boninsegna (37th).

Brazil—Felix, C.Alberto, Everaldo, Clodoaldo, Brito, Piazza, Jairzinho, Gerson, Tostao, Pele, Rivelino.

Italy—Albertosi, Burgnich, Facchetti, Bertini (Juliano, 73rd), Rosato, Cera, Domenghini, Mazzola, Boninsegna (Rivera, 84th), De Sisti, Riva.

Attendance: 107,412. **Referee:** Gloeckner (E. Germany).

1974
West Germany 2, Holland 1
(at Munich)

	1	2—T
July 7 West Germany (6-1)	2	0—2
Holland (5-1-1)	1	0—1

Goals: West Germany—Paul Breitner (25th minute, penalty kick), Gerd Mueller (43rd); Holland—Johan Neeskens (1st, penalty kick).

West Germany—Maier, Beckenbauer, Vogts, Breitner, Schwarzenbeck, Overath, Bonhof, Hoeness, Grabowski, Mueller, Holzenbein.

Holland—Jongbloed, Suurbier, Rijsbergen (De Jong, 58th), Krol, Haan, Jansen, Van Hanegem, Neeskens, Rep, Cruyff, Rensenbrink (R.Van de Kerkhof, 46th).

Attendance: 77,833. **Referee:** Taylor (England).

World Cup Finals (Cont.)

1978

Argentina 3, Holland 1 (OT)
(at Buenos Aires)

	1	2	OT—T
June 25 Argentina (5-1-1)	1	0	2—3
Holland (3-2-2)	0	1	1—1

Goals: Argentina—Mario Kempes (37th minute), Kempes (104th), Daniel Bertoni (114th); Holland—Dirk Nanninga (81st).

Argentina—Fillol, Olguin, L.Galvan, Passarella, Tarantini, Ardiles (Larrosa, 65th), Gallego, Kempes, Luque, Bertoni, Ortiz (Houseman, 77th).

Holland—Jongbloed, Jansen (Suurbier, 72nd), Brandts, Krol, Poortvliet, Haan, Neeskens, W.Van de Kerkhof, R.Van de Kerkhof, Rep (Nanninga, 58th), Rensenbrink.

Attendance: 77,000. **Referee:** Gonella (Italy).

1982

Italy 3, West Germany 1
(at Madrid)

	1	2—T
July 11 Italy (4-0-3)	0	3—3
West Germany (4-2-1)	0	1—1

Goals: Italy—Paolo Rossi (57th minute), Marco Tardelli (68th), Alessandro Altobelli (81st); West Germany—Paul Breitner (83rd).

Italy—Zoff, Scirea, Gentile, Cabrini, Collovati, Bergomi, Tardelli, Oriali, Conti, Rossi, Graziani (Altobelli, 8th, and Causio, 89th).

West Germany—Schumacher, Stielike, Kaltz, Briegel, K.H.Foerster, B.Foerster, Breitner, Dremmler (Hrubesch, 61st), Littbarski, Fischer, Rummenigge (Mueller, 69th).

Attendance: 90,080. **Referee:** Coelho (Brazil).

1986

Argentina 3, West Germany 2
(at Mexico City)

	1	2—T
June 29 Argentina (6-0-1)	1	2—3
West Germany (4-2-1)	0	2—2

Goals: Argentina—Jose Brown (22nd minute), Jorge Valdano (55th), Jorge Burruchaga (83rd); West Germany—Karl-Heinz Rummenigge (73rd), Rudi Voeller (81st).

Argentina—Pumpido, Cuciuffo, Olarticoechea, Ruggeri, Brown, Batista, Burruchaga (Trobbiani, 89th), Giusti, Enrique, Maradona, Valdano.

West Germany—Schumacher, Jakobs, K.H.Foerster, Berthold, Briegel, Eder, Brehme, Matthaeus, Rummenigge, Magath (Hoeness, 61st), Allofs (Voeller, 46th).

Attendance: 114,580. **Referee:** Filho (Brazil).

1990

West Germany 1, Argentina 0
(at Rome)

	1	2—T
July 8 West Germany (6-0-1)	0	1—1
Argentina (4-2-1)	0	0—0

Goals: West Germany—Andreas Brehme (85th minute, penalty kick).

West Germany—Illgner, Berthold (Reuter, 75th), Kohler, Augenthaler, Buchwald, Brehme, Haessler, Matthaeus, Littbarski, Klinsmann, Voeller.

Argentina: Goycoechea, Ruggeri (Monzon, 46th), Simon, Serrizuela, Lorenzo, Basualdo, Troglio, Burruchaga (Calderon, 53rd), Sensini, Dezotti, Maradona.

Attendance: 73,603. **Referee:** Codesal (Mexico).

OTHER WORLDWIDE COMPETITION

The Olympic Games

Held every four years since 1896, except during World War I (1916) and World War II (1940-44). Soccer was not a medal sport in 1896 at Athens or in 1932 at Los Angeles. By agreement between FIFA and the IOC, Olympic soccer competition is currently limited to players 23 years old and under.

Multiple winners: England and Hungary (3); USSR and Uruguay (2).

Year		Year		Year		Year	
1896	Not held	1920	Belgium	1948	Sweden	1972	Poland
1900	England	1924	Uruguay	1952	Hungary	1976	East Germany
1904	Canada	1928	Uruguay	1956	Soviet Union	1980	Czechoslovakia
1906	Denmark	1932	Not held	1960	Yugoslavia	1984	France
1908	England	1936	Italy	1964	Hungary	1988	Soviet Union
1912	England	1940-44	Not held	1968	Hungary	1992	Spain
1916	Not held						

The Under-20 World Cup

Held every two years since 1977. Officially, The World Youth Championship for the FIFA/Coca-Cola Cup.

Multiple winners: Brazil and Portugal (2).

Year		Year	
1977	Soviet Union	1985	Brazil
1979	Argentina	1987	Yugoslavia
1981	West Germany	1989	Portugal
1983	Brazil	1991	Portugal

Five-a-Side Championship

First held in 1989. FIFA's only indoor tournament.

Year		Year	
1989	Brazil	1992	at Hong Kong

The Under-17 World Cup

Held every two years since 1985. Officially, The FIFA U-17 World Tournament for the JVC Cup.

Year		Year	
1985	Nigeria	1989	Saudi Arabia
1987	Soviet Union	1991	Ghana

Women's World Championship

First held in 1991. Officially, the FIFA World Championship for Women's Football for the M&M's Cup.

Year	
1991	United States

CONTINENTAL COMPETITION

European Championship

Held every four years since 1960. Officially, the European Football Championship.
Multiple winner: West Germany (2).

Year		Year		Year		Year	
1960	Soviet Union	1972	West Germany	1980	West Germany	1988	Holland
1964	Spain	1976	Czechoslovakia	1984	France	1992	Denmark
1968	Italy						

Copa America

Held irregularly since 1916. Unofficially, the championship of South America.
Multiple winners: Argentina and Uruguay (13), Brazil (4), Paraguay and Peru (2).

Year		Year		Year		Year	
1916	Uruguay	1926	Uruguay	1946	Argentina	1963	Bolivia
1917	Uruguay	1927	Argentina	1947	Argentina	1967	Uruguay
1919	Brazil	1929	Argentina	1949	Brazil	1975	Peru
1920	Uruguay	1935	Uruguay	1953	Paraguay	1979	Paraguay
1921	Argentina	1937	Argentina	1955	Argentina	1983	Uruguay
1922	Brazil	1939	Peru	1956	Uruguay	1987	Uruguay
1923	Uruguay	1941	Argentina	1957	Argentina	1989	Brazil
1924	Uruguay	1942	Uruguay	1958	Argentina	1991	Argentina
1925	Argentina	1945	Argentina	1959	Uruguay		

African Nations' Cup

Contested since 1957 and held every two years since 1968.
Multiple winners: Ghana (4); Egypt (3); Cameroon and Congo (2).

Year		Year		Year		Year	
1957	Egypt	1968	Congo Kinshasa	1978	Ghana	1986	Egypt
1959	Egypt	1970	Sudan	1980	Nigeria	1988	Cameroon
1962	Ethiopa	1972	Congo	1982	Ghana	1990	Algeria
1963	Ghana	1974	Zaire	1984	Cameroon	1992	Ivory Coast
1965	Ghana	1976	Morocco				

CONCACAF Gold Cup

The Confederation of North, Central American and Caribbean Football (CONCACAF) Championship. First held in Los Angeles in 1991 and won by the United States.

CLUB COMPETITION

Toyota Cup

Contested annually in December between the winners of the previous year's European Cup and Libertadores Copa (see below). On four occasions, the European Cup winner has refused to participate. In each case, the European Cup runner-up went instead—Panathinaikos (Greece) in 1971, Juventus (Italy) in 1973, Atletico Madrid (Spain) in 1974, and Malmo (Sweden) in 1979.

Originally the **Intercontinental Cup** (1960-79). Best-of-three game format until 1968, then two-game/total-goal format was used. Toyota became sponsor in 1980, changed the format to one-game championship and moved it to Tokyo.

Multiple winners: AC Milan, Nacional and Penarol (3); Independiente, Inter Milan and Santos (2).

Year		Year		Year	
1960	Real Madrid (Spain)	1972	Ajax Amsterdam (Holland)	1982	Penarol (Uruguay)
1961	Penarol (Uruguay)	1973	Independiente (Argentina)	1983	Gremio (Brazil)
1962	Santos (Brazil)	1974	Atletico Madrid (Spain)	1984	Independiente (Argentina)
1963	Santos (Brazil)	1975	Not held	1985	Juventus (Italy)
1964	Inter Milan (Italy)	1976	Bayern Munich (W.Germany)	1986	River Plate (Argentina)
1965	Inter Milan (Italy)	1977	Boca Juniors (Argentina)	1987	FC Porto (Portugal)
1966	Penarol (Uruguay)	1978	Not held	1988	Nacional (Uruguay)
1967	Racing Club (Argentina)	1979	Olimpia (Paraguay)	1989	AC Milan (Italy)
1968	Estudiantes (Argentina)				
1969	AC Milan (Italy)	1980	Nacional (Uruguay)	1990	AC Milan (Italy)
		1981	Flamengo (Brazil)	1991	Red Star (Yugoslavia)
1970	Feyenoord (Holland)				
1971	Nacional (Uruguay)				

Club Competition (Cont.)
European Champions' Cup

Contested annually since the 1955-56 season by the league champions of the member countries of the Union of European Football Associations (UEFA).

Multiple winners: Real Madrid (6); AC Milan and Liverpool (4); Ajax Amsterdam and Bayern Munich (3); Benfica, Inter Milan and Nottingham Forest (2).

Year		Year		Year	
1956	Real Madrid (Spain)	1968	Manchester United (England)	1980	Nottingham Forest (England)
1957	Real Madrid (Spain)	1969	AC Milan (Italy)	1981	Liverpool (England)
1958	Real Madrid (Spain)			1982	Aston Villa (England)
1959	Real Madrid (Spain)	1970	Feyenoord (Holland)	1983	SV Hamburg (W.Germany)
		1971	Ajax Amsterdam (Holland)	1984	Liverpool (England)
1960	Real Madrid (Spain)	1972	Ajax Amsterdam (Holland)	1985	Juventus (Italy)
1961	Benfica (Portugal)	1973	Ajax Amsterdam (Holland)	1986	Steaua Bucharest (Romania)
1962	Benfica (Portugal)	1974	Bayern Munich (W.Germany)	1987	FC Porto (Portugal)
1963	AC Milan (Italy)	1975	Bayern Munich (W.Germany)	1988	PSV Eindhoven (Holland)
1964	Inter Milan (Italy)	1976	Bayern Munich (W.Germany)	1989	AC Milan (Italy)
1965	Inter Milan (Italy)	1977	Liverpool (England)		
1966	Real Madrid (Spain)	1978	Liverpool (England)	1990	AC Milan (Italy)
1967	Glasgow Celtic (Scotland)	1979	Nottingham Forest (England)	1991	Red Star (Yugoslavia)
				1992	Barcelona (Spain)

European Cup Winners' Cup

Contested annually since the 1960-61 season by the cup winners of the member countries of the Union of European Football Associations (UEFA).

Multiple winners: Barcelona (3); AC Milan, Anderlecht and Dynamo Kiev (2).

Year		Year		Year	
1961	Fiorentina (Italy)	1972	Glasgow Rangers (Scotland)	1983	Aberdeen (Scotland)
1962	Atletico Madrid (Spain)	1973	AC Milan (Italy)	1984	Juventus (Italy)
1963	Tottenham Hotspur (England)	1974	FC Magdeburg (E.Germany)	1985	Everton (England)
1964	Sporting Lisbon (Portugal)	1975	Dinamo Kiev (USSR)	1986	Dynamo Kiev (USSR)
1965	West Ham United (England)	1976	Anderlecht (Belgium)	1987	Ajax Amsterdam (Holland)
1966	Borussia Dortmund (W.Germany)	1977	SV Hamburg (W.Germany)	1988	Mechelen (Belgium)
1967	Bayern Munich (W.Germany)	1978	Anderlecht (Belgium)	1989	Barcelona (Spain)
1968	AC Milan (Italy)	1979	Barcelona (Spain)		
1969	Slovan Bratislava (Czech.)			1990	Sampdoria (Italy)
		1980	Valencia (Spain)	1991	Manchester United (England)
1970	Manchester City (England)	1981	Dynamo Tbilisi (USSR)	1992	Werder Bremen (Germany)
1971	Chelsea (England)	1982	Barcelona (Spain)		

UEFA Cup

Contested annually since the 1957-58 season by teams other than league champions and cup winners of the Union of European Football Associations (UEFA). Teams selected by UEFA based on each country's previous performance in the tournament. Teams from England were banned from UEFA Cup play from 1985-90 for the criminal behavior of their supporters.

Multiple winners: Barcelona (3); Borussia Moenchengladbach, IFL Gothenburg, Juventus, Leeds United, Liverpool, Real Madrid, Tottenham Hotspur and Valencia (2).

Year		Year		Year	
1958	Barcelona (Spain)	1970	Arsenal (England)	1980	Eintracht Frankfurt (W.Germany)
1959	Not held	1971	Leeds United (England)	1981	Ipswich Town (England)
		1972	Tottenham Horspur (England)	1982	IFK Gothenburg (Sweden)
1960	Barcelona (Spain)	1973	Liverpool (England)	1983	Anderlecht (Belgium)
1961	AS Roma (Italy)	1974	Feyenoord (Holland)	1984	Tottenham Hotspur (England)
1962	Valencia (Spain)	1975	Borussia Moenchen-	1985	Real Madrid (Spain)
1963	Valencia (Spain)		gladbach (W.Germany)	1986	Real Madrid (Spain)
1964	Real Zaragoza (Spain)	1976	Liverpool (England)	1987	IFK Gothenburg (Sweden)
1965	Ferencvaros (Hungary)	1977	Juventus (Italy)	1988	Bayer Leverksen (W.Germany)
1966	Barcelona (Spain)	1978	PSV Eindhoven (Holland)	1989	Napoli (Italy)
1967	Dinamo Zagreb (Yugoslavia)	1979	Borussia Moenchen-		
1968	Leeds United (England)		gladbach (W.Germany)	1990	Juventus (Italy)
1969	Newcastle United (England)			1991	Inter Milan (Italy)
				1992	Ajax-Amsterdam (Holland)

Copa Libertadores

Contested annually since the 1955-56 season by the league champions of South America's football union.

Multiple winners: Independiente (7); Penarol (5); Estudiantes and Nacional-Uruguay (3); Boca Juniors, Olimpia and Santos (2).

Year		Year		Year	
1960	Penarol (Uruguay)	1964	Independiente (Argentina)	1968	Estudiantes (Argentina)
1961	Penarol (Uruguay)	1965	Independiente (Argentina)	1969	Estudiantes (Argentina)
1962	Santos (Brazil)	1966	Penarol (Uruguay)		
1963	Santos (Brazil)	1967	Racing Club (Argentina)	1970	Estudiantes (Argentina)
				1971	Nacional (Uruguay)

Year		Year		Year	
1972	Independiente (Argentina)	1980	Nacional (Uruguay)	1988	Nacional (Uruguay)
1973	Independiente (Argentina)	1981	Flamengo (Brazil)	1989	Nacional Medellin (Colombia)
1974	Independiente (Argentina)	1982	Penarol (Uruguay)		
1975	Independiente (Argentina)	1983	Gremio (Brazil)	1990	Olimpia (Paraguay)
1976	Cruzeiro (Brazil)	1984	Independiente (Argentina)	1991	Colo Colo (Chile)
1977	Boca Juniors (Argentina)	1985	Argentinos Jrs.(Argentina)	1992	Sao Paolo (Brazil)
1978	Boca Juniors (Argentina)	1986	River Plate (Argentina)		
1979	Olimpia (Paraguay)	1987	Penarol (Uruguay)		

Annual Awards
European Player of the Year

Officially, the "Ballon d'Or" and presented by *France Football* magazine since 1956. Candidates are limited to European players in European leagues and winners are selected by a panel of 29 European soccer journalists.
Multiple winners: Johan Cruyff and Michel Platini (3); Franz Beckenbauer, Alfredo di Stefano, Kevin Keegan, Karl-Heinz Rummenigge and Marco Van Basten (2).

Year		Nat'l Team	Year		Nat'l Team
1956	Stanley Matthews, Blackpool	England	1974	Johan Cruyff, Barcelona	Holland
1957	Alfredo di Stefano, Real Madrid	Arg./Spain	1975	Oleg Blokhin, Dinamo Kiev	Soviet Union
1958	Raymond Kopa, Real Madrid	France	1976	Franz Beckenbauer, Bayern Munich	W.Ger.
1959	Alfredo di Stefano, Real Madrid	Arg./Spain	1977	Allan Simonsen, B.M'chengladbach	Denmark
1960	Luis Suarez, Barcelona	Spain	1978	Kevin Keegan, SV Hamburg	England
1961	Enrique Sivori, Juventus	Arg./Italy	1979	Kevin Keegan, SV Hamburg	England
1962	Josef Masopust, Dukla Praque	Czech.	1980	K.H.Rummenigge, Bayern Munich	W.Ger.
1963	Lev Yachin, Dynamo Moscow	Soviet Union	1981	K.H.Rummenigge, Bayern Munich	W.Ger.
1964	Denis Law, Manchester United	Scotland	1982	Paolo Rossi, Juventus	Italy
1965	Eusebio, Benfica	Portugal	1983	Michel Platini, Juventus	France
1966	Bobby Charlton, Manchester United	England	1984	Michel Platini, Juventus	France
1967	Florian Albert, Ferencvaros	Hungary	1985	Michel Platini, Juventus	France
1968	George Best, Manchester United	N.Ireland	1986	Igor Belanov, Dinamo Kiev	Soviet Union
1969	Gianni Rivera, AC Milan	Italy	1987	Ruud Gullit, AC Milan	Holland
1970	Gerd Mueller, Bayern Munich	W.Ger.	1988	Marco Van Basten, AC Milan	Holland
1971	Johan Cruyff, Ajax Amsterdam	Holland	1989	Marco Van Basten, AC Milan	Holland
1972	Franz Beckenbauer, Bayern Munich	W.Ger.	1990	Lothar Matthaeus, Inter Milan	W. Ger.
1973	Johan Cruyff, Barcelona	Holland	1991	Jean-Pierre Papin, Marseille	France

South American Player of the Year

Presented by *El Pais* of Uruguay since 1971. Candidates are limited to South American players in South American leagues and winners are selected by a panel of 83 Latin American sports editors.
Multiple winners: Elias Figueroa and Zico (3); Diego Maradona (2).

Year		Nat'l Team	Year		Nat'l Team
1971	Tostao, Cruzeiro	Brazil	1982	Zico, Flamengo	Brazil
1972	Teofilo Cubillas, Alianza Lima	Peru	1983	Socrates, Corinthians	Brazil
1973	Pelé, Santos	Brazil	1984	Enzo Francescoli, River Plate	Uruguay
1974	Elias Figueroa, Internacional	Chile	1985	Julio Cesar Romero, Fluminense	Paraguay
1975	Elias Figueroa, Internacional	Chile	1986	Antonio Alzamendi, River Plate	Uruguay
1976	Elias Figueroa, Internacional	Chile	1987	Carlos Valderrama, Deportivo Cali.	Colombia
1977	Zico, Flamengo	Brazil	1988	Ruben Paz, Racing Buenos Aires	Uruguay
1978	Mario Kempes, Valencia	Argentina	1989	Bebeto, Vasco da Gama	Brazil
1979	Diego Maradona, Argentinos Juniors	Argentina			
1980	Diego Maradona, Boca Juniors	Argentina	1990	Raul Amarilla, Olimpia	Paraguay
1981	Zico, Flamengo	Brazil	1991	Oscar Ruggeri, Velez Sarsfield	Argentina

African Player of the Year

Officially, the African "Ballon d'Or" and presented by France Football magazine since 1970. All African players are eligible for the award and winners are selected by a panel of 41 African soccer journalists.
Multiple winners: Roger Milla and Thomas N'kona (2).

Year		Year		Year	
1970	Salif Keita, Mali	1978	Abdul Razak, Ghana	1985	Mohamed Timoumi, Morocco
1971	Ibrahim Sunday, Ghana	1979	Thomas N'Kono, Cameroon	1986	Badou Zaki, Morocco
1972	Cherif Souleymane, Guinea			1987	Rabah Madjer, Algeria
1973	Tshimimu Bwanga, Zaire	1980	Jean Manga Onguene, Cameroon	1988	Kalusha Bwalya, Zambia
1974	Paul Moukila, Congo	1981	Lakhdar Belloumi, Algeria	1989	George Weah, Liberia
1975	Ahmed Faras, Morocco	1982	Thomas N'Kono, cameroon		
1976	Roger Milla, Cameroon	1983	Mahmoud Al-Khatib, Egypt	1990	Roger Milla, Cameroon
1977	Dhiab Tarak, Tunisia	1984	Theophile Abega, Cameroon	1991	Abedi Pele, Ghana

U.S. Pro Leagues
OUTDOOR
National Professional Soccer League (1967)

Not sanctioned by FIFA, the international soccer federation. The NPSL recruited individual players to fill the rosters of its 10 teams. The league lasted only one season.

		Playoff Final			Regular Season			
Year	Winner	Score(s)	Loser	Leading Scorer		G	A	Pts
1967	Oakland Clippers	0-1,4-1	Baltimore Bays	Yanko Daucik, Toronto		20	8	48

United Soccer Association (1967)

Sanctioned by FIFA. Originally called the North American Soccer League, it became the USA to avoid being confused with the National Professional Soccer League (see below). Instead of recruiting individual players, the USA imported 12 entire teams from Europe to represent its 12 franchises. It, too, only lasted a season. The league champion Los Angeles Wolves were actually Wolverhampton of England and the runner-up Washington Whips were Aberdeen of Scotland.

		Playoff Final			Regular Season			
Year	Winner	Score	Loser	Leading Scorer		G	A	Pts
1967	Los Angeles Wolves	6-5 (OT)	Washington Whips	Roberto Boninsegna, Chicago		10	1	21

North American Soccer League (1968-84)

The NPSL and USA merged to form the NASL in 1968 and the new league lasted until 1985. The NASL championship was known as the Soccer Bowl from 1975-84. One game decided the NASL title every year but five. There were no playoffs in 1969; a two-game/aggregate goals format was used in 1968 and '70; and a best-of-three games format was used in 1971 and '84; (*) indicates overtime and (†) indicates tie-breaker.
Multiple winners: NY Cosmos (5); Chicago (2).

		Playoff Final			Regular Season			
Year	Winner	Score(s)	Loser	Leading Scorer		G	A	Pts
1968	Atlanta Chiefs	0-0,3-0	San Diego Toros	John Kowalik, Chicago		30	9	69
1969	Kansas City Spurs	No game	Atlanta Chiefs	Kaiser Motaung, Atlanta		16	4	36
1970	Rochester Lancers	3-0,1-3	Washington Darts	Kirk Apostolidis, Dallas		16	3	35
1971	Dallas Tornado	1-2*,4-1,2-0	Atlanta Chiefs	Carlos Metidieri, Rochester		19	8	46
1972	New York Cosmos	2-1	St.Louis Stars	Randy Horton, New York		9	4	22
1973	Philadelphia Atoms	2-0	Dallas Tornado	Kyle Rote, Jr., Dallas		10	10	30
1974	Los Angeles Aztecs	4-3†	Miami Toros	Paul Child, San Jose		15	6	36
1975	Tampa Bay Rowdies	2-0	Portland Timbers	Steve David, Miami		23	6	52
1976	Toronto Metros	3-0	Minnesota Kicks	Giorgio Chinaglia, New York		19	11	49
1977	New York Cosmos	2-1	Seattle Sounders	Steve David, Los Angeles		26	6	58
1978	New York Cosmos	3-1	Tampa Bay Rowdies	Giorgio Chinaglia, New York		34	11	79
1979	Vancouver Whitecaps	2-1	Tampa Bay Rowdies	Oscar Fabbiani, Tampa Bay		25	8	58
1980	New York Cosmos	3-0	Ft.Laud.Strikers	Giorgio Chinaglia, New York		32	13	77
1981	Chicago Sting	1-0†	New York Cosmos	Giorgio Chinaglia, New York		29	16	74
1982	New York Cosmos	1-0	Seattle Sounders	Giorgio Chinaglia, New York		20	15	55
1983	Tulsa Roughnecks	2-0	Toronto Blizzard	Roberto Cabanas, New York		25	16	66
1984	Chicago Sting	2-1,3-2	Toronto Blizzard	Steve Zungul, Golden Bay		20	10	50

Regular Season MVP

Regular season Most Valuable Player as designated by the NASL.
Multiple winner: Carlos Metidieri (2).

Year		Year		Year	
1967	Rueben Navarro, Phila (NPSL)	1973	Warren Archibald, Miami	1979	Johan Cruyff, LA
1968	John Kowalik, Chicago	1974	Peter Silvester, Baltimore	1980	Roger Davis, Seattle
1969	Cirilio Fernandez, KC	1975	Steve David, Miami	1981	Giorgio Chinaglia, NY
1970	Carlos Metidieri, Rochester	1976	Pele, New York	1982	Peter Ward, Seattle
1971	Carlos Metidieri, Rochester	1977	Franz Beckenbauer, NY	1983	Roberto Cabanas, NY
1972	Randy Horton, New York	1978	Mike Flanagan, N.Eng.	1984	Steve Zungul, San Jose

American Professional Soccer League

Formed in 1990 after the merger of the Western Soccer League (WSL) and New American Soccer League (NASL). The APSL was officially sanctioned as an outdoor professional league in 1992.

Year		Year		Year	
1990	Maryland Bays	1991	SF Bay Blackhawks	1992	Colorado Foxes

INDOOR
Major Soccer League (1978-92)

Originally the Major Indoor Soccer League from 1978-90. The MISL championship was decided by one game in 1980 and 1981; a best-of-three games series in 1979, best-of-five games in 1982 and 1983; and best-of-seven games since 1984. The MSL folded after the 1991-92 season.

Multiple winners: San Diego (8); New York (4).

	Playoff Final			Regular Season			
Year	Winner	Series	Loser	Leading Scorer	G	A	Pts
1979	New York Arrows	2-0 (WW)	Philadelphia	Fred Grgurev, Philadelphia	46	28	74
1980	New York Arrows	7-4 (1 game)	Houston	Steve Zungul, New York	90	46	136
1981	New York Arrows	6-5 (1 game)	St. Louis	Steve Zungul, New York	108	44	152
1982	New York Arrows	3-2 (LWWLW)	St. Louis	Steve Zungul, New York	103	60	163
1983	San Diego Sockers	3-2 (WWLLW)	Baltimore	Steve Zungul, NY/Golden Bay	75	47	122
1984	Baltimore Blast	4-1 (LWWWW)	St. Louis	Stan Stamenkovic, Baltimore	34	63	97
1985	San Diego Sockers	4-1 (WWLWW)	Baltimore	Steve Zungul, San Diego	68	68	136
1986	San Diego Sockers	4-3 (WLLLWWW)	Minnesota	Steve Zungul, Tacoma	55	60	115
1987	Dallas Sidekicks	4-3 (LLWWLWW)	Tacoma	Tatu, Dallas	73	38	111
1988	San Diego Sockers	4-0	Cleveland	Eric Rasmussen, Wichita	55	57	112
1989	San Diego Sockers	4-3 (LWWWLLW)	Baltimore	Preki, Tacoma	51	53	104
1990	San Diego Sockers	4-2 (LWWWLW)	Baltimore	Tatu, Dallas	64	49	113
1991	San Diego Sockers	4-2 (WLWLWW)	Cleveland	Tatu, Dallas	78	66	144
1992	San Diego Sockers	4-2 (WWWLLW)	Dallas	Zoran Karic, Cleveland	39	63	102

MSL Playoff MVPs

MSL playoff Most Valuable Players, selected by a panel of soccer media covering the playoffs.

Multiple winners: Zungul (4); Quinn (2).

Year		Year	
1979	Shep Messing, NY	1986	Brian Quinn, SD
1980	Steve Zungul, NY	1987	Tatu, Dallas
1981	Steve Zungul, NY	1988	Hugo Perez, SD
1982	Steve Zungul, NY	1989	Victor Nogueira, SD
1983	Juli Veee, SD	1990	Brian Quinn, SD
1984	Scott Manning, Bal.	1991	Ben Collins, SD
1985	Steve Zungul, SD	1992	Thompson Usiyan, SD

MSL Regular Season MVPs

MSL regular season Most Valuable Players, selected by a panel of soccer media from every city in the MISL.

Multiple winner: Zungul (6); Nogueira (2).

Year		Year	
1979	Steve Zungul, NY	1986	Steve Zungul, SD/Tac.
1980	Steve Zungul, NY	1987	Tatu, Dallas
1981	Steve Zungul, NY	1988	Erik Rasmussen, Wich.
1982	Steve Zungul, NY	1989	Preki, Tacoma
	& Stan Terlecki, Pit.	1990	Tatu, Dallas
1983	Alan Mayer, G, SD	1991	Victor Nogueira, SD
1984	Stan Stamenkovic, Bal.	1992	Victor Nogueira, SD
1985	Steve Zungul, SD		

NASL Indoor Champions (1979-83)

The North American Soccer League had both outdoor and indoor schedules from 1979-83. The indoor version of the NASL folded midway through the 1982-83 season, while the outdoor closed down after the 1984 season (see above).

Year		Year		Year		Year	
1980	Tampa Bay Rowdies	1981	Edmonton Drillers	1982	San Diego Sockers	1983	San Diego Sockers

Colleges
NCAA Division I Champions

NCAA Division I champions since the first title was contested in 1959. The championship game has ended in a tie three times—in 1967, 1968 and 1989.

Multiple winners: St.Louis (10); San Francisco (5); Indiana (3); Clemson, Howard, Michigan St. and Virginia (2).

Year	Winner	Head Coach	Score	Runner-up	Host/Site	Semifinalists
1959	St.Louis	Bob Guelker	5-2	Bridgeport	UConn	West Chester, CCNY
1960	St.Louis	Bob Guelker	3-2	Maryland	Brooklyn	West Chester, UConn
1961	West Chester	Mel Lorback	2-0	St.Louis	St.Louis	Bridgeport, Rutgers
1962	St.Louis	Bob Guelker	4-3	Maryland	St.Louis	Mich.St., Springfield
1963	St.Louis	Bob Guelker	3-0	Navy	Rutgers	Army, Maryland
1964	Navy	F.H. Warner	1-0	Mich.St.	Brown	Army, St.Louis
1965	St.Louis	Bob Guelker	1-0	Mich.St.	St.Louis	Army, Navy
1966	San Francisco	Steve Negoesco	5-2	LIU-Bklyn	California	Army, Mich. St.
1967-a	Michigan St. & St. Louis	Gene Kenney Harry Keough	0-0	—	St.Louis	LIU-Bklyn, Navy
1968-b	Michigan St. & Maryland	Gene Kenney Doyle Royal	2-2 (2 OT)	—	Ga.Tech	Brown, Sam Jose St.
1969	St.Louis	Harry Keough	4-0	San Fran.	S.Jose St.	Harvard, Maryland
1970	St.Louis	Harry Keough	1-0	UCLA	So.Ill.	Nartwick, Howard
1971-c	Howard	Lincoln Phillips	3-2	St.Louis	Miami	Harvard, San Fran.
1972	St.Louis	Harry Keough	4-2	UCLA	Miami	Cornell, Howard
1973	St.Louis	Harry Keough	2-1 (OT)	UCLA	Miami	Brown, Clemson

Colleges (Cont.)
NCAA Division I Champions

Year	Winner	Head Coach	Score	Runner-up	Host/Site	Semifinalists
1974	Howard	Lincoln Phillips	2-1*	St. Louis	St. Louis	Hartwick 3, UCLA 1
1975	San Francisco	Steve Negoesco	4-0	So.Ill.	So.Ill.	Brown 2, Howard 0
1976	San Francisco	Steve Negoesco	1-0	Indiana	Penn	Hartwick 4, Clemson 3
1977	Hartwick	Jim Lennox	2-1	San Francisco	California	So.Ill. 3, Brown 2
1978-d	San Francisco	Steve Negoesco	4-3 (OT)	Indiana	Tampa	Clemson 6, Phi.Textile 2
1979	So.Illinois	Bob Guelker	3-2	Clemson	Tampa	Penn St. 2, Columbia 1
1980	San Francisco	Steve Negoesco	4-3 (OT)	Indiana	Tampa	Ala.A&M 2, Hartwick 0
1981	Connecticut	Joe Morrone	2-1 (OT)	Alabama A&M	Stanford	East.Ill. 4, Phi.Textile 2
1982	Indiana	Jerry Yeagley	2-1 (8 OT)	Duke	Ft.Lauderdale	UConn, So.Ill.
1983	Indiana	Jerry Yeagley	1-0 (2 OT)	Columbia	Ft.Lauderdale	UConn, Virginia
1984	Clemson	I.M. Ibrahim	2-1	Indiana	Seattle	Hartwick, UCLA
1985	UCLA	Sigi Schmid	1-0 (8 OT)	American	Seattle	Evansville, Hartwick
1986	Duke	John Rennie	1-0	Akron	Tacoma	Fresno St., Harvard
1987	Clemson	I.M. Ibrahim	2-0	San Diego St.	Clemson	Harvard, N. Carolina
1988	Indiana	Jerry Yeagley	1-0	Howard	Indiana	Portland, S.Carolina
1989-e	Santa Clara	Steve Sampson	1-1 (2 OT)	—	Rutgers	Indiana, Rutgers
	& Virginia	Bruce Arena		—		
1990-f	UCLA	Sigi Schmid	0-0 (PKs)	Rutgers	South Fla.	Evansville, N.C.St.
1991-g	Virginia	Bruce Arena	0-0 (PKs)	Santa Clara	Tampa	Indiana, St. Louis

Notes: a—game declared a draw due to inclement weather after regulation time; **b**—game declared a draw after two overtimes; **c**—Howard vacated title for using ineligible player; **d**—San Francisco vacated title for using ineligible player; **e**—game declared a draw due to inclement weather after two overtimes; **f**—UCLA wins on penalty kicks (4-3) after four overtimes; **g**—Virginia wins on penalty kicks (3-1) after four overtimes.

Women's NCAA Division I Champions

NCAA Division I women's champions since the first title was contested in 1982.
Multiple winner: North Carolina (9).

Year		Score	Runner-up	Year		Score	Runner-up
1982	North Carolina	2-0	Central Florida	1987	North Carolina	1-0	Massachusetts
1983	North Carolina	4-0	George Mason	1988	North Carolina	4-1	N.C.State
1984	North Carolina	2-0	Connecticut	1989	North Carolina	2-0	Colorado College
1985	George Mason	2-0	North Carolina	1990	North Carolina	6-0	Connecticut
1986	North Carolina	2-0	Colorado College	1991	North Carolina	3-1	Wisconsin

Hermann Trophy

Voted on by Division I college coaches and selected sportswriters and first presented in 1967 in the name of Robert Hermann, one of the founders of the North American Soccer League.
Multiple winners: Mike Seerey, Ken Snow and Al Trost (2).

Year		Year		Year	
1967	Dov Markus, LIU	1976	Glenn Myernick, Hartwick	1984	Amr Aly, Columbia
1968	Manuel Hernandez, S.Jose St.	1977	Billy Gazonas, Hartwick	1985	Tom Kain, Duke
1969	Al Trost, St.Louis	1978	Angelo DiBernardo, Indiana	1986	John Kerr, Duke
1970	Al Trost, St.Louis	1979	Jim Stamatis, Penn St.	1987	Bruce Murray, Clemson
1971	Mike Seerey, St.Louis	1980	Joe Morrone, Jr., UConn	1988	Ken Snow, Indiana
1972	Mike Seerey, St.Louis	1981	Armando Betancourt, Ind.	1989	Tony Meola, Virginia
1973	Dan Counce, St.Louis	1982	Joe Ulrich, Duke	1990	Ken Snow, Indiana
1974	Farrukh Quraishi, Oneonta	1983	Mike Jeffries, Duke	1991	Alexi Lalas, Rutgers
1975	Steve Ralbovsky, Brown				

Missouri Athletic Club Award

Voted on by 1,100 college and junior college coaches. First presented to the U.S. College Player of the Year in 1986 by the Missouri Athletic Club of St.Louis.
Multiple winner: Ken Snow (2).

Year		Year		Year	
1986	John Kerr, Duke	1988	Ken Snow, Indiana	1990	Ken Snow, Indiana
1987	John Harkes, Virginia	1989	Tony Meola, Virginia	1991	Alexi Lalas, Rutgers

Women's Hermann Trophy

Women's Division I Player of the year. Voted on by Division I college coaches and selected sportswriters and first presented in 1988 in the name of Robert Hermann, one of the founders of the North American Soccer League.

Year		Year		Year	
1988	Michelle Akers, Central Fla.	1990	April Kater, Massachusetts	1991	Kristine Lilly, N.Carolina
1989	Shannon Higgins, N.Carolina				

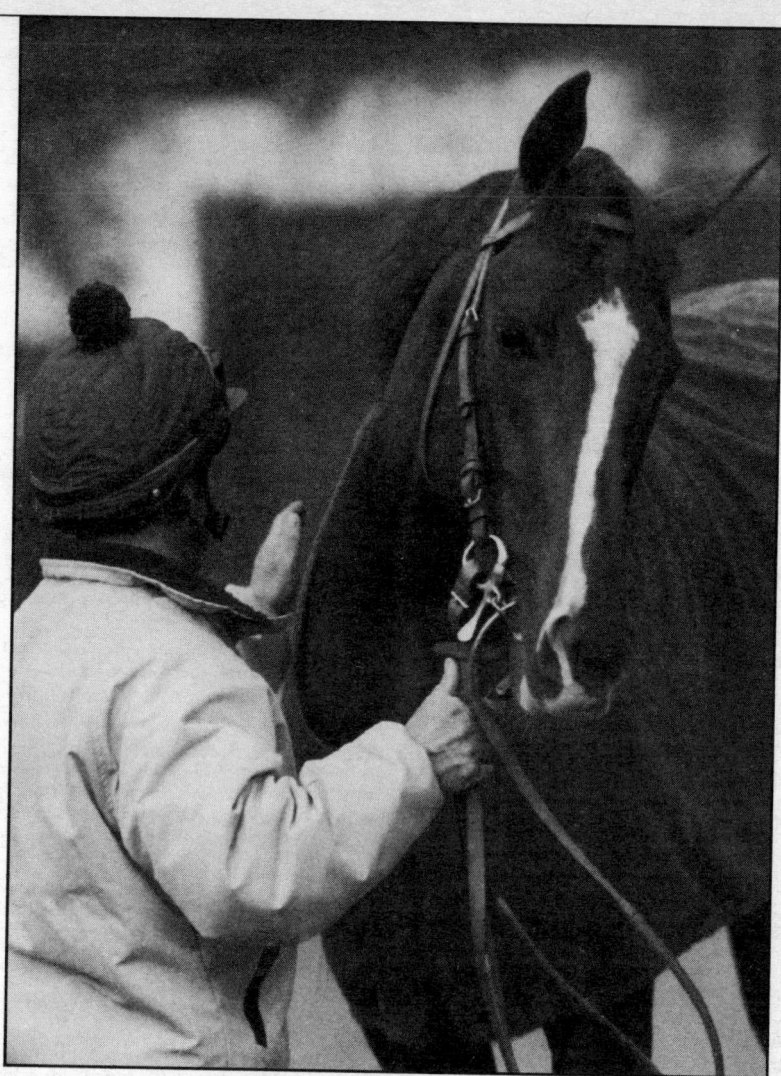

Wide World Photos

French wonder horse **Arazi** is groomed by his exercise rider after an early morning workout before the Kentucky Derby. A heavy favorite, he finished eighth.

HORSE RACING

Meltdown

Highly-touted French wonder horse Arazi fails to live up to his press clippings, finishing 8th in the Kentucky Derby.

The legend of Icarus is one of the favorite stories of classical mythology. The boy Icarus, with wings made of wax and feathers, soars skyward from Crete, ignoring warnings and his own common sense that wings of wax won't survive close contact with the sun. The legend describes how Icarus soars a little too high, his wings melt from the heat of the sun, and he plunges to his death in the sea.

No horse in recent years has soared higher than the flame-colored Arazi. The American-bred, French-trained colt arrived at Churchill Downs for the Breeders' Cup in November, 1991, after so dominating French two-year-old racing that some observers seemed to be convinced they saw wings sprouting from his flanks. Arazi's performance in the Juvenile had the rest of the world seeing wings, too. A startling burst of speed hurtled the colt past most of the top American two-year-olds and on to the most dominant victory in the race's history.

"Best since Secretariat," some people said. "Secretariat? Best since Man o'War!" others said. The glare of publicity intensified over the winter when Arazi's owners let it be known that he would return to Louisville in May for the Kentucky

Derby, and the other colts prepping for the big race seemed only to be preparing to compete for second place.

By May, the glare was a full-scale conflagration. Arazi had won a good prep race in France, and that was enough to further fan the flames. A record number of European and American journalists descended on Churchill Downs. They, and ordinary fans, thronged the track to watch his most routine workouts. Every move was chronicled and Arazi's wings seemed to lengthen by the minute.

But wings created in newspapers tend to be of the wax and feather variety, and the glare of publicity produces a heat that rivals that of the sun. Few horses could have lived up to the kind of expectations that were aroused, and Arazi proved not to be one of them.

Arazi broke well in the 118th Kentucky Derby, settled into 17th place, then began to move quickly on the far turn—all according to expectations. Pat Day, riding Lil E. Tee, had been through that six months before in the Breeders' Cup aboard another horse. On Derby Day, it seemed to be happening again.

"I thought, maybe I'm running for second," Day said after the race. "But this time he didn't sprint away from me." Where Arazi had once roared past rivals, this time he stalled. He crossed the finish line a tired eighth, and the wings were gone.

Sharon Smith is the author of *The Performance Mare* (Howell Book House) which is due out in the summer of 1993.

Wide World Photos

Lil E. Tee outruns **Casual Lies** down the stretch at Churchill Downs to win the 118th Kentucky Derby. The victory was jockey **Pat Day's** first at the Derby.

The winner was the 17-1 Lil E. Tee, who finished ahead of two other longshots, Casual Lies and Dance Floor. What happened to Arazi? Trainer François Boutin talked about the difficulty of the trip from France and the inability of Arazi to settle in at Churchill Downs. When reporters asked Boutin why such a horse failed so badly, the Fox of Chantilly responded, "You made him a superhorse, not me. So you explain."

Rider Pat Valenzuela thought the colt was working well during the week before the race. "I didn't think he could lose," he said. But lose he did.

Arazi flew back to France the next day, rested, and then started in the St. James Palace Stakes in England in early summer. He failed badly again. The wings seemed gone for good.

Meanwhile, Derby fifth place finisher Pine Bluff won the Preakness, besting the Canadian Alydeed and the Shelley Riley trained-and-owned Casual Lies. Lil E. Tee was fifth. The sport was still looking for a potential three-year-old champion.

After the Belmont Stakes, one appeared to have arrived. A.P. Indy, a son of Seattle Slew who'd been scratched from the Derby and hadn't made the Preakness, won a hard-fought victory over the Irish colt My Memoirs and Pine Bluff in 2:26 for the mile and a half, equaling the second-fastest time ever for America's most challenging classic race. Pine Bluff took home the million-dollar bonus for the best composite finish in the Triple Crown races, but A.P. Indy took home the honors as the top three-year-old in North America.

Over the summer, his position solidified, even though he rested. Pine Bluff retired with a leg injury, Casual Lies went out of action with a hoof injury suffered in the Belmont, Lil E. Tee underwent knee surgery, and Alydeed—after a superb victory in Canada's Queen's Plate—ran a couple of poor races and failed to win the Canadian Triple Crown that seemed his for the asking. A.P. Indy stood, not just at the top of the three-year-old rankings, but at the summit of the Top Ten list of best horses in the country.

But Technology won the Haskell at Monmouth and Thunder Rumble won the Travers at Saratoga, suggesting that they

Wide World Photos

After missing both the Kentucky Derby and the Preakness, **A.P. Indy** showed up at the Belmont and carried jockey **Eddie Delahoussaye** to the winner's circle.

weren't quite ready to concede a championship to A.P. Indy. Their performances were not enough to vault them to the top of the standings, but with big fall races and the Breeders' Classic to come on Oct. 31, none of their people had given up hope.

Their optimism seemed justified after the September 13 Molson Export Million at Woodbine in Ontario. Returning to the track for the first time in three months, A.P. Indy ran a feeble fifth to the Canadian gelding Benburb. Still, nobody was accusing the season's three-year-olds of being a weak group, as often happens when the crop isn't dominated by one or two horses.

The quality of American three-year-olds seemed to be confirmed in Europe over the summer, when the Irish-bred Dr Devious, a poor seventh in the Kentucky Derby, won the Epsom Derby. Second in that race was St. Jovite, an American-bred son of 1981 Kentucky Derby winner Pleasant Colony. A month later, St. Jovite turned the tables in the Irish Derby, beating Dr Devious by 12 lengths. A six-length victory over older horses in the King George VI and Queen Elizabeth Stakes at

Ascot in July made St. Jovite the unquestioned leader of the three-year-old crop as well as the most celebrated horse of any age in Europe.

St. Jovite lost little of his status when Dr Devious reversed the results again in the Champion Stakes in Dublin in September. The two raced head-and-head through a long stretch, with Dr Devious emerging as the nose victor. The rest of the field, most of them older horses, finished far behind. In Europe, 1992 was the year of the 3-year-old.

In America, the position at the top of the heap belonged to an older horse through the summer, although the identity of that horse changed from month to month. First up was the fast and consistent Best Pal. He had been a top three-year-old in 1991, and nobody was surprised when he won the final two legs of the rich Strub Series for four-year-olds at Santa Anita.

Best Pal earned the favorite's role for the $1 million Santa Anita Handicap and rewarded his supporters with a five length victory. When he added the Oaklawn Handicap to his list of wins, his position at the top seemed assured.

Trainer Gary Jones had nothing but admiration for his fine horse. "He's just an athlete and a half," Jones said. "He knows what he's supposed to do and he's the ultimate professional on the track."

Elsewhere, one of 1991's other top three-year-olds, Kentucky Derby winner Strike the Gold, was moving in the other direction. He was working on a 12-race losing streak, having lost every race he started in the year since the Derby. To be fair, Strike the Gold had earned nearly a million dollars in checks for finishing second, third, and fourth in major races, but even a million dollars couldn't quite erase the loser label.

An acrimonious partnership among his three owners resulted in Strike the Gold's sale at auction in May. Two of the three owners bought him back for $2.9 million. He began to pay them back four days later with a win over Fly So Free, Twilight Agenda, and Best Pal in the Pimlico Special.

Another win three weeks later in the Nassau County Handicap pushed Strike the Gold higher in the esteem of racing fans. With Best Pal sitting out the rest of the year with an injury, he became a primary contender for top horse. With his two wins and a respectable second in the Suburban Handicap, Strike the Gold clinched the $750,000 bonus for most points in the 9-race American Championship Racing Series. But subsequent losses in the Iselin and the Whitney left him far from the top of the heap.

Meanwhile, the mare Paseana moved directly to the top, thanks to seven straight wins over fillies and mares. Jolie's Halo became a contender, on the strength of a victory in the Iselin, as did Sultry Song, winner of the Hollywood Gold Cup and the Whitney. In the final race of the ACRS series, neither Paseana nor Jolie's Halo solidified a position. Jolie's Halo stumbled and lost his rider at the start, and Paseana finished a tired fifth to longshot Missionary Ridge.

Top performers in other divisions remained contenders for season-end honors: the grass runner Sky Classic, the three-year-old fillies Turnback the Alarm and November Snow, and the two-year-old filly Sky Beauty. But at summer's end, the resting three-year old A.P. Indy and the out-of-commission Best Pal were back on top—the likely contenders for Horse of the Year honors.

In harness racing, 1992 was a year for older horses to shine. The four-year-old pacing stallion Artsplace was undefeated through September, with two world records and four track records for his owners to boast about. In one of those efforts, in the Driscoll Series at The Meadowlands, Artsplace paced the fastest racing mile in harness history: 1:49⅖. His other wins included the U.S. Pacing Championship at Yonkers and the American-National at Sportsman's Park.

An older trotter also earned headlines. The five-year-old Canadian gelding Billyjojimbob had won fourteen of sixteen races, including the prestigious Elitlopp in Sweden, going into the 34th International Trot at Yonkers. But just past the half mile, Billyjo's driver Murray Bethour, trying to slow the eager horse, slowed him too much. The horse dropped to the ground, setting off a chain reaction that resulted in half the field dropping out. Although Billyjojimbob lay on the track for several minutes, he suffered only a cut and returned to training a few weeks later. Nor did psychological trauma result from the choking accident. Billyjo won his required qualifying heat by 21 lengths to prove that he was ready for more racing.

The three-year-old trotters tend to get the lion's share of publicity in harness racing, thanks largely to the fame and prestige of the Hambletonian, the sport's most celebrated event. A lot of fans expected 31-year-old Swede Per Eriksson, the trainer of the top three-year-old King Konch, to visit the winner's circle a second straight time in 1992. As the horses came down the stretch in the final, Erikkson cheered as he watched King Conch try to hold a lead he'd taken shortly after the start.

"I was hoarse from cheering," Eriksson said afterwards. "I was hoping for King Conch to hold. I didn't see the other one coming." The other one was Alf Palema, the forgotten half of Eriksson's two-horse entry. Alf snuck up on the rail, edging his more famous stablemate by a head. "I was surprised," Eriksson added, "but it was a good surprise."

Later in the summer, two more young trotting heroes emerged. Sierra Kosmos won the Beacon Course and the filly Imperfection, who once beat Sierra Kosmos, had taken over trotting headlines from the Hambletonian horses. But Alf Palema, nearly forgotten again after the Hambletonian, came back to beat them both at DuQuoin in September, securing his position at the top of the three-year-old trotting ladder.

On the pacing side, Western Hanover emerged as the star of summer with a win in the rich Cane Pace at Yonkers. The three-year-old colt added to his laurels with a victory in the Messenger Pace at Rosecroft Raceway in September. The victory pushed him to the top of the money earnings list, with more than a million dollars in purse money through August.

On the economic front, 1992 proved to be a year of mixed signals. Several years of recession even worse than that suffered by the country as a whole had left track operators, horse owners, and breeders reeling. But signs of optimism were everywhere. Del Mar in California, Hialeah in Florida, and Foxboro Park in Massachusetts all either opened or re-opened with multimillion dollar renovations and closed meets with attendance and handle statistics the operators claimed to be promising.

Still other racing jurisdictions seemed inclined to self-destruct. Florida faced potential disaster in July, when legislative inaction led to the expiration of most of the state's parimutuel laws. The Breeders' Cup, scheduled for Oct. 31 at Gulfstream Park, was threatened. Organizers began to look for a new site, but after legal assurances that sufficient law remained to allow a relatively normal parimutuel operation to continue, Cup officials decided to stay put.

Other tracks simply couldn't work out their problems. Longacres Park in Renton, Wash., was forced to close down after sixty years in operation. The track turned a $3 million profit in 1991, but that was not enough to prevent the property's owners from turning one of the country's most beautiful racetracks into an office park.

Even though the two major Thoroughbred yearling auctions saw yet another year of declining prices, there were nonetheless glimmers of hope. The July yearling sale at Keeneland in Lexington was disastrous for some breeders, with average prices down 19 percent over the previous year and 30 percent of the yearlings

Cordero Dismounts At Age 49

Basic contradictions exist in the sport of race riding. Few activities are more physically demanding than the process of controlling animals who weigh ten times what you do while urging them to run, in close company, at a speed of 35 miles an hour. You wear nothing more protective than a hard hat, and you repeat the exercise as many as nine times a day, six or seven days a week.

What's more, the sport doesn't forgive the few extra pounds of middle age. It's a dangerous, sometimes deadly, business. Yet no sport—not even golf—has enjoyed so many fine athletes performing so well at the highest levels into middle age and beyond. No other major sport has the equivalent of Bill Shoemaker winning a Kentucky Derby at the age of 54 and a $3 million Breeder's Cup at the age of 56. Laffit Pincay Jr. still adds to his title as the all-time money-winning jockey at the age of 46.

At 49, Angle Cordero, Jr. was not quite at his peak, but he wasn't far from it. Three times the leading American jockey, he was also a 14-time winner of the Saratoga riding title, and second only to Pincay in money earnings. Then on Jan. 12, Cordero was involved in the kind of accident that horrifies racing fans and makes a man pushing 50 reevaluate his career.

A four-horse spill at Aqueduct left Cordero hospitalized with severe internal injuries, including the loss of his spleen, as well as a broken arm and broken ribs. When he realized that he was facing a year off from race riding, he made the decision to retire. Cordero had always planned to turn to training horses when he stopped riding them, but the change came a little sooner than he had hoped.

"I'm really going to miss racing," he said. "Riding has been my life." At 5 feet 3 inches and 114 pounds, Cordero had remained in such good condition during the latter years of his career that some people found it hard to believe that he would stay retired, once the injuries of the terrible accident had fully healed.

Would he consider a comeback? "The only way I'll ever ride a horse in my life," he said, "will be if I have a horse in the

Wide World Photos

Angel Cordero Jr. throws some Black-Eyed Susans to the crowd after winning the 1980 Preakness aboard Codex. Cordero retired on May 7, with 7,077 career wins.

Kentucky Derby or the Breeder's Cup and the jockey gets sick before the race."

Racing loses a superb athlete with an incomparable will to win with the retirement of Angel Cordero, Jr. When asked how he would describe his riding, he said, "I always went out to win and I did my best." Cordero's best was good enough for 7,077 wins and $164,571,847 in purse money in 32 years of race riding.

In that time, he won the Kentucky Derby three times (1974, '76 and '85), the Preakness twice (1980 and '84) and the Belmont once (1976). He also won consecutive Eclipse Awards as the nation's top jockey in 1982 and '83.

Although Cordero rode such champions as Seattle Slew, Slew o' Gold, and Pleasant Colony to victory in some of North America's most prestigious races, history will probably remember him most for the tough ones—the bold, smart rides that had people talking more about the jockey than the horse.

There was the 1980 Preakness, when Cordero, aboard Codex, moved very wide entering the stretch, intimidating Kentucky

Derby winner Genuine Risk. Fans accused Cordero of "mugging" the popular filly, but Cordero's number was not taken down after Codex cruised to victory.

People are still trying to figure out how Cordero managed to go wire-to-wire with the sprinter Bold Forbes in the 1976 Belmont Stakes, personally exploding the myth that a horse has to be a distance-loving, come-from-behind horse to win the 1½-mile classic. Cordero fans are convinced that his biggest problem as a trainer will come in finding jockeys who ride with his own audacity.

Traditionally, top jockeys who have turned to training have struggled, notwithstanding John Longden's success with Majestic Prince, the 1969 Kentucky Derby winner. Cordero may also get inspiration from Bill Shoemaker. In spite of a car accident in April of 1991 that left him paralyzed from the neck down, Shoemaker has begun a successful training career. Through the summer of 1992, Shoemaker, the all-time winningest jockey who retired in 1990, had sent out eight different stakes winners—a record that long-time trainers might envy.

Wide World Photos

Artsplace, with **Catello Nanzi** in the sulky, paces a blistering 1:49⅖ mile at the Meadowlands on June 20, breaking the record set by Nihilator back in 1985.

failing to reach the reserve prices placed on them. The Saratoga sale in August also saw a 19 percent decrease in average price, but only 18 percent went home unsold. The figures compared favorably with the last few years, when plunging prices and soaring owner buy-backs pushed many breeders to the brink of bankruptcy.

But the trend of recent years that saw fewer European and Arab buyers spend millions on individual horses continued in 1992. The reasons: world-wide recession, better breeding stock in Europe, and the loss of the stallions that most appealed to overseas buyers. There was an additional loss on that front in April, when the 25-year-old Nijinsky II was destroyed in Kentucky due to the complications of advanced age. The son of the late Northern Dancer was the first of the truly international horses, a Canadian-bred who raced in Europe, then spent his stud career in Kentucky. He sired nearly 150 stakes winners in his brilliant career, and some of his offspring who never won stakes races were nearly as important to the economics of racing. It was a Nijinsky colt that brought the all-time record auction price of $13.1 million.

On Feb. 7, 1992, after less than a year in operation, *The Racing Times* ceased publication. Media mogul Robert Maxwell had promised to give the new past performance daily five years to break even, but the British publishing baron's mysterious death on Nov. 5, 1991, had cast doubt on that likelihood. The end came for editor Steven Crist's innovative and widely-admired paper after just 274 editions.

A brighter day for racing dawned six weeks later, when the bankrupt Calumet Farm was auctioned. Fears that the historic property might be subdivided or otherwise exploited were dispelled when prominent Thoroughbred owner and breeder Henryk de Kwiatkowski entered a winning bid of $17 million for the 763-acre farm, plus an additional $210,000 for the use of the Calumet name. De Kwiatkowski, who owned 1982 Horse of the Year Conquistador Cielo, promised to maintain the legendary name and property in the manner it deserves.

"The crowning achievement of my life," de Kwiatkowski said of his purchase of Calumet. Other people in the industry called it a happy ending to a very sad story. □

THE 1993 SPORTS ALMANAC — INFORMATION PLEASE

HORSE RACING STATISTICS

SEC A

THE SEASON IN REVIEW
1991–1992
THOROUGHBRED • HARNESS

PAGE 655

Thoroughbred Racing
Major Stakes Races

Winners of major stakes races from Sept. 22, 1991 through Sept. 19, 1992; (T) indicates turf race course; (F) indicates furlongs. See "Updates" for later results.

LATE 1991

Date	Race	Location	Miles	Winner	Jockey	Value to Winner
Sept. 22	Man o'War Stakes	Belmont	1⅜	Solar Splendor	Herb McCauley	$ 240,000
Sept. 22	Super Derby XII	La. Downs	1¼	Free Spirit's Joy	Calvin Borel	600,000
Oct. 5	Jockey Club Gold Cup	Belmont	1¼	Festin (ARG)	Eddie Delahoussaye	510,000
Oct. 6	Oak Tree Invitational	Santa Anita	1½ (T)	Filago	Pat Valenzuela	300,000
Oct. 6	Turf Classic	Belmont	1½ (T)	Solar Splendor	Herb McCauley	300,000
Oct. 6	L'arc de Triomphe	Longchamp	1½ (T)	Suave Dancer	Cash Asmussen	987,000
Oct. 12	Champagne Stakes	Belmont	1	Tri to Watch	Angel Cordero, Jr.	300,000
Oct. 18	Meadowlands Cup	Meadowlands	1⅛	Twilight Agenda	Chris McCarron	300,000
Oct. 19	Budweiser International	Laurel	1¼ (T)	Leariva	Edgar Prado	450,000
Oct. 20	Rothmans International	Woodbine	1½ (T)	Sky Classic	Paty Day	624,750
Oct. 26	NYRA Mile	Aqueduct	1	Rubiano	Jose Santos	300,000
Nov. 2	Breeders' Cup Classic	Churchill Downs	1¼	Black Tie Affair (IRE)	Jerry Bailey	1,560,000
Nov. 2	Breeders' Cup Turf	Churchill Downs	1½ (T)	Miss Alleged	Eric Legrix	1,040,000
Nov. 2	Breeders' Cup Distaff	Churchill Downs	1⅛	Dance Smartly	Pat Day	520,000
Nov. 2	Breeders' Cup Mile	Churchill Downs	1	Opening Verse	Pat Valenzuela	520,000
Nov. 2	Breeders' Cup Juvenile	Churchill Downs	1 1/16	Arazi	Pat Valenzuela	520,000
Nov. 2	Breeders' Cup Fillies	Churchill Downs	1 1/16	Pleasant Stage	Eddie Delahoussaye	520,000
Nov. 2	Breeders' Cup Sprint	Churchill Downs	6 F	Sheikh Albadou (GB)	Pat Eddery	500,000
Nov. 23	Hawthorne Gold Cup	Hawthorne	1¼	Sunny Sunrise	Chris Antley	309,840
Nov. 24	Japan Cup	Tokyo Racecourse	1½	Golden Pheasant	Gary Stevens	1,160,328
Dec. 15	Hollywood Turf Cup	Hollywood	1½	Miss Alleged	Chris McCarron	275,000
Dec. 21	Hollywood Starlet	Hollywood	1 1/16	Magical Maiden	Gary Stevens	138,105
Dec. 22	Hollywood Futurity	Hollywood	1 1/16	A.P. Indy	Eddie Delahoussaye	329,780

1992 (through Sept. 19)

Date	Race	Location	Miles	Winner	Jockey	Value to Winner
Jan. 4	Flamingo Stakes	Hialeah	1⅛	Pistols and Roses	H. Castillo, Jr.	$ 280,000
Jan. 25	El Camino Real Derby	Bay Meadows	1 1/16	Casual Lies	Alan Patterson	165,000
Feb. 1	Donn Handicap*	Gulfstream	1⅛	Sea Cadet	Alex Solis	300,000
Feb. 9	Charles H. Strub Stakes	Santa Anita	1¼	Best Pal	Kent Desormeaux	275,000
Feb. 22	Fountain of Youth St.	Gulfstream	1 1/16	Dance Floor	Chris Antley	150,258
Mar. 7	Santa Anita Handicap*	Santa Anita	1¼	Best Pal	Kent Desormeaux	550,000
Mar. 7	Gulfstream Park Hand.	Gulfstream	1¼	Sea Cadet	Alex Solis	180,000
Mar. 14	Florida Derby	Gulfstream	1⅛	Technology	Jerry Bailey	300,000
Mar. 28	Jim Beam Stakes	Turfway	1⅛	Lil E. Tee	Pat Day	300,000
Mar. 29	San Luis Rey Stakes	Santa Anita	1½	Fly Till Dawn	Laffit Pincay, Jr.	179,000
Apr. 4	Santa Anita Derby	Santa Anita	1⅛	A.P. Indy	Eddie Delahoussaye	275,000
Apr. 11	Blue Grass Stakes	Keeneland	1⅛	Pistols and Roses	Jacinto Vasquez	325,000
Apr. 11	California Derby	Golden Gate	1⅛	Treekster	Gary Boulanger	165,000
Apr. 11	Oaklawn Handicap*	Oaklawn	1⅛	Best Pal	Kent Desormeaux	300,000
Apr. 17	Apple Blossom Handicap	Oaklawn	1 1/16	Paseana (ARG)	Chris McCarron	300,000
Apr. 18	Wood Memorial Invit.	Aqueduct	1⅛	Devil His Due	Mike Smith	300,000
Apr. 18	Arkansas Derby	Oaklawn	1⅛	Pine Bluff	Jerry Bailey	300,000
Apr. 26	San Juan Capistrano	Santa Anita	1¾ (T)	Fly Till Dawn	Pat Valenzuela	275,000

Thoroughbred Racing (Cont.)
Major Stakes Races

Date	Race	Location	Miles	Winner	Jockey	Value to Winner
May 2	Kentucky Derby	Churchill Downs	1¼	Lil E. Tee	Pat Day	$ 724,800
May 9	Pimlico Special*	Pimlico	1³⁄₁₆	Strike The Gold	Craig Perret	420,000
May 16	Preakness Stakes	Pimlico	1	Pine Bluff	Chris McCarron	484,120
May 23	Acorn Stakes	Belmont	1	Prospectors Delite	Pat Day	113,400
May 25	Hollywood Turf Handicap	Hollywood	1¼ (T)	Quest for Fame	Gary Stevens	275,000
May 25	Jersey Derby	Garden State	1⅛	American Chance	Pat Day	180,000
June 3	EverReady English Derby	Epsom Downs	1½ (T)	Dr Devious (IRE)	John Reid	662,075
June 6	Belmont Stakes	Belmont	1½	A.P. Indy	Eddie Delahoussaye	458,880
June 6	Nassau County Handicap*	Belmont	1⅛	Strike the Gold	Craig Perret	300,000
June 7	Mother Goose Stakes	Belmont	1⅛	Turnback the Alarm	Chris Antley	120,000
June 27	Hollywood Gold Cup*	Hollywood	1¼	Sultry Song	Jerry Bailey	550,000
June 28	Caesars Int'l Handicap	Atlantic City	1³⁄₁₆(T)	Sky Classic	Pat Day	300,000
June 28	Budweiser Irish Derby	Curragh	1½	St. Jovite	Christy Roche	616,615
July 5	Queen's Plate	Woodbine	1¼	Alydeed	Craig Perret	228,900
July 11	Coaching Club Am. Oaks	Belmont	1¼	Turnback the Alarm	Chris Antley	150,000
July 18	Suburban Handicap*	Belmont	1¼	Pleasant Tap	Eddie Delahoussaye	300,000
July 25	King George VI and Queen Elizabeth Diamond Stakes	Ascot	1½	St. Jovite	Stephen Craine	487,168
July 26	Prince of Wales Stakes	Fort Erie	1³⁄₁₆	Benburb	Larry Attard	109,700
Aug. 2	Haskell Invitational	Monmouth	1⅛	Technology	Jerry Bailey	300,000
Aug. 8	Philip Iselin Handicap*	Monmouth	1⅛	Jolie's Halo	Edgar Prado	300,000
Aug. 15	Alabama Stakes	Saratoga	1¼	November Snow	Chris Antley	120,000
Aug. 16	Breeders' Stakes	Woodbine	1½ (T)	Blitzer	Don Seymour	180,000
Aug. 22	Travers Stakes	Saratoga	1¼	Thunder Rumble	Herb McCauley	600,000
Aug. 29	Whitney Handicap	Saratoga	1⅛	Sultry Song	Jerry Bailey	150,000
Aug. 30	Pacific Classic*	Del Mar	1¼	Missionary Ridge (GB)	Kent Desormeaux	550,000
Sept. 5	Beverly D. Stakes	Arlington	1³⁄₁₆	Kostroma (IRE)	Kent Desormeaux	300,000
Sept. 6	Arlington Million	Arlington	1¼	Dear Doctor (FR)	Cash Asmussen	600,000
Sept.13	Molson Export Million	Woodbine	1⅛	Benburb	Richard Dos Ramos	600,000
Sept.19	Woodward Stakes	Belmont	1⅛	Sultry Song	Jerry Bailey	300,000
Sept.19	Man o'War Stakes	Belmont	1⅜ (T)	Solar Splendor	Herb McCauley	240,000

*One of nine races in the 2nd annual American Championship Racing Series.

TRC National Thoroughbred Poll
(Released Sept. 21, 1992)

Through Week 34 of the 1992 racing season. Poll taken by Thoroughbred Racing Communications, Inc., and based on the votes of sports and Thoroughbred racing media. First place votes are in parentheses.

	Pts	Owner (Trainer)	'92 Record Sts—1-2-3	Earnings	Last Start (Date, Distance)
1. Sultry Song (12)	265	Live Oak Plantation (Pat Kellly)	6—3-1-1	$1,067,700	1st—Woodward Stakes (9/19, 1⅛ mi.)
2. Sky Classic (6)	240	Sam-Son Farms (Jim Day)	7—4-2-0	955,482	2nd—Arlington Million (9/6, 1¼ mi.-T)
3. Best Pal (10)	224	Golden Eagle Farm (Gary Jones)	5—4-0-0	1,297,000	4th—Pimlico Special (5/9, 1³⁄₁₆ mi.)
4. Paseana-ARG	203	Sidney Craig (Ron McAnally)	7—6-0-0	905,575	5th—Pacific Classic (8/30, 1¼ mi.)
5. A.P. Indy (4)	196	Tomonori Tsurumaki (Neil Drysdale)	5—4-0-0	960,560	5th—Molson Million (9/13, 1⅛ mi.)
6. Pleasant Tap	165	Buckland Farm (Christopher Speckert)	8—3-4-0	812,414	2nd—Woodward Stakes (9/19, 1⅛ mi.)
7. Flawlessly	96	Harbor View Farm (Charlie Whittingham)	2—2-0-0	371,500	1st—Ramona Handicap (8/15, 1⅛ mi.-T)
8. Thunder Rumble	65	Braeburn Farm (Richard O'Connell)	8—5-0-1	850,902	5th—Woodward Stakes (9/19, 1⅛ mi.)
9. Kosrroma—IRE	63	deBurgh & Sangster (Gary Jones)	5—3-1-0	597,000	1st—Beverly D. Stakes (9/5, 1³⁄₁₆ mi.-T)
10. Sky Beauty	45	Georgia Hofmann (Allan Jerkens)	5—4-0-1	197,640	1st—Matron Stakes (9/19, 7 furlongs)

Others receiving votes: 11. Strike the Gold (20); **12.** Dear Doctor-FRA and Jolie's Halo (18); **14.** Rubiano and Versailles Treaty (17); **16.** Benbarb (15); **17.** Solar Splendor (14); **18.** Pine Bluff (12); **19.** Missy's Mirage (10); **20.** Out of Place and Sea Cadet (8); **22.** Dr Devious, Gilded Time, Missionary Ridge, November Snow and Strolling Along (5); **27.** Furiously and Lil E. Tee (4); **29.** Bolulight and Fly Till Dawn (3); **31.** Eliza and Navarone (1).

The 1992 Triple Crown

Thoroughbred racing's Triple Crown for 3-year-olds consists of the Kentucky Derby, Preakness Stakes and Belmont Stakes run over six weeks in May and June. Pine Bluff won the 1992 Triple Crown Challenge (and a $1 million bonus) as the best overall performer entered in all three races by winning the Preakness and finishing 3rd in the Belmont after coming in 4th in the Derby. Casual Lies was the only other horse to run in all three races, finishing 2nd in the Derby, 3rd in the Preakness and 5th in the Belmont.

118TH KENTUCKY DERBY

Grade I for three-year-olds; 8th race at Churchill Downs in Louisville. **Date**—May 2, 1992; **Distance**—1 1/4 miles; **Stakes purse**—$974,800 ($724,800 to winner); **Track**—fast; **Off**—5:34 P.M. EDT.

Winner—Lil E. Tee; **Time**—2:03; **Won**—Driving; **Sire**—At the Threshold; **Dam**—Eileen's Moment (by For the Moment); **Breeder**—Littman Larry (Pa.).

Finish		PP	To $1	Jockey	Trainer	Owner
1—1	Lil E. Tee	10	16.80	Pat Day	Lynn Whiting	W. Cal Partee
2—3 1/4	Casual Lies	4	29.90	Gary Stevens	Shelley Riley	Shelley Riley
3—2	Dance Floor	16	33.30	Chris Antley	D. Wayne Lukas	Oaktown Sable
4—1	Conte Di Savoya	8	21.30	Shane Sellers	Leroy Jolley	Jaime Carrion
5—3/4	Pine Bluff	12	10.50	Craig Perret	Tom Bohannan	Loblolly Stable
6—head	Al Sabin	1	33.30	Cory Nakatani	D. Wayne Lukas	Henryk de Kwiatkowski
7—head	Dr Devious	15	20.80	Chris McCarron	Ron McAnally	Sidney Craig
8—2	Arazi	17	.90	Pat Valenzuela	Francois Boutin	Allen Paulson & Sheikh Moh. al Maktoum
9—2 1/4	My Luck Runs North	14	12.80	Ricardo Lopez	Angel Medina	Melvin Benitez
10—2	Technology	2	4.20	Jerry Bailey	Sonny Hine	Scott Savin
11—nose	West by West	11	12.80	Jean-Luc Samyn	Rusty Arnold	John Peace
12—6	Devil His Due	6	21.60	Mike Smith	Allen Jerkens	Lion Crest Stable
13—3/4	Thyer	5	12.80	Christy Roche	James Bolger	Sheikh Maktoum al Maktoum
14—neck	Ecstatic Ride	13	12.80	Julie Krone	Hal Griffitt	Dandar Farm & Joan Rich
15—3 1/2	Sir Pinder	9	12.80	Randy Romero	Emanuel Tortora	James Lewis
16—1 1/2	Pistols and Roses	7	13.40	Jacinto Vasquez	George Gianos	Willis Stables
17—2 3/4	Snappy Landing	3	12.80	Jorge Velasquez	Dennis Manning	Frederick McNeary
18	Disposal	18	12.80	Alex Solis	Bruce Headley	Bramble Farm

Times—0:23 2/5; 0:47; 1:12; 1:37; 2:03.
$2 Mutuel Prices—#7 Lil E. Tee ($35.60, 12.60, 7.60); #3 Casual Lies ($22.00, 11.60); #1 Dance Floor ($12.80).
Scratched—A.P. Indy; **Overweights**—none; **Attendance**—132,543; **TV Rating**—10.3/30 share (ABC).

117TH PREAKNESS STAKES

Grade I for three-year-olds; 10th race at Pimlico in Baltimore. **Date**—May 16, 1992; **Distance**—1 3/16 miles; **Stakes purse**—$744,800 ($484,120 to winner); **Track**—good; **Off**—5:34 P.M. EDT.

Winner—Pine Bluff; **Time**—1:55 3/5; **Won**—Driving; **Sire**—Danzig; **Dam**—Rowdy Angel (By Halo); **Breeder**—Loblolley Stable (Ky.).

Finish		PP	To $1	Jockey	Trainer	Owner
1—3/4	Pine Bluff	4	3.50	Chris McCarron	Tom Bohannan	Loblolly Stable
2—1 1/2	Alydeed	12	5.40	Craig Perret	Roger Attfield	Kinghaven Farms
3—3/4	Casual Lies	8	5.60	Gary Stevens	Shelley Riley	Shelley Riley
4—2	Dance Floor	14	9.20	Chris Antley	D. Wayne Lukas	Oaktown Stable
5—8 1/2	Lil E. Tee	9	4.20	Pat Day	Lynn Whiting	W. Cal Partee
6—1 3/4	Technology	2	6.80	Jerry Bailey	Sonny Hine	Scott Savin
7—1 1/4	Agincourt	1	70.10	Art Madrid, Jr.	Nick Zito	Robert Perez
8—1 1/4	Dash for Dotty	10	42.10	Tommy Turner	Bill Donovan	Rainbow Stable
9—4	Careful Gesture	6	68.00	Bobby Lester	Elbert Dixon	Elbert Dixon
10—1 1/2	Fortune's Gone	11	79.50	Rene Douglas	Angel Medina	R.W. Tweed
11—neck	Big Sur	5	30.70	Mike Smith	D. Wayne Lukas	W.T. Young
12—1 1/2	My Luck Runs North	7	33.10	Edgar Prado	Angel Medina	Melvin Benitez
13—1 3/4	Conte Di Savoya	3	10.50	Shane Sellers	Leroy Jolley	Jaime Carrion
14—	Speakerphone	13	17.90	Jo Jo Ladner	Dean Gaudet	Israel Cohen

Times—0:23 1/5; 0:46 1/5; 1:10 4/5; 1:36; 1:55 3/5.
$2 Mutuel Prices—#4 Pine Bluff ($9.00, 5.80, 4.40); #12 Alydeed ($7.60, 3.80); #8 Casual Lies ($4.20).
Scratched—none; **Overweights**—none; **Attendance**—96,865; **TV Rating**—6.5/19 share (ABC).

The 1992 Triple Crown (Cont.)

124TH BELMONT STAKES

Grade I for three-year-olds; 8th race at Belmont Park in Elmont, NY. **Date**—June 6, 1992; **Distance**—1½ miles; **Stakes purse**—$1,764,800 ($458,880 to winner); **Track**—good; **Off**—5:31 P.M. EDT.
Winner—A.P. Indy; **Time**—2:26; **Won**—Driving; **Sire**—Seattle Slew; **Dam**—Weekend Surprise (by Secretariat); **Breeder**—William S. Farish and W.S. Kilroy (Ky.).

Finish		PP	To $1	Jockey	Trainer	Owner
1—¾	A.P. Indy	1	1.10	Eddie Delahoussaye	Neil Drysdale	Tomonori Tsurumaki
2—neck	My Memoirs	9	18.00	Jerry Bailey	Richard Hannon	Team Valor
3—13¼	Pine Bluff	3	3.80	Chris McCarron	Tom Bohannan	Loblolly Stable
4—1¾	Cristofori	6	7.50	Steve Cauthen	Andre Fabre	Sheikh Mohammed al Maktoum
5—4	Casual Lies	2	4.60	Gary Stevens	Shelley Riley	Shelley Riley
6—6½	Colony Light	11	20.70	Julie Krone	Rusty Arnold	John Peace
7—3	a-Agincourt	7	24.30	Art Madrid, Jr.	Nick Zito	Robert Perez
8—23	Montreal Marty	10	24.20	Jose Santos	Scotty Schulhofer	Vendome Stable
9—9½	a-Robert's Hero	8	24.30	Jorge Chavez	David Monaci	Robert Perez
10—	Al Sabin	4	21.90	Laffit Pincay, Jr.	D. Wayne Lukas	Henryk de Kwiatkowski
11—Eased	Jacksonport	5	44.40	Jean Cruguet	Murray Garren	Murray Garren

Times—0:23⅕; 0:47; 1:11⅘; 1:36⅕; 2:01⅕; 2:26.
$2 Mutuel Prices—#1 A.P. Indy ($4.20, 3.80, 3.00); #9 My Memoirs ($11.60, 6.60), #3 Pine Bluff ($4.20).
Scratched—none; **Overweights**—none; **(a)**—coupled; **Attendance**—50,204; **TV Rating**—5.1/16 share (ABC).

1991-92 Money Leaders

Official Top 10 standings for 1991 and unofficial Top 10 standings for 1992, through Sept.20, as compiled by *The Daily Racing Form*.

FINAL 1991

Horses	Age	Sts	1st	Earnings
Dance Smartly	3	8	8	$2,876,821
Farma Way	4	11	5	2,598,350
Hansel	3	9	4	2,565,680
Black Tie Affair (IRE)	5	10	7	2,483,540
Festin (ARG)	5	11	3	2,003,250
Twilight Agenda	5	11	6	1,563,600
Strike the Gold	3	12	2	1,443,850
Miss Alleged	4	3	2	1,345,000
In Excess (IRE)	4	8	5	1,328,800
Golden Pheasant	5	4	1	1,302,125

Jockeys	Mts	1st	Earnings
Chris McCarron	1440	265	$14,456,073
Pat Day	1405	430	14,400,348
†Gary Stevens	1499	241	13,652,132
Eddie Delahoussaye	1363	214	11,751,061
Jerry Bailey	1111	204	11,290,461
Mike Smith	1759	339	10,808,036
†Angel Cordero, Jr	1341	238	9,383,904
Corey Nakatani	1514	213	8,991,276
Laffit Pincay, Jr	1435	217	8,326,627
Pat Valenzuela	1055	197	8,269,924

†Includes foreign racing.

Trainers	Sts	1st	Earnings
D.Wayne Lucas	1497	289	$15,942,223
Ron McAnally	620	106	8,339,830
Jim Day	285	77	6,991,902
Bobby Frankel	309	63	6,186,966
Charlie Whittingham	443	61	5,378,204
Scotty Schulhofer	460	80	4,347,432
Gary Jones	403	80	4,233,932
Bill Mott	417	83	3,918,346
Frank Brothers	247	41	3,484,108
Jack Van Berg	775	102	3,403,972

1992 (through Sept.20)

Horses	Age	Sts	1st	Earnings
Pine Bluff	3	6	3	$1,970,896
*Strike the Gold	4	11	2	1,733,176
Best Pal	4	5	4	1,672,000
Lil E. Tee	3	6	3	1,148,000
Sultry Song	4	6	3	1,067,700
A.P. Indy	3	5	4	960,560
Sky Classic	5	7	4	955,482
Paseana (ARG)	5	7	6	930,550
Technology	3	9	4	869,390
Thunder Rumble	3	8	5	850,902

*Includes ACRS bonus money.

Jockeys	Mts	1st	Earnings
Kent Desormeaux	1236	280	$10,450,236
Chris McCarron	891	150	9,397,588
Eddie Delahoussaye	1071	218	8,445,289
Jerry Bailey	871	185	8,437,079
Pat Day	956	225	8,391,987
Gary Stevens	1163	183	7,681,645
Mike Smith	1189	231	7,486,045
Julie Krone	1149	230	6,580,999
Alex Solis	1250	183	6,508,651
Pat Valenzuela	894	164	6,236,097

Trainers	Sts	1st	Earnings
D.Wayne Lucas	1010	176	$6,837,193
Ron McAnally	483	81	5,584,762
Bobby Frankel	247	41	4,795,754
Gary Jones	293	62	4,029,200
Jim Day	232	49	3,031,021
Allen Jerkens	305	65	2,833,752
Tom Bohannan	131	23	2,514,524
Scotty Schulhofer	308	61	2,504,148
Richard Mandella	285	61	2,469,605
Charlie Whittingham	269	28	2,375,250

Harness Racing
Major Stakes Races

Winners of major stakes races from Sept. 19, 1991 through Sept. 12, 1992; all paces and trots cover one mile; (BC) indicates year-end Breeders' Crown series.

LATE 1991

Date	Race	Raceway	Winner	Driver	Value to Winner
Sept.21	Little Brown Jug	Delaware,OH	Precious Bunny	Jack Moiseyev	$228,334
Oct. 6	Kentucky Futurity	The Red Mile	Whiteland Janice	Michel Lachance	67,514
Oct. 11	BC Aged Horse/Geld.Pace	The Meadows	Camluck	Michel Lachance	173,625
Oct. 11	BC Aged Horse/Geld.Trot	The Meadows	Billyjojimbob	Paul MacDonell	197,000
Oct. 11	BC Aged Mare Pace	The Meadows	Delinquent Account	Bill O'Donnell	150,000
Oct. 11	BC Aged Mare Trot	The Meadows	Me Maggie	Berndt Lindstedt	150,000
Oct. 25	BC 2-Yr-Old Colt/Geld.Trot	Pompano	King Conch	Bill Gale	150,000
Oct. 25	BC 3-Yr-Old Colt/Geld.Trot	Pompano	Giant Victory	Ron Pierce	182,703
Oct. 25	BC 2-Yr-Old Filly Trot	Pompano	Armbro Keepsake	John Campbell	150,000
Oct. 25	BC 3-Yr-Old Filly Trot	Pompano	Twelve Speed	Ron Waples	155,027
Oct. 25	BC 2-Yr-Old Filly Pace	Pompano	Hazelton Kay	John Campbell	158,000
Oct. 25	BC 3-Yr-Old Filly Pace	Pompano	Miss Easy	John Campbell	150,000
Oct. 25	BC 2-Yr-Old Colt/Geld.Pace	Pompano	Digger Almahurst	Doug Brown	188,500
Oct. 25	BC 3-Yr-Old Colt/Geld.Pace	Pompano	Three Wizzards	Bill Gale	178,703
Nov. 23	Governor's Cup	Garden St.	Western Hanover	Bill Fahy	292,150

1992 (through Sept. 12)

Date	Race	Raceway	Winner	Driver	Value to Winner
May 31	Elitlopp (SWE)	Solvalla	Billyjojimbob	Murray Brethour	$161,440
June 20	North America Cup	Greenwood	Safely Kept	Michel Lachance	500,000
July 10	Meadowlands Pace	Meadowlands	Carlsbad Cam	Rod Allen	500,000
July 11	Yonkers Trot	Yonkers	Magic Lobell*	Lorenzo Baldi	138,849
			& McCluckey*	Michel Lachance	138,849
Aug. 1	Hambletonian	Meadowlands	Alf Palema	Mickey McNichol	575,000
Aug. 16	Woodrow Wilson Pace	Meadowlands	America's Pastime	Wally Hennessey	389,400
Aug. 16	Sweetheart Pace	Meadowlands	Immortality	John Campbell	334,375
Aug. 29	Cane Pace	Yonkers	Western Hanover	Bill Fahy	182,175
Sept.12	Messenger Stakes	Rosecroft	Western Hanover	Bill Fahy	183,375

1991-92 Money Leaders

Official Top 10 standings for 1991 and unofficial Top 10 standings for 1992 through Sept.22, as compiled by the U.S.Trotting Association.

FINAL 1991

Horses	Age	Sts	1st	Earnings
Precious Bunny	3pc	25	20	$2,217,222
Giant Victory	3tc	20	9	1,130,488
Die Laughing	3pc	15	7	1,022,064
Artsplace	3pc	18	10	972,487
Sportsmaster	2pc	16	8	727,563
Western Hanover	2pc	14	8	697,332
Somatic	3tc	24	9	659,427
Miss Easy	3pf	15	10	648,700
Crowns Invitation	3tc	21	13	566,377
Odds Against	Aph	21	8	546,890

1992 (through Sept.22)

Horses	Age	Sts	1st	Earnings
Western Hanover	3pc	17	12	$1,326,330
Alf Palema	3tc	15	5	1,038,746
Carlsbad Cam	3pc	17	3	896,554
Safely Kept	3pc	15	4	682,890
Artsplace	Aph	14	14	648,275
Immortality	2pf	11	9	630,235
Direct Flight	3pc	14	6	577,566
Shore Patrol	3pc	17	5	511,400
King Conch	3tc	11	6	493,360
Imperfection	3tf	16	8	468,004

Drivers	Sts	1st	Purses
Jack Moiseyev	3896	769	$9,568,468
John Campbell	2133	441	9,340,737
Michel Lachance	2050	290	5,887,933
Cat Manzi	3350	548	4,793,239
Ron Pierce	2162	309	4,115,407
Herve Filion	3891	646	4,096,053
Doug Brown	1697	353	3,976,375
Ron Waples	1261	193	3,893,375
Dave Magee	2354	452	3,567,019
Bill Gale	1206	199	3,285,364

Drivers	Sts	1st	Purses
Jack Moiseyev	2905	579	$6,116,803
John Campbell	1835	328	6,092,535
Michel Lachance	1790	273	5,446,350
Cat Manzi	2597	392	3,938,439
Bill Fahy	1131	157	3,593,943
Doug Brown	1421	271	3,159,415
Dave Magee	2052	415	3,072,926
Ron Pierce	1757	232	2,986,067
Walter Case, Jr	2044	583	2,817,334
Mickey McNichol	1677	163	2,549,038

THE 1993 INFORMATION PLEASE SPORTS ALMANAC

HORSE RACING
STATISTICS
THROUGH THE YEARS
1867-1992
THOROUGHBRED • HARNESS

SEC B

PAGE 660

Thoroughbred Racing
The Triple Crown

The term "Triple Crown" was coined by sportswriter Charles Hatton while covering the 1930 victories of Gallant Fox in the Kentucky Derby, Preakness Stakes and Belmont Stakes. Before then, only Sir Barton (1919) had won all three races in the same year. Since then, nine horses have won the Triple Crown. Two trainers, James (Sunny Jim) Fitzsimmons and Ben A.Jones, have saddled two Triple Crown champions, while Eddie Arcaro is the only jockey to ride two champions.

Year		Jockey	Trainer	Owner	Sire/Dam
1919	**Sir Barton**	Johnny Loftus	H.Guy Bedwell	J.K.L.Ross	Star Shoot/Lady Sterling
1930	**Gallant Fox**	Earle Sande	J.E. Fitzsimmons	Belair Stud	Sir Gallahad III/Marguerite
1935	**Omaha**	Willie Saunders	J.E. Fitzsimmons	Belair Stud	Gallant Fox/Flambino
1937	**War Admiral**	Chas.Kurtsinger	George Conway	Samuel Riddle	Man O'War/Brushup
1941	**Whirlaway**	Eddie Arcaro	Ben A.Jones	Calumet Farm	Blenheim II/Dustwhirl
1943	**Count Fleet**	Johnny Longden	Don Cameron	Mrs.J.D.Hertz	Reigh Count/Quickly
1946	**Assault**	Warren Mehrtens	Max Hirsch	King Ranch	Bold Venture/Igual
1948	**Citation**	Eddie Arcaro	Ben A.Jones	Calumet Farm	Bull Lea/Hydroplane II
1973	**Secretariat**	Ron Turcotte	Lucien Laurin	Chenery Estate	Bold Ruler/Somethingroyal
1977	**Seattle Slew**	Jean Cruguet	Billy Turner	Karen Taylor	Bold Reasoning/My Charmer
1978	**Affirmed**	Steve Cauthen	Laz Barrera	Harbor View Farm	Exclusive Native/Won't Tell You

Note: Gallant Fox (1930) is the only Triple Crown winner to sire another Triple Crown winner, Omaha (1935). Wm.Woodward Sr., owner of Belair Stud, was breeder-owner of both horses and both were trained by Sunny Jim Fitzsimmons.

Triple Crown Near Misses

Thirty-nine horses have won two legs of the Triple Crown. Of those, a dozen won the Kentucky Derby (KD) and Preakness Stakes (PS) only to be beaten in the Belmont Stakes (BS). Two others, Burgoo King (1932) and Bold Venture (1936), each won the Derby and Preakness but were forced out of the Belmont with the same injury—a bowed tendon—that effectively ended their racing careers. In 1978, Alydar finished second to Affirmed in all three races, the only time that has happened; (*) indicates won on disqualification.

Year		KD	PS	BS	Year		KD	PS	BS
1877	**Cloverbrook**	DNS	won	won	1958	**Tim Tam**	won	won	2nd
1878	**Duke of Magenta**	DNS	won	won					
1880	**Grenada**	DNS	won	won	1961	**Carry Back**	won	won	7th
1881	**Saunterer**	DNS	won	won	1963	**Chateaugay**	won	2nd	won
1895	**Belmar**	DNS	won	won	1964	**Northern Dancer**	won	won	3rd
					1966	**Kauai King**	won	won	4th
1920	**Man O'War**	DNS	won	won	1967	**Damascus**	3rd	won	won
1922	**Pillory**	DNS	won	12th	1968	**Forward Pass**	won*	won	2nd
1923	**Zev**	won	12th	won	1969	**Majestic Prince**	won	won	2nd
1931	**Twenty Grand**	won	2nd	won	1971	**Canonero II**	won	won	4th
1932	**Burgoo King**	won	won	DNS	1972	**Riva Ridge**	won	4th	won
1936	**Bold Venture**	won	won	DNS	1974	**Little Current**	5th	won	won
1939	**Johnstown**	won	5th	won	1976	**Bold Forbes**	won	3rd	won
					1979	**Spectacular Bid**	won	won	3rd
1940	**Bimelech**	2nd	won	won					
1942	**Shut Out**	won	5th	won	1981	**Pleasant Colony**	won	won	3rd
1944	**Pensive**	won	won	2nd	1984	**Swale**	won	7th	won
1949	**Capot**	2nd	won	won	1987	**Alysheba**	won	won	4th
1950	**Middleground**	won	2nd	won	1988	**Risen Star**	3rd	won	won
1953	**Native Dancer**	2nd	won	won	1989	**Sunday Silence**	won	won	2nd
1955	**Nashua**	2nd	won	won	1991	**Hansel**	10th	won	won
1956	**Needles**	won	2nd	won					

The Triple Crown Challenge

Seeking to make the Triple Crown more than just a media event and to insure that owners would not be attracted to more lucrative races, officials at Churchill Downs, the Maryland Jockey Club and the New York Racing Association created Triple Crown Productions in 1985 and announced that a $1 million bonus would be given to the horse that performs best in the Kentucky Derby, Preakness Stakes and Belmont Stakes. Furthermore, a bonus of $5 million would be presented to any horse winning all three races. Chrysler Motors has been the sponsor since 1987.

Revised in 1991, the rules state that the winning horse must: 1. finish all three races; 2. earn points by finishing first, second, third or fourth in at least one of the three races; and 3. earn the highest number of points based on the following system—10 points to win, five to place, three to show and one to finish fourth. In the event of a tie, the $1 million is distributed equally among the top point-getters.

From 1987-90, the system was five points to win, three to place and one to show.

Year		KD	PS	BS	Pts	Year		KD	PS	BS	Pts
1987	1. **Bet Twice**	2nd	2nd	1st — 11		1990	1. **Unbridled**	1st	2nd	4th — 8
	2. Alysheba	1st	1st	4th — 10			2. Summer Squall	2nd	1st	DNR — 8
	3. Cryptoclearance	4th	3rd	2nd — 4			3. Go and Go	DNR	DNR	1st — 5
							(Unbridled was only horse to run all three races.)				
1988	1. **Risen Star**	3rd	1st	1st — 11		1991	1. **Hansel**	10th	1st	1st — 20
	2. Winning Colors	1st	3rd	6th — 6			2. Strike the Gold	1st	6th	2nd — 15
	3. Brian's Time	6th	2nd	3rd — 4			3. Mane Minister	3rd	3rd	3rd — 9
1989	1. **Sunday Silence**	1st	1st	2nd — 13		1992	1. **Pine Bluff**	5th	1st	3rd — 13
	2. Easy Goer	2nd	2nd	1st — 11			2. Casual Lies	2nd	3rd	5th — 8
	3. Hawkster	5th	5th	5th — 0			(No other horses ran all three races.)				

Kentucky Derby

For three-year-olds. Held the first Saturday in May at Churchill Downs in Louisville, Ky. Inaugurated in 1875. Originally run at 1½ miles (1875-95), shortened to present 1¼ miles in 1896.

Trainers with most wins: Ben A. Jones (6); Dick Thompson (4); Sunny Jim Fitzsimmons and Max Hirsch (3).
Jockeys with most wins: Eddie Arcaro and Bill Hartack (5); Bill Shoemaker (4); Angel Cordero, Jr, Issac Murphy and Earl Sande (3).
Winning fillies: Regret (1915), Genuine Risk (1980) and Winning Colors (1988).

Year		Time	Jockey	Trainer	2nd place	3rd place
1875	**Aristides**	2:37¾	Oliver Lewis	Andy Anderson	Volcano	Verdigris
1876	**Vagrant**	2:38¼	Bobby Swim	James Williams	Creedmoor	Harry Hill
1877	**Baden-Baden**	2:38	Billy Walker	Ed Brown	Leonard	King William
1878	**Day Star**	2:37¼	Jimmy Carter	Lee Paul	Himyar	Leveler
1879	**Lord Murphy**	2:37	Charlie Shauer	George Rice	Falsetto	Strathmore
1880	**Fonso**	2:37½	George Lewis	Tice Hutsell	Kimball	Bancroft
1881	**Hindoo**	2:40	Jim McLaughlin	James Rowe, Sr.	Lelex	Alhambra
1882	**Apollo**	2:40¼	Babe Hurd	Green Morris	Runnymede	Bengal
1883	**Leonatus**	2:43	Billy Donohue	Raleigh Colston	Drake Carter	Lord Raglan
1884	**Buchanan**	2:40¼	Isaac Murphy	William Bird	Loftin	Audrain
1885	**Joe Cotton**	2:37¼	Babe Henderson	Alex Perry	Bersan	Ten Booker
1886	**Ben Ali**	2:36½	Paul Duffy	Jim Murphy	Blue Wing	Free Knight
1887	**Montrose**	2:39¼	Isaac Lewis	John McGinty	Jim Gore	Jacobin
1888	**MacBeth II**	2:38¼	George Covington	John Campbell	Gallifet	White
1889	**Spokane**	2:34½	Thomas Kiley	John Rodegap	Proctor Knott	Once Again
1890	**Riley**	2:45	Isaac Murphy	Edward Corrigan	Bill Letcher	Robespierre
1891	**Kingman**	2:52¼	Isaac Murphy	Dud Allen	Balgowan	High Tariff
1892	**Azra**	2:41½	Lonnie Clayton	John Morris	Huron	Phil Dwyer
1893	**Lookout**	2:39¼	Eddie Kunze	Wm. McDaniel	Plutus	Boundless
1894	**Chant**	2:41	Frank Goodale	Eugene Leigh	Pearl Song	Sigurd
1895	**Halma**	2:37½	Soup Perkins	Byron McClelland	Basso	Laureate
1896	**Ben Brush**	2:07¾	Willie Simms	Hardy Campbell	Ben Eder	Semper Ego
1897	**Typhoon II**	2:12½	Buttons Garner	J.C. Cahn	Ornament	Dr. Catlett
1898	**Plaudit**	2:09	Willie Simms	John Madden	Lieber Karl	Isabey
1899	**Manuel**	2:12	Fred Taral	Robert Walden	Corsini	Mazo
1900	**Lieut. Gibson**	2:06¼	Jimmy Boland	Charles Hughes	Florizar	Thrive
1901	**His Eminence**	2:07¾	Jimmy Winkfield	F.B. VanMeter	Sannazarro	Driscoll
1902	**Alan-a-Dale**	2:08¾	Jimmy Winkfield	T.C. McDowell	Inventor	The Rival
1903	**Judge Himes**	2:09	Hal Booker	J.P. Mayberry	Early	Bourbon

Kentucky Derby (Cont.)

Year		Time	Jockey	Trainer	2nd place	3rd place
1904	**Elwood**	2:08½	Shorty Pryor	C.E. Durnell	Ed Tierney	Brancas
1905	**Agile**	2:10¾	Jack Martin	Robert Tucker	Ram's Horn	Layson
1906	**Sir Huon**	2:08⅕	Roscoe Troxler	Pete Coyne	Lady Navarre	James Reddick
1907	**Pink Star**	2:12⅗	Andy Minder	W.H.Fizer	Zal	Ovelando
1908	**Stone Street**	2:15⅕	Arthur Pickens	J.W.Hall	Sir Cleges	Dunvegan
1909	**Wintergreen**	2:08⅕	Vincent Power	Charles Mack	Miami	Dr. Barkley
1910	**Donau**	2:06⅖	Fred Herbert	George Ham	Joe Morris	Fighting Bob
1911	**Meridian**	2:05	Geo.Archibald	Albert Ewing	Governor Gray	Colston
1912	**Worth**	2:09⅖	C.H.Schilling	Frank Taylor	Duval	Flamma
1913	**Donerail**	2:04⅘	Roscoe Goose	Thomas Hayes	Ten Point	Gowell
1914	**Old Rosebud**	2:03⅖	John McCabe	F.D.Weir	Hodge	Bronzewing
1915	**Regret**	2:05⅖	Joe Notter	James Rowe, Sr.	Pebbles	Sharpshooter
1916	**George Smith**	2:04	Johnny Loftus	Hollie Hughes	Star Hawk	Franklin
1917	**Omar Khayyam**	2:04⅗	Charles Borel	C.T.Patterson	Ticket	Midway
1918	**Exterminator**	2:10⅘	William Knapp	Henry McDaniel	Escoba	Viva America
1919	**SIR BARTON**	2:09⅘	Johnny Loftus	H.Guy Bedwell	Billy Kelly	Under Fire
1920	**Paul Jones**	2:09	Ted Rice	Billy Garth	Upset	On Watch
1921	**Behave Yourself**	2:04⅕	Chas.Thompson	Dick Thompson	Black Servant	Prudery
1922	**Morvich**	2:04⅗	Albert Johnson	Fred Burlew	Bet Mosie	John Finn
1923	**Zev**	2:05⅖	Earl Sande	Samuel Hildreth	Martingale	Vigil
1924	**Black Gold**	2:05⅕	John Mooney	Hedley Webb	Chilhowee	Beau Butler
1925	**Flying Ebony**	2:07⅗	Earl Sande	William Duke	Captain Hal	Son of John
1926	**Bubbling Over**	2:03⅘	Albert Johnson	Dick Thompson	Bagenbaggage	Rock Man
1927	**Whiskery**	2:06	Linus McAtee	Fred Hopkins	Osmond	Jock
1928	**Reigh Count**	2:10⅖	Chick Lang	Bert Michell	Misstep	Toro
1929	**Clyde Van Dusen**	2:10⅘	Linus McAtee	Clyde Van Dusen	Naishapur	Panchio
1930	**GALLANT FOX**	2:07⅗	Earl Sande	Jim Fitzsimmons	Gallant Knight	Ned O.
1931	**Twenty Grand**	2:01⅘	Chas.Kurtsinger	James Rowe, Jr.	Sweep All	Mate
1932	**Burgoo King**	2:05⅕	Eugene James	Dick Thompson	Economic	Stepenfetchit
1933	**Brokers Tip**	2:06⅘	Don Meade	Dick Thompson	Head Play	Charley O.
1934	**Cavalcade**	2:04	Mack Garner	Bob Smith	Discovery	Agrarian
1935	**OMAHA**	2:05	Willie Saunders	Jim Fitzsimmons	Roman Soldier	Whiskolo
1936	**Bold Venture**	2:03⅗	Ira Hanford	Max Hirsch	Brevity	Indian Brown
1937	**WAR ADMIRAL**	2:03⅕	Chas.Kurtsinger	George Conway	Pompoon	Reaping Reward
1938	**Lawrin**	2:04⅘	Eddie Arcaro	Ben Jones	Dauber	Can't Wait
1939	**Johnstown**	2:03⅖	James Stout	Jim Fitzsimmons	Challedon	Heather Broom
1940	**Gallahadion**	2:05	Carroll Bierman	Roy Waldron	Bimelech	Dit
1941	**WHIRLAWAY**	2:01⅖	Eddie Arcaro	Ben Jones	Staretor	Market Wise
1942	**Shut Out**	2:04⅖	Wayne Wright	John Gaver	Alsab	Valdina Orphan
1943	**COUNT FLEET**	2:04	Johnny Longden	Don Cameron	Blue Swords	Slide Rule
1944	**Pensive**	2:04⅕	Conn McCreary	Ben Jones	Broadcloth	Stir Up
1945	**Hoop Jr**	2:07	Eddie Arcaro	Ivan Parke	Pot O'Luck	Darby Dieppe
1946	**ASSAULT**	2:06⅗	Warren Mehrtens	Max Hirsch	Spy Song	Hampden
1947	**Jet Pilot**	2:06⅘	Eric Guerin	Tom Smith	Phalanx	Faultless
1948	**CITATION**	2:05⅖	Eddie Arcaro	Ben Jones	Coaltown	My Request
1949	**Ponder**	2:04⅕	Steve Brooks	Ben Jones	Capot	Palestinian
1950	**Middleground**	2:01⅗	William Boland	Max Hirsch	Hill Prince	Mr. Trouble
1951	**Count Turf**	2:02⅗	Conn McCreary	Sol Rutchick	Royal Mustang	Ruhe
1952	**Hill Gail**	2:01⅗	Eddie Arcaro	Ben Jones	Sub Fleet	Blue Man
1953	**Dark Star**	2:02	Hank Moreno	Eddie Hayward	Native Dancer	Invigorator
1954	**Determine**	2:03	Raymond York	Willie Molter	Hasty Road	Hasseyampa
1955	**Swaps**	2:01⅘	Bill Shoemaker	Mesh Tenney	Nashua	Summer Tan
1956	**Needles**	2:03⅖	David Erb	Hugh Fontaine	Fabius	Come On Red
1957	**Iron Liege**	2:02⅕	Bill Hartack	Jimmy Jones	Gallant Man	Round Table
1958	**Tim Tam**	2:05	Ismael Valenzuela	Jimmy Jones	Lincoln Road	Noureddin
1959	**Tomy Lee**	2:02⅕	Bill Shoemaker	Frank Childs	Sword Dancer	First Landing
1960	**Venetian Way**	2:02⅖	Bill Hartack	Victor Sovinski	Bally Ache	Victoria Park
1961	**Carry Back**	2:04	John Sellers	Jack Price	Crozier	Bass Clef
1962	**Decidedly**	2:00⅖	Bill Hartack	Horatio Luro	Roman Line	Ridan
1963	**Chateaugay**	2:01⅘	Braulio Baeza	James Conway	Never Bend	Candy Spots
1964	**Northern Dancer**	2:00	Bill Hartack	Horatio Luro	Hill Rise	The Scoundrel
1965	**Lucky Debonair**	2:01⅕	Bill Shoemaker	Frank Catrone	Dapper Dan	Tom Rolfe

Year	Time	Jockey	Trainer	2nd place	3rd place
1966 **Kauai King**	2:02	Don Brumfield	Henry Forrest	Advocator	Blue Skyer
1967 **Proud Clarion**	2:00⅗	Bobby Ussery	Loyd Gentry	Barbs Delight	Damascus
1968 **Forward Pass***	—	Ismael Valenzuela	Henry Forrest	Francie's Hat	T.V. Commercial
1969 **Majestic Prince**	2:01⅘	Bill Hartack	Johnny Longden	Arts and Letters	Dike
1970 **Dust Commander**	2:03⅖	Mike Manganello	Don Combs	My Dad George	High Echelon
1971 **Canonero II**	2:03⅕	Gustavo Avila	Juan Arias	Jim French	Bold Reason
1972 **Riva Ridge**	2:01⅘	Ron Turcotte	Lucien Laurin	No Le Hace	Hold Your Peace
1973 **SECRETARIAT**	1:59⅖	Ron Turcotte	Lucien Laurin	Sham	Our Native
1974 **Cannonade**	2:04	Angel Cordero, Jr.	Woody Stephens	Hudson County	Agitate
1975 **Foolish Pleasure**	2:02	Jacinto Vasquez	LeRoy Jolley	Avatar	Diabolo
1976 **Bold Forbes**	2:01⅗	Angel Cordero, Jr.	Laz Barrera	Honest Pleasure	Elocutionist
1977 **SEATTLE SLEW**	2:02⅕	Jean Cruguet	Billy Turner	Run Dusty Run	Sanhedrin
1978 **AFFIRMED**	2:01⅕	Steve Cauthen	Laz Barrera	Alydar	Believe It
1979 **Spectacular Bid**	2:02⅖	Ron Franklin	Buddy Delp	General Assembly	Golden Act
1980 **Genuine Risk**	2:02	Jacinto Vasquez	LeRoy Jolley	Rumbo	Jaklin Klugman
1981 **Pleasant Colony**	2:02	Jorge Velasquez	John Campo	Woodchopper	Partez
1982 **Gato Del Sol**	2:02⅕	E. Delahoussaye	Eddie Gregson	Laser Light	Reinvested
1983 **Sunny's Halo**	2:02⅕	E. Delahoussaye	David Cross	Desert Wine	Caveat
1984 **Swale**	2:02⅖	Laffit Pincay, Jr.	Woody Stephens	Coax Me Chad	At The Threshold
1985 **Spend A Buck**	2:00⅕	Angel Cordero, Jr.	Cam Gambolati	Stephan's Odyssey	Chief's Crown
1986 **Ferdinand**	2:02⅘	Bill Shoemaker	Chas.Whittingham	Bold Arrangement	Broad Brush
1987 **Alysheba**	2:03⅖	Chris McCarron	Jack Van Berg	Bet Twice	Avies Copy
1988 **Winning Colors**	2:02⅕	Gary Stevens	D.Wayne Lukas	Forty Niner	Risen Star
1989 **Sunday Silence**	2:05	Pat Valenzuela	Chas. Whittingham	Easy Goer	Awe Inspiring
1990 **Unbridled**	2:02	Craig Perret	Carl Nafzger	Summer Squall	Pleasant Tap
1991 **Strike the Gold**	2:03	Chris Antley	Nick Zito	Best Pal	Mane Minister
1992 **Lil E. Tee**	2:04	Pat Day	Lynn Whiting	Casual Lies	Dance Floor

*Dancer's Image finished first (in 2:02 ⅕), but was disqualified after traces of prohibited medication were found in his system.

Preakness Stakes

For three-year-olds. Held two weeks after the Kentucky Derby at Pimlico Race Course in Baltimore, Md. Inaugurated 1873.

Originally run at 1½ miles (1873-88), then at 1¼ miles (1889), 1½ miles (1890), 1 1/16 miles (1894-1900), 1 mile & 70 yards (1901-07), 1 1/16 miles (1908), 1 mile (1909-10), 1⅛ miles (1911-24), and the present 1 3/16 miles since 1925.

Trainers with most wins: Robert W.Walden (7); T.J. Healey (5); Sunny Jim Fitzsimmons and Jimmy Jones (4); J. Whalen (3).

Jockeys with most wins: Eddie Arcaro (6); G. Barbee, Bill Hartack and Lloyd Hughes (3).

Winning fillies: Flocarline (1903), Whimsical (1906), Rhine Maiden (1915) and Nellie Morse (1924).

Year	Time	Jockey	Trainer	2nd place	3rd place
1873 **Survivor**	2:43	G.Barbee	A.D.Pryor	John Boulger	Artist
1874 **Culpepper**	2:56½	W.Donohue	H.Gaffney	King Amadeus	Scratch
1875 **Tom Ochiltree**	2:43½	L.Hughes	R.W.Walden	Viator	Bay Final
1876 **Shirley**	2:44¾	G.Barbee	W.Brown	Rappahannock	Algerine
1877 **Cloverbrook**	2:45½	C.Holloway	J.Walden	Bombast	Lucifer
1878 **Duke of Magenta**	2:41¾	C.Holloway	R.W.Walden	Bayard	Albert
1879 **Harold**	2:40½	L.Hughes	R.W.Walden	Jericho	Rochester
1880 **Grenada**	2:40½	L.Hughes	R.W.Walden	Oden	Emily F.
1881 **Saunterer**	2:40½	T.Costello	R.W.Walden	Compensation	Baltic
1882 **Vanguard**	2:44½	T.Costello	R.W.Walden	Heck	Col. Watson
1883 **Jacobus**	2:42½	G.Barbee	R.Dwyer	Parnell	—
1884 **Knight of Ellerslie**	2:39½	S.Fisher	T.B.Doswell	Welcher	—
1885 **Tecumseh**	2:49	Jim McLaughlin	C.Littlefield	Wickham	John C.
1886 **The Bard**	2:45	S.Fisher	J.Huggins	Eurus	Elkwood
1887 **Dunboyne**	2:39½	W.Donohue	W.Jennings	Mahoney	Raymond
1888 **Refund**	2:49	F.Littlefield	R.W.Walden	Judge Murray	Glendale
1889 **Buddhist**	2:17½	W.Anderson	J.Rogers	Japhet	—
1890 **Montague**	2:36¾	W.Martin	E.Feakes	Philosophy	Barrister
1891–93 Not held					
1894 **Assignee**	1:49¼	F.Taral	W.Lakeland	Potentate	Ed Kearney
1895 **Belmar**	1:50½	F.Taral	E.Feakes	April Fool	Sue Kittie

Preakness Stakes (Cont.)

Year		Time	Jockey	Trainer	2nd place	3rd place
1896	**Margrave**	1:51	H.Griffin	Byron McClelland	Hamilton II	Intermission
1897	**Paul Kauvar**	1:51¼	T.Thorpe	T.P.Hayes	Elkins	On Deck
1898	**Sly Fox**	1:49⅗	W.Simms	H.Campbell	The Huguenot	Nuto
1899	**Half Time**	1:47	R.Clawson	F.McCabe	Filigrane	Lackland
1900	**Hindus**	1:48⅖	H.Spencer	J.H.Morris	Sarmation	Ten Candles
1901	**The Parader**	1:47⅕	F.Landry	T.J.Healey	Sadie S.	Dr. Barlow
1902	**Old England**	1:45⅘	L.Jackson	G.B.Morris	Maj.Daingerfield	Namtor
1903	**Flocarline**	1:44⅘	W.Gannon	H.C.Riddle	Mackey Dwyer	Rightful
1904	**Bryn Mawr**	1:44⅕	E.Hildebrand	W.F.Presgrave	Wotan	Dolly Spanker
1905	**Cairngorm**	1:45⅘	W.Davis	A.J.Joyner	Kiamesha	Coy Maid
1906	**Whimsical**	1:45	Walter Miller	T.J.Gaynor	Content	Larabie
1907	**Don Enrique**	1:45⅖	G.Mountain	J.Whalen	Ethon	Zambesi
1908	**Royal Tourist**	1:46⅖	Eddie Dugan	A.J.Joyner	Live Wire	Robert Cooper
1909	**Effendi**	1:39⅘	Willie Doyle	F.C.Frisbie	Fashion Plate	Hilltop
1910	**Layminster**	1:40⅗	R.Estep	J.S.Healy	Dalhousie	Sager
1911	**Watervale**	1:51	Eddie Dugan	J.Whalen	Zeus	The Nigger
1912	**Colonel Holloway**	1:56⅗	C.Turner	D.Woodford	Bwana Tumbo	Tipsand
1913	**Buskin**	1:53⅖	James Butwell	J.Whalen	Kleburne	Barnegat
1914	**Holiday**	1:53⅘	A.Schuttinger	J.S.Healy	Brave Cunarder	Defendum
1915	**Rhine Maiden**	1:58	Douglas Hoffman	F.Devers	Half Rock	Runes
1916	**Damrosch**	1:54⅘	Linus McAtee	A.G.Weston	Greenwood	Achievement
1917	**Kalitan**	1:54⅖	E.Haynes	Bill Hurley	Al M. Dick	Kentucky Boy
1918	**War Cloud**	1:53⅗	Johnny Loftus	W.B.Jennings	Sunny Slope	Lanius
1918	**Jack Hare Jr**	1:53⅖	Charles Peak	F.D.Weir	The Porter	Kate Bright
1919	**SIR BARTON**	1:53	Johnny Loftus	H.Guy Bedwell	Eternal	Sweep On
1920	**Man o'War**	1:51⅗	Clarence Kummer	L.Feustel	Upset	Wildair
1921	**Broomspun**	1:54⅕	F.Coltiletti	James Rowe, Sr.	Polly Ann	Jeg
1922	**Pillory**	1:51⅗	L.Morris	Thomas Healey	Hea	June Grass
1923	**Vigil**	1:53⅗	B.Marinelli	Thomas Healey	General Thatcher	Rialto
1924	**Nellie Morse**	1:57⅕	John Merimee	A.B.Gordon	Transmute	Mad Play
1925	**Coventry**	1:59	Clarence Kummer	William Duke	Backbone	Almadel
1926	**Display**	1:59⅘	John Maiben	Thomas Healey	Blondin	Mars
1927	**Bostonian**	2:01⅗	Whitey Abel	Fred Hopkins	Sir Harry	Whiskery
1928	**Victorian**	2:00⅕	Sonny Workman	James Rowe, Jr.	Toro	Solace
1929	**Dr. Freeland**	2:01⅗	Louis Schaefer	Thomas Healey	Minotaur	African
1930	**GALLANT FOX**	2:00⅗	Earl Sande	Jim Fitzsimmons	Crack Brigade	Snowflake
1931	**Mate**	1:59	George Ellis	J.W.Healey	Twenty Grand	Ladder
1932	**Burgoo King**	1:59⅘	John Maiben	Dick Thompson	Tick On	Boatswain
1933	**Head Play**	2:02	Chas.Kurtsinger	Thomas Hayes	Ladysman	Utopian
1934	**High Quest**	1:58⅕	Robert Jones	Bob Smith	Cavalcade	Discovery
1935	**OMAHA**	1:58⅖	Willie Saunders	Jim Fitzsimmons	Firethorn	Psychic Bid
1936	**Bold Venture**	1:59	George Woolf	Max Hirsch	Granville	Jean Bart
1937	**WAR ADMIRAL**	1:58⅖	Chas.Kurtsinger	George Conway	Pompoon	Flying Scot
1938	**Dauber**	1:59⅘	Maurice Peters	Dick Handlen	Cravat	Menow
1939	**Challedon**	1:59⅘	George Seabo	Louis Schaefer	Gilded Knight	Volitant
1940	**Bimelech**	1:58⅗	F.A.Smith	Bill Hurley	Mioland	Gallahadion
1941	**WHIRLAWAY**	1:58⅘	Eddie Arcaro	Ben A. Jones	King Cole	Our Boots
1942	**Alsab**	1:57	Basil James	Sarge Swenke	Requested/ Sun Again (dead heat)	
1943	**COUNT FLEET**	1:57⅖	Johnny Longden	Don Cameron	Blue Swords	Vincentive
1944	**Pensive**	1:59⅕	Conn McCreary	Ben A. Jones	Platter	Stir Up
1945	**Polynesian**	1:58⅘	W.D.Wright	Morris Dixon	Hoop Jr.	Darby Dieppe
1946	**ASSAULT**	2:01⅖	Warren Mehrtens	Max Hirsch	Lord Boswell	Hampden
1947	**Faultless**	1:59	Doug Dobson	Jimmy Jones	On Trust	Phalanx
1948	**CITATION**	2:02⅖	Eddie Arcaro	Jimmy Jones	Vulcan's Forge	Boyard
1949	**Capot**	1:56	Ted Atkinson	J.M.Gaver	Palestinian	Noble Impulse
1950	**Hill Prince**	1:59⅕	Eddie Arcaro	Casey Hayes	Middleground	Dooley
1951	**Bold**	1:56⅖	Eddie Arcaro	Preston Burch	Counterpoint	Alerted
1952	**Blue Man**	1:57⅖	Conn McCreary	Woody Stephens	Jampol	One Count
1953	**Native Dancer**	1:57⅘	Eric Guerin	Bill Winfrey	Jamie K.	Royal Bay Gem
1954	**Hasty Road**	1:57⅖	Johnny Adams	Harry Trotsek	Correlation	Hasseyampa
1955	**Nashua**	1:54⅗	Eddie Arcaro	Jim Fitzsimmons	Saratoga	Traffic Judge

Year		Time	Jockey	Trainer	2nd place	3rd place
1956	**Fabius**	1:58⅖	Bill Hartack	Jimmy Jones	Needles	No Regrets
1957	**Bold Ruler**	1:56⅕	Eddie Arcaro	Jim Fitzsimmons	Iron Liege	Inside Tract
1958	**Tim Tam**	1:57⅕	Ismael Valenzuela	Jimmy Jones	Lincoln Road	Gone Fishin'
1959	**Royal Orbit**	1:57	Wm.Harmatz	R. Cornell	Sword Dancer	Dunce
1960	**Bally Ache**	1:57⅗	Bobby Ussery	Jimmy Pitt	Victoria Park	Celtic Ash
1961	**Carry Back**	1:57⅗	Johnny Sellers	Jack Price	Globemaster	Crozier
1962	**Greek Money**	1:56⅕	John Rotz	V.W.Raines	Ridan	Roman Line
1963	**Candy Spots**	1:56⅕	Bill Shoemaker	Mesh Tenney	Chateaugay	Never Bend
1964	**Northern Dancer**	1:56⅘	Bill Hartack	Horatio Luro	The Scoundrel	Hill Rise
1965	**Tom Rolfe**	1:56⅕	Ron Turcotte	Frank Whiteley	Dapper Dan	Hail To All
1966	**Kauai King**	1:55⅖	Don Brumfield	H. Forrest	Stupendous	Amberoid
1967	**Damascus**	1:55⅕	Bill Shoemaker	Frank Whiteley	In Reality	Proud Clarion
1968	**Forward Pass**	1:56⅘	Ismael Valenzuela	Henry Forrest	Out Of the Way	Nodouble
1969	**Majestic Prince**	1:55⅗	Bill Hartack	Johnny Longden	Arts and Letters	Jay Ray
1970	**Personality**	1:56⅕	Eddie Belmonte	John Jacobs	My Dad George	Silent Screen
1971	**Canonero II**	1:54	Gustavo Avila	Juan Arias	Eastern Fleet	Jim French
1972	**Bee Bee Bee**	1:55⅗	Eldon Nelson	Red Carroll	No Le Hace	Key To The Mint
1973	**SECRETARIAT**	1:54⅖	Ron Turcotte	Lucien Laurin	Sham	Our Native
1974	**Little Current**	1:54⅗	Miguel Rivera	Lou Rondinello	Neapolitan Way	Cannonade
1975	**Master Derby**	1:56⅖	Darrel McHargue	Smiley Adams	Foolish Pleasure	Diabolo
1976	**Elocutionist**	1:55	John Lively	Paul Adwell	Play The Red	Bold Forbes
1977	**SEATTLE SLEW**	1:54⅖	Jean Cruguet	Billy Turner	Iron Constitution	Run Dusty Run
1978	**AFFIRMED**	1:54⅖	Steve Cauthen	Laz Barrera	Alydar	Believe It
1979	**Spectacular Bid**	1:54⅕	Ron Franklin	Buddy Delp	Golden Act	Screen King
1980	**Codex**	1:54⅕	Angel Cordero, Jr.	D.Wayne Lukas	Genuine Risk	Colonel Moran
1981	**Pleasant Colony**	1:54⅗	Jorge Velasquez	John Campo	Bold Ego	Paristo
1982	**Aloma's Ruler**	1:55⅖	Jack Kaenel	John Lenzini	Linkage	Cut Away
1983	**Deputed Testamony**	1:55⅖	Donald Miller	Bill Boniface	Desert Wine	High Honors
1984	**Gate Dancer**	1:53⅗	Angel Cordero, Jr.	Jack Van Berg	Play On	Fight Over
1985	**Tank's Prospect**	1:53⅖	Pat Day	D.Wayne Lukas	Chief's Crown	Eternal Prince
1986	**Snow Chief**	1:54⅘	Alex Solis	Melvin Stute	Ferdinand	Broad Brush
1987	**Alysheba**	1:55⅘	Chris McCarron	Jack Van Berg	Bet Twice	Cryptoclearance
1988	**Risen Star**	1:56⅕	E.Delahoussaye	Louie Roussel	Brian's Time	Winning Colors
1989	**Sunday Silence**	1:53⅘	Pat Valenzuela	Chas.Whittingham	Easy Goer	Rock Point
1990	**Summer Squall**	1:53⅗	Pat Day	Neil Howard	Unbridled	Mister Frisky
1991	**Hansel**	1:54	Jerry Bailey	Frank Brothers	Corporate Report	Mane Minister
1992	**Pine Bluff**	1:55⅗	Chris McCarron	Tom Bohannan	Alydeed	Casual Lies

Belmont Stakes

For three-year-olds. Held three weeks after Preakness Stakes at Belmont Park in Elmont, N.Y. Inaugurated in 1867 at Jerome Park, moved to Morris Park in 1890 and Belmont Park in 1905.

Originally run at 1 mile and 5 furlongs (1867-89), then 1¼ miles (1890-1905), 1⅜ miles (1906-25), and the present 1½ miles since 1926.

Trainers with most wins: James Rowe, Sr.(8); Sam Hildreth (7); Sunny Jim Fitzsimmons (6); Woody Stephens (5); Max Hirsch and Robert W. Walden (4); Elliott Burch, Lucien Laurin, F. McCabe and D. McDaniel (3).

Jockeys with most wins: Eddie Arcaro and Jim McLaughlin (6); Earl Sande and Bill Shoemaker (5); Braulio Baeza, Laffit Pincay, Jr and James Stout (3).

Winning fillies: Ruthless (1867) and Tanya (1905).

Year		Time	Jockey	Trainer	2nd place	3rd place
1867	**Ruthless**	3:05	J.Gilpatrick	A.J.Minor	De Courcey	Rivoli
1868	**General Duke**	3:02	Bobby Swim	A.Thompson	Northumberland	Fanny Ludlow
1869	**Fenian**	3:04¼	C.Miller	J.Pincus	Glenelg	Invercauld
1870	**Kingfisher**	2:59½	W.Dick	R.Colston	Foster	Midday
1871	**Harry Bassett**	2:56	W.Miller	D.McDaniel	Stockwood	By-the-Sea
1872	**Joe Daniels**	2:58¼	James Roe	D.McDaniel	Meteor	Shylock
1873	**Springbok**	3:01¾	James Roe	D.McDaniel	Count d'Orsay	Strachino
1874	**Saxon**	2:39½	G.Barbee	W.Prior	Grinstead	Aaron Pennington
1875	**Calvin**	2:42¼	Bobby Swim	A.Williams	Aristides	Milner
1876	**Algerine**	2:40½	Billy Donohue	T.B.Doswell	Fiddlesticks	Barricade
1877	**Cloverbrook**	2:46	C.Holloway	J.Walden	Loiterer	Baden-Baden

Belmont Stakes (Cont.)

Year		Time	Jockey	Trainer	2nd place	3rd place
1878	**Duke of Magenta**	2:43½	L.Hughes	R.W.Walden	Bramble	Sparta
1879	**Spendthrift**	2:42¾	George Evans	T.Puryear	Monitor	Jericho
1880	**Grenada**	2:47	L.Hughes	R.W.Walden	Ferncliffe	Turenne
1881	**Saunterer**	2:47	T.Costello	R.W.Walden	Eole	Baltic
1882	**Forester**	2:43	Jim McLaughlin	L.Stuart	Babcock	Wyoming
1883	**George Kinney**	2:42½	Jim McLaughlin	James Rowe, Sr.	Trombone	Renegade
1884	**Panique**	2:42	Jim McLaughlin	James Rowe, Sr.	Knight of Ellerslie	Himalaya
1885	**Tyrant**	2:43	Paul Duffy	C.Claypool	St.Augustine	Tecumseh
1886	**Inspector B**	2:41	Jim McLaughlin	F.McCabe	The Bard	Linden
1887	**Hanover**	2:43½	Jim McLaughlin	F.McCabe	Oneko	—
1888	**Sir Dixon**	2:40¼	Jim McLaughlin	F.McCabe	Prince Royal	—
1889	**Eric**	2:47¼	W.Hayward	J.Huggins	Diablo	Zephyrus
1890	**Burlington**	2:07¾	Pike Barnes	A.Cooper	Devotee	Padishah
1891	**Foxford**	2:08¾	Ed Garrison	M.Donavan	Montana	Laurestan
1892	**Patron**	2:12	W.Hayward	L.Stuart	Shellbark	—
1893	**Commanche**	1:53¼	Willie Simms	G.Hannon	Dr.Rice	Rainbow
1894	**Henry of Navarre**	1:56½	Willie Simms	B.McClelland	Prig	Assignee
1895	**Belmar**	2:11½	Fred Taral	E.Feakes	Counter Tenor	Nanki Poo
1896	**Hastings**	2:24½	H.Griffin	J.J.Hyland	Handspring	Hamilton II
1897	**Scottish Chieftain**	2:23½	J.Scherrer	M.Byrnes	On Deck	Octagon
1898	**Bowling Brook**	2:32	F.Littlefield	R.W.Walden	Previous	Hamburg
1899	**Jean Beraud**	2:23	R.Clawson	Sam Hildreth	Half Time	Glengar
1900	**Ildrim**	2:21¼	Nash Turner	H.E.Leigh	Petruchio	Missionary
1901	**Commando**	2:21	H.Spencer	James Rowe, Sr.	The Parader	All Green
1902	**Masterman**	2:22⅗	John Bullman	J.J.Hyland	Renald	King Hanover
1903	**Africander**	2:21¾	John Bullman	R.Miller	Whorler	Red Knight
1904	**Delhi**	2:06⅗	George Odom	James Rowe, Sr.	Graziallo	Rapid Water
1905	**Tanya**	2:08	E.Hildebrand	J.W.Rogers	Blandy	Hot Shot
1906	**Burgomaster**	2:20	Lucien Lyne	J.W.Rogers	The Quail	Accountant
1907	**Peter Pan**	N/A	G.Mountain	James Rowe, Sr.	Superman	Frank Gill
1908	**Colin**	N/A	Joe Notter	James Rowe, Sr.	Fair Play	King James
1909	**Joe Madden**	2:21⅗	E.Dugan	Sam Hildreth	Wise Mason	Donald MacDonald
1910	**Sweep**	2:22	James Butwell	James Rowe, Sr.	Duke of Ormonde	—
1911–12	Not held					
1913	**Prince Eugene**	2:18	Roscoe Troxler	James Rowe, Sr.	Rock View	Flying Fairy
1914	**Luke McLuke**	2:20	Merritt Buxton	J.F.Schorr	Gainer	Charlestonian
1915	**The Finn**	2:18⅖	George Byrne	E.W.Heffner	Half Rock	Pebbles
1916	**Friar Rock**	2:22	E.Haynes	Sam Hildreth	Spur	Churchill
1917	**Hourless**	2:17⅘	James Butwell	Sam Hildreth	Skeptic	Wonderful
1918	**Johren**	2:20⅖	Frank Robinson	A.Simons	War Cloud	Cum Sah
1919	**SIR BARTON**	2:17⅖	John Loftus	H.Guy Bedwell	Sweep On	Natural Bridge
1920	**Man o'War**	2:14⅕	Clarence Kummer	L.Feustel	Donnacona	—
1921	**Grey Lag**	2:16⅘	Earl Sande	Sam Hildreth	Sporting Blood	Leonardo II
1922	**Pillory**	2:18⅘	C.H.Miller	T.J.Healey	Snob II	Hea
1923	**Zev**	2:19	Earl Sande	Sam Hildreth	Chickvale	Rialto
1924	**Mad Play**	2:18⅘	Earl Sande	Sam Hildreth	Mr.Mutt	Modest
1925	**American Flag**	2:16⅘	Albert Johnson	G.R.Tompkins	Dangerous	Swope
1926	**Crusader**	2:32⅕	Albert Johnson	George Conway	Espino	Haste
1927	**Chance Shot**	2:32⅖	Earl Sande	Pete Coyne	Bois de Rose	Flambino
1928	**Vito**	2:33⅕	Clarence Kummer	Max Hirsch	Genie	Diavolo
1929	**Blue Larkspur**	2:32⅘	Mack Garner	C.Hastings	African	Jack High
1930	**GALLANT FOX**	2:31⅗	Earl Sande	Jim Fitzsimmons	Whichone	Questionnaire
1931	**Twenty Grand**	2:29⅗	Chas.Kurtsinger	James Rowe,Jr	Sun Meadow	Jamestown
1932	**Faireno**	2:32⅘	Tom Malley	Jim Fitzsimmons	Osculator	Flag Pole
1933	**Hurryoff**	2:32⅗	Mack Garner	H.McDaniel	Nimbus	Union
1934	**Peace Chance**	2:29⅕	W.D.Wright	Pete Coyne	High Quest	Good Goods
1935	**OMAHA**	2:30⅗	Willie Saunders	Jim Fitzsimmons	Firethorn	Rosemont
1936	**Granville**	2:30	James Stout	Jim Fitzsimmons	Mr.Bones	Hollyrood
1937	**WAR ADMIRAL**	2:28⅗	Chas.Kurtsinger	George Conway	Sceneshifter	Vamoose
1938	**Pasteurized**	2:29⅖	James Stout	George Odom	Dauber	Cravat
1939	**Johnstown**	2:29⅗	James Stout	Jim Fitzsimmons	Belay	Gilded Knight

Year		Time	Jockey	Trainer	2nd place	3rd place
1940	**Bimelech**	2:29⅗	Fred Smith	Bill Hurley	Your Chance	Andy K.
1941	**WHIRLAWAY**	2:31	Eddie Arcaro	Ben Jones	Robert Morris	Yankee Chance
1942	**Shut Out**	2:29⅕	Eddie Arcaro	John Gaver	Alsab	Lochinvar
1943	**COUNT FLEET**	2:28⅕	Johnny Longden	Don Cameron	Fairy Manhurst	Deseronto
1944	**Bounding Home**	2:32⅕	G.L.Smith	Matt Brady	Pensive	Bull Dandy
1945	**Pavot**	2:30⅕	Eddie Arcaro	Oscar White	Wildlife	Jeep
1946	**ASSAULT**	2:30⅘	Warren Mehrtens	Max Hirsch	Natchez	Cable
1947	**Phalanx**	2:29⅖	R.Donoso	Syl Veitch	Tide Rips	Tailspin
1948	**CITATION**	2:28⅕	Eddie Arcaro	Jimmy Jones	Better Self	Escadru
1949	**Capot**	2:30⅕	Ted Atkinson	John Gaver	Ponder	Palestinian
1950	**Middleground**	2:28⅗	William Boland	Max Hirsch	Lights Up	Mr.Trouble
1951	**Counterpoint**	2:29	David Gorman	Syl Veitch	Battlefield	Battle Morn
1952	**One Count**	2:30⅕	Eddie Arcaro	Oscar White	Blue Man	Armageddon
1953	**Native Dancer**	2:28⅗	Eric Guerin	Bill Winfrey	Jamie K.	Royal Bay Gem
1954	**High Gun**	2:30⅘	Eric Guerin	Max Hirsch	Fisherman	Limelight
1955	**Nashua**	2:29	Eddie Arcaro	Jim Fitzsimmons	Blazing Count	Portersville
1956	**Needles**	2:29⅘	David Erb	Hugh Fontaine	Career Boy	Fabius
1957	**Gallant Man**	2:26⅗	Bill Shoemaker	John Nerud	Inside Tract	Bold Ruler
1958	**Cavan**	2:30⅕	Pete Anderson	Tom Barry	Tim Tam	Flamingo
1959	**Sword Dancer**	2:28⅖	Bill Shoemaker	Elliott Burch	Bagdad	Royal Orbit
1960	**Celtic Ash**	2:29⅗	Bill Hartack	Tom Barry	Venetian Way	Disperse
1961	**Sherluck**	2:29⅕	Braulio Baeza	Harold Young	Globemaster	Guadalcanal
1962	**Jaipur**	2:28⅘	Bill Shoemaker	B.Mulholland	Admiral's Voyage	Crimson Satan
1963	**Chateaugay**	2:30⅕	Braulio Baeza	James Conway	Candy Spots	Choker
1964	**Quadrangle**	2:28⅖	Manuel Ycaza	Elliott Burch	Roman Brother	Northern Dancer
1965	**Hail to All**	2:28⅖	John Sellers	Eddie Yowell	Tom Rolfe	First Family
1966	**Amberoid**	2:29⅗	William Boland	Lucien Laurin	Buffle	Advocator
1967	**Damascus**	2:28⅘	Bill Shoemaker	F.Y.Whiteley	Cool Reception	Gentleman James
1968	**Stage Door Johnny**	2:27⅕	Gus Gustines	John Gaver	Forward Pass	Call Me Prince
1969	**Arts and Letters**	2:28⅘	Braulio Baeza	Elliott Burch	Majestic Prince	Dike
1970	**High Echelon**	2:34	John Rotz	John Jacobs	Needles N Pins	Naskra
1971	**Pass Catcher**	2:30⅖	Walter Blum	Eddie Yowell	Jim French	Bold Reason
1972	**Riva Ridge**	2:28	Ron Turcotte	Lucien Laurin	Ruritania	Cloudy Dawn
1973	**SECRETARIAT**	2:24	Ron Turcotte	Lucien Laurin	Twice A Prince	My Gallant
1974	**Little Current**	2:29⅕	Miguel Rivera	Lou Rondinello	Jolly Johu	Cannonade
1975	**Avatar**	2:28⅕	Bill Shoemaker	Tommy Doyle	Foolish Pleasure	Master Derby
1976	**Bold Forbes**	2:29	Angel Cordero, Jr.	Laz Barrera	McKenzie Bridge	Great Contractor
1977	**SEATTLE SLEW**	2:29⅗	Jean Cruguet	Billy Turner	Run Dusty Run	Sanhedrin
1978	**AFFIRMED**	2:26⅘	Steve Cauthen	Laz Barrera	Alydar	Darby Creek Road
1979	**Coastal**	2:28⅗	Ruben Hernandez	David Whiteley	Golden Act	Spectacular Bid
1980	**Temperence Hill**	2:29⅘	Eddie Maple	Joseph Cantey	Genuine Risk	Rockhill Native
1981	**Summing**	2:29	George Martens	Luis Barerra	Highland Blade	Pleasant Colony
1982	**Conquistador Cielo**	2:28⅕	Laffit Pincay, Jr.	Woody Stephens	Gato Del Sol	Illuminate
1983	**Caveat**	2:27⅘	Laffit Pincay, Jr.	Woody Stephens	Slew o'Gold	Barberstown
1984	**Swale**	2:27⅕	Laffit Pincay, Jr.	Woody Stephens	Pine Circle	Morning Bob
1985	**Creme Fraiche**	2:27	Eddie Maple	Woody Stephens	Stephan's Odyssey	Chief's Crown
1986	**Danzig Connection**	2:29⅘	Chris McCarron	Woody Stephens	Johns Treasure	Ferdinand
1987	**Bet Twice**	2:28⅕	Craig Perret	Jimmy Croll	Cryptoclearance	Gulch
1988	**Risen Star**	2:26⅖	E.Delahoussaye	Louie Roussel	Kingpost	Brian's Time
1989	**Easy Goer**	2:26	Pat Day	Shug McGaughey	Sunday Silence	Le Voyageur
1990	**Go And Go**	2:27⅕	Michael Kinane	Dermot Weld	Thirty Six Red	Baron de Vaux
1991	**Hansel**	2:28	Jerry Bailey	Frank Brothers	Strike the Gold	Mane Minister
1992	**A.P. Indy**	2:26	E.Delahoussaye	Neil Drysdale	My Memoirs	Pine Bluff

Fastest/Slowest Winning Times

The fastest and slowest winning times at the current distances of the three Triple Crown races.

	Distance	Fastest	Time	Slowest	Time
Kentucky Derby	1¼ mi.	Secretariat (1975)	1:59⅖ F	Stone Sheet (1908)	2:15⅕ H
Preakness Stakes	1 3/16 mi.	Tank's Prospect (1985)	1:53⅖ F	Citation (1948)	2:02⅖ H
Belmont Stakes	1½ mi.	Secretariat (1975)	2:24 F	Vito (1928)	2:33⅕ F

F—Fast track; H—Heavy track.

Note: Secretariat's time of 2:24 in the Belmont is a world record for a mile and a half distance on a dirt track.

Breeders' Cup

Inaugurated on Nov. 10, 1984, the Breeders' Cup consists of seven races at one track on one day late in the year to determine thoroughbred racing's principal champions.

Breeders' Cup Day has been held at Hollywood Park (Calif.) in 1984, Aqueduct Racetrack (N.Y.) in 1985, Santa Anita Park (Calif.) in 1986, Hollywood Park in 1987, Churchill Downs (Ky.) in 1988 and '91, Gulfstream Park (Fla.) in 1989 and Belmont Park (N.Y.) in 1990.

The steeplechase was added to the Breeders' Cup championship roster in 1986, and has been held at Fair Hill Race Course (Md.) in 1986–88 and '91, Moreland Farms (N.J.) in 1989 and Belmont Park in 1990.

Trainers with most wins: D.Wayne Lukas (10); François Boutin, Neil Drysdale and Shug McGaughey (3).

Jockeys with most wins: Pat Day and Laffit Pincay, Jr. (6); Jose Santos (5); Angel Cordero, Jr. and Pat Valenzuela (4); Eddie Delahoussaye, Chris McCarron, Craig Perret and Randy Romero (3).

Juvenile

Distances: one mile (1984-85, 87); 1 1/16 miles (1986 and since 1988).

Year		Time	Jockey	Trainer	2nd place	3rd place
1984	Chief's Crown	1:36 1/5	Don MacBeth	Roger Laurin	Tank's Prospect	Spend A Buck
1985	Tasso	1:36 1/5	Laffit Pincay, Jr.	Neil Drysdale	Storm Cat	Scat Dancer
1986	Capote	1:43 3/5	Laffit Pincay, Jr.	D.Wayne Lukas	Qualify	Alysheba
1987	Success Express	1:35 1/5	Jose Santos	D.Wayne Lukas	Regal Classic	Tejano
1988	Is It True	1:46 3/5	Laffit Pincay, Jr.	D.Wayne Lukas	Easy Goer	Tagel
1989	Rhythm	1:43 3/5	Craig Perret	Shug McGaughey	Grand Canyon	Slavic
1990	Fly So Free	1:43 2/5	Jose Santos	Scotty Schulhofer	Take Me Out	Lost Mountain
1991	Arazi	1:44 3/5	Pat Valenzuela	Francois Boutin	Bertrando	Snappy Landing

Juvenile Fillies

Distances: one mile (1984-85, 87); 1 1/16 miles (1986 and since 1988).

Year		Time	Jockey	Trainer	2nd place	3rd place
1984	Outstandingly	1:37 4/5	Walter Guerra	Pancho Martin	Dusty Heart	Fine Spirit
1985	Twilight Ridge	1:35 4/5	Jorge Velasquez	D.Wayne Lukas	Family Style	Steal A Kiss
1986	Brave Raj	1:43 1/5	Pat Valenzuela	Melvin Stute	Tappiano	Saros Brig
1987	Epitome	1:36 2/5	Pat Day	Phil Hauswald	Jeanne Jones	Dream Team
1988	Open Mind	1:46 3/5	Angel Cordero, Jr.	D.Wayne Lukas	Darby Shuffle	Lea Lucinda
1989	Go for Wand	1:44 1/5	Randy Romero	William Badgett	Sweet Roberta	Stella Madrid
1990	Meadow Star	1:44	Jose Santos	LeRoy Jolley	Private Treasure	Dance Smartly
1991	Pleasant Stage	1:46 2/5	Eddie Delahoussaye	Chris Speckert	La Spia	Cadillac Women

Note: in 1984, winner **Fran's Valentine** was disqualified for interference in the stretch and placed 10th.

Sprint

Distance: six furlongs (since 1984).

Year		Time	Jockey	Trainer	2nd place	3rd place
1984	Eillo	1:10 1/5	Craig Perret	Budd Lepman	Commemorate	Fighting Fit
1985	Precisionist	1:08 2/5	Chris McCarron	R.Fenstermaker	Smile	Mt.Livermore
1986	Smile	1:08 2/5	Jacinto Vasquez	Scotty Schulhofer	Pine Tree Lane	Bedside Promise
1987	Very Subtle	1:08 4/5	Pat Valenzuela	Melvin Stute	Groovy	Exclusive Enough
1988	Gulch	1:10 2/5	Angel Cordero, Jr.	D.Wayne Lukas	Play The King	Afleet
1989	Dancing Spree	1:09	Angel Cordero, Jr.	Shug McGaughey	Safely Kept	Dispersal
1990	Safely Kept	1:09 3/5	Craig Perret	Alan Goldberg	Dayjur	Black Tie Affair
1991	Sheikh Albadou	1:09 1/5	Pat Edderly	Alexander Scott	Pleasant Tap	Robyn Dancer

Mile

Year		Time	Jockey	Trainer	2nd place	3rd place
1984	Royal Heroine	1:32 3/5	Fernando Toro	John Gosden	Star Choice	Cozzene
1985	Cozzene	1:35	Walter Guerra	Jan Nerud	Al Mamoon	Shadeed
1986	Last Tycoon	1:35 1/5	Yves St.-Martin	Robert Collet	Palace Music	Fred Astaire
1987	Miesque	1:32 4/5	Freddie Head	Francois Boutin	Show Dancer	Sonic Lady
1988	Miesque	1:38 3/5	Freddie Head	Francois Boutin	Steinlen	Simply Majestic
1989	Steinlen	1:37 1/5	Jose Santos	D.Wayne Lukas	Sabona	Most Welcome
1990	Royal Academy	1:35 1/5	Lester Piggott	M.V. O'Brien	Itsallgreektome	Priolo
1991	Opening Verse	1:37 2/5	Pat Valenzuela	Dick Lundy	Val des Bois	Star of Cozzene

Note: in 1985, 2nd place finisher **Palace Music** was disqualified for interference and placed 9th.

Distaff

Distances: 1 1/4 miles (1984-87); 1 1/8 miles (since 1988).

Year		Time	Jockey	Trainer	2nd place	3rd place
1984	Princess Rooney	2:02 3/5	E.Delahoussaye	Neil Drysdale	Life's Magic	Adored
1985	Life's Magic	2:02	Angel Cordero, Jr.	D.Wayne Lukas	Lady's Secret	DontstopThemusic
1986	Lady's Secret	2:01 1/5	Pat Day	D.Wayne Lukas	Fran's Valentine	Outstandingly
1987	Sacahuista	2:02 4/5	Randy Romero	D.Wayne Lukas	Clabber Girl	Queee Bebe
1988	Personal Ensign	1:52	Randy Romero	Shug McGaughey	Winning Colors	Goodbye Halo
1989	Bayakoa	1:47 3/5	Laffit Pincay, Jr.	Ron McAnally	Gorgeous	Open Mind
1990	Bayakoa	1:49 1/5	Laffit Pincay, Jr.	Ron McAnally	Colonial Waters	Valay Maid
1991	Dance Smartly	1:50 4/5	Pat Day	Jim Day	Versailles Treaty	Brought to Mind

Turf

Distance: 1½ miles (since 1984).

Year		Time	Jockey	Trainer	2nd place	3rd place
1984	**Lashkari**	2:25⅕	Yves St.-Martin	De Royer-Dupre	All Along	Raami
1985	**Pebbles**	2:27	Pat Eddery	Clive Brittain	Strawberry Rd.II	Mourjane
1986	**Manila**	2:25⅖	Jose Santos	Leroy Jolley	Theatrical	Estrapade
1987	**Theatrical**	2:24⅖	Pat Day	Bill Mott	Trempolino	Village Star II
1988	**Grt.Communicator**	2:35⅕	Ray Sibille	Thad Ackel	Sunshine Forever	Indian Skimmer
1989	**Prized**	2:28	E.Delahoussaye	Neil Drysdale	Sierra Roberta	Star Lift
1990	**In The Wings**	2:29⅗	Gary Stevens	Andre Fabre	With Approval	El Senor
1991	**Miss Alleged**	2:30⅘	Eric Legrix	Pascal Bary	Itsallgreektome	Quest for Fame

Classic

Distance: 1¼ miles (since 1984).

Year		Time	Jockey	Trainer	2nd place	3rd place
1984	**Wild Again**	2:03⅖	Pat Day	V.Timphony	Slew O'Gold	Gate Dancer
1985	**Proud Truth**	2:00⅘	Jorge Velasquez	John Veitch	Gate Dancer	Turkoman
1986	**Skywalker**	2:00⅖	Laffit Pincay, Jr.	M.Whittingham	Turkoman	Precisionist
1987	**Ferdinand**	2:01⅖	Bill Shoemaker	C.Whittingham	Alysheba	Judge Angelucci
1988	**Alysheba**	2:04⅘	Chris McCarron	Jack Van Berg	Seeking the Gold	Waquoit
1989	**Sunday Silence**	2:00⅕	Chris McCarron	C.Whittingham	Easy Goer	Blushing John
1990	**Unbridled**	2:02⅕	Pat Day	Carl Nafzger	Ibn Bey	Thirty Six Red
1991	**Black Tie Affair**	2:02⅘	Jerry Bailey	Ernie Poulos	Twilight Agenda	Unbridled

Note: in 1984, 2nd place finisher **Gate Dancer** was disqualified for interference and placed 3rd.

Steeplechase

Distances: 2⅜ miles (1986); 2⅝ miles (since 1987).

Year		Time	Jockey	Trainer	2nd place	3rd place
1986	**Census**	4:27⅗	Jeff Teter	Janet Elliott	Kesslin	Pont du Loup
1987	**Gacko**	5:15⅕	Roger Duchene	Xavier Guigand	Inlander	Gateshead
1988	**Jimmy Lorenzo**	5:12⅖	Graham McCourt	J.E.Sheppard	Kalankoe	Polar Pleasure
1989	**Highland Bud**	4:58⅘	Rich. Dunwoody	J.E.Sheppard	Polar Pleasure	Victorian Hill
1990	**Morley Street**	4:53⅕	Jimmy Frost	Toby Balding	Summer Colony	Moonstruck
1991	**Morley Street**	5:10⅗	Jimmy Frost	Toby Balding	Declare Your Wish	Cheering News

Annual Money Leaders

Horses

Annual money-leading horses since 1910, according to *The American Racing Manual.*

Multiple leaders: Round Table, Buckpasser and Alysheba (2).

Year		Age	Sts	1st	Earnings
1910	Novelty	2	16	11	$72,630
1911	Worth	2	13	10	16,645
1912	Star Charter	4	17	6	14,655
1913	Old Rosebud	2	14	12	19,057
1914	Roamer	3	16	12	29,105
1915	Borrow	7	9	4	20,195
1916	Campfire	2	9	6	49,735
1917	Sun Briar	2	9	5	59,505
1918	Eternal	2	8	6	56,173
1919	Sir Barton	3	13	8	88,250
1920	Man o'War	3	11	11	166,140
1921	Morvich	2	11	11	115,234
1922	Pillory	3	7	4	95,654
1923	Zev	3	14	12	272,008
1924	Sarazen	3	12	8	95,640
1925	Pompey	2	10	7	121,630
1926	Crusader	3	15	9	166,033
1927	Anita Peabody	2	7	6	111,905
1928	High Strung	2	6	5	153,590
1929	Blue Larkspur	3	6	4	153,450
1930	Gallant Fox	3	10	9	308,275
1931	Gallant Flight	2	7	7	219,000
1932	Gusto	3	16	4	145,940
1933	Singing Wood	2	9	3	88,050
1934	Cavalcade	3	7	6	111,235
1935	Omaha	3	9	6	142,255
1936	Granville	3	11	7	110,295
1937	Seabiscuit	4	15	11	168,580
1938	Stagehand	3	15	8	189,710
1939	Challedon	3	15	9	184,535

Year		Age	Sts	1st	Earnings
1940	Bimelech	3	7	4	$110,005
1941	Whirlaway	3	20	13	272,386
1942	Shut Out	3	12	8	238,872
1943	Count Fleet	3	6	6	174,055
1944	Pavot	2	8	8	179,040
1945	Busher	3	13	10	273,735
1946	Assault	3	15	8	424,195
1947	Armed	6	17	11	376,325
1948	Citation	3	20	19	709,470
1949	Ponder	3	21	9	321,825
1950	Noor	5	12	7	346,940
1951	Counterpoint	3	15	7	250,525
1952	Crafty Admiral	4	16	9	277,225
1953	Native Dancer	3	10	9	513,425
1954	Determine	3	15	10	328,700
1955	Nashua	3	12	10	752,550
1956	Needles	3	8	4	440,850
1957	Round Table	3	22	15	600,383
1958	Round Table	4	20	14	662,780
1959	Sword Dancer	3	13	8	537,004
1960	Bally Ache	3	15	10	445,045
1961	Carry Back	3	16	9	565,349
1962	Never Bend	2	10	7	402,969
1963	Candy Spots	3	12	7	604,481
1964	Gun Bow	4	16	8	580,100
1965	Buckpasser	2	11	9	568,096
1966	Buckpasser	3	14	13	669,078
1967	Damascus	3	16	12	817,941
1968	Forward Pass	3	13	7	546,674
1969	Arts and Letters	3	14	8	555,604

Annual Money Leaders (Cont.)
Horses

Year		Age	Sts	1st	Earnings	Year		Age	Sts	1st	Earnings
1970	Personality	3	18	8	$ 444,049	1981	John Henry	6	10	8	$1,798,030
1971	Riva Ridge	2	9	7	503,263	1982	Perrault (GB)	5	8	4	1,197,400
1972	Droll Role	4	19	7	471,633	1983	All Along (FRA)	4	7	4	2,138,963
1973	Secretariat	3	12	9	860,404	1984	Slew o'Gold	4	6	5	2,627,944
1974	Chris Evert	3	8	5	551,063	1985	Spend A Buck	3	7	5	3,552,704
1975	Foolish Pleasure	3	11	5	716,278	1986	Snow Chief	3	9	6	1,875,200
1976	Forego	6	8	6	401,701	1987	Alysheba	3	10	3	2,511,156
1977	Seattle Slew	3	7	6	641,370	1988	Alysheba	4	9	7	3,808,600
1978	Affirmed	3	11	8	901,541	1989	Sunday Silence	3	9	7	4,578,454
1979	Spectacular Bid	3	12	10	1,279,334	1990	Unbridled	3	11	4	3,718,149
1980	Temperence Hill	3	17	8	1,130,452	1991	Dance Smartly	3	8	8	2,876,821

Jockeys

Annual money-leading jockeys since 1910, according to *The American Racing Manual.*

Multiple leaders: Bill Shoemaker (10); Laffit Pincay, Jr. (7); Eddie Arcaro (6); Braulio Baeza (5); Chris McCarron and Jose Santos (4); Angel Cordero, Jr. and Earl Sande (3); Ted Atkinson, Laverne Fator, Mack Garner, Bill Hartack, Charles Kurtsinger, Johnny Longden, Sonny Workman and Wayne Wright (2).

Year		Mts	Wins	Earnings	Year		Mts	Wins	Earnings
1910	Carroll Shilling	506	172	$ 176,030	1952	Eddie Arcaro	807	188	$1,859,591
1911	Ted Koerner	813	162	88,308	1953	Bill Shoemaker	1683	485	1,784,187
1912	Jimmy Butwell	684	144	79,843	1954	Bill Shoemaker	1251	380	1,876,760
1913	Merritt Buxton	887	146	82,552	1955	Eddie Arcaro	820	158	1,864,796
1914	J.McCahey	824	155	121,845	1956	Bill Hartack	1387	347	2,343,955
1915	Mack Garner	775	151	96,628	1957	Bill Hartack	1238	341	3,060,501
1916	John McTaggart	832	150	155,055	1958	Bill Shoemaker	1133	300	2,961,693
1917	Frank Robinson	731	147	148,057	1959	Bill Shoemaker	1285	347	2,843,133
1918	Lucien Luke	756	178	201,864	1960	Bill Shoemaker	1227	274	2,123,961
1919	John Loftus	177	65	252,707	1961	Bill Shoemaker	1256	304	2,690,819
1920	Clarence Kummer	353	87	292,376	1962	Bill Shoemaker	1126	311	2,916,844
1921	Earl Sande	340	112	263,043	1963	Bill Shoemaker	1203	271	2,526,925
1922	Albert Johnson	297	43	345,054	1964	Bill Shoemaker	1056	246	2,649,553
1923	Earl Sande	430	122	569,394	1965	Braulio Baeza	1245	270	2,582,702
1924	Ivan Parke	844	205	290,395	1966	Braulio Baeza	1341	298	2,951,022
1925	Laverne Fator	315	81	305,775	1967	Braulio Baeza	1064	256	3,088,888
1926	Laverne Fator	511	143	361,435	1968	Braulio Baeza	1089	201	2,835,108
1927	Earl Sande	179	49	277,877	1969	Jorge Velasquez	1442	258	2,542,315
1928	Linus McAtee	235	55	301,295	1970	Laffit Pincay, Jr.	1328	269	2,626,526
1929	Mack Garner	274	57	314,975	1971	Laffit Pincay, Jr.	1627	380	3,784,377
1930	Sonny Workman	571	152	420,438	1972	Laffit Pincay, Jr.	1388	289	3,225,827
1931	Chas.Kurtsinger	519	93	392,095	1973	Laffit Pincay, Jr.	1444	350	4,093,492
1932	Sonny Workman	378	87	385,070	1974	Laffit Pincay, Jr.	1278	341	4,251,060
1933	Robert Jones	471	63	226,285	1975	Braulio Baeza	1190	196	3,674,398
1934	Wayne Wright	919	174	287,185	1976	Angel Cordero, Jr.	1534	274	4,709,500
1935	Silvio Coucci	749	141	319,760	1977	Steve Cauthen	2075	487	6,151,750
1936	Wayne Wright	670	100	264,000	1978	Darrel McHargue	1762	375	6,188,353
1937	Chas.Kurtsinger	765	120	384,202	1979	Laffit Pincay, Jr.	1708	420	8,183,535
1938	Nick Wall	658	97	385,161	1980	Chris McCarron	1964	405	7,666,100
1939	Basil James	904	191	353,333	1981	Chris McCarron	1494	326	8,397,604
1940	Eddie Arcaro	783	132	343,661	1982	Angel Cordero, Jr.	1838	397	9,702,520
1941	Don Meade	1164	210	398,627	1983	Angel Cordero, Jr.	1792	362	10,116,807
1942	Eddie Arcaro	687	123	481,949	1984	Chris McCarron	1565	356	12,038,213
1943	Johnny Longden	871	173	573,276	1985	Laffit Pincay, Jr.	1409	289	13,415,049
1944	Ted Atkinson	1539	287	899,101	1986	Jose Santos	1636	329	11,329,297
1945	Johnny Longden	778	180	981,977	1987	Jose Santos	1639	305	12,407,355
1946	Ted Atkinson	1377	233	1,036,825	1988	Jose Santos	1867	370	14,877,298
1947	Douglas Dodson	646	141	1,429,949	1989	Jose Santos	1459	285	13,847,003
1948	Eddie Arcaro	726	188	1,686,230	1990	Gary Stevens	1504	283	13,881,198
1949	Steve Brooks	906	209	1,316,817	1991	Chris McCarron	1440	265	14,456,073
1950	Eddie Arcaro	888	195	1,410,160					
1951	Bill Shoemaker	1161	257	1,329,890					

All-Time Leaders

The all-time winning horses and jockeys of North America through 1991, according to *The American Racing Manual*. Records include all available information on races in foreign countries.

Top 25 Horses—Money Won

Note that horses who raced in 1991 are in **bold** type; (†) indicates foreign-bred; and (f) indicates female.

		Sts	1st	2nd	3rd	Earnings
1	Alysheba	26	11	8	2	$6,679,242
2	John Henry	83	39	15	9	6,597,947
3	Sunday Silence	14	9	5	0	4,968,554
4	Easy Goer	20	14	5	1	4,873,770
5	Spend A Buck	15	10	3	2	4,220,689
6	Creme Fraiche	64	17	12	13	4,024,727
7	**Unbridled**	24	8	6	6	4,489,475
8	Ferdinand	29	8	9	6	3,777,978
9	Slew o'Gold	21	12	5	1	3,533,534
10	Precisionist	46	20	10	4	3,485,393
11	Snow Chief	24	13	3	5	3,383,210
12	Cryptoclearance	44	12	10	7	3,376,327
13	**Black Tie Affair**†	45	18	9	6	3,370,694
14	Bet Twice	26	10	6	4	3,308,599
15	Steinlent	45	20	10	7	3,300,100
16	Gulch	32	13	8	4	3,095,521
17	**Dance Smartly** (f)	13	11	1	1	3,083,456
18	Lady's Secret (f)	45	25	9	3	3,021,425
19	All Along† (f)	21	9	4	2	3,015,764
20	Theatrical†	22	10	4	2	2,943,627
21	**Hansel**	14	7	2	2	2,936,586
22	Gt. Communicator	56	14	10	7	2,922,615
23	Symboli Rudolf	16	13	1	1	2,909,593
24	**Farma Way**	23	8	5	2	2,897,176
25	With Approval	23	13	5	1	2,863,540

Top 20 Jockeys—Races Won

Note that jockeys active in 1991 are in **bold** type.

		Yrs	Wins	Earnings
1	Bill Shoemaker	42	8833	$123,375,524
2	**Laffit Pincay, Jr.**	26	7694	162,986,471
3	**Angel Cordero, Jr.**	30	7050	164,328,056
4	**Jorge Velasquez**	29	6442	116,501,629
5	**Larry Snyder**	32	6205	44,920,466
6	Johnny Longden	40	6032	24,665,800
7	**David Gall**	35	5910	16,905,764
8	**Sandy Hawley**	24	5906	74,940,141
9	**Carl Gambardella**	36	5894	26,096,512
10	**Chris McCarron**	17	5569	142,281,817
11	**Pat Day**	19	5436	113,695,307
12	**Earlie Fires**	27	5181	56,274,594
13	**Jacinto Vasquez**	32	4941	74,503,815
14	Eddie Arcaro	31	4779	30,039,543
15	**Eddie Delahoussaye**	22	4720	106,518,527
16	Don Brumfield	37	4573	43,567,861
17	Steve Brooks	34	4451	18,239,817
18	Walter Blum	22	4382	26,497,189
19	Bill Hartack	22	4272	26,466,758
20	Avelino Gomez	34	4081	11,777,297
21	Hugo Dittfach	33	4000	13,506,052
22	**Eddie Maple**	24	3956	87,783,200
23	Ted Atkinson	22	3795	17,449,360
24	**David Whited**	34	3784	25,064,766
25	Ralph Neves	21	3772	13,786,239

Retired: Arcaro (1961); Atkinson (1959); Blum (1975); Brooks (1975); Brumfield (1989); Dittfach; Gomez (1980); Hartack (1974); Longden (1966); Neves (1964); Shoemaker (1990).

Horse of the Year (1936–70)

In 1971, the *Daily Racing Form*, the Thoroughbred Racing Associations, and the National Turf Writers Assn. joined forces to create the Eclipse Awards. Before then, however, the *Racing Form* (1936–70) and the TRA (1950-70) issued separate selections for Horse of the Year. Their picks differed only four times from 1950-70 and are so noted. Horses listed in CAPITAL letters are Triple Crown winners; (f) indicates female.

Multiple winners: Kelso (5); Challedon, Native Dancer and Whirlaway (2).

Year		Year		Year		Year	
1936	Granville	1946	ASSAULT	1955	Nashua	1964	Kelso
1937	WAR ADMIRAL	1947	Armed	1956	Swaps	1965	Roman Brother (DRF)
1938	Seabiscuit	1948	CITATION	1957	Bold Ruler (DRF)		Moccasin (TRA)
1939	Challedon	1949	Capot		Dedicate (TRA)	1966	Buckpasser
1940	Challedon	1950	Hill Prince	1958	Round Table	1967	Damascus
1941	WHIRLAWAY	1951	Counterpoint	1959	Sword Dancer	1968	Dr. Fager
1942	Whirlaway	1952	One Count (DRF)	1960	Kelso	1969	Arts and Letters
1943	COUNT FLEET		Native Dancer (TRA)	1961	Kelso	1970	Fort Marcy (DRF)
1944	Twilight Tear (f)	1953	Tom Fool	1962	Kelso		Personality (TRA)
1945	Busher (f)	1954	Native Dancer	1963	Kelso		

Eclipse Awards

The Eclipse Awards, honoring the Horse of the Year and other champions of the sport, are sponsored by the *Daily Racing Form*, the Thoroughbred Racing Associations and the National Turf Writers Assn.

The awards are named after the 18th century racehorse and sire, Eclipse, who began racing at age five and was unbeaten in 18 starts (eight wins were walkovers). As a stallion, Eclipse sired winners of 344 races, including three Epsom Derby champions.

Horses listed in CAPITAL letters won the Triple Crown that year. Age of horse in parentheses where necessary.

Multiple winners (horses): Forego (8); John Henry (7); Affirmed and Secretariat (5); Flatterer, Seattle Slew and Spectacular Bid (4); Ack Ack, Susan's Girl and Zaccio (3); All Along, Alysheba, Bayakoa, Black Tie Affair, Cafe Prince, Conquistador Cielo, Desert Vixen, Ferdinand, Go for Wand, Housebuster, Lady's Secret, Life's Magic, Miesque, Morley Street, Open Mind, Riva Ridge, Slew o'Gold and Spend A Buck (2).

Multiple winners (people): Laffit Pincay, Jr.(5); Laz Barrera and Pat Day (4); Steve Cauthen, Pat Day, Harbor View Farm, Fred W. Hooper, Nelson Bunker Hunt, Mr.& Mrs. Gene Klein, Dan Lasater, D.Wayne Lucas, Ogden Phipps, Bill Shoemaker, Edward Taylor and Charlie Whittingham (3); Braulio Baeza, C.T.Chenery, Claiborne Farm, Angel Cordero, Jr., Kent Desormeaux, John Franks, John W.Galbreath, Chris McCarron and Paul Mellon.

Horse of the Year

Year		Year		Year		Year	
1971	Ack Ack (5)	1976	Forego (6)	1982	Conquistador Cielo (3)	1987	Ferdinand (4)
1972	Secretariat (2)	1977	SEATTLE SLEW (3)	1983	All Along (4)	1988	Alysheba (4)
1973	SECRETARIAT (3)	1978	AFFIRMED (3)	1984	John Henry (9)	1989	Sunday Silence (3)
1974	Forego (4)	1979	Affirmed (4)	1985	Spend A Buck (3)	1990	Criminal Type (5)
1975	Forego (5)	1980	Spectacular Bid (4)	1986	Lady's Secret (4)	1991	Black Tie Affair (5)
		1981	John Henry (6)				

Older Colt, Horse or Gelding

Year		Year		Year		Year	
1971	Ack Ack (5)	1977	Forego (7)	1982	Lemhi Gold (4)	1987	Ferdinand (4)
1972	Autobiography (4)	1978	Seattle Slew (4)	1983	Bates Motel (4)	1988	Alysheba (4)
1973	Riva Ridge (4)	1979	Affirmed (4)	1984	Slew o' Gold (4)	1989	Blushing John (4)
1974	Forego (4)	1980	Spectacular Bid (4)	1985	Vanlandingham (4)	1990	Criminal Type (5)
1975	Forego (5)	1981	John Henry (6)	1986	Turkoman (4)	1991	Black Tie Affair (5)
1976	Forego (6)						

Older Filly or Mare

Year		Year		Year		Year	
1971	Shuvee (5)	1977	Cascapedia (4)	1982	Track Robbery (6)	1987	North Sider (5)
1972	Typecast (6)	1978	Late Bloomer (4)	1983	Amb. of Luck (4)	1988	Personal Ensign (4)
1973	Susan's Girl (4)	1979	Waya (5)	1984	Princess Rooney (4)	1989	Bayakoa (5)
1974	Desert Vixen (4)	1980	Glorious Song (4)	1985	Life's Magic (4)	1990	Bayakoa (6)
1975	Susan's Girl (6)	1981	Relaxing (5)	1986	Lady's Secret (4)	1991	Queena (5)
1976	Proud Delta (4)						

3-Year-Old Colt

Year		Year		Year		Year	
1971	Canonero II	1977	SEATTLE SLEW	1982	Conquistador Cielo	1987	Alysheba
1972	Key to the Mint	1978	AFFIRMED	1983	Slew o' Gold	1988	Risen Star
1973	SECRETARIAT	1979	Spectacular Bid	1984	Swale	1989	Sunday Silence
1974	Little Currant	1980	Temperence Hill	1985	Spend A Buck	1990	Unbridled
1975	Wajima	1981	Pleasant Colony	1986	Snow Chief	1991	Hansel
1976	Bold Forbes						

3-Year-Old Filly

Year		Year		Year		Year	
1971	Turkish Trousers	1977	Our Mims	1982	Christmas Past	1987	Sacahuista
1972	Susan's Girl	1978	Tempest Queen	1983	Heartlight No. One	1988	Winning Colors
1973	Desert Vixen	1979	Davona Dale	1984	Life's Magic	1989	Open Mind
1974	Chris Evert	1980	Genuine Risk	1985	Mom's Command	1990	Go for Wand
1975	Ruffian	1981	Wayward Lass	1986	Tiffany Lass	1991	Dance Smartly
1976	Revidere						

2-Year-Old Colt

Year		Year		Year		Year	
1971	Riva Ridge	1977	Affirmed	1982	Roving Boy	1987	Forty Niner
1972	Secretariat	1978	Spectacular Bid	1983	Devil's Bag	1988	Easy Goer
1973	Protagonist	1979	Rockhill Native	1984	Chief's Crown	1989	Rhythm
1974	Foolish Pleasure	1980	Lord Avie	1985	Tasso	1990	Fly So Free
1975	Honest Pleasure	1981	Deputy Minister	1986	Capote	1991	Arazi
1976	Seattle Slew						

2-Year-Old Filly

Year		Year		Year		Year	
1971	Numbered Account	1977	Lakeville Miss	1982	Landaluce	1987	Epitome
1972	La Prevoyante	1978	Candy Eclair	1983	Althea	1988	Open Mind
1973	Talking Picture		& It's in the Air	1984	Outstandingly	1989	Go for Wand
1974	Ruffian	1979	Smart Angle	1985	Family Style	1990	Meadow Star
1975	Dearly Precious	1980	Heavenly Cause	1986	Brave Raj	1991	Pleasant Stage
1976	Sensational	1981	Before Dawn				

Champion Turf Horse

Year		Year		Year		Year	
1971	Run the Gantlet (3)	1973	Secretariat (3)	1975	Snow Knight (4)	1977	Johnny D (3)
1972	Cougar II (6)	1974	Dahlia (4)	1976	Youth (3)	1978	Mac Diarmida (3)

Champion Male Turf Horse

Year		Year		Year		Year	
1979	Bowl Game (5)	1983	John Henry (8)	1986	Manila (3)	1989	Steinlen (6)
1980	John Henry (5)	1984	John Henry (9)	1987	Theatrical (5)	1990	Itsallgreektome (3)
1981	John Henry (6)	1985	Cozzene (4)	1988	Sunshine Forever (3)	1991	Tight Spot (4)
1982	Perrault (5)						

Champion Female Turf Horse

Year		Year		Year		Year	
1979	Trillion (5)	1983	All Along (4)	1986	Estrapade (6)	1989	Brown Bess (7)
1980	Just A Game II (4)	1984	Royal Heroine (4)	1987	Miesque (3)	1990	Laugh and Be Merry (5)
1981	De La Rose (3)	1985	Pebbles (4)	1988	Miesque (4)	1991	Miss Alleged (4)
1982	April Run (4)						

Sprinter

Year		Year		Year		Year	
1971	Ack Ack (5)	1977	What a Summer (4)	1982	Gold Beauty (3)	1987	Groovy (4)
1972	Chou Croute (4)	1978	Dr.Patches (4)	1983	Chinook Pass (4)	1988	Gulch (4)
1973	Shecky Greene (3)		& J.O.Tobin (4)	1984	Eillo (4)	1989	Safely Kept (4)
1974	Forego (4)	1979	Star de Naskra (4)	1985	Precisionist (4)	1990	Housebuster (3)
1975	Gallant Bob (3)	1980	Plugged Nickle (3)	1986	Smile (4)	1991	Housebuster (4)
1976	My Juliet (4)	1981	Guilty Conscience (5)				

Steeplechase or Hurdle Horse

Year		Year		Year		Year	
1971	Shadow Brook (7)	1977	Cafe Prince (7)	1982	Zaccio (6)	1987	Inlander (6)
1972	Soothsayer (5)	1978	Cafe Prince (8)	1983	Flatterer (4)	1988	Jimmy Lorenzo (6)
1973	Athenian Idol (5)	1979	Martie's Anger (4)	1984	Flatterer (5)	1989	Highland Bud (4)
1974	Gran Kan (8)	1980	Zaccio (4)	1985	Flatterer (6)	1990	Morley Street (6)
1975	Life's Illusion (4)	1981	Zaccio (5)	1986	Flatterer (7)	1991	Morley Street (7)
1976	Straight & True (6)						

Outstanding Jockey

Year		Year		Year		Year	
1971	Laffit Pincay, Jr.	1977	Steve Cauthen	1982	Angel Cordero, Jr.	1987	Pat Day
1972	Braulio Baeza	1978	Darrel McHargue	1983	Angel Cordero, Jr.	1988	Jose Santos
1973	Laffit Pincay, Jr.	1979	Laffit Pincay, Jr.	1984	Pat Day	1989	Kent Desormeaux
1974	Laffit Pincay, Jr.	1980	Chris McCarron	1985	Laffit Pincay, Jr.	1990	Craig Perret
1975	Braulio Baeza	1981	Bill Shoemaker	1986	Pat Day	1991	Pat Day
1976	Sandy Hawley						

Outstanding Apprentice Jockey

Year		Year		Year		Year	
1971	Gene St. Leon	1977	Steve Cauthen	1982	Alberto Delgado	1987	Kent Desormeaux
1972	Thomas Wallis	1978	Ron Franklin	1983	Declan Murphy	1988	Steve Capanas
1973	Steve Valdez	1979	Cash Asmussen	1984	Wesley Ward	1989	Michael Luzzi
1974	Chris McCarron	1980	Grank Lovato, Jr.	1985	Art Madrid, Jr.	1990	Mark Johnston
1975	Jimmy Edwards	1981	Richard Migliore	1986	Allen Stacy	1991	Mickey Walls
1976	George Martens						

Eclipse Awards (Cont.)
Outstanding Trainer

Year		Year		Year		Year	
1971	Charlie Whittingham	1977	Laz Barrera	1982	Charlie Whittingham	1987	D.Wayne Lukas
1972	Lucien Laurin	1978	Laz Barrera	1983	Woody Stephens	1988	Shug McGaughey
1973	H.Allen Jerkens	1979	Laz Barrera	1984	Jack Van Berg	1989	Charlie Whittingham
1974	Sherrill Ward	1980	Bud Delp	1985	D.Wayne Lukas	1990	Carl Nafzger
1975	Steve DiMauro	1981	Ron McAnally	1986	D.Wayne Lukas	1991	Ron McAnally
1976	Laz Barrera						

Outstanding Owner

Year		Year		Year		Year	
1971	Mr.& Mrs. E.E. Fogleson	1976	Dan Lasater	1981	Dotsam Stable	1987	Mr.& Mrs. Gene Klein
1972	No award	1977	Maxwell Gluck	1982	Viola Sommer	1988	Ogden Phipps
1973	No award	1978	Harbor View Farm	1983	John Franks	1989	Ogden Phipps
1974	Dan Lasater	1979	Harbor View Farm	1984	John Franks	1990	Frances Genter
1975	Dan Lasater	1980	Mr.& Mrs. Bertram Firestone	1985	Mr.& Mrs. Gene Klein	1991	Sam-Son Farms
				1986	Mr.& Mrs. Gene Klein		

Outstanding Owner-Breeder

Year		Year		Year	
1971	Paul Mellon	1972	C. T. Chenery	1973	C. T. Chenery

Outstanding Breeder

Year		Year		Year		Year	
1974	John W.Galbreath	1979	Claiborne Farm	1984	Claiborne Farm	1988	Ogden Phipps
1975	Fred W.Hooper	1980	Mrs. Henry Paxson	1985	Nelson Bunker Hunt	1989	North Ridge Farm
1976	Nelson Bunker Hunt	1981	Golden Chance Farm	1986	Paul Mellon	1990	Calumet Farm
1977	Edward P. Taylor	1982	Fred W.Hooper	1987	Nelson Bunker Hunt	1991	Mr. & Mrs. John Mabee
1978	Harbor View Farm	1983	Edward P.Taylor				

Man of the Year

Year		Year		Year		Year	
1972	John W.Galbreath	1973	Edward P. Taylor	1974	William L.McKnight	1975	John A. Morris

Outstanding Achievement

Year		Year	
1971*	Charles Engelhard	1972*	Arthur B.Hancock, Jr

*Awarded posthumously

Award of Merit

Year		Year		Year		Year	
1976	Jack J.Dreyfus	1980	John D.Schapiro	1986	Herman Cohen	1989	Michael Sandler
1977	Steve Cauthen	1981	Bill Shoemaker	1987	J.B.Faulconer	1990	Warner L. Jones
1978	Dinny Phipps	1984	John Gaines	1988	John Forsythe	1991	Fred W. Hooper
1979	Jimmy Kilroe	1985	Keene Daingerfield				

Special Award

Year		Year		Year		Year	
1971	Robert J.Kleberg	1980	John T.Landry & Pierre E. Bellocq	1985	Arlington Park	1988	Edward J. DeBartolo, Sr.
1974	Charles Hatton	1984	C.V.Whitney	1987	Anheuser-Busch	1989	Richard Duchossois
1976	Bill Shoemaker						

Harness Racing
Triple Crown Winners
TROTTERS

Six 3-year-olds have won the Yonkers Trot, Hambletonian and Kentucky Futurity in the same year since the Trotting Triple Crown was established in 1955. Stanley Dancer is the only driver/trainer to win it twice.

Year		Driver/Trainer	Owner
1955	**Scott Frost**	Joe O'Brien	S.A. Camp Farms
1963	**Speedy Scot**	Ralph Baldwin	Castleton Farms
1964	**Ayres**	John Simpson, Sr.	Charlotte Sheppard
1968	**Nevele Pride**	Stanley Dancer	Nevele Acres & Lou Resnick
1969	**Lindy's Pride**	Howard Beissinger	Lindy Farms
1972	**Super Bowl**	Stanley Dancer	Rachel Dancer & Rose Hild Breeding Farm

PACERS

Seven 3-year-olds have won the Cane Pace, Little Brown Jug and Messenger Stakes in the same year since the Pacing Triple Crown was established in 1956. No trainer or driver has won it more than once.

Year		Driver	Trainer	Owner
1959	**Adios Butler**	Clint Hodgins	Paige West	Paige West & Angelo Pellillo
1965	**Bret Hanover**	Frank Ervin	Frank Ervin	Richard Downing
1966	**Romeo Hanover**	Bill Myer & George Sholty*	Jerry Silverman	Lucky Star Stable & Morton Finder
1968	**Rum Customer**	Billy Haughton	Billy Haughton	Kennilworth Farms & L.C. Mancuso
1970	**Most Happy Fella**	Stanley Dancer	Stanley Dancer	Egyptian Acres Stable
1980	**Niatross**	Clint Galbraith	Clint Galbraith	Niagara Acres, Niatross Stables & Clint Galbraith
1983	**Ralph Hanover**	Ron Waples	Stan Firlotte	Waples Stable, Pointsetta Stable, Grant's Direct Stable & P.J. Baugh

*Myer drove Romeo Hanover in the Cane, Sholty in the other two races.

Triple Crown Near Misses

TROTTERS

Five horses have won the first two legs of the Triple Crown—the Yonkers Trot (YT) and the Hambletonian (Ham)—but not the third. The eventual winner of the Ky. Futurity (KF) is listed.

Year		YT	Ham	KF
1962	**AC's Viking**	won	won	Safe Mission
1976	**Steve Lobell**	won	won	Quick Pay
1977	**Green Speed**	won	won	Texas
1978	**Speedy Somolli**	won	won	Doublemint
1987	**Mack Lobell**	won	won	Napoletano

Note: Green Speed (1977) not eligible for Ky. Futurity.

PACERS

Seven horses have won the first two legs of the Triple Crown, but not the third. The Cane Pace (CP), Little Brown Jug (LBJ), and Messenger Stakes (MS) have not always been run in the same order so numbers after races won indicate sequence for that year.

Year		CP	LBJ	MS
1957	**Torpid**	won, 1	won, 2	DNF
1960	**Countess Adios**	won, 2	NE	won, 1
1971	**Albatross**	won, 2	2nd*	won, 1
1976	**Keystone Ore**	won, 1	won, 2	2nd*
1986	**Barberry Spur**	won, 1	won, 2	2nd*
1990	**Jake and Elwood**	won, 1	NE	won, 2
1992	**Western Hanover**	won, 1	2nd*	won, 2

Winning horses: Nansemond (1971), Windshield Wiper (1976), Amity Chef (1986), Fake Left (1992).

Note: Torpid (1957) scratched before the final heat; Countess Adios (1960) not eligible for Messenger; Jake and Elwood (1990) not eligible for Little Brown Jug.

The Hambletonian

For three-year-old trotters. Inaugurated in 1926 and has been held in Syracuse, N.Y.; Lexington, Ky.; Goshen, N.Y, Yonkers, N.Y.; Du Quoin, Ill.; and, since 1981 at The Meadowlands in East Rutherford, N.J.

Run at one mile since 1947. Winning horse must win two heats.

Drivers with most wins: Ben White, Stanley Dancer and Bill Haughton (4); Howard Beissinger, Del Cameron, John Campbell and Henry Thomas (3).

Year		Driver	Fastest Heat	Year		Driver	Fastest Heat
1926	**Guy McKinney**	Nat Ray	2:04¾	1950	**Lusty Song**	Del Miller	2:02
1927	**Iosola's Worthy**	Marvin Childs	2:03¾	1951	**Mainliner**	Guy Crippen	2:02.3
1928	**Spencer**	W.H.Lessee	2:02½	1952	**Sharp Note**	Bion Shively	2:02.3
1929	**Walter Dear**	Walter Cox	2:02¾	1953	**Helicopter**	Harry Harvey	2:01.3
1930	**Hanover's Bertha**	Tom Berry	2:03	1954	**Newport Dream**	Del Cameron	2:02.4
1931	**Calumet Butler**	R.D.McMahon	2:03¼	1955	**Scott Frost**	Joe O'Brien	2:00.3
1932	**The Marchioness**	Wm. Caton	2:01¼	1956	**The Intruder**	Ned Bower	2:01.2
1933	**Mary Reynolds**	Ben White	2:03¾	1957	**Hickory Smoke**	John Simpson Sr.	2:00.1
1934	**Lord Jim**	Doc Parshall	2:02¾	1958	**Emily's Pride**	Flave Nipe	1:59.4
1935	**Greyhound**	Sep Palin	2:02¼	1959	**Diller Hanover**	Frank Ervin	2:01.1
1936	**Rosalind**	Ben White	2:01¾	1960	**Blaze Hanover**	Joe O'Brien	1:59.3
1937	**Shirley Hanover**	Henry Thomas	2:01½	1961	**Harlan Dean**	James Arthur	1:58.2
1938	**McLin Hanover**	Henry Tomas	2:02¼	1962	**A.C.'s Viking**	Sanders Russell	1:59.3
1939	**Peter Astra**	Doc Parshall	2:04¼	1963	**Speedy Scot**	Ralph Baldwin	1:57.3
1940	**Spencer Scott**	Fred Egan	2:02	1964	**Ayres**	John Simpson Sr.	1:56.4
1941	**Bill Gallon**	Lee Smith	2:05	1965	**Egyptian Candor**	Del Cameron	2:03.4
1942	**The Ambassador**	Ben White	2:04	1966	**Kerry Way**	Frank Ervin	1:58.4
1943	**Volo Song**	Ben White	2:02½	1967	**Speedy Streak**	Del Cameron	2:00
1944	**Yankee Maid**	Henry Thomas	2:04	1968	**Nevele Pride**	Stanley Dancer	1:59.2
1945	**Titan Hanover**	Harry Pownall,Sr.	2:04	1969	**Lindys Pride**	Howard Beissinger	1:57.3
1946	**Chestertown**	Thomas Berry	2:02½	1970	**Timothy T.**	John Simpson, Jr.	1:58.2
1947	**Hoot Mon**	Sep Palin	2:00	1971	**Speedy Crown**	Howard Beissinger	1:57.2
1948	**Demon Hanover**	Harrison Hoyt	2:02	1972	**Super Bowl**	Stanley Dancer	1:56.2
1949	**Miss Tilly**	Fred Egan	2:01.2	1973	**Flirth**	Ralph Baldwin	1:57.1

The Hambletonian (Cont.)

Year		Driver	Fastest Heat	Year		Driver	Fastest Heat
1974	Christopher T.	Bill Haughton	1:58.3	1984	Historic Freight	Ben Webster	1:56.2
1975	Bonefish	Stanley Dancer	1:59	1985	Prakas	Bill O'Donnell	1:54.3
1976	Steve Lobell	Bill Haughton	1:56.2	1986	Nuclear Kosmos	Ulf Thoresen	1:55.2
1977	Green Speed	Bill Haughton	1:55.3	1987	Mack Lobell	John Campbell	1:53.3
1978	Speedy Somolli	Howard Beissinger	1:55	1988	Armbro Goal	John Campbell	1:54.3
1979	Legend Hanover	George Sholty	1:56.1	1989	Park Avenue Joe & Probe	Ron Waples Bill Fahy	1:54.3
1980	Burgomeister	Bill Haughton	1:56.3				
1981	Shiaway St. Pat	Ray Remmen	2:01.1	1990	Harmonious	John Campbell	1:54.1
1982	Speed Bowl	Tommy Haughton	1:56.4	1991	Giant Victory	Jack.Moiseyev	1:55
1983	Duenna	Stanley Dancer	1:57.2	1992	Alf Palema	Mickey McNichol	1:56.3

Note: In 1989, Park Avenue Joe and Probe finished in a dead heat in the race-off. They were later declared co-winners, but Park Avenue Joe was awarded 1st place money because his three-race summary (2-1-1) was better than Probe's (1-9-1).

All-Time Leaders

The all-time winning trotters, pacers and drivers through 1990, according to *The Trotting and Pacing Guide*. Purses for horses include races in foreign countries. Purses, starts and wins for drivers include only races held in North America.

Top 10 Horses—Money Won

Note that (*) indicates horse raced in 1991.

		T/P	Sts	1st	Purses
1	Ourasi (FRA)*	T	N/A	32	$4,010,105
2	Peace Corps*	T	41	34	3,923,806
3	Mack Lobell*	T	86	65	3,917,594
4	Reve d'Udon*	T	23	18	3,611,351
5	Nihilator	P	38	35	3,225,653
6	Matt's Scooter	P	61	37	2,944,591
7	On the Road Again	P	61	44	2,819,102
8	Ideal du Gazeau (FRA)	T	N/A	21	2,744,777
9	Grades Singing	T	101	66	2,607,552
10	Beach Towel	P	36	29	2,570,357

Top 10 Drivers—Races Won

All drivers were active in 1991.

		Yrs	Wins	Earnings	(Rank)
1	Herve Filion	31	13,313	$ 75,102,112	(2)
2	Carmine Abbatiello	36	7,078	48,923,444	(5)
3	Michel Lachance	24	6,194	59,619,032	(4)
4	John Campbell	20	5,577	100,822,498	(1)
5	Walter Paisley	34	5,494	32,870,864	(12)
6	Joe Marsh, Jr	37	5,408	32,856,113	(13)
7	Buddy Gilmour	37	5,366	43,741,229	(7)
8	Ron Waples	26	5,277	47,690,620	(6)
9	Eddie Davis	28	5,197	24,478,213	(28)
10	Bill Gale	22	5,042	25,549,145	(23)

Annual Awards

Horse of the Year

Selected since 1947 by U.S. Trotting Association and the U.S. Harness Writers Association; age of winning horse is noted; (t) indicates trotter and (p) indicates pacer. USTA added Trotter and Pacer of the Year awards in 1970.

Multiple winners: Bret Hanover and Nevele Pride (3); Adios Butler, Albatross, Cam Fella, Good Time, Mack Lobell, Niatross and Scott Frost (2).

Year		Year		Year		Year	
1947	Victory Song (4t)	1959	Bye Bye Byrd (4p)	1970	Fresh Yankee (7t)	1981	Fan Hanover (3p)
1948	Rodney (4t)			1971	Albatross (3p)	1982	Cam Fella (4p)
1949	Good Time (3p)	1960	Adios Butler (4p)	1972	Albatross (4p)	1983	Cam Fella (4p)
		1961	Adios Butler (5p)	1973	Sir Dalrai (4p)	1984	Fancy Crown (3t)
1950	Proximity (8t)	1962	Su Mac Lad (8t)	1974	Delmonica Hanover (5t)	1985	Nihilator (3t)
1951	Pronto Don (6t)	1963	Speedy Scot (3t)	1975	Savoir (7t)	1986	Forrest Skipper (4p)
1952	Good Time (6t)	1964	Bret Hanover (2p)	1976	Keystone Ore (3p)	1987	Mack Lobell (3t)
1953	Hi Lo's Forbes (5p)	1965	Bret Hanover (3p)	1977	Green Speed (3t)	1988	Mack Lobell (4t)
1954	Stenographer (3t)	1966	Bret Hanover (4p)	1978	Abercrombie (3p)	1989	Matt's Scooter (4p)
1955	Scott Frost (3t)	1967	Nevele Pride (2t)	1979	Niatross (2p)		
1956	Scott Frost (4t)	1968	Nevele Pride (3t)	1980	Niatross (3p)	1990	Beach Towel (3p)
1957	Torpid (3p)	1969	Nevele Pride (4t)			1991	Precious Bunny (3p)
1958	Emily's Pride (3t)						

Driver of the Year

Determined by Universal Driving Rating System (UDR) and presented by the Harness Tracks of America since 1968. Eligible drivers must have at least 1000 starts for the season.

Multiple winners: Herve Filion (10); John Campbell and Michel Lachance (3); Bill O'Donnell and Ron Waples (2).

Year		Year		Year		Year	
1968	Stanley Dancer	1975	Joe O'Brien	1980	Ron Waples	1986	Michel Lachance
1969	Herve Filion	1976	Herve Filion	1981	Ron Waples	1987	Michel Lachance
		1977	Donald Dancer	1982	Bill O'Donnell	1988	John Campbell
1970	Herve Filion	1978	Carmine Abbatiello	1983	John Campbell	1989	Herve Filion
1971	Herve Filion		& Herve Filion	1984	Bill O'Donnell		
1972	Herve Filion	1979	Ron Waples	1985	Michel Lachance	1990	John Campbell
1973	Herve Filion					1991	Walter Case, Jr.
1974	Herve Filion						

Erik Mahr/Belleville (Ill.) News-Democrat

It was a year for new faces, but PBA legend **Dick Weber** made news when his victory in the Senior/Touring Pro Doubles stretched his decade winning streak to five.

BOWLING

New Kids

A bunch of unknown players and first-time winners leave longtime pro bowling fans wondering, "Who are those guys?"

The 1992 PBA season was less than two months old before long-time fans of ABC-TV's "Pro Bowlers Tour" were asking, "Who are those guys?" Gone, it seemed, were the familiar faces of Saturday afternoons past.

Enter pro bowling's New Kids on the Block. Thirty-four different players made the first seven telecasts of 1992 and 16 were unknowns outside of their home areas. The only PBA veteran able to make as many as two TV appearances in that stretch was six-time champion Dave Ferraro, and he finished fifth both times.

Five players who had never won before—Mike Scroggins, Alan Bishop, Eric Forkel, Bruce Hamilton and Bob Learn, Jr.—combined to win five consecutive tournaments from Jan. 25 to Feb. 22. And on March 28, Forkel walked off with the PBA National Championship after beating another unknown, Bob Vespi, in the final.

Did the New Kids' invasion worry the often too-set-in-its-ways Professional Bowlers Association? Not at all, according to commissioner Mike Connor, a new kid himself after succeeding outgoing PBA boss Joe Antenora on Jan. 1. "We have so many good young bowlers on tour," says Connor, "that anybody can beat any-

body. The depth of our talent, thanks to collegiate bowling, is unbelievable."

All this was an early indication that the 1992 bowling season was going to be vastly different from 1991.

For one thing, 1991 Bowler of the Year Dave Ozio was nowhere to be found on TV during the 16-week Winter and eight-week Spring tours. After winning four titles in '91 and topping the tour money list with $225,585, Ozio didn't make a single '92 telecast through the Summer tour and entered the Fall schedule with winnings of just $19,495.

And he wasn't the only veteran missing in action. PBA bad boy Pete Weber—who won the 1991 U.S. Open and came close to earning Bowler of the Year honors despite serving a six-month suspension—was winless through the summer, reaching the championship round in only two tournaments. And two-time Bowler of the Year Amleto Monacelli won only once—beating Weber in the final of the Choice Hotels Summer Classic in July.

Another big difference between 1992 and the year before was the absence of bomb scares like the ones that plagued three '91 telecasts.

There was, however, an earthquake. More than 250 senior bowlers were in Lakewood, Calif., June 28, for the Cal Bowl Open when a quake rumbled through Southern California. It lasted only 47 seconds, but seemed like an eternity.

Dick Evans has covered bowling for *The Miami Herald* since 1957. He is also a member of both the PBA and ABC halls of fame.

Allan Detrich/The Toledo Blade

Eric Forkel, who entered 1992 winless on the PBA tour, won two tournaments during the winter, including his first major at the PBA National in Toledo on March 28.

Nevertheless, it didn't scare off any of the contestants.

Senior tour regular Gene Stus, who has overcome two heart bypass operations, shook things up by himself five days later by bowling a perfect game on the ESPN telecast. Stus, a 51-year-old righthander from Allen Park, Mich., who had taken early retirement from General Motors in 1990, received $13,000 for winning the tournament and a record $110,000 in bonus money for the 300 game.

For a long time, the PBA had a standing offer of $10,000 for any senior who bowled a perfect game on live TV. Then, on June 19, the Brunswick Corp. announced it would give $50,000 to any bowler rolling a 300 game on live TV with a Brunswick ball and another $50,000 to any bowler rolling a perfect game on live TV in a Brunswick shirt.

Another senior making national headlines was Dick Weber, the Hall of Famer with 26 regular PBA titles, five senior PBA titles and four National All-Stars to his credit.

Weber, 62, had suffered a mild stroke in October at the last 1991 PBA senior stop in Lady Lake, Fla. He remained hospitalized for a week in nearby Leesburg, not knowing whether he would ever bowl again. But eight months later, on June 20, Weber was among the record 420 seniors who showed up for the opening of the '92 season at the Showboat Hotel's 106-lane center in Las Vegas.

Two months after that, at the Senior/Touring Pro Doubles tournament in Belleville, Ill., a coin flip helped Weber become the only player in PBA history to win a title in five different decades.

Justin Hromek and Tony Westlake of the regular PBA Tour had tied after 18 qualifying rounds and flipped a coin to decide who would pick between Weber and Don Johnson—who, like Weber, had 26 regular tour victories to his credit.

Hromek won the toss, picked Weber, and they never looked back until picking up the $28,000 winners' check. The only athletes who can match Weber's five-decade winning streak against major

Allan Detrich/The Toledo Blade

Home run hitter **Bob Vespi** reached three finals during the winter tour, but didn't finally win until July 4.

Leanne Barrette, who shared Bowler of the Year honors with Johnson in 1990, was the unanimous choice for the award in '91—winning three titles, topping the money list with $87,618, and averaging 211.48 a game. In 1992, however, she was winless through the summer and fourth on the money list with $31,600.

Things were much tighter in the PBA as the tour prepared to start up again in October. Six bowlers—New Kids Forkel and Vespi, along with veterans Ballard, Ferraro, Marc McDowell and Parker Bohn III—all had won two times, with Forkel out front in money won with $150,530.

In addition, Mike Aulby picked up his 20th tour title—the Green Bay Classic on Aug. 13—putting him in the elite company of fellow 20-title winners Earl Anthony (41), Mark Roth (33), Don Johnson and Dick Weber (26 each), Marshall Holman (21) and Dick Ritger (20).

Four bowlers also became PBA millionaires in 1992, as Monacelli, Wayne Webb, Brian Voss and Dave Husted all reached seven figures in career winnings—doubling the size of an exclusive club that also includes Holman ($1.6 million), Roth ($1.4), Anthony ($1.3) and Aulby ($1.2).

Voss joined the club in the most impressive fashion. At the Paula Carter's Homestead Classic on March 7, he defeated—in order—Ferraro (235-207), McDowell (211-207), Danny Wiseman (225-218) and Harry Sullins (225-209) to win the tournament and the $20,000 first prize.

"I wanted to hit the million-dollar mark the same way Earl Anthony did—with a win," said Voss after his 12th career win. "This was the best tournament of my life. It means so much more when you need the shots in the 10th frame to win and you make them like a true champion."

Five and half months later, the new Paula Carter's Pro Bowl-Homestead became the old Paula Carter's Pro-Bowl when Hurricane Andrew barrelled through Homestead, Fla., on Aug. 24, and leveled the establishment.

Of all the New Kids making names for themselves in 1992, perhaps none arrived with the impact of Vespi, who led three of the year's first 12 tournaments—the Las Vegas Showboat in January, the Florida Open in February and the PBA

national competition are two all-time greats: golfer Jack Nicklaus and retired jockey Bill Shoemaker.

"It's a thrill to win national titles in five decades," said Weber, recalling his first PBA triumphs at Paramus, N.J., and Dayton, Ohio, in 1959. "Last year it ran through my mind that I might never have a chance to win again after the stroke I suffered."

Stus and Weber's accomplishments may not have produced the TV highlight reel feeding frenzy that came in the wake of Del Ballard Jr.'s 1991 gutter ball, but it did generate headlines. And in Weber's case, nobody was asking, "Who's he?"

While the New Kids and Old-Timers were making news on the two men's tours, Tish Johnson was dominating the 1992 women's circuit.

Entering the Fall, the 1990 co-Bowler of the Year from Panorama City, Calif., was the LPBT leader in tournament wins (3), money won ($59,085) and average (212.62). She also won her first U.S. Open on March 1, beating Aleta Sill, 216-213, in the championship round.

National in March. He bowled poorly in two—losing in Las Vegas to Sullins (175-150) and to Forkel in Toledo (217-133)—but in Winter Park, Fla., he did better against Chris Warren, losing by 211-208.

Warren and Vespi are both cocky, excitable and talkative players, so it came as no surprise that sparks flew in their match. After Warren rolled his final strike for a come-from-behind victory, he appeared to point his finger at Vespi as he screamed, "I'm the man, I'm the man."

Later, Warren explained that it was nothing personal. "Bob Vespi is very aggressive," said Warren, "and that puts a lot of people off. But I don't mind at all because I'm pretty aggressive, too. That's what puts excitement into this game. We don't need a bunch of robots throwing balls down the lane."

McDowell is certainly no robot. Rookie of the Year in 1986, he also happens to be, at 29, the PBA's youngest president ever. And he's open to ideas. After winning the AC Delco Classic on Jan. 11, he revealed that he had been seeing a hypno-therapist who made a tape for him to strengthen his mental game. "One of the things he says on [the tape] is that I can be Player of the Year," McDowell said. "Winning the first tournament of the year is the best way to start."

The second best way is to win your first major championship at the Firestone Tournament of Champions in Akron, Ohio—the final stop on the 16-week winter tour.

McDowell did that on April 25, even though the crowd at the Riviera Lanes was pulling for Wiseman and Don Genalo. Wiseman was trying to win a major in front of his dying father, Albert; while Genalo reached the championship round despite being only a part-time player.

"It was unbelievable with Danny and his father," said McDowell after eliminating Wiseman in the semifinals, 248-236. "I'm an emotional guy and I felt bad about beating him, but I couldn't let my feelings overcome what I was here to do, and that's win."

In two other major tournaments, Robert Lawrence defeated Scott Devers to win the BPAA U.S. Open on Apr. 11. And Ken Johnson, an unknown from North Richland Hills, Tex., beat Dave D'Entremont to win the ABC Masters on May 2.

Russ Vitale/Bowlers Journal

Marc McDowell revealed that visits to a hypno-therapist helped his confidence. To prove it, he won the Firestone.

Meanwhile, Ferraro, who lost his first game on TV four straight times, beat four opponents to win the Johnny Petraglia Open at North Brunswick, N.J., on Mar. 14.

"Winning my first game was the key," said Ferraro. "When you get going, you can build up a head of steam on TV. But I'd still rather bowl as the top-seeded player rather than have to win four consecutive games."

On June 13, as the top qualifier at the Active West Open in Riverside, Calif., he got his wish—beating David Traber, 217-202, in his only game.

Ferraro's argument that the stepladder TV finals seem to favor the first bowler to win a match or the last player to appear on the telecast is a valid one. In the first 29 events of 1992, the top-seeded player came away with 10 victories and the player who survived the opening match wound up winning the championship trophy seven times.

Forkel, the first player to win twice in '92, also won from the bottom and the top. In his third TV appearance ever on Feb. 8, he was seeded first and defeated

Mort Luby, Jr./Bowlers Journal

While no dominant player emerged on the men's tour through the summer, **Tish Johnson**, seen here after winning her first U.S. Open championship in March, was the leader of the pack on the LPBT circuit with three wins and the top average.

veteran Dave Husted, 204-192, to win the Flagship City Open.

Seven weeks later at the PBA National, Forkel won four matches, including the 217-133 championship laugher over Vespi, the John Daly of pro bowling. Forkel explained the lopsided victory this way: "Bob lives and dies with the home run ball. Sometimes a singles and doubles hitter overcomes the player who swings for the fences."

At the Tucson Open on July 4, Vespi finally produced enough fireworks to win his first PBA tournament. He went for the fences again and it paid off with wins over Webb (244-225), Traber (259-226), Norm Duke (244-187) and Ron Williams (234-203).

"It feels great to finally accomplish my goal of winning a title," said Vespi, who averaged better than 244. "I might even be close to a 200 average on TV now."

A month later Vespi won ABC West Lanes Open from the top qualifying position, beating Jim Pencak, 279-205, with 11 strike balls. That gave him six national TV appearances—two behind Ferraro, one more than McDowell and two ahead of Ballard and Bohn.

Ballard finally won a game and a tournament on April 4, when he successfully defended his Long Island Open title in Sayville, N.Y. "I don't know why, but I had a lot of people behind me," said Ballard. "Who would've thought a bowler from Texas would consider Long Island his second home?"

Ballard's second victory came two months later across country at the Oregon Open in Portland.

Bohn, a lefthander like Forkel, won both of his '92 titles in Texas during the summer. The first came at the El Paso Open in June and the second in July when he teamed with fellow lefty Hugh Miller to win the Beaumont PBA Doubles Classic.

Finally, the PBA introduced the "Kool Shootouts" in 1992. The one-game exhibiton matches were fun for the fans and financially rewarding for the players selected to participate.

Some of the interesting match-ups included Dick Weber and son Pete against Don Johnson and his son Jimmy; good guys Brian Voss and Mike Aulby; and all-time PBA money leaders Marshall Holman and Mark Roth.

Holman beat Pete Weber in the Shoot-out of Champions before the start of the Firestone tournament in April to win $6,000. At the four-player Shootout of Legends in June, Carmen Salvino put on one of his best vaudeville acts and also got the only strike of the match in the 10th frame to win $10,500. □

BOWLING
STATISTICS

THE SEASON IN REVIEW
1991-1992

PBA • SENIORS • LPBT

SEC
A

PAGE
683

THE 1993 *SPORTS ALMANAC* INFORMATION PLEASE

Tournament Results

Winners of stepladder finals in all PBA, Seniors and LPBT tournaments from the Fall Tours of 1991 through the Summer Tours of 1992; major tournaments in **bold** type; (a) indicates amateur.

PBA

1991 Fall Tour

Final	Event	Winner	Earnings	Score	Runner-up
Oct. 5	Toyota Classic	Danny Wiseman	$27,000	204-200	John Mazza
Oct. 13	Japan Cup '91 (Tokyo)	Walter R. Williams Jr.	18,500	211-189	John Mazza
Nov. 16	Brunswick World Open	Jess Stayrook	34,120	234-215	Ron Palombi, Jr.
Nov. 23	Chevy Truck Classic	David Ozio	27,000	235-160	Marc McDowell
Nov. 30	Touring Players Championship	Dave Ferraro	27,000	213-212	Roger Bowker
Dec. 8	Cambridge Mixed Doubles	Del Ballard Jr./ Nikki Giannulias	40,000	+69 pins	Robert Lawrence/ Rene Fleming
Dec. 15	National Resident Championship	Kevin McGerr	6,000	218-215	Bob Vespi

1992 Winter Tour

Final	Event	Winner	Earnings	Score	Runner-up
Jan. 11	AC-Delco Classic	Marc McDowell	$37,000	216-190	Wayne Webb
Jan. 18	Showboat Invitational	Harry Sullins	35,000	175-150	Bob Vespi
Jan. 25	ARC Sacramento PBA Open	Mike Scroggins	23,000	242-202	Robert Lawrence
Feb. 1	Quaker State Open	Alan Bishop	36,000	223-190	Jess Stayrook
Feb. 8	Flagship City Open	Eric Forkel	27,000	204-192	Dave Husted
Feb. 15	True Value Open	Bruce Hamilton	40,000	224-180	Amleto Monacelli
Feb. 22	Fair Lanes Open	Bob Learn Jr.	31,000	253-163	Dave D'Entremont
Feb. 29	Florida Open	Chris Warren	23,000	211-208	Bob Vespi
Mar. 7	Paula Carter's Homestead Classic	Brian Voss	20,000	225-209	Harry Sullins
Mar. 14	Johnny Petraglia Open	Dave Ferraro	28,000	216-200	Joe Salvemini
Mar. 21	Cleveland Open	Steve Cook	21,000	214-201	Mike Aulby
Mar. 28	**PBA National Championship**	Eric Forkel	55,000	217-133	Bob Vespi
Apr. 4	Toyota Long Island Open	Del Ballard Jr.	27,000	244-201	Dave Ferraro
Apr. 11	**BPAA U.S. Open**	Robert Lawrence	40,000	226-221	Scott Devers
Apr. 18	Tums Classic	Jimmy Keeth	31,000	234-217	Walter Williams Jr.
Apr. 25	**Firestone Tourn. of Champions**	Marc McDowell	60,000	223-193	Don Genalo
May 2	**Bud Light ABC Masters**	Ken Johnson	43,600	235-207	Dave D'Entremont

Note: The American Bowling Congress Masters tournament is not a PBA Tour event.

1992 Spring/Summer Tour

Final	Event	Winner	Earnings	Score	Runner-up
May 23	Earl Anthony Open	Mike Shady	$18,000	247-178	Parker Bohn III
May 30	Seattle Open	Eric Adolphson	18,000	234-161	Dave D'Entremont
June 6	Oregon PBA Open	Del Ballard Jr.	20,000	256-204	Mark Thayer
June 13	Active West PBA Open	Dave Ferraro	18,000	217-202	David Traber
June 20	Fresno Open	Dave D'Entremont	18,000	258-195	Marc McDowell
June 27	El Paso Open	Parker Bohn III	20,000	247-212	Derek Williams
July 4	Tuscon Open	Bob Vespi	18,000	234-203	Ron Williams
July 11	Wichita Open	Mike Miller	20,000	202-198	Ron Williams
July 18*	Choice Hotels Summer Classic	Amleto Monacelli	38,000	241-212	Pete Weber
July 23	PBA Doubles Classic	Parker Bohn III/ Hugh Miller	28,000	268-182	Mike Scroggins/ Mark Scroggins
July 30	Columbia 300 Open	Roger Bowker	21,000	228-208	Butch Soper
Aug. 6	Senior Touring Pro Doubles	Justin Hromek/ Dick Weber	28,000	248-200	Bob Benoit/ Nelson Burton Jr.
Aug. 13	Green Bay Classic	Mike Aulby	18,000	289-172	Bill Oakes
Aug. 20	ABC West Lanes Open	Bob Vespi	18,000	279-205	Jim Pencak

*Monacelli defeated Gene Stus in Choice Challenge $25,000 Winner-Take-All match.

Tournament Results (Cont.)
SENIOR PBA
1991 Fall Tour

Final	Event	Winner	Earnings	Score	Runner-up
Oct. 3	Woodside Open	Robert Gibbs	$ 5,000	203-196	John Hricsina
Oct. 10	Villages Open	John Handegard	5,000	259-254	Teata Semiz

1992 Summer Tour

Final	Event	Winner	Earnings	Score	Runner-up
June 25	Showboat Invitational	Larry Galloway	$14,000	170-153	Gene Stus
July 2	Pacific Cal Bowl Open	Gene Stus	9,000*	225-216	John Handegard
July 9	Escondido Open	Mike Samardzija	8,000	193-188	John Handegard
July 16	Rocky Mountain Open	John Handegard	8,000	251-201	Gene Stus
Aug. 6	Senior Touring Pro Doubles	Dick Weber/ Justin Hromek	28,000	248-200	Nelson Burton Jr./ Bob Benoit
Aug. 12	Jackson Open	a-Lon Marshall	5,000	214-192	Tommy Evans
Aug. 19	Lansing Open	Barry Gurney	5,000	243-166	Tommy Evans
Aug. 29	**Ebonite Senior Championship**	Gene Stus	20,000	192-166	Teata Semiz
Sept. 5	Canadian Open	Tommy Evans	5,000	235-214	Jim Lewis

*Stus bowled a 300-game on live national TV in his first match of the finals to earn bonuses of $110,300 ($10,000 from the PBA, $300 from the Cal Bowl, and $100,000 from Brunswick for using the sponsor's ball and shirt).

LPBT
1991 Fall Tour

Final	Event	Winner	Earnings	Score	Runner-up
Oct. 9	Hammer Eastern Open	Tish Johnson	$ 9,000	187-174	Dana Miller-Mackie
Oct. 16	Columbia 300 Delaware Open	Donna Adamek	12,600	195-189	Carol Norman
Oct. 23	Brunswick Open	Leanne Barrette	9,000	234-171	Donna Adamek
Oct. 30	Hammer Midwest Open	Carol Norman	9,000	195-193	AnneMarie Duggan
Nov. 6	Denver Classic	Leanne Barrette	6,000	269-197	Robin Romeo
Nov. 13	Ebonite Fall Classic	Dana Miller-Mackie	10,800	228-178	Donna Adamek
Nov. 23	**Sam's Town Invitational**	Lorrie Nichols	18,000	235-223	Dana Miller-Mackie
Dec. 8	Cambridge Mixed Doubles	Nikki Gianulias/ Del Ballard Jr.	40,000	+69 pins	Rene Fleming/ Robert Lawrence

1992 Winter Tour

Final	Event	Winner	Earnings	Score	Runner-up
Feb. 2	Las Vegas Western Open	Tish Johnson	$ 6,000	203-180	Cheryl Daniels
Feb. 9	Yuba City Open	Anne Marie Duggan	6,000	206-171	Tish Johnson
Feb. 16	Hemet Open	Sue Neidig	6,000	257-181	AnneMarie Duggan
Feb. 23	Santa Maria Classic	Carol Norman	6,000	203-175	SandraJo Shiery
Mar. 1	**BPAA U.S. Open**	Tish Johnson	18,000	216-213	Aleta Sill
Mar. 8	Yuma Open	Michelle Mullen	9,000	265-237	Dede Davidson

1992 Spring/Summer Tour

Final	Event	Winner	Earnings	Score	Runner-up
Apr. 9	Robby Open	Linda Kelly	$ 7,000	191-190	Wendy Macpherson
Apr. 16	New Orleans Classic	Carol Gianotti	5,000	182-161	Donna Adamek
Apr. 23	Central Florida Classic	Cheryl Daniels	5,000	209-187	Leanne Barrette
Apr. 30	Athens Open	Robin Romeo	5,000	184-178	AnneMarie Duggan
May 7	Blue Ribbon Ladies Classic	Jackie Sellers	7,000	193-170	Lisa Wagner
May 14	**WIBC Queens**	Cindy Coburn-Carroll	12,525	184-170	Dana Miller-Mackie
May 21	Michigan Ladies Classic	Tish Johnson	5,000	221-190	Leanne Barrette
May 28	Brunswick Open	Nikki Gianulias	9,000	204-184	Tish Johnson
Aug. 15	Gold Rush Mixed Doubles	Robin Romeo/ Rick Easley	10,000	437-414	Sharon Todd/ Steve Todd
Aug. 19	National Doubles	Stacy Rider/ Anne Marie Duggan	11,000	191-166	Maria Lewis/ Darris Street

Note: The Women's International Bowling Congress Queens tournament is not an LPBT Tour event.

1992 Fall Tour Schedules
PBA
Events (5): Japan Cup '92 (Oct. 8-11); Touring Players Championship (Oct. 17-21); Rochester Open (Oct. 24-28); Greater Detroit Open (Oct. 31-Nov. 4); Brunswick World Open (Nov. 5-11).

SENIOR PBA
Events (3): Don Carter Classic (Sept. 27-30); Naples Hammer Open (Oct. 3-7); Pinellas Suncoast Open (Oct. 10-14).

LPBT
Events (7): Columbia 300 Delaware Open (Oct. 3-7); Hammer Eastern Open (Oct. 10-14); Princess Lanes—no title (Oct. 21-25); Hammer Midwest Open (Oct. 28-Nov. 1); Ebonite Fall Classic (Nov. 4-8); River Valley Recreation—no title (Nov. 11-15); Sam's Town Invitational (Nov. 15-22).

Tour Leaders

Official Top 10 standings for 1991 and unofficial Top 10 standings (including summer tours) for 1992. PBA, Seniors and LPBT figures for 1992 reflect performances through Sept. 5.

Final 1991

PBA

Top 10 Money Winners

		Tourn	Titles	Earnings
1	David Ozio	32	4	$225,585
2	John Mazza	31	3	154,280
3	Amleto Monacelli	27	2	146,315
4	Del Ballard, Jr.	28	4	146,150
5	Pete Weber	19	3	144,945
6	Norm Duke	25	2	144,175
7	Walter Ray Williams Jr.	32	1	120,030
8	Bob Benoit	32	2	116,965
9	Jess Stayrook	34	2	101,895
10	Mike Miller	21	1	99,663

Note: Earnings include ABC Masters.

Top 5 Averages

		Gm	Pinfall	Avg
1	Norm Duke	883	192,678	218.21
2	Pete Weber	730	158,277	216.82
3	Walter R. Williams Jr	998	215,417	215.85
4	David Ozio	1053	227,072	215.64
5	John Mazza	1070	230,098	215.05

SENIOR PBA

Top 10 Money Winners

		Tourn	Titles	Earnings
1	John Handegard	12	3	$52,220
2	Gene Stus	11	2	40,900
3	John Hricsina	12	0	28,580
4	Teata Semiz	11	1	27,100
5	Tommy Evans	12	0	22,653
6	Jimmy Certain	12	0	21,418
7	Robert Gibbs	12	1	20,810
8	Mickey Spiezio	12	1	20,483
9	Dave Soutar	11	0	17,838
10	Don Johnson	12	0	16,890

Top 5 Averages

		Gm	Pinfall	Avg
1	Gene Stus	420	93,023	221.48
2	John Handegard	443	98,070	221.38
3	John Hricsina	422	92,496	219.19
4	Robert Gibbs	363	78,877	217.29
5	Jimmy Certain	375	81,362	216.97

LPBT

Top 10 Money Winners

		Tourn	Titles	Earnings
1	Leanne Barrette	20	3	$87,618
2	Donna Adamek	20	2	78,170
3	Dana Miller-Mackie	17	2	73,135
4	Nikki Gianulias	20	4	61,409
5	Anne Marie Duggan	20	1	51,720
6	Tish Johnson	19	2	51,263
7	Lorrie Nichols	19	1	49,605
8	Sandra Jo Shiery	19	1	47,368
9	Carol Norman	17	1	41,660
10	Aleta Sill	18	1	41,270

Note: Earnings include WIBC Queens.

Top 5 Averages

		Gm	Pinfall	Avg
1	Leanne Barrette	798	168,760	211.4787
2	Donna Adamek	769	162,627	211.4785
3	Sandra Jo Shiery	710	149,173	210.10
4	Wendy Macpherson	743	155,251	208.95
5	Dana Miller-Mackie	647	135,091	208.79

1992 (through Sept. 5)

PBA

Top 10 Money Winners

		Tourn	Titles	Earnings
1	Eric Forkel	29	2	$150,530
2	Marc McDowell	26	2	139,155
3	Dave Ferraro	24	2	126,115
4	Bob Vespi	27	2	125,785
5	Dave D'Entremont	28	1	108,525
6	Amleto Monacelli	23	1	107,150
7	Del Ballard Jr	24	2	88,035
8	Parker Bohn III	27	2	85,340
9	Robert Lawrence	27	1	84,445
10	Harry Sullins	30	1	74,065

Note: Earnings include ABC Masters.

Top 5 Averages

		Gm	Pinfall	Avg
1	Dave Ferraro	897	197,466	220.14
2	Eric Forkel	870	190,180	218.60
3	Amleto Monacelli	695	151,737	218.33
4	Ron Williams	829	180,639	217.90
5	Dave D'Entremont	853	185,774	217.79

SENIOR PBA

Top 10 Money Winners

		Tourn	Titles	Earnings
1	Gene Stus	9	2	$58,525
2	John Handegard	9	1	30,425
3	Teata Semiz	8	0	22,300
4	Dick Weber	9	1	22,030
5	Tommy Evans	9	1	19,500
6	Ron Winger	8	0	17,480
7	John Hricsina	9	0	17,045
8	Nelson Burton Jr.	4	0	15,750
9	Larry Galloway	6	1	15,230
10	Dave Davis	7	0	12,885

Top 5 Averages

		Gm	Pinfall	Avg
1	John Handegard	381	84,142	220.85
2	Gene Stus	381	83,833	220.03
3	Teata Semiz	274	60,037	219.11
4	Tommy Evans	307	67,153	218.74
5	Dave Davis	278	60,727	218.44

LPBT

Top 10 Money Winners

		Tourn	Titles	Earnings
1	Tish Johnson	15	3	$59,960
2	Anne Marie Duggan	15	2	47,490
3	Carol Gianotti	14	1	32,735
4	Leanne Barrette	15	0	32,600
5	Michelle Mullen	14	1	28,330
6	Jackie Sellers	14	1	27,050
7	Cindy Coburn-Carroll	13	1	26,590
8	Dede Davidson	15	0	24,520
9	Cheryl Daniels	13	1	24,440
10	Lisa Wagner	15	0	24,375

Note: Earnings include WIBC Queens.

Top 5 Averages

		Gm	Pinfall	Avg
1	Tish Johnson	559	118,408	211.82
2	Leanne Barrette	539	114,168	211.81
3	Aleta Sill	237	50,071	211.27
4	Anne Marie Duggan	588	124,140	211.12
5	Wendy Macpherson	467	98,133	210.13

THE 1993 SPORTS ALMANAC — INFORMATION PLEASE

BOWLING STATISTICS

THROUGH THE YEARS 1942-1992

CHAMPIONS • AWARDS

SEC B

PAGE 686

Major Championships
MEN
BPAA U.S. Open

Started in 1941 by the Bowling Proprietors' Association of America, 18 years before the founding of the Professional Bowlers Association. Originally the BPAA All-Star Tournament, it became the U.S. Open in 1971. There were two BPAA All-Star tournaments in 1955, in January and December.

Multiple winners: Don Carter and Dick Weber (4); Marshall Holman, Junie McMahon, Connie Schwoegler, Andy Varipapa and Pete Weber (2).

Year		Year		Year		Year	
1942	John Crimmons	1955	Steve Nagy	1968	Jim Stefanich	1980	Steve Martin
1943	Connie Schwoegler	1956	Bill Lillard	1969	Billy Hardwick	1981	Marshall Holman
1944	Ned Day	1957	Don Carter			1982	Dave Husted
1945	Buddy Bomar	1958	Don Carter	1970	Bobby Cooper	1983	Gary Dickinson
1946	Joe Wilman	1959	Billy Welu	1971	Mike Limongello	1984	Mark Roth
1947	Andy Varipapa			1972	Don Johnson	1985	Marshall Holman
1948	Andy Varipapa	1960	Harry Smith	1973	Mike McGrath	1986	Steve Cook
1949	Connie Schwoegler	1961	Bill Tucker	1974	Larry Laub	1987	Del Ballard, Jr
		1962	Dick Weber	1975	Steve Neff	1988	Pete Weber
1950	Junie McMahon	1963	Dick Weber	1976	Paul Moser	1989	Mike Aulby
1951	Dick Hoover	1964	Bob Strampe	1977	Johnny Petraglia		
1952	Junie McMahon	1965	Dick Weber	1978	Nelson Burton, Jr	1990	Ron Palombi, Jr
1953	Don Carter	1966	Dick Weber	1979	Joe Berardi	1991	Pete Weber
1954	Don Carter	1967	Les Schissler			1992	Robert Lawrence

ABC Masters Tournament

Sponsored by the American Bowling Congress. The Masters is not a PBA event, but is considered one of the four major tournaments on the men's tour and is open to qualified pros and amateurs.

Multiple winners: Earl Anthony, Billy Golembiewski, Dick Hoover and Billy Welu (2).

Year		Year		Year		Year	
1951	Lee Jouglard	1962	Billy Golembiewski	1973	Dave Soutar	1984	Earl Anthony
1952	Willard Taylor	1963	Harry Smith	1974	Paul Colwell	1985	Steve Wunderlich
1953	Rudy Habetler	1964	Billy Welu	1975	Eddie Ressler	1986	Mark Fahy
1954	Red Elkins	1965	Billy Welu	1976	Nelson Burton, Jr.	1987	Rick Steelsmith
1955	Buzz Fazio	1966	Bob Strampe	1977	Earl Anthony	1988	Del Ballard, Jr.
1956	Dick Hoover	1967	Lou Scalia	1978	Frank Ellenburg	1989	Mike Aulby
1957	Dick Hoover	1968	Pete Tountas	1979	Doug Myers		
1958	Tom Hennessey	1969	Jim Chestney			1990	Chris Warren
1959	Ray Bluth	1970	Don Glover	1980	Neil Burton	1991	Doug Kent
		1971	Jim Godman	1981	Randy Lightfoot	1992	Ken Johnson
1960	Billy Golembiewski	1972	Bill Beach	1982	Joe Berardi		
1961	Don Carter			1983	Mike Lastowski		

Firestone Tournament of Champions

The Tournament of Champions has been held in Akron, Ohio, since it began in 1965.

Multiple winners: Mike Durbin (3); Earl Anthony, Jim Godman, Marshall Holman and Mark Williams (2).

Year		Year		Year		Year	
1965	Billy Hardwick	1972	Mike Durbin	1980	Wayne Webb	1987	Pete Weber
1966	Wayne Zahn	1973	Jim Godman	1981	Steve Cook	1988	Mark Williams
1967	Jim Stefanich	1974	Earl Anthony	1982	Mike Durbin	1989	Del Ballard, Jr.
1968	Dave Davis	1975	Dave Davis	1983	Joe Berardi		
1969	Jim Godman	1976	Marshall Holman	1984	Mike Durbin	1990	Dave Ferraro
		1977	Mike Berlin	1985	Mark Williams	1991	David Ozio
1970	Don Johnson	1978	Earl Anthony	1986	Marshall Holman	1992	Marc McDowell
1971	Johnny Petraglia	1979	George Pappas				

PBA National Championship

The Professional Bowlers Association was formed in 1958 and its first national championship tournament was held in Memphis in 1960. The tournament has been held in Toledo, Ohio, since 1981.

Multiple winners: Earl Anthony (6); Mike Aulby, Dave Davis, Mike McGrath and Wayne Zahn (2).

Year		Year		Year		Year	
1960	Don Carter	1969	Mike McGrath	1977	Tommy Hudson	1985	Mike Aulby
1961	Dave Soutar	1970	Mike McGrath	1978	Warren Nelson	1986	Tom Crites
1962	Carmen Salvino	1971	Mike Limongello	1979	Mike Aulby	1987	Randy Pedersen
1963	Billy Hardwick	1972	Johnny Guenther			1788	Brian Voss
1964	Bob Strampe	1973	Earl Anthony	1980	Johnny Petraglia	1989	Pete Weber
1965	Dave Davis	1974	Earl Anthony	1981	Earl Anthony		
1966	Wayne Zahn	1975	Earl Anthony	1982	Earl Anthony	1990	Jim Pencak
1967	Dave Davis	1976	Paul Colwell	1983	Earl Anthony	1991	Mike Miller
1968	Wayne Zahn			1984	Bob Chamberlain	1992	Eric Forkel

WOMEN
BPAA U.S.Open

Started by the Bowling Proprietors' Association of America in 1949, 11 years before the founding of the Professional Women's Bowling Association. Originally the BPAA Women's All-Star Tournament, it became the U.S. Open in 1971. There were two BPAA All-Star tournaments in 1955, in January and December. Note that (a) indicates amateur.

Multiple winners: Marion Ladewig (8); Donna Adamek, Paula Sperber Carter, Pat Costello, Dotty Fothergill, Dana Miller-Mackie and Sylvia Wene (2).

Year		Year		Year		Year	
1949	Marion Ladewig	1960	Sylvia Wene	1972	a-Lorrie Koch	1983	Dana Miller
1950	Marion Ladewig	1961	Phyllis Notaro	1973	Millie Martorella	1984	Karen Ellingsworth
1951	Marion Ladewig	1962	Shirley Garms	1974	Pat Costello	1985	Pat Mercatanti
1952	Marion Ladewig	1963	Marion Ladewig	1975	Paula Sperber Carter	1986	Wendy Macpherson
1953	Not held	1964	LaVerne Carter	1976	Patty Costello	1987	Carol Norman
1954	Marion Ladewig	1965	Ann Slattery	1977	Betty Morris	1988	Lisa Wagner
1955	Sylvia Wene	1966	Joy Abel	1978	Donna Adamek	1989	Robin Romeo
1955	Anita Cantaline	1967	Gloria Bouvia	1979	Diana Silva		
1956	Marion Ladewig	1968	Dotty Fothergill			1990	Dana Miller-Mackie
1957	Not held	1969	Dotty Fothergill	1980	Pat Costello	1991	Anne Marie Duggan
1958	Merle Matthews	1970	Mary Baker	1981	Donna Adamek	1992	Tish Johnson
1959	Marion Ladewig	1971	a-Paula Sperber	1982	Shinobu Saitoh		

WIBC Queens

Sponsored by the Women's International Bowling Congress, the Queens is a double elimination, match play tournament. It is not an LPBT event, but is open to qualified pros and amateurs. Note that (a) indicates amateur.

Multiple winners: Mille Martorella (3); Donna Adamek, Dotty Fothergill, Aleta Sill and Katsuko Sugimoto (2).

Year		Year		Year		Year	
1961	Janet Harman	1970	Millie Martorella	1979	Donna Adamek	1986	Cora Fiebig
1962	Dorothy Wilkinson	1971	Millie Martorella			1987	Cathy Almeida
1963	Irene Monterosso	1972	Dotty Fothergill	1980	Donna Adamek	1988	Wendy Macpherson
1964	D.D. Jacobson	1973	Dotty Fothergill	1981	Katsuko Sugimoto	1989	Carol Gianotti
1965	Betty Kuczynski	1974	Judy Soutar	1982	Katsuko Sugimoto		
1966	Judy Lee	1975	Cindy Powell	1983	Aleta Sill	1990	a-Patty Ann
1967	Millie Martorella	1976	Pam Buckner	1984	Kazue Inahashi	1991	Dede Davidson
1968	Phyllis Massey	1977	Dana Stewart	1985	Aleta Sill	1992	Cindy Coburn-Carroll
1969	Ann Feigel	1978	Loa Boxberger				

Sam's Town Invitational

Originally held in Milwaukee as the Pabst Tournament of Champions, but discontinued after one year (1981). The event was revived in 1984, moved to Las Vegas and renamed Sam's Town Tournament of Champions. Since then it has been known as the LPBT Tournament of Champions (1985), the Sam's Town National Pro/Am (1986-88) and the Sam's Town Invitational (since 1989).

Multiple winner: Aleta Sill (2).

Year		Year		Year		Year	
1981	Cindy Coburn	1985	Patty Costello	1988	Donna Adamek	1990	Wendy Macpherson
1982-83	Not held	1986	Aleta Sill	1989	Tish Johnson	1991	Lorrie Nichols
1984	Aleta Sill	1987	Debbie Bennett				

Major Championships (Cont.)
WOMEN
WPBA National Championship (1960-1980)

The Women's Professional Bowling Association National Championship tournament was discontinued when the WPBA broke up in 1981. The WPBA changed its name from the Professional Women Bowlers Association (PWBA) in 1978.

Multiple winners: Patty Costello (3); Dotty Fothergill (2).

Year		Year		Year		Year	
1960	Marion Ladewig	1966	Judy Lee	1972	Patty Costello	1977	Vesma Grinfelds
1961	Shirley Garms	1967	Betty Mivelaz	1973	Betty Morris	1978	Toni Gillard
1962	Stevie Balogh	1968	Dotty Fothergill	1974	Pat Costello	1979	Cindy Coburn
1963	Janet Harman	1969	Dotty Fothergill	1975	Pam Buckner	1980	Donna Adamek
1964	Betty Kuczynski	1970	Bobbe North	1976	Patty Costello		
1965	Helen Duval	1971	Patty Costello				

Annual Leaders
Average
PBA Tour

The George Young Memorial Award, named after the late ABC Hall of Fame bowler. Based on at least 16 national PBA tournaments from 1959-78, and at least 400 games of tour competition since 1979.

Multiple winners: Mark Roth (6); Earl Anthony (5); Marshall Holman (3); Billy Hardwick, Don Johnson and Wayne Zahn (2).

Year		Avg	Year		Avg	Year		Avg
1962	Don Carter	212.84	1972	Don Johnson	215.29	1982	Marshall Holman	216.15
1963	Bill Hardwick	210.35	1973	Earl Anthony	215.80	1983	Earl Anthony	216.65
1964	Ray Bluth	210.51	1974	Earl Anthony	219.34	1984	Marshall Holman	213.91
1965	Dick Weber	211.90	1975	Earl Anthony	219.06	1985	Mark Baker	213.72
1966	Wayne Zahn	208.63	1976	Mark Roth	215.97	1986	John Gant	214.38
1967	Wayne Zahn	212.14	1977	Mark Roth	218.17	1987	Marshall Holman	216.80
1968	Jim Stefanich	211.90	1978	Mark Roth	219.83	1988	Mark Roth	218.04
1969	Billy Hardwick	212.96	1979	Mark Roth	221.66	1989	Pete Weber	215.43
1970	Nelson Burton Jr.	214.91	1980	Earl Anthony	218.54	1990	Amleto Monacelli	218.16
1971	Don Johnson	213.98	1981	Mark Roth	216.70	1991	Norm Duke	218.21

LPBT Tour

Based on at least 282 games of tour competition.

Multiple winners: Nikki Gianulias and Lisa Rathgeber Wagner (3); Leanne Barrette and Aleta Sill (2).

Year		Avg	Year		Avg	Year		Avg
1981	Nikki Gianulias	213.71	1985	Aleta Sill	211.10	1989	Lisa Wagner	211.87
1982	Nikki Gianulias	210.63	1986	Nikki Gianulias	213.89	1990	Leanne Barrette	211.53
1983	Lisa Rathgeber	208.50	1987	Wendy Macpherson	211.11	1991	Leanne Barrette	211.48
1984	Aleta Sill	210.68	1988	Lisa Wagner	213.02			

Money Won
PBA Tour

Multiple winners: Earl Anthony (6); Dick Weber and Mark Roth (4); Mike Aulby and Don Carter (2).

Year		Earnings	Year		Earnings
1959	Dick Weber	$7,672	1976	Earl Anthony	$110,833
1960	Don Carter	22,525	1977	Mark Roth	105,583
1961	Dick Weber	26,280	1978	Mark Roth	134,500
1962	Don Carter	49,972	1979	Mark Roth	124,517
1963	Dick Weber	46,333	1980	Wayne Webb	116,700
1964	Bob Strampe	33,592	1981	Earl Anthony	164,735
1965	Dick Weber	47,675	1982	Earl Anthony	134,760
1966	Wayne Zahn	54,720	1983	Earl Anthony	135,605
1967	Dave Davis	54,165	1984	Mark Roth	158,712
1968	Jim Stefanich	67,375	1985	Mike Aulby	201,200
1969	Billy Hardwick	64,160	1988	Walter Ray Williams, Jr.	145,550
1970	Mike McGrath	52,049	1987	Peter Weber	179,516
1971	Johnny Petraglia	85,065	1988	Brian Voss	225,485
1972	Don Johnson	56,648	1989	Mike Aulby	298,237
1973	Don McCune	69,000	1990	Amleto Monacelli	204,775
1974	Earl Anthony	99,585	1991	David Ozio	225,585
1975	Earl Anthony	107,585			

WPBA and LPBT Tours

WPBA leaders through 1980; LPBT leaders since 1981.

Multiple winners: Aleta Sill (4); Donna Adamek, Patty Costello and Betty Morris (3); Dotty Fothergill and Nikki Gianulias (2).

Year		Earnings	Year		Earnings	Year		Earnings
1965	Betty Kuczynski	$3,792	1974	Betty Morris	$30,037	1983	Aleta Sill	$42,525
1966	Joy Abel	5,795	1975	Judy Soutar	20,395	1984	Aleta Sill	81,452
1967	Shirley Garms	4,920	1976	Patty Costello	39,585	1985	Aleta Sill	52,655
1968	Dotty Fothergill	16,170	1977	Betty Morris	23,802	1988	Aleta Sill	36,212
1969	Dotty Fothergill	9,220	1978	Donna Adamek	31,000	1987	Betty Morris	55,095
1970	Patty Costello	9,317	1979	Donna Adamek	26,280	1988	Lisa Wagner	105,500
1971	Vesma Grinfelds	4,925	1980	Donna Adamek	31,907	1989	Robin Romeo	113,750
1972	Patty Costello	11,350	1981	Nikki Gianulias	41,270	1990	Tish Johnson	94,420
1973	Judy Cook	11,200	1982	Nikki Gianulias	45,875	1991	Leanne Barrette	87,618

All-Time Leaders

All-time leading money winners on the PBA and LPBT tours, through 1991. PBA figures date back to 1959, while LPBT figures include Women's Pro Bowlers Association (WPBA) earnings through 1980.

Money Won

PBA Top 15

		Titles	Earnings
1	Marshall Holman	21	$1,555,851
2	Mark Roth	33	1,400,881
3	Earl Anthony	41	1,361,931
4	Pete Weber	18	1,319,142
5	Mike Aulby	19	1,194,905
6	Wayne Webb	17	984,691
7	Brian Voss	11	971,353
8	Amleto Monacelli	11	964,866
9	Dave Husted	7	964,441
10	Walter Ray Williams Jr	6	854,449
11	Dick Weber	26	842,604
12	Joe Berardi	10	822,889
13	Del Ballard Jr	9	814,867
14	Dave Ozio	10	799,410
15	George Pappas	10	793,234

WPBA-LPBT Top 15

		Titles	Earnings
1	Lisa Wagner	26	$464,444
2	Aleta Sill	17	444,351
3	Donna Adamek	19	440,434
4	Lorrie Nichols	15	418,796
5	Nikki Gianulias	17	416,311
6	Robin Romeo	12	386,046
7	Tish Johnson	14	346,753
8	Betty Morris	17	326,920
9	Cindy Coburn-Carroll	13	309,563
10	Leanne Barrette	13	294,756
11	Jeanne Maiden	8	277,748
12	Dana Miller-Mackie	10	251,487
13	Pat Costello	11	241,196
14	Patty Costello	25	240,705
15	Cheryl Daniels	4	237,812

Annual Awards
MEN
BWAA Bowler of the Year

Winners selected by Bowling Writers Association of America.

Multiple winners: Earl Anthony and Don Carter (6); Mark Roth (4); Dick Weber (3); Mike Aulby, Buddy Bomar, Ned Day, Billy Hardwick, Don Johnson, Steve Nagy (2).

Year		Year		Year		Year	
1942	Johnny Crimmins	1955	Steve Nagy	1968	Jim Stefanich	1980	Wayne Webb
1943	Ned Day	1956	Bill Lillard	1969	Billy Hardwick	1981	Earl Anthony
1944	Ned Day	1957	Don Carter	1970	Nelson Burton Jr.	1982	Earl Anthony
1945	Buddy Bomar	1958	Don Carter	1971	Don Johnson	1983	Earl Anthony
1946	Joe Wilman	1959	Ed Lubanski	1972	Don Johnson	1984	Mark Roth
1947	Buddy Bomar			1973	Don McCune	1985	Mike Aulby
1948	Andy Varipapa	1960	Don Carter	1974	Earl Anthony	1986	Walter Ray Williams Jr.
1949	Connie Schwoegler	1961	Dick Weber	1975	Earl Anthony	1987	Marshall Holman
		1962	Don Carter	1976	Earl Anthony	1988	Brian Voss
1950	Junie McMahon	1963	Dick Weber	1977	Mark Roth	1989	Mike Aulby
1951	Lee Jouglard	1964	Billy Hardwick	1978	Mark Roth		
1952	Steve Nagy	1965	Dick Weber	1979	Mark Roth	1990	Amleto Monacelli
1953	Don Carter	1966	Wayne Zahn			1991	David Ozio
1954	Don Carter	1967	Dave Davis				

Annual Awards (Cont.)
PBA Player of the Year

Winners selected by members of Professional Bowlers Association. The PBA Player of the Year has differed from the BWAA Bowler of the Year three times—in 1963, '64 and '89.

Multiple winners: Earl Anthony (6); Mark Roth (4); Billy Hardwick, Don Johnson and Amleto Monacelli (2).

Year		Year		Year		Year	
1963	Billy Hardwick	1971	Don Johnson	1979	Mark Roth	1986	Walter Ray Williams Jr.
1964	Bob Strampe	1972	Don Johnson	1980	Wayne Webb	1987	Marshall Holman
1965	Dick Weber	1973	Don McCune	1981	Earl Anthony	1988	Brian Voss
1966	Wayne Zahn	1974	Earl Anthony	1982	Earl Anthony	1989	Amleto Monacelli
1967	Dave Davis	1975	Earl Anthony	1983	Earl Anthony		
1968	Jim Stefanich	1976	Earl Anthony	1984	Mark Roth	1990	Amleto Monacelli
1969	Billy Hardwick	1977	Mark Roth	1985	Mike Aulby	1991	David Ozio
1970	Nelson Burton, Jr.	1978	Mark Roth				

PBA Rookie of the Year

Winners selected by members of Professional Bowlers Association.

Year		Year		Year		Year	
1964	Jerry McCoy	1972	Tommy Hudson	1980	Pete Weber	1987	Ryan Shafer
1965	Jim Godman	1973	Steve Neff	1981	Mark Fahy	1988	Rick Steelsmith
1966	Bobby Cooper	1974	Cliff McNealy	1982	Mike Steinbach	1989	Steve Hoskins
1967	Mike Durbin	1975	Guy Rowbury	1983	Toby Contreras		
1968	Bob McGregor	1976	Mike Berlin	1984	John Gant	1990	Brad Kiszewski
1969	Larry Lichstein	1977	Steve Martin	1985	Tom Crites	1991	Ricky Ward
1970	Denny Krick	1978	Joseph Groskind	1986	Marc McDowell		
1971	Tye Critchlow	1979	Mike Aulby				

WOMEN
BWAA Bowler of the Year

Winners selected by Bowling Writers Association of America.

Multiple winners: Marion Ladewig (9); Donna Adamek (4); Betty Morris and Lisa Rathgeber Wagner (3); Patty Costello, Dotty Forthergill, Shirley Garms, Val Mikiel, Aleta Sill, Judy Soutar and Sylvia Wene (2).

Year		Year		Year		Year	
1948	Val Mikiel	1960	Sylvia Wene	1972	Patty Costello	1982	Nikki Gianulias
1949	Val Mikiel	1961	Shirley Garms	1973	Judy Soutar	1983	Lisa Rathgeber
1950	Marion Ladewig	1962	Shirley Garms	1974	Betty Morris	1984	Aleta Sill
1951	Marion Ladewig	1963	Marion Ladewig	1975	Judy Soutar	1985	Aleta Sill
1952	Marion Ladewig	1964	LaVerne Carter	1976	Patty Costello	1986	Lisa Wagner
1953	Marion Ladewig	1965	Betty Kuczynski	1977	Betty Morris	1987	Betty Morris
1954	Marion Ladewig	1966	Joy Abel	1978	Donna Adamek	1988	Lisa Wagner
1955	Marion Ladewig	1967	Millie Martorella	1979	Donna Adamek	1989	Robin Romeo
1956	Sylvia Wene	1968	Dotty Fothergill	1980	Donna Adamek	1990	Tish Johnson
1957	Anita Cantaline	1969	Dotty Fothergill	1981	Donna Adamek	1991	Leanne Barrette
1958	Marion Ladewig	1970	Mary Baker				
1959	Marion Ladewig	1971	Paula Sperber				

LPBT Player of the Year

Winners selected by members of Ladies Professional Bowlers Tour. The LPBT Player of the Year has differed from the BWAA Bowler of the Year twice—in 1985 and '86.

Multiple winner: Leanne Barrette and Lisa Rathgeber Wagner (2).

Year		Year		Year		Year	
1983	Lisa Rathgeber	1986	Jeanne Maiden	1988	Lisa Wagner	1990	Leanne Barrette
1984	Aleta Sill	1987	Betty Morris	1989	Robin Romeo	1991	Leanne Barrette
1985	Patty Costello						

WPBA and LPBT Rookie of the Year

Winners selected by members of Women's Professional Bowlers Association (1978-80) and the Ladies Professional Bowlers Tour (since 1981).

Year		Year		Year		Year	
1978	Toni Gillard	1982	Carol Norman	1986	Wendy Macpherson	1989	Kim Terrell
1979	Nikki Gianulias	1983	Anne Marie Pike	1987	Paula Drake	1990	Debbie McMullen
1980	Lisa Rathgeber	1984	Paula Vidad	1988	Mary Martha Cerniglia	1991	Kim Kahrman
1981	Cindy Mason	1985	Dede Davidson				

David Leah/Allsport

Australian Open

Chris Cole/Allsport

French Open

Bob Martin/Allsport

Wimbledon

Simon Bruty/Allsport

U.S. Open

For the second year in a row, 18-year-old **Monica Seles** won three out of four Grand Slam tournaments, but Wimbledon wasn't one of them.

TENNIS

Young Guns

*In a year where youth was truly served, the oldest winner
of a Grand Slam tournament was 26-year-old Stefan Edberg.*

The night before the semifinals at the U.S. Open, a clothing company sponsored a bash in Manhattan with former tennis star Yannick Noah of France serving as host and lead entertainer. Noah, who has a recording contract in France, played guitar and sang several reggae numbers.

Halfway into the show, he was joined on stage by the noisemaker of tennis himself—John McEnroe—who had played guitar with several rock groups before. But, lo, McEnroe *sang* this time on a couple of rock songs. Mac 'n roll.

Two years earlier on this night, McEnroe was in bed early because he played the next day in the semifinals. And on the eve of the 1991 semifinals, his fellow American left-handed basher Jimmy Connors also was resting in his Run for the Ages at Flushing Meadows.

But at the 1992 U.S. Open, McEnroe and Connors were long gone before the semifinals; so was Martina Navratilova, who exited in the second-round. As a result, there was no nostalgia run at the U.S. Open or any other major tennis event in 1992, save for 32-year-old Ivan Lendl's courageous march to the semifinals during the Flushing fortnight and McEnroe's

dash to the Australian Open semis. This was the year youth truly was served.

Jim Courier won the Australian Open and French Open titles before turning 22 in August.

Andre Agassi, also 22, finally delivered in a Grand Slam final by winning at Wimbledon of all places.

Eighteen-year-old Monica Seles, her hairdos and tint seemingly changing at every major tournament and her grunting drawing the ire of opponents and the press, captured three-quarters of the women's Grand Slam—the Australian, French and U.S. opens—for the second year in a row.

And Steffi Graf, 23, once the dominant force in the game, reasserted herself after a long lull and silenced Seles at the Wimbledon final.

Stefan Edberg became the year's oldest major champion at age 26 as he successfully and heroically defended his U.S. Open title. In 1991, Edberg was denied the accolades he deserved at Flushing Meadows when he was upstaged by the 39-year-old Connors' headline-grabbing strut to the semifinals. But this time Edberg rated the spotlight alone in a herculean effort in which he was down a service break in the fifth set of matches against Richard Krajicek, Lendl and Michael Chang. Then he was down a set against Pete Sampras before prevailing in four to win his sixth Grand Slam title.

Jim Martz, the former tennis writer for *The Miami Herald*, is editor and publisher of *Florida Tennis* magazine.

Richard Martin/Allsport

Jim Courier (right), seen here with legendary Musketeers **Rene Lacoste** (left) and **Jean Borotra** (behind trophy), charmed both the French and Johnny Carson in winning his second straight title on the red clay at Roland Garros.

Edberg also wrested the No. 1 ranking away from Courier, who had supplanted him at the top of the heap in February.

This also was a year of vindication, in part for Agassi, who had been labeled as being afraid to win the big one, and for Nick Bollettieri, his coach and the former mentor of Courier and Seles.

Courier, Agassi and Seles spent their formative years under the tutelage of Bollettieri, the controversial coach who triggered the wave of junior academies when he launched his in the late 1970s in Florida. Seles left Bollettieri in 1990, claiming she had never really been coached by Nick. Courier decided to go his own way after he saw Bollettieri sitting with the Agassi entourage when they met at the French Open in 1989. Agassi's Wimbledon triumph marked the first time a Bollettieri protege won a Grand Slam singles title while still under Bollettieri's coaching.

One of the highlights of the 1991 tennis calendar came in the Davis Cup final between the U.S. and France in Lyon, the weekend of Nov. 29-Dec. 1. With team captain Noah stoking the patriotic fever of 7,000 fans at the Palais des Sports, Guy Forget and Henri Leconte teamed up to pull off one of the most surprising victories in 91 years of Cup play.

After an opening day split that saw Agassi defeat Forget and Leconte beat Sampras, Forget and Leconte stunned the seasoned doubles team of Ken Flach and Robert Seguso to take a 2-1 lead into the final day. Forget then clinched France's first Davis Cup championship since 1932 with an emotional 7-6 (8-6), 3-6, 6-3, 6-4 triumph over Sampras that touched off an hour-long celebration featuring a conga line of players and spectators and the singing of the "Marseillaise."

Six weeks later, McEnroe launched the 1992 season at the Australian Open by electrifying Flinders Park fans in Melbourne as he knocked off Boris Becker and Emilio Sanchez. A few weeks shy of his 33rd birthday and showing impeccable behavior two years after being thrown out of the tournament because of a temper tantrum, McEnroe made a run to the semifinals that nearly mirrored Connors' at the 1991 U.S. Open. However, Wayne Ferriera, a 21-year-old South African, kept McEnroe out of the final, 6-4, 6-4, 6-4.

Meanwhile, Courier quietly worked his way into the final, where he overcame Edberg in four sets for his second Grand Slam crown. He celebrated by jumping into the Yarra River.

Seles, like Courier a baseline bombardier, defended her Australian title without tangling with Graf, Jennifer Capriati or Gabriela Sabatini. America's Mary Joe Fernandez, buoyed with a more aggressive game honed by new coach and former tour pro Harold Solomon, ousted Sabatini in the semifinals before falling to Seles, 6-2, 6-3.

McEnroe's choir boy demeanor didn't make it through one match at the next Grand Slam event. He was fined $7,500 for swearing during a first-round loss to 21-year-old Swede Nicklas Kulti in the French Open. That meant McEnroe, who was in what he said would be his final full year on the tour, would have to keep his temper in check or risk being barred from Wimbledon if he committed another offense.

"I suppose I'm a little bit sad," McEnroe said, knowing this might have been his last appearance on the red clay at Roland Garros Stadium.

Courier and Agassi met for the fourth consecutive year at Paris—this time in the semifinals on a chilly, windy day with temperatures dipping into the 50s. Courier was hot, though, and apparently ruffled by a comment earlier in the week by Agassi, who said Courier's game was built on hard work and mental strength because, "I don't think he has a lot of natural ability to fall back on."

Courier replied with a 6-3, 6-2, 6-2 dissecting of Agassi and said, "There are many different talents besides hitting a tennis ball. Having guts on the court is a talent; having desire is a talent; having courage to go for a shot when you are love-40 down is a talent."

Petr Korda, the seventh seed from Czechoslovakia, ruined the hopes of local hero Henri Leconte, 6-2, 7-6, 6-3, in the other semifinal to reach his first Grand Slam final. Courier then showed

he has mastered the French Open and is now working on the language; he trounced a jittery Korda, 7-5, 6-2, 6-1, to successfully defend his title, and delighted spectators by speaking to them in French as he accepted the trophy. Just after match point, Courier turned toward Johnny Carson in a front-row box and imitated the golf swing that the recently retired Tonight Show host made famous. Carson laughed.

"It was kind of impromptu," Courier said. "Every time Petr would serve to me, I would see Johnny right behind him."

The women's final was a compelling 2-hour and 43-minute war between the world's two top players—Seles and Graf. Seles finally won the match and her third straight French Open title, 6-2, 3-6, 10-8. Seles thus had won six of the past nine Grand Slam titles, and she had won her six in just 11 appearances—the fastest in open-era history. Chris Evert needed 15 Grand Slam tournaments to win her first six, Graf needed 19 and Martina Navratilova 30.

So at the midway point in 1992, Courier and Seles were halfway toward winning the Grand Slam. Both were seeking their first Wimbledon, and it proved elusive again.

Courier lost to 193rd-ranked Andrei Olhovskiy of Russia in a third-round shocker, 6-4, 4-6, 6-4, 6-4. Seles, meanwhile, played amid an outcry from the British media because of her grunting on most shots (a London tabloid claimed its "grunt-o-meter" compared her shrieks to diesel engines). She managed to grunt her way to the final, but then muffled herself and was drubbed by Graf, 6-2, 6-1.

Navratilova, playing in her 20th Wimbledon and seeking her 10th singles championship at the All England Lawn Tennis and Croquet Club, said she was physically ready but that her confidence was waning. She reached the semis where she met the still-grunting Seles and lost in three sets.

"I think she would have beaten me even without the grunt," Navratilova said.

Goran Ivanisevic, a 1990 Wimbledon semifinalist and the No. 8 seed, said he knew why Courier wouldn't be the men's champion—"On the grass, you cannot stay back." Indeed, the last four Wimbledon men's champions have been serve-

Bob Martin/Allsport

Defying gravity and the logic that baseliners can't win at Wimbledon, **Andre Agassi** survived a record 37 aces by Goran Ivanisevic and won their five-set final.

and-volley players—Edberg (1988 and 1990), Boris Becker (1989) and Michael Stich (1991).

But Agassi, the 12th seed and a baseline basher à la Courier, didn't get the message. Ironically, he met Ivanisevic in the final, and both deserved to be there. Agassi, who shunned Wimbledon for three years after a humbling first-round loss in 1987, upended three-time Wimbledon champions Becker and McEnroe in the quarterfinals and semifinals. Ivanisevic, a free-wheeling Croatian with a sizzling 130-miles-per-hour serve, ousted two-time champion Edberg in the quarterfinals and Sampras in the semifinals.

In the final, Agassi joined Bjorn Borg and Connors in defying the logic that men can't win from the baseline at Wimbledon. He withstood the record 37 aces that whizzed past him (Ivanisevic blasted 206 in the tournament), responded with a superb return game and hung on to win, 6-7 (8-10), 6-4, 6-4, 1-6, 6-4. The teen idol with the punk rock hair and the "Image is everything" ad campaign was both jubilant and humbled after sinking to his knees in celebration.

"To do it here is more than I could ask for," Agassi said. "If my career was over tomorrow, I had a lot more than I deserved."

Then it was on to the Olympic gold rush for many of the top players. And that proved to be a grueling task because the red clay courts at Barcelona were slower than those at the French Open. Moreover, the men had to play best-of-five sets and the weather was sultry.

Edberg lost in the first round to Andrei Chesnokov and Courier, the top seed, lost in the third round to eventual champion Marc Rosset of Switzerland. Becker, who in a second-round match with Younes El Aynaoui of Morocco snapped his racquet on his knee in a rage, also lost in the third round to France's Fabrice Santoro.

The story of the Olympics, though, was Jennifer Capriati, the 16-year-old Floridian who had spent the year going through inevitable growing pains. She had lost in three consecutive Grand Slam quarterfinals, had played poorly in some other events, had changed coaches, put on weight and sometimes looked sullen or uninterested on the court.

But the bubbly Jen-Jen of old was back at Barcelona. She turned the year around by defeating Sanchez Vicario and Graf in succession to win her first tournament of the year and the women's singles gold medal. She reveled in the atmosphere of the Olympic Village, where she sent computer messages back and forth to athletes in various sports.

"It was so emotional," Capriati said of being on the medal stand. "I had chills the whole time. For two weeks, I was watching the other athletes up there who won gold medals and was thinking that it would be so cool to be up there. Right now this means more to me than any of the Grand Slams."

By defeating top-seed Graf in the final, 6-3, 3-6, 6-4, Capriati beat the only top rival she had never conquered.

Rosset, No. 43 in the world, won the men's singles gold medal with a 7-6, 6-3, 3-6, 4-6, 8-6 victory over Jordi Arrese of Spain. Doubles gold medals went to Germany's Becker and Stich and Americans Gigi Fernandez and Mary Joe Fernandez.

Seles, Navratilova and Sabatini could not compete in the Summer Games because they had not played for their nations in the 1991 Federation Cup, a requisite for Olympic eligibility. The 1992 Fed Cup in Frankfurt served as an early July tuneup for the Olympics, with the Germans beating Spain in the final, 2-1.

Both Courier and Seles entered the U.S. Open amid summer slumps, or "a lull," as Courier called it. He had failed to win a title in five straight tournaments, and she had dropped three consecutive finals—including the Canadian Open, where Sanchez Vicario beat her for the first time in 11 meetings.

The U.S. Open reflected what was happening all year in tennis—that American men and women were going in opposite directions. Mary Joe Fernandez was the only American to reach the women's quarterfinals. At the French Open, Capriati was the lone American in the round of 16; and at Wimbledon only Capriati and former Czech Navratilova made it as far as the quarterfinals.

On the other hand, three American men moved into the U.S. Open semifinals—Courier, Sampras and Chang. McEnroe, Sampras and Agassi were in the Wimbledon semifinals, and Courier

Reluctant Ashe Goes Public

In his 1981 autobiography, *Off The Court*, Arthur Ashe wrote, "I believe I was destined to do more than hit tennis balls."

A new autobiography is due out in June 1993, and there will be plenty for Ashe to update—his second open heart surgery in 1983; brain surgery in 1988, which revealed he had contracted the AIDS virus from a blood transfusion during the 1983 surgery; his reluctant public disclosure on April 8, 1992, that he has AIDS; and within a two-day period in early September, his arrest in front of the White House for protesting the Bush administration's policy toward Haitian refugees, which was followed by another heart attack.

At 49, Ashe has spent his life overcoming obstacles on and off the tennis court. He was a reluctant pioneer in a sport played mainly at country clubs when he was growing up in Richmond, Va. An All-America at UCLA, he went on to become the first black to win the men's championship at the U.S. Open (1968), Australian Open (1970) and Wimbledon (1975). He was also the first black on the U.S. Davis Cup team and later served as captain from 1981-85, winning two titles.

He was clearly an athlete who cared. He helped found the Association of Tennis Professionals—the players' union on the men's tour—and served as ATP president from 1974-79. He also helped form the National Junior Tennis League, a program designed to involve inner-city youths in the sport.

Away from tennis, he has written several books, including the acclaimed three-volume *A Hard Road to Glory*, which chronicles the history of the African-American athlete. He has also been quietly influential in promoting many causes, from ridding South Africa of apartheid to serving as national campaign chairman for the American Heart Association and working for the Cystic Fibrosis Foundation.

Soon after he learned he had the AIDS virus, he told about a dozen family members and friends, including some journalists. His fellow ABC-TV commentator Cliff Crysdale knew for two years.

But his days of leaving the public spotlight to others ended on April 8, when, after

Wide World Photos

An emotional **Arthur Ashe** announcing at an April 8 news conference that he had been infected by the AIDS virus through a blood transfusion in 1983.

inquiries by *USA Today*, he called a press conference and made the disclosure himself.

The following is a partial transcript:

"Some of you have heard that I had tested positive for HIV, the virus that causes AIDS.

"That is indeed the case. It was transmitted through a blood transfusion after one of my open-heart bypass operations. . . . I have known since . . . September 1988 that I have AIDS. . . . So some people may ask why not go public earlier. The answer to me and my family was simple. Any admission of HIV infection at that time would have seriously, permanently, and my wife and I firmly believe, unnecessarily infringed upon our family's right to privacy.

"I have had it on good authority that my status was common knowledge in the medical community, especially here in New York City, and I am truly grateful to all of you, medical and otherwise, who knew, but either didn't even ask me or never made it public.

"What I actually came to feel about a year ago was that there was a silent and a generous conspiracy to assist me in maintaining my privacy.

"Then sometime last week, someone phoned *USA Today* and told the paper. Af-

ter several days of checking it out, *USA Today* decided to confront me with the rumors. It put me in the unenviable position of having to lie if I wanted to protect our privacy. No one should have to make that choice. I am sorry that I have been forced to make this revelation now at this time. After all, I am not running for some office of public trust, nor do I have stockholders to account to. It is only that I fall in the dubious umbrella of, quote, public figure, end of quote.

"I am not sick. And I can function very well. . . . I have been an activist on many issues in the past, against apartheid, for education and the athlete, the need for a faster change in tennis. I will continue with those projects in progress and will certainly get involved with the AIDS crisis. . . .

"The quality of one's life changes irrevocably when something like this becomes public. Reason and rational thought are too often waived out of fear, out of caution, or out of just plain ignorance. My family and I must now learn a new set of behavioral standards to function in the everyday world. And, sadly, there really was not good reason for this to have happened now. But it has happened, and we will adjust and go forward."

and Agassi reached the French semis.

A victory by Courier, Sampras or Chang would have given the U.S. the distinction of sweeping all four of the Grand Slam singles titles in 1992. The last time the U.S. achieved that feat was when Don Budge won the Slam by himself in 1938.

As the tournament developed, the men's side of the draw began to look like it might become the 1992-93 U.S. Open. Lengthy five-set matches abounded, as a weary Edberg could attest. In the fourth round against Krajicek of the Netherlands, he overcame a fifth-set service break to win, 6-4, 6-7, 6-3, 3-6, 6-4. Next, he met Ivan Lendl, whose so-so year seemed to turn around right after he gained his American citizenship on July 7.

Lendl ousted sentimental favorite Connors in the second round, 3-6, 6-3, 6-2, 6-0, two days after Connors celebrated his 40th birthday with a three-set victory over Jaime Oncins. And, suddenly becoming a crowd favorite himself, Lendl sent Becker packing in the fourth round, 6-7, 6-2, 6-7, 6-3, 6-4.

Edberg and Lendl met in a quarterfinal showdown that took two days to complete. Edberg was leading on serve at 2-1 in the fifth when rain halted play for the night. The next afternoon, Lendl broke for 4-3, but Edberg broke back and held on to win, 6-3, 6-3, 3-6, 5-7, 7-6.

That, however, was just a tuneup. In the semis, Edberg and Chang hooked up for what is believed to be the longest match in U.S. Open history—a 5-hour-and-26-minute test of endurance that saw Edberg overcome a 2-4 deficit in the final set to survive, 6-7, 7-5, 7-6, 5-7, 6-4.

As usual, the women's final was sandwiched between the men's semifinals on Saturday to accommodate CBS television coverage of "Super Saturday," and there were several empty seats at the stadium court following the Edberg-Chang marathon. Seles, who dusted off the grunt while fighting off a virus most of the second week of the Open, outclassed Sanchez Vicario, 6-3, 6-3. In the second men's semifinal, Sampras beat Courier in four sets, but his strength was sapped because of a stomach virus that struck toward the end of the match.

The next afternoon, Edberg had to fight from behind one more time to win, 3-6,

Simon Bruty/Allsport

Stefan Edberg won the U.S. Open and regained his No. 1 ranking by rallying from behind to beat Lendl, Chang, and Sampras in consecutive matches.

6-4, 7-6, 6-2.

"It has been a bumpy road," Edberg said. "I mean, I really earned it this year. The more important thing was to defend my title. Becoming No. 1 again is a nice present."

Not so pleasant was the American squad of Courier, Agassi, Sampras and McEnroe that awaited Edberg and the Swedes two weeks later in the Davis Cup semifinals at Minneapolis.

The U.S. jumped out to a 2-0 lead after the first day with Courier beating Nicklas Kulti and Edberg losing to Agassi in four sets. The next day, a fired-up McEnroe teamed with Sampras to rally from a set down and beat Edberg and Anders Jarryd, 6-1, 6-7 (2-7), 4-6, 6-3, 6-3, to clinch the round.

The final is scheduled for Dec. 4-6, at Fort Worth, where the U.S. will try for its 30th Davis Cup championship against Switzerland. The Swiss have never won the Cup and McEnroe, for one, doesn't expect them to this time.

"We're ready for the finals," said McEnroe. "I see us beating them 5-0." □

THE 1993 INFORMATION PLEASE SPORTS ALMANAC

TENNIS STATISTICS

SEC A

THE SEASON IN REVIEW
1991-1992
MEN • WOMEN • LEADERS

PAGE 699

Tournament Results

Winners of men's and women's pro singles championships from Nov. 3, 1991 through Sept. 20, 1992.

Men's Tour

LATE 1991

Finals	Tournament	Winner	Earnings	Loser	Score
Nov. 3	Paris Open	Guy Forget	$270,000	P.Sampras	76 46 57 64 64
Nov. 3	Kolynos Cup (Buzios)	Jordi Allese	21,240	J.Oncins	16 64 60
Nov. 10	Diet Pepsi Indoor (Birmingham, EN)	Michael Chang	65,000	G.Roux	63 62
Nov. 10	Bayer Kremlin Cup (Moscow)	Andrei Cherkasov	32,000	J.Hlasek	76 36 76
Nov. 10	Banespa Open (Sao Paulo)	Christian Minussi	32,400	J.Oncins	26 63 64
Nov. 17	ATP World Championship (Frankfort)	Pete Sampras	625,000	J.Courier	36 76 63 64
Nov. 24	ATP Doubles Champs.(Johannesburg)	Anders Jarryd/ John Fitzgerald	325,000	K.Flach/ R.Seguso	64 64 26 64
Dec. 15	ITF Grand Slam Cup (Munich)	David Wheaton	2,000,000	M.Chang	75 62 64

Note: The Grand Slam Cup is not an ATP Tour event.

1992 (through Sept. 20)

Finals	Tournament	Winner	Earnings	Loser	Score
Jan. 5	BP Nationals (Wellington)	Jeff Tarango	$ 22,600	A.Volkov	61 60 63
Jan. 5	West End Open (Adelaide)	Goran Ivanisevic	22,600	C.Bergstrom	16 76 64
Jan. 12	Benson & Hedges Open (Auckland)	Jaime Yzaga	22,600	M.Washington	76 64
Jan. 12	New South Wales Open (Sydney)	Emilio Sanchez	33,800	G.Forget	63 64
Jan. 26	**Australian Open** (Melbourne)	Jim Courier	278,850	S.Edberg	63 36 64 62
Feb. 9	Muratti Time Indoor (Milan)	Omar Camporese	81,200	G.Ivanisevic	36 63 64
Feb. 9	Volvo/Sanfrancisco	Michael Chang	33,800	J.Courier	63 63
Feb. 9	Chevrolet Classic (Maccio)	Tomas Carbonell	18,700	C.Miniussi	36 75 64
Feb. 16	Federal Express International (Memphis)	MaliVai Washington	103,000	W.Ferreira	63 62
Feb. 16	Donnay Indoor (Brussels)	Boris Becker	111,000	J.Courier	67 26 76 76 75
Feb. 23	Eurocard Classics (Stuttgart)	Goran Ivanisevic	144,000	S.Edberg	67 63 64 64
Feb. 23	U.S. Pro Indoor (Philadelphia)	Pete Sampras	141,500	A.Mansdorf	61 76 26 76
Mar. 1	ABN/AMRO World (Rotterdam)	Boris Becker	68,400	A.Volkov	76 46 62
Mar. 1	Purex Championships (Scottsdale)	Stefano Pescosolido	33,800	B.Gilbert	60 16 64
Mar. 8	Copenhagan Open	Magnus Larsson	18,700	A.Jarryd	64 76
Mar. 8	Newsweek Champions Cup (Indian Wells)	Michael Chang	137,500	A.Chesnokov	63 64 75
Mar. 22	Lipton International (Key Biscayne)	Michael Chang	197,000	A.Mancini	75 75
Mar. 22	Grand Prix Hassan II (Casablanca)	Guillermo Perez-Rolden	18,700	G.Lopez	26 75 63
Apr. 5	Estoril Open (Lisbon)	Carlos Costa	34,500	S.Bruguera	46 62 62
Apr. 5	Epson Singapore Super Tennis	Simon Youl	34,500	P.Haarhuis	64 61
Apr. 5	South African Open (Johannesburg)	Aaron Krickstein	38,800	A.Volkov	64 64
Apr. 12	Suntory Japan Open (Tokyo)	Jim Courier	144,000	R.Krajicek	64 64 76
Apr. 12	Trofeo Conde De Godo (Barcelona)	Carlos Costa	110,000	M.Gustafsson	64 76 64
Apr. 19	Salem Open (Hong Kong)	Jim Courier	38,800	M.Chang	75 63
Apr. 19	Philips Open (Nice)	Gabriel Markus	33,800	J.Sanchez	64 64
Apr. 19	USTA (Tampa)	Jaime Yzaga	33,800	M.Washington	46 64 61
Apr. 26	Volvo Monte Carlo Open	Thomas Muster	170,200	A.Krickstein	63 61 63
Apr. 26	KAL Cup Korea Open (Seoul)	Shuzo Matsuoka	20,800	T.Woodbridge	63 46 75
May 3	XXI Trofeo Grupo Zeta (Madrid)	Sergi Bruguera	100,800	C.Costa	76 62 62
May 3	BMW Open (Munich)	Magnus Larsson	39,600	P.Korda	64 46 61
May 3	AT&T Challenge (Atlanta)	Andre Agassi	33,800	P.Sampras	75 64
May 10	U.S. Clay Court (Charlotte)	MaliVai Washington	32,400	C.Mezzadri	63 63
May 11	German Open (Hamburg)	Stefan Edberg	166,600	M.Stich	57 64 61
May 17	Italian Open (Rome)	Jim Courier	179,700	C.Costa	76 60 64
May 24	Muratti Time Classic (Bologna)	Jaime Oncins	34,500	R.Furlan	62 64

Tournament Results (Cont.)

MEN

Finals	Tournament	Winner	Earnings	Loser	Score
June 7	**French Open** (Paris)	Jim Courier	490,618	P.Korda	75 62 61
June 14	Stella Artois Grass Court (London)	Wayne Ferreira	68,800	S.Matsuoka	63 64
June 14	Continental Grass Court (Rosmalen)	Michael Stich	33,800	J.Stark	64 75
June 14	Tomeo Internazionale (Florence)	Thomas Muster	33,800	R.Furlan	63 16 61
June 20	Manchester Open	Jacco Eltingh	33,800	M.Washington	63 64
June 23	IP Cup (Genova)	Andrei Medvedev	33,800	G.Perez-Roldan	63 64
July 5	**Wimbledon** (London)	Andre Agassi	501,514	G.Ivanisevic	67 64 64 16 64
July 12	Hall of Fame Championship (Newport)	Bryan Shelton	25,000	A.Antonitsch	64 64
July 12	Swedish Open (Bastad)	Magnus Gustafsson	33,800	T.Carbonell	57 75 64
July 13	Swiss Open (Gstaad)	Sergi Bruguera	43,800	F.Clavet	61 64
July 19	Mercedes Cup (Stuttgart)	Andrei Medvedev	141,500	W.Ferreira	61 64 67 26 61
July 19	Nations Bank Classic (Washington)	Petr Korda	81,600	H.Holm	64 64
July 25	Canadian Open (Toronto)	Andre Agassi	170,800	I.Lendl	36 62 60
July 26	Philips Head Cup (Kitzbuhel)	Pete Sampras	50,000	A.Mancini	63 75 63
July 26	Dutch Open (Hilversum)	Karel Novacek	32,400	J.Arrese	62 63 26 75
Aug. 2	San Marino Open	Karel Novacek	33,800	F.Clavet	75 62
Aug. 7	**Summer Olympics** (Barcelona) Doubles	Boris Becker/ Michael Stich	—	W.Ferreira/ P.Norval	76 46 76 63
Aug. 8	**Summer Olympics** (Barcelona) Singles	Marc Rosset	—	J.Arrese	76 64 36 46 86
Aug. 9	Volvo/Los Angeles	Richard Krajicek	33,800	M.Woodforde	64 26 64
Aug. 16	ATP Championship (Cincinnati)	Pete Sampras	187,500	I.Lendl	63 36 63
Aug. 16	Czechoslovak Open (Prague)	Karel Novacek	46,000	F.Davin	61 61
Aug. 23	RCA Championships (Indianapolis)	Pete Sampras	144,000	J.Courier	64 64
Aug. 24	Volvo International (New Haven)	Stefan Edberg	144,000	M.Washington	76 61
Aug. 30	Croatia Open (Umag)	Thomas Muster	33,800	F.Davin	61 46 64
Aug. 30	Waldbaum's Hamlet Cup (Long Island)	Peter Korda	33,800	I.Lendl	62 62
Aug. 30	OTB International (Schenectady)	Wayne Ferreira	18,700	J.Morgan	62 67 62
Sept.13	**U.S. Open** (New York)	Stefan Edberg	500,000	P.Sampras	36 64 76 62
Sept.20	Cologne Open	Bernd Karbacher	43,000	M.Ondruska	76 64
Sept.20	Grand Prix Passing Shot (Bordeaux)	Andrei Medvedev	43,000	S.Bruguera	63 16 62

Women's Tour

LATE 1991

Finals	Tournament	Winner	Earnings	Loser	Score
Nov. 3	Arizona Classic (Phoenix)	Sabine Appelmans	$ 27,000	C.Rubin	75 61
Nov. 10	Va.Slims/California (Oakland)	Martina Navratilova	70,000	M.Seles	63 36 63
Nov. 10	Va.Slims/Nashville	Sabine Appelmans	27,000	K.Adams	62 64
Nov. 16	Va.Slims/Philadelphia	Monica Seles	70,000	J.Capriati	75 61
Nov. 17	Jell-o Classic (Indianapolis)	Katerina Maleeva	27,000	A.Keller	76 62
Nov. 24	Va.Slims Championships (New York)	Monica Seles	250,000	M.Navratilova	64 36 75 60

1992 (through Sept. 20)

Finals	Tournament	Winner	Earnings	Loser	Score
Jan. 12	New South Wales Open (Sydney)	Gabriela Sabatini	$ 45,000	A.S-Vicario	61 61
Jan. 26	**Australian Open** (Melbourne)	Monica Seles	242,614	M.J.Fernandez	62 63
Feb. 2	Toray Pan Pacific Open (Tokyo)	Gabriela Sabatini	70,000	M.Navratilova	62 46 62
Feb. 2	Nutri-Metics Bendon Classic (Auckland)	Robin White	18,000	A.Strnadova	26 64 63
Feb. 9	Nokia Grand Prix (Essen)	Monica Seles	70,000	M.J.Fernandez	60 63
Feb. 9	Fernleaf Butter Classic (Wellington)	Noelle Van Lottum	18,000	D.Faber	64 60
Feb. 9	Mizuno World Ladies (Osaka)	Helena Sukova	27,000	L.Gildemeister	62 46 61
Feb. 16	Va.Slims/Chicago	Martina Navratilova	70,000	J.Novotna	76 46 75
Feb. 16	Austrian Indoors (Linz)	Natalia Medvedeva	18,000	P.P-Mangon	64 62
Feb. 23	VaSlims/Oklahoma (Oklahoma City)	Zina Garrison	27,000	L.McNeil	75 36 76
Feb. 23	Cesena Championship	Mary Pierce	18,000	C.Tanvier	61 61
Mar. 1	Evert Cup (Indian Wells)	Monica Seles	70,000	C.Martinez	63 61
Mar. 8	Va.Slims/Florida (Boca Raton)	Steffi Graf	110,000	C.Martinez	36 62 60
Mar. 22	Lipton International (Key Biscayne)	Arantxa Sanchez Vicario	120,000	G.Sabatini	61 64
Mar. 29	U.S. Hardcourts (San Antonio)	Martina Navratilova	45,000	N.Tauziat	62 61
Mar. 29	Light n'Lively Doubles (Wesley Chapel)	Jana Novotna/ Larisa S-Neiland	65,000	N.Zvereva/ A.S-Vicario	64 62
Apr. 5	Family Circle Cup (Hilton Head)	Gabriela Sabatini	110,000	C.Martinez	61 64
Apr. 12	Bausch & Lomb Champs. (Amelia Island)	Gabriela Sabatini	70,000	S.Graf	62 16 63
Apr. 12	Suntory Japan Open (Tokyo)	Kimiko Date	27,000	S.Appelmans	75 36 63
Apr. 19	VaSlims/Houston	Monica Seles	70,000	Z.Garrison	61 61
Apr. 19	Volvo Open (Pattaya City)	Sabine Appelmans	18,000	A.Strnadova	75 36 75
Apr. 26	Int'l Champs. of Spain (Barcelona)	Monica Seles	45,000	A.Vicario	36 62 63
Apr. 26	Malaysia Open (Kuala Lumpur)	Yayuk Basuki	18,000	A.Strnadova	63 60

Finals	Tournament	Winner	Earnings	Loser	Score
May 3	Citizen Cup (Hamburg)	Steffi Graf	70,000	G.Sabatini	76 62
May 3	Ilva Trophy (Taranto)	Julie Halard	18,000	E.Zardo	60 75
May 10	Italian Open (Rome)	Gabriela Sabatini	110,000	M.Seles	75 64
May 10	Belgian Open (Waregem)	Wiltrud Probst	18,000	M.Babel	62 63
May 17	Lufthansa Cup (Berlin)	Steffi Graf	110,000	A.S-Vicario	46 75 62
May 24	Lucerne European Open	Amy Frazier	27,000	R.Zrubakova	64 46 75
May 24	Strasborg International	Judith Wiesner	27,000	N.Sawamatsu	61 63
June 7	**French Open** (Paris)	Monica Seles	372,896	S.Graf	62 36 108
June 14	Dow Classic (Birmingham)	Brenda Schultz	27,000	J.Byrne	62 62
June 21	Pilkington Glass Champs. (Eastbourne)	Lori McNeil	70,000	L.H-Wild	64 64
July 5	**Wimbledon** (London)	Steffi Graf	421,584	M.Seles	62 61
July 12	Torneo Internazionale (Palermo)	Mary Pierce	18,000	B.Schultz	61 67 61
July 12	Austrian Open (Kitzbuhel)	Conchita Martinez	27,000	M.M-Fragniere	60 36 62
July 26	HTC Pragne Open	Radka Zrubakova	18,000	K.Kroupova	63 75
July 26	San Marino Open	Magdalena Maleeva	18,000	F.Bonsignori	76 64
Aug. 7	**Summer Olympics** (Barcelona) Singles	Jennifer Capriati	—	S.Graf	36 63 64
Aug. 8	**Summer Olympics** (Barcelona) Doubles	Mary Joe Fernandez/ Gigi Fernandez	—	C.Martinez/ A.S.Vicario	75 26 62
Aug. 16	VaSlims/Los Angeles	Martina Navratilova	70,000	M.Seles	64 62
Aug. 23	Canadian Open (Montreal)	Arantxa Sanchez Vicario	110,000	M.Seles	63 46 64
Aug. 30	Mazda Tennis Classic (San Diego)	Jennifer Capriati	45,000	C.Martinez	63 62
Aug. 30	OTB International (Schenectady)	Barbara Rittner	18,000	B.Schultz	76 63
Sept.12	**U.S. Open** (New York)	Monica Seles	500,000	A.S-Vicario	63 63
Sept.20	Clarins Open (Paris)	Sandra Cecchini	27,000	E.Zaedo	62 61

1992 Grand Slam Tournaments

Australian Open

MEN'S SINGLES

Final Eight—#1 Stefan Edberg; #2 Jim Courier; #4 Michael Stich; #5 Ivan Lendl; plus unseeded Wayne Ferreira, Richard Krajicek, Amos Mansdorf and John McEnroe.

Quarterfinals

Edberg def. Lendl .... 46 75 61 67(5-7) 61
Ferreira def. McEnroe 64 64 64
Krajicek def. Stich .... 57 76(7-2) 67(1-7) 64 64
Courier def. Mansdorf 63 62 62

Semifinals

Edberg def. Ferreira .... 76(7-2) 61 62
Courier def. Krajicek .... walkover

Final

Courier def. Edberg 63 36 64 62

WOMEN'S SINGLES

Final Eight—#1 Monica Seles; #3 Gabriela Sabatini; #4 Arantxa Sanchez Vicario; #5 Jennifer Capriati; #7 Mary Joe Fernandez; #9 Manuela Maleeva-Fragniere; #12 Anke Huber; plus unseeded Amy Frazier.

Quarterfinals

Seles def. Huber 75 63
Sabatini def. Capriati .... 64 76(7-1)
Sanchez Vicario def. Maleeva-Fragniere ..... walkover
M.J. Fernandez def. Frazier .... 64 76(8-6)

Semifinals

Seles def. Sanchez Vicario 62 62
M.J. Fernandez def. Sabatini 61 64

Final

Seles def. M.J. Fernandez 62 63

DOUBLES FINALS

Men—#4 Todd Woodbridge & Mark Woodforde def. #11 Kelly Jones and Rick Leach, 6-4, 6-3, 6-4.

Women—#4 Helena Sukova & Arantxa Sanchez Vicario def. #5 Mary Joe Fernandez & Zina Garrison, 6-4, 7-6 (7-3).

Mixed—#3 Nicole Provis & Mark Woodforde def. #1 Arantxa Sanchez Vicario & Todd Woodbridge, 6-3, 4-6, 11-9.

French Open

MEN'S SINGLES

Final Eight—#1 Jim Courier; #3 Pete Sampras; #7 Petr Korda; #8 Goran Ivanisevic; #11 Andre Agassi; plus unseeded Andrei Cherkasov, Nicklas Kulti and Henri Leconte.

Quarterfinals

Courier def. Ivanisevic 62 61 26 75
Korda def. Cherkasov .... 64 67(3-7) 62 64
Agassi def. Sampras .... 76(8-6) 62 61
Leconte def. Kulti .... 67(8-10) 36 63 63 63

Semifinals

Courier def. Agassi 63 62 62
Korda def. Leconte .... 62 76(7-4) 63

Final

Courier def. Korda 75 62 61

WOMEN'S SINGLES

Final Eight—#1 Monica Seles; #2 Steffi Graf; #3 Gabriela Sabatini; #4 Arantxa Sanchez Vicario; #5 Jennifer Capriati; #7 Conchita Martinez; plus unseeded Manon Bollegraf and Natalia Zvereva.

Quarterfinals

Seles def. Capriati 62 62
Graf def. Zvereva .... 63 67(4-7) 63
Sabatini def. Martinez 36 63 62
Sanchez Vicario def. Bollegraf 62 63

Semifinals

Seles def. Sabatini 63 46 64
Graf def. Sanchez Vicario 06 62 62

Final

Seles def. Graf 62 36 10-8

DOUBLES FINALS

Men—Jakob Hlasek & Marc Rosset def. David Adams & Andrei Olhovsky, 7-6(7-4), 6-7(3-7), 7-5.

Women—#2 Gigi Fernandez & Natalia Zvereva def. #4 Conchita Martinez & Arantxa Sanchez Vicario, 6-3, 6-2.

Mixed—#2 Arantxa Sanchez Vicario & Todd Woodbridge def. Lori McNeil & Bryan Shelton, 6-2, 6-3.

1992 Grand Slam Tournaments (Cont.)

Wimbledon

MEN'S SINGLES

Final Eight—#2 Stefan Edberg; #3 Michael Stich; #4 Boris Becker; #5 Pete Sampras; #8 Goran Ivanisevic; #9 Guy Forget; #12 Andre Agassi; plus unseeded John McEnroe.

Quarterfinals

McEnroe def. Forget .... 62 76(11-9) 63
Agassi def. Becker 46 62 62 46 63
Sampras def. Stich......................... 63 62 64
Ivanisevic def. Edberg .... 67(10-12) 75 61 36 63

Semifinals

Ivanisevic def. Sampras........ 67(4-7) 76(7-5) 64 62
Agassi def. McEnroe 64 62 63

Final

Agassi def. Ivanisevic.......... 67(8-10) 64 64 16 64

WOMEN'S SINGLES

Final Eight—#1 Monica Seles; #2 Steffi Graf; #3 Gabriela Sabatini; #4 Martina Navratilova; #6 Jennifer Capriati; #12 Katerina Maleeva; #14 Nathalie Tauziat; plus unseeded Natalia Zvereva.

Quarterfinals

Seles def. Tauziat............................... 61 63
Navratilova def. Maleeva................. 63 76(7-2)
Graf def. Zvereva............................. 63 61
Sabatini def. Capriati 61 36 63

Semifinals

Seles def. Navratilova.................. 62 67(3-7) 64
Graf def. Sabatini 63 63

Final

Graf def. Seles 62 61

DOUBLES FINALS

Men—John McEnroe & Michael Stich def. #4 Jim Grabb and Richey Reneberg, 5-7, 7-6(5-7), 6-3, 6-7(5-7), 19-17.

Women—#2 Gigi Fernandez & Natalia Zvereva def. #1 Jana Novotna & Larisa Savchenko-Neiland, 6-4, 6-1.

Mixed—#3 Larisa Savchenko-Neiland & Cyril Suk def. Miriam Oremans & Jacco Eltingh, 76(7-2), 6-2.

U.S. Open

MEN'S SINGLES

Final Eight—#1 Jim Courier; #2 Stefan Edberg; #3 Pete Sampras; #4 Michael Chang; #8 Andre Agassi; #9 Ivan Lendl; #12 Wayne Ferreira; plus unseeded Alexander Volkov.

Quarterfinals

Edberg def. Lendl .... 63 63 36 57 76(7-3)
Chang def. Ferreira .... 75 26 63 67(4-7) 61
Sampras def. Volkov....................... 64 61 60
Courier def. Agassi .... 63 67(6-8) 61 64

Semifinals

Edberg def. Chang .... 67(3-7) 75 76(7-3) 57 64
Sampras def. Courier...................... 61 36 62 62

Final

Edberg def. Sampras .... 36 64 76(7-5) 62

WOMEN'S SINGLES

Final Eight—#1 Monica Seles; #2 Steffi Graf; #4 Gabriela Sabatini; #5 Arantxa Sanchez Vicario; #7 Mary Joe Fernandez; #9 Manuela Maleeva-Fragniere; plus unseeded Patricia Hy and Magdalena Maleeva.

Quarterfinals

Seles def. Hy.......................... 61 76(7-2)
M.J. Fernandez def. Sabatini 62 16 64
Sanchez Vicario def. Graf................ 76(7-5) 63
Maleeva-Fragniere def. Maleeva........... 62 53(ret)

Semifinals

Seles def. M.J. Fernandez 63 62
Sanchez Vicario def. Maleeva-Fragniere........ 62 61

Final

Seles def. Sanchez Vicario..................... 63 63

DOUBLES FINALS

Men—#2 Jim Grabb & Richey Reneberg def. #4 Kelly Jones & Rick Leach, 3-6, 7-6(7-2), 6-3, 6-3.

Women—#3 Gigi Fernandez & Natalia Zvereva def. #1 Jana Novotna & Larisa Savchenko-Neiland, 7-6(7-4), 6-1.

Mixed—#6 Nicole Provis & Mark Woodforde def. #5 Helena Sukova & Tom Nijssen, 4-6, 6-3, 6-3.

1992 Grand Slam Champions

Australian Open

Men's Singles	Jim Courier
Men's Doubles	Todd Woodbridge/
	Mark Woodforde
Women's Singles....................	Monica Seles
Women's Doubles..............	Helena Sukova/
	A.Sanchez Vicario
Mixed Doubles....	Nicole Provis/Mark Woodforde

French Open

Men's Singles	Jim Courier
Men's Doubles	Jakob Hlasek/Marc Rosset
Women's Singles....................	Monica Seles
Women's Doubles	Gigi Fernandez/
	Natalia Zvereva
Mixed Doubles..	A.Sanchez Vicario/T.Woodbridge

Wimbledon

Men's Singles.......................	Andre Agassi
Men's Doubles	John McEnroe/Michael Stich
Women's Singles	Steffi Graf
Women's Doubles	Gigi Fernandez/
	Natalia Zvereva
Mixed Doubles....	L.Savchenko-Neiland/Cyril Suk

U.S. Open

Men's Singles	Stefan Edberg
Men's Doubles	Jim Grabb/Richey Reneberg
Women's Singles...................	Monica Seles
Women's Doubles	Gigi Fernandez/
	Natalia Zvereva
Mixed Doubles....	Nicole Provis/Mark Woodforde

Singles Leaders

Official Top 20 computer rankings and money leaders of men's and women's tours for 1991 and unofficial rankings and money leaders for 1992 (through Sept.20), as compiled by ATP (Association of Tennis Professionals) and WTA (Women's Tennis Association). Note that money list includes doubles earnings.

Final 1991 Computer Rankings and Money Won

Listed are titles won (1st), record (W-L) and earnings for the year with rank on earnings list in parentheses.

MEN

		1st	W-L	Earnings	(No.)
1	Stefan Edberg	6	76-17	$2,363,575	(1)
2	Jim Courier	3	58-19	1,748,171	(3)
3	Boris Becker	2	50-12	1,228,708	(5)
4	Michael Stich	4	71-25	1,220,116	(6)
5	Ivan Lendl	3	53-17	1,438,983	(4)
6	Pete Sampras	4	52-19	1,908,413	(2)
7	Guy Forget	6	62-20	1,101,772	(7)
8	Karel Novacek	4	57-31	650,350	(11)
9	Petr Korda	2	45-24	573,970	(13)
10	Andre Agassi	2	39-17	982,611	(8)
11	Sergi Bruguera	3	51-22	527,320	(17)
12	Magnus Gustafsson	3	52-17	538,792	(16)
13	Derrick Rostagno	2	39-24	399,729	(23)
14	Emilio Sanchez	3	43-25	672,071	(10)
15	Michael Chang	1	44-19	461,730	(19)
16	Goran Ivanisevic	1	41-23	562,795	(15)
17	David Wheaton	0*	29-19	479,239	(18)
18	Goran Prpic	0	39-30	411,068	(20)
19	Brad Gilbert	0	37-24	343,803	(27)
20	Jakob Hlasek	1	49-26	573,642	(14)

*Neither Wheaton's victory in the ITF Grand Slam Cup nor his winnings of $2 million are considered official by the ATP.

WOMEN

		1st	W-L	Earnings	(No)
1	Monica Seles	10	74- 6	$2,457,758	(1)
2	Steffi Graf	7	65- 8	1,468,336	(2)
3	Gabriela Sabatini	5	62-11	1,192,971	(3)
4	Martina Navratilova	5	53- 9	989,986	(4)
5	Arantxa Sanchez Vicario	1	61-15	799,340	(5)
6	Jennifer Capriati	2	42-12	535,617	(9)
7	Jana Novotna	2	47-16	766,369	(6)
8	Mary Joe Fernandez	0	49-19	672,035	(7)
9	Conchita Martinez	3	40-13	304,790	(15)
10	M. Maleeva-Fragniere	3	45-15	316,003	(14)
11	Katerina Maleeva	1	36-17	299,693	(16)
12	Zina Garrison	0	38-18	435,859	(11)
13	Nathalie Tauziat	0	37-20	280,304	(18)
14	Anke Huber	1	33-14	196,629	(21)
15	Leila Meskhi	1	30-14	223,168	(20)
16	Judith Wiesner	1	36-14	167,361	(26)
17	Helena Sukova	1	34-18	396,824	(12)
18	Sabine Appelmans	2	34-15	192,871	(22)
19	Lori McNeil	2	39-21	253,565	(19)
20	Julie Halard	1	44-23	187,677	(23)

1992 Computer Rankings (through Sept.20)

For Men's Tour, listed are tournaments played (TP), titles won (1st), record (W-L), and computer points earned (Pts). For Women's Tour, listed are tournaments played (TP), titles won (1st), record (W-L), and average computer points per game (Avg).

MEN

ATP/IBM singles rankings based on total computer points from each player's 14 best tournaments covering the last 12 months. Tournaments, titles and match won-lost records, however, are for 1992 only.

		TP	1st	W-L	Pts
1	Stefan Edberg	15	3	56-16	3577
2	Jim Courier	15	5	58-11	3574
3	Pete Sampras	15	4	59-15	3442
4	Michael Chang	18	3	48-16	2447
5	Goran Ivanisevic	16	2	41-15	2103
6	Andre Agassi	15	2	38-12	2067
7	Petr Korda	21	2	44-21	2066
8	Boris Becker	14	2	34-12	1944
9	Ivan Lendl	20	0	39-21	1867
10	Wayne Ferreira	21	2	46-20	1806
11	Carlos Costa	18	2	37-16	1610
12	MaliVai Washington	19	2	46-17	1548
13	Guy Forget	16	0	31-18	1513
14	Richard Krajicek	19	1	35-17	1477
15	Michael Stich	17	1	37-18	1466
16	Alexander Volkov	24	0	41-27	1364
17	Aaron Krickstein	17	1	31-15	1293
18	Sergi Bruguera	17	2	36-18	1283
19	Thomas Muster	21	3	34-18	1253
20	John McEnroe	14	0	27-14	1250

WOMEN

WTA/Va.Slims Slimstat singles rankings based on average computer points awarded for each tournament played during the last 12 months. Tournaments, titles and match won-lost records, however, are for 1992 only.

		TP	1st	W-L	Avg
1	Monica Seles	12	7	58-5	277.4
2	Steffi Graf	9	4	52-6	242.6
3	Gabriela Sabatini	13	5	54-8	189.3
4	Martina Navratilova	8	3	23-5	172.3
5	A. Sanchez-Vicario	14	2	59-14	169.0
6	Jennifer Capriati	10	1	32-9	110.7
7	Mary Joe Fernandez	12	0	43-13	109.6
8	Conchita Martinez	13	1	43-15	90.6
9	M. Maleeva-Fragniere	10	0	29-10	87.6
10	Anke Huber	10	0	26-11	83.1
11	Jana Novotna	13	0	26-15	70.4
12	Nathalie Tauziat	14	0	33-16	68.3
13	Helena Sukova	12	1	30-12	63.4
14	Zina Garrison	15	1	31-15	61.2
15	Mary Pierce	9	1	27-9	59.3
16	Amanda Coetzer	11	0	30-13	57.5
17	Katerina Maleeva	12	0	21-14	57.2
18	Sabine Appelmans	13	1	26-14	54.6
19	Amy Frazier	14	1	32-13	53.7
20	Lori McNeil	16	1	32-17	53.6

Singles Leaders (Cont.)
Money Won
Amounts include singles and doubles earnings.

MEN

		Earnings			Earnings			Earnings
1	Jim Courier	$1,550,045	6	Michael Chang	$754,597	11	Ivan Lendl	$553,366
2	Stefan Edberg	1,367,029	7	Goran Ivanisevic	708,371	12	Carlos Costa	550,747
3	Pete Sampras	1,131,372	8	Michael Stich	628,976	13	John McEnroe	529,537
4	Andre Agassi	1,000,484	9	Emilio Sanchez	586,668	14	Sergi Bruguera	521,023
5	Petr Korda	793,823	10	Wayne Ferreira	585,560	15	Boris Becker	510,987

WOMEN

		Earnings			Earnings			Earnings
1	Monica Seles	$1,732,352	6	Mary Joe Fernandez	$483,083	11	L.Savchenko-Neiland	$338,577
2	A.Sanchez Vicario	1,093,155	7	Martina Navratilova	403,233	12	Helena Sukova	307,662
3	Steffi Graf	1,068,026	8	Gigi Fernandez	401,137	13	Lori McNeil	301,266
4	Gabriela Sabatini	824,065	9	Jana Novotna	344,934	14	Zina Garrison	279,747
5	Natalia Zvereva	519,144	10	Conchita Martinez	343,618	15	Jennifer Capriati	272,001

National Team Competition
Davis Cup

France won the 1991 Davis Cup, beating the defending champion United States, 3-1, in Lyon. The victory marked the seventh time the French have won the Cup, but it was their first title since 1932 and the heyday of the Four Musketeers.

Henri Leconte and Guy Forget each won in singles against Pete Sampras of the U.S., and teamed to beat Ken Flach and Robert Seguso in doubles.

1991 Final

France 3, United States 1
(at Lyon, France, Nov.29-Dec.1)

Day One—Andre Agassi (USA) def. Guy Forget (FRA), 6-7 (7-9), 6-6.2, 6-1, 6-2; Henri Leconte (FRA) def. Pete Sampras (USA), 6-4, 7-5, 6-4. Match tied, 1-1.

Day Two—Forget & Leconte (FRA) def. Ken Flach & Robert Seguso (USA), 6-1, 6-4, 4-6, 6-2. France leads, 2-1.

Day Three—Forget (FRA) def. Sampras (USA), 7-6 (8-6), 3-6, 6-3, 6-4. France clinches, 3-1 (second singles match cancelled by mutual consent).

1992 Early Rounds

The United States will host Switzerland in the Davis Cup final, Dec. 4-6, at Ft. Worth. The U.S. has won the Cup 29 times and appeared in 56 finals. The Swiss have never reached the final before.

1st ROUND
(Jan. 29-Feb. 2)

Winner	Loser
Australia 5	Yugoslavia 0 (at Cyprus)
at Brazil 3	Germany 1
at Czechoslovakia 5	Belgium 0
at France 5	Britain 0
at Italy 4	Spain 1
Sweden 3	at Canada 0
Switzerland 4	at Holland 1
at United States 5	Argentina 0

QUARTERFINALS
(Mar.27-30)

Winner	Loser
at Brazil 3	Italy 1*
at Sweden 5	Australia 2
Switzerland 3	at France 2
at United States 3	Czechoslovakia 2

*Last singles of Brazil-Italy match cancelled by rain.

SEMIFINALS
United States 4, Sweden 1
(Sept. 25-27, at Minneapolis)

Day One—Jim Courier (USA) def. Nicklas Kulti (SWE), 4-6, 7-6 (7-2), 6-3, 7-5; Andre Agassi (USA) def. Stefan Edberg (SWE), 5-7, 6-3, 7-6 (7-1), 6-3. U.S. leads, 2-0.

Day Two—Pete Sampras & John McEnroe (USA) def. Edberg & Anders Jarryd (SWE), 6-1, 6-7 (2-7), 4-6, 6-3, 6-3. U.S. clinches, 3-0.

Day Three—Magnus Larsson (SWE) def. Jim Courier (USA), 2-6, 7-6 (8-6), 7-6 (7-5); Andre Agassi (USA) def. Nicklas Kulti (SWE), 6-7 (7-4), 6-2, 6-4.

Switzerland 5, Brazil 0
(Sept. 25-27, at Geneva)

Day One—Marc Rosset (SWI) def. Jaime Oncins (BRA), 6-3, 7-5, 7-5; Jakob Hlasek (SWI) def. Luiz Mattar (BRA), 6-2, 6-3, 6-7 (5-7), 6-3. Swiss lead, 2-0. Switerland leads, 2-0.

Day Two—Rosset & Hlasek (SWI) def. Cassio Motta & Fernando Roese (BRA), 6-3, 6-4, 6-3. Switzerland clinches, 3-0.

Day Three—Hlasek (SWI) def. Oncins (BRA), 6-4, 6-2; Rosset (SWI) def. Mattar (BRA), 7-6 (7-2), 6-3.

FINAL
Switzerland vs USA at Ft. Worth (Dec. 4-6)

1992 Federation Cup

Germany defeated defending champion Spain, 2-1, to win the women's Federation Cup for the second time (West Germany won in 1987). The week-long tournament featuring 32 international teams was held in Frankfurt, July 12-19.

FINAL
Germany 2, Spain 1

Singles—Anke Huber (GER) def. Conchita Martinez (SPA), 6-3, 6-7 (0-7), 6-1; Steffi Graf (GER) def. Arantxa Sanchez Vicario (SPA), 6-4, 6-2.

Doubles—Martinez & Vicario (SPA) def. Huber & Barbara Rittner (GER), 6-1, 6-2.

Grand Slam Championships
Australian Open
MEN

Became an Open Championship in 1969. Two tournaments were held in 1977; the first in January, the second in December. Tournament moved back to January in 1987, so no championship was decided in 1986.
Surface: Synpave Rebound Ace (hardcourt surface composed of polyurethane and synthetic rubber).
Multiple winners: Roy Emerson (6); Jack Crawford and Ken Rosewall (4); James Anderson, Rod Laver, Adrian Quist, Mats Wilander and Pat Wood (3); John Bromwich, Ashley Cooper, Stefan Edberg, Rodney Heath, Johan Kriek, Ivan Lendl, John Newcombe, Frank Sedgman, Guillermo Vilas and Tony Wilding (2).

Year	Winner	Loser	Score	Year	Winner	Loser	Score
1905	Rodney Heath	A.Curtis	46 63 64 64	1953	Ken Rosewall	M. Rose	60 63 64
1906	Tony Wilding	H.Parker	60 64 64	1954	Mervyn Rose	R. Hartwig	62 06 64 62
1907	Horace Rice	H.Parker	63 64 64	1955	Ken Rosewall	L. Hoad	97 64 64
1908	Fred Alexander	A.Dunlop	36 36 60 62 63	1956	Lew Hoad	K. Rosewall	64 36 64 75
1909	Tony Wilding	E.Parker	6175 62	1957	Ashley Cooper	N. Fraser	63 911 64 62
1910	Rodney Heath	H.Rice	64 63 62	1958	Ashley Cooper	M. Anderson	75 63 64
1911	Norman Brookes	H.Rice	61 62 63	1959	Alex Olmedo	N. Fraser	61 62 36 63
1912	James Parke	A.Beamish	36 63 16 61 75	1960	Rod Laver	N. Fraser	57 36 63 86 86
1913	Ernie Parker	H.Parker	26 61 62 63	1961	Roy Emerson	R. Laver	16 63 75 64
1914	Pat Wood	G.Patterson	64 63 57 61	1962	Rod Laver	R. Emerson	86 06 64 64
1915	Francis Lowe	H.Rice	46 61 61 64	1963	Roy Emerson	K. Fletcher	63 63 61
1916-18	Not held			1964	Roy Emerson	F. Stolle	63 64 62
1919	A.R.F.Kingscote	E.Pockley	64 60 63	1965	Roy Emerson	F. Stolle	79 26 64 75 61
1920	Pat Wood	R. Thomas	63 46 68 61 63	1966	Roy Emerson	A. Ashe	64 68 62 63
1921	Rhys Gemmell	A. Hedeman	75 61 64	1967	Roy Emerson	A. Ashe	64 61 61
1922	James Anderson	G. Patterson	60 36 36 63 62	1968	Bill Bowrey	J. Gisbert	75 26 97 64
1923	Pat Wood	C.B. St. John	61 61 63	1969	Rod Laver	A. Gimeno	63 64 75
1924	James Anderson	R. Schlesinger	63 64 36 57 63	1970	Arthur Ashe	D. Crealy	64 97 62
1925	James Anderson	G. Patterson	119 26 62 63	1971	Ken Rosewall	A. Ashe	61 75 63
1926	John Hawkes	J. Willard	61 63 61	1972	Ken Rosewall	M. Anderson	76 63 75
1927	Gerald Patterson	J. Hawkes	36 64 36 1816 63	1973	John Newcombe	O. Parun	63 67 75 61
1928	Jean Borotra	R.O. Cummings	64 61 46 57 63	1974	Jimmy Connors	P. Dent	76 64 46 63
1929	John Gregory	R. Schlesinger	62 62 57 75	1975	John Newcombe	J. Connors	75 36 64 75
1930	Gar Moon	H. Hopman	63 61 63	1976	Mark Edmondson	J. Newcombe	67 63 76 61
1931	Jack Crawford	H. Hopman	64 62 26 61	1977	Roscoe Tanner	G. Vilas	63 63 63
1932	Jack Crawford	H. Hopman	46 63 36 63 61		Vitas Gerulaitis	J. Lloyd	63 76 57 36 62
1933	Jack Crawford	K. Gledhill	26 75 63 62	1978	Guillermo Vilas	J. Marks	64 64 36 63
1934	Fred Perry	J. Crawford	63 75 61	1979	Guillermo Vilas	J. Sadri	76 63 62
1935	Jack Crawford	F. Perry	26 64 64 64	1980	Brian Teacher	K. Warwick	75 76 63
1936	Adrian Quist	J. Crawford	62 63 46 36 97	1981	Johan Kriek	S. Denton	62 76 67 64
1937	V.B. McGrath	J. Bromwich	63 16 60 26 61	1982	Johan Kriek	S. Denton	63 63 62
1938	Don Budge	J. Bromwich	64 62 61	1983	Mats Wilander	I. Lendl	61 64 64
1939	John Bromwich	A. Quist	64 61 63	1984	Mats Wilander	K. Curran	67 64 76 62
1940	Adrian Quist	J. Crawford	63 61 62	1985	Stefan Edberg	M. Wilander	64 63 63
1941-45	Not held			1986	Not held		
1946	John Bromwich	D. Pails	57 63 75 36 62	1987	Stefan Edberg	P. Cash	63 64 36 57 63
1947	Dinny Pails	J. Bromwich	46 64 36 75 86	1988	Mats Wilander	P. Cash	63 67 36 61 86
1948	Adrian Quist	J. Bromwich	64 36 63 26 63	1989	Ivan Lendl	M. Mecir	62 62 62
1949	Frank Sedgman	K. McGregor	63 63 62	1990	Ivan Lendl	S. Edberg	46 76 52 (ret)
1950	Frank Sedgman	K. McGregor	63 64 46 61	1991	Boris Becker	I. Lendl	16 64 64 64
1951	Richard Savitt	K. McGregor	63 26 63 61	1992	Jim Courier	S. Edberg	63 36 64 62
1952	Ken McGregor	F. Sedgman	75 1210 26 62				

Grand Slam Championships (Cont.)
Australian Open
WOMEN

Became an Open Championship in 1969. Two tournaments were held in 1977, the first in January, the second in December. Tournament moved back to January in 1987, so no championship was decided in 1986.

Multiple winners: Margaret Smith Court (11); Nancye Wynne Bolton (6); Daphne Akhurst (5); Evonne Goolagong Cawley (4); Steffi Graf, Jean Hartigan and Martina Navratilova (3); Coral Buttsworth, Chris Evert Lloyd, Thelma Long, Hana Mandlikova, Mall Molesworth, Mary Carter Reitano and Monica Seles (2).

Year	Winner	Loser	Score	Year	Winner	Loser	Score
1922	Mall Molesworth	E. Boyd	63 108	1960	Margaret Smith	J. Lehane	75 62
1923	Mall Molesworth	E. Boyd	61 75	1961	Margaret Smith	J. Lehane	61 64
1924	Sylvia Lance	E. Boyd	63 36 64	1962	Margaret Smith	J. Lehane	60 62
1925	Daphne Akhurst	E. Boyd	16 86 64	1963	Margaret Smith	J. Lehane	62 62
1926	Daphne Akhurst	E. Boyd	61 63	1964	Margaret Smith	L. Turner	63 62
1927	Esna Boyd	S. Harper	57 61 62	1965	Margaret Smith	M. Bueno	57 64 52 (ret)
1928	Daphne Akhurst	E. Boyd	75 62	1966	Margaret Smith	N. Richey	walkover
1929	Daphne Akhurst	L. Bickerton	61 57 62	1967	Nancy Richey	L. Turner	61 64
				1968	Billie Jean King	M. Smith	61 62
1930	Daphne Akhurst	S. Harper	108 26 75	1969	Margaret Court	B. Jean King	64 61
1931	Coral Buttsworth	M. Crawford	16 63 64				
1932	Coral Buttsworth	K. LeMessurier	97 64	1970	Margaret Court	K. Melville	63 61
1933	Joan Hartigan	C. Buttsworth	64 63	1971	Margaret Court	E. Goolagong	26 76 75
1934	Joan Hartigan	M. Molesworth	61 64	1972	Virginia Wade	E. Goolagong	64 64
1935	Dorothy Round	N. Bolton	16 61 63	1973	Margaret Court	E. Goolagong	64 75
1936	Joan Hartigan	N. Bolton	64 64	1974	Evonne Goolagong	C. Evert	76 46 60
1937	Nancye Wynne	E. Westacott	63 57 64	1975	Evonne Goolagong	M. Navratilova	63 62
1938	Dorothy Bundy	D. Stevenson	63 62	1976	Evonne Cawley	R. Tomanova	62 62
1939	Emily Westacott	N. Hopman	61 62	1977	Kerry Reid	D. Balestrat	75 62
					Evonne Cawley	H. Gourlay	63 60
1940	Nancye Bolton	T. Coyne	57 64 60	1978	Chris O'Neill	B. Nagelsen	63 76
1941-45	Not held			1979	Barbara Jordan	S. Walsh	63 63
1946	Nancye Bolton	J. Fitch	64 64				
1947	Nancye Bolton	N. Hopman	63 62	1980	Hana Mandlikova	W. Turnbull	60 75
1948	Nancye Bolton	M. Toomey	63 61	1981	Martina Navratilova	C. Evert Lloyd	67 64 75
1949	Doris Hart	N. Bolton	63 64	1982	Chris Evert Lloyd	M. Navratilova	63 26 63
				1983	Martina Navratilova	K. Jordan	62 76
1950	Louise Brough	D. Hart	64 36 64	1984	Chris Evert Lloyd	H. Sukova	67 61 63
1951	Nancye Bolton	T. Long	61 75	1985	Martina Navratilova	C. Evert Lloyd	62 46 62
1952	Thelma Long	H. Angwin	62 63	1986	Not held		
1953	Maureen Connelly	J. Sampson	63 62	1987	Hana Mandlikova	M. Navratilova	75 76
1954	Thelma Long	J. Staley	63 64	1988	Steffi Graf	C. Evert	61 76
1955	Beryl Pemrose	T. Long	64 63	1989	Steffi Graf	H. Sukova	64 64
1956	Mary Carter	T. Long	36 62 97				
1957	Shirley Fry	A. Gibson	63 64	1990	Steffi Graf	M.J. Fernandez	63 64
1958	Angela Mortimer	L. Coghlan	63 64	1991	Monica Seles	J. Novotna	57 63 61
1959	Mary Reitano	T. Schuman	62 63	1992	Monica Seles	M.J. Fernandez	62 63

French Open
MEN

Prior to 1925, entry was restricted to members of French clubs. From 1941-45, tournament was closed to all foreigners. Became an Open Championship in 1968, but closed to contract pros in 1972.

Surface: Red clay.

First year: 1891. **Most wins:** Max Decugis (8).

Multiple winners (since 1925): Bjorn Borg (6); Henri Cochet (4); Rene Lacoste, Ivan Lendl, Yvon Petra and Mats Wilander (3); Jim Courier, Bernard Destremau, Jaroslav Drobny, Roy Emerson, Jan Kodes, Rod Laver, Frank Parker, Nicola Pietrangeli, Ken Rosewall, Manuel Santana, Tony Trabert and Gottfried von Cramm (2).

Year	Winner	Loser	Score	Year	Winner	Loser	Score
1925	Rene Lacoste	J. Borotra	75 61 64	1936	Gottfried von Cramm	F. Perry	60 26 62 26 60
1926	Henri Cochet	R. Lacoste	62 64 63	1937	Henner Henkel	H. Austin	61 64 63
1927	Rene Lacoste	B. Tilden	64 46 57 63 119	1938	Don Budge	R. Menzel	63 62 64
1928	Henri Cochet	R. Lacoste	57 63 61 63	1939	Don McNeill	B. Riggs	75 60 63
1929	Rene Lacoste	J. Borotra	63 26 60 26 86	1940	Not held		
1930	Henri Cochet	B. Tilden	36 86 63 61	1941	Bernard Destremau		Not available
1931	Jean Borotra	C. Boussus	26 64 75 64	1942	Bernard Destremau		Not available
1932	Henri Cochet	G. de Stefani	60 64 46 63	1943	Yvon Petra		Not available
1933	Jack Crawford	H. Cochet	86 61 63	1944	Yvon Petra		Not available
1934	Gottfried von Cramm	J. Crawford	64 79 36 75 63	1945	Yvon Petra	B. Destremau	75 64 62
1935	Fred Perry	G. von Cramm	63 36 61 63	1946	Marcel Bernard	J. Drobny	36 26 61 64 63

Year	Winner	Loser	Score	Year	Winner	Loser	Score
1947	Joseph Asboth	E. Sturgess	86 75 64	1970	Jan Kodes	Z. Franulovic	62 64 60
1948	Frank Parker	J. Drobny	64 75 57 86	1971	Jan Kodes	I. Nastase	86 62 26 75
1949	Frank Parker	Budge Patty	63 16 61 64	1972	Andres Gimeno	P. Proisy	46 63 61 61
				1973	Ilie Nastase	N. Pilic	63 63 60
1950	Budge Patty	J. Drobny	61 62 36 57 75	1974	Bjorn Borg	M. Orantes	67 60 61 61
1951	Jaroslav Drobny	E. Sturgess	63 63 63	1975	Bjorn Borg	G. Vilas	62 63 64
1952	Jaroslav Drobny	F. Sedgman	62 60 36 64	1976	Adriano Panatta	H. Solomon	61 64 46 76
1953	Ken Rosewall	V. Seixas	63 64 16 62	1977	Guillermo Vilas	B. Gottfried	60 63 60
1954	Tony Trabert	A. Larsen	64 75 61	1978	Bjorn Borg	G. Vilas	61 61 63
1955	Tony Trabert	S. Davidson	26 61 64 62	1979	Bjorn Borg	V. Pecci	63 61 67 64
1956	Lew Hoad	S. Davidson	64 86 63				
1957	Sven Davison	H. Flam	63 64 64	1980	Bjorn Borg	V. Gerulaitis	64 61 62
1958	Mervyn Rose	L. Ayala	63 64 64	1981	Bjorn Borg	I. Lendl	61 46 62 36 61
1959	Nicola Pietrangeli	I. Vermaak	36 63 64 61	1982	Mats Wilander	G. Vilas	16 76 60 64
				1983	Yannick Noah	M. Wilander	62 75 76
1960	Nicola Pietrangeli	L. Ayala	36 63 64 46 63	1984	Ivan Lendl	J. McEnroe	36 26 64 75 75
1961	Manuel Santana	N. Pietrangeli	46 61 36 60 62	1985	Mats Wilander	I. Lendl	36 64 62 62
1962	Rod Laver	R. Emerson	36 26 63 97 62	1986	Ivan Lendl	M. Pernfors	63 62 64
1963	Roy Emerson	P. Darmon	36 61 64 64	1987	Ivan Lendl	M. Wilander	75 62 36 76
1964	Manuel Santana	N. Pietrangeli	63 61 46 75	1988	Mats Wilander	H. Leconte	75 62 61
1965	Fred Stolle	T. Roche	36 60 62 63	1989	Michael Chang	S. Edberg	61 36 46 64 62
1966	Tony Roche	I. Gulyas	61 64 75				
1967	Roy Emerson	T. Roche	61 64 26 62	1990	Andres Gomez	A. Agassi	63 26 64 64
1968	Ken Rosewall	R. Laver	63 61 26 62	1991	Jim Courier	A. Agassi	36 64 26 61 64
1969	Rod Laver	K. Rosewall	64 63 64	1992	Jim Courier	P. Korda	75 62 61

WOMEN

Prior to 1925, entry was restricted to members of French clubs. Became an Open Championship in 1968, but closed to contract pros in 1972.

First year: 1897. **Most wins:** Chris Evert Lloyd (7) and Suzanne Lenglen (6).

Multiple winners (since 1920): Chris Evert Lloyd (7); Margaret Smith Court (5); Helen Wills Moody (4); Monica Seles and Hilde Sperling (3); Maureen Connolly, Steffi Graf, Margaret Osborne duPont, Doris Hart, Ann Haydon Jones, Suzanne Lenglen, Simone Mathieu, Margaret Scriven, Martina Navratilova and Lesley Turner (2).

Year	Winner	Loser	Score	Year	Winner	Loser	Score
1925	Suzanne Lenglen	K. McKane	61 62	1962	Margaret Smith	L. Turner	63 36 75
1926	Suzanne Lenglen	M. Browne	61 60	1963	Lesley Turner	A. Jones	26 63 75
1927	Kea Bouman	I. Peacock	62 64	1964	Margaret Smith	M. Bueno	57 61 62
1928	Helen Wills	E. Bennett	61 62	1965	Lesley Turner	M. Smith	63 64
1929	Helen Wills	S. Mathieu	63 64	1966	Ann Jones	N. Richey	63 61
				1967	Francoise Durr	L. Turner	46 63 64
1930	Helen Moody	H. Jacobs	62 61	1968	Nancy Richey	A. Jones	57 64 61
1931	Cilly Aussem	B. Nuthall	86 61	1969	Margaret Court	A. Jones	61 46 63
1932	Helen Moody	S. Mathieu	75 61				
1933	Margaret Scriven	S. Mathieu	62 46 64	1970	Margaret Court	H. Niessen	62 64
1934	Margaret Scriven	H. Jacobs	75 46 61	1971	Evonne Goolagong	H. Gourlay	63 75
1935	Hilde Sperling	S. Mathieu	62 61	1972	Billie Jean King	E. Goolagong	63 63
1936	Hilde Sperling	S. Mathieu	63 64	1973	Margaret Court	C. Evert	67 76 64
1937	Hilde Sperling	S. Mathieu	62 64	1974	Chris Evert	O. Morozova	61 62
1938	Simone Mathieu	N. Landry	60 63	1975	Chris Evert	M. Navratilova	26 62 61
1939	Simone Mathieu	J. Jedrzejowska	63 86	1976	Sue Barker	R. Tomanova	62 06 62
				1977	Mima Jausovec	F. Mihai	62 67 61
1940-45	Not held			1978	Virginia Ruzici	M. Jausovec	62 62
1946	Margaret Osborne	P. Betz	16 86 75	1979	Chris Evert Lloyd	W. Turnbull	62 60
1947	Patricia Todd	D. Hart	63 36 64				
1948	Nelly Landry	S. Fry	62 06 60	1980	Chris Evert Lloyd	V. Ruzici	60 63
1949	Margaret duPont	N. Adamson	75 62	1981	Hana Mandlikova	S. Hanika	62 64
				1982	Martina Navratilova	A. Jaeger	76 61
1950	Doris Hart	P. Todd	64 46 62	1983	Chris Evert Lloyd	M. Jausovec	61 62
1951	Shirley Fry	D. Hart	63 36 63	1984	Martina Navratilova	C. Evert Lloyd	63 61
1952	Doris Hart	S. Fry	64 64	1985	Chris Evert Lloyd	M. Navratilova	63 67 75
1953	Maureen Connolly	D. Hart	62 64	1986	Chris Evert Lloyd	M. Navratilova	26 63 63
1954	Maureen Connolly	G. Bucaille	64 61	1987	Steffi Graf	M. Navratilova	64 46 86
1955	Angela Mortimer	D. Knode	26 75 108	1988	Steffi Graf	N. Zvereva	60 60
1956	Althea Gibson	A. Mortimer	62 1210	1989	Arantxa Sanchez	S. Graf	76 36 75
1957	Shirley Bloomer	D. Knode	61 63				
1958	Zsuzsi Kormoczy	S. Bloomer	64 16 62	1990	Monica Seles	S. Graf	76 64
1959	Christine Truman	Z. Kormoczy	64 75	1991	Monica Seles	A. Vicario	63 64
				1992	Monica Seles	S. Graf	62 36 108
1960	Darlene Hard	Y. Ramirez	63 64				
1961	Ann Hayden	Y. Ramirez	62 61				

Grand Slam Champions (Cont.)
Wimbledon
MEN

Officially called "The Lawn Tennis Championships" at the All-England Club, Wimbledon. Challenge round system (defending champion qualified for following year's final) used from 1877-1921. Became an Open Championship in 1968, but closed to contract pros in 1972.

Surface: Grass.

Multiple winners: William Renshaw (7); Bjorn Borg and Laurie Doherty (5); Reggie Doherty, Rod Laver and Tony Wilding (4); Wilfred Baddeley, Boris Becker, Arthur Gore, John McEnroe, John Newcombe, Fred Perry and Bill Tilden (3); Jean Borotra, Norman Brookes, Don Budge, Henri Cochet, Jimmy Connors, Stefan Edberg, Roy Emerson, John Hartley, Lew Hoad, Rene Lacoste, Gerald Patterson and Joshua Pim (2).

Year	Winner	Loser	Score	Year	Winner	Loser	Score
1877	Spencer Gore	W.Marshall	61 62 64	1935	Fred Perry	G. von Cramm	62 64 64
1878	Frank Hadow	S.Gore	75 61 97	1936	Fred Perry	G. von Cramm	61 61 60
1879	John Hartley	V.St.L.Gould	62 64 62	1937	Don Budge	G. von Cramm	63 64 62
				1938	Don Budge	H. Austin	61 60 63
1880	John Hartley	H.Lawford	60 62 26 63	1939	Bobby Riggs	E. Cooke	26 86 36 63 62
1881	William Renshaw	J.Hartley	60 62 61				
1882	William Renshaw	E.Renshaw	61 26 46 62 62	1940-45	Not held		
1883	William Renshaw	E.Renshaw	26 63 63 46 63	1946	Yvon Petra	G. Brown	62 64 79 57 64
1884	William Renshaw	H.Lawford	60 64 97	1947	Jack Kramer	T. Brown	61 63 62
1885	William Renshaw	H.Lawford	75 62 46 75	1948	Bob Falkenburg	J. Bromwich	75 06 62 36 75
1886	William Renshaw	H.Lawford	60 57 63 64	1949	Ted Schroeder	J. Drobny	36 60 63 46 64
1887	Herbert Lawford	E.Renshaw	16 63 36 64 64				
1888	Ernest Renshaw	H.Lawford	63 75 60	1950	Budge Patty	F. Sedgman	61 810 62 63
1889	William Renshaw	E.Renshaw	64 61 36 60	1951	Dick Savitt	K. McGregor	64 64 64
				1952	Frank Sedgman	J. Drobny	46 63 62 63
1890	William Hamilton	W.Renshaw	68 62 36 61 61	1953	Vic Seixas	K. Nielsen	97 63 64
1891	Wilfred Baddeley	J.Pim	64 16 75 60	1954	Jaroslav Drobny	K. Rosewall	1311 46 62 97
1892	Wilfred Baddeley	J.Pim	46 63 63 62	1955	Tony Trabert	K. Nielsen	63 75 61
1893	Joshua Pim	W.Baddeley	36 61 63 62	1956	Lew Hoad	K. Rosewall	62 47 75 61
1894	Joshua Pim	W.Baddeley	108 62 86	1957	Lew Hoad	A. Cooper	62 61 62
1895	Wilfred Baddeley	W.Eaves	46 26 86 62 63	1958	Ashley Cooper	N. Fraser	36 63 64 1311
1896	Harold Mahoney	W.Baddeley	62 68 57 86 63	1959	Alex Olmedo	R. Laver	64 63 64
1897	Reggie Doherty	H.Mahoney	64 64 63				
1898	Reggie Doherty	L.Doherty	63 63 26 57 61	1960	Neale Fraser	R. Laver	64 36 97 75
1899	Reggie Doherty	A.Gore	16 46 62 63 63	1961	Rod Laver	C. McKinley	63 61 64
				1962	Rod Laver	M. Mulligan	62 62 61
1900	Reggie Doherty	S.Smith	68 63 61 62	1963	Chuck McKinley	F. Stolle	97 61 64
1901	Arthur Gore	R.Doherty	46.75 64 64	1964	Roy Emerson	F. Stolle	64 1210 46 63
1902	Laurie Doherty	A.Gore	64 63 36 60	1965	Roy Emerson	F. Stolle	62 64 64
1903	Laurie Doherty	F.Riseley	75 63 60	1966	Manuel Santana	D. Rolston	64 119 64
1904	Laurie Doherty	F.Riseley	61 75 86	1967	John Newcombe	W. Bungert	63 61 61
1905	Laurie Doherty	N.Brookes	86 62 64	1968	Rod Laver	T. Roche	63 64 62
1906	Laurie Doherty	F.Riseley	64 46 62 63	1969	Rod Laver	J. Newcombe	64 57 64 64
1907	Norman Brookes	A.Gore	64 62 62				
1908	Arthur Gore	R.Barrett	63 62 46 36 64	1970	John Newcombe	K. Rosewall	57 63 62 36 61
1909	Arthur Gore	M.Ritchie	68 16 62 62 62	1971	John Newcombe	S. Smith	63 57 26 64 64
				1972	Stan Smith	I. Nastase	46 63 63 46 75
1910	Tony Wilding	A.Gore	64 75 46 62	1973	Jan Kodes	A. Metreveli	61 98 63
1911	Tony Wilding	R.Barrett	64 46 26 62 Ret	1974	Jimmy Connors	K. Rosewall	61 61 64
1912	Tony Wilding	A.Gore	64 64 46 64	1975	Arthur Ashe	J. Connors	61 61 57 64
1913	Tony Wilding	M.McLoughlin	86 63 108	1976	Bjorn Borg	I. Nastase	64 62 97
1914	Norman Brookes	T.Wilding	64 64 75	1977	Bjorn Borg	J. Connors	36 62 61 57 64
1915-18	Not held			1978	Bjorn Borg	J. Connors	62 62 63
1919	Gerald Patterson	N.Brookes	63 75 62	1979	Bjorn Borg	R. Tanner	67 61 36 63 64
1920	Bill Tilden	G. Patterson	26 63 62 64	1980	Bjorn Borg	J. McEnroe	16 75 63 67 86
1921	Bill Tilden	B. Norton	46 26 61 60 75	1981	John McEnroe	B. Borg	46 76 76 64
1922	Gerald Patterson	R. Lycett	63 64 62	1982	Jimmy Connors	J. McEnroe	36 63 67 76 64
1923	Bill Johnston	F. Hunter	60 63 61	1983	John McEnroe	C. Lewis	62 62 62
1924	Jean Borotra	R. Lacoste	61 36 61 36 64	1984	John McEnroe	J. Connors	61 61 62
1925	Rene Lacoste	J. Borotra	63 63 46 86	1985	Boris Becker	K. Curran	63 67 76 64
1926	Jean Borotra	H. Kinsey	86 61 63	1986	Boris Becker	I. Lendl	64 63 75
1927	Henri Cochet	J. Borotra	46 46 63 64 75	1987	Pat Cash	I. Lendl	76 62 75
1928	Rene Lacoste	H. Cochet	61 46 64 62	1988	Stefan Edberg	B. Becker	46 76 64 62
1929	Henri Cochet	J. Borotra	64 63 64	1989	Boris Becker	S. Edberg	60 76 64
1930	Bill Tilden	W. Allison	63 97 64	1990	Stefan Edberg	B. Becker	62 62 36 36 64
1931	Sidney Wood	F. Shields	walkover	1991	Michael Stich	B. Becker	64 76 64
1932	Ellsworth Vines	H. Austin	64 62 60	1992	Andre Agassi	G.Ivanisevic	67 64 64 16 64
1933	Jack Crawford	E. Vines	46 119 62 26 64				
1934	Fred Perry	J. Crawford	63 60 75				

WOMEN

Officially called "The Lawn Tennis Championships" at the All-England Club, Wimbledon. Challenge round system (defending champion qualified for following year's final) used from 1886-1921. Became an Open Championship in 1968, but closed to contract pros in 1972.

Multiple winners: Martina Navratilova (9); Helen Wills Moody (8); Dorothea Douglass Chambers (7); Blanche Bingley Hillyard, Billie Jean King and Suzanne Lenglen (6); Lottie Dod and Charlotte Cooper Sterry (5); Louise Brough and Steffi Graf (4); Maria Bueno, Maureen Connolly, Margaret Smith Court and Chris Evert Lloyd (3); Evonne Goolagong Cawley, Althea Gibson, Dorothy Round, May Sutton and Maud Watson (2).

Year	Winner	Loser	Score
1884	Maud Watson	L.Watson	68 63 62
1885	Maud Watson	B.Bingley	61 75
1886	Blanche Bingley	M.Watson	63 63
1887	Lottie Dod	B.Bingley	62 60
1888	Lottie Dod	B.Hillyard	63 63
1889	Blanche Hillyard	L.Rice	46 86 64
1890	Lena Rice	L.Jacks	64 61
1891	Lottie Dod	B.Hillyard	62 61
1892	Lottie Dod	B.Hillyard	61 61
1893	Lottie Dod	B.Hillyard	68 61 64
1894	Blanche Hillyard	L.Austin	61 61
1895	Charlotte Cooper	H.Jackson	75 86
1896	Charlotte Cooper	W.Pickering	62 63
1897	Blanche Hillyard	C.Cooper	57 75 62
1898	Charlotte Cooper	L.Martin	64 64
1899	Blanche Hillyard	C.Cooper	62 63
1900	Blanche Hillyard	C.Cooper	46 64 64
1901	Charlotte Sterry	B.Hillyard	62 62
1902	Muriel Robb	C.Sterry	75 61
1903	Dorothea Douglass	E.Thomson	46 64 62
1904	Dorothea Douglass	C.Sterry 60 63	
1905	May Sutton	D.Douglass	63 64
1906	Dorothea Douglass	M.Sutton	63 97
1907	May Sutton	D.Chambers	61 64
1908	Charlotte Sterry	A.Morton	64 64
1909	Dora Boothby	A.Morton	64 46 86
1910	Dorothea Chambers	D.Boothby	62 62
1911	Dorothea Chambers	D.Boothby	60 60
1912	Ethel Larcombe	C.Sterry	63 61
1913	Dorothea Chambers	R.McNair	60 64
1914	Dorothea Chambers	E.Larcombe	75 64
1915-18 Not held			
1919	Suzanne Lenglen	D.Chambers	108 46 97
1920	Suzanne Lenglen	D. Chambers	63 60
1921	Suzanne Lenglen	E. Ryan	62 60
1922	Suzanne Lenglen	M. Mallory	62 60
1923	Suzanne Lenglen	K. McKane	62 62
1924	Kathleen McKane	H. Wills	46 64 64
1925	Suzanne Lenglen	J. Fry	62 60
1926	Kathleen Godfree	L. de Alvarez	62 46 63
1927	Helen Wills	L. de Alvarez	62 64
1928	Helen Wills	L. de Alvarez	62 63
1929	Helen Wills	H. Jacobs	61 62
1930	Helen Moody	E. Ryan	62 62
1931	Cilly Aussem	H. Kranwinkel	75 75
1932	Helen Moody	H. Jacobs	63 61
1933	Helen Moody	D. Round	64 68 63
1934	Dorothy Round	H. Jacobs	62 57 63
1935	Helen Moody	H. Jacobs	63 36 75
1936	Helen Jacobs	H.K. Sperling	62 46 75
1937	Dorothy Round	J. Jedrzejowska	62 26 75

Year	Winner	Loser	Score
1938	Helen Moody	H. Jacobs	64 60
1939	Alice Marble	K. Stammers	62 60
1940-45	Not held		
1946	Pauline Betz	L. Brough	62 64
1947	Margaret Osborne	D. Hart	62 64
1948	Louise Brough	D. Hart	63 86
1949	Louise Brough	M. duPont	108 16 108
1950	Louise Brough	M. duPont	61 36 61
1951	Doris Hart	S. Fry	61 60
1952	Maureen Connolly	L. Brough	64 63
1953	Maureen Connolly	D. Hart	86 75
1954	Maureen Connolly	L. Brough	62 75
1955	Louise Brough	B. Fleitz	75 86
1956	Shirley Fry	A. Buxton	63 61
1957	Althea Gibson	D. Hard	63 62
1958	Althea Gibson	A. Mortimer	86 62
1959	Maria Bueno	D. Hard	64 63
1960	Maria Bueno	S. Reynolds	86 60
1961	Angela Mortimer	C. Truman	46 64 75
1962	Karen Susman	V. Sukova	64 64
1963	Margaret Smith	B.J. Moffitt	63 64
1964	Maria Bueno	M. Smith	64 79 63
1965	Margaret Smith	M. Bueno	64 75
1966	Billie Jean King	M. Bueno	63 36 61
1967	Billie Jean King	A. Jones	63 64
1968	Billie Jean King	J. Tegart	97 75
1969	Ann Jones	B.J. King	36 63 62
1970	Margaret Court	B.J. King	1412 119
1971	Evonne Goolagong	M. Court	64 61
1972	Billie Jean King	E. Goolagong	63 63
1973	Billie Jean King	C. Evert	60 75
1974	Chris Evert	O. Morzova	60 64
1975	Billie Jean King	E. Cawley	60 61
1976	Chris Evert	E. Cawley	63 46 86
1977	Virginia Wade	B. Stove	46 63 61
1978	Martina Navratilova	C. Evert	26 64 75
1979	Martina Navratilova	C. Evert Lloyd	64 64
1980	Evonne Cawley	C. Evert Lloyd	61 76
1981	Chris Evert Lloyd	H. Mandlikova	62 62
1982	Martina Navratilova	C. Evert Lloyd	61 36 62
1983	Martina Navratilova	A. Jaeger	60 63
1984	Martina Navratilova	C. Evert Lloyd	76 62
1985	Martina Navratilova	C. Evert Lloyd	46 63 62
1986	Martina Navratilova	H. Mandlikova	76 63
1987	Martina Navratilova	S. Graf	75 63
1988	Steffi Graf	M. Navratilova	57 62 61
1989	Steffi Graf	M. Navratilova	62 67 61
1990	Martina Navratilova	Z. Garrison	64 61
1991	Steffi Graf	G. Sabatini	64 36 86
1992	Steffi Graf	M. Seles	62 61

Grand Slam Champions (Cont.)
U.S. Open
MEN

Challenge round system (defending champion qualified for following year's final) used from 1884–1911. Amateur and Open Championships held in 1968 and '69. Became an exclusively Open Championship in 1970.

Surface: Decoturf II (acrylic cement). Known as Patriotic Tournament in 1917 during WWI.

Multiple winners: William Larned, Richard Sears and Bill Tilden (7); Jimmy Connors (5); John McEnroe and Robert Wrenn (4); Oliver Campbell, Ivan Lendl, Fred Perry and Malcolm Whitman (3); Wilmer Allison, Don Budge, Stefan Edberg, Roy Emerson, Neale Fraser, Pancho Gonzalez, Bill Johnston, Jack Kramer, Rene Lacoste, Rod Laver, Maurice McLoughlin, R.L. Murray, John Newcombe, Frank Parker, Bobby Riggs, Ken Rosewall, Frank Sedgman, Henry Slocum, Tony Trabert, Ellsworth Vines and Richard Williams (2).

Year	Winner	Loser	Score	Year	Winner	Loser	Score
1881	Richard Sears	W.Glyn	60 63 62	1937	Don Budge	G. von Cramm	61 79 61 36 61
1882	Richard Sears	C.Clark	61 64 60	1938	Don Budge	G. Mako	63 68 62 61
1883	Richard Sears	J.Dwight	62 60 97	1939	Bobby Riggs	S. van Horn	64 62 64
1884	Richard Sears	H.Taylor	60 16 60 62	1940	Don McNeill	B. Riggs	46 68 63 63 75
1885	Richard Sears	G.Brinley	63 46 60 63	1941	Bobby Riggs	F. Kovacs	57 61 63 63
1886	Richard Sears	R.Beeckman	46 61 63 64	1942	Fred Schroeder	F. Parker	86 75 36 46 62
1887	Richard Sears	H.Slocum	61 63 62	1943	Joseph Hunt	J. Kramer	63 68 108 60
1888	Henry Slocum	H.Taylor	64 61 60	1944	Frank Parker	B. Talbert	64 36 63 63
1889	Henry Slocum	Q.Shaw	63 61 46 62	1945	Frank Parker	B. Talbert	1412 61 62
1890	Oliver Campbell	H.Slocum	62 46 63 61	1946	Jack Kramer	T. Brown, Jr.	97 63 60
1891	Oliver Campbell	C.Hobart	26 75 79 61 62	1947	Jack Kramer	F. Parker	46 26 61 60 63
1892	Oliver Campbell	F.Hovey	75 36 63 75	1948	Pancho Gonzalez	E. Sturgess	62 63 1412
1893	Robert Wrenn	F.Hovey	64 36 64 64	1949	Pancho Gonzalez	F. Schroeder	1618 26 61 62 64
1894	Robert Wrenn	M.Goodbody	68 61 64 64	1950	Arthur Larsen	H. Flam	63 46 57 64 63
1895	Fred Hovey	R.Wrenn	63 62 64	1951	Frank Sedgman	V. Seixas	64 61 61
1896	Robert Wrenn	F.Hovey	75 36 60 16 61	1952	Frank Sedgman	G. Mulloy	61 62 63
1897	Robert Wrenn	W.Eaves	46 86 63 26 62	1953	Tony Trabert	V. Seixas	63 62 63
1898	Malcolm Whitman	D.Davis	36 62 62 61	1954	Vic Seixas	R. Hartwig	36 62 64 64
1899	Malcolm Whitman	P.Paret	61 62 36 75	1955	Tony Trabert	K. Rosewall	97 63 63
1900	Malcolm Whitman	W.Larned	64 16 62 62	1956	Ken Rosewall	L. Hoad	46 62 63 63
1901	William Larned	B.Wright	62 68 64 64	1957	Mal Anderson	A. Cooper	108 75 64
1902	William Larned	R.Doherty	46 62 64 86	1958	Ashley Cooper	M. Anderson	62 36 46 108 86
1903	Laurie Doherty	W.Larned	60 63 108	1959	Neale Fraser	A. Olmedo	63 57 62 64
1904	Holcombe Ward	W.Clothier	108 64 97	1960	Neale Fraser	R. Laver	64 64 97
1905	Beals Wright	H.Ward	62 61 119	1961	Roy Emerson	R. Laver	75 63 62
1906	William Clothier	B.Wright	63 60 64	1962	Rod Laver	R. Emerson	62 64 57 64
1907	William Larned	R.LeRoy	62 62 64	1963	Rafael Osuna	F. Froehling	75 64 62
1908	William Larned	B.Wright	62 62 86	1964	Roy Emerson	F. Stolle	64 62 64
1909	William Larned	W.Clothier	61 62 57 16 61	1965	Manuel Santana	C. Drysdale	62 79 75 61
1910	William Larned	T.Bundy	61 57 60 68 61	1966	Fred Stolle	J. Newcombe	42 1210 63 64
1911	William Larned	M.McLoughlin	64 64 62	1967	John Newcombe	C. Graebner	64 64 86
1912	Maurice McLoughlin	W.F.Johnson	36 26 62 64 62	1968	Arthur Ashe	T. Okker	1412 57 63 36 63
1913	Maurice McLoughlin	R.Williams	64 57 63 61	1969	Rod Laver	T. Roche	79 61 63 62
1914	Richard Williams	M.McLoughlin	63 86 108	1970	Ken Rosewall	T. Roche	26 64 76 63
1915	Bill Johnston	M.McLoughlin	16 60 75 108	1971	Stan Smith	J. Kodes	36 63 62 76
1916	Richard Williams	B.Johnston	46 64 06 62 64	1972	Ilie Nastase	A. Ashe	36 63 67 64 63
1917	R.L.Murray	N.Niles	57 86 63 63	1973	John Newcombe	J. Kodes	64 16 46 62 63
1918	R.L.Murray	B.Tilden	63 61 75	1974	Jimmy Connors	K. Rosewall	61 60 61
1919	Bill Johnston	B.Tilden	64 64 63	1975	Manuel Orantes	J. Connors	64 63 63
1920	Bill Tilden	B. Johnston	61 16 75 57 63	1976	Jimmy Connors	B. Borg	64 36 76 64
1921	Bill Tilden	W. Johnson	61 63 61	1977	Guillermo Vilas	J. Connors	26 63 76 60
1922	Bill Tilden	B. Johnston	46 36 62 63 64	1978	Jimmy Connors	B. Borg	64 62 62
1923	Bill Tilden	B. Johnston	64 61 64	1979	John McEnroe	V. Gerulaitis	75 63 63
1924	Bill Tilden	B. Johnston	61 97 62	1980	John McEnroe	B. Borg	76 61 67 57 64
1925	Bill Tilden	B. Johnston	46 119 63 46 63	1981	John McEnroe	B. Borg	46 62 64 63
1926	Rene Lacoste	J. Borotra	64 60 64	1982	Jimmy Connors	I. Lendl	63 62 46 64
1927	Rene Lacoste	B. Tilden	119 63 119	1983	Jimmy Connors	I. Lendl	63 67 75 60
1928	Henri Cochet	F. Hunter	46 64 36 75 63	1984	John McEnroe	I. Lendl	63 64 61
1929	Bill Tilden	F. Hunter	36 63 46 62 64	1985	Ivan Lendl	J. McEnroe	76 63 64
1930	John Doeg	F. Shields	108 16 64 1614	1986	Ivan Lendl	M. Mecir	64 62 60
1931	Ellsworth Vines	G. Lott Jr.	79 63 97 75	1987	Ivan Lendl	M. Wilander	67 60 76 64
1932	Ellsworth Vines	H. Cochet	64 64 64	1988	Mats Wilander	I. Lendl	64 46 63 57 64
1933	Fred Perry	J. Crawford	63 1113 46 60 61	1989	Boris Becker	I. Lendl	76 16 63 76
1934	Fred Perry	W. Allison	64 63 16 86	1990	Pete Sampras	A. Agassi	64 63 62
1935	Wilmer Allison	S. Wood	62 62 63	1991	Stefan Edberg	J. Courier	62 64 60
1936	Fred Perry	D. Budge	26 62 86 16 108	1992	Stefan Edberg	P. Sampras	36 64 76 62

Note: In the last two U.S. championships open only to amateurs, Arthur Ashe def. Bob Lutz (4-6, 6-3, 8-10, 6-0, 6-4) in 1968; and Stan Smith def. Lutz (9-7, 6-3, 6-1) in 1969.

WOMEN

Amateur and Open Championships held in 1968 and '69. Became an exclusively Open Championship in 1970. Known as Patriotic Tournament in 1917 during WWI.

Multiple winners: Molla Mallory Bjurstedt (8); Helen Wills Moody (7); Chris Evert Lloyd (6); Margaret Smith Court (5); Pauline Betz, Mario Bueno, Helen Jacobs, Billie Jean King, Alice Marble, Elisabeth Moore, Martina Navratilova and Hazel Hotchkiss Wightman (4); Juliette Atkinson, Mary Browne, Maureen Connolly and Margaret Osborne duPont (3); Tracy Austin, Mabel Cahill, Sarah Palfrey Cooke, Darlene Hard, Doris Hart, Althea Gibson, Steffi Graf, Monica Seles and Bertha Townsend (2).

Year	Winner	Loser	Score
1887	Ellen Hansell	L.Knight	61 60
1888	Bertha Townsend	E.Hansell	63 65
1889	Bertha Townsend	L.Voorhes	75 62
1890	Ellen Roosevelt	B.Townsend	62 62
1891	Mabel Cahill	E.Roosevelt	64 61 46 63
1892	Mabel Cahill	E.Moore	57 63 64 46 62
1893	Aline Terry	M.Cahill	default
1894	Helen Hellwig	A.Terry	75 36 60 36 63
1895	Juliette Atkinson	H.Hellwig	64 62 61
1896	Elisabeth Moore	J.Atkinson	64 46 62 62
1897	Juliette Atkinson	E.Moore	63 63 46 36 63
1898	Juliette Atkinson	M.Jones	63 57 64 26 75
1899	Marion Jones	J.Atkinson	default
1900	Myrtle McAteer	E.Parker	62 6260
1901	Elizabeth Moore	M.McAteer	64 36 75 26 62
1902	Marion Jones	E.Moore	61 10(ret)
1903	Elizabeth Moore	M.Jones	75 86
1904	May Sutton	E.Moore	61 62
1905	Elizabeth Moore	M.Sutton	default
1906	Helen Homans	E.Moore	default
1907	Evelyn Sears	C.Neely	63 62
1908	Maud B.Wallach	Ev.Sears	63 16 63
1909	Hazel Hotchkiss	M.Wallach	60 61
1910	Hazel Hotchkiss	L.Hammond	64 62
1911	Hazel Hotchkiss	F.Sutton	811 61 97
1912	Mary Browne	El.Sears	64 62
1913	Mary Browne	D.Green	- 62 75
1914	Mary Browne	M.Wagner	62 16 61
1915	Molla Bjurstedt	H.Wightman	46 62 60
1916	Molla Bjurstedt	L.Raymond	60 61
1917	Molla Bjurstedt	M.Vanderhoef	46 60 62
1918	Molla Bjurstedt	E.Gross	64 63
1919	Hazel Wightman	M.Zinderstein	61 62
1920	Molla Mallory	M. Zinderstein	63 61
1921	Molla Mallory	M. Browne	46 64 62
1922	Molla Mallory	H. Wills	63 61
1923	Helen Wills	M. Mallory	62 61
1924	Helen Wills	M. Mallory	61 63
1925	Helen Wills	K. McKane	36 60 62
1926	Molla Mallory	E. Ryan	46 64 97
1927	Helen Wills	B. Nuthall	61 64
1928	Helen Wills	H. Jacobs	62 61
1929	Helen Wills	P. Watson	64 62
1930	Betty Nuthall	A. Harper	61 64
1931	Helen Moody	E. Whitingstall	64 61
1932	Helen Jacobs	C. Babcock	62 62
1933	Helen Jacobs	H. Moody	86 36 30(ret)
1934	Helen Jacobs	S. Palfrey	61 64
1935	Helen Jacobs	S. Fabyan	62 64
1936	Alice Marble	H. Jacobs	46 63 62
1937	Anita Lizana	J. Jedrzejowska	64 62
1938	Alice Marble	N. Wynne	60 63
1939	Alice Marble	H. Jacobs	60 810 64
1940	Alice Marble	H. Jacobs	62 63
1941	Sarah Cooke	P. Betz	75 62
1942	Pauline Betz	L. Brough	46 61 64
1943	Pauline Betz	L. Brough	63 57 63
1944	Pauline Betz	M. Osborne	63 86
1945	Sarah Cooke	P. Betz	36 86 64
1946	Pauline Betz	P. Canning	119 63
1947	Louise Brough	M. Osborne	86 46 61
1948	Margaret duPont	L. Brough	46 64 15 13
1949	Margaret duPont	D. Hart	64 61
1950	Margaret duPont	D. Hart	64 63
1951	Maureen Connolly	S. Fry	63 16 64
1952	Maureen Connolly	D. Hart	63 75
1953	Maureen Connolly	D. Hart	62 64
1954	Doris Hart	L. Brough	68 61 86
1955	Doris Hart	P. Ward	64 62
1956	Shirley Fry	A. Gibson	63 64
1957	Althea Gibson	L. Brough	63 62
1958	Althea Gibson	D. Hard	36 61 62
1959	Maria Bueno	C. Truman	61 64
1960	Darlene Hard	M. Bueno	64 1012 64
1961	Darlene Hard	A. Haydon	63 64
1962	Margaret Smith	D. Hard	97 64
1963	Maria Bueno	M. Smith	75 64
1964	Maria Bueno	C. Graebner	61 60
1965	Margaret Smith	B.J. Moffit	86 75
1966	Maria Bueno	N. Richey	63 61
1967	Billie Jean King	A. Haydon Jones	119 64
1968	Virginia Wade	B. Jean King	64 62
1969	Margaret Court	N. Richey	62 62
1970	Margaret Court	R. Casals	62 26 61
1971	Billie Jean King	R. Casals	64 76
1972	Billie Jean King	K. Melville	63 75
1973	Margaret Court	E. Goolagong	76 57 62
1974	Billie Jean King	E. Goolagong	36 63 75
1975	Chris Evert	E. Cawley	57 64 62
1976	Chris Evert	E. Cawley	63 60
1977	Chris Evert	W. Turnbull	76 62
1978	Chris Evert	P. Shriver	75 64
1979	Tracy Austin	C. Evert Lloyd	64 63
1980	Chris Evert Lloyd	H. Mandlikova	57 61 61
1981	Tracy Austin	M. Navratilova	16 76 76
1982	Chris Evert Lloyd	H. Mandlikova	63 61
1983	Martina Navratilova	C. Evert Lloyd	61 63
1984	Martina Navratilova	C. Evert Lloyd	46 64 64
1985	Hana Mandlikova	M. Navratilova	76 16 76
1986	Martina Navratilova	H. Sukova	63 62
1987	Martina Navratilova	S. Graf	76 61
1988	Steffi Graf	G. Sabatini	63 36 61
1989	Steffi Graf	M. Navratilova	36 75 61
1990	Gabriela Sabatini	S. Graf	62 76
1991	Monica Seles	M. Navratilova	76 61
1992	Monica Seles	A. Sanchez Vicario	63 63

Note: In the last two U.S. championships open only to amateurs, Margaret Court def. Maria Bueno (6-2, 6-2) in 1968 and Virginia Wade (4-6, 6-3, 6-0) in 1969.

Grand Slam Summary

Men's and Women's singles winners of the four Grand Slam tournaments—Australian, French, Wimbledon and United States—since the French was opened to all comers in 1925. Note that there were two Australian Open championships in 1977 and none in 1986.

MEN

Only two men have won the Grand Slam—all four events in a single year: Don Budge in 1938 and Rod Laver in both 1962 and 1969.

Three wins in one year: Jack Crawford (1933); Fred Perry (1934); Tony Trabert (1955); Lew Hoad (1956); Ashley Cooper (1958); Roy Emerson (1964); Jimmy Connors (1974); Mats Wilander (1988).

Two wins in one year: Roy Emerson (4 times); Bjorn Borg (3 times); Rene Lacoste, Ivan Lendl, John Newcombe and Fred Perry (twice); Boris Becker, Don Budge, Henri Cochet, Jimmy Connors, Jim Courier, Neale Fraser, Jack Kramer, John McEnroe, Alex Olmedo, Budge Patty, Bobby Riggs, Ken Rosewall, Dick Savitt, Frank Sedgman and Guillermo Vilas (once).

Year	Australia	French	Wimbledon	US	Year	Australia	French	Wimbledon	US
1925	Anderson	Lacoste	Lacoste	Tilden	1960	Laver	Pietrangeli	Fraser	Fraser
1926	Hawkes	Cochet	Borotra	Lacoste	1961	Emerson	Santana	Laver	Emerson
1927	Patterson	Lacoste	Cochet	Lacoste	1962	**Laver**	**Laver**	**Laver**	**Laver**
1928	Borotra	Cochet	Lacoste	Cochet	1963	Emerson	Emerson	McKinley	Osuna
1929	Gregory	Lacoste	Cochet	Tilden	1964	Emerson	Santana	Emerson	Emerson
					1965	Emerson	Stolle	Emerson	Santana
1930	Moon	Cochet	Tilden	Doeg	1966	Emerson	Roche	Santana	Stolle
1931	Crawford	Borotra	Wood	Vines	1967	Emerson	Emerson	Newcombe	Newcombe
1932	Crawford	Cochet	Vines	Vines	1968	Bowrey	Rosewall	Laver	Ashe
1933	Crawford	Crawford	Crawford	Perry	1969	**Laver**	**Laver**	**Laver**	**Laver**
1934	Perry	vonCramm	Perry	Perry	1970	Ashe	Kodes	Newcombe	Rosewall
1935	Crawford	Perry	Perry	Allison	1971	Rosewall	Kodes	Newcombe	Smith
1936	Quist	vonCramm	Perry	Perry	1972	Rosewall	Gimeno	Smith	Nastase
1937	McGrath	Henkel	Budge	Budge	1973	Newcombe	Nastase	Kodes	Newcombe
1938	**Budge**	**Budge**	**Budge**	**Budge**	1974	Connors	Borg	Connors	Connors
1939	Bromwich	McNeill	Riggs	Riggs	1975	Newcombe	Borg	Ashe	Orantes
					1976	Edmondson	Panatta	Borg	Connors
1940	Quist	—	—	McNeill	1977	Tanner	Vilas	Borg	Vilas
1941	—	Destremau	—	Riggs		& Gerulaitis			
1942	—	Destremau	—	Schroeder	1978	Vilas	Borg	Borg	Connors
1943	—	Petra	—	Hunt	1979	Vilas	Borg	Borg	McEnroe
1944	—	Petra	—	Parker	1980	Teacher	Borg	Borg	McEnroe
1945	—	Petra	—	Parker	1981	Kriek	Borg	McEnroe	McEnroe
1946	Bromwich	Bernard	Petra	Kramer	1982	Kriek	Wilander	Connors	Connors
1947	Pails	Asboth	Kramer	Kramer	1983	Wilander	Noah	McEnroe	Connors
1948	Quist	Parker	Falkenburg	Gonzalez	1984	Wilander	Lendl	McEnroe	McEnroe
1949	Sedgman	Parker	Schroeder	Gonzalez	1985	Edberg	Wilander	Becker	Lendl
1950	Sedgman	Patty	Patty	Larse	1986	—	Lendl	Becker	Lendl
1951	Savitt	Drobny	Savitt	Sedgman	1987	Edberg	Lendl	Cash	Lendl
1952	McGregor	Drobny	Sedgman	Sedgman	1988	Wilander	Wilander	Edberg	Wilander
1953	Rosewall	Rosewall	Seixas	Trabert	1989	Lendl	Chang	Becker	Becker
1954	Rose	Trabert	Drobny	Seixas	1990	Lendl	Gomez	Edberg	Sampras
1955	Rosewall	Trabert	Trabert	Trabert	1991	Becker	Courier	Stich	Edberg
1956	Hoad	Hoad	Hoad	Rosewall	1992	Courier	Courier	Agassi	Edberg
1957	Cooper	Davidson	Hoad	Anderson					
1958	Cooper	Rose	Cooper	Cooper					
1959	Olmedo	Pietrangeli	Olmedo	Fraser					

WOMEN

Only three women have won the Grand Slam—all four events in a single year: Maureen Connolly in 1953, Margaret Smith Court in 1970 and Steffi Graf in 1988.

Three in one year: Helen Wills Moody (1928 and '29); Margaret Smith Court (1962, '65, '69 and '73); Billie Jean King (1972); Martina Navratilova (1983 and '84); Steffi Graf (1989); and Monica Seles (1991 and '92).

Two in one year: Chris Evert Lloyd (5 times); Helen Wills Moody and Martina Navratilova (3 times); Maria Bueno, Maureen Connolly, Margaret Smith Court, Althea Gibson, Billie Jean King (twice); Cilly Aussem, Pauline Betz, Louise Brough, Evonne Goolagong Cawley, Shirley Fry, Darlene Hard, Margaret Osborne duPont, Suzanne Lenglen and Alice Marble.

Year	Australia	French	Wimbledon	US	Year	Australia	French	Wimbledon	US
1925	Akhurst	Lenglen	Lenglen	Wills	1930	Akhurst	Moody	Moody	Nuthall
1926	Akhurst	Lenglen	Godfree	Mallory	1931	Buttsworth	Aussem	Aussem	Moody
1927	Boyd	Bouman	Wills	Wills	1932	Buttsworth	Moody	Moody	Jacobs
1928	Akhurst	Wills	Wills	Wills	1933	Hartigan	Scriven	Moody	Jacobs
1929	Akhurst	Wills	Wills	Wills	1934	Hartigan	Scriven	Round	Jacobs

Year	Australia	French	Wimbledon	US	Year	Australia	French	Wimbledon	US
1935	Round	Sperling	Moody	Jacobs	1965	Smith	Turner	Smith	Smith
1936	Hartigan	Sperling	Jacobs	Marble	1966	Smith	Jones	King	Bueno
1937	Bolton	Sperling	Round	Lizana	1967	Richey	Durr	King	King
1938	Bundy	Mathieu	Moody	Marble	1968	King	Richey	King	Wade
1939	Westacott	Mathieu	Marble	Marble	1969	Court	Court	Jones	Court
1940	Bolton	—	—	Marble	**1970**	**Court**	**Court**	**Court**	**Court**
1941	—	—	—	Cooke	1971	Court	Goolagong	Goolagong	King
1942	—	—	—	Betz	1972	Wade	King	King	King
1943	—	—	—	Betz	1973	Court	Court	King	Court
1944	—	—	—	Betz	1974	Goolagong	Evert	Evert	King
1945	—	—	—	Cooke	1975	Goolagong	Evert	King	Evert
1946	Bolton	Osborne	Betz	Betz	1976	Cawley	Barker	Evert	Evert
1947	Bolton	Todd	Osborne	Brough	1977	Reid & Cawley	Jausovec	Wade	Evert
1948	Bolton	Landry	Brough	duPont	1978	O'Neil	Ruzici	Navratilova	Evert
1949	Hart	duPont	Brough	duPont	1979	Jordan	Lloyd	Navratilova	Austin
1950	Brough	Hart	Brough	duPont	1980	Mandlikova	Lloyd	Cawley	Evert
1951	Bolton	Fry	Hart	Connolly	1981	Navratilova	Mandlikova	Evert	Austin
1952	Long	Hart	Connolly	Connolly	1982	Lloyd	Navratilova	Navratilova	Evert
1953	**Connolly**	**Connolly**	**Connolly**	**Connolly**	1983	Navratilova	Lloyd	Navratilova	Navratilova
1954	Long	Connolly	Connolly	Hart	1984	Lloyd	Navratilova	Navratilova	Navratilova
1955	Penrose	Mortimer	Brough	Hart	1985	Navratilova	Evert	Navratilova	Mandlikova
1956	Carter	Gibson	Fry	Fry	1986	—	Evert	Navratilova	Navratilova
1957	Fry	Bloomer	Gibson	Gibson	1987	Mandlikova	Graf	Navratilova	Navratilova
1958	Mortimer	Kormoczy	Gibson	Gibson	**1988**	**Graf**	**Graf**	**Graf**	**Graf**
1959	Reitano	Truman	Bueno	Bueno	1989	Graf	Sanchez	Graf	Graf
1960	Smith	Hard	Bueno	Hard	1990	Graf	Seles	Navratilova	Sabatini
1961	Smith	Hayden	Mortimer	Hard	1991	Graf	Seles	Graf	Seles
1962	Smith	Smith	Susman	Smith	1992	Seles	Seles	Graf	Seles
1963	Smith	Turner	Smith	Bueno					
1964	Smith	Smith	Bueno	Bueno					

All-Time Grand Slam Singles Champions

Men and Women with the most singles championships in the Australian, French, Wimbledon and U.S. championships, through 1991. Note that (*) indicates player did not play in that particular Grand Slam event; players active in 1991 are in **bold** type.

Top 10 Men

		Aus	Fre	Wim	US		Total
1	Roy Emerson	6	2	2	2	—	12
2	Bjorn Borg	0	6	5	0	—	11
	Rod Laver	3	2	4	2	—	11
4	Bill Tilden	*	0	3	7	—	10
5	**Jimmy Connors**	1	0	2	5	—	8
	Ivan Lendl	2	3	0	3	—	8
	Fred Perry	1	1	3	3	—	8
	Ken Rosewall	4	2	0	2	—	8
9	Rene Lacoste	3	2	2	2	—	7
	William Larned	*	*	*	7	—	7
	John McEnroe	0	0	3	4	—	7
	John Newcombe	2	0	3	2	—	7
	William Renshaw	*	*	7	*	—	7
	Richard Sears	*	*	*	7	—	7
	Mats Wilander	3	3	0	1	—	7

Top 10 Women

		Aus	Fre	Wim	US		Total
1	Margaret Smith Court	11	5	3	5	—	24
2	Helen Wills Moody	*	4	8	7	—	19
3	Chris Evert Lloyd	2	7	3	6	—	18
	Martina Navratilova	3	2	9	4	—	18
5	Billie Jean King	1	1	6	4	—	12
	Suzanne Lenglen	*	6	6	0	—	12
7	**Steffi Graf**	3	2	4	2	—	11
8	Maureen Connolly	1	2	3	3	—	9
9	Molla Bjurstedt Malloy	*	*	0	8	—	8
10	Maria Bueno	0	0	3	4	—	7
	Evonne G. Cawley	4	1	2	0	—	7
	Dorothea L. Chambers	*	*	7	*	—	7
	Monica Seles	2	3	0	2	—	7

Maiden & Married Names of Women Champions

Maiden Name	Married Name	Maiden Name	Married Name
Blanche Bingley	Blanche Hillyard	Hazel Hotchkiss	Hazel Wightman
Molla Bjurstedt	Molla Mallory	Hilde Krahwinkel	Hilde Sperling
Patricia Canning	Patricia Todd	Kerry Melville	Kerry Reid
Mary Carter	Mary Raitano	Kathleen McKane	Kathleen Godfree
Charlotte Cooper	Charlotte Sterry	Billie Jean Moffitt	Billie Jean King
Thelma Coyne	Thelma Long	Margaret Osborne	Margaret duPont
Dorothea Douglass	Dorothea Lambert Chambers	Sarah Palfrey	Sarah Fabyan Cooke
Chris Evert	Chris Evert Lloyd	Margaret Smith	Margaret Court
Evonne Goolagong	Evonne Cawley	Helen Wills	Helen Moody
Louise Hammond	Louise Raymond	Nancye Wynne	Nancye Bolton
Ann Haydon	Ann Jones		

Year-end Tournaments
MEN
The Masters (1970–89)

The year-end championship of the men's tour from 1970-89. Contested by the year's top eight players. Originally a round-robin, the Masters was revised in 1972 to include a round-robin to decide the four semifinalists then a single elimination format after that. Held at Madison Square Garden in New York from 1978-89. Replaced by ATP Tour World Championship in 1990.

Multiple Winners: Ivan Lendl (5); Ilie Nastase (4); John McEnroe (3); Bjorn Borg (2).

Year	Winner	Runner-Up
1970	Stan Smith (4-1)	Rod Laver (4-1)
1971	Ilie Nastase (6-0)	Stan Smith (4-2)

Year	Winner	Loser	Score
1972	Ilie Nastase	S. Smith	63 62 36 26 63
1973	Ilie Nastase	T. Okker	63 75 46 63
1974	Guillermo Vilas	I. Nastase	76 62 36 36 64
1975	Ilie Nastase	B. Borg	62 62 61
1976	Manuel Orantes	W. Fibak	57 62 06 76 61
1978*	Jimmy Connors	B. Borg	64 16 64
1979	John McEnroe	A. Ashe	67 63 75

Year	Winner	Loser	Score
1980	Bjorn Borg	V. Gerulaitis	62 62
1981	Bjorn Borg	I. Lendl	64 62 62
1982	Ivan Lendl	V. Gerulaitis	67 26 76 62 64
1983	Ivan Lendl	J. McEnroe	64 64 62
1984	John McEnroe	I. Lendl	63 64 64
1985	John McEnroe	I. Lendl	75 60 64
1986	Ivan Lendl	B. Becker	62 76 63
1986*	Ivan Lendl	B. Becker	64 64 64
1987	Ivan Lendl	M. Wilander	62 62 63
1988	Boris Becker	I. Lendl	57 76 36 62 76
1989	Stefan Edberg	B. Becker	46 76 63 61

*Tournament switched from December to January in 1977-78, then back to December in 1986.
Note: In 1970, Smith was declared the winner because he beat Laver in their round-robin match (4-6, 6-3, 6-4).

ATP Tour World Championship

Replaced The Masters in 1990 as the year-end championship tournament for the Association of Tennis Professionals (ATP). Field made up of top eight players on ATP Tour (according to ATP computer rankings).

Year	Winner	Loser	Score
1990	Andre Agassi	S.Edberg	57 76 75 62
1991	Pete Sampras	J. Courier	36 76 63 64

ITF Grand Slam Cup

Inaugurated in 1990 by the International Tennis Federation to compete directly with the ATP Tour Championship. Field made up of top performers in year's Grand Slam events.

Year	Winner	Loser	Score
1990	Pete Sampras	B. Gilbert	63 64 62
1991	David Wheaton	M. Chang	75 62 64

WOMEN
Virginia Slims Championships

The year-end championship of the women's tour since 1977. Contested by the year's top 16 players. Since 1983, the tournament has featured the tour's only best-of-five set final.

Multiple winners: Martina Navratilova (6); Tracy Austin, Steffi Graf, Chris Evert Lloyd and Monica Seles (2).

Year	Winner	Loser	Score
1977	Chris Evert	B.J. King	62 62
1978	Chris Evert	M. Navratilova	63 63
1979	M. Navratilova	T. Austin	62 61
1980	Tracy Austin	A. Jaeger	62 62
1981	Tracy Austin	M. Navratilova	26 64 62
1982	M. Navratilova	C. Evert Lloyd	46 61 62
1983	M. Navratilova	C. Evert Lloyd	63 75 64
1984	M. Navratilova	H. Sukova	63 75 64

Year	Winner	Loser	Score
1985	M. Navratilova	H. Mandlikova	62 60 36 61
1986	M. Navratilova	S. Graf	76 63 62
1987	Steffi Graf	G. Sabatini	46 64 60 64
1988	Gabriela Sabatini	P. Shriver	75 62 62
1989	Steffi Graf	M. Navratilova	64 75 26 62
1990	Monica Seles	G. Sabatini	64 57 36 64 62
1991	Monica Seles	M. Navratilova	64 36 75 60

Annual Number One Players

Unofficial world rankings for men and women determined by the London Daily Telegraph from 1914-72. Since then, official world rankings computed by men's and women's tours. Rankings included only amateur players from 1914 until the arrival of open (professional) tennis in 1968. No rankings were released during World Wars I and II.

MEN

Multiple winners: Bill Tilden (6); Jimmy Connors (5); Henri Cochet, Rod Laver, Ivan Lendl and John McEnroe (4); John Newcombe and Fred Perry (3); Bjorn Borg, Don Budge, Ashley Cooper, Stefan Edberg, Roy Emerson, Neale Fraser, Jack Kramer, Rene Lacoste, Ilie Nastase, Frank Sedgman and Tony Trabert (2).

Year		Year		Year		Year	
1914	Maurice McLoughlin	1925	Bill Tilden	1933	Jack Crawford	1946	Jack Kramer
1915-18	No rankings	1926	Rene Lacoste	1934	Fred Perry	1947	Jack Kramer
1919	Gerald Patterson	1927	Rene Lacoste	1935	Fred Perry	1948	Frank Parker
1920	Bill Tilden	1928	Henri Cochet	1936	Fred Perry	1949	Pancho Gonzalez
1921	Bill Tilden	1929	Henri Cochet	1937	Don Budge		
1922	Bill Tilden			1938	Don Budge	1950	Budge Patty
1923	Bill Tilden	1930	Henri Cochet	1939	Bobby Riggs	1951	Frank Sedgman
1924	Bill Tilden	1931	Henri Cochet			1952	Frank Sedgman
		1932	Ellsworth Vines	1940-45	No rankings	1953	Tony Trabert

Year		Year		Year		Year	
1954	Jaroslav Drobny	1964	Roy Emerson	1974	Jimmy Connors	1983	John McEnroe
1955	Tony Trabert	1965	Roy Emerson	1975	Jimmy Connors	1984	John McEnroe
1956	Lew Hoad	1966	Manuel Santana	1976	Jimmy Connors	1985	Ivan Lendl
1957	Ashley Cooper	1967	John Newcombe	1977	Jimmy Connors	1986	Ivan Lendl
1958	Ashley Cooper	1968	Rod Laver	1978	Jimmy Connors	1987	Ivan Lendl
1959	Neale Fraser	1969	Rod Laver	1979	Bjorn Borg	1988	Mats Wilander
						1989	Ivan Lendl
1960	Neale Fraser	1970	John Newcombe	1980	Bjorn Borg		
1961	Rod Laver	1971	John Newcombe	1981	John McEnroe	1990	Stefan Edberg
1962	Rod Laver	1972	Ilie Nastase	1982	John McEnroe	1991	Stefan Edberg
1963	Rafael Osuna	1973	Ilie Nastase				

WOMEN

Multiple winners: Helen Wills Moody (9); Margaret Smith Court and Martina Navratilova (7); Chris Evert Lloyd (5); Margaret Osborne duPont, Steffi Graf and Billie Jean King (4); Maureen Connolly (3); Maria Bueno, Althea Gibson and Suzanne Lenglen (2).

Year		Year		Year		Year	
1925	Suzanne Lenglen	1946	Pauline Betz	1962	Margaret Smith	1978	Martina Navratilova
1926	Suzanne Lenglen	1947	Margaret Osborne	1963	Margaret Smith	1979	Martina Navratilova
1927	Helen Wills	1948	Margaret duPont	1964	Margaret Smith		
1928	Helen Wills	1949	Margaret duPont	1965	Margaret Smith	1980	Chris Evert Lloyd
1929	Helen Wills			1966	Billie Jean King	1981	Chris Evert Lloyd
		1950	Margaret duPont	1967	Billie Jean King	1982	Martina Navratilova
1930	Helen Wills Moody	1951	Doris Hart	1968	Billie Jean King	1983	Martina Navratilova
1931	Helen Wills Moody	1952	Maureen Connolly	1969	Margaret Court	1984	Martina Navratilova
1932	Helen Wills Moody	1953	Maureen Connolly			1985	Martina Navratilova
1933	Helen Wills Moody	1954	Maureen Connolly	1970	Margaret Court	1986	Martina Navratilova
1934	Dorothy Round	1955	Louise Brough	1971	Evonne Goolagong	1987	Steffi Graf
1935	Helen Wills Moody	1956	Shirley Fry	1972	Billie Jean King	1988	Steffi Graf
1936	Helen Jacobs	1957	Althea Gibson	1973	Margaret Court	1989	Steffi Graf
1937	Anita Lizana	1958	Althea Gibson	1974	Billie Jean King		
1938	Helen Wills Moody	1959	Maria Bueno	1975	Chris Evert	1990	Steffi Graf
1939	Alice Marble			1976	Chris Evert	1991	Monica Seles
		1960	Maria Bueno	1977	Chris Evert		
1940-45	No rankings	1961	Angela Mortimer				

All-Time Leaders
Overall Wins

All-time tournament wins for men and women, from the arrival of open tennis in 1968 through 1991. Totals include doubles earnings. Note that Billie Jean King and Margaret Smith Court started their careers before Open tennis, so their records are incomplete. Players active in 1991 in **bold** type.

MEN	Total		WOMEN	Total
1 **Jimmy Connors**	109	1	Chris Evert	157
2 **Ivan Lendl**	91		**Martina Navratilova**	157
3 **John McEnroe**	77	3	Evonne Goolagong Cawley	88
4 Bjorn Borg	62	4	Margaret Smith Court	79
5 Guillermo Vilas	61	5	Billie Jean King	71
6 Ilie Nastase	57	6	**Steffi Graf**	61
7 Rod Laver	47	7	Virginia Wade	52
8 Stan Smith	39	8	Helga Masthoff	37
9 Arthur Ashe	33	9	Olga Morozova	31
Stefan Edberg	33	10	Tracy Austin	29
Mats Wilander	33	11	Hana Mandlikova	27
12 John Newcombe	32	12	Nancy Richey	25
Manuel Orantes	32	13	Kerry Melville Reid	22
Ken Rosewall	32	14	Sue Barker	21
15 **Boris Becker**	31		**Pam Shriver**	21
16 Tom Okker	30	16	Julie Heldman	20
17 Vitas Gerulaitis	27		**Gabriela Sabatini**	20
18 Jose-Luis Clerc	25		**Monica Seles**	20
Brian Gottfried	25	19	Dianne Fromholst Balestrat	19
20 Yannick Noah	23	20	Rosie Casals	18

All-Time Leaders (Cont.)
Money Won

All-time money winners for men and women from the arrival of open tennis in 1968 through 1991. Totals include doubles earnings.

	MEN	Earnings		WOMEN	Earnings
1	Ivan Lendl	$18,211,061	1	Martina Navratilova	$17,664,593
2	John McEnroe	11,586,545	2	Chris Evert	8,896,195
3	Stefan Edberg	10,997,271	3	Steffi Graf	8,641,534
4	Boris Becker	9,376,755	4	Gabriela Sabatini	4,849,107
5	Jimmy Connors	8,332,004	5	Pam Shriver	4,616,058
6	Mats Wilander	7,377,193	6	Monica Seles	4,349,041
7	Guillermo Vilas	4,904,922	7	Helena Sukova	3,869,921
8	Andre Agassi	4,255,449	8	Hana Mandlikova	3,340,959
9	Andres Gomez	4,140,425	9	Zina Garrison	3,219,629
10	Anders Jarryd	3,986,703	10	Wendy Turnbull	2,769,024
11	Tomas Smid	3,697,243	11	Manuela Maleeva-Fragniere	2,282,682
12	Bjorn Borg	3,609,896	12	Claudia Kohde-Kilsch	2,143,048
13	Brad Gilbert	3,561,749	13	Jana Novotna	2,116,473
14	Yannick Noah	3,295,395	14	Arantxa Sanchez Vicario	2,059,757
15	Emilio Sanchez	3,247,148	15	Billie Jean King	1,966,487
16	Pete Sampras	3,012,138	16	Tracy Austin	1,925,415
17	Guy Forget	2,989,554	17	Natalia Zvereva	1,706,135
18	Jakob Hlasek	2,892,962	18	Mary Joe Fernandez	1,647,613
19	Kevin Curren	2,792,780	19	Lori McNeil	1,646,629
20	Brian Gottfried	2,782,514	20	Kathy Jordan	1,592,111

National Team Competition
Davis Cup

Established in 1900 as an annual international tournament by American player Dwight Davis. Originally called the International Lawn Tennis Challenge Trophy. Challenge round system until 1972. Since 1981, the top 16 nations in the world have played a straight knockout tournament over the course of a year. The format is a best-of-five match of two singles, one doubles and two singles over three days.

Multiple winners: USA (29); Australia (20); France (7); Australasia (6); British Isles (5); Britain and Sweden (4); West Germany (2).

Challenge Rounds

Year	Winner	Loser	Score	Site	Year	Winner	Loser	Score	Site
1900	USA	British Isles	3-0	Boston	1933	Britain	France	3-2	Paris
1901	Not held				1934	Britain	USA	4-1	Wimbledon
1902	USA	British Isles	3-2	New York	1935	Britain	USA	5-0	Wimbledon
1903	British Isles	USA	4-1	Boston	1936	Britain	Australia	3-2	Wimbledon
1904	British Isles	Belgium	5-0	Wimbledon	1937	USA	Britain	4-1	Wimbledon
1905	British Isles	USA	5-0	Wimbledon	1938	USA	Australia	3-2	Philadelphia
1906	British Isles	USA	5-0	Wimbledon	1939	Australia	USA	3-2	Philadelphia
1907	Australasia	British Isles	3-2	Wimbledon					
1908	Australasia	USA	5-0	Melbourne	1940-1945	Not held			
1909	Australasia	USA	5-0	Sydney	1946	USA	Australia	5-0	Melbourne
					1947	USA	Australia	4-1	New York
1910	Not held				1948	USA	Australia	5-0	New York
1911	Australasia	USA	5-0	N. Zealand	1949	USA	Australia	4-1	New York
1912	British Isles	Australasia	3-2	Melbourne	1950	Australia	USA	4-1	New York
1913	USA	British Isles	3-2	Wimbledon	1951	Australia	USA	3-2	Sydney
1914	Australasia	USA	3-2	New York	1952	Australia	USA	4-1	Adelaide
1915-18	Not held				1953	Australia	USA	3-2	Melbourne
1919	Australasia	British Isles	4-1	Sydney	1954	USA	Australia	3-2	Sydney
					1955	Australia	USA	5-0	New York
1920	USA	Australasia	5-0	N. Zealand	1956	Australia	USA	5-0	Adelaide
1921	USA	Japan	5-0	New York	1957	Australia	USA	3-2	Melbourne
1922	USA	Australasia	4-1	New York	1958	USA	Australia	3-2	Brisbane
1923	USA	Australasia	4-1	New York	1959	Australia	USA	3-2	New York
1924	USA	Australia	5-0	Philadelphia	1960	Australia	Italy	4-1	Sydney
1925	USA	France	5-0	Philadelphia	1961	Australia	Italy	5-0	Melbourne
1926	USA	France	4-1	Philadelphia	1962	Australia	Mexico	5-0	Brisbane
1927	France	USA	3-2	Philadelphia	1963	USA	Australia	3-2	Adelaide
1928	France	USA	4-1	Paris	1964	Australia	USA	3-2	Cleveland
1929	France	USA	3-2	Paris	1965	Australia	Spain	4-1	Sydney
1930	France	USA	4-1	Paris	1966	Australia	India	4-1	Melbourne
1931	France	Britain	3-2	Paris	1967	Australia	Spain	4-1	Brisbane
1932	France	USA	3-2	Paris					

Final Rounds

Year	Winner	Loser	Score	Site	Year	Winner	Loser	Score	Site
1968	USA	Australia	4-1	Adelaide	1980	Czech.	Italy	4-1	Prague
1969	USA	Romania	5-0	Cleveland	1981	USA	Argentina	3-1	Cincinnati
					1982	USA	France	4-1	Grenoble
1970	USA	W. Germany	5-0	Cleveland	1983	Australia	Sweden	3-2	Melbourne
1971	USA	Romania	3-2	Charlotte	1984	Sweden	USA	4-1	Gothenburg
1972	USA	Romania	3-2	Bucharest	1985	Sweden	W.Germany	3-2	Munich
1973	Australia	USA	5-0	Cleveland	1986	Australia	Sweden	3-2	Melbourne
1974	So. Africa	India	walkover	—	1987	Sweden	India	5-0	Gothenburg
1975	Sweden	Czech.	3-2	Stockholm	1988	W.Germany	Sweden	4-1	Gothenburg
1976	Italy	Chile	4-1	Santiago	1989	W.Germany	Sweden	3-2	Stuttgart
1977	Australia	Italy	3-1	Sydney					
1978	USA	Britain	4-1	Palm Springs	1990	USA	Australia	3-2	St. Petersburg
1979	USA	Italy	5-0	San Francisco	1991	France	USA	3-1	Lyon

Federation Cup

Started in 1963 by the International Lawn Tennis Federation as the Davis Cup of women's tennis. The major difference is that all competing countries gather at one site to decide the Cup winner in one week.
Multiple winners: USA (14); Australia (7); Czechoslovakia (5); Germany (2).

Year	Winner	Loser	Score	Site	Year	Winner	Loser	Score	Site
1963	USA	Australia	2-1	London	1978	USA	Australia	2-1	Melbourne
1964	Australia	USA	2-1	Philadelphia	1979	USA	Australia	3-0	Spain
1965	Australia	USA	2-1	Melbourne					
1966	USA	Germany	3-0	Italy	1980	USA	Australia	3-0	W.Germany
1967	USA	Britain	2-0	W.Germany	1981	USA	Britain	3-0	Tokyo
1968	Australia	Holland	3-0	Paris	1982	USA	W.Germany	3-0	Santa Clara
1969	USA	Australia	2-1	Athens	1983	Czech.	W.Germany	2-1	Zurich
					1984	Czech.	Australia	2-1	Brazil
1970	Australia	Britain	3-0	W.Germany	1985	Czech.	USA	2-1	Japan
1971	Australia	Britain	3-0	Perth	1986	USA	Czech.	3-0	Prague
1972	So. Africa	Britain	2-1	Africa	1987	W.Germany	USA	2-1	Vancouver
1973	Australia	So. Africa	3-0	W.Germany	1988	Czech.	USSR	2-1	Melbourne
1974	Australia	USA	2-1	Italy	1989	USA	Spain	3-0	Tokyo
1975	Czech.	Australia	3-0	France					
1976	USA	Australia	2-1	Philadelphia	1990	USA	USSR	2-1	Atlanta
1977	USA	Australia	2-1	Eastbourne	1991	Spain	USA	2-1	Nottingham
					1992	Germany	Spain	2-1	Frankfurt

Colleges

The NCAA recognizes men's individual tennis champions since 1883, but team titles were not sanctioned until 1946. NCAA women's individual and team championships started in 1982.

Men's NCAA Individual Champions (1883-1945)

Multiple winners: Malcolm Chace and Pancho Segura (3); Edward Chandler, George Church, E.B.Dewhurst, Fred Hovey, Frank Guernsey, W.P.Knapp, Robert LeRoy, P.S.Sears, Cliff Sutter, Ernest Sutter and Richard Williams (2).

Year		Year		Year	
1883	J.Clark, Harvard (spring)	1904	Robert LeRoy, Columbia	1925	Edward Chandler, Calif.
	H.Taylor, Harvard (fall)	1905	E.B.Dewhurst, Penn	1926	Edward Chandler, Calif.
1884	W.P.Knapp, Yale	1906	Robert LeRoy, Columbia	1927	Wilmer Allison, Texas
1885	W.P.Knapp, Yale	1907	G.P.Gardner Jr, Harvard	1928	Julius Seligson, Lehigh
1886	G.M.Brinley, Trinity,CT	1908	Nat Niles, Harvard	1929	Berkeley Bell, Texas
1887	P.S.Sears, Harvard	1909	Wallace Johnson, Penn		
1888	P.S.Sears, Harvard			1930	Cliff Sutter, Tulane
1889	R.P.Huntington Jr, Yale	1910	R.A.Holden Jr, Yale	1931	Keith Gledhill, Stanford
		1911	E.H.Whitney, Harvard	1932	Cliff Sutter, Tulane
1890	Fred Hovey, Harvard	1912	Geo.Church, Princeton	1933	Jack Tidball, UCLA
1891	Fred Hovey, Harvard	1913	Richard Williams, Harv.	1934	Gene Mako, USC
1892	William Larned, Cornell	1914	Geo.Church, Princeton	1935	Wilbur Hess, Rice
1893	Malcolm Chace, Brown	1915	Richard Williams, Harv.	1936	Ernest Sutter, Tulane
1894	Malcolm Chace, Yale	1916	G.C.Caner, Harvard	1937	Ernest Sutter, Tulane
1895	Malcolm Chace, Yale	1917	Not held	1938	Frank Guernsey, Rice
1896	Malcolm Whitman, Harvard	1918	Not held	1939	Frank Guernsey, Rice
1897	S.G.Thompson, Princeton	1919	Charles Garland, Yale		
1898	Leo Ware, Harvard			1940	Don McNeill, Kenyon
1899	Dwight Davis, Harvard	1920	Lascelles Banks, Yale	1941	Joseph Hunt, Navy
		1921	Philip Neer, Stanford	1942	Fred Schroeder, Stanford
1900	Ray Little, Princeton	1922	Lucien Williams, Yale	1943	Pancho Segura, Miami-FL
1901	Fred Alexander, Princeton	1923	Carl Fischer, Phi.Osteo.	1944	Pancho Segura, Miami-FL
1902	William Clothier, Harvard	1924	Wallace Scott, Wash.	1945	Pancho Segura, Miami-FL
1903	E.B.Dewhurst, Penn				

Colleges (Cont.)

Men's NCAA Division I Champions

Multiple winners (teams): UCLA (15); USC (13); Stanford (12); Georgia and William & Mary (2). **Multiple winners** (players): Alex Olmedo, Mikael Pernfors, Dennis Ralston and Ham Richardson (2).

Year	Team winner	Individual Champion	Year	Team winner	Individual Champion
1946	USC	Bob Falkenburg, USC	1970	UCLA	Jeff Borowiak, UCLA
1947	Wm.& Mary	Garner Larned, Wm.& Mary	1971	UCLA	Jimmy Connors, UCLA
1948	Wm.& Mary	Harry Likas, San Francisco	1972	Trinity-TX	Dick Stockton, Trinity-TX
1949	San Francisco	Jack Tuero, Tulane	1973	Stanford	Alex Mayer, Stanford
1950	UCLA	Herbert Flam, UCLA	1974	Stanford	John Whitlinger, Stanford
1951	USC	Tony Trabert, Cinncinati	1975	UCLA	Bill Martin, UCLA
1952	UCLA	Hugh Stewart, USC	1976	USC & UCLA	Bill Scanlon, Trinity-TX
1953	UCLA	Ham Richardson, Tulane	1977	Stanford	Matt Mitchell, Stanford
1954	UCLA	Ham Richardson, Tulane	1978	Stanford	John McEnroe, Stanford
1955	USC	Jose Aguero, Tulane	1979	UCLA	Kevin Curren, Texas
1956	UCLA	Alex Olmedo, USC	1980	Stanford	Robert Van't Hof, USC
1957	Michigan	Barry MacKay, Michigan	1981	Stanford	Tim Mayotte, Stanford
1958	USC	Alex Olmedo, USC	1982	UCLA	Mike Leach, Michigan
1959	Tulane	Whitney Reed, San Jose St.	1983	Stanford	Greg Holmes, Utah
	& Notre Dame		1984	UCLA	Mikael Pernfors, Georgia
1960	UCLA	Larry Nagler, UCLA	1985	Georgia	Mikael Pernfors, Georgia
1961	UCLA	Allen Fox, UCLA	1986	Stanford	Dan Goldie, Stanford
1962	USC	Rafael Osuna, USC	1987	Georgia	Andrew Burrow, Miami-FL
1963	USC	Dennis Ralston, USC	1988	Stanford	Robby Weiss, Pepperdine
1964	USC	Dennis Ralston, USC	1989	Stanford	Donni Leaycraft, LSU
1965	UCLA	Arthur Ashe, UCLA	1990	Stanford	Steve Bryan, Texas
1966	USC	Charlie Pasarell, UCLA	1991	USC	Jared Palmer, Stanford
1967	USC	Bob Lutz, USC	1992	Stanford	Alex O'Brien Stanford
1968	USC	Stan Smith, USC			
1969	USC	Joaquin Loyo-Mayo, USC			

Women's NCAA Champions

Multiple winners (teams): Stanford (8); USC (2). **Multiple winners** (players): Sandra Birch and Patty Fendick (2).

Year	Team winner	Individual Champion	Year	Team winner	Individual Champion
1982	Stanford	Alycia Moulton, Stanford	1988	Stanford	Shaun Stafford, Florida
1983	USC	Beth Herr, USC	1989	Stanford	Sandra Birch Stanford
1984	Stanford	Lisa Spain, Georgia	1990	Stanford	Debbie Graham, Stanford
1985	USC	Linda Gates, Stanford	1991	Stanford	Sandra Birch, Stanford
1986	Stanford	Patty Fendick, Stanford	1992	Florida	Lisa Raymond, Florida
1987	Stanford	Patty Fendick, Stanford			

Wide World Photos

Masters champion **Fred Couples** (right) embraces runner-up **Ray Floyd** after beating the ageless Floyd by two strokes to finally win his first major tournament.

GOLF

by Marino Parascenzo

Major Wins

Fred Couples and Tom Kite win at Augusta and Pebble Beach, while Seniors rookie Ray Floyd is the toast of two tours.

It was as if Fred Couples had swum the Piranha River, won the Sahara Super Marathon and sat in a locked room watching nothing but Geraldo reruns for a week.

By the end of March, it seemed there wasn't anything the 1991 PGA Tour Player of the Year couldn't do.

Couples, known as "Boom-Boom" for his power and also for shooting himself in the foot more often than not, was on a roll the likes of which the tour hadn't seen in a while.

In 24 starts from mid-June 1991 up to the 1992 Masters, he won five tournaments, finished second twice, and logged 10 other top-six finishes all around the world. They always said he'd be great, but this was something else.

All the while, however, there was the unanswered question: If Couples is so great, how come, at age 32, he's never won a major?

It was the same question that cast a shadow over the otherwise brilliant career of Tom Kite, who entered '92 as the Tour's all-time leading money winner. The 42-year-old Kite had over $6.5 million in the bank, but no majors in his trophy case.

Couples and Kite both got the no-major monkey off their backs in 1992—Couples winning the Masters in April and Kite following two months later with a victory in the U.S. Open at Pebble Beach.

Two foreign Nicks—Faldo and Price—won the other two majors, Faldo rallying to take his third British Open (and second at Muirfield) in July, while Price captured the PGA Championship (and his first major) in St.Louis in August.

But first came the Masters, and the story of how Freddie Couples finally got great—thanks to the Miracle at No. 12.

It happened during the final round at golf's loveliest graveyard, Augusta National's wicked little 12th hole.

"I knew if I could get past that hole," Couples said later, "I would win."

The gods of golf saw to it. They repealed the Law of Gravity just for him. Couples' two-shot lead caught in his throat when his tee shot fell short on the bank and trickled backward toward the water. But somehow it stopped and perched there in the crew-cut grass, maybe 18 inches above the water.

"That's the most nervous I've ever been on a golf course," Couples said. "I don't know what would have happened if the ball had gone in the water."

Thus saved at the water's edge, Couples regained his composure and popped a chip shot to within gimme range and saved his par, his Masters and

Marino Parascenzo has been the *Pittsburgh Post-Gazette's* golf writer since 1975. He is also a contributing editor to *Golf Digest*.

Dave Cannon/Allsport

Wide World Photos

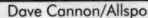
Major championship hardware came **Tom Kite's** way, at last, at the U.S. Open in June,
while **Nick Price** carried off the Wannamaker trophy by winning the PGA in August.

his first major. In the process, he also ended the British seige of Augusta—halting the four-year run of Sandy Lyle, Faldo (twice) and Ian Woosnam.

No sooner had Woosnam helped Couples on with his new green blazer than the Seattle native was being hailed by the media as the best golfer in the world.

"Forget it," Couples said. "I'm not even close."

"If he's not close," said 1993 Ryder Cup captain Tom Watson, "who the hell is?"

The Masters opened with fireworks. On opening day, Lanny Wadkins birdied the entire Amen Corner, and Jeff Sluman started birdie-birdie-par-ace to share the lead with 65s. Twenty-four hours later, they were gone, replaced by defending champ Woosnam and promising young Australian Craig Parry who tied at 135. Parry had the lead all to himself after three rounds, but then blew up with a 78 on the final day. That opened the door for Couples, who shot 70 to go along with rounds of 69, 67, and 69. His 275 score won by two strokes.

"It's a great feeling," Couples said. "I was just thinking—it's over, it's finally over, and we won."

Finishing second was 49-year-old Ray Floyd, Couples' old Ryder Cup coach (in 1989) and playing partner (in '91). Floyd won the Masters in 1976, but lost his attempt to become the tournament's oldest winner in 1990 when he lost to Faldo in a playoff. He left Augusta that year deeply disappointed and doubtful that he would ever get that close again.

This time, however, Floyd was more proud than frustrated when his putting let him down on the back nine.

"It was at my expense, but I predicted this," Floyd said afterward. "Fred had another level to go, and now he's there. I believe he will go on to be known as a really great player. He's already a great player."

Then it was Kite's turn.

Despite 16 wins and all that money won in 21 years on the tour, Kite seemed doomed to play out his career as "the best player who never won a major." He lost that tag in mid-June when he conquered heavy winds and Pebble Beach to win the U.S. Open.

Actually, it was Gil Morgan's Open to win or lose. And Morgan lost gruesomely. He started 66-69, and in the third round became the first player ever to reach 10 under par in a U.S. Open. In fact, he got to 12 under after birdies on the sixth and seventh holes and was leading by seven. Then he blew sky-high and finished with a 77.

"Will you all bow your heads?" he joked, greeting the media corps after his ill-fated round. The next day it got worse. He closed with an 81.

In the wind-whipped final round, Kite holed a long chip shot for a birdie at the par-3 No. 7 and was on his way. He shot 71-72-70-72—285, three under par, beating Jeff Sluman by two, and Scotland's Colin Montgomerie by three. The wind was so tough that Jack Nicklaus, doing commentary for ABC-TV, congratulated Montgomerie as the winner while Kite was still out on the course. Nicklaus forgot to tell Kite.

"How do you describe the emotions I'm going through now?" Kite said. "I don't know. We're talking about dreams that have been around many, many years. And there are an awful lot of dreams left."

At the British Open at Muirfield, England's Faldo nearly won his old title of "El Faldo" back.

Floyd and Steve Pate tied for the first-round lead at 64, then Faldo took over with a 64 in the second. Come the final round, he started with a four-shot lead and was cruising comfortably. But he cracked down the final stretch. He made three bogeys in a four-hole span, and suddenly John Cook found himself within reach of his first major. Not to worry. Once again, American foreign aid came to Faldo's rescue.

"Sure, I thought I had blown it," Faldo said.

Said Cook: "I definitely let one slip away. Absolutely. I gave away the championship."

Cook was leading by two with only two holes to play when he sprang a fatal leak. At the cushy 17th, where a par-5 is like a bogey, Cook was putting for an eagle from 30 feet. He missed. Then he was putting for a birdie from two feet. He missed again. He settled for a par, and left the green visibly shaken. At the 18th, he missed the green badly and bogeyed.

Faldo, meantime, playing behind Cook, pulled himself together brilliantly. He birdied the 15th and the 17th, then parred the 18th to nip Cook by a stroke.

Golf Hall Welcomes Chi Chi

Lots of golfers have come up the hard way—Sam Snead, Lee Trevino and Calvin Peete, to name three. But the odds are that no golfer came from so far down and soared as high as a fragile-looking Puerto Rican best known by his nickname, Juan "Chi Chi" Rodriguez.

"In my day," Chi Chi has said, recalling his dirt poor youth, "You drank milk with a fork because you didn't want that glass of milk to run out." He also remembers going out on the street picking his teeth, so his friends would think he'd had meat for dinner. Do it too often, though, and they'd know he was bluffing. Nobody had that much meat.

That hardscrabble kid from the streets reached the top of his profession in 1992 when he was inducted into the World Golf Hall of Fame. The voters probably weren't looking at Chi Chi's record, although goodness knows it's better than most. He won eight tournaments and $1,037,105 on the PGA Tour from 1960-84. He then moved on to the Senior Tour in 1985 and, through Sept. 20 of this year, has been a winner 20 times with earnings of $3,498,967. That's over $4.5 million in total career money won and doesn't include the $540,000 he's come away with in the Senior Skins Games.

But of the 41 male golfers who preceded him, all had won at least one major pro championship—a Masters, U.S. Open, British Open, or PGA—or a U.S. or British Amateur. Chi Chi never came close. He didn't get there for playing to the gallery, either; although many have been charmed by his wit and entertained with a trademark sword dance or two after a big putt.

What got Chi Chi to Pinehurst was something else. Something sensed rather than defined.

For want of an official label, let's call it service to humanity. A lot of grateful kids can tell you what Chi Chi has meant to them. After he'd made it on the PGA Tour in the early 1960s, Rodriguez returned to Puerto Rico to bail out his impoverished family first, then began a career of charitable works with a pro-am for a local children's hospital, and he's still going strong.

Mike Powell/Allsport

In 33 years on the PGA and Senior golf tours, **Chi Chi Rodriguez** has entertained countless galleries and raised millions of dollars for poor kids.

Some golfers might consider it a snub not to be recognized for their game. Not Chi Chi.

"I just love it," he says. "Just think—having my name up there with Snead and Hogan and Palmer and Nicklaus. I'm only 5-7, but now I feel like I'm 10 feet tall."

Chi Chi thanks God a lot.

"Every morning," he says. "I ask God, 'Why me? Why am I the lucky one?'"

The answer is in a photo taken at Arnold Palmer's Bay Hill Classic some years ago. It shows Chi Chi walking down the fairway, his hand on the shoulder of some little kid. He had brought in a bunch of hard cases from a nearby youth home to walk with him in the pro-am, to show them another side of life.

That was the seed. Some time later, Chi Chi and a friend took over an old municipal golf course and turned it into a place for rescuing troubled kids. The Chi Chi Rodriguez Youth Foundation has since raised over $1 million for Florida youth.

How does a poor Puerto Rican kid become a professional golfer?

First, you sit up in a banyan tree and watch the swells drive into the country club where you caddie for pennies, and you vow you're going to have one of those big cars someday.

To learn the game, you get a tin can and pound it down into a ball, and cut yourself a limb from a guava tree. You can't really work this ball, but you sure can get strong trying. Then you get tired of the cane fields, tired of scrubbing pots in that psychiatric hospital, and you decide golf is the way out.

But Puerto Ricans don't make it in golf. They make it in baseball. Chi Chi might have too, if he hadn't loved golf so much. He played ahead of island hero Roberto Clemente one year when they were kids ("That manager," chuckles Chi Chi, "what a genius.")

The Hall of Fame was about the only honor Rodriguez hadn't won. He leads the world in "good guy" awards. All told, at least 15 of them, including the U.S. Golf Association's Bob Jones Award, the golfing equivalent of the Nobel Peace Prize.

Chi Chi, who turned 57 on Oct. 23, is now in his 33rd year following the sun. His drives are still long and his short game is still to be marveled at. But when the time comes to put the clubs aside, he knows what he's going to do.

"Go back to Puerto Rico," he says, "and teach poor kids how not to be poor."

Wide World Photos

Cigar-smoking **Larry Laoretti** shot a 3-under par 68 the day after his 53rd birthday to win the U.S. Senior Open championship by four strokes over Jim Colbert.

He shot 66-64-69-73—272, 12 under.

"I should have become a fishing pro," Faldo said, quivering and sobbing. "There's no pressure dragging out trout."

True, Faldo had played well enough. But it was like winning when the other team's pitcher walks in the winning run with two outs. In addition to the 1992 British Open, he has now won the '87 British Open, the '89 Masters, and the '90 Masters thanks to grievous late errors by, in order, Paul Azinger, Scott Hoch, and Ray Floyd.

Nick Price, an All-World Mr. Nice Guy from Zimbabwe, also might prefer fishing. He blew the 1982 British Open over the last few holes. This time, in the PGA at Bellerive near St. Louis, it was the others who threw a shoe. Price, 35, shot 70-70-68-70 for a six-under-par 278, beating Cook by three.

The two best chances to catch Price self-destructed in the final round—would-be wire-to-wire winner Gene Sauers on the front nine, and Jeff Maggert on the back. Price was no cherry-picker, though. He made 10 straight pars, birdied the 11th, bogeyed the 15th, birdied the 16th, then salvaged a heart-stopping par on the 17th, holing a 12-footer for his 5. Then he got up and down at the 18th for the win.

"It's been a long wait—10 years—but it's been well worth it," Price said. "It did me more good than harm by not winning that British Open. It strengthened my determination."

Couples might have hogged the entire spotlight for 1992 if it hadn't been for a few scene-stealers. Among them, his good buddy and fellow big-hitter Davis Love III. Both had won three times by late summer and were 1-2 on the PGA Tour money list with over $1 million apiece.

Then there was Floyd, whose year got off to a crushing start when a Feb. 16 fire destroyed his sprawling suburban Miami home of 14 years. Nevertheless, there he was three weeks later winning the Doral-Ryder Open, becoming only the second man, after Sam Snead, to win in four different decades. He then finished second in the Masters and the Byron Nelson Classic, third in the Honda Classic, and challenged Faldo in the British Open. He was playing the best golf of his 30-year career.

The big question was whether he'd join the Senior PGA Tour when he turned 50 on Sept. 4. The answer was predictable: He would play both. He was too hot to give up the regular tour, and the pickings on the senior tour were too easy to pass up.

Sure enough, on Sept. 20, Floyd won the second senior tournament he entered—the GTE North Classic—and became the first golfer to win on both tours in the same year.

Then Floyd did something remarkable. He donated his winner's check of $67,500 to the Hurricane Andrew Relief Fund in Florida. "I feel very strongly about donating these winnings to the people of Miami," he said. "You can't imagine the devastation down there."

Elsewhere, an unlikely guy had already carved out a place for himself on the Senior Tour. This was cigar-smoking Larry Laoretti, 53, an unknown former club pro who hadn't won a tour event of any kind. Then came the U.S. Senior Open in July at Saucon Valley, in Bethlehem, Pa. He took the lead in the third round, and won by four shots, shooting 68-72-67-68—275, nine under. His secret: "Smoke six or seven cigars, enjoy a little wine at night, have a beautiful wife who loves you, and have a great caddie like mine, that's all."

Laoretti's win upstaged Lee Trevino, who was playing gorilla. Trevino won the PGA Seniors and three other events, and teamed with Mike Hill to win the Legends. That put him atop the money list with over $771,000 as autumn approached.

On the LPGA Tour, Dottie Mochrie, who had won twice since joining the tour in 1988, established herself as the world's top female golfer with four wins by early September. The outburst started in March, with her first major—the Nabisco Dinah Shore—when she beat Juli Inkster in a sudden-death playoff. It was an experience Inkster would come to know and hate.

In the U.S. Women's Open in July, Patty Sheehan tied Inkster in the final round, then beat her in an 18-hole playoff the next day. It was Sheehan's third win of the year, and also her career 29th and second major. Under the LPGA's formula, that left her just one victory away from automatic induction into the LPGA Hall of Fame.

Also Hall-bound was Betsy King, who ran off with the LPGA Championship by 11 shots with a 17-under 267. Said her

Wide World Photos

Dottie Mochrie won four LPGA titles by early September, including her first major at the Nabisco Dinah Shore.

caddie, Gary Harrison: "The way Betsy is playing, Rin Tin Tin could carry her clubs and it wouldn't make any difference." It was her fifth major and her 26th career win. She got No. 27 at the Phar-Mor in Youngstown (Ohio), in a four-way playoff.

Sherri Steinhauer, 29 and winless in seven years on tour, finally put it all together in mid-August and won the LPGA's final major of the season, the du Maurier Classic.

Elsewhere on the LPGA Tour, Danielle Ammaccapane and Colleen Walker each won three times, and Hall of Famer Nancy Lopez, a three-time runner-up, broke through for back-to-back wins in September. Sweden's Helen Alfredsson, though not winning, piled up enough points to take the Rookie of the Year Award.

The European Tour was as volatile as the European Common Market. In fact, it didn't even start in Europe. It opened in Thailand, with the Johnnie Walker Asian Classic. For another piece of history, it was won by a South African, Ian Palmer. With South Africa easing its apartheid policies, all European doors swung open to South African athletes after being closed for years.

The tour turned into a reign of Spain—six wins in the first 10 events, with Seve Ballesteros and Jose Marie Olazabal winning two each before they flamed out. After that it was the Swedes, with Cussin' Anders Forsbrand winning the Cannes Open, and a bunch of others—none named Sven—finishing second everywhere.

Then it settled down into a Faldo kind of year. Faldo was relatively quiet in 1991, winning only the Irish Open. He repeated in '92, then went on to win the British Open, the Scandinavian Masters and the European Open. He also had two seconds in the United States, in the Players Championship and the PGA.

Maybe the greatest success on the Euro tour was that of Ireland's Christy O'Connor Jr. He survived a helicopter crash, and a week later won the Dunhill British Masters. "My putting has got better," O'Connor said. "I probably just don't care anymore."

And out and about in the world of golf:

▶ Hottest newcomer. Big, blond Ernie Els, 22, regarded as the best South African since Gary Player surfaced in the 1950s. "Great potential—best I've seen for someone that young, by far," said Arnold Palmer. Els is aiming for the American tour.

▶ Arrival of the Year. Phil Mickelson, 22, ballyhooed lefthander out of Arizona State. He won an unprecedented third NCAA individual championship, then turned pro. "The difference can best be felt," he said, "when the check arrives in the mail." He debuted in the U.S. Open and missed the cut with 68-81. By mid-September he had won $132,800.

▶ Comeback of the Year I. Bill Glasson, 32, Kemper Open winner, just for being able to walk. Glasson looks like a beach boy, but he has the knees (four surgeries) and back (basic agony) of a linebacker. "I went into therapy in March," he said, "because I couldn't stand up for more than 10 minutes."

▶ Comebacks of the Year II and III. Former British Open champions Mark Calcavecchia, who won the Phoenix Open after 2½ years without a victory, and Greg Norman, whose Canadian Open win was his first since the Memorial in 1990. Said Norman: "This is bigger than the British Open. I needed it—I needed it bad."

▶ The Prince of Pebble Beach. Mark O'Meara, winning his fourth Pebble

Stephen Munday/Allsport

After a relatively quiet 1991, **Nick Faldo** dominated the European tour and won his third British Open in '92.

Beach national Pro-Am, boosting his winnings there alone to $705,752. "I ought to buy this place," he said.

▶ Long John Daly. The golden boy of 1991 took on a coat of tarnish in '92. He was still winless by summer's end, and he was living a soap opera. The most public episodes included having legal papers served on him during practice at the Masters, and being put off a plane in Denver. "Media hype," he said.

▶ Kids stuff. University of Georgia sophomore Vicki Goetze, 19, won the NCAA individual, the U.S. Women's Amateur, and was low amateur in the U.S. Women's Open, then said she wasn't turning pro. And Eldrick "Tiger" Woods, 16, of Cypress, Calif., who extended a sensational junior record with a second straight U.S. Junior championship.

▶ Decline and Fall? Jack Nicklaus, 52, missed the cut in three consecutive majors for the first time in his 30-year professional career. He made it only in the Masters.

▶ The Bloodless Sack—Washington Redskins quarterback Mark Rypien got a sponsor's exemption into the Kemper Open, and missed the cut with 80-91-171, 29 over par.   □

THE 1993 SPORTS ALMANAC · INFORMATION PLEASE · GOLF STATISTICS · THE SEASON IN REVIEW · 1991-1992 · PGA · SENIORS · LPGA · SEC A · PAGE 727

Tournament Results

Winners of PGA, European PGA, Senior PGA and LPGA tournaments from Nov. 3, 1991 through Sept. 20, 1992.

PGA Tour

LATE 1991

Last Rd	Tournament	Winner	Earnings	Runner-Up
Nov. 3	Tour Championship	Craig Stadler (279)*	$360,000	R.Cochran (279)
Nov. 10	Asahi 4 Tours WCOG (Adelaide)	PGA Europe (8 pts)	480,000	AUS/NZE (4 pts)
Nov. 16	Ping Kapalua International	Mike Hulbert (276)*	150,000	D.Love III (276)
Nov. 24	Shark Shoot-out	Tom Purtzer/	125,000	G.Norman/
		Lanny Wadkins (189)	125,000	J.Nicklaus (193)
Dec. 1	Skins Game #9	Payne Stewart (8)	260,000	J.Daly (7)
Dec. 8	JCPenney Classic	Billy Andrade/	110,000	E.Humenik/
		Kris Tschetter (266)*	110,000	E.Crosby (266)

*Playoffs (3): **Tour Championship**—Stadler won on 2nd hole; **Kapalua**— Hulbert won on 1st hole; **JCPenney**—Andrade/Tschetter won on 2nd hole.

1992 (through Sept. 20)

Last Rd	Tournament	Winner	Earnings	Runner-Up
Jan. 12	Infiniti Tournament of Champions	Steve Elkington (279)*	$144,000	B.Faxon (279)
Jan. 19	Bob Hope Chrysler Classic	John Cook (336)*	198,000	4-way tie (336)
Jan. 26	Phoenix Open	Mark Calcavecchia (264)	180,000	D.Waldorf (269)
Feb. 2	AT&T Pebble Beach Nat'l Pro-Am	Mark O'Meara (275)*	198,000	J.Sluman (269)
Feb. 9	United Hawaiian Open	John Cook (265)	216,000	P.Azinger (267)
Feb. 16	Northern Telecom Open	Lee Janzen (270)	198,000	B.Britton (271)
Feb. 23	Buick Invitational	Steve Pate (200)#	180,000	C.Beck (201)
Mar. 1	Nissan Los Angeles Open	Fred Couples (269)*	180,000	D.Love III (269)
Mar. 8	Doral Ryder Open	Ray Floyd (271)	252,000	K.Clearwater & F.Couples(273)
Mar. 15	Honda Classic	Corey Pavin (273)*	198,000	F.Couples (273)
Mar. 22	Nestle Invitational	Fred Couples (269)	180,000	G.Sauers (278)
Mar. 29	The Players Championship	Davis Love III (273)	324,000	4-way tie (277)
Apr. 5	Freeport-McMoRan Classic	Chip Beck (276)	180,000	G.Norman & M.Standly (277)
Apr. 12	**The Masters** (Augusta)	Fred Couples (275)	270,000	R.Floyd (277)
Apr. 12	Deposit Guaranty Classic	Richard Zokol (267)	54,000	4-way tie (268)
Apr. 19	MCI Heritage Classic	Davis Love III (269)	180,000	C.Beck (273)
Apr. 26	K mart Greater Greensboro Open	Davis Love III (272)	225,000	J.Cook (273)
May 3	Shell Houston Open	Fred Funk (272)	216,000	K.Triplett (274)
May 10	BellSouth Atlanta Classic	Tom Kite (272)	180,000	J.D.Blake (275)
May 17	GTE Byron Nelson Classic	Billy Ray Brown (199)*†	198,000	3-way tie (199)
May 24	Southwestern Bell Colonial	Bruce Lietzke (267)*	234,000	Corey Pavin (267)
May 31	Kemper Open	Bill Glasson (276)	198,000	4-way tie (277)
June 7	Memorial Tournament	David Edwards (273)*	234,000	R.Fehr (273)
June 14	Federal Express St.Jude Classic	Jay Haas (263)	198,000	D.Forsman & R.Gamez (266)
June 21	**U.S. Open** (Pebble Beach)	Tom Kite (285)	275,000	J.Sluman (287)
June 28	Buick Classic	David Frost (268)	180,000	D.Waldorf (276)
July 5	Centel Western Open	Ben Crenshaw (276)	198,000	G.Norman (277)
July 12	Anheuser-Busch Classic	David Peoples (271)	198,000	3-way tie (273)
July 19	**British Open** (Muirfield)	Nick Faldo (272)	190,000	J.Cook (273)
July 19	Chattanooga Classic	Mark Carnevale (269)	144,000	E.Dougherty & D.Forsman (271)
July 26	New England Classic	Brad Faxon (268)	180,000	P.Mickelson (270)

Tournament Results (Cont.)
PGA Tour

Last Rd	Tournament	Winner	Earnings	Runner-Up
Aug. 2	Greater Hartford Open..................	Lanny Wadkins (274)	$180,000	3-way tie (276)
Aug. 9	Buick Open	Dan Forsman (276)*	180,000	S.Elkington & B. Faxon (276)
Aug. 16	**PGA Championship** (St.Louis)	Nick Price (278)	280,000	4-way tie (281)
Aug. 23	The International	Brad Faxon (+14)	216,000	L.Janzen (+12)
Aug. 30	World Series of Golf	Craig Stadler (273)	252,000	C.Pavin (274)
Sept. 6	Greater Milwaukee Open...............	Richard Zokol (269)	180,000	D.Mast (271)
Sept.13	Canadian Open	Greg Norman (280)*	198,000	B.Lietzke (280)
Sept.20	Hardee's Golf Classic	David Frost (266)	180,000	L.Roberts & T.Leman (269)

#Fog-shortened.
†Rain-shortened.

*Playoffs (10): **Infiniti**—Elkington won on 1st hole; **Bob Hope**—Cook won on 4th hole; **AT&T Pebble Beach**—O'Meara won on 1st hole; **LA Open**—Couples won on 2nd hole; **Honda**—Pavin won on 2nd hole; **Byron Nelson**—Brown won on 1st hole; **Colonial**—Lietzke won on 1st hole; **Memorial**—Edwards won on 2nd hole; **Buick**—Forsman won on 2nd hole; **Canadian**—Norman won on 2nd hole.

Second-place ties (3 players or more): 4-WAY—**Bob Hope** (R.Fehr, T.Kite, G.Sauers, M.O'Meara); **Players** (T.Watson, I.Baker-Finch, N.Faldo, P.Blackmar); **Deposit** (B.Eastwood, G.Twiggs, M.Donald, M.Nicolette); **Kemper** (H.Twitty, M.Springer, K.Green, J.Daly); **PGA Champs.** (J.Gallagher, J.Cook, G.Sauers, N.Faldo). 3-WAY—**Byron Nelson** (R.Floyd, B.Crenshaw, B.Lietzke); **Anheuser-Busch** (J.Gallagher, B.Britton, E.Dougherty); **Hartford** (N.Price, D.Forsman, D.Hammond).

1992 PGA Majors

The Masters

Edition: 56th   **Dates:** April 9-12
Site: Augusta National GC, Augusta, Ga.
Par: 36-36—72 (6905 yards)   **Purse:** $1,350,000

		1	2	3	4	Tot	Earnings
1	Fred Couples	72	66	67	72	275	$270,000
2	Ray Floyd	69	68	69	71	277	162,000
3	Corey Pavin	72	71	68	67	278	102,000
4	Mark O'Meara	74	67	69	70	280	66,000
	Jeff Sluman...........	65	74	70	71	280	66,000
6	Nolan Henke	70	71	70	70	281	43,829
	Ted Schulz	68	69	72	72	281	43,829
	Steve Pate	73	71	70	67	281	43,829
	Greg Norman	70	70	73	68	281	43,829
	Larry Mize	73	69	71	68	281	43,829
	Nick Price	70	71	67	73	281	43,829
	Ian Baker-Finch	70	69	68	74	281	43,829

Early round leaders: 1st—Jeff Sluman, Lanny Wadkins (65); 2nd—Craig Parry, Ian Woosnam (135); 3rd—Craig Parry (204).
Top amateur: Manny Zerman (294).

British Open

Edition: 121st   **Dates:** July 16-19
Site: Muirfield Golf Links, Guilland, Scotland
Par: 36-35—71 (6970 yards) **Purse:** $1,805,000 (US)

		1	2	3	4	Tot	Earnings
1	Nick Faldo	66	64	69	73	272	$190,000
2	John Cook	66	67	70	70	273	150,000
3	Jose Maria Olazabal ..	70	67	69	68	274	128,000
4	Steve Pate	64	70	69	73	276	106,000
5	Malcolm MacKenzie ..	71	67	70	71	279	63,000
	Robert Karlsson	70	68	70	71	279	63,000
	Ian Woosnam	65	73	70	71	279	63,000
	Gordan Brand, Jr...	65	68	72	74	279	63,000
	Donnie Hammond....	70	65	70	74	279	63,000
	Ernie Els	66	69	70	74	279	63,000
	Andrew Magee........	67	72	70	70	279	63,000

Early round leaders: 1st—Steve Pate, Ray Floyd (64); 2nd—Nick Faldo (130); 3rd—Nick Faldo (199).
Top amateur: Darren Lee (293).

U.S. Open

Edition: 92nd   **Dates:** June 18-21
Site: Pebble Beach (CA) Golf Links
Par: 36-36—72 (6809 yards)   **Purse:** $1,500,000

		1	2	3	4	Tot	Earnings
1	Tom Kite.............	71	72	70	72	285	$275,000
2	Jeff Sluman...........	73	74	69	71	287	137,500
3	Colin Montgomerie	70	71	77	70	288	84,245
4	Nick Price	71	72	77	71	291	54,924
	Nick Faldo	70	76	68	77	291	54,924
6	Billy Andrade	72	74	72	74	292	32,316
	Jay Don Blake	70	74	75	73	292	32,316
	Bob Gilder	73	70	75	74	292	32,316
	Mike Hulbert........	74	73	70	75	292	32,316
	Tom Lehman	69	74	72	77	292	32,316
	Joey Sindelar	74	72	68	78	292	32,316
	Ian Woosnam	72	72	69	79	292	32,316

Early round leaders: 1st—Gil Morgan (66); 2nd—Gil Morgan (135); 3rd—Gil Morgan (212).
Top amateur: None.

PGA Championship

Edition: 74th   **Dates:** Aug. 13-16
Site: Bellerive Country Club, St. Louis
Par: 36-35—71 (7148 yards)   **Purse:** $1,600,000

		1	2	3	4	Tot	Earnings
1	Nick Price	70	70	68	70	278	$280,000
2	Jim Gallagher, Jr.......	72	66	72	10	281	101,250
	John Cook	71	72	67	71	281	101,250
	Gene Sauers	67	79	70	75	281	101,250
	Nick Faldo	68	70	76	67	281	101,250
6	Jeff Maggert........	71	72	65	74	282	60,000
7	Dan Forsman	70	73	70	70	283	52,500
	Russ Cochran	69	69	76	69	283	52,500
9	Duffy Waldorf.......	74	73	68	69	284	40,000
	Anders Forsbrand	73	71	70	70	284	40,000
	Brian Claar...........	68	73	73	70	284	40,000

Early round leaders: 1st—Gene Sauers, Craig Stadler (67); 2nd—Gene Sauers (136); 3rd—Gene Sauers (206).
Top Amateur: None.

European PGA Tour

Earnings listed in pounds sterling (£).

LATE 1991

Last Rd	Tournament	Winner	Earnings	Runner-Up
Nov. 3	World Cup of Golf	Sweden (563)	£137,694	Wales (564)
Nov. 8	Asahi 4 Tours WCOG (Adelaide)	PGA Europe (8 pts)	271,186	AUS/NZE (4 pts)
Nov. 10	Benson & Hedges Mixed Team	Anders Forsbrand/ Helen Alfredsson (275)	33,900	Mackenzie/Whitaker & Norton/Sinn (277)

*Playoff: German Masters—Langer won on 1st hole.

1992 (through Sept. 20)

Last Rd	Tournament	Winner	Earnings	Runner-Up
Feb. 2	Johnny Walker Asian Classic	Ian Palmer (268)	£ 83,330	3-way tie (269)
Feb. 9	Dubai Desert Classic	Seve Ballesteros (272)*	58,330	R.Rafferty (272)
Feb. 16	Turespana Masters	Vijay Singh (277)	50,000	G.Evans (279)
Feb. 23	Turespana Open de Tenerife	Jose Maria Olazabal (268)	50,000	M.Martin (273)
Mar. 1	Open Mediterrania	Jose Maria Olazabal (276)	66,660	J.Rivero (278)
Mar. 8	Turespana Open de Baleares	Seve Ballesteros (277)*	41,660	J.Parnevik (277)
Mar. 14	Open Catalonia	Jose Rivero (280)	50,000	3-way tie (281)
Mar. 22	Portugese Open	Ronan Rafferty (273)	37,500	A.Forsbrand (274)
Mar. 29	Volvo Open di Firenze	Anders Forsbrand (271)	37,500	P.Senior (272)
Apr. 5	Roma Masters	Jose Maria Canizares (286)*	37,500	B.Lane (286)
Apr. 12	Jersey European Airways Open	Daniel Silva (277)	37,500	C.Moody (279)
Apr. 19	Moroccan Open	David Gilford (287)*	41,660	R.Karlsson (287)
Apr. 26	Credit Lyonnais Cannes Open	Anders Forsbrand (273)	58,330	P.Johansson (274)
May 3	Lancia Martini Italian Open	Sandy Lyle (270)	61,038	C.Montgomerie (271)
May 10	Benson & Hedges Int'l. Open	Peter Senior (287)*	83,330	T.Johnstone (287)
May 17	Peugeot Spanish Open	Andrew Sherborne (271)	66,660	N.Faldo (272)
May 25	Volvo PGA Championship	Tony Johnstone (272)	100,000	J.M.Olazabal & G.Brand,Jr.(274)
May 31	Dunhill British Masters	Christy O'Connor (270)*	100,000	T.Johnstone (270)
June 7	Carrolls Irish Open	Nick Faldo (274)*	76,275	W.Westner (274)
June 14	Mitsubishi Austrian Open	Peter Mitchell (271)	58,330	3-way tie (272)
June 21	Open de Lyon Trophee V33	David Russell (267)	37,500	B.Ogle (273)
June 28	Peugeot French Open	Miguel Angel Martin (276)	66,660	M.Poxon (278)
July 4	European Monte Carlo Golf Open	Ian Woosnam (261)	73,475	J.Rystrom & M.McNulty (263)
July 11	Bell's Scottish Open	Peter O'Malley (262)	100,000	C.Montgomerie (264)
July 19	British Open	Nick Faldo (272)	95,000	J.Cook (273)
July 26	Heineken Dutch Open	Bernhard Langer (277)*	100,000	G.Brand,Jr.(277)
Aug. 2	Scandinavian Masters	Nick Faldo (277)	100,000	6-way tie (280)
Aug. 9	BMW International Open	Paul Azinger (266)*	83,330	4-way tie (266)
Aug. 23	Volvo German Open.	Vijay Singh (262)	87,500	J.M.Carriles (273)
Aug. 31	Murphy's English Open	Vicente Fernandez (283)	91,660	P.Johansson & F.Lindgren (284)
Sept. 6	Canon European Masters	James Spence (271)*	93,859	A.Forsbrand (271)
Sept.13	GA European Open	Nick Faldo (262)	100,000	R.Karlsson (265)
Sept.20	Lancôme Trophy	Mark Roe (267)	79,000	V.Fernandez (269)

*Playoffs (10): Dubai—Ballesteros won on 2nd hole; Turespana—Ballesteros won on 6th hole; Roma—Canizares won on 4th hole; Morocco—Gilford won on 3rd Hole; Benson & Hedges—Senior won on 1st hole; Dunhill—O'Connor won on 1st hole; Irish Open—Faldo won on 4th hole; Dutch Open—Langer won on 2nd hole; BMW Open—Azinger won on 1st hole; European Open—Spence won on 2nd hole.

Second-place ties (3 players or more): 6-WAY—Scandinavian (D.Mijovic, F.Nobilo, R.Allenby, P.Baker, J.M. Olazabal, P.O'Malley). 4-WAY—BMW Open (G.Day, B.Langer, A.Forsbrand, M.James). 3-WAY—Walker (B.Ogle, B.Langer, R.Rafferty); Catalonia (H.Selby-Green, J.M.Canizares, J.Rystrom); Austrian (J.Spence, D.Russell, P.Fowler).

Sony World Rankings

Begun in 1986, the Sony World Rankings combine the best golfers on the PGA and European PGA tours. Rankings are based on a rolling three-year period and weighted in favor of more recent results. Points are awarded after each worldwide tournament according to finish. Final point averages are determined by dividing a player's total points by the number of tournaments played in.

1992 (Through Sept.20)

		Avg			Avg			Avg
1	Nick Faldo	22.46	8	John Cook	10.38	15	Bruce Lietzke	8.57
2	Fred Couples	16.31	9	Nick Price	10.25	16	Ray Floyd	8.47
3	Bernhard Langer	13.50	10	Seve Ballesteros	10.08	17	Mark McNulty	7.91
4	Jose Maria Olazabal	13.47	11	Tom Kite	9.92	18	Masashi Ozaki	7.77
5	Ian Woosnam	12.39	12	David Love III	9.87	19	Rodger Davis	7.36
6	Greg Norman	11.92	13	Mark O'Meara	9.33	20	Payne Stewart	7.22
7	Paul Azinger	10.47	14	Corey Pavin	8.58			

Tournament Results (Cont.)
Senior PGA Tour
LATE 1991

Last Rd	Tournament	Winner	Earnings	Runner-Up
Nov. 17	DuPont Cup (Japan)	USA (24 pts)	$360,000	Japan (8)
Dec. 8	Kaanapali Classic	Jim Colbert (195)	90,000	D.Douglass (197)
Dec. 15	N.Y.Life Champions (Puerto Rico)	Mike Hill (202)	150,000	J.Colbert (204)

1992 (through Sept. 20)

Last Rd	Tournament	Winner	Earnings	Runner-Up
Jan. 12	Infiniti Tournament of Champions	Al Geiberger (282)	$ 52,500	C.C.Rodriguez & B.Crampton (285)
Jan. 26	Senior Skins Game #5	Arnold Palmer (7)	205,000	C.C.Rodriquez (3)
Feb. 2	Royal Caribbean Classic	Don Massengale (205)	75,000	G.Player (206)
Feb. 9	Aetna Challenge	Jimmy Powell (197)	67,500	L.Trevino (201)
Feb. 16	Suncoast Classic	Jim Colbert (200)*	67,500	G.Archer (200)
Mar. 1	Chrysler Cup	United States (54 pts)	405,000	Int'l Team (46)
Mar. 8	GTE West Classic	Bruce Crampton (195)	67,500	C.C.Rodriquez (198)
Mar. 15	Vantage At The Dominion	Lee Trevino (201)	60,000	C.C.Rodriquez (203)
Mar. 22	Vintage Arco Invitational	Mike Hill (203)*	75,000	T.Aaron & J.Colbert (203)
Mar. 29	Fuji Electric Grand Slam	Ray Floyd (197)	69,000	G.Player (204)
Apr. 5	**The Tradition** (Scottsdale)	Lee Trevino (274)	120,000	J.Nicklaus (275)
Apr. 19	**PGA Seniors** (Palm Beach Gardens)	Lee Trevino (278)	100,000	M.Hill (279)
Apr. 26	Liberty Mutual Legends of Golf	Lee Trevino/ Mike Hill (251)	70,000 70,000	J.Colbert/ T.Aaron (254)
May 3	Las Vegas Classic	Lee Trevino (206)	67,500	O.Moody (207)
May 10	Murata Reunion Pro-Am	George Archer (211)*	60,000	T.Aaron (211)
May 17	Doug Sanders Celebrity Classic	Mike Hill (134)†	52,500	L.Mowry & G.Gilbert (136)
May 24	Bell Atlantic Classic	Lee Trevino (205)	82,500	G.Gilbert (206)
May 31	NYNEX Commemorative	Dale Douglass (133)*†	60,000	T.Dill (133)
June 7	Paine Webber Invitational	Don Bies (203)	67,500	L.Trevino (204)
June 14	**Senior Players Champs.**(Dearborn)	Dave Stockton (277)	150,000	L.Trevino & J.C.Snead (278)
June 28	Southwestern Bell Classic	Gibby Gilbert (193)	67,500	J.Colbert (202)
July 5	Kroger Senior Classic	Gibby Gilbert (198)*	90,000	J.C.Snead (198)
July 12	**U.S. Senior Open** (Bethlehem)	Larry Laoretti (275)	130,000	J.Colbert (279)
July 19	Ameritech Open	Dale Douglass (201)	75,000	J.Dent (205)
July 26	Newport Cup	Jim Dent (204)	60,000	J.Powell (205)
Aug. 2	Northville Long Island Classic	George Archer (205)	67,500	J.Albus (207)
Aug. 9	Digital Classic	Mike Hill (136)*†	75,000	W.Zembriski (136)
Aug. 16	Bruno's Memorial Classic	George Archer (208)	105,000	J.Kiefer & R.Thompson (209)
Aug. 23	GTE Northwest Classic	Mike Joyce (204)	67,500	M.Hill (206)
Aug. 30	Franklin Showdown Classic	Orville Moody (137)*†	60,000	B.Betley (137)
Sept. 7	First of America Classic	Gibby Gilbert (202)	60,000	4-way tie (203)
Sept.13	Bank One Classic	Terry Dill (203)	75,000	B.Crampton & D.Douglass (207)
Sept.20	GTE North Classic	Ray Floyd (199)	67,500	M.Hill (201)

†Rain-Shortened
  *Playoffs (7): **Suncoast**—Colbert won on 4th hole: **Vintage**—Hill won on 1st hole: **Reunion**—Archer won on 3rd hole; **Commemorative**—Douglass won on 1st hole; **Kroger**—Gilbert won on 2nd hole; **Digital**—Hill won on 2nd hole; **Showdown**—Moody won on 8th hole.
  Second-place ties (3 Players or More): 4-WAY—**First of America**—(H.Henning, D.Stockton, D.Hendrickson, T.Aaron).

LPGA Tour
LATE 1991

Last Rd	Tournament	Winner	Earnings	Runner-Up
Nov. 3	Nichierei International (Japan)	USA (21.5 Pts)	—	Japan (10.5)
Nov. 10	Mazda Japan Classic	Liselotte Neumann (211)	$ 82,500	C.Keggi & D.Mochrie (213)
Dec. 8	JCPenney Classic	Kris Tschetter/ Billy Andrade (266)*	110,000 110,000	E.Crosby/ E.Humenik (266)
Dec. 15	JBP Cup Match Play Championship	Deb Richard (2&1)	100,000	K.Tschetter

  *Playoff: **JCPenney**—Tschetter/Andrade won on 2nd hole.

1992 (through Sept. 20)

Last Rd	Tournament	Winner	Earnings	Runner-Up
Feb. 2	Oldsmobile LPGA Classic	Colleen Walker (279)*	$ 60,000	D.Coe (279)
Feb. 9	Phar-Mor at Inverrary	Shelley Hamlin (206)	75,000	3-way tie (207)
Feb. 22	Itoki Hawaiian Ladies Open	Lisa Walters (208)	60,000	K.Albers & M.Verteotti (209)
Feb. 29	Women's Kemper Open	Dawn Coe (275)	75,000	D.Mochrie (276)
Mar. 8	Inamori Classic	Judi Dickinson (277)	63,750	M.Mallon (279)
Mar. 15	Ping-Welch's Championship	Brandie Burton (277)	60,000	D.Eggeling & B.Daniel (278)
Mar. 22	Standard Register Ping	Danielle Ammaccapane (279)	82,500	K.Albers (281)
Mar. 29	**Nabisco Dinah Shore** (Rancho Mirage)	Dottie Mochrie (279)*	105,000	J.Inkster (279)
Apr. 5	Desert Inn International	Dana Lofland (212)	67,500	3-way tie (214)
Apr. 19	SEGA Championships	Dottie Mochrie (277)	90,000	D.Ammaccapane (278)
Apr. 26	Sara Lee Classic	Maggie Will (207)*	78,750	A.Benz & B. Burton (207)
May 3	Centel Classic	Danielle Ammaccapane (275)	180,000	3-way tie (276)
May 10	Crestar-Farm Fresh Classic	Jennifer Wyatt (208)	63,750	D.Andrews (210)
May 17	**LPGA Championship** (Bethesda)	Betsy King (267)	150,000	3-way tie (268)
May 24	Corning Classic	Colleen Walker (276)	67,500	A.Miller & B.Daniel (281)
May 24	JCPenney Skins Game	Pat Bradley (8)	200,000	N.Lopez (5)
May 31	Oldsmobile Classic	Barb Mucha (276)	75,000	D.Mochrie (277)
June 7	McDonald's Championship	Ayako Okamoto (205)	112,500	3-way tie (208)
June 14	ShopRite Classic	Anne Marie Palli (207)*	60,000	L.Davies (207)
June 21	Lady Keystone Open	Danielle Ammaccapane (208)	60,000	3-way tie (210)
June 28	Rochester International	Patty Sheehan (269)	60,000	N.Lopez (278)
July 5	Jamie Farr Toledo Classic	Patty Sheehan (209)	60,000	4-way tie (210)
July 12	Phar-Mor in Youngstown	Betsy King (209)*	75,000	3-way tie (209)
July 19	Big Apple Classic	Juli Inkster (273)	75,000	N.Lopez (275)
July 26	**U.S. Women's Open** (Oakmont)	Patty Sheehan (280-72)*	130,000	J.Inkster (280-74)
Aug. 2	Welch's Classic	Dottie Mochrie (278)	63,750	S.Farwig (281)
Aug. 9	Stratton Mountain Classic	Florence Descampe (278)	75,000	D.Mochrie (280)
Aug. 16	**du Maurier Classic** (Winnipeg)	Sherri Steinhaur (277)	105,000	J.Dickinson (279)
Aug. 23	Northgate Computer Classic	Kris Tschetter (211)	63,750	D.Richard (214)
Aug. 30	Sun-Times Challenge	Dottie Mochrie (216)*	67,500	J.Dickinson & B.Daniel (216)
Sept. 6	Rail Charity Classic	Nancy Lopez (199)*	67,500	L.Davies (199)
Sept.13	Ping-Cellular One Champs	Nancy Lopez (209)*	67,500	J.Crafter (209)
Sept.20	Safeco Classic	Colleen Walker (277)	67,500	V.Fergon & R.Jones (279)

*Playoffs (9): **Oldsmobile**—Walker won on 1st hole; **Dinah Shore**—Mochrie won on 1st hole; **Sara Lee**—Will won on 1st hole; **ShopRite**—Palli won on 1st hole; **Youngstown**—King won on 1st hole; **U.S. Open**—Sheehan won 18-hole playoff (72-74); **Sun-Times**—Mochrie won on 6th hole; **Rail Charity**—Lopez won on 1st hole; **Ping-Cellular**—Lopez won on 2nd hole.

Second-place ties (3 players or more): 4-WAY—**Jamie Farr** (B.Burton, H.Drew, T.Green, D.Richard). 3-WAY—**Inverrary** (B.Burton, D.Lofland, J.Carner); **Desert Inn** (M.Berteoti, J.Dickinson, B.Daniel); **Centel** (C.Waler, M. Estill, L.Neumann); **LPGA Championship** (K.Noble, L.Neumann, J.Carner); **McDonald's** (P.Bradley, D.Richard, B.Burton); **Lady Keystone** (M.Spencer-Devlin, L.West, N.Lopez); **Youngstown** (B.Daniel, D.Andrews, M.Mallon).

Money Leaders

Official money leaders of men's, seniors, European and women's tours for 1991 and unofficial money leaders for 1992 (through Sept.20), as compiled by the PGA, European PGA and LPGA. All European amounts are in pound sterling (£).

PGA

Listed are tournaments played (TP), titles won (1st) and earnings for the year.

FINAL 1991

		TP	1st	Earnings
1	Corey Pavin	25	2	$979,430
2	Craig Stadler	21	1	827,628
3	Fred Couples	21	2	791,749
4	Tom Purtzer	25	2	750,568
5	Andrew Magee	28	1	750,082
6	Steve Pate	26	1	727,997
7	Nick Price	23	2	714,389
8	Davis Love III	28	1	686,361
9	Paul Azinger	21	1	685,603
10	Russ Cochran	30	1	684,851
11	Mark Brooks	30	2	667,263
12	Lanny Wadkins	23	1	651,495
13	Ian Baker-Finch	21	1	649,513
14	Billy Andrade	29	2	615,765
15	Rocco Mediate	25	1	597,438

1992 (through Sept.20)

		TP	1st	Earnings
1	Fred Couples	20	3	$1,254,473
2	Davis Love III	22	3	1,084,714
3	Nick Price	24	1	930,659
4	Tom Kite	21	2	909,236
5	John Cook	18	2	885,971
6	Corey Pavin	21	1	757,134
7	Brad Faxon	23	2	749,893
8	Dan Forsman	27	1	700,190
9	Jeff Sluman	27	0	672,199
10	Ray Floyd	14	1	665,918
11	Chip Beck	22	1	643,606
12	Bruce Lietzke	16	1	642,405
13	Mark O'Meara	21	1	619,248
14	Greg Norman	15	1	617,443
15	Steve Elkington	21	1	613,152

Money Leaders (Cont.)
EUROPEAN PGA

The Volvo Order of Merit; listed are tournaments played (TP), titles won (1st) and earnings for the year; earnings listed are in pounds sterling (£).

FINAL 1991	TP	1st	Earnings	1992 (through Sept.20)	TP	1st	Earnings
1 Seve Ballesteros	15	3	£545,354	1 Nick Faldo	12	4	£571,245
2 Steven Richardson	28	2	393,155	2 Anders Forsbrand	25	3	367,206
3 Bernhard Langer	14	2	372,703	3 Jose Maria Olazabal	12	2	341,627
4 Colin Montgomerie	28	1	343,576	4 Tony Johnstone	15	1	289,137
5 Craig Parry	18	2	328,116	5 Colin Montgomerie	21	0	285,568
6 Rodger Davis	19	1	317,442	6 Bernhard Langer	12	1	271,098
7 Jose Maria Olazabal	17	2	302,270	7 Jamie Spence	23	1	255,881
8 Ian Woosnam	12	3	257,434	8 Vijay Singh	20	2	252,407
9 David Gilford	26	1	249,241	9 Jose Rivero	21	1	233,998
10 Nick Faldo	11	1	245,892	10 Gordon Brand, Jr	24	0	211,124
11 Mark McNulty	10	1	230,061	11 Peter Senior	14	1	210,485
12 Mike Harwood	14	1	223,857	12 Vicente Fernandez	18	1	204,473
13 Vijay Singh	29	0	221,998	13 Ian Woosnam	13	1	194,964
14 David Feherty	23	1	218,390	14 Barry Lane	24	0	191,067
15 Paul Broadhurst	26	1	217,751	15 Peter O'Malley	18	1	190,096

SENIOR PGA

Listed are tournaments played (TP), titles won (1st) and earnings for the year.

FINAL 1991	TP	1st	Earnings	1992 (through Sept.20)	TP	1st	Earnings
1 Mike Hill	32	5	$1,065,657	1 Lee Trevino	22	5	$789,708
2 George Archer	32	3	963,455	2 Mike Hill	22	2	614,768
3 Jim Colbert	22	3	880,749	3 George Archer	25	3	556,149
4 Chi Chi Rodriguez	32	4	794,013	4 Chi Chi Rodriguez	25	0	469,795
5 Lee Trevino	28	3	723,163	5 Jim Colbert	21	1	465,131
6 Bob Charles	28	1	673,910	6 Dave Stockton	24	1	439,203
7 Dale Douglass	31	1	606,949	7 Dale Douglass	24	2	437,266
8 Charles Coody	31	2	543,326	8 Gibby Gilbert	23	3	428,357
9 Jim Dent	32	0	529,315	9 Larry Laoretti	28	1	369,309
10 Al Geiberger	25	1	519,926	10 Bruce Crampton	27	1	360,142
11 Bruce Crampton	34	1	514,509	11 Jim Dent	23	1	302,479
12 Rocky Thompson	35	2	435,794	12 J.C. Snead	23	0	296,774
13 Harold Henning	34	1	394,803	13 Tommy Aaron	23	0	286,359
14 Gibby Gilbert	31	0	392,351	14 Rocky Thompson	28	0	282,211
15 Larry Laoretti	33	0	371,097	15 Al Geiberger	19	0	277,237

Note: Jack Nicklaus played in three events, with no wins and earnings of $110,708.

LPGA

Listed are tournaments played (TP), titles won (1st) and earnings for the year.

FINAL 1991	TP	1st	Earnings	1992 (through Sept.20)	TP	1st	Earnings
1 Pat Bradley	26	4	$763,118	1 Dottie Mochrie	26	4	$693,335
2 Meg Mallon	26	4	633,802	2 Danielle Ammaccapane	25	3	508,125
3 Dottie Mochrie	28	0	477,767	3 Betsy King	26	2	443,743
4 Beth Daniel	18	2	469,501	4 Patty Sheehan	22	3	418,622
5 Deb Richard	26	2	376,640	5 Brandie Burton	22	1	413,755
6 Danielle Ammaccapane	25	1	361,925	6 Juli Inkster	24	1	392,063
7 Ayako Okamoto	16	0	349,437	7 Nancy Lopez	20	2	372,051
8 Patty Sheehan	22	1	342,204	8 Colleen Walker	24	3	364,507
9 Betsy King	26	2	341,785	9 Judy Dickinson	25	1	351,559
10 Jane Geddes	27	2	315,240	10 Meg Mallon	22	0	343,672
11 Colleen Walker	26	1	294,845	11 Beth Daniel	21	0	324,582
12 Rosie Jones	23	1	281,089	12 Sherri Steinhauer	25	1	291,373
13 Amy Alcott	23	1	258,269	13 Donna Andrews	24	0	266,911
14 Judy Dickinson	28	0	251,017	14 Dana Lofland	26	1	261,888
15 Tammie Green	26	0	237,073	15 Deb Richard	25	0	253,875

THE 1993 INFORMATION PLEASE SPORTS ALMANAC

GOLF STATISTICS

THROUGH THE YEARS 1860-1992

MAJOR TITLES • LEADERS

SEC B

PAGE 733

Major Championships
MEN
The Masters

The Masters has been played every year since 1934 at the Augusta National Golf Club in Augusta, GA. Both the course (6905 yards, par 72) and the tournament were created by Bobby Jones; (*) indicates playoff winner.

Multiple winners: Jack Nicklaus (6); Arnold Palmer (4); Jimmy Demaret, Gary Player and Sam Snead (3); Seve Ballesteros, Nick Faldo, Ben Hogan, Byron Nelson, Horton Smith and Tom Watson (2).

Year		Year		Year		Year	
1934	Horton Smith	1952	Sam Snead	1966	Jack Nicklaus*	1980	Seve Ballesteros
1935	Gene Sarazen*	1953	Ben Hogan	1967	Gary Brewer	1981	Tom Watson
1936	Horton Smith	1954	Sam Snead*	1968	Bob Goalby	1982	Craig Stadler*
1937	Byron Nelson	1955	Cary Middlecoff	1969	George Archer	1983	Seve Ballesteros
1938	Henry Picard	1956	Jack Burke, Jr.			1984	Ben Crenshaw
1939	Ralph Guldahl	1957	Doug Ford	1970	Billy Casper*	1985	Bernhard Langer
1940	Jimmy Demaret	1958	Arnold Palmer	1971	Charles Coody	1986	Jack Nicklaus
1941	Craig Wood	1959	Art Wall, Jr.	1972	Jack Nicklaus	1987	Larry Mize*
1942	Byron Nelson*			1973	Tommy Aaron	1988	Sandy Lyle
1943–45	Not held	1960	Arnold Palmer	1974	Gary Player	1989	Nick Faldo*
1946	Herman Keiser	1961	Gary Player	1975	Jack Nicklaus		
1947	Jimmy Demaret	1962	Arnold Palmer*	1976	Raymond Floyd	1990	Nick Faldo*
1948	Claude Harmon	1963	Jack Nicklaus	1977	Tom Watson	1991	Ian Woosnam
1949	Sam Snead	1964	Arnold Palmer	1978	Gary Player	1992	Fred Couples
		1965	Jack Nicklaus	1979	Fuzzy Zoeller*		
1950	Jimmy Demaret						
1951	Ben Hogan						

*PLAYOFFS

1935: Sarazen (144) def. Craig Wood (149) in 36 holes. **1942:** Nelson (69) def. Ben Hogan (70) in 18 holes. **1954:** Snead (70) def. Ben Hogan (71) in 18 holes. **1962:** Palmer (68) def. Gary Player (71) and Dow Finsterwald (77) in 18 holes. **1966:** Nicklaus (70) def. Tommy Jacobs (72) and Gay Brewer (78) in 18 holes. **1970:** Casper (69) def. Gene Littler (74) in 18 holes. **1979:** Zoeller (4-3) def. Ed Sneed (4-4) and Tom Watson (4-4) on 2nd hole of sudden death. **1982:** Stadler (4) def. Dan Pohl (5) on 1st hole of sudden death. **1987:** Mize (4-3) def. Greg Norman (4-4) and Seve Ballesteros (5) on 2nd hole of sudden death. **1989:** Faldo (5-3) def. Scott Hoch (5-4) on 2nd hole of sudden death. **1990:** Faldo (4-4) def. Raymond Floyd (4-x) on second hole of sudden death.

U.S. Open

Played at a different course each year, the U.S. Open was launched by the new U.S. Golf Association in 1895. The Open switched from a 3-day, 36-hole Saturday finish to 4 days of play in 1965; (*) indicates playoff winner and (a) indicates amateur winner.

Multiple winners: Willie Anderson, Ben Hogan, Bobby Jones and Jack Nicklaus (4); Hale Irwin (3); Julius Boros, Billy Casper, Ralph Guldahl, Walter Hagen, John McDermott, Cary Middlecoff, Andy North, Gene Sarazen, Alex Smith, Curtis Strange and Lee Trevino (2).

Year		Year		Year		Year	
1895	Horace Rawlins	1904	Willie Anderson	1913	a-Francis Ouimet*	1923	a-Bobby Jones*
1896	James Foulis	1905	Willie Anderson	1914	Walter Hagen	1924	Cyril Walker
1897	Joe Lloyd	1906	Alex Smith	1915	a-Jerry Travers	1925	Willie Macfarlane*
1898	Fred Herd	1907	Alex Ross	1916	a-Chick Evans	1926	a-Bobby Jones
1899	Willie Smith	1908	Fred McLeod*	1917–18	Not held	1927	Tommy Armour*
		1909	George Sargent	1919	Walter Hagen*	1928	Johnny Farrell*
1900	Harry Vardon			1920	Edward Ray	1929	a-Bobby Jones*
1901	Willie Anderson*	1910	Alex Smith*	1921	Jim Barnes		
1902	Laurie Auchterlonie	1911	John McDermott*	1922	Gene Sarazen	1930	a-Bobby Jones
1903	Willie Anderson*	1912	John McDermott			1931	Billy Burke*

Major Championships (Cont.)
MEN
U.S. Open

Year		Year		Year		Year	
1932	Gene Sarazen	1950	Ben Hogan*	1965	Gary Player*	1980	Jack Nicklaus
1933	a-John Goodman	1951	Ben Hogan	1966	Billy Casper*	1981	David Graham
1934	Olin Dutra	1952	Julius Boros	1967	Jack Nicklaus	1982	Tom Watson
1935	Sam Parks, Jr.	1953	Ben Hogan	1968	Lee Trevino	1983	Larry Nelson
1936	Tony Manero	1954	Ed Furgol	1969	Orville Moody	1984	Fuzzy Zoeller*
1937	Ralph Guldahl	1955	Jack Fleck*			1985	Andy North
1938	Ralph Guldahl	1956	Cary Middlecoff	1970	Tony Jacklin	1986	Raymond Floyd
1939	Byron Nelson*	1957	Dick Mayer*	1971	Lee Trevino*	1987	Scott Simpson
		1958	Tommy Bolt	1972	Jack Nicklaus	1988	Curtis Strange*
1940	Lawson Little*	1959	Billy Casper	1973	Johnny Miller	1989	Curtis Strange
1941	Craig Wood			1974	Hale Irwin		
1942–45	Not held	1960	Arnold Palmer	1975	Lou Graham*	1990	Hale Irwin*
1946	Lloyd Mangrum*	1961	Gene Littler	1976	Jerry Pate	1991	Payne Stewart*
1947	Lew Worsham*	1962	Jack Nicklaus*	1977	Hubert Green	1992	Tom Kite
1948	Ben Hogan	1963	Julius Boros*	1978	Andy North		
1949	Cary Middlecoff	1964	Ken Venturi	1979	Hale Irwin		

*PLAYOFFS

1901: Anderson (85) def. Alex Smith (86) in 18 holes. **1903:** Anderson (82) def. David Brown (84) in 18 holes. **1908:** McLeod (77) def. Willie Smith (83) in 18 holes. **1910:** A.Smith (71) def. John McDermott (75) & Macdonald Smith (77) in 18 holes. **1911:** McDermott (80) def. Mike Brady (82) & George Simpson (85) in 18 holes. **1913:** Ouimet (72) def. Harry Vardon (77) & Edward Ray (78) in 18 holes. **1919:** Hagen (77) def. Mike Brady (78) in 18 holes. **1923:** Jones (76) def. Bobby Cruickshank (78) in 18 holes. **1925:** Macfarlane (75-72) def. Bobby Jones (75-73) in 36 holes. **1927:** Armour (76) def. Harry Cooper (79) in 18 holes. **1928:** Farrell (143) def. Bobby Jones (144) in 36 holes. **1929:** Jones (141) def. Al Espinosa (164) in 36 holes. **1931:** Burke (149-148) def. George Von Elm (149-149) in 72 holes. **1939:** B.Nelson (68-70) def. Craig Wood (68-73) in 36 holes. **1940:** Little (70) def. Gene Sarazen (73) in 18 holes. **1946:** Mangrum (72-72) def. Byron Nelson (72-73) and Vic Ghezzi (72-73) in 36 holes. **1947:** Worsham (69) def. Sam Snead (70) in 18 holes. **1950:** Hogan (69) def. Lloyd Mangrum (73) & George Fazio (75) in 18 holes. **1955:** Fleck (69) def. Ben Hogan (72) in 18 holes. **1957:** Mayer (72) def. Cary Middlecoff (79) in 18 holes. **1962:** Nicklaus (71) def. Arnold Palmer (74) in 18 holes. **1963:** Boros (70) def. Jacky Cupit (73) & Arnold Palmer (73) in 18 holes. **1965:** Player (71) def. Kel Nagle (74) in 18 holes. **1966:** Casper (69) def. Arnold Palmer (73) in 18 holes. **1971:** Trevino (68) def. Jack Nicklaus (71) in 18 holes. **1975:** L.Graham (71) def. John Mahaffey (73) in 18 holes. **1984:** Zoeller (67) def. Greg Norman (75) in 18 holes. **1988:** Strange (71) def. Nick Faldo (75) in 18 holes. **1990:** Irwin (74-3) def. Mike Donald (74-4) on 1st hole of sudden death after 18 holes. **1991:** Stewart (75) def. Scott Simpson (77) in 18 holes.

Playing Sites

1895—Newport GC, (R.I.); **1896**—Shinnecock Hills GC (N.Y.); **1897**—Chicago GC (Ill.); **1898**—Myopia Hunt Club (Mass.); **1899**—Baltimore CC (Md.).

1900—Chicago GC (Ill.); **1901**—Myopia Hunt Club (Mass.); **1902**—Garden City GC (N.Y.); **1903**—Baltusrol GC (N.J.); **1904**—Glen View Club (Ill.); **1905**—Myopia Hunt Club (Mass.); **1906**—Onwentsia Club (Ill.); **1907**—Phila. Cricket Club (Pa.); **1908**—Myopia Hunt Club (Mass.); **1909**—Englewood GC (N.J.).

1910—Phila. Cricket Club (Pa.); **1911**—Chicago GC (Ill.); **1912**—CC of Buffalo (N.Y.); **1913**—The Country Club (Mass.); **1914**—Midlothian CC (Ill.); **1915**—Baltusrol GC (N.J.); **1916**—Minikahda Club (Minn.); **1917-18**—Not held; **1919**—Brae Burn CC (Mass.).

1920—Inverness CC (Ohio); **1921**—Columbia CC (Md.); **1922**—Skokie CC (Ill.); **1923**—Inwood CC (N.Y.); **1924**—Oakland Hills (Mich.); **1925**—Worcester CC (Mass.); **1926**—Scioto CC (Ohio); **1927**—Oakmont CC (Pa.); **1928**—Olympia Fields CC (Ill.); **1929**—Winged Foot GC (N.Y.).

1930—Interlachen (Minn.); **1931**—Inverness Club (Ohio); **1932**—Fresh Meadows CC (N.Y.); **1933**—North Shore CC (Ill.); **1934**—Merion Cricket (Pa.); **1935**—Oakmont CC (Pa.); **1936**—Baltusrol GC (N.J.); **1937**—Oakland Hills CC (Mich.); **1938**—Cherry Hills CC (Colo.); **1939**—Philadelphia CC (Pa.).

1940—Canterbury GC (Ohio); **1941**—Colonial Club (Tex.); **1942-45**—Not held; **1946**—Canterbury CC (Ohio); **1947**—St. Louis CC Mo.); **1948**—Riviera CC (Calif.); **1949**—Medinah CC (Ill.).

1950—Merion GC (Pa.); **1951**—Oakland Hills CC (Mich.); **1952**—Northwood Club (Tex.); **1953**—Oakmont CC (Pa.); **1954**—Baltusrol GC (N.J.); **1955**—Olympic Club (Calif.); **1956**—Oak Hill CC (N.Y.); **1957**—Inverness Club (Ohio); **1958**—Southern Hills CC (Okla.); **1959**—Winged Foot GC (N.Y.).

1960—Cherry Hills CC (Colo.); **1961**—Oakland Hills CC (Mich.); **1962**—Oakmont CC (Pa.); **1963**—The Country Club (Mass.); **1964**— Congressional CC (Md.); **1965**—Bellerive CC (Mo.); **1966**—Olympic Club (Calif.); **1967**—Baltusrol GC (N.J.); **1968**—Oak Hill CC (N.Y.); **1969**—Champions GC (Tex.).

1970—Hazeltine GC (Minn.); **1971**—Merion GC (Pa.); **1972**—Pebble Beach GL (Calif.); **1973**—Oakmont CC (Pa.); **1974**—Winged Foot GC (N.Y.); **1975**—Medinah CC (Ill.); **1976**—Atlanta AC (Ga.); **1977**—Southern Hills CC (Okla.); **1978**—Cherry Hills CC (Colo.); **1979**—Inverness Club (Ohio).

1980—Baltusrol GC (N.J.); **1981**—Merion GC (Pa.); **1982**—Pebble Beach GL (Calif.); **1983**—Oakmont CC (Pa.); **1984**—Winged Foot CC (N.Y.); **1985**—Oakland Hills (Mich.); **1986**—Shinnecock Hills GC (N.Y.); **1987**—Olympic Club (Calif.); **1988**—The Country Club (Mass.); **1989**—Oak Hill CC (N.Y.).

1990—Medinah (Ill.) CC; **1991**—Hazeltine National GC (Minn.); **1992**—Pebble Beach GL (Calif.).

British Open

The oldest of the Majors, the British Open began in 1860 to determine "the champion golfer of the world." Conducted by the Royal and Ancient Golf Club of St. Andrews, The Open is rotated among select golf courses in England; (*) indicates playoff winner and (a) indicates amateur winner.

Multiple winners: Harry Vardon (6); James Braid, J.H.Taylor, Peter Thomson and Tom Watson (5); Walter Hagen, Bobby Locke, Tom Morris, Sr., Tom Morris, Jr., and Willie Park (4); Jamie Anderson, Seve Ballesteros, Henry Cotton, Nick Faldo, Robert Ferguson, Bobby Jones, Jack Nicklaus and Gary Player (3); Harold Hilton, Bob Martin, Arnold Palmer, Willie Park, Jr., and Lee Trevino (2).

Year		Year		Year		Year	
1860	Willie Park	1892	a-Harold Hilton	1927	a-Bobby Jones	1963	Bob Charles*
1861	Tom Morris, Sr.	1893	Wm.Auchterlinie	1928	Walter Hagen	1964	Tony Lema
1862	Tom Morris, Sr.	1894	J.H.Taylor	1929	Walter Hagen	1965	Peter Thomson
1863	Willie Park	1895	J.H.Taylor			1966	Jack Nicklaus
1864	Tom Morris, Sr.	1896	Harry Vardon*	1930	a-Bobby Jones	1967	Roberto de Vicenzo
1865	Andrew Strath	1897	a-Harold Hilton	1931	Tommy Armour	1968	Gary Player
1866	Willie Park	1898	Harry Vardon	1932	Gene Sarazen	1969	Tony Jacklin
1867	Tom Morris, Sr.	1899	Harry Vardon	1933	Denny Shute*		
1868	Tom Morris, Jr.			1934	Henry Cotton	1970	Jack Nicklaus*
1869	Tom Morris, Jr.	1900	J.H.Taylor	1935	Alf Perry	1971	Lee Trevino
		1901	James Braid	1936	Alf Padgham	1972	Lee Trevino
1870	Tom Morris, Jr.	1902	Sandy Herd	1937	Henry Cotton	1973	Tom Weiskopf
1871	Not held	1903	Harry Vardon	1938	Reg Whitcombe	1974	Gary Player
1872	Tom Morris, Jr.	1904	Jack White	1939	Dick Burton	1975	Tom Watson*
1873	Tom Kidd	1905	James Braid			1976	Johnny Miller
1874	Mungo Park	1906	James Braid	1940–45	Not held	1977	Tom Watson
1875	Willie Park	1907	Arnaud Massy	1946	Sam Snead	1978	Jack Nicklaus
1876	Bob Martin*	1908	James Braid	1947	Fred Daly	1979	Seve Ballesteros
1877	Jamie Anderson	1909	J.H.Taylor	1948	Henry Cotton		
1878	Jamie Anderson			1949	Bobby Locke*	1980	Tom Watson
1879	Jamie Anderson	1910	James Braid			1981	Bill Rogers
		1911	Harry Vardon*	1950	Bobby Locke	1982	Tom Watson
1880	Bob Ferguson	1912	Ted Ray	1951	Max Faulkner	1983	Tom Watson
1881	Bob Ferguson	1913	J.H.Taylor	1952	Bobby Locke	1984	Seve Ballesteros
1882	Bob Ferguson	1914	Harry Vardon	1953	Ben Hogan	1985	Sandy Lyle
1883	Willie Fernie*	1915–19	Not held	1954	Peter Thomson	1986	Greg Norman
1884	Jack Simpson			1955	Peter Thomson	1987	Nick Faldo
1885	Bob Martin	1920	George Duncan	1956	Peter Thomson	1988	Seve Ballesteros
1886	David Brown	1921	Jock Hutchison*	1957	Bobby Locke	1989	Mark Calcavecchia
1887	Willie Park, Jr.	1922	Walter Hagen	1958	Peter Thomson*		
1888	Jack Burns	1923	Arthur Havers	1959	Gary Player	1990	Nick Faldo
1889	Willie Park, Jr.*	1924	Walter Hagen			1991	Ian Baker-Finch
		1925	Jim Barnes	1960	Kel Nagle	1992	Nick Faldo
1890	a-John Ball	1926	a-Bobby Jones	1961	Arnold Palmer		
1891	Hugh Kirkaldy			1962	Arnold Palmer		

*PLAYOFFS

1876: Martin awarded title when David Strath refused playoff. **1883:** Fernie (158) def. Robert Ferguson (159) in 36 holes. **1889:** Park (158) def. Andrew Kirkaldy (163) in 36 holes. **1896:** Vardon (157) def. John H.Taylor (161) in 36 holes. **1911:** Vardon won when Arnaud Massy conceded at 35th hole. **1921:** Hutchison (150) def. Roger Wethered (159) in 36 holes. **1933:** Shute (149) def. Craig Wood (154) in 36 holes. **1949:** Locke (135) def. Harry Bradshaw (147) in 36 holes. **1958:** Thomson (139) def. Dave Thomas (143) in 36 holes. **1963:** Charles (140) def. Phil Rodgers (148) in 36 holes. **1970:** Nicklaus (72) def. Doug Sanders (73) in 18 holes. **1975:** Watson (71) def. Jack Newton (72) in 18 holes. **1989:** Calcavecchia (4-3-3-3—13) def. Wayne Grady (4-4-4-4—16) and Greg Norman (3-3-4-x) in 4 holes.

Playing Sites

1860-69—Prestwick, Scotland; **1870**—Prestwick; **1871**—Not held; **1872**—Prestwick; **1873**—St. Andrews, Scotland; **1874**—Musselburgh, Scotland; **1875**—Prestwick; **1876**—St. Andrews; **1877**—Musselburgh; **1878**—Prestwick; **1879**—St. Andrews.

1880—Musselburgh; **1881**—Prestwick; **1882**—St. Andrews; **1883**—Musselburgh; **1884**—Prestwick; **1885**—St. Andrews; **1886**—Musselburgh; **1887**—Prestwick; **1888**—St. Andrews; **1889**—Musselburgh; **1890**—Prestwick; **1891**—St. Andrews; **1892**—Muirfield, Scotland; **1893**—Prestwick; **1894**—Royal St. George's, England; **1895**—St. Andrews; **1896**—Muirfield; **1897**—Hoylake, England; **1898**—Prestwick; **1899**—Royal St. George's.

1900—St. Andrews; **1901**—St. Andrews; **1902**—Hoylake; **1903**—Prestwick; **1904**—Royal St. George's; **1905**—St. Andrews; **1906**—Muirfield; **1907**—Hoylake; **1908**—Prestwick; **1909**—Deal, England; **1910**—St. Andrews; **1911**—Royal St. George's; **1912**—Muirfield; **1913**—Hoylake; **1914**—Prestwick; **1915-19**—Not held.

1920—Deal; **1921**—St. Andrews; **1922**—Royal St. George's; **1923**—Troon, Scotland; **1924**—Hoylake; **1925**—Prestwick; **1926**—Royal Lytham and St. Annes, England; **1927**—St. Andrews; **1928**—Royal St. George's; **1929**—Muirfield.

1930—Hoylake; **1931**—Carnoustie, Scotland; **1932**—Prince's, England; **1933**—St. Andrews; **1934**—Royal St. George's; **1935**—Muirfield; **1936**—Hoylake; **1937**—Carnoustie; **1938**—Royal St. George's; **1939**—St. Andrews. **1940-45**—Not held; **1946**—St. Andrews; **1947**—Hoylake; **1948**—Muirfield; **1949**—Royal St. George's.

1950—Troon; **1951**—Royal Portrush, Ireland; **1952**—Royal Lytham and St. Annes; **1953**—Carnoustie; **1954**—Royal Birkdale, England; **1955**—St. Andrews; **1956**—Hoylake; **1957**—St. Andrews; **1958**—Royal Lytham and St. Annes; **1959**—Muirfield.

Major Championships (Cont.)
MEN
British Open

1960—St. Andrews; **1961**—Royal Birkdale; **1962**—Troon; **1963**—Royal Lytham and St. Annes; **1964**—St. Andrews; **1965**—Royal Birkdale; **1966**—Muirfield; **1967**—Hoylake; **1968**—Carnoustie; **1969**—Royal Lytham and St. Annes.

1970—St. Andrews; **1971**—Royal Birkdale; **1972**—Muirfield; **1973**—Troon; **1974**—Royal Lytham and St. Annes; **1975**—Carnoustie; **1976**—Royal Birkdale; **1977**—Turnberry, Scotland; **1978**—St. Andrews; **1979**—Royal Lytham and St.Annes.

1980—Muirfield; **1981**—Royal St. George's; **1982**—Royal Troon; **1983**—Royal Birkdale; **1984**—St. Andrews; **1985**—Royal St. George's; **1986**—Turnberry; **1987**—Muirfield; **1988**—Royal Lytham and St. Annes; **1989**—Royal Troon.

1990—St. Andrews; **1991**—Royal Birkdale; **1992**—Muirfield.

PGA Championship

The PGA Championship began in 1916 as a professional golfers match play tournament, but switched to stroke play in 1958. Conducted by the PGA of America, the tournament is played on a different course each year.

Multiple winners: Walter Hagen and Jack Nicklaus (5); Gene Sarazen and Sam Snead (3); Jim Barnes, Leo Diegel, Raymond Floyd, Ben Hogan, Byron Nelson, Larry Nelson, Gary Player, Paul Runyan, Denny Shute, Dave Stockton and Lee Trevino (2).

Year		Year		Year		Year	
1916	Jim Barnes	1936	Denny Shute	1955	Doug Ford	1974	Lee Trevino
1917–18	Not held	1937	Denny Shute	1956	Jack Burke, Jr.	1975	Jack Nicklaus
1919	Jim Barnes	1938	Paul Runyan	1957	Lionel Hebert	1976	Dave Stockton
1920	Jock Hutchison	1939	Henry Picard	1958	Dow Finsterwald	1977	Lanny Wadkins*
1921	Walter Hagen	1940	Byron Nelson	1959	Bob Rosburg	1978	John Mahaffey*
1922	Gene Sarazen	1941	Vic Ghezzi			1979	David Graham*
1923	Gene Sarazen	1942	Sam Snead	1960	Jay Hebert		
1924	Walter Hagen	1943	Not held	1961	Jerry Barber*	1980	Jack Nicklaus
1925	Walter Hagen	1944	Bob Hamilton	1962	Gary Player	1981	Larry Nelson
1926	Walter Hagen	1945	Byron Nelson	1963	Jack Nicklaus	1982	Raymond Floyd
1927	Walter Hagen	1946	Ben Hogan	1964	Bobby Nichols	1983	Hal Sutton
1928	Leo Diegel	1947	Jim Ferrier	1965	Dave Marr	1984	Lee Trevino
1929	Leo Diegel	1948	Ben Hogan	1966	Al Geiberger	1985	Hubert Green
1930	Tommy Armour	1949	Sam Snead	1967	Don January*	1986	Bob Tway
1931	Tom Creavy	1950	Chandler Harper	1968	Julius Boros	1987	Larry Nelson*
1932	Olin Dutra	1951	Sam Snead	1969	Raymond Floyd	1988	Jeff Sluman
1933	Gene Sarazen	1952	Jim Turnesa			1989	Payne Stewart
1934	Paul Runyan	1953	Walter Burkemo	1970	Dave Stockton		
1935	Johnny Revolta	1954	Chick Harbert	1971	Jack Nicklaus	1990	Wayne Grady
				1972	Gary Player	1991	John Daly
				1973	Jack Nicklaus	1992	Nick Price

*PLAYOFFS

1961: J.Barber (67) def. Don January (68) in 18 holes. **1967:** January (69) def. Don Massengale (71) in 18 holes. **1977:** L.Wadkins (4-4-4) def. Gene Littler (4-4-5) on 3rd hole of sudden death. **1978:** Mahaffey (4-3) def. Jerry Pate (4-4) and Tom Watson (4-5) on 2nd hole of sudden death. **1979:** D.Graham (4-4-2) def. Ben Crenshaw (4-4-4) on 3rd hole of sudden death. **1987:** Nelson (4) def. Lanny Wadkins (5) on 1st hole of sudden death.

Playing Sites

1916—Siwanoy CC (N.Y.); **1917**—Engineers CC (N.Y.); **1918**—Flossmoor CC (Ill.); **1919**—Inwood CC (N.Y.).

1920—Flossmoor CC (Ill.); **1921**—Inwood CC (N.Y.); **1922**—Oakmont CC (Pa.); **1923**—Pelham CC (N.Y.); **1924**—French Lick CC (Ind.); **1925**—Olympia Fields (Ill.); **1926**—Salisbury GC (N.Y.); **1927**—Cedar Crest (Tex.); **1928**—Five Farms CC (Md.); **1929**—Hillcrest CC (Calif.).

1930—Fresh Meadow CC (N.Y.); **1931**—Wannamoisett CC (R.I.); **1932**—Keller GC (Minn.); **1933**—Blue Mound CC (Wisc.); **1934**—Park CC (N.Y.); **1935**—Twin Hills CC (Okla.); **1936**—Pinehurst CC (N.C.); **1937**—Pittsburgh FC (Pa.); **1938**—Shawnee CC (Pa.); **1939**—Pomonok CC (N.Y.).

1940—Hershey CC (Pa.); **1941**—Cherry Hills CC (Colo.); **1942**—Seaview CC (N.J.); **1943**—Not held; **1944**—Manito G&CC (Wash.); **1945**—Morraine CC (Ohio); **1946**—Portland GC (Ore.); **1947**—Plum Hollow CC (Mich.); **1948**—Norwood Hills CC (Md.); **1949**—Hermitage CC (Va.).

1950—Scioto CC (Ohio); **1951**—Oakmont CC (Pa.); **1952**—Big Spring CC (Ky.); **1953**—Birmingham CC (Mich.); **1954**—Keller GC (Minn.); **1955**—Meadowbrook CC (Mich.); **1956**—Blue Hill CC (Mass.); **1957**—Miami Valley CC (Ohio); **1958**—Llanerch CC (Pa.); **1959**—Minneapolis GC (Minn.).

1960—Firestone CC (Ohio); **1961**—Olympia Fields CC (Ill.); **1962**—Aronomink GC (Pa.); **1963**—Dallas AC (Tex.); **1964**—Columbus CC (Ohio); **1965**—Laurel Valley CC (Pa.); **1966**—Firestone CC (Ohio); **1967**—Columbine CC (Colo.); **1968**—Pecan Valley CC (Tex.); **1969**—NCR CC (Ohio).

1970—Southern Hills CC (Okla.); **1971**—PGA National CC (Fla.); **1972**—Oakland Hills CC (Mich.); **1973**—Canterbury GC (Ohio); **1974**—Tanglewood CC (N.C.); **1975**—Firestone CC (Ohio); **1976**—Congressional CC (Md.); **1977**—Pebble Beach GL (Calif.); **1978**—Oakmont CC (Pa.); **1979**—Oakland Hills CC (Mich.).

1980—Oak Hill CC (N.Y.); **1981**—Atlanta AC (Ga.); **1982**—Southern Hills CC (Okla.); **1983**—Riviera CC (Calif.); **1984**—Shoal Creek (Ala.); **1985**—Cherry Hills CC (Colo.); **1986**—Inverness CC (Ohio); **1987**—PGA National (Fla.); **1988**—Oak Tree GC (Okla.); **1989**—Kemper Lakes CC (Ill.).

1990—Shoal Creek (Ala.) **1991**—Crooked Stick GC (Ind.); **1992**—Bellerive CC (Mo.).

U.S. Amateur

Match play from 1895-64, stroke play from 1965-72, match play since 1972.

Multiple winners: Bobby Jones (5); Jerry Travers (4); Walter Travis (3); Deane Beman, Charles Coe, Gary Cowan, H.Chandler Egan, Chick Evans, Lawson Little, Jack Nicklaus, Francis Ouimet, Jay Sigel, William Turnesa, Bud Ward, Harvie Ward and H.J.Whigham (2).

Year		Year		Year		Year	
1895	Charles Macdonald	1920	Chick Evans	1947	Skee Riegel	1970	Lanny Wadkins
1896	H.J.Whigham	1921	Jesse Guilford	1948	William Turnesa	1971	Gary Cowan
1897	H.J.Whigham	1922	Jess Sweetser	1949	Charles Coe	1972	Vinny Giles
1898	Findlay Douglas	1923	Max Marston	1950	Sam Urzetta	1973	Craig Stadler
1899	H.M.Harriman	1924	Bobby Jones	1951	Billy Maxwell	1974	Jerry Pate
1900	Walter Travis	1925	Bobby Jones	1952	Jack Westland	1975	Fred Ridley
1901	Walter Travis	1926	George Von Elm	1953	Gene Littler	1976	Bill Sander
1902	Louis James	1927	Bobby Jones	1954	Arnold Palmer	1977	John Fought
1903	Walter Travis	1928	Bobby Jones	1955	Harvie Ward	1978	John Cook
1904	H.Chandler Egan	1929	Harrison Johnston	1956	Harvie Ward	1979	Mark O'Meara
1905	H.Chandler Egan	1930	Bobby Jones	1957	Hillman Robbins	1980	Hal Sutton
1906	Eben Byers	1931	Francis Ouimet	1958	Charles Coe	1981	Nathanial Crosby
1907	Jerry Travers	1932	Ross Somerville	1959	Jack Nicklaus	1982	Jay Sigel
1908	Jerry Travers	1933	George Dunlap	1960	Deane Beman	1983	Jay Sigel
1909	Robert Gardner	1934	Lawson Little	1961	Jack Nicklaus	1984	Scott Verplank
1910	W.C.Fownes, Jr.	1935	Lawson Little	1962	Labron Harris	1985	Sam Randolph
1911	Harold Hilton	1936	John Fischer	1963	Deane Beman	1986	Buddy Alexander
1912	Jerry Travers	1937	John Goodman	1964	Bill Campbell	1987	Billy Mayfair
1913	Jerry Travers	1938	William Turnesa	1965	Bob Murphy	1988	Eric Meeks
1914	Francis Ouimet	1939	Bud Ward	1966	Gary Cowan	1989	Chris Patton
1915	Robert Gardner	1940	Richard Chapman	1967	Bob Dickson	1990	Phil Mickelson
1916	Chick Evans	1941	Bud Ward	1968	Bruce Fleisher	1991	Mitch Voges
1917-18	Not held	1942-45	Not held	1969	Steve Melnyk	1992	Justin Leonard
1919	Davidson Herron	1946	Ted Bishop				

British Amateur

Match play since 1885.

Multiple winners: John Ball (8); Michael Bonallack (5); Harold Hilton (4); Joe Carr (3); Horace Hutchinson, Ernest Holderness, Trevor Homer, Johnny Laidley, Lawson Little, Peter McEvoy, Dick Siderowf, Frank Stranahan, Freddie Tait and Cyril Tolley (2).

Year		Year		Year		Year	
1885	Allen MacFie	1912	John Ball	1947	William Turnesa	1970	Michael Bonallack
1886	Horace Hutchinson	1913	Harold Hilton	1948	Frank Stranahan	1971	Steve Melnyk
1887	Horace Hutchinson	1914	J.L.C.Jenkins	1949	Samuel McCready	1972	Trevor Homer
1888	John Ball	1915-19	Not held	1950	Frank Stranahan	1973	Dick Siderowf
1889	Johnny Laidley	1920	Cyril Tolley	1951	Richard Chapman	1974	Trevor Homer
1890	John Ball	1921	William Hunter	1952	Harvie Ward	1975	Vinny Giles
1891	Johnny Laidlay	1922	Ernest Holderness	1953	Joe Carr	1976	Dick Siderowf
1892	John Ball	1923	Roger Wethered	1954	Douglas Bachli	1977	Peter McEvoy
1893	Peter Anderson	1924	Ernest Holderness	1955	Joe Conrad	1978	Peter McEvoy
1894	John Ball	1925	Robert Harris	1956	John Beharrell	1979	Jay Sigel
1895	Leslie Balfour	1926	Jesse Sweetser	1957	Reid Jack	1980	Duncan Evans
1896	Freddie Tait	1927	William Tweedell	1958	Joe Carr	1981	Phillipe Ploujoux
1897	Jack Allen	1928	Thomas Perkins	1959	Deane Beman	1982	Martin Thompson
1898	Freddie Tait	1929	Cyril Tolley	1960	Joe Carr	1983	Philip Parkin
1899	John Ball	1930	Bobby Jones	1961	Michael Bonallack	1984	Jose-Maria Olazabal
1900	Harold Hilton	1931	Eric Smith	1962	Richard Davies	1985	Garth McGimpsey
1901	Harold Hilton	1932	John deForest	1963	Michael Lunt	1986	David Curry
1902	Charles Hutchings	1933	Michael Scott	1964	Gordon Clark	1987	Paul Mayo
1903	Robert Maxwell	1934	Lawson Little	1965	Michael Bonallack	1988	Christian Hardin
1904	Walter Travis	1935	Lawson Little	1966	Bobby Cole	1989	Stephen Dodd
1905	Arthur Barry	1936	Hector Thomson	1967	Bob Dickson	1990	Rolf Muntz
1906	James Robb	1937	Robert Sweeny, Jr.	1968	Michael Bonallack	1991	Gary Wolstenholme
1907	John Ball	1938	Charles Yates	1969	Michael Bonallack	1992	Stephen Dundas
1908	E.A.Lassen	1939	Alexander Kyle				
1909	Robert Maxwell	1940-45	Not held				
1910	John Ball	1946	James Bruen				
1911	Harold Hilton						

Major Championship Leaders
Through 1991; active players in **bold** type.

	US Open	British Open	PGA	Masters	US Am	British Am	Total
Jack Nicklaus	4	3	5	6	2	0	**20**
Bobby Jones	4	3	0	0	5	1	**13**
Walter Hagen	2	4	5	0	0	0	**11**
Ben Hogan	4	1	2	2	0	0	**9**
Gary Player	1	3	2	3	0	0	**9**
John Ball	0	1	0	0	0	8	**9**
Arnold Palmer	1	2	0	4	1	0	**8**
Tom Watson	1	5	0	2	0	0	**8**
Harold Hilton	0	2	0	0	1	4	**7**
Gene Sarazen	2	1	3	1	0	0	**7**
Sam Snead	0	1	3	3	0	0	**7**
Harry Vardon	1	6	0	0	0	0	**7**
Lee Trevino	2	2	2	0	0	0	**6**

Tournaments: U.S. Open, British Open, PGA Championship, Masters, U.S. Amateur, and British Amateur.

Grand Slam Summary

The only golfer ever to win a recognized Grand Slam—four major championships in a single season—was Bobby Jones in 1930. That year, Jones won the U.S. and British Opens as well as the U.S. and British Amateurs.

The men's professional Grand Slam—the Masters, U.S. Open, British Open and PGA Championship—did not gain acceptance until 30 years later when Arnold Palmer won the 1960 Masters and U.S. Open. The media wrote that the popular Palmer was chasing the "new" Grand Slam and would have to win the British Open and the PGA to claim it. He did not, but then nobody has before or since.

Three wins in one year: Ben Hogan (1953).

Two wins in one year (16): Jack Nicklaus (5 times); Ben Hogan, Arnold Palmer and Tom Watson (twice); Nick Faldo, Gary Player, Sam Snead, Lee Trevino and Craig Wood (once).

Year	Masters	US Open	Brit.Open	PGA	Year	Masters	US Open	Brit.Open	PGA
1934	H.Smith	Dutra	Cotton	Runyan	1964	Palmer	Venturi	Lema	Nichols
1935	Sarazen	Parks	Perry	Revolta	1965	Nicklaus	Player	Thomson	Marr
1936	H.Smith	Manero	Padgham	Shute	1966	Nicklaus	Casper	Nicklaus	Geiberger
1937	B.Nelson	Guldahl	Cotton	Shute	1967	Brewer	Nicklaus	DeVicenzo	January
1938	Picard	Guldahl	Whitcombe	Runyan	1968	Goalby	Trevino	Player	Boros
1939	Guldahl	B.Nelson	Burton	Picard	1969	Archer	Moody	Jacklin	Floyd
1940	Demaret	Little	—	B.Nelson	1970	Casper	Jacklin	Nicklaus	Stockton
1941	Wood	Wood	—	Ghezzi	1971	Coody	Trevino	Trevino	Nicklaus
1942	B.Nelson	—	—	Snead	1972	Nicklaus	Nicklaus	Trevino	Player
1943	—	—	—	—	1973	Aaron	J.Miller	Weiskopf	Nicklaus
1944	—	—	—	Hamilton	1974	Player	Irwin	Player	Trevino
1945	—	—	—	B.Nelson	1975	Nicklaus	L.Graham	T.Watson	Nicklaus
1946	Keiser	Mangrum	Snead	Hogan	1976	Floyd	J.Pate	Miller	Stockton
1947	Demaret	Worsham	F.Daly	Ferrier	1977	T.Watson	H.Green	T.Watson	L.Wadkins
1948	Harmon	Hogan	Cotton	Hogan	1978	Player	North	Nicklaus	Mahaffey
1949	Snead	Middlecoff	Locke	Snead	1979	Zoeller	Irwin	Ballesteros	D.Graham
1950	Demaret	Hogan	Locke	Harper	1980	Ballesteros	Nicklaus	T.Watson	Nicklaus
1951	Hogan	Hogan	Faulkner	Snead	1981	T.Watson	D.Graham	Rogers	L.Nelson
1952	Snead	Boros	Locke	Turnesa	1982	Stadler	T.Watson	T.Watson	Floyd
1953	**Hogan**	**Hogan**	**Hogan**	Burkemo	1983	Ballesteros	L.Nelson	T.Watson	Sutton
1954	Snead	Furgol	Thomson	Harbert	1984	Crenshaw	Zoeller	Ballesteros	Trevino
1955	Middlecoff	Fleck	Thomson	Ford	1985	Langer	North	Lyle	H.Green
1956	Burke	Middlecoff	Thomson	Burke	1986	Nicklaus	Floyd	Norman	Tway
1957	Ford	Mayer	Locke	L.Hebert	1987	Mize	S.Simpson	Faldo	L.Nelson
1958	Palmer	Bolt	Thomson	Finsterwald	1988	Lyle	Strange	Ballesteros	Sluman
1959	Wall	Casper	Player	Rosburg	1989	Faldo	Strange	Calcavecchia	Stewart
1960	Palmer	Palmer	Nagle	J.Hebert	1990	Faldo	Irwin	Faldo	Grady
1961	Player	Littler	Palmer	J.Barber	1991	Woosnam	Stewart	Baker-Finch	J.Daly
1962	Palmer	Nicklaus	Palmer	Player	1992	Couples	Kite	Faldo	Price
1963	Nicklaus	Boros	Charles	Nicklaus					

Major Championships
WOMEN
U.S. Women's Open

The U.S. Women's Open began under the direction of the defunct Women's Professional Golfers Assn. in 1946, passed to the LPGA in 1949 and to the U.S.GA in 1953. The tournament used a match play format its first year then switched to stroke play; (*) indicates playoff winner and (a) indicates amateur winner.

Multiple winners: Betsy Rawls and Mickey Wright (4); Susie M.Berning, Hollis Stacy and Babe Zaharias (3); JoAnne Carner, Donna Caponi, Betsy King and Louise Suggs (2).

Year		Year		Year		Year	
1946	Patty Berg	1958	Mickey Wright	1970	Donna Caponi	1982	Janet Anderson
1947	Betty Jameson	1959	Mickey Wright	1971	JoAnne Carner	1983	Jan Stephenson
1948	Babe Zaharias	1960	Betsy Rawls	1972	Susie M.Berning	1984	Hollis Stacy
1949	Louise Suggs	1961	Mickey Wright	1973	Susie M.Berning	1985	Kathy Baker
1950	Babe Zaharias	1962	Murle Lindstrom	1974	Sandra Haynie	1986	Jane Geddes*
1951	Betsy Rawls	1963	Mary Mills	1975	Sandra Palmer	1987	Laura Davies*
1952	Louise Suggs	1964	Mickey Wright*	1976	JoAnne Carner*	1988	Liselotte Neumann
1953	Betsy Rawls*	1965	Carol Mann	1977	Hollis Stacy	1989	Betsy King
1954	Babe Zaharias	1966	Sandra Spuzich	1978	Hollis Stacy	1990	Betsy King
1955	Fay Crocker	1967	a-Catherine Lacoste	1979	Jerilyn Britz	1991	Meg Mallon
1956	Kathy Cornelius*	1968	Susie M.Berning	1980	Amy Alcott	1992	Patty Sheehan
1957	Betsy Rawls	1969	Donna Caponi	1981	Pat Bradley		

*PLAYOFFS

1953: Rawls (71) def. Jackie Pung (77) in 18 holes. **1956:** Cornelius (75) def. Barbara McIntire (82) in 18 holes. **1964:** Wright (70) def. Ruth Jessen (72) in 18 holes. **1976:** Carner (76) def. Sandra Palmer (78) in 18 holes. **1986:** Geddes (71) def. Sally Little (73) in 18 holes. **1987:** Davies (71) def. Ayako Okamoto (73) and JoAnne Carner (74) in 18 holes. **1992:** Sheehan (72) def. Juli Inkster (74) in 18 holes.

LPGA Championship

Officially the Mazda LPGA Championship since 1987, the tournament began in 1955 and has had extended stays at the Stardust CC in Las Vegas (1961-66), Pleasant Valley CC in Sutton, MA (1967-68,70-74) and the Jack Nicklaus Sports Center at Kings Island, Ohio (1978-89); (*) indicates playoff winner.

Multiple winners: Mickey Wright (4); Nancy Lopez and Kathy Whitworth (3); Donna Caponi, Sandra Haynie, Mary Mills, Betsy Rawls and Patty Sheehan (2).

Year		Year		Year		Year	
1955	Beverly Hanson	1965	Sandra Haynie	1975	Kathy Whitworth	1985	Nancy Lopez
1956	Marlene Hagge*	1966	Gloria Ehret	1976	Betty Burfeindt	1986	Pat Bradley
1957	Louise Suggs	1967	Kathy Whitworth	1977	Chako Higuchi	1987	Jane Geddes
1958	Mickey Wright	1968	Sandra Post*	1978	Nancy Lopez	1988	Sherri Turner
1959	Betsy Rawls	1969	Betsy Rawls	1979	Donna Caponi	1989	Nancy Lopez
1960	Mickey Wright	1970	Shirley Englehorn*	1980	Sally Little	1990	Beth Daniel
1961	Mickey Wright	1971	Kathy Whitworth	1981	Donna Caponi	1991	Meg Mallon
1962	Judy Kimball	1972	Kathy Ahern	1982	Jan Stephenson	1992	Betsy King
1963	Mickey Wright	1973	Mary Mills	1983	Patty Sheehan		
1964	Mary Mills	1974	Sandra Haynie	1984	Patty Sheehan		

*PLAYOFFS

1956: Hagge def. Patti Berg in sudden death. **1968:** Post (68) def. Kathy Whitworth (75) in 18-holes. **1970:** Englehorn def. Kathy Whitworth in sudden death.

Nabisco Dinah Shore

Formerly known as the Colgate Dinah Shore from 1972-81, the tournament become the LPGA's fourth designated major championship in 1983. Named after the entertainer, this tourney has been played at Mission Hills CC in Rancho Mirage, CA since it began; (*) indicates playoff winner.

Multiple winners (as a major): Amy Alcott (3); Juli Inkster and Betsy King (2).

Year		Year		Year		Year	
1972	Jane Blalock	1978	Sandra Post	1983	Amy Alcott	1988	Amy Alcott
1973	Mickey Wright	1979	Sandra Post	1984	Juli Inkster*	1989	Juli Inkster
1974	Jo Ann Prentice	1980	Donna Caponi	1985	Alice Miller	1990	Betsy King
1975	Sandra Palmer	1981	Nancy Lopez	1986	Pat Bradley	1991	Amy Alcott
1976	Judy Rankin	1982	Sally Little	1987	Betsy King*	1992	Dottie Mochrie*
1977	Kathy Whitworth						

*PLAYOFFS

1984: Inkster def. Pat Bradley in sudden death. **1987:** King def. Patty Sheehan in sudden death. **1992:** Mochrie def. Juli Inkster in sudden death.

Major Championships (Cont.)
WOMEN
du Maurier Classic

Formerly known as La Canadienne in 1973 and the Peter Jackson Classic from 1974-83, this Canadian stop on the LPGA Tour became the third designated major championship in 1979; (*) indicates playoff winner.

Multiple winner (as a major): Pat Bradley (3); JoAnne Carner (2).

Year		Year		Year		Year	
1973	Jocelyne Bourassa	1978	JoAnne Carner	1983	Hollis Stacy	1988	Sally Little
1974	Carole Jo Skala	1979	Amy Alcott	1984	Juli Inkster	1989	Tammie Green
1975	JoAnne Carner	1980	Pat Bradley	1985	Pat Bradley	1990	Cathy Johnston
1976	Donna Caponi	1981	Jan Stephenson	1986	Pat Bradley*	1991	Nancy Scranton
1977	Judy Rankin	1982	Sandra Haynie	1987	Jody Rosenthal	1992	Sherri Steinhaur

*PLAYOFF
1986: Bradley def. Ayako Okamoto in sudden death.

Titleholders Championship (1937–72)

The Titleholders was considered a major title on the women's tour until it was discontinued after the 1972 tournament.

Multiple winners: Patty Berg (7); Louise Suggs (4); Babe Zaharias (3); Dorothy Kirby, Marilynn Smith, Kathy Whitworth and Mickey Wright (2).

Year		Year		Year		Year	
1937	Patty Berg	1947	Babe Zaharias	1955	Patty Berg	1963	Marilynn Smith
1938	Patty Berg	1948	Patty Berg	1956	Louise Suggs	1964	Marilynn Smith
1939	Patty Berg	1949	Peggy Kirk	1957	Patty Berg	1965	Kathy Whitworth
1940	Betty Hicks	1950	Babe Zaharias	1958	Beverly Hanson	1966	Kathy Whitworth
1941	Dorothy Kirby	1951	Pat O'Sullivan	1959	Louise Suggs	1967-71	Not held
1942	Dorothy Kirby	1952	Babe Zaharias	1960	Fay Crocker	1972	Sandra Palmer
1943-45	Not held	1953	Patty Berg	1961	Mickey Wright		
1946	Louise Suggs	1954	Louise Suggs	1962	Mickey Wright		

Western Open (1937–67)

The Western Open was considered a major title on the women's tour until it was discontinued after the 1967 tournament.

Multiple winners: Patty Berg (7); Louise Suggs and Babe Zaharias (4); Mickey Wright (3); Betty Jameson and Betsy Rawls (2).

Year		Year		Year		Year	
1937	Betty Hicks	1945	Babe Zaharias	1953	Louise Suggs	1961	Mary Lena Faulk
1938	Bea Barrett	1946	Louise Suggs	1954	Betty Jameson	1962	Mickey Wright
1939	Helen Dettweiler	1947	Louise Suggs	1955	Patty Berg	1963	Mickey Wright
1940	Babe Zaharias	1948	Patty Berg	1956	Beverly Hanson	1964	Carol Mann
1941	Patty Berg	1949	Louise Suggs	1957	Patty Berg	1965	Susie Maxwell
1942	Betty Jameson	1950	Babe Zaharias	1958	Patty Berg	1966	Mickey Wright
1943	Patty Berg	1951	Patty Berg	1959	Betsy Rawls	1967	Kathy Whitworth
1944	Babe Zaharias	1952	Betsy Rawls	1960	Joyce Ziske		

U.S. Women's Amateur

Stroke play in 1895, match play since 1896.

Multiple winners: Glenna Collett Vare (6); JoAnne Gunderson Carner (5); Margaret Curtis, Beatrix Hoyt, Dorothy Campbell Hurd, Juli Inkster, Alexa Stirling, Virginia Van Wie, Anne Quast Decker Welts (3); Kay Cockerill, Beth Daniel, Vicki Goetze, Katherine Harley, Genevieve Hecker, Betty Jameson and Barbara McIntire (2).

Year		Year		Year		Year	
1895	Mrs.Chas.S. Brown	1912	Margaret Curtis	1930	Glenna Collett	1950	Beverly Hanson
1896	Beatrix Hoyt	1913	Gladys Ravenscroft	1931	Helen Hicks	1951	Dorothy Kirby
1897	Beatrix Hoyt	1914	Katherine Harley	1932	Virginia Van Wie	1952	Jacqueline Pung
1898	Beatrix Hoyt	1915	Florence Vanderbeck	1933	Virginia Van Wie	1953	Mary Lena Faulk
1899	Ruth Underhill	1916	Alexa Stirling	1934	Virginia Van Wie	1954	Barbara Romack
1900	Frances Griscom	1917	Not held	1935	Glenna Collett Vare	1955	Patricia Lesser
1901	Genevieve Hecker	1918	Not held	1936	Pamela Barton	1956	Marlene Stewart
1902	Genevieve Hecker	1919	Alexa Stirling	1937	Estelle Lawson	1957	JoAnne Gunderson
1903	Bessie Anthony	1920	Alexa Stirling	1938	Patty Berg	1958	Anne Quast
1904	Georgianna Bishop	1921	Marion Hollins	1939	Betty Jameson	1959	Barbara McIntire
1905	Pauline Mackay	1922	Glenna Collett	1940	Betty Jameson	1960	JoAnne Gunderson
1906	Harriot Curtis	1923	Edith Cummings	1941	Elizabeth Hicks	1961	Anne Quast Decker
1907	Margaret Curtis	1924	Dorothy C. Hurd	1942-45	Not held	1962	JoAnne Gunderson
1908	Katherine Harley	1925	Glenna Collett	1946	Babe D. Zaharias	1963	Anne Quast Welts
1909	Dorothy Campbell	1926	Helen Stetson	1947	Louise Suggs	1964	Barbara McIntire
1910	Dorothy Campbell	1927	Miriam Burns Horn	1948	Grace Lenczyk	1965	Jean Ashley
1911	Margaret Curtis	1928	Glenna Collett	1949	Dorothy Porter	1966	JoAnne G. Carner
		1929	Glenna Collett			1967	Mary Lou Dill

Year		Year		Year		Year	
1968	JoAnne G. Carner	1974	Cynthia Hill	1980	Juli Inkster	1987	Kay Cockerill
1969	Catherine Lacoste	1975	Beth Daniel	1981	Juli Inkster	1988	Pearl Sinn
1970	Martha Wilkinson	1976	Donna Horton	1982	Juli Inkster	1989	Vicki Goetze
1971	Laura Baugh	1977	Beth Daniel	1983	Joanne Pacillo	1990	Pat Hurst
1972	Mary Budke	1978	Cathy Sherk	1984	Deb Richard	1991	Amy Fruhwirth
1973	Carol Semple	1979	Carolyn Hill	1985	Michiko Hattori	1992	Vicki Goetze
				1986	Kay Cockerill		

Major Championship Leaders

Through 1991; active players in **bold** type.

	US Open	LPGA	duM	Dinah	Title-holders	Western	US Am	Brit Am	Total
Patty Berg	1	0	0	0	7	7	1	0	16
Mickey Wright	4	4	0	0	2	3	0	0	13
Louise Suggs	2	1	0	0	4	4	1	1	13
Babe Zaharias	3	0	0	0	3	4	1	1	12
Betsy Rawls	4	2	0	0	0	2	0	0	8
JoAnne Carner	2	0	0	0	0	0	5	0	7
Kathy Whitworth	0	3	0	0	2	1	0	0	6
Pat Bradley	1	0	3	1	0	0	0	0	6
Juli Inkster	0	0	1	2	0	0	3	0	6
Glenna C. Vare	0	0	0	0	0	0	6	0	6

Tournaments: U.S. Open, LPGA Championship, du Maurier Classic, Nabisco Dinah Shore, Titleholders (1937-72), Western Open (1937-67), U.S. Amateur, and British Amateur.

Grand Slam Summary

The women's Grand Slam has consisted of four tournaments only 19 years. From 1955-66, the U.S. Open, LPGA Championship, Western Open and Titleholders tournaments served as the major events. Since 1983, the U.S. Open, LPGA, du Maurier Classic in Canada and Nabisco Dinah Shore have been the major events. No one has won a four-event Grand Slam on the women's tour.

Three wins in one year (3): Babe Zaharias (1950), Mickey Wright (1961) and Pat Bradley (1986).

Two wins in one year (14): Patty Berg and Mickey Wright (3 times); Louise Suggs (twice); Sandra Haynie, Juli Inkster, Betsy King, Meg Mallon, Betsy Rawls and Kathy Whitworth (once).

Year	LPGA	US Open	T'holders	Western
1937	—	—	Berg	Hicks
1938	—	—	Berg	Barrett
1939	—	—	Berg	Dettweiler
1940	—	—	Hicks	Zaharias
1941	—	—	Kirby	Berg
1942	—	—	Kirby	Jameson
1943	—	—	—	Berg
1944	—	—	—	Zaharias
1945	—	—	—	Zaharias
1946	—	Berg	Suggs	Suggs
1947	—	Jameson	Zaharias	Suggs
1948	—	Zaharias	Berg	Berg
1949	—	Suggs	Kirk	Suggs
1950	—	Zaharias	Zaharias	Zaharias
1951	—	Rawls	O'Sullivan	Berg
1952	—	Suggs	Zaharias	Rawls
1953	—	Rawls	Berg	Suggs
1954	—	Zaharias	Suggs	Jameson
1955	Hanson	Crocker	Berg	Berg
1956	Hagge	Cornelius	Suggs	Hanson
1957	Suggs	Rawls	Berg	Berg
1958	Wright	Wright	Hanson	Berg
1959	Rawls	Wright	Suggs	Rawls
1960	Wright	Rawls	Crocker	Ziske
1961	**Wright**	**Wright**	**Wright**	Faulk
1962	Kimball	Breer	Wright	Wright
1963	Wright	Mills	M.Smith	Wright
1964	Mills	Wright	M.Smith	Mann
1965	Haynie	Mann	Whitworth	Berning

Year	LPGA	US Open	T'holders	Western
1966	Ehret	Spuzich	Whitworth	Wright
1967	Whitworth	a-LaCoste	—	Whitworth
1968	Post	Berning		
1969	Rawls	Caponi		
1970	Englehorn	Caponi	—	—
1971	Whitworth	Carner	—	—
1972	Ahern	Berning	Palmer	—
1973	Mills	Berning	—	—
1974	Haynie	Haynie	—	—
1975	Whitworth	Palmer	—	—
1976	Burfeindt	Carner	—	—
1977	Higuchi	Stacy	—	—
1978	Lopez	Stacy	—	—

Year	LPGA	US Open	duMaurier	D.Shore
1979	Caponi	Britz	Alcott	—
1980	Little	Alcott	Bradley	—
1981	Caponi	Bradley	Stephenson	—
1982	Stephenson	Anderson	Haynie	—
1983	Sheehan	Stephenson	Stacy	Alcott
1984	Sheehan	Stacy	Inkster	Inkster
1985	Lopez	Baker	Bradley	Miller
1986	**Bradley**	Geddes	**Bradley**	**Bradley**
1987	Geddes	Davies	Rosenthal	King
1988	Turner	Neumann	Little	Alcott
1989	Lopez	King	Green	Inkster
1990	Daniel	King	Johnston	King
1991	Mallon	Mallon	Scranton	Alcott
1992	King	Sheehan	Steinhaur	Mochrie

Major Championships (Cont.)

SENIOR PGA

PGA Seniors Championship

First played in 1937. Two championships played in 1979 and 1984.

Multiple winners: Sam Snead (6); Gary Player and Eddie Williams (3); Julius Boros, Jock Hutchison, Don January, Arnold Palmer, Paul Runyan, Gene Sarazen and Al Watrous (2).

Year		Year		Year		Year	
1937	Jock Hutchison	1952	Ernest Newnham	1967	Sam Snead	1980	Arnold Palmer*
1938	Fred McLeod*	1953	Harry Schwab	1968	Chandler Harper	1981	Miller Barber
1939	Not held	1954	Gene Sarazen	1969	Tommy Bolt	1982	Don January
		1955	Mortie Dutra			1983	Not held
1940	Otto Hackbarth*	1956	Pete Burke	1970	Sam Snead	1984	Arnold Palmer
1941	Jack Burke	1957	Al Watrous	1971	Julius Boros	1984	Peter Thomson
1942	Eddie Williams	1958	Gene Sarazen	1972	Sam Snead	1985	Not held
1943	Not held	1959	Willie Goggin	1973	Sam Snead	1986	Gary Player
1944	Not held			1974	Robert de Vicenzo	1987	Chi Chi Rodriguez
1945	Eddie Williams	1960	Dick Metz	1975	Charlie Sifford*	1988	Gary Player
1946	Eddie Williams*	1961	Paul Runyan	1976	Pete Cooper	1989	Larry Mowry
1947	Jock Hutchison	1962	Paul Runyan	1977	Julius Boros		
1948	Charles McKenna	1963	Herman Barron	1978	Joe Jiminez*	1990	Gary Player
1949	Marshall Crichton	1964	Sam Snead	1979	Jack Fleck*	1991	Jack Nicklaus
		1965	Sam Snead	1979	Don January	1992	Lee Trevino
1950	Al Watrous	1966	Fred Haas				
1951	Al Watrous*						

*PLAYOFFS

1938: McLeod def. Otto Hackbarth in 18 holes. **1940:** Hackbarth def. Jock Hutchison in 36 holes. **1946:** Williams def. Jock Hutchison in 18 holes. **1951:** Watrous def. Jock Hutchison in 18 holes. **1975:** Sifford def. Fred Wampler on 1st extra hole. **1978:** Jiminez def. Joe Cheves and M.de la Torre on 1st extra hole. **1979:** Fleck def. Bill Johnston on 1st extra hole. **1980:** Palmer def. Paul Harney on 1st extra hole.

U.S. Senior Open

Established in 1980 for senior players 55 years-old and over, the minimum age was dropped to 50 (the PGA Seniors Tour entry age) in 1981. Arnold Palmer, Billy Casper, Orville Moody, Jack Nicklaus and Lee Trevino are the only golfers who have won both the U.S. Open and U.S. Senior Open.

Multiple winners: Miller Barber (3); Gary Player (2).

Year		Year		Year		Year	
1980	Roberto deVicenzo	1984	Miller Barber	1987	Gary Player	1990	Lee Trevino
1981	Arnold Palmer*	1985	Miller Barber	1988	Gary Player*	1991	Jack Nicklaus*
1982	Miller Barber	1986	Dale Douglass	1989	Orville Moody	1992	Larry Laoretti
1983	Bill Casper*						

*PLAYOFFS

1981: Palmer (70) def. Bob Stone (74) and Billy Casper (77) in 18 holes. **1983:** Tied at 75 after 18-hole playoff, Casper def. Rod Funseth with a birdie on the 1st extra hole. **1988:** Player (68) def. Bob Charles (70) in 18 holes. **1991:** Nicklaus (65) def. Chi Chi Rodriguez (69) in 18 holes.

Senior Players Championship

First played in 1983 and contested in Cleveland (1983-86), Ponte Vedra, Fla. (1987-89), and Dearborn, Mich. (since 1990).

Multiple winner: Arnold Palmer (2).

Year		Year		Year		Year	
1983	Miller Barber	1986	Chi Chi Rodriguez	1989	Orville Moody	1991	Jim Albus
1984	Arnold Palmer	1987	Gary Player	1990	Jack Nicklaus	1992	Lee Trevino
1985	Arnold Palmer	1988	Billy Casper				

The Tradition

First played in 1989 and played every year since at the Golf Club at Desert Mountain in Scottsdale, Ariz.

Multiple winner: Jack Nicklaus (2).

Year		Year		Year		Year	
1989	Don Bies	1990	Jack Nicklaus	1991	Jack Nicklaus	1992	Lee Trevino

Grand Slam Summary

Officially, the Senior Slam of Golf; sanctioned in 1992 by the PGA Tour to promote a year-end (tentatively set for January, 1993) match involving the winners of the Senior Tour's top 72-hole events—The Tradition, the PGA Senior Championship, the Senior Players Championship and the U.S. Senior Open. Jack Nicklaus won three of the four events in 1991, but no one has won all four in one season.

Three wins in one year: Jack Nicklaus (1991).

Two wins in one year: Gary Player (twice); Orville Moody, Jack Nicklaus, Arnold Palmer and Lee Trevino (once).

Year	Tradition	PGA Sr.	Players	US Open	Year	Tradition	PGA Sr.	Players	US Open
1983	—	—	M. Barber	Casper	1988	—	Player	Casper	Player
1984	—	Palmer*	Palmer	M. Barber	1989	Bies	Mowry	Moody	Moody
1985	—	Thomson	Palmer	M. Barber	1990	Nicklaus	Player	Nicklaus	Trevino
1986	—	Player	Rodriguez	Douglass	1991	Nicklaus	Nicklaus	Albus	Nicklaus
1987	—	Rodriguez	Player	Player	1992	Trevino	Trevino	Stockton	Laboretti

Annual Money Leaders

Annual money leaders on the PGA, European PGA, Senior PGA and LPGA tours. European PGA earnings listed in pounds sterling (£).

PGA

Multiple leaders: Jack Nicklaus (8); Ben Hogan and Tom Watson (5); Arnold Palmer (4); Sam Snead and Curtis Strange (3); Julius Boros, Billy Casper, Tom Kite and Byron Nelson (2).

Year		Earnings	Year		Earnings	Year		Earnings
1934	Paul Runyan	$ 6,767	1954	Bob Toski	$ 65,820	1973	Jack Nicklaus	$308,362
1935	Johnny Revolta	9,543	1955	Julius Boros	63,122	1974	Johnny Miller	353,021
1936	Horton Smith	7,682	1956	Ted Kroll	72,836	1975	Jack Nicklaus	298,149
1937	Harry Cooper	14,139	1957	Dick Mayer	65,835	1976	Jack Nicklaus	266,438
1938	Sam Snead	19,534	1958	Arnold Palmer	42,608	1977	Tom Watson	310,653
1939	Henry Picard	10,303	1959	Art Wall	53,168	1978	Tom Watson	362,429
						1979	Tom Watson	462,636
1940	Ben Hogan	10,655	1960	Arnold Palmer	75,263			
1941	Ben Hogan	18,358	1961	Gary Player	64,540	1980	Tom Watson	530,808
1942	Ben Hogan	13,143	1962	Arnold Palmer	81,448	1981	Tom Kite	365,699
1943	No records kept		1963	Arnold Palmer	128,230	1982	Craig Stadler	446,462
1944	Byron Nelson	37,968	1964	Jack Nicklaus	113,285	1983	Hal Sutton	426,668
1945	Byron Nelson	63,336	1965	Jack Nicklaus	140,752	1984	Tom Watson	476,260
1946	Ben Hogan	42,556	1966	Billy Casper	121,945	1985	Curtis Strange	542,321
1947	Jimmy Demaret	27,937	1967	Jack Nicklaus	188,998	1986	Greg Norman	653,296
1948	Ben Hogan	32,112	1968	Billy Casper	205,169	1987	Curtis Strange	925,941
1949	Sam Snead	31,594	1969	Frank Beard	164,707	1988	Curtis Strange	1,147,644
1950	Sam Snead	35,759				1989	Tom Kite	1,395,278
1951	Lloyd Mangrum	26,089	1970	Lee Trevino	157,037			
1952	Julius Boros	37,033	1971	Jack Nicklaus	244,490	1990	Greg Norman	1,165,477
1953	Lew Worsham	34,002	1972	Jack Nicklaus	320,542	1991	Corey Pavin	979,430

Note: In 1944-45, Nelson's winnings were in War Bonds.

EUROPEAN PGA

Multiple leaders: Seve Ballesteros (6); Sandy Lyle (3); Gay Brewer, Bernard Hunt, Bernhard Langer, Peter Thomson and Ian Woosnam (2).

Year		Earnings	Year		Earnings	Year		Earnings
1961	Bernard Hunt	£ 4,492	1972	Bob Charles	£18,538	1983	Nick Faldo	£140,761
1962	Peter Thomson	5,674	1973	Tony Jacklin	24,839	1984	Bernhard Langer	160,883
1963	Bernard Hunt	7,209	1974	Peter Oosterhuis	32,127	1985	Sandy Lyle	199,020
1964	Neil Colos	7,890	1975	Dale Hayes	20,507	1986	Seve Ballesteros	259,275
1965	Peter Thomson	7,011	1976	Seve Ballesteros	39,504	1987	Ian Woosnam	439,075
1966	Bruce Devlin	13,205	1977	Seve Ballesteros	46,436	1988	Seve Ballesteros	502,000
1967	Gay Brewer	20,235	1978	Seve Ballesteros	54,348	1989	Ronan Rafferty	465,981
1968	Gay Brewer	23,483	1979	Sandy Lyle	49,233			
1969	Billy Casper	23,483	1980	Greg Norman	74,829	1990	Ian Woosnam	737,977
1970	Christy O'Connor	31,532	1981	Bernhard Langer	95,991	1991	Seve Ballesteros	744,236
1971	Gary Player	11,281	1982	Sandy Lyle	86,141			

SENIOR PGA

Multiple leaders: Don January (3); Miller Barber and Bob Charles (2).

Year		Earnings	Year		Earnings	Year		Earnings
1980	Don January	$44,100	1984	Don January	$328,597	1988	Bob Charles	$533,929
1981	Miller Barber	83,136	1985	Peter Thomson	386,724	1989	Bob Charles	725,887
1982	Miller Barber	106,890	1986	Bruce Crampton	454,299	1990	Lee Trevino	1,190,518
1983	Don January	237,571	1987	Chi Chi Rodriguez	509,145	1991	Mike Hill	1,065,657

Annual Money Leaders (Cont.)

LPGA

Multiple leaders: Kathy Whitworth (8); Mickey Wright (4); Patty Berg, JoAnne Carner and Nancy Lopez (3); Pat Bradley, Beth Daniel, Betsy King, Judy Rankin, Betsy Rawls, Louise Suggs and Babe Zaharis (2).

Year		Earnings	Year		Earnings	Year		Earnings
1950	Babe Zaharias	$14,800	1965	Kathy Whitworth	$ 28,658	1980	Beth Daniel	$231,000
1951	Babe Zaharias	15,087	1966	Kathy Whitworth	33,517	1981	Beth Daniel	206,978
1952	Betsy Rawls	14,505	1967	Kathy Whitworth	32,937	1982	JoAnne Carner	310,399
1953	Louise Suggs	19,816	1968	Kathy Whitworth	48,379	1983	JoAnne Carner	291,404
1954	Patty Berg	16,011	1969	Carol Mann	49,152	1984	Betsy King	266,771
1955	Patty Berg	16,497				1985	Nancy Lopez	416,472
1956	Marlene Hagge	20,235	1970	Kathy Whitworth	30,235	1986	Pat Bradley	492,021
1957	Patty Berg	16,272	1971	Kathy Whitworth	41,181	1987	Ayako Okamoto	466,034
1958	Beverly Hanson	12,639	1972	Kathy Whitworth	65,063	1988	Sherri Turner	350,851
1959	Betsy Rawls	26,774	1973	Kathy Whitworth	82,864	1989	Betsy King	654,132
			1974	JoAnne Carner	87,094			
1960	Louise Suggs	16,892	1975	Sandra Palmer	76,374	1990	Beth Daniel	863,578
1961	Mickey Wright	22,236	1976	Judy Rankin	150,734	1991	Pat Bradley	763,118
1962	Mickey Wright	21,641	1977	Judy Rankin	122,890			
1963	Mickey Wright	31,269	1978	Nancy Lopez	189,814			
1964	Mickey Wright	29,800	1979	Nancy Lopez	197,489			

All-Time Leaders

PGA, Senior PGA and LPGA leaders through 1991.

Tournaments Won

	PGA	No		**SENIOR PGA**	No		**LPGA**	No
1	Sam Snead	81	1	Miller Barber	24	1	Kathy Whitworth	88
2	Jack Nicklaus	70	2	Don January	22	2	Mickey Wright	82
3	Ben Hogan	63	3	Chi Chi Rodriguez	20	3	Patty Berg	57*
4	Arnold Palmer	60	4	Bruce Crampton	18	4	Betsy Rawls	55
5	Byron Nelson	52	5	Bob Charles	16	5	Louise Suggs	50
6	Billy Casper	51		Gary Player	16	6	Nancy Lopez	44
7	Walter Hagen	40	7	Peter Thomson	11	7	JoAnne Carner	42
	Cary Middlecoff	40	8	Mike Hill	10		Sandra Haynie	42
9	Gene Sarazen	38		Orville Moody	10	9	Carol Mann	38
10	Lloyd Mangrum	36		Arnold Palmer	10	10	Babe Zaharias	31
11	Horton Smith	32		Lee Trevino	10	11	Pat Bradley	30
	Tom Watson	32	12	Billy Casper	9	12	Amy Alcott	29
13	Harry Cooper	31	13	George Archer	8		Jane Blaylock	29
	Jimmy Demaret	31		Lee Elder	8	14	Beth Daniel	27
15	Leo Diegel	30		Gene Littler	8	15	Judy Rankin	26
							Patty Sheehan	26

Note: Patty Berg's total includes 13 official pro wins prior to formation of LPGA in 1950.

Money Won

	PGA	Earnings		**SENIOR PGA**	Earnings		**LPGA**	Earnings
1	Tom Kite	$6,655,474	1	Bob Charles	$3,168,642	1	Pat Bradley	$4,109,165
2	Tom Watson	5,729,108	2	Chi Chi Rodriguez	3,029,172	2	Beth Daniel	3,362,984
3	Curtis Strange	5,629,225	3	Miller Barber	2,777,540	3	Betsy King	3,355,322
4	Jack Nicklaus	5,294,261	4	Bruce Crampton	2,662,039	4	Nancy Lopez	3,180,243
5	Lanny Wadkins	5,265,876	5	Gary Player	2,449,180	5	Patty Sheehan	3,172,668
6	Payne Stewart	5,059,959	6	Dale Douglass	2,375,069	6	Amy Alcott	2,750,125
7	Ben Crenshaw	4,690,831	7	Mike Hill	2,373,439	7	JoAnne Carner	2,473,762
8	Greg Norman	4,571,466	8	Orville Moody	2,364,006	8	Ayako Okamoto	2,391,903
9	Hale Irwin	4,488,732	9	Harold Henning	2,153,218	9	Jan Stephenson	1,881,552
10	Paul Azinger	4,372,987	10	Don January	2,075,981	10	Kathy Whitworth	1,722,440
11	Ray Floyd	4,165,562	11	Al Geiberger	2,034,115	11	Hollis Stacy	1,585,384
12	Fred Couples	4,122,727	12	Charles Coody	1,964,457	12	Jane Geddes	1,568,378
13	Craig Stadler	4,090,523	13	Lee Trevino	1,922,940	13	Rosie Jones	1,544,306
14	Chip Beck	4,011,553	14	George Archer	1,811,208	14	Juli Inkster	1,447,943
15	Bruce Lietzke	4,008,896	15	Dave Hill	1,741,837	15	Sally Little	1,412,038

EUROPEAN PGA

Earnings listed in pounds sterling (£).

	Earnings			Earnings			Earnings
1 Seve Ballesteros	£2,889,973	6 Sandy Lyle	£1,677,769		11 Rodger Davis	£1,372,033
2 Ian Woosnam	2,613,578	7 Ronan Rafferty	1,665,886		12 Gordon Brand Jr	1,229,439
3 Nick Faldo	2,190,222	8 Sam Torrance	1,635,474		13 Howard Clark	1,226,089
4 Bernhard Langer	2,085,420	9 Mark McNulty	1,604,106		14 David Feherty	1,116,500
5 Jose Maria Olazabal	1,753,744	10 Mark James	1,428,931		15 Eammon Darcy	1,059,951

Annual Awards
PGA of America Player of the Year

Awarded by the PGA of America; based on points scale that weighs performance in major tournaments, regular events, money earned and scoring average.

Multiple winners: Tom Watson (6); Jack Nicklaus (5); Ben Hogan (4); Julius Boros, Billy Casper and Arnold Palmer (2).

Year		Year		Year		Year	
1948	Ben Hogan	1960	Arnold Palmer	1972	Jack Nicklaus	1982	Tom Watson
1949	Sam Snead	1961	Jerry Barber	1973	Jack Nicklaus	1983	Hal Sutton
1950	Ben Hogan	1962	Arnold Palmer	1974	Johnny Miller	1984	Tom Watson
1951	Ben Hogan	1963	Julius Boros	1975	Jack Nicklaus	1985	Lanny Wadkins
1952	Julius Boros	1964	Ken Venturi	1976	Jack Nicklaus	1986	Bob Tway
1953	Ben Hogan	1965	Dave Marr	1977	Tom Watson	1987	Paul Azinger
1954	Ed Furgol	1966	Billy Casper	1978	Tom Watson	1988	Curtis Strange
1955	Doug Ford	1967	Jack Nicklaus	1979	Tom Watson	1989	Tom Kite
1956	Jack Burke	1968	No award	1980	Tom Watson	1990	Nick Faldo
1957	Dick Mayer	1969	Orville Moody	1981	Bill Rogers	1991	Corey Pavin
1958	Dow Finsterwald	1970	Billy Casper				
1959	Art Wall	1971	Lee Trevino				

PGA Tour Player of the Year

Awarded by the PGA Tour starting in 1990. Winner voted on by tour members from list of nominees.

Year		Year	
1990	Wayne Levi	1991	Fred Couples

PGA Senior Player of the Year

Awarded by the PGA Seniors Tour starting in 1990. Winner voted on by tour members from list of nominees.

Year		Year	
1990	Lee Trevino	1991	George Archer & Mike Hill

European Golfer of the Year

Officially, the Ritz Club Trophy; voting done by panel of European golf writers and tour members.

Multiple winners: Seve Ballesteros (3); Nick Faldo (2).

Year		Year		Year		Year	
1985	Bernhard Langer	1987	Ian Woosnam	1989	Nick Faldo	1991	Seve Ballesteros
1986	Seve Ballesteros	1988	Seve Ballesteros	1990	Nick Faldo		

Sony World Rankings

Begun in 1986, the Sony World Rankings combine the best golfers on the PGA and European PGA tours. Rankings are based on a rolling three-year period and weighed in favor of more recent results. While annual winners are not announced, certain players reaching No. 1 have dominated each year.

No. 1 players (through Sept., 1992): Greg Norman (6 times for 181 weeks); Seve Ballesteros (5 times, 60 weeks); Ian Woosnam (1 time, 50 weeks); Nick Faldo (4 times, 28 weeks); Fred Couples (2 times, 16 weeks); Bernhard Langer (1 time, 3 weeks).

Year		Year		Year		Year	
1986	Seve Ballesteros	1989	Seve Ballesteros	1990	Nick Faldo	1991	Ian Woosnam
1987	Greg Norman		& Greg Norman		& Greg Norman	1992	Fred Couples
1988	Greg Norman						& Nick Faldo

LPGA Player of the Year

Awarded by the LPGA; based on performance points accumulated during the year.

Multiple winners: Kathy Whitworth (7); Nancy Lopez (4); JoAnne Carner (3); Pat Bradley, Beth Daniel, Betsy King and Judy Rankin (2).

Year		Year		Year		Year	
1966	Kathy Whitworth	1973	Kathy Whitworth	1980	Beth Daniel	1987	Ayako Okamoto
1967	Kathy Whitworth	1974	JoAnne Carner	1981	JoAnne Carner	1988	Nancy Lopez
1968	Kathy Whitworth	1975	Sandra Palmer	1982	JoAnne Carner	1989	Betsy King
1969	Kathy Whitworth	1976	Judy Rankin	1983	Patty Sheehan	1990	Beth Daniel
1970	Sandra Haynie	1977	Judy Rankin	1984	Betsy King	1991	Pat Bradley
1971	Kathy Whitworth	1978	Nancy Lopez	1985	Nancy Lopez		
1972	Kathy Whitworth	1979	Nancy Lopez	1986	Pat Bradley		

The Skins Game

The Skins Game is a made-for-TV, $450,000 shootout between four premier golfers playing 18 holes over two days (nine each day). Each hole is counted as a skin with the first six skins worth $15,000 apiece, the second six worth $25,000, and the last six worth $35,000. If a hole is tied, the money is added to the worth of the next hole. The PGA Skins Game was started in 1983, followed by the Senior Skins in 1988 and the LPGA Skins in 1990. Due to scheduling conflicts, the LPGA Skins was not played in 1991.

PGA Skins

Played in late November.

Total Winnings: Jack Nicklaus ($650,000); Fuzzy Zoeller ($625,000); Curtis Strange ($605,000); Lee Trevino ($435,000); Raymond Floyd ($350,000); Payne Stewart ($260,000); Arnold Palmer ($245,000); Tom Watson ($230,000); Gary Player ($170,000); and John Daly ($120,000).

Year	Winner	Earnings	Outskinned	
1983	Gary Player	$170,000	Palmer	$140,000
			Nicklaus	40,000
			Watson	10,000
1984	Jack Nicklaus	$240,000	Watson	$120,000
			Palmer	0
			Player	0
1985	Fuzzy Zoeller	$225,000	Watson	$100,000
			Palmer	80,000
			Nicklaus	15,000
1986	Fuzzy Zoeller	$370,000	Trevino	$55,000
			Palmer	25,000
			Nicklaus	0
1987	Lee Trevino	$310,000	Nicklaus	$70,000
			Zoeller	70,000
			Palmer	0
1988	Ray Floyd	$290,000	Nicklaus	$125,000
			Trevino	35,000
			Strange	0
1989	Curtis Strange	$265,000	Nicklaus	$90,000
			Floyd	60,000
			Trevino	35,000
1990	Curtis Strange	$220,000	Norman	$90,000
			Faldo	70,000
			Nicklaus	70,000
1991	Payne Stewart	$260,000	Daly	$160,000
			Strange	120,000
			Nicklaus	0

Senior Skins

Played in early January.

Total Winnings: Arnold Palmer ($550,000); Jack Nicklaus ($545,000); Chi Chi Rodriguez ($540,000); Lee Trevino ($225,000); Gary Player ($130,000); Billy Casper ($80,000); and Sam Snead (0).

Year	Winner	Earnings	Outskinned	
1988	C.C.Rodriguez	$300,000	Player	$40,000
			Palmer	20,000
			Snead	0
1989	C.C.Rodriguez	$120,000	Player	$90,000
			Casper	80,000
			Palmer	70,000
1990	Arnold Palmer	$240,000	Nicklaus	$140,000
			Trevino	70,000
			Player	0
1991	Jack Nicklaus	$310,000	Trevino	$125,000
			Palmer	15,000
			Player	0
			Rodriguez	0
1992	Arnold Palmer	$205,000	Rodriguez	$120,000
			Nicklaus	95,000
			Trevino	30,000

LPGA Skins

Played in late May.

Total Winnings: Jan Stephenson ($270,000); Nancy Lopez ($210,000); Pat Bradley ($200,000); JoAnne Carner ($110,000); Meg Mallon ($65,000); and Betsy King ($45,000).

Year	Winner	Earnings	Outskinned	
1990	Jan Stephenson	$200,000	Carner	$110,000
			Lopez	95,000
			King	45,000
1991	Not held.			
1992	Pat Bradley	$200,000	Lopez	$115,000
			Stephenson	70,000
			Mallon	65,000

National Team Competition

MEN

Ryder Cup

The Ryder Cup was presented by British businessman Samuel Ryder in 1927 for competition between professional golfers from Great Britain and the United States. Since 1979, the British have been joined by the rest of Europe in challenging the U.S. The U.S. leads the series with a 22-5-2 record after 29 matches.

Year		Year		Year	
1927	United States, 9½-2½	1953	United States, 6½-5½	1973	United States, 19-13
1929	Britain-Ireland, 7-5	1955	United States, 8-4	1975	United States, 21-11
1931	United States, 9-3	1957	Britain-Ireland, 7½-4½	1977	United States, 12½-7½
1933	Britain-Ireland, 6½-5½	1959	United States, 8½-3½	1979	United States, 17-11
1935	United States, 9-3	1961	United States, 14½-9½	1981	United States, 18½-9½
1937	United States, 8-4	1963	United States, 23-9	1983	United States, 14½-13½
1939–45	Not held	1965	United States, 19½-12½	1985	Europe, 16½-11½
1947	United States, 11-1	1967	United States, 23½-8½	1987	Europe, 15-13
1949	United States, 7-5	1969	Draw, 16-16	1989	Draw, 14-14
1951	United States, 9½-2½	1971	United States, 18½-13½	1991	United States, 14½-13½

Playing Sites

1927—Worcester CC (Mass.); **1929**—Moortown, England; **1931**—Scioto CC (Ohio); **1933**—Southport & Ainsdale, England; **1935**—Ridgewood CC (N.J.); **1937**—Southport & Ainsdale, England; **1939-45**—Not held.

1947—Portland CC (Ore.); **1949**—Ganton GC, England; **1951**—Pinehurst CC (N.C.); **1953**—Wentworth, England; **1955**—Thunderbird Ranch & CC (Calif.); **1957**—Lindrick GC, England; **1959**—Eldorado CC (Calif.).

1961—Royal Lytham & St. Annes, England; **1963**—East Lake CC (Ga.); **1965**—Royal Birkdale, England; **1967**—Champions GC (Tex.); **1969**—Royal Birkdale, England; **1971**—Old Warson CC (Mo.); **1973**—Muirfield, Scotland; **1975**—Laurel Valley GC (Pa.); **1977**—Royal Lytham & St. Annes, England; **1979**—Greenbrier (W.Va.). **1981**—Walton Health GC, England; **1983**—PGA National GC (Fla.); **1985**—The Belfry, England; **1987**—Muirfield Village GC (Ohio); **1989**—The Belfry, England; **1991**—Ocean Course (S.C.).

Walker Cup

The Walker Cup was presented by American businessman George Herbert Walker in 1922 for competition between amateur golfers from Great Britain and the United States. The U.S. leads the series with a 29-3-1 record after 33 matches.

Year		Year		Year	
1922	United States, 8-4	1949	United States, 10-2	1971	Britain-Ireland, 13-11
1923	United States, 6-5	1951	United States, 7½-4½	1973	United States, 14-10
1924	United States, 9-3	1953	United States, 9-3	1975	United States, 15½-8½
1926	United States, 6½-5½	1955	United States, 10-2	1977	United States, 16-8
1928	United States, 11-1	1957	United States, 8½-3½	1979	United States, 15½-8½
1930	United States, 10-2	1959	United States, 9-	1981	United States, 15-9
1932	United States, 9½-2½	1961	United States, 11-1	1983	United States, 13½-10½
1934	United States, 9½-2½	1963	United States, 14-10	1985	United States, 13-11
1936	United States, 10½-1½	1965	Draw, 12-12	1987	United States, 16½-7½
1938	Britain-Ireland, 7½-4½	1967	United States, 15-9	1989	Britain-Ireland, 12½-11½
1940-46	Not held	1969	United States, 13-11	1991	United States, 14-10
1947	United States, 8-4				

WOMEN
Solheim Cup

The Solheim Cup was presented by the Karsten Manufacturing Co. in 1990 for competition between women professional golfers from Europe and the United States. The Cup was contested for the first time in 1990 in Orlando.

Year		Year	
1990	United States, 11½-4½	1992	Europe, 11½-6½

Curtis Cup

Named after British golfing sisters Harriot and Margaret Curtis, the Curtis Cup was first contested in 1932 between teams of women amateurs from the United States and the British Isles.

Competed for every other year since 1932 (except during World War II). The U.S. leads the series with a 20-5-2 record after 26 matches.

Year		Year		Year	
1932	United States, 5½-3½	1954	United States, 6-3	1974	United States, 13-5
1934	United States, 6½-2½	1956	British Isles, 5-4	1976	United States, 11½-6½
1936	Draw, 4½-4½	1958	Draw 4½-4½	1978	United States, 12-6
1938	United States, 5½-3½	1960	United States, 6½-2½	1980	United States, 13-5
1940	Not held	1962	United States, 8-1	1982	United States, 14½-3½
1942	Not held	1964	United States, 10½-7½	1984	United States, 9½-8½
1944	Not held	1966	United States, 13-5	1986	British Isles, 13-5
1946	Not held	1968	United States, 10½-7½	1988	British Isles, 11-7
1948	United States, 6½-2½	1970	United States, 11½-6½	1990	United States, 14-4
1950	United States, 7½-1½	1972	United States, 10-8	1992	British Isles, 10-8
1952	British Isles, 5-4				

Colleges
Men's NCAA Division I Champions

College championships decided by match play from 1897-1964, and stroke play since 1965.

Multiple winners (teams): Yale (21); Houston (16); Princeton (12); Oklahoma St.(7); Harvard and Stanford (6); LSU abd North Texas (4); Wake Forest (3); Florida, Michigan, Ohio St. and Texas (2).

Multiple winners (individuals): Ben Crenshaw and Phil Mickelson (3); Dick Crawford, Dexter Cummings, G.T.Dunlop, Fred Lamprecht, and Scott Simpson (2).

Year	Team winner	Individual champion	Year	Team winner	Individual champion
1897	Yale	Louis Bayard, Princeton	1900	Not held	—
1898	Harvard (spring)	John Reid, Yale	1901	Harvard	H.Lindsley, Harvard
1898	Yale (fall)	James Curtis, Harvard	1902	Yale (spring)	Chas.Hitchcock, Jr., Yale
1899	Harvard	Percy Pyne, Princeton	1902	Harvard (fall)	Chandler Egan, Harvard

Colleges (Cont.)
Men's NCAA Division I Champions

Year	Team winner	Individual champion	Year	Team winner	Individual champion
1903	Harvard	F.O.Reinhart, Princeton	1950	North Texas	Fred Wampler, Purdue
1904	Harvard	A.L.White, Harvard	1951	North Texas	Tom Nieporte, Ohio St.
1905	Yale	Robert Abbott, Yale	1952	North Texas	Jim Vichers, Oklahoma
1906	Yale	W.E.Clow Jr., Yale	1953	Stanford	Earl Moeller, Oklahoma St.
1907	Yale	Ellis Knowles, Yale	1954	SMU	Hillman Robbins, Memphis St.
1908	Yale	H.H.Wilder, Harvard	1955	LSU	Joe Campbell, Purdue
1909	Yale	Albert Seckel, Princeton	1956	Houston	Rick Jones, Ohio St.
1910	Yale	Robert Hunter, Yale	1957	Houston	Rex Baxter Jr., Houston
1911	Yale	George Stanley, Yale	1958	Houston	Phil Rodgers, Houston
1912	Yale	F.C.Davison, Harvard	1959	Houston	Dick Crawford, Houston
1913	Yale	Nathaniel Wheeler, Yale	1960	Houston	Dick Crawford, Houston
1914	Princeton	Edward Allis, Harvard	1961	Purdue	Jack Nicklaus, Ohio St.
1915	Yale	Francis Blossom, Yale	1962	Houston	Kermit Zarley, Houston
1916	Princeton	J.W.Hubbell, Harvard	1963	Oklahoma St.	R.H. Sikes, Arkansas
1917-18	Not held	—	1964	Houston	Terry Small, San Jose St.
1919	Princeton	A.L.Walker, Jr., Columbia	1965	Houston	Marty Fleckman, Houston
1920	Princeton	Jess Sweetster, Yale	1966	Houston	Bob Murphy, Florida
1921	Dartmouth	Simpson Dean, Princton	1967	Houston	Hale Irwin, Colorado
1922	Princeton	Pollack Boyd, Dartmouth	1968	Florida	Grier Jones, Oklahoma St.
1923	Princeton	Dexter Cummings, Yale	1969	Houston	Bob Clark, Cal St.-LA
1924	Yale	Dexter Cummings, Yale	1970	Houston	John Mahaffey, Houston
1925	Yale	Fred Lamprecht, Tulane	1971	Texas	Ben Crenshaw, Texas
1926	Yale	Fred Lamprecht, Tulane	1972	Texas	Ben Crenshaw, Texas
1927	Princeton	Watts Gunn, Georgia Tech			& Tom Kite, Texas
1928	Princeton	Maurice McCarthy, G'town	1973	Florida	Ben Crenshaw, Texas
1929	Princeton	Tom Aycock, Yale	1974	Wake Forest	Curtis Strange, W.Forest
1930	Princeton	G.T.Dunlap Jr., Princeton	1975	Wake Forest	Jay Haas, Wake Forest
1931	Yale	G.T.Dunlap Jr., Princeton	1976	Oklahoma St.	Scott Simpson, U.S.C
1932	Yale	J.W.Fischer, Michigan	1977	Houston	Scott Simpson, U.S.C
1933	Yale	Walter Emery, Oklahoma	1978	Oklahoma St.	David Edwards, Okla.St.
1934	Michigan	Charles Yates, Ga.Tech	1979	Ohio St.	Gary Hallberg, Wake Forest
1935	Michigan	Ed White, Texas	1980	Oklahoma St.	Jay Don Blake, Utah St.
1936	Yale	Charles Kocsis, Michigan	1981	Brigham Young	Ron Commans, U.S.C
1937	Princeton	Fred Haas, Jr., LSU	1982	Houston	Billy Ray Brown, Houston
1938	Stanford	John Burke, Georgetown	1983	Oklahoma St.	Jim Carter, Arizona St.
1939	Stanford	Vincent D'Antoni, Tulane	1984	Houston	John Inman, N.Carolina
1940	Princeton & LSU	Dixon Brooke, Virginia	1985	Houston	Clark Burroughs, Ohio St.
1941	Stanford	Earl Stewart, LSU	1986	Wake Forest	Scott Verplank, Okla.St.
1942	LSU & Stanford	Frank Tatum Jr., Stanford	1987	Oklahoma St.	Brian Watts, Oklahoma St.
1943	Yale	Wallace Ulrich, Carleton	1988	UCLA	E.J.Pfister, Oklahoma St.
1944	Notre Dame	Louis Lick, Minnesota	1989	Oklahoma	Phil Mickelson, Ariz.St.
1945	Ohio State	John Lorms, Ohio St.	1990	Arizona St.	Phil Mickelson, Ariz.St.
1946	Stanford	George Hamer, Georgia	1991	Oklahoma St.	Warren Schuette, UNLV
1947	LSU	Dave Barclay, Michigan	1992	Arizona	Phil Mickelson, Ariz.St.
1948	San Jose St.	Bob Harris, San Jose St.			
1949	North Texas	Harvie Ward, N.Carolina			

Women's NCAA Champions

College championships decided by stroke play since 1982.
   Multiple winners (teams): Florida, San Jose St. and Tulsa (2).

Year	Team winner	Individual champion	Year	Team winner	Individual champion
1982	Tulsa	Kathy Baker, Tulsa	1988	Tulsa	Melissa McNamara, Tulsa
1983	TCU	Penny Hammel, Miami	1989	San Jose St.	Pat Hurst, San Jose St.
1984	Miami-FL	Cindy Schreyer, Georgia	1990	Arizona St.	Susan Slaughter, Arizona
1985	Florida	Danielle Ammaccapane, Ariz.St.	1991	UCLA	Annika Sorenstam, Ariz.
1986	Florida	Page Dunlap, Florida	1992	San Jose St.	Vicki Goetze, Georgia
1987	San Jose St.	Caroline Keggi, N.Mexico			

Steve Swope/Allsport

Al Unser (left) and **Al Unser Jr.** became the first father and son winners of the Indianapolis 500 when Little Al won the race for the first time on May 24.

AUTO RACING

Sons Shine

*Al Unser Jr. and Davey Allison follow in their fathers'
footsteps with 500-mile wins at Indianapolis and Daytona.*

Sons of great drivers were the biggest auto racing stories of 1992, with Al Unser Jr. winning the Indianapolis 500 and Davey Allison taking the checkered flag at the Daytona 500.

Unser, whose father, Al Sr., won a record-tying four Indy 500s, and Allison, son of three-time Daytona 500 winner Bobby Allison, earned the biggest wins of their still-young careers after coming frustratingly close once before.

Little Al, whose boyish features belie his 30 years, lost one of the toughest Indy finishes ever in 1989 when he and eventual winner Emerson Fittipaldi battled wheel-to-wheel through the turns at 200 mph going into the final 10 miles of the race.

Going through Turn 3 on the 2.5-mile oval, their wheels bumped together and Unser skidded into the concrete wall. He was not injured, but losing a race like that after coming so close to winning weighed heavily on the youngster, whose family legacy also includes three-time Indy-winning uncle Bobby.

When he did finally get the elusive victory on May 24, it was in the closest finish in the storied history of the Indianapolis Motor Speedway as Unser held off a determined effort by unsung Canadian driver Scott Goodyear to win by just 43-hundredths of a second.

For cars traveling at close to 240 mph on the final straightaway, that amount of time is quicker than an eye-blink, but a victory nevertheless.

To get to that final showdown, Unser had to outwait Michael Andretti—the son of Indy winner Mario—and the driver who had dominated the 200-lap race, seemingly on the way to becoming the first second-generation Indy champion until his engine simply quit 10 laps from the end as he cruised toward the finish with a half-lap lead.

Adding to his dismay, Andretti's father and younger brother, Jeff, were among 13 crash victims in the wreck-filled race that saw more than half the laps run under caution flags. Jeff Andretti was the worst injured, suffering serious ankle and lower leg injuries that kept him hospitalized for more than a month.

As crushed as Michael was by the loss, Little Al, his boyhood playmate, was emotionally charged.

Father and son hugged during a tear-filled celebration and the younger Unser said, "I'd never been in Victory Lane. My dad won this race four times and I had never been there. This is just the greatest feeling in the world."

Unser and his team won a record $1,244,184 from the record purse of $7.52 million.

Mike Harris has been Motorsports Editor for the Associated Press since 1980. He has been covering the Indianapolis 500 since 1969 and covers more auto races during the year than any other writer in the country.

© C.D. Stouffer

Al Unser Jr. wins the closest race in the 76-year history of the Indianapolis 500 as he crosses the finish line just 43-hundredths of a second before Scott Goodyear.

It was a historic Indy for several other reasons, as well.

Not only did 57-year-old A.J. Foyt decide not to retire and run instead in his record 35th consecutive Indy 500, finishing 10th, but Lyn St. James finished 11th and earned Rookie of the Year honors after becoming only the second woman to race at Indy.

Roberto Guerrero, who set a qualifying record of 232.482 mph in his four-lap time trial—with a record single lap of 232.618—two weeks earlier, never even made the start of the race from his pole position. He lost control on a warmup lap, crashed and was unable to continue.

Sadly, the Brickyard was also the site of the first fatality in Indy-car racing since 1982, when Jovy Marcello, a rookie from the Philippines, died instantly in a crash during practice, 10 days before the race.

Indy runner-up Goodyear, who had been well on the way to becoming known as simply a journeyman, said he drove the last few laps of the race with tears in his eyes and disbelief in his mind.

But that near victory proved something to the 32-year-old racer and his team, who later in the season won the other Indy-car 500-miler—the Marlboro 500 at Michigan. The runner-up in that race was Paul Tracy, a budding 23-year-old star who helped give Canadian drivers a one-two Indy-car finish for the first time.

Meanwhile, the 31-year-old Allison had to deal with a stock car season that knocked his body and mind around like a ping-pong ball.

After several other top contenders in the Daytona 500 were eliminated in a crash early in the Feb. 16 race, Allison drove on to what was basically an easy victory, winning $244,050 after leading the last 30 laps on the 2.5-mile oval and beating Morgan Shepherd by two car-lengths.

His joy was similar to Unser's several months later at Indianapolis as Allison celebrated with his father, whose last Daytona victory came in 1988 when he barely held off a late charge by Davey.

"Really," the younger Allison said, "that second-place finish was even more exciting than winning this time because I followed my lifelong idol across the finish line. But having him with me after winning it is a real big thrill, too."

The senior Allison, whose career ended in a brutal crash at Pocono in July of '88, had to help his elder son find the courage to get through the next few months after those moments of elation at Daytona.

Davey twice was battered in race crashes early in the season that caused him physical pain. Then, in July at the same Pocono track where his father nearly lost his life, the younger Allison, too, was nearly killed in a wild crash in which his car barrel-rolled 11 times before nearly going over the wall.

Allison, who by that time had forged a lead in NASCAR's Winston Cup point standings over former champion Bill Elliott, spent five nights in a Pennsylvania hospital being treated for a variety of injuries that included a broken right collarbone, broken right forearm and a broken bone in his right hand. Nevertheless, he was back in a stock car by the following weekend at Talladega, Ala.

"There are just some things that you feel an obligation to do," Allison said. "As long as the doctors tell me it's okay to drive, and I feel I can do it without doing myself any more damage, I want to be in that race car. What else would I be doing if I wasn't driving?"

Even though Allison was quickly back up to speed, Elliott took control of the points race and appeared late in the season to be on the way to adding another title to the one he earned in 1988.

In his first year teamed with car-owner Junior Johnson, Elliott won four straight races early in the season and continued to drive consistently at or near the front into the late stages of the championship battle, with Allison tenaciously hanging on to the runner-up spot.

But Allison's troubles weren't over after the Pocono crash. Three days before the Aug. 16 NASCAR race at Michigan International Speedway, his younger brother, 27-year-old Clifford Allison, died of injuries received while practicing for the race.

Davey drove in that event, finishing fifth and saying, "Clifford died doing what he always wanted to do—driving a race car. Our family is devastated, but racing is something that has been our lives. I've been around it all my life, and you always know in your mind what can happen. But you go on because that's what Clifford would have wanted, and that's what we all want."

Allison, who added the Winston 500 on May 3 to his Daytona triumph to earn a $100,000 bonus from the series sponsor, failed in two chances to raise that bonus to $1 million.

King Richard Takes Final Victory Lap

The seemingly endless line of people stretched across the big room and out the door.

In it were people of just about every age, from three-year-olds to senior citizens. Most were talking excitedly and occasionally peering across the room at the table that marked their destination. At that table, the object of all this excitement was a man who appeared tall even sitting down.

Wearing his trademark feathered cowboy hat, dark glasses and white-toothed grin, Richard Petty talked and wrote, and wrote and talked.

There was no rush in his movements, no sign of irritation when someone asked for a special notation along with his name on the glossy picture that the King of stock car racing was signing.

This was Richard Petty at his best—the man of the people, the idol of stock car fans everywhere and a Southern icon.

Longtime friend and public relations man Harvey Duck says Petty has signed more than a million autographs. And he doesn't scribble, either. His signature is distinctive—even flowery—and it takes around 10 seconds to produce.

"I worked on that (signature) for the time it takes," Petty says. "In that time, there's just me and the fan. I have a chance to say something and so does the fan."

Looking at the endless line on this particular night, an observer asked Petty how he would ever end the evening without leaving some people without an autograph and angry at the long, unfulfilled wait.

"Well, I hate for that to happen," he said, looking away from the next fan for only a moment. "So, what I do is ask somebody to tell me when the time we've set aside for the appearance has about 15 minutes to run. Then I send somebody out to the end of the line and tell 'em not to let anybody else get in line after that last person. Then I just sit there and sign until that last person gets what they want."

Is it any wonder that Richard Petty's final season as a NASCAR stock car driver is filled with as much excitement and energy as a tour by some famous rock band?

752

Wide World Photos

At another stop on his 1992 farewell tour, NASCAR legend **Richard Petty** holds up a street sign presented to him by the City of Daytona Beach, Fla., at a ceremony naming a boulevard in his honor on July 4.

Petty announced in October of 1991 that 1992 was going to be his last as a driver, but that he would spend the season catering to his fans with a 29-race "Richard Petty Fan Appreciation Tour."

It has been some ride for the man generally acknowledged to be the greatest driver in NASCAR history. He has more Winston Cup championships (seven) and Daytona 500s (seven) than anyone else and his 200 career victories lap the field. Long-retired Dave Pearson is second on the all-time list with 105.

"This year hasn't been an easy thing because our time is so filled that it's almost impossible to get everything done that needs to be done," Petty said. "But meeting the people has been really nice. I just appreciate so much what they have done for me and for stock car racing over the years."

As much as the 55-year-old North Carolinian appreciates his fans, it can't be anywhere near as much as those millions of people appreciate the man who made modern stock car racing live.

Just as Arnold Palmer hitched up his pants and shot golf into the nation's consciousness in the 1960s, or Babe Ruth made people forget the 1919 Black Sox scandal and turned baseball into the American pastime, Petty put on his helmet and drove racing into a major sport over the past 34 years.

Bill Elliott, the 1988 Winston Cup champion and a current star on the NASCAR circuit, understands exactly how much Petty has meant to the sport that has been his life.

"He's been a role model for every driver and his sponsor and NASCAR," Elliott said. "I've always tried to work hard and be understanding of people and the fans because that's what Richard has always done."

Petty hasn't won since July 4, 1984 at Daytona, but that really doesn't matter because he remains beloved and will as long as people remember him.

Beginning in 1993, Petty will concentrate on his role as team owner, leaving the driving to somebody else.

"No matter how much I miss it, nobody's going to know it but me," the King said of his retirement from driving. "I just think that all the things that Richard Petty has done from a driver's standpoint should be a closed book.

"Then, what Richard Petty does as a car owner should be another book."

Jean-Pierre Lenfant/Allsport

Daytona 500 winner **Davey Allison** (right) shares the spotlight with father **Bobby**, who won the race three times, after Davey's victory on Feb. 16.

At Charlotte Motor Speedway later in May, Allison finished fourth in the Coca-Cola 600—won by two-time defending series champion Dale Earnhardt—despite suffering a concussion earlier that week in a crash after winning the Winston all-star event there.

Allison finished fifth at the last of NASCAR's Crown Jewel events—the Southern 500 in September, which was shortened by rain and gave three-time Winston Cup champion Darrell Waltrip his first Southern 500 victory in 18 tries.

It was the last major event Waltrip had failed to win and gave him his 84th career victory, tying him with Bobby Allison for third on the all-time victory list. It also was Davey Allison's final chance to win the Winston Million, which only Elliott has won (in 1985).

The all-time leader in NASCAR victories—Richard Petty—also made news in 1992 (see box).

While he was not a part of the championship battle, the 55-year-old Petty was in the headlines and on TV at every stop in the elite stock car series.

The seven-time series champion was calling it a career at the end of the season and used the 29-race schedule as a year-long "Fan Appreciation Tour."

Just three years Petty's junior, Harry Gant continued to amaze one and all, winning two more races, each time raising his record as the oldest man ever to win a Winston Cup event.

"Age is only a number," the 52-year-old Gant said. "I don't even think about that. I've got two more years on my contract."

Englishman Nigel Mansell, who had finished second in the Formula One championship a frustrating three times, finally put together a dream season and became the first citizen of Great Britain to win the world championship since James Hunt in 1976.

And Mansell did it in overwhelming fashion, driving his Williams-Renault race car to victory in the first five races of the season and clinching the championship on Aug. 30 at Budapest, Hungary in the 12th of 16 races with a second-place finish to defending series champion Ayrton Senna of Brazil.

Mansell's eight victories in the first 13 races of 1992 tied the single-season record set by Senna last year.

Ironically, only a week after wrapping up his first series title, Mansell, saying he could no longer deal with team owner Fran Williams, bid adieu to Formula One and signed a contract for 1993 with the Newman-Haas Racing team in the American-based Indy-car series.

He will take the ride vacated by Michael Andretti, who just days before Mansell's move announced he will drive in 1993 for Team McLaren in Formula One.

"Indy-car racing is a wonderful new challenge to me," Mansell said. "I've seen quite a few races on television and the competition clearly is good. Indianapolis and the other ovals will be a new experience. I'm ready to give it a go."

Andretti, who turned 30 in October, has dreamed of driving in Formula One since watching his father race in the international grand prix series as a youngster.

Mario Andretti won the Formula One title in 1978 with Lotus and two years later was teamed at Lotus with a rookie named Nigel Mansell. Now the elder Andretti, who is 52 and has one more year on his current contract, will team again with the Englishman.

"I have very mixed emotions about this," Mario said. "I've totally enjoyed driving with my son as my teammate since 1989. We've traveled together and worked together and I'm going to miss him, of course. But I'm also happy for him because I know how much he has wanted this."

Michael, who remained locked in the Indy-car championship battle late in the season with Unser, Bobby Rahal and Fittipaldi, was excited by the big move.

"I consider it a major challenge to prove I can be competitive over there," he said. "Let's face it, I'm very, very fortunate to be driving for McLaren, which is the best team in the world. When this opportunity came along, there was no turning back.

"I'm looking forward to carrying the American flag over there," added Michael, who said he will make sure there is a replica of the American flag affixed to his helmet. "Formula One has been in desperate need of an American driver, and I hope I can do the job."

Andretti said his biggest regret in leaving the Indy-car series at this point in his career is that he has not yet won the Indy

Mike Hewitt/Allsport

England's **Nigel Mansell** ran off with the Formula One driving championship in 1992, then quit to race Indy-cars.

500, although he has come close twice. But Ron Dennis, managing director of McLaren, said the possibility remained open that Andretti could be back at Indianapolis in '93, if the schedule permits and he can find a competitive ride.

"The problem in the past is that all the top drivers have wanted to have a complete season in CART [now IndyCar]," Dennis said. "Therefore, that opportunity has never presented itself. I do not think that bringing a Formula One driver to race at Indianapolis would be a smart thing. I do think that Michael could well be seen in a McLaren at Indianapolis sometime in the future. Highly unlikely next year, but a definite possibility in the future."

Since there is no conflict between Formula One and Indy on the tentative 1993 schedule, Dennis was asked if Andretti could possibly drive in the 500 for someone else.

"If Michael asked to participate at Indianapolis next year, we would carefully consider it and it is not ruled out. It is a possibility, but it is not a contractual right."

Marlboro Racing Team

Michael Andretti, the 1991 Indy-car champion, will drive for Team McLaren on the Formula One circuit in 1993.

Unser, too, appeared determined to try Formula One, although his father never ventured on to the world's glamour circuit. The younger Unser was negotiating late in the season to move into the seat vacated on the Williams team by Mansell.

Rahal, a two-time Indy-car champion and now co-owner of his own team, has no intention of leaving the series, but he did blow a big points lead for the second straight season.

The usually consistent Rahal lost the Indy-car PPG Cup title to Michael Andretti a year ago when Andretti won eight of the last 13 races to overcome the older driver's nearly season-long lead.

This season, Rahal built a margin of 34 points over Andretti, with Unser even further off the pace, then began to stumble, failing to finish races while the two younger drivers sliced into the margin.

"You want to win races, but you have to finish," said Unser, who took the lead late in the season with a string of 21 straight finishes in the points, dating to early in the 1991 season.

Elsewhere, NASCAR star Ricky Rudd earned the 1992 International Race of Champions title as an IROC rookie, winning the $175,000 first-place prize by taking a pair of seconds and a pair of thirds in the four-race all-star series.

The race victories went to Earnhardt at Daytona, Allison at Talladega, IMSA road-racing star Geoff Brabham at Michigan and Unser in another Michigan race. For Allison and Brabham those were their first IROC wins, while Unser became the all-time series leader with six wins.

As the season wound toward its close, Juan Manuel Fangio II of Argentina, the nephew of the five-time Formula One champion, was just one point from clinching his first IMSA Camel GT Prototype championship. With two races remaining, Fangio had six victories in his Toyota Eagle GTP and was ready to unseat Brabham as the four-time defending series champion.

Also in sports car racing, there were firsts in the two most important endurance races in the world, with an all-Japanese team winning the 24 Hours of Daytona in a Nissan prototype, and Peugeot giving France its first victory in 12 years at the 24 Hours of Le Mans.

Japanese drivers had never won a major 24-hour event, but that was remedied by Massahiro Hasemi, Kazuyoshi Hoshino and Toshio Suzuki, who set a Daytona record by averaging 112.897 mph as they covered 762 laps and 2,712.72 miles.

Peugeot, with Derek Warwick of England, Yannick Dalmas of France and Mark Blundell of England sharing the driving chores, went on to win the World Sports Car Championship.

Kenny Bernstein, an entrepreneur who owns a NASCAR team, an Indy-car team, a NHRA drag racing team and four Funny Car championships (as a driver), on Mar. 20, 1992 became the first drag racer in a piston-driven car to surpass 300 mph.

Bernstein, who made the switch to a Top Fuel dragster last season, had a terminal speed of 301.70 mph on the quarter-mile at Gainesville, Fla. He added two more 300 mph runs at the U.S. Nationals in Indianapolis on Labor Day weekend and remained the only man to have climbed the magic 300 barrier. □

THE 1993 SPORTS ALMANAC — INFORMATION PLEASE

AUTO RACING STATISTICS

THE SEASON IN REVIEW 1991-1992

NASCAR • INDYCAR • FORMULA 1

SEC A

PAGE 757

NASCAR Results

Winners of NASCAR Winston Cup races from Sept. 29, 1991 through Sept. 20, 1992.

LATE 1991

Date	Event	Winner (Pos.)	Avg.mph	Earnings	Pole	Qual.mph
Sept. 29	Tyson Holly Farms 400	Dale Earnhardt (16)	94.113	$69,350	H.Gant	116.871
Oct. 6	Mello Yello 500	Geoff Bodine (6)	138.984	92,200	M.Martin	176.499
Oct. 20	AC Delco 500	Davey Allison (10)	127.292	66,050	K.Petty	149.461
Nov. 3	Pyroil 500(K)	Davey Allison (13)	95.746	78,500	G.Bodine	127.58
Nov. 17	Hardee's 500	Mark Martin (4)	137.968	88,950	B.Elliott	177.937

Winning Cars: Ford Thunderbird (4)—Allison 2, Bodine and Martin; Chevy Lumina—Earnhardt.

1992 (through Sept. 20)

Date	Event	Winner (Pos.)	Avg.mph	Earnings	Pole	Qual.mph
Feb. 16	**Daytona 500**	Davey Allison (6)	160.256	$244,050	S.Marlin	192.213
Mar. 1	Goodwrench 500	Bill Elliott (2)	126.125	57,800	K.Petty	149.926
Mar. 8	Pontiac Excitement 400	Bill Elliott (1)	104.378	272,200*	B.Elliott	121.337
Mar. 15	Motorcraft 500	Bill Elliott (4)	147.746	71,000	M.Martin	179.923
Mar. 29	Transouth 500	Bill Elliott (2)	139.364	64,290	S.Marlin	163.067
Apr. 5	Food City 500	Alan Kulwicki (1)	86.316	83,360*	A.Kulwicki	122.474
Apr. 12	First Union 400	Davey Allison (7)	90.652	51,740	A.Kulwicki	117.242
Apr. 26	Hanes 500	Mark Martin (14)	78.086	59,300	D.Waltrip	92.956
May 3	**Winston 500**	Davey Allison (2)	167.608	89,325	E.Irvan	192.831
May 16	The Winston	Davey Allison (1)	132.678	300,000†	D.Allison	135.265
May 24	**Coca-Cola 600**	Dale Earnhardt (13)	132.980	125,100	B.Elliott	175.479
May 31	Budweiser 500	Harry Gant (15)	109.389	65,145	B.Bodine	147.408
June 7	Save Mart 300km	Ernie Ivan (2)	81.403	61,810	R.Rudd	90.985
June 14	Champion Spark Plug 500	Alan Kulwicki (6)	144.069	74,255	K.Schrader	162.165
June 21	Miller Genuine Draft 400	Davey Allison (1)	152.672	150,665*	D.Allison	176.268
July 4	Pepsi 400	Ernie Irvan (6)	170.495	86,300	S.Marlin	189.366
July 19	Miller Genuine Draft 500	Darrell Waltrip (8)	134.058	63,445	D.Allison	162.022
July 26	Diehard 500	Ernie Irvan (7)	176.308	81,815	S.Marlin	190.586
Aug. 9	Bud at the Glen	Kyle Petty (2)	85.895	50,895	D.Earnhardt	118.662
Aug. 16	Champion 400	Harry Gant (24)	143.056	71,545	A.Kulwicki	178.196
Aug. 29	Bud 500	Darrell Waltrip (9)	91.198	73,050	E.Irvan	120.535
Sept. 6	**Mountain Dew Southern 500**	Darrell Waltrip (5)	129.114	66,030	S.Marlin	162.249
Sept. 12	Miller Genuine Draft 400	Rusty Wallace (3)	104.662	47,115	E.Irvan	120.787
Sept. 20	Peak Antifreeze 500	Rickey Rudd (6)	115.289	64,965	A.Kulwicki	145.267

Note: The Winston (May 16) is a non-points race.
*Includes carryover Unocal 76 bonus for winning race from the pole—Elliott ($197,600); Kulwicki ($22,800); Allison ($60,800).
†Includes the following bonuses: pole ($50,000), first leg winner ($50,000) and sponsor R.J.Reynolds' bonus of $100,000 for winning both the Daytona 500 and The Winston in same year.
  Winning Cars: Ford Thunderbird (11)—Allison 4, Elliott 4, Kulwicki 2 and Martin; Chevy Lumina (7)—Irvan 3, Waltrip 3, and Earnhardt; Olds Cutless (2)—Gant 2; Pontiac Grand Prix (2)—Petty and Wallace.
  Remaining Races (6): Goody's 500 (Sept. 27); Tyson Holly Farms 400 (Oct. 4); Mello Yello 400 (Oct. 11); AC Delco 500 (Oct. 25); Pyroil 500 (Nov. 1); Hooter's 500 (Nov. 15).

1992 Race Locations

February—Daytona 500 at Daytona (Fla.) International Speedway. **March**—Goodwrench 500 at North Carolina Motor Speedway in Rockingham; Pontiac Excitement 400 at Richmond (Va.) International Speedway; Motorcraft 500 at Atlanta International Speedway; TranSouth 500 at Darlington (S.C.) International Raceway. **April**—Food City 500 at Bristol (Tenn.) International Raceway; First Union 400 at North Wilkesboro (N.C.) Speedway; Hanes 500 at Martinsville (Va.) Speedway. **May**—Winston 500 at Talladega (Ala.) Superspeedway; The Winston at Charlotte (N.C.) Motor Speedway; Coca-Cola 600 at Charlotte (N.C.) Motor Speedway; Budweiser 500 at Dover (Del.) Downs International Speedway. **June**—Save Mart 300km at Sears Point (Calif.) International Raceway; Champion Spark Plug 500 at Pocono (Pa.) International Raceway.
July—Miller Draft 400 at Michigan International Speedway in Brooklyn; Pepsi 400 at Daytona; Miller Draft 500 at Pocono; DieHard 500 at Talladega. **August**—Bud at the Glen at Watkins Glen (N.Y.) International; Champion 400 at Richmond; Bud 500 at Bristol. **September**—Mountain Dew Southern 500 at Darlington; Miller Genuine Draft 400 at Richmond; Peak 500 at Dover; Goody's 500 at Martinsville. **October**—Tyson Holly Farms 400 at North Wilkesboro; Mello-Yello 500 at Charlotte; AC Delco 500 at Rockingham. **November**—Pyroil 500 at Phoenix International Raceway; Hooters 500 at Atlanta.

NASCAR Results (Cont.)
1992 Daytona 500

Date—Sunday, Feb.16, 1992, at Daytona,FL International Speedway. **Distance**—500 miles; **Course**—2.5 miles; **Field**—42 cars; **Average speed**—160.256 mph; **Margin of victory**—two car lengths; **Time of race**—3 hours, 7 minutes, 12 seconds; **Caution flags**—4 for 22 laps; **Lead changes**—15 among 7 drivers; **Lap leader**—Davey Allison (127 laps); **Pole sitter**—Sterling Marlin at 192.213 mph; **Attendance**—150,000 (estimated); **TV Rating**—9.3/25 share (CBS).

	Driver (Pos.)	Hometown	Car	Laps	Ended	Earnings
1	Davey Allison (6)	Hueytown, Ala.	Ford Thunderbird	200	Running	$244,050
2	Morgan Shepherd (4)	Conover, N.C.	Ford Thunderbird	200	Running	161,300
3	Geoff Bodine (16)	Julian, N.C.	Ford Thunderbird	200	Running	116,250
4	Alan Kulwicki (41)	Concord, N.C.	Ford Thunderbird	200	Running	87,500
5	Dick Trickle (28)	Iron Station, N.C.	Olds Cutlass	200	Running	78,800
6	Kyle Petty (33)	High Point, N.C.	Pontiac Grand Prix	199	Running	67,700
7	Terry Labonte (34)	Archdale, N.C.	Chevy Lumina	199	Running	58,575
8	Ted Musgrave (40)	Franklin, Wisc.	Chevy Lumina	199	Running	52,750
9	Dale Earnhardt (3)	Doolie, N.C.	Chevy Lumina	199	Running	87,000
10	Phil Parsons (19)	Denver, N.C.	Ford Thunderbird	199	Running	49,150
11	Buddy Baker (24)	Sherrill's Ford, N.C.	Olds Cutlass	199	Running	38,375
12	Harry Gant (11)	Taylorsville, N.C.	Olds Cutlass	199	Running	51,100
13	Rick Mast (13)	Rockbridge Baths, Va.	Olds Cutlass	199	Running	40,355
14	Greg Sacks (9)	Winter Park, Fla.	Chevy Lumina	199	Running	38,790
15	Wally Dallenbach (37)	Basalt, Colo.	Ford Thunderbird	198	Running	29,700
16	Richard Petty (32)	Randleman, N.C.	Pontiac Grand Prix	198	Running	32,530
17	Phil Barkdoll (25)	Phoenix	Olds Cutlass	198	Running	27,960
18	Michael Waltrip (10)	Huntersville, N.C.	Pontiac Grand Prix	197	Running	37,140
19	Dorsey Schroeder (31)	Ballwin, Mo.	Ford Thunderbird	196	Running	25,720
20	Dave Marcis (23)	Avery's Creek, N.C.	Chevy Lumina	195	Running	26,210
21	A.J. Foyt (39)	Houston	Olds Cutlass	195	Running	23,055
22	Stanley Smith (30)	Chelsea, Ala.	Chevy Lumina	195	Running	24,150
23	Rick Wilson (38)	Mooresville, N.C.	Ford Thunderbird	195	Running	24,045
24	Hut Stricklin (42)	Calera, Ala.	Chevy Lumina	188	Running	27,740
25	Delma Cowart (27)	Savannah, Ga.	Ford Thunderbird	188	Running	23,285
26	Darrell Waltrip (12)	Franklin, Tenn.	Chevy Lumina	180	Running	33,580
27	Bill Elliott (2)	Dawsonville, Ga.	Ford Thunderbird	178	Running	60,225
28	Ernie Irvan (7)	Mooresville, N.C.	Chevy Lumina	166	Running	43,370
29	Mark Martin (5)	Jamesburg, N.C.	Ford Thunderbird	162	Running	49,675
30	Mike Potter (29)	Johnson City, Tenn.	Chevy Lumina	151	Fuel Pump	21,710
31	Rusty Wallace (17)	Concord, N.C.	Pontiac Grand Prix	150	Running	30,455
32	Bobby Hamilton (22)	Nashville	Olds Cutlass	125	Piston	27,350
33	Kerry Teague (21)	Harrisburg, N.C.	Olds Cutlass	122	Crash	22,445
34	Derrike Cope (20)	Kings Mountain, N.C.	Chevy Lumina	120	Radiator	23,115
35	Sterling Marlin (1)	Columbia, Tenn.	Ford Thunderbird	91	Crash	34,435
36	Dale Jarrett (35)	Conover, N.C.	Chevy Lumina	91	Crash	19,780
37	Ken Schrader (15)	Concord, N.C.	Chevy Lumina	91	Crash	30,500
38	Bobby Hillin Jr. (26)	Harrisburg, N.C.	Chevy Lumina	91	Crash	20,370
39	Chad Little (14)	Spokane, Wash.	Ford Thunderbird	90	Crash	22,760
40	Ricky Rudd (8)	Chesapeake, Va.	Chevy Lumina	79	Engine	34,350
41	Brett Bodine (18)	Harrisburg, N.C.	Ford Thunderbird	13	Distributor	25,150
42	Bob Schacht (36)	Elmhurst, Ill.	Olds Cutlass	7	Fuel Pump	18,250

NASCAR Point Standings

Official Top 10 NASCAR Winston Cup point leaders and Top 15 money leaders for 1991 and unofficial Top 10 point leaders and Top 15 money leaders for 1992 (through Sept. 20). Points awarded for places 1 to 40 and lap leaders. Earnings include bonuses. Listed are starts (Sts), races won (1st), top five finishes (Top5), poles won (PW) and points (Pts).

	FINAL 1991	Sts	1st	Top5	PW	Pts		1992 (thru Sept.20)	Sts	1st	Top5	PW	Pts
1	Dale Earnhardt	29	4	14	0	4287	1	Bill Elliott	23	4	12	2	3417
2	Ricky Rudd	29	1	9	1	4092	2	Davey Allison	23	4	14	2	3263
3	Davey Allison	29	5	12	3	4088	3	Harry Gant	23	2	10	0	3178
4	Harry Gant	29	5	15	1	3985	4	Alan Kulwicki	23	2	7	4	3139
5	Ernie Irvan	29	2	11	1	3925	5	Mark Martin	23	1	7	1	3065
6	Mark Martin	29	1	14	5	3914	6	Kyle Petty	23	1	5	1	3029
7	Sterling Marlin	29	0	7	2	3839	7	Ricky Rudd	23	1	7	1	3002
8	Darrell Waltrip	29	2	5	0	3711	8	Darrell Waltrip	23	3	9	1	2976
9	Ken Schrader	29	2	10	0	3690	9	Dale Earnhardt	23	1	6	1	2911
10	Rusty Wallace	29	2	9	2	3582	10	Morgan Shepard	23	0	3	0	2910

Money Leaders

FINAL 1991

		Earnings
1	Dale Earnhardt	$2,396,685
2	Davey Allison	1,732,924
3	Harry Gant	1,194,033
4	Ricky Rudd	1,093,765
5	Ernie Irvan	1,079,017

		Earnings
6	Mark Martin	$1,039,991
7	Ken Schrader	772,434
8	Bill Elliott	705,605
9	Sterling Marlin	633,690
10	Geoff Bodine	625,256

		Earnings
11	Darrell Waltrip	$604,854
12	Alan Kulwicki	595,614
13	Morgan Shepherd	521,147
14	Rusty Wallace	502,073
15	Dale Jarrett	444,256

1992 (through Sept.20)

		Earnings
1	Davey Allison	$1,474,190
2	Bill Elliott	1,085,465
3	Ernie Irvan	753,145
4	Dale Earnhardt	750,545
5	Alan Kulwicki	718,500

		Earnings
6	Harry Gant	$693,185
7	Darrell Waltrip	688,225
8	Mark Martin	624,255
9	Kyle Petty	621,500
10	Ricky Rudd	549,345

		Earnings
11	Morgan Sheperd	$517,235
12	Ken Schrader	483,995
13	Sterling Marlin	477,640
14	Rusty Wallace	475,840
15	Geoff Bodine	473,475

IndyCar Results

Winners of IndyCar (formerly CART) races from Oct. 6, 1991 through Sept 13, 1992.

LATE 1991

Date	Event	Winner (Pos.)	Avg.mph	Earnings	Pole	Qual.mph
Oct. 6	Bosch Spark Plug GP	Arie Luyendyk (11)	131.310	$63,452	R.Mears	178.74
Oct. 20	Toyota Monterey GP	Michael Andretti (1)	103.604	83,700	Ma.Andretti	110.555

Winning car: Lola-Chevrolet (2)—Mi.Andretti and Luyendyk.

1992 (through Sept. 13)
IndyCar did not release per race winnings in 1992.

Date	Event	Winner (Pos.)	Time	Avg.mph	Pole	Qual.mph
Mar. 22	Daikyo Indy Car GP	Emerson Fittipaldi (3)	2:20:33	77.561	A.Unser, Jr.	100.831
Apr. 5	Valvoline 200	Bobby Rahal (2)	1:31:56	130.526	Mi.Andretti	171.825
Apr. 12	Toyota GP of Long Beach	Danny Sullivan (2)	1:48:56.7	91.945	Mi.Andretti	106.251
May 24	**Indianapolis 500**	Al Unser, Jr. (12)	3:43:04.9	134.479	R.Guerrero	232.482
June 7	ITT Automotive Detroit GP	Bobby Rahal	1:58:20	81.988	Mi.Andretti	101.694
June 21	Budweiser/GI Joe's 200	Michael Andretti (2)	1:55:25.2	105.219	E.Fittipaldi	115.730
June 28	Miller Genuine Draft 200	Michael Andretti (5)	1:26:56.2	138.031	B.Rahal	162.924
July 5	New England 200	Bobby Rahal (1)	1:35:00.9	133.621	B.Rahal	170.956
July 19	Molson Indy Toronto	Michael Andretti (3)	1:52:21.9	97.898	B.Rahal	108.505
Aug. 2	Marlboro 500	Scott Goodyear (3)	2:48:53.7	177.625	Ma.Andretti	230.150
Aug. 9	Budweiser Cleveland GP	Emerson Fittipaldi (1)	1:30:38.5	133.292	E.Fittipaldi	142.778
Aug. 23	Texaco/Havoline 200	Emerson Fittipaldi (2)	1:48:26.7	110.656	P.Tracy	133.069
Aug. 30	Molson Indy Vancouver	Michael Andretti (1)	1:41:50.8	98.796	Mi.Andretti	110.746
Sept. 13	Pioneer Electronics 200	Emerson Fittipaldi (3)	1:51:23.4	107.352	Mi.Andretti	117.790

Winning cars: Lola Chevrolet (4)—Rahal 3 and Goodyear; Lola Ford (4)—Mi. Andretti 4; Penske Chevrolet (4)—Fittipaldi 4; Galmer Chevrolet (2)—Sullivan and Unser, Jr.
Remaining races (2): Bosch Spark Plug GP (Oct. 4); Toyota Monterery GP (Oct. 18).

1992 Race Locations

March—Daikyo Gold Coast GP at Surfers Paradise, Australia. **April**—Valvoline 200 at Phoenix International Raceway; Toyota GP at Long Beach, Calif. **May**—Indianapolis 500 at Indianapolis Motor Speedway. **June**—Detroit GP at Belle Isle, Mich.; Budweiser/G.I.Joe's 200 at Portland (Ore.) International Raceway; Miller 200 at Wisconsin State Fair Park Speedway in West Allis. **July**—New England 200 at New Hampshire International Speedway in Loudon; Molson Indy Toronto at Exhibition Place.

August—Marlboro 500 at Michigan International Speedway in Brooklyn; Budweiser Cleveland GP at Burke Lakefront Airport; Texaco/Havoline 200 at Road America in Elkart Lake, Wisc.; Molson Indy Vancouver at Pacific Place.

September—Pioneer 200 at Mid-Ohio Sports Car Course in Lexington. **October**—Bosch Spark Plug GP at Pennsylvania International Raceway in Nazareth; Toyota Monterey (Calif.) GP at Laguna Seca Raceway.

IndyCar Point Standings

Official Top 10 CART PPG Cup point leaders and Top 15 money leaders for 1991 and unofficial Top 10 point leaders (through Sept. 13) and Top 15 money leaders (through July 5) for 1992. CART changed its name to IndyCar in '92 and only released money figures periodically during the year. Points awarded for places 1 to 12, fastest qualifier and overall lap leader. Listed are starts (Sts), races won (1st), races running on finish (RAF), poles won (PW), and points.

FINAL 1991

		Sts	1st	RAF	PW	Pts
1	Michael Andretti	17	8	12	8	234
2	Bobby Rahal	17	1	13	1	200
3	Al Unser, Jr.	17	2	14	0	197
4	Rick Mears	17	2	11	6	144
5	Emerson Fittipaldi	17	1	11	2	140
6	Arie Luyendyk	17	2	12	0	134
7	Mario Andretti	17	0	12	0	132
8	John Andretti	17	1	13	0	105
9	Eddie Cheever	17	0	11	0	91
10	Scott Pruett	17	0	7	0	67

1992 (thru Sept.13)

		Sts	1st	RAF	PW	Pts
1	Al Unser, Jr.	14	1	14	1	163
2	Bobby Rahal	14	3	11	3	162
3	Michael Andretti	14	4	9	5	152
4	Emerson Fittipaldi	14	4	9	2	145
5	Scott Goodyear	14	1	10	0	96
6	Danny Sullivan	14	1	13	0	93
7	John Andretti	14	0	11	0	84
8	Mario Andretti	13	0	9	1	79
9	Raul Boesel	11	0	7	0	64
	Eddie Cheever	14	0	8	0	64

IndyCar Results (Cont.)
1992 Indianapolis 500

Date—Sunday, May 24, 1992, at Indianapolis Motor Speedway. **Distance**—500 miles; **Course**—2.5 mile oval; **Field**—33 cars; **Winner's average speed**—134.479 mph; **Margin of victory**—0.043 seconds; **Time of race**—3 hours, 43 minutes, 04.991 seconds; **Caution flags**—13 for 85 laps; **Lead changes**—18 by 6 drivers; **Lap leader**—Michael Andretti (161 laps); **Pole sitter**—Roberto Guerrero at 232.482 mph (course record); **Attendance**—400,000 (estimated); **TV Rating**—9.8/31 share (ABC).

	Driver (Pos.)	Hometown	Car	Laps	Ended	Earnings
1	Al Unser, Jr. (12)	Albuquerque, N.M.	Galmer-Chevy	200	Running	$1,244,184
2	Scott Goodyear (33)	Toronto	Lola-Chevy	200	Running	609,333
3	Al Unser (22)	Albuquerque, N.M.	Lola-Buick	200	Running	368,533
4	Eddie Cheever(2)	Aspen, Colo.	Lola-Ford Cosworth	200	Running	271,103
5	Danny Sullivan (8)	Aspen, Colo.	Galmer-Chevy	199	Running	211,803
6	Bobby Rahal (10)	Dublin, Oh.	Lola-Chevy	199	Running	237,703
7	Raul Boesel (25)	Miami/Brazil	Lola-Chevy	198	Running	191,503
8	John Andretti (14)	Indianapolis	Lola-Chevy	195	Running	186,203
9	A.J. Foyt (23)	Houston	Lola-Chevy	195	Running	189,883
10	John Paul Jr. (18)	West Palm Beach, Fla.	'90 Lola-Buick	194	Running	171,403
11	r-Lyn St. James (27)	Ft. Lauderdale, Fla.	'91 Lola-Chevy	193	Running	187,953
12	Dominic Dobson (29)	Fairfax, Calif.	'91 Lola-Chevy	193	Running	179,983
13	Michael Andretti (6)	Nazareth, Pa.	Lola-Ford Cosworth	189	Engine	295,383
14	Buddy Lazier (24)	Vail, Colo.	'91 Lola-Buick	139	Engine	164,283
15	Arie Luyendyk (4)	Scottsdale, Ariz.	Lola-Ford Cosworth	135	Crash	166,953
16	r-Ted Prappas (32)	Los Angeles	'91 Lola-Chevy	135	Gearbox	163,253
17	Gary Bettenhausen (5)	Martinsville, Ind.	Lola-Buick	112	Crash	150,803
18	Jeff Andretti (20)	Nazareth, Pa.	'91 Lola-Chevy	109	Crash	153,703
19	r-Brian Bonner (26)	Boston	'91 Lola-Buick	97	Crash	156,953
20	r-Paul Tracy (19)	West Hill, Ont.	'91 Penske-Chevy	96	Engine	160,053
21	r-Jimmy Vasser (28)	Discovery Bay, Calif.	'91 Lola-Chevy	94	Crash	170,853
22	Scott Brayton (7)	Coldwater, Mich.	Lola-Buick	93	Engine	173,683
23	Mario Andretti (3)	Nazareth, Pa.	Lola-Ford Cosworth	78	Crash	156,633
24	Emerson Fittipaldi (11)	Miami/Brazil	Penske-Chevy	75	Crash	138,703
25	Jim Crawford (21)	Tierra Verde, Fla.	Lola-Buick	74	Crash	167,503
26	Rick Mears (9)	Jupiter, Fla.	Penske-Chevy	74	Crash	136,403
27	Stan Fox (13)	Janesville, Wisc.	'91 Lola-Buick	63	Crash	136,683
28	r-Philippe Gache (16)	France	'91 Lola-Chevy	61	Crash	136,128
29	Gordon Johncock (31)	Hastings, Mich.	'91 Lola-Buick	60	Engine	136,003
30	Scott Pruett (17)	Dublin, Oh.	Truesports-Chevy	52	Engine	143,503
31	Tom Sneva (30)	Paradise Valley, Ariz.	'91 Lola-Buick	10	Crash	139,778
32	r-Eric Bachelart (15)	Brussels, Belgium	'90 Lola-Buick	4	Engine	144,228
33	Roberto Guerrero (1)	S.J.Capristrano, Calif.	Lola-Buick	0	Crash	286,378

Money Leaders
FINAL 1991

		Earnings			Earnings			Earnings
1	Michael Andretti	$2,461,734	6	Arie Luyendyk	$1,142,194	11	Danny Sullivan	$753,156
2	Rick Mears	2,369,865	7	Mario Andretti	1,037,217	12	Scott Brayton	722,234
3	Bobby Rahal	1,514,473	8	John Andretti	904,855	13	Jeff Andretti	685,335
4	Al Unser,Jr.	1,464,752	9	Eddie Cheever	797,652	14	Tony Bettenhausen	632,757
5	Emerson Fittipaldi	1,201,473	10	Scott Pruett	779,214	15	Scott Goodyear	632,610

1992 (through July 5)

		Earnings			Earnings			Earnings
1	Al Unser, Jr.	$1,553,266	6	Emerson Fittipaldi	$519,052	11	Al Unser	$368,533
2	Scott Goodyear	853,348	7	Danny Sullivan	504,816	12	Scott Pruett	357,791
3	Bobby Rahal	742,458	8	John Andretti	431,407	13	Raul Boesel	348,136
4	Michael Andretti	684,536	9	Scott Brayton	387,031	14	Mario Andretti	347,468
5	Eddie Cheever	537,602	10	Rick Mears	386,406	15	Ted Prappas	322,470

Formula One Results

Winners of Formula One Grand Prix races from Sept. 29, 1991 through Sept. 13, 1992.

LATE 1991

Date	Grand Prix	Winner (Pos.)	Time	Avg.mph	Pole	Qual.mph
Sept. 29	Spain	Nigel Mansell (2)	1:38:41.541	116.561	G.Berger	134.839
Oct. 20	Japan	Gerhard Berger (1)	1:32:10.695	125.702	G.Berger	138.515
Nov. 3	Australia	Ayrton Senna (1)	24:34.899	80.262	A.Senna	114.202

Note: Heavy rain shortened the Australian GP to just 32.858 miles.
Winning Constructors: McLaren-Honda (2)—Berger and Senna; Williams-Renault—Mansell.

1992 (through Sept. 13)

Date	Grand Prix	Winner (Pos.)	Time	Avg.mph	Pole	Qual.mph
Mar. 1	South Africa	Nigel Mansell (1)	1:36:45.320	118.251	N.Mansell	126.088
Mar 22	Mexico	Nigel Mansell (1)	1:31:51.587	123.762	N.Mansell	129.531
Apr 5	Brazil	Nigel Mansell (1)	1:36:51.856	118.191	N.Mansell	127.778
May 3	Spain	Nigel Mansell (1)	1:56:10.674	99.017	N.Mansell	132.435
May 17	San Marino	Nigel Mansell (1)	1:28:40.927	127.130	N.Mansell	137.372
May 31	Monaco	Ayrton Senna (3)	1:50:59.372	87.196	N.Mansell	93.651
June 14	Canada	Gerhard Berger (4)	1:37:08.299	117.318	A.Senna	124.233
July 5	France	Nigel Mansell (1)	1:38:08.459	111.401	N.Mansell	126.689
July 12	Britain	Nigel Mansell (1)	1:25:42.991	134.109	N.Mansell	148.030
July 26	Germany	Nigel Mansell (1)	1:18:22.032	145.897	N.Mansell	155.194
Aug 16	Hungary	Ayrton Senna (3)	1:46:19.216	107.139	R.Patrese	117.631
Aug 30	Belgium	Michael Schumacher (3)	1:36:10.721	118.948	N.Mansell	140.424
Sept. 13	Italy	Ayrton Senna (2)	1:18:15.349	146.450	N.Mansell	157.797

Winning Constructors: Williams-Renault (8)—Mansell 8; McLaren-Honda (4)—Senna 3 and Ber ger; Benetton-Ford—Schumacher.
Remaining Races (3): Portugal (Sept. 27); Japan (Oct. 25); Australia (Nov. 8).

1992 Race Locations

March—South African GP at Johannesburg; Mexican GP at Mexico City. **April**—Brazilian GP at Sao Paulo. **May**—Spanish GP at Barcelona; San Marino GP at Imola, Italy; Monaco GP in downtown Monte Carlo. **June**—Canadian GP at Montreal. **July**—French GP at Nevers; British GP at Silverstone in Towcester; German GP at Hockenheim. **August**—Hungarian GP at Hungaroring in Budapest; Belgian GP at Spa-Francorchamps. **September**—Italian GP at Monza in Milan; Portuguese GP at Estoril. **October**—Japanese GP at Suzuka. **November**—Australian GP at Adelaide.

Formula One Point Standings

Official Top 10 Formula One World Championship point leaders for 1991 and unofficial Top 10 point leaders for 1992 (through Sept. 13). Points awarded for places 1 to 6. Listed are starts (Sts), races won (1st), top six finishes (T/6), poles won, and points.

Note: Formula One does not keep Money Leader standings.

	FINAL 1991	Sts	1st	T/6	PW	Pts
1	Ayrton Senna, BRA	16	7	14	8	96
2	Nigel Mansell, GBR	16	5	10	2	72
3	Riccardo Patrese, ITA	16	2	11	4	53
4	Gerhard Berger, AUT	16	1	9	2	43
5	Alain Prost, FRA	15	0	8	0	34
6	Nelson Piquet, BRA	16	1	8	0	26½
7	Jean Alesi, FRA	16	0	7	0	21
8	Stefano Modena, ITA	16	0	3	0	10
9	Andrea De Cesaris, ITA	15	0	4	0	9
10	Roberto Moreno, BRA	14	0	4	0	8

	1992 (thru Sept. 13)	Sts	1st	T/6	PW	Pts
1	Nigel Mansell, GBR	13	8	11	11	98*
2	Michael Shumacher, GER	13	1	10	0	47
3	Ayrton Senna, BRA	13	3	7	1	46
	Riccardo Patrese, ITA	13	0	9	1	46
5	Gerhard Berger, AUT	13	1	7	0	27
	Martin Brundle, GBR	13	0	8	0	27
7	Jean Alesi, FRA	13	0	4	0	13
8	Mika Hakkinen, FIN	13	0	5	0	9
9	Michele Alboreto, ITA	13	0	3	0	5
	Andrea De Cesaris, ITA	13	0	3	0	5

*Clinches World Championship.

1992 Endurance Races

24 Hours of Daytona
Feb. 1-2 at Daytona Beach FL

Officially the Rolex 24 Hours of Daytona and first held in 1962 (as a 3-hour race). An IMSA Camel GT race for exotic prototype sports cars and contested over a 3.56-mile road course at Daytona International Speedway. Listed are drivers, home countries, car, prize money, and laps completed. Starting positions in parentheses.

1 (2) Masahiro Hasemi, Kazuyoshi Hoshino and Toshio Suzuki (JPN); NISSAN R91CP; $73,000; 762 laps (2,712.720) miles) at 112.897 mph.

2 (7) Davy Jones (USA), David Brabham (GBR), Scott Pruett (USA) and Scott Goodyear (CAN); JAGUAR XJR-12; 753 laps.

3 (9) Hurley Haywood (USA), Eje Elgh (SWE), Roland Ratzenberger (AUT) and Scott Brayton (USA); PORSCHE 962; 749 laps.

4 (6) Rocky Moran, P.J. Jones and Mark Dismore (USA); TOYOTA Eagle MKIII; 739 laps.

5 (14) Parker Johnstone, Dan Marvin, Jim Vasser and Steve Cameron (USA); ACURA Spice; 681 laps.

Fastest lap: Hasemi (JPN), Nissan R91CP; 130.118 mph (1:38.495).

24 Hours of Le Mans
June 20-21 at Le Mans, France

Officially the Le Mans Grand Prix d'Endurance and first held in 1923. Contested over the 8.451-mile circuit in Le Mans, France. Listed are drivers, countries, car, and laps completed.

1 Derek Warwick (GBR), Yannick Dalmas (FRA) and Mark Blundell (GBR); PEUGEOT 905; 352 laps (2,974.40 miles) at 123.89 mph.

2 Masanori Sekiya (JPN), Pierre-Henri Raphanel (FRA)and Kenny Acheson (IRE); TOYOTA TS010; 346 laps.

3 Mauro Baldi (ITA), Philippe Alliot and Jean-Pierre Jabouille (FRA); PEUGEOT 905; 345 laps.

4 Johnny Herbert (GBR), Volker Weidler (GER), Bertrand Gachot (FRA) and Maurizio Sala (BRA); MAZDA MX-R01; 336 laps.

5 Georges Fouche (SAF), Steven Andskar and Stefan Johansson (SWE); TOYOTA 92C-V; 336 laps.

Fastest lap: Jan Lammers (HOL), Toyota TS010; 143.208 mph (3:32.295).

THE 1993 INFORMATION PLEASE SPORTS ALMANAC

AUTO RACING STATISTICS

THROUGH THE YEARS
1911-1992
MAJOR RACES • LEADERS

SEC B

PAGE 762

NASCAR Circuit
The Crown Jewels

The four biggest races on the NASCAR circuit are the Daytona 500, the Winston 500, the Coca-Cola 600 and the Mountain Dew Southern 500. The Winston Cup Media Guide lists them as the richest (Daytona), the fastest (Winston), the longest (Coca-Cola) and the oldest (Southern). Winston has offered a $1 million bonus since 1985 to any driver who can win three of the four races. The only drivers to win three of the races in a single year are Lee Roy Yarbrough (1969), David Pearson (1976) and Bill Elliott (1985).

Daytona 500

Held early in the NASCAR season; 200 laps around a 2.5-mile high-banked oval at Daytona International Speedway in Daytona Beach, FL. First race in 1959, although stock car racing at Daytona dates back to 1936. Winning drivers who started from pole positions are in **bold** type.

Multiple winners: Richard Petty (7); Cale Yarborough (4); Bobby Allison (3); Bill Elliott (2).
Multiple poles: Buddy Baker and Cale Yarborough (4); Bill Elliott, Fireball Roberts and Ken Schrader (3); Donnie Allison (2).

Year	Winner	Car	Owner	MPH	Pole Sitter	MPH
1959	Lee Petty	Oldsmobile	Petty Enterprises	135.521	Bob Welborn	140.121
1960	Junior Johnson	Chevrolet	Ray Fox	124.740	Cotton Owens	149.892
1961	Marvin Panch	Pontiac	Smokey Yunick	149.601	Fireball Roberts	155.709
1962	**Fireball Roberts**	Pontiac	Smokey Yunick	152.529	Fireball Roberts	156.999
1963	Tiny Lund	Ford	Wood Brothers	151.566	Fireball Roberts	160.943
1964	Richard Petty	Plymouth	Petty Enterprises	154.344	Paul Goldsmith	174.910
1965-a	Fred Lorenzen	Ford	Holman-Moody	141.539	Darel Dieringer	171.151
1966-b	**Richard Petty**	Plymouth	Petty Enterprises	160.627	Richard Petty	175.165
1967	Mario Andretti	Ford	Holman-Moody	149.926	Curtis Turner	180.831
1968	**Cale Yarborough**	Mercury	Wood Brothers	143.251	Cale Yarborough	189.222
1969	Lee Roy Yarbrough	Ford	Junior Johnson	157.950	Buddy Baker	188.901
1970	Pete Hamilton	Plymouth	Petty Enterprises	149.601	Cale Yarborough	194.015
1971	Richard Petty	Plymouth	Petty Enterprises	144.462	A.J.Foyt	182.744
1972	A.J.Foyt	Mercury	Wood Brothers	161.550	Bobby Issac	186.632
1973	Richard Petty	Dodge	Petty Enterprises	157.205	Buddy Baker	185.662
1974-c	Richard Petty	Dodge	Petty Enterprises	140.894	David Pearson	185.017
1975	Benny Parsons	Chevrolet	L.G.DeWitt	153.649	Donnie Allison	185.827
1976	David Pearson	Mercury	Wood Brothers	152.181	Ramo Stott	183.456
1977	Cale Yarborough	Chevrolet	Junior Johnson	153.218	Donnie Allison	188.048
1978	Bobby Allison	Ford	Bud Moore	159.730	Cale Yarborough	187.536
1979	Richard Petty	Oldsmobile	Petty Enterprises	143.977	Buddy Baker	196.049
1980	**Buddy Baker**	Oldsmobile	Ranier Racing	177.602*	Buddy Baker	194.099
1981	Richard Petty	Buick	Petty Enterprises	169.651	Bobby Allison	194.624
1982	Bobby Allison	Buick	DiGard Racing	153.991	Benny Parsons	196.317
1983	Cale Yarborough	Pontiac	Ranier Racing	155.979	Ricky Rudd	198.864
1984	**Cale Yarborough**	Chevrolet	Ranier Racing	150.994	Cale Yarborough	201.848
1985	**Bill Elliott**	Ford	Melling Racing	172.265	Bill Elliott	205.114
1986	Geoff Bodine	Chevrolet	Hendrick Motorsports	148.124	Bill Elliott	205.039
1987	**Bill Elliott**	Ford	Melling Racing	176.263	Bill Elliott	210.364†
1988	Bobby Allison	Buick	Stavola Bros.Racing	137.531	Ken Schrader	193.823
1989	Darrell Waltrip	Chevrolet	Hendrick Motorsports	148.466	Ken Schrader	196.996
1990	Derrike Cope	Chevrolet	Whitcomb Racing	165.761	Ken Schrader	196.515
1991	Ernie Irvan	Chevrolet	Morgan McClure Racing	148.148	Davey Allison	195.955
1992	Davey Allison	Ford	Robert Yates	160.256	Sterling Martin	192.213

*Track and race record for Winning Time.
†Track and race record for Qualifying Time.
Notes: a—rain shortened 1965 to 332 + miles; **b**—rain shortened 1966 race to 495 miles; **c**—in 1974, race shortened 50 miles due to energy crisis.
Also: Pole sitters determined by pole qualifying race (1959-65); by two-lap average (1966-68); by fastest single lap (since 1969).

Winston 500

Held at Talladega (Ala.) Superspeedway. **Multiple winners:** Bobby Allison, Davey Allison, Buddy Baker and David Pearson (3); Darrell Waltrip and Cale Yarborough (2).

Year		Year		Year		Year	
1970	Pete Hamilton	1977	Darrell Waltrip	1983	Richard Petty	1988	Phil Parsons
1971	Donnie Allison	1978	Cale Yarborough	1984	Cale Yarborough	1989	Davey Allison
1972	David Pearson	1979	Bobby Allison	1985	Bill Elliott	1990	Dale Earnhardt
1973	David Pearson	1980	Buddy Baker	1986	Bobby Allison	1991	Harry Gant
1974	David Pearson	1981	Bobby Allison	1987	Davey Allison	1992	Davey Allison
1975	Buddy Baker	1982	Darrell Waltrip				
1976	Buddy Baker						

Coca-Cola 600

Held at Charlotte (N.C.) Motor Speedway. **Multiple winners:** Darrell Waltrip (5); Bobby Allison, Buddy Baker, David Pearson (3); Neil Bonnett, Dale Earnhardt, Fred Lorenzen, Jim Paschal, Richard Petty (2).

Year		Year		Year		Year	
1960	Joe Lee Johnson	1969	Lee Roy Yarbrough	1977	Richard Petty	1985	Darrell Waltrip
1961	David Pearson	1970	Donnie Allison	1978	Darrell Waltrip	1986	Dale Earnhardt
1962	Nelson Stacy	1971	Bobby Allison	1979	Darrell Waltrip	1987	Kyle Petty
1963	Fred Lorenzen	1972	Buddy Baker	1980	Benny Parsons	1988	Darrell Waltrip
1964	Jim Paschal	1973	Buddy Baker	1981	Bobby Allison	1989	Darrell Waltrip
1965	Fred Lorenzen	1974	David Pearson	1982	Neil Bonnett	1990	Rusty Wallace
1966	Marvin Panch	1975	Richard Petty	1983	Neil Bonnett	1991	Davey Allison
1967	Jim Paschal	1976	David Pearson	1984	Bobby Allison	1992	Dale Earnhardt
1968	Buddy Baker						

Mountain Dew Southern 500

Held at Darlington (S.C.) International Raceway. **Multiple winners:** Cale Yarborough (5); Bobby Allison (4); Buck Baker, Dale Earnhardt, David Pearson and Herb Thomas (3); Bill Elliott, Harry Gant and Fireball Roberts (2).

Year		Year		Year		Year	
1950	Johnny Mantz	1962	Larry Frank	1973	Cale Yarborough	1983	Bobby Allison
1951	Herb Thomas	1963	Fireball Roberts	1974	Cale Yarborough	1984	Harry Gant
1952	Fonty Flock	1964	Buck Baker	1975	Bobby Allison	1985	Bill Elliott
1953	Buck Baker	1965	Ned Jarrett	1976	David Pearson	1986	Tim Richmond
1954	Herb Thomas	1966	Darel Dieringer	1977	David Pearson	1987	Dale Earnhardt
1955	Herb Thomas	1967	Richard Petty	1978	Cale Yarborough	1988	Bill Elliott
1956	Curtis Turner	1968	Cale Yarborough	1979	David Pearson	1989	Dale Earnhardt
1957	Speedy Thompson	1969	Lee Roy Yarbrough	1980	Terry Labonte	1990	Dale Earnhardt
1958	Fireball Roberts	1970	Buddy Baker	1981	Neil Bonnett	1991	Harry Gant
1959	Jim Reed	1971	Bobby Allison	1982	Cale Yarborough	1992	Darrell Waltrip
1960	Buck Baker	1972	Bobby Allison				
1961	Nelson Stacy						

All-Time Leaders

NASCAR's all-time Top 20 drivers in victories, pole positions and earnings, based on records through 1991. Drivers active in 1991 in **bold** type.

	Victories			Pole Positions			Earnings	
1	**Richard Petty**	200	1	**Richard Petty**	127	1	**Dale Earnhardt**	$15,244,319
2	David Pearson	105	2	David Pearson	113	2	**Darrell Waltrip**	11,130,141
3	Bobby Allison	84	3	Cale Yarborough	70	3	**Bill Elliott**	10,958,644
4	Cale Yarborough	83	4	Bobby Allison	57	4	**Richard Petty**	7,406,539
5	**Darrell Waltrip**	81		**Darrell Waltrip**	57	5	Bobby Allison	7,102,233
6	Lee Petty	54	6	Bobby Isaac	51	6	**Rusty Wallace**	6,837,732
7	**Dale Earnhardt**	52	7	Junior Johnson	47	7	**Terry Labonte**	6,638,077
8	Ned Jarrett	50	8	Buck Baker	44	8	**Ricky Rudd**	6,094,705
	Junior Johnson	50	9	**Bill Elliott**	41	9	**Harry Gant**	5,986,476
10	Herb Thomas	48	10	**Buddy Baker**	40	10	**Geoff Bodine**	5,625,227
11	Buck Baker	46	11	Herb Thomas	38	11	Cale Yarborough	5,003,716
12	Tim Flock	40	12	Tim Flock	37	12	**Davey Allison**	4,237,761
13	Bobby Isaac	37		Fireball Roberts	37	13	**Ken Schrader**	4,053,128
14	**Bill Elliott**	34	14	Ned Jarrett	36	14	Benny Parsons	3,926,539
	Fireball Roberts	34		Rex White	36	15	**Mark Martin**	3,850,154
16	Rex White	28	16	Fred Lorenzen	33	16	Neil Bonnett	3,847,146
17	Fred Lorenzen	26	17	Fonty Flock	30	17	**Kyle Petty**	3,660,767
18	Jim Paschal	25	18	**Geoff Bodine**	29	18	**Dave Marcis**	3,595,429
19	Joe Weatherly	24	19	Marvin Panch	25	19	**Buddy Baker**	3,582,221
20	Benny Parsons	21	20	Jack Smith	24	20	**Morgan Shepherd**	3,210,033
	Jack Smith	21						

NASCAR Circuit (Cont.)

Winston Cup Champions

Originally the Grand National Championship, 1949-70, and based on official NASCAR (National Association for Stock Car Auto Racing) records through the 1991 racing season.

Multiple winners: Richard Petty (7); Dale Earnhardt (5); David Pearson, Lee Petty, Darrell Waltrip and Cale Yarborough (3); Buck Baker, Tim Flock, Ned Jarrett, Herb Thomas and Joe Weatherly (2).

Year		Year		Year		Year	
1949	Red Byron	1960	Rex White	1971	Richard Petty	1982	Darrell Waltrip
1950	Bill Rexford	1961	Ned Jarrett	1972	Richard Petty	1983	Bobby Allison
1951	Herb Thomas	1962	Joe Weatherly	1973	Benny Parsons	1984	Terry Labonte
1952	Tim Flock	1963	Joe Weatherly	1974	Richard Petty	1985	Darrell Waltrip
1953	Herb Thomas	1964	Richard Petty	1975	Richard Petty	1986	Dale Earnhardt
1954	Lee Petty	1965	Ned Jarrett	1976	Cale Yarborough	1987	Dale Earnhardt
1955	Tim Flock	1966	David Pearson	1977	Cale Yarborough	1988	Bill Elliott
1956	Buck Baker	1967	Richard Petty	1978	Cale Yarborough	1989	Rusty Wallace
1957	Buck Baker	1968	David Pearson	1979	Richard Petty	1990	Dale Earnhardt
1958	Lee Petty	1969	David Pearson	1980	Dale Earnhardt	1992	Dale Earnhardt
1959	Lee Petty	1970	Bobby Issac	1981	Darrell Waltrip		

NASCAR Rookie of the Year

Award presented to rookie driver who accumulates the most Winston Cup points based on his best 15 finishes.

Year		Year		Year		Year	
1958	Shorty Rollins	1967	Donnie Allison	1976	Skip Manning	1984	Rusty Wallace
1959	Richard Petty	1968	Pete Hamilton	1977	Ricky Rudd	1985	Ken Schrader
1960	David Pearson	1969	Dick Brooks	1978	Ronnie Thomas	1986	Alan Kulwicki
1961	Woodie Wilson	1970	Bill Dennis	1979	Dale Earnhardt	1987	Davey Allison
1962	Tom Cox	1971	Walter Ballard	1980	Jody Ridley	1988	Ken Bouchard
1963	Billy Wade	1972	Larry Smith	1981	Ron Bouchard	1989	Dick Trickle
1964	Doug Cooper	1973	Lennie Pond	1982	Geoff Bodine	1990	Rob Moroso
1965	Sam McQuagg	1974	Earl Ross	1983	Sterling Marlin	1991	Bobby Hamilton
1966	James Hylton	1975	Bruce Hill				

IndyCar Circuit

Indianapolis 500

Held every Memorial Day weekend; 200 laps around a 2.5-mile oval at Indianapolis Motor Speedway. First race was held in 1911. Winning drivers are listed with starting positions. Winners who started from pole position are in **bold** type.

Multiple wins: A.J.Foyt, Rick Mears and Al Unser (4); Louis Meyer, Mauri Rose, Johnny Rutherford, Wilbur Shaw and Bobby Unser (3); Gordon Johncock, Tommy Milton, Bill Vukovich and Rodger Ward (2).

Multiple poles: Rick Mears (6); Mario Andretti, A.J.Foyt and Tom Sneva (4); Rex Mays (3); Billy Arnold, Ralph DePalma, Walt Faulkner, Parnelli Jones, Jack McGrath, Jimmy Murphy, Duke Nalon, Johnny Rutherford and Jimmy Snyder (2).

Year	Winner (Pos.)	Car	MPH	Pole Sitter	MPH
1911	Ray Harroun (28)	Marmon Wasp	74.602	Lewis Strang	—
1912	Joe Dawson (7)	National	78.719	Gil Anderson	—
1913	Jules Goux (7)	Peugeot	75.933	Caleb Bragg	—
1914	Rene Thomas (15)	Delage	82.474	Jean Chassagne	—
1915	Ralph DePalma (2)	Mercedes	89.840	Howard Wilcox	98.90
1916-**a**	Dario Resta (4)	Peugeot	84.001	John Aitken	96.69
1917-18	Not held				
1919	Howard Wilcox (2)	Peugeot	88.050	Rene Thomas	104.78
1920	Gaston Chevrolet (6)	Monroe	88.618	Ralph DePalma	99.15
1921	Tommy Milton (20)	Frontenac	89.621	Ralph DePalma	100.75
1922	**Jimmy Murphy** (1)	Murphy Special	94.484	Jimmy Murphy	100.50
1923	**Tommy Milton** (1)	H.C.S. Special	90.954	Tommy Milton	108.17
1924	L.L.Corum & Joe Boyer (21)	Duesenberg Special	98.234	Jimmy Murphy	108.037
1925	Peter DePaolo (2)	Duesenberg Special	101.127	Leon Duray	113.196
1926-**b**	Frank Lockhart (20)	Miller Special	95.904	Earl Cooper	111.735
1927	George Souders (22)	Duesenberg	97.545	Frank Lockhart	120.100
1928	Louis Meyer (13)	Miller Special	99.482	Leon Duray	122.391
1929	Ray Keech (6)	Simplex Piston Ring Special	97.585	Cliff Woodbury	120.599
1930	**Billy Arnold** (1)	Miller-Hartz Special	100.448	Billy Arnold	113.268
1931	Louis Schneider (13)	Bowes Seal Fast Special	96.629	Russ Snowberger	112.796
1932	Fred Frame (27)	Miller-Hartz Special	104.144	Lou Moore	117.363

Year	Winner (Pos.)	Car	MPH	Pole Sitter	MPH
1933	Louis Meyer (6)	Tydol Special	104.162	Bill Cummings	118.530
1934	William Cummings (10)	Boyle Products Special	104.863	Kelly Petillo	119.329
1935	Kelly Petillo (22)	Gilmore Speedway Special	106.240	Rex Mays	120.736
1936	Louis Meyer (28)	Ring-Free Special	109.069	Rex Mays	119.644
1937	Wilbur Shaw (2)	Shaw-Gilmore Special	113.580	Bill Cummings	123.343
1938	**Floyd Roberts** (1)	Burd Piston Ring Special	117.200	Floyd Roberts	125.681
1939	Wilbur Shaw (3)	Boyle Special	115.035	Jimmy Snyder	130.138
1940	Wilbur Shaw (2)	Boyle Special	114.277	Rex Mays	127.850
1941	Floyd Davis & Mauri Rose(17)	Noc-Out Hose Clamp Special	115.117	Mauri Rose	128.691
1942-45	Not held				
1946	George Robson (15)	Thorne Engineering Special	114.820	Cliff Bergere	126.471
1947	Mauri Rose (3)	Blue Crown Spark Plug Spl.	116.338	Ted Horn	126.564
1948	Mauri Rose (3)	Blue Crown Spark Plug Spl.	119.814	Duke Nalon	131.603
1949	Bill Holland (4)	Blue Crown Spark Plug Spl.	121.327	Duke Nalon	132.939
1950-c	Johnnie Parsons (5)	Wynn's Friction Proofing	124.002	Walt Faulkner	134.343
1951	Lee Wallard (2)	Belanger Special	126.244	Duke Nalon	136.498
1952	Troy Ruttman (7)	Agajanian Special	128.922	Fred Agabashian	138.010
1953	**Bill Vukovich** (1)	Fuel Injection Special	128.740	Bill Vukovich	138.392
1954	Bill Vukovich (19)	Fuel Injection Special	130.840	Jack McGrath	141.033
1955	Bob Sweikert (14)	John Zink Special	128.209	Jerry Hoyt	140.045
1956	**Pat Flaherty** (1)	John Zink Special	128.490	Pat Flaherty	145.596
1957	Sam Hanks (13)	Belond Exhaust Special	135.601	Pat O'Connor	143.948
1958	Jim Bryan (7)	Belond AP Parts Special	133.791	Dick Rathmann	145.974
1959	Rodger Ward (6)	Leader Card 500 Roadster	135.857	Johnny Thomson	145.908
1960	Jim Rathmann (2)	Ken-Paul Special	138.767	Eddie Sachs	146.592
1961	A.J.Foyt (7)	Bowes Seal-Fast Special	139.131	Eddie Sachs	147.481
1962	Rodger Ward (2)	Leader Card 500 Roadster	140.293	Parnelli Jones	150.370
1963	**Parnelli Jones** (1)	Agajanian-Willard Special	143.137	Parnelli Jones	151.153
1964	A.J.Foyt (5)	Sheraton-Thompson Special	147.350	Jim Clark	158.828
1965	Jim Clark (2)	Lotus Ford	150.686	A.J.Foyt	161.233
1966	Graham Hill (15)	American Red Ball Special	144.317	Mario Andretti	165.899
1967-d	A.J.Foyt (4)	Sheraton-Thompson Special	151.207	Mario Andretti	168.982
1968	Bobby Unser (3)	Rislone Special	152.882	Joe Leonard	171.559
1969	Mario Andretti (2)	STP Oil Treatment Special	156.867	A.J.Foyt	170.568
1970	**Al Unser** (1)	Johnny Lightning 500 Spl.	155.749	Al Unser	170.221
1971	Al Unser (5)	Johnny Lightning Special	157.735	Peter Revson	178.696
1972	Mark Donohue (3)	Sunoco McLaren	162.962	Bobby Unser	195.940
1973-e	Gordon Johncock (11)	STP Double Oil Filters	159.036	Johnny Rutherford	198.413
1974	Johnny Rutherford (25)	McLaren	158.589	A.J.Foyt	191.632
1975-f	Bobby Unser (3)	Jorgensen Eagle	149.213	A.J.Foyt	193.976
1976-g	**Johnny Rutherford** (1)	Hy-Gain McLaren/Goodyear	148.725	Johnny Rutherford	188.957
1977	A.J.Foyt (4)	Gilmore Racing Team	161.331	Tom Sneva	198.884
1978	Al Unser (5)	FNCTC Chaparral Lola	161.363	Tom Sneva	202.156
1979	**Rick Mears** (1)	The Gould Charge	158.899	Rick Mears	193.736
1980	**Johnny Rutherford** (1)	Pennzoil Chaparral	142.862	Johnny Rutherford	192.256
1981-h	**Bobby Unser** (1)	Norton Spirit Penske PC-9B	139.084	Bobby Unser	200.546
1982	Gordon Johncock (5)	STP Oil Treatment	162.029	Rick Mears	207.004
1983	Tom Sneva (4)	Texaco Star	162.117	Teo Fabi	207.395
1984	Rick Mears (3)	Pennzoil Z-7	163.612	Tom Sneva	210.029
1985	Danny Sullivan (8)	Miller American Special	152.982	Pancho Carter	212.583
1986	Bobby Rahal (4)	Budweiser/Truesports/March	170.722	Rick Mears	216.828
1987	Al Unser (20)	Cummins Holset Turbo	162.175	Mario Andretti	215.390
1988	**Rick Mears** (1)	Penske-Chevrolet V-8	149.809	Rick Mears	219.198
1989	Emerson Fittipaldi (3)	Penske-Chevrolet PC-18	167.581	Rick Mears	223.885
1990	Arie Luyendyk (3)	Domino's Pizza Chevrolet	185.981*	Emerson Fittipaldi	225.301
1991	**Rick Mears** (1)	Penske-Chevrolet	176.457	Rick Mears	224.113
1992	Al Unser, Jr. (12)	Galmer-Chevrolet	134.479	Roberto Guerrero	232.482†

*Track record for Winning Time.
†Track record for Qualifying Time.

Notes: a—1916 race scheduled for 300 miles; **b**—rain shortened 1926 race to 400 miles; **c**—rain shortened 1950 race to 345 miles; **d**—1967 race postponed due to rain after 18 laps (May 30), resumed next day (May 31); **e**—rain shortened 1973 race to 332+ miles; **f**—rain shortened 1975 race to 435 miles; **g**—rain shortened 1976 race to 255 miles; **h**—in 1981, runner-up Mario Andretti was awarded 1st place when winner Bobby Unser was penalized a lap after the race was completed for passing cars illegally under the caution flag. Unser and car-owner Roger Penske appealed the race stewards' decision to the U.S. Auto Club. Four months later, USAC overturned the ruling, saying that the penalty was too harsh and Unser should be fined $40,000 rather than stripped of his championship.

IndyCar Circuit (Cont.)

Indy 500 Rookie of the Year

Voted on by a panel of auto racing media. Award does not necessarily go to highest-finishing first year driver. Graham Hill won the race on this first try in 1966, but the rookie award went to Jackie Stewart.

Father and son winners: Mario and Michael Andretti (1965 and 1984); Bill and Billy Vukovich (1968 and 1988).

Year		Year		Year		Year	
1952	Art Cross	1963	Jim Clark	1974	Duane Carter, Jr	1984	Michael Andretti
1953	Jimmy Daywalt	1964	Johnny White	1975	Bill Puterbaugh		& Robt. Guerrero
1954	Larry Crockett	1965	Mario Andretti	1976	Vern Schuppan	1985	Arie Luyendyk
1955	Al Herman	1966	Jackie Stewart	1977	Jerry Sneva	1986	Randy Lanier
1956	Bob Veith	1967	Denis Hulme	1978	Rick Mears	1987	Fabrizio Barbazza
1957	Don Edmunds	1968	Bill Vukovich		& Larry Rice	1988	Billy Vukovich III
1958	George Amick	1969	Mark Donohue	1979	Howdy Holmes	1989	Bernard Jourdain
1959	Bobby Grim						& Scott Pruett
1960	Jim Hurtubise	1970	Donnie Allison	1980	Tim Richmond		
1961	Parnelli Jones	1971	Denny Zimmerman	1981	Josele Garza	1990	Eddie Cheever
	& Bobby Marshman	1972	Mike Hiss	1982	Jim Hickman	1991	Jeff Andretti
1962	Jimmy McElreath	1973	Graham McRae	1983	Teo Fabi	1992	Lyn St.James

All-Time Leaders

IndyCar's all-time Top 20 drivers in victories, pole positions and earnings, based on records through 1991. Drivers active in 1991 are in **bold** type.

	Victories			Pole Positions			Earnings	
1	**A.J. Foyt**	67	1	**Mario Andretti**	64	1	**Rick Mears**	$10,638,430
2	**Mario Andretti**	51	2	**A.J. Foyt**	53	2	**Mario Andretti**	8,951,853
3	**Al Unser**	39	3	Bobby Unser	49	3	**Bobby Rahal**	8,931,280
4	Bobby Unser	35	4	**Rick Mears**	40	4	**Al Unser, Jr.**	8,386,936
5	**Rick Mears**	29	5	**Al Unser**	27	5	**Michael Andretti**	8,293,931
6	Johnny Rutherford	27	6	Johnny Rutherford	23	6	**Emerson Fittipaldi**	7,740,365
7	Rodger Ward	26	7	**Gordon Johncock**	20	7	**Danny Sullivan**	6,763,995
8	**Gordon Johncock**	25		**Michael Andretti**	20	8	**Al Unser**	6,150,151
9	Ralph DePalma	24	9	**Danny Sullivan**	19	9	**A.J. Foyt**	5,150,206
10	Tommy Milton	23		Rex Mays	19	10	**Arie Luyendyk**	5,015,317
11	**Michael Andretti**	22	11	**Bobby Rahal**	15	11	**Tom Sneva**	4,253,215
12	Tony Bettenhausen	21		Don Branson	15	12	**Johnny Rutherford**	4,209,232
	Earl Cooper	21	13	Tony Bettenhausen	14	13	**Gordon Johncock**	3,295,411
14	**Bobby Rahal**	20		**Tom Sneva**	14	14	**Roberto Guerrero**	3,291,157
15	Jimmy Bryan	19		Parnelli Jones	12	15	**Kevin Cogan**	2,996,253
	Jimmy Murphy	19	16	**Emerson Fittipaldi**	11	16	**Scott Brayton**	2,988,006
17	Ralph Mulford	17		Danny Ongais	11	17	**Pancho Carter**	2,698,733
	Al Unser, Jr.	17		Rodger Ward	11	18	Bobby Unser	2,674,516
19	**Danny Sullivan**	15	19	Dan Gurney	10	19	**Raul Boesel**	2,609,858
20	**Emerson Fittipaldi**	13		Johnny Thomson	10	20	**Geoff Brabham**	2,393,123
	Tom Sneva	13						

PPG Cup Champions

Officially the PPG Indy Car World Series Championship since 1979 and based on official AAA (American Automobile Assn., 1909-55), USAC (U.S. Auto Club, 1956-79), and CART (Championship Auto Racing Teams, 1979-91) records through the 1990 racing season. CART was renamed IndyCar in 1992.

Multiple titles: A.J.Foyt (7); Mario Andretti (4); Jimmy Bryan, Earl Cooper, Ted Horn, Rick Mears, Louis Meyer and Al Unser (3); Tony Bettenhausen, Ralph DePalma, Peter DePaolo, Joe Leonard, Rex Mays, Tommy Milton, Jimmy Murphy, Bobby Rahal, Wilbur Shaw, Tom Sneva, Bobby Unser and Rodger Ward (2).

AAA

Year		Year		Year		Year	
1909	George Robertson	1921	Tommy Milton	1932	Bob Carey	1946	Ted Horn
1910	Ray Harroun	1922	Jimmy Murphy	1933	Louis Meyer	1947	Ted Horn
1911	Ralph Mulford	1923	Eddie Hearne	1934	Bill Cummings	1948	Ted Horn
1912	Ralph DePalma	1924	Jimmy Murphy	1935	Kelly Petillo	1949	Johnnie Parsons
1913	Earl Cooper	1925	Peter DePaolo	1936	Mauri Rose		
1914	Ralph DePalma	1926	Harry Hartz	1937	Wilbur Shaw	1950	Henry Banks
1915	Earl Cooper	1927	Peter DePaolo	1938	Floyd Roberts	1951	Tony Bettenhausen
1916	Dario Resta	1928	Louis Meyer	1939	Wilbur Shaw	1952	Chuck Stevenson
1917	Earl Cooper	1929	Louis Meyer			1953	Sam Hanks
1918	Ralph Mulford			1940	Rex Mays	1954	Jimmy Bryan
1919	Howard Wilcox	1930	Billy Arnold	1941	Rex Mays	1955	Bob Sweikert
		1931	Louis Schneider	1942-45	No racing		
1920	Tommy Milton						

USAC

Year		Year		Year		Year	
1956	Jimmy Bryan	1962	Rodger Ward	1968	Bobby Unser	1974	Bobby Unser
1957	Jimmy Bryan	1963	A.J.Foyt	1969	Mario Andretti	1975	A.J.Foyt
1958	Tony Bettenhausen	1964	A.J.Foyt	1970	Al Unser	1976	Gordon Johncock
1959	Rodger Ward	1965	Mario Andretti	1971	Joe Leonard	1977	Tom Sneva
1960	A.J.Foyt	1966	Mario Andretti	1972	Joe Leonard	1978	Tom Sneva
1961	A.J.Foyt	1967	A.J.Foyt	1973	Roger McCluskey	1979	A.J.Foyt

CART

Year		Year		Year		Year	
1979	Rick Mears	1983	Al Unser	1986	Bobby Rahal	1989	Emerson Fittipaldi
1980	Johnny Rutherford	1984	Mario Andretti	1987	Bobby Rahal	1990	Al Unser, Jr.
1981	Rick Mears	1985	Al Unser	1988	Danny Sullivan	1991	Michael Andretti
1982	Rick Mears						

IndyCar Rookie of the Year

Award presented to rookie who accumulates the most PPG Cup points among first year drivers. Originally the CART Rookie of the Year; CART was renamed IndyCar in 1992.

Year		Year		Year		Year	
1979	Bill Alsup	1983	Teo Fabi	1986	Dominic Dobson	1989	Bernard Jourdain
1980	Dennis Firestone	1984	Roberto Guerrero	1987	Fabrizio Barbazza	1990	Eddie Cheever
1981	Bob Lazier	1985	Arie Luyendyk	1988	John Jones	1991	Jeff Andretti
1982	Bobby Rahal						

Formula One Circuit

United States Grand Prix

There have been 54 official Formula One races held in the United States since 1950, including the Indianapolis 500 from 1950-60. FISA sanctioned two annual U.S. Grand Prix—USA/East and USA/West—from 1976-80 and 1983. Phoenix has been the site of the U.S. Grand Prix since 1989.

Indianapolis 500

Officially sanctioned as Grand Prix race from 1950-60 only. See IndyCar Circuit for further details.   ·

Year		Car	Year		Car
1950	Johnnie Parsons, USA	Wynn's Curtis	1956	Pat Flaherty, USA	Zink Special
1951	Lee Wallard, USA	Belanger Special	1957	Sam Hanks, USA	Belond Special
1952	Troy Ruttman, USA	Agajanian Special	1958	Jim Bryan, USA	Belond Special
1953	Bill Vukovich, USA	Fuel Injec.Special	1959	Rodger Ward, USA	Leader Roadster
1954	Bill Vukovich, USA	Fuel Injec.Special	1960	Jim Rathmann, USA	Ken-Paul Special
1955	Bob Sweikert, USA	Zink Special			

U.S. Grand Prix—East

Held from 1959-80 and 1981-88 at the following locations: Sebring, Fla. (1959); Riverside, Calif. (1960); Watkins Glen, N.Y. (1961-80); and Detroit (1982-88). There was no race in 1981.

Multiple winners: Jim Clark, Graham Hill and Ayrton Senna (3); James Hunt, Carlos Reutemann and Jackie Stewart (2).

Year		Car	Year		Car
1959	Bruce McLaren, NZE	Cooper Climax	1974	Carlos Reutemann, ARG	Brabham Ford
1960	Stirling Moss, GBR	Lotus Climax	1975	Niki Lauda, AUT	Ferrari
1961	Innes Ireland, GBR	Lotus Climax	1976	James Hunt, GBR	McLaren Ford
1962	Jim Clark, GBR	Lotus Climax	1977	James Hunt, GBR	McLaren Ford
1963	Graham Hill, GBR	BRM	1978	Carlos Reutemann, ARG	Ferrari
1964	Graham Hill, GBR	BRM	1979	Gilles Villeneuve, CAN	Ferrari
1965	Graham Hill, GBR	BRM	1980	Alan Jones, AUS	Williams Ford
1966	Jim Clark, GBR	Lotus BRM	1981	Not held	
1967	Jim Clark, GBR	Lotus Ford	1982	John Watson, GBR	McLaren Ford
1968	Jackie Stewart, GBR	Matra Ford	1983	Michele Alboreto, ITA	Tyrrell Ford
1969	Jochen Rindt, AUT	Lotus Ford	1984	Nelson Piquet, BRA	Brabham BMW Turbo
1970	Emerson Fittipaldi, BRA	Lotus Ford	1985	Keke Rosberg, FIN	Williams Honda Turbo
1971	Francois Cevert, FRA	Tyrrell Ford	1986	Ayrton Senna, BRA	Lotus Renault Turbo
1972	Jackie Stewart, GBR	Tyrrell Ford	1987	Ayrton Senna, BRA	Lotus Honda Turbo
1973	Ronnie Peterson, SWE	Lotus Ford	1988	Ayrton Senna, BRA	McLaren Honda Turbo

Formula One Circuit (Cont.)
U.S. Grand Prix—West

Held from 1976-83 at Long Beach, Calf. Races also held in Las Vegas (1981-82), Dallas (1984) and Phoenix (since 1989).

Multiple winners: Ayrton Senna (2) at Phoenix.

Long Beach

Year	Car
1976 Clay Regazzoni, SWI.	Ferrari
1977 Mario Andretti, USA	Lotus Ford
1978 Carlos Reutemann, ARG	Ferrari
1979 Gilles Villeneuve, CAN	Ferrari
1980 Nelson Piquet, BRA	Brabham Ford
1981 Alan Jones, AUS	Williams Ford
1982 Niki Lauda, AUT	McLaren Ford
1983 John Watson, GBR	McLaren Ford

Las Vegas

Year	Car
1981 Alan Jones, AUS	Williams Ford
1982 Michele Alboreto, ITA	Tyrrell Ford

Dallas

Year	Car
1984 Keke Rosberg, FIN	Williams Honda Turbo

Phoenix

Year	Car
1989 Alain Prost, FRA	McLaren Honda
1990 Ayrton Senna, BRA	McLaren Honda
1991 Ayrton Senna, BRA	McLaren Honda

All-Time Leaders

The all-time Top 20 Grand Prix winning drivers, based on records through 1991. Listed are starts (Sts), poles won (Pole), wins (1st), second place finishes (2nd), and thirds (3rd). Drivers active in 1991 in **bold** type.

	Sts	Pole	1st	2nd	3rd			Sts	Pole	1st	2nd	3rd
1 **Alain Prost**	184	20	**44**	32	18		13 Alberto Ascari	32	14	**13**	4	0
2 **Ayrton Senna**	126	60	**33**	20	13		14 Mario Andretti	128	18	**12**	2	5
3 Jackie Stewart	99	17	**27**	11	5		Alan Jones	116	6	**12**	8	5
4 Jim Clark	72	33	**25**	1	6		Carlos Reutemann	146	6	**12**	13	20
Niki Lauda	171	24	**25**	20	9		17 James Hunt	92	14	**10**	6	7
6 Juan-Manuel Fangio	51	28	**24**	11	1		Ronnie Peterson	123	14	**10**	10	6
7 **Nelson Piquet**	204	24	**23**	20	17		Jody Scheckter	112	3	**10**	14	9
8 **Nigel Mansell**	165	17	**21**	14	11		20 Denis Hulme	112	1	**8**	9	16
9 Stirling Moss	66	16	**16**	5	3		Jacky Ickx	116	13	**8**	7	10
Graham Hill	176	13	**14**	15	7							

Note #1: The following drivers either died or were killed in their final year of competition—**Clark** in a Formula Two race in W.Germany in 1968; **Hill** in a plane crash in 1975; **Ascari** in a private practice run in 1955; and **Peterson** following an accident in the 1978 Italian Grand Prix.

Note #2: Fittipaldi and Andretti are still active, but driving on the CART circuit.

World Champions

Officially called the World Championship of Drivers and based on Formula One (Grand Prix) records through the 1990 racing season.

Multiple winners: Juan-Manuel Fangio (5); Jack Brabham, Niki Lauda, Nelson Piquet, Alain Prost, Ayrton Senna and Jackie Stewart (3); Alberto Ascari, Jim Clark, Emerson Fittipaldi and Graham Hill (2).

Year	Car
1950 Giuseppe Farina, ITA	Alfa Romeo
1951 Juan-Manuel Fangio, ARG	Alfa Romeo
1952 Alberto Ascari, ITA	Ferrari
1953 Alberto Ascari, ITA	Ferrari
1954 Juan-Manuel Fangio, ARG	Maserati/Mercedes
1955 Juan-Manuel Fangio, ARG	Mercedes
1956 Juan-Manuel Fangio, ARG.	Ferrari
1957 Juan-Manuel Fangio, ARG	Maserati
1958 Mike Hawthorn, GBR	Ferrari
1959 Jack Brabham, AUS	Cooper Climax
1960 Jack Brabham, AUS	Cooper Climax
1961 Phil Hill, USA	Ferrari
1962 Graham Hill, GBR	BRM
1963 Jim Clark, GBR.	Lotus Climax
1964 John Surtees, GBR.	Ferrari
1965 Jim Clark, GBR.	Lotus Climax
1966 Jack Brabham, AUS	Brabham Climax
1967 Denis Hulme, NZE	Brabham Repco
1968 Graham Hill, GBR	Lotus Ford
1969 Jackie Stewart, GBR	Matra Ford
1970 Jochen Rindt, AUT	Lotus Ford
1971 Jackie Stewart, GBR	Tyrrell Ford

Year	Car
1972 Emerson Fittipaldi, BRA	Lotus Ford
1973 Jackie Stewart, GBR	Tyrrell Ford
1974 Emerson Fittipaldi, BRA	McLaren Ford
1975 Niki Lauda, AUT	Ferrari
1976 James Hunt, GBR	McLaren Ford
1977 Niki Lauda, AUT	Ferrari
1978 Mario Andretti, USA	Lotus Ford
1979 Jody Scheckter, SAF	Ferrari
1980 Alan Jones, AUS	Williams Ford
1981 Nelson Piquet, BRA	Brabham Ford
1982 Keke Rosberg, FIN	Williams Ford
1983 Nelson Piquet, BRA	Brabham BMW Turbo
1984 Niki Lauda, AUT	McL. TAG Porsche Turbo
1985 Alain Prost, FRA	McL. TAG Porsche Turbo
1986 Alain Prost, FRA	McL. TAG Porsche Turbo
1987 Nelson Piquet, BRA	Williams Honda Turbo
1988 Ayrton Senna, BRA.	McLaren-Honda Turbo
1989 Alain Prost, FRA	McLaren-Honda
1990 Ayrton Senna, BRA	McLaren-Honda
1991 Ayrton Senna, BRA	McLaren-Honda
1992 Nigel Mansell, GBR	Williams-Renault

Endurance Races
The 24 Hours at Le Mans

Officially, the Le Mans Grand Prix d'Endurance. First run May 22-23, 1923, and won by Andre Lagache and Rene Leonard in a 3-litre Chenard & Walcker. All subsequent races have been held in June, except in 1956 (July) and 1968 (September). Originally contested over a 10.73-mile track, the circuit was shortened to its present 8.451-mile distance in 1932. The original start of Le Mans, where drivers raced across the track to their unstarted cars, was discontinued in 1970.

Multiple winners: Jacky Ickx (6); Derek Bell (5); Oliver Gendebien and Henri Pescarolo (4); Woolf Barnato, Luigi Chinetti, Phil Hill, Klaus Ludwig and Al Holbert (3); Sir Henry Birkin, Ivoe Bueb, Ron Flockhart, Hurley Haywood, Jean-Pierre Jaussaud, Gerard Larrousse, Andre Rossignol, Raymond Sommer, Hans Stuck, Gijs van Lennep and Jean-Pierre Wimille (2).

Year	Drivers	Car	Speed (mph)
1923	Andre Lagache & Rene Leonard	Chenard & Walcker	57.21
1924	John Duff & Francis Clement	Bentley	53.78
1925	Gerard de Courcelles & Andre Rossignol	La Lorraine	57.84
1926	Robert Bloch & Andre Rossignol	La Lorraine	66.08
1927	J.D. Benjafield & Sammy Davis	Bentley	61.35
1928	Woolf Barnato & Bernard Rubin	Bentley	69.11
1929	Woolf Barnato & Sir Henry Birkin	Bentley	73.63
1930	Woolf Barnato & Glen Kidston	Bentley	75.88
1931	Earl Howe & Sir Henry Birkin	Alfa Romeo	78.13
1932	Raymond Sommer & Luigi Chinetti	Alfa Romeo	76.48
1933	Raymond Sommer & Tazio Nuvolari	Alfa Romeo	81.40
1934	Luigi Chinetti & Philippe Etancelin	Alfa Romeo	74.74
1935	John Hindmarsh & Louis Fontes	Lagonda	77.85
1936	Not held		
1937	Jean-Pierre Wimille & Robert Benoit	Bugatti	85.13
1938	Eugene Chaboud & Jean Tremoulet	Delahaye	82.36
1939	Jean-Pierre Wimille & Pierre Veyron	Bugatti	86.86
1940-48	Not held		
1949	Luigi Chinetti & Lord Selsdon	Ferrari	82.28
1950	Louis Rosier & Jean-Louis Rosier	Talbot-Lago	89.71
1951	Peter Walker & Peter Whitehead	Jaguar	93.50
1952	Herman Lang & Fritz Reiss	Mercedes-Benz	96.67
1953	Tony Rolt & Duncan Hamilton	Jaguar	98.65
1954	Froilan Gonzalez & Maurice Trintignant	Ferrari	105.13
1955	Mike Hawthorn & Ivor Bueb	Jaguar	107.05
1956	Ron Flockhart Ninian Sanderson	Jaguar	104.47
1957	Ron Flockhart & Ivor Bueb	Jaguar	113.83
1958	Oliver Gendebien & Phil Hill	Ferrari	106.18
1959	Roy Salvadori & Carroll Shelby	Aston Martin	112.55
1960	Oliver Gendebien & Paul Frere	Ferrari	109.17
1961	Oliver Gendebien & Phil Hill	Ferrari	115.88
1962	Oliver Gendebien & Phil Hill	Ferrari	115.22
1963	Lodovico Scarfiotti & Lorenzo Bandini	Ferrari	118.08
1964	Jean Guichel & Nino Vaccarella	Ferrari	121.54
1965	Masten Gregory & Jochen Rindt	Ferrari	121.07
1966	Bruce McLaren & Chris Amon	Ford	125.37
1967	A.J. Foyt & Dan Gurney	Ford	135.46
1968	Pedro Rodriguez & Lucien Bianchi	Ford	115.27
1969	Jacky Ickx & Jackie Oliver	Ford	129.38
1970	Hans Herrmann & Richard Attwood	Porsche	119.28
1971	Gijs van Lennep & Helmut Marko	Porsche	138.13
1972	Graham Hill & Henri Pescarolo	Matra-Simca	121.45
1973	Henri Pescarolo & Gerard Larrousse	Matra-Simca	125.67
1974	Henri Pescarolo & Gerard Larrousse	Matra-Simca	119.27
1975	Derek Bell & Jacky Ickx	Gulf-Cosworth	118.98
1976	Jacky Ickx & Gijs van Lennep	Porsche	123.49
1977	Jacky Ickx, Jurgen Barth & Hurley Haywood	Porsche	120.95
1978	Jean-Pierre Jaussaud & Didier Pironi	Renault-Alpine	130.60
1979	Klaus Ludwig, Bill Wittington & Don Whittington	Porsche	108.10
1980	Jean-Pierre Jaussaud & Jean Rondeau	Rondeau-Cosworth	119.23
1981	Jacky Ickx & Derek Bell	Porsche	124.94
1982	Jacky Ickx & Derek Bell	Porsche	126.85
1983	Vern Schuppan, Hurley Haywood & Al Holbert	Porsche	130.70
1984	Klaus Ludwig & Henri Pescarolo	Porsche	126.88

Endurance Races (Cont.)
The 24 Hours at Le Mans

Year	Drivers	Car	Speed (mph)	Year	Drivers	Car	Speed (mph)
1985	Klaus Ludwig, Paolo Barilla & John Winter	Porsche	131.75	1989	Jochen Mass, Manuel Reuter & Stanley Dickens	Sauber-Mercedes	136.39
1986	Derek Bell, Hans Stuck & Al Holbert	Porsche	128.75	1990	John Nielsen, Price Cobb & Martin Brundle	Jaguar	126.71
1987	Derek Dell, Hans Stuck & Al Holbert	Porsche	124.06	1991	Volker Weider, Johnny Herbert & Bertrand Gachof	Mazda	127.31
1988	Jan Lammers, Johnny Dumfries & Andy Wallace	Jaguar	137.75	1992	Derek Warwick, Yannick Dalmas & Mark Blundell	Peugeot	123.89

The 24 Hours of Daytona

Officially, the Rolex 24 Hours of Daytona. First run in 1962 as a three-hour race and won by Dan Gurney in a Lotus 19 Ford. Contested over a 3.56-mile course at Daytona (Fla.) International Speedway. There have been several distance changes since 1962: the event was a three-hour race (1962-63); a 2,000-kilometer race (1964-65); a 24-hour race (1966-71); a six-hour race (1972) and a 24-hour race again since 1973. The race was canceled in 1974 due the national energy crisis.

Multiple winners: Hurley Haywood (5); Peter Gregg, Pedro Rodriguez and Bob Wollek (4); Derek Bell and Rolf Stommelen (3); A.J. Foyt, Al Holbert, Ken Miles, Lloyd Ruby and Al Unser, Jr. (2).

Year	Drivers	Car	Speed (mph)	Year	Drivers	Car	Speed (mph)
1962	Dan Gurney	Lotus Ford	104.101	1981	Bobby Rahal, Brian Redman & Bob Garretson	Porsche	113.153
1963	Pedro Rodriguez	Ferrari	102.074				
1964	Pedro Rodriguez & Phil Hill	Ferrari	98.230	1982	John Paul Sr., John Paul Jr. & Rolf Stommelen	Porsche	114.794
1965	Ken Miles & Lloyd Ruby	Ford	99.944	1983	A.J. Foyt, Preston Henn & Bob Wollek	Porsche	98.781
1966	Ken Miles & Lloyd Ruby	Ford	108.020				
1967	Lorenzo Bandini & Chris Amon	Ferrari	105.688	1984	Sarel van der Merwe, Tony Martin & Graham Duxbury	Porsche	103.119
1968	Vic Elford & Jochen Neerpasch	Porsche	106.697	1985	A.J. Foyt, Bob Wollek Al Unser Sr. & Thierry Boutsen	Porsche 962	104.162
1969	Mark Donohue & Chuck Parsons	Lola Chevrolet	99.268				
1970	Pedro Rodriguez & Leo Kinnunen	Porsche	114.866	1986	Al Holbert, Derek Bell & Al Unser Jr.	Porsche 962	105.484
1971	Pedro Rodriguez & Jackie Oliver	Porsche	109.203	1987	Al Holbert, Derek Bell, Chip Robinson & Al Unser Jr.	Porsche 962	111.599
1972	Mario Andretti & Jacky Ickx	Ferrari	122.573				
1973	Peter Gregg & Hurley Haywood	Porsche	106.225	1988	Raul Boesel, Martin Brundle & John Nielsen	Jaguar XJR-9	107.943
1974	Not held			1989	John Andretti, Derek Bell & Bob Wollek	Porsche 962	92.009
1975	Peter Gregg & Hurley Haywood	Porsche	108.531				
1976	Peter Gregg & Brian Redman	BMW	104.040	1990	Davy Jones, Jan Lammers & Andy Wallace	Jaguar XJR-12	112.857
1977	Hurley Haywood, John Graves & Dave Helmick	Porsche	108.801	1991	Hurley Haywood, John Winter, Frank Jelinski, Henri Pescarolo & Bob Wollek	Porsche 962-C	106.633
1978	Peter Gregg, Rolf Stommelen & Antoine Hezemans	Porsche	108.743				
1979	Hurley Haywood, Ted Field & Danny Ongais	Porsche	109.249	1992	Masahiro Hasemi, Kazuyoshi Hoshino & Toshio Suzuki	Nissan R-91	112.897
1980	Rolf Stommelen, Volkert Merl & Reinhold Joest	Porsche	114.303				

Gary Mook/Allsport

Mike Tyson arriving at the Marion County (Ind.) Courthouse during his February trial for rape. With him is his stepmother **Camille Ewald**, the companion of his late manager Cus D'Amato.

BOXING

BOXING

by Bernard Fernandez

On the Ropes

*Mike Tyson's conviction for rape ends a sordid chapter
and further weakens an unexciting heavyweight division.*

One can only imagine what it would have been like for Jack Johnson, the last great heavyweight boxer involved in a major scandal, had he lived in an age of cable television, satellite communications and call-in sports radio shows.

Johnson, the first black heavyweight champion, was notorious by the standards of the era in 1913, when he was forced to flee to Europe for an infringement of the Mann Act, under which he was charged with transporting a white woman for "immoral purposes." Johnson eventually returned to America and served a prison term.

But the furor over Johnson's violation was minor in comparison to that which surrounded former heavyweight champion Mike Tyson's conviction for rape. In fact, along with basketball star Magic Johnson's revelation that he had tested positive for the HIV virus, the Tyson case was the most closely followed, intensely scrutinized out-of-the-arena sports story of 1992.

Tyson's subsequent incarceration in the Indiana Youth Center, where he is serving a six-year sentence, underscores the fragile hold boxing has on an increasingly skeptical public. Although there are those who saw him as an unhealthy influ-

ence, and thus applauded the guilty verdict, Tyson's forced removal from the scene left a collection of decidedly less enthralling fighters to carry a torch whose flame is flickering lower than at any time in recent years.

As holder of the World Boxing Council, World Boxing Association and International Boxing Federation versions of the title (Michael Moorer is champion of the lightly regarded World Boxing Organization), "undisputed" heavyweight champion Evander Holyfield is the man primarily responsible for keeping the sport visible and exciting. But while Holyfield is undeniably a fine fellow, a role model in a manner Tyson, a fatherless street thug out of the Brooklyn ghetto, never could be, his reign to date has been anything but riveting.

After winning the title on a one-punch knockout of Tyson's conqueror, Buster Douglas, on Nov. 25, 1990, Holyfield has plodded to unanimous-decision victories over 42-year-old ex-champs George Foreman and Larry Holmes, sandwiched around a tougher-than-it-should-have-been TKO of Bert Cooper, a substitute for a substitute. In that one, Cooper had Holyfied on the canvas for the first time in his professional career before the window of opportunity closed.

The hope of many fight fans is that a heavyweight "Final Four," involving Holyfield and highly ranked contenders Riddick Bowe, Donovan "Razor" Ruddock

Bernard Fernandez joined the *Philadelphia Daily News* in 1974 and has been the paper's boxing writer since 1987.

Holly Stein/Allsport

Evander Holyfield (left) backs up challenger **Larry Holmes** with a left jab
in the third round of their heavyweight title fight on June 19.
Holmes was Holyfield's second 42-year-old opponent in 14 months.

and Lennox Lewis, will give boxing's most prestigious division the air of electricity that always charged Tyson's ring appearances. Ruddock and Lewis were to have met in a WBC elimination bout Oct. 31 in London, followed by a Holyfield-Bowe title fight Nov. 13 in Las Vegas. The two winners presumably would square off in the spring, although rumors persist that Bowe, agitated that the WBC placed Ruddock above him as its No. 1 contender, might go in another direction should he and Ruddock emerge victorious from their big fall bouts.

Emergence of a heavyweight superstar, be it Holyfield or someone else, would seem to be an absolute necessity given the scarcity of box-office draws in the '90s. Not only is Tyson in the slammer, but almost all of the long-time kings of boxing have bid farewell or are on the verge of doing so. Sugar Ray Leonard retired—this time, probably for good—after taking a savage beating from Terry Norris on Feb. 9, 1991. Roberto Duran, 41, and Thomas Hearns, 34, are still hanging on, but as shadowy ghosts of their luminescent former selves. Hearns,

who gave his fans a last blast from the past when he won the WBA light heavyweight title from Virgil Hill on June 3, 1991, didn't much resemble the "Hit Man" of old in losing it nine months later to Iran Barkley.

Foreman continues to be a beloved figure at 43, so much so that he signed a three-fight, $18 million deal with HBO for 1993. But Foreman, whose face was punched lopsided in an April 11 split-decision win over Alex Stewart, has proved the exception to many rules.

The best of the current practitioners —Norris, Julio Cesar Chavez and Pernell Whitaker—all have flaws in their makeup which, despite their undeniable talents, have kept them from stepping up to the plateau occupied by the legendary likes of Muhammad Ali and Leonard. Their fights are just that, fights, enjoyed mostly by boxing purists. With Ali and Leonard— and, yes, Tyson—you got grand events, anticipated as much by fringe and non-fans as by boxing nuts who can quote the *Ring Record Book* chapter and verse.

And as if the charisma gap weren't enough for boxing to contend with, the standard drains on the sport's popularity continued. Despite a mild increase in network boxing dates, it was a rare occasion in 1992 when a fight was seen on free television. A number of used-up former standouts, including Ray "Boom Boom" Mancini, Leon Spinks, Danny "Little Red" Lopez and Donny Lalonde, attempted comebacks that did nothing to enhance their stature. Perhaps most critically, the Barcelona Olympics, which yielded only one American gold medal winner—lightweight Oscar De La Hoya—and three U.S. medalists overall, failed to produce a bumper crop of can't-miss prospects.

The sum total of the rest of the year's boxing stories, though, barely registered on the Richter scale in comparison to the natural disaster imposed upon the sport by Tyson's conviction for the rape of an 18-year-old beauty contestant during the Miss Black America contest in the summer of 1991.

This much is indisputable: In the early morning hours of July 19, 1991, Desiree Washington and Tyson both were in his bedroom in suite 606 of the Canterbury Hotel in Indianapolis.

What really happened there was left to the interpretation of 12 jury members who, after hearing two weeks of testimony involving 49 witnesses, decided that the story presented by Washington, a model citizen, honor student and Sunday school teacher from Coventry, R.I., was far more plausible than that offered by Tyson, whose coarse, meandering account of the incident was loaded with contradictions.

Although the believability, or lack of it, of other witnesses on either side contributed to the guilty verdict, the four key players in the trial were the accused, the accuser and the heads of their respective legal teams.

In a risky gambit, given the difficulty of proving date rape, Tyson's $5,000-a-day lead defense attorney, Vincent Fuller, decided to put Tyson on the stand. Tyson proved to be his own worst witness, and Fuller's presentation of Tyson as a voracious sexual predator, whose sleazy reputation should have been enough to keep Washington or any other self-respecting woman from placing herself in a position of being alone with him, hardly scored points with the jury.

Washington and her mother, on the other hand, painted a portrait of Tyson that was so terrifying that at least two jurors had tears in their eyes as the older woman related how the alleged attack had become her daughter's recurring nightmare.

Fuller's fumbling defense left many courtroom observers wondering how he had come by his reputation as one of the finest legal minds in the country, but prosecutor Greg Garrison's performance was nothing less than brilliant.

Charley Steiner, who covered the trial for ESPN, said Garrison vs. Fuller was as noncompetitive as say, Tyson vs. Michael Spinks.

"As the trial unfolded, I just got the sense that it was a mismatch from the opening arguments," Steiner said. "Greg Garrison is as good an orator as anyone in the country. He held that courtroom spellbound.

"I'll never forget his closing argument to wrap the trial. You got chills. That's how good he was."

Steiner cites two scenes that illustrated the shift from Tyson, the wealthy and powerful former heavyweight champion, to Tyson, the about-to-be convicted rapist.

"The first four or five days of the trial, Tyson would arrive each morning at the courthouse and go up those steps almost as if he were on his way to the ring," Steiner said. "People were cheering, cameras were rolling and flashbulbs were popping.

"During a lunch break early in the trial, Tyson was signing autographs in the courtroom. I overheard one spectator say 'Good luck, Mike, you're going to get off.' And Tyson said, 'Oh, I'll win. I always win.' That was his attitude.

"But after the prosecution rested, Tyson was in the courtroom during another lunch break and he was all by himself at the defense table, chin in hand, looking down. I got the sense that for the first time in his life—certainly for the first time in the last ten years—he was truly alone. There was nobody left to pick up his mess."

As might be expected, the guilty verdict didn't close the book on the Tyson story; it merely ended one chapter. Another high-priced attorney, Harvard law professor Alan Dershowitz, the renowned defender of Claus von Bulow and Leona Helmsley,

Holly Stein/Allsport

Unbeaten WBC super lightweight champion **Julio Cesar Chavez** drills a right hand into the face of **Hector (Macho) Camacho** on the way to a unanimous 12-round decision on Sept. 12 in Las Vegas.

joined Team Tyson and filed an appeal. It is Dershowitz's contention that a later civil suit filed against Tyson by Washington is proof that she is, as Fuller had attempted to prove during the criminal proceedings, a scheming gold-digger. Washington's suit asks for reimbursement for medical and other expenses as well as punitive monetary damages for assault, battery, false imprisonment and emotional distress.

"The (civil) lawsuit finally disclosed Desiree Washington's true motive behind her accusation —money, lots of it," Dershowitz said.

Not that Tyson is a prince.

Former Tyson employee Rudy Gonzalez, interviewed by the *New York Post*, contended that Tyson was a man whose sexual appetite was so intense that he "would have four or five girls, sometimes 10 or 15 a night." Gonzalez added that Tyson had 1,300 names of sex partners filed in a pocket computer.

Given the wide variety of willing women available to him, one might think Tyson wouldn't force himself on anyone inclined to reject his advances. But, in addition to Washington, the former champion must also answer to charges brought against him by former Miss Black America Rosie Jones, who has a $100

million lawsuit pending. Jones alleges that Tyson, "assaulted, battered and humiliated" her during the same beauty pageant in which Tyson had his fateful encounter with Washington.

Should substantial judgments be rendered for the plaintiffs in the civil suits, Tyson, who has earned $70 million during his boxing career to date, might not be able to pay up. Court documents showed him to have assets totaling only $4.6 million, much of which can be expected to go to future legal fees.

The rapidly diminishing state of Tyson's finances gave rise to speculation that his flamboyant promoter, Don King, had systematically bilked him out of millions of dollars. King denied the charges and Tyson, in a handwritten letter released to the media by King, said, "I approved every exspense (sic). Don never stole from me."

In any case, it would now seem that the blockbuster Holyfield-Tyson title bout, which was to have taken place Nov. 8, 1991, might have brought Tyson fiscal solvency as well as a possible place in boxing history. That fight, which was to have paid Holyfield $30 million and Tyson $15 million, was postponed when Tyson suffered an injury in training, and canceled altogether after Tyson's conviction.

Should Tyson be paroled after three years, as many believe, he would be only 29, still young enough to resume his career. But three years away from his trade might be too much for him to overcome in any bid to achieve his former level of domination.

"If he loses that speed, that will take all the fight out of him," says Holyfield's trainer, George Benton. "Without speed, he'll be easy to beat. He's never had stamina."

Holyfield has continued to maintain that he would have upset Tyson, who was an early-line 13-5 favorite in the Nevada sports books, had their fight gone off as scheduled. But "The Real Deal," as the 29-year-old Holyfield is known, did little in the interim to convince the public that he is, in fact, the best heavyweight in the world.

Holyfield was to have faced Italy's Francesco Damiani while waiting for Tyson's legal situation to be resolved, but Damiani pulled out with an injury and Cooper was brought in on six days' notice. Fighting before a hostile crowd in Holyfield's hometown of Atlanta, Cooper knocked the champion down in the third round of their Nov. 23, 1993, fight and seemingly was on the verge of the biggest shocker in boxing since Douglas dethroned Tyson.

"My heart started to go boom, boom, boom," Cooper said. "I thought I was the heavyweight champion of the world. I said to myself, 'Oh, boy, this is it.' " Instead, Holyfield surged back to score an eighth-round TKO.

Next up for Holyfield was a June 19 date with Holmes, a grandfather who, after coming out of retirement, had made himself a viable challenger with a Feb. 7 unanimous decision over one of the so-called "young lions," Ray Mercer. But Holyfield, after sustaining a cut over his right eye in the sixth round, fought cautiously the rest of the way and had to settle for a less-than-satisfying decision over Holmes.

It was imperative for Holyfield, in order to maintain credibility, to stop fighting geezers and go up against a top-flight heavyweight in his prime. Promoter Dan Duva then orchestrated a series of fights, beginning with a July 18 WBA elimination bout in which Bowe registered a seventh-round TKO of South African Pierre Coetzer. Bowe thus moved on to the Nov. 13 show

Senate Probe Finds Little Has Changed

As bad decisions in boxing go, Dave Tiberi's split-decision loss to IBF middleweight champion James Toney on Feb. 8 is far down the list of real or perceived injustices.

But don't tell that to U.S. Sen. William Roth of Delaware, who represents Toberi's home state. Roth watched his constituent's long-shot bid to dethrone Toney on TV and was outraged when the champion left the ring in Atlantic City still in possession of his title. Never mind that 14 ringside reporters were evenly split over who deserved to win; to Roth, Tiberi's misfortune symbolized all victims in a sport in which the athletes have comparatively little say over their destinies.

Roth subsequently introduced Senate Bill 2852, which would create a non-profit Professional Boxing Corporation.

Five months into the most extensive government probe of boxing since the late Sen. Estes Kefauver decried the "racketeers and hoodlums who infest professional boxing" in 1960, Roth and other members of the Senate Permanent Subcommittee on Investigations convened in Washington in August to pick up Kefauver's torch.

"I am convinced that uniform rules and strong investigative powers of a centralized authority are essential if professional boxing is to regain its credibility," Roth said in a prepared statement before hearing two days of open testimony.

Many of the witnesses called before the subcommittee addressed standard concerns: the lack of comprehensive physical and neurological examinations, as well as health insurance and a pension plan; the need for a uniform drug and alcohol testing policy; rigid training procedures for officials; the elimination of shoddy record-keeping that too often results in mismatches.

But the questioning kept returning to those old standbys—boxing's alleged links to organized crime, and the shenanigans of high-profile promoters like Don King.

King and IBF president Bob Lee invoked the Fifth Amendment rather than answer questions on corruption in boxing. The refusal to answer questions, under oath, on the grounds that their testimony might incriminate them would seem to indicate King

Boxers **Bobby Czyz** (left), **Dave Tiberi** (center) and **James Pritchard** are sworn in on Aug. 11, prior to their testimony before the U.S. Senate Permanent Subcommittee on Investigations.

and Lee have something to hide. But Lee's attorney said that isn't necessarily the case.

"It's great theater," Carl Rowan Jr., son of the nationally syndicated columnist, said of the hearings. "Maybe it'll convince a few members of Congress that the federal government needs to regulate boxing, but I find the conduct of the Senate shameful. If the evidence is so compelling, where are the charges? If they're relying on ancient history to make a case, they haven't made a case."

Many of the Lee and King accusations were aired in the early 1980s during a failed FBI investigation into corruption involving King. That undercover operation brought charges against King and others, a point Lee made in harsh terms after refusing to answer questions.

"No one in the whole scam was indicted or convicted," Lee said. "Not one. And now they're bringing it all back again."

But while the subcommittee appeared to lack hard proof of wrongdoing by individuals, there is little question the system in general could stand a massive overhaul.

World Boxing Association cruiserweight champion Bobby Czyz testified that there is "more honesty and integrity among criminals and street thieves than among managers and promoters."

Noting that major promoters often hold options on both fighters in title bouts, Tiberi likened the practice to a "private, legalized slave industry" in which the promoters are in a no-lose situation and losing boxers routinely are discarded like yesterday's trash.

The Senate subcommittee did not list many specifics as to how the "Professional Boxing Corporation" would regulate the sport, but Lee said the first step he anticipated was the appointment of a commissioner with wide-ranging powers.

"It's not going to be a boxing person they pick, it's going to be someone with political connections," Lee complained. "I give him five, maybe six years before he ruins boxing."

One boxing person with political connections is Sig Rogich, previously the chairman of the Nevada State Athletic Commission, who recently was appointed U.S. Ambassador to Iceland by President Bush. Rogich, however, is not in favor of a federal boxing commission.

"I don't feel that the government wants to get involved in the governing of sports," Rogich said. As long as you have people of integrity and a strong attorney general and local entities, you can administer and oversee (at the state level)."

Holly Stein/Allsport

Terry Norris savors the moment with handlers after successfully defending his WBC super welterweight title against Meldrick Taylor on May 9.

courage in going the distance, but it was obvious his skills had largely deserted him.

Norris, the WBC super welterweight champ, followed up his routs of Leonard and Donald Curry with a fourth-round TKO of highly regarded WBA welterweight king Meldrick Taylor on May 9. But, like Chavez, Norris never seems to get as much credit as he deserves; critics claimed Taylor lacked the firepower to fully test the larger man.

Other notable bouts saw WBC super featherweight champ Azumah Nelson notch an eighth-round knockout of Jeff Fenech March 1 in Sydney, Australia, which removed the cloud that had hung over the Ghanan's head since he and Fenech fought to a controversial draw eight months earlier; Buddy McGirt claim the WBC welterweight crown with a dazzling, unanimous decision over Simon Brown Nov. 29, 1991, in Las Vegas; and IBF middleweight king James Toney retain his title on a rousing draw with Mike McCallum Dec. 13, 1991, in Atlantic City. Toney subsequently took a majority decision over McCallum Aug. 29 in Reno, Nev., in a sequel that was far less action-packed than the original.

At least none of the pro bouts were scored by computer, which was the case during the Barcelona Olympics. Chief victim of the newfangled gadgetry was American Eric Griffin, a four-time world amateur champion in the light-flyweight division, who somehow managed to come out ahead on all five judges' individual scoresheets yet dropped a 6-5 second-round decision to Spain's Rafael Lozano.

Griffin's ouster was one of many disappointments for a U.S. squad that was limited to one gold for De La Hoya, a silver by middleweight Chris Byrd and a bronze by flyweight Tim Austin. Cuba, meanwhile, dominated the competition, winning seven golds and two silvers.

The poor showing by the American team led Foreman, the 1968 heavyweight gold medalist, to call for a boxing "Dream Team" comprised of U.S. pros. "I'd go for a nickel," Foreman said.

Which poses a couple of questions: If pros are eligible to compete in the 1996 Olympics in Atlanta, will Tyson be free to punch for his country? And if so, would anyone want him to? □

down with Holyfield while Ruddock, who made his reputation off two knock-down, drag-out fights (both losses) with Tyson in 1991, was paired against Lewis, the 1988 Olympic super heavyweight champion.

Barring an early release of Tyson, the best of the rest of the heavyweights would seem to be Moorer, who captured the vacant WBO crown in an entertaining slugfest with Cooper on May 16 in Atlantic City. Like Tyson, though, Moorer has legal problems: He faces aggravated assault charges for punching a Monessen, Pa., police officer in 1991. The two most widely anticipated non-heavyweight fights of the year were hardly classics, despite terrific performances by the winners.

Undefeated WBC super lightweight champ Julio Cesar Chavez retained his title Sept. 12 with a lopsided, unanimous decision over Hector "Macho" Camacho in Las Vegas. Chavez, a Mexican national hero whose limited use of the English language and low-key demeanor have kept him from getting his proper due in this country, demonstrated why he is widely believed to be the best fighter, pound for pound, in the world. Camacho showed

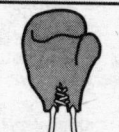

THE 1993 INFORMATION PLEASE SPORTS ALMANAC

BOXING STATISTICS

THE SEASON IN REVIEW
1991-1992
CHAMPIONS • TITLE BOUTS

SEC A
PAGE 779

Current Champions
WBA, WBC and IBF Titleholders (through Sept. 30, 1992)

The champions of professional boxing's 17 principal weight divisions, as recognized by the World Boxing Association (WBA), World Boxing Council (WBC) and International Boxing Federation (IBF). Heavyweight champion Evander Holyfield is the only fighter currently holding all three titles.

	Weight Limit	WBA Champion	WBC Champion	IBF Champion
Heavyweight	—	Evander Holyfield 28-0-0, 22 KO	Evander Holyfield 28-0-0, 22 KO	Evander Holyfield 28-0-0, 22 KO
Jr.Heavyweight	190 lbs	Bobby Czyz 40-5-0, 26 KO	Anaclet Wamba 35-2-0, 13 KO	Alfred Cole 20-1-0, 10 KO
Light Heavyweight	175 lbs	Virgil Hill 33-1-0, 18 KO	Jeff Harding 22-1-0, 17 KO	Charles Williams 33-4-2, 23 KO
Super Middleweight	168 lbs	Michael Nunn 38-1-0, 24 KO	Mauro Galvano 18-1-2, 3 KO	Iran Barkley 29-8-0, 17 KO
Middleweight	160 lbs	Reggie Johnson 31-2-1, 22 KO	Julian Jackson 45-1-0, 42 KO	James Toney 31-0-2, 21 KO
Jr.Middleweight	154 lbs	Vacant	Terry Norris 32-3-0, 18 KO	Gianfranco Rosi 55-3-0, 17 KO
Welterweight	147 lbs	Meldrick Taylor 29-2-1, 15 KO	Buddy McGirt 54-2-1, 44 KO	Maurice Blocker 34-2-0, 19 KO
Jr.Welterweight	140 lbs	Morris East 15-2-0, 10 KO	Julio Cesar Chavez 82-0-0, 67 KO	Pernell Whitaker 30-1-0, 14 KO
Lightweight	135 lbs	Joey Gamache 29-0-0, 18 KO	Miguel A.Gonzalez 26-0-0, 24 KO	Vacant
Jr.Lightweight	130 lbs	Genaro Hernandez 26-0-0, 18 KO	Azumah Nelson 33-2-1, 25 KO	John John Molina 26-3-0, 18 KO
Featherweight	126 lbs	Yung-Kyun Park 23-1-1, 13 KO	Paul Hodkinson 21-1-1, 20 KO	Manuel Medina 44-3-0, 21 KO
Jr.Featherweight	122 lbs	Wilfredo Vasquez 32-6-3, 27 KO	Tracy Harris Patterson 46-2-0, 34 KO	Welcome Ncita 31-0-0, 14 KO
Bantamweight	118 lbs	Eddie Cook 17-1-0, 15 KO	Victor Rabanales 33-10-2, 18 KO	Orlando Canizales 22-1-1, 24 KO
Jr.Bantamweight	115 lbs	Katsuya Onizuka 20-0-0, 17 KO	Sung-Kil Moon 17-1-0, 14 KO	Robert Quiroga 20-0-0, 11 KO
Flyweight	112 lbs	Aquiles Guzman 13-5-1, 5 KO	Yuri Arbachakov 11-0-0, 10 KO	Rodolfo Blanco 26-6-1, 19 KO
Jr.Flyweight	108 lbs	Hiroki Ioka 20-2-1, 9 KO	Humberto Gonzalez 34-1-0, 26 KO	Michael Carbajal 24-0-0, 13 KO
Strawweight	105 lbs	Hi-Yong Choi 14-0-0, 7 KO	Ricardo Lopez 30-0-0, 21 KO	Manny Melchor 20-14-5, 5 KO

Note: the following weight divisions are also known by these names—**Jr.Heavyweight** as Cruiserweight; **Jr.Middleweight** as Super Welterweight; **Jr.Welterweight** as Super Lightweight; **Jr.Lightweight** as Super Featherweight; **Jr.Featherweight** as Super Bantamweight; **Jr.Bantamweight** as Super Flyweight; **Jr. Flyweight** as Light Flyweight; and **Strawweight** as Minimum.

Evander Holyfield's Career Record

Going into his fourth title defense, against Riddick Bowe on Nov. 13, 1992 in Las Vegas, undisputed heavyweight champion Evander Holyfield was 28-0 with 22 knockouts.

1984

Date	Opponent, location	Result
Nov. 15	Lionel Byarm, New York	Wu 6

1985

Date	Opponent, location	Result
Jan. 20	Eric Winbush, Atlantic City	Wu 6
Mar. 13	Freddie Brown, Norfolk	KO 1
Apr. 20	Mark Rivera, Corpus Christi	KO 2
July 20	Tyrone Booze, Norfolk	Wu 8
Aug. 29	Rick Myers, Atlanta	KO 1
Oct. 30	Jeff Meachem, Atlantic City	KO 5
Dec. 21	Anthony Davis, Virginia Beach	KO 4

1986

Date	Opponent, location	Result
Mar. 1	Chisanda Mutti, Lancaster, Pa	KO 3
Apr. 6	Jesse Shelby, Corpus Christi	KO 3
May 28	Terry Mims, Metairie, LA	KO 5
July 12	Dwight M. Qawi, Atlanta	Ws 15
	(Won WBA & IBF Jr. Heavyweight titles)	
Dec. 8	Mike Brothers, Paris	KO 3

1987

Date	Opponent, location	Result
Feb. 14	Henry Tillman, Reno	TKO 7
May 15	Rickey Parkey, Las Vegas	TKO 3
Aug. 15	Ossie Ocasio, St.Tropez, France	TKO 11
Dec. 5	Dwight M.Qawi, Atlantic City	TKO 4

1988

Date	Opponent, location	Result
Apr. 9	Carlos DeLeon, Las Vegas	KO 8
	(Won WBC Jr.Heavyweight title)	
July 16	James Tillis, Lake Tahoe	KO 5
Dec. 9	Pinklon Thomas, Atlantic City	TKO 7

1989

Date	Opponent, location	Result
Mar. 11	Michael Dokes, Las Vegas	TKO 10
July 15	Adilson Rodrigues, Lake Tahoe	KO 2
Nov. 4	Alex Stewart, Atlantic City	TKO 8

1990

Date	Opponent, location	Result
June 1	Seamus McDonagh, Atlantic City	TKO 4
Oct. 25	Buster Douglas, Las Vegas	KO 3
	(Won undisputed Heavyweight title)	

1991

Date	Opponent, location	Result
Apr. 19	George Foreman, Atlantic City	Wu 12
Nov. 23	Bert Cooper, Atlanta	TKO 7

1992

Date	Opponent, location	Result
June 19	Larry Holmes, Las Vegas	Wu 12

Major Bouts

Division by division, from Oct. 15, 1991 through Sept. 30, 1992.

WBA, WBC and IBF champions are listed in **bold** type. Note the following Result columm abbreviations: KO (knockout); TKO (technical knockout); Wu (won by unanimous decision); Ws (won by split decision); Wm (won by majority decision); TW (won by majority technical decision); No Dec. (no decision).

Heavyweights

Date	Winner	Loser	Result	Title	Site
Oct. 18	Ray Mercer	Tommy Morrison	TKO 5	Non-title	Atlantic City
Oct. 29	Riddick Bowe	Elijah Tillery	TKO 1	Non-title	Washington, D.C.
Nov. 12	Larry Holmes	Jamie Howe	TKO 1	Non-title	Jacksonville, Fla.
Nov. 23	Lennox Lewis	Tyrell Biggs	TKO 3	Non-title	Atlanta
Nov. 23	**Evander Holyfield**	Bert Cooper	TKO 7	**WBA/WBC/IBF**	Atlanta
Dec. 7	George Foreman	Jimmy Ellis	TKO 3	Non-title	Las Vegas
Feb. 1	Michael Moorer	Mike White	Wu 10	Non-title	Las Vegas
Feb. 7	Larry Holmes	Ray Mercer	Wu 12	Non-title	Atlantic City
Feb. 15	Razor Ruddock	Greg Page	TKO 8	Non-title	Las Vegas
Apr. 7	Riddick Bowe	Conroy Nelson	KO 1	Non-title	Atlantic City
Apr. 11	George Foreman	Alex Stewart	Wm 10	Non-title	Las Vegas
Apr. 30	Lennox Lewis	Derek Williams	TKO 3	Non-title	London
May 8	Riddick Bowe	Everett Martin	TKO 5	Non-title	Las Vegas
May 15	Michael Moorer	Bert Cooper	TKO 5	Non-title	Atlantic City
June 19	**Evander Holyfield**	Larry Holmes	Wu 12	**WBA/WBC/IBF**	Las Vegas
June 26	Razor Ruddock	Phil Jackson	KO 4	Non-title	Cleveland
July 18	Riddick Bowe	Pierre Coetzer	TKO 7	Non-title	Las Vegas
Aug. 11	Lennox Lewis	Mike Dixon	KO 4	Non-title	Atlantic City

Junior Heavyweights
(Cruiserweights)

Date	Winner	Loser	Result	Title	Site
Nov. 15	**James Warring**	Donnell Wingfield	KO 5	IBF	Roanoke, Va.
Dec. 13	**Anaclet Wamba**	Massimiliano Duran	TKO 11	WBC	Paris
Apr. 30	**Anaclet Wamba**	Juan Polance	KO 2	Non-title	Pointe-a-Pitre
May 8	**Bobby Czyz**	Don Lalonde	Wu 12	WBA	Las Vegas
May 16	**James Warring**	Johnny Nelson	Wu 12	IBF	Bealeton, Va.
June 13	**Anaclet Wamba**	Andrei Rudenko	TKO 5	WBC	Levallois, France
July 30	Alfred Cole	**James Warring**	Wu 12	IBF	Waterloo Village, N.J.

Light Heavyweights

Date	Winner	Loser	Result	Title	Site
Oct. 19	**Charles Williams**	Fred Delgado	TKO 2	IBF	Williamson, W.Va.
Jan. 10	Frank Tate	Andrew Maynar	TKO 11	Non-title	New York City
Mar. 1	Virgil Hill	Aundrey Nelson	Wu 10	Non-title	Melbourne
Mar. 20	Iran Barkley*	**Thomas Hearns**	Ws 12	**WBA**	Las Vegas
Mar. 27	Frank Tate	Tim Johnson	TKO 6	Non-title	Countryside, Ill.
Apr. 11	Virgil Hill	Lotte Mwale	KO 4	Non-title	Bismarck, N.D.
June 5	**Jeff Harding**	Christophe Tiozzo	TKO 8	**WBC**	Marseilles, France
Sept.29	Virgil Hill	Frank Tate	Wu 12	vacant **WBA**	Bismarck, N.D.

*Barkley, the IBF super middleweight champion, stepped up a weight class to fight Hearns. He won, but resigned the heavier title on April 3, 1992, to remain as a super middleweight.

Super Middleweights

Date	Winner	Loser	Result	Title	Site
Dec. 13	**Victor Cordova**	Vicenzo Nardiello	KO 11	**WBA**	Paris
Jan. 10	Iran Barkley	**Darrin Van Horn**	TKO 2	IBF	New York City
Feb. 6	**Mauro Galvano**	Juan Carlos Gimenez	Wu 12	**WBC**	Marino, Italy
Apr. 25	Chris Eubank	John Jarvis	TKO 3	Non-title	Manchester, England
Apr. 25	**Mauro Galvano**	Eladio Centurion	Wu 8	Non-title	Grosseto, Italy
June 27	Chris Eubank	Ron Essett	Wu 12	Non-title	Quinta DoLago, Port.
June 30	Darrin Van Horn	Nicky Walker	Wu 10	Non-title	Pensacola, Fla.
Sept.12	Michael Nunn	**Victor Cordova**	Ws 12	**WBA**	Las Vegas

Note: IBF champion Barkley defeated Thomas Hearns for the WBA light heavyweight championship on Mar. 20, 1992. He then resigned that title on April 3, 1992, to retain his super middleweight championship.

Middleweights

Date	Winner	Loser	Result	Title	Site
Dec. 17	Reggie Johnson	Melvin Wynn	KO 2	Non-title	Pensacola, Fla.
Jan. 10	Roy Jones, Jr.	Jorge Vaca	KO 1	Non-title	New York City
Feb. 8	**James Toney**	Dave Tiberi	Ws 12	IBF	Atlantic City
Feb. 15	**Julian Jackson**	Ismael Negron	TKO 1	**WBC**	Las Vegas
Apr. 3	Roy Jones, Jr.	Art Serwano	TKO 1	Non-title	Reno
Apr. 10	**Julian Jackson**	Ron Collins	TKO 5	**WBC**	Mexico City
Apr. 11	**James Toney**	Glenn Wolfe	Wu 12	IBF	Las Vegas
Apr. 22	Reggie Johnson	Steve Collins	Ws 12	vacant **WBA**	E.Rutherford, N.J.
May 21	Mike McCallum	Fermino Chirino	Wu 10	Non-title	Las Vegas
May 26	**James Toney**	Ricky Stackhouse	KO 3	Non-title	Auburn Hills
June 26	Simon Brown	Melvin Wynn	KO 2	Non-title	Cleveland
June 30	Roy Jones Jr.	Jorge Castro	Wu 10	Non-title	Pensacola, Fla.
Aug. 1	**Julian Jackson**	Thomas Tate	Wu 12	**WBC**	Las Vegas
Aug. 29	**James Toney**	Mike McCallum	Wm 12	IBF	Reno

Junior Middleweights
(Super Welterweights)

WBA champion Vinny Pazienza was forced to give up his title in 1992 after being sidelined with neck and back injuries suffered in a car accident on Nov. 12, 1991, in Rhode Island.

Date	Winner	Loser	Result	Title	Site
Nov. 21	**Gianfranco Rosi**	Gilbert Baptist	Wu 12	IBF	Perugia, Italy
Jan. 10	Roy Jones, Jr.	Jorge Vaca	KO 1	Non-title	New York City
Feb. 22	**Terry Norris**	Carl Daniels	TKO 9	**WBC**	San Diego
Apr. 9	**Gianfranco Rosi**	Angel Hernandez	TKO 6	IBF	Celano, Italy
May 9	**Terry Norris**	Meldrick Taylor*	TKO 4	**WBC**	Las Vegas
May 21	Gilbert Dele	Eric Rhinehart	KO 4	Non-title	Paris
June 9	John David Jackson	Pat Lawlor	TKO 9	Non-title	San Francisco
July 11	**Gianfranco Rosi**	Gilbert Dele	Ws 12	IBF	Monte Carlo

*Taylor, the WBA welterweight champion, stepped up a weight class to fight Norris.

Welterweights

Date	Winner	Loser	Result	Title	Site
Nov. 29	Buddy McGirt	**Simon Brown**	Wu 12	**WBC**	Las Vegas
Dec. 14	Manning Galloway	Nika Khuhalo	Ws 12	Non-title	Cape Town, S.Africa
Jan. 18	**Meldrick Taylor**	Glenwood Brown	Wu 12	**WBA**	Philadelphia
Mar. 27	Glenwood Brown	Miguel Santana	Ws 10	Non-title	Catskill, N.Y.
May 2	**Buddy McGirt**	Delfino Marin	TKO 7	Non-title	Fort Worth
June 4	Glenwood Brown	Roque Montoya	TKO 2	Non-title	Atlantic City
June 19	Ramon Campas	Roger Turner	Wm 12	Non-title	Las Vegas
June 25	**Buddy McGirt**	Patrizio Oliva	Wu 12	**WBC**	Licola, Italy
Aug. 28	**Maurice Blocker**	Luis Garcia	Ws 12	IBF	Atlantic City

Junior Welterweights
(Super Lightweights)

Date	Winner	Loser	Result	Title	Site
Nov. 11	**Julio Cesar Chavez**	Jorge Melian	TKO 4	Non-title	Mexico City
Dec. 7	Rafael Pineda	Roger Mayweather	KO 10	vacant **IBF**	Reno
Jan. 14	Terrance Alli	Alfredo Rojas	TKO 5	Non-title	Atlantic City
Jan. 18	Pernell Whitaker	Harold Brazier	Wu 10	Non-title	Philadelphia
Jan. 24	Joey Gamache	Rick Souce	TKO 3	Non-title	Paris
Mar. 13	**Julio Cesar Chavez**	Ramos Soberanes	KO 4	Non-title	La Paz, Mex.
Apr. 3	Greg Haugen	Ray Mancini	TKO 7	Non-title	Reno
Apr. 10	Akinobu Hiranaka	**Edwin Rosario**	TKO 1	**WBA**	Mexico City
Apr. 10	**Julio Cesar Chavez**	Angel Hernandez	TKO 5	**WBC**	Mexico City
May. 1	Terrence Alli	Primo Ramos	Wu 8	Non-title	Sete, France
May 22	Pernell Whitaker	Jerry Lee Smith	TKO 1	Non-title	Mexico City
May 22	**Rafeal Pineda**	Clarence Coleman	TKO 7	**IBF**	Mexico City
June 13	Terrence Alli	Steve Larrimore	TKO 5	Non-title	Georgetown, Guyana
July 18	Pernell Whitaker	**Rafael Pineda**	Wu 12	**IBF**	Las Vegas
Aug. 1	**Julio Cesar Chavez**	Frankie Mitchell	TKO 4	**WBC**	Las Vegas
Sept. 9	Morris East	**Akinobu Hiranaka**	TKO 11	**WBA**	Tokyo
Sept. 12	**Julio Cesar Chavez**	Hector Camacho	Wu 12	**WBC**	Las Vegas

Lightweights

Champion Pernell Whitaker gave up his unified title in January 1992, and moved up to the Junior Welterweight division.

Date	Winner	Loser	Result	Title	Site
Jan. 11	Darryl Tyson	Leo Mancillas	KO 5	Non-title	Washington, D.C.
Jan. 16	Tracy Spann	Darryl Richardson	TKO 3	Non-title	Elizabeth, N.J.
Mar. 16	Miguel A. Gonzalez	Ramon Marchena	TKO 5	Non-title	Mexico City
May 22	Miguel A. Gonzalez	Tomas da Cruz	TKO 3	Non-title	Mexicali, Mex.
May 29	Jorge Paez	Eduardo Perez	Wu 10	Non-title	Atlantic City
June 4	Darryl Tyson	Roberto Medina	TKO 3	Non-title	Portland, Ore.
June 13	Joey Gamache	Chil-Sung Chun	TKO 9	vacant **WBA**	Portland, Ore.
Aug. 24	Miguel A. Gonzalez	Wilfrido Rocha	TKO 10	vacant **WBC**	Mexico City
Aug. 28	Fred Pendleton	Tracy Spann	No Dec.*	vacant **IBF**	Reno

*Pendleton and Spann fought to a 2-round technical draw after the fight was stopped when Pendleton was severely cut by a head butt.

Junior Lightweights
(Super Featherweights)

IBF champion Brian Mitchell retired in January, 1992.

Date	Winner	Loser	Result	Title	Site
Nov. 22	Genaro Hernandez	Daniel Londas	TKO 9	vacant **WBA**	Epernay, France
Jan. 14	John John Molina	Francisco Ortiz	KO 2	Non-title	San Juan, P.R.
Feb. 12	John John Molina	Jackie Gunguluza	TKO 4	vacant **IBF**	Sun City, S.Africa
Feb. 24	**Genaro Hernandez**	Omar Catari	Wu 12	**WBA**	Inglewood
Mar. 1	**Azumah Nelson**	Jeff Fenech	TKO 8	**WBC**	Melbourne
July 15	**Genaro Hernandez**	Masuaki Takeda	Wu 12	**WBA**	Fukuoka, Japan
Aug. 22	**John John Molina**	Fernando Caicedo	TKO 4	**IBF**	San Juan, P.R.

Featherweights

Date	Winner	Loser	Result	Title	Site
Nov. 13	Paul Hodkinson	**Marcos Villasana**	Wu 12	**WBC**	Liverpool
Nov. 18	**Manuel Medina**	Tom Johnson	TW 9	**IBF**	Inglewood
Jan. 25	**Yung-Kyun Park**	Seiji Asakawa	KO 9	**WBA**	Inchon, S.Kor.
Mar. 14	**Manuel Medina**	Fabrice Benichou	Ws 12	**IBF**	Antibes, France
Apr. 4	Tom Johnson	Mario Lozano	TKO 1	Non-title	Eldorado, Ill.
Apr. 25	**Yung-Kyun Park**	Koji Matsumoto	KO 11	**WBA**	Seoul
Apr. 25	**Paul Hodkinson**	Steve Cruz	TKO 3	**WBC**	Belfast
May 29	Fabrice Benichou	John Davidson	Wm 12	Non-title	Amneville, France
June 10	Tom Johnson	Kelvin Seabrooks	TKO 7	Non-title	New York City
July 22	**Manuel Medina**	Fabrizio Cappai	TKO 10	**IBF**	Capo d'Orlando, Italy
Aug. 29	**Yung-Kyun Park**	Giovanni Nieves	Wu 12	**WBA**	Seoul
Sept. 12	**Paul Hodkinson**	Fabrice Benichou	TKO 10	**WBC**	Toulouse, France

Junior Featherweights
(Super Bantamweights)

Date	Winner	Loser	Result	Title	Site
Dec. 9	**Daniel Zaragoza**	Paul Banke	Wu 12	**WBC**	Inglewood
Mar. 11	Tracy Harris Patterson	Angel Levi-Mayor	TKO 1	Non-title	New York City
Mar. 20	Thierry Jacob	**Daniel Zaragoza**	Wu 12	**WBC**	Calais, France
Mar. 27	Wilfredo Vasquez	**Raul Perez**	TKO 3	**WBA**	Mexico City
June 23	Tracy Harris Patterson	**Thierry Jacob**	TKO 2	**WBC**	Albany, N.Y.
June 27	**Wilfredo Vasquez**	Freddy Cruz	Wu 12	**WBA**	Gorle, Italy

Bantamweights

WBC champion Joichiro Tatsuyoshi underwent eye surgery in December, 1991, and was sidelined for nine months. An interim champion was decided on Mar. 30, 1992, when Victor Rabanales scored a majority technical decision over Yong-Hoon Lee in Ingelwood, Calif. Rabanales (in CAPITAL letters) was interim champion until he knocked out Tatsuyoshi for the official title on Sept. 17.

Date	Winner	Loser	Result	Title	Site
Oct. 21	Israel Contreras	**Luisito Espinosa**	KO 5	WBA	Quezon City, Phi.
Dec. 21	**Orlando Canizales**	Ray Minus	TKO 11	IBF	Laredo, Tex.
Mar. 15	Eddie Cook	**Israel Contreras**	KO 5	WBA	Las Vegas
Mar. 30	Victor Rabanales	Yong-Hoon Lee	TW 9	interim **WBC**	Inglewood
Apr. 23	**Orlando Canizales**	Francisco Alvarez	Wu 12	IBF	Paris
May 16	VICTOR RABANALES	Luis Ocampo	TKO 4	interim **WBC**	Tuxtla Gutierrez
July 27	VICTOR RABANALES	Chang-Kyun Oh	Wu 12	interim **WBC**	Inglewood
Sept.17	VICTOR RABANALES	**Joichiro Tatsuyoshi**	KO 9	WBC	Osaka, Japan
Sept.18	**Orlando Canizales**	Samuel Duran	Wu 12	IBF	Bozeman, Mont.

Junior Bantamweights
(Super Flyweights)

Date	Winner	Loser	Result	Title	Site
Dec. 22	**Sung-Kil Moon**	Torsak Pongsupa	TKO 6	WBC	Inchon, S.Kor.
Dec. 22	**Khaosai Galaxy**	Armando Castro	Wu 12	WBA	Bangkok
Feb. 15	**Robert Quiroga**	Carlos Mercado	Wu 12	IBF	Salerno, Italy
Feb. 22	Jose Quirino	Jose Ruiz	Wu 12	Non-title	Las Vegas
Apr. 10	Katsuya Onizuka	Thanomsak Sithboabey	Wu 12	vacant **WBA**	Tokyo
July 4	**Sung-Kil Moon**	Armando Salazar	TKO 8	WBC	Inchon, S.Kor.
July 11	**Robert Quiroga**	Jose Ruiz	Wu 12	IBF	Las Vegas
Sept.11	**Katsuya Onizuka**	Kenichi Matsumura	TKO 5	WBA	Tokyo

Flyweights

Date	Winner	Loser	Result	Title	Site
Oct. 25	**Muangchai Kittikasem**	Alberto Jimez	Wm 12	WBC	Bangkok
Feb. 28	**Muangchai Kittikasem**	Sot Chitalada	TKO 9	WBC	Samut Prakan, Thai.
Mar. 16	Yuri Arbachakov	S. Chalermsri	Wu 10	Non-title	Tokyo
Mar. 27	**Yong-Kang Kim**	Jonathan Penaloza	KO 6	WBA	Inchon, S.Kor.
Apr. 20	Yuri Arbachakov	S. Chalermsri	KO 3	Non-title	Tokyo
Apr. 30	Michael Carbajal*	Jose L. Velarde	Wu 10	Non-title	Albuquerque
May 27	**Muangchai Kittikasem**	Tarman Garzim	Wu 10	Non-title	Pathum Thani, Thai.
June 11	Rodolfo Blanco	**Dave McAuley**	Wu 12	IBF	Bilbao, Spain
June 23	Yuri Arbachakov	**Muangchai Kittikasem**	KO 8	WBC	Tokyo
Sept.26	Aquiles Guzman	**Yong-Kang Kim**	Wu 12	WBA	Pohan, S.Kor.

*Carbajal, the IBF junior flyweight champion, stepped up a weight class to fight Velarde.

Junior Flyweights
(Light Flyweights)

Date	Winner	Loser	Result	Title	Site
Oct. 18	**Michael Carbajal**	Jesus Chong	Wu 10	Non-title	Atlantic City
Dec. 17	Hiroki Ioka	**Myung-Woo Yuh**	Ws 12	WBA	Osaka, Japan
Jan. 27	**Humberto Gonzalez**	Domingo Sosa	Wu 12	WBC	Inglewood
Feb. 15	**Michael Carbajal**	Marcos Pacheco	Wu 12	IBF	Phoenix
Mar. 31	**Hiroki Ioka**	Noel Tunacao	Wu 12	WBA	Kitakyushu, Japan
June 7	**Humberto Gonzalez**	Kwang-Sun Kim	TKO 12	WBC	Seoul
June 15	**Hiroki Ioka**	Bong-Jun Kim	Wu 12	WBA	Osaka, Japan
Sept.14	**Humberto Gonzalez**	Napa Kiatwanchai	KO 2	WBC	Inglewood

Strawweights
(Minimum)

Date	Winner	Loser	Result	Title	Site
Oct. 21	**Phalan Lukmingkwan**	Andy Tabanas	Wu 12	IBF	Bangkok
Oct. 26	**Hi-Yong Choi**	Bong-Jun Kim	Wu 12	WBA	Seoul
Dec. 22	**Ricardo Lopez**	Kyung-Yun Lee	Wu 12	WBC	Inchon, S.Kor.
Feb. 22	**Hi-Yong Choi**	Yuichi Hosono	TKO 10	WBA	Seoul
Feb. 23	**Phalan Lukmingkwan**	Felix Naranjo	KO 2	IBF	Naknon Pathon, Thai.
Mar. 16	**Ricardo Lopez**	Pretty Boy Lucas	Wu 12	WBC	Mexico City
June 13	**Hi-Yong Choi**	Rommel Lawas	TKO 3	WBA	Inchon, S.Kor.
June 14	**Phalan Lukmingkwan**	Said Iskandar	TKO 8	IBF	Bangkok
Aug. 22	**Ricardo Lopez**	Singprasert Kittikasem	KO 5	WBC	Tampico, Mex.
Sept. 6	Manny Melchor	**Phalan Lukmingkwan**	Wu 12	IBF	Bangkok

THE 1993 INFORMATION PLEASE SPORTS ALMANAC

BOXING STATISTICS

THROUGH THE YEARS
1884-1992
WORLD CHAMPIONS

SEC B

PAGE 784

World Heavyweight Championship Fights

Widely accepted world champions in **bold** type. Note following result abbreviations: KO (knockout), TKO (technical knockout), Wu (unanimous decision), Wm (majority decision), Ws (split decision), Ref (referee's decision), ND (no decision), Disq (won on disqualification).

Year	Date	Winner	Age	Wgt	Loser	Wgt	Result	Location
1892	Sept. 7	James J.Corbett	26	178	**John L. Sullivan**	212	KO 21	New Orleans
1894	Jan. 25	**James J.Corbett**	27	184	Charley Mitchell	158	KO 3	Jacksonville, FL
1897	Mar. 17	Bob Fitzsimmons	34	167	**James J.Corbett**	183	KO 14	Carson City, NV
1899	June 9	James J. Jeffries	24	206	**Bob Fitzsimmons**	167	KO 11	Coney Island, NY
1899	Nov. 3	**James J. Jeffries**	24	215	Tom Sharkey	183	Ref 25	Coney Island, NY
1900	Apr. 6	**James J. Jeffries**	24	NA	Jack Finnegan	NA	KO 1	Detroit
1900	May 11	**James J. Jeffries**	25	218	James J.Corbett	188	KO 23	Coney Island, NY
1901	Nov. 15	**James J. Jeffries**	26	211	Gus Ruhlin	194	TKO 6	San Francisco
1902	July 25	**James J. Jeffries**	27	219	Bob Fitzsimmons	172	KO 8	San Francisco
1903	Aug. 14	**James J. Jeffries**	28	220	James J.Corbett	190	KO 10	San Francisco
1904	Aug. 25	**James J. Jeffries**	29	219	Jack Munroe	186	TKO 2	San Francisco
1905	July 3	Marvin Hart	28	190	Jack Root	171	KO 12	Reno, NV
1906	Feb. 23	Tommy Burns	24	180	**Marvin Hart**	188	Ref 20	Los Angeles
1906	Oct. 2	**Tommy Burns**	25	NA	Jim Flynn	NA	KO 15	Los Angeles
1906	Nov. 28	**Tommy Burns**	25	172	Phila.Jack O'Brien	163½	Draw 20	Los Angeles
1907	May 8	**Tommy Burns**	25	180	Phila.Jack O'Brien	167	Ref 20	Los Angeles
1907	July 4	**Tommy Burns**	26	181	Bill Squires	180	KO 1	Colma, Calif
1907	Dec. 2	**Tommy Burns**	26	177	Gunner Moir	204	KO 10	London
1908	Feb. 10	**Tommy Burns**	26	NA	Jack Palmer	NA	KO 4	London
1908	Mar. 17	**Tommy Burns**	26	NA	Jem Roche	NA	KO 1	Dublin
1908	Apr. 18	**Tommy Burns**	26	NA	Jewey Smith	NA	KO 5	Paris
1908	June 13	**Tommy Burns**	26	184	Bill Squires	183	KO 8	Paris
1908	Aug. 24	**Tommy Burns**	27	181	Bill Squires	184	KO 13	Sydney
1908	Sept. 2	**Tommy Burns**	27	183	Bill Lang	187	KO 6	Melbourne
1908	Dec. 26	Jack Johnson	30	192	**Tommy Burns**	168	TKO 14	Sydney
1909	Mar. 10	**Jack Johnson**	30	NA	Victor McLaglen	NA	ND 6	Vancouver
1909	May 19	**Jack Johnson**	31	205	Phila.Jack O'Brien	161	ND 6	Philadelphia
1909	June 30	**Jack Johnson**	31	207	Tony Ross	214	ND 6	Pittsburgh
1909	Sept. 9	**Jack Johnson**	31	209	Al Kaufman	191	ND 10	San Francisco
1909	Oct. 16	**Jack Johnson**	31	205½	Stanley Ketchel	170¼	KO 12	Colma, Calif.
1910	July 4	**Jack Johnson**	32	208	James J.Jeffries	227	KO 15	Reno, Nev.
1912	July 4	**Jack Johnson**	34	195½	Jim Flynn	175	TKO 9	Las Vegas, NM
1913	Dec. 19	**Jack Johnson**	35	NA	Jim Johnson	NA	Draw 10	Paris
1914	June 27	**Jack Johnson**	36	221	Frank Moran	203	Ref 20	Paris
1915	Apr. 5	Jess Willard	33	230	**Jack Johnson**	205½	KO 26	Havana
1916	Mar. 25	**Jess Willard**	34	225	Frank Moran	203	ND 10	NYC (Mad.Sq.Garden)
1919	July 4	Jack Dempsey	24	187	**Jess Willard**	245	TKO 4	Toledo, Ohio
1920	Sept. 6	**Jack Dempsey**	25	185	Billy Miske	187	KO 3	Benton Harbor, Mich.
1920	Dec. 14	**Jack Dempsey**	25	188¼	Bill Brennan	197	KO 12	NYC (Mad.Sq.Garden)
1921	July 2	**Jack Dempsey**	26	188	Georges Carpentier	172	KO 4	Jersey City, N.J.

Year	Date	Winner	Age	Wgt	Loser	Wgt	Result	Location
1923	July 4	**Jack Dempsey**	28	188	Tommy Givvons	175½	Ref 15	Shelby, Montana
1923	Sept. 14	**Jack Dempsey**	28	192½	Luis Firpo	216½	KO 2	NYC (Polo Grounds)
1926	Sept. 23	Gene Tunney	29	189½	**Jack Dempsey**	190	Wu 10	Philadelphia
1927	Sept. 22	**Gene Tunney**	30	189½	Jack Dempsey	192½	Wu 10	Chicago
1928	July 26	**Gene Tunney**	31	192	Tom Heeney	203½	TKO 11	NYC (Yankee Stadium)
1930	June 12	Max Schmeling	24	188	Jack Sharkey	197	Foul 4	NYC (Yankee Stadium)
1931	July 3	**Max Schmeling**	25	189	Young Stribling	186½	TKO 15	Cleveland
1932	June 21	Jack Sharkey	29	205	**Max Schmeling**	188	Ws 15	Long Island City, N.Y.
1933	June 29	Primo Carnera	26	260½	**Jack Sharkey**	201	KO 6	Long Island City, N.Y.
1933	Oct. 22	**Primo Carnera**	26	259½	Paulino Uzcudun	229¼	Wu 15	Rome
1934	Mar. 1	**Primo Carnera**	27	270	Tommy Loughran	184	Wu 15	Miami
1934	June 14	Max Baer	25	209½	**Primo Carnera**	263¼	TKO 11	Long Island City, N.Y.
1935	June 13	James J.Braddock	29	193¾	**Max Baer**	209½	Wu 15	Long Island City, N.Y.
1937	June 22	Joe Louis	23	197¼	**James J.Braddock**	197	KO 8	Chicago
1937	Aug. 30	**Joe Louis**	23	197	Tommy Farr	204¼	Wu 15	NYC (Yankee Stadium)
1938	Feb. 23	**Joe Louis**	23	200	Nathan Mann	193½	KO 3	NYC (Mad.Sq.Garden)
1938	Apr. 1	**Joe Louis**	23	202½	Harry Thomas	196	KO 5	Chicago
1938	June 22	**Joe Louis**	24	198¼	Max Schmeling	193	KO 1	NYC (Yankee Stadium)
1939	Jan. 25	**Joe Louis**	24	200¼	John Henry Lewis	180¾	KO 1	NYC (Mad.Sq.Garden)
1939	Apr. 17	**Joe Louis**	24	201¼	Jack Roper	204¾	KO 1	Los Angeles
1939	June 28	**Joe Louis**	25	200¾	Tony Galento	233¾	TKO 4	NYC (Yankee Stadium)
1939	Sept. 20	**Joe Louis**	25	200	Bob Pastor	183	KO 11	Detroit
1940	Feb. 9	**Joe Louis**	25	203	Arturo Godoy	202	Ws 15	NYC (Mad.Sq.Garden)
1940	Mar. 29	**Joe Louis**	25	201½	Johnny Paychek	187½	KO 2	NYC (Mad.Sq.Garden)
1940	June 20	**Joe Louis**	26	199	Arturo Godoy	201¼	TKO 8	NYC (Yankee Stad.)
1940	Dec. 16	**Joe Louis**	26	202¼	Al McCoy	180¾	TKO 6	Boston
1941	Jan. 31	**Joe Louis**	26	202½	Red Burman	188	KO 5	NYC (Mad.Sq.Garden)
1941	Feb. 17	**Joe Louis**	26	203½	Gus Dorazio	193½	KO 2	Philadelphia
1941	Mar. 21	**Joe Louis**	26	202	Abe Simon	254½	TKO 13	Detroit
1941	Apr. 8	**Joe Louis**	26	203½	Tony Musto	199½	TKO 9	St. Louis
1941	May 23	**Joe Louis**	27	201½	Buddy Baer	237½	Disq 7	Washington, DC
1941	June 18	**Joe Louis**	27	199½	Billy Conn	174	KO 13	NYC (Polo Grounds)
1941	Sept. 29	**Joe Louis**	27	202¼	Lou Nova	202½	TKO 6	NYC (Polo Grounds)
1942	Jan. 9	**Joe Louis**	27	206¾	Buddy Baer	250	KO 1	NYC (Mad.Sq.Garden)
1942	Mar. 27	**Joe Louis**	27	207½	Abe Simon	255½	KO 6	NYC (Mad.Sq.Garden)
1942–45		World War II						
1946	June 9	**Joe Louis**	32	207	Billy Conn	187	KO 8	NYC (Yankee Stadium)
1946	Sept. 18	**Joe Louis**	32	211	Tami Mauriello	198½	KO 1	NYC (Yankee Stadium)
1947	Dec. 5	**Joe Louis**	33	211½	Jersey Joe Walcott	194½	Ws 15	NYC (Mad.Sq.Garden)
1948	June 25	**Joe Louis**	34	213½	Jersey Joe Walcott	194¾	KO 11	NYC (Yankee Stadium)
1949	June 22	Ezzard Charles	27	181¾	Jersey Joe Walcott	195½	Wu 15	Chicago
1949	Aug. 10	**Ezzard Charles**	28	180	Gus Lesnevich	182	TKO 8	NYC (Yankee Stadium)
1949	Oct. 14	**Ezzard Charles**	28	182	Pat Valentino	188½	KO 8	San Francisco
1950	Aug. 15	**Ezzard Charles**	29	183¼	Freddie Beshore	184½	TKO 14	Buffalo
1950	Sept. 27	**Ezzard Charles**	29	184½	Joe Louis	218	Wu 15	NYC (Yankee Stadium)
1950	Dec. 5	**Ezzard Charles**	29	185	Nick Barone	178½	KO 11	Cincinnati
1951	Jan. 12	**Ezzard Charles**	29	185	Lee Oma	193	TKO 10	NYC (Mad.Sq.Garden)
1951	Mar. 7	**Ezzard Charles**	29	186	Jersey Joe Walcott	193	Wu 15	Detroit
1951	May 30	**Ezzard Charles**	29	182	Joey Maxim	181½	Wu 15	Chicago
1951	July 18	Jersey Joe Walcott	37	194	**Ezzard Charles**	182	KO 7	Pittsburgh
1952	June 5	**Jersey Joe Walcott**	38	196	Ezzard Charles	191½	Wu 15	Philadelphia
1952	Sept. 23	Rocky Marciano	29	184	**Jersey Joe Walcott**	196	KO 13	Philadelphia
1953	May 15	**Rocky Marciano**	29	184½	Jersey Joe Walcott	197¾	KO 1	Chicago
1953	Sept. 24	**Rocky Marciano**	30	185	Roland LaStarza	184¾	TKO 11	NYC (Polo Grounds)
1954	June 17	**Rocky Marciano**	30	187½	Ezzard Charles	185½	Wu 15	NYC (Yankee Stadium)
1954	Sept. 17	**Rocky Marciano**	31	187	Ezzard Charles	192½	KO 8	NYC (Yankee Stadium)
1955	May 16	**Rocky Marciano**	31	189	Don Cockell	205	TKO 9	San Francisco
1955	Sept. 21	**Rocky Marciano**	32	188¼	Archie Moore	188	KO 9	NYC (Yankee Stadium)

World Heavyweight Championship Fights (Cont.)

Year	Date	Winner	Age	Wgt	Loser	Wgt	Result	Location
1956	Nov. 30	Floyd Patterson	21	182¼	Archie Moore	187¾	KO 5	Chicago
1957	July 29	**Floyd Patterson**	22	184	Tommy Jackson	192½	TKO 10	NYC (Polo Grounds)
1957	Aug. 22	**Floyd Patterson**	22	187¼	Pete Rademacher	202	KO 6	Seattle
1958	Aug. 18	**Floyd Patterson**	23	184½	Roy Harris	194	TKO 13	Los Angeles
1959	May 1	**Floyd Patterson**	24	182½	Brian London	206	KO 11	Indianapolis
1959	June 26	Ingemar Johansson	26	196	**Floyd Patterson**	182	TKO 3	NYC (Yankee Stadium)
1960	June 20	Floyd Patterson	25	190	**Ingemar Johansson**	194¾	KO 5	NYC (Polo Grounds)
1961	Mar. 13	**Floyd Patterson**	26	194¾	Ingemar Johansson	206½	KO 6	Miami Beach
1961	Dec. 4	**Floyd Patterson**	26	188½	Tom McNeeley	197	KO 4	Toronto
1962	Sept. 25	Sonny Liston	30	214	**Floyd Patterson**	189	KO 1	Chicago
1963	July 22	**Sonny Liston**	31	215	Floyd Patterson	194½	KO 1	Las Vegas
1964	Feb. 25	Cassius Clay*	22	210½	**Sonny Liston**	218	TKO 7	Miami Beach
1965	Mar. 5	Ernie Terrell WBA	25	199	Eddie Machen	192	Wu 15	Chicago
1965	May 25	**Muhammad Ali**	23	206	Sonny Liston	215¼	KO 1	Lewiston, Me.
1965	Nov. 1	Ernie Terrell WBA	26	206	George Chuvalo	209	Wu 15	Toronto
1965	Nov. 22	**Muhammad Ali**	23	210	Floyd Patterson	196¾	TKO 12	Las Vegas
1966	Mar. 29	**Muhammad Ali**	24	214½	George Chuvalo	216	Wu 15	Toronto
1966	May 21	**Muhammad Ali**	24	201½	Henry Cooper	188	TKO 6	London
1966	June 28	Ernie Terrell WBA	27	209½	Doug Jones	187½	Wu 15	Houston
1966	Aug. 6	**Muhammad Ali**	24	209½	Brian London	201½	KO 3	London
1966	Sept. 10	**Muhammad Ali**	24	203½	Karl Mildenberger	194¼	TKO 12	Frankfurt, W.Ger.
1966	Nov. 14	**Muhammad Ali**	24	212¾	Cleveland Williams	210½	TKO 3	Houston
1967	Feb. 6	**Muhammad Ali**	25	212¼	Ernie Terrell WBA	212½	Wu 15	Houston
1967	Mar. 22	**Muhammad Ali**	25	211½	Zora Folley	202½	KO 7	NYC (Mad.Sq.Garden)
1968	Mar. 4	Joe Frazier	24	204½	Buster Mathis	243½	TKO 11	NYC (Mad.Sq.Garden)
1968	Apr. 27	Jimmy Ellis	28	197	Jerry Quarry	195	Wm 15	Oakland
1968	June 24	Joe Frazier NY	24	203½	Manuel Ramos	208	TKO 2	NYC (Mad.Sq.Garden)
1968	Aug. 14	Jimmy Ellis WBA	28	198	Floyd Patterson	188	Ref 15	Stockholm
1968	Dec. 10	Joe Frazier NY	24	203	Oscar Bonavena	207	Wu 15	Philadelphia
1969	Apr. 22	Joe Frazier NY	25	204½	Dave Zyglewicz	190½	KO 1	Houston
1969	June 23	Joe Frazier NY	25	203½	Jerry Quarry	198½	TKO 8	NYC (Mad.Sq.Garden)
1970	Feb. 16	Joe Frazier NY	26	205	Jimmy Ellis WBA	201	TKO 5	NYC (Mad.Sq.Garden)
1970	Nov. 18	Joe Frazier	26	209	Bob Foster	188	KO 2	Detroit
1971	Mar. 8	Joe Frazier	27	205½	**Muhammad Ali**	215	Wu 15	NYC (Mad.Sq.Garden)
1972	Jan. 15	**Joe Frazier**	28	215½	Terry Daniels	195	TKO 4	New Orleans
1972	May 26	**Joe Frazier**	28	217½	Ron Stander	218	TKO 5	Omaha, Neb.
1973	Jan. 22	George Foreman	24	217½	**Joe Frazier**	214	TKO 2	Kingston, Jamaica
1973	Sept. 1	**George Foreman**	24	219½	Jose (King) Roman	196½	KO 1	Tokyo
1974	Mar. 26	**George Foreman**	25	224¼	Ken Norton	212¼	TKO 2	Caracas, Venezuela
1974	Oct. 30	Muhammad Ali	32	216½	**George Foreman**	220	KO 8	Kinshasa, Zaire
1975	Mar. 24	**Muhammad Ali**	33	223½	Chuck Wepner	225	TKO 15	Cleveland
1975	May 16	**Muhammad Ali**	33	224½	Ron Lyle	219	TKO 11	Las Vegas
1975	July 1	**Muhammad Ali**	33	224½	Joe Bugner	230	Wu 15	Kuala Lumpur, Malaysia
1975	Oct. 1	**Muhammad Ali**	33	224½	Joe Frazier	215	TKO 15	Manila, Philippines
1976	Feb. 20	**Muhammad Ali**	34	226	Jean Pierre Coopman	206	KO 5	San Juan, P.R.
1976	Apr. 30	**Muhammad Ali**	34	230	Jimmy Young	209	Wu 15	Landover, Md.
1976	May 24	**Muhammad Ali**	34	230	Richard Dunn	206½	TKO 5	Munich, W.Ger.
1976	Sept. 28	**Muhammad Ali**	34	221	Ken Norton	217½	Wu 15	NYC (Yankee Stadium)
1977	May 16	**Muhammad Ali**	35	221¼	Alfredo Evangelista	209¼	Wu 15	Landover, Md.
1977	Sept. 29	**Muhammad Ali**	35	225	Earnie Shavers	211¼	Wu 15	NYC (Mad.Sq.Garden)
1978	Feb. 15	Leon Spinks	24	197¼	**Muhammad Ali**	224¼	Ws 15	Las Vegas
1978	June 9	Larry Holmes	28	209	Ken Norton WBC†	220	Ws 15	Las Vegas
1978	Sept. 15	Muhammad Ali	36	221	**Leon Spinks**	201	Wu 15	New Orleans
1978	Nov. 10	Larry Holmes WBC	29	214	Alfredo Evangelista	208¼	KO 7	Las Vegas

*Muhammad Ali was known as Cassius Clay when he stopped Sonny Liston on Feb. 25, 1964.

Year	Date	Winner	Age	Wgt	Loser	Wgt	Result	Location
1979	Mar. 23	Larry Holmes WBC	29	214	Osvaldo Ocasio	207	TKO 7	Las Vegas
1979	June 22	Larry Holmes WBC	29	215	Mike Weaver	202	TKO 12	NYC (Mad.Sq.Garden)
1979	Sept. 28	Larry Holmes WBC	29	210	Earnie Shavers	211	TKO 11	Las Vegas
1979	Oct. 20	John Tate	24	240	Gerrie Coetzee	222	Wu 15	Pretoria, S.Africa
1980	Feb. 3	Larry Holmes WBC	30	213½	Lorenzo Zanon	215	TKO 6	Las Vegas
1980	Mar. 31	Mike Weaver	27	232	John Tate WBA	232	KO 15	Knoxville, Tenn.
1980	Mar. 31	Larry Holmes WBC	30	211	Leroy Jones	254½	TKO 8	Las Vegas
1980	July 7	Larry Holmes WBC	30	214¼	Scott LeDoux	226	TKO 7	Minneapolis
1980	Oct. 2	Larry Holmes WBC	30	211¼	Muhammad Ali	217½	TKO 11	Las Vegas
1980	Oct. 25	Mike Weaver WBA	28	210	Gerrie Coetzee	226½	KO 13	Sun City, Boph'swana
1981	Apr. 11	**Larry Holmes**	31	215	Trevor Berbick	215½	Wu 15	Las Vegas
1981	June 12	**Larry Holmes**	31	212¼	Leon Spinks	200¼	TKO 3	Detroit
1981	Oct. 3	Mike Weaver WBA	29	215	Quick Tillis	209	Wu 15	Rosemont, Ill.
1981	Nov. 6	**Larry Holmes**	32	213¼	Renaldo Snipes	215¾	TKO 11	Pittsburgh
1982	June 11	**Larry Holmes**	32	212½	Gerry Cooney	225½	TKO 13	Las Vegas
1982	Nov. 26	**Larry Holmes**	33	217½	Randall (Tex) Cobb	234¼	Wu 15	Houston
1982	Dec. 10	Michael Dokes	24	216	Mike Weaver WBA	209¾	TKO 1	Las Vegas
1983	Mar. 27	**Larry Holmes**	33	221	Lucien Rodriguez	209	Wu 12	Scranton, Pa.
1983	May 20	Michael Dokes WBA	24	223	Mike Weaver	218½	Draw 15	Las Vegas
1983	May 20	**Larry Holmes**	33	213	Tim Witherspoon	219½	Ws 12	Las Vegas
1983	Sept. 10	**Larry Holmes**	33	223	Scott Frank	211¼	TKO 5	Atlantic City
1983	Sept. 23	Gerrie Coetzee	28	215	Michael Dokes WBA	217	KO 10	Richfield, Ohio
1983	Nov. 25	**Larry Holmes**	34	219	Marvis Frazier	200	TKO 1	Las Vegas
1984	Mar. 9	Tim Witherspoon**	26	220¼	Greg Page	239½	Wm 12	Las Vegas
1984	Aug. 31	Pinklon Thomas	26	216	Tim Witherspoon WBC	217	Wm 12	Las Vegas
1984	Nov. 9	**Larry Holmes** IBF	35	221½	Bonecrusher Smith	227	TKO 12	Las Vegas
1984	Dec. 1	Greg Page	26	236½	Gerrie Coetzee WBA	218	KO 8	Sun City, Boph'swana
1985	Mar. 15	**Larry Holmes**	35	223½	David Bey	233¼	TKO 10	Las Vegas
1985	Apr. 29	Tony Tubbs	26	229	Greg Page WBA	239½	Wu 15	Buffalo
1985	May 20	**Larry Holmes**	35	222¼	Carl Williams	215	Wu 15	Las Vegas
1985	June 15	Pinklon Thomas	27	220¼	Mike Weaver	221¼	KO 8	Las Vegas
1985	Sept. 21	Michael Spinks	29	200	**Larry Holmes** IBF	221½	Wu 15	Las Vegas
1986	Jan. 17	Tim Witherspoon	28	227	Tony Tubbs WBA	229	Wm 15	Atlanta
1986	Mar. 22	Trevor Berbick	33	218½	Pinklon Thomas WBC	222¾	Wu 15	Las Vegas
1986	Apr. 19	**Michael Spinks**	29	205	Larry Holmes	223	Ws 15	Las Vegas
1986	July 19	Tim Witherspoon	28	234¾	Frank Bruno	228	TKO 11	Wembley, England
1986	Sept. 6	**Michael Spinks**	30	201	Steffen Tangstad	214¾	TKO 4	Las Vegas
1986	Nov. 22	Mike Tyson	20	221¼	Trevor Berbick WBC	218½	TKO 2	Las Vegas
1986	Dec. 12	Bonecrusher Smith	33	228½	Tim Witherspoon WBA	233½	TKO 1	NYC (Mad.Sq.Garden)
1987	Mar. 7	Mike Tyson WBC	20	219	James Smith WBA	233	Wu 12	Las Vegas
1987	May 30	Mike Tyson	20	218¾	Pinklon Thomas	217¾	TKO 6	Las Vegas
1987	May 30	Tony Tucker‡	28	222¼	Buster Douglas	227¼	TKO 10	Las Vegas
1987	June 15	**Michael Spinks**	30	208¾	Gerry Cooney	238	TKO 5	Atlantic City
1987	Aug. 1	Mike Tyson	21	221	Tony Tucker IBF	221	Wu 12	Las Vegas
1987	Oct. 16	Mike Tyson	21	216	Tyrell Biggs	228¾	TKO 7	Atlantic City
1988	Jan. 22	Mike Tyson	21	215¾	Larry Holmes	225¾	TKO 4	Atlantic City
1988	Mar. 20	Mike Tyson	21	216¼	Tony Tubbs	238¼	KO 2	Tokyo
1988	June 27	Mike Tyson	21	218¼	**Michael Spinks**	212¼	KO 1	Atlantic City
1989	Feb. 25	**Mike Tyson**	22	218	Frank Bruno	228	TKO 5	Las Vegas
1989	July 21	**Mike Tyson**	23	219¼	Carl Williams	218	TKO 1	Atlantic City
1990	Feb. 10	Buster Douglas	29	231½	**Mike Tyson**	220½	KO 10	Tokyo
1990	Oct. 25	Evander Holyfield	28	208	**Buster Douglas**	246	KO 3	Las Vegas
1991	Apr. 19	**Evander Holyfield**	28	208	George Foreman	257	Wu 12	Atlantic City
1991	Nov. 23	**Evander Holyfield**	29	210	Bert Cooper	215	TKO 7	Atlanta
1992	June 19	**Evander Holyfield**	29	210	Larry Holmes	233	Wu 12	Las Vegas

†WBC recognized Ken Norton as world champion when Leon Spinks refused to meet Norton before Spinks' rematch with Muhammad Ali. Norton had scored a 15-round split decision over Jimmy Young on Nov. 5, 1977 in Las Vegas.
**WBC recognized winner of Mar. 9, 1984 fight between Tim Witherspoon and Greg Page as world champion after Larry Holmes relinquished title in dispute. IBF then recognized Holmes.
‡IBF recognized winner of May 30, 1987 fight between Tony Tucker and James (Buster) Douglas as world champion after Michael Spinks relinquished title in dispute.

Muhammad Ali's Career Pro Record

Born Cassius Marcellus Clay, Jr. on Jan. 17, 1942, in Louisville; Amateur record of 100-5; won light-heavyweight gold medal at 1960 Olympic Games; Pro record of 56-5-0 with 37 KOs in 61 fights.

1960

Date	Opponent (location)	Result
Oct. 29	Tunney Hunsaker, Louisville	Wu 6
Dec. 27	Herb Siler, Miami Beach	TKO 4

1961

Date	Opponent (location)	Result
Jan. 17	Tony Esperti, Miami Beach	TKO 3
Feb. 7	Jim Robinson, Miami Beach	TKO 1
Feb. 21	Donnie Fleeman, Miami Beach	TKO 7
Apr. 19	Lamar Clark, Louisville	KO 2
June 26	Duke Sabedong, Las Vegas	Wu 10
July 22	Alonzzo Johnson, Louisville	Wu 10
Oct. 7	Alex Miteff, Louisville	TKO 6
Nov. 29	Willi Besmanoff, Louisville	TKO 7

1962

Date	Opponent (location)	Result
Feb. 10	Sonny Banks, New York	TKO 4
Feb. 28	Don Warner, Miami Beach	TKO 4
Apr. 23	George Logan, Los Angeles	TKO 4
May 19	Billy Daniels, Los Angeles	TKO 7
July 20	Alejandro Lavorante, Los Angeles	KO 5
Nov. 15	Archie Moore, Los Angeles	KO 4

1963

Date	Opponent (location)	Result
Jan. 24	Charlie Powell, Pittsburgh	KO 3
Mar. 13	Doug Jones, New York	Wu 10
June 18	Henry Cooper, London	TKO 5

1964

Date	Opponent (location)	Result
Feb. 25	Sonny Liston, Miami Beach	TKO 7

(won World Heavyweight title)
After the fight, Clay announces he is a member of the Black Muslim religious sect and has changed his name to Muhammad Ali.

1965

Date	Opponent (location)	Result
May 25	Sonny Liston, Lewiston, Me	KO 1
Nov. 22	Floyd Patterson, Las Vegas	TKO 12

1966

Date	Opponent (location)	Result
Mar. 29	George Chuvalo, Toronto	Wu 15
May 21	Henry Cooper, London	TKO 6
Aug. 6	Brian London, London	KO 3
Sept.10	Karl Mildenberger, Franfurt	TKO 12
Nov. 12	Cleveland Williams, Houston	TKO 3

1967

Date	Opponent (location)	Result
Feb. 6	Ernie Terrell, Houston	Wu 15
Mar. 22	Zora Folley, New York	KO 7
Apr. 28	Refuses induction into U.S. Army and is stripped of world title by WBA and most state commissions the next day.	
June 20	Found guilty of draft evasion in Houston; fined $10,000 and sentenced to 5 years; remains free pending appeals, but is barred from the ring.	

1968-69
(Inactive)

1970

Date	Opponent (location)	Result
Feb. 3	Announces retirement	
Oct. 26	Jerry Quarry, Atlanta	TKO 3
Dec. 7	Oscar Bonavena, New York	TKO 15

1971

Date	Opponent (location)	Result
Mar. 8	Joe Frazier, New York	Lu 15

(for World Heavyweight title)

June 28	U.S. Supreme Court unanimously reverses Ali's 1967 conviction saying he had been drafted improperly.	
July 26	Jimmy Ellis, Houston	TKO 12

(won vacant NABF Heavyweight title)

Nov. 17	Buster Mathis, Houston	Wu 12
Dec. 26	Jurgen Blin, Zurich	KO 7

1972

Date	Opponent (location)	Result
Apr. 1	Mac Foster, Tokyo	Wu 15
May 1	George Chuvalo, Vancouver	Wu 12
June 27	Jerry Quarry, Las Vegas	TKO 7
July 19	Al (Blue) Lewis, Dublin, Ire	TKO 11
Sept.20	Floyd Patterson, New York	TKO 7
Nov. 21	Bob Foster, Stateline, Nev	TKO 8

1973

Date	Opponent (location)	Result
Feb. 14	Joe Bugner, Las Vegas	Wu 12
Mar. 31	Ken Norton, San Diego	Ls 12

(lost NABF Heavyweight title)

Sept.10	Ken Norton, Inglewood, Calif.	Ws 12

(regained NABF Heavyweight title)

Oct. 20	Rudi Rubbers, Jakarta, Indonesia	Wu 12

1974

Date	Opponent (location)	Result
Jan. 28	Joe Frazier, New York	Wu 12
Oct. 30	George Foreman, Kinshasa, Zaire	KO 8

(regained World Heavyweight title)

1975

Date	Opponent (location)	Result
Mar. 24	Chuck Wepner, Cleveland	TKO 15
May 16	Ron Lyle, Las Vegas	TKO 11
June 30	Joe Bugner, Kuala Lumpur, Malaysia	Wu 15
Sept.30	Joe Frazier, Manila	TKO 14

1976

Date	Opponent (location)	Result
Feb. 20	Jean-Pierre Coopman, San Juan	KO 5
Apr. 30	Jimmy Young, Landover, Md	Wu 15
May 24	Richard Dunn, Munich	TKO 5
Sept.28	Ken Norton, New York	Wu 15

1977

Date	Opponent (location)	Result
May 16	Alfredo Evangelista, Landover	Wu 15
Sept.29	Earnie Shavers, New York	Wu 15

1978

Date	Opponent (location)	Result
Feb. 15	Leon Spinks, Las Vegas	Ls 15

(lost World Heavyweight title)

Sept.15	Leon Spinks, New Orleans	Wu 15

(regained World Heavyweight title)

1979

Date		
June 27	Announces retirement	

1980

Date	Opponent (location)	Result
Oct. 2	Larry Holmes, Las Vegas	TKO by 11

1981

Date	Opponent (location)	Result
Dec. 11	Trevor Berbick, Nassau	Lu 10

All-Time Heavyweight Upsets

Buster Douglas' Feb. 10, 1990, knockout of unbeaten heavyweight champion Mike Tyson ranks as the biggest upset in boxing history. It tops 11 other well-known upsets in the annals of the heavyweight division. All were fights for the world championship except the Max Schmeling-Joe Louis bout.

Note the following abbreviations: KO (knockout), Wu (unanimous decision), TKO (technical knockout, fight stopped), WS (split decision).

Date	Winner	Loser	Result	KO Time	Location
9/7/1892	James J.Corbett	John L.Sullivan	KO 21	1:30	Olympic Club, New Orleans
4/5/1915	Jess Willard	Jack Johnson	KO 26	1:26	Mariano Race Track, Havana
9/23/26	Gene Tunney	Jack Dempsey	Wu 10	—	Sesquicentennial Stadium, Phila.
6/13/35	James J.Braddock	Max Baer	Wu 15	—	Mad.Sq.Garden Bowl, L.I.City
6/19/36	Max Schmeling	Joe Louis	KO 12	2:29	Yankee Stadium, New York
7/18/51	Jersey Joe Walcott	Ezzard Charles	KO 7	0:55	Forbes Field, Pittsburgh
6/26/59	Ingemar Johansson	Floyd Patterson	TKO 3	2:03	Yankee Stadium, New York
2/25/64	Cassius Clay†	Sonny Liston	TKO 7	*	Convention Hall, Miami Beach
10/30/74	Muhammad Ali	George Foreman	KO 8	2:58	20th of May Stadium, Zaire
2/15/78	Leon Spinks	Muhammad Ali	Ws 15	—	Hilton Pavilion, Las Vegas
9/21/85	Michael Spinks	Larry Holmes	Wu 15	—	Riviera Hotel, Las Vegas
2/10/90	Buster Douglas	Mike Tyson	KO 10	1:23	Korakuen Stadium, Tokyo

*Liston failed to answer bell for Round 7.
†Cassius Clay changed his name to Muhammad Ali after winning title.

Major Titleholders

Note the following sanctioning body abbreviations: NBA (National Boxing Association), WBA (World Boxing Association), WBC (World Boxing Council), GBR (Great Britain), IBF (International Boxing Federation), plus other national and state commissions.

Fighters who retired as champion are indicated by (*) and champions who abandoned or relinquished their titles are indicated by (†).

Heavyweights

Widely accepted champions in CAPITAL letters. Current champions in **bold** type.

Champion	Held Title	Champion	Held Title
JOHN L.SULLIVAN	1885-92	Jimmy Ellis (WBA)	1968-70
JAMES J.CORBETT	1892-97	JOE FRAZIER	1970-73
BOB FITZSIMMONS	1897-99	GEORGE FOREMAN	1973-74
JAMES J.JEFFRIES	1899-1905*	MUHAMMAD ALI	1974-78*
MARVIN HART	1905-06	LEON SPINKS	1978
TOMMY BURNS	1906-08	Ken Norton (WBC)	1978
JACK JOHNSON	1908-15	Larry Holmes (WBC)	1978-80
JESS WILLARD	1915-19	MUHAMMAD ALI	1978-79
JACK DEMPSEY	1919-26	John Tate (WBA)	1979-80
GENE TUNNEY	1926-28*	Mike Weaver (WBA)	1980-82
MAX SCHMELING	1930-32	LARRY HOLMES	1980-85
JACK SHARKEY	1932-33	Michael Dokes (WBA)	1982-83
PRIMO CARNERA	1933-34	Gerrie Coetzee (WBA)	1983-84
MAX BAER	1934-35	Tim Witherspoon (WBC)	1984
JAMES J.BRADDOCK	1935-37	Pinklon Thomas (WBC)	1984-86
JOE LOUIS	1937-49*	Greg Page (WBA)	1984-85
EZZARD CHARLES	1949-51	MICHAEL SPINKS	1985-87
JERSEY JOE WALCOTT	1951-52	Tim Witherspoon (WBA)	1986
ROCKY MARCIANO	1952-56*	Trevor Berbick (WBC)	1986
FLOYD PATTERSON	1956-59	Mike Tyson (WBC)	1986-87
INGEMAR JOHANSSON	1959-60	James (Bonecrusher) Smith (WBA)	1986-87
FLOYD PATTERSON	1960-62	Tony Tucker (IBF)	1987
SONNY LISTON	1962-64	Mike Tyson (WBC,WBA,IBF)	1987-88
CASSIUS CLAY (MUHAMMAD ALI)	1964-70	MIKE TYSON	1988-90
Ernie Terrell (WBA)	1965-67	BUSTER DOUGLAS (WBC, WBA, IBF)	1990
Joe Frazier (NY)	1968-70	**EVANDER HOLYFIELD** (WBC, WBA, IBF)	1990-

Note: John L.Sullivan held the Bare Knuckle championship from 1882-85.

Light Heavyweights

Widely accepted champions in CAPITAL letters. Current champions in **bold** type.

Champion	Held Title	Champion	Held Title
JACK ROOT	1903	BATTLING SIKI	1922-23
GEORGE GARDNER	1903	MIKE McTIGUE	1923-25
BOB FITZSIMMONS	1903-05	PAUL BERLENBACH	1925-26
PHILADELPHIA JACK O'BRIEN	1905-12*	JACK DELANEY	1926-27†
JACK DILLON	1914-16	Jimmy Slattery (NBA)	1927
BATTLING LEVINSKY	1916-20	TOMMY LOUGHRAN	1927-29
GEORGES CARPENTIER	1920-22	JIMMY SLATTERY	1930

Light Heavyweights (Cont.)

Champion	Held Title
MAXIE ROSENBLOOM	1930-34
George Nichols (NBA)	1932
Bob Godwin (NBA)	1933
BOB OLIN	1934-35
JOHN HENRY LEWIS	1935-38
MELIO BETTINA (NY)	1939
Len Harvey (GBR)	1939-42
BILLY CONN	1939-40†
ANTON CHRISTOFORIDIS (NBA)	1941
GUS LESNEVICH	1941-48
Freddie Mills (GBR)	1942-46
FREDDIE MILLS	1948-50
JOEY MAXIM	1950-52
ARCHIE MOORE	1952-62
Harold Johnson (NBA)	1961
HAROLD JOHNSON	1962-63
WILLIE PASTRANO	1963-65
Eddie Cotton (Mich.)	1963-64
JOSE TORRES	1965-66
DICK TIGER	1966-68
BOB FOSTER	1968-74*
Vicente Rondon (WBA)	1971-72
John Conteh (WBC)	1974-77
Victor Galindez (WBA)	1974-78
Miguel A.Cuello (WBC)	1977-78
Mate Parlov (WBC)	1978

Champion	Held Title
Mike Rossman (WBA)	1978-79
Marvin Johnson (WBC)	1978-79
Matthew (Franklin) Saad Muhammad (WBC)	1979-81
Marvin Johnson (WBA)	1979-80
Eddie (Gregory) Mustapha Muhammad (WBA)	1980-81
Michael Spinks (WBA)	1981-83
Dwight (Braxton) Muhammad Qarvi (WBC)	1981-83
MICHAEL SPINKS	1983-85†
J.B.Williamson (WBC)	1985-86
Slobodan Kacar (IBF)	1985-86
Marvin Johnson (WBA)	1986-87
Dennis Andries (WBC)	1986-87
Bobby Czyz (IBF)	1986-87
Leslie Stewart (WBA)	1987
Virgil Hill (WBA)	1987-91
Prince Charles Williams (IBF)	1987-
Thomas Hearns (WBC)	1987
Donny Lalonde (WBC)	1987-88
Sugar Ray Leonard (WBC)	1988
Dennis Andries (WBC)	1989
Jeff Harding (WBC)	1989-90, 1991-
Dennis Andries (WBC)	1990-91
Thomas Hearns (WBA)	1991-92
Iran Barkley (WBA)	1992†
Virgil Hill (WBA)	1992-

Middleweights

Widely accepted champions in CAPITAL letters. Current champions in **bold** type.

Champion	Held Title
JACK (NONPAREIL) DEMPSEY	1884-91
BOB FITZSIMMONS	1891-97
CHARLES (KID) McCOY	1897-98
TOMMY RYAN	1898-1907
STANLEY KETCHEL	1908
BILLY PAPKE	1908
STANLEY KETCHEL	1908-10
FRANK KLAUS	1913
GEORGE CHIP	1913-14
AL McCOY	1914-17
Jeff Smith (AUS)	1914
Mick King (AUS)	1914
Jeff Smith (AUS)	1914-15
Lee Darcy (AUS)	1915-17
MIKE O'DOWD	1917-20
JOHNNY WILSON	1920-23
Wm.Bryan Downey (Ohio)	1921-22
Dave Rosenberg (NY)	1922
Jock Malone (Ohio)	1922-23
Mike O'Dowd (NY)	1922
Lou Bogash (NY)	1923
HARRY GREB	1923-26
TIGER FLOWERS	1926
MICKEY WALKER	1926-31†
GORILLA JONES	1931-32
MARCEL THIL	1932-37
Ben Jeby (NY)	1932-33
Lou Brouillard (NBA,NY)	1933
Vince Dundee (NBA,NY)	1933-34
Teddy Yarosz (NBA,NY)	1934-35
Babe Risko (NBA,NY)	1935-36
Freddie Steele (NBA,NY)	1936-38
FRED APOSTOLI	1937-39
Al Hostak (NBA)	1938
Solly Krieger (NBA)	1938-39
Al Hostak (NBA)	1939-40
CEFERINO GARCIA	1939-40
KEN OVERLIN	1940-41

Champion	Held Title
Tony Zale (NBA)	1940-41
BILLY SOOSE	1941
TONY ZALE	1941-47
ROCKY GRAZIANO	1947-48
TONY ZALE	1948
MARCEL CERDAN	1948-49
JAKE LA MOTTA	1949-51
SUGAR RAY ROBINSON	1951
RANDY TURPIN	1951
SUGAR RAY ROBINSON	1951-52*
CARL (BOBO) OLSON	1953-55
SUGAR RAY ROBINSON	1955-57
GENE FULLMER	1957
SUGAR RAY ROBINSON	1957
CARMEN BASILIO	1957-58
SUGAR RAY ROBINSON	1958-60
Gene Fullmer (NBA)	1959-62
PAUL PENDER	1960-61
TERRY DOWNES	1961-62
PAUL PENDER	1962-63
Dick Tiger (WBA)	1962-63
DICK TIGER	1963
JOEY GIARDELLO	1963-65
DICK TIGER	1965-66
EMILE GRIFFITH	1966-67
NINO BENVENUTI	1967
EMILE GRIFFITH	1967-68
NINO BENVENUTI	1968-70
CARLOS MONZON	1970-77*
Rodrigo Valdez (WBC)	1974-76
RODRIGO VALDEZ	1977-78
HUGO CORRO	1978-79
VITO ANTUOFERMO	1979-80
ALAN MINTER	1980
MARVELOUS MARVIN HAGLER	1980-87
SUGAR RAY LEONARD	1987
Frank Tate (IBF)	1987-88
Sumbu Kalambay (WBA)	1987-89

Champion	Held Title	Champion	Held Title
Thomas Hearns (WBC)	1987-88	Mike McCallum (WBA)	1989-91
Iran Barkley (WBC)	1988-89	**Julian Jackson** (WBC)	1990-
Michael Nunn(IBF)	1988-91	**James Toney** (IBF)	1991-
Roberto Duran (WBC)	1989-90*	**Reggie Johnson** (WBA)	1992-

Welterweights

Widely accepted champions in CAPITAL letters. Current champions in **bold** type.

Champion	Held Title	Champion	Held Title
PADDY DUFFY	1888-90	KID GAVILAN	1951-54
MYSTERIOUS BILLY SMITH	1892-94	JOHNNY SAXTON	1954-55
TOMMY RYAN	1894-98	TONY DeMARCO	1955
MYSTERIOUS BILLY SMITH	1898-1900	CARMEN BASILIO	1955-56
MATTY MATTHEWS	1900	JOHNNY SAXTON	1956
EDDIE CONNOLLY	1900	CARMEN BASILIO	1956-57†
JAMES (RUBE) FERNS	1900	VIRGIL AKINS	1958
MATTY MATHEWS	1900-01	DON JORDAN	1958-60
JAMES (RUBE) FERNS	1901	BENNY (KID) PARET	1960-61
JOE WALCOTT	1901-04	EMILE GRIFFITH	1961
THE DIXIE KID	1904-05	BENNY (KID) PARET	1961-62
HONEY MELLODY	1906-07	EMILE GRIFFITH	1962-63
Mike (Twin) Sullivan	1907-08	LUIS RODRIGUEZ	1963
FRANK MANTELL	1907-08	EMILE GRIFFITH	1963-66†
HARRY LEWIS	1908-13	Charlie Shipes (Calif.)	1966-67
Jimmy Gardner	1908-09	CURTIS COKES	1966-69
Jimmy Clabby	1910-11	JOSE NAPOLES	1969-70
WALDEMAR HOLBERG	1914	BILLY BACKUS	1970-71
TOM McCORMICK	1914	JOSE NAPOLES	1971-75
MATT WELLS	1914-15	Hedgemon Lewis (NY)	1972-73
MIKE GLOVER	1915	Angel Espada (WBA)	1975-76
JACK BRITTON	1915	JOHN H. STRACEY	1975-76
TED (KID) LEWIS	1915-16	CARLOS PALOMINO	1976-79
JACK BRITTON	1916-17	Pipino Cuevas (WBA)	1976-80
TED (KID) LEWIS	1917-19	WILFREDO BENITEZ	1979
JACK BRITTON	1919-22	SUGAR RAY LEONARD	1979-80
MICKEY WALKER	1922-26	ROBERTO DURAN	1980
PETE LATZO	1926-27	Thomas Hearns (WBA)	1980-81
JOE DUNDEE	1927-29	SUGAR RAY LEONARD	1980-82
JACKIE FIELDS	1929-30	Donald Curry (WBA)	1983-85
YOUNG JACK THOMPSON	1930	Milton McCrory (WBC)	1983-85
TOMMY FREEMAN	1930-31	DONALD CURRY	1985-86
YOUNG JACK THOMPSON	1931	LLOYD HONEYGHAN	1986-87
LOU BROUILLARD	1931-32	JORGE VACA (WBC)	1987-88
JACKIE FIELDS	1932-33	LLOYD HONEYGHAN (WBC)	1988-89
YOUNG CORBETT III	1933	Mark Breland (WBA)	1987
JIMMY McLARNIN	1933-34	Marlon Starling (WBA)	1987-88
BARNEY ROSS	1934	Tomas Molinares (WBA)	1988-89
JIMMY McLARNIN	1934-35	Simon Brown (IBF)	1988-91
BARNEY ROSS	1935-38	Mark Breland (WBA)	1989-90
HENRY ARMSTRONG	1938-40	MARLON STARLING (WBC)	1989-90
FRITZIE ZIVIC	1940-41	Aaron Davis (WBA)	1990-91
Izzy Jannazzo (Md.)	1940-41	Maurice Blocker (WBC)	1990-91
Freddie (Red) Cochrane	1941-46	**Meldrick Taylor** (WBA)	1991-
MARTY SERVO	1946*	Simon Brown (WBC)	1991
SUGAR RAY ROBINSON	1946-51†	**Maurice Blocker** (IBF)	1991-
JOHNNY BRATTON	1951	**Buddy McGirt** (WBC)	1991-

Lightweights

Widely accepted champions in CAPITAL letters. Current champions in **bold** type.

Champion	Held Title	Champion	Held Title
JACK McAULIFFE	1886-94	FREDDIE WELSH	1915-17
GEORGE (KID) LAVIGNE	1896-99	BENNY LEONARD	1917-25*
FRANK ERNE	1899-02	JIMMY GOODRICH	1925
JOE GANS	1902-04	ROCKY KANSAS	1925-26
JIMMY BRITT	1904-05	SAMMY MANDELL	1926-30
BATTLING NELSON	1905-06	AL SINGER	1930
JOE GANS	1906-08	TONY CANZONERI	1930-33
BATTLING NELSON	1908-10	BARNEY ROSS	1933-35†
AD WOLGAST	1910-12	TONY CANZONERI	1935-36
WILLIE RITCHIE	1912-14	LOU AMBERS	1936-38

Lightweights (Cont.)

Champion	Held Title	Champion	Held Title
HENRY ARMSTRONG	1938-39	Ishimatsu Suzuki (WBC)	1974-76
LOU AMBERS	1939-40	Esteban DeJesus (WBC)	1976-78
Sammy Angott (NBA)	1940-41	Jim Watt (WBC)	1979-81
LEW JENKINS	1940-41	Ernesto Espana (WBA)	1979-80
SAMMY ANGOTT	1943-44	Hilmer Kenty (WBA)	1980-81
Beau Jack (NY)	1942-43	Sean O'Grady (WBA,WAA)	1981
Slugger White (Md.)	1943	Alexis Arguello (WBC)	1981-82
Bob Montgomery (NY)	1943	Claude Noel (WBA)	1981
Sammy Angott (NBA)	1943-44	Andrew Ganigan (WAA)	1981-82
Beau Jack (NY)	1943-44	Arturo Frias (WBA)	1981-82
Bob Montgomery (NY)	1944-47	Ray Mancini (WBA)	1982-84
Juan Zurita (NBA)	1944-45	ALEXIS ARGUELLO	1982-83
IKE WILLIAMS	1947-51	Edwin Rosario (WBC)	1983-84
JAMES CARTER	1951-52	Choo Choo Brown (IBF)	1984
LAURO SALAS	1952	Livingstone Bramble (WBA)	1984-86
JAMES CARTER	1952-54	Harry Arroyo (IBF)	1984-85
PADDY DeMARCO	1954	Jose Luis Ramirez (WBC)	1984-85
JAMES CARTER	1954-55	Jimmy Paul (IBF)	1985-86
WALLACE (BUD) SMITH	1955-56	Hector Camacho (WBC)	1985-86
JOE BROWN	1956-62	Edwin Rosario (WBA)	1986-87
CARLOS ORTIZ	1962-65	Greg Haugen (IBF)	1986-87
Kenny Lane (Mich.)	1963-64	Julio Cesar Chavez (WBA)	1987-88
ISMAEL LAGUNA	1965	Jose Luis Ramirez (WBC)	1987-88
CARLOS ORTIZ	1965-68	JULIO CESAR CHAVEZ (WBC,WBA)	1988-89
CARLOS TEO CRUZ	1968-69	Vinny Pazienza (IBF)	1987-88
MANDO RAMOS	1969-70	Greg Haugen (IBF)	1988-89
ISMAEL LAGUNA	1970	Pernell Whitaker (IBF,WBC)	1989-90
KEN BUCHANAN	1970-72	Edwin Rosario (WBA)	1989-90
Pedro Carrasco (WBC)	1971-72	Juan Nazario (WBA)	1990
Mando Ramos (WBC)	1972	PERNELL WHITAKER (IBF, WBC, WBA)	1990-92†
ROBERTO DURAN	1972-79†	**Joey Gamache** (WBA)	1992-
Chango Carmona (WBC)	1972	**Miguel A. Gonzalez** (WBC)	1992-
Rodolfo Gonzalez (WBC)	1972-74		

Featherweights

Widely accepted champions in CAPITAL letters. Current champions in **bold** type.

Champion	Held Title	Champion	Held Title
TORPEDO BILLY MURPHY	1890	JOEY ARCHIBALD	1939-40
YOUNG GRIFFO	1890-92	Petey Scalzo (NBA)	1940-41
GEORGE DIXON	1892-97	Jimmy Perrin (La.)	1940-41
SOLLY SMITH	1897-98	HARRY JEFFRA	1940-41
Ben Jordan (GBR)	1898-99	JOEY ARCHIBALD	1941
Eddie Santry (GBR)	1899-1900	Richie Lemos (NBA)	1941
DAVE SULLIVAN	1898	CHALKY WRIGHT	1941-42
GEORGE DIXON	1898-1900	Jackie Wilson (NBA)	1941-43
TERRY McGOVERN	1900-01	WILLIE PEP	1942-48
YOUNG CORBETT II	1901-03	Jackie Callura (NBA)	1943
ABE ATTELL	1903-04	Phil Terranova (NBA)	1943-44
BROOKLYN TOMMY SULLIVAN	1904-05	Sal Bartolo (NBA)	1944-46
ABE ATTELL	1906-12	SANDY SADDLER	1948-49
JOHNNY KILBANE	1912-23	WILLIE PEP	1949-50
Jim Driscoll (GBR)	1912-13	SANDY SADDLER	1950-57*
EUGENE CRIQUI	1923	HOGAN (KID) BASSEY	1957-59
JOHNNY DUNDEE	1923-24†	DAVEY MOORE	1959-63
LOUIS (KID) KAPLAN	1925-26†	ULTIMINIO (SUGAR) RAMOS	1963-64
Dick Finnegan (Mass.)	1926-27	VICENTE SALDIVAR	1964-67*
BENNY BASS	1927-28	Howard Winstone (GBR)	1968
TONY CANZONERI	1928	Raul Rojas (WBA)	1968
ANDRE ROUTIS	1928-29	Jose Legra (WBC)	1968-69
BATTLING BATTALINO	1929-32†	Shozo Saijyo (WBA)	1968-71
Tommy Paul (NBA)	1932-33	JOHNNY FAMECHON (WBC)	1969-70
Kid Chocolate (NY)	1932-33	VICENTE SALDIVAR (WBC)	1970
Freddie Miller (NBA)	1933-36	KUNIAKI SHIBATA (WBC)	1970-72
Baby Arizmendi (MEX)	1935-36	Antonio Gomez (WBA)	1971-72
Mike Belloise (NY)	1936-37	CLEMENTE SANCHEZ (WBC)	1972
Petey Sarron (NBA)	1936-37	Ernesto Marcel (WBA)	1972-74
HENRY ARMSTRONG	1937-38†	JOSE LEGRA (WBC)	1972-73
Joey Archibald (NY)	1938-39	EDER JOFRE (WBC)	1973-74
Leo Rodak (NBA)	1938-39	Ruben Olivares (WBA)	1974

Champion	Held Title
Bobby Chacon (WBC)	1974-75
ALEXIS ARGUELLO (WBA)	1974-76†
Ruben Olivares (WBC)	1975
David (Poison) Kotey (WBC)	1975-76
DANNY (LITTLE RED) LOPEZ (WBC)	1976-80
Rafael Ortega (WBA)	1977
Cecilio Lastra (WBA)	1977-78
Eusebio Pedroza (WBA)	1978-85
SALVADOR SANCHEZ (WBC)	1980-82
Juan LaPorte (WBC)	1982-84
Wilfredo Gomez (WBC)	1984
Min-Keun Oh (IBF)	1984-85
Azumah Nelson (WBC)	1984-88

Champion	Held Title
Barry McGuigan (WBA)	1985-86
Ki-Young Chung (IBF)	1985-86
Steve Cruz (WBA)	1986-87
Antonio Rivera (IBF)	1986-88
Antonio Esparragoza (WBA)	1987-91
Calvin Grove (IBF)	1988
Jorge Paez (IBF)	1988-91†
Jeff Fenech (WBC)	1988-90†
Marcos Villasana (WBC)	1990-91
Yung-Kyun Park (WBA)	1991-
Troy Dorsey	1991
Manuel Medina (IBF)	1991-
Paul Hodkinson (WBC)	1991-

Bantamweights

Widely accepted champions in CAPITAL letters. Current champions in **bold** type.

Champion	Held Title
HUGHEY BOYLE	1887-88
CHAPPIE MORAN	1889-90
TOMMY (SPIDER) KELLY	1890-92
BILLY PLIMMER	1892-95
PEDLAR PALMER	1895-99
TERRY McGOVERN	1899-1900
DANNY DOUGHERTY	1900-01
HARRY FORBES	1901-03
FRANKIE NEIL	1903-04
JOE BOWKER	1904-05
JIMMY WALSH	1905-06†
OWEN MORAN	1907-08
MONTE ATTELL	1909-10
FRANKIE CONLEY	1910-11
JOHNNY COULON	1911-14
Digger Stanley (GBR)	1910-12
Charles Ledoux (GBR)	1912-13
Eddie Campi (GBR)	1913-14
KID WILLIAMS	1914-17
Johnny Ertle	1915-18
PETE HERMAN	1917-20
Memphis Pal Moore	1918-19
JOE LYNCH	1920-21
PETE HERMAN	1921
JOHNNY BUFF	1921-22
JOE LYNCH	1922-24
ABE GOLDSTEIN	1924
CANNONBALL EDDIE MARTIN	1924-25
PHIL ROSENBERG	1925-27
Teddy Baldock (GBR)	1927
BUD TAYLOR (NBA)	1927-28†
Willie Smith (GBR)	1927-28
Bushy Graham (NY)	1928-29
PANAMA AL BROWN	1929-35
Sixto Escobar (NBA)	1934-35
BALTAZAR SANGCHILLI	1935-36
Lou Salica (NBA)	1935
Sixto Escobar (NBA)	1935-36
TONY MARINO	1936
SIXTO ESCOBAR	1936-37
HARRY JEFFRA	1937-38
SIXTO ESCOBAR	1938-39*
Georgie Pace (NBA)	1939-40
LOU SALICA	1940-42
MANUEL ORTIZ	1942-47
HAROLD DADE	1947
MANUEL ORTIZ	1947-50
VIC TOWEEL	1950-52

Champion	Held Title
JIMMY CARRUTHERS	1952-54*
ROBERT COHEN	1954-56
Raul Macias (NBA)	1955-57
MARIO D'AGATA	1956-57
ALPHONSE HALIMI	1957-59
JOE BECERRA	1959-60*
Johnny Caldwell (EBU)	1961-62
EDER JOFRE	1961-65
MASAHIKO FIGHTING HARADA	1965-68
LIONEL ROSE	1968-69
RUBEN OLIVARES	1969-70
CHUCHO CASTILLO	1970-71
RUBEN OLIVARES	1971-72
RAFAEL HERRERA	1972
ENRIQUE PINDER	1972-73
ROMEO ANAYA	1973
Rafael Herrera (WBC)	1973-74
ARNOLD TAYLOR	1973-74
SOO-HWAN HONG	1974-75
Rodolfo Martinez (WBC)	1974-76
ALFONSO ZAMORA	1975-77
Carlos Zarate (WBC)	1976-79
JORGE LUJAN	1977-80
Lupe Pintor (WBC)	1979-83
JULIAN SOLIS	1980
JEFF CHANDLER	1980-84
Albert Davila (WBC)	1983-85
RICHARD SANDOVAL	1984-86
Satoshi Shingaki (IBF)	1984-85
Jeff Fenech (IBF)	1985
Daniel Zaragoza (WBC)	1985
Miguel (Happy) Lora (WBC)	1985-88
GABY CANIZALES	1986
BERNARDO PINANGO	1986-87
Wilfredo Vasquez (WBA)	1987-88
Kevin Seabrooks (IBF)	1987-88
Kaokor Galaxy (WBA)	1988
Moon Sung-Kil (WBA)	1988-89
Kaokor Galaxy (WBA)	1989
Raul Perez (WBC)	1988-91
Orlando Canizales (IBF)	1988-
Luisito Espinosa (WBA)	1989-91
Greg Richardson	1991
Joichiro Tatsuyoshi (WBC)	1991-92
Israel Contreras (WBA)	1991-92
Eddie Cook (WBA)	1992-
Victor Rabanales (WBC)	1992-

Flyweights

Widely accepted champions in CAPITAL letters. Current champions in **bold** type.

Champion	Held Title
SID SMITH	1913
BILL LADBURY	1913-14
PERCY JONES	1914
JOE SYMONDS	1914-16
JIMMY WILDE	1916-23
PANCHO VILLA	1923-25
FIDEL LoBARBA	1925-27*
FRENCHY BELANGER (NBA,IBU)	1927-28
Izzy Schwartz (NY)	1927-29
Johnny McCoy (Calif.)	1927-28
Newsboy Brown (Calif.)	1928
FRANKIE GENARO (NBA,IBU)	1928-29
Johnny Hill (GBR)	1928-29
SPIDER PLADNER (NBA,IBU)	1929
FRANKIE GENARO (NBA,IBU)	1929-31
Willie LaMorte (NY)	1929-30
Midget Wolgast (NY)	1930-35
YOUNG PEREZ (NBA,IBU)	1931-32
JACKIE BROWN (NBA,IBU)	1932-35
BENNY LYNCH	1935-38†
Small Montana (NY,Calif.)	1935-37
PETER KANE	1938-43
Little Dado (NBA,Calif.)	1938-40
JACKIE PATERSON	1943-48
RINTY MONAGHAN	1948-50*
TERRY ALLEN	1950
SALVADOR (DADO) MARINO	1950-52
YOSHIO SHIRAI	1953-54
PASCUAL PEREZ	1954-60
PONE KINGPETCH	1960-62
MASAHIKO (FIGHTING) HARADA	1962-63
PONE KINGPETCH	1963
HIROYUKI EBIHARA	1963-64
PONE KINGPETCH	1964-65
SALVATORE BURRINI	1965-66
Horacio Accavallo (WBA)	1966-68
WALTER McGOWAN	1966
CHARTCHAI CHIONOI	1966-69
EFREN TORRES	1969-70
Hiroyuki Ebihara (WBA)	1969
Bernabe Villacampo (WBA)	1969-70
CHARTCHAI CHIONOI	1970
Berkrerk Chartvanchai (WBA)	1970
Masao Ohba (WBA)	1970-73
ERBITO SALAVARRIA	1970-73
Betulio Gonzalez (WBC)	1972
Venice Borkorsor (WBC)	1972-73
VENICE BORKORSOR	1973

Champion	Held Title
Chartchai Chionoi (WBA)	1973-74
Betulio Gonzalez (WBA)	1973-74
Shoji Oguma (WBC)	1974-75
Susumu Hanagata (WBA)	1974-75
Miguel Canto (WBC)	1975-79
Erbito Salavarria (WBA)	1975-76
Alfonso Lopez (WBA)	1976
Guty Espadas (WBA)	1976-78
Betulio Gonzalez (WBA)	1978-79
Chan-Hee Park (WBC)	1979-80
Luis Ibarra (WBA)	1979-80
Tae-Shik Kim (WBA)	1980
Shoji Oguma (WBC)	1980-81
Peter Mathebula (WBA)	1980-81
Santos Laciar (WBA)	1981
Antonio Avelar (WBC)	1981-82
Luis Ibarra (WBA)	1981
Juan Herrera (WBA)	1981-82
Prudencio Cardona (WBC)	1982
Santos Laciar (WBA)	1982-85
Freddie Castillo (WBC)	1982
Eleoncio Mercedes (WBC)	1982-83
Charlie Magri (WBC)	1983
Frank Cedeno (WBC)	1983-84
Soon-Chun Kwon (IBF)	1983-85
Koji Kobayashi (WBC)	1984
Gabriel Bernal (WBC)	1984
Sot Chitalada (WBC)	1984-88
Hilario Zapate (WBA)	1985-87
Chong-Kwan Chung (IBF)	1985-86
Bi-Won Chung (IBF)	1986
Hi-Sup Shin (IBF)	1986-87
Dodie Penalosa (IBF)	1987
Fidel Bassa (WBA)	1987-89
Choi Chang-Ho (IBF)	1987-88
Rolando Bohol (IBF)	1988
Yong-Kang Kim (WBC)	1988-89
Duke McKenzie (IBF)	1988-89
Dave McAuley (IBF)	1989-92
Sot Chitalada (WBC)	1989-91
Jesus Rojas (WBA)	1989-90
Yul-Woo Lee (WBA)	1990
Leopard Tamakuma (WBA)	1990-91
Muangchai Kittikasem (WBC)	1991-92
Yong-Kang Kim (WBA)	1991-92
Rodolfo Blanco (IBF)	1992-
Yuri Arbachakov (WBC)	1992-
Aquiles Guzman (WBA)	1992-

Triple Champions

Sugar Ray Leonard (5)—WBC Welterweight (1979-80,80-82); WBA Jr.Middleweight (1981); WBC Middleweight (1987); WBC Super Middleweight (1988-90); WBC Light Heavyweight (1988).

Thomas Hearns (5)—WBA Welterweight (1980-81); WBC Jr.Middleweight (1982-84); WBC Light Heavyweight (1987); WBC Middleweight (1987-88); WBA Light Heavyweight (1991).

Roberto Duran (4)—Lightweight (1972-79); WBC Welterweight (1980); WBA Jr.Middleweight (1983); WBC Middleweight (1989-90).

Alexis Arguello (3)—WBA Featherweight (1974-77); WBC Jr.Lightweight (1978-80); WBC Lightweight (1981-82).

Henry Armstrong (3)—Featherweight (1937-38); Welterweight (1938-40); Lightweight (1938-39).

Wilfredo Benitez (3)—Jr.Welterweight (1976-79); Welterweight (1979); WBC Jr.Middleweight (1981-82).

Tony Canzoneri (3)—Featherweight (1928); Lightweight (1930-33); Jr.Welterweight (1931-32,33).

Julio Cesar Chavez (3)—WBC Jr.Lightweight (1984-87); WBA/WBC Lightweight (1987-89); WBC/IBF Jr.Welterweight (1989-91); WBC Jr.Welterweight (1991).

Jeff Fenech (3)—IBF Bantamweight (1985); WBC Jr.Featherweight (1986-88); WBC Featherweight (1988-90).

Bob Fitzsimmons (3)—Middleweight (1891-97); Light Heavyweight (1903-05); Heavyweight (1897-99).

Emile Griffith (3)—Welterweight (1961,62-63,63-66); Jr.Middleweight (1962-63); Middleweight (1966-67,67-68).

Stanley Ketchel (3)—Welterweight (1908,08-10); Middleweight (1908-10); Light Heavyweight (1909-10).

Terry McGovern (3)—Bantamweight (1889-1900); Featherweight (1900-01); Lightweight (1900-01).

Barney Ross (3)—Lightweight (1933-35); Jr.Welterweight (1933-35); Welterweight (1934-38).

Note that (*) indicates title claimant.

Stephen Dunn/Allsport

*America*³ successfully defended the America's Cup in May, defeating Italian challenger *Il Moro di Venezia* in five races off the coast of San Diego.

MISCELLANEOUS SPORTS

Capt. Koch Keeps the Cup
by Bill Center

Bill Koch's *America³*, with Buddy Melges as helmsman, successfully defended the America's Cup off San Diego in May, defeating Italian challenger *Il Moro di Venezia*, 4-1, in the best-of-seven match racing series.

The victory was the first for a defending nation against a multinational challenge since Dennis Conner's *Freedom* defeated *Australia* off Newport, R.I., in 1980.

America³ had beaten Conner's *Stars & Stripes* for the right to defend the America's Cup against the Italian boat, which had upset favored *New Zealand* in the finals of the challenger trials.

The 28th Cup defense attracted only two defense candidates and eight challengers from seven nations, including first-time bids from Japan and Spain.

Koch was the last entry in the competition, taking over remnants of two other failed defense efforts in what became a successful bid to unseat Conner, a three-time Cup winner.

As Conner struggled with financing this time and was unable to raise enough sponsorship funding to build a second boat, Koch, a multimillionaire from Kansas, personally bankrolled most of a $64 million campaign that produced an armada of four, 75-foot, carbon-fiber composite International America's Cup Class sloops in a span of 17 months.

Narrower and lighter than the year-old *Stars & Stripes, America³* emerged as Koch's best all-around performer, beating *Stars and Stripes* in 15 of 22 races, including a 7-4 advantage in the best-of-13 defense finals.

Meanwhile, the challenger trials divided into two fleets, split along financial lines. The four teams with the biggest budgets—*Il Moro di Venezia, New Zealand, Nippon* from Japan and France's *Ville de Paris*—advanced to the challenger semifinals while the four boats operating on smaller budgets failed.

New Zealand (7-2) and *Il Moro di Venezia* (5-4) advanced to the finals with the two best records in the round-robin challenger semifinals.

Skippered by Rod Davis, the radical New Zealand boat featured a rudderless twin-post keel that seemed to do well in San

Ken Levine/Allsport

Owner-skipper **Bill Koch** signals victory after defending the Cup.

Diego's prevailing light winds and heavy seas. Favored to defeat *Il Moro di Venezia*, the Kiwis built a quick 4-1 lead in the best-of-nine challenger finals.

But *Il Moro* skipper Paul Cayard, a San Francisco native, successfully protested New Zealand's use of its bowsprit, getting one New Zealand victory thrown out. The Italians then won four straight races against the disheartened Kiwis, who couldn't reverse their slide despite replacing Davis with Russell Coutts for the final two losses.

Il Moro, however, was no match for *America³.* The defender was slightly faster and its crew out-performed their Italian counterparts in all but the second race. That race resulted in the closest finish in the Cup's 141-year history—a winning margin for *Il Moro* of just three seconds or the length of the bow.

The Americans then won the next three races over the 20.3-mile course. In all, *America³*'s winning margins were 30 seconds, 1:58, 1:04 and 44 seconds in a series the produced three of the seven closest finishes in the event's 103-race history.

Bill Center covers America's Cup yacht racing for the *San Diego Union.*

AMERICA'S CUP YACHTING

International yacht racing was launched in 1851 when England's Royal Yacht Squadron staged a 60-mile regatta around the Isle of Wight and offered a silver trophy to the winner. The 101-foot schooner **America**, sent over by the New York Yacht Club, won the race and the prize. Originally called the Hundred-Guinea Cup, the trophy was renamed The America's Cup after the winning boat's owners deeded it to the NYYC with instructions to defend it whenever challenged.

From 1870-1980, the NYYC successfully defended the Cup 25 straight times; first in large schooners and J-class boats that measured up to 140 feet in overall length, then in 12-meter boats.

A foreign yacht finally won the Cup in 1983 when **Australia II** beat defender **Liberty** in the seventh and deciding race off Newport, R.I. Four years later, the San Diego Yacht Club's **Stars & Stripes** won the Cup back, sweeping the four races of the final series off Fremantle, Australia.

Then in 1988, New Zealand's Mercury Bay Boating Club, unwilling to wait the usual three- to four-year period between Cup defenses, challenged the SDYC to a match race, citing the Cup's 102-year-old Deed of Gift, which clearly stated that every challenge had to be honored. Mercury Bay announced it would race a 133-foot monohull. San Diego countered with a 60-foot catamaran. The resulting best-of-three series (Sept.7-8) was a mismatch as the SDYC's catamaran **Stars & Stripes** won two straight by margins of better than 18 and 21 minutes.

Mercury Bay syndicate leader Michael Fay protested the outcome and took the SDYC to court in New York State (where the Deed of Gift was first filed) claiming San Diego had violated the spirit of the deed by racing a catamaran instead of a monohull. N.Y.State Supreme Court judge Carmen Ciparick agreed and on March 28, 1989, ordered the SDYC to hand the Cup over to Mercury Bay. The SDYC refused, but did consent to the court's appointment of the New York Yacht Club as custodian of the Cup until an appeal was ruled on.

On Sept.19, 1989, the Appellate Division of the N.Y.Supreme Court overturned Ciparick's decision and awarded the Cup back to the SDYC. An appeal by Mercury Bay was denied by the N.Y.Court of Appeals on April 26, 1990, ending three years of legal wrangling.

To avoid the chaos of 1988–90, a new class of boat—75-foot monohulls with 110-foot masts—was used by all competing countries in the 1992 races.

The America's Cup will be contested again in 1995 off San Diego.

Note that (*) indicates skipper was also owner of the boat.

Schooners and J-Class Boats

Year	Winner	Skipper	Series	Loser	Skipper
1851	America	Richard Brown	—	—	—
1870	Magic	Andrew Comstock	1-0	Cambria, GBR	J.Tannock
1871	Columbia (2-1) & Sappho (2-0)	Nelson Comstock Sam Greenwood	4-0	Livonia, GBR	J.R.Woods
1876	Madeleine	Josephus Williams	2-0	Countess of Dufferin, CAN	J.E.Ellsworth
1881	Mischief	Nathanael Clock	2-0	Atalanta, CAN	Alexander Cuthbert*
1885	Puritan	Aubrey Crocker	2-0	Genesta, GBR	John Carter
1886	Mayflower	Martin Stone	2-0	Galatea, GBR	Dan Bradford
1887	Volunteer	Henry Haff	2-0	Thistle, GBR	John Barr
1893	Vigilant	William Hansen	3-0	Valkyrie II, GBR	Wm.Granfield
1895	Defender	Henry Haff	3-0	Valkyrie III, GBR	Wm.Granfield
1899	Columbia	Charles Barr	3-0	Shamrock I, GBR	Archie Hogarth
1901	Columbia	Charles Barr	3-0	Shamrock II, GBR	E.A.Sycamore
1903	Reliance	Charles Barr	3-0	Shamrock III, GBR	Bob Wringe
1920	Resolute	Charles F.Adams	3-2	Shamrock IV, GBR	William Burton
1930	Enterprise	Harold Vanderbilt*	4-0	Shamrock V, GBR	Ned Heard
1934	Rainbow	Harold Vanderbilt*	4-2	Endeavour, GBR	T.O.M.Sopwith
1937	Ranger	Harold Vanderbilt*	4-0	Endeavour II, GBR	T.O.M.Sopwith

12-Meter Boats

Year	Winner	Skipper	Series	Loser	Skipper
1958	Columbia	Briggs Cunningham	4-0	Sceptre, GBR	Graham Mann
1962	Weatherly	Bus Mosbacher	4-1	Gretel, AUS	Jock Sturrock
1964	Constellation	Bob Bavier & Eric Ridder	4-0	Sovereign, AUS	Peter Scott
1967	Intrepid	Bus Mosbacher	4-0	Dame Pattie, AUS	Jock Sturrock
1970	Intrepid	Bill Ficker	4-1	Gretel II, AUS	Jim Hardy
1974	Courageous	Ted Hood	4-0	Southern Cross, AUS	John Cuneo
1977	Courageous	Ted Turner	4-0	Australia	Noel Robins
1980	Freedom	Dennis Conner	4-1	Australia	Jim Hardy
1983	Australia II	John Bertrand	4-3	Liberty, USA	Dennis Conner
1987	Stars & Stripes	Dennis Conner	4-0	Kookaburra III, AUS	Iain Murray

60-ft Catamaran vs 133-ft Monohull

Year	Winner	Skipper	Series	Loser	Skipper
1988	Stars & Stripes	Dennis Conner	2-0	New Zealand, NZE	David Barnes

75-ft International America's Cup Class

Year	Winner	Skipper	Series	Loser	Skipper
1992	America[3]	Bill Koch* & Buddy Melges	4-1	Il Moro di Venezia, ITA	Paul Cayard

CHESS

World Champions

The big news in chess in 1992 happened in September on the Adriatic island of Sveti Stevan in war-weary Yugoslavia. That's where former world champion Bobby Fischer, 49, of the U.S. emerged from self-imposed exile to play Boris Spassky, 55, the Russian he beat for the world title in 1972 at Reykjavik, Iceland. The winner's share of the $5 million exhibition match will be $3.35 million and will go to the first player to gain 10 victories (draws do not count). Fischer led Spassky, 5-2, after the first 11 games.

Meanwhile, current world champion Garry Kasparov of Russia is negotiating to defend his championship in August of 1993 at one or two North American sites, most likely Los Angeles and a Canadian city.

Years		Years		Years	
1866-94	Wilhelm Steinitz, Austria	1937-46	Alexander Alekhine, France	1963-69	Tigran Petrosian, USSR
1894-		1948-57	Mikhail Botvinnik, USSR	1969-72	Boris Spassky, USSR
1921	Emanuel Lasker, Germany	1957-58	Vassily Smyslov, USSR	1972-75	Bobby Fischer, USA
1921-27	Jose Capablanca, Cuba	1958-59	Mikhail Botvinnik, USSR	1975-85	Anatoly Karpov, USSR
1927-35	Alexander Alekhine, France	1960-61	Mikhail Tal, USSR	1985–	Garry Kasparov, USSR
1935-37	Max Euwe, Holland	1961-63	Mikhail Botvinnik, USSR		

Note: Fischer defaulted Championship in 1975.

U.S. Champions (since 1900)

United States champion Gata Kamsky, the 18-year-old emigre from the former Soviet Union who won the U.S. Invitational title in 1991, was scheduled to defend his crown, Dec. 1-20, in Durango, Colo. Kamsky is the youngest American champion since Fischer, who won the title at age 14 in 1957.

Years		Years		Years	
1857-71	Paul Morphy	1946-48	Samuel Reshevsky	1981-83	Walter Browne
1871-76	George Mackenzie	1948-51	Herman Steiner		& Yasser Seirawan
1876-80	James Mason	1951-54	Larry Evans	1983	Roman Dzindzichashvili,
1880-89	George Mackenzie	1954-57	Arthur Bisguier		Larry Christiansen
1889-90	Samuel Lipschutz	1957-61	Bobby Fischer		& Walter Browne
1890	Jackson Showalter	1961-62	Larry Evans	1984-85	Lev Alburt
1890-91	Max Judd	1962-68	Bobby Fischer	1986	Yasser Seirawan
1891-92	Jackson Showalter	1968-69	Larry Evans	1987	Joel Benjamin
1892-94	Samuel Lipschutz	1969-72	Samuel Reshevsky		& Nick DeFirmian
1894	Jackson Showalter	1972-73	Robert Byrne	1988	Michael Wilder
1894-95	Albert Hodges	1973-74	Lubomir Kavalek	1989	Roman Dzindzichashvili,
1895-97	Jackson Showalter		& John Grefe		Stuart Rachels
1897-1906	Harry Pillsbury	1974-77	Walter Browne		& Yasser Seirawan
1906-09	Vacant	1978-80	Lubomir Kabalek	1990	Lev Alburt
1909-36	Frank Marshall	1980-81	Larry Evans,	1991	Gata Kamsky
1936-44	Samuel Reshevsky		Larry Christiansen,		
1944-46	Arnold Denker		& Walter Browne		

DOGS

Iditarod Trail Sled Dog Race

Martin Buser, a 33-year-old Swiss-born musher who sings to his dogs, won the 20th Iditarod Trail Sled Dog Race on March 11, 1992, and did it in record time. Shoving off from Anchorage on Feb. 29, Buser and his dogs covered the 1,159-mile course to Nome in 10 days, 19 hours and 17 minutes, shaving six hours off the 1990 record set by four-time champion Susan Butcher. The victory earned Buser $50,000 and a new pick-up truck valued at $25,000.

The annual 1,159-mile race stretches from Anchorage to Nome, Alaska. Begun in 1973, the course follows an old frozen river mail route and is named after a deserted mining town along the way. The Iditarod also commemorates a famous midwinter emergency mission to get medical supplies to Nome during a 1925 diptheria epidemic. Men and women mushers compete together.

Multiple winners: Rick Swenson (5); Susan Butcher (4); Rick Mackey (2).

Year		Elapsed Time	Year		Elapsed Time
1973	Dick Wilmarth	20 days, 00:49:41	1983	Rick Mackey	12 days, 14:10:44
1974	Carl Huntington	20 days, 15:02:07	1984	Dean Osmar	12 days, 15:07:33
1975	Emmitt Peters	14 days, 14:43:45	1985	Libby Riddles	18 days, 00:20:17
1976	Gerald Riley	18 days, 22:58:17	1986	Susan Butcher	11 days, 15:06:00
1977	Rick Swenson	16 days, 16:27:13	1987	Susan Butcher	11 days, 02:05:13
1978	Dick Mackey	14 days, 18:52:24	1988	Susan Butcher	11 days, 11:41:40
1979	Rick Swenson	15 days, 10:37:47	1989	Joe Runyan	11 days, 05:24:34
1980	Joe May	14 days, 07:11:51	1990	Susan Butcher	11 days, 01:53:23
1981	Rick Swenson	12 days, 08:45:02	1991	Rick Swenson	12 days, 16:34:39
1982	Rick Swenson	16 days, 04:40:10	1992	Martin Buser	10 days, 19:17:00*

*Course record.

Westminster Kennel Club
Best in Show

Ch. Registry's Lonesome Dove, a 4-year-old wire fox terrier whose more familiar name is Lacey, was judged Best-in-Show, Feb. 11, 1992, at the 116th Westminster Kennel Club show at Madison Square Garden in New York. Lacey, who is owned by Marion and Sam Lawrence of Orlando, Fla., was the nation's top-winning show dog in 1991, winning 120 groups and 82 best-in-show honors.

The Westminster show is the most prestigious canine event in America. Held every year since 1877, it is one of the oldest annual sporting events in the country.

Multiple winners: Ch.Warren Remedy (3); Ch.Chinoe's Adamant James, Ch.Comejo Wycollar Boy, Ch.Flornell Spicy Piece of Halleston; Ch.Matford Vic, Ch.My Own Brucie, Ch.Pendley Calling of Blarney, Ch.Rancho Dobe's Storm (2).

Year		Breed	Year		Breed
1907	Warren Remedy	Fox Terrier	1950	Walsing Winning Trick of Edgerstoune	Scot.Terrier
1908	Warren Remedy	Fox Terrier	1951	Bang Away of Sirrah Crest	Boxer
1909	Warren Remedy	Fox Terrier	1952	Rancho Dobe's Storm	Doberman
			1953	Rancho Dobe's Storm	Doberman
1910	Sabine Rarebit	Fox Terrier	1954	Carmor's Rise and Shine	Cocker Spaniel
1911	Tickle Em Jock	Scottish Terrier	1955	Kippax Fearnought	Bulldog
1912	Kenmore Sorceress	Airedale	1956	Wilber White Swan	Toy Poodle
1913	Strathway Prince Albert	Bulldog	1957	Shirkhan of Grandeur	Afghan Hound
1914	Brentwood Hero	Old English Sheepdog	1958	Puttencove Promise	Standard Poodle
1915	Matford Vic	Old English Sheepdog	1959	Fontclair Festoon	Miniature Poodle
1916	Matford Vic	Old English Sheepdog			
1917	Comejo Wycollar Boy	Fox Terrier	1960	Chick T'Sun of Caversham	Pekingese
1918	Haymarket Faultless	Bull Terrier	1961	Cappoquin Little Sister	Toy Poodle
1919	Briergate Bright Beauty	Airedale	1962	Elfinbrook Simon	W.Highland Terrier
			1963	Wakefield's Black Knight	English Springer Spaniel
1920	Comejo Wycollar Boy	Fox Terrier	1964	Courtenay Fleetfoot of Pennyworth	Whippet
1921	Midkiff Seductive	Cocker.Spaniel	1965	Carmichaels Fanfare	Scottish Terrier
1922	Boxwood Barkentine	Airedale	1966	Zeloy Mooremaides Magic	Fox Terrier
1923	No best-in-show award		1967	Bardene Bingo	Scottish Terrier
1924	Barberryhill Bootlegger	Sealyham	1968	Stingray of Derryabah	Lakeland Terrier
1925	Governor Moscow	Pointer	1969	Glamoor Good News	Skye Terrier
1926	Signal Circuit	Fox Terrier			
1927	Pinegrade Perfection	Sealyham	1970	Arriba's Prima Donna	Boxer
1928	Talavera Margaret	Fox Terrier	1971	Chinoe's Adamant James	E.S.Spaniel
1929	Land Loyalty of Bellhaven	Collie	1972	Chinoe's Adamant James	E.S.Spaniel
			1973	Acadia Command Performance	Standard Poodle
1930	Pendley Calling of Blarney	Fox Terrier	1974	Gretchenhof Columbia River	German SH Pointer
1931	Pendley Calling of Blarney	Fox Terrier	1975	Sir Lancelot of Barvan	Old Eng.Sheepdog
1932	Nancolleth Markable	Pointer	1976	Jo Ni's Red Baron of Crofton	Lakeland Terrier
1933	Warland Protector of Shelterock	Airedale	1977	Dersade Bobby's Girl	Sealyham
1934	Flornell Spicy Bit of Halleston	Fox Terrier	1978	Cede Higgens	Yorkshire Terrier
1935	Nunsoe Duc de la Terrace of Blakeen	Standard Poodle	1979	Oak Tree's Irishtocrat	Irish Water Spaniel
1936	St.Margaret Magnificent of Clairedale	Sealyham			
1937	Flornell Spicy Bit of Halleston	Fox Terrier	1980	Sierra Cinnar	Siberian Husky
1938	Daro of Maridor	English Setter	1981	Dhandy Favorite Woodchuck	Pug
1939	Ferry v.Rauhfelsen of Giralda	Doberman	1982	St.Aubrey Dragonora of Elsdon	Pekingese
			1983	Kabik's The Challenger	Afghan Hound
1940	My Own Brucie	Cocker Spaniel	1984	Seaward's Blackbeard	Newfoundland
1941	My Own Brucie	Cocker Spaniel	1985	Braeburn's Close Encounter	Scottish Terrier
1942	Wolvey Pattern of Edgerstoune	W.Highland Terrier	1986	Marjetta National Acclaim	Pointer
1943	Pitter Patter of Piperscroft	Miniature Poodle	1987	Covy Tucker Hill's Manhattan	German Sheperd
1944	Flornell Rarebit of Twin Ponds	Welsh Terrier	1988	Great Elms Prince Charming II	Pomeranian
1945	Shieling's Signature	Scottish Terrier	1989	Royal Tudor's Wild As The Wind	Doberman
1946	Hetherington Model Rhythm	Fox Terrier			
1947	Warlord of Mazelaine	Boxer	1990	Wendessa Crown Prince	Pekingese
1948	Rock Ridge Night Rocket	Bedling.Terrier	1991	Whisperwind on a Carousel	Stan. Poodle
1949	Mazelaine's Zazarac Brandy	Boxer	1992	Lonesome Dove	Fox Terrier

FISHING
IGFA All-Tackle World Records

All-tackle records are maintained for the heaviest fish of any species caught on any line up to 130-lb (60 kg) class and certified by the International Game Fish Association. **Address:** 3000 East Las Olas Blvd., Ft.Lauderdale, FL, 33316. **Telephone:** 305-467-0161.

FRESHWATER FISH

Species	Lbs-Oz	Where Caught	Date	Angler
Barramundi	63- 2	Queensland, Australia	April 28,1991	Scott Barnsley
Bass, largemouth	22- 4	Montgomery Lake, GA	June 2,1932	George W.Perry
Bass, peacock	26- 8	Matevini River, Colombia	Jan.26,1982	Rod Neubert

Fishing (cont.)
FRESHWATER FISH

Species	Lbs-Oz	Where Caught	Date	Angler
Bass, redeye	8- 3	Flint River, GA	Oct.23,1977	David A.Hubbard
Bass, rock	3- 0	York River, Ontario	Aug. 1,1974	Peter Gulgin
Bass, smallmouth	11-15	Dale Hollow Lake, KY	Jul. 9,1955	David L.Hayes
Bass, spotted	9- 4	Parris Lake, CA	Jan.24,1987	Steven West
	9- 4	Lake Perris, CA	Apr. 1,1987	Gilbert Rowe
Bass, striped (landlocked)	67- 8	O'Neill Forebay, San Luis, CA	May 7,1992	Hank Ferguson
Bass, Suwannee	3-14	Suwannee River, FL	Mar. 2,1985	Ronnie Everett
Bass, white	6-13	Lake Orange, VA	Jul.31,1989	Ronald L.Sprouse
Bass, whiterock	24- 3	Leesville Lake, VA	May 12,1989	David N.Lambert
Bass, yellow	2- 4	Lake Monroe, IN	Mar.27,1977	Donald L.Stalker
Bluegill	4-12	Ketona Lake, AL	Apr. 9,1950	T.S.Hudson
Bowfin	21- 8	Florence, SC	Jan.29,1980	Robert L.Harmon
Buffalo, bigmouth	70- 5	Bussey Brake, Bastrop, LA	Apr.21,1980	Delbert Sisk
Buffalo, black	55- 8	Cherokee Lake, TN	May 3,1984	Edward H.McLain
Buffalo, smallmouth	68- 8	Lake Hamilton, AR	May 16,1984	Jerry L.Dolezal
Bullhead, black	8- 0	Lake Waccabuc, NY	Aug. 1,1951	Kani Evans
Bullhead, brown	5- 8	Veal Pond, GA	May 22,1975	Jimmy Andrews
Bullhead, yellow	4- 4	Mormon Lake, AZ	May 11,1984	Emily Williams
Burbot	18- 4	Pickford, MI	Jan.31,1980	Tom Courtemanche
Carp	75-11	Lac de St.Cassien, France	May 21,1987	Leo van der Gugten
Catfish, blue	109- 4	Cooper River, SC	Mar.14,1991	George Lijewski
Catfish, channel	58- 0	Santee-Cooper Res., SC	Jul. 7,1964	W.B. Whaley
Catfish, flathead	91- 4	Lake Lewisville, TX	Mar.28,1982	Mike Rogers
Catfish, white	18-14	Inverness, FL	Sept.21,1991	Jim Miller
Char, Arctic	32- 9	Tree River, Canada	Jul.30,1981	Jeffery Ward
Crappie, black	4- 8	Kerr Lake, VA	Mar. 1,1981	L.Carl Herring,Jr.
Crappie, white	5- 3	Enid Dam, MS	Jul.31,1957	Fred L.Bright
Dolly Varden	16-12	Mashutuk River, AL	July 21,1991	Gary King, Jr.
Dorado	51- 5	Corrientes, Argentina	Sep.27,1984	Armando Giudice
Drum, freshwater	54- 8	Nickajack Lake, TN	Apr.20,1972	Benny E.Hull
Gar, alligator	279- 0	Rio Grande, TX	Dec. 2,1951	Bill Valverde
Gar, Florida	21- 3	Boca Raton, FL	June 3,1981	Jeff Sabol
Gar, longnose	50- 5	Trinity River, TX	Jul.30,1954	Townsend Miller
Gar, shortnose	5- 0	Sally Jones Lake, OK	Apr.26,1985	Buddy Croslin
Gar, spotted	8-12	Tennessee River, AL	Aug.26,1987	Winston H.Baker
Goldfish	3- 0	Southland Pk., Livingston, TX	May 8,1988	Kenneth R.Kinsey
Grayling, Arctic	5-15	Katseyedie River, N.W.T.	Aug.16,1967	Jeanne P.Branson
Inconnu	53- 0	Pah River, AK	Aug.20,1986	Lawrence E.Hudnall
Kokanee	9- 6	Okanagan Lake, Brit.Columbia	Jun.18,1988	Norm Kuhn
Muskellunge	69-15	St. Lawrence River, NY	Sep.22,1957	Arthur Lawton
Muskellunge, tiger	51- 3	Lac Vieux-Desert, WI-MI	Jul.16,1919	John A.Knobla
Perch, Nile	191- 8	Lake Victoria, Kenya	Sept.5,1991	Andy Davison
Perch, white	4-12	Messalonskee Lake, ME	Jun. 4,1949	Mrs.Earl Small
Perch, yellow	4- 3	Bordentown, NJ	May, 1865	Dr.C.C.Abbot
Pickerel, chain	9- 6	Homerville, GA	Feb.17,1961	Baxley McQuaig, Jr.
Pike, northern	55- 1	Lake of Grefeern, W.Germany	Oct.16,1986	Lothar Louis
Redhorse, greater	9- 3	Salmon River, Pulaski, NY	May 11,1985	Jason Wilson
Redhorse, silver	11- 7	Plum Creek, WI	May 29,1985	Neal D.G.Long
Salmon, Atlantic	79- 2	Tana River, Norway	1928	Henrik Henriksen
Salmon, chinook	97- 4	Kenai River, AK	May 17,1985	Les Anderson
Salmon, chum	32- 0	Behm Canal, AK	Jun. 7,1985	Fredrick Thynes
Salmon, coho	33- 4	Salmon River, Pulaski, NY	Sep.27,1989	Jerry Lifton
Salmon, pink	12- 9	Morse & Kenai Rivers, AK	Aug.17,1974	Steven Alan Lee
Salmon, sockeye	15- 3	Kenai River, AK	Aug. 9,1987	Stan Roach
Sauger	8-12	Lake Sakakawea, ND	Oct. 6,1971	Mike Fischer
Shad, American	11- 4	Conn.River, S.Hadley, MA	May 19,1986	Bob Thibodo
Sturgeon, lake	92- 4	Kettle River, MN	Sep. 11,1986	James M.DeOtis
Sturgeon, white	468- 0	Benicia, CA	Jul. 9,1983	Joey Pallotta 3rd
Tigerfish	97- 0	Zaire River, Kinshasa, Zaire	Jul. 9,1988	Raymond Houtmans
Tilapia	6- 0	Lake Okeechobee, FL	Jun.24,1989	Joseph M.Tucker
Trout, Apache	4-15	Christmas Tree Lake, AZ	May 5,1990	Arthur L. Pearce II
Trout, brook	14- 8	Nipigon River, Ontario	July, 1916	Dr. W.J.Cook
Trout, brown	37- 7	Lake Storsjon, Lappland, Sweden	Oct.16,1991	Kurt Stenlund
Trout, bull	32- 0	Lake Pond Orielle, ID	Oct.27,1949	N.L.Higgins
Trout, cutthroat	41- 0	Pyramid Lake, NV	Dec., 1925	John Skimmerhorn
Trout, golden	11- 0	Cooks Lake, WY	Aug. 5,1948	Charles S.Reed
Trout, lake	66- 8	Great Bear Lake, N.W.T.	July 19,1991	Rodney Harback

Species	Lbs-Oz	Where Caught	Date	Angler
Trout, rainbow	42- 2	Bell Island, AK	Jun.22,1970	David Robert White
Trout, tiger	20-13	Lake Michigan, WI	Aug.12,1978	Peter M.Friedland
Walleye	25- 0	Old Hickory Lake, TN	Apr. 1,1960	Mabry Harper
Warmouth	2- 7	Guess Lake, Holt, FL	Oct.19,1985	Tony D.Dempsey
Whitefish, lake	14- 6	Meaford, Ontario	May 21,1984	Dennis M.Laycock
Whitefish, mountain	5- 6	Rioh River, Saskatchewan	Jun.15,1988	John R.Bell
Whitefish, river	11- 2	Skrabean, Nymoua, Sweden	Dec. 9,1984	Jorgen Larsson
Whitefish, round	6- 0	Putahow River, Manitoba	Jun.14,1984	Allan J.Ristori
Zander	25- 2	Trosa, Sweden	Jun.12,1986	Harry Lee Tennison

SALTWATER FISH

Species	Lbs-Oz	Where Caught	Date	Angler
Albacore	88- 2	Gran Canaria, Canary Islands	Nov.19,1977	Siegfried Dickemann
Amberjack, greater	155-10	Challenger Bank, Bermuda	Jun.24,1981	Joseph Dawson
Amberjack, pacific	104- 0	Baja Calif., Mexico	Jul. 4,1984	Richard Cresswell
Barracuda, great	83- 0	Lagos, Nigeria	Jan.13,1952	K.J.W.Hackett
Barracuda, Mexican	21- 0	Phantom Island, Costa Rica	Mar.27,1987	E.Greg Kent
Barracuda, slender	17- 4	Sitra Channel, Bahrain	Nov.21,1985	Roger Cranswick
Bass, barred sand	13- 3	Huntington Beach, CA	Aug.29,1988	Robert Halal
Bass, black sea	9- 8	Virginia Beach, VA	Jan. 9,1987	Joe Mizelle, Jr.
Bass, European	20-11	Stes Maries de la Mer, France	May. 6,1986	Jean Baptiste Bayle
Bass, giant sea	563- 8	Anacapa Island, CA	Aug.20,1968	J.D.McAdam, Jr.
Bass, striped	78- 8	Atlantic City, NJ	Sep.21,1982	Albert R.McReynolds
Bluefish	31-12	Hatteras, NC	Jan.30,1972	James M.Hussey
Bonefish	19- 0	Zululand, South Africa	May 26,1962	Brian W.Batchelor
Bonito, Atlantic	18- 4	Faial Island, Azores	Jul. 8,1953	D.Gama Higgs
Bonito, Pacific	23- 8	Victoria, Mahe, Seychelles	Feb.19,1975	Anne Cochain
Cabezon	23- 0	Juan de Fuca Strait, WA	Aug. 4,1990	Wesley Hunter
Cobia	135- 9	Shark Bay, W.Australia	Jul. 9,1985	Peter W.Goulding
Cod, Atlantic	98-12	Isle of Shoals, NH	Jun. 8,1969	Alphonse Bielevich
Cod, Pacific	30- 0	Andrew Bay, AK	Jul. 7,1984	Donald R.Vaughn
Conger	110- 0	English Channel, Plymouth, England	Aug.20,1991	Hans Christian Clausen
Dolphin	87- 0	Papagallo Gulf, Costa Rica	Sep.25,1976	Manuel Salazar
Drum, black	113- 1	Lewes, DE	Sep.15,1975	Gerald M.Townsend
Drum, red	94- 2	Avon, NC	Nov. 7,1984	David G.Deuel
Eel, African mottled	36- 1	Durban, S. Africa	Jun.10,1984	Ferdie van Nooten
Eel, American	8- 8	Cliff Pond, Brewster, MA	May 17,1992	Gerald G. Lapierre, Sr.
Flounder, southern	20- 9	Nassau Sound, FL	Dec.23,1983	Larenza Mungin
Flounder, summer	22- 7	Montauk, NY	Sep.15,1975	Charles Nappi
Grouper, warsaw	436-12	Gulf of Mexico, Destin, FL	Dec.22,1985	Steve Haeusler
Haddock	11-11	Perkins Cove, Ogunquit, ME	Sept.12,1991	Jim Mailea
Halibut, Atlantic	255- 4	Gloucester, MA	Jul.28,1989	Sonny Manley
Halibut, California	53- 4	Santa Rosa Island, CA	Jul. 7,1988	Russell J.Harmon
Halibut, Pacific	368- 0	Gustavus, AL	July 5,1991	Celia H.Dueitt
Jack, almaco (Pacific)	132- 0	La Paz, Baja Calif., Mexico	Jul.21,1964	Howard H.Hahn
Jack, crevalle	54- 7	Port Michel, Gabon	Jan.15,1982	Thomas F.Gibson, Jr.
Jack, horse-eye	24- 8	Miami, FL	Dec.20,1982	Tito Schnau
Jewfish	680- 0	Fernandina Beach, FL	May 20,1961	Lynn Joyner
Kawakawa	29- 0	Clarion Island, Mexico	Dec.17,1986	Ronald Nakamura
Lingcod	66- 0	Granite Island, AK	Jul. 31,1990	James A. McKenzie
Mackerel, cero	17- 2	Islamorada, FL	Apr. 5,1986	G.Michael Mills
Mackerel, king	90- 0	Key West, FL	Feb.16,1976	Norton I.Thomton
Mackerel, Spanish	13- 0	Ocracoke Inlet, NC	Nov. 4,1987	Robert Cranton
Marlin, Atlantic blue	1282- 0	St.Thomas, Virgin Islands	Aug. 6,1977	Larry Martin
Marlin, Black	1560- 0	Cabo Blanco, Peru	Aug. 4,1953	A.C.Glassell, Jr.
Marlin, Pacific blue	1376- 0	Kaaiwi Point, Kona, HI	May 31,1982	Jay W.deBeaubien
Marlin, striped	494- 0	Tutakaka, New Zealand	Jan.16,1986	Bill Boniface
Marlin, white	181-14	Vitoria, Brazil	Dec. 8,1979	Evandro Luiz Coser
Permit	51- 8	Lake Worth, FL	Apr.28,1978	William M. Kenney
Pollack	27- 6	Salcombe, Devon, England	Jan.16,1986	Robert S. Milkins
Pollock	46-10	Perkins Cove, Ogunquit, ME	Oct.24,1990	Linda M. Paul
Pompano, African	50- 8	Daytona Beach, FL	Apr.21,1990	Tom Sargent
Roosterfish	114- 0	La Paz, Baja Calif., Mexico	Jun. 1,1960	Abe Sackheim
Runner, blue	8- 4	Bimini, Bahamas	Sep. 9,1990	Brent Rowland
Runner, rainbow	37- 9	Clarion Island, Mexico	Nov.21,1991	Tom Pfleger
Sailfish, Atlantic	135- 5	Lago, Nigeria	Nov.10,1991	Ron King
Sailfish, Pacific	221- 0	Santa Cruz Is., Ecuador	Feb.12,1947	C.W.Stewart
Seabass, white	83-12	San Felipe, Mexico	Mar.31,1953	L.C.Baumgardner
Seatrout, spotted	16- 0	Mason's Beach, VA	May 28,1977	William Katko
Shark, blue	437- 0	Catherine Bay, NSW, Australia	Oct. 2,1976	Peter Hyde
Shark, great white	2664- 0	Ceduna, S.Australia	Apr.21,1959	Alfred Dean

Fishing (Cont.)
SALTWATER FISH

Species	Lbs-Oz	Where Caught	Date	Angler
Shark, greenland	1708- 9	Trondheimsfjord, Norway	Oct.18,1987	Terje Nordtvedt
Shark, hammerhead	991- 0	Sarasota, FL	May 30,1982	Allen Ogle
Shark, mako	1115- 0	Black River, Mauritius	Nov.16,1988	Patrick Guillanton
Shark, porbeagle	465- 0	Padstow, Cornwall, England	Jul.23,1976	Jorge Potier
Shark, thresher	802- 0	Tutukaka, New Zealand	Feb. 8,1981	Dianne North
Shark, tiger	1780- 0	Cherry Grove, SC	Jun.14,1964	Walter Maxwell
Snapper, cubera	121- 8	Cameron, LA	Jul. 5,1982	Mike Hebert
Snapper, red	46- 8	Destin, FL	Oct. 1,1985	E.Lane Nichols, III
Snook	53-10	Parismina Ranch, Costa Rica	Oct.18,1978	Gilbert Ponzi
Spearfish	90-13	Madeira Island, Portugal	Jun. 2,1980	Joseph Larkin
Swordfish	1182- 0	Iquique, Chile	May 7,1953	L.Marron
Tarpon	283- 0	Lake Maracaibo, Venezuela	Mar.19,1956	M.Salazar
Tautog	24- 0	Wachapreague, VA	Aug.25,1987	Gregory R.Bell
Tuna, Atlantic bigeye	375- 8	Ocean City, MD	Aug.26,1977	Cecil Browne
Tuna, blackfin	42- 0	Bermuda	Jun.2,1978	Alan J. Card
	42- 0	Challenger Bank, Bermuda	Jul.18,1989	Gilbert C.Pearman
Tuna, bluefin	1496- 0	Aulds Cove, Nova Scotia	Oct.26,1979	Ken Fraser
Tuna, longtail	79- 2	Montague Is., NSW, Australia	Apr.12,1982	Tim Simpson
Tuna, Pacific bigeye	435- 0	Cabo Blanco, Peru	Apr.17,1957	Dr.Russell Lee
Tuna, skipjack	41-14	Pearl Beach, Mauritius	Nov.12,1985	Edmund Heinzen
Tuna, southern bluefin	348- 5	Whakatane, New Zealand	Jan.16,1981	Rex Wood
Tuna, yellowfin	388-12	San Benedicto Island, Mexico	Apr. 1,1977	Curt Wiesenhutter
Tunny, little	35- 2	Cape de Garde, Algeria	Dec.14,1988	Jean Yves Chatard
Wahoo	155- 8	San Salvador, Bahamas	Apr. 3,1990	William Bourne
Weakfish	19- 2	Jones Beach, Long Island, NY	Oct.11,1984	Dennis R.Rooney
	19- 2	Delaware Bay, DE	May 20,1989	William E.Thomas

LITTLE LEAGUE BASEBALL

World Series

Less than a month after beating Long Beach, Calif., 15-4, to win the 1992 Little League World Series, Zamboanga City of the Philippines became the first champion in the 46-year history of the tournament to be stripped of its title.

Little League Baseball's international tournament committee announced on Sept. 12, that Zamboanga City had been disqualified for using several players from other teams outside the city limits. As a result, the '92 title was forfeited to Long Beach, which enters the record book as a 6-0 winner (one run for each inning of the game).

Said Long Beach pitcher Randall Shelley after the decision was handed down: "I think this is a big thing. But it would've been better if we'd won it on the field."

Multiple winners: Taiwan (15); California, Connecticut and Pennsylvania (4); Japan and New Jersey (3); Mexico, New York, South Korea and Texas (2).

Year	Winner	Score	Loser	Year	Winner	Score	Loser
1947	Williamsport, PA	16-7	Lock Haven, PA	1970	Wayne, NJ	2-0	Campbell, CA
1948	Lock Haven, PA	6-5	St. Petersburg, FL	1971	Tainan, Taiwan	2-3	Gary, IN
1949	Hammonton, NJ	5-0	Pensacola, FL	1972	Taipei, Taiwan	6-0	Hammond, IN
				1973	Tainan City, Taiwan	12-0	Tucson, AZ
1950	Houston, TX	2-1	Bridgeport, CT	1974	Kao Hsiung, Taiwan	7-2	El Cajun, CA
1951	Stamford, CT	3-0	Austin, TX	1975	Lakewood, NJ	4-3*	Tampa, FL
1952	Norwalk, CT	4-3	Monongahela, PA	1976	Tokyo, Japan	10-3	Campbell, CA
1953	Birmingham, AL	1-0	Schenectady, NY	1977	Kao Hsiung, Taiwan	7-2	El Cajun, CA
1954	Schenectady, NY	7-5	Colton, CA	1978	Pin-Tung, Taiwan	11-1	Danville, CA
1955	Morrisville, PA	4-3	Merchantville, NJ	1979	Hsien, Taiwan	2-1	Campbell, CA
1956	Roswell, NM	3-1	Merchantville, NJ				
1957	Monterrey, Mex.	4-0	LaMesa, CA	1980	Hua Lian, Taiwan	4-3	Tampa, FL
1958	Monterrey, Mex.	10-1	Kankakee, IL	1981	Tai-Chung, Taiwan	4-2	Tampa, FL
1959	Hamtramck, MI	12-0	Auburn, CA	1982	Kirkland, WA	6-0	Hsien, Taiwan
				1983	Marietta, GA	3-1	Barahona, D.Rep.
1960	Levittown, PA	5-0	Ft. Worth, TX	1984	Seoul, S.Korea	6-2	Altamonte Sgs, FL
1961	El Cajon, CA	4-2	El Campo, TX	1985	Seoul, S.Korea	7-1	Mexicali, Mex.
1962	San Jose, CA	3-0	Kankakee, IL	1986	Tainan Park, Taiwan	12-0	Tucson, AZ
1963	Granada Hills, CA	2-1	Stratford, CT	1987	Hua Lian, Taiwan	21-1	Irvine, CA
1964	Staten Island, NY	4-0	Monterrey, Mex.	1988	Tai-Chung, Taiwan	10-0	Pearl City, HI
1965	Windsor Locks, CT	3-1	Stoney Creek, Can.	1989	Trumbull, CT	5-2	Kaohsiung, Taiwan
1966	Houston, TX	8-2	W.New York, NJ				
1967	West Tokyo, Japan	4-1	Chicago, IL	1990	Taipei, Taiwan	9-0	Shippensburg, PA
1968	Osaka, Japan	1-0	Richmond, VA	1991	Taichung, Taiwan	11-0	San Ramon Vly, CA
1969	Taipei, Taiwan	5-0	Santa Clara,CA	1992	Long Beach, CA	6-0	Zamboanga, Phil.

*Foreign teams were banned from the tournament in 1975. The ban was lifted the next year.

POWER BOAT RACING
APBA Gold Cup

Despite a collision with defending champion Winston Eagle in the championship heat, Chip Hanauer piloted Miss Budweiser to victory in the APBA Gold Cup, June 14, on the Detroit River. The bump of rival hydroplanes left Winston Eagle dead in the water, but only splintered Miss Budweiser's tail section as Hanauer was able to join Bill Muncey as the Gold Cup's only eight-time winning pilots. Miss Budweiser's average speed over four heats was 136.282 mph.

The American Power Boat Association Gold Cup for unlimited hydroplane racing is the oldest active motor sports trophy in North America. The first Gold Cup was competed for on the Hudson River in New York in June and September of 1904. Since then several cities have hosted the race, led by Detroit (27 times, including 1990) and Seattle (14). Note that (*) indicates driver was also owner of the winning boat.

Drivers with multiple wins: Chip Hanauer and Bill Muncey (8); Gar Wood (5); Dean Chenoweth (4); Caleb Bragg, Tom D'Eath, Lou Fageol, Ron Musson, George Reis and Jonathon Wainwright (3); Danny Foster, George Henley, Vic Kliesrath, E.J.Schroeder, Bill Schumacher, Zalmon G.Simmons Jr., Joe Taggart and George Townsend (2).

Year	Boat	Driver	Avg. MPH	Year	Boat	Driver	Avg. MPH
1904	Standard (June)	*Carl Riotte	23.160	1948	Miss Great Lakes	Danny Foster	46.845
1904	Vingt-Et-Un II (Sept.)	*W.Sharpe Kilmer	24.900	1949	My Sweetie	Bill Cantrell	73.612
1905	Chip I	*J.Wainwright	15.000	1950	Slo-Mo-Shun IV	Ted Jones	78.216
1906	Chip II	*J.Wainwright	25.000	1951	Slo-Mo-Shun V	Lou Fageol	90.871
1907	Chip II	*J.Wainwright	23.903	1952	Slo-Mo-Shun IV	Stan Dollar	79.923
1908	Dixie II	*E.J.Schroeder	29.938	1953	Slo-Mo-Shun IV	Joe Taggart & Lou Fageol	99.108
1909	Dixie II	*E.J.Schroeder	29.590	1954	Slo-Mo-Shun IV	Joe Taggart & Lou Fageol	92.613
1910	Dixie III	*F.K.Burnham	32.473	1955	Gale V	Lee Schoenith	99.552
1911	MIT II	*J.H.Hayden	37.000	1956	Miss Thriftaway	Bill Muncey	96.552
1912	P.D.Q. II	*A.G.Miles	39.462	1957	Miss Thriftaway	Bill Muncey	101.787
1913	Ankle Deep	*Cas Mankowski	42.779	1958	Hawaii Kai III	Jack Regas	103.000
1914	Baby Speed Demon II	Jim Blackton & Bob Edgren	48.458	1959	Maverick	Bill Stead	104.481
1915	Miss Detroit	Johnny Milot & Jack Beebe	37.656	1960	Not held		
1916	Miss Minneapolis	Bernard Smith	48.860	1961	Miss Century 21	Bill Muncey	99.678
1917	Miss Detroit II	*Gar Wood	54.410	1962	Miss Century 21	Bill Muncey	100.710
1918	Miss Detroit II	Gar Wood	51.619	1963	Miss Bardahl	Ron Musson	105.124
1919	Miss Detroit III	*Gar Wood	42.748	1964	Miss Bardahl	Ron Musson	103.433
1920	Miss America I	*Gar Wood	62.022	1965	Miss Bardahl	Ron Musson	103.132
1921	Miss America I	*Gar Wood	52.825	1966	Tahoe Miss	Mira Slovak	93.019
1922	Packard Chriscraft	*J.G.Vincent	40.253	1967	Miss Bardahl	Bill Shumacher	101.484
1923	Packard Chriscraft	Caleb Bragg	43.867	1968	Miss Bardahl	Bill Shumacher	108.173
1924	Baby Bootlegger	*Caleb Bragg	45.302	1969	Miss Budweiser	Bill Sterett	98.504
1925	Baby Bootlegger	*Caleb Bragg	47.240	1970	Miss Budweiser	Dean Chenoweth	99.562
1926	Greenwich Folly	*Geo.Townsend	47.984	1971	Miss Madison	Jim McCormick	98.043
1927	Greenwich Folly	*Geo.Townsend	47.662	1972	Atlas Van Lines	Bill Muncey	104.277
1928	Not held			1973	Miss Budweiser	Dean Chenoweth	99.043
1929	Imp	*Richard Hoyt	48.662	1974	Pay 'n Pak	George Henley	104.428
1930	Hotsy Totsy	*Vic Kliesrath	52.673	1975	Pay 'n Pak	George Henley	108.921
1931	Hotsy Totsy	*Vic Kliesrath	53.602	1976	Miss U.S.	Tom D'Eath	100.412
1932	Delphine IV	Bill Horn	57.775	1977	Atlas Van Lines	*Bill Muncey	111.822
1933	El Lagarto	*George Reis	56.260	1978	Atlas Van Lines	*Bill Muncey	111.412
1934	El Lagarto	*George Reis	55.000	1979	Atlas Van Lines	*Bill Muncey	100.765
1935	El Lagarto	*George Reis	55.056	1980	Miss Budweiser	Dean Chenoweth	106.932
1936	Impshi	Kaye Don	45.735	1981	Miss Budweiser	Dean Chenoweth	116.932
1937	Notre Dame	Clell Perry	63.675	1982	Atlas Van Lines	Chip Hanauer	120.050
1938	Alagi	*Theo Rossi	64.340	1983	Atlas Van Lines	Chip Hanauer	118.507
1939	My Sin	*Z.G.Simmons,Jr	66.133	1984	Atlas Van Lines	Chip Hanauer	130.175
1940	Hotsy Totsy III	*Sidney Allen	48.295	1985	Miller American	Chip Hanauer	120.643
1941	My Sin	*Z.G.Simmons,Jr	52.509	1986	Miller American	Chip Hanauer	116.523
1942	Not held			1987	Miller American	Chip Hanauer	127.620
1943	Not held			1988	Miss Circus Circus	Chip Hanauer & Jim Prevost	123.756
1944	Not held			1989	Miss Budweiser	Tom D'Eath	131.209
1945	Not held			1990	Miss Budweiser	Tom D'Eath	143.176
1946	Tempo VI	*Guy Lombardo	68.132	1991	Winston Eagle	Mark Tate	137.771
1947	Miss Peps V	Danny Foster	57.000	1992	Miss Budweiser	Chip Hanauer	136.282

PRO RODEO
All-Around Champion Cowboy

Ty Murray, of Stephenville, Texas, won his third consecutive professional rodeo cowboy All-Around championship on Dec. 13, 1991, in Las Vegas. Murray, 22, qualified for the National Finals in three events—bareback, saddle bronc and bull riding—and set another single season earnings record with $258,750.

The Professional Rodeo Cowboys Association (PRCA) title of All-Around World Champion Cowboy goes to the rodeo athlete who wins the most prize money in two or more events. Only prize money earned in sanctioned PRCA rodeos is counted. From 1929-44, All-Around champions were named by the Rodeo Association of America (earnings for those years is not available).

Multiple winners: Tom Ferguson and Larry Mahan (6); Jim Shoulders (5); Lewis Feild, Ty Murray and Dean Oliver (3); Everett Bowman, Lewis Brooks, Clay Carr, Bill Linderman, Phil Lyne, Gerald Roberts, Casey Tibbs and Harry Tompkins (2).

Year		Year		Year		Year	
1929	Earl Thode	1934	Leonard Ward	1938	Burel Mulkey	1942	Gerald Roberts
1930	Clay Carr	1935	Everett Bowman	1939	Paul Carney	1943	Louis Brooks
1931	John Schneider	1936	John Bowman	1940	Fritz Truan	1944	Louis Brooks
1932	Donald Nesbit	1937	Everett Bowman	1941	Homer Pettigrew	1945-46	No award
1933	Clay Carr						

Year		Earnings	Year		Earnings	Year		Earnings
1947	Todd Whatley	$18,642	1963	Dean Oliver	$31,329	1978	Tom Ferguson	$83,734
1948	Gerald Roberts	21,766	1964	Dean Oliver	31,150	1979	Tom Ferguson	96,272
1949	Jim Shoulders	21,495	1965	Dean Oliver	33,163	1980	Paul Tierney	105,568
1950	Bill Linderman	30,715	1966	Larry Mahan	40,358	1981	Jimmie Cooper	105,861
1951	Casey Tibbs	29,104	1967	Larry Mahan	51,996	1982	Chris Lybbert	123,709
1952	Harry Tompkins	30,934	1968	Larry Mahan	49,129	1983	Roy Cooper	153,391
1953	Bill Linderman	33,674	1969	Larry Mahan	57,726	1984	Dee Picket	122,618
1954	Buck Rutherford	40,404	1970	Larry Mahan	41,493	1985	Lewis Feild	130,347
1955	Casey Tibbs	42,065	1971	Phil Lyne	49,245	1986	Lewis Feild	166,042
1956	Jim Shoulders	43,381	1972	Phil Lyne	60,852	1987	Lewis Feild	144,335
1957	Jim Shoulders	33,299	1973	Larry Mahan	64,447	1988	Dave Appleton	121,546
1958	Jim Shoulders	32,212	1974	Tom Ferguson	66,929	1989	Ty Murray	134,806
1959	Jim Shoulders	32,905	1975	Tom Ferguson	50,300	1990	Ty Murray	213,772
1960	Harry Tompkins	32,522	1976	Tom Ferguson	87,908	1991	Ty Murray	258,750
1961	Benny Reynolds	31,309	1977	Tom Ferguson	65,981			
1962	Tom Nesmith	32,611						

SOAP BOX DERBY
All-American Soap Box Derby

Girls swept all three titles at the 1992 All-American Soap Box Derby on Aug. 8, in Akron, Ohio. Bonnie Eileen Thornton, 12, of Redding, Calif., won the Masters Division; Carolyn Renee Fox, 11, of Sublimity, Ore., won the Kit Division; and 10-year-old Loren Marie Hurst of Hudson, Ohio, was the winner in the new Stock Car Division for novices. More than 200 regional champions competed in the races.

The All-American Soap Box Derby is a coasting race for small gravity-powered cars built by their drivers and assembled within strict guidelines on size, weight and cost. The Derby got its name in the 1930s when most cars were built from wooden soap boxes. Held every summer on the second Saturday of August at Derby Downs in Akron, the Soap Box Derby is open to all boys and girls from 9 to 16 years old who qualify.

There are three competitive divisions: Stock Cars (ages 9-16), made up of generic, prefab racers that come in Derby-approved kits and can be assembled in four hours; Kit Cars (ages 9-16), made up of racers assembled from Derby-approved kits that do not include wood shells; and Masters (ages 11-16), made up of racers designed by drivers, but constructed with Derby-approved hardware. The racing ramp at Derby Downs is 953.75 feet with an 11 percent grade.

One champion was determined at the All-American Soap Box Derby each year from 1934-75; Junior and Senior division champions from 1976-87; Kit and Masters champions from 1988-91; and Stock, Kit and Masters champions starting in 1992.

Year		Hometown	Age	Year		Hometown	Age
1934	Robert Turner	Muncie, IN	11	1940	Thomas Fisher	Detroit	12
1935	Maurice Bale, Jr.	Anderson, IN	13	1941	Claude Smith	Akron, OH	14
1936	Herbert Muench, Jr.	St.Louis	14	1942-45	Not held		
1937	Robert Ballard	White Plains, NY	12	1946	Gilbert Klecan	San Diego	14
1938	Robert Berger	Omaha, NE	14	1947	Kenneth Holmboe	Charleston, WV	14
1939	Clifton Hardesty	White Plains, NY	11	1948	Donald Strub	Akron, OH	13
				1949	Fred Derks	Akron, OH	15

Year		Hometown	Age	Year		Hometown	Age
1950	Harold Williamson	Charleston, WV	15	1979	JR: Russell Yurk	Flint, MI	10
1951	Darwin Cooper	Williamsport, PA	15		SR: Craig Kitchen	Akron, OH	14
1952	Joe Lunn	Columbus, GA	11	1980	JR: Chris Fulton	Indianapolis	11
1953	Fred Mohler	Muncie, IN	14		SR: Dan Porul	Sherman Oaks, CA	12
1954	Richard Kemp	Los Angeles	14	1981	JR: Howie Fraley	Portsmouth, OH	11
1955	Richard Rohrer	Rochester, NY	14		SR: Tonia Schlegel	Hamilton, OH	13
1956	Norman Westfall	Rochester, NY	14	1982	JR: Carol A.Sullivan	Rochester, NH	10
1957	Terry Townsend	Anderson, IN	14		SR: Matt Wolfgang	Lehigh Val., PA	12
1958	James Miley	Muncie, IN	15	1983	JR: Tony Carlini	Del Mar, CA	10
1959	Barney Townsend	Anderson, IN	13		SR: Mike Burdgick	Flint, MI	14
1960	Fredric Lake	South Bend, IN	11	1984	JR: Chris Hess	Hamilton, OH	11
1961	Dick Dawson	Wichita, KS	13		SR: Anita Jackson	St.Louis	15
1962	David Mann	Gary, IN	14	1985	JR: Michael Gallo	Danbury, CT	12
1963	Harold Conrad	Duluth, MN	12		SR: Matt Sheffer	York, PA	14
1964	Gregory Schumacher	Tacoma, WA	14	1986	JR: Marc Behan	Dover, NH	9
1965	Robert Logan	Santa Ana, CA	12		SR: Tami Jo Sullivan	Lancaster, OH	13
1966	David Krussow	Tacoma, WA	12	1987	JR: Matt Margules	Danbury, CT	11
1967	Kenneth Cline	Lincoln, NE	13		SR: Brian Drinkwater	Bristol, CT	14
1968	Branch Lew	Muncie, IN	11	1988	KIT: Jason Lamb	Des Moines, IA	10
1969	Steve Souter	Midland, TX	12		MAS: David Duffield	Kansas City	13
1970	Samuel Gupton	Durham, NC	13	1989	KIT: David Schiller	Dayton, OH	12
1971	Larry Blair	Oroville, CA	13		MAS: Faith Chavarria	Ventura, CA	12
1972	Robert Lange, Jr.	Boulder, CO	14	1990	KIT: Mark Mihal	Valparaiso, IN	12
1973	Bret Yarborough	Elk Grove, CA	11		MAS: Sami Jones	Salem, OR	13
1974	Curt Yarborough	Elk Grove, CA	11	1991	KIT: Paul Greenwald	Saginaw, MI	13
1975	Karren Stead	Lower Bucks, PA	11		MAS: Danny Garland	San Diego, CA	14
1976	JR: Phil Raber	Sugarcreek, OH	11	1992	KIT: Carolyn Fox	Sublimity, OR	11
	SR: Joan Ferdinand	Canton, OH	14		MAS: Bonnie Thornton	Redding, CA	12
1977	JR: Mark Ferdinand	Canton, OH	10		STK: Loren Hurst	Hudson, OH	10
	SR: Steve Washburn	Bristol, CT	15				
1978	JR: Darren Hart	Salem, OR	11				
	SR: Greg Cardinal	Flint, MI	13				

SOFTBALL

Men's and women's national champions since 1933 in Major Fast Pitch, Major Slow Pitch and Super Slow Pitch (men only). Sanctioned by the Amateur Softball Association of America.

MEN

Major Fast Pitch

Multiple winners: Clearwater Bombers (10); Raybestos Cardinals (5); Sealmasters (4); Briggs Beautyware, Pay'n Pak and Zollner Pistons (3); Billard Barbell, Hammer Air Field, Penn Corp and Peterbilt Western (2).

Year		Year		Year	
1933	J.L.Gill Boosters, Chicago	1955	Raybestos Cardinals, Stratford, CT	1976	Raybestos Cardinals
1934	Ke-Nash-A, Kenosha, WI			1977	Billard Barbell, Reading, PA
1935	Crimson Coaches, Toledo, OH	1956	Clearwater Bombers	1978	Billard Barbell
1936	Kodak Park, Rochester, NY	1957	Clearwater Bombers	1979	McArdle Pontiac/Cadillac, Midland, MI
1937	Briggs Body Team, Detroit	1958	Raybestos Cardinals		
1938	The Pohlers, Cincinnati	1959	Sealmasters, Aurora, IL	1980	Peterbilt Western, Seattle
1939	Carr's Boosters, Covington, KY	1960	Clearwater Bombers	1981	Archer Daniels Midland, Decatur, IL
1940	Kodak Park, Rochester, NY	1961	Sealmasters		
1941	Bendix Brakes, South Bend, IN	1962	Clearwater Bombers	1982	Peterbilt Western
1942	Deep Rock Oilers, Tulsa, OK	1963	Clearwater Bombers	1983	Franklin Cardinals, Stratford, CT
1943	Hammer Air Field, Fresno, CA	1964	Burch Tool, Detroit		
1944	Hammer Air Field	1965	Sealmasters	1984	California Kings, Merced, CA
1945	Zollner Pistons, Ft.Wayne, IN	1966	Clearwater Bombers	1985	Pay'n Pak, Seattle
1946	Zollner Pistons	1967	Sealmasters	1986	Pay'n Pak
1947	Zollner Pistons	1968	Clearwater Bombers	1987	Pay'n Pak
1948	Briggs Beautyware, Detroit	1969	Raybestos Cardinals	1988	TransAire, Elkhart, IN
1949	Tip Top Tailors, Toronto	1970	Raybestos Cardinals	1989	Penn Corp, Sioux City, IA
1950	Clearwater (FL) Bombers	1971	Welty Way, Cedar Rapids, IA	1990	Penn Corp
1951	Dow Chemical, Midland, MI	1972	Raybestos Cardinals	1991	Gianella Bros., Rohnert Park, CA
1952	Briggs Beautyware	1973	Clearwater Bombers		
1953	Briggs Beautyware	1974	Gianella Bros, Santa Rosa, CA	1992	National Health Care, Sioux City, IA
1954	Clearwater Bombers	1975	Rising Sun Hotel, Reading, PA		

Softball (Cont.)
MEN
Major Slow Pitch

Multiple winners: Gatliff Auto Sales and Skip Hogan A.C. (3); Campbell Carpets, Hamilton Tailoring and Howard's Furniture (2).

Year		Year		Year	
1953	Shields Construction, Newport, KY	1966	Michael's Lounge, Detroit	1980	Campbell Carpets
1954	Waldneck's Tavern, Cincinnati	1967	Jim's Sport Shop, Pittsburgh	1981	Elite Coating, Gordon, CA
1955	Lang Pet Shop, Covington, KY	1968	County Sports, Levittown, NY	1982	Triangle Sports, Minneapolis
1956	Gatliff Auto Sales, Newport, KY	1969	Copper Hearth, Milwaukee	1983	No.1 Electric & Heating, Gastonia, NC
1957	Gatliff Auto Sales	1970	Little Caesar's, Southgate, MI	1984	Lilly Air Systems, Chicago
1958	East Side Sports, Detroit	1971	Pile Drivers, Va.Beach, VA	1985	Blanton's Fayetteville, NC
1959	Yorkshire Restaurant, Newport, KY	1972	Jiffy Club, Louisville, KY	1986	Non-Ferrous Metals, Cleveland
		1973	Howard's Furniture, Denver, NC	1987	Stapath, Monticello, KY
1960	Hamilton Tailoring, Cincinnati	1974	Howard's Furniture	1988	Bell Corp/FAF, Tampa, FL
1961	Hamilton Tailoring	1975	Pyramid Cafe, Lakewood, OH	1989	Ritch's Salvage, Harrisburg, NC
1962	Skip Hogan A.C., Pittsburgh	1976	Warren Motors, J'ville, FL		
1963	Gatliff Auto Sales	1977	Nelson Painting, Okla.City	1990	New Construction, Shelbyville,IN
1964	Skip Hogan A.C.	1978	Campbell Carpets, Concord, CA	1991	Riverside Paving, Louisville
1965	Skip Hogan A.C.	1979	Nelco Mfg.Co., Okla.City	1992	Vernon's, Jacksonville, FL

Super Slow Pitch

Multiple winners: Howard's/Western Steer and Steele's Sports (3).

Year		Year		Year	
1981	Howard's/Western Steer, Denver, NC	1986	Steele's Sports	1990	Steele's Silver Bullets
1982	Jerry's Catering, Miami	1987	Steele's Sports	1991	Sun Belt/Worth, Atlanta
1983	Howard's/Western Steer	1988	Starpath, Monticello, KY	1992	Rich's/Superior, Windsor Locks, CT
1984	Howard's/Western Steer	1989	Ritch's Salvage, Harrisburg, NC		
1985	Steele's Sports, Grafton, OH				

WOMEN
Major Fast Pitch

Multiple winners: Raybestos Brakettes (21); Orange Lionettes (9); Jax Maids (4); Arizona Ramblers (3); Hi-Ho Brakettes, J.J. Krieg's and National Screw & Manufacturing (2).

Year		Year		Year	
1933	Great Northerns, Chicago	1954	Leach Motor Rockets, Fresno, CA	1973	Raybestos Brakettes
1934	Hart Motors, Chicago	1955	Orange Lionettes	1974	Raybestos Brakettes
1935	Bloomer Girls, Cleveland	1956	Orange Lionettes	1975	Raybestos Brakettes
1936	Nat'l Screw & Mfg., Cleveland	1957	Hacienda Rockets, Fresno, CA	1976	Raybestos Brakettes
1937	Nat'l Screw & Mfg.	1958	Raybestos Brakettes, Stratford, CT	1977	Raybestos Brakettes
1938	J.J.Krieg's, Alameda, CA			1978	Raybestos Brakettes
1939	J.J.Krieg's	1959	Raybestos Brakettes	1979	Sun City (AZ) Saints
1940	Arizona Ramblers, Phoenix	1960	Raybestos Brakettes	1980	Raybestos Brakettes
1941	Higgins Midgets, Tulsa, OK	1961	Gold Sox, Whittier, CA	1981	Orlando (FL) Rebels
1942	Jax Maids, New Orleans	1962	Orange Lionettes	1982	Raybestos Brakettes
1943	Jax Maids	1963	Raybestos Brakettes	1983	Raybestos Brakettes
1944	Lind & Pomeroy, Portland, OR	1964	Erv Lind Florists, Portland, OR	1984	Los Angeles Diamonds
1945	Jax Maids	1965	Orange Lionettes	1985	Hi-Ho Brakettes, Stratford, CT
1946	Jax Maids	1966	Raybestos Brakettes	1986	So.California Invasion, LA
1947	Jax Maids	1967	Raybestos Brakettes	1987	Orange County Majestics, Anaheim, CA
1948	Arizona Ramblers	1968	Raybestos Brakettes	1988	Hi-Ho Brakettes (CT)
1949	Arizona Ramblers	1969	Orange Lionettes	1989	Whittier (CA) Raiders
1950	Orange (CA) Lionettes	1970	Orange Lionettes	1990	Raybestos Brakettes
1951	Orange Lionettes	1971	Raybestos Brakettes	1991	Raybestos Brakettes
1952	Orange Lionettes	1972	Raybestos Brakettes	1992	Raybestos Brakettes
1953	Betsy Ross Rockets, Fresno, CA				

Major Slow Pitch

Multiple winners: Dana Gardens and Spooks (4); Cannan's Illusions, Bob Hoffman's Dots and Marks Brothers Dots (2).

Year		Year		Year	
1959	Pearl Laundry, Richmond, VA	1971	Gators, Ft.Lauderdale, FL	1981	Tifton (GA) Tomboys
1960	Carolina Rockets, High Pt., NC	1972	Riverside Ford, Cincinnati	1982	Richmond (VA) Stompers
1961	Dairy Cottage, Covington, KY	1973	Sweeney Chevrolet, Cincinnati	1983	Spooks, Anoka, MN
1962	Dana Gardens, Cincinnati	1974	Marks Brothers Dots, Miami	1984	Spooks
1963	Dana Gardens	1975	Marks Brothers Dots	1985	Key Ford Mustangs,
1964	Dana Gardens	1976	Sorrento's Pizza, Cincinnati		Pensacola, FL
1965	Art's Acres, Omaha, NE	1977	Fox Valley Lassies,	1986	Sur-Way Tomboys, Tifton, GA
1966	Dana Gardens		St.Charles, IL	1987	Key Ford Mustangs
1967	Ridge Maintenance, Cleveland	1978	Bob Hoffman's Dots, Miami	1988	Spooks
1968	Escue Pontiac, Cincinnati	1979	Bob Hoffman's Dots	1989	Cannan's Illusions, Houston
1969	Converse Dots, Hialeah, FL	1980	Howard's Rubi-Otts,	1990	Spooks
1970	Rutenschruder Floral, Cincinnati		Graham, NC	1991	Cannan's Illusions, San Antonio
				1992	Universal Plastics, Cookeville, TN

TRIATHLON
Ironman Championship

Contested in Hawaii since 1978, the Ironman Triathlon Championship consists of a 2.4-mile swim, a 112-mile bike ride and 26.2-mile run. The race begins at 7 A.M. and continues all day until the course is closed at midnight.

MEN

Multiple winners: Dave Scott (6); Mark Allen (3); Scott Tinley (2).

Year	Date	Winner	Time	Runner-up	Margin	Start	Finish	Location
I	2/18/78	Gordon Haller	11:46	John Dunbar	34:00	15	12	Waikiki Beach
II	1/14/79	Tom Warren	11:15:56	John Dunbar	48:00	15	12	Waikiki Beach
III	1/10/80	Dave Scott	9:24:33	Chuck Neumann	1:08	108	95	Ala Moana Park
IV	2/14/81	John Howard	9:38:29	Tom Warren	26:00	326	299	Kailua-Kona
V	2/6/82	Scott Tinley	9:19:41	Dave Scott	17:16	580	541	Kailua-Kona
VI	10/9/82	Dave Scott	9:08:23	Scott Tinley	20:05	850	775	Kailua-Kona
VII	10/22/83	Dave Scott	9:05:57	Scott Tinley	0:33	964	835	Kailua-Kona
VIII	10/6/84	Dave Scott	8:54:20	Scott Tinley	24:25	1036	903	Kailua-Kona
IX	10/25/85	Scott Tinley	8:50:54	Chris Hinshaw	25:46	1018	965	Kailua-Kona
X	10/18/86	Dave Scott	8:28:37	Mark Allen	9:47	1039	951	Kailua-Kona
XI	10/10/87	Dave Scott	8:34:13	Mark Allen	11:06	1380	1284	Kailua-Kona
XII	10/22/88	Scott Molina	8:31:00	Mike Pigg	2:11	1277	1189	Kailua-Kona
XIII	10/15/89	Mark Allen	8:09:15	Dave Scott	0:58	1285	1231	Kailua-Kona
XIV	10/6/90	Mark Allen	8:28:17	Scott Tinley	9:23	1386	1255	Kailua-Kona
XV	10/19/91	Mark Allen	8:18:32	Greg Welch	6:01.9	1386	1235	Kailua-Kona

WOMEN

Multiple winners: Paula Newby-Fraser (4); Erin Baker and Sylviane Puntous (2).

Year	Winner	Time	Runner-up	Year	Winner	Time	Runner-up
1978	No finishers			1985	Joanne Ernst	10:25:22	Liz Bulman
1979	Lyn Lemaire	12:55.00	None	1986	Paula Newby-Fraser	9:49:14	Sylviane Puntous
1980	Robin Beck	11:21:24	Eve Anderson				
1981	Linda Sweeney	12:00:32	Sally Edwards	1987	Erin Baker	9:35:25	Sylviane Puntous
1982	Kathleen McCartney	11:09:40	Julie Moss	1988	P.Newby-Fraser	9:01:01	Erin Baker
				1989	P.Newby-Fraser	9:00:56	Sylviane Puntous
1982	Julie Leach	10:54:08	Joann Dahlkoetter	1990	Erin Baker	9:13:42	P.Newby-Fraser
1983	Sylviane Puntous	10:43:36	Patricia Puntous	1991	P.Newby-Fraser	9:07:52	Erin Baker
1984	Sylviane Puntous	10:25:13	Patricia Puntous				

World Championship

Contested since 1989, the Triathlon World Championship consists of a 1.5 kilometer swim, a 40-kilometer bike ride and a 10-kilometer run. Race sites have included Avignon, France (1989), Orlando, Fla. (1990), Surfers Paradise in Queensland, Australia (1991), and Huntsville, Ontario (1992).

MEN

Year		Time
1989	Mark Allen, United States	1:58.46
1990	Greg Welch, Australia	1:51.37
1991	Miles Stewart, Australia	1:48.20
1992	Simon Lessing, Great Britain	1:49.04

WOMEN

Year		Time
1989	Erin Baker, New Zealand	2:10.01
1990	Karen Smyers, United States	2:03.33
1991	Joanne Ritchie, Canada	2:02.04
1992	Michelle Jones, Australia	2:02.08

Other 1992 Champions

Championships decided in 1992 unless otherwise indicated.

American Football

Arena Football League Championship
Detroit Drive 56 .... Orlando Predators 38

WLAF World Bowl
Sacramento Surge 21 .... Orlando Thunder 17

Australian Rules Football

AFL Grand Final
Perth West Coast Eagles 113 .... Geelong Cats 85

Billiards

World Championships
Men's Pro 9-ball .... Johnny Archer, USA
Women's Pro 9-ball .... Franziska Stark, GER

U.S. Open 14.1 Champions
Men .... Mike Sigel, Baltimore
Women .... Loree Jon Jones, Hillsboro, NJ

Cricket

World Cup Final
Pakistan 249 .... England 227

England vs. Australia
The Ashes .... at England (1993)

West Indies vs. Australia
Sir Frank Worrell Trophy .... at Australia (1993)

Curling

World Champions
Men .... Switzerland (skip: Markus Eggler)
Women .... Sweden (skip: Elisebet Johansson)

U.S. Champions
Men .... Seattle (skip: Doug Jones)
Women .... Madison, WI (skip: Lisa Schoeneberg)

Drag Racing

NHRA U.S. Nationals
Top Fuel .... Ed McCulloch
Funny Car .... Cruz Pedregon
Pro Stock .... Warren Johnson

1991 NHRA Overall Champions
Top Fuel .... Joe Amato
Funny Car .... John Force
Pro Stock .... Darrell Alderman

Equestrian

Volvo World Cup
Show Jumping .... Thomas Fruhmann, AUT
Dressage .... Isabell Werth, GER

U.S. Champions
Show Jumping . Norman Dello Joio, W.Palm Beach, FL
Dressage .... Carol Lavel, Fairfax, VT

Handball

U.S. Championships
FOUR-WALL
Men .... Octavio Silveyra, Commerce, CA
Women .... Lisa Fraser, Winnipeg
Open doubles ..... David Chapman, Long Beach, CA
& Naty Elvarado, Jr., Hesperia, CA

Horseshoe Pitching

World Champions
Men .... Kevin Cone, Alta, IA
Women .... Sue Snyder, Grandview, IN

Lacrosse

Major Indoor League Championship
Buffalo Bandits 11 .... OT .... Philadelphia Wings 10

Motorcycle Racing

ROAD RACING

Grand Prix Champions
125 cc .... Alessandro Gramigni, ITA
250 cc .... Luca Cadalora, ITA
500 cc ... Wayne Rainey, USASuper Bike ... undecided

MOTORCROSS

Motorcross des Nations
Team ..... USA (Jeff Eming, Mike LaRocco & Billy Liles)

Grand Prix Champions
125 cc .... Greg Albertijn, SAF
250 cc .... Donny Schmidt, USA
500 cc .... Georges Jobe, BEL

Racquetball

U.S. Amateur Champions
Men .... Chris Cole, Davison, MI
Women .... Michelle Gould, Boise, ID

U.S. Pro Champions
Men .... Drew Kachtik, Carrollton, TX
Women .... Jackie Paraiso-Gibson, San Diego

Rugby

International Champions
1991 World Cup .... Australia
1995 World Cup .... at South Africa
1992 Five Nations .... England

U.S. Champions
Club .... Old Blues Rugby Club, Berkeley, CA
College .... California (Berkeley)

Volleyball

International Champions
1991 World Cup: Men .... Soviet Union
Women .... Cuba
1994 World Championship: Men .... at Greece
Women .... at Italy

U.S. Open Champions
Men's Gold Div .... Creole Six Pack, Elmhurst, NY
Women's Gold Div .... Nick's Kronies, Chicago

Pro Beach Tours

MEN (AVP)
Manhattan Beach Open ... Karch Kiraly & Kent Steffes
U.S. Championships ...... Karch Kiraly & Kent Steffes
Tourn. of Champions ...... Karch Kiraly & Kent Steffes

WOMEN (WPVA)
Las Vegas Shootout.... Linda Carillo & Liz Masakayan
World Championships ... Karolyn Kirby & Nancy Reno
U.S.Open .... Angela Rock & Jackie Silva

Water Skiing

World Championships
Men/Women .... Singapore (1993)

U.S. Open Champions
Overall: Men .... Patrice Martin, FRA
Women .... Julie Petrus, Hartville, MO

Bud Water Ski Tour
Overall: Men .... Sammy Duvall, Windermere, FL
Women .... Kristi Overton, Greenville, NC

Wide World Photos

Former New York Jets owner **Sonny Werblin** (left) looks on as Alabama quarterback **Joe Namath** signs his first pro football contract on Jan. 2, 1965, for a then staggering $427,000. Werblin died of a heart attack on Nov. 21, 1991.

DEATHS

(November 1991 through October 1992)

Daytona International Speedway   Wide World Photos   Baseball Hall of Fame

Clifford Allison   **Lyle Alzado**   **Sandy Amoros**

Richard Affils, 62; former pro football player who gained fame as pro wrestling's Dick the Bruiser; got his nickname as an offensive lineman for the Green Bay Packers from 1951-54; left NFL to become a pro wrestler for four decades; known for his scowl, crew-cut hair and gravelly voice, the result of a football injury to the larynx; of internal bleeding; in Largo, Fla., Nov. 10, 1991.

Clifford Allison, 27; stock car race driver, who was the youngest son of 1983 NASCAR Winston Cup champion Bobby Allison and brother of current NASCAR star Davey Allison; began racing in 1983 in street stocks, advanced to All-Pro, IMSA sports car and ARCA; joined Grand National tour in 1990; of injuries suffered in crash during practice laps; in Brooklyn, Mich., Aug. 13.

Lyle Alzado, 43; two-time All-Pro defensive end with Denver, who was the NFL defensive player of the year in 1977, also played for Cleveland and the LA Raiders; helped lead Raiders to 1984 Super Bowl title; known for his ferocious style of play, but later became a symbol of the dangers of steroid use with his July 8, 1991, *Sports Illustrated* cover story; after retiring from football, he became an actor, appearing in commercials and action films; of brain cancer, brought on, Alzado maintained, by his steroid use; in Portland, Ore., May 14.

Sandy Amoros, 62; Cuban-born Dodgers outfielder from 1952-60, who earned a place in baseball history with a spectacular double play catch against the New York Yankees that helped Brooklyn win its one and only World Series championship in 1955; a .255 career hitter, he was sent in as a defensive replacement in the sixth inning of Game 7 at Yankee Stadium; with the Dodgers ahead, 2-0, and men on first and second with no outs, Yankee catcher Yogi Berra hit a ball that sliced down the left field line and appeared to be a game-tying hit until Amoros, regarded as the fastest man in the majors, snagged the ball on the run; in that same series, he hit a two-run homer that helped the Dodgers win Game 5; of pneumonia; in Miami, June 27.

Eric Andolsek, 25; Detroit Lions offensive lineman; fifth round pick in 1988 NFL Draft after three standout years at LSU; from injuries suffered after being hit by a truck on the lawn in front of his house; in Thibodaux, La., June 23.

Scott Appleton, 50; former All-America football tackle at Texas, who led the Longhorns to the national championship in 1963; also won the Outland Trophy in '63 as the nation's outstanding interior lineman; went on to play six years in the NFL with Houston and San Diego; of heart failure; in Austin, Tex., Mar. 2.

"Gorgeous George" Arena, 84; pro wrestler in the 1940s and '50s; a primping and platinum-haired villain on the circuit, he was the first of many "Gorgeous Georges" (the most famous of whom was George Raymond Wagner, who gained fame as TV wrestling's biggest draw in the '50s); after a long illness; in Boca Raton, Fla., July 16.

Irvin (Ace) Bailey, 88; NHL Hall of Fame left wing, who scored 111 goals and 193 points in 313 games for Toronto from 1926-33; NHL scoring leader in 1928-29 and member of the Maple Leafs Stanley Cup-winning team in 1933; nearly died after a vicious check by Boston's Eddie Shore that fractured his skull and ended his career on Dec. 12, 1933; in an effort to raise money to cover his hospital expenses, the Maple Leafs played a benefit game against a team of NHL all-stars and collected $20,000; that game was the forerunner of the NHL All-Star Game; of a stroke; in Toronto, Apr. 1.

Josy Barthel, 65; unheralded distance runner from Luxembourg, who was the surprise winner of the 1,500 meters at the 1952 Olympics in Helsinki; his time of 3:45.1 was an Olympic record and a personal best; was ranked No. 1 in the world that year; cause of death not disclosed; in Luxembourg, in June.

Nan Gindele Bauman, 81; one of only two American women to hold the world record in the javelin; her throw of 153-4 in 1932 was the world standard until 1942 and the U.S. record until '55; finished fifth behind gold medalist Babe Didrikson in the 1932 Olympics; after a long illness; Mar. 26.

Danny Biasone, 83; former bowling alley proprietor and owner of the NBA's Syracuse Nationals, who persuaded the league to introduce the 24-second clock in 1954; his innovation is credited with rescuing pro basketball at a time when it was not uncommon for five minutes or more to pass without a shot from the floor; the Nats won the NBA championship in 1954 and Biasone sold the franchise in 1963 (the team was subsequently moved to Philadelphia and renamed the 76ers); of a blood infection; in Syracuse, N.Y., May 25.

Glenn Brenner, 44; former minor league baseball pitcher and award-winning TV sportscaster in Washington, D.C.; joined WUSA-TV as sports director in 1977 and worked there for 15 years; known for his irreverent sense of humor; hosted popular weekly Redskins report with Sonny Jurgensen and was said to be one of the few people who could make Redskin head coach Joe Gibbs laugh; of a malignant brain tumor; in Washington, D.C., Jan. 14.

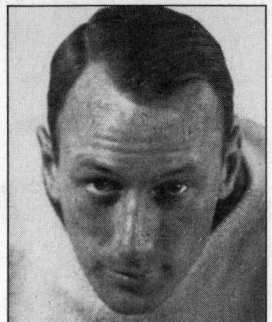

Toronto Maple Leafs

Irvin (Ace) Bailey

Philadelphia Eagles

Jerome Brown

Wide World Photos

Buck Buchanan

Al Brightman, 68; former basketball and baseball coach at the University of Seattle, who was hired for both jobs in 1949 at the age of 24; guided the Chieftains to four straight NCAA basketball tournament appearances from 1953-56; an original member of the Boston Celtics, he compiled a 108-68 record at Seattle; after a two-year battle with cancer; in Seattle, June 10.

Jerome Brown, 27; two-time All-Pro defensive tackle and anchor of the Philadelphia Eagles' defense; registered 150 tackles and nine sacks as the Eagles ranked first in the NFL in pass, run and total defense in 1991; first-round pick in 1987 NFL Draft; an All-America at Miami in 1986 and member of Hurricanes' 1983 national championship team; leader of Canes' bad-attitude defense and instigator of the infamous fish-fry walkout before 1987 Fiesta Bowl with Penn State; Philadelphia retired his number 99 before the 1992 season opener; from injuries suffered in a one-car accident that also claimed the life of his 12-year-old nephew; in Brooksville, Fla., June 25.

Robert (Red) Brown, 85; former West Virginia athletics director (1954-72) who was instrumental in the building of the WVU Coliseum, which opened in 1970; coached the Mountaineer basketball team to a 73-31 record from 1951-54 before giving way to Fred Schaus; after a long illness; in Morgantown, W. Va., June 8.

John Bruno, 27; walk-on punter at Penn State whose 43.4-yard average on nine punts in the 1987 Fiesta Bowl helped the No. 2 Nittany Lions defeat No. 1 Miami-FL and win the national championship; of skin cancer; in Pittsburgh, Apr. 13.

Josephine Hartford Bryce, 88; philanthropist and sportswoman, who owned a racing yacht and thoroughbred horses, piloted planes and played tournament tennis; granddaughter of George Huntington Hartford, the founder of the Great Atlantic and Pacific Tea Company (A&P); after a long illness, June 8.

Buck Buchanan, 51; outstanding lineman at Grambling, who was selected by the Dallas Texans as the first overall selection in the American Football League's 1963 draft; also one of the first black players ever chosen in the first round of the NFL Draft (by the N.Y. Giants); signed with Dallas, which moved to Kansas City and became the Chiefs before the '63 season; at 6-8 and 300 lbs., he was a six-time All-Pro defensive end in the AFL and played in 181 of 182 regular season games; helped lead Chiefs to AFL titles in 1966 and '69 and their only Super Bowl title on Jan. 11, 1970; became a defensive-line coach at New Orleans and Cleveland; inducted into the Pro Football Hall of Fame in 1990; of lung cancer; in Kansas City, July 16.

Joe Burke, 68; president of the Kansas City Royals since 1981 after serving as executive V.P. and general manager from 1974-81; assembled teams that won six American League Western Division championships, two AL pennants and the 1985 World Series; of cancer of the lymph nodes; in Kansas City, May 12.

Frank Carideo, 83; five-foot-seven All-America quarterback of 1929 and 1930 Notre Dame teams that won consecutive national championships under Knute Rockne; unbeaten Irish went 19-0 over both years; later was an assistant football coach at Mississippi State from 1935-38 and coached the MSU men's basketball team to a 27-31 record from 1936-39; a member of the College Football Hall of Fame; after a long illness; in Ocean Springs, Miss., Mar. 17.

Sherm Chavoor, 73; former swimming coach whose Arden Hills Swimming and Tennis Club in Carmichael, Calif., launched the careers of Olympic champions such as Mark Spitz, Debbie Meyer and Mike Burton; his swimmers set 100 world and American records and won a total of 31 Olympic medals, including 20 golds; Meyer and Spitz won five gold medals between them at Mexico City in 1968, while Spitz alone won seven golds four years later in Munich; of cancer; in Sacramento, Calif., Sept. 3.

John Cherberg, 81; former head football coach at the University of Washington, who compiled a 10-18-2 career record from 1953-55; of natural causes; in Olympia, Wash., April 8.

Arkady Chernyshev, 78; former coach of the Soviet national hockey team, who guided the USSR to four Olympic gold medals from 1956-72; cause of death not disclosed; in Moscow, Apr. 18.

Harlong Clift, 79; All-Star third baseman for the St. Louis Browns in 1937 when he hit .306 with 29 homers and 118 RBI; his 34 home runs the following season stood as the major league record for third basemen until Eddie Mathews of Milwaukee hit 47 in 1953; hit .272 with 178 HRs over 12-year career from 1934-45; later became a scout for the Detroit Tigers; after a long illness; in Yakima, Wash., Apr. 27.

John Clune, 59; former athletic director at Air Force and president of the National Assn. of Collegiate Directors of Athletics; a retired U.S. Air Force colonel who served as AD from 1975-91; of cancer; in San Antonio, Tex., Apr. 4.

Tommy Colella, 73; former Canisius halfback, who played pro football for Detroit and the Cleveland Rams of the NFL during World War II and then with the Cleveland Browns and Buffalo of the All-America Football Conference after the war; after a long illness; May 15.

University of Notre Dame   Wide World Photos   Wide World Photos

Frank Carideo   **Clint Frank**   **Bernice Gera**

Bob Commings, 59; former guard and head football coach at Iowa; played for the third-ranked Hawkeyes team that went 9-1 in 1956 for Forest Evashevski and beat Oregon State in the Rose Bowl; his Iowa teams went 18-37 while he was head coach from 1974-78; coached at Glen Oak High School in Canton since 1980; of cancer; in Canton, Ohio, Feb. 20.

Larry Craig, 75; quarterback of Green Bay Packer teams that beat the New York Giants to win NFL championships in both 1939 and 1944; played in Green Bay from 1939-49 after an outstanding college career at South Carolina; of cancer; in Ninety Six, S.C., May 30.

Max Crowder, 62; head basketball trainer at Duke from 1966-78 and head athletics trainer since 1978; had a hand in more than 600 of the Blue Devils' victories and nine of their 10 Final Four appearances; of cancer; in Durham, N.C., May 28.

Shane Curry, 24; Indianapolis Colts defensive end, who was a member of the 1989 national championship team at Miami of Florida; shot and killed by a 15-year-old boy during an argument outside a bar in his hometown of Cincinnati; May 3.

Dallas Times Herald; three-time Pulitzer Prize-winning newspaper and the city's oldest daily; known for its well-written and entertaining sports section; ceased publication after losing advertising and circulation battle with archrival, The _Dallas Morning News;_ said columnist Molly Ivins: "The _Herald_ had the guts and the writers; The _News_ had the money and the circulation"; in Dallas, Dec. 9, 1991.

Howie Dallmar, 69; former All-America basketball guard at Stanford, who was named Most Outstanding Player of the 1942 NCAA tournament when he led the (then) Indians to a 53-38 victory over Dartmouth in the championship game; after two NBA seasons with the Philadelphia Warriors, he became the basketball and baseball coach at Penn for six years; he returned to Stanford as head basketball coach in 1955 and compiled a record of 264-264 in 21 seasons, but never made it back to the NCAA tournament; of congestive heart failure; in Menlo Park, Calif., Dec. 19, 1991.

Howard Davis, 73; founder and coach of the Harlem Wizards comedy basketball team, which showcased such future NBA stars as Connie Hawkins and Nate (Tiny) Archibald; formed the Wizards in 1961 with friend and former Harlem Globetrotter Goose Tatum; promoted a team called the Kokomo Clowns in the 1930s, playing teams from the National Basketball League, the predecessor to today's NBA; of a heart attack; in North Bergen, N.J., Sept. 3.

John Dromo, 76; head basketball coach at Louisville from 1967-71, when he suffered a heart attack after a game in Tulsa; had a record of 80-31 over four seasons, then handed the program over to Denny Crum in 1971; of congestive heart failure; in Louisville, Sept. 29.

Sara C. Farrington, 84; internationally known angler and writer, whose work appeared under the pen name of Chisie Farrington; her fishing articles in the 1930s and '40s helped to establish women as sporting participants; owner of seven world angling records, she married noted outdoorsman and author, Selwyn Kip Farrington, Jr.; once caught a 674-pound tuna off Watch Hill, R.I., and traveled in a circle of big-game adventurers that included Ernest Hemingway and Alfred Glassell; of pneumonia after suffering a stroke; in Southampton, N.Y., Apr. 23.

Frank Finnigan, 91; former right wing and last surviving member of the 1927 Stanley Cup champion Ottawa Senators; scored 115 goals in 558 games over 14 NHL seasons from 1923-37; also won the Stanley Cup with Toronto in 1932; big booster of efforts to return an NHL team to Ottawa, but died before the new Senators could take the ice in 1992; of a heart attack; in Shawville, Que., Dec. 26, 1991.

Len Fontes, 54; brother of Detroit head coach Wayne Fontes and the Lions' defensive backs coach since 1990; played defensive back at Ohio State from 1958-59, but did not play in the pros; of a heart attack; in Rochester Hills, Mich., May 8.

Bill France, 82; the preeminent figure in the creation of stock-car racing, who founded NASCAR in 1947 and ran it until his retirement in 1972; known as Big Bill, the 6-foot-5 former mechanic moved to Daytona Beach, Fla., in 1934, during the heyday of beach racing; later, he built Daytona International Speedway and made the Daytona 500 stock car racing's biggest race; also built Talladega (Ala.) Superspeedway; of complications from Alzheimer's disease a few months after the death of his wife Anne; in Ormond Beach, Fla., June 7.

Clint Frank, 76; two-time All-America halfback at Yale, who won the Heisman Trophy in 1937—beating out former Colorado halfback and current U.S. Supreme Court justice Byron (Whizzer) White; Frank's Heisman came the year after teammate Larry Kelley won the award in 1936; inducted into the College Football Hall of Fame in 1955 and received the National Football Foundation's highest award, the Gold Medal, in 1988; after a brief illness; in Evanston, Ill., July 7.

Bill France
1909-92
by Herman Hickman

Big Bill France strode onto the scene of stock car racing's rough and tumble era in the 1940s and '50s much like the hero in a John Wayne movie.

In short order, he established himself as the main man by creating and presiding over NASCAR, the sanctioning body for a sport that would spread nationwide five years after its creation in 1947.

The 6-foot-5-inch France took on all comers—from the sport's greatest stars, like Fireball Roberts and Richard Petty, to the powerful automobile manufacturers in Detroit. And he won every encounter. It got so, as time went by, dissidents didn't even bother to challenge him.

His dream of making NASCAR a major league sport changed this nation's concept of stock car racing.

True, his dedication and unwillingness to bend the rules led to his being referred to as a dictator. But he would just smile and say, "Well, let's make that a benevolent dictator. What I'm doing is best for the sport, not just me."

NASCAR's early stars came from a variety of backgrounds—from moonshine haulers to refugees of weekend bullring racing. There were shade-tree mechanics and more accomplished car builders like Smokey Yunick and Ray Fox.

France rode herd over all of them. He treated them the same and faced down anyone or any group who dared challenge his authority.

In 1961, when Curtis Turner, Fireball Roberts, Tim Flock and Buck Baker spearheaded an effort to form a union with the backing of the Teamsters, France called a meeting at the next event in Winston-Salem, N.C.

Brandishing a handgun, he told them: "No known union member will be permitted to compete in a NASCAR race from this day forward, and I'll use my pistol to enforce it."

He then banned Turner, Roberts, and Flock for life. Roberts recanted and was reinstated, but Turner's ban stuck for four years despite Ford Motor Company pleas to reinstate him.

When France finally reinstated Turner in 1965, the Virginian immediately left the scene of a non-NASCAR event, declaring:

Daytona Racing Archives

Bill France founded NASCAR and built the speedways at Daytona and Talladega.

"I'm taking no chances on getting that man mad again. NASCAR racing is where it's at."

France stunned the racing world by introducing Daytona International Speedway, a 2½-mile high-banked facility, in 1959. Shortly afterward, super speedways sprang up at Charlotte, Atlanta, Rockingham, Dover (Del.), Michigan and Pocono. France came back in 1969 with the 2.66-mile Talladega Superspeedway in Alabama.

"Senior didn't worry about the details of running NASCAR," says Bill France Jr., who has been NASCAR president since his father's retirement in 1972. "His role was making contacts, building and reaching out for greater things—like Talladega Superspeedway."

When Richard Petty, as president of a newly formed drivers' organization, opposed running in Talladega's first race because his group feared the tires wouldn't take the 195 m.p.h. speeds, France borrowed a car and ran 176 m.p.h. "Surely," he said, "the young pros can run 20 m.p.h. faster than I can."

Petty would later say, "France was tough. I didn't always agree with him, but what he did for stock car racing can't be denied."

Herman Hickman has covered stock car racing for over 30 years as former racing writer for the *Winston-Salem Journal* and a past PR director at North Carolina Motor Speedway.

Baseball Hall of Fame

George Giles

UPI/Bettmann

Kathleen (Kitty) Godfree

Wide World Photos

Billy Graham

Thomas J. Frericks, 59; former Dayton athletic director from 1964-1991 and chairman of the NCAA's Division I Men's Basketball Committee; also served as NCAA secretary-treasurer from 1987-89, supervised the construction of Dayton's $4.5 million arena in 1977 and was honored by having the renovated field house named after him; of cancer; in Dayton, Ohio, Jan. 31.

Bernice Gera, 61; the first female umpire in professional baseball; gained national attention on June 24, 1972, when she officiated a Class A minor league game between Geneva and Auburn in the New York-Penn League; despite a five-year legal battle that resulted in a New York State Supreme Court ruling allowing her to umpire, Gera quit after just that one game, saying the other umpires refused to cooperate with her on the field; of cancer; in Pembroke Pines, Fla., Sept. 23.

George Giles, 82; All-Star first baseman for several teams in the Negro Leagues; originally signed by the Kansas City Monarchs at age 16; his grandson, Brian Giles, played for the New York Mets, Milwaukee and Chicago White Sox from 1981-86; after a long illness, in Manhattan, Kan., March 3.

Kathleen (Kitty) Godfree, 96; Wimbledon singles champion as Kitty McKane in 1924 and Kitty Godfree in '26; only woman to defeat eight-time winner Helen Wills Moody in a Wimbledon final (1924); also won five Grand Slam doubles championships and was the first woman to be elected a vice president of the All-England Club; from the effects of old age; in Wimbledon, June 19.

Billy Graham, 70; former welterweight boxer, who never hit the canvas in 126 fights from 1941-55; had a career record of 102-15-9, but the closest he got to the title was losing a controversial 15-round decision to welterweight champion Kid Gavilan on Aug. 29, 1951 at Madison Square Garden; wrote A.J. Liebling: "He was as good as a fighter can be without being a hell of a fighter"; of cancer; in West Islip, N.Y., Jan. 22.

Jack Gray, 81; former All-America basketball player at Texas—the Longhorns' first—who is often credited with developing the one-handed jump shot; returned to Texas as head coach in 1937 and from 1937-42 and 1946-51, compiled a record of 194-97 with Southwest Conference titles in 1939, '40, '47 and '51; in Austin, Tex., Mar. 7.

David Greenspan, 68; film narrator who, under the professional name of David Perry, was known as "the voice of the Olympics," for his work on his brother Bud's "Olympiad" series; collaborated on other sports projects with his brother as well as doing voice-overs for the popular TV program, "Lifestyles of the Rich and Famous"; of lung cancer; in New York, Dec. 29, 1991.

Raymond Guest, 84; horse breeder, champion polo player and former U.S. Ambassador to Ireland; among his champion horses were 1962 Epsom Derby winner Larkspur, 1965 Preakness winner Tom Rolfe, 1968 Epsom winner Sir Ivor and 1975 Grand National Steeplechase winner L'Escargot; named Irish ambassador by President Lyndon Johnson in 1965; of pneumonia after a long illness; in King George, Va., Dec. 31, 1991.

Chick Harbert, 77; golfer, whose nine career victories on the PGA Tour included the 1954 PGA Championship at Keller Golf Club in St. Paul, Minn., where he beat Walter Burkemo 4 & 3 for the title; served as captain of the successful U.S. Ryder Cup team in 1955 and was elected to the old PGA Hall of Fame in 1968; of a cerebral hemorrhage; in Ocala, Fla., Sept. 1.

Reg Harris, 72; bicycle racer who captured the British sprint title in 1974 at age 54; won two silver medals at the 1948 Summer Olympics in London and was the world professional sprint champion from 1949-51 and again in 1954; of a stroke while cycling near his home; in London, June 22.

Bob Hazel, 61; rookie outfielder who hit .403 for Milwaukee over the last two months of the 1957 season to help the Braves win the NL pennant; called up from the minors in July, he got 54 hits in 134 at bats including seven HRs and 27 RBI in 41 games; his performance earned him the nickname, "Hurricane Hazel"; the following year he hit just .179 in the Braves' first 20 games and was traded to Detroit; of a heart attack; in Columbia, S.C., Apr. 26.

Mel Hein, 82; Durable center-linebacker for the New York football Giants, who was an NFL All-Pro selection for eight consecutive seasons from 1933-40; led Giants as captain to seven division titles and two league championships in 1934 and '38; was the NFL's first official MVP in 1938; also an All-America at Washington State, where he led the Cougars to the Rose Bowl in 1931; served as an assistant coach at Southern Cal for 15 years after a four-year stay at Union (N.Y.) College as head coach; of stomach cancer; in San Clemente, Calif., Jan. 31.

Don Heinrich, 62; a two-time All-America quarterback at Washington in 1950 and '52; also played in the pros for the NY Giants, Dallas and Oakland from 1954-62; member of the College Football Hall of Fame; also served as an NFL assistant coach and sportscaster; of cancer; Saratoga, Fla., Feb. 29.

UPI/Bettmann
Chick Harbert

UPI/Bettmann
Mel Hein

Wide World Photos
Billy Herman

Billy Herman, 83; Hall of Fame second baseman who played in 10 All-Star Games over 15 seasons with the Chicago Cubs and Brooklyn; traded to the Dodgers in 1941 and helped lead them to their first NL pennant in 21 years; participated in four World Series—three with the Cubs and one with the Dodgers—but never won; ended his playing career with a .304 batting average and 2,345 hits; managed Pittsburgh in 1947 and the Boston Red Sox from 1964-66 for a career record of 189-274; of cancer; in West Palm Beach, Fla., Sept 5.

Wilbur Hess, 79; collegiate tennis player at Rice, who won both the Southwest Conference and NCAA singles championships in 1935; cause of death not disclosed; on Jan. 27.

Raymond Hickok, 74; co-creator of the S. Rae Hickok belt, a $35,000 trophy belt made of leather and diamond-studded gold that was awarded annually from 1950-76 to the year's outstanding professional athlete; similar Hickok belts were made for boxing champions; of heart failure; in Rochester, N.Y., Sept. 9.

Tony Hinkle, 92; three-sport athlete and coach; won nine letters in football, basketball and track at the University of Chicago from 1918-20; at Butler, his football, basketball and baseball teams won more than 1,000 games from 1921 until his retirement in 1970; he was also Butler's athletic director for nearly 40 years and a member of the Basketball Hall of Fame; the school's 10,800-seat gym was renamed Hinkle Fieldhouse in 1965; in his sleep; in Indianapolis, Sept. 21.

Dick Huffman, 69; All-America tackle at Tennessee in 1946, who went on to become a three-time All-Pro for the LA Rams from 1947-49; jumped to the CFL in 1951 and played eight seasons with Winnipeg and Calgary; member of the Canadian Football Hall of Fame; after a short illness; Sept. 13.

Denis Hulme, 56; former Formula One race driver from New Zealand, who raced on the Grand Prix circuit from 1965-74 and won the world driving championship in 1967; was also Rookie of the Year in the 1967 Indianapolis 500 where he finished fourth; after suffering an apparent heart attack while racing in a 1,000-kilometer event in Bathhurst, Australia; Sept. 27.

David H. Jacobs, 71; real estate developer and majority owner of the Cleveland Indians; purchased the team and its $11 million debt on Dec. 9, 1986, with brother Richard; a major backer of downtown Cleveland's Gateway complex, where the Indians will move into a new stadium in 1994; of pneumonia; in Westlake, Ohio, Sept. 17.

Larry Jennings, 74; thoroughbred trainer who saddled more than 1,100 winners in 38 years on the New Jersey, Maryland and Florida circuits; of cancer; July 6.

Bob Johnson, 60; became only the second American coach to win hockey's Stanley Cup, and the first since World War II, when he guided Pittsburgh to a 4-2 series victory over Minnesota in 1991; remembered for his favorite phrase: "It's a great day for hockey"; nicknamed "Badger Bob" at the University of Wisconsin where he won NCAA titles in 1973, '77 and '81; also coached U.S. Olympic team in 1976; moved up to the NHL in 1982, where he coached the Calgary Flames from 1982-87; resigned to become executive director of USA Hockey before joining the Penguins in 1990; won 367 games in college and 275 (including playoffs) in the NHL; of brain cancer on the eve of the 1991 Canada Cup; in Colorado Springs, Colo.; Nov. 26, 1991.

Deron Johnson, 53; baseball slugger who led the NL with 130 RBI in 1965 with Cincinnati and tied a major league record with home runs in four straight plate appearances on July 10-11, 1971, with Philadelphia; hit 245 HRs and knocked in 923 runs with eight different teams over his 16-year career; won the World Series with Oakland in 1973; was later a coach with California and four other clubs; of lung cancer; in Powa, Calif., Apr. 23.

Mort Kaer, 88; All-America back at Southern Cal in 1926, who led the Trojans in rushing and scoring each of his last two seasons; inducted into the College Football Hall of Fame in 1972; cause of death not disclosed; on Jan. 12.

Robert Kane, 81; former president of the U.S. Olympic Committee and athletic director at Cornell for 36 years; presided over the USOC from 1977-81 during which time he ended years of bickering between the USOC and AAU and organized the first Olympic Festival; forced to keep U.S. athletes home during the 1980 Summer Olympics when U.S. President Jimmy Carter ordered a boycott of the Games in Moscow as punishment for the Soviets' invasion of Afghanistan; of heart and respiratory failure; in Ithaca, N.Y., May 31.

Ken Keltner, 75; former Cleveland third baseman best known for his backhanded stops of two hard-hit ground balls that helped end Joe DiMaggio's 56-game hitting streak before a crowd of 67,468 at Municipal Stadium on the night of July, 17, 1941; hit 31 home runs with 119 RBI to help lead the Indians to the 1948 World Series title; named to the AL All-Star team seven times in his 13-year career; retired in 1950 with a career average of .276 and 161 HRs; of a heart attack; in Milwaukee, Dec. 12, 1991.

Basketball Hall of Fame

Tony Hinkle

Hockey Hall of Fame

Bob Johnson

Wide World Photos

Robert Kane

Earnest Killum, 20; sophomore guard on Oregon State's basketball team, who had been previously diagnosed with a blood-clotting disorder; a few nights prior to his death, he scored 13 points in 16 minutes against Southern Cal; sat out his first season with the Beavers after suffering a stroke in a pick-up game; after lapsing into a coma; in Inglewood, Calif., Jan. 20.

John Kissell, 68; former All-Pro defensive tackle who played on the Cleveland Browns' NFL championship teams of 1950, '54 and '55; anchored the Boston College defense that played in the 1943 Orange Bowl; of cancer; in Nashua, N.H., Apr. 3.

John Kordic, 27; veteran right wing and enforcer for four NHL teams; picked up 997 penalty minutes in 245 games from 1985 until his release by Quebec during the 1991-92 season; alcohol abuser who went berserk on the night of his death and had to be subdued by eight police officers; his condition worsened en route to the hospital where he died of lung failure related to a malfunctioning heart (unused syringes and anabolic steroids were found in his motel room); in L'Ancienne-Lorette, Que., Aug. 8.

Greene (Red) Laird, 89; former baseball and basketball coach at Virginia Tech; in 30 years as baseball coach he amassed a 343-275-4 record that included 18 winning seasons; his basketball teams were not as successful, going 77-120 from 1947-55; of natural causes; in Montgomery County, Va., Apr. 10.

Ron Lapointe, 42; former head coach of the Quebec Nordiques from December 1987 to December 1988, who was forced to resign after a cancerous tumor was found in one of his kidneys; was a scout with Vancouver during the 1991-92 season; after a four-year battle with cancer; in Quebec, Mar. 23.

Tippy Larkin, 74; former junior-welterweight boxing champion, who never lost a fight that went the distance in the last 13 years of his career; he fought 153 bouts over a span of 20 years, appearing in 19 main events at Madison Square Garden; born Anthony Pilleteri, but took the name Tippy from the initials for Tony Pilleteri and the name Larkin from his older brother Frank, who boxed professionally as Bobby Larkin; of kidney failure; in Passaic, N.J., Dec. 10, 1991.

Michel (Bunny) Larocque, 40; former goaltender who played on four Stanley Cup-winning teams in Montreal from 1976-79; shared the Vezina Trophy three times with starting Canadiens' goalie Ken Dryden; also played for Toronto, Philadelphia and St. Louis in his 11-year career, which ended in 1984; of brain cancer; Hull, Que., July 29.

Jimmy Lennon, Sr, 79; boxing's best known ring announcer, who appeared in over 75 movies including "Raging Bull" and "Rocky III"; uncle of the singing Lennon Sisters, remembered for eloquent delivery and trademark tuxedo; of heart failure; in Santa Monica, Calif., Apr. 20.

Eddie Lopat, 73; combined with fellow Yankee pitchers Vic Raschi and Allie Reynolds to hurl New York to five consecutive World Series championships from 1949-53; was 113-59 as a Yankee and 166-112 overall in 12 years in the majors; earned the nickname The Junk Man, by keeping batters off balance with his variable speed pitches; Lopat's pitches, wrote Red Smith, "never exceeded the speed limit"; born Edmund Walter Lopatynaski; in his sleep; in Darien, Conn., June 15.

Aurelio Lopez, 44; Mexican relief pitcher whose 10-1 record, 14 saves and 2.94 ERA helped lead Detroit to an AL pennant and World Series title in 1984; ended his 11-year baseball career in 1987 with a record of 62-36 and 93 saves; from injuries suffered in an auto accident; 300 miles north of Mexico City, Sept. 22.

George Lott, 85; DePaul tennis coach, who won more than 40 national and international tennis titles during his playing career and went unbeaten in seven straight years playing Davis Cup; won both doubles and mixed doubles titles at Wimbledon in 1931 and captured the doubles title again in 1934; inducted into the Tennis Hall of Fame in 1964—one of seven halls of fame that claim him as a member; still coaching at DePaul at the time of his death; cause of death not reported; in Chicago, Dec. 3, 1991.

Horatio Luro, 90; Argentine-born thoroughbred trainer, who saddled Kentucky Derby winners Decidedly in 1962 and Northern Dancer in 1964; known as Señor Luro, he was inducted into the National Museum of Racing Hall of Fame in 1980; of pancreatic cancer; in Bal Harbour, Fla., Dec. 12.

Jay MacDowell, 72; defensive end who helped Philadelphia win back-to-back NFL championships in 1948-49 with consecutive shutouts over the Chicago Cardinals (7-0) and LA Rams (14-0); was also a first-team All-America at Washington University in 1940; of cancer; in Springfield, Pa., June 15.

Major Soccer League, 14; crisis-plagued professional indoor soccer league, originally known as the MISL; enjoyed its best years in the early 1980s when it boasted 14 teams and robust attendance figures; failed when league officials could not come up with a sixth team to compete in 1992-93; in Overland Park, Kan., July 10.

Baseball Hall of Fame

Ken Keltner

Wide World Photos

Eddie Lopat

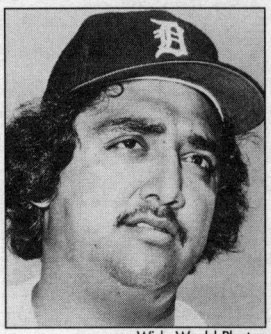

Wide World Photos

Aurelio Lopez

Jovy Marcelo, 27; Philippine race car driver who won the Toyota Atlantic championship in 1991; stepped up to Indy-cars in 1992 when he joined Antonio Ferrari's Euromotorsports team in time for the first race of the season at Surfers Paradise in Australia; of injuries suffered in a crash during practice for the Indianapolis 500; in Indianapolis, May 15.

Joe Marconi, 59; former fullback at West Virginia who helped the Mountaineers win 31 of 38 games between 1952-55 and reach the Sugar Bowl in 1953; drafted by the LA Rams in 1956, he also played five seasons for Chicago and started on the Bears' 1963 NFL championship team; of a heart attack; in Chicago, Aug. 22.

Robert Maxwell, 68; flamboyant British press baron, whose international media empire included the *Daily News* in New York and the *Daily Mirror* in London; an ardent soccer fan, he owned several clubs at one time or another in Britain and Israel; also bankrolled *The Racing Times*, the U.S. horse racing newspaper that ceased publication in 1992; estimated to have drained at least $1.4 billion from his public companies to prop up his overextended empire; died under mysterious circumstances after falling from his yacht off the Canary Islands in the Atlantic Ocean, Nov. 5, 1991.

Rob McCall, 33; Canadian Olympic figure skater who teamed with Tracy Wilson to win the ice dancing bronze medal at Calgary in 1988; of AIDS related brain cancer; in Toronto, Nov. 15.

A.J. McClane, 69; highly regarded angling writer and sport fisherman; joined *Field & Stream* magazine in 1947 and was fishing editor and then executive editor until he retired in 1977; wrote more than 20 books including *The Practical Fly Fisherman* and *McClane's New Standard Fishing Encyclopedia* and *International Angling Guide*, both considered foremost reference sources of their kind; of congestive heart failure; in Palm Beach, Fla., Dec. 19, 1991.

Jay McGillis, 21; starting safety on the 1991 Boston College football team who was diagnosed with cancer last fall; after a six-month battle with the disease; in Boston, July 3.

Frank McKinney, Jr, 53; former Indiana high school swimming standout, who won a bronze medal in the 100-meter backstroke at the 1956 Olympics in Melbourne; four years later in Rome, he won a silver in the 100-meter backstroke and led the U.S. 400-meter medley relay team to a gold medal in world record time (4:05.4); swam for Doc Counsilman at Indiana University and led the Hoosiers to their first Big Ten championship in 1961; inducted into the International Swimming Hall of Fame in 1975; father, Frank Sr., owned the Pittsburgh Pirates from 1947-51; killed in a collision of two small planes; near Indianapolis, Sept. 11.

Chuck Minker, 42; former fight judge and executive director of the Nevada Athletic Commission since 1987; as supervisor of all boxing activity in Nevada, he was regarded as a man of integrity in an otherwise unsavory business; of lung cancer; in Las Vegas, May 17.

Earnest B. Morris, 83; former owner of Saratoga (N.Y.) Raceway harness track from 1963-87, and a member of harness racing's Hall of Fame; also a former president of the Harness Tracks of America and a board member and counsel for the U.S. Trotting Assn.; cause of death not disclosed; in Manchester, N.H.; Dec. 22, 1991.

Charles (Stretch) Murphy, 85; Purdue's first three-time basketball All-America, who teamed with the Boilmakers' second three-time All-America, John Wooden, to win Big Ten championships in 1928 and '30; set Big Ten scoring records for a single game (26 points) and a single season (143) in 1929; after a long illness; in Tampa, Fla., Aug. 24.

Don Murphy, 61; former minor league catcher, who later became an NBA referee for 17 seasons; worked memorable Game 5 of the 1976 NBA Finals between Boston and Phoenix, which went into triple overtime before the Celtics won, 128-126; cause of death not disclosed; in Cincinnati, May 22.

Jim Nance, 49; college football star at Syracuse, where he also won the NCAA heavyweight wrestling title in 1963 and '65; went on to set an AFL rushing record with 1,458 yards for the Boston Patriots in 1966; AFL Most Valuable Player in 1966 and All-Pro again in '67; traded to Philadelphia after the 1971 season, but only played one more year—with the NY Jets in 1973; of acute cardiac arrhythmia; in Quincy, Mass., June 16.

Davey Nelson, 71; longtime athletic director (1951-84) and football coach (1951-66) at the University of Delaware; his football teams went 84-42-2 over 16 years, including an unbeaten season in 1963; influential secretary-rules editor of the NCAA Football Rules Committee since 1962; was also commissioner of the Yankee Conference at the time of his death; of a heart attack; in Newark, Del., Nov. 30, 1991.

Nijinsky II, 25; winner of 11 of 13 career starts and the last horse to win the English Triple Crown (the 2,000 Guineas, Epsom Derby and St. Leger Stakes in 1970); did all his racing in Europe, earning the equivalent of $677,118 U.S. dollars; produced 88 graded stakes winners as one of thoroughbred racing's greatest stallions; at Keenland's Selected Sale in 1985, nine of his yearlings averaged a cost of $2.9 million; son of Northern Dancer, out of the mare Flaming Page; troubled by chronic leg problems and destroyed; at Claiborne Farm in Lexington, Ky., Apr. 15.

Wide World Photos

Robert Maxwell

Wide World Photos

Frank McKinney, Jr.

Wide World Photos

Jim Nance

Pat O'Callaghan, 85; two-time Olympic gold medalist in the hammer throw, winning at Amsterdam in 1928 and again at Los Angeles in '32; his toss of 195-feet 5-inches in 1937 exceeded the existing world record by almost six feet; after a long illness; in Clonmell, Ire., Dec. 1, 1991.

Red Patterson, 83; a pioneer in the art of baseball publicity; joined the NY Yankees in 1946 after 17 years as a sportswriter for the *New York Herald-Tribune;* credited with inventing promotions like old-timers' games, cap days and team yearbooks, that are still in use today; created the "tape measure home run" on Apr. 17, 1953, when he claimed that Mickey Mantle's titanic homer off Washington pitcher Chuck Stobbs fell to earth 565 feet from home plate at Griffith Stadium; he came up with that figure after running across the street, finding the kid who recovered the ball, asking him where it landed and then pacing off the distance; Patterson later worked for the LA Dodgers and was president of the California Angels for two years in the mid-1970s; of cancer; in Fullerton, Calif., Feb. 14.

Peter Pavia, 53; former college basketball official who worked 14 NCAA tournaments and two Final Fours (1986 and '91); gained notoriety in the 1991 Final Four semifinal between Kansas and North Carolina when he ejected Tar Heels' coach Dean Smith for leaving the coaching box with 35 seconds left in the game; won NASO Golden Whistle award in 1990; of cancer; in Rochester, N.Y., Oct. 9.

Angel Penna, Sr, 69; thoroughbred horse trainer who won over 250 stakes races in a career that spanned 50 years; began U.S. career training horses owned by Gustave Ring and William Levine, which included 1971 Travers Stakes winner Bold Reason; won the Prix de l'Arc de Triomphe with Allez France in 1974; inducted into Horse Racing Hall of Fame in 1988; of cancer; in Garden City, N.Y., Jan. 15.

Doyt Perry, 82; former Bowling Green football coach from 1955-64, whose 77-11-5 career record included five Mid-American Conference titles and the 1959 small-college national championship; after a long illness; in Bowling Green, Oh., Feb. 10.

Vern Plagenhoef, 45; highly-regarded sportswriter for 18 years, who covered the Detroit Tigers for the Booth Newspapers chain; former president of the Baseball Writers Association of America; of a heart attack following a United States-Portugal soccer match he covered at Soldier Field; in Chicago, June 3.

Otto Pommerening, 86; former tackle at Michigan, and consensus All-America selection in 1928; after a long illness; in Bloomfield Hills, Mich., Feb. 2.

Adrian Quist, 78; Australian tennis star who won the Australian Open singles title three times between 1936 and 1948; also won two Wimbledon doubles titles fifteen years apart (1935 and '50) and captured 10 straight Australian Open doubles titles, teaming with John Bromwich eight times and D.P. Turnbull twice; played in 54 Davis Cup doubles matches and served as Australia's team captain in 1948; of cancer; in Sydney, Nov. 18, 1991.

***The Racing Times,* 10 mos.;** respected racing daily edited by former New York Times turf writer Steven Crist; debuted in April 1991 as an upstart challenger to the entrenched *Daily Racing Form,* folded with the collapse of publisher Robert Maxwell's media empire (see above); in New York; Feb. 6.

Jim Rathschmidt, 79; a Princeton, N.J., native who was the Yale crew coach from 1951-70; guided an eight-oared Eli crew to the Olympic gold medal at Melbourne in 1956; known as Genial Jim, he returned to Princeton in the early 1970s to coach the university's first women's crew; of a heart attack; in Boynton Beach, Fla., Aug. 25.

Gaston Reiff, 71; Belgian distance runner who held world records at 2,000 meters, 3,000 meters and two miles during his 15-year career; best remembered, however, for his dramatic dash to hold off the legendary Emile Zatopek in the 5,000 meters at the 1948 London Olympics; his gold medal was Belgium's first ever in track and field; cause of death not disclosed; in Brussels, May 7.

Samuel Reshevsky, 80; Polish-born chess prodigy and grandmaster, who won the U.S. championship seven times from 1936-72; came to America as an eight-year-old immigrant in 1920 and became a national celebrity on coast-to-coast tours where he took on and defeated up to 75 opponents at a time; held the U.S. championship from 1936-44, 1946-48, and 1969-72; closest he came to the world title was a third-place finish in a special 1948 playoff to decide who would succeed world champion Alexander Alekhine, who had died in 1946; beat the new world champion, Mikhail Botvinnik, in a 1955 exhibition match, but was soon eclipsed as America's top player by 14-year-old Bobby Fischer (Fischer went on to win the world championship in 1972); of a heart attack; in Suffern, N.Y., Apr. 4.

Wide World Photos

Davey Nelson

Baseball Hall of Fame

Red Patterson

UPI/Bettmann

Adrian Quist

Douglas Roby, 94; former Michigan halfback, who played one season with the NFL's Cleveland Indians in 1923 and later served as president of both the Amateur Athletic Union (AAU) from 1951-53, and the U.S. Olympic Committee from 1965-68; no stranger to controversy, as USOC president he suspended Olympic 200-meter gold and bronze medalists Tommie Smith and John Carlos after their Black Power salute on the victory stand in 1968 and ordered them to leave Mexico City in 48 hours; as one of two U.S. members of the International Olympic Committee from 1952-84, he voted against the admission of China in 1979 and for the readmission of South Africa in 1984; of heart failure; in Ann Arbor, Mich., Mar. 31.

Alan Roth, 74; a native of Montreal and statistician for the Canadiens of the NHL, who talked Brooklyn Dodgers president Branch Rickey into hiring him in 1947 as the first full-time statistician for a major league baseball club; his stats changed the whole approach managers had towards the game; insisted on working by hand or with a simple calculator instead of more advanced computers; moved to Los Angeles with the Dodgers in 1958, then left the team in 1964 to join NBC and later ABC on their national game-of-the- week broadcasts; of a heart attack; in Los Angeles, Mar. 3.

Joe Sapora, 87; former college wrestling champion at Illinois, who won back-to-back NCAA titles at 115 pounds in 1929 and '30, then went on to coach at City College of New York from 1932-68; guided 29-year-old New York policeman Henry Wittenberg to an Olympic gold medal in the light heavyweight division at London in 1948, and helped Jacob Twersky, a blind wrestler, make it to the NCAA finals in 1942; of pneumonia; in Ormond Beach, Fla., Jan. 6.

Joe Scibelli, 52; former Notre Dame tackle, who went on to anchor the offensive line for the Los Angeles Rams from 1961-75; was Rams' captain the last 10 years of his career; played in the 1969 Pro Bowl; of cancer; in Boston, Dec. 11, 1991.

Field Scovell, 85; courtly Texas A&M graduate and Cotton Bowl official, who is credited with securing an automatic berth for Southwest Conference champion in the Cotton Bowl; also convinced Notre Dame officials to end their self-imposed, 45-year bowl prohibition in 1970 and play No. 1 Texas in Dallas on New Year's Day (the No. 6 Irish won the game, 24-11); gained a measure of hardball negotiation fame in the 1980s when he frowned on a low CBS bid to purchase the exclusive rights to the Cotton Bowl, by telling CBS Sports president Van Gordon Sauter: "I'm sorry, sir. That dog won't hunt"; CBS came up with the additional money; of cancer; in Dallas, June 25.

Harold Seymour, 82; former Brooklyn Dodgers bat boy in the 1920s, who grew up to become one of baseball's foremost historians; his extensive research helped debunk the myth that the game was invented by Abner Doubleday at Cooperstown, N.Y. in 1839; while a college teacher, he received his doctorate in 1956 when Cornell accepted what many believe to be the first dissertation devoted to the history of baseball; his books include "Baseball: The Early Years," and a three-volume history of the sport, written between 1971 and 1991; had recently served as a consultant on filmmaker Ken Burns' upcoming television documentary on the history of baseball; after a long illness complicated by Alzheimer's disease; in Keene, N.H., Sept. 26.

John Sirica, 88; federal judge whose relentless pursuit of the facts behind the Watergate break-in made him a national hero and eventually led to the resignation of President Richard Nixon in 1974; after graduating from Georgetown law school in 1926, the 5-foot-6, 150-pound Sirica returned home to Miami and took up a brief career as a boxer, defeating a 6-foot-1 professional named Tommy Thompson in one of his few recorded fights; during World War II, he met and became close friends with former heavyweight champion Jack Dempsey and the two toured the country together selling war bonds; of pneumonia; in Georgetown, Aug. 14.

Terry Slater, 54; Colgate hockey coach, whose 15-year record of 251-180-23 was the best in the school's skating history; started coaching the Red Raiders in 1977, and later led them to an ECAC championship and a berth in the NCAA finals in 1990 (Colgate lost the title game, 7-3, to Wisconsin); of a stroke; in Hamilton, N.Y., Dec. 5, 1991.

C.M. (Tad) Smith, 86; former halfback and athletic director at Mississippi; played for Ole Miss from 1926-29, then returned to serve as AD from 1946-70; the school's Rebel Coliseum was renamed in 1972 in his honor; after a long illness; in Oxford, Miss., May 27.

Vernon Smith, 33; former star forward at Texas A&M, who was the Aggies' all-time leading scorer and rebounder; helped lead A&M to the 1980 Southwest Conference championship and a victory over third-seeded North Carolina in the Midwest Regional semifinals of the NCAA tournament (the Aggies lost to eventual NCAA champion Louisville in the regional final); shot to death by a gunman who apparently mistook him for someone else; in Dallas, July 7.

USOC Photo Library   Cotton Bowl Athletic Association   UPI/Bettmann

Douglas Roby   **Field Scovell**   **Carl Stotz**

C.C. Johnson Spink, 75; former editor and publisher of *The Sporting News* from 1962-77, when he sold the weekly to the Times-Mirror Corporation; the fourth member of the Spink family—following father J.G. Taylor Spink, grandfather Charles C. Spink and great uncle Alfred Henry Spink—to edit *The Sporting News* since the first eight-page issue came out in 1886; under his direction, the paper expanded its all-baseball coverage to include football, basketball and hockey; other innovations included the addition of color photos, elimination of column rules, and simpler one-line headlines; *TSN's* first four-color cover (April 8, 1967) featured Baltimore Orioles player Frank Robinson; after a brief illness; in St. Louis, Mar. 26.

Carl Stotz, 82; lifetime resident of Williamsport, Pa., who founded Little League baseball there in 1939; today, 2.5 million boys and girls in nearly 45 countries play the sport; the idea to start a league for kids came to Stotz while he was having a catch with his nephews in 1938; a year later, after downsizing the dimensions of the field to suit younger players (60 feet between the bases and 46 feet from the mound to the plate), he recruited sponsors and played the first official Little League game on June 6, 1939 (Lundy Lumber beat Lycoming Dairy, 23-8); the inaugural Little League World Series was played in 1947, but by 1955, Stotz had grown disenchanted with the manner in which his brainchild had outgrown its neighborhood roots; he filed suit against what had become Little League, Inc. and walked away from the organization after an out-of-court settlement; of a heart attack; in Williamsport, Pa., June 4.

Mikhail Tal, 55; daring Latvian chess grandmaster, who became the youngest person in this century to win the world chess championship when he defeated Mikhail Botvinnik in 1960 to capture the title at age 23; a year later, however, Botvinnik beat Tal to win the title back and Tal never played for the championship again; after a long illness; in Moscow, June 28.

Gabriel Tiaoch, 28; won the first Olympic medal ever for the Ivory Coast when he took a silver in the 400-meters at the 1984 Summer Games in Los Angeles; Alonzo Babers of the U.S. won the gold in 44.27 seconds with Tiaoch next at 44.54; two years later, as a college student at Washington State, Tiaoch won the 400 at the NCAA Championships with a personal best of 44.30; of viral meningitis; in Atlanta, Apr. 2.

James Van Fleet, 100; retired U.S. Army General and head football coach at Florida from 1923-24; led Gators to 12-3-4 record in those two seasons; West Point classmate of President Dwight Eisenhower and Gen. Omar Bradley; of natural causes; Sept. 23.

Ramon Velazquez, 93; an important figure in the early days of professional boxing in Mexico; was a founding member of the Boxing Committee of the Federal District in 1922, the Amateur Boxing Assn. of Mexico in 1924, the National School of Physical Education in 1936 and the World Boxing Council in 1963; served as WBC president from 1971-75; of natural causes; in Mexico City, June 10.

Gene Ward, 78; former sportswriter with the *New York Daily News,* who rose from copy boy to nationally-known columnist in 46 years at the paper; a Marine Corps combat correspondant for three-and-a-half years during World War II, his reports were often read on radio by Lowell Thomas; later, wrote "Ward to the Wise" sports column from 1960-79; of complications following colon surgery; in Glen Cove, L.I., March 28.

Jim Weatherall, 62; former two-time All-America tackle for Bud Wilkinson at Oklahoma and winner of the 1951 Outland Trophy as the nation's outstanding interior lineman; also did the place kicking on the Sooners' 1950 national championship team that went 10-0 during the regular season, but was upset, 13-7, in the Sugar Bowl by Bear Bryant's Kentucky squad; after a three-year stint with the Marines, Weatherall played one season with Edmonton in the CFL then signed with the Philadelphia Eagles in 1955; also played for Washington and Detroit before retiring in 1960; inducted into the College Football Hall of Fame in December 1992; of a heart attack; in Oklahoma City, Okla., August 2.

Sonny Werblin, 81; sports and entertainment impresario, who stunned the pro football world in 1965 by signing Alabama quarterback Joe Namath to a $427,000 contract with the New York Jets; the deal was the making of the American Football League and set in motion a chain of events that would result in the Jets' even more surprising 16-7 upset of the Baltimore Colts in Super Bowl III; Werblin established himself in show business as an agent with Music Corporation of America and built MCA's television division into a powerhouse with programs like the Ed Sullivan and Jackie Gleason shows; transferring his show business acumen to sports in the 1960s, Werblin, at one time or another, owned Monmouth Park race track in New Jersey, turned the pathetic New York Titans into the hip, new New York Jets, took over Madison Square Garden and revived the fortunes of its prime tenants, the Rangers and Knicks, and then supervised the construction of the $340 million Meadowlands Sports Complex in East Rutherford, N.J.; said Howard Cosell after Werblin's death: "He single-handedly changed the face of sports in America"; of a heart attack; in Manhattan, Nov. 21, 1991.

Jean Yawkey
1909-92
by George Sullivan

She was baseball's Garbo and likely will be the first woman enshrined at Cooperstown, where she would join her husband, Tom, making them the first couple to be reunited in the Summer Game's Valhalla.

The "Yawkey Tradition"—long on quality and privacy, short on championships—spanned 60 seasons. During those six decades the Red Sox won only four pennants (1946, 1967, 1975 and 1986) and no world championships, losing late in the seventh game of each World Series.

The most powerful woman in baseball history came within one haunting strike of the championship in 1986, her first World Series as Red Sox president after being widowed in 1976.

National Baseball Library, Cooperstown, N.Y.

Jean Yawkey's death ended 60 years of one-family ownership at Fenway Park.

There is a lingering image of Jean Yawkey standing on a television platform in the visiting-team clubhouse at New York's Shea Stadium as Game 6 wound down. Sparkling in the klieg lights, baseball's ultimate trophy sat on a table nearby awaiting presentation to the Red Sox matriarch as soon as her team, leading by two runs with two out in the 10th inning, wrapped up the franchise's first world title since 1918. All the years of near-miss frustration would soon be over.

Incredibly, the final out never came. Three Mets singled and—while Mrs. Yawkey watched a TV monitor in horror—a Bob Stanley pitch skipped to the backstop before a feeble grounder found its way through Bill Buckner's bowed legs.

Without a word, Jean Yawkey turned and left as workmen hastily wheeled away cases of champagne. The Red Sox would not taste the championship bubbly that night—or any other during the Yawkey years.

"It's a shame Mrs. Yawkey never got that championship," Carl Yastrzemski said upon her death Feb. 26 at age 83. "She loved the Red Sox and wanted that title so badly for Boston. As much as I wanted it, the Yawkeys wanted it even more."

"It's sad the Yawkeys never got their championship," Ted Williams said. "But it sure wasn't from lack of trying."

The Yawkeys were the last of a breed—of sufficient mind and wealth to run their team more as a sport than a business. "It was never a player-owner relationship," Yaz said. "The Yawkeys treated the players like family."

Together the Yawkeys directed a first-class operation that has become one of baseball's showcase franchises, and among its most profitable. And they did it with that fierce privacy, always shunning the spotlight. Tom rarely mixed with the media, and Jean refused all interview requests beyond fielding an occasional question on the run when ambushed by reporters.

After Tom Yawkey died of leukemia at age 73, his widow ignored higher bids and sold the club to herself in partnership with Haywood Sullivan and Buddy LeRoux, the team's onetime third-string catcher and trainer, respectively. Unhappily, each partner would later fall out of favor with Mrs. Yawkey. Her fight with LeRoux ended up in court, and she had to testify ("Garbo Talks!"). She bought him out in 1987. That regained her majority ownership—two shares to Sullivan's one—and they reportedly didn't speak during her last three years.

Red Sox ownership could end up in the courts again. Sullivan contends that as surviving general partner he has refusal rights when the franchise is put up for sale. Lawyers for Mrs. Yawkey's estate disagree. The dispute could be an ugly postscript to the Yawkey era.

George Sullivan is a former Boston sportswriter who has been writing about the Red Sox since the mid-1950s.

The Sporting News

C.C. Johnson Spink

Wide World Photos

Sonny Werblin

Wide World Photos

Alex Wojciechowicz

Edwin (Dib) Williams, 82; shortstop who played six seasons with Connie Mack's Philadelphia A's; hit .320 in the 1931 World Series, which the A's lost in seven games to the St. Louis Cardinals; retired in 1935 with a career batting average of .267; played football and basketball at Oklahoma A&M (now Oklahoma State), but left to play baseball when the school dropped that sport; of natural causes; in Conway, Ark., Apr. 2.

Tommy Williams, 51; youngest member of the 1960 U.S. Olympic hockey team that won the gold medal at Squaw Valley, Calif., and one of the first American-born players to make it in the NHL; in the Olympic semifinal against the Soviet Union, he assisted on Billy Christian's winning goal at 14:59 of the third period, enabling the U.S. to eliminate the favored Russians, 3-2; the Americans then beat Czechoslovakia, 9-4, to win the gold; played 16 seasons in the NHL with Boston, Minnesota, Washington and California, scoring 161 goals and 269 assists before he retired in 1976; inducted into the U.S. Hockey Hall of Fame in 1981; of a heart attack; in Hudson, Mass., Feb. 8.

Windell Williams, 69; former Rice end, whose winning touchdown reception against Texas in 1946 is remembered as the "Cyclone Fence Play"; after making the catch that put Rice ahead 18-13 late in the game, Williams crashed through a fence just outside the end-zone and left a hole in it; the 10th-ranked Owls went on to share the Southwest Conference title with Arkansas and then beat Tennessee in the Orange Bowl; of a gunshot wound in an apparent burglary at his home; in Houston, May 5.

Bert Wilson, 42; journeyman hockey player who scored 37 goals and 81 points in eight NHL seasons with the New York Rangers, Los Angeles, St. Louis and Calgary; retired in 1981; of liver cancer; in Toronto, Feb. 28.

Paul Winter, 86; French discus thrower, who won the bronze medal at the 1932 Olympics in Los Angeles with a toss of 156 feet 11 inches (John Anderson of the U.S. won the event with an Olympic record of 162-4); Winter, who is the only Frenchman ever to medal in the discus, got off a throw of 166-4 later in 1932, making him No. 4 on the all-time list; of natural causes; in France, April 12.

Mike Wise, 28; highly-regarded lineman at University of California-Davis who was the fourth round pick of the LA Raiders in the 1986 NFL Draft; played three games in 1991 and started two; became a Plan B free agent and was picked up and then waived by Cleveland prior to the start of the 1992 season; of a self-inflicted gunshot wound to the head; in Davis, Calif., Aug. 21.

Alex Wojciechowicz, 76; two-time All-America center at Fordham in 1936 and 1937, who would later gain entry to both the college and pro football halls of fame; anchored the Seven Blocks of Granite—Fordham's storied offensive line that also included future NFL head coach Vince Lombardi; in the pros, he was a two-way center with Detroit from 1938-46, but midway through the 1946 season he was traded to Philadelphia and turned into a linebacker by Eagles' coach Greasy Neale; a member of back-to-back NFL championship teams with the Eagles in 1948 and 1949; retired in 1950 after 13 years; of heart failure; in South River, N.J., July 13.

Jean R. Yawkey, 83; majority owner of the Boston Red Sox and a fixture at Fenway Park since her 1944 marriage to multi-millionaire sportsman Tom Yawkey, who bought the Red Sox for $1.5 million in 1933 and died in 1976; as owner, Mrs. Yawkey saw the Sox win the AL Eastern Division three times and lose the 1986 World Series to the NY Mets; she was also a major benefactor of the Baseball Museum and Hall of Fame and the only woman ever to serve on its board; after suffering a severe stroke; in Boston, Feb. 26.

Louis Young, Jr, 73; captain of the Dartmouth football team that defeated Cornell in the famous "Fifth-Down Game" at Hanover, N.H., on Nov. 16, 1940; outplayed most of the contest, Cornell rallied to score on a pass play in the final two seconds and seemed to have won, 7-3; Dartmouth protested that Cornell had been given an extra chance to score—a fifth down—and the touchdown shouldn't count; a study of the game films proved the protest valid and Cornell magnanimously forfeited the victory, giving Dartmouth a 3-0 win; it is the only time in college football history that a final score has been reversed; Young was later decorated for valor during the Allied invasion of Normandy in World War II; cause of death not disclosed; in Bryn Mawr, Pa., July 25.

Hy Zausner, 84; founder of the Port Washington, (N.Y.) Tennis Academy, whose graduates include John McEnroe and Vitas Gerulaitis; a successful dairyman and cheese importer, Zausner first got interested in tennis in 1964 after taking a series of lessons from a young pro in Puerto Rico named Nick Bollettieri; he recruited Bollettieri as the academy's first chief instructor; when Bollettieri left after one year to start his own school in Florida, Zausner replaced him with former Australian Davis Cup coach Harry Hopman; in 28 years, the academy has helped more than 10,000 youths learn tennis; of a stroke; in Manhasset, N.Y., Feb. 12.

National Baseball Library, Cooperstown, N.Y.

Though he later became a legend as a home run-hitting outfielder with the New York Yankees, in 1918 **Babe Ruth** led the Boston Red Sox to victory in the World Series as a pitcher.

TIME-OUT

1918

It's been 75 years since a pitching slugger named Ruth led the Boston Red Sox to their last World Series triumph.

Harry Frazee's Boston Red Sox had already won world championships in 1912, 1915 and 1916 when they faced the Chicago Cubs in the World Series following the stunted season of 1918. Some of the best baseball talents had gone off to join the fighting overseas, and, due to war restrictions, baseball's National Commission had voted to end the season after only 130 games on Labor Day. The Red Sox reached the Series with a meager but adequate 75 victories.

It had been the year Babe Ruth, the Red Sox star pitcher, was outshone on his off-days by Ruth the slugging outfielder and, afterward, there really was no going back. The gifted lefthander had been a 23-game winner with a league-leading 1.75 earned run average in 1916, after which he tossed a 14-inning shutout at Brooklyn in the World Series. In 1917, he won 24 games with a 2.01 ERA. He was 13-7 in 1918, but working increasingly as an outfielder, he also hit .300 in 95 games and tied Philadelphia's Tilly Walker for the American League lead in home runs with 11. After boosting the Sox to their early pennant with his slugging, Ruth took the mound to face the Cubs.

In the World Series opener on Sept. 5th, Chicago pitcher Hippo Vaughn held Boston to just two hits, but Ruth artfully scattered six Cub safeties for a 1-0 victory, extending his Series shutout streak to 23 innings. After Chicago broke up an equally tight second game with a triple in the ninth inning, Vaughn barely lost Game 3 by a 2-1 score. Ruth entered Game 4 hoping to prolong his Series shutout streak indefinitely. Although Boston won 3-2, the Cubs had the pleasure of ending Ruth's grand streak at 29⅔ innings. While sometimes crowded out by his later hitting feats, Ruth's scoreless record for World Series play lived on another 42 years.

An insurrection among the players almost prevented Game 5 when the Cubs and Red Sox voted to strike over what they considered an unfair division of World Series spoils by the National Commission. The players had hoped to appeal directly to commissioner Ban Johnson, but abandoned this idea when he arrived at Fenway Park drunk beyond sympathy. Instead, the game was played as scheduled, and Vaughn finally had a win over Boston, 3-0. The Sox still took it all in the sixth and final game, 2-1, led by the submariner Carl Mays, who allowed three hits and profited from a two-run outfielder's error. Mays and Ruth had two victories apiece in the Series.

Nathan Ward is an assistant editor of *American Heritage* magazine where he writes "The Time Machine" column each month.

The BOSTON RED SOX 1918

National Baseball Library, Cooperstown, N.Y.

Nothing was ever the same for the Red Sox after the soldiers came home from the World War in 1919. The heart of the great Boston teams left town with the dozen or more star players—most notably Ruth and Mays—that Harry Frazee sold to the Yankees to cover his Broadway investments.

By using brewery tycoon Jacob Ruppert's Yankee organization as a kind of pawn shop, Frazee helped build the indomitable New York powerhouse of the 1920s even as he decimated his own club. Mays was sold to the Yanks for $40,000 in 1919, followed by Ruth a year later for $125,000 plus a $300,000 personal loan. His last season in Boston, Ruth was 9-5 as a pitcher, but batted .322 with 29 home runs—17 more than any other player in either league.

But by the start of the 1920 season the Babe was gone. What remained of Frazee's Red Sox watched as their former mates—now wearing the pin-stripped livery of the Yankees—roared through the Twenties winning six pennants and three World Series.

Boston hasn't won a World Series since. At Fenway Park, the drought is known simply as the Curse of the Bambino.

1893
One Hundred Years Ago

Forty-six nations and most of the American states were represented in Chicago's World Columbian Exposition from May to November. Overshadowed by 150 examples of fanciful architecture from Stanford White and Louis Sullivan among others and by showcased inventions such as the ferris wheel, the debut tournament of the Chicago Fly Casting Club did not get the press it deserved. It was, however, the first such national casting tournament in America.

* * *

Although a strong argument can be made that a kind of ice hockey was being played at St. Paul's School in Concord, N.H., in the 1880s, Yale and Johns Hopkins universities are usually credited with importing the sport to the United States in 1893. That's when a Canadian student-organizer arranged a face-off in Baltimore between his Johns Hopkins squad and a willing team from Quebec. Two Yale tennis players who liked what they'd seen of the strange ice game while in Canadian tennis tournament brought hockey back to New Haven at about the same time.

1943
Fifty years ago.

With more than 300 colleges sacrificing their football programs for the war's duration, it came as no surprise that seven service teams cracked the Associated Press Top 20. An undefeated season eluded Notre Dame in the last 33 seconds of its final game when Great Lakes (Ill.) Naval Station won, 19-14, on a 46-yard Steve Lach to Paul Anderson touchdown pass. Nevertheless, the Irish were named national champion and quarterback Angelo Bertelli, who only played the first six games of the season before being called to boot camp by the Marines, won the Heisman Trophy.

1968
Twenty-five years ago.

Peggy Fleming took home the only American gold medal from the Winter Olympics at Grenoble, France, then after winning the World Championship for the third straight year, retired before she could even vote—at age 19.

Although she had been born in Pasadena, Calif., Fleming discovered skating while the family lived briefly under the raw winters of Cleveland. She was nine years old when she "started skating as though she had been at it for a long time," her mother later recalled, and even after the family moved back to California, Fleming kept at it and began competing at age eleven. She was sixth at the 1964 Winter Olympics at Innsbruck and claimed five consecutive national championships with her mesmerizing style before conquering Grenoble. Lloyd Garrison called her Olympic performance "a victory of the ballet over the Ice Follies approach to figure skating."

* * *

For pitchers, the 1968 baseball season was a magnificent pinnacle in which Oakland's Catfish Hunter hurled the American League's first regular-season perfect game since 1922; Bob Gibson of St. Louis overwhelmed and frightened enough NL batters to pitch 13 shutouts and post the league's second lowest ERA (1.12) since 1893; Don Drysdale of Los Angeles achieved 58 scoreless innings for a new record, surpassing Walter

Wide World Photos

Quarterback **Angelo Bertelli** of Notre Dame and the U.S. Marine Corps was college football's top player in 1943.

Johnson's 56-inning mark of 1913; and Denny McLain won 31 games for Detroit, missing a chance at 32 when he lost by 2-1 scores in each of his final two starts.

Major league batters as a class fared little better in the All-Star Game, which was a stirring 1-0 pitchers' duel won by the Nationals. In the fall classic, Gibson twice outdueled McLain, who returned after only two days off to win Game 6. Gibson then lost to Detroit's Mickey Lolich in the final game and the Year of the Pitcher was over. After 1968, the mound was lowered slightly in hopes that offense might return to the sport. For whatever combination of reasons, it did.

* * *

Unlike its disappointments at Grenoble only months earlier, the United States led all nations at the Summer Olympics in Mexico City with 45 gold medals. Bob Beamon leaped an unheard-of 29 feet, 2½ inches in the long jump; Al Oerter won the discus for an unprecedented fourth straight gold medal; and Dick Fosbury popularized his backwards "Fosbury

Flop" over the high jump bar for a gold medal at 7 feet 4¼ inches.

But the most potent images of the Games were political, at least one of them deliberately. American 200-meter medalists Tommie Smith and John Carlos, their gloved fists raised and heads bowed during the national anthem in a "black power" salute, mystified and angered millions of Americans and were later suspended for their silent protest.

Meanwhile, heavyweight boxing gold medalist George Foreman later waved a small American flag in the ring after pounding his Russian opponent unconscious. "Nobody told me to do it," Foreman said. "I told myself, 'Uncle Sam paid my way here, fed me, and gave me a chance. He deserves something.' " His personal gesture was much exploited at home, however, to counterpoint the runners' defiance. To California governor Ronald Reagan, Foreman's comportment in victory was "proof that the American dream is just as real as it was 192 years ago." Others at home called him a stooge and a "Tom."

* * *

In the NBA playoffs, Bill Russell's Boston Celtics trailed Philadelphia three games to one in the Eastern finals, but rallied to win three straight to win the series and the right to meet Los Angeles in the NBA Finals. Russell, John Havlicek, Sam Jones and company were no strangers to the big post-season series: after all, the Celtics had won the NBA title 10 out of 12 years since their star center came to town. But this was their first Final since Russell had replaced general manager Red Auerbach as coach after the 1966 season. Not to worry. The Celtics took the Lakers four games to two, and thumped them loudly in the last game, 124-109.

* * *

Wilt Chamberlain, who had led Philadelphia to a regular season record of 62-20, led the league in rebounds and assists, increased his record career scoring total to 25,434 points, and added to another growing record of 706 consecutive games in which he failed to foul out, was nevertheless traded to Los Angeles after the playoffs.

Chamberlain had supposedly asked to be paid one million dollars over three

Wide World Photos

Tommie Smith (left) and **John Carlos** give the "black power" salute that got them suspended from the 1968 Olympics.

years (his arch-rival, Russell of the Celtics, was making $200,000 a year for three years as player and coach). In exchange for the Sixers' star center, the Lakers sent Archie Clark, Jerry Chambers, and Darrall Imhoff to Philadelphia. The question of Chamberlain's worth was argued not only by fans and sportswriters, but even turned up in the landmark philosophical text *Anarchy, State and Utopia* by the libertarian philosopher Robert Nozick, who determined that such an exciting player was worth whatever fans were willing to "cheerfully" pay to see him.

* * *

In 1968, the pros arrived at center court in international tennis and the money was finally above the table. The often hypocritical distinctions between amateur and professional players on the circuit began to break down starting with the British Lawn Tennis Association the previous December, and led to the first U.S. Open championship at Forest Hills with a record number of entrants, both amateur and professional, in August.

Wide World Photos

Billie Jean King (left) and **Bobby Riggs** at the press conference announcing their $100,000, winner-take-all "Battle of the Sexes" tennis match in 1973. The 29-year-old King trounced Riggs, 55, in three sets.

Virginia Wade of England defeated her favored American opponent, Billie Jean King, in the women's finals, while a lithe, thoughtful American named Arthur Ashe (still considered an amateur, or "registered," player) defeated Tom Okker in five sets to win the men's title. With his steady, graceful play the reticent Ashe had earlier in the summer become the first black male champion at the U.S. Amateur Championships in Brookline, Mass. Following his military service as a computer specialist at West Point in 1968, Ashe went pro. In 1975, he would become the first black champion at Wimbledon.

1973
Twenty years ago.

Orenthal James (O.J.) Simpson, the former Heisman Trophy-winning running back for the Buffalo Bills, ran for 2,003 yards in one season, surpassing Jim Brown's old record of 1,863. Ten minutes into the final game of the year against the New York Jets at Shea Stadium, O.J. spotted a hole and slipped through for six yards and the new record.

After the game, Simpson shared the credit with his doting offensive line. Like a headline singer introducing his band, he said, "I hope to stay in the league until all these guys get old, so no young back can get behind them and break the record." Of Brown, Simpson noted, "Jim hasn't called me or anything this season, but then he hasn't called me in any other season."

* * *

Billie Jean King answered the challenge of a loudmouthed former Wimbledon champion named Bobby Riggs, whose put-downs of women's tennis and feminism had revived his career.

The 55-year-old Riggs had proclaimed that any male weekend hacker could defeat a women's tennis champion, and then beat 1970 Grand Slam winner Margaret Smith Court in May for $10,000. He next arranged to play King, the reigning women's champion at Wimbledon in a $100,000, winner-take-all "Battle of the Sexes" at the Houston Astrodome on Sept. 20. King upstaged Riggs by being carried Cleopatra-like onto the court. She then proceeded to dismantle him, 6-4, 6-3, 6-3, before an estimated 48 million people watching on television.

Other Milestones

1873
(120 years ago)

On May 27, a crowd of 12,000, including Maryland Gov. William Pinkney White, gathers at Pimlico Race Course in Baltimore to watch the first running of the **Preakness Stakes**. John Chamberlain's bay colt, Survivor, wins the Tuesday afternoon race by 10 lengths over John Boulger. Named in honor of the powerful three-year-old colt who won the first stakes race ever run at Pimlico in 1870, the Preakness was discontinued by the Maryland Jockey Club in 1891, then revived by the Brooklyn Jockey Club and moved to New York in 1894 before returning to Pimlico in 1909.

1903
(90 years ago)

Although baseball's established National League (founded in 1876) and upstart American League (founded in 1901) are feuding, owners Barney Dreyfuss of Pittsburgh and Henry Killilea of Boston agree to match their pennant-winning clubs in a best-of-nine "world championship." The Boston Pilgrims (they would be renamed the Red Sox by 1907) win the **first modern World Series**, five games to three, boosting the junior circuit's claim to major league status. A year later, Boston is denied a chance to defend its title when the NL's New York Giants refuse to play them.

1908
(85 years ago)

At the IVth Olympic Games in London, U.S. flag bearer and discus champion **Martin Sheridan** establishes an American opening ceremony tradition when he refuses to lower the Stars and Stripes before King Edward VII's box. "This flag dips to no earthly king," says Sheridan.

"**Merkle's Boner**" enters baseball's vernacular when 19-year-old New York Giants baserunner Fred Merkle fails to advance from first to second as Al Bridwell singles in Harry McCormick from third to beat Chicago in the bottom of the ninth inning. By turning for the clubhouse when the winning run scored instead of touching second, Merkle's mental lapse would eventually cost the Giants the pennant. The Cubs protested and when the teams finished the season within a game of each other in the standings, the Sept. 23 contest was replayed. This time Chicago won, 4-2.

1913
(80 years ago)

Twenty-year-old Boston amateur golfer **Francis Ouimet** upsets British professionals Harry Vardon and Ted Ray in a three-way playoff to win the U.S. Open at the Country Club in Brookline, Mass. Ouimet, who grew up across the street from the Country Club and used to sneak on to the course to play, shoots a 72 and beats Varden by five strokes and Ray by six. Ouimet's caddy on that rainy Sept. 20, is 10-year-old Eddie Lowery.

1923
(70 years ago)

Fifty-seven thousand spectators jam Pasadena's brand new horseshoe-shaped **Rose Bowl** stadium on New Year's Day to watch Southern Cal defeat Penn State, 14-3, in the ninth Rose Bowl game. The first eight games had been played at Tournament Park.

Babe Ruth slugs a three-run homer as the New York Yankees defeat (who else?) the Boston Red Sox, 4-1, to officially open Yankee Stadium on April 18. Opening Day attendance at "the House that Ruth Built" is 74,217 with another 20,000 turned away.

Amateur **Bobby Jones**, 21, defeats professional Bobby Cruikshank by two strokes in an 18-hole playoff to win his first U.S. Open on July 15. Jones, who never turned pro, went on to win the Open three more times in the next six years.

1933
(60 years ago)

Johnny Goodman of Omaha, an amateur, wins the U.S. Open golf championship by a stroke over Ralph Guldahl on June 10. No amateur has won the Open since. Guldahl went on to win back-to-back Opens in 1937-38.

On July 6, the **American League** captures baseball's first All-Star Game with a 4-2 trimming of the Nationals at Comiskey Park in Chicago. Thirty-eight-year-old **Babe Ruth** belts a two-run homer in the third off Wild Bill Hallahan of the St. Louis Cardinals to provide the margin of victory.

The **Chicago Bears** rally in the fourth quarter to beat the New York Giants, 23-21, and win in the first NFL championship game between regular season division champions. The game is played at Wrigley Field on Dec. 17.

1938
(55 years ago)

Temple thrashes Colorado, 60-36, on Mar. 16 to win the inaugural **National Invitation Basketball Tournament** (NIT) at Madison Square Garden. Don Shields of the Owls is the tourney MVP, while Byron (Whizzer) White scores 10 points for Colorado. The previous fall, White, a future U.S. Supreme Court justice, had led the Buffaloes' football team to the Cotton Bowl and finished second in the voting for the Heisman Trophy.

On June 15, Cincinnati pitcher **Johnny Vander Meer** hurls his second no-hitter in two starts, blanking Brooklyn, 6-0, at Ebbets Field. The game, attended by 38,748, is also the first night game ever played in the New York area. The first of Vander Meer's unprecedented back-to-back gems, a 3-0 win over Boston, came at home on the afternoon of June 11.

1948
(45 years ago)

Gretchen Fraser wins the first Olympic skiing gold medal ever for the United States with a victory in the women's slalom at the Winter Games in St. Moritz, Switzerland. Fraser also picks up a silver medal in the Alpine combined.

Citation, with Eddie Arcaro aboard, beats Better Self by eight lengths in the June 12 Belmont Stakes to become the fourth three-year-old to win the Triple Crown in the 1940s. The others were Whirlaway (also ridden by Arcaro) in 1941, Count Fleet in 1943 and Assault in 1946.

Heavyweight champion **Joe Louis** knocks out challenger Jersey Joe Walcott in the 11th round at Yankee Stadium on June 25. Following the fight, Louis announces his retirement from the ring after holding the title continuously since 1935.

1953
(40 years ago)

Ben Hogan beats Sam Snead by six strokes to win his fourth U.S. Open in six years. Hogan also wins the Masters and the British Open to become the only golfer ever to win all three in one year.

In their first season in Milwaukee, **the former Boston Braves** lead the major leagues in attendance with over 1.8 million paid admissions at County Stadium. The Braves, who finished seventh in the NL in 1952 with a record of 64-89, rise to second in 1953 with a 92-62 mark under new manager Charlie Grimm.

1953
(40 years ago)

On Sept. 29, American League owners approve the sale and transfer of the **St. Louis Browns** to Baltimore, where the team will become the Orioles in 1954.

Second baseman **Billy Martin** gets 12 hits and knocks in eight runs as the New York Yankees defeat Brooklyn in six games to win the 50th annual World Series. The victory is also a record-breaking fifth title in a row for the Bronx Bombers.

The **U.S. Supreme Court** decides by a 7-2 vote that baseball is a sport, not a business, and is therefore not subject to antitrust laws (Nov. 9).

1958
(35 years ago)

Sugar Ray Robinson, who had lost the world middleweight championship to Carman Basilio at Yankee Stadium on Sept. 23, 1957, wins back the title on Mar. 25 at Chicago Stadium. Both bouts were 15-round split decisions. Robinson's victory gives him the middleweight crown for a record fifth time.

1963
(30 years ago)

Boston guard **Bob Cousy** retires at age 34 after the Celtics defeat the Los Angeles Lakers in six games to win their sixth NBA championship in seven years. In a career covering 13 seasons, Cousy led the league in assists eight times, was a first team All-Star 10 times and was named MVP in 1957.

St. Louis outfielder-first baseman **Stan (the Man) Musial** retires at age 42 after 22 seasons, 3,630 hits and a career batting average of .331. He also played on three World Series championship teams and was voted National League MVP three times (1943, '46 and '48).

1968
(25 years ago)

Trailing, 32-29, late in the fourth quarter of a critical AFL game with the New York Jets, the Oakland Raiders score two touchdowns in the final minute and five seconds to win, 43-32. Unfortunately, the national TV audience watching the game on NBC never sees the Raider comeback because the network switches from the game to begin the children's movie, **"Heidi"** (Nov.17).

1973
(20 years ago)

A group of investors, headed by Cleveland shipbuilder **George Steinbrenner** purchases the New York Yankees from CBS for $10 million (Jan. 3).

On Jan. 14, the **Miami Dolphins** defeat the Washington Redskins, 14-7, in Super Bowl VII, becoming the first and only team in NFL history to go through an entire season with a perfect record (17-0).

Challenger **George Foreman**, a 3-to-1 underdog, knocks down heavyweight champion **Joe Frazier** six times in the first two rounds, to win the title in Kingston, Jamaica (Jan. 22).

UCLA beats Notre Dame, 82-63, in South Bend on Jan. 27, to set a new NCAA basketball winning streak record of 61 straight. A year later, the Irish would host the Bruins again and beat them, 71-70, to end the streak at 88.

With the start of spring training less than a week away, **baseball players and owners** agree on a new, three-year Basic Agreement that calls for a $15,000 minimum salary, salary arbitration and a "10 and 5" trade rule that allows a player with 10 years service in the majors and the last five with the same team to veto any trade involving him.

The Chicago White Sox sign AL MVP **Dick Allen** to a three-year contract worth $250,000, making him the highest-paid player in baseball history (Feb. 27).

Musher **Dick Wilmarth** and his team of huskies win the inaugural Iditarod Sled Dog Race, covering the 1,160-mile course from Anchorage to Nome, Alaska, in 20 days, 49 minutes and 41 seconds.

The first comprehensive agreement between **NBA players and owners** is reached with the players getting pension benefits and the highest minimum annual salary in professional sports—$20,000.

Secretariat, with jockey Ron Turcotte along for the ride, wins the Belmont Stakes in record time (2:24) and by a record margin (31 lengths) to become the first three-year-old in 25 years to claim horse racing's Triple Crown (June 9).

Willie Mays announces his retirement at age 42 on Sept. 20. Mays, who starred with the New York and San Francisco Giants before joining the Mets in 1972, bows out with 660 home runs, 3,283 hits and MVP awards in 1954 and '65.

1978
(15 years ago)

With only seven professional fights under his belt, **Leon Spinks** stuns the boxing world with a 15-round split decision over heavyweight champion **Muhammad Ali** in Las Vegas on Feb. 15. Seven months later, Ali wins the title back for an unprecedented third time, with a unanimous 15-round decision in New Orleans.

Affirmed, with Steve Cauthen in the saddle, beats **Alydar** by a head to win the Belmont Stakes and the Triple Crown. Alydar, ridden by Jorge Velasquez, becomes the first and only three-year-old to finish second in all three Triple Crown races (June 10).

Pete Rose singles off Montreal's Steve Rogers to become the 13th and youngest (at 37) player to reach 3,000 career hits (May 5).

Jimmy Connors beats Bjorn Borg, 6-4, 6-2, 6-2, to win the first U.S. Open played at the new National Tennis Center at Flushing Meadow Park. The victory gives Connors the distinction of winning the Open on three different surfaces—grass (1974) and clay (1976) at Forest Hills and cement at Flushing.

In a one-game playoff at Fenway Park for the AL's Eastern Division title, light-hitting New York shortstop **Bucky Dent** hits a three-run homer in the seventh inning off Boston's Mike Torrez as the Yankees beat the Red Sox, 5-4. The Yanks go on to beat Kansas City in the ALCS and Los Angeles in the World Series.

1983
(10 years ago)

After coming close several times, **Penn State** finally wins its first college football national championship as the second-ranked Nittany Lions defeat No. 1 Georgia, 27-23, in the Sugar Bowl (Jan. 1).

The **United States Football League** begins its first spring season on Mar. 6 with 12 teams, two TV contracts and 21-year-old Heisman Trophy winner Herschel Walker, who leaves Georgia a year early to join the USFL's New Jersey Generals.

North Carolina State upsets No. 1 Houston, 54-52, on a last-second basket by Lorenzo Charles to win the NCAA men's basketball championship at Albuquerque on Apr. 4. The Wolfpack ended the regular season with a record of 17-10, then won nine games in a row.

Australia II defeats Liberty in the seventh and deciding race for the America's Cup, ending the longest winning streak in sport on Sept. 26. The U.S. had held the Cup for 132 years and through 24 defenses before finally losing to the Aussies.

Major League Cities & Teams

At the end of 1992, there were 115 major league sports teams playing or scheduled to play baseball, basketball, football and hockey in 62 cities in the United States and Canada. Listed below are the cities and the teams that play there. If a team actually plays in a nearby suburb, that town is in parentheses.

Anaheim
AL   California Angels
NFL   Los Angeles Rams

Arlington
AL   Texas Rangers

Atlanta
NL   Braves
NBA   Hawks
NFL   Falcons

Baltimore
AL   Orioles

Boston
AL   Red Sox
NBA   Celtics
NFL   N.E.Patriots (Foxboro)
NHL   Bruins

Buffalo
NFL   Bills (Orchard Park)
NHL   Sabres

Calgary
CFL   Stampeders
NHL   Flames

Charlotte
NBA   Hornets

Chicago
AL   White Sox
NL   Cubs
NBA   Bulls
NFL   Bears
NHL   Blackhawks

Cincinnati
NL   Reds
NFL   Bengals

Cleveland
AL   Indians
NBA   Cavaliers (Richfield)
NFL   Browns

Dallas
NBA   Mavericks
NHL   Cowboys (Irving)

Denver
NL   Colorado Rockies (1993)
NBA   Nuggets
NFL   Broncos

Detroit
AL   Tigers
NBA   Pistons (Auburn Hills)
NFL   Lions (Pontiac)
NHL   Red Wings

East Rutherford
NBA   New Jersey Nets
NFL   New York Giants
NFL   New York Jets
NHL   New Jersey Devils

Edmonton
CFL   Eskimos
NHL   Oilers

Green Bay
NFL   Packers

Hamilton
CFL   Tiger-Cats

Hartford
NHL   Whalers

Houston
NL   Astros
NBA   Rockets
NFL   Oilers

Indianapolis
NBA   Pacers
NFL   Colts

Kansas City
AL   Royals
NFL   Chiefs

Los Angeles
NL   Dodgers
NBA   Clippers
NBA   Lakers (Inglewood)
NFL   Raiders
NHL   Kings (Inglewood)

Miami
NL   Florida Marlins (1993)
NBA   Heat
NFL   Dolphins

Milwaukee
AL   Brewers
NBA   Bucks

Minneapolis
AL   Minnesota Twins
NBA   Minnesota Timberwolves
NFL   Minnesota Vikings
NHL   Minnesota North Stars
        (Bloomington)

Montreal
NL   Expos
NHL   Canadiens

New Orleans
NFL   Saints

New York
AL   Yankees
NL   Mets
NBA   Knicks
NHL   Rangers

Oakland
AL   Athletics
NBA   Golden St. Warriors

Orlando
NBA   Magic

Ottawa
CFL   Rough Riders
NHL   Senators

Philadelphia
NL   Phillies
NBA   76ers
NFL   Eagles
NHL   Flyers

Phoenix
NBA   Suns
NFL   Cardinals (Tempe)

Pittsburgh
NL   Pirates
NFL   Steelers
NHL   Penguins

Portland
NBA   Trail Blazers

Quebec City
NHL   Nordiques

Regina
CFL   Saskatchewan Roughriders

Sacramento
NBA   Kings

St.Louis
NL   Cardinals
NHL   Blues

Salt Lake City
NBA   Jazz

San Antonio
NBA   Spurs

San Diego
NL   Padres
NFL   Chargers

San Francisco
NL   Giants
NFL   49ers

San Jose
NHL   Sharks

Seattle
AL   Mariners
NBA   SuperSonics
NFL   Seahawks

Tampa
NFL   Buccaneers
NHL   Lightning

Toronto
AL   Blue Jays
CFL   Argonauts
NHL   Maple Leafs

Uniondale
NHL   New York Islanders

Vancouver
CFL   B.C. Lions
NHL   Canucks

Washington
NBA   Bullets (Landover)
NFL   Redskins
NHL   Capitals (Landover)

Winnipeg
NHL   Jets
CFL   Blue Bombers

Olympics
Winter Games

Year	No.	Host city	Dates
1994	XVII	Lillehammer, Norway.............	Feb.12-27
1998	XVII	Nagano, Japan	TBA

Summer Games

Year	No.	Host city	Dates
1996	XXVI	Atlanta, Georgia.............	July 20-Aug.4
2000	XXVII	TBA (Sept., 1993)	

All-Star Games
Baseball

Year	Site	Date
1993	Camden Yards, Baltimore	July 13
1994	Three Rivers Stadium, Pittsburgh..............	TBA
1995	New Stadium, Texas......................	TBA

NBA Basketball

Year	Site	Date
1993	Delta Center, Salt Lake City................	Feb.21
1994	Target Center, Minneapolis	Feb.13

NFL Pro Bowl

Year	Site	Date
1993	Aloha Stadium, Honolulu....................	Feb.7
1994	Aloha Stadium, Honolulu....................	Feb.6
1995	Aloha Stadium, Honolulu....................	Feb.5

NHL Hockey

Year	Site	Date
1993	Montreal Forum...........................	Feb.6
1994	Madison Square Garden......................	TBA

Auto Racing

The Daytona 500 stock car race is usually held on the Sunday before the third Monday in February, while the Indianapolis 500 is usually held on the Sunday of Memorial Day weekend in May. Except for 1993, the following dates are tentative.

Year	Daytona 500	Indianapolis 500
1993	Feb.14	May 30
1994	Feb.20	May 29
1995	Feb.19	May 28
1996	Feb.18	May 26

NCAA Basketball
Men's Final Four

Year	Site	Dates
1993	Superdome, New Orleans	April 3-5
1994	Charlotte (N.C.) Coliseum	April 2-4
1995	The Kingdome, Seattle	April 1-3
1996	Meadowlands (N.J.) Arena	Mar.30-Apr.1
1997	Hoosier Dome, Indianapolis	March 29-31

Women's Final Four

Year	Site	Dates
1993	The Omni, Atlanta........................	April 3-4
1994	Richmond (Va.) Coliseum	April 2-3
1995	Target Center, Minneapolis................	April 1-2

NFL Football
Super Bowls

No.	Site	Date
XXVII	Rose Bowl, Pasadena	Jan.31,1993
XXVIII	Georgia Dome, Atlanta	Jan.30,1994
XXIX	Joe Robbie Stadium, Miami	Jan.29,1995
XXX	Sun Devil Stadium, Tempe....................	TBA

Golf
The Masters

Year	Site	Dates
1993	Augusta National, Ga....................	April 8-11
1994	Augusta National, Ga....................	April 7-10
1995	Augusta National, Ga....................	April 6-9
1996	Augusta National, Ga....................	April 11-14

U.S. Open

Year	Site	Dates
1993	Baltusrol GC, Springfield, N.J	June 17-20
1994	Oakmont (Pa.) CC	June 16-19
1995	Shinnecock Hills (N.Y.) GC	TBA
1996	Oakland Hills CC, Birmingham, Mich.....	June 13-16

U.S. Women's Open

Year	Site	Dates
1993	Crooked Stick GC, Carmel, Ind	July 22-25
1994	Indian Wood GC, Lake Orion, Mich.......	July 21-24
1995	Broadmoor GC, Colorado Springs........	July 13-16

U.S. Senior Open

Year	Site	Dates
1993	Cherry Hills, CC, Engelwood, Colo........	July 8-11
1994	Pinehurst (N.C.) CC....................	Jun.30-Jul.3
1995	Congressional CC, Bethesda, Md	Jun.29-Jul.2

PGA Championship

Year	Site	Dates
1993	Inverness Club, Toledo, Ohio	Aug.12-15
1994	Southern Hills CC, Tulsa, Okla..........	Aug.11-14
1995	Riviera CC, Pacific Palisades, Cailf	TBA
1996	Valhalla GC, Louisville........................	TBA

British Open

Year	Site	Dates
1993	Royal St. George's, England	July 15-18
1994	Turnberry, Scotland.....................	July 14-17
1995	St. Andrews, Scotland	July 20-23
1996	Royal Lytham & St. Annes, England	July 18-21

Ryder Cup

Year	Site	Dates
1993	The Belfry, England	Sept.24-26
1995	Oak Hill CC, Rochester, N.Y.	TBA

Horse Racing
The Triple Crown Races

The Kentucky Derby is always held at Churchill Downs in Louisville on the first Saturday in May, followed two weeks later by the Preakness Stakes at Pimlico Race Course in Baltimore and three weeks after that by the Belmont Stakes at Belmont Park in Elmont, NY.

Year	Ky Derby	Preakness	Belmont
1993	May 1	May 15	June 5
1994	May 7	May 21	June 11
1995	May 6	May 20	June 10
1996	May 4	May 18	June 8

Tennis
U.S. Open

Usually held from the last Monday in August through the second Sunday in September, with Labor Day weekend the midway point in the tournament.

Year	Site	Dates
1993	U.S. Tennis Center, NYC...........	Aug.30-Sept.12
1994	U.S. Tennis Center, NYC...........	Aug.29-Sept.11
1995	U.S. Tennis Center, NYC...........	Aug.28-Sept.10
1996	U.S. Tennis Center, NYC...........	Aug.26-Sept.8

Proof of
Purchase
1993 Information
Please Sports Almanac